P9-DVE-039

Routledge
Encyclopedia of
PHILOSOPHY

General Editor
EDWARD CRAIG

London and New York

First published 1998
by Routledge
11 New Fetter Lane, London EC4P 4EE
Simultaneously published in the USA and Canada
by Routledge
29 West 35th Street, New York, NY 10001

©1998 Routledge

Typeset in Monotype Times New Roman by
Routledge

Printed in England by
T J International Ltd, Padstow, Cornwall, England

Printed on acid-free paper which conforms to ANS1.Z39, 48-1992 and ISO 9706 standards

British Library Cataloguing-in-Publication Data
A catalogue record for this book is available from the British Library

The Library of Congress Cataloguing-in-Publication data is given in volume 10.

ISBN: 0415-07310-3 (10-volume set)
ISBN: 0415-18706-0 (volume 1)
ISBN: 0415-18707-9 (volume 2)
ISBN: 0415-18708-7 (volume 3)
ISBN: 0415-18709-5 (volume 4)
ISBN: 0415-18710-9 (volume 5)
ISBN: 0415-18711-7 (volume 6)
ISBN: 0415-18712-5 (volume 7)
ISBN: 0415-18713-3 (volume 8)
ISBN: 0415-18714-1 (volume 9)
ISBN: 0415-18715-X (volume 10)

ISBN: 0415-16916-X (CD-ROM)
ISBN: 0415-16917-8 (10-volume set and CD-ROM)

Contents

Using the *Encyclopedia*

List of entries

Volume 1   A posteriori – Bradwardine, Thomas

Volume 2   Brahman – Derrida, Jacques

Volume 3   Descartes, René – Gender and science

Volume 4   Genealogy – Iqbal, Muhammad

Volume 5   Irigaray, Luce – Lushi chunqiu

Volume 6   Luther, Martin – Nifo, Agostino

Volume 7   Nihilism – Quantum mechanics, interpretation of

Volume 8   Questions – Sociobiology

Volume 9   Sociology of knowledge – Zoroastrianism

Volume 10   Index

Using the *Encyclopedia*

The *Routledge Encyclopedia of Philosophy* is designed for ease of use. The following notes outline its organization and editorial approach and explain the ways of locating material. This will help readers make the most of the *Encyclopedia*.

SEQUENCE OF ENTRIES

The *Encyclopedia* contains 2,054 entries (from 500 to 19,000 words in length) arranged in nine volumes with a tenth volume for the index. Volumes 1–9 are arranged in a single alphabetical sequence, as follows:

Volume 1: A posteriori *to* Bradwardine, Thomas

Volume 2: Brahman *to* Derrida, Jacques

Volume 3: Descartes, René *to* Gender and science

Volume 4: Genealogy *to* Iqbal, Muhammad

Volume 5: Irigaray, Luce *to* Lushi chunqiu

Volume 6: Luther, Martin *to* Nifo, Agostino

Volume 7: Nihilism *to* Quantum mechanics, interpretation of

Volume 8: Questions *to* Sociobiology

Volume 9: Sociology of knowledge *to* Zoroastrianism

Alphabetical order

Entries are listed in alphabetical order by word rather than by letter with all words including *and*, *in*, *of* and *the* being given equal status. The exceptions to this rule are as follows:

- biographies: where the forenames and surname of a philosopher are inverted, the entry takes priority in the sequence, for example:

Alexander, Samuel (1859–1938)
Alexander of Aphrodisias (*c.* AD 200)
Alexander of Hales (*c.* 1185–1245)

- names with prefixes, which follow conventional alphabetical placing (see Transliteration and naming conventions below).

A complete alphabetical list of entries is given in each of the Volumes 1 to 9.

Inverted titles

Titles of entries consisting of more than one word are often inverted so that the key term (in a thematic or signpost entry) or the surname (in a biographical entry) determines the place of the entry in the alphabetical sequence, for example:

Law, philosophy of *or*
Market, ethics of the *or*
Hart, Herbert Lionel Adolphus (1907–93)

Conceptual organization

Several concerns have had a bearing on the sequence of entries where there is more than one key term.

In deciding on the sequence of entries we have tried, wherever possible, to integrate philosophy as it is known and studied in the USA and Europe with philosophy from around the world. This means that the reader will frequently find entries from different philosophical traditions or approaches to the same topic close to each other, for example, in the sequence:

Political philosophy [signpost entry]
Political philosophy, history of
Political philosophy in classical Islam
Political philosophy, Indian

Similarly, in entries where a philosophical tradition or approach is surveyed we have tried, whenever appropriate, to keep philosophical traditions from different countries together. An example is the sequence:

Confucian philosophy, Chinese
Confucian philosophy, Japanese
Confucian philosophy, Korean
Confucius (551–479 BC)

Finally, historical entries are usually placed with contemporary entries under the topic rather than the historical period. For example, in the sequence:

Language, ancient philosophy of
Language and gender
Language, conventionality of
Language, early modern philosophy of
Language, Indian theories of
Language, innateness of

DUMMY TITLES

The *Encyclopedia* has been extensively cross-referenced in order to help the reader locate their topic of interest. Dummy titles are placed throughout the alphabetical sequence of entries to direct the reader to the actual title of the entry where a topic is discussed. This may be under a different entry title, a synonym or as part of a larger entry. Wherever useful we have included the numbers of the sections (§§) in which a particular topic or subject is discussed. Examples of this type of cross-reference are:

AFRICAN AESTHETICS *see*
AESTHETICS, AFRICAN

CANGUILHEM, GEORGES *see*
FRENCH PHILOSOPHY OF SCIENCE §§3–4

TAO *see* DAO

GLOSSARY OF LOGICAL AND MATHEMATICAL TERMS

A glossary of logical and mathematical terms is provided to help users with terms from formal logic and mathematics. 'See also' cross-references to the glossary are provided at the end of entries where the user might benefit from help with unfamiliar terms. The glossary can be found in Volume 5 under L (LOGICAL AND MATHEMATICAL TERMS, GLOSSARY OF).

THE INDEX VOLUME

Volume 10 is devoted to a comprehensive index of key terms, concepts and names covered in Volumes 1–9, allowing readers to reap maximum benefit from the *Encyclopedia*. A guide to the index can be found at the beginning of the index. The index volume includes a full listing of contributors, their affiliations and the entries they have written. It also includes permission acknowledgements, listed in publisher order.

STRUCTURE OF ENTRIES

The *Routledge Encyclopedia of Philosophy* contains three types of entry:

- 'signpost' entries, for example, METAPHYSICS; SCIENCE, PHILOSOPHY OF; EAST ASIAN PHILOSOPHY. These entries provide an accessible overview of the sub-disciplines or regional coverage within the *Encyclopedia*; they provide a 'map' which directs the reader towards and around the many entries relating to each topic;
- thematic entries, ranging from general entries such as KNOWLEDGE, CONCEPT OF, to specialized topics such as VIRTUE EPISTEMOLOGY;
- biographical entries, devoted to individual philosophers, emphasizing the work rather than the life of the subject and with a list of the subject's major works.

Overview

All thematic and biographical entries begin with an overview which provides a concise and accessible summary of the topic or subject. This can be referred to on its own if the reader does not require the depth and detail of the main part of the entry.

Table of contents

All thematic and biographical entries over 1000 words in length are divided into sections and have a numbered table of contents following the overview. This gives the headings of each of the sections of the entry, enabling the reader to see the scope and structure of the entry at a glance. For example, the table of contents in the entry on HERACLITUS:

1 Life and work
2 Methodology
3 Unity of opposites and perspectivism
4 Cosmology
5 Psychology, ethics and religion
6 Influence

Cross-references within an entry

Entries in the *Encyclopedia* have been extensively cross-referenced in order to indicate other entries that may be of interest to the reader. There are two types of cross-reference in the *Encyclopedia*:

1. 'See' cross-references

Cross-references within the text of an entry direct the reader to other entries on or closely related to the topic under discussion. For example, a reader may be directed from a conceptual entry to a biography of the philosopher whose work is under discussion or vice versa. These internal cross-references appear in small capital letters, either in parentheses, for example:

Opponents of naturalism before and since Wittgenstein have been animated by the notion that the aims of social science are not causal explanation and improving prediction, but uncovering rules that make social life intelligible to its participants (see EXPLANATION IN HISTORY AND SOCIAL SCIENCE).

or sometimes, when the reference is to a person who

has a biographical entry, as small capitals in the text itself, for example:

> Thomas NAGEL emphasizes the discrepancy between the objective insignificance of our lives and projects and the seriousness and energy we devote to them.

For entries over 1,000 words in length we have included the numbers of the sections (§) in which a topic is discussed, wherever useful, for example:

> In *Nicomachean Ethics*, Aristotle criticizes Plato's account for not telling us anything about particular kinds of goodness (see ARISTOTLE §§ 21–6).

2. 'See also' cross-references

At the end of the text of each entry, 'See also' cross-references guide the reader to other entries of related interest, such as more specialized entries, biographical entries, historical entries, geographical entries and so on. These cross-references appear in small capitals in alphabetical order.

References

References in the text are given in the Harvard style, for example, Kant (1788), Rawls (1971). Exceptions to this rule are made when presenting works with established conventions, for example, with some major works in ancient philosophy. Full bibliographical details are given in the 'List of works' and 'References and further reading'.

Bibliography

List of works

Biographical entries are followed by a list of works which gives full bibliographical details of the major works of the philosopher. This is in chronological order and includes items cited in the text, significant editions, dates of composition for pre-modern works (where known), preferred English-language translations and English translations for the titles of untranslated foreign-language works.

References and further reading

Both biographical and thematic entries have a list of references and further reading. Items are listed alphabetically by author's name. (Publications with joint authors are listed under the name of the first author and after any individual publications by that author). References cited in the text are preceded by an asterisk (*). Further reading which the reader may find particularly useful is also included.

The authors and editors have attempted to provide the fullest possible bibliographical information for every item.

Annotations

Publications in the 'List of works' and the 'References and further reading' have been annotated with a brief description of the content so that their relevance to readers' interests can be quickly assessed.

EDITORIAL STYLE

Spelling and punctuation in the *Encyclopedia* have been standardized to follow British English usage.

Transliteration and naming conventions

All names and terms from non-roman alphabets have been romanized in the *Encyclopedia*. Foreign names have been given according to the conventions within the particular language.

Arabic

Arabic has been transliterated in a simplified form, that is, without macrons or subscripts. Names of philosophers are given in their Arabic form rather than their Latinate form, for example, IBN RUSHD rather than AVERROES. Arabic names beginning with the prefix 'al-' are alphabetized under the substantive part of the name and not the prefix, for example:

> KILWARDBY, ROBERT (d. 1279)
> AL-KINDI, ABU YUSUF YAQUB IBN ISHAQ (d. *c.*866–73)
> KNOWLEDGE AND JUSTIFICATION, COHERENCE THEORY OF

Arabic names beginning with the prefix 'Ibn' are alphabetized under 'I'.

Chinese, Korean and Japanese

Chinese has been transliterated using the Pinyin system. Dummy titles in the older Wade–Giles system are given for names and key terms; these direct the reader to the Pinyin titles.

Japanese has been transliterated using a modified version of the Hepburn system.

Chinese, Japanese and Korean names are given in Asian form, that is, surname preceding forenames, for example:

> WANG FUZHI
> NISHITANI KEIJI

The exception is where an author has chosen to present their own name in conventional Western form.

Hebrew

Hebrew has been transliterated in a simplified form, that is, without macrons or subscripts.

Russian

Cyrillic characters have been transliterated using the Library of Congress system. Russian names are usually given with their patronymic, for example, BAKUNIN, MIKHAIL ALEKSANDROVICH.

Sanskrit

A guide to the pronunciation of Sanskrit can be found in the INDIAN AND TIBETAN PHILOSOPHY signpost entry.

Tibetan

Tibetan has been transliterated using the Wylie system. Dummy titles in the Virginia system are given for names and key terms. A guide to Tibetan pronunciation can be found in the INDIAN AND TIBETAN PHILOSOPHY signpost entry.

European names

Names beginning with the prefixes 'de', 'von' or 'van' are usually alphabetized under the substantive part of the name. For example:

BEAUVOIR, SIMONE DE
HUMBOLDT, WILHELM VON

The exception to this rule is when the person is either a national of or has spent some time living or working in an English-speaking country. For example:

DE MORGAN, AUGUSTUS
VON WRIGHT, GEORG HENRIK

Names beginning with the prefix 'de la' or 'le' are alphabetized under the prefix 'la' or 'le'. For example:

LA FORGE, LOUIS DE
LE DOEUFF, MICHÈLE

Names beginning with 'Mc' or 'Mac' are treated as 'Mac' and appear before Ma.

Historical names

Medieval and Renaissance names where a person is not usually known by a surname are alphabetized under the forename, for example:

GILES OF ROME
JOHN OF SALISBURY

List of entries

Below is a complete list of entries in the order in which they appear in the *Routledge Encyclopedia of Philosophy*.

A posteriori
A priori
'Abduh, Muhammad
Abelard, Peter
Aberdeen Philosophical Society
Abhinavagupta
Abravanel, Isaac
Abravanel, Judah ben Isaac
Absolute, the
Absolutism
Abstract objects
Academy
Action
Adorno, Theodor Wiesengrund
Adverbs
Aenesidemus
Aesthetic attitude
Aesthetic concepts
Aesthetics
Aesthetics, African
Aesthetics and ethics
Aesthetics, Chinese
Aesthetics in Islamic philosophy
Aesthetics, Japanese
Affirmative action
al-Afghani, Jamal al-Din
African philosophy
African philosophy, anglophone
African philosophy, francophone
African traditional religions
Agnosticism
Agricola, Rudolph
Agricultural ethics
Agrippa
Agrippa von Nettesheim, Henricus
  Cornelius
Ailly, Pierre d'
Ajdukiewicz, Kazimierz
Akan philosophical psychology
Akrasia
Albert of Saxony
Albert the Great
Albo, Joseph
Alchemy

Alcinous
Alcmaeon
Alemanno, Yohanan ben Isaac
D'Alembert, Jean Le Rond
Alexander, Samuel
Alexander of Aphrodisias
Alexander of Hales
Alienation
Alighieri, Dante
Alison, Archibald
Alterity and identity, postmodern
  theories of
Althusser, Louis Pierre
Ambedkar, Bimrao Ramji
Ambiguity
American philosophy in the 18th and
  19th centuries
al-'Amiri, Abu'l Hasan Muhammad
  ibn Yusuf
Ammonius, son of Hermeas
Amo, Anton Wilhelm
Analysis, nonstandard
Analysis, philosophical issues in
Analytic ethics
Analytical philosophy
Analytical philosophy in Latin
  America
Analyticity
Anaphora
Anarchism
Anaxagoras
Anaxarchus
Anaximander
Anaximenes
Ancient philosophy
Anderson, John
Animal language and thought
Animals and ethics
Anomalous monism
Anscombe, Gertrude Elizabeth
  Margaret
Anselm of Canterbury
Anthropology, philosophy of
Antiochus

Antiphon
Anti-positivist thought in Latin
  America
Antirealism in the philosophy of
  mathematics
Anti-Semitism
Antisthenes
Applied ethics
Apuleius
Aquinas, Thomas
Arama, Isaac ben Moses
Arcesilaus
Archaeology, philosophy of
Archē
Architecture, aesthetics of
Archytas
Arendt, Hannah
Aretē
Argentina, philosophy in
Aristippus the Elder
Ariston of Chios
Aristotelianism in Islamic
  philosophy
Aristotelianism in the 17th century
Aristotelianism, medieval
Aristotelianism, Renaissance
Aristotle
Aristotle commentators
Arithmetic, philosophical issues in
Armstrong, David Malet
Arnauld, Antoine
Art, abstract
Art and morality
Art and truth
Art criticism
Art, definition of
Art, performing
Art, understanding of
Art, value of
Art works, ontology of
Artificial intelligence
Artistic expression
Artistic forgery
Artistic interpretation

Artistic style
Artistic taste
Artist's intention
Arya Samaj
Asceticism
Ash'ariyya and Mu'tazila
Asmus, Valentin Ferdinandovich
Astell, Mary
Atheism
Atomism, ancient
Atonement
Augustine
Augustinianism
Aureol, Peter
Aurobindo Ghose
Austin, John
Austin, John Langshaw
Australia, philosophy in
Authority
Autonomy, ethical
Avenarius, Richard
Averroism
Averroism, Jewish
Awakening of Faith in Mahāyāna
Awareness in Indian thought
Axiology
Axiom of choice
Ayer, Alfred Jules
Bachelard, Gaston
Bacon, Francis
Bacon, Roger
al-Baghdadi, Abu'l-Barakat
Bakhtin, Mikhail Mikhailovich
Bakunin, Mikhail Aleksandrovich
Báñez, Domingo
Bar Hayya, Abraham
Barth, Karl
Barthes, Roland
Bartolus of Sassoferrato (or
    Saxoferrato)
Bataille, Georges
Baudrillard, Jean
Bauer, Bruno
Baumgardt, David
Baumgarten, Alexander Gottlieb
Bayle, Pierre
Beattie, James
Beauty
Beauvoir, Simone de
Beck, Jacob Sigismund
Behaviourism, analytic
Behaviourism in the social sciences
Behaviourism, methodological and
    scientific
Being

Belief
Belief and knowledge
Belinskii, Vissarion Grigorievich
Bell's theorem
Benjamin, Walter
Bentham, Jeremy
Bentley, Richard
Berdiaev, Nikolai Aleksandrovich
Bergson, Henri-Louis
Berkeley, George
Berlin, Isaiah
Bernard of Clairvaux
Bernard of Tours
Bernier, François
Bernstein, Eduard
Beth's theorem and Craig's theorem
Bhartṛhari
Bible, Hebrew
Biel, Gabriel
Bioethics
Bioethics, Jewish
Blackstone, William
Blair, Hugh
Blanchot, Maurice
Blasius of Parma
Bloch, Ernst Simon
Bobbio, Norberto
Bodily sensations
Bodin, Jean
Boehme, Jakob
Boethius, Anicius Manlius Severinus
Boethius of Dacia
Bogdanov, Aleksandr
    Aleksandrovich
Bohr, Niels
Bold, Samuel
Bolzano, Bernard
Bonaventure
Bonhoeffer, Dietrich
Bonnet, Charles
Boole, George
Boolean algebra
Bosanquet, Bernard
Bourdieu, Pierre
Boutroux, Emile
Bowne, Borden Parker
Boyle, Robert
Bradley, Francis Herbert
Bradwardine, Thomas
Brahman
Brahmo Samaj
Brazil, philosophy in
Brentano, Franz Clemens
Bridgman, Percy William
Brinkley, Richard

Brito, Radulphus
Broad, Charlie Dunbar
Brown, Thomas
Browne, Peter
Brunner, Emil
Bruno, Giordano
Brunschvicg, Léon
Bryce, James
Buber, Martin
Büchner, Friedrich Karl Christian
    Ludwig (Louis)
Buddha
Buddhism, Ābhidharmika schools of
Buddhism, Mādhyamika: India and
    Tibet
Buddhism, Yogācāra school of
Buddhist concept of emptiness
Buddhist philosophy, Chinese
Buddhist philosophy, Indian
Buddhist philosophy, Japanese
Buddhist philosophy, Korean
Buffier, Claude
Buffon, Georges Louis Leclerc,
    Comte de
Bulgakov, Sergei Nikolaevich
Bultmann, Rudolf
Buridan, John
Burke, Edmund
Burley, Walter
Burthogge, Richard
Bushi philosophy
Business ethics
Butler, Joseph
Byzantine philosophy
Cabanis, Pierre-Jean
Cabral, Amílcar
Cajetan (Thomas de Vio)
Calcidius
Callicles
Calvin, John
Cambridge Platonism
Campanella, Tommaso
Campbell, George
Campbell, Norman Robert
Camus, Albert
Cantor, Georg
Cantor's theorem
Capreolus, Johannes
Cardano, Girolamo
Carlyle, Thomas
Carmichael, Gershom
Carnap, Rudolf
Carneades
Carolingian renaissance
Cassirer, Ernst

Casuistry
Categories
Category theory, applications to the foundations of mathematics
Category theory, introduction to
Cattaneo, Carlo
Causality and necessity in Islamic thought
Causation
Causation, Indian theories of
Cavell, Stanley
Cavendish, Margaret Lucas
Celsus
Certainty
Certeau, Michel de
Chaadaev, Pëtr Iakovlevich
Chaldaean Oracles
Change
Chaos theory
Charity
Charity, principle of
Charleton, Walter
Charron, Pierre
Chartres, School of
Chatton, Walter
Chemistry, philosophical aspects of
Cheng
Cheng Hao
Cheng Yi
Chernyshevskii, Nikolai Gavrilovich
Chillingworth, William
Chinese classics
Chinese philosophy
Chinese Room Argument
Chinul
Chisholm, Roderick Milton
Chomsky, Noam
Chŏng Yagyong
Christine de Pizan
Chrysippus
Church, Alonzo
Church's theorem and the decision problem
Church's thesis
Cicero, Marcus Tullius
Cieszkowski, August von
Citizenship
Civil disobedience
Civil society
Cixous, Hélène
Clandestine literature
Clarembald of Arras
Clarke, Samuel
Clauberg, Johannes
Cleanthes

Clement of Alexandria
Cleomedes
Cockburn, Catharine
Coercion
Cognition, infant
Cognitive architecture
Cognitive development
Cognitive pluralism
Cohen, Hermann
Coleridge, Samuel Taylor
Collegium Conimbricense
Collier, Arthur
Collingwood, Robin George
Collins, Anthony
Colour and qualia
Colour, theories of
Combinatory logic
Comedy
Comenius, John Amos
Common Law
Common Sense School
Common-sense ethics
Common-sense reasoning, theories of
Commonsensism
Communication and intention
Communicative rationality
Communism
Community and communitarianism
Complexity, computational
Compositionality
Computability and information
Computability theory
Computer science
Comte, Isidore-Auguste-Marie-François-Xavier
Concepts
Conceptual analysis
Condillac, Etienne Bonnot de
Condorcet, Marie-Jean-Antoine-Nicolas Caritat de
Confirmation theory
Confucian philosophy, Chinese
Confucian philosophy, Japanese
Confucian philosophy, Korean
Confucius
Connectionism
Conscience
Consciousness
Consent
Consequence, conceptions of
Consequentialism
Conservation principles
Conservatism
Constant de Rebeque, Henri-Benjamin

Constitutionalism
Constructible universe
Constructivism
Constructivism in ethics
Constructivism in mathematics
Content, indexical
Content, non-conceptual
Content: wide and narrow
Contextualism, epistemological
Contingency
Continuants
Continuum hypothesis
Contractarianism
Conventionalism
Conway, Anne
Copernicus, Nicolaus
Cordemoy, Géraud de
Corruption
Cosmology
Cosmology and cosmogony, Indian theories of
Counterfactual conditionals
Cournot, Antoine Augustin
Cousin, Victor
Crathorn, William
Cratylus
Creation and conservation, religious doctrine of
Crescas, Hasdai
Crime and punishment
Criteria
Critical legal studies
Critical realism
Critical theory
Croce, Benedetto
Crucial experiments
Crusius, Christian August
Cudworth, Ralph
Cultural identity
Culture
Culverwell, Nathaniel
Cumberland, Richard
Cynics
Cyrenaics
Czech Republic, philosophy in
Dai Zhen
Damascius
Damian, Peter
Dance, aesthetics of
Dao
Daodejing
Daoist philosophy
Darwin, Charles Robert
David of Dinant
Davidson, Donald

al-Dawani, Jalal al-Din
Daxue
De
De Man, Paul
De Morgan, Augustus
De re/de dicto
Death
Decision and game theory
Deconstruction
Dedekind, Julius Wilhelm Richard
Deductive closure principle
Definition
Definition, Indian concepts of
Deism
Deleuze, Gilles
Delmedigo, Elijah
Demarcation problem
Democracy
Democritus
Demonstratives and indexicals
Dennett, Daniel Clement
Denys the Carthusian
Deontic logic
Deontological ethics
Depiction
Derrida, Jacques
Descartes, René
Descriptions
Desert and merit
Desgabets, Robert
Desire
Determinism and indeterminism
Development ethics
Dewey, John
Dharmakīrti
Dialectical materialism
Dialectical school
Dialogical logic
Dicey, Albert Venn
Diderot, Denis
Dietrich of Freiberg
Digby, Kenelm
Dignāga
Dilthey, Wilhelm
Diodorus Cronus
Diogenes Laertius
Diogenes of Apollonia
Diogenes of Oenoanda
Diogenes of Sinope
Discourse semantics
Discovery, logic of
Discrimination
Dissoi logoi
Dodgson, Charles Lutwidge (Lewis Carroll)

Dōgen
Dong Zhongshu
Dooyeweerd, Herman
Dostoevskii, Fëdor Mikhailovich
Double effect, principle of
Doubt
Doxography
Dreaming
Du Bois-Reymond, Emil
Du Châtelet-Lomont, Gabrielle-Émilie
Dualism
Ducasse, Curt John
Duhem, Pierre Maurice Marie
Dühring, Eugen Karl
Dummett, Michael Anthony Eardley
Duns Scotus, John
Duran, Profiat
Duran, Simeon ben Tzemach
Durandus of St Pourçain
Durkheim, Emile
Duty
Duty and virtue, Indian conceptions of
Dworkin, Ronald
Dynamic logics
East Asian philosophy
Eberhard, Johann August
Ecological philosophy
Ecology
Economics and ethics
Economics, philosophy of
Education, history of philosophy of
Education, philosophy of
Edwards, Jonathan
Egoism and altruism
Egyptian cosmology, ancient
Egyptian philosophy: influence on ancient Greek thought
Einstein, Albert
Electrodynamics
Eliade, Mircea
Eliminativism
Eliot, George
Elisabeth of Bohemia
Emerson, Ralph Waldo
Emotion in response to art
Emotions, nature of
Emotions, philosophy of
Emotive meaning
Emotivism
Empedocles
Empiricism
Encyclopedists, eighteenth-century
Encyclopedists, medieval

Engels, Friedrich
Engineering and ethics
Enlightenment, continental
Enlightenment, Jewish
Enlightenment, Russian
Enlightenment, Scottish
Enthusiasm
Environmental ethics
Epicharmus
Epictetus
Epicureanism
Epicurus
Epiphenomenalism
Epistemic logic
Epistemic relativism
Epistemology
Epistemology and ethics
Epistemology, history of
Epistemology in Islamic philosophy
Epistemology, Indian schools of
Equality
Erasmus, Desiderius
Eriugena, Johannes Scottus
Erotic art
Error and illusion, Indian conceptions of
Eschatology
Essentialism
Eternity
Eternity of the world, medieval views of
Ethical systems, African
Ethics
Ethics in Islamic philosophy
Ethiopia, philosophy in
Ethnophilosophy, African
Eudaimonia
Eudoxus
Eurasian movement
Eusebius
Evans, Gareth
Events
Evil
Evil, problem of
Evolution and ethics
Evolution, theory of
Evolutionary theory and social science
Examples in ethics
Existence
Existentialism
Existentialist ethics
Existentialist theology
Existentialist thought in Latin America

Experiment
Experiments in social science
Explanation
Explanation in history and social
  science
Fa
Fackenheim, Emil Ludwig
Facts
Fact/value distinction
Faith
Fallacies
Fallibilism
Family, ethics and the
Fanon, Frantz
al-Farabi, Abu Nasr
Fardella, Michelangelo
Farrer, Austin Marsden
Fascism
Fatalism
Fatalism, Indian
Fazang
Fechner, Gustav Theodor
Federalism and confederalism
Fëdorov, Nikolai Fëdorovich
Feminism
Feminism and psychoanalysis
Feminism and social science
Feminist aesthetics
Feminist epistemology
Feminist ethics
Feminist jurisprudence
Feminist literary criticism
Feminist political philosophy
Feminist theology
Feminist thought in Latin America
Fénelon, François de Salignac de la
  Mothe
Ferguson, Adam
Ferrier, James Frederick
Feuerbach, Ludwig Andreas
Feyerabend, Paul Karl
Fichte, Johann Gottlieb
Ficino, Marsilio
Fiction, semantics of
Fictional entities
Fictionalism
Field theory, classical
Field theory, quantum
Film, aesthetics of
Filmer, Sir Robert
Florenskii, Pavel Aleksandrovich
Fludd, Robert
Fodor, Jerry Alan
Folk psychology
Fonseca, Pedro da

Fontenelle, Bernard de
Forcing
Forgiveness and mercy
Formal and informal logic
Formal languages and systems
Formalism in art
Foucault, Michel
Foucher, Simon
Foundationalism
Francis of Meyronnes
Frank, Jerome
Frank, Semën Liudvigovich
Frankfurt School
Franklin, Benjamin
Free logics
Free logics, philosophical issues in
Free will
Freedom and liberty
Freedom, divine
Freedom of speech
Frege, Gottlob
Frei, Hans
French philosophy of science
Freud, Sigmund
Friendship
Fries, Jacob Friedrich
Fujiwara Seika
Fuller, Lon Louvois
Functional explanation
Functionalism
Functionalism in social science
Future generations, obligations to
Fuzzy logic
Gadādhara
Gadamer, Hans-Georg
Gaius
Galen
Galilei, Galileo
Gandhi, Mohandas Karamchand
Gaṅgeśa
Garrigou-Lagrange, Réginald
Gassendi, Pierre
Gaudīya Vaiṣṇavism
Gautama, Akṣapāda
Gender and science
Genealogy
General relativity, philosophical
  responses to
General will
Genetics
Genetics and ethics
Gentile, Giovanni
Gentzen, Gerhard Karl Erich
Geology, philosophy of
Geometry, philosophical issues in

George of Trebizond
Gerard, Alexander
Gerard of Cremona
Gerard of Odo
Gerbert of Aurillac
Gerdil, Giancinto Sigismondo
German idealism
Gerson, Jean
Gersonides
Gestalt psychology
Gettier problems
Geulincx, Arnold
al-Ghazali, Abu Hamid
Gilbert of Poitiers
Giles of Rome
Gioberti, Vincenzo
Glanvill, Joseph
Gnosticism
God, arguments for the existence of
God, concepts of
God, Indian conceptions of
Gödel, Kurt
Gödel's theorems
Godfrey of Fontaines
Godwin, William
Goethe, Johann Wolfgang von
Good, theories of the
Goodman, Nelson
Goodness, perfect
Gorgias
Grace
Gramsci, Antonio
Greek philosophy: impact on Islamic
  philosophy
Green political philosophy
Green, Thomas Hill
Gregory of Rimini
Grice, Herbert Paul
Grosseteste, Robert
Grote, John
Grotius, Hugo
Guanzi
Gurney, Edmund
Ha'am, Ahad
Habermas, Jürgen
Haeckel, Ernst Heinrich
Hägerström, Axel Anders Theodor
Halakhah
Halevi, Judah
Hamann, Johann Georg
Hamilton, William
Han Feizi
Han Wŏnjin
Han Yu
Hanslick, Eduard

Hanson, Norwood Russell
Happiness
Hare, Richard Mervyn
Harrington, James
Hart, Herbert Lionel Adolphus
Hartley, David
Hartmann, Karl Robert Eduard von
Hartmann, Nicolai
Hasidism
Hayek, Friedrich August von
Heaven
Heaven, Indian conceptions of
Hedonism
Hegel, Georg Wilhelm Friedrich
Hegelianism
Hegelianism, Russian
Heidegger, Martin
Heideggerian philosophy of science
Heisenberg, Werner
Hell
Hellenistic medical epistemology
Hellenistic philosophy
Helmholtz, Hermann von
Helmont, Franciscus Mercurius van
Help and beneficence
Helvétius, Claude-Adrien
Hempel, Carl Gustav
Henricus Regius
Henry of Ghent
Henry of Harclay
Heraclides of Pontus
Heraclitus
Herbart, Johann Friedrich
Herbert Edward (Baron Herbert of
    Cherbury)
Herbrand's theorem
Herder, Johann Gottfried
Hermeneutics
Hermeneutics, Biblical
Hermetism
Herrera, Abraham Cohen de
Hertz, Heinrich Rudolf
Hervaeus Natalis
Herzen, Aleksandr Ivanovich
Heschel, Abraham Joshua
Hesiod
Hess, Moses
Hessen, Sergei Iosifovich
Heytesbury, William
Hierocles
Hilbert's Programme and
    Formalism
Hildegard of Bingen
Hillel ben Samuel of Verona
Hindu philosophy

Hippias
Hippocratic medicine
Historicism
History, Chinese theories of
History, philosophy of
Hobbes, Thomas
Hohfeld, Wesley Newcomb
Holcot, Robert
Hölderlin, Johann Christian
    Friedrich
Holism and individualism in history
    and social science
Holism: mental and semantic
Holmes, Oliver Wendell, Jr
Holocaust, the
Home, Henry (Lord Kames)
Homer
Honour
Hooker, Richard
Hope
Horkheimer, Max
Huainanzi
Huet, Pierre-Daniel
Hugh of St Victor
Human nature
Human nature, science of, in the
    18th century
Humanism
Humanism, Renaissance
Humboldt, Wilhelm von
Hume, David
Humour
Hungary, philosophy in
Hus, Jan
Husserl, Edmund
Hutcheson, Francis
Huxley, Thomas Henry
Hypatia
Iamblichus
Ibn 'Adi, Yahya
Ibn al-'Arabi, Muhyi al-Din
Ibn ar-Rawandi
Ibn Bajja, Abu Bakr Muhammad
    ibn Yahya ibn as-Say'igh
Ibn Daud, Abraham
Ibn Ezra, Abraham
Ibn Ezra, Moses ben Jacob
Ibn Falaquera, Shem Tov
Ibn Gabirol, Solomon
Ibn Hazm, Abu Muhammad 'Ali
Ibn Kammuna
Ibn Khaldun, 'Abd al-Rahman
Ibn Massara, Muhammad ibn 'Abd
    Allah
Ibn Miskawayh, Ahmad ibn

Muhammad
Ibn Paquda, Bahya
Ibn Rushd, Abu'l Walid Muhammad
Ibn Sab'in, Muhammad ibn 'Abd al-
    Haqq
Ibn Sina, Abu 'Ali al-Husayn
Ibn Taymiyya, Taqi al-Din
Ibn Tufayl, Abu Bakr Muhammad
Ibn Tzaddik, Joseph ben Jacob
Idealism
Idealizations
Ideals
Identity
Identity of indiscernibles
Ideology
Ikhwan Al-Safa'
Il'enkov, Eval'd Vasil'evich
Il'in, Ivan Aleksandrovich
Illuminati
Illumination
Illuminationist philosophy
Imagery
Imagination
Immanuel ben Solomon of Rome
Immutability
Impartiality
Imperative logic
Implicature
Incarnation and Christology
Incommensurability
Indian and Tibetan philosophy
Indicative conditionals
Indirect discourse
Induction, epistemic issues in
Inductive definitions and proofs
Inductive inference
Inference, Indian theories of
Inference to the best explanation
Infinitary logics
Infinity
Information technology and ethics
Information theory
Information theory and
    epistemology
Ingarden, Roman Witold
Inge, William Ralph
Innate knowledge
Innocence
Institutionalism in law
Intensional entities
Intensional logics
Intensionality
Intention
Intentionality
Internalism and externalism in

epistemology
International relations, philosophy of
Interpretation, Indian theories of
Introspection, epistemology of
Introspection, psychology of
Intuitionism
Intuitionism in ethics
Intuitionistic logic and antirealism
Iqbal, Muhammad
Irigaray, Luce
Isaac of Stella
Islam, concept of philosophy in
Islamic fundamentalism
Islamic philosophy
Islamic philosophy, modern
Islamic philosophy: transmission
  into Western Europe
Islamic theology
Israeli, Isaac Ben Solomon
Italy, philosophy in
Itō Jinsai
Jacobi, Friedrich Heinrich
Jaina philosophy
James of Viterbo
James, William
Japanese philosophy
Jaspers, Karl
Jefferson, Thomas
Jewish philosophy
Jewish philosophy, contemporary
Jewish philosophy in the early 19th
  century
Jhering, Rudolf von
Jia Yi
Joachim of Fiore
John of Damascus
John of Jandun
John of La Rochelle
John of Mirecourt
John of Paris
John of Salisbury
John of St Thomas
Johnson, Alexander Bryan
Johnson, Dr Samuel
Johnson, Samuel
Journalism, ethics of
Judah ben Moses of Rome
Jung, Carl Gustav
Jungius, Joachim
Jurisprudence, historical
Justice
Justice, equity and law
Justice, international
Justification, epistemic
Justification, religious

Justinian
al-Juwayni, Abu'l Ma'ali
Kabbalah
Kaibara Ekken
Kant, Immanuel
Kantian ethics
Kaplan, Mordecai
Karaism
Karma and rebirth, Indian
  conceptions of
Katharsis
Kauṭilya
Kautsky, Karl Johann
Keckermann, Bartholomew
Kelsen, Hans
Kemp Smith, Norman
Kepler, Johannes
Keynes, John Maynard
Kierkegaard, Søren Aabye
Kilvington, Richard
Kilwardby, Robert
al-Kindi, Abu Yusuf Ya'qub ibn
  Ishaq
Knowledge and justification,
  coherence theory of
Knowledge by acquaintance and
  description
Knowledge, causal theory of
Knowledge, concept of
Knowledge, defeasibility theory of
Knowledge, Indian views of
Knowledge, tacit
Knutzen, Martin
Kojève, Alexandre
Kokoro
Kotarbiński, Tadeusz
Koyré, Alexandre
Krause, Karl Christian Friedrich
Kripke, Saul Aaron
Kristeva, Julia
Krochmal, Nachman
Kronecker, Leopold
Kropotkin, Pëtr Alekseevich
Kuhn, Thomas Samuel
Kūkai
Kuki Shūzō
Kumazawa Banzan
Kyoto school
La Forge, Louis de
La Mettrie, Julien Offroy de
Labriola, Antonio
Lacan, Jacques
Lachelier, Jules
Lacoue-Labarthe, Philippe
Lakatos, Imre

Lambda calculus
Lambert, Johann Heinrich
Lange, Friedrich Albert
Langer, Susanne Katherina Knauth
Language, ancient philosophy of
Language and gender
Language, conventionality of
Language, early modern
  philosophy of
Language, Indian theories of
Language, innateness of
Language, medieval theories of
Language of thought
Language, philosophy of
Language, Renaissance
  philosophy of
Language, social nature of
Lassalle, Ferdinand
Latin America, colonial thought in
Latin America, philosophy in
Latin America, pre-Columbian and
  indigenous thought in
Latitudinarianism
Lavrov, Pëtr Lavrovich
Law and morality
Law and ritual in Chinese
  philosophy
Law, economic approach to
Law, Islamic philosophy of
Law, limits of
Law, philosophy of
Law, William
Laws, natural
Le Clerc, Jean
Le Doeuff, Michèle
Le Grand, Antoine
Le Roy, Edouard Louis Emmanuel
  Julien
Learning
Lebensphilosophie
Lefebvre, Henri
Legal concepts
Legal discourse
Legal evidence and inference
Legal hermeneutics
Legal idealism
Legal positivism
Legal realism
Legal reasoning and interpretation
Legalist philosophy, Chinese
Legitimacy
Leibniz, Gottfried Wilhelm
Leibowitz, Yeshayahu
Lenin, Vladimir Il'ich
Leont'ev, Konstantin Nikolaevich

Leśniewski, Stanisław
Lessing, Gotthold Ephraim
Leucippus
Levinas, Emmanuel
Lévi-Strauss, Claude
Lewis, Clarence Irving
Lewis, Clive Staples
Lewis, David Kellogg
Li
Liber de causis
Liberalism
Liberalism, Russian
Liberation philosophy
Liberation theology
Libertarianism
Libertins
Lichtenberg, Georg Christoph
Life and death
Life, meaning of
Life, origin of
Limbo
Linear logic
Linguistic discrimination
Linji
Linnaeus, Carl von
Lipsius, Justus
Literature, philosophy in Latin American
Literature, philosophy in modern Japanese
Llewellyn, Karl Nickerson
Llull, Ramon
Locke, John
Logic, ancient
Logic in China
Logic in Islamic philosophy
Logic in Japan
Logic in the 17th and 18th centuries
Logic in the 19th century
Logic in the early 20th century
Logic machines and diagrams
Logic, medieval
Logic of ethical discourse
Logic, philosophy of
Logic, Renaissance
Logical atomism
Logical constants
Logical form
Logical laws
Logical positivism
Logical and mathematical terms, glossary of
Logicism
Logos
Loisy, Alfred

Lombard, Peter
Lonergan, Bernard Joseph Francis
Lorenzen, Paul
Losev, Aleksei Fëdorovich
Lossky, Nicholas Onufrievich
Lotze, Rudolf Hermann
Love
Löwenheim-Skolem theorems and non-standard models
Lu Xiangshan
Lucian
Lucretius
Lukács, Georg
Łukasiewicz, Jan
Lushi chunqiu
Luther, Martin
Luxemburg, Rosa
Lyotard, Jean-François
Mach, Ernst
Machiavelli, Niccolò
MacIntyre, Alasdair
McTaggart, John McTaggart Ellis
Mādhava
Madhva
Mahāvīra
Maimon, Salomon
Maimonides, Abraham ben Moses
Maimonides, Moses
Maine de Biran, Pierre-François
Major, John
Malebranche, Nicolas
Mamardashvili, Merab Konstantinovich
Mandeville, Bernard
Manicheism
Manifoldness, Jaina theory of
Many-valued logics
Many-valued logics, philosophical issues in
Marcel, Gabriel
Marcus Aurelius
Marcuse, Herbert
Marginality
Maritain, Jacques
Marius Victorinus
Market, ethics of the
Marsilius of Inghen
Marsilius of Padua
Marston, Roger
Martineau, Harriet
Marx, Karl
Marxism, Chinese
Marxism, Western
Marxist philosophy of science
Marxist philosophy, Russian and

Soviet
Marxist thought in Latin America
Masaryk, Thomáš Garrigue
Masham, Damaris
Mass terms
Materialism
Materialism in the philosophy of mind
Materialism, Indian school of
Mathematics, foundations of
Matter
Matter, Indian conceptions of
Matthew of Aquasparta
Mauthner, Fritz
Maxwell, James Clerk
Mead, George Herbert
Meaning and communication
Meaning and rule-following
Meaning and truth
Meaning and understanding
Meaning and verification
Meaning in Islamic philosophy
Meaning, Indian theories of
Measurement, theory of
Mechanics, Aristotelian
Mechanics, classical
Medical ethics
Medicine, philosophy of
Medieval philosophy
Medieval philosophy, Russian
Megarian School
Meinecke, Friedrich
Meinong, Alexius
Meister Eckhart
Melanchthon, Philipp
Melissus
Memory
Memory, epistemology of
Mencius
Mendelssohn, Moses
Mental causation
Mental illness, concept of
Mental states, adverbial theory of
Mereology
Merleau-Ponty, Maurice
Mersenne, Marin
Messer Leon, Judah
Metaphor
Metaphysics
Methodological individualism
Mexico, philosophy in
Meyerson, Emile
Mi bskyod rdo rje
Midrash
Mikhailovskii, Nikolai

Konstantinovich Miki Kiyoshi
Mill, James
Mill, John Stuart
Millar, John
Mīmāṃsā
Mimēsis
Mind, bundle theory of
Mind, child's theory of
Mind, computational theories of
Mind, identity theory of
Mind, Indian philosophy of
Mind, philosophy of
Mir Damad, Muhammad Baqir
Miracles
mKhas grub dge legs dpal bzang po
Modal logic
Modal logic, philosophical issues in
Modal operators
Model theory
Models
Modernism
Modularity of mind
Mohist philosophy
Molecular biology
Molina, Luis de
Molinism
Molyneux problem
Momentariness, Buddhist doctrine of
Monboddo, Lord (James Burnett)
Monism
Monism, Indian
Monotheism
Montague, Richard Merett
Montaigne, Michel Eyquem de
Montesquieu, Charles Louis de Secondat
Moore, George Edward
Moral agents
Moral development
Moral education
Moral expertise
Moral judgment
Moral justification
Moral knowledge
Moral luck
Moral motivation
Moral particularism
Moral pluralism
Moral psychology
Moral realism
Moral relativism
Moral scepticism
Moral sense theories
Moral sentiments

Moral standing
Moralistes
Morality and emotions
Morality and ethics
Morality and identity
More, Henry
Moscow-Tartu School
Motoori Norinaga
Mozi
Mujō
Mulla Sadra (Sadr al-Din Muhammad al-Shirazi)
Multiculturalism
Multiple-conclusion logic
al-Muqammas, Daud
Music, aesthetics of
Musonius Rufus
Mystical philosophy in Islam
Mysticism, history of
Mysticism, nature of
Næss, Arne
Nāgārjuna
Nagel, Ernest
Nagel, Thomas
Nahmanides, Moses
Nancy, Jean-Luc
Narrative
Nation and nationalism
Native American philosophy
Nativism
Natural deduction, tableau and sequent systems
Natural kinds
Natural Law
Natural philosophy, medieval
Natural theology
Naturalism in ethics
Naturalism in social science
Naturalized epistemology
Naturalized philosophy of science
Nature, aesthetic appreciation of
Nature and convention
Naturphilosophie
Necessary being
Necessary truth and convention
Neckham, Alexander
Needs and interests
Negative facts in classical Indian philosophy
Negative theology
Nemesius
Neo-Confucian philosophy
Neo-Kantianism
Neo-Kantianism, Russian
Neoplatonism

Neoplatonism in Islamic philosophy
Neo-Pythagoreanism
Neumann, John von
Neurath, Otto
Neutral monism
Neutrality, political
Newman, John Henry
Newton, Isaac
Nichiren
Nicholas of Autrecourt
Nicholas of Cusa
Niebuhr, Helmut Richard
Niebuhr, Reinhold
Nietzsche, Friedrich
Nietzsche, impact on Russian thought
Nifo, Agostino
Nihilism
Nihilism, Russian
Nirvāṇa
Nishi Amane
Nishida Kitarō
Nishitani Keiji
Nominalism
Nominalism, Buddhist doctrine of
Non-constructive rules of inference
Non-monotonic logic
Normative epistemology
Norms, legal
Norris, John
Nous
Nozick, Robert
Numbers
Numenius
Nursing ethics
Nyāya-Vaiśeṣika
Nygren, Anders
Oakeshott, Michael Joseph
Objectivity
Obligation, political
Observation
Occasionalism
Ogyū Sorai
Oken, Lorenz
Olivecrona, Karl
Olivi, Peter John
Oman, John Wood
Omnipotence
Omnipresence
Omniscience
Ontological commitment
Ontology
Ontology in Indian philosophy
Opera, aesthetics of
Operationalism

Optics
Ordinal logics
Ordinary language philosophy
Ordinary language philosophy,
    school of
Oresme, Nicole
Orientalism and Islamic philosophy
Origen
Orphism
Ortega y Gasset, José
Oswald, James
Other minds
Otto, Rudolf
Overton, Richard
Owen, Gwilym Ellis Lane
Oxford Calculators
Paine, Thomas
Paley, William
Panaetius
Pan-Africanism
Panpsychism
Pan-Slavism
Pantheism
Paracelsus (Philippus Aureolus
    Theophrastus Bombastus von
    Hohenheim)
Paraconsistent logic
Paradoxes, epistemic
Paradoxes of set and property
Paranormal phenomena
Parapsychology
Pareto principle
Parmenides
Particulars
Partiinost'
Pascal, Blaise
Passmore, John Arthur
Patañjali
Paternalism
Patočka, Jan
Patristic philosophy
Patrizi da Cherso, Francesco
Paul of Venice
Pecham, John
Peirce, Charles Sanders
Pelagianism
Perception
Perception, epistemic issues in
Perfectionism
Performatives
Peripatetics
Personal identity
Personalism
Persons
Peter of Auvergne

Peter of Spain
Petrarca, Francesco
Petrażycki, Leon
Phenomenalism
Phenomenological movement
Phenomenology, epistemic issues in
Phenomenology in Latin America
Phenomenology of religion
Philip the Chancellor
Philo of Alexandria
Philo of Larissa
Philo the Dialectician
Philodemus
Philolaus
Philoponus
Photography, aesthetics of
Physis and nomos
Piaget, Jean
Pico della Mirandola, Giovanni
Pietism
Planck, Max Karl Ernst Ludwig
Platform Sutra
Plato
Platonism, Early and Middle
Platonism in Islamic philosophy
Platonism, medieval
Platonism, Renaissance
Pleasure
Plekhanov, Georgii Valentinovich
Plotinus
Pluralism
Plutarch of Chaeronea
Pneuma
Poetry
Poincaré, Jules Henri
Poland, philosophy in
Polanyi, Michael
Polish logic
Political philosophy
Political philosophy, history of
Political philosophy in classical
    Islam
Political philosophy, Indian
Political philosophy, nature of
Pomponazzi, Pietro
Popper, Karl Raimund
Population and ethics
Pornography
Porphyry
Port-Royal
Posidonius
Positivism in the social sciences
Positivism, Russian
Positivist thought in Latin America
Possible worlds

Post, Emil Leon
Postcolonial philosophy of science
Postcolonialism
Postmodern theology
Postmodernism
Postmodernism and political
    philosophy
Postmodernism, French critics of
Post-structuralism
Post-structuralism in the social
    sciences
Potentiality, Indian theories of
Pothier, Robert Joseph
Pound, Roscoe
Power
Practical reason and ethics
Pragmatics
Pragmatism
Pragmatism in ethics
Praise and blame
Praxeology
Prayer
Predestination
Predicate calculus
Predication
Prescriptivism
Presocratic philosophy
Presupposition
Price, Richard
Prichard, Harold Arthur
Priestley, Joseph
Primary-secondary distinction
Prior, Arthur Norman
Privacy
Private language argument
Private states and language
Probability, interpretations of
Probability theory and epistemology
Process philosophy
Process theism
Processes
Proclus
Prodicus
Professional ethics
Projectivism
Promising
Proof theory
Proper names
Property
Property theory
Prophecy
Propositional attitude statements
Propositional attitudes
Propositions, sentences and
    statements

Protagoras
Proudhon, Pierre-Joseph
Provability logic
Providence
Prudence
Pseudo-Dionysius
Pseudo-Grosseteste
Psychē
Psychoanalysis, methodological issues in
Psychoanalysis, post-Freudian
Psychology, theories of
Ptolemy
Public interest
Pufendorf, Samuel
Purgatory
Putnam, Hilary
Pyrrho
Pyrrhonism
Pythagoras
Pythagoreanism
Qi
Qualia
Quantification and inference
Quantifiers
Quantifiers, generalized
Quantifiers, substitutional and objectual
Quantum logic
Quantum measurement problem
Quantum mechanics, interpretation of
Questions
Quine, Willard Van Orman
Rabelais, François
Race, theories of
Radbruch, Gustav
Radhakrishnan, Sarvepalli
Radical translation and radical interpretation
Rahner, Karl
Ramakrishna movement
Rāmānuja
Ramsey, Frank Plumpton
Ramsey, Ian Thomas
Ramus, Petrus
Rand, Ayn
Randomness
Rashdall, Hastings
Rational beliefs
Rational choice theory
Rationalism
Rationality and cultural relativism
Rationality of belief
Rationality, practical

Ravaisson-Mollien, Jean-Gaspard Félix Lacher
Rawls, John
al-Razi, Abu Bakr Muhammad ibn Zakariyya'
al-Razi, Fakhr al-Din
Realism and antirealism
Realism in the philosophy of mathematics
Reasons and causes
Reasons for belief
Reciprocity
Recognition
Rectification and remainders
Recursion-theoretic hierarchies
Reduction, problems of
Reductionism in the philosophy of mind
Reference
Régis, Pierre-Sylvain
Reichenbach, Hans
Reid, Thomas
Reinach, Adolf
Reincarnation
Reinhold, Karl Leonhard
Relativism
Relativity theory, philosophical significance of
Relevance logic and entailment
Reliabilism
Religion and epistemology
Religion and morality
Religion and political philosophy
Religion and science
Religion, critique of
Religion, history of philosophy of
Religion, philosophy of
Religious experience
Religious language
Religious pluralism
Renaissance philosophy
Renner, Karl
Renouvier, Charles Bernard
Representation, political
Reprobation
Reproduction and ethics
Republicanism
Respect for persons
Responsibilities of scientists and intellectuals
Responsibility
Resurrection
Revelation
Revolution
rGyal tshab dar ma rin chen

Rhetoric
Richard of Middleton
Richard of St Victor
Richard Rufus of Cornwall
Ricoeur, Paul
Right and good
Rights
Risk
Risk assessment
Ritual
Rohault, Jacques
Roman law
Romanticism, German
Rorty, Richard McKay
Roscelin of Compiègne
Rosenzweig, Franz
Rosmini-Serbati, Antonio
Ross, Alf
Ross, William David
Rousseau, Jean-Jacques
Royce, Josiah
Rozanov, Vasilii Vasil'evich
Ruge, Arnold
Rule of law (Rechtsstaat)
Russell, Bertrand Arthur William
Russian empiriocriticism
Russian literary formalism
Russian Materialism: 'The 1860s'
Russian philosophy
Russian religious-philosophical renaissance
Ryle, Gilbert
Sa skya paṇḍita
Saadiah Gaon
al-Sabzawari, al-Hajj Mulla Hadi
Sacraments
Saint-Simon, Claude-Henri de Rouvroy, Comte de
Salvation
Sanches, Francisco
Sanctification
Śaṅkara
Sāṅkhya
Santayana, George
Sapir-Whorf hypothesis
Sartre, Jean-Paul
Saussure, Ferdinand de
Savigny, Friedrich Karl von
Scandinavia, philosophy in
Scepticism
Scepticism, Renaissance
Scheler, Max Ferdinand
Schelling, Friedrich Wilhelm Joseph von
Schellingianism

Schiller, Ferdinand Canning Scott
Schiller, Johann Christoph Friedrich
Schlegel, Friedrich von
Schleiermacher, Friedrich Daniel
    Ernst
Schlick, Friedrich Albert Moritz
Schmitt, Carl
Schopenhauer, Arthur
Schumpeter, Joseph Alois
Schurman, Anna Maria van
Schütz, Alfred
Science in Islamic philosophy
Science, 19th century philosophy of
Science, philosophy of
Scientific method
Scientific realism and antirealism
Scientific realism and social science
Scope
Searle, John
Second- and higher-order logics
Second-order logic, philosophical
    issues in
Secondary qualities
Selden, John
Self, Indian theories of
Self-control
Self-cultivation in Chinese
    philosophy
Self-deception
Self-deception, ethics of
Self-realization
Self-respect
Sellars, Wilfrid Stalker
Semantic paradoxes and theories of
    truth
Semantics
Semantics, conceptual role
Semantics, game-theoretic
Semantics, informational
Semantics, possible worlds
Semantics, situation
Semantics, teleological
Semiotics
Seneca, Lucius Annaeus
Sengzhao
Sense and reference
Sense perception, Indian views of
Sense-data
Sergeant, John
Set theory
Set theory, different systems of
Sextus Empiricus
Sexuality, philosophy of
Shaftesbury, Third Earl of (Anthony
    Ashley Cooper)

Shah Wali Allah (Qutb al-Din
    Ahmad al-Rahim)
Shao Yong
Shem Tov Family
Shestov, Lev (Yehuda Leib
    Shvartsman)
Shinran
Shintō
Shōtoku Constitution
Shpet, Gustav Gustavovich
Sidgwick, Henry
Siger of Brabant
Signposts movement
al-Sijistani, Abu Sulayman
    Muhammad
Silvestri, Francesco
Simmel, Georg
Simplicity (in scientific theories)
Simplicity, divine
Simplicius
Sin
Sirhak
Situation ethics
Skinner, Burrhus Frederick
Skovoroda, Hryhorii Savych
Slavery
Slavophilism
Slovakia, philosophy in
Smart, John Jamieson Carswell
Smith, Adam
Social action
Social choice
Social democracy
Social epistemology
Social laws
Social norms
Social relativism
Social science, contemporary
    philosophy of
Social science, history of
    philosophy of
Social science, methodology of
Social sciences, philosophy of
Social sciences, prediction in
Social theory and law
Socialism
Society, concept of
Socinianism
Sociobiology
Sociology of knowledge
Sociology, theories of
Socrates
Socratic dialogues
Socratic schools
Solidarity

Solipsism
Soloveitchik, Joseph B.
Solov'ëv, Vladimir Sergeevich
Sophists
Sorel, Georges
Sôsan Hyujông
Soto, Domingo de
Soul in Islamic philosophy
Soul, nature and immortality of the
South Slavs, philosophy of
Sovereignty
Space
Spacetime
Spain, philosophy in
Species
Speech acts
Spencer, Herbert
Speusippus
Spinoza, Benedict de
Split brains
Sport and ethics
Sport, philosophy of
Staël-Holstein, Anne-Louise-
    Germaine, Mme de
Stair, James Dalrymple, Viscount
State, the
Statistics
Statistics and social science
Steiner, Rudolf
Stevenson, Charles Leslie
Stewart, Dugald
Stirner, Max
Stoicism
Strato
Strauss, David Friedrich
Strauss, Leo
Strawson, Peter Frederick
Structuralism
Structuralism in linguistics
Structuralism in literary theory
Structuralism in social science
Suárez, Francisco
Subject, postmodern critique of the
Sublime, the
Substance
Suchon, Gabrielle
Suffering
Suffering, Buddhist views of
    origination of
al-Suhrawardi, Shihab al-Din Yahya
Suicide, ethics of
Sunzi
Supererogation
Supervenience
Supervenience of the mental

Suso, Henry
Swedenborg, Emanuel
Symbolic interactionism
Syntax
Systems theory in social science
Tagore, Rabindranath
Taine, Hippolyte-Adolphe
Tanabe Hajime
Tarski, Alfred
Tarski's definition of truth
Tauler, John
al-Tawhidi, Abu Hayyan
Taxonomy
Taylor, Charles
Taylor, Harriet
Technology and ethics
Technology, philosophy of
Teilhard de Chardin, Pierre
Tel Quel School
Teleological ethics
Teleology
Telesio, Bernardino
Temple, William
Tennant, Frederick Robert
Tense and temporal logic
Tertullian, Quintus Septimus
    Florens
Testimony
Testimony in Indian philosophy
Tetens, Johann Nicolaus
Thales
Themistius
Theological virtues
Theology, political
Theology, Rabbinic
Theophrastus
Theoretical (epistemic) virtues
Theories, scientific
Theory and observation in social
    sciences
Theory and practice
Theory of types
Theosophy
Thermodynamics
Thielicke, Helmut
Thierry of Chartres
Thomas à Kempis
Thomas of York
Thomasius (Thomas), Christian
Thomism
Thoreau, Henry David
Thought experiments
Thrasymachus
Thucydides
Ti and yong

Tian
Tibetan philosophy
Tillich, Paul
Time
Time travel
Timon
Tindal, Matthew
Tocqueville, Alexis de
Todorov, Tzvetan
Toland, John
Toleration
Toletus, Franciscus
Tolstoi, Count Lev Nikolaevich
Tominaga Nakamoto
Tonghak
Totalitarianism
Tradition and traditionalism
Tragedy
Transcendental arguments
Translators
Trinity
Troeltsch, Ernst Peter Wilhelm
Trotsky, Leon
Trust
Truth, coherence theory of
Truth, correspondence theory of
Truth, deflationary theories of
Truth, pragmatic theory of
Truthfulness
Tschirnhaus, Ehrenfried Walther von
Tsong kha pa Blo bzang grags pa
Tucker, Abraham
Turing, Alan Mathison
Turing machines
Turing reducibility and Turing
    degrees
Turnbull, George
al-Tusi, Khwajah Nasir
Twardowski, Kazimierz
Type/token distinction
Udayana
Uddyotakara
Ûisang
Ulrich of Strasbourg
Unamuno y Jugo, Miguel de
Unconscious mental states
Underdetermination
Unity of science
Universal language
Universalism in ethics
Universals
Universals, Indian theories of
Use/mention distinction and
    quotation
Utilitarianism

Utopianism
Vagueness
Vaihinger, Hans
Valla, Lorenzo
Vallabhācārya
Value judgements in social science
Value, ontological status of
Values
Vasubandhu
Vātsyāyana
Vedānta
Venn, John
Vernia, Nicoletto
Vico, Giambattista
Vienna Circle
Villey, Michel
Violence
Virtue epistemology
Virtue ethics
Virtues and vices
Vision
Vital du Four
Vitalism
Vitoria, Francisco de
Vives, Juan Luis
Vlastos, Gregory
Voegelin, Eric
Voltaire (François-Marie Arouet)
Voluntarism
Voluntarism, Jewish
Von Wright, Georg Henrik
Vulnerability and finitude
Vygotskii, Lev Semënovich
Vysheslavtsev, Boris Petrovich
Wallace, Alfred Russel
Wang Chong
Wang Fuzhi
Wang Yangming
War and peace, philosophy of
Watsuji Tetsurō
Weber, Max
Weil, Simone
Weinberger, Ota
Welfare
Weyl, Hermann
Weyr, František
Whewell, William
White, Thomas
Whitehead, Alfred North
Will, the
William of Auvergne
William of Auxerre
William of Champeaux
William of Conches
William of Ockham

William of Sherwood
Williams, Bernard Arthur Owen
Wisdom
Witherspoon, John
Wittgenstein, Ludwig Josef Johann
Wittgensteinian ethics
Wodeham, Adam
Wolff, Christian
Wollaston, William
Wollstonecraft, Mary
Wônch'ũk
Wônhyo
Work, philosophy of
Wróblewski, Jerzy
Wundt, Wilhelm
Wyclif, John
Xenocrates

Xenophanes
Xenophon
Xin (heart and mind)
Xin (trustworthiness)
Xing
Xunzi
Yang Xiong
Yangzhu
Yi Hwang
Yi Kan
Yi Yulgok
Yijing
Yin-yang
Yoruba epistemology
You-wu
Zabarella, Jacopo
Zeami

Zeno of Citium
Zeno of Elea
Zermelo, Ernst
Zhang Zai
Zheng Xuan
Zhi
Zhi Dun
Zhiyi
Zhongyong
Zhou Dunyi
Zhu Xi
Zhuangzi
Zionism
Zongmi
Zoroastrianism

An alphabetical list of contributors, their affiliations and the entries they have written can be found in the index volume (Volume 10).

QUESTIONS

Some theorists hold that a question is an interrogative sentence; others that a question is what is meant or expressed by an interrogative sentence. Most theorists hold that each question has two or more answers, and that the point of asking a question is to have the respondent reply with one of the answers. Most hold that each question has an assertive core or presupposition that is implied by each of the answers; if it is false, then no answer is true, so we say that the question commits the fallacy of many questions and we regard the negation of the presupposition as a corrective reply to the question (it corrects the question).

For example, consider the question 'Has Adam stopped sinning?' Its answers are 'Adam has stopped sinning' and 'Adam has not stopped sinning'. It presupposes 'Adam has sinned'; thus 'Adam has not sinned' is a corrective reply. The 'safe' way to ask this question is via the conditional 'If Adam has sinned, then has Adam stopped sinning?'

We can construct formal systems for asking whether and which questions in an effective way. Other types of question (for example, who and why) are still problematic. It can be proved that some questions are reducible to others, some questions raise others, and some systems for the logic of questions can never be complete in certain ways.

1   **Concepts and theories**
2   **Effective systems**
3   **Some problems**
4   **Epistemic analysis of questions**
5   **Intensional analysis of questions**
6   **Erotetic logic**

1   Concepts and theories

Questions have been discussed since Aristotle, although formal, systematic study did not begin until the 1950s. Theorists disagree on basic concepts, and there are at least three approaches to theorizing about questions. In one, the essence of a question is its set of answers, in another the essence is the questioner's intentions, and in another the essence is an objective intensional entity.

The 'reduction-to-answers' view holds that every question has direct answers, these direct answers are statements, and to know what counts as a direct answer to the question is to understand the question. A question presupposes any statement that is implied by every direct answer. A complete answer is a statement that implies a direct answer; a partial answer is a statement that is implied by a direct answer. The reduction-to-answers view is exemplified in most of the systems noted in §2 below.

The 'reduction-to-*intentions*' view holds that to know the questioner's intentions is to understand the question (see §4 below). The 'reduction-to-*intensions*' view holds that questions are intensional entities that are not relative to language and might or might not be expressible by sentences in a language (see §5 below and INTENSIONAL ENTITIES).

2   Effective systems

For many purposes (for example, conversation with strangers, courtroom procedure, automated information retrieval systems), it is desirable to have systems for question and answer that are effective in the following sense: for any expression of the given language, we can effectively tell whether it is an interrogative sentence and, if it is one, tell what question it expresses. In the reduction-to-answers view this implies that, given an interrogative sentence, we can effectively tell what counts as a direct answer to the question that is expressed.

Beginning with G. Stahl and T. Kubiński in the 1950s, logicians have constructed systems that provide for *whether* and *which* questions and that satisfy the effectiveness condition. The system of Belnap and Steel (1976) is exemplary. In it, *whether* and *which* questions are expressed by interrogatives of the form *?RS*. Here the subject part *S* indicates a set of statements, which are the alternatives presented by the question. (For *whether* questions *S* is a finite list of statements; for *which* questions *S* is a formula indicating all the statements that result when names are substituted for the queriables (the free variables) in the formula.) Given *S*, the request part *R* indicates how many of the true alternatives are to be put into each direct answer and indicates whether the answer is to claim that it contains all of the true alternatives and (in the case of *which* questions) claim that the various names given in the answer denote distinct entities. The system provides for *who, when, where, why, what* questions – if these are construed as asking which person, which time, which place, which reason, which thing. It allows the questioner to call for a complete list or just some examples or an answer of the form at-least-*m*-but-at-most-*n*.

3   Some problems

Systems such as those noted above are good models for some question-asking situations but not for others. First consider 'What is in the box?' and 'Some of John's things are in the box'. If the latter is a complete answer, as some theorists say, then this *what* question cannot be construed as a *which things* question, and the system must be altered or extended to provide for it. Similar examples exist for *who* and other so-called 'wh-questions'.

Why questions pose special problems. Consider 'Why did this apple fall?'. We may construe this as 'What is a good explanation of why this apple fell?', but we will not know what counts as an answer until we know what counts as a good explanation. S. Bromberger (1992) has proposed that some types of *why* question can be adequately answered by citing (1) a general rule, (2) an abnormic law – that is, a law that specifies exceptions to the rule, and (3) some exception mentioned by the law. For example: 'An apple remains on the tree unless it becomes ripe or a wind blows or the tree dies, and in this case the wind blew.' It is reasonable to require that the abnormic law be empirical and true, but then (because we cannot always recognize truth) we cannot always recognize the admissible direct answers.

Effective systems have some intrinsic limitations. Suppose that the interrogatives of a system can be effectively recognized and hence listed by some algorithm and that, for each interrogative, its direct answers can be recognized and hence listed. Then it can be shown by Cantor's diagonal method that the system is incomplete in the sense that there is a set of sentences that might be the answers to some question but cannot be the answers for any interrogative in the given list (Harrah 1984).

4 Epistemic analysis of questions

L. Åqvist (1965) proposed that questions are requests concerning epistemic states, expressible by imperatives such as 'Let it be the case that I know that *A* or I know that *B*' or 'Let it be the case that, for some *x*, I know that *Px*'. In this approach there may be a variety of imperative operators, and reference made to different knowers, so that, for example, a teacher can put questions to a class in the form 'Bring it about that I know that you know...' J. Hintikka (1983) has developed this approach further to elaborate its pragmatic dimension. Hintikka has extended his game-theoretic semantics to provide a semantics for epistemically construed questions and rules for conducting various types of rational question-and-answer dialogue (see SEMANTICS, GAME-THEORETIC).

In this approach every question has a presupposition (in the first example above: '*A* or *B*'), a desideratum ('I know that *A* or I know that *B*') and direct answers (*A*, *B*). If an answer meets certain conditions of relevance and conclusiveness, guaranteeing that the desideratum is satisfied, then it is a conclusive answer. The conditions vary with the type of question. In the case of a *which* question, quantified variables should range over entities with which the questioner is acquainted, and the answer should specify a noun phrase only if the questioner knows what that phrase denotes. There is no guarantee that the respondent can effectively tell from the imperative sentence what the range of the variables is supposed to be, or what noun phrases will suffice, so, in this approach, the concept of conclusive answer in general is not effective.

5 Intensional analysis of questions

P. Tichý (1978) proposed that a question is a function defined on possible worlds. Propositions, individual concepts and properties are such functions, and they are the common types of question. For any given world the value of such a function is a truth-value, an individual or a set of individuals, respectively. In general the right answer to a question is the value of the function in the actual world.

This idea can be developed on its own; it can also be combined fruitfully with the ideas of Richard MONTAGUE. In Montague's analysis of declaratives, meanings are higher-order intensional entities. These are assigned to linguistic expressions according to Frege's principle that the meaning of a syntactical compound is the corresponding semantic compound of the meanings of the parts of the syntactical compound. Some linguists and logicians have developed analyses of this sort that treat both declaratives and interrogatives. In most, an interrogative expresses a question and denotes its true direct answers (see FREGE, G.).

6 Erotetic logic

In a general sense erotetic logic is the logic of utterance and reply (Harrah 1984). In the strict sense it is the logic of question and answer.

For most systems, especially those noted in §2 above, an important concept is that of containment. One question contains (or covers, or obviates) another if and only if every direct answer to the first implies some direct answer to the second, and two questions are equivalent if and only if each contains the other.

For analysis of the raising of questions, the implying of questions and arguing to questions, Wiśniewski (1995) has defined some useful concepts. For example: A set of declarative sentences evokes a question if and only if the set implies that the question has a true direct answer but does not imply the truth of any particular direct answer. Also, one question implies another if and only if each direct answer to the first implies that some direct answer to the second is true and for each direct answer to the second there is a proper subset (that is, a small selection) of direct answers to the first such that the given direct answer to the second implies that a true direct answer to the first is contained in that subset (so each true answer to the second helps us find a true answer to the first).

Another of Wiśniewski's concepts is that one question is reducible to a set of other questions (call it the reducing set) if and only if each direct answer to the given question implies that all the questions in the reducing set have true direct answers; and each collection of sentences that contains exactly one direct answer to each question in the reducing set implies some direct answer to the given question; and no question in the reducing set has more direct answers than the given question does. One result is that, if a question is 'safe' (that is, in every interpretation of the language the question has a true direct answer), then the question is reducible to some set of simple yes-no questions.

References and further reading

All the works cited contain some technical material. All contain useful bibliographies.

* Åqvist, L. (1965) *A New Approach to the Logical Theory of Interrogatives*, Uppsala: Almqvist & Wiksell. (Referred to in §4. Outlines an approach based on commands about knowledge. Technical and difficult.)
* Belnap, N.D., Jr and Steel, T.B., Jr (1976) *The Logic of Questions and Answers*, New Haven, CT: Yale University Press. (Referred to in §2. Presents many useful concepts.)
* Bromberger, S. (1992) *On What We Know We Don't Know: Explanation, Theory, Linguistics, and How Questions Shape Them*, Chicago, IL: University of Chicago Press. (Referred to in §3. Good discussion of *why* questions.)
  Groenendijk, J. and Stokhof, M. (1984) *Studies on the Semantics of Questions and the Pragmatics of Answers*, Amsterdam: Academisch Proefschrift. (Gives an intensional analysis with a pragmatic dimension.)
* Harrah, D. (1984) 'The Logic of Questions', in D. Gabbay and F. Guenthner (eds) *Handbook of Philosophical Logic, Vol. II: Extensions of Classical Logic*, Dordrecht: Reidel, 715–64. (Referred to in §§3, 6. Introduction, some history and a survey of various theories.)
  —— (1985) 'A Logic of Message and Reply', *Synthèse* 65: 275–94. (§3 presents a general erotetic logic.)
* Hintikka, J. (1983) 'New Foundations for a Theory of Questions and Answers', in Kiefer, F. (ed.) *Questions and Answers*, Dordrecht: Reidel, 1983, 159–90. (Referred to in §4. Outlines an approach based on a modification of Åqvist (1965).)
  —— (ed.) (1988) 'Knowledge-Seeking by Questioning', *Synthèse* 74: 1–262. (Papers by various authors, mainly on Hintikka's approach.)
  —— (1992) 'The Interrogative Model of Inquiry as a General Theory of Argumentation', *Communication and Cognition* 25: 221–42. (Brief introduction to Hintikka-style systems.)
  Kiefer, F. (ed.) (1983) *Questions and Answers*, Dordrecht: Reidel. (Papers presenting several approaches and discussing many aspects.)
* Tichý, P. (1978) 'Questions, Answers, and Logic', *American Philosophical Quarterly* 15: 275–84. (Referred to in §5. Outlines an approach based on a theory of possible worlds.)
* Wiśniewski, A. (1995) *The Posing of Questions: Logical Foundations of Erotetic Inferences*, Dordrecht: Kluwer. (Concerned mainly with raising and implying, as described in §6; technical and rigorous in some chapters but very clear throughout; has useful expositions, surveys and bibliography, and can serve as an introduction to the entire field.)

DAVID HARRAH

QUINE, WILLARD VAN ORMAN (1908–)

Quine is the foremost representative of naturalism in the second half of the twentieth century. His naturalism consists of an insistence upon a close connection or alliance between philosophical views and those of the natural sciences. Philosophy so construed is an activity within nature wherein nature examines itself. This contrasts with views which distinguish philosophy from science and place philosophy in a special transcendent position for gaining special knowledge. The methods of science are empirical; so Quine, who operates within a scientific perspective, is an empiricist, but with a difference. Traditional empiricism, as in Locke, Berkeley, Hume and some twentieth-century forms, takes impressions, ideas or sense-data as the basic units of thought. Quine's empiricism, by contrast, takes account of the theoretical as well as the observational facets of science. The unit of empirical significance is not simple impressions (ideas) or even isolated individual observation sentences, but systems of beliefs. The broad theoretical constraints for choice between theories, such as explanatory power, parsimony, precision and so on, are foremost in this empiricism. He is a fallibilist, since he holds that each individual belief in a system is in principle revisable. Quine proposes a new conception of observation sentences, a naturalized account of our knowledge of the external world, including a rejection of a priori knowledge, and he extends the same empiricist and fallibilist account to our knowledge of logic and mathematics.

Quine confines logic to first-order logic and clearly demarcates it from set theory and mathematics. These are all empirical subjects when empiricism is understood in its Quinian form. They are internal to our system of beliefs that make up the natural sciences. The language of first-order logic serves as a canonical notation in which to express our ontological commitments. The slogan 'To be is to be the value of a variable' ([1953] 1961: 15) encapsulates this project. Deciding which ontology to accept is also carried out within the naturalistic constraints of empirical science – our ontological commitments should be to those objects to which the best scientific theories commit us. On this basis Quine's own commitments are to physical objects and sets. Quine is a physicalist and a Platonist, since the best sciences require physical objects and the mathematics involved in the sciences requires abstract objects, namely, sets.

The theory of reference (which includes notions such as reference, truth and logical truth) is sharply demarcated from the theory of meaning (which includes notions such as meaning, synonymy, the analytic–synthetic distinction and necessity). Quine is the leading critic of notions from the theory of meaning, arguing that attempts to make the distinction between merely linguistic (analytic) truths and more substantive (synthetic) truths has failed. They do not meet the standards of precision which scientific and philosophical theories adhere to and which are adhered to in the theory of reference. He explores the limits of an empirical theory of language and offers a thesis of the indeterminacy of translation as further criticism of the theory of meaning.

1   Life
2   Epistemology naturalized – nature know thyself
3   Dethroning the a priori
4   Logic as first-order logic
5   Canonical notation and ontological commitment
6   Competing ontologies
7   Indeterminacy of reference and global structuralism
8   The theory of meaning: its myths and dogmas
9   Indeterminacy of translation

1   Life

Willard Van Orman Quine was born on 25 June 1908. He was an undergraduate at Oberlin College and a graduate student at Harvard, where he studied with A.N. Whitehead, C.I. Lewis and Sheffer. In his dissertation 'The Logic of Sequences: A Generalization of *Principia Mathematica*' there already appears a prominent theme of Quine's philosophy – a concern with matters of ontology (Quine 1934).

In 1931, Quine had what he has described as his 'most dazzling exposure to greatness', when Bertrand RUSSELL came to lecture at Harvard. Russell is one of the most influential figures on Quine's thought. Both share a preoccupation with questions concerning what there is. For example, Quine adopted and improved upon Russell's view of how we express ontological claims. More significantly, as the dissertation already reveals, Russell's influence was that of a rival whose theories spur Quine on to the creation of more acceptable alternatives. Wherever possible, Quine tries to get on with the fewest and most precise assumptions which will suffice to do the job at hand. Whereas *Principia Mathematica* is constructed on the basis of an ontology that comprises propositional functions, which are properties of a sort, Quine's revision tries to accomplish the same goals with concrete physical objects and sets or classes. In addition, some of Quine's most famous systems of logic and set theory are designed to achieve the same effects as *Principia Mathematica*, while avoiding Russell's theory of types (see THEORY OF TYPES).

A travelling fellowship to Europe in 1932 exposed Quine to the latest developments in logic and in philosophy. In Vienna he attended meetings of the Vienna Circle, and described the following weeks spent in Prague and Warsaw as 'the intellectually most rewarding months I have known' (see VIENNA CIRCLE). In Prague, Quine met Rudolf CARNAP, one of the most careful expositors of prominent themes of analytic philosophy and especially those of the logical empiricists, such as the verifiability criterion for the empirical meaningfulness of sentences, the linguistic (analytic) character of a priori knowledge, as in mathematics and logic, and the triviality or meaninglessness of ontology as a species of metaphysics. Quine subjected each of these themes to severe criticism, resulting in some of the most important philosophical debates of the century. In Warsaw, he attended the lectures of Lesniewski, Łukasiewicz and Tarski and in the next few years was to adopt Tarski's and GÖDEL's 'classic' formulation of logic in formulating his most famous works. Quine was quite sympathetic to the extensionalist and the nominalist side of the Warsaw school.

At Harvard in the period prior to the Second World War, Quine worked out some of his most distinctive positions: his conception of ontological commitment (best known from his 1948 essay 'On

What There Is'); his two most distinctive systems of logic and set theory 'New Foundations for Mathematical Logic' (1937) and *Mathematical Logic* (1940); and his criticisms of the position that a priori knowledge as it purportedly exists in logic and mathematics is merely linguistic. These criticisms began to appear in 1934, when Quine lectured on Carnap's work. Some of this material can be found in 'Truth by Convention' (1936) and his most famous paper, 'Two Dogmas of Empiricism' (1951).

Quine served as a naval officer in the Second World War, and after continued his work on the above topics (see *From a Logical Point of View* (1953)). Much of his most original work since then has been the formulation of a new holistic variety of empiricism and the exploration of its consequences: 'The point of holism, stressed by Pierre Duhem..., is that the observable consequence by which we test a scientific hypothesis is ordinarily not a consequence of the hypothesis taken by itself; it is a consequence only of a whole cluster of sentences...' (1987: 141). Beginning with 'Two Dogmas', and eventually in *Word and Object* (1960), Quine employed this new holistic empiricism to criticize the concepts of meaning, synonymy and analyticity. In *Word and Object* he presented a thesis of the indeterminacy of translation as a further criticism of these notions. Later, in *Ontological Relativity* (1969), *The Roots of Reference* (1974), *Pursuit of Truth* (1992) and *From Stimulus to Science* (1995) he took a similar critical stance on concepts from the theory of reference. In essays dating from this period Quine's naturalism also comes to the fore. Though the theme of the continuity of philosophy and science is found in earlier works, he explores it more explicitly in 'Epistemology Naturalized' (1969), *Theories and Things* (1981), *Pursuit of Truth* and *From Stimulus to Science*.

2 Epistemology naturalized – nature know thyself

The problem of our knowledge of the external world is traditionally stated as one of how a self with private mental states can come to have knowledge of the external world. Quine's restatement is strikingly more naturalistic:

> I am a physical object sitting in a physical world. Some of the forces of this physical world impinge on my surface. Light rays strike my retinas; molecules bombard my eardrums and fingertips. I strike back, emanating concentric air waves. These waves take the form of a torrent of discourse about tables, people, molecules, light rays, retinas, air waves, prime numbers, infinite classes, joy and sorrow, good and evil.
>
> (1966: 215)

In its traditional statement the problem lies in how, starting with 'experience' in the form of immediately given impressions or sense-data, we justify our claims to know objects such as tables, chairs or molecules. This vantage point was that of a first philosophy, intended as providing a foundation of certainty for the sciences by standing outside of them and legitimizing their accomplishments. Quine rejects this formulation. His naturalized epistemology rephrases the problem as one of how we learn to talk about or refer to objects (ordinary as well as scientific). What are the conditions that lead to reference? How is scientific discourse possible?

The traditional accounts of the linkage between 'experience' and our knowledge vary from mentalistic conceptions, like that of Hume, in which all our ideas are copies of sense impressions, to more neutral linguistic formulations, in which cognitive claims are to be translated into observation sentences. On Quine's holistic account, one cannot deal with the empirical content of sentences, much less of terms – the linguistic correlates of ideas – one by one, either via definition, translation or some other sort of linkage. To study the relation of knowledge and science to observation sentences is to trace the psychological and linguistic development of the knower, that is, the potential user of scientific language. Observation sentences serve as both the starting point in human language learning as well as the empirical grounds for science. The problem of knowledge now is how, starting with observation sentences, we can proceed to talk of tables, chairs, molecules, neutrinos, sets and numbers. One of the reasons for doing epistemology by studying the roots of reference is simply the failure of the traditional empiricists' programme mentioned above. Another is that it enables one to dispense with mentalistic notions such as 'experience' or 'observation'. One relies instead on two components which are already part of a naturalist's ontology: the physical happening at the nerve endings, the neural input or stimulus; and the linguistic entity, the observation sentence. These two serve as naturalistic surrogates for 'experience' and 'observation'. On Quine's empiricist and behaviourist account, observation sentences are those that can be learned independently of other language acquisition. They are the sentences that can be learned purely by ostension and as such are causally most proximate to the stimulus. This account is not vulnerable to attacks on the notion of observation as dependent on the theories one holds, since observation sentences are precisely those which are learnable without any background information. Another point of difference with empiricists concerns the alleged certainty or incorrigibility of observation. Though

5

Quine's observation sentences are assented to with a minimum of background information and are thus included among those sentences less likely to be revised, they are not in principle immune from revision.

Unlike traditional epistemology, then, Quine's epistemology is naturalistic: we cannot stand apart from our place as part of nature and make philosophical judgments (see NATURALIZED EPISTEMOLOGY). This is part of the theme that philosophy is continuous with science, science being the part of nature most suitable for knowing itself.

The naturalistic philosopher begins his reasoning within the inherited world theory as a going concern. He tentatively believes all of it, but believes also that some unidentified portions are wrong. He tries to improve, clarify and understand the system from within.

(1981: 72)

3 Dethroning the a priori

A purported stumbling block for empiricism is a priori knowledge in logic and mathematics and in such purportedly conceptual truths as 'All bachelors are unmarried' and 'Nothing is larger than itself'. Such subject matter appears to defy justification in terms of observation. J.S. Mill's empiricist programme foundered on this point, and the various forms of rationalism are unacceptable to an empiricist. A proposed solution, the dominant one favoured by analytic philosophers, involved the analytic–synthetic distinction: all a priori knowledge was said to be analytic, in the sense that the truth of sentences claimed to be known independent of experience was reducible to matters of language, for example, linguistic convention, definitions, and truth in virtue of the meaning of the expressions involved.

Quine's critique is that of an empiricist reforming empiricism, supplanting reductionist-atomistic empiricism with Duhemian holism. Experimental testing is a juncture where observation ('experience') enters as a factor in deciding whether to accept or reject a claim. An oversimplified model of how observation counts in testing is that given a hypothesis and a statement of initial conditions, we deduce by logic and/or mathematics some observation sentence as an observable consequence. If the expected observation occurs, we take this as evidence for the hypothesis. If it does not, we take this as evidence that the hypothesis is false. Such a model makes use of the dogma of reductionism by assuming that individual sense experiences-observation sentences function unequivocally for or against isolated sentences-hypotheses. Pierre DUHEM showed that this model is flawed and Quine extends Duhem's point into a holistic one that embodies a critique of reductionism and the a priori.

Duhem had pointed out that where the observation fails to occur, one has leeway in dealing with the situation. All serious testing involves background assumptions, implicit in the hypothesis or in the statement of the initial conditions. A test situation underdetermines which factor should be revised and there is no way of knowing in advance where the revision should be made. Quine's insight was to take cognizance of all the assumptions that can be questioned in a test situation. The underdetermination of theory by observation does not stop with revising background assumptions relative to the hypothesis and the initial conditions. Both the purportedly disconfirming observation made and the principles involved in deriving the observable consequence can also be revised. In test situations whole systems of beliefs go into the hopper and we have leeway as to how we make the consistency-preserving revisions. We can edit the observation. We can even question the logic and or mathematics used in deriving the observable conclusion. No sentence is in principle immune from being revised. In this spirit, all knowledge is empirical; there is no a priori knowledge. The quest for certainty is replaced by fallibilism, the associated foundationalist programmes are abandoned, as is the verifiability theory of the logical empiricists. Instead, the broad constraints on what to do in a test situation are the natural scientist's criteria for preferring one hypothesis, theory or system of beliefs over another. These criteria include explanatory power, simplicity or parsimony, conservatism, modesty and precision (1970: 54). Conservatism cautions, other things being equal, that we should accept that hypothesis-theory which clashes least with our other beliefs. This 'maxim of minimal mutilation' comes into play in explaining why logic, while in principle revisable (for example, some suggest adopting a three-valued logic), is the least likely item to be revised. Doing so would have far-reaching consequences for our other beliefs. Modesty says that all other things being equal we should hypothesize as little as is necessary for the job at hand. Precision mandates standards on introducing and explaining philosophical or scientific concepts. It requires that philosophical explications be couched in acceptable terms, the extensional or empirical notions of logic, set theory and the sciences. For example, abstract objects should not be posited without a precise account of what they are, that is to say, 'no entity without identity' (see A PRIORI §1; ANALYTICITY §§1–3; FALLIBILISM).

4 Logic as first-order logic

Quine distinguishes the theory of reference from the theory of meaning. He is sceptical of notions associated with the theory of meaning, such as those of meaning, intension, synonymy, analyticity and necessity. By contrast, he relies on and makes contributions to the theory of reference, for example, to the understanding of logical truth, truth, reference and ontological commitment.

For Quine, the notion of logical truth falls squarely in the theory of reference. His most characteristic definition of logical truth is that a sentence is a logical truth if it is true and if it remains true when one uniformly replaces its nonlogical parts. The logical parts are the logical constants, signs for negation, disjunction, quantification and identity. 'Brutus killed Caesar or it is not the case that Brutus killed Caesar' is such a logical truth. In Quine's terminology the logical constants 'or' and 'it is not the case that' occur essentially, while the nonlogical part 'Brutus killed Caesar' can be uniformly varied and the resulting sentence will still be true. In other words a logical truth cannot be changed into a falsehood by varying the nonlogical expressions, whereas an ordinary truth can be.

The same concept of logical truth is found in BOLZANO and AJDUKIEWICZ. One of its virtues lies in its being parsimonious, that is, in what it does not say. Logical truth and related notions are often explained in modal terms. That is, logical truths are said to be distinguished by being 'necessary' or 'true in all possible worlds', and a valid argument is defined as one in which, if the premises are true, the conclusion 'must be true'. These accounts make logic presuppose modal notions. Quine's definition leaves logic autonomous in this respect. Indeed Quine is a critic of modal logic, challenging various attempts to explain the notion of necessity. Logical truth, as defined by Quine, is a precisely explained species of truth, fitting squarely inside the theory of reference. Quine relies on the concept of truth, which he construes along the lines of Tarski's theory (see TARSKI'S DEFINITION OF TRUTH).

If logical truths are those in which only logical constants occur essentially, then the scope of logic is in part determined by what we take to be a logical constant. Quine lists as the logical constants the truth-functional connectives 'not', 'and', 'or', 'if...then', 'if and only if'; the quantifiers 'all' and 'some'; and the identity predicate '$a = b$'. The language of logic so construed is that of sentences formed out of truth-functional connectives, quantifiers, identity, schematic predicate letters and individual variables. Quantificational logic of this sort is

also known as first-order logic. For Quine, logic *is* first-order logic with identity. Ruled out as logic on this construal are modal logic, because 'necessity' is not taken as a logical constant. Also excluded is higher-order logic, which has quantifiers for predicate positions (it is 'set theory in sheep's clothing' (1986: 66)). On other grounds other proposals such as intuitionist logic are also ineligible. Set theory, and with it mathematics, are not logic (see LOGICAL CONSTANTS §§1–2).

Quine falls in the camp of the Logicist programme in holding that mathematics is reducible to set theory. Set theory is the theory of the 'is a member of' predicate and is stated in the language of first-order logic. Given the theory of membership and logic as first-order logic plus identity, Quine introduces mathematical notions as definitional abbreviations: for example, a number is defined as a special set, addition as a special function on these sets and so on. He argues that logic does not include set theory because membership should not be considered a logical constant for the following reasons: (1) There is a general consensus about elementary logic, which, given paradoxes such as Russell's, is lacking in the case of set theory. Alternative set theories have the status of so many tentative hypotheses. This lends credence to Quine's view that mathematics based on set theory is not very different from other sciences. (2) The incompleteness of set theory contrasts sharply with the completeness of elementary logic. (3) The ontology of set theory is not as topic neutral as that of logic. The second item in the membership relation is restricted to sets. Logic is the most general of subjects, since the variables of logic are not restricted to any one category of objects (see LOGICISM §1).

5 Canonical notation and ontological commitment

Ever since Frege and Russell, existential quantification has been the prevalent way in which existence assertions have been understood. The idea is that existence sentences in natural language can be paraphrased in the language of logic and 'existence' explicated by the existential quantifier of predicate logic. 'Existence is what existential quantification expresses' (1969: 97). The functions that the predicate 'exists' performs in English can be accomplished by the '$\exists x$' quantifier. Quine's version of this theme is incorporated into his account of ontological commitment. The language of first-order predicate logic in which our ontological commitments are made is his 'canonical notation'.

Taking the canonical notation thus austerely...we have just these basic constructions: predication, quantification...and the truth functions...What thus confronts us as a scheme for systems of the world is that structure so well understood by present-day logicians, the logic of quantification or calculus of predicates.

Not that the idioms thus renounced are supposed to be unneeded in the market place or in the laboratory...The doctrine is only that such a canonical idiom can be abstracted and then adhered to in the statement of one's scientific theory. The doctrine is that all traits or reality worthy of the name can be set down in an idiom of this austere form if in any idiom.

It is in spirit a philosophical doctrine of categories,...philosophical in its breadth however continuous with science in its motivation.

(1960b: 228–9)

A key reason for regarding this language as canonical is that in it one's use of the existential quantifier is explicit. To discover the existence assumptions or ontological commitments of a theory, we first state it in the language of truth-functional connectives and quantification, and then look at the existential quantifications we have made. The logic of '$\exists x$' is the logic of existence, and a notation that makes '$\exists x$' explicit accordingly makes our existence assumptions or ontological commitments explicit.

One of Quine's most famous remarks, 'to be is to be the value of a variable' ([1953] 1961: 15), sums up this criterion of ontological commitment. The slogan also incorporates one of Quine's elaborations on Russell's theory of definite descriptions. Russell held that in most sentences ordinary names are disguised definite descriptions, which on his theory are analysed as existential generalizations. Thus 'Socrates is human' becomes 'The one husband of Xanthippe is human' which in turn becomes the existential generalization 'There is one and only one husband of Xanthippe and he is human'. Quine's elaboration dispenses with names entirely. Wherever a name occurs in the original sentence, we can get by in the canonical notation with variables, predicates and the logical constants. If we do not have a definite description on hand to put in place of the name, we can form a predicate, such as 'Socratizes', then encapsulate the coined predicate in a definite description and define away the descriptions via Russell's theory. So names disappear and are not part of the canonical notation. Dispensing with names not only has the virtue of a more parsimonious notation: it also specifies that variables are the vehicles of reference and as such the grounds of ontological commitment. Being the value of a variable is what 'being' is all about (see LOGICAL FORM; ONTOLOGICAL COMMITMENT).

6 Competing ontologies

Some important philosophical differences concern competing ontologies. Physicalists, for instance, have as their basic objects physical objects, while phenomenalists have sense-data. A twentieth-century version of the problem of universals involves a dispute over the relative merits of (1) a nominalistic ontology according to which only concrete individuals exist; and (2) realist ontologies, such as those of Platonists, which involve the existence of abstract objects. The issue of nominalism versus Platonism arises for Quine in connection with the mathematics required for science and the question whether it requires hypothesizing abstract objects such as sets. Another area of ontological controversy is whether Platonist assumptions should include only extensional objects such as sets or intensional ones such as properties or propositions (see ABSTRACT OBJECTS §3; NOMINALISM §4).

While we look to the existential generalizations of a theory stated in canonical notation to see what its ontological commitments are, this does not answer the question of which ontological commitments we should have. As a naturalist and scientific realist, Quine regards this as a matter of epistemology. It is the question of which theory we ought to accept. Deciding on a theory (scientific or philosophical) and its attendant ontology is once again done within a scientific perspective. Appeal is made to the same theoretical concerns mentioned earlier, that is, explanatory power, parsimony, conservatism, precision and so on. Quine's own ontological commitments are the result of just such considerations. He is a physicalist, no longer taking seriously the phenomenalist programme; partly on grounds connected with the dogma of reductionism and partly on the grounds that sense-data are not needed in a naturalized epistemology (the functions performed by sense-data are accomplished by nerve hits and observation sentences which are already part of our physicalist ontology). But he is a Platonist (a reluctant one) because of the mathematics that is required by our best scientific theories. In canonical notation, this mathematics requires quantifying over at least as many extensional abstract objects, namely sets, as there are real numbers. In an early essay co-authored with Nelson GOODMAN, 'Steps Towards A Constructive Nominalism' (1947), the possibilities of taking a nominalist stance were surveyed. But unlike Goodman, Quine reluctantly concluded that the nominalist programme failed. He has considered later attempts at nominalism such as by an appeal to substitutional quantification. The success of these attempts depends on whether impredicative notions are required by the mathematics embedded in the natural sciences. Others

(Field 1980) try to make the case for nominalism by abiding by some and abandoning other of Quine's constraints.

However, Quine has consistently argued against theories which require abstract objects of an intensional sort. An intensional notion might provisionally be characterized as one requiring for its explanation notions which do not conform to certain basic assumptions of first-order logic and standard set theories. Intensional contexts are not truth-functional, or do not allow the substitutability of coextensive singular terms or predicates. Modal notions are a case in point. 'Necessarily P' is not a truth-functional operation; we cannot replace singular terms or predicates in P, or the whole sentence P, with coextensive expressions and be guaranteed that if the original sentence is true then the subsequent one will also be true. In non-intensional contexts, that is, extensional contexts, such replacements are truth-preserving. Intensional objects are those that require intensional notions to account for them, such as properties or propositions. Extensional objects are those that do not require intensional notions to account for them, such as sets or sentences. So sets are identical if they have the same members, for example, the set of humans is the same as the set of featherless bipeds. Properties, on the other hand, are identical only if they necessarily belong to the same objects. So the properties of being human and being a rational animal are identical, but differ from the property of being a featherless biped.

Given Quine's views on the precision of notions from first-order logic and set theory, it is not surprising that he is critical of intensional notions which are not based on standard assumptions of first-order logic and set theory. His arguments against hypothesizing intensional objects are numerous and can be sketchily listed as cases where their explanatory power is questioned, where parsimony is invoked and where precise accounts of the identity conditions of such items is lacking ('no entity without identity'). Sometimes he argues that extensional ersatz constructions can achieve the same purpose for which the intensional objects were introduced: for instance, eternal sentences rather than propositions, sets rather than properties, ordered pairs rather than relations (construed intensionally), non-modal notions rather than modal ones, and so on (see INTENSIONAL ENTITIES § I).

7 Indeterminacy of reference and global structuralism

Quine's views on ontology undergo refinements in his later writings. Most important is the recognition that empiricism does not uniquely determine which objects are required as the values of our variables. There is an indeterminacy of reference which is in keeping with empiricist strictures on deciding which ontology to accept.

The thesis of ontological relativity, also known as the inscrutability or indeterminacy of reference, is in accord with Quine's naturalistic empiricism. It has been generalized into a view which he refers to as global structuralism. Since it is only at the observation sentences construed holophrastically as indissoluble wholes that the system is externally constrained, there are different but equally plausible ways of meeting these observational constraints and these can involve diverse ontologies, such as an ontology of rabbits or of rabbit parts. It is the structural part of the system that must be saved in order to meet the observational constraints. But this can be accomplished with quite different objects being the values of the variables. Quine endorses this global structuralist perspective by generalizing from his own cases and by noting a less global structuralist argument from the philosophy of mathematics. Quite different objects can be taken as the values of the variables for arithmetic, for example, numbers can be taken as Frege–Russell sets or as von Neumann sets without changing the truths of arithmetic. For Quine the question of whether we are really committed to rabbits as opposed to sums of rabbit parts, or to a given number as the set of all sets equinumerous to a given set (as on the Frege–Russell account) or to some different set (as on von Neumann's view) is without sense. It is without sense in that there is no natural-empirical way of raising this question. Global structuralism is a consequence of the denial of a first philosophy – a point of view in nature that transcends all natural points of view.

Quine's best-known cases which serve as evidence for his global structuralism are his rabbits case and his proxy functions, especially that of cosmic complements. Intertwined with his discussion in *Word and Object* of a linguist translating a native speaker's utterance of 'Gavagai', Quine points out that construing that expression as a referring expression leaves no empirical way of deciding whether it is used to refer to rabbits, rabbit parts, or rabbit stages and so on. As a later example he asks us to consider how sentences about concrete objects can be reinterpreted in terms of different ontologies assigned as values of the variables so that there is no empirical way of saying which is the correct one. Indeed the message of structuralism is that it is an error to speak as though there were a uniquely correct referent. The sentence 'This rabbit is furry' is true and is usually interpreted as being about individual rabbits and individual furry things. However, if we reinterpret the referring portions in terms of mereological cosmic complements the sentence remains true and there is no empirical way if we do this uniformly to say which is the correct ontology. Thus assign to 'This rabbit' the entire cosmos less this rabbit (imagine a complete jigsaw puzzle with a rabbit piece removed; the cosmic complement would be the puzzle without the rabbit piece). Assign to the predicate 'is furry' each of the cosmic complements of individual furry things. The sentence 'This rabbit is furry' is true under such an interpretation because the cosmos less this rabbit is a member of the set of cosmic complements of individual furry things (that is, that set includes the cosmic complement of that individual rabbit). One can extend this treatment of singular sentences to the remaining referential sentences.

8 The theory of meaning: its myths and dogmas

Quine's reaction in the 1930s to Carnap's work was a sceptical critique of the prevalent view among analytic philosophers that logic and mathematics are justified in some distinctively linguistic way, that is, that they are based on merely analytic-linguistic truths – truths by convention. The scepticism then and later questions proposed accounts of the distinction. Linguistic truth or truth by convention, as opposed to non-conventionally based empirical truths, appears in the end to be a purported distinction without a real difference. Of special importance is the failure to satisfy the requirement of precision in explaining the distinction. In 'Truth By Convention' (1936) and 'Carnap on Logical Truth' (1960a), Quine takes up different attempts to characterize such truths and finds that for the most part they are either too broad – not distinctive of logic or mathematics – or require non-linguistically based truth. There are as many of these characterizations as there are different senses of 'convention'. Quine considers truth by convention as based on the following: the arbitrary factor in axiomatization; formalization-disinterpretation; the arbitrary element in hypothesizing; and definition. But neither logic nor mathematics is distinguished by being axiomatized, or formalized-disinterpreted. The same can be done for other disciplines, such as physics and biology. The somewhat arbitrary choice of which sentences to take as axioms, so long as we can prove the right sentences, is also not distinctive of them. If truth by convention is taken as the somewhat arbitrary element in framing hypotheses, then this too is not distinctive of logic or mathematics. Nor are the formulas involved distinguished by being true by definition. Thus, if '$p \rightarrow p$' is defined in terms of '$-p \lor p$', then the truth of the defined formula depends on the truth of the defining formula, and that formula's truth is not a matter of definition or convention. For Quine, logic and mathematics can be precisely characterized in terms from the theory of reference. Logic is described in terms of truth, the logical constants and interchange of the extralogical elements; mathematics can be characterized in terms of set theory. But neither of these subjects is distinct in having a different epistemological basis which results in their being in some interesting sense 'analytic' or mere 'linguistic truths'.

The 'Two Dogmas' of Quine's 1951 essay were the dogma of reduction (see §3 above) and the dogma of the analytic/synthetic distinction. In discussing the dogma of analyticity, Quine questions, as he did in 'Truth by Convention', whether the distinction can be well made. Here he rejects five ways of explaining analyticity. These involve appeals to: (1) meanings, (2) definition, (3) interchangeability, (4) semantic rules and (5) the verifiability theory of meaning.

(1) 'Bachelors are unmarried men' might be regarded as analytic, where that notion is explained as truth in virtue of the meanings of its words. One suggestion is that the meaning of 'unmarried man' is included in the meaning of 'bachelor'. Another approach would hypothesize the existence of meanings to explain synonymy and then use synonymy in turn to show how the above sentence is a synonymous instance of a logical truth. The success of the above explanations requires assuming that there are such things as precisely characterizable meanings. Quine is sceptical of this assumption. He rejects three accounts of meanings: (a) referential theories – meanings as referents; (b) mentalism – meanings as ideas; and (c) intensionalism – meanings as intensional entities. Meaning (or sense), as Frege taught, must be distinguished from reference. The notion of meaning that is to explain synonymy and analyticity cannot simply be reference, because coreferential terms need not be synonymous and so will not distinguish analytic sentences from true non-analytic ones. Truth in virtue of meaning where meaning is simply reference is too broad as all truths would then be analytic. As to meanings as ideas, Quine brings to bear empiricist and behaviourist qualms. The account of meanings as abstract intensional entities is found in Frege, Carnap and Church. Quine maintains that such intensional objects are neither required as posits by our theories of language, nor are they precisely accounted for. The attempt to explain intensional notions is either circular or unhelpful. There is a circle of intensional notions, meaning, synonymy, analyticity, necessity, and we can define one in terms of another. Quine's criticism is that if we do not break out of this intensional circle, then the account has

failed to clarify the matter. For example, if the meaning of a predicate 'is human' is the property of being human, how would one go about identifying whether 'being a rational animal' or 'being a featherless biped' stood for the same property or had the same meaning? One answer is that the sentence 'humans are rational animals' is analytic, while the sentence 'humans are featherless bipeds' is not. But this relies on the notion of 'analytic' – which we haven't yet defined. Another approach at giving an identity condition uses modal notions and says that the first sentence is a necessary truth while the second is not. This, however, raises the problem of giving a precise account of modal notions. Explaining modal claims in terms of analyticity, for example, 'Necessarily humans are rational' as explained by '"Humans are rational" is analytic', will not do – since we have not defined 'analytic'. Quine's challenge is that one break out of this intensional circle and explain notions from the theory of meaning in more acceptable terms.

(2) He next rejects accounts of analyticity in terms of logical truth and synonymy. On this account a sentence is analytic if it is a synonymous instance of a logical truth, that is, 'All bachelors are unmarried men' is analytic in that it is derivable from the first-order logical truth 'All bachelors are bachelors' by putting a synonym 'unmarried man' for the second occurrence of 'bachelor'. One account attempts to explain synonymy in terms of definition. However, the various forms of definition either presuppose synonymy or stipulate it; none explain it. Quine is sceptical of definitions or philosophical analysis when thought of as capturing or analysing some concept or meaning. Instead philosophical explication is thought of in terms of the theory of reference and scientific hypothesizing and thus again embodying the naturalistic theme of the continuity of science and philosophy. One does not capture 'the meaning' of an expression; one explicates or proposes a theory of the referential features one is interested in preserving.

(3) Another attempt to define synonymy asserts that two expressions are synonymous if they are interchangeable. But it is not enough to say expressions are synonymous when the interchange of the one with the other within extensional contexts does not change the truth value of the sentences involved. This has the unacceptable consequence that merely coextensive terms would be synonyms. To do better one has to require interchangeability within intensional contexts. However, this raises the problem of breaking out of the circle of intensional notions.

(4) The fourth approach is another of Carnap's. It consists in constructing an artificial language and then defining 'analytic' for it. While it is possible to construct a language and specify that relative to it logic, mathematics and such truths as 'All bachelors are unmarried men' and 'Nothing is larger than itself' are analytic, this language-relative specification of analyticity does not clarify matters. It does not help to be told that in one language, language 1 (artificial or otherwise), we have a list of sentences that are analytic 1, and that in another language, language 2, we have the list analytic 2 and so on. What we want of an explication of analyticity is an account of what analytic 1, analytic 2 and so on have in common. The appeal to artificial languages fails to provide this characterization. Moreover, the problem is precisely why 'All bachelors are unmarried' is on the list and 'No bachelors are six-legged' is not. To be told that a sentence is analytic because it is on a list (even the list of an artificial language) provides no real distinction.

(5) The last attempt to define analyticity that Quine considers appeals to the verification theory of meaning. According to this theory, 'the meaning of a statement is the method of empirically confirming or infirming it'; 'statements are synonymous if and only if they are alike in point of method of empirical confirmation or infirmation' ([1953] 1961: 37). Though sympathetic towards the empiricist thrust of this theory Quine does not think it survives the holistic criticism of the dogma of reductionism.

Quine's critique of the theory of meaning has amounted to a challenge to provide precise accounts of its notions. What counts as precise could take the form of reducing intensional notions to extensional ones. His criticisms of modal concepts has spurred a generation of responses in what is known as possible world semantics (see MODAL LOGIC, PHILOSOPHICAL ISSUES IN §3), which in one of its variations can be seen as trying to provide a reduction of intensional modal notions via extensional metalinguistic truth conditions for modal statements. The success of this reduction is still challenged by Quinians (1981: 113–24). More in keeping with Quine's challenge to explicate the theory of meaning is Davidson's work on letting a Tarskian theory of truth serve as surrogate for a theory of meaning. Another way in which scepticism about the theory of meaning might be overcome would be by an empirical and behaviouristically constrained account of such notions. Carnap took up this challenge and sketched a programme for empirically identifying meanings by testing translation hypotheses, for example, a linguist's hypotheses for translating the terms 'Pferd' from German to English as 'horse'. Quine's response was the topic of radical translation and his thesis of the indeterminacy of translation.

9 Indeterminacy of translation

How much of language is susceptible to empirical analysis? Like Carnap, Quine takes the case of linguists hypothesizing about translations as the subject matter for empirical inquiry. Both take as their data a native speaker's response to appropriate stimuli. Quine introduces the concept of the stimulus meaning of a sentence for a person as the class of stimulations which would prompt them to assent to it. But Quine deals with the stimulus meaning of whole sentences, such as 'This is a horse', and not terms, such as 'horse'. Quine's linguist offers a hypothesis equating two sentences (one is the native's and the other the linguist's) and checks it against a native speaker's assenting or dissenting to the native sentence in the presence of some nonverbal stimulus. Carnap considered translation for languages such as German and English which are known to have much in common. For Quine, the critical case is that of radical translation, that is, translations between languages that have little or nothing in common. Think of a linguist among some radically foreign tribe. The linguist observes a certain correlation between a native utterance of 'Gavagai' and the presence of rabbits, and proceeds to frame a hypothesis which equates 'Gavagai' and the one-word sentence 'Rabbit', short for 'Here's a rabbit'. The linguist could, on learning how to recognize the native's assent and dissent, question the native by uttering 'Gavagai' when a rabbit appears and seeing whether the native assents. Carnap would presumably want this to count as evidence that 'Gavagai' and 'Rabbit' have the same meaning. But does the evidence really go that far? All that we have as data is the native's expression and the rabbit stimulation. Quine claims that on these grounds one could equally well translate 'Gavagai' as 'rabbit stage' or 'temporal part of a rabbit' or something else. For wherever there are rabbit stimulations there are also rabbit-stage stimulations, and so on. On what basis, then, would one decide between these different translations? In the case of culturally similar languages one assumes a stock of more theoretical guides to translations, and thus one can ask the German whether all horses are *Pferde* and all *Pferde* are horses. In the case of radical translation, the linguist is not in a position to pose these more theoretical questions. At this point hypotheses less directly connected to the data – to the stimulus conditions – may be introduced by the linguist. These, which Quine calls analytical hypotheses, can be framed so as to do justice to quite different translations. Thus radical translation provides evidence for the thesis of the indeterminacy of translation (see RADICAL TRANSLATION AND RADICAL INTERPRETATION §§2–5).

To illustrate this matter for the Gavagai case we must note that in order to ask the question 'Is this rabbit the same as that?' the linguist must have decided how to translate articles, pronouns, identity predicates and so on. To translate these sentences is to go far beyond the data provided by the stimuli and involves selecting from different sets of analytical hypotheses, that is, different possible manuals of translation. On one set of these we translate the question as 'Is this the same rabbit as that?', while on another as 'Is this rabbit stage of the same series as that?' Each of these translations is equally good, yet they are mutually incompatible. Since neither of these has any immediate connection with the Gavagai stimulation there is no way of deciding between them.

This indeterminacy provides further grounds for discrediting the notion of meaning. Philosophers have talked as if meanings are related to expressions in somewhat the same way as paintings in a museum are related to their labels. Quine dubs this 'the myth of the museum' (1969: 27). According to this view, two expressions are synonymous when they are related to a unique meaning, like two labels for the same painting. In the case of translation, one English expression is a translation of another in a different language when the two bear a relation to one and the same interlinguistic object which is their meaning. Quine is attempting to dislodge this model for thinking about language and to put in its place a more empirically based conception. According to the museum model, an expression has its meaning, pure and simple, and two synonymous expressions relate uniquely to one meaning which, as interlinguistic, is independent of the languages in which it is expressed. What Quine has shown is that it makes no sense to speak of language-independent meanings. Translation from one language to another is relative to a set of analytical hypotheses. There is no independent meaning of 'Gavagai' which the linguist can link to 'This is a rabbit' and not 'This is a rabbit stage'. The linguist is at best in a position of saying that 'Gavagai' and 'This is a rabbit' are synonymous relative to the assumption of certain analytical hypotheses. We have to study language in terms of linguistic behaviour in the face of stimulus conditions; in turn this behaviour must be interpreted in relation to more theoretical background assumptions. With the exception of observation sentences, we have at best relative notions of meaning (synonymy and analyticity), and these will not do the job philosophers have frequently assigned to them according to the myth of the museum.

Quine insists on behaviourism as the required method for studying language learning. He argues that we learn language by observing verbal behaviour and having our verbal behaviour reinforced by others.

But there are naturalistic accounts of language learning which are scientifically respectable and not behaviourist (see CHOMSKY, N. §3). Yet although Quine insists on behaviourism as the method for studying and acquiring languages, he is not a behaviourist in psychology or the philosophy of mind. On the mind–body problem he endorses Davidson's anomalous monism – the view that our ways of speaking of the mental, for example, of perceptions and beliefs, cannot be stated in terms of the natural laws which govern the underlying physiological states, even though our mental states just are such states. Quine construes the matter so that mental ascriptions have a role in everyday life and the social sciences that cannot be precisely specified in purely physiological or physicalist terms.

See also: ANALYTICAL PHILOSOPHY §4;
BEHAVIOURISM, METHODOLOGICAL AND SCIENTIFIC

List of works

Quine, W.V. (1934) *A System of Logistic*, Cambridge, MA: Harvard University Press. (A revised version of Quine's dissertation.)

—— (1936) 'Truth by Convention', in O.H. Lee (ed.) *Philosophical Essays for A.N. Whitehead*, New York: Longmans. (Critique of attempts to justify logical and mathematical truth in some distinctively non-empirical way – for example, as grounded in conventions.)

—— (1937) 'New Foundations for Mathematical Logic', *American Mathematical Monthly* 44: 70–80. (One of Quine's most famous alternatives to issues in the foundations of mathematics such as Russell's paradox.)

—— (1940) *Mathematical Logic*, Cambridge, MA: Harvard University Press. (One of Quine's most systematic logic texts, including another alternative account of the foundation of mathematics.)

Quine, W.V. and Goodman, N. (1947) 'Steps Towards a Constructive Nominalism', *Journal of Symbolic Logic* 12: 97–122. (An early examination of the prospects for a nominalist programme in mathematics and its limitations.)

Quine, W.V. (1948) 'On What There Is', *Review of Metaphysics* 2: 21–38. (The classic statement of Quine's view on ontological commitment.)

—— (1951) 'Two Dogmas of Empiricism', *Philosophical Review* 60: 20–43. (Quine's classic critique of the analytic–synthetic distinction and of reductionist-atomistic empiricism.)

—— (1953) *From a Logical Point of View*, Cambridge, MA: Harvard University Press, revised, 1961. (An early collection of some of his most famous essays, including 'New Foundations for Mathematical Logic', 'On What There Is' and 'Two Dogmas of Empiricism'. The 1961 edition incorporates many important revisions.)

—— (1960a) 'Carnap on Logical Truth', *Synthèse* 12: 350–74. (Continues criticism of the attempt to give a distinctly linguistic justification of logical truth.)

—— (1960b) *Word and Object*, New York: Wiley & Sons. (A major source for Quine's views on meaning, translation, reference, modality and propositional attitudes.)

—— (1966) *The Ways of Paradox and Other Essays*, New York: Random House. (A collection of essays on various topics, including 'Truth by Convention' and 'Three Grades of Modal Involvement'.)

—— (1969) *Ontological Relativity and Other Essays*, New York: Columbia University Press. (Collection of essays including the title essay and others such as 'Epistemology Naturalized'.)

Quine, W.V. and Ullian, J.S. (1970) *The Web of Belief*, New York: Random House. (An introduction to the scientific method from a Quinian perspective.)

Quine, W.V. (1974) *The Roots of Reference*, La Salle, IL: Open Court. (A Quinian, methodologically behaviourist account of how we get to talk about objects.)

—— (1981) *Theories and Things*, Cambridge, MA: Harvard University Press. (Essays, mainly from this period, on positing objects and what it means.)

—— (1985) *The Time of My Life: An Autobiography*, Cambridge, MA: MIT Press. (Quine's very readable autobiography.)

—— (1986) *Philosophy of Logic*, Cambridge, MA: Harvard University Press. (An introduction to the subject via a discussion of truth, modalities and propositional attitudes, logic – its nature, scope and justification.)

—— (1987) *Quiddities*, Cambridge, MA: Harvard University Press. (Introduction to various philosophical topics via a dictionary format.)

—— (1992) *Pursuit of Truth*, Cambridge, MA: Harvard University Press. (A survey and update of Quine's views on cognitive meaning, objective reference and the grounds of knowledge.)

—— (1995) *From Stimulus to Science*, Cambridge, MA: Harvard University Press. (A distinctive short tour of the history of philosophy, followed by an exploration of topics such as epistemology naturalized, reference, empirical content and the philosophy of mind.)

References and further reading

Barrett, R.B. and Gibson, R. (eds) (1990) *Perspectives on Quine*, Oxford: Blackwell. (Papers given at a conference for Quine's 80th birthday, followed by his replies.)

Davidson, D. and Hintikka, J. (eds) (1975) *Words and Objections*, Dordrecht: Reidel. (A collection of essays followed by Quine's comments.)

* Field, H. (1980) *Science Without Numbers*, Princeton, NJ: Princeton University Press. (An important attempt at a nominalistic approach to mathematics.)

Gibson, R. (1982) *The Philosophy of W.V. Quine*, Gainesville, FL: University Presses of Florida. (An extremely fine secondary source on Quine.)

Hahn, L.E. and Schilpp, P.A. (eds) (1986) *The Philosophy of W.V. Quine*, La Salle, IL: Open Court. (The Quine volume in a distinguished series, containing an intellectual autobiography by Quine, essays on his work and his replies; also contains an excellent bibliography of Quine's works.)

Inquiry 37 (1994) Symposium on Quine. (A journal issue with Quine's comments on the essays.)

Leonardi, P. and Santambroggia, M. (eds) (1995) *On Quine*, Cambridge: Cambridge University Press. (A conference volume on Quine with his comments.)

Orenstein, A. (1977) *Willard Van Orman Quine*, Boston, MA: G.K. Hall. (An introduction to Quine's thought and its place in twentieth-century philosophy.)

Orenstein, A. and Kotatko, P. (eds) (1998) *Knowledge, Language and Logic: Questions for Quine*, Boston Studies in the Philosophy of Science, Dordrecht: Kluwer. (A collection of essays followed by Quine's comments.)

Revue Internationale de Philosophie (January 1998), ed. P. Gochet. (A special Quine issue with papers on his work followed by his comments.)

Russell, B.A.W. and Whitehead, A.N. (1910–13) *Principia Mathematica*, Cambridge: Cambridge University Press, 3 vols; 2nd edn, 1925–7. (A groundbreaking classic of modern logic and of the logicist programme of reducing mathematics to higher-order logic.)

ALEX ORENSTEIN

QUOTATION *see* USE/MENTION DISTINCTION AND QUOTATION

R

RABBINIC LAW *see* HALAKHAH

RABBINIC THEOLOGY
see THEOLOGY, RABBINIC

RABELAIS, FRANÇOIS (*c.*1483–1553)

Rabelais, a French humanist and comic writer of the Renaissance, is best known for his chronicles of Gargantua and Pantagruel, in which coarse popular humour, fine Lucianic irony and staggering erudition are uniquely blended, and which claim to reveal, first appearances notwithstanding, 'certain very high sacraments and dread mysteries, concerning not only our religion, but also our public and private life' ([1532–52] 1955: 38).

Rabelais has been subjected to the most contradictory interpretations and judgments. Like Erasmus, whom he admired, Rabelais was attacked in his own time by schismatic Protestants (most notably Calvin) and by reactionary Catholics (most notably the faculty of theology at Paris), as an obscene Lucianic atheist and a heretic. At the same time he was admired and supported by high-minded patrons including Francis I, the king's devout sister Marguerite de Navarre, and Cardinal Jean Du Bellay. Even today Rabelais' religion and philosophy are the subject of debate among scholars, while his work is known to non-specialists more for the 'Rabelaisian' ribaldry of a few pages than for the complex irony and profoundly humanistic design that characterize his works as a whole.

1 Intellectual orientation
2 Early works: *Pantagruel* and *Gargantua*
3 Late works: *Tiers Livre* and *Quart Livre*

1 Intellectual orientation

Rabelais himself was a man of multiple talents and professions, prodigiously learned in all disciplines that were currently being transformed under the influence of humanism: classical languages (Latin, Greek, Hebrew), ancient and modern literatures, history,

moral philosophy, medicine, law, theology. Son of a lawyer in Chinon, he served in the orders of St Francis and St Benedict before becoming a lay priest, a doctor and professor of medicine, an accomplished student of Roman law, an amateur biblical humanist, and a member of French diplomatic missions to the Holy See in the years leading up to the Gallican crisis (1534, 1535–6, 1547–9). His humanist preoccupations are clearly evident in the serious works he published in Latin and Greek in 1532. These include an annotated edition and Latin translation of medical treatises by Hippocrates and Galen, an edition of documents he took to be a will and a contract of sale dating from Roman Republican times, and an edition of a contemporary treatise on the topography of Ancient Rome. Equally revealing are several parodic almanacs Rabelais published in the vernacular, most notably the *Pantagrueline prognostication* (1533), in which astrology and prognostication generally are humorously debunked in the name of Christian scepticism.

Rabelais stated his intellectual loyalties explicitly in admiring letters to humanists like Guillaume Budé (1521) and ERASMUS (1532). To the latter in particular he declared, addressing the aged humanist as his spiritual father and mother, that: 'whatever I am, whatever I am good for, it is to you alone that I owe it'. Rabelais' works in the vernacular give considerable substance to this extravagant claim, championing as they do Erasmian causes like the restoration of classical learning and the return to a non-doctrinal, eirenic, paleo-Christian church.

2 Early Works: *Pantagruel* and *Gargantua*

Rabelais' first two books, *Pantagruel* (1532) and *Gargantua* (*c.*1534), were published anonymously in Lyons under the anagrammatic pseudonym Alcofrybas Nasier. These vigorous mock epics relate the birth, education and 'horrific' exploits of two giant heroes drawn from popular tradition. Masquerading as penny chapbooks to be sold at the commercial fairs of Lyons, they adopt the format and superficial trappings of medieval popular literature in order to satirize all things medieval and represent the triumph of an enlightened Christian humanism over gothic darkness.

The principal focus of *Pantagruel* is political. Set in

Utopia, the political non-place invented a mere sixteen years earlier by Thomas More (see UTOPIANISM §1), and visibly inspired by pacificist writings like *Institutio principis christiani* (Education of a Christian Prince) (1516) by ERASMUS (§3), *Pantagruel* narrates the failure of an imperialistic war of aggression. When Gargantua's realm is invaded by an usurping tyrant named Anarche (meaning 'non-rule') the eponymous hero repels the invaders, and inaugurates a new Golden Age of peace and harmony resembling Christ's kingdom of heaven (Matthew 20: 25–7 and 23: 12). He does this by abolishing the hierarchical political and religious institutions of the old order (empire and church). Pantagruel is prepared for this messianic role by a humanistic education. After a fruitless tour of the gothic universities he rejects the likes of Duns Scotus and Ockham and incorporates instead the entire curriculum of newly restored humanist disciplines, described by Gargantua in a justly famous letter to his son ([1532–52] 1955: ch.8).

Appearing two years later, *Gargantua* rehearses the same basic plot as *Pantagruel* but in a more realistic and satirical mode. The unjust invader, Picrochole (which means 'bitter bile'), resembles the Holy Roman Emperor Charles V in his incursions against Francis I. The scholastic old guard is represented by the 'sophists' of the Sorbonne, whose syllogistic illogic and wretched Latin are brilliantly parodied in a muddled speech by the unforgettable Master Janotus Bragmardo (see MAJOR, J. §4). To these familiar themes *Gargantua* adds a sustained attack against monasticism, focusing on what Erasmus called the *constitutiones humanae* of the modern church (that is, traditions and practices unauthorized by Scripture). The most sympathetic character of the book is an anti-monk named Frère Jean des Entommeures, whose febrile activity and good-natured spontaneity are favourably contrasted with the monastic ideal of a contemplative life governed by rules and regulations. The book concludes with the founding of a utopian anti-monastery, the Abbaye de Thélème, in which the Benedictine Rule is abolished in favour of the Pauline principle of Christian freedom, expressed in the single non-rule, 'Fay ce que vouldras' ('Do as you wish').

3 Late works: *Tiers Livre* and *Quart Livre*

Many years later Rabelais wrote a sequel to *Pantagruel*, the *Tiers Livre* (*Third Book of Pantagruel*) (1546), followed by a sequel to the sequel, the *Quart Livre* (*Fourth Book of Pantagruel*) (1552). Published in Paris under the author's own name, printed in beautiful Roman type and humanistic format, these more mature works are of a very different character.

Massive humanistic learning overwhelms attenuated vestiges of popular humour and comic effects depend less on the reader's recognition of well-known biblical and Virgilian tags, as before, than on a good first-hand knowledge of works of moral philosophy by PLUTARCH and LUCIAN, CICERO and SENECA, as well as the Hebrew Bible, the Greek New Testament, Pliny's *Natural History* and the Justinian *Digest*. The sequels relate a pseudo-Socratic quest undertaken by Pantagruel's foolish companion, Panurge. In both books the quest ends in failure and appears to serve chiefly as a loose structuring device for an open-ended series of episodes in which political, theological and philosophical ideologies and institutions are brilliantly satirized.

The focal character of the *Tiers Livre*, Panurge, is a sophistical egotist first seen justifying his profligacy by praising debts as the *anima mundi* in terms borrowed directly from Ficino's *De amore* (On Love) (1469) (see FICINO, M. §4). Suspended between the desire to take a wife and the fear of being cuckolded, he tries in vain throughout the book to decide whether or not to marry. Whereas the Socratic Pantagruel would have him do this simply by knowing his own will, the gnostic Panurge insists that he must first know things above and beyond himself, believing that such knowledge will allow him to eliminate future contingents. His misguided quest leads him to consult burlesque sources of divination as well as experts in various fields of learning, none of which provides the certainty he seeks. In the lengthy discussions surrounding many of these consultations Pantagruel speaks the language of Neoplatonism in such a way as to mock the Hermetic tendencies of his wayward companion. Panurge's thirteen consultants include a sinister astrologer, Her Trippa, in whom many have seen a caricature of Henricus Cornelius AGRIPPA and an exasperatingly elusive philosopher, Trouillogan, in whom Rabelais ridicules 'ephectic' Pyrrhonians a full decade and a half before the works of Sextus Empiricus first appeared in print.

The *Quart Livre* prolongs the quest of the *Tiers Livre* in a fantastical sea voyage to Cathay where Panurge hopes to consult the oracle of Bacbuc, the Holy Bottle. But Panurge's personal dilemma is soon displaced by the political and religious crises of contemporary Christendom as the principal focus of the continuation. Modelled roughly on Lucian's *True History* and profoundly influenced by Plutarch's *On the Obsolescence of Oracles*, this bitter odyssey narrates Pantagruel's encounters with the inhabitants of fourteen islands, which satirize the social and political institutions of modern Europe. The harshest episodes condemn the Council of Trent and the doctrines and practices it was even then legislating as dogma. The un-Christian fanaticism and intransigence of both Catholics and Protestants is a recurring theme.

The *Quart Livre* ends even more abruptly than the *Tiers Livre*, far from its ostensible goal. This deliberately non-teleological structure was so unsettling that it provoked an anonymous editor to publish an apocryphal, posthumous *Cinquiesme Livre* (*Fifth Book of Pantagruel*) (1564), which concludes with the Holy Bottle and the oracular word ('Trinch') vainly sought by Panurge in the *Quart Livre*. Although this final revelation completes Panurge's personal quest it adds nothing to the meaning of the preceding books and seriously detracts from their formal and ideological coherence.

See also: Erasmus, D.; Humanism, Renaissance §7; Political philosophy, history of §5–6; Scepticism, Renaissance §4

List of works

Rabelais, F. (*c.*1483–1553) *The Complete Works of François Rabelais*, trans. D. Frame, Berkeley and Los Angeles, CA: University of California Press, 1991. (The only English translation that includes minor works and letters, all helpfully annotated by the translator and R.C. La Charité. The letters to Budé (1521) and Erasmus (1532) and the *Pantagrueline prognostication* (1533) appear in this edition, as well as the five books of Gargantua and Pantagruel.)
—— (*c.*1483–1553) *Oeuvres complètes*, ed. M. Huchon, Bibliothèque de la Pléiade, Paris: Gallimard, 1994. (The complete works in French and Latin, superbly edited and annotated by the leading expert on Rabelais' language and the evolution of his text. Destined to supersede the standard but incomplete edition begun by Abel Lefranc in 1913. Contains a useful chronology and a full bibliography of recent books on Rabelais.)
—— (1532–52) *Gargantua and Pantagruel*, trans. J.M. Cohen, London and New York: Penguin, 1955. (The most accessible and faithful of modern English versions, unfortunately virtually unannotated. Like all editions includes the posthumous *Cinquiesme Livre* (1564) along with the authentic four books, *Pantagruel* (1532), *Gargantua* (*c.*1534), *Tiers Livre* (1546) and *Quart Livre* (1552).)

References and further reading

Cooper, R. (1991) *Rabelais et l'Italie*, Études Rabelaisiennes, Geneva: Droz. (Presents most extant documents pertaining to Rabelais' personal and civic life, expertly edited. Introduction helps to fill some gaps in our sketchy knowledge of Rabelais' life and partially fills the need for an up-to-date biography.)
Defaux, G. (1973) *Pantagruel et les sophistes: Contribution à l'histoire de l'humanisme chrétien au XVIe siècle*, The Hague: Nijhoff. (An extremely erudite analysis of the conflict between scholasticism and Christian scepticism in Rabelais' works, especially *Pantagruel*. An important, rewarding study, but hard reading for those with little Latin.)
Desrosiers-Bonin, D. (1992) *Rabelais et l'humanisme civil*, Études Rabelaisiennes, Geneva: Droz. (Insightful, thorough thematic treatment of the ethical and political dimensions of Rabelais' works. Includes a complete bibliography of modern Rabelais scholarship up to 1990.)
Duval, E.M. (1991) *The Design of Rabelais's Pantagruel*, New Haven, CT and London: Yale University Press. (Demonstrates the formal and ideological coherence of Rabelais' first book as they are revealed through an overarching epic and messianic pattern.)
—— (1997) *The Design of Rabelais's Tiers Livre de Pantagruel*, Études Rabelaisiennes, Geneva: Droz. (Discovers the coherence and intention of Rabelais' most ambiguous book in the hero's ironic design for his companion and in the author's corresponding design for his reader, both of which turn on the oracular 'Know thyself' uttered by Panurge at the centre of a symmetrically-ordered work.)
—— (1998) *The Design of Rabelais's Quart Livre de Pantagruel*, Études Rabelaisiennes, Geneva: Droz. (Examines the religious basis for Rabelais' critique of the ideologies and institutions of sixteenth-century Europe, and the nature of Pantagruel's ethical stance in confronting them.)
Febvre, L. (1982) *The Problem of Unbelief in the Sixteenth Century: The Religion of Rabelais*, trans. B. Gottlieb, Cambridge, MA: Harvard University Press. (Translation of a book by the great Annales School historian, first published in 1942 to refute the then current view that Rabelais was a rationalist and an atheist. A milestone in Rabelais scholarship still useful for its analysis of Rabelais' intellectual and religious culture and for background on humanist circles in Lyons.)
Screech, M.A. (1959) *L'Évangélisme de Rabelais: Aspects de la satire religieuse au seizième siècle*, trans. by the author as *Rabelais and the Challenge of the Gospel: Evangelism, Reformation, Dissent*, Baden-Baden: Koerner, 1992. (Treats theological questions like the nature of faith, the efficacy of works, predestination and freedom of the will, and so on, according to Rabelais. Occasionally mistakes

the intention of the text by reading it as a theological treatise.)

—— (1979) *Rabelais*, London, Duckworth and Ithaca, NY: Cornell University Press. (A useful, accessible episode-by-episode commentary on all of Rabelais' literary works, distilling the fruits of a lifetime of scholarship by the most learned of modern Rabelais scholars.)

Weinberg, F.M. (1972) *The Wine and the Will: Rabelais's Bacchic Christianity*, Detroit, MI: Wayne State University Press. (Analyses the ubiquitous wine motif in terms of a syncretistic fusing of Bacchic mysteries and Christian eucharist.)

EDWIN M. DUVAL

RACE, THEORIES OF

The first theories of race were attempts to explain why the peoples of Europe (or sometimes particular peoples within Europe) had developed a higher civilization than the peoples of other regions. They attributed inequality in development to different biological inheritance, undervaluing the importance of the learning process. Between the world wars social scientists demonstrated how many apparently natural differences, and attitudes towards other groups, were not inherited but learned behaviour. They asked instead why people should entertain false ideas about members of other groups. As the twentieth century comes to an end, it is claimed on the one hand that processes of racial group formation can be explained in the same terms as those used for explaining group phenomena in general. On the other hand it is maintained that the only possible theories are those explaining why, in particular societies and at particular times, racism assumes a given form.

1 **Unequal development**
2 **Early social science**
3 **Recent social science**

1 Unequal development

The word race entered west European languages in the sixteenth century to designate a set of humans of common ancestry. The end of the eighteenth century saw the first attempts to utilize it as a scientific concept. These ultimately failed, but much confusion was generated by the lack of clarity in its scientific use and by the interaction between popular and scientific usage. The French anatomist Cuvier in 1817 divided *Homo sapiens* into three subspecies (or varieties) which he called races: they were Caucasians, Mon-

golians and Ethiopians. He maintained that differences in human physique produced differences in culture and mental quality. This explained why whites had gained dominion over the world and made the most rapid progress in the sciences. 'Yellows' were less advanced, and blacks degraded. So race was used as a taxon, but if it meant the same as subspecies it was redundant. It was also employed as an *explanans* of unequal development. At much the same time the idiom of race was popularized in historical novels, notably in Sir Walter Scott's description of Normans and Saxons as races in his best-selling *Ivanhoe* (1820). Racial designations were used as a way of identifying group differences within Europe that was later extended to describe differences between Europeans and the peoples of other regions colonized by Europeans.

Any understanding of the causes of variation within the human species in the pre-Darwinian era was bedevilled by the near-impossibility of explaining how that variation could have come about if, as was generally believed, humanity had descended from Adam and Eve in the space of some six thousand years. One answer was the claim that humanity consisted of a limited number of permanent racial types (as argued by Charles Hamilton Smith in England, Robert Knox in Scotland, Arthur de Gobineau in France, J.C. Nott and G.R. Gliddon in the USA, Karl Vogt in Germany). This doctrine has often been called scientific racism. Its exponents tended to equate race with species and claimed that it constituted a scientific explanation of human history.

Darwin's theory of natural selection was applied to human affairs by the eugenists and by writers such as Sir Arthur Keith. Their arguments in certain respects prefigured modern sociobiology. They presented races as units in the course of evolution which developed their distinctiveness by in-breeding. Racial prejudice was seen as an inherited character that helped them do this. This has also been seen as scientific racism, but whereas the typological theory looked to the past in assuming that there had once been pure races, the selectionist theory looked to the future in presenting ethnic and national groups as prospective species.

The further development of Darwinian theory put an end to the notion of race as an *explanans* of human history. If one publication marks the transition, it is *We Europeans* (1935) by Sir Julian Huxley and A.C. Haddon. This separated human physical variation, as an *explanandum* to be explained by population genetics, from the variation between national groups (now named ethnic groups) to be addressed by historians and social scientists (see EVOLUTIONARY THEORY AND SOCIAL SCIENCE).

2   Early social science

Not until the 1920s was there evidence that racial prejudice was a form of learned rather than inherited behaviour. How then were the physical differences that people in western Europe and North America called 'racial' used to construct social categories?

The ecological theory developed by Robert E. Park in Chicago maintained that migration brought distinctive peoples into contact; competition made them conscious of what distinguished them, and those in a superior status developed prejudice as a defensive reaction.

The Freudian theory maintained that social life built up frustration which individuals released on to scapegoats in the form of displaced aggression; this added to the direct aggression that sprang from the conflict of interests.

The first empirical studies of the relations between blacks and whites in the USA of the 1930s were cast in a structural-functionalist framework. US society was said to be founded on distinctive values that stressed the social equality of citizens. Racial discrimination conflicted with these values and generated an 'American dilemma'.

This orthodoxy was attacked most vigorously in *Caste, Class and Race* (1948) by Oliver Cromwell Cox, a black Trinidad-born sociologist. He contended that as European capitalism expanded into territories where natural resources were abundant, demand increased for labour, especially unfree labour. So beliefs justifying black subordination were built into the structure of capitalist societies, dividing white from black workers. Cox distinguished racism and anti-Semitism as distinct social forms. The former justified exploitation. The latter was directed to the conversion, expulsion or eradication of the alien group. That the two might share a common psychological component was irrelevant.

Many subsequent writers have similarly chosen to start from postulates about power relations within and between states. While conceding that in some societies the main conflicts derived from the relation of groups to the means of production, Leo Kuper maintained that there were states (like apartheid South Africa) in which political power influenced the relation to the means of production much more than any influence in the reverse direction. These were 'plural societies' in which racial conflict pre-empted or preceded class conflict.

3   Recent social science

Recent theoretical writing is at one in recognizing the political significance of race as a folk concept underlying group boundaries and in denying that this concept has any value for the explanation of why humans draw racial boundaries in particular ways. To simplify what can otherwise be a confusing picture, it can be helpful to focus upon the sharp division of opinion about what are the most important *explananda* and about the kind of *explanantia* to be sought. These are expressed in two 'problematics' (meaning by this sets of questions of interest to scholars who share views about the best ways to answer the questions). The racial discrimination problematic (a revised version of the frequently-criticized race relations problematic) holds that the attitudes and behaviour which in popular speech are called racial are to be explained in the same terms as other forms of attitude and behaviour. The racism problematic, by contrast, holds that there is a distinctive historical phenomenon known as racism that has to be seen for itself and related to the social processes that produce it. Underlying these contentions are two contrasting epistemologies; there is no agreement on the best names for these, though the writer has called them Kant-inspired and Hegel-inspired.

The first problematic is primarily concerned with the causes of racial discrimination as a feature of individual behaviour. It holds that discrimination, like crime, is a normal feature of every kind of society. Discrimination is not necessarily unlawful or immoral, and individuals are to be held morally responsible for any social distinctions they draw. Because it starts from the individual, this approach leads to a rational choice theory that borrows from neoclassical economics and the analysis of the means–end relationship in sociology. The name has led some into assuming that it is a theory of rational choices alone, whereas the theory takes rationality (or optimization) purely as a criterion against which to assess the consequences of choices of whatever motivation or character (see RATIONAL CHOICE THEORY). The attitudes and behaviour that are popularly called racial are then explained as the product of shared tastes or values which individuals seek to satisfy in situations of scarcity and constraint. Outward differences, like those which are called racial, may be used to identify persons as belonging to particular social categories. A person's appearance may create an expectation that they will possess or lack some social quality. Through such expectations social inequalities in one generation may be transmitted to succeeding generations. This approach attempts, within a single conceptual framework, to analyse processes of group inclusion and exclusion based upon ethnic origin in all historical periods and geographical regions.

The contrasting problematic is primarily concerned

with racism as a pathological feature of society that generates structural and ideological pressures upon individuals, thereby diminishing the degree of their personal responsibility for any discriminatory action. Its starting point is with the collectivity, confining the analysis of group inclusion and exclusion to particular societies and their spheres of influence. The utility for research of the postulate that racism is manifested in changing forms is dependent upon the reliability of the method for identifying what lies behind the form. The political dimension of the problem was illustrated in 1975 when the UN General Assembly resolved that 'Zionism is a form of racism and racial discrimination' (a resolution revoked in 1991). Whether Zionism is such a form depends upon the definitions of Zionism and racism.

The approach from racial discrimination follows Kant's view of the Copernican revolution in science. The observer does not seek to comprehend objects in their entirety as things in themselves, but, by standing apart from them, to develop concepts that will help explain selected features of the observations. Definitions have to be adapted to research methods (see KANT, I. §6). The approach from racism follows Hegel's view of the observer as part of the world they study, but able to ascertain the principles underlying the development of that world and to reach a knowledge validated by history (see HEGEL, G.W.F. §8). Definitions are sought that will express the true nature of objects. There is a fundamental difference of opinion about the kinds of knowledge that are possible and the task of the social scientist.

French sociologists have recently revived and reformulated one of Cox's arguments. They contend that whereas racial ideology in Europe used to follow a logic of inferiorization and exploitation, it now follows a logic of differentiation directed to the expulsion or destruction of groups perceived as alien. The structures of industrial society based upon stratification and the welfare state have been weakened. In the West the old nationalism has lost its appeal so that people have been turning to regional, ethnic, religious and life-style identities. These conditions stimulate racist exclusions. In the UK and North America, as in France, it is now said to be necessary to distinguish a variety of racisms that are expressed in coded language. Crucially, they can produce a racist effect while denying that this effect is the result of racism. For example, certain arguments about defending a national way of life against the pressures of immigration have been described as coded expressions of racist sentiment. 'Race' is said to be a political construct and the sociologist's choice of an *explanandum* a political decision. But there remains the problem of how to delimit the number of possible racisms. For example, the Catholic Church contends that *in vitro* fertilization and genetic manipulation could give rise to a new form of racism; others might argue that whether or not such possibilities are matters of concern, their origins are not those of racial ideology. Since racism is assumed to be a hidden essence, there is no sure way of establishing any cause-and-effect relationship.

Racial differentiation has been a subject for research in other social sciences. In social psychology there is now no distinctive branch of 'racial' theory. Racial distinctions are explained by reference to the principles used in accounting for other forms of group behaviour, such as attitudes, attributions, identity, and so on. Geographers have studied processes of racial segregation, including the spatial dimension to the emergence of new identities based upon racial or ethnic origin. Political scientists have studied the influence of racial identification upon voting behaviour and the ways in which racial problems and policies are handled by national and international political institutions. Since the collapse of Soviet control over eastern Europe many older ethnic conflicts have reappeared, so that for some fields of research theories of racial or ethnic tensions have to entail theories of nationalism.

See also: ANTI-SEMITISM; MULTICULTURALISM

References and further reading

Banton, M. (1983) *Racial and Ethnic Competition*, Cambridge: Cambridge University Press; repr. Aldershot: Gregg Revivals, 1992. (Pages 15–31 for the development of ideas on race in the New World, 42–50 and 78–99 for early social science theories.)

Banton, M. (1987) *Racial Theories*, Cambridge: Cambridge University Press, 2nd edn, 1998. (A history, covering the change from biological to social theories.)

Bataille, P., Couper, K., Martucelli, D. and Peralva, A. (1994) *Racisme et xénophobie en Europe: une comparaison internationale* (Racism and Xenophobia in Europe: an International Comparison), with intro. and conclusion by M. Wieviorka, Paris: La Découverte. (Includes sections on the UK, Belgium, Germany and Italy against a background of French experience.)

* Cox, O.C. (1948) *Caste, Class and Race: A Study in Social Dynamics*, New York: Monthly Review Press. (A wide-ranging and pioneering study influenced by Marxist theory.)

* Huxley, J.S. and Haddon, A.C. (1935) *We Europeans: A Survey of Racial Problems*, London: Jonathan

Cape. (Important to the history of thought on the subject.)

Omi, M. and Winant, H. (1986) *Racial Formation in the United States*, New York: Routledge. (An influential US work that emphasizes political and legal relations.)

Miles, R. (1989) *Racism*, London: Routledge. (Attacks the conceptual inflation resulting from over-extensive use of 'racism' and relates it more closely to class relations.)

Rex, J. and Mason, D. (1986) *Theories of Race and Ethnic Relations*, Cambridge: Cambridge University Press. (A collection of essays about the main approaches current in 1984.)

* Scott, Sir W. (1820) *Ivanhoe*, Harmondsworth: Penguin, 1984. (One of the nineteenth-century's most widely-read novels.)

Solomos, J. and Back, L. (1994) 'Conceptualizing Racisms: Social Theory, Politics and Research', *Sociology* 28 (1): 143–61. (Reviews recent writing in the light of a claim that new forms of racism have emerged, requiring a revision of concepts.)

MICHAEL BANTON

RACONIS, CHARLES D'ABRA DE see ARISTOTELIANISM IN THE 17TH CENTURY

RADBRUCH, GUSTAV (1878–1949)

Gustav Radbruch is an emblematic figure in twentieth-century German legal philosophy and legal science. His particular blending of legal philosopher, dogmatist and politician, and his personal history, interwoven with the tragedy of the Weimar Republic and the rebirth of a democratic Germany after the Nazi horror, have given him special prestige and influence on both constitutional and ordinary jurisprudence in Germany. Some of Radbruch's theses, like the one in his well-known article 'Gesetzliches Unrecht und übergesetzliches Recht' (1946 – translatable as 'Statutory Non-law and Suprastatutory Law'), remain highly topical in German universities and courts.

Radbruch was born in Lübeck to a family of the mercantile bourgeoisie. He completed high school there, and entered the Munich law faculty in 1898, later studying also in Leipzig and Berlin. In Berlin he was a pupil of Franz von Liszt, probably the most influential scholar of criminal law in the new unitary German state, who upheld the line of liberal thought inaugurated by P.A. Feuerbach. Under Liszt's guidance, Radbruch took his doctorate in 1902. The following year, at Heidelberg University, Radbruch secured his *Habilitation* with a study on the relevance of the concept of action to the doctrine of criminal law. He filled various teaching posts between 1906 and 1914, took part in the First World War, and in 1919 secured a chair in criminal law at the University of Kiel.

In 1920 he was elected to the Reichstag, the German parliament, as a socialist member, and in 1921 became Minister of Justice in the Wirth cabinet, subsequently serving again as a minister in the first and second Stresemann cabinets. In November 1923, after Stresemann's withdrawal, he went back to Kiel University, where he stayed till autumn 1926 when he was called to a chair at Heidelberg University. Shortly after Hitler came to power, in May 1933, he was among the first university teachers to be removed from their posts on political grounds. In the twelve years of the Nazi regime, Radbruch retreated to the so-called *innere Emigration*, condemned to silence in his own country even though he did not leave it, devoting himself to historical and humanistic studies and publishing abroad. In September 1945, after the Nazis' defeat, he was appointed Dean of Law at Heidelberg, returning to teaching with renewed enthusiasm.

Radbruch's oeuvre is bracketed by two works, the book *Grundzüge der Rechtsphilosophie* (1914, with a definitive revised edition in 1932) and the 'Gesetzliches Unrecht und übergesetzliches Recht' ('Statutory Non-law and Suprastatutory Law') of 1946 (see Radbruch 1973). This article overturns the main thesis of the *Grundzüge*, namely a radically noncognitivist meta-ethical position, denying claims to knowledge or to objective rightness in moral values (see MORAL JUDGMENT §1). For such an ethical relativism, to which all possible moralities seem acceptable, positive law is independent of moral values. The point is then to arrive at a formula or a conception of positive law not committed a priori to any ethical position, but permitting all of them. Radbruch considered this possible only if a positivistic conception of law is assumed. Here, then, as is also the case *mutatis mutandis* in Hans Kelsen's work, the endpoint of ethical relativism is legal positivism (see KELSEN, H.; LEGAL POSITIVISM §§1, 2).

Noncognitivism is also used by Radbruch to found or justify democracy: if no conception of any faction is capable of proof, then every conception should be fought from the viewpoint of an opposite conception;

but since none of them can be refuted, each of them ought accordingly to be respected even within the viewpoint of the opposing conception (Radbruch 1934). Although he maintained that the concept of law 'is a cultural concept, that is, the concept of a reality oriented to values, which has the object of serving a value' (Radbruch 1973: 29), for Radbruch, at least until 1933, a law whose promulgation is formally and procedurally correct is valid and binding even where its content is morally reprehensible. This conclusion has, however, also a moral basis, grounded in the idea of legal certainty: 'However unjust the law may become in its content, it always, from its mere existence, meets one aim: that of legal certainty' (Radbruch 1914: 183).

Experience of the Nazi horror changed Radbruch's view radically. First and foremost, he accused legal positivism, understood more as a psychological attitude than as a legal philosophical doctrine, of having prepared, aided, or failed to obstruct the affirmation of Nazism. Jurists, accustomed to the motto 'Gesetz ist Gesetz', that is, to regard any duly enacted statute as valid and binding law, however it be promulgated, were incapable of showing resistance to Hitler's injustice and despotism. There must therefore be a change of attitude by jurists, starting from, or at least not neglecting, requirements of substantive justice, so that – this is the 'Radbruch formula' still applied by the German Constitutional Court – where a formally valid law proves intolerably unjust, it is no longer to be regarded as valid or binding. The 'Radbruch formula' breaks down into three parts: (1) first, it is asserted that in general positive law prevails over substantive requirements of justice, even when, while formally valid, it is unjust and irrational; (2) this primacy stops at breaches of principles of justice that are of intolerable proportions; (3) intolerable breaches of justice exist where the positive law explicitly and systematically does not have as its goal the realization or pursuit of aims of justice, and especially where the principles of formal equality (the equal treatment of equal cases) are deliberately and constantly ignored (see JUSTICE, EQUITY AND LAW §1; LAW AND MORALITY §1).

In German culture between the nineteenth and twentieth centuries, in particular in the stormy years of the Weimar Republic, Radbruch represents the enlightened, democratic tradition, all too rare in those times among German philosophers and jurists, often seduced by irrationalist, communitarian and authoritarian slogans. It is the Germany of Kant and of Anselm Feuerbach, the Zivilisation of reason and of rights, whose courageous interpreter he is. 'The expression of a spirit that has become profoundly sterile' was how he was contemptuously dismissed by the Nazi Karl Larenz. But in the end it is Radbruch's, not Larenz's, spirit that has proved fertile.

See also: LAW, PHILOSOPHY OF; LEGAL POSITIVISM

List of works

Radbruch, G. (1914) Grundzüge der Rechtsphilosophie, Leipzig: Duncker & Humblot. (Examines legal certainty.)

—— (1934) 'Le relativisme dans la philosophie du droit', Archives de philosophie du droit.

—— (1973) Rechtsphilosophie, Stuttgart: K.F. Koehler Verlag. (His principal work on legal philosophy in its final edition, with appendices added after the war. 'Anhang 4' is the essay 'Gesetzliches Unrecht und übergesetzliches Recht' (Statutory Non-law and Suprastatutory Law).)

—— (1980) Legal Philosophy of Lask, Radbruch, and Dabin, trans. H. Wilk, with intro. by E.W. Patterson, 20th Century Legal Philosophy, vol. 4, Cambridge, MA: Harvard University Press. (A translation of the 1936 edition of Radbruch's Rechtsphilosophie is to be found at pp. 45–224, capturing his thought before the later post-war revisions and adjustments.)

—— (1996a) Der Mensch im Recht. Ausgewählte Vorträge und Aufsätze über Grundfragen des Rechts, Göttingen: Vandenhoeck & Ruprecht, 3rd edn. (A selection of the author's essays and papers on fundamental questions about law.)

—— (1996b) Einführung in die Rechtswissenschaft, Stuttgart: K.F. Koehler Verlag, 12th edn. (An introductory text on jurisprudence and legal system, discussing the main branches of law.)

—— (1996c) Paul Anselm Feuerbach, ein Juristenleben, Göttingen: Vandenhoeck & Ruprecht, 3rd edn. (This life of Feuerbach gives valuable insights into Radbruch's approach and his sense of indebtedness to Kant and Feuerbach.)

References and further reading

Baratta, A. (1959) 'Relativismus und Naturrecht, im Denken Gustav Radbruchs', Archiv für Rechts- und Sozialphilosophie 45: 505. (A useful analysis of the tension between ethical relativism and natural law inclinations in Radbruch's work.)

Kaufmann, A. (1987) Gustav Radbruch. Rechtsdenker, Philosoph, Sozialdemokrat, Munich/Zurich: Pieper. (A valuable intellectual and philosophical biography of Radbruch by one of his leading successors as a critic of legal positivism in German jurisprudence.)

Stone, J. (1965) Human Law and Human Justice,

London: Stevens and Sons. (A thoughtful account of Radbruch's work, especially on justice in relation to law, is to be found at pp. 231–57, with further useful references.)

MASSIMO LA TORRE

RADHAKRISHNAN, SARVEPALLI (1888–1975)

As a modern interpreter of Indian thought to Western scholars and a major influence on later Indian thinkers, Sarvepalli Radhakrishnan's teaching, writing and worldwide lecturing introduced the West to Indian religion and philosophy as essentially an all-inclusive monism. He was actively committed to participation in Indian and international society as an educator, states-man and leader of the Indian republic and defended Hinduism against Western critics as essentially toler-ant, world-affirming, progressive and socially and politically conscious. Radhakrishnan's neo-Advaita was based on one major strand of Indian monism with modifications based on assumptions from his education in Christian institutions. While maintaining that the Absolute is identical with one's true self, he emphasized the reality of the universe. The truly religious person, he argued, does not flee the world but withdraws to attain personal realization and returns to apply the insight thereby gained to better society.

1   Life and influences
2   Metaphysics
3   Ethics
4   Inclusivism

1   Life and influences

Sarvepalli Radhakrishnan's life was that of a philo-sopher, definer and apologist for Hinduism and an active educator, statesman and world figure. Born in 1888 in south India, he was educated at Christian missionary schools. He received his BA and MA in philosophy from Madras Christian College. He studied under the Christian missionary and ethicist A.G. Hogg (1856–1931) who was a student at Edinburgh University of A.S. Pringle-Pattison and was influenced by A. Ritschl's school of German theology. Trained as an ethicist, Radhakrishnan emerged with the ethical concern of his teachers, but argued that this concern was found in his own tradition, which he traced back to early Indian scriptures and called Vedānta. The major influence in his definition of his tradition was the writings of

the modern Indian leader Swami Vivekananda (see RAMAKRISHNA MOVEMENT), whose response to critics and definition of Hinduism resolved a number of Radhakrishnan's existential dilemmas. Radhakrish-nan chose it as his own definition and devoted his thinking to explicating it as a philosophy and proclaiming it in his life and writings.

After a number of university appointments in south India, Radhakrishnan was appointed in 1921 to the most prestigious philosophical position in India, the King George V Chair of Mental and Moral Science of Calcutta University. From 1936 to 1941 he was the Spalding Professor of Eastern Religions and Ethics at Oxford University. His many posts include chief executive officer at a number of Indian universities, president of the executive board of UNESCO, a member of independent India's constituent assembly, India's second ambassador to the Soviet Union, vice president of India (1952–62) and president of India (1962–7). He lectured throughout the world, retired in 1967 and died in April 1975, having written over three dozen books. These included commentaries on four Indian religious texts and over one hundred articles on philosophy and religion.

2   Metaphysics

In his two-volume *Indian Philosophy* (1923) Radhak-rishnan surveys and evaluates the major Indian philosophical traditions, but from his early writings he clearly identifies his approach and evaluation of others with the tradition of Advaita Vedānta of the eighth-century thinker ŚAŃKARA and the early Indian scriptures called the Upaniṣads which, he believes, show evidence of that tradition. Thus, reality is ultimately a unity in which the One is the indescrib-able, impersonal Absolute, Brahman (see BRAHMAN; MONISM, INDIAN). This One is also the true self, a state of pure consciousness which is a subject rather than an object to us. In traditional terms it is *saccidānanda*, being itself, pure consciousness and unlimited bliss. Knowledge of this One is possible through rational analysis of the empirical data, but certainty comes from an intuitive, immediate aware-ness of Brahman. Science gradually confirms what religions have intuitively understood. This monism does not negate the world, Radhakrishnan insisted, and Śaṅkara has thus been gravely misunderstood when interpreted as teaching that the world is an illusion. When Śaṅkara declared all but the unqua-lified Brahman to be *māyā*, he meant that the world's reality is not independent, for its cause is Brahman. Only Brahman is independently real and the world is one particular manifestation of Brahman, although the actual nature of the relationship between the world and Brahman is logically inconceivable. Radhakrishnan's concern is to affirm the reality of a place in which to live the ethical life and to embrace the universe itself as a cosmic process which has meaning and value. This position he calls 'idealism' (see IDEALISM).

Others have understood the Absolute to be a personal, divine being. This is not a false understanding, he asserted, but a reference to the impersonal Absolute in its relationship to the world. The gods of India are personifications and symbols of the Absolute and three major deities form the *trimūrti*, the three forms of the One Brahman, at times called the Hindu Trinity. Brahma is the Divine as creator, Vishnu as preserver and Shiva as destroyer.

3   Ethics

The goal of human existence, Radhakrishnan asserts, is not a flight from this world for mere personal salvation. Hinduism has been falsely accused of teaching this. Human beings find themselves in ignorance in the rounds of karma and rebirth, but karma is not a mechanical principle; it is an ethical one. It should not be understood fatalistically, as has often been the popular understanding in India. Although actions from past lives have conditioned the present life, humanity can overcome the conditioning through choosing to live the good life. There is no mercy or grace to be sought, only human responsibility. The goal of Hinduism and true religion is *sarvamukti*, the liberation of all. One may withdraw from life in the world for a period to attain an intuitive experience of the One. However, in the spirit of the Buddhist *bodhisattva*, who refuses to enter liberation until all beings are brought in together (see DUTY AND VIRTUE, INDIAN CONCEPTIONS OF §3), the realized individual returns to the world, with the insights gained thereby, to provide a religious, moral and social influence which leads all to liberation. Since all human beings are one in spirit, sacrifice and a life of service follows. Radhakrishnan chooses the *Bhagavad Gītā* (second century BC) with its call to an active lifestyle, as his major support for an ethic of unselfish action.

He does not reject the class system in India, but argues that its correct understanding is as the ordering of society, which he understands to be more like an organism. The four classes are necessary for the life of society, but these divisions are not based on birth but on ethical personality types without one being any higher, purer or more important than another. Therefore, in Radhakrishnan's opinion, this is not the corrupted system of castes found in contemporary India. The intention of the system is to solve the problem of race in India by allowing separate divisions without extermination or subordination.

4   Inclusivism

Radhakrishnan argued for the future of religion against those who proclaimed its modern irrelevance. That future faith, he said, must be consistent with the discoveries and experiential approach of science, morally active so as to solve the world's social problems and inclusive of all the world's religious viewpoints so as to promote world unity. In his later writings he advocated this 'religion of the spirit' or 'spiritual religion' which he defined in terms similar to his earlier definitions of Vedānta and Hinduism.

Radhakrishnan made religious tolerance a major theme of his work, defining it not as merely bearing with others, but as a hierarchic, subordinating inclusivism. He affirmed the truth of religious positions in terms of a hierarchy. He believed in an impersonal Absolute, identical with the self to be the highest understanding of reality as it is and that theistic positions of the highest reality as a Divine being are subordinate doctrinal understandings. These should be accepted as expressions which are relative to the historical environment of the believer (see RELIGIOUS PLURALISM; TOLERATION).

Radhakrishnan quoted widely from the literature of the world's religions to support his contention that at the heart of all religions is a common religious experience which is understood differently by the religions according to their particular cumulative traditions. Hinduism, he argued, understands this best and allows for a variety of doctrinal interpretations. However, the nondual experience of the impersonal Absolute as the true Self within is, in fact, the nature of that experience.

As spokesman for the Indian state, Radhakrishnan argued that this understanding of monistic idealism provided the basis for democracy. The individual's value is rooted in its essential identity with the Absolute. Applied to economics, Radhakrishnan spoke in general terms of the value of a socialism which is 'economic democracy'. Likewise, the correct understanding of political secularism was not the indifference or rejection of religion by the state, but a nonsectarianism which affirms the essence of all religions. That essence is the 'religion of the spirit', he affirmed. Radhakrishnan's general approach to political thought and his public role as a detached teacher while president of India, positioned him as the ideal public *rājaguru*, the traditional scholar-teacher of the king, for India's first two prime ministers, Jawaharlal Nehru and Lal Bahadur Shastri.

See also: POLITICAL PHILOSOPHY, INDIAN; VEDĀNTA

List of works

Radhakrishnan, S. (1920) *The Reign of Religion in Contemporary Philosophy*, London: Macmillan. (An early argument defending monistic idealism against theism.)

—— (1923) *Indian Philosophy*, London: Allen & Unwin; 2nd edn, 1927. (A two-volume critical analysis of major traditions from his monistic perspective.)

—— (1927) *The Hindu View of Life*, London: Allen & Unwin. (Collected lectures defending Hinduism for the modern world.)

—— (1929) *An Idealist View of Life*, London: Allen & Unwin. (Collected lectures which present his most systematic argument.)

—— (1939) *Eastern Religions and Western Thought*, London: Oxford University Press. (Collected lectures analysing religion and philosophy comparing East and West.)

—— (1947) *Religion and Society*, London: Allen & Unwin. (Lectures applying religious ideals to social reconstruction.)

—— (1955) *Recovery of Faith*, New York: Harper. (A defence of the need for a new religion for the modern world.)

References and further reading

Arapura, J.G. (1966) *Radhakrishnan and Integral Experience*, New York: Asia Publishing House. (Philosophical analysis of Radhakrishnan's thought.)

Minor, R.N. (1987) *Radhakrishnan: A Religious Biography*, Albany, NY: State University of New York Press. (Introduces his thought by placing it in the context of his life with a complete bibliography of Radhakrishnan's writings and secondary literature.)

Schilpp, P.A. (1952) *The Philosophy of Sarvepalli Radhakrishnan*, New York: Tudor. (Collection of critical, scholarly essays on a variety of topics in Radhakrishnan's thought.)

ROBERT N. MINOR

RADICAL ARISTOTELIANISM
see AVERROISM

RADICAL TRANSLATION AND RADICAL INTERPRETATION

Radical translation *is the setting of a thought experiment conceived by W.V. Quine in the late 1950s. In that setting a linguist undertakes to translate into English some hitherto unknown language – one which is neither historically nor culturally linked to any known language. It is further supposed that the linguist has no access to bilinguals versed in the two languages, English and (what Quine called) 'Jungle'. Thus, the only empirical data the linguist has to go on in constructing a 'Jungle-to-English' translation manual are instances of the native speakers' behaviour in publicly recognizable circumstances. Reflecting upon the fragmentary nature of these data, Quine draws the following conclusions:*

(1) It is very likely that the theoretical sentences of 'Jungle' can be translated as wholes into English in incompatible yet equally acceptable ways. In other words, translation of theoretical sentences is indeterminate. On the assumption that a sentence and its translation share the same meaning, the import of indeterminacy of translation is indeterminacy of meaning: the meanings of theoretical sentences of natural languages are not fixed by empirical data. The fact is, the radical translator is bound to impose about as much meaning as they discover. This result (together with the dictum 'no entity without identity') undermines the idea that propositions are meanings of sentences.

(2) Neither the question of which 'Jungle' expressions are to count as terms nor the question of what object(s), if any, a 'Jungle' term refers to can be answered by appealing merely to the empirical data. In short, the empirical data do not fix reference.

The idea of radical interpretation was developed by Donald Davidson in the 1960s and 1970s as a modification and extension of Quine's idea of radical translation. Quine is concerned with the extent to which empirical data determine the meanings of sentences of a natural language. In the setting of radical interpretation, Davidson is concerned with a different question, the question of what a person could know that would enable them to interpret another's language. For example, what could one know that would enable the interpretation of the German sentence 'Es regnet' as meaning that it is raining? The knowledge required for interpretation differs from the knowledge required for translation, for one could know that 'Es regnet' is translated as 'Il pleut' without knowing the meaning (the interpretation) of either sentence. Beginning with the knowledge that the native speaker holds certain sentences true when in certain publicly recognizable circumstances, Davidson's radical interpreter strives to understand the meanings of those sentences. Davidson argues that this scenario reveals that interpretation centres on one's having knowledge comparable to an empirically verified, finitely based, recursive specification of the truth-conditions for an infinity of sentences – a Tarski-like truth theory. Thus, Quine's radical translation and Davidson's radical interpretation should not be regarded as competitors, for although the methodologies employed in the two contexts are similar, the two contexts are designed to answer different questions. Moreover, interpretation is broader than translation; sentences that cannot be translated can still be interpreted.

1   **Radical translation**
2–3 **Indeterminacy of translation**
4   **Criticism**
5   **Indeterminacy of reference**
6   **Criticism**
7   **Radical interpretation**
8–9 **Truth theory**
10   **Criticism**

1   Radical translation

Suppose that children, in the normal course of events, acquire their native tongue (for example, English) by observing their parents and others talking in publicly observable circumstances. A corollary of this common sense supposition is that whatever there is to linguistic meaning can be manifested in behaviour in publicly observable circumstances. However, one might ask, just how far do empirical data go toward fixing the meanings of the sentences being spoken? Quine's thought experiment of radical translation is designed to answer this question.

In the context of radical translation, the field linguist sets out to construct a manual for translating the newly discovered language of 'Jungle' into English. Of course, the linguist has a prior knowledge of English, and will exploit that knowledge in constructing a 'Jungle-to-English' translation manual. Obviously, a child learning a first language has no prior language to exploit. So, there is this fundamental difference in psychological readiness to learn 'Jungle' between the linguist and the child of native-speakers of the language. However, this difference does not affect the central fact that the ultimate empirical data available to both linguist and child are the same: facts about behaviour. The poverty of these ultimate data is what the context of radical translation is meant to bring out.

2   Indeterminacy of translation

The primary reference for indeterminacy of translation is 'Translation and Meaning', the second chapter of Quine's *Word and Object* (1960). According to that account, the linguist first compiles a list of phonemes of the native-speakers' language (which Quine dubbed 'Jungle'), and then they settle on some expressions used by native speakers for assent and dissent.

A rabbit scurries by; the native speaker utters 'Gavagai'. Having noticed the rabbit, and that the native speaker noticed it too, and suspecting that the rabbit probably prompted the native speaker's utterance of 'Gavagai', the linguist tentatively enters into their 'Jungle-to-English' translation manual that the native speaker's 'Gavagai' might well be translated as 'Lo, a rabbit'. On later occasions, some rabbited, some rabbitless, the linguist will volunteer 'Gavagai?' with the intention of eliciting the native speaker's assent, dissent, or neither. In this way, the linguist can assess whatever inductive support there may be for their hypothesis that 'Gavagai' translates as 'Lo, a rabbit'.

The distal stimulus, in this case a rabbit, serves as the criterion for the linguist's inductive hypothesis that 'Gavagai' can be translated as 'Lo, a rabbit'. However, what a sentence (even a one word sentence) and its translation share is the same meaning. In the case at hand, is the rabbit the meaning of 'Gavagai'? No; that would be to confuse meaning with reference. What, then, is its meaning? Quine's answer to this question (what he calls 'stimulus meaning') is given in terms of the proximal stimulus, namely, patterns of a subject's activated nerve endings. Affording the native speaker a global pattern of non-verbal stimulation for a specific duration together with the linguist's query 'Gavagai?' will elicit from the native speaker either assent, dissent, or neither. Patterns of stimulation which would prompt assent and patterns which would prompt dissent belong, respectively, to the affirmative stimulus meaning and negative stimulus meaning for that sentence and native speaker at that time. Stimulus meaning *simpliciter* is the ordered pair of the two. Patterns which would prompt neither assent nor dissent are irrelevant.

Given stimulus meaning, one might say that what 'Gavagai' and its translation 'Lo, a rabbit' share is the same stimulus meaning. However, this too would be wrong, for stimulus meaning (as just defined) is private: the native speaker's nerves are distinct from the linguist's nerves. It would be more accurate, but still problematic, to say that the native speaker's stimulus meaning for 'Gavagai' and the linguist's for 'Lo, a rabbit' are approximately the same. This is Quine's approach in *Word and Object* (although he subsequently altered this account, as we shall see).

In the context of radical translation, it is stipulated that there are no bilinguals for the linguist to consult. So, the linguist must go about compiling the translation manual by observing the behaviour of native speakers, verbal and otherwise, and querying them with sentences for assent/dissent under various publicly observable circumstances. Thus, the criteria of translation remain keyed to distal stimuli, though the definition of stimulus meaning remains keyed to proximal stimuli. After all, one cannot plausibly expect the linguist to know anything about the native speakers' or their own global patterns of activated nerve endings.

Given the behavioural limits of the empirical data of radical translation, Quine maintains in *Word and Object* that (1) observation sentences, like 'Gavagai', can be determinately translated; (2) truth functions (for example, 'and', 'or', 'not') can be determinately translated; (3) stimulus-analytic and stimulus-contradictory sentences can be identified, but not translated; and (4) questions regarding the intrasubjective stimulus synonymy of occasion sentences can be settled, if raised. (A stimulus-analytic sentence is one that a person would assent to after every stimulation: 'There have been black dogs', for example. A stimulus-contradictory sentence is one that a person would dissent from after every stimulation. The occasion sentences 'Bachelor' and 'Unmarried man' could count as intrasubjectively stimulus synonymous for a person, if they have the same stimulus meaning for him.)

However, if the linguist were to become bilingual (for example, if they forgot about translation and simply acquired 'Jungle' as a native speaker might, or nearly so), then according to Quine (1') they could determinately translate all occasion sentences, not just observation sentences, and (4) above becomes superfluous. (Non-observational occasion sentences are those that require a new prompting stimulus each time they are queried, but lack the community-wide agreement characteristic of observation sentences, such as 'There goes John's old tutor'.) This leaves the linguist of *Word and Object* with determinate translations for (1'), (2) and (3).

However, in *Roots of Reference* (1974), Quine explains that the truth functions cannot be determinately translated after all. One barrier concerns conjunction ('and'): if each of a pair of sentences commands neither assent nor dissent, their conjunction can sometimes command dissent and sometimes neither dissent nor assent. If (to use Quine's examples) 'It's a mouse' and 'It's a chipmunk' are neither affirmed nor denied, still their conjunction will be denied. Whereas if the components are 'It's a mouse' and 'It's in the kitchen' and neither is affirmed or denied, their conjunction will be neither affirmed nor denied. An analogous barrier stands in the way of determinately translating alternation ('or').

3   Indeterminacy of translation (cont.)

In discussing the translation of observation sentences and truth functions in Word and Object, Quine makes use of Neil Wilson's principle of charity (see Wilson 1959). The central idea of the principle is that any proffered translation that construes the native speaker as holding some patently silly belief (for example, that the law of non-contradiction is false) is less likely than that the proffered translation is a bad one (see CHARITY, PRINCIPLE OF §4). Thus, there is a sound methodological reason for translating a native speaker so as to construe them as holding true beliefs (true by the linguist's own standards). However, Quine augments this principle with another: maximize psychological plausibility. This latter principle permits the linguist to translate a native speaker's sentence by some patently false English sentence if, given the native speaker's 'outlandish' rites and taboos or whatever, doing so is more plausible than translating the sentence in question by some true English sentence.

Putting the matter overly schematically, the next steps the linguist takes in constructing a manual of translation are as follows: (a) segmenting newly heard sentences uttered by native speakers into short recurrent parts ('words') which these sentences share with some of the observation sentences already translated; (b) segmenting further new sentences in ways that reflect the 'words' of the previous step, so that a lexicon and grammar begin to emerge; (c) generating new sentences in the native speaker's language as recursion sets in; (d) continuing to fine tune the manual. Steps (a) to (d) make use of analytical hypotheses, hypotheses that go beyond the behavioural data: though analytical hypotheses should not contravene those data, neither are they supported by them.

In 'Indeterminacy of translation again' (1987), Quine articulates some constraints of a pragmatic nature which help to guide the linguist's conjectures in this area, but clearly the linguist's latitude for conjecture remains enormous. In fact, two linguists working independently of one another might well come up with equally successful 'Jungle-to-English' manuals which, despite being consistent with all the behavioural data, differ from one another in assigning to countless 'Jungle' sentences different English sentences as translations. Of these, countless different English sentences would not be interchangeable in English contexts. But which of these rival translation manuals is the correct one? There is no fact of the matter here; they are both correct. Such is the thesis of indeterminacy of translation.

Quine sums up the philosophical import of radical translation and of indeterminacy as follows:

> The point of my thought experiment in radical translations was philosophical: a critique of the uncritical notion of meanings and, therewith, of introspective semantics. I was concerned to expose its empirical limits. A sentence has a meaning, people thought, and another sentence is its translation if it has the same meaning. This, we see, will not do.
>
> (Quine 1987: 9)

The truth is more nearly the reverse: if some sentence is the translation of another, then it is proper to say that it has the same meaning. So, the idea of propositions as objectively valid translation relations, or as meanings of sentences, cannot be maintained. Furthermore:

> The critique of meaning leveled by my thesis of indeterminacy of translation is meant to clear away misconceptions, but the result is not nihilism. Translation remains, and is indispensable. Indeterminacy means not that there is no acceptable translation, but that there are many. A good manual of translation fits all checkpoints of verbal behavior, and what does not surface at any checkpoint can do no harm.
>
> (Quine 1987: 9)

So, the radical translator imposes about as much meaning as they discover.

Before surveying some criticisms of Quine's indeterminacy thesis, we need to clear up an ancillary matter. In *Word and Object*, Quine claims that the native speaker's stimulus meaning for 'Gavagai' and the linguist's stimulus meaning for 'Lo, a rabbit' are approximately the same. But Quine realized as early as 1960 that such intersubjective comparisons of stimulus meanings are problematic, for no two people's nerve nets are isomorphic. Consequently, in *Pursuit of Truth* (1990) Quine proposes to do without intersubjective comparisons of stimulus meaning. Empathy fills the gap. A rabbit scurries by; the native speaker utters 'Gavagai'. Empathizing with the native speaker, the linguist conjectures that were they in the native speaker's place they would have uttered 'Lo, a rabbit'. Thus, the linguist forms the tentative inductive hypothesis that 'Gavagai' translates as 'Lo, a rabbit'. Appealing to empathy instead of to approximate sameness of stimulus meaning forces Quine to reformulate his definition of 'observation sentence' (see Quine [1990] 1992: 43), but he does not drop the

concept of stimulus meaning from his scientific semantics. Quine leaves to the neuropsychologists the task of accounting for the mechanisms underlying humans' ability to empathize.

4 Criticism

Indeterminacy of translation has been hotly debated by philosophers ever since the publication of *Word and Object*, and it is probably fair to say that more philosophers reject what they take to be the thesis than accept it. Some of the more widespread criticisms are: (a) Quine does not prove the thesis; (b) linguistics is underdetermined, but not indeterminate; (c) the thesis is unintelligible; and (d) the evidence for actual translation is not limited to that of radical translation. Let us briefly examine each of these criticisms in turn:

(a) *In 'Word and Object' Quine does not provide a deductive proof of his thesis of indeterminacy.* This is correct, but in addition to the more or less inductive argument presented there, Quine elsewhere offers two other arguments for indeterminacy. One of these, found in 'Epistemology naturalized' (1969a), takes Peirce's verificationism and Duhem's holism as premises supporting indeterminacy:

> If we recognize with Peirce that the meaning of a sentence turns purely on what would count as evidence for its truth, and if we recognize with Duhem that theoretical sentences have their evidence not as single sentences but only as larger blocks of theory, then the indeterminacy of translation of theoretical sentences is the natural conclusion.
>
> (Quine 1969a: 80–1)

A second argument is to be found in 'On the reasons for indeterminacy of translation' (Quine 1970: 179–81). There Quine argues for indeterminacy on the grounds of underdetermination of physical theory. He argues that translation of a foreign physicist's theory which is underdetermined by observable evidence will itself be underdetermined by translation of the theory's observation sentences. Thus, the translator will have to rely on analytical hypotheses, and different systems of analytical hypotheses can result in equally good, but incompatible, translations. Thus, the extent to which a physical theory is underdetermined by observation is a measure of the extent to which its translation is indeterminate. (But see Quine 1979: 66–7 for a reservation about this way of arguing for indeterminacy.)

(b) *It is true that scientific theory is underdetermined by all possible observations, and in so far as linguistic theory is a part of scientific theory it too is under-*

determined, but there is no special indeterminacy that afflicts linguistics. Quine responds to this criticism by pointing out that once one accepts some single physical theory from among its competitors as the whole truth about what there is, still, within that theory, indeterminacy of translation can occur. The reason is that all that matters to translation are the behavioural facts, and since behavioural facts do not fix translation, no further physical theory, not even the whole truth about nature, would do so.

(c) *The thesis of indeterminacy is unintelligible, for it repudiates meanings and at the same time claims that there can be rival manuals of translation assigning to some 'Jungle' sentence English sentences which diverge in meaning. But if there are no meanings, then how can English sentences diverge in meaning? And if they can diverge in meaning, then how can there be no meanings?* The response to this criticism is to explain how two English sentences can diverge in meaning without reifying meanings. Quine responds as follows:

> A manual of Jungle-to-English translation constitutes a recursive, or inductive, definition of a *translation relation* together with a claim that it correlates sentences compatibly with the behavior of all concerned. The thesis of indeterminacy of translation is that these claims on the part of two manuals might both be true and yet the two translation relations might not be usable in alternation, from sentence to sentence, without issuing in incoherent sequences. Or, to put it another way, the English sentences prescribed as translation of a given Jungle sentence by two rival manuals might not be interchangeable in English contexts.
>
> (Quine [1990] 1992: 48)

Once again, Quine's solution to the difficulty is along behaviourist lines.

(d) *There may well be indeterminacy of translation in the context of radical translation, but in the context of actual translation there is more evidence available to fix the meanings of sentences.* For example, it is a fact of established usage, that is, verbal dispositions, that we translate the French sentence *'Il y a peut-être des êtres intelligents sur Mars'* as the English sentence *'There may be intelligent beings on Mars'*. It is true that the context of radical translation was designed to expose the ultimate empirical data for translation, where the word 'ultimate' excludes verbal behaviour linked to systems of analytical hypotheses that over time have become customary. But the point remains, even for languages as close as French and English, that some uncustomary system of analytical hypotheses could produce different translation relations between French and English which are just as effective as the customary one. Indeed, as Quine points out, inde-

terminacy of translation begins with the translator's home language. English, for example, could be mapped into itself by using one 'Jungle-to-English' manual to translate English into 'Jungle', then using a rival 'Jungle-to-English' manual to translate 'Jungle' back into English.

The four criticisms dealt with above are by no means the only criticisms philosophers have levelled against Quine's thesis of indeterminacy of translation, but they are some of the more interesting and widespread ones.

5 Indeterminacy of reference

As we have seen, given the empirical data, the 'Jungle' observation sentence 'Gavagai' can be determinately translated by the English observation sentence 'Lo, a rabbit'. May we conclude from this that 'gavagai' is therefore a 'Jungle' term, and if so, that it can be determinately translated as 'rabbit'? According to Quine, the answer is 'no' on both counts. Termhood and reference are matters that can be settled only by appealing to analytical hypotheses. For example, assuming the linguist decides to construe 'gavagai' as a term, is it to be construed as an abstract singular term (for example 'rabbithood'), or as a concrete general term? If the latter, then 'undetached rabbit part' could serve just as well as 'rabbit' as a translation of 'gavagai'. After all, the same portions of space-time as are occupied by undetached rabbit parts are occupied by rabbits.

The only way to settle such questions is, according to Quine, by relying upon the 'Jungle' equivalents of English plural endings, pronouns, numerals, the 'is' of identity and its adaptations 'same' and 'other'. These constitute the cluster of interrelated grammatical particles and constructions with which the individuation of terms of divided reference in English is connected. Once a linguist has fixed these equivalences, they can put to the native speaker questions like 'Is this gavagai the same as that one?', 'Is this one gavagai or two?', and so on. Once the linguist is able to ask such questions, they can begin to determine whether to translate 'gavagai' as 'rabbit' or as 'undetached rabbit part'. However, before they can ask such questions, the linguist will have to formulate a system of analytical hypotheses in connection with some other 'Jungle' expressions, namely, those playing the role of that cluster of interrelated grammatical particles and constructions of English which govern reference. But that cluster is itself susceptible to indeterminacy of translation. Thus, if one overall system of analytical hypotheses works for translating some 'Jungle' expression into 'is the same as', perhaps some other workable but systematically different system would translate the same 'Jungle' expression as 'belongs with'. Therefore, when the linguist attempts to ask 'Is this gavagai the same as that?', they could unwittingly be asking 'Does this gavagai belong with that?'. So the native speaker's assent cannot be used to settle the reference of 'gavagai' absolutely. Consequently, even though this method of translation is the best the linguist can manage, it is not sufficient for settling absolutely the indeterminacy between translating 'gavagai' as 'rabbit' or as 'undetached rabbit part', and so on. The linguist can say only that 'gavagai' refers to rabbits relative to one manual, and to undetached rabbit parts relative to a rival manual. So long as these manuals are consistent with the behaviour of all concerned, there is no fact of the matter of what is 'really' referred to by 'gavagai'.

Quine has also argued for indeterminacy of reference independent of the indeterminacy of holophrastic translation. In what he calls his 'proxy function argument', Quine explains how:

> we might reinterpret every reference to a physical object arbitrarily as a reference rather to its cosmic complement, the rest of the physical universe. The old names and predicates would be introduced by ostension as usual, but it would be deferred ostension: pointing to what was not part of the intended object. Sensory associations would carry over similarly. The word 'rabbit' would now denote not each rabbit but the cosmic complement of each, and the predicate 'furry' would now denote not each furry thing but the cosmic complement of each. Saying that rabbits are furry would thus be reinterpreted as saying that complements-of-rabbits are complements-of-furry things, with 'complements-of-rabbits' and 'complements-of-furry' seen as atomic predicates. The two sentences are obviously equivalent.
>
> (Quine 1995: 71)

Quine goes on to explain that 'cosmic complement of' expresses what he calls a 'proxy' function: a one-to-one reinterpretation of objective reference. Such proxy functions leave the truth-values of the containing sentences undisturbed.

> It is a matter of reconstruing all terms and predicates as designating or denoting the proxies of what they had designated or denoted. A term that had designated an object x now designates the proxy of x, and a predicate that had denoted x now denotes the proxy of x. No big deal; we are proxying both sides of the predication, and it cancels out. We appreciated the triviality where the proxy was the cosmic complement.
>
> (Quine 1995: 72)

Thus, unlike the conjectural status Quine accords indeterminacy of translation of theoretical sentences as wholes, indeterminacy of reference has the apodictic certainty of a proof.

6 Criticism

As with indeterminacy of translation, indeterminacy of reference (or inscrutability of reference) has been vigorously criticized. The most widespread criticism is, perhaps, that Quine's doctrine is inconsistent: it maintains that reference is and is not determinate. For example, it asserts that the native speaker's 'gavagai' is indeterminate, since it can be adequately translated by 'rabbithood', by 'undetached rabbit part', by 'rabbit', and so on, while taking the reference of these English terms to be determinate. A full Quinian response to this criticism would take us far afield, but perhaps the following two quotations will suffice:

> To say that 'gavagai' denotes rabbits is to opt for a manual of translation in which 'gavagai' is translated as 'rabbit', instead of opting for any of the alternative manuals.
>
> And does the indeterminacy or relativity extend also somehow to the home language? In 'Ontological relativity' I said it did, for the home language can be translated into itself by permutations that depart materially from the mere identity transformation, as proxy functions bear out. But if we choose as our manual of translation the identity transformation, thus taking the home language at face value, the relativity is resolved. Reference is then explicated in disquotational paradigms analogous to Tarski's truth paradigm...; thus 'rabbit' denotes rabbits, whatever *they* are, and 'Boston' designates Boston.
>
> (Quine [1990] 1992: 52; for his essay 'Ontological relativity', see Quine 1969b)

and:

> The very freedom vouchsafed us by the indeterminacy of reference allows us to *adopt* ostension as decisive for reference to observable concrete objects. We end up as we began, then, agreeing on the denotations of 'rabbit' after all: rabbits for all concerned. We may then merely differ on the deeper nature of rabbits: they are spatio temporal for some... sui generis for most. Adaptation of our usage must not, however, be allowed to obscure the lesson of proxy functions. Namely, a language-wide one-to-one reassignment of values to our variables has no effect on the truth of falsity of our statements.
>
> (Quine 1995: 75)

We turn, now, to a consideration of radical interpretation.

7 Radical interpretation

Mary utters 'It's raining'; Tom interprets her utterance to mean that it is raining. How is this possible? What could Tom know that would enable him to interpret the sentences of a natural language? Donald Davidson argues that we would have answers to these questions – a theory of meaning – if we had a theory meeting two requirements. First, the theory must provide an interpretation for a potential infinity of utterances of a speaker or group of speakers; second, the theory must be verifiable without assuming a detailed knowledge of the speaker's propositional attitudes. The first requirement recognizes the holistic nature of linguistic understanding; the second requirement recognizes that the theory must not beg questions by assuming too much of what it is supposed to explain.

Davidson hypothesizes that a Tarski-like truth theory, suitably modified to apply to natural languages, just might meet these two conditions. To test his hypothesis, Davidson envisages a context of radical interpretation wherein an interpreter is faced with interpreting in one idiom talk in another. (For example, Kurt utters 'Es regnet' and Mary interprets his utterance to mean that it is raining.)

As Davidson points out in his essay 'Radical interpretation':

The term 'radical interpretation' is meant to suggest strong kinship with Quine's 'radical translation'. Kinship is not identity, however, and 'interpretation' in place of 'translation' marks one of the differences: a greater emphasis on the explicitly semantic in the former.

(Davidson 1984b: 126, n.1)

Or, as Quine has put the difference:

Translation is not the field linguist's goal. His goal is to command the native language and perhaps to teach it, whether for reasons of ethnography and philology or simply to implement fluent dialogue and successful negotiation with the natives. His undertaking, broader than translation, is *interpretation*. An untranslatable sentence, such as the one about neutrinos ['Neutrinos lack mass.'] can still be interpreted, and that indeed is how we have learned it ourselves. For broadly semantic purposes, as Donald Davidson appreciates, interpretation is the thing. Translation is the narrower project, pertinent specifically to my concern over

the fancied concepts of proposition and sameness of meaning.

(Quine 1995: 80–1)

Thus, Quine's radical translation and Davidson's radical interpretation are devoted to different issues. Quine wants to discover the extent to which the empirical data determine meanings of sentences of a natural language; Davidson wants to discover what one could know that would enable one to understand the sentences of a natural language. Furthermore, the knowledge required for interpretation differs from the knowledge required for translation, for one could know that 'Es regnet' is translated as 'Il pleut' without knowing the interpretation (meaning) of either sentence. Davidson is fully aware of these differences, of course:

The idea of a translation manual with appropriate empirical constraints as a device for studying problems in the philosophy of language is, of course, Quine's. This idea inspired much of my thinking on the present subject, and my proposal is in important respects very close to Quine's. Since Quine did not intend to answer the questions I have set, the claim that the method of translation is not adequate as a solution to the problem of radical interpretation is not a criticism of any doctrine of Quine's.

(Davidson 1984b: 129, n.3)

What, then, is the nature of the Tarski-like theory that Davidson believes might serve as a theory of meaning?

8 Truth theory

Alfred Tarski's theory of truth is designed to apply only to artificial languages meeting certain formal requirements: extensional languages like first-order predicate logic with relations and identity. According to Davidson:

What characterizes a theory of truth in Tarski's style is that it entails, for every sentence s of the object language, a sentence of the form:

s is true (in the object language) if and only if p.

Instances of the form (which we shall call T-sentences) are obtained by replacing 's' by a canonical description of s, and 'p' by a translation of s. The important undefined semantical notion in the theory is that of *satisfaction* which relates sentences, open or closed, to infinite sequences of objects, which may be taken to belong to the range of the variables of the object language. The axioms which are finite in number, are of two kinds: some give the conditions under which a sequence satisfies a complex sentence on the basis of the conditions of satisfaction of simpler sentences, others give the conditions under which the simplest (open) sentences are satisfied. Truth is defined for closed sentences in terms of the notion of satisfaction.

(Davidson 1984b: 130–1)

Following Tarski's lead, Davidson's blueprint for a theory of meaning consists of axioms, rules and theorems. A finite set of axioms state satisfaction conditions for each of the object language's *semantical primitives* (basic terms and various other basic non-sentential expressions). An example might be: '*chien* applies to a thing if and only if it is a dog'. A finite set of rules allows proving T-sentences as theorems from the axioms. The resulting theorems are a potential infinity of T-sentences stating the truth-conditions for each object-language sentence. The proof of a T-sentence amounts to an analysis of how the truth or falsity of the object-language sentence depends on how it is composed from the semantical primitives. (These axioms, rules and T-sentences are, of course, stated in the language of the theory – the metalanguage.)

This general form of Davidson's theory of meaning reflects certain features of natural languages. First, since natural languages are learnable by finite beings, they must have a finite number of semantical primitives. Second, since natural languages consist of a potential infinity of sentences, the semantic features of such sentences must ultimately depend upon those of the semantical primitives. However, this does not imply that 'word' meaning is known somehow prior to sentence meaning. In fact, Davidson argues just the opposite: sentence meaning is known prior to word meaning. Words have whatever meanings they do as a result of their functioning in meaningful sentences. Third, like the axioms, the number of rules for proving T-sentences must be finite, and for the same reason. Finally, it is noteworthy that this Tarski-like theory of meaning has several obvious ontological advantages in that it makes no use of meanings as entities, nor of properties as denotatations of predicates, nor of states of affairs as denotatations of sentences.

Tarski's *Convention T* is that a theory of truth should entail T-sentences, in which descriptions of object-language sentences are linked to translations of those sentences in the metalanguage. For his own purposes, Davidson modifies Convention T in two fundamental ways. Tarski's Convention T relies on the notion of meaning (or translation) in order to explain truth. But meaning (or translation) is just the semantic notion that Davidson wants to explain, so he cannot, without begging questions, interpret Convention T in the manner of Tarski. Rather, Davidson construes Convention T as claiming that:

> an acceptable theory of truth must entail, for every sentence *s* of the object language, a sentence of the form: *s* is true if and only if *p*, where '*p*' is replaced by any sentence that is true if and only if *s* is.
>
> (Davidson 1984b: 134)

Thus, Davidson reverses Tarski's priorities: instead of assuming meaning in order to explain truth, he assumes truth in order to explain meaning.

Furthermore, since Davidson wants to apply the theory to natural languages (something which, as Davidson reports, Tarski explicitly denies can be done), he must allow for the fact that the object language contains a wide diversity of expressions, including proper names, functional expressions, indexicals, demonstratives, and so on. Admitting indexicals and demonstratives into the object language provides for the possibility of sentences which vary in truth-value according to time and speaker. Thus, Davidson's version of a Tarskian theory must take utterances of sentences, not sentences themselves, as truth vehicles. Davidson modifies Convention T accordingly:

s is true in *L* when spoken by *x* at *t* if and only if *p*.

Recall that Davidson believes we would have an answer to the question of what a person could know that would enable them to interpret the sentences of a natural language, if we had a theory meeting two requirements. First, the theory must provide an interpretation for a potential infinity of utterances of a speaker or group of speakers – a potential infinity of T-sentences. Davidson's modified version of Tarski's theory of truth is a blueprint for constructing such a theory. Second, since that theory is to be an empirical theory about a speaker's (or speakers') behaviour, it must be verifiable – without assuming a detailed knowledge of the speaker's (or speakers') propositional attitudes. So, how is this second requirement to be met?

This is where the notion of a radical interpreter (like Quine's radical translator) serves as a useful heuristic. By imagining the routine of a radical interpreter at work, we come to appreciate that a theory of meaning is supported by verifying its T-sentences, and we come to see what ultimate evidence there is for verifying T-sentences.

9 Truth theory (cont.)

Imagine a radical interpreter who speaks only English, does not have access to bilinguals or dictionaries, and is attempting to interpret Kurt, who speaks only German. The interpreter has no prior detailed knowledge of the meanings of Kurt's utterances nor of Kurt's beliefs. Kurt utters 'Es regnet' at a time when it is raining near him. Judging that Kurt's utterance is both linguistic and intentional, the interpreter conjectures that Kurt holds 'Es regnet' to be true. The important methodological point to note, according to Davidson, is that the interpreter can spot such utterances purely on the basis of the speaker's observable behaviour, independently of knowing anything of the utterance's meaning or the speaker's beliefs. It is those utterances that a speaker (or speakers) hold true, at a time, under publicly observable circumstances, which constitute the ultimate evidence for T-sentences.

This ultimate evidence, about what sentences a speaker holds-true, is evidence not specifically about meaning, but about a combination of meaning and belief: a speaker believes whatever it is that they mean by the sentences. However, if the interpreter knew not only that Kurt holds a certain utterance true, but also what Kurt believes at the time, then the interpreter could extract the meaning of Kurt's utterance. Similarly, if the interpreter knew both that Kurt held a certain utterance true and its meaning, then they could extract Kurt's current belief. The problem is that there is no way to discover meaning which is independent of belief, and no way to discover belief which is independent of meaning. Thus, the central problem of interpretation is simultaneously to disentangle meaning and belief. How can a radical interpreter accomplish this task?

Suppose the interpreter, to use one of Davidson's examples (1984b: 135), can formulate the following T-sentence:

(T) 'Es regnet' is true-in-German when spoken by x at time t if and only if it is raining near x at t.

The interpreter's evidence for this T-sentence is:

(E) Kurt belongs to the German speech community and Kurt holds-true 'Es regnet' on Saturday at noon and it is raining near Kurt on Saturday at noon.

The interpreter's next step is to gather generalized evidence:

(GE)$(x)(t)$ (if x belongs to the German speech community then (x holds-true 'Es regnet' at t if and only if it is raining near x at t)).

The interpreter can take (E) as evidence for (T) and for (GE), if they assume Kurt believes it is raining nearby at noon on Saturday, and if they assume that particular belief played a role in the causal chain prompting Kurt's utterance, 'Es regnet'. By using this procedure of holding belief constant as far as possible while solving for meaning, the interpreter can hope to solve the problem of the interdependence of belief and meaning.

But what justifies this procedure? After all, Kurt could be in error about it raining near him, and the interpreter could be in error about what distal stimulus is prompting Kurt's utterance and, hence, about the belief that is ascribed to Kurt. 'What justifies the procedure is the fact that disagreement and agreement alike are intelligible only against a background of massive agreement' (Davidson 1984b: 137). For example, if two people agree or disagree that what they see is a rabbit in tall grass, they must be in agreement regarding an indefinite number of other beliefs about rabbits, grass, distance, and so on. Furthermore:

> The methodological advice to interpret in a way that optimizes agreement should not be conceived as resting on a charitable assumption about human intelligence that might turn out to be false. If we cannot find a way to interpret the utterances and other behavior of a creature as revealing a set of beliefs largely consistent and true by our own standards, we have no reason to count that creature as rational, as having beliefs, or as saying anything.
> (Davidson 1984b: 137)

This mandatory principle of charity indicates that the verification of ascriptions of meaning and of belief are holistic in character. So while the principle of charity (namely, 'optimize agreement') does not guarantee that Kurt's acceptance of 'Es regnet', or any other sentence considered in isolation, is to be deemed correct (in that it will be interpreted to mean something we accept), Davidson contends that the principle does guarantee that most of Kurt's acceptances are in that sense correct.

> The method is rather one of getting a best fit. We want a theory that satisfies the formal constraints on a theory of truth, and that maximizes agreement, in the sense of making Kurt (and others) right, as far as we can tell, as often as possible.
> (Davidson 1984b: 136)

Unlike Quine, who advocates the principle of charity at the level of translating 'Jungle' observation sentences like 'Gavagai' and the 'Jungle' equivalents of truth functions like 'and', 'or' and 'not', Davidson advocates the principle at every level of interpretation (see Davidson 1984b: 136, n.16). However, his principle of charity definitely involves more than the basic methodological precept 'optimize agreement':

> It is impossible to simplify the considerations that

are relevant [for dealing with disagreements], for everything we know or believe about the way evidence supports belief can be put to work in deciding where the theory can best allow error, and what errors are least destructive of understanding. The methodology of interpretation is, in this respect, nothing but epistemology seen in the mirror of meaning.

(Davidson 1984c: 169)

It is Davidson's contention that for a theory that satisfies the formal constraints on a theory of truth, and which optimally fits the evidence about utterances held true, each of its T-sentences will yield an acceptable interpretation. Moreover, Davidson believes – and for Quinian reasons – that if there is one such theory for some object language, then there are many. Thus, Davidson's theory of meaning possesses its own forms of indeterminacy and inscrutability.

10 Criticism

Davidson's theory of radical interpretation has precipitated a tremendous amount of discussion of the topic among philosophers. Two of the more general criticisms of Davidson's programme are: (a) the construction of a Tarski-like theory of meaning for an entire natural language is implausible; and (b) Davidson's rendering of Convention T is too weak to yield interpretations.

(a) *The construction of a Tarski-like theory of meaning for an entire natural language is seen to be implausible when one considers the number and variety of idioms whose truth-conditions are not fully understood; idioms like 'knows that' and 'believes that', contrary to fact conditionals, and so on.* Citing some of his own work on attributions of attitudes and performatives, as well as other philosophers' work on proper names, mass terms, 'ought', and so on, Davidson remains optimistic that many of these problems will be solved in ways consistent with his Tarski-like theory of meaning (see Davidson 1984b: 132–3).

(b) *Davidson's rendering of Convention T is too weak to yield interpretations.* Recall, for Davidson, Convention T says that *s* is true if and only if *p*, where '*p*' is replaced by any sentence that is true if and only if *s* is. Hence, we get the following T-sentence:

(1) 'John is a renate' is true if and only if John is a renate.

But, since all renates are cordates, and vice versa, we also get the following T-sentence:

(2) 'John is a renate' is true if and only if John is a cordate.

But even if (1) is an interpretation of the object-language sentence 'John is a renate', surely (2) is not. So Convention T is too weak.

Davidson's response to this problem is two-fold: he emphasizes that T-sentences are verified not individually but holistically, and he recognizes that T-sentences (and axioms) must be viewed as empirical laws. In accord with the latter point, T-sentences which yield interpretations must not only be true, they must also be capable of supporting counterfactual claims. Presumably (1) supports the counterfactual:

(1′) If 'John is a renate' were false, then John would not be a renate.

But (2) does not support the counterfactual:

(2′) If 'John is a renate' were false, then John would not be a cordate.

Davidson would explain this difference, presumably, by claiming that (1) does, but (2) does not depend ultimately on certain causal relations between speakers and the world (see Davidson 1984a: xiv).

These criticisms of Davidson's programme are by no means the only ones; many questions have been raised about his handling of indexicals, ambiguity, word-meaning versus sentence-meaning, the principle of charity, and so on.

See also: DAVIDSON, D.; HERMENEUTICS; MEANING AND TRUTH; QUINE, W.V.; REFERENCE

References and further reading

Davidson, D. (1980) *Essays on Actions and Events*, Oxford: Clarendon Press. (A collection of Davidson's essays on the philosophy of action.)

* —— (1984a) *Inquiries into Truth and Interpretation*, Oxford: Clarendon Press. (A collection containing some of Davidson's key essays on radical interpretation.)

* —— (1984b) 'Radical interpretation', in *Inquiries into Truth and Interpretation*, Oxford: Clarendon Press, 125–39. (One of the most important of Davidson's essays for understanding radical interpretation.)

* —— (1984c) 'Thought and talk', in *Inquiries into Truth and Interpretation*, Oxford: Clarendon Press, 155–70. (One of the most important of Davidson's essays for understanding his views on the principle of charity.)

Føllesdal, D. (1988) 'Indeterminacy and mental states', in R. Barrett and R. Gibson (eds) *Perspectives on Quine*, Oxford: Blackwell, 98–109. (Føllesdal gives a clear statement of Quine's indeterminacy doctrine.)

Gibson, R. (1986) 'Translation, physics, and facts of

the matter', in L. Hahn and P. Schilpp (eds) *The Philosophy of W. V. Quine*, La Salle, IL: Open Court Press, 139–54. (Gives a clear statement of the difference between indeterminacy of translation and underdetermination of physical theory; excellent bibliography of Quine's writings.)

LePore, E. (ed.) (1986) *Truth and Interpretation*, Oxford: Blackwell. (A collection of twenty-eight essays on Davidson's philosophy, including three by Davidson.)

LePore, E. and B. McLaughlin (eds) (1985) *Actions and Events*, Oxford: Blackwell. (A collection of thirty essays on Davidson's philosophy of action and psychology, including three by Davidson; excellent bibliography.)

Quine, W.V. (1959) 'Meaning and translation', in R.A. Brower (ed.) *On Translation*, Cambridge, MA: Harvard University Press, 148–71. (An earlier version of Chapter 2 of *Word and Object*.)

* —— (1960) *Word and Object*, Cambridge, MA: MIT Press. (See Chapter 2, 'Translation and meaning', for discussion of radical translation.)

* —— (1969a) 'Epistemology naturalized', in *Ontological Relativity and Other Essays*, New York: Columbia University Press, 69–70. (Contains the argument for indeterminacy from holism and verificationism.)

* —— (1969b) 'Ontological relativity', in *Ontological Relativity and Other Essays*, New York: Columbia University Press, 26–68. (Quine explains inscrutability of reference.)

* —— (1970) 'On the reasons for indeterminacy of translation', *The Journal of Philosophy* 67 (6): 178–83. (Clarifies and expands upon earlier material.)

* —— (1974) *Roots of Reference*, La Salle, IL: Open Court Press. (See pages 75–8 for discussion of barriers to translating truth functions.)

* —— (1979) 'Comment on Newton-Smith', *Analysis* 39 (3): 66–7. (Quine expresses a reservation regarding the argument from underdetermination to indeterminacy.)

* —— (1987) 'Indeterminacy of translation again', *The Journal of Philosophy* 84 (1): 5–10. (An excellent exposition of Quine's reasons for indeterminacy of translation.)

* —— (1990) *Pursuit of Truth*, Cambridge, MA: Harvard University Press; revised edn, 1992. (Excellent discussions of indeterminacy of translation and indeterminacy of reference.)

* —— (1995) *From Stimulus to Science*, Cambridge, MA: Harvard University Press. (Excellent discussions of Quine's naturalism, reification and objects of thought.)

* Wilson, N. (1959) 'Substances without substrata',

Review of Metaphysics 12: 521–39. (Originator of the principle of charity.)

ROGER F. GIBSON

RADISCHEV, A *see* ENLIGHTENMENT, RUSSIAN; LIBERALISM, RUSSIAN

AL-RAHIM, QUTB AL-DIN AHMAD *see* SHAH WALI ALLAH (QUTB AL-DIN AHMAD AL-RAHIM)

RAHNER, KARL (1904–84)

Rahner sought to offer an account of the Christian faith that would be credible to the modern mind. His early philosophical works lay the foundation for this theological project. Using both the method and categories of the early Heidegger, Rahner placed the thought of the medieval philosopher and theologian Thomas Aquinas in conversation with modern philosophy. He asked of Aquinas' epistemology Kant's question about the conditions of human subjectivity which make knowledge possible. Rahner argued that Aquinas' description of knowledge and human freedom requires, as its necessary condition, that the subject possess an openness to a universal horizon of being, an openness to God. There is, in the structure of subjectivity, a constitutive, experiential, a priori relationship with the divine mystery. While this openness occurs within an individual's self-awareness, it is always mediated by and interpreted through the objects, people, language and ideas that make up one's historical context (the categorical). In his theology, Rahner argued that the true nature of humanity's relationship with God had been revealed by Jesus to be one of absolute nearness. Rahner rendered Christian doctrines credible by correlating them with the transcendental experience of a God who is near.

1   **Life**
2   **Context and project**
3   **Fundamental ontology**
4   **Freedom**
5   **Theology**

1 Life

Karl Rahner was born near Freiburg, Germany, on 5 March 1904. He entered the Society of Jesus in April 1922 and, as a Jesuit seminarian, studied the Thomistic philosophy which then dominated Roman Catholic thought. In personal study he read the works of the Belgian Jesuit Joseph Maréchal.

In 1934, two years after ordination to the priesthood, Rahner was sent to Freiburg University to take a doctorate in philosophy. While he pursued his degree under the Thomist Martin Honecker, Rahner attended Martin Heidegger's lectures and seminars. He wrote a dissertation on Aquinas' epistemology which Honecker rejected because Rahner's interpretation of Aquinas was too much influenced by Heidegger. The dissertation was published in 1939 as *Geist in Welt* (*Spirit in the World* (1968)). Its perspective is the philosophical ground for Rahner's later theology. Rahner left Freiburg in 1936. In 1937, he satisfied the doctoral and post-doctoral requirements in theology at the University of Innsbruck and lectured there until the theology faculty was abolished by the Nazis in July 1938. He spent the war years at the Pastoral Institute in Vienna and later as a pastor in Bavaria. His philosophy of religion, *Hearers of the Word*, appeared in 1941.

After the Second World War, Rahner returned to teach theology at Innsbruck. He became one of the most influential and prolific Roman Catholic theologians. During the Second Vatican Council, he served as theological advisor to Cardinal König of Vienna. He also held positions at the Universities of Munich (1963–7) and Münster (1967–71). Most of Rahner's theological publications appear as essays collected in the sixteen volumes of *Schriften zur Theologie* (1954–84) (*Theological Investigations* (1961–92)). His *Grundkurs des Glaubens* (1976) (*Foundations of Christian Faith* (1978)) offers a systematic though incomplete presentation of his thought. Rahner also edited and contributed to theological dictionaries and published a number of significant works in spiritual theology. After retiring in 1971, he continued to lecture and write until his death on 30 March 1984.

2 Context and project

Rahner is primarily a Roman Catholic theologian. The aim and content of his thought emerge from the context of the Church's intellectual life in the mid-twentieth century. In 1879, Pope Leo XIII published the encyclical *Aeterni Patris*, which granted the thought of Thomas Aquinas a privileged status within the Catholic Church. Against the scepticism of modern thought, the philosophy of Aquinas represents a realism which both offers rational proof of God's existence and establishes the divine attributes necessary to ground historical revelation. In this way it illuminates Christian revelation and serves Catholic theology (see THOMISM).

Leo XIII's encyclical led to a revival of Thomistic thought within the Church. By the middle of the twentieth century, this revival had produced an unanticipated pluralism in interpretations of Aquinas. Some saw Aquinas as an alternative to the errors of modern philosophy. Others, such as the Jesuits Pierre Rousselot and Joseph Maréchal, interpreted Aquinas in the light of modern questions and insights. In *Le point de départ de la métaphysique* (The Starting Point of Metaphysics) Maréchal began a dialogue between the epistemologies of Kant and Aquinas. By Rahner's own account, the basic and decisive philosophical direction of his thought came from Maréchal.

The neo-Kantianism that dominated German university philosophy at the beginning of the twentieth century assumed the correctness of Kant's critique of metaphysics. In his *Critique of Pure Reason* (1781), Kant argued that human knowledge is properly directed towards the objects of sensation. Efforts to know transcendent realities such as being, human freedom and God, while inevitable, are futile. The human capacity for knowledge is properly employed only when directed towards the physical world presented in sensation. Metaphysics and natural theology do not fall within reason's competence (see KANT §§4–8).

Pursuing Maréchal's project and influenced by Heidegger's efforts to retrieve the question of being, Rahner sought a Thomistic response to Kant's critique of metaphysics. Rather than eschewing modernity's turn to the subject as the abandonment of realism, Rahner offers a transcendental interpretation of Aquinas which leads to an epistemology, an ontology, and an argument for the existence of God. His thought not only offers a Thomistic response to modern philosophical questions, it also serves as the foundation for his theology. The notion of God which Rahner draws from Aquinas serves as an experiential reference in his existential interpretation of Catholic doctrine. In sum, Rahner's thought retrieves a Thomistic ontology within the context of modern thought and, in doing so, grounds a credible account of Christian faith.

3 Fundamental ontology

Rahner observes that Aquinas, like Kant, roots all knowledge in sensation. The proper object of human knowing is the physical world perceived by the senses. Rahner's rejected doctoral dissertation *Spirit in the*

World is an interpretation of *Summa theologiae* Ia, question 84, article 7, in which Aquinas asserts that there is nothing in the human intellect apart from what is attained by turning to phantasms (that is, to objects sensed and imagined). Rahner's interpretation of Aquinas is not a literal rendering of Aquinas' historical position. Rather Rahner adopts Heidegger's interpretive method of retrieval. He uncovers possibilities in Aquinas' thought (in response to Kant) which could not have occurred to a medieval thinker. If human knowledge is properly directed towards objects of sensation, as Kant and Aquinas hold, how are metaphysics and natural theology possible?

Knowledge is more than sensation (after all, animals sense the same things as humans). Knowing is the work of what Aquinas calls the agent or active intellect. Attending to sense data, one forms a concept or idea, such as the concept of 'dog'. But having concepts is not yet knowing. Ideas are the means by which the human intellect comes to the intelligibility of sensed objects. One attains truth (that is, what is) in the act of judgment that, for example, this concrete object is a dog. Thus for Aquinas, knowledge consists of sensation, conceptualization (abstraction) and judgment (see AQUINAS, T. §11).

Rahner then asks of this account of knowledge Kant's transcendental question. What are the conditions that make knowing possible? What must be true of the human intellect for it to move from sensation through conceptualization to judgment? Rahner thereby follows Kant's transcendental approach and attends to the a priori conditions of subjectivity for knowing. He is a transcendental Thomist in that he asks Kant's question of Aquinas' description of knowledge.

Using a term from Heidegger, he contends that the intellect must possess a *Vorgriff*, a pre-grasp of universal being as the necessary condition for the activities of forming universal concepts and judging. The *Vorgriff* is crucial to Rahner's metaphysics and philosophy of religion. For the intellect to form universal concepts from the particular objects of sensation it must have an a priori openness to universality. Again, for the intellect to judge that this object is a dog and nothing else requires a pre-grasp of the nothing else, of a universal horizon of all other beings. The *Vorgriff* of universality is not itself a concept or an object of direct experience. It is a dynamism towards all being, manifest and experienced in the activity of the intellect as the necessary condition for that activity.

What is this universality? In judgment, one asserts what a thing is against an infinite horizon of what it is not. Judgment requires, as its necessary condition, an anticipation of the absolute range of all knowable objects. The range of the intellect is unlimited. It is ordered towards knowing everything that is, all being. If judgment attains what is (being), the absolute range of universality must be absolute being. Absolute being is what a Thomist means by God.

Furthermore, in judgment one asserts what a thing is. One attains the intelligibility of an object (for example, 'that is a dog'). Being, what is, and intelligibility coincide. Being and knowledge must constitute an original unity. Thus absolute being is pure intelligibility, a knower knowing itself, subject and object, absolute and pure self-presence. Pure being is a pure luminosity in which knower and known are identical. There is a hierarchy of being which is a hierarchy of self-possession, of intelligibility, of knowledge. God is one simple act of self-knowledge in which God knows all that is, all being. Humans, lower in the hierarchy, come to self-possession by knowing particular beings. Every act of knowledge involves an encounter with the other in sensation, in-the-world, and the return to self in judgment ('This is a dog and not I'). One possesses the known in the return to self. Human truth is an increase in being, in that the knower possesses more of what is. Knowledge is an existential occurrence in which the knower becomes.

4 Freedom

Human nature is not static. Rahner adopts the early Heidegger's notion of human existence as freedom-in-the-world. To be human is to be handed over to oneself to become. The capacity to make specific choices is rooted in this primordial being as becoming. Human freedom is finite in that persons become through their commerce with other people and objects in-the-world, and through the possibilities offered by a particular time and place. But the performance of freedom requires, as its necessary condition, the *Vorgriff* of unlimited being. Human freedom is unavoidable transcendence, a becoming without limit. To set limits to human becoming – to assert, for example, that human beings are creatures of their environment and no more – is already to transcend those limits. To know oneself is already to transcend, to stand beyond self. Like knowing, the performance of human freedom requires as its necessary condition the subject's openness to an unlimited horizon of being. Human freedom is exercised within the ever mysterious horizon of infinite being. One determines one's being before absolute mystery.

Thus Rahner argues that an experiential openness to absolute being (God) is the necessary condition for human knowledge and freedom. But God remains a mystery. In *Hearers of the Word*, Rahner states that the divine may be merely the mysterious horizon within which human transcendence occurs. It is also possible, though, for God to establish and reveal a more intimate relationship with human creatures.

5 Theology

Rahner's fundamental ontology is the enduring context for the theology which constitutes the bulk of his work. He distinguishes two poles of human experience – object and subject, the categorical and the transcendental. The things, events, possibilities and people one encounters are the categorical. All these encounters happen to a transcendental subject. The *Vorgriff* occurs in the transcendental. Locating the experiential reference for God in the transcendental determines the direction of Rahner's theology.

Speech about God, religious and philosophical, employs categories from historical contexts (for example, horizon, depth, father, creator) to point towards and interpret humanity's transcendental relationship with the divine. Rahner concludes his philosophy of religion described in *Hearers of the Word* with the suggestion that we search history to see if God has, in fact, revealed the character of humanity's constitutive relationship with the divine mystery.

The core truth of the Christian faith is that in Jesus, God has revealed the nature of humanity's relationship with the divine to be one of absolute nearness. God is offering God's very self to each human person for eternal communion. Borrowing a Heideggerian term, Rahner asserts that God's self-offer is an existential, constitutive element of human existence. The transcendental experience is revealed to be an experience of this offer. Human freedom is the capacity to determine who one is before God, to affirm or negate the divine self-offer. Specific Christian teachings give expression to this one core truth and its implications. This truth is proclaimed by the Church within history and can be grasped by all people because it calls them to what they already are.

An example can clarify how Rahner's theology works. Belief in the resurrection of Jesus is the foundation of Christian faith. Yet many find it difficult to believe because they think of Jesus' resurrection as a categorical event, the resuscitation of a dead body within history. Setting aside historical and categorical questions about what happened to Jesus after his death, Rahner suggests that the meaning of Jesus' resurrection is attained by correlating this doctrine with the transcendental experience of God's nearness. Again following Heidegger, Rahner describes human existence as freedom-toward-death. Human beings know they will die, and in the anticipation of death the question inevitably occurs as to whether how one lives, who one becomes in freedom, makes any difference. Does human existence have any meaning or are we simply freedom becoming towards nothing? Since we are helpless to maintain ourselves in existence at death, the question of meaning raises the possibility that what we have achieved in freedom might be granted some final, enduring validity. This possibility of meaning, which Rahner calls transcendental hope, necessarily occurs to everyone. Even the assertion that life is meaningless implies a grasp of what meaningful existence might be. This hope is the experiential manifestation of God's self-gift to every human being. Hope occurs because humanity exercises its freedom within the horizon of God's self-offer.

Transcendental hope is the horizon for hearing and believing the proclamation that Jesus is risen. God has granted final, enduring validity to Jesus' life. From this side of the grave, understanding of the resurrection is rooted in freedom's option that life is meaningful. This option occurs in a life of generosity and service. Hope is rejected in selfishness. Freedom's 'yes' to the divine self-offer may or may not take the form of explicitly religious and Christian categories. But any individual who opts for meaning implicitly affirms the truth of Jesus' resurrection and Christian revelation.

See also: HEIDEGGER, M.

List of works

Rahner, K. (1939) *Spirit in the World*, trans. W. Dych, New York: Herder & Herder, 1968. (This difficult text is Rahner's early interpretation of Aquinas, an interpretation which underlies all his later work.)

—— (1941) *Hearers of the Word*, trans. M. Richards, New York: Herder & Herder, 1969. (This translation of *Hörer des Wortes* is frequently inaccurate. A good translation may be obtained through the journal *Philosophy and Theology* from Marquette University, Milwaukee. The anthology *A Rahner Reader* includes well-translated sections.)

—— (1954–84) *Theological Investigations*, New York: Crossroad, 23 vols, 1961–92. (The essays in these volumes, published originally in the sixteen-volume *Schriften zur Theologie*, contain the core of Rahner's work.)

—— (1975) *A Rahner Reader*, ed. G. McCool, New York: Seabury. (An anthology, with excellent introductions by the editor, of Rahner's philosophical and theological works.)

—— (1976) *Foundations of Christian Faith*, trans. W.

Dych, New York: Seabury, 1978. (A synthetic presentation of Rahner's theology.)

References and further reading

* Aquinas, T. (1266–73) *Summa theologiae*, Blackfriars edn, New York: McGraw-Hill, 1964. (Thomas Aquinas' comprehensive treatise, which remains the most influential work in Roman Catholic theology.)

Carr, A.E. (1984) 'Karl Rahner', in D.G. Peerman and M.E. Marty (eds) *A Handbook of Christian Theologians*, Nashville, TN: Abingdon Press, 519–542. (A good introductory essay which deals with both Rahner's philosophy and theology.)

* Kant, I. (1781) *Critique of Pure Reason*, trans. N. Kemp Smith, London: Macmillan, 1963. (Kant's epistemology and his most influential work.)

* Maréchal, J. (1927–49) *Le point de départ de la métaphysique* (The Starting Point of Metaphysics), Paris: Desclée de Brouwer, and Brussels: L'Édition Universelle, 5 vols. (Maréchal places the thought of Aquinas in conversation with Kant, seeking a Thomistic response to Kant's method and conclusions.)

—— (1970) *A Maréchal Reader*, ed. and trans. J. Doncell, New York: Herder & Herder. (This is an anthology of Maréchal's writings taken almost entirely from his major work, *Le point de départ de la métaphysique*.)

McCool, G. (1989) *From Unity to Pluralism: The Internal Evolution of Thomism*, New York: Fordham University Press. (A history of the Thomistic revival in the early twentieth century that formed the context for Rahner's philosophical and theological work.)

—— (1989) *Nineteenth-Century Scholasticism: The Search for a Unitary Method*, New York: Fordham University Press. (An account of the origins of the Thomistic revival within Roman Catholicism that gave rise to the intellectual context for Rahner's thought.)

Schüssler-Fiorenza, F. (1968) 'Karl Rahner and the Kantian Problematic', introduction to *Spirit in the World*, New York: Herder & Herder, xix–xlv. (A clear essay setting forth the philosophical context for Rahner's early work.)

Sheehan, T. (1987) *Karl Rahner: The Philosophical Foundations*, Athens, OH: Ohio University Press. (An excellent though difficult study of the philosophical background, especially Heidegger, for Rahner's *Spirit in the World*.)

Tallon, A. (1989–90) 'Rahner Studies, 1939–1989: Part I, 1939–73', *Theology Digest* 36 (4): 321–46; 'Rahner Studies, 1939–1989: Part II, 1974–89', *Theology Digest* 37 (1): 17–41; 'Rahner bibliography supplement', *Theology Digest* 38 (2): 131–40. (A fairly comprehensive bibliography of works about Rahner. Tallon's bibliography is to be kept current by the journal *Philosophy and Theology* from Marquette University, Milwaukee.)

Vorgrimler, H. (1986) *Understanding Karl Rahner: An Introduction to His Life and Thought*, New York: Crossroad. (An excellent introduction to Rahner's thought.)

JACK A. BONSOR

RALBAG *see* GERSONIDES

RAMAKRISHNA MOVEMENT

Although the Ramakrishna Movement was born in Bengal and influenced by Christian missionary activity and Western Orientalism, its understanding of Hinduism has become the standard for modern educated Indians. Drawing on the spiritual inspiration of its guru, Sri Ramakrishna (1836–86), and the dynamic preaching of his main disciple, Swami Vivekananda (1863–1902), the Ramakrishna Order has founded centres throughout India and the West. Calling his system 'Practical Vedānta', Vivekananda laid claim to the classical Advaita Vedānta associated with Śaṅkara. Unlike Śaṅkara, though, Vivekananda elevated selfless social work to a spiritual path equal in value to meditation, devotion and gnosis. The swamis of the order combine traditional Hindu religious practice with the administration of educational and medical institutions on the model of Christian missions. Vivekananda's vision of Indian culture as united and renewed by his humanistic Hinduism has inspired other gurus as well as Hindu nationalists.

1 Background
2 Principal tenets

1 Background

The Ramakrishna Movement, a highly successful Hindu religious and missionary order, was first propagated by Swami Vivekananda (1863–1902), a disciple of Sri Ramakrishna (1836–86), in the 1890s. Vivekananda received training in Western philosophy at a college of the Scottish Free Church in Calcutta, capital of the British Raj. Before joining Sri Ramakrishna during his college years, Vivekananda belonged to the Brahmo Samaj, the first major Hindu reform movement (see BRAHMO SAMAJ). Wounded by the scathing attacks on Hindu tradition by Christian missionaries, by the triumphalist histories of Anglo-centric Orientalists, and by discriminatory policies in the colonial civil service and the courts, members of the emerging Bengali Western-educated middle class took refuge in literature, the arts and religion. A few, like Vivekananda, sought to represent their culture in a way that would integrate their conflict-torn identities within and, at the same time, stand up to Western scrutiny. By the time of Lord Curzon's partition of Bengal in 1905, a mark of Vivekananda's success was that his new Hinduism was feeding the resistance movement against British colonialism.

Those educated Bengalis who did not completely forsake their cultural tradition took heart from a long line of sympathetic Orientalists – from Sir William Jones in the late eighteenth century to Max Müller in the late nineteenth. Both the Brahmo Samaj and Vivekananda's Ramakrishna Movement felt empowered by such work to imagine a reconciliation of the conflict, as they saw it, between East and West. Both Keshub Chunder Sen, leader of the Brahmo Samaj, and Swami Vivekananda took inspiration also from Sri Ramakrishna, who seemed to offer a liberal outreach from the authentic depths of the indigenous tradition (see BRAHMO SAMAJ §2). Keshub preached a New Dispensation based on a personal mixture of Indian and Western traditions; Vivekananda convinced his contemporaries that his synthesis was fully rooted in Hinduism, that he 'spoke nothing but the Upaniṣads'. Vivekananda followed Orientalists in presenting the classic Hindu systems in Western terms. His ultimate intention, however, was to universalize key Vedāntic concepts such as Brahman, *ātman* and *mokṣa* into a controlling framework of norms and values for the entire world.

Vivekananda assumed that each culture represents a unique national spirit which complemented that of other nations. Here Vivekananda combined European romanticism with the caste theory of *jātidharma* – the notion that each class of persons has an inherent and unique role in society. Vivekananda tried to divine this intercultural cosmology by weighing the strengths and weaknesses of each nation's religion and society:

> Which is better, the social freedom of America, or the social system of India with all its restrictions? The American method is individualistic. It gives an opportunity to the lowest. There can be no growth except in freedom, but it also has obvious dangers. Still, the individual gets experience even through mistakes. Our Indian system is based entirely upon the good of the *samāj* [society]. The individual must fit into the system at any cost. There is no

freedom for the individual unless he renounces society and becomes a *sannyāsin* (monk). This system has produced towering individuals, spiritual giants. Has it been at the expense of those less spiritual than themselves? Which is better for the race? Which? The freedom of America gives opportunities to masses of people. It makes for breadth, whilst the intensity of India means depth. How to keep both, that is the problem.
>
> (Eastern and Western Admirers 1964: 218–9)

This dialectic was typical of Vivekananda's thought process. Romantic Orientalism assumed that the great cosmic struggle of the time pitted a materialist West against a spiritually gifted but weakened East. Vivekananda assimilated these two entities to the primary *guṇas* (qualities) of Sāṅkhya cosmology: *rajas* (passion, power) and *tamas* (inertia) respectively. When *rajas* and *tamas* regain balance with each other, the universe attains to *sattva* (a salvific equilibrium) (see SĀṄKHYA §2). Through a cultural exchange of qualities, the East would regain its vitality and teach the West its spiritual insights.

2 Principal tenets

Although Ramakrishna introduced Vivekananda to Advaita Vedānta, Vivekananda's readings in Herbert SPENCER, Ernst HAECKEL and Paul Deussen confirmed the viability of metaphysical nondualism as a framework for cross-cultural apologetics and assimilation. Knowledge of the Absolute equalized all competing doctrines and symbols by uniformly nullifying them, but the penultimate perception of One-and-Many equally exalted them:

> All we know about things now or may know in future are but relative truths. It is impossible for our limited mind to grasp the absolute truth. Hence, though truth be absolute, it appears variously to diverse minds and intellects. All these facets or modes of truth belong to the same class as truth itself, they being based on the same absolute truth. This is like the different photographs of the same sun taken from various distances. Each of them seems to represent a different sun. The diverse relative truths have the same kind of relation with the absolute truth. Each religion is thus true, just because it is a mode of presentation of the absolute religion.
>
> (Eastern and Western Admirers 1964: 28)

Vivekananda wanted especially to include the materialist viewpoint – 'The materialist is right! There is but One. Only he calls that One Matter, and I call it God!' (Nivedita 1910: 23). Vivekananda wanted to claim like

Herbert Spencer that he had reconciled religion and science. But the styling of philosophical differences as mere terminological distinctions recalls Ramakrishna's simple dictum that the different gods of the various religions are like the different names for water in various languages.

Following the Orientalist Sir William Hunter, Vivekananda linked Vedānta cosmology with Western evolutionism. For him evolution was a soteriological process:

> From the lowest form of life to man, the soul is manifesting itself through nature. The highest manifestation of the soul is involved in the lowest form of manifest life and is working itself outward through the process called evolution. The whole process of evolution is the soul's struggle to maintain itself.
>
> (Vivekananda 1977 vol. 6: 35–6)

Vivekananda maintained that the Indian theory taught that the process did not occur through competition (Spencer's survival of the fittest) but by the 'infilling of nature' (prakṛtyāpūrāt). Among humans, evolution took place not by overcoming obstacles but by letting the obstacles 'give way' through 'education and culture'. This theory is more 'consonant with reason' and less 'evil'. Darwin's theory applied to plants and animals; human culture advanced not by means of human competition and cooperation with Natural Law, as Spencer argued, but rather on the basis of a struggle against Nature, as Thomas HUXLEY argued, and self-sacrifice for the good of society.

Vivekananda used evolutionism also to frame his philosophy of history. He endorsed the views of Spencer and Müller that religions and nations evolve and progress in history, though not without cyclical periods of decay or regression. In the case of India, he postulated a Golden Age followed by degeneration, and he looked forward to a national renewal. Vivekananda was not promoting historical determinism, however. In March 1899 he said to his main Western disciple, Sister Nivedita (the Irishwoman and Indian nationalist Margaret Noble):

> I say, Margot, I have been thinking for days about [Spencer's] line of least resistance; it is a base fallacy. It is a comparative thing.... The history of the world is the history of a few earnest men, and when one man is earnest the world must just come to his feet. I am not going to water down my ideals, I am going to dictate terms.
>
> (Eastern and Western Admirers 1964: 278)

Thomas Carlyle's Great Man theory, another favourite of Vivekananda's, here overcame Spencer's Natural Law.

Vivekananda also questioned Western progressivism from a more traditional Indian view. Ramakrishna taught that 'The world is like a dog's curly tail ... people have been striving to straighten it out for years ... when they let it go, it has curled up again' (Vivekananda 1977 vol. 1: 79). Vivekananda preached that people should aspire to progress, to do some good for society, but with the goal in mind of spiritual progress rather than worldly perfection: 'You cannot overcome the idea of progress. But things do not grow better. They remain as they were, and we grow better, by the changes we make in them' (Nivedita 1910: 148).

The goal of religion in classic Advaita Vedānta was mokṣa, a state in which the self frees itself from consciousness of both self and world. Ramakrishna privileged the state of exalted devotion in which one retains consciousness of one's self in order to play in the consciousness of God. Vivekananda combined Advaita Vedānta and Western humanism to preach that because every ātman was truly Brahman, service to humanity was service to God.

See also: VEDĀNTA

References and further reading

Bharati, A. [Fischer, L.] (1970) 'The Hindu Renaissance and Its Apologetic Patterns', *Journal of Asian Studies* 29 (February): 267–88. (Biting Western view of Vivekananda as a facile nationalist ideologue by a former member of the Ramakrishna Order.)

Burke, M.L. (1957) *Swami Vivekananda in the West: New Discoveries*, Calcutta: Advaita Ashrama, 3rd edn, 1983–7, 6 vols. (Detailed documentation by a Western devotee of Vivekananda's tour of the West, especially the USA.)

Chatterjee, P. (1993) *The Nation and Its Fragments: Colonial and Postcolonial Histories*, Princeton, NJ: Princeton University Press. (Secular Indian view of Vivekananda as a cultural nationalist.)

Dhar, S.N. (1975) *A Comprehensive Biography of Swami Vivekananda*, Madras: Vivekananda Prakashan Kendra, 2 vols. (More historically orientated than the official 'Life', but underplays Western influences.)

* Eastern and Western Disciples (1964) *Reminiscences of Swami Vivekananda*, Calcutta: Advaita Ashrama, 5th edn, 1979. (Uncritical but comprehensive.)

Gupta, M. [M] (1969) *The Gospel of Sri Ramakrishna*, trans. Swami Nikhilananda, New York: Ramakrishna–Vivekananda Center. (Abridged, but well-written edition of a canonical Bengali original by M, a Western-educated devotee who transcribed his conversations with Ramakrishna.)

Halbfass, W. (1981) *Indien und Europa*, trans. W. Halbfass and J. Baker, *India and Europe: An Essay in Understanding*, Albany, NY: State University of New York Press, 1988. (Sophisticated hermeneutical and philosophical analysis of the East–West encounter, with sections on Vivekananda and contemporaries.)

Jackson, C.T. (1994) *Vedānta for the West: The Ramakrishna Movement in the United States*, Bloomington, IN: Indiana University Press. (Survey of the Order's Mission to America.)

Kripal, J.J. (1995) *Kali's Child: The Mystical and the Erotic in the Life and Teachings of Ramakrishna*, Chicago: University of Chicago Press. (Argues for the centrality of tantra in this tradition.)

Mahadevan, T.M.P. (1961) *Outlines of Hinduism*, Bombay: Chetana. (Representative presentation of neo-Vedānta in philosophical mode.)

Müller, F.M. (1899) *Ramakrishna: His Life and Sayings*, Calcutta: Advaita Ashrama, 1984. (Reprint of Müller's understanding and digest of the movement as it was forming in the 1890s.)

* Nivedita [Margaret Noble] (1910) *The Master as I Saw Him: Being Pages from the Life of the Swami Vivekananda by his Disciple Nivedita*, Calcutta: Udbodhan Office, 3rd edn, 1923. (Record of her training by Vivekananda's main Western disciple.)

—— (1913) *Notes of Some Wanderings with the Swami Vivekananda*, ed. Swami Saradananda, Calcutta: Udbodhan Office. (Sister Nivedita describes her travels with Vivekananda on pilgrimage in northern India.)

Rambachan, A. (1994) *The Limits of Scripture: Vivekananda's Reinterpretation of the Vedas*, Honolulu: University of Hawaii Press. (Reveals contradictions within Vivekananda's reinterpretations and in their claims to continuity with Śaṅkara's philosophy.)

Raychaudhuri, T. (1988) *Europe Reconsidered: Perceptions of the West in 19th Century Bengal*, Delhi: Oxford University Press. (Analysis of Vivekananda's 'reconsideration' of the West.)

Rolland, R. (1931) *Life of Vivekananda and the Universal Gospel*, trans. E.M. Smith, Calcutta: Advaita Ashrama, 1965. (Classic Western idealization of the new movement.)

* Vivekananda (1977) *The Complete Works of Swami Vivekananda*, Calcutta: Advaita Ashrama, 8 vols. (Collection of letters, lectures, interviews and published writings, with little or no contextualization.)

THOMAS L. BRYSON

RĀMĀNUJA (d. *circa* 1137)

A south Indian Brahman, Rāmānuja was the theistic exegete of the Vedānta who propounded a doctrine which came to be known as viśiṣṭādvaita or 'qualified monism'. As such, he is often said to be the founder of the most prominent of the four schools of the Vaishnava religion, the Śrīsampradāya, although in fact he considered himself to be a participant in an already ancient tradition. Rāmānuja's version of Vedānta challenges the uncompromising nondualism of Śaṅkara.

1   **Life and works**
2   **Epistemology**
3   **Theology**
4   **Soteriology**

1   Life and works

Nine works are ascribed to Rāmānuja by his biographers: three are commentaries on the *Vedānta-sūtra* of which the extensive *Śrībhāṣya* is the most important; *Vedāntasāra* (The Essence of Vedānta) and *Vedāntadīpa* (Light on the Vedānta) are shorter commentaries on the same text. His other philosophical works are a commentary on the *Bhagavad Gītā* and an independent summary of his doctrine, *Vedārthasaṃgraha* (A Compendium of the Meaning of *the Veda*) (*c*.1016–1137). *Nityagrantha* (A manual of Daily Worship), as well as three shorter devotional works are also ascribed to Rāmānuja. Of these nine, only *Śrībhāṣya*, *Bhagavad Gītābhāṣya* and *Vedārthasaṃgraha* are accepted without dispute to be his own. Of the remaining six, scholarly consensus leans towards accepting the two shorter commentaries on Vedānta as genuine and the others as later ascriptions.

Rāmānuja first took instruction in the Vedānta aphorisms from Yādavaprakāśa, who himself had composed a commentary on them in the *bhedābheda* ((simultaneous) difference and identity) tradition. Following Bhāskara (*c*.900), Yādavaprakā śa gave equal ontological status to both Brahman, the ultimate reality, and the phenomenal universe. However, in Rāmānuja's opinion, his teacher was inclined towards a monistic interpretation as he considered īśvara, the personal god, to be part of the phenomenal universe and not identical with Brahman. After his break with Yādavaprakāśa, Rāmānuja transferred his loyalties to Yāmunācārya, the head priest of the Viṣṇu temple at Śrīraṅgam and representative of the devotional creed of the Āḷvārs. Although he had no personal contact with Yāmuna, legend has it that Rāmānuja was given a posthumous order to undertake several tasks, including that of presenting a systematic commentary on the Vedānta which was in opposition to that of Śaṅkara, through which commentary a philosophical basis would be given to the devotional religion presented in the hymns of the Āḷvārs. This Rāmānuja was able to do through combining a realistic metaphysic with a theology of revelation.

2 Epistemology

Like Śaṅkara, Rāmānuja accepted three sources of knowledge: direct perception, inference and revelation (See KNOWLEDGE, INDIAN VIEWS OF). Although immediate experience of Brahman is the ultimate proof of its truth, revelation is the only dependable source of knowledge for the aspiring seeker, direct perception being subject to various sensory defects and inference to other human failings (see BRAHMAN). Among the sources of revelation, Rāmānuja follows Śaṅkara in giving precedence to the Upaniṣads, the *Brahmasūtras* and the *Bhagavad Gītā*, as the measure of all revelatory sources. In addition, he made extensive use of the Purāṇas, primarily the *Viṣṇupurāṇa* (*c.* fourth century AD).

3 Theology

According to Śaṅkara, Brahman, the supreme truth, is pure existence with no qualities; it is consciousness alone without differentiation of subject and object (see ŚAṄKARA). Rāmānuja understood that an eternal distinction between the individual soul and Brahman is essential to monotheistic religion. The religious relationship between God and the individual which Śaṅkara considered to be conventional, that is, merely an aspect of the phenomenal existence, had to be shown to be ultimate. Rāmānuja thus rejected Śaṅkara's theory of two levels of revelation, claiming that all revealed statements should be given equal status. Just as certain Upaniṣadic passages illustrating the ultimacy of the monotheistic position presented a problem to Śaṅkara, Rāmānuja had to accept and deal with others which showed that the individual souls and the supreme truth were not different. This he did by showing that the distinctions between the selves, the phenomenal world of matter and God were maintained even while they formed a unity. Thus, the nondual (*advaita*) ultimate reality was shown to be qualified (*viśiṣṭa*) by the existence of the finite conscious living beings and the unconscious universe. All objects of experience are characterized by generic and specific properties. Therefore, Śaṅkara's characterization of Brahma as pure existence which has no properties was seen as a figment of the imagination. Yāmunācārya had argued persuasively for the existence of the soul by showing that despite the changes in the objects of knowledge, the knower remains essentially the same. Individual consciousness remains constant and unchanging despite the changes in the body. This is further confirmed by the sense of difference between the self and the body, as evidenced by a statement such as 'this is my body'. Rāmānuja expands on this idea with his doctrine of inseparability through which he argues that no soul can be without a body, for there is no such thing as consciousness without a field of consciousness, that is, a body. Similarly, God or Brahman cannot be pure consciousness (as is held by Śaṅkara), because such a thing lies outside the realm of experience. Since nothing exists outside of Brahman, that of which he is conscious is also himself. The object of God's consciousness, that is, the creation consisting of both unconscious matter and individual souls, is thus considered, by analogy with the individual consciousness, to be his body. Despite the changes in the universe, his body, he, as the soul of the universe, remains unchanged and unchanging. Through this reasoning, the universe is given the same ontological status as the ever-constant eternal ground of being, because the one is dependent on the other. Just as changes in the body of the individual do not accrue to that individual, similarly the various transformations of the universe do not constitute a change in the essence of Brahman.

4 Soteriology

The individual soul has been confounded through his association with unconscious matter and so identifies with his material body. Through surrender and devotion he can attain a body which is suitable for directly experiencing and eternally serving the personal God. This is the ultimate goal of life. After Rāmānuja's death, his followers split over whether surrender, with its implication of complete dependence on the grace of God, or devotion, interpreted as a type of doctrine of works, was the more important aspect in the path of attaining God.

See also: BRAHMAN; GOD, INDIAN CONCEPTIONS OF; MONISM, INDIAN; VEDĀNTA

List of works

Rāmānuja (*c.*1016–*c.*1137) *Vedārthasaṃgraha of Śrī Rāmānujacārya*, trans. S.S. Raghavachar, Mysore: Sri Ramakrishna Ashram, 1968. (Without dispute, this text is accepted to be the author's own.)

References and further reading

Buitenen, J.A.B. von (1953) *Rāmānuja and the Bhagavad Gītā*, The Hague: Ned Boek en Steendrukkerij. (A condensed translation of Rāmānuja's *Bhagavad Gītā Bhāṣya*.)

* *Bhagavad Gītā* (200 BC–AD 200, disputed), trans. with text in Devanagari and English S. Adidevananda, Madras: Sri Ramakrishna Math, 1991. (A more recent translation.)

Carman, J.B. (1974) *The Theology of Rāmānuja: An Essay in Interreligious Understanding*, New Haven, NJ and London: Yale University Press. (Comparisons of Rāmānuja's theology with that of the Christians.)

Dasgupta, S.N. (1940) *A History of Indian Philosophy*, Cambridge: Cambridge University Press, vol. 3. (An exposition of varieties of classical Vedānta; in five volumes.)

Devamani, B.S. (1990) *The Religion of Rāmānuja: A Christian Appraisal*, Madras: Christian Literature Society. (Rāmānuja's theology is compared with Christian theology.)

Lacombe, O. (1937) *L'Absolu selon le Vedānta: Les notions de Brahman et d'Atman dans les systèmes de Çankara et Rāmānuja* (The Absolute According to Vedānta: The Notions of Brahman and Atman in the Systems of Śaṅkara and Rāmānuja), Paris: Librairie orientaliste Paul Geuthner. (Comparative study of Rāmānuja and Śaṅkara.)

Lipner, J.J. (1986) *The Face of Truth: A Study of Meaning and Metaphysics in the Vedāntic Theology of Rāmānuja*, Albany, NY: State University of New York Press. (An interesting read.)

Lott, E.J. (1976) *God and the Universe in the Vedāntic Theology of Rāmānuja*, Madras: Rāmānuja Research Society. (An in-depth discussion of Rāmānuja's theology.)

Radhakrishnan, S. (1928) *The Vedānta According to Śaṅkara and Rāmānuja*, London: Allen & Unwin. (This book has not lost its value.)

Raghavachar, S.S. (1972) *Śrī Rāmānuja on the Upaniṣads*, Madras: Professor M. Rangacharya Memorial Trust. (Rāmānuja shows the Upaniṣads to be a revelatory source.)

Srinivasachari, S.M. (1956) 'Advaita and Viśiṣṭādvaita', Adyar Library Series, vol. 39, Madras: Adyar Library and Research Center, 2nd edn. (A study of Rāmānuja's doctrine.)

Thibaut, G. (1904) 'The *Vedāntasūtras* with Commentary by Rāmānuja', *The Sacred Books of the East Series*, vol. 48, ed. F.M. Müller, Oxford: Clarendon Press. (Numerous summaries of Rāmānuja's thought have been written, although translations of primary sources are rare. Thibaut's English translation of the *Vedāntasūtras* (*Brahmasūtras*) commentary, the *Śrībhāṣya* is considered to be adequate to the task.)

Varadachari, K.C. (1956) *Rāmānuja's Theory of Knowledge*, Tirupati: Tirumalai–Tirupati Devasthanams Press, 2nd edn. (An examination of Rāmānuja theory of the three sources of knowledge.)

* *Viṣṇupurāṇa* (*c*.4th century AD), trans. Nag Sharan Singh, Delhi: Nag Publishers, 1980. (Rāmānuja made extensive use of this text in his philosophy.)

JAN K. BRZEZINSKI

RAMBAM *see* MAIMONIDES, MOSES

RAMEE, PIERRE DE LA *see* RAMUS, PETRUS

RAMIFIED TYPE THEORY *see* THEORY OF TYPES

RAMMOHUN ROY, RAJA *see* BRAHMO SAMAJ

RAMSEY, FRANK PLUMPTON (1903–30)

Before Ramsey died at the age of 26 he did an extraordinary amount of pioneering work, in economics and mathematics as well as in logic and philosophy. His major contributions to the latter are as follows. (1) He produced the definitive version of Bertrand Russell's attempted reduction of mathematics to logic. (2) He produced the first quantitative theory of how we make decisions, for example about going to the station to catch a train. His theory shows how such decisions depend on the strengths of our beliefs (that the train will run) and desires (to catch it), and uses this dependence to define general measures of belief and desire. This theory also underpins his claim that what makes induction reasonable is its being a reliable way of forming true beliefs, and it underpins his equation of knowledge generally with reliably formed true beliefs. (3) He used the equivalence between believing a proposition and believing that it is true to define truth in terms of beliefs. These in turn he proposed to define by how they affect our actions and whether those actions fulfil our desires. (4) He produced two theories of laws of nature. On the first of these, laws are the generalizations that would be axioms and theorems in the simplest true theory of everything. On the second, they are generalizations that lack exceptions and would if known be used to support predictions ('I'll starve if I don't eat') and hence decisions ('I'll eat'). (5) He showed how established, for example optical, phenomena can be explained by theories using previously unknown terms, like 'photon', which they introduce. (6) He showed why no grammatical distinction between subjects like 'Socrates' and predicates like 'is wise' entails any intrinsic difference between particulars and universals.

1 **Mathematics**
2 **Probability and knowledge**
3 **Belief and truth**
4 **Laws and causation**
5 **Theories**
6 **Universals**

1 Mathematics

The British philosopher Frank Plumpton Ramsey graduated in mathematics from Trinity College Cambridge in 1923, became a Fellow of King's College in 1924 and a University Lecturer in Mathematics in 1926. In his short life he did work in mathematics and economics which created new branches of those subjects. But his vocation and greatest achievements were in philosophy, influenced by and influencing his Cambridge colleagues, especially RUSSELL, WITTGENSTEIN and KEYNES. His first major work, on 'The Foundations of Mathematics' (1925) (this can be found, as can all his other works cited in this entry, in Ramsey (1990a)), makes two key improvements to the attempted reduction of mathematics to logic in Whitehead and Russell's *Principia Mathematica* (see LOGICISM). First, Ramsey tightens *Principia*'s definition of mathematical propositions as purely general by requiring them also to be tautologies in the sense of Wittgenstein's *Tractatus*. Second, he shows that it need deal only with purely logical paradoxes, like that of the class of all classes which are not members of themselves, not semantic ones like 'this is a lie', which depend on the meanings of words like 'lie'. This lets Ramsey simplify *Principia*'s complex hierarchy of propositions, since it no longer needs to make 'this is a lie' ill-formed by making '*p*' and '*p* is a lie' propositions of different types. This in turn lets him drop the 'axiom of reducibility' (of propositions of higher types to equivalent ones of lower types) that *Principia* needs to validate 'many important mathematical arguments' (1990a: 190). Dropping this axiom is essential to logicism, since 'there is no reason to suppose [it] true; and if it were true, this would be a happy accident and not a logical necessity, for it is not a tautology' (1990a: 191) (see THEORY OF TYPES; SEMANTIC PARADOXES AND THEORIES OF TRUTH).

In 'Mathematical Logic' (1926) Ramsey defends his logicism against 'the Bolshevik menace of Brouwer and Weyl' (1990a: 219) (see INTUITIONISM) and the formalism of Hilbert (see HILBERT'S PROGRAMME AND FORMALISM). The former he attacks for denying that all propositions are either true or false – 'Brouwer would refuse to agree that either it was raining or it was not raining, unless he had looked to see' (1990a: 228) – and the latter for reducing mathematics to 'a meaningless game with marks on paper' (1990a: 233). But he remains embarrassed by logicism's need to assume that there are infinitely many things; and R.B. Braithwaite, introducing his edition of Ramsey's papers in 1931, reports that in 1929 Ramsey 'was converted to a finitist view which rejects the existence of any actual infinite aggregate'. Despite this, and logicism's general rejection by mathematicians, Ramsey's version of it remains of great interest to logicians (Chihara 1980).

2 Probability and knowledge

If Russell and Wittgenstein prompted Ramsey's work on mathematics, Keynes prompted his work on economics and probability. The latter was provoked especially by Keynes' *A Treatise on Probability* (1921), which extends the deductive logic of conclusive inference to an inductive logic of inconclusive inference by postulating a relation of 'partial entailment', knowable a priori. This, when measurable, enables a probability measure of the strength of an inference from one proposition to another. But in 'Truth and Probability' (1926) Ramsey attacked the idea of an a priori inductive logic so effectively that Keynes abandoned it, although it was later revived (see CARNAP; PROBABILITY, INTERPRETATIONS OF).

Ramsey's main achievement in 'Truth and Probability' is his probability measure of the strength (degree) of a belief. This starts from 'the old-established way of measuring a person's belief, [that is,] to propose a bet, and see what are the lowest odds which he will accept' (1990a: 68). Refining this by invoking 'the theory that we act in the way we think most likely to realise the objects of our desires' (1990a: 69), Ramsey derives measures both of desires (subjective utilities) and of beliefs (subjective probabilities), thereby founding the now standard use of these concepts (see DECISION AND GAME THEORY).

Ramsey himself uses his theory to extend 'the lesser

logic...of consistency' (1990a: 82) from full to partial beliefs. Thus to the injunction not to believe both *p* and not-*p* he adds, for example, that anyone who believes *p* to degree 1/3 must believe not-*p* to degree 2/3. Otherwise what these beliefs will make him do 'would depend on the precise form in which the options were offered him, which would be absurd': that is, they would make him bet at different odds on *p* and against not-*p*, so that 'he could have a book made against him by a cunning better and would then stand to lose in any event' (1990a: 78).

Ramsey also uses his theory to develop 'the larger logic...of discovery', applied (following PEIRCE) to belief-forming 'habits of inference...observation and memory' (1990a: 92). He shows why such a habit is good or bad 'as the degree of belief it produces is near or far from the actual proportion in which the habit leads to truth', and hence why the fact that 'the world is so constituted that inductive arguments lead on the whole to true opinions' makes our inductive habits reasonable (1990a: 93).

Hence also Ramsey's claim in 'Knowledge' (1929) that 'a belief [is] knowledge if it is (i) true, (ii) certain [that is, a full belief], (iii) obtained by a reliable process...[that is, one] that can be more or less relied on to give true beliefs' (1990a: 110). This claim anticipates later accounts of knowledge (see INTERNALISM AND EXTERNALISM IN EPISTEMOLOGY; RELIABILISM), showing amongst other things how we can know things we do not know we know. This in particular enables Ramsey to evade several well-known objections to knowledge, conceived of as true belief that the believer could justify, which need to assume that I can only know something if I know I know it (Sahlin 1991).

In 'Truth and Probability' Ramsey does not apply his subjective reading of probability to physics. Unfortunately he later, in 'Chance' (1928), anticipates de Finetti (1937) by taking even physical chances to be only 'in another sense objective, in that everyone agrees about them' (1990a: 106). To this we may reply by adding to his objection to Keynes, that determining the right probabilities 'in molecular mechanics...is a matter of physics rather than pure logic' (1990a: 85), that it takes more than mass psychology to explain (for example) the random decay of radioactive atoms.

Fortunately Ramsey does not make all his successors' mistakes. In particular, unlike many later decision theorists (for example, Jeffrey 1983), he never *prescribes* acting 'in the way we think most likely to realise the objects of our desires'. He claims only that the theory that we do so is 'a useful approximation to the truth...like Newtonian mechanics' (1990a: 69). Here he is right: for even when I

in fact do something because 'it seemed a good idea at the time', this fact about my action does not suffice to make it rational.

3 Belief and truth

In defining a belief's strength by its effects on our actions, Ramsey foreshadows later theories which define mental states by their causes, effects and interactions (see FUNCTIONALISM). In 'Facts and Propositions' (1927) he extends this idea from degrees to contents of beliefs, taking (for example) 'the equivalence between believing "not-*p*" and disbelieving "*p*"...to be defined [by their sharing] many of their causes and...effects' (1990a: 44). But after failing to define the contents of beliefs as effectively as their degrees, Ramsey concludes that his view, that 'the meaning of a sentence [expressing a belief] is to be defined by reference to the actions to which asserting it would lead', remains 'very vague and undeveloped' (1990a: 51).

It is, however, developed enough to stop Ramsey's theory of truth being, as is usually supposed, that truth is definable by the fact that for all *p*, it is true that *p* iff *p* (see TRUTH, DEFLATIONARY THEORIES OF). He does say that 'there is really no separate problem of truth' since (for example) '"it is true that Caesar was murdered" means no more than that Caesar was murdered', so that 'if we have analysed [belief] we have solved the problem of truth' (1990a: 38–9). But the solution will not be the so-called redundancy theory if our analysis of beliefs includes a substantive analysis of their truth conditions, as Ramsey's needs to do.

Ramsey starts by observing that we can 'say that a chicken believes a certain sort of caterpillar to be poisonous, and mean by that merely that it abstains from eating such caterpillars on account of unpleasant experiences connected with them'. Since this action is 'such as to be useful if, and only if, the caterpillars were actually poisonous...any set of actions for whose utility *p* is a necessary and sufficient condition might be called a belief that *p*, and so would be true if *p*, i.e. if they were useful' (1990a: 40, see TRUTH, PRAGMATIC THEORY OF).

Unfortunately Ramsey drops this idea when dealing 'with those beliefs which are expressed in words...or other symbols, consciously asserted', although it can apply to them too. In fact its only fault is to identify a belief with a set of actions, like abstaining from eating caterpillars, instead of with one of their causes. But any theory that makes beliefs entail causal functions from desires to actions can remedy this. For then the 'set of actions' of a full belief *b* will be all those that *b* would combine with some desire to cause; and p will be the condition in which every such action would succeed – that is, achieve the object of the desire involved, say to eat without dying. But this is obviously the condition that b be true, that is, b's truth condition.

Ramsey can therefore let this 'success semantics' (Whyte 1990) give the truth condition of any belief definable by 'the actions to which ... it would lead'. Indeed he must do so, since a belief's truth condition cannot be given just by how it makes us act, for that will be the same whether it is true or false. What does depend on a belief's truth is whether the actions it causes succeed: hence success semantics. But this, while vindicating Ramsey's claim that analysing belief solves the problem of truth, rules out the redundancy theory: for success semantics, since its contribution to the analysis of beliefs is to say what makes them true, is itself a substantive theory of truth.

4 Laws and causation

Ramsey produced two theories of laws of nature (see LAWS, NATURAL). Both are Humean in distinguishing law statements from accidentally true generalizations not by what they say but by how we use them. In 'Universals of Law and of Fact' (1928) Ramsey says they are 'consequences of those [general] propositions which we should take as axioms if we knew everything and organised it as simply as possible in a deductive system' (1990a: 150). Although Ramsey soon abandoned this 'systematic theory' (Armstrong 1983), it remains the best Humean account of laws.

Ramsey's second theory, in 'General Propositions and Causality' (1929), is that law statements like 'all men are mortal' are 'variable hypotheticals', which 'are not judgments but rules for judging "If I meet a ϕ I shall regard it as a ψ"' (1990a: 149). Thus 'a causal generalization is not ... one which is simple, but one we trust' (1990a: 150), while to believe there are unknown laws is to believe there are 'such singular facts ... as would lead us, did we know them, to assert a variable hypothetical [which must] be also asserted to hold within ... the scope of our possible experience' (1990a: 152).

This theory explains why we invoke causation and laws in assessing action, since 'we cannot blame a man except by considering what would have happened if he had acted differently; and this ... depends essentially on variable hypotheticals' (1990a: 154). But its account of why 'the deduction of effect from cause is conceived to be so radically different from that of cause from effect' (1990a: 157) will not do. For here Ramsey relies on our view that causes precede their effects, a view he identifies with the fact 'that any present volition of ours is (*for us*) irrelevant to any past event ... *to us* now what we do affects only the probability of the future' (1990a: 158; emphasis added). But this implies that the only reason we can't affect the past is that we think we can't, which is absurd. Only the fact, not the view, that effects never precede their causes can explain why gluttons should believe 'I will starve if I don't eat' but not 'I will have starved if I don't eat': *pace* Ramsey, some variable hypotheticals need to be made true by facts (see CAUSATION; COUNTERFACTUAL CONDITIONALS).

5 Theories

Scientific theories apply new predicates to unobservable entities, like photons, to explain observable, for example optical, phenomena. How do these predicates acquire empirical meaning? Ramsey's drastic answer in 'Theories' (1929) is that there are no such predicates: we use 'is a photon', 'has frequency n', and so on not as predicates but as existentially bound variables. That is, a theory tacitly starts with quantifiers, 'properties exist – call them "being a photon", etc. – such that ...', followed by the explicit theory, in two parts. Its *axioms* link its predicate variables to each other, while its *dictionary* (see CAMPBELL, N.R.) links them to observable predicates like 'is red' (1990a: 112). Thus if 'a', 'b' and 'g' are our theoretical predicates, 'the best way to write our theory seems to be ... ($\exists$ a,b,g):dictionary.axioms' (1990a: 131). This, which is now called the 'Ramsey sentence' of the theory, eliminates its problematic predicates while keeping its structure and observable consequences.

Although this account has been widely accepted – and explicitly applied to functionalist theories of the mind (Lewis 1972) – its explanations of other striking facts about theories are rarely noticed. It entails for example that parts of theories, since they contain variables, are not 'strictly propositions by themselves' and their meaning 'can only be given when we know to what stock of "propositions" ... [they are] to be added' (1990a: 131). Since this makes theoretical statements in rival theories incomparable, 'the adherents of two such theories could quite well dispute, although neither affirmed anything the other denied' (1990a: 133). This both explains the phenomenon of 'incommensurability' (see KUHN, T.S.; INCOMMENSURABILITY) and limits its consequences, for example for deductive accounts of theoretical explanation (see HEMPEL, C.G.): for as Ramsey remarks, it does not affect reasoning within the scope of a single theory's quantifiers.

Because Ramsey sentences say that certain universals (properties or relations) exist, nominalists, who deny this, must reject them (see NOMINALISM).

Realists about universals, however, can use Ramsey sentences to determine what empirical universals exist, as follows. Since not only *un*observable properties exist, we treat *all* predicates in law statements as variables. The Ramsey sentence of all such statements then quantifies over all universals that occur in laws, which are all the empirical universals there are (Mellor 1991).

6 Universals

What lets Ramsey ignore nominalism in 'Theories' is his denial in 'Universals' (1925) that our distinction between particulars and universals shows any intrinsic difference between them. First, it cannot be based on the subject–predicate distinction, e.g. between 'Socrates' and 'is wise' in 'Socrates is wise': for the subject of the equivalent 'wisdom is a characteristic of Socrates' is wisdom, which is not a particular (1990a: 14). Also, in molecular propositions like 'Socrates is wise or Plato is foolish', the subject–predicate distinction generates complex universals, like being wise unless Plato is foolish. But Ramsey argues that if these existed, then (for example) that a universal R relates a to b, that a has the complex property Rb and that b has aR would 'be three different propositions because they have different sets of constituents, and yet they are ... but one, namely that a has R to b. So the theory of complex universals is responsible for an incomprehensible trinity, as senseless as that of theology' (1990a: 14). Similarly with Socrates' apparent property of being wise-unless-Plato-is-foolish and Plato's of being foolish-unless-Socrates-is-wise. If, as Ramsey assumes, the proposition that Socrates is wise or Plato is foolish can have only one set of constituents, there can be no such complex properties.

Predicates can therefore distinguish universals from particulars only in atomic propositions, and even then the distinction will not imply an intrinsic difference unless that difference would explain our impression that (for example) 'Socrates is a real independent entity, wisdom ... a quality of something else' (1990a: 19). But no such difference will do this. For our impression comes from associating 'wise' only with propositions of the atomic form 'x is wise' while associating 'Socrates' with *all* propositions containing it, including the molecular 'Socrates is neither wise nor just'. Yet we could as easily associate 'wise' with this and all other propositions containing it, and restrict 'Socrates' to the atomic form 'Socrates is q', where q is a universal: a form which, without complex universals, can no more include 'Socrates is neither wise nor just' than 'x is wise' can include 'neither Socrates nor Plato is wise' (1990a: 20–1). So no

intrinsic difference between universals and particulars can be inferred from – since none will explain – our associating atomic forms with predicates but not subjects.

Why then do we do that, thus making universals seem less 'real and independent' than particulars? Ramsey's explanation is this. A predicate symbol 'ϕ' can stand alone only if it names a real universal, not if it abbreviates (for example) 'has R to a or S to b'. This we must abbreviate to 'ϕx', to distinguish it from the two-place '... has R to a or ... has S to b', written '$\phi(x,y)$'. But since it is irrelevant to an extensional logic whether or not 'ϕ' names a universal, we always write 'ϕ' as 'ϕx', '$\phi(x,y)$', etc., thus associating all predicates with atomic forms (1990a: 26–8).

We cannot therefore infer from this practice that particulars differ intrinsically from universals. A logician can take 'any type of objects whatever as the subject of his reasoning, and call them individuals, meaning by that simply that he has chosen this type to reason about' (1990a: 30). We naturally choose easily discriminable objects, such as those with locations in space and time, to quantify over first; but what makes them particulars is simply *that* we choose them, not why. But then the fact that objects of certain types fail to count as particulars, just because we choose to exclude them from the range of our *first*-order quantifiers, is no reason to deny, as nominalists do, that they exist. The existence of universals – that is, of whatever we leave for our second-order quantifiers to range over – is no more problematic than that of particulars.

See also: BELIEF; FREGE, G.; MIND, IDENTITY THEORY OF; PROBABILITY THEORY AND EPISTEMOLOGY; UNIVERSALS

List of works

Ramsey, F. P. (1931) *The Foundations of Mathematics and other Logical Essays*, ed. R.B. Braithwaite, London: Routledge & Keegan Paul. (Referred to in §1. The first published collection of Ramsey's papers.)

—— (1990a) *Philosophical Papers*, ed. D. H. Mellor, Cambridge: Cambridge University Press. (Contains all Ramsey's major philosophical papers. By permission of Cambridge University Press, this entry draws on the editor's Introduction to this book. Page references for the quotations from Ramsey's work refer to this edition; the dates given are those of first publication or, if published posthumously, of composition.)

—— (1990b) 'Weight or the Value of Knowledge, ed. N.-E. Sahlin, *British Journal for the Philosophy of*

Science 41: 1–3. (Previously unpublished note calculating the value of collecting evidence for the truth or falsity of a proposition.)
—— (1990c) *Notes on Philosophy, Probability and Mathematics*, ed. M.C. Gavalotti, Naples: Bibliopolis. (Previously unpublished notes.)
—— (1991) *On Truth*, ed. N. Rescher and U. Majer (1991), Dordrecht: Kluwer. (Previously unpublished notes for an uncompleted book on truth and related matters.)

References and further reading

* Armstrong, D.M. (1983) *What is a Law of Nature?*, Cambridge: Cambridge University Press, ch. 5.4. (Referred to in §4. Argues that Ramsey's first theory of laws of nature is the best Humean account of them and then attacks it.)
* Chihara, C.S. (1980) 'Ramsey's Theory of Types: Suggestions for a Return to Fregean Sources', in *Prospects for Pragmatism: Essays in Memory of F. P. Ramsey*, ed. D.H. Mellor, Cambridge: Cambridge University Press, 21–47. (Referred to in §1. Defends a Fregean reading of Ramsey's theory of types.)
* de Finetti, B. (1937) 'Foresight: its Logical Laws, its Subjective Sources', ch. VI, trans. H. E. Kyburg, in *Studies in Subjective Probability*, eds H. E. Kyburg Jr and H. E. Smokler (1964), New York: Wiley, 93–158. (Referred to in §2. Argues on operationalist grounds – see OPERATIONALISM – against objective interpretations of probability even in physics.)
* Jeffrey, R.C. (1983) *The Logic of Decision*, 2nd edn, Chicago: University of Chicago Press, ch. 3. (Referred to in §2. Interprets Ramsey's *'Truth and Probability'* as a prescriptive subjective decision theory.)
* Keynes, J.M. (1921) *A Treatise on Probability*, London: Macmillan. (Referred to in §2. Gives the interpretation of probability as a measure of a logical relation of partial entailment attacked by Ramsey and later revived by Carnap.)
* Lewis, D. (1972) 'Psychophysical and Theoretical Identifications', in *Readings in Philosophy of Psychology*, vol. I, ed. N. Block, London: Methuen, 1980, 207–22. (Referred to in §5. Uses Ramsey sentences to define mental states by their causes and effects.)
Mellor, D.H. (ed.) (1980) *Prospects for Pragmatism: Essays in Memory of F. P. Ramsey*, Cambridge: Cambridge University Press. (Contains eleven original essays on different aspects of Ramsey's philosophy.)
* Mellor, D.H. (1991) 'Properties and Predicates', *Matters of Metaphysics*, Cambridge: Cambridge University Press, 170–82. (Referred to in §5. Uses the Ramsey sentence of all laws to determine what empirical universals exist.)
Sahlin, N.-E. (1990) *The Philosophy of F. P. Ramsey*, Cambridge: Cambridge University Press. (A comprehensive introduction to Ramsey's philosophy and also to his mathematics and economics, not dealt with in this entry.)
* Sahlin, N.-E. (1991) 'Obtained by a Reliable Process and always Leading to Success', *Theoria* 57: 132–49. (Referred to in §2. Develops and defends Ramsey's reliabilist theory of knowledge.)
* Whitehead, A.N. and Russell, B. (1927) *Principia Mathematica*, Cambridge: Cambridge University Press, 2nd edn. (Referred to in §1. The basis of Ramsey's attempt to reduce mathematics to logic.)
* Whyte, J.T. (1990) 'Success Semantics', *Analysis* 50 (3): 149–57. (Referred to in §3. Gives the truth conditions of beliefs as the conditions in which the actions they combine with desires to cause achieve the objects of those desires.)
* Wittgenstein, L. (1922) *Tractatus Logico-Philosophicus*, London: Routledge, §4.46. (Referred to in §1. The theory of tautology used by Ramsey to strengthen *Principia*'s definition of mathematical propositions.)

D.H. MELLOR

RAMSEY, IAN THOMAS (1915–72)

Ramsey's work developed within two parameters. One concerned God and language: he held that no literal statement could be true of God; all language concerning God must be metaphorical. Another concerned his epistemology: knowledge, he held, comes ultimately from experience – sensory, introspective, but also religious. Evidence that God exists comes from experience, and claims about God must be cast in nonliteral terms.

Born in 1915, Ramsey earned firsts in mathematics, moral sciences and theology at Cambridge University. He was chaplain of Christ's College, Cambridge, from 1943, and Nolloth Professor of the Philosophy of the Christian Religion at Oxford from 1951–66. In 1966, he was appointed Bishop of Durham.

Ramsey maintained that any use of religious language needs to be understood in terms of its context. He described the experiential contexts in which the word 'God' is used as a referring term. To do this, it is necessary to map the relationships between the term 'God' (and the concept it expresses) and other terms endemic to the same context. This constitutes Ramsey's 'logical empiricism'.

In endeavouring to understand and express experiences of divine activity, believers use models. For Ramsey, in no sentence of the form 'God is...' is the predicate term that fills in the blank used either univocally, equivocally or analogically. The relation between 'God' and the predicate term will be that between the key word of a model and a term qualifying that model. Thus his analysis of religious experience is offered in the formal rather than the material mode.

As an example of how Ramsey's account works, consider the word 'wave', which is a key term in a model used to record regularities in the behaviour of light. Otherwise isolated phenomena thereby become conceptually organized, and prediction of further regularities is possible. Second-order models organize first-order models into a comprehensive theory. Without first- and second-order models, science would be impossible.

Logical positivism and its verification principle dominated Ramsey's academic setting. The plausibility and the destructive implications of the verification principle were vastly overrated, but to be heard, Ramsey had to respond to positivism's challenge. The positivists prized formal philosophy, science and sensory experience. Ramsey offered a formal mode account of models, and an analysis of science as the task of constructing appropriate first-order reportive models and second-order theoretical models. He added that theology does for religious experience what science does for sensory experience. In both cases, the relevant story is formal, experiential and model-governed. Ramsey's view was that the nature of religious experience justified his type of approach to it, and that the approach of science to observation was analogous; thus in so far as positivist concerns were legitimate, they could be met. What Ramsey called a 'disclosure model' of some thing X is isomorphic with X (shares X's structure), but shares no quality with X and justifies no description of X beyond the claim that the model and X are structurally analogous.

Ramsey's account of self-knowledge is central to his theory. Each of us has experiences in which we know ourselves distinctively as ourselves. In such experiences, there is self-disclosure; we apply to ourselves a model in which 'I' is the key term. We may discern ourselves in circumstances in which we fall in love, fear death, or recognize an obligation. The disclosure is to the effect that the self (construed as indescribable) bears a relation to its states in a manner structurally analogous to the relation between 'I' and 'my states' in a conceptual model in which these serve as key terms. We may experience God in situations in which we are impressed by ceaseless changes in nature or note the existential dependence of what we experience, discerning a changeless being or an independent being. This amounts to the claim that God and changing or dependent things are related to one another as the 'Unchanging Independent Cause' and 'changing dependent things' in a conceptual model in which these serve as key terms.

Ramsey, then, claimed that in our recognition of change, dependence and demise we discern the presence of something unchanging, independent and unending. He held that God cannot be described in literal terms, and endeavoured to hold these ideas together by viewing the relevant experiences as properly capturable in models whose structure (and nothing else) is ascribable to dependent things and God. Disclosure experiences are for Ramsey epistemologically primitive, needing no justification. Theological reasoning is a matter of placing collective disclosure models, which integrate particular experiences or types of experiences, under a second-order model, and theological statements 'point to' rather than describe God.

Ramsey tried to combine a stringent empiricism with an acceptance of the cognitive significance of theology. He thought that scientific theories and Christian theology were similarly dependent on the use of nonpicturing models. His work helped keep alive a stream of philosophical theology which nearly dried up during the times of positivism's dominance, but which again flourishes today.

List of works

Ramsey, I. (1960) *Freedom and Immortality*, London: SCM Press. (Presents an argument for human transcendence of empirical conditions.)

—— (ed.) (1961) *Prospect for Metaphysics*, New York: The Philosophical Library. (An excellent collection of essays, including one by Ramsey on the prospects of metaphysical theology.)

—— (1963a) *On Being Sure in Religion*, London: Athlone Press. (Develops Ramsey's religious epistemology.)

—— (1963b) *Religious Language*, New York: Macmillan. (Defends Ramsey's view of religious language.)

—— (1964a) *Religion and Science: Conflict and Synthesis*, London: SPCK. (Gives Ramsey's account of the similarities and differences between religion and science, arguing that both are cognitively significant.)

—— (1964b) *Models and Mystery*, London: Oxford University Press. (Presents Ramsey's views concerning what he sees as a delicate balance, mediated by models, between the incomprehensibility and intelligibility of what matters most.)

—— (1964c) *Christian Empiricism*, ed. J. Gill, London: Sheldon Press. (An excellent collection of Ramsey's writings, with a good bibliography.)

—— (1965) *Christian Discourse: Some Logical Explorations*, London, Oxford University Press. (An account of Ramsey's view of Christian religious language.)

—— (ed.) (1966) *Christian Ethics and Contemporary Philosophy*, London, SCM Press. (Has an introduction, an essay on moral judgment and divine commands, and an essay on natural law, by Ramsey.)

—— (eds) (1971) *Personality and Science*, London: Churchill Livingstone. (Introduction, epilogue, and essay on human personality, by Ramsey.)

References and further reading

Edwards, D.L. (1973) *Ian Ramsey, Bishop of Durham*, London: Oxford University Press. (A memoir.)

Lucier, P. (1976) *Empirisme logique et langage réligieux: trois approches anglo-saxones contemporaines* (Logical Empiricism and Religious Language: Three Contemporary Anglo-Saxon Approaches), Tournai: Desclée & Cie. (Deals with R.B. Braithwaite and R.M. Hare as well as Ramsey.)

Pye, J. (1979) *A Bibliography of the Works of Ian Thomas Ramsey*, Durham: Abbey House Publications. (A useful resource.)

KEITH E. YANDELL

RAMUS, PETRUS (1515–72)

Petrus Ramus, for many years a professor of philosophy and eloquence at the University of Paris, wrote textbooks and controversial works in grammar, logic, rhetoric, mathematics, physics and philosophy. He was also a university reformer. His followers were prolific with commentaries, Ramist analyses of classical texts and handbooks of their own. His logical works and those of his school exercised a large influence between 1550 and 1650.

His formation was humanist, in that he attacked scholasticism and encouraged the study (and logical analysis) of classical texts, as Agricola, Sturm and Melanchthon had done. But he was far more independent-minded than them, a stern critic of the textbooks of Aristotle and Cicero, as well as an admirer of their style and intellect. His most important innovation was the method, a theory of organization which he used to simplify his textbooks. He emphasized the need for learning to be comprehensible and useful, with a particular stress on the practical aspect of mathematics. His critics would say he oversimplified. He was also a student of Gaulish pseudo-antiquities and an important proponent of the French language. His Dialectique (1555) was the first book on dialectic in French.

1 Life and educational reforms
2 Logic and rhetoric
3 Method
4 Mathematics, physics and science

1 Life and educational reforms

Petrus Ramus (born Pierre de la Ramée at Cuts, near Noyon) came from a family which had lost its wealth but not its patent of nobility with the sack of Liège in 1468. He studied in Paris at the Collège de Navarre, where he took his MA in 1536, allegedly defending the thesis that 'everything which Aristotle said was arbitrarily fabricated'. Even if this prophetic story is true, it should be pointed out that the theses chosen for MA disputations were often humorous or paradoxical. At this stage of his life, Ramus had already been influenced by Johann Sturm, who introduced the teaching of Rudolph AGRICOLA to Paris. Ramus began teaching at the Collège du Mans, before moving to the Collège de l'Ave Maria. As a young teacher he reread the texts of the arts course and began to formulate his response to them in his earliest books *Dialecticae partitiones* (Divisions of Dialectic), *Dialecticae institutiones* (The Teaching of Dialectic) and *Aristotelicae animadversiones* (Notes on Aristotle) (all published in 1543). These books attacking Aristotle's approach to dialectic were condemned by the university authorities and Ramus was forbidden to teach or publish in philosophy. He turned his attention to rhetoric and mathematics, but the shortage of teachers enabled him to evade the ban, by teaching at the Collège de Presles, and he soon became head of the college. He published a new version of his dialectic under the name of his friend Omer Talon. In 1547 he was released from the ban owing to the influence of the Cardinal de Guise on the new king, Henry II. In 1551 he was named professor of philosophy and eloquence at the Collège Royal. He continued to teach and publish on rhetoric, dialectic, Latin literature, philosophy and mathematics. He became involved in many controversies with his critics, notably Jacques Charpentier, both over his attacks on Aristotle and in relation to university appointments. In 1562 he became a Calvinist. Persecution forced him to flee Paris in 1562 and 1567. From 1568 he travelled in Germany and Switzerland. He was persuaded to return to Paris in 1570, but even explicit royal protection was unable to save him from the wrath of his enemies during the St Bartholomew's Day Massacre of 1572. That he died a Protestant martyr had considerable consequences for his later reputation. His works were massively reprinted and became very influential in Protestant parts of Germany, in Britain and in New England well into the seventeenth century.

Ramus composed several orations and prefaces on the reform of the University of Paris, in practical matters as well as in the curriculum. The main force of his curricular changes was to support and extend the growth of humanism in Paris. He wanted to purge Aristotle as well as the accretions of scholastic logic. He proposed (in 1546) that rhetoric and dialectic should be taught simultaneously, and involve composition by the pupils. Both subjects were to be illustrated through the analysis of literary texts. In 1551 he suggested a more orthodox linear syllabus, but argued for the study of mathematics and physics in the last two years (though these were also to involve literature, including Virgil's *Georgics* and Lucretius in the final year). In 1562 he called for more practical work in physics and medicine, referring particularly to botany and dissection. Ramus' reforms were humanist, they were methodical (in the sense of §3 below), but above all they were intended to increase the usefulness of what is learnt in the university.

2 Logic and rhetoric

For Ramus logic was the subject which organized the rest of the curriculum. Ramus published several different versions of his major works in dialectic and rhetoric, all of which were reprinted many times. Bruyère (1984) proposes five stages for the development of the dialectic; Meerhoff (1986) proposes eight for the rhetoric. Moreover, earlier versions continued to be reprinted after later ones. These facts present the student of Ramus with large bibliographical problems. It is essential to study different states of each text and to make use of the work of Bruyère, Meerhoff and Ong (1958a).

Ramus produced works of two main kinds in each subject. Where *Dialecticae institutiones* (later called *Dialectica*) is a textbook, setting out the main doctrines of the subject, *Aristotelicae animadversiones* (Notes on Aristotle) and its successors – later incorporated in the *Scholae in liberales artes* (Lectures on the Liberal Arts) – are works of controversy, attacking Aristotle's teachings. Discoveries in the

controversial works, often prompted by Ramus' critics, are absorbed in the textbooks, and materials dropped from the textbooks often turn up later in the commentaries to the textbooks, while materials dropped from the commentaries can reappear in the controversial works. What follows is inevitably a statement of the general tendencies of Ramus' dialectic rather than an analysis of any particular text.

Ramus aimed at clarity, simplicity and usefulness. His textbooks proceed by definition and division and they are full of examples. Ramus' method obliged him to avoid overlaps between subjects. Accordingly a good deal of the traditional material of Aristotelian dialectic, for example the predicables and the categories, was rejected as belonging to metaphysics. For Ramus dialectic is the art of discoursing well. It consists of invention, which finds the matter for arguments through the topics (see AGRICOLA, R. §2), and judgment, which forms arguments into propositions, syllogisms and larger structures. Within invention Ramus proceeds by a series of dichotomies to the individual topics. His list is shorter than most earlier versions; it is organized into groups and it avoids duplication. So, for example, there is no topic of definition or substance, since Ramus considers that Agricola's new topic of subject covers the same arguments. Ramus regarded the topics as the classes of arguments (whereas his predecessors had called them the places where the arguments are found) and he left it to his examples to show how particular topical arguments function. He followed Agricola in emphasizing the usefulness of the topics and in illustrating them with passages from poetry and oratory, but he explained much less, preferring a more austere and systematic exposition.

Ramus divided judgment into axiomatic judgment, which concerns the parts, qualities, quantities and connections of the proposition (corresponding to Aristotle's *De interpretatione*), and dianoetic judgment, which comprises the syllogism (including all three figures, and the hypothetical syllogism) and the overall shape of the piece. At first Ramus called the latter 'disposition', indicating a link with rhetoric and with Agricola, but later he called it 'method'. This integration of dialectical judgment and overall organization represents an improvement on Agricola. Thus, in earlier versions Ramus sets out the imperfect method (or method of prudence) of poets and orators alongside the perfect method (from general to particular), but later the perfect method overwhelms its counterpart. In early versions of the dialectic Ramus gives a worked example of analysing a literary text into its argumentative structure, in the way Agricola had, but later this becomes part of the commentary or an exercise for the teacher. The general tendency is for the dialectic textbook to become briefer and tighter.

For Ramus rhetoric is the art of speaking well (see RHETORIC §3). It involves ornate and correct speaking and skilful delivery. Since invention and disposition belong to dialectic they are not part of rhetoric. Since correct speaking is the concern of grammar, rhetoric can begin with a discussion of the ornate, which consists of a drastically shortened account of the tropes and figures. Thus there are only four tropes (metonymy, irony, metaphor and synecdoche). Figures of diction include the rules of prose and poetic metre as well as a selection of the figures of repetition, while figures of thought are connected with the attitude of the speaker, either alone or in an imagined dialogue with the audience. The discussion of delivery is divided into suggestions on the tones of voice to be used for different effects and on suitable gestures for head and hands. Ramus carried out a thorough reduction and simplification of rhetoric. His reduced and reorganized figures are undoubtedly easier to remember, but there is also a loss of expressive force. In the rush to simplify, many valuable observations were lost along with the repetitions and the points which apply only to the Roman courtroom.

Ramus' controversial works tend to survey selected texts from ARISTOTLE (for dialectic), and CICERO (§2) and Quintilian (for rhetoric), pointing out what has been omitted and what is superfluous compared with a strict view of the subject. Ramus nearly always begins by complaining that the author has not defined his subject and divided it. He often criticizes work for confused organization and for including material which is useless or which belongs to other subjects. He attacks other authors for not having written his books, rather than trying to understand what they have to say. As a result he misses Quintilian's wisdom and Aristotle's philosophical subtlety. Still, some of his remarks are well-founded: Cicero's *Orator* is badly organized; Quintilian's *Training in Oratory* does contain a considerable amount of reduplication and a good deal of material that applies mainly to Roman lawcourts; the early books of Aristotle's Organon are more metaphysical than logical, and his *Topics* is very hard to understand. It is also true that many of Ramus' criticisms are based on a consistent position outlined in his theory of method. By the end of the revisions Ramus comes to display a good knowledge of Aristotle's work, much of it owed to his opponents.

3 Method

Ramus regards method as the key to the presentation of all arts and sciences. Method first appears in Ramus' textbook in 1546 as 'the organization of

different things in such a way that the whole subject may be more easily perceived and taught'. It is mainly related to the presentation of a subject and seems to derive from Ramus' former teacher Johann Sturm. Sturm had begun his 1539 commentary on Cicero's *Divisons of Rhetoric* by defining method as 'the certain, brief, correct and comprehensive way of teaching an art'. He distinguished three types of method: from general to particular, from particular to general, and by definition and division. Sturm is probably basing himself on Galen, who in turn relies on Plato's and Aristotle's remarks on method. Between them Melanchthon, Sturm, Ramus and the commentators on Aristotle's *Posterior Analytics* raised method to an issue of major significance in the mid-sixteenth century.

Ramus adopted method as the principal form of organization for an art and he developed three laws of method, which appear after 1566 and in the *Scholae*: (1) only things which are true and necessary may be included, (2) all and only things which belong to the art in question must be included, (3) general things must be dealt with in a general way, particular things in a particular way. The first two laws are mainly used to exclude material, the third to prescribe the organization of an art, from the most general principles to the most specific instances. Ramus came to see this method as the true interpretation of Aristotle's *Posterior Analytics* and himself as Aristotle's only true follower. This did not prevent him from using the laws of method to attack the content and organization of Aristotle's own writings. Equally the laws of method gave him the confidence to streamline his own textbooks, so that what began as a humanist project based on literature became (at least on the page) a structured series of definitions and divisions, almost a set of axioms, as in modern formal logic. It also enabled the whole content of a subject to be set out in the famous pictorial dichotomies which were popularized by Ramus and his followers. The austerity of his textbooks was complemented by his emphasis on usefulness and his continuing to comment on literary texts in his own teaching. Ramus' followers produced tree diagrams to express the content and organization of literary and scriptural texts. For the future Ramus increased the importance of method as a subject, emphasized the need to select material, according to what we would now call disciplinary boundaries, and encouraged the critique of Aristotle (see LOGIC, RENAISSANCE §7).

4 Mathematics, physics and science

Ramus promoted mathematics. In his orations and prefaces he cited the Bible to establish the religious duty of studying mathematics and he argued that it was the oldest of the sciences. He included it in his syllabus reforms and he left a considerable part of his wealth to endow a chair of mathematics in Paris. He insisted on the practical usefulness of mathematics and argued that it should be taught in relation to practice. He proposed a new division of the subject, into the mathematics of *intelligibilia* (arithmetic, from which geometry is also derived) and the mathematics of *sensibilia* (mechanics, astronomy and optics). Although Ramus undoubtedly taught mathematics, and regarded it as an important aspect of his reforms, he did not make original contributions to the subject. He made acute criticisms of the organization of earlier mathematics texts, according to his precepts of method, but he relied on his collaborators to provide original mathematical material.

In his lectures on physics, Ramus rejected Aristotle's conception of the subject, because much of the subject-matter is not found in nature and because of Aristotle's confusions and contradictions. He wanted less on logical issues and more on problems of mechanics, astronomy and biology. Though he preferred to derive these facts from classical texts, such as Pliny's *Natural History* and Virgil's *Georgics*, he called for observation as the basis of physics and astronomy. In particular he argued for astronomy without hypotheses, an idea which involves a rejection of traditional astronomy, and which Tycho Brahe, whom he consulted, regarded as impossible. Ramus' followers extended his methodical approach to other curriculum subjects. Theodore Zwinger produced an analysis of moral philosophy, and Johannes Freigius wrote a huge *Quaestiones physicae* (1579) which provides a systematic account of learning about the natural world (including acoustics, music, hydrography and geography), drawing on many sources besides Aristotle.

See also: AGRICOLA, R.; LOGIC, RENAISSANCE; PLATONISM, RENAISSANCE §5

List of works

There is no edition (modern or otherwise) of the collected works of Ramus, but the facsimiles which follow include some of the most important texts. Otherwise refer to the bibliographies of Ong (1958a) and Bruyère-Robinet (1986).

Ramus, P. [Ramée, P. la] (1543) *Dialecticae institutiones, Aristotelicae animadversiones* (Teaching of Dialectic, Notes on Aristotle), Paris; repr. Stuttgart: Frommann, 1964. (Early versions of Ramus' dialectic textbooks and his critique of Aristotle.)

—— (1549) *Rhetoricae distinctiones in Quintilianum*, trans. J. Murphy and C. Newlands, *Arguments in Rhetoric: Against Quintilian*, De Kalb, IL: Northern Illinois University Press, 1986. (Ramus' attack on classical Latin rhetoric.)

—— (1569) *Scholae in liberales artes* (Lectures on the Liberal Arts), Basle; repr. Hildesheim: Olms, 1970. (Lectures which collect Ramus' criticism of previous writers across the university syllabus.)

—— (1569) *Dialectica*, Basle; English trans. *The Logike*, London, 1574; repr. Menston: Scolar Press, 1970. (First English translation of Ramus' logic.)

—— (1577) *Praefationes, Epistolae, Orationes* (Prefaces, Letters, Orations), Paris; repr. as P. la Ramée, *Oeuvres Diverses*, Geneva: Slatkine, 1971. (Useful collection of Ramus' prefaces and programmatic writings.)

References and further reading

* Bruyère, N. (1984) *Méthode et dialectique dans l'oeuvre de La Ramée* (Method and Dialectic in Ramus' Works), Paris: Vrin. (Good account of the development of Ramus' dialectic, which overstates his Platonism. Referred to in §2.)

Bruyère-Robinet, N. (1986) 'Les fonds Pierre de la Ramée des bibliothèques de France' (Holdings of Ramus' Works in French Libraries), *Nouvelles de la République des lettres* 6: 71–97. (A survey of locations for early editions of Ramus' works.)

—— (ed.) (1986) *Revue des sciences philosophiques et théologiques* 70 (1), special issue. (Useful collection of recent articles about Ramus.)

Hooykaas, R. (1958) *Humanisme, Science et réforme: Pierre de la Ramée*, Leiden: Brill. (A useful overview of Ramus' approach to mathematics and science.)

Mack, P. (1993) *Renaissance Argument: Valla and Agricola in the Traditions of Rhetoric and Dialectic*, Leiden: Brill, 334–55. (Details Agricola's influence on Ramus.)

* Meerhoff, K. (1986) *Rhétorique et poétique au XVIe siècle en France*, Leiden: Brill, 175–348. (Excellent account of Ramus' rhetoric, with particular attention to prose rhythm, French poetics and Latin rhetoric. Referred to in §2.)

* Ong, W. (1958a) *Ramus and Talon Inventory*, Cambridge, MA: Harvard University Press. (Useful list of editions. Referred to in §2.)

—— (1958b) *Ramus, Method and the Decay of Dialogue*, Cambridge, MA: Harvard University Press. (Useful account but excessively dismissive of Ramus.)

Risse, W. (1964) *Die Logik der Neuzeit. I Band. 1500–1640* (The Logic of the Modern Period),

Stuttgart and Bad Cannstatt: Frommann. (A survey of sixteenth-century schools of logic.)

Sharratt, P. (1986) 'Recent Work on Petrus Ramus', *Rhetorica* 5: 7–58. (An invaluable guide to recent studies, which extends his earlier survey in *Studi francesi* 47–8: 201–13.)

—— (ed.) (1991) *Argumentation* 5 (4), special issue. (Collection of articles on Ramus.)

Vasoli, C. (1967) *La dialettica e la retorica dell'Umanesimo* (Humanist Dialectic and Rhetoric), Milan: Feltrinelli. (A very good account of humanist rhetoric and dialectic, including a section on Ramus.)

Verdonk, J.J. (1966) *Petrus Ramus en de wiskunde* (Petrus Ramus and the Sciences), Assen: Van Gorcum. (The best account of Ramus' contribution to mathematics.)

Waddington, C. (1855) *Ramus: sa vie, ses écrits et ses opinions* (Ramus: his Life, his Writings and Opinions), Paris: Meyrveis. (The fullest Ramus biography.)

PETER MACK

RAND, AYN (1905–82)

Ayn Rand was a Russian-born US novelist and philosopher who exerted considerable influence in the conservative and libertarian intellectual movements in the post-war USA. Rand's ideas were expressed mainly through her novels; she set forth a view of morality as based in rational self-interest and in political philosophy defended an unrestrained form of capitalism.

Ayn Rand was born Alyssa Rosenbaum into a middle-class Jewish family in St Petersburg. Her family's expropriation by the Bolsheviks and subsequent poverty had a profound effect on her; her first novel, *We the Living* (1936), describes the tragedy of a Russian student struggling against an evil society in the 'vast prison' that was the USSR in the 1920s. Her work was marked not only by a hostility to communism but also by a strong antipathy towards any form of compromise among competing values.

Popular success came in 1943 with the publication of her philosophical novel, *The Fountainhead*, the story of an architect who refuses to compromise his independence or his integrity while good people despair in the face of evil. A deeply moral work, its theme is integrity which, for Rand, was at the root of the idea of freedom. Even greater success came with *Atlas Shrugged* (1957), Rand's final work of fiction. More explicitly political than her earlier work, it tells

of the breakdown of a society of evil as the captains of capitalist industry withdraw from a world marked by political and moral corruption. As with her earlier works, the hero is uncompromising in his integrity and confidence in the value of the moral path; the bulk of the novel charts the rise of those who begin in despair. However, Rand also turns more explicitly to philosophical problems in ethics in an attempt to set morals on a more secure epistemological footing. The book contains many long philosophical speeches by characters speaking for Rand.

The popular success of her fiction brought discipleship and the 1960s and 1970s saw the growth of an 'objectivist' movement. The influence of Rand's ideas was strongest among college students in the USA but attracted little attention from academic philosophers. Her outspoken defence of capitalism in works like *Capitalism: The Unknown Ideal* (1967), and her characterization of her position as a defence of the 'virtue of selfishness' in her novel of the same title (published in 1974), also brought notoriety, but kept her out of the intellectual mainstream.

The central philosophical argument of Rand's thought is an attempt to show that the good life is itself a substantial ethical value from which may be derived important moral conclusions. In this she is self-consciously Aristotelian, although most commentators have concluded that her argument falls victim to the same difficulties, relying on a morally substantive and controversial account of human nature to generate ethical conclusions.

Rand's political theory is of little interest. Its unremitting hostility towards the state and taxation sits inconsistently with a rejection of anarchism, and her attempts to resolve the difficulty are ill-thought out and unsystematic. Of more enduring interest is her fiction, belonging to a genre she labelled 'romantic realism'. Despite her attack on altruism and insistence on the virtue of selfishness, her real concerns were the defence of the value of integrity (to the point of self-sacrifice) in the face of evil and moral despair.

List of works

Rand, A. (1936) *We the Living*, New York: Macmillan.

—— (1943) *The Fountainhead*, New York: Bobbs-Merrill.

—— (1957) *Atlas Shrugged*, New York: Random House.

—— (1967) *Capitalism: The Unknown Ideal*, New York: New American Library.

—— (1974) *The Virtue of Selfishness*, New York: New American Library.

—— (1990) *Introduction to Objectivist Epistemology*, New York: New American Library.

References and further reading

Den Uyl, D.J. and Rasmussen, D. (eds) (1984) *The Philosophic Thought of Ayn Rand*, Chicago, IL: University of Illinois Press.

Merrill, R.E. (1993) *The Ideas of Ayn Rand*, Chicago and La Salle, IL: Open Court.

CHANDRAN KUKATHAS

RANDOMNESS

The fundamental intuition underlying randomness is the absence of order or pattern. To cash out this intuition philosophers and scientists employ five approaches to randomness.

(1) Randomness as the output of a chance process. Thus an event is random *if it is the output of a chance process. Moreover, a sequence of events constitutes a* random sample *if all events in the sequence derive from a single chance process and no event in the sequence is influenced by the others.*

(2) Randomness as mimicking chance. Statisticians frequently wish to obtain a random sample (in the sense of (1)) according to some specified probability distribution. Unfortunately, a chance process corresponding to this probability distribution may be hard to come by. In this case a statistician may employ a computer simulation to mimic the desired chance process (for example, a random number generator). Randomness qua mimicking chance is also known as pseudo-randomness.

(3) Randomness via mixing. Consider the following situation: particles are concentrated in some corner of a fluid; forces act on the fluid so that eventually the particles become thoroughly mixed throughout the fluid, reaching an equilibrium state. Here randomness is identified with the equilibrium state reached via mixing.

(4) Randomness as a measure of computational complexity. Computers are ideally suited for generating bit strings. The length of the shortest program that generates a given bit string, as well as the minimum time it takes for a program to generate the string, both assign measures of complexity to the strings. The higher the complexity, the more random the string.

(5) Randomness as pattern-breaking. Given a specified collection of patterns, an object is random if it breaks all the patterns in the collection. If, on the other hand, it fits at least one of the patterns in the collection, then it fails to be random.

1   **Chance**
2   **Simulation**
3   **Mixing**
4   **Complexity**
5   **Pattern-breaking**

1   Chance

The most common conception of randomness identifies randomness with chance. Indeed, much of probability theory and statistics does not distinguish the two. Thus for a probabilist or statistician a *random event* and an *event due to chance* are typically the same thing. Moreover, processes giving rise to such events are referred to indiscriminately as *random, chance,* or *stochastic* processes.

Within statistics the adjective 'random' assumes a technical sense when it occurs in the phrase 'random sample'. Given a chance process, one may wish to consider not just a single random event from this process, but rather an entire sequence of such events. Such a sequence is then said to constitute a random sample if: first, the same chance process is responsible for each event in the sequence; and, second, the occurrence of any event in the sequence is unaffected by the occurrence of other events in the sequence. If the first condition is satisfied one says that the events are 'identically distributed'; if the second, that the events are 'independent'.

Identifying randomness with chance now raises the obvious question, what is chance? While there exists a metaphysics of chance related to causation, determinism and free will, this entry approaches chance instrumentally in terms of those processes, like coin tossing and radioactive decay, for which our best understanding is irreducibly probabilistic (see CHAOS THEORY for comparison, where the probabilities are artifacts of underlying deterministic systems).

2   Simulation

Scientific research consists increasingly of computer simulations that generate vast amounts of data. Presumably, if scientists had sufficient time and resources to examine nature directly, computer simulations that imitate nature would be unnecessary. Practical limitations, however, seem to render computer simulations indispensable to scientific research.

A dilemma now confronts the scientist. For many purposes the data a scientist wishes to obtain should properly be the output of a chance process characterized by some well-defined probability distribution.

Practical limitations, however, often prevent the scientist from actually sampling such a process and obtaining the desired data set (imagine a scientist who desires as data the sequence of heads and tails attained by flipping a coin one billion times – the scientist will expire before the billion flips can be accomplished). In this case, the scientist will want to simulate the chance process computationally.

The dilemma then is this. On the one hand computers are fully deterministic devices – specify an algorithm, and the behaviour of the machine is fixed. It follows that any probabilistic features of the data generated by a computer simulation are strictly eliminable. Yet, on the other hand, such data are to substitute for data generated by a genuine chance process, data which cannot be characterized except in probabilistic terms. As the output of a chance process, truly random data (in the sense of §1) are supposed to defy all but *post hoc* characterizations. As the output of an algorithm the (pseudo-) random data generated by a computer simulation are fully characterized in advance. How can the twain meet?

Strictly speaking they cannot. If randomness is identified with chance, then an event is random just in case it has the right sort of causal history and it was generated by a chance process. A computer is not a chance process. Ergo the data generated by a computer cannot be random. John von Neumann summed up the matter: 'Anyone who considers arithmetical methods of producing random digits is, of course, in a state of sin' (Knuth 1981: 1).

Nonetheless, the incongruity of using not merely deterministic systems, but systems whose entire behaviour can be precisely specified in advance has not dampened the proliferation of random number generators (RNGs). What then justifies using the data generated in a computer simulation in place of data generated by a chance process? In practice what happens is this. Given an RNG statisticians, as it were, set up a gauntlet of statistical tests that serve to vet it. The tests specify properties which the overwhelming majority of numerical sequences should have if they were generated by the chance process that the RNG is attempting to mimic. If the numerical sequences generated by the RNG do not have these properties, the RNG is rejected. Otherwise it is considered adequate.

Although in practice RNGs do a lot of useful work, there remains a theoretical problem in justifying RNGs in this way (which unfortunately is the only way RNGs can be justified): any RNG is only as good as the last statistical test that it passed. Indeed, history is strewn with RNGs that were for a time considered adequate, and then shown to be deficient. The problem is that we can never be sure that an RNG incorporates biases which the statistical tests we have thrown at it have simply failed to detect. This is bad. Practically speaking this means that the scientific literature may contain errors which we shall be unable to root out until appropriate statistical tests are found to detect the biases. For instance, cosmologists whose computer simulations of the early universe rely on RNGs may find their models overturned if the RNGs they employ are subsequently found to be badly biased.

3 Mixing

Take a fresh deck of playing cards and begin to riffle-shuffle them. How many riffle-shuffles are required before the deck is thoroughly mixed? Persi Diaconis has shown that seven riffle-shuffles are needed. What it means for the deck to be thoroughly mixed is that any configuration of the deck is as likely as any other. The deck starts in a specified configuration. A single shuffle mixes the deck, but not enough to break all connection with the previous configuration. Only after multiple shuffles does the configuration of the deck lose its connection with the starting configuration. At this point one says that the deck has attained a random state.

Shuffling a deck of cards is an example of a group action. Group actions provide one way of mixing things up, but not the only way. Imagine a gas concentrated in one corner of a box. The particles that make up the gas are in motion. Over time the gas will reach an equilibrium state, filling the entire box uniformly. This is an example of a dynamical system from statistical mechanics. The system starts out in a low entropy state, with the particles concentrated in one corner, and eventually reaches a maximal entropy state (an equilibrium state), with the particles evenly distributed throughout the box. The system is said to be random once it reaches the maximal entropy state (see THERMODYNAMICS).

The preceding examples illustrate several features that are common to systems which attain randomness via mixing: (1) such a system starts out from a specified configuration that is highly ordered or constrained (for example, the opposite of what we would intuitively want to call random); (2) a mixing process (for example, a group action) acts on the system, over time continually transforming the configuration of the system; (3) eventually an equilibrium state is reached after which further mixing does not affect the equilibrium. When the equilibrium state is reached, the system is said to be random.

It is worth noting that uniform probabilities frequently characterize the equilibrium states signalling randomness. What it means for a deck of playing cards to be thoroughly shuffled is that no configuration of the deck is more likely than any other. Shuffling has therefore randomized the deck only if each possible configuration of the deck is equiprobable. Similarly, a gas within a box has reached equilibrium if temperature throughout the box is uniform and the particles are evenly distributed. Uniform probabilities are therefore intimately connected with this understanding of randomness.

4 Complexity

Consider the following two sequences of a hundred coin tosses (heads = 1, tails = 0):

(R) 1100001101011000110111111
     1010001100011011001110111
     0001100100001011110111011
     0011111010010100101011110

and

(N) 1111111111111111111111111
     1111111111111111111111111
     1111111111111111111111111
     1111111111111111111111111

It seems clear that any theoretical account of randomness had better make (R) more random than (N). For instance, since (R) was obtained by actually flipping a coin whereas (N) was artificially contrived, according to the causal account of randomness sketched in §1, (R) would be random, but (N) nonrandom.

If, however, we prescind from our knowledge of the causal process responsible for these sequences, could we still distinguish these sequences in terms of randomness? We could, for instance, try to find a statistical test whose rejection region includes (N) and excludes (R), and thereby justify calling (N) nonrandom and (R) random. But for every such test it is possible to find a corresponding test whose rejection region includes (R) and excludes (N). Nor do probabilities help distinguish the sequences, since both (R) and (N), and indeed all such sequences of length 100, have the same small probability of occurring by chance, namely, 2^{-100} or approximately 1 in 10^{30}.

Starting in the 1960s a group of researchers that included Gregory Chaitin and Andrei Kolmogorov proposed a way around these difficulties (Earman 1986). Instead of characterizing randomness probabilistically, they took the very different tack of characterizing randomness computationally. What they said was that a string of 0s and 1s becomes

increasingly random as the shortest computer program that generates the string becomes increasingly long. In the 1980s cryptographers proposed a variant of this characterization: a string of 0s and 1s becomes increasingly random as the most efficient computer program that generates the string requires increasingly long computation times. The first approach characterizes randomness in terms of space complexity (that is, the amount of memory the program occupies); the second, in terms of time complexity (that is, the computation time the program requires). The space complexity approach to randomness is referred to in the literature as 'algorithmic information theory'.

It is now intuitively obvious why (R) is more random than (N). The shortest program that computes (N) has the form 'repeat "1" 100 times'. On the other hand, (R) seems to have no shorter description than the string itself. (N) can be drastically compressed, (R) cannot. Thus from the point of view of algorithmic information theory (R) is more random than (N) (see INFORMATION THEORY).

Although complexity approaches to randomness represent a genuine advance in the theoretical study of randomness, there is a limitation to these approaches that is often lost in the initial enthusiasm: all complexity approaches to randomness are relativized to a given computational environment. What this means is that even though a sequence may be random when its generating program is running in PASCAL on a standard mainframe computer, with respect to another computational device it may be nonrandom, and vice versa. In fact, since mappings between finite sets are always computable (recursion theory on finite sets is trivial), any finite string will be random with respect to certain programming environments, nonrandom with respect to others (see COMPUTABILITY AND INFORMATION; COMPUTABILITY THEORY).

5 Pattern-breaking

Having now surveyed four distinct approaches to randomness, one is tempted to ask whether a common thread runs through these approaches? There is a common thread, but one that at first sight will seem counterintuitive. In a dictionary definition of 'randomness', the term characterizes objects or events brought about without method, plan, purpose, forethought, pattern, principle, order or design. Random objects are supposed to be higgledy-piggledy, evincing no patterns.

But what does it mean for an object to evince no patterns? Consider a spy who eavesdrops on a communication channel in which encrypted messages are being relayed. If the spy has yet to break the cryptosystem, the encrypted messages traversing the communication channel will, as far as the spy is concerned, fail to display any patterns. Yet as soon as the cryptosystem is broken, all the patterns hidden by the cryptosystem become apparent.

The point is this: what determines the patterns that must be broken for an object to be random is not some objective feature of the world – randomness is not a natural kind. Rather, what is random depends on the patterns that are specified within a given context and that must then be broken for an object to be random. What is counterintuitive about this approach is that randomness becomes thoroughly parasitic on the patterns with respect to which it is defined. Randomness on this view does not make sense until a given collection of patterns is specified.

How then does this pattern-breaking approach to randomness relate to the four preceding approaches? For the computational complexity approach to randomness, the low complexity programs specify the patterns. For the mixing approach to randomness, far-from-equilibrium-states specify the patterns. For the simulation approach to randomness, statistical tests specify the patterns. The pattern-breaking approach to randomness also makes clear why chance is so often a dependable route to randomness: in many applications the patterns specified in advance identify a set of very small probability (for example, a full complement of statistical tests used to vet an RNG will typically designate as nonrandom only a tiny proportion of possible numerical sequences). Since small probability events are rare, chance will typically deliver objects or events that break all such patterns, that is, objects that are random in the pattern-breaking sense.

References and further reading

Bayer, D. and Diaconis, P. (1989) 'Trailing the Dovetail Shuffle to its Lair', Technical Report 329, Stanford, CA: Department of Statistics, Stanford University. (See §3.)
Borel, E. (1963) *Probability and Certainty*, trans. D. Scott, New York: Walker. (Treats the problem of small probabilities. See §5.)
Dembski, W.A. (1991) 'Randomness by Design', *Nous* 25 (1): 75–106. (See §5. An exposition of the pattern-breaking approach to randomness.)
Diaconis, P. (1988) *Group Representations in Probability and Statistics*, Hayward, CA: Institute of Mathematical Statistics. (The road to randomness via group actions. See §3.)
* Earman, J. (1986) *A Primer on Determinism*, Dordrecht: Reidel. (Gives a general treatment of algorithmic information theory. See §4.)
Garey, M.R. and Johnson, D.S. (1979) *Computers and Intractability: A Guide to the Theory of NP-Completeness*, New York: Freeman. (An introduction to computational complexity in which computation time serves as the measure of complexity. See §4.)
Hacking, I. (1965) *Logic of Statistical Inference*, Cambridge: Cambridge University Press. (A good discussion of what statisticians mean by randomness in the sense of chance. See §1.)
* Knuth, D.E. (1981) *Seminumerical Algorithms*, 2nd edn; in *The Art of Computer Programming*, vol. 2, Reading, MA: Addison-Wesley. (Includes Knuth's classic treatment of random number generators. See §2.)
Kranakis, E. (1986) *Primality and Cryptography*, Stuttgart: Wiley-Teubner. (Treats random number generators as well as the time complexity approach to randomness. See §§2, 4.)
Lambalgen, M. van (1989) 'Algorithmic Information Theory', *Journal of Symbolic Logic* 53 (4): 1389–400. (Technical treatment of algorithmic information theory.)
Lasota, A. and Mackey, M.C. (1985) *Probabilistic Properties of Deterministic Systems*, Cambridge: Cambridge University Press. (The road to randomness via dynamical systems. See §3.)
Mises, R. von (1957) *Probability, Statistics, and Truth*, New York: Dover, 2nd edn. (Develops many seminal ideas about randomness; although much of what von Mises did has since had to be modified or corrected.)

WILLIAM A. DEMBSKI

RASHDALL, HASTINGS (1858–1924)

Hastings Rashdall was a utilitarian in ethics, an idealist in metaphysics and a Christian monotheist in religion. His history of medieval universities became a classic. His revisions of utilitarianism are an important part of the development of that ethical theory beyond its original version in Bentham and Mill. His religious metaphysic strongly opposed the influential nonmonotheistic idealism of F.H. Bradley.

Born in 1858, and educated at Harrow and New College, Oxford, Hastings Rashdall was a lecturer in St David's College (for clergy), a theology tutor at University College, Durham, chaplain and divinity tutor at Balliol College, and Fellow, tutor and dean at New College. He became a canon of Hereford

Cathedral in 1910, and dean of Carlisle in 1917. He died in 1924.

In ethics, Rashdall rejected the hedonism of Jeremy Bentham and John Stuart Mill. He none the less accepted the general utilitarian perspective that Bentham and Mill developed. He agreed with them that an action is right only if it best serves (or, in the worst case, least harms) human wellbeing. But he refused to define the good that action should pursue in terms of pleasure alone; his utilitarianism is hence ideal rather than hedonistic. He held that rational moral judgments are possible concerning the moral worth of particular ends or goals, and it is these, rather than moral intuitions of general principles defining the nature of right action independently of consequences, that should be basic in moral reflection. A tendency to promote human wellbeing is part of the good that our actions should promote.

Rashdall held that there is a deep link between morality and monotheism:

> Belief in God ... is the logical presupposition of an 'objective' or absolute Morality. Our moral ideal can only claim objective validity in so far as it can rationally be regarded as the revelation of a moral ideal eternally existing in the mind of God.
>
> (1907, vol. 2: 212)

In metaphysics, Rashdall was an idealist, maintaining that only minds and their states and characteristics exist, and that there are no spatially extended and consciousness-independent physical objects. Because, as BERKELEY (§§3, 5–7) argued, neither secondary qualities nor primary qualities can exist without consciousness, what we refer to as matter is the perceptual content of mental states.

Our efficacious willing is the only causality that we experience, and thus order in nature (that is, among our perceptual states) is best explained by reference to a Mind that causes regularities among our experiences. By analogy with our minds, presumably that Mind also has thought, feeling and will. Each mind is a mental substance, and none is to be thought of as merely a mode of a divine mind.

In philosophy of religion, Rashdall was a monotheist, maintaining that God is a self-conscious, independently existing mental substance on whom all other minds depend for their existence. Our knowledge of God comes, not from religious experience, but from the arguments of natural theology, particularly the moral argument for God's existence, and from revelation in so far as it is supported by reason (see RELIGION, HISTORY OF PHILOSOPHY OF §5). Our moral consciousness makes us aware that only if a preventable evil serves a greater good is its existence morally permissible.

Rashdall held that there are goods for whose existence evil is necessary: for example, he suggested that evolving 'highly organized beings without a struggle for existence' and training 'human beings in unselfishness without allowing the existence of both sin and of pain' was impossible (1909: 82).

It was Rashdall's contention, then, that there are goods that not even God can elicit without allowing evil. This, he said, follows from God's nature. He seems to have meant two things. First, he meant that regarding some actual goods G and evils E, 'G exists and E does not' is self-contradictory and G outweighs E; some evils are allowed because they are logically necessary conditions for important goods. Second, he meant that in some manner the ground of logical necessity lies in God's nature. No divine defect was implied when Rashdall said that it follows from God's nature that not even God can elicit certain goods without also allowing evil. God, being good, would not have created at all if evil were going to triumph.

Rashdall was a determinist: he held that human actions occur as the result of factors over which their agents have no effective control. Hence the existence of evil cannot even in part be ascribed to free and wrong human choices. God, however, is not blameworthy for the evil in the world, for God must allow certain evils in order for there to be certain goods.

See also: EVIL, PROBLEM OF

List of works

Rashdall, H. (1895) *The Universities of Europe in the Middle Ages*, London: Oxford University Press. (Rashdall's classic study of medieval universities.)

—— (1905) *Conscience and Christ*, London: Duckworth. (Six lectures on Christian ethics.)

—— (1907) *The Theory of Good and Evil*, London: Oxford University Press, 2 vols. (The fullest statement of Rashdall's ideal utilitarianism.)

—— (1909) *Philosophy and Religion*, London: Duckworth. (Six lectures on metaphysics, ethics and revelation.)

—— (1912) *The Problem of Evil*, Manchester: Manchester University Press. (Rashdall's discussion of the thorniest problem for monotheists.)

—— (1920) *The Moral Argument for Personal Immortality*, London: Duckworth. (Rashdall's discussion of the moral argument for the existence of God.)

—— (1930) *God and Man*, Oxford: Blackwell. (Chapters, historical and systematic, on various issues in philosophical theology.)

References and further reading

Elliot-Binns, J.E. (1956) *English Thought 1860–1900: The Theological Aspect*, London: Longmans, Green & Company. (Discusses the historical, philosophical, theological and social setting of English theology in the indicated period.)

Langford, T. (1969) *In Search of Foundations: English Theology 1900–1920*, Nashville, TN: Abington Press. (Presentation of English theological thought in its cultural and philosophical context; good bibliography.)

Mozley, J.K. (1951) *Some Tendencies in British Theology*, London: SPCK. (Discussion of British theology from *Lux mundi* (1889) to the thought of Oman.)

KEITH E. YANDELL

RATIONAL BELIEFS

To the extent that a belief is rational, it ought to be held, other things being equal; irrational beliefs should not be held. From traditional epistemological perspectives, the obligation here is narrow, concerning only good reasons for acceptance that constitute sufficient justification or warrant. Recent epistemological trends broaden the viewpoint to include also practical considerations that enter into other rational decisions, such as best use of the agent's limited resources.

A related but weaker conception of rationality appears in philosophy of mind as a necessary coherence requirement on personal identity – roughly, 'No rationality, no agent'. Such agent-constitutive rationality standards are more lenient than normative epistemic standards, since agents' belief sets can and often do fall short of epistemically uncriticizable rationality without the agents thereby ceasing to qualify as having minds.

Finally, at the widest perspective, long-standing sceptical lines of challenge to rationality of the entire structure of human belief-forming procedures conclude that we can never have the slightest good reason to accept even our most central beliefs. Recent approaches that 'naturalize' epistemology into a branch of science tend to exclude such general doubts as insignificant or meaningless; but if distinctively philosophical questions in fact do not fully reduce to regular scientific ones, sceptical-type rationality challenges may instead remain a permanent part of the human condition.

1 A priori belief
2 A posteriori belief
3 Philosophy, science and ordinary life

1 A priori belief

What rational belief is can be best conveyed through some major types of example. The simplest, and most extreme, case of irrationality is accepting a proposition that is inconsistent. Indeed, attribution to a person of such irrationality has sometimes been regarded as self-defeating, in that we purportedly cannot even make sense of so severe a reasoning failure. In this way charity principles of Quine and Davidson dictate that 'better translation imposes our logic' – and our rationality generally – upon the beliefs of any agent we undertake to interpret (see CHARITY, PRINCIPLE OF §4). Such in-principle exclusion of the very possibility of inconsistency may seem like an overreaction, since human beings (unlike God) must often lack the insight to identify the less obvious inconsistencies in propositions they accept. To idealize away these failures as mere occasional, corrigible slips is to deny a basic fact of existence for a finite creature, human or otherwise, and to deny much of the project of the deductive sciences. We understand all too well how Gottlob Frege could genuinely accept his axioms for naïve set theory, even though they turned out to harbour Russell's Paradox; inconsistency is always with us (see FREGE, G. §§8–9; RUSSELL, B. §4).

Granting the possibility (indeed, pervasiveness) of inconsistencies, they are, as paradigmatic irrationality, conventionally viewed as disasters to be avoided or remedied at all costs. As Frege responded to Russell on the status of inconsistent foundations of mathematics, 'Arithmetic totters'. Indeed, the history of the rise of modern logic can be viewed as conditioned in large part by the discovery of, and response to, the paradoxes. However, in contrast to the traditional picture of antinomies as symptoms of disease, alternative accounts have emerged along the lines of Wittgenstein's apophthegm, 'A contradiction is not a germ which shows a general illness'. Some of these go further, to propose that inconsistency may in fact sometimes be positively healthy, as in the familiar way that inconsistent naïve set theory can be used for informal purposes than later, more complicated formulations devised to avoid the paradoxes.

Psychological studies of recent decades provide some evidence that everyday human reasoning – inductive as well as deductive – might be formally incorrect to a surprising extent (see RATIONALITY OF BELIEF; COMMON-SENSE REASONING, THEORIES OF). From the perspective of more 'realistic' theories of rationality that take account of an agent's actual cognitive processes and resources, such incorrectness need not be mysterious reasoning pathology. Such local irrationality could be made sense of as the trade-off cost of a globally rational strategy to avoid cognitive paralysis: use of 'quick but dirty', formally incorrect heuristic procedures that are more computationally efficient in many contexts than formally adequate ones can be. These accounts suggest that human beings have a multiplicity of overlapping special-purpose reasoning strategies – some formally correct, some not – that they can switch among. In this way, reasoning is evaluated in terms of, not only preservation of truth, but also wider practical issues of, for example, actual human usability of procedures given a limited cognition-budget. Paradoxes such as Russell's then appear not necessarily as symptoms of dysfunction at the core of the human conceptual scheme, but rather as signs of fundamentally rational speed–reliability trade-offs.

2 A posteriori belief

For the empirical domain, accounts of rational belief develop along lines independent of, but still parallel to, the evolution of accounts for a priori belief. At the start of modern epistemology, Descartes proposes among rules for direction of the mind, 'I should hold back my assent from opinions which are not completely certain and indubitable just as carefully as I do from those which are patently false' (Descartes [1641] 1984: 12). He then points out that, for any belief, wide-scale sceptical doubts are always possible that would undermine any of my reasons for accepting it – for example, I might be experiencing a perfectly realistic hallucination rather than anything of a mind-independent world. Consequently, Descartes recommends a method of universal doubt, reconstructing our entire belief system from a blank slate; rational belief-management strategy must start by rejecting everything (see DESCARTES, R. §4; DOUBT §2). However, history's majority verdict seems to be that universal doubt is not in fact advisable, that it would leave us in an epistemological tragicomedy of total, irreversible cognitive paralysis, which is rarely a rational option (see SCEPTICISM).

Pragmatism first introduces and defines itself in terms of rejection of the Cartesian programme. Its inventor, C.S. Peirce, proposes instead 'critical commonsensism': while no belief can be immune to doubt, we can never begin with suspension of all our beliefs (see COMMONSENSISM). From this anti-Cartesianism stems a neo-pragmatist leitmotif of much epistemology of the twentieth century. Quine (1960), for example, following Neurath, explains that Cartesian universal doubt is not only a psychological impossibility for human beings, but also self-defeating because self-undermining; to try to practise it is from the outset to sink the scientific-philosophical enterprise. The thesis that, while we must begin from whatever belief scheme with which we find ourselves, any belief can still be doubted, raises a natural next question: *Which* beliefs ought in fact to be challenged, and when?

One line of reply is that an agent is held responsible for ruling out those counter-possibilities to a belief that satisfy a 'special reasons requirement': specific, relevant ones that there is definite basis for thinking might now apply. In an example of J.L. Austin's, normally it would be humorous to criticize as hasty someone's belief that there is a goldfinch in the garden on grounds that he had not checked that the objects he glimpsed were not stuffed toys – unless, for instance, he had already been in a position to find out the neighbours' children had lately been playing with toy birds. In this way, epistemic responsibility resembles traditional doctrines of general culpable negligence, of legal responsibility for taking the due care in actions that a 'reasonable person' would. However, a thesis that the epistemic agent must take due care that falls somewhere between total irresponsibility and perfection in turn raises questions about how particular levels of required vigilance are set. Just because people in certain situations are in fact found subject to criticism if they do not maintain certain levels of care does not completely answer this question – unless actual practices are guaranteed to be optimal (see §3 below).

Thus, there has been an evolution from a simple if perfectionistic view that beliefs cannot be rational if *any* challenges to them are imaginable, to a more realistic or pragmatic type of account, where rationality of beliefs is subject to challenge only when a circumscribed set of appropriate counter-possibilities can be raised. However, if the agent is responsible for eliminating challenges whose seriousness is obviously implied by the current belief system, then formation of new rational beliefs crucially depends upon the agent's current background beliefs. Yet the background belief-set must inevitably be incomplete, particularly at cutting edges of the belief system, themselves inevitable for finite creatures like ourselves. And so breakdown scenarios can still arise where appropriateness of a counter-possibility cannot be evaluated. Even if recognition of a counter-possibility-filter in our knowledge-gathering processes may block the traditional embarrassment of sceptical paralysis, history still threatens to repeat itself in a new guise.

3 Philosophy, science and ordinary life

More generally, we seem unable to avoid posing distinctively philosophical challenges regarding adequacy of our doubt-screening procedures themselves. A question inappropriate in ordinary or scientific contexts may still not be inappropriate *simpliciter*. Rationality consists of more than just playing according to the rules of our belief-forming games; an essential part of rationality concerns the advisability of deciding to play the games in the first place. Recognition of the latter type of rationality-domain can be discerned in Kant's distinction between the concepts of (scientific) understanding and the extrascientific ideas of reason that guide the scientific enterprise (see KANT, I. §§6–7), in Carnap's separation of internal questions of science from external questions concerning acceptance of a whole framework for settling internal questions (see CARNAP, R. §5), and in Kuhn's distinguishing 'normal' scientific activity from debate about paradigms or disciplinary matrices within which that activity proceeds (see KUHN, T. §§2–3). *Prima facie*, we seem able to put our most basic knowledge-gathering mechanisms themselves in question and ask whether the actual is the ideal: just because a procedure is part of the system we in fact actually use, does it follow that the procedure must be perfect or otherwise uncriticizable?

One response to the intractability of such philosophical questions is to make a virtue of necessity, and to exchange impending scepticism for relativism. Basic principles cannot themselves be rationally justified without courting circularity; hence, their acceptance can be no more than a matter of epistemic taste, about which ultimately one cannot dispute or judge (see COGNITIVE PLURALISM §2; EPISTEMIC RELATIVISM). Our own procedures may happen to be the only ones we have encountered, but they ought not to serve as a Procrustean Bed into which genuine cognitive differences must be forced. Without parochial a priori constraints on rationality, possibilities for radical cognitive diversity become wide open. However, questions in turn arise about whether radical relativism itself can even be coherently articulated. In their extreme form, these concerns tend towards a conservative conclusion that also aims to block sceptical-type challenges. One recurring argument to this effect (used, for example, by Quine) is that there is no cosmic exile from which we can take the God's-eye view required to evaluate our own basic conceptual scheme; we need a *pou sto*, a standpoint from which and by which to judge our scheme, and our actual one is the only one we have. External questions perforce become internal (see RATIONALITY AND CULTURAL RELATIVISM).

However, one reply has been that, while we may have to employ the only system we possess, our system itself may furnish the basis for large-scale doubts about its own adequacy. For example,

'naturalized' epistemology seeks vindication of our actual procedures in a core part of the scientific worldview, evolutionary theory: natural selection has engineered cognitive structures of human beings just as it has the biological structures, and the validation of our belief-forming systems is that evolution has designed them to function well. But then in turn a natural concern is that what is efficient for information-processing tasks conducive to survival need not be epistemically sound – for instance, as mentioned in §1 above, speed and correctness are often outright antagonistic. Thus, naturalism can engender its own challenges to our scheme; such self-evaluations do not guarantee happy endings. Apparently, when sceptical challenges are eliminated by attempting to assimilate distinctively philosophical questions to those of science or ordinary life, they reintroduce themselves in new form. In this way, articulation of our conception of rationality seems a task never completed, only set aside.

See also: JUSTIFICATION, EPISTEMIC; NATURALIZED EPISTEMOLOGY; REASONS FOR BELIEF

References and further reading

Austin, J. (1946) 'Other Minds', in *Philosophical Papers*, Oxford: Oxford University Press, 3rd edn, 1990. (The 'special reasons requirement' on challenges of rationality of empirical knowledge claims.)

Carnap, R. (1956) 'Empiricism, semantics, and ontology', in *Meaning and Necessity*, Chicago: University of Chicago Press, 2nd edn. (A positivist account of the science-philosophy division, with Kantian affinities.)

Cherniak, C. (1986) *Minimal Rationality*, Cambridge, MA: MIT Press. (Exposition of a 'resource-realistic' model of rationality.)

* Descartes, R. (1641) *Meditations*, in J. Cottingham, R. Stoothoff, and D. Murdoch (eds) *Philosophical Writings of Descartes*, vol. 2, Cambridge: Cambridge University Press, 1984. (On the method of universal doubt, which pragmatism attacks. See especially Meditation I.)

Kant, I. (1783) *Prolegomena to Any Future Metaphysics*, trans. L. Beck, New York: Bobbs-Merrill, 1950. (On the relation between the domains of science and philosophy. Sections 40–4 and 56–7 are especially relevant; see §3 above.)

Peirce, C.S. (1868) 'Some consequences of four incapacities', in *Collected Papers*, vol. 5, Cambridge, MA: Harvard University Press, 1932. (The original statement of the pragmatist anti-Cartesian doctrine of 'critical commonsensism'; see §2 above.)

* Quine, W.V. (1960) *Word and Object*, Cambridge,

MA: MIT Press. (The starting point of much recent neopragmatist epistemology, and naturalized epistemology in particular. Chapter 1 is especially relevant.)

Simon, H. (1982) *Models of Bounded Rationality*, vol. 2, Cambridge, MA: MIT Press. (An early and important critique of extreme rationality-idealizations of the agent in economics. See especially chapters 8.2 and 8.4.)

Stich, S. (1990) *The Fragmentation of Reason*, Cambridge, MA: MIT Press. (A relativist theory of rationality; a good overview.)

Tversky, A. and Kahneman, D. (1974) 'Judgment under uncertainty: heuristics and biases', *Science* 185 (4157): 1124–31. (Experimental studies of human use of formally incorrect inductive reasoning procedures; see §1 above.)

CHRISTOPHER CHERNIAK

RATIONAL CHOICE THEORY

Rational choice theory is the descendant of earlier philosophical political economy. Its core is the effort to explain and sometimes to justify collective results of individuals acting from their own individual motivations – usually their own self interest, but sometimes far more general concerns that can be included under the rubric of preferences. The resolute application of the assumption of self-interest to social actions and institutions began with Hobbes and Machiavelli, who are sometimes therefore seen as the figures who divide modern from early political philosophy. Machiavelli commended the assumption of self interest to the prince; Hobbes applied it to everyone. Their view of human motivation went on to remake economics through the work of Mandeville and Adam Smith. And it was plausibly a major factor in the decline of virtue theory, which had previously dominated ethics for many centuries.

Game theory was invented almost whole by the mathematician von Neumann and the economist Morgenstern during the Second World War. Their theory was less a theory that made predictions or gave explanations than a framework for viewing complex social interactions. It caught on with mathematicians and defence analysts almost immediately, with social psychologists much later, and with economists and philosophers later still. But it has now become almost necessary to state some problems game theoretically in order to keep them clear and to relate them to other analyses. The game-theory framework represents ranges of payoffs that players can get from their simultaneous or sequential moves in games in which

they interact. Moves are essentially choices of strategies, and outcomes are the intersections of strategy choices. If you and I are in a game, both of us typically depend on our own and on the other's choices of strategies for our payoffs.

The most striking advance in economics in the twentieth century is arguably the move from cardinal to ordinal value theory. The change had great advantages for resolving certain classes of problems but it also made many tasks more difficult. For example, the central task of aggregation from individual to collective preferences or utility could be done – at least in principle – as a matter of mere arithmetic in the cardinal system. In that system, Benthamite utilitarianism was the natural theory for welfare economics. In the ordinal system, however, there was no obvious way to aggregate from individual to collective preferences. We could do what Pareto said was all that could be done: we could optimize by making those (Pareto) improvements that made at least one person better off but no one worse off. But we could not maximize. In his impossibility theorem, Arrow (1951) showed that, under reasonable conditions, there is no general method for converting individual to collective orderings.

After game theory and the Arrow impossibility theorem, the next major contribution to rational choice theory was the economic theory of democracy of Downs (1957). Downs assumed that everyone involved in the democratic election system is primarily self interested. Candidates are interested in their own election; citizens are interested in getting policies adopted that benefit themselves. From this relatively simple assumption, however, he deduced two striking results that ran counter to standard views of democracy. In a two-party system, parties would rationally locate themselves at the centre of the voter distribution; and citizens typically have no interest in voting or in learning enough to vote in their interests even if they do vote.

The problem of the rational voter can be generalized. Suppose that I am a member of a group of many people who share an interest in having some good provided but that no one of us values its provision enough to justify paying for it all on our own. Suppose further that, if every one of us pays a proportionate share of the cost, we all benefit more than we pay. Unfortunately, however, my benefit from my contribution alone might be less than the value of my contribution. Hence, if our contributions are strictly voluntary, I may prefer not to contribute a share and merely to enjoy whatever follows from the contributions of others. I am then a free-rider. If we all rationally attempt to be free-riders, our group fails and none of us benefits.

A potentially disturbing implication of the game theoretic understanding of rationality in interactive choice contexts, of the Arrow impossibility theorem, of the economic theory of democracy and of the logic of collective action is that much of philosophical democratic theory, which is usually normative, is irrelevant to our possibilities. The things these theories often tell us we should be doing cannot be done.

1 **Historical background**
2 **Game theory**
3 **Mixed-motive games**
4 **The Arrow problem**
5 **Voting and democracy**
6 **The logic of collective action**
7 **Further applications**
8 **Intentional behaviour**
9 **Value theory**
10 **Preliminary conclusions**

1 Historical background

Of course, the role of self interest in explaining behaviour was not a discovery of the Renaissance and Reformation. From Socrates to the beneficent utilitarians, interest has been of central concern. Indeed, it has long been common to view morality as action against one's own interest in the interest of others or for otherwise good ends or good reasons. For example, SIDGWICK saw beneficence and self-interest as often contrary dual motivations. MACHIAVELLI and HOBBES were merely more insistent than many earlier philosophers on seeing the world as dominated by self-interest, and they were less ready to salvage social order in theory by supposing individuals just would or do behave well or public spiritedly.

The history of the slow invention of rational choice theory may be best told in the account of the role of fallacies of composition in political philosophy. Such fallacies in the aggregation from individual to collective choice or good are a standard background problem for rational choice theory. We are guilty of a fallacy of composition when, without argument, we assume that the attributes of an entity are the attributes of its constituents. This is a form of metaphorical or analogical reasoning that might sometimes yield correct results, but it often leads us astray. For example, we argue from the premise that every individual is rational to the conclusion that a nation or a group of individuals is rational in the same sense. It is only a slight exaggeration to say that rational-choice political theory is essentially an effort to block conclusions that are fallacies of composition. The three biggest bodies of work in rational-choice political theory – the aggregation of individual into collective preferences in the Arrow problem (§4), the rational-choice theory of voting and democracy (§5), and the logic of collective action (§6) – are deflations

of fallacies of composition, as is the prisoner's dilemma game (§3), which is related to the collective action and voting problems.

Perhaps the central claim in Socrates' political philosophy is that it is in an individual's interest to act justly, to be just. This claim contradicts appearances that we, Glaucon in Plato's *Republic*, and others cannot deny. Socrates denies that there is a fallacy of composition in going from what is best for the individual to what is best for the community. It takes a great deal of devious argument and an adoring audience for him to seem convincing. Many teenage university students have since been hectored into accepting Socrates' conclusion and have therefore misconceived politics and group action from the beginnings of their supposed understanding. Perhaps it does not take more hectoring than it does merely because the fallacy is remarkably easy and seemingly natural.

After Socrates, Aristotle began his *Politics* with his own variant fallacy of composition. He supposed that, because every man acts with the intention of producing something that is a good, the polis, the most sovereign association of men, must pursue the most sovereign of goods. Aristotle's views have often been taught less with hectoring than with the weight of authority, but they too have set beginners on the path of confusion. Long after the reign of Greek philosophy, Aristotle came back into favour in a church that secured a match between individual interest and morality by inventing everlasting punishment for immorality. In effect, the church established a causal connection between individual and collective good to replace the failed conceptual connection. The causal connection it created was to make full use of self-interest.

Eventually Hobbes and others demolished the fallacy of composition at the heart of Socrates' and Aristotle's claims. In his allegory of the state of nature, Hobbes explicitly supposed that individuals would follow their own interests and that the result would be collective misery. This result gave licence to his invocation of an all-powerful governor to bring harmony and wellbeing because it can generally be in my interest to act well toward others only if there is a government prepared to coerce both me and the others to behave well. In three short chapters (*Leviathan*, chapters 13–15) Hobbes laid the foundations for rational choice theory and for political philosophy thereafter. A rational choice theorist might finally wish to say that Hobbes is the first modern political philosopher because he was the first to recognize and be persistent in avoiding fallacies of composition inherent in much of political philosophy before him (and, alas, since).

Nearly a century after Hobbes, MANDEVILLE (§3) argued that private vices beget public virtues. In particular, universal avarice produces wide prosperity. This is a grim thought for virtue theory. All of us must wish others were avaricious because then they would serve our interests well. Avarice, the worst of all vices, has good results and its contrary virtue might have bad results. Smith, after writing his own book of near-virtue theory, *The Theory of Moral Sentiments*, then went on to write an economic theory in *The Wealth of Nations* that matched Mandeville's and severely undercut virtue theory (see SMITH, A. §3). The central move, again, was to cut the supposedly conceptual connection between self interest and collective interest. There could be no conceptual, but only a causal, connection, if any.

2 Game theory

Game theory is typically not about the source of the incentives we face but about the force of them, as is also true of rational-choice theory more generally. For most of its use, game theory is applied to actual payoff structures or to idealized structures. The payoffs are simply given. An economic theory of knowledge and preference formation can be brought to bear to explain preferences and, hence, to determine payoffs.

In social thought and in rational choice theory, games may be associated with three broad classes. There are games that involve pure conflict, games that involve pure coordination, and games that mix these two. If the only way for you to do better is for me to do worse, as when we play chess, we are in a game of *pure conflict*. If the way for each of us to do best is for both of us to do the same thing (in some sense), we are in a game of *pure coordination*, as when we drive our cars in North America and hope that every other driver stays to the right as we do (or in the UK, to the left). If I can sometimes do better only when you do worse and sometimes we can both do better by doing the same thing, we are in a *mixed-motive* game, which involves a mixture of conflict and coordination.

These three kinds of game can be represented very simply in two-person formats; each intersection of strategy choices yields a pair of payoffs. The first payoff in each pair is to Row, the second is to Column. The payoffs here are ordinal, with 1 as the first (best) choice, 4 the last (worst) choice. In the coordination and mixed-motive games, each player has two strategies from which to choose. In the pure conflict game, Column has no choice but will get whichever payoff Row chooses.

There could be any number of strategies available to both players in all categories of games. Moreover,

the payoffs could be in almost anything, such as money, position, goods, or abstract utility. In most of social theory and of rational choice theory, ordinal games are adequate because there is no good sense of any quantity that could cover the range of payoffs. Even in games in which one might state what the payoffs are in each cell, one might be unable sensibly to assign them weights in anything like monetary or utility terms, so that ordinal representations still are adequate. However, ordinal representations lose important information that might alter the way people choose in a game, for example if the difference between one's first and second ranked outcome is trivial while that between the second and third is enormous.

Game theory first grew out of games of pure conflict (see game 1), perhaps especially on the model of poker. In a pure conflict game there is nothing to be gained by cooperation. When there are more than two players, there is typically the possibility of cooperation that makes the game not pure conflict. Then the analysis of the game becomes an analysis of coalitions of players that can form. Poker can be played under rules that block collusion or cooperation between players, and other games can be contrived that have more than two players but that are still games of pure conflict between every pair of players. Von Neumann's saddle-point or *maximin* theorem for two-person pure conflict games shows that one cannot do better against a symmetrically rational player than to choose a strategy that includes the so-called maximin payoff. That payoff is the best of the set of worst payoffs one could get from each strategy choice, or the maximum minimum (see NEUMANN, JOHN VON).

One might think that pure conflict games are a very large and important class for social interaction. However, most social interactions that seem superficially to be pure conflict actually involve extensive opportunity for mutual benefit. For example, war might be seen as a game for victory or defeat, an analogue of chess. But actual wars, other than wars of attempted annihilation, can be fought in restricted ways that make all potentially better off. Hence, there is room for coordination as well as conflict.

Virtually the opposite of games of pure conflict are games of pure coordination, in which the incentive is

Game 1. Pure conflict

	Column	
	I	II
Row		
	II	2,1

to achieve harmony. Indeed, these games have been called common-interest games. Harmony can often be achieved without communication or anything even vaguely approaching agreement. The players need only recognize that their jointly best payoffs are in one or more outcomes and that there is some reason for choosing some particular strategy that includes one of those outcomes. If I am playing you in game 2 without opportunity for communication, I might choose strategy I instead of strategy II simply because the I-I outcome would come first for anyone reading English, which starts at the top left of the page – and I presume you might think the same way. Thomas Schelling (1960) has shown that people are remarkably good at coordinating in such ways without conversation.

In the pure coordination game of game 2, note that there are two outcomes with equally good payoffs for each player. Row does not care whether Column chooses strategy I or strategy II, but only cares whether both of them choose strategy I or strategy II. So long as they both choose the same strategy, they do well. Because there are two possible coordination outcomes, it is possible for the players to miscue and to finish in one of the second best payoffs. Hence, even pure coordination problems, as sanguine and simple as they may seem, can pose difficult personal and social choice problems. When such games in practical life are iterated, they are often resolved by convention (Hume 1739–40; Lewis 1969). Once we reach one of the best outcomes in an iterated class of interactions, we thereafter stick with the successful strategy, thereby establishing a *convention*.

3 Mixed-motive games

The mixed-motive game of game 3 merits extended discussion. The mixed-motive category includes many strategically distinct games. Game 3 is specifically a variant of the prisoner's dilemma game, which is by far the most studied of all games. In the 1960s it captured the imagination of social psychologists, for whom it became a lasting focus of research. It is central in theoretical and simulation studies of altruism. And it has been associated more generally with the problem of collective action (§6). Despite all

the attention it has got, however, it may have been relatively neglected in many circles because it has a misleading name.

As can be seen from the order of payoffs in game 3, prisoner's dilemma has two striking features that suggest a conflict of motivations for the players. Suppose you are Column and I am Row. You can readily see that you rank your payoff from defection higher than your payoff from cooperation no matter what I do. If I cooperate, you get your best outcome in defecting. If I defect, you get your third best rather than your fourth best if you defect. Hence, you have a *dominant strategy*: defect no matter what. My position is symmetrically equivalent to yours, so that I have the same dominant strategy. If we both follow our dominant strategy, we both defect and we reach an *equilibrium* in the game. But it is also obvious in game 3 that we both will be better off if we both cooperate than if we both defect. If we have any device outside the payoffs of game 3 to enable us to contract to insure mutual cooperation, we would benefit from doing so.

The prisoner's dilemma is unique among the seventy-eight strategically distinct two-person ordinal games in that it has an equilibrium that is Pareto inferior to some other outcome (Rapoport and Guyer 1966). (One outcome is Pareto inferior to another if moving from it to the other makes at least one person better off while hurting no one.) Defection dominates cooperation individually but mutual cooperation is better than mutual defection. The crossed incentives are maddening. But they are nothing new – we face them daily in our lives. Moreover, resolving their large-number analogue is the crux of political order (§6).

The discoverers of prisoner's dilemma were Flood and Dresher at the Rand Corporation around 1950. Flood had been trying to represent the sale of a used car as a game. Perhaps from a sense of that game's peculiarity, he and Dresher then designed the original prisoner's dilemma to test how people involved in an interaction repeatedly would behave. In essence, the first prisoner's dilemma experiment was of an iterated game. The game was sufficiently peculiar in comparison to other games, as noted, that they showed it to many people, including the Princeton mathematician, A.W. Tucker, speculating on what it might mean or

Game 2. Pure coordination

		Column	
		I	II
Row	I	1,1	2,2
	II	2,2	1,1

Game 3. Mixed motive (Prisoner's dilemma or exchange)

		Column	
		Cooperate	Defect
Row	Cooperate	2,2	4,1
	Defect	1,4	3,3

represent. Tucker proposed the morality tale of two prisoners caught up in the American legal system. Kept in separate rooms, the prisoners are offered a chance at a reduced sentence if they will turn state's evidence against their partner. If both turn state's evidence, both will get lighter than the maximum sentences. If only one does, the other will get the maximum sentence, while the confessor will get a very light sentence. If both refuse to talk, both will get a mild sentence for a corollary crime (illegal possession of a firearm). The individual incentive is to turn state's evidence, but the prisoners could jointly do better if they both keep silence. The terms 'cooperate' and 'defect' correspond, for the prisoners, to keeping silence and turning state's evidence.

Unfortunately, this story of the two prisoners seems to have been more captivating than the game. Yet the real structure of that game is so common in life that, had it been properly identified in its name, it might have entered political philosophy and economics a decade or two sooner. In its payoff structure, prisoner's dilemma is fundamentally the model of ordinary *exchange*. The tale of two prisoners blurs the generality and import of the game. As is instantly obvious from their identical payoff structures, the morality tale of two prisoners and ordinary exchange are *strategically* identical. If there are morals to be drawn, they will first have to be inserted.

A particularly important variant of the prisoner's dilemma is the game in iterated play. When you and I are in an interaction beyond the immediate play of the game, we might both have incentives for action that derive from the further interaction as well as from our immediate game structure. In general, we may expect to see cooperative play in a prisoner's dilemma that is iterated many times, even into the distant future. Because much of our social life involves ongoing relationships, we will be able to map it into game theory only through iterated games. If the prisoner's dilemma is played once only between players who do not expect to meet again and without external constraints that would, for example, permit enforceable contracts, then virtually all game theorists think the players should rationally defect. What we face in real life commonly violates these pristine conditions enough to make it our interest to cooperate in manifold exchange relations (Hardin 1982; Axelrod 1984).

Game theory is a natural ground on which to investigate the plausible meaning of rationality in interactive choice. The standard statement is that it is rational to maximize (or optimize) one's own payoff against another player (or other players) who simultaneously maximizes. This is a patently circular or self-referential definition. But it sometimes works, as in pure conflict games. It also sometimes fails, as in many mixed-motive games. When it fails, we are left free to proclaim various solution concepts for games because we cannot stipulate that a particular one is rational in this natural but circular sense – and the literature is cluttered with variant solution concepts. We might conclude that rationality is ill-defined and merely wants more analysis. But we might sooner conclude that rationality is inherently indeterminate in many interactive choice contexts.

Note also that rational choice in the context of strategic interaction does not fit well with much of philosophical action theory. In philosophical action theory, I typically produce outcomes directly from my own action. My action when I choose one strategy rather than another is, of course, motivated by my concern with outcomes. But the choice and the outcome are not directly connected. Rather, the outcome is the joint result of choices of strategy by me and by as many others as there are in the interaction. I might choose a strategy that includes some dreadful outcomes because my choice joined with strategies that I expect others to choose would produce a very good outcome. In the terminology of rational choice and standard decision theory, when I do not choose against nature but choose in combination with others with whom I interact, the meanings of my choices can be very complex.

4 The Arrow problem

The basic move from cardinal to ordinal value theory was completed in the 1930s when J.R. Hicks and R.G.D. Allen (1934) worked out the formal structure of an ordinal theory that could then be put to work in standard economic accounts. The next challenge was to move from Benthamite aggregate welfare to ordinal social welfare, still based on aggregation from individual, but now ordinal, preferences. Arrow took on this problem with the apparent expectation of resolving it positively. In a retrospective account, Arrow (1983) implicitly acknowledged that he had expected to demonstrate that it was not a fallacy of composition that we could move from individual to collective preferences of the same kind. Instead, he soon showed that it was a fallacy of composition and that Pareto was *de facto* right. He proved what is now called Arrow's *impossibility theorem*: that there is no general way to aggregate individual ordinal preferences into collective ordinal preferences over the possible whole states of affairs.

The limited Pareto principle is often indeterminate because in many social contexts all plausible changes would make someone worse off and because, when there is more than one available Pareto improvement (a common state of affairs), the Pareto principle typically cannot say which is better. Similarly, ordinal social choice is indeterminately related to individual preference.

Arrow's theorem is based on several assumptions that sound relatively benign and acceptable. First, he stipulates that only ordinal preference rankings be considered (the ordering condition, O). Then he stipulates that no individual's preference ordering will be the ordering of the society (nondictatorship, D), no restrictions can be placed on any individual's choice of orderings (universal domain, U), if everyone prefers one state of affairs to another, society prefers that state to the other (unanimity or Pareto, P), and if individuals' rankings over the social choices are changed but no individual reverses the order of two possible choices, then the collective ordering over those two choices cannot change (irrelevance of independent alternatives, I). Finally, he implicitly assumes, reasonably enough, that our society has a finite number of individuals.

One might quarrel with each of these assumptions. But there is no point in quarrelling with O, since it is the point of Arrow's exercise. There is also no point in quarrelling with Arrow's unstated but implicitly invoked condition of finitude of the citizenry. And few have ever quarrelled with condition D – except to suggest it be made even stronger. Similarly, few argue against condition P, although Amartya Sen (1970) has campaigned hard against it. It is easy, however, to imagine states of affairs that everyone would rank below some other state (thus violating U). And many, perhaps most, commentators do not really know what to think of condition I. Is it naturally compelling? Or does it merely represent the lazy way we think through the problem of aggregation? In his own proof of the impossibility theorem, Arrow did not explicitly invoke the condition – although he did implicitly assume it.

As will be discussed further in §9, there is another fundamental issue that seems bothersome for Arrow's theorem: the ranking of whole states of affairs. As Arrow says, a whole state of affairs means everything is determined. We can avoid the burden of such inclusiveness only if ordinal preferences over some things can be stated with a *ceteris paribus* clause that declares these things to be decoupled from all else. Why? Because ordinal preferences resolve two important and nearly intransigent problems of the older cardinal value theory. Under the older theory, I should apparently value two dinners tonight at twice the value of one – but clearly I do not. Indeed, I might even pay not to have to eat one of them. The two dinners would be *substitutes* for each other and therefore the second one need add no welfare to me.

Also under the older theory, I should apparently value anything independently of what else there is or what else I have – but this is patently false. Some things are *complements*, and their value might be enhanced or reduced by my having something else with them, as my dinner and my glass of wine might be better enjoyed jointly than separately.

Now if the value to me of some consumption depends on whether there are substitutes or complements in my bundle of consumptions, I cannot rank some part of the whole package. I can only rank whole packages in comparison to other whole packages. That is, as a citizen, I can only rank whole states of affairs fully determined.

Despite this relatively daunting thought, there is a reduced form of Arrow's theorem that is of great practical importance. It was recognized by the Marquis de Condorcet and by C.L. Dodgson. It is called the Condorcet paradox or the problem of cyclic majorities. If three or more people must choose from three candidates by majority rule, candidate A can defeat B, B can defeat C, and C can defeat A. There is then no outright majority winner (see CONDORCET §2). Many voting systems in wide use avoid this problem by various random or controlled devices that sometimes bias outcomes. For example, legislatures commonly consider amendments to a piece of legislation one at a time. An amendment that wins a majority vote is added to the legislation; one that loses is dropped from further consideration. In the end, there is a decisive vote for or against the amended legislation, which is pitted only against the *status quo* and not against other possible variants. The *status quo* is therefore given privileged status because, if there are cyclic preferences over the *status quo*, the final piece of legislation and the same legislation with an alternative amendment, the *status quo* wins by virtue of not having to face the alternative. One might wish to say this is the best of plausible resolutions. But one cannot say any such thing with coherent meaning – that is the point of Arrow's theorem. Our presumptive notions of 'the best' are vacuous in this context.

5 Voting and democracy

Game theory and Arrow's theorem were very slow to enter debates in political philosophy and political science. Downs' economic theory of democracy, however, immediately became the starting point for most subsequent debate. Again, there are two main results of the theory. First, candidates, needing a majority of votes for election in two-party contests, would have to locate themselves near the middle of the range of popular preferences. Hence, in a catch phrase of 1950s US politics, the Democratic and Republican parties put up candidates who were close twins, Tweedledum and Tweedledee. This tendency inspired a massive literature on so-called responsible parties, a literature that argued that parties must emphasize their differences and must take strong positions. Downs' theory virtually killed that literature.

Second, the more crucial deduction was that voters have little interest in actually voting if the act of voting has real costs associated with it. If there are millions of voters and victory goes to the majority candidate, then my vote has little or no chance of affecting the outcome. Indeed, if elections were as close as a single vote, they would sometimes be voided and repeated simply because the counting of votes could not be accurate enough to yield a determinate outcome. But, in any case, genuinely close elections are extremely rare above the level of minor local offices. Hence, to weigh the value of my vote to me in affecting policies in my interest, I must discount my vote by the exceedingly low probability that it could matter. Its discounted value to me must be vanishingly small. This is the benefit side of my vote. Now consider the cost side. Suppose it takes a couple of hours out of my hard day for me to vote. This cost is not vanishingly small. On balance, it is therefore unlikely to be in my interest to vote.

Suppose voting costs could be reduced to nearly nothing. Would it then be in my interest to vote? Only if I can be reasonably sure that I know enough to vote in my interest. Karl Marx (1852) thought the French peasants of the mid nineteenth century did not know enough and that they harmed themselves with their votes. US air-traffic controllers might soon have concluded that their voting for Ronald Reagan in the presidential election of 1980 was stupid (he fired them when they went on strike). Some people know enough to judge the relation between elections and their interests accurately. Most people may have too limited knowledge and theory to judge that relation. If they are to vote rationally, therefore, they must acquire information. Typically it is costly to acquire information, and often the costs of relevant information for voting would far outweigh the discounted value to oneself of one's vote.

It is sometimes suggested that we can overcome the logic of Downs' rational voter by imposing sanctions on those who do not register and vote. But this is not a full solution – indeed, it might have perverse effects on elections because it may typically still not be rational for a voter to learn enough to make intelligent decisions. A requirement that people register and vote could be monitored relatively easily and cheaply. A requirement that they be prepared to vote intelligently could probably not be monitored without becoming massively intrusive. Moreover, the collective benefit from having everyone be well informed might be reckoned less than the collective costs of the required study. Hence, it seems reasonable to conclude from the rational-choice theory of citizen participation in democratic politics that democracy faces severe constraints and that much of philosophical democratic theory is outside the realm of real-world politics (see DEMOCRACY §4).

Suppose the logic of the economic theory of democracy is correct and that the assumptions about individual capacities are roughly right. If ought implies can, it follows that most so-called democracies should not be the democracies of the democratic theorists. Hence, a theory that is about possibilities and that is based on simple assumptions of the weights of costs and benefits to individuals and groups yields fundamentally normative conclusions.

Unfortunately for simple, stable visions of democracy, there is a third major result in the economic theory. One of the obvious simplifications of Downs' theory was his assumption of a one-dimensional policy space along which voters are arrayed from left to right. If the world is more complex than this and there are two or more policy dimensions that do not collapse into each other, the results can be chaotic. Slight changes in location of candidates can entail radical changes in election outcomes. If candidates attempt to respond to each other, the winning policy position can be anywhere in the entire policy space. Every outcome is democratic – or none is.

6 The logic of collective action

Suppose we are members of a group who share an interest in having some policy adopted but that every one of us would rather be a free-rider on the efforts of others than contribute toward providing our common benefit. If we all attempt to be free-riders, we will none of us enjoy any collective provision. It is in the group's interest to have the good provided even at its costs; but it is in no individual member's interest to provide any part of the good. The economist Olson has called this the logic of collective action (Olson 1965; Hardin 1982).

It is commonly said that doing something is in *our* interest and therefore in the interest of *each* of us. Indeed, this is the central argument of distressingly many newspaper editorials on such problems as pollution, urban blight, war and peace, and ending poverty. The argument is wrong. Before Olson, the standard theory of groups fallaciously supposed that what was in a group's interest was in the individual group member's interest. In one very influential theory, it was supposed that, in order to predict policy, we need only do a vector sum of the force of all the relevant groups, with each group's vector length given by its number of members and its vector direction given by its policy preference. Hence, if there was a very large group with an interest, there would be policies adopted to satisfy much of the interest. This was a fallacy of composition – perhaps best called a fallacy of decomposition – but it is hard to read the error directly in traditional group theories. Anyone who stated the matter articulately would plausibly have recognized its illogic.

The full panoply of possible groups includes, in Olson's terms, privileged, latent, and intermediate groups. In a privileged group at least one person values provision (of some good that benefits a group) enough to pay fully for its provision – and therefore we might expect provision. In a latent group, every member has the preferences of the free-rider and therefore we expect no provision. In an intermediate group, every member has the preferences of a free-rider but the group is small enough and close enough for interactions that might produce greater cooperativeness and therefore, possibly, provision. In political contexts it is often seemingly true that small, well organized industrial groups can succeed in acting collectively for their political benefit, as in lobbying for privileged legislation or helping the relevant candidate win election. At the same time, the large group of much, even most, of the public is latent and fails to organize well enough to lobby for or against legislation of interest to the group or to support relevant candidates. The rational-choice theory of group behaviour therefore suggests that government outputs will be biased in favour of concentrated interests and against wider public interests.

7 Further applications

The rational choice theory of democracy suggests that we should want to understand the relation of individuals to the institutions in which they have roles and with which they have to deal in social life. If an institution is comprised of individuals in some structure of roles, then we should be able to give an individual-choice theory of institutions. This has long been a major programme, as in the work of Smith, Bentham, and Mill. It is the reputed next project for bringing Rawls' theory of justice to bear in a real world. It is a frequent worry in jurisprudence and in the resurgence of constitutional thinking after the extraordinary events of 1989 in eastern Europe. And it is a major industry in organization theory in economics, psychology, and sociology.

The modern public-choice programme in economics is often attributed to the judgment of Joseph Schumpeter that standard economics applies as well to public as to market choice because it is essentially a theory of the effects of incentives (see SCHUMPETER, J.A. §3). One could generalize Schumpeter's recommendation that we apply standard economic theory to government as well as the market and recommend that we apply it to all of human behaviour. This would be audacious, perhaps, and possibly misguided. But the recommendation has been taken up by many theorists, who have applied rational choice, game theory, standard price theory, equilibrium analysis, and other devices of economics to family relations, altruism, racism, crime and sex (Becker 1976), to theory of knowledge, norms, and group identification (Hardin 1995), to the rise of states (Levi 1988), to agency, religion, addiction, war, trust, and whatever ails or moves us. Rational choice theorists commonly treat motivation from anything other than interest or personal preference as an anomaly to be explained, not only for actions in the province of public choice but, increasingly, for action across the broad spectrum of life. In return, economics has benefited from feedback from social concerns in the information economics of Stigler and others, theories of cognitive limits associated with Herbert Simon and concerns with fairness and distributive justice.

8 Intentional behaviour

In rational-choice explanations there are commonly generalizations that do not turn on asking every relevant person in a decision-making group why they act as they do. Instead of asking, the rational choice theorist simply assumes a pattern of interests or of costs and benefits. Sometimes, it would be wrong to take people's claims for their actions and motives as compelling. Twentieth-century social and psychological thought has been receptive to the supposition that much of our motivation is not recognized by us. From Freudian psychology to mass movement sociology to economic and rational choice, it is commonly assumed that people act intelligibly but with poor understanding of their own actions.

Much of twentieth-century psychology and, to a lesser degree, other social sciences, was a reaction to this assumption. Since it has often been assumed that we cannot know what is going on in other people's minds many psychologists and others have insisted on considering only behavioural data, not putative mental events. In face of the Freudian vision of mental processes, one can imagine that behaviourism was appealing to many psychologists in the early twentieth century. Behaviourism has sometimes been identified with logical positivism in the philosophy of science, but the identification fails for those who are otherwise positivist but are none the less interested in mental explanations that involve such notions as rationality, instinct, or moral commitment (see BEHAVIOURISM IN THE SOCIAL SCIENCES; BEHAVIOURISM, METHODOLOGICAL AND SCIENTIFIC).

The social sciences in which behaviourism has had the least impact are economics and anthropology. There may be many reasons for the relative paucity of behaviourist theory in economics. First, and arguably the most important, is that much of economics hardly makes sense as anything but a theory of choice, and much of choice hardly makes sense as anything but mental events. Ideally, a chooser should be able to justify a choice, as must a theorist. In a similar way, rational choice explanations of behaviour cannot be merely behaviourist. They involve attributions of rationality to actors. Second, it may be true that for many problems of interest, economists can safely enough assume that behaviour is fully indicative of preference – typically a mental notion – because some preferences are virtually objective or universal. Much of what is called behavioural economics is about such quasi-objective or universal preferences. For such objects of choice, behaviour is a good proxy for mental preference. Third, economists may often find that attempting to ground theory in strictly behavioural assumptions, as in revealed preference theory, is less fruitful than relying on mental notions.

The grievous problem for explanations based on the mental notion of rationality is that, if the theory is worth doing, the explanations go beyond what the actors themselves understand of their actions. For example, when Olson presented his logic of collective action, when Flood and Dresher presented the game that is now known as the prisoner's dilemma, when Hume and, much later, David Lewis presented their theory of coordination, and when economists argue for rational expectations, they all go beyond what the subjects of their theories have recognized. If all these things had already been understood by the actors, there would be little point of doing social science, which would lead not to discoveries but merely to catalogues. Yet it seems absurd to say that people who cannot or who have never yet had occasion to understand these theories are not acting according to them. Indeed, the astonishing thing about these and many other theories is that they make sense of commonplace behaviour in *de facto* mental terms – for example, by showing that the behaviour is rational.

9 Value theory

There are several problems at the foundations of rational choice. In addition to the problem of indeterminacy discussed above (§§3–4), there are problems in the underlying value theory. I will discuss only two categories of these: variant rationality assumptions and the relations between interests, consumptions, and utility.

First consider variant rationality assumptions. When game theory first appeared it was praised as brilliant but damned as irrelevant by economists in the vanguard of the ordinal revolution. They held two counts against the von Neumann-Morgenstern utility theory. It was interpersonally comparable and it was cardinal. Decades earlier, Pareto had argued forcefully against interpersonal comparability and most economists agreed with him in principle (although they also regularly did cost–benefit analyses that violated Pareto's view). With cardinality, payoffs could be added or combined in probabilistic functions. As discussed above (§4), cardinality violated evident sense – and, perhaps worse, it was unnecessary for economic theory.

Immediately, von Neumann responded to economist critics with his proof that anyone with complete ordinal preferences, including preferences over probabilistic combinations of outcomes, has preferences that are cardinal up to a linear transformation. This claim mirrors an earlier claim by the philosopher Frank Ramsey (1931). Around this view there has risen a vast body of theory about individual decision making under uncertainty and the Bayesian theory of decision. Even a rejected value theory seems to bear fruit. Still, the ordinalists may note that Bayesian or von Neumann value theory is seemingly restricted to contexts in which there are no major effects of substitutability and complementarity among the elements of an outcome.

In the longer run, game theory and the utility theory of von Neumann and Morgenstern were seen as separable, and ordinal games are widely used. For much of game theory even in the original tradition, the use of cardinal, interpersonally additive preferences may often be little more than a mathematical crutch to ease the way to a solution.

Now turn to interests, consumptions and utility. Satisfying interests enables consumptions, which produce or have utility. Interest is therefore merely proxy for the utility of eventual consumption. If we include all consumptions now and into the future in our choice function, as in Arrow's fully determined states of affairs, interest drops out. Note that interests and consumptions trade off against each other. It is against my interest to consume an opera tonight; but if I could not do such things, I would have little interest in living. It is the very point of my interest in various resources that they enable me to consume and enjoy.

To do rational choice theory with interests instead of the full complexity of consumptions superficially might seem to simplify the account. But the costs of consumptions need not be linearly related to their utility or the enjoyment of them. Using interests as a proxy for consumptions is therefore potentially misleading, although it might often be relatively sensible. The cardinal value theory of von Neumann and Thomas Bayes might apply to simply conceived interests but not so readily to a panoply of consumptions. To put this the other way around, focusing on interests allows us to think cardinally; focusing on consumptions virtually forces us to think ordinally.

10 Preliminary conclusions

Two conclusions from the rational choice theory and one conclusion about it seem evident. The first two of these are the grievous problem of indeterminacy and the difficulties of democratic theory. Indeterminacy seems to inhere in the problems we face: aggregation from individual to social choice. It is a large part of the cause of difficulty for democratic theory. If certain choice procedures were not indeterminate, we could plausibly reach strong conclusions about the relation of democratic procedures to best outcomes. But if the category of 'best outcomes' is conceptually empty or meaningless, we may have no ground from which to judge particular procedures.

The third conclusion is that rational choice theory has been remarkably successful in the sense of systematically addressing and, in its own terms, resolving an enormous number and variety of issues. This success poses an interesting question in the philosophy of the social sciences. Why has rational choice theory been so successful? A first answer might be that it is like utilitarianism and economics – it has a programmatic approach that is broadly applicable and it has a highly refined value theory. Or rather it has several highly refined value theories, each developed over centuries by many of the best social theorists. Even in the central disagreement over the relevance of ordinal and cardinal utility theories, there is programmatic and sustained focusing of the issues.

A second answer might look instead to the standard against which the theory seems to be successful: the relative success of other approaches to social theory. Social theory often seems to be faddish – we go from one perspective to another. In many other branches of knowledge there may also be fads, but these seem to be about marginal matters while the core continues. A summary account of twentieth-century social theory would be dizzying in its rollicking from one fad to another. Many of these have gone to the core of one or more of the social

sciences. A striking feature of many of the faddish movements is that they are critical, they are not constructive. Once its criticism is adequately made, each critical theory goes into decline. If rational choice theory is to go into decline, it will not be from exhaustion but from failure, which can probably happen only if a more successful approach is invented. Rational choice theory has had the advantage of centuries of coherent development that cannot soon be matched by a new approach.

See also: DECISION AND GAME THEORY; SOCIAL CHOICE; SOCIAL NORMS

References and further reading

* Aristotle (384–322 BC) *Politics*, trans. E. Barker, New York: Oxford University Press, 1958. (Sprawling normative account of politics in the polis.)
* Arrow, K.J. (1951) *Social Choice and Individual Values*, New Haven, CT: Yale University Press, 2nd edn, 1963. (The master's presentation, with responses to early criticisms and extensions.)
* —— (1983) *Collected Papers*, vol. 1: *Social Choice and Justice*, Cambridge, MA: Harvard University Press. (Many important papers on varied topics plus a note, pp. 1–4, on Arrow's meeting with his fundamental impossibility theorem.)
* Axelrod, R. (1984) *The Evolution of Cooperation*, New York: Basic Books. (On the possibility of establishing cooperative relations in dyadic interactions in large societies.)
  Barry, B. (1989) *Theories of Justice*, Berkeley, CA: University of California Press. (Includes a game theoretic account of theories of distributive justice.)
  Barry, B. and Hardin, R. (eds) (1982) *Rational Man and Irrational Society?*, Beverly Hills, CA: Sage Publications. (A collection of papers on the Arrow, collective action, and voting problems with commentaries and an extensive bibliography.)
* Becker, G.S. (1976) *The Economic Approach to Human Behavior*, Chicago, IL: University of Chicago Press. (Collection of essays on broad range of issues. Sometimes technically demanding.)
  Breton, A. and Wintrobe, R. (1982) *The Logic of Bureaucratic Conduct: An Economic Analysis of Competition, Exchange, and Efficiency in Private and Public Organizations*, Cambridge: Cambridge University Press. (A rational choice account with a strong emphasis on the sources and role of trust, esp. pp. 4–6, 61–88.)
  Buchanan, J.M. and Tullock, G. (1962) *The Calculus of Consent: Logical Foundations of Constitutional Democracy*, Ann Arbor, MI: University of Mich-

igan Press. (Rational choice applied to government institutions and to democratic theory.)

Coleman, J.S. (1990) *Foundations of Social Theory*, Cambridge, MA: Harvard University Press. (Occasionally technically demanding sociological theory as grounded in principles of individual rational choice.)

* Downs, A. (1957) *An Economic Theory of Democracy*, New York: Harper & Row. (On the problem of collective action that undercuts individual incentive to vote and on the incentives of parties and their candidates to adopt policies that produce winning votes.)

Eatwell, J., Milgate, M. and Newman, P. (1987) *The New Palgrave: A Dictionary of Economics*, 4 vols, London: Macmillan. (Includes many articles, often technical, on Arrow's problem, game theory, utility theory, and economists who have made major contributions to these issues, with extensive bibliographies.)

Elster, J. (1989) *The Cement of Society: A Study of Social Order*, Cambridge: Cambridge University Press. (On collective action, norms, and bargaining, all with some scepticism toward rational choice.)

Gauthier, D. (1986) *Morals by Agreement*, Oxford: Oxford University Press. (A rational choice theory of morality.)

* Hardin, R. (1982) *Collective Action*, Baltimore, MD: Johns Hopkins University Press. (Game theoretic treatment of Prisoner's Dilemma, collective action, and convention with substantial bibliography.)

—— (1988) *Morality within the Limits of Reason*, Chicago, IL: University of Chicago Press. (Applies game theoretic reasoning to utilitarian moral theory, esp. in chapter 2, and presents an account of institutional utilitarianism in chapters 3 and 4.)

* —— (1995) *One for All: The Logic of Group Conflict*, Princeton, NJ: Princeton University Press. (Rational choice account of individual identification with a group or community and of group conflict.)

* Hicks, J.R. and Allen, R.G.D. (1934) 'A Reconstruction of the Theory of Value, Parts I and II', *Economica*, new series, 1: 52–76, 196–219. (The original presentation of now standard ordinal utility theory.)

* Hobbes, T. (1651) *Leviathan*, C.B. Macpherson (ed.), Harmondsworth: Penguin, 1968. (Chapters 13–15 present a tight, bare-bones theory of government.)

* Hume, D. (1739–40) *A Treatise of Human Nature*, L.A. Selby-Bigge and P.H. Nidditch (eds), Oxford: Oxford University Press, 3rd edn, 1978. (Book 3, part 2, §2 gives the original statement of convention as a resolution of a coordination interaction.)

Kavka, G. (1986) *Hobbesian Moral and Political Theory*, Princeton, NJ: Princeton University Press. (A game theoretic analysis.)

* Levi, M. (1988) *Of Rule and Revenue*, Berkeley, CA: University of California Press. (Discusses how revenue policies drive state evolution.)

* Lewis, D.K. (1969) *Convention*, Cambridge, MA: Harvard University Press. (Defines convention as the spontaneous resolution of a repeated coordination interaction.)

Luce, R.D. and Raiffa, H. (1957) *Games and Decisions*, New York: Wiley. (Dated but still valuable general survey of fundamental issues in game theory. Often quite demanding.)

* Marx, K. (1852) *The 18th Brumaire of Louis Bonaparte*, New York: World Publishing, 1963. (Discusses the rational choice problems of French peasants, pp. 118–35.)

Mueller, D. (1989) *Public Choice II*, 2nd edn, Cambridge: Cambridge University Press. (An economist's textbook survey of rational choice theory with an extensive bibliography.)

Neumann, J. von and Morgenstern, O. (1944) *Theory of Games and Economic Behavior*, Princeton, NJ: Princeton University Press, 3rd edn, 1953. (Original presentation of game theory; mathematical but generally not difficult. Later editions include, as an appendix, von Neumann's proof that complete ordinal preferences yield cardinal preferences.)

* Olson, M., Jr (1965) *The Logic of Collective Action*, Cambridge, MA: Harvard University Press. (Original presentation of the problem of collective action.)

* Plato (*c.*428–*c.*348 BC) *The Republic*, trans. G.M.A. Grube, Indianapolis, IN: Hackett, 1974. (Hierarchical theory of the state. Glaucon argues for freeriding in book 2.)

* Ramsey, F.P. (1931) 'Truth and Probability', in F.P. Ramsey, *Foundations: Essays in Philosophy, Logic, Mathematics and Economics*, London: Routledge & Kegan Paul, expanded edn 1978, 58–100. (Philosopher's development of Baysian decision theory.)

* Rapoport, A. and Guyer, M. (1966) 'A Taxonomy of 2X2 Games', *General Systems* 11: 203–14. (Presentation of the seventy-eight strategically nonequivalent 2X2 games.)

Rawls, J. (1971) *A Theory of Justice*, Cambridge, MA: Harvard University Press. (Most important modern work on distributive justice.)

Samuelson, P. (1974) 'Complementarity: An Essay on the 40th Anniversary of the Hicks-Allen Revolution in Demand Theory', *Journal of Economic Literature* 12: 1255–89. (Account of development of ordinal utility theory from early beginnings with an extensive bibliography.)

* Schelling, T. (1960) *The Strategy of Conflict*, Cam-

bridge, MA: Harvard University Press, esp. pp. 83–118, 267–90. (Splendid, very accessible discussion of the real-world relevance of game theory.)

* Sen, A.K. (1970) *Collective Choice and Social Welfare*, San Francisco, CA: Holden-Day. (Survey of the Arrow problem and related issues with an extensive but dated bibliography; has alternating verbal and technical chapters, the former quite accessible, the latter often difficult. The presentation in §4 uses Sen's notation.)

Skyrms, B. (1990) *The Dynamics of Rational Decision*, Cambridge, MA: Harvard University Press. (Attempts to bring Bayesian theory and classical game theory together. Useful bibliography.)

* Smith, A. (1759) *The Theory of Moral Sentiments*, D.D. Raphael and A.L. Macfie (eds), Oxford: Oxford University Press, 1976. (Presents an impartial spectator theory of morality.)

* —— (1776) *An Inquiry into the Nature and Causes of the Wealth of Nations*, R.H. Campbell and A.S. Skinner (eds), Oxford: Oxford University Press, 1976. (Economic theory that severly undercut virtue theory.)

Taylor, M. (1987) *The Possibility of Cooperation*, Cambridge: Cambridge University Press. (Rational-choice vision of anarchy, collective action, and the state with discussions of Hobbes and other classical thinkers.)

RUSSELL HARDIN

RATIONALISM

Rationalism is the view that reason, as opposed to, say, sense experience, divine revelation or reliance on institutional authority, plays a dominant role in our attempt to gain knowledge. Different forms of rationalism are distinguished by different conceptions of reason and its role as a source of knowledge, by different descriptions of the alternatives to which reason is opposed, by different accounts of the nature of knowledge, and by different choices of the subject matter, for example, ethics, physics, mathematics, metaphysics, relative to which reason is viewed as the major source of knowledge. The common application of the term 'rationalist' can say very little about what two philosophers have in common.

Suppose we mean by reason our intellectual abilities in general, including sense experience. To employ reason is to use our individual intellectual abilities to seek evidence for and against potential beliefs. To fail to employ reason is to form beliefs on the basis of such non-rational processes as blind faith, guessing or unthinking obedience to institutional authority. Suppose too that we conceive of knowledge as true, warranted belief, where warrant requires that a belief be beyond a reasonable doubt though not beyond the slightest doubt. Here, then, is a version of rationalism: reason is the major source of knowledge in the rational sciences. This is a weak version of rationalism which simply asserts that our individual intellectual abilities, as opposed to blind faith and so on, are the major source of knowledge in the natural sciences. It is clearly not very controversial and is widely accepted.

Suppose, however, we take reason to be a distinct faculty of knowledge distinguished from sense experience in particular. To employ reason is to grasp self-evident truths or to deduce additional conclusions from them. Suppose we conceive of knowledge as true, warranted belief, where warrant now requires that a belief be beyond even the slightest doubt. Let us also extend our attention to metaphysics and issues such as the existence of God, human free will and immortality. Here is a much stronger version of rationalism which asserts that the intellectual grasp of self-evident truths and the deduction of ones that are not self-evident is the major source of true beliefs warranted beyond even the slightest doubt in the natural sciences and metaphysics. Clearly it is highly controversial and not very widely accepted.

The term 'rationalism' has been used to cover a range of views. Scholars of the Enlightenment generally have in mind something like the first example – a general confidence in the powers of the human intellect, in opposition to faith and blind acceptance of institutional authority, as a source of knowledge – when they refer to the rationalist spirit of the period and the work of such philosophers as Voltaire. Most frequently, the term 'rationalism' is used to refer to views, like the second one above, which introduce reason as a distinct faculty of knowledge in contrast to sense experience. Rationalism is then opposed to empiricism, the view that sense experience provides the primary basis for knowledge. This entry concentrates on this still very general form of rationalism, reserving the term 'rationalism' for it alone.

1　**Continental Rationalism and British Empiricism**
2　**Innate ideas**
3–4　**Intuition and demonstration**

1　**Continental Rationalism and British Empiricism**

The rationalist–empiricist division has traditionally played a major role in our understanding of the history of philosophy, particularly that of the modern period of the seventeenth and eighteenth centuries leading up to Kant. The major philosophers of the period are regularly grouped into two sets of three: DESCARTES, SPINOZA and LEIBNIZ are the Continental Rationalists, in opposition to LOCKE, BERKELEY and HUME, the British Empiricists. Philosophy department curricula, textbooks, scholarly anthologies and conference programmes have all incorporated the classification for years and are likely to continue to do so.

None the less, scholars have at least five basic reservations about its accuracy. First, a close study of the three Continental Rationalists, especially their work in the natural sciences, reveals they had a great respect for the role played by experience in scientific knowledge. Second, the British Empiricists, especially Locke and Berkeley, stress, in one way or another, the importance of reason as a source of knowledge; consider Locke's account of a priori knowledge and Berkeley's acceptance of innate ideas. Third, the division encourages us to overlook important areas of agreement between philosophers on different sides of the divide, such as the views of Descartes and Locke on the nature, though not the source, of our ideas. Fourth, the division encourages us to associate irrelevant differences in language and geography – those who do not write in English against those who do; the Continent against England and Scotland – with a supposed difference in philosophical views. Fifth, the grouping of the six philosophers in epistemological terms encourages an incorrect grouping of them in metaphysical ones. The Continental Rationalists are mistakenly seen as attempting to apply their reason-centred epistemology to pursue a common metaphysical programme, each trying to improve on the efforts of those before him; the British Empiricists are incorrectly seen as gradually rejecting those metaphysical claims, with each again consciously trying to improve on the efforts of predecessors. Defenders of the Continental Rationalists–British Empiricists distinction generally admit many, if not all, of these shortcomings but treat them as minor anomalies.

This entry does not attempt to resolve the controversy or even to lay out each side's supporting evidence from the works of the philosophers involved. A few points deserve mention, however. First, in evaluating whether it is appropriate to classify these philosophers in this way, we must consider what purpose the classification is supposed to serve. The classification might well be acceptable for pedagogical purposes at a certain level of instruction in the history of philosophy in order to initiate consideration of their views, but not at another level or for other purposes.

Second, attempts to group philosophers into such families as the rationalists and the empiricists are best

understood as attempts to classify them by shared family resemblances. The question to ask, then, is not whether there is a list of interesting claims the acceptance of which is definitive of being a Continental Rationalist and the rejection of which is definitive of being a British Empiricist, so that Descartes, Spinoza and Leibniz may each be classified as a Continental Rationalist just so long as all those claims are accepted, and Locke, Berkeley and Hume may each be classified as a British Empiricist just so long as one rejects them. Critics of the classification sometimes present the issue in this way but few, if any, proponents see it in these terms. We need to consider whether there is an interesting list of claims emphasizing reason as a source of knowledge of the external world, a sufficiently large number of which are accepted by each of Descartes, Spinoza and Leibniz and rejected by each of Locke, Berkeley and Hume, though the first three may not accept all the same claims and the second three may not reject all the same ones.

Third, independently of the historical accuracy of the classification, the terms 'rationalist' and 'empiricist' are associated with some basic claims which define the family resemblance for each category. The rest of this entry focuses on the innate idea thesis and the demonstrative knowledge thesis. Minimal attention will be given to the sometimes complex scholarly questions of whether and why the claims are actually adopted by Descartes, Spinoza and Leibniz, and rejected by Locke, Berkeley and Hume, though some of these philosophers will be cited as examples where the attribution is fairly uncontroversial.

2 Innate ideas

To gain knowledge about the external world we need to think about it and thus we need the appropriate concepts. How do we gain them? One of the central theses associated with rationalism is that at least some of our concepts are not gained from experience but are instead innate. Descartes, for example, divided our ideas into three categories: adventitious ideas, such as our idea of red, are gained through sense experience; fictitious ideas, such as our idea of a hippogriff, are manufactured by us from other ideas we possess; innate ideas, such as our idea of God, of extended matter and of a perfect triangle, are placed in our minds by God at creation.

It is important to distinguish the innate-idea thesis from some other ones. The term 'innate' is often associated with things other than concepts. Some rationalists, for example Descartes and Leibniz, write of innate propositions as well as innate concepts. They seem to have in mind that we have beliefs, in particular true propositions, as part of our initial mental make-up rather than as a result of experience; the propositions are presumably constructed of innate concepts. Whether and just how such true beliefs might constitute knowledge is not clear. Some philosophers have also claimed that we have innate knowledge, though it is not always clear whether this is 'knowing that' or 'knowing how' (see INNATE KNOWLEDGE; NATIVISM). It has been maintained by contemporary philosophers, for example, that learning a natural language requires a knowledge of grammar which is 'innate' in that learners could not have inferred it from their experience. The focus in this section is solely on the thesis that some of our concepts are innate (see CONCEPTS). The central rationalist positions on knowledge are considered in the next.

Some defences of the innate idea thesis are based in claims peculiar to particular philosophers. Leibniz's view that all substances are causally isolated monads implies a general rejection of sense experience as a source of any ideas and so supports the claim that all ideas are innate. ('It is a bad habit we have of thinking as though our minds receive certain messengers, as it were, or as if they had doors or windows. We have in our minds all those forms for all periods of time because the mind at every moment expresses all its future thoughts and already thinks confusedly of all that of which it will ever think distinctly,' Leibniz 1685: Section 26.) The most common defence of the innate-idea thesis, however, takes the form of admitting experience as a source of ideas but then arguing that some concepts could not have been gained directly or indirectly from experience; that these concepts are innate is then offered as the best explanation of their existence. That the concepts could not have been gained from experience is generally defended in one or both of two ways. First, the content of the concepts is beyond what we directly gain in experience as well as anything we could gain by performing the available mental operations on what experience provides. Second, our possession of the concepts is presupposed by our ability to employ the very empirical concepts that might be thought to provide a basis for them in experience.

Consider, for example, Descartes' defence of the claim that our concept of God, as an infinitely perfect being, is innate. This concept is not directly gained in experience, as a particular sensation of pain might be. Its content is far beyond any we could ever construct by applying available mental operations to what experience provides. Our empirical concepts include the concept of a finitely knowledgeable, powerful and good being; we can even construct the concept of a finitely but *very* knowledgeable, powerful and good

being, but we cannot move on to the concept of an infinite one. We cannot, for example, gain the idea of infinite perfection by simply negating our concept of finite perfection. ('I must not think that, just as my conceptions of rest and darkness are arrived at by negating movement and light, so my perception of the infinite is arrived at not by means of a true idea but merely by negating the finite' (Descartes 1641: Third Meditation).)Moreover, we must possess the concept of infinite perfection in order to employ the concept of finite perfection gained from experience. ('For how could I understand that... I was not wholly perfect, unless there were in me some idea of a more perfect being which enabled me to recognize my own defects by comparison' (Descartes 1641: Third Meditation).)

Objections to the standard arguments for the innate-idea thesis generally take two forms. The less radical line of objection, exemplified by Locke, is to argue that the supposedly innate concepts are indeed gained by sense experience and to offer an account of the mental processes involved. The more radical critique, exemplified by Hume, is to agree that the supposedly innate concept could not be gained by experience and to argue that we do not in fact have the concept as understood by the innate-idea theorists in the first place; a failure to find an experiential source for a supposed concept should not lead to us to the innate idea thesis but to a critical examination of our concepts themselves (see LOCKE, J. §2; HUME, D. §2).

Besides defending their theory, innate-idea theorists face the task of explaining exactly what it is for an idea to be innate. Innate concepts are in the mind from creation but are not present in consciousness until we actually conceive them. How are these concepts 'in the mind' prior to being present to consciousness? How too can any of them, prior to being present to consciousness, serve as a precondition of our employing other ideas gained from experience?

Finally, innate idea theorists often assume that the ways in which we conceive of the external world using our innate concepts actually correspond to how it is, and they thus face the question of what justification, if any, there can be for this assumption. A frequent strategy is to find a non-deceptive source for our innate concepts – be it a non-deceiving God, as for Descartes, or a non-sensory experience by the soul prior to its union with the body, as in Plato's doctrine of recollection (see PLATO §§11–14).

3 Intuition and demonstration

A second thesis generally identified with rationalism is the claim that reason alone can provide us with at least some knowledge of the external world through our intuition of self-evident propositions and our subsequent deduction of additional information from those starting points. Intuition is understood as a kind of intellectual 'grasping' by which we comprehend a proposition in such a way as to recognize its truth; in a demonstration we reason through a series of intuited premises to a logically entailed conclusion. Propositions known by intuition are self-evident, while those known by demonstration are evidenced by the intuited premises; in either case the knowledge is a priori, independent of evidence gained from sense experience (see A PRIORI).

It is essential to the rationalist account of knowledge by intuition and demonstration that the knowledge gained in this way is knowledge of the external world. Many empiricists, indeed even Hume, are willing to admit that an intellectual grasping of our concepts can provide us with a priori knowledge, but they limit that knowledge to knowledge of the relations of our ideas: when we intuit that that two plus three make five, we gain knowledge about how the concepts involved are related, but we do not learn anything about the world as it exists independently of our mind.

The rationalist commitment to intuitive and demonstrative knowledge of the external world is not necessarily a commitment to have such knowledge of propositions affirming the existence of particular concrete objects. It may take the form of a commitment to have such knowledge of abstract objects which none the less exist, and are as they are, independently of our thought. Descartes, for example, claimed that while he had no knowledge of the existence of any particular triangle, he none the less had an intuitive and demonstrative knowledge of propositions about the properties of a triangle and that the content of his knowledge was a 'determinate nature' independent of his mind.

The rationalist account of knowledge under consideration involves a version of foundationalism. It endorses the view that we know some propositions independently of their being evidenced for us by any other propositions; these basic propositions provide us with the evidential base for additional knowledge (see FOUNDATIONALISM). Rationalists generally adopt a strong view about the strength of our intuitive and demonstrative knowledge. When we intuit a proposition we know it to be true with certainty. Our intuitive grasp places it beyond even the slightest doubt. This extreme degree of epistemic justification can only be transferred to other beliefs by deductive inference which precludes the possibility of the conclusion being false while the premise is true. Even our ability to gain additional knowledge by demonstration is

limited. Once our demonstrations get so lengthy as to rely on memory, the possibility of a mistake in recall weakens our degree of justification. (On some interpretations of Descartes' epistemology, a major aim of his epistemic programme is to remove the limitation that this reliance on memory placed on the certainty of our demonstrations.)

Rationalism is sometimes identified with the view that every science has the same deductive structure in which knowledge moves from the intuition of self-evident axioms to the demonstration of theorems. It is thus seen as endorsing a single method for all sciences and as asserting the priority of the knower over the known: as we move from one subject to another – from mathematics to physics – the subject matter changes, but so long as the nature of the knower's mind remains constant the same method of intuition and demonstration may be used in each case. The Continental Rationalists were all impressed by the rigour and certainty associated with the deductive method of mathematics and they stressed the importance of meeting such standards in other areas. So too, Descartes and Leibniz, like Galileo, were quite concerned with the application of mathematics to the natural sciences. Yet, it is clearly a mistake to attribute to them individually, or to rationalism generally, the view that all science proceeds by intuition and demonstration. Even though Descartes, for example, attempted to use intuition and demonstration to establish some basic laws of nature (that whatever is in motion continues in motion in so far as it can, that all motion is rectilinear, and so on), he admitted that we need to use experiments to move beyond very basic principles.

Just as the innate idea thesis is partially motivated by the belief that sense experience can not provide some concepts we clearly have, so too the rationalist belief in knowledge of the external world by intuition and demonstration is often at least partly motivated by the conviction that sense experience falls short of providing us with knowledge in some areas. Our claims in mathematics, metaphysics and ethics, for example, seem to outstrip the content of our sense experiences. We experience lots of imperfect triangles but no perfect ones, we may experience the effects of God's creative powers but not God, and we experience how things are but not how they ought to be. So how can we have knowledge in such areas? Intuition and demonstration provide an alternative account; one that becomes increasingly attractive when the other main option seems to be scepticism (see SCEPTICISM).

The rationalist appeal to intuition and deduction is also at times motivated by a demanding conception of knowledge that seems to require more than experience can provide. Descartes' conception of knowledge as permanent supported his requirement that it be absolutely certain which in turn placed it beyond sense experience. Whenever we form beliefs on the basis of sense experience, the possibility that our senses are deceiving us keeps us from absolute certainty (see CERTAINTY; DOUBT; FALLIBILISM). Here again, intuition and demonstration provide an attractive alternative, especially given their apparently successful use in mathematics with its high degree of epistemic justification.

4 Intuition and demonstration (cont.)

Some of the difficulties for the rationalist appeal to intuition and deduction arise out of the reasons for rejecting sense experience. If knowledge requires certainty, what makes our intuitions and subsequent demonstrations certain? We have already noted the worry about the use of memory in extended demonstrations (see MEMORY, EPISTEMOLOGY OF). What makes our intuitions a source of certainty even while we are having them? Could not a deceitful God have us intuit false propositions, just as easily as we might deceive ourselves in a dream? Do not such epistemic possibilities as a deceitful God give us at least a slight reason to doubt our intuition that two plus three make five, preventing it from being absolutely certain?

One rationalist strategy for responding to this difficulty is to offer an argument for the veridicality of our intuitions. Once we establish that our intuitions are non-deceptive, we can gain certainty by them, and we can establish the universal veridicality of our intuitions while we cannot establish the universal veridicality of our sense experiences. Yet, the argument for the truth of our intuitions will only meet the sceptical challenge if it establishes its conclusion with certainty, and the demand for certainty thus requires the rationalists to rely on intuition to support the premises of their argument for the veridicality of intuition. They thus fall into an apparently vicious form of circular reasoning (sometimes called the 'Cartesian Circle' in recognition of Descartes' struggle with the problem). A second strategy is to claim that all our intuitions are certain, even when we have not gained certain knowledge that the faculty never deceives. Whenever we intuit a proposition, we are certain of it; such hypotheses as that of a deceiving God do not give us a reason to doubt it, even if they are epistemic possibilities for us. This strategy risks being *ad hoc*: why should we accept intuition as an automatic source of certainty?

Appeals to intuition carry a related methodological problem. Let us assume that real intuitions are always true and always certain. How do we distinguish between real intuitions and only apparent ones, and how do we get ourselves in a position to have the former but not the latter? People have taken themselves to 'just see' the truth of all sorts of contradictory claims; they cannot all be correct (see PYRRHONISM). Descartes' method of doubt is intended to help us gain a psychological state where we will have real intuitions, but his own extravagant list of 'intuited' propositions in the course of following his method illustrates its ineffectiveness.

Another difficulty for the rationalist reliance on intuition and demonstration takes us back to the view that some claims about the external world fall beyond the range of our sense experience but within that of intuition and demonstration. The rationalist must argue that the contents of intellectual intuition are independent of us in such a way that, as in Descartes' theory of simple natures, our knowledge of how they are related is not just knowledge about the structure of our own thoughts. Rationalism, while primarily an epistemological position, thus involves its proponents in at least some metaphysical commitments (see INTROSPECTION, EPISTEMOLOGY OF).

According to many contemporary epistemologists, rationalism, like such related theories as foundationalism, is dead. It surely is beset with problems in both the innate idea thesis and the demonstrative knowledge thesis. Yet, a complete evaluation of rationalism must involve more than an examination of these two central points. It must also include an overall examination of the nature and extent of our knowledge and the nature and extent of our experience. Rationalism, in one form or another, will remain attractive so long as we find that we have knowledge of the external world which appears to go beyond what experience can provide.

See also: EMPIRICISM; ENLIGHTENMENT, CONTINENTAL

References and further reading

Chisholm, R. (1966) *Theory of Knowledge*, Englewood Cliffs, NJ: Prentice Hall, 3rd edn, 1989. (General introduction to epistemology containing a detailed analysis of the rationalist view that reason alone can provide knowledge of the external world.)

* Descartes, R. (1641) *Meditations on First Philosophy*, in *The Philosophical Writings of Descartes*, vol. 2, trans J. Cottingham, R. Stoothoff and D. Murdoch, Cambridge: Cambridge University Press, 1984. (Along with the *Discourse on Method* (1637) and *The Principles of Philosophy* (1644), this work provides a fine introduction to Descartes' thought.)

Kenny, A. (1986) *Rationalism, Empiricism and Idealism*, Oxford: Oxford University Press. (Several articles in this collection question the correctness of the traditional distinction between the Continental Rationalists and the British Empiricists with regard to specific comparisons between philosophers.)

* Leibniz, G.W. (1686) *Discourse on Metaphysics, Correspondence with Arnauld, Monadology*, trans. G. Montgomery, La Salle, IL: Open Court, 1973. (These three works provide a fine introduction to Leibniz.)

Loeb, L. (1981) *From Descartes to Hume: Continental Metaphysics and the Development of Modern Philosophy*, Ithaca, NY: Cornell University Press. (One of the best general challenges to the traditional distinction between the Continental Rationalists and the British Empiricists.)

Malebranche, N. (1688) *Dialogue on Metaphysics and on Religion*, trans. W. Doney, New York: Abaris, 1980. (The works of Malebranche represent an interesting development on the Cartesian tradition. This work offers the best introduction to his views.)

Quine, W.V. (1951) 'Two Dogmas of Empiricism', in *From a Logical Point of View*, Cambridge, MA: Harvard University Press, 1953. (The rationalism–empiricism dispute over intuitive knowledge of the external world is sometimes conceived as involving a distinction between analytic and synthetic truths: the rationalists' commitment to such knowledge is understood as a commitment to synthetic a priori knowledge; the empiricists' rejection of such knowledge is understood as a denial of synthetic a priori knowledge; this piece contains an influential critique of the analytic–synthetic distinction.)

Rorty, R. (1979) *Philosophy and the Mirror of Nature*, Princeton, NJ: Princeton University Press. (Attack on epistemic foundationalism and more generally on epistemology as done in a tradition based in Descartes on the rationalist side, and Locke on the empiricist side.)

Spinoza, B. de (1677) *The Ethics, in The Collected Works of Spinoza*, vol. 1, ed. and trans. E. Curley, Princeton, NJ: Princeton University Press, 1985. (The best introduction to Spinoza's philosophy.)

Stich, S. (1975) *Innate Ideas*, Berkeley, CA: University of California Press. (A discussion of innate ideas and related topics.)

PETER J. MARKIE

RATIONALITY AND CULTURAL RELATIVISM

Under what conditions may we judge the practices or beliefs of another culture to be rationally deficient? Is it possible that cultures can differ so radically as to embody different and even incommensurable modes of reasoning? Are norms of rationality culturally relative, or are there culture-independent norms of rationality that can be used to judge the beliefs and practices of all human cultures?

In order to be in a position to make judgments about the rationality of another culture, we must first understand it. Understanding a very different culture itself raises philosophical difficulties. How do we acquire the initial translation of the language of the culture? Can we use our categories to understand the social practices of another culture, for instance, our categories of science, magic and religion? Or would the mapping of our categories on to the practices of culturally distant societies yield a distorted picture of how they construct social practices and institutions?

A lively debate has revolved around these questions. Part of the debate involves clarifying the difficult concepts of rationality and relativism. What sort of judgments of rationality are appropriate? Judgments about how agents' reasons relate to their actions? Judgments about how well agents' actions and social practices conform to the norms of their culture? Or judgments about the norms of rationality of cultures as such? Can relativism be given a coherent formulation that preserves the apparent disagreements for which it is meant to account?

Can there be incommensurable cultures, such that one culture could not understand the other? According to Donald Davidson's theory of interpretation, radical translation requires the use of a principle of charity that in effect rules out the possibility of incommensurable cultures. If this result is accepted, then a strong form of cultural relativism concerning norms of rationality is also ruled out.

Davidson's theory, some argue, does not eliminate the possibility of attributing irrational beliefs and practices to agents in other cultures, and thus still leaves some room for debate about how to understand and evaluate such beliefs and practices. Three positions frame the debate. The intellectualist position holds that judgments of rationality are in order across cultures. The symbolist and functionalist positions, here taken together, try to avoid such judgments by attributing functions or symbolic meanings to cultural practices that are generally not understood as such by the agents. The fideist position, wary of too easily being ethno-

centric, assumes a more relativist stance with regard to cross-cultural judgments of rationality.

1 Background to the debate
2 Rationality
3 Relativism
4 Interpretation and translation
5 The debate and its errors
6 The intellectualist position
7 The functionalist and symbolist positions
8 The fideist position

1 Background to the debate

Interest in questions of cross-cultural understanding and judgment can be found among the Greeks, in Herodotus for instance. At the beginning of the modern period, Giambattista Vico in *The New Science* (1744) in effect raised many of these issues in his attempt to develop a new science of human history (see VICO, G. §§4–6). The modern preoccupation with these questions, however, began only with the development of anthropology in the late nineteenth century. Evidence began to accumulate of apparently irrational beliefs and associated practices in diverse cultures. How was this evidence to be assessed and explained? The founders of anthropology, including Sir Edward Tylor, Sir James Frazer, Bronislaw Malinowski and Lucien Levy-Bruhl, reacting to the encounter between European and non-European civilizations and noting the diversity of cultural practices and beliefs, debated these issues largely in terms of the now suspect categories of 'civilized' versus 'savage' or 'primitive' societies, or of 'pre-logical' and 'pre-scientific' versus 'logical' and 'scientific' cultures. While largely rejecting this terminology, a later generation of philosophers and anthropologists carried on a debate about essentially the same issues, with a particularly intense period of discussion occurring in the 1960s, 1970s and into the 1980s. Some argued that the best account of the apparent irrationalities found in other cultures was in terms of a theory of cultural relativism. Others rejected relativism of any sort (see ANTHROPOLOGY, PHILOSOPHY OF §1). Rather than reaching a resolution, the debate about rationality and cultural relativism continues and draws closer to parallel debates in the history and philosophy of science and epistemology generally.

The participants in this debate use a number of difficult concepts and not always in the same way. Clarification of the concepts of rationality and relativism is required before the various positions in the debate can be presented.

2 Rationality

A wide variety of things can be said to be rational or irrational. In the context of the debate about the rationality of distant cultures, the most important are beliefs, individual actions and cultural practices. Rationality, in general, has to do with how people acquire beliefs from evidence and connect reasons to actions. At the most basic level, rationality concerns the standards for truth, consistency and deductive and inductive inference. The concept of rationality is standardly used in a normative sense, that is, one that conveys commendation or endorsement. To call an action rational is to certify that there is good reason to do the action or to judge that the action was brought about in a suitably correct way. Likewise, to describe an action as irrational is to indicate that there is not good reason to do the action or to judge that there was some error or fault in how the action came about and to criticize it (or rather, the agent performing the action) in that regard (see RATIONALITY OF BELIEF; PRACTICAL REASON AND ETHICS; REASONS FOR BELIEF).

Focusing on the rationality of action, we can usefully distinguish three levels where judgments of rationality may be made. The first level regards individual actions. According to the model of rational action suggested by Davidson, a rational action is one that stands in a certain relation to the agent's beliefs and desires, that is, their reasons for acting. For example, if a person has a desire, all things considered, to bring about goal X, and believes, all things considered, that action A is the most effective means to goal X, then the person acts rationally if they bring about action A for those reasons. This formulation simplifies things considerably. In some instances, it may be rational to choose an action that is suitably effective, but not the most effective one. Thus, there may be more than one action that would be rational, given an agent's reasons. In this case, the concept of rationality would limit but not uniquely determine the action to be chosen.

On this level, an agent would be acting irrationally if they did not choose the action that was the most effective (or at least a suitably effective) means to goal X; that is, if the agent's reasons were not good reasons for the action chosen. This failure might occur for a number of complicated reasons, most of which involve some sort of failure of critical thinking or consistency. While capturing the standard notion of instrumental rationality, this model, in this context, is meant to apply to more than what might be thought of as narrowly instrumental action. Thus, actions oriented towards successful communication or successful participation in a ritual can be understood in terms of the model with suitably adjusted notions of effective means towards those goals.

The second level where judgments of rational action may be appropriate involves questions about the agent's reasons (beliefs and desires), in particular, questions about how the agent acquired the reasons. Is the belief appropriately related to the available evidence? Does the evidence come from a reliable source? Is the evidence reliable such that the agent has good reasons for the action undertaken?

One way to understand what makes the relationships of evidence to beliefs and of reasons to action good or appropriate is to ask: (1) whether a belief was acquired by an agent in a way that conformed to the epistemic norms of the agent's culture, and (2) whether the agent's reasons (beliefs and desires) provide good reasons for the action according to the canons of reasoning of the agent's culture. Putting the questions in this way allows space for what seems to be a form of cultural relativism. If different cultures have different and conflicting epistemic norms and/or canons of reasoning, then a belief might be rationally acquired according to the norms of one culture but not according to those of another, or provide good reasons for an action in one culture but not in another. For instance, if a certain way of reading omens is considered a reliable means of evidence gathering in one culture but not in another, then reading omens to acquire evidence for beliefs and acting on those beliefs would be considered rational by the standards of the first but not the second culture. Likewise, inductive counter-evidence might be assigned different weight in different cultures, affecting what is considered a good reason for action. Thus, at this level, judgments of the rationality or irrationality of an agent's action can be regarded as intersubjective judgments relative to the norms of the agent's culture.

The move from the second level, thus construed, to the third is readily apparent. Can one make judgments of the rationality or irrationality of the norms of a culture? If we can make such judgments, then the action of an agent might on analysis turn out to be rational on the first two levels but still be irrational from the point of view of the third. For instance, if omen reading is judged not to be epistemically rational, then omen reading, and actions based on omen reading, could still be judged irrational even if they took place in a culture that endorsed the practice. (It should be noted that an action that was judged irrational on the second level because it was not properly related to the norms of the agent's culture in a way that the culture would regard as rational, might still turn out to be rational on the third level if the agent's individual norms were judged rational.)

Given this analysis of rationality, we can restate some of the questions central to the debate. From what point of view might we make such third level judgments of the rationality or irrationality of a culture's norms? Is the only available position that of the norms of rationality of our culture? If so, should we restrict ourselves to second level judgments only? If we make third level judgments, are we really judging the other culture to be irrational, or only different? And what would we mean by such a judgment of cultural irrationality? What sort of mistake would a culture so judged be making?

3 Relativism

Relativism is a notoriously difficult concept. The form of relativism of primary concern here is cultural relativism with regard to norms of rationality. What such a relativist theory typically holds is that (1) norms of rationality differ across cultures; that (2) judgments of the rationality of a given action are relative to the governing norms of the local particular culture; such that (3) two people, depending on their cultural locations, might disagree about the rationality of the same action, one judging it to be rational and the other irrational, and both judgments would be equally correct.

One implication of this form of cultural relativism is that it denies the existence of a universal or 'objective' system of rationality that could be used to judge the rationality of actions in all cultures. In the terms used above, relativism denies that there is a culture-independent position from which to make third level judgments about the rationality of a culture's norms. The most we can say is that an action seems irrational to us, by the norms of our culture, even while recognizing that by the norms of the culture in which is occurs, the action may be rational.

There is an ongoing debate about whether relativism can be stated coherently in a way that saves the phenomenon for which it is meant to account. The relativist, at least in certain versions of the position, seems to want to endorse as correct propositions that are apparently logically incompatible. On the other hand, where claims are clearly relativized to particular theories or cultures, thus eliminating the appearance of logical inconsistency, it is not clear that genuine disagreement remains. Some maintain that if disagreement is resolved by relativizing apparently competing claims, then part of the phenomenon that relativism is meant to analyse is dissolved rather than accounted for. Also, part of the point of making normative judgments, especially critical ones, is often to offer people reasons for changing their behaviour.

If judgments of rationality were thoroughly relativized to particular cultures, however, one could no longer recommend reasons in this way. The critical judgment would seemingly be simply out of place.

Despite the problems that some see with relativism, the position has enough intuitive appeal to have some purchase on us. In matters of taste, for instance, we seem ready to concede that two cultures could have very different standards such that one culture could judge an object beautiful, the other judge it ugly, and the best analysis be that each judgment is correct according to the standards of that culture. It is this sort of analysis that raises the problem of relativism concerning judgments of rationality across cultures.

4 Interpretation and translation

In order to make judgments of the rationality or irrationality of actions in other cultures, one must first understand the actions involved. If one is dealing with distant cultures where the native language is poorly understood or even not understood at all, problems of understanding are obvious, although the same problems occur much closer to home.

Could there be a culture so distant from ours, using norms of rationality so different from ours, that we could not successfully interpret it? In such a case, our culture and the other culture could be said to be incommensurable.

Davidson (1984), building on Quine's work on the radical indeterminacy of translation, argues that there could not be incommensurable human cultures (see RADICAL TRANSLATION AND RADICAL INTERPRETATION). When confronted with the task of translating the language, hitherto unknown, of another culture, we should, counsels Davidson, proceed according to a principle of charity such that most of the beliefs of the people whose language is being translated come out true (see CHARITY, PRINCIPLE OF §4). This would require, among other things, that the speakers of the translated language reason at least roughly as we do.

Some have argued that Davidson's theory of radical translation leads to what may be called a problem of the attribution of irrationality, for it might seem that according to the principle of charity, it is improper to attribute any appreciable irrationality to those whose language is being translated. When faced with what seem provisionally to be irrational beliefs and practices, one should question the validity of the translation. If this is what Davidson's theory implies, then it is ruling out irrationality in effect on purely conceptual grounds. This result would seem unduly strong to many, especially in light of the accumulated evidence from social anthropology. Others, however, feel that this interpretation of Davidson is itself uncharitable and that Davidson does not mean to deny the possibility of translating beliefs that may seem irrational to us.

We can assume for present purposes that the principle of charity might be amended into what is sometimes called the principle of humanity. The directive of the principle of humanity is to attempt to make the beliefs and practices of those translated intelligible rather than true. In certain circumstances at least, irrational beliefs could be intelligible, if within the context we could understand how the speakers could acquire them, but still not true. Practices informed by intelligible but false beliefs would thus be intelligible in light of the beliefs. Accordingly, Davidson's approach thus understood would not rule out the attribution of some kinds of irrationality to those being translated. However, it would rule out translating a language of another culture as involving a radically different system of rationality, that is, different standards of truth and deductive and inductive inference. Attributing to a culture different standards on this basic level would make many of their beliefs and practices appear massively irrational to us, and such massive irrationality could no longer be made intelligible. Thus a strong form of cultural relativism would not be countenanced by a Davidsonian.

5 The debate and its errors

The debate over rationality and cultural relativism has focused on several related questions. The first asks whether we should apply the categories we (in the West) use to divide up cultural practices (for example, science, magic, or religion) to other, significantly different cultures? Do our categories enhance or distort our understanding of others? This question raises the subsidiary question of what has been called the pragmatics of belief: What are people using certain beliefs to do? Are they using the beliefs to explain part of the world, or are they using them to express participation in some aspect of their social reality or religious rituals, or something else again? The other question central to the debate asks when, if at all, and from what standpoint, can we judge the rationality of the beliefs, actions and practices in other cultures?

A variety of positions have been taken in answer to these questions. Before turning to the positions, however, we should note three especially contentious moves that often divide the field. The first is what many would consider a form of ethnocentrism; it holds in effect that our (Western) norms are objectively correct and may be used to assess the rationality of any and all cultures. Many find this position to be culturally insensitive and lacking sound epistemological grounding.

A second view that many reject as inadequate is the opposite of ethnocentrism, namely, a strong relativism. Apart from the various logical and epistemological problems of which relativism is accused, this view appears to many to paralyse judgment, preventing us from making the kinds of judgments about the rationality or irrationality of other cultures that seem intuitively in place.

The third contentious move in effect severs the link between agents' reasons and actions by explaining the action in terms not immediately available to the agents. This is done in an effort to avoid making others seem manifestly irrational. For many, however, this move merely displaces the problem by reducing away the rationality of other cultures.

6 The intellectualist position

Horton classified the main positions in the debate in a way that will be largely adopted here. The first position is the intellectualist. Among the participants in the early phases of the debate, this position can be associated with Tylor and Frazer. Although their views differed somewhat, Tylor and Frazer sought to explain apparently irrational beliefs in terms of their purpose. For both, the general purpose of belief systems, as they understood them, is to explain, predict and control the world. On this view, systems of beliefs informing practices such as magic, witchcraft and primitive religion are seen as primitive theories, similar to Western science but for the most part inferior to it, proto-sciences one might say.

Horton (1993) has developed the most sophisticated rendering of the neo-intellectualist position. In his analysis of traditional West African belief systems, Horton finds norms of reasoning and attempts at theory building that are similar to those at work in Western science. African systems often display considerable sophistication and explanatory prowess. Still, for the most part, their explanations are not as successful as those of our sciences. However, in certain instances, Horton notes, African systems provide arguably superior accounts of some phenomena.

By and large, the intellectualist position imports our categories such as science and magic and puts them to work in analysing other cultures. In addition, the position allows for cross-cultural judgments of rationality. Thus, in instances where the norms of a culture appear to countenance the seeming disregard of relevant evidence, or where certain inductive inferences are not drawn upon, for example, the non-efficacy of a rain dance, we can make the third

level judgment that the norms are rationally deficient compared to our own.

The intellectualist takes the belief and desire statements of the members of other cultures literally as translated. The beliefs and desires are then construed as the agents' reasons for action and a corresponding attempt is made to understand how the agents act in their cultural context. Beliefs that, when translated, appear wrong or irrational are judged false and seen as perhaps acquired in an irrational way.

7 The functionalist and symbolist positions

The second position to be examined does not approach the problem in this way. According to this position, beliefs that appear initially to be false or irrational or that appear not to offer good reasons for the associated action are not subject to rational evaluation. Rather, an alternative interpretation is offered that makes the actions rational, even if it means decoupling the actions from the reasons for it offered by the agents. Actions or practices are understood as rational in terms of their function, according to one alternative of this position, or in terms of their symbolic meaning, according to the other. Beliefs are either not considered as part of the explanation of the action or practice, or taken as expressive but not descriptive, as having a predominantly symbolic meaning. In either case, beliefs are not subject to assessment in terms of their literal meaning.

The two variants of this position, the functionalist and the symbolist, should not be entirely conflated, of course. For a functionalist, such as Radcliffe-Brown, the problem of rationality does not come up in the standard form discussed in this entry. The functionalist focuses on explaining the existence and persistence of certain social practices in terms of the effects they produce, understood against a theory of necessary social functions (see FUNCTIONALISM IN SOCIAL SCIENCE §2). Questions of the rationality of belief as informing the practices is at best of secondary interest.

In contrast, symbolists, such as Beattie, and with some qualifications, Sperber, are primarily concerned with understanding beliefs. They typically see human actions as having an expressive dimension. Beliefs that taken literally as translated seem to be indicative propositions, and problematically rational as such, symbolists interpret as having essentially symbolic meaning. They argue that this dimension of meaning can only be fully recovered by understanding the symbolic or expressive content of the ritual or practice in which the belief is embedded. Once the symbolic meanings of the belief and practice are recovered, there are no further issues of rational evaluation to be raised.

Many see a basic problem with the functionalist and symbolist approaches. In neither view is it clear how to connect the agents' reasons to their actions. Rational agents act for reasons, expressed in terms of their beliefs and desires as they understand them. They do not typically act to satisfy the function assigned to a practice by the functionalist. Nor, for the most part, do they understand their beliefs as primarily expressive or symbolic utterances. However, reasons as understood by the agents themselves do not enter into the functionalist's or symbolist's explanation of the rationality of the action. Thus, agents do not appear as rational actors on the first level noted above, where actions are brought about for and in light of reasons. Practices may be understood as rational, given these approaches, but we lose our grip on the agents as rational actors.

8 The fideist position

The third position, the fideist, is most associated with Winch and influenced by Wittgenstein's remarks on Frazer's *The Golden Bough* (Wittgenstein 1979). Wittgenstein criticized Frazer in rather harsh terms for interpreting early magical and religious accounts as if they were putting forth theories to explain the world, and then judging them to be inferior, mistaken accounts at best. It is nonsense, Wittgenstein argued, to treat, as he thought Frazer did, magical accounts as a kind of false physics. Rather, we should attempt to appreciate their ritualistic and spiritual meanings as part of a culture. According to the fideist, the intellectualist imposes Western categories on other cultures too uncritically and reaches judgments of irrationality too easily. What is crucial for the fideist is attempting to understand, to as great an extent as possible, beliefs and practices as they are understood from within the other culture, or to use the Wittgensteinian term, the other form of life. Unlike the symbolist, the fideist does not want to impose a level of symbolic meaning on beliefs that is not accessible to the speakers themselves. We are to assume that agents act for reasons that they understand, but we have to be very careful about how we establish the meanings of propositions stating the agents' beliefs and desires.

Furthermore, the fideist is reluctant to make judgments of rationality or irrationality. Just as we have to understand meaning from the point of view of the agents, so we have to understand their concepts and norms of rationality. Those are the only norms that can properly be used to evaluate their beliefs and practices. Even such basic logical concepts as consistency and contradiction cannot be assumed to be held in common with us and we should not impose our concepts on others who may have very different ones. Thus, the fideist position seems to endorse a form of cultural relativism.

The fideist, then, would argue that we must stop at level two judgments of rationality, that is, judgments of the rationality of actions relative to the norms of the culture in which they occur. For the fideist, level three judgments are either incoherent, wrong, or pointless. They are incoherent if it is thought that there can be culture-independent judgments. For the fideist, all judgments are relative to a culture or form of life; we simply have to give up the idea of 'the view from nowhere', to use Nagel's phrase. Third level judgments are wrong if, thinking we are being neutral, we merely impose our norms on others. Norms and concepts cannot, according to the fideist, be exported beyond the boundaries of the form of life in which they function and have meaning. And such judgments are pointless if all we are doing is using the norms of the agents' own culture. In that case, there is no distinction between level two and level three judgments, for the norms of rationality of a culture are of course going to be judged rational from within that culture.

In so far as fideists endorse some form of relativism, they will have to contend with the various criticisms aimed at relativism in general. For instance, it is not clear that the fideists' relativism is consistent with a Davidsonian approach to interpretation. Fideists have served the important function of warning the intellectualist, and in a different way, the symbolist against uncritical use of our categories to understand others. If other cultures do have very different cultural norms and practices, we have to attempt to understand them in their own terms. It may be, for instance, that a very different culture has nothing quite analogous to Western science, or for that matter, to the practice of Western religion. What may seem initially like a rather irrational form of science might be better understood in very different terms. In cases where practices seem all but incommensurable, judgments of comparative rationality may be out of place.

Still, despite the objections of some fideists, judgments of rationality may have their place even here. What is needed is a way of comparing across cultures practices that initially seem to resist being placed in the same categories. Some have suggested that a properly developed theory of human interests might afford such common ground. Furthermore, to the degree that one is convinced by Davidson's theory of interpretation, one cannot allow for different basic norms of rationality. It would follow, then, that there are norms of rationality with which one can judge the beliefs and practices of others (and of ourselves), once the beliefs and practices are properly understood.

See also: EPISTEMIC RELATIVISM; MORAL RELATIVISM; RELATIVISM; SOCIAL RELATIVISM

References and further reading

* Davidson, D. (1984) *Truth and Interpretation*, Oxford: Oxford University Press. (A collection including most of Davidson's important essays on radical interpretation.)

Hollis, M. and Lukes, S. (eds) (1982) *Rationality and Relativism*, Cambridge, MA: MIT Press. (An important collection including papers by Hollis, Taylor, Sperber, Horton and Lukes. Good bibliography.)

* Horton, R. (1993) *Patterns of Thought in Africa and the West*, Cambridge: Cambridge University Press. (A collection of Horton's papers stating his neo-intellectualist position. Good bibliography.)

Skorupski, J. (1976) *Symbol and Theory: A Philosophical Study of Theories of Religion in Social Anthropology*, Cambridge: Cambridge University Press. (An interesting philosophical discussion centring on the intellectualist position.)

Tambiah, S.J. (1990) *Magic, Science, Religion, and the Scope of Rationality*, Cambridge: Cambridge University Press. (An interesting survey of the debate by a leading anthropologist. Useful bibliography.)

* Vico, G.B. (1744) *The New Science of Giambattista Vico*, revised trans. of 3rd edn, T.G. Bergin and M.H. Fisch, Ithica, NY and London: Cornell University Press, 1968. (Vico's attempt to develop a new science of human history.)

Wilson, B.R. (ed.) (1970) *Rationality*, Oxford: Blackwell. (An important collection of papers from the debate, mostly from the 1960s. Contributors include: Winch, MacIntyre, Horton, Beattie, Lukes and Hollis.)

Winch, P. (1958) *The Idea of a Social Science and its Relation to Philosophy*, London: Routledge & Kegan Paul. (The classic statement of Winch's views.)

* Wittgenstein, L. (1979) *Remarks on Frazer's 'Golden Bough'*, ed. R. Rhees, trans. A.C. Miles and R. Rhees, Atlantic Heights, NJ: Humanities Press. (Wittgenstein's criticism of Fraser.)

LAWRENCE H. SIMON

RATIONALITY OF BELIEF

Humans, claimed Aristotle, are rational animals. However, recent psychological studies purport to show that people systematically deviate from canons of logic, probability theory, decision theory and statistics. Interpretations of these studies differ about the nature of the errors: on some views, there are no real errors at all; on others, subjects are distracted from applying the proper formal rules by, for example, the influence of conversational expectations. A common suggestion is that the reasoning subjects display is nearly optimal, once we take account of our severe cognitive limits in realistic circumstances or in our evolutionary history.

These diverse views reveal two opposed tendencies in constructing a theory of rationality. One favours the formal rules which, if violated in real life, could have serious consequences. The other holds that people's actual practice provides the only standard. A popular model, incorporating both tendencies, holds that those principles or norms are justified that yield the best balance between our reasoning intuitions and the demands of theory or system.

1 Empirical studies of reasoning
2 Interpretation

1 Empirical studies of reasoning

Reasoning is central to the acquisition and improvement of our beliefs. If a belief is recognized as sustained through defective reasoning, it is not rational to maintain the belief. Consequently, a good deal of interest attends recent psychological studies (for example, Wason and Johnson-Laird 1972; Kahneman *et al.* 1982) that purport to show serious and systematic deviation from canons of logic, probability theory, decision theory and statistics. Although these canons do not function as theories of what *should* be believed (Harman 1986), they do provide serious *constraints* on reasoning and inference. Because these recent studies seem to show people violating these constraints, they are troubling and important.

Four of the best known of these studies are: the 'selection task', which investigates deductive reasoning with conditionals; the 'conjunction problem', the 'base rate' problem, and the 'preference reversal' problem, all of which involve features of probabilistic reasoning. (The reader is advised to try each one, before reading the results.)

The selection task. Four cards are placed in front of each subject.

$$E \quad K \quad 4 \quad 7$$

The subjects know that on one side of each card is a

letter and on the other a number. The following rule is presented: if a card has a vowel on one side, then it has an even number on the other. The task is to pick out just those cards that need to be turned over in order to determine whether the rule is true or false. Almost all subjects turn over the E card, and many the 4. More crucially, few turn over the 7 card (Wason and Johson-Laird 1972).

Conjunction. Subjects are offered the following personality sketch:

> Linda is 31 years old, single, outspoken and very bright. She majored in philosophy. As a student, she was deeply concerned with issues of discrimination and social justice, and also participated in anti-nuclear demonstrations.

They are then asked to rate the probability of the following statements:

(1) Linda is a psychiatric social worker.

(2) Linda is a bank clerk.

(3) Linda is an insurance salesperson.

(4) Linda is a bank clerk and is active in the feminist movement.

The main finding in the conjunction study is that 'Linda is a bank clerk and a feminist' is judged more probable than that 'Linda is a bank clerk' (Tversky and Kahneman 1983).

Base rates. Subjects are told that a cab has been involved in a hit-and-run accident at night. They are given the following data:

(1) 85% of the cabs in the city are green and 15% are blue.

(2) A witness identified the cab as blue.

(3) The court tested the reliability of the witness under the same circumstances that existed on the night of the accident and concluded that the witness correctly identified each one of the two colours 80% of the time and failed 20% of the time.

What is the probability that the cab involved in the accident was blue rather than green? Subjects largely assign the probability 0.8; that is, their judgment is based wholly on the reliability of the witness. But if the base rates (0.85 and 0.15) are used as prior probabilities, then the answer is 0.41 (Kahneman *et al.* 1982: 156–7).

Preference reversal. Subjects are offered two gambles (at different times):

(a) Choose between

gamble 1. £500,000 with probability 1; and

gamble 2. £2,500,000 with probability 0.1, £500,000 with probability 0.89.

(b) Choose between

gamble 3. £500,000 with probability 0.11; and

gamble 4. £2,500,000 with probability 0.1.

The study is cited as of 'preference reversal' because it is generally found that subjects prefer gamble 1 to gamble 2 in situation (a), while they prefer gamble 4 to gamble 3 in situation (b). Yet, one should prefer gamble 1 to 2 if and only if one prefers gamble 3 to 4, since they are equivalent. (See essays by Allais, Ellsberg, Kahneman and Tversky, and Savage in Moser (1990).)

In each case the violation is of a simple and familiar formal principle. In the selection task, a statement of the form 'If *p*, then *q*' is incompatible with one of the form '*p* and not-*q*' (for example, a vowel on one side, and an odd number on the other). In the conjunction task, the probability that someone satisfies a *conjunction* of properties (being both a feminist and a bank clerk) cannot be greater than the probability of their satisfying one of the conjuncts *separately* (being a bank clerk alone).

The correct way to calculate the probability in the base-rate case is by using Bayes' theorem, which says that the posterior (or, conditional) probability of a hypothesis *h* (the cab was blue) given evidence *e* (the witness saw a blue cab) is determined by how likely *e* and *h* are to be true simultaneously and by the probability of *e* being true at all. But subjects ignore the likely colour of the cab and judge only on the basis of the reliability of the witness, disregarding the probability of the cab's actually being blue. In the 'preference reversal' case, one is assigning a utility to an outcome in one gamble that is inconsistent with the utility assigned to it in the other (see RATIONAL CHOICE THEORY; RATIONALITY, PRACTICAL).

2 Interpretation

Some hold that we should not treat these results as deserving a uniform account. In particular, dispute has focused on whether in the base-rate studies, subjects' answers are, in fact, incorrect. For example, in an article that generated much controversy, Cohen (1981) argued that the Bayesian analysis using the base rates as prior probabilities would be correct, if the question concerned repeated or long-run samplings. But subjects reasonably interpret their task as the determination of the colour in this particular accident. From the information given, only the reliability of the witness is relevant to that determination. The base rates would also be relevant if they were not mere frequencies, but reflected causal factors involved in an accident, for example, if the 85–15 difference was a difference in respective accident rates. In fact, when the base rates have a natural causal explanation, it was found that subjects *do* incorporate them into their answers (Kahneman *et al.* 1982: essays 8, 10).

Among further interpretational questions, four deserve mention.

(1) The task may generate conversational implicatures that lead subjects away from the target formal representation (see Grice 1989; Sperber *et al.* 1995; IMPLICATURE). For example, the statement 'Linda is a bank clerk' in the context would appear conversationally to implicate that Linda is a bank clerk *and not a feminist*. Experimenters try to control for conversational inferences. For example, instead of offering 'Linda is a bank clerk' they might offer the alternative of 'Linda is a bank clerk, who may or may not be a feminist'. Even so, it remains questionable whether habitual conversational expectations are so easily set aside (Adler 1991).

(2) Some variant presentations yield different patterns of response. In the base-rate or conjunction studies, presentation in a *frequency* format (citing *number* of cases, rather than *ratios* or *probabilities*) leads to many more subjects responding according to a straightforward probabilistic analysis (Girgerenzer 1991).

(3) In the case of preference reversal, alternative understandings may be legitimate so that, for example, the achievement of certainty is itself valued, rather than being treated as just another degree of belief (Schick 1991).

(4) Most dramatically, at least in the selection task, when the problem is posed for a natural setting, there is enormous improvement. In one set-up there is an array of envelopes (face down and sealed; face down and unsealed; face up with a 50 lire stamp on it; face up with a 40 lire stamp on it) and the rule 'If a letter is sealed, then it has a 50 lire stamp on it'. Once subjects are presented with a realistic model, they readily recognize that the envelope with the 40 lire stamp on it (the analogue of the '7' card) must be turned over. What is crucial is the realism of the conditional, not its familiarity (Wason and Johnson-Laird 1972). In particular, striking improvement occurs when the conditional captures a connection or rule of practices involving permissions or obligations. Recent work treats such rules as modularized, products of social exchange important in our hunter-gatherer evolutionary history (Cosmides and Tooby 1996).

These interpretational questions suggest that subjects orient the problems to common expectations or habits, rather than representing their task as clearly calling on formal principles. What is it about the task or set-up that directs subjects away from representing the problem so that the familiar formal rules are seen as applicable?

The guiding thought in most answers is that these results actually reveal near optimal reasoning, given the demands on us for cognitive economy in the environments in which our reasoning capacities evolved. If subjects formed the logically equivalent contrapositive of the above rule, they would turn over the '7' card: since 'If that bird is a raven then it is black' is equivalent to 'If that bird is non-black then it is a non-raven'. But normally the contrapositive of an ordinary conditional as it involves the complement class of a natural class is not itself a natural class: black ravens form a natural class, but non-black, non-ravens do not. We do not ordinarily test whether ravens are black by examining non-black things (for example, pennies) to see whether they are non-ravens (see CONFIRMATION THEORY; HEMPEL, C.G. §2).

Nor do we ordinarily reason with the kind of *static* information characteristic of these studies. Although other studies do reveal a tendency towards belief perseverance or conservatism (Kahneman *et al.* 1982: essays 9, 15, 25), in general dynamic or continuous reasoning is much less investigated. Where feedback from the environment is expected, the cost of initial errors may be compensated for, so long as we remain open to subsequent modification or correction (Hogarth 1986).

In reflecting on what these studies reveal about the rationality of our beliefs, there are two opposed tendencies. One says that to violate or bypass the formal rules is to commit errors, whose analogues in real life can be serious. The other says that the formal rules, and the experts in the corresponding formal systems, are not authoritative on how it is reasonable to understand the problems: we are. Suggestive of a 'naturalized epistemology', there is no authority about reason apart from the actual reasoning processes or intuitive judgments of human beings (see NATURALIZED EPISTEMOLOGY).

A popular model, incorporating both tendencies, holds that those principles or norms are justified that yield the best balance between our reasoning intuitions and the demands of theory or system. The model has been especially attractive to those who hold that it is an a priori truth that canons for human reasoning must reveal its rationality, since they are derived from human judgment, at least when suitably idealized (Cohen 1981). However, the balance model supports this strong a priori rational view only if the judgments in these studies do count as telling intuitions and these intuitions are sufficiently systematic. But given the dependence on changes in content, this is disputable. Moreover, formalization allows the generation of powerful theories based on very weak axioms: the resulting gains in systematicity could quickly outweigh any appeals to the kinds of intuitions revealed by these psychological studies.

See also: CONFIRMATION THEORY; INDUCTIVE INFERENCE; RATIONAL BELIEFS; RATIONALITY AND CULTURAL RELATIVISM

References and further reading

* Adler, J.E. (1991) 'An Optimist's Pessimism: Conversation and Conjunction', in E. Eells and T. Maruszewski (eds) *Probability and Rationality*, Amsterdam: Poznan, 251–82. (The first part explores conversational influences on reasoning, especially in regard to the conjunction studies.)
* Cohen, L.J. (1981) 'Can Human Irrationality be Experimentally Demonstrated?', *Behavioral and Brain Sciences* 4: 317–70. (With commentary in this and subsequent issues. A comprehensive critique of the experimental literature, sparking a lively debate. The nonstandard base-rate analysis is defended, via an alternative notion of probability, and an a priori balance argument is offered for the necessity of our competence in reasoning.)
* Cosmides, L. and Tooby, J. (1996) 'Are Humans Good Intuitive Statisticians After All? Rethinking Some Conclusions from the Literature on Judgments under Uncertainty', *Cognition* 58: 1–73. (Building on Cosmides' demonstration of great improvement on the Wason selection task through content corresponding to realistic problems faced by our ancestors, the two authors of this paper propose an evolutionary approach to the mind with particular application to the above studies.)
 Fischhoff, B. (1982) 'For Those Condemned to Study the Past: Heuristics and Biases in Hindsight', repr. in D. Kahneman, P. Slovic and A. Tversky (eds) *Judgment under Uncertainty: Heuristics and Biases*, Cambridge: Cambridge University Press, 335–51. (One of a number of the author's important studies of overconfidence due to knowledge after the fact.)
* Girgerenzer, G. (1991) 'How to Make Cognitive Illusions Disappear: Beyond "Heuristics and Biases"', *European Review of Social Psychology* 2: 83–115. (One of many studies by this author showing how variations emphasizing more extensional or frequentist representations facilitate judgments in line with probabilistic analyses.)
 Goldman, A. (1986) *Epistemology and Cognition*, Cambridge, MA: Harvard University Press. (Critically examines research in cognitive psychology,

generally, through application of an epistemological framework. Forceful commitment to interdisciplinary research. A good deal of part 2 is devoted to the above studies.)
* Grice, H.P. (1989) *Studies in the Way of Words*, Cambridge, MA: Harvard University Press, esp. essays 2, 3, 7, 17. (Classic presentation of influential theory of conversational reasoning and pragmatics. Methodologically fundamental for analytical philosophy and cognitive psychology.)
* Harman, G. (1986) *Change in View*, Cambridge, MA: MIT Press. (An elegant approach to reasoning and change of belief, sensitive to our cognitive limits and the empirical literature, while adding novel ideas.)
* Hogarth, R.M. (1986) 'Beyond Discrete Biases: Functional and Dysfunctional Aspects of Judgmental Heuristics', repr. in H.R. Arkes and K.R. Hammond (eds) *Judgment and Decision Making: An Interdisciplinary Reader*, Cambridge: Cambridge University Press, 680–704. (Argues for the importance of studying reasoning in continuous, not just static, environments.)
 Johnson-Laird, P.N. (1983) *Mental Models*, Cambridge, MA: Harvard University Press. (An original approach to reasoning, especially deductive, turning on our interpretation of formal or syntactic presentations of inferences.)
* Kahneman, D., Slovic, P. and Tversky, A. (eds) (1982) *Judgment under Uncertainty: Heuristics and Biases*, Cambridge: Cambridge University Press. (A basic source book containing most of the research on probabilistic reasoning and many related topics, including overconfidence, risk perception and corrective procedures. Extensive references.)
* Moser, P. (ed.) (1990) *Rationality in Action: Contemporary Approaches*, Cambridge: Cambridge University Press. (Includes some of the most important early and recent essays on the nature and applicability of decision theory and related problems, including the prisoner's dilemma, Newcomb's problem, and the Arrow-Sen results on social choice.)
 Nisbett, R. (1993) *Rules for Reasoning*, Hillsdale, NJ: Erlbaum. (Studies defects in reasoning with attention to both what content in problems facilitates success and what teaching will lead to improvement.)
 Nisbett, R. and Ross, L. (1980) *Human Inference: Strategies and Shortcomings of Social Judgment*, Englewood Cliffs, NJ: Prentice Hall. (Highly readable. A classic and comprehensive account of social judgment research, including work on heuristics, attribution and limits on our self-knowledge. Extensive references.)

Piattelli-Palmarini, M. (1994) *Inevitable Illusions*, New York: Wiley & Sons. (Highly engaging and accessible presentation of most of the problems studied in the above literature on reasoning. Argues that the results display serious, even if natural, failings of reason. Helpful guide to readings.)

Rips, L. (1994) *The Psychology of Deductive Reasoning*, Cambridge, MA: MIT Press. (Comprehensive and sophisticated studies of deductive reasoning, powerfully arguing for a large role for a syntactic, ruled-based account.)

* Schick, F. (1991) *Understanding Action*, Cambridge: Cambridge University Press. (Defends different understandings of the same problem.)

* Sperber, D., Cara, F. and Girotto (1995) 'Relevance Theory Explains the Selection Task', *Cognition* 57: 31–95. (Thorough attempt to explain the 'selection task' in terms of Sperber's influential theory of conversational reasoning.)

Stich, S. (1990) *The Fragmentation of Reason: Preface to a Pragmatic Theory of Cognitive Evaluation*, Cambridge, MA: MIT Press. (Failure of the balance model as an account of these studies, among other reasons, leads to a renouncing of any a priori epistemology in favour of a relativism and pragmatism.)

* Tversky, A. and Kahneman, D. (1983) 'Extensional Versus Intuitive Reasoning: The Conjunction Fallacy Improbability Judgment', *Psychological Review* 90: 293–315. (The conjunction study, with many variations and extensive discussion.)

* Wason, P.C. and Johnson-Laird, P.N. (1972) *Psychology of Reasoning: Structure and Content*, Cambridge, MA: Harvard University Press. (Especially good on studies of deductive reasoning, including the selection task, which one of the authors invented. Out of date now, but still a very helpful presentation of studies on reasoning from the early 1930s until the late 1960s.)

JONATHAN E. ADLER

RATIONALITY, PRACTICAL

Whereas theoretical reason is that form of reason that is authoritative over belief, practical reason is that form of reason that applies, in some way, to action: by either directing it, motivating it, planning it, evaluating it or predicting it. Accounts of practical reason include theories of how we should determine means to the ends we have; how we should define the ends themselves; how we should act given that we have a multiplicity of ends; how requirements of consistency should govern our actions; and how moral considerations should be incorporated in our deliberations about how to act.

Economics has provided, in recent times, what many regard as the most compelling portrait of practical reason, called 'expected utility theory' (hereafter 'EU theory'). On this theory, rational action is that action which yields the highest expected utility, which is calculated by measuring the utility – or the 'goodness' or 'badness' – of the possible outcomes of the action, multiplying the utility of each outcome by the probability that it will occur, and, finally, adding together the results for all the possible outcomes of each action. The action that has the highest expected utility is the rational action. Other technical representations of practical reason have been explored in the branch of social science called 'game theory', which studies 'strategic' situations in which the action that is rational for any agent depends in part on what other agents do.

A theory of practical reason can have one or more of several different goals. If it sets out how human beings actually reason, it functions as a descriptive theory of reasoning. If it sets out a conception of how our reasoning ought to proceed, it functions as a normative theory of reasoning. Theories of reason can also be about actions themselves: if a theory presents a conception of the way our actions should be intelligible or consistent or useful (regardless of the quality of the deliberation that preceded it), it functions as a (normative) theory of behavioural rationale. If it merely presents an account of consistent action that allows us to predict the behaviour of an agent whose previous actions fit this account of consistency, it functions as a descriptive theory.

One might say that whereas theoretical reason is supposed to pursue truth, practical reason is supposed to pursue some sort of good or value in human action. Theories that take rational action to be that which achieves, furthers or maximizes (what is regarded as) good, are consequentialist or teleological theories. Theories that believe rational action must sometimes be understood as action that has an intrinsic value or 'rightness' regardless of how much good it will accomplish or manifest, are non-consequentialist or non-teleological conceptions of reason. If the theory defines reason as that which serves ends defined by something other than itself, it is an instrumental conception. If it allows reason to have a non-instrumental role, itself capable of establishing at least some of our ends of action, it is setting out a non-instrumental conception. Theories of practical reason that recognize the existence of a special moral reasoning procedure tend to represent that procedure as non-instrumental.

Philosophers have disagreed about whether practical reason gives us a way of reasoning prior to choice that can actually motivate us to behave in the way that it directs. Many believe it lacks motivational power, so that it can only give us authoritative directives that must be motivated by something else (for example, by our desires). Finally, the study of practical reason also considers the variety of ways in which one can fall short of being rational; and issues about the nature and possibility of irrational 'weakness of will' have been central to this discussion.

1   **Representations of practical reasoning**
2   **Categories of theories of practical reason**
3   **The interpretation of EU**
4   **The axioms of EU**
5   **Challenges to expected utility theory**
6–7 **Contemporary non-maximizing alternatives to expected utility theory**
8   **Game theory**
9   **Practical reasoning and standards**
10 **Moral reasoning and weakness of will**

1   Representations of practical reasoning

Historical suggestions. There have been many theories of the nature of practical reason over the years, going back to the Ancient Greeks.

Aristotle, although never offering a detailed theory of practical reason, made certain remarks in various of his writings that assimilated practical reasoning to a kind of logical reasoning. One example of (what are called) Aristotelian practical syllogisms appearing in Aristotle's *Nicomachean Ethics* (1147a5) goes as follows:

> Dry food suits any human.
>
> Such-and-such food is dry.
>
> I am human.
>
> This is a bit of such-and-such food.
>
> Therefore, this food suits me.

But why is this syllogism an example of practical reasoning? On the face of it, it is a logical deduction, which is a form of theoretical reasoning. Aristotle can only claim it to be a form of practical reasoning if this logical deduction eventuates in some kind of imperative with authority over action. But in the argument presented above, the conclusion is not in imperative form, and the argument makes no direct connection between the conclusion (that this food suits me) and any actions or intentions to act that I do or should have. Nor does Aristotle tell us how reasoning, operating practically, would produce a connection between the conclusion of this syllogism and my actions or intentions.

In more recent times, philosophers have argued that practical reason produces imperatives of the form 'If you desire *x*, then since *y* is a means to *x*, do *y*'. Immanuel Kant (1785) refers to these as 'hypothetical imperatives' (see KANT, I. §9). So on this view, a hypothetical imperative that is authoritative over action eventuates from practical reasoning, understood as a process by which we work out effective means to the given ends of an agent. To use Aristotle's example, if I were hungry, I would engage in practical reasoning to determine a kind of food that suits me, where my reasoning would (if I had sufficient information about the world) eventuate in a hypothetical imperative of the form 'If I am hungry, I should eat such-and-such dry food'.

But if this is how we understand practical deliberation, it seems little different from theoretical reasoning. On this view, deliberation is primarily a matter of working out causes and effects, and if that is all reason is doing, it appears to be functioning merely theoretically, using the principles of causal reasoning. Indeed, one interpretation of the theory of reason offered by David Hume (1739–40) is that reason only has a theoretical function, and thus is a purely informational faculty, working out relations of ideas and causal connections, with no authority or motivational efficacy with respect to action (see HUME, D.). So interpreted, Hume is saying that there is no such thing as a form of reason that chooses or judges action – but only a form of reason by which we form and judge belief that is (merely) informational with respect to action. However, even among those who accept the validity of both practical and theoretical reason, there has been ongoing dispute about whether these forms of reason are genuinely distinct; even assuming that they are not, there is disagreement: some – including Plato (in the *Republic*) – have held that practical reason derives from theoretical, others (for example, Goldman 1986) have said that the theoretical derives from the practical, and still others (for example, Kant 1785) have claimed that practical reason and theoretical reason are two forms of the same thing.

Expected utility theory: the basic idea. Defenders of the reality of practical reason have attempted to define practical reasoning so as to show how it differs from theoretical reasoning. The most popular of these theories in modern times is highly mathematical, in ways that highlight how complicated and intricate idealized decision making with respect to action might be. Called 'expected utility theory', it was developed by John von Neumann, Oskar Morgenstern and Leonard Savage.

To get a rough idea of what the theory says, imagine yourself in a situation where you do not know for certain what the results of your various alternative courses of action might be. Suppose, for example, that you have the option to buy a lottery ticket: if it is the winning ticket, you will receive a million dollars; if it is not, you will receive nothing and you will lose the money (let us say $10) that it cost you to purchase the ticket. If you do not buy the ticket at all, you will not win, but neither will you lose. So you have a choice between a risky action (buying the ticket) and an action the results of which you know for sure, which avoids both losses and gains. What do you do? The idea behind expected utility theory is that for each possible action available to you, you develop some measure of the 'goodness' or 'badness' of that action by, first, evaluating the goodness or badness of each possible alternative outcome, second, multiplying this value by the probability of that outcome's occurring and, finally, adding together the products for all the possible outcomes of each action.

So, in our lottery example, you proceed, first, by developing a measure of the goodness of winning the lottery prize and the badness of losing the prize and being $10 out of pocket. As we shall discuss in §3 below, there is more than one way that people who have endorsed expected utility theory have thought such a measure should be constructed; the result is standardly referred to as the 'utility' of the outcome. In general, positive, pleasurable or beneficial outcomes of an action are represented using a positive number, whereas negative, costly or painful results are represented with a negative number.

Second, you should multiply each of these numbers by the probability of winning the lottery or losing the lottery. The probability of a sure thing is taken to be 1; in our lottery case, this means that the probability of gaining nothing if you do not buy a ticket is 1. Note also, however, that if you do buy a ticket, it is a sure thing that you will either win the lottery or not win the lottery, meaning that the sum of the probabilities of these mutually exclusive outcomes should equal 1. Hence if p is the probability of winning the lottery, we can express the probability of not winning the lottery as $1-p$ (see PROBABILITY THEORY AND EPISTEMOLOGY).

Third, you should add together the products of the utility and probability numbers to get the 'expected utility of the action of buying the lottery ticket'. So, if the probability of winning the lottery is p, and the probability of not winning the lottery is $1-p$, and if (as economists often do) we identify utility with money, so that the utility of winning the lottery is 1,000,000 and the utility of not winning the lottery is -10, the expected utility (EU) of buying the lottery ticket is

$$(1,000,000)p + (-10)(1-p).$$

After determining the EU of buying the ticket, you then compare it to the expected utility of not buying the ticket. Since you will not win or lose anything if you do not buy the ticket, the utility of the result of this action is 0. That number is multiplied by the probability 1 (since it is a sure thing that you will neither win nor lose if you buy the ticket), making the expected utility of not buying the ticket equal to 0. So if the expected utility of buying the ticket is greater than 0, you should buy the ticket, despite the risk of losing, and if the expected utility of buying the ticket is less than 0, you should not buy the ticket despite the chance of making great gains. In a way, one can think of expected utility theory as telling you how to determine, in each of life's risky situations, when and if a certain course of action is a 'good bet' or a 'bad bet' given the possibilities.

2 Categories of theories of practical reason

Descriptive v. normative theories of reasoning and rationale. In evaluating whether expected utility theory is a successful theory of practical reason, we should consider, first, what a theory of practical reason should be expected to do.

There have been a number of distinctive tasks that philosophers have thought their theories of practical reason must perform. For example, it is commonly thought that there is a kind of deliberation or reasoning process that does or should occur in the minds of agents prior to action, which authorizes that action and may also motivate it. Theories that describe how we *actually* deliberate prior to action are *descriptive* theories of reasoning. Theories that prescribe how we *ought* to deliberate prior to action (where this may diverge substantially from our actual reasoning process) are *normative* (or *prescriptive*) theories of reasoning.

Theories of behavioural *rationale* are a kind of normative theory that specifies one or more standards by which the behaviour of an agent is evaluated. It is a common (and understandable) presumption of many that the principle(s) used to judge behaviour should be the same as the principle(s) on which human reasoning is based prior to choice, and normative versions of theories of reasoning often function as theories of behavioural rationale. None the less, it may be that the correct conception of behavioural rationale is one that, given human constraints and limitations, is too difficult for us to use as a reasoning process, in which case, the theory used to judge the rationality of behaviour would diverge from the (less complicated) reasoning procedure human beings would be able to use prior to action.

A *predictive* theory of reason predicts the behaviour of an agent who satisfies certain consistency requirements. Such a theory may be (and often has been) linked to a theory of rationale when these consistency requirements are taken to manifest a certain normatively desirable consistency in choice. Some might speculate that if a predictive theory made successful predictions of an agent's choices, then that success would provide evidence that the agent (in some way) mentally followed the procedure described by that theory to make those choices, so that it was (in some way) a description of the reasoning processes upon which the agent operated. But the success of these predictions does not require that one draw this descriptive conclusion, and might be explained in other ways.

Two further distinctions in practical reason. There are important further issues concerning how a theory of practical reason should bear upon action. For example, should rational actions be understood as those actions that promote (what are regarded as) good objects or good states of affairs? Or as those actions that are, in some way, intrinsically valuable or right, regardless of the good they generate? Those theorists who believe that rational actions must be defined as those actions that maximize, achieve or promote the good have a *consequentialist* or *teleological* conception of reason. In contrast, *non-consequentialist* theorists believe that a rational action has certain characteristics that make it rational other than its tendency to promote the good. They try to define rational action, at least in part, by reference to principles of what might be called inherent rightness.

Different from this distinction is that between *instrumental* and *non-instrumental* conceptions of reason itself. An instrumental conception takes reason to serve ultimate goals that are set by something *other than reason itself.* (Hume is often considered to be the source of this idea.) An instrumental theory can allow the possibility that reasoning can set goals by functioning instrumentally. That is, we can distinguish between *motivated* ends, that is, ends that are means to the attainment of other ends, and unmotivated ends, that is, ends that are not means to the attainment of other ends. Many instrumental theories accept that reason can at least fix our motivated ends; others deny even this possibility. All of them, however, agree that our unmotivated ends are fixed by non-rational forces within us, for example, our basic or innate passions or desires (see DESIRE).

Nor need an instrumental theory be committed to the claim that the only form of reasoning is means/ end reasoning; there are other tasks that reason can perform consistent with a denial of a non-instrumental role for reason. For example, practical reasoning can include not only deliberation about instrumentally effective means to ends, but also deliberation concerning the most convenient, economical, or pleasant way of satisfying some element in an agent's motivational set, as well as deliberations with respect to time-ordering, or weighting of conflicting desires. It is only the non-instrumental fixing of ends that the instrumental theory leaves beyond the province of rational criticism.

Non-instrumental theories of reasoning or rationale, while admitting reason has an instrumental component, also ascribe to reason a role in defining unmotivated ends of action. Such views may hold, for example, that certain things are worth having for their own sake (for example, appetitive pleasure, comfort, aesthetic appreciation, certain sorts of accomplishment) and that practical reason is capable of recognizing their appropriateness as (unmotivated) ends of human action or activity.

3 The interpretation of EU

With these distinctions between kinds of reasons in mind, we can ask whether EU theory is a successful portrayal of practical reason. It all depends upon how one interprets the theory and, surprisingly, it has been interpreted in many different ways.

EU theory can be either an instrumental or a non-instrumental theory of reason, depending upon how one understands the source of the measure of the 'utility' or goodness of the outcomes used to evaluate the expected utility of the actions being assessed. Suppose, for now, that we adopt the account of Jeremy Bentham (1823) that regards this measure as a way of assessing the amount of pleasure or pain that one will receive from the results of an action. In this case, the goodness or badness of any outcome is defined by the way the agent experiences that outcome, where this experience has nothing to do with the agent's reasoning process. Pleasure and the absence of pain can therefore be understood as the agent's good (a good that, with each action, the agent attempts to achieve or maximize), where the content of this good is not in any way determined by reason operating non-instrumentally. Expected utility theory, on this view, is merely an account of the reasoning process we use in attempting to maximize this good, and thus should be understood as an instrumental theory.

However, von Neumann and Morgenstern (1944) developed a notion of 'utility' that is deliberately not meant to refer to an experiential state or to be an interpersonal measure of such an experiential state. The notion of preference can be (and has been) understood either as a mental state (for example, a kind of disposition to choose), or as something not merely revealed by, but actually consisting in, a person's publicly observable behaviour (commonly referred to by economists as the idea of 'revealed preference'). In their development of EU theory, an agent's utility function attempts (merely) to represent an agent's preferences understood in either of these ways, but the theory does not offer any explanation of why the agent has these preferences. Hence the theory leaves open the possibility that what an agent prefers may be the result of reason operating non-instrumentally. Only a psychological theory of preference formation could tell us whether reason does or does not play a role in determining an agent's preferences (interpreted in either of the ways just mentioned). This means that von Neumann and Morgenstern's EU theory can receive either an instrumental or a non-instrumental interpretation, depending upon the kind of psychological theory of preference formation appended to it.

Interestingly, however, von Neumann and Morgenstern appended no such psychological theory to their theory. Both were influenced by the philosophical position called logical positivism, which advocates that theories, to be scientific, must concern only that which is publicly verifiable – something that behaviour and choices seem to be, unlike deliberation or inner experiences (see BEHAVIOURISM, ANALYTIC; LOGICAL POSITIVISM). However, a behaviouristic interpretation of the theory (which would embrace the idea of revealed preference) precludes us from developing it in a way that determines whether it is instrumental or non-instrumental.

Von Neumann and Morgenstern's non-psychological understanding of their theory is connected to their interest in developing a theory that could function *predictively*, regardless of any use it might have as a theory of reasoning or behavioural rationale. On their view, we interview or observe a person in order to get them to (arbitrarily) assign utility numbers to certain outcomes which they know they will get. Call these 'riskless prizes'. Once we know a person's assignments and once we know that their preferences satisfy certain seemingly weak axioms (defined more fully below), we can predict their preferences in situations where risk is involved. That is, we do not have to ask them what their preferences are in these risky situations – this can be determined for them from our computation. Moreover, our computations do not require that they actually reason using the expected utility formula – indeed, they may be agents that do not engage in reasoning at all. As long as we know

that their preferences conform to certain axioms, we know they will make their choices as if they were such a reasoner, and that is good enough for us to predict their choices, regardless of whether or not they actually use the EU reasoning process.

4 The axioms of EU

There have been two important types of axiomatization of expected utility theory: the one that was originally developed by von Neumann and Morgenstern (1944), which relies on objective probabilities, and a second kind developed by Savage (1954), using Frank Ramsey's idea (1931) that we can define probabilities subjectively from information about the agent's preferences (see RAMSEY, F.P. §2). We will consider here only the following rough, non-technical statement of von Neumann and Morgenstern's axioms relying on the idea of objective probabilities.

(1) The *completeness* (or ordering) axiom specifies that all the objects over which we have preferences can be compared or ordered. To be precise: for any prizes a and b, $a > b$ or $b > a$ or they are indifferent.

(2) The *transitivity* axiom tells us that if you prefer, say, apples to oranges, and oranges to bananas, you will also prefer apples to bananas. To be precise: for any prizes a, b and c, if $a > b$ and $b > c$, then $a > c$.

(3) Suppose you can participate in a compound lottery (that is, a lottery that has another lottery as at least one of its prizes), where there is some chance that you will ultimately win a million dollars rather than nothing. Suppose you figure out the chance you will get the million. Call this probability p. The *reduction of compound lotteries* axiom says that you will be indifferent between this compound lottery and a simple lottery in which the chance that you will win the million rather than nothing is also p. This axiom is mathematically necessary in order for von Neumann and Morgenstern to prove their conclusion.

(4) Suppose there are three prizes a, b and c. The *continuity* axiom says that if a is preferred to b, and b is preferred to c, then there will be probabilities such that a person will be indifferent between b and a lottery with a and c as prizes. This indifference depends upon the probability of getting a being great enough to outweigh the risk of only getting c, but not so great that the person would prefer the lottery over b, nor so small that the person would prefer b over the lottery.

(5) The *independence* (or substitutability) axiom says, very roughly, that if a person is indifferent

between two prizes, *a* and *b*, considered alone, they are also indifferent between two lotteries that are exactly the same, with the exception that in one of them prize *b* is substituted for prize *a*. (This axiom is roughly equivalent to what Savage calls the 'sure thing' principle in his axiomatization of EU theory. The only difference is that Savage's principle does not assume objective probabilities, allowing for the determination of a decision-maker's subjective probabilities from his utilities.)

(6) The *monotonicity* axiom says that, between any two lotteries involving only the most and least preferred alternatives, you should not prefer the lottery that renders the least preferred alternative more probable.

Many philosophers, economists and social scientists have wanted to revise von Neumann and Morgenstern's theory explicitly to make it into a theory of reasoning or a theory of behavioural rationale. These theorists have added psychological theories or normative interpretations of the axioms, so as to transform EU theory into what they regard as a plausible descriptive or normative theory. For example, Savage considers the theory a normative conception of both reasoning and rationale, whatever predictive value it might have. Other theorists (such as Kahneman and Tversky 1990) have explored the extent to which the theory might succeed as a descriptive account of human reasoning, generally reaching the conclusion that some of EU's axioms are not widely followed (especially the independence axiom, which assumes that what we do is not affected by whether, for example, we see a glass as half full or half empty), meaning that the theory, on their view, is best construed as a normative rather than a descriptive conception of reasoning (see RATIONALITY OF BELIEF).

If this theory is construed either as a theory of reasoning or as a theory of rationale, is it an instrumental or a non-instrumental theory? As noted earlier, it can only be construed as instrumental if its supporters introduce a psychological theory that specifies that all ultimate or unmotivated ends of action are set by something other than reason. Yet the addition of such a theory may seem initially precluded by the structure of EU theory, which makes it easy to give it a non-instrumental interpretation. Consider that EU theory makes a subject's preferences the definers of the ends of their action. However, it would seem the theory does not permit just any preference to be end-defining, but rather, only those preferences that satisfy the axioms of expected utility theory explicated above. But this appears to mean that the axioms play a role in fixing the ends of action by

acting as a normative 'sieve' through which our preferences must pass in order to be considered 'end-defining'. Therefore, if these principles are part of what we mean by practical reason, does this not mean that reason is playing a role in setting our ends of action? If so, EU theory, in so far as it is defined in terms of these axioms, cannot be considered an implementation of the instrumental theory of reasoning. A number of theorists who regard EU theory as a normative account of human reasoning characterize the theory in ways that strongly suggest this non-instrumental interpretation – this even includes some who elsewhere treat it as an instrumental theory of reasoning.

Some philosophers, loyal to the instrumental characterization of practical reason, have argued that EU theory's reliance on these axioms is not really enough to make it a non-instrumental theory. For example, R. Nozick (1993) argues that admitting that these axioms play a role in defining our ends is only introducing consistency standards into our preference set, which is just 'one tiny step beyond Hume'. Yet by taking this 'tiny step' we invite the possibility that there are normative standards other than those of consistency (for example, moral standards) to which our desires ought to be subject (for on what grounds can we argue for some non-instrumental standards and against others?).

How might we argue that the EU axioms can be defended within a pure instrumental theory? One obvious way to try to do so is to claim that EU axioms can be instrumentally justified. On this view, the EU axioms prescribe consistency, and agents must have consistent preferences if they are to achieve the maximal satisfaction of whatever preferences they have. But even if the principle 'To satisfy ends, one must be consistent' is true, the EU axioms are not the only representation of consistency, so it seems one could satisfy the principle by using other reasoning theories with rather different axioms. Furthermore, an instrumentalist argument must avoid circularity: to defend the axioms as instrumentally justified, the argument cannot appeal to the desirable consequences of following the axioms, if that very appeal presupposes that these consequences are desirable as the objects of preferences that satisfy the axioms to be defended. Alternatively, the axioms of EU, or some other set of axioms, might be non-instrumentally justified as intuitively compelling or as cohering well with other intuitive principles of reason.

5 Challenges to expected utility theory

Many theorists have maintained, on the basis of empirical evidence, that human beings consistently violate some of the EU axioms (see, for example, Kahneman and Tversky 1990; Allais 1979; Ellsberg 1951; RATIONALITY OF BELIEF). That evidence appears to show that, at the very least, EU theory fails as a *descriptive* account of our practical reasoning. And the violations of some of the EU axioms seem so intuitively reasonable that many theorists believe they show EU theory fails as a *normative* account of our reasoning. While the examples are too complicated to discuss here, it is important to note that there is a pattern to many of the purported violations. Peter Hammond (1988) and others have argued that the axioms of EU theory articulate the idea that we choose actions (solely) by assessing the consequences of those actions, but violations of these axioms occur when people's choice of action results from certain non-consequential preferences they have – for example, preferences for the situation, action or process from which the consequences will result. Economists have called these *state-dependent* preferences. Does the existence of these preferences show not only that EU theory is the wrong portrayal of practical reason but also, more fundamentally, that any successful descriptive or normative theory of practical reason will have to be non-consequentialist, relying on axioms of choice that recognize that sometimes we choose to act for reasons other than the desirability of the consequences of these actions?

Some advocates of the idea that we are consequentialist reasoners answer this last question negatively. They have proposed that purported counterexamples to EU theory can be accommodated once we reinterpret them to show that hidden in the examples are possible consequences to which people have positive or negative attitudes. If this strategy works, it would support the idea that, if we understand the consequences in any choice situation in an appropriately broad way, no human being whom we would consider rational will violate the (consequentialist) EU axioms in their choices. One worry that even the defenders of this strategy have voiced is that it might work too well – allowing us to redeem any violation of the axioms by finding some hidden consequence to which the purported violator is actually responding. Some theorists (particularly John Broome 1991) try to avoid the problem by arguing for principles that specify when a rational agent must be indifferent between two outcomes. Such principles prohibit us from postulating hidden consequentialist attitudes that, if recognized, would mean the agent was not violating the axiom after all.

Those theorists who believe that the purported counterexamples cannot be explained away have advocated rejecting one or more of EU theory's axioms, so as to develop a revised theory that attempts to be a better descriptive or normative theory of reasoning or behavioural rationale. For example, Mark Machina (1991) rejects the independence axiom, and Graham Loomes and Robert Sugden (1982) drop the transitivity axiom. These revised theories are not, however, radical departures from EU theory, and retain much of the structure of that theory.

6 Contemporary non-maximizing alternatives to expected utility theory

One central assumption of EU theory is that rational action is maximizing action: faced with a multiplicity of ends, we are supposed to try to maximize their satisfaction. But some critics of the theory insist that rational action with respect to a multiplicity of ends often permits, and sometimes even requires, that we refrain from maximizing.

For example, Herbert Simon (1982) has argued that we should understand reason in a non-maximizing way because human beings operate subject to limitations and constraints that make effective maximization impossible. These limitations and constraints come in two varieties: constraints on information-gathering relevant to action (for example, limited access, high costs of obtaining, and limited time), and constraints on computational ability (for example, limited memory, intellectual disabilities, high costs of difficult calculations, and slowness of calculation relative to time allowed). Because of these constraints, Simon argues that human beings do not (and should not) reason by straightforwardly maximizing. Instead he says they do (and should) use certain shorthand reasoning procedures that yield good results given these constraints and limitations. Simon calls reasoning using these shorthand procedures 'satisficing'.

However, Simon's satisficing can be understood as consistent with a maximizing conception of reasoning if it is defended as a form of reasoning used by agents interested in maximizing preference satisfaction while subject to the above constraints. On this view, agents maximize to the best of their ability if they use these shorthand satisficing procedures. This position therefore represents a maximizing form of reasoning as a 'meta-rational' procedure that assesses possible operational reasoning procedures for those agents who are subject to certain constraints that make maximization too costly or too difficult to operate upon directly.

A more radical anti-maximizing theory that cannot be reconciled with an overall maximizing theory of reason is proposed by Isaac Levi (1986), who argues that our decision making must sometimes contend with unresolved conflict. On Levi's view, there are times when different options available to us are good in quite different ways (reflecting different moral, aesthetic, prudential, cognitive or political values), such that we cannot conclude that one of them is, all things considered, better than the other(s). Levi argues that when such conflict between values cannot be resolved, a rational agent cannot act so as to maximize one unified conception of the good (since there is no such thing in these circumstances), but must instead act in a way that, given their evaluation of the options, is at least admissible. Levi's non-maximizing theory is none the less still a teleological or consequentialist portrayal of practical reasoning, in so far as rational action is construed as that which serves a goal.

An even more radical anti-maximizing portrayal of practical reason has been proposed by Michael Slote (1989). Slote holds that self-regarding rationality often permits or requires maximization with respect to our own good, but he also insists that we are sometimes rationally permitted and even have positive reason, on balance, to abstain from performing actions that we know will maximize our own good. On his view, if we are moderate in our desires, we can, for example, reasonably turn down a second dessert or a luxurious house – not because we think we would not enjoy or be better off with them – but because we consider our situation to be good enough and fine just as it is. Since it says that there can sometimes be reason on balance to prefer an action whose results are *less* good for one, Slote's conception of rationality is, strictly speaking, neither consequentialist nor teleological.

Jon Elster (1979) thinks about the issue of maximization in another way. Elster distinguishes between (what he calls) a *global* maximizer conception of practical reason and a *local* maximizer conception of practical reason. Local maximizers do whatever they judge best at the time of choice, but this means they have a 'myopic eye fixed to the ground' and cannot take into account 'what happens behind the next hill'. In contrast, a global maximizer can choose the worse option now, in order to be in a position to realize a far better outcome than the presently better option would yield. Unlike theorists who think of us as reflecting in some piecemeal fashion about how to satisfy effectively a set of desires as they present themselves to us at any given time, Elster's discussion points out that human beings need, and use, a conception of means/end reasoning that stretches out over time, permitting the rationality of enduring short-term losses in order to realize long-term gains.

The importance of reasoning long-term is, in the view of many theorists, connected to the idea of prudence. It is commonly (but not universally)

thought that the practically rational person can not only choose effective means to ends, but also resolve on a course of action that will advance their interests in the long run, not merely the short run. Much of the literature in this area is inspired by the work of Thomas Nagel (1970). Some of it (see, for example, Derek Parfit 1984) explores the extent to which our conception of our own identity as persons is connected to reasoning with respect to the future (see MORALITY AND IDENTITY).

How the idea of global rationality should be developed is controversial; some, such as David Gauthier (1986) and Edward McClennen (1990), have proposed that fully rational agents should sometimes remain 'resolute' in their intention to perform an action in order to achieve some desirable end, even in situations where conventional maximizing forms of reasoning would endorse another tempting alternative. Such resolution is rational on their view, when it would make possible benefits that can only be realized if the agent maintains the intention to perform this action. Gregory Kavka's 'toxin puzzle' (1983) gives us a way to illustrate their view: imagine that there is a millionaire who will give you a million dollars if you form the intention to drink a toxin that will not kill you but will make you ill, where this millionaire will give you the money before you have to drink the toxin, as long as they are satisfied that you have formed the intention to do so. Resolute theorists argue that, to get the money, you should form the intention to drink the toxin, and then drink it. However, other theorists dispute the rationality of resoluteness, and argue that a rational agent in the toxin example would conclude that it would be irrational to drink the toxin, and thus irrational to form the intention to do so (even though this means losing a million dollars). This view presupposes a theory of rational intention that makes resoluteness irrational. Theorists on both sides of this issue believe that intentions and actions must be linked, on pain of irrationality. However, resolute theorists believe that as long as it is rational to intend to perform an action, then it is rational to perform it, whereas critics of the idea of resoluteness maintain that one can only rationally intend to perform an action when it is actually rational to perform it.

7 Contemporary non-maximizing alternatives to expected utility theory (cont.)

Elster and others have also argued that conceptions of reasoning must go beyond maximization in order to reckon with the phenomenon of 'endogenous preference formation'. This term refers to the process by which agents modify or revise what they prefer in response to constraints their environment places upon them. For example, in Aesop's fable, the fox, who cannot reach the grapes he desires, finally decides that they must be sour anyway, so that he does not want them. Thus the fox changes his preferences when he discovers that he cannot satisfy them as they are. Endogenous preference formation may not only be a fact, but a normatively desirable response to our environment. (Consider the advice given by Crosby, Stills and Nash in a popular song: 'If you can't be with the one you love, love the one you're with'.) Note that this phenomenon would seem to be neither explained nor endorsed by EU theory, since it involves a (non-instrumental) form of reasoning explicitly concerned with establishing our ends of action, in ways that have nothing to do with the axioms of consistency that define EU theory.

Theorists have also proposed non-maximizing conceptions of reasoning for situations of complete uncertainty, that is, situations in which we cannot assign probabilities to the possible outcomes. In such cases, we cannot reason as expected utility maximizers, since doing so precisely requires that we know, or be able to estimate, the probabilities of possible outcomes of alternative actions. Some theorists (such as John Harsanyi 1976) have proposed that we should use the 'principle of insufficient reason' to derive probabilities that enable us to use an expected utility calculation. This principle tells us to estimate as equiprobable the possible outcomes of alternative actions most relevant to our decision making, and then use these probabilities in an expected utility calculation. However, other theorists (such as John Rawls 1971) have proposed the rationality of a 'maximin rule' of choice in at least some situations of complete uncertainty. This rule tells us to choose that action whose worst possible outcome is better than, or at least as good as, the worst possible outcomes of all the other alternative actions. This is generally considered a very conservative principle of choice under uncertainty.

Many theorists (for example, Bratman 1987) believe progress in understanding human reasoning should be made not by concentrating on maximization, but by thinking about the way our deliberation standardly involves planning. Constructing a plan involves a complicated and interconnected series of intentions about how to act. Plans would seem to be necessary in order to achieve a wide variety of ends, and in order to ensure that the achievement of one end does not foreclose the possibility of securing ends that are as important as, or more important than, the one we are presently concerned to achieve. This suggests that part of what it means to say that a person is practically rational is that they are a good

planner, so that understanding practical reasoning involves specifying what 'good planning' is. This requires specifying, for example, what a 'feasible' plan is, when sub-plans are necessary, how extensive a good plan should be, and so forth. Those who are interested in constructing artificially intelligent beings are trying to specify the nature of rational planning in a way sufficiently detailed to allow the construction of a rational planner. Such a project, involving both philosophers and researchers in artificial intelligence, attempts to produce a form of practical reasoning that we would expect any agent to perform such that we would regard their operation in the world as 'successful' from a rational point of view (see Pollock 1995; ARTIFICIAL INTELLIGENCE).

8 Game theory

Other technical representations of practical reason exist within a subject called 'game theory', also invented by John von Neumann and Oscar Morgenstern (see DECISION AND GAME THEORY). To understand game theory, consider another distinction made by Jon Elster (1979), between 'parametric' and 'strategic' forms of reasoning. Consider the parametric reasoner Harry, who treats the environment in which he will act as a 'given', estimating how his actions will affect it. In contrast, the strategic reasoner Harriet regards her environment as containing agents whose choice of behaviour will depend in part on what they believe she will do, even while her choice of behaviour depends in part on what she believes they will do. Game theory concerns strategic reasoning because it depicts situations in which the ultimate payoffs to each player from possible actions available to them depend upon what the other player(s) will do. These situations can involve pure conflict – in which each player will only gain if the other(s) lose(s); or pure cooperation, in which each player will only gain if the other(s) gains; or games of mixed conflict and cooperation. In general, what counts as a rational solution in game theory has been the subject of considerable controversy.

A particularly famous game is the 'prisoner's dilemma' or 'PD game'. The name for this game comes from an early example of it in which the two players are prisoners who have jointly participated in a crime, and who are separately encouraged by the police to confess, thereby informing on their partner. If neither confesses they can only be convicted of a crime that yields 1 year in jail; if both confess they will both get 5 years in jail; if one confesses and the other does not, the confessor gets no years in jail but the person who fails to confess will get 10. In a game of this sort, each player prefers most the situation where he confesses but his partner does not, he prefers second the situation where neither he nor his partner confesses, he prefers third the situation where he and his partner both confess, and he prefers least the situation where he does not confess but his partner does. While this fanciful example may make the game seem arcane, social scientists have argued that the PD game is very common in a variety of social situations, especially in a free market. For example, consider two companies, who each have the choice between colluding on prices (the equivalent of not confessing in the original example) or competing rather than colluding (the equivalent of confessing). The payoffs to each company make this a prisoner's dilemma. The seeming ubiquity of this game has persuaded many social scientists of the importance of studying it (see RATIONAL CHOICE THEORY §§2–3).

Many theorists have proposed that rational players in a prisoner's dilemma should reason using the idea of a 'dominant strategy'. According to this form of reasoning, the only rational choice is the non-cooperative action because no matter what the other player does, each player is better off not cooperating (if the other player cooperates, he gets his favourite outcome if he fails to cooperate; if the other player fails to cooperate, he avoids his worst outcome if he fails to cooperate). In this sense, not cooperating 'dominates' over cooperating. However, whether this is the right strategy for dealing with the prisoner's dilemma has been debated, and some theorists have proposed other ways of solving it. These include using expected utility reasoning and impartial (moral) reasoning – both of which may sometimes recommend that the parties in a PD game choose the cooperative option.

The PD game has also been compared to a puzzle called 'Newcomb's paradox'. Imagine that you are given the choice between taking the contents of an opaque box, or taking the contents of that box plus the contents of another, transparent box which you can see contains $1,000. The opaque box contains either a million dollars or nothing. Which of these it contains depends upon whether a powerful being (for example, some kind of god) capable of predicting behaviour with virtually 100 per cent reliability has predicted how you will behave. If the predictor has previously determined that you will choose only the opaque box, it has put a million dollars in it. If the predictor has previously determined you will choose both boxes, it has put nothing in the opaque box. How should you rationally choose? Some theorists (for example, David Lewis 1985) maintain that the prisoner's dilemma is an instance of Newcomb's paradox. More generally, those who discuss the paradox recommend different strategies for its resolu-

tion, including dominance reasoning and expected utility reasoning, that not only generate opposing advice, but also reflect different conceptions of the structure and aim of practical reasoning.

Another game much discussed in recent years is related to the prisoner's dilemma, and the resolution proposed for it seems interestingly suggestive of a kind of moral thinking. Imagine a situation in which a prisoner's dilemma between two or more players repeatedly recurs over time, and where the last recurrence is unknown. This is called an *iterated* prisoner's dilemma. Whereas, in a single-play prisoner's dilemma, the dominant strategy is not to cooperate, in an iterated prisoner's dilemma, cooperation is rational as long as each player has reasonable assurance that the other player will also cooperate (and will not lose too much by acting on the expectation that the other cooperates, and is wrong). Some theorists have argued on the basis of computer models that agents who follow this 'tit for tat' strategy (cooperating with cooperative partners, not cooperating with non-cooperative partners) do better, overall, than players who follow other, less cooperative strategies. This strategy strikes many as having moral overtones (cooperation is rewarded, non-cooperation is punished), and some have speculated that moral responses and emotions, and moral ways of thinking, may well be explained by the way in which certain cooperative or non-cooperative forms of behaviour can be beneficial or harmful to human beings in common game-theoretic situations. Such reflections on the nature of strategic reasoning encourage the hope that future theorizing in game theory may serve to link rational and moral forms of reasoning. This link is also suggested by the work of theorists (such as J.F. Nash 1951; Gauthier 1986) who have explored the extent to which the rational resolution of some of these games might be understood to mimic the results of an ideal bargaining process.

9 Practical reasoning and standards

Most of the preceding theories of reason, including both the maximizing and the non-maximizing conceptions, assume that reason involves weighing the values of various considerations (for example, outcomes, actions) pertinent to our making a choice. This idea is naturally suggested by a teleological or consequentialist conception of reason. However, there are theories that represent rational action as involving the idea of satisfying principles or standards. On this view, a rational agent is one who, at least on some occasions, chooses how to act by applying the appropriate principle to their situation. Such principle-based reasoning can be assimilated to a consequentialist conception of practical reason if the justification for applying these principles is that doing so will help an agent to achieve or maximize the good. Non-consequentialist theorists who reject this assimilation believe that at least some of these principles of right action cannot be justified by reference to any goal or conception of the good. On this view, in addition to whatever concerns an agent might have about how much good or bad an action might produce, they must none the less deliberate or act so as to satisfy these principles in order to be considered rational.

Some non-consequentialists believe that, to be rational, an action or policy must satisfy certain moral or political principles that prescribe 'right conduct' (some of which we will discuss in §10 below). Moreover, although some feminists (such as Lloyd 1984) have questioned whether the whole concept of practical reason reflects the assumptions and biases of our patriarchal society, Ruddick has argued that, in order to bring up their children, mothers must engage in reasoning that determines how to act so as to satisfy different and often conflicting principles (see, for example, Ruddick 1989). Apart from presenting a principle-based view of reasoning, her argument suggests there may be distinctive forms of reasoning appropriate for different practical activities (see FEMINISM; FEMINIST ETHICS).

Finally, Onora O'Neill (1989) has suggested that even though the object of instrumental reasoning is a goal, *how* that reasoning ought to proceed is defined by a variety of 'principles of rational intending', none of which is captured by EU's axioms. Her account clearly implies the possibility of a non-consequentialist theory of instrumental reason.

10 Moral reasoning and weakness of will

A variety of moral theorists insist that practical reason has a moral aspect. Some theorists believe moral reasoning can be accommodated within the confines of expected utility theory since, on their view, moral reasoning is simply EU reasoning with other-regarding preferences. However, others insist that moral reasoning is not merely about how we satisfy our actual other-regarding preferences, but also (and more importantly) about defining how our preference set *ought* to take others' interests into account.

For example, KANT (1785) believed that reason structurally involves a moral reasoning procedure that indirectly defines our ends of action. Kant calls this reasoning procedure the 'moral law' and one of his formulations of it is: 'Act only on that maxim through which you can at the same time will that it will be a universal law'. When I follow this procedure, I

universalize my maxim of action, converting it from the form 'I will do x in circumstances c in order to achieve y' to the form 'Everyone does x in circumstances c in order to achieve y'. Then I evaluate that universalized maxim by determining, first, whether I will be able to achieve y by doing x in circumstances c in a world where everyone does x in c to get y; and second, whether I can 'will' the world in which everyone does x in c to get y. If a maxim meets this test, then I am permitted to act on it – otherwise, I have an obligation not to do so. This test procedure generates what Kant calls 'categorical imperatives', that is, imperatives that (in contrast to hypothetical imperatives) direct us to engage in certain forms of action, or direct us to refrain from certain forms of action, regardless of the desires or interests we happen to have (see KANTIAN ETHICS).

Kant's account of moral reasoning is non-instrumental. The moral law acts as a kind of moral 'filtering device' through which maxims generated by our desires must pass, and his account is also non-consequentialist, because it presents reason not as that which weighs competing goods, but as that which answers to a certain principle of right conduct.

Another representation of moral reasoning is put forward by contractarian theorists. Contractarian reasoning procedures ask us to deliberate about a course of action, plan or policy by determining whether those affected by it (understood so that they are suitably impartial and equal in power) could agree to it or, alternatively, whether it would be something none of them could reasonably reject. This type of reasoning procedure is explicitly presented by John Rawls (1971) as a non-teleological or non-consequentialist form of reasoning, and the way in which it could be used to define ends of action also makes it a non-instrumental conception of reason. Other philosophers, such as David Gauthier (1986) and Thomas Scanlon (1982), have also insisted that contractarian forms of reasoning can define and illuminate the content, and perhaps even the motivational source, of moral behaviour (see CONTRACTARIANISM).

Many contemporary moral philosophers called 'utilitarians', following Bentham, have endorsed various forms of a moral reasoning procedure labelled utilitarian, in which actions and policies are evaluated by determining whether they maximize the welfare (understood by different theorists in different ways, for example, as happiness or preference-satisfaction) of members of a community (see UTILITARIANISM). Some utilitarians (for example, Harsanyi 1976) have linked a form of a utilitarian reasoning procedure (for example, the kind called 'average utilitarianism') to expected utility theory. Utilitarian forms of reasoning are classic examples of consequentialist theories of reasoning, in so far as actions or policies are determined by attempting to maximize a certain conception of the good, construed as human welfare (see CONSEQUENTIALISM; WELFARE).

Particularly when an agent's preferences are formed by social or political processes that seem unjust (for example, practices such as slavery, or institutional discrimination), some theorists have argued that the agent's preferences may have a content that we can evaluate as violating reason. Such an evaluation requires a non-instrumental moral reasoning procedure that determines not only the content of the preferences a rational agent ought to have, but also the ways in which such preferences are rightly formed.

Even if practical reason is the source of normatively authoritative directives (or imperatives) governing our conduct, philosophers disagree about whether these directives can (solely by virtue of that authority) motivate us to act (see MORAL MOTIVATION). Hume argues that reason is motivationally inert, so that only our passions can motivate us. Reason, according to Hume, is a mere slave to our passions that never itself defines or precipitates action directly.

In contrast, Kant insists that his 'moral law' can move us to action, and this belief in the motivational efficacy of practical reason arises in part from his concern to show that, no matter what our interests, desires or emotions, each of us as a rational being always has the capacity not only to understand what the moral course of action is, but also to perform that action, by virtue of the fact that our reason is always in a position to comprehend and initiate appropriate moral conduct.

However, there is a related issue about how to describe cases where passion or desire seemingly leads us to act against our 'better judgment'. There has long been controversy about how to conceive such irrational 'weakness of will' and even about whether the idea of such weakness is really logically coherent (see AKRASIA). But it is not surprising that philosophers and others who disagree about the foundations and content of practical reason should in this way (and others) also disagree about the nature and forms of human irrationality.

See also: ECONOMICS AND ETHICS; ECONOMICS, PHILOSOPHY OF; IMPERATIVE LOGIC; RATIONALITY AND CULTURAL RELATIVISM; RATIONALITY OF BELIEF

References and further reading

* Allais, M. (1979) 'The So-Called Allais Paradox and Rational Decision Under Uncertainty', in M. Allais and O. Hagen (eds) *Expected Utility Hypothesis and the Allais Paradox*, Dordrecht: Reidel, 437–681. (Presents a counterexample to EU theory's independence axiom; discussed in §5.)

* Bentham, J. (1823) *Introduction to the Principles of Morals and Legislation*, ed. J.H. Burns and H.L.A. Hart, London: Methuen, 1982. (Seminal work introducing utilitarian reasoning, discussed in §10; and the idea of utility as a measure of the pleasure or pain of an object or event, discussed in §3.)

* Bratman, M. (1987) *Intentions, Plans and Practical Reason*, Cambridge, MA: Harvard University Press. (Expounds a conception of intention and links it to planning and practical reason; discussed in §7.)

* Broome, J. (1991) *Weighing Goods*, Oxford: Blackwell. (Exploration of EU theory as a consequentialist conception of reasoning; concerned to defend EU theory from counterexamples challenging its adequacy as a normative theory, as discussed in §5.)

Campbell, R. and Sowden, L. (1985) *Paradoxes of Rationality and Cooperation: Prisoner's Dilemma and Newcomb's Problem*, Vancouver, BC: University of British Columbia Press. (Collection of articles, plus a useful summary by the editors, of literature on the prisoner's dilemma and Newcomb's paradox, and thus expands on the discussion in §8.)

Dworkin, R. (1977) *Taking Rights Seriously*, Cambridge, MA: Harvard University Press. (Classic work in philosophy of law; includes extensive exploration of legal reasoning.)

* Ellsberg, D. (1951) 'Risk, Ambiguity and the Savage Axioms', *Quarterly Journal of Economics* 75: 653–6; repr. in Gardenfors and Sahlin (1988). (Presents counterexamples to the Savage axiomatization of EU theory; mentioned in §5.)

* Elster, J. (1979) *Ulysses and the Sirens: Studies in Rationality and Irrationality*, Cambridge: Cambridge University Press. (A work that distinguishes between global and local reasoning, discussed in §§6–7; and between parametric and strategic reasoning, discussed in §8.)

—— (1983) *Sour Grapes: Studies in the Subversion of Rationality*, Cambridge: Cambridge University Press. (Includes an exploration of endogenous preference formation, discussed in §7.)

Frank, R. (1988) *Passions within Reason: The Strategic Role of the Emotions*, New York: Norton. (Expounds on the idea that our passions are allies in our attempts to solve certain game-theoretic problems, and may have evolved within us because of this function.)

Gardenfors, P. and Sahlin, N. (1988) *Decision, Probability and Utility: Selected Readings*, Cambridge: Cambridge University Press. (A collection of classic essays in rational choice theory, including works by Allais, Ellsberg, Savage, Ramsey and later theorists. An excellent resource.)

* Gauthier, D. (1986) *Morals by Agreement*, Oxford: Oxford University Press. (Presents a kind of contractarian moral theory; also a conception of rationality that interprets EU theory as an instrumental theory as discussed in §3; and develops a bargaining-like solution to certain game-theoretic problems.)

Gibbard, A. and Harper, W.L. (1985) 'Counterfactuals and Two Kinds of Expected Utility', in R. Campbell and L. Sowden (eds) *Paradoxes of Rationality and Cooperation*, Vancouver, BC: University of British Columbia Press; repr. in Gardenfors and Sahlin (1988). (In response to Newcomb's paradox, discussed in §8, these authors develop two conceptions of decision-theoretic reasoning, 'evidential' and 'causal'; quite technical and ill-suited for beginners.)

* Goldman, A. (1986) *Epistemology and Cognition*, Cambridge, MA: Harvard University Press. (Explores epistemic norms, and suggests that norms of theoretical reason may be related to or derived from norms of practical reason; discussed in §1.)

* Hammond, P. (1988) 'Consequentialist Foundations for Expected Utility Theory', *Theory and Decision* 25: 25–78. (Expounds the way in which EU theory expresses a consequentialist conception of reason, discussed in §5. Highly technical and ill-suited for beginners.)

Hampton, J. (1994) 'The Failure of Expected Utility Theory as a Theory of Reason', *Economics and Philosophy* 10: 195–242. (Expands on the discussion in §§3–5 of the extent to which EU theory is an instrumental conception of reason, and argues that EU theory fails as a descriptive and normative conception of reasoning, and as a theory of behavioural rationale, because it is too consequentialist.)

* Harsanyi, J. (1976) *Essays on Ethics, Social Behavior and Scientific Explanation*, Dordrecht: Reidel. (A collection of essays that, among other things, expresses the author's conception of utilitarianism, influenced by EU theory, mentioned in §10, and defends the use of the principle of insufficient reason in situations of complete uncertainty, discussed in §7.)

Hart, H.L.A. (1961) *The Concept of Law*, Oxford: Clarendon Press. (A classic work in philosophy of law; considers questions about the nature of moral reasoning.)

* Hume, D. (1739–40) *A Treatise of Human Nature*, ed. L.A. Selby-Bigge, revised P.H. Nidditch, Oxford: Clarendon Press, 1975. (A major work in the history of philosophy, including the thesis that reason is motivationally inert (discussed in §10) and suggesting that reasoning prior to action may be nothing but theoretical reasoning (§1); also influential in the development of the instrumental theory of practical reason (discussed in §§2–3).)

* Kahneman, D. and Tversky, A. (1990) 'Rational Choice and the Framing of Decisions', in K. Cook and M. Levi (eds) *The Limits of Rationality*, Chicago, IL: Chicago University Press, 60–89. (An important article that uses empirical studies to show that people frequently violate some of the EU axioms. The collection in which it appears includes a number of classic works in decision theory.)

* Kant, I. (1785) *The Groundwork of the Metaphysics of Morals*, trans. H.J. Paton, London: Harper Torchbooks, 1964. (A major work in the history of philosophy presenting a theory of moral reasoning discussed in §10. It is also the source of the distinction between categorical imperatives, discussed in §10, and hypothetical imperatives, discussed in §1.)

—— (1793) 'On the Common Saying, "This May Be True in Theory, But It Does Not Apply In Practice"', in *Kant's Political Writings*, ed. H. Reiss, Cambridge: Cambridge University Press, 1970. (An essay that proposes a contractarian reasoning procedure for political decision making; see §10.)

* Kavka, G. (1983) 'The Toxin Puzzle', *Analysis* 43: 33–6. (Sets out a puzzle that some theorists have used to expound different conceptions of global reasoning; discussed in §6.)

* Levi, I. (1986) *Hard Choices: Decision-Making under Unresolved Conflict*, New York: Cambridge University Press. (Proposes a non-maximizing but consequentialist account of practical reason; discussed in §6.)

* Lewis, D. (1985) 'Prisoner's Dilemma is a Newcomb Problem', in R. Campbell and L. Sowden (eds) *Paradoxes of Rationality and Cooperation: Prisoner's Dilemma and Newcomb's Problem*, Vancouver, BC: University of British Columbia Press. (Relates the prisoner's dilemma to Newcomb's problem, both discussed in §8.)

* Lloyd, E. (1984) *The Man of Reason*, Minneapolis, MN: University of Minnesota Press. (Explores the extent to which conceptions of reason are generated by western patriarchal society in which men have dominated the academy; discussed in §9.)

* Loomes, G. and Sugden, R. (1982) 'Regret Theory: An Alternative Theory of Rational Choice Under Uncertainty', *Economic Journal* 92: 805–24. (Uses

empirical evidence to argue that people violate EU theory's transitivity axiom; discussed in §5.)

Luce, R.D. and Raiffa, H. (1957) *Games and Decisions: Introduction and Critical Survey*, New York: Dover, 1985. (Classic statement of EU theory and a superb reference work for those wishing to study EU theory and game theory. Expands on the discussions of these fields, and includes a technical statement of the EU axioms.)

* Machina, M. (1991) 'Dynamic Consistency and Non-Expected Utility Models of Choice under Uncertainty', in M. Bacharach and S. Hurley (eds) *Foundations of Decision Theory: Issues and Advances*, Oxford: Blackwell. (Uses empirical evidence to challenge EU's independence axiom; discussed in §5.)

* McClennen, E. (1990) *Rationality and Dynamic Choice*, Cambridge: Cambridge University Press. (Presents a conception of rationality as resoluteness, discussed in §6; also challenges the idea that some of the EU axioms can be defended instrumentally – see §5.)

* Nagel, T. (1970) *The Possibility of Altruism*, Princeton, NJ: Princeton University Press. (Important work that explores and develops conceptions of prudential and moral reasoning; mentioned in §6.)

* Nash, J.F. (1951) 'Non-Cooperative Games', *Annals of Mathematics* 54: 286–95. (Develops a bargaining-like solution to some games.)

* Neumann, J. von and Morgenstern, O. (1944) *Theory of Games and Economic Behavior*, Princeton, NJ: Princeton University Press, 1953. (Classic and seminal work creating both EU theory and game theory. Most parts of the book are highly technical but the first chapter is fairly accessible to the non-specialist.)

* Nozick, R. (1993) *The Nature of Rationality*, Princeton, NJ: Princeton University Press. (Wide-ranging discussion of issues in the study of rationality; highly readable. Expands upon the discussion in §4 of the extent to which the EU axioms can be interpreted consistently with the idea that EU reasoning is instrumental.)

* O'Neill, O. (1989) *Constructions of Reason*, Cambridge: Cambridge University Press. (An exploration of Kantian moral theory; proposes a principle-based conception of instrumental reasoning discussed in §9.)

* Parfit, D. (1984) *Reasons and Persons*, Oxford: Clarendon Press. (A wide-ranging discussion of practical reason that explores instrumental and prudential reasoning, and personal identity; mentioned in §6.)

* Pollock, J. (1995) *Cognitive Carpentry*, Cambridge, MA: MIT Press. (A presentation of practical reasoning as planning, discussed in §7, for the purpose of developing an artificial person.)

* Ramsey, F. (1931) 'Truth and Probability', in D.H. Mellor (ed.) *Foundations of Mathematics*, London: Routledge & Kegan Paul, 1978; repr. in Gardenfors and Sahlin (1988). (Sets out a way of deriving subjective probabilities from an agent's utility, relevant to Savage's version of EU theory.)

* Rawls, J. (1971) *A Theory of Justice*, Cambridge, MA: Harvard University Press. (This classic work in modern political theory develops an influential version of a contractarian reasoning procedure (discussed in §10) and includes an endorsement of maximin reasoning in some situations of complete uncertainty, as discussed in §7.)

* Ruddick, S. (1989) *Maternal Thinking: Toward A Politics of Peace*, Boston, MA: Beacon Press. (Proposes a standard-based conception of the reasoning that mothers engage in when they bring up their children; discussed in §9.)

* Savage, L. (1954) *The Foundations of Statistics*, New York: Wiley & Sons; 2nd edn, New York: Dover, 1972. (A seminal work in the development of EU theory, with an axiomatization that is an alternative to that of von Neumann and Morgenstern. Not for beginners.)

* Scanlon, T. (1982) 'Contractualism and Utilitarianism', in A. Sen and B. Williams (eds) *Utilitarianism and Beyond*, Cambridge: Cambridge University Press. (Develops a kind of contractarian moral reasoning procedure; discussed in §10.)

* Simon, H. (1982) *Models of Bounded Rationality*, Cambridge, MA: MIT Press. (Expounds the idea that the reasoning upon which we operate is not concerned with maximizing but with 'satisficing'; discussed in §6.)

* Slote, M. (1989) *Beyond Optimizing: A Study of Rational Choice*, Cambridge, MA: Harvard University Press. (Proposes a non-maximizing and non-consequentialist conception of practical reason; discussed in §6.)

Williams, B. (1981) 'Internal and External Reasons', in *Moral Luck*, Cambridge: Cambridge University Press, 101–13. (Influential article that develops a conception of practical reason indebted to Hume.)

JEAN HAMPTON

RAVAISSON-MOLLIEN, JEAN-GASPARD FÉLIX LACHER (1813–1900)

Félix Ravaisson was a French philosopher, born in Namur. Apart from his three main works – Rapport sur la philosophie en France au dix-neuvième siècle (Report on Philosophy in France in the Nineteenth Century) (1863), Métaphysique d'Aristote (Metaphysics of Aristotle) (1837, 1846) and De l'habitude (On Habit) (1838) – his ideas can mainly be found in articles, fragments and short passages, such as those collected in Testament philosophique (Philosophical Testament) (1901) or others that are still unpublished. None the less, Henri-Louis Bergson, who succeeded him at the Academy of Moral and Political Sciences, according to custom gave a synthetic account of Ravaisson's work, in his Notice sur la vie et les oeuvres de M. Félix Ravaisson-Mollien (Account of the Life and Works of Mr Félix Ravaisson-Mollien) (1934). Bergson insisted on the importance of artistic research in Ravaisson's thought, and one can indeed explain his philosophy as beginning from a meditation on works of art and on beauty. The importance of this starting point can be seen in the privileged role he gives to synthesis in all explanation, for in an artistic masterpiece, it is the whole that allows for comprehension of the parts. Ravaisson gave this idea a metaphysical dimension.

In 1832 Ravaisson was awarded a prize by the Academy of Moral and Political Sciences in a competition on the study of Aristotle's metaphysics. The first volume of his *Essai sur la métaphysique d'Aristote* (On Aristotle's Metaphysics) appeared in 1837, the second in 1846. In 1838 he defended his doctoral thesis, *De l'habitude* (On Habit). However, Ravaisson never became a professor of philosophy. In 1839 he was made Inspector of Libraries, and fifteen years later he became Inspector General of Higher Education. In 1852, the Minister of Public Education considered the issue of the teaching of drawing in schools. Ravaisson was chairman on the commission set up to report to the minister, while Delacroix and Ingres were among its members. In 1863, at the request of the government, Ravaisson wrote a *Rapport sur la philosophie en France au dix-neuvième siècle* (Report on Philosophy in France in the Nineteenth Century), which exercised an important influence on academic philosophy. In 1893 he put forward an overview of his philosophy in an article titled 'Métaphysique et morale' (Metaphysics and Morals), which appeared as the introduction to the philosophical journal of that name. A complete exposition of his doctrine appeared in the unpublished fragments put together after his death under the title *Testament philosophique* (Philosophical Testament) (1901).

Ravaisson's most original work is *De l'habitude*, in which, according to Bergson, he broadly sets out a philosophy of nature. He refused to limit habit to its negative aspect, claiming, indeed, that it allows the mind to liberate itself more easily from nature. Nature, according to Ravaisson, is essentially spontaneity. Just as habit is voluntarily acquired, and spirit is thereby made nature, so freedom makes itself into necessity.

Ravaisson also developed a personal conception of the teaching of drawing. In his research on the Venus de Milo, he emphasized the spiritual significance of a pose that expresses love and peace. Finding the paradigm of all the stages of thought in aesthetic intuition, Ravaisson believed that the method goes back to ARISTOTLE in his attempt to make teleological explanation the basis for all true understanding. Indeed, in his studies on the metaphysics of Aristotle, Ravaisson insisted on the fact that Aristotle saw philosophy as a bringing to completion of reality. According to Ravaisson, the essential claim in Aristotle's philosophy is that attention must be focused on the individual, and not dispersed in the general. Philosophy must not stay in the abstract, which is why Aristotle finds the highest truth in the contemplation of works of art.

Rapport sur la philosophie en France au dix-neuvième siècle gives the most complete account of Ravaisson's thought. Having distinguished the mechanical and organic modes of apprehension, he returns to the origin of things, and claims that God created the universe by a process of 'condescension' and love in a way that resembles the creation of art.

Ravaisson begins the *Rapport* by examining the ancient philosophers, and shows that Aristotle is the founder of metaphysics. After a rapid overview of pre-nineteenth-century thinkers, he summarizes the eclecticism of Victor COUSIN and insists on his debt to SCHELLING. His examination of COMTE suggests that Comte passed from physical to moral positivism, and, from the same point of view, his study of Paul Janet's works leads him to conclude that true materialism is impossible.

The *Rapport* ends with the examination of two works that seem best to express Ravaisson's fundamental ideas: those of Anthelme-Edouard Chaignet and Jean-Charles Leveque on the theory of beauty. In commenting on them, he shows that beauty, charm and grace spring from souls that are capable of goodness and love. These qualities are the essential driving forces of the world, and as a result the realm of the aesthetic blends with that of philosophy. In short, while materialism finds its origins in the mathematical and physical sciences, living things reveal the spiritual, or rather the moral and aesthetic order, being dominated more by considerations of the order and harmony of the whole than by the detail of its parts; they are more concerned with form than with content. According to Ravaisson, this leaves two main routes for philosophy: analysis and synthesis. The perspective of synthesis is essentially that of art, which consists primarily of composition and construction, and thus also of science, when it is inventive. In other words, synthesis is the main method of philosophy. We judge the whole against the model of perfection which we carry in ourselves. Synthesis strives to explain everything through the absolute perfection that nothing limits; it strives by degrees towards the infinite. Similarly, in the order of wisdom, the wise man freely chooses the good. This also leads to a reconciliation of spirit and nature, which is one way of linking the classical belief that Eros was the first of all the gods with the Christian dictum, 'God is love'.

Testament philosophique repeats the essential themes of the *Rapport*. Ravaisson once more shows the importance of the role of feeling in the search for truth and restates the claim that beauty can only be created where there is enthusiasm. He underlines the values of generosity and love as the proper foundation of education and social morality. In addition to these claims, Ravaisson adds one for a natural belief in immortality.

See also: BEAUTY

List of works

Ravaisson, F. (1837) *Essai sur la Métaphysique d'Aristote* (On Aristotle's Metaphysics), vol. 1, Paris: Imprimerie royale; vol. 2, Paris, de Joubert, 1846; vol. 1, repr. 1963, Hildesheim, Georg Olms Verlagsbuchandlung. (Ravaisson here criticizes the philosophy of Aristotle, because he sees it as analytic philosophy, while he himself sought a synthetic position.)

—— (1838) *De l'habitude* (On Habit), Paris: H. Fournier; repr. in *Revue de métaphysique et de morale*, (2), 1–35, 1894; and as *De l'habitude*, with intro. by J. Baruzi, Paris, Alcan, 1933; repr. Paris, Vrin, 1981. (Ravaisson posits that habit is not simply a negative force, but allows the mind to free itself. In this way free will can be seen as part of the spontaneity of nature.)

—— (1863) *La philosophie en France au dix-neuvième siècle*, Paris: Imprimerie impériale. (Ravaisson shows that French nineteenth-century philosophy consists of two schools of thought – materialism and spiritualism – and concludes his work with the triumph of the latter, the philosophy of spirit. This work is often referred to as the *Rapport* after some later editions, entitled *Rapport sur la philosophie en France au dix-neuvième siècle*.)

—— (1893) 'Métaphysique et morale' (Metaphysics and Morals), introduction to *Revue de métaphysique et de morale*. (Overview of Ravaisson's philosophy, in which he claims that metaphysical truth transcends conventional thought processes and that it is necessary 'to love in order to understand'.)

—— (1901) *Testament philosophique*, ed. X. Léon, in *Revue de métaphysique et de morale*, 1–31. (This work consolidates the fragments of Ravaisson's thought and brings to light the philosophical importance of free will, emotion and love.)

—— (1933) *Testament philosophique et fragments*, revised and presented by C. Devivaise, Paris: Boivin. (Revised edition of *Testament philosophique* (1901).)

—— (1953) *Essai sur la métaphysique d'Aristote, fragments du tome III (Héllénisme, Judaisme, Christianisme)*, ed. C. Devivaise, Paris: Vrin. (Ravaisson's unfinished third volume on Aristotle, posthumously assembled from manuscripts.)

References and further reading

* Bergson, H.-L. (1934) 'La vie et l'oeuvre de Ravaisson', in *La pensée et le mouvant*, Paris: P.U.F., ch. 9; trans. M.L. Andison in *The Creative Mind*, New York: Philosophical Library, 1946. (A clear, complete, brilliant and perfectly accessible exposition, which can perhaps only be criticized for 'bergsonifying' Ravaisson.)

* Chaignet, A.E. (1882–93) *Histoire de la psychologie des Grecs*, Paris, 2 vols. (In analysing the questions of Plato and Greek philosophy, Chaignet distinguishes the idea of beauty from that of the Good, and the idea of benevolence from that of moral perfection.)

Dopp, J. (1933) *Félix Ravaisson, la formation de sa pensée d'après des documents inédits*, Louvain: Institut supérieur de Philosophie. (Dopp shows how Ravaisson, starting from his thoughts on Aristotle, Kant and Schelling, worked towards unifying mind and nature in concrete terms.)

Janicaud, D. (1969) *Une généalogie du spiritualisme français. Aux sources du bergsonisme: Ravaisson et la métaphysique*, The Hague: Martinus Nijhoff. (Janicaud criticizes the Bergsonian interpretation of Ravaisson, while recognizing that it illuminates the real difficulties of a philosophy which explains through life what cannot be explained through thought.)

—— (1985) *F. Ravaisson. L'art et les mystères grecs*,

Paris: L'Herme. (Texts collected and edited by Janicaud, with an interview with Alain Pasquier, head of the Department of Antiquities at the Louvre. This collection presents the original aspects of Ravaisson's personality that led him to be both a philosopher and lover of art.)

* Lévêque, J.C. (1861) *La science du beau étudiée dans ses principles, dans ses applications et dans son histoire*, Paris, 2 vols. (Dissatisfied by theories in which beauty consists in proportion, Lévêque rediscovers the principles of order and strength through the works of Malebranche and Leibniz. He gives a precise definition of what beauty consists in: it is greatness tempered by order, and expresses strength and will.)

Translated by Robert Stern

PIERRETTE BONET

RAWLS, JOHN (1921–)

Rawls' main work, A Theory of Justice *(1971), presents a liberal, egalitarian, moral conception – 'justice as fairness' – designed to explicate and justify the institutions of a constitutional democracy. The two principles of justice outlined in this text affirm the priority of equal basic liberties over other political concerns, and require fair opportunities for all citizens, directing that inequalities in wealth and social positions maximally benefit the least advantaged. Rawls develops the idea of an impartial social contract to justify these principles: Free persons, equally situated and ignorant of their historical circumstances, would rationally agree to them in order to secure their equal status and independence, and to pursue freely their conceptions of the good.*

In Political Liberalism *(1993), his other major text, Rawls revises his original argument for justice as fairness to make it more compatible with the pluralism of liberalism. He argues that, assuming that different philosophical, religious and ethical views are inevitable in liberal society, the most reasonable basis for social unity is a public conception of justice based in shared moral ideas, including citizens' common comception of themselves as free and equal moral persons. The stability of this public conception of justice is provided by an overlapping consensus; all the reasonable comprehensible philosophical, religious and ethical views can endorse it, each for their own specific reasons.*

1 Justice as fairness
2 Democratic institutions
3 Stability
4 Political liberalism

1 Justice as fairness

Rawls' overriding aim is 'to provide the most appropriate moral basis for a democratic society' (1971: viii). Despite its many strengths, he sees the dominant utilitarian tradition as providing deficient foundations for democracy. Rawls begins with a normative conception of persons, whom he describes as free, equal, rational and endowed with a moral capacity for a sense of justice. Because of differences in knowledge and situations, free persons inevitably will develop different conceptions of the good. To pursue their good, they make conflicting claims on scarce resources. Principles of justice regulate the division of benefits and burdens resulting from social cooperation. Rawls contends that the appropriate way to decide principles for a democratic society is by conjecturing what principles free persons would agree to among themselves to regulate basic social institutions (the political constitution, property, markets and the family). But to ensure this agreement is fair, they must abstract knowledge of their own situations – of their talents and social positions and their conceptions of the good. Since these principles will be used to assess the justice of existing institutions and the reasonableness of existing desires and claims, Rawls further envisages that contracting parties abstract not just awareness of their own, but everyone's historical circumstances, desires and conceptions of the good. They are to be placed behind a thick 'veil of ignorance'. What such free individuals do know are general social, economic, psychological, and physical theories of all kinds. They also know there are certain all-purpose means that are essential to achieving their good, whatever it might be. These 'primary social goods' are rights and liberties, powers and opportunities, income and wealth, and the basis of self-respect.

The effect of these restrictions on knowledge is to render Rawls' parties strictly equal. This enables Rawls to carry to the limit the intuitive idea of the democratic social contract tradition: that justice is what could, or would, be agreed to among free persons from a position of equality (see CONTRACTARIANISM). Rawls sees his strong equality condition, along with other moral conditions on agreement (that principles be universal, general, publicly known, final, and so on), as reasonable restrictions on arguments for principles of justice for the basic structure of society. These conditions define the 'original position', the perspective from which rational agents are to unanimously agree. Parties to the original position are presented with a list of all known feasible conceptions of justice and consider them in pairwise comparisons. The parties are rational, in that all utilize effective means to secure their ends, and are motivated by their interests, and so are moved to acquire an adequate share of the primary social goods needed to pursue their interests. The parties are also assumed to be rationally prudent (with zero time-preference), mutually disinterested (of limited altruism) and without envy.

Given these conditions, Rawls argues that the parties would unanimously agree to justice as fairness over the classical and average principles of utility, perfectionist and intuitionistic conceptions, and rational egoism. Its main principles state: (1) each person has an equal right to a fully adequate scheme of equal basic liberties, compatible with a similar scheme of liberties for all; and (2) social and economic inequalities must be attached to offices and positions open to all under conditions of fair equality of opportunity and must be to the greatest benefit of the least advantaged members of society (the 'difference principle'). The basic liberties of the first principle are liberty of conscience, freedom of thought, equal political rights, freedom of association, freedoms specified to maintain the liberty and integrity of the person (including rights to personal property), and the rights and liberties covered by the rule of law. These liberties are basic in that they have priority over the difference principle; their equality cannot be infringed, even if inequalities would increase the opportunities or wealth of those least advantaged. Moreover, the rights implied by both principles have priority over all other social values: they cannot be infringed or traded for the sake of efficiency, others' likes and dislikes or perfectionist values of culture.

Rawls' argument for these principles is that, given complete ignorance of everyone's position, it would be irrational to jeopardize one's good to gain whatever marginal advantages might be promised by other alternatives. For included in one's conception of the good are the religious and philosophical convictions and ethical ways of life that give one's existence meaning. It is fundamentally irrational, Rawls contends, to gamble with these given complete ignorance of risks and probabilities. In his later work, Rawls contends that parties in the original position are also moved by 'higher-order interests' to develop and exercise the 'moral powers' that enable them to engage in social cooperation – the capacity to form, revise and rationally pursue a conception of the good, and the capacity to understand, apply and act from a sense of justice. Parties agree on the two principles underlying justice as fairness since they provide each

with primary goods adequate to realize these powers; other alternatives jeopardize these conditions.

One objection to Rawls' theory is that the parties' 'maximin' strategy of choice is too conservative. Harsanyi (1982) contends that Rawls' parties should assume an equal probability of being any member in society. Given sympathetic identification with each person's interests, they should choose (as if they were following) the principle of average utility (see UTILITARIANISM). But Harsanyi's ideal chooser, although ignorant of their own identity, still has full knowledge of everyone's desires and situations; Harsanyi views such knowledge as necessary for sympathetic identification. But Rawls' parties are without knowledge of anyone's desires and circumstances, and thus are rendered incapable of sympathetic identification, as well as making interpersonal comparisons of utility. Rawls also finds that, especially under conditions of radical uncertainty, gambling freedom to practise one's conscientious convictions against added resources betrays a failure to understand what it is to have a conception of the good. For these and other reasons Rawls contends that it is difficult to see how the argument for average utility can arise from his original position. More important, assuming publicity of basic principles, a utilitarian society will not command the willing allegiance of everyone (especially those made worse off), and so will not evince stability (see §3). That basic political principles be publicly known is required by democratic freedom; otherwise citizens are under illusions about the bases of their social relations and are manipulated by forces placed beyond their control. With Rawls' liberal egalitarian principles, nothing is, nor need be, hidden from public view in order to maintain social stability.

2 Democratic institutions

For Rawls the role of democratic legislation is not to register citizens' unconstrained preferences and let majority preferences rule, but to advance the interests of all citizens, so that each has the status of equal citizen, is suitably independent and can freely pursue a good consistent with justice. The two principles of justice as fairness designate a common good that provides the end of democratic legislation. Ideally it should not be individual or group interests voting, but citizens and legislators, whose judgments are based on laws that best realize the common good of justice, as defined by the two principles. These principles imply a liberal constitution that specifies basic liberties immune from majority infringement. The first principle also requires maintaining the fair value of each citizen's political rights, thereby establishing a limit on inequalities in wealth allowable by the difference principle. The second principle, the 'difference principle', preserves the 'fair value' of the remaining basic liberties. It suggests a criterion for deciding the basic minimum of resources each citizen needs to fairly and effectively exercise the basic liberties: property and economic institutions are to be so designed that those least advantaged have resources exceeding what the worst off would acquire under any alternative economic scheme (consistent with the first principle). This implies (depending on historical conditions) either a property-owning democracy (with widespread private ownership of the means of production) or liberal socialism. In either case, Rawls assumes markets are needed for efficient *allocation* of factors of production; but use of markets for *distribution* of output is constrained by the difference principle. Whatever effect redistributions from the market have on allocative efficiency is not a problem for Rawls, since justice has priority over efficiency. The end of justice is not to maximize productive output whatever the distributive effects, any more than it is to maximize aggregate utility (see JUSTICE §5).

3 Stability

The argument from the original position aims to show that justice as fairness best coheres with our considered judgments of justice (in 'reflective equilibrium'). But why should we care about justice enough to allow its requirements to outweigh our other aims? Stability addresses this issue of motivation. A conception of justice is 'stable' whenever departures from it call into play forces within a just system that tend to restore the arrangement. Unstable conceptions are utopian, not realistic possibilities. HOBBES argued that stability required a nearly absolute sovereign. This is incompatible with Rawls' democratic aim. To argue that justice as fairness is stable, Rawls appeals to principles of moral psychology to show how citizens in a 'well-ordered society' can acquire a settled disposition to act on and from the principles of justice. He then argues that justice as fairness is compatible with human nature, and is even 'congruent' with citizens' good in a society well-ordered by justice as fairness.

A person's good is the plan of life they would rationally choose based on their considered interests from an informed position of 'deliberative rationality'. Rawls' congruence argument contends that it is rational, part of a person's good, to be just and reasonable for their own sake in a well-ordered society. Assuming citizens there have a sense of justice, it is instrumentally rational for them to cultivate this capacity by doing justice, in order to

achieve the benefits of social cooperation. On the Kantian interpretation of justice as fairness, the capacity for justice is among the powers that define our nature as rational agents; by developing and exercising this power for its own sake, citizens realize their nature and achieve moral autonomy. The Aristotelian principle is a psychological law which implies that it is rational to want to develop the higher capacities implicit in one's nature. Since the circumstances of a well-ordered society describe optimal conditions for exercising one's sense of justice, it is rational to want to cultivate the virtue of justice for its own sake and achieve moral autonomy. Justice and moral autonomy are then intrinsic and supreme goods in a well-ordered society, so the Right and the Good are 'congruent'. If so, it is not rational to depart from justice, and a well-ordered society manifests inherent stability.

HEGEL argued that Rousseau's social contract, like Hobbes's, was individualistic and incompatible with the values of community. Contemporary communitarians (for example, Sandel 1982) re-state Hegel's criticism, contending that Rawls' original position presupposes abstract individualism, with a metaphysical conception of persons as essentially devoid of the final ends and commitments that constitute their identity (see COMMUNITY AND COMMUNITARIANISM). In *Political Liberalism* (1993) Rawls contends that this is mistaken. In *A Theory of Justice* he presupposes, not a metaphysical conception of persons, but a practical account of the conditions of political agency, as grounded in the moral powers. Given congruence, maintaining justice and just institutions is the shared good that underwrites the values of community (or 'social union') among free and equal moral persons.

Rawls' Kantian congruence argument addresses the classical aim of showing how justice can be compatible with the human good. It is one of Rawls' most original contributions to moral philosophy. It also bears implications that led Rawls subsequently to revise his view.

4 Political liberalism

The problem with congruence is that it conflicts with the 'reasonable pluralism' of liberal societies, which should tolerate a wide range of religious, philosophical and moral views. The 'burdens of judgment' imply certain limitations on judgment, so that under free institutions we cannot expect agreement upon a comprehensive metaphysical, religious, or moral doctrine or conception of the good. But congruence implies that widespread acceptance of the intrinsic good of moral autonomy is a condition of liberal stability. By hypothesis, most conceptions of the good in a well-ordered society can endorse Rawls' principles of justice. The problem is, some may not accept the intrinsic goodness of moral autonomy. Teleological views, such as liberal Thomism or a reasonable utilitarianism, will gain adherents in a well-ordered society, and for these views justice and autonomy are at best but instrumental to the one rational and intrinsic good (the Vision of God, and aggregate or average utility, respectively). The incompatibility of congruence with reasonable pluralism then undermines Rawls' original argument for stability.

In *Political Liberalism* Rawls reformulates the justification of justice as fairness as a 'freestanding' political conception. He aims to provide a public justification for justice as fairness acceptable to all citizens of a well-ordered democracy. This requires an argument that is not grounded in Kant's or some other comprehensive ethical doctrine, but rather in certain fundamental intuitive ideas implicit in democratic culture. Rawls argues that the features of the original position can be construed as a 'procedural representation' of the idea of social cooperation among free and equal citizens implicit in a democracy. The principles of justice can then be represented as 'constructed' from a 'model conception' of democratic citizens as free, equal and possessed of the two moral powers that enable them to participate in social cooperation. These principles are politically justified since they are presented, not as true, but as most reasonable; they fit best with the considered political convictions of justice shared by democratic citizens, at all levels of generality, in wide reflective equilibrium (see LIBERALISM §5).

To complete this freestanding political justification, however, Rawls needs an alternative stability argument, one that, unlike congruence, does not rely upon premises peculiar to Kant's moral philosophy. The idea of 'overlapping consensus' says that the conception of justice that is politically justified as reasonable on grounds of individuals' shared conception of themselves as democratic citizens, will also be judged most reasonable or true on independent grounds, specific to each of the reasonable comprehensive doctrines gaining adherents in a well-ordered society. For its own particular reasons, each comprehensive view (for example, Kantians, utilitarians, pluralists, and religions accepting a doctrine of free faith) can endorse justice as fairness as true or reasonable. Justice as fairness then has one public, but many nonpublic, justifications in a well-ordered society. Assuming an overlapping consensus of reasonable comprehensive views exists there, justice as fairness evinces willing compliance, and hence stability.

See also: EQUALITY; FREEDOM AND LIBERTY; RIGHTS

List of works

Rawls, J. (1971) *A Theory of Justice*, Cambridge, MA: Harvard University Press. (Rawls' major work.)
—— (1975a) 'The Independence of Moral Theory', *Proceedings and Addresses of the American Philosophy Association* 48 (November): 5–22. (Argues that justice as fairness relies on a moral conception of the person, not a metaphysical conception of personal identity.)
—— (1975b) 'Fairness to Goodness', *Philosophical Review* 84 (4): 536–54. (Response to early critics.)
—— (1980) 'Kantian Constructivism in Moral Philosophy', *Journal of Philosophy* 77 (9): 512–72. (Important transitional work, in which Rawls introduces an account of Kantian constructivism.)
—— (1982) 'Social Unity and Primary Goods', in A. Sen and B. Williams (eds) *Utilitarianism and Beyond*, Cambridge: Cambridge University Press, 159–85. (Contends that primary social goods are basic needs of free and equal moral persons.)
—— (1985) 'Justice as Fairness: Political, not Metaphysical', *Philosophy and Public Affairs* 14 (3): 223–51. (Begins the transition to political liberalism.)
—— (1993) *Political Liberalism*, New York: Columbia University Press. (Significant reworking of the basis of justification for 'justice as fairness'.)

References and further reading

Barry, B. (1973) *The Liberal Theory of Justice*, Oxford: Oxford University Press. (Early assessment of *A Theory of Justice*.)
Daniels, N. (ed.) (1989) *Reading Rawls*, Stanford, CA: Stanford University Press. (Collection of the major critical reactions to *A Theory of Justice* in the early 1970s by Hart, Dworkin, Daniels, Scanlon, Nagel, Hare, Sen and others.)
* Harsanyi, J. (1982) 'Morality and the Theory of Rational Behaviour', in A. Sen and B. Williams (eds) *Utilitarianism and Beyond*, Cambridge: Cambridge University Press. (Argues that behind a veil of ignorance, rational agents would choose, not Rawls' principles of justice, but maximizing average utility.)
Hegel, G.W.F. (1821) *Philosophy of Right*, trans. H.B. Nisbet, ed. A. Wood, Cambridge: Cambridge University Press, 1991. (Critical of liberal democracy and the social contract tradition on the grounds that they undermine community.)
Martin, R. (1985) *Rawls and Rights*, Lawrence, KS: University Press of Kansas. (Focuses on the centrality of basic rights in Rawls' view.)
Pogge, T. (1989) *Realizing Rawls*, Ithaca, NY: Cornell

University Press. (Defends justice as fairness against libertarian and communitarian criticisms, and argues for applying Rawls to global justice.)

* Sandel, M. (1982) *Liberalism and the Limits of Justice*, Cambridge: Cambridge University Press. (Communitarian criticism of Rawls.)

Symposium on *Political Liberalism* (1994), *Chicago-Kent Law Review* 69 (3). (Contains articles by Cohen, Freeman and Greenawalt, among others, on Rawls' *Political Liberalism*.)

SAMUEL FREEMAN

AL-RAZI, ABU BAKR MUHAMMAD IBN ZAKARIYYA' (D. 925)

Perhaps the most famous and widely respected Islamic authority on medicine in the medieval period, al-Razi also aspired to a comparable achievement in philosophy and the other sciences such as alchemy. His success in these other subjects, however, was seldom recognized either in his own time or later; in philosophy, for example, more writers cite him for purposes of rejection and refutation than for admiration and emulation. However, his ideas were and are important. Chief among his positive contributions is his advocacy of a doctrine of equal aptitude in all humans, which grants no special role for unique and divinely favoured prophets and which recognizes the possibility of future progress in the advancement of knowledge. Philosophically, al-Razi was by his own admission a disciple of Socrates and Plato, much of whose teaching he knew on the basis of the latter's Timaeus. *Accordingly, he was noted for upholding the eternity of five primary principles, God, soul, time, matter and space, and for a concept of pleasure that sees it as the return to a normal harmony following a serious deviation or disruption which is itself pain.*

1 Life and work
2 Metaphysics
3 Ethical and moral philosophy

1 Life and work

Al-Razi's main career was that of a physician, and in that field he earned great respect and wide acclaim even from his most vociferous detractors in other matters. He directed two major hospitals, one in Baghdad, the capital of the Islamic empire at that time, and another in his native city of Rayy in northern Iran. His voluminous writings on medicine were universally admired. Despite advancing infirmities, he continued his research and writing into old age, still surrounded by students and assistants when he died in AH 313/AD 925. In Christian Europe he was known as Rhazes, and his works on medicine were highly respected.

The whole of al-Razi's work, both in medicine and the physical sciences and in philosophy, derives its central concern from his naturalistic view of the universe as like a 'visible animal' which, in contrast to almost all of the other philosophers in his era, he regarded as a subject of empirical scrutiny. At the heart of his philosophy lies Plato's *Timaeus*, which seems to have been al-Razi's ultimate inspiration (see PLATO). He displayed almost no interest in the rest of Plato, although curiously he was the most avowedly loyal follower of Plato in Arabic and Islamic literature. His other idol was, as might be expected, SOCRATES, whose way of life he attempted to emulate, advocate and defend; although al-Razi's Socrates was not the extreme ascetic of an earlier period in Socrates' life but rather a later, fully participating social being. For Aristotle he had little use, rejecting outright commonly accepted doctrines that had deeply influenced his philosophical contemporaries (see ARISTOTELIANISM IN ISLAMIC PHILOSOPHY). Unusually for his time, al-Razi boldly claimed that he could and had moved beyond his ancient philosophical predecessors and that neither the religious prophets nor the Greek masters (nor even al-Razi himself) possessed the final word or ultimate truth. Others in the future can and will surpass the achievements already realized by the great minds of the past and present.

Although denying prophetic religion, al-Razi's own ethical philosophy suggests a kind of religion that encompasses God and the universal soul, and hints at the salvation of particular souls. Nevertheless, writings of his on the falsity of prophets were broadly and specifically condemned and he was branded an archheretic for them. An opponent quotes him as claiming that the Qur'an yields no information of particular value in comparison with the books of Ptolemy, Euclid, Hippocrates, Galen, Plato or even Aristotle. It is clear that al-Razi would not accommodate revealed religion, which he saw as both particularistic and divisive. There is thus no harmony to be found between such religion and philosophy – a dangerous and certainly radical stance to take in his day. Al-Razi's metaphysical doctrines received no approval from later scholars. As a consequence, with the exception of two treatises on ethics, few of his non-medical works survive, thereby making a fair and detailed judgment of his ideas now difficult and often impossible.

2 Metaphysics

The metaphysical doctrine of al-Razi, insofar as it can be reconstructed, derives from his concept of the five eternal principles. God, for him, does not 'create' the world from nothing but rather arranges a universe out of pre-existing principles. His account of the soul features a mythic origin of the world in which God out of pity fashions a physical playground for the soul in response to its own desires; the soul, once fallen into the new realm God has made for it, requires God's further gift of intellect in order to find its way once more to salvation and freedom (see SOUL IN ISLAMIC PHILOSOPHY).

In this scheme, intellect does not appear as a separate principle but is rather a later grace of God to the soul; the soul becomes intelligent, possessed of reason and therefore able to discern the relative value of the other four principles. Whereas the five principles are eternal, intellect as such is apparently not. Such a doctrine of intellect is sharply at odds with that of all of al-Razi's philosophical contemporaries, who are in general either adherents of some form of Neoplatonism or of Aristotelianism.

The remaining three principles, space, matter and time, serve as the non-animate components of the natural world. Space is defined by the relationship between the individual particles of matter, or atoms, and the void that surrounds them. The greater the density of material atoms, the heavier and more solid the resulting object; conversely, the larger the portion of void, the lighter and less solid. Time and matter have both an absolute, unqualified form and a limited form (see MATTER; TIME). Thus there is an absolute matter – pure extent – that does not depend in any way on place, just as there is a time, in this sense, that is not defined or limited by motion. The absolute time of al-Razi is, like matter, infinite; it thus transcends the time which Aristotle confined to the measurement of motion. Al-Razi, in the cases of both time and matter, knew well how he differed from Aristotle and also fully accepted and intended the consequences inherent in his anti-Peripatetic positions.

3 Ethical and moral philosophy

More can be said about al-Razi's ethical doctrines because two of his treatises that contain elements of a moral philosophy – al-Tibb al-ruhani (The Spiritual Physick) and al-Sira al-falsafiyya (The Philosophical Life) – have survived. On the one hand, al-Razi saw ethics as a kind of psychological medicine. The restoration of equilibrium following upon dislocation is the goal of spiritual or psychic healing, and preventing such disruptions is ethics. For him,

pleasure is not a positive or cumulative affection but instead the result of a prior pain that was itself caused by a rupture or departure from the normal state and which thereafter ceases as the normal condition returns or is restored. Passion and appetites will occur naturally but they must be restrained by reason from growing to excess; they should be neither served nor encouraged. True virtue lies in satisfying every need only so far as is indispensable. Al-Razi was against all forms of asceticism, specifically those practised by Muslims. In comparison to the ascetic model of Socrates, contemporaries faulted him for leading a public existence, marrying and having children, earning a living and enjoying the company of princes. Al-Razi, however, vigorously denied that such asceticism was true of his ancient master; Socrates, he insisted, eventually did return to public life and thereafter avoided the extremes of his earlier position.

Equally al-Razi denied excesses of commission as well as abstinence. The merciful Lord, he said, does not approve the causing of pain and injustice; hence inflicting hurt either on oneself or on any other being is wrong unless necessary or inevitable. All must be in accord with nature and thus, on occasion, the greater good or benefit may require it. In this way al-Razi warned against the needless slaughter of animals (except in the case of wild, carnivorous creatures whose own extinction may spare their victims' death and also provide for the release of the beast's own soul).

On the other hand, al-Razi, in line with his emphasis on the controlling role of reason, believed that philosophy and the philosophic life yields the only salvation that is ultimately possible (see SALVATION). Pursuit of that life is to imitate God in the way possible for humankind. The ultimate end for which humans were created does not comprise a physical existence but another world, one without death and pain. The human soul will achieve its hold on that world in proportion to the quality of its previous life while in the body. Those who practise justice and seek to acquire knowledge – that is, to lead the philosophical life – become habituated to reason, living free of the body and accustomed to unceasing joy. Upon death this will be their permanent state. In contrast, those who cling to a physical existence will, as Plato said, fail to depart this world of generation and corruption and will therefore continue to suffer pain and unending distress.

See also: ETHICS IN ISLAMIC PHILOSOPHY; PLATONISM IN ISLAMIC PHILOSOPHY; SOUL IN ISLAMIC PHILOSOPHY

List of works

al-Razi (before 925) *al-Tibb al-ruhani* (The Spiritual Physick), ed. P. Kraus in *Rasa'il falsafiyya li-Abu Bakr Muhammad b. Zakariyya' al-Razi*, Cairo: Fouad I University Faculty of Letters, 1939; repr. Beirut: Dar al-Afaq al-Jadida, 1973; trans A. Arberry, *The Spiritual Physick of Rhazes*, London: John Murray, 1950. (An account of al-Razi's philosophical and ethical psychology.)

—— (before 925) *al-Sira al-falsafiyya* (The Philosophical Life), ed. P. Kraus in *Rasa'il falsafiyya li-Abu Bakr Muhammad b. Zakariyya' al-Razi*, Cairo: Fouad I University Faculty of Letters, 1939; repr. Beirut: Dar al-Afaq al-Jadida, 1973; trans. A. Arberry, 'Apologia Pro Vita Sua', in *Aspects of Islamic Civilization*, London: George Allen & Unwin, 1964. (Al-Razi's own philosophical autobiography.)

References and further reading

Goodman, L. (1971) 'The Epicurean Ethic of M. b. Zakariya' al-Razi', *Studia Islamica* 34: 5–26. (An account of the links between Epicureanism and al-Razi.)

—— (1972) 'Razi's Psychology', *Philosophical Forum* 4: 26–48. (An explanation of the implications and background of his psychological views.)

—— (1975) 'Razi's Myth of the Fall of the Soul: Its Function in His Philosophy', in G. Hourani (ed.) *Essays in Islamic Philosophy and Science*, Albany, NY: State University of New York Press, 25–40. (A detailed account of the doctrine of the soul.)

—— (1994) 'Al-Razi, Abu Bakr Muhammad b. Zakariya'', *Encyclopaedia of Islam*, new edn. vol. VIII: 474–77. (An excellent summary of all that is known about al-Razi and his work.)

—— (1996) 'Muhammad ibn Zakariyya' al-Razi', in S.H. Nasr and O. Leaman (eds) *History of Islamic Philosophy*, London: Routledge, ch. 13, 198–215. (Description of the life and thought of the thinker, and the wider relevance of his ideas.)

Walker, P. (1992) 'The Political Implications of al-Razi's Philosophy', in C. Butterworth (ed.) *The Political Aspects of Islamic Philosophy*, Cambridge, MA: Harvard University Press, 61–94. (The standard work on al-Razi's political theory.)

PAUL E. WALKER

AL-RAZI, FAKHR AL-DIN (1149–1209)

Imam Fakhr al-Din al-Razi was one of the outstanding figures in Islamic theology. Living in the second half of the sixth century AH (twelfth century AD), he also wrote on history, grammar, rhetoric, literature, law, the natural sciences and philosophy, and composed one of the major works of Qur'anic exegesis, the only remarkable gap in his output being politics. He travelled widely in the eastern lands of Islam, often engaging in heated polemical confrontations. His disputatious character, intolerant of intellectual weakness, frequently surfaces in his writings, but these are also marked by a spirit of synthesis and a profound desire to uncover the truth, whatever its source. A number of his metaphysical positions became well known in subsequent philosophical literature, being cited more often than not for the purposes of refutation. His prolixity and pedantic argumentation were often criticized, but he was widely considered the reviver of Islam in his century.

1 Theology and philosophy
2 Metaphysics

1 Theology and philosophy

Fakhr al-Din al-Razi was born in Rayy near present-day Tehran in AH 543 or 544/AD 1149–50. Like his predecessor al-Ghazali, he was an adherent of the Shafi'i school in law and of the theology of Ash'arism (see ASH'ARIYYA AND MU'TAZILA). He was attracted at an early age to the study of philosophy, in which he soon became proficient. In his late twenties, he visited Khwarazm and Transoxania, where he came in contact with some of the last theologians in the Mu'tazilite tradition. Although he endured hardship and poverty at the beginning of his career, on returning to Rayy from Transoxania he entered into the first of a series of patronage relations with rulers in the east which contributed to his reputedly considerable wealth and authority.

Al-Razi's skill in polemic ensured that controversy followed him in his subsequent sojourns in Khurasan, Bukhara, Samarqand and elsewhere (he is said to have visited India). He consequently made several dangerous enemies, including among them the Karramiyyah (an activist ascetic sect, staunch defenders of a literal interpretation of scripture and of anthropomorphism), the Isma'ilis, and the Hanbalites, each of whom apparently threatened his life at various points. Al-Razi settled finally in Herat, where he had a teaching *madrasa* built for him, and where he died in AH 606/AD 1209.

In the religious sciences, AL-GHAZALI had legitimized the use of logic, while at the same time attacking those key metaphysical doctrines of the philosophers which most offended against orthodox doctrine. This move prepared the ground for the subsequent incorporation of philosophical argumentation into theology. It was through al-Razi that this marriage was most completely effected in the Sunni world. His major theological works all begin with a section on metaphysics, and this was to become the pattern for most later writers.

The problem of how far al-Razi should be considered a philosopher (rather than a theologian) is complicated by changes of view during the course of his life, and by his highly disputatious and often intemperate personality, which he himself acknowledged. His style is marked by an extensively ramifying dialectic, often ending in highly artificial subtleties, and is not easy to follow. The relentlessness and sometimes obvious delight with which al-Razi used this method to home in on his victims earned him among philosophers the sobriquet of Iman al-Mushakkikin (Leader of the Doubters). Nevertheless, al-Razi was scrupulous in representing the views he set out to criticize, manifesting his concern to lay out a rigorous dialectic in which theological ideas could be debated before the arbitration of reason. This predictably brought him under subsequent attack from those who believed that upholding orthodox doctrine was the primary task of theology, one of whom remarked that in al-Razi's works 'the heresy is in cash, the refutation on credit'.

One of al-Razi's major concerns was the self-sufficiency of the intellect. His strongest statements show that he believed proofs based on Tradition (*hadith*) could never lead to certainty (*yaqin*) but only to presumption (*zann*), a key distinction in Islamic thought. On the other hand, his acknowledgement of the primacy of the Qur'an grew with his years. A detailed examination of al-Razi's rationalism has never been undertaken, but he undoubtedly holds an important place in the debate in the Islamic tradition on the harmonization of reason and revelation. In his later years he seems to have shown some interest in mysticism, although this never formed a significant part of his thought.

Al-Razi's most important philosophical writings were two works of his younger days, a commentary (*sharh*) on the physics and metaphysics of Ibn Sina's *Kitab al-isharat wa-'l-tanbihat* (Remarks and Admonitions) (see IBN SINA) and another work on the same subject, *al-Mabahith al-mashriqiyya* (Eastern Studies), which is based in large part on the latter's *al-Shifa'* and *al-Najat* as well as *al-Isharat*, but in which al-Razi frequently preferred the views of Abu 'l-Barakat AL-

BAGHDADI (d. after AH 560/AD 1164–5). Also of great philosophical interest is his theological text *Muhassal al-afkar* (The Harvest of Thought). Perhaps al-Razi's greatest work, however, is the *Mafatih al-ghayb* (The Keys to the Unknown), one of the most extensive commentaries on the Qur'an, running to eight volumes in quarto and known more popularly as simply *al-Tafsir al-kabir* (The Great Commentary). As its more orthodox detractors have been happy to point out, this work, which occupied al-Razi to the end of his life and was completed by a pupil, contains much of philosophical interest.

The person who did the most to defend Ibn Sina, and philosophy in general, against the criticisms of al-Razi was Nasir al-Din AL-TUSI, whose commentary on the *Kitab al-isharat* was in large measure a refutation of al-Razi's opinions. Al-Tusi also wrote a *Talkhis al-muhassal al-afkar* (Abridgement of the *Muhassal al-afkar*), where he likewise undertook a criticism of many of the philosophical criticisms in the *Muhassal al-afkar*.

2 Metaphysics

Al-Razi was associated by later authors with the view that existence is distinct from, and additional to, essence, both in the case of creation and in the case of God, and that pure existence is merely a concept (see EXISTENCE). This view is at variance with the Ash'arite and Mu'tazilite positions, as well as with that of Ibn Sina and his followers. Al-Razi only departed from this view in his commentary on the Qur'an, where he went back to a more traditional view that in God essence and existence are one.

Another challenge to the philosophers for which al-Razi achieved fame was his refutation of the emanationist principle *ex uno non fit nisi unum* (only one can come from one.) In Ibn Sina's formulation, if an indivisible single thing were to give rise to two things, *a* and *b*, this would result in a contradiction, for the same single thing would be the source of both *a* and of not-*a* (= *b*). Al-Razi's refutation was based on the claim that the contradictory of 'the emanation of *a*' is 'the non-emanation of *a*', not 'the emanation of not-*a*'. On a related point, he originally denied the possibility of a vacuum, but in his *Mafatih* he argues for its existence, and for the power of the Almighty to fill it with an infinity of universes.

The philosophers, following Ibn Sina, held knowledge to be an inhering in the knower of the form of the thing known, and that consequently God knew only universals and not particulars, knowledge of the latter implying inadmissible changes in God's essence as particulars changed (see IMMUTABILITY). For the most part theologians were opposed to thus restrict-

113

ing God's knowledge, on the grounds that he was omniscient (see OMNISCIENCE). Al-Razi upheld the theological side of the debate through postulating that knowledge involved a relation between the knower and the thing known, so that a change in the thing known would produce a change in the relation but not in the essence of the knower. This notion of a relation involved the substitution of a philosophical term, *idafa* (relation), for a theological one, *ta'alluq* (connection), in an argument about the attribute of knowledge which belonged essentially to Abu 'l-Husayn al-Basri's Mu'tazilite school.

In ethics, al-Razi held that God alone, through revelation, determines moral values for man, it being these which give rise to praise and blame. God himself was beyond the moral realm and acted from no purpose extraneous to himself, be it out of pure goodness or for the benefit of his creation. Following AL-GHAZALI, and before him AL-JUWAYNI, al-Razi's solution to the problem posed for divine subjectivists by God's threats of punishment and reward was to acknowledge a subjective rational capacity within man allowing him to understand what causes him pleasure and pain and thus enabling him to perceive where his advantage lies. In his *'Ilm al-akhlaq* (Science of Ethics) al-Razi built upon al-Ghazali's ethical writings, particularly from the *Ihya' 'ulum al-din*, providing a systematic framework based on psychology, again under the influence of al-Baghdadi (see ETHICS IN ISLAMIC PHILOSOPHY).

On the question of free will, al-Razi took a radical determinist position and rejected outright the Ash'arite doctrine of *kasb* (acquisition). Al-Razi postulated two factors necessary for the production of an action: the power to do it or not to do it, and a preponderating factor, the motivation, which leads to the action being performed or not. Once the preponderating factor exists together with the power, either the act comes about necessarily or else it becomes impossible. Al-Razi pushed this essentially Mu'tazilite thesis, which is also similar to Ibn Sina's thinking, to its logical conclusion, arguing that both the power and the preponderating factor had to be created by God for the result to exist necessarily, and hence that all human actions have been produced through God's determination. We thus appear to be free agents because we act according to our motives, but in reality we are constrained. A consequence of this theory when it is applied to God's own acts is that since God acts through his power, he must himself either act through constraint (if there is a preponderating factor in this case) or else by chance (if there is not), both of which conclusions violate the central Sunnite position that God is a totally free agent. Those who came after al-Razi felt that he had never

adequately solved this difficulty, and he himself confessed that, whether from the point of view of reason or of tradition, there was in the end no satisfactory solution to the free will problem (see FREE WILL).

Al-Razi held the Ash'arite position that God could re-create what had been made inexistent, and this formed the basis of his literal understanding of bodily resurrection. However, he also expressed views which were influenced by the theory of the late Mu'tazili Ibn al-Malahimi, who held the contrary position on the restoration of non-existence, that the world did not pass into non-existence but its parts were dissociated, and that the essential of these parts were reassembled on the resurrection. This ambivalence on al-Razi's part perhaps reflects the changes in his position on atomism, which he vehemently denied in his earlier purely philosophical works but of which he was more supportive towards the end of his life.

See also: AL-GHAZALI; IBN SINA; ISLAMIC THEOLOGY; AL-TUSI

List of works

al-Razi, Fakhr al-Din (before 1185) *al-Mabahith al-mashriqiyya fi 'ilm al-ilahiyyat wa-'l-tabi'iyyat* (Eastern Studies in Metaphysics and Physics), Hyderabad: Da'irat al-Ma'arif al-Nizamiyyah, 1923–4, 2 vols; repr. Tehran, 1966. (One of al-Razi's most important philosophical texts.)

—— (before 1239) *al-Tafsir al-kabir* (The Great Commentary), Cairo: al-Matba'ah al Bahiyyah al-Misriyyah, 1938, 32 vols in 16; several reprints. (Al-Razi's commentary on the Qur'an, completed by his pupil al-Khuwayyi; useful in many places as in indication of his later philosophical positions.)

—— (before 1209) *Muhassal afkar al-mutaqaddimin wa-'l-muta'akhkhirin min al-'ulama' wa-'l-hukama' wa-'l-mutakallimin* (The Harvest of the Thought of the Ancients and Moderns), Cairo: al-Matba'ah al Bahiyyah al-Misriyyah, 1905. (Printed with al-Tusi's *Talkhis al-Muhassal* at the bottom of the page and al-Razi's *al-Ma'alim fi usul al-din* (The Waymarks and Principles of Religion) in the margin.)

—— (before 1209) *Kitab al-nafs wa-'l-ruh wa sharh quwa-huma* (Book on the Soul and the Spirit and their Faculties), ed. M.S.H. al-Ma'sumi, Islamabad: Islamic Research Institute, 1968; trans. M.S.H. al-Ma'sumi, *Imam Razi's 'Ilm al-akhlaq*, Islamabad: Islamic Research Institute, 1969. (Al-Razi's work on ethics.)

—— (before 1209) *Sharh al-Isharat* (Commentary on the *Isharat*). (No critical edition of al-Razi's commentary on Ibn Sina's *Kitab al-isharat* has appeared. Portions can be found in S. Dunya (ed.) *al-Isharat wa-'l-tanbihat*, Cairo: Dar al-Ma'arif, 1957–60, 4 parts, 3 vols in 2; also in *al-Isharat wa-'l-tanbihat*, Tehran: Matba'at al-Haydari, 1957–9, 3 vols. Both these editions contain al-Tusi's commentary as well as parts of Fakhr al-Din al-Razi's commentary, to which al-Tusi is responding. The Tehran edition also contains Qutb al-Din al-Razi's commentary, which set out to adjudicate between al-Tusi and al-Razi.)

—— (before 1209) *Lubab al-Isharat* (The Pith of the *Isharat*), ed. M. Shihabi in *al-Tanbihat wa-'l isharat*, Tehran: Tehran University Press, 1960; ed. A. 'Atiyah, Cairo: Maktabat al-Kharji, 1936/7. (Al-Razi's epitome of Ibn Sina's work, written after he had completed his commentary.)

References and further reading

Abrahamov, B. (1992) 'Fakhr al-Din al-Razi on God's Knowledge of Particulars', *Oriens* 33: 133–55. (Discussion of a key point of difference between Islamic theologians and philosophers.)

Arnaldez, R. (1960) 'L'oeuvre de Fakhr al-Din al-Razi commentateur du Coran et philosophe' (The Works of Fakhr al-Din al-Razi, Qu'ranic Commentator and Philosopher), *Cahiers du Civilization médiévale, Xe–XIIe siècles* 3: 307–23. (In this article, Arnaldez has dug into al-Razi's enormous commentary on the Qur'an to come up with his mature philosophical ideas. Can be compared with McAuliffe (1990) and Mahdi's response to McAuliffe.)

—— (1989) 'Trouvailles philosophiques dans le commentaire coranique de Fakhr al-Dîn al-Râzî', *Études Orientales* 4: 17–26. (A follow-up to Arnaldez (1960).)

Ibn Sina (980–1037) *Kitab al-Isharat wa-'l-tanbihat* (Remarks and Admonitions), trans. A.-M. Goichon, *Livre des directives et remarques*, Beirut and Paris, 1951. (Introduction and notes by the translator. Contained in the notes are a number of al-Razi's comments from his commentary on this work, as well as some of al-Tusi's criticisms of al-Razi.)

Kholeif, F. (1966) *A Study on Fakhr al-Din al-Razi and His Controversies in Transoxania*, Pensée Arabe et Musulmane 31, Beirut: Dar al-Machreq Éditeurs. (Arabic text and English translation of al-Razi's text of sixteen questions (philosophical, logical, legal) broached with scholars in Transoxania; gives a good idea of al-Razi's style. Also contains a list of al-Razi's works.)

Kraus, P. (1936–7) 'Les "Controverses" de Fakhr al-Din Razi' (The 'Controversies' of Fakhr al-Din al-Razi), *Bulletin de l'Institut d'Egypte* 19: 187–214. (An important early study of the 'controversies' translated in Kholeif (1966). An English translation appears in 'The controversies of Fakhr al-Din Razi', *Islamic Culture* 12, 1938: 131–53.)

McAuliffe, J.D. (1990) 'Fakhr al-Din al-Razi on God as al-Khaliq', in D.B. Burrell and B. McGinn (eds) *God and Creation: An Ecumenical Symposium*, Notre Dame, IN: University of Notre Dame Press, 276–96. (An examination of al-Razi's late philosophical theology, with particular reference to the problem of creation; see also M. Mahdi's response in the same volume (297–303) on the general question of al-Razi as philosopher.)

JOHN COOPER

REALISM *see* MORAL REALISM; REALISM IN THE PHILOSOPHY OF MATHEMATICS; REALISM AND ANTIREALISM; SCIENTIFIC REALISM AND ANTIREALISM; SCIENTIFIC REALISM AND SOCIAL SCIENCE

REALISM AND ANTIREALISM

The basic idea of realism is that the kinds of thing which exist, and what they are like, are independent of us and the way in which we find out about them; antirealism denies this. Most people find it natural to be realists with respect to physical facts: how many planets there are in the solar system does not depend on how many we think there are, or would like there to be, or how we investigate them; likewise, whether electrons exist or not depends on the facts, not on which theory we favour. However, it seems natural to be antirealist about humour: something's being funny is very much a matter of whether we find it funny, and the idea that something might really be funny even though nobody ever felt any inclination to laugh at it seems barely comprehensible. The saying that 'beauty is in the eye of the beholder' is a popular expression of antirealism in aesthetics. An obviously controversial example is that of moral values; some maintain that they are real (or 'objective'), others that they have no existence apart from human feelings and attitudes.

115

This traditional form of the distinction between realism and its opposite underwent changes during the 1970s and 1980s, largely due to Michael Dummett's proposal that realism and antirealism (the latter term being his own coinage) were more productively understood in terms of two opposed theories of meaning. Thus, a realist is one who would have us understand the meanings of sentences in terms of their truth-conditions (the situations that must obtain if they are to be true); an antirealist holds that those meanings are to be understood by reference to assertability-conditions (the circumstances under which we would be justified in asserting them).

1   **Facets of the debate**
2   **Ontological realism/antirealism**
3   **Epistemological versions**
4   **Logical and semantic versions**

1   Facets of the debate

Realism became a prominent topic in medieval times, when it was opposed to nominalism in the debate concerning whether universals were independent properties of things or if classification was just a matter of how people spoke or thought (see NOMINALISM). The impetus for the debate in modern times comes from Kant's doctrine that the familiar world is 'empirically real' but 'transcendentally ideal', that is to say a product of our ways of experiencing things, not a collection of things as they are 'in themselves' or independently of us. Kant's 'empirical realism', confusingly, is thus a form of antirealism (see KANT, I. §5).

Closely related is 'internal realism', as represented by Hilary Putnam, according to which something may be real from the standpoint marked out by a particular theoretical framework, while the attempt to ask whether it is real *tout court* without reference to any such framework is dismissed as nonsensical (see PUTNAM, H. §§7–8). This re-affirms the thesis propounded earlier by Rudolf Carnap, that there are 'internal' and 'external' questions about existence or reality (see CARNAP, R. §5). An internal question is asked by someone who has adopted a language of a certain structure and asks the question on that basis. Only philosophers attempt to ask external questions (are there really – independently of the way we speak – physical objects?). But this is either nonsense or a misleading way of asking whether our linguistic framework is well suited to our practical purposes. 'Internal realism', it should be noted, is certainly not a form of realism, since it admits only language- or theory-relative assertions of existence.

By the mid-1980s, largely as a result of the work of

Putnam and DUMMETT, it had become common to formulate the distinction between realism and antirealism in a variety of what are *prima facie* quite different ways. A realist, it was said, thinks of truth in terms of correspondence with fact, whereas an antirealist defines truth 'in epistemic terms', for instance as 'what a well-conducted investigation under ideal circumstances would lead us to believe'. A realist holds that there are, or could be, 'recognition-transcendent facts', whereas an antirealist denies this. Also present was the idea that an antirealist believes that there can be a 'reductive analysis' (see §2 below) of whatever subject matter their antirealism relates to, whereas a realist holds such analysis to be impossible. Seemingly still further from the origins of the distinction, it was said to be characteristic of realism to accept, and of antirealism to deny, the general validity of the law of excluded middle. Yet another version located the basic difference in the respective theories of meaning: a realist gave the meaning of a sentence by specifying its truth-conditions, an antirealist by specifying the conditions under which it could properly be asserted.

To come to terms with this debate, the reader therefore needs an awareness of the interrelations of the many definitions of the realism–antirealism distinction, and of the inexactness of fit between some of them and others.

2   Ontological realism/antirealism

The primary form of the definition deals directly in terms of what really exists. A realist about Xs, for example, maintains that Xs (or facts or states of affairs involving them) exist independently of how anyone thinks or feels about them; whereas an antirealist holds that they are so dependent. We are not speaking here of causal (in)dependence: the fact that there would be no houses if people had not had certain thoughts should not force us into antirealism about houses. So the point of the definition is better brought out by saying that *what it is for an X to exist* does not involve any such factors (whatever their causal role in the production of Xs may be). Nor does the definition entail an antirealist stance towards the mental. Realism about mental states is a *prima facie* plausible option, holding that our mental states are what they are whatever we think they are, or whatever we would come to think they were if we investigated.

Where philosophers have argued for realism about some particular subject matter (for example, universals, ethical value, the entities of scientific theory), one particular argument is repeatedly found. For the subject matter in question, it is claimed, we find that everyone's opinion is the same, or tends to become the same if they investigate, or that (in science) theory seems to 'converge', later theories appearing to account for the partial success of their predecessors. Why should this be, unless it is the effect of a reality independent of us, our opinions and our theorizing? (See UNIVERSALS; SCIENTIFIC REALISM AND ANTIREALISM.)

In consequence, there are two broad antirealist strategies, both common. One is to argue that the supposed conformity of opinion, actual or potential, does not exist – so we hear of the diversity of ethical or aesthetic judgements, for instance, or the extent to which judgements of colour depend on viewing conditions and the state of the observer. The other is to accept the conformity, but explain it as arising from a uniformity of *our* nature rather than the independent nature of things. Thus it is argued that moral 'objectivity' is really 'inter-subjectivity' – that is, a result of shared human psychological responses rather than of independent moral properties in the world – or that the similarity between different languages' schemes of classification is a product of shared basic human interests, not something forced on us by 'real' universals.

In modern times nobody has made a more radical use of this method of explaining conformity of judgement in terms of intersubjectivity than Kant. He argued that even the experience of our environment as extended in space and time was a human reaction to things that were in themselves not of a spatiotemporal nature, and to which other beings might just as legitimately react altogether differently. In the face of this it may be felt that the argument from conformity is better used to establish a very abstract realism, namely that there must be *something* independent of us, rather than that any specific property or type of thing must be so.

Two other objections have been used against certain forms of realism. One is that the realist provides no account of how the supposed real things or properties can actually have an effect on our experience. What sense do we have, it is asked, that is affected by the ethical properties of the moral realist, or by the real properties of necessity and possibility that the modal realist posits? The common realist practice of speaking of 'intuition' in these contexts is rejected as providing only a word, not an answer. The second type of objection (christened the 'argument from queerness' by John Mackie (1977), who used it in the moral context) claims that the things or properties in which the realist believes would need to be too strange to be credible (see MORAL REALISM; MODAL LOGIC, PHILOSOPHICAL ISSUES IN).

A closely related definition of the realism–antirealism distinction focuses not on the independence of things but on the truth of judgements about them: realism takes truth to be correspondence with fact and our knowledge of truth to be a separate matter, whereas antirealism defines truth 'in epistemic terms', that is to say as what human beings would believe after the best possible application of their cognitive faculties. This is much more a change of perspective than of substance. It is natural to think that if some object exists independently of us, then judging truly must consist in getting our judgement to match the way the object is; while if the object is determined by (perhaps a projection of) our cognitive and/or affective faculties, judging truly can only mean judging as those very faculties lead us to judge.

Harder to assess is the position of *reductive analysis* in the debate. A reductive analysis exists where what makes statements about one kind of thing, *A*, true or false are the facts about another kind *B*. (*A*s are then said to be reducible to *B*s.) Classically, phenomenalism claims that statements about physical objects are thus reducible to statements about sensory experiences; behaviourism holds that propositions about mental states are reducible to ones about dispositions to physical behaviour. Does accepting such a reduction mean accepting antirealism about the *A*s, while rejecting reduction of *A*-statements mean accepting realism? Some philosophers speak in this way, and there is a clear point to doing so: if a reduction is possible, then a complete statement of everything there 'really is' would not need to mention *A*s – it could speak of *B*s instead. Besides, reductive analyses have usually been offered in opposition to a different conception of what *A*s are, and in relation to *that* (rejected) conception of an *A* the reducer is certainly saying that there are no *A*s. But it is not thereby said that *A*s and facts about them are dependent upon us – only that they are really certain sorts of fact about *B*s; our attitude to their independence is therefore a question of whatever we think about the latter (see REDUCTION, PROBLEMS OF).

3 Epistemological versions

It is common to hear realism characterized in terms of the limits of knowledge as the belief that there are, or could be, 'recognition-transcendent facts' (meaning thereby facts which lie beyond *our* cognitive powers – there is no intention to saddle the realist with the view that there may be facts which simply could not be recognized at all). Antirealism then becomes the view that no such facts are possible.

The motivation for this epistemic version of the realism–antirealism divide is not hard to see. If the way something is is independent of the way we are, what could rule out the possibility that there should be facts about it beyond our powers of knowledge? Conversely, if its whole nature is due to the way we 'construct' it through our style of experience and investigation, how could there be anything about it that our cognitive faculties cannot recover? Although understandable, this is quick and imprecise. Consider someone who holds that the nature of the physical world is utterly independent of what human beings may believe it to be, but also has such anthropocentric theological inclinations as to hold that God must have given us cognitive powers equal, in principle, to discovering every fact about it. If we call this philosopher an antirealist on these grounds, we have surely changed the original subject, not just drawn it from another perspective.

This brings out the significance of formulating the epistemic criterion in terms of mere possibility (there *could be* recognition-transcendent facts) rather than actuality, thus allowing the philosopher who thinks, for whatever reason, that our cognitive powers are in fact a match for reality, still to be a realist by virtue of accepting that our powers might have been more limited without reality being any different.

It is one thing to suggest that there may be facts beyond our powers of recognition, quite another to hold that this is true of certain specific facts; the former is just modesty about our cognitive capacities, the latter a positive scepticism. So to imply an intrinsic connection between realism and scepticism, as some do, is very different from identifying realism with a belief in the possibility of recognition-transcendent facts.

Again, there is a plausible line of thought linking realism closely to scepticism. If a certain type of fact is as it is quite independently of us, then our knowledge of it must depend on an intermediary, namely the effect that it has upon us. But then we encounter the sceptical argument of which Descartes' fiction of a malicious demon represents the classic formulation: how are we ever to know that this intermediary effect is produced by the sort of thing we think it is produced by, and not rather by something completely different? Hence, starting with realism, we arrive at scepticism.

However, it seems undesirable to use scepticism (and the absence of it) to characterize the realism–antirealism distinction. The classic argument from realism (as independence of the subject) to scepticism may be a formidable one, but it nevertheless involves substantial assumptions which can be challenged; to adopt terminology which makes it sound as if its conclusion were true by definition invites confusion. Besides, scepticism is not itself a precise notion, and there may be forms of it which apply even under

certain antirealist conceptions. For instance, one who thinks that truth is to be understood as the opinion that would be reached under ideal conditions may still be a sceptic, because they remain sceptical of our ability to recognize ideal conditions or know how closely we have approximated to them.

4 Logical and semantic versions

It is often said that realism and antirealism can be distinguished by their attitude towards the law of excluded middle (the logical principle that, given two propositions one of which is the negation of the other, one of them must be true): the realist accepts it, the antirealist does not. Again, we can understand this if we think back to the original characterization of the distinction in terms of what is independently there and what we 'construct', what is the case 'in itself' and what is so because of our ways of experiencing (see INTUITIONISTIC LOGIC AND ANTIREALISM).

For explanatory purposes we may consider the world of literary fiction. Most people will be happy enough with the idea that, in so far as anything can be said to be true of the world of Macbeth, just those things are true which Shakespeare wrote into it. But in that case neither 'Lady Macbeth had two children' nor its negation 'Lady Macbeth did not have two children' is true, since Shakespeare's text (we may suppose) does not touch on that question; the law of excluded middle fails in this 'constructed' world.

Passing now to a genuinely disputed case, there are those who think that whether a mathematical statement is true is one thing, whether it can be proved quite another; and there are those who think that truth in mathematics can only mean provability. For the latter the law of excluded middle is unsafe. From the fact that not-p cannot be proved, it does not follow that p can be proved; perhaps neither is provable and hence, on this view of mathematical truth, perhaps neither is true. And anyone who equates truth, in whatever sphere, with verifiability-in-principle by us will be liable to the parallel conclusion: only for those propositions p where failure to refute p is *ipso facto* to verify p may we rely on the law of excluded middle. Where verifying p and verifying not-p are distinct procedures, excluded middle fails. (It is because they are characteristically distinct when the proposition in question makes some claim about an infinite totality that we hear so much about infinite totalities and the rejection of excluded middle.) This explains why some writers (in particular Dummett) often say that the difference between realist and antirealist lies in the difference between their conceptions of truth (see ANTIREALISM IN THE

PHILOSOPHY OF MATHEMATICS; REALISM IN THE PHILOSOPHY OF MATHEMATICS).

It can also be seen why it should have become common to express the realism–antirealism opposition as an opposition between theories of meaning, and why philosophers should be found speaking of realist and antirealist semantics. Any theory which ties meaning to verification, which equates the understanding of a sentence with a knowledge of those conditions that would verify it or would justify us in asserting it, promotes the view that we have no other idea of what it is for it to be true than for these conditions to be satisfied. Hence the realism–antirealism debate often exhibits neo-verificationist features; sometimes (especially by Dummett) antirealism is presented as the outcome of Wittgensteinian ideas about meaning, sometimes (especially by Putnam) of the alleged impossibility of explaining how our language could ever come to refer to the mind-independent items that realism posits (see MEANING AND VERIFICATION).

References and further reading

Carnap, R. (1956) 'Empiricism, Semantics and Ontology', in *Meaning and Necessity*, 2nd edn, Chicago, IL: University of Chicago Press, 205–21. (Carnap expounds his distinction between 'external' and 'internal' questions, as mentioned above in §1.)

Dummett, M.A.E. (1963) 'Realism', in *Truth and Other Enigmas*, London: Duckworth, 145–65. (Seminal – and fairly difficult – paper, shifting the debate from the perspectives of §2 above to those of §4.)

Goodman, N. (1978) *Ways of Worldmaking*, Hassocks: Harvester Press. (Chapters I, VI and VII are especially relevant. Entertainingly written presentation of an all-inclusive antirealist position. Grows a little harder and more technical in chapter VII; full understanding of some points calls for knowledge of other works by Goodman.)

James, W. (1907) 'Pragmatism's Conception of Truth', Lecture VI of *Pragmatism* in *Pragmatism and the Meaning of Truth*, Cambridge, MA, and London: Harvard University Press, 1978. (Popular, polemical presentation of the doctrine that 'truth is *made*'.)

* Mackie, J. (1977) *Ethics – Inventing Right and Wrong*, London: Penguin. (Ch.1.9 is especially relevant. Contains the 'argument from queerness' against realism over moral value, referred to in §2 above.)

Putnam, H. (1981) 'Two Philosophical Perspectives', in *Reason, Truth and History*, Cambridge: Cambridge University Press. (Putnam links the traditional form of the debate to the question of the rival accounts of truth and problems about linguistic reference. For the most part not difficult reading; full understanding of some points calls for acquaintance with the two preceding chapters.)

Wright, C.J.G. (1987) *Realism, Meaning and Truth*, Oxford: Blackwell, 1–43. (The Introduction provides a wide-ranging survey of the issues, with antirealist slant; at times quite intricate. Useful bibliography.)

EDWARD CRAIG

REALISM AND ANTIREALISM, SCIENTIFIC

see SCIENTIFIC REALISM AND ANTIREALISM

REALISM IN THE PHILOSOPHY OF MATHEMATICS

Mathematical realism is the view that the truths of mathematics are objective, which is to say that they are true independently of any human activities, beliefs or capacities. As the realist sees it, mathematics is the study of a body of necessary and unchanging facts, which it is the mathematician's task to discover, not to create. These form the subject matter of mathematical discourse: a mathematical statement is true just in case it accurately describes the mathematical facts.

An important form of mathematical realism is mathematical Platonism, the view that mathematics is about a collection of independently existing mathematical objects. Platonism is to be distinguished from the more general thesis of realism, since the objectivity of mathematical truth does not, at least not obviously, require the existence of distinctively mathematical objects.

Realism is in a fairly clear sense the 'natural' position in the philosophy of mathematics, since ordinary mathematical statements make no explicit reference to human activities, beliefs or capacities. Because of the naturalness of mathematical realism, reasons for embracing antirealism typically stem from perceived problems with realism. These potential problems concern our knowledge of mathematical truth, and the connection between mathematical truth and practice. The antirealist argues that the kinds of objective facts posited by the realist would be inaccessible to us, and would bear no clear relation to the procedures we have for determining the truth of mathematical statements. If this is right, then realism implies that mathematical knowledge is inexplicable. The challenge to the realist is to show that the objectivity of mathematical facts does not conflict with our knowledge of them, and to show in particular how our ordinary proof-procedures can inform us about these facts.

1   Platonism and intuitionism
2   Platonism and epistemology
3   Anti-Platonist realism

1   Platonism and intuitionism

Platonism, probably the most popular form of realism (and sometimes itself called 'realism'), is the view that mathematics is the study of a collection of distinctively mathematical objects which exist independently of us: numbers, functions, sets, lines and so on. Thus the Platonist takes mathematical discourse at face value: to say that there exists a prime number between seven and twelve is to make a straightforward existential claim; and to say that nine is greater than seven is to make a comparison between two objects. Mathematical objects, on the Platonist account, are abstract; they occupy no particular position in space or time. They are immutable and eternal, which explains the unchanging character of mathematical truth. They are related to one another in essential and also unchanging ways: the fact that nine is greater than seven, for instance, is no mere accident, but is part of the nature of the system of natural numbers.

On the Platonist account, reasoning about mathematical objects is just like reasoning about ordinary concrete objects, in that the objects, and collections of them, are simply 'out there' waiting to be investigated and described. There are of course many more mathematical than concrete objects, and the abstractness of the mathematical objects sets them apart, but they are none the less like concrete objects in their relation to our cognitive processes: in both cases the objects would exist, bearing the properties and relations they currently bear, whether or not we had ever given them any thought. And in both cases, it is reasonable to suppose that there are facts about the objects which we do not yet know, and even facts which we may be incapable of discovering.

At the other end of the realist/antirealist spectrum from Platonism is the position of 'intuitionism', according to which it makes no sense to speak of true-yet-undiscoverable mathematical facts. According to L.E.J. Brouwer, the twentieth century's paradigm intuitionist, our knowledge of mathematical objects is best explained by the view that these objects

are actually *created*, not discovered, by us: mathematical objects are the products of human mental activity. As the intuitionist sees it, to say, for instance, that there is a natural number with such-and-such property is to say that we can mentally construct such a number. To say that every natural number has a given property is not to make a claim about some pre-existing infinite collection, but is rather to assert the existence of a particular kind of proof-procedure (see INTUITIONISM; CONSTRUCTIVISM IN MATHEMATICS).

Reasoning about infinite collections in general is a much more cautious affair under the intuitionist's strictures than under the Platonist's, since the only true universal claims, according to the intuitionist, are those which come with effective proof-procedures. And because the only states of affairs relevant to the truth of mathematical statements are those given by our own mental constructions, a statement is counted true by the intuitionist just in case it is provable. As a result, the kinds of mathematical reasoning accepted by the intuitionist differ from those accepted by the Platonist, and the intuitionist must reject some of the truths of classical mathematics.

Though the original motivation for intuitionism was a view about the creative powers of the human mind, a quite different motivation stems, in the work of Michael Dummett, from general views about the relationship between meaning, truth and verification (see DUMMETT, M.A.E. §3). As Dummett sees it, to grasp the meaning of a statement is to understand how it is used, and in particular to know what counts as a verification or falsification of it. Since mathematical statements are verified via mathematical proof, the view as applied to mathematics is that the meaning of a mathematical statement is given not in terms of facts which it purportedly represents, but rather in terms of the procedures which would count as a proof of it. Again, the upshot is that truth reduces to provability, and the idea of a realm of independent mathematical facts is rejected as incomprehensible.

The Platonist response to the intuitionist is that the revisionary picture recommended by the latter is under-motivated. Against Dummett, the argument is that we have a perfectly good conception of verification-transcendent truth-conditions, and hence of meaning which is given in terms of objective truth, and independently of provability. With respect to the original intuitionists' conception of mathematical objects, the Platonist's claim is that there is no reason to think of the objects of mathematics as dependent on us, and that the view of the mathematician's activity as one of creation, rather than discovery, does not do justice to this activity. An important complaint made by the Platonist in this regard is that the picture of mathematical objects as mental constructions fails to do justice to the communal nature of mathematical research, since it makes each mathematical object accessible only to its creator.

2 Platonism and epistemology

The strength of the Platonist position is that only the Platonist can hold that the ordinarily-accepted statements of classical mathematics are strictly and literally true. We all want to affirm, in some sense, that there is a prime number between three and six. But having said this, the non-Platonist must add when pressed that the claim is not to be taken quite literally, or is at least not to be taken to have objective truth-conditions. Only the Platonist can say what in weaker moments almost all of us would like to say, which is that there simply *is* a prime number between three and six.

But the literal reading of mathematical discourse does come at a price. Particularly problematic, at least on the face of it, is the explanation of mathematical knowledge. The mathematical objects posited by the Platonist are, unlike concrete objects, entirely divorced from human experience; we cannot perceive them, nor do they bring about any perceptible effects. It is therefore not easy to see how we might be in a position to know anything about them. A central challenge to the Platonist is to show that Platonism does not leave our mathematical knowledge a mystery.

There are two main lines of Platonist response to this epistemological challenge. The first is to claim that we bear a relationship to mathematical objects which is analogous to the perceptual relation we bear to concrete objects: as empirical data are to knowledge of concrete objects, so mathematical intuition is to knowledge of numbers, functions and sets. Such a position is held by Kurt Gödel (1944), who points out that even our knowledge of concrete objects is not direct, but is inferred from immediately evident sensations; so too, on this view, knowledge of mathematical objects is inferred from the immediate knowledge of simple mathematical truths. The primary challenge facing the mathematical-intuition theorist is to give a clear account of the nature of mathematical intuition, and of how, precisely, it relates us to the objects in question.

The second Platonist approach is to argue that knowledge about mathematical objects is simply knowledge of propositions, or perhaps of entire theories, in which those objects figure. The problem of explaining knowledge about the objects is then reduced to the problem of explaining the justification of those propositions or theories. Thus, for instance, Gottlob Frege (1884) holds that knowledge about numbers is simply knowledge of the propositions of arithmetic, which is explained in terms of more general capacities, and not in terms of individual contacts with the objects. An important question facing such an account is whether it is really Platonist; whether, that is, knowledge of propositions of the right form should count as, at bottom, knowledge about objects.

An explanation which attempts to reduce knowledge of mathematical objects to knowledge of entire theories is found in the work of W.V. Quine (1960) and Hilary Putnam (1971). On this account, we know about mathematical objects in exactly the same way that we know about non-mathematical objects. Consider, for instance, the subatomic particles of modern physics. We know about these things, as Quine sees it, not in virtue of direct contact with them, but rather in virtue of the fact that our best theory includes the claim that these objects exist, and contains specific assertions about them. The evidence for the existence of these objects is just the empirical evidence we have for the truth of the theory as a whole. Similarly for ordinary concrete objects like tables and chairs, on this account: we posit these objects in order to make sense of the brute sensory data before us, and the success of the theory that posits them is the evidence we have that they exist. Given this picture of objectual knowledge, mathematical objects pose no special problem: the claim that there are such objects, and that they have the usual mathematical properties, is an indispensable part of our best theory of the world, since mathematics is an essential part of modern physics. Thus we have just as much reason to believe in the objects of mathematics as we do to believe in the existence of pieces of furniture. Whether such an account is successful will turn largely on the tenability of the holist account of knowledge in general.

An interesting response to such indispensability arguments is the 'instrumentalist' position, according to which the usefulness of mathematical statements in science is no evidence of their truth, and hence is no evidence of the existence of mathematical objects. As argued by Hartry Field (1980), the central claim is that the statements of mathematics offer a conservative extension of (say) physics, which is to say that, useful as mathematics is as a tool, it allows us to reach only those conclusions in physics which we would have been able to reach (albeit less efficiently) anyway. On this reading, the ordinary mathematical existence-assertions turn out to be useful but not true. The viability of this project turns on whether the conservativeness result can in fact be demonstrated and whether physics can in fact be reformulated in Field's 'nominalistic' terms.

3 Anti-Platonist realism

A different response to the problems surrounding mathematical objects is to view the apparent object-directedness of mathematical discourse as just a mode of speaking, and not an indication that the truths of mathematics really are about objects. On this picture, mathematics is concerned rather with general features of collections, structures, potential measurements, or some such thing. Just as talk involving such phrases as 'Emily's sake', or 'the average family' are easily seen to be rephrasable without the use of these terms, and to be free of commitment to any objects meeting the descriptions, so too statements purportedly about mathematical objects can be rephrased, it is argued, in such a way as to remove any *prima facie* commitment to such objects. As long as the rephrasings have objective truth-conditions which render them true or false independently of our ability to recognize whether or not they obtain, such an account is fully realist, though anti-Platonist.

One example of such a rephrasing is as follows. In recognition of the close connection between arithmetic and cardinality, one might hold that claims apparently about natural numbers can be cashed out as claims about collections and their sizes. Thus, for example, the sentence 'Every natural number has a successor' is taken to mean 'For every possible finite collection, there is a possible collection with one more member', where the phrase 'one more' is itself cashed out without reference to the number one. (The reference to possibility will be required in order for the claim to remain true even if the world happens to be finite.)

A more widely applicable reduction is the 'structuralist' account, on which mathematical statements are taken to be either about all collections of entities exhibiting the appropriate structure, or about those abstract structures themselves. Thus, the sentence 'Every natural number has a successor' can be taken to mean that for every (possible) collection whose members exhibit the pattern N (which we describe in terms of the successor-like relation S), for each member x of the collection there is a member y of that collection such that $S(x,y)$.

With even these simple examples, a number of important issues arise. The first is that the quantification over 'possible collections' may involve ontological commitments at least as strong as the commitment to numbers. Thus despite avoiding a commitment to numbers, one does not by such a strategy obviously obtain ontological parsimony, or avoid the difficulties associated with knowledge about abstract objects. Similarly, the usual ways of cashing out the necessary relations between structures or collections will involve quantification over functions; thus in the attempt to avoid one kind of mathematical object, the analysis is apparently committed immediately to another. On the other hand, such reductionist approaches have the benefit of construing arithmetical knowledge in a way which requires no epistemic relation to particular individuals (such as natural numbers), but only to whole classes of collections or patterns. This is an advantage if general properties of such collections or patterns are in principle accessible to a priori reflection in a way in which distinguishing properties of individuals are not.

An important question about non-Platonist realism is whether it is coherent. Can one simultaneously maintain that the ordinarily accepted statements of mathematics are indeed true, but that there are no mathematical objects? The difficulty in this position is that it requires one to hold that statements such as 'There are prime numbers between ten and twenty' are true, while maintaining that there are no numbers. It is not enough to say that the quoted sentence can be rephrased in a way which apparently avoids mention of numbers. For if the rephrasing simply tells us what it means to say that there are prime numbers between ten and twenty, then its truth implies that there are such numbers. (See Alston (1958).)

It is tempting to try to avoid Platonism by saying that statements such as 'There are prime numbers between ten and twenty', and hence 'There are numbers' are true in some secondary sense – perhaps true 'within mathematics', but that they are not *really* true. But it is not clear whether this can be made sense of, since it is not clear what it is for a mathematical statement to be true in one sense and not in the other. In sum: a successful analysis of mathematical discourse which appears to eliminate reference to and quantification over particular mathematical objects does not by itself establish the claim that mathematical statements are free of commitment to mathematical objects. For all that has been said so far, such an analysis may well be regarded as an account of what it is to be committed to those objects. Whether there is more to Platonism than the acceptance of the objective truth of certain mathematical statements – and hence whether there is sense to be made of a non-Platonist realism – will turn, then, on the answers to some extra-mathematical questions concerning ontological commitment and the nature of objects in general.

See also: ANTIREALISM IN THE PHILOSOPHY OF MATHEMATICS; OBJECTIVITY; LOGICAL AND MATHEMATICAL TERMS, GLOSSARY OF; REALISM AND ANTIREALISM

References and further reading

* Alston, W.P. (1958) 'Ontological Commitments', *Philosophical Studies* 9: 8–17. (Argues that ontological commitment cannot be avoided by 'translating away' explicit reference to or quantification over purported entities.)

Benacerraf, P. (1973) 'Mathematical Truth', *Journal of Philosophy* 70: 661–80; repr. in P. Benacerraf and H. Putnam (eds) *Philosophy of Mathematics: Selected Readings*, Cambridge: Cambridge University Press, 2nd edn, 1983, 403–20. (A clear account of tensions between a Platonist account of mathematical content and acceptable theories of mathematical knowledge and reference.)

Benacerraf, P. and Putnam, H. (eds) (1964) *Philosophy of Mathematics: Selected Readings*, Cambridge: Cambridge University Press, 2nd edn, 1983. (A useful collection of central papers in the field.)

Bernays, P. (1935) Sur le platonisme dans les mathématiques, *L'Enseignement mathématique*, 1st series, 34: 52–69; trans. C.D. Parsons (1964), 'On Platonism in Mathematics', in P. Benacerraf and H. Putnam (eds) *Philosophy of Mathematics: Selected Readings*, Cambridge: Cambridge University Press, 2nd edn, 1983, 258–71. (Classic discussion of Platonism and its alternatives.)

Brouwer, L.E.J. (1912) *Intuitionisme et Formalisme*, Groningen: Noordhoff; trans. A. Dresden, 'Intuitionism and Formalism', *Bulletin of the American Mathematical Society* 20: 81–96, 1913; repr. in P. Benacerraf and H. Putnam (eds) *Philosophy of Mathematics: Selected Readings*, Cambridge: Cambridge University Press, 2nd edn, 1983, 77–89. (Gives an account of some of the central tenets of intuitionism.)

Dedekind, R. (1888) *Was Sind und was Sollen die Zahlen?*, Brunswick: Vieweg; trans. W.W. Beman, 'The Nature and Meaning of Numbers', in *Essays on the Theory of Numbers*, Chicago, IL: Open Court, 1901; repr. New York: Dover, 1963. (A classic of nineteenth-century foundations of mathematics. Gives an early non-eliminative but arguably structuralist account of the natural numbers.)

Dummett, M.A.E. (1967) 'Platonism', in *Truth and Other Enigmas*, Cambridge, MA: Harvard University Press, 1978, 202–14. (A criticism of the Platonist's claim that our relation to mathematical objects is analogous to our perception of concrete objects.)

—— (1973) 'The Philosophical Basis of Intuitionist Logic', in H.E. Rose and J.C. Shepherdson (eds) *Proceedings of the Logic Colloquium, Bristol, July 1973*, Amsterdam: North Holland, 1975, 5–40; repr. in *Truth and Other Enigmas*, Cambridge, MA: Harvard University Press, 1978, 215–47; and in P. Benacerraf and H. Putnam (eds) *Philosophy of Mathematics: Selected Readings*, Cambridge: Cambridge University Press, 2nd edn, 1983, 97–129. (Argues, from general principles about the theory of meaning, that classical logic should be replaced by intuitionistic logic within mathematical reasoning.)

* Field, H. (1980) *Science Without Numbers*, Oxford: Blackwell. (An argument that the usefulness of mathematics in physical science is no reason to hold that mathematical statements are true, as discussed in §2.)

* Frege, G. (1884) *Die Grundlagen der Arithmetik: eine logisch-mathematische Untersuchung über den Begriff der Zahl*, Breslau: Koebner; trans. J.L. Austin, *The Foundations of Arithmetic: A Logico-Mathematical Enquiry into the Concept of Number*, Evanston, IL: Northwestern University Press, 2nd edn, 1980. (This classic statement of the logicist position is also an excellent introduction to many issues concerning mathematical realism. Defends the view that numbers are 'self-subsistent objects', as discussed in §2.)

* Gödel, K. (1944) 'Russell's Mathematical Logic', in P.A. Schilpp (ed.) *The Philosophy of Bertrand Russell*, Evanston, IL: Northwestern University Press, 125–53; repr. in Benacerraf, P. and Putnam, H. (eds) *Philosophy of Mathematics: Selected Readings*, Cambridge: Cambridge University Press, 2nd edn, 1983, 447–69. (Gödel's view that the reasons for believing in mathematical objects are analogous to the reasons for believing in concrete objects, as discussed in §2.)

Hart, W.D. (ed.) (1996) *The Philosophy of Mathematics*, Oxford: Oxford University Press. (A collection of important recent papers.)

Parsons, C. (1990) 'The Structuralist View of Mathematical Objects', *Synthese* 84: 303–46; repr. in W.D. Hart (ed.) *The Philosophy of Mathematics*, Oxford: Oxford University Press, 1996. (A survey and critique of the structuralist treatment of mathematics.)

* Putnam, H. (1971) *Philosophy of Logic*, New York: Harper. (Includes a clear statement of the 'indispensability' argument for the existence of mathematical objects, as discussed in §2.)

* Quine, W.V. (1960) *Word and Object*, Cambridge, MA: MIT Press. (A classic. Includes the outline of Quine's views on ontological commitment and theoretical posits, as discussed in §2.)

Resnik, M. (1981) 'Mathematics as a Science of Patterns: Ontology and Reference', *Noûs* 15 (4):

123

529–50. (An explanation and defence of a modern structuralist account of mathematics.)

PATRICIA A. BLANCHETTE

REALISM, MORAL *see* MORAL REALISM

REASONING, COMMON-SENSE

see COMMON-SENSE REASONING, THEORIES OF

REASONS AND CAUSES

Imagine being told that someone is doing something for a reason. Perhaps they are reading a spy novel, and we are told that their reason for doing so is that they desire to read something exciting and believe that spy novels are indeed exciting. We then have an explanation of the agent's action in terms of the person's reasons. Those who believe that reasons are causes think that such explanations have two important features. First, they enable us to make sense of what happens. Reading a spy novel is the rational thing for an agent to do if they have that particular desire and belief. Second, such explanations tell us about the causal origins of what happens. They tell us that the desires and beliefs that allow us to make sense of actions cause those actions as well.

The idea that reasons are causes has evident appeal. We ordinarily suppose that our reasons make a difference to what we do. In the case just described, for example, we ordinarily suppose that had the agent had appropriately different desires and beliefs then they would have acted differently: had the person desired to read something romantic instead of exciting, or had the person believed that spy novels are not exciting, a spy novel would not have been chosen. But if what they desire and believe makes a difference to what they do then the desires and beliefs that are those reasons must, it seems, be the cause of the person's actions.

Despite its evident appeal, however, the view that reasons are causes is not without its difficulties. These all arise because of the manifest differences between explanations in terms of reasons and causal explanations.

1 **The normative character of reason explanations**
2 **The logical connection argument**
3 **The problem of wayward causal chains**

1 The normative character of reason explanations

If we are told that a person acts because of a desire and belief they have then we have an explanation of their action in terms of their reasons; a rationalization, as it is sometimes called. Those who think that reasons are causes claim that such rationalizations are a kind of causal explanation. This view has evident plausibility, as it allows us to make straightforward sense of the idea that our desires and beliefs make a difference to what we do. If we had had different desires and beliefs then we would have behaved differently because the cause of our behaviour would itself have been different.

Even so, many anti-causalists think that reasons are not causes. One problem, as they see it, is that if reasons were causes then there would have to be underlying causal generalizations connecting desires and beliefs on the one hand, with actions on the other. For causal explanations are derived from, grounded in, such generalizations. However, they argue, rationalizations have a normative aspect which eludes capture in the purely descriptive terms in which causal generalizations deal. No such generalizations can therefore be found. An example will help to make the problem more vivid.

Suppose someone wants to illuminate the room and believes that they can do so by flicking a particular switch. Provided nothing else is wanted, and provided there are no interfering factors that it make it pointless for the person to try to do anything, it follows that they should flick the switch. Flicking the switch would be the rational thing to do, in one perfectly ordinary sense of the term rational; it is what we would expect to happen if we are to make sense of what is going on. However, say the anti-causalists, we cannot go on to conclude that the individual will flick the switch. For that would be to move illicitly from an 'ought' to an 'is'. In this respect, they insist, causal generalizations are therefore quite different from rationalizations. Causal generalizations purport to tell us what will happen without regard to what should. If one billiard ball moves towards another at a certain speed, and if nothing else interferes, then the other ball will move off in a certain direction at a certain speed. Whether or not it should is neither here nor there.

According to these anti-causalists, the fact that rationalizations have a normative aspect means that they serve a quite different function from that of causal explanation. Of course they agree that if, in the case just described, the agent does flick the switch then it will be useful to think of her as having done so for a reason; but they insist that it is a mistake to suppose that we thereby give the cause of what happened, because the function of such a rationalization is to give a useful interpretation of what happened, not a causal explanation. We interpret each other as creatures with desires and beliefs who act in various ways, and so instantiate the various rational norms, because doing so helps us to understand what we have done, are doing, and will do; it helps us to make sense of each other. However these interpretations no more presuppose that our desires and beliefs are states that play a causal role than do the similar interpretations we give of the behaviour of desktop computers, electronic calculators and telephone exchanges in terms of the desires and beliefs that they possess – or so say these anti-causalists. In each case we simply work with a useful fiction or manner of speaking.

Note that two crucial claims have been made. First, talk of an agent's desires and beliefs is not unlike talk of similar states in electronic calculators and the like, a fiction or manner of speaking. Second, this manner of speaking is useful because it helps us understand what has happened, does happen and will happen. The question is: how are we to put these two claims together? If desire and belief talk is indeed useful then we need to know why this is so, and the most straightforward explanation available is surely that our desires and beliefs causally explain what we do. For then our understanding of what has happened, does happen and will happen is the familiar sort of understanding that comes from knowing about the causal origins of the events in question. On this way of looking at things there is therefore a crucial difference between human beings on the one hand, and electronic calculators, telephone exchanges and the rest on the other. Desire and belief talk really is a mere manner of speaking in the latter case, but not in the former. Electronic calculators and telephone exchanges are like human beings, but not the same as them, for they do not really have desires and beliefs, whereas human beings do. We must therefore ask why anti-causalists resist giving this most straightforward explanation of the usefulness of rationalizations, at least in the case of human beings. Why do they think that all desire and belief talk is a mere manner of speaking?

The answer is that they think the normative character of rationalizations makes it impossible to state rationalizations in the form of causal generalizations. It is, however, difficult to see why they think that this is so. For whenever we explain what someone does by appeal to their reasons we in fact make an additional, descriptive assumption, one which is

perfectly suited to turn the normative claim anti-causalists accept into a descriptive causal generalization: namely, the assumption that the agent in question is a rational agent, in the relevant sense of rational. Thus, even though the claim 'If an agent wants to illuminate the room, and believes that they can do so by flicking the switch, and wants nothing else more, and there are no interfering factors present, then the agent should flick the switch' does not look at all like a causal generalization, the claim 'If an agent desires to illuminate the room, and believes that they can do so by flicking the switch, and wants nothing else more, and there are no interfering factors present, and the agent is rational, then they will flick the switch' most certainly does. Seen in this light, being rational is itself a substantive disposition agents possess, a disposition which makes its own difference to what they do.

In conclusion, it seems that anti-causalists are right that rationalizations have a normative aspect, but wrong that we are therefore unable to state them in the form of causal generalizations. We have seen no reason to disagree with the causalist that the usefulness of rationalizations lies in the fact that they offer us causal explanations.

2   The logical connection argument

Anti-causalists have another objection. Hume taught us that cause and effect are logically distinct. Causal generalizations like 'If one billiard ball moves towards another at a certain speed, and if nothing else interferes, then the other ball will move off in a certain direction at a certain speed' thus report substantive facts about the world. This is because, logically speaking, we can imagine the cause with an entirely different effect, or without any effect at all. The second billiard ball might have gone in any of a number of different directions, or disappeared, or stayed precisely where it was (see CAUSATION).

However, anti-causalists point out, in the generalizations causalists suppose ground our rationalizations the so-called cause and effect are not logically distinct. The claim 'If someone wants to illuminate the room, and believes that they can do so by flicking the switch, and wants nothing else more, and nothing else interferes, and the person is rational, then they will flick the switch' does not report a substantive fact about the world because, if the agent is indeed rational, we cannot imagine these desires and beliefs having different effects. Imagining them with different effects – imagining the agent doing something different – is to imagine an agent with different desires and beliefs. The generalization linking desires and beliefs on the one hand, and doings on the other, unlike the claim linking the separate movements of billiard balls, thus reports a logical truth, not a substantive causal generalization.

The key idea behind this logical connection argument, as it is known, is plausible enough. We can indeed define desires and beliefs as states that occupy certain functional roles: that is, desires and beliefs are states that are caused by various perceptual inputs, and which in turn cause various sorts of behavioural and other mental outputs (see FUNC- TIONALISM). Those who propose the logical connec- tion argument are right that the cause and effect in a rationalization are not logically distinct in at least this sense: in describing the cause as a desire – that is, as a state that occupies a certain functional role – we thereby mention events of the effect kind, for we must mention behaviour in characterizing the relevant functional role.

However, if this is right, then it becomes clear that the anti-causal thrust of the logical connection argument is undermined. For the states of an agent that occupy the functional roles characteristic of desire and belief – presumably complex states of an agent's brain – are logically distinct from the behaviour they help to produce. It is our descriptions of these states as states that are occupiers of certain functional roles – that is, as states that, inter alia, cause certain sorts of behaviour – that are logically connected with facts about behaviour, not the states themselves. Even though the generalization connecting desires and beliefs with behaviour is indeed a logical truth, it thus follows that the desires and beliefs themselves – that is, the states that occupy the functional roles character- istic of desire and belief – are still logically distinct from the behaviour that they cause, just as Hume insisted cause and effect should be.

Moreover, despite the fact that there is this sort of logical connection between desires and beliefs and behaviour at the level of description, note that it is still appropriate to cite an agent's desires and beliefs in giving a causal explanation of what they do. In order to see why, consider an analogy. To say that a glass is fragile is similarly to ascribe to it a state with a certain functional role. A fragile glass is one which is in a state that causes it to break when struck in the appropriate circumstances. The generalization 'If a glass is fragile, and it is struck in the appropriate circumstances, and nothing else interferes, then it will break' is thus a logical truth, just like the general- ization connecting desires and beliefs with behaviour. However we can still cite the fact that a glass is fragile in giving a causal explanation of its breaking. For we get information about how a glass broke when we learn that it broke because it was fragile. A fragile glass that breaks need not break because it is fragile,

after all. (Just imagine that it breaks when we explode a nuclear bomb next to it.) To say that a glass broke because it was fragile thus gives us causal information because it narrows down the possible ways in which the breakage was caused to those that implicate the state of the glass that occupies the functional role characteristic of fragility.

Likewise, even though desires and beliefs are themselves just states that occupy certain functional roles, including the role of producing behaviour, we can still cite the fact that an agent has certain desires and beliefs in giving a causal explanation of what they do. For when someone who, say, desires to illuminate a room and believes that a room can be illuminated by flicking a switch does indeed flick it, they need not flick it because they have those desires and beliefs. (Just imagine that they flick the switch as the result of being hit by a falling chandelier.) To say that the agent flicked the switch because they had these desires and beliefs thus gives us causal information because it narrows down the possible ways in which the flicking of the switch was caused to those that implicate the states of the agent that occupy the functional roles characteristic of desire and belief.

Those who propose the logical connection argu- ment are right that desires and beliefs are logically connected with behaviour, but wrong to draw the conclusion that they are therefore ineligible to be causes of behaviour. Desires and beliefs may not only cause behaviour; they may also be cited in giving causal explanations of behaviour.

3 The problem of wayward causal chains

Suppose we accept that reasons are causes. Do we thereby commit ourselves to the view that it is necessary and sufficient for an agent's having acted for reasons that they had certain desires and beliefs that caused them to behave in the appropriate way, or are we merely committed to the weaker claim that it is a necessary condition? In order to support the fundamental idea mentioned earlier – the idea that our reasons make a difference to what we do – we need only commit ourselves to the weaker claim. The stronger claim is worth considering, however, for it would be a striking victory for the causalist if we could spell out the content of a rationalization in purely causal terms.

There is, however, a well-known objection to this idea. Imagine an actor playing a role that calls for them to shake as if extremely nervous. We can readily suppose that, despite the fact that the actor wants to play the role and believes that it can be done by making certain movements, once they get on stage they are so overwhelmed by their desire and belief that they are overcome by nerves and rendered totally incapable of action. Instead of playing the role as required, the actor just stands there, shaking nervously. What this case suggests is that it is therefore insufficient for an agent's having acted for a reason that they have desires and beliefs that cause appropriate behaviour. For an agent may well have desires and beliefs that cause such behaviour, and yet, because these states cause that behaviour in the wrong way, as in this case, it would be wrong to say that they act for a reason. In order to give necessary and sufficient conditions for an agent's having acted for a reason in purely causal terms we therefore need to rule out the possibility of such wayward causal chains. In this particular case, we need to rule out the possibility of the agent's desires and beliefs causing them to shake via causing them to become nervous.

Some causalists think that it is plain what is needed. The crucial feature in all such cases, they say, is that the match between what the agent does and the content of her desires and beliefs is entirely accidental. In the case just described, for example, it is entirely an accident that the actor wanted to make just the movements that their nervousness subsequently caused. These causalists therefore suggest that, in order to state a sufficient condition for an agent's having acted for a reason, we need simply to ensure that their behaviour is especially sensitive to the content of their desires and beliefs, as opposed to being sensitive to the operation of wayward factors like nerves. An agent acts for a reason, they suggest, only if, in addition to the other conditions, over a range of desires and beliefs that differ ever so slightly in their content – suppose the actor had desired to act nervously and believed that they could do so making their teeth chatter, or desired to act nervously and believed that they could do so by walking around wringing their hands, they would still have behaved in an appropriate way. This condition is clearly violated in the case described because, no matter what the content of the actor's desires and beliefs, nervousness would still have caused them to shake.

See also: ACTION; INTENTION; AKRASIA; MENTAL CAUSATION

References and further reading

Bishop, J. (1989) *Natural Agency*, Cambridge: Cambridge University Press. (States and attempts a solution to the problem of wayward causal chains.)
Davidson, D. (1963) 'Actions, Reasons and Causes', repr. in D. Davidson *Essays on Actions and Events*, Oxford: Oxford University Press, 1981. (Classic statement and defence of the claim that reasons are causes.)
Dennett, D.C. (1987) *The Intentional Stance*, Cambridge, MA: Bradford Books. (Argues that we rationalize behaviour in order to make sense of what happens, but not in order to find out about the causal origins of what we do.)
Hempel, C.G. (1962) 'Rational Action', *Proceedings and Addresses of the American Philosophical Association* XXXV. (Explains how we can state a rationalization in the form of a causal generalization.)
Jackson, F. and Pettit, P. (1990) 'Program Explanation: A General Perspective', *Analysis* 50: 107-17. (Explains how states that are functionally characterized may still figure in causal explanations.)
Melden, A.I. (1961) *Free Action*, London: Routledge & Kegan Paul. (Classic statement and defence of the logical connection argument.)

MICHAEL SMITH

REASONS FOR BELIEF

Reasons for believing something are one or another kind of ground for believing it. Some grounds provide evidence for a belief; others explain it; some are consciously known, others not. Philosophers are concerned with these and other aspects of reason, including the questions of whether reasons are also causes, whether they yield beliefs only by inference, and whether, by suitable reflection, believers can always become aware of the reasons for a belief they hold.

1 **Varieties**
2 **Reasons and reason states**
3 **Pragmatic reasons**
4 **Dimensions of appraisal**
5 **Reasons versus grounds**

1 Varieties

To see the several kinds of reasons for believing, consider these examples:

(1) There *is reason* for believing (to believe) that Israeli–Palestinian negotiations will affect the United States' standing in the Middle East.
(2) You seem to be suggesting there is (some) *reason for me* to believe he will not represent us well at the meeting – ah, you are thinking of his previous blunder – I had forgotten.
(3) She *has reason* to believe the referee was unfair.
(4) The *reason why* he believes (the reason for his

believing) this myth is not evidential; it is an emotional commitment to his father's views.

(5) Despite the reliable indications that her husband will survive, the only *reason for which* she actually believes this is his saying so, not the favourable statistics.

Case (1) illustrates a normative reason, a reason there *is* to believe the proposition in question (*p*). Such a reason can also be called impersonal, since its status as a reason does not depend on anyone's being aware of it or believing the evidential proposition (the reason): I might have, in the form of propositions I know or believe, the kind of political evidence in question, but the reason could also be merely implicit in what is known by experts. Case (2) illustrates a person-relative normative reason, one there is *for S* (the person in question) to believe. Case (3) exhibits a possessed reason, one *S has*, for believing *p*. In (4) we have an explanatory reason, a reason *why S* believes *p*. And case (5) illustrates a grounding reason, one *for which S* believes *p*. Here, *S* believes *p* on the *basis* of the reason. The belief that *p* thus stands in the (epistemic) basis (or basing) relation to the reason, which is a ground *on account of which S* believes *p*. Such reasons are at least psychological grounds sustaining the belief that *p*, what might be called 'pillars of conviction'. They may also be justifying grounds for *p* itself.

2 Reasons and reason states

Reasons as just described are propositions (conceived as meeting certain conditions, for example being true or believed by *S*). But whereas a proposition *q*, an obvious truth implying *p*, may be a reason there *is* to believe *p* whether or not anyone believes *q* – and thus *q* is in that sense an *external reason* for believing *p* – *q* must be believed by *S* in order to be a reason *for* which *S* believes *p* (case 5). That an accurate thermometer says a child has fever is a reason *to* think so, but this proposition is not a reason *for* which I believe this, until I come to believe the proposition and thereby come to believe the child has fever.

Given that we do not believe *for* reasons until they enter our minds, and given the obvious truth that one belief of *S*'s can be a reason *why S* holds another belief, some philosophers speak of (certain) beliefs themselves as reasons for believing. We can preserve these points, however, and achieve greater clarity, by construing reasons for believing as propositions and using 'reason state' for a belief *expressing* such a reason, in the sense that its content constitutes the reason. Reasons proper, as abstract entities, are presumably not causes. In so far as denials that

reasons are causes make this point, they are plausible. But reason states, as concrete psychological elements, are good candidates to be causes (of a certain kind). Granted, a proposition can be cited as a reason why *S* believes *p* (case 4) and this *appears* to attribute causal power to it; but the proposition can *be* a reason why *S* believes *p* only if either its truth, or at least *S*'s believing it, actually explains why *S* believes *p*: these elements, *not* the proposition itself, play the relevant causal role. That the thermometer says the child has fever is the reason *why* I believe so, because it is my *believing* that the thermometer says this that *explains* my belief that the child has fever. A reason why I believe it, such as brain manipulation that implants the belief, could, however, explain why I believe the child has fever, without being a reason *for* anyone's believing this. Explaining reasons need not be reason states.

We can illustrate all five cases of a reason progressively and in relation to the same proposition: that the thermometer says the child has fever is (1) a reason (for anyone) to believe so; (2) a reason for me – but not the child, who is too young to understand thermometers – to believe so; (3) a reason I have to believe so – once I see the mercury above normal; (4) a reason why I believe so – provided the mercury level, as opposed to, say, my feeling the burning forehead, explains my believing so; and (5) a reason for which I believe so, when my belief is *based on* my reading of the thermometer.

3 Pragmatic reasons

Suppose I desperately need a loan and that, to be persuasive, I must believe I deserve it. Some philosophers would say I thereby have a reason for believing I deserve the loan. In one tradition, deriving from Blaise Pascal and William James, this might be considered a reason for believing that I deserve the loan, even though it provides no evidence of desert. On this view, a reason for believing *p* can be a consideration – not necessarily an evidential one – that, in a certain way, makes believing *p* useful. Such non-evidential considerations are perhaps better regarded as reasons to *cause* oneself to believe, and hence reasons for *acting* rather than for believing. These pragmatic reasons regarding belief are not among the kinds discussed below.

4 Dimensions of appraisal

Among the important questions concerning the relation between believing *p* and reasons for believing it are these: Are such reasons *evidential* (providing some degree of justification of *p*), *explanatory* (at least when combined with information implicit in the context of their ascription to S), *causal* (in sustaining or producing the belief that p), *internal* (in the sense that S can, by suitable reflection, become aware of them, as with one's sensations), *conscious* (in being present to awareness), *inferential* (in providing a kind of premise for the belief that p), and psychologically *connected* (linked in S's mind to p, for example, as evidence for it)? Consider these questions for our five kinds of reasons.

(1) Impersonal normative reasons are evidential: if there is a reason to believe the child has fever, then that reason (the thermometer's indicating fever) provides some evidence for the proposition that the child has fever. Impersonal normative reasons need not be internal. Perhaps, however, they must be *accessible*, in the sense that someone could, by suitable investigation, become aware of them: normally, in speaking of reasons there are for believing p, one is referring to what is known or justifiedly believed, or can be discovered or justifiedly believed, for example, by reconsidering the data or searching the literature.

(2) Person-relative normative reasons are evidential at least *for S* (for example, for me as opposed to people lacking the relevant information). Neither these nor impersonal normative reasons need be explanatory, causal, conscious, inferential or psychologically connected; for they require no belief that p: I may, for example, never see the thermometer, and thus may have no belief to be explained, conscious or inferential, nor any occasion to connect the normative reason with p as, say, good evidence for p. (I might be disposed to make this connection if the reason is highlighted in association with p; but there can be a reason for me to believe p even if no such psychological connection exists.) Person-relative reasons for believing are usually internal and apparently must be accessible: the thermometer's indicating fever is not a reason *for me* if I cannot become aware of that reading.

(3) Possessed reasons may be normative, as where there is an evidential reason for believing p, *and* one acquires it; they can also be explanatory and causal; and they apparently must be internal. If they are internal, then although they need not be *in* consciousness and in that sense conscious, they cannot be unconscious in the sense that only external help, such as testimony from others, can bring them to S's awareness. But reasons one has can be unconscious in the common sense (associated, for example, with self-deception and buried prejudices) that they are accessible to one only by systematic self-reflection. As to psychological connectedness, perhaps if S *has a*

reason for believing p and is not merely in possession of information that *is* a reason for believing it, then S somehow takes the reason to support p. This would not imply a specific belief, say that the reason justifies p; one might just see the two in a familiar pattern, like 'If q then p; and q. Hence, p'. However, the view that having a reason for believing implies psychological connectedness makes it difficult to explain such self-reproach as 'I had reasons all along to believe it; why did I not see the connections sooner?'

(4) Explanatory reasons for believing are usually possessed and are often, but not necessarily, normative. Arguably, they must be causal. How, without playing some causal role in S's believing p, would such reasons explain *why* S believes it? Explanatory reasons can certainly be unconscious; they need not imply any inference – since manipulation of S's brain could explain why S believes p; and, as that case also shows, they need not be psychologically connected.

(5) Grounding reasons must be possessed, explanatory and, arguably, causal, internal and psychologically connected. There is better warrant for thinking them connected than for merely possessed reasons, since here S believes p on the *basis* of the ground. This basis relation is not merely a causal one that might occur as, say, an accidental effect of rays hitting the brain; believing on the basis of a reason implies a response to the reason *as* some kind of support for p. If grounding reasons are connected, however, they still need not be evidential, at least if one can believe for bad reasons *and* such reasons can constitute not just inadequate evidence but none. Grounding reasons are unlike all the others in that they must be inferential, in the broad sense that they exist only if S actually believes p on the basis of another belief – a premise belief for p. This does not require *drawing* an inference; one can have a grounding reason for p either without going through an inferential process or after doing so, and thereby continue to hold the belief that p on the basis of the inferential ground in question.

5 Reasons versus grounds

Not all grounds for belief are themselves beliefs. Perceptions, for example seeing blue, are grounds for colour beliefs. Some philosophers call such grounds 'reasons for believing'. These non-inferential reasons can certainly be reasons *why* S believes; but in more perspicuous (and perhaps prevailing) usage, non-inferential grounds for beliefs are not called reasons *for* believing. It may be significant that such grounds are naturally expressible without a 'that'-clause: the reason *why* I believe – what explains my believing – that there is something blue before me is my seeing it, whereas at best I can say that my reason *for* believing this is that I see something blue. This reason is not the perception we started with but a self-ascription of that perception; and offering the reason suggests, misleadingly, that I believe there is something blue before me on the basis of *believing* I see something blue. A further advantage of the stricter terminology is that it allows us to leave open whether some grounds of our beliefs, including justifying grounds, may be external and inaccessible to reflection, as well as to hold that people's reasons for believing (as opposed to reasons why they believe) are always internally accessible to them – which best accords with the plausible idea that, on careful reflection, we can give the reasons for which we actually believe.

See also: INFERENCE TO THE BEST EXPLANATION; INTERNALISM AND EXTERNALISM IN EPISTEMOLOGY; JUSTIFICATION, EPISTEMIC; RATIONALITY OF BELIEF; RATIONAL BELIEFS; RELIABILISM

References and further reading

Alston, W.P. (1993) *The Reliability of Sense Perception*, Ithaca, NY: Cornell University Press. (Defends a social practice theory of justification on which justifying reasons must be, in the terminology above, both internal and evidentially adequate.)

Audi, R. (1993) 'Belief, Reason, and Inference', in *The Structure of Justification*, Cambridge: Cambridge University Press. (A detailed account of what it is to believe for a reason and of how so believing is connected with inference, explanation and justification.)

Chisholm, R.M. (1966) *Theory of Knowledge*, Englewood Cliffs, NJ: Prentice Hall, 3rd edn, 1989. (Systematic statement of an internalist epistemology that construes reasons for believing as ultimately deriving from foundations in self-presenting psychological states.)

Foley, R.A. (1987) *The Theory of Epistemic Rationality*, Cambridge, MA: Harvard University Press. (Detailed defence of a subjectivist conception of justification and, thereby, of reasons for believing.)

Goldman, A.I. (1986) *Epistemology and Cognition*, Cambridge, MA: Harvard University Press. (A well-developed reliabilist theory of justification, which argues that grounds of beliefs need not be internal and that reasons for believing can justify only if they are objectively adequate.)

Moser, P.K. (1989) *Knowledge and Evidence*, Cambridge: Cambridge University Press. (A theory of the nature of reasons and evidence, how they justify, and how justification is connected with explanation.)

Plantinga, A. (1993) *Warrant and Proper Function*, New York: Oxford University Press. (A theory of warrant that construes reasons, especially those actually sufficient for knowledge, as meeting conditions of proper cognitive function for human beings.)

ROBERT AUDI

REBIRTH, INDIAN THEORIES OF *see* KARMA AND REBIRTH, INDIAN CONCEPTIONS OF

RECHTSSTAAT *see* RULE OF LAW

RECIPROCITY

To reciprocate is to return good in proportion to the good one has received, or to retaliate proportionately for harms. The central, contested philosophical issues surrounding reciprocity are whether reciprocity is a fundamental moral principle or a subsidiary one; how we are to measure fittingness and proportionality; and whether the norm of reciprocity requires that we reciprocate for all the goods we receive, or only for the ones we invite. While most philosophers believe that reciprocity is a subsidiary principle which is unproblematic only in the context of fully voluntary transactions, there are significant minority views on this matter.

To some political philosophers, reciprocity appears to be the linchpin of a theory of justice that stands midway between an altruistic concern for the welfare of everyone (justice as impartiality) and an egoistic concern for reaping the benefits of cooperation (justice as mutual advantage). On this intermediate view justice involves a commitment to impartial principles that further the welfare of everyone, but only when others have reciprocal commitments. It thus defines a unique conception of justice, distinct from standard utilitarian and contractualist ones (see JUSTICE). Other philosophers, however, see reciprocity as derived from more fundamental moral principles.

Interest in reciprocity as a separate, fundamental principle of social life and morality arose in the twentieth century. Early anthropological studies of gift-giving rituals were developed into comprehensive theories of social exchange, and integrated into structuralist accounts of social life. Stated abstractly, reciprocity appears to social scientists to be a universal social norm, implicated in a wide array of social practices from the most trivial aspects of etiquette to the most lethal aspects of retribution. To evolutionary theorists it seemed plausible to suppose that norms of reciprocity were genetically encoded. Moreover, the development of rational choice theory, and the mathematical manipulation of collective action problems, gave support to the notion that reciprocity (tit-for-tat, beginning with a beneficent opening move) was the best strategy for dealing with (rational) non-cooperative behaviour (see RATIONAL CHOICE THEORY).

Philosophical efforts to find a rational foundation for morality and justice have often alluded to reciprocity – or at least to related notions such as mutuality and fair play. There are, however, some thorny philosophical issues buried in the concept and practice of reciprocity. One is the question of measurement. In order to reciprocate we need to rank goods (and bads), so as to determine the fitting and proportional response in each case. On the good-for-good side of things, for example, 'fittingness' might be determined by what the potential recipients will accept as similar goods. Thus if I make you a gift of a delicacy (say a double chocolate cake) just to delight you, though I do not myself like it or other sweet desserts, you will have to find some other sort of thing – something I do like – if you want to make a fitting return to me. Further, the quantity that will count as a proportional return still needs to be decided, and it is clear that equal money value is not an adequate principle. (I may like emeralds, but giving me the market value of a chocolate cake in emerald chips is a joke, not a reciprocal response.) Besides, the declining marginal utility of money means that an equal market value rule would be oppressive for the poor. Equal marginal sacrifice is a more plausible principle. We could set proportionality to how much the gift 'costs' the giver on the margin. Then the reciprocator, if poor, will not 'suffer' more from making the return than the giver did, and if rich, will not be able to reciprocate painlessly (unless the gift was painless).

Unfortunately, this rather tidy metric does not look very plausible on the negative side of things (that is, in implementing the policy of returning bad for bad). Victims who want compensation demand plausibly to be made whole; victims who want to exact punishment demand plausibly that the malefactor's punishment be proportional to the wrongful

intent, not to the actual harm done. (People die from negligence as well as from premeditated murder. The harm done is the same; the suffering might even be greater for some victims of negligence.) So the doubts about a coherent account of fittingness and proportionality remain.

Perhaps the deepest philosophical issue raised by reciprocity, however, concerns the scope of the norm. A great deal of the good we receive from others comes to us uninvited and unavoidable. Some of it (like the care of loving parents for their young children) is given to us directly, intentionally. Some of it (like a rich cultural environment) is merely a public good from which we cannot be excluded. The 'wide' view of reciprocity holds that the norm covers all of one's interactions with others; it holds that one owes a fitting and proportional return for all the good one receives, and not merely for the good actually accepted or invited. The 'narrow' view argues that at most we owe a return only for the good we have accepted or invited by voluntary participation in the relevant social practices. On the wide view, reciprocity has important contributions to make to solving general cooperation problems, to giving accounts of obligations to parents, to the state, and to future generations (see FUTURE GENERATIONS, OBLIGATIONS TO; OBLIGATION, POLITICAL). But even in its narrow form, reciprocity speaks to fundamental issues of justice and fair play.

See also: DESERT AND MERIT; EGOISM AND ALTRUISM; RECTIFICATION AND REMAINDERS

References and further reading

Axelrod, R. (1984) *The Evolution of Cooperation*, New York: Basic Books. (Covers rational choice theory, sociobiology and tit-for-tat as a cooperative strategy.)

Barry, B. (1995) *Justice as Impartiality*, Oxford: Oxford University Press, 46–51. (Criticizes justice as reciprocity.)

Becker, L. (1986) *Reciprocity*, Boston, MA and London: Routledge; repr. Chicago, IL: University of Chicago Press, 1990. (Argues for the 'wide' view of reciprocity, namely that one owes a fitting and proportional return for all the good one receives, and not merely for the good actually accepted or invited.)

Buchanan, A. (1990) 'Justice as Reciprocity versus Subject-Centered Justice', *Philosophy and Public Affairs* 19: 227–52. (Addresses the question of whether reciprocity generates a distinct theory of justice.)

Gibbard, A. (1991) 'Constructing Justice', *Philosophy*

and *Public Affairs* 20: 264–79. (Defends justice as reciprocity as a distinct theory.)

Gouldner, A. (1960) 'The Norm of Reciprocity', *American Sociological Review* 25: 161–78. (Classic sociological thesis about the universality of reciprocity.)

Mauss, M. (1923/4) 'Essai sur le don, forme et raison de l'échange dans les sociétés archaïques', *L'année sociologique* 2 (1): 30–186; trans. W.D. Halls, foreword by M. Douglas, *The Gift: Forms and Functions of Exchange in Archaic Societies*, New York: W.W. Norton, 1990. (The anthropology of primitive exchange.)

Rawls, J. (1993) *Political Liberalism*, New York: Columbia University Press. (Views reciprocity as an element of fairness in the norms of cooperation and justice.)

Sahlins, M. (1981) *Stone Age Economics*, New York: Aldine. (The sociology of primitive exchange; includes extensive bibliography on anthropology.)

Sidgwick, H. (1874) *The Methods of Ethics*, London: Macmillan; 7th edn, 1907; 7th edn repr. Chicago, IL: University of Chicago Press, 1962, books III, IV. (Material on gratitude.)

Simmons, J. (1979) *Moral Principles and Political Obligations*, Princeton, NJ: Princeton University Press. (Raises objections to using the principle of fair play as a basis for political obligation.)

LAWRENCE C. BECKER

RECOGNITION

The concept of recognition has played an important role in philosophy since ancient times, when the good life was thought to depend partly on being held in regard by others. Only Hegel, however, made recognition fundamental to his practical philosophy. He claimed that human self-consciousness depends on recognition, and that there are different levels of recognition: legal or moral recognition, and the forms of recognition constituted by love and the state. A similar tripartite distinction can be used to ground a plausible modern account of ethics.

1   The history of recognition
2   Hegel and recognition
3   An ethic of recognition

1   The history of recognition

In one way or another the concept of recognition has always played a major role in practical philosophy: in ancient ethics the conviction was predominant that only someone whose conduct met with high regard in the *polis* could lead a good life; Scottish moral philosophy was led by the idea of public recognition or disapproval as a social mechanism through which the individual was motivated to attain the desirable virtues; with Kant the term *Achtung* (respect) eventually takes over the function of a highest moral principle in the sense that it contains the nucleus of the categorical imperative: to treat any other human being only as an 'end in themselves'. None of these authors, however, made the principle of recognition itself the foundation of an ethic; the term was eclipsed by others, regarded as more fundamental. Only Hegel, in this respect a solitary pioneer, used the concept of recognition as a foundation of his practical philosophy.

2   Hegel and recognition

When Hegel undertook the project of reconstructing the development of human morality with the aid of the term recognition, he based it on Fichte's explanation of the possibility of human consciousness of freedom in terms of a theory of recognition: by examining Kant and Schelling on the foundations of natural law, Fichte (1796/7) became convinced that subjects can only achieve consciousness of their freedom if they challenge each other to exercise their autonomy and accordingly recognize each other (and themselves) as free persons (see AUTONOMY, ETHICAL; FREEDOM AND LIBERTY; FICHTE, J.; HEGEL, G.; KANT, I.; SCHELLING, F.; NATURAL LAW).

If the idea so outlined was bolstered with elements of Hobbes' and Rousseau's political anthropology, Hegel could use the result as the foundation of his theory of recognition: human self-consciousness depends on the interpersonal experience of being recognized by other human beings (see HOBBES, T.; ROUSSEAU, J.-J.).

For Hegel's purposes, however, the bare assertion of a necessary connection between self-consciousness and interpersonal recognition was not enough. To explain how the experience of recognition could bring about progress in morality, it was necessary in addition to explain the dynamic interrelationship that had to exist between the attainment of self-consciousness and the moral development of whole societies. Hegel's answers to these complex questions form the nucleus of his model of a 'struggle for recognition', according to which moral progress takes place in three different stages of recognition, each of them reached through an interpersonal struggle. Subjects engage in this struggle to confirm their claims to identity.

Peculiar to this approach is a thesis reaching far beyond Fichte, namely the classification into three different types of recognition once the interpersonal basis of self-consciousness had been understood. The mechanism that concedes reciprocally a sphere of individual freedom (which Fichte had in mind in his account of natural law) in fact explains the formation of a subjective consciousness of rights, but by no means does it comprehend the full positive self-understanding of a free person (see RIGHTS).

Hegel therefore adds to legal recognition, which was to include something like what Kant understood as moral respect, two more types of reciprocal recognition which have also to correspond with particular stages of the individual's self-awareness: in love, the subjects recognize each other reciprocally in the unique nature of their desires in order to attain emotional security in the articulation of their desires (see LOVE). Finally, in the moral environment of the state, a type of recognition unfolds which is to allow the subjects to further their esteem for each other through the very qualities which contribute to the maintenance of social order (see STATE).

In his early works Hegel seems to have been convinced that the transition between these different areas of recognition is characterized by a struggle, conducted among persons in order to be respected in their gradually growing self-esteem: the claim to be recognized in more and more dimensions of one's own personality leads to an inter-subjective conflict, the solution of which can only be the establishment of yet another sphere of recognition (Honneth 1992: ch. 1).

Hegel is not sociologist enough to think of this process as actually constituting modern societies. Still very much limited by the horizons of German Idealism, he sees it as the totality of the intellectual work which the subjects together have to perform in order to build a common world of the 'objective spirit' (see IDEALISM).

None the less, Hegel's early model of a struggle for recognition has proved complex enough still to be able to stimulate much present thought in moral philosophy and social theory (Siep 1979; Wildt 1982; Honneth 1992). Yet as early as the *Phänomenologie des Geistes (Phenomenology of Spirit)* (1807) Hegel replaced his initial programme with a concept in which the assumptions of the later system came more and more to fruition; from now on the constitution of social reality is no longer explained through an interpersonal process of conflict-formation, but seen as a result of a dialectic advance of the mind.

However, Hegel's divisions into family, civic society and state in *Grundlinien der Philosophie des Rechts (Philosophy of Right)* (1821) reflect once more the earlier distinction of three types of recognition; and it is this division into three which today allows the

development of Hegel's mature system into a practical philosophy (Hardimon 1994).

3 An ethic of recognition

Somewhat as it was for Hegel, today the first step towards a contemporary ethic of recognition is to show that the potential for moral injury arises from the inter-subjectivity of the human form of life: human beings are vulnerable in that specific way we call 'moral', because their identity is constructed out of practical self-awareness which is dependent on the assistance and approval of other human beings from the very beginning (Habermas 1983: 53–67).

If we are to draw a positive idea of morals from this anthropological premise, then the 'moral standpoint' is to be defined by the network of attitudes we have to adopt in order to save other human beings from injuries resulting from the communicative nature of their self-awareness. Positively defined, morality consists of those types of recognition that we are obliged reciprocally to take up if we are to secure together the preconditions of our personal freedom.

Hegel assumed that the differentiation of types of recognition is a matter of which levels of personal self-awareness, or of the human consciousness of freedom, can sensibly be distinguished: for each stage of positive self-awareness on which we have to rely in constructing our autonomy, another type of inter-personal recognition was required, so that the differentiation into family, civil/civic society and state defined three necessary conditions of personal freedom (see MORALITY AND ETHICS).

If we follow this proposition and detach it from any restriction to particular institutions, a division into three emerges, which appears plausible even today; the three types of recognition then define interpersonal conditions of personal identity as well as moral attitudes, which form together the 'moral point of view': (1) the individual is recognized as someone whose wishes and desires are of unique value to another person; for this type of recognition, which has the character of unquestioning care, the moral philosophical tradition offers terms like 'love' or 'care'; (2) the individual is recognized as a person deserving the same moral responsibility as all others; for this type of recognition, which is characterized by universally equal treatment, the Kantian term 'moral respect' has become established (see KANTIAN ETHICS; RESPECT FOR PERSONS; UNIVERSALISM IN ETHICS); (3) the individual is recognized as a person whose abilities are of constitutive value to a community; for this type of recognition, which is characterized by special esteem, philosophical tradition lacks adequate moral terms; it may however be appropriate to have recourse here to categories like 'solidarity' or 'loyalty' (see SOLIDARITY).

To specify these three different patterns of recognition in their moral content, and if possible even to interpret them as moral duties, is the task of any theory of morality which aspires to be heir to the Hegelian theory of recognition.

See also: FRIENDSHIP; MORAL AGENTS; MORALITY AND IDENTUTY; RECTIFICATION AND REMAINDERS; FINITUDE AND VULNERABILITY

References and further reading

Bernstein, J.M. (1996) 'Confession and Forgiveness: Hegel's Poetics of Action', in R. Eldridge (ed.) *Beyond Representation: Philosophy and Poetic Imagination*, Cambridge: Cambridge University Press. (Argues for transgressive actions and misrecognition – strife – as constitutive of the recognitive relations of modern subjects.)

* Fichte, J.G. (1796/7) *Grundlage des Naturrechts nach Principien der Wissenschaftslehre*, trans. A.E. Kroeger, *The Science of Rights*, Philadelphia, PA: Lippincott, 1869. (A less than reliable translation. Elegantly argues that recognizing the rights of another free self is a necessary condition for self-consciousness. Probably the first fully worked out account of a recognitive analysis of self-consciousness.)

* Habermas, J. (1983) *Moralbewußtsein und kommunikatives Handeln*, Frankfurt: Suhrkamp; trans. C. Lenhardt and S. Nicholsen, *Moral Consciousness and Communicative Action*, Cambridge, MA: MIT Press, 1990. (See 'Discourse Ethics: Notes on a Program of Philosophical Justification' in Lenhardt and Nicholsen's translation (43–50). This portion of Habermas' argument builds towards an account of normative recognitive relations between selves from the example of emotional responses to actions, such as feeling resentment, only available in a performative attitude.)

* Hardimon, M.O. (1994) *Hegel's Social Philosophy: The Project of Reconciliation*, Cambridge: Cambridge University Press. (Reconstructs the argument of Hegel's *Grundlinien der Philosophie des Rechts* as arguing that reconciliation between self and society is only possible if strong conditions of individuality and strong conditions of social membership are satisfied simultaneously.)

* Hegel, G.W.F. (1807) *Phänomenologie des Geistes*, trans. A.V. Miller, *Phenomenology of Spirit*, Oxford: Oxford University Press, 1977. (Hegel's most systematic attempt to ground self-consciousness in structures of recognition, beginning with the dialectic of master and slave.)

* —— (1821) *Grundlinien der Philosophie des Rechts*, trans. H.B. Nisbet, *Elements of the Philosophy of Right*, Cambridge: Cambridge University Press. (Hegel's analysis of right in terms of the recognitive structures of family, civil society and the state.)

* Honneth, A. (1992) *Kampf um Anerkennung*, Frankfurt: Suhrkamp; trans. J. Anderson, *The Struggle for Recognition: the Moral Grammar of Social Conflicts*, Oxford: Polity Press, 1995. (An attempt to provide a formal reconstruction of Hegel's conception of self-consciousness and recognition through a series of stages: love, rights and solidarity.)

Siep, L. (1974) 'Der Kampf um Anerkennung: Zu Hegels Auseinandersetzung mit Hobbes in den Jenaer Schriften', *Hegel-Studien* 9: 155-207; trans. C. Dudas, 'The Struggle for Recognition: Hegel's Dispute with Hobbes in the Jena Writings', repr. in J. O' Neill (ed.) *Hegel's Dialectic of Desire and Recognition: Texts and Commentary*, Albany, NY: State University of New York Press, 1996. (Tracks the transformation of Hobbes' notion of honour into recognition in Hegel's early writings.)

* —— (1979) *Anerkennung als Prinzip der praktischen Philosophie. Untersuchungen zu Hegels Jenaer Philosophie des Geistes* (Recognition as the Principle of Practical Philosophy: Investigations of Hegel's Jena Philosophy of Spirit), Freiburg: Alber Verlag. (Provides clarification on the distinction between intersubjective and social forms of recognition in Hegel, and argues that recognition is a synthesis of love and strife.)

* Wildt, A. (1982) *Autonomie und Anerkennung. Hegels Moralitätskritik im Lichte seiner Fichte-Rezeption* (Autonomy and Recognition: Hegel's Critique of Morality in Light of his Reception of Fichte), Stuttgart: Klett-Cotta. (Influential analysis of Hegel's critique of Kantian moral theory as grounded in appropriation of Fichte's doctrine of recognition.)

Williams, R. (1992) *Recognition: Fichte and Hegel on the Other*, Albany, NY: Sate University of New York Press. (An analysis of the concept of recognition in Hegel's *Phänomenologie des Geistes* as it emerges out of Fichte's writings.)

Translated by Ferdinand Knapp

AXEL HONNETH

RECTIFICATION AND REMAINDERS

Forgiveness, mercy and gratitude are rectifications, attempts to correct imbalances or set things right between us. Guilt is a moral remainder, a residue acknowledging an unexpiated wrong. Remainders offer us a limited redemption in revealing our appreciation that not everything has been made right.

Forgiveness manifests compassion for wrongdoers, who may or may not deserve it. Questions arise about when, what and whom we can forgive, what forgiving achieves, and when we ought or ought not to forgive. Forgiveness has special value in personal relationships, enabling their renewal. Connections among punishment, repentance, forgiveness and regret (another remainder) are complex, sometimes paradoxical.

Mercy often manifests forgiveness, as in pardons and amnesties. Yet we can also show mercy in administering rules where there has been no wrong. Is mercy unjust? Answers vary according to whether the case resembles a criminal offence or a civil suit. Grounded in others' sufferings rather than their deeds, mercy has us see ourselves in them, but the value of doing so can be qualified by considerations of justice and of self-respect.

Mercy and forgiveness sometimes evoke gratitude, appreciative acknowledgement of another's goodwill. Gratitude can be deserved or misplaced. Debts of gratitude are paradoxical, giving rise to ethical questions. When do we owe more than emotional response? What does reciprocity require between unequals? Some paradoxes may be solved by understanding obligations of gratitude as like those of a trustee rather than those of a debtor.

Guilt is emotional self-punishment (often relievable by forgiveness) which continues even after compensation, restitution or punishment by others. Questions arise about when it is rational and how it is related to shame, remorse, regret and repentance, which are also remainders.

1 **Rectification and remainders**
2 **Forgiveness**
3 **Mercy**
4 **Gratitude**
5 **Guilt**

1 Rectification and remainders

Rectification is setting matters right, redressing wrongs, correcting imbalances, settling scores. Remainders are rectificatory feelings that go some way towards morally redeeming us for what we cannot

rectify by our actions and sometimes for actions that not even others can rectify.

Apart from punishment, praise and blame, rectificatory actions most explored in philosophy are forgiveness, mercy and gratitude (see PRAISE AND BLAME; CRIME AND PUNISHMENT). Other rectificatory actions – amnesty, apology, compensation, pardon, repentance, restitution and reward – are considered here in terms of their relationships to these three. Because we cannot claim forgiveness, mercy or gratitude as a right, these actions resemble what Kant (1797) called 'imperfect duties', which allow the agent some latitude regarding when, where, towards whom and how much (as in our duty to help others) instead of specifying exactly what must be done (see KANT, I. §10). And yet, as with 'perfect duties', such as the duty to keep a promise, these rectifications can be due specific individuals, who deserve them from us (see PROMISING). Omissions of gratitude, mercy or forgiveness can make us as vulnerable to moral criticism as failures of honesty, fidelity or integrity. As character traits, ingratitude, being unforgiving and being unmerciful are grave faults, while gratitude, forgiveness and mercy are cherished virtues of the moral life (see VIRTUES AND VICES §§2–3).

Ever since Bernard Williams observed that 'moral conflicts are neither systematically avoidable, nor all soluble without remainder' (1965: 179), certain emotional residues have been referred to as 'moral remainders' (see WILLIAMS, B.A.O. §5). These include guilt, remorse, regret and sometimes shame, rectificatory responses of feeling rather than action. They reveal relevant positive values of an agent who has acted wrongly or is identified with a bad action or state of affairs. Aristotle said of shame, explaining its status as a 'quasi-virtue', that ideally the occasion for it would not arise, but if it does, we do better to have shame than to be shameless. Remainders can survive rectificatory action as well as hard choices in complex situations where inevitably someone will be wronged and the best we can do is seek the least of evils. Guilt is a paradigm remainder. Other remainders – shame, remorse, regret – are discussed here in terms of their relationships to guilt, and guilt takes us back to rectificatory action.

2 Forgiveness

Forgiveness is a liberal response to those who have wronged us. Like mercy it characteristically (but not necessarily) manifests compassion for others. It can be offered as a gift, which another may accept or reject. The questions arise when, what and whom we can forgive, what forgiveness does and implies, when we ought to forgive, when it is deserved, when it is a free choice, even when if ever it would be wrong.

We can forgive what we can resent: persons and deeds, wrongs done us and the agents of those wrongs. Hannah Arendt (1958) said we cannot forgive ourselves, that only others can forgive us. Joseph Butler (1726) presented forgiveness as a renunciation of resentment, a view that explains Arendt's observation, as we cannot resent ourselves. Although, like Butler, Arendt emphasizes the liberality of forgiveness, presenting it as letting go of the deed, she also presents it as charitable, claiming that we forgive the offence for the sake of the offender (1958: 241) (see CHARITY). To forgive is not simply to forget (even if we forget) nor simply to cease resenting with time. It is a choice producing a change of heart from defensive hostility at feeling disrespected or neglected to a friendlier, more pacific attitude of no longer emotionally holding against the offender what we had once resented. It is a natural response to another's sincere apology, expression of contrition, or offer to make amends or atone for an offence.

Forgiveness is of special value in personal relationships (friendships, family, work relationships), where we are most vulnerable to offence, and needs for forgiveness are probably greatest. Arendt called the power to forgive a 'redemption from the predicament of irreversibility' (1958: 237), namely past deeds. Forgiveness enables renewal of relationships but frees us to move on even if we do not renew relations.

Does forgiveness imply at least a willingness to renew relations? In the jointly authored *Mercy and Forgiveness* (1988), Jean Hampton suggests that normally it does, at least with repentant offenders, except when such renewal would be dangerous (as for a battered intimate who rightly believes the offender unregenerate), while Jeffrie Murphy regards renewal as an open question depending on many factors.

If punishment is in question, does forgiveness imply mercy? Arendt called forgiveness and punishment alternative ways of trying to put an end to what is past but also said they are not opposites (1958: 241). Hastings Rashdall (1907) found the two in tension (see RASHDALL, H.). Others, including Murphy, find no incompatibility, arguing that punishment need not manifest resentment but may be required out of justice to other offenders and for deterrence to protect the innocent. Mabbott (1939) argued that duties of forgiveness and punishment fall upon different parties. If they are right, forgiveness need not imply total absolution. If it frees one only from the forgiver's resentment and not from the blame of others or the guilt that justifies punishment, it is but a limited redemption of the past's irreversibility.

If then we ought to support punishment of some

forgiven offenders, we may also rightly regret that necessity. Such regret is a 'moral remainder'. This example shows, incidentally, that regret does not presuppose that the regretter acted wrongly or was even responsible for what is regretted. Such regret is primarily a sense of loss – here, loss of a permissible opportunity to engage in such otherwise natural manifestations of a forgiving attitude as remitting or not supporting punishment.

Ought we to forgive the unrepentant? Ordinarily, repentant offenders deserve forgiveness. Paradigmatically, a repentant offender apologizes and asks forgiveness, which is then granted, or a victim offers forgiveness, which is accepted and followed by repentance. Yet many find they can forgive the dead who never asked it nor even admitted wrongdoing. We can cease to resent the dead and choose to remember them for their good qualities. Forgiving the dead may be easiest. With the living, problems arise. How can we distinguish forgiving the unrepentant from condoning their offences, tacitly approving them, thus tacitly encouraging their continuation? And if an offender does repent and regenerate, what remains to forgive? Aurel Kolnai (1987) presented these questions as a paradox of forgiveness. Together they suggest that forgiveness is either inappropriate or redundant.

One way to avoid condonation is to withhold forgiveness from the unrepentant. Another may be to combine forgiveness with punishment. What remains to be forgiven even a transformed offender is the offence, for which the offender, however changed, remains responsible.

Are some deeds unforgivably heinous, however deeply repented? Atrocities of slavery and genocide are prime candidates. Survivors and descendants of survivors find the issues complex. Arendt observed that we are unable to forgive what we cannot punish nor can we punish what turns out to be unforgivable (1958: 241). Howard McGary (1992) argues that rational self-interest offers African-Americans powerful reason to move beyond resentment regarding histories of slavery, advocating such forgiveness (in the liberal sense of letting go) for the sake of the forgiver. Simon Wiesenthal, in *Die Sonnenblume (The Sunflower)* (1969), portrays his dilemma in a concentration camp when a dying, horribly wounded German soldier Karl confessed to having participated in a mass murder of Jews and then begged forgiveness from Wiesenthal as a Jew. Wiesenthal's solution was to listen, appreciate the repentance, even not withdraw his hand when Karl took it but also finally to leave without speaking. Later, upon visiting Karl's mother (under the pretence of having been one of her son's friends), and realizing from what she told him that Karl had been truthful in his account of his early years, Wiesenthal decided not to tell her about Karl's murderous deed. By refraining from this, Wiesenthal granted Karl's wish that his mother be spared disillusionment about her son's honour. Wiesenthal circulated his meditations on these events to respected contemporaries who wrote their reflections, and he published them as a symposium with his essay. Together, they cover most ethical questions that have been asked about forgiveness.

Can forgiveness be wrong? Too ready to forgive, we may be suspected of deficiencies of the self-respect that resentment emerges to defend (see SELF-RESPECT). Forgiveness can also be misplaced, as in arrogantly or mistakenly judging that there was anything to forgive. Many of Wiesenthal's symposiasts argued that it would be presumptuous to forgive in the name of others or to forgive an offence done an entire group to which one belongs.

3 Mercy

A natural manifestation of forgiveness in some cases is to mercifully reduce or remit punishment. Mercy is compassionately withholding or mitigating a hardship or penalty that one has authority or power to inflict on another. Leniency and clemency suggest indulgence, softness, mildness. Mercy, however, can issue from strength of character.

Pardons and amnesties can exemplify mercy, although they need not. Pardons remit punishment, or the portion remaining. Ordinarily they are issued after a guilt finding, whereas amnesties preclude such findings. Mercy need not presuppose an offence, however. We can be merciful in administering requirements that can impose hardships and when we can release others from commitments that would impose unforeseen hardships.

The most difficult cases concern mercy for offenders who retributively deserve punishment (what Twambley (1975/6) calls 'the criminal court model') or who deserve to be held liable for compensation or restitution for harm to others (Twambley's 'civil court model') (see DESERT AND MERIT).

The criminal court model raises the question whether administrators of the law (or other public systems) can be merciful without being unjust. If one offender is shown mercy, every relevantly similar offender should likewise receive it. But then the reduced penalty has become an offender's right and is no longer merciful. Showing mercy to some and not others on the basis of personal inclinations is unjust favouritism. Reducing penalties for all beyond what justice requires may be unjust to the innocent who depend on deterrence for protection. Thus some

philosophers hold that criminals should not be shown mercy by agents of the law (although heads of state may occasionally pardon), and others conclude that mercy for criminals is permissible only when contrary obligations (such as support of a criminal's family) require mitigation of the penalty anyhow.

A satisfactory principle setting out conditions under which offenders deserve mercy would enable administrators to discriminate among offenders without arbitrariness or favouritism. If repentant offenders deserve forgiveness, some may also (or instead) deserve mercy. The desert basis for mercy, however, is not the same. We deserve mercy when we deserve compassion even from those we have wronged or harmed, because of extraordinarily severe undeserved misfortunes in our lives, relative to the lives of our victims and others who depend for protection on enforcement of rules we violated. Such a principle helps distinguish the bases of mercy from the bases of excuse and justification, which rest on facts about the commission of the offence. Excuses remove or reduce responsibility; justifications remove or soften judgments of wrongness (see RESPONSIBILITY). By contrast, a case for mercy rests primarily on what offenders have suffered, rather than simply on what they have done. It need not cite their offences, although it can, as when the crime recoils upon the perpetrator causing worse suffering than justifiable punishment would have done. The offender's undeserved misfortunes might include such things as having been victimized by yet worse crimes of others or having suffered severe natural disasters. Deserved mercy, so understood, moves towards cosmic moral compensation for inequalities in undeserved misfortune. Such deserved mercy is also a kind of equity and thus a point at which justice and charity come together.

There appears no rightful place for undeserved mercy in criminal court, no way to be merciful to those who do not deserve it without being unjust to other offenders and to the innocent who deserve protection – at least, if the laws are just. Where laws are deeply unjust, judges and juries may be lenient and heads of state issue pardons. Such compassion can respond to both injustice and undeserved misfortune.

On the civil court model (as in Shakespeare's *The Merchant of Venice* (1596/7)), mercy may be permissible or even morally required without being deserved through special misfortune. Just as one had a choice whether to bring a suit, the choices remain whether to call it off or settle. The questions are when such actions are consistent with self-respect and would not condone abuse. As with forgiveness, the offender's evident repentance and apology may obviate the problem of condonation and vindicate one's self-respect. Here mercy is a natural consequence of deserved forgiveness. Yet on the civil as on the criminal court model, offenders who have suffered extraordinary undeserved misfortune may still deserve mercy even if, as unrepentant, they do not deserve forgiveness.

Everyday situations can resemble either criminal or civil court models. Administrative positions allow us discretion in enforcing requirements on others, thus suggesting the criminal court model. Informal relations with friends, neighbours and family suggest the civil court model. In neither is mercy totally arbitrary. It is grounded in the suffering and moral responses of others, calling upon us to see ourselves in them, and it can be restricted by formal justice and by demands of self-respect.

4 Gratitude

Forgiveness and mercy, commonly motivated by compassion for wrongdoers, may evoke gratitude. Gratitude is an appreciative acknowledgement of another's goodwill (or more), often manifesting joy and accompanied normally by dispositions to reciprocate. Fred Berger (1975) argued that gratitude demonstrates that we do not value the beneficiary simply as useful for our own ends. Paradigmatically, gratitude is deserved by a benefactor from a beneficiary who was the intended recipient of the benefactor's freely bestowed (and freely accepted) goodwill. We may be grateful for gifts, favours, support and encouragement, recognition, sympathy, many things others do for us or give us beyond what they owed us or were constrained to offer (see SUPEREROGATION).

In an extended (nonmoral) sense, we can be grateful that something occurred, such as good weather, without being grateful to anyone for it. Henry Sidgwick even suggested that gratitude universalized yields the principle that good deeds ought to be rewarded (1874: 279).

Undeserved forgiveness and undeserved mercy can be virtuous, but undeserved gratitude to others is misplaced and suggests deficiencies of respect or self-respect. Gratitude is misplaced when the ostensible benefactor was only refraining from abuse or was compelled to provide the benefit or when the recipient was forced by the donor to accept it. Gratitude is misplaced for 'offers one cannot refuse', as the phrase is used regarding organized crime and likewise for a spouse's refraining from spouse battering. Gratitude for basic decencies is ordinarily misplaced. It risks offending others as well as betraying deficient self-respect.

Deserved gratitude can involve a special obligation, a 'debt' that goes beyond acknowledging appreciation and giving thanks. Richard Brandt (1974) noted that we incur obligations of two kinds, one in undertaking commitments (contracts, promises), the other in accepting benefactions. Ethical questions regarding gratitude tend to be connected with this special incurred obligation: how great the benefit must be to impose a debt, what its measure of value is, how much one should do in return, whether one can ever be done with it, even whether knowingly creating such a debt undermines desert of gratitude.

Is gratitude due one who tries but does not succeed in benefiting us? Some gratitude may be due for good intentions, but what if the would-be benefactor went to some expense or trouble? Do we measure the worth of the deed by what it cost the doer? Or by what it was worth to the recipient? Sidgwick found 'no clear accepted principle' here but noted that if either effort or benefit were great, we tend to feel strong gratitude. Aristotle said that if our relationship to the doer is based on utility, the value to the recipient is what counts, but that in true friendship, the purpose of the doer is what counts (*Nicomachean Ethics* 1163a10–24). What if the value of the effort is high but the benefit meagre, or the donor well-off and the recipient poor? Sidgwick thought that for such discrepancies reciprocating 'something between' is what 'seems to suit our moral taste' (1874: 261).

Do we owe gratitude where need compels us to accept a benefit? Such cases can create mixed feelings, gratitude undermined by humiliation. It is more considerate, as some religions teach, to give alms anonymously. Reciprocity for anonymous giving may be replaced by recipients' dispositions to do likewise for still others.

The idea of a debt of gratitude is paradoxical. Ideally, gratitude expresses gratification. Yet debts are burdensome, and paying them off a relief. Further, how can we owe for a benefit bestowed freely? How can we pay without so transforming the transaction that there is nothing for which to be grateful, and without needing to disguise the relief to avoid offending the benefactor?

These paradoxes arise from the borrower or debtor paradigm of duty or obligation. Borrowers who are granted credit occupy 'inferior' positions in relation to their creditors. Such debtors prove their reliability by paying off the debt, discharging the obligation to the creditor, terminating it. Unpayable debts of gratitude, the fear of which was expressed by Kant in his lecture 'Duties to Oneself' (1780–81), are depressing on this model, as they suggest that one can never adequately prove one's reliability.

The debtor paradigm does not cohere well with

obligations of gratitude. A trustee or guardianship paradigm works better. Trustees who accept a deposit owe but are not in debt; they incur obligations but are not 'inferior' and do not have to prove their honour. It can already be an honour to be entrusted. Living up to obligations of a trustee does not terminate them. Terminating trusteeships is what others do when trustees fail to come through.

Accepting a beneficiary's goodwill is more like accepting a deposit (another's good will) than like borrowing. It can be an honour to be so 'indebted', which we express by saying we are happy to be obliged. As the anthropologist Mauss (1967) has shown, entire cultures have been built on the gift relationship, rather than on the economic relationship of buyer and seller.

Thomas Hobbes captured the basic obligation of gratitude in his 'natural law', that '[you are to] suffer him not to be the worse for you, who out of the confidence he had in you, first did you a good turn' and that one should 'endeavour, that the giver shall have no just occasion to repent him of his gift' (1642: 47). Ingratitude, a major moral failing, consists in failing to live up to this basic obligation. More than simple ungratefulness (lack of appreciation, sometimes justified), it gives the benefactor cause for regret.

Gratitude is also among the things for which gratitude is felt, which fits with the observation of Max Scheler that 'love (once it is somehow perceived) evokes a loving response' (1923: 164) (see SCHELER, M.F. §7).

5 Guilt

Failure to be forgiving, merciful or even grateful can produce guilt. Unlike guilt for many offences, this guilt cannot be expiated by punishment, because forgiveness, mercy and gratitude cannot be rightfully compelled. Until we are forgiven this guilt may stay as a moral remainder.

'Guilt' is ambiguous between emotional self-punishment for having wronged others (internal guilt; guilt feelings) and the fact or finding of a transgression (objective guilt; a verdict). Internal guilt is associated with the voice of conscience, what Nietzsche (1887) called 'bad conscience' (see NIETZSCHE, F. §9). The debtor paradigm makes sense of guilt in both senses. Borrowers receive loans, the guilty steal; both are in debt. Borrowers need to demonstrate reliability; the guilty need to reclaim honour. Nietzsche noted that in German 'Schuld' means both 'guilt' and 'debt'. He speculated that guilt was originally a substitute payment extracted from debtors who defaulted and that this idea was

carried into punishment when legal offenders were seen as having defaulted on what they owed society (obedience).

Internal guilt is a 'moral remainder' when it continues after punishment, compensation or restitution, when no more remains to be done to set things right. Removing guilt feelings is a major point of forgiveness. Whether internal guilt is understood as the offender's introjections of victim resentment or, as Nietzsche suggested, as the offender's emotional enactments of introjected victim desires for the compensating pleasure of making the offender suffer, forgiveness naturally cancels the emotional 'debt' by communicating the victim's change of heart. It does not cancel objective verdicts of 'guilty'. Still, if accepted, it removes barriers (internal guilt and victim resentment) to renewals of relationship, barriers that might otherwise remain after punishment.

Are our guilt feelings irrational when they are not based on the belief that we culpably committed an offence? Herbert Morris (1987) has argued that three kinds of such 'blameless guilt' are not irrational: survivor guilt (or guilt over unjust enrichment, involuntarily benefiting from injustice to others); guilt over acts of one's country or other groups to which one belongs (even though one had no effective say over those acts); and guilt for feelings and desires that one did not act upon. Guilt over unjust enrichment is what we may feel instead of gratitude for benefits made possible by injustice. Here the debtor model of obligation makes sense and suggests a way to alleviate the guilt in some cases. One may feel obliged to use the benefits to help or enrich those treated unjustly, or if that is impossible, to help or enrich their descendants.

Is internal guilt necessary? Neither guilt feelings nor the voice of conscience occur in Aristotle's ethics, although he discussed the fault of *akrasia* (acting contrary to one's better judgment) (see AKRASIA). The disposition to feel guilt, as something distinct from shame, may not be learned in all cultures. Ruth Benedict (1946) characterized Japanese culture as a shame culture by contrast with guilt cultures of Europe and North America. Shame is a response to falling short of aims or standards we set ourselves, whereas guilt responds to boundary transgressions (see Piers and Singer 1971; Rawls 1971). Shame is moral when the aim or standard we fail to reach is moral; such shame injures our self-respect (see MORAL SENTIMENTS §3).

Guilt differs also from remorse, regret and repentance. Repentance is that change of heart whereby a transgressor becomes contrite, remorseful. It is appropriate for major offences. Remorse is intense, often lasting, moral regret regarding our own conduct. Regret, more generally, is sorrow over a fault, offence, mistake or loss, ranging in intensity from mild to deep. It does not presuppose responsibility for what is regretted, although remorse does. More painful than guilt, remorse is emotional gnawing at oneself over one's wrongdoing. Etymologically, it means 'to bite again', suggesting continual reopening of wounds as one rehearses again and again a vivid appreciation of one's wrongdoing. By contrast, internal guilt, as emotional self-flagellation, can actually dull one's appreciation of the wrong. Remorse is often accompanied by shame, and forgiveness removes neither.

Remainders remind us that not everything can be made right, rectified. Yet they offer us a limited redemption in revealing our moral appreciation of that very fact.

References and further reading

The following works are accessible, with the exception of those marked as demanding a higher level of comprehension.

* Arendt, H. (1958) *The Human Condition*, Chicago, IL: University of Chicago Press, 236–43. (Discusses forgiveness as a remedy for the irreversibility of past deeds.)
* Aristotle (*c.* mid 4th century BC) *Nicomachean Ethics*, trans. W.D. Ross, London: Oxford University Press, 1925. (Books 1108a30–35 and 1128b10–15 focus on shame; 1145a15–1152a35 deal with acting against one's better judgment; regarding gratitude, see 1123a34–1125a35 on pride and 1162a34–1163a24 on requiting services.)
* Benedict, R. (1934) *The Chrysanthemum and the Sword: Patterns of Japanese Culture*, Boston, MA, and New York: Houghton Mifflin; repr. New York: New American Library, 1946. (On Japanese culture as a shame culture.)
* Berger, F. (1975) 'Gratitude', *Ethics* 85: 298–309. (Classic article, presenting a nonutilitarian analysis of gratitude.)
* Brandt, R. (1974) 'The Concepts of Duty and Obligation', *Mind* 73: 374–93. (Notes two kinds of incurred obligations, those from commitments, such as promises, and those from accepting benefactions.)
* Butler, J. (1726) 'Upon Forgiveness of Injuries', in *Fifteen Sermons Preached at the Rolls Chapel*, London: G. Bell & Sons, 1967, Sermon IX. (Classic analysis of forgiveness as a remedy for the excesses of resentment.)
Card, C. (1972) 'On Mercy', *Philosophical Review* 81 (2): 182–207. (Offers a principle for distinguishing criminals who deserve mercy from those who do not; presents mercy as a virtue of persons rather than of institutions; argues for compatibility of charity and justice.)
—— (1988) 'Gratitude and Obligation', *American Philosophical Quarterly* 25 (2): 115–27. (On debts of gratitude as paradoxical; debtor and trustee paradigms of obligation; misplaced gratitude; gratitude in relation to friendship; and gratitude between unequals; many references.)
Emerson, R.W. (1883) 'Gifts', in *Essays*, Boston, MA: Houghton Mifflin; repr. in *The Essays of Ralph Waldo Emerson*, Harvard, MA: Belknap, 1987, 311–4. (Short classic discussing ideal gifts and pitfalls of giving; helpful for thinking about gratitude.)
Feinberg, J. (1970) 'Justice and Personal Deserts' in *Doing and Deserving: Essays in the Theory of Responsibility*, Princeton, NJ: Princeton University Press, 55–94. (Distinguishes between deserts and rights; moderately difficult but rewarding.)
* Hobbes, T. (1642) 'Of the Other Laws of Nature', *De cive (The Citizen)*, New York: Appleton, Century, Crofts, 1949, 43–59. (Includes law of gratitude as third law of nature; often cited as a basis of political obligation; moderately difficult.)
* Kant, I. (1780–81) 'Duties to Oneself', 'Friendship' in *Lectures on Ethics*, trans. L. Infield, New York: Harper & Row, 1963, 116–261, 200–9. (The first essay argues that accepting unnecessary favours violates a duty to oneself, the second, that ideal friends do not do material favours.)
* —— (1797) 'On Duties of Love to Other Men', in *Metaphysische Anfangsgründe der Tugendlehre*, trans. M.J. Gregor, *The Doctrine of Virtue: Part II of The Metaphysic of Morals*, New York: Harper & Row, 1964, 115–38. (Presents gratitude as a sacred duty that can never be completely discharged; difficult.)
* Kolnai, A. (1973/4) 'Forgiveness', *Proceedings of the Aristotelian Society*, new series, 74: 91–106; repr. in *Ethics, Value, and Reality: Selected Papers*, Indianapolis, IN: Hackett Publishing Company, 1987, 211–24. (Discusses paradoxes of forgiveness; difficult.)
* Mabbott, J.D. (1939) 'Punishment', *Mind* 48: 152–67. (Classic defence of retributive theory of punishment; finds forgiveness compatible with punishment.)
* Mauss, M. (1923/4) 'Essai sur le don, forme et raison de l'échange dans les sociétés archaïques', *L'année sociologique* 2 (1): 30–186; trans. I. Cunnison, *The Gift: Forms and Functions of Exchange in Archaic Societies*, New York: W.W. Norton, 1967. (Classic anthropological study of societies structured

around giving rather than around buying and selling; moderately difficult.)

McConnell, T. (1993) *Gratitude*, Philadelphia, PA: Temple. (Comprehensive examination and survey of literature; chapters on political obligation and filial obligations.)

* McGary, H. (1992) 'Forgiveness and Slavery', in H. McGary and B. Lawson, *Between Slavery and Freedom: Philosophy and American Slavery*, Bloomington, IN: Indiana University Press, 90–112. (Develops a case for forgiveness for the forgiver's own sake and independently of repentance by perpetrators.)

Moore, K.D. (1989) *Pardons: Justice, Mercy, and the Public Interest*, New York: Oxford University Press. (Comprehensive and illuminating discussion, rich with examples.)

Morris, H. (ed.) (1971) *Guilt and Shame*, Belmont, CA: Wadsworth. (Selections by Dostoevskii, Jaspers, Freud, Buber, Fingarette, Nietzsche, Rawls, Piers and Singer, Erikson, and Lynd; excellent place to begin.)

* —— (1987) 'Nonmoral Guilt', in F. Schoeman (ed.) *Responsibility, Character, and the Emotions: New Essays in Moral Psychology*, Cambridge: Cambridge University Press. (Discusses survivor guilt, guilt feelings for what other members of one's country or other group have done, and guilt feelings for emotions not acted on.)

* Murphy, J.G. and Hampton, J. (1988) *Mercy and Forgiveness*, Cambridge: Cambridge University Press. (Alternate essays by each author; topics include retribution, forgiveness, Christianity, resentment, hatred, mercy, and legal justice.)

* Nietzsche, F. (1887) '"Guilt", "Bad Conscience", and the Like', in *Zur Genealogie der Moral*, trans. W. Kaufmann and R.J. Hollingdale, *On the Genealogy of Morals*, New York: Vintage Books, 1969. (Discusses punishment, responsibility, justice, law and Christian guilt; difficult but rewarding.)

* Piers, G. and Singer, M.B. (1953) *Shame and Guilt: A Psychoanalytic and a Cultural Study*, Springfield, IL: Charles C. Thomas; repr. New York: W.W. Norton, 1971. (A classic by a psychologist and an anthropologist contrasting shame as a response to failure of achievement with guilt as a response to transgression, and contrasting shame cultures with guilt cultures. Very accessible.)

* Rashdall, H. (1907) *The Theory of Good and Evil: A Treatise on Moral Philosophy*, Oxford: Clarendon Press; 2nd edn, London: Humphrey Milford, 1924, vol. 1, 306–12. (On tensions between forgiveness and punishment.)

* Rawls, J. (1971) *A Theory of Justice*, Cambridge, MA:

Harvard University Press, ch. 8. (Discusses guilt and shame; moderately difficult.)

* Scheler, M.F. (1923) *Wesen und Formen der Sympathie*, Bonn: Friedrich Cohen; trans. P. Heath, *The Nature of Sympathy*, London, Routledge & Kegan Paul, 1954; repr. Hamden, CT: Archon Books, 1970. (A classic phenomenological examination of sympathy and related emotions; helpful for thinking about forgiveness, mercy and gratitude; difficult.)

* Shakespeare, W. (1596/7) *The Merchant of Venice*, New York: Bantam, 1988, act IV, scene 1. (See Portia's speech, beginning 'The quality of mercy is not strained', on the elective nature of showing mercy.)

* Sidgwick, H. (1874) *The Methods of Ethics*, London: Macmillan; 7th edn, 1907; 7th edn repr. Chicago, IL: University of Chicago Press, 259–61, 279. (Discusses common sense views on the ethics of gratitude; presents reward as gratitude universalized.)

Smart, A. (1968) 'Mercy', *Philosophy* 43 (166): 345–59. (Classic discussion of mercy on the criminal court model; interesting examples; good place to begin.)

* Twambley, P. (1975/6) 'Mercy and Forgiveness', *Analysis* 36 (2): 84–90. (Argues against mercy in the criminal court model and presents the civil court model as an appropriate forum; moderately difficult.)

* Wiesenthal, S. (1969) *Die Sonnenblume*, Paris: Opera Mundi; trans. H.A. Pichler and C.P. Pinto, *The Sunflower*, New York: Schocken, 1976. (Written with a symposium of many authors, this work comprises memoirs and meditation on the lived dilemma of forgiveness in a death camp; excellent place to begin.)

* Williams, B. (1965) 'Ethical Consistency', *Proceedings of the Aristotelian Society*, supplementary vol. 39; repr. in *Problems of the Self: Philosophical Papers 1956–72*, Cambridge: Cambridge University Press, 1973. (Introduces the concept of 'moral remainders'; difficult.)

CLAUDIA FALCONER CARD

RECURSION-THEORETIC HIERARCHIES

In mathematics, a hierarchy is a 'bottom up' system classifying entities of some particular sort, a system defined inductively, starting with a 'basic' class of such entities, with further ('higher') classes of such entities defined in terms of previously defined ('lower') classes. Such a classification reflects complexity in some respect, one entity being less complex than another if it appears 'earlier' ('lower') then that other. Many of the hierarchies studied by logicians construe complexity as complexity of definition, placing such hierarchies within the purview of model theory; but even such notions of complexity are closely tied to species of computational complexity, placing them also in the purview of recursion theory.

1 Hierarchies of formulas
2 The arithmetical hierarchy
3 The analytical hierarchy
4 Two more hierarchies of relation on ω
5 Hierarchies of relations between reals
6 Other hierarchies

1 Hierarchies of formulas

Consider a formal language L with quantifiers $\forall$ and $\exists$ (see FORMAL LANGUAGES AND SYSTEMS). Let B be a class of formulas of L such that by adding a $\forall$- or $\exists$-prefix to any member of B we get a non-member. We define a hierarchy of formulas of L that treats members of B as 'basic'. Set $\Pi_0^B = \Sigma_0^B = B$. Suppose that classes Π_n^B and Σ_n^B have been defined. Let Π_{n+1}^B = the class of all formulas of L of the form $\forall v_1 \ldots \forall v_m \varphi$ for $m \geqslant 1$, distinct variables $v_1, \ldots, v_m$ and $\varphi \in \Sigma_{n+1}^B$; let Σ_{n+1}^B = the class of all formulas of L of the form $\exists v_1 \ldots \exists v_m \varphi$ for $m \geqslant 1$, distinct variables $v_1, \ldots, v_m$, and $\varphi \in \Pi_n^B$. This classifies all formulas of L that consist of a string of quantifier-prefixes attached to a member of B.

Motivation The complexity of a minimally complex formula (complexity understood as above) defining a given relation may be identified with the complexity of that relation. We can now 'transfer' this hierarchy to a hierarchy of the relations defined by such formulas over an appropriate structure. This was first done by S. Kleene (1943) with first-order formulas over the standard model of arithmetic to get the arithmetical hierarchy.

2 The arithmetical hierarchy

Let L_0 = the first-order language based on function-constants for successor, addition and multiplication, an individual-constant of 0, and a two-place predicate for $<$; variables range over ω. For $\varphi(x_0, \ldots, x_m)$ a formula of L_0 with free-variables among those indicated, φ defines $\{<a_0, \ldots, a_m> \in \omega^m : \varphi(a_0, \ldots, a_m)\}$. A relation R is arithmetic iff R is defined by some formula of L_0.

Let a formula φ of L_0 be bounded iff each occurrence of $\forall$ in φ is in a context of the form $\forall v$ (if $v < t$ then $\ldots$) and each occurrence of $\exists$ in φ is in a context of the form $\exists v$ ($v < t$ and $\ldots$), for t a term and v a variable; take B = the set of bounded formulae, $\Pi_n^0 = \Pi_n^B, \Sigma_n^0 = \Sigma_n^B$. For any $m, n \in \omega, m \geqslant 1$, and any $R \subseteq \omega^m$, we will also let: $R \in \Sigma_n^0$ iff R is defined by some Σ_n^0 formula of $\mathfrak{L}_0$; $R \in \Pi_n^0$ iff R is defined by some Π_n^0 formula; $R \in \Delta_n^0$ iff $R \in \Sigma_n^0 \cap \Pi_n^0$. Context should make it clear whether Σ_n^0 and Π_n^0 is a set of formulas or a set of relations. This is the arithmetical hierarchy of relations; since any defining formula has an equivalent in prenex form, it classifies all arithmetical relations. It looks like this (with rightward = up):

$$\Sigma_0^0 = \Pi_0^0 = \Delta_0^0 \subset \Delta_1^0 \begin{matrix} \subset \Sigma_1^0 \subset \\ \\ \subset \Pi_1^0 \subset \end{matrix} \Delta_2^0 \begin{matrix} \subset \Sigma_2^0 \subset \\ \\ \subset \Pi_2^0 \subset \end{matrix} \Delta_3^0 \begin{matrix} \subset \Sigma_3^0 \subset \\ \\ \subset \Pi_3^0 \subset \end{matrix} \Delta_4^0 \cdots$$

Any tuple of natural numbers can be effectively coded by a single natural number; so we lose nothing by restricting the arithmetical hierarchy to reals. The 'arithmetical hierarchy theorem' states that each class contains infinitely many 'new' reals (that is, for each new $n \in \omega$ $\Sigma_{n+1}^0 - \Pi_{n+1}^0$, $\Pi_{n+1}^0 - \Sigma_{n+1}^0$ and $\Delta_{n+1}^0 - (\Sigma_n^0 \cup \Pi_n^0)$ are all non-empty). The definitional complexity of an arithmetic relation is indicated by the class in which it 'first' appears.

This hierarchy is related to classification by recursion-theoretic properties. Most significantly: Δ_1^0 = the class of recursive relations; Σ_1^0 = the class of r.e. relations: Δ_2^0 = the class of relations recursive in Post's set K (i.e. those of T-degree $\leqslant O'$). H. Putnam and Y. Ershov independently proved that Δ_2^0 is also the class of 'trial-and-error' relations: R is trial-and-error iff there is a recursive $m + 1$-place function f such that given any $\vec{a} = <a_0, \ldots, a_m> f$ guesses forever as to whether $\vec{a} \in R(f(\vec{a}, k) =$ the kth guess), and eventually f guesses correctly for ever after. In fact, they found and studied a fine-grained hierarchy within Δ_2^0 (see Putnam 1965).

These facts generalize 'up' the hierarchy. For a real X, set $X^{(n+1)}$ = the jump of $X^{(n)}$, with $X^{(0)} = X$. We then have: $X \in \Delta_{n+1}^0$ iff $X \leqslant_T \{\}^{(n)}$ for $\{\}$ = the empty set; furthermore, $X \in \Sigma_{n+1}^0$ iff X is r.e. relative to $\{\}^{(n)}$. (H. Rogers credits these basic results to Kleene and Post; see Rogers 1967.)

For $R \subseteq \omega^m$ and real $Y: R \leqslant_1 Y$ iff there is a $1 - 1$ recursive function $f: \omega^m \to \omega$ so that for any $\vec{a} \in \omega^m: \vec{a} \in R$ iff $f(\vec{a}) \in Y$. 1-reducibility (that is,

$\leqslant_1$) is the strongest of the recursion-theoretic reducibilities. For $\mathcal{C}$ a class of relations on ω: Y is $\mathcal{C}$-complete iff $Y \in \mathcal{C}$ and for any $R \in \mathcal{C}, R \leqslant_1 Y$. Fact: $\{\}^{(n)}$ is Σ_n^0-complete and $\omega - \{\}^{(n)}$ is Π_n^0-complete for each $n \leqslant 1$. Let T_{Σ_n} and T_{Π_n} be the sets of all and only the true Σ_n^0 and Π_n^0 sentences respectively. These sets have Σ_n^0 and Π_n^0 definitions respectively. (There is no paradox here: 'I am not a true Σ_n^0 sentence' requires negation of the truth predicate for Σ_n^0, making it Π_n^0 rather that Σ_n^0, and thus trivially true!) In fact, these two sets are also Σ_n^0-complete and Π_n^0-complete respectively, and thus (by a theorem of J. Myhill) are recursively isomorphic to $\{\}^{(n)}$ and to $\omega - \{\}^{(n)}$ respectively; this expresses the sense in which the jump is the recursion-theoretic analog of $\exists$ in arithmetic, and connects recursion-theory to truth-theory (see TARSKI'S DEFINITION OF TRUTH; SEMANTIC PARADOXES AND THEORIES OF TRUTH).

Let us contrast the arithmetical hierarchy with classification of reals by T-degree. Each real has a T-degree; the arithmetical hierarchy only classifies arithmetic reals. In one respect T-degrees are finer than the 'compartments' of the arithmetical hierarchy (that is, $\Sigma_n^0 - \Delta_n^0$ and $\Pi_n^0 - \Delta_n^0$ for $n > 0$, $\Delta_{n+1}^0 - (\Sigma_n^0 \cup \Pi_n^0)$ for $n \geqslant 0$): for example, there are countably many T-degrees with members from $\Sigma_1^0 - \Delta_1^0$ (see Post's problem in TURING REDUCIBILITY AND TURING DEGREES). On the other hand, for a real $X \in \Sigma_1^0$ with $\deg(X) = a, \omega - X \in a$; but if $X \notin \Delta_1^0$ then $\omega - X \notin \Sigma_1^0$; so except for the T-degree 0 no T-degree is a subset of Σ_1^0; similarly for the other compartments of the arithmetical hierarchy. So in another respect these classifications are orthogonal.

3 The analytical hierarchy

Expand L_0 to L_1 by introducing infinitely many predicate- (that is, second-order) variables, allowing $\forall$ and $\exists$ to bind them; without loss of generality let us require them all to be one-place. A relation on ω is analytical iff it is defined by a formula (containing no free predicate-variables), taking each predicate-variable to range over the class of all reals, with individual-variables ranging over ω. ('Analytical' alludes to quantification over reals, as in 'Analysis' in its mathematical sense.)

Now take B = the class of formula of L_1 containing no bound predicate-variables and no free individual-variables (though by coding tricks we could restrict B further). Set $\Sigma_0^1 = \Sigma_0^B, \Pi_n^1 = \Pi_0^B$. For any m, $n \in \omega, m \geqslant 1$, and any $R \subseteq \omega^m$, let: $R \in \Sigma_n^1$ iff R is

defined by some Σ_n^1 formula of L_1 (with predicate variables ranging as above); $R \in \Pi_n^1$ iff R is defined by some Π_n^1 formula: $R \in \Delta_n^1$ iff $R \in \Sigma_n^1 \cap \Pi_n^1$; again, context disambiguates this double-usage. This is the analytical hierarchy. Using prenexing, it classifies all analytical relations. A picture of this hierarchy with regard to subsethood would look just like that of the arithmetic hierarchy, with superscripts changed from '0' to '1'. Again, each class contains infinitely many new reals, there are Σ_n^1-complete and Π_n^1-complete reals, and among those are the truth-set for Σ_n^1 and Π_n^1 respectively.

4 Two more hierarchies of relation on ω

Set RA_0 = the set of arithmetic relations on ω. Suppose RA_α has been defined, for α an ordinal. A formula $\varphi(x_0, \ldots, x_m)$ (all free variables first-order and among those shown) defines R over RA_α iff for any $\vec{a} \in \omega^m : \vec{a} \in R$ iff $\varphi(a_0, \ldots, a_m)$, with predicate-variable ranging over RA_α; note this change from §3. Let $RA_{\alpha+1}$ = the set of relations defined by such formulas over RA_α. For a limit ordinal $\lambda : RA_\lambda$ = the union of all RA_α for $\alpha < \lambda$. This sequence is the ramified-analytical (hereafter RA) hierarchy: 'ramified' because the definitions used allow predicate-variables to range only over entities that were 'previously' defined. Note: if $\alpha \leqslant \beta$ then $RA_\alpha \subseteq RA_\beta$. This hierarchy is to reals what Gödel's constructible hierarchy is to arbitrary sets (see CONSTRUCTIBLE UNIVERSE); indeed work by R. Jensen shows that the latter can be construed as a recursion-theoretic hierarchy (see Devlin 1973). Note one difference between these hierarchies: the RA hierarchy 'peters out' (at the countable ordinal β_0 = least ordinal β such that $RA_{\beta+1} = RA_\beta$). In a natural sense the constructible relations on ω appearing the β_0-stage of the constructible hierarchy extend the RA hierarchy; see Odifreddi (1989) for details.

The RA hierarchy can be further refined by breaking up each stage $RA_{\alpha+1} - RA_\alpha$ in terms of the quantifier-prefix of the defining formulae (in prenex-form, of course): $\Sigma_{\omega \cdot \alpha + n}^0$ = the set of relations defined over RA_α by Σ_n^1 formulas of L_1; now $\Pi_{\omega \cdot \alpha + n}^0$ = the set of relations defined over RA_α by Π_n^1 formulas; $\Delta_{\omega \cdot \alpha + n}^0 = \Sigma_{\omega \cdot \alpha + n}^0 \cap \Pi_{\omega \cdot \alpha + n}^0$. For $n \geqslant 1$ we again have a hierarchy theorem: each such class contains infinitely many new reals. There are connections between the RA hierarchy, the jump operation, and truth in arithmetic.

An ordinal is recursive if it is order-isomorphic to some recursive well-ordering of natural numbers. There is a countable ordinal ω_1^{CK} = the least non-recursive ordinal ('CK' for Church and Kleene, who first studied it). $\omega_1^{CK} < \beta_0$, and if we cut off the RA hierarchy at ω_1^{CK} we get the hyperarithmetical (hereafter HA) hierarchy, introduced independently by M. Davis, A. Mostowski and S. Kleene (in Davis (1950), Mostowski (1951), Kleene (1955)). For $\alpha = \omega_1^{CK}$, RA_α = the class of hyperarithmetical relations.

The so-called Souslin/Kleene theorem connects the HA hierarchy to the analytical hierarchy: Δ_1^1 = the class of the hyperarithmetic relations; so the HA hierarchy is a classification of the Δ_1^1 relations. Δ_1^1 can be thought of as the class of relations on ω that would be computable by a super-mind capable of completing an effectively specified ω-sequence of tasks, in which case Δ_1^1 is to Δ_1^0 as Π_1^1 is to Σ_1^0; this analogy was one of the starting points for generalized recursion theory. The class of ramified-analytical sets (= RA_α for $\alpha = \beta_0$) is a proper subset of Δ_2^1.

5 Hierarchies of relations between reals

So far we have only considered relations on ω defined by formulae of L_1; but a formula of L_1 whose only free-variables are one-place predicate-variables defines a relation between reals, that is, on Power(ω) = the class of reals. Such a relation is analytical iff it is defined in this way, allowing bound predicate-variables to range over Power(ω); it is arithmetical iff it is defined by such a formula with no bound predicate-variables (which formula may be classified like one of L_0). Thus we have an arithmetical and analytical hierarchy of such relations; for $i \in \{0,1\}, R \subseteq \text{Power}(\omega)^m$: $R \in \Sigma_n^i$ iff R is so defined by a Σ_n^i formula of L_1; $R \in \Pi_n^i$ iff R is so defined by a Π_n^i formula.

Similarly, if we use 'ramified' definitions we obtain the HA hierarchy, and, going further, the RA hierarchy, of relations between reals. In the 1950s J. Addison (in his 1954 doctoral dissertation and in Addison (1959)) pointed out that the HA and analytical hierarchies of such relations where the 'effective analogues' of the so-called Borel and projective hierarchies, studied by French and Russian analysts (for example, E. Borel, H. Lesbesgue, M. Suslin and N. Lusin) in the early twentieth century. Their work, usually labelled 'descriptive set-theory', was thought of as a part of topology; apparently the logicians (except for Mostowski) had worked in complete ignorance of it. Contemporary descriptive set-theory emerged from this cross-pollination as a hybrid of recursion theory and topology.

6 Other hierarchies

There is at least one interesting hierarchy within the class of recursive relations, the so-called Grzegorczyk hierarchy. Even further 'low-down' (within the class of primitive-recursive relations) hierarchies have been proposed by computer-scientists, though here as this writing (1993) ignorance outstrips knowledge (see COMPLEXITY, COMPUTATIONAL). The study of such animals is usually called 'subrecursion theory'.

All hierarchies discussed here classify relation on ω or on Power(ω). Practitioners of generalized recursion theory have generalized some of these hierarchies to classify relations on other classes of mathematical objects.

See also: LOGICAL AND MATHEMATICAL TERMS, GLOSSARY OF

References and further reading

* Addison, J. (1959) 'Separation Principles in the Hierarchies of Classical and Effective Descriptive Set Theory', *Fundamenta Mathematica* 46: 123–135. (Apparently the first bridge between recursion theory and descriptive set theory.)
* Davis, M. (1950) *On the Theory of Recursive Unsolvability*, Ph.D. thesis, Princeton University. (The first definition of the *HA* hierarchy.)
* Devlin, K. (1973) 'Aspects of Constructibility', *Lecture Notes in Mathematics* no. 354, Berlin: Springer Verlag. (For the Jensen hierarchy, in effect Gödel's Constructible hierarchy of sets viewed recursion-theoretically.)
  Hinman, P. (1978) *Recursion-Theoretic Hierarchies*, Berlin: Springer-Verlag. (A good text introducing a lot of this subject to the novice.)
* Kleene, S. (1943) 'Recursive Predicates and Quantifiers', *Translations of the American Mathematical Society* 53: 41–73; repr. in M. Davis (ed.) *The Undecidable*, Raven Press, 1965, 255–287. (The first work on the arithmetical hierarchy.)
* Kleene, S. (1955) 'Hierarchies of Number-theoretic Predicates', *Bulletin of the American Mathematical Society* 61: 193–213. (Kleene's first work on the HA hierarchy.)
  Mosschovakis, Y. (1980) *Descriptive Set Theory*, Amsterdam: North-Holland Publishing Company. (An excellent text, connecting descriptive set theory and recursion theory.)
* Mostowski, A. (1951) ' A Classification of Logical

Systems, *Studia Philosophia* 4: 237– 274. (Another first paper on the HA hierarchy.)

* Odifreddi, P. (1989) *Classical Recursion Theory*, Amsterdam: North-Holland Publishing. (An excellent introductory text on classical recursion theory as of 1989, with a lot on the arithmetical and analytical hierarchies, and some on the others.)

* Putnam, H. (1965) 'Trial and Error Predicates and the Solution to a Problem of Mostowski', *Journal of Symbolic Logic* 30: 49–57. (A hierarchy within Δ_2^0.)

* Rogers, H. (1967) *The Theory of Recursive Functions and Effective Computability*, New York: McGraw Hill Inc. (The original textbook on recursion theory, a good complement to Odifreddi (1989), with excellent exercises.)

HAROLD HODES

REDUCTION, PROBLEMS OF

Reduction is a procedure whereby a given domain of items (for example, objects, properties, concepts, laws, facts, theories, languages, and so on) is shown to be either absorbable into, or dispensable in favour of, another domain. When this happens, the one domain is said to be 'reduced' to the other. For example, it has been claimed that numbers can be reduced to sets (and hence number theory to set theory), that chemical properties like solubility in water or valence have been reduced to properties of molecules and atoms, and that laws of optics are reducible to principles of electromagnetic theory. When one speaks of 'reductionism', one has in mind a specific claim to the effect that a particular domain (for example, the mental) is reducible to another (for example, the biological, the computational). The expression is sometimes used to refer to a global thesis to the effect that all the special sciences, for example chemistry, biology, psychology, are reducible ultimately to fundamental physics. Such a view is also known as the doctrine of the 'unity of science'.

1 **Reduction by derivation and definition**
2 **The Nagel model of reduction**
3 **Emendations to the Nagel model: the Kemeny–Oppenheim model**
4 **Microreduction and microdeterminism**
5 **Multiple (or variable) realization and reduction**
6 **The primacy of physical theory**

1   Reduction by derivation and definition

Unity and simplicity are often touted as important virtues achieved through reduction (see UNITY OF SCIENCE). By reducing one domain to another, we show the reduced domain to be either part of the second or eliminable in favour of it. Depending on the nature of the entities reduced, reduction will, therefore, promote ontological or conceptual economy and unity. When numbers have been reduced to sets, numbers no longer need be countenanced over and above sets; numerical concepts can be explained in terms of notions involving only sets; and laws about numbers follow from principles about sets. There will often be an explanatory gain as well: when gas laws are reduced to principles of statistical mechanics, via the kinetic theory of gases, we have an explanation of why these gas laws hold to the extent that they do – why the pressure, temperature and volume of gases behave (roughly) in accordance with the gas laws. Furthermore, reduction is sometimes thought of as a way of vindicating or grounding a possibly suspect domain of entities; if number theory is successfully reduced to logic, as Frege claimed, that would show number theory to be as firm and well-grounded as laws of logic. If the mental realm is reducible to the physical-biological domain, this would remove whatever problems and doubts might becloud the scientific status of the mental. Such are the thoughts and aspirations that inspire and sustain reductive projects and reductionisms.

There are apparently simple cases of reduction in which logical-mathematical derivation alone suffices for reduction. When Galileo's law of free fall or Kepler's laws of planetary motion are derived from the principles of Newtonian mechanics in conjunction with applicable force laws (see MECHANICS, CLASSICAL §2), they are reductively absorbed into a more general and comprehensive theoretical framework.

According to logical behaviourism, mental expressions are definable – that is, given synonymous translations – in terms of expressions referring to actual or possible behaviour ('behaviour dispositions'). Logical behaviourism, therefore, exemplifies an attempt to reduce the mental to the physical-behavioural through definition (see BEHAVIOURISM, ANALYTIC). Thus, one way to reduce a domain of expressions, or concepts, is to provide each expression with a definition couched solely in the expressions of the base domain. On the assumption that synonymous expressions refer to the same entities, a definitional reduction would also accomplish an ontological reduction: entities referred to by the first group of expressions have been shown to be among those referred to by the second group.

Reduction becomes more complex for domains that do not yield to direct derivational or definitional relationships, as in the case of reductions involving theories each with its own distinctive vocabulary, for example the reduction of thermodynamics to statistical mechanics.

2 The Nagel model of reduction

Ernest NAGEL (1961) articulated a model of reduction for scientific theories that has served as the principal reference point in discussions of reduction (see THEORIES, SCIENTIFIC). The guiding idea of this model remains derivation, but Nagel saw that to derive laws of a theory from another which does not share the same vocabulary, certain 'bridge principles' must be assumed as additional premises. Consider two theories, T_1 and T_2, each with its distinctive vocabulary, V_1 and V_2, where T_2 is the candidate for reduction and T_1 the reduction base. Theories in this context are construed as sets of laws. Nagel's model requires that there be connecting laws, standardly called 'bridge laws', correlating terms of V_2 with terms of V_1. What form do such laws take and how many are needed for reduction? The simple answer is that they must be available in sufficient numbers and be sufficiently powerful to enable the derivation of T_2-laws from T_1-laws. But that depends on the strengths of the specific theories involved. The only general requirement worth considering, therefore, is the following:

The condition of connectibility: For each primitive n-place predicate F of V_2, there is a predicate G of V_1, such that for any $x_1, \ldots, x_n$ (in the domain of entities covered by the two theories), it is a law that $F(x_1, \ldots, x_n)$ if and only if $G(x_1, \ldots, x_n)$.

Thus, each predicate of the theory to be reduced must be connected, via a *biconditional law*, with a nomologically coextensive predicate of the reducer. These bridge laws in effect licence the rewriting of every T_2-law as a T_1-statement; in general, they enable the translation of T_2-statements into the language of T_1. Thus, the only difference between Nagel reduction and definitional reduction is that in the former the translation is underwritten by empirical laws whereas in the latter it is based on meaning equivalences.

There is a sense in which the condition of connectibility alone guarantees reduction: if any T_1-rewrite of a T_2-law is not derivable from the laws of T_1 as they stand, simply add it to T_1 as a new law (assuming it, as well as the original T_1-laws, to be true). This would extend the base theory, but not its vocabulary; and the extension would be warranted since the base theory was incomplete in failing to capture a true law statable in its vocabulary: namely, the T_1-rewrite of the T_2-law.

It is evident that when a theory has been derivationally reduced, it is conserved as part of the base theory; its laws are shown to be 'derivative laws' of a more comprehensive theory. Moreover, the condition of connectibility ensures that the properties posited by the reduced theory find their nomic equivalents in the reduction base, with which they may ultimately be identified when a successful reduction becomes entrenched. Thus, Nagel reduction is a species of 'conservative' (or 'retentive') reduction, which conserves, and can legitimize, that which is reduced; it contrasts with 'eliminative' reduction which dispenses with what has been reduced.

3 Emendations to the Nagel model: the Kemeny–Oppenheim model

Nagel's model has been criticized on various grounds, of which the following three are perhaps the most important. First, biconditional bridge laws are too weak, and must be strengthened into identities if they are to yield genuine reductions (Sklar 1967; Causey 1977). We need, it is argued, the identity 'temperature = mean molecular kinetic energy', not just a law that merely affirms covariance of the two magnitudes. As long as the reduction falls short of identifying them, there would be temperatures as properties of physical systems 'over and above' their microstructural properties. Moreover such correlations ('nomological danglers') cry out for an explanation: why does temperature covary in just this way with mean molecular kinetic energy? By identifying them we provide a short and conclusive answer: because they are in fact one and the same.

Second, the reduced theory is often only approximately true, and its laws are derivable only under special simplifying assumptions (which, strictly speaking, are false). For example, in deriving the gas laws in kinetic theory of gases, one has to make various assumptions, such as that collisions between molecules are perfectly elastic, that molecules are point masses, and so on. And the laws hold only approximately and within a fairly narrow range of conditions. Third, it is often pointed out that the condition of connectibility, which requires biconditional bridge laws, is unrealistic and can seldom be satisfied. Thus, temperature cannot, it is claimed, be uniformly correlated, or identified, with a single micro-based property; it may be mean kinetic energy of molecules for gases, but something else for solids or in vacuums.

As a response to the second criticism, it has been suggested (Schaffner 1967; Churchland 1986) that the reduction of T_2 to T_1 should require only that a *corrected version* of T_2 (or its 'image' in T_1), rather than T_2 itself, be derivable from T_1. We may also explicitly allow special limiting assumptions of the sort mentioned earlier. But to what extent can we correct or revise a theory without turning it into another theory? Obviously, the required corrections must be such as to yield the necessary bridge laws or identities, but there is no guarantee that any reasonable amount of tinkering will suffice to accomplish this. This takes us back to the last of the objections mentioned above.

Kemeny and Oppenheim (1956) proposed a model of reduction that departs extensively from the Nagel model, giving us a broader conception of reduction that does not require connecting principles between the theories involved. The gist of the new model can be stated thus: T_2 is *Kemeny–Oppenheim reduced* to T_1 just in case all observational data explainable by T_2 are explainable by T_1. This definition can, and should, be understood in a way that does not presuppose a context-independent theory–observation distinction or any special conception of explanation. The core idea here is that anything, be it an observation or a low-level empirical generalization or law, that the reduced theory can explain, or predict, should be explainable and predictable by the base theory. The base theory, then, is at least as powerful, as an explanatory and predictive instrument, as the theory being reduced, making the latter at best otiose. This means that the reduced theory is ripe for elimination – unless, that is, it is also Nagel-reducible, and hence conserved as a subtheory of the reducer. Notice that any case of Nagel reduction is also a case of Kemeny–Oppenheim reduction (at least, on the standard deductive-nomological account of explanation; see EXPLANATION §2). Unlike the Nagel model, the Kemeny–Oppenheim model requires no direct relationship between the reduced theory and its reducer; in particular, it involves no bridge laws of any form. In fact, the reduced theory may be false and the reducer true. However, it assumes that the two theories concern the same domain of phenomena (at least, that the domain of the reduced theory is included in that of the reducer). In any case, the Kemeny–Oppenheim model allows the replacement, or elimination, of the reduced theory, and hence can serve as a model of 'eliminative' reduction.

4 Microreduction and microdeterminism

A pervasive trend in modern science has been to explain macrophenomena in terms of their micro-structures, and reduce theories about the former to theories about the latter. Examples abound in the physical and biological sciences. The reduction of thermodynamics to statistical mechanics (see THERMODYNAMICS), the reduction of optics to electromagnetic theory (see OPTICS §1), the successes in

solid-state physics and molecular biology (see GENETICS; MOLECULAR BIOLOGY; SOCIOBIOLOGY), and a host of other examples appear to attest to the fruitfulness of microreduction as a research strategy (Oppenheim and Putnam 1958).

Both the Nagel and the Kemeny–Oppenheim models can be applied to microreduction. What is needed is the idea that one theory is a *microtheory* in relation to another. The rough idea is that the microtheory deals with objects that are *proper parts* of the objects in the domain of the macro-theory. More specifically, the domain of the microtheory will include objects that are parts of the objects in the domain of the macrotheory; in addition it will include aggregates of these micro-objects, and aggregates of aggregates, and so on. And the objects of the macrotheory are identified with certain complex aggregates in this domain. Moreover, the microtheory has a set of properties and relations characterizing its basic micro-objects, and will generate complex properties for aggregates of these objects from the basic properties and relations. These micro-based properties (for example, mean molecular kinetic energy of a gas) of aggregative structures of micro-objects are important for reduction: in Nagel reductions, it is these micro-based properties that will be correlated (or identified) by bridge laws with the properties of the macrotheory; in Kemeny–Oppenheim reductions, they will be needed in providing explanations of the data explained by the macrotheory.

The metaphysical underpinning of microreduction is the principle of *microdeterminism* or *mereological supervenience*: properties of a whole are wholly determined by, or supervenient on, the properties and relations characterizing its proper parts. No matter how complex an object (say, a human being, a planetary system) may be, if you put together qualitatively indistinguishable parts in the same structural relationship, you will get an exact duplicate of that object (barring basic physical indeterminacies). It is the task of science, then, to identify a physically significant decomposition of a whole into parts and develop a microtheory about these parts that will explain why the whole has the properties it has.

5 Multiple (or variable) realization and reduction

One influential objection often deployed against the claim that a given theory is reducible to another is 'the multiple realization argument'. This argument was initially developed as an objection against mind–body reduction, but has been used to argue for the impossibility of reduction almost everywhere (Fodor

1974). Consider a higher level property, such as pain: pain as a psychological state is 'realized' by diverse physical-biological processes in widely divergent organisms and structures. The neural realizer of pain in humans probably has little in common with its realizer in octopuses; nor can we a priori exclude the nomological possibility of pain in inorganic electro-mechanical systems. This means that there is no single physical-biological state which could be correlated, or identified, with pain in a biconditional bridge law, and this defeats Nagel reduction of any theory of pain to an underlying physical-biological theory, as well as reductive identification of pain with a physical-biological state. The same argument is often applied to biological concepts, such as 'heart' and 'digestive system', functionally defined physical concepts like 'carburettor' and 'thermometer', and dispositional concepts like 'transparency' and 'water solubility'.

Notice that the multiple realization argument does not touch Kemeny–Oppenheim reduction in general, but works only against Nagel reduction which, as we saw, aims to conserve the reduced higher level properties. In any case, one reply that is usually rejected is this: why not reduce pain to a *disjunction* of its diverse physical realizers? But given the kind of extreme diversity involved, such disjunctive states are unlikely to be projectible nomic properties and there cannot, it seems, be a unitary theory dealing with them (Kim 1992). Another, more plausible, way of dealing with the phenomenon of multiple realization is to lower our reductive aspirations: the argument perhaps shows that *uniform* or *global reduction* of pain is not feasible, but not that human pain, octopus pain and Martian pain cannot each be *locally reduced* to human physiology, octopus physiology and Martian electrochemistry, respectively (Kim 1992). Thus, multiple realization is consistent with (in fact, it arguably entails) the local reducibility of higher level sciences: for example, human psychology to human neurobiology, octopus psychology to octopus neurobiology, and so on. One possible difficulty with this approach is that pain, when considered multiply reduced to a set of diverse physical-biological bases, seems to lose its integrity as a single mental state; pain as such appears either eliminated or else remains unreduced outside the ontology of the lower level theories.

6 The primacy of physical theory

Physics is generally thought to be our basic science, the only science that aspires to 'full coverage' of all of the natural world. But what does this mean? Does it mean that all the special sciences – that is, laws and generalizations of these sciences and the properties posited by them – are reducible to the basic laws of physics and fundamental physical properties? It used to be thought that the primacy of physical theory was equivalent to global physical reductionism. This view will be rejected by most philosophers. Many now doubt the possibility of reduction in almost all areas of science, and downplay the scientific and philosophical significance of reductions (although of course no one has seriously suggested that we would ever actually achieve a single unified science in the vocabulary of basic microphysics). Some have argued that even where reductions are possible, we lose important explanatory information about phenomena in a given domain when we focus only on their microstructures and neglect the larger 'patterns' that emerge at macrolevels. These macropatterns are claimed to cut across microstructures, and be capturable only by higher level laws (Fodor 1974). These remain controversial issues, however.

Views of this kind resemble the position of emergentism (Morgan 1923) on higher level 'emergent' properties. Those who hold these or related views often try to explain the primacy of physical theory in a thesis of supervenience or determination, the claim that physical facts (including physical laws) determine all the facts, or that worlds that are indiscernible in respect of all physical features are one and the same world (Hellman and Thompson 1975; Kim 1984). However, the relationship between reductionism and various forms of the supervenience thesis remains controversial and continues to be debated (Kim 1984).

See also: LAWS, NATURAL; LOGICAL POSITIVISM; REDUCTIONISM IN THE PHILOSOPHY OF MIND; SIMPLICITY (IN SCIENTIFIC THEORIES); SUPERVENIENCE; SUPERVENIENCE OF THE MENTAL

References and further reading

Benacerraf, P. (1965) 'What Numbers Could Not Be', *Philosophical Review* 74: 47– 73. (Raises important ontological issues concerning the set-theoretic reduction of numbers.)

Carnap, R (1938–55) 'Logical Foundations of the Unity of Science', in O. Neurath, R. Carnap and C. Morris (eds) *International Encyclopedia of Unified Science*, Chicago, IL: University of Chicago Press, vol. 1, 42–62. (A classic positivist statement on reductionism.)

* Causey, R.L. (1977) *Unity of Science*, Dordrecht: Reidel. (A useful and comprehensive account of reduction in science.)

* Churchland, P.S. (1986) *Neurophilosophy*, Cambridge, MA: MIT Press. (Contains discussion of reductive strategies in cognitive neuroscience.)

* Fodor, J.A. (1974) 'Special Sciences – or the Disunity of Science as a Working Hypothesis', *Synthèse* 28: 97–115. (Presents the multiple realization argument against reduction and reductionism discussed in §5, and defends the autonomy of the special sciences.)

* Hellman, G. and Thompson, F. (1975) 'Physicalism: Ontology, Determination, and Reduction', *Journal of Philosophy* 72: 551–64. (Presents a version of physicalism that rejects reductionism in favour of a supervenience thesis.)

Hooker, C. (1981) 'Toward a General Theory of Reduction', *Dialogue* 20: 38–60, 201–35, 496–529. (A detailed survey and critical examination of the literature on reduction up to the late 1970s.)

* Kemeny, J. and Oppenheim, P. (1956) 'On Reduction', *Philosophical Studies* 7: 6–18. (Presents the classic replacement model of reduction as discussed in §3.)

* Kim, J. (1984) 'Concepts of Supervenience', *Philosophy and Phenomenological Research* 45: 153–76. (Distinguishes various forms of supervenience and discusses the relationship between supervenience and reduction.)

* —— (1992) 'Multiple Realization and the Metaphysics of Reduction', *Philosophy and Phenomenological Research* 52: 1–26. (An assessment of the multiple realization argument against reduction.)

* Morgan, C.L. (1923) *Emergent Evolution*, London: Williams & Norgate. (A classic statement of emergentism.)

* Nagel, E. (1961) *The Structure of Science*, New York: Harcourt Brace. (The classic source of Nagel's derivational model of theory reduction as discussed in §2, and which also includes discussion of emergentism.)

* Oppenheim, P. and Putnam, H. (1958) 'Unity of Science as a Working Hypothesis', *Minnesota Studies in the Philosophy of Science*, vol. 2. (A useful presentation of the doctrine of physical reductionism through microreduction.)

Quine, W.V. (1964) 'Ontological Reduction and the World of Numbers', *Journal of Philosophy* 61: 209–16. (Reviews some ontological issues in the reduction of number theory, but the discussion has wider implications.)

* Schaffner, K.F. (1967) 'Approaches to Reduction', *Philosophy of Science* 34: 137–47. (Stresses the point that the reduced theory must be appropriately corrected.)

* Sklar, L. (1967) 'Types of Intertheoretic Reduction', *British Journal for the Philosophy of Science* 18: 109–24. (Argues that 'bridge laws' should be construed as identities.)

JAEGWON KIM

REDUCTIONISM IN THE PHILOSOPHY OF MIND

Reductionism in the philosophy of mind is one of the options available to those who think that humans and the human mind are part of the natural physical world. Reductionists seek to integrate the mind and mental phenomena – fear, pain, anger and the like – with the natural world by showing them to be natural phenomena. Their inspirations are the famous reductions of science: of the heat of gases to molecular motion, of lightning to electric discharge, of the gene to the DNA molecule and the like. Reductionists hope to show a similar relationship between mental kinds and neurophysiological kinds.

1   The road to functionalism
2   Functionalism
3   'No problem' theories
4   What does physicalism require?

1   The road to functionalism

Reductionism in the philosophy of mind is generated by an apparent conflict between two conceptions of persons. The first we inherit from our general culture, and is often called folk psychology. Folk psychology portrays humans as having experiences, emotions, purposes, thoughts about and expectations of the world: humans are conscious intentional agents (see FOLK PSYCHOLOGY). According to the picture we derive from the natural sciences, humans are evolved animals, and animals are nothing more than complex physical systems. Reductionist strategies in the philosophy of mind all start from a firm commitment to this second conception: the idea that humans are part of the natural order. That natural order is not essentially mysterious or occult. So reductionists accept some version of physicalism (see MATERIALISM IN THE PHILOSOPHY OF MIND).

Reductionist programmes in the philosophy of mind face three problems. (1) Are humans part of the natural order – is the physicalist conception true? (2) If we are part of the natural order, does folk psychology fit, or fail to fit, with that conception? (3) What do we need to do in order to integrate folk psychology within the naturalistic conception?

It has often been thought that no physicalist theory of consciousness or subjective experience is possible; these phenomena show the outright falsity of physicalism. For example, there seems to be a fundamental contrast between my knowledge of my own mind and my knowledge of the physical world. The latter is error-prone: it is conceivable that we could be wrong in any belief about the physical world. But it is not even conceivable, the idea runs, that I am wrong in thinking that I feel sleepy. I could be wrong about the causes of the feeling, but not that I have that feeling (see INTROSPECTION; QUALIA).

There are three options available for those who think humans are part of an unmysterious natural order. One idea (the 'No real problem' option) is that the dualists' puzzles of how thought and consciousness fit into the natural order evaporate on a proper understanding of the nature of folk psychology. Properly understood, the folk conception of the mental is unproblematic. The strategy seeks to show that mental concepts are equivalent to, or translate into, concepts for quite innocent phenomena. The most famous variant of this line is behaviourism. Behaviourists think that mental kinds have behavioural signatures; the essence of anger, for instance, is not a particular kind of internal mental event, but a way of behaving. A claim that a person is conscious, or intelligent, or is purposive is not about their inner workings or organization. It is not a claim about the causal structure that produces behaviour; but rather about the pattern of that behaviour. It is a claim that therefore cannot, of its very nature, traffic in weird causes or weird stuff (see BEHAVIOURISM, ANALYTIC).

The eliminativist option takes the conflict between folk psychology and the idea that humans are part of the natural order to be irresolvable. They think we cannot accept the view that we are conscious intentional agents and the view that we are part of the natural order. They furthermore suggest that the folk conception must be rejected, forced as we are to choose between them. So the eliminativist proposes to abandon the folk conception of the mind (see ELIMINATIVISM).

That leaves the reductionists. They accept (1) that folk conceptions of the mental do make claims about the causal structures that produce behaviour, and (2) that folk psychologists' inventory of mental events, processes and kinds must be shown to be compatible with the view that the mind is a wholly natural phenomenon. If folk psychology offers an incomplete but more or less correct account of some of the causal structure underlying human behaviour, and if humans are just complex physical systems, then the events, processes and properties named in folk psychology must be physical events, processes and properties.

Identity theorists developed for philosophy of mind ideas then current in the philosophy of science about the relationship between less and more fundamental sciences (see MIND, IDENTITY THEORY OF). The idea was that a less fundamental domain could be reduced to a more fundamental domain via bridge laws that linked the domains. Thus the chemical property of valency might be linked to atomic physics via bridge laws that identified different elements' valencies with properties of their electron structure. In the philosophy of mind, this became the identity theory, holding that

Mental states = states of the central nervous system.

In J.J.C. Smart's most famous example, perhaps pain just is C-fibre stimulation. If identity hypotheses can be defended for all mental states, events and processes, then facts about the mental would be reduced to facts about neural structures, events and processes.

When the identity theory was formulated in the 1950s, it had to fight against the idea that it was conceptually confused. How could physicalism be true without being obviously true? The defenders of the theory had to show that one could master and understand the language of folk psychology without any mastery of the language of the neurosciences. They had to show how it is possible to know that you are in pain without knowing, say, that your C-fibres are being stimulated.

Identity theorists met these challenges through example and analysis. Though lightning is nothing but the discharge of static electricity we can understand lightning and know plenty about lightning without knowing its physical nature. Until the discovery of the structure of DNA, population geneticists talked of genes without knowing their chemical nature. Genes were identified by their role in inheritance and development. We can understand concepts for kinds, and know something about these kinds without knowing about their intrinsic characteristics. Smart re-reinforced these examples with a 'topic neutral analysis' of mental concepts. To say that you are experiencing blue visual sensations, for example, is just to say that the experiences you are now having are similar to those you have when you see a blue wall in good light. It is obviously possible both to learn and correctly deploy topic neutral sensation concepts without knowing anything about the intrinsic nature of those sensations.

The identity theory however proved to be chauvinist in Ned Block's terminology. If pain is C-fibre stimulation, then if you have no C-fibres, you cannot feel pain. Yet it is surely possible, and perhaps even actual, for organisms with different neurophysiologies to feel pain. It seemed to be a mistake to tie our account of what cognition is too closely to the details of how our brain works. So the identity theory does not quite show how it is possible to be both a folk psychologist and a reductionist.

2 Functionalism

So most current reductionists accept some version of functionalism. The many forms of that doctrine are united in holding that the essential feature of any mental state is its causal role (see FUNCTIONALISM). For example, all instances of fear have a distinctive causal role: fear has a characteristic profile of causes and effects. But functionalists also claim that fear is realized by a physiological state: most probably a complex of hormonal activity and arousal of the nervous system. The functional role of fear is occupied by a physiological state. If functionalists are right, our mental life can be described in complementary ways. A functional description tells us the causal roles of the full range of human psychological states. A physical description specifies the physical states which have those causal roles. The attraction of functionalism as a theory of mind is its attempt to reconcile physicalism with folk psychology.

The relationship between functional kinds and their physical realizations is complex. Two different people can be in the same mental state, hold the same belief, for instance. A functional description specifying a certain causal role is true of them both. Psychological kinds can be multiply realized. The neural organization of our memory is flexible and shows a good deal of individual variation, so the same mental state can have different physical realizations in different people, or in the same person at different times. These complications are magnified when we consider psychological states – fear, for example – that we share with other animals. Furthermore, if there are intelligent aliens or robots, then there are systems whose intelligence has a very different physical basis from ours. So the one mental state might have wildly varied physical realizations.

The functionalist pictures psychological kinds as realized by neural kinds in complex and varied ways. So the natural kinds of psychology are not identical to the natural kinds of the physical basis of the mind. Hence, despite the fact that we are nothing but complex physical systems, functionalists often claim that psychology is relatively independent of the sciences of the brain. The functionalist programme needs to show (1) that a reductionist strategy of some kind is needed, that against the no real problem option it really is necessary to demonstrate the connection between the folk psychological and the natural science picture; (2) that folk psychology can be properly built into the physicalist world view through the idea of functional kinds as merely realized by physical kinds, and (3) that it really is plausible that all psychological kinds are some species of functional kind.

3 'No problem' theories

Behaviourism is no longer widely accepted, but it is still argued that there is no potential for conflict between folk psychology and the natural sciences because folk psychology is an instrument: its use is instrumental or practical rather than theoretical. The contrast here is with the so-called 'theory-theory': folk psychology as an implicit theory of the causes of human behaviour. Like other theories, such a theory would need to be integrated with the rest of the natural sciences; like other theories, it could be wrong and shown to be wrong by its conflict with, or isolation from, the rest of our picture of nature.

The theory-theory may well over-intellectualize folk psychology. Folk psychology is not part of a conscious research programme into the structure of the human mind. Our use of it may be as much knowing how as knowing that. Nevertheless, folk psychology is full of claims about human minds, and about the causes of human behaviour: about, for instance, beliefs and desires causing behaviour ('They went because they believed that they would enjoy themselves'), and about perceptions causing beliefs ('Seeing is believing'). Paul Churchland has given one set of arguments for the theory-theory: folk psychology can be assembled into a package of generalizations connecting perceptions, thought and behaviour. Folk psychology can be organized in such a way that there are structural similarities between it and paradigm scientific theories. But a potential for conflict between the natural sciences and folk psychology does not depend on accepting a full-blooded version of the theory-theory. An analogy with other folk crafts should make that clear. The folk agriculture of, say, a New Zealand Maori tribe is not research science. It includes as much knowledge how as knowledge that. Its uses are practical. Yet none of that made it invulnerable to advances in scientific knowledge. Its central categories might turn out to be empty, to be misconceived, if their failure to correspond to the causes of growth are radical enough. Potential for conflict depends only on the idea that practices, modes of practical knowledge and skill, can depend on or presuppose conceptions of the causal structure of a domain. Even if folk psychology has different goals or purposes from the scientific behavioural sciences the demand that folk psychology be shown to be compatible with a naturalistic conception of human nature is still reasonable. An analogy with folk medicine is compelling. What would we think of a claim for the therapeutic value of some practice where we could find no physiological mechanism that would explain that value? Or, still worse, where our physiological sciences seem to

151

show that the practice could not have therapeutic value?

4   What does physicalism require?

Though the matter remains very controversial, in my view the 'no real problem' option is not attractive. Folk psychology seems to make claims about the working of the human mind, about its causal structure, whose relation to the natural sciences requires explanation. But it has proved very difficult to formulate precisely this idea of demonstrating compatibility between two conceptions of human nature. At the very least, folk psychological states must supervene on the physical world. There can be no change in my folk psychological state – say, from fear to calm – without some change in my intrinsic or relational physical properties (see SUPERVENIENCE OF THE MENTAL). But the eliminativists argue for a much stronger condition, something close to the original idea of the identity theory's bridge laws between the domains of psychology and neurophysiology. They argue that without a strong condition, spurious compatibility is too easy to construct, and the debris of intellectual history will escape appropriate rejection.

Despite the eliminativists' claims, the idea that folk psychology requires bridge laws for its vindication is clearly much too strong. The double descriptions characteristic of the functionalist idea is not a fancy trick dreamed up just for the philosophy of mind. The distinction between a role and its occupant is not restricted to psychology. We can make the same distinction in politics between, say, the chief justice and the particular person who occupies that role. We can ask questions about that role; about the legal and constitutional powers of the chief justice. We can ask questions about the occupier: about their political background and skills; about size, sex or place of birth. We can make the same distinction in biology. Zoologists investigate the causal role echo-location plays in the life of the bat. They measure the discriminatory capacities and range of the system, test its role in hunting, courtship and mating. Neuroethologists investigate the physical systems that occupy that causal role in the bat.

The idea of multiple realization is not restricted to the relationship between mental state types and the neural states realizing those types. There are no simple bridge laws between classical genetics and molecular genetics, the science which is rightly seen as vindicating classical genetics. The bodily effects of DNA sequences depend very much on the cellular environment of those DNA sequences plus many other factors. So the geneticists' fruit-fly gene for red

eyes is not identical to a particular DNA sequence: there is no DNA sequence that always and only produces red-eyed fruit-flies (see GENETICS). So the complexity of the relationship between functional state and physical realization is not a feature just of the relationship between folk psychology and neuroscience; it is common to many of these other domains as well.

Nonetheless if folk psychological kinds are parts of causal explanations within human psychology, an explanation of their capacity to play that causal role does seem needed. Causal powers stand in need of explanation. There is a tree of explanatory dependence that links together causal mechanisms. That tree is rooted in fundamental physical kinds and processes. Through various different branchings, all scientific kinds depend on that taproot. The kinds (and the processes in which they take part) further out in the branches need to be explained by kinds and laws closer to the root.

The importance of this idea is seen in its regulative role in scientific debate. For example, the biogeographic and geological evidence for continental drift was quite impressive even before the Second World War. But continental drift remained marginalized in the profession, in part because the proposed mechanisms to shift continents were impossible. The drifters of the 1930s conceived of continents as ploughing through somewhat less dense ocean floor rather as a concrete slab might be pushed half through, half over the top, of a layer of earth. The proposed forces were too weak, and the stresses on continental crusts would be far too great for them to survive the passage. Until drift could be plausibly placed in the explanatory tree, driftist explanations of movement were hard to accept.

There have been similar problems with mechanism in recent debates within evolutionary theory. From time to time there are announcements of counterexamples to Crick's central dogma of molecular biology, nucleic acids code proteins, but not vice versa; changes in the protein envelope of the nuclear material do not result in reverse transcription, changing RNA and thence DNA (though reverse transcription form RNA to DNA is possible). There is no plausible mechanism through which three dimensional form can be transcribed into two dimensional form, hence no mechanism through which acquired characteristics can be inherited through changes in DNA. A discoverer of the inheritance of acquired characteristics would need to give some account of a mechanism of inheritance.

The reductionist debate has not been concluded. A precise and plausible formulation of the physicalist constraint remains elusive. Many psychological kinds continue to resist functionalist theory: if they have a characteristic causal role, that causal role has been difficult to characterize. The appropriate formulation of functionalism remains a matter of intense debate.

See also: REDUCTION, PROBLEMS OF

References and further reading

Armstrong, D.M. (1968) *A Materialist Theory of Mind*, London: Routledge & Kegan Paul. (An early functionalist classic, but written before the distinction between functionalism and the identity theory was clearly drawn. So Armstrong describes the book as a defence of the identity theory.)

* Block, N. (1978) 'Troubles with Functionalism' in C. Wade Savage (ed.) *Minnesota Studies in the Philosophy of Science*, vol. 9, *Perception and Cognition*, Minneapolis. MN: University of Minnesota Press, 261-325. (Block describes the problems for the identity theory, but spends most of this paper showing how hard it is to specify the functional profile of most mental kinds.)

* Churchland, P.M. (1981) 'Eliminative Materialism and the Propositional Attitudes', *Journal of Philosophy* 78: 67-90. (A clear and classic exposition of eliminativism, reprinted in W.G Lycan, 1990.)

Dennett, D.C. (1987) *The Intentional Stance*, Cambridge, MA.: MIT Press. (A very sophisticated version of the 'No problem' approach to the cognitive aspects of the mind.)

Dennett, D.C. (1991) *Consciousness Explained*, Boston, MA: Little, Brown. (A very sophisticated version of the 'No problem' strategy applied to the problems of consciousness. The first two chapters give a good account of the attractions of dualism.)

Fodor, J.A. (1968) *Psychological Explanation*, New York: Random House. (An early and very clear version of functionalism.)

—— (1975) *The Language of Thought*, New York: Thomas Crowell. (A classic and very accessible paradigm of functionalism focused on thought and thinking rather than consciousness.)

Lycan, W.G. (1987) *Consciousness*, Cambridge, MA: MIT Press. (A fine and very clearly written example of contemporary functionalism.)

Lycan, W.G. (1990) *Mind and Cognition: a Reader*, Oxford: Blackwell. (A well-organized and well-chosen anthology with good introductions.)

Ryle, G. (1949) *The Concept of Mind*, London: Hutchinson. (The first clear statement of the behaviourist programme.)

* Smart, J.J.C. (1959) 'Sensations and Brain Processes', *Philosophical Review* 68: 141-56. (An early and very

important defence of the identity theory; available in many collections.)

KIM STERELNY

REFERENCE

It is usual to think that referential relations hold between language and thoughts on one hand, and the world on the other. The most striking example of such a relation is the naming relation, which holds between the name 'Socrates' and the famous philosopher Socrates. Indeed, some philosophers in effect restrict the vague word 'reference' to the naming relation, or something similar. Others use 'reference' broadly (as it is used in this entry) to cover a range of semantically significant relations that hold between various sorts of terms and the world: between 'philosopher' and all philosophers, for example. Other words used for one or other of these relations include 'designation', 'denotation', 'signification', 'application' and 'satisfaction'.

Philosophers often are interested in reference because they take it to be the core of meaning. Thus, the fact that 'Socrates' refers to that famous philosopher is the core of the name's meaning and hence of its contribution to the meaning of any sentence – for example, 'Socrates is wise' – that contains the name. The name's referent contributes to the sentence's meaning by contributing to its truth-condition: 'Socrates is wise' is true if and only if the object referred to by 'Socrates' is wise.

The first question that arises about the reference of a term is: what does the term refer to? Sometimes the answer seems obvious – for example, 'Socrates' refers to the famous philosopher – although even the obvious answer has been denied on occasions. On other occasions, the answer is not obvious. Does 'wise' refer to the property wisdom, the set of wise things, or each and every wise thing? Clearly, answers to this should be influenced by one's ontology, or general view of what exists. Thus, a nominalist who thinks that properties do not really exist, and that talk of them is a mere manner of speaking, would not take 'wise' to refer to the property wisdom.

The central question about reference is: in virtue of what does a term have its reference? Answering this requires a theory that explains the term's relation to its referent. There has been a great surge of interest in theories of reference in this century.

What used to be the most popular theory about the reference of proper names arose from the views of Gottlob Frege and Bertrand Russell and became known as 'the description theory'. According to this theory, the meaning of a name is given by a definite description – an expression of the form 'the F' – that competent speakers associate with the name; thus, the meaning of 'Aristotle' might be given by 'the last great philosopher of antiquity'. So the answer to our central question would be that a name refers to a certain object because that object is picked out by the name's associated description.

Around 1970, several criticisms were made of the description theory by Saul Kripke and Keith Donnellan; in particular, they argued that a competent speaker usually does not have sufficient knowledge of the referent to associate a reference-determining description. Under their influence, many adopted 'the historical–causal theory' of names. According to this theory, a name refers to its bearer in virtue of standing in an appropriate causal relation to the bearer.

Description theories are popular also for words other than names. Similar responses were made to many of these theories in the 1970s. Thus, Kripke and Hilary Putnam rejected description theories of natural-kind terms like 'gold' and proposed historical–causal replacements.

Many other words (for example, adjectives, adverbs and verbs) seem to be referential. However we need not assume that all other words are. It seems preferable to see some words as syncategorematic, contributing structural elements rather than referents to the truth-conditions and meanings of sentences. Perhaps this is the right way to view words like 'not' and the quantifiers (like 'all', 'most' and 'few').

The referential roles of anaphoric (cross-referential) terms are intricate. These terms depend for their reference on other expressions in their verbal context. Sometimes they are what Peter Geach calls 'pronouns of laziness', going proxy for other expressions in the context; at other times they function like bound variables in logic. Geach's argument that every anaphoric term can be treated in one of these two ways was challenged by Gareth Evans.

Finally, there has been an interest in 'naturalizing' reference, explaining it in scientifically acceptable terms. Attempted explanations have appealed to one or more of three causal relations between words and the world: historical, reliable and teleological.

1   **Millian and description theories of proper names**
2   **Three arguments against description theories of proper names**
3   **General terms and mass terms**
4   **Historical–causal theories**
5   **Indexicals**
6   **Descriptions**
7   **Other terms**
8   **Naturalizing reference**
9   **Further issues**

1   Millian and description theories of proper names

The description theory of proper names stands in sharp contrast to the age-old and attractive theory that there is no more to a name's meaning than its role of designating something. Thus, John Stuart Mill claimed that 'proper names are not connotative: they denote the individuals who are called by them; but they do not indicate or imply any attributes as belonging to those individuals' ([1843] 1867: 20) (see MILL, J.S. §2). One problem for this theory is that it makes answering our central question seem hard: if a name does not 'imply any attributes' of its bearer, as the description theory claims it does, what determines which object is the bearer?

It was not primarily concern with this question, however, that led most philosophers to abandon the Millian theory and adopt the description theory. They did this largely as a result of the criticisms and counter-proposals of Frege (1893) and Russell (1911).

The most famous criticism of the Millian theory concerns identity statements. The ancient Greeks observed what they took to be a star rising in the evening and called it 'Hesperus', and what they took to be another star rising in the morning and called it 'Phosphorus'. In fact these 'two stars' were the planet Venus. Consider the following two statements:

(1) Hesperus is Phosphorus.
(2) Hesperus is Hesperus.

Sentence (1) is true. A comparison of (1) and (2) seems to indicate that they differ sharply in meaning. Various reasons have been adduced in favour of this view. Some philosophers have argued that whereas (1) is synthetic, (2) is analytic; others that whereas (1) is known empirically, (2) is known a priori; still others that whereas (1) is contingent, (2) is necessary. However, probably the most influential reason for thinking that the statements differ in meaning has been Frege's claim that they differ in 'cognitive value': (1) is highly informative, revealing an important astronomical discovery, whereas (2) is uninformative, a trivial piece of logical knowledge (see FREGE, G. §3). In any case, it was generally agreed that the two statements do differ in meaning. If so, the only way to explain this seemed to be to attribute different meanings to 'Hesperus' and 'Phosphorus'. Yet, according to the Millian theory, they must have the same meaning as they both have the role of designating Venus. So the Millian theory must be wrong: a name's role of designating its bearer does not exhaust its meaning.

Another important criticism concerns existence statements. 'Vulcan does not exist' is true. Because it is true, 'Vulcan' does not designate anything. So, according to the Millian theory, 'Vulcan' should be meaningless. So, 'Vulcan does not exist' should be partly meaningless. Yet, it is perfectly meaningful. Indeed, if it were not, it could not be true. So, once again, the Millian theory must be wrong (see FICTION, SEMANTICS OF).

The description theory provides neat solutions to what are problems for the Millian theory. According to the description theory, a name in effect abbreviates the definite description that competent speakers associate with the name: thus 'Aristotle' might abbreviate 'the last great philosopher of antiquity'. So it is easy to see why (1) and (2) differ in meaning: 'Hesperus' might be associated with the description 'the star that rises in the evening', and 'Phosphorus' with 'the star that rises in the morning'. And 'Vulcan does not exist' is fully meaningful because 'Vulcan' abbreviates the meaningful description 'the planet in orbit between Mercury and the Sun' (see PROPER NAMES §§1, 5).

More importantly for our purposes, the description theory provides an answer to our central question. A name designates a certain object because that object is denoted by the definite description associated with the name; 'Aristotle' designates Aristotle because 'the last great philosopher of antiquity' denotes him. Of course, this answer raises another question (see §6): in virtue of what does the description denote that object? Still, progress has clearly been made because we had that problem anyway.

Some obvious problems with this 'classical' description theory – including the problem that speakers differ in the descriptions that they associate with a name – led some philosophers, notably John Searle (1958) and Peter Strawson (1959), to modify the theory. A name is not tied tightly to one description but loosely to many. It can designate its bearer despite the failure of some in its 'cluster' of associated descriptions to denote that object: it designates whatever object most of the descriptions in the cluster denote.

2 Three arguments against description theories of proper names

Description theories dominated for half a century until challenged by three arguments around 1970: the unwanted necessity and rigidity arguments, both due largely to Kripke (1980), and the argument from ignorance and error, due to Kripke and to Donnellan (1972).

Unwanted necessities were one of the obvious problems for the classical description theory. If 'the last great philosopher of antiquity' is synonymous with 'Aristotle', then 'Aristotle is a philosopher' should be necessarily true (provided Aristotle exists). Yet it is not: Aristotle might have died young, long before his philosophical fulfilment. The cluster theory avoided this version of the problem. The description 'the last great philosopher of antiquity' is just one among many in the cluster that expresses the meaning of 'Aristotle'. Aristotle need not have any particular one of the many properties specified by the cluster. The cluster theory does require, however, that Aristotle have *most* of the properties specified by the cluster. Kripke points out how implausible this is. Aristotle might not have had any of the properties commonly associated with him: he might not have been a pupil of Plato, taught Alexander the Great, and so on. So 'Aristotle' cannot be synonymous with the cluster of associated descriptions (see KRIPKE, S.A. §2).

The rigidity argument deploys the notion of 'rigid designation'. This is explained as follows: for a term *a* to be a rigid designator is for it to designate the same object in every possible world (in which it designates at all), or, less picturesquely, for it to be such that '*a* is *F*' would truly characterize some non-actual situation if and only if the object that the term *actually* designates were *F* in that situation. Kripke argues that names are rigid designators whereas the descriptions alleged to be synonymous with them are not. So description theories are wrong. Consider:

(3) Aristotle was fond of dogs.
(4) The last great philosopher of antiquity was fond of dogs.

Suppose that Aristotle had indeed died young. Then Plato, not Aristotle, would have been the last great philosopher of antiquity. In those circumstances the truth of (4) would depend on whether Plato was fond of dogs. But the truth of (3) would still depend, just as it does depend in the actual world, on whether Aristotle was fond of dogs. The name 'Aristotle' designates Aristotle in a non-actual situation just as it does in the actual situation, whereas the description 'the last great philosopher of antiquity' designates whoever is the last great philosopher of antiquity in that situation, whether Aristotle or not. So the name is not synonymous with the description. Similarly, it is not synonymous with any other description, or cluster of descriptions, that is a candidate to give its meaning. (Note that in assessing rigidity we are evaluating the truth and reference of our expressions with the meanings that they actually have as a result of our usage, but we consider them as used to characterize hypothetical situations. Of course, any expression could have a different meaning as a result of different usage in a non-actual situation – language is 'arbitrary' – but that is beside the point) (see PROPER NAMES §§2–3).

Statements (3) and (4) are not modal statements (although we have been evaluating them as characterizations of non-actual situations). Other versions of the rigidity argument concern modal statements. For example, whereas 'Hesperus is necessarily Hesperus' is true, 'Hesperus is necessarily the star that rises in the evening' is not: had the solar system been differently arranged, Hesperus might not have been visible in the evening but it still would have been Hesperus. This sort of difference between descriptions and names in modal statements had been emphasized earlier by other philosophers, particularly Ruth Barcan Marcus (1961).

Some philosophers, notably Michael Dummett (1973), resisted Kripke's two arguments by focusing on modal statements. These philosophers exploited the well-known ambiguities of scope in these statements to undermine the apparent difference between names and descriptions. Whatever the truth of this matter, the apparent difference in nonmodal statements remains.

These two arguments challenge the description theory as a theory of the meaning of a name, a meaning that determines the name's reference. This is how the theory is naturally understood. However, as Kripke points out, the theory could be understood as simply a theory of reference: the reference of a name is fixed by a description, but the name is not synonymous with that description. This weaker theory is impervious to the two arguments. Of course, the weak theory has a defect: because it is no longer a theory of meaning, it no longer solves the problems that troubled the Millian theory. Indeed, the relation between meaning and reference becomes a pressing issue on the basis of this theory.

There is another way of saving the description theory from the two arguments while avoiding this defect. Instead of weakening the original theory into a mere theory of reference, we revise it along the following lines: a name is synonymous with a 'rigidified' description. Our language already seems to have descriptions that contain 'rigidity operators'; for example, the italicized part of 'the person who, *in the actual world*, is the last great philosopher of antiquity' seems to make this description designate Aristotle in every possible world. If descriptions of this sort are indeed rigid, the revised theory claims that a name is synonymous with such a description. If such descriptions are not rigid, the revised theory can claim that the name itself supplies the rigidity operator and so would be synonymous with an ordinary nonrigid description governed by that operator.

All of these description theories – original, weak and revised – have the consequence that the users of a name associate with it a description that identifies its bearer. The third argument against description theories, the argument from ignorance and error, challenges this. So, if the argument is good, it counts against all description theories.

The argument shows that people who seem perfectly able to designate with a name are very often too ignorant to supply an identifying description. Thus some may fail with the name 'Cicero' because they associate with it only the description 'a famous Roman orator', which applies to many people. Others may fail because they associate 'the man who denounced Catiline' with 'Cicero' and are unable to supply an appropriate description for 'Catiline': the description that they associate with 'Catiline' is 'the man denounced by Cicero', which takes us in a circle and leaves both names without reference, according to the description theory.

The argument shows also that people often associate with a name a description that identifies something other than the name's bearer: they are simply wrong about the bearer. Thus some associate 'the inventor of the atomic bomb' with 'Einstein' and some associate 'the first person to realize that the world was round' with 'Columbus'. Almost everyone who has heard of Peano associates 'the discoverer of Peano's axioms' with 'Peano', but the axioms were actually discovered by Dedekind. Despite such errors, people succeed in designating Einstein, Columbus and Peano by their names.

The description theory can be improved by allowing people to 'borrow' their reference from others. So the description Martha associates with 'Einstein' might be 'the person Joe referred to yesterday as "Einstein"'. Provided Joe can supply an appropriate description – either one that describes Einstein directly or one that borrows reference from someone who can supply an appropriate description – Martha will succeed in designating Einstein. There is a danger of a circle, of course. Apart from that, there are problems of ignorance and error once more. Perhaps Martha cannot remember the reference lender; or she can remember the lender by his name, 'Joe', but cannot supply the identifying description that the theory requires; or the lender is identified but he cannot identify Einstein, perhaps identifying something else instead. The description theory still seems to place too great an epistemic burden on speakers.

An argument from ignorance and error can also be brought against another, more general, theory that some – for example, Dummett – have taken from Frege. This is the theory that to understand a name a person must be able to 'identify' its bearer. This ability is usually evidenced by providing a description, but it may be evidenced by 'recognizing' the bearer.

The epistemic burden that this more general theory places on speakers still seems too great.

Various moves have been made to save the description theory in the face of these difficulties. Most popular, perhaps, have been theories that the reference of, for example, 'Einstein' is determined by a description along the lines of 'the person referred to by (called, named and so on) "Einstein"', for this description does identify Einstein and speakers surely associate it with the name. However, such theories still risk circularity.

3 General terms and mass terms

Just as there are description theories of names, so also there are description theories of general terms like 'tiger', 'hammer' and 'bachelor', and of mass terms like 'gold' and 'paper' (see MASS TERMS). Speakers of the language associate various descriptions with a term. One of these descriptions, or most of a cluster of them, expresses the meaning of the term and determines what it applies to. If only one description does the job, the view is analogous to the classical description theory of names. If a cluster of descriptions does, the view is analogous to the cluster theory of names.

Kripke (1980) and Putnam (1975) argued that description theories are false of general and mass terms that apply to natural kinds. So they are false of 'tiger' and 'gold'. The arguments are like the three against description theories of names (see §2). First, the theories yield unwanted necessities. The description we associate with 'tiger' is along the lines of 'large carnivorous quadrupedal feline, tawny yellow in colour with blackish transverse stripes and white belly'. Yet it is not necessary that a tiger has four legs and is striped: a tiger might lose a leg, or in a different environment tigers might not be striped. Second, the term 'gold' is a rigid designator, applying to the same kind of stuff in every possible world. In contrast, an associated description like 'dense yellow metal' is nonrigid. Third, people who seem perfectly able to use a term are often too ignorant or misguided about the things to which it applies to supply an appropriate identifying description. Thus, some who use 'elm' and 'beech' cannot supply descriptions that distinguish elms from beeches; many who use 'gold' cannot distinguish gold from fool's gold; it was once common to associate 'fish' with 'whale'.

Putnam added a further argument built around the following fantasy. Imagine that somewhere in the galaxy there is a planet, Twin Earth. Twin Earth, as its name suggests, is very like Earth. In particular, each Earthling has a *doppelgänger* on Twin Earth who is a cell for cell duplicate of the Earthling. Twin Earth differs from Earth in one respect, however: the stuff that the Twin Earthians who appear to speak English call 'water', stuff that is superficially indistinguishable from what we call 'water', is not H_2O but a very different compound XYZ. So Oscar on Earth and Twin Oscar on Twin Earth are referring to different stuff by 'water'. Yet Oscar and Twin Oscar are *doppelgängers*, associating exactly the same descriptions with 'water' (which is more plausible if we place Oscar and Twin Oscar in 1750 before the chemical composition of water was known). So those associations are not sufficient to determine reference and the description theory is wrong. Indeed, nothing happening in the head is sufficient to determine reference. As Putnam put it, 'meanings just ain't in the head' (see CONTENT: WIDE AND NARROW; PUTNAM, H. §3).

We have considered criticisms of description theories of proper names and natural-kind words. Do these criticisms extend to description theories of other words? Putnam took the arguments to apply to almost all words, including 'pencil' and 'paediatrician'. Tyler Burge (1979) took a similar line, arguing that the meanings (contents) and references of a wide range of a person's words and accompanying thoughts are not 'individualistic' in that they are not determined simply by that person's intrinsic states. To a large extent they are determined by the person's social context. Burge's examples include 'arthritis', 'sofa', 'brisket', 'clavichord' and 'contract' (see METHODOLOGICAL INDIVIDUALISM).

The Twin Earth fantasy brings out an important feature of description theories in general: even if a description theory gives the right answer to our central question for some word, its answer is incomplete. Thus, consider a description theory of 'tiger'. According to the theory, the reference of 'tiger' is determined by the reference of such words as 'carnivorous' and 'striped'. Suppose, contrary to the arguments above, that this were so. We then need to explain the reference of those words to complete the explanation of the reference of 'tiger'. Description theories might be offered again. But then the explanation will still be incomplete. At some point we must offer a theory of reference that does not make the reference of one word parasitic on that of other words. We need an 'ultimate' explanation of reference that relates some words directly to the world, if there is to be any reference at all.

4 Historical–causal theories

Kripke and Donnellan followed their criticism of description theories of names with an alternative view. This became known as the 'causal' or 'historical' theory, although Kripke and Donnellan regarded

157

their view as more of a 'picture' than a theory (see PROPER NAMES §4).

The basic idea of this theory is that a name designates whatever is causally linked to it in an appropriate way, a way that does not require speakers to associate an identifying description of the bearer with the name. Reference is initially fixed at a dubbing, either by perception or description of the referent. The name is then passed on from person to person in communicative exchanges. People succeed in designating an object with a name because underlying their uses of the name are causal chains stretching back to the dubbing of the object with the name. People borrow their reference from people earlier in the chain but borrowers do not have to remember lenders; it is enough that borrowers are, as a matter of historical fact, appropriately linked to their lenders in communication. So people can designate Cicero despite their ignorance of him, or designate Einstein despite their errors about him.

Similarly, Kripke and Putnam proposed an historical–causal theory of natural-kind words. Reference is initially fixed at a dubbing, either by description or perception of samples of the kind. The reference is then to all those objects, or all that stuff, having an internal structure of the same sort as the samples: for example, in the case of gold having the atomic number 79. People at a dubbing lend their reference to others, who can then lend it to still others. People who are ignorant about the kind can use the word to refer to the kind's members because underlying the use of the word are causal chains stretching back to a dubbing.

In thus removing the epistemic burden on speakers, historical–causal theories are a radical departure from the Frege–Russell tradition. That tradition assumes that those who understand a name must know about its meaning and reference, so that if its reference is determined in a certain way, they must know that it is. The historical–causal theory must reject the assumption that speakers have this privileged 'Cartesian' access to semantic facts: the reference of a name is determined by causal chains that are likely to be beyond the ken of the ordinary speaker. Once again, we must conclude with Putnam that 'meanings just ain't in the head'. This very feature of the theory has led many to reject it and to work hard to preserve the description theory (or the more general 'identification theory' favoured by Dummett; see §3). From the traditional Cartesian perspective, the causal theory's failure to impose an epistemic burden rules it out as a candidate to explain reference.

The historical–causal theory nicely captures the rigidity of names: the reference of a name is determined by its *actual* causal relations, something that cannot change when we consider other possible worlds. Less pleasingly, by rejecting any descriptive element to the meaning of a name, the theory may seem to leave no alternative but to resurrect the Millian view, identifying a name's meaning with its role of designating its bearer. Many philosophers, influenced by the 'direct reference' approach to indexicals (see §5), have taken this route, despite the problems for the Millian view (see §1). To avoid this it seems that we must explain a name's meaning in terms of the particular sort of causal chain that determines the name's reference.

The theory faces problems arising from various confusions and mistakes that can play a role in forming the causal network underlying a name. And it must explain how the reference of a name can change even though the historical fact of the dubbing cannot change. In developing the theory to deal with these problems, Michael Devitt (1981) has emphasized that a name is typically 'grounded' in its bearer in many perceptual confrontations after the initial dubbing: it is 'multiply' grounded in its bearer.

The historical–causal theory is returned to in §8.

5 Indexicals

To answer our central question for indexicals – terms like 'I', 'now', 'here', 'you', 'she', 'that' and 'this table' – we need to consider how the context of their utterance determines their reference.

Both Russell (1918) and Hans Reichenbach (1947) explain the reference of all indexicals (called 'egocentric particulars' by Russell and 'token-reflexive words' by Reichenbach) in terms of the reference of 'this'. Thus, Reichenbach claims that '"I" means the same as "the person who utters this token"; "now" means the same as "the time at which this token is uttered"; "this table" means the same as "the table pointed to by a gesture accompanying this token"' (1947: 284). This amounts to a description theory of reference for all indexicals except 'this token' in terms of the reference of 'this token'.

Any description theory of an indexical may face arguments of the usual three sorts: unwanted necessities, rigidity, and ignorance and error. The theory is particularly vulnerable to the argument from rigidity, as David Kaplan (1989) showed. (Kaplan prefers to talk of the closely related notion of 'direct reference' rather than 'rigidity'.) Thus, compare:

(5) This table is green

and Reichenbach's interpretation of it:

(6) The table pointed to by a gesture accompanying this token is green.

Suppose that the table referred to is in fact green, so that (5) and (6) both assert true propositions. Consider now a situation in which that table was still green but the furniture had been moved around so that a different table, a brown one, would be the subject of the gesture. Would those propositions asserted by (5) and (6) still be true? (Note that this question concerns the propositions actually asserted by (5) and (6), not the propositions that would have been asserted by the sentences in that non-actual situation.) Kaplan argues that whereas what (6) asserts would be false, what (5) asserts would still be true. The indexical 'this table' is rigid, referring to the same table in each possible world, whereas the description 'the table pointed to by a gesture accompanying this token' is nonrigid, referring to whatever table fits that description in the possible world. So the demonstrative is not synonymous with the description.

Apart from this, a general theoretical consideration counts against a description theory of indexicals. We have noted the essential incompleteness of description theories (see §3): even if a description theory is right for some word, the theory's explanation must rest ultimately on the reference of some other words which must be explained nondescriptively. Indexicals seem to be the most plausible candidates for nondescriptive explanation, more so even than proper names or natural-kind words: indexicals seem to be the place where language stands in its most direct relationship to the world.

In seeking a nondescriptive theory, it helps to follow Kaplan in dividing indexicals into two groups: 'pure indexicals' like 'I', 'here' and 'now', and 'demonstratives' like 'she', 'that' and 'this table'. The nondescriptive explanations of pure indexicals are fairly simple: 'I' designates the speaker of the utterance, 'here' the place of the utterance, 'now' the time of the utterance, and so on. (These explanations may seem to be description theories once again, but they are crucially different. For example, the last explanation is not that 'now' designates the time of the utterance because it is synonymous with an associated description 'the time of this utterance', but rather, because it is governed by the rule that it designates that time.) Demonstratives are more difficult to explain.

There are three basic ideas for a nondescriptive explanation of demonstratives. According to the first, a demonstrative designates the object demonstrated by the speaker. One problem with this idea is that a demonstration is often so vague that it alone would not distinguish one object from many others in the environment. A more serious problem is that demonstratives are not always accompanied by a demon-

stration. Thus, where only one table is prominent in the environment, the speaker may use 'this table' without a demonstration. And reference is often to an object that is not around to be demonstrated: for example, 'That drunk at the party last night was offensive'.

According to the second idea for a nondescriptive explanation, a demonstrative designates the object that the speaker intends to refer to. Even if this is so, it does not take us far because it raises the question: in virtue of what does the speaker intend to refer to that object? This is very similar to the original problem.

According to the third idea – urged, for example, by Edmund Husserl (1900–1) – a demonstrative designates the object in which it is based perceptually (compare the perceptually based grounding of a name according to the historical–causal theory). So 'this table' designates a certain table in virtue of the fact that it was perception of that table that led to the utterance; similarly 'that drunk at the party' designates the person that caused the remark (see DEMONSTRATIVES AND INDEXICALS).

6 Descriptions

Definite descriptions have the form, 'the F', and indefinite descriptions the form, 'a/an F'. In his theory of descriptions, Russell (1905) claimed that 'the F is G' is equivalent to 'there is something that is alone in being an F and it is G'; and 'an F is G' is equivalent to 'there is something that is an F and it is G'. So the descriptions are to be understood in terms of the general term, 'F' and the existential quantifier, 'there is something'.

Under the influence particularly of Donnellan (1966), many now think that a description is 'ambiguous', having not only this 'attributive' meaning captured by Russell but also a 'referential' meaning like that of a name or demonstrative.

It has been generally agreed that descriptions have a referential use as well as an attributive use. Used attributively, 'the F' conveys a thought about whatever is alone in being F; 'an F' conveys a thought about some F or other. Used referentially, each description conveys a thought about a particular F that the speaker has in mind, a thought about a certain F. Thus, consider:

(7) The murderer of Smith is insane

used in the following two contexts. (a) We come upon Smith foully murdered. We have no idea who is responsible but the brutal manner of the killing leads us to utter (7). Its description is used attributively. (b) We observe Jones on trial for Smith's murder. The oddity of his behaviour leads us to utter (7). Its description is used referentially. Next, consider:

(8) A man in a red cap stole Anne's computer

used in the following two contexts. (c) Anne's computer is discovered missing in the morning. We find signs that the burglar made a hasty escape dropping a red cap in the alley. This leads us to utter (8). Its description is used attributively. (d) After discovering that Anne's computer is missing we remember noticing a man in a red cap behaving suspiciously earlier in the day. We utter (8) to report our suspicions to the boss. Its description is used referentially.

Despite agreement that there are these two uses, there is no agreement that descriptions are ambiguous. Appealing to ideas prominent in the work of H.P. GRICE (1989), many have defended Russell. They argue that a speaker can use a description referentially, thus making the object in mind the 'speaker referent', even though that object is not the semantic referent. Whether a speaker has an object in mind or not, the truth-conditions of the sentence are as specified by Russell. The referential use is pragmatically, but not semantically, different from the attributive use (see PRAGMATICS §§3–4, 8). Thus, in context (b), although Jones is the speaker referent, the truth of (7) will depend on the sanity of whoever murdered Smith, whether Jones or not. And in context (d), although the man behaving suspiciously is the speaker referent, the truth of (8) will depend on whether some man or other in a red cap stole the computer.

Against this, many have found reasons for thinking that in contexts like (b) and (d) the speaker referent is also the semantic referent and hence that descriptions are semantically ambiguous after all. Some of these reasons – for example, those arising from failures to describe correctly the object in mind and from the behaviour of descriptions in opaque contexts – have not stood up well. Others seem more promising. First, we are not just able to use descriptions referentially, it seems that we regularly do so. This regularity suggests that there is a convention of so using descriptions. If there is, then it is hard to see why the convention is not semantic. Second, in their referential uses descriptions seem to have roles just like demonstratives: 'the F' and 'an F' function like 'that F', and are similarly based on perception of a particular object. To try to treat these demonstratives like Russellian descriptions would be to give a description theory of them, and we have already noted problems for this (see §5). Third, definite (but not indefinite) descriptions seem to have the same range of anaphoric roles as a pronoun like 'she' (see §7). We might then expect them also to share the pronoun's role as a demonstrative which, as has already been pointed out, seems not to be Russellian. Fourth, consider the utterance, 'The book is on the table'. In the right circumstances, this will seem true and yet, according to the Russellian view, it must be false: since the world is full of books and tables the two definite descriptions fail to describe unique objects. The obvious modification to save the Russellian view is to treat these 'incomplete' descriptions as elliptical. But this modification has problems. A speaker may have many ways to complete the description and there may be no basis for saying that any one is the correct way. Alternatively, trying to complete the description may lead to the familiar problems of ignorance and error.

Another argument against the ambiguity thesis appeals to rigidity. If referential uses of descriptions were semantically significant then, it is claimed, they should be rigid like names and demonstratives. Yet they do not seem to be. Consider the use of 'Smith's murderer' in context (b) above. 'Smith's murderer is insane' does not seem to be true in a world where Smith is alive and well, even if Jones is insane. However, this argument has a problem: the referential use of the demonstrative 'that murderer' would equally seem to fail this rigidity test in these circumstances (hence suggesting a need to revise Kaplan's claims about demonstratives; see §5). Yet a demonstrative surely has a semantically significant referential use. If so, then a description may have one too, despite not being rigid (see DESCRIPTIONS).

7 Other terms

Many terms that we have not discussed – like adjectives, adverbs and verbs – are naturally taken to refer. It is certainly no easier to explain reference for these terms than for the terms discussed, but we may hope that doing so will not pose sharply different problems (see ADVERBS; PREDICATION).

We must also consider sentential operators like 'and' and 'not', and quantifiers like 'every pen', 'some stones', 'most dogs' and 'few bachelors'. Perhaps these should be seen as largely syncategorematic (see LOGICAL CONSTANTS; QUANTIFIERS). If we are prepared to accept the existence of certain abstract entities, however, we can take these expressions as referential also. Thus we can take 'and' as denoting a 'truth function' *conjunction* which is such that the sentence 'p and q' is true if and only if 'p' is true and 'q' is true. The quantifiers involve a 'determiner' and a general term, and can be taken as applying to sets. Thus 'most dogs' involves the determiner 'most' and the general term 'dogs' and can be taken as applying to any set that contains more than half the dogs; and the sentence 'most dogs bark' is true if and only if there is such a set and 'bark' applies to all its members.

In virtue of what do these expressions have these referents? The most promising answer for the sentential operators has two stages. We start by describing the 'conceptual role' of the operator in deductive, inductive and practical inferences. For a token to denote 'conjunction' it must have the appropriate conceptual role. But in virtue of what should we assign to a token with that role the denotation 'conjunction' rather than, say, 'disjunction'? Because, under that assignment, deductive inferences are truth-preserving, inductive inferences are reliable, and so on. A similar line is presumably part of the answer for the quantifiers: 'most dogs' applies to any set containing most dogs (rather than, say, to any set containing a few cats) partly because of the reference of 'dogs' and partly because of the conceptual role of the determiner 'most' and the reliability of inferences. A worrying feature of both these answers is that they seem to make widespread irrationality impossible (see SEMANTICS, CONCEPTUAL ROLE).

Finally, we must consider anaphoric terms. Pronouns, and even definite descriptions, often depend for their reference on other expressions in their verbal context. Thus 'one' in 'John owns a car and Alice owns one too' is (using Geach's term) a 'pronoun of laziness', going proxy for the noun phrase 'a car' in the preceding conjunct. And consider 'he' in 'John is happiest when he is alone' and in 'Every man knows a woman that he admires'. In the former sentence 'he' is naturally seen as coreferential with 'John', in the latter as 'bound by' the quantifier 'every man' and so functioning like a bound variable in logic.

Geach (1962) has argued that all anaphoric pronouns are either pronouns of laziness or bound by quantifier antecedents. Against this Evans (1985) has argued that some pronouns with quantifier antecedents are unbound. He calls these 'E-type'. (a) Consider:

(9) Few congressmen admire the president, and they are very junior.

If 'they' were bound by 'few congressmen', (9) should mean that few congressmen both admire the president and are very junior. But it does not. The first clause of (9) entails that few congressmen admire the president; the second that all of those who do admire him are very junior. (b) If 'they' were bound in (9), then we should be able to substitute any quantifier for 'few congressmen' and still make sense. But 'No congressmen admire the president, and they are very junior' does not make sense. (c) Last, consider:

(10) If many men come to the ball, Mary will dance with them.

The quantifier 'many men' could bind 'them' only if (10) meant 'Many men are such that if they come to the ball Mary will dance with them', which is not the natural reading. As a result of these considerations and others – particularly pronouns in one person's sentence that are anaphoric on quantifiers in another person's – it is generally agreed that Evans has identified a distinct type of pronoun.

However, Evans' view of this type has been challenged. He thinks that the reference of such a pronoun is determined in a Russellian way by a definite description that can be derived from its quantified antecedent; thus, the reference of 'they' in (9) is determined by 'the few congressmen who admire the president', and that of 'them' in (10) by 'the many men who come to the ball'. Because these are definite descriptions, for (9) to be true *all* the Kennedy admirers must be junior, and for (10) to be true Mary must dance with *all* the men who come. This consequence does not seem to generalize. 'Some congressmen admire the president, and they are very junior' seems to be compatible with some other congressmen admiring him and not being very junior. The problem is more acute in singular cases: 'Socrates owned a dog and it bit him' seems to be compatible with Socrates owning another dog which did not bite him. Finally, there are the formidably difficult 'donkey sentences': 'Every man that owns a donkey beats it' and 'If John owns a donkey, he beats it'. On one reading, these sentences concern not simply the unique donkey of each donkey owner but *all* the owner's donkeys (see ANAPHORA).

8 Naturalizing reference

From a naturalistic perspective, reference must ultimately be explained in scientifically acceptable terms. Attempted explanations have appealed to one or more of three causal relations between words and the world: historical, reliable and teleological.

Historical–causal theory of reference. Kripke, Donnellan and Putnam (see §4) did not claim to be naturalizing reference, but their theories – together with the role that perception of an object may play in determining the reference of demonstratives and referential descriptions (see §§5–6) – suggest the idea that reference might be explained naturalistically in historical–causal terms: a token refers to the object that played the appropriate role in causing it. But this idea, developed by Devitt, faces the *qua*-problem. In virtue of what is 'Aristotle', say, perceptually grounded in a 'whole object' and not a time-slice or undetached part of the object, each of which is equally present and causally efficacious? The problem is more pressing for natural-kind words. 'Horse' is grounded in a few horses. But those objects are not only horses, they are mammals, vertebrates and so on; they are members of very many natural kinds. Indeed, any horse is a member of indefinitely many *non-natural* kinds: it may be a pet, an investment and so on. In virtue of what is 'horse' grounded in an object *qua* horse, rather than *qua* mammal, pet, or whatever? So in virtue of what does it refer, as a result of such groundings, to all and only horses rather than all and only mammals, pets, or whatever?

Reliabilist theory of reference. Under the influence particularly of Fred Dretske (1981) and Jerry FODOR (1990), 'reliabilist', 'informational', or 'indicator' theories have been popular. The basic idea is that a token refers to objects of a certain sort because tokens of that type are reliably correlated with the presence of those objects; the tokens are 'caused by' those objects. The token 'carries the information' that a certain situation holds in much the same way that tree rings carry information about the age of a tree. There is a problem. How can the theory allow for error? Occasionally we see a muddy zebra and wrongly think 'horse'. So, some zebras are among the things that would cause tokens of 'horse'. What 'horse' is reliably correlated with is really the presence of horses, muddy zebras, the odd cow in bad light and so forth. So according to reliabilism, it should refer to horses, muddy zebras, the odd cow and so on (with the result that it was not wrong to think 'horse' after all). The problem is that many things that a token of a certain type does not refer to, including some denizens of Twin Earth, would cause a token of that type (see SEMANTICS, INFORMATIONAL).

Teleological theory of reference. Most fully developed by Ruth Millikan (1984), teleological theories explain the reference of a token in terms of its function, where that function is explained causally along Darwinian lines: a token's function is what tokens of that type do that explains why they exist. This theory deals neatly with the problem of error because something – for example, sperm – can have a function which it does not reliably perform. An immediate consequence of the theory is that a token of a type that has not evolved will lack a referent. So the 'thoughts' and 'utterances' of an exact replica of Russell created by some cosmic accident would have no reference. This strikes many as implausible but is accepted by the theory's proponents. To complete the theory it must be shown that tokens – even a belief like 'computers make writing easier' which could not plausibly be taken as innate – have a function in the required biological sense and that this function does

indeed relate the token to its referent. Millikan has attempted this formidable task (see SEMANTICS, TELEOLOGICAL).

9 Further issues

Terms in opaque or intensional contexts cannot be seen as having their usual referential roles. For, in these contexts, particularly those of propositional attitude ascriptions (see PROPOSITIONAL ATTITUDE STATEMENTS), the replacement of a term by a coreferential term may not preserve truth.

There are a range of what might be called 'negative' views of reference. (a) Some philosophers have a 'deflationary' view according to which there is nothing more to referential notions than is captured by all instances of a schema like '*e* designates *a*', where what is substituted for '*a*' 'translates' what is named by the term substituted for '*e*'; '"Socrates" designates Socrates' is a typical instance. This view accompanies a similarly deflationary view of truth (see TRUTH, DEFLATIONARY THEORIES OF). (b) W.V. Quine (1960) argues that even once the translation of a sentence has been fixed the reference of any part of the sentence is inscrutable; thus there is no fact of the matter whether an alien's 'Gavagai' in response to an environment of rabbits refers to rabbits, undetached rabbit parts, time-slices of rabbits, and so on (see RADICAL TRANSLATION AND RADICAL INTERPRETATION §§1–4). Related to this, Donald Davidson (1984) takes an instrumentalist attitude to reference, denying both the need for, and the possibility of, a theory of reference. Putnam (1983) gives a model-theoretic argument that reference is indeterminate because any theory has unintended models. (c) Kripke (1982) presents an argument (which he finds in Ludwig Wittgenstein's discussion of rule-following) that the meanings and references of terms are not determinate (see MEANING AND RULE-FOLLOWING). (d) Less sweepingly, Hartry Field (1973) has argued that in some cases there is no determinate matter of fact whether a term refers to one thing or another and we should see it as 'partially referring' to both: for example, 'mass' as used by Newtonians does not determinately refer to either proper mass or relativistic mass but partially refers to both. (e) Finally, those in the 'structuralist' tradition reject reference, and hence its role in meaning, altogether. They apparently think that the only possible theory of reference is one according to which a word resembles what it refers to. But this theory is refuted by the fact that language is arbitrary, by the fact that anything could be used to mean anything. Reference is thus left as simply 'God-given', which is unacceptable (see STRUCTURALISM IN LINGUISTICS).

Finally, views on reference can bear on realist notions about the external world (see REALISM AND ANTIREALISM). Putnam, for example, draws antirealist conclusions from his model-theoretic argument. And consider the consequences of a holistic description theory for scientific terms. When, in time, we come to replace one scientific theory with another, it is natural to think that part of the reason we do so is that the theory does not accurately describe reality. Combine this thought with the holistic view that the reference of each term in the theory is determined by its associations with all other terms in the theory, and we get the consequence that all terms in the theory fail to refer. So, it was a mistake to believe in the entities apparently referred to by that theory. Worse, it is probably a mistake to believe in the entities of our present theory, for that theory will surely be replaced in time too. So we should not be scientific realists. Indeed, these considerations lead Thomas S. KUHN (1970) and others to constructivism, a radically relativistic antirealism: rather than saying that the replaced theory does not describe reality, they say that it describes *its* reality, a reality that only exists relative to that theory (see CONSTRUCTIVISM). Each theory has its own reality and no sense can be made of scientific entities existing 'absolutely'. This line of thought can be resisted by rejecting the holistic description theory of reference in favour of a localist theory, perhaps one explaining reference in terms of causal relations to reality (see HOLISM: MENTAL AND SEMANTIC).

See also: SEMANTICS

References and further reading

* Burge, T. (1979) 'Individualism and the Mental', in P.A. French, T.E. Uehling, Jr. and H.K. Wettstein (eds) *Midwest Studies in Philosophy*, vol. 10, *Studies in the Philosophy of Mind*, Minneapolis, MN: University of Minnesota Press. (Argues that reference for many terms is determined by the social context; referred to in §3.)

Chastain, C. (1975) 'Reference and Context', in K. Gunderson (ed.) *Minnesota Studies in the Philosophy of Science*, vol. 7, *Language, Mind and Knowledge*, Minneapolis, MN: University of Minnesota Press. (A long paper on singular reference and anaphora. A source for the view that indefinite descriptions have two uses.)

* Davidson, D. (1984) *Inquiries into Truth and Interpretation*, Oxford: Oxford University Press, 215–25. (Argues against the need for, and possibility of, theories of reference; referred to in §9.)

* Devitt, M. (1981) *Designation*, New York: Columbia University Press. (Develops a causal-historical theory of proper names, demonstratives and referential descriptions along naturalistic lines; referred to in §§4 and 8.)

Devitt, M. and Sterelny, K. (1998) *Language and Reality: An Introduction to the Philosophy of Language*, Oxford: Blackwell, 2nd edn. (Provides an introductory discussion of reference and of its significance for issues such as realism. Also includes an annotated guide to further reading.)

* Donnellan, K.S. (1966) 'Reference and Definite Descriptions', *Philosophical Review* 75: 281–304. (Influential work proposing a distinction between referential and attributive descriptions and criticizing Russell and Strawson; referred to in §6.)

* —— (1972) 'Proper Names and Identifying Descriptions', in D. Davidson and G. Harman (eds) *The Semantics of Natural Language*, Dordrecht: Reidel. (Criticizes the description theory of proper names and proposes a historical theory; referred to in §§2 and 4.)

* Dretske, F. (1981) *Knowledge and the Flow of Information*, Cambridge, MA: MIT Press. (Most influential proposal of a reliabilist theory of reference; referred to in §8.)

* Dummett, M.A.E. (1973) 'Appendix: Note on an Attempted Refutation of Frege', in *Frege: Philosophy of Language*, London: Duckworth. (A defence of a Fregean view of proper names from Kripke's criticisms; referred to in §2.)

Evans, G. (1982) *The Varieties of Reference*, ed. J. McDowell, Oxford: Clarendon Press. (Defends 'Russell's Principle' that to think about an object a person must know which object is in question.)

* —— (1985) *Collected Papers*, Oxford: Clarendon Press. (Chapters 4, 5 and 8 argue for the view that some anaphoric pronouns are 'E-type' rather than bound; referred to in §7.)

* Field, H. (1973) 'Theory Change and the Indeterminacy of Reference', *Journal of Philosophy* 70: 462–81. (Argues that the reference of scientific terms is sometimes indeterminate and that they should be seen as 'partially referring'; referred to in §9.)

* Fodor, J.A. (1990) *A Theory of Content and Other Essays*, Cambridge, MA: MIT Press. (Chapters 3 and 4 propose a reliabilist theory of reference appealing to 'asymmetric counterfactuals'; referred to in §8.)

* Frege, G. (1893) 'On Sense and Reference', in P. Geach and M. Black (eds) *Translations from the Philosophical Writings of Gottlob Frege*, Oxford: Blackwell, 1952. (Classic work raising the problem of identity statements for a Millian theory of

proper names and proposing the theory that names have 'senses'; referred to in §1.)

* Geach, P. (1962) *Reference and Generality*, Ithaca, NY: Cornell University Press. (Argues that all anaphoric pronouns are either like bound variables or are 'pronouns of laziness'; referred to in §7.)

* Grice, H.P. (1989) *Studies in the Way of Words*, Cambridge, MA: Harvard University Press. (Proposes the distinction between speaker meaning and semantic meaning that has been influential in discussions of definite descriptions; referred to in §6.)

* Husserl, E. (1900–1) *Logical Investigations*, trans. J.N. Findley, London: Routledge & Kegan Paul, 1970, part 1, §26; part 6, §§1–5. (Proposes a theory of demonstratives based on perception; referred to in §5.)

* Kaplan, D. (1989) 'Demonstratives: An Essay on the Semantics, Logic, Metaphysics, and Epistemology of Demonstratives and Other Indexicals', in J. Almog, J. Perry and H. Wettstein (eds) *Themes from Kaplan*, New York: Oxford University Press. (Influential work arguing that the reference of a demonstrative is 'direct' not via a Fregean sense; referred to in §5.)

* Kripke, S.A. (1980) *Naming and Necessity*, Cambridge, MA: Harvard University Press. (Very influential work criticizing the description theory of proper names and natural-kind terms and proposing a causal 'picture'; first presented in lectures in the late 1960s; referred to in §§2–4.)

* —— (1982) *Wittgenstein on Rules and Private Language: An Elementary Exposition*, Cambridge, MA: Harvard University Press. (Argues from a consideration of rule-following that the meanings and references of terms are not determinate; referred to in §9.)

* Kuhn, T.S. (1970) *The Structure of Scientific Revolutions*, Chicago, IL: Chicago University Press, 2nd edn. (In this brilliant work on scientific change, a description theory of reference leads to antirealist constructivism; referred to in §9.)

* Marcus, R.B. (1961) 'Modalities and Intensional Language', *Synthèse* 13: 303–22. (Argues that proper names are Millian and that true identity statements involving them are always necessary; referred to in §2.)

* Millikan, R. (1984) *Language, Thought, and Other Biological Categories*, Cambridge, MA: MIT Press. (The most detailed proposal of a teleological theory of reference; referred to in §8.)

* Mill, J.S. (1843) *A System of Logic*, London: Longmans, 1867. (Book 1, Chapter 2 proposes his theory of both 'general and singular' names – referred to in §1.)

Neale, S. (1990) *Descriptions*, Cambridge, MA: MIT Press. (A thorough defence of the Russellian approach to definite descriptions. Includes an excellent bibliography.)

Papineau, D. (1987) *Reality and Representation*, Oxford: Blackwell. (Proposes a teleological theory of reference.)

* Putnam, H. (1975) *Mind, Language and Reality: Philosophical Papers*, Cambridge: Cambridge University Press, vol. 2, 196–290. (Very influential argument against description theories and for causal theories of natural-kind and other terms; referred to in §§3 and 4.)

* —— (1983) *Realism and Reason: Philosophical Papers*, Cambridge: Cambridge University Press, vol. 3, 1–25. (Presents his model-theoretic argument that reference is indeterminate; referred to in §9.)

* Quine, W.V. (1960) *Word and Object*, Cambridge, MA: MIT Press. (Section 12 argues for the inscrutability of reference in the context of arguing for the indeterminacy of translation; referred to in §9.)

* Reichenbach, H. (1947) *Elements of Logic*, London: Macmillan. (Section 50 proposes a theory of 'token-reflexive' words; referred to in §5.)

* Russell, B. (1905) 'On Denoting', *Mind* 14: 479–93. (A classic paper proposing his famous theory of descriptions; referred to in §6.)

* —— (1911) 'Knowledge by Acquaintance and Knowledge by Description', in *Mysticism and Logic*, London: Allen & Unwin, 1917. (A classic source for the description theory of proper names; referred to in §1.)

—— (1912) *The Problems of Philosophy*, London: Oxford University Press, 1959. (Chapter 5 gives a brief and accessible account of Russell's theory of proper names and descriptions.)

* —— (1918) 'The Philosophy of Logical Atomism', in R.C. Marsh (ed.) *Logic and Knowledge*, London: Allen & Unwin, 1956. (Discusses the referential properties of many terms, including 'egocentric particulars'; referred to in §§1, 5 and 6.)

* Searle, J. (1958) 'Proper Names', *Mind* 67: 166–73. (A very clear presentation of a cluster description theory of names; referred to in §1.)

Strawson, P.F. (1950) 'On Referring', *Mind* 59: 320–44. (A critique of Russell's theory of descriptions.)

* —— (1959) *Individuals: An Essay in Descriptive Metaphysics*, London: Methuen, 180–3, 190–4. (Proposes a cluster description theory of names; referred to in §1.)

MICHAEL DEVITT

REFERENTIAL OPACITY

see PROPOSITIONAL ATTITUDE
STATEMENTS (§2)

REFERENTIAL/ATTRIBUTIVE

see DESCRIPTIONS; REFERENCE

RÉGIS, PIERRE-SYLVAIN (1632–1707)

Régis helped to define and disseminate Cartesianism. He proselytized on its behalf, defended it against its critics and innovators, and wrote the systematic textbook for which Descartes had hoped. Although primarily an expositor of Descartes' views, he sometimes developed them in creative ways that tended towards empiricism. He seems to have been led in this direction by Robert Desgabets who, while adhering to Descartes' principles, consciously departed from what Descartes actually said in order to be 'more Cartesian than Descartes himself'. The same may often be said of Régis.

'One of the ornaments and pillars of the Cartesian sect', as Pierre BAYLE called him, Régis was born near Agen, France. After his education by the Jesuits at Cahors, he studied theology in Paris, where he became interested in the philosophy of Descartes. A clearly important influence was the weekly lectures given by the leading proponent of Cartesianism, Jacques ROHAULT. A more important influence came from Robert DESGABETS, who may have introduced Régis to Descartes' philosophy. Desgabets would have provided him with an understanding of those of its principles, particularly the doctrine of created eternal truths, that gave it a quasi-empiricist complexion.

Around 1665, Rohault sent Régis to Toulouse to spread the gospel of Cartesianism. There, at Montpellier (where he met Locke), at Aigues-Mortes and finally back in Paris in 1680 after the death of Rohault, Régis' lectures enjoyed enormous success. However, given the official opposition to Cartesianism because of the theological controversies it generated, the lectures were suppressed by the Archbishop of Paris, and the publication of Régis' first, longest and most important work, the *Système de philosophie* (1690), was delayed for ten years.

Régis was less a creative thinker than an expositor of what he took to be Cartesianism (even if he sometimes developed it in surprising ways), which he defended in a number of polemical works. His *Système* criticized Malebranche on several topics, on three of which Malebranche and he then exchanged 'Replies': the nature of sensual pleasure, the problem of the horizontal versus meridional moon (on which Régis was demonstrably mistaken), and, most importantly, the nature of ideas (see MALEBRANCHE, N. §§1, 2).

As had been the case in Malebranche's much longer debate with Arnauld over the nature of ideas, the central issue was whether the soul's modifications are essentially representative (as Arnauld and Régis held), or whether ideas different from those modifications are required for knowledge of material things (as Malebranche held). Many of the same arguments from the Arnauld debate reappear – for example, Malebranche's contention that a modification of the soul, which is a particular, cannot represent a circle in general (see ARNAULD, A. §3). But novel points also emerge, one of the most important being Régis' contention that the exemplary cause of an idea is the thing it represents, which he deduces from the principle that a representation cannot be of nothing. Régis and Malebranche, in fact, share this principle but draw different conclusions from it: Malebranche sees perception mediated by God, while Régis has it directly of objects. Malebranche's problem is to explain how we know material things; Régis' problem is to explain how we can fail to do so.

Malebranche's cause in general was taken up by his disciple Henri Lelevel, who found Régis committed both to Spinozism and to scepticism (see SPINOZA, B. DE). Régis tried to respond to the charge of Spinozism by condemning in no uncertain terms the view that there is only one substance, which is God, but he seems not to have rejected or modified his earlier view that individual minds are modes of thought, just as individual material things are modes of extension. Thus, while holding with Desgabets that substances are indefectible, the basis for personal immortality seems none the less upset.

In other debates, Régis defended Cartesianism against the sceptical attacks of P.-D. HUET, against the objections of Jean Du Hamel on a range of issues beginning with the theory of ideas, and finally against the misgivings of LEIBNIZ, with whom he also exchanged 'Replies' concerning the consequences of Cartesianism for religion and piety. In his last work, *L'usage de la raison et de la foi* (1704), Régis sought to establish the compatibility of faith and reason, essentially by establishing their independence. He was one of the few Cartesians to subscribe to Descartes' doctrine of the created eternal truths, which he thought followed from God's omnipotence (see DESCARTES, R. §6). He held, moreover, that anything dependent on God's will can be known only through experience or revelation, and thus the apriorism usually associated with Cartesianism is contrary to the central thrust of Régis' philosophy. This thrust is clear, too, in his conception of the soul, which thinks through the body.

Régis disavowed the occasionalism that he might have been expected to hold (see OCCASIONALISM). His emphasis on divine omnipotence led him to the principle on which Malebranche had based his occasionalism: 'there is such a necessary connection between His will and the existence of the thing He wills to produce that it is incomprehensible that God should will a thing to be produced and that it not be' (1690: 110). But the created things between which this necessary connection fails to occur are none the less real secondary causes, and not just occasional causes of God's operation. As occasional causes determining God to act, they would violate his immutability. It is open to question, however, whether Régis really understood the doctrine of occasionalism, and whether the occasional causes of Malebranche really differ from Régis' secondary causes, which he describes as having 'no proper causality' and as 'contributing to the production of things only by serving as instruments by which God modifies His action' (1690: 125).

In accordance with the arboreal metaphor in the introduction to his *Principles*, Descartes thought that all philosophy was connected and based on metaphysics. Aside from the earlier sketchy effort of François Bayle, however, Régis' *Système* was the first attempt to produce a systematic and comprehensive account of the Cartesian view of things that Descartes had only imperfectly realized. In addition to logic and metaphysics, an extended physics, biology and so on, the *Système* also offers ethical, political, legal and theological theories. The title of its second edition (1691) seems fully justified: *Cours entier de philosophie ou système général selon les principes de Mr. Descartes.*

List of works

Régis, P.-S. (1690) *Système de philosophie contenant la logique, la métaphysique, la physique et la morale* (System of philosophy containing logic, metaphysics, physics and morality), Paris; 2nd edn, Amsterdam, 1691; repr. with introduction by R.A. Watson, New York and London: Johnson, 1970. (A textbook account of the Cartesian system, but one that departs from the views of Descartes in a number of crucial respects, for example in holding that individual minds are modes of a single substance.)

—— (1691) *Réponse au livre qui a pour titre P. Danielis*

Huetii censura philosophiae cartesianae (Response to book which has as its title P. Daniel Huet's critique of philosophy), Paris. (A defence of Cartesianism against the sceptical attack of Pierre-Daniel Huet.)

—— (1692) *Réponse au réflexions critiques de Du Hamel* (Response to the critical reflections of Du Hamel), Paris. (Important for Regis' views on, among other things, the creation of the eternal truths.)

—— (1694) *Première réplique á... Malebranche [Seconde... Troisième...]* (First reply to Malebranche [second... third...]), Paris. (Polemical works directed against Malebranche on three topics: the nature of ideas, the problem of the horizontal versus meridional sun, and the nature of sensual pleasure.)

—— (1697) 'Réflexions sur... Leibniz...' (Reflections on Leibniz), and 'Réflexions pour... réplique...' (Reflections for... response...), *Journal des savants* 17 June and 16 November. (A defence of Cartesianism against Leibniz's criticisms with respect to religion and piety. Compare Leibniz's *Die philosophischen Schriften*, ed. C.I. Gerhardt, Berlin: Weidmannsche Buchhandlung, vol. 4, pages 333–42.)

—— (1704) *L'usage de la raison et de la foy ou l'accord de la foy et de la raison* (The use of reason and faith or the relation of faith and reason), Paris. (Important for the author's views on causation, immortality, the mind–body connection, as well as the relation between faith and reason; a refutation of Spinoza is appended.)

References and further reading

Rodis-Lewis, G. (1993) 'Régis', in R.W. Meyer (ed.) *Friedrich Ueberwegs Gundriss der Geschichte der Philosophie* (Friedrich Ueberweg's outline of the history of philosophy), Basel: Verlag Schwabe, 431–9. (The most comprehensive account of both the primary and the secondary literature.)

Watson, R.A. (1988) *The Breakdown of Cartesian Metaphysics*, Atlantic Highlands, NJ: Humanities Press, 89–93. (Sees Régis as sharing the Cartesian failure to reconcile dualism with causal and epistemological likeness principles.)

THOMAS M. LENNON

REICHENBACH, HANS (1891–1953)

Philosophy of science flourished in the twentieth century, partly as a result of extraordinary progress in the sciences themselves, but mainly because of the efforts of philosophers who were scientifically knowledgeable and who remained abreast of new scientific achievements. Hans Reichenbach was a pioneer in this philosophical development; he studied physics and mathematics in several of the great German scientific centres and later spent a number of years as a colleague of Einstein in Berlin. Early in his career he followed Kant, but later reacted against his philosophy, arguing that it was inconsistent with twentieth-century physics.

Reichenbach was not only a philosopher of science, but also a scientific philosopher. He insisted that philosophy should adhere to the same standards of precision and rigour as the natural sciences. He unconditionally rejected speculative metaphysics and theology because their claims could not be substantiated either a priori, on the basis of logic and mathematics, or a posteriori, on the basis of sense-experience. In this respect he agreed with the logical positivists of the Vienna Circle, but because of other profound disagreements he was never actually a positivist. He was, instead, the leading member of the group of logical empiricists centred in Berlin.

Although his writings span many subjects Reichenbach is best known for his work in two main areas: induction and probability, and the philosophy of space and time. In the former he developed a theory of probability and induction that contained his answer to Hume's problem of the justification of induction. Because of his view that all our knowledge of the world is probabilistic, this work had fundamental epistemological significance. In philosophy of physics he offered epoch-making contributions to the foundations of the theory of relativity, undermining space and time as Kantian synthetic a priori categories.

1 Life
2 Epistemology
3 Induction and probability
4 Space and time
5 Other topics

1 Life

Hans Reichenbach was born in Hamburg, Germany, on 26 September 1891, where he grew up and received his primary and secondary education. In 1910 he went to Stuttgart to study engineering, but found the subject intellectually unsatisfying. He soon shifted to mathematics, physics and philosophy, which he pursued at the Universities of Berlin, Göttingen and Munich under such teachers as Max Born, Ernst Cassirer, David Hilbert and Max Planck. During the First World War he served in the German Signal Corps at the Russian front, but returned to his academic work after suffering a severe illness.

Reichenbach wrote his doctoral dissertation (1916) on the applicability of mathematical probability to the physical world; he received his degree at Erlangen in 1915. In the following year he passed a state examination in physics and mathematics at Göttingen. From then until 1920 he held a regular job in the radio industry, while pursuing academic work on a part-time basis. During that time Einstein offered his first seminar in the theory of relativity in Berlin; Reichenbach attended and established a lasting relationship with him. In 1920 he returned to Stuttgart to teach at the Technische Hochschule. In 1926, due mainly to Einstein's influence, he became Professor of Philosophy of Physics in Berlin, where he remained until Hitler's rise to power in 1933. At that time he fled to Turkey, where he taught philosophy at the University of Istanbul. In 1938 he moved to the University of California at Los Angeles, where he remained until his death from a heart attack on 9 April 1953.

2 Epistemology

Early in the twentieth century, many scientifically minded philosophers, impressed by new developments in logic and other epistemological considerations, maintained that the entire world could be viewed as a logical construction from sensations (see PHENOMENALISM §1; NEUTRAL MONISM). This view appealed strongly to some of the logical positivists, especially Rudolf Carnap, who attempted to carry out the construction in detail (1928); it represented the epitome of logical positivism (see CARNAP, R. §1). In his review of this book, Reichenbach (1933) praised its precision and scope, but expressed one misgiving. He could see no place for probability in the positivistic approach (see LOGICAL POSITIVISM §2).

Reichenbach (1938) developed the issue of probability into a full-scale attack on logical positivism. He elaborated three major points. First, whereas the positivists had insisted that a statement must be fully verifiable in principle to be cognitively meaningful, Reichenbach enunciated a principle that required only probabilistic support (see DEMARCATION PROBLEM §3). Second, he denied that our factual knowledge must be based on incorrigible reports of sensory experience; he maintained that it is founded on fallible perceptions of middle-sized physical objects and is probabilistic from the ground up. Third, he maintained that we can have probabilistic knowledge of unobservable physical entities. The atom is not a construct out of sense impressions; it is a physical object whose reality we can infer probabilistically (see SCIENTIFIC REALISM AND ANTIREALISM §4). Atoms would exist even if there were no sentient beings in the universe. This was his refutation of logical positivism.

3 Induction and probability

The concept of probability was one of Reichenbach's major concerns throughout his career; his main treatise on the subject is *The Theory of Probability* (1949). He argued that probability should be understood as the limit of a sequence of relative frequencies. Suppose, for example, that we have a coin that can be flipped in the standard way. We begin flipping the coin, and keeping track of the result (heads or tails) of each toss: H T T H T H H H T H .... This generates a sequence of fractions m/n representing the number of times m that heads has shown in n tosses of the coin: $\frac{1}{1}$, $\frac{1}{2}$, $\frac{1}{3}$, $\frac{2}{4}$, $\frac{2}{5}$, $\frac{3}{6}$, $\frac{4}{7}$, $\frac{5}{8}$, $\frac{5}{9}$, $\frac{6}{10}$, ... If this sequence of fractions has a limit, that is, if the members of this sequence become and remain arbitrarily close to some value (say $\frac{1}{2}$) as the sequence is extended indefinitely, then that limit *constitutes* the probability of heads on flips of that coin.

This concept of probability leads to many problems. First, we have no guarantee that such a limit exists; these fractions can continue fluctuating forever without approaching any particular value. Aware of this problem, Reichenbach noted its relationship to Hume's problem of justifying induction. Hume argued correctly that we have no guarantee that nature is uniform – that the future will be like the past. Similarly, since we have no guarantee that our particular sequence of coin tosses will exhibit the statistical regularity of converging to a limit, we have no guarantee that the probability in question exists. Nevertheless, we are justified in *positing* that the observed frequency in an initial section of the sequence approximates the limiting frequency, even though that posit may be incorrect. The justification is pragmatic. First, if no limit exists, we will be wrong in our posits, but no other method would succeed, for there is no limit to be discovered. Second, there may be a limit, but it may be quite different from the frequency in the observed initial portion of the sequence. It follows from the definition of 'limit', however, that persistent use of this method, 'the rule of induction', will eventually lead to posits that are accurate to any desired degree of approximation. In ascertaining probabilities (that is, limiting frequencies) we have everything to gain and nothing to lose by using the inductive method (see INDUCTION, EPISTEMIC ISSUES IN §2; INDUCTIVE INFERENCE §§1–2; PROBABILITY THEORY AND EPISTEMOLOGY §1).

Why should we want to ascertain probabilities? According to Reichenbach, all of our knowledge, scientific or common-sensical, is probabilistic; moreover the frequency interpretation is the only legitimate interpretation of probability. Thus, the ascertainment of probabilities (limiting frequencies) is fundamental to all our knowledge. Unfortunately, as Reichenbach acknowledged, his justification applies to an infinite class of other rules – asymptotic rules – that direct us to posit $m/n + c_n$ where c_n is a 'corrective term' that approaches zero as n approaches infinity. He had no satisfactory way of showing that his rule is superior to any other asymptotic rule. The best we can say, perhaps, is that the addition of an arbitrary c_n to the observed frequency would be epistemologically unsupportable.

Reichenbach's claim that the frequency interpretation is the only legitimate one poses two other major problems. First, in many practical situations we must deal with single events rather than long sequences – for example, buying an insurance policy. Reichenbach argued that such cases can be handled by assigning the single case to an appropriate sequence and transferring the probability in the sequence, as a weight, to the single case. This will be a successful strategy if one deals with large numbers of diverse single cases. The second major problem – a special case of the first – is the probabilities of hypotheses. A given hypothesis is either true or false, just as a given toss of a coin comes up heads or tails. How can probabilities of hypotheses be construed in terms of relative frequencies? Reichenbach stated that Bayes' theorem in the probability calculus enables us to handle this problem, but he never clearly explained how.

4 Space and time

Reichenbach wrote four major treatises on space and time (1920, 1924, 1928, 1956); in the first he attempted a compromise between KANT and EINSTEIN, but in the later works he severed his ties with Kant completely. In his classic work, *Philosophie der Raum-Zeit-Lehre* (The Philosophy of Space and Time) (1928), he argued that the question of the geometrical structure of physical space is a matter to be decided, not a priori, but by empirical science. The situation is, however, rather complicated. The discovery of non-Euclidean geometries early in the nineteenth century did not refute Kant, even after the proof of relative consistency (if the non-Euclidean geometries are self-contradictory then so is Euclidean geometry). Kant had claimed that Euclidean geometry is synthetic; if its denial were logically inconsistent, then it would be analytic. Kant's view had been that Euclidean geometry is epistemologically, not logically, privileged; it is a necessary form of visualization of the physical world. Reichenbach argued in detail that the non-Euclidean geometries are possible forms of visualization. (Recall that Einstein had chosen non-Euclidean geometry to formulate his General Theory of Relativity before 1920.) The question is which geometry provides the most suitable one (see SPACE; SPACETIME).

Certain facts about two-dimensional geometry were well-known in the nineteenth century. For example, in Euclidean geometry the sum of the angles of a triangle is exactly 180°; in non-Euclidean geometries this sum is either greater or less than 180°, and the value of the sum differs for triangles of different areas. It might seem that we could ascertain the geometry of physical space by measuring angular sums of triangles with various orientations in three-dimensional space. However, at the turn of the century Henri POINCARÉ had realized that to determine geometrical features of physical space we must use physical measuring instruments, and the results will depend upon the behaviour of these instruments (Poincaré 1902). According to Reichenbach, Poincaré held that the geometry of space is a matter of pure convention; although we could use any geometry we wished to describe physical space, we actually choose Euclidean geometry because it is simpler than non-Euclidean geometries.

Although Reichenbach has often been called a 'conventionalist', he was actually an anti-conventionalist regarding physical geometry (see CONVENTIONALISM §1). To interpret mathematical geometry for application to physical space we must of course adopt certain conventions, such as deciding that a certain type of measuring instrument retains its length unchanged as it is transported from place to place. By calling such decisions 'coordinative definitions' he emphasized their status as conventions. Once such a decision is made, however, the structure of physical space becomes a matter of empirical fact. A different choice of a coordinative definition, employed in the same space, may yield a different geometry, but the descriptions based on these different coordinative definitions are physically equivalent. According to Reichenbach's 'theory of equivalent descriptions', then, one set of equivalent descriptions (rather than a single description) correctly describes physical space, but other logically possible sets of equivalent descriptions give false descriptions of physical space (see GEOMETRY, PHILOSOPHICAL ISSUES IN).

On one aspect of time, Reichenbach took a more strongly conventionalistic position. According to special relativity, no signal can travel faster than light *in vacuo*. The fact that this speed is finite places limits on our ability to synchronize clocks located at different places in any inertial frame of reference. Given two spatially separated clocks A and B, if we send a light signal at t_1 from A to B where it is reflected back to A, arriving at t_3, then we can choose any time t_2 between t_1 and t_3 as its time of arrival at B. This amounts to saying that, while the round-trip speed of light is a matter of physical fact, the one-way speed of light is (within limits) a matter of convention. An important result by David Malament (1977) indicates that causal constraints imply that the two one-way speeds are equal (see RELATIVITY THEORY, PHILOSOPHICAL SIGNIFICANCE OF §3).

One of Reichenbach's fundamental purposes in developing his theories of space and time was to implement a causal theory. He believed that causal processes, such as light pulses and moving material objects, as well as causal interactions, such as reflections of light pulses by mirrors or collisions of material particles, constitute verifiable features of the world, whereas the abstract structure of spacetime by itself does not. In his posthumously published work, *The Direction of Time* (1956), Reichenbach seeks to ground the direction of time – the difference between past and future – in causal aspects of the universe that are also probabilistic. This book contains pioneering work on the concept of probabilistic causality.

5 Other topics

Reichenbach also made significant contributions to other subjects. A major scientific revolution of the twentieth century was the advent of quantum mechanics. Reichenbach's book on this development, *Philosophic Foundations of Quantum Mechanics* (1944), emphasizes causal anomalies, and introduces a three-valued logic (in which a statement can have the value indeterminate as well as true or false) to deal with these problems (see MANY-VALUED LOGICS; QUANTUM LOGIC; QUANTUM MECHANICS, INTERPRETATION OF §3). Additional discussions of quantum mechanics are included in *The Direction of Time*.

Reichenbach's *Elements of Symbolic Logic* (1947), his major work on symbolic logic, contains an extended analysis of conversational language, as well as an analysis of laws of nature, physical modalities (necessity, possibility and impossibility) and counterfactual conditionals (see LAWS, NATURAL §2; COUNTERFACTUAL CONDITIONALS). These three topics receive a fuller treatment in his monograph, *Nomological Statements and Admissible Operations* (1954).

Although he never wrote a book on the subject,

discussions of causality can be found in his writings throughout his career. He wrote very little explicitly on the nature of scientific explanation, but his work on causality contains many valuable hints (see EXPLANATION §4).

Finally, on the basis of his verifiability criterion of meaning, Reichenbach adopted a non-cognitivist ethical theory in *The Rise of Scientific Philosophy* (1951). For him, ethical utterances were expressions of 'volitional decisions'. Fundamental value judgments cannot be considered true or false, but scientific knowledge and logic are extremely useful in dealing with 'entailed decisions', that is, hypothetical value judgments about the compatibility or incompatibility of various basic value judgments and about the selection of appropriate means to reach desired ends.

See also: SCIENTIFIC METHOD

List of works

Reichenbach, H. (1977–) *Hans Reichenbach: Gesammelte Werke in 9 Bänden* (Hans Reichenbach: Collected Works in Nine Volumes), ed. A. Kamlah and M. Reichenbach, Wiesbaden: Friedr. Vieweg and Sohn. (All works appear in German, including those originally written or published in other languages.)

—— (1978) *Hans Reichenbach: Selected Writings, 1909–1953*, ed. R. Cohen and M. Reichenbach, Dordrecht: Reidel. (All works appear in English; contains an excellent bibliography of Reichenbach's writings.)

—— (1916) 'Der Begriff der Wahrscheinlichkeit für die mathematische Darstellung der Wirklichkeit' (The Concept of Probability for the Mathematical Representation of Reality), *Zeitschrift für Philosophie und philosophische Kritik* 161: 210–39; 162: 98–112, 223–53. (A reprint of Reichenbach's doctoral dissertation.)

—— (1920) *Relativitätstheorie und Erkenntnis Apriori*, Berlin: Springer; trans. M. Reichenbach, *The Theory of Relativity and A Priori Knowledge*, Berkeley and Los Angeles, CA: University of California Press, 1965. (Reichenbach's first major challenge to Kant's theory of space and time. Translation contains a comprehensive introductory essay on Reichenbach's philosophy of space and time by M. Reichenbach.)

—— (1924) *Axiomatik der Relativistischen Raum-Zeit-Lehre*, Braunschweig: Vieweg; trans. M. Reichenbach, *Axiomatization of the Theory of Relativity*, Berkeley and Los Angeles, CA: University of California Press, 1969. (A rather technical work in which Reichenbach attempts to clarify logical features of Einstein's theories by means of an axiomatic approach.)

—— (1928) *Philosophie der Raum-Zeit-Lehre*, Berlin and Leipzig: de Gruyter; trans. M. Reichenbach, *The Philosophy of Space and Time*, New York: Dover, 1957. (The central classic in twentieth-century philosophy of space and time.)

—— (1933) 'Rudolf Carnap, Der logische Aufbau der Welt' (Rudolf Carnap's The Logical Structure of the World), *Kantstudien* 38: 199–201. (A review of Carnap's *Aufbau* (1928), and Reichenbach's first challenge to logical positivism; it is fully developed in Reichenbach (1938).)

—— (1935) *Wahrscheinlichkeitslehre* (Theory of Probability), Leiden: A.W. Sijthoff's Uitgeversmattschappij; 2nd enlarged edn, trans. E.H. Hutton and M. Reichenbach, *The Theory of Probability*, Berkeley and Los Angeles, CA: University of California Press, 1949. (Reichenbach's major treatise on probability and induction.)

—— (1938) *Experience and Prediction*, Chicago, IL: University of Chicago Press. (Reichenbach's treatise on epistemology, containing his refutation of logical positivism.)

—— (1944) *Philosophic Foundations of Quantum Mechanics*, Berkeley and Los Angeles, CA: University of California Press. (Reichenbach's attempt to resolve problems of quantum mechanics using the nonstandard (3-valued) logic.)

—— (1947) *Elements of Symbolic Logic*, New York: Macmillan. (Reichenbach's analysis of conversational language (including verb tenses) in chapter 7 is especially interesting.)

—— (1951) *The Rise of Scientific Philosophy*, Berkeley and Los Angeles, CA: University of California Press. (Reichenbach's popularized account of his philosophy.)

—— (1954) *Nomological Statements and Admissible Operations*, Amsterdam: North-Holland. (Reissued in 1976 (see below) and with a new foreword; the title later describes the topics covered in this work.)

—— (1956) *The Direction of Time*, Berkeley and Los Angeles: University of California Press. (Contains many valuable ideas concerning causality and explanation, along with important approaches to problems of temporal symmetry.)

—— (1976) *Laws, Modalities, and Counterfactuals*, Berkeley and Los Angeles, CA: University of California Press. (The new foreword attempts to make Reichenbach's convoluted theory accessible to a wide audience of philosophers.)

References and further reading

* Carnap, R. (1928) *Der logische Aufbau der Welt* (The

Logical Structure of the World), Berlin-Schlachtenesee: Weltkreis-Verlag; trans. R. George, *The Logical Structure of the World*, Berkeley and Los Angeles, CA: University of California Press, 1967. (Carnap's monumental attempt to implement the programme of logical positivism.)

Grünbaum, A. (1963) *Philosophical Problems of Space and Time*, New York: Alfred A. Knopf; 2nd enlarged edn, Dordrecht: Reidel, 1973. (Detailed and often technical discussions of Reichenbach's views.)

* Malament, D. (1977) 'Causal Theories of Time and the Conventionality of Simultaneity', *Nous* 11: 293–300. (A serious challenge to Reichenbach's doctrine of conventionality of simultaneity.)

* Poincaré, H. (1902) *La science et l'hypothèse*, Paris: E. Flammarion; trans. *Science and Hypothesis*, New York: Dover, 1952. (Part 2, composed of chapters 3–5, provides the point of departure for twentieth-century discussions of the conventionality of geometry.)

Salmon, W. (1967) *The Foundations of Scientific Inference*, Pittsburgh, PA: University of Pittsburgh Press. (An elementary survey of problems of induction and probability from a Reichenbachian perspective.)

—— (ed.) (1979) *Hans Reichenbach: Logical Empiricist*, Dordrecht: Reidel. (A collection of critical essays on Reichenbach, with an extended introductory essay, 'The Philosophy of Hans Reichenbach', by the editor.)

—— (1975) *Space, Time, and Motion: A Philosophical Introduction*, Encino, CA: Dickenson; 2nd edn, Minneapolis, MN: University of Minnesota Press, 1980. (An elementary exposition of some of Reichenbach's theories of space and time.)

WESLEY C. SALMON

REID, THOMAS (1710–1796)

Thomas Reid, born at Strachan, Aberdeen, was the founder of the Scottish school of Common Sense philosophy. Educated at Marishal College, Aberdeen, he taught at King's College, Aberdeen until appointed professor of moral philosophy at Glasgow. He was the co-founder of the Aberdeen Philosophical Society or 'Wise Club', which counted among its members George Campbell, John Stewart, Alexander Gerard and James Beattie. His most noteworthy early work, An Inquiry into the Human Mind: Or the Principles of Common Sense attracted the attention of David Hume and secured him his professorship. Other important works are Essays on the Intellectual Powers of Man (1785) and Essays on the Active Powers of the Human Mind (1788).

Reid is not the first philosopher to appeal to common sense; Berkeley and Butler are notable British predecessors in this respect, in the discussions of perception and of free will respectively. It fell to Reid, however, to collect and systematize the deliverances of common sense – the first principles, upon the acceptance of which all justification depends – and to provide adequate criteria for that status. Reid insists we rightly rely on our admittedly fallible faculties of judgment, including the five senses, as well as memory, reason, the moral sense and taste, without need of justification. After all, we have no other resources for making judgments, to call upon in justification of this reliance. We cannot dispense with our belief that we are continually existing and sometimes fully responsible agents, influenced by motives rather than overwhelmed by passions or appetites. In Reid's view major sceptical errors in philosophy arise from downgrading the five senses to mere inlets for mental images – ideas – of external objects, and from downgrading other faculties to mere capacities for having such images or for experiencing feelings. This variety of scepticism ultimately reduces everything to a swirl of mental images and feelings. However we no more conceive such images than perceive or remember them; and our discourse, even in the case of fiction, is not about them either. Names signify individuals or fictional characters rather than images of them; when I envisage a centaur it is an animal I envisage rather than the image of an animal. In particular the information our five senses provide in a direct or non-inferential manner is, certainly in the case of touch, about bodies in space.

Reid thus seems to be committed to the position that our individual perceptual judgments are first principles in spite of his admission that our perceptual faculties are fallible. Moreover, moral and aesthetic judgments cannot be mere expressions of feeling if they are to serve their purposes; a moral assessor is not a 'feeler'. Reid is therefore sure that there are first principles of morals, a view that scarcely fits the extent and degree of actual moral disagreement.

Reid offers alternative direct accounts of perception, conception, memory and moral and aesthetic judgment. He stoutly defends our status as continuing responsible agents, claiming that the only genuine causality is agency and that although natural regularities are held to be causes they cannot be full-blooded causes. Continuing persons are not reducible to material entities subject to laws of nature, (pace Priestley); nor does the proper study of responsible agents belong within natural philosophy. Morals may be adequately systematized on a human rights basis according to

171

which private property is not sacrosanct, once moral judgment is recognised to be based on first principles of morals. Judgments of beauty likewise rest on a body of first principles, even though Reid readily allows that there are no properties that all beautiful objects must have in common.

1   Life
2   Perception and sensation
3   Causality
4   Motivation and action
5   Language and conception
6   The beautiful and the sublime
7   Moral judgment, rights and right bearers
8   Common sense and first principles

1   Life

Thomas Reid, the founder of the Scottish school of Common Sense Philosophy, was born in Strachan near Aberdeen, Scotland. His mother, Margaret Gregory, was a member of a very scientifically gifted Scottish family. Her brother, David Gregory, was Savilian professor of Astronomy at Oxford and close friend of Sir Isaac Newton. After a formative period in the grammar school and Marischal College, Aberdeen, where George Turnbull was his regent, marrying, and a period as minister at New Machar, Reid was appointed a regent at King's College, Aberdeen, in 1751. While there he co-founded the Aberdeen Philosophical Society or 'Wise Club' whose members included George Campbell, John Stewart, Alexander Gerard and James Beattie. He also produced his Latin 'Philosophical Orations' and wrote his first major work 'An Inquiry into the Human mind on the Principles of Common Sense', published in 1764. Hume found it challenging and it secured Reid the professorship of Moral Philosophy in Glasgow College that year, as successor to Adam Smith. Here his activities culminated in two major works after his retirement from teaching in 1780, 'Essays on the Intellectual Powers of Man', published in 1785, and 'Essays on the Active Powers of the Human Mind', published in 1788, a controversy with Joseph Priestly and a fascinating correspondence, particularly with Lord Kames and James Gregory. He died in 1796, survived by one daughter from nine children.

2   Perception and sensation

Reid attacks the view of David HUME that nothing can ever be present to the mind but an image or perception and that the senses are only inlets through which these images are conveyed. According to Hume, the table which we see, and which appears to diminish as we move further from it, is not the real table that exists independently of us and undergoes no alteration as we move away from it; it is the image of the table that is immediately present to the mind, or seen. Reid claims that we have no good grounds for accepting the existence of such images or ideas, arguing that in perceiving something the mind has an immediate acquaintance with it. Perception of an external object involves some conception or notion of the object and an irresistible conviction of its present existence; the conviction is immediate and not inferential (1785: II.v).

But consider smelling a rose and the agreeable sensation raised when the rose is smelled. Reid allows that he is led, by his nature, to conclude some quality to be in the rose, which is the cause of this sensation. However in sensation there is no object distinct from the act of mind as there is in the cases of perception and memory; in 'I feel pain' the distinction between act and object is merely grammatical. Moreover the firm cohesion of the parts of a body is quite unlike that sensation by which I perceive it to be hard. And so sensations are not suitable as bases for inferences to qualities in objects. Given this firm rejection of the doctrine that we can have no conception of any material thing which is not like some sensation, it is hard to see how sensations can be more than occasional causes of conceptions. Reid even raises doubts about the existence of sensations in certain cases of perception (1764: VI). Thus there is no sensation for what he calls visible figure. The different positions on a visually perceived body facing an observer make a two-dimensional figure with length and breadth only. This visible figure represents the three-dimensional form of the perceived body which has length, breadth and thickness.

Sensation is an important ingredient of Reid's distinction between primary and secondary qualities. He states that our senses give us a direct and distinct notion of the primary qualities of objects, in spite of the obstacles mentioned above, but only a relative and obscure notion of secondary qualities: they are unknown qualities that produce certain sensations in us. Yet Reid freely admits (1785: II.xviii) that in seeing a coloured body the sensation is indifferent, drawing no attention, and that the (unknown) quality which we call its colour is the only object of our attention. Presumably we should follow Reid in distinguishing between the colour of a body, conceived to be a fixed and permanent quality in the body, and the appearance of colour to the eye which may be varied in a thousand ways, while not following him in his view that it is the former that we attend to when we look at a coloured object.

Reid thinks there is no visual perception of spherical objects without perception of their visible figure and colour; these are all that is originally perceived by sight even though we learn to perceive by the eye almost anything, including sphericality, that we can originally perceive by touch. It should be clear that this Berkelian view of vision sits uncomfortably with Reid's position that perception of something includes an immediate conviction of its present existence, even though it enables him to dismiss many cases of fallacy of vision as rash inferences.

Reid does not deny that there is no perception unless some impression is made upon the organ of sense either directly or through a medium which is then communicated to the nerves and by them to the brain (1785: II). However, he insists upon the following points. First, there is nothing more ridiculous than to imagine that any motion or modification of matter should produce thought. Second, when I look upon the wall of my room the wall does not act at all and is incapable of action; rather the perceiving of it is an act or operation in me, albeit an involuntary one.

3 Causality

Reid maintains that only beings which, by their active power, produce some change in themselves or in some other being are properly called causes and agents (1788: I). Moreover, whatever is the effect of active power must be something that is contingent, dependent upon the power and will of its cause. Power to produce an effect supposes power not to produce it, otherwise it is necessity, which is incompatible with power taken in the strict sense. Reid concedes that there is another sense of the term cause, so well authorized by custom that we cannot always avoid using it. He proposes to James Gregory (see Reid 1895) that we call it the 'physical' sense, as when we say that heat is the cause that turns water into vapour. A cause, in this sense, means only something which, by the laws of nature, the effect always follows. There is yet another sense of the term 'cause' that Reid allows to have currency and which he distinguishes from the sense just explained. Specifically, laws of nature may be called 'physical' causes too; but note that they do not bring about anything unless put to work either by some agent or by some physical cause.

Why does Reid maintain that physical causes are not true causes? One reason is that they cannot be ultimate. Thus, that a body put in motion continues to move until stopped might be viewed as an effect of an inherent property of matter, and so as not physically ultimate. If so, we may say that that property of matter is the physical cause of the continuing motion;

but surely the ultimate cause of this is the being who gave the inherent property to matter. Alternatively the continuing motion may be viewed as an arbitrary appointment of the Deity, and may then be called a law of nature and a physical cause. But such a law requires a being to enact it.

Must that being be an agent? Reid answers (1788: IV.ii) by invoking as a first principle the thesis 'that neither existence, nor any mode of existence, can begin without an efficient cause', from which it follows 'that everything which undergoes any change must either be the efficient cause of that change in itself, or it must be changed by some other efficient'. Reid adds that we can only conceive kinds of active power similar or analogous to the kind we attribute to ourselves, which is exerted by will and with understanding.

Again, consider the notion of a physical cause as something which, by the laws of nature, the effect always follows. Now given this account it would seem that, on Reid's view, the existence of such causes is, at best, contingent. Thus he says that the conjunction between a physical cause and its effect must be constant, unless in the case of a miracle, or suspension of the laws of nature. Moreover, processes such as evaporation are frequently interrupted in quite ordinary ways. Finally, it is clear that this account of physical causes will not, of itself, suffice to deal with the problem that Reid left for regularity accounts of physical causation, namely that, according to them, day is the cause of night and night of day.

Let us now turn to consider Reid's account of how physical causes are to be discovered. Reid (1785: I) adopts a Newtonian view on this question (see NEWTON, I.), maintaining that if anyone claims to show us the cause of any natural effect, whether pertaining to matter or to mind, we must first consider whether there is sufficient evidence that the cause really exists. If there is not, it should be rejected as a fiction. If it does really exist, we are to consider next whether the effect necessarily follows from it. And, Reid adds, conjectures about causes should be treated as 'reveries of the vain'. However, writing to Kames (see HOME, H.), he allows that such conjectures can have definite value in the following way. Attending to a given phenomenon, I conjecture that it may be owing to a certain cause. This may lead me to make the experiments or observations appropriate for discovering whether that is really the cause or not; and if I discover that it is or that it is not, my knowledge is improved and it is clear then that my conjecture was a means to that improvement.

The establishing of efficient causes is not within the sphere of natural philosophy, the method of which is experimental and leads to the establishing of physical causes at best. Indeed, Reid writes to Kames (see Reid 1965), apart from the fact that our nature leads us to believe ourselves to be the efficient causes of our own actions, and that from analogy we judge the same of other intelligent beings (with the result that attributions of human action are outside the sphere of natural philosophy) we are left, for the establishing of efficient causes, with nothing but resort to such first principles as that every beginning of existence has an efficient cause, and that an effect which has the most manifest marks of intelligence, wisdom and goodness, must have an intelligent, wise and good efficient cause. And with final causes, apparently so pervasive, it is similar (see CAUSATION).

4 Motivation and action

Faced with a deterministic universe the particles of which are initially set in motion by a Deity who prescribes Newton's laws of motion for them, it is hard to see how anything that happens to particles can be an action of mine. What I call my actions would seem to become mere movements of masses of particles, given that I am such a mass. But even if we do not accept this simple picture, problems remain. To say that people act is, Reid thinks, to say that we are efficient causes. How might that status be established for us? Reid responds by claiming (1788: I.vi) that it is a first principle that I am the cause that has power to produce certain motions of my body and directions of my thought.

Reid admits the fact of an established harmony between our willing certain motions of our bodies and the operations of the appropriate nerves and muscles. Now the willing is an act of the mind; but whether it has any physical effect upon the nerves and muscles, or whether it is only an occasion of their being acted upon by some other efficient cause according to established laws of nature, is not known to us. 'This may leave some doubt whether we be, in the strictest sense, the efficient cause of the voluntary motions of our own body' (1788: I.vii). He continues: 'The man who knows that such an event depends upon his will, and who deliberately wills to produce it is, in the strictest moral sense the *cause* of the event; and the event is justly imputed to him, no matter what physical causes may have concurred in its production.' However Reid has just shown that it is far from clear that the motion depends upon his will. For he has correctly pointed out that, for all we can know, the volition is at best an occasional cause of the operations of the nerves and muscles. Moreover, he holds that occasional causation, as in the case of night following day, does not of itself amount to physical causation. So unless Reid is willing to allow that

dependency can be instanced by occasional causation, there is no clear sense in which the bodily movement depends upon the will.

Reid maintains (1788: IV) that for a bodily movement to be rated as an action of a free agent it is not sufficient that there arise a determination of the will that the movement be produced; it is also required that the agent deliberately willed to produce it. Indeed if they cannot discern one determination to be preferable to another, and thereby exercise their power to choose, their determinations can be neither right nor wrong, wise nor foolish. It is when an agent exercises their active power to determine, or decide upon, their course of action that they act with the liberty of a moral agent. Now the difficulty about whether we are in the strictest sense the cause of so-called voluntary bodily movements emerges once again at the level of voluntary determinations of the will.

The determination of the will the fulfilment of which is my bodily movement must have a cause which had power to produce it. Now the cause is either myself or some other being. But we must ask in what circumstances a determination of will to move my right arm up rates as caused by me. Clearly, first, I must have the power to bring about the determination. Second, the only way in which the exercise of power is conceivable is via a determination of the will. So the only way in which I can conceive of a determination of the will being caused by me is via a prior determination of my will. But what if that prior determination of the will is not brought about by me? Then it would appear that the prior determination – the determination via which my decision to raise my arm up was formed – was either the product of another agent or of myself. In the former case the decision to raise my arm up was not an exercise of moral liberty. Let us remember, however, that it does not follow from the contention that an exercise of active power without will is not clearly conceivable by us that it is impossible.

What is the alternative to the belief that we are efficient causes with moral liberty? We might think that every event, including thoughts and actions, has a physical cause, arguing that if thinking and behaviour are not governed by universal exceptionless laws, they must be random, and consequently that rewards and punishments are without effect. Arguably every deliberate action must have a motive. When there is no conflicting motive this motive must cause us to act. When there are contrary motives the strongest must prevail.

Reid confronts such positions vigorously in (1788: IV.iv). Whether every deliberate action must have a motive depends upon how we understand deliberation. If deliberation means the weighing of motives, then there must be motives – and conflicting ones at that. But if a deliberate action means only an action done through a cool and calm determination, it is not clear that such determinations must be reached by weighing. Consider a case where an end of some importance may be achieved equally well by various means, none of which has any special appeal to the agent. Again the position that when there is a motive on only one side that motive must determine the action ignores such factors as caprice, quite apart from its presumption that motives are the sole causes of actions. But many motives, such as money, or success, are often not even things that exist, but *entia rationis* (mental constructions), which may best be compared to advice or exhortation, leaving the agent still at liberty to choose. However, we can find entities to serve as occasional causes of determinations such as the desire for money.

When it is said of conflicting motives that the strongest always prevails, Reid rightly points out that this cannot be affirmed or denied with understanding until we know what is meant by the strongest motive. Reid allows that when the contrary motives are of the same kind and differ only in quantity it may be easy to say which is the strongest. Thus a bribe of a thousand pounds is a stronger inducement than one of a hundred pounds. But when the motives are of different kinds, as are money and integrity, we have no rule by which to judge which is the stronger. If we go for prevalence, then the strongest motive would simply be the one that prevailed and the maxim would be trivially true.

These remarks would seem to apply to motives such as hunger and lust, which we have in common with 'the brutes'. Reid maintains that in their case the strongest motive always prevails, since brutes lack self-command. But this must be so on the trivial interpretation of the maxim. Reid claims that in contrast humankind judges the strength of its appetites by the conscious effort which is needed to resist them. And since it is possible for a person to resist with effort a strong appetite, the strongest appetite does not always prevail (see DESIRE).

What of rational motives? An interesting example is our good 'upon the whole' – that which, taken with all its discoverable connections and consequences, brings more good than ill. Another is our duty. No sooner do we have the former conception than we are 'led by our constitution' to seek the good and avoid the ill. So perhaps rational principles of action motivate by themselves. Reid characterises some rational motives as the conviction of what we ought to do in order to achieve some end we have judged fit to be pursued. Such motives may very properly be compared to advocates pleading at the bar. To say

that an advocate was the more powerful pleader because judgment was given on their side would be unsatisfactory; once again strength does not guarantee prevalence (see ACTION).

5 Language and conception

Reid distinguishes proper names and general words in (1785:V). A general word signifies either an attribute or a combination of attributes; a proper name signifies an individual. By affirming a singular substantive (for example, 'horse') of an individual we claim it to have all the attributes each of which must be possessed by any member of the class named by its plural ('horses'). From the infinite number of combinations of attributes that might be formed, we choose for purposes of classification only those that are useful for arranging our thoughts in discourse and in reasoning.

Concerning the conception of individual things that really exist, Reid says (1785: IV), that the things conceived are the *actual* things, which need not act upon him, nor him on them, in order to be conceived. Such conceptions are called 'true' when they agree with the thing conceived in respect of its attributes and relations. In 'general conception' what is conceived is the meaning of the general term, attribute or combination of attributes – the conception affixed to it by those who best understand the language.

There are conceptions which Reid calls 'fancy pictures'. Such are the conceptions which Swift formed of Laputa, and Cervantes of Don Quixote and his squire. We can give names to such creatures of the imagination, conceive them distinctly, and reason consequentially concerning them (1785: IV.i), although there are no bearers for these names outside the story. Reid insists that he can conceive a centaur (1785: IV.ii). Conceiving is an operation of the mind. The sole object in this case is a centaur, an animal which has never existed. Reid rightly insists that what he conceives is not the image of an animal but an animal. It is a body of a certain figure and colour, having life and spontaneous motion. It would seem to be an individual nonexistent. Thus, for Reid the question of how conceiving of nonexistents is possible is, arguably, equivalent to that of how the conceiving of nonexistent individuals is possible.

'Suppose I conceive a triangle, that is, a plain figure terminated by three right lines. He that understands this definition distinctly has a distinct conception of a triangle. But a triangle is not an individual; it is a species. . . . the thing conceived is general, and cannot exist without other attributes' (1785: V.ii). A triangle that really exists must have a certain length of sides and measure of angles, a fixed time and place; the definition of a triangle includes neither existence nor any of these other attributes. Such passages suggest that Reid thinks that an *ens rationis* is a combination of attributes lacking certain members. But does Reid really think that Don Quixote is a universal?

Reid readily allows that one may conceive of a plan of government which is never put into practice (1785: V.iv). Such compositions are things conceived in the mind of the author, not individuals that really exist; the same general conception which the author had may be communicated to others by language. This seems to support the view that Don Quixote is general. And a mere combination of attributes lacks real existence, although Reid allows that we may ascribe existence to a universal in the sense of its being actually instantiated.

Reid insists that we have clear and distinct conceptions of attributes. He certainly maintains that the attributes of individuals are all we can distinctly conceive about them; but he also holds (1785: V.ii) that the whiteness of this sheet is one thing and whiteness another thing, and that, unlike whiteness, it is not a universal. Attributes are expressed by general words. The other class of general terms is of those terms that signify the genera and species into which we divide and subdivide things. This division neglects certain substantive-like expressions such as 'entity'; if these are genuine substantives they can scarcely be said to signify a finite collection of attributes, where things that possess them all belong to one kind. Reid himself notices that the adjective 'beautiful' is applied to things of such different kinds that he is unable to conceive any quality that is in all the different things to which it applies (see CONCEPTS).

6 The beautiful and the sublime

For Reid, taste is a power of the mind by which we are capable of discerning and enjoying both the beauties of nature and whatever is excellent in the fine arts (1785:VIII) (see ARTISTIC TASTE). In the end, we always judge that there is some real excellence in beautiful objects. In some cases that excellence is distinctly conceived and can be pointed out (for example, a primary quality), while in other cases objects appear beautiful at first encounter without our being able to specify any excellence (for example, a secondary or occult quality).

When confronted by a beautiful object we should distinguish the pleasure produced in us from the quality in the object that causes it. Nevertheless, Reid emphasizes that since beauty is found in things so various and so very different in kind, it is at least difficult to say in what beauty consists. 'What can it be that is common to the thought of a mind, and the form of a piece of matter, to an abstract theorem, and a stroke of wit?' If the beauty of a stroke of wit were its excellence, and the beauty of a proof its excellence, there would be a negative answer to this question. However, since 'excellent' does not express an attribute or combination of attributes save when conjoined with a genuine substantive, this answer poses no problem for Reid's account of significance for full-blooded general terms.

Reid holds that the excellence of an object justifies the judgment of beauty. Our taste ought to be accounted most just and perfect when we are pleased with things most excellent of their kind, and displeased with the contrary. Every excellence has a real beauty and charm that makes it an agreeable object to those of good taste. Of course, Reid thinks that since judgments of taste are either true or false, there must be first principles of taste. But does every judgment of beauty depend for its truth on some excellence the object has (pace KANT)?

Reid does indeed allow that some objects appear beautiful at first sight without our being able to specify any excellence that could justify our judgment, citing the plumage of birds and butterflies as examples. But he claims that by a careful examination of such objects we may perhaps discover some real excellence in them. This claim is implausible. For I may rightly exclaim, 'What a lovely butterfly!', confronted by a less than perfect specimen. Moreover in some cases, such as the starry heavens, any excellence to be found in the object upon deeper investigation may be in a respect quite unconnected with the features of it that first impressed me. But then if an ugly object shares that excellence, why may it not count as beautiful too?

Might a basis for my exclamation be found in the novelty of seeing such a specimen? We are so constituted, claims Reid, that what is new to us commonly gives pleasure upon that account, provided it be not in itself disagreeable. However, if 'beautiful' can be properly used in a case of novelty, Reid is in difficulties. For some uses of 'beautiful' would not then serve to represent anything in the object.

Reid avoids such difficulties by accepting the common division of the objects of taste into novelty, grandeur and beauty. In order to understand his views on the nature of beauty we should consider his thoughts on grandeur. True grandeur is such a degree of excellence as is fit to raise enthusiastic admiration; it is found originally and properly in certain qualities of mind, and only derivatively in objects of sense. (One immediately wants to ask why it is not a department of beauty.) There is no grandeur in mere matter. There is, according to Reid, a real intrinsic excellence in such qualities of mind as power, knowledge, wisdom, virtue and magnanimity. These in every degree deserve esteem, but in an outstanding degree merit admiration, and lead to imitation of what is admired. When we contemplate such vast objects as the earth, the sea or the planetary system, it seems absurd to deny there is grandeur in them; yet it deserves to be considered whether all the grandeur we ascribe to such objects is not derived from some qualities of mind of which they are the effects or signs. Thus a great work such as the *Iliad*, is a work of great power, wisdom and goodness, well contrived for some important end; but power wisdom and goodness belong to the work figuratively, being really in its author.

It cannot be without reason that things as different as a flower and a song are called 'beautiful'. The grand is the proper object of admiration. The beautiful is the proper object of love and kind affection. A distinction can analogously be made between original and derived beauty. Original beauty is to be found in certain qualities of mind, such as innocence, gentleness and humanity, which are amiable from their very nature. Knowledge, good sense, wit and cheerfulness draw our love as do many other useful qualities. Clearly Reid needs to establish the claim that what we call beautiful among humankind, inferior animals and the inanimate, are either signs or expressions of such amiable qualities of mind or else the effects of design, art and wise contrivance (see BEAUTY; SUBLIME, THE).

7   Moral judgment, rights and right bearers

As via the external senses we have both the original conceptions of the various qualities of bodies and the original judgment that this body is hard, so via our moral faculty we have the conceptions of right and wrong and the original judgment that this conduct is right and that conduct wrong. If moral approbation were simply expression of feeling and did not involve moral judgment, then quite ordinary sentences would have either no meaning or one inconsistent with all rules of grammar and rhetoric in all languages throughout all the ages (1788: V.vii).

Reid offers examples of first principles of morals (1788: V. iv and III.iii.6). The latter examples include the maxim that we ought not to do to another what we should think wrong if done to us in like circumstances. Clearly application of the maxim presupposes some basis for distinguishing right from wrong. Happily other examples such as 'no human being is born for themselves only' contain the basis of many more particular familiar moral directives.

Reid does not claim that all persons must perceive the truth of their first principles of morals. The immature may not reach the moral starting points of the mature. Just as we may rely upon the clear and distinct testimony of our eyes concerning the colours and shapes of the bodies around us, so we may rely upon the clear and unbiased testimony of our moral faculty with regard to what we ought to do. But testimony is not invariably satisfactory. Reid (1788: III.iii.6) claims that someone who in a cool moment does not accept the maxim about not doing to another what is unacceptable to us does not possess a moral outlook. He also claims that one can be misled by prejudice and bad example (III.iii.8). Consider someone brought up to pursue injury with unrelenting malice. If they have the virtues of clemency, generosity and forgiveness laid before them, and are in a suitably calm and fair frame of mind, they can come to see, Reid believes, that it is more noble to subdue vengeance than to destroy an enemy. Finally, since the exercise of moral judgment depends on how actions are classified, we cannot expect moral judgments to coincide among people who classify them differently. Reid recognizes the first point when he remarks that our first moral conceptions are probably acquired by attending coolly to the conduct of others, and by observing what moves our approval or our indignation.

The need for moral instruction justifies systematic presentations of morals. Such presentations are not accounts of the structure of the powers of our mind by which we have our moral conceptions and make moral assessments. Reid prefers a presentation in terms of rights – a system of Natural Jurisprudence (1788: V.iii). Whereas a 'right action' is an action conformable to our duty, a 'right' is a technical term from law and covers all that a person may lawfully do, all that they may lawfully possess and use, and all that they may lawfully claim of any other person.

A system of the rights of persons can be as adequate a presentation of morals as a system of their duties. What I have a liberty right to do, it is everyone's duty not to hinder me from doing. What is my property right, no one ought to take from me; or to molest me in the use and enjoyment of it. And what I have a right to demand of any one it is their duty to perform.

However it may be my duty to do a kindness to a person who has no claim of right to it. Here Reid resorts to the notion of an imperfect right. They are not owed the kindness, but it would be a wrong act on the part of the agent not to do them the kindness. Again, if my neighbour possesses a horse which he has stolen, as long as I am ignorant of the theft it is my duty to treat the horse as I would any lawful possession of theirs. Reid seems inclined to allow that the thief has a claim to the stolen goods while the theft is unknown, calling the right 'external'. But while I indisputably have the duty not to take the horse until the theft is known, the thief's claim is groundless all along.

Reid is clear that the right of liberty extends to what I am obliged to do, to refraining from all unlawful actions and to all actions that are indifferent. The rights of liberty and property are perfect – their violation is an injury. Some claim, citing competitive sports, that Reid should not say (see 1788: V.iii) that it is the duty of all persons not to hinder me from doing what I have the liberty right to do. Clearly, if I parry and thereby thwart your thrust, I have not violated your right to thrust.

Reid holds that, although perfect, the right of property is subject to limitations and restrictions. Thus the right of an innocent individual to the necessities of life is superior to that which the rich individual has to their honestly acquired riches. Reid argues that the Utopian order of society, in which there is no private property, offers the least temptation to bad conduct (see DUTY; RIGHTS).

If someone has a limb cut off they are still the same person (1785: III.iv). The limb is no part of that person with a right to a part of their estate. My personal identity implies the continued existence of that indivisible thing which I call myself. Is it immaterial? Reid says that the changes which in common language are consistent with bodily identity differ merely in number and degree from those that are thought to undermine it; whereas personal identity does not admit of degree. Yet he allows that the testimony of witnesses to the identity of a person is commonly grounded on the same factors as our judgments of bodily identity. Nor does he think that the sole means of establishing that there is a permanent self which has a claim to all its thoughts and actions is its memory. Persons are the immediate objects of love or resentment. They are, in that respect, as far from being immediately present to the mind as other external objects.

However, Reid also argues that when I say, I see, I hear, I feel, I remember, this implies that it is one and the same self that performs all these operations. If the faculty of seeing were in the eye, that of hearing in the ear, and so on, the thinking principle, which I call myself, would be not one but many. And Kames is asked in a letter of 1775 (see Reid 1895), whether, given that we say with Joseph Priestley that mental powers are the result of brain structure, several intelligent beings formed out of Reid's brain and having its structure will all be Reid (see PERSONS)?

8 Common sense and first principles

Reid is not the first philosopher to have argued that

since a view is contrary to common sense it should be rejected. But he is among the earliest post-medievals to reflect systematically on that argument (1785: VI). Common sense is that degree of judgment which is common to those members of humankind with whom we can converse and transact business. The same degree of understanding makes one capable of discovering what is true and what is false in matters that are self-evident. What is contrary to common sense is contrary to what is self-evident.

Sometimes Reid's characterizations of self-evidence are fairly neutral. Thus whenever we examine the evidence of any proposition either we find it self-evident, or it rests upon one or more propositions that support it, which, in turn, rest upon propositions that support them. But we cannot go back in this way to infinity. Clearly this can only come to a halt when we reach propositions which support all that are built upon them but are not themselves supported. Sometimes his characterizations serve as marks of self-evidence. One mark is that the principle be expressed in a proposition which is no sooner understood than believed. This runs the risk of fielding only trifling propositions. Another mark is that of an opinion's appearing so early in the minds of people that it cannot be the effect of education or reasoning. But this applies to a great number of beliefs that are simply false, such as the belief that parents know everything that the child wants to know, as well as to others that are true but need justification. Another mark is universality of an opinion, revealed by the tenor of human conduct. This, Reid thinks, will apply to such opinions as the existence of a material world and that there is a right and a wrong in human conduct, and no doubt many others. Another is the indispensability of the belief to our daily conduct of affairs. Yet another is the ridiculous as applied to the contraries of first principles. And, arguably, by the neutral criterion all the deliverances of the senses and of memory are self-evident, although Reid allows that the faculties in question are fallible. Clearly it is far from obvious that just any person with common sense is competent effectively to employ all of these criteria, although that is not to express doubts about their capacity to acquire the competence.

Reid is inclined to withhold the title of 'axiom' from the individual deliverances of the senses since philosophers call only necessary truths axioms. He divides his candidates for first principles into first principles of necessary truths and first principles of contingent truths. Such principles appear to serve as starting points from which other truths can be derived – necessary truths from the former kind and contingent truths from the latter. But it is not Reid's view that necessarily true first principles are intrinsically more certain or more surely known than contingently true first principles. Indeed Reid argues (1785: VII) that probable evidence of the highest degree – consisting of an accumulation of different arguments based on first principles of contingent truths – often leads to a degree of assurance as great as fits a proposition of Euclid.

The first principles of contingent truths concerning the reliability of the senses and of memory, of which Reid offers as direct an account as that (1785: III) for the senses, are almost immediate consequences of the principle that our faculties – senses, memory, consciousness and reasoning – are not fallacious.

In reply to a sceptic who objects that we are prone to error, Reid contends that to claim that our faculties are not fallacious is not to say that they are infallible; only by using them can we establish anything at all, including their proneness to error. But that our faculties are not fallacious is not something that can be established by using them; it is rather a presupposition of their use.

Another sceptic might resolve to withhold assent to anything until it is established that our faculties are not fallacious. Reid remarks that it would be impossible to move them out of this position by argument. Indeed, it is not possible to enter into a dispute with someone who does not share our first principles. For the procedure by which the truth of a proposition is discovered, or its falsehood detected, is to show its necessary connection with first principles or its incompatibility with them; hence one cannot reason with someone who denies one's first principles. Indeed, if many key terms are implicitly defined by acceptance of first and derived principles it is hard to see how we can even communicate with someone who does not share our first principles.

It might be thought that Reid's view that first principles are the voice of God should be taken as a possible justification for adhering to them, or for thinking them true. But if it is not self-evident that they are from God (even if it be evident that their acceptance is, in some instances, a part of human nature), it requires use of our faculties to establish the point that they are from God. Only then can that point be used on behalf of their acceptability.

See also: ABERDEEN PHILOSOPHICAL SOCIETY; BUFFIER, C.; CERTAINTY; COMMON SENSE SCHOOL; COMMONSENSISM; ENLIGHTENMENT, SCOTTISH; MORAL SENSE THEORIES; PRIMARY–SECONDARY DISTINCTION

List of works

Reid, T. (1764) *An Inquiry into the Human Mind, On the Principles of Common Sense*, Edinburgh; repr. as 'An Abstract of the Inquiry into the Human Mind on the Principles of Common Sense', ed. D.F. Norton, in S.F. Barker and T. Beauchamp (eds) *Thomas Reid: Critical Interpretations*, Philadelphia, PA: Philosophical Monographs.

—— (1780) *Lectures on Natural Theology*, repr. in *Thomas Reid's Lectures on Natural Theology*, ed. E.H. Duncan, Washington, DC: University Press of America, 1981.

—— (1785) *Essays on the Intellectual Powers of Man*, Edinburgh.

—— (1788) *Essays on the Active Powers of the Human Mind*, Edinburgh.

—— (1895) *The Correspondence of Dr. Reid in The Works of Thomas Reid, D.D.*, ed. W. Hamilton, Edinburgh: Thin, 8th edn.

—— (1937) *Philosophical Orations of Thomas Reid*, ed. W.R. Humphries, Aberdeen: Aberdeen University Press.

—— (1965) 'Unpublished Letters of Thomas Reid to Lord Kames', ed. I.S. Ross, *Texas Studies in Literature and Language* 7: 17–65.

—— (1976) 'An Abstract of the Inquiry into the Human Mind on the principles of Common Sense', ed. D.F. Norton, in S.F. Barker and T. Beauchamp (eds) *Thomas Reid: Critical Interpretations*, Philadelphia, PA: Philosophical Monographs.

—— (1982) *Cura Prima*, ed. D.F. Norton, appended to L. Marcil-Lacoste, *Claude Buffier and Thomas Reid: Two Common Sense Philosophers*, Kingston and Montreal, Que.: McGill-Queens University Press.

—— (1988) *The Philosophical Orations of Thomas Reid*, ed. D.D. Todd, trans. S.D. Sulivan, Carbondale, IL: Southern Illinois University Press.

—— (1990) *Thomas Reid: Practical Ethics*, ed. K. Haakonssen, Princeton, NJ: Princeton University Press.

References and further reading

* Dalgarno, M. (1984) 'Reid's Natural Jurisprudence: The Language of Rights and Duties', in V. Hope (ed.) *Philosophers of the Scottish Enlightenment*, Edinburgh, 13–31. (A clear and helpful introductory paper, discussed in 6.)

Dalgarno, M. and Matthews, E. (eds) (1989) *The Philosophy of Thomas Reid*, Dordrecht, Boston, MA and London: Kluwer. (Contains useful papers on perception, sensation, common sense, mind and action, aesthetics, moral and political obligation, as well as material on the historical context and a helpful bibliography. Invaluable for the serious intending student.)

* Daniels, N. (1974) *Thomas Reid's Inquiry: The Geometry of Visibles and the Case for Realism*, New York: Franklin. (A simple exposition of Reid's non-euclidean geometry of visibles.)

* Ferreira, M.J. (1986) *Scepticism and Reasonable Doubt*, Oxford: Clarendon Press. (Ably expounds and discusses Reid on first principles and probable reasoning.)

* Gallie, R.D. (1989) *Thomas Reid and 'The Way of Ideas'*, Dordrecht, Boston, MA and London: Kluwer. (Contains useful discussions of perception, conception, signification, active power, continuity and the self, and first principles.)

* Gracyk, T. (1987) 'The Failure of Thomas Reid's Aesthetics', *Monist* 70 (4): 465–82. (A stimulating paper on this subject discussed in 4 and 5. There are other interesting papers on Reid in the same number.)

Haldane, J. (1993) 'Whose Theory? Which Representations?', *Pacific Philosophical Quarterly* 74 (3): 247–57. (Further valuable discussion on Reid and modern representationalism in response to Stecker (1992).)

Kivy, P. (1973) *Thomas Reid's Lectures on the Fine Arts*, The Hague: Martinus Nijhoff. (Although the lecture notes on which the text is based are not in Reid's hand the text is an invaluable source for the serious student of Reid's aesthetics.)

* Lehrer, K. (1989) *Thomas Reid*, London and New York: Routledge. (Ingeniously applies a computational mind model approach to Reid in order to illuminate important areas of Reid's thought-perception, memory and conception, first principles and morality. Contains useful bibliographical information. A stimulating analytical introduction to much of Reid's philosophy suitable for advanced undergraduate students and beyond.)

Stecker, R. (1992) 'Thomas Reid's Philosophy of Action', *Philosophical Studies* 66 (2): 197–208. (Able discussion of whether Reid's insights into decision and action require a libertarian framework.)

Stecker, R. (1992) 'Does Reid Reject/Refute the Representational Theory of Mind?', *Pacific Philosophical Quarterly* 73 (2): 174–84. (Argues clearly that Lehrer's contention that there are sufficient materials in Reid to refute modern representationalism is not well founded.)

Rowe, W.L. (1991) *Thomas Reid on Freedom and Morality*, Ithaca, NY and London: Cornell University Press. (Clear and thorough exposition and discussion of Reid, as well as of Locke, Collins and Clarke, in the areas of decision, free action, causation and motivation.)

Schulthess, D. (1983) *Philosophie et Sens Commun chez Thomas Reid*, Berne: Lang. (A clear and readable exposition of nearly all aspects of Reid's philosophy.)

ROGER GALLIE

REINACH, ADOLF (1883–1917)

Adolf Reinach, a German philosopher of Jewish extraction, was born in Mainz and died on the battlefield in Flanders. He is of principal note as the inventor, in 1913, of a theory of speech acts (or 'social acts' to use Reinach's own terminology) which in some respects surpasses the later work of thinkers such as J.L. Austin and Searle. Reinach was a leading member of the so-called Munich–Göttingen school of phenomenologists who were inspired by Husserl's early realism and who rejected Husserl's subsequent turn to 'transcendental idealism', drawing their inspiration rather from the more analytic orientation of thinkers such as Franz Brentano and other Austrian philosophers.

1   **The legal a priori**
2   **Promises and other acts**
3   **The theory of social acts**

1   The legal a priori

Reinach and his fellows conceived phenomenology as a method for describing the 'essential structures' manifested in different realms of objects of experience, in terms of the dependent and independent parts and moments which are the constituent elements of such structures (see the third of Husserl's *Logical Investigations* (1900–01)). This method led Reinach to embrace an extreme version of 'apriorism' in legal theory. All creations of positive law, according to Reinach, presuppose certain basic legal or institutional categories prior to any human convention and subject to certain 'material a priori laws', laws which would obtain even though never recognized by any human subject. Examples of such laws are: a promise gives rise to a mutually correlated claim and obligation; a promise gives rise to a defeasible tendency on the part of the promiser to fulfil the content of the promise. Such laws are analogous to the a priori laws which obtain in other spheres – for example, laws to the effect that nothing can be red and green all over, that red is darker than orange, and so on. Only against the background of this fabric of basic legal structures and associated laws, Reinach argues, can we understand the peculiar phenomena of convention and of positive law-making – phenomena whereby uses of language give rise to certain real changes in the legal and institutional world.

2   Promises and other acts

That uses of language not only can, but even normally do, have the character of actions was a fact largely unrealized by those engaged in the study of language before the present century, not least in virtue of the influence of ARISTOTLE, who in *De Interpretatione* (17a1–5) relegates the study of non-statement-making sentences to the disciplines of rhetoric and poetry. The first philosopher to have fought against the Aristotelian conception seems to have been Thomas REID, who saw that in addition to judgments there are also other types of sentence permitting of a theoretical treatment (see Schuhmann and Smith 1990). Reid's remarks on social acts were, however, uninfluential, and it was not until the end of the nineteenth century that the idea of linguistic action began to rear its head once more, in the tradition initiated by BRENTANO and HUSSERL. Brentano defended the thesis that all mental acts are intentional – that is, that they are directed towards some precisely tailored object. Husserl exploited this thesis in the *Logical Investigations*, above all in the principle: every intentional experience is either an objectifying act or is dependent upon such an act for its existence. Non-objectifying acts such as feelings and emotions, Husserl held, need objectifying acts to supply them with their objects.

Husserl's theory of linguistic meaning is based on this theory of objectifying acts. For Husserl all uses of language approximate to referential uses. More precisely: all expressions are associated either with nominal acts or with acts of judgment. How, on this basis, can Husserl account for the meaningfulness of uses of language involved in asking questions, issuing commands, expressing requests, and so on? Answer: by conceiving the corresponding utterances as disguised statements about certain associated experiences on the part of the language-using subject. The command 'Sit down on the chair!', for example, is a disguised statement to the effect that 'your sitting down on the chair is my current request'. It was in response to the perceived inadequacies of this position that Reinach formulated his theory of social acts.

3   The theory of social acts

The rejection by the Munich phenomenologists of Husserl's theory of linguistic meaning was a cumulative process, instigated by Johannes Daubert (1877–1947) and culminating in the theory of speech acts put forward by Reinach in his monograph on *The*

A Priori Foundations of the Civil Law (1913). On the traditional account the action of promising is seen as the expression of an act of will or as the declaration of an intention to act in the interests of the promisee. Such an account, however, throws no light on how an utterance of the given sort can give rise to a mutually correlated obligation and claim. The bare intention to do something has, after all, no quasi-legal consequences of this sort, and it is difficult to see why things should be different just because such an intention is brought to expression in language.

Both promising and communicating one's intention to do something, according to Reinach, belong to the category of what he calls 'spontaneous' acts – that is, acts which involve a subject's bringing something about within his own psychic sphere, as contrasted with passive experiences of, say, feeling a pain or hearing an explosion (Reinach [1913: 706] 1983: 18). Certain specific types of spontaneous acts require as a matter of necessity a linguistic utterance or some other overt performance of a non-natural (rule-governed) sort. This does not hold of judging or deciding, nor even of forgiving, but it does hold of apologizing, commanding, accusing. We may accordingly divide spontaneous acts into two classes, which we might call 'internal' and 'external', according to whether the act's being brought to overt expression is a separable or inseparable moment of the relevant complex whole.

Acts are divided further into self-directable and non-self-directable. Self-directable acts are such that the subject towards whom they are directed may be identical with the subject of the act (as in cases of self-pity, self-hatred and so on). Non-self-directable acts, on the other hand, such as forgiving or praying, demand an alien subject. A peculiarity of certain external and non-self-directable acts is that the relevant utterance must of necessity not only be directed towards a certain subject but also registered or grasped by this subject in a further act: a command must be received and understood by those to whom it is addressed (something which does not apply, for example, to an act of blessing or cursing). What has been said of commands holds also for requests, admonishments, questionings, informings, answerings, and many other types of act (Reinach [1913: 707] 1983: 19). Each such 'social' act constitutes a unity of deliberate execution and utterance; the utterance is not something added as an incidental extra. Certainly there exist also incidental statements relating to social acts: 'I have just issued the command'. But such statements then relate to the whole social act, with its external aspect, as an independent unity (Reinach [1913: 708] 1983: 20).

The closeness to J.L. Austin and later speech act

theorists is unmistakable. For Reinach, as for Austin, a promise is not just the expression of an act of will; it is a social act with an essential external dimension embracing utterance and execution (see AUSTIN, J.L. §3). Reinach's treatment of social acts includes also an account of conditional acts, of sham and incomplete and otherwise defective acts, of acts performed jointly and severally, and of that sort of impersonality of social acts that we find in the case of legally issued norms and in official declarations such as are involved in marriage and baptismal ceremonies (see SPEECH ACTS).

Reinach's theory is embedded within a larger theory of legal formations and includes a subtle treatment of the ways in which basic legal categories may become modified in their instantiations as a result of the contingent and pragmatically motivated issuances of the positive law. It is embedded also within a larger (non-Kantian, ontological) theory of the a priori, on the one hand, and of the relation between is and ought, as well as between linguistic phenomena and legal and ethical and institutional phenomena, on the other. His brilliance and originality were greatly admired by early phenomenologists, including Husserl himself, but his influence was cut short by an early death and by a shift of direction in the phenomenological movement away from the logico-linguistic, ontological and psychological concerns manifested by Husserl himself and by his earliest followers in Munich and Göttingen.

See also: PHENOMENOLOGICAL MOVEMENT; SEARLE, J. §1

List of works

Reinach, A. (1911a) 'Zur Theorie des negativen Urteils', in Pfänder, A. (ed.) *Münchener Philosophische Abhandlungen*, *Festschrift* for Theodor Lipps, Leipzig: Barth, 196–254; trans. B. Smith, 'On the Theory of the Negative Judgment', in *Parts and Moments*, Munich: Philosophia, 1982, 315–77. (Account of a theory of truth and meaning based on an ontology of states of affairs.)
—— (1911b) 'Kants Auffassung des Humeschen Problems', *Zeitschrift für Philosophie und philosophische Kritik* 141: 176–209; trans. J.N. Mohanty, 'Kant's Interpretation of Hume's Problem', *Southwestern Journal of Philosophy* 7 (1976): 161–88. (Criticism of Kant's misunderstanding of Hume's theory of relations of ideas and defence of an ontological theory of the a priori of which traces are found in Hume.)
—— (1913) 'Die apriorischen Grundlagen des bürgerlichen Rechtes', *Jahrbuch für Philosophie und*

phänomenologische Forschung I/2: 685–847; trans. as 'The Apriori Foundations of the Civil Law', *Aletheia* 3 (1983): 1–142. (First systematic theory of speech acts, with special attention to the structure of the promise, presented as part of a general theory of the foundations of law.)
—— (1989) *Sämtliche Werke: Kritische Ausgabe mit Kommentar* (Diverse Works: Critical Edition With Commentary), ed. K. Schuhmann and B. Smith, Munich and Vienna: Philosophia, 2 vols. (Critical edition of Reinach's works.)

References and further reading

* Husserl, E. (1900–1) *Logische Untersuchungen*, Halle: Niemeyer; repr. in *Husserliana*, vol. 17, ed. E. Holenstein, 1975, and vols 19 (1) and 19 (2), ed. U. Panzer, 1984, The Hague: Nijhoff; trans. J.N. Findlay, *Logical Investigations*, London: Routledge & Kegan Paul, 1970. (Husserl's magnum opus.)
Mulligan, K. (ed.) (1987) *Speech Act and Sachverhalt: Reinach and the Foundations of Realist Phenomenology*, The Hague: Nijhoff. (Essays on Reinach's work, particularly on his philosophy of language and law, with extensive bibliography.)
Pfänder, A. (ed.) (1911) *Münchener Philosophische Abhandlungen*, *Festschrift* for Theodor Lipps, Leipzig: Barth. (Early collection of papers by leading Munich phenomenologists.)
Schuhmann, K. and Smith, B. (1990) 'Elements of Speech Act Theory in the work of Thomas Reid', *History of Philosophy Quarterly* 7: 47–66.
Smith, B. (1993) 'An Essay on Material Necessity', *Canadian Journal of Philosophy*, supplementary vol. 18: 301–22. (Comparison of the views of Hume, Reinach and Searle on speech acts and the is–ought problem.)
Spiegelberg, H. (1960) *The Phenomenological Movement: A Historical Introduction*, The Hague: Nijhoff, 2 vols. (Extensive historical survey.)

BARRY SMITH

REINCARNATION

The doctrine of reincarnation teaches that each human being has been born and died, and again been born and died, over and over again in a beginningless process that will never end unless they become enlightened. The doctrine of karma asserts that right and wrong actions bring, respectively, positive and negative consequences. For monotheistic religious traditions that accept reincarnation and karma, each person beginninglessly

*depends on God, and karmic consequences are under
God's providential control; repentance and faith may
lead to God graciously cancelling negative consequences. Nonmonotheistic religious traditions that
embrace reincarnation and karma doctrine see karma
as operating in terms of what is, in effect, a moral
version of natural or causal law. Both sorts of religious
tradition view escape from the reincarnation cycle – 'the
wheel' – as the ultimate goal of one's existence and as
possible only if one can escape from having karmic
consequences still coming at one of one's deaths.
Monotheistic traditions see escape as continuance of
personal identity, and living in the presence of God (as
in monotheistic Hinduism). Nonmonotheistic traditions
range from seeing escape as continuance of personal
identity in a disembodied condition of omniscience
(Jainism, an atheistic religion), loss of all personal
identity in entering a changeless nirvāṇa, or annihilation of all undesirable states but continued existence
composed of only desirable states (as in different
Buddhist traditions), or simply the realization of
identity with a qualityless ultimate reality, so that
there only apparently are either persons or reincarnations (as in Mahāyāna voidism and Advaita Vedānta).*

1   Karma and Brahman
2   The importance of escape
3   Persons and enlightenment
4   Reincarnation and evil

1   Karma and Brahman

Karmic consequences accrue over lifetimes. A right or
wrong action performed by an agent *A* in one lifetime
may only result in consequences to *A* in *A*'s next
lifetime or in *A*'s next lifetime plus one, or later still.
One's circumstances of birth (one's sex, caste,
economic status, place in society, health, psychological structure, and so on) are functions of one's karmic
history. While popularly humans are thought sometimes to be reborn as animals, scholarly Hindu
tradition tends to take the idea of a person being
reborn as something other than a person as under-
lining the importance of acting rightly, and accounts
of human persons being reborn as animals as stories
warning against wrong actions, not literal accounts of
the future fate of wicked people.

Within Hindu monotheistic traditions, Brahman or
God is held to superintend the reincarnation cycle
and its karmic distributions; karma is thought of as
God's way of acting justly, parcelling out the
appropriate rewards for right action and punishments
for misdeeds. Further, repentance of one's sin and
trust in God's forgiving mercy is held to provide a way
of escape from one's bearing the full brunt of one's

negative karma, as well as from the cycle of
reincarnation (see BRAHMAN; KARMA AND REBIRTH,
INDIAN CONCEPTIONS OF).

Nonmonotheistic South Asian (Indian) traditions
– Jainism and, in so far as it takes reincarnation and
karma literally, Buddhism – of course have no notions
of divine forgiveness or of God providing release from
the wheel of rebirth. Their account of what makes
escape possible is that if one becomes enlightened in a
given lifetime, this signals that at the moment of
enlightenment one is free both from karmic credit
and karmic debit. Taking one's life would be wrong,
so following enlightenment by suicide is not regarded
as a solution. One can keep oneself from deserving
negative consequences in a future life by not acting
wrongly. It is possible, we are told, to perform right
actions in a way that does not bring positive consequences, namely by performing them disinterest-
edly, without emotional investment in their outcome.
Thus by maintaining a detached attitude regarding
right actions and avoiding wrong actions, an enlightened person can avoid piling up further karmic
credits and debits. 'Becoming enlightened' for these
traditions is a matter of having an esoteric religious
experience; such an experience is a pre-*nirvāṇa* state –
an event in one's current lifetime that promises final
nirvāṇa at this lifetime's end (see NIRVĀṆA).

2   The importance of escape

One might consider the doctrines of reincarnation
and karma as exceedingly good news, since if they are
true then apparently one could improve one's overall
lifestyle and status by being a morally decent person
until one reached a lifetime in which one enjoyed
highly satisfactory circumstances. Then, one might
think, one could maintain that level of happy life
while being born into various healthy bodies and
living in sundry pleasant surroundings. Yet any such
entrepreneurial alternative is universally rejected by
the reincarnation and karma traditions.

There are two reasons why the entrepreneurial
perspective is nowhere taken in Indian thought. The
more superficial reason is that the nature of
reincarnation is not such as to allow one, in one
lifetime, to make an efficacious decision regarding
one's moral efforts in all future lifetimes. Thus one's
decision now to be decent ever after, even if it holds
for one's current lifetime, does not guarantee that one
will make a similar choice the next time around or
guarantee the effectiveness of that new choice should
it be made. The more important reason is that human
existence within the reincarnation cycle is itself held
not to be worthy of one's continued attachment. A
Hindu text reads as follows:

In this body, which is afflicted with desire, anger, covetousness, delusion, fear, despondency, envy, separation from the desirable, union with the undesirable, hunger, thirst, senility, disease, sorrow, and the like, what is the good of the enjoyment of desires... we see that this whole world is decaying.... In this sort of cycle of existence, what is the good of the enjoyment of desires, when after a man has fed on them there is seen repeatedly his return here to earth?... [I]n this cycle of existence I am a frog in a waterless well.

(Maitri Upaniṣad, I, 3–4)

It is basic Theravāda Buddhist doctrine that this world is a place of suffering and 'unsatisfactoriness'. No unenlightened state that a human can be in is satisfactory or worthy of being clung to. The basic religious problem is that of escaping the round of birth and rebirth, and the way to do so is through enlightenment. Theravāda, and Indian Buddhism generally, is nonmonotheistic; there is no doctrine of a creator and providence, and what gods and goddesses there may be are themselves involved in the reincarnation cycle and seeking their own way out.

3   Persons and enlightenment

The Theravāda Buddhist account of what a person is contends that *at* a single time a person is nothing more or other than a bundle of nonconscious and conscious, or physical and mental, states; *over* time a person is nothing more or other than a series of such bundles. An individual person is a set of elements, each momentary and transitory, and everything else is made up of momentary, transitory states. Much of the intellectual context within which Buddhism developed held that each person (*ātman*) is a mental substance that endures throughout its reincarnation history and (should that person become enlightened) on into the enlightenment state. It also held that Brahman is a supreme person who exists everlastingly, is not subject to reincarnation or karma, and gives aid in escaping the reincarnation cycle to those who seek it. For the Buddhist (save for a heretical personalist school) there is no enduring self (*ātman*), nor is there an unchanging ultimate reality (Brahman). It is basic Buddhist doctrine that nothing noncomposite endures even two moments; everything is impermanent. The person, or self, of everyday experience – the 'empirical self' – is held to be unreal or illusory, since we ordinarily or commonsensically take ourselves to be enduring self-conscious things – mental substances – and Buddhist doctrine is adamantly nonsubstantialist. For the Theravādin, there is only a stream of successive, causally linked bundles of momentary physical and mental states. Later Indian Buddhism, for example Mahāyāna, retains the structure of this analysis, but, as an idealist tradition, rejects the view that there are physical states. Causal and (potential) memory connections link one series of bundles in one lifetime to another series in another to constitute reincarnation. Reincarnation is simply a matter of this stream continuing.

If one becomes enlightened, one has a pre-*nirvāṇa* experience in which one learns the truth concerning 'impermanence' and 'selflessness'; final, postmortem *nirvāṇa* is the cessation of even this transitory self with consequent release from all desire and unsatisfactoriness. For the Theravāda tradition, the goal is simply to achieve *nirvāṇa*, and no one who has the sort of pre-*nirvāṇa* experience that makes final *nirvāṇa* an option could rationally turn down reaching the final goal upon death. The Mahāyāna tradition, however, holds that one who becomes enlightened in the sense of attaining the relevant pre-*nirvāṇa* state will put off achieving *nirvāṇa* upon death and opt to return to the reincarnation cycle in order to help others become enlightened. Final *nirvāṇa* will be accepted by such a person only when everyone has become enlightened, a condition that for some schools is far off and for others will never arise. Other Mahāyāna schools hold 'voidist' doctrines and contend that even the doctrines of reincarnation and karma presuppose the existence of distinct elements, whereas all reality is seamless; since no distinction that can be made corresponds to anything real, there is no reincarnation cycle and no karma, and coming to see that all is void is *nirvāṇa* (see BUDDHIST CONCEPT OF EMPTINESS).

The Jaina tradition holds that 'modifications cannot exist without an abiding or eternal something – a permanent substance' (Radhakrishnan and Moore 1957: 269). A 'substance' in this sense is something that has qualities, is not itself a quality or a bundle of qualities, remains the same through change, and endures over time; indeed, on the Jaina view, a substance is indestructible. On this account, then, persons are mental substances, self-conscious souls whose existence neither begins nor ends. The participation of a soul in the reincarnation cycle involves its embodiment, with the undesirable consequence that its inherent omniscience is not realized and it appears to itself to be destructible. By achieving an esoteric religious experience, one can come to a true notion of one's personhood and, upon one's next death, attain *nirvāṇa*. Both embodiment and karmic consequences, positive and negative, become things of the past, and, with full retention of personal identity (remaining numerically the same self-conscious substance that one has always been), one is freed from all errors and need never return to the wheel. For the Jaina, then, there is an infinite number of real (nonillusory) things which are eternally distinct from one another. Most important among these distinct things are persons (souls, *jīvas*), who can attain enlightenment in which their inherent omniscience is no longer dimmed by embodiment and their individuality is not lost but enhanced. Though the Jainas believe in individual immortality, they do not believe in a supreme deity.

Advaita Vedānta is a nonmonotheistic, monistic variety of Hinduism, according to which only Brahman without qualities exists (see VEDĀNTA). Each person (*ātman*) is identical to the qualityless Brahman. Freedom from the reincarnation cycle involves coming to see that this identity holds. For the Advaitin, ultimate reality (that which does not depend on anything else for its existence) is apersonal and eternal, unchanging and permanent. The real self is identical to this ultimate reality and in a this-life esoteric religious experience, one learns this truth, thereby escaping the cycle of rebirth, losing all individuality, and being 'absorbed' into Brahman. There are obvious similarities between Buddhist 'voidism' and Advaita Vedānta, as was noted by those Hindus who accused Śaṅkara, perhaps the greatest of Advaita Vedānta thinkers, of being a crypto-Buddhist. Critics of Advaita Vedānta have argued that if reincarnation and karma are illusions, then there must be someone whose illusions they are, and since by nature Brahman cannot be subject to illusion there must be persons who are not identical to Brahman.

Reincarnation and karma doctrines, then, vary as notions of what a person is and what is ultimately real vary. Agreement on the desirability of escape from the cycle of reincarnation coexists with quite different notions of what sort of thing is in the cycle, what exactly the cycle is and whether the cycle is itself guided by an intelligent and gracious hand.

4 Reincarnation and evil

It is sometimes said that the doctrines of reincarnation and karma make it clear why there is evil in the world and why apparently innocent people suffer. A baby born with disease or defect cannot deserve its fate due to anything it has done in its lifetime. Very bad things happen to very good people and very good things happen to very bad people in ways that seem quite unjust in the light of their current conduct and character. The 'luck of the draw' regarding one's family, intelligence, social status, economic position and the like can powerfully affect the degree to which one is healthy and happy. Wellbeing seems poorly correlated with personal merit or character. In sum, the world plainly seems not to be characterized by a just distribution of goods or of (what might be seen as) rewards and punishments.

If the doctrines of reincarnation and karma are true, however, each person now reaps what they have sown in the past. One deserves whatever one gets, though perhaps not because of anything one has done in one's current lifetime. If a person exists before each of their embodied lifetimes, then the conditions of embodiment and the pleasures and sufferings they undergo may reflect their character in previous lives; so the apparently unjust distribution of goods, or of rewards and punishments, may in fact be exquisitely matched to their deserts.

The claim is that whatever circumstances a person is born into, and whatever befalls that person, are what is morally appropriate in the sense that they are the sort of circumstances and consequences that a morally perfect being, fully informed and capable, would provide them with. For the monotheistic reincarnation traditions, things are this way precisely because such a being has so acted; for the non-monotheistic traditions, the universe is so structured that this happens by law.

On this account, a person's life-conditions in a given lifetime are a function of their moral conduct and character in a previous lifetime, and so on back forever. The resulting situation is perfectly analogous to that in which the existence of one dependent thing is explained by reference to another, and that to another, without ever coming to anything that exists independently. In this latter case, one always has, by hypothesis, an answer to 'What caused this particular thing to exist?' but never, in principle, an answer to the question 'Why does anything at all exist?' In the former (reincarnation and karma) case, there is always, by hypothesis, an answer to the question 'Why does this particular evil exist?' but never, in principle, an answer to the question 'Why is there any evil at all?' The reincarnation and karma explanation simply assumes the existence of evil, and then goes on to present its blueprint for explaining the fact that evils are distributed as they are. Of course, it involves the general claim that there are such explanations without providing specific explanations in particular cases. Hence no explanation of the fact of evil is forthcoming from a reincarnation and karma perspective.

See also: SALVATION; SOUL, NATURE AND IMMORTALITY OF THE

References and further reading

O'Flaherty, W.D. (1985) *Karma and Rebirth in Classical Indian Traditions*, Berkeley, CA: University of California Press. (Collection on the historical, social, religious and philosophical settings of re-incarnation and karma doctrines; includes a long bibliography.)

* Radhakrishnan, S. and Moore, C.A. (eds) (1957) *A Sourcebook in Indian Philosophy*, Princeton, NJ: Princeton University Press. (Still the standard anthology of Indian philosophy.)

Smart, N. (1964) *Doctrine and Argument in Indian Philosophy*, London: Allen & Unwin. (Clear general discussion of Indian philosophy.)

Reichenbach, B. (1990) *The Law of Karma*, London: Macmillan. (A philosophical discussion of karma.)

Warren, H.C. (1962) *Buddhism in Translations*, New York: Atheneum Publications. (Standard collection of Buddhist texts.)

KEITH E. YANDELL

REINHOLD, KARL LEONHARD (1757–1823)

A catalyst in the rise of post-Kantian idealism, Reinhold popularized Kant's critical philosophy by systematizing it in the form of a theory of consciousness. Reinhold shifted from one position to another, however, each time declaring his latest philosophical creed as ultimate. For this he was ridiculed by his more famous contemporaries, including Fichte, Schelling and Hegel, and his historical reputation suffered accordingly. Recent re-evaluations, however, suggest that there was considerable coherence to his philosophical wanderings.

A sometime priest who converted to Protestantism, active freemason and popular teacher, Reinhold advocated political intervention in the promotion of enlightened practices. He steadfastly defended the French Revolution.

A secret promoter of the Austrian Enlightenment while still a priest and monk in Vienna, Reinhold eventually left the Church and fled to Protestant Germany in 1783. There he continued his campaign against 'monkish' obscurantism, mostly in C.M. Wieland's journal, *Der Teutsche Merkur*. Appointed to the chair of Kantian philosophy at Jena in 1787, he later took up a professorship in Kiel (1794), where he remained – popular teacher and voluminous writer – to the end.

In 1784 Reinhold defined the Enlightenment as the effort to accelerate through political and educational means the otherwise slow natural advance of the masses towards rational life. This advance, though retarded by priestly and political reaction, is unstoppable. It is also subject to an inner logic discernible in the history of metaphysics – itself only a reflective, specialized expression of common sense. But metaphysics, Reinhold later repeatedly declared, had run the full gamut of logically possible one-sided views concerning truth. The time was therefore ripe for the revelation of the one true position that would reconcile all past ones.

In 1786–7, this belief led Reinhold, in the midst of the Jacobi–Mendelssohn dispute (see JACOBI, F.H. §2), to portray Kant as the philosopher who, in response to the needs of the time, had cut across old dividing lines with a few new and bold distinctions. Kant was therefore capable of reconciling such extreme opposites as Mendelssohn's rationalism and Jacobi's faith, thereby satisfying the full aspirations of common sense (see KANT, I. §4; MENDELSSOHN, M. §1).

Reinhold drew this portrait of Kant in *Der Teutsche Merkur*, in eight 'Kantian Letters' which won immediate popularity for critical philosophy and notoriety for himself. However, since Reinhold held that truth cannot but be recognized and accepted as such by all immediately upon display, he had to explain the failure of critique to win universal following. The reason was that Kant – a pioneer – had neither declared his principles explicitly nor systematized his philosophy accordingly. To remedy this failure, in 1789 Reinhold developed a theory of the faculty of representation in which he expounded Kantianism in 88 propositions, all based on a statement of supposedly the most simple fact of consciousness, to wit: 'Representation is distinguished in consciousness by the subject from both subject and object, and is referred to both' (*Beyträg* 1790: 167). Reinhold's new theory, though presented as a systematization of Kant's position, differed from it substantially. Behind its veneer of deductions, it was a description of presumed facts of consciousness – a phenomenology rather than critique. Moreover, Reinhold introduced a form–content distinction at every representational level, and explained each level as the product of a reflection upon a more elementary one – the 'form' in one providing the 'content' of the next.

In two volumes of essays (1790–4) Reinhold sought to refine his *Elementarphilosophie* (Philosophy of the elements), as his theory came to be known. There, and in the second of two other volumes of new 'Kantian Letters' (1790–2, the first incorporating the original eight), he also reacted to recent attacks on critical moral theory. He rejected Kant's identification of 'will' with 'reason', and sought to establish in the faculty of choice the basis of 'personality'. However, Reinhold's efforts in the promotion of Kantianism proved counterproductive, precipitating G.E. Schulze's successful sceptical attack on critical philosophy in 1792.

But Reinhold began to study Fichte's new *Wissenschaftslehre* (which his own theory had influenced) and, for a brief period, even declared himself for it (1797) (see FICHTE, J.G. §3). He then tried, in 1799, to position himself between Jacobi and Fichte by defining philosophy as the artificial (religiously neutral) conceptual reconstruction of truths already possessed through faith, only to turn his attention to the 'rational realism' of C.G. Bardili. Bardili held that it is possible by means of a reflection upon pure thought to establish the first predicates of 'being as such', and the necessity of a First Being. But the abstract categories thereby obtained only yield a science of nature when applied to a matter that must be presupposed independently of all thought. Reinhold refined and defended this dualism in six volumes of essays (1801–3). After 1800, however, he gravitated ever closer to Jacobi, criticizing idealism and expressing sympathy for the synthesis of empirical and critical elements which younger philosophers such as F. Bouterwek, in part inspired by Jacobi, were formulating. Reinhold accepted Jacobi's claim that the first access to truth is through faith, but staunchly defended reason's independent ability to grasp and express this truth scientifically.

Reinhold sided with Jacobi in the latter's final attack on Schelling (see JACOBI, F.H. §3). In 1812, inspired by Jacobi and indirectly by the later J.G. HAMANN (§2), he tried his hand at a meta-critique of reason by means of an analysis of language. He attributed all past philosophical errors to confusions (to which reason is held hostage) which are inherent in accepted usages of language. Critique must dispel these confusions. Accordingly Reinhold identified eight 'families of words', in an effort to define the relations of meaning that obtain within each and the irreversible (linear and non-dialectical) order connecting one group to the other. True to his Enlightenment heritage, Reinhold assumed that underlying language is a natural system of universal meanings which now lie hidden under the sedimentation of historically determined usages, but which, once brought to consciousness as they inevitably shall, cannot but be universally recognized and accepted.

See also: ENLIGHTENMENT, CONTINENTAL; GERMAN IDEALISM

List of works

Reinhold, K.L. (1977) *Karl Leonhard Reinhold: Schriften zur Religionskritik und Aufklärung, 1782–1784*, ed. Z. Batscha, Bremen: Jacobi. (Includes Reinhold's anonymous polemical reviews of theological literature written in 1782–3 while he was still a monk in Vienna, the 1784 essay on Enlightenment and an informative introductory study.)

—— (1786–7) 'Briefe über die Kantische Philosophie' (Letters Concerning Kant's Philosophy), *Der Teutscher Merkur* 3 (1786): 99–127, 127–41; 1 (1787): 3–39, 117–42; 2 (1787): 167–85; 3 (1787): 67–88, 142–65, 247–78. (The original eight 'Kantian Letters' that helped popularize Kant's *Critique*.)

—— (1789a) 'Über das bisherige Schicksal der Kantischen Philosophie' (On Kantian Philosophy's Present Fortune), *Der Teutscher Merkur* 2: 3–37, 113–35. (An attempt to place Kant's *Critique* in a historical context; republished by Reinhold in various places.)

—— (1789b) *Versuch einer neuen Theorie des menschlichen Vorstellungsvermögen* (Attempt at a New Theory of the Human Faculty of Representation), Prague and Jena: Widtmann & Mauke. (Reinhold's attempt at systematizing Kant's philosophy. Reprinted 1963, Darmstadt: wissenschaftliche Buchgesellschaft.)

—— (1790, 1792) *Briefe über die Kantische Philosophie* (Letters Concerning Kantian Philosophy), Leipzig: Göschen, 2 vols. (Two volumes of twelve 'Kantian Letters' each. The first volume, which incorporates the original eight Letters, deals with theoretical issues; the second, with moral issues. Both volumes republished 1923, ed. R. Schmidt, Leipzig: Reclam.)

—— (1790, 1794) *Beyträge zur Berichtigung bisheriger Mißverständnisse der Philosophen* (Contributions to the Correction of Present Misunderstandings by the Philosophers), Jena: Mauke, 2 vols. (Two volumes of essays – the first containing some refinements of the Theory of Representation and Reinhold's reaction to his critics; the second, reflections on a variety of topics including common sense, scepticism, morality, religion and taste.)

—— (1791) *Über das Fundament des philosophischen Wissens* (Concerning the Foundation of Philosophical Knowledge), Jena: Mauke; republished 1978, ed. W.H. Schrader, Hamburg, Meiner. (The translation of a substantial excerpt is included in G. di Giovanni and H.S. Harris (1985) *Between Kant and Hegel: Texts in the Development of Post-Kantian Idealism*, Albany, NY: State University of New York.)

—— (1797) *Auswahl vermischter Schriften* (Miscellaneous Writings: A Selection), Jena: Mauke, 2 vols. (Reinhold declared himself for Fichte's *Wissenschaftslehre* in the Preface of vol. 2.)

—— (1799) *Über die Paradoxien der neuesten Philosophie* (Concerning the Paradoxes of the Most Recent Philosophy), Hamburg: Perthes. (Reflections on post-critical idealism.)

—— (1799) *Sendschreiben an J.C. Lavater und J.G.*

Fichte über den Glauben an Gott (Letter to Lavater and Fichte Concerning Faith in God), Hamburg: Perthes. (Reflections on the relation of faith to reason occasioned by the then ongoing dispute regarding atheism. Critical edition in *Fichte-Gesamtausgabe*, ed. R. Lauth and H. Gliwitzky, Stuttgart/Bad Cannstat: Frommann, 1972, 3: 3.)

—— (1801–3) *Beyträge zur leichtern Übersicht der Philosophie beym Anfange des 19. Jahrhunderts* (Contributions to an Easier Overall View of Philosophy at the Beginning of the Nineteenth Century), Hamburg: Perthes, 6 vols. (These volumes include essays on a variety of topical subjects, some polemical tracts against idealism and Reinhold's exposition of Bardili's philosophy.)

—— (1812) *Grundlegung einer Synonymik für den allgemeinen Sprachgebrauch in den philosophischen Wissenschaften* (Groundwork of a Synonymy for Universal Language Usage in the Philosophical Sciences), Kiel: Schmidt. (Reinhold's linguistic turn. Reprint in preparation, Frankfurt/Main: Minerva.)

—— (1816) *Das menschliche Erkenntnißvermögen, aus dem Gesichtspunkte des durch die Wortsprache vermittelten Zusammenhangs zwischen der Sinnlichkeit und dem Denkvermögen* (The Human Cognitive Faculty, from the Standpoint of the Connection between Sensibility and the Faculty of Thought as Mediated through Language), Kiel: Academische Buchhandlung. (Reprint in preparation, Frankfurt am Main: Minerva.)

Lauth, R., Heller, E. and Hiller, K. (eds) (1983) *Karl Leonhard Reinhold: Korrespondenz 1773–1788*, Stuttgart/Bad Cannstatt: Frommann, Holzbook, Österreichische Akademie der Wissenschaften. (The first of a planned six-volume edition of Reinhold's correspondence.)

Schonborn, A. von (1991) *Karl Leonhard Reinhold: Eine annotierte Bibliographie*, Stuttgart/Bad Cannstatt. (A critical bibliography of authenticated works with a very informative introductory study.)

References and further reading

* Bardili, C.G. (1800) *Grundriß der ersten Logik gereiniget von den Irrhümmern bisherigen Logiken überhaupt, der kantischen insbesondere; keine Kritik sondern eine Medicina mentis, brauchbar hauptsächlich für Deutschlands kritische Philosophie* (Outline of First Logic, Purified of the Mistakes of All Prior Logics, the Kantian in Particular; Not a Critique But a *Medicina mentis*, of use Chiefly for Germany's Critical Philosophy), Stuttgart. (Reinhold studied this text even before its official publication date of 1800. It was instrumental to his conversion to 'rational realism'. Reprinted 1970, Brussels: Culture et Civilisation.)

Beiser, F.C. (1987) *The Fate of Reason*, Cambridge: Harvard. (Includes a very readable chapter on the *Elementarphilosophie*.)

Bondeli, M. (1995) *Das Anfangsproblem bei Karl Leonhard Reinhold* (The problem of a beginning in K.L. Reinhold), Frankfurt/Main: Vittorio Klostermann. (Scholarly, detailed presentation of the development of Reinhold's philosophy from 1789 to 1803.)

* Bouterwek, F. (1799) *Idee einer Apodiktic. Ein Beytrag zur menschlichen Selbstverständigung und zur Entscheidung des Streits über Metaphysik, kritische Philosophie und Skepticismus* (Idea of an Apodictic. A Contribution to Human Self-Understanding and to the Resolution of the Conflict over Metaphysics, Critical Philosophy and Scepticism), Halle: Renger, 2 vols. (An example of traditional empiricism modified by the importation of Kantian critical elements.)

Breazeale, D. (1981–2) 'Between Kant and Fichte: Karl Leonhard Reinhold's "Elementary Philosophy"', *The Review of Metaphysics* 35 (4): 785–821. (Very readable and informative.)

Cloeren, J.-J. (1972) 'Philosophie als Sprachkritik bei K.L. Reinhold. Interpretive Bemerkungen zu seiner Spätphilosophie' (Philosophy as Critique of Language in K.L. Reinhold. Interpretive Comments on His Late Philosophy), *Kant-Studien* 63 (2): 225–36. (An interpretation of Reinhold's late linguistic turn.)

Giovanni, G. di (1985) 'The Facts of Consciousness', in G. di Giovanni and H.S. Harris, *Between Kant and Hegel: Texts in the Development of Post-Kantian Idealism*, Albany, NY: State University of New York, 1985, 2–50. (Reinhold in the context of the early reception of Kantian Critique.)

Klemmt, A. (1958) *Karl Leonhard Reinholds Elementarphilosophie* (Karl Leonhard Reinhold's Philosophy of the Elements), Hamburg: Meiner. (A detailed and readable study of the 'Philosophy of the Elements' as transition point from Kantian Critique to subsequent Idealism.)

—— (1961) 'Die philosophische Entwicklung Karl Leonhard Reinholds nach 1800' (Karl Leonhard Reinhold's Philosophical Development After 1800), *Zeitschrift fur philosophische Forschung* 15 (1–2): 79–101, 250–77. (Reinhold's development after 1800.)

König, A. (1980) *Denkformen in der Erkenntnis. Die Urteilstafel Immanuel Kants in der Kritik der reinen Vernunft und in Karl Leonhard Reinhold Versuch einer neuen Theorie des menschlichen Vorstellungsvermögen* (Forms of Thought in

Cognition. Immanuel Kant's Table of Judgments in the *Critique of Pure Reason* and in Karl Leonhard Reinhold's *Attempt at a New Theory of the Human Faculty of Representation*), Bonn: Bouvier. (A technical examination of Reinhold's difference with respect to Kant.)

Lauth, R. (ed.) (1974) *Philosophie aus einem Prinzip Karl Leonhard Reinhold* (Philosophy on One Principle: Karl Leonhard Reinhold), Bonn: Bouvier. (Seven important specialized essays and a catalogue of letters.)

Pupi, A. (1966) *La formazione della filosofia di K.L. Reinhold, 1784–1794* (The Fashioning of K.L. Reinhold's Philosophy, 1784–1794), Milan: Vita & Pensiero. (A careful and readable historical study of Reinhold's Kantian period, with special attention to the debates and the journal literature of the day.)

Reichner, W. (1976) *Rekonstrucktion oder Reproduktion des Grundes. Die Begründung der Philosophie als Wissenschaft durch Kant und Reinhold* (Ground Reconstruction v. Ground Reproduction. The Grounding of Philosophy as Science by Kant and Reinhold), Bonn: Bouvier. (Kant's and Reinhold's contrasting strategies in the founding of science.)

* Schulze, G.E. (1792) *Aenesidemus oder über die Fundamente der von dem Herrn Prof. Reinhold in Jena gelieferte Elementar-Philosophie. Nebst einer Vertheidigung des Skepticismus gegen die Anmaa ungen der Vernunftkritik* (Aenesidemus or Concerning the Foundations of The Philosophy of the Elements Delivered in Jena by Prof. Reinhold, Together with a Defence of Scepticism Against the Pretensions of the Critique of Reason), n.p.p.; substantial excerpts trans. G. di Giovanni and H.S. Harris in *Between Kant and Hegel: Texts in the Development of Post-Kantian Idealism*, Albany, NY: State University of New York, 1985. (The attack on Critical Philosophy precipitated by Reinhold's attempt at reforming it.)

Valenza, P. (1994) *Reinhold e Hegel. Ragione storica e inizio assoluto della filosofia* (Reinhold and Hegel. Historical Reason and Philosophy's Absolute Beginning), Padua: CEDAM. (An instructive study of possible points of contact between the philosophy of history of Reinhold and of Hegel.)

GEORGE DI GIOVANNI

RELATIVISM

Someone who holds that nothing is simply good, but only good for someone or from a certain point of view, holds a relativist view of goodness. Protagoras, with his dictum that 'man is the measure of all things', is often taken to be an early relativist. Quite common are relativism about aesthetic value, about truth in particular areas such as religious truth, and (arising from anthropological theory) about rationality. There are also a number of ways of answering the question 'relative to what?' Thus something might be said to be relative to the attitudes or faculties of each individual, or to a cultural group, or to a species. Relativism therefore has many varieties; some are very plausible, others verge on incoherence.

1 **Grades of relativism**
2 **The credibility of relativism**

1 Grades of relativism

What people believe is affected by their circumstances. A twentieth-century business executive will probably not hold the same views on morality as a medieval peasant, nor a medieval monk the same views on the nature of the physical world as a twentieth-century physicist. An Indian is unlikely to have the same religious opinions as an Italian. This rather commonplace point is hardly exciting enough to deserve the name of 'relativism'. Admittedly, some have concluded from it that there is no one truth about these things, only what seems true from certain perspectives. This argument has proved especially appealing in the case of morality, but it is quite certainly invalid. From the fact that two people hold (even predictably hold) different opinions on a question, it does not follow that there is no truth of the matter – only that, if there is, at least one of them has got it wrong.

But at least the idea that there is no one truth about things sounds closer to something which we might pointfully call 'relativism'. And perhaps there are in some cases (morality looks, *prima facie*, a more promising candidate than physics) better reasons for believing it than this crude and manifestly invalid reasoning. For suppose two people each set themselves to think of a moral code, conformity to which will, in their differing cultural and economic environments, result in as much good as possible – may we not expect that the codes will differ? In widely differing circumstances, the same practices may have widely differing results.

The (moral) relativism which this argument yields is still a rather dilute one. It is fully compatible with there being utterly objective moral principles on which both our protagonists agree. The difference arises only when each asks what these principles dictate when applied to their own situation. Similarly, we can imagine circumstances in which certain procedures were irrational (in the sense of being unlikely to lead to true beliefs) which are rational in ours. In a society whose members were much more wary and suspicious of strangers than they are in our own, it might be irrational to believe information from anybody one does not know. Again, the (epistemic) relativism here is superficial.

A fully-blown relativism denies that there is any such deeper unity beneath the diversity. There is simply what *they* consider right (or rational), and what *we* consider right, what passes for true among them, and what so passes among us.

2 The credibility of relativism

Relativism in its strong form is a version of anti-realism, and how credible it is will depend very much on what we are asked to be relativists about (see REALISM AND ANTIREALISM). Few will have difficulty about 'gastronomic relativism': whether peaches taste nice or not is just a matter of how individuals respond to eating peaches. Many will not object to relativism about colour, according to which the colour of something is a matter of how an observer's visual system responds to it (see SECONDARY QUALITIES). Even if this does involve accepting that in some sense grass is not 'really' green, we can still react to colours, enjoy certain combinations of colour, attach emotive associations to colours, stop at red traffic lights, and in short go on as we always have.

With moral relativism things are more difficult. To hold that something is wrong for you, or in your society, but perfectly permissible for someone else, or in their society, and that *that is all there is to be said about it*, comes very close to giving up one's own moral view. Are you really to think that there is nothing morally objectionable going on in that other society, just because it is that society? How are you to judge its members if their conduct comes to affect you? An uninvolved Olympian spectator (this may be why relativism sometimes seems easier while we are philosophizing!) might be able to see that there is no more to it than the different reactions and feelings of members of the two societies, but whether that can be believed from within the melée – even if it is actually true – is quite a different question.

Trickier still is the relativist doctrine that 'true' always really means 'true-by-the-standards-of-X', where X is some individual or group. An example might be a theory which understands truth in terms of what it is satisfactory to believe (see TRUTH, PRAG-MATIC THEORY OF). Such a theory allows that truth may differ from group to group or from person to person, since social conditions, and individual psychology, may affect the satisfaction to be had from a given belief. Proponents of this kind of theory face

various problems: have they anything at all to say to someone who questions whether the standards adopted by their chosen X are good ones? And are they offering their theory of truth as being itself true, or merely 'true-by-the-standards-of-X'?

One response, favoured by many postmodernists, is to flit ironically from perspective to perspective, espousing none (see POSTMODERNISM). Another response would be to say nothing. How many postmodernists have adopted this latter alternative is, from the nature of the case, hard to determine.

See also: ANTHROPOLOGY, PHILOSOPHY OF; EPISTEMIC RELATIVISM; MORAL RELATIVISM; PLURALISM; PROTAGORAS; RATIONALITY AND CULTURAL RELATIVISM; SOCIAL RELATIVISM

References and further reading

Barnes, J. (1979) *The Presocratic Philosophers*, London and New York: Routledge & Kegan Paul, 1982. (Chapters 23 and 24 discuss some ancient forms of relativism, moral and epistemic, including that ascribed to Protagoras.)

Hollis, M. (1994) *The Philosophy of Social Science*, Cambridge: Cambridge University Press. (Chapter 11 provides an introduction to relativism about rationality. Quite accessible, given that this is not an easy topic.)

Morton, A. (1996) *Philosophy in Practice: An Introduction to the Main Questions*, Oxford: Blackwell. (Written in quite an unusual style for a philosophy textbook, with 'reader-participation'. See pages 105–23 for an introduction to moral relativism.)

Williams, B.A.O. (1972) *Morality: An Introduction to Ethics*, Cambridge: Cambridge University Press. (Pages 34–9 offer a brisk and hostile introduction to moral relativism.)

EDWARD CRAIG

RELATIVISM, EPISTEMIC *see* EPISTEMIC RELATIVISM

RELATIVISM, MORAL *see* MORAL RELATIVISM

RELATIVITY THEORY *see*
General relativity, philosophical responses to

RELATIVITY THEORY, PHILOSOPHICAL SIGNIFICANCE OF

There are two parts to Albert Einstein's relativity theory, the special theory published in 1905 and the general theory published in its final mathematical form in 1915. The special theory is a direct development of the Galilean relativity principle in classical Newtonian mechanics. This principle affirms that Newton's laws of motion hold not just when the motion is described relative to a reference frame at rest in absolute space, but also relative to any reference frame in uniform translational motion relative to absolute space. The class of frames relative to which Newton's law of motion are valid are referred to as inertial frames. It follows that no mechanical experiment can tell us which frame is at absolute rest, only the relative motion of inertial frames is observable. The Galilean relativity principle does not hold for accelerated motion, and also it does not hold for electromagnetic phenomena, in particular the propagation of light waves as governed by Maxwell's equations. Einstein's special theory of relativity reformulated the mathematical transformations for space and time coordinates between inertial reference frames, replacing the Galilean transformations by the so-called Lorentz transformations (they had previously been discovered in an essentially different way by H.A. Lorentz in 1904) in such a way that electromagnetism satisfied the relativity principle. But the classical laws of mechanics no longer did so. Einstein next reformulated the laws of mechanics so as to make them conform to his new relativity principle. With Galilean relativity, spatial intervals, the simultaneity of events and temporal durations, did not depend on the inertial frame, although, of course, velocities were frame-dependent. In Einstein's relativity the first three now become frame-dependent, or 'relativized' as we may express it, while for the fourth, namely velocity, there exists a unique velocity, that of the propagation of light in vacuo, whose magnitude c is invariant, that is, the same for all inertial frames. It can be argued that c also represents the maximum speed with which any causal process can be propagated. Moreover in Einstein's new mechanics inertial mass m becomes a relative notion and is associated via the equation

$m = E/c^2$ with any form of energy E. Reciprocally inertial mass can be understood as equivalent to a corresponding energy mc^2.

In the general theory Einstein ostensibly sought to extend the relativity principle to accelerated motions of the reference frame by employing an equivalence principle which claimed that it was impossible to distinguish observationally between the presence of a gravitational field and the acceleration of a reference frame. Einstein here elevated into a fundamental principle the known but apparently accidental numerical equality of the inertial and the gravitational mass of a body (which accounts for the fact that bodies move with the same acceleration in a gravitational field, independent of their inertial mass). By extending the discussion to gravitational fields which could be locally, but not globally, transformed away by a change of reference frame, Einstein was led to a new theory of gravitation, modifying Newton's theory of gravitation, which could explain a number of observed phenomena for which the Newtonian theory was inadequate. This involved a law (Einstein's field equations) relating the distribution of matter in spacetime to geometrical features of spacetime associated with its curvature, considered as a four-dimensional manifold. The path of an (uncharged spinless) particle moving freely in the curved spacetime was a geodesic (the generalized analogue in a curved manifold of a straight line in a flat manifold).

Einstein's theories have important repercussions for philosophical views on the nature of space and time, and their relation to issues of causality and cosmology, which are still the subject of debate.

1 The Lorentz transformations
2 The relativity of simultaneity, duration and length
3 Causality and the conventionality of simultaneity
4 General covariance
5 Determinism and substantivalism in general relativity
6 Mach's principle
7 Supersubstantivalism

1 The Lorentz transformations

Consider two inertial reference frames K and K', where the spatial origin of the K'-frame moves along the positive X-axis with velocity v as viewed from the K-frame. If we introduce Cartesian spatial coordinates x, y, z and a time coordinate t to locate some arbitrary event relative to the K-frame, and similarly use x', y', z' and t' to locate the event relative to the K'-frame, where we suppose the spatial axes are parallel in the two frames, and the origins of the frames coincide at time $t = t' = 0$, then the classical

Galilean transformations (see MECHANICS, CLASSI-CAL §1) read:

$$x' = x - vt$$
$$y' = y$$
$$z' = z$$
$$t' = t \qquad (1)$$

The corresponding Lorentz transformations of special relativity are:

$$x' = \frac{1}{\sqrt{1 - v^2/c^2}}(x - vt)$$
$$y' = y$$
$$z' = z$$
$$t' = \frac{1}{\sqrt{1 - v^2/c^2}}\left(t - \frac{vx}{c^2}\right) \qquad (2)$$

where c is the magnitude of the velocity of light *in vacuo*.

For sufficiently small values of v/c the Lorentz transformations are approximately the same as the Galilean transformations.

Einstein argued for (2) by considering the propagation of a spherical light wave centred on the origin of the K and K' frames at the time $t = t' = 0$. He employed two principles:

(i) the 'light constancy principle', that the velocity of light was a constant independent of the motion of the source; and

(ii) the 'special principle of relativity', that the laws of nature are invariant (take the same form) in all inertial reference frames.

From (i) and (ii) Einstein inferred:

(iii) the 'light invariance principle', that the velocity of light was the same in any direction and had the same numerical magnitude as viewed from the K and K'-frames.

By invoking various other 'homogeneity' and 'symmetry' properties of space and time, Einstein proceeded to derive the Lorentz transformation equations. Since Einstein's 1905 paper there have been many other derivations of the Lorentz transformations from various combinations of plausible principles. In particular it has been argued that the principle of relativity only licences a weak form of the light invariance principle, committed just to invariance of the shape of the light wave, not also the magnitude of the light velocity, but it turns out that the Lorentz transformations can still be derived without invoking the strong form of the light invariance principle. Returning to Einstein's own derivation, the light constancy principle already follows from assuming that light propagates in accordance with Maxwell's equations (see MAXWELL, J.C.; OPTICS §1; ELECTRODYNAMICS), and the light invariance principle would follow from assuming the invariance of Maxwell's equations. But Einstein did not want to assume the full validity of Maxwell's equations, but rather to base his relativity theory on specific principles that he thought would survive possible alterations to Maxwell's theory that would be engendered by the quantum theory.

It is easily checked that the light invariance principle is satisfied by the Lorentz transformation equations, whereas the Galilean transformations clearly violate it. It also turns out that the full set of Maxwell's equations *are* invariant under the Lorentz transformations although, as we have just mentioned, this was not built into Einstein's derivation.

H. Minkowski (1909) gave a geometrical interpretation of the Lorentz transformations in terms of a four-dimensional geometry equipped with an indefinite metric, which defined the four-dimensional interval between two punctiform events located at x_1, y_1, z_1, t_1 and x_2, y_2, z_2, t_2 relative to the K-frame as:

$$s = (t_2 - t_1)^2 - \frac{1}{c^2}\left[(x_2 - x_1)^2 + (y_2 - y_1)^2 + (z_2 - z_1)^2\right]$$

The events are said to be time-like separated, light-like separated, or space-like separated according as s is greater than zero, equal to zero or less than zero.

The metric corresponding to this interval is said to have Lorentzian signature, which distinguishes it from a four-dimensional *Euclidean* space, where the interval would be positive definite.

The interval between two events is then invariant under the Lorentz transformations. That $s = 0$ corresponds to the fact that the two events are connectable by a light signal. Time-like separated events are connectable by a signal travelling slower than light, while for space-like separated events they can only be connected by signals travelling faster than light. If we adopt a limiting velocity principle and take the velocity of light *in vacuo* to be the maximum velocity with which any signal can be propagated, then space-like separated events cannot be connected by a signal. The status of the limiting velocity principle *vis-à-vis* the light invariance principle will be discussed in §3.

If connectibility by a physically propagating signal is identified with causal connectibility, then the causal structure imposed on events in Minkowski spacetime comprises a double light-cone constructed at any point P in spacetime which divides the whole of spacetime into the locations of three classes of event: those that can be causally influenced by an event at P, bounded by the future-directed light-cone; the events which can causally effect an event at P, bounded by the past-directed light-cone, points on the light-cone being connectable with P by light signals; while the third region comprises the locations of events external to the light-cone, which are causally isolated from an event at P (see SPACETIME §2). These facts about Minkowski spacetime have been employed by philosophers such as Hans Reichenbach and Adolf Grünbaum to provide a causal underpinning for Einstein's light invariance principle (see §3).

2 The relativity of simultaneity, duration and length

From the point of view of the Galilean transformations all inertial reference frames agree on which events are simultaneous with one another. The simultaneity relationship is an equivalence relation which partitions the set of all actual and possible events in spacetime into equivalence classes, which are indexed by the absolute time at which they occur. Absolute time can be understood as the linearly ordered quotient set associated with this equivalence relation, corresponding to Leibniz's order of succession, while the equivalence classes themselves, the spatial slices at a given time, correspond to Leibniz's order of coexistence (see LEIBNIZ, G.W. §11).

In the case of the Lorentz transformations, however, simultaneity becomes a three-place relation, the third place being filled by the inertial reference frame relative to which the simultaneity of events is being assessed. Thus, referring to the transformation equations, (2), the locus of events simultaneous with the origin according to the K'-frame, that is, events satisfying the condition $t' = 0$, correspond according to the K-frame to the locus $t = vx/c^2$, which is a straight line inclined at a slope v/c^2 to the X-axis, which is the locus $t = 0$ of events judged to be simultaneous with the origin by the K-frame (for simplicity we ignore the y and z spatial dimensions for the time being). This has immediate repercussions for reconciling the A-theory of time (see TIME §1) with the special theory of relativity. For the A-theorists the present is a distinguished simultaneity class of events which alone are co-real. The future comprises unrealized possibilities, the past, events that were actual when their occurrence coincided with the then present, but are no longer actual now. According to special relativity theory, if we assume that the relation of co-reality is *not* frame-dependent, then it is easy to prove that all events in spacetime are co-real. This arises simply because if we take any two events A and B in spacetime there always exists a possible event C which is simultaneous with A according to one frame of reference K and simultaneous with B according to another frame of reference K'. If A occurs now, then

C is co-real with A according to K; so C is now real, while B is co-real with C, according to K'; so B is also real now, but since B is an arbitrary event it follows that all events in spacetime are real now.

Such an argument has also been used to claim that special relativity is inconsistent with indeterminism, since the occurrence of all events has a determinate truth-value now. The latter argument can be resisted by distinguishing determinateness from determinism (see DETERMINISM AND INDETERMINISM). The former argument shows, however, that special relativity is inconsistent with a unique global frame-independent notion of becoming and hence is fundamentally opposed to the underlying intuition of the A-theorists, which requires a uniquely distinguished present. The best that can be done in rescuing a notion of becoming is to relativize it to individual time-like worldlines, but the local 'nows' cannot be assembled into a global 'now'.

We turn now to the relativity of temporal duration. Reverting to the transformation equations, (2), it follows immediately that a time interval T' assessed by a clock at rest in the frame K' is assigned an interval T by the frame K, where T and T' are related by

$$T = \frac{1}{\sqrt{1 - v^2/c^2}} T' \qquad (3)$$

So the moving clock suffers a dilatation of its time-scale in accordance with equation (3).

But it also follows from (2) that clocks stationary in the K-frame suffer the *same* dilatation in time-scale as assessed relative to the K'-frame. This reciprocity of clock dilatation I shall refer to as the *clock paradox* of special relativity. How can two clocks each run slow as assessed by each other? It has even been claimed that the clock paradox shows special relativity to be a logically inconsistent theory. But the resolution is simple when proper account is taken of the relativity of simultaneity. Each clock is not being assessed by the other clock in isolation, but only in conjunction with the relevant standard of simultaneity, which changes according to which reference frame is being used to assess the rate of the clock.

The clock paradox is closely related to another famous paradox in special relativity, the twin paradox. Here one considers two twins (biological clocks), one of which remains at rest in the K-frame, the other moves away and then returns to meet up again with the stationary twin. On comparing clock readings (biological ageing), the stay-at-home twin shows a greater lapse of time than the travelling twin. This follows from the time dilatation formula of equation (3). But from the reciprocity of time dilatation would it not follow that, describing the situation from a reference frame in which the traveller is at rest, the original stay-at-home twin would be the younger when they meet up again? Once more a logical contradiction seems to threaten.

The resolution of the twin paradox arises from noting that there is no single *inertial* reference frame relative to which the travelling twin is always at rest. And the reciprocity result only holds between inertial frames. Does this mean that the resolution of the twin paradox requires consideration of accelerated (that is, non-inertial) reference frames for a complete elucidation, as has been widely claimed in the literature? We shall return to this matter in §3.

Just as temporal duration becomes a relative notion in special relativity, the same is also true of spatial lengths. In place of the dilatation formula, (3), it is easy to derive a corresponding contraction formula for length:

$$L = \sqrt{1 - v^2/c^2} \, L'$$

where L' is the length of a moving rod as assessed by K', and L the length assessed by K.

But the relativization of simultaneity, temporal duration and spatial length does not mean that *all* spatial-temporal quantities are relativized to reference frames. The central idea in special relativity is that there is a unique velocity, whose magnitude is the *same* as assessed by all inertial referenced frames. In its geometrical interpretation by Minkowski, the invariant notion in the geometry is the interval s, and relativity theory should more accurately be called the invariance theory of the interval, that is, the theory of transformations under which the interval is invariant. The attempt to use Einstein's theory to motivate a general thesis of the relativity of local particulars to their global context, as in the philosophy of Alfred Whitehead, is thus seen to be misguided (see WHITEHEAD, A.N. §3).

The question is often asked, do clocks really run slower, or rods really contract, when they move, or do they only *appear* to do so? The answer according to the presentation of the theory we are adopting in this section (but for a quite different answer see §3), is that if the behaviour of the clocks and rods is governed by the laws of *relativistic* mechanics, then it is a consequence of those laws that clocks will run slower, and rods contract, as a result of the detailed mechanics of what happens when they are suitably set in motion. There is thus a harmonious consistency between relativistic kinematics and relativistic mechanics. But at a deeper level we may ask, are the moving rods and clocks *measuring* relativized features of space and time, so is special relativity a theory about space and time *per se*, or is it a theory about

how measuring instruments behave when in motion, and not a revision of our concepts of space and time at all? In particular, does the invariance of the speed of light, as measured by different observers in relative motion to each other, arise as a remarkable conspiracy of compensating effects in the instruments which prevent us from ever being able to know our state of absolute motion? The thoroughgoing relativist rejects such conspiracies, and moves directly to new metaphysical theses about the nature of space and time. The compensating theories were espoused by H.A. Lorentz and H. Poincaré and in that sense the real conceptual revolution must be ascribed to Einstein. But was Einstein genuinely a relativist in the sense we have been describing in this section? In the next section a quite different outlook on the theory will be described, the origins of which can also be traced to Einstein's 1905 paper.

3 Causality and the conventionality of simultaneity

Einstein (1915) recognized that the light invariance principle (see §1) could not be directly verified by measurement. With a single clock it would be possible to measure the average two-way speed of light by emitting a light signal at spatial location A (marked as event a in the figure) reflecting it at location B (event b) and noting the time of the event a'' when the signal returns to A. If d is the spatial separation of A and B, then the average two-way speed of light would be equal to $2d/t_{a''} - t_a$, where the time interval $t_{a''} - t_a$ between the events a and a'' is measured by a single clock stationary at A throughout the experiment. But how could we measure the one-way speed of light from A to B or from B to A? This would require recording the time of event b by a clock located at B. But this means we would first of all have to synchronize the clocks at A and B. Einstein assumed that this was done by defining b to be simultaneous with the event a', midway in time, according to the clock at A, between a and a''. This is equivalent to assuming that light propagates with the same speed from A to B as from B to A. But Einstein states that this is a matter of *definition*, the one-way speed cannot be measured independently of a decision as to how to synchronize spatially separated clocks.

The line of argument was further developed by Hans REICHENBACH (1928) who claimed that one could set

$$t_b = t_a + \varepsilon(t_{a''} - t_a) \tag{5}$$

where the parameter ε has any value between 0 and 1, the choice being a matter of convention, the Einstein convention corresponding to the choice $\varepsilon = 1/2$. What Reichenbach is claiming then is that b can be

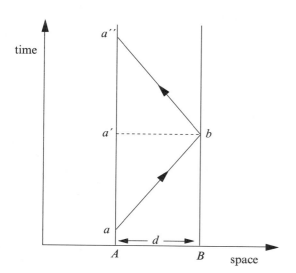

time

a''

a' - - - - - - - - - - - - - b

a

A $\longleftrightarrow$ d $\longrightarrow$ B space

Measuring the speed of light by sending a signal from A to B and back again

identified as simultaneous with any event in the closed interval $[a, a'']$. The conventionality thesis is based, not just on the invariance of the light speed, but on the limiting velocity principle, that light is the fastest possible signal, thus preventing us from using a faster signal to narrow down the conventional latitude $[a, a'']$ of events at A ascribed simultaneity with the event b at B.

Adolf Grünbaum expressed the matter somewhat differently by defining a concept of topological simultaneity which relates any two events not connectable by a causal signal. Thus any two events at space-like separation are topologically simultaneous. Grünbaum claimed that any more precise identification of distant simultaneity could have no ontological status, since it could not be specified in purely causal terms.

It is easy to show that any two events which are topologically simultaneous can be made metrically simultaneous relative to the Einstein convention applied in a suitably moving inertial reference frame. In other words the range of events, such as $[a, a'']$ in the figure which are topologically simultaneous with the distant event (such as b in the figure) in a *given* frame of reference is exactly the same as the range of events that are declared metrically simultaneous with the distant event in *different* frames of reference, according to the relativity of simultaneity (which, of course, follows from the Einstein convention).

By exploiting the conventionality of simultaneity in a given frame, we can actually eliminate the relativity of simultaneity, temporal duration and length as between different frames! So, from this point of view, these effects are not 'real', as opposed to effects such as the invariance of the average two-way speed of light which do not depend on any simultaneity convention.

The conventionality thesis has attracted considerable discussion in the literature. First it has been argued that Einstein synchrony *is* causally definable. To explain this, we can note that Einstein synchrony in a given reference frame is equivalent to the locus of events which are orthogonal in Minkowski geometry to the world-line of the origin of the reference frame. There has been a series of results in the literature showing that Minkowski-orthogonality is causally definable. So given the world-line of the origin of a reference frame, then Einstein synchrony in that frame can be defined causally. But the conventionalist response is just to note that relative to a given frame we are free to use the causally defined Einstein synchrony relative to a moving frame, but as we have seen this is the same as using nonstandard synchrony in the given frame. The same argument can be used to resist the admitted fact that, in the limit of a sufficiently slow transport of a clock, such transport can be used to pick out Einstein synchrony. But again the conventionalist retorts that in a given frame we can use clock transport which is sufficiently slow relative to a moving frame to establish Einstein synchrony relative to that frame, and hence non-standard synchrony relative to the original frame.

It is a remarkable fact that in four-dimensional Minkowski spacetime the causal structure determines the complete metric structure (*modulo* dilatations). From a point of view which emphasizes the geometrical structure of spacetime the issue of how we coordinatize the spacetime can appear trivial, but from the causal point of view the conventional latitude in simultaneity in a given frame can be regarded as licensing the discordant ascriptions of simultaneity relative to moving frames in the orthodox interpretation.

The limiting velocity principle is a logically stronger principle than the light invariance principle. Indeed the latter is consistent with the possibility of tachyons, particles which *always* travel faster than light. However it has been argued by Redhead that there are inherent limitations in the use of tachyons as a signalling device that arise out of their relativistic properties, and that a suitable emendation of Grünbaum's causal criterion for simultaneity can still yield his same notion of topological simultaneity even in the presence of tachyons.

Finally we may note that the conventionality approach can be usefully applied to the twin paradox, avoiding the use of accelerated reference frames (Redhead 1993).

4 General covariance

We turn now to the development of the general theory of relativity (GR). Historically Einstein believed this to be an extension of the relativity principle from inertial frames to arbitrary reference frames. However subsequent analysis has shown that GR is a quite different sort of theory from special relativity (SR) as we shall now attempt to explain. GR considers spacetime as a semi-Riemannian manifold. By a manifold one means that spacetime can be coordinatized by quadruples of real numbers and this can be carried out in many different ways, different possible coordinates being related by smooth mathematical transformations. This generality of description replaces the coordinates supplied by inertial reference frames and their relationship via the linear transformations of the Lorentz group. Just as in Minkowski spacetime there is defined an invariant interval between events specified by a metric with a Lorentzian signature, so in GR we assume spacetime to be equipped with a variable metric, but still with the property that by a suitable smooth transformation the metric can be reduced to the Lorentzian form at a given spacetime point, but in general this cannot be achieved over a region of spacetime, only at a single point. As first shown by Bernhard Riemann this corresponds to the fact that the manifold is curved as opposed to flat over that region (see SPACE §4; SPACETIME §3). Moreover local inertial reference frames can be introduced relative to which gravitational effects can be (locally) eliminated, and Einstein assumed a generalized equivalence principle according to which *all* physical phenomena reduced to their SR description relative to such frames.

Einstein's field equations can be written symbolically in the form

$$G = \kappa T \qquad (6)$$

where G is a quantity related to the curvature of spacetime and T represents the distribution of matter and electromagnetic energy throughout spacetime; κ is a fundamental constant representing the coupling of the geometry to the distribution of mass/energy.

The fact that the field equations can be written in so-called component form using *any* system of coordinates in spacetime was called by Einstein the principle of general covariance. But the fact that we can redescribe spacetime points in many different ways does not of itself have any physical content, as was pointed out by E. Kretschmann in 1917. In no sense is the principle of general covariance a generalization of the principle of Lorentz invariance that arises in SR.

Important clarification of this issue was introduced by J. Anderson in 1967, who expressed covariance and invariance principles in terms of active point transformations on the spacetime manifold M instead of the passive coordinate transformations. Smooth point transformations are known to mathematicians as diffeomorphisms. Coordinate transformations induce diffeomorphisms according to the rule that corresponding points have the *same* numerical coordinates in the two coordinate systems. A geometric object field 0 is transformed to a new object field, the 'drag-along' of 0, written d_*0, under the diffeomorphism d, where d_*0 evaluated at the transformed point $d(p)$ has the same numerical components with respect to the new coordinate system as does 0 evaluated at p, with respect to the old coordinate system.

Anderson partitions the geometric objects into absolute objects A_i which characterize the fixed geometrical spacetime background and dynamical objects P_j which characterize the physical contents of spacetime. The active version of general covariance then states that if $\langle M, A_i, P_j \rangle$ is a model of a spacetime theory T, then so also is $\langle M, d_*A_i, d_*P_j \rangle$. The diffeomorphisms are said to comprise the covariance group of T. A spacetime symmetry is a diffeomorphism for which $d_*A_i = A_i$, for all values of i. SR then is a spacetime theory in which the Minkowski metric is the absolute object, and the spacetime symmetries are the Lorentz transformations that maintain the invariance of the metric. But in GR there are no absolute objects: the geometrical structure characterized by the metric is itself a dynamical object. In a degenerate sense all diffeomorphisms become spacetime symmetries, so the spacetime symmetry group and the covariance group are formally identical, but the symmetry no longer has physical content just because it provides no *restriction* on the covariance group.

Anderson failed to provide a precise mathematical definition of absolute object, although the intuitive meaning seems clear enough. This technical problem has still not been given a satisfactory solution, despite a notable attempt by Friedman (1983) to clarify Anderson's ideas.

General covariance is not the distinctive feature of GR. Indeed Newtonian gravitational theory can also be expressed in generally covariant form. The distinctive feature of GR is the dynamic interplay between the geometrical structure of the spacetime and the distribution of mass and energy in the spacetime, and the fact that the geometric structures (curvature, affine connection, and so on) are all specifiable in terms of a metric.

Solutions of the Einstein field equations tell us how

the geometric structure (the metric and associated curvature) vary throughout spacetime. Einstein originally augmented the field equations with a principle stating that an uncharged test-particle introduced into the spacetime would follow a geodesic path defined by the metric field. So, in a crisp slogan, a test-particle according to Einstein moves in a straight line in a curved spacetime, whereas in Newtonian gravitational theory it would move in a curved line, in a flat spacetime. In GR the metric does 'double duty', defining both the local spacetime geometry, and also specifying the effective gravitational field acting on a test-particle. It was later shown that the geodesic equation of motion is not an independent principle, but actually is a consequence of the field equations themselves.

5 Determinism and substantivalism in general relativity

We shall now examine a number of arguments concerned with the question of whether GR is consistent with a substantival interpretation of spacetime or with a relationist interpretation (see SPACE §3).

We begin with an ingenious argument that if we assume determinism then GR is inconsistent with a substantivalist conception of spacetime points. Suppose $\langle M, g, T \rangle$ is a model of GR with metric g and mass/energy distribution T. M is the spacetime manifold whose points are treated by the substantivalist as 'individuals' to which properties, the values of the g- and T-fields, can be attributed. Then, according to general covariance, for an arbitrary diffeomorphism d, $\langle M, d_*g, d_*T \rangle$ is also a model. Now consider an arbitrary proper neighbourhood in spacetime, which we refer to as a 'hole', and take for d a diffeomorphism such that it is the identity map everywhere outside the hole, but unequal to the identity inside the hole. The original model and the new model produced by dragging inside the hole with such a so-called hole diffeomorphism are distinct spacetimes, in the sense that inside the hole the same manifold points are associated with different values of the metric field and mass/energy field. But the two models agree everywhere outside the hole, so what has been shown is that there can be no unique physics *inside* the hole that is controlled by the state of affairs *outside* the hole, so determinism in the weakest possible sense is violated.

Notice that the argument fails in SR, where the symmetry group is sufficiently restrictive that hole diffeomorphisms, which are also symmetries of the Minkowski metric, cannot be constructed.

In standard modern text books of GR, spacetimes are specified only up to diffeomorphism on the grounds that diffeomorphically related spacetimes are empirically equivalent. This of course is true, but does not help the thoroughgoing substantivalist, who does not believe that empirical equivalence implies ontological equivalence. The worrying point is that the failure of determinism demonstrated is a pervasive feature of GR spacetimes, and does not depend on the detailed physics of field equations, equations of motion, and so on.

There has been much discussion of the 'hole' argument in the philosophical literature. Possible responses include just accepting the failure of determinism as a metaphysical discovery about GR spacetimes, or giving up a version of substantivalism in which the identity of spacetime points is independent of properties instantiated at those points, and allowing the identity of spacetime points to follow the dragged metric field (metrical essentialism). Another approach is to resort to counterpart theory and refuse to allow that the dragged model refers to the *same* points of spacetime as the original model, but just to counterparts of those points, the counterparthood relation being formulated so as to rescue a definition of determinism that does not fall foul of the hole argument.

No completely satisfactory solution of the problem has been proposed by the substantivalists, but as we shall argue in the next section, this does not mean that GR should be interpreted relationally; that is, that spacetime just expresses relational properties of the contents of spacetime as encoded in the T-field.

6 Mach's principle

In GR we can raise the question: what determines the local inertial reference frames relative to which the laws of SR hold, according to the generalized equivalence principle? The local inertial frames are themselves determined by the g-field, so we can rephrase the question as: what determines the g-field? Looking at Einstein's field equations the possible answer suggests itself that it is the T-field, that is, that matter (or other forms of energy) is the source of the g-field. This would suggest that mass/energy is the ultimate origin of inertia, rather than spacetime itself. If correct this would demonstrate the implementation in GR of the principle enunciated by Ernest Mach in his critique of classical mechanics at the end of the nineteenth century (1893), that inertial effects in a terrestrial laboratory arise from motion relative to the average matter in the whole universe. If the matter were removed, inertia would disappear, since there would be no chimerical absolute Newtonian space surviving the removal of the contents of the space. Einstein certainly anticipated that GR would support a relationist conception of spacetime, and that Mach's principle would be a crucial feature of his theory. This turned out not to be the case, for a number of reasons we shall now try to explain.

First we should note that in the field equations the specification of the density of the T-field on the right-hand side of the equation already involves the g-field, so that the T-field cannot be regarded as an independent input to the equations, independent, that is, of the spacetime geometry. Second, the solutions of the field equations involve in general boundary conditions, which again have to be specified in terms of the behaviour of the g-field (Einstein tried to obviate this difficulty by requiring the universe to be spatially closed, thus eliminating the need to specify boundary conditions at spatial infinity). Third, it is possible to define the rotation of the matter field with respect to the local inertial frames specified by the g-field. So it makes sense in GR to talk of matter rotating locally relative to spacetime, rather than with respect to the rest of the material contents of spacetime. A nice example is the rotating universe discovered by Kurt Gödel (see SPACETIME §4). Fourth, we can ask what happens if we set $T = 0$ throughout spacetime. In the spirit of Mach's principle, the vacuum equations $G = 0$ should admit of no solutions. However, many non-flat matter-free solutions of the field equations exist, in which, informally speaking, gravitational energy provides the source of the curvature (note that in the Einstein field equations gravitational energy is *not* included in the T-field).

So one concludes that GR is quite inimical to a relationist conception of spacetime. Far from reducing spacetime to matter, one may indeed envisage spacetime as the primary ontological category, and regard matter (and electromagnetism) as reducible to certain geometrical features of the spacetime.

7 Supersubstantivalism

Supersubstantivalism is the view that spacetime is not just *a* substance but the only substance. What we regard as matter is just a region endowed with certain sorts of geometrical structure, and other candidates for physical reality, such as electromagnetic fields, are also to be given a geometrical interpretation. Precursors of this view include Isaac Newton, who interpreted matter in terms of a property of impenetrability impressed on a region of space, and Rudjer Boscovich and Michael Faraday who regarded material atoms as centres of active force, rather than substantial bodies. William Kingdon Clifford applied Riemann's theory of curved manifolds to suggest a geometrical interpretation of matter in terms of local regions of curvature impressed on physical space. Einstein in his own later work sought geometrical explanation of electromagnetic forces in terms of additional geometric structure such as asymmetric connections or higher dimensions of the spacetime manifold. But in terms of orthodox GR, a theory known as geometrodynamics was especially espoused by John Wheeler (1962) and his associates. This exploited an identification of the electromagnetic field with aspects of the four-dimensional geometry, due originally to G. Rainich, electric charges being associated with novel small-scale topology in the spacetime structure, while mass was identified with local concentrations of curvature in the style of Clifford (1876). Technically geometrodynamics foundered in the 1960s due to the pervasive existence of singularities in the solutions of the GR field equations, and problems associated with formulating the initial value problem for the time-evolution of the metric. Nevertheless the spirit of supersubstantivalism has continued to exercise a strong hold on further developments in theoretical physics associated with the programme of quantizing gravitation and unifying it with the other fundamental interactions of electromagnetism and nuclear physics in the general framework of a geometrically interpreted quantum field theory.

See also: COSMOLOGY; GENERAL RELATIVITY, PHILOSOPHICAL RESPONSES TO

References and further reading

* Anderson, J.L. (1967) *Principles of Relativity Physics*, New York: Academic Press. (Stresses important distinction between covariance principles and symmetry principles – see §4.)
* Clifford, W.K. (1876) 'On the Space-Theory of Matter', *Proceedings of the Cambridge Philosophical Society* 2: 157–8. (Interprets matter as the curvature of space.)
Earman, J. (1989) *World Enough and Space-Time: Absolute versus Relational Theories of Space and Time*, Cambridge, MA: MIT Press. (Comprehensive discussion of absolute versus relational theories of space and time.)
—— (1995) *Bangs, Crunches, Whimpers and Shrieks: Singularities and Acausality in Relativistic Spacetimes*, Oxford: Oxford University Press. (Discussion of spacetime singularities and their significance.)
Earman, J., Glymour, C. and Stachel, J. (eds) (1977) *Foundations of Space-Time Theories*, Minneapolis, MN: University of Minnesota Press. (Papers on philosophy of relativity expressing the state-of-the-art in the late 1970s.)

* Einstein, A. (1905) 'Zur Electrodynamik bewegter Körper', *Annalen der Physik* 17: 891–921; trans. W. Perrett and G.B. Jeffery, *The Principle of Relativity: A Collection of Original Memoirs on the Special and General Theory of Relativity*, London: Methuen, 1923. (Classic paper introducing the special theory of relativity.)

* —— (1915) 'Die Feldgleichungen der Gravitation', *Preussische Akademie der Wissenschaften*, Berlin: Sitzungsberichte, 844–7. (Statement of the final form of the Einstein field equations without the so-called cosmological constant, introduced by Einstein in 1917 to secure a static bounded universe – see §6.)

—— (1916) 'Die Grundlagen der Allgemeinen Relativitätstheorie', *Annalen der Physik* 49: 769–822; trans. W. Perrett and G.B. Jeffery, *The Principle of Relativity: A Collection of Original Memoirs on the Special and General Theory of Relativity*, London: Methuen, 1923. (Einstein's own views on the foundations of general relativity.)

* Friedman, M. (1983) *Foundations of Space-Time Theories*, Princeton, NJ: Princeton University Press. (A modern classic – a good deal of mathematical technicality.)

Grünbaum, A. (1973) *Philosophical Problems of Space and Time*, Dordrecht: Reidel, 2nd enlarged edn. (Classic philosophical discussion of Einstein's theories.)

* Kretschmann, E. (1917) 'Ueber den Physikalischen Sinn der Relativitätspostulaten', *Annalen der Physik* 53: 575–614. (Important critique of the principle of general covariance.)

* Lorentz, H.A. (1904) 'Electromagnetic Phenomena in a System Moving with any Velocity Less than that of Light', *Proceedings of the Royal Academy of Amsterdam* 6: 809–31. (Pre-Einstein derivation of the Lorentz transformations.)

Lucas, J.R. and Hodgson, P.E. (1990) *Spacetime and Electromagnetism: An Essay on the Philosophy of the Special Theory of Relativity*, Oxford: Clarendon Press. (Comprehensive discussion of different approaches to deriving the Lorentz transformations.)

* Mach, E. (1893) *Die Mechanik in ihrer Entwickelung, historischkritisch dargestellt*, Leipzig: Brockhaus; trans. T.J. McCormack, *The Science of Mechanics: A Critical and Historical Account of its Development*, La Salle, IL: Open Court, 1960. (Mach's formulation of his principle – see §6.)

Malament, D. (1977) 'Causal Theories of Time and the Conventionality of Simultaneity', *Nous* 11: 293–300. (Influential attack on the conventionality of simultaneity.)

* Minkowski, H. (1909) 'Raum und Zeit', *Physikalische Zeitschrift* 10: 104–11; trans. W. Perrett and G.B.

Jeffery, *The Principle of Relativity: A Collection of Original Memoirs on the Special and General Theory of Relativity*, London: Methuen, 1923. (Introduces the four-dimensional geometrical interpretation of special relativity.)

Nagel, E. (1980) 'Relativity and Twentieth-Century Intellectual Life', in H. Woolf (ed.) *Some Strangeness in the Proportion: A Centennial Symposium to Celebrate the Achievements of Albert Einstein*, Reading, MA: Addison-Wesley, 38–45. (Nontechnical introduction to the general philosophical import of relativity theory.)

Perrett, W. and Jeffery, G.B. (1923) *The Principle of Relativity: A Collection of Original Memoirs on the Special and General Theory of Relativity*, London: Methuen; repr. New York: Dover, 1952. (Useful collection of English translations of the classic papers on relativity theory.)

Poincaré, H. (1905) 'Sur la Dynamique de l'Electron', *Comptes Rendus de l'Academie des Sciences* 140: 1,504–8. (Summarizes Poincaré's version of relativity theory – see §2.)

* Redhead, M.L.G. (1993) 'The Conventionality of Simultaneity', in J. Earman, A.I. Janis, G.J. Massey and N. Rescher (eds) *Philosophical Problems of the Internal and External Worlds: Essays on the Philosophy of Adolf Grünbaum*, Pittsburg, PA: University of Pittsburg Press, 103–28. (Critical assessment of the conventionality thesis in special relativity and its application to the twin paradox – also discusses the significance of tachyons in special relativity.)

* Reichenbach, H. (1928) *Philosophie der Raum-Zeit-Lehre*, Berlin: de Gruyter; trans. M. Reichenbach and J. Freund, *The Philosophy of Space and Time*, New York: Dover, 1957. (Important philosophical commentary on Einstein's theories.)

Salmon, W.C. (1975) *Space, Time and Motion: A Philosophical Introduction*, Encino, CA: Dickenson. (Clear nontechnical discussion of special relativity in the Reichenbach–Grünbaum tradition.)

Sklar, L. (1976) *Space, Time, and Space-Time*, Berkeley, CA: University of California Press. (General introduction to the philosophy of relativity theory.)

—— (1985) *Philosophy of Spacetime Physics*, Berkeley, CA: University of California Press. (Collection of papers by Sklar updating his 1976 book.)

Stein, H. (1991) 'On Relativity Theory and the Openness of the Future', *Philosophy of Science* 58: 147–67. (Defends a notion of becoming in special relativity, but relativized locally to the here and now, rather than the global 'now'.)

Torretti, R. (1983) *Relativity and Geometry*, Oxford: Pergamon Press. (Philosophical discussion of both the special and general theory, with much technical detail.)

* Wheeler, J.A. (1962) *Geometrodynamics*, New York: Academic Press. (Comprehensive collection of papers on geometrodynamics – see §7.)

MICHAEL REDHEAD

RELEVANCE LOGIC AND ENTAILMENT

'Relevance logic' came into being in the late 1950s, inspired by Wilhelm Ackermann, who rejected certain formulas of the form $A \rightarrow B$ on the grounds that 'the truth of A has nothing to do with the question whether there is a logical connection between B and A'.

The central idea of relevance logic is to give an account of logical consequence, or entailment, for which a connection of relevance between premises and conclusion is a necessary condition. In both classical and intuitionistic logic, this condition is missing, as is highlighted by the validity in those logics of the 'spread law', $A \& {\sim}A \rightarrow B$; a contradiction 'spreads' to every proposition, and simple inconsistency is equivalent to absolute inconsistency. In relevance logic the spread law fails, and the simple inconsistency of a theory (that a set of formulas entails a contradiction) is distinguished from absolute inconsistency (or triviality: that a set of formulas entails every proposition). The programme of relevance logic is to characterize a logic, or a range of logics, satisfying the relevance condition, and to study theories based on such logics, such as relevant arithmetic and relevant set theory.

1   The calculus of entailment
2   The calculus of relevant implication
3   The systems of relevance logic
4   Relevant predication and arithmetic

1   The calculus of entailment

'Relevance logic' (also known as 'relevant logic') was born in the late 1950s, when Alan Ross Anderson and Nuel D. Belnap were inspired by reading a paper by Wilhelm Ackermann (1956). In that paper, 'Begründung einer strengen Implikation' (A Foundation for a Rigorous Implication), Ackermann set out to characterize an implication relation, or connective, $A \rightarrow B$ in which there was always a connection between A and B. 'Rigorous implication', he wrote, 'is intended to express the idea that a logical connection holds between A and B, that the content of B is part of the content of A' (1956: 113). Formulas which, though valid in classical logic, were rejected by Ackermann on the grounds that 'the truth of A has nothing to do with the question whether there is a logical connection between B and A' included

$$A \rightarrow (B \rightarrow A) \qquad A \rightarrow (B \rightarrow A \& B)$$
$$A \rightarrow ({\sim}A \rightarrow B) \qquad A \rightarrow ((A \rightarrow B) \rightarrow B)$$
$$B \rightarrow (A \rightarrow A) \qquad A \rightarrow (A \rightarrow A)$$
$$A \& {\sim}A \rightarrow B.$$

Ackermann began his paper by recalling C.I. Lewis' reasons for developing his calculus of strict implication as a calculus expressing a more reasonable notion of 'implication' or 'entailment' than was current at the time (see Lewis 1914). (That the quest for a relevant notion of entailment goes back well before Lewis has been demonstrated more recently by C.J. Martin (1986) in his investigations into twelfth-century logic.) But Ackermann believed Lewis had not gone far enough. Although the first four formulas above fail when '$\rightarrow$' is interpreted as strict implication, the last three still hold. Moreover, taking '$\Box$' to represent 'is necessary', $\Box A \rightarrow (B \rightarrow A)$ and $\Box {\sim}A \rightarrow (A \rightarrow B)$ were theses of Lewis' system of strict implication. Ackermann added '$\Box$' to his calculus of rigorous implication (via an absurdity constant '$\bot$' and a definition of 'A is impossible' as $A \rightarrow \bot$) and showed that the above so-called 'paradoxes of strict implication' fail when '$\rightarrow$' is taken as rigorous implication.

Belnap reports returning to Yale University from a year in Europe working with Feys on composing a Gentzen system for Ackermann's system, to write up his Ph.D. dissertation, and ingenuously asking Anderson if he knew anyone in the United States who was interested in Ackermann's work. Anderson, feeling equally isolated in his fascination with Ackermann's ideas, having reviewed them in the *Journal of Symbolic Logic*, was delighted to find, as Belnap put it, a 'fellow Strengenite'. Together they started the research programme which led to more than thirty years' creative work on every aspect of a logic of relevance.

How does their work relate to Ackermann's? The initial motivation was the same, and the same goal which had inspired Lewis: to find a satisfactory explication of the concept of entailment, or (formal) logical consequence. Therefore, in the first decade of work, the focus was on the calculus of entailment (E) incorporating aspects of both relevance and necessity. E validates the same theses as Ackermann's system, and differs from it in several apparently minor ways, which in fact are quite significant. First, '$\Box A$' can be defined directly in the basic system as $(A \rightarrow A) \rightarrow A$, yielding the same theses, so '$\bot$' and the associated apparatus can be removed. '$\rightarrow$' is itself a modal connective (the '$\rightarrow$'-fragment of E is a subsystem of the arrow fragment of S4). Second, two of Ackermann's four rules of inference, namely (γ) and (δ), though unproblematic in the pure logic, are unacceptable when the logic is extended to a substantive theory. Anderson and Belnap showed that they could be dispensed with. Ackermann's rule of inference (γ) says that a proof of B results immediately from proofs of $A \lor B$ and $\sim A$. The point is this: whenever $A \lor B$ and $\sim A$ are provable in the pure logic of E, so too is B, that is, (γ) is an admissible rule of E, and so is redundant. (Conjectured in 1958, the first proof was not found until ten years later.) But in a theory based on E, there might be proofs of $A \lor B$ and $\sim A$ (that is, these formulas might belong to the theory, extending E by non-logical axioms) without there necessarily being a proof of B (or of $\sim B$ – the theory need not be negation-complete). One major task in the research programme of relevance logic became to show the admissibility of (γ) for various E-theories, once E was shown to admit (γ) itself. We will note later the major disappointment in this search, the failure of (γ) for relevant arithmetic.

The problem with the rule (δ) is similar, but less deep and seminal. (δ) says that from $A \rightarrow (B \rightarrow C)$ and a proof of B one can infer $A \rightarrow C$. Again, the proof of B must be logical. Even if $A \rightarrow (B \rightarrow C)$ and B belong to a theory, $A \rightarrow C$ might not. Indeed, (δ) seems to promise a permutation, from $A \rightarrow (B \rightarrow C)$ to $B \rightarrow (A \rightarrow C)$, and that is unacceptable in the modal logic E, being a fallacy of modality. (Let A be $B \rightarrow C$ itself, and consider how the permutation would fail in S4 with '$\rightarrow$' as strict implication.) Such a move is legitimate only if B is appropriately modal, which we can capture with the connective '$\Box$'. (δ) can therefore be replaced by an axiom,

$$(A \rightarrow (B \rightarrow C)) \rightarrow (\Box B \rightarrow (A \rightarrow C)),$$

or, equivalently, as Anderson and Belnap chose to do in E,

$$(\Box A \,\&\, \Box B) \rightarrow \Box(A \,\&\, B),$$

with '$\Box$' defined as above.

E, the calculus of entailment, had thus been born; its study was to reveal new worlds in logic, and, before long, to shift attention to a range of related logics. (See Anderson and Belnap 1975, 1992.)

2 The calculus of relevant implication

Anderson and Belnap called E the logic of relevance and necessity. However, it is important to understand that the programme they embarked on did not try to give any general characterization of relevance, or even

of relevance as a logical notion. What they identified were what they called fallacies of modality and of relevance. Fallacies of modality were first characterized by them for the '$\rightarrow$'-fragment as taking as valid any formula of the form $B \rightarrow (A \rightarrow C)$, where B was a propositional variable. Ackermann had suggested the criterion for his full calculus that neither '$\rightarrow$' nor '$\bot$' should belong to B.

Arguably, neither characterization really identifies what a modal fallacy is. For one thing, neither condition easily generalizes beyond the propositional language given. Adding further connectives or quantifiers and the language of predicates, one must generalize the condition, yet that means one needs some understanding of what motivates it. Pottinger tried to capture a notion suitable for E (see Anderson and Belnap 1975: 348), but again, how it would generalize further is unclear. These are technical criteria, not proper philosophical analyses. Moreover, while separating the modal from the relevance fallacies is a promising idea, a natural consequence is that the modal fallacies should equally be rejected in S4. Yet $B \rightarrow (A \rightarrow C)$ is a thesis of S4 whenever $A \rightarrow C$ is, regardless of the nature of B, even if it is a propositional variable. The answer is that a modal fallacy is essentially a permutation move, promoting B from its secondary position to a primary one: from $A \rightarrow (B \rightarrow C)$ to $B \rightarrow (A \rightarrow C)$. Such a permutation will permit, *inter alia*, validation of formulas $B \rightarrow (A \rightarrow C)$ where B is a propositional variable (or contains neither '$\rightarrow$' nor '$\bot$'). Checking that such formulas are not theses is a useful test that a system does not commit any modal fallacies. But it is not an adequate explication of the notion.

Fallacies of relevance were also characterized by Anderson and Belnap only in technical terms, without any wider elaboration of what was really wrong with them. Their formal tests of relevance were variable-sharing and derivational utility. The former again only applies to the propositional fragment. The idea was that $A \rightarrow B$ is valid only if A and B share a propositional variable. Belnap presented matrices which test for this condition. The other criterion arose from an attempt by Anderson and Belnap to prove a deduction theorem for Ackermann's system, and led to the creation of a (Fitch-style) natural deduction formulation of E. They developed sets of indices which kept track of relevance through the proof. Conditional proof (the analogue in the natural deduction formulation of the deduction theorem as a result about axiomatic formulations) was permissible only when in the proof of B from A, B's index contained that assigned to the assumption of A. The idea has been fecund in the development of relevance logic, especially when one realizes that the indices play the role of the assumption lists in a Gentzen-style formulation of the logic as a natural deduction calculus of sequents. But it is still a restricted and technical idea: how will it generalize when we extend the calculus to, say, second-order, and outstrip proof theory? In brief, what is really meant here by relevance?

But separating ideas of relevance from those of modality permitted the creation of the system R of relevant implication. This results from E by relaxing the restriction on permutation. The '→' of R is a non-modal relevant conditional. It was seen as relating to the '→' of E as material implication relates to strict implication. Yet in this development lay the effective death-knell of E. If one now starts with R and adds an S4-necessity operator '□', there are theses containing '□' only in the position $\Box(A \rightarrow B)$ which do not result from theses of E in which $A \rightarrow B$ has been replaced by $\Box(A \rightarrow B)$. Since this discovery in 1973 (see Anderson and Belnap 1975: 351–2), work on R and its extensions and subsystems has put E in the shade.

3 The systems of relevance logic

With the creation of R, and more so with its eclipse of E, the stage was set for a study of a full range of systems of relevance logic. Immediate neighbours of E and R were the system T of 'ticket entailment' and the 'mingle' systems EM and RM. Ticket entailment picked up an idea of Ryle's; that conditionals are a kind of inference-ticket, licensing the inference from one factual (non-conditional) statement to another. T is a subsystem of E which effectively restricts even the permutation of conditional antecedents which is allowed in E.

The mingle systems extend E and R by the addition of the axiom $A \rightarrow (A \rightarrow A)$. This looks harmless, lacking the obvious irrelevance of $A \rightarrow (B \rightarrow A)$. But adding the mingle axiom to R leads to the validity of $(A \rightarrow B) \lor (B \rightarrow A)$, and we find one of the classic paradoxes of material implication has returned. RM is an interesting source of study; but it is, in Meyer's phrase, a 'semi-relevant logic'.

With hindsight, one can see the study of E and R as the start of research into a range of systems which in the early 1990s came to be called 'substructural logics'. Two insights led to this development. One was recognition of the Curry–Howard correspondence, the treatment of formulas as types (see LAMBDA CALCULUS). This reveals that the '→'-fragment of R was being studied even in the 1930s by Church, in his λ-I calculus. In the λ-calculus one studies functions, developing a framework for the general treatment of functional abstraction and application. The reductions and equivalences of functional expressions are governed by combinators, so that, for example, the combinator B asserts that the composition of functions is associative: $B(fg)h$ reduces to $f(gh)$ (see COMBINATORY LOGIC §1). Correlating functional abstraction with conditional proof, functional application with *modus ponens*, there is a natural correlation of the definability of λ-terms, or combinators, with the provability of '→'-formulas (which extends to Cartesian product and conjunctions, and so on). R (or at least, its '→'-fragment) is then seen as BCW-logic, the logic of associativity, permutation and contraction, placed in a family with BCK-, BCI- and other logics. BCI-logic, otherwise known as the '→'-fragment of RW (R without contraction) corresponds to Church's λ-I calculus. The relevance logics can then be classed as those representing functions that 'really depend on their arguments', rejecting the combinators such as K, corresponding to the λ-term $\lambda x, y.x$ (see COMBINATORY LOGIC §1).

The other development was 'correspondence theory', the study of the correlation between logical principles and constraints on corresponding relations in the model theory. It started in the study of semantics for modal logics, whereby different conditions on accessibility in possible worlds semantics are seen to match various axioms for necessity, '□', in the logic modelled. The semantics for relevance logic began to be worked out in the late 1960s and early 1970s by Dunn, the Routleys, Meyer, Maximova and Fine, working largely independently. There were two aspects needing special attention. First, a way of invalidating the spread law had to be found, and that seemed to require modelling A and $\sim A$ simultaneously. One solution was the negation-shift operation, pairing each world w with w^*, whereby $\sim A$ is true at w if and only if A is true at w^*. Suitable constraints on '*' give the right involute properties to '$\sim$'. The other aspect was the relevance '→' itself, whether for E or R (or related logics). The approach which has come to dominate uses a three-place relation on worlds, R, whereby $A \rightarrow B$ is true at x if B is true at b whenever A is true at a and $Rxab$. Again, suitable constraints on R give the desired properties of '→'. Fine's version used a pre-ordering of worlds (as in S4) and an operation of fusion, '∘', such that $A \rightarrow B$ is true at x if B is true at $x \circ a$ whenever A is true at a. This operational semantics makes more transparent the correspondence with the combinators. The correspondences thus set up identify a range of logics, the substructural logics (logics with restricted structural rules), which differ essentially only in their structural rules.

This assumes, however, the invariance of the Boolean apparatus of '&' and '∨' erected on the underlying calculus of '$\sim$', '→', and perhaps fusion

'∘', with $A \circ B$ true at $a \circ b$ whenever A is true at a and B at b. '∘' is a 'relevant conjunction', $A \circ B \rightarrow C$ being equivalent to $A \rightarrow (B \rightarrow C)$. '&' and '∨' need not be so invariant, however. Ackermann noted that distribution of '&' over '∨' no longer followed from the other axioms when restricted to yield rigorous implication, and so added it as a separate axiom. Anderson and Belnap followed him, supporting the case by yet another criterion of relevance, applied to first-degree entailments ($A \rightarrow B$ where A and B contain only '∼', '&' and '∨'); that they be tautological: putting A in disjunctive normal form (DNF) and B in conjunctive (CNF), every disjunct on the left shares an atom with every conjunct on the right, roughly, B is 'contained in' A. But some have argued that dropping the combinator K ('weakening') as the source of irrelevance in full classical logic, should yield a non-distributive calculus. Interestingly, every classical tautology (in '∼', '&' and '∨') is provable in R. But this fact fails for the non-distributive calculus. For example, the axiom 'sum' of *Principia Mathematica*,

$$(Q \supset R) \supset ((P \vee Q) \supset (P \vee R)),$$

with '$A \supset B$' for '$\sim A \vee B$', is unprovable in LR (R without distribution). LR was the focus of much research in automated theorem proving in the 1980s.

Dropping W ('contraction') from LR yields a fragment of Girard's linear logic (1987), as does dropping distribution from RW (see LINEAR LOGIC). Girard's rich theory, encompassing additive connectives ('&' and '∨' – there written '&' and '⊕'), multiplicatives ('→' and '∘' – there '⊸' and '⊗') and exponentials (the modal operators '!' and '?'), tracking the essential and profligate use of resources, picks up Church's original interest in BCI and has played a central role recently in theoretical computer science.

Those relevance logics (Ackermann's system is one exception) which reject the spread law in the form $A \,\&\, \sim A \vdash B$, are paraconsistent logics (see PARACONSISTENT LOGIC). For some, they even share a motivation, namely, to allow logical treatment of inconsistent theories without making them trivial (their deductive closure does not embrace everything, as in classical logic). But for others, their motivation is different: many paraconsistent logics arise from an interest in dialetheism, the belief that some inconsistent theories are true. Wider still run the 'sociative logics' (a term of Sylvan's), encompassing relevance, connexive, non-transitive and a whole range of, as he puts it, 'broadly relevant' logics.

4 Relevant predication and arithmetic

This survey of relevance logics suggests an undue concentration on the zero-order (propositional) fragment, and that reflects the facts. But important results have been established for first-order relevance logic, relevant arithmetic and so on. For too long, perhaps, it was thought that the extension to first-order was straightforward. Fine's discovery that plausible ways of extending the proof theory and semantics to first-order quantifiers led to incompleteness was a surprise, not really softened by his later elaboration of a semantics which did not validate the unprovable formulas (see Anderson and Belnap 1992: §§52–3). Urquhart's demonstration of undecidability for propositional T, E and R settled an open problem of twenty years' standing, again in a surprising way (1992: §65). (The non-distributive logics are decidable.) The failure of (γ) for the formulation $R^{\#}$ of relevant arithmetic was another surprise, blocking a natural line of research.

The exposure of these negative results in the 1980s was not unlike the exposure of the limitative results for classical mathematics (incommensurability, uncountability, incompleteness). At first, relevance logic lost momentum as they were settled, and settled in such surprising and negative ways. Nonetheless, limitative results notoriously give rise, once assimilated, to new avenues of research. They are appearing in relevance logic, two notable ones being the attempt to characterize a notion of relevant predication by Dunn and others (Anderson and Belnap 1992: §74) – recognizing that the extension to first-order is not straightforward; and the search for a relevant arithmetic which admits (γ) (1992: §72) – perhaps by strengthening the rule of induction.

See also: CONSEQUENCE, CONCEPTIONS OF; LOGICAL LAWS; LOGICAL AND MATHEMATICAL TERMS, GLOSSARY OF; MODAL LOGIC

References and further reading

* Ackermann, W. (1956) 'Begründung einer strengen Implikation' (A Foundation for a Rigorous Implication), *Journal of Symbolic Logic* 21: 113–28. (The original paper which started it all.)
* Anderson, A.R. and Belnap, N.D. (eds) (1975, 1992) *Entailment: The Logic of Relevance and Necessity*, Princeton, NJ: Princeton University Press, 2 vols. (The classic source for their work and others'; includes an extensive bibliography.)
Došen, K. and Schroeder-Heister, P. (eds) (1993) *Substructural Logics*, Oxford: Clarendon Press. (Places relevance logic in the framework of wider study of logics with restricted structural rules.)
Dunn, J.M. (1986) 'Relevance Logic and Entailment', in D. Gabbay and F. Guenthner (eds) *Handbook of*

Philosophical Logic, vol. 3, *Alternatives to Classical Logic*, Dordrecht: Reidel, 117–229. (A very useful technical survey.)

Friedman, H. and Meyer, R.K. (1992) 'Whither Relevant Arithmetic?', *Journal of Symbolic Logic* 57: 824–31. (Shows the failure of (γ) for relevant arithmetic.)

Girard, J.-Y. (1987) 'Linear Logic', *Theoretical Computer Science* 50: 1–102. (The first and definitive presentation of linear logic.)

* Lewis, C.I. (1914) 'The Calculus of Strict Implication', *Mind* 23: 240–7. (One of Lewis' early papers in which he described his project of formalizing a logic of entailment.)

* Martin, C.J. (1986) 'William's Machine', *Journal of Philosophy* 83: 564–72. (The debate over relevance in twelfth century logic.)

Read, S. (1988) *Relevant Logic*, Oxford: Blackwell. (An elementary presentation of the philosophical basis of relevance logic and a formal system for a range of relevance logics.)

Sylvan, R. [née Routley] with Plumwood, V., Meyer, R.K. and Brady, R. (1982) *Relevant Logics and Their Rivals*, vol. 1, *The Basic Philosophical and Semantical Theory*, Atascadero, CA: Ridgeview. (Places zero-order relevance logic in a setting of non-classical intensional logics.)

Sylvan, R. and Norman, J. (eds) (1989) *Directions in Relevant Logic*, Dordrecht: Kluwer. (A collection of papers including those given at a memorial conference for Alan Anderson in 1974, some updated and others additional.)

Thistlewaite, P.B., McRobbie, M.A. and Meyer, R.K. (1988) *Automated Theorem-Proving in Non-Classical Logics*, London: Pitman. (The computer program KRIPKE, using a search tree based on models for non-distributive relevance logic.)

STEPHEN READ

RELEVANT ALTERNATIVES

see SCEPTICISM

RELIABILISM

Reliabilism is an approach to the nature of knowledge and of justified belief. Reliabilism about justification, in its simplest form, says that a belief is justified if and only if it is produced by a reliable psychological process, meaning a process that produces a high proportion of true beliefs. A justified belief may itself be false, but its

mode of acquisition (or the way it is subsequently sustained) must be of a kind that typically yields truths. Since random guessing, for example, does not systematically yield truths, beliefs acquired by guesswork are not justified. By contrast, identifying middle-sized physical objects by visual observation is presumably pretty reliable, so beliefs produced in this manner are justified. Reliabilism does not require that the possessor of a justified belief should know that it was reliably produced. Knowledge of reliability is necessary for knowing that a belief is justified, but the belief can be justified without the agent knowing that it is.

A similar reliabilist account is offered for knowledge, except that two further conditions are added. First, the target belief must be true and, second, its mode of acquisition must rule out all serious or 'relevant' alternatives in which the belief would be false. Even an accurate visual identification of Judy does not constitute knowledge unless it is acute enough to exclude the possibility that it is her twin sister Trudy instead.

One major virtue of reliabilism is its ability to secure knowledge against threats of scepticism. In place of excessive requirements often proposed by sceptics, reliabilism substitutes more moderate conditions. People do not need infallible or certainty-producing processes to have justified beliefs, according to reliabilism, only fairly reliable ones. Processes need not exclude radical alternatives like Descartes' evil demon in order to generate knowledge; they need only exclude realistic possibilities like the presence of an identical twin.

1   **Reliabilism and naturalistic epistemology**
2   **Reliabilism as a species of externalism**
3   **A variant form of reliabilism**

1   Reliabilism and naturalistic epistemology

Reliabilism is often regarded as a species of naturalistic epistemology (see NATURALIZED EPISTEMOLOGY). There are various properties of an epistemology that might invite the label 'naturalistic', and reliabilism has most if not all of them. First, an epistemological theory may be called naturalistic if it holds that normative epistemic properties are reducible to natural, non-epistemic properties and relations. The reliabilist theory of justified belief sketched above fits this description. It tries to reduce the normative property of 'justifiedness' to three types of 'natural' properties: psychological properties (for example, being a psychological process), causal relations and truth. It is generally agreed that psychological properties are non-normative (certainly not epistemically normative, at any rate), and similarly for causation. Although some philosophers maintain that truth is an epistemic concept, which should be defined in terms of justification or rationality, reliabilism typically rejects epistemic analyses of truth in favour of a realist, non-epistemic account, such as a correspondence theory (see TRUTH, CORRESPONDENCE THEORY OF). If the latter approach is correct, then only natural properties are invoked by reliabilism.

Reliabilism is also naturalistic in portraying the cognitive agent as a natural – that is, physical or biological – system and interpreting epistemic accomplishments as the products of natural processes or mechanisms. Psychological operations, processes or mechanisms may be conceptualized as input-output devices, where the inputs are doxastic or nondoxastic states and the outputs are beliefs. One variant of reliabilism, the information-theoretic approach, views the cognitive system as an 'information-processing' system. Knowledge that s is F is acquired when the system receives the 'information' that s is F, that is, when it receives a signal that eliminates all (relevant) counter-possibilities. Since the concept of information transmission has been applied to a variety of physical systems, this approach has a strong naturalistic flavour (see INFORMATION THEORY AND EPISTEMOLOGY).

Epistemologies are called naturalistic in a third sense when they appeal to empirical science for the execution of certain epistemological tasks. Under one brand of reliabilism, for example, it is a task for cognitive science to identify the specific psychological operations available to human cognizers and to determine their reliability. Of course, ordinary people must have rough and intuitive notions of our psychological processes; otherwise they could not segregate beliefs into the categories of justified and unjustified. But cognitive science may be expected to produce more revealing and refined accounts of belief-forming processes.

At what age, for example, are children able to form reliable beliefs about the number of objects in a collection, and what mental operations enable them to do so? Surprisingly, it appears that infants as young as five months are sensitive to numbers and can calculate the results of small additions and subtractions. Judging by the amount of time infants stare at a display, psychologists have determined that they expect one item added to one item to yield two items, and expect the subtraction of one item from two items to leave one item. The plausibility of early – indeed, innate – counting abilities in humans is strengthened by the discovery of impressive feats of counting in non-human animals. Rats, for example, can identify the number of times they have pressed a lever, up to at least twenty-four presses, when they are trained to press a specified number of times on a particular lever before pressing once on a second lever for a reward (see INNATE KNOWLEDGE).

What operation or mechanism might subserve reliable counting? One possibility proposed by researchers is an accumulator device. A hypothesized pacemaker puts out pulses at a constant rate, which can be passed into an accumulator by the closing of a mode switch. Every time an entity is experienced that is to be counted, the mode switch closes for a fixed interval, passing energy into the accumulator. The accumulator fills up in equal increments, one for each entity counted. A device of this sort would be a reliable counter. If animals have some such mechanism, their numerical beliefs generated by it would qualify as knowledge according to reliabilism.

Reliabilism does not claim, of course, that knowledge depends exclusively on specialized innate mechanisms. Culturally acquired methods, such as a method for deriving square roots, can also breed knowledge if they are reliable. Although native resources must be employed to mentally represent and execute learned methods, the methods themselves need not be 'hard-wired'.

According to reliabilism the epistemic status of a belief depends on its mode of causation (see KNOWLEDGE, CAUSAL THEORY OF). This contrasts with purely evidentialist theories, which consider a belief to be justified as long as it is logically or probabilistically supported by a corpus of evidence that the agent possesses (see PROBABILITY THEORY AND EPISTEMOLOGY). Reliabilism contends that mere possession of strong evidence is not enough for justified belief. A detective, for example, may possess assorted strands of evidence that jointly incriminate a certain suspect, but the slow-witted detective may not notice that these disparate strands of evidence can be woven into an airtight case. If the detective is prompted to accept the suspect's guilt for entirely different and illegitimate reasons – for example, the suspect's unsavoury appearance – then the belief is unwarranted.

Not only is mere possession of adequate evidence insufficient for justification, but it is also unnecessary. At least the *current* possession of adequate evidence is not required for justification. Suppose you once had excellent evidence for p (having heard it from a trustworthy source) but you no longer recall this evidence: your belief in p may still be justified. A person's failure to keep track of his original evidence does not destroy the justifiedness of a belief, as long as the belief in fact had a suitable provenance, namely a history of reliable belief-forming and belief-preserving steps.

2 Reliabilism as a species of externalism

Reliabilism is a species of epistemological externalism rather than internalism (see INTERNALISM AND EXTERNALISM IN EPISTEMOLOGY). Although there is no unanimity in defining these terms, the rough idea is that a theory is internalist if and only if all of the factors it requires for a belief to be justified are directly accessible to the cognizer, whereas a theory is externalist if and only if some of the justificatory factors are beyond the cognizer's (direct) ken. Since neither the truth-propensity of a belief-forming process nor the history of a belief's acquisition is directly accessible to the cognizer, reliabilism is a form of externalism. Externalism is often criticized for departing from traditional epistemology, which is allegedly internalist. It is debatable, however, whether the dominant tradition in epistemology is really internalist. In fact, many historical epistemologies can be interpreted as having strong elements of reliabilism, including the epistemologies of Plato, Descartes, Hume, Reid and Peirce – see, for example, Schmitt (1992).

Historical epistemology aside, it is clear that the concept of knowledge (as contrasted with justification) has externalist elements. First, knowledge requires the truth of what is known, and truth is the quintessential externalist element. Second, a satisfactory solution to the Gettier problem about knowledge seems to require a further externalist component (see GETTIER PROBLEMS). For example, a person might have a justified belief that the object they see in the nearby field is a barn, and this may be true. But if, entirely unknown to them, there are papier-mâché barn facsimiles in the neighbourhood which they would mistake for a barn if one of them were there instead, then intuitively they do not know what they see to be a barn. This seems to show that the external situation of the cognizer, and not just their internal mental condition, is relevant to the possession or non-possession of knowledge. The reliabilist theory of knowledge covers this by saying that knowledge is only acquired when all relevant alternatives are excluded, and the external situation – such as the presence of papier-mâché facsimiles in the neighbourhood – helps to determine which alternatives are relevant.

Although knowledge clearly has externalist components, the concept of justification may yet be thoroughly internalist, as internalists contend. But what, more precisely, is required by internalism? The typical internalist requirement of cognitive accessibility can be interpreted in at least two ways: as requiring that the believer actually should be aware of the justifying factors (at the time of the belief), or as requiring only the capacity to become aware of these factors by appropriate focusing of attention, without any change of position, new information, and so on. Either of these criteria, however, is probably unsatisfiable by many traditional theories of justification. One brand of coherentism, for example, says that a belief is justified only if it coheres with the totality of the cognizer's other current beliefs (see KNOWLEDGE AND JUSTIFICATION, COHERENCE THEORY OF). The justifying factors in this theory cannot meet the direct-accessibility requirement (in either version) because it is psychologically impossible to retrieve and examine the totality of one's beliefs. The beliefs of a normal adult number in the thousands or even millions, are mostly stored in long-term memory and are often difficult to recall without appropriate retrieval cues. Furthermore, many brands of coherentism, as well as other forms of evidentialism, impose complex demands in terms of the probabilistic relations that a justified belief must bear to the background corpus of beliefs. Whether a target belief satisfies these demands is not readily accessible to ordinary people who lack training in probability theory. So coherentism, no less than reliabilism, will turn out to be a brand of externalism.

Is it so bad for a theory of justification to be externalist? A common objection is that externalism, at least in its reliabilist incarnation, renders mistaken classifications. Imagine a person with a reliable clairvoyance faculty, who occasionally forms beliefs 'out of the blue' (that is, unguided by any sense-like appearances) about properties and locations of far-off objects; and these are usually correct. This person never checks up on these beliefs, and therefore has no independent evidence that the faculty is reliable; or we may suppose that the person has evidence to the contrary. Would a clairvoyantly-formed belief of that person's be justified? Reliabilism in its simplest form says yes, because the belief would be caused by a reliable process; but critics reject this assessment as intuitively mistaken.

Reliabilists may respond by complicating their theory. A standard gambit is to add a 'non-undermining' requirement, namely, a provision that the cognizer must neither believe nor possess evidence supporting the proposition that the target belief is *un*reliably caused (see KNOWLEDGE, DEFEASIBILITY THEORY OF). In at least one version of the clairvoyance case, the agent has evidence against his possession of a (reliable) clairvoyance faculty. This might give him evidence that his belief is unreliably caused (since it has no other familiar mode of causation), which would violate the new requirement. Even in the variant of the example in which the cognizer merely lacks positive evidence in support of his possessing a clairvoyance faculty, it might be argued that background scientific information makes the existence of such a faculty highly improbable; so if one lacks specific evidence of this power, the overall evidence cuts against it. The non-undermining condition would again be violated, and hence the revised version of reliabilism would declare the belief to be unjustified. Addition of the non-undermining condition does not transform reliabilism into a form of internalism, for it retains the reliability element that would violate the direct-accessibility requirement.

Whereas the clairvoyance counterexample tries to show that reliability is not sufficient for justification, a second type of objection claims that it is not necessary. Imagine a person regularly deceived by a Cartesian demon. They have the same patterns of sensory experiences as you or I, but in this case the resulting perceptual beliefs are systematically mistaken. Despite the unreliability of their perceptual belief-forming processes, surely their beliefs are as justified as yours or mine, since subjectively the grounds for belief are exactly the same. This challenges the very core of externalism by suggesting that only subjective, internal factors matter to justification, not external ones.

Reliabilists may respond by first pointing out that reliabilism also makes internal factors such as sensory experiences and background beliefs relevant to justification. These internal states are the inputs to mental processes, and only in combination with them can mental processes yield accurate output-beliefs. Furthermore, mental processes themselves are internal events, so reliabilism cannot justly be accused of ignoring internal matters completely. But these points do not blunt the force of the objection. After all, reliabilism does appeal to 'external' truth-ratios to distinguish justified from unjustified beliefs, and yet the demon case seems to show that this appeal is misplaced.

The objection assumes, however, that the reliability of a process is assessed by its performance in the world of the example. If this assumption is correct – if reliability is determined by a process's performance in the example world – then reliabilism does imply the unjustifiedness of the demon-world beliefs. But some alternate interpretations of reliability might be proposed under which the epistemic status of the beliefs (as judged by reliabilism) may be different. For example, a reliabilist might propose that what counts is reliability in the *actual* world. Since perceptual belief-formation is reliable in the actual world, use of the same process or processes would yield justified beliefs even in a demon world. This particular reformulation of reliabilism may not quite succeed,

but it shows how reliabilism has greater flexibility than might initially be supposed.

A third kind of problem for reliabilism – one not directly related to the internalism–externalism issue – is the 'generality' problem. Reliabilism says that a belief's justificational status depends on the truth-conduciveness of the psychological processes that cause it. But processes can be individuated in many ways; indeed, each token belief can be viewed as the outcome of numerous process types of differing grain or generality, with widely varying truth-ratios. What principle selects the appropriate process type, or set of process types, for each case?

3   A variant form of reliabilism

In light of these problems, different variants of reliabilism have been proposed. Let us examine one such variant and see how it addresses two of the foregoing problems. As a preliminary point, we should be clearer about what is expected of a theory of knowledge or justified belief. On one approach, such a theory should reveal the 'nature' or 'essence' of knowledge or justification, where these are construed as something like natural kinds, independent of our human conceptualization of them. On another approach, the aim of a theory is to reveal the concepts or mental representations associated with these epistemic predicates, and to reveal the ways that these representations are deployed by epistemic evaluators when they make epistemic judgments. This latter approach is the one that is pursued here.

The form of reliabilism considered in this section starts with a familiar idea in cognitive science, namely that a great deal of cognitive activity consists of 'pattern matching'. A pupil doing algebra problems, for instance, will try to match a new problem with some familiar pattern or structure of problems. It is much easier to solve a problem with a familiar solution pattern than an entirely novel one. The view considered here is that epistemic evaluation similarly proceeds by pattern matching. Evaluators are assumed to represent, in their heads, various patterns (or prototypes) of belief formation, some categorized as good patterns and some as bad. Examples of good patterns might include the use of various types of perception and the use of the 'straight rule' in inductive reasoning (see THEORETICAL (EPISTEMIC) VIRTUES §1). Examples of bad patterns might include forming beliefs by guesswork and ignoring relevant evidence. Good patterns may be called epistemic 'virtues' and bad patterns epistemic 'vices'. The present hypothesis is that when an evaluator is presented with a real or imagined case of belief, they consult their mentally stored list of virtues and vices, and judge the belief to be justified or unjustified by seeing whether its own mode of production matches virtues or vices. If its mode of production matches virtues only, it is categorized as justified; otherwise it is categorized as unjustified. If a mode of production is unfamiliar or non-standard, the epistemic judgment will depend on the judged similarity of the process to the antecedently stored patterns of virtue or vice.

How would this approach apply to our previously discussed examples? In the demon-world case, beliefs are produced by standard perceptual belief-forming processes. So these are matched to patterns that are clearly virtues. In the clairvoyance cases, matters are somewhat less clear. In one version of this case, the epistemic agent is described as having evidence against possessing a reliable clairvoyance power; but they apparently ignore this evidence, since they still rely on the clairvoyance faculty. If ignoring relevant evidence is on an evaluator's list of epistemic vices, it is predictable that the evaluator would judge the belief to be unjustified. Furthermore, the process of clairvoyance might seem very similar to a process of guesswork, since there are no appearances or sensory presentations associated with clairvoyance as there are with sight, hearing, smell and so forth. Thus, a clairvoyantly formed belief might be assimilated to the 'vice' of guesswork, and judged to be unjustified on that basis.

Thus far, nothing in the present approach invokes reliability. The reliability element is now introduced to explain how 'patterns' come to be classified as good or bad. The theory suggests that evaluators form opinions about the truth-ratios associated with sundry belief-forming processes. Those thought to have high truth-ratios are treated as good patterns and those with low truth-ratios as bad patterns. Thus, reliability is the criterion to which evaluators appeal in establishing patterns as good or bad. Evaluators might not do this purely individually. They might inherit some evaluative prototypes from others in the linguistic community. Whether individually or socially, however, the good and bad prototypes are selected by considerations of (judged) reliability.

The theory that emerges, then, is a two-level theory, somewhat analogous to rule-utilitarianism (see UTILITARIANISM §3). Judgments of justifiedness in particular cases do not appeal directly to the reliability of the belief's generating processes. Rather, such judgments involve pattern-matching to stored prototypes of good and bad belief-generating processes. Reliability enters the theory as the basis for classifying these processes as epistemically good or bad.

Recalling the demon-world example, it may be asked whether the basis for process evaluation is performance in the actual world or performance in other possible worlds as well. Presumably, evaluators appeal to real-world track records in making their evaluations, but they may also tend to assume that these observed track records can be extrapolated to non-observed and non-actual cases. In general, it is doubtful that ordinary evaluators, who lack ways of thinking systematically about 'possible worlds', use any sharply defined, world-relativized basis for reliability assessments. The crucial point, however, is that evaluators do not directly apply reliability considerations to novel cases. According to the present theory, they do not say (or think): 'Since perception is unreliable in the demon world, therefore perception-based beliefs in that world are unjustified'. Instead, they use pattern-matching to previously entrenched prototypes to arrive at an epistemic assessment of the target belief. With this understood, we have a form of reliabilism that has notable success in explaining evaluators' judgments in 'hard' cases, that is, cases that are hard for simple reliabilism.

See also: JUSTIFICATION, EPISTEMIC; KNOWLEDGE, CONCEPT OF; NORMATIVE EPISTEMOLOGY; VIRTUE ETHICS

References and further reading

All of the following works involve intricate argument but little or no technicality.

Alston, W.P. (1989) *Epistemic Justification: Essays in the Theory of Knowledge*, Ithaca, NY: Cornell University Press. (Contains several essays defending a form of reliabilism and discussing background meta-epistemological issues.)

—— (1996) 'How to Think about Reliability', *Philosophical Topics* 23 (1): 1–29. (Attempts to resolve the generality problem for reliabilism.)

Dretske, F.I. (1981) *Knowledge and the Flow of Information*, Cambridge, MA: MIT Press. (Expounds the information-theoretic version of reliabilism mentioned in §1 above.)

Feldman, R. (1985) 'Reliability and Justification', *Monist* 68 (2): 159–74. (Presses the generality problem for reliabilism.)

Goldman, A.I. (1986) *Epistemology and Cognition*, Cambridge, MA: Harvard University Press. (Systematic exposition of reliabilism plus an examination of psychological processes and their reliability.)

—— (1992) *Liaisons: Philosophy Meets the Cognitive and Social Sciences*, Cambridge, MA: MIT Press. (The essay 'What Is Justified Belief?' is a standard formulation of reliabilism; a second, 'Epistemic

Folkways and Scientific Epistemology', presents the two-tiered version of reliabilism sketched in §3 above.)

—— (1994) 'Naturalistic Epistemology and Reliabilism', in P.A. French, T.E. Uehling, Jr and H.K. Wettstein (eds) *Midwest Studies in Philosophy, XIX, Naturalism*, Notre Dame, IN: University of Notre Dame Press. (Expansion of some of the material in §§1–2 of this entry.)

Nozick, R. (1981) *Philosophical Explanations*, Cambridge, MA: Harvard University Press. (Chapter 3 presents a 'tracking' theory of knowledge.)

* Schmitt, F.F. (1992) *Knowledge and Belief*, London: Routledge. (The historical section examines reliabilist themes in the epistemologies of Plato, Descartes and Hume.)

Sosa, E. (1991) *Knowledge in Perspective: Selected Essays in Epistemology*, Cambridge: Cambridge University Press. (Several essays defend a form of reliabilism, including a virtues/vices approach similar to the one sketched in §3 above.)

Wynn, K. (1992) 'Evidence against empiricist accounts of the origins of numerical knowledge', *Mind and Language* 7 (4): 315–32. (Expansion of the material on counting in §1 above.)

ALVIN I. GOLDMAN

RELIGION AND EPISTEMOLOGY

Epistemology is theory of knowledge; one would therefore expect epistemological discussions of religion to concentrate on the question as to whether one could have knowledge of religious beliefs. However, discussions of religious belief have tended to focus on arguments for and against the existence of God: the traditional theistic arguments on the one hand and, on the other, such arguments against the existence of God as the argument from evil.

To see why, we must think about evidentialism with respect to religious belief ('evidentialism' for short), the doctrine that a religious believer must have evidence for their beliefs if they are to be rationally justified. In particular, they must have propositional evidence: evidence from other things they believe, evidence that can be put forward in the form of argument. And going with evidentialism is the evidentialist objection to religious belief: the objection that religious belief is unjustified because there is not enough evidence for it. Evidentialism begins with the classical foundationalists René Descartes and (especially) John Locke. According to Descartes and Locke, some beliefs are certain for

us. There are two kinds of certain belief: first, self-evident beliefs, such as '2 + 1 = 3', and second, beliefs about one's own mental life, such as 'it now seems to me that I see a hand'. According to Locke, I am, of course, clearly justified in accepting those beliefs that are certain; indeed, it is not within my power to reject them. For any belief that is not certain, however, I am justified in accepting it only if I can see that it is probable or likely with respect to beliefs that are *certain for me.*

What is this 'justification' and why does it matter whether or not my beliefs have it? Locke believed that human beings are rational creatures: creatures capable of forming, holding and criticizing beliefs. And rational creatures, he thought, have an intellectual duty to believe only those propositions they can see to be probable with respect to beliefs that are certain for them. This is our duty as rational agents. And justification, as Locke thinks of it, is simply the condition of being within your rights, of not having gone against your duties. You are justified in doing a given thing if it is not contrary to duty for you to do it.

Locke's view of this matter has been extremely influential among epistemologists in general and among those who think about the epistemology of religious belief in particular. Furthermore, given his views it is easy to see why there should be so much concern with proofs or arguments for the existence of God. It is not self-evident that God exists – otherwise there would be no atheists and agnostics – and of course the belief that God exists is not about one's own mental life. But then, according to this Lockean way of thinking, anyone who accepts this belief must see that it is probable with respect to what is certain for them, else they will be going contrary to their duty and deserve blame and disapprobation. And proofs or arguments are just the vehicles by means of which one sees (and shows) that a given belief is *probable with respect to what is certain.*

Evidentialism has come to seem less compelling. First, the whole history of Western philosophy from Descartes to Hume shows that there is little one can really see to be probable with respect to what is certain. If we may only believe propositions that meet that condition, then most of what we believe – that there is an external world, that there are other people, that there has been a past – will not be (or will not clearly be) justified. And second, on sober reflection it just does not seem that there really is a duty to restrict belief to what is probable with respect to what is certain.

If we step back for a broader look, we can distinguish two different kinds of question about religious belief, and two corresponding kinds of criticism or objection. First, there are the claims that religious belief – Christianity, say – is not true: it simply is not true, for example, that there is such a person as God, or that Jesus Christ is the divine son of God. We may call such an objection a de facto *objection: the claim is that the religious belief in question is false, is not factual. But there is another kind of criticism or objection as well. Here the claim is not that religious belief is false, but that whether or not it is false, it is in some way improper – unjustified, irrational or in some way not worthy of belief. The evidentialist objection to religious belief is one version of such a* de jure *criticism of religious belief, and it has been the most prominent objection. But there is another* de jure *objection that has been increasingly important. This is the objection, raised by Freud, Marx and Nietzsche, that religious belief is irrational. What does that mean? According to Freud, religious belief arises out of illusion or wish-fulfilment: we find ourselves confronted by a cruel and heartless nature that delivers pain, fear and hurt, and in the end demands our death. As a response, we (subconsciously) invent a father in heaven who loves us and is really in charge of nature; otherwise we would sink into depression, stupor and death.*

According to Freud, therefore, religious belief arises out of illusion. And the reason this constitutes a criticism of such belief is that this mechanism of illusion is not aimed at the production of true *belief, but rather at belief that has some other, non-truth-related property – in this case, the property of enabling us to carry on in this otherwise discouraging world. It is for this reason that religious belief, on this account, is irrational.*

This is an intriguing criticism of religious belief. But perhaps the most important thing to see about it is that while it is an allegedly de jure *objection to religious belief, it is not really independent of the* de facto *question. For if Christianity is true, then Christian belief pretty clearly is not irrational in Freud's sense at all. If it is true, then indeed there is such a person as God, who intends that we should have knowledge of him; and the cognitive processes that produce belief in God and in the other truths of the Christian religion very likely have as their function the production of true belief in us. On the other hand, if Christianity is false, then it is very likely that Christian belief is not produced by cognitive processes whose purpose it is to produce true belief. This* de jure *criticism of Christian belief, therefore, presupposes that Christian belief is not true; it is viable only if Christian belief is false. If it is intended as a reason for rejecting Christian belief, it is question-begging.*

More generally, it seems that there is no sensible de jure *epistemic criticism of religious belief that is independent of the* de facto *question as to the truth of the belief in question. (The evidentialist criticism is a failure and Freud's complaint is not independent of the* de facto *question whether the religious belief in question is true.) One fairly common critical attitude*

towards religious belief can be expressed as follows: 'As to whether religious belief is true I am completely agnostic – but I do know this: religious belief is irrational.' The above considerations show that this attitude is at best problematic.

1 **Evidentialism**
2 **Evidentialism characterized**
3 **Evidentialism criticized**
4 ***De facto* and *de jure***
5 **Freud and Marx**
6 **The religious riposte**
7 ***De jure* reduced to *de facto***

1 Evidentialism

Epistemology is theory of knowledge: an inquiry into whatever it is that distinguishes knowledge from mere true belief. (For example: due to pathological optimism, you are convinced that you will win the lottery; if by some fluke it turns out you *do* win, your belief will be an example of true belief that is not knowledge.) We need a name for that quality or quantity, whatever precisely it is, that makes the difference between knowledge and mere true belief: call it 'warrant'. Then one would expect the epistemology of religious belief to centre on whether religious belief has warrant, and if so, how much and how it gets it. As a matter of fact, however, epistemological discussion of religious belief, at least since the Enlightenment (and in the Western world), has mostly focused not on the question as to whether religious belief has warrant, but on arguments – in particular, on arguments for and against theistic belief. This is the belief that there exists a person like God as conceived in traditional Christianity, Judaism and Islam: an almighty, all-knowing, wholly benevolent and loving immaterial person who created the world, created human beings in his own image, and continues to act in the world by way of providential care for his creatures.

The most popular theistic proofs or arguments have been the traditional big three – the ontological, cosmological and teleological arguments, to use Kant's terms for them – together with the moral argument (see GOD, ARGUMENTS FOR THE EXISTENCE OF). Of these, the teleological argument, the argument from design (as in Swinburne 1979), is perhaps both the most popular and the most convincing. On the other side, the anti-theistic side, the principal argument has traditionally been the deductive argument from evil: the argument that the existence of an omnipotent, omniscient, wholly good God is logically inconsistent with the existence of evil, or with all the pain, suffering and human wickedness actually found

210

in the world (see EVIL, PROBLEM OF). The deductive argument has fallen out of favour over the last quarter-century as philosophers have come to think that there is no inconsistency here; it has been replaced by the probabilistic argument, according to which it is *unlikely* that there is such a person as God, given all the evil the world displays. The argument from evil is flanked by subsidiary arguments, such as the claim that the very concept of God is incoherent (because, for example, it is thought to be impossible that there be an omnipotent person, or an omniscient person, or a transcendent person who can act in the world, or a person without a body). (As we shall see below, in the nineteenth century Freud and Marx introduced a different style of argument against theistic belief, one according to which such belief is irrational in that it arises out of cognitive malfunction or wish-fulfilment.)

Which of these groups of arguments is the stronger? According to *evidentialism*, belief in God is justifiable only if the former is stronger than the latter.

2 Evidentialism characterized

Why has discussion centred on these arguments, and why does it matter which group is stronger? Indeed, suppose there are no good arguments for religious or theistic belief at all: why should that be thought to create a problem for the believer? To see why we must understand evidentialism with respect to religious belief ('evidentialism' for short). Evidentialism has been the dominant (though not the sole) way of thinking about these matters from the Enlightenment to the present (again, in the Western world). The evidentialist thinks a person who accepts a religious belief must have evidence for that belief. In particular, they must have propositional evidence for it – evidence from other things they believe. And this is why arguments are crucially important: an argument is simply a way of organizing and presenting your propositional evidence for some belief or other. Just to simplify matters, let us follow current custom and think for the most part about theistic belief, belief in God; later we can think also about beliefs that go beyond theism, such as beliefs that distinguish Christianity from Islam and Judaism.

The evidentialist, therefore, thinks a believer in God must have evidence for that belief – but must for what? What will be the matter with them if they do not? The answer, according to the evidentialist, is twofold. In the first place, if they have no (or insufficient) evidence, then the belief will not constitute knowledge. The believer will know that there is such a person as God (that belief will have warrant for

them) only if they have propositional evidence for it – only if they have a good argument for it. But the stakes here are considerably higher than that. For if the believer does not have evidence, then, according to the evidentialist, not only will they lack knowledge, they will also be unjustified in holding this belief; they will not be rationally justified.

But what *is* this justification, and why do we need it? Why is lacking it a problem? And why should the justification of theistic belief be so closely linked to the discussion of theistic and anti-theistic arguments? To answer these questions, we must go back to the beginnings of modern and Enlightenment thought on these questions, to the genesis of Locke's *Essay Concerning Human Understanding* (1689), one of the most influential sources of thought on these topics (see LOCKE, J. §7).

Locke lived through one of the most turbulent periods of British intellectual and spiritual history; it was in particular the religious ferment and diversity, the enormous variety of divergent religious opinion, that caught his attention. There was the Catholic–Protestant debate, and within Protestantism there were countless disagreements and controversies and many warring factions. Locke was deeply concerned about this blooming, buzzing confusion of religious opinion and the civil unrest that went with it. His *Essay* is at least in part designed to ameliorate this problem.

The source of this confusing welter of inconsistent religious opinion, Locke thought, was the propensity of people to indulge themselves in unjustified belief. But what is it to be justified (or unjustified) in holding a belief? According to Locke (as well as René DESCARTES (§7), the other of the twin towers of modern Western epistemology), there are epistemic or intellectual duties, or obligations, or requirements:

Faith is nothing but a firm assent of the mind: which if it be regulated, as is our duty, cannot be afforded to anything, but upon good reason; and so cannot be opposite to it. He that believes, without having any reason for believing, may be in love with his own fancies; but neither seeks truth as he ought, nor pays the obedience due his maker, who would have him use those discerning faculties he has given him, to keep him out of mistake and error. He that does not this to the best of his power, however he sometimes lights on truth, is in the right but by chance; and I know not whether the luckiness of the accident will excuse the irregularity of his proceeding. This at least is certain, that he must be accountable for whatever mistakes he runs into: whereas he that makes use of the light and faculties God has given him, and seeks sincerely to discover truth, by those helps and abilities he has, may have this satisfaction in doing his duty as a rational creature, that though he should miss truth, he will not miss the reward of it. For he governs his assent right, and places it as he should, who in any case or matter whatsoever, believes or disbelieves, according as reason directs him. He that does otherwise, transgresses against his own light, and misuses those faculties, which were given him.

(1689: IV.xvii.24)

We have a duty to regulate our belief a certain way. If we do not, we are accountable. One who regulates belief in this way has the satisfaction of 'doing his duty as a rational creature'; such a person 'governs his assent right and places it as he should'. Rational creatures, creatures capable of holding and with-holding belief, have duties and obligations with respect to the regulation of their belief or assent. And the central core of the notion of justification (as the etymology of the term indicates) is this: a person is justified in an action or belief if, in taking that action or holding that belief, they violate no duties or obligations, conform to the relevant requirements, are within their rights. To be justified in believing something is to be *responsible* in forming and holding those beliefs; it is to be flouting no duty in holding them. This way of thinking of justified belief (together with analogical extensions of one kind or another) has remained dominant from Locke's day to this.

Now Locke believed that if only everyone could be persuaded to restrict assent to those beliefs in which they were justified, we would no longer be confronted with this confusing welter of religious belief. His reasoning is as follows. A belief is justified for me, he says, just if I am within my epistemic rights, am flouting no duties or obligations in holding that belief. But what are my duties or obligations in this area? According to Locke, the central epistemic duty is this: to believe a proposition only to the degree that it is probable with respect to what is *certain* for you. Which beliefs are certain for you? There are two kinds. First, according to Locke (here again he concurs with Descartes), there are propositions about your own immediate experience that are certain for you: that you have a mild headache, for instance, or that you are thinking about dinosaurs. And second, there are propositions that are self-evident for you: necessarily true propositions so obvious that you cannot so much as entertain them without seeing that they must be true. (Examples would be simple arithmetical and logical propositions, together with such propositions as that red is a colour, and that whatever exists has properties.) Propositions of these two sorts are certain for you, and you are auto-

matically justified in believing them; as for other propositions, you are justified in believing any one of them, says Locke, only to the degree to which that proposition is probable with respect to what is certain for you. (Here he differs from Descartes, who seems to say that you are justified in believing a proposition that is not certain for you only if that proposition follows deductively from propositions that are certain for you.) According to the whole modern founda-tionalist tradition initiated by Locke and Descartes, therefore, you have a duty not to accept a proposition unless either it is certain for you, or it is (at least) probable with respect to what is certain for you. If a proposition is not certain for you, you have a duty to refrain from believing it unless you have propositional evidence for it. But it was Locke's belief that if we all did our epistemic duty and believed only propositions we could see to be probable with respect to what is certain for us, we would not find ourselves in disagreement, or at least would not disagree nearly as often.

Returning to theistic belief, we can see how the above thought about justification applies. First, this belief is not certain for us: it is neither self-evident (since there are atheists and agnostics, it is not such that grasping or understanding it guarantees accept-ing it); nor is it about one's own mental states. Therefore theistic belief, on Locke's way of thinking, is justified only if there is propositional evidence for it – more exactly, a person is justified in accepting theistic belief only if they believe it on the basis of a good argument for it, an argument whose premises are certain for them. And this is the linchpin of the way of thinking about the justification of theistic belief that has prevailed from Locke's time to ours. Theistic belief is justified only if it is probable with respect to what is certain; it is probable with respect to what is certain only if there are good arguments for it; therefore theistic belief is justified only if there are good arguments for it. But then of course it is very easy to see why discussion of theistic belief has tended to focus on the arguments for and against theism.

Now Locke does not *argue* for this position; he simply *announces* it. Subsequent thinkers who have discussed the justification of theistic belief have for the most part followed him here, both in announcing the position and in failing to argue for it. Thus W.K. Clifford trumpets that 'it is wrong, always, every-where, and for anyone to believe anything upon insufficient evidence' (1879: 183); his is perhaps the most prominent in a considerable chorus of voices insisting that there is an intellectual duty not to believe in God unless you have a good argument for that belief. (A few others in the choir are Brand Blanshard (1974: 400–), H.H. Price, Bertrand Russell and Michael Scriven.) According to all these thinkers, if you accept theistic belief without having a good argument for it, you are going contrary to epistemic duty, are therefore unjustified in accepting it, and are living in epistemic sin.

3 Evidentialism criticized

It is widely thought that there are several important problems with this approach to the epistemology of theistic belief. First, the standards for theistic arguments have traditionally been set absurdly high (and perhaps part of the responsibility for this must be laid at the door of some who have offered these arguments and claimed that they constitute wholly demonstrative proofs). The idea seems to be that a good theistic argument must start from what is self-evident or utterly obvious and proceed majestically by way of self-evidently valid argument forms to its conclusion. It is no wonder that few if any theistic arguments meet that lofty standard – after all, almost no philosophical arguments of any sort meet it.

Second, attention has been mostly confined to three theistic arguments: the traditional ontological, cosmological and teleological arguments. But in fact there are many more theistic arguments. For example, there are arguments from the nature of proper function, and from the nature of propositions, numbers and sets. There are arguments from intentionality, from counterfactuals, from the confluence of epistemic reliability with epistemic justification, from reference, simplicity, intuition and love. There are arguments from colours and flavours, from miracles, play and enjoyment, from morality, from beauty and from the meaning of life. There is even a theistic argument from the existence of horrifying evil.

But there is a third and much deeper problem. The basic assumption underlying traditional thought about the justification of theistic belief is that such belief is justified only if there is a good argument for it from other propositions you believe. But why believe that? Perhaps *some* beliefs are like that. Scientific hypotheses – special relativity or the theory of evolution, for example – are such that if you believe them without evidence you are irresponsible. For such theories have been devised to explain certain phenomena, and they get all their warrant from their success in so doing. (Even so, would you really be irresponsible in believing such a proposition without evidence, or just foolish or irrational?) But other beliefs – such as memory beliefs, or belief in other minds – are not like that at all; they are not hypotheses, and are not accepted because of their explanatory powers. Now why assume that theistic belief, belief in God, is in this

regard more like a scientific hypothesis than like, say, a memory belief? Why think that the justification of theistic belief depends upon the evidential relation of theistic belief to other things one believes?

According to Locke, it is because there is a duty not to assent to a proposition unless you can see that it is probable with respect to what is certain to you; but is there really any such duty? No one has succeeded in showing that, say, belief in other minds or the belief that there has been a past is probable with respect to what is certain for us. Suppose it is not: does it follow that you are living in epistemic sin if you believe that there are other minds? Or a past? Nearly everyone recognizes such duties as that of shunning gratuitous cruelty, of taking care of one's children and one's aged parents, and the like; but do we also find ourselves recognizing that there is a duty not to believe what is not probable (or what we cannot see to be probable) with respect to what is certain for us? Hardly. But then it is hard to see why being justified in believing in God requires that the existence of God be probable with respect to some such body of evidence as the set of propositions certain for you. Perhaps theistic belief is properly basic – that is, such that one can be justified in accepting it without accepting it on the evidential basis of other propositions one believes.

For consider a typical Christian believer: they have been brought up as a Christian, and for the most part Christian belief has always seemed to them clearly true. While they have never looked carefully into the alleged objections to Christian belief, what they have heard of them does not seem promising; those whom they respect on these matters tell them the objections are without foundation and they accept this. Such a person, surely, is not to be censured; they are not a proper subject of moral disapprobation. They may be mistaken, deluded, even foolish; they may be insufficiently critical; but there is no reason to think them unjustified or derelict in their epistemic duties.

On the other hand, consider someone sophisticated in these matters and very well aware of the critics. This person does not believe on the basis of propositional evidence; they therefore believe in the basic way. Can they be justified? They read the critics, but on careful reflection do not find them compelling; likewise, although they are aware of theistic arguments and find some of them not without value, they do not believe on the basis of them. Rather, this person has a rich inner spiritual life; it seems to them that they sometimes catch a glimpse of the overwhelming beauty and loveliness of God; they are often aware, as it strongly seems to them, of the work of the Holy Spirit in their heart, comforting, encouraging, teaching, and leading them to accept the 'great things of the gospel' as Jonathan Edwards (1746) calls them. After long, hard, conscientious reflection, they find all this enormously more convincing than the complaints of the critics. Are they then going contrary to duty in believing as they do? Are they being irresponsible? Clearly not. There could be something defective about them, some malfunction not apparent on the surface. They could be mistaken, a victim of an illusion; they could be a victim of wishful thinking, despite their best efforts. They could be wrong, desperately wrong, pitiably wrong, in thinking these things. But they are not flouting any discernible duty; they are doing their level best to fulfil their epistemic responsibilities. They are certainly justified.

Taking justification in that original etymological sense, therefore, there is every reason to doubt that one is justified in holding theistic belief only if one has evidence for it. Of course, the term 'justification' has undergone various analogical extensions in the work of various philosophers. Thus it is sometimes used just to mean propositional evidence; then to say that a belief is justified for someone is to say that they have (sufficient) propositional evidence for it. In that sense of 'justified', of course, a person will be justified only if they have evidence. But you cannot settle a substantive question just by giving a definition. If you accept that definition, then the real question is whether there is anything amiss with holding beliefs that are unjustified. Perhaps one does not have propositional evidence for one's memory beliefs; if so, those beliefs would be unjustified in that sense, but none the worse for that; it would not suggest that there is something wrong with holding them. And the same goes for theistic belief.

4   De facto and de jure

Suppose we try to set evidentialism in a broader perspective. Ever since the Enlightenment, there have been two kinds of critical question about religious belief. On the one hand, there are those who argue that religious beliefs are false or at any rate improbable: it is at best unlikely that (say) there is such a person as God, or that, if there is, Jesus Christ is his divine Son. (Here typical arguments would include the anti-theistic arguments mentioned above.) Since this question is about the truth or factual character of Christian belief, we may call it the *de facto* question. On the other hand, there is the question of the propriety, or reasonability, or justification, or rationality, or to combine those last two, the rational justification of Christian belief. Christian belief may be true and it may be false; but even if it happens to be true, so these critics say, there are

serious questions as to whether it is rational or rationally justifiable to accept it. Call this the *de jure* question. The claim that belief in God is unjustified (that is, irresponsible) because there is insufficient evidence for it, is an example of a *de jure* criticism; as we have seen, however, this claim has very little to be said for it. This claim has been the dominant *de jure* criticism of religious belief; but the nineteenth century saw the rise of another kind of *de jure* criticism, one associated with those three great 'masters of suspicion', Nietzsche, Freud and Marx.

Freud and Marx insisted that Christian belief is irrational. (Of course it was not only Christian belief that drew their fire). Nietzsche's complaint could also be examined here: that religion originates in slave morality, in the *ressentiment* of the oppressed (see NIETZSCHE, F. §§8–9). As Nietzsche puts it, Christianity both arises from and fosters a sort of weak, snivelling, cowardly, servile and generally disgusting sort of character, which is at the same time envious, self-righteous and full of hate disguised as loving kindness. In what follows, we shall ignore Nietzsche, considering the objection Freud and Marx bring against religious belief, with the emphasis upon Freud.

5   Freud and Marx

Some of Freud's treatment of religious belief is perhaps rather fanciful – for example, his suggestion that religion originated in a remarkable transaction among the 'primal horde'. (The sons of the dominant male, jealous of their father because he had seized all the women for himself, killed and ate him; religion somehow emerged from the resulting guilt and remorse.) But he also makes a much more sober claim about the 'psychical origin of religious ideas':

These, which are given out as teachings, are not precipitates of experience or end-results of thinking: they are illusions, fulfilments of the oldest, strongest and most urgent wishes of mankind. The secret of their strength lies in the strength of those wishes. As we already know, the terrifying impression of helplessness in childhood aroused the need for protection – for protection through love – which was provided by the father; and the recognition that this helplessness lasts throughout life made it necessary to cling to the existence of a father, but this time a more powerful one. Thus the benevolent rule of a divine Providence allays our fear of the dangers of life; the establishment of a moral world-order ensures the fulfilment of the demands of justice, which have so often remained unfulfilled in human civilization; and the prolongation of earthly existence in a future life provides the local and temporal framework in which these wish-fulfilments shall take place.

(1927: 30)

The idea is that theistic belief arises from a psychological mechanism FREUD (§4) calls 'wish-fulfilment'; in this case, the wish is father, not to the deed, but to the belief. Nature rises up against us, cold, pitiless, implacable, and blind to our needs and desires. It delivers hurt, fear and pain, and in the end demands our death. Paralysed and appalled, we invent (unconsciously, of course) a Father in Heaven who exceeds our earthly fathers as much in power and knowledge as in goodness and benevolence; we believe he loves and cares for us. The alternative would be to sink into depression, stupor and finally death. According to Freud, belief in God is an illusion, in a semi-technical use of the term: a belief that arises from the mechanism of wish-fulfilment. But if Freud intends this as a criticism of religious belief, he must be thinking that what he says in some way discredits it, casts doubt upon it, and, in a word, shows that there is something wrong with it. So what, precisely, is the problem? We can put it by saying that religious belief (specifically theistic belief) is irrational; but what does that mean? Irrational in what way? In order to understand what is really involved in that complaint, we must make a brief excursion into the assumptions underlying the sort of criticism it represents.

It is natural to think that there are intellectual, or cognitive, or rational powers or faculties – for example, perception and memory. These powers or processes produce in us the myriad beliefs we hold. They are something like instruments; and like instruments, they have a function or purpose. If we thought of ourselves as created and designed either by a Master Craftsman or by Evolution, these cognitive faculties would be the parts of our total cognitive establishment whose purpose it is to produce beliefs in us. Their purpose, furthermore, is presumably to produce true beliefs in us; to put it a bit less passively, they are designed in such a way that by using them properly we can come to true belief. Our cognitive faculties work over an immensely large area to deliver beliefs on many different topics: beliefs about our immediate environment, about the external world at large, about the past, about numbers, propositions and other abstract objects and the relations between them, about other people and what they are thinking and feeling, about what the future will be like, about right and wrong, about what is necessary and impossible, and about God himself.

These faculties are aimed at the truth in the sense that their purpose or function is to furnish us with true belief. And like any other instruments or organs,

they can work either well or ill; they can function properly or malfunction. A wart or a tumour does not function properly, but nor does it malfunction (although it might be by virtue of malfunction that the tumour is present). That is because it has no function or purpose. But an organ – such as your heart, liver or pancreas – does have a function, and does either work properly or malfunction. And the same goes for cognitive faculties or capacities: they too can function well or badly. Further, we ordinarily take it for granted that when our cognitive faculties are functioning properly, when they are not subject to dysfunction or malfunction, then for the most part the beliefs they produce are at least close to the truth. There is, we might say, a presumption of reliability for properly functioning faculties; we are inclined (rightly or wrongly) to take it that properly functioning cognitive faculties for the most part deliver true belief. No doubt there will be mistakes and disagreements, and we may be inclined to scepticism about certain special areas of belief – political beliefs, for example, as well as beliefs formed at the very limits of our ability, as in cosmology and subatomic physics – but the bulk of the everyday beliefs delivered by our rational faculties, so we think, are true.

But when our cognitive faculties malfunction, they do not fulfil their purpose of furnishing us with true belief – or if they do, it is by accident. Insanity is an extreme case of malfunction of the rational faculties. But there are more subtle ways in which irrational or non-rational beliefs can be formed in us. First, there are belief-forming mechanisms that are not aimed at the formation of true belief, but at the formation of belief with some other property – contributing to survival, perhaps, or peace of mind or psychological comfort. Someone with a lethal disease may believe their chances of recovery much higher than the statistics in their possession warrant; their so believing itself improves their chances of recovery. The function of the process producing this belief is not that of furnishing true beliefs, but beliefs that make it more likely that the believer will recover. A person may be blinded (as we say) by ambition, failing to see that a certain course of action is wrong or stupid, even though it is obvious to everyone else. Our idea is that the inordinately ambitious person fails to recognize something they would otherwise recognize; the normal functioning of some aspect of their cognitive powers is inhibited or overridden or impeded by that excessive ambition. You may be blinded also by fear, lust, anger, pride, grief, social pressure, and even loyalty, continuing to believe in the honesty of your friend long after an objective look at the evidence would have dictated a reluctant change of mind.

So there are at least three ways in which a belief can

fail to be a proper deliverance of our rational faculties: it may be produced by malfunctioning faculties, or it may be produced by cognitive processes aimed at something other than the truth, or the proper function of rational faculties can be impeded and overridden by lust, mother love, ambition, greed, grief, fear, low self-esteem and other emotional conditions. And here we come to the heart of Freud's objection: when Freud says that theistic belief is irrational, his basic idea is that belief of this sort is not produced by the unimpeded proper function of belief-producing processes whose purpose it is to furnish us with true belief. This means that the presumption of reliability attaching to properly functioning cognitive faculties does not apply to the processes that yield belief in God. The idea is that theistic belief has a source distinct from those of our faculties that are aimed at the truth – or, if such belief does somehow issue from those truth-aimed faculties, their operation, in producing such belief, is impeded by other factors. It is therefore irrational; and it is also irrational in the further sense that it is inconsistent with rational belief. For this reason the presumption of reliability does not attach to religious belief.

Marx's views differ from Freud's here in an interesting way. MARX (§3) thinks that religion arises from cognitive malfunction: 'Man is *the world of man*, the state, society. This state, this society, produce religion, *a perverted world consciousness*, because they are a *perverted* world' (Marx and Engels [1844] 1964: 41–2; original italics). So Marx's idea, fundamentally, is that religious belief is produced by *malfunctioning* cognitive faculties – malfunctioning in response to social and political malfunction. Freud, on the other hand, thinks theistic belief is an *illusion* in his special sense of a cognitive mechanism that is aimed, not at the truth, but at psychological wellbeing. But illusions have their functions; they may serve important ends (such as the end Freud thinks religious belief does serve). When our cognitive faculties produce illusions, therefore, they are not necessarily malfunctioning. So Marx thinks theistic belief is the product of malfunctioning cognitive faculties, whereas Freud thinks it is the product of cognitive processes not aimed at the truth. They concur in thinking that theistic belief is irrational in the double sense that it is not produced by unimpeded properly functioning cognitive faculties aimed at the truth, and it runs counter to the deliverances of our rational powers. As Freud puts it, religious belief is 'patently infantile', and 'foreign to reality'.

6 The religious riposte

Of course, Christians and other theists will not agree

that theistic belief is irrational in this sense; they will have their own views as to how it is that belief in God is formed, their own candidates for the sources of belief in God. Thomas AQUINAS (§11), for example, speaks of a 'natural (and confused)' knowledge of God. John CALVIN (§2) develops this idea, suggesting that we human beings have a *sensus divinitatis* (a sense of divinity) whereby under a wide variety of circumstances – danger, perception of the beauties and wonders of nature, perception of our own sinful condition – we form true beliefs about God. The *sensus divinitatis*, according to Calvin, is a natural, inborn faculty with which human beings have been created; in this respect it resembles perception, memory, reason and other cognitive faculties. What is important in all these views is that our beliefs about God are produced by cognitive faculties aimed at the truth and functioning properly; hence on these views such belief is not at all irrational in the sense intended by Freud and Marx.

There is a complication here: according to Christianity, our natural knowledge of God has been compromised by sin, which has cognitive or noetic as well as moral and spiritual results. As a result, God, as Anselm says, is obscured by the smoke of our wrongdoing. But (again, according to Christianity) God has made a gracious response to our human sinful condition. There is the offer of salvation and eternal life, available through the sacrificial death and resurrection of Jesus Christ, the divine Son of God. But there is also a cognitive component to the divine response. This is God's providing a way by which we human beings can come to know and appropriate the gracious offer of salvation. Here Christians will think of the Scripture, the Church, and perhaps above all, the inward testimony of the Holy Spirit. The doctrine of the work of the Holy Spirit was developed perhaps most fully in the Reformed tradition and in particular by the great Puritan divines. According to John Calvin, the principal work of the Holy Spirit in the life of a Christian is the production of faith, which includes at the least a deep acceptance of the gracious offer of salvation, and a deep conviction of the truth of the essentials of Christian teaching. In so far as Christian belief (including belief in God) is a result of the work of the Holy Spirit, it is not a product just of natural faculties; the activity of the Holy Spirit is supernatural. But of course it is not at all irrational in the sense of the objection from Freud and Marx: it is not produced by cognitive faculties that are malfunctioning or aimed at something other than the truth. Instead, these beliefs are produced in us (with our concurrence) by the work of God himself, as part of his gracious response to the human sinful condition. From this point of view, then, Christian faith is in no way irrational, and, indeed, is a form of knowledge (given most accounts of knowledge), so that it is an error to *contrast* faith with knowledge; for faith is one kind of knowledge.

7 *De jure* reduced to *de facto*

Freud, Marx, Nietzsche and their confrères claim that theistic belief is irrational (in the sense explained); Christians and other believers in God deny this. Who is right? Here it is important to see that this question cannot really be settled apart from the question as to whether Christian or theistic belief is true. First, it is clear that if Christian belief is true, then very likely it is rational; it is produced by unimpeded cognitive faculties functioning properly and aimed at the production of true belief. For if Christian belief is true, then we have been created by God and created in his image, one aspect of which involves our being able to resemble him with respect to knowledge. Further, God has instituted a way of salvation for human beings, and has also made available to us the means to know of and apprehend that salvation. When Christians form these beliefs, therefore, they do so by way of mechanisms that are working properly and successfully aimed at the production of true belief. So if Christian belief is true, it is rational. On the other hand, if Christian or theistic belief is false (if, for example, naturalism is true), then these beliefs constitute massive error, and it is hard to see how cognitive faculties functioning properly and aimed at the truth could produce them. Whatever mechanisms do produce them then, those mechanisms must be either malfunctioning or, like wishful thinking, be aimed at something other than the truth.

Once we see this, however, we see an important point about the version of the *de jure* criticism offered by Freud and Marx. What we see is that this question as to the rationality (or lack thereof) of Christian belief is not really just an epistemological question at all; it is at bottom a metaphysical, or theological, or religious question. For it is to be answered in terms of the answer to another question: what sort of beings are human persons, and what sorts of belief do their noetic faculties produce when they are functioning properly? Your view as to what sort of creature a human being is will determine or at any rate heavily influence your views as to what it is rational or irrational for human beings to believe. But the answer to that question depends on whether or not Christian theism is true. And so the dispute as to whether theistic belief is rational, in the present sense, cannot be settled just by attending to epistemological considerations; it is at bottom not merely an epistemological dispute, but a metaphysical or theological dispute.

You may think humankind is created by God in the image of God – and created both with a natural tendency to see God's hand in the world about us, and with a natural tendency to recognize that we have indeed been created and are beholden to our creator, owing him worship, obedience and allegiance. You may add that the source of distinctively Christian belief lies in the work of God himself. Then of course you will not think of belief in God or Christian belief as (in the typical case) a manifestation of cognitive dysfunction or any other kind of intellectual defect; nor is it a product of some mechanism not aimed at the truth. (It is then more like a deliverance of sense perception, or memory, or sympathy – or perhaps the faculty responsible for a priori knowledge.) On the other hand, you may think we human beings are the product of blind evolutionary forces; you may think that we are part of a Godless universe. Then you will no doubt be inclined to go along with Freud and Marx in seeing belief in God as either a product of cognitive dysfunction or of a mechanism whose function is not that of the production of true belief. If you adopt the former view, you will of course think Christian belief eminently rational; if you adopt the latter you will think it irrational. But the important thing to see is that this dispute cannot be settled by attending only to epistemology: at bottom it is a dispute about the truth of Christian belief. To determine whether Christian theism is rational, therefore, one must first determine whether it is true. But then this *de jure* question – the one associated with Freud and Marx – is not after all independent of the *de facto* question. To answer the former, we must already know the answer to the latter.

What we have seen so far is that there are fundamentally two *de jure* criticisms of Christian theism: the evidentialist objection and that from Freud and Marx. The first is easily seen to be mistaken and the second is not independent of the *de facto* question of the truth of Christian belief. But then it seems that there are no any sensible *de jure* questions or criticisms that are independent of the *de facto* question of the truth of Christianity. And this means that the only possibly successful objections to Christian or theistic belief will have to be to the *truth* of such belief, not to its rationality, or justification, or intellectual respectability, or rational justification, or whatever. The only possibly successful objections are *de facto* objections; the *de jure* objections drop away.

See also: AGNOSTICISM; ATHEISM; DEISM; EPISTEMOLOGY, HISTORY OF; FAITH; NATURAL THEOLOGY; RELIGION, HISTORY OF PHILOSOPHY OF §8

References and further reading

Alston, W. (1991) *Perceiving God*, Cornell, NY: Cornell University Press. (Powerful and probing inquiry into the justification of Christian belief; it concludes that religious belief can receive justification by way of *perceiving* God. Requires a little preliminary work in epistemology.)

* Blanshard, B. (1974) *Reason and Belief*, London: Allen & Unwin, 400–. (Elegant statement of a rationalist position with respect to the justification of religious belief.)

* Clifford, W.K. (1879) 'The Ethics of Belief', Lectures and Essays, London: Macmillan. (Classic statement of the position that belief without evidence is unjustifiable and contrary to duty.)

* Edwards, J. (1746) *Religious Affections*, ed. J.E. Smith, New Haven, CT: Yale University Press, 1959. (Not explicitly on the topic of the epistemology of religious belief, but contains a wealth of suggestions about the work of the Holy Spirit in producing Christian belief.)

* Freud, S. (1927) *Die Zukunft einer Illusion*, Leipzig and Zurich: Internationaler Psychoanalytischer Verlag; trans. and ed. J. Strachey, *The Future of an Illusion*, New York and London: W.W. Norton. (Freud's account of the nature and prospects of religious belief.)

Gale, R. (1991) *On the Nature and Existence of God*, Cambridge: Cambridge University Press. (An inquiry into the question as to whether there are any good arguments for or against the existence of God. Technical in places.)

* Locke, J. (1689) *An Essay Concerning Human Understanding*, with Locke's 'Prolegomena', ed. A. Fraser, Oxford: Oxford University Press, 1894; New York: Dover, 1959, bk IV. (An influential source of the dominant contemporary way of thinking about the justification of religious belief.)

Mackie, J. (1982) *The Miracle of Theism*, Oxford: Clarendon Press. (Perhaps the best contemporary argument for the position that theistic belief is unjustified.)

* Marx, K. and Engels, F. (1844) *Contribution to the Critique of Hegel's Philosophy of Right*, in R. Niebuhr (ed.) *On Religion*, Chicago, IL: Scholars Press, 1964. (Contains Marx's and Engels' account and criticism of religious belief.)

Plantinga, A. (1974) *God, Freedom and Evil*, Grand Rapids, MI: Eerdmans. (Argues that there is no inconsistency in the propositions that God exists and that there is evil.)

—— (1998) *Warranted Christian Belief*, New York: Oxford University Press. (Argues that the epistemological objections to Christian belief fail, that Christian belief is warranted if true, and that belief in naturalism is irrational.)

* Swinburne, R. (1979) *The Existence of God*, Oxford: Clarendon Press; revised edn, 1991. (Detailed and powerful development of the theistic argument from design.)

Wolterstorff, N. and Plantinga, A. (eds) (1983) *Faith and Rationality*, Notre Dame, IN: University of Notre Dame Press. (An influential collection of essays by the editors and others on the rationality or justification of Christian and theistic belief; for the most part the essays reject classical foundationalism with respect to theistic belief.)

Wykstra, S. (1989) 'Towards a Sensible Evidentialism: On the Notion of "Needing Evidence"', in W. Rowe and W. Wainwright (eds) *Philosophy of Religion: Selected Readings*, New York: Harcourt Brace Jovanovich. (Argues that the sort of evidentialism associated with classical foundationalism is extravagant and clearly mistaken, but that there is a more restrained variety of evidentialism that makes much better sense.)

ALVIN PLANTINGA

RELIGION AND MORALITY

The relationship between religion and morality has been of special and long-standing concern to philosophers. Not only is there much overlap between the two areas, but how to understand their proper relationship is a question that has stimulated much debate. Of special interest in philosophical discussions has been the question of divine authority and the moral life. If there is a God, how are we to understand the moral status of his commands? Are there moral standards that even God must acknowledge? Or does God's commanding something make it morally binding? Secular thinkers have insisted that these questions pose a serious dilemma for any religiously based ethic: either the moral standards are independent of God's will, with the result that God's authority is not supreme, or God's will is arbitrary, which means that what appears to be a morality is really a worship of brute power. Many religious ethicists have refused to acknowledge the dilemma, arguing for an understanding of divine moral directives as expressions of the complexities and excellences of God's abiding attributes.

The impact of religion on moral selfhood has also been much disputed. Secularists of various stripes have insisted that religion is not conducive to moral maturity. Religious thinkers have responded by exploring the ways in which one's notion of moral maturity is shaped by one's larger worldview. If we believe that there is a God who has provided us with important moral information, then this will influence the ways we understand what is to count as a 'mature' and 'rational' approach to moral decision making.

Religious ethicists have had a special interest in the ways in which worldviews shape our understandings of moral questions. This interest has been necessitated by the fact of diversity within religious communities. Different moral traditions coexist in Christianity, for example, corresponding to the rich diversity of theological perspectives and the plurality of cultural settings in which Christian beliefs have taken shape. This complexity has provided some resources for dealing with the 'postmodern' fascination with moral relativism and moral scepticism.

The relationship between religion and morality is also important for questions of practical moral decision. Religious ethical systems have often been developed with an eye to their 'preachability', which means that religious ethicists have a long record of attempting to relate theory to practice in moral discussion. The ability of a moral system to provide practical guidance is especially important during times of extensive moral confusion.

1   **God and moral authority**
2   **Moral maturity**
3   **Morality and worldview**
4   **Practical ethics**

1   God and moral authority

It is not surprising that philosophers have devoted considerable attention to the relationship between religion and morality. Both areas of discourse address the issue of how people are to order their lives so as to promote human flourishing in the light of 'ultimate concerns'. The relationship is also one that easily generates controversies. The notion that morality has a close link to religion has been deeply offensive to those philosophers who have wanted to protect the 'autonomy' of ethics. Their passion in addressing the topic has often been matched by those philosophers who have been convinced that the moral life requires a commitment to 'absolutes' that can only be provided by a religious perspective.

Religious activity extends, of course, well beyond the range of specifically moral concerns. Believers have typically insisted, however, that religious teachings provide the larger context in which the claims of morality find their proper place. Most religious systems portray the good life, including the morally good life, as grounded in obedience to the will of God. (Some religious perspectives are polytheistic,

and a few are even properly characterized as atheistic; here, however, we will focus on monotheistic religion (see ATHEISM §1; MONOTHEISM §§1–2).) It is often argued from a religious perspective that the moral convictions of all human beings, whether or not they consciously acknowledge God's moral authority, presuppose, or are in some other sense dependent upon, a divinely instituted moral ordering of reality. Philosophers who have been critical of religious belief as such have often focused on this alleged connection in arguing for the independence of morality from religious teachings.

The terms of the debate over these issues were established early on in the Western philosophical tradition, when Plato asked in the *Euthyphro* whether the gods themselves must honour the standards of 'the pious or holy'. The issues at stake here have loomed large in philosophical discussions of religion and morality. Are there standards of goodness and obligation that even God must acknowledge, since they are independent of the divine will? Or are we to view divine directives as morally binding simply because they are willed by God? For many religious thinkers, neither option has been especially attractive as stated. If moral standards have their own reality, independent of the divine will, then God's supreme moral authority is called into question. If, on the other hand, moral standards are themselves created by God, then the divine will would seem to be arbitrary: God could have created a moral order that conflicts in very basic ways with the convictions acknowledged by existing religious systems (see VOLUNTARISM).

Philosophical critics of religious belief have persistently pressed these points. On occasion, they have done so in the hope of demonstrating the basic incoherence of any attempt to provide a religious grounding for morality. If God's will is viewed as arbitrary, then it is difficult to see, the argument goes, how we can rescue the *moral* enterprise. In such a universe, human obedience to divine directives is essentially a subjection to brute power; here, it would seem, duty and moral deliberation have no obvious role to play. Some believers have been willing to concede this point. Peter Geach once gave a blunt answer to the charge that obedience to the will of God is 'plain power worship': indeed it is, he responded, 'but it is worship of Supreme power, and as such is wholly different from, and does not carry with it, a cringing attitude toward earthly powers' (1969: 127).

Many religious ethicists have stopped short of that kind of unnuanced understanding of the situation. In formulating their alternatives, they have generally opted for one of two strategies. The first is to defend a *compatibilist* perspective. Here it is argued that the acceptance of religiously based ethical directives is compatible with adherence to a more generally accepted philosophical perspective. A number of major philosophical ethicists have encouraged such an approach. For example, Jeremy BENTHAM (§2) defended the ultimacy of the utilitarian principle by attempting to show that the principle of utility was simply an explication of that which is accepted by all human beings, 'wheresoever they have a clear view of their own interest'. He immediately applied this to religious believers: those who submit to the commands of God are aiming at that kind of personal happiness that can best be attained 'by God's appointment, either in this life, or in a life to come' ([1823] 1961: 40). Similarly, John Stuart MILL (§§8–11) attacked the notion that utilitarians advocate 'a *godless* doctrine' by suggesting that to submit to the will of a God who wants his creatures to be happy is to 'fulfil the requirement of utility in a supreme degree' ([1861] 1961: 423). Adopting a very different approach to moral justification, Immanuel KANT (§§9–11) held that many of the moral directives found in the Bible can be viewed as conforming to the categorical imperative. Ethicists working within specific religious traditions have sometimes seized on the opportunities offered by such accounts, arguing that engaging in religious moral practices is quite consistent with the acceptance of one or another of the perspectives in the philosophical tradition. One of the more sophisticated attempts along these lines can be found in William Frankena's 'Ideal Observer' theory of moral justification (Frankena 1976). Frankena contends that in the making of moral judgments we are implicitly claiming a consensus for what we are advocating: to say that something is right or good is to insist, in effect, that we would be sustained in our verdict by everyone who takes the moral point of view, and who thinks about the subject in a clear-headed and rational way in the light of all relevant facts. In short, as Frankena puts it, it is to insist that our position is the one that would hold up on 'the Day of Judgment'. This is not to prove, of course, that the making of moral judgments entails the existence of a divine Judge. But it does suggest that a wise, omniscient and benevolent deity would be in the best position to determine questions of moral value.

A second strategy is to take a *distinctivist* approach, portraying religious ethics as a unique alternative to the standard options in philosophical understandings of moral justification. On such a view, God is not simply a Platonic contemplator of rationally discernible ideals, nor is he a utilitarian calculator, a Kantian universalizer or an Ideal Observer. None of these philosophical perspectives,

it is insisted, can do justice to God's moral authority as we experience it from within the religious life. A common line of argument here is that God's will is not arbitrary, but is an expression of his attributes. For example, Eleonore Stump and Norman Kretzmann (1991) have defended such a view by appealing to Thomas Aquinas' thesis that God is essential goodness itself; on this understanding of God's nature, the relationship between God and moral principles is neither one of subjective divine arbitrariness nor of God subscribing to standards that are independent of the divine nature (see SIMPLICITY, DIVINE).

A 'third way' approach of this sort points to the need for a somewhat fluid understanding of the process of moral formation. To the obvious question, for example, of how we know that God's attributes are morally good unless we employ some independent standard of moral value, the answer can be given that the ways in which we learn, refine and employ moral standards and beliefs are complicated. The adult convert to a religious perspective surely brings certain moral notions to the initial encounter with God; but these notions can themselves be transformed as the person internalizes a new and complex belief system. In such a process, it is not always clear where we apply 'independent' standards of evaluation in assessing divine directives and where we submit our previous moral commitments to divine scrutiny for correction and even transformation. Basil Mitchell makes this case by observing that while submission to God's moral authority does require that 'we can recognize what is excellent', it surely is not the case 'that the only sufficient reason for believing God to be good is our own ability, independently, to think up the divine decrees for ourselves' (1980: 150).

2 Moral maturity

Critics of religiously based moral perspectives have not only focused on divine moral authority. They have also objected strenuously to the notion that submission to divine authority is a way of promoting human flourishing. The objection takes many forms. Some have argued that a morality based on obedience to a divine will is 'infantile' (Patrick Nowell-Smith 1966); others see it as 'prehuman' (Erich Fromm) or 'bad faith' (Simone de Beauvoir), or as promoting a 'loss of self' (Karl MARX (§3)). These various formulations embody a common core objection: that the posture of obedience to a will that is 'external' to, or 'higher' than, one's own is an impediment to human flourishing. Moral maturity requires the development of a healthy sense of freedom, as autonomous selves chart their own moral courses without coercion. To accept God's moral directives, however 'benevolent' they might be, is destructive in a very fundamental way to the moral enterprise.

One prominent religious response to this analysis is to challenge the ways in which concepts such as autonomy and maturity are being used. Autonomous selfhood does not require the creation of moral principles and values *ex nihilo*. It is enough to take responsibility for the standards one accepts and the decisions one makes. And such a sense of responsible freedom is not alien to a life that centres on obedience to the will of God. For example, the biblical notion of the 'covenantal' framework for the believer's relationship to God highlights the importance of responsible selfhood in the religious life.

Obedience to the divine will can be viewed as an important manifestation of moral maturity. To be a mature person requires a willingness to take the facts seriously. If one happens to believe that God in fact exists, and is infinitely greater than human beings in his knowledge, goodness and power, then it would be immature, even self-deceptive, to ignore God's moral greatness. If God is in fact a loving Creator, who desires that human beings experience the divine peace, then to serve such a God is to realize new dimensions of mature human selfhood. Someone might insist, of course, that the factual claims that are basic to a religious perspective – that there is a God, that God has revealed important information about moral reality, that human beings are sinners who are very much in need of moral guidance – are so outlandish that their endorsement is itself a sign of immaturity. While these are important issues to raise, to do so is to shift the discussion away from specifically moral themes to more general philosophical topics having to do with the ways in which we form and justify our beliefs.

A religious understanding of morality, then, cannot be criticized without also challenging the larger complex of beliefs with which it is intimately associated. To criticize such a perspective in the name of autonomy or moral maturity only raises broader questions about the 'thick' theoretical frameworks in which those terms can be understood. Ultimately, one is led to issues that have to do not only with the existence and nature of the deity, but with the contours of the human condition, the character and extent of divine revelation, the proper locus of moral authority, and the ways in which religious teachings actually bear on the rich diversity of human practices.

3 Morality and worldview

Religion and morality interact in many different ways. For one thing, the moral universe of the believer is typically more densely populated than it is for other perspectives: even if the believer is, for example, a fairly straightforward utilitarian in their understanding of moral justification, they would still have to take the concerns of saints and angels, to say nothing of God, into account in ascertaining what will promote 'the greatest good for the greatest number'. Believers also regularly operate with a lengthier sense of the temporal context for thinking about the implications of moral activity, since in most religious traditions moral decisions have eternal significance. Religious teachings are also narratively rich: the believer is provided with abundant examples of spiritual saints, heroes, heroines and villains, stories of people who live out their moral lives in response to a variety of challenges and temptations. These same narratives provide the believer with an expanded sense of what is morally possible: the belief in miracles and a Final Judgment, and a sense of access to divine sources of strength and blessing, can have an important impact on moral motivation.

If these 'thick' relationships are to be explored properly, the philosophical discussion of religion and morality cannot be confined to formulating philosophical responses to the critics of religious ethics. What is also required is the more positive, constructive task described by Marilyn McCord Adams (1988): she has challenged Christian philosophers to engage in a 'mapping of . . . alternative positions' that will inevitably lead to the 'mounting of theological theories' about the nature of 'moral value and the human good'. For some religious ethicists, this more constructive dimension of their work has been partially fulfilled by demonstrating the ways in which a religious understanding of morality can be seen as more comprehensive, and/or more satisfactory, than the secular ethical alternatives. One common strategy is to portray non-religious schools of thought as emphasizing, in a reductionistic manner, some aspect of morality that is an integral component of a larger religious scheme. Thus deontologists are attempting to account for what religionists view as God's 'intrinsic' ordering of moral reality; utilitarians are sensitive, albeit in a distorted manner, to the moral universe's divinely ordained *telos*; secularist treatments of virtue and moral character are probing the contours of the Creator's designs for human flourishing; and so on. Some religious ethicists, especially in the Christian tradition, have also delineated the ways in which the biblical call to a life of self-giving love offers a richer understanding of the good life than any non-religious alternative theory.

The mandate to engage in more constructive efforts has also motivated many religious ethicists to explore a rather broad interdisciplinary territory, looking at the ways in which the general patterns of 'the good life' relate to even larger philosophical and theological topics. One way of viewing this broader constructive endeavour in moral thought is to see it as an exercise in a more expanded understanding of the scope of the work of philosophical theologians. Philosophical theology has often been construed too narrowly, as a discipline that focuses exclusively on epistemological questions regarding faith and reason, and metaphysical questions about the nature of God. Philosophical theology can be viewed more broadly, as encompassing the whole theological curriculum, so that it addresses philosophical topics relating to biblical studies, human nature, evangelism and the like. In this sense, moral philosophical theology can be treated as a sub-discipline of philosophical theology, just as moral theology is seen as a sub-discipline of theology proper in standard theological curricula.

Needless to say, these topics are much debated among theologians. The constructive task of religious moral thought, then, must pay considerable attention to the different ways in which specific theological perspectives shape understandings of moral topics. The ethics of Reform Judaism, for example, differ significantly from the moral teachings of the Hasidim. Similar differences exist within, say, Buddhism and Islam. Comparative moral thought has, in fact, been a major preoccupation of Christian thinkers. The Eastern and Western Churches developed divergent understandings of the metaphysics of 'spirit' and 'matter', which has led to alternative prescriptions regarding many significant moral issues (see SANCTIFICATION §§1–2). Within Protestantism, to cite just one contrast, thinkers in the Anabaptist tradition have developed an ethical perspective that emphasizes 'simple living' and pacifism, whereas those in the Calvinist tradition have often emphasized 'work ethic' themes and a 'just war' perspective on the use of violence. In Roman Catholicism, where ecclesiastical authorities officially function as a moral magisterium, a significant body of practical moral teachings has been developed, although the fostering of a variety of special 'religious communities' (Benedictine, Dominican, Franciscan, Jesuit, Carmelite, and the like) has also resulted in a diversity of spiritualities (contemplative, activist, eremitic, liberationist, and so forth) that correspond, in turn, to differing patterns of living.

The comparative study of diverse moral perspectives within religious traditions has also focused heavily on cross-cultural issues. Again, this has been a special emphasis within the Christian community, where the phenomenon of 'contextualization' has been emphasized by thinkers who want to draw sympathetic attention to the different ways in which the Christian message is received, appropriated and interpreted in a variety of cultural contexts. Moral matters have loomed large in these investigations, especially when missionary efforts have forced Christians to think about how cultural factors contribute to the shaping of moral differences, even when there is a common core of religious convictions.

The question, though, of how a traditional religious moral outlook can shed light on 'postmodern' discussions of moral relativism and moral pluralism raises new challenges for philosophical theology. The widespread conviction that 'the Enlightenment project', with its strong assumption of the sufficiency of autonomous human reason to address basic issues of human concern, has failed to deliver on its promises, has generated a quest for alternatives. For some, both in academia and popular culture, this has stimulated a renewed interest in 'premodern' metaphysical schemes; for others, it has meant some sort of fundamental accommodation to radical pluralism, whether in the form of a thoroughgoing, 'deconstructing' epistemological and moral scepticism, or a more modest advocacy of a 'perspectivalist' approach.

One significant attempt to address this complex of issues has been the emergence in the late twentieth century of a strong interest in the role of 'narrative' in the moral life. This interest has been especially strong among religious ethicists. In his elaboration of a Christian narrativism, Stanley Hauerwas (Hauerwas and MacIntyre 1983) has been very explicit about the anti-Enlightenment motives at work. We are not 'noumenal selves' who best actualize our natures by formulating moral universals that strip us of our particularities; rather we are 'historically formed' communal beings whose selfhood is realized only in the telling of our particularized narratives. The good life, as Hauerwas views it, is most effectively attained when we immerse ourselves in communities whose narratives embody social practices that enable us to be 'faithful to the one true God of the universe'.

An important question for religious narrativism is, of course, how we know which communities are the ones whose practices are 'true' to the will of God. In addressing this question, religious narrativists refuse to join those who express great scepticism about the plausibility of 'meta-narratives'. They insist on the importance of formulating a 'larger story' that makes sense of more particular stories – where 'making sense of' includes the ability to expose weaknesses and inadequacies. Here divine revelation is viewed as a resource that provides not primarily a set of commands or moral principles, but a larger worldview, embedded in an elaborate narrative of God's dealings with humankind.

Discussions of the larger context for understanding the relation between religion and morality have also been strongly influenced by developments in feminist thought. Unlike nineteenth-century feminist reformers, who often took traditional theism for granted in their campaigns for equality, the emergence of feminism in the twentieth century featured a critical re-examination of widely accepted metaphysical and epistemological assumptions. Many issues raised in these explorations focused on topics fundamental to a religious understanding of reality. Some feminists argue, for example, that any notion of a 'hierarchy', including the idea that God has transcendent being and power 'over' humankind, is designed to reinforce gender oppression.

To be sure, not all feminist thought is critical of divine authority or religious transcendence as such. But even where feminist philosophers and theologians have worked within the general contours of a traditional religious perspective, they have probed deeply entrenched patterns of construing some basic moral themes. In doing so, they have called attention to long-neglected thinkers, such as medieval women mystics, and highlighted less 'masculine' motifs (the 'ethics of care', relationality) in religiously based moral reflection (see FEMINIST ETHICS; FEMINIST THEOLOGY).

4 Practical ethics

The relationship between religion and morality has also been highlighted in the late twentieth century by an intense concern with practical moral questions. Alasdair MACINTYRE has suggested that there are 'periods in the history of morality when the deepest moral divisions exist in areas of central human concern: social justice, war, sexuality, the uses of technology' (Hauerwas and MacIntyre 1983: 1). When these times come, many people who are not themselves professional philosophers see a need to discuss practical moral concerns 'with an unusual degree of articulateness and theoretical depth', and they want very much to know what academic moral philosophy 'has to contribute at the level of practice'. Of course, the capacity to generate practical guidance is not by itself a test of the truth of a theoretical perspective on morality. But practical relevance is certainly one factor that is to be taken into account in the overall assessment of an ethical system.

Both theologians and philosophers are notable for the degree of abstraction that characterizes their investigations. But the theological enterprise has typically been closely connected with efforts to 'preach' theories in popular settings dominated by practical concerns. These religious efforts have often been characterized by an unusual degree of 'thickness'. In discussions of medical ethics, for example, religious ethicists have regularly insisted that the 'ought' topics addressed by medical ethics are seldom simply questions of moral rightness and wrongness. Since they also have to do with our larger worldview, we must pay explicit attention to a broad range of philosophical and theological topics: metaphysical, epistemological and anthropological questions concerning the genesis and cessation of human life; dualistic and monistic accounts of human composition, as they touch on basic issues concerning the significance of medical treatments in the lives of human persons; and many others. What is true for medical ethics will also hold for other areas where practical moral guidance is offered, although it is not only religious believers who will insist on calling attention to these complexities. Proponents of a variety of non-religious points of view, such as Marxists, Freudians, deconstructionists and secular feminists, have their own reasons for insisting on the recognition of theoretical 'thickness'. Here, as in other discussions of moral topics, though, the religious believer has a special role in pointing to the unique and important ways in which religious questions enter the picture.

See also: HALAKHAH; MORALITY AND ETHICS

References and further reading

* Adams, M.M. (1988) 'Problems of Evil: More Advice to Christian Philosophers', *Faith and Philosophy* 5 (April): 121–43. (Cited above for the case it makes for placing philosophical analyses of specific issues in the larger context of theologically informed theories of reality.)

Adams, R.M. (1987) *The Virtue of Faith and Other Essays in Philosophical Theology*, New York: Oxford University Press. (Includes several essays that have been highly influential in discussions of religion and morality.)

Alcoff, L. and Potter, E. (eds) (1993) *Feminist Epistemologies*, New York: Routledge. (An anthology of essays setting forth feminist perspectives on basic philosophical questions, including religious and ethical ones.)

Benhabib, S. (1992) *Situating the Self: Gender, Community and Postmodernism in Contemporary Ethics*, New York: Routledge. (Essays covering a broad range of themes in postmodern and feminist moral thought.)

* Bentham, J. (1823) *An Introduction to the Principles of Morals and Legislation*, in *The Utilitarians*, Garden City, NJ: Doubleday, 1961. (Cited above for its

argument for utilitarianism's compatibility with a religious belief in the afterlife.)

* Frankena, W.K. (1976) *Perspectives on Morality: Essays by William K. Frankena*, ed. K. Goodpaster, Notre Dame, IN: University of Notre Dame Press. (Includes several essays in which Frankena elaborates on his 'Ideal Observer' theory of moral justification.)

* Geach, P. (1969) *God and the Soul*, New York: Schocken Books. (Argues in favour of obeying divine commands that are backed by 'supreme power'.)

* Hauerwas, S. and MacIntyre, A. (eds) (1983) *Revisions: Changing Perspectives in Moral Philosophy*, Notre Dame, IN: University of Notre Dame Press. (The collected essays explore various links between religion and morality; the editors' essays provide helpful overviews.)

Helm, P. (ed.) (1981) *Divine Commands and Morality*, New York: Oxford University Press. (A helpful anthology setting forth various perspectives on the relevance of God's directives for the moral life.)

* Mill, J.S. (1861) *Utilitarianism*, in *The Utilitarians*, Garden City, NJ: Doubleday, 1961. (Cited above for its argument that utilitarianism is not 'a godless doctrine'.)

* Mitchell, B. (1980) *Morality: Religious and Secular*, Oxford: Clarendon Press. (A broad-ranging discussion of philosophical and theological themes in ethics.)

* Nowell-Smith, P.H. (1966) 'Morality: Religious and Secular', in I.T. Ramsey (ed.) *Christian Ethics and Contemporary Philosophy*, New York: Macmillan. (Cited above for its critique of religious ethics as 'infantile'.)

Quinn, P.L. (1978) *Divine Commands and Moral Requirements*, Oxford: Clarendon Press. (A careful study of issues at stake in formulating a divine-command ethics.)

* Stump, E. and Kretzmann, N. (1991) 'Being and Goodness' in S. MacDonald (ed.) *Being and Goodness: The Concept of the Good in Metaphysics and Philosophical Theology*, Ithaca, NY: Cornell University Press. (Develops Aquinas' thesis regarding the relationship between God's being and goodness; the collection includes several essays on morality and the divine nature.)

RICHARD J. MOUW

RELIGION AND POLITICAL PHILOSOPHY

Political philosophy began in Athens, but the large-scale impact of religion upon it had to await Christianity. Biblical Christianity portrays human beings as subjects of a kingdom of God, destined for a supernatural end and bound to love one another. This view is potentially in tension with the demands of the various political societies to which Christians belong. The requirement of devotion to God might conflict with the allegiance that temporal government demands; human beings' attempts to attain their supernatural end can bring them into conflict with civil laws. The power and structure of the Church in the Middle Ages opened the possibility of tensions between the authority of the institutional Church and of various national states. These tensions, potential and actual, set much of political philosophy's agenda from the fourth to the fourteenth century.

The tension between membership of the kingdom of God and of an earthly polity was forcefully described by Augustine. He likened faithful Christians to pilgrims journeying through the world, who avail themselves of the peace temporal authority provides. Political thinkers of the early Middle Ages examined the conditions under which war, regicide and disobedience were permissible, and queried whether the Pope had authority over temporal rulers. Thomas Aquinas elaborated a theory of natural law according to which valid human law cannot conflict with the dictates of morality. Temporal rulers, he argued, are responsible for promoting their subjects' common good and eternal salvation.

Since the sixteenth century, political philosophy has been concerned with problems set by the religious developments that ushered in the modern period. The Reformation brought religious diversity to European nations on a large scale. It thereby raised questions about how policy could be set and unity maintained without a shared religion to provide common goals and social bonds. The seventeenth-century philosopher Thomas Hobbes opposed the toleration of religious diversity and argued that states could remain unified only if their religious unity were maintained by an absolute sovereign. John Locke, on the other hand, argued for the right to religious liberty. Locke and other liberals associated with the movement of thought known as the Enlightenment were opposed by classical conservatives such as Edmund Burke. Burke argued that human society depended upon willing adherence to traditional customs and social institutions, including an established national Church. More recently, liberalism has also been opposed by Marxism. Marxists argue that religion helps to maintain social stability under modern conditions by masking the exploitation of the working class.

Contemporary political philosophy in the English-speaking world is descended from the Enlightenment liberalism of Locke. John Rawls argues that social cooperation must be based only upon what citizens of liberal democracies can reasonably affirm under ideal conditions. Religious critics of contemporary liberalism argue that it unduly restricts religiously inspired political argument and activism.

1 **Political philosophy in the Middle Ages**
2 **Political philosophy in the modern period**
3 **Contemporary political philosophy**

1 Political philosophy in the Middle Ages

Classical Athens was the birthplace of systematic philosophical reflection on politics, but Greek religion made little impact upon it. There have been bodies of political thought associated with Judaism, Islam and Byzantine Christianity, but these religions too exercised little lasting influence on the development of political philosophy. By contrast, the development of the subject has been profoundly influenced by the doctrinal and institutional developments of Latin Christianity and the religions descended from it.

The Christian Scriptures portray all human beings as equal members of God's kingdom, bound to love God with their whole hearts and their neighbours as themselves. The Scriptures are also standardly interpreted as promising righteous people eternal life with God. The demands of the Christian life portrayed in the Scriptures are potentially in tension with the demands of membership of political society. Conformity with God's commands might require disobedience to human law. The demands of Christian charity may conflict with the requirements of armed military service. National unity may seem to depend less upon mutual love than upon patriotism or economic reciprocity. Laws, it might seem, are more often used to promote national purposes than eternal salvation. During the Middle Ages, the increasing power, wealth and organization of the Church paved the way for jurisdictional controversies between political authorities and the institutional Church. These controversies centred on the relative primacy of the pope and various secular rulers, the government of Church property, the power to appoint bishops, and the laws governing the clergy. Political philosophy between the fourth and the fourteenth centuries was concerned in large part with addressing these tensions, both potential and actual.

Augustine, the fourth-century North African bishop, was the first great Christian social thinker.

His political thought is unsystematic, but he frequently touched on political subjects in his greatest work, *The City of God* (413–27). There Augustine argued that political authority is inherently coercive and would be unnecessary had the Fall not occurred. Pride, Augustine thought, is the legacy of this original sin and the source of actual sin. God ordained that humans be subject to political authority in part to teach them humility. Augustine enjoins Christians not to take pride in the glory of the state to which they belong. Christians are, he said, pilgrims journeying through a sinful world as through an alien land. They are to make use of the peace earthly authority makes possible, but are not to love the things of this world. They may hold positions of authority, but ought not covet them. Political authority, Augustine argued, should sometimes be used to suppress heresy and to force schismatics to return to the Church.

The adoption of Christianity as the official religion of the Roman Empire by the emperor Constantine (*c.*275–337) and the Empire's later collapse brought the Church a power and wealth which required increasingly complex administration. This increasing organizational complexity set the stage for both conflict and cooperation between ecclesiastical and political institutions. Potential conflicts of jurisdiction between ecclesiastical and civil authorities, the power of the Pope to depose temporal rulers, and the permissibility of killing tyrants were among the subjects that engaged political thinkers between Augustine and the thirteenth century. The political thought of this period was largely occasional in character. It was more a product of immediate political circumstance than an element of larger philosophical enterprises.

Political philosophy was reinvigorated in western Europe in the thirteenth century. This occurred when the works of Aristotle were rediscovered by the Latin-speaking world and introduced into the medieval universities. Thomas Aquinas, the greatest of Aristotle's followers in the Middle Ages, was a practitioner of the method of inquiry known as scholasticism. It was characteristic of scholastics to integrate the truths they found in diverse sources into systematic wholes. Thus Aquinas sought to combine the truths he found in the Scriptures and in patristic sources with the insights of Aristotle's writings.

Aquinas touched on a number of political questions while constructing his own philosophical and theological system. In his treatment of politics, as of other subjects, he attempted to combine what he learned from Aristotle and from the Christian tradition. Thus he argued, following ARISTOTLE (§27), that the purpose of political society is to make the good life available to its members. Political authorities, he concluded, are responsible for promoting the common good and eternal salvation of their subjects. Because he thought that political authority had these positive functions, he disagreed with Augustine's view that subjection to political authority is merely a consequence of sin.

Aquinas' most famous contribution to political philosophy is his theory of law (*c*.1270) (see AQUINAS, T. §13). He argued that the precepts of human morality are found in what he called 'the natural law'. The natural law is ordained by God to lead human beings to their good and is accessible to human reason. It consists of injunctions such as 'Parents are to be honoured' and prohibitions such as 'Innocents should not be killed'. Human law, Aquinas argued, must be consistent with natural law. A law enjoining the ritual killing of the innocent, for example, would be inconsistent with the natural law. Aquinas would therefore argue that such a law is not, properly speaking, a law at all, and that no-one is obliged to obey it. Aquinas also thought that some societies – various Christian societies, for example, and the Israelites of the Hebrew Scriptures – enjoy the benefit of God's revelation. Through revelation, these societies have access to what Aquinas called 'divine law'. The divine law includes precepts about how God is to be worshipped. Authorities in societies to which God has revealed such precepts should enact laws which promote proper worship, where such laws are feasible. They also have a duty to suppress heresy where possible.

Another of Aquinas' important contributions to political philosophy is his account of the conditions under which a war is just. He argued that wars must be declared by proper authority rather than be the result of private initiative. He also agreed with Augustine that combatants must have the right motives. They ought not be moved by belligerence or desire for revenge. The war must be fought for a just cause, such as self-defence or the defence of the innocent. Finally, the damage done and casualties inflicted must be proportionate to the offence done by the enemy and must be necessary to achieve the just aims of the war.

In the fourteenth century, questions about the proper extent of Papal authority provoked bitter political controversy and philosophical debate. WILLIAM OF OCKHAM (§11) and MARSILIUS OF PADUA, a follower of Aristotle, argued for severe limitations on papal authority over political rulers and political matters.

During much of the Middle Ages, political philosophers thought of Europe as a single entity unified by religion. The common religion was Christianity, headed by the pope, whose proper relationship to various temporal rulers remained a matter of debate. The ascendancy of Holy Roman Emperors, such as Charlemagne in the ninth century and Frederick II in the thirteenth, kindled hopes for a Europe that would be politically as well as religiously unified. In such a world, it was natural for political theorists to argue that religion grounded the legitimacy of political authorities. Rulers, it was sometimes thought, derived their moral authority from the fact that they were doing God's will. Thus Charlemagne was crowned by the pope on Christmas Day. He was often portrayed holding a copy of Augustine's *The City of God* and thought of his empire as an attempt to realize the city of which Augustine wrote. Much later, Frederick II employed highly religious imagery to legitimate his authority. He portrayed himself as a Christlike figure who pronounced law on God's behalf.

The Reformation early in the sixteenth century brought large-scale religious diversity to Europe and effectively ended the hope of a unified Christendom. It thereby posed new questions for political philosophy, questions about how social unity could be maintained in the face of religious diversity, about what the proper ends of politics should be, and about what gives rulers their political legitimacy.

2 Political philosophy in the modern period

One challenge to the claim that human beings naturally form a spiritual unity came with the discovery of the Americas. The native peoples of the Americas had had no previous exposure to Christianity and lived very differently from Europeans. European political thinkers of the sixteenth century therefore asked what the status of the native peoples was and how Europeans were obliged to treat them. Some argued that the native peoples were either animals or natural slaves who could be deprived of their property. Most religious political philosophers, notably the Spaniards Francisco de VITORIA, Luis de MOLINA (§4) and Domingo de SOTO (§4), argued that the native peoples of the Americas were fully human, that they should not be compelled to accept Christianity, that their property rights should be respected and that the *conquistadores* should return what they had taken. These arguments, sadly, had little practical impact.

The last great defender of a unified Christendom was Robert Bellarmine, a cardinal of the Roman Catholic Church and opponent of the Reformation. In his *De summo pontifice*, Bellarmine argued that human beings have a common human nature and common supernatural end, and are thus spiritually united. He concluded that all human beings are subject to a single ultimate spiritual authority, whom he identified as the pope. Because the pope has ultimate authority over spiritual matters, he also has authority over those political matters that affect people's spiritual welfare. Bellarmine concluded that the pope has the power to declare laws invalid that endanger the one true faith and to depose rulers who fall into heresy or who leave the one true Church.

Like Bellarmine, the English philosopher Thomas HOBBES (§7) recognized that religious diversity was a source of political conflict. Religious diversity, Hobbes recognized, carries with it a diversity of religious authorities. Members of political societies who owe their allegiance to different religious authorities can find themselves under obligations which bring them into conflict. Some, for example, may be obliged to worship in ways that others find intolerable. Rulers who follow different religions can think themselves obliged to spread their religion to other nations. Like Bellarmine, Hobbes therefore located the source of religiously based conflict in the potentially conflicting demands of diverse authorities. Where Hobbes and Bellarmine disagreed was on how these problems were to be addressed.

In *Leviathan* (1651), Hobbes denied Bellarmine's claim that all human beings naturally form a spiritual unity which has but one spiritual leader. Instead, he argued, groups of human beings unite themselves by subjecting themselves to a common sovereign. Hobbes thought that the toleration of religious diversity within a state was an invitation to civil war. He also thought that recognizing a spiritual authority (such as the pope) not subject to the national sovereign would breed political division. A sovereign, Hobbes argued, can maintain the unity and peace of the subjects only if the sovereign has absolute authority in both political and spiritual matters. Therefore each national state is to have a Church of its own. The doctrine and practices of a national Church should, in Hobbes' view, be dictated by a political ruler with the power to punish dissenters.

According to Hobbes' analysis of moral obligation, individuals can have obligations only when there is someone with absolute power to ensure compliance. A contract between two people is morally binding, for example, only if there is someone with absolute power to enforce its terms. It follows that members of one society, with religious and political obligations to its absolute sovereign, cannot have any conflicting obligations to a foreign religious authority such as the Pope. Moreover, no one exercises absolute sovereignty over the world. It follows, therefore, that no national sovereign can have an obligation to spread religion to other nations, since there is no one to compel the sovereign to fulfil that obligation.

John LOCKE (§7) endorsed a different solution: religious toleration. This is the doctrine that state power should not be used to enforce religious conformity. Locke's defence of this doctrine, as found in his *A Letter Concerning Toleration* (1689), rests upon two arguments. First, Locke argued that religious belief is a mental state into which people cannot be forced. It is therefore irrational to employ coercive force in an attempt to secure religious conformity. Second, Locke held that religious diversity is not itself a source of social and political conflict. What leads to such conflict is religious persecution. Cease persecuting dissent, and religiously based political conflict will largely disappear.

The toleration Locke defended was limited in scope. He was suspicious of Catholics because of their allegiance to the pope. He was also suspicious of atheists who, he thought, lacked sufficient motivation to perform their civic duty because they lacked a belief in eternal punishment. Locke was therefore reluctant to extend religious toleration to members of either of these groups.

Locke said that public officials may prohibit religious conduct if it interferes with valid political purposes, but denied that they may promote or discourage religion as such. His view, as he lays it out in his *Letter*, therefore contains the germ of an important idea: the separation of Church and state. However, Locke did not explicitly develop and defend this view himself. Church–state separation and religious toleration were, however, very important ideas to the founders of the American republic a century later. Some, such as Thomas Jefferson, defended religious freedom because of the importance they attached to individual liberty. James Madison (1785) argued against establishing the Church of the majority. He thought that establishment and the governmental support that came with it conferred too privileged a position on the Church in question, which in turn led to complacency and even corruption among the clergy. Thus disestablishment, Madison concluded, benefited the Church of the majority as well as minority denominations.

Historians of philosophy commonly associate Locke and Jefferson with the movement of thought known as the Enlightenment. Its most prominent philosophers were Locke, Montesquieu, Rousseau and Kant. These Enlightenment liberals reposed great confidence in the power of human reason to understand the natural world and to solve social and ethical problems. This confidence in human reason was central to the political philosophies of Enlightenment philosophers. Political thinkers of the Enlightenment typically argued that political authority is legitimate only if society is organized in ways that each individual could understand and approve, at least under proper circumstances.

The Enlightenment account of legitimacy was not only a reaction to those such as Hobbes who thought that rulers should have absolute power. It was also a reaction against earlier thinkers in the modern period who invoked religion to legitimate political authority. According to the doctrine of the divine right of kings, for example, monarchs were entitled to rule by the grace of God and were responsible only to God for their rule. Divine-right theory was at its height in England in the century prior to the Civil Wars of 1642–51 and in France under Louis XIV.

The insistence that the legitimacy of a political order rests upon the rational consent of individuals who live under it has provoked charges that Enlightenment liberalism is unduly individualistic and rationalistic. Enlightenment liberalism has also been criticized as overly hostile to religion, in part because it purposely excludes religion from its account of the foundations of government. Whether or not the charge of hostility can be sustained, the fact remains that the theological doctrines of Catholic and Protestant Christianity had little impact on the substantive views of Enlightenment political philosophers. These thinkers were, however, concerned with the power of ecclesiastical institutions. They generally advocated religious toleration and favoured restricting the political influence of the clergy and of institutions such as the Catholic Church.

Among the critics of Enlightenment liberalism was the British thinker and political figure Edmund BURKE (§3). Burke is considered a classical conservative. While contemporary conservatives are usually identified by the value they attach to the operation of free markets and to minimalist government, classical conservatives are identified by the value they accord to tradition. Thus Burke argued that emphasis on individual rational consent neglects the importance of tradition in maintaining political unity and in setting social aims. He claimed that social unity and peace depend upon the willing adherence to traditional mores, social arrangements and institutions. These institutions should, in Burke's view, include an established national Church such as the Church of England.

More recently, liberalism has also been criticized by Karl MARX (§3) and his followers. Marxists argue that religion is an ideology. It helps to maintain social stability under conditions of industrial capitalism by obscuring the operations of an economic system that exploits the working classes. It does so by systematically encouraging false social analysis. Its emphasis on individual charity as an ideal human motivation masks the fundamental character of economic forces in human history. More importantly, its other-worldly emphasis distracts members of the working class from their condition and makes them more content with it than they would otherwise be. A fully communist society would abolish exploitation of the working class and vest political power in its hands. In such a society, religion would wither away because the felt need for it would disappear. Twentieth-century countries that have purported to be Marxist – such as China, the former Soviet Union, the former East Germany, and Albania – have discouraged or prohibited organized religion, ostensibly to help realize full communist society.

3 Contemporary political philosophy

The first half of the twentieth century saw a revival of interest in the thought of Thomas Aquinas among Catholic scholars. With this Thomistic revival came a renewed interest in natural law political philosophy (see NATURAL LAW; THOMISM). Natural law theory has traditionally emphasized the common good as the goal of government. Pursuit of the common good, it is sometimes thought, must come at the expense of individuals whose opinions and ways of life are at odds with it. Natural law theory has therefore been criticized for an inability to accommodate the rights of individuals. This is a criticism that twentieth-century natural law thinkers have tried to meet. Jacques MARITAIN (§3), for example, argued that natural law theory could lend philosophical support to the UN's Declaration of Human Rights. John Courtney Murray, an American Jesuit, used natural law reasoning to argue that the Catholic Church should accept freedom of conscience (1960). The Catholic Church endorsed Murray's position in 1965 at the Second Vatican Council. John Finnis' *Natural Law and Natural Rights* (1980) is an attempt to ground natural rights in an original, and controversial, account of natural law.

Most contemporary political philosophy in the English-speaking world is descended from the Enlightenment liberalism of Locke and Kant. Contemporary liberalism finds its most sophisticated expression in *A Theory of Justice* (1971) by the American political philosopher John RAWLS. Rawls claims that liberal democracies must conform with moral principles that would be acceptable to every individual. This claim raises questions about the circumstances under which hypothetical consent must be registered. Rawls argues that it should be rendered under circumstances of freedom and equality.

Consent to moral principles cannot, Rawls says, depend upon the religious or philosophical beliefs of the consenting parties. Therefore the moral foundations of liberal democracy are, on Rawls' view, independent of religion. He also believes that religion should play only a very restricted role in debates about legislation and public policy. He argues, for example, that using *only* religious considerations to justify sharp legal restrictions on abortion compromises the reasonableness and civility of public debate. Other contemporary liberals, such as Robert Audi, have defended even more severe moral (not legal) restrictions than Rawls endorses. Audi argues that it is wrong to participate in political debate from religious motives, even if the arguments introduced into debate are thoroughly secular (Audi 1989). Such religiously motivated participation, Audi says, compromises reasonableness and civility.

Some religious thinkers (Wolterstorff 1997, for example) have criticized Rawls and other liberals for these restrictions. They argue that religion is so important to its adherents that they should be able to express their convictions in public debate. They also point out that religious themes and stories have a political appeal that transcends denominational lines. Use of religious imagery and argumentation, they maintain, is therefore not as unreasonable as they think Rawls, Audi and other liberals take it to be.

See also: LIBERATION THEOLOGY; POLITICAL PHILOSOPHY, NATURE OF: RELIGION AND MORALITY

References and further reading

* Aquinas, T. (*c.*1270) *The Treatise on Law*, trans. R.J. Henle, Notre Dame, IN: University of Notre Dame Press, 1993. (A recent translation of Aquinas' discussion of law in the *Summa theologiae*.)

Audi, R. (1989) 'The Separation of Church and State and the Obligations of Citizenship', *Philosophy and Public Affairs* 18 (3): 259–96. (Defends normative constraints on the role of religion in liberal democracies committed to separating Church and state.)

* Augustine (413–27) *The City of God*, trans. H. Bettenson, New York: Penguin, 1972. (Augustine's most important work of social theory; see especially Book XIX.)

* Bellarmine, R. (1581–92) *De summo pontifice*, V, in *Opera omnia*, vols 1–2, ed. J. Fèvre, Paris: Louis Vives, 1870–4. (This is the third of Bellarmine's *General Controversies*.)

Black, A. (1992) *Political Thought in Europe 1250–1450*, Cambridge: Cambridge University Press. (A brief and historically sensitive discussion of the political thought of the late Middle Ages.)

Bossuet, J. (1709) *Politics Drawn from the Very Words of Holy Scripture*, trans. and ed. P. Riley, Cambridge: Cambridge University Press, 1990. (The *locus classicus* of divine-right theory.)

Carlyle, R.W. (1950) *A History of Medieval Political Theory in the West*, New York: Barnes & Noble. (Accessible and thorough history of medieval political philosophy.)

Filmer, Sir R. (1680) *Patriarcha*, ed. J.P. Sommerville, Cambridge: Cambridge University Press, 1991. (This work, the classical source of English divine-right theory, was composed sometime between 1636–40 and enjoyed wide circulation in manuscript form until its publication in 1680. Locke wrote his *First Treatise of Government* in the late 1670s in reply.)

* Finnis, J. (1980) *Natural Law and Natural Rights*, Oxford: Oxford University Press. (Contemporary statement of natural law political philosophy.)

* Hobbes, T. (1651) *Leviathan*, ed. C.B. MacPherson, New York: Penguin, 1985. (A summary and definitive statement of Hobbes' political philosophy.)

* Locke, J. (1689) *A Letter Concerning Toleration*, ed. J. Tully, Indianapolis, IN: Hackett, 1983. (Locke's defence of religious toleration.)

* Madison, J. (1785) 'A Memorial and Remonstrance', in S. Padover (ed.) *The Complete Madison*, New York: Harper, 1953. (Madison's argument against establishment.)

* Murray, J.C. (1960) *We Hold These Truths*, New York: Sheed & Ward. (An influential example of a natural law argument.)

* Rawls, J. (1971) *A Theory of Justice*, Cambridge, MA: Harvard University Press. (The major contemporary statement of the liberal position.)

—— (1993) *Political Liberalism*, New York: Columbia University Press. (A collection of Rawls' papers; essay 6 addresses the place of religious considerations in political debate.)

Skinner, Q. (1978) *The Foundations of Modern Political Thought*, Cambridge: Cambridge University Press. (A history of political philosophy from the late middle ages to the seventeenth century. Contains an excellent bibliography.)

Wallace Hadrill, J.M. (1965) 'The *Via Regia* of the Carolingian Age', in B. Smalley (ed.) *Trends in Medieval Political Thought*, Oxford: Blackwell, 22–41. (A useful and accessible essay on the political thought of Charlegmagne's time.)

Walzer, M. (1965) *The Revolution of the Saints*, Cambridge, MA: Harvard University Press. (A study of the Puritan origins of radical politics.)

* Wolterstorff, N. (1997) 'Why We Should Reject What Liberalism Tells Us About Thinking and Acting in Public for Religious Reasons', in P.J. Weithman (ed.) *Religion and Contemporary Liberalism*, Notre Dame, IN: University of Notre Dame Press. (An

accessible criticism of the restrictions on religion in political debate desired by some liberals.)

PAUL J. WEITHMAN

RELIGION AND SCIENCE

Philosophical discussion of the relation between modern science and religion has tended to focus on Christianity, because of its dominance in the West. The relations between science and Christianity have been too complex to be described by the 'warfare' model popularized by A.D. White (1896) and J.W. Draper (1874). An adequate account of the past two centuries requires a distinction between conservative and liberal positions. Conservative Christians tend to see theology and science as partially intersecting bodies of knowledge. God is revealed in 'two books': the Bible and nature. Ideally, science and theology ought to present a single, consistent account of reality; but in fact there have been instances where the results of science have (apparently) contradicted Scripture, in particular with regard to the age of the universe and the origin of the human species.

Liberals tend to see science and religion as complementary but non-interacting, as having concerns so different as to make conflict impossible. This approach can be traced to Immanuel Kant, who distinguished sharply between pure reason (science) and practical reason (morality). More recent versions contrast science, which deals with the what and how of the natural world, and religion, which deals with meaning, or contrast science and religion as employing distinct languages. However, since the 1960s a growing number of scholars with liberal theological leanings have taken an interest in science and have denied that the two disciplines can be isolated from one another. Topics within science that offer fruitful points for dialogue with theology include Big-Bang cosmology and its possible implications for the doctrine of creation, the 'fine-tuning' of the cosmological constants and the possible implications of this for design arguments, and evolution and genetics, with their implications for a new understanding of the human individual.

Perhaps of greater import are the indirect relations between science and theology. Newtonian physics fostered an understanding of the natural world as strictly determined by natural laws; this in turn had serious consequences for understanding divine action and human freedom. Twentieth-century developments such as quantum physics and chaos theory call for a revised view of causation. Advances in the philosophy of science in the second half of the twentieth century provide a much more sophisticated account of knowledge than was available earlier, and this has important implications for methods of argument in theology.

1 **Religion and Western predecessors of science**
2 **Early modern science and worldview**
3 **Indirect relations**
4 **Geology, evolution and the age of the earth**
5 **Biological sciences**
6 **Cosmology**
7 **Physics and metaphysics**
8 **Epistemology and language**
9 **Religion's implications for science**

1 Religion and Western predecessors of science

Western interest in a systematic account of the natural world is an inheritance from the ancient Greeks rather than from the Hebrew tradition, which tended to focus on the human world. The Greek concept of nature was not set over against a concept of super-nature, as it has been in more recent centuries, so it is possible to say that Greek philosophy of nature was inherently theological. Early Christian scholars were divided in their approach to Greek natural philosophy, some making great use of it for apologetic purposes (see ORIGEN §3; AUGUSTINE §§1, 4, 8), others rejecting it (see TERTULLIAN).

After the fall of Rome, the centre of scholarship shifted eastward. Islamic scholars in the Middle Ages were largely responsible for preserving the learning of the Greeks, as well as for significant scientific developments of their own in the fields of optics, medicine, astronomy and mathematics. It was through Muslims in Spain that important scientific works by Aristotle were introduced to western Europe in the twelfth century. The influence of these works on Christian thought culminated in Thomas Aquinas' two Summas (see AQUINAS, T. §§5–6; ARISTOTELIANISM, MEDIEVAL §§3–4).

2 Early modern science and worldview

At the end of the nineteenth century, White (1896) and Draper (1874) promoted the view of science and religion as traditional enemies. However, revisionist history at the end of the twentieth century presents a much more complex picture. It is true that the Catholic Church silenced GALILEO (§§1, 4) in 1633, that René Descartes' mechanicist conception of matter was condemned, and that fear of censorship had a generally chilling effect on scientific theorizing throughout the seventeenth century (see DESCARTES, R. §11). However, it must be noted that not all of the

Catholic officials were opposed to Galileo. In addition, a number of the century's greatest scientists were Catholic: Pierre GASSENDI (§1), Marin MERSENNE (§§1, 2), Blaise PASCAL (§§3, 6) and Nicolas Steno, as well as Galileo and Descartes. The Jesuit order was home to a number of scientists who were not outstanding theorists but contributed significantly to experimental science.

In the early modern period, it is difficult to distinguish conflicts between science and religion on the one hand from intra-theological conflicts and conflicts between the new science and the Aristotelian scholastic synthesis on the other. The Galileo affair needs to be interpreted in the light of both these complications, since it is not possible to understand the resistance to Galileo's astronomy without recognizing the fact that it called into question an entire socio-political order founded on a picture of the cosmos and of the place of humans in it. The affair was also an internal church struggle concerning the proper interpretation of Scripture. Galileo followed Augustine's rule that an interpretation of Scripture should be revised when it is found to conflict with other knowledge. This put him in conflict with conservative church officials who adopted a more literalist interpretive strategy. A further complication is the fact that the new science was often liberally mixed with magic and astrology, which the Catholic Church condemned both because they dabbled with the demonic and because of suspicion that they confirmed Calvinist views of determinism against the Catholic view of free will.

Robert Merton (1938) argued that Puritanism promoted the scientific revolution, a thesis still debated over half a century later. While Merton's thesis was overstated, it is likely that a particular Reformed doctrine of the sovereignty of God – that God's sovereignty excludes all active contributions of lesser beings to his work – made the modern scientific and philosophical conception of matter as inert or passive more acceptable to Isaac NEWTON, Robert BOYLE (§4) and other Protestants than it would otherwise have been. Here again it is important to recognize the interplay of Aristotelianism and intra-theological disputes. The mechanicist conception of matter was a direct rejection both of Neoplatonic magical conceptions and of the Aristotelian teleological and organicist view, that 'forms' inherent in substances provided built-in powers and goals. At the same time, it furthered theological convictions first expressed by late medieval nominalist theologians (see NOMINALISM §§1–2). It is one of the great ironies of history, then, that Newton's mechanicist conception of the material universe so quickly evolved into Pierre Simon de Laplace's purely materialist and determinist view, the latter being absolutely incompatible with religion.

3 Indirect relations

If direct conflicts between Christian theology and the various theories of modern science have often been overemphasized, the deleterious effects on theology of indirect conflicts between religion and science have received too little attention. These indirect interactions can be considered under the headings of metaphysics and epistemology.

Metaphysics. Descartes' mechanicist view of matter as pure extension, accompanied by a view of mind as 'thinking substance', inaugurated a metaphysical dualism that has replaced older and more nuanced views of Christian anthropology. In so far as this dualism has been shown to be philosophically untenable, Christianity, with its view of the soul and afterlife, has appeared untenable as well (see DUALISM).

The clockwork image of the universe as a closed system of particles in motion, strictly governed by the laws of physics (the image epitomized in the nineteenth century by the work of Laplace), created insuperable problems in accounting for divine action. A popular variety of deism offered the most reasonable account: God was the creator of the universe, and responsible for the laws of nature, but has no ongoing interaction with the natural world or with human history (see DEISM §1). The alternatives for theists were accounts of miraculous interventions or an account of God as an immanent sustainer of natural processes (see MIRACLES §§1–2). The former seemed to make God irrational (contradicting God's own decrees) or inept (needing to readjust the system). The latter view made it difficult to maintain any more sense of God's personal involvement in human life than was possible for the deists. Much of the difference between liberal and conservative Christianity can be traced to theories of divine action: conservatives tend to take an interventionist, liberals an immanentist, view.

Epistemology. Medieval theologians had two sets of epistemological categories at their disposal, those relating to *scientia* (demonstrative or scientific knowledge) and those relating to *opinio* ('probable' beliefs, including those based on authority). So those theological conclusions that could not be deduced from first principles could, happily, be based on unimpeachable authority, the very word of God. However, in the modern period, the range of *scientia* contracted to the spheres of mathematics and formal logic; HUME (§6) and KANT (§8) both provided powerful critiques of deductive arguments for the existence of God and of natural theology generally. Furthermore, when probable knowledge took on its contemporary sense of knowledge based on the weight of empirical evidence, appeals to authority became irrelevant, and most judged it impossible to provide empirical evidence for theological claims. Thus the central question for modern liberal theologians has been how, if at all, theology is possible.

Liberal theology diverged from more traditional accounts as a result of its strategies for meeting the problems raised directly or indirectly by science. Following Friedrich SCHLEIERMACHER (§7), many liberal theologians have understood religion to constitute its own sphere of experience, unrelated to that of scientific knowledge. Theological doctrines are expressions of religious awareness, not accounts of a supernatural realm. God works immanently, not by interventions in either the natural world or human history. Thus liberal theology has avoided direct conflict with modern science, at the cost (or with the beneficial consequence) of a radical revision of the very concepts of religion and theology. However, Ian Barbour's *Issues in Science and Religion* (1966) presented an encyclopedic overview of the points at which scientific claims *are* relevant to religious thought, and in *Myths, Models, and Paradigms* (1974) he argued for significant epistemological similarities between science and religion. Since then, a growing number of scholars from the liberal wing of Christianity have begun to call the modern division of territory into question.

4 Geology, evolution and the age of the earth

Physics and astronomy were the main scientific foci for theologians in the seventeenth and eighteenth centuries; geology and biology held an analogous place in the nineteenth and twentieth. For centuries, the biblical narrative from creation to Christ and the projected Last Judgment provided the skeletal outline for accounts of natural as well as human history. For instance, the story of Noah and the Flood served as a useful explanation for marine fossils found high above sea level. However, by the seventeenth century, the short span of history calculated from the Bible was being challenged from a number of directions. (James Ussher, a seventeenth-century Irish archbishop, has been credited with the calculation that creation took place a mere 4004 years before Christ.) Although sporadic attempts to reconcile geological history with Genesis continue up to the present, in the eighteenth century a large number of geologists already recognized that the Flood hypothesis could not explain the growing body of knowledge regarding rock stratification and the placement of fossils. A much longer

history of the Earth, prior to human history, had to be presumed. At the same time, Egyptian and Chinese records were calling into question the short span of human history calculated from the Bible.

While some contemporary opposition to evolutionary theory involved 'young earth' chronology, negative reactions in the nineteenth century to Charles Darwin's *The Origin of Species* (1859) were more often objections to social Darwinism and to the claim that humans were kin to the 'lower animals'; other negative reactions focused on the fact that natural selection provided an alternative to divine design for explaining the fit of organisms to their environments, thus undermining an important apologetic argument. Nonetheless, many theologians and other believers readily accepted the theory and judged the changes it required in theology to be salutary rather than mere accommodation (see DARWIN, C. §§2–4; EVOLUTION, THEORY OF).

5 Biological sciences

The theory of evolution is a surprisingly hot issue again at the end of the twentieth century. A Gallup poll published in the magazine *US News and World Report* (December 23, 1991) reported that a majority of North American Christians are sceptical of the macroevolutionary paradigm. The best explanation for this resistance is probably the fact that the issue has come to be framed in terms of creation *versus* chance as an account of the origin of the human species. That the issues can be formulated in these terms is due in part to a (defective) theory of divine action that contrasts God's creative acts with natural processes, rather than allowing that God may work through natural processes, including those that involve random events. The controversy is exacerbated by the use made of evolutionary biology by proselytizing atheists.

Genetics provides a new area for dialogue between religion and the biological sciences. Studies showing a genetic basis for human characteristics and behaviour raise questions about the status of the human person – for example, questions about free will and determinism – that have been the province of philosophy and religion. Of particular interest are studies of twins suggesting a genetic factor in religious behaviour (for example, Eaves *et al.* 1990).

Genetic research in general and genetic engineering in particular have raised a number of ethical questions that relate to theological ethics. For example, while most people favour genetic treatment for illnesses, many are opposed to germ-line intervention, which would affect all succeeding generations. Some objections are based on quasi-religious positions: scientists should not 'play God'. This line of thinking calls for theological scrutiny: are not human beings themselves created in order to participate in God's ongoing creative process? It is noteworthy that in 1991, the US National Institutes of Health awarded its first grant ever to a theological institution to the Center for Theology and the Natural Sciences (Berkeley, California) to study the theological and ethical implications of the Human Genome Initiative, the project to map human DNA (see GENETICS AND ETHICS; RELIGION AND MORALITY §4).

6 Cosmology

Physical cosmology is the branch of science that studies the universe as a whole. Beginning in the 1920s, developments in this field have sparked lively debate at the interface between theology and science. The Big-Bang theory, based on the expansion of the universe and a variety of other data, postulates that the universe originated in an extremely dense, extremely hot 'singularity' some 15 to 20 billion years ago (see COSMOLOGY §3). Many Christians, including Pope Pius XII, greeted this theory as a confirmation of the biblical doctrine of creation. It was not only religious people who saw it as such; Frederick Hoyle defended a steady-state model of the universe, in which hydrogen atoms come into being throughout an infinite time span, partly because he saw it as more compatible with his atheism.

The discussion among theologians on the relevance of Big-Bang cosmology to the doctrine of creation involves controversy over the very nature of theology. As mentioned above, it has been common among liberal theologians since Schleiermacher to claim that religious meaning is entirely independent of scientific fact. Theologians who hold this position claim that the doctrine of creation, having to do only with the relation of all that exists to God, says nothing about the temporal origin of the universe, and is therefore equally compatible with any cosmological model.

A more recent area of research that has occasioned theological speculation can be referred to as the issue of the anthropic principle. A number of factors in the early universe had to be adjusted in a remarkably precise way to produce the universe we have. These factors include the mass of the universe, the strengths of the four basic forces (electromagnetism, gravitation, and the strong and weak nuclear forces), and others. Calculations show that if any of these numbers had deviated even slightly from its actual value, the universe would have evolved in a radically different manner, making life as we know it – and probably life of any sort – impossible. An example of the 'fine-tuning' required is that if the ratio of the strength of

electromagnetism to gravity had varied by as much as one part in 10^{40}, there would be no stars like our sun.

Many claim that this apparent fine-tuning of the universe for life calls for explanation. To some, it appears to provide grounds for a new design argument (see GOD, ARGUMENTS FOR THE EXISTENCE OF §5). Others believe that it can be explained in scientific terms – for example, by suggesting that there are vastly many universes, either contemporaneous with our own or in succession, each of which instantiates a different set of fundamental constants. One or more of these universes would be expected to support life, and it is only in such a universe that observers would be present to raise the question of fine-tuning. Whether or not the fine-tuning is taken as evidence for the existence of God, it has important consequences for theology in that some philosophers believe that it argues against an interventionist account of continuing creation and divine action, since the prerequisites for human existence were built into the universe from the very beginning.

7 Physics and metaphysics

A variety of developments in physics since the end of the nineteenth century have called into question the determinist worldview. Quantum physics has introduced indeterminacy into the worldview of physics. Quantum theory generally allows only for probabilistic predictions regarding classes of events, not for prediction of individual events. It is unclear whether this limitation represents only a limit of human knowledge, or whether it signifies genuine indeterminacy in nature (see QUANTUM MECHANICS, INTERPRETATION OF §3). However, scholarly opinion tends towards the latter view. Thus, most physicists reject the determinism of the Newtonian worldview, at least at this level. 'Quantum non-locality' refers to the peculiar fact that electrons and other sub-atomic entities that have once interacted continue to behave in coordinated ways, even when they are too far apart for any known causal interaction in the time available. This phenomenon calls radically into question the Newtonian picture of the universe as discrete particles in motion, interacting by means of familiar physical forces. If Newtonian determinism had strong implications for theories of divine action, it is surely the case that these developments in quantum physics must have theological implications as well. What these implications are is still very much an open question.

A more recent development, which cuts across physics and the other natural sciences, is chaos theory (see CHAOS THEORY). This is the study of systems whose behaviour is highly sensitive to changes in initial conditions. What this means can be illustrated with an example from classical dynamics: the movements of a billiard ball are governed in a straightforward way by Newton's laws, but very slight differences in the angle of impact of the cue stick have greatly magnified effects after several collisions; moreover, initial differences that make for large differences in later behaviour are too small to measure, so the system is intrinsically unpredictable. Chaotic systems are found throughout nature – in thermodynamic systems far from equilibrium, in weather patterns and even in animal populations. Chaos theory is relevant to discussions of divine action not because chaotic systems are indeterminate (that is, not causally determined) and thus open to divine action without violation of laws of nature. Rather, the recognition of the ubiquity of chaotic systems shows the intrinsic limitations of human knowledge, and leads to the negative but important conclusion that one is rarely (or never) in a position to know that God is not acting in natural processes.

Another development throughout science with important implications for the issue of determinism and divine action is the recognition of 'top–down causation'. The sciences can be conceived as a hierarchy in which higher sciences study progressively more complex systems: physics studies the smallest, simplest components of the universe; chemistry studies complex organizations of physical particles (atoms and molecules); biochemistry studies the extremely complex chemical compounds making up living organisms, and so on. The dream of the logical positivists was to provide an account of the sciences wherein the laws of the higher-level sciences could all be reduced to the laws of physics (see LOGICAL POSITIVISM). This concept of explanatory reductionism followed naturally from the ontological reductionism that has become an important tenet of the modern scientific worldview: if all entities and systems are ultimately made up of the entities studied by physics, their behaviour ought to be understandable in terms of the laws of physics. So ontological and explanatory reductionism entail causal reductionism, or 'bottom–up causation'. If the laws of physics are deterministic, we have a deterministic account of the whole of nature. However, it has become apparent that the behaviour of entities at various levels of the hierarchy of complexity cannot always be understood entirely in terms of the behaviour of their parts; attention to their interaction with non-reducible features of their environments is also required. Thus, the state or behaviour of a higher-level system exercises top–down causal influence on its components.

Arthur Peacocke (1990) has used this development in scientific thought to propose new directions for understanding divine action. In his 'panentheist' view, the universe is 'in' God, and God's influence on the cosmos can then be understood by analogy with top–down causation throughout the hierarchy of natural levels (see GOD, CONCEPTS OF §8). While this proposal does not answer questions about how God affects specific events within the cosmos, it does dissolve the long-standing problem of causal determinism.

8 Epistemology and language

The shift from medieval epistemology to modern empiricism required radical revision of religious epistemology. Various strategies were employed during the modern period to show theology to be epistemologically respectable. However, the increasing prevalence of atheism in scholarly circles suggests that these strategies have not been successful. At a point in intellectual history that some would call the end of the modern period, theories of knowledge have changed enough that the question of the epistemic status of theology needs to be examined afresh. Our concern here will be only with changes relating directly to science.

Theologians' statements have sometimes been dismissed on the grounds that they describe states of affairs that are unimaginable or non-picturable. However, quantum theory and other recent scientific developments describe a physical reality that is equally unimaginable and, some would say, calls into question traditional two-valued logic. This line of argument is intended to point out that a view of knowledge more humble than that of the modern period is called for; reality is more complex and mysterious than anything our language and concepts allow us to capture.

It has often been said (especially by theologians) that theology differs radically from science in that science is objective while all religious knowledge is self-involving, the product of an interaction between God and the human subject. Another way in which science has tempered older views of knowledge, and narrowed the difference between science and theology, is in its recognition that scientific knowledge itself is interactive. Measurements are interactions with the phenomena being measured, especially at the subatomic level.

Most modern thinkers have judged it impossible to provide empirical support for theology. However, beginning with the work of Ian Barbour (1974), there has been an investigation of the ways in which theological reasoning resembles that of science, including accounts of suitable data for theology. This development was made possible by advances in philosophy of science that show science itself to be a more complicated, and more human, enterprise than the positivists assumed (see KUHN, T.; LAKATOS, I. §3).

9 Religion's implications for science

Most of this entry has focused on the implications of science for religion. However, it is also the case that religion has implications for science. It has been argued that Christian doctrine was an important contributor to the rise of modern science: God's freedom entailed that features of the natural world could not be deduced a priori from rational principles, yet God's goodness and faithfulness suggested that the world would not be so chaotic as to be unintelligible. The very existence of religion is a valuable reminder that there are boundaries beyond which scientific explanation cannot go, and its doctrines help to answer questions that lie beyond those boundaries. The Newtonian era saw the separation of natural philosophy (science) from natural theology, and since then it has been a methodological presupposition of science that it should provide purely natural explanations. Science has thereby set boundaries on its own competence, but this does not mean that what is beyond its competence is therefore unimportant (or non-existent). Cosmology and physics raise questions they cannot answer: Why is the behaviour of natural processes law-like? What caused the Big Bang? Why is there a universe at all? While theology and science may interact in minor ways within each of their proper domains, it is here that theological explanation comes into its own.

See also: CREATION AND CONSERVATION, RELIGIOUS DOCTRINE OF §6; PERSONALISM §2; RELIGION AND EPISTEMOLOGY; SCIENCE IN ISLAMIC PHILOSOPHY; WITTGENSTEIN, L.J. §15

References and further reading

* Barbour, I. (1966) *Issues in Science and Religion*, New York: Harper & Row. (Very accessible survey of relations between science and Christianity, beginning in the modern period.)

* —— (1974) *Myths, Models and Paradigms*, New York: Harper & Row. (Methodological comparison of science and religion, making use especially of Thomas Kuhn's philosophy of science. Very accessible.)

—— (1990) *Religion in an Age of Science: The Gifford Lectures, 1989–1991*, San Francisco, CA: Harper-Collins, vol. 1. (Combines and updates material

from previous books. A particularly good introduction.)

* Darwin, C. (1859) *The Origin of Species*, London: John Murray. (Classic statement of Darwin's thesis.)

* Draper, J.W. (1874) *History of the Conflict between Religion and Science*, New York: D. Appleton. (A once-popular denunciation of Catholicism for its interference with scientific development.)

* Eaves, L.J., Martin, N.G. and Heath, A.C. (1990) 'Religious Affiliation in Twins and Their Parents: Testing a Model of Cultural Inheritance', *Behaviour Genetics* 20 (1): 1–21. (Provides some evidence for a genetic component in religious behaviour.)

Hefner, P. (1993) *The Human Factor: Evolution, Culture, and Religion*, Minneapolis, MN: Fortress Press. (Example of theological use of the theory of evolution.)

Leslie, J. (1989) *Universes*, London: Routledge. (An accessible account of the anthropic or fine-tuning issue.)

Lindberg, D.C. (1992) *The Beginnings of Western Science: The European Scientific Tradition in Philosophical, Religious, and Institutional Context, 600* BC *to* AD *1450*, Chicago, IL: University of Chicago Press. (Accessible.)

Lindberg, D.C. and Numbers, R.L. (eds) (1986) *God and Nature: Historical Essays on the Encounter between Christianity and Science*, Berkeley, CA: University of California Press. (Criticizes accounts of the history of science and religion that presuppose the warfare model.)

* Merton, R. (1938) *Science, Technology and Society in Seventeenth-Century England*, New York: Harper & Row, repr. 1970. (Presents the thesis that the development of science was encouraged by Puritanism.)

Murphy, N. (1990) *Theology in the Age of Scientific Reasoning*, Ithaca, NY: Cornell University Press. (On the relation between theological method and philosophy of science. Presupposes some knowledge of philosophy.)

Murphy, N. and Ellis, G.F.R. (1996) *On the Moral Nature of the Universe: Theology, Cosmology, and Ethics*, Minneapolis, MN: Fortress Press. (Comprehensive model for relating natural and social sciences to theology and ethics. Moderate technicality.)

Peacocke, A.R. (1979) *Creation and the World of Science: The Bampton Lectures, 1978*, Oxford: Clarendon Press. (Thorough survey of issues in the relation of contemporary science to Christian theology. Expands on issues of evolution and creation, and the hierarchical ordering of the sciences. Less accessible than Barbour.)

* —— (1990) *Theology for a Scientific Age*, Oxford: Blackwell; enlarged edn, Minneapolis, MN: Fortress Press, 1993. (Relates top–down causation to divine action.)

Rolston, H. (1987) *Science and Religion: A Critical Survey*, New York: Random House. (A good introduction to the field; less readable than Barbour, but aesthetically pleasing.)

Russell, R.J., Murphy, N. and Peacocke, A. (eds) (1994) *Chaos and Complexity: Scientific Perspectives on Divine Action*, Vatican City State: Vatican Observatory; distributed by University of Notre Dame Press. (A series of articles on divine action, of various levels of technicality.)

* White, A.D. (1896) *A History of the Warfare of Science with Theology in Christendom*, New York: D. Appleton, 2 vols. (Referred to in introduction and §2.)

NANCEY MURPHY

RELIGION, CRITIQUE OF

During the Enlightenment a new philosophy of religion arose, one which was not connected with metaphysics or philosophical theology. It asked to what extent religion could be legitimated philosophically, to what extent it could be shown to be reasonable.

*The reasonableness of religion was taken to be significant for the political as well as the confessional clash between Christian denominations in Europe, all of which tried to justify their conflicting religious doctrines by reference to a supernatural revelation. The philosophical debate that began in the Enlightenment with regard to the criteria and arguments for a religion connected either to human nature or to public reason can be called a 'critique of religion' (*Religionskritik*), although the expression is not common before the critical philosophy of Kant and his school. Hegel followed the programme of Kant's philosophy, maintaining a philosophical concept of religion as falling 'within the limits of reason alone'. The radical left-wing school of Hegelianism transformed Hegel's approach, which was a critical legitimation of religion, into its destruction. Presupposing materialism in ontology and atheism, Feuerbach held that religion should be interpreted as a kind of anthropology. Marx claimed that religion is an expression of a certain sort of ideology and a necessary illusion within a class-structured society.*

In twentieth-century philosophy, the critique of religion can be found in two positions. The first is a rational reconstruction of the practical intentions or semantic content of religious belief; the second is a continuation of the interpretation of religion as ideological or illusory. In addition, we can identify certain other varieties of the critique of religion, including the theological critique of religion (found, for example, in the work of Barth and Bonhoeffer) and the philosophical critique of particular religious traditions (found, for example, in the romantic and postmodern rejections of Christian monotheism by Hölderlin, Nietzsche, Klages and Heidegger).

1   **The concept of the critique of religion**
2   **Critique of religion after Hegel**
3   **Critique of religion in the twentieth century**

1   The concept of the critique of religion

In the history of Western philosophy, the specific contents of mythologies and religions as well as the forms of religious representations and practices have always been the subject of philosophical reflection. But only at the time of the European Enlightenment do we find the term 'critique of religion' (*Religionskritik*). This may indicate that the philosophy of the seventeenth and eighteenth centuries discovered the problem of a general philosophical theory of religion as such beyond the earlier metaphysical theories of a first cause or highest good. The immediate cause of the Enlightenment reflection was concern regarding the conflicting claims of reason and faith, of rational human insight and of divine revelation. While Pierre BAYLE maintained the fundamental incompatibility of reason and religion, the rationalist LEIBNIZ (§3) claimed a conformity of faith with reason. But in so far as the religious confessions had to refer to historical events or traditions, Leibniz's belief in such a conformity lost its plausibility. The search for a natural religion as a common property of all human beings sought to overcome the uncertainties of the particular confessions, their conflicting claims and their recourse to revelation. Belief in a 'natural religion' by thinkers such as Reimarus, Lessing and WOLFF (§6) was clearly a criticism of the unrestrained claims of the historical religions based on revelation. None the less, it was the philosophy of KANT that first introduced the concept of a critique of religion into the philosophical debate. His special critique of religious belief is part of the general critical task he defined as essential for philosophy. In the preface to the first edition of his *Critique of Pure Reason*, Kant describes the duty of philosophy as 'a call to reason to undertake anew the most difficult of all its tasks, namely that of self-knowledge, and to institute a tribunal which will assure to reason its lawful claims, and dismiss all groundless pretensions' (1781: A11).

According to that account of the task of philosophy, all historical forms of religion have to be examined in the light of a general and public reason. Kant presupposes a concept of reason which is able to develop the criteriology to judge by its own competence. This critical approach is clearly distinct from the earlier positions. In defining the essence of religion as the recognition of the duties of human beings discovered by pure practical reason 'as divine commands', Kant is able to escape from the conceptual choice offered by deism, between a natural religion and a historical and revealed one. For Kant, it is not the origin of a religion but its 'qualification to be universal' which defines religious legitimacy. As he explains in *Religion within the Limits of Reason Alone*:

Such a religion can be natural, and at the same time revealed, when it is so constituted that men could and ought to have discovered it of themselves merely through the use of their reason, although they would not have come upon it so nearly, or over so wide an area, as is required.

(1793/1794: A219/B233)

2   Critique of religion after Hegel

In Hegel's idealistic philosophical system, religion and philosophy have the same subject, namely God or the Absolute Idea. One difference between religion and philosophy has to do with how each is able to express or to comprehend that subject. While Hegel defines religion as a system of symbolization or a 'form of imagination', it lacks a specific stage of conceptual reflection and self-awareness. It is the task of philosophy to reflect the imaginative form of the religious representation of the Absolute and, in doing so, to overcome its limits. Therefore, Hegel concludes that philosophy can claim the higher insight (see HEGEL, G.W.F. §8).

This idealistic critique of religion was the immediate cause for a series of severe controversies after Hegel's death (1831). Karl Marx's famous opening statement in his *Critique of Hegel's Philosophy of Law* (1844), that 'the critique of religion is the precondition for all further criticism', has to be seen as a reaction to Hegel's idealistic view of religion's function and limits and the identical content of philosophy and religion (see MARX, K. §§2–3). On the other hand, Kierkegaard's existentialist protest against Hegel must be understood as criticism of the devaluation of religion and its interpretation within the idealistic system of philosophy (see KIERKEGAARD, S.A. §2). Feuerbach's theory of the anthropological content of religion and his critique of religion as an illusory projection of human attributes onto God participates in the general rejection of Hegel's philosophy by the critical movement of the 'Hegelian left' (see FEUERBACH, L.A.). One of the consequences of this programme to reduce the idealistic philosophy to its true – that is, social-historical – origin and its practical human content is found in Marx's work. Religion for Marx is no longer the symbolic expression of the Absolute Idea, but the 'sigh' of the oppressed creature, a necessary illusion in a class society and a protest against injustice and exploitation.

3   Critique of religion in the twentieth century

The philosophical critique of religion in the twentieth century reflects the broader interest and engagement of philosophers in the field of philosophy of religion. In addition to a continuation of a rational critique of religion in the tradition of the Enlightenment, Kant and Hegel (examples are the Neo-Kantian philosophers Paul Natorp, W. Windelband, Hermann COHEN (§3) and Ernst CASSIRER, and the philosophers of religion Paul TILLICH and R. Schaeffler), and a tradition of a more or less Marxist critique (examples are R. Garaudy and Ernst BLOCH), we can identify various new types of philosophy of religion. These often include new categories of a critique of religion, with both affirmative and disapproving statements of religion. In the tradition of psychoanalysis, there are the works of Freud and Mitscherlich. In the context of historicism we find Ernst TROELTSCH. In the philosophical school of phenomenology there are Rudolf OTTO and Max Scheler, and in the analytical tradition there are Russell, Carnap, Wittgenstein, Ayer and Hare. In addition to these, we can recognize two further contributions to the critique of religion, especially in Germany. First, there is the dialectical theology of Karl BARTH, in which religion is supposed to be a work of human beings which is opposed to the 'word of God', and the position of Dietrich BONHOEFFER, who favours a Christian belief without religious qualities (*religionsloses Christentum*); second, there is the (neo-)romantic proposal to resuscitate elements of ancient Greek mythology and a polytheistic view of the world in the tradition of Hölderlin, Nietzsche, Klages and Heidegger.

See also: ATHEISM; ENLIGHTENMENT, CONTINENTAL; DEISM; EXISTENTIALIST THEOLOGY; NATURAL THEOLOGY; RELIGION AND EPISTEMOLOGY

237

References and further reading

Bayle, P. (1695–7) *Dictionnaire historique et critique* (Historical and Critical Dictionary), ed. J.C. Gottsched, Hildesheim: Olms, 1973–. (A very influential critique of prejudice and ignorance in the early European Enlightenment.)

Bloch, E. (1968) *Atheismus im Christentum* (Atheism in Christianity), Frankfurt: Suhrkamp Verlag. (A Neo-Marxist critique of Christianity.)

Feuerbach, L. (1841) *Das Wesen des Christentums* (The Essence of Christianity), Stuttgart: Reclam Verlag, 1971. (The classical critique of religion in the post-Hegelian era of German philosophy in the nineteenth century.)

Hegel, G.W.F. (1832) *Vorlesungen zur Philosophie der Religion* (Lectures on the Philosophy of Religion), in *Werke in 20 Bänden*, vols 16–17, Frankfurt: Suhrkamp Verlag, 1971. (Contains Hegel's doctrine concerning the relation between reason and religious belief.)

* Kant, I. (1781) *Critique of Pure Reason*, trans. N. Kemp Smith, New York: St Martin's Press, 1965. (The most important work of modern German philosophy, in which Kant intended to construct a critical metaphysics on the basis of a critique of human understanding.)

* —— (1793) *Religion within the Limits of Reason Alone*, trans. T.M. Greene and H.H. Hudson, New York: Harper & Row, 1960. (This text contains the basic assumptions of Kant's doctrine of religion.)

Leibniz, G.W. (1710) 'Discours préliminaire de la conformité de la foi avec la raison' (Introductory Discourse on the Conformity of Faith with Reason), in C.J. Gerhardt (ed.) *Essais de Théodicée*, Hildesheim: Olms, 1961. (An important early-Enlightenment reflection on the possibility of a fundamental harmony between religious belief and philosophical reason.)

Lutz-Bachmann, M. (1977) *Kritische Theorie und Religion* (Critical Theory and Religion), Würzburg: Echter Verlag. (A collection of articles on the critique of religion in Critical Theory.)

* Marx, K. (1844) *Critique of Hegel's Philosophy of Law*, in *Collected Works of Marx and Engels*, vol. 3, London: Lawrence & Wishart, 1975–. (The introduction to this book contains Marx's critique of religion.)

Post, W. (1969) *Kritik der Religion bei K. Marx* (Marx's Critique of Religion), Munich: Kösel Verlag. (A brilliant dissertation on Marx's critique of religion.)

Reimarus, H.S. (1754) *Die vornehmsten Wahrheiten der natürlichen Religion* (The Most Exalted Truths of Natural Religion), Hamburg. (An important document of the German enlightenment.)

Thielicke, H. (1957) *Offenbarung, Vernunft und Existenz, Studien zur Religionsphilosophie Lessings* (Revelation, Reason and Existence, Studies in Lessing's Philosophy of Religion), Gütersloh: Gütersloher Verlagshaus Gerd Mohn. (A qualified summary of the philosophical thought of Lessing, the most influential German poet of the Enlightenment.)

MATTHIAS LUTZ-BACHMANN

RELIGION, HISTORY OF PHILOSOPHY OF

The philosophy of religion comprises any philosophical discussion of questions arising from religion. This has primarily consisted in the clarification and critical evaluation of fundamental beliefs and concepts from one or another religious tradition. Major issues of concern in the philosophy of religion include arguments for and against the existence of God, problems about the attributes of God, the problem of evil, and the epistemology of religious belief.

Of arguments for the existence of God, the most prominent ones can be assigned to four types. First, cosmological arguments, which go back to Plato and Aristotle, explain the existence of the universe by reference to a being on whom all else depends for its existence. Second, teleological arguments seek to explain adaptation in the world, for example, the way organisms have structures adapted to their needs, by positing an intelligent designer of the world. Third, ontological arguments, first introduced by Anselm, focus on the concept of a perfect being and argue that it is incoherent to deny that such a being exists. Finally, moral arguments maintain that objective moral statuses, distinctions or principles presuppose a divine being as the locus of their objectivity.

Discussions of the attributes of God have focused on omniscience and omnipotence. These raise various problems, for example, whether complete divine foreknowledge of human actions is compatible with human free will. Moreover, these attributes, together with God's perfect goodness give rise to the problem of evil. If God is all-powerful, all-knowing and perfectly good, how can there be wickedness, suffering and other undesirable states of affairs in the world? This problem has been repeatedly discussed from ancient times to the present.

The epistemology of religious belief has to do with the questions of what is the proper approach to the assessment of religious belief (for rationality, justification, or whatever) and with the carrying out of such assessments. Much of the discussion has turned on the contrast between the roles of human reason and God's revelation to us. A variety of views have been held on this. Many, such as Aquinas, have tried to forge a synthesis of the two; Kant and his followers have sought to ground religion solely on reason; others, most notably Kierkegaard, have held that the subjecting of religious belief to rational scrutiny is subversive of true religious faith. Recently, a group of 'Reformed epistemologists' (so-called because of the heavy influence of the Reformed theology of Calvin and his followers on their thinking) has attacked 'evidentialism' and has argued that religious beliefs can be rationally justified even if one has no reasons or evidence for them.

1   **What is philosophy of religion?**
2–5 **Arguments for the existence of God**
6   **Divine attributes**
7   **The problem of evil**
8   **The epistemology of religious belief**

1   What is philosophy of religion?

The term 'philosophy of religion' is a relative newcomer, dating only from the late eighteenth century. It became widespread under the influence of Hegel, whose system of philosophy featured various 'philosophy of' components – history, mind, art, as well as religion. But philosophical reflection on religious issues is as old as philosophy itself. One of the earliest spurs to philosophy in ancient Greece was the emergence of doubts concerning the religious tradition. The present article construes 'philosophy of religion' as the philosophical discussion of questions growing out of religion, whether conducted under that title or not.

These discussions are highly diverse. Different religions give rise to different issues, depending, for example, on whether the religion is centred around faith in a personal deity. The philosophizing that is done will reflect the thinker's conception of the philosophical task. The philosophy of religion of a speculative metaphysician such as Hegel will differ widely from that produced by an analytic philosopher who thinks of philosophy as concerned primarily with the clarification of concepts. And even when these two variables are assigned specific values, there are different views as to how philosophy can best contribute to the understanding of religion. The main concern has been the clarification and critical evaluation of fundamental beliefs and concepts from some particular religious tradition. But some philo-

sophers in the last two centuries, influenced by Hegel and by phenomenology, have set out to produce a synoptic view of religion in all its aspects, not only the doctrinal and conceptual ones, and to survey and interrelate the different forms in which it is realized (see van der Leeuw 1963).

Faced with this bewildering diversity and long history, an article of this length can provide only a brief sample. It will therefore concentrate on the attempts of Western philosophy to deal with philosophical questions arising from the Judaeo-Christian tradition, and, among these attempts, on what can more specifically be called *philosophical theology*. This involves the attempt to deal with fundamental religious concepts and beliefs in a philosophical way, where 'philosophical' implies two restrictions. First, when our aim is philosophical, we are concerned with *understanding* (clarifying, explicating) the material, and critically evaluating it for truth, coherence and rationality, rather than with *describing* it or discovering laws that govern it. (This distinguishes philosophy of religion from the history, sociology or psychology of religion.) Second, the enterprise is not conducted from the standpoint of any religious commitments. It appeals only to what is (claimed to be) available to any rational person who reflects carefully on the matter. (This distinguishes philosophical theology from dogmatic theology.)

Even with this restriction there is an enormous choice of topics on which to concentrate. Here is a list of those that most frequently appear in current treatises and textbooks on the subject:

(1) arguments for and against the existence of God;
(2) problems concerning the various attributes of God;
(3) the problem of evil;
(4) religious issues concerning human nature, particularly the possibility of human life after death, and free will;
(5) the bearing of religion on ethics;
(6) how to understand basic religious concepts, such as faith, salvation, creation and spirituality;
(7) questions about divine action, particularly the notion that God 'intervenes' in the world, bringing about events that would not have occurred had only purely natural causes been involved (miracles);
(8) the epistemology of religious belief.

The present entry deals with the most significant elements in the histories of topics (1), (2), (3) and (8); this choice is prompted by the main areas of interest among contemporary philosophers of religion.

2 Arguments for the existence of God: the cosmological argument

Philosophical theology goes back to the ancient Greeks, to a time at which intellectual dissatisfaction with the polytheistic religious tradition led to attempts by philosophers to develop a more rational religious orientation. Plato, in the *Laws*, may be said to have inaugurated the project of giving philosophical arguments for the existence of God. Interestingly enough, it occurs in a political context. Arguing that the denial of certain theological truths is a grave offence against the social order, he proceeds to demonstrate those truths, beginning with the existence of God. He presents a form of the cosmological argument that turns on the cause of motion. Briefly put, the argument is that motion produced by something else presupposes a self-mover, a being that spontaneously moves. This is identified by Plato with soul (*psychē*). He does not seek to show that all change can be traced to a single self-changing source. On the contrary, he holds that there must be at least two, though he takes the 'best soul' to be supreme.

A more elaborate argument from motion is found in Book XII of Aristotle's *Metaphysics* (see ARISTOTLE §16). Time is necessarily everlasting, for if it came into being, that would presuppose a time before which there was time; and if it were to cease there would be a time after that, a time with no time. Aristotle also thinks that there cannot be time without motion. Therefore motion is everlasting. And since motion presupposes substances that move, it is necessary that there are always substances in motion. But if all substances were destructible (had a potentiality for nonexistence), it would be possible that at some time there were no substances. Hence there must exist at least one substance that is pure actuality, with no unrealized potentialities, and it is this that guarantees the eternality of moving substances. Since it is pure actuality, it does not move, and since all matter involves potentiality it is immaterial. As the source of all motion, it is the 'first mover unmoved'. Since the first mover is immune to any kind of change, it can be the source of motion only as what Aristotle calls a 'final cause', the end or goal towards which a process tends. It moves the heavens (which in turn move all else) as an object of desire or love. As unmoved, it does not enter into causal interaction with the world, as the Judaeo-Christian God does, but confines itself to pure thought. It is 'thought thinking itself'.

Neither Plato nor Aristotle thought of God as creating the physical universe, but Plato's God is somewhat more active than Aristotle's. In the *Timaeus*, Plato depicts God as a 'Demiurge' who introduces order into the chaos with which he is initially confronted. But it was left to Christian theology to develop the radical idea of the divine creation of everything other than God *ex nihilo*, from nothing.

Neoplatonism, as developed most fully by PLOTINUS in the *Enneads*, involved a more mystical view, in which the supreme reality is an absolute One, devoid of any distinctions whatever, and accessible only to a unitive mystical experience in which even the distinction between subject and object is obliterated. Neoplatonism profoundly influenced Christian theology, primarily through the thinker who wrote mystical treatises around AD 500 under the name of 'Dionysius' (see PSEUDO-DIONYSIUS). His influence is evident even in thinkers who were not primarily mystical theologians, including Anselm and Aquinas, both of whom held the doctrine of the absolute simplicity of God.

Neoplatonism was the main philosophical basis of Christian theology from Augustine to the twelfth century, when Aristotle's works were rediscovered in western Europe. By the latter half of the thirteenth century the philosophical thought of the West was thoroughly Aristotelian. As for arguments for the existence of God, the 'five ways' of Thomas Aquinas, in his *Summa theologiae* Ia, q.2, came to dominate Roman Catholic philosophical theology up to our own day. Three of the five ways can be viewed as cosmological. There is an argument, reminiscent of Aristotle, to a first mover unmoved, a parallel argument to a first cause (of existence) uncaused, and an argument, again reminiscent of Aristotle, that is designed to show that the universe cannot consist merely of contingent beings (beings that may or may not exist), but must contain a necessary being, one that exists by the necessity of its own nature. But though these arguments are heavily, and admittedly, indebted to Aristotle, Aquinas draws from them conclusions much more congenial to Christian theology. Like Aristotle, he argues that the first cause uncaused must be pure actuality, since it is prior to all other beings and actuality is prior to potentiality. But he also maintains that the first cause must contain all the perfections of those things that depend on it for their existence, since causality consists in actualizing potentialities, and an agent can bestow only those actualities it already possesses. That is the thin end of the wedge Aquinas needs to show that the first cause is absolutely perfect, and from that he proceeds to derive the basic attributes of the Christian God – omniscience, omnipotence, perfect goodness, love, and so on.

Aquinas' first mover and first cause arguments involve the thesis that an infinite series of causes or movers is impossible; hence any such series must stem from a first member, on which all succeeding members depend for their efficacy. It is natural to read Aquinas as denying that a *temporally* infinite series of causes is possible, in which case his conclusion would be that there is a temporally first cause of the universe, and hence that the universe came into existence some finite period of time ago. But since he elsewhere denies that it can be shown by reason that the world had a beginning, this cannot be his intention. His claim is rather that there cannot be an infinite hierarchy of levels of dependence. Such a series would begin, for example, with the motion of a pencil being dependent on the simultaneous motion of my hand, which in turn is dependent on my will, which in turn . . . . However, Aquinas' development of this way of thinking was in terms of medieval physics, which is far removed from anything taken seriously today. Hence there have been repeated attempts in the modern period to free the argument from entanglement with outmoded science. A notable example is Samuel CLARKE (§1) (1738). A brilliant contemporary critical discussion of this argument is put forward by Rowe (1975). Avoiding the sometimes labyrinthine details of Clarke's presentation, the basic idea can be presented as follows:

(1) The physical universe is temporally either finite or infinite.
(2) If finite, the beginning of its existence must have been due to some cause.
(3) If infinite, there must be some cause, the activity of which is responsible for the fact that this universe exists rather than some other or none at all.
(4) Even if the cause of the existence of our universe owes its existence to some other cause, an infinite regress of such causes is impossible.
(5) Therefore, the entire system ultimately owes its existence to an uncaused first cause, one that exists by the necessity of its own nature (a necessary being).

In this version, the series of causes that is claimed to be necessarily non-infinite is wholly outside the spatiotemporal universe. And since the argument begins with the universe as a whole, it does not depend on any particular scientific view of the internal economy of that universe.

In this version, the argument's dependence on what has come to be called the Principle of Sufficient Reason is apparent. According to that principle, for any fact (state of affairs) there must be a sufficient reason for its obtaining, a reason either in itself or in some external cause. Much discussion of the argument has centred around that principle, which

received a historically important defence by LEIBNIZ (§§3, 11).

3 Arguments for the existence of God: the teleological argument

Here the crucial claim is that a cosmic designer is required to explain the design or adaptation we find in the world, the way in which things are fitted to achieve certain ends. Aquinas' fifth way is an early example. He thought in terms of a teleological physics in which all physical processes were explained by an orientation to goal states. For example, each type of matter was thought of as seeking its proper place in the universe – solids the centre (identified with the centre of the earth), fire the periphery, and so on. He then argued that such goal direction is possible for inanimate beings only if they are directed to these goals by an intelligent being. But with the demise of teleological physics in the modern period the main examples of design are found in the organic realm, in the ways in which the structure and function of organisms are nicely adapted to the satisfaction of their needs. For example, the outer ears that land animals, but not fish, possess are fitted to focus sound waves that are weaker in air than in water. And the ears of predators are fitted to receive sounds from in front, while their intended victims have ears that pick up sounds better from the rear. A famous example of this argument is found in Paley's *Natural Theology* (1802), in which he imagines coming across a watch on the ground and becoming convinced, from the way in which its design is conducive to keeping the time, that it was produced by an intelligent designer. He then argues that we must say the same of the human eye (see PALEY, W. §2).

The argument was subjected to a variety of criticisms in the *Dialogues Concerning Natural Religion* (1779) of David HUME (§6), many of which involve doubts that the universe as a whole is enough like a watch or other artefact to sustain the argument. In the last century and a half, the chief criticism of the argument has been that the theory of evolution provides a superior, naturalistic explanation for the cases of organic adaptation on which the argument is based. Organisms are well adapted to survive in the environments in which they find themselves because otherwise they would die out. It is the fittest that survive in the competition for scarce resources. In the face of such criticism, the argument has shifted in a way analogous to the shift noted above in the cosmological argument. Instead of starting with particular cases of adaptation, for which scientific explanations might be advanced, we start with the universe as a whole and ask why it is so constituted as to be fitted for life, however particular forms of life are to be explained in terms of factors within the universe. To that question no science could possibly provide an answer, since science is concerned with the internal economy of the universe, how one part or aspect is related to another. With recent developments in the study of the origin and development of the physical universe, this more cosmic form of the argument has received a shot in the arm from considerations concerning the 'fine tuning' that is required of basic physical constants if the universe is to be supportive of life (see Leslie 1989) (see RELIGION AND SCIENCE §6). The argument has also been extended to include a larger variety of features said to require a designer, such as mathematical order and beauty (see Tennant 1930).

4 Arguments for the existence of God: the ontological argument

This is the final member of the classic trio of arguments. It was first stated clearly by ANSELM OF CANTERBURY (§4), the most important thinker of the eleventh century, in his *Proslogion* (1077–8). It differs from the other two in not seeking an explanation of empirical facts. It is purely a priori, consisting in the analysis of concepts. In Anselm's version, it is a *reductio ad absurdum*. Suppose, he says, that the being than which no greater can be conceived ('the perfect being', for short) exists only in the mind and not in reality. Then we could conceive a greater being, one just like the former except that it also exists in reality. But it is impossible that we should conceive a being greater than a being than which none greater can be conceived. Hence the supposition with which we began – that the perfect being does not exist in reality – must be rejected.

A monk named Gaunilo sent Anselm a criticism of the argument, in which one of the points he made was that there must be something wrong with it, since one could use an exactly parallel argument to show that a perfect island, or a perfect anything else, exists. Aquinas rejected the argument on the grounds that it wrongly assumes that we know the essence of God. However, the most persistent criticism, classically expressed by Immanuel Kant in his *Critique of Pure Reason* (1781), is that the argument falsely assumes that existence is a property, whereas we do not add anything to our concept of a being (to the list of its properties) when we point out that it exists.

The argument has had a number of supporters through the centuries, including DESCARTES (§6) and LEIBNIZ (§3), as well as a number of critics. Leibniz realized that questions could be raised about the *possibility* of a perfect being, and he undertook to

establish that. A major step forward occurred in this century when Charles Hartshorne (1962) and Norman Malcolm (1963) independently discovered that there are two versions of the argument in the *Proslogion*. The first, the one presented above, is designed to show that a perfect being exists, the second that a perfect being necessarily exists. Both Hartshorne and Malcolm point out that the second version is immune to the charge of treating existence as a predicate. There are not the same objections to treating necessary existence as a predicate. More recently, Alvin Plantinga (1974) has made use of contemporary modal logic to develop the most sophisticated formulation of the second form of the argument.

5 Arguments for the existence of God: the moral argument

This argument takes its start from premises concerning moral obligation, moral principles, moral goodness, and the like. It is a more recent arrival than the three just discussed. It was first given prominence by KANT (§11) in his *Critique of Practical Reason* (1788), where we find the following argument: Moral endeavour presupposes that the virtuous will eventually attain happiness, for only in the union of virtue and happiness do we have the supreme good, and it is a fundamental moral obligation to strive to realize the good. But this can be an obligation only if it is possible to attain the supreme good. And this is possible only if the universe is under the control of a morally good personal being. Therefore the existence of God is a necessary presupposition of morality. Kant did not claim that this reasoning enables us to *know* that God exists; it only shows the existence of God to be a presupposition of the moral life.

Other thinkers in the nineteenth and twentieth centuries have presented more straightforward moral arguments. The most common form starts from the claim that moral distinctions – between right and wrong, between what we are and are not obliged to do – are objective. It is an objective fact that it is wrong wantonly to inflict suffering on another human being, and that one is obliged to care for one's children. But this can be so only if there is a God to 'anchor' these facts. According to the argument, there is no other possible objective locus for morality. In some versions it is the divine will – what God commands us to do and not to do – that renders moral facts objective. In others it is the goodness of God that plays this role. God *is* the good, and human morality constitutes the approximation to the divine goodness that is most appropriate for human beings (see Adams 1987).

There have been some interesting recent reformulations of traditional arguments for the existence of

God. Chief among them is the restatement of cosmological and teleological arguments in terms of probability and confirmation theory by Swinburne (1979).

6 Divine attributes

As Christian theology developed, the nature of God was thought of in terms of various attributes, such as omnipotence, omniscience and perfect goodness. He was also thought of as a personal agent, one who has purposes and who acts to carry them out in the light of his knowledge. The attempt to think all this through gives rise to various difficulties with which philosophical theologians have been concerned since the early centuries of our era.

Omnipotence. It is not difficult to see that this attribute must be limited in some way if we are to avoid paradoxes and contradictions. For one thing, we have to avoid the idea that God could bring about contradictory states of affairs. If he could, then he could both save Jones and damn Jones, an inconceivable result. Aquinas put this by saying that God can do only what is possible absolutely. Since a contradiction is not a possible state of affairs, it is no limitation on God's power that he cannot bring it about. From the middle ages the 'paradox of the stone' has exercised philosophers. Can God create a stone so heavy he cannot lift it? If we say 'Yes', then there is something he cannot do, namely, lift such a stone. If we say 'No', there is still something he cannot do, namely, create such a stone (see Rosenkrantz and Hoffman 1980).

A more obviously religiously important problem has to do with God's ability to do wrong. If God is essentially perfectly good, it is impossible that he should act wrongly. But then this is something he cannot do, so how can he be omnipotent? Both Anselm and Aquinas answer this by maintaining that since to do wrong is to fall short of a perfect action, omnipotence implies the inability to do wrong rather than the ability to do it. But this looks like fudging. A better answer would be that since God's doing wrong is an inherently impossible state of affairs, there would be no lapse from omnipotence in not being able to realize it, any more than in not being able to realize any other impossible state of affairs (see Pike 1969) (see OMNIPOTENCE).

Omniscience. The most widely discussed problem in this area concerns divine foreknowledge and its relation to human free will. If God is omniscient, he knows everything there is to know, including future human actions. But then how can any of those actions be free? If God knows now that I will accept a certain invitation tomorrow, how can it be that I have any

choice in the matter? Surely I can't do anything contrary to what God knows; and so it is not within my power to do anything on this point except accept the invitation. I have no choice; I am not free. But if I never have a choice about what I do, how can I be responsible for my actions?

The problem is given classic expression in Book V of *The Consolation of Philosophy* (525–6) by BOETHIUS (§5). His solution, which was accepted by Anselm, Aquinas, and many other medieval philosophers, was that God's being is not temporal. God does not live through a succession of moments but enjoys, in Boethius' memorable phrase, 'the complete possession all at once of illimitable life' (*The Consolation of Philosophy* V, pr. 6). Hence God does not know in advance what choices I will make, for God never occupies any temporal standpoint. As eternal rather than temporal, he is all at once simultaneous with every moment of time. Hence he knows what I do because, so to say, he 'sees' me doing it when I do it. Therefore there is no threat to human free will (see ETERNITY).

Though the doctrine of divine atemporality was widely held in the Middle Ages, as well as by many modern theologians, including Schleiermacher, the father of liberal Protestant theology, it has been severely criticized in this century as being unbiblical and as rendering incoherent any notion of divine action in the world (see Pike 1970). It has been vigorously defended recently by Stump and Kretzmann (1981), and by Leftow (1991). However, various attempts have been made to reconcile divine omniscience and human free will without denying divine temporality. One of the most influential is that of William of Ockham, whose seminal idea ran something like this: Even though God's knowing today that I will wash the windows tomorrow entails that I will wash the windows tomorrow, that does not mean that his foreknowledge renders it *necessary* that I will wash the windows tomorrow, and hence does not imply that I have no choice. It is all a question of what depends on what. The past is necessary in the sense that nothing we can do now can alter it. But God's knowledge of future contingent facts is not a 'pure' past fact. It depends for what it is on the future. God knows that I will wash the windows tomorrow because I will wash the windows tomorrow. That is, God's knowledge of what will happen tomorrow is partly a function of what will happen tomorrow. So that leaves me free to have a choice. It is because of the choice that I will make at that time that God's past state is one of knowledge (see Ockham's *Predestination, God's Foreknowledge, and Future Contingents*, q.1, M). A number of contemporary philosophers – for example Plantinga (1986) and

Freddoso (1983) – have developed these Ockhamist ideas in new and fruitful ways. Various other solutions to the problem have been developed recently. Some have suggested a limitation of divine omniscience to exclude foreknowledge of free actions, on analogy with limitations on omniscience mentioned above (Swinburne 1977; Hasker 1989). Freddoso has revived Luis de Molina's doctrine of 'middle knowledge', knowledge of what free creatures would freely do if placed in a certain situation (see MOLINA, L. DE §3; OMNISCIENCE). The problem of divine foreknowledge and human free will has been widely debated in contemporary philosophy of religion; a useful selection of articles can be found in the anthology edited by Fischer (1989).

7 The problem of evil

'Evil' as understood here ranges over anything undesirable, anything we would be better off without. It is not restricted, as it is in ordinary usage, to wrong actions, or wickedness. It also includes the suffering of sentient creatures, which is termed 'natural evil', in contrast to 'moral evil'. Evil is a serious, perhaps the most serious, problem for theistic religion just because it seems obvious at first sight that an omnipotent and perfectly good God would not allow any evil in his creation (see EVIL, PROBLEM OF). Being omnipotent, he could prevent it, and being perfectly good, he would do so. How then can there be evil if the world is governed by such a deity?

This problem has been with us since the beginning of philosophy in ancient Greece, and it has been extensively discussed in Christianity and other theistic traditions (see EVIL). The most common line in Christian theology has been that moral evil is the result of wrong choices (sins) by free created agents (angels and humans), and that natural evil is either a divine punishment for sin or is involved in the corruption of nature that is consequent on angelic and human sin. Here, however, we are concerned with treatments of the problem that are philosophical rather than theological. The most prominent of these can be traced back at least as far as St AUGUSTINE (§9), and they were taken up by many of his successors. Their exposition in Aquinas' *Summa theologiae* Ia, qq.48–9, will be utilized here. First, all evil is a *privation* of something a being would have naturally, like blindness, which is a lack of normal sight. (Only a naturally sighted being can be called 'blind'; a stone is not blind.) Thus evil is not a positive 'nature' or attribute. Everything positive is good, and since there can only be a privation where there is something with a positive (good) nature to be deprived, evil always presupposes good and is

parasitic on it. This is not to say that evil is unreal or an illusion; it is only to say what kind of metaphysical status it has. And since evil is real, we are still faced with the question of why God brings it about, or at least permits it. Here Aquinas treats moral and natural evil separately. Wrongdoing is in no sense the work of God, though he permits it, because he has chosen to create free agents who have the power of choice between right and wrong, and sometimes choose the wrong. As for natural evil, that is the work of God, and his (allegedly sufficient) reason for including it is the Principle of Plenitude:

> The perfection of the universe requires that there should be inequality in this, so that every grade of goodness may be realized. Now, one grade of goodness is that of the good which cannot fail. Another grade of goodness is that of the good which can fail in goodness.... Now it is in this that evil consists, namely, in the fact a thing fails in goodness.
>
> (*Summa theologiae* Ia, q.48, a.2)

It is for the perfection of the universe as a whole that God brings it about that there are creatures subject to privation as well those that are not. This has felicitously been termed an 'aesthetic' approach to the problem, since it depicts God as a supreme artist, aiming at the most perfect composition of the whole universe.

These Augustinian themes have persisted in discussions of the problem up to the present, though they fail to convince many contemporary thinkers. One of the most famous post-medieval treatments is that of LEIBNIZ (§3) in his *Theodicy* (1710). This is most famous for Leibniz's insistence that God created the best of all possible worlds, since otherwise he would not be perfectly good. (It is noteworthy that Aquinas (*Summa theologiae* Ia, q.25, a.6) denies that God's goodness has this implication. He argues that since whatever the state of creation, God could make it better by adding goods, there can be no best possible creation.) By holding there to be no alternative to regarding this as the best world possible, Leibniz raised the stakes even higher, making it more difficult to understand why there is evil in the world. He makes many suggestions as to how things that are undesirable in themselves can lead to goods that far outweigh them, but he makes no major advances in this beyond the medieval tradition.

A contemporary thinker, John Hick (1978), has unearthed and developed an important alternative to the Augustinian approach, one which he traces to the second-century Christian theologian Irenaeus. The point of natural evil in the divine plan is its usefulness in 'soul making', giving people the opportunity to develop morally and spiritually in dealing with the suffering and misery in their lives (see also Stump 1985).

Since evil arises in its acutest form only if God is regarded as omnipotent, it is not surprising that it has occurred to some to challenge that assumption. A relatively early example is Mill (1874). In this century, Charles Hartshorne (1941, 1984), following the lead of Alfred North WHITEHEAD (§4), has forged a highly influential 'process theology', in which God is far and away the most powerful being, but is not omnipotent. Instead, God and the world are coexistent and equally necessary. What God does is to work for order, harmony and fulfilment in the world, but without an absolute ability to bring any of this about by a simple act of will. For anything undesirable in the world, we can say that God is doing the best he can to bring good from it (see PROCESS THEISM).

8   The epistemology of religious belief

Though it is only recently that this topic has been a major preoccupation in philosophy of religion, it is not without historical roots. The question of the nature and status of religious faith has concerned theologians and philosophers at least since the early Christian centuries. Faith is a multifaceted attitude, involving affective and behavioural as well as cognitive components. Concentrating here on the belief component, what are the appropriate standards by which to assess religious belief for rationality, justification, knowledge, and the like? A major issue from the beginning has been the place of reason in all this. Must one have adequate reasons for a religious belief in order to hold it justifiably? Or is that the wrong way to look at the matter? Views on this issue range all the way from that of TERTULLIAN (160–225), who is famous for the dictum concerning the Incarnation, 'I believe it because it is absurd', thus hurling his opponents' reproach into their teeth, to Kant's rationalism, which expresses itself in the title of his major work in the field, *Religion Within the Bounds of Reason Alone* (1793). Most treatments fall somewhere between these extremes. On the one hand, when we look at the full range of the beliefs of an actual religion, there is general agreement that not all those beliefs can be established by unaided human reason. If we are to have any basis for them they must be disclosed to us by God, by divine revelation. In Christianity this is true of the Incarnation, as well as beliefs about divine purposes for, requirements on, and interaction with human beings. Though it is often held that God accompanied his major revelations with miracles to indicate their status, it is also widely held that these indications do not constitute a decisive proof of that status. Hence it has been thought that divine assistance is required for a person to have firm faith in divine revelation, that faith is, at least in part, a gift of God. On the other hand, there are basic beliefs that are often regarded as susceptible of rational proof – the existence and nature of God, and the immortality of the soul, for example. During the first Christian millennium no sharp distinction was made between these two groups of beliefs. With Augustine, for example, it is difficult to say whether he meant to give rational arguments for the doctrine of the Trinity, or only to explain its meaning. By the thirteenth century, however, we find AQUINAS (§14) making a clear distinction between the preambles of faith that could be established by philosophical argument and the remainder that rested on divine testimony.

The Thomistic synthesis fell apart in the modern period under the impact of increasing doubts about both of Aquinas' divisions. David HUME (§2), in the chapter on miracles in his *Enquiry Concerning Human Understanding* (1748) argued that since in order to count as a miracle an event must be contrary to our general experience, and since that experience makes it extremely unlikely that such a thing should happen, a report of a miracle would need an enormous weight of testimony to outweigh that intrinsic improbability, a weight that no report of the miraculous ever displays. Thus, said Hume, we can never be justified in accepting a report of a miracle. As for faith as a gift of God, believing in the absence of sufficient reasons has often been deemed unworthy of a rational agent. This attitude was given classic expression in the late nineteenth century in W.K. Clifford's 'The Ethics of Belief', where he says that 'It is wrong always, everywhere, and for every one, to believe anything upon insufficient evidence' (1879: 183). Finally, with the rejection of the Aristotelian philosophy on which Aquinas' arguments for the existence and nature of God rest, those arguments lost their appeal. The enterprise of providing other arguments for the existence and nature of God was continued by such thinkers as Descartes, Leibniz, LOCKE (§§6–7) and BERKELEY (§§3, 6–7), but by the latter part of the eighteenth century Kant was arguing that it is impossible that any such arguments could be productive of knowledge, though, as pointed out above, he held that we could exhibit the existence of God as a necessary presupposition of morality. Since Kant, although many thinkers have continued to propound arguments for the existence of God, the enterprise has not regained its former prestige.

Not everyone took the failings of natural theology to reflect badly on religion. The nineteenth-century

Danish religious thinker Søren KIERKEGAARD (§§4–5) was a modern Tertullian who passionately argued that rational argument, so far from being required by faith, is incompatible with it. Faith requires a leap, a risk. Seeking the security of rational proof is a snare and a deception; it is a way of avoiding the trust that God requires of us. Though Kierkegaard has been enormously influential, especially in this century, other voices have also been heard. John Henry NEWMAN, in his *An Essay in Aid of a Grammar of Assent* (1870), stressed the continuity of religious belief with other areas in which trained sensitive judgment is needed to assess the bearing of a complex set of diverse considerations. This approach has been continued in this century in the work of Basil Mitchell (1981).

The most prominent position on the current scene is 'Reformed epistemology', so called because its advocates are self-consciously working in the Reformed tradition stemming from John Calvin. A notable example is Alvin Plantinga (1983), who attacks 'evidentialism', the view that religious belief is irrational unless supported by adequate evidence (see RELIGION AND EPISTEMOLOGY §§1–3). In this he sounds like Kierkegaard, but the alternatives they suggest are quite different. Plantinga argues that religious beliefs can be 'properly basic', that is, rationally justified even though based on no reasons whatever. Thus he is no more irrationalist than the evidentialists he opposes. He simply has a different theory as to the conditions for rational religious belief.

See also: GOD, ARGUMENTS FOR THE EXISTENCE OF; GOD, CONCEPTS OF

References and further reading

* Adams, R.M. (1987) 'Moral Arguments for Theistic Belief', in *The Virtue of Faith*, New York: Oxford University Press. (A useful survey of moral arguments for the existence of God.)
* Anselm of Canterbury (1077–8) *Proslogion*, trans. S.N. Deane, Chicago, IL: Open Court, 1939. (The classic source for the ontological argument.)
* Aquinas, T. (1266–73) *Summa theologiae*, London: Eyre & Spottiswoode, 60 vols, 1964. (Question 2 of Part I contains the celebrated five ways of proving the existence of God, and questions 3–26 draw out the consequences of that for the divine nature.)
* Aristotle (mid 4th-century BC) *Metaphysics*, trans. W.D. Ross, in R. McKeon (ed.) *The Basic Works of Aristotle*, New York: Random House, 1941. (Book XII contains Aristotle's philosophical theology.)
* Boethius, A.M.S. (525–6) *The Consolation of Philosophy*, Indianapolis, IN: Bobbs-Merrill, 1962. (A classic late ancient work, containing an influential discussion of divine foreknowledge.)
* Clarke, S. (1738) *A Discourse Concerning the Being and Attributes of God, The Obligations of Natural Religion and the Truth and Certainty of the Christian Revelation*, London: John & Paul Knapton. (Classic presentation of the eighteenth-century version of the cosmological argument. Not easy going.)
* Clifford, W.K. (1879) 'The Ethics of Belief', in *Lectures and Essays*, London: Macmillan. (Trenchant statement of 'evidentialism', the view that it is irrational to believe without adequate evidence.)
* Fischer, J.M. (ed.) (1989) *God, Foreknowledge, and Freedom*, Stanford, CA: Stanford University Press. (A good selection of essays on the subject.)
* Freddoso, A.J. (1983) 'Accidental Necessity and Logical Determinism', *Journal of Philosophy* 80 (5): 257–78. (Contemporary version of Ockhamism.)
* Hartshorne, C. (1941) *Man's Vision of God*, Hamden, CT: Archon Books. (A primary source for 'process theology'.)
* —— (1962) *Anselm's Discovery: A Re-examination of the Ontological Proof for God's Existence*, La Salle, IL: Open Court. (Launched the concentration on a modal version of the ontological argument.)
* —— (1984) *Omnipotence and Other Theological Mistakes*, Albany, NY: State University of New York Press. (The case for a God of limited power.)
* Hasker, W. (1989) *God, Time, and Knowledge*, Ithaca, NY: Cornell University Press. (Fine survey of issues concerning God's knowledge of future contingent events.)
* Hegel, G.W.F. (1984–7) *Lectures on the Philosophy of Religion*, trans. C.P. Hodgson and R.F. Brown, Berkeley, CA: University of California Press, 3 vols. (Religion as a pictorial version of Hegelian metaphysics.)
* Hick, J. (1978) *Evil and the God of Love*, New York: Harper & Row, revised edn. (The classic presentation of natural evil as a contribution to 'soul making'.)
* Hume, D. (1748) *An Enquiry Concerning Human Understanding*, La Salle, IL: Open Court, 1907. (Section 10 contains Hume's famous attack on the credibility of miracles.)
* —— (1779) *Dialogues Concerning Natural Religion*, London: Penguin Books, 1990. (The classic critique of the teleological argument.)
* Kant, I. (1781) *Critique of Pure Reason*, trans. N.K. Smith, New York: St Martin's Press, 1929. (One of the major landmarks in the history of philosophy. Difficult.)

* —— (1788) *Critique of Practical Reason*, trans. T.K. Abbott, London: Longmans, Green & Co., 1898. (Kant's major work on ethics, and the source of his moral argument for the existence of God.)

* —— (1793) *Religion Within the Limits of Reason Alone*, trans. T.H. Greene and H.H. Hudson, New York: Harper & Row, 1960. (Kant's major philosophical treatment of religion.)

Kierkegaard, S. (1846) *Concluding Unscientific Postscript*, trans. D.F. Swenson, Princeton, NJ: Princeton University Press, 1944. (A major source of Kierkegaard's radical views on religious faith.)

* Leeuw, G. van der (1963) *Religion in Essence and Manifestation*, New York: Harper & Row. (Classic work on the phenomenology of religion.)

* Leftow, B. (1991) *Time and Eternity*, Ithaca, NY: Cornell University Press. (The latest major work on divine eternity and a rich treatment of the subject. Difficult.)

* Leibniz, G.W. (1710) *Theodicy*, trans. E.M. Huggard, La Salle, IL: Open Court, 1985. (Leibniz's extended treatment of the problem of evil.)

* Leslie, J. (1989) *Universes*, London: Routledge. (The teleological argument in the light of contemporary science.)

* Malcolm, N. (1963) 'Anselm's Ontological Arguments', in *Knowledge and Certainty*, Englewood Cliffs, NJ: Prentice-Hall. (A discovery of a modal ontological argument in Anselm.)

* Mill, J.S. (1874) *Three Essays on Religion*, New York: Liberal Arts Press, 1958. (A powerfully argued case for a God of limited power.)

* Mitchell, B. (1981) *The Justification of Religious Belief*, New York: Oxford University Press. (A 'cumulative case' defence of belief in God.)

Molina, L. de (1588) *On Divine Foreknowledge*, Part IV of the *Concordia*, trans. A.J. Freddoso, Ithaca, NY: Cornell University Press, 1988. (An important sixteenth-century view on divine foreknowledge and human free will.)

* Newman, J.H. (1870) *An Essay in Aid of a Grammar of Assent*, Notre Dame, IN: University of Notre Dame Press, 1979. (A major nineteenth-century work on the epistemology of religious belief. Not easy going.)

* Paley, W. (1802) *Natural Theology, or Evidences of the Existence and Attributes of the Deity Collected from the Appearances of Nature*, London: R. Faulder & Son; ed. F. Ferré, Indiana, IN: Bobbs-Merrill, 1964. (Important statement of the teleological argument.)

* Pike, N. (1969) 'Omnipotence and God's Ability to Sin', *American Philosophical Quarterly* 6 (3): 208–16. (Important discussion of this problem.)

* —— (1970) *God and Timelessness*, London: Routledge & Kegan Paul. (Powerful case for the temporality of God.)

Plantinga, A. (1967) *God and Other Minds*, Ithaca, NY: Cornell University Press. (A masterful discussion of various arguments for the existence of God.)

* —— (1974) *The Nature of Necessity*, Oxford: Clarendon Press. (Very technical, but worth the effort for the latest word on the ontological argument.)

* —— (1983) 'Reason and Belief in God', in A. Plantinga and N. Wolterstorff (eds.) *Faith and Rationality*, Notre Dame, IN: University of Notre Dame Press. (Important statements of new trends in the epistemology of religious belief.)

* —— (1986) 'On Ockham's Way Out', *Faith and Philosophy* 3 (3): 235–69. (A sophisticated 'Ockhamist' way of reconciling divine foreknowledge and human freedom. Difficult.)

* Plato (366–360 BC; 360–347 BC) *Laws* and *Timaeus*, in E.Hamilton and H. Cairns (eds.) *The Collected Dialogues of Plato*, Princeton, NJ: Princeton University Press, 1961. (The main sources for Plato's conception of God and arguments for the existence of God.)

* Plotinus (*c*.250–66) *Enneads*, Cambridge, MA: Harvard University Press, 1966–88. (The fountainhead of Neoplatonism.)

* Rosenkrantz, G. and Hoffman, J. (1980) 'The Omnipotence Paradox, Modality, and Time', *The Southern Journal of Philosophy* 18 (4): 473–9. (A brilliant solution of the paradox of the stone.)

* Rowe, W.L. (1975) *The Cosmological Argument*, Princeton, NJ: Princeton University Press. (The best survey of the topic. Rather difficult.)

* Stump, E. (1985) 'The Problem of Evil', *Faith and Philosophy* 2 (4): 392–423. (Natural evil as a device by God to 'fix' human wills. Very readable.)

* Stump, E. and Kretzmann, N. (1981) 'Eternity', *Journal of Philosophy* 78: 429–57. (An essay that sparked the contemporary revival of interest in divine eternity.)

* Swinburne, R. (1977) *The Coherence of Theism*, Oxford: Clarendon Press. (Impressive discussion of divine attributes.)

* —— (1979) *The Existence of God*, Oxford: Clarendon Press. (Reformulation of traditional arguments for the existence of God in terms of modern probability theory.)

* Tennant, F.R. (1930) *Philosophical Theology*, Cambridge: Cambridge University Press. (Important twentieth-century formulation of the arguments for the existence of God.)

Whitehead, A.N. (1929) *Process and Reality*, New York: Macmillan. (A major metaphysical work, and the source of 'process philosophy' and 'process theology'.)

* William of Ockham (after 1317) *Predestination, God's Foreknowledge, and Future Contingents*, trans. M. Adams and N. Kretzmann, New York: Appleton–Century–Crofts, 1969. (One of the most important approaches to this problem.)

WILLIAM P. ALSTON

RELIGION, PHILOSOPHY OF

Philosophy of religion is philosophical reflection on religion. It is as old as philosophy itself and has been a standard part of Western philosophy in every period (see RELIGION, HISTORY OF PHILOSOPHY OF). In the last half of the twentieth century, there has been a great growth of interest in it, and the range of topics philosophers of religion have considered has also expanded considerably.

Philosophy of religion is sometimes divided into philosophy of religion proper and philosophical theology. This distinction reflects the unease of an earlier period in analytic philosophy, during which philosophers felt that reflection on religion was philosophically respectable only if it confined itself to mere theism and abstracted from all particular religions; anything else was taken to be theology, not philosophy. But most philosophers now feel free to examine philosophically any aspect of religion, including doctrines or practices peculiar to individual religions. Not only are these doctrines and practices generally philosophically interesting in their own right, but often they also raise questions that are helpful for issues in other areas of philosophy. Reflection on the Christian notion of sanctification, for example, sheds light on certain contemporary debates over the nature of freedom of the will (see SANCTIFICATION).

1 Philosophy and belief in God

As an examination of mere theism, the core of beliefs common to Western monotheisms, philosophy of religion raises and considers a number of questions. What would anything have to be like to count as God? Is it even possible for human beings to know God's attributes (see GOD, CONCEPTS OF; NEGATIVE THEOLOGY)? And if so, what are they? Traditionally, God has been taken to be a necessary being, who is characterized by omniscience, omnipotence, perfect goodness, immutability and eternity (see NECESSARY BEING; OMNISCIENCE; OMNIPOTENCE; GOODNESS, PERFECT; IMMUTABILITY; ETERNITY), who has freely created the world (see CREATION AND CONSERVA-

TION, RELIGIOUS DOCTRINE OF; FREEDOM, DIVINE), and who is somehow specially related to morality (see RELIGION AND MORALITY).

This conception of God takes God to be unique (see MONOTHEISM), unlike anything else in the world. Consequently, the question arises whether our language is capable of representing God. Some thinkers, such as Moses MAIMONIDES, have argued that it is not and that terms applied to God and creatures are equivocal. Others have argued that our language can be made to apply to God, either because some terms can be used univocally of God and creatures, or because some terms used of creatures can be applied to God in an analogical sense (see RELIGIOUS LANGUAGE).

Not everyone accepts the traditional characterization of God, of course. Pantheists, for example, reject the distinction between God and creation (see PANTHEISM). Certain philosophers have objected to the traditional conception on the grounds that it leaves certain philosophical problems, such as the problem of evil, insoluble (see PROCESS THEISM). And many feminists reject it as patriarchal (see FEMINIST THEOLOGY).

Given the traditional conception of God, can we know by reason that such a God exists? There are certain arguments that have been proposed to demonstrate the existence of God so understood (see GOD, ARGUMENTS FOR THE EXISTENCE OF; NATURAL THEOLOGY). The ontological argument tries to show that a perfect being must exist (see ANSELM OF CANTERBURY). The cosmological argument argues that the existence of the world demonstrates the existence of a transcendent cause of the world. And the teleological argument argues from design in nature to the existence of a designer. Some philosophers have maintained that the widespread phenomenon of religious experience also constitutes an argument for the existence of a supernatural object of such experience (see RELIGIOUS EXPERIENCE; MYSTICISM, HISTORY OF; MYSTICISM, NATURE OF). Most contemporary philosophers regard these arguments as unsuccessful (see ATHEISM; AGNOSTICISM).

But what exactly is the relation between reason and religious belief? Do we need arguments? Or is faith without argument rational? What is faith? Is it opposed to reason? Some philosophers have argued that any belief not based on evidence is defective or even culpable. This position is not much in favour any more. On the other hand, some contemporary philosophers have suggested that evidence of any sort is unnecessary for religious belief. This position is also controversial (see FAITH; RELIGION AND EPISTEMOLOGY).

Some philosophers have supposed that these

questions are obviated by the problem of evil (see EVIL, PROBLEM OF), which constitutes an argument against God's existence. In their view, God and evil cannot coexist, or at any rate the existence of evil in this world is evidence which disconfirms the existence of God. In response to this challenge to religious belief, some philosophers have held that religious belief can be defended only by a theodicy, an attempt to give a morally sufficient reason for God's allowing evil to exist. Others have thought that religious belief can be defended without a theodicy, by showing the weaknesses in the versions of the argument from evil against God's existence. Finally, some thinkers have argued that only a practical and political approach is the right response to evil in the world (see LIBERATION THEOLOGY).

Those who use the existence of evil to argue against the existence of God assume that God, if he existed, could and should intervene in the natural order of the world. Not everyone accepts this view (see DEISM). But supposing it is right, how should we understand God's intervention? Does he providentially intervene to guide the world to certain ends (see PROVIDENCE)? Would an act of divine intervention count as a miracle? What is a miracle, and is it ever rational to believe that a miracle has occurred (see MIRACLES)? Some people have supposed that a belief that miracles occur is incompatible with or undermined by a recognition of the success of science. Many people also think that certain widely accepted scientific views cast doubt on particular religious beliefs (see RELIGION AND SCIENCE).

2 Philosophy and religious doctrines and practices

In addition to the issues raised by the traditional conception of God, there are others raised by doctrines common to the Western monotheisms. These include the view that the existence of a human being does not end with the death of the body but continues in an afterlife (see SOUL, NATURE AND IMMORTALITY OF THE; REINCARNATION; RESURRECTION). Although there is wide variation in beliefs about the nature of the afterlife, typically the afterlife is taken to include heaven and hell. For some groups of Christians, it also includes limbo and purgatory. All of these doctrines raise an array of philosophical questions (see HEAVEN; HELL; LIMBO; PURGATORY).

There is equally great variation in views on what it takes for a human being to be accepted into heaven (see SALVATION). Christians generally suppose that faith is a necessary, if not a sufficient, requirement (see JUSTIFICATION, RELIGIOUS). But they also suppose that faith is efficacious in this way because of the suffering and death of Jesus Christ (see

INCARNATION AND CHRISTOLOGY; TRINITY). Christians take sin to be an obstacle to union with God and life in heaven, and they suppose that Christ's atonement is the solution to this problem (see SIN; ATONEMENT). Because of Christ's atonement, divine forgiveness and mercy are available to human beings who are willing to accept it (see FORGIVENESS AND MERCY). Most Christians have supposed that this willingness is itself a gift of God (see GRACE), but some have supposed that human beings unassisted by grace are able to will or even to do what is good (see PELAGIANISM). How to interpret these doctrines, or whether they can even be given a consistent interpretation, has been the subject of philosophical discussion.

The religious life is characterized not only by religious belief and experience but by many other things as well (see PHENOMENOLOGY OF RELIGION). For many believers, ritual and prayer structure religious life (see RITUAL; PRAYER). Christians also suppose that sacraments are important, although Protestants and Catholics differ on the nature and number of the sacraments (see SACRAMENTS). For Christians, the heart of the religious life, made possible by the atonement and the believer's acceptance of grace, consists in the theological virtues – faith, hope, and charity (see THEOLOGICAL VIRTUES).

Many religious believers suppose they know that these and other things are essential to the religious life because God has revealed them (see REVELATION). This revelation includes or is incorporated in a book, the Qur'an for Muslims, the Hebrew Bible for Jews, and the Old and New Testaments for Christians. How the texts in this book are to be understood and the way in which religious texts are to be interpreted raise a host of philosophical issues (see HERMENEUTICS, BIBLICAL).

Certain thinkers who are not themselves philosophers are none the less important for the philosophy of religion and so are also included in this encyclopedia. These include, for example, John CALVIN and Martin LUTHER, whose views on such issues as justification and atonement significantly influenced the understanding of these notions, and Jacques MARITAIN and Pierre TEILHARD DE CHARDIN, whose influence on contemporary philosophical theology has been significant.

See also: AFRICAN TRADITIONAL RELIGIONS; AQUINAS, T.; AUGUSTINE; BARTH, K.; BOEHME, J.; BOWNE, B.P.; BRAHMAN; BUDDHIST PHILOSOPHY, CHINESE; BUDDHIST PHILOSOPHY, INDIAN; BUDDHIST PHILOSOPHY, JAPANESE; BUDDHIST PHILOSOPHY, KOREAN; EAST ASIAN PHILOSOPHY; EDWARDS, J.; ESCHATOLOGY; EXISTENTIALIST

THEOLOGY; GNOSTICISM; GOD, INDIAN CONCEPTIONS OF; ILLUMINATION; INDIAN AND TIBETAN PHILOSOPHY; ISLAMIC PHILOSOPHY; ISLAMIC THEOLOGY; JAINA PHILOSOPHY; JEWISH PHILOSOPHY; MANICHEISM; NIEBUHR, R.; OCCASIONALISM; OMNIPRESENCE; OTTO, R.; PERSONALISM; PIETISM; POSTMODERN THEOLOGY; PREDESTINATION; PROPHECY; RAHNER, K.; RELIGION AND POLITICAL PHILOSOPHY; RELIGION, CRITIQUE OF; RELIGIOUS PLURALISM; REPROBATION; SHINTŌ; SIMPLICITY, DIVINE; THEOLOGY, RABBINIC; THEOSOPHY; TILLICH, P.; TINDAL, M.; TONGHAK; VOLUNTARISM; ZOROASTRIANISM

Further reading

Murray, M. and Stump, E. (eds) (1999) *Philosophy of Religion: The Big Questions*, Oxford: Blackwell. (A broad and inclusive anthology of readings in philosophy of religion.)
Quinn, P. and Taliaferro, C. (1997) *A Companion to Philosophy of Religion*, Oxford: Blackwell. (A helpful and comprehensive reference work for philosophy of religion.)

ELEONORE STUMP

RELIGIONSKRITIK *see*
RELIGION, CRITIQUE OF

RELIGIOUS EXPERIENCE

Philosophy is interested in religious experience as a possible source of knowledge of the existence, nature and doings of God. The experiences in question seem to their possessors to be direct, perceptual awarenesses of God. But they may be wrong about this, and many philosophers think they are. Many philosophers think that such experiences are never what they seem, and that no one has a veridical experience of the presence and/or activity of God. The main philosophical reason for supposing that such experiences are in fact sometimes veridical is a principle according to which any apparent experience of something is to be regarded as veridical unless we have sufficient reasons to the contrary. Experiences are innocent until proven guilty. If we do not accept that principle, we will never have sufficient grounds for taking any experience to be veridical – religious, sensory or whatever.

There are critics who think that we do have sufficient reasons to the contrary in the case of religious experience. For one thing, we do not have the same capacity for intersubjective checks of religious experiences that we have with sense perceptions. But to this it can be replied that we should not suppose that sense perception represents the only way in which we can achieve genuine cognitive contact with objective reality. For another thing, it is widely supposed that religious experience can be adequately explained by psychological and social factors, without bringing God into the picture. But even if this-worldly factors are the only immediate causes of the experience, God could figure as a cause farther back in the causal chain. Finally, the disagreements between alleged experiences of God, especially across different religions, provide a reason for doubting the deliverances of religious experience. But it is possible for a number of people to be genuinely experiencing the same thing, even though they disagree as to what it is like. This is a common occurrence in sense perception.

1 **The experience of God**
2 **Mystical experience as a basis for beliefs about God**
3 **Objections to regarding experiences of God as veridical**

1 The experience of God

The term 'religious experience' is properly used for any experiences one has in connection with one's religious life, including a sense of guilt or release, joys, fears, longings, a sense of gratitude, and so on. But the usual philosophical concern with religious experience has a much narrower focus. It is concerned with experiences taken by the subject to be an experiential awareness of God. To cast the net as widely as possible, and to avoid restricting the discussion to one kind of religion, such as 'theistic' religions that think of God in personal terms, let us understand 'God' here to range over any supreme reality, however construed.

Here is an anonymous report of such an experience:

All at once I . . . felt the presence of God – I tell of the thing just as I was conscious of it – as if his goodness and his power were penetrating me altogether. . . . Then, slowly, the ecstasy left my heart; that is, I felt that God had withdrawn the communion which he had granted . . . I asked myself if it were possible that Moses on Sinai could have had a more intimate communication with God. I think it well to add that in this ecstasy of mine God had neither form, color, odor, nor taste; moreover, that the feeling of his presence was accompanied by no determinate localization . . . .

But the more I seek words to express this intimate intercourse, the more I feel the impossibility of describing the thing by any of our usual images. At bottom the expression most apt to render what I felt is this: God was present, though invisible; he fell under no one of my senses, yet my consciousness perceived him.

(James [1902] 1982: 68)

This report is typical in several respects. First, the awareness of God is experiential, as contrasted with abstract thought (thinking of God, reasoning about God, or asking questions about God). Like sense experience it seems to involve a presentation of the object. The subject takes God to have been present, to have been given to the subject's awareness, in something like the way in which a tree is presented to one's awareness when one sees it.

Second, the experience is direct. The subject feels immediately aware of God, rather than being aware of God through being aware of something else. That is, it seems to be analogous to directly seeing another human being in front of you, rather than seeing that person on television, where one is aware of the person through being aware of something else, in this case the television screen. People also report indirect experiences of God:

There was a mysterious presence in nature and sometimes met within the communion and in praying by oneself, which was my greatest delight, especially when as happened from time to time, *nature became lit up from inside* with something that came from beyond itself (or seemed to do so to me).

(Beardsworth 1977: 19; original italics)

Third, the experience is completely lacking in sensory content. It is a wholly non-sensory presentation of God. But there are also experiences of God that involve seeing or hearing something:

I awoke and looking out of my window saw what I took to be a luminous star which gradually came nearer, and appeared as a soft slightly blurred white light. I was seized with violent trembling, but had no fear. I knew that what I felt was great awe. This was followed by a sense of overwhelming love coming to me, and going out from me, then of great compassion from this Outer Presence.

(Beardsworth 1977: 30)

Many find it incredible that a non-sensory experience should involve a presentation of something, but this seems a baseless prejudice. Why should we suppose that our modes of sensory receptivity constitute the only possible vehicles of an experiential awareness of external reality?

Finally, it is a focal experience, one in which the awareness of God attracts one's attention so strongly as to blot out all else for the moment. But there are also lower-intensity experiences that persist over long periods of time as a background to everyday experiences, as in this report from James: 'God surrounds me like the physical atmosphere. He is closer to me than my own breath. In him literally I live and move and have my being' ([1902] 1982: 71–2).

The present discussion will be limited to direct, non-sensory, focal experiences, since they constitute the most distinctive and striking claims to be experientially aware of God.

A great deal of the literature on this subject concentrates on mystical experience, understood as a state in which all distinctions are transcended, even the distinction between subject and object. The person is aware of a seamless unity. Such experience falls under our general category, for it is typically taken by the mystic to be a direct awareness of supreme reality. But since experiences like this pose special problems of their own, the present entry will focus primarily on more moderate cases like the ones cited, in which subjects do not seem to lose their own identity. In spite of this, the term 'mystical experience' will be used as a convenient way of designating what is taken by the subject to be a direct experience of God. Since these subjects suppose themselves to be aware of God in a way analogous to that in which one is aware of things in the physical environment by sense perception, the term 'mystical perception' will be used.

2 Mystical experience as a basis for beliefs about God

The chief philosophical interest in mystical experience concerns the possibility that it serves as a source of knowledge, or justified belief, about God. Those who have such experiences typically take themselves to have learned something from them, as well as receiving additional confirmation of beliefs already held. Usually they suppose only a limited set of beliefs to be justified in this way. These include the belief that God exists, certain beliefs about his nature (for example, that he is loving or powerful), and beliefs about what God is doing vis-à-vis the subject at the moment – comforting, condemning, forgiving, inspiring, communicating a certain message. It is rare, at best, for someone to think it possible to come to know that God delivered the Israelites from slavery in Egypt or that he is three persons in one substance just from an experience of God (unless that is something that the subject takes God to be saying). But the beliefs that are derived from such experiences typically play a central role in one's religious life. In another anonymous report, the writer, after speaking of an experience in which he 'felt the perfect unison of my spirit with His' goes on to say: 'My highest faith in God and truest idea of him were then born in me.... My most assuring evidence of his existence is deeply rooted in that hour of vision, in the memory of that supreme experience' (James [1902] 1982: 66–7).

The fact that subjects take themselves to acquire knowledge of God from mystical perception does not guarantee that they do. One can be misled even by sense experience. One can suppose that one saw, at dusk, that there was a car in the distance when it was actually a cow. And in extreme cases one can be subject to complete hallucinations, like Macbeth falsely taking there to be a dagger in front of him. With both sense experience and mystical experience, contradictions between reports prevent us from taking all of them to be veridical. As for mystical experience, we need look no further than the many cases in which someone supposes that God commanded the murder of as many people of a certain sort as possible, in contrast to those instances in which one is aware of God as supremely loving. In both areas of experience there are two ways in which one can acquire false beliefs. One may not be experiencing the thing, or sort of thing, one supposes one is experiencing. The two cases of sensory illusion just mentioned illustrate this, as do the cases of people supposing themselves to be aware of God telling them to do things that God would not tell anyone to do. But second, even if one is genuinely aware of the sort of thing in question, the beliefs one forms about it may be mistaken. I may genuinely see a car in the distance, but mistakenly think it is moving. I may genuinely be aware of the presence of God, but mistakenly suppose that he refuses to forgive me. A comprehensive discussion would go into both these ways in which experiences can be misleading. But since sceptics about religious experience usually take it that no one is ever genuinely aware of a really existing God, we will concentrate on the former, more radical criticism. The main issue will be whether mystical experiences are significantly often genuine experiences of God, are veridical experiences.

Reasons for a positive answer can be divided into theological and philosophical ones. The former comprise any components of the belief system of a given religion that give us reason for thinking either that God is in principle accessible to human experience, or that particular persons have experienced God's presence on one or another occasion. Theological considerations are out of bounds here. As for philosophical reasons, the most important one, perhaps the only important one, goes as follows.

Any supposition that one perceives something to be the case – that there is an elephant in front of one or that God is strengthening one – is *prima facie* justified. That is, one is justified in supposing this unless there are strong enough reasons to the contrary, strong enough overriders. Overriders can be divided into *rebutters*, strong enough reasons for the falsity of the belief, and *underminers*, strong enough reasons for supposing that the experience, in this instance, does not sufficiently support the belief. In the elephant case, strong reasons for thinking that there is no elephant in the vicinity would be a rebutter. A reason for supposing oneself to be subject to hallucinations, perhaps because of some drug, would be an underminer. According to this position, beliefs formed on the basis of experience possess an initial credibility by virtue of their origin. They are innocent until proven guilty.

This position has been widely advocated for sense perception (see Chisholm 1977, ch. 4). Swinburne (1979, ch. 13) applies it to mystical experience, terming it 'The Principle of Credulity'. Alston (1991) gives it a more social twist; the claim is that any socially established 'doxastic (belief-forming) practice' is to be accepted as a source of (generally) true beliefs unless there are sufficient reasons against its reliability. The position is usually supported by the claim that unless we accord a *prima facie* credibility to all experiential reports, we can have no sufficient reason to trust any experiential source of beliefs. This is the only alternative to a thoroughgoing scepticism.

As applied to mystical experience, this '*prima facie* credibility' position implies that whenever anyone reports having perceived God as being or doing so-and-so, the report is to be accepted as true unless we have sufficient reasons for refusing to do so. Lest one fear that this lets in any crackpot report, remember that we wouldn't regard reports as 'crackpot' unless we had reasons, from other reports of mystical perception or from other theological sources, for denying that what the 'crackpot' believes about God is correct.

3   Objections to regarding experiences of God as veridical

A large number of contemporary philosophers deny that anyone ever genuinely perceives the presence or activity of God. Most of the reasons for this are based on differences, real or alleged, between sense experience and mystical experience. Since we are all, in practice, completely confident of the by-and-large reliability of sense perception, positive analogies between the two will be taken to support a positive epistemic assessment of mystical perception, whereas differences between them will be taken to support a negative assessment (see Alston 1991, chaps 5–7, for further discussion; also Wainwright 1981, ch. 3).

The first and most obvious reason for a negative assessment concerns certain striking differences between sense experience and mystical experience. Sense experience is a common possession of all human beings, whereas, so far as we can tell, mystical experience is not. Even if we are careful to include dim, background experiences in the reckoning, it is foreign to a considerable proportion of the population. Moreover, even for those who are privileged with both, they play vastly different roles in one's life. Sense experience is continuously, insistently and unavoidably present during all our waking hours, while mystical experience, except for a few choice souls, is a rare phenomenon. Sense experience, especially vision, is vivid and richly detailed, bursting with information, more than we can possibly encode; while mystical experience, by comparison, is meagre and obscure. These differences can lead one to deny that mystical experience is a conduit of information about objective reality.

The differences certainly render mystical experience much less useful as a source of information, but that is quite different from saying that, where it exists, it is never or seldom a veridical experience of God, or that it provides no information about God. Regarding the partial distribution in the population, the defence can point out that there is no a priori reason to suppose that a doxastic practice engaged in by only a part of the population is less likely to be a source of truth than one we all engage in. There are many reliable practices engaged in by only a small minority – for example, research in the physical sciences and wine tasting. We have to learn from experience which features of the world are open to all and which are open only to some people who satisfy special requirements. And it would beg the question to think that experience tells us that no aspect of reality is disclosed in mystical experience. Similar points can be made about the lesser frequency and lesser detail of mystical experience. That shows that it provides less information than sense experience, but not that it provides none.

A second common charge is that the mystic is simply reading prior religious beliefs into a cognitively indifferent (perhaps purely affective) experience, rather than being directly aware of supreme reality. By and large, only Christians report experiences of Christ, only Hindus of Vishnu, and only Buddhists of *nirvāṇa*. Nevertheless, the charge is a serious oversimplification. There are many conversions on the basis of an alleged experience of God. In these cases, subjects do not suppose themselves to be aware of what they were antecedently expecting; quite the contrary. To be sure, one cannot report what one was aware of except by using concepts one has (what else?). But this is as true of sense perception as of mystical perception. When I report what I saw from the train window, I use my conceptual repertoire; I say that I saw houses, trees, a river, and so on. Sense perception and mystical perception would not seem to differ in this respect.

A third reason for partiality is the supposition that mystical experience can be adequately explained in purely naturalistic terms, and that this fact shows it not to constitute an experience of a supernatural reality (see Mackie 1982). It is a basic principle of perception that we cannot be genuinely perceiving an entity that does not make a significant causal contribution to the experience involved. If a tree on the other side of a high stone wall plays no role in eliciting my present visual experience, then I cannot be *seeing* that tree, whatever my experience is like. But if the causes of a religious experience are purely this-worldly, then God plays no role in producing it. Hence I am not really perceiving God in that experience, however it might seem.

There are a number of points the defence might make. First, the claim to an adequate naturalistic causal explanation can be challenged. We are certainly not in possession of any such explanation. At most there are programmatic suggestions – from psychoanalysis, social psychology, and other quarters – as to the general form such an explanation might take. Second, the causal requirement for genuine perception might be challenged, though not with much plausibility. The most impressive defence would be the following. A consideration of sense perception shows that even there the object perceived need not be among the *proximate* causes of the experience. The immediate causes of a sense experience are all within the subject's brain, which is not perceived. When the causal requirement is satisfied in sense perception, it is by the perceived object's figuring further back along the causal route leading to the experience. Hence, even if the immediate causes of a mystical experience are all natural, that leaves open the possibility that God figures among the more remote causes of the experience, and in such a way as to qualify as what is perceived. Hence a proximate naturalistic explanation of mystical experience poses no threat to the veridicality of (some) mystical perception.

A fourth important difference between sensory and mystical perception is that there are effective tests for accuracy in the case of the former but not the latter. When someone claims to have seen something – for example, an aeroplane overhead – there are procedures that can yield a conclusive verdict on that claim.

We can look into whether suitably qualified observers saw an aeroplane, and check appropriate sources to find whether there are any records of an aeroplane being there at that time. But nothing like this is available for mystical perception. There are checks that are commonly applied in established mystical communities, such as conformity with the background system of religious doctrine, and conducivity to spiritual development and purity of life. But they are far from yielding comparable results. Moreover, there is nothing like the check of other observers we have for sense perceptual reports. If I claim to have been aware of God's sustaining me in being, there are no conditions such that if someone else who satisfies those conditions is not (at that time or any time) aware of being sustained in being by God, I will take that as showing that I was mistaken. And the argument of the critic is that this discredits the claim of the mystic to be aware of an objective reality. If my claims to perceive something objective cannot be validated by intersubjective agreement, they have no standing (Martin 1959; Rowe 1982).

The best response to this criticism is to charge the critic with what we might call 'epistemic imperialism', unwarrantedly subjecting the outputs of one doxastic practice to the requirements of another. The complaint is that a mystical perception cannot lay claim to putting its subject into effective touch with objective reality because the subject cannot validate this status in the same way as with sense perceptions. But there are various sources of belief that work quite differently from sense experience in this respect. Consider introspection, one's awareness of one's own conscious states. My report that I feel relieved cannot be validated by considering whether someone else, who satisfies certain conditions, feels my relief. But it would be absurd to reject introspection as a source of knowledge because of the unavailability of such tests. Unless critics can give a convincing reason for supposing that the criteria available for sense perception constitute a necessary condition for *any* experiential access to objective reality, they are guilty of epistemic chauvinism (to change the metaphor) in rejecting mystical perception for this reason. Epistemic chauvinism is also exhibited by the first criticism in this section, to which the response was to ask why one should suppose that a mode of experience different from sense experience in the ways specified should be less likely to be a source of knowledge.

Another disability of some of the above criticisms is the use of a double standard, whereby mystical perception is taken to be discredited by some feature it shares with sense perception. This is exhibited by the second and third criticisms above. We saw that both modes of perception use antecedent conceptual schemes to report what is perceived, and that both locate the object perceived among remote rather than proximate causes of the experience.

The final criticism concerns the fact of religious pluralism, probably the most epistemologically significant difference between mystical perception and sense perception. Human beings at all times and places and in all cultures use pretty much the same conceptual scheme to specify what they perceive by the senses. The extent to which there is less than complete agreement is a matter of controversy among anthropologists and historians, but the commonality is clearly much greater than it is with mystical experience. The full range of religions, past and present, differ widely in their conceptions of ultimate reality, and their beliefs about it differ even more widely. This point still holds if we confine ourselves to contemporary major world religions. Since the conceptions and beliefs of the various religions are the ones used by people to articulate what they take themselves to be aware of in mystical experience, those articulations are correspondingly different and often contradict each other. 'Theistic' religions such as Judaism, Christianity and Islam think of supreme reality as a personal creator who enters into personal relationships with us. Buddhism and certain forms of Hinduism think of ultimate reality in more impersonal terms, as an undifferentiated unity of which nothing can literally be said, or as a void or 'Nothingness'. The theistic religions also differ in what they believe about what God has done in history, what his plans are and what he requires of us. In the face of this unresolved diversity, how can we think that mystical experience is a conduit of objective truth?

It is important to be clear as to what is and is not involved in this problem. It was pointed out earlier that it would not be sensible to think that mystical perception can generate a complete system of religious belief. Hence the experiential reports of Christians and Muslims might not contradict each other, even though there are contradictions between the two complete bodies of belief. But even if the experiential reports are contradictory to a certain extent, mystical perception could still constitute a genuine awareness of a supreme reality. Two people can both genuinely perceive something even if they disagree as to what it is like. Two witnesses to a car accident might both have really seen the accident, though their accounts of what happened are importantly different. By the same token, mystics from widely different religions might genuinely perceive the same ultimate reality, even if what they perceive it as is quite different.

Still, it must be admitted that the unresolved incompatibilities in mystical perceptual reports count as negative evidence for the claim that mystical perception is, often, a genuine awareness of supreme reality, though for the reasons just given it can hardly be regarded as conclusive evidence against that claim. On this point there would seem to be a standoff between the mystic and the critic, a standoff that would be resolved by strong enough reasons for regarding one of the competing religious traditions to be closest to the truth or, contrariwise, by strong enough reasons for regarding no religions to have any truth about supernatural dimensions of reality.

See also: MYSTICISM, NATURE OF; RELIGION AND EPISTEMOLOGY; REVELATION

References and further reading

* Alston, W.P. (1991) *Perceiving God: The Epistemology of Religious Experience*, Ithaca, NY: Cornell University Press. (A defence of the thesis that mystical experience is a source of justification for certain kinds of religious beliefs. Rather advanced.)
—— (1993) *The Reliability of Sense Perception*, Ithaca, NY: Cornell University Press. (A critical analysis of attempts to show that sense perception is a reliable source of belief.)
* Beardsworth, T. (1977) *A Sense of Presence*, Oxford: Religious Experience Research Unit. (A fine collection of reports of experiences of God.)
* Chisholm, R.M. (1977) *Theory of Knowledge*, Englewood Cliffs, NJ: Prentice-Hall, 2nd edn. (A concise presentation of the epistemology of one of America's leading philosophers. Difficult.)
* James, W. (1902) *The Varieties of Religious Experience*, New York: Penguin, 1982. (The classic work on the subject. Very readable, as always with James.)
* Mackie, J. (1982) *The Miracle of Theism*, Oxford: Clarendon Press. (Critical of theistic religion. Fairly accessible.)
* Martin, C.B. (1959) *Religious Belief*, Ithaca, NY: Cornell University Press. (An unsympathetic treatment of many aspects of religious belief, including the claims of mystical experience. Not very difficult.)
Poulain, A. (1950) *The Graces of Interior Prayer*, trans. L.Y. Smith and J.V. Bainvel, London: Routledge & Kegan Paul. (A classic of Catholic mystical theology which presents a strong case for the veridicality of mystical perception. Very readable.)
* Rowe, W.L. (1982) 'Religious Experience and the Principle of Credulity', *International Journal for Philosophy of Religion* 13 (2): 85–92. (Fairly technical.)
* Swinburne, R. (1979) *The Existence of God*, Oxford: Clarendon Press. (A contemporary classic. Moderately difficult.)
* Wainwright, W. (1981) *Mysticism*, Brighton: Harvester Press. (Clearly written.)
Yandell, K.E. (1993) *The Epistemology of Religious Experience*, Cambridge: Cambridge University Press. (A defence of the claim that religious experience provides evidence for religious belief. Difficult.)

WILLIAM P. ALSTON

RELIGIOUS LANGUAGE

The main philosophical interest in religious language is in the understanding of what purport to be statements about God. Can they really be what they seem to be – claims to say something true about a divine reality? There are several reasons for denying this. The most prominent of these stems from the verifiability criterion of meaning, according to which an utterance can be a statement that is objectively true or false only if it is possible to verify or falsify it empirically. It is claimed that this is not possible for talk about God. However, the verifiability criterion itself has been severely criticized. Moreover, many religious beliefs do have implications that are, in principle, empirically testable, though not conclusively.

If one is moved to reject the idea that statements about God are what they seem to be, they can be taken as expressions of feelings and attitudes, and/or as guides to a life orientation. To be sure, religious utterances can have these functions even if they are also genuine statements of fact.

If one believes there to be genuine true-or-false statements about God, there are still problems as to how to understand them. We can focus on the construal of the predicates of such statements – for example, 'made the heavens and the earth' and 'commissioned Moses to lead the Israelites out of Egypt'. There is a serious problem here because of two basic features of the situation. First, the terms we apply to God got their meaning from their application to creatures, particularly human beings. Second, God is so radically different from us that it seems that these terms cannot have the same meaning in the two uses. One possibility here is that all these terms are used metaphorically when applied to God, which obviously often happens ('The Lord is my shepherd'). But are there some terms that can be literally true of God? This may be the case if some abstract aspect of the creaturely meaning of a term can be literally applied to God. For example, if one aspect of the meaning of 'makes' when applied to one of us is 'brings about some state of affairs by an act of will', the term 'makes' with that particular meaning might be truly applied to God.

1 The topic
2 Reasons for denying that there are genuine statements about God
3 Nonassertive construals of theological statements
4 Theological predicates

1 The topic

The title of this entry is a misnomer. There is no language peculiar to religion ('Do you speak English, French or religious?'), nor is religion restricted to any particular type of language. A more accurate term for the topic would be 'religious uses of language'. Here we find an enormous diversity. Worshippers engage in praise, thanksgiving, petition, confession, instruction and exhortation. Sacred writings contain cosmological speculations, fictional narratives, historical records, predictions, commandments, theological pronouncements and legal codes. In devotional literature there are biographical reminiscences, theologizing, rules for the spiritual life and descriptions of religious experience. Philosophers of religion have concentrated on a very restricted portion of this plenitude, namely on statements about God or, more generally, about the objects of religious devotion and worship.

There is more than one reason for this selectivity. First, it is the belief aspect of religion with which philosophy is most concerned. This is partly an occupational bias. Philosophy is largely taken up with a critical examination of beliefs, assumptions and presuppositions in all areas. When the inquiry takes a linguistic turn, it is deflected to the linguistic formulations of beliefs. Since the most central statements in a religion are statements about God, they get most of the philosophical attention. Second, the belief system of a religion underlies everything else. Religious believers pray as they do, worship as they do, lead, or try to lead, their lives as they do, take up the attitudes they do, because of what they believe about God. If we are concerned to evaluate a religion, we are well advised to evaluate the belief system of that religion, since its pluses and minuses will have implications for the evaluative status of the whole.

Philosophers raise questions of various degrees of generality about religious statements. Some pose difficulties of understanding. The Christian doctrines of the Trinity (God is three persons in one substance) and the dual nature of Christ (the divine and human natures of one person), the Buddhist doctrine of *nirvāṇa* as the ultimate human fulfilment (is it pure nothingness, or does it have a positive aspect?), and the Hindu doctrine of Brahman (the absolute undifferentiated unity that constitutes all reality) are famous cases. But philosophers have also been concerned with more general questions as to how religious statements are to be understood. Traditionally this investigation has centred on the question of how predicates are to be understood in their application to God, predicates such as 'made the heavens and the earth' and 'knows the inmost secrets of our hearts'. For our grasp of the subject, 'God', presumably comes from some predicates or other. Even if reference to God is at least partly on the basis of experience of God (Alston 1989, ch. 5), still it is also at least partly on the basis of what predicates we apply to him. Thus the question of how to understand predicates as applied to God is the most fundamental issue here.

It has generally been assumed that most apparent statements about God really do have that status, that they are used to make truth claims about a reality that is what it is independently of us, our beliefs, attitudes and conceptual schemes. But in the twentieth century that assumption has frequently been questioned. Hence, before tackling issues about the understanding of theological predicates, the reasons that have been given for denying the credentials of religious statements will be considered, along with the alternative construals of such utterances that have been proposed.

2 Reasons for denying that there are genuine statements about God

These reasons can be ranked under three headings: *metaphysical* – if treated as statements that are true or false, they are all false; *epistemological* – we have no effective way of determining their truth value; and *semantic* – because of the previous epistemological criticism, sentences predicating properties of God do not satisfy necessary conditions for having the kind of meaning (factual meaning) that would fit them for being used to make statements that are true or false.

The *metaphysical* claim is based on a naturalistic or materialistic metaphysics that takes reality to be confined to the 'natural' order, that is, to the physical universe in space and time (see NATURALIZED PHILOSOPHY OF SCIENCE §1). Since that leaves no room for God, as usually conceived in religion, all statements that purport to refer to such a being are false. To be sure, this is quite compatible with taking what appear to be religious statements to have that status; they just all happen to be false. But if, while embracing naturalism, one is still motivated to hang on to something like traditional religion, the only option is to give religious utterances some nonstandard interpretation.

This line of thought can be no better than the naturalistic metaphysics on which it is based. Though materialists can claim some support from the developments of modern science for the thesis that everything in the spatiotemporal universe is purely physical in nature, it is not clear that they have any significant reason for denying that there are realities of a different order altogether, such as God is typically taken as being.

The *epistemological* reason is that we lack sufficient grounds for supposing that religious statements are true. Whether this is so is an extremely complicated issue that is treated elsewhere (see GOD, ARGUMENTS FOR THE EXISTENCE OF; RELIGION AND EPISTEMOLOGY; RELIGIOUS EXPERIENCE). But even if it is so, that only implies that they must be accepted on faith. If one feels uncomfortable with that, it would be another motive for holding that apparent religious statements are not what they seem.

The *semantic* approach draws a stronger conclusion from an epistemological claim like the foregoing. The principle on which this reasoning is based is the verifiability criterion of meaningfulness. According to this principle, a sentence has factual meaning (the kind of meaning that renders it usable to make a statement with a truth value) only if it is in principle possible to verify it or falsify it empirically, on the basis of observations (see MEANING AND VERIFICATION §§2–3). The argument is that alleged statements about God fail this test and hence are not genuine statements of fact. In a famous passage, Antony Flew (1955) posed the rhetorical question, 'What would have to occur or to have occurred to constitute for you a disproof of the love of, or of the existence of, God?'. The implied answer is that nothing would fit this bill, and, by the same token, nothing would amount to a proof either. Alleged statements about God are only pretend-statements because they are not empirically testable.

It is this argument against the genuineness of statements about God that has received the most press. Again, it can be no stronger than the principle on which it is based, and the verifiability criterion has repeatedly been severely criticized (see Plantinga 1967). But in any case, do statements about God really fall foul of the requirement? That depends on a number of things. First, it depends on what counts as an 'observation' or 'empirical datum'. It makes a big difference whether mystical experience is allowed to count as 'observation'. Second, it depends on the

viability of arguments for the existence of God, such as the teleological argument, that are based on observable features of the universe. And, on the other side, many thinkers take it that massive and apparently undeserved suffering constitutes empirical evidence against the existence of God. Third, it depends on details of the particular religious belief system in question. Many such systems involve fairly straightforward predictions as to what the gods will do under certain conditions, where these divine actions manifest themselves in sensorily observable changes. In many primitive religions it has been believed that the gods will bring rain or military victory if they are approached through certain rites. In the Judaeo-Christian tradition it is believed that God will see to it that the Church or the chosen people will be finally victorious on earth and that prayers, made in the right spirit and in the right conditions, will be effective. It is true that such predictions come with severe qualifications. We cannot say *when* the Church will be victorious or when the second coming of Christ will inaugurate a new era. And it is impossible to be sure that one has prayed in the right spirit. Thus it is rare to find a decisive empirical test for religious beliefs. (But it is often held that this is true of science as well.) In any event, the issue of whether belief about God is empirically testable to some extent is by no means easily answered.

3 Nonassertive construals of theological statements

If one is convinced that talk of God can be meaningful only if it does not involve statements that are assessable as true or false, there are several options. Here are two:

Expressivism-instrumentalism. This is an analogue of 'noncognitivism' or 'emotivism' in ethics, a view that also springs from attachment to verificationism and which takes ethical utterances to be expressions of attitudes and emotions, or as recommendations of a policy of action, rather than as statements of fact. A classic version of the application to religion is found in Santayana (1905). On his view, there are two components to a religious doctrine, or 'myth'. There is (a) an evaluation of some sort, which is (b) expressed in the form of a picture or story. Thus the Christian myth of God's incarnation in Jesus Christ, and his death on the cross to atone for our sins can be regarded as an expression of the moral value of self-sacrifice. That is the expressive side of the position, but Santayana also thinks of religious myths as *guiding* our lives, our responses to the world. This side of the matter is indicated by the term 'instrumentalism', taken from the philosophy of science. The function for which religious beliefs are 'instrumental' is not predictive, as in science, but rather 'life-orienting' (see Braithwaite 1955).

Symbolisticism. Here a leading figure is Paul TILLICH (§§3–5), according to whom it is misguided to ask whether religious doctrines are true or false of God. Since God (the true God, Being-Itself) is beyond any conceptualization (1953: 264–5), it is hopeless to seek any correspondence between what we say about God, and God. Instead, our 'God-talk' is made up of symbols of God, which 'point to' his reality by 'participating' in his power and being. Not only what are commonly recognized as symbols – the lamb, water, the shepherd, and so on – are to be so construed; anything concrete or conceptualizable is a symbol, including Christ, God the Father, and the Holy Spirit. Speaking of God the Father is an appropriate way of symbolizing Being-Itself because fatherhood is one of the 'places' in the world where we are 'grasped' by the power of Being. But any literal correspondence of our religious utterances with the divine is out of the question.

It must be noted that even if what seem to be factual religious statements do genuinely have that status, they can also function in an expressive-instrumental and a symbolic role.

4 Theological predicates

In discussing the question of how to understand predicates in their application to God we will assume that the arguments of §2 against the genuineness of statements about God are not cogent, and that such statements are to be understood as what they appear to be. Each such statement can be thought of as applying a certain predicate to God. Here is a sample:

(1) made the heavens and the earth;
(2) became incarnate in Jesus of Nazareth;
(3) is omnipotent (perfectly good, loving, wise, omniscient);
(4) forgives the sins of those that repent and turn to him;
(5) told me not to worry so much about trifles;
(6) wills that all people should be saved.

We can roughly divide this list into attributes (3), actions (1, 2, 4, 5) and intentional psychological states (6). The attributes can be seen as derivative from the other types, being properties of God that fit him for actions (loving, omnipotent) or for psychological states (omniscient, wise). Discussions of the topic have tended to concentrate on attributes, perhaps because they can be more concisely formulated, but this tends to distort the subject.

Why should there be a special problem here? We know what it is to tell someone something, to know

something, to comfort someone, and so on. Is that not what we are saying of God in these cases?

There is a problem because, first, as the last paragraph suggests, we get our terms (concepts) for talking (thinking) about God from our talk and thought about creatures, particularly human beings, and, second, God is so different from human beings as to make the use of these terms problematic.

Regarding the first point, does it just happen that all the terms we use to specify God's attributes, actions and psychological states are terms we also use for human beings, or is there some deep reason for this? The latter alternative is supported by the following considerations. We have the kind of cognitive access to each other that makes it possible to establish a common language for talking about us. But we do not have the same resources for setting up an independent language for talking of God. To put it roughly, the parent can know when the child is perceiving another person talking or hugging someone or criticizing someone, and this makes it possible to introduce the child to the publicly shared meanings of those terms in application to human beings. But we cannot do anything analogous in the case of God. Even if the child can be aware of being spoken to or forgiven or comforted by God, the parent cannot tell when the child is aware of this unless the child tells the parent, which presupposes that the child already has learned how to apply the terms to God.

The second point is that creaturely terms cannot, in general, be used of God in exactly the same sense because of the ways in which God is different from creatures. There is no universal agreement as to just what these ways are, but some of those most commonly cited are as follows. God is infinite in power, knowledge and goodness; each of us is very limited in these respects. God is purely spiritual; we are embodied. God is omnipresent; we are severely restricted in spatial location. According to some theologies, God enjoys an atemporal mode of being – the simultaneous and complete possession of illimitable life; we live our lives successively, one moment at a time.

These differences have implications for what it is for God to be or do the various things we believe of him. God's knowledge is a very different thing from human knowledge. It is not built up by inference from the deliverances of perception. God has no sense organs, and no need to infer some truths from others. He knows everything directly. Since God is immaterial, divine overt action is a fundamentally different thing from human overt action. The only things we can effect directly are changes in our bodies; we bring about changes in the external world only by moving our bodies in certain ways. But God, having no body, will directly bring about changes in the world. Finally, if God's mode of being is atemporal, the picture will be still more different. Virtually every aspect of our activity is deeply imbued with temporality. We acquire information, think, deliberate and act by a temporal succession of stages.

This makes it clear that predicates cannot be truly applied to God in just the sense in which they apply to creatures. They cannot be used univocally of God and creatures. But that leaves several alternatives. They can be used metaphorically of God. That is very common in religious discourse. When we say 'His *hands* prepared the dry land' or 'The Lord is my *rock* and my *fortress*', the italicized terms are obviously used metaphorically. We do not think that God literally has hands or is a rock. And some people take all, or virtually all, theology to be metaphorical (see McFague 1982). But most theologians have supposed that we can make some literally true statements about God, and that it is important for the foundations of faith that we are able to do so. This has led them to explore other alternatives. A popular tack is that classically taken by Aquinas and developed in various ways by his successors. On this view, (some) creaturely terms are used analogically of God. There is an important analogy between their creaturely and theological import. According to AQUINAS (§9), there is not even a partial univocity between 'know', for example, as applied to humans and God, even though there is enough analogy between their senses to enable us to understand what is said of God when he is said to know something. Aquinas' denial of partial univocity stems from his belief in a particularly radical divine–human difference, namely that God is absolutely simple. There is no difference of any sort between 'aspects' of the divine being. Since God is not different from any of his attributes or actions, no term as applied to God can mean even partly the same as to it does when applied to creatures (see SIMPLICITY, DIVINE §§1–2).

Contrary to Aquinas, there is a way in which, for some terms, there can be a partial overlap of meaning in the divine and human applications. The crucial point here is that the meaning of a term often includes more abstract, generic aspects and more concrete, specific ones. The term might carry over its more abstract meaning, though not its more concrete meaning, from one application to another. This would make it possible for the more abstract component of the concept of knowledge to be common to God and humans, even though the way this is realized (and so the more concrete meaning of the term) would be different in the two cases. Consider an action term, such as 'makes'. It seems reasonable to suppose that the full concrete meaning

of this term, as it is used of human beings in saying 'John made a bookcase', includes 'transforming some pre-existing material' and 'effecting this by moving his body in certain ways'. If so, that full meaning does not carry over to 'God made the universe', assuming that we mean this to involve creation *ex nihilo* and take God to be immaterial. But there could be a more abstract component of the meaning that is carried over, for example, 'brings it about by one or more acts of will that a certain state of affairs obtains'. In this way, some parts of the creaturely meanings of some terms can be used literally to make statements about God that have a chance of being true.

See also: NEGATIVE THEOLOGY

References and further reading

* Alston, W.P. (1989) *Divine Nature and Human Language: Essays in Philosophical Theology*, Ithaca, NY: Cornell University Press. (Philosophical essays on the nature of God and our talk of God.)

Aquinas, T. (1259–65) *Summa contra gentiles*, trans. V.J. Bourke, Garden City, NY: Doubleday, 1956, I, chaps 29–36. (See next item.)

—— (1266–73) *Summa theologiae*, London: Eyre & Spottiswoode, 60 vols, 1964, Ia, q.13. (This and the preceding item provide the classic statement of the view that terms applied to God have an analogical mode of meaning.)

Barbour, I.G. (1974) *Myths, Models, and Paradigms*, New York: Harper & Row. (Religious belief as based on models. Very readable.)

* Braithwaite, R.B. (1955) *An Empiricist's View of the Nature of Religious Belief*, Cambridge: Cambridge University Press. (An interpretation of religious beliefs in terms of stories told for their moral point. Influenced by the verifiability criterion of meaningfulness.)

Crombie, I.M. (1957) 'The Possibility of Theological Statements', in B. Mitchell (ed.) *Faith and Logic*, London: Allen & Unwin. (A rich and complex view of the understanding of talk about God.)

* Flew, A. (1955) 'Theology and Falsification', in A. Flew and A. MacIntyre (eds) *New Essays in Philosophical Theology*, London: SCM Press. (Classic application of the verifiability criterion to religious discourse.)

* McFague, S. (1982) *Metaphorical Theology*, Philadelphia, PA: Fortress Press. (A stimulating presentation.)

* Plantinga, A. (1967) *God and Other Minds*, Ithaca, NY: Cornell University Press. (A classic in philosophy of religion. Advanced.)

* Santayana, G. (1905) *Reason in Religion*, New York:

Charles Scribner's Sons. (An early account of religious discourse as non-factual.)

* Tillich, P. (1953) *Systematic Theology*, vol. 1, London: Nisbet & Co. (Sets forth his view of theological discourse as symbolic; see also his 'Theology and Symbolism', in F.E. Johnson (ed.) *Religious Symbolism*, New York: Harper & Bros, and 'Religious Symbols and Our Knowledge of God', *Christian Scholar* 38 (3): 189–97, both published in 1955.)

WILLIAM P. ALSTON

RELIGIOUS PLURALISM

Religion displays a luxuriant diversity of beliefs and practices. Crusades and colonialism, preaching and proselytizing, argument and apologetics have failed to produce worldwide agreement. In order to understand this situation, four possibilities are worth considering. The first is reductive naturalism. On this view, religious beliefs about a supernatural or transcendent dimension of existence are all false. They are to be explained as products of a merely human projection mechanism. The writings of such naturalistic philosophers and scientists as Feuerbach, Marx, Freud, and Durkheim suggest ways in which such projections might occur. A second possibility is exclusivism. Doctrinal exclusivism is the view that the doctrines of one religion are completely true; the doctrines of all others are false whenever there is conflict. Soteriological exclusivism is the view that only one religion offers an effective path to salvation or liberation. Though the two kinds of exclusivism are logically independent, they are usually held together. A third option, which has found increasing favour in the second half of the twentieth century, is inclusivism: one religion contains the final truth and others contain only approaches to or approximations of it; the privileged religion offers the most effective path to salvation, but those outside it can somehow be saved or liberated. The final option, pluralism, is a relative newcomer. According to pluralism, a single ultimate religious reality is being differently experienced and understood in all the major religious traditions; they all, as far as we can tell, offer equally effective paths to salvation or liberation.

These options raise interesting questions. What accounts for the growing popularity of inclusivism and pluralism? How are we to articulate pluralism? Does exclusivism remain a rational option in spite of what is known about the whole range of religious traditions? Is pluralism, once clearly stated, a rational option?

1 The emergence of inclusivism and pluralism
2 The pluralistic hypothesis
3 The rationality of exclusivism
4 The rationality of pluralism

1 The emergence of inclusivism and pluralism

Many Westerners will best understand the emergence of inclusivism and pluralism in terms of the history of Christianity. For most of its history Christianity has been resolutely exclusivist. In late antiquity it was a new religion, struggling to establish itself in the face of criticism and persecution. It is not surprising to find it making exclusive claims on behalf of its charismatic founder, Jesus of Nazareth. Support for exclusivism was derived from sayings attributed to Jesus in scripture, such as 'No one comes to the Father except through me' (John 14: 6). By the third century many Christians held that there was no salvation outside their church (*extra ecclesiam, nulla salus*). During the Middle Ages, Christian Europe had little direct contact with the non-theistic religions of Asia. Islamic civilization was at the height of its powers and so posed a cultural and sometimes a military threat to Christian civilization. Jews were often despised and persecuted. To be sure, thinkers such as Thomas Aquinas managed to learn from Maimonides and Ibn Sina (Avicenna), but there were few opportunities for Christians, Muslims and Jews to interact on a footing of equality and develop mutual religious respect. And when in the modern era Christian Europe became the dominant world power, colonial expansion began and Christian missionaries, whose chief aim was conversion, spread over the face of the earth.

Of course, Christianity is not the only religion to have fostered exclusivist attitudes. In their more militant moments, Muslims have done the same. Some Jews cherish an ethnically exclusive identity as God's chosen people, and some Hindus revere the Vedas as a source of absolute truth. Buddhists often see in the teachings of Guatama the only *dharma* that can liberate humans from illusion and suffering. Still, the exclusivist strain in Christianity has been unusually strong and persistent.

The turn away from exclusivism on the part of many but not all Christians in the latter half of the twentieth century is therefore a dramatic development. No doubt the full explanation of it will be complex, but it seems clear that at least the following three factors will figure in it. First, many Christians have learned tolerance for other religions. Christian denominations learned tolerance for one another in the aftermath of the Wars of Religion; Christianity is learning tolerance of other religions in the aftermath of colonialism and the Holocaust. In retrospect, many Christians have come to see in exclusivist attitudes both a source of complicity in the evils of colonialism and a stimulus for the anti-Semitism that contributed causally to the Holocaust. Second, many Christians have also come to understand (at least to some extent) other religions, a benefit often conferred on them by the modern academic study of religion. When one can read the important texts of other religious traditions in good translations with helpful commentaries, one can experience for oneself their power, nobility and allure. When one learns that the beliefs of other religious traditions are supported by experiences and arguments similar to those that support the beliefs of one's own tradition, one is apt to acknowledge the epistemic rationality of the participants in other traditions. And one is likely to acknowledge their practical rationality once one comes to see that their traditions, judged by the fruits they yield, are comparable to one's own in helping people to live well and in producing saintly people.

The third and most important factor is the increasing frequency of intense and cooperative personal interaction among participants in diverse religious traditions. Exclusivist attitudes are under pressure in such contexts. Such interactions have played a major role in the careers of two of the leading pluralist thinkers, Wilfred Cantwell Smith and John Hick. Smith has written about the influence on his thought of having taught for some years at a small Christian college in Lahore in which the majority of the teaching staff and students were Hindus, Muslims or Sikhs (Smith 1963). He also organized and worked for several years in the Institute for Islamic Studies at McGill University, which is structured by the proviso that half the faculty and half the graduate students should be Muslims. Hick has written of the impression made on him by cooperating with Muslims, Jews, Hindus and Sikhs in campaigns for tolerance in Birmingham, England, during the 1960s (Hick 1993). As religious diversity increases within our societies, more and more Christians are involved in and being influenced by such personal interactions, and the influence in many cases has operated to undermine exclusivist attitudes.

If one moves away from exclusivism, the step to pluralism is larger than the step to inclusivism. Since the Second Vatican Council in the 1960s, inclusivists among Roman Catholic theologians have proposed that human salvation depends entirely on the sacrificial death of Christ, but that all humans can somehow be united with Christ and so share in his redemption. To pluralists, this view seems to be an unsatisfactory halfway house. If one is going to allow that people in religious traditions other than

Christianity can be saved, it appears to be simpler and more natural to claim that their salvation is mediated by their traditions than to insist that it is mediated by Christ. Thinking that something more radical than inclusivism is called for, Smith, himself a Christian theologian, argues that it is an urgent task for us to work out a world theology or a theology of comparative religion. He suggests that such a theology would involve discourse about the transcendent dimension of human life and of the universe, to which the history of religion bears witness and which it elucidates (Smith 1981). However, this suggestion raises philosophical problems. According to Muslims, the transcendent dimension of the universe is a personal deity, Allah; according to Advaitic Hindus, it is an impersonal absolute, Brahman. These claims seem to be logical contraries. Hence it appears that any theology that takes a stand on the specific nature of the transcendent dimension of the universe will be unable to escape doctrinal exclusivism.

2   The pluralistic hypothesis

Appearances, however, can deceive. Hick has set forth a philosophically sophisticated pluralistic hypothesis that may avoid problems of this sort (1987, 1989). As he sees it, each of the major religious traditions offers a path to salvation or liberation that involves a transformation of human existence from self-centredness to reality-centredness. Judged by their results, all of these traditions are, as far as we can tell, of roughly equal effectiveness in producing this transformation. This suggests that a single ultimate reality is being differently conceived, experienced and responded to from within different traditions. Following KANT (§3), Hick develops the suggestion using the distinction between the phenomenal and the noumenal. His hypothesis is that the noumenal Real is experienced and conceived within different religious traditions as the range of gods and absolutes reported by the phenomenology of religion. Being phenomenal, such gods and absolutes are not illusory but are empirically real manifestations of the noumenal Real.

There are two ways of interpreting these claims. According to the first, the pluralistic hypothesis postulates a single noumenal Real and diverse ways in which it appears and is experienced within different religious traditions. On this interpretation, apparently conflicting claims about ultimate reality are to be understood as truths about how the noumenal Real appears to various groups, but as falsehoods about how it is in itself. It is not contradictory to suppose that the noumenal Real appears as and is experienced as personal by Muslims and impersonal by Advaitic Hindus. Moreover, if we assume that being personal

261

and being impersonal are contraries rather than contradictories, it is consistent to suppose that the noumenal Real is in itself neither personal nor impersonal. On this view, the major religions will be on a par in two senses: they are all equally correct if their apparently conflicting claims are taken to be about the ways in which the noumenal Real appears to them, and they are all equally mistaken if those claims are taken to be about the ways in which it is in itself.

According to the second interpretation, the pluralistic hypothesis postulates not only a single noumenal Real but also many phenomenal Reals that are joint products of the interaction of the noumenal Real and various human religious traditions. On this interpretation, apparently conflicting claims about ultimate reality are to be understood as truths about the attributes of the diverse phenomenal Reals of the various religious traditions, but falsehoods about the attributes of the noumenal Real. It is not contradictory to suppose that the phenomenal Real of Islam is personal, the distinct phenomenal Real of Advaitic Hinduism is impersonal, and the noumenal Real, which is yet a third thing, has neither of the contrary attributes of being personal and being impersonal. On this view, the major religions will also be on a par in two senses: they are all equally correct if their apparently conflicting claims are taken to be about the attributes of their diverse phenomenal Reals, and they are all equally mistaken if those claims are taken to be about the attributes of the noumenal Real.

It should be noted that, on either interpretation, Hick's pluralistic hypothesis purchases such parity at a high price. It is a rival to the main lines of self-understanding within the major religious traditions. Most members of such traditions would reject the claim that their beliefs are true only of ways in which ultimate reality appears to them, or of phenomenal objects it contributes to producing, and are not true of that reality as it is in itself. If they employed the distinction between the phenomenal and the noumenal, Muslims would be likely to insist that the noumenal Real is personal, and Advaitic Hindus would be likely to insist that it is impersonal. Hick can attribute only mythological truth to such claims, and he takes mythological truth to be nothing more than literal falsity plus a tendency to evoke appropriate dispositional attitudes. So Hick's version of pluralism attributes massive literal error to both Muslims and Advaitic Hindus. This is not surprising, because their traditions remain, for the most part, stoutly pre-Kantian in their self-understandings. Of course, Hick's pluralism attributes equally large literal error to all the other major religious traditions. Hence it will be unacceptable to most people who at this time

participate in any of the major religions; such people will prefer to hang on to their doctrinal exclusivism. Is it rational for them to do so in the face of what is known about religious diversity?

3 The rationality of exclusivism

A positive answer to this question is contained in the religious epistemology of William P. Alston. He operates within a doxastic practice approach to epistemology. A doxastic practice is a way of forming beliefs and evaluating them epistemically in terms of a background system of beliefs that furnishes potential overriders. For example, forming beliefs on the basis of sense perception is a doxastic practice. Alston (1991) argues at length that it is practically rational to engage in socially established doxastic practices that are not demonstrably unreliable or otherwise unqualified for rational acceptance.

In the religious sphere, mystical perception is defined by Alston as religious experience in which a presentation or appearance to the subject of something the subject identifies as ultimate reality occurs (see RELIGIOUS EXPERIENCE). As he sees it, there are different socially established mystical doxastic practices in the major religious traditions because there are substantial differences in their overrider systems of background beliefs. One such practice is Christian mystical practice. Alston argues that it is not demonstrably unreliable, and parallel arguments can be made for the mystical practices of other major religions. However, both the outputs of Christian mystical practice and its overrider system are massively inconsistent with their counterparts in the mystical practices of other religious traditions, and those mystical practices are in turn massively inconsistent with one another. Hence at most one of them can be a reliable way of forming beliefs about ultimate reality. But why should one suppose that Christian mystical practice is the one that is reliable if any is?

Of course, Christian mystical practice can come up with internal reasons for supposing that it is more reliable than its rivals. But each of them can do the same. Moreover, as Alston points out, Christian mystical practice enjoys significant self-support from the way in which promises it represents God as making are fulfilled in the spiritual lives of its practitioners. But each of its rivals enjoys similar self-support. Thus it seems that Christian mystical practice is disqualified for rational acceptance unless it can come up with sufficient independent reasons for supposing that it is reliable or, at least, more reliable than its rivals. By parity of reasoning, the same thing seems to be true of the mystical practices of other religious traditions.

Alston does not try to provide independent reasons for the reliability of Christian mystical practice, and he acknowledges that its epistemic efficacy is weakened in the absence of such reasons. However, he denies that it is reduced to the point at which it is no longer qualified for rational acceptance, and supports this denial with an analogical argument. It proceeds by comparing the actual diversity of mystical perceptual practices and a hypothetical diversity of sensory perceptual practices. Suppose that in certain cultures there were a socially established Cartesian practice of seeing what is visually perceived as an indefinitely extended medium that is more or less concentrated at various points, rather than (as in our actual Aristotelian practice) as made up of more or less discrete objects scattered about in space. Further suppose that both these practices are equal in terms of the fruits they produce in terms of enabling their practitioners to deal successfully with their physical environment. Imagine also that in this scenario we are as firmly wedded to our Aristotelian practice as we are in fact, yet can find no independent reasons for supposing that it is more reliable than the rival Cartesian practice. According to Alston, in the absence of independent reasons for thinking that the Cartesian practice is more reliable than our own, the rational thing for us to do is to stick with our Aristotelian practice, of which we are masters and which serves us well in guiding our activity in the world. But the imagined situation is precisely parallel to our actual situation with respect to Christian mystical practice. Therefore, by analogy, the rational thing for those engaged in Christian mystical practice to do is to stick with it and continue to accept the Christian system of belief. Since that system of belief as currently constituted is exclusivist, it follows that it is rational for its adherents to remain Christian exclusivists. And, of course, by parity of reasoning, similar conclusions hold for those engaged in the mystical practices of other religious traditions. Leaving aside independent reasons for thinking that alternatives are more reliable than their own practices, the rational thing for them to do is also to stick with those practices and to accept their exclusivist systems of belief.

4 The rationality of pluralism

Even if it is granted that Alston has convincingly argued for the practical rationality of sticking with the exclusivist beliefs of one's own mystical practice, the claim that this is the only rational thing to do can be challenged. To return to his analogy, sticking with our own Aristotelian practice and switching to the rival Cartesian practice are not the only options. We can also revise our Aristotelian practice from within and try to get the revised practice socially established. Revisions might proceed in a Kantian direction. Suppose it occurs to us that the success of both Aristotelian and Cartesian sensory perceptual practices in the imagined situation can be explained by the hypothesis that each is reliable with respect to the appearances things present to its practitioners, but neither is reliable with respect to how things are in themselves. Moved by this consideration, we decide to modify our perceptual practice so that it comes to map sensory inputs onto doxastic outputs about the appearances things present to us, but not about how things really are independent of us. Precedent for such modifications is found in the way people respond to learning that such things as phenomenal colours are not mind-independent. It seems that it would be rational to proceed in accordance with this scenario. In the imagined situation, then, it would be rational to stick with our Aristotelian practice, but it would also be rational to transform it into a Kantian practice.

The imagined situation is, of course, relevantly parallel to the actual situation with regard to competing mystical practices. Hence, by analogy, though it is rational for those engaging in Christian mystical practice to continue to do so, it is not the only rational thing to do, there being more than one thing it is rational to do in the face of competing mystical practices. Another such thing would be to modify Christian mystical practice from within to make it more Kantian. Each of these courses of action is rationally permissible in the light of religious diversity. Neither is irrational, but neither is rationally required. And setting aside any relevant dissimilarities, the lesson applies not only for those engaged in Christian mystical practice, but also for those engaged in other socially established mystical practices with significant self-support.

See also: MYSTICISM, HISTORY OF; MYSTICISM, NATURE OF

References and further reading

* Alston, W.P. (1991) *Perceiving God: The Epistemology of Religious Experience*, Ithaca, NY and London: Cornell University Press. (Chapter 7 provides full details of the argument summarized in §3.)
* Hick, J. (1987) 'Religious Pluralism', in M. Eliade (ed.) *The Encyclopedia of Religion*, New York: Macmillan. (A brief and informal summary of the position discussed in §2.)
* —— (1989) *An Interpretation of Religion: Human Responses to the Transcendent*, New Haven, CT and

London: Yale University Press. (Detailed presentation of the position discussed in §2.)

* —— (1993) *Disputed Questions in Theology and the Philosophy of Religion*, New Haven, CT: Yale University Press. (Essay 8, 'A Personal Note', contains the autobiographical information referred to in §1.)

Plantinga, A. (1995) 'Pluralism: A Defense of Religious Exclusivism', in T. Senor (ed.) *The Rationality of Belief and the Plurality of Faith*, Ithaca, NY and London: Cornell University Press. (Presents a critique of Hick's religious pluralism. The volume also contains interesting essays on religious pluralism by George Mavrodes, Peter van Inwagen and William Wainwright.)

Quinn, P.L. (1995) 'Towards Thinner Theologies: Hick and Alston on Religious Diversity', in E.T. Long (ed.) *God, Reason and Religions*, Dordrecht, Boston, MA and London: Kluwer Academic Publishers. (Expansion of the material of §§2–4 of this entry.)

Smith, H. (1991) *The World's Religions*, San Francisco, CA: Harper. (A readable and informative overview of the major religious traditions.)

* Smith, W.C. (1963) *The Faith of Other Men*, New York: New American Library. (The introduction contains the autobiographical information referred to in §1.)

—— (1976) *Religious Diversity*, New York: Harper & Row. (Essays on various issues connected with religious diversity.)

* —— (1981) *Towards a World Theology*, Philadelphia, PA: The Westminster Press. (Contains details of the proposal for a theology of comparative religion mentioned in §1.)

PHILIP L. QUINN

REN *see* CONFUCIAN PHILOSOPHY, CHINESE; CONFUCIUS

RENAISSANCE HUMANISM

see HUMANISM, RENAISSANCE

RENAISSANCE PHILOSOPHY

The term 'Renaissance' means rebirth, and was originally used to designate a rebirth of the arts and literature that began in mid-fourteenth century Italy (see HUMANISM, RENAISSANCE). Here the term is simply used to refer to the period from 1400 to 1600, but there are ways in which Renaissance philosophy can be seen as a rebirth, for it encompasses the rediscovery of Plato and Neoplatonism (see PLATONISM, RENAISSANCE), the revival of such ancient systems as Stoicism and scepticism (see SCEPTICISM, RENAISSANCE; STOICISM), and a renewed interest in magic and the occult. Continuity with the Middle Ages is equally important. Despite the attacks of humanists and Platonists, Aristotelianism predominated throughout the Renaissance, and many philosophers continued to work within the scholastic tradition (see ARISTOTELIANISM, RENAISSANCE).

1 Historical and social factors

Three historical events were of particular importance. First is the Turkish advance, culminating in the capture of Constantinople in 1453. This advance produced a migration of Greek scholars (like GEORGE OF TREBIZOND) and Greek texts into the Latin-speaking West (see HUMANISM, RENAISSANCE §4; PLATONISM, RENAISSANCE §3). It also led to a search for new trade routes. The European discovery of the Americas and the first voyages to China and Japan widened intellectual horizons through an awareness of new languages, religions and cultures (see SCEPTICISM, RENAISSANCE §2). New issues of colonialism, slavery and the rights of non-Christian peoples had an impact on legal and political philosophy (see LATIN AMERICA, COLONIAL THOUGHT IN §1; VITORIA, F. DE; SOTO, D. DE; SUÁREZ, F.). The study of mathematics and science (especially astronomy) was also affected by developments in navigation, trade and banking, by new technology such as the telescope and other instruments (see KEPLER, J.; GALILEI, GALILEO), as well as by the recovery of Greek mathematics and the favourable attitude of Plato towards mathematical studies (see PLATONISM, RENAISSANCE §6).

Second is the development of printing in the mid-fifteenth century (see HUMANISM, RENAISSANCE §6). This allowed for the publication of scholarly text editions, for the expansion of learning beyond the universities, and for the increased use of vernacular languages for written material (see HUMANISM, RENAISSANCE §4). These changes particularly affected women, who were most often literate only in the vernacular. CHRISTINE DE PIZAN, PARACELSUS, RAMUS, MONTAIGNE, BRUNO and CHARRON are among those who used vernacular languages in at least some of their works.

Third is the Protestant reformation in the first part of the sixteenth century (see LUTHER, M.;

CALVIN, J.). Protestant insistence on Bible reading in the vernacular strengthened both the use of the vernacular and the spread of literacy (see MELANCHTHON, P. §1). The Catholic Counter-Reformation also affected education, particularly through the work of the Jesuit Order (founded 1540), which set up educational institutions throughout Europe, including the Collegio Romano in Rome (founded 1553) and the secondary school at La Flèche, where DESCARTES was educated (for further examples, see COLLEGIUM CONIMBRICENSE; ARISTOTELIANISM IN THE 17TH CENTURY §2). Political philosophy took new directions (see HOOKER, R., for example) and theological studies changed. As the Protestants abandoned the *Sentences* of PETER LOMBARD and emphasized the church fathers, so the Catholics replaced the *Sentences* with the *Summa theologiae* of Thomas AQUINAS. In turn, these changes affected the undergraduate curriculum, which (for other reasons as well) became less technically demanding, especially in relation to logic studies (see LOGIC, RENAISSANCE). Personal liberties, too, were affected. Both Catholics and Protestants censored undesirable views, and the first Roman Catholic Index of Prohibited Books was drawn up in 1559. BRUNO was burnt for heresy, and CAMPANELLA was imprisoned. Calls for tolerance by such men as MONTAIGNE and LIPSIUS were not always favourably received. The books of all these men, and others such as ERASMUS, MACHIAVELLI and RABELAIS, were placed on the Index or required to be revised. At the same time, Calvinist Geneva prohibited the printing of Thomas AQUINAS and RABELAIS.

Social factors also affected philosophy which, as an academic discipline, was tied to the universities. These continued to accept only male students, and to teach in Latin, the universal language of learning and of the Roman Catholic Church, but more students came from higher social classes than during the Middle Ages. They expected a curriculum with less emphasis on technical logic and natural science and more on rhetoric, modern languages, history and other practical disciplines. Such curricular changes owed much to humanism, as did the spread of new secondary schools (see HUMANISM, RENAISSANCE §7; MONTAIGNE, M. DE §1).

The Renaissance was also notable for the spread of learning outside the university. Some men largely relied on the patronage of nobles, princes and popes (among them VALLA, FICINO, PICO DELLA MIRANDOLA and ERASMUS), some were medical practitioners (including PARACELSUS and CARDANO), some had private resources (like MONTAIGNE). Nor was it only men that were involved: CHRISTINE DE PIZAN, for example, was a court poet.

2 Humanism and the recovery of ancient texts

Humanism was primarily a cultural and educational programme (see HUMANISM, RENAISSANCE; PETRARCA, F.; AGRICOLA, R.; Erasmus, D.; VIVES, J.L.; Rabelais, F.). Humanists were very much concerned with classical scholarship, especially the study of Greek, and with the imitation of classical models. Despite their frequent criticisms of scholastic jargon and techniques, they were not direct rivals of scholastic philosophers, except in so far as changes to the university curriculum brought about by the influence of humanist ideals diluted or squeezed out scholastic subjects. It was humanism that led to the rediscovery of classical texts, and their dissemination in printed form, in Greek and in Latin translation. Plato is the most notable example, but he was rediscovered with the Neoplatonists, and was often read through Neoplatonic eyes (see FICINO, M.; PLATONISM, RENAISSANCE §1). The so-called ancient wisdom of Hermeticism (also known as HERMETISM) was also recaptured within a Neoplatonic framework (see FICINO, M. §2; PATRIZI DA CHERSO, F.), and, along with the Kabbalah (see KABBALAH), led to a revived interest in magic and the occult (see ALCHEMY §5; AGRIPPA VON NETTESHEIM, H.C.; BRUNO, G.; PARACELSUS). These streams also fed into the new vitalistic philosophy of nature (in such thinkers as PARACELSUS, BRUNO, CAMPANELLA, CARDANO and TELESIO). Other ancient schools of thought that were revived include Epicureanism (see VALLA, L. §2), scepticism (see AGRIPPA VON NETTESHEIM, H.C.; ERASMUS, D. §4; SANCHES, F.; MONTAIGNE, M. DE; CHARRON, P.) and Stoicism (see LIPSIUS, J.).

Some humanists wrote important works on education, including the education of women (see ERASMUS, D. §2; VIVES, J.L. §§1, 4). The Lutheran Aristotelian MELANCHTHON was also an educational reformer; and the Jesuits drew up the *Ratio Studiorum* (Plan of Studies) which prescribed texts for all Jesuit institutions (see COLLEGIUM CONIMBRICENSE; FONSECA, P. DA §1). Humanism also affected Bible studies (see ERASMUS, D. §1; LUTHER, M. §3; HUMANISM, RENAISSANCE §6) and Aristotelianism itself (see ARISTOTELIANISM, RENAISSANCE §1).

3 Scholasticism and Aristotle

Scholastic philosophy was the philosophy of the schools, the philosophy which was taught in institutions of higher learning, whether the secular universities or the institutions of religious orders. The association of late scholastic philosophy with institutions of higher learning carried with it a certain method of presentation, one which is both highly organized and argumentative, with a clear account of views for and against a given thesis. It also carried with it a focus on Aristotle, for it was Aristotle who provided most of the basic textbooks in the sixteenth- and even the seventeenth-century university. Nor was the study of Aristotle necessarily carried on in a rigidly traditional manner, for many different Aristotelian-isms were developed (see ARISTOTELIANISM, RENAISSANCE). Moreover, particularly within the Jesuit order, there was a strong inclination to include new developments in mathematics and astronomy within the framework of Aristotelian natural philosophy (see ARISTOTELIANISM IN THE 17TH CENTURY §1).

Aristotelians include PAUL OF VENICE, GEORGE OF TREBIZOND, VERNIA, NIFO, POMPONAZZI, MELANCHTHON, ZABARELLA and the Thomists (see below). Anti-Aristotelians include Petrarch (see PETRARCA, F.), BLASIUS OF PARMA, VALLA, RAMUS, SANCHES, TELESIO, PATRIZI DA CHERSO and CAMPANELLA. Some philosophers sought to reconcile Platonism and Aristotelianism (see PICO DELLA MIRANDOLA, G. §4; PLATONISM, RENAISSANCE §§3, 6).

A very important characteristic of late scholastic philosophy is its use of medieval terminology, along with its continued, explicit, concern both with problems stemming from medieval philosophy and with medieval philosophers themselves. There are fashions here as elsewhere. Albertism (the philosophy of ALBERT THE GREAT) was important in the fifteenth century (see ARISTOTELIANISM, MEDIEVAL §6); nominalism more or less disappeared after a final flowering in the early sixteenth-century (see BIEL, G.; MAJOR, J.). Scotism declined significantly, but was still present in the seventeenth century (see ARISTOTELIANISM IN THE 17TH CENTURY §§2–4; LATIN AMERICA, COLONIAL THOUGHT IN §2). Thomism underwent a strong revival especially through the work of the Dominicans (CAPREOLUS, CAJETAN, SILVESTRI, VITORIA, SOTO, BÁÑEZ and JOHN OF ST THOMAS) and the Jesuits (FONSECA, TOLETUS, SUÁREZ and Rubio: see LATIN AMERICA, COLONIAL THOUGHT IN §§2, 5).

4 Philosophical themes

It is difficult to map the interests of Renaissance philosophers on to the interests of contemporary philosophers, especially as the main form of writing remained the commentary, whether on Aristotle or Aquinas. SUÁREZ is the first well-known author to write a major systematic work of metaphysics that is not a commentary, though earlier authors (such as NIFO and POMPONAZZI) had written shorter works on particular themes. Nonetheless, certain general themes can be isolated:

4.1 Logic and language. Logic was basic to the curriculum of all educational institutions, and many Renaissance philosophers wrote on logic (see LOGIC, RENAISSANCE; LANGUAGE, RENAISSANCE PHILOSOPHY OF; ARISTOTELIANISM, RENAISSANCE §2; LOGIC IN THE 17TH AND 18TH CENTURIES §§1–2). Individual humanists who worked in this field include VALLA (§4), AGRICOLA, VIVES; MELANCHTHON (§2) and RAMUS (§2); individual scholastics include SOTO (§2), TOLETUS and FONSECA (§2). Theories of logic and language were often closely related to metaphysics and philosophy of mind, as well as to science.

4.2 Metaphysics and philosophy of mind. Among the themes that overlapped with theories of logic and language were: (i) mental language (see LANGUAGE, RENAISSANCE PHILOSOPHY OF §2; LANGUAGE, MEDIEVAL PHILOSOPHY OF §2; see also LANGUAGE OF THOUGHT); (ii) analogy (see LANGUAGE, RENAISSANCE PHILOSOPHY OF §4; CAPREOLUS, J.; CAJETAN §2; SILVESTRI, F.; FONSECA, P. DA §3); (iii) objective and formal concepts (see CAPREOLUS, J.; FONSECA, P. DA §3; SUÁREZ, F. §2; LANGUAGE, RENAISSANCE PHILOSOPHY OF §4); (iv) beings of reason (see LANGUAGE, RENAISSANCE PHILOSOPHY OF §3; FONSECA, P. DA §3; JOHN OF ST THOMAS §4). A specifically Thomistic theme in metaphysics was the relation between essence and existence (see AQUINAS, T. §9; CAJETAN §5; FONSECA, P. DA §3; BÁÑEZ, D.; SUÁREZ, F. §2). Other metaphysical issues include: (i) universals (see PAUL OF VENICE; BIEL, G. §4; SUÁREZ, F. §2); (ii) individuation (see CAPREOLUS, J.; CAJETAN §3; SUÁREZ, F. §2); and (iii) the Great Chain of Being (see PAUL OF VENICE; FICINO, M. §3; POMPONAZZI, P. §4; BRUNO, G. §5; ARISTOTELIANISM, RENAISSANCE §6). Issues in the philosophy of mind included the existence of an agent sense (see BLASIUS OF PARMA §3; NIFO, A. §3; ARISTOTELIANISM, RENAISSANCE §4) and of intelligible species (CAJETAN §4; NIFO, A. §3; TOLETUS, F. §5; ARISTOTELIANISM, RENAISSANCE §4).

4.3 Immortality. The biggest single issue was the nature of the intellectual soul, whether it was immortal, and if so, whether its immortality could be proved (see PAUL OF VENICE; BLASIUS OF PARMA §2; FICINO, M. §3; CAJETAN §4; SILVESTRI, F.; POMPONAZZI, P. §2; NIFO, A. §3; TOLETUS, F. §5; SUÁREZ, F. §3; JOHN OF ST THOMAS §3; ARISTOTELIANISM, RENAISSANCE §5; see also SOUL, NATURE AND IMMORTALITY OF THE).

4.4 Free will. Free will was a topic closely connected with the religious issues of grace, predestination and God's foreknowledge (see VALLA, L. §3; BIEL, G. §3; POMPONAZZI, P. §4; LUTHER, M. §3; ERASMUS, D. §1; CALVIN, J. §4; MOLINA, L. DE; MOLINISM; BÁÑEZ, D.; PROVIDENCE §3).

4.5 Science and philosophy of nature. The discussion

of scientific method also overlaps with logic (see LOGIC, RENAISSANCE §7; ARISTOTELIANISM, RENAISSANCE §2; VERNIA, N. §2; ZABARELLA, J. §§4–5; LATIN AMERICA, COLONIAL THOUGHT IN §5). Themes include (i) traditional Aristotelian discussions about the object of natural philosophy (see ARISTOTELIANISM, RENAISSANCE §3; VERNIA, N. §3; ZABARELLA, J. §6, JOHN OF ST THOMAS §3); (ii) Anti-Aristotelian materialism (see BLASIUS OF PARMA); (iii) the new philosophies of nature which saw the universe as full of life (see PARACELSUS; BRUNO, G.; CAMPANELLA, T.; CARDANO, G.; TELESIO, B.) or as explicable in terms of light-metaphysics (see PATRIZI DA CHERSO, F.); (iv) tentative approaches to empiricism (see VIVES, J.L. §4; RAMUS, P. §4; SANCHES, F. §3). Finally, there are the thinkers who set science on a new path by using a combination of mathematical description and experiment (such as COPERNICUS, KEPLER and GALILEO).

4.6 Moral and political philosophy. Humanists were deeply concerned with moral and political philosophy (see HUMANISM, RENAISSANCE §2; ERASMUS, D. §3; VIVES, J.L. §2), as were Protestant reformers (see MELANCHTHON, P. §3; CALVIN, J. §5). Although the central focus remained on Aristotle (see ARISTOTELIANISM, RENAISSANCE §7), Epicurean moral philosophy was taken up by VALLA and Stoic moral philosophy was also influential (see LIPSIUS, J.; CHARRON, P. §3). Major political thinkers included MACHIAVELLI, VITORIA and BODIN. Many discussions of forms of government, the status of law, and the notion of a just war grew out of the Aristotelian–Thomistic tradition – prominent contributors to this tradition include CHRISTINE DE PIZAN, VITORIA, SOTO (§4), TOLETUS (§2), SUÁREZ (§4), MOLINA (§4) and HOOKER (see also LATIN AMERICA, COLONIAL THOUGHT IN §1). Other significant types of Renaissance political philosophy include: (i) conciliarism (see AILLY, P. D'; GERSON, J.; NICHOLAS OF CUSA; MAJOR, J. §3); (ii) utopianism (see UTOPIANISM; RABELAIS, F. §2; CAMPANELLA, T. §3); (iii) Neostoicism (see LIPSIUS, J.). (See also POLITICAL PHILOSOPHY, HISTORY OF; RELIGION AND POLITICAL PHILOSOPHY; NATURAL LAW.)

4.7 The human being. Themes related to the human being that were prominent in the Renaissance include: (i) the distinction between microcosm and macrocosm (NICHOLAS OF CUSA; PICO DELLA MIRANDOLA, G. §2; PARACELSUS §2; CAMPANELLA, T. §2); (ii) love (FICINO, M. §4; PICO DELLA MIRANDOLA, G. §2); (iii) the ability to shape one's own nature (PICO DELLA MIRANDOLA, G. §3; POMPONAZZI, P. §4).

E.J. ASHWORTH

RENNER, KARL (1870–1950)

Karl Renner was a leading contributor to democratic-socialist legal theory within the Neo-Kantian 'Austro-Marxist' interpretation of socialism that developed in late nineteenth-century Vienna. For Renner and his associates, law is a fundamental and universal institution in any ordered human society. Given the universal necessity of law, the development of socialism may well proceed in an evolutionary rather than a revolutionary manner – and certainly, within the context of Viennese social democracy, it would proceed better by evolution.

A view of Soviet Marxism is expressed by such as E.B. Pashukanis, for whom law in its full bourgeois development is simply the commodity structure reflected, while the juridical subject is an ideological representation of *homo economicus*. Law can neither contribute to nor survive the revolution. By contrast, Renner analyses human society in terms of three universal 'orders': the orders of power, of labour and of goods. Without power-relations, he holds, there can be no order in society; without social labour, there can be no material means for survival; goods for use and consumption are the product of labour and a necessity for social existence. So Marx's analysis of capitalist society can be recast in terms of the subordination of power and labour to property: the order of goods dominates the order of power and the order of labour. Any transformation in fundamental social forms will be expressed through a reshaping of the three orders (see SOCIAL THEORY AND LAW §3).

Though it may seem paradoxical, the institutions of private law, at the level of their formal constitutive and regulative rules, persist in a superficially unchanged way through economic and societal change. The slave-owner, the subsistence farmer, and the joint-stock company of different epochs and modes of production enjoy property rights expressible in substantially unchanging juridical terms. But the institution's function in society will be transformed by shifts in the three orders. This in turn is reflected in development of 'complementary institutions', earlier of private law, later of labour law, welfare law, and planning law. The development through public law of institutions that subordinate the order of goods to those of labour and power is the evolutionary route to socialism.

As well as contributing significantly to legal theory, Renner played a large and important part in Austrian public life, with the obvious exception of the years 1934–45. One of the founding fathers of the Austrian republican constitution in 1919, he was first Chancellor of the Republic in 1919, and remained active in law and legal politics until the troubled thirties. After

1945, he became briefly Chancellor of the restored Republic, and was subsequently its President till his death in 1950. At the end of the twentieth century, his work is in something of an eclipse; but it remains worthy of attention as an attempt to state a democratic-socialist conception of law outside the sphere of the socio-legal ideas discredited in the revolutions of 1989.

See also: LAW, PHILOSOPHY OF

List of works

Renner, K. (1949) *The Institutions of Private Law and their Social Functions*, trans. A. Schwarzschild, ed. with intro. O. Kahn-Freund, London: Routledge & Kegan Paul. (An excellent and clear translation of Renner's *magnum opus*, his only substantial work available in English. Kahn-Freund's introduction, though somewhat dated, remains of real value for the contemporary reader with an English-speaking or common-law background and approach.)

References and further reading

Robson, P. (1977) 'Renner Revisited', in E. Attwooll (ed.), *Perspectives in Jurisprudence*, Glasgow: Glasgow University Press, 221–35. (A critical rereading of Renner's work which looks at it in terms of a socialist perspective in legal theory of the 1970s in the UK.)

Kinsey, R. (1983) 'Karl Renner on Socialist Legality', in D. Sugarman (ed.), *Legality, Ideology and the State*, London: Academic Press, 11–42. (A very clear account of Renner's theory, setting it properly in the context of the debate between Austro-Marxism and Soviet Marxism, and explaining the 'three orders' briefly sketched in the present article.)

RICHARD KINSEY
NEIL MacCORMICK

RENOUVIER, CHARLES BERNARD (1815–1903)

Charles Renouvier is the main representative of French Neo-Kantianism in the nineteenth century. Following Kant, he delimited the conditions for the legitimate exercise of the faculty of knowledge, and denounced the illusions of past metaphysics. Wishing to go further than Kant in this direction, he criticized the notions of substance and of actual infinity. According to him, relation is the basis of all our representations, reality is finite, and certainty rests on liberty. In ethics, he took into consideration, beyond the ideal of duty, the existence of the desires and interests to which history testifies.

Renouvier became known shortly after leaving the École polytechnique through an academic treatise on Cartesianism. His first philosophy, known as 'the philosophy of manuals', is marked by the attempt to reconcile contradictories in being and by republicanism in political thought.

The discovery of contradictions of the actual infinite led to the real system of 'neo-criticism', a doctrine combining phenomenalism, finitism and apriorism. Neo-criticism rests on the principle of relativity: our knowledge is restricted to things as they appear to us, as they enter into our representations, which are subject to the laws that govern our experience a priori. Thus things of which we have no representation do not exist, or are as nothing to us. Agreeing with Auguste COMTE, Renouvier substitutes the investigation into phenomena and laws for the investigation into essences. He formulates the 'principle of number', according to which everything given is numbered, and shows that space, time, matter and movement could not be posited in themselves without implying the contradictory notion of an actual infinity of parts. He undertakes to destabilize metaphysics, which he calls an 'idology', by refuting its illusions or 'idols' (the Absolute, the Substance, the Infinite, pure Oneness, pure Being) and to refine the Kantian system, in which he perceives a remnant of the substantialism of pre-critical philosophy. His criticisms are many: KANT makes the mistake of identifying the real with the unknowable thing in itself, and of relegating liberty to the noumenal sphere; sensibility is not a separate faculty from the understanding; relation is the principle law of representation, which underlies all the other categories (number, position, succession, quality, becoming, causality, finality, personality); the enumeration of these categories is not justifiable, but they must be simply submitted to the verification of each person; finally, the system of antinomies juxtaposes theses of unequal value, as the antitheses are contradictory in themselves, while the theses are simply incomprehensible.

The affirmation of liberty marks the transition from theoretical to practical reason. Following his friend Jules Lequier, Renouvier maintains that liberty is the basis of certainty. The scope of evidence is limited to the perception of actual phenomena. Certainty rests on belief, and belief on liberty. Our affirmations are governed, at bottom, by free acts. Thus the existence of external things, pushed back beyond the limits of knowledge, is rehabilitated in the field of belief. Opposed to the doctrine of 'inevitable progress', Renouvier proposes an 'analytic' philosophy of history, proceeding from complex data to elementary facts, without claiming that these facts could not be combined in another way, and explaining rise and decline in history through the free actions of individuals and societies. He proposes on the other hand a 'science of ethics', comprising a pure morality, with the notions of justice and obligation or the categorical imperative, and an applied morality, understood as a collection of principles inspired by pure morality, but taking into account the interests and desires revealed by experience and history. Renouvier considered that morality, like mathematics, must be based on pure concepts, but by confronting the ideal and the real, the state of peace and the state of war, and in formulating a right distinct from pure rationality and adapted to real humanity, he escapes from formalism, and constructs a morality that deals with concrete questions, such as marriage, property, taxation, universal suffrage and the death penalty.

Renouvier's final philosophy of 'personalism' is characterized by a metaphysics inspired by Leibniz and by new postulates concerning the divine and the origin of evil. Being, that is not in itself, *is* nevertheless, as it is representation for itself; it is composed of monads, defined by the functions of spontaneous activity, perception and appetition. Man, in so far as he is disposed towards a reflective consciousness and freedom, is a person. God is a person also, but the first and creator of the universe, understood in reference to the world and to our consciousness, which constitute the sole data by which we can formulate the idea of him, through acts of induction and generalizations. By admitting the fact of a first cause, Renouvier avoided the thesis, which to him was contradictory, of the infinite regress of phenomena; he recognized that it was a question of a limit for understanding, but notes that the beginning of a series of phenomena due to our will is no less incomprehensible. In this period, Renouvier applied himself to summarizing the conflict of philosophical doctrines in the form of dilemmas, and opposed, on each subject, the 'doctrine of consciousness' to the 'doctrine of things'. The postulate required by practical reason to account for the existence of evil leads to an astonishing cosmogony: primitive humanity, a happy society instituted in a perfect natural order, was taken to collapse due to the effects of self-love and injustice; once the harmony of cosmic forces and human ends was corrupted, the whole was doomed to break up, forming the nebula, which is the probable origin of the present world.

See also: NEO-KANTIANISM §1; PERSONALISM

List of works

Renouvier, C.B. (1842) *Manuel de philosophie moderne* (Manual of Modern Philosophy), Paris: Paulin. (A manual of philosophy, including a close study of Cartesianism.)

—— (1844) *Manuel de philosophie ancienne* (Manual of Ancient Philosophy), Paris: Paulin. (A study of ancient philosophy.)

—— (1848) *Manuel républicain de l'Homme et du Citoyen* (Republican Manual of Man and Citizen), Paris: Pagnerre; ed. J. Thomas, Paris: Colin, 1904. (A work on politics.)

—— (1854) *Essais de critique générale. Premier Essai* (Essays of General Critique. First Essay), Paris: Ladrange; 2nd edn, expanded, *Traité de logique générale et de logique formelle* (Treatise on General and Formal Logic), Paris: Bureau de la Critique philosophique, 1875; reprinted, Paris: Colin, 1912. (Renouvier's theory of knowledge.)

—— (1859) *Essais de critique générale. Deuxième Essai* (Essays of General Critique. Second Essay), Paris: Ladrange; 2nd edition, expanded, *Traité de psychologie rationnelle* (Treatise on Rational Psychology), Paris: Bureau de la Critique philosophique, 1875; reprinted, Paris: Colin, 1912. (Renouvier's theory of faculties of mind, certainty and human freedom.)

—— (1864a) *Essais de critique générale. Troisième Essai* (Essays of General Critique. Third Essay), Paris: Ladrange; 2nd edn, modified, *Les principes de la nature* (The Principles of Nature), Paris: Alcan, 1892; reprinted, Paris: Colin, 1912. (Renouvier's philosophy of nature.)

—— (1864b) *Essais de critique générale. Quatrième Essai* (Essays of General Critique. Fourth Essay), Paris: Ladrange; 2nd edn, modified, *Introduction à la philosophie analytique de l'histoire* (Introduction to the Analytic Philosophy of History), Paris: E. Leroux, 1896. (Renouvier's philosophy of history.)

—— (1869) *Science de la morale* (Science of Ethics), Paris; Ladrange; 2nd edn, Paris: Alcan, 1908. (Renouvier's theory of ethics, a response to fundamental problems in political theory, concerning justice and democracy.)

—— (1876) *Uchronie*, Paris: Bureau de la Critique philosophique; recent edn, Paris: Fayard, 1988. (A fictitious reconstruction of European history.)

—— (1885–6) *Esquisse d'une classification systématique des doctrines philosophiques* (Sketch of a Systematic Classification of Philosophical Doctrines), Paris: Bureau de la Critique philosophique. (A history of philosophy based on logical alternatives, including Renouvier's intellectual autobiography.)

—— (1896–7) *Philosophie analytique de l'histoire* (Analytic Philosophy of History), Paris: E. Leroux. (A history of ideas, religions and philosophical systems.)

Renouvier, C.B. and Prat, L. (1899) *La Nouvelle Monadologie* (The New Monadology), Paris: Colin. (A theory of being along Leibnizian lines, but free of infinitism.)

Renouvier, C.B. (1901a) *Les dilemmes de la métaphysique pure* (The Dilemmas of Pure Metaphysics), Paris: Alcan. (A further history of philosophy based on dilemmas.)

—— (1901b) *Histoire et solution des problèmes métaphysiques* (History and the Solution of Metaphysical Problems), Paris: Alcan. (A history of major philosophical systems.)

—— (1903) *Le Personnalisme* (Personalism), Paris: Alcan. (A theory of creation, of divinity and of the existence of evil.)

Prat, L. (1904) *Les Derniers Entretiens de C. Renouvier* (The Last Conversations of C. Renouvier), Paris: Colin. (Renouvier's last conversation about his theories.)

Renouvier, C.B. (1906) *Critique de la doctrine de Kant* (Critique of Kant's Philosophy), Paris: Alcan. (A critical analysis of the *Critique of Pure Reason*.)

References and further reading

Foucher, L. (1927) *La jeunesse de Renouvier et sa première philosophie (1815–54)* (Renouvier's Youth and His First Philosophy (1815–54)), Paris: Vrin. (A study of the 'philosophie des Manuels'.)

Hamelin, O. (1927) *Le système de Renouvier* (Renouvier's System), ed. P. Mouy, Paris: Vrin. (A series of lectures given at the Sorbonne.)

Séailles, G. (1905) *La philosophie de Renouvier* (Renouvier's Philosophy), Paris: Alcan. (A critical study that has become a reference work.)

Verneaux, R. (1945) *L'idéalisme de Renouvier* (Renouvier's Idealism), Paris: Vrin. (A study of the problem of knowledge in Renouvier's philosophy.)

Translated by Robert Stern

LAURENT FEDI

RENUNCIATION IN INDIAN PHILOSOPHY *see* DUTY AND VIRTUE, INDIAN CONCEPTIONS OF

REPRESENTATION IN ART
see DEPICTION

REPRESENTATION, POLITICAL

Political representation – the designation of a small group of politically active citizens to serve as representatives of the political community as a whole – is a central feature of contemporary states, especially of those that claim to be democratic. But what does it mean to say that one person or one group of people represents a larger group? Representatives are sometimes understood as agents of those they represent, sometimes symbolizing them, sometimes typifying their distinctive qualities or attitudes. Although political representation has something in common with each of these, it has its own special character. The missing idea here may be that the group represented authorizes the representative to make decisions on its behalf. This still leaves open one crucial question, however: how far should political representatives remain answerable to those they represent, and how far should they have the freedom to act on their own judgment?

1 The concept of representation
2 Representation, election and authorization
3 The limits of representation

1 The concept of representation

In what sense or senses (if any) can one person represent another? Apart from the philosophical problems involved, there is also a problem about the political relevance of any of the senses identified. This may be brought out by considering the approach of Anthony Birch. In three books, Birch has analysed the notion of representation and its political application. He identifies three senses of 'representation', in relation to the general issue of how one person may be thought to represent another. The first is manifest in the relationship between a principal and an agent. For example, a person may employ others, such as lawyers and accountants, to act on their behalf with respect to a particular facet of their affairs. The second is when one person (or sometimes an institution or even an item like a flag) may be thought of as representing persons in a symbolic sense. A flag may be seen as a symbol of a nation; or a sports team may be regarded as representing the country for which it competes. Third, a person may represent others by being in some way typical of them. A jury may represent a wider community because it reflects in some way the composition of the general public. Birch, however, holds that none of these three logically distinct senses of what it is to be a 'representative' is a good guide to the meaning of the term applied in a political setting. This consideration reverts to the question of 'political relevance'.

On the face of it, it is not difficult to provide political analogies to Birch's three senses of representation. A person who votes for a candidate in an election might be thought to empower that person to act on their behalf, reproducing the relationship between principal and agent. Just as persons might arrange for their affairs to be dealt with by an accountant or lawyer, so they might pass the expression of their political concerns to someone for whom they vote. Again, symbolic representation seems to have a clear application with respect to heads of state: a monarch or a president may be thought of as representing the nation (or state) of which they are the titular head. Finally, a political representative may have characteristics, such as class, domicile, attitude and policy preference, which are shared with those persons represented.

Nevertheless, Birch maintains that these three senses of representation do not capture the meaning of political representation. He claims that there is a fourth sense of representation, applied to members of a representative assembly, 'because they have been appointed by a particular process of election to occupy that role', which authorizes them to 'exercise certain powers' (1993: 74).

2 Representation, election and authorization

This perspective introduces two important considerations: the relation between representation and election, and the relation between authorization and representation.

Despite the historical importance of arguments about the role of elections in a system of representation, there is no straightforward logical connection between election and representation. This is clear from a review of the three central understandings of 'representation' identified above. In the relation between a principal and an agent, in the usual case, an agent is selected rather than elected. This is because one person is choosing another to pursue their interests or to look after their affairs. The powers that each has as a result of their agreement are primarily a matter of the contract between them. For example, someone might allow a lawyer to pursue a case for them as the lawyer saw fit; but another individual might reserve judgment on the suggestions made by the lawyer and thus make any 'final'

decisions. The amount of discretion enjoyed by an agent varies according to the agreement with the principal.

In political terms, there is a distinction between a representative conceived of as a delegate and a representative conceived less narrowly. Delegates are bound by a prior decision of those for whom they speak; a delegate is to carry out the wishes, already determined, of the principals. The distinction was explored by Edmund BURKE in his famous speech in Bristol in 1774. He contrasted the role of the representative, who uses his best judgment about the issue in hand, with the role of the delegate, who was expected to carry out the instructions of those who had chosen him, whatever the 'delegate's' own opinion. The 'political relevance' of this notion of representation depends on the space for negotiation between principal and agent. While it is true that a representative might be thought of as an agent, nothing much follows about the relative powers of the parties until the relation between them is understood. On the one side, the representative could be seen as having *carte blanche*; on the other, as having no role other than to register the decisions of those represented. Clearly, the understanding of this relation will impinge on how the representative is selected. If the representative is a delegate, then the delegate might be chosen at random. If the representative is expected to use judgment, then a procedure enabling those represented to register their acceptance of that potential for judgment, such as election, might seem more appropriate. Some specifications of the principal–agent relation will support the appropriateness of election; others will not.

Symbolic representation is connected with elections in an even more contingent manner. Many political systems have an elected head of state, but these systems vary widely in the amount of executive power which that head enjoys. On the other hand, many political systems have non-elected heads of state: for example, a hereditary monarch. Whatever powers are enjoyed, and irrespective of election, the head of state's claim to represent the nation as a whole, symbolically, can be advanced.

The last notion of representation – as related to typicality – is obviously the one which allows the greatest space for political argument; chiefly, disputes about the political relevance of the representative's various characteristics, on the one side, and the political relevance of various distinctions between those represented on the other. For example, recent feminist arguments have advocated the importance of quotas to ensure that allegedly relevant distinctions are properly reproduced in the representative body. The contingency of the connection between election and representation is also clear: in any election, the individual voter may aim not to support a candidate who possesses similar characteristics to the elector.

3 The limits of representation

The question arises, therefore, as to whether Birch is correct in claiming that none of the three understandings of representation helps in giving meaning to political representation. As we have seen, it is possible to produce political examples of the three general interpretations; on the other hand, there are limits as to how far such examples illuminate the special circumstances of politics. Birch's preferred solution is to rely on the idea that electors authorize their representatives to exercise particular powers. This is to tie the theory of representation to a particular theory of representative democracy, which has been historically contested (see DEMOCRACY).

The concept of authorization can indeed illuminate some difficulties. For example, the election of a pope may be seen as authorizing his role in the apostolic succession, thereby legitimizing his claim to the papacy. There is nevertheless considerable scope for political argument about the nature of authorization: when, and in what circumstances, may it be withdrawn? Which voting system is best equipped to sustain claims that those who are successful have been authorized (or have a mandate)? Representative government has been promoted as a political system solving many problems: for James Mill, that of harnessing the interests of the governed to those of the decision makers; for J.S. Mill (1861), that of balancing expertise with participation; for the Founding Fathers of the American Republic, that of balancing virtue with improving popular sentiment, or perhaps, again, restraining power. ROUSSEAU (§§2–3) objected to political representation because the general will of the people (which was the proper source of legislation) could not be represented. Whatever the (no doubt considerable) merits of representative government, there are likely to be tensions between any government's claim to representativeness and the policy preferences of those they claim to represent.

References and further reading

* Birch, A.H. (1972) *Representation*, London: Macmillan. (A conceptual exploration rooted in the writings of specific authors.)

* —— (1993) *Concepts and Theories of Modern Democracy*, London: Routledge. (Relates representative government to the development of political

science; especially useful for those without a background in political science.)

* Burke, E. (1774) 'Speech at the Conclusion of the Poll, Bristol, 1774', vol. III, *The Works of Edmund Burke*, ed. F. Lawrence and W. King, London, 16 vols, 1815–27. (Eloquent argument defending the view that elected representatives should use their own judgment, rather than merely transmit the opinions of the represented.)

Dunn, J. (ed.) (1993) *Democracy – The Unfinished Journey 508 BC to AD 1993*, corrected edn, Cambridge: Cambridge University Press. (An excellent collection of essays with enormous historical sweep)

Lively, J. and Lively, A. (eds) (1994) *Democracy in Britain: A Reader*, Oxford: Blackwell and The British Council. (An anthology of debate, from both literary and political sources, about the development of representative institutions in the UK.)

* Mill, J.S. (1861) *Considerations of Representative Government*, London: Dent, 1910. (Classic statement of the benefits of representative government when it combines expertise with participation.)

Phillips, A. (1995) *The Politics of Presence*, Oxford: Clarendon Press. (Most recent writing of an author who has been concerned with the relationship between democracy and feminism.)

Phillips Griffiths, A. (1960) 'How Can One Person Represent Another?', *The Aristotelian Society*, supplementary volume 34: 187–208. (A philosophical enquiry into the question posed.)

Pitkin, H. (1967) *The Concept of Representation*, Berkeley and Los Angeles, CA: University of California Press. (Another exploration of ideas about representation drawn from a criticism of theorizing presented by important writers in the historical canon.)

ANDREW REEVE

REPROBATION

Reprobation is an eternal decision by God that results in everlasting death and punishment for some persons. The doctrine of reprobation typically takes one of three forms: (1) that God from eternity decreed to elect some without regard to faith or works and to reprobate others without regard to sin or unbelief, both to display his glory and for reasons we do not know (sometimes called double predestination); (2) that God from eternity decreed to elect some, despite their sin, and to abandon the rest, with the cause of their reprobation being sin and unbelief; or (3) that God from eternity elected those he foreknew would believe in Christ and reprobated those he foreknew would persist in sin and unbelief.

Reprobation doctrine was developed by Augustine and appears in the theology of Thomas Aquinas, Martin Luther and John Calvin, who were deeply indebted to Augustine's thought. Although some Lutheran and Roman Catholic theologians have defended reprobation doctrine since the sixteenth century, Reformed theologians have stressed it and made it the occasion of controversy.

1 **Predestination, election and reprobation**
2 **Augustine and the Middle Ages**
3 **The Reformation and post-Reformation period**
4 **The twentieth century**

1 Predestination, election and reprobation

Reprobation is closely linked to election and predestination. Election is an eternal divine decision to choose some people to be the recipients of special saving grace. Sometimes the term predestination is synonymous with election, and sometimes it encompasses both election and reprobation.

Since the Middle Ages, many theologians have identified two aspects of reprobation. Negative reprobation, or preterition, is God's decision to 'pass by', or withhold saving grace from, certain individuals, thereby permitting them to sin, to reject the gospel, and to undergo eternal punishment for their sin and unbelief. Positive reprobation is the divine decision or will to punish eternally those who sin and do not receive saving grace.

The doctrine of reprobation is rooted in the Bible's statements that God loved Jacob and hated Esau 'even before they had been born or had done anything good or bad' (Malachi 1: 2–3; Romans 9: 10–13), that God hardened Pharaoh's heart (Exodus 4: 21, 7: 3, 9: 12, 10: 27, 11: 10; Romans 9: 14–18), and that God, who is like a potter working with clay, has the right to make some individuals for destruction in order to demonstrate his wrath, power and glory (Romans 9: 19–24). The most troublesome biblical text for reprobation doctrine is the statement that God 'desires everyone to be saved and to come to knowledge of the truth' (1 Timothy 2: 4).

2 Augustine and the Middle Ages

In opposition to Pelagian teachings that God gives grace to some and punishes others according to their merits, Augustine of Hippo affirmed the existence of an eternal divine decision, not based on merit, to give faith and eternal life to some but not to others (see

AUGUSTINE §§6, 10, 13). Predestination is God's preparation of kindnesses that certainly deliver the elect, while the rest are denied the means of believing and left to God's righteous judgment upon their sin.

Recognizing that speaking of some who are foreordained to damnation might make God seem unjust, Augustine argued that reprobation is deserved, while election in Christ occurs by grace, not by merit. Even if no human being had been redeemed, God's justice would have been untarnished. Moreover, by showing what the whole race deserved, the everlasting punishment of the reprobate impresses upon the elect the benefits they have received by grace. Basing his argument on the parable of the labourers in the vineyard (Matthew 20: 1–16), Augustine said that God is not unjust if he is just towards some and benevolent towards others. Still, God's ways are past finding out, and Augustine cannot say why God mercifully chooses one person and abandons another in his justice even though both could have been saved if God had so willed it. Nevertheless, the will of the omnipotent God is never evil, and is never defeated, 'because even when it inflicts evil it is just, and what is just is certainly not evil' (*Enchiridion*, 102). By interpreting the biblical statement that God desires all people to be saved to mean that God desires every *sort* of person to be saved, Augustine avoided saying that 'the omnipotent God has willed anything to be done which was not done' (*Enchiridion*, 103).

In the ninth century, Gottschalk of Orbais (*c*.804–69), who defended double predestination (the doctrine that God from eternity decreed to elect some without regard to faith or works and to reprobate others without regard to sin or unbelief), was condemned by the council of Mainz (848) and by the first and second councils of Quiercy (849 and 853), which held that God predestines certain individuals to life only. The decisions of these councils were repudiated by the council of Valence (855), which upheld the notion of double predestination.

Thomas Aquinas said that God predestines some to eternal life through his providence, and reprobates others by *permitting* them to fall into sin and suffer its consequence. Reprobation is more than simply knowing that a person will sin and not reach eternal life; it also includes God's *will* 'to permit a person to fall into sin, and to impose the punishment of damnation on account of that sin' (*Summa theologiae* Ia, q.23, a.3). So predestination (or election) causes both saving grace and eternal salvation, whereas reprobation causes abandonment by God and future eternal punishment, but not sin in the present life. Still, God's will alone determines which individuals are elect and which are reprobate.

Aquinas responded to the objection that God is

unjust because he treats equals unequally, electing some and reprobating others. First, God can justly deny something to someone to whom it is not owed. Since all are equally undeserving of salvation, God is free to give grace to one person but not to another. Second, God elects some and reprobates others, not on the basis of foreknowing their good and evil actions, but to display his goodness, which is one and undivided in himself, but must be manifested in many ways in creatures. God manifests his goodness by mercifully sparing the elect and justly punishing the reprobate.

Rejecting Aquinas' position, Henry of Ghent argued that God elects those he foreknows will accept grace freely and reprobates those he foreknows will not. John Duns Scotus, drawing his doctrine of election from Aquinas and his doctrine of reprobation from Henry of Ghent, held that God eternally wills salvation for the elect apart from divine foreknowledge, but eternally wills damnation for the reprobate only on the basis of foreseeing their sin. WILLIAM OF OCKHAM (§10) came close to Henry of Ghent's view of reprobation, although his view that there are no standards of justice independent of God's policies led him to hold that God's free choice determined that obedience leads to eternal life while ultimate and unrepentant sinning results in eternal punishment.

Thomas BRADWARDINE (§3) revived the notion of double predestination, saying that reprobation is a sovereign act of God's will and is not based on foreknowledge of sin. In response to the objection that it would be unjust for God to predestine anyone to damnation apart from foreknown guilt, Bradwardine argued both that the reprobate serve the purpose of leading the elect to flee from sin and choose the good and that, since God's will alone is the righteous law for all creation, no creaturely lump of clay can dispute the divine potter's actions.

3 The Reformation and post-Reformation period

Martin LUTHER taught that God predestines some individuals to salvation and others to damnation. In his treatise *The Bondage of the Will*, Luther based his view on statements in Romans 9 that God loved Jacob and hated Esau prior to their birth and apart from any merits or demerits of their free actions, and also that the clay has no right to question the actions of the potter. He attacked human reason for holding that God, in order to qualify as good, 'may damn none but those who in our judgment have deserved it'. Even if God should send all people to perdition, says Luther, he is nevertheless good. Still, God's hardening or working evil in people does not involve 'creating evil in us from scratch' ([1525] 1972: 178). Rather, God

allows a person's evil will to proceed according to its own bent and confronts the person with words and actions with which this evil bent will clash. Departing from Luther's view of unconditional reprobation, the Lutheran Formula of Concord (1577) says that predestination causes the salvation of the elect, whereas the non-elect perish because of their own sinfulness, not because of God's will or foreordination.

John CALVIN (§4) held that God, on the basis of his will alone and not on the basis of foreknown holiness or sinfulness, foreordains eternal life for some and eternal damnation for others. God's sovereign election of some and reprobation of others reveals his glory by showing his justice as well as by impressing upon the elect God's infinite mercy to them.

The Roman Catholic Council of Trent (1545–63) responded to Protestants' renewed emphasis on election and reprobation by anathematizing anyone who says that the grace of justification extends only to those who are predestined to life and that others who are called do not receive grace because they are by divine power predestined to evil.

In the seventeenth century, a dispute arose in the Reformed churches, sparked by Jacob Arminius (1559–1609) and his followers, the Remonstrants. Arguing against the view of Calvin and others that God reprobates without giving any consideration to sin and unbelief, the Remonstrants held that God elects those he foreknows will respond to grace and reprobates those he foreknows to be unrepentant unbelievers. In response, the Reformed Synod of Dort (1618–19) declared that God's eternal decision is the reason he softens the hearts of some, giving them the gift of faith, and leaves others 'in their wickedness and hardness of heart' (*Canons*, I, art. 6). Election to salvation is based not on foreseen faith, but exclusively in God's good pleasure in adopting as his own certain persons 'from among the common mass of sinners' (*Canons*, I, arts 9–10). Reprobation, according to Dort, is God's free and irreproachable decision not to grant 'saving faith and the grace of conversion' to some, but rather to leave them in the misery into which, 'by their own fault, they have plunged themselves'; and finally to condemn and eternally punish them for their sin and unbelief 'in order to display his justice' (*Canons*, I, art. 15). By reflecting the medieval distinction between negative and positive reprobation, Dort followed a more moderate line than Calvin on the doctrine of reprobation. Dort defended God's justice by arguing that God would have done no one an injustice if he had condemned the entire human race on account of their sin and also by pointing out, on the basis of Romans 9: 20, that we human beings have no place finding fault with God.

4 The twentieth century

Karl Barth emphasized and recast the doctrines of election and reprobation. For Barth, Jesus Christ is both the elect one in whom all humanity is elect and the reprobate or rejected one. Arguing that morality disallows ascribing to God a justice that would lead to the reprobation or rejection of individuals, Barth said that God in love from eternity transfers to Jesus Christ his rejection of and wrath against all humanity. So in Jesus Christ, the rejected one who suffers the wrath of God, we see that rejection means being cast out from the presence of God and suffering eternal death.

The Reformed theologian Louis Berkhof (1874–1957) and the Thomist Réginald Garrigou-Lagrange held kindred views regarding reprobation. Both distinguished preterition, or negative reprobation, and condemnation, or positive reprobation, arguing that positive reprobation is based on foreseen sin, while negative reprobation is not. Although both held that there is no reason other than God's will for God's decision to predestine some to salvation and to pass by others, Garrigou-Lagrange added that the motive for negative reprobation is God's will to manifest his goodness by his justice as well as by his mercy, while Berkhof said that God alone knows his reason for preterition.

See also: ETERNITY; GRACE; HEAVEN; HELL; JUSTIFICATION, RELIGIOUS; OMNISCIENCE §§3–4; PREDESTINATION; PROVIDENCE; SALVATION

References and further reading

Adams, M.M. (1987) *William Ockham*, Notre Dame, IN: University of Notre Dame Press, 2 vols. (Contains a very good chapter on election and reprobation in thirteenth- and fourteenth-century theology.)

Aquinas, T. (1256–9) *The Disputed Questions on Truth*, trans. R.W. Mulligan, Chicago, IL: Henry Regnery, 1952. (An early treatise by Aquinas that discusses reprobation.)

* —— (1266–73) *Summa theologica*, trans. Fathers of the English Dominican Province, New York: Benziger, 1948. (Includes a classic statement of Aquinas' position on predestination and reprobation.)

* Augustine (*c.*421) *Enchiridion*, in P. Schaff (ed.) *Nicene and Post-Nicene Fathers of the Christian Church*, series 1, 1886–9; reprint, Grand Rapids, MI: Eerdmans, 1978. (Includes Augustine's anti-Pelagian works.)

Barth, K. (1956–77) *Church Dogmatics*, ed. G.W. Bromiley and T.F. Torrance, Edinburgh: T. & T. Clark. (Election and reprobation are dealt with in volume 2, part 2.)

Berkhof, L. (1939) *Systematic Theology*, Grand Rapids, MI: Eerdmans, 4th edn. (Includes a classic Reformed definition and defence of the doctrine of reprobation.)

* *The Book of Concord: The Confessions of the Evangelical Lutheran Church* (1580), trans. and ed. T.G. Tappert, Philadelphia, PA: Fortress Press, 1959. (Includes the Formula of Concord, discussed in §3.)

Bradwardine, T. (*c.*1344) *The Cause of God Against the Pelagians*, in H. Oberman (trans. and ed.) *Forerunners of the Reformation: The Shape of Late Medieval Thought Illustrated by Key Documents*, 1966; reprint, Philadelphia, PA: Fortress, 1981. (An important document by Bradwardine on predestination and reprobation.)

Calvin, J. (1552) *Concerning the Eternal Predestination of God*, trans. and ed. J.K.S. Reid, London: James Clarke & Co, 1961. (An important treatise by Calvin on election and reprobation.)

—— (1559) *Institutes of the Christian Religion*, The Library of Christian Classics, ed. J.T. McNeill, trans. F.L. Battles, Philadelphia, PA: Westminster, 1960. (A summary of Calvin's theology, including his views on reprobation.)

Garrigou-Lagrange, R. (1939) *Predestination*, trans. B. Rose, St Louis, MO: Herder. (Includes a summary of Roman Catholic teaching on, and a restatement of, the doctrine of reprobation.)

Klooster, F.H. (1984) *Calvin's Doctrine of Predestination*, Grand Rapids, MI: Baker, 2nd edn. (Includes a good summary of Calvin's views on reprobation.)

* Luther, M. (1525) *The Bondage of the Will*, in P.S. Watson (ed.), *Luther's Works*, vol. 33, general eds J. Pelikan and H.T. Lehmann, St Louis, MO: Concordia and Philadelphia, PA: Fortress, 1972. (Contains Luther's most extensive comments on reprobation.)

Muller, R.A. (1986) *Christ and the Decree: Christology and Predestination in Reformed Theology from Calvin to Perkins*, Durham, NC: Labyrinth Press. (An important study of predestination and reprobation in sixteenth-century Reformed theology.)

* Schaff, P. (ed.) (1931) *The Creeds of Christendom*, revised D. Schaff, 6th edn; reprint, Grand Rapids, MI: Baker, 1983. (Contains the Canons and Decrees of the Council of Trent, the summary Epitome of the Lutheran Formula of Concord, and the Canons of the Synod of Dort.)

Sinnema, D.W. (1985) *The Issue of Reprobation at the Synod of Dort (1618–1619) in Light of the History of This Doctrine*, PhD dissertation, Toronto, Ont.:

University of St Michael's College. (A thorough study of the history of the doctrine of reprobation, with an emphasis on Reformed theology.)

William of Ockham (*c.*1320–3) *Predestination, God's Foreknowledge, and Future Contingents,* trans. and ed. M.M. Adams and N. Kretzmann, Indianapolis, IN: Hackett. (Both the introduction and the translated material deal with reprobation.)

RONALD J. FEENSTRA

REPRODUCTION AND ETHICS

The first reproductive issue debated extensively by philosophers was abortion. Debates about its morality were, and still are, dominated by the issue of the moral status of the foetus, on which a wide variety of views has been defended. The most 'conservative' view is usually associated with very restrictive abortion policies, inconsistent with 'a woman's right to choose' (though the connection has been challenged by Judith Jarvis Thomson). However, all but the most conservative find it hard to ground prevailing moral intuitions concerning the newer issue of using human embryos for research purposes. Embryos, and even gametes, also assume importance in the context of methods for overcoming infertility (artificial insemination by donor (AID), egg and embryo donation involving in vitro fertilization (IVF), surrogacy) where issues about rights and ownership may arise. Considerations of 'the welfare of the child', often used to settle surrogacy disputes, also bear on questions of what should, or may, be done to avoid bringing a child with a genetic abnormality into the world. Current philosophical literature on reproductive issues is largely limited to a vocabulary of rights and little attention is paid to the social and familial contexts in which reproductive decisions are usually made

1 The status of the foetus
2 Embryonic and foetal research
3 The right over one's own body
4 Rights and ownership
5 Welfare considerations
6 Morality, legislation and rights

1 The status of the foetus

A wide range of views on the moral status of the foetus, and whether it is the sort of thing that may, or may not, be killed has been defended. (1) According to the 'conservative' position, the foetus has, from the moment of conception, the same moral status as an adult human being. (2) At the other, 'liberal', extreme, the foetus is claimed to be nothing but a collection of cells, part of the pregnant woman's body, like her appendix, until the moment of birth. Oddly enough, these diametrically opposed views share two assumptions; both assume that the moral status of the foetus remains unchanged from conception to birth and both assume that the foetus is, morally speaking, like something else – an adult or an appendix. Three other views reject at least one of these assumptions. (3) A 'moderate' view claims that the moral status changes at some determinate 'cut off point' such as motility or viability. (4) According to the 'gradualist' view, the moral status changes gradually, increasing as the foetus develops. (5) According to the 'potentiality' view, the foetus has a unique moral status, being quite unlike anything else, that of a potential human being, from the moment of conception. Minor variations on these views exist, beyond the scope of this entry; however, a well-known sixth must be mentioned. (6) According to Michael Tooley and his followers, whatever the foetus is, it is not a person, that is, does not have a right to life; and the same is true of infants (see RIGHTS; MORAL STANDING §3).

Each of these views has been not only defended, but contested. None has an argument to establish what the moral status of the foetus is that its opponents regard as conclusive and each has difficulties concerning its *prima facie* consequences, which may be seized upon by opponents as unacceptable. So, for example, the potentiality view's 'difficulty' is that it hardly counts as yielding any consequences at all. The conservative view appears to yield the consequence that if you can save only a baby or a two-day-old embryo in vitro from certain death, you are faced with just the same moral dilemma as when you can save only one of two babies in cradles. Tooley's view, notoriously, licenses infanticide, and so on. The difficulties become even more acute when we come to consider the treatment of foetuses not *in utero*.

Embryonic and foetal research

The debate about the status of the foetus assumed prominence in the days when abortion came to be seen as an issue of women's rights, and this was well before we had acquired the technique of fertilizing extracted ova in vitro, or discovered that foetal brain tissue might help adult human beings suffering from Parkinson's disease, or started on the 'genome project' (see GENETICS AND ETHICS §1). The gradualist or moderate positions were, perhaps, gaining ground, as the views that underpinned the legislation governing abortion in many Western countries, wherein increasingly 'serious' reasons for abortion are required as the pregnancy develops but abortion 'on demand' is allowed in the first trimester, until the new questions about the treatment of first-trimester-age foetuses (or embryos) hit the headlines, and people started manifesting qualms. In fact, research on quite well-developed – even viable – foetuses had been going on, but few people knew about it, and, in many countries, there was no legislation that covered it. Now there is, but the substantial restrictions laid down seem to fit badly with the policies which are fairly 'liberal' about first trimester abortions. If the moral status of a ten-week-old foetus is so minimal that abortion 'on demand' is morally permissible, why do we insist on laws restricting the use of even two- or three-day-old embryos for research? In particular, why is it always assumed (as it is) that embryos may only be used as a last resort (when, that is, no other animals can be used to further the research), a restriction that those concerned about our exploitation of other animals rightly point out calls for some justification (see ANIMALS AND ETHICS).

In fact, the debates about these issues tend to dodge questions about morality and centre instead around legislation where considerations of the general consequences of allowing or forbidding certain practices become obviously relevant. Hence *prima facie* inconsistent positions which combine liberal abortion legislation with very restrictive legislation on the use of embryos and foetuses may be defended on the grounds that, as things are at the moment, liberal abortion legislation is a necessary evil, the only available way of avoiding desperate women resorting to backstreet abortionists or suffering the emotional and economic hardship of having babies they did not want and could not afford. However, this is hardly a defence that conservatives about the moral status of the foetus can employ; nor does it tend to recommend itself to those who defend 'a woman's right to choose'.

3   The right over one's own body

The prevailing emphasis on the status of the foetus has an odd effect; one could, if ignorant of the facts of human reproduction, read hundreds of articles written on abortion and be left wondering what they were. Those who maintain that, at least in the early stages, the foetus is just a growth in the woman's body, fail to mention the fact that it is a growth like no other, namely a growth that, uniquely, results from the cells of two human beings, and is a growth that will usually become a baby, someone's child, if allowed to develop. Those who hold the 'conservative' or 'potential' view emphasize the fact that a fertilized ovum naturally develops into a baby; some mention the fact that an ovum is fertilized by a male cell and

that this usually happens as a result of sexual intercourse, but remarkably few mention the fact that the nine-month development into a baby standardly – and arduously – takes place in a woman's body. If one did not know better, one might reasonably infer that parthenogenesis was common and that many of the results of sexual intercourse were raised in incubators as in Aldous Huxley's *Brave New World*.

Conservatives about not only the status of the foetus, but also abortion do not deny that we all have some sort of right over our own bodies; they merely claim that it is restricted, or outweighed, by the foetus' right to life. This initially plausible move has been challenged, however, in a deservedly famous article by Judith Jarvis Thomson (1971), which, despite its age, still stands almost alone in its attempt to take account of what is special about abortion, namely that it is the termination of a (human) pregnancy. A human pregnancy, regardless of one's views about the status of the foetus, is a condition of a human body, and usually results from sexual inter-course, voluntary or involuntary, in the hope, or not, of conceiving. Thomson daringly allows the conser-vatives their premise about the moral status of the foetus and argues that, even if this is granted, the impermissibility of abortion does not follow in many cases. Her argument depends on the claim that the right to life does not, as such, include the right to the use of another person's body to survive. If you can survive only by being connected to my circulatory system for nine months, then my right to decide what happens to my body allows me not only to refuse and let you die, but, moreover, to disconnect us and thereby kill you if I have not granted you the right to use my body but have been kidnapped and connected up to you while unconscious.

The wild unlikelihood of the latter scenario reflects Thomson's heroic attempt to describe something that is not a pregnancy but is like at least unintended pregnancies in the (assumed) relevant respects, namely that one person (the foetus, granting the conservative view) needs the use of another person's body to survive, while the second person has not done anything that can be construed as giving them the right to use it. The strained nature of Thomson's analogies has attracted much criticism, but few of her critics have paused to reflect that any analogies to pregnancy are bound to be strained because there simply is not any other condition of the human body remotely like it.

Her article manages to take cognizance of remark-ably many of the unique features of pregnancy but still leaves several out. When we turn from the issue of abortion to those of surrogacy, artificial insemination by donor (AID) and in vitro fertilization (IVF), the fact that a fertilized ovum has resulted from the cells of two human beings, a man and a woman, and the fact that it would become a baby, someone's child, if enabled and allowed to develop *in utero*, assume unavoidable prominence. Moreover, questions about what is involved in 'the right to decide what happens to my body' and, more generally, what counts as 'mine', become increasingly problematic.

4 Rights and ownership

AID, IVF and surrogacy, as moral and political issues, revolve around those people who very much want to have a child; hence the question of whether the foetus has the moral status of something that may be killed tends to fade into the background, and passionate feelings about parenthood, families and 'my (our) child' come to the foreground. Those who espouse the conservative view on the status of the foetus do indeed object to the current practice of IVF on the ground that it tends to involve producing 'spare' embryos, which must either be allowed to die or be frozen and stored; but the various methods of alleviating infertility involve many further problems.

Feminists have found themselves divided over what to say about surrogacy, inclined, on the one hand, to defend the view that a woman's right to decide what happens to her body surely extends to deciding whether or not to act as a surrogate mother but inclined, on the other, to liken surrogacy to female prostitution, regarding both as practices in which the woman's body is *used* in an exploitative and degrading manner, even if she has, in some sense, freely consented.

Anyone who is, for whatever reason, inclined to defend at least some forms of surrogacy, has to consider what should be done when the agreement between the parties concerned breaks down – when, say, the surrogate mother changes her mind, and wants to keep the child, or the commissioning couple change theirs and do not want to take it. Some aim to settle these unhappy questions by arguing that surrogacy is a form of 'pre-natal adoption', whereby the commissioning couple acquire parental rights (and duties) to the embryo as soon as fertilization takes place; the surrogate mother cannot abort it, nor claim it, nor can the commissioning couple refuse to take it without this counting as their immorally abandoning it. Others aim to settle them by considering who owned the sperm and ovum involved initially, who can be said to have 'donated' or given up their rights to these gametes and who has retained them, whether the surrogate mother acquires a right to the baby by (in a new sense of the phrase) 'mixing her labour with it', and hence who 'owns' the baby, as

though gametes, foetuses and children were like any other possessions. But, like the two most extreme positions on the moral status of the foetus, each of these approaches takes cognizance of only some of the facts relevant to human reproduction, ignoring those emphasized by the other side and leaving some out entirely.

5 Welfare considerations

What about, in particular, 'the welfare of the child', the consideration which, in practice, has preeminently been appealed to in resolving disputes when surrogacy agreements have broken down? This undoubtedly goes beyond the debates about the various adults' rights but it is not, thereby, a consideration independent of the facts that are appealed to in those debates. For, it may be said, it is in the best interests of any child not only to be wanted and loved by two adults, but also for its mother's love to spring from the natural bond that exists between the child and the mother who carries it and gives birth to it and, even further, for it to have the opportunity to know, and, we hope, love, its genetic parents. But these considerations resolve a surrogacy-agreement breakdown adequately (if that) only in the particular case in which the surrogate child is the genetic offspring of the surrogate mother and her partner and they decide mutually they want to keep the child. Otherwise, the decision has to be over the circumstances in which the child will be least disadvantaged.

That surrogacy and, indeed, AID, egg and embryo donation are all methods of overcoming infertility that, arguably, lead to the production of a disadvantaged child probably forms the strongest basis for those who are morally opposed to them all. Common claims that they are all unnatural, or introduce a third party into what should be 'the exclusive relationship between wife and husband', thus undermining the family, tend to fall foul of the obvious counter that few things are more 'natural', or more affirmative of the value of family life, than a couple's desire to have a child. But no-one thinks that this natural, proper, and in some cases, quite consuming, desire can, morally, be satisfied by any means. You cannot steal a child in order to have one, and, it may be said, you cannot set about bringing a disadvantaged child into the world in order to have one either.

The extent to which different methods of overcoming infertility produce, or would produce, a disadvantaged child is usually thought to vary. As I write, many people in Britain have said that it would be a terrible thing for a child to know that its 'mother' was an aborted foetus and, on those grounds, supported legislation designed to forbid any future use of the ova already present in female foetuses. It is important to remember in cases such as these that the very existence of the child whose welfare would be at stake depends on the decision taken. The choice here, for example, is not between existence with a foetus as mother and existence without, but between existence with a foetus as mother and nonexistence. However, egg donation by mature women, embryo donation and AID, when uncomplicated by surrogacy, often pass unquestioned – though the recent discovery that an unscrupulous doctor at an infertility clinic in America was the genetic father of hundreds of children, having used his own sperm to fertilize all his patients, gave some people pause for thought.

Considerations of what sort of life a child produced in certain circumstances will have may also form the basis of adverse moral judgments of people's self-ishness and irresponsibility. Many condemned a fifty-nine-year-old woman who chose to have a child by IVF (though the same judgment is rarely passed on even older men who father children), and some insist that people carrying certain genes should get them-selves sterilized and resign themselves to childlessness or adoption. It is sometimes even said that it is selfish and irresponsible of pregnant women to reject screening for genetic abnormality or to reject abortion when it is identified; but whether this is so surely depends on their reasons for the rejections. If they think, for instance, that the genetic abnormality does not prevent one's life being a good one (perhaps because they or their partner have it themselves), or if they think that abortion, at least in their circum-stances, is wrong, then they have a good reason for not trying to 'maximize happiness' on this occasion (see UTILITARIANISM).

6 Morality, legislation and rights

At this point we return to the abortion debate, but now under a new aspect and in a way that brings questions about infanticide more clearly to the fore. The most fundamental objection to the conservative position on the status of the foetus is that it puts abortion, at any stage, on a par with infanticide, and, in the usual context of the abortion debate, infanticide equals murder; on the conservative view, abortion in the case of rape is not one whit more justifiable than murdering a child conceived through rape, and arguably less justifiable or excusable (given the innocence of the child) than the woman's murdering the rapist. But in the context of euthanasia, killing an infant, or allowing it to die, without its consent, may well not be counted as murder, even on a conservative view; not because, quite generally, infants fail to be

'persons' with a right to life, who can thereby be killed for any old reason (as Tooley suggests), but because, when a human being is by virtue of extreme youth (or perhaps extreme impairment) incapable of autonomy, 'paternalistic' considerations of their welfare form, quite properly, the determining factor (see LIFE AND DEATH).

So even on the conservative view on the status of the foetus, abortion in the form of 'foetal euthanasia' may be justified, as infant euthanasia may be; and on any view that ranks the foetus as somehow not quite the same as a born baby, the possibilities of justification increase. But a new twist has been added; 'euthanasia' has its motivation built in, since it is done for the sake of the one who dies. Morally speaking, there is all the difference in the world between seeking an abortion because one wants a 'designer baby', and seeking it because one thinks it is wrong to bring a disadvantaged child into the world, just as there is a difference between my instructing the doctors to take my mother off life support for her sake, and my doing it to save myself the medical bills. But, given that people can and will lie about their motives, there is no way in which legislation can effectively permit the well-motivated cases but prohibit the callous ones.

Much of the literature devoted to reproductive ethics in fact vacillates between discussing morality and legislation, frequently leaving it unclear which is at issue. This is, no doubt, in part the result of the current tendency to talk almost exclusively in terms of rights, for we tend to think of (moral) rights as things that should be protected by good legislation. But we too readily forget that, particularly within families, it may be morally quite wrong for me to exercise a right that I certainly have and, more generally, that there is much opportunity within families for acting morally well or ill where questions of rights, and even duties, do not arise. Most reproductive decisions are made by couples who love each other, who discuss what 'their' decision will be; the discussion is often extended to other members of the family who will say 'we' decided; most of the couples want to be good parents, and morally good people. This is, indeed, how things should mostly be, but none of it can be brought about by legislation, and all of it is almost universally ignored in the current literature (see FAMILY, ETHICS AND THE §5).

See also: APPLIED ETHICS; BIOETHICS; NURSING ETHICS

References and further reading

Alpern, K.D. (1992) *The Ethics of Reproductive Technology*, Oxford: Oxford University Press. (A wide range of readings, not exclusively modern, with useful case studies.)

Dyson, A. and Harris, J. (1991) *Experiments on Embryos*, London: Routledge. (Articles by lawyers, scientists and theologians as well as philosophers; more appropriate for a British audience than a North American one.)

Feinberg, J. (1984) *The Problem of Abortion*, Belmont, CA: Wadsworth, 2nd edn. (Still the most comprehensive collection of articles on the topic, including Judith Jarvis Thomson's and Michael Tooley's, with a helpful introduction.)

O'Neill, O. and Ruddick, W. (1979) *Having Children, Philosophical and Legal Reflections on Parenthood*, New York: Oxford University Press. (Too early to contain any articles specifically concerned with surrogacy, but still the best collection of readings on parenthood.)

* Thomson J.J. (1971) 'Defense of Abortion', *Philosophy and Public Affairs* 1. (Despite its age, still the most original article on abortion available.)

ROSALIND HURSTHOUSE

REPUBLICANISM

Significant divisions exist in all societies and communities of any size. The expression of these divisions in politics takes many forms, one of them republican. The hallmark of republican politics is the subordination of different interests to the common weal, or what is in the interest of all citizens. To ensure this outcome, government in a republic can never be the exclusive preserve of one interest or social order; it must always be controlled jointly by representatives of all major groups in a society. The degree of control exercised by representatives of different social elements may not be equal, and different styles of government are compatible with republican objectives. However, all republican governments involve power-sharing in some way. Even in a democratic republic political majorities must share power with minorities for the common good to be realized.

Maintaining an appropriate balance of political power is the chief problem of republicans. One or another faction may obtain control of government and use it to further its own interests, instead of the common weal. To prevent this republicans have developed a variety of strategies. Some rely on constitutional 'checks and balances' to cure the mischief of factionalism. Others seek to minimize factionalization itself by regulating the causes of faction – for example, the distribution of land and other forms of property. Still

others promote civic religions in order to bind diverse people together. All these methods accept the inevitability of conflicting interests, and see the need to accommodate them politically. Hence, civic life is at the heart of republicanism.

1 **Political diversity of republicans**
2 **Mixed forms of government**
3 **Republicanism and majoritarianism**
4 **Maintaining the republic**

1 Political diversity of republicans

Republicanism is a remarkably protean sentiment. It embraces the most famous republic of all, Plato's *politeia*, wherein philosophers rule. It includes Cicero's Rome under Numa and Servius Tullius, statesmen of the highest rank. It encompasses Machiavelli's Florence under the financial dominance of the Medici family. Republicanism includes Harrington's Oceana, and the representative government of Thomas Paine, wherein the common sense of ordinary people holds sway. It even includes Jean-Jacques Rousseau's vision of a polity ruled by the *volonté générale*, or general will, not to mention most contemporary regimes.

In terms of their politics, then, republicans are a diverse lot: they stand to the left of absolutism, to the right of majoritarianism, and at every point between these extremes. The political diversity of republicans arises from different conceptions of the public good, the object of republicans in all times and places. Plato's *politeia* was meant to be good for all residents of the city, not just for those who ruled (see PLATO §14). For that reason Cicero called it *res publica*, a Latin term referring to 'the public affair'. Cicero's own version of the just regime, *De re publica, de legibus* (54–51 BC), or *On the Commonwealth* as the work is known in English, likewise stressed the ways in which the different peoples of a vast empire might be served by a common legal order. It highlighted the sense in which persons differentiated by rank, privilege and duty nevertheless might be unified in spirit, law and political allegiance (see CICERO).

Republicans of all stripes are committed to a public order in which every citizen has a definite standing or place. Associated with this place in the community are specific responsibilities, for example, the defence of the homeland, as well as certain rights or legal protections for citizens and their property. As long as all citizens assume their proper place and perform their appointed role in civic life, the public good is served. Justice prevails, in the sense that each person receives their due, whatever that may be (and it need not be the same for all). Conversely, if citizens fail to act as they should, or when they step out of place and exercise prerogatives rightly belonging to others, injustice occurs. The public order is disturbed, and if it cannot be restored the sense of commonality will unravel and the republic will expire.

Although republicans are committed to justice, they are divided over its meaning. They also disagree about the most telling signs of injustice and the best means of preventing harm to the common weal. Such differences are reflected in preferences for various forms of government and strategies for insulating government from factional strife.

2 Mixed forms of government

Classical republicans had a strong affinity for mixed government, an ideal that dominated Western political thought after Plato. According to this way of thinking, all pure forms of government tend to degenerate. Monarchy generally gives way to tyranny, aristocracy becomes oligarchy, and democracy declines into ochlocracy, or mob rule. In each case, the interests of a single order or faction prevail at the expense of others' interests, and at the expense of the common weal. Mixed government is a solution to the problem, in so far as it combines elements of all three forms of rule: the one, the few and the many, each influences mixed government. Since all interests must be taken into account in policy making; justice is the necessary outcome of this balance of power.

In a mixed government, the power of one, few and many need not be equal. Historically, monarchic republicans favoured a mixture that gave kings the upper hand, on the presumption that only a strong monarch was capable of constraining ambitious nobles, on the one hand, and intemperate masses bent on furthering their own interests, on the other. Thus, Cicero preferred 'that there should be a dominant and royal element in the commonwealth' ([54–51 BC]1976: 151). The sixteenth-century historian Guicciardini was of the same opinion; his Bernardo mourned the passing reign of the Medici in Florence. And in England, the Reverend Philip Hunton, Provost of Durham University, defended what he called 'mixed monarchy' against those who would oppose Charles I in the Civil War.

Aristocratic republicans preferred mixed governments dominated by the few, as long as they exhibited proper republican virtues: courage in military affairs, skill in diplomacy and a commitment to order and justice at home. Where such aristocrats held the balance of power, they resisted tyrannically inclined monarchs – and unruly peoples. This was the version of republicanism favoured by MACHIAVELLI (§§5–6), who saw it as the most stable form of polity (Machiavelli 1531). In England, aristocratic republicanism was the choice of Algernon Sidney, who was executed for his role in a plan to assassinate Charles II and James II, although his democratic inclinations were exaggerated for political purposes by opponents and proponents of monarchy alike.

For their part, democratic republicans sought a larger role for the many in defining the public good and pursuing it by political means. Publius Valerius (friend of the plebians in Rome), Savonarola (religious and political reformer in Florence) and James HARRINGTON (utopian writer in England), all favoured republics in which the people or their representatives exercised control over policy makers. In fact, it was during Harrington's life that 'republican' and 'republicanism' first entered the English language as an appellation for 'Commonwealth men' and anyone else who wanted to reduce the power of hereditary rulers in England. Few of these republicans were democrats in a modern sense, although most remained dedicated to mixed government with a strong popular element. Not until the late eighteenth and early nineteenth century did republicanism come to be associated exclusively with the cause of popular sovereignty and majoritarianism, and applied to large, commercially-oriented nations (as distinct from the urban polities of the Renaissance or ancient Rome and Greece).

3 Republicanism and majoritarianism

Opponents of popular sovereignty always assumed that democratic republicanism led straight to majoritarianism, a form of rule that was suspect on two grounds. First, majoritarianism was a form of class rule, and therefore unjust on its face; and second, it was rule by the class least suited for political rule – ordinary folk, who were apt to place the interest of commoners above the common interest of all. Radicals such as Thomas PAINE (§1) seemed to confirm this suspicion when they rejected the very idea of mixed rule in favour of a government composed solely of representatives elected by 'the people'. Paine's vision of simple government, infused with common sense and beholden to the majority, became the rallying cry for opponents of monarchy and aristocracy in Europe. In the subsequent political struggle against hereditary rule a modern conception of republicanism took root and flourished.

Interestingly, democratic republicanism stopped short of outright majoritarianism. Even Paine admitted that the first principle of the republic is justice, which rules out 'any species of despotism over each other, or doing a thing, not right in itself, because a majority of them may have the strength of number sufficient to accomplish it' (1989: 233). In other words, in a republic there must exist a balance between the will of a majority and the interests of political minorities. Majorities should defer to the legitimate rights of minorities, who must nevertheless accept the right of majorities to determine the direction of communal affairs. Thus, majorities and minorities each have a recognized place in the political order of democratic republics, which are not only more egalitarian, but also much larger, than the city-states of an earlier era (see DEMOCRACY).

Whereas classical republicans sought a balance of more or less immutable social orders, Paine and other modern republicans, such as the US statesman James Madison, wanted a balance of political interests that might change places, so to speak. The composition of political majorities is not fixed; they may decline into minorities, just as minorities may ascend to majority status over time. To preserve this fluidity it was necessary to prevent majorities from abusing minorities, and to do so without undermining popular sovereignty. In the USA the Federalists' plan to 'extend the republic' was meant to encompass a broader range of interests, inhibiting the formation of majorities of the moment, the most likely source of abuse in a popular regime. Should this kind of majority ever form, the constitutional system of 'checks and balances' was supposed to frustrate any tyrannical impulses that might appear (see CONSTITUTIONALISM).

On the other hand, power in the US system could be exercised by extraordinary majorities, which were much less likely to behave tyrannically than majorities of the moment (since the formation of large majorities depends on moderation and a regard for a broad spectrum of opinion, without which the coalition will not grow to the necessary size). In other nations the same effect has been achieved under political arrangements that require the concurrence of important linguistic, ethnic or religious minorities for policies to be adopted and implemented by numerical majorities. The presumption is that larger, more comprehensive majorities have a better view of the common good than bare majorities, who in turn see the common good more clearly than minorities of any sort.

4 Maintaining the republic

The preservation of a balance of interests is the leitmotif of republicanism. The constitutional plans of the Federalists were preceded by Harrington's reliance on the Agrarian Law as a means of stabilizing relations between diverse interests in the republic. Before that, republicans emphasized the importance of civic virtue as the foundation of order and political stability. Civic virtue implied a willingness to place one's talents in service to the republic. For most citizens this meant temporary service in militias raised to repel invaders. For a select few it meant a longer stint of public service, perhaps as political leaders, or in some other important capacity. The performance of various kinds of public service was deemed patriotic, and in that sense it was self-sacrificing. But in another sense it was self-serving; by contributing to the maintenance of the republic, citizens defended their place in the republic and whatever liberty it conveyed upon them (see CITIZENSHIP §2).

For many classical republicans instilling a love of ordered liberty among citizens required something like a civil religion. Certainly this is what Plato had in mind when he endorsed the propagation of a 'noble lie' concerning the origin of human differences and their embodiment in the division of political labour outlined in *Republic* (c.380–367 BC). Other republics had comparable myths of origin or founding, the purpose of which was to reconcile people to their place in a social order. The idea of a 'social contract' performs the same function in modern republicanism, which rests on a 'civic culture' that acknowledges different interests even as it stresses the importance of balancing them by political means. An even stronger version of this sentiment may be found today in communitarian thought, which stresses the bonds that unite different members of a polity (see COMMUNITY AND COMMUNITARIANISM §2).

Perhaps that is why Marx and other radicals of the nineteenth century favoured democracy over republicanism. For them the primary division in a society is between classes, defined in terms of their relationship to the means of production. With the abolition of private property, classes were expected to disappear and the state would no longer be a site of class struggle. In that sense radical democrats looked forward to the elimination of divisions among citizens, and hence an end to politics. Their solution promised to remove the entire *raison d'être* of republicanism: the reconciliation or accommodation of powerful and persistent divisions of interest in human communities.

References and further reading

* Cicero, M.T. (54–51 BC) *De re publica, de legibus*, trans. and intro. G.H. Sabine and S.B. Smith, *On the Commonwealth*, Indianapolis, IN: Bobbs-Merrill, 1976. (Translation of Cicero's dialogue on republicanism in Rome.)

Fontana, B. (ed.) (1994) *The Invention of the Modern Republic*, Cambridge: Cambridge University Press. (Intellectual historians discuss the adaptation of republicanism in revolutionary America and France, and its subsequent emergence in large, commercial societies in western European nations; complements Rahe (1994).)

Harrington, J. (1656) *The Commonwealth of Oceana and A System of Politics*, ed. J.G.A. Pocock, New York: Cambridge University Press, 1992. (Description of a democratic republic based on the widespread ownership of land and frequent rotation of crops.)

* Machiavelli, N. (1531) *The Discourses*, ed. B. Crick, Harmondsworth: Penguin, 1981. (The single best explication of classical republicanism in the context of mixed government.)

* Paine, T. (1989) *Political Writings*, ed. B. Kuklick, Cambridge: Cambridge University Press. (A stirring statement of modern republicanism and the need for simple government.)

* Plato (*c.*380–367 BC) *Republic*, trans., with notes and an interpretive essay, by A. Bloom, New York: Basic Books, 1968. (Socrates explains why the just city is ruled by philosopher kings, protected by a class of guardians, and economically sustained by farmers and craftsmen..)

Pocock, J.G.A. (1975) *The Machiavellian Moment: Florentine Political Thought and the Atlantic Tradition*, Princeton, NJ: Princeton University Press. (The best single-volume discussion of classical republican thought and its modern variants.)

Rahe, P. (1994) *Republics Ancient and Modern*, Chapel Hill, NC: University of North Carolina Press. (A compendious, and at times tendentious, history of republics and republicanism in the West; anticipates Fontana (1994).)

Skinner, Q. (1978) *The Foundations of Modern Political Thought*, Cambridge: Cambridge University Press, 2 vols. (A treatise on political thinking in Europe during the Renaissance and Reformation, with particular stress on the evolution of republicanism and notions of the state.)

RUSSELL L. HANSON

RESPECT FOR PERSONS

The idea that one should treat persons with due *respect is an important part of common sense morality, but opinions differ about when respect is called for, what it requires, and why. Respect for persons is also a central concept in many ethical theories. Some theories even hold respect for persons to be the foundation of all other moral duties and obligations.*

Respect is distinguished commonly, on one side, from fear and submission, and on another, from admiration, liking and affection. Respect for all persons as such is distinguished normally from esteem or special regard for persons of unusual merit. Some philosophers identify respect with agape, a special kind of love, but respect is perhaps most often regarded as a distinct attitude that should constrain and complement the promptings of love. Kant, for example, held that the requirements of respect and love are different, though compatible, and that both are dependent upon the more general and fundamental idea that humanity in every person is an end in itself.

Other key issues in discussions of respect for persons include: what moral requirement, if any, there is to respect all persons; what the grounds, scope, and theoretical status are of that requirement; whether one can forfeit all claim to respect as a person; what 'respect for persons' demands with regard to specific problems, such as conflicts rooted in race and gender differences; and whether there is the same ground and obligation to respect oneself as to respect others.

1 **Aspects and kinds of respect**
2 **Respect for persons in Kant's ethics**
3 **Some later developments and applications**

1 Aspects and kinds of respect

The root idea of the word 'respect' is 'to look back' or 'to look again'. People speak of respecting a variety of things in addition to persons, for example, talents, achievements, character, laws, authorities, social positions, opinions, powerful forces, and even nature. A common thread seems to be the idea of 'paying heed' or 'giving proper attention' to the object of respect. Respect is generally an acknowledgement of the value or importance of something (or someone) from some perspective (presupposed in the context). It is often associated with awe, reverence, uncoerced willingness to obey or conform, or at least symbolic recognition of status, excellence or power. Depending on the situation, we can show respect *for persons* in a variety of ways: for example, by praising, giving tokens of honour, and accepting orders or advice, or merely by maintaining an appropriate social distance and refraining from expressions of contempt and arrogance. We may respect enemies without necessarily liking them, agreeing with their opinions, approving of their projects, or obeying them; but respecting them is incompatible with regarding them as utterly 'worthless' or 'insignificant'.

Is respect a feeling, a belief, a behavioural pattern, a disposition to act, or an attitude? Respect is often felt, for example, towards persons, standards, or institutions, but a mere feeling or sentiment would not count as respect without some corresponding disposition to *treat* the object in appropriate ways ('respectfully') and a *belief* that the object is worth such treatment. Respect is also more than merely respectful behaviour, for one can show respect deceptively when one does not feel or have it. In discussions of the morality of respect for persons, respect seems most often treated as an *attitude* that might be analysed as a combination of elements: beliefs, evaluative judgments, and policy commitments, as well as dispositions of behaviour and feeling, towards the person who is respected.

Respect for persons *as persons* is to be distinguished from respect for persons as professionals, officials, or members of more specific groups. We might, for example, respect an individual as a musician though not as person, if we thought that the person, though dishonest, is an extraordinarily talented and creative pianist. Even if we regard someone as both professionally inept and morally corrupt, we might, in a sense, respect the person as an official (such as a judge, a priest, or a prime minister) within an institution the authority of which we acknowledge. Here what is respected primarily is the office itself; but in other cases when we say we respect someone as, say, a judge, a priest, or a prime minister, we mean to imply that the person is a good official who fulfils the specified role well. Thus 'respecting a person as a –', where the blank is filled with a reference to a role or office, is ambiguous between, on the one hand, an attitude of due regard to the rights and privileges of the person's position and, on the other hand, an attitude appreciative of the excellence of the person's ability and performance in the position.

Although being a person is not the same as having a specific profession or public office, there is an ambiguity, similar to the one above, in the expression 'respect for a person as a person'. In one sense, this indicates an appreciation that the person has good traits of character or personality, that is, traits that are generally considered desirable in persons whatever their particular roles and circumstances. For example, one might say of persons of known integrity, 'They may be ineffective lawyers, but I respect them highly as persons'. In another sense, however, we might respect individuals as persons, even though we believe them to be immoral and lacking in most other human excellences. Here, 'being a person' is treated as if it were a widely inclusive, nonconventional status, analogous to holding a public office, with at least some minimum rights (or consideration due) independently of individual merit. To illustrate with an extreme and controversial example, some might say

even of unrepentant Nazi war criminals that although their outrageous crimes deserve nothing but condemnation and they have forfeited their right to liberty, perhaps even life, we cannot simply discard them as worthless rubbish but must continue to respect them as persons (see GOOD, THEORIES OF THE §3).

Darwall (1977) introduced the now common term, 'appraisal respect', for respect based on a positive assessment of the merits of individuals, whether as persons or as professionals. This is contrasted with 'recognition respect', which is a disposition to give appropriate weight in one's deliberations to the fact that someone is a person (whether meritorious or not). It is obvious that we need not, and indeed cannot, respect every person as a person in the first sense, for in that sense respect implies a belief that the person in question has individual merits that deserve respect. What is controversial is whether we should respect all persons in the second sense – regardless of their individual merits – and if so, why.

When we say that persons should be respected *as persons*, the qualification 'as persons' may reflect, ambiguously and indefinitely, our view of the scope of the requirement, its grounds, how it is to be fulfilled, or several of these. That is, first, the point could be merely to say that *all* persons should be respected, without saying how or why. Alternatively, the suggestion could be, instead or in addition, that persons should be respected *because* they are persons. That is, the fact that people have the various features constitutive of persons might be seen as the pivotal premise in some argument, presupposed but not yet spelled out, to justify the claim that they should be respected. Finally, the point might be to give clues as to how respect is to be shown. Assuming a background of shared understanding about how various other things are treated appropriately, the injunction to respect persons as persons offers at least negative counsel: for example, persons should not be treated as mere expendable commodities, as instruments or playthings existing solely for our convenience or pleasure, as dogs, vermin, or dirt, or, more metaphorically, as mere statistics (as opposed to individuals with rights, feelings and particular interests). Again, assuming a common agreement on positive requirements for the appropriate treatment of persons, the injunction to treat persons as persons can serve rhetorically as a reminder to apply those standards to a particular case at hand. Here it says, in effect, 'Treat these individuals in the manner that, as you know, is befitting their status as persons.'

Since commonly accepted standards for the appropriate treatment of persons and other things may be challenged, there is an obvious need for further thinking. Some ethical theories raise and respond to the following natural questions. Why must I respect all persons? What argument can justify the inference from 'They are persons' to 'They should be treated in such-and-such a manner'? What, specifically, are reasonable, and not merely widely shared, standards for how persons should be treated (see MORAL STANDING §2)?

2 Respect for persons in Kant's ethics

The historical roots of most contemporary discussion of respect for persons are in the moral philosophy of Immanuel Kant (see KANT, I. §§9–11; KANTIAN ETHICS §1). Previous practice and theory often called for proper respect for individuals according to their social rank and individual merit, but Kant (1785, 1788), influenced by Rousseau, argued that all human beings have a dignity that is independent of rank and merit. All moral agents, by virtue of their rationality and autonomy of will, are jointly 'authors' of moral law, bearers of fundamental rights, and pursuers of ends that others may not ignore (see AUTONOMY, ETHICAL; MORAL AGENTS). Moral duties are categorical imperatives, that is, rational requirements to which we are subject independently of the various personal ends that we choose to set for ourselves. According to Kant, there could be categorical imperatives only if there is something of absolute value; and only persons, as the source of all other values, could have this status. Persons exist as 'ends in themselves', of unconditional and incomparable worth, in contrast to things valuable merely as means or as objects of affection. All rational persons, Kant thought, attribute this special value to themselves. Furthermore, he argued, they must acknowledge, on due reflection, that the ground for this self-attribution is not something unique to them but something they have in common with all other persons, namely, 'humanity' or the special human capacities identified with reason and freedom. Accordingly, a version of the categorical imperative, which is supposed to be a basic, comprehensive, and universal requirement of reason, is, 'Act so that you treat humanity, whether in your own person or in that of another, always as an end, and never as a means only.'

In *Die Metaphysik der Sitten* (*The Metaphysics of Morals*) (1797), Kant used this idea as a basis for both legally enforceable rights and ethical duties to respect others and oneself. In his theory of justice he implied that the status of persons as ends in themselves underlies all rights and, in particular, imposes limits on what legal punishments are permissible. In his theory of virtue Kant maintained that proper self-respect requires one to avoid drunkenness, gluttony, and servility and that respect for others is incompatible with arrogance, defamation, and ridicule. He also held that respect, together with love, is an essential element in friendship.

What is required morally, according to Kant, is to act with due respect, not to have or cultivate a mere 'feeling' of respect. This is partly because we cannot in general control our feelings by will in the way we can and must control our behaviour. Another reason is that respect for persons is derivative from respect for the moral law, and respect for the moral law, in Kant's view, is not something we choose to have or not but rather is something that, as human moral agents, we cannot help but feel. It is the humbling feeling that moral requirements reasonably impose limits on our attempts to satisfy our desires and pursue our personal ends. In so far as it is a form of respect for morality, then, the imperative to respect persons does not ask us to try to conjure up immediately, or even to cultivate over time, an 'affect' or sentiment that we might lack. Rather, what is required is that we choose to act so that, in practice, we live up to our own rational assessment of the worth (dignity) of humanity, a worth that all human moral agents (to some degree) recognize and feel.

3 Some later developments and applications

The idea of respect for persons has been interpreted in various ways, and has served different functions, in philosophical discussions before and after Kant. Contemporary moral philosophers often appeal to principles of respect in support of their judgments regarding practical issues, and some have attempted to develop ethical theories with respect for persons as the basic moral requirement. Downie and Telfer (1969), for example, treat the attitude of respect as morally basic. This attitude is characterized as 'valuing and cherishing persons for what they are'. It is identified as a kind of love, *agape*, which requires 'active sympathy'. The concept of 'persons' itself is viewed as an evaluative concept, though not in a way that makes the injunction to respect persons trivial. What is morally salient about persons is that they have 'rational wills'; that is, they are 'self-determining and rule-following'. This is understood in a sense, taken to be different from Kant's, that includes affective and emotional capacities. Respect for persons requires that we make the ends of others our own and be ready at least to consider how others' rules apply to them and ourselves. This requirement is supposed to be consistent with utilitarianism, but not derived from it; to the contrary, Downie and Telfer (1969) have argued that utilitarianism is in fact derivable from a principle of respect for persons (see UTILITARIANISM).

Alan Donagan (1977) also presented respect for persons as the core of morality. He interpreted Kant's imperative to treat humanity as an end in itself as the principle, 'It is impermissible not to respect every human being, oneself or any other, as a rational creature.' This, he claimed, is the basic principle of those aspects of traditional Western morality not based on theological beliefs. Respect for persons 'as rational creatures', in Donagan's view, is a descriptive term, difficult to define, but familiar in social science and everyday life. Thus he thought it possible to spell out the meaning of the phrase in 'specificatory premises' which enable one to derive from the basic principle a system of intermediate moral principles regarding truth-telling, promise-keeping, non-injury, charity, family, property, obedience to law, and cultivation of one's own health and mental powers. Guided by prior work of Jewish and Christian casuists, he argued that the resulting principles would incorporate more flexibility for exceptional circumstances than Kant admitted but far less latitude than advocated by contemporary consequentialists (see CASUISTRY; CONSEQUENTIAL-ISM). The system of principles, he claimed, is grounded in reason, not faith. Although he presented morality as a system of principles derived deductively from a first principle, he disclaimed the 'foundationalist' idea that the first principle is 'self-evident' or more certainly rational than the intermediate principles (see FOUNDATIONALISM).

Attempts to make respect for persons a comprehensive standard invite various sceptical responses (see, for example, Cranor 1975; Frankena 1986; Hill 1993). It is questionable, for example, whether the idea of respect is sufficiently substantive and descriptive to serve the role it has in Donagan's theory. Further, common usage suggests, and many philosophers agree, that respect is not at issue in all moral contexts, even though it is an important consideration in many. Rather than an all-encompassing first principle, it is one moral consideration along with many others (such as beneficence and gratitude) (see MORAL PLURALISM). Treating respect for persons as the comprehensive source of all moral duties also raises serious questions about the grounds for decent treatment of nonrational animals and human beings with severe mental incapacities (see ANIMALS AND ETHICS). Also, most utilitarians would deny the primacy of respect for persons, and, to be consistent, all of them must object to principles of respect if they demand acts, rules, and motives that promote less than maximum utility.

Not all contemporary discussions of respect for persons, however, are focused on this controversy about the primacy and scope of respect principles.

Many concentrate instead on the implications of respect for persons with regard to particular moral issues, such as racism and sexism, violent protest, pornography, punishment, privacy, legal enforcement of community values, and paternalism in medicine. Self-respect has also been a common theme. Most notably, Rawls (1971) has argued that his theory of justice is morally preferable to utilitarian theories because it better affirms and supports the self-respect of citizens. Sachs (1981) and others have noted significant distinctions between self-respect and self-esteem, and the idea that one should respect oneself is a common premise in recent moral arguments, for example, that no one should passively tolerate humiliation and oppression.

See also: SELF-RESPECT

References and further reading

* Cranor, C. (1975) 'Toward a Theory of Respect for Persons', *American Philosophical Quarterly* 12: 309–19. (Reviews previous accounts, offers a complex analysis of respect, and argues that respect for persons alone cannot be an adequate basis for moral theory.)
* Darwall, S. (1977) 'Two Kinds of Respect', *Ethics* 88: 36–49. (A discussion of the distinction between 'appraisal respect' and 'recognition respect'.)
Dillon, R. (1992) 'Respect and Care: Toward Moral Integration', *Canadian Journal of Philosophy* 22: 105–31. (A discussion of how moral considerations of respect for persons might be combined with a feminist ethics of care.)
* Donagan, A. (1977) *The Theory of Morality*, Chicago, IL and London: University of Chicago Press. (A systematic attempt to derive moral duties from a basic and comprehensive principle of respect for persons.)
* Downie, R.S. and Telfer, E. (1969) *Respect for Persons*, London: Allen & Unwin. (Develops the idea of the supreme worth of the individual person as the basis for a comprehensive requirement of respect.)
* Frankena, W.E. (1986) 'The Ethics of Respect for Persons', *Philosophical Topics* 14: 149–67. (A clear critique of the project of grounding all of morality on respect for persons.)
Fried, C. (1978) *Right and Wrong*, Cambridge, MA: Harvard University Press. (Employs the idea of respect for persons in discussions of many particular moral problems.)
Green, O.H. (ed.) (1982) *Respect for Persons*, Tulane Studies in Philosophy, vol. 31, New Orleans, LA: Tulane University. (A collection of twelve short

essays on respect for persons in relation to moral theory, self-respect, and various moral problems.)

Hill, T.E., Jr (1993) 'Donagan's Kant', *Ethics* 104: 22–52. (A comparative and critical discussion of Donagan and Kant on respect for persons and humanity as an end in itself.)

Hudson, S.D. (1980) 'The Nature of Respect', *Social Theory and Practice* 6: 69–90. (A detailed analysis of four kinds of respect.)

* Kant, I. (1785) *Grundlegung zur Metaphysik der Sitten*, trans. with notes by H.J. Paton, *Groundwork of the Metaphysics of Morals* (originally *The Moral Law*), London: Hutchinson, 1948; repr. New York: Harper & Row, 1964. (Kant's classic, but not easy, work on the foundations of ethics, important here especially for its discussion of humanity as an end in itself.)

* —— (1788) *Critik der practischen Vernunft*, trans. L.W. Beck, *Critique of Practical Reason*, New York: Macmillan, 1965; 3rd edn, 1993. (Another important but difficult work on the foundations of morals, with an extended treatment of respect for moral law, which underlies respect for persons.)

* —— (1797) *Die Metaphysik der Sitten*, trans M.J. Gregor, *The Metaphysics of Morals*, Cambridge: Cambridge University Press, 1991. (Kant's late work on the intermediate principles of morals, including quite readable sections on respect for others, respect in friendship, and, under 'duties to oneself', self-respect.)

* Rawls, J. (1971) *A Theory of Justice*, Cambridge, MA: Harvard University Press. (Now a classic of moral and political theory, this work argues that self-respect is a primary good better secured by Rawls' two principles of justice than by utilitarian principles.)

* Sachs, D. (1981) 'How to Distinguish Self-Respect from Self-Esteem', *Philosophy and Public Affairs* 10 (4): 346–60. (A subtle account of self-respect and ways in which it differs from self-esteem.)

THOMAS E. HILL, JR

RESPONSIBILITIES OF SCIENTISTS AND INTELLECTUALS

Do scientists and intellectuals bear responsibilities peculiar to them? If an 'intellectual' is whoever has a committed interest in the truth or validity of ideas for their own sake and a 'scientist' anyone possessing a special competence in the natural or social sciences, they may indeed be more likely to find themselves in certain characteristic positions of responsibility. In the case of intellectuals, the importance of providing checkable justification of claims made in their pursuit of truth brings certain responsibilities. Scientists may be said to have responsibilities for pursuing truth in their own areas of competence, for wielding their social power appropriately, for making their results generally accessible and for using resources properly. But these apparently special responsibilities are nevertheless to be understood as rooted ultimately in those which any human being may, in the relevant circumstances, be thought to bear to their fellows.

1   The terms of debate
2   Intellectuals
3   Scientists

1   The terms of debate

In what sense might scientists and intellectuals have responsibilities different from those of any other member of society (see RESPONSIBILITY)? Clearly the question is not one of their strictly contractual responsibilities. Anyone employed to teach or to engage in research on the basis of a contract of service will legally have whatever responsibilities are specified in their contract. Of course, teachers, doctors, priests and plumbers among many others will be widely assumed to have responsibilities stemming from the roles that they occupy going far beyond any that may be set out in their contracts of employment. In that sense one might say that all members of society have an obligation to fulfil whatever responsibilities are generally taken to be incumbent upon them in virtue of the roles that they may occupy, whether specified in their contracts or not. But there are wide differences between different types of role in different types of society. In most contemporary societies, for example, nobody can qualify as a doctor or lawyer without passing certain well-defined tests. One can be expelled from these roles by the appropriate authorities acting in accordance with recognized procedures, or one may cease to occupy them of one's own accord. Moreover, lawyers, doctors and many others have produced for themselves fairly elaborate codes of ethics designed to make explicit many of their most recognizably important responsibilities, which does not mean that it always puts their proper line of conduct beyond all possible doubt (see PROFESSIONAL ETHICS). (Among lawyers' chief responsibilities are those of seeking always to do their best for their clients and of never knowingly misleading the court. What to do when these responsibilities clash is, very sensibly perhaps, left open to potentially divergent judgment.) Other social roles, however, may differ in a whole variety of ways. The institution of marriage, for instance, differs notoriously from one society to another (and even within some overall societies) not least in the degrees of freedom, if any, with which those concerned may or may not enter upon or renounce that state – as also in the diverse responsibilities which may be considered to go with it. The same is true of many other socially recognizable roles.

Problematic as the search for common agreement as to the responsibilities attendant upon such roles and institutions may be, there are at least generally clear criteria for determining whether or not someone actually is a doctor or lawyer, husband or wife. This is somewhat less clear in the case of so-called common-law husbands and wives, much less clear in the case of scientists and very much less so in that of intellectuals. Is the term 'scientist' to be reserved for those working as teachers or researchers in the area of the natural sciences? What exactly is the extent of that area? What level must they have achieved to be entitled to this appellation? What of those who once worked in that area, but who have moved to other fields or have simply retired? Nevertheless, if anyone asked me, as a university teacher, which of my colleagues were scientists, I should not expect many of them to disagree with my response. If asked how many were intellectuals, however, I should first need to settle on what exactly we might both understand by that expression.

For present purposes, then, we need to stipulate some guiding definitions. The term 'intellectual' I take to refer to anyone who takes a committed interest in the validity and truth of ideas for their own sake independently of their causal relationships to whatever other ends. The term 'scientist' I take to refer to anyone possessing a specialized competence in the natural or social sciences, leaving open questions as to which of the social studies at what stage of their development should be treated as sciences (in whatever sense of that term) and what level of competence should here be counted as sufficiently specialized. Thus defined, the classes of intellectuals and of scientists will, of course, show a substantial, if indeterminate, overlap. They are nevertheless by no means identical, for not only will there be many nonscientific intellectuals, but many scientists will be interested in the truth and validity of their ideas not so much for their own sake as for that of what can be done with them.

However, in so far as scientists and intellectuals (thus defined) occupy social roles, they do not do so in such explicitly determinable manner as do doctors or barristers. Moreover, there are no constituted bodies who might properly take it upon themselves to draw up a code of ethics for them. If, then, we attribute to them certain special responsibilities, it must be in virtue of certain generally recognizable characteristics of their roles rather than of any formally defining constitution.

2 Intellectuals

Let us take first the case of intellectuals, whether they be scientists or not. Our definition is, of course, cast in terms that reflect the relative indeterminacy of the concept of an intellectual itself. There is much room for debate and disagreement about what might count as validity and truth in the assessment not just of statements, propositions or sentences, which is complicated enough, but even more so of something as indefinite as 'ideas'. Still, such debates are themselves typical of intellectual concerns. And whatever its degree of indeterminacy on the margins, the overall difference is clear enough between those whose interest in ideas is primarily from the point of view, say, of their history or that of imaginative play, but for whom consideration of their validity or truth remains firmly in brackets, and those for whom that consideration is their first preoccupation. In other words, intellectuals, according to our definition, are interested not only in ideas, but also in questions concerning their possible justification.

Justification, however, is a fundamentally serious matter. If one genuinely wants to assure oneself whether a given set of ideas is justified or not, one cannot knowingly rest content with only half-thought-out approximations. One is, so to speak, responsible to oneself, to others and before the tribunal of whatever ideas are under consideration for the seriousness of one's endeavour to probe the matter of their justification. There is nothing essentially secret about this responsibility to oneself. On the contrary, the first responsibilities, which in a sense underpin all others, are those reciprocally reflexive responsibilities generally incumbent on every speaker of a language to respect those overall norms of truth and reference on which the stability of its meanings depends. To that not insignificant extent all participants in meaningful discourse have an implicit share of responsibility for the validity, even indirectly the truth, of the meanings and concepts on which their discourse is based; and to that same extent, however surprising it may appear to them, all participants in discourse have at least an implicit foot within the terrain of intellectuals. Those who have come to occupy positions which may justify their being picked out as intellectuals, however, can justly be said to have a more special and explicit responsibility; they may rightly be called upon to answer to their communities of common communication for the truth or validity of what they may have to say. This is no light responsibility; for, as Vaclav Havel has shown so well in his essay on *The Power of the Powerless* (1985), a society which has lost the most fundamental capacities for 'living in the truth' is one which has exposed itself to the most fundamental forms of corruption and demoralization.

It should be noted, incidentally, that it is not only intellectuals as such who bear a special responsibility for truth and validity. It falls also upon teachers to a very special degree. (Of course, all participants in human discourse may, at times and often willy-nilly, also find themselves fulfilling some of the functions of a teacher; but again the more explicit responsibilities fall upon those who openly occupy such a role.) Naturally, many teachers will also be intellectuals, just as many intellectuals will be teachers; but again the two classes are not coextensive, and neither is wholly included in the other.

3 Scientists

To those (very many) scientists who are also intellectuals the same responsibilities may be ascribed as to any other intellectual as such. What other questions of responsibility arise? They may seem to fall in the main under three heads, none concerning scientists alone, but all perhaps presenting themselves to scientists with an often peculiar urgency.

First, scientists may be held responsible, by others but more particularly by the scientific community itself, not simply for respecting the truth about whatever their domain of research may be, but, more positively, for remaining uncompromisingly active in their pursuit of as yet undiscovered truth. Many would say that this respect for truth must include a commitment to make the results of their research publicly available. Some scientists, indeed, would maintain that this is, strictly speaking, their only responsibility *qua* scientists.

Second, however, in the world as it now is, scientists, or at any rate certain among them, are in a position to furnish it with its most powerfully necessary and perhaps sometimes sufficient means of life and death – not to mention many of its other most powerful instruments for the ongoing transformation of our environment and of our lives together. (One may think of nuclear research and of its applications to nuclear weapons, or of research into the human genome; but there are many other examples (see TECHNOLOGY AND ETHICS; GENETICS AND ETHICS §1).) Scientists may thus possess very real social power. Should they be held peculiarly responsible – as

scientists – for the ways in which that power may be exercised?

Third, certain scientific research programmes may cost sums of money that are already very large in themselves, but, more to the point, quite enormous as a proportion of the money socially available. Of course, the results of such research may bring enormous more or less long-term returns – to society at large maybe, but also to more restricted sectional interests, perhaps even to the scientists concerned themselves. At all events, those seeking such investment, whether from public or from private sources, will be expected to justify their requests, and may naturally be held responsible for their proper seriousness as well as for the honest and non-wasteful use of the resources allocated to them. They may also find that their sponsors, whether governmental or commercial, will make it a condition of their support for research that its results should not be made public.

In principle, however, none of these issues and dilemmas really concerns scientists alone. Power is distributed widely in society in all sorts of complex and interconnected ways. In particular, other non-scientific intellectuals, teachers or researchers may also occupy positions of diverse forms and degrees of power. Indeed, as Michel FOUCAULT persistently pointed out, knowledge and culture themselves constitute formidable resources for the exercise of power. Again, many nonscientific researchers also may seek and receive substantial financial support – not to mention all those other forms of cultural activity which can flourish only on the basis of such subsidy. Nor is it scientists alone who may be held responsible for continuing unremittingly in the search for as yet undiscovered truths. Historians furnish just one among a whole number of other possible examples.

There are also important connections, including potential trade-offs, between these three groups of issues. For example, the (presumed) importance of whatever one is seeking to discover as the result of any given research has to be measured against its likely cost. Again, the more money one has at one's disposal in mounting a research programme, the greater one's potential power for all sorts of purposes. Conversely, the stronger one's initial position in the field, the greater one's chances of obtaining substantial financial and other institutional support.

None of these responsibilities, of course, exists as pure indisputable fact. The questions of their exact nature and weight, of whom they should fall on and even of their very existence, are all open to controversy. In the end, however, it is fair to say that they all derive ultimately from the reciprocal moral responsibilities of human beings as such – of human beings who may find themselves in one role or another, endowed with one set of capacities or powers or another, but whose responsibilities in the exercise of those roles or powers derive fundamentally from the general responsibilities which human beings may be thought to have to one another in so far as they are able to think of themselves as moral beings at all (see MORAL AGENTS; UNIVERSALISM IN ETHICS).

See also: ANIMALS AND ETHICS; RISK

References and further reading

Gordon, C. (ed.) (1980) *Power/Knowledge: selected interviews and other writings, 1972–1977*, New York: Pantheon. (Selection of interviews with, and excerpts from the major works of, Michel Foucault; illustrates his views on the relation of knowledge to power.)

* Havel, V. (1985) *The Power of the Powerless*, London: Hutchinson. (A remarkable analysis of the pervasively demoralizing effects on society of a ruthless totalitarian insistence on lip service to the 'truth' of what all concerned know to be false.)

Kieffer, G.H. (1979) *Bioethics: A Textbook of Issues*, Reading, MA: Addison-Wesley. (A clear discussion of ethical issues arising in the biomedical sciences, with a final chapter on science and society and the moral responsibility of scientists.)

MacLean, I., Montefiore, A. and Winch, P. (eds) (1990) *The Political Responsibility of Intellectuals*, Cambridge: Cambridge University Press. (A collection of essays by writers from a number of different countries.)

Singer, P. (ed.) (1991) *A Companion to Ethics*, Oxford: Blackwell. (A good collection of papers covering abstract issues of ethical theory as well as a number of practical examples.)

Various, *Science and Engineering Ethics*. (A relatively new journal, which first appeared in 1995 and whose nature is well indicated by its title.)

ALAN MONTEFIORE

RESPONSIBILITY

To be responsible for something is to be answerable for it. We have prospective *responsibilities, things it is up to us to attend to: these may attach to particular roles (the responsibilities of, for instance, parents or doctors), or be responsibilities we have as moral agents, or as human beings. We have* retrospective *responsibilities, for what we have done or failed to do, for the effects of*

our actions or omissions. Such responsibilities are often (but not always) moral or legal responsibilities.

The scope of our retrospective moral responsibilities is controversial. We are responsible for the intended results of our actions, but how far we are responsible for their foreseen effects, or for harms that we do not prevent when we could, depends on how we should define our prospective responsibilities, that is, on how far we should regard such foreseen effects, or such preventable harms, as our business. To say that I am responsible for some foreseen effect, or for a harm which I did not prevent, is to say that I should have attended to that effect or to that harm in deciding how to act; our retrospective responsibilities are partly determined by our prospective responsibilities.

I am responsible for something only if it is within my control. It is sometimes argued that I am therefore not responsible for that whose occurrence is a matter of luck; but it is not clear that we can or should try to make responsibility wholly independent of matters of luck.

We have responsibilities not merely as individuals, but also as members of organizations (organizations themselves have responsibilities in so far as they can be seen as agents). This raises the question of how far we are responsible for the actions of groups or organizations to which we belong.

1 Prospective and retrospective responsibility
2 The scope of responsibility
3 Responsibility and luck
4 Collective responsibility

1 Prospective and retrospective responsibility

Our concern is with responsibility-ascriptions of the form '*A* is [was] responsible for *x*'. Such locutions may ascribe merely causal responsibility ('the earthquake was responsible for the damage'); but our concern is with normative ascriptions which hold an agent answerable for something.

My *prospective* responsibilities are those I have before the event, those matters that it is up to me to attend to or take care of. These are often tied to specific roles: I may have responsibilities as a teacher, or parent, or doctor (see PROFESSIONAL ETHICS). But we also have responsibilities as friends, as citizens, perhaps even as human beings (to pay some attention to the interests of other human beings), or as inhabitants of this planet (to have some practical concern for its future) (see HELP AND BENEFICENCE; FUTURE GENERATIONS, OBLIGATIONS TO; ENVIRONMENTAL ETHICS). My prospective responsibilities are those I have in virtue of satisfying some description – 'teacher', 'parent', 'human being'; and we may disagree about just what responsibilities, if any, belong with particular descriptions.

My *retrospective* responsibilities are those I have after the event, for events or outcomes which can be ascribed to me as an agent. I am retrospectively responsible for what I do, or fail to do, in discharging my prospective responsibilities. A doctor who cures a patient is responsible for that cure; one whose treatment (or lack of it) causes death is responsible for that death. More generally, though, we are responsible for at least some of the results of our actions, most obviously for those we bring about intentionally (see INTENTION). If I kill *V* intentionally, I am responsible for *V*'s death (see §§2–3).

To hold *A* responsible for an event is not yet to say that *A* should be blamed for it, partly because praise, rather than blame, may be due; and partly because I can avoid blame for an untoward event by justifying my action (I killed *V* intentionally, but did so in self-defence) (see PRAISE AND BLAME). To be responsible for *x* is to be answerable for it. I can be called to account for it: to explain, justify or admit my culpability for bringing it about or failing to prevent it. Retrospective responsibilities may also bring liabilities. If I am responsible for the harm that someone suffered, I may be liable to censure or punishment for causing that harm, to make compensation for it, or to apologize for it.

Such responsibilities, prospective and retrospective, flow from a conception of our moral duties and relationships, or are ascribed by a legal system. But they may be neither moral nor legal: a sports referee, for instance, has prospective and retrospective responsibilities, but they are not all a matter either of morality or of law.

Only responsible agents, those with the capacities necessary for accepting and discharging responsibilities, can be held prospectively or retrospectively responsible. Just what those capacities are depends on the kind of responsibility at stake. Only moral agents can have moral responsibilities (see MORAL AGENTS; FREE WILL); but the law specifies its own criteria of responsible agency, which might differ between criminal and civil law. However, in so far as criminal responsibility entails liability to punishment, which itself involves censure, we can hold that the criteria of criminal responsibility should match those of moral responsibility (see CRIME AND PUNISHMENT §1).

A responsible agent is one who can be held prospectively or retrospectively responsible. A different use of 'responsible' concerns the agent's attitude to their responsibilities. A responsible person is someone who can be trusted to discharge their prospective responsibilities, and to accept their retrospective responsibilities; an irresponsible person is not one who has no responsibilities, but one who does not take their responsibilities seriously.

2 The scope of responsibility

One general question about retrospective moral responsibility concerns its scope: what are we responsible *for*? An answer to this question depends partly on an account of the scope of our prospective responsibilities.

I am most obviously responsible for the directly intended results of my actions. I make myself responsible for them by directing my action towards bringing them about. I am also responsible for at least many events which I am certain will ensue from my actions. An arsonist who realizes that the fire they start will kill someone is responsible for that death, whether or not they directly intend it (but see §3).

Those who deny any intrinsic moral difference between direct intention and foresight argue that I am as responsible for any certainly foreseen consequence of my action as I am for its directly intended results (see DOUBLE EFFECT, PRINCIPLE OF). Those who deny any intrinsic moral difference between 'acts' and 'omissions' also argue that I am as responsible for events which I could but do not prevent as I am for effects which I actively bring about. For whether I act with the intention of bringing *x* about, or simply knowing that x will ensue if I act thus; whether I actively bring *x* about, or do not do what I know would prevent *x*; in each case I know that I can determine, by my action or inaction, whether *x* occurs or not.

To deny any intrinsic moral difference between direct intention and foresight, or between acts and omissions, is to hold that I am retrospectively responsible for whatever was within my control; and *x* was within my control if I knew that it was within my power to determine, by my action or inaction, whether *x* occurred or not. More precisely, control as thus strictly defined is held to be a *sufficient* condition of responsibility. I am responsible for at least what I thus control. It is not a necessary condition of responsibility. I am responsible for harm I cause recklessly or negligently; but a reckless agent realizes only that their action might cause harm, while a negligent agent is unaware even of a risk that harm will ensue. A weaker 'control' requirement still holds here, however. I act recklessly or negligently only if I know, or could and should have realized, that my conduct might cause harm and that I could avoid that risk by acting differently. (Such retrospective responsibility depends on prospective responsibility. I act recklessly or negligently as to some harm only if I should have taken care with regard to it.)

But is control sufficient for responsibility? To argue that it is, that I am retrospectively responsible for all that lay within my control, is to take a particular moral view of our prospective responsibilities as moral agents. If we believe that agents should attend to all the foreseen effects of their projected actions (in particular that they should see the fact that some harm will ensue from an action as a reason against acting thus), we will hold them responsible for all such foreseen effects; if we believe that agents have a general, stringent duty of care towards all others, to save them from harm, we will hold them responsible for any harms which they knew they could have prevented. But such beliefs are morally controversial. If I believe in the free market, I might deny responsibility for my competitor's ruin, which I knew would ensue from my commercial activities. Such an outcome of my legitimate commercial activity, I may say, is not my concern; it is not something I should attend to as a reason against acting thus. But a critic of the free market might insist that I am responsible for my competitor's ruin; that I can avoid blame for it only if I can justify my action of ruining them (see MARKET, ETHICS OF THE). Likewise, while I may recognize some general responsibility towards others, simply in virtue of our common humanity, to help them if they are in grave distress, I might insist that that responsibility is limited. If I fail to save the lives of distant strangers, my responsibility for their deaths is less than it would be if I made myself fully responsible for their deaths by deliberately killing them; if I do not prevent some trivial harm befalling another, I may deny any (retrospective) responsibility for that harm, by denying any (prospective) responsibility to take such care for their interests. So to determine the scope of our retrospective responsibilities, we must determine the scope of our prospective responsibilities; where moral responsibility is at stake, that must be a moral determination.

Our particular roles, which help determine our prospective responsibilities, thus also help determine our retrospective responsibilities, most obviously by extending them. I could, but do not, stop a child committing a minor act of vandalism. If the child is a stranger, I might deny responsibility for the damage – it was not my business to control the child; but if the child is in my care, I cannot thus deny responsibility. Our roles may also, however, limit our responsibilities. I know that if I fail this thesis, the candidate will lose their academic job. But I might insist that my responsibility as an examiner is to judge the thesis on its merits; the further effects of my decision are not my concern (the candidate's prospective dismissal is not something I should attend to as a reason against failing the thesis), and I am not responsible for them.

Conceptions of prospective and retrospective responsibility help to determine our very descriptions of people's actions or omissions. As a free marketeer I might deny, but others might insist, that I 'ruined my competitor', since whether that is an appropriate description depends on whether I am responsible for my competitor's ruin. Likewise, we can say that someone 'let x happen', or 'failed to do y', only if there was some expectation that they would or should prevent x or do y.

3 Responsibility and luck

The connection noted above between responsibility and control underpins the idea that moral responsibility is incompatible with luck. How can I be morally responsible for some harm if its occurrence was a matter of luck, and thus not within my control?

But this idea threatens to undermine my responsibility for the actual (intended or foreseen) effects of my actions. For the occurrence of such effects depends on factors outside my control, and is thus arguably a matter of luck. The success of an attempt depends not merely on the agent, but on external factors which they do not control; if it fails because of one of those factors, that failure is a matter of luck. Similarly, it is a matter of luck whether a reckless or negligent action causes harm. How then can I be held morally responsible for the actual effects of my actions, if their occurrence is a matter of luck?

Those who argue in this way do not typically argue that the intrusion of luck precludes every kind of responsibility: I am responsible for the actual harm that I cause in that I may be liable to pay compensation for it. But luck does, they insist, preclude responsibility as *blameworthiness*. I am blameworthy only for what is strictly within my control, and not for that whose occurrence depends on luck. One who attempts to do harm is blameworthy for the attempt, but their culpability is not affected by the chance fact of success or failure; those who act recklessly or negligently are culpable for their reckless or negligent acts, but are no more culpable if they actually cause harm than if they do not.

To assess this argument, we must attend to three matters. First, it seems to misuse the contrastive concepts of control and luck. We do not normally think that we lack control over all the effects of our actions, or that those effects always depend on chance. One confusion here is to think that if the occurrence of x depends on any factors outside my control, I do not (really) control it; another is to move from the true claim that my control over anything is not invulnerable (I could lose it) to the false conclusion that I therefore do not (really) have control.

Second, it might be argued that our ordinary talk of control and luck is loose or metaphysically shallow. There is a deeper sense in which all that we do is vulnerable to chance, which captures a deeper truth about our lack of (real) control over the external world. But this metaphysical thought (if it is coherent) threatens any idea of control. If for this reason I do not (really) control the effects of my actions, I do not control my actions or intentions either. For these too are vulnerable to chance, and depend on factors outside my control.

Third, we must none the less admit that the actual outcome of an action is sometimes a matter of luck. It might be a matter of luck that an attempt fails, or succeeds; that a reckless action causes harm, or does not. Should we then, in ascribing moral blame, ignore such matters of luck; draw no distinction between the successful and the failed assailant, or between lucky and unlucky reckless agents? This suggestion, however, requires us to draw a sharp distinction between moral blame, or judgments of moral culpability, and those other aspects of our understanding of and responses to a person's action which are structured by its actual effects; it is not clear whether that distinction can be drawn (see MORAL LUCK).

4   Collective responsibility

We must also attend to collective, or shared, responsibilities: the responsibilities of organizations or groups; the responsibilities individuals have as members of organizations; and whether such membership can make us responsible for the actions of others.

We can talk of the responsibilities of organizations such as corporations, universities, governments and nations in so far as we can see such collectives as agents – as capable of acting purposively, as being potentially answerable for what they do or fail to do. The actions of such organizations involve, of course, the actions of individual agents within them; but that is not to say that descriptions of corporate actions can be reductively analysed without loss into descriptions of individual actions of individual agents (see HOLISM AND INDIVIDUALISM IN HISTORY AND SOCIAL SCIENCE).

Our prospective and retrospective responsibilities, as individuals, are often defined partly by our roles within organizations: I may have responsibilities, for instance, as a teacher, as an employee, as a director, as a minister. Such responsibilities are defined initially by the organization itself, in the light of its purposes and values. But there is obviously room for controversy (often moral controversy) about what our

role-responsibilities ought to be, and about when and whether they may be overridden by moral responsibilities which transcend our particular roles.

In so far as I have responsibilities within an organization, I share, with other members of the organization, responsibility for what the organization does. But is that responsibility limited to the part which I play directly, or could and should play, in the organization's actions? Or can I properly be held responsible for the actions of others in the organization even though I did not myself have authority or control over them? Can I be held responsible for actions of the organization to which I did not contribute directly, and which I could not control? If the government of my country behaves despicably, can I disavow responsibility by pointing out that I voted against that party or that measure; or must I still see that action as being in some sense 'mine', as a citizen of this country? Indeed, can or should I accept responsibility for my country's actions before I was born?

Answers to such questions depend on getting clear about what it is to be a member of a group, and about what it is to be responsible. It would, for instance, be absurd to blame myself for governmental actions over which I had no control, or which were done before I was born; but it is not obviously absurd to feel shame for them, or think that it is up to me (though not of course up only to me) to apologize for them, or to try to find some way of making up for them.

See also: ACTION; CONFUCIAN PHILOSOPHY, CHINESE §5; LEGAL CONCEPTS

References and further reading

Ashworth, A.J. (1987) 'Belief, Intent and Criminal Liability', in J. Eekelaar and J. Bell (eds) *Oxford Essays in Jurisprudence*, 3rd series, Oxford: Oxford University Press, 1–31. (An account of retrospective criminal responsibility which tries to eliminate the role of luck.)

Casey, J. (1971) 'Actions and Consequences', in J. Casey (ed.) *Morality and Moral Reasoning*, London: Methuen, 155–205. (A sophisticated discussion of the ways in which descriptions of actions and omissions depend on ascriptions of prospective responsibility.)

Duff, R.A. (1990) *Intention, Agency and Criminal Liability*, Oxford: Blackwell, chaps 4–5. (Discusses competing conceptions of our retrospective responsibility for the foreseen effects of our actions.)

Hart, H.L.A. (1968) *Punishment and Responsibility*, Oxford: Oxford University Press. (See especially 'Intention and Punishment', on attempted crimes and on intention and foresight; and 'Postscript: Responsibility and Retribution', on different aspects of responsibility.)

Lucas, J.R. (1993) *Responsibility*, Oxford: Oxford University Press. (Analyses responsibility as answerability; discusses omissions, the responsibilities attaching to roles, and collective responsibility.)

Nagel, T. (1976) 'Moral Luck', *Proceedings of the Aristotelian Society*, supplementary vol. 50: 137–51; repr. in *Mortal Questions*, Cambridge: Cambridge University Press, 1979, 24–38. (A seminal discussion of the ways in which our actions are vulnerable to luck, and their implications for responsibility.)

Wells, C. (1993) *Corporations and Criminal Responsibility*, Oxford: Oxford University Press. (Argues that corporations can and should be seen as criminally responsible agents.)

Williams, B. (1976) 'Moral Luck', *Proceedings of the Aristotelian Society*, supplementary vol. 50: 115–36; repr. in *Moral Luck: Philosophical Papers 1973–80*, Cambridge: Cambridge University Press, 1981, 20–39. (Another key discussion of the significance of luck for responsibility.)

—— (1993) *Shame and Necessity*, Berkeley, CA: University of California Press, ch. 3. (An account of the central elements of retrospective responsibility, comparing our conception with those of the ancient Greeks.)

Zimmerman, M.J. (1988) *An Essay on Moral Responsibility*, Totowa, NJ: Rowman & Littlefield. (An exhaustive analysis of retrospective moral responsibility, covering most of the topics discussed in this entry; has a useful bibliography.)

R.A. DUFF

RESURRECTION

The Judaeo-Christian belief in a future general resurrection of the dead arose in late second-temple Judaism (see, for example, Daniel 12: 2 and John 11: 24). (Whether there would be a resurrection of the dead was one of the main points that divided the Pharisees and the Sadducees.) When the new Christian movement appeared – before it was clearly something other than a party or sect within Judaism – it centred on the belief that the crucified Jesus of Nazareth had been, in a literal, bodily sense, raised from the dead (resurrectus) and that his resurrection was, in some way, the means by which the expected general resurrection of the dead would be accomplished. Indeed, resurrection was so pervasive a theme in early Christian preaching that it was apparently sometimes thought that Christians worshipped two gods called 'Jesus' and 'Resurrection' (Anastasis). The early Christians generally said that 'God raised Jesus from the dead'. In post-New Testament times, it became more common for Christians to say that 'Jesus rose from the dead'. Belief in the resurrection of Jesus and a future general resurrection continue to be central to Christianity. Christians have always insisted that resurrection is not a mere restoration of what the resurrected person had before death (as in the story in the fourth Gospel of the raising of Lazarus) but is rather a doorway into a new kind of life. The status of a belief in the general resurrection in rabbinic Judaism is difficult to summarize. It should be noted, however, that a belief in the resurrection of the dead is one of Maimonides' 'thirteen principles', which some Jews regard as a summary of the essential doctrines of Judaism. A belief in a general resurrection of the dead is one of many Judaeo-Christian elements that have been incorporated into Islam.

1   The concept of resurrection
2   Philosophical difficulties

1   The concept of resurrection

The concept of the resurrection of the body (or of the dead) is most easily explained by laying out the ways in which it differs from the most important competing picture of the survival of death, the Platonic picture. According to PLATO (§13), when one dies (that is, when one's body dies), one will continue to be what one has been all along, a soul: an immaterial centre of consciousness, reason and action. One's death is, therefore, an extrinsic change in one: being dead means simply no longer having a body to animate. Since one's death is an extrinsic change in one, one's survival of death is something that happens in the natural course of events: one continues to exist after death by the continued exercise of the same powers or capacities that enabled one to exist when one still animated a body. (This inference is natural and plausible, but, as Descartes would later point out, it is not logically valid: for all logic can tell us, animating a body might be essential to the existence of a soul.) Death is, moreover, not a bad thing, as the vulgar believe, but a liberation, for the body is a prison of the soul – or it might be likened to a millstone that drags the soul down into the world of flux and impermanence. The liberation of the soul by death will not, unfortunately, be permanent, for the soul is destined repeatedly to suffer the misfortune of embodiment.

Christians, Jews and Muslims who believe in the resurrection of the dead will accept two of Plato's theses about death: that the person does survive death, and that dead persons will not be forever disembodied. But everyone who believes in resurrection will dispute the following elements of Plato's metaphysic of body, soul and death: that the body is a prison; that the soul must by its very nature survive the death of the body; and that the embodied soul has been disembodied in the past and will experience a large, perhaps infinite, number of 'reincarnations' in the future. Christians, moreover, will insist that the new bodily life that awaits the soul (the saved soul, at least; perhaps this is not true of the damned) will not be of the same sort as its earlier life. The doctrine of resurrection, however, is no more than a doctrine. It is not a worked-out metaphysic of body, soul and death. (The primary biblical data concerning the metaphysics of resurrection are found in 1 Corinthians 15: 35–55. This passage, however, is open to a variety of interpretations.)

There are several competing philosophical theories of the metaphysics of resurrection. Some who accept the doctrine of resurrection deny the existence of a separable, immaterial soul. Examples include TER-TULLIAN, who argued in his *De anima* (c. 210–13) that the soul is corporeal, and, in the twentieth century, the Scottish computer scientist D.M. MacKay (1987) and the English physicist J.C. Polkinghorne (1994). Others accept the existence of an immaterial soul, but differ on the question whether the person, the 'I', *is* the immaterial soul. AQUINAS (§10), for example, sees the human person as essentially a composite of a human soul and a human body. According to the 'composite' theory, a person cannot exist without a body: to exist is for one's soul (always numerically the same) to animate some human body or other. (In the interval between one's death and one's receiving a new body at the time of the general resurrection, one's soul exists and thinks and has experiences, but *one* does not, strictly speaking, exist.) However, others who believe in a separable soul – most of the Fathers of the Church and, probably, most Christians who have not given the matter much thought – accept a metaphysic of soul and body that is deceptively similar to Plato's: one *is* an immaterial soul, and one will exist and think and have experiences throughout the interval during which one is without a body. But even the members of this party – the theologically well instructed among them, at any rate – would accept the following anti-Platonic theses: that the death of one's 'first' body is not a natural consequence of the impermanence of material things, but is rather a result of the Fall; that the soul's survival of death is not a natural consequence of its immateriality or simplicity, but is rather a miracle, a special gift from God; that existing without a body is not a good thing for the soul, an essential part of the *telos* of which is to animate a body; and that the life of the 'spiritual' or 'glorified' body that the saved soul will be given at the general resurrection will be qualitatively different from (and superior to) the life of the soul's first or 'natural' body. (It must be emphasized that, whatever 'spiritual body' may mean, it does not mean 'immaterial body'.)

2 Philosophical difficulties

Each of these metaphysical theories of resurrection faces philosophical problems. Believers in resurrection who are dualists face the problems any dualist faces (see DUALISM). Since these problems are the same whether or not the dualist believes in resurrection, they will not be discussed here. Believers in resurrection who are materialists (as regards human beings) face the problems any materialist faces (see MATERIALISM IN THE PHILOSOPHY OF MIND). Since these problems are the same whether or not the materialist believes in resurrection, they will not be discussed here. In addition, however, believers in resurrection who are materialists face a special philosophical problem about personal identity. The remainder of this entry will discuss this special problem.

It can be plausibly argued that the doctrine of the resurrection of the dead presupposes some form of dualism. For if human persons are not immaterial souls, if they are living animals, then it would seem that death must be the end of them. A living animal is a material object. A material object is composed, at any given moment, of certain atoms. But if one is composed of certain atoms today, it is clear from what we know about the metabolisms of living things that one was not composed of those same atoms a year ago: one must then have been composed of a set of atoms that hardly overlaps the set of atoms that composes one today – and so for any living organism. This fact, the fact that the atoms of which a living organism is composed are in continuous flux, is a stumbling block for the materialist who believes in resurrection.

Suppose, then, that God proposes to raise Socrates from the dead. How shall he accomplish this? How shall even omnipotence bring back a particular person who lived long ago and has returned to the dust? – whose former atoms have been, for millennia, spread pretty evenly throughout the biosphere? This question does not confront the dualist, who will say either that there is no need to bring Socrates back (because, so to speak, Socrates has never left), or else that Socrates can be brought back simply by providing his soul (which still exists) with a newly created human body. But what will the materialist say? From the point of view of the materialist, it looks as if asking God to bring Socrates back is like asking him to bring back the snows of yesteryear or the light of other days. For what can even omnipotence do but reassemble? What else is there to do? And reassembly is not enough, for Socrates was composed of different atoms at different times. If someone says, 'If God now reassembles the atoms that composed Socrates at the moment of his death, those reassembled atoms will once more compose Socrates', there is an obvious objection to the thesis. If God can reassemble the atoms that composed Socrates at the moment of his death in 399 BC – and no doubt he can – he can also reassemble the atoms that composed Socrates at some particular instant in 409 BC. In fact, if there is no overlap between the two sets of atoms, God could do both of these things, and set the two resulting men side by side. And which would be Socrates? Neither or both, it would seem, and, since not both, neither.

It might be objected that God would not do such a frivolous thing, and this may indeed be so. Nevertheless, if God were to reassemble either set of atoms, the resulting man would be who he was, and it is absurd, it is utterly incoherent, to suppose that his identity could depend on what might happen to some atoms other than the atoms that composed him (for this is what a materialist who holds that the reassembled '399 BC' atoms compose Socrates just so long as the '409 BC' atoms are not also reassembled is committed to). In the end, there would seem to be no way round the following requirement: if Socrates was a material thing, a living organism, then, if a man who lives at some time after Socrates' death and physical dissolution is to be *Socrates*, there will have to be some sort of material and causal continuity between the matter that composed Socrates at the moment of his death and the matter that at any time composes that man. (St Paul seems to suggest, in the passage from 1 Corinthians cited above, that this will indeed be the case.) But 'physical dissolution' and 'material and causal continuity' are hard to reconcile. To show how the continuity requirement can be satisfied, despite appearances – or else to show that the continuity requirement is illusory – is a problem that must be solved if a philosophically satisfactory 'materialist' theory of resurrection is to be devised.

See also: ESCHATOLOGY; PERSONAL IDENTITY; REINCARNATION §3; SOUL, NATURE AND IMMORTALITY OF THE

References and further reading

Cullmann, O. (1958) *Immortality of the Soul or Resurrection of the Dead?*, London: Epworth; also in K. Stendahl (ed.) *Immortality and Resurrection*, New York: Macmillan, 1965. (A classic and much discussed essay that contrasts the two concepts of its title and argues that the concept of the immortality of the soul is foreign to the New Testament.)

Edwards, P. (ed.) (1992) *Immortality*, New York: Macmillan. (A very useful collection, which contains an extensive bibliographical essay. Includes the relevant passages from Plato's *Phaedo* and Thomas Aquinas' *Summa theologiae*.)

Geach, P. (1969) *God and the Soul*, London: Routledge. (A modern defence of the 'composite' thesis; see especially chapter 2, 'Immortality', which is reprinted in Edwards.)

* MacKay, D. (1987) 'Computer Software and Life after Death', in R. Gregory (ed.) *Oxford Companion to the Mind*, Oxford: Oxford University Press. (Argues that the distinction between computer hardware and software may be used to defend a 'materialist' account of resurrection. Reprinted in Edwards.)

* Polkinghorne, J. (1994) *The Faith of a Physicist: Reflections of a Bottom-up Thinker*, Princeton, NJ: Princeton University Press. (Recent defence of a broadly 'materialist' account of resurrection; see especially chapter 6, 'Crucifixion and Resurrection', and chapter 9, 'Eschatology'.)

Tertullian, Q.S.F. (*c.*210–13) *De anima* (On the Soul), in R. Arbesman, E.J. Daly and E.A. Quain (eds) *Tertullian: Apologetical Works*, New York, 1950. (Contains Tertullian's account of the soul as a corporeal entity.)

Van Inwagen, P. (1978) 'The Possibility of Resurrection', *International Journal for Philosophy of Religion* 9: 114–21. (This essay (which is reprinted in Edwards) and the following essay attempt to devise a metaphysic of resurrection that presupposes that human beings are living organisms.)

—— (1995) 'Dualism and Materialism: Athens and Jerusalem?', *Faith and Philosophy* 12: 475–88. (See previous item.)

Wolfson, H.A. (1961) 'Immortality and Resurrection in the Philosophy of the Church Fathers', in *Religious Philosophy: A Group of Essays*, Cambridge, MA: Belnap; also in K. Stendahl (ed.) *Immortality and Resurrection*, New York: Macmillan, 1965. (A very learned account of the positions of the Church Fathers on the metaphysics of resurrection.)

PETER VAN INWAGEN

REVELATION

All major theistic religions have claimed that God has revealed himself in some way, both by showing something of himself in events and also by providing some true, important and otherwise unknowable propositions. Event-revelation may include both general revelation (God revealing himself in very general events, observable by all, such as the existence of the universe and its conformity to natural laws), and special revelation (God revealing himself in certain particular historical events). The events are a revelation in the sense that God has brought them about and they show something of his character. Thus Judaism teaches that God manifested his nature and his love for Israel when he brought his people out of Egypt and led them to the promised land through the agency of Moses. Christianity traditionally affirms that God has revealed himself in a much fuller sense in Jesus Christ – because Jesus did not merely show us something of the character of God but was God himself. God reveals propositions by some chosen prophet or society telling us truths orally or in writing which we would not have adequate grounds for believing unless they had been announced to us by persons who showed some mark of God-given authority. Thus Islam teaches that God inspired Muhammad to write the Qur'an in the seventh century AD, and that its success (its proclamation throughout a large part of the civilized world), content and style (deep thoughts expressed in a beautiful way, not to be expected of an uneducated person) show its divine origin.

1   Event revelation
2   Propositional revelation: its grounds
3   Propositional revelation: its content

1   Event revelation

Any event brought about by an agent reveals something of that agent's character. If God made the world, one would expect its general character to show something about its Creator. The prophet Jeremiah represented God as speaking of his 'covenant of day and night', the regular succession of day after night and night after day, as showing the reliability of God and providing a reason why his solemn undertakings should be believed (Jeremiah 33: 20–6). Some recent writers have seen the focus of God's general revelation as the general progress of humanity in its understanding of the world and moral truth and in its working together for the advancement of all the human race. Most theologians have believed in special, as well as general revelation. But some recent 'neo-orthodox' Christian theologians, inspired by Karl BARTH (§2), have held that God does not reveal

himself in any comprehensible way in the natural world or secular history – he is too 'other' and too different from such things. By contrast, the eighteenth-century deist movement denied that God had manifested his presence in some historical events more than others; and this spirit has been in evidence in much recent liberal Christian theology (see DEISM). It has been characterized by a denial that Christianity is in any unique way the true religion and so has held that if some events manifest God's nature more than others, they include events within the histories of all the great religious traditions and secular cultures. This is contrary to unanimous Christian tradition from the first to the eighteenth century, that God has manifested his presence pre-eminently in Christian history and above all in Jesus Christ (see INCARNATION AND CHRISTOLOGY §1).

If one has any reason to believe that there is a God, one would expect the natural world to reveal to some extent what he is like. Only if one has other beliefs about what God is like would one deny this; and those other beliefs would require justification. Why believe that certain historical events reveal God better than others? Perhaps reason, and in particular our understanding of moral goodness, might lead us to see that if God is at work in the world, he is at work in some places more than others. Our private religious experience or the miraculous nature of the special events might also show us this. But if one allows general as well as special revelation, one can learn something about what God is like from the natural world; one can then use that to recognize in which particular events God was at work and, by reflecting on them, gain more knowledge of him.

Theistic religions have generally maintained that God manifests his presence not merely publicly in the natural order or in events within human history, but privately to particular individuals. But such events, except when they involve the conveying of information, are more naturally called religious experiences than instances of revelation.

If God reveals himself in particular events of human history and these are events of significance for the human race, then if later generations are to benefit from them, they will presumably need to know about them. Some Scripture or Church proclamations will presumably be needed. Many twentieth-century theologians have been unwilling to regard such written records – for example, the Bible – as themselves items of revelation. Barth preferred to call them 'witnesses' to revelation. Such theologians have regarded the scriptural texts as not always true but as useful and inspiring signposts to what is true. Earlier Christian centuries generally regarded the Bible as containing only truths, some reporting significant historical events, others conveying God's commandments and truths about his nature.

2 Propositional revelation: its grounds

The major theistic religions have all held that God has revealed certain propositions, which are incorporated in written works. For Christians, they are in the Bible; for Jews, in the Hebrew Bible (known to Christians as 'The Old Testament' of their Bible); for Muslims, in the Qur'an. Why should anyone believe this?

As most theologians have supposed, there must be two kinds of relevant evidence. The first is the consonance of the propositions purportedly revealed with what is known by other routes of the nature of God (including the evidence of other propositions purportedly revealed). God is supposed, by definition, to be morally good. If the purportedly revealed propositions commend what is not morally good, they cannot be the commands of God (see RELIGION AND MORALITY §1). Again, God is supposed to be non-embodied and omnipotent (and natural theology claims that arguments from the natural world show this). If the propositions purportedly revealed speak of God having arms and legs, and being unable to do various actions, they cannot be revealed.

But if the propositions are to reveal anything to us, they must go beyond our prior knowledge while remaining consonant with it. Why believe one rather than another claim consonant with prior knowledge? The normal answer is that the purported revelation is accompanied by miracles, events contrary to natural laws, which, since God keeps natural laws operative, God alone could bring about (see MIRACLES). Miracles are thus the second kind of relevant evidence. If the miracles produce or forward the teaching of a purportedly revealed book, that is reasonably understood as an act of God (like a nod or a signature) authenticating that teaching. The major theistic religions have all claimed evidence of this sort for their revealed documents. The Qur'an was to be recognized as of divine origin by its 'inimitability' – it was a document of a kind that an uneducated person could not have written unless God had intervened to give him knowledge and literary ability beyond his education. The Hebrew Bible was to be recognized as of divine origin because it was the record of miraculous events (such as the parting of the Red Sea) and of the people founded as a result of those events. The Christian Bible was to be recognized as of divine origin because it was founded upon the resurrection of Jesus from the dead and other miracles which accompanied the foundation and growth of Christianity. That miracles are vital to authenticate claims to revelation was the normal teaching of

Christian theologians, at least until the last century or two, when many have tried to dispense with any appeal to the miraculous.

Analogy with human cases explains why we look for these two kinds of evidence. If I receive a letter purportedly from John, my grounds for believing it to come really from John are first, that everything written in it is the sort of thing John could be expected to write; it is in character and shows knowledge of our previous meetings. And, second, it is written in a way or comes by a route that letters from John, and very few others, alone would do. Thus it may be that the handwriting is almost exactly like previous specimens of John's handwriting, and very few others can write in that way. Or it may be that the letter is given to me by a friend who says that John gave it to him, a friend whom in the past I have found to be completely trustworthy. The two kinds of evidence are sometimes called respectively internal and external evidence of authorship. We rightly look for both kinds of evidence of the divine authorship of purportedly revealed propositions.

A private religious experience had by the prophet writing the teaching down could perhaps provide him with the requisite authentication; and quite a few Christian writers, especially Protestants, have stressed the importance of the inner conviction that God is speaking to us through the text as grounds for believing its truth. But in view of the conflicting revelations purportedly inspired by God to which 'inner conviction' has seemed to testify, and the danger of self-deception in such matters, it would be dangerous for those other than the prophet to rely too much on inner conviction to authenticate such detailed claims about God as a revelation purports to give. There is need for public miracles.

How are you to know that a purported miracle took place and was indeed a miracle? We need to have evidence that if the event in question took place, it would have been contrary to natural laws; for example, that if the Red Sea parted in the way described in Exodus, that could not have been produced by natural processes of wind and tide operating normally. We also need evidence that the event in question took place. Evidence that some event took place will always include both historical evidence of its purported effects – testimony of witnesses and any physical traces of its occurrence – and also evidence from any well-authenticated general theory of how likely such an event is to occur. The more evidence we have from overall theory that a certain kind of event is likely to happen some time or other, the less we need in the way of detailed historical evidence to show that it has happened. If your theory of astronomy leads you to suppose that sometimes stars will explode, then it is reasonable to interpret what you see through your telescope as the debris of a stellar explosion. The better justified your overall theory, the better justified your interpretation of the data. But if a well-justified theory tells you that these things cannot happen, then you need a great deal of detailed historical evidence to outweigh the countervailing theory. Similarly, the better established is theism, and the better established is the view that God has reason to intervene in history, the less you need by way of historical evidence to show that he has done so (see ATHEISM; GOD, ARGUMENTS FOR THE EXISTENCE OF). We must consider here whether if there is a God, he has reason to give us a revelation and so to authenticate it by miracle. If so, we need less in the way of detailed historical evidence to show that he has done so.

Some have supposed revelation to be unnecessary, since reason or natural theology can show us what God is like and which acts are morally good or bad, and that is all we need to know. The theistic religions have, however, generally claimed that while natural theology can show us quite a bit, there is also a lot that it cannot show us and that we need to know in order to have the right relation to God and to live the right sort of life on earth. St Thomas AQUINAS (§14) in particular claimed that while natural theology can show us God's existence and the most general moral truths, we need revelation to show us in much more detail what God is like (*Summa contra gentiles* I, chaps 2–13). Revelation also fleshes out our general duty of conformity to the will of God, by showing us, for example, that God wills us to worship him in particular ways on particular occasions. Even with respect to the former truths which, Aquinas claims, reason can discover, many humans may simply not have the time and ability to discover them; and revelation could also inform us about them. It is plausible to suppose that if there is a God, he wants us to know a lot more about him than pure reason can discover in order to enter into a personal relationship with him. And if he has provided some sort of community and institutions to help us to do this, he will need to inform us. The Catholic tradition has generally followed Aquinas, and seen Christian faith as involving the acceptance of the Christian revelation. The First Vatican Council (1870) declared that faith is a supernatural virtue whereby 'we believe that what has been revealed by God is true'.

But if God dictates a book, it may get destroyed or misinterpreted, and with the passage of centuries any book can get badly misinterpreted. So it is plausible to suppose that a propositional revelation would need to be backed up by the provision of an institution or tradition of interpretation itself based on a miracu-lous foundation, which authenticated the book and its subsequent interpretation. Both Islam and Judaism have claimed that there are authorized interpreters of revelation. Catholic and Eastern Orthodox Christianity claim the Christian Church to be such a divinely authorized interpreter; and even many Protestants have held that the Christian tradition in a wide sense is a divinely guided tradition for interpreting the Bible.

3 Propositional revelation: its content

How is the Qur'an or the Hebrew Scriptures or the Bible to be interpreted? The Qur'an was written down at the dictation of a single human author, Muhammad, allegedly inspired by God. The Hebrew Scriptures were a collection of books compiled over many centuries, having different human authors; and the Bible was put together over even more centuries with even more human authors. How these Scriptures are to be interpreted depends on the genres to which we suppose their various parts to belong.

There are many kinds of literary genre: history, historical novel, narrative poetry, philosophical dialogue, science fiction, moral fable, and so on; and there are many genres known to the ancient world which are unfamiliar today, such as wisdom literature, apocalyptic, allegory, and Greek tragedy. They differ in various stylistic respects, and above all in the respect of whether they have a truth-value. Furthermore, in varying ways, for some but not all genres the truth-value of the whole is a function of the truth-value of the component sentences. Thus a newspaper story is true to the extent to which its component sentences are true. The whole is more or less true according to how many of the component sentences are true, and even the truth of individual sentences may be a matter of degree; some sentences may be only approximately true. By contrast, a simple modern novel is neither true nor false. But literary works may also have a true message, even though that is not a matter of having most of their sentences true. Poems or fables, such as Aesop's fables, often tell us things deep and important about human nature or moral worth by means of fictional stories (about historical or non-existent persons), each of whose sentences taken on its own is false or lacks a truth-value.

So in interpreting an ancient work, purportedly revealed, we need to inquire about the genre of the whole and the way in which it affects the genre of the constituent books. Is, for example, the Book of Jonah, a constituent of the Hebrew Scriptures and the Bible, to be taken as straight history or as a moral fable? Our judgments about the genre of a work (and so how its sentences are to be interpreted) must depend on our judgments about who is the author and who are the intended audience. For the authorship of the Qur'an, there are only two possible candidates – Muhammad (if he was not inspired by God) and God. For the Bible, there are very many candidates, for the Bible is a patchwork; small passages written by one human author or group were put together into larger strands and then into 'Books', and those eventually into the whole Bible. Passages may have one meaning when written by one author on their own, a different meaning when used as part of a larger work by another author, and so on. Thus the central part of the Book of Ecclesiastes is an atheistic work, but this was sandwiched by another author within chapters having a theistic tone, which – if you think of the work as a whole – leads to reinterpretation of the central parts; the later author having taken over the central chapters, they must be interpreted as having a meaning consistent with the other chapters.

The document of revelation is, for Jews, the Hebrew Scriptures; for Christians, their whole Bible, Old and New Testaments. The Christian Church promulgated that work as having a central core, condensed into the Christian creeds, in the light of which the whole must be interpreted. It declared that Scripture was totally true and that God was the author of the Bible. It was meant for one Church of many centuries. What is the genre of the Bible? There is little with which to compare it. But there is one obvious principle of interpretation: that, like any other work, it must be interpreted in the light of other things we know about the author's beliefs. Hence there grew up in the Christian Church a tradition of biblical interpretation, first stated explicitly by ORIGEN (§2), and continued in many writers of the first 1500 years AD: that passages are to be taken literally (as well, perhaps, as in other senses) where that is consonant with other things known about God, both through natural reason and as part of the central core of Christian revelation, and otherwise they are to be taken only in figurative senses (see Origen's *On First Principles*, 4.3). This led to books and passages of the Bible being interpreted in analogical, allegorical or metaphorical ways. For example, any passages at variance with the best science of the day or suggesting that God had a body were not to be taken literally; much in the early chapters of the book of Genesis needed to be taken in figurative senses.

What then is at stake with respect to any purported propositional revelation is whether the evidence of its content and any accompanying miracle suggests that God is its author and so that it is a genuine revelation. Competing claims to provide a revelation must be weighed against each other. But in judging what the content of a purported revelation is, the inquirer must do so on the assumption that God is its author.

See also: HERMENEUTICS, BIBLICAL; JEWISH PHILOSOPHY IN THE EARLY 19TH CENTURY §4; NATURAL THEOLOGY; PROPHECY; RELIGIOUS EXPERIENCE

References and further reading

* Aquinas, T. (1259–65) *Summa contra gentiles* I, trans. A.C. Pegis, *On the Truth of the Catholic Faith*, bk I, Garden City, NY: Doubleday., 1955. (Statement of Aquinas' distinctions between natural and revealed theology; see chapters 2–13.)

Arberry, A.J. (1957) *Revelation and Reason in Islam*, London: Allen & Unwin. (Useful guide to the history of Islamic thought on the issue.)

Butler, J. (1736) *The Analogy of Religion*, London: George Bell & Sons, 1902, pt 2, 'Of Revealed Religion'. (A classic statement of the need for propositional revelation and for miracles as evidence for it.)

Dulles, A. (1983) *Models of Revelation*, Dublin: Gill & Macmillan. (A survey of twentieth-century theological accounts of revelation.)

Duns Scotus, J. (c.1305) *Ordinatio*, Prologus, 2, 100–19, vol. 1 of *Omnia opera*, Vatican City: Scotistic Commission, 1950–. (A very clear fourteenth-century account of the grounds for believing what is revealed in the Bible. There is no available English translation.)

Newman, J.H. (1845) *An Essay on the Development of Christian Doctrine*, London: Longmans, Green & Co. (Newman's classic statement of the view that Christianity involves a progressive development in understanding the doctrines originally revealed.)

* Origen (c.225) *On First Principles*, trans. G.W. Butterworth, New York: Harper & Row, 1966, 4.3. (First and classic Christian statement of the principles of biblical interpretation.)

Pannenberg, W. (1991) *Systematic Theology*, trans. G.W. Bromley, Edinburgh: T. & T. Clark, vol. 1, ch. 4. (A history of Christian understanding of revelation, including an exposition of revelation as God acting through historical events.)

Swinburne, R. (1992) *Revelation: From Metaphor to Analogy*, Oxford: Clarendon Press. (Develops an account of the meaning and justification of Christian propositional revelation.)

RICHARD SWINBURNE

REVOLUTION

There have been revolutions in politics, science, philosophy and most other spheres of human life. This entry discusses revolution mainly through concepts pertaining especially to the political realm. Attempts to define political revolution have been controversial; as a consequence there is dispute about whether specific occurrences were revolutions, rebellions, coups d'état or reformations.

If we define revolution as the illegal introduction of a radically new situation and order for the sake of obtaining or increasing individual or communal freedom, we may list those characteristics most often ascribed to it. These characteristics distinguish it from its earlier use where revolution referred to the return of an original state of affairs, as in astronomy; they also allow its distinction from related concepts such as reformation. At least at a superficial level this definition can do justice to early modern (seventeenth and eighteenth) as well as late modern (nineteenth and twentieth century) revolutions. Through these periods there has, however, been sufficient change in concepts closely related to revolution to require the definition's openness to nuances for it to apply to both periods. It is unclear whether even such a nuanced definition can apply in postmodern thought.

1   **Related concepts**
2   **Defining characteristics**
3   **Revolution and reason**

1   Related concepts

Revolution should be distinguished from *reformation, rebellion* and *coup d'état. Coup d'état* refers to attempts to change the rulers of a system, often with the intent of making more accessible or changing the benefits derivable from that same system; and rebellion indicates attempts to redress specific grievances within a particular system without necessarily a change of that system's leadership. Reformation denotes events potentially more extensive than either of these; it aims at general overhaul by insisting that pre-existing fundamental norms judge both rulers and systems. If a system is not structured by these norms and its rulers refuse their implementation, reformers take it as their task to change the system to conformity, if necessary against the rulers' wishes. Not infrequently, one result is a split in the system, with part remaining unreformed under the old leadership and part claiming successful confirmation of old norms under new leadership. Revolution designates events more radical than any of these; its

intent is not modification but uprooting and transformation.

To clarify the difference between reformation and revolution, consider two events whose traditional labels correctly mark it: the early sixteenth-century Lutheran Reformation and the late eighteenth-century French Revolution. Although they share their stress on the individual and its concomitant rejection of certain kinds of authority, there are profound dissimilarities reflecting an essential distinction.

Notwithstanding Luther's stress on individuals in his rejection of the church's mediating role between individual and God, he insists primarily on extra-personal unchanging norms – revealed by God and codified in the Scriptures – which are to judge both church and individual. Since he believed these norms no longer characterized institutional and individual practice, their practice needed re-formation in order to restore institutional legitimacy and secure the individuals' justification. Underlying Luther's slogan 'through faith alone' is the requirement that we should return to intended and traditional ways. Equality before God includes equal individual responsibility for implementing God's unchanging edicts (see LUTHER).

Of the French Revolution's slogans 'no God, no master' and 'freedom, equality, brotherhood', the first demands extirpation of all external religious and secular hierarchical power, while the second indicates the outcome of heeding that call. Liberation from divine and royal edicts enfranchises a common humanity expressed through each free and equal individual. The norms which are to structure life now find their source in each individual's reason; and the assumed commonality of human nature, including reason's universal sameness, guarantees the uniformity and authorizes the universally compelling force of these rules. The Revolution meant to effect a total reversal: institutions sanctioned in the past through extra-individual powers are found wanting when judged by new norms demanding a new order derived from its subjects.

This comparison distinguishes reformation from revolution through their different radicalism. Whereas reformers return to roots, insisting that institutions and actions conform to root situations, revolutionaries pluck up and discard roots. Reformers reinstitute old norms, revolutionaries establish new ones. When they aim to re-establish a quite probably mythical past golden age, reformers are appropriately called 'utopian reactionaries'. In contrast to reformers, revolutionaries are anti-tradition in their suspicion and rejection of whatever their cultural present or past would have them accept on trust.

Both rebellion and *coup d'état* can function in

reforming and revolutionary movements. Rebellions may occur when a reforming movement's leadership is deemed to effect change too quickly or too slowly, or to aim at reinstitution of the wrong norms. If the leadership resist the rebels' demands a coup may follow – although often not, strictly speaking, a *coup d'état*, since the leaders of a reformation need not be leaders of a state. The success of a *coup* allows for continuing reformation at a different pace or in a different direction. Similarly for revolutions: rebellions or coups are then not themselves revolutionary to the extent that the revolution is already under way; rebels then demand a change of pace or of direction (that is, new ideals different from those pursued by the current leadership). If the current revolutionary leadership rejects such demands a *coup* may follow. Regimes that revolutionaries want to depose seldom leave quietly; revolutions tend to be violent events. Similarly for *coups* within revolutionary movements: of the French Revolution it was said that it devoured its children.

2 Defining characteristics

The definition introduced above contains three characteristics of revolution: (1) radical novelty, (2) illegality, and (3) freedom. These three are both essential and most frequently present in writings on revolution, and will remain focal.

Radical novelty is generally seen as fundamental to revolution; both illegality and freedom presuppose it. Writers speak of revolution as involving 'drastic substitution', 'fundamental change', 'the speaking of a new, unheard of language, another logic, a revaluation of all values', a change 'affecting the fundamental laws' and expressing itself in 'radical transformation' (Brinton 1952; Friedrich 1966). This radical novelty as fundamental change makes revolutions typically modern phenomena. Pre-modern times accepted a transcendent reality (as in the Greeks' Platonic Good or the Medievals' Christian God) which characteristically imposed eternally and universally binding norms for human institutions and actions. The appearance of revolutions coincides with the irrelevance (at least in principle) of the transcendent in some of the most important events of human history.

Not all alteration of fundamental laws or constitutions is illegal; constitutions often include directives for their legal amendments. Revolutionary change is illegal change of fundamental laws, unconstitutional change of constitutions. Because revolutionary change is meant to be sweeping and fundamental, it intends to remove whatever opposes it which is, primarily, the current order. Since the order to be

instituted is radically different from the order it means to replace, the latter contains no provision for sanctioning the former.

Revolutions occur for the sake of promoting human freedom (Arendt 1963). This freedom is both positive and negative, freedom from a current order creating room for freedom to institute a new order. The pertaining order is always seen as constricting, its revolutionary abolition as enfranchising, the new order as guaranteeing greater freedom. Like illegality so also is freedom intrinsically connected with radical novelty: what is completely swept away has lost all power to prevent the revolutionaries' establishment of their new order. Freedom is connected, as well, with passion, for revolutionaries are persons chafing under constraints which they want removed; they are driven by anger about the present, confidence in the possibility of progress and hence hope for a better future. Passion precipitates revolutions, while reason serves as an instrument to direct both liberating activity and the establishment of new freedom.

3 Revolution and reason

An intimate relationship between revolution and reason in the early modern period raises the question whether a single definition of revolution is possible given changing views of the nature and role of reason as we move from this period through historicism into postmodernism (see HISTORICISM; POSTMODERNISM).

Influential early modern thinkers took reason to dictate the revolutionary stance of plucking up and discarding roots. DESCARTES was the first to present this stance as integral to all systematic thinking. In his *Discourse on the Method* (1637) reductionistic reason dictates non-acceptance of whatever experience initially provides as true or good unless the individual is able to free such items from their given contexts and then fit them into a new rational scheme. His *Meditations* (1641) provide the new foundation for this rational scheme in the activity of the individual's autonomous thought. Descartes's project displays all the major characteristics of revolutionary activity: it opposes predominant systems of his day which upheld the absolute necessity of tradition and so could not possibly legitimate its uprooting; it introduces the radical novelty of locating the criteria of truth in each individual thinker; its initial rejection of all givens aims to free thinkers from historical contexts to enable their progress in knowledge, power and freedom. In the following century figures important to the French Revolution spoke of Descartes as their precursor in breaking the tyranny of tradition.

With HEGEL (§8), MARX (§8) and ENGELS, historicism, for which anything must be understood in its past-dependent changing context, becomes part of the Western outlook. Marx and Engels therefore locate initiating revolutionary force in material and economic conditions rather than in persons no longer characterized by reductionistic reason. *The Communist Manifesto* (1848) states as conditions for revolution: exploitation of the suppressed class to the degree that it understands and becomes ready to shake off institutional shackles; and incapacity of the oppressors to continue exploitation competently. Both conditions appear through the historically inexorable development of class antagonism under changing forms of economic production. Reason still has a place – revolution is a rational attempt by the oppressed to achieve change – but economic forces expressed as macro-historical laws are primary in determining the possibility of revolutionary activity. Economic forces, argues *The German Ideology* (1846), cause changes in material production and alter the oppressed's thinking and products of their thinking so that, generally, it is not thought which determines life but life which determines thought. Nevertheless, chief characteristics of the earlier definition remain. The socialist revolution is seen as introducing novelty greater than that of the French Revolution, for it will abolish classes as well as the old division of labour; it will certainly be illegal in the eyes of both oppressors and oppressed, for it will annul the oppressing legal system and thereby progress towards new forms of freedom.

Postmodernism considers itself free from all forms of modern rationality; in its rejection of both reductionistic and holistic past narratives it embraces epistemic, moral and cultural relativism. Consequently, postmodernism neither advocates a particular political stance nor identifies an overarching cause for revolution (see POSTMODERNISM IN POLITICAL PHILOSOPHY §2). It rejects 'the *foundational* character of the revolutionary act, the institution of a point of concentration of power from which society could be "rationally" reorganized' (Laclau and Mouffe 1985: 177; original emphasis). Nevertheless, the term revolution is ubiquitous in its political, sociological and artistic writings and 'revolutionary' now conveys no less praise than during late-modernity's struggles for liberation. But can revolution retain any of its modern content given a radical diversity of values? Are the dislocated selves of postmodernity still capable of deliberate revolutionary activity in a relativistic culture? Or is it only possible to rebel against contingent structures, or perpetrate *coups* at best resulting in transfer of control from one group to another without a fuller realization of individual or communal freedom?

Modernity's revolution became possible given its concepts of rationality, freedom, radical novelty and progress, where at least some of the meaning of these terms carried over from its earlier to its later phase. Postmodernity's questioning the meaning of each of these terms makes the univocal use of revolution more problematic when we move from modernity to postmodernity than from early to late modernity.

References and further reading

* Arendt, H. (1963) *On Revolution*, Westport, CT: Greenwood Press, 140–1, 235–6. (Referred to in §2. A classic modern introduction to the topic, illustrated with reference to major European events.)
* Brinton, C. (1952) *Anatomy of Revolution*, New York: Vintage Books, esp. its opening pages and 277–8. (Referred to in §2. Presents a comparative historical study of major Western revolutions with the French Revolution as an archetypical phenomenon.)
  Calvert, P. (1990) *Revolution and Counter-Revolution*, Milton Keynes: Open University Press. (Useful general introduction to theoretical accounts of the concept.)
* Descartes, R. (1637) *Discourses on the Method*, in J. Cottingham, R. Stoothoff and D. Murdoch (eds) *The Philosophical Writings of Descartes*, vol. 1, Cambridge: Cambridge University Press, 1985. (Introduces the modern stance for which reductionistic human reason dictates that, fundamentally, truth is known non-contextually.)
* —— (1641) *Meditations*, in J. Cottingham, R. Stoothoff and D. Murdoch (eds) *The Philosophical Writings of Descartes*, vol. 2, Cambridge: Cambridge University Press, 1985. (Presents the influential early-modern argument for the autonomy of the individual's thought which places the criteria for truth in each individual thinker.)
  Dunn, J. (1989) *Modern Revolutions: An Introduction to the Analysis of a Political Phenomenon*, Cambridge: Cambridge University Press, 2nd edn. (An important theoretical introduction followed by an analysis of eight twentieth-century revolutions; provides an extensive bibliography.)
* Friedrich, C.J. (1966) *Revolution*, New York: Atherton Press, esp. 4, 37, 124. (Referred to in §2. Contains various useful articles on theories of revolution.)
  Kristeva, J. (1984) *Revolution in Poetic Language*, New York: Columbia University Press. (Explores the meaning of revolution in postmodernist semiotic and aesthetic terms.)
* Kuhn, T.S. (1970) *The Structure of Scientific Revolutions*, Enlarged, Chicago, IL: University of Chicago

Press, 2nd edn. (Classic treatment of revolutions in science, which argues that the characteristics of radical novelty and illegality hold for scientific as well as political revolutions.)

Laclau, E. (1991) *New Reflections on the Revolution of Our Time*, London: Verso. (Argues that, free from modern notions of rationality, certain kinds of revolution are still possible in a postmodern world).

* Laclau, E. and Mouffe, C. (1985) *Hegemony and Socialist Strategy: Towards a Radical Democratic Politics*, London: Verso. (Referred to in §3. Defines 'radical democracy' in the postmodern condition of social and cultural relativism, a definition which displaces the old leftist understanding of and commitment to revolution.)

* Marx, K. and Engels F. (1846) *The German Ideology*, ed. C.J. Arthur, London: Lawrence & Wishart, 1970. (Refrred to in §3. Explores relationships among material and economic conditions, modes of thought and sociopolitical activity.)

* —— (1848) *The Communist Manifesto*, London: Lawrence & Wishart, 1983. (Referred to in §3. A popular tract which states the conditions for, and urges the working class to, revolution.)

PETER A. SCHOULS

RGYAL TSHAB DAR MA RIN CHEN (1364– 1432)

rGyal tshab dar ma rin chen (Gyeltsap darma rinchen) was a disciple of the great Tsong kha pa. Like much Tibetan philosophy, his work is commentarial in style. In his commentaries on the work of Dharmakīrti he developed a moderate realist position with regard to abstract entities, claiming that this was what Dharmakīrti (apparently an antirealist) really intended. Properties, rGyal tshab maintained, do exist, but not independently of things; universals are separable from particulars in thought, but never in perception. Perception straightforwardly presents us with real objects; inference, on the other hand, tends to present reality in a distorted way.

rGyal tshab dar ma rin chen (Gyeltsap darma rinchen) was one of the foremost disciples of TSONG KHA PA BLO BZANG GRAGS PA (Dzongkaba, 1357–1419), the founder of the dGa'-ldan (Ganden) school, later known as dGe-lugs-pa (Geluk). rGyal tshab was born in Western Tibet at Ri-nang and moved to Sa-skya, where he acquired a solid scholarly reputation prior to meeting Tsong kha pa. He became one of Tsong kha pa's closest disciples. After his teacher passed away, rGyal tshab succeeded him to the throne of dGa'-ldan monastery.

Even more than other Tibetan thinkers, rGyal tshab discusses classical problems both on the basis of their philosophical merits and in relation to, and under the form of, commentaries on basic texts formative of the tradition. He does not examine philosophical propositions independently of the traditional framework, but always examines other systems from within his own and defends or develops his own from within. This he sees as responsible philosophizing, as distinguished from irresponsible sophistry. rGyal tshab offers a number of clear expositions of important Buddhist commentaries omitted by his master, and among his commentaries those elucidating the texts of Maitreya and Dharmakīrti are his greatest contributions.

A peculiarity of the way rGyal tshab interprets Dharmakīrti's epistemology is that he presents a realist version of a system that is fundamentally antirealist. Although DHARMAKĪRTI (§2) describes universals as unreal conceptual constructs, rGyal tshab does not accept this description as representing Dharmakīrti's true thought. Following a realist tradition of interpretation that goes back to at least Phya pa chos kyi seng ge (Chaba chögyi sengge, 1109–69), rGyal tshab holds that Dharmakīrti's many passages that seem to reject universals must be reinterpreted, for they lead to unacceptable philosophical consequences.

rGyal tshab's position is a form of moderate realism. Like its Western counterparts, it is born from the attempt to find a middle ground between the extreme realists and the antirealists. Moderate realists are sympathetic to the antirealist's rejection of the extreme realist assertion that properties exist independently of the particulars that instantiate them. They are unwilling, however, to take the next antirealist step, namely the complete rejection of abstract entities. If abstract entities were totally dependent on our conceptual schemata, as argued by the antirealists, our concepts would be arbitrary. To avoid this unwanted consequence, moderate realists hold that we must admit that properties exist independently of the mind. This does not mean, argue the moderate realists, that they exist independently of their instances. How, they ask, can properties exist without any support in empirical reality? Consequently, moderate realists hold that universals exist in things (see ABSTRACT OBJECTS).

The problem with this position is that it makes it difficult to spell out the relation between universals and their instances. Since they do not exist apart, they cannot be different. And yet they cannot be identical either, since the former are not reducible to the latter.

rGyal tshab and his tradition respond to this predicament, which seems inherent in moderate realism, by positing a new type of relation: particulars and universals are described as being distinct and yet the same entity (*ngo bo gcig la ldog pa tha dad*). Suffice it to say here that, for rGyal tshab, particulars and universals are distinct because they can be separated by thought. Hence they can be thought of as apart, but, since they cannot be taken apart by perceptual experience, they are the same entity.

Epistemologically, the consequence of rGyal tshab's realism is that he presents a picture of perception that differs markedly from that of Sa skya Paṇḍita (Sagya paṇḍita, 1182–1251). For rGyal tshab, perception presents us with a fully fledged common-sense object. When we perceive, for example, a jar, we do not merely sense a presence that we interpret as a jar. Rather, we directly see the object as being a jar. This common-sense account of perception is possible for rGyal tshab because of his acceptance of real universals. Because they exist in reality, perception, which accurately reflects reality, can perceive them and deliver a cognitively articulated vision of reality.

A similar realist streak is present in rGyal tshab's account of inference. He accepts that conceptual cognition in general, and inference in particular, are distorted. They do not apprehend the object as it is. This does not mean, argues rGyal tshab, that they are totally mistaken, as antirealist interpreters wrongly assume. Conceptuality should not be thought of as being cut off from reality, but rather as putting us in touch with reality, albeit in an indirect and distorted way.

See also: NOMINALISM, BUDDHIST DOCTRINE OF; TIBETAN PHILOSOPHY

List of works

rGyal tshab dar ma rin chen (1364–1432) *tshad ma rnam 'grel gyi tshig le'ur byas pa'i rnam bshad thar lam phyin ci ma log par gsal bar byed pa* (The Faultless Revealing of the Path to Liberation, a Complete Explanation of the Stanzas of [Dharmakīrti's] *Pramāṇavārttika*), Varanasi: Ge-luk-ba Press, 1974–5; second chapter trans. R. Jackson, *Is Enlightenment Possible? Dharmakīrti and rGyal tshab on Knowledge, Rebirth, No-Self and Liberation*, Ithaca, NY: Snow Lion Publications, 1993. (rGyal tshab's major commentary on Dharmakīrti's main work on epistemology and logic, the 'Commentary on Valid Cognition'.)

—— (1364–1432) *tshad ma rigs pa'i gter gyi rnam bshad legs par tshad pa'i snying po* (Essence of Good Sayings, an Explanation of [Sa skya Paṇḍita's] *tshad ma rigs gter*), in G. Dreyfus and S. Onoda, *A Recent Rediscovery: rGyal tshab's Rigs gter rnam bshad*, Kyoto: Biblia Tibetica, 1994. (This commentary on Sa skya Paṇḍita's work on logic and epistemology – the 'Treasure on the Science of Valid Cognition' – was not included in rGyal tshab's collected works, but then resurfaced in Tibet.)

—— (1364–1432) *phar phyin rnam bshad snying po rgyan* (The Essential Ornament, a Complete Explanation of the Perfection [of Wisdom Sūtra]), Varanasi: Ge-luk-ba Press, 1980. (rGyal tshab's main commentary on Maitreya's *Abhismayālaṃkara*.)

—— (1364–1432) *Commentary on Āryadeva's Catuḥśataka*, trans. R. Sonam and Geshe Sonam Rinchen, *The Yogic Deeds of Bodhisattvas; Gyeltsap on Āryadeva's Four Hundred*, Ithaca, NY: Snow Lion Publications, 1994. (Being an explanation of Buddhist practice according to the Madhayamaka school by Nāgārjuna's main disciple.)

References and further reading

Dreyfus, G. (1996) *Recognizing Reality*, New York: State University of New York Press. (A philosophical discussion of Sa skya Paṇḍita's epistemology in the context of the Tibetan reception of Dharmakīrti.)

GEORGES B.J. DREYFUS

RHAZES *see* AL-RAZI, ABU BAKR MUHAMMAD IBN ZAKARIYYA'

RHETORIC

Rhetoric is the power to persuade, especially about political or public affairs. Sometimes philosophy has defined itself in opposition to rhetoric – Plato invented the term 'rhetoric' so that philosophy could define itself by contrast, and distinctions like that between persuasion and knowledge have been popular ever since. Sometimes philosophy has used rhetorical techniques or materials to advance its own projects. Some of its techniques, especially topics of invention, the classification of issues, and tropes or figures of speech, are occasionally employed by philosophers. The philosophical question is whether these techniques have any interest beyond efficacy. What is the relation between techniques effective in persuading others and methods for making up one's own mind? Is there any connection

305

between the most persuasive case and the best decision? Is there a relation between the judgments of appropriateness and decorum exercised by the rhetorician, and the judgments of appropriateness exercised by the person of practical wisdom? Do judgments about probability, ambiguity and uncertainty, and judgments under constraints of time or the need for decision, aspire to the ideal of perfect rationality, to which they are doomed to fall short, or do these kinds of judgment have an integrity of their own? Apart from supplying useful techniques, an art of persuasion also raises philosophic questions concerning the relation between rhetoric and logic, rhetoric and ethics, and rhetoric and poetics.

1   **Philosophy and rhetoric at their beginning**
2   **Philosophical problems posed by rhetoric**
3   **Rhetorical methods and philosophy**

1   Philosophy and rhetoric at their beginning

Plato invented the term 'rhetoric' as a contrast term against which philosophy could define itself. Philosophy and rhetoric both proposed new truths and apparently powerful methods that threatened existing moral codes and authorities. As modes of empowerment, self-making and self-consciousness they could as easily become enemies as allies. Thus while philosophy attempted to achieve self-consciousness and power through an awareness of thought and being, rhetoric focused on an awareness of language and the circumstances of speaking and acting. Cicero interpreted the Platonic separation of philosophy from rhetoric as that of Socrates dividing wisdom from eloquence, and saw that the task of philosophical rhetoric was to overcome this separation. Prior to Socrates, he says in *de Oratore*, 'the same teaching seems to have imparted education both in right conduct and in good speech . . . the same masters gave instruction in both ethics and rhetoric' (see CICERO §§1, 2). From the beginning, then, rhetoric already had the pejorative connotation it continues to have, in spite of periodic attempts to speak in its defence.

Rhetoric's importance for philosophy seems greatest in periods of political and cultural confrontation and pluralism, for example, during Roman expansion, the Renaissance and today. These are all times of 'linguistic turns' in philosophy and, in addition, of fruitful interactions between philosophic and legal argumentation and interpretation. Linguistic, legal and pragmatic turns are rhetorical phenomena that direct attention to effective reasoned communication. In such times, the revival of rhetoric is motivated by a sense that philosophy itself has become too professionalized and too remote from human concerns. Rhetoric is then invoked, as in Cicero, to bring philosophy back down to earth. That neither Rome nor the Renaissance is considered a golden age of philosophy is probably a reflection of their rhetorical character.

Whether or not the history of philosophy is a series of footnotes to Plato, the history of the philosophical issues of rhetoric certainly can be read that way. The *Gorgias* begins by showing the difficulty in defining rhetoric. Gorgias finds it hard not only to define rhetoric logically, but to offer a definition in the more serious sense of keeping it within its proper sphere. In Socrates' hands the universality of rhetoric becomes a sign of emptiness, not power, and its flexibility turns from resourcefulness into slavishness. The conversation between Socrates and Polus make this philosophy of rhetoric the first example of 'applied ethics', in which one searches for ethical constraints on an activity. The conversation between Socrates and Callicles originates the tradition of 'professional ethics' which relates the internal norms of a practice to the sort of person the practitioner is.

Other Platonic dialogues amplify these considerations and raise further questions. The same rhetoric that appears in the *Gorgias* as a power of domination appears in the *Protagoras* in a context of mutual agreement. The most obvious use of rhetoric – arguing both sides of a question – can be either to exercise power unilaterally or to provide the basis of community, just as competitive Homeric virtues either underlie or are transformed into the cooperative virtues of the polis. In the twentieth century, Kenneth Burke (1950) highlights this shift by changing the central occupation of rhetoric from persuasion to 'identification'. The relation between the competitive and cooperative facets of rhetorical argument sets another philosophic problem for rhetoric: Under what conditions can the power to argue both sides of a question become the power to uncover truth through the free competition or marketplace of ideas? (In *On Liberty*, Mill develops his vision of truth emerging through controversy by reference to Cicero, 'the second greatest orator in antiquity'.) The introductory conversation in the *Protagoras* between Hippocrates and Socrates raises questions about the relation between learning from the sophists and being a sophist oneself. The dialogue then presents Socrates in conversation with the sophists Protagoras, Hippias and Prodicus. Protagoras limits the domain of rhetoric to political questions, justice and civic virtue, while Hippias would expand it to cover the natural sciences, and Prodicus would extend it to literary interpretation. Whether rhetoric is restricted to political questions, whether there is a 'rhetoric of science' or further uses of rhetoric outside politics all become standard questions for rhetoric from then onwards.

The *Phaedrus* turns to a third possible alliance which defines rhetoric in relation to poetics. In addition to rhetoric and logic (what does the rhetorician know?) and rhetoric and ethics (what are the uses and abuses of this power, and what sort of person does one become in practising rhetoric?) there is the relation between rhetoric and poetry, another activity that either employs charms not available to more rational approaches or operates at a further remove from reality. The *Phaedrus* raises further questions concerning the relation between written and spoken language, and so between the production and reception of discourse, a line of investigation that eventually leads from rhetoric to hermeneutics. Questions from the *Gorgias* concerning rhetoric and knowledge are formulated in the *Phaedrus* in a pointed manner as the relation between rhetoric and sincerity and deception, or between persuasion, *eros*, beauty, and seduction. Burke's investigations of the relations between serious and playful uses of language are a modern rediscovery of this set of questions, as are the recent revivals of rhetoric in DE MAN and DERRIDA.

The *Phaedrus* ends with Socrates asking whether there is a rhetoric for philosophy – that is, whether there are modes of communication that are especially suited for philosophy. But Socrates' questions about written versus spoken language, and long speeches versus questions and answers, at the same time pose the parallel problem of whether rhetoric has a philosophy, whether it has ethical or metaphysical commitments. The answer is parallel to that for the analogous question about mathematics: does the mathematical enterprise inherently have a 'philosophy'. There seems to be a natural affinity between mathematics and one type of philosophy, namely Platonism. On the other hand there are as many philosophies of mathematics as there are types of philosophy. Similarly, there are affinities of rhetoric with scepticism and relativism, and there are as many philosophies of rhetoric as there are kinds of philosophy (see PLATO §§4, 5).

2 Philosophical problems posed by rhetoric

Rhetoric is persuasive communication, especially about practice and politics. Whether rhetoric is a subject for philosophy depends on whether persuasion raises issues of its own apart from those exhausted by logic, ethics and psychology. If the way people were persuaded had nothing at all to do with logical cogency or ethical responsibility, or if it was simply reducible to one of them, there would be nothing philosophic about rhetoric. It is only because there seems to be some connection between logical cogency and rhetorical persuasiveness, between the trust accorded a persuasive speaker and the confidence we have in good ethical agents, and between figurative language and something more than mere ornament, that rhetoric is a subject for philosophy. While rhetorical theory has had negligible influence on the history of philosophy, the problems raised by rhetorical practice are significant philosophical problems.

All the issues raised by Plato's dialogues could have become philosophical problems in a variety of ways, but they were disciplined by Aristotle's organization of knowledge. The details of Aristotle's *Rhetoric* have had little impact on the history of either philosophy or rhetoric, but his placement of rhetoric relative to other arts and sciences has organized the trajectory of the relation of philosophy and rhetoric. Rhetoric, he says, is the offshoot of dialectic and politics. There are three ends and kinds of rhetoric: political or deliberative rhetoric directed towards utility; judicial or forensic rhetoric which determines justice and injustice; and epideictic or demonstrative rhetoric which concerns worthiness and blameworthiness. There are three sources of persuasion or belief (*pistis*) in rhetoric – the character (*êthos*) of the speaker, the passions of the audience, and the 'speech (*logos*) itself, in so far as it proves or seems to prove' – generating the trio implicit in Plato: rhetoric and logic, rhetoric and ethics, rhetoric and poetics.

The meaning and scope of all these terms of opposition (logic, ethics and poetics) shifts as the domain of rhetoric itself expands and contracts. Rhetoric is potentially about everything that can be communicated, and so about all thought and language. But the use of speech in deliberation about the concrete and practical particular is always at its core. As ethics after Aristotle became less political, so too did rhetoric. In Plato's dialogue, Protagoras defines his subject politically as the abilities without which men could not be citizens. Others softened the definition to the ability to speak on those matters on which people would be ashamed not to have an opinion, that is, the field of common sense and common understanding. Austin's (1962) inquiry captures part of the idea of persuasive communication apart from a political context, and shows the alliance between the linguistic and the rhetorical turns of philosophy (see AUSTIN, J.L.). Some argue that rhetoric is as broad as human speech in general, with extensions to general rhetorics like the 'rhetoric of inquiry' or 'rhetoric of the human sciences' or, as with Burke, to all strategies for encompassing situations. Others would restrict it to public or political affairs. The broadening of rhetoric is sometimes a reflection of the lack of political, or even practical, functioning for rhetoric, and sometimes a corrective to the impractical specialization and professionalization of rhetoric itself. The logic, ethics and poetics against which rhetoric defines itself are usually much broader than the three sources of proof in Aristotle's account.

3 Rhetorical methods and philosophy

As rhetoric developed, it elaborated specific techniques for persuasion, and even if rhetorical activity had no philosophic dimensions, the history of rhetoric would still offer a usable history of persuasion. The first rhetorical method with philosophic import is that of topical invention, which brings into focus the relation between rhetoric and logic. *Topos* is the Greek word for place, translated into Latin as *locus*. *Koinoi topoi* became *loci communi* and then, in English, 'commonplaces,' places to find arguments, pigeon-holes for classifying appeals, or major premises from which to derive particular conclusions. Topics are the means for finding something persuasive to say in a practical situation. Aristotle defines rhetoric as an art of finding in any case the available means of persuasion. Subsequent rhetoricians make invention (*heuresis*, *inventio*) the first of five parts of rhetoric, alongside judgment (sometimes called disposition or arrangement), style, memory and delivery. Any of these can be a merely verbal technique or an art with philosophical significance. The topics can range from the logical ('similar effects have similar causes') to more substantive considerations ('follow the money'; *'cherchez la femme'*; 'we all know that Athenians are acquisitive'). Often there is a connection between methods for finding arguments and systems of artificial memory for recalling them. When the rhetorical invention of arguments is replaced by a scientific discovery of things, only style remains in rhetoric's domain. Ramus' (1574) division of labour between a topical dialectic or logic and a rhetoric confined to style and arrangement in the early modern period is perhaps the most historically influential of such moves.

Scientific method might supplant rhetorical invention, but the methods of scientific discovery which replace rhetorical invention were themselves derived from topical invention. Much of the meaning of necessity in seventeenth-century science, for example, derives from pleas of necessity as an excuse or justification in legal proceedings. Stephen Toulmin's (1964) 'inference warrants', which supply the connection between grounds and claims, is one recent reappearance of the topics; Chaim Perelman's (1969) *loci* for establishing connections is another.

Hume finds the meaning of 'personal merit' through epideictic rhetoric by 'displaying the praises of any humane, beneficent man'. He refers to the considerations used as the 'topics of praise'. The inter-relations among the three kinds of rhetoric, and the kinds of argument appropriate to each, generate significant philosophical problems. Why, as Hume asks, does utility please? What is the relation between the impartial spectator whose judgment is the focus of epideictic rhetoric, the judge whose verdicts are the end of forensic rhetoric, and the ideal deliberative agent? What is the relation between the right and the good, or between what is best and what should be done? What is the connection between action-guiding and agent-evaluating reasons?

The other two philosophically interesting rhetorical methods besides topical invention can trace their ancestry back to Plato and Aristotle, but were really developed in later rhetorics which emphasized judicial oratory and the performance values associated primarily with demonstrative rhetoric. Issues – *staseis* in Greek and *constitutiones* in Latin – were rhetoric's central technique for most of its history. The classification of issues evolved out of practices of judicial rhetoric, which is always the most systematic of the three kinds of rhetoric, and they draw attention to the relation between rhetoric and ethics. There are, usually, four *staseis*: (1) the question of fact or conjectural issue; (2) the definitive stasis; (3) the qualitative issue concerning mitigating or aggravating circumstances; and (4) the translative issue of whether a given court is the appropriate forum for judgment. Kant, not long after Hume, explains the 'principles of any transcendental deduction' by referring to stasis theory: 'Jurists, when speaking of rights and claims, distinguish in a legal action the question of right (*quid juris*) from the question of fact (*quid facti*)' (1787: B116–7). His question of right is the translative issue, by what right knowledge can be judged to have a 'legal title', so the foundations of knowledge cannot be secured by pointing to facts about the success of science. Austin's 'plea for excuses' and contemporary arguments about responsibility invite reconsideration of the rich problems that revolve around the qualitative issue.

If the topics emphasize the relations between rhetoric and logic, and the theory of issues or *staseis* develops the relation between rhetoric and ethics, the third rhetorical method, that of figures or tropes, concerns the relation of rhetoric to poetics. Augustine, in the *de Doctrina Christiana*, used rhetoric to teach Christians to read their Bible figuratively and to adjust contradictory passages by considering the circumstances to which speakers and authors adapted their statements and meanings. For Vico (1744), a near contemporary of Hume and Kant, the 'tropes are corollaries of poetic logic'. Borrowing from a formulation that seems to originate with Ramus, Vico names four primary tropes: metaphor, metonymy, synecdoche and irony. These tropes are not merely elegant variations on things that could be expressed more directly, but reveal original truths hidden by more sophisticated and professionalized philosophy. In the hands of our own contemporaries such as Kenneth Burke (1950) and Hayden White (1973), the figures move from methods of description or redescription into methods of seeing and encompassing situations, as rhetoric is expanded from a verbal to a universal art. Perelman, similarly, constructs a relation between argumentative forms and figures of speech and thought. Vico has become a hero to those who think that progress will come in philosophy from being anti-Cartesian, and championing conversation and communication over more limited, anti-rhetorical, forms of rationality. These examples show how even the most language-centred or poetic dimension of rhetoric has an ethical agenda. The rhetorical emphasis on saying what is appropriate provides the connection between ethical and poetic demands for timeliness and decorum. The current revival and popularity of rhetoric in philosophy often takes the form of a programme to replace science by conversation as the model for community and rationality and the hope for democracy.

See also: LANGUAGE, MEDIEVAL THEORIES OF; LANGUAGE, RENAISSANCE PHILOSOPHY OF; LEGAL REASONING AND INTERPRETATION

References and further reading

* Aristotle (*c.* mid 4th century BC) *On Rhetoric: A Theory of Civic Discourse*, trans. with introduction, notes and appendices by G.A. Kennedy, New York and Oxford: Oxford University Press, 1991. (The most readable and reliable English translation available.)
* Augustine (*c.*396–427) *De Doctrina Christiana (On Christian Doctrine)*, trans. D.W. Robertson, Jr, Indianapolis, IN: Bobbs-Merrill, 1958. (The most influential work explicitly adapting rhetoric to Christian religious and theological purposes.)
* Austin, J.L. (1962) *How to do things with words*, Cambridge, MA: Harvard University Press. (A recovery of the rhetorical dimension of language under the title 'performative utterance'.)
Barthes, R. (1970) 'L'Ancienne Rhetorique: Aide-mémoire', *Communications* 16 (1970): 172–229; 'The Old Rhetoric: An Aide-Mémoire', in *The Semiotic Challenge*, trans. R. Howard, New York: Hill & Wang, 1988, 11–94. (Designed as a summary of the history of rhetoric for students of contemporary literary criticism.)
* Burke, K. (1950) *A Rhetoric of Motives*, New York: Prentice Hall. (A cataloguing of the formal techniques for persuasion.)
—— (1965) *Permanence and Change: An Anatomy of Purpose*, Indianapolis, IN: Bobbs-Merill. (An analysis of uses of poetry to solve ethical conflicts through rhetoric as 'an art of appeal'.)
* Cicero (55 BC) *de Oratore*, trans. E.W. Sutton and H. Rackham, London: Loeb Classical Library, 1959. (Cicero's most philosophical treatment of rhetoric. Not a practical handbook but a dialogue on the place of rhetoric in ethical and political life.)
Conley, T.M. (1990) *Rhetoric in the European Tradition*, New York and London: Longman; Chicago, IL: University of Chicago Press, 1994. (A textbook, full of summaries and bibliographies; the best one-volume history of rhetoric.)
Garver, E. (1994) *Aristotle's Rhetoric: An Art of Character*, Chicago, IL: University of Chicago Press. (A philosophical analysis of Aristotle's Rhetoric.)
* Hume, D. (1748, 1751) *Enquiries Concerning the Human Understanding and Concerning the Principles of Morals*, ed. L.A. Selby-Bigge, Oxford: Clarendon Press, 1966. (A moral theory based on the inference patterns of epideicic rhetoric.)
* Kant, I. (1787) *Critique of Pure Reason*, trans. N. Kemp Smith, London: Macmillan, 1929. (A critical philosophy rooted in justificatory rhetoric.)
Kennedy, G. (1980) *Classical rhetoric and its Christian and secular tradition from ancient to modern times*, Chapel Hill, NC: University of North Carolina Press. (One of a series of informative histories of rhetoric by this author.)
McKeon, R. (1987) *Rhetoric: Essays in Invention and Discovery*, Woodbridge, CT: Oxbow Press. (Contains the influential 'Rhetoric in the Middle Ages' and other articles by an important but difficult historian and philosopher of rhetoric.)
* Mill, J.S. (1859) *On Liberty*, New York: Bobbs-Merrill, 1956. (Chapter 2, in particular, concerns the power of controversy and discussion to reveal truth.)
* Perelman, C. and Olbrecht-Tyteca, L. (1969) *The New Rhetoric: A Treatise on Argumentation*, Notre Dame, IN: University of Notre Dame Press. (A treatment of the argumentative force of figures of speech and the topics or *loci communes*.)
* Plato (*c.*390–347BC) *The Collected Dialogues of Plato*, ed. E. Hamilton and H. Cairns, Princeton, NJ: Princeton University Press, 1971. (All Plato's dialogues collected in one volume, with an introduction and prefatory notes.)
* Ramus, P. (1574) *Logikē*, trans. M. Roll, London:

Scholar Press, 1966. (The only edition available in English of this highly influential work.)

Richards, I.A. (1936) *The Philosophy of Rhetoric*, New York and London: Oxford University Press. (Proposes a new rhetoric that studies misunderstandings and their remedies.)

Ricoeur, P. (1977) *The Rule of Metaphor*, Toronto, Ont.: University of Toronto Press. (A historical and philosophical investigation of the interrelations between rhetorical and poetic approaches to language and literature.)

Trimpi, W. (1983) *Muses of One Mind: The Literary Analysis of Experience and Its Continuity*, Princeton, NJ: Princeton University Press. (Traces the competition and joint contributions of philosophy and rhetoric to literary theory, from the Greeks to the Renaissance.)

* Toulmin, S. (1964) *The Uses of Argument*, Cambridge: Cambridge University Press. (A re-discovery, under the name 'inference warrants', of the topics of classical rhetoric.)

* Vico, G. (1744) *The New Science*, trans. T. Bergin and M. Fish, Ithaca, NY: Cornell University Press, 1984. (A defence of rhetoric against philosophy, and in particular the epistemic and ethical value of figurative over literal language.)

* White, H. (1973) *Metahistory: The Historical Imagination in Nineteenth-Century Europe*, Baltimore, MD and London: Johns Hopkins University Press. (Uses of Kenneth Burke's theory of tropes to analyse historical narratives and philosophies of history.)

EUGENE GARVER

RICHARD OF MIDDLETON (*c.*1249–1302)

Richard was a Franciscan philosopher and theologian. In general he followed the tradition flowing from Bonaventure, although on some questions he sided with Thomas Aquinas. However, there is also a strong anti-Thomist reaction in his work. Many of the questions raised in the condemnations of 1277 at Paris and Oxford are central in Richard's works. His answers often echo Bonaventure, William of Ware and Matthew of Aquasparta; yet his argumentation carries his personal stamp and shows him deeply engaged with the definitions and arguments of the authors of his own era.

Richard studied in Paris during the intellectually exciting years 1276–87, probably under William of Ware and MATTHEW OF AQUASPARTA. In general, the *Doctor solidus* (Solid Doctor) followed the tradition flowing from BONAVENTURE, although on some questions he sided with Thomas AQUINAS, at least in his sober commentary on Peter Lombard's *Sentences* (probably begun in 1281 and completed in 1284). However, while regent master of the Franciscan house of studies in Paris from 1284–87, his *Quodlibeta (Quodlibetal Questions)* manifest a strong anti-Thomist reaction, as do his earlier *Quaestiones disputatae* (Disputed Questions) (disputed after 1277 but before the *Sentences* commentary). In 1295 he was elected Provincial Minister of France, and he died at Reims in 1302.

When Aquinas, for instance, argued that philosophical reason cannot show the impossibility of an eternal creation, Richard was quick to point out the ambiguity hidden in Aquinas' portrait of creation. When the latter speaks of *creatio ex nihilo* (creation out of nothing), he correctly stresses the absolute dependence of creatures on God for existence. Richard charged, however, that Aquinas' definition had excluded any consideration of the issue of duration. By neglecting a treatment of the temporal or eternal character of creation, Aquinas, according to Richard, had built a prejudice in favour of the possibility of an eternal world into his very definition of the term 'creation' (see ETERNITY OF THE WORLD, MEDIEVAL VIEWS OF).

Richard likewise rejects Aquinas' theory of individuation by matter. For him, the singular is singular by its proper essence, since this concrete essence is of its very nature indivisible. He thus follows in the footsteps of Bonaventure, for whom the ultimate cause of individuation is the very 'act of existence'. Richard agrees with the opinion that 'by the very fact that a thing actually exists, it is numerically one... Because a being in actual existence is composed of essence and actual existence, its being one adds nothing positive to such an actually existing being but only a negation of division' (*Sententiarum* I, d. 24, a. 1, q. 2).

By holding that in each of the elements there is only one substantial form, Richard disagreed with Bonaventure. However, as he moved on to consider the substantial forms in more complex beings, and especially in man, he reaffirmed the arguments of Bonaventure and John PECHAM for the plurality of substantial forms. Richard could not see how, for instance, those who argued for the unicity of substantial form or the dominance of the intellective or rational soul in man could explain why the accidents of the body remain the same in number after the recession of the intellective soul at death. The unicity-of-form theory, defended by Aquinas, Giles of Lessines, GILES OF ROME and many others, is also incapable of explaining human generation.

310

Richard taught that if there is to be any meaning to the phrase 'man generates man', then the vegetative and sensitive forms of the human being must exist before, and must continue to exist after, the arrival of the rational soul created directly by God. There must, therefore, be a plurality of substantial forms in composite beings.

In his theory of universals and in his theory of knowledge, Richard comes close to Aquinas: 'Whatever God has created is singular. A universal exists only through an act of the intellect' (*Sententiarum* I, d. 36, a. 1, q. 1) Intellectual knowledge arises from the singulars of experience by means of the abstraction performed by the agent intellect in human beings. Richard rejects the need for special divine illumination, defended by Bonaventure, to account for our intellectual knowledge. Human beings know, and they know by means of their own proper intellectual efforts.

This Aristotelian bent continues in Richard's discussion of man's knowledge of God. There is no innate or immediate knowledge of God. He can be known only in starting with creatures and by our reasoning about their origins or purposes: 'We only come to a knowledge of spiritual beings by means of sensible things... and to a knowledge of God only through sensible and intelligible effects...' (*Sententiarum* II, d. 25, a. 5, q. 1).

Richard's teaching on the primacy of the will returns him to the Augustinian camp. 'The will', he declares, 'is unqualifiedly more noble than the intellect' (*Sententiarum* II, d. 24, a. 1, q. 5). Richard argues that it is more noble to love God than to understand him, since such understanding, if not linked with love, keeps us aloof from God' (*Quaestiones disputatae* q. 10, a. 3). The nobility of our will, furthermore, is found in its freedom. Unlike the intellect, which can be forced by evidence, the will remains free except in the case of its end, the good. This object the will must pursue by the radical tendency built into it by its creator. However, the will is free in regard to all the means leading to that predetermined goal. There is no parallel between the case of the intellect, in connection with which we are forced to accept a logically drawn conclusion once we have accepted the premises, and the will in regard to those things that lead to our end. Even when our intellect shows us the best means to our end, we do not have to adopt them: 'For although the intellect, like a servant with a lamp, points out the way, the will, like the master, makes the decisions and can go in any direction it pleases' (*Sententiarum* II, d. 38, a. 2, q. 4).

Richard, with a questioning spirit, most often follows the tradition of Bonaventure. His commentary on the *Sentences* in particular represents a solid, searching mind in an age of great philosophical challenge and confusion.

See also: AQUINAS, T.; AUGUSTINIANISM; BONAVENTURE; GILES OF ROME

List of works

Richard of Middleton (1284–7) *Quodlibeta quaestiones octuaginta* (Eighty Quodlibetal Questions), Brescia, 1590; repr. Frankfurt: Minerva, 1963. (The reprinted edition also includes the *Sententiarum*.)

—— (1281–4) *Super IV libros Sententiarum Petri Lombardi quaestiones subtilissimae* (Questions on the Four Books of Peter Lombard's *Sentences*), Brescia, 1591; repr. Frankfurt: Minerva, 1963, 4 vols. (The reprinted edition also includes the *Quodlibeta*.)

—— (1277–84) *Quaestio de gradu formarum* (A Question on the Hierarchy of Forms), ed. R. Zavalloni, *Richard de Mediavilla et la controverse sur la pluralité des formes*, Louvain: Éditions de l'Institut Supérieur de Philosophie, 1951, 35–169. (On the hierarchy and plurality of forms.)

—— (1277–84) *Quaestiones disputatae* (Disputed Questions). (The following few questions have been edited: *Quaestio de unitate formae* (Question on the Unity of Form), ed. R. Zavalloni, *Richard de Mediavilla et la controverse sur la pluralité des formes*, Louvain: Éditions de l'Institut Supérieur de Philosophie, 1951, 173–80; *Quaestio de immortalitate animae* (Question on the Immortality of the Soul), ed. S. Vanni Rovighi, *L'immortalità dell'anima nel maestri francescani del secolo XIII*, Milan: Pubblicazioni dell'Università Cattolica del Sacro Cuore, 1936, 349–70; *Quaestio disputata: Utrum voluntas angeli possit movere se ipsam* (A Disputed Question: Can an Angel's Will Move Itself?), ed. O. Lottin, *Psychologie et morale aux XIIe et XIIIe siécles*, Louvain: Abbaye du Mont César, 1942, vol. I, 293–9; *Quaestio: Utrum angelus vel homo naturaliter intelligat verum creatum in veritate aeterna* (A Question: Can an Angel or a Human Being Naturally Understand Created Truth in Eternal Truth?), ed. Patres Franciscani, *De humanae cognitionis ratione anecdota*, Quaracchi: Ad Claras Aquas, 1883, 221–45.)

References and further reading

Cova, L. (1984) *Originale peccatum e concupiscentia in Riccardo di Mediavilla: vizio ereditario e sessualità nell'antropologia teologia del XIII secolo*, Rome: Edizioni dell'Ateneo. (Studies man's hereditary corruption and sensuality according to Richard.)

Cunningham, F.A. (1970) 'Richard of Middleton, O.F.M. on *esse* and Essence', *Franciscan Studies* 30: 49–76. (Richard's views on essence and existence.)

Henninger, M.G. (1994) 'Hervaeus Natalis (b. 1250/60; d. 1323) and Richard of Mediavilla (b. 1245/49; d. 1302/07)', in J.J.E. Gracia (ed.) *Individuation in Scholasticism: The Later Middle Ages and the Counter-Reformation, 1150–1650*, Albany, NY: State University of New York Press, 299–318. (Compares Richard's views with those of Hervaeus.)

Hocedez, E. (1916) 'Les "Quaestiones disputatae" de Richard de Middleton', *Recherches de science religieuse* 6: 493–513. (Provides a clear portrait of the content of Richard's disputed questions.)

—— (1925) *Richard de Middleton: sa vie, ses oeuvres, sa doctrine (Richard of Middleton: His Life, His Works and His Teaching)*, Louvain: Spicilegium Sacrum Lovaniense, and Paris: Librairie Ancienne Honoré Champion, Edouard Champion. (Provides a solid overview of Richard's life, works and teaching.)

Lampen, W. (1930) 'Richard de Mediavilla', *La France Franciscaine* 13: 388–90. (Updates two earlier articles concerning nationality of Richard.)

Lippens, H. (1944) 'De modo celebrandi Capitulum deque observantia Regulae in Provincia Franciae post annum 1517 (iuxta documenta inexplorata)', *Archivum Franciscanum Historicum* 37: 3–47. (Concerns the election of Richard as Provincial Minister of France: notes that this election does not determine his nationality.)

Sharp, D.E. (1930) 'Richard of Middleton', *Franciscan Philosophy at Oxford in the Thirteenth Century*, London: Oxford University Press; repr. Farnborough: Gregg Press, 1966, 211–76. (Summarizes the main doctrinal positions.)

Van Veldhuijsen, P. (1990) 'Richard of Middleton contra Thomas Aquinas on the Question Whether the Created World Could Have Been Eternally Produced by God', in J.B.M. Wissink (ed.) *The Eternity of the World in the Thought of Thomas Aquinas and his Contemporaries*, Studien und Texte zur Geistesgeschichte des Mittelalters 24, Leiden: Brill, 69–81. (Richard's views on eternity and creation.)

Zavalloni, R. (1951) *Richard de Mediavilla et la controverse sur la pluralité des formes* (Richard of Middleton on the Plurality of Forms), Philosophes médiévaux 2, Louvain: Éditions de l'Institut Supérieur de Philosophie. (Details Richard's role in the controversy over the unicity and plurality of forms in man.)

STEPHEN F. BROWN

RICHARD OF ST VICTOR (d. 1173)

Richard is most famous for his contemplative doctrine, which is based on a biblical anthropology that involves a philosophical psychology and noetic theory. Richard's writings should be understood in the context of Hugh of St Victor's programme for a complete theological pedagogy, organized according to the threefold sense of Scripture (literal, allegorical, tropological). Richard's specifically exegetical works include an encyclopedic introduction to the methods of interpreting Scripture, the Liber exceptionum, *and important commentaries on the Apocalypse and Ezekiel. Like Hugh, he stresses that the literal sense of Scripture is the foundation of its spiritual senses.*

Richard of St Victor was a native of Scotland or Ireland. He became an Augustinian Canon Regular at the Abbey of St Victor in Paris, where he was a student of HUGH OF ST VICTOR. He later served as sub-prior and prior of the monastery and was the master of its famous school. He died in 1173.

Richard's most important speculative work is *De trinitate* (On the Trinity). In the manner of ANSELM OF CANTERBURY, through a 'faith seeking understanding' he discovers 'necessary reasons' for God's existence, the divine attributes and the Trinity. Richard does not 'demonstrate' the Trinity, but through a conceptual logic of perfection considers the divine being as it is revealed in Scriptures. The reasons for the Trinity are intrinsic to God's 'necessary' being and attributes. God is love or Goodness itself, which by nature is wholly self-giving. God is also Glory itself and Felicity itself, which likewise communicate themselves wholly. This three-fold communicative fullness requires that there be one who gives himself exhaustively, one who receives and gives back himself exhaustively and one who from both receives exhaustively. A further existential category of 'one who gives nothing and receives nothing' is inconceivable. Therefore the circle of self-giving and receiving is consummated in three 'persons', each of whom possesses divine existence incommunicably and independently. Richard's account of the Trinity had considerable influence on ALEXANDER OF HALES, BONAVENTURE and John DUNS SCOTUS (see TRINITY).

According to Richard's contemplative teaching, union with God is possible because the soul's rational 'force' is created in the 'image' of God, and its affective 'force' is made in the 'likeness' of God. Originally the human body also reflected the divine nature. By the Fall, human reason was corrupted by ignorance, the affections by concupiscence and the body by infirmity and death. The light of divine wisdom heals the soul's ignorance, divine charity heals its concupiscence and the virtues alleviate the body's infirmity, although they cannot prevent its death. Within this dynamic of sin and grace, Richard develops a philosophical psychology of contemplation and spiritual perfection (see GRACE).

In *De duodecim patriarchis* (The Twelve Patriarchs), or *Benjamin minor*, Richard interprets the affiliations among the wives and sons of Jacob tropologically (that is, morally and mystically), as signifying relations among powers and virtues of the soul. In *De arca mystica* (The Mystical Ark), or *Benjamin major*, he tropologically interprets the features of the Ark revealed to Moses, as signifying cognitive powers of the soul. The soul's imaginative, reasonable and 'intelligent' powers apprehend, respectively, sensible, intelligible and transcendent 'intellectible' realities. These modes of apprehension diversify into six genera of contemplation. The first four are 'in the imagination according to imagination', or wonder at the order and form of sensible realities; 'in the imagination but according to reason', whereby the spirit discerns the principles underlying sensible realities; 'in reason according to imagination', whereby one discovers the similitudes of invisible realities in visible symbols; and 'in reason according to reason', whereby one contemplates purely spiritual created beings (for example, the human soul and its operations, angelic beings). These kinds of contemplation are attainable by human 'industry' aided by God, but the last two depend solely on the light of grace shining in the 'fine point of the intelligence'. The fifth kind, which contemplates the divine unity and attributes, is 'above reason but not without it'. The sixth 'is above and beyond reason' and seemingly against it, inasmuch as it regards mysteries (the Trinity, the Eucharist) that elude the priniciples of human thought.

Richard's philosophical psychology derives ultimately from Neoplatonic sources. The human soul is able to know itself immediately. Its rational and affective 'forces' are reciprocal and not really distinct, but are simply different modes of its operation. Hence love and desire motivate the search for wisdom, and understanding elicits love and desire. The soul's highest cognitive power, the 'intelligence', transcends discursive reasoning and penetrates spiritual realities intuitively (see PLATONISM, MEDIEVAL).

Richard of St Victor's contemplative writings profoundly influenced Bonaventure's *Journey of the Mind into God* and Dante's *Comedy* (see ALIGHIERI, DANTE). Bonaventure designates Richard (with PSEUDO-DIONYSIUS) as the exemplar of 'anagogic' or mystical theology. Accordingly, in the later Middle Ages Richard was a standard authority among mystical writers.

See also: HUGH OF ST VICTOR; PLATONISM, MEDIEVAL

List of works

Richard of St Victor (before 1173) *Opera omnia*, ed. F. Hugonin and J.-P. Migne, Patrologia Latina, Paris: 1855; repr. 1880, vol. 196. (A re-presentation of the seventeenth century edition prepared under the care of Victorine fathers. The volume contains some spurious works and omits some authentic ones. The text is often faulty.)

—— (before 1173) *De quatuor gradibus violentae caritatis* (The Four Degrees of Fervent Charity), ed. and trans. G. Dumeige, *Épître à Séverin sur la charité; Le quatre degrés de la violente charité (De quatuor gradibus violentae caritatis)*, Textes philosophiques du moyen âge 3, Paris: Vrin, 1955. (An edition of the Latin texts, with French translations, of a small treatise by a 'Brother Ivo', falsely attributed to Richard, and of *De quatuor gradibus*.)

—— (before 1173) *Liber exceptionum*, ed. J. Châtillon, *Liber exceptionum: Texte critique avec introduction, notes et tables*, Paris: Vrin, 1958. (A critical edition of the Latin text of Richard's methodological introduction to the reading of Scripture.)

—— (before 1173) *De trinitate* (On the Trinity), ed. J. Ribaillier, Textes philosophiques du moyen âge 6, Paris: Vrin, 1958. (A critical edition of the Latin text of Richard's most important speculative work. A French translation can be found in *La Trinité: Texte latin, introduction et notes*, ed. and trans. G. Salet, Sources Chrétiennes 63, Paris: Éditions du Cerf, 1959, which includes a Latin text with the French translation on facing pages. A reliable English translation of Book III only can be found in *The Twelve Patriarchs, The Mystical Ark, Book Three of The Trinity*, trans. G.A. Zinn, New York: Paulist Press, 1979.)

—— (before 1273) *De duodecim patriarchis* (The Twelve Patriarchs) or *Benjamin minor*, trans. G.A. Zinn, *The Twelve Patriarchs, The Mystical Ark, Book Three of The Trinity*, New York: Paulist Press, 1979. (A reliable English translation, with a good introduction to Richard's spiritual teaching.)

—— (before 1273) *De arca mystica (The Mystical Ark)* or *Benjamin major*, trans. G.A. Zinn, *The Twelve Patriarchs, The Mystical Ark, Book Three of The Trinity*, New York: Paulist Press, 1979. (A reliable English translation, with a good introduction to Richard's spiritual teaching.)

—— (before 1273) Theological Works, in J. Châtillon

and W.J. Tulloch (eds), J. Barthelemy (trans.) *Sermons et opuscules spirituels inédits 1: Texte latin, introduction et notes*, Paris: Desclée de Brouwer, 1951. (This volume presents the first edition of Richard's *Exiit edictum* or *De tribus processionibus*, with a French translation. The work gives spiritual interpretations of the processions celebrated on the feasts of the Purification, Palm Sunday and the Ascension.)

—— (before 1273) Theological Works, in J. Ribaillier (ed.) *Opuscules theologiques: Texte critique avec notes et tables*, Textes philosophiques du moyen âge 15, Paris: Vrin, 1967. (A critical edition of the Latin texts of speculative treatises by Richard concerning the power of absolving sins, the spirit of blasphemy, the final judgment, the Holy Spirit, the appropriations of the Trinity, the incarnate Word, the difference between venial and mortal sin and the explanation of difficult passages in Scripture.)

—— (before 1273) Three Treatises, in J. Châtillon (ed.) *Trois opuscules spirituels de Richard de Saint-Victor. Textes inedits accompagnes d'etudes critiques et de notes*, Paris: Études augustiniennes, 1986. (A critical edition of the Latin texts of three previously unedited treatises concerning the inner life of the soul.)

References and further reading

Châtillon, J. (1987) 'Richard de Saint-Victor', *Dictionnaire de spiritualité ascétique et mystique, histoire et doctrine*, Paris: Beauchesne, 1987, 13: 593–654. (An excellent, ample and detailed introduction to Richard's life, works, doctrine and influence, with a full bibliography of publications since 1952, by the leading student of Richard's texts and thought.)

DiLorenzo, R.D. (1982) 'Imagination as the First Way to Contemplation in Richard of St. Victor's *Benjamin minor*', *Medievalia et Humanistica* 11: 77–96. (An interesting study of the high value Richard places on the imagination and on its power to envision suprasensible realities. The essay lays the groundwork for assessing Richard's influence on Dante.)

Dumeige, G. (1952) *Richard de Saint-Victor et l'idée chrétienne de l'amour* (Richard of St Victor and the Christian Idea of Love), Paris: Presses universitaires de France, 1952. (A study of the central importance of the idea of love in every aspect of Richard's thought, especially important for a critical bibliography of publications on Richard until 1952.)

Lubac, H. de (1959–64) *Exégèse médiévale: Les quatre sens de l'Écriture* (Medieval Exegesis: The Four Senses of Scripture), Paris: Aubier, 4 vols. (In vol. 3, 361–435, de Lubac treats Richard's method of biblical interpretation and its place in the history of exegesis.)

Robilliard, J.A. (1939) 'Les six genres de contemplation chez Richard de Saint-Victor et leur origene platonicienne' (Richard of St Victor's Six Kinds of Contemplation and their Platonic Origin), *Revue des sciences philosophiques et théologiques* 28: 229–33. (A brief but important article tracing the Neoplatonic sources of Richard's genera of contemplation.)

Zinn, G.A. (1977) 'Personification, Allegory and Visions of Light in Richard of St. Victor's Teaching on Contemplation', *University of Toronto Quarterly* 46: 190–214. (A study of Richard's 'historical' personification allegory, distinct from rhetorical techniques of personification and allegory.)

KENT EMERY, JR

RICHARD RUFUS OF CORNWALL (d. after 1259)

A thirteenth-century philosopher and theologian, Rufus was among the first Western medieval authors to study Aristotelian metaphysics, physics and epistemology; his lectures on Aristotle's Physics *are the earliest known surviving Western medieval commentary. In 1238, after writing treatises against Averroes and lecturing on Aristotle – at greatest length on the* Metaphysics *– he joined the Franciscan Order, left Paris and became a theologian.*

Rufus' lectures on Peter Lombard's Sentences *were the first presented by an Oxford bachelor of theology. Greatly influenced by Robert Grosseteste, Rufus' Oxford lectures were devoted in part to a refutation of Richard Fishacre, the Dominican master who first lectured on the* Sentences *at Oxford. Though much more sophisticated philosophically than Fishacre, Rufus defended the more exclusively biblical theology recommended by Grosseteste against Fishacre's more modern scholasticism.*

Rufus' Oxford lectures were employed as a source by Bonaventure, whose lectures on the Sentences *were vastly influential. Returning to Paris shortly after Bonaventure lectured there, Rufus took Bonaventure's lectures as a model for his own Parisian* Sentences *commentary. Rufus' Paris lectures made him famous. According to his enemy Roger Bacon, when he returned to Oxford after 1256 as the Franciscan regent master, his influence increased steadily. It was at its height forty years later in the 1290s, when John Duns Scotus was a bachelor of theology. Early versions of many important positions developed by Duns Scotus can be found in Rufus' works.*

1 **Natural philosophy**
2 **Epistemology**
3 **Metaphysics**
4 **Logic**
5 **Influence**

1 Natural philosophy

As far as we know, the earliest work we have by Rufus is a set of lectures on Aristotle's *Physics*, presented at Paris shortly before the ban against teaching the *libri naturales* was formally lifted. A series of brief questions on issues raised by the Aristotelian text, they have never been published. The published works they most closely resemble are Roger Bacon's post-1237 question–commentaries.

Rufus' *Physics* commentary is important in part because of his unorthodox approach, often departing from Averroes' interpretation of Aristotle. Those departures Bacon consciously rejects. A case in point is the explanation of projectile motion. Rufus is the first Western scholastic to declare Aristotle's account of projectile motion inadequate. No explanation involving only the medium could be adequate because there can be projectile motion in opposite directions in a uniform medium, and because different projectiles move through the same medium at different speeds. To explain projectile motion, Rufus posits an imprint of violent motion in the projectile, but he does not completely reject Aristotle's account. Arguing that the projector affects the medium as well as the projectile, he explains projectile motion in terms of the effect of violent motion both on the projectile and on the medium. Postulating an imprint of violent motion on the projectile, he also accepts *antiperistasis* as an account of the effect of violent motion on the medium. By contrast, BACON rejects imprint theory, arguing that there is constant substantial contact between mover and moved object; 'everything that moves is moved by another'. Other contemporaries rejected imprint theory on the grounds that Rufus could not precisely explain what was imprinted. However, Rufus' views had continued currency and were cited, accepted and given a fuller exposition in the fourteenth century by Franciscus de Marchia (see NATURAL PHILOSOPHY, MEDIEVAL).

Among the first medieval Western philosophers to encounter Aristotle's arguments for the eternity of the world, Rufus also presented some of the most cogent counter-arguments. One argument is based on a contradiction between the definitions of 'past' and 'infinity'. It is impossible to traverse an infinity, but it

pertains to the nature of the past to have been traversed; therefore, past time cannot be infinite. Rufus presents the argument with characteristic brevity: 'Having been traversed' is incompatible with the definition of 'infinity', but 'having been traversed' belongs to the definition of the past. Therefore, being past is incompatible with the definition of infinity.

This argument, first presented in late antiquity by John PHILOPONUS, is now associated with Immanuel KANT; in medieval philosophy, it is ordinarily ascribed to BONAVENTURE, who advanced it in 1250 or 1251. It occurs in different versions, some more persuasive than others. GROSSETESTE, for example, mistakenly seeks to apply it to the future as well as the past, claiming that the argument can be used to show that time could not be infinite *a parte post*. Rufus sees even more clearly than Philoponus that the direction of time is an important part of this argument. He notices that the argument needs to be based on the fact that the *whole* of past time has been traversed, rather than on the claim that the whole of the past and the future will have been traversed. In his later work he seeks to force his opponents to see that they are committed to the claim that some past days are not now and never were present. By contrast, Philoponus sees this as an argument about the impossibility of completely counting an infinite series, with no particular focus on the direction of time.

Rufus' version of another of Philoponus' arguments is based on our concept of priority. If the number of days before today is infinite, and the number of days before tomorrow is infinite, then the number of days before today is not less than the number of days before tomorrow. Consequently, today does not arrive sooner than tomorrow, which is absurd. Rufus assumes here that unequal infinities are impossible. Following Georg CANTOR, modern mathematicians reject this assumption. However, Rufus needs only the uncontroversial claim that mappable infinities are equal: if we postulate beginningless time, the number of days before today and the number of days before tomorrow are mappable infinite series. Rufus might still argue that if the world has no beginning, then we must give up the belief that less time elapses before earlier events than before later events.

Philoponus' original version of this argument is not based on the claim that more time transpires before later events than before earlier events. The absurdities he asks us to reject are mathematical: that it is possible to add to an infinity, or that one infinity can be multiplied by another, so that one infinity would be greater than another by a determinate proportion. By contrast, the absurd conclusion Rufus asks us to reject is that 'today does not come sooner than tomorrow'; he emphasizes the unique properties of time (see ETERNITY OF THE WORLD, MEDIEVAL VIEWS OF).

2 Epistemology

The fullest statement of Rufus' epistemological views now known is a treatise entitled *Speculum animae* (A Mirror of the Soul), probably written to explain problems in Aristotelian philosophy to his Franciscan confrères. In this ambitious treatise, Rufus attempts to explain what Aristotle means when he says that 'in some manner the soul is every thing'. Rufus asks in what sense the soul becomes an object when it understands or senses that object. He rejects the view his predecessors based on patristic authorities: the soul is everything because it shares being with rocks, life with animals and understanding with angels. He also rejects a literal interpretation of the dictum. This leaves Rufus in a difficult position, since he holds that species in the soul are really identical with the common natures exemplified in external objects. If the material in the sensory soul combines with the sensible species, why does not the soul become green when it perceives something green? There are two elements in Rufus' reply: one is to postulate a different kind of being for sensible and intelligible species. Sensible species are not natural beings, in the sense that they are not included in the Aristotelian categories; they are neither substances nor accidents. Because they are different kinds of entities, when they combine with the soul, what is produced is not the object itself but cognition. The second element of Rufus' reply is to argue that what is formally distinct may be really identical. Species have the same real nature, but are not formally identical with, or predicable of, the objects they represent in the soul. This safeguards the claim that what we perceive is really the same as external objects; in some sense the soul really is all things.

3 Metaphysics

Postulating a kind of identity which permits real but not formal predication is a conceptual tool which Rufus employs when discussing a variety of philosophical topics, for example, the problem of individuation. Like DUNS SCOTUS in his *Metaphysics* commentary, Rufus postulates individual forms to explain individuation. Individual forms are really, but not formally, the same as specific forms. Specific forms are principles of shared identity; they pertain to common natures capable of instantiation (*multiplicabilis*). By contrast, individual forms pertain to the same individual natures as are actually instantiated (*actu multiplicata*).

Rufus' arguments against alternative theories were initially more influential than his own views. He holds that the cause of individuation cannot be an accident or an aggregation of accidents, since individual primary substances are ontologically prior to accidents. Though he allows a role for matter as an occasional cause of individuation, Rufus argues that even determinate matter could not by itself be the principle of individuation. Being an individual means being distinct and united, both of which are functions of form, the active principle of substance, not matter, the passive principle.

Holding that individual forms added to an aggregate of matter and specific form must be the principle of individuation, Rufus denies that the ultimate constituents of individuals are knowable. He is not sure whether what is added to the common nature can be located within an Aristotelian category. He suggests that, strictly speaking, the cause of individuation may be neither a substance nor an accident. Identifying individual forms as perfections of the specific form, he suggests that they may be substantial without being substances. Specific and individual forms provide different degrees of unity: specific unity is less than individual unity and greater than generic unity.

Like Rufus' views on individuation, his argument for the existence of God was accepted and modified by John Duns Scotus. Rufus rejected Anselm's famous ontological argument as sophistical (though subtle) (see ANSELM OF CANTERBURY). In its place he advanced a modal argument based on the concept of God as an independent being (*a se et non ab alio*). The existence of independent beings is either necessary or impossible. Therefore, if an independent being can exist, it does exist. Rufus employs logically sophisticated arguments to show that an independent being can exist.

4 Logic

Rufus' works are all characterized by rigour and logical subtlety, but whether he wrote any independent treatise in logic is not yet clear. One such treatise, called *Abstractiones*, has been plausibly attributed to him. It is a guide to the proper exposition of ambiguous propositions, often propositions including syncategorematic words such as 'only' and 'every' or modal operators such as 'possible' and 'necessary'. If this attribution is correct, Rufus was known to fourteenth century Franciscans such as WILLIAM OF OCKHAM as the 'Magister Abstractionum'.

5 Influence

Rufus' importance has long gone unrecognized, in part because he preferred not to take credit for his own work and in part because, unlike his contemporaries, he provided lengthy quotations of the positions he treated seriously. Since his own views were often stated briefly, historians who overlooked his critical bent saw him as a derivative figure. Now that Bonaventure's borrowing from Rufus has been discovered, and we are beginning to appreciate the significance of citations by Robert Grosseteste (Magister Richardus), John Duns Scotus (*Doctor antiquus*) and Franciscus de Marchia (Richardus), the question of Rufus' influence will have to be reconsidered. The first prerequisite is a critical edition of his works.

See also: ARISTOTELIANISM, MEDIEVAL; BACON, R.; ETERNITY OF THE WORLD, MEDIEVAL VIEWS OF; GROSSETESTE, R.

List of works

As noted, there is no critical edition of Richard Rufus' works, most of which survive only in a single manuscript. Extant works include commentaries on the *Physics* and *Metaphysics* of Aristotle; two treatises against Averroes (*De ideis (On Ideas)* and *De causa individuationis* (On the Basis of Individuation); disputed questions; two commentaries on Peter Lombard's *Sentences*, lectures given at Oxford and Paris; and an epistemological treatise (*Speculum animae* (A Mirror of the Soul)). Lost or unidentified is a commentary on Aristotle's *Meteorology*, cited by Bartolomeus Anglicus.

References and further reading

Callus, D. (1939) 'Two Early Oxford Masters on the Problem of Plurality of Forms: Adam of Buckfield – Richard Rufus of Cornwall', *Revue Néoscolastique de Philosophie* 42: 425–9. (Notes that Rufus does not support the doctrine of plurality of forms.)

Dales, R.C. (1971) 'The Influence of Grosseteste's *Hexaemeron* on the *Sentences* Commentaries of Richard Fishacre, O.P. and Richard Rufus of Cornwall, O.F.M.', *Viator* 2: 270–300. (Considers Rufus a derivative figure.)

de Libera, A. (1983) 'La littérature des *Abstractiones* et la tradition logique d'Oxford' (The Abstractiones Literature and the Oxford Logical Tradition), in O. Lewry (ed.) *The Rise of British Logic*, Toronto, Ont.: Pontifical Institute of Mediaeval Studies, 63–114. (Discusses the evidence for identifying Richard Rufus as Richardus Sophista, the Magister Abstractionum.)

Doucet, V. (1948) 'Prolegomena', in *Summa Halesiana* IV part 1, Quaracchi: Typographia Collegii S. Bonaventurae, 243–5. (A discussion of Rufus' life and works, not rendered obsolete by the works of Raedts or Wood.)

Gál, G. (1950) 'Commentarius in Metaphysicam Aristotelis cod. Vat. lat. 4538, fons doctrinae Richardi Rufi' (Cod. Vat. lat. 4538, a Commentary on Aristotle's *Metaphysics* and a Richard Rufus Source), *Archivum Franciscanum Historicum* 43: 209–42. (Concludes prematurely on the basis of Rufus' misleading references to this as the work of a secular author that Rufus is not the author of the *Metaphysics* commentary. Provides an outline of the contents of the work and publishes excerpts. Best introduction to the *Metaphysics* commentary.)

—— (1956) 'Viae ad exsistentiam Dei probandum in doctrina Richari Rufi' (Proofs for the Existence of God in Richard Rufus), *Franziskanische Studien* 38: 177–202. (Publishes substantial excerpts from Rufus' Oxford commentary and briefer excerpts from Assisi 138. Excellent study of Rufus' Oxford theology lectures, which does not include Book IV of the *Sentences*.)

—— (1975) 'Opiniones Richardi Rufi Cornubiensis a Censore Reprobatae' (Richard Rufus of Cornwall's Censored Opinions), *Franciscan Studies* 35: 136–93. (Correctly attributes the *Metaphysics* commentary to Rufus and documents his influence on Scotus. As Bacon notes, Rufus' Paris theology lectures brought him censure as well as fame. Gál prints substantial excerpts from the Paris commentary as well as marginal notes criticizing Rufus, and points outs that many of the censured opinions were not asserted but recited. Of special interest are Rufus' views on relations and on the human soul. Best introduction to Rufus' Paris theology lectures.)

Noone, T. (1987) *An Edition and Study of the Scriptum super Metaphysicam, Book 12, Dist. 2: A Work Attributed to Richard Rufus of Cornwall*, Ottawa, Ont.: National Library of Canada, 1989. (Correctly attributes the *Metaphysics* commentary to Rufus and publishes substantial portions of the text. A good exploration of the relation to Robert Grosseteste.)

—— (1989) 'Richard Rufus of Cornwall and the Authorship of the *Scriptum super Metaphysicam*', *Franciscan Studies* 49: 79–80. (Notes Adam Buckfield's debt to Richard Rufus; despite statements in early Franciscan sources that Rufus was a Parisian master when he joined the Order, suggests that his pre-Franciscan *Metaphysics* commentary originated in Oxford.)

Pelster, F. (1926) 'Der älteste Sentenzenkommentar aus der Oxforder Franziskanerschule', *Scholastik* 1: 50–80. (Establishes that Rufus was the author of the first surviving Oxford *Sentences* commentary by a bachelor of theology, and also the first Franciscan commentary from Oxford.)

—— (1950) 'Richardus Rufus Anglicus O.F.M. (c. 1250), ein Vorläufer des Duns Scotus in der Lehre von Wirkung der priestlichen Lossprechung', *Scholastik* 25: 550. (Notes Rufus' rejection of priestly character and his influence on Scotus.)

Plevano, R. (1993) 'Richard Rufus of Cornwall and Geoffrey of Aspall: Two Questions on the Instant of Change', *Medioevo* 19: 167–232. (The only recent discussion of Rufus' disputed questions, includes an edition.)

Raedts, P. (1987) *Richard Rufus of Cornwall and the Tradition of Oxford Theology*, Oxford: Clarendon Press. (A survey of the literature on Rufus' life and works published before 1987, this book deals chiefly with Rufus' Oxford lectures. Rufus is compared with Richard Fishacre and Robert Grosseteste; no notice is taken of another major source, Alexander of Hales.)

Wood, R. (1992a) 'Richard Rufus of Cornwall and Aristotle's Physics', *Franciscan Studies* 53: 247–81. (Presents the evidence for attributing the *Physics* commentary preserved in Erfurt, Quarto 312 to Rufus; publishes his account of projectile motion.)

—— (1992b) 'Richard Rufus on Creation: The Reception of Aristotle's Physics in the West', *Medieval Philosophy and Theology* 2: 7–30. (Discusses the development of Rufus' view on the eternity of the world from 1235–55.)

—— (1994) 'Richard Rufus: Physics at Paris before 1240', *Documenti e Studi sulla Tradizione Filosofica Medievale* 5: 87–127. (Summarizes Wood's earlier work on the *Physics* commentary. Concentrates on Rufus' discussion of place. Trying to answer the question how the heavens can be in a place, Rufus argues that in its most general sense place indicates a fixed relation of a surface to the center of the earth.)

—— (1995) 'Richard Rufus' *Speculum animae*: Epistemology and the Introduction of Aristotle in the West', in A. Speer (ed.) *Die Bibliotheca Amploniana ihre Bedeutung im Spannungsfeld von Aristotelismus, Nominalismus und Humanismus*, Miscellanea Mediaevalia 23, Leiden: Brill, 86–109. (Identifies the manuscript sources of the *Speculum* and summarizes its contents.)

—— (1996a) 'Richard Rufus and English Scholastic Discussion of Individuation', in J. Marenbon (ed.), *Aristotle in Britain in the Middle Ages*, Rencontres de Philosophie Médieévale 5, Turnhout: Brepols 117–143 . (Shows the influence of Rufus' theories of individuation prior to Scotus; argues against accounts of English scholasticism which minimize continental influences.)

—— (1996b) 'Angelic Individuation: According to Richard Rufus, St. Bonaventure and St. Thomas Aquinas', in *Individuum und Individualität in Mittelalter*, ed. A. Speer, *Miscellanea Mediaevalia* 24: 209–29. (Shows Bonaventure's borrowing from Rufus, and presents Aquinas' views in the context of Rufus' Aristotelianism.)

Zimmermann, A. (1992) 'Some Aspects of the Reception of Aristotle's *Physics* and *Metaphysics* in the Thirteenth Century', in M. Jordan and K. Emery (eds) *Ad Litteram*, Notre Dame, IN: University of Notre Dame Press. (Notes Bacon's use of Rufus' *Metaphysics* commentary. Includes a discussion of Rufus on the subject of metaphysics.)

REGA WOOD

RICKERT, H. *see* NEO-KANTIANISM

RICOEUR, PAUL (1913–)

Paul Ricoeur is one of the leading French philosophers of the second half of the twentieth century. Along with the German philosopher Hans-Georg Gadamer, Ricoeur is one of the main contemporary exponents of philosophical hermeneutics: that is, of a philosophical orientation which places particular emphasis on the nature and role of interpretation. While his early work was strongly influenced by Husserl's phenomenology, he became increasingly concerned with problems of interpretation and developed – partly through detailed inquiries into psychoanalysis and structuralism – a distinctive hermeneutical theory. In his later writings Ricoeur explores the nature of metaphor and narrative, which are viewed as ways of creating new meaning in language.

1   **Early work**
2   **Psychoanalysis and structuralism**
3   **Text and interpretation**
4   **Metaphor and narrative**

1   Early work

Born in Valence in 1913, Ricoeur began his philosophical career at a time when phenomenology and existentialism were influential in French intellectual circles. As a student in Paris in the late 1930s, and subsequently as a prisoner of war in Germany during the Second World War, Ricoeur read the work of HUSSERL, HEIDEGGER, JASPERS and MARCEL. Following the war, Ricoeur and Mikel Dufrenne published a lengthy study of Jaspers, *Karl Jaspers et la philosophie de l'existence* (1947); in the same year, Ricoeur published his own comparative study of Jaspers and Marcel. Ricoeur also translated Husserl's *Ideen I* into French, thereby establishing himself as a leading authority on phenomenology (see PHENOMENOLOGICAL MOVEMENT).

In 1948 Ricoeur was elected to a chair in the history of philosophy at the University of Strasbourg. During the following decade Ricoeur sought to develop an ambitious project on the 'philosophy of the will': that is, a systematic reflection on the affective and volitional aspects of human existence. In the first volume of this project, *Freedom and Nature* (1950), Ricoeur employed a phenomenological method to explore the interplay between the voluntary and the involuntary features of life, such as the way in which action is mediated by the organs of the body and by a range of factors which lie beyond the individual's control. The second volume of the philosophy of the will was published in 1960 as two separate books: *Fallible Man* and *The Symbolism of Evil*. In these books Ricoeur moved away from a strict phenomenological method and began to develop a more interpretative approach to symbols and myths, as a way of gaining access to problems of human fallibility and fault. Ricoeur sketched the plan for a third volume which would be concerned with the 'poetics of the will', but postponed this project while he turned his attention to other matters.

2 Psychoanalysis and structuralism

In 1957 Ricoeur was elected Professor of Philosophy at the Sorbonne where he remained until 1966, when he was appointed Dean at the University Paris X, Nanterre – a position he currently holds in conjunction with Professorships in the Department of Philosophy and the Divinity School at the University of Chicago. In the late 1950s and early 1960s, the intellectual climate in Paris was changing in significant ways: there was a growing interest in psychoanalysis, and structuralist ideas were beginning to have a significant impact. Ricoeur responded to this change by undertaking a detailed inquiry into the work of FREUD and by engaging critically with some of the key texts underpinning the structuralist approach (see PSYCHOANALYSIS, METHODOLOGICAL ISSUES IN; STRUCTURALISM).

Freud and Philosophy appeared in 1965 and is one of Ricoeur's best-known works. Ricoeur provides a thorough analysis of the development of Freud's work, with the aim of bringing out its philosophical relevance. Unlike philosophical orientations (like phenomenology) which take the contents of consciousness as a starting point, Freud begins by questioning the primacy of consciousness and looking elsewhere, at the level of the unconscious, for the key processes that shape psychic life. But, as Ricoeur shows, Freud's postulation of unconscious processes is inseparable from the activity of interpretation. Psychoanalysis is, on Ricoeur's account, a form of hermeneutics in which the analyst employs a specialized set of rules, assumptions and models in order to make sense of actions and utterances that are initially difficult to understand. Hence psychoanalysis should be regarded, not as a natural science like physics or chemistry, but rather as an interpretative discipline similar in character to history and literary criticism; it is a discipline concerned with deciphering symbols and signs in relation to the expression of desire.

Ricoeur's critical discussions of structuralism appeared in a series of essays which were brought together in a volume entitled *The Conflict of Interpretations* (1969). There were many thinkers in France and elsewhere who argued that the principles of structural linguistics – especially as elaborated by the Swiss linguist Ferdinand de Saussure – provided a generalizable model that could be used for the analysis of social and cultural phenomena (see STRUCTURALISM IN LINGUISTICS). Ricoeur had serious reservations about this line of argument. He wanted to show that, while structuralist methods of analysis could be useful for certain purposes, they were based on a number of assumptions which limited their validity. Hence structuralist methods could not provide a comprehensive and self-sufficient approach; they had to be integrated into a broader hermeneutical theory (see HERMENEUTICS).

Ricoeur developed this argument through a rigorous analysis of the work of some of the authors who were influential in the rise of structuralism. This included the work of structural linguists, such as Saussure, Jakobson and Hjelmslev, as well as the work of the anthropologist Claude LÉVI-STRAUSS – one of the few thinkers who explicitly and consistently described himself as a structuralist. Through a brilliant analysis of Lévi-Strauss's writings on myth, Ricoeur showed that Lévi-Strauss was constantly overstepping the limits of validity of the structuralist approach, ending up in what Ricoeur described as 'a Kantianism without a transcendental subject'. Ricoeur also argued that the structuralist analysis of myth was at best a partial account, since it neglected, among other things, the ways in which myths were embedded in historical traditions that were handed down from one generation to the next.

3   Text and interpretation

Ricoeur's critique of LÉVI-STRAUSS and others remains one of the best accounts available of the strengths and weaknesses of the structuralist approach. It also formed the backcloth against which Ricoeur developed his own hermeneutical theory. In a short text called *Interpretation Theory* (1976) and in a series of essays reprinted in *Hermeneutics and the Human Sciences* (1981), Ricoeur worked out a systematic theory of interpretation based on a distinctive notion of the text. A text, according to Ricoeur, is an instance of written discourse; it involves four forms of 'distanciation' which differentiate it from the conditions of speech. First, in spoken discourse there is an interplay between the event of saying (the utterance) and the meaning of what is said; but in the case of written discourse, the event of saying is eclipsed by the meaning of what is said: it is the meaning which is inscribed in the text. Second, whereas in spoken discourse there is an overlap between the intention of the speaking subject and the meaning of what is said, in the case of written discourse these two dimensions of meaning drift apart: the meaning of the text does not coincide with what the author meant. Third, whereas spoken discourse is addressed to a specific recipient, written discourse is addressed to an unknown audience and potentially to anyone who can read. Fourth, whereas the shared circumstances of the speech situation provide some degree of referential specificity for spoken discourse, in the case of written discourse these shared circumstances no longer exist.

These various characteristics of the text provide the basis upon which Ricoeur elaborates his theory of interpretation. Like earlier thinkers within the tradition of hermeneutics, Ricoeur treats the text as a privileged object of interpretation. But unlike earlier thinkers, Ricoeur argues that the process of interpretation can be facilitated and enriched by the use of explanatory methods of analysis. Since a text is a structured totality of meaning which has been distanced from its conditions of production, it can be analysed fruitfully and legitimately by means of structuralist methods. But this type of analysis can never be an end in itself. It can only be a step along the path of interpretation – that is, a partial contribution to the broader hermeneutical task of unfolding the 'world' of the text and the significance it has for its readers.

While Ricoeur's theory of interpretation is formulated with regard to texts, he argues that it can be extended to non-textual phenomena like action (see *Hermeneutics and the Human Sciences* (1981) and *From Text to Action* (1986)). Ricoeur's argument is that action involves the four forms of distanciation characteristic of written discourse; and hence, for the purposes of analysis, action can be treated as a text. One advantage of this approach is that it enables Ricoeur to propose a novel solution to the problem of the relation between explanation and understanding in the social sciences. Just as the interpretation of texts can be facilitated by the structuralist analysis of their contents, so too the understanding of action can be enriched by an explanatory account. Hence explanation and understanding are not necessarily opposed to one another, as some philosophers of social science have suggested (see SOCIAL SCIENCE, CONTEMPORARY PHILOSOPHY OF). Rather, the explanation of action can be treated as an integral part of a process of understanding.

4   Metaphor and narrative

Throughout his writings Ricoeur has been interested in the phenomena of creativity and imagination, and in the 1970s and 1980s he pursued this interest through his extensive studies of metaphor and narrative. *The Rule of Metaphor* was published in 1975, and the three volumes of *Time and Narrative* appeared in 1983, 1984 and 1985. Metaphor and narrative are particularly interesting for Ricoeur because they are sites of creativity in language: they are works of displacement and synthesis in which the productive imagination is expressed.

On Ricoeur's account, the creative character of metaphor stems from the fact that a metaphorical utterance sets up a tension between two terms in a sentence through the violation of a linguistic code. The metaphor emerges through a creative semantic pertinence which reduces the tension established by the incongruous attribution. Metaphor thus operates not simply at the level of words, but rather at the level of the sentence. The emergent meaning can be grasped only through a constructive interpretation, an imaginative restructuring of semantic fields, which makes sense of the sentence as a whole. The creative character of metaphor does not destroy the referential dimension of language but rather endows metaphor with a new kind of referential power: the power to redescribe reality (see METAPHOR).

In the case of narrative, the semantic innovation consists in the invention of a plot. By bringing together characters, goals, causes and chance, the plot of a narrative creates something new: a new pattern in the organization of events. To understand this pattern, one must use the imagination to grasp the diverse elements of the plot, integrating them into a complete and intelligible whole. Moreover, just as metaphor has the referential power to redescribe reality, so too narrative has what Ricoeur calls, following ARISTOTLE, a 'mimetic function'. The invention of plots – or, more generally, the telling of stories – is the means by which we refashion the field of human action and refigure the temporality of human existence. In this respect, suggests Ricoeur, the difference between fictional narratives (such as novels) and historical narratives (that is, works of historical scholarship) is not as great as it might at first appear to be. Of course, historians generally assume that their narratives bear some relation to a past that is presumed to be 'real'. But, at a more general level, both historical narratives and works of fiction are concerned with the refiguration of the temporality of human existence.

As his writings on metaphor and narrative illustrate, Ricoeur addresses problems which are of interest not only to philosophers but also to individuals in other disciplines. His work has had a significant impact on debates in literary criticism, theology, sociology, anthropology and history. There is a consistent vision that animates Ricoeur's work, a vision that emphasizes creativity, interpretation and the social-historical embeddedness of human action and existence. But Ricoeur's work is also distinguished by its generous assessment of other thinkers and its openness to other disciplines and traditions of thought.

See also: HERMENEUTICS

List of works

Ricoeur, P. (1947) *Gabriel Marcel et Karl Jaspers: Philosophie du mystère et philosophie du paradoxe.* Paris: Temps Présent.

Ricoeur, P. and Dufrenne, M. (1947) *Karl Jaspers et la philosophie de l'existence*, Paris: Éditions du Seuil.

Ricoeur, P. (1950) *Philosophie de la volont, I: Le Volontaire et l'involontaire*, Paris: Aubier; trans. E.V. Kohk, *Freedom and Nature: The Voluntary and the Involuntary*, Evanston, IL: Northwestern University Press, 1966.

—— *Histoire et vérité.* (1955) Paris: Éditions du Seuil; trans. C.A. Kelbley, *History and Truth*, Evanston, IL: Northwestern University Press, 1965.

—— (1960a) *Philosophie de la volonté. Finitude et culpabilité, I: L'homme fallible*, Paris: Aubier; trans. C.A. Kelbley, *Fallible Man*, Chicago: Henry Regnery, 1965.

—— (1960b) *Philosophie de la volonté: Finitude et culpabilité, II: La symbolique du mal*, Paris: Aubier;

trans. E. Buchanan, *The Symbolism of Evil*, New York: Harper & Row, 1967.

—— (1965) *De l'interprétation: Essai sur Freud*, Paris: Éditions du Seuil; trans. D. Savage, *Freud and Philosophy: An Essay on Interpretation*, New Haven, CT: Yale University Press, 1970.

—— (1967) *Husserl: An Analysis of his Phenomenology*, trans. E.G. Ballard and L.E. Embree, Evanston, IL: Northwestern University Press.

—— (1969) *Le conflit des interprétations: Essais d'hermneutique*, Paris: Éditions du Seuil; trans. W. Domingo et al., *The Conflict of Interpretations: Essays in Hermeneutics*, ed. D. Ihde, Evanston, IL: Northwestern University Press, 1974.

—— (1974) *Political and Social Essays*, ed. D. Stewart and J. Bien, Athens, OH: Ohio University Press.

—— (1975) *La métaphore vive*, Paris: Éditions du Seuil; trans. R. Czerny, *The Rule of Metaphor: Multi-Disciplinary Studies of the Creation of Meaning in Language*, London: Routledge, 1978.

—— (1976) *Interpretation Theory: Discourse and the Surplus of Meaning*, Fort Worth, TX: Texas Christian University Press.

—— (1981) *Hermeneutics and the Human Sciences: Essays on Language, Action and Interpretation*, ed. and trans. J.B. Thompson, Cambridge: Cambridge University Press.

—— (1983) *Temps et récit, I*, Paris: Éditions du Seuil, 1983; trans. K. McLaughlin and D. Pellauer, *Time and Narrative, Volume I*, Chicago: University of Chicago Press, 1984.

—— (1984) *Temps et récit, II: La configuration du temps dans le récit de fiction*, Paris: Éditions du Seuil; trans. K. McLaughlin and D. Pellauer, *Time and Narrative, Volume 2*, Chicago: University of Chicago Press, 1985.

—— (1985) *Temps et récit, III: Le Temps raconté*, Paris: Éditions du Seuil; trans. K. Blamey and D. Pellauer, *Time and Narrative, Volume 3*, Chicago: University of Chicago Press, 1988.

—— (1986) *Du texte à l'action: Essais d'hermeneutique, II*, Paris: Éditions du Seuil; trans. K. Blamey and J.B. Thompson, *From Text to Action: Essays in Hermeneutics, II*, Evanston, IL: Northwestern University Press, 1991.

—— (1986) *Lectures on Ideology and Utopia*, ed. George H. Taylor, New York: Columbia University Press.

—— (1990) *Soi-Même comme un autre*, Paris: Éditions du Seuil; trans. K. Blamey, *Oneself as Another*, Chicago: University of Chicago Press, 1992.

References and further reading

Bourgeois, P.L. (1973) *Extension of Ricoeur's*

Hermeneutic, The Hague: Martinus Nijhoff. (A study of Ricoeur's earlier work for the advanced student.)

Clarke, S.H. (1990) *Paul Ricoeur*, London: Routledge. (A general and accessible introduction to Ricoeur's work, placing particular emphasis on its relevance to debates in literary theory.)

Ihde, D. (1971) *Hermeneutic Phenomenology: The Philosophy of Paul Ricoeur*, Evanston, IL: Northwestern University Press. (An authoritative work on Ricoeur, which deals with his writings up to 1970.)

Kemp, T.P. and Rasmussen, D. (eds) (1989) *The Narrative Path: The Later Works of Paul Ricoeur*, Cambridge, MA: MIT Press. (A collection of essays on Ricoeur's later work, for the advanced student. This volume contains an excellent bibliography of Ricoeur's publications in English up to 1987.)

Klemm, D.E. (1983) *The Hermeneutical Theory of Paul Ricoeur: A Constructive Analysis*, East Brunswick, NJ: Associated University Presses, 1983. (An introduction to Ricoeur's work for students with an interest in religious language and theology.)

Madison, G.B. (ed.) (1975) *Sens et existence: En hommage Paul Ricoeur*, Paris: Éditions du Seuil. (A collection of essays for the advanced student.)

Palmer, R.E. (1969) *Hermeneutics: Interpretation Theory in Schleiermacher, Dilthey, Heidegger, and Gadamer*, Evanston, IL: Northwestern University Press. (An excellent introduction to the tradition of hermeneutics.)

Philibert, M. (1971) *Paul Ricoeur ou la liberté selon l'espérance*, Paris: Seghers. (A study of Ricoeur's earlier work for the advanced student.)

Rasmussen, D. (1971) *Mythic-Symbolic Language and Philosophical Anthropology*, The Hague: Martinus Nijhoff. (A study of Ricoeur's earlier work, for the advanced student.)

Reagan, C.E. (ed.) (1979) *Studies in the Philosophy of Paul Ricoeur*. Athens, OH: Ohio University Press. (A collection of essays for the advanced student. This volume includes an excellent bibliography of Ricoeur's writings up to 1976.)

Thompson, J.B. (1981) *Critical Hermeneutics: A Study in the Thought of Paul Ricoeur and Jürgen Habermas*, Cambridge: Cambridge University Press. (A comparative study of the work of Ricoeur and Habermas, aimed at the advanced student.)

Valdz, M.J. (ed.) (1991) *A Ricoeur Reader: Reflection and Imagination*, Toronto: University of Toronto Press. (A selection of essays by, and interviews with, Ricoeur. The volume has a good introduction which highlights the relevance of Ricoeur's work to literary theory and criticism.)

Vanhoozer, K.J. (1990) *Biblical Narrative in the Philosophy of Paul Ricoeur: A Study in Herme-neutics and Theology*, Cambridge: Cambridge University Press. (A study of Ricoeur's philosophy of religion, for the advanced student.)

Wood, D. (ed.) (1991) *On Paul Ricoeur: Narrative and Interpretation*, London: Routledge. (A collection of essays on Ricoeur's later work, for the advanced student.)

JOHN B. THOMPSON

RIGHT AND GOOD

'Right' and 'good' are the two basic terms of moral evaluation. In general, something is 'right' if it is morally obligatory, whereas it is morally 'good' if it is worth having or doing and enhances the life of those who possess it.

Acts are often held to be morally right or wrong in respect of the action performed, but morally good or bad in virtue of their motive: it is right to help a person in distress, but good to do so from a sense of duty or sympathy, since no one can supposedly be obliged to do something (such as acting with a certain motive) which cannot be done at will.

Henry Sidgwick distinguished between two basic conceptions of morality. The 'attractive' conception, favoured by the ancient Greeks, views the good as fundamental, and grounds the claims of morality in the self-perfection to which we naturally aspire. The 'imperative' conception, preferred in the modern era, views the right as fundamental, and holds that we are subject to certain obligations whatever our wants or desires.

1 **Meaning of the terms**
2 **Ancient and modern ethics**
3 **Contemporary problems**

1 Meaning of the terms

There are two different ideas of moral value, which the everyday usage of 'right' and 'good' comes close to matching (see MORALITY AND ETHICS). The idea of right refers to what is obligatory, to a prescription to which we ought to conform (see DUTY). The idea of good, by contrast, refers to what is desirable; it applies to whatever is worth having or doing and enhances the life of which it is a part. Clearly, the obligatory and the desirable are not the same. Pleasure at the sight of another's success may well be morally admirable without being obligatory; so, too, some duties are ours, it seems, whatever their performance may mean for the quality of our lives. Each of these fundamental notions plays an essential role in our moral thinking, and morality as a whole turns on the relations assumed to exist between them.

W.D. Ross' classic study, *The Right and the Good* (1930), explains the difference between moral right and good along these lines. But Ross wrongly supposed that it is as easy to determine which things are morally right and which things morally good as it is to distinguish conceptually between the obligatory and the desirable. What counts as obligatory and what as desirable are often controversial. Like Kant before him, Ross held that acts are morally right or wrong in respect of the action performed, but morally good or bad in virtue of their motive (see KANTIAN ETHICS §2). In Ross' view, it cannot be obligatory or morally right that I act with a certain motive – that I keep my promise, not out of fear for my reputation, but because I believe it the proper thing to do. For 'I ought' implies 'I can', whereas I cannot by choice produce a certain motive.

Though near-canonical, this analysis of moral action rests on shaky ground. True, it is often said that we cannot have an obligation to do what it is not in our power to do, and the feelings or convictions that may move us to act cannot be brought about at will. Yet there is also the common thought that it is right, not just to acknowledge our benefactors, but to do so with a sense of gratitude. In addition, the principle that 'ought' implies 'can' is not really so evident as sometimes believed. It does not even seem to fit every case of obligatory action. As Aristotle observed, people may pursue a life of injustice for so long that they become unable to do what justice still requires. No doubt, these conflicting commitments can be qualified so as to hang together with some coherence. But we should not suppose that reasonable people will agree upon the way to do it.

2 Ancient and modern ethics

Another question has to do with how the right and the good are themselves to be related at the foundations of ethics. Henry SIDGWICK gave this problem a probing analysis in *The Methods of Ethics* (1874). The nature of moral value, he suggested, assumes two different forms, depending on whether the right or the good is considered the more basic notion. In the one case, he wrote, morality has an *imperative* form, in the other an *attractive* one. In addition, these two views were in his eyes historically distinct: the priority of the good was central to Greek ethics, whereas modern ethics has largely embraced the priority of the right. Sidgwick's remarks contain important insights, both philosophical and historical.

Sidgwick distinguished the imperative and attract-

ive conceptions of morality in the following way. To suppose that the right is fundamental is to hold that there are principles of conduct which are binding or obligatory, whatever our wants or desires may be. By contrast, to assume that the good is basic is to believe that proper conduct is what we would display if we were sufficiently informed about what at bottom we really desire. Of course, each conception makes use of the other moral notion as well, though in a subordinate position. If the right is fundamental, then, to be good, what the agent wants must conform to the demands of obligation; the good is the object of right desire. If the good is fundamental, then the right is what one ought to do in order to attain what one would want if adequately informed. Thus, the imperative view of morality makes the right prior to the good, whereas the attractive view makes the good prior to the right.

These two theoretical conceptions become clearer if we look at the evidence which led Sidgwick to correlate them with the different outlooks of ancient and modern ethics. The ethical thought of Plato and Aristotle drew upon an attractive notion of good, for they regarded the exercise of moral virtue as an intrinsic part of the 'happy' or fulfilled life that by nature each human being desires as the ultimate end (see EUDAIMONIA). For them, morality is the agent's interest well-understood. This does not mean that their ethical outlook was a species of egoism, at least as that position is usually defined (see EGOISM AND ALTRUISM). For they believed that the agent's self-fulfilment consists in the exercise of virtue (instead of being a condition instrumentally advanced by it), so that we achieve the fulfilled life we want only by being generous, courageous, and so on, for their own sakes. But the crucial point is that, though both philosophers indeed referred to what we 'ought' to do, they appealed nowhere to the idea that there are obligations binding on all agents unconditionally (or 'categorically', as Kant would say). Theirs was an ethics in which the good is prior to the right.

The priority of the right over the good is an expression that comes from Kant. But Sidgwick rightly maintained that the imperative conception is in reality a broad one, encompassing much of modern ethics. It seems to have first appeared among late medieval Franciscans such as Scotus and Ockham. Rejecting the idea of a perspicuous natural order in the name of God's inscrutable omnipotence, they shifted the source of moral principles from what human beings naturally desire to what God commands (see DUNS SCOTUS, J. §14; WILLIAM OF OCKHAM §10). In fact, Scotus anticipated developments we associate with Kant, arguing that the Christian rule of loving others for their own sake and thus the idea of justice in its fullest sense cannot rest on the natural desire for self-perfection that underlies Aristotelian and Thomistic ethics, but only on a freedom of will that can suspend that desire (see PERFECTIONISM; AUTONOMY, ETHICAL §2). Christian theology, with its image of God as moral legislator and its ideal of disinterested love, played a decisive role in the rise of an ethics of the right (see LOVE §2).

Freed from a theological idiom, the imperative conception of morality has dominated modern moral philosophy. The utilitarian tradition, at least since Sidgwick himself, is no exception (see UTILITARIANISM). In *Ethics* (1963), William Frankena wrongly, but influentially, described the difference between deontological and utilitarian theories as lying in whether the right or the good is made the fundamental moral concept (see DEONTOLOGICAL ETHICS). In reality, both sorts of theory turn on the priority of the right over the good. The essential principle of any 'consequentialist' theory (utilitarianism being the version that conceives of the good as subjective happiness) is that right action consists in bringing about the most good overall, for all those affected by the action, each 'counting for one and only one' (see CONSEQUENTIALISM). This principle does not subordinate the idea of right action to an independent notion of the good. For it defines the good to be maximized by reference to a categorical principle of right: the maximizand is determined by considering everyone's good impartially, as it is claimed we ought to do, so that the pursuit of the greatest good overall is a duty binding on us unconditionally, whatever the direction in which our own interests would lead us (see IMPARTIALITY).

Deontological theories generally hold that we are bound by certain obligations even if an alternative course of action is known to bring about more good overall. But it is not this principle that expresses the priority of the right characteristic of modern ethics. It is rather the view such theories share with consequentialism, namely, the view that moral duty is independent of the agent's own good. This common assumption is foreign to the spirit of ancient ethics, which is why the unending debate between deontological and consequentialist outlooks, so central to modern ethics, never engaged the Greek moralists and their successors.

3 Contemporary problems

Two important qualifications must be made to Sidgwick's account of the difference between ancient and modern ethics. First, even if we agree that we are subject to categorical duties and thus continue to understand ourselves as 'modern', we need not suppose that morality as a whole must fit the imperative conception. A more plausible view would have a place, not just for a core morality unconditionally binding on all, but also for duties arising from friendship, the ties of place and culture, and membership of particular associations (see FRIENDSHIP; FAMILY, ETHICS AND THE; SOLIDARITY). Such duties are ours only so long as we remain interested in maintaining these social relations. It would be a hollow idea of friendship that implied that we owe our friends the special concern they deserve whatever we may feel about them.

Second, we should note that some important modern philosophers have denied that 'right' or 'ought' should play the fundamental role in moral theory. In *An Enquiry Concerning the Principles of Morals* (1751), Hume suggests that the idea of morality as a system of laws is an invention of Christian theology, which, focusing moral approval on what can be performed at will, misses the central importance of the virtues. Schopenhauer (1840) took Kant to task for assuming that ethics must have an imperative form (see SCHOPENAUER, A. §6). That assumption makes sense, he insisted, only within a theological framework, so that the practical postulate of belief in God which Kant drew from his ethics was really its guiding premise all along. And in the twentieth century, G.E.M. Anscombe argued that the modern emphatic sense of 'ought' has its home only within the conception of a divine legislator (see ANSCOMBE, G.E.M. §2). While we may feel unconditionally bound by certain obligations, without thinking of any theological framework, these convictions are in her view only 'survivals'. Having lost all intelligible meaning, they urge themselves upon us with the authority of conscience only because we have been shaped by a tradition in which, however, we no longer believe.

These dissenting voices do not refute Sidgwick's thesis about the difference between ancient and modern ethics. For all three philosophers understood themselves as protesting against what had become the dominant conception of ethics in modern times. Indeed, Hume and Anscombe urged a return to ancient models. Anscombe's essay, 'Modern Moral Philosophy' (1958), is a charter document of recent neo-Aristotelianism or 'virtue ethics', which seeks to conceive of the virtues as fundamentally forms of human flourishing (see VIRTUE ETHICS). Whether the good should thus be regarded as prior to the right, or whether the modern priority of the right should be maintained, is a cardinal debate of contemporary ethics.

See also: CONFUCIAN PHILOSOPHY, CHINESE §6; GOOD, THEORIES OF THE

References and further reading

* Anscombe, G.E.M. (1958) 'Modern Moral Philosophy', *Philosophy* 33 (1): 1–19; repr. in *Collected Philosophical Papers*, Minneapolis, MN: University of Minnesota Press, 1981, vol. 3, 26–42. (An influential critique of the modern emphasis on the notion of right.)
* Frankena, W. (1963) *Ethics*, Englewood Cliffs, NJ: Prentice Hall, 2nd edn, 1973. (Contains an influential, if erroneous, account of the distinction between 'teleological' and 'deontological' theories.)
* Hume, D. (1751) *An Enquiry Concerning the Principles of Morals*, in *Enquiries Concerning the Human Understanding and Concerning the Principles of Morals*, ed. L.A. Selby-Bigge, revised by P.H. Nidditch, Oxford: Clarendon Press, 3rd edn, 1975, appendix IV. (Discusses the difference between ancient and modern ethics.)
  Larmore, C. (1996) 'The Right and the Good', in *The Morals of Modernity*, Cambridge: Cambridge University Press. (Explores the roles of the right and the good at the foundations of ethics.)
* Ross, W.D. (1930) *The Right and the Good*, Oxford: Oxford University Press. (A classic work containing an acute analysis of the moral notions of right and good.)
* Schopenhauer, A. (1840) *Über die Grundlage der Moral*, trans. E.F.J. Payne, *On the Basis of Morality*, Indianapolis, IN: Bobbs-Merrill, 1965, section 4. (Contains his critique of Kant's imperative conception of morality.)
* Sidgwick, H. (1874) *The Methods of Ethics*, Macmillan: London; 7th edn, 1907; repr. Indianapolis, IN: Hackett Publishing Company, 1981, book I, ch. 9. (Contains his insightful contrast between ancient and modern ethics.)
  Wolter, A.B. (1990) *The Philosophical Theology of John Duns Scotus*, Ithaca, NY: Cornell University Press. (Excellent treatment of Scotus' ethics, bringing out those elements which anticipate modern conceptions.)

CHARLES LARMORE

RIGHTS

There is widespread consensus that rights are ways of acting or of being treated that are beneficial to the rightholder. Controversy begins, however, when one attempts to specify the notion of rights further.

(1) It is sometimes said, perhaps too casually, that all rights carry with them correlated obligations – things that other persons are supposed to do or refrain from doing when some given person is said to have a right to something. The question is: how is it best to state this relationship between rights and correlated obligations?

(2) Most people think that rights are, in some sense, justified. But there is considerable controversy as to what, precisely, is the proper focus of justification. Some say that rights are practices (certain ways of acting or of being treated) that are established, typically socially established. Thus, the issue for them is whether the fact of social recognition and enforcement is justified (or could be). Others say that rights themselves are claims; hence a right is a justified claim or principle of some sort (whether the practice identified in that claim exists or not). This dispute, between rights as justified practices and rights as justified claims, needs to be explored and, if possible, resolved.

Other topics need addressing beyond the question of the initial characterization of rights. One of them is the question of the function of rights: what good are they anyway? what can one do with rights? Another is the question of how best to justify particular kinds of rights, such as human rights and basic constitutional rights. Is there a substantive theory of critical morality that can do the job? Many people are concerned, especially, with whether utilitarianism (one of the dominant ethical theories in the West today) is up to this task. Finally, mention should be made of one other issue much talked about of late: what kinds of beings can have rights, and under what conditions of possession and dispossession?

1 Initial characterization and some points of consensus
2 Normative direction
3 Accreditation
4 Functions of rights
5 Critical justification

1 Initial characterization and some points of consensus

Rights are an important issue in contemporary social and political philosophy. For it is widely held that rights, by providing a significant protection of important interests of individuals against the state and against other persons (even a majority), give a person something to stand on. One may not want to go so far as to say that rights are 'trumps' (as some have), but it is none the less clear that rights are valuable things. So it seems natural to ask: 'what, then, is a right?'

Rights are socially established ways of acting or ways of being treated (or, alternatively, such ways as ought to be so established). More specifically, a right so understood is a right *to* something that is (1) fairly determinate and that (2) can be similarly distributed on an individual basis to each and all of those who are said to be rightholders. A right is always regarded as (3) a beneficial way of acting or of being treated both for the rightholder and, more generally, for society. Thus, (4) it is or should be something socially accepted – recognized and protected in given societies. Such acceptance would be (5) deemed reasonable, even by outsiders, in that it made explanatory sense. For the way of acting or of being treated in question could be exhibited, plausibly, as a means to or as a part of accomplishing some interest or perceived benefit or other good (or desirable) thing. Accordingly, (6) directives could be issued to others, to those who are not rightholders. And (7) further initiatives could be taken as a feature of any such successful claim to rights status.

This initial characterization constitutes common ground in the arguments people make about rights. Indeed, several of its features are not particularly controversial at all. Thus, there would today be widespread consensus on the idea that rights are ways of acting or ways of being treated that are (1) appropriately determinate, (2) equitably distributable on an individual basis and (3) beneficial. Even the central characterization, concerning social acceptability in (4), is not unduly contestable as stated; but dispute would break out as soon as we tried to determine what to emphasize – whether rights are *socially established* or merely *ought* to be. Finally, the idea (6) that rights always involve some sort of normative direction of the behaviour of others might also appear to be universally agreed upon; but there are problems with alleging consensus on this particular point.

2 Normative direction

The view in question in (6) is often put by saying that rights correlate with duties – meaning thereby that a right always implies or has attached some distinctive and closely related duty of others. But serious difficulties arise for the thesis in this precise form.

The most interesting arguments against such correlations derive from Wesley Hohfeld's highly influential classification of rights (Hohfeld 1964) (see HOHFELD, W.N.). On his view a legal right could be constituted by any one of four elements: a claim; a liberty; a power; or an immunity. And each type of

right has a unique second-party correlative. Thus, for a legal *claim right* to some thing the correlative element is a legal duty of some second party. Analogously, a person's *immunity right* from some thing is necessarily correlated with a lack of power – with a legal disability – on the part of others to do that thing (for example, the constitutional inability of the US Congress to 'abridge' free political speech). Hohfeld's point is simply that a legal duty and a no-power (a legal inability) are significantly different. Accordingly, the existence of immunity rights tells against the view that the correlative of every right is always going to be a closely related second-party duty (see DUTY).

Thus, the thesis that rights logically correlate with specific duties is not sound. A weaker but more defensible view is that any genuine right must involve some normative direction of the behaviour of persons other than the holder. Even this weaker thesis, however, seems to run up against the authority of HOBBES (in his account of rights in the state of nature) and of Hohfeld. We can see this most clearly by looking at the Hohfeldian liberty right.

Here the legal *liberty right* to do some thing – which consists in the absence of any duty on the agent's part to refrain from doing that thing – is matched with other people's lack of a claim that such a thing not be done by the agent. The point is, this is the *only* directive incumbent on the conduct of second parties in the case of a liberty. They can make no claim on the duties of a liberty-rightholder (to refrain); beyond that their own action is relatively unencumbered.

A liberty right, so conceived, is indeed an odd one. For it fails to capture the common-sense notion that when one has a liberty right to do a thing someone else is directed not to interfere with that doing. The problem is that literally *no* normative direction at all is involved for second parties (in Hobbes' case) and no *significant* normative direction against interference is involved (in Hohfeld's).

If the common-sense notion of a liberty right is correct, there ought always to be some sort of strong mandate for non-interference, either explicitly stated in our formulation of a given liberty or present at least in the context in which that liberty normally occurs. Thus, to take the latter case, certain standing duties of second parties (such as the duty not to assault or batter others or to trespass on their property), even though these are relatively independent of a given liberty (for example, the liberty to paint one's barn a shocking purple), would none the less afford the exercise of that liberty a considerable degree of protection. Without some such fairly robust mandates against interference (either closely connected to the liberty in question or permanently and independently in place on the 'perimeter' of its usual exercise), we would probably be inclined to call that liberty, not a right, but a *mere* liberty or a privilege.

The upshot, then, is that we should state our main contention so as to emphasize *significant* normative direction (on the conduct of second parties). This is the focal point of what appears to be an emerging consensus on the matter at issue.

3 Accreditation

No real consensus has emerged, however, on the point we now turn to: whether rights, in order to be rights, require social recognition (and beyond that, social maintenance). In considering this issue one school of thought – embracing both classical natural rights theorists and contemporary advocates of human rights – has tended to emphasize that individuals can have rights independently of organized society, of social institutions, and hence of social recognition and maintenance in any form. The rather common characterization that rights are essentially claims can be taken as a way of emphasizing that rights hold irrespective of whether they have been acknowledged, either in the society or, more specifically, by that person against whom the claim is made.

Against the view that rights are essentially claims are ranged a number of philosophers. BENTHAM (§5) comes most readily to mind, and his polemic on this very point against natural rights as 'nonsense' still adds relish to philosophical discussions. T.H. GREEN, in his insistence that rights require social recognition and that without it they are something less than rights, would be another. And, oddly enough, LENIN would be a third.

The problem we are examining arises, in part, because the procedure for deciding whether something is a right is not wholly settled. We find that the vocabulary of rights, in particular, of human rights, may actually be used at any of several steps: that of mere claim, that of entitlement (where only the claim-to element is really settled), that of fully validated claim (where we have the idea both of a justified claim *to* something and of a justified claim *against* someone for it) and, finally, that of satisfied or enforced claim (where the appropriate measures required to support or to fulfil the claim have been given effective embodiment as well). The presence of these possible stages has introduced a degree of ambiguity into assertions that a right exists.

Accordingly, we find a significant variety of contemporary opinion as to the point at which such assertions can most plausibly be thought to take hold. While some have said simply that rights are *claims*

(Mayo 1965), others say they are *entitlements* (McCloskey 1965), and yet others (most notably, Feinberg 1973, 1980) say they are *valid claims*. Ranged against them have been those (such as Sumner 1987; Martin 1993) who emphasize that rights, even human rights, are basically established ways of acting or being treated. And, last of all, some (for example, Rawls 1971; Melden 1988) have treated rights as legitimate expectations and, hence, have landed more or less in the middle (see RAWLS, J.).

The main backdrop to the view that rights are (valid) claims is, I think, the common opinion (emphasized by Dworkin (1978), Raz (1986), Mac-Cormick (1977) and Held (1984) among others) that to have a right is to have a justification for acting in a certain way, or a justification for being treated in a certain way (see DWORKIN, R.). Now, suppose that a candidate for rights status had all the rights-making features (mentioned in §1) but one. Although accredited (in the sense of justified), it was not established; it lacked the *social* recognition which it ought to have.

Why should the lack of such recognition deprive it of rights status? For, clearly, if we modelled the rights-making features on what was justified (what was accredited in *that* sense), the thing was already a right even before it was recognized, even before it became a practice. And when it was recognized it would be recognized as a *right* (as something that was fully justified) and would not simply become a right in being recognized.

The opposing view, that rights are socially recognized practices, rests on three main contentions. The first of these is the contention that the notions of authoritative recognition (if not explicit, then at least implicit, as evidenced by conduct) and of governmental promotion and maintenance (usually on a wide variety of occasions) are themselves part of the standard notion of a *legal* right, that is, when we are concerned with rights that are more than merely nominal ones.

Thus, on the social recognition view, the fatal flaw in the theory of rights as valid claims (in any of its formulations) is the suggestion that practices of governmental recognition and enforcement in law can be dispensed with in the case of legal rights. Indeed, this is the very point at which both Dworkin and Raz, who might otherwise be taken to be supporters of some form of the valid claims thesis, desert that thesis for one that emphasizes the necessity of institutionally establishing ways of acting/being treated, if these are to count as *legal* rights (see Dworkin 1978; Raz 1984).

The second point put forward by the social recognition view is that it is desirable to have, if possible, a single, unequivocal sense of 'rights': one that is capable of capturing both legal rights and human (and other moral) rights under a single generic heading. Now, if the argument just sketched is to be credited, then the view of rights as valid claims does not provide an adequate generalized notion of rights, one that can comfortably include both legal and human rights. For we have already seen that legal rights cannot be satisfactorily accounted for under the heading of valid claims.

This brings us to the third point urged by the social recognition view. Here the argument is that *all* moral rights can, indeed must, be construed as involving established practices of recognition and maintenance. Since human rights (as a special case of moral rights) are thought to be addressed to governments in particular, we must regard practices of governmental recognition and promotion as being the form for such recognition and maintenance to take for these rights. Here we have, in brief compass, then, the social recognition view that opposes the contention that rights are essentially justified or valid claims.

4 Functions of rights

Rights have many functions. Two in particular are emphasized in the contemporary literature: the conferring of liberty or autonomy (on rightholders) and the protection of their interests, especially their basic interests.

Rights in the seventeenth and eighteenth centuries were largely discussed as if they were simply liberties and, hence, ways of acting on the part of the rightholder. Indeed, this tendency is deeply rooted in the tradition of rights discourse. It is hard to say when 'a right' was first spoken of in a way continuous with current usage, but many careful expositors locate that first recognizable use with WILLIAM OF OCKHAM (§11), when he talked of a right (*ius* or *jus*) as a power or capacity (*potestas*) to act in accordance with 'right reason' or, in the special case of a legal right (*ius fori*), with an agreement. Such a usage was well established by the seventeenth century (with Hobbes and, some would say, with Locke) and has been widespread ever since.

It constitutes, none the less, a drastic oversimplification – even if the rights referred to are, as they often are, the classic rights of the eighteenth-century declarations. For these rights include important rights to ways of being treated and such rights are not things the rightholder does or can do. Even so, the oversimplification continues to prevail in philosophical literature (for example, Hart 1973; Rawls 1971, 1993). Thus, Rawls' 'equal basic liberties' (enshrined in his first principle of justice) include both liberties of action and ways of being treated, typically ways of not being injured by the actions of others (see FREEDOM AND LIBERTY §3).

It is clearly possible to have both important functions (the conferring of liberty on rightholders and the protection of their interests) as functions of rights, often of a single right. Thus it seems arbitrary, where both functions are normally served by almost all rights, to single out just one of these functions (typically the function of conferring autonomy) and to give it *definitional* weight (see Sumner 1987).

In fact, in line with the contemporary understanding of rights (as expressed, for example, in the UN's *Universal Declaration of Human Rights* of 1948), it might be best to stress three main functions of rights. Thus, the central content of some rights will be a way of acting (for example, a liberty of conduct of some sort). But at the core of other rights will be a way of being treated: a non-injury of some sort or, alternatively, the provision of a service.

Corresponding to each main heading or class of rights (as determined by these central cores), there is an appropriate or characteristic normative response enjoined for the conduct of others. But the essential character of this normative direction of the conduct of second parties shifts from main case to main case. Allowing or even encouraging a piece of conduct is what these parties are normatively directed to do in the case of a liberty; prohibiting their doing of an injury to the rightholder or requiring of them a service, again to the rightholder, is the incumbent directive in the other two cases.

5 Critical justification

Rights are eminently plausible candidates for justification, an idea that I tried to capture in §1 with the notion that rights are *accredited* ways of acting or of being treated. This section will consider some of the main full-blown theories offered to justify rights. One proviso is that the most important rights are universal rights – in particular, human rights and constitutional rights, which are fundamental or basic civil rights of all persons (or all citizens) within a given politically organized society. My account is limited to theories that attempt to justify such universal rights.

All civil rights are important rights and all reflect a high level of social commitment. But not all can be justified as representing individuated and practicable and universal moral claims which serve as proper conclusions to sound arguments from objective principles of critical morality (or at least from principles widely regarded as reasonable).

Some can be, however. Indeed, in the social recognition view (described in §3), human rights would be, simply, constitutional rights that embodied precisely such morally valid claims. These claims, then, when on their own, could be described (relatively noncontroversially and giving due weight to both the opposing views canvassed in §3) as human rights *norms*.

We can ask: what might be involved, then, in the justification of human rights – or human rights norms – and of those constitutional rights susceptible of the same sort of justification? One thing seems clear: the norms which constitute or back up human rights are moral norms. Thus human rights can exist only if substantive moral norms in some sense exist (or, at least, can be objectively described and argued for). Now, it is possible for moral, and hence human, rights to exist even if moral norms are conventional or are relative to culture. But if human rights – or human rights norms – are to serve their role as international standards of political criticism then such a conventional morality would have to include some norms that are accepted worldwide. More important, if such norms are to have weight and bearing for future human beings in societies not yet existing (and this much would seem to be involved if we are to call these norms *universal* in any significant sense), then these norms cannot be merely conventional (see UNIVERSALISM, ETHICAL).

Thus, in classifying human rights as moral rights one may wish to distinguish between actual and critical moralities. What seems especially crucial to human rights, then, is the belief that there are objectively correct, or objectively reasonable, critical moral principles. Often, human rights – or human rights norms – are traced back to such foundational ideas as human dignity or moral personality or moral agency or moral community (for example, Melden 1988). But the exploration of such possibilities has failed to gain widespread support, perhaps because such notions as moral agency do not themselves seem sufficiently distinct from the very norms or rights they are being called upon to justify. Or perhaps because such notions seem, in the end, to stand in need of a more basic sort of justification themselves. Thus, we might do well to consider other grounding principles, principles that could be regarded as rock bottom and, arguably, as objectively reasonable.

One appropriate way to narrow the field among these is to consider first those substantive theories of critical justification that have grown up in proximity to serious talk about human and constitutional rights. Three important contemporary theories fit this description: utilitarianism (in particular, the theory developed by J.S. MILL (§10) and advocated recently under the name of 'indirect' utilitarianism), the theory of John Rawls, and rational-choice ethical theory, especially that of David Gauthier (1986) (see

CONTRACTARIANISM §3). I will confine the discussion to one example.

Rawls' theory (like Dworkin's) emphasizes the standing priority of basic liberties and other constitutional rights over such things as the common good or perfectionist values (for example, the value of holiness, as religiously conceived, or the values of Nietzschean elitism). In his 1993 book Rawls sketches a complex theory of justification; it has two main parts. He starts with what he calls a 'freestanding' justification of the political conception of justice, drawing here on certain fundamental ideas which he finds 'implicit' in the contemporary democratic tradition. Next he claims that this political conception will also be endorsed and supported as the focus of an 'overlapping consensus' among the proponents of various comprehensive religious and moral doctrines that exist in the Western world today. Historic utilitarianism is prominently mentioned as one of these doctrines.

But it is doubtful that the utilitarian principle of general happiness could support the assignment of basic rights – constitutionally guaranteed benefits – to individuals if such rights prevented the utilitarian politician from allowing policies favourable to corporate or aggregate interests to override or supersede constitutional rights when those interests could be seen to conduce to greater benefit. In that sense, then, philosophical utilitarianism is incompatible with the notion of basic rights developed by Rawls, Dworkin and others. For utilitarianism cannot possibly accept a critical justification of a scheme of basic institutions in which constitutional civil rights have a standing priority over policies favouring corporate goods or aggregate welfare.

Much hinges, it would seem, then, on how discussion of the critical justification of rights is set up and conducted. And if questions regarding the distribution of rights are best taken up *after* successful or at least plausible attempts at justification, then such issues as what kinds of beings can have rights are seen to hang in the balance as well.

Currently, we find highly agitated discussions about whether foetuses have rights or whether animals can have them or about limits to the right to life (in cases of mercy killing, for example, or in requests for assisted suicide). But a serious attempt to give answers to questions such as these, questions of distribution and of scope and of defeasibility, cannot be clearly addressed until they can be considered in the light of adequate accounts of the function of rights and with one or more substantive theories of critical justification in hand (see ANIMALS AND ETHICS; REPRODUCTION AND ETHICS).

See also: LAW, LIMITS OF

References and further reading

* Dworkin, R. (1978) *Taking Rights Seriously*, Cambridge, MA: Harvard University Press, ch. 4. (Referred to in §§3, 5. Originally published 1977; important appendix added in 1978. Essays vary in difficulty; some are intended for a popular audience, others are law review articles. Essays 2–4, 6, 7, 12 and 13 are especially relevant to rights.)

—— (1985) *A Matter of Principle*, Cambridge, MA: Harvard University Press. (Essays, with a similar range of difficulty to Dworkin 1978. Essays 2, 5 and 17 are especially relevant to rights.)

* Feinberg, J. (1973) *Social Philosophy*, Foundations of Philosophy series, Englewood Cliffs, NJ: Prentice Hall. (Referred to in §3. Feinberg is probably the leading US writer on the concept of rights; his argument – also found in Feinberg 1980 – that rights are valid claims has been especially influential. This book is intended for introductory reading by students in political studies. Chapters 4–6 are relevant to rights.)

* —— (1980) *Rights, Justice, and the Bounds of Liberty*, Princeton, NJ: Princeton University Press. (Referred to in §3. A collection of Feinberg's writings, originally published in scholarly journals. Feinberg is an unusually clear writer. Essays 6–8 and 11 are relevant to rights.)

* Gauthier, D. (1986) *Morals by Agreement*, Oxford: Oxford University Press. (Referred to in §5. An impressive attempt to ground morality in rational choice theory. It is elegantly written; some parts are quite technical. Chapters 7 and 9 are especially relevant to rights.)

* Hart, H.L.A. (1973) 'Bentham on Legal Rights', in A. W. Simpson (ed.) *Oxford Essays in Jurisprudence*, Oxford: Clarendon Press, 2nd series, 171–201; repr. unchanged, in H.L.A. Hart, *Essays on Bentham: Studies in Jurisprudence and Political Theory*, Oxford: Oxford University Press, 1982, ch. 7, 162–93. (Referred to in §4. A very influential paper.)

* Held, V. (1984) *Rights and Goods: Justifying Social Action*, New York and London: Free Press. (Referred to in §3. Well-written book, with many interesting examples.)

* Hohfeld, W.N. (1964) *Fundamental Legal Conceptions*, New Haven, CT: Yale University Press. (Referred to in §2. The two papers printed under the above title first appeared as articles in the *Yale Law Journal*, one in 1913, the other in 1917. Earlier editions of this book appeared in 1919 and 1923. Hohfeld's idea of four distinct rights patterns has left an indelible impression on Anglo-American theory.)

* MacCormick, D.N. (1977) 'Rights in Legislation', in P.M.S. Hacker and J. Raz (eds) *Law, Morality and Society: Essays in Honour of H.L.A. Hart*, Oxford: Oxford University Press, ch. 11, 189–209. (Referred to in §3. Criticizes Hart's idea of rights as protected choices, discussed in §4.)

* McCloskey, H.J. (1965) 'Rights', *Philosophical Quarterly* 15 (59): 115–27. (Referred to in §3; this paper is one of the foremost interpretations of rights as entitlements. See also McCloskey's 1976 paper 'Rights – Some Conceptual Issues', *Australasian Journal of Philosophy* 54 (2): 99–115.)

* Martin, R. (1993) *A System of Rights*, Oxford: Clarendon Press. (Expansion of the material of this entry, esp. of §§1, 5; referred to in §3. See chapter 13 for a discussion and criticism, with extensive citation, of utilitarian attempts at a critical justification of rights and those of Rawls', especially his 1982 article and his writings from 1985 onwards. This book contains a considerable bibliography relevant to rights.)

Martin, R. and Nickel, J.W. (1980) 'Recent Work on the Concept of Rights', *American Philosophical Quarterly* 17 (3): 165–80. (Expansion of the material of §§2–4 of this entry. The 1980 paper contains lengthy discussions of human rights and of the defeasibility of rights. It contains a useful bibliography. For an even more extensive bibliography, with some annotations, by the same authors, see their 1978 piece 'A Bibliography on the Nature and Foundations of Rights, 1947–77', *Political Theory* 6 (3): 395–413.)

* Mayo, B. (1965) 'Symposium on "Human Rights", II', *Proceedings of the Aristotelian Society Supplementary Volume* 39: 219–36. (Referred to in §3. Well-written exposition of the idea that rights are simply claims.)

* Melden, A.I. (1988) *Rights in Moral Lives: A Historical–Philosophical Essay*, Berkeley, CA: University of California Press. (Referred to in §§3 and 5. Some parts are easy going, others not. Interesting attempt to justify our current set of rights by moving along two main lines: through considering relations of persons in a moral community and through comparing rights, or their absence, in moral communities at different times in history.)

* Rawls, J. (1971) *A Theory of Justice*, Cambridge, MA: Harvard University Press. (Referred to in §§3, 4. A magisterial treatise. Not easy going – Rawls' prose is reminiscent of the high Victorian philosophical style of Green and Sidgwick. Rawls' characterization of rights is vague, but the book contains one of the most impressive attempts at a critical justification of rights.)

* —— (1993) *Political Liberalism*, New York: Columbia

University Press. (Although Rawls here attempts a more conversational style, this book is ultimately no easier than his 1971 book. In his 1993 book Rawls attempts to rework his theory of justice as a political theory. It also contains, unrevised, his important 1982 essay on 'The Basic Liberties and Their Priority'. Rawls' 1993 theory of critical justification is described and criticized in §5.)

* Raz, J. (1984) 'Legal Rights', *Oxford Journal of Legal Studies* 4 (1): 1–21. (Cited in §3. Raz is a principal representative of the jurisprudential tradition of Hart. The essay, although difficult, repays close reading.)

* —— (1986) *The Morality of Freedom*, Oxford: Oxford University Press. (Referred to in §3. Chapter 7 is on rights.)

* Sumner, L.W. (1987) *The Moral Foundation of Rights*, Oxford: Oxford University Press. (Referred to in §§3 and 4. This well-written book also represents one of the most important attempts to provide a critical justification of rights on a utilitarian basis.)

Tuck, R. (1979) *Natural Rights Theories: Their Origins and Development*, Cambridge: Cambridge University Press. (A major study – provides a brief early history of rights and an indispensable background to seventeenth-century thought, in particular Hobbes.)

Waldron, J. (ed.) (1987) *Nonsense Upon Stilts: Bentham, Burke and Marx on the Rights of Man*, New York and London: Methuen. (This book consists mainly of excerpts from the three theorists named plus introductions to each by Waldron and, also, a lengthy general introduction and a lengthy concluding essay by him. Valuable for background to discussions on rights in the eighteenth and nineteenth centuries – although weak on Rousseau and on the US contribution. Includes a very useful bibliographical essay.)

REX MARTIN

RISK

Every day persons face threats from natural disasters such as hurricanes and from technological hazards such as exposure to more than 60,000 different chemicals. The increase of pervasive, human-caused hazards raises a number of philosophical issues, most notably in the areas of ethics and epistemology. There are three main classes of ethical issue associated with risk. (1) Who should define risk, and how should it be defined? (2) Who should evaluate risk, and according to which rules? (3) What are the conditions under which it is ethically

acceptable to impose societal risk? Societal risks (such as those from liquefied natural gas facilities) tend to be involuntarily imposed, whereas individual risks (such as those from dietary consumption of saturated fats) are more voluntarily chosen. This discussion addresses societal, rather than individual, risks because they involve less individual choice and hence more ethical controversy.

1 **Ethics and risk definition**
2 **Ethics and risk evaluation**
3 **Ethics and risk imposition**

1 Ethics and risk definition

Moral philosophers use the term 'risk' in at least five distinct ways. In the context of ordinary language analysis and normative ethics, a 'risk' is the possibility that some harm will occur. In the (second) context of Bayesian decision theory, a 'risk' is the probability of an undesirable outcome (see DECISION AND GAME THEORY). Risks are thus distinguished from certain outcomes (having probability 1) and from uncertain outcomes (to which no probabilities can be assigned). In the (third) context of quantitative risk assessment (QRA), a 'risk' is the probability that some consequence will occur. Typically a risk is expressed in QRA as the average annual probability of fatality that a particular situation imposes on an individual, such as a coal miner (see RISK ASSESSMENT). In the (fourth) context of risk-benefit analysis (RBA), a 'risk' is the monetary value assigned to some probable negative outcome such as loss of life. A variant of cost-benefit analysis, RBA is used commonly to evaluate whether some risk (such as the use of a pesticide) is worth the benefits. In the (fifth) context of insurance, a 'risk' is the chance of loss, often financial loss.

One of the most basic ethical issues associated with risk is how and by whom it is to be defined. Scientists and engineers who study societal risks – such as those associated with toxic waste dumps – typically define 'risk' in the third way just mentioned, as the probability that some harm, like death, will occur (National Research Council 1983). Social scientists and philosophers often argue that risk cannot be reduced to a mathematical expression, as in the third definition, because it also is a function of qualitative components (captured by the first definition) such as citizen consent and trust in government risk managers (MacLean 1986). Some moral philosophers also argue that typical definitions of risk exhibit a 'naturalistic fallacy' in the sense that they attempt to reduce ethical to purely scientific concepts (Shrader-Frechette 1985).

Much ethical debate focuses on whether societal risk ought to be defined (as in the second, third and fourth senses) by members of the scientific community, or by laypersons (as in the first sense) who are most likely to be its victims. Scientists tend to treat risk definition as the paternalistic prerogative of experts, in part because they claim that the definitions of irrational, ignorant, or risk-averse laypersons could impede social progress (Douglas and Wildavsky 1982) (see PATERNALISM). Many moral philosophers argue, in return, that rationality is a matter not merely of scientifically defensible outcomes but – because risk affects public welfare – also of just procedures for defining and evaluating risk (Cranor 1992; Shrader-Frechette 1991). Ethicists also claim that because there are no established hazard frequency records for new risks and because scientists have well-known heuristic biases in defining and estimating risks – such as the overconfidence biases in estimates of nuclear risk (Cooke 1993; Kahneman *et al*. (eds) 1982) – it is important to shape risk definitions through participatory democracy as well as by scientific fiat.

2 Ethics and risk evaluation

Still other ethical controversies concern how one ought to evaluate risks. A major issue is whether one ought to judge risk acceptability according to Bayesian or maximin rules. Should one maximize average expected utility (where 'utility' is the ability to satisfy some human want and where 'expected utility' is the subjective probability of some state multiplied by its ability to satisfy some human want)? Or should one minimize the likelihood of the worst outcome (consequences)? Utilitarians like Harsanyi (1975) argue for the Bayesian position on the grounds that 'worst cases' of technological risk occur rarely. They say that maximin decisions are overly conservative, impede social progress, and overemphasize small probabilities of harm. Egalitarians, many influenced by Rawls (1971), argue for maximin on the ground that the subjective risk probabilities are both uncertain and dwarfed by potentially catastrophic consequences, such as global warming, toxic leaks, or nuclear core melts. They also point out that a small (close to zero) probability of catastrophe does not outweigh infinitely serious risk consequences (see RATIONALITY, PRACTICAL §§6–7).

Other ethical controversies regarding risk evaluation concern whether, in cases of uncertainty where both cannot be avoided, one ought to minimize false positives (false assertions of harm) or false negatives (false assertions of no harm). Following traditional norms, many scientists argue for minimizing false positives on grounds that this stance is conservative, avoids positing an effect where there may be none, and places the burden of proof on those attempting to confirm some harm. Many moral philosophers, however, claim that traditional, pure-science norms for dealing with uncertainty are inapplicable to societal risk decisions because they affect human welfare. They argue for minimizing false negatives because doing so gives greater protection to public health and places the burden of proof on risk imposers rather than risk victims (Shrader-Frechette 1991). More generally, ethicists have challenged the traditional legal dictum that a potentially hazardous substance (such as a carcinogen) is 'innocent until proved guilty'. In cases involving 'toxic torts', they argue that fairness and equal treatment require risk evaluators and decision-makers to reverse the burden of proof, in part because causal chains of harm are difficult to prove and in part because risk victims are less able than risk imposers to bear the costs of faulty risk evaluations (Cranor 1992).

3 Ethics and risk imposition

Apart from the quantitative and scientific rules (such as expected utility) for evaluating risk, the most significant set of ethical issues regarding risk concerns the qualitative criteria under which it is acceptable to impose some hazard (such as chemical effluents) on workers or the public. One important criterion is the equity of distribution of the risks and benefits associated with some activity. Parfit (1983), for example, argues that temporal differences among persons/generations are not a relevant basis for discriminating against them with respect to risk. He and others maintain that a risk imposition is less acceptable to the degree that it imposes costs on future persons but awards benefits to present persons. Commercial nuclear fission, for example, benefits mainly present generations, whereas its risks and costs will be borne by members of future generations (see FUTURE GENERATIONS, OBLIGATIONS TO). Many economists, however, question notions of distributive equity and continue to discount future costs such as deaths caused by hazardous technologies. They also question whether 'geographical equity' (Shrader-Frechette 1993) or 'environmental justice' (Bullard 1993) requires risks to be distributed equally across generations, regions and nations. Proponents of siting hazardous facilities – for example, toxic dumps – in economically and socially disenfranchised areas argue that such risks have been accepted voluntarily and that they provide employment as well as tax benefits. They say that a bloody loaf of bread is better than no loaf at all.

Opponents of such risk impositions argue that life-threatening risks rarely bring substantial benefits. They maintain that economically and socially disenfranchised persons typically bear larger burdens of societal and workplace risk.

Economically, educationally, or socially disfranchised persons also are less likely than others to be able to give genuine free informed consent to public and workplace risk (MacLean 1986; Rescher 1983) (see CONSENT). Some utilitarian ethicists have argued, however, that no instances of consent are perfect, that workers and members of the public have the moral right to trade bodily security for higher wages or economic benefits, and that the greater good is achieved by risk-for-money trade-offs (see UTILITARIANISM). Ethical debate over such trade-offs focuses on opposed views about rights, paternalism, human dignity, equal treatment, and adequate compensation for risk. On the one hand, many utilitarians and traditional economists believe that the 'compensating wage differential', for example, gives workers in riskier occupations fair or equitable treatment. They also argue that overall economic prosperity justifies the imposition of industry-generated risks and that allowing companies to buy and sell legal rights to pollute leads to the greater good of all. Moreover, they claim that the contemporary federalist economy requires a 'politics of sacrifice' within which guaranteeing free informed consent to all societal and workplace risks is unrealistic and unattainable. On the other hand, MacLean (1986) and others claim that some things (like bodily health and environmental security) ought not be traded for compensation. Gewirth (1982), for example, argues that persons have a moral and legal right not to be caused to have cancer. Philosophers who argue for the ethical justifiability of the economics-safety trade-off tend to be utilitarians, to have more lenient conceptions of free informed consent, to underemphasize sociological differences among those who accept risky jobs and living conditions, and to believe that pursuing neoclassical economics leads overall to social and ethical benefits. Philosophers who argue against the economics-safety trade-off tend to be egalitarians or social-contract theorists, to have more stringent conceptions of free informed consent, to overemphasize the sociological differences among persons allegedly choosing different levels of societal risks, and to be more critical of the ethical assumptions underlying neoclassical economics.

Another aspect of the consent and compensation debate over risk imposition concerns liability for societal risks. Current US laws, for example, excuse nuclear power plant licensees from full liability for accidents on grounds of economic efficiency and the greater good. Many ethicists argue that such exclusions violate rights such as due process (Shrader-Frechette 1993), legal rights to full administration of the law and to redress under the law.

Apart from the question whether risk victims deserve due process, a related ethical issue is the magnitude of societal risks that ought to be subject to regulation. How far do legal or moral rights to bodily security extend? Ought government or industry be allowed to impose even a minimal risk on persons without their consent (MacLean 1986)? The Delaney Clause to the US food additive amendments, for example, demands a zero-risk level and prohibits the direct addition of any amount of carcinogens to food. For US hazards not related to food, the maximum level of societal risk that can be imposed on the public, without any government regulation, is 10^{-6} (the risk imposes on each person an average annual chance of death of 1 in 1 million). The comparable level for workplace risks is approximately 10^{-3}. Proponents of uniform standards argue that zero risk is unachievable and unrealistic and that economic efficiency and fairness require such standards. Opponents of uniform standards argue that because the public is more averse to some risks, like cancer, different standards (including zero risk) are necessary for different risks. They also argue that all societal and workplace risks should be kept as low as possible, perhaps below the 10^{-6} level, and that uniform standards are too lenient in protecting only 'average' persons rather than especially sensitive individuals such as children (Shrader-Frechette 1991).

Apart from the particular norms one accepts for societal risk definition, evaluation and imposition, there is consensus on several general conclusions. Not all societal risks can be reduced by a technological 'fix'. Not all can be resolved by a legislative 'fix' that imposes a hazardous facility on a group without its consent. Not all societal risks can be ameliorated by a public-relations 'fix'. Most risk problems can be solved only by ethical analysis and democratic process: the most important aspect of risk is not scientific but ethical.

See also: PUBLIC INTEREST

References and further reading

* Bullard, R.D. (1993) *Confronting Environmental Racism*, Boston, MA: South End Press. (Criticism of distributive inequities regarding risk.)
* Cooke, R. (1993) *Experts in Uncertainty: Opinion and Subjective Probability in Science*, New York: Oxford University Press. (Provides suggestions for more reliable estimates of probabilistic risk.)

* Cranor, C. (1992) *Regulating Toxic Substances: A Philosophy of Science and the Law*, New York: Oxford University Press. (An argument for changing the burden of proof to the plaintiff in toxic-tort cases.)

* Douglas, M. and Wildavsky, A. (1982) *Risk and Culture*, Berkeley, CA: University of California. (Provides arguments that risk is a social construct.)

* Gewirth, A. (1982) *Human Rights*, Chicago, IL: University of Chicago Press. (Explanation and defence of a theory of human rights.)

* Harsanyi, J. (1975) 'Can the Maximin Principle Serve as a Basis for Morality?', *American Political Science Review* 69: 594–605. (Arguments in favour of utilitarian risk evaluations.)

* Kahneman, D., Slovic, P. and Tversky, A. (eds) (1982) *Judgment Under Uncertainty: Heuristics and Biases*, Cambridge: Cambridge University Press. (Criticism of traditional scientific accounts of risk estimates and probabilistic reasoning.)

Kneese, A.V., Ben-David, S. and Schulze, W.D. (1982) 'The Ethical Foundations of Benefit-Cost Analysis Techniques', in D. MacLean and P. Brown (eds) *Energy and the Future*, Totowa, NJ: Rowman and Littlefield. (Argues that economic methods ought to take account of ethical values.)

* MacLean, D. (ed.) (1986) *Values at Risk*, Totowa, NJ: Rowman and Allanheld. (Argues that risk decisions ought to take account of social and ethical values.)

* National Research Council (1983) *Risk Assessment in the Federal Government: Managing the Process*, Washington, DC: National Academy Press. (Classic survey of how to manage/control societal risks.)

* Parfit, D. (1983) 'The Further Future: The Discount Rate', in D. MacLean and P. Brown (eds) *Energy and the Future*, Totowa, NJ: Rowman and Littlefield, 31–7. (Argues against economists' use of discount rates.)

* Rawls, J. (1971) *A Theory of Justice*, Cambridge, MA: Harvard University Press. (Classic contemporary defence of social-contract ethics and egalitarian views of risk.)

* Rescher, N. (1983) *Risk: A Philosophical Introduction*, Washington, DC: University Press of America. (Readable philosophical survey of problems related to risk.)

Sagoff, M. (1988) *The Economy of the Earth*, Cambridge: Cambridge University Press. (Criticism of traditional scientific accounts of economic methods for dealing with risk.)

* Shrader-Frechette, K. (1985) *Science Policy, Ethics, and Economic Methodology*, Boston, MA: Kluwer. (Analysis of the values issues underlying risk-benefits analysis.)

* —— (1991) *Risk and Rationality: Philosophical Foundations for Populist Reforms*, Berkeley, CA: University of California Press. (Presents arguments for lay, as well as expert, evaluations of risk.)

* —— (1993) *Burying Uncertainty: Risk and the Case Against Geological Disposal of Nuclear Waste*, Berkeley, CA: University of California Press. (Criticism of risk evaluation methods that ignore ethical and social values.)

KRISTIN SHRADER-FRECHETTE

RISK ASSESSMENT

Probabilistic or quantitative risk assessment (QRA) aims to identify, estimate and evaluate a variety of threats to human health and safety. These threats arise primarily from particular technologies (such as commercial nuclear fission) or from environmental impacts (such as deforestation). Defined in terms of the probability that some consequence will occur, 'risk' typically is expressed as the average annual probability of fatality that a particular activity imposes on one individual. For example, because of normal lifetime exposure to dichloromethane (DCM), a multipurpose solvent, the average member of the public has an annual probability of dying from cancer of 0.0000041 or (4.1×10^{-6}). Or, for every million persons exposed to DCM throughout their lifetimes, on average the chemical will cause four cancer deaths each year.

Although risks may be individual (such as those from consuming saturated fats) or societal (such as those from liquified natural gas facilities), government typically regulates only societal risks. By definition, they are largely involuntarily imposed, whereas individual risks affect only the persons voluntarily choosing them. Most QRAs address societal risks, either because a government seeks a scientific basis for particular risk regulations, because some industry wishes to determine possible liability for its processes or products, or because actual or potential victims want to protect themselves or to allocate risks by means other than market mechanisms.

Philosophical contributions to QRA are of three main types: assessments of particular risks, criticisms of existing assessments, and clarifications of important QRA concepts, methods or theories. Such contributions usually focus on either epistemology (including philosophy of science) or ethics. Epistemological analyses address, for example, the adequacy and appropriateness of some scientific, probabilistic or policy technique used in QRA; the status of a specific causal hypothesis about risk; or the rationality of alternative decision rules for evaluating risks. Ethical analyses investigate, for instance, the equity of the risk distributions presupposed in a specific QRA or by general QRA methodology; the degree to which a particular method of risk evaluation accounts for crucial social values, such as free informed consent and due process; and the extent to which a given QRA technique, such as discounting the future (see Parfit 1983), begs important ethical questions such as rights of future generations.

1 **The need for risk assessment**
2 **Three tasks of assessment**
3 **Epistemological issues in risk assessment**

1 The need for risk assessment

Agricultural, military and industrial technologies typically cause occupational and public fatalities. The World Health Organization estimates, for instance, that normal use of pesticides kills 40,000 persons every year in developing countries. Even in developed nations like the USA, approximately 100,000 workers die annually from accidents or exposure to compounds such as toluene or chromium. Members of the public also are at risk, as shown by catastrophes in Bhopal (India), Seveso (Italy) and Chernobyl (Ukraine). For example, experts predict that the 1986 Chernobyl nuclear-reactor accident will cause between 25,000 and 475,000 premature deaths from cancer worldwide.

Recognizing the enormity of societal hazards, and spurred by environmental legislation, in the 1960s many governments intensified their efforts in quantitative risk assessment (QRA). By the early 1980s, most regulatory agencies, industries and environmental groups – at least in developed nations – employed decision theorists, economists, engineers, epidemiologists, mathematicians, philosophers, various physical and social scientists, and toxicologists to assess risks associated with many technological activities and environmental impacts. In the USA during the 1980s committees of the National Academy of Sciences and the National Science Foundation developed both methodological standards and research priorities for QRA. Their goals were assisting society in determining which societal risks, relative to others, are likely to be most dangerous or most in need of regulation; protecting public health and safety; distributing societal risks and benefits equitably; and providing a framework for efficient and wise risk management.

2 Three tasks of assessment

Most QRAs include three tasks: risk identification, risk estimation and risk evaluation (National Research Council 1983, 1993; National Academy of Engineering 1986). Assessors perform *risk identification* by looking for clusters of harm associated with some environmental impact or technological activity. In the 1970s, for example, risk assessors identified vinyl chloride as hazardous by noticing the liver cancers occurring among rubber workers exposed to the chemical. To identify vinyl chloride or other substances as hazardous, assessors need to be able to make a number of causal inferences and to show that particular clusters of disease or death are neither random occurrences nor the result of hidden variables (see CAUSATION).

At the step of *risk estimation* scientists employ sensitive toxicological, biostatistical and epidemiological methods to estimate the population at risk (from a particular hazard), its level of exposure and the associated dose-response curve. By gathering data among affected persons, risk assessors were able to determine, for example, the average vinyl-chloride exposure for rubber-industry workers. Using exposure data, assessors develop a dose-response curve by determining which of many possible curves best explains and predicts the numbers of cases of disease, injury or death as a function of a particular dose of (or exposure to) a substance like vinyl chloride. Because data on humans frequently are not available, assessors usually interpolate and extrapolate from animal data to arrive at a dose-response curve. Particular curves are controversial because data are almost always incomplete and because different curves have different consequences for human health, for government regulations and for industry expenditures to control hazards.

Performing *risk evaluation*, assessors analyse whether a given societal activity – for example, use of commercial nuclear fission – is socially and ethically acceptable, relative to other risks associated with similar benefits. To determine risk acceptability, assessors generally employ economic methods (such as risk-cost-benefit analysis), psychometric techniques (such as expressed preferences or revealed preferences), and ethical analyses (such as weighting risk parameters on the basis of Paretian or Rawlsian rules (Kneese, Ben-David and Schulze 1982)) (see APPLIED ETHICS). A major problem with risk-evaluation conclusions, however, is their sensitivity to specific assumptions about measuring preferences, determining social choices, or quantifying risks, costs and benefits. For example, when risk assessors include the value of government subsidies for radioactive waste storage/disposal in their calculations of the costs of nuclear-generated electricity, it is virtually impossible to show a favourable benefit–cost ratio for this technology. Studies that assert the cost-effectiveness of commercial nuclear energy, however, typically ignore the effects of government subsidies – on the grounds that they are external to normal market processes. As this nuclear example illustrates, reliably assessing a particular risk-evaluation conclusion requires one to know both the methodological assumptions and the factual parameters to which the conclusion is most sensitive.

3 Epistemological issues in risk assessment

Because of its emphasis on methodological assumptions, QRA provides a new and important context for investigating traditional questions in epistemology and philosophy of science. Some of these questions, for example, address the realist-versus-antirealist debate over the status of scientific knowledge (see SCIENTIFIC REALISM AND ANTIREALISM). A central controversy in QRA concerns the degree to which both general and particular risk estimates are realistic. Natural scientists, more traditionally oriented philosophers of science, and proponents of normative epistemology tend to be more realist. They argue that although all risk estimates are assumption-laden, they are based on actual characteristics of phenomena that can, in principle, be analysed by mathematicians and scientists. Risk assessors in more realist camps also defend their claims by arguing that obtaining new data (such as accident frequencies) forces analysts to modify their risk estimates and illustrates that their assessments are not purely subjective (National Research Council 1983). Social scientists, more sociologically oriented philosophers of science, and proponents of naturalized epistemology tend to be more conventionalist. Arguing that all risk estimates are socially constructed and that no risk knowledge is unbiased, they claim that all risks are assessed on the basis of social, cultural and methodological values. More conventionalist assessors also maintain that, even if risk estimation were objective, risk evaluation would nevertheless be determined by our perceptions and constructs (Johnson and Covello 1987; Douglas and Wildavsky 1982).

Other epistemological debates over risk assessment mirror continuing metascientific controversies concerning the nature of rationality and the reliability of inductive inferences (see INDUCTION, EPISTEMIC ISSUES; INDUCTIVE INFERENCE). Does Bayesian rationality adequately characterize successful risk evaluation? Are given data adequate to estimate a particular risk? Do expert or lay opinions provide better evaluations of risk acceptability (as opposed to risk magnitude)? Some assessors argue that they, not members of the public, have more reliable knowledge of various risk probabilities and therefore are able to make more rational decisions about risk acceptability (Douglas and Wildavsky 1982). More populist assessors respond that, although laypersons may have inaccurate knowledge of risk probabilities, lay ignorance in this regard is beside the point. They claim that members of the public have 'the right to be wrong' because rational decisions about risk acceptability are less a function of *knowledge* of risk *probabilities* than a function of the *value* they attach to avoiding potentially catastrophic *consequences* and to obtaining benefits from taking some risk (Shrader-Frechette 1985, 1991; MacLean 1986).

Philosophical debates over subjective probabilities and the role of expert judgment are central to QRA because risk controversies typically arise as a result of new technologies and activities. For example, roughly 60,000 different chemicals are used annually in developed nations. For the 10,000 new chemicals introduced each year, there are no established frequency records regarding potential hazards. Without such records, there are numerous debates over which estimates and models accurately represent particular risks. It is often not easy to settle these conflicts because of the many inferences, extrapolations and interpolations associated with QRA methods; because ethical sanctions against human experimentation limit available data; because of the expenses associated with long-term epidemiological testing and the large sample sizes or time periods needed to detect small effects, for example, of low-level exposures to toxic substances. In response to conflicts over the estimation of risk probabilities, philosophers of science have proposed new techniques for calibrating the subjective estimates of different assessors (Cooke 1992).

In addition to problems with risk estimation, empirical underdetermination in QRA also causes many metascientific and philosophical controversies over risk evaluation. One conflict, for example, concerns which decision-theoretic rules are more appropriate to risk evaluation – those based on average expected utility, on maximin, or on some other rule (Giere 1991)? Proponents of expected utility would maximize average welfare in making risk decisions because any other procedure assigns too much weight to small risk probabilities. Proponents of maximin rules argue, in response, that in cases involving probabilistic uncertainty and potentially catastrophic risks, it is more rational to avoid the worst possible outcomes. Defending maximin rules, they claim that rational persons would accept neither potentially catastrophic consequences, even if their probability were low, nor risks with uncertain probabilities (Slovic 1987). Other risk debates focus on whether, in a situation of uncertainty, one ought to make the 'equiprobability assumption' that all unknown probabilities have the same value. What is appropriate risk/scientific behaviour in a situation of uncertainty?

Some of the most basic questions raised by philosophers of science interested in risk assessment concern the adequacy of particular causal inferences or predictions. What causal accounts explain a given number of fatalities? When should a scientist claim that the evidence of harm is adequate and therefore abandon the search for confounders (Cranor 1992)? When are analogies between animal models and human models close enough to infer that similar causal processes create similar risks? Or, which scientific accounts (such as hydrogeological models for groundwater flow at hazardous waste sites) adequately explain and predict phenomena relevant to risk estimation and risk evaluation (Shrader-Frechette 1993)? When is a particular scientific model too idealized to be useful in the practical work of risk estimation and evaluation? Why does one risk-estimation curve fit the dose-response data better than another? Is predictive power a necessary condition for explaining risk phenomena? Are assessors justified, especially in cases of potential catastrophe, in making an inference to the best explanation (see IDEALIZATIONS; INFERENCE TO THE BEST EXPLANATION; STATISTICS AND SOCIAL SCIENCE)?

As the disputes over causal inferences reveal, epistemological controversies regarding QRA frequently concern the methodological adequacy of various techniques of risk assessment. These controversies are likely to persist, so long as we continue to purchase societal progress at the price of increasing particular risks and costs.

See also: CONFIRMATION THEORY; ENVIRONMENTAL ETHICS; OBSERVATION; PROBABILITY, THEORY AND EPISTEMOLOGY; RISK; SCIENTIFIC METHOD

References and further reading

* Cooke, R. (1992) *Experts in Uncertainty: Opinion and Subjective Probability in Science*, New York: Oxford University Press. (Mathematical and philosophical analysis of how to take account of differing subjective probabilities used in risk assessment by one of the prominent European risk assessors.)

* Cranor, C. (1992) *Regulating Toxic Substances: A Philosophy of Science and the Law*, New York: Oxford University Press. (Philosophical and ethical arguments for putting the burden of proof, in legal controversies over toxic substances, on the alleged perpetrators of the risk.)

* Douglas, M. and Wildavsky, A. (1982) *Risk and Culture*, Berkeley, CA: University of California. (Analysis of risk behaviour in terms of three main constructivist or relativist accounts of risk, and an attack on environmentalist views of risk.)

Freudenburg, W. (1988) 'Perceived Risk, Real Risk: Social Science and the Art of Probabilistic Risk Assessment', *Science* 242 (7 October): 44–9. (Classical analysis and defence of the position that all risks are perceived, and that experts do not really know real risk, independent of their perceptions.)

* Giere, R. (1991) 'Knowledge, Values, and Technological Decisions: A Decision-Theoretic Approach', in D. Mayo and R. Hollander (eds) *Acceptable Evidence: Science and Values in Risk Management*, New York: Oxford University Press. (Example of how to use decision-theoretic rules in risk assessment.)

Hornstein, D.T. (1992) 'Reclaiming Environmental Law: A Normative Critique of Comparative Risk Analysis', *Columbia Law Review* 92: 501–71. (Classic legal and ethical criticism of risk assessment.)

Humber, J. and Almeder, R. (eds) (1987) *Quantitative Risk Assessment*, Clifton, NJ: Humana Press. (An early philosophical analysis of some key issues in risk assessment.)

* Johnson, B. and Covello, V. (eds) (1987) *The Social and Cultural Construction of Risk*, Boston, MA: Kluwer. (An early sociological analysis of risk assessment.)

Kahneman, D., Slovic, P. and Tvesky, A. (eds) (1982) *Judgment Under Uncertainty: Heuristics and Biases*, Cambridge: Cambridge University Press. (Classic analysis of the ways in which subjective judgements of probabilities err, even among experts.)

* Kneese, A.V., Ben-David, S. and Schulze, W.D. (1982) 'The Ethical Foundations of Benefit–Cost Analysis Techniques', in D. MacLean and P. Brown (eds) *Energy and the Future*, Totowa, NJ: Rowman & Littlefield. (Economists' analysis of how results of benefit–cost analysis and risk assessment can change if one employs ethical weighting criteria.)

Krimsky, S. and Golding, D. (1992) *Social Theories of Risk*, London: Praeger. (Well-known social and philosophical views of risk.)

* MacLean, D. (ed.) (1986) *Values at Risk*, Totowa, NJ: Rowman & Allanheld. (Analysis of how risk assessment challenges some important values, especially ethical values.)

* National Academy of Engineering (1986) *Hazards:*

Technology and Fairness, Washington, DC: National Academy Press. (Important survey of risk-assessment problems that arise in connection with engineering risk assessment.)

* National Research Council (1983) *Risk Assessment in the Federal Government: Managing the Process*, Washington, DC: National Academy Press. (Known as the 'Redbook', this is the 'how to' manual for all risk assessors.)

* —— (1993) *Issues in Risk Assessment*, Washington, DC: National Academy Press. (Work on several important problems in ecological risk assessment.)

* Parfit, D. (1983) 'The Further Future: The Discount Rate', in D. MacLean and P. Brown (eds) *Energy and the Future*, Totowa, NJ: Rowman & Littlefield, 31–7. (Well known argument against the use of discount rates in benefit–cost analysis and risk assessment.)

Rescher, N. (1983) *Risk: A Philosophical Introduction*, Washington, DC: University Press of America. (Good mathematical and philosophical survey of risk assessment: key methods and issues.)

Schultze, W. and Kneese, A. (1981) 'Risk and Benefit–Cost Analysis', *Risk Analysis* 1: 81–8. (Overview of how one applies benefit–cost analysis to risk assessment.)

* Shrader-Frechette, K. (1985) *Risk Analysis and Scientific Method*, Boston, MA: Kluwer. (Analysis of some of the main epistemological, scientific and ethical problems in quantative risk assessment.)

* —— (1991) *Risk and Rationality: Philosophical Foundations for Populist Reforms*, Berkeley, CA: University of California Press. (Argument against letting the expert and scientific community make decisions about acceptable risk, and argument in favour of more populist, procedural and ethical accounts of acceptable risk.)

* —— (1993) *Burying Uncertainty: Risk and the Case Against Geological Disposal of Nuclear Waste*, Berkeley, CA: University of California Press. (Scientific, ethical and logical analysis of arguments for the world's first permanent geological repository for nuclear waste.)

* Slovic, P. (1987) 'Perception of Risk', *Science* 236: 280–5. (Explanation of how and why people perceive risks in particular ways.)

KRISTIN SHRADER-FRECHETTE

RITUAL

Ritual, present throughout human affairs and central to many religious and cultural traditions, presents per- plexities. One important question concerns the worth of such repetition and fixety – for example, in prayer, in human interaction, sometimes even in eating and drinking. To consider prayer, why not encourage the direct expression of religious thought and affect – from the heart, as it were, rather than in prescribed ways? It is sometimes suggested, and tempting to suppose, that to regularize such expression is to constrict it, ultimately to demean it. It is difficult to locate value in such apparently unnecessary regulation of human affairs.

In the context of philosophy the question becomes striking. None of the prevailing approaches to ethics makes it easy to see how ritual might possess ethical value or figure crucially in the ethical life. Yet this is precisely how ritualized ways are often seen within communities of practitioners.

1 **The ethical import of ritual and traditional Judaism**
2–3 **Developed religious character**
4 **Ritual: linguistic and nonlinguistic**
5 **Conclusion**

1 The ethical import of ritual and traditional Judaism

Ethical theory, as we have it, seems unfriendly to ritual. For the Kantian, what distinguishes moral norms is their applicability to all rational agents. Rituals, however, are owned by communities, in whose highly particular and idiosyncratic idioms they speak. Indeed, rituals are sometimes optional even within the community. Nor does ritual come to mind when utilitarians reflect on behaviour that contributes to human betterment. Finally, engagement with ritual does not suggest itself to us, nor did it to Aristotle, as a trait that figures crucially in flourishing.

It will be helpful to examine a tradition or cultural setting in which ritual is taken seriously, in which it has a weighty, even a central, role. The present entry will focus upon traditional Judaism, a highly ritualized, comprehensive system of practice, indeed an inclusive legal system in which ritual permeates areas such as torts, contracts and divorce law. Ritual is pervasive, and since communal customs attain something of the status of law, the domain of ritual increases over time. How are we to think about the ethical status of ritual in the Jewish context?

A striking and suggestive feature of Jewish ritual is its essential role in the tradition's distinctive approach to human flourishing. Flourishing, of course, is the pivotal ethical notion, at least according to Aristotle and his followers.

Aristotle himself did not see ritual as essential to flourishing. Different cultural settings and traditions, however, may yield different ideas about human flourishing. And while not just anything should count as flourishing, a broadly Aristotelian view will want to allow for some latitude. The Aristotelian project as understood here – the empirical study of flourishing, and of the traits of character that contribute to and partly constitute human flourishing – thus becomes applicable to a wide range of cultural settings. Carried out in connection with traditional Judaism, the project yields the conclusion that ritual observance is ethically of the first importance. It is noteworthy that MENCIUS, in the Confucian tradition, counted *li* – often translated as 'propriety', a trait that centrally involved engagement with ritual – among the virtues.

What is the distinctive approach of traditional Judaism to human flourishing, and how is it that ritual is essential? At the heart of that approach is the conception of developed religious character. Ritual plays an essential role in the growth and sustenance of religious character.

2 Developed religious character: the role of awe

We are apt to think of a deeply religious person as a 'true believer'. However, there is no expression in biblical Hebrew that corresponds to our term, 'believer'. The phrase that comes closest is *Y'rei Adonai*, which means 'one who stands in awe of the Lord'. (The Hebrew expression *yirah*, translated here as 'awe', also means 'fear'. As A.J. Heschel notes, the term and its cognates are used in the Bible primarily in the sense of awe.) This suggests an emphasis on affect, orientation and responsiveness, rather than on the doxastic. Specifically, this Hebrew expression suggests that awe plays a central role. 'Awe rather than faith is the cardinal attitude of the religious Jew', writes A.J. HESCHEL (1959: 77).

One can see why awe might be of special interest by an examination even of quite ordinary – not religiously charged – experiences. Particularly important is a curious duality. In the grip of awe, one feels humbled; in the extreme case, overwhelmed. At the same time, remarkably, one does not feel crushed or diminished, but rather elevated, exhilarated. This duality – humbled yet elevated – is of great importance for the religious orientation at which Judaism aims. (Needless to say, the features of awe experiences highlighted here and below vary in intensity and relative prominence from experience to experience.)

Awe experiences, perhaps as a consequence of the elevation-cum-humility, characteristically engender generosity of spirit, lack of pettiness, and increased ability to forgive and to contain anger and disappointment. The tradition notably associates just such

affect and behaviour with God. Turning to the cognitive, awe experiences engender a Godlike perspective, the ability to see things, or almost see things, under the aspect of eternity, as Spinoza put it. One often also feels a powerful sense of gratitude.

Reflection on awe provides an entry point into the concept of holiness, a concept that is as important to Judaeo-Christian (as opposed to Greek) thinking about flourishing as it is difficult. In the grip of powerful awe, one often feels oneself to be in the presence of something sacred. To destroy the object of such an experience – the Grand Canyon, say – or to allow it to be destroyed, would be sacrilege. If 'holy' and 'sacred' have any natural application for non-theists, it is in connection with such moments. It is sometimes suggested that such reactions on the part of non-theists reflect the lingering presence of a religious upbringing, or an earlier time in our history. Instead, such reactions might be taken at face value, and as shedding light on the concept of holiness by providing a beginning point for reflection: awe seems to engender a sense of the holy.

These considerations provide a sense of what we might call the religious content of awe, and thus provide motivation for Heschel's making awe pivotal. At the same time, powerful awe experiences are relatively rare and transitory. How can such uncommon and fleeting experiences bear so great a weight?

It is here that the concept of the *y're Adonai*, one who stands in awe of God, comes to the fore. What is distinctive about such a religiously developed person is not only the object of awe. Perhaps even more important is the habitual quality, the steadiness, of awe. The *y're Adonai* is one who has made awe a regular, albeit not a constant, companion. And with awe comes its concomitants: the sense of being humbled and yet elevated, the Godlike tendencies of thought, feeling and behaviour, the perspective *sub specie aeternitatis*, the gratitude, the sense of being confronted by the holy in all sorts of unlikely places. 'Ordinary' experiences, interactions with other human beings, for example, or with nature, become encounters with the holy. It has been said that close to the core of the Jewish religious attitude – and this perhaps represents an important contribution of Judaism to culture – is the idea of the sanctification of the ordinary.

To say that awe goes to the heart of the religious attitude is not to say that there are no other important aspects. A more complete treatment than is possible here would need to explore other such features, for example, the love of God, an aspect of the religious attitude that seems related, but not reducible to, awe.

3 Developed religious character: the role of ritual

To attain the heightened responsiveness of the *y're Adonai* is quite an achievement. What is called for is a substantial change of orientation, a heightened responsiveness, and a deepening of wonder, of appreciation and of one's character. Effecting such change is intrinsically difficult, and external factors often make it more so. The frailties and limitations of one's fellows often inhibit their support for such development. And the distractions, discouragements, frustrations and sufferings of the human situation only increase the difficulty.

How then is such character development and sustenance possible? What are the tools by which the tradition means to effect its exceedingly ambitious plan? One often said to be the most fundamental is study of the tradition. Indeed, 'study' is not adequate, for it fails to convey the intensity of intellectual engagement. Jewish liturgy highlights an adaptation of Deuteronomy 30: 20, 'For they [the words and teachings of the Torah] are our lives and the length of our days, and with them we are engaged [or we meditate] day and night'. Saintly personalities throughout post-biblical Jewish history are paradigmatically giants of scholarship, those who quite literally are engaged day and night.

Ritual plays a major role in effecting and sustaining the transformation. Consider the practice of saying blessings: on eating and drinking, on smelling fragrant spices, herbs, plants, on seeing lightning, shooting stars, vast deserts, high mountains, a sunrise, the ocean, on seeing trees blossoming for the first time in the year, on seeing natural objects (including creatures) of striking beauty, on meeting a religious scholar, on meeting a secular scholar, on seeing a head of state, on hearing good news, on hearing bad news.

Heschel suggests that the practice of saying blessings is training in awe. One develops the habit, before so much as sipping water, to reflect and appreciate. In addition to the blessings' training function, blessings also function as reminders. Ordinary experience is distracting, and the tradition has assembled reminders to assist in maintaining focus.

In addition to occasion-related blessings, Jewish practice includes thrice-daily fixed prayer. Whatever one thinks of the practice of saying occasion-related blessings, the thrice-daily fixed prayer is likely to appear highly constricting. The blessings, at least, are appropriate to one's current experience.

We should remember, however, the magnitude and ambition of the tradition's project. While fixed prayer can degenerate into mechanical, unthinking, unfeeling performance, it offers great opportunities. Some of the usual translations notwithstanding, Jewish liturgy is a compilation of passages of literary magnificence. That such literature, the Psalms, for example, has survived the ages is a tribute to its expressive power, its ability to articulate and illuminate religious experience. To engage regularly with such literature – not merely to read the words but to declare them, to wrestle with them – is to occupy oneself with the tradition's project. The encounter with literature of such power encourages regularization of the attitudes to which it so ably gives voice. Indeed, ritualization turns out to be a great virtue: the agent need not wait until the appropriate experiences present themselves.

Ritualized prayer has another distinct advantage over spontaneous prayer. Spontaneous expressions – for example, of awe – are limited by the expressive capacities of the agent. How many among us are capable of summoning words adequate to powerful experiences and their concomitant thoughts and emotions?

Ritualized prayer does indeed present challenges of its own. The challenge is presented not by the repetition, but rather by the difficulty, the sheer hard work, involved in summoning up the thoughts and feelings appropriate to such literary magnificence. The founder of Hasidism, the Ba'al Shem Tov, is reputed to have said that it would be easier to deliver two advanced Talmudic lectures than to offer a single *amidah*, a fixed prayer of a few pages.

4 Rituals: linguistic and nonlinguistic

The examples of ritual we have been exploring all involve ritualized speech. Rituals need not involve linguistic performance, however, even in the highly word-oriented context of Judaism. Some may involve nonlinguistic behaviour that accompanies speech, as in bowing at appropriate times during prayer. Some may involve pure behaviour, that is behaviour not accompanying a linguistic performance – for example, the donning of a prayer shawl, or of phylacteries, or the burning of the leaven before Passover. These performances are accompanied by blessings (expressive, *inter alia*, of appreciation for the opportunity to perform the ritual), but the blessing accompanies them (and not vice versa). These are distinct from examples in which the action is a mere adjunct to the linguistic performance, for example, in bowing during prayer. Still other nonlinguistic rituals may involve no overt behaviour, as in the practice of hearing the searing call of the ram's horn every day during a month of the year devoted to reflection on the direction of one's life.

Ritualized prayer is ritualized engagement with dramatic and literary representation. It might seem that nonlinguistic ritual is distinctive in that it involves the actual performance of a dramatic representation, as opposed to merely engaging with one, as in prayer. There is, no doubt, something to this. Dramatic representations of ideas, for example, have a power beyond mere discursive articulations of the ideas themselves. It would be difficult to find a verbal equivalent of, say, wrapping oneself in a prayer shawl (where part of what this may mean to the agent is the wrapping of oneself in the tradition). Similarly, the call of the ram's horn is simply not to be equalled by any discursive substitute. Still, we should not forget that to engage in the prayer of Jewish tradition is not simply to read the text. It is rather to declare it, to make it one's own in speech and thought.

For the stranger to ritual, ritual will seem like rote performance, constricting rather than expansive, mechanical rather than expressive. One of the things lacking in such an attitude, according to the advocate of ritual, is a healthy respect for repetition. One who regularly engages with prayer, for example, can come not only to take comfort in the familiar, but also to see, in the repeated sentences, new depths. Since we are speaking of great literature, it will inevitably be the case that different sentences, or different turns of phrase, leap off the page, as will different emphases, and different meanings and levels of meaning. And what is true of prayer is also true for the nonlinguistic rituals.

For the stranger to ritual, multiplication of ritual forms will seem like a burden. But for one's day to be sprinkled with such dramatic representations is for one's day to be sprinkled with powerful expressions of the attitudes and ethical motifs in question. It is also to be in possession of a multiplicity of reminders, mechanisms by means of which one may retain one's focus.

5 Conclusion

Our look at traditional Judaism suggests that in the right cultural setting, ritual can figure importantly in human flourishing. Having come this far, we can extend the point: whether ritual is ethically relevant for the utilitarian depends upon what counts as well-being. A different sense of what counts as flourishing may indeed yield a different sense of well-being. Even for Kantians, community-based ritual might well come to be seen as ethically relevant, as conducing, say, to an increased respect for persons.

The foregoing suggests that ethical relevance is not a purely formal matter, but depends upon the particulars of the culture or tradition. One might conclude that although ritual may indeed be ethically relevant, it is not so in our cultural setting. One may

wonder, however, whether ritualized ways of acquiring, sustaining and celebrating values might play a more useful role than we have allowed.

See also: PRAYER; RELIGIOUS EXPERIENCE; SACRAMENTS; SHINTŌ

References and further reading

Douglas, M. (1970) *Natural Symbols: Explorations in Cosmology*, New York: Pantheon Books. (An argument for the indispensability of ritual.)

Durkheim, É. (1912) *Elementary Forms of the Religious Life*, trans. J.W. Swain, London: Allen & Unwin, 1915. (Classic discussion of the ritual nature of society and religion.)

Frank, D.H. (ed.) (1993) *A People Apart: Chosenness and Ritual in Jewish Philosophical Thought*, Albany, NY: State University of New York Press. (Contemporary discussion, including some discussion of historical figures. See especially Part 2, 'Ritual', and chapter 4, 'Rational Law/Ritual Law' by L.E. Goodman.)

* Heschel, A.J. (1959) *God in Search of Man*, New York: Meridian Books, and Philadelphia, PA: Jewish Publication Society. (See especially chapter 4 (43–53), which is a discussion of wonder and its role in the religious life, of wonder and blessings, and of the ordinary as wondrous; chapter 7 (73–9, especially note 6), which examines awe and its relation to and primacy over faith; and chapter 15 (152–7), which characterizes faith as steady and heightened responsiveness.)

HOWARD WETTSTEIN

RITUAL IN CHINESE PHILOSOPHY *see* LAW AND RITUAL IN CHINESE PHILOSOPHY

ROHAULT, JACQUES (1617–72)

Rohault belongs (with Régis and de Cordemoy) to a generation which did much to consolidate the position of Cartesian physics in France. He is particularly famous for his experimental attitude. He contributed to the debate over the physical interpretation of the Eucharist.

Jacques Rohault was born in France at Amiens. Although he obtained a degree at Paris University, he seems to have been an autodidact in philosophy. He

341

was a friend of Cyrano de Bergerac, of Molière and Clerselier (the best-known Cartesian philosopher of his time often cited in conjunction with the editor of Descartes' works), whose daughter Geneviève he married in 1664. Rohault was most famous for his public lectures on Cartesian philosophy, which from 1665 he held in his own house every Wednesday. In 1670 Rohault published *Traité de physique* Treatise on Physics, probably based on these lectures, followed by *Entretiens sur la philosophie* Conversations on Philosophy (1671). This book is essentially a defence of DESCARTES, dealing with controversial topics such as the relation between Descartes and Aristotle, Descartes' interpretation of the Eucharist and Descartes' ideas on the animal soul. Both of these works remained influential until the second quarter of the eighteenth century. Other works by Rohault, mostly on mathematics, were published posthumously by Clerselier in 1682.

According to Rohault, traditional natural philosophy is too 'metaphysical'. His own physics, on the other hand, is experimental. Indeed, the experiments and demonstrations were the great attraction of his Wednesday lectures. His concepts, however, are unmistakably Cartesian, although he does believe that Aristotelian concepts like 'matter' and 'form' can be made more precise: matter is extended matter, and forms are the various ways in which matter is modified into particular things. Apart from the fact that Rohault's physics is more complete (at least in terms of contemporary notions) than Descartes' (the *Treatise on Physics* also contains a part on animated bodies), it is also more overtly experimental (he even has a theory of experimentation) and therefore more attractive for students. Moreover, Rohault never claims more than probability for his theories. Physical explanations have the status of scientific hypotheses. They are true not because they are metaphysically warranted but because they provide the best account of experience.

One of the classical objections to Cartesian philosophy in Catholic countries was that Descartes' rejection of 'real accidents' makes it impossible to account for the fact that in the Eucharist the accidents belonging to the bread and the wine continue to exist independently from the original substance (which was changed into the body and blood of Christ). Also the definition of matter as extension (which implies that wherever there is any extension there is matter) would be contrary to the idea that Christ is really present under the dimensions of bread and wine. Rohault's general answer, to which he devoted his first 'Entretien' is that his theory is not contrary to that of Aristotle, so that, given that the traditional theory was based on Aristotle, there is nothing to worry about. Further, that theology and philosophy are mutually independent, so that no philosophical theory can ever be dangerous for theology. His specific reply is twofold. First he maintains that, since 'real accidents' cannot exist independently from a mind that perceives them, there is nothing strange in the fact that after the Consecration, God continues to give us the sensations connected with the bread and wine, although their substance is no longer there. Next he repeats what Descartes himself had said in the Fourth Set of Replies, namely, that the body of Christ affects the senses in the same way as the bread and the wine did because, in replacing them, its physical limits are formed by the same surface. This surface however is not part of the substance as such. Accordingly, the substance can change (the bread can change into the body of Christ), while the impression its surface makes on the senses remains the same.

See also: SACRAMENTS §§2–3

List of works

Rohault, J. (1670) *Traité de physique*, Paris; Latin trans. *Tractus physicus*, 1674; English trans. J. Clarke as *Rohault's System of physics*, London, 1728–9, 2 vols; repr. with intro. L. Laudan, New York and London, 1969.

—— (1671) *Entretiens sur la philosophie*, Paris; repr. ed. P. Clair in *Recherches sur le XVIIe siècle*, vol. 3, Paris, 1978, 101–64.

—— (1682) *Oeuvres posthumes*, Paris; new edn, The Hague, 1690, 2 vols. (Of the items published in this collection, Rohault's treatise on mechanics was also published separately, first in Latin (*De arte mechanica tractatus mathematicus*, London, 1692), then in English (*A treatise of mechanicks*, London, 1716) and finally in French (*Traité de mécanique*, 1723).)

References and further reading

Armogathe, J.-R. (1977) *Theologia cartesiana*, The Hague: Nijhoff, 108–10. (A good – and the only – work on the physical interpretation of transubstantiation.)

Balz, A.G.A. (1951) *Cartesian Studies*, New York, 28–41.

Bouillier, F. (1868) *Histoire de la philosophie cartésienne*, 3rd edn, Paris: Delagrave, vol. 1, 508–11. (Fundamental on the history of Cartesian philosophy in general; still useful, but on the whole now outdated.)

Clair, O. (1978) *Jacques Rohault (1618–1672): Biobibliographie avec l'édition critique des 'Entretiens sur la philosophie'*, *Recherches sur le XVIIe siècle*, vol. 3, Paris: CNRS. (Critical edition of an important text of Rohault; definitive on biography.)

Clarke, D. (1983) *Occult Powers and Hypotheses: Cartesian Natural Philosophy under Louis XIV*, Oxford: Clarendon Press. (Fundamental on Cartesian natural philosophy in France at the end of the seventeenth century.)

Gouhier, H. (1978) *Augustinisme et cartésianisme*, Paris: Vrin, 71–88.

Martinet, M. 'Jacques Rohault', in *Grundriß der Geschichte der Philosophie* (Überweg): Die Philosophie des 17. Jahrhunderts, Basel: Schwabe, Bd.2/2, 660–70. (Reliable, but short.)

Mouy, P. (1937) *Le développement de la physique cartésienne*, Paris: Vrin, 113–45.

THEO VERBEEK

ROMAN LAW

Law was Rome's greatest gift to the intellect of modern Europe. Even today the Roman law library, and the achievements of the jurists who built it up, live on in the law of the Continental jurisdictions and of other countries farther afield. It is true that over the past two centuries codification has largely interrupted the long tradition of direct recourse to the Roman materials, but the concepts applied in civilian jurisdictions and the categories of legal thought which they use are still in large measure those of the Roman jurists. In England, perhaps for no better reason than that from the late thirteenth century the judges of the King's Bench and Common Pleas happened to come from a background which cut them off from the clerical education which had given their predecessors access to the Roman library, there was no reception of Roman law. Post-Norman England thus became the second Western society to set about building up a mature law library from scratch. The common law (being the law common to the whole realm of England) and the civil law (being the ius civile, the law pertaining to the civis, the citizen, initially of course the Roman citizen) thus became the two principal families within the Western legal tradition. It is wrong, however, to suppose that the development of the common law was constantly isolated. There have on the contrary been important points of contact at almost all periods. One result is that the categories of English legal thought are not in fact dissimilar to those of the jurisdictions of continental Europe. The study of Roman law has contributed immeasurably to the idea of a rational normative order, an idea fundamental to legal philosophy as indeed to all practical philosophy.

1 **Markers in time**
2 **The *Corpus iuris civilis***
3 **Intellectual achievements**

1 Markers in time

The first life of Roman law, when it was the law of the Romans themselves, is conventionally allotted to the millennium which is almost exactly divided by the change of era, five hundred years before and five hundred years after Christ. There are convenient markers. Emerging from its prehistory, the tough agricultural society which had recently expelled the last of its kings enacted a crude code, the Twelve Tables, in 451 BC. Nearly a thousand years later, and no longer in Rome but in the predominantly Greek capital of the eastern Roman empire, the Emperor JUSTINIAN and his chief minister, Tribonian, carried through a task which to lesser men would have seemed intellectually and administratively impossible. They set up Commissions to read the whole law library and to compact it. The result was two huge volumes and one small one, the *Digest*, the *Codex* and the *Institutes*. These came out in the early 530s AD. Private collections of the emperor's subsequent pronouncements later added a fourth volume, the *Novels*. The four make up what we call the whole body of the civil law, the *Corpus iuris civilis*.

Within this thousand years, the focus of most modern scholarship has been the age of the greatest names, from the reign of Hadrian to that of Alexander Severus, roughly the century from AD 125 to 225. It is sometimes said that the strongest court that ever sat in England sat in York in AD 211, the year that the Emperor Septimius Severus died there, on campaign against the Scots. Papinian was certainly there, possibly also both Paul and Ulpian. One cannot but wish that the three greatest Roman jurists were there. The end of the golden age, the classical period of Roman law, is usually marked by the murder of Ulpian in the summer of AD 223. At the time of the assassination he was the first man in the empire below only the Emperor Alexander Severus himself.

Hardly less interest attaches to the preceding periods, since it is of them that the question has to be asked why Rome, and no other ancient society, managed to develop a mature law library. The end of the beginning was the work of Servius Sulpicius Rufus, who died in AD 43, in the tense months which followed the murder of Julius Caesar, on a mission to Marcus Antonius in Mutina. Pomponius' account of the history of Roman jurisprudence shows that Servius, both a prolific writer and an innovator in methods, more than doubled the number of law books which had been written before his time. He and his distinguished pupils prepared the way for the exponential improvement and expansion of the law library in the pre-classical or, as some would prefer, early classical first century AD, from Augustus to Hadrian.

After the assassination of Ulpian, the great names soon dry up, and in terms of military and political history the empire runs into deeply troubled times, from which it was saved, albeit at the cost of sowing the seeds of later division, by the Diocletianic settlement at the end of the third century. Whether the post-classical period was a time of steep and absolute decline in legal science is now doubtful. The form certainly changed. The responsibility for the interpretive development of the law shifted decisively to the emperor and the imperial bureaucracy, whose characteristic utterance was the rescript, the written reply to a request for a ruling on the problems arising from a given fact-situation. The jurists who in earlier times would have been the great names achieving personal immortality through their books were now civil servants working in the anonymity of the imperial chancery. Decline and vulgarization cannot be denied, especially in the collapsing West, but the phenomena are more complex than was previously supposed. Although the *Codex Theodosianus*, a collection of imperial pronouncements put together and published in the early fifth century, does evidence a failing grip on the precise use of language, it is broadly true that the centre held. In the sixth century Justinian's Commissions are themselves evidence of complete recovery, based largely on the great law schools of the East at Beirut and Constantinople. Professors of law from those schools were leading members of the Commissions and had without doubt been vigorous advocates of the seemingly superhuman task of renewing the law library.

The western empire is taken to have ended with the abdication of an emperor whose name seems with specious elegance to close a great cycle of history, Romulus Augustulus (475–6). The second life of the Roman law, when its library was taken back into the foundations of western Europe, began about five hundred years after that collapse. From the embers of the western empire there ultimately sprang the European unity of the middle ages, that pre-Reformation Catholic civilization which is now most obviously attested by the great cathedrals and universities. The secular learning of that civilization was law, the law of Justinian's *Corpus iuris civilis*. The University of Oxford owes its existence in large measure to the fact that the Church happened to make Oxford a centre of jurisdiction and administration. By 1150 Roman law was being studied there, if not from the great Bolognese jurist Vacarius then at least from his

writings. Oxford was not unique. In the twelfth century law was the study of the age. The appetite of both spiritual and secular powers for competent administrators meant that there were careers to be made by those who knew their law, and this in turn drew jurists out across Europe to spread the learning which was so much in demand. The centre from which this learning radiated was northern Italy. In the universities there a legal renaissance had begun. The study of the *Corpus iuris*, in particular of the *Digest*, had not merely been restarted but had quickly been raised to a remarkably high scholarly level. This legal renaissance is usually dated from the work of Irnerius in the University of Bologna. He died about 1125.

By 1100 the authors whose works contributed to the *Digest* had mostly been dead for upwards of eight hundred years. The generations of medieval professors of law, first the glossators and then the commentators, did not expound their texts as historians, revealing the law of a lost society which had itself changed as it developed through the centuries of its first life. On the contrary, they used the texts for their own time, as though they had all been written yesterday or outside time, and with scriptural authority. With brilliant ingenuity they explained away contradictions which we would recognize as due to juristic disagreement or to historical development. In some areas, though in remarkably few, no intellectual somersaults would suffice, and the Roman materials then had to be supplemented from more recent materials. Feudal land-tenure is one such case. The Romans knew nothing of feudalism.

In short the medieval expositors treated the Roman texts as a law library ready made for themselves and their own conditions of life, supplementing where absolutely necessary. In the sixteenth century humanist scholars reacted both against the scriptural authority of the Roman texts, with its tendency to stifle thought and undervalue contemporary experience, and against the intellectual dishonesty implicit in an unhistorical approach to the texts. Scholars such as Cujas (1522–90) and Hotman (1524–90) advocated and pursued a more critical and historical approach, more in the style of modern Roman lawyers who, relieved of the burden of adapting and applying the Roman law library to contemporary conditions, aim chiefly to rediscover the Roman law as it was and as it differed between, say, Sabinus in the first century, Julian in the second and Ulpian in the early third. Since the dissident humanists were mostly French, their critical historicism became known as 'the French way' (*mos Gallicus*) as opposed to 'the Italian way' (*mos Italicus*).

2 The *Corpus iuris civilis*

The work of Justinian's Commissions is the fulcrum upon which the story turns. The *Corpus iuris* sums up the first life of Roman law, and its rebirth in the West begins the second. Certain aspects of the work come as a surprise. The *Digest*, twice the size of the Bible, has 432 titles. One, for example, is 'Marriage', another 'Formation of the Contract of Sale' and another 'Theft'. Under those and the other headings the law was stated, not in the words of the Commissioners, but by their choice of extracts from the works written by the classical and pre-classical authors. The book is thus a classified anthology of excerpts, each one carefully attributed.

The excerpts from the jurists as we see them have to a certain extent been managed. Many have been abbreviated, or doctored so as to be able to stand alone. Some routine modernizations have been introduced. Some imperfections and impurities in the manuscript tradition have survived. But, while these species of interpolation or disfigurement are not to be denied, few scholars now believe in the wholesale rewriting by the Commissioners that was suspected by many Romanists earlier in this century.

The *Codex* is somewhat less huge than the *Digest*. It is also a classified collection of material, but the matter collected, and once again managed by abbreviation and so on, is different. The *Codex* collects the pronouncements of the emperors, chiefly rescripts. The relationship between the two great books is chronological. The *Digest* compacts the library of the classical and pre-classical periods, while the *Codex* is the book of the post-classical period, when the imperial chancery monopolized all forms of authoritative utterance. Because in reality there was no abrupt transition from classical to post-classical or from private to nationalized utterance, there is some chronological overlap between the two volumes. The word 'codex' has nothing to do with codes and codification. It means 'book' and, in particular, the kind of book with pages and a spine. The transition from scrolls to that kind of book, the greatest revolution in information storage before printing and the computer, was complex but is generally located in the third century. The codex was thus the medium of the age which is represented in Justinian's 'Book'.

The *Institutes* was by comparison tiny. In size it is to the *Digest* much as St Matthew to the Bible. The genre can be traced back to GAIUS in the second half of the second century. Indeed Justinian's *Institutes* is essentially a new edition of the work of Gaius and actually re-uses substantial parts of the original. Gaius himself was long denied the full credit, because through the whole second life of Roman law no copy of his *Institutes* was known to have survived until in Verona in 1816 one was miraculously discovered, overwritten, by Niebuhr. Of Gaius himself we know only what can be wrung from his writings. It seems likely that he was a teacher of law. He certainly had a strong interest in legal history and believed that full understanding of an area of law could only be achieved by trying to go back to the beginning.

The function of the Institutes was to provide a coherent map of the whole law. It had a fixed place in Justinian's scheme of legal education. Most of the first year was to be spent studying this overview of the whole law. Even deep in the jungle of the *Digest* and *Codex*, the mind thus formed would never be lost. This is an educational lesson that the contemporary study of law, throughout the civilized word, had taken to neglecting. However, in that the mind cannot dispense with categories, least of all the legal mind, jurisprudence cannot safely continue to neglect the fundamental categories of legal thought and their relation one with another (see LEGAL CONCEPTS).

3 Intellectual achievements

There are many negatives. The jurists were not interested in jurisprudence in the narrow modern sense, meaning legal philosophy. CICERO (§2) engaged in some discussion of the nature of law and its relation with the state and political theory, but Cicero, a contemporary of Servius Sulpicius, lived in the period before the law library had put on any weight; and he was, anyhow, not a jurist. Roman law produced no Austins, Kelsens, Harts or Dworkins. Next, from the standpoint of social science there was little to admire. Slavery was an unchallenged feature of the Roman legal landscape. Again, access to justice was not obviously of much concern. It was a rich man's system. Politically, the picture is equally grim. Though lawyers could fairly claim to have been a moderating and a stablizing influence, the constitutional structure within which they worked had no democratic aspirations. Indeed as time went on its tendency was to ever more absolute autocracy.

What can there be left? The question needs to be answered against an awareness of two facts. First, the requirement of justice that like cases be treated alike requires that legal science achieve stable analyses and solutions of a multitude of problems of responsibility, problems over which moral philosophers have the luxury of continual debate and uncertainty. The requirement of stability, not, be it noted, morbid rigidity, adds a dimension of intellectual difficulty to law which is absent from ethics and goes some way to explain why BLACKSTONE presented law as the highest branch of ethics. Second, there is the not unrelated fact, perhaps naïve-seeming but none the less true, that there is a vast amount of law which is to a large extent politically neutral. For example, unless the very concept of private property is rejected, it is necessary to know what interests in land and material goods can be held by individuals and how they are acquired, transferred and inherited. Again, raising the level of magnification, a mature legal system must be able to say exactly how a sale works, how the contract is formed, how it differs from neighbouring transactions such as hire and exchange, what obligations as to quality and title the seller undertakes, when the risk of damage passes to the buyer, at what moment and by virtue of what acts the buyer becomes owner. These and many other questions need stable answers applicable or adaptable to all imaginable versions of the facts. The analyses and their implications for litigation are likely to be more or less immune to politico-moral upheavals in the larger structures of society. If this were not so, it would be difficult to explain how it could be possible for medieval and early modern Europe to borrow the law library of an ancient and largely alien society.

The intellectual achievement of Roman law has to be seen at two levels. One is represented by the *Digest* and the *Codex*, the other by the *Institutes*. In large matters these great volumes are thoroughly disordered, rather as the English common law of the nineteenth century was, and today largely remains, in structural disarray. Nevertheless, when focused on matters of detail – when is legacy invalid, what if a neighbour's activities threaten damage or if he refuses you access to the aqueduct which brings your water across his land, what if a buyer is mistaken as to the thing bought, can an owner ever steal his own property, is it possible for a person to own a wild animal? – the jurists achieved a level of stable analysis unsurpassed by modern legal science. The acid test is whether, and how often, the intellect of the law is defeated by novel or unusual facts and driven back to abstract appeals to justice and good sense, alias gut reaction or mere personal prejudice. Although there were of course disagreements and uncertainties, some of them long unresolved, the ordered intellect of jurists such as Papinian, Paul and Ulpian was rarely defeated in matters of detail. Their concepts and methods set a standard of legal rationality which both challenges modern law and legal philosophy and explains the continuing importance of these practical and untheoretical jurists.

The second great intellectual achievement is represented by the *Institutes*. When he wrote his book, or delivered his lectures, Gaius developed a way of looking at the whole law in such a way that all the parts related intelligibly to each other. Mediated through Justinian's *Institutes* with some minor modifications, Gaius' scheme has dominated legal thinking ever since, and, though there have been bold attempts to escape it or improve it, it has by and large survived. Like many great intellectual advances it has about it a simplicity which almost defies attempts to recreate the pre-existing situation in which people had to do without it. Common lawyers, no strangers to serious disorder, can probably do it better than civilians (see COMMON LAW).

One kind of disorder, of which English law is overfond, is the alphabetical list of topics, but that was not quite how Roman law was before Gaius. It should rather be conceived as a historically determined list of actions (that is, of claims claimable), each having attracted its own packet of juristic interpretation. Thus the action of debt, called the *condictio*, was, only slightly simplified, 'I say you ought to give me 1000'. Generations of juristic tradition then built up a detailed commentary on that claim, showing who could make it, against whom, and, especially, what facts would as a matter of law substantiate it. Models of all the claims were set out and publicly displayed in the edict of the minister responsible for litigation, called the Urban Praetor. And if you knew all that the law library had to say about each one you knew virtually the whole law, albeit thrown together in a heap.

The institutional scheme put that heap in order. In Justinian's version, only minutely different from that of Gaius, it affirmed that the law was either public or private. Public law had the barest toe-hold in the *Institutes*, represented by the pages on the constitutional sources of law at the very beginning and the single chapter on crime at the end. Private law, the meat of the book, was first divided into three: all private law was about persons, things or actions – persons who make and defend claims, things claimed, and claiming. The law of things, essentially the law relating to assets of all kinds, was the largest of the three divisions of private law: assets were either corporeal, like land or a ship, or incorporeal. Incorporeal things were different kinds of right, rights over other people's property, such as a right of way or water, the right of inheritance, and rights to compel another person to make a performance, called (from the other end of the relationship) obligations. Obligations in turn arose from contracts or from wrongs or as though from a contract or as though from a wrong. Of course the *Institutes* is not just a diagrammatic representation of the law, like a family tree. At every level of classification it introduces the reader to the substance, so that it both reveals how the different areas of the law fit together and introduces the reader to the general nature of each one.

In the early modern period jurists who considered themselves emancipated from dependence on the Roman texts and wanted to write in their own language and of the contemporary law of their own country still used the scheme of the *Institutes* to provide their structure. In the seventeenth century GROTIUS did so in his *Introduction to the Jurisprudence of Holland*; and in Scotland Mackenzie did the same, as in the next century did Erskine. Scotland also provides a particularly fine example of a jurist who wrestled with the Roman scheme and hoped to improve it. Viscount STAIR, a contemporary of Mackenzie, argued that the law of persons should be eliminated and, since the different conditions of persons were reflected in the different incidence of obligations, absorbed into the law of obligations.

Just as the *Institutes* either provided the structure of law books or the structure against which the author reacted, so also, when from the late eighteenth century the movement for codification gathered momentum on the continent of Europe, the codifiers either followed the institutional scheme, as in France, or sought to improve upon it, as in Germany. In fact, however, even the improvers, whether codifiers or authors, always left a good deal of the Roman scheme intact. It thus remains true that one who knows the *Institutes* is instantly at home in any of the civil codes, as also in the legal bookshops of the Continent. More remarkably, but rarely noticed, the categories of English legal thought and the curricula of English law schools reflect the same enduring influence. It is not by fortuitous parallelism that English law students read books and attend courses on contract and tort (or, as is becoming fashionable, on obligations), on property and on succession, and, on the public law side, on criminal law and constitutional law.

Classification lies at the foundation of legal rationality. The best evidence of the Roman genius for law is that the lawyers of Europe still use their scheme. It is a tribute both to Gaius and to the power of the teacher of law that if today we want to understand the categories of modern legal thought, or to improve them, we still have to follow generations of earlier lawyers in making ourselves thoroughly conversant with the *Institutes*.

See also: BARTOLUS OF SASSOFERRATO; LAW, PHILOSOPHY OF; LEGAL HERMENEUTICS; POTHIER, R.J.

References and further reading

Cairns, J.W. (1984) 'Blackstone, an English Institutist: Legal Literature and the Rise of the Nation State', *Oxford Journal of Legal Studies* 4: 318. (Studies the influence of the *Institutes* on early modern law. Cairns shows how in Blackstone English law flirted with the same systematizing tradition.)

Gaius (*c.* AD 161) *The Institutes of Gaius*, ed. and trans W.M. Gordon and O.F. Robinson, London: Duckworth. (Gives the Latin text of the *Institutes*, with a parallel English translation.)

Honoré, T. (1981) *Emperors and Lawyers*, 2nd edn, Oxford: Oxford University Press, 1994. (This is a detailed study of the transition from the juristic tradition of classical Roman law to the bureaucratic law-making of the post-classical period, when jurists became anonymous civil servants in the ministry of justice.)

—— (1982) *Ulpian*, Oxford: Oxford University Press. (The first chapter tells us all we know of the life and times of the early third-century jurist whose work contributed more than any other to the *Corpus iuris civilis*. The rest of the book is an advanced study of the jurist's style and pattern of work.)

Justinian (533) *Justinian's Institutes*, trans. with intro. P. Birks and G. McLeod, London: Duckworth, 1987. (Gives the Latin text of the *Institutes*, with a parallel English translation. Also gives a substantial introduction explaining the importance of the *Institutes* in the later development of the Western legal tradition.)

Luig, K. (1972) 'The Institutes of National Law in the Seventeenth and Eighteenth Centuries', *Juridical Review* 17: 193. (Studies the influence of the *Institutes* on early modern law.)

Nicholas, B. (1962) *Introduction to Roman Law*, 3rd edn, Oxford: Oxford University Press, 1987. (This is a marvellous introduction not only to Roman law but to law in general. Read with the *Institutes* it provides the best foundation for further study of Roman law and legal thought and, incidentally, the best point from which any aspiring lawyer can get to know the concepts which law school takes for granted.)

Watson, A. (1981) *The Making of the Civil Law*, Cambridge, MA, and London: Harvard University Press. (Provides a way into the story of the second life of Roman law, its reception into modern private law.)

Wieacker, F. (1967) *Privatrechtsgeschichte der Neuzeit*, 2nd edn, Göttingen: Vandenhoeck and Ruprecht; trans. T. Weir, *The History of Private Law in Europe*, Oxford: Oxford University Press, 1995. (Provides a way into the story of the second life of Roman law, its reception into modern private law. A classic, to some extent requiring modification as a result of more recent research but still the most powerful and subtle account of the formation of modern European law.)

Zimmermann, R. (1990) *The Law of Obligations: Roman Foundations of the Civilian Tradition*, Cape Town: Juta. (This is a great work of comparative legal history which, confining itself to the law of obligations, shows how the Roman law was developed into the *ius commune* of Europe and then fixed in different forms by Continental fashion for codification. The author makes constant reference to parallels in the development of the common law. Though long and detailed, the book is extremely accessible even to the reader from the Anglo-American tradition.)

P.B.H. BIRKS

ROMAN STOICISM

see EPICTETUS; MARCUS AURELIUS; MUSONIUS RUFUS; SENECA; STOICISM

ROMANO, JUDAH *see* JUDAH BEN MOSES OF ROME

ROMANTICISM, GERMAN

Because Romanticism has many meanings which vary according to time and place, it is best to examine the movement in a specific culture and period. Of all the phases of Romanticism, early German Romanticism is of special importance in the history of Western philosophy. The early German Romantics – Friedrich Schlegel, Friedrich von Hardenberg, Schleiermacher and Schelling – developed influential ideas in the fields of metaphysics, ethics, aesthetics and politics. The aim of their movement was essentially social and political: to overcome the alienation and disenchantment created by modernity, and to restore unity with oneself, others and nature. In accord with this aim, the Romantics advocated an ethics of love and self-realization, in opposition to hedonism and the Kantian ethic of duty. They championed an ideal of community against the competitive egoism of modern society; and, finally, they developed an organic concept of nature against the mechanistic worldview of Cartesian physics. Romantic ethics, politics and aesthetics should all be seen in the light of their essential cultural goal: to cure humanity of homesickness and to make people feel at home in the world again.

1 **Intellectual geography**
2 **The early Romantic agenda**
3 **Aestheticism**
4 **Ethics**
5 **Politics**
6 *Naturphilosophie*

1 Intellectual geography

Romanticism was a European-wide literary and artistic movement, appearing chiefly in Germany, England, Italy and France, but also in virtually every other country. It began in the late eighteenth century, fully blossomed by the 1830s and began to dissipate by mid-century; some currents continued until the late nineteenth century. Although Romanticism is usually understood as an artistic or literary movement, it also has an important place in the history of philosophy. While rarely systematic, the Romantics developed original and influential ideas in epistemology, metaphysics, ethics and politics.

Considered in all its breadth, it is impossible to generalize about Romanticism. The movement differed from country to country and underwent many changes, one stage often contradicting another. To make any generalization about Romanticism, therefore, it is necessary to limit oneself to a specific time and place. It is best to begin with German Romanticism, partly because its ideas were deeply influential elsewhere, and partly because, in many respects, it marks the beginning of the movement as a whole.

German Romanticism is often divided into three phases: *Frühromantik* (early Romanticism) from 1797 to 1802; *Hochromantik* (high Romanticism) from 1803 to 1815; and *Spätromantik* (late Romanticism) from 1816 to 1830. From a philosophical viewpoint, the most important phase was *Frühromantik*, which flourished chiefly in the literary salons of Berlin and Jena. The leading figures of the early Romantic circle were August Wilhelm Schlegel (1767–1845), his brother Friedrich SCHLEGEL (1772–1829), Ludwig Tieck (1773–1853), Wilhelm Heinrich Wackenroder (1773–1801), Friedrich SCHLEIERMACHER (1768–1834), and Friedrich von Hardenberg (1772–1801), chiefly known by his pseudonym 'Novalis'. Other important thinkers on the fringes of this circle and connected with it in various ways and from time to time include Wilhelm von HUMBOLDT (1767–1835), Friedrich HÖLDERLIN (1770–1843) and August Ludwig Hülsen (1765–1810). The most important philosophers of the circle were Friedrich Schlegel, SCHELLING, Schleiermacher and Novalis. It is chiefly their views that are summarized below.

2 The early Romantic agenda

Early German Romanticism grew out of a disillusionment with some of the fundamental tendencies of modernity, more specifically the growth of science and technology, the division of labour, and a competitive market economy. For the Romantics, these tendencies had created the fundamental malaise of modern culture: alienation or disenchantment. There were three facets to this alienation: that people had become divided from themselves, from others and from nature. Each facet was the result of one of the tendencies of modernity. People became divided from themselves because of the increasing division of labour, which forced them to ignore their inner selves for the demands of productive labour, and which made them neglect the diverse sides of their humanity to specialize in one activity. They became divided from others because they had to compete in the market place rather than cooperate with them in a community. And they became divided from nature because the sciences treated it as an object to be dominated and controlled instead of a realm of beauty, mystery and magic (see ALIENATION).

The Romantics' reaction to modernity has to be placed within the context of their general philosophy of history. They see history, along the lines of the Biblical myth, as a drama of innocence, fall and redemption. KANT and SCHILLER had shown how this myth could be rationalized and secularized in explaining moral development; the Romantics duly followed this lead, applying the myth to all history. Innocence consists in unity with oneself, others and nature; the fall starts with division and alienation; and redemption consists in re-achieving unity after division. The present modern epoch is the depth of the fall. The task of the modern human is to achieve redemption by recovering unity with the self, others and nature.

The Romantics saw the rise of modernity as tragic, as the inevitable product not just of capitalism but of civilization. They looked back with nostalgia to earlier cultures, such as those of ancient Greece and the High Middle Ages, which enjoyed much greater unity. But their pessimism was also tempered by the optimism of their utopian belief that it was still possible for modern humans to approach redemption, even if they could not achieve it. If people directed their energies in the right direction, they would be able to recreate through reason that unity with the self, nature and society given to earlier humans through nature.

Hence the Romantic agenda sought to heal the wounds of modernity: to restore unity with the self, with others and with nature. They wanted everybody to become a whole person again, so that each realizes their unique individuality and all their distinctively human characteristics. They championed a community based on love and cooperation, rather than a society torn by self-interest and competition. And, finally, they hoped to restore the beauty, magic and mystery of nature in the aftermath of the ravages of science and technology.

3 Aestheticism

Early German Romanticism has often been understood as an aesthetic or literary movement. The Romantics indeed saw art as the highest form of human experience and self-expression, making it their instrument for the education and redemption of humanity. Romantic art had a definite objective, set by the Romantics' social and political agenda to restore the unity with the self, society and nature that had been destroyed by modernity. In this regard, the Romantics were deeply influenced by Schiller's programme for the aesthetic education of humankind, which gives primacy to art as the means to restore humanity to wholeness.

The early Romantic aesthetic, especially as defined by Friedrich Schlegel, has its origins in Schiller's reflections on naïve and sentimental poetry. According to Schiller, the poetry of the ancients was naïve because it simply and directly imitated nature; naïve poetry thus reflected the ancients' harmony with the world around them. The poetry of the moderns, however, is sentimental because it expresses a sentiment or feeling: the *longing* to return to that unity with nature that had once been given to the ancients.

Schlegel believed that Romantic poetry should adopt some of the characteristics which Schiller had attributed to sentimental poetry. It should be free of all the constraints of classicism, allowing the poet to express the freedom characteristic of modernity; but it should above all express the feeling and longing of the poet, the striving to return to unity with the self, society and nature.

Novalis' definition of Romantic art should also be understood in the same context. The aim of the artist, Novalis wrote, is *to romanticize* the world, to see the infinite in the finite, the extraordinary in the common place, the wonderful in the banal. Here again the mission of Romantic art was to restore unity: its purpose was to restore the magic, mystery and beauty of nature that had been lost with the growth of science and technology.

Romantic aestheticism has often been dismissed as quixotic, because it seems to exaggerate the power of art to motivate human action and to reform morals. But the Romantic faith in art should not be understood simply as a claim about the influence of the arts, and still less as a claim about their autonomy. Rather, Romantic aestheticism is based on the classical equation of the good with the beautiful. The Romantics believe that beauty should have a central role in culture because they think that beauty is involved in all forms of perfection, whether individual, social or political. The Romantic ideal of a self-realized person, of the ideal society and of the perfect state is that they should be aesthetic wholes. Hence the aim of the Romantic was not only to produce good poems, plays and novels, but first and foremost to make the individual, society and the state into works of art.

4   Ethics

The Romantic ethic is best understood in terms of a response to the classical question of the highest good, to the problem of the supreme value of life. The Romantics saw the highest good as *Bildung*, loosely translatable as education or personal development. Theirs was an ethic of self-realization, which stressed the development not only of one's individuality but also of all one's characteristic human traits. This view of the highest good should be seen as a reaction against the two prevalent views in the late eighteenth century: hedonism and the Kantian-Fichtean ethic. According to the hedonists, the highest good is pleasure, while according to Kant and FICHTE it is happiness in accord with virtue.

The Romantics rejected pleasure as the highest good because it would not develop those powers characteristic of our humanity and individuality. Their critique of hedonism is most apparent in their indictment of the philistines, those who devote themselves to a life of comfort and security at the expense of the real self.

The Romantics saw two fundamental difficulties for the Kantian ethic. First, Kant and Fichte had stressed reason at the expense of sensibility, ignoring how our senses are just as much a part of our humanity and just as in need of cultivation and development. It is not simply a purely rational being who acts morally but the whole individual who does their duty not contrary to but from their inclination. Second, by emphasizing action according to universal laws, Kant and Fichte had failed to see the importance of individuality.

The fundamental ethical value for the Romantics was love, which they believed should be the basis of social life and the heart of personal development. They pitted their ethic of love against the egoism of modern society, and the abstract and artificial commands of the Kantian-Fichtean ethic. They saw no conflict between the demands of love and individualism: the individual could become a unique whole only in virtue of love, which is the source of all personal development. Love rather than law was the chief social bond, holding that the state could become secure only through ties of affection and brotherhood.

5   Politics

The early Romantics came of age in the 1790s, a decade dominated by the French Revolution. Not surprisingly, their social and political ideals were formed in the crucible of that epochal event. At first they celebrated the Revolution as the dawn of a new age, embracing the ideals of liberty, equality and fraternity. As moderate republicans they believed that an ideal constitution should be a mixture of democracy, aristocracy and monarchy. They became progressively disillusioned with the Revolution, however, when they fully realized its cultural implications, and were horrified by the egoism, materialism and anomie of modern French civil society, which seemed to leave no place for community and spiritual values.

Because of its reaction against modernity, it would seem that Romanticism was, or at least became, an essentially conservative movement. Some of the Romantics were indeed eager to preserve some traditional aspects of European society, such as guilds and monarchy, because they saw these as a source of community and as a bulwark against materialism. Some looked back with nostalgia upon the society of the Middle Ages, which was more devoted to communal and spiritual values.

It is necessary, however, to place the Romantics' traditionalism in the context of their general social and political values. What they especially wished to maintain in traditional society was its pluralistic structure, its autonomous guilds and local corporations. They valued such a pluralistic structure chiefly because they saw it as a safeguard of liberty and a bulwark against tyranny. They were critical of all forms of political centralization and absolutism, whether it came from a revolutionary dictator or an absolute prince. In this regard they were moderates, as critical of the *ancien régime* as of the Revolution in France.

For all their disillusionment with modernity, the early Romantics endorsed one of its fundamental values: freedom of the individual. They never ceased to embrace this ideal, seeking to liberate the individual from all forms of oppression, whether political, social or cultural, so that people could fully realize and develop their individuality. Friedrich Schlegel, Humboldt and Schleiermacher were early champions of sexual liberation, of the right to divorce and to love without marriage. The main political problem for the young Romantics was how to square the freedom of individuality with the need for community. Their solution was a pluralistic society, whose autonomous groups would provide for community while serving as a defence of liberty.

6 Naturphilosophie

One of the characteristic products of early Romanticism was *Naturphilosophie*, which flourished in the first decade of the nineteenth century (see NATURPHILOSOPHIE). Its chief representative was Schelling, but it is important to see that he was only one figure in a much wider movement. Other important *Naturphilosophen* include Carl August Eschenmeyer (1771–1852), Lorenz Oken (1779–1851), Franz von Baader (1765–1841), Johann Wilhelm Ritter (1776–1810) and Gotthilf Schubert (1780–1860). It would be wrong to see all these thinkers as forming a single school, for they usually worked independently and were often critical of one another. Nevertheless, they did have some common characteristics: the vision of humans and nature as a unity, the attempt to see all the various phenomena of nature (magnetism, gravity and electricity) as manifestations of a single fundamental force, and a rejection of the old mechanical physics. The impetus for *Naturphilosophie* came from several sources: Kant's dynamic concept of nature, Herder's vitalistic pantheism, Goethe's natural investigations, and the vital materialist tradition of the English freethinkers and French *philosophes* (see HERDER, J.G.; GOETHE, J.W.).

Naturphilosophie developed from the Romantic concern to overcome the alienation between humans and nature. It saw the fundamental expression for this alienation in the Cartesian mental–physical dualism. The ultimate source of this dualism lay with the concept of matter and the mechanical model of explanation of Cartesian physics. According to Descartes, the essence of matter consists in inert extension; and we explain matter only if we show how the motion of one body is caused by the motion of another body upon it. This concept of matter and paradigm of explanation seemed to make the explanation of the mind impossible according to natural laws. Consciousness is not within space, and hence we cannot explain its changes by the impact of other bodies on it. If we follow Descartes' paradigm of explanation, the only options then seem to be dualism or materialism (see DESCARTES, R. §8).

Responding to this dilemma, Schelling developed a dynamic concept of matter, according to which the essence of matter consists in living force or power. The advantage of this concept of nature is that it

seemed to surmount the dualism between the mental and the physical: they are now simply differing degrees of organization and development of living force. Mind is the highest degree of organization and development of the living forces of matter, while matter is simply the lowest degree of organization and development of the living forces of the mind (see PANPSYCHISM).

For Schelling, the fundamental category of *Naturphilosophie* is that of an organism. He extends this metaphor to all nature, so that we should regard all nature as one vast organism, and mechanism itself as only an appearance of it. In his 1798 *Von der Weltseele* (Of the world-soul) Schelling explicitly revived the ancient Stoic doctrine of a single soul pervading all of nature. His general vision of nature could be described as a vitalistic monism or as a monistic vitalism.

References and further reading

Collected works, critical editions and English translations of philosophers mentioned in the text can be found in the individual biographical entries throughout the *Encyclopedia*.

Ayrault, R. (1961) *La Genèse du romantisme allemand* (The genesis of German Romanticism), Paris: Aubier, 3 vols. (A thorough historical account of the origins of Romanticism.)

Beiser, F. (1992) *Enlightenment, Revolution and Romanticism: the Genesis of Modern German Political Thought, 1790–1800*, Cambridge, MA: Harvard University Press. (Chapters 8 to 11 place early German Romanticism in its social and political context.)

Behler, E. (1992) *Frühromantik* (Early Romanticism), Berlin: Walter de Gruyter. (A useful survey that treats Romanticism as a literary movement.)

Bowie, A. (1997) *From Romanticism to Critical Theory*, London: Routledge. (Explores the origin of German Romanticism and the development of Romantic literary theory, tracing its continuation into the work of Heidegger, Benjamin and Adorno.)

Haym, R. (1870) *Die romantische Schule* (The Romantic School), Berlin: Gaertner. (A brilliant classic, still the most substantial work on the early history of Romanticism.)

Heine, H. (1833) *Die romantische Schule* (The Romantic School), Stuttgart: Reclam, 1976. (Witty and provocative critique of the Romantic movement.)

Huch, R. (1924) *Die Romantik* (The Romantic), Leipzig: Haessel. (Perceptive study of central themes of Romanticism from its birth to its decline.)

351

Izenberg, G. (1992) *Impossible Individuality: Romanticism, Revolution, and the Origins of Modern Selfhood*, Princeton, NJ: Princeton University Press. (A study of the early Romantic concept of the self in Germany, France and England.)

Kluckhohn, P. (1941) *Das Ideengut der deutschen Romantik* (The ideas of German Romanticism), Tübingen: Niemeyer. (Introductory thematic treatment of central philosophical themes of early Romanticism.)

Pikulik, L. (1992) *Frühromantik (Early Romanticism)*, Munich: Beck. (Very useful survey of some of the basic works and themes of early Romanticism.)

Prang, H. (ed.) (1968) *Begriffsbestimmung der Romantik* (Conceptual determination of the Romantic), Darmstadt: Wissenschaftliche Buchgesellschaft. (Useful anthology of essays dealing with the definition and historiography of Romanticism.)

Prawer, S. (ed.) (1970) *The Romantic Period in Germany*, New York: Schocken. (A helpful anthology on the literary and aesthetic dimension of Romanticism.)

* Schelling, F.W.J. (1798) *Von der Weltseele, eine Hypothese der höheren Physik zur Erklärung des allgemeinen Organismus* (On the world-soul: a hypothesis of higher physics in order to explain the general organism), Hamburg: Perthes; repr. in *Sämmtliche Werke*, ed. K.F.A. Schelling, Stuttgart 1856–61, vol. 2, 345–583. (Explanation of organic nature in terms of a general dualism of opposing forces.)

Schmitt, C. (1925) *Politische Romantik* (The Political Romantic), Munich: Duncker & Humblot. (Influential and controversial interpretation of Romanticism arguing that the movement was essentially apolitical.)

Seyhan, A. (1992) *Representation and its Discontents: The Critical Legacy of German Romanticism*, Berkeley, CA: University of California Press. (An incisive treatment of the aesthetic and critical dimension of Romanticism.)

Silz, W. (1929) *Early German Romanticism*, Cambridge, MA: Harvard University Press. (A clear and straightforward account of early Romanticism that exposes many anachronistic interpretations.)

Walzel, O. (1918) *Deutsche Romantik*, Leipzig: Teubner; trans. A.E. Lussky as *German Romanticism*, New York: Putnam. (Incisive treatment of the philosophical aspects of early Romanticism.)

FREDERICK BEISER

RORTY, RICHARD McKAY (1931–)

Richard Rorty is a leading US philosopher and public intellectual, and the best-known contemporary advocate of pragmatism. Trained in both analytic and traditional philosophy, he has followed Dewey in attacking the views of knowledge, mind, language and culture that have made both approaches attractive, drawing on arguments and views of the history of philosophy from sources ranging from Heidegger and Derrida to Quine and Wilfrid Sellars. He takes pragmatism to have moved beyond Dewey by learning from analytical philosophy to make 'the linguistic turn', and from Thomas Kuhn that there is no such thing as 'scientific method'. Language and thought are tools for coping, not representations mirroring reality. Rorty's characteristic philosophical positions are what might be called 'anti-isms', positions defined primarily by what they deny. In epistemology he endorses anti-foundationalism, in philosophy of language anti-representationalism, in metaphysics anti-essentialism and anti- both realism and antirealism, in meta-ethics ironism. He extols pragmatism as the philosophy that can best clear the road for new ways of thinking which can be used to diminish suffering and to help us find out what we want and how to get it. In the public arena, he is a leading exponent of liberalism and critic of both left and right.

1   **Life**
2   **Metaphilosophy**
3   **Knowledge and truth**
4   **Mind and society**

1   Life

Rorty's philosophical training at the University of Chicago and Yale University grounded him in the history of philosophy and the main currents of pragmatism and traditional philosophy dominant in the USA in the first half of the twentieth century, as well as the techniques and goals of the analytical philosophy then winning the allegiance of younger philosophers. Starting in the 1960s, he published articles and reviews addressing a wide range of philosophical subjects, the philosophies of thinkers as disparate as Whitehead, Dewey, Royce, Austin and Wilfrid Sellars, and, always, the metaphilosophical issues that arise from the multiplicity of conceptions of philosophy and its methods. He surveyed these metaphilosophical issues from a pragmatist point of view in the introduction to his anthology *The Linguistic Turn: Recent Essays in Philosophical Method* (1967). During the later 1960s and the

1970s he won wide recognition as a leading contributor to debates in the philosophy of mind, metaphysics, epistemology and the philosophy of language, staking out radical positions in each of these fields and drawing on the attacks on the philosophical tradition in Heidegger, Derrida, the later Wittgenstein and especially Dewey. He reached the first rank of US philosophers and won international attention outside philosophical circles with the publication of his major work *Philosophy and the Mirror of Nature* (1979). This book brought together all his lines of thought in an attempt to get philosophers, and those who look to philosophy to lend authority to their own cultural activity, to abandon the views of knowledge, mind, language and culture which give appeal to movements like analytic philosophy that claim to put philosophy on the true path of a science. Since then he has, in many articles, reviews and lectures, extended his attack on that philosophical tradition. He has defended his version of pragmatism as the best way of thinking about those things philosophers should still be thinking about; he has sought to place his thought in relation to an ever-widening range of other twentieth-century writers both within and outside philosophy (for example, Castoriadis, Davidson, Dennett, Foucault, Freud, Habermas, Lyotard, Nabokov, Orwell, Putnam and Roberto Unger) and to make pragmatism useful to workers in other areas (for example, feminism, education, jurisprudence and literary criticism). And he has taken up the role, well-established in Europe but rare among philosophers in the United States after Dewey's death, of a public intellectual, commenting in articles and interviews in journals of general circulation on affairs of common interest in democratic societies. Rorty's wide command of modern philosophy is remarkable, as is his dialogue with a broad spectrum of philosophical movements, and he is unusual also in giving credit to a number of other thinkers (Dewey, Heidegger, Davidson, Freud, Kuhn, Dennett, Quine, Sellars, Derrida, Nietzsche) for most of the key ideas in his writings. (Dennett, however, has enunciated the *Rorty Factor*: 'Take whatever Rorty says about anyone's views and multiply it by .742' to derive what they actually said.) Many of his most important papers and lectures have been collected in four volumes (listed below). Having urged a break with the traditional project of philosophy, he left the philosophy department at Princeton University to become a professor of humanities at the University of Virginia in 1982.

2 Metaphilosophy

Rorty takes the three models of philosophy most attractive to contemporary philosophers to be the scientistic (Carnap), the poetic (Heidegger) and the political (Dewey); he endorses the last as most congenial to pragmatism. Philosophers should emulate the moral virtues which scientific communities have exemplified, but give up belief in 'scientific method' as well as philosophical method. They should foster the invention of new metaphors that is the work of poets and prophets, creating new vocabularies and social hopes; but philosophers have no special mission to be either poets or prophets. Philosophy should be hermeneutic, helping different areas of culture to make contact with each other and to sort out conflicts, just as liberal politics tries to find a working relationship among the different and conflicting desires and hopes at play in the world (see HERMENEUTICS). Its most important task now is to clear away past bad philosophy and bad ideas that are getting in the way of thinking usefully about, and doing, what can be done to make people happier.

As his metaphilosophy suggests, Rorty's characteristic philosophical positions are what might be called 'anti-isms', positions defined primarily by what they deny. In epistemology he endorses anti-foundationalism, in philosophy of language anti-representationalism, in metaphysics anti-essentialism and anti- both realism *and* antirealism, in meta-ethics ironism (see FOUNDATIONALISM; ESSENTIALISM; REALISM AND ANTIREALISM). None of these is a theory but, rather, a collection of considerations for the rejection of theorizing in these areas.

3 Knowledge and truth

Rorty's anti-foundationalism, drawing on arguments of QUINE and Wilfrid SELLARS, denies that the justification of our knowledge claims must or can terminate in beliefs or statements that provide a foundation for knowledge. Nor does Rorty think that knowledge has any other overall structure. On his view (epistemological behaviourism), one justifies a belief or statement by adducing other beliefs or statements that do not require justification in that context, so as to satisfy the standards implicit in our social practice of justification (see CONTEXTUALISM, EPISTEMOLOGICAL). He consequently denies both that scepticism is a problem for philosophy and the theories whose appeal is that they purport to solve the problem of scepticism (see SCEPTICISM). Rorty's anti-foundationalism also denies that there is some particular discipline or part of culture that has the job of providing justification for, or making sense of, all the rest. In particular, he insists that it is a mistake to try to justify practices and institutions like liberal democracy, academic freedom and scientific research by appeal to philosophical theories that show them to correspond to or be in touch with the ultimate nature of reality or the human self or the will of God or something else bigger or deeper than our actual practices. This is not the view that such practices do not need any justification, which some critics have accused Rorty of holding, but rather that appropriate justifications will always be piecemeal and local (see JUSTIFICATION, EPISTEMIC §7).

Epistemological behaviourism is an account of justification but not a theory of truth. Rorty denies that there is any interesting theory of truth, that is, any general account of what makes beliefs and sentences true. He endorses James' dictum that the true is just the good in the realm of belief; there is no general account of why beliefs are true any more than there is a general account of why things are good. He rejects correspondence theories and coherence theories of truth alike. His anti-representationalism denies that the essence of language is to represent or picture reality in such a way that bits of language match up with bits of reality; languages – the noises, gestures and marks we humans make – and thoughts – the brain states we get into – are part of the repertory of devices we have accumulated for coping with the world (including ourselves). While some stretches of language or thought might work by such matching-up techniques, these stretches have no special privilege or philosophical importance. Rorty rejects both realism and antirealism (or idealism) as products of a misguided representational view of language. No class of truths has foundational status with respect to the rest of the truths. While we usually call beliefs true when they are better justified than their competitors, 'true' does not *mean* 'justified' or 'warranted'; it is indefinable and ineliminable.

Since there is no foundation for truth or knowledge, there is nothing outside our social practices to ground them, according to Rorty. Hence, he has sometimes rejected objectivity as a goal of inquiry (and objective–subjective as a relevant dimension of appraisal in the cognitive realm) in favour of solidarity with our community of inquirers; less provocatively, he urges that objectivity be understood as intersubjectivity or taken as shorthand for practices, like not taking bribes, that we have found very helpful in most kinds of inquiry.

Rorty is often accused of relativism and as often rejects the accusation. He claims that relativism about truth is easily refutable. The alternative to relativism about justification that he espouses is 'ethnocentrism', the view that justification is relative to *our* practices.

The defence of our beliefs against challenges by other communities (Nazis, religious fundamentalists, the Nuer) must always be question-begging, but this does not vitiate the defence, since no other kind of defence is better or even as good, and appraisal must always be against relevant alternatives (see COGNITIVE PLURALISM).

Opponents with epistemological and political concerns have regarded Rorty's ethnocentrism and epistemological behaviourism as viciously circular and conservative, making existing practices and institutions self-justifying and impervious to rational criticism, an objection also brought against other epistemological behaviourists such as Wittgenstein. Rorty's response has been to appeal to Kuhn and Davidson. According to Kuhn's account of scientific revolutions, relatively large-scale changes in the standards and practices of rhetorical communities are not justifiable by criteria available to those in the community before the change, but one result of the change is that new criteria become available to the reconstituted community after the revolution. Rational justification of the new beliefs and vocabulary, and rational criticism of the old beliefs and old vocabulary are available, but only when the new vocabulary and its attendant standards are established. According to Davidson's account of metaphor, metaphorical uses of old words to make new judgments that are false and even irrational by existing practices of justification, can change people's practices so that, as dead metaphors, the sentences are true and justified. Our accounts of the development of thought to its present (or future) achievements are always 'Whiggish'. The recognition that our most important values and practices are without foundation or non-question-begging justification is *ironism*.

4 Mind and society

As a social philosopher, Rorty advances two different lines of thought: on the one hand, he is a bourgeois liberal democrat celebrating 'the end of ideology' and advocating an incremental meliorism; on the other hand, he tries to keep the field open for, and even to cheer on, radically imaginative utopianism (for example, by feminists), however uncongenial to the stodginess of his first line of thought, provided it does not actually clash with either his liberalism or his anti-foundationalism. This has made him a target for political thinkers from all points on the political spectrum, who accuse him, even when he agrees with them, of giving comfort to the enemy.

In philosophy of mind, Rorty, following RYLE and DENNETT, takes our talk of beliefs, desires and so on to be a way of talking which we find useful for predicting, controlling, imagining and making sense of some of the things that we and some other things do, just as physics and neurology give us ways of talking which are useful for predicting, and so on, other things that we and some other things do. No one of these is primary or needs to be reduced to the others, though we need not suppose that when we mention someone's beliefs and desires we are talking about something other than what we are talking about when we mention their neural processes (non-reductive physicalism). The mind as a philosophical subject Rorty takes to be a monstrous fiction cobbled together by Descartes out of thoughts and sensations; philosophers should drop talk of the mind, as it is confusing and unhelpful (eliminative physicalism).

Many strands in Rorty's thought have been neglected in the preceding sketch – his continuing skirmishes with philosophy as a profession, his ideas on the historiography of philosophy and his attacks on socialism, for example. Rorty has exhibited the virtues of modesty and willingness to learn from sympathetic criticism, and he has modified and extended his thought considerably throughout his career. He will undoubtedly have added new twists by the time you read this.

See also: LIBERALISM; PRAGMATISM

List of works

Rorty's output runs to hundreds of articles and grows by a dozen or more items each year, often published in out-of-the-way places. A nearly complete list up to 1994 may be found in Saatkamp's 1995 work. I have listed his books and a few of the most influential or representative articles that have not, at the time of publication, yet appeared in his books.

Rorty, R. (1965) 'Mind-Body Identity, Privacy and Categories', *Review of Metaphysics* 19 (1): 24–54. (Much anthologized early defence of eliminative materialism with metaphilosophical corollaries.)

—— (ed.) (1967) *The Linguistic Turn: Recent Essays in Philosophical Method*, Chicago, IL, and London: The University of Chicago Press, 2nd edn, 1992. (Anthology of metaphilosophical essays by ordinary language and ideal language analytic philosophers; long introduction by Rorty.)

—— (1979) *Philosophy and the Mirror of Nature*, Princeton, NJ: Princeton University Press. (His major work; see §1 above.)

—— (1982a) *Consequences of Pragmatism (Essays: 1972–1980)*, Minneapolis, MN: University of Minnesota Press. ('Essays which might have some interest for readers outside of philosophy'.)

—— (1982b) 'Contemporary Philosophy of Mind', *Synthese* 53 (2): 323–48. (Places his views in the context of views of contemporary analytic philosophers.)

—— (1984) 'Diskussion/Discussion: A Reply to Six Critics', *Analyse & Kritik* 6: 78–98. (A good example of Rorty's responses to criticisms.)

—— (1987) 'Thugs and theorists: A Reply to Bernstein', *Political Theory* 15 (4): 564–80. (Defence of Rorty's anti-Marxist social democratic liberalism.)

—— (1989) *Contingency, Irony, and Solidarity*, Cambridge: Cambridge University Press. (Lectures on language, selfhood and politics plus interpretations of other writers.)

—— (1991a) *Objectivity, Relativism, and Truth: Philosophical Papers*, vol. 1, Cambridge: Cambridge University Press. (Papers, 1980–89, dealing with issues and figures within analytic philosophy, especially Davidson.)

—— (1991b) *Essays on Heidegger and Others: Philosophical Papers*, vol. 2, Cambridge: Cambridge University Press. (Papers, 1980–89, dealing with Heidegger, Derrida and Foucault.)

—— (1993a) 'Feminism, ideology, and deconstruction: a pragmatist view', *Hypatia* 8 (Spring): 96–103. (What Rorty thinks pragmatism can contribute to feminism.)

—— (1993b) 'Putnam and the relativist menace', *Journal of Philosophy* 90 (9): 443–61. (An attempt to settle some differences with Putnam.)

—— (1994) 'Does Academic Freedom Have Philosophical Presuppositions?', *Academe* 80 (6): 52–63. (Consequences of anti-foundationalism for academic freedom.)

—— (1996) 'Who are we? Moral Universalism and Economic Triage', *Diogenes* 44 (1): 5–15. (Consequences of ethnocentrism for the politics of rich and poor.)

References and further reading

Geras, N. (1995) *Solidarity in the Conversation of Humankind: The Ungroundable Liberalism of Richard Rorty*, London: Verso. (Criticism of Rorty's ethnocentrism.)

Hall, D.L. (1994) *Richard Rorty: Prophet and Poet of the New Pragmatism*, Albany NY: State University of New York Press. (Good survey of Rorty's philosophy.)

Kolenda, K. (1990) *Rorty's Humanistic Pragmatism: Philosophy Democratized*, Tampa, FL: University of South Florida Press. (Sympathetic exposition of Rorty's philosophy.)

Malachowski, A. (ed.) (1990) *Reading Rorty: Critical*

Responses to Philosophy and the Mirror of Nature (and Beyond), Oxford: Blackwell. (Articles, mostly attacking Rorty's views; good bibliography.)

Saatkamp, H.J., Jr (ed.) (1995) *Rorty & Pragmatism: The Philosopher Responds to His Critics*, Nashville, TN, and London: Vanderbilt University Press. (Articles, mostly attacking Rorty's views, with Rorty's responses; good bibliography.)

MICHAEL DAVID ROHR

ROSCELIN OF COMPIÈGNE (c.1050–after 1120)

Roscelin of Compiègne was one of a group of logicians in late eleventh and early twelfth-century Europe who, in defiance of most of their predecessors in the field, treated logic as dealing with the concrete physical things that serve as verbal signs of realities rather than the realities those signs signified. This meant that although the things logic talks about are part of the physical world, it talks about them not as things referred to by language but as parts of language itself. All the technical notions of Aristotelian logic, for example 'universal', 'individual', 'category', 'genus' and 'species', apply only to those linguistic signs themselves qua signs.

Very little is known of Roscelin's life beyond the facts that he was born in Brittany around 1050, taught in France, was forced in 1092 to renounce certain positions he had taken on the doctrine of the Holy Trinity, and died after 1120. Of his work, only a letter to Peter ABELARD is known to have survived. Consequently, what knowledge we have of his views comes to us second-hand, and in this case from the witness of two thinkers, Abelard and ANSELM OF CANTERBURY, known to be unsympathetic to his positions. Anselm tells us that Roscelin thought of universals, such as genera and species, as mere 'puffs of air', by which was meant the air expelled in uttering a word such as 'animal' or 'donkey' (see UNIVERSALS). Also according to Anselm, Roscelin denied that qualities such as colours are anything over and above the subjects that possess them.

Roscelin's view of universals as concrete physical things used as verbal signs goes along with his apparent refusal to allow that anything could be common to many things independently of being a signifier of many. Abelard reports that Roscelin was 'insane' enough to draw from this view that wholes should not be thought of as divided into parts. This opposition to commonness is probably what led him

to a form of tritheism in which there is no room for a divine essence that is genuinely common to all three divine Persons. He characterized the doctrine that the three Persons have but one substance as 'a manner of speaking', and such remarks were sufficient to bring down on him the charge of heresy.

What we know of Roscelin's views in logic entirely coincides with some positions adopted in a work entitled *Dialectica* dating from the mid or late eleventh century and ascribed to a certain 'Garland'. Professor L.M. de Rijk (1959) in his edition of this work has made a case for the work being by Garland 'the Computist', the author of an astronomical work called *Compotus*, probably a native of Lorraine and eventually a master at Besançon in 1084; but the authorship of the *Dialectica* is still very much in doubt. On the assumption that 'Garland' is the author's name, we can note that his overall approach to logic is probably very close to what Roscelin accepted. For example, when discussing the Aristotelian categories (see CATEGORIES), Garland equates a given category, such as substance, with the physical thing that serves as the category-word, for example, 'substance', plus all the words which are its species and individuals, such as 'body', 'human' and 'Socrates'. Any word 'signifies' the items it is true of, that is, those we would now say are in its extension. 'Animal', for example, signifies each and every animal. As for the intensional side of meaning, Garland speaks of 'modes of signifying' rather than anything signified. Thus both 'human' and 'wise' signify Socrates, but they do so in different modes. On this basis Garland draws the conclusion that of the category-words, that is, the ten highest genera serving to name the ten Aristotelian categories, each signifies everything, but in different modes. 'Substance', 'quantity', 'quality' and so on all signify the individual things named by the proper names in the category of substance; in other words, their extensions entirely coincide. It is very likely that something close to this was Roscelin's position as well. This relegation of the intensional side of signification to mere 'modes' removes from logic the temptation to posit real entities common to many individuals prior to any signification, the real universals we know Roscelin abhorred. Although Roscelin agreed that universals were things – that is, uttered puffs of air – their universality resulted from the use of those things as signs, and in that sense he was an anti-realist on the question of universals (see REALISM AND ANTI-REALISM).

This anti-realism doubtless had an effect on Roscelin's pupil, Peter Abelard, who in the early twelfth century conducted a sustained polemic against the various forms of realism which were current in his day. However, Abelard never credits his former teacher with having been right about anything, perhaps because he wished to distance himself as much as possible from a suspected heretic. Nevertheless, Roscelin's position that universals were only words and that commonness is a result, not a presupposition, of signification remained an important option on this question throughout the medieval period, indeed throughout all subsequent philosophy in the West.

See also: ABELARD, P.; REALISM AND ANTI-REALISM; UNIVERSALS

List of works

Of Roscelin's works, only a letter to Abelard is still extant; the text of this can be found in the appendix of F. Picavet *Roscelin philosophe et theologien d'après la légende et d'après l'histoire; sa place dans l'histoire generale et comparée des philosophies medievales*, Paris: Alcan, 1911. The further readings suggested for this entry offer further sources for Roscelin's thought.

References and further reading

* de Rijk, L.M. (1959) *Garlandus Compotista: Dialectica*, Assen: Van Gorcum. (Contains the Latin text of a logical work which sustains positions very like those ascribed to Roscelin, as well as de Rijk's defence of the work's being ascribed to Garland 'the Computist'.)

Kluge, E-H. (1976) 'Roscelin and the Medieval Problem of Universals', *Journal of the History of Philosophy* 14 (4): 405–14. (The best attempt so far to reconstruct Roscelin's philosophical views.)

Meier, H.C. (1974) *Macht und Wahnwitz der Begriffe: der Ketzer Roscellinus* (The Power and Madness of Concepts: Roscelin the Heretic), Aalen: Spieth Verlag. (An imaginative presentation of Roscelin's conflict with the church authorities.)

Mews, C.J. (1992) 'Nominalism and Theology Before Abaelard: New Light on Roscelin of Compiègne', *Vivarium* 30 (1): 4–33. (Claims Roscelin was not anti-realist about universals after all. Relates him to the theological and grammatical discussions of his day.)

Picavet, F. (1911) *Roscelin philosophe et theologien d'après la légende et d'après l'histoire; sa place dans l'histoire generale et comparée des philosophies medievales* (The Philosopher and Theologian Roscelin, in Legend and History: His Place in History Generally as well as in the Comparative History of Medieval Philosophies), Paris: Alcan. (The appendix contains Roscelin's surviving letter and other important texts.)

Tweedale, M.M. (1988) 'Logic(i): From the Late Eleventh Century to the Time of Abelard', in P. Dronke (ed.) *A History of Twelfth Century Western Philosophy*, Cambridge: Cambridge University Press, 196–226. (Gives an overview of the trends in logic and grammar at the time Roscelin taught.)

MARTIN M. TWEEDALE

ROSENKRANZ, KARL
see HEGELIANISM

ROSENZWEIG, FRANZ (1886–1929)

An outstanding Hegel scholar – his Hegel und der Staat *(Hegel and the State) (1920) remains a standard work on Hegel's political philosophy – Franz Rosenzweig elaborated, in* Der Stern der Erlösung *(The Star of Redemption) (1921) and several articles – notably, his 1925 article 'Das neue Denken' (The New Thinking) – a philosophy of revelation that breaks with the systematic and rationalistic premises of German Idealism. The nisus of Rosenzweig's New Thinking was formulated as early as 1917, in a letter containing the germ (*Urzelle*) of* Der Stern*: 'after reason, "philosophical reason", has absorbed everything in itself', Rosenzweig writes, 'after it has proclaimed its sole existence, man suddenly discovers that he is still here, although he was digested long ago.... I am still here, I – plain, private subject, with first and last name, I – dust and ashes.... Individuum ineffabile triumphans'. How can this be? The human being, Rosenzweig explains, can acquire personal identity as an individual only through the call, that is, the revelation of the Other: God – but also, some other human being. Dialogue, communication in language, comes to the fore in this philosophy, developed around the same time as Martin Buber's* Ich und Du *(I and Thou) (1923). Often treated as a common ground and basis for understanding between Jews and Christians,* Der Stern der Erlösung *is a major source of inspiration for such contemporary philosophers as Lévinas and is widely regarded as a masterpiece of Jewish philosophy.*

1 Life
2 German Idealism
3 The New Thinking

1 Life

Born in Cassel, Germany, Rosenzweig studied history (under Friedrich Meinecke) and philosophy (under Heinrich Rickert) at Freiburg and Berlin. His dissertation on Hegel's political philosophy became the first part of *Hegel und der Staat* (Hegel and the State) (1920). While in Berlin Rosenzweig discovered a manuscript in Hegel's hand, *Das älteste System-programm des deutschen Idealismus* (The Earliest Programmatic System of German Idealism), which he thought to be Hegel's copy of an original sent to Hegel by Schelling. The manuscript and Rosenzweig's analysis of it are still at the core of many discussions of German Idealism. But Rosenzweig himself turned in another direction. In July 1913, after intense discussions with friends and relatives who had converted from Judaism to Christianity, Rosenzweig resolved to become a convert himself. Determined to enter Christianity as a Jew and not 'a pagan', he attended the worship services of Rosh ha-Shanah and Yom Kippur and found there a spirituality he had not expected to find in his ancestral faith. Abandoning his planned conversion, he committed himself to the Jewish religious tradition. Drawing nearer to the Jewish Neo-Kantian philosopher Hermann COHEN, Rosenzweig wrote *Der Stern der Erlösung* (The Star of Redemption) (1921), most of it in the trenches during his years of military service in the First World War, completing the book in 1918. He settled in Frankfurt in 1920, where he founded the *Freies Jüdisches Lehrhaus* (Independent House of Judaic Studies). From 1922 until his death he battled with a severe illness which progressively paralysed him, but he continued to write on the New Thinking, Jewish thought, Jewish life in Germany, and the problems of translating the Hebrew Bible into German, a project which he undertook in collaboration with Martin Buber.

2 German Idealism

Rosenzweig's *Hegel und der Staat* shows the influence of his teacher, Meinecke. But it also breaks with Meinecke's widely influential reading of Hegel and evinces a pioneering independence of mind. In *Weltbürgertum und Nationalstaat* (Cosmopolitanism and the National State) (1907), Meinecke had made Hegel an early advocate of the Machtstaat, or power-state, a Machiavellian entity grounded in *Realpolitik* and exempt from all moral obligations towards the individual. In *Hegel und der Staat*, Rosenzweig breaks with this reading of Hegel's political philosophy. He offers a meticulously documented and still author-itative analysis of Hegel's intellectual development.

Adopting a stance that has been enlarged and deepened but broadly confirmed by later research, Volume II interprets Hegel's mature idea of the state as a counter to both revolutionist and royalist/legitimist claims, owing much more to British parliamentary models than to prevailing Prussian traditions (see HEGEL, G.W.F. §8).

Rosenzweig's reading of Hegel still holds to many of Meinecke's ideas (see Bienenstock 1992a). For example, it takes over Meinecke's definition of *Macht*, power, in terms of *Gewalt*, violence. Hegel in fact identified *Macht* with *Geist* (spirit). Rosenzweig notes that fact but never elucidates the true sense that Hegel gives the idea of Geist. Rather, he interprets Hegel's assertion of a link between the *Volksgeist* and the state in terms of a distinction borrowed, once again, from Meinecke: between *Staatsnationen* and *Kultur-nationen*; that is, nations, founded on the unifying force of a common political history and constitution, and those founded on some common cultural experience – linguistic, literary, or religious. To Rosenzweig it seemed clear that Hegel, who claimed that there can be no universal history without the state – that is, without a common *political* history – would have been able to account for the nation state but not for the *Kulturnation*, in which a common language or religion grounds a common history.

The idea of culture that Rosenzweig used here is again heavily indebted to Meinecke and tinged with a non-Hegelian, romantic conception of culture as the irrational source of a people's life. The manuscript that Rosenzweig had found in Berlin contains sharp criticism of the very idea of the state, this 'mechanical thing', and ends with a call for the foundation of a 'new mythology' among the people. It was because he saw these ideas as more in keeping with Schelling's project than with Hegel's that Rosenzweig ascribed the work to Schelling, but he felt deep affinities with the Programme. In a letter to his mother (3 July 1918) he remarks with approbation that the Jewish people is now 'the only people with a national myth' – and, for this reason, the only people beyond the state and beyond history. The remark sheds light on Rosen-zweig's attitude toward German idealism in the *Der Stern der Erlösung*. Reacting there against Hegel's logocentrism, Rosenzweig draws upon Schelling's late, 'positive' philosophy. It was Schelling's *Philoso-phie der Offenbarung* (Philosophy of Revelation) (1856–8) and *Die Weltalter* (The Ages of the World) (1811–15) (read by Rosenzweig in the 1913 version) that helped him find his way back to a Jewish reading of the Bible.

3 The New Thinking

Rosenzweig's New Thinking originates in his rejection of Hegel's philosophy, which he sees as the climax of the philosophical enterprise at large, 'from Ionia to Jena'. This tradition, which endeavours to grasp the All, Rosenzweig argues, always reduces reality, in the end, to a single element, whether world (in ancient Greek philosophy), God (in the medieval period), or human spirit (in the modern). The New Thinking sets in with a broken totality. It speaks for the irreducibility of each element: God, world, the human being. Drawing on Kierkegaard, but also on Schopenhauer and Nietzsche, Rosenzweig writes at the very beginning of *Der Stern* that when I, as a human being, am confronted with death, my own personal death, I experience the impossibility of reducing it to nought (*Nichts*), and the corresponding impossibility of reducing the world to some rationally comprehensible 'being' (see KIERKEGAARD, S.A.).

Being, Rosenzweig insists, is not identical with thought or, for that matter, with God conceived as *logos*. Setting himself against the opening verse of John's Gospel, 'In the beginning was the Word', he contends that the Word (*logos*) comes second: 'The beginning is: *God Created*'. Here Rosenzweig returns not just to Genesis but to one of the great issues tackled in Jena around 1800 by Hölderlin, the young Schelling and Hegel: the problem of the nexus of myth and language. To ascribe the creation of all things to the Word, he argues, confines us to myth, to a world produced by a 'creative' activity like that of the poet or artist. Such an activity, he insists, involves no real language. For, instead of using words as symbols denoting things and thus different from those things, it presumes the identity of words with things; that is, it relies upon myth. To account for language, one must break with myth and so with the logos-philosophy grounded on the identification of word and thing, thought and being. For Rosenzweig this requires us to acknowledge the reality of Creation, and the main part of *Der Stern* – its 'heart' in Rosenzweig's words (Book II) – thus begins with Creation. Here Rosenzweig describes Creation – like Schelling in the *Philosophie der Offenbarung* – as a 'birth from the ground' (*Geburt aus dem Grunde*), manifesting itself through the 'alternation' (*Wechsel*) of two 'primal Words' (*Urworte*), irreducible to one another: Yes and No, 'Being' (*Sein*) and 'Nought' (*Nichts*), one principle through which God's 'essence' will assert itself, and another through which it will negate or restrain itself.

These Words, Rosenzweig insists, constitute no real language. The close affinity some have seen in Rosenzweig's conception of a *creatio ex nihilo*

(*Schöpfung aus Nichts*) to Kabbalistic ideas is open to question (see Scholem 1930; Idel 1988). But its conceptual roots in Schelling should not be overlooked. Like Schelling, Rosenzweig aims at exposing the failure of any kind of idealistic dialectic that would arrogate to itself the power of explaining Creation – the emanationist doctrines elaborated in the Middle Ages and their culmination in the more recent, idealistic attempts of philosophers to produce the Many from the One. Against Hegel's 'pantheism', Rosenzweig builds upon Schelling's understanding of the relationship between myth and language and argues in *Der Stern* that myth, which is typical of paganism, remains alive in us all. To a mythical consciousness, he writes, the world appears endowed with life, animated by forces perceived as both natural and divine. Such a consciousness resists distinctions between nature and culture, but also between past and present. To it, past events are still here, still living, permanently present in consciousness (see SCHELLING, F.W.J.).

For consciousness to distinguish between past, present and future, it must break loose from the mythical world in which it first lives. This, Rosenzweig claims, is what Revelation achieves. It replaces the mythic past, in which neither past nor present exist, with a past comprehended as such, thus making possible both a present and a future. Here Rosenzweig draws on the opening sentences of Schelling's *Weltalter*: 'the past is known (*gewußt*), the present is understood (*erkannt*), the future is foreseen (*geahndet*). That which is known is narrated (*erzählt*), that which is understood is described (*dargestellt*), that which is foreseen is prophesied (*geweissagt*)'. Building on these distinctions, Rosenzweig makes the past the age of Creation, the present the age of Revelation, and the future the age of Redemption (the three parts of the 'heart' of *Der Stern*). Creation is *narrated*, in the Bible; the present is *described*, and Redemption is *prophesied*.

In 'Das neue Denken' (The New Thinking) (1925), Rosenzweig urges that the human experience of past, present and future, is existential; it grows out of the inner life of consciousness; and its temporality, therefore, cannot be erased by thought. Thus the error of all philosophical systems in which thought is made timeless. Rosenzweig's insistence on temporality (*Zeitlichkeit*) anticipates Heidegger's *Sein und Zeit* (Being and Time) (published six years after *Der Stern*; see Löwith 1942). But where Heidegger acknowledges only 'existential' (temporal) truths, Rosenzweig discovers a truth beyond time, eternal, revealed truth. Revelation, he argues in *Der Stern*, enables us to apprehend Creation as an event belonging to the past, but is not itself an event in the past. Rather, revelation takes the form of a command issued to us in the present: the command to love God and, through God, our fellow human beings. To explain why this command dawns upon us as a revelation, Rosenzweig goes back beyond the Revelation at Mount Sinai, to God's call to Adam in Genesis (1: 9): 'Where are you?'. God's original Revelation occurs through this call. For Revelation is made to all human beings, not only to Israelites; and it dawns upon us from the outside. It is the revelation of a 'Thou', of an Other issuing a command. There is at first no 'I' to answer. Adam does not answer God's call. He tries to escape his responsibility – to evade the summons made to him personally, to him as an individual, who has a 'private name' – by hiding behind a pronoun: 'it', 'she' or 'he' (did it). An answer to God's call becomes audible in Abraham's 'Here am I' (Genesis 22: 1) – then, louder, in Israel's acceptance, renewed each day, of God's command. Only so does the revelation of a 'Thou' issue in a true dialogue with an 'I'.

Rosenzweig elaborates here, almost simultaneously with the Catholic teacher Ferdinand Ebner in *Das Wort und die geistigen Realitäten* (The Word and the Spiritual Realities) (1921) and with Martin Buber in *Ich und Du* (1923), what may be considered the first systematic presentation of the philosophy of dialogue (see BUBER, M.). Rosenzweig, who knew both works, also criticized them. According to him, both Ebner and Buber so narrowed the 'I–Thou' relation that they lost sight of the 'We' and of nature.

Rosenzweig himself also drew on the work of his friend Eugen Rosenstock-Huessy, a historian and sociologist of Jewish origin who had converted to Christianity and who was then teaching at the University of Leipzig. In his *Angewandte Seelenkunde* (Practical Knowledge of the Soul) (1924), a text Rosenstock-Huessy sent to Rosenzweig as early as 1916, the former had argued that the Cartesian *cogito ergo sum* should be replaced with a so-called 'grammatical' proposition: 'God called me, therefore I am. I am given a private name, therefore I exist'. He had made the human being 'a being that is spoken to' (*ein angeredtes Wesen*). He had sought to establish on this basis a true 'science of the soul' (*Seelenkunde*), a discipline that would do justice to the soul, instead of just giving up the word, as William James had done in his *Psychology*. According to Rosenstock, those who reduce the science of the soul to a 'science of the mind' (*Geisteswissenschaft*), turn language to logic and cannot understand what a 'community' (*Gemeinschaft*) is. They reduce it either to a mere collection of individuals moved by private interests, or to an entity understandable only as an 'it'. Such reductions are politically dangerous.

Rosenzweig fully agreed with his friend's diagnosis.

He saw in the Jewish people a true community in Rosenstock's sense. Making much use of the Song of Songs, where 'strong as death is love' (8: 6), he contends in *Der Stern* that the dialogue of the 'lover' (God) with the 'beloved' (Israel) announces a Redemption already lived by the Jewish people in the present, although it is pregnant with the future. The eternal people are 'beyond history' – always and already 'with God'. In this sense, Israel is the true incarnation of Eternity in time. Other peoples, particularly Christian ones, are 'on the way to God', that is, invested with the responsibility to realize the divine mission in history.

In keeping with this model, Rosenzweig opposed Zionism, thinking that Judaism can be lived only in Exile, at least as long as the history of the peoples of the earth has not ended. This conviction of his, much criticized for its seeming acceptance of the notion and the myth of the Wandering Jew, may also be seen as a variant of Hegel's idea that eternity itself is in time. Despite all his criticism of German Idealism, Rosenzweig remained enmeshed in it.

See also: HEGELIANISM; JEWISH PHILOSOPHY IN THE EARLY 19TH CENTURY

List of works

Rosenzweig, F. (1976–) *Franz Rosenzweig: Der Mensch und sein Werk: Gesammelte Schriften* (Franz Rosenzweig: The Man and his Work: Collected Writings), The Hague, Dordrecht, Boston, MA and Lancaster: Martinus Nijhoff. (Collected works; four volumes published so far, under various editors.)

—— (1917) *Das älteste Systemprogramm des deutschen Idealismus: Ein handschriftlicher Fund* (The Earliest Programmatic System of German Idealism: A Manuscript Find), Heidelberg: Winter; repr. in *Franz Rosenzweig: Der Mensch und sein Werk: Gesammelte Schriften*, vol. III, 3–44. (Rosenzweig's first, scholarly publication. Also sheds light upon his later thought.)

—— (1917) '"Urzelle" des *Stern der Erlösung*' ('Germ' of The Star of Redemption), in *Franz Rosenzweig: Der Mensch und sein Werk: Gesammelte Schriften*, vol. III, 125–38. (First formulation of Rosenzweig's main ideas.)

—— (1920) *Hegel und der Staat* (Hegel and the State), Munich and Berlin: Oldenbourg; repr. Aalen: Scientia, 1962. (Rosenzweig's scholarly study of Hegel's political thought.)

—— (1921a) *Der Stern der Erlösung* (The Star of Redemption), Frankfurt: Kauffmann; trans. W.W. Hallo, New York: Holt, Rinehart & Winston, 1970;

paperback edn, Boston: Beacon Press, 1972. (Rosenzweig's main work, in which he sets out a 'new thinking' to outline a history of culture and proposes a philosophical theology of Judaism and Christianity.)

—— (1921b) *Das Büchlein vom gesunden und kranken Menschenverstand*, Düsseldorf: Melzer; trans. and ed. N.N. Glatzer, *Understanding the Sick and the Healthy: A View of World, Man and God*, New York: Noonday Press, 1954. (Rosenzweig's world view.)

—— (1925) 'Das neue Denken: Einige nachträgliche Bemerkungen zum *Stern der Erlösung*' (The New Thinking: Some additional remarks to The Star of Redemption), *Der Morgen* 1 (4); repr. in *Franz Rosenzweig: Der Mensch und sein Werk: Gesammelte Schriften*, vol. III, 139–61. (Rosenzweig's own synopsis of his masterpiece.)

—— (1937) *Kleinere Schriften* (Smaller Writings), Berlin: Schocken. (Contains many of Rosenzweig's 'smaller' but important writings, such as the 'Urzelle', 'Atheistiche Theologie' and 'Das neue Denken'.)

References and further reading

Anckaert, L. and Casper B. (1990) *An Exhaustive Rosenzweig Bibliography: Primary and Secondary Writings*, Leuven: Library of the Faculty of Theology; 2nd edn, 1995. (Comprehensive bibliography.)

Bergman, S.H. (1991) *Dialogical Philosophy from Kierkegaard to Rosenzweig*, New York: State University of New York Press, 173–214. (Vivid introduction to Rosenzweig.)

* Bienenstock, M. (1992a) 'Rosenzweig's Hegel', *The Owl of Minerva* 23 (2): 177–82. (Detailed discussion of Rosenzweig's relationship to Hegel.)

—— (1992b) 'Mythe et révélation dans *l'Étoile de la rédemption*: Contemporanéité de Franz Rosenzweig' (Myth and Revelation in The Star of Redemption: Rosenzweig, Our Contemporary), *Archives de Philosophie* 55: 17–34. (Analysis of the philosophical and historical context of Rosenzweig's thought.)

* Buber, M. (1923) *Ich und Du*, Leipzig: Insel; trans. R.G. Smith, *I and Thou*, New York: Charles Scribner's Sons, 1958. (Buber's most famous presentation of his philosophy of dialogue.)

Cohen, R.A. (1994) *Elevations: The Height of the Good in Rosenzweig and Levinas*, Chicago, IL: University of Chicago Press. (Comparative study.)

* Ebner, F. (1921) *Das Wort und die geistigen Realitäten: Pneumatologische Fragmente* (The Word and the Spiritual Realities: Pneumatological Fragments), Innsbruck: Brenner; trans. H.J. Green, The Word and the Spiritual Realities, Evanston, IL: Northwestern University Press, 1980. (The philosophy of dialogue, by one of Rosenzweig's contemporaries.)

Freund, E. (1933) *Die Existenzphilosophie Franz Rosenzweigs: Ein Betrag zur Analyse seines Werkes Der Stern der Erlösung* (Franz Rosenzweig's Philosophy of Existence: An analysis of The Star of Redemption), Berlin and Leipzig: Felix Meiner; trans. S.L. Weinstein and R. Israel, The Hague, Boston, MA and London: Martinus Nijhoff. (General introduction.)

Glatzer, N.N. (1953) *Franz Rosenzweig: His Life and Thought*, New York: Schocken; 2nd edn, 1961. (The classic English introduction to Rosenzweig. Contains extracts from Rosenzweig's works in English translation.)

* Idel, M. (1988) 'Franz Rosenzweig and the Kabbalah', in P. Mendes-Flohr (ed.) *The Philosophy of Franz Rosenzweig*, Hanover, NH and London: University Press of New England, 162–71. (The classic English introduction to Rosenzweig. Contains extracts from his works in English translation.)

Levinas, E. (1961) *Totalité et infini: Essai sur l'extériorité* (Totality and Infinity: An Essay on Exteriority), The Hague: Nijhoff; trans. A. Lingis, Pittsburgh, PA: Duquesne University Press, 1969. (The work in which Levinas explicitly acknowledges his debt to Rosenzweig.)

* Löwith, K. (1942) 'M. Heidegger and F. Rosenzweig, or Temporality and Eternity', *Philosophy and Phenomenological Research* 3 (1): 53–77. (Comparison between Heidegger's and Rosenzweig's philosophical points of departure.)

* Meinecke, F. (1907) *Weltbürgertum und Nationalstaat* (Cosmopolitanism and the Nation State), Munich and Berlin: Oldenbourg. (The work of the great German historian who was Rosenzweig's teacher.)

* Rosenstock-Huessy, E. (1924) *Angewandte Seelenkunde* (Practical Knowledge of the Soul), Darmstadt: Roether; trans. Jericho, VT: Argo Books, 1988. (A text written for Rosenzweig and sent to him as early as 1916, in which it is argued that the Cartesian *cogito ergo sum* should be replaced with a so-called 'grammatical' proposition: 'God called me, therefore I am. I am given a private name, therefore I exist'.)

—— (ed.) (1969) *Judaism despite Christianity: The letters on Christianity and Judaism between Eugen Rosenstock-Huessy and Franz Rosenzweig*, Tuscaloosa, AL: University of Alabama Press. (Contains a good introductory article by A. Altmann, and several other contributions.)

* Schelling, F.W.J. (1811–15) *Die Weltalter* (The Ages of the World), ed. L. Kuhlenbeck, Leipzig: Reclam, 1913; trans. with introduction and notes by F. de W. Bolman, Jr, *The Ages of the World*, New York: Columbia University Press, 1967. (Rosenzweig probably used the Kuhlenbeck edition. Schelling wrote several drafts of the text from 1810 onwards. The major source of Schelling's later philosophy, in which he outlines God's progressive realization of the divine self through self-consciousness of ideas within himself.)

* —— (1856–8) *Philosophie der Offenbarung* (Philosophy of Revelation), Stuttgart: Cotta. (Posthumously published on the basis of numerous lecture notes. In this work, he outlines his belief that revelation, the incursion of the divine into history, is the point around which persons organize their world and experiences.)

Schmied-Kowarzik, W. (ed.) (1988) *Der Philosoph Franz Rosenzweig (1886–1926)*, Freiburg and Munich: Alber. (The Proceedings, in two volumes, of the International 1986 Conference on Rosenzweig in Kassel. An extensive collection, containing articles on most aspects of Rosenzweig's thought, with useful bibliographical indications.)

Scholem, G. (1930) 'Franz Rosenzweig and His Book *The Star of Redemption*', in P. Mendes-Flohr (ed.) *The Philosophy of Franz Rosenzweig*, Hanover, NH and London: University Press of New England, 1988, 20–41. (Scholem's speech at the Hebrew University of Jerusalem, thirty days after Rosenzweig's death.)

M. BIENENSTOCK

ROSMINI-SERBATI, ANTONIO (1797–1855)

In the reactionary, anti-Enlightenment, spiritualistic climate of Italy and Europe in the first decades of the nineteenth century, the Italian philosopher Rosmini set out to elaborate a Christian, Catholic system of philosophy which drew elements from Platonic, Augustinian and Thomist thought, while also taking account of recent philosophical developments, especially Kantian ones, as well as of the new liberal political trends in the culture of the time. His aim was to restore the principle of objectivity in the field of gnoseology, as well as in ethics, law and political thought.

Rosmini studied at Padua and was ordained in 1821. In 1826 he settled in Milan and two years later founded a religious congregation, the Istituto della Carità (Institute of Charity). In 1830 he published his first and most important philosophical work, the *Nuovo saggio sull'origine delle idee* (New Essay on the Origins of Ideas), in which he distanced himself from empiricism and sensism, on the one hand, and idealism and rationalism, on the other. Empiricism and sensism, for Rosmini, offer less than what is needed, in that they attempt to derive knowledge and spirituality exclusively from experience. Idealism and rationalism, by contrast, offer more than is necessary, claiming, as Kant did, the innateness of all ideas as formal elements of knowledge. Both positions are characterized by subjectivism and thus lead to scepticism.

To get beyond subjectivism and scepticism, Rosmini argues, it is necessary to proceed from the proposition that the human intellect contains an original, essential idea, which does not derive from experience but is innate and thus imprinted by God, and which can be sensed through intuition. This idea is the idea of being in general: of indeterminate, possible being, in the sense that it can take on any determination and that it is the presupposition of all ideas and all judgments. It is this idea of being, this light of reason, that guarantees the objectivity of knowledge. This owes a great deal to the doctrines of Plato, Augustine and Aquinas, especially where the elements of 'innatism' and the illumination of reason are concerned. In the part of his system that deals with the processes of knowledge, however, Rosmini accepts certain fundamental aspects of Kant's critical philosophy.

One notion he derives from Kant is the distinction between material and formal elements and the need for a synthesis between them in the act of knowing (which, for Rosmini, as for Kant, is essentially the act of judging) (see KANT, I. §6). He departs sharply from Kantian tradition, however, regarding Kant's a priori synthesis – what Rosmini calls '*percezione intellettiva*' ('intellective perception'). For Rosmini, the formal element is represented not by a mere transcendental category, but by the idea of being. Although this idea guarantees the objective validity of knowledge, it is not sufficient in itself to form the basis for determinate knowledge, to allow us to apprehend the reality of things. A direct encounter between the intellect and the sensible world is needed. This 'intellective perception' is the product of the synthesis between form, given by the idea of being and intuited by the intellect, and matter, which derives from sensations and from the '*sentimento fondamentale*': the underlying sense that all human beings have of their own life in its entirety and of which sensations are merely modifications.

The above notion of being or ideal being was

particularly central to Rosmini's thought, supplying a philosophical foundation for his reconstruction of a spiritualistic metaphysics in his posthumously published *Teosofia* (Theosophy) (1859–74). In particular, it provided a grounding for the essential principle of that metaphysics, the existence of God. For Rosmini, ideal being is in fact merely one divine element of a personal Being, God. Ideal being thus postulates the real and absolute Being of God. In addition, Rosmini sees general ideas, such as identity, non-contradiction, and substance and cause, as deriving from the same notion of being through a process of abstraction and universalization. In this way, he constructs a comprehensive philosophical system, spanning the 'ideological' sciences, whose object is ideal being; the metaphysical sciences; and the deontological sciences, which concern themselves with ethics, law and politics.

In ethics, as in metaphysics, with such works as *Antropologia in servizio della scienza morale* (Anthropology at the Service of Ethics) (1838), Rosmini aims to restore the principle of objectivity, which he regards as having been abandoned in favour of subjectivism by both utilitarians and hedonists and by Kant. From the notion of being, which for him was the premise of gnoseological truth, there also stemmed the notion of the Good, which is the end of morality and the object towards which our love should be directed, according to a scale of values that has God at its summit, but which also has a place for persons, who have the status of ends in themselves, as they do in Kant. The Good, which translates into moral law, not only can be known by the intellect, but should also be pursued by the will. The achievement of this objective can be impeded by the senses and by our instincts, as well as by individuals' free choice.

Rosmini's contributions to jurisprudence and political philosophy are closely bound up with his moral thought. It is moral law, in fact, which justifies personal rights – the ends to which society and state are the means. Civil society should under all circumstances adhere to the model provided by ecclesiastical society, which aims at a happiness lying beyond this world. In other words, it should look to the Church, which Rosmini considered was in need of reform, as he argues in his *Delle cinque piaghe della santa Chiesa* (The Five Wounds of the Holy Church) (1848a). From 1836, Rosmini lived in Piedmont, where, under the influence of liberal trends in political thought, he underwent an intellectual evolution that took him as far as a moderate constitutionalism and support for the notion of a federation of Italian states against Austria, expressed in his *Costituzione secondo la giustizia sociale* (The Constitution According to Principles of Social Justice) (1848b).

Rosmini was accused of psychologism (that is, subjectivism) by Vincenzo GIOBERTI, and he came under attack from Catholic critics (in 1888, the *Congregazione del Saint'Uffizio* condemned forty propositions drawn from his works). Idealists, however, considered him an Italian and Catholic version of Kant, and a point of transition to Neapolitan neo-Hegelianism. His attempt at a modern synthesis of Catholic philosophy has influenced modern Christian spiritualism.

See also: ITALY, PHILOSOPHY IN §2

List of works

Rosmini-Serbati, A. (1934–) *Opere edite e inedite di Antonio Rosmini* (Complete Works), ed. E. Castelli and M.F. Sciacca. (The National Edition of Rosmini's works is published with the collaboration of the Istituto di studi filosofici, Rome and the Centro di studi rosminiani, Stresa.)

—— (1830) *Nuovo saggio sull'origine delle idee* (New Essay On The Origin Of Ideas), ed. F. Orestano, Rome: Anonima Romana Editoriale, 1934. (Rosmini's central work, this forms the basis for his entire theoretic, metaphysical, moral and legal-political system of philosophy. Vols 3–4 of the *Complete Works*.)

—— (1831, 1837) *Principi della scienza morale e storia comparativa e critica dei sistemi intorno al principio della morale* (Principles of Ethics, with a Comparative Critical History of Systems Concerned with the Principle of Morality), ed. D. Morando, Milan: Fratelli Bocca, 1941; trans. D. Cleary and T. Watson, *Principles of Ethics*, Durham, Rosmini House, 2nd edn, 1989. (The first work in which Rosmini uses the foundations laid by the philosopher di Rovereto to re-establish, on an objective basis, a universally valid moral science. Vol. 21 of the *Complete Works*.)

—— (1838) *Antropologia in servizio della scienza morale* (Anthropology at the Service of Ethics), ed. C. Riva, Roma and Milan: Fratelli Bocca, 1954. (Complements and enlarges on his principles of moral science. Vol. 25 of the *Complete Works*.)

—— (1841–5) *Filosofia del diritto*, ed. R. Orecchia, Rome: Città nuova, 1967–8, 2 vols; vol. 1, trans. D. Cleary and T. Watson, *The Philosophy of Right*, Durham, Rosmini House, 1993. (In this work Rosmini illustrates the essential human rights – rights to truth and justice, rights regarding ones body and life, and property rights – which cannot be postponed, even for the sake of public welfare. Vols 35 and 36 of the *Opere edite e inedite*.)

—— (1848a) *Delle cinque piaghe della Santa Chiesa*

(The Five Wounds of the Holy Church), ed. A. Valle, Rome: Città nuova, 1981. (In perhaps his best-known work, Rosmini illustrates what he perceived as the worst evils of the Church at the time and proposes remedies, from a liberal-catholic viewpoint.)

—— (1848b) *Progetti di Costituzione. La Costituzione secondo la giustizia sociale* (Constitutional Projects. The Constitution According to Principles of Social Justice), ed. C. Gray, Milan: Fratelli Bocca, 1952. (These reflect the constitutional phase of Rosmini's political thought, in which he forces himself to accept as fully as possible, with limitations of a confessional catholic nature, the aspirations of the moderate liberal movement. Vol. 24 of the *Opere edite e inedite*.)

—— (1859–74) *Teosofia* (Theosophy), ed. C. Gray, Rome: Edizioni Rome and Milan, Fratelli Bocca, 1938–9, 1940–1. (A posthumous work in which Rosmini brings out the first and most important consequence of the construction of his philosophical system, namely the restoration of a spiritualistic metaphysics. Vols 7–14 of the *Complete Works*.)

References and further reading

Bergamaschi, C. (1967–82) *Bibliografia rosminiana* (Bibliography of Works by and on Rosmini), Milan: Marzorati, 6 vols. (Very ample and helpful.)

Bulferetti, L. (1942) *A. Rosmini nella Restaurazione* (Rosmini during the Restoration), Florence: Le Monnier. (On the evolution of Rosmini's philosophical and political thought.)

De Giorgi, F. (1995) *La scienza del cuore. Spiritualità e cultura religiosa in Antonio Rosmini* (The science of the heart. Spirituality and religious culture in Antonio Rosmini), Bologna: Il Mulino. (In depth study of the spirituality and religious culture of Rosmini, set against the larger picture of contemporary agnosticism; with an extensive bibliography.)

Gentile, G. (1898) *Rosmini e Gioberti* (Rosmini and Gioberti), Florence: Sansoni, 3rd edn, 1958. (Presents the idealist intepretation of Rosmini's thought.)

Piovani, P. (1957) *La teodicea sociale di Rosmini* (Rosmini's Social Theodicy), Padua: Milani. (On the relation between theology and society in Rosmini's thought.)

Solari, G. (1957) *Studi rosminiani* (Studies on Rosmini), Milan: Giuffrè. (A rigorous and scholarly study relating the development of Rosmini's thought to the cultural climate in which he lived.)

Traniello, F. (1966) *Società religiosa e società civile in Rosmini* (Religious society and civil society in Rosmini), Bologna: Il Mulino. (An acute study of

Rosmini's life and thought, from a fundamentally ecclesiastical and religious perspective.)

Translated by Virginia Cox

GUIDO VERUCCI

ROSS, ALF (1899–1979)

Famous for his contribution to Scandinavian legal realism, Alf Niels Christian Ross was among the major philosophers of the latter half of the twentieth century. He was Kelsen's ideal successor and on a par with H.L.A. Hart in terms of notoriety and international influence.

Ross opposed equally natural law theories and formalistic legal positivism and, following Hans KELSEN whose Vienna seminars he attended in 1924–5, he insisted that the central questions of law were epistemological (what is law? what is legal knowledge?) yet rejected the 'two-world' dichotomy of *Sein* and *Sollen* ('is' and 'ought') with their separate methods of investigation. The rejection of dualism and dilemmas on how to characterize the interplay of law's normative and factual character condition his entire life's work (see LEGAL POSITIVISM §5; NATURAL LAW).

Under the influence of Axel HÄGERSTRÖM (§4) Ross found the philosophical basis on which to ground his need for realism. Ross embraced the theory that a concept of reality is not logically conceivable outside the context of space and time, the emotivistic concept of values and the noncognitive notion of value judgments, and the rejection of voluntarism as a theory of positive law. Ross claimed that 'legal phenomena' rather than 'positive law' must be investigated. These comprise mental impulses and attitudes of impartial behaviour, rationalized in the use of normative and evaluative linguistic expressions (validity), as well as attitudes of biased behaviour, construed as the subjectivization of coercion. Although formally distinguishing them, Ross equates legal and moral validity, both understood as psychological phenomena of rationalization. Naturally he now abandoned his previous view that specific normative knowledge is possible. Legal science, including legal dogmatics, was to be subsumed in the wider sphere of psychological and sociological sciences which study human behaviour. Yet the concern did not abandon the need to explain at least the feeling of obligation, being bound by law.

In the final and most famous phase of his work, Ross turned to logical positivism. In the preface to the

English edition of *On Law and Justice*, Ross coupled Anglo-American jurisprudence from John Austin to Oliver Wendell Holmes with the Scandinavian tradition from Anders Sandoe Orsted to Hägerström. Ross declared that his aim was to trace empiricist principles to their ultimate conclusions in the field of law. The principle of verifiability provided the means to do this: any statement has a meaning in so far as it implies that, following certain procedures, certain results can be obtained, the set of results representing the 'real content' of the statement. Hence legal statements of the type 'Directive D is a valid law' signifies that 'by applying the system of norms as a scheme of interpretation, we are enabled to comprehend the actions of the courts as meaningful responses to given conditions' (Ross 1958: 39). The procedure of verifying such propositions will be the behaviour of the courts which settle legal disputes (see MEANING AND VERIFICATION).

In *Directives and Norms* (1968) Ross adopts and modifies R.M. Hare's distinction between phrastic and neustic in order to ascribe to norms a semantic meaning denied earlier. Legal dogmatics none the less remains an empirical science, no longer a branch of sociology since this discipline is concerned with law in action while legal dogmatics studies the abstract ideal content of legal norms. Now too the biased and impartial attitudes are separated out, no longer construed as part of the reality of law, but rather, part of the phenomenon of reasons that induce people to obey the law.

See also: LAW, PHILOSOPHY OF; LEGAL REALISM §1; VOLUNTARISM

List of works

Ross, A. (1933) *Kritik der sogenannten praktischen Erkenntnis* (Critique of So-called Practical Knowledge), Copenhagen and Leipzig: Munksgaard. (A critique of theories about 'so-called practical cognition', presenting a strongly anti-cognitivist moral and legal theory.)
—— (1946) *Towards a Realistic Jurisprudence: A Criticism of Dualism in Law*, Copenhagen: Munksgaard. (An attack on the dualism of norms and facts, arguing that in a scientific perspective norms are merely psychological contents of thought which have a causal impact on behaviour.)
—— (1957) 'Tû-Tû', *Harvard Law Review* 70: 812–25. (A witty and influential essay, using imaginary anthropology to suggest that legal terms like 'right' and 'ownership' have no semantic meaning, serving in legal discourse only as a link between conditioning facts and conditioned consequences.)
—— (1958) *On Law and Justice*, London: Stevens and Sons. (Readable statement of ethical noncognitivism coupled with legal realism, reducing legal statements in the last resort to predictions of behaviour and emotive utterances tending to affect behaviour.)
—— (1968) *Directives and Norms*, London: Routledge & Kegan Paul. (Final and most mature statement of Ross' position, modifying it to take into account the work of R.M. Hare and other analytical moral philosophers, developing a theory of norms that makes it possible to ascribe meaning to them.)

References and further reading

Harris, J.W. (1978) *Law and Legal Science*, London: Butterworth. (Advanced discussion of leading positions in modern jurisprudence, containing a sympathetic account of Ross' psychological approach to the explanation of law, but preferring a more Kelsenian thesis about the nature of legal norms and legal science.)
MacCormack, G.D. (1971) 'Scandinavian Realism', *Juridical Review*, new series, 14: 259–81. (Discussion of realist accounts of law in terms of 'facts', criticizing the psychologism of Ross and Karl Olivecrona.)
Marshall, G. (1957) 'Law in a Cold Climate: the Scandinavian Realism', *Juridical Review*, new series, 1: 259–81. (Discussion in dialogue form of some main points of Scandinavian realism, with prominent attention to Ross.)
Simpson, A.W.B (1964) 'The Analysis of Legal Concepts', *Law Quarterly Review* 80: 535–58. (Critical account of certain leading discussions of legal concepts, notably those of H.L.A. Hart and of Ross.)

ENRICO PATTARO

ROSS, WILLIAM DAVID (1877–1971)

W.D. Ross was a British ancient and moral philosopher. In terms of his moral thinking, he was a pluralist, who held that there are several distinct moral considerations which bear on the rightness of an action. Among the things we need to take into account are promises we have made, the need to avoid harming others, gratitude to benefactors, and the amount of good our action will produce. That these considerations are morally relevant is something we can know, but which action is the right one is a matter of fallible judgment, because that will depend upon how these considerations are to be weighed against each other in the particular case. Ross' contributions to the study of ancient philosophy mainly concerned Aristotle. He is now best known, however, for his moral philosophy.

W.D. Ross was a Fellow of Merton College, Oxford, before moving to Oriel College, where he became Provost. He was knighted in 1938. Ross made contributions to the study of ancient philosophy and in particular Aristotle, though he also published a book on the Platonic Forms (1951). He edited the Oxford Translation of Aristotle, wrote an influential book on Aristotle, and published several important editions of Aristotelian texts, with commentaries. Now, though, he is best known for his moral philosophy.

In his two major ethical works, *The Right and the Good* (1930) and *The Foundations of Ethics* (1939), Ross offers the clearest and most ably defended account of a pluralist deontology in the twentieth century (see DEONTOLOGICAL ETHICS; MORAL PLURALISM). One of Ross' main targets is the consequentialism of G.E. Moore (1903), which held that, in determining whether an action is right, there is just one consideration that is relevant, namely the amount of good that will result from doing that action (see CONSEQUENTIALISM; MOORE, G.E.). Ross held, by contrast, that a number of features of actions are morally significant, and that which action is right will depend on which of these features carries the most weight in a particular case.

Deontology thus distinguishes itself from consequentialism in claiming that the right is independent of the good (see RIGHT AND GOOD); the right action is not necessarily the one that produces the most good. Ross defends this claim by arguing that being productive of the most good is neither what it *is* for an action to be right, nor what *makes* an action right. The right action is also distinct from the morally good action; the latter depends on the agent's motives, whereas the former does not. His method throughout is to appeal to our ordinary reflective consciousness, which for Ross is the final arbiter on all ethical issues. He is confident that reflection on attempts to define 'right' will reveal that it is an irreducible notion. It cannot be analysed, but it can be elucidated: Ross suggests that rightness is a species of the relational property of fittingness or suitability. Just as a telling word or phrase may be called for at a particular juncture in a poem, so a particular moral response may be called for by various features of a situation, and the right action will be the act which constitutes the most suitable response to all the factors in that situation, taken as a whole.

Which features of an action are relevant to its rightness? Ross offers a list of what he terms '*prima facie* duties', each of which may have a bearing on the rightness of an action. These are duties of fidelity (promise-keeping), reparation, gratitude, justice, beneficence, self-improvement and nonmaleficence (not injuring others). Ross thus agrees with the consequentialist that we have a duty to do as much good as possible (beneficence) but he maintains that this is merely one duty among several, and one or more of the others might outweigh the duty of beneficence on some particular occasion (see HELP AND BENEFICENCE).

Despite having passed into common philosophical parlance, the phrase '*prima facie* duty' is, as Ross is quick to point out, doubly misleading. First, this is not strictly a list of duties, of things I ought to do, since, for example, it may precisely be my duty not to act in the way which will do the most good if I have promised to do something else. In here allowing considerations of fidelity to override those of beneficence I am not failing to carry out any sort of duty. Second, the term '*prima facie*' might suggest that we are speaking only of an appearance which a moral situation presents at first sight and which might turn out to be illusory. But even where some morally significant consideration is overridden by others, it does not cease to be relevant. (For this reason, some writers now prefer to use the term '*pro tanto*' duty.) It is perhaps best to think of Ross' list of *prima facie* duties as a list of fundamental moral considerations, or right-making characteristics, which always count in favour of an action (see DUTY §2).

Ross' list is not an arbitrary one. He offers it as a list of the most basic morally relevant features. He does not claim that it is final – he is perfectly prepared to consider the possibility, for example, that one of the general features on the list might turn out not to be basic, or to be genuinely distinct from the others – but he does hold that what should be on the list is a subject for reasoned debate, drawing again on careful reflection on our moral beliefs.

That certain features of actions are right-making features is self-evident, according to Ross, in much the way that a mathematical axiom or the validity of a form of inference is self-evident. It is not that they are immediately obvious, but that, since they are basic, we cannot appeal to anything more fundamental to justify them. What we ought to do in any particular case is, by contrast, something of which we can never be certain, according to Ross, but only have a better or worse founded opinion. This pessimism about the possibility of moral knowledge in the particular case is perhaps over-stated, but it rests on a structural difference between knowledge of a general moral principle and appreciation of the particular case. Ross holds that, in all but the most trivial cases, whether an action is right will depend on the way that conflicting moral considerations bear on the particular case. There is no mechanical method, no algorithm, for calculating which of these considerations is the weightiest in some specific case. In most cases, there will be just one action that is the right one, but deciding which that is calls for judgment and practical wisdom (see MORAL JUDGMENT §4).

See also: AXIOLOGY; INTUITIONISM IN ETHICS; VALUES

List of works

Ross, W.D. (1923) *Aristotle*, London: Methuen. (A general introduction to Aristotle.)
—— (ed.) (1924) *Aristotle: Metaphysics*, Oxford: Clarendon Press, 2 vols. (Contains Greek text and introduction by Ross.)
—— (1930) *The Right and the Good*, Oxford: Clarendon Press. (The finest modern systematic exposition of a moderate deontology.)
—— (ed.) (1936) *Aristotle: Physics*, Oxford: Clarendon Press. (Contains Greek text and introduction by Ross.)
—— (1939) *The Foundations of Ethics*, Oxford: Clarendon Press. (Ross' further thoughts on these matters, being the Gifford Lectures 1935–6.)
—— (1951) *Plato's Theory of Ideas*, Oxford: Clarendon Press. (A discussion of Platonic metaphysics.)
—— (1954) *Kant's Ethical Theory*, Oxford: Clarendon Press. (A commentary on Kant's *Groundwork of the Metaphysics of Morals* (1785).)
—— (ed.) (1955) *Aristotle: Parva Naturalia*, Oxford: Clarendon Press. (Contains Greek text and introduction by Ross.)
—— (ed.) (1957) *Aristotle: Prior and Posterior Analytics*, Oxford: Clarendon Press. (Contains Greek text and introduction by Ross.)
—— (ed.) (1961) *Aristotle: De Anima*, Oxford: Clarendon Press. (Contains Greek text and introduction by Ross.)

References and further reading

Audi, R. (1996) 'Intuitionism, Pluralism, and the Foundations of Ethics', in W. Sinnott-Armstrong and M. Timmons (eds) *Moral Knowledge?: New Readings in Moral Epistemology*, Oxford: Oxford University Press, 101–36. (A full-scale examination and defence of an intuitionist epistemology.)
Dancy, J. (1993) 'An Ethic of *Prima Facie* Duties', in P. Singer (ed.) *A Companion to Ethics*, Oxford:

Blackwell, 230–40. (Offers a number of serious challenges to Ross' account of a *prima facie* duty.)
Gaut, B. (1993) 'Moral Pluralism', *Philosophical Papers* 22: 17–40. (A forceful defence of moral pluralism.)
McNaughton, D. (1996) 'An Unconnected Heap of Duties?', *Philosophical Quarterly* 46: 433–47. (Argues that deontology, in the form advocated by Ross, can offer a systematic account of our distinct duties.)
* Moore, G.E. (1903) *Principia Ethica*, ed. T. Baldwin, Cambridge: Cambridge University Press, revised edn, 1993. (Moore here makes consequentialism true by definition by defining the right action as the action which produces the most good. This claim is vigorously rebutted by Ross.)
—— (1912) *Ethics*, London: Oxford University Press. (By the time he wrote this book, Moore had abandoned the view that the right could be *defined* in terms of the good, but he still held that what made an action right was solely that it produced the greatest amount of good. Ross also vigorously rebutted this claim.)
Urmson, J.O. (1975) 'A Defence of Intuitionism', *Proceedings of the Aristotelian Society* 75: 111–19. (A lively defence of moral pluralism of a Rossian kind.)

DAVID McNAUGHTON

ROUSSEAU, JEAN-JACQUES (1712–78)

Rousseau was born in Geneva, the second son of Isaac Rousseau, watchmaker. His mother died a few days after his birth. From this obscure beginning he rose to become one of the best known intellectual figures of the eighteenth-century French Enlightenment, taking his place alongside Diderot, Voltaire and others as one of the emblematic figures of this period, for all that he came to differ violently in view from them. He died in 1778 and in 1794 his body was transferred to the Panthéon in Paris.

Rousseau always maintained that he regretted taking up a career of letters. His first love was music and he composed a number of operas in the 1740s with some success. The turning point in his life occurred in July 1749. He was on his way to see his then friend Diderot who was imprisoned at Vincennes. He read in the newspaper a prize essay question, asking whether advances in the sciences and arts had improved morals. So overcome was he by the flood of ideas that this question aroused in him the realization that he had to break his journey. The rest of his life's work was, he claimed, determined for him at that moment. Rousseau's primary claim to fame depends on his ideas about morals, politics and society. Perhaps his best-known remark is 'Man is born free; and everywhere he is in chains'; this reveals his preoccupation with issues of freedom in the state.

In answer to the prize essay question Rousseau argued that men and morals were corrupted and debilitated by advances in higher learning. The goal of prestigious distinction is substituted for that of doing useful work for the good of all. This theme, of people seeking invidious ascendancy by doing others down – the effect of exacerbated amour-propre *– pervades Rousseau's social theorizing generally. His essay,* Discourse on the Sciences and Arts *(1750), won the prize; related concerns shape the more profound* Discourse on the Origin of Inequality *of 1755. In his most famous work of political theory,* The Social Contract *(1762), Rousseau presents an alternative approach to how we might achieve a just and legitimate civil order. All members of society should take an equal place as members of the sovereign authority and societal laws should come from the general will by which a people gives rules to itself. Only under such a system, Rousseau argues, will humankind live on equal terms bound by fraternal ties, enjoying as much freedom and rights of self-determination as is possible in a stable community. Speaking up in this way for the equal political standing of all, regardless of birth or wealth, Rousseau points the way towards the dissolution of the* ancien régime *and the emergence of more democratically based polities. Precisely what influence his ideas had on the French Revolution is impossible to determine, although his name was often invoked.*

Rousseau also wrote extensively on education. In his Émile *(subtitled* On Education, *1762) he tries to show how a child could be brought up free of the aggressive desire to dominate others. Instead that child can be caused to want to cooperate with others on a footing of mutual respect. He hopes by this to show that his social proposals are not an unrealizable dream. In this work there are also criticisms of religious dogma and church practices which brought severe condemnation onto Rousseau. He had to flee Paris in 1762 to avoid imprisonment. This, and other related experiences, plunged him into a protracted period of mental distress in which he feared he was the object of the plotting of others. These others came to include David Hume, with whom Rousseau had hoped to find refuge in England in 1766.*

Still troubled in mind, Rousseau returned to France the next year, and during the last decade of his life he wrote several works of self-explanation and self-justification. The greatest of these is his autobiography, Confessions *(written between 1764 and 1775, published posthumously), but there are other more prolix writings. After an accident in 1776, the worst of Rousseau's mental disturbance seems to have cleared and his last substantive work, an album of miscellaneous reflections on his life, ideas and experiences (*Reveries of the Solitary Walker, *written 1776–8), has a clarity and balance which had been absent for so long.*

1 **Life and writings**
2 **Works leading up to** *The Social Contract*
3 *The Social Contract*
4 *Émile* **(or** *On Education***)**
5 **Controversial works**
6 *La Nouvelle Héloïse* **and other literary works**
7 **Autobiography and other personal works**

1 Life and writings

Brought up by his father for the first ten years of his life after the death of his mother, Rousseau traced his love of republican Rome to the reading of Plutarch that he and his father used to do. This love, along with the idolization of his native Geneva, provided the inspiration for many of his political ideas. After being involved in a fight, Rousseau's father fled Geneva in 1722 and Rousseau was sent to live with his cousin not far from Geneva for a couple of years. This period in his youth is exquisitely evoked by Rousseau in Book One of *Confessions* (1764–75). When he returned to Geneva his more lowly social station became apparent and he was indentured to an engraver, Abel Ducommun, a brutal and ill-educated man.

Restless and dissatisfied, Rousseau was more than glad to take advantage of the mischance of being locked out of the city on a Sunday in 1728. He walked away from that life, seeking the help of a Catholic priest who sent him to see Françoise-Louise de la Tour, Baronne de Warens, who was in receipt of money to secure more Catholic converts. She sent him, in turn, to Turin for instruction and Rousseau was admitted to the Church in April 1728. It is doubtful that Rousseau had any deep spiritual involvement in this process; he was more anxious to retain others' interest in him. He had a number of shortlived jobs in Turin. In one of these, he lied about stealing a ribbon and put the blame on a servant girl. This wicked deed preyed on his mind for the rest of his life.

The next year, he made his way back to Madame de Warens. He learned the rudiments of music and his passion for music was a dominant force in his life at this time. By the Autumn of 1731 he had moved in permanently with Madame de Warens. They lived a life of innocent delight for some years, she calling him *petit* and he calling her *maman*. He became her lover in 1733, although he appears never to have enjoyed this almost incestuous relationship. He read avidly during this time, laying a foundation for many of his later writings.

This idyll did not endure, however. Rousseau was displaced in Madame de Warens's affections in 1738. Considerably aggrieved, he took up the post of tutor to the two sons of Jean Bonnot de Mably in Lyons in 1740. Not an adept teacher, he gave up the post after a year determined to make his way in the larger world of Paris where he moved in 1742 (two short essays on education date from this time).

Once there, he presented a paper on musical notation to the Academy of Sciences; this was published in 1743 as *Dissertation on Modern Music*. In that year, Rousseau went to Venice as secretary to the French Ambassador. They quarrelled and Rousseau returned to Paris to resume his musical compositions. About this time he set up home with his mistress, Thérèse Levasseur, who was to be his lifelong companion. He had a number of children by her, whom he abandoned to his later shame. Rousseau had also begun to keep the company of the rising Parisian intelligensia. DIDEROT was a personal friend and it was while on the way to visit him during one of his periodic bouts of imprisonment that Rousseau had the experience that fixed the course of the rest of his life. The Academy at Dijon had advertised a prize essay question asking whether the advancements in the sciences and arts had improved morals. Rousseau saw this and was so overwhelmed by a flood of insights evoked by it that (he said) he spent the rest of his life trying to put into words what he had seen in one hour. Rousseau, answering the question with a firm 'No', won the prize and his essay was published in 1750 under the title *Discourse on the Sciences and Arts*. He was poised to begin a new career as social critic, moralist and philosopher, but his last triumphs as a composer and musical theoretician also occur about this time. His opera *Le Devin du Village* was performed before the King at Fontainebleau in 1752 and his *Letter on French Music* (1753) created an enormous stir as part of a large-scale argument over the relative merits of the French and Italian styles.

Rousseau was soon to turn his back on Parisian society. He wrote a further, very original, essay on social questions, *Discourse on the Origin of Inequality* (1755) but then withdrew to the countryside the better to meditate and write about his new concerns, attracting the scorn of many of his erstwhile friends. Around this time he returned to the protestant faith of his childhood, and reclaimed his citizenship of Geneva. The *Discourse on the Origin of Inequality* has a passionate dedication to Geneva.

During the next six years, Rousseau wrote the bulk of his greatest work: his masterpiece of educational theory, *Émile* (1762); of political theory, *The Social Contract* (1762); but also a best-selling novel, *La Nouvelle Héloïse* (1761) and a host of smaller pieces: the *Letter to M. d'Alembert on the Theatre* (1758); the *Letter to Voltaire on Providence* (1756), the *Moral Letters* (1757–8), written to Sophie d'Houdetot with whom Rousseau was then desperately in love.

Catastrophe befell Rousseau in 1762 after the publication of *Émile*. A section of it, the so-called *Creed of a Savoyard Vicar*, was judged unacceptable by the religious authorities and out of fear of being imprisoned Rousseau fled Paris in June 1762. Unsettled years followed, mostly spent in different parts of Switzerland. Rousseau wrote extensively in defence of himself and his work during this time, including his *Letter to Christophe de Beaumont, Archbishop of Paris* (1763) written in reply to the condemnation of the *Creed of a Savoyard Vicar*; and his *Lettres Écrites de la Montagne* (Letters Written from the Mountain) (1764), a response to criticism of him made by Geneva's attorney-general. From January 1766 Rousseau spent just over a year in England at the invitation and in the company of David HUME. Rousseau, almost always a touchy and suspicious person, was at that time in the grip of a severe paranoiac breakdown and he became convinced Hume was plotting to humiliate him. An account of this sorry episode was given by Hume (*A Concise Account*, 1766). Exhausted and ill, Rousseau returned to France in early 1767 and sought refuge well away from the public gaze near Grenoble where he married Thérèse.

The tide of public opinion was slowly turning, and in 1770 he returned to Paris very much a celebrated figure and object of curiosity, even though he was banned from writing and speaking on controversial matters. Despite his grave mental distress, Rousseau had, from around 1764, been working on his great autobiography, *Confessions*. He completed part one by 1770. He gave some private readings of parts of the text; these also were banned. Other personal works occupied the bulk of the last decade of his life. There is an extensive essay in self-justification and defence, *Rousseau Judge of Jean-Jacques: Dialogues* (1772–6). Its completion was marked by another episode of desperate mental anguish as Rousseau attempted to place the manuscript on the altar at Nôtre Dame. Later in 1776, returning home from a walk, Rousseau was knocked down by a dog. This accident seems, miraculously, to have cleared his mind and his last work, *Reveries of the Solitary Walker* (1776–8) has a simplicity and clarity of manner missing from the writings of the preceding years.

Not all his work was in self-vindication however. He wrote at length on the political problems of Poland (*Considerations on the Government of Poland* (1769–70); he prepared a *Dictionary of Music* (1767) and he botanized extensively, also writing some short works on botany (*Elementary Letters on Botany and Dictionary of Botanical Terms*, uncompleted). He died at Ermenonville in June 1778, outlived by Thérèse for twenty-two years.

It is useful to give more information about Rousseau's life than is usual for most philosophers or political theorists, since so much of his work arises from events in his life or is directly about himself. This is, however, not so true of his principal works of social and political theory, just because they are works more purely of theory. They provide the most solid basis for Rousseau's reputation, and an account of these follows.

2 Works leading up to *The Social Contract*

From 1750 onwards, Rousseau developed increasingly deeper and more sophisticated ideas about the origin and nature of the condition of man in society and about what could and should be done to ameliorate that condition. His discussion of these themes in his first serious work, *Discourse on the Sciences and Arts*, is fairly shallow. He argues that increasing scientific knowledge and refinement of arts and letters does not at all produce an improvement of morals either in individuals or in society at large. On the contrary, such sophistication is the offshoot of luxury and idleness and it has developed principally to feed people's vanity and desire for ostentatious and aggressive self-display. All these features work against the moral virtues of loyalty to one's country, courage in its defence and dedication to useful callings. Rousseau allows for the fact that there are a few people of genius who genuinely enrich humanity by their ideas. But the majority of us are not improved, but harmed, by exposure to the 'higher learning'.

This essay attracted considerable notice and a number of replies, to which Rousseau responded with care. But he did not continue immediately with his works of social criticism. His musical interests intervened, although with some of these his social and moral ideas became entwined. In his *Letter on French Music* (1753), Rousseau criticizes French music as monotonous, thin and without colour because the spoken language (in which all music is rooted) is thus also. This is because, as Rousseau explains in his *Essay on the Origin of Languages* (1755–60, but never completed), the French language has been shaped by the imperatives of calling for help and controlling other people, which require harshness

and clarity above all else. In warmer southern climes it is the sweet accents of love and passion which colour the language and hence the supremacy of Italian opera. Thus social and political demands shape even the nature of music, according to Rousseau. Effective government also requires sharp, impressive utterance, he maintains, and it is to the origin and function of government that Rousseau turns in his so-called second *Discourse*, the *Discourse on the Origin and Foundations of Inequality*, to give it its full title. This is a very substantial essay and one of Rousseau's most important works.

In *Discourse on the Origin and Foundations of Inequality* Rousseau gives an account of the 'fall' of natural humankind, its degeneration and corruption as it joins together with others to make up tribes, societies and eventually states. Natural man (the 'noble savage') left alone in his natural environment is self-sufficient, largely absorbed in present feeling without foresight or recollection, solitary, peaceable and, in fact, most often asleep. (Rousseau may well have had the orang-utan in view here.) Inclement circumstances, increase in numbers (arising from hasty couplings in the forest devoid of all the artificial trappings of romantic love), force people to live together. Sexual jealousy, the desire for domination, vindictive resentments grow up as men come to demand esteem and deference. *Amour-propre*, an anxious concern for tribute to be paid to one's status, replaces *amour de soi*, a simple healthy concern for one's own natural wellbeing. Men begin to compete for precedence and life is tainted by aggression and spite. Those who have acquired dominance then conspire together to consolidate their position. They argue that everyone needs a more peaceable and stable society, which can only be achieved through the apparatus of government, law, punishments. Thus it is that they consolidate the *status quo*, but without right or justice and acting only to perpetuate unfair privilege and the oppression of the weak.

This extraordinarily subversive essay seems to have attracted no official censure; that came later in connection with other works. Rousseau's other significant essay on political themes from this period is the so-called *Discourse on Political Economy* (1755, first published separately 1758), which began life as an entry for Diderot and D'Alembert's *Encyclopaedia* (1751–72; see D'ALEMBERT). A very eloquently written piece, it shows clear signs of being a preliminary study for *The Social Contract*. Much play is made with the idea of the sovereignty of all the people over themselves, expressing their legislative intent through the general will. Emphasis is laid on the need to cultivate patriotic republican loyalties in citizens if a just society of equals united by common care and respect is ever to arise and to survive. The essay ends with a discussion of taxation and fiscal issues, but the principal force of the argument lies in the discussion of the source of legitimate law in 'the people'. It is this same issue which Rousseau places at the centre of his now most famous work, *The Social Contract*.

3 *The Social Contract*

This work is generally regarded as an essential entry in the canon of classic works in political theory and as Rousseau's masterpiece. Many people read nothing else of his. This is a pity, for many of the themes in it are rendered unnecessarily hard to understand by being taken in isolation. Also, the work is in some ways poorly constructed and uses idea drawn from different times in Rousseau's development. As he says in a prefatory note to the work, it is the only residue remaining of a project begun many years before. However, we must take the work as we find it. Its present reputation would perhaps have surprised contemporary readers. *Émile* was considered a more seditious work; and *La Nouvelle Héloïse* regarded as the most perfect exhibition of Rousseau's genius. Certainly Hume regarded Rousseau's own good opinion of *The Social Contract* as quite absurd.

The Social Contract is divided into four parts. Roughly speaking, Book One concerns the proper basis for the foundation of a legitimate political order; Book Two the origin and functions of the sovereign body within that order; Book Three considers the role of government, which Rousseau treats as a subsidiary body in the state deriving its powers from the sovereign; and Book Four considers more issues regarding a just society, treating of the Roman republic at some length and of the functions of civil religion. It is important always to remember that the book is subtitled: *The Principles of Political Right*. Rousseau's paramount concerns are normative, with the nature and basis of legitimacy, justice and right and not simply with *de facto* political structures. A useful brief summary of the principal themes of the work is given in Book Five of *Émile*, as part of Émile's political education.

Rousseau argues that it is our lack of individual self-sufficiency that requires us to associate together into society. But, when we do so, we do not want to have to accept a condition of enslavement as the price of our survival. Freedom is an essential human need and the mark of humanity; mere survival without that does not constitute a human life. Rousseau holds that freedom and association can only be combined if all the persons of the association make up the sovereign body for that association, that is, the final author-

itative body which declares the law by which the people wish to bind themselves. This law is a declaration of the 'general will'.

The notion of the general will is wholly central to Rousseau's theory of political legitimacy (see GENERAL WILL). It is, however, an unfortunately obscure and controversial notion. Some commentators see it as no more than the dictatorship of the poletariat or the tyranny of the urban poor (such as may perhaps be seen in the French Revolution). Such was not Rousseau's meaning. This is clear from the *Discourse on Political Economy* where Rousseau emphasizes that the general will exists to protect individuals against the mass, not to require them to be sacrificed to it. He is, of course, sharply aware that men have selfish and sectional interests which will lead them to try to oppress others. It is for this reason that loyalty to the good of all alike must be a supreme (although not exclusive) commitment by everyone, not only if a truly general will is to be heeded, but also if it is to be formulated successfully in the first place.

This theme is taken up in Book Two. Here Rousseau appeals to the charisma of a quasi-divine legislator to inspire people to put the good of their whole community above their own narrow selfish interest and thereby gain a greater good for themselves. In the course of this Book, Rousseau alludes to Corsica as having a people who have the sentiments and capacities to establish just laws and a good state (Book Two, ch. 10). His passing remark that 'I have the feeling that some day that little island will astonish Europe' has caused some fancifully to suppose that he foresaw the emergence of Napoléon.

Book Three of *The Social Contract* concerns the role of government. Rousseau knows that governors often rule in their own interest, not in the interests of their community. For this reason he argues that governmental functions must be thoroughly subordinate to the sovereign judgment of the people and that it is essential to adjust the form and powers of government to suit the different circumstances (size, dispersion and so on) of different states. It still surprises some readers that Rousseau has no particular enthusiasm for democratic government. Of course, the constitution and functions of the sovereign body are a different matter.

Book Four has something of a disjointed character. Rousseau discusses the Roman republic at considerable length, principally to hold it up as a model from which, in his opinion, there has been a terrible falling away. But he also discusses civil religion, arguing that divine sanctions should be joined to civil laws the better to procure obedience to them and people's loyalty to the common good of all in their nation.

Rousseau made wholly central to his vision of

political right the union of free and equal men devising for themselves the laws under which they shall then proceed to live their lives as citizens one with another of their own state. In doing so he depicted a form of political community which exerts a very great appeal and influence on the modern imagination. We are still learning to live with the consequences of that appeal.

Rousseau's political concerns were not confined to theory alone. On two occasions he was approached for help with the political affairs and constitutional problems of countries. In 1764 he wrote an unfinished fragment, A *Project for a Constitution for Corsica*, in response to a plea for help and guidance from the Corsican rebels. Then again, in 1769–70, Rousseau wrote extensively on the constitutional and legislative problems facing Poland (*Considerations on the Government of Poland*) in response to a request from persons opposed to Russian domination. This work (not properly published in Rousseau's lifetime) is a substantial essay which throws a lot of light on how Rousseau envisaged his theoretical notions working out in historically specific situations. He reveals many shrewd and hard-headed practical insights.

4 *Émile* (or *On Education*)

There is some evidence that Rousseau regarded *Émile* as his most mature and well-achieved work. In his self-evaluating *Rousseau Judge of Jean-Jacques: Dialogues* (1772–6) he specifies it as the book in which someone who is truly concerned to understand him will find his ideas most deeply and comprehensively expressed. Posterity has, perhaps unfortunately, not generally endorsed this evaluation.

Precisely when he began work on *Émile* is unclear, but it must have been around 1759 when Rousseau was at the peak of his creative powers. Its immediate occasion seems to have been a request from certain of his distinguished women friends to give them his advice about the upbringing of their children; and indeed, the subtitle of the book is *On Education*. However, within this framework Rousseau gives us his deepest ideas about the origins of human evil and wickedness and about the prospects for a whole and happy life.

Émile is structured as the narrative of the upbringing of a young man (Émile himself) who is to be spared the pain and loss of human corruption but made whole and entire by following the teachings of 'nature'. The work also includes in Book Four, a long more-or-less self-contained essay on the basis and nature of religious belief, called the *Creed of a Savoyard Vicar*. Rousseau puts his religious ideas into the mouth of a fictitious priest, although one modelled on priests he had previously known. It was this section which attracted the condemnation of the Catholic authorities and led to the burning of the book in June 1762. Rousseau then fled Paris, condemned to almost ten years of distress and displacement. He wrote at some length in defence of these religious ideas, in his *Letter to Christophe de Beaumont, Archbishop of Paris* of 1763 (see §5).

Rousseau held that most men and women in contemporary society were corrupted and their lives deformed because of the nature and basis of their social relationships and of the civil order (see §2). That man is good by nature, but is perverted by society is perhaps the dominant theme of *Émile*. Thus, if a person is to live a whole and rewarding life they must first be protected from such damaging influences and then be given the personal resources and emotional and moral dispositions to enable them to develop in a creative, harmonious and happy way once they do enter society. The principal discussions in *Émile* are devoted to studying the deepest causes of health or sickness in human development, both those internal to the individual and those coming from external influences, at each stage in the growth and maturation of a person from infancy to adulthood.

In early life it is the tendency to imperious rage and the petulant demand for others' immediate compliance to one's wishes that must be checked. Children must certainly not be tormented, but neither must they be indulged since that gives rise to both misplaced expectations and to even less capacity to cope with setbacks. Children need to be treated in a steady, predictable and methodical way, as if not in contact with other humans at all at first. Thus they learn to manage in a practical and efficacious way with concrete issues and not to engage in a battle of wills and in contention for dominance.

This motif of living according to nature – that is, according to the actualities of our powers and real circumstances – continues as Émile matures. As and when he needs to find a place for himself in society he will not try to control all that is around him and be aggrieved if he cannot as if he were a despot. Rather, he will seek to establish relations grounded in friendship, mutual respect and cooperation proper to finite and needy beings. Our capacity to feel compassion for each other and our acceptance of compassion with gratitude forms, in Rousseau's view, the fundamental basis for human union and the true explanation of the Golden Rule. Real moral demands are not imposed on us from outside, nor are they precepts discovered by reason. Rather, they express the requirements by which a bond of creative respect can be sustained between equals. This same issue of maintaining self-possession and mutual respect shapes Rousseau's treatment of marriage and sexual relations in Book Five. Such intimate union holds out the greatest hopes of human happiness, but can also lead to enslavement to the whims of the beloved. Feminist critics have found Rousseau's depiction of the character and role of Émile's intended, Sophie, objectionable, in that she appears to be stereotyped as largely passive and destined for traditional domestic occupations.

In the controversial material on religious belief Rousseau argues that we know God not by reason, but through simple feelings and convictions much deeper and more permanent than any theorems of reason. Such feelings teach us that the world is animated by a loving and powerful intelligence, who is God. Rousseau spends some time denouncing religious factionalism and intolerance which he sees as wholly incompatible with Christ's message of love and forgiveness. There can be no serious doubt that these are Rousseau's own thoughts. The rhetorical distance provided by the figure of the vicar is very slight.

In his deep and subtle psychological insights into the damage aggression does, not just simply to the victims of aggression, but in a complex and concealed way to the aggressors themselves, Rousseau shows the greatness of his mind in *Émile*.

5 Controversial works

Rousseau did not take the condemnation of the *Creed of a Savoyard Vicar* lightly. Almost as soon as he had settled again after his flight from Paris, he wrote a lengthy reply to the criticism of his work made by Christophe de Beaumont, Archbishop of Paris. Written in the form of a letter, Rousseau defends the fundamental tenets of his work. He has always held, he says, that man is naturally good, but corrupted by society. It is therefore a mystery why his work should only now be singled out for condemnation. He then mounts a point-by-point reply to the Archbishop's criticisms, arguing that the religion of the priests and the dogmas of the church must never be confused with the true gospel of charity and love taught by Christ. This *Letter to Christophe de Beaumont, Archbishop of Paris* was published in 1763. It ends on a note of self-aggrandizement. So far from being reviled, Rousseau says, statues of himself should be erected throughout Europe.

Just a year later, Rousseau published his extensive *Lettres Écrites de la Montagne* (Letters Written from the Mountain). In 1763, the Genevan attorney-general, Jean-Robert Tronchin, had written in defence of the authorities in their condemnation of Rousseau's works in his *Letters Written from the Country* (hence Rousseau's oppositional title). Rousseau again replies

at length, arguing that the Geneval political system had become very corrupt, but also defending once more the basic principles of his thought.

These two works date from the period just after the condemnation of Rousseau's most famous works. But prior to that he had also been engaged in some controversial exchanges. In 1758 he wrote the *Letter to M. d'Alembert on the Theatre* in which he argues that to establish a theatre in Geneva would corrupt the honest morals and civil integrity of that city-state. This was in opposition to D'Alembert's argument, presented in an article on Geneva for the *Encyclopaedia*, that a theatre would improve the cultural life of that city. However, such sophistication is not a benefit, in Rousseau's opinion; it goes along with deceit and the abandonment of morally commendable activities. Rousseau writes with great verve in this essay, harking back to some of his themes in his first discourse, *Discourse on the Sciences and Arts*.

A similar clash between urbane civilization and (what Rousseau liked to see as his own) plainness and simplicity of heart occurs in the exchange with VOLTAIRE on the providence of God (written in 1756; Voltaire may also have been an influence on D'Alembert). Voltaire, in his poem on the Lisbon earthquake, had written scornfully of Leibnizian optimism that all is for the best in the best of all possible worlds. Rousseau retorts that one must rest one's certainty of God's providence in feeling, not on the subtleties of philosophical reasoning. More personally, he says that it is surprising to find the wealthy and successful Voltaire complaining against God when he, Rousseau, who lives in poverty and obscurity, sees only the blessings of existence. This *Letter to Voltaire on Providence* also makes some very sharp points against religious intolerance, prefiguring the ideas of the *Creed of a Savoyard Vicar*. Rousseau's controversial writings are among his most eloquent, even though they do not generally add much to our appreciation of his overall intellectual achievement.

6 *La Nouvelle Héloïse* and other literary works

Outside the narrow circle of the intelligentsia and his aristocratic patrons, Rousseau was probably best known during his lifetime for his novel of illicit passion, reconciliation and self-transcendence, *Julie, ou La Nouvelle Héloïse*. At a time when works in different genres were not so sharply compartmentalized, David Hume for one saw in this novel the most perfect expression of Rousseau's genius and could not understand why Rousseau seemed to value *The Social Contract* more.

Rousseau professed himself surprised and dismayed to be writing the work. In 1756 he had turned his back on the hot-house world of fashionable Parisian society, wishing to dedicate the rest of his life to working for the good of humankind. However, as he took solitary walks in the forest of Montmorency, be became absorbed in an imaginary world of passion and illicit love. In a fever of erotic ecstasy he wrote the first of the letters between Julie, her tutor-lover Saint-Preux and her friend and cousin Claire. Saint-Preux confesses his love for Julie; a love which she tries to fend off through intimate conversations instructing him to be virtuous and pure. Of course, this does not work and she finally gives herself over to him in a passion. But her father has other plans for her. She is betrothed to the Baron de Wolmar; Saint-Preux leaves and not until much later does he return to become tutor once more, but now to Julie's two young sons. Wolmar (who has come to know of their earlier intimacy), leaves Julie and Saint-Preux alone on his model estate at Clarens. Saint-Preux confesses that he had never ceased to love Julie, but the novel ends tragically with the death of Julie, who has contracted pneumonia after having saved one of her children from drowning.

As Rousseau wrote this work nature seemed to imitate art. Sophie d'Houdetot, the sister-in-law of Madame d'Épinay whose house Rousseau was then living in, visited him and Rousseau fell in love with her. He saw in her the incarnation of his imaginary Julie. The relationship did not endure. Rousseau became morbidly suspicious that his middle-aged love was being mocked behind his back by his erstwhile friends.

La Nouvelle Héloïse was published in 1761 and was a bestseller. It is seldom read these days, except to be mined for ideas which might illuminate Rousseau's social and political philosophy. Wolmar's model estate is sometimes argued to be Rousseau's own vision of an ideal community, with rigid paternalistic control and substantial manipulation of the inhabitants by the all-seeing, all-knowing Wolmar. It is scarcely clear that this was Rousseau's intention. The fact that Julie dies, despite living at Clarens, may be taken to imply that it provides no adequate human habitation.

The rest of Rousseau's literary output is slight. It includes a number of mostly short poems, dating from the early 1740s, some plays (also mostly early), one of which *Narcissus* (Self-Lover), received performance in 1752 and for which Rousseau wrote a substantial preface explaining how his theatrical writing could be squared with his then political and social polemic against civilized letters.

7 Autobiography and other personal works

The last ten or so years of Rousseau's life were primarily given over to the writing of works of autobiography and other substantial essays of self-explanation and justification. These were presaged in his four *Letters to Malesherbes* written in 1762, just before the catastrophe of the banning of *Émile* and *The Social Contract*. Malesherbes, although official censor and likely to be suspicious of Rousseau's subversive ideas, in fact took a highly intelligent and sympathetic interest in his work. Rousseau became fearful that the printing of *Émile* was being held up by Jesuit plotting. Through Madame de Luxembourg, Malesherbes was contacted and able to put Rousseau's mind to rest. Rousseau expressed his gratitude by writing to Malesherbes four semi-confessional letters, setting out the principal events of his life and trying to make his motives and character plain to Malesherbes. Rousseau writes that he is not a misanthrope; he seeks the country only because he can live there more freely and fully as himself. He wants, in fact, nothing more than to serve humankind, but he can best do this by keeping himself apart and not getting embroiled in quarrels and back-stabbing.

Around this time Rousseau began to assemble materials towards writing an autobiography. He worked on and off at this until 1767, by which time part one of what we now know as *Confessions* was completed. This still extraordinary work of self-disclosure and candour is one of the most remarkable books ever written. It includes some beautiful writing about childhood and about his travels, but also revelations of a most intimate and shameful kind. Part one covers the period up to 1741–2, when Rousseau left Madame de Warens to make his way in Paris. Part two (1769–70) is less successful. Rousseau's morbid fears sometimes surface here as he describes the events of the years 1742–65, including his foolish passion for Sophie d'Houdetot, the writing and publication of *Émile*, and so on. The book breaks off in 1765, just as Rousseau is about to leave for England in the company of Hume, there (he believed) further to be ensnared. As the revelation of the quality of being of another human soul, *Confessions* is almost without equal.

Another lengthy work of self-explanation is *Rousseau Judge of Jean-Jacques: Dialogues* (published, like *Confessions*, posthumously). This is in three parts, cast in the form of dialogues between 'Rousseau' and 'a Frenchman', who together try to delve beneath the surface to find out the true nature of 'Jean-Jacques', the real Rousseau. The innumerable lies put about regarding Jean-Jacques are considered and exposed in the first part; in the second, a visit is paid to him and his true character is revealed; in the third part, a careful reading of his works is made and their true meaning explained. Although sometimes obsessively detailed and very repetitive, this work has considerable interest for the light it throws on Rousseau's own estimate of his achievement. The overall tone is, it is thought, marred by lengthy self-justification.

Rousseau's last work of self-accounting is *Reveries of the Solitary Walker* (left unfinished at his death). Cast in the form of 'Walks', it comprises a series of reflections, ideas and meditations which supposedly occurred to Rousseau as he went on his perambulations in and around Paris. Rousseau returns to special moments in his life – his love for Mme de Warens; the episode of the stolen ribbon; his 'illumination' on the way to see Diderot. But he also reflects for one last time on some of his major intellectual preoccupations – on the depth of *amour-propre*; on the sources of malice and on the nature of happiness. There is a clear steadiness of vision which pervades this work which contrasts markedly with the often distressed and distressing writing of the preceding five years.

After his death, Rousseau's grave on the Île des Peupliers at Ermenonville became a place of pilgrimage for Parisians and Rousseau was embraced as one of the great sons of France. His influence remains very great, not only because of his political writings which have become part of the permanent canon of works in political theory, but also because of his more imponderable effect on sensibility and attitudes. His love of nature and stress on the value of the simple life, as well as his far-reaching explorations of his own character and feelings, make him a central figure in the development of romanticism. The emphasis in his educational writings on discouraging the coercion of the child into tasks which are apparently pointless, undoubtedly influenced the work of Montessori and A.S. Neill (see EDUCATION, HISTORY OF PHILOSOPHY OF). Even Rousseau's musical writings and compositions, seldom studied these days, made a marked impact on the history of opera in particular. His place as one of the major figures of Western civilization is secure, even though he can still attract violent differences of opinion.

See also: CONTRACTARIANISM; ENLIGHTENMENT, CONTINENTAL; LANGUAGE, EARLY MODERN PHILOSOPHY OF; POLITICAL PHILOSOPHY, HISTORY OF; SOCIETY, CONCEPT OF

List of works

There is no complete standard English translation of Rousseau's works. The most ambitious undertaking (edited by Masters and Kelly) is still in progress. It is listed here with two French editions of Rousseau's complete works, followed by selected works in French and English and individual works in English.

Collected works:

Cole, G.D.H. (ed. and trans.) (1973) *The Social Contract and Discourses*, London: Dent. (Revised and augmented by J.H. Brumfitt and J.C. Hall. Contains principal writings on political theory; an excellent selection in English.)
Gagnebin, B. and Raymond, M. (eds) (1959–95) *Jean-Jacques Rousseau: Oeuvres Complètes*, Paris: Gallimard, 5 vols. (The standard modern edition.)
Grimsley, R. (ed.) (1970) *Rousseau: Religious Writings*, Oxford: Clarendon Press. (Selected works in French.)
Launay, M. (ed.) (1967–71) *Rousseau: Oeuvres Complètes*, Paris: Éditions du Seuil, 3 vols. (Also valuable.)
Leigh, R.A. (ed.) (1965–89) *Correspondance Complète de Jean-Jacques Rousseau*, Geneva and Banbury: Voltaire Foundation, 50 vols. (One of the greatest scholarly achievements of this century and an indispensable source for Rousseau studies.)
Mason, J.H. (ed.) (1979) *The Indispensable Rousseau*, London: Quartet. (Offers selections in English from across the total range of Rousseau's writings.)
Masters, R.D. and Kelly, C. (eds) (1990–) *The Collected Writings of Rousseau*, Hanover, NH and London: University Press of New England, 5 vols to date. (Vol. 1: *Rousseau Judge of Jean-Jacques* (1990); vol. 2: *Discourse on the Sciences and Arts and Polemics* (1992); vol. 3: *Discourse on the Origin of Inequality, Polemics and Political Economy* (1992); vol. 4: *The Social Contract and short pieces* (1994); vol. 5: *Confessions* (1995) – the most up-to-date English translation, with excellent notes.)
Vaughan, C.E. (ed.) (1915) *The Political Writings of Jean-Jacques Rousseau*, Cambridge: Cambridge University Press, 2 vols. (Selected works in French.)

Individual works:

Rousseau, J.-J. (1743) *Dissertation on Modern Music*, trans. L. Hewitt, in *Project Concerning New Symbols for Music*, Kilkenny, 1982.
—— (1750) *Discourse on the Sciences and Arts*, in G.D.H. Cole (ed. and trans.) *The Social Contract and Discourses*, London: Dent, 1973; also in V. Gourevitch (ed.) *The First and Second Discourses together with the Replies to Critics*, New York: Harper & Row, 1986.
—— (1753) *Letter on French Music*, trans. in part in *Source Readings in Music History*, O. Strunk (ed.) London: Faber & Faber, 1950.
—— (1755) *Discourse on the Origin of Inequality*, in G.D.H. Cole (ed. and trans.) *The Social Contract and Discourses*, London: Dent, 1973; also in V.

Gourevitch (ed.) *The First and Second Discourses together with the Replies to Critics*, New York: Harper & Row, 1986.

—— (1755) *A Discourse on Political Economy*, in G.D.H. Cole (ed. and trans.) *The Social Contract and Discourses*, London: Dent, 1973; also in R.D. Masters (ed.) *On The Social Contract with Geneva Manuscript and Political Economy*, New York: Harper & Row, 1978.

—— (1755–60) *Essay on the Origin of Languages*, in J.H. Moran and A. Gode (eds) *On the Origin of Languages*, New York: University of Chicago Press, 1966; also in V. Gourevitch (ed.) *The First and Second Discourses together with the Replies to Critics*, New York: Harper & Row, 1986. (Written around 1755–60, but not completed.)

—— (1756) *Letter to Voltaire on Providence*, trans. in part in *The Indispensible Rousseau*, J.H. Mason (ed.) London: Quartet, 1979.

—— (1757–8) *Moral Letters*. (No English translation currently available.)

—— (1758) *Letter to M. d'Alembert on the Theatre*, in A. Bloom (ed. and trans.) *Politics and the Arts: Rousseau's Letter to M. d'Alembert*, Ithaca, NY: Cornell University Press, 1960.

—— (1761) *La Nouvelle Héloïse*, abridged and trans. J.H. McDowell, Philadelphia, PA: Pennsylvania State University Press, 1968; also trans. W. Kenrick, *Eloisa, or a Series of Original Letters*, Oxford: Woodstock Books, 1989. (Facsimile reprint of an 1803 translation).

—— (1762) *Letters to Malesherbes*, in C.W. Hendel (ed. and trans.) *Citizen of Geneva*, Oxford: Oxford University Press, 1937.

—— (1762) *Émile, or On Education*, trans. A. Bloom, New York: Basic Books, 1979; repr. London: Penguin, 1991.

—— (1762) *The Social Contract*, in G.D.H. Cole (ed. and trans.) *The Social Contract and Discourses*, London: Dent, 1973; also in R.D. Masters (ed.) *On the Social Contract with Geneva Manuscript and Political Economy*, New York: St Martin's Press, 1978; also in M. Cranston (ed.) *The Social Contract*, Harmondsworth: Penguin, 1968.

—— (1763) *Lettre à Christophe de Beaumont* (Letter to Christophe de Beaumont), in J.H. Mason (ed.) *The Indispensable Rousseau*, London: Quartet, 1979. (Parts only; this work does not exist in whole in English translation.)

—— (1764) *Lettres Écrites de la Montagne* (Letters Written from the Mountain), in J.H. Mason (ed.) *The Indispensable Rousseau*, London: Quartet, 1979. (Parts only; this work does not exist in whole in English translation.)

—— (1764–5) *Project for a Constitution for Corsica*, in

F. Watkins (ed.) *Rousseau: Political Writings*, Edinburgh: Thomas Nelson, 1953.

—— (1764–75) *Confessions*, trans. J.M. Cohen, Harmondsworth: Penguin, 1954.

—— (1769–70) *Considerations on the Government of Poland*, in F. Watkins (ed.) *Rousseau: Political Writings*, Edinburgh: Thomas Nelson, 1953; also trans. W. Kendall, *Considerations: The Government of Poland*, Indianapolis, IN: Hackett, 1985.

—— (1767) *Dictionary of Music*. (Published posthumously; no English translation currently available.)

—— (1771–3) *Elementary Letters on Botany and Dictionary of Botanical Terms*, in *Botany: A Study of Pure Curiosity*, trans. P.J. Redouté, London: Michael Joseph, 1979. (The *Dictionary* is unfinished.)

—— (1772–6) *Rousseau Judge of Jean-Jacques: Dialogues*, trans. J.R. Bush, C. Kelly and R.D. Masters, ed. R.D. Masters and C. Kelly, Hanover, NH and London: University Press of New England, 1990.

—— (1776–8) *Reveries of the Solitary Walker*, trans. P. France, Harmondsworth: Penguin, 1979; trans. C.E. Butterworth, New York: Hackett, 1979.

References and further reading

Bloom, A. (1979) 'Introduction', *Émile, or On Education*, New York: Basic Books; repr. Harmondsworth: Penguin, 1991. (Revised edition of 'The education of democratic man', *Daedalus*, 107 (1978). An outstanding essay on *Émile*.)

Charvet, J. (1974) *The Social Problem in the Philosophy of Rousseau*, Cambridge: Cambridge University Press. (A lively analysis of Rousseau's social philosophy.)

Cranston, M. (1983–97) *Jean-Jacques*, vol. 1, London: Allen Lane, 1983; *The Noble Savage*, vol. 2, London: Allen Lane, 1991; *The Solitary Self*, vol. 3, London: Viking and Penguin, 1997. (A beautifully written and very insightful work.)

Crocker, L.G. (1968) *Jean-Jacques Rousseau: The Quest (1712–58)*; *The Prophetic Voice (1758–78)*, New York: Macmillan; 2nd edn 1973. (A very thorough treatment by a fairly hostile critic.)

Dent, N.J.H. (1988) *Rousseau*, Oxford: Blackwell. (Covers most of the psychological and political works.)

Gay, P. (1964) 'Reading about Rousseau', in *The Party of Humanity: Studies in the French Enlightenment*, London: Weidenfeld & Nicolson. (An exceptional essay on the reception and assessment of Rousseau's work.)

Grimsley, R. (1973) *The Philosophy of Rousseau*,

Oxford: Oxford University Press. (The best short introduction to Rousseau's work overall.)

Guehenno, J. (1966) *Jean-Jacques Rousseau*, London: Routledge, 2 vols. (An engaging biography, making good use of the correspondence.)

Lovejoy, A.O. (1948) 'Rousseau's supposed primitivism', in *Essays on the History of Ideas*, Baltimore, MD: John Hopkins Press, 1948. (A remarkable study of the *Discourse on the Origin of Inequality*.)

Masters, R.D. (1968) *The Political Philosophy of Jean-Jacques Rousseau*, Princeton: NJ, Princeton University Press. (A ground-breaking study of Rousseau's political ideas.)

Plamenatz, J. (1992) *Man and Society*, vol. 2, London: Longman. (A judicious and elegant short study of the political ideas.)

Shklar, J. (1969) *Men and Citizens*, Cambridge: Cambridge University Press. (A subtle and insightful study of the psychology and politics.)

Starobinski, J. (1971) *Jean-Jacques Rousseau: La Transparence et l'Obstacle*, trans. A. Goldhammer, *Transparency and Obstruction*, Chicago, IL: University of Chicago Press, 1988. (A very influential study by one of France's foremost critics.)

Wokler, R. (1987) *Rousseau on Society, Politics, Music and Language*, New York: Garland. (An exemplary scholarly work, particularly on the *Essay on the Origin of Languages*.)

N.J.H. DENT

ROYCE, JOSIAH (1855–1916)

Josiah Royce rose from a humble background in the California of the Gold Rush period to become Professor of the History of Philosophy at Harvard University and one of the most influential American philosophers of the so-called 'period of classical American philosophy' from the late nineteenth to the early twentieth century. He was also (along with F.H. Bradley) one of the two most important English-speaking philosophers of the period who defended philosophical idealism: the doctrine that in some sense or other all things either are minds or else are the contents of minds. Royce remained loyal to his own idealist commitments throughout his life, despite the fact that his friend and Harvard colleague William James was extremely hostile to idealism, and that his intellectual environment was increasingly dominated by the 'pragmatism' of which James was an outspoken champion. In later years, however, under the influence of another pragmatist, Charles S. Peirce, Royce gave the themes of his idealist thought a naturalistic social foundation rather than the abstract metaphysical foundation of his earliest writings. Royce's entire corpus is perhaps best seen as representing a bridge from the German world of Neo-Kantianism and various varieties of philosophical idealism to the American world of pragmatism and of philosophical naturalism.

1   Life
2   Ethical theory
3   Metaphysics
4   Mathematical logic
5   Ultimate position

1   Life

Josiah Royce was born on 20 November 1855 in Grass Valley, California. In the spring of 1866 Royce's family moved to San Francisco, where he attended grammar school and high school. From 1870 to 1875 Royce was a student at the University of California. From 1875 to 1876 he studied in Germany, principally among thinkers who were revitalizing Kant's thought or defending and modifying Hegel's thought. From 1876 to 1878 Royce did graduate work at The Johns Hopkins University, where he gave a series of lectures entitled *On the Return to Kant*, in which he both expounded and defended Kant. Royce received the Ph.D. degree from Johns Hopkins in 1878.

From 1878 to 1882 Royce taught English at the University of California at Berkeley, and during this period he married. In 1882, taking his wife and their new child with him, Royce went to Harvard University to replace William James, who was on temporary leave. This appointment developed into an assistant professorship in 1885; eventually, in 1892, Royce obtained a full professorship in the history of philosophy. In 1914 Royce was appointed Alford Professor at Harvard. Except for brief excursions, Royce remained at Harvard from his initial appointment in 1882 until his death on 14 September 1916.

In American philosophy prior to the First World War, Royce was an even greater force than James. He had many distinguished students, among them George Santayana, W.E.B. Du Bois, T.S. Eliot, and C.I. Lewis.

2   Ethical theory

Besides his work in mathematical logic, Royce's philosophical thought concentrated on ethics and on metaphysics, which latter topic included philosophy of religion. In both ethics and metaphysics Royce's thought was heavily influenced by Kant, much of whose philosophy Royce absorbed from Neo-Kantians during his year of study in Germany.

In his ethical theory, espoused for example in his book *The Philosophy of Loyalty* (1908a), Royce's highest ethical principle appealed to the idea of acting from 'loyalty to loyalty', a formula in which Royce captured an ethical notion closely akin to Kant's notion of acting 'from duty'. Just as Kant held that acting from duty meant acting in such a way that one's motive for acting is to be in accord with the ideal of duty itself, so Royce held that acting out of loyalty to loyalty meant acting in such a way that one's motive for acting is to be consistent with the ideal of loyalty in general (see KANTIAN ETHICS). With the beginning of the First World War the ethical dimensions of Royce's thinking took on a pronounced social and geopolitical air. Royce even wrote a treatise in 1914 on geopolitical morality, published as *War and Insurance*. Shocked by the German sinking of the *Lusitania* in 1915, Royce became a vehement supporter of the Allies, and 'loyalty' acquired in his usage a certain patriotic flavour. In general, however, the meaning of 'loyalty' in Royce's ethical thought is akin to that of 'commitment', and not to any especially patriotic or chauvinistic notion.

In his ethical thinking during the last four or five years before his death, Royce was going beyond a mere ethics of duty and freedom and was pressing towards a more general ethics of responsibility and the 'fitting'. The very last of Royce's ethical thoughts were devoted not so much to an attempt to specify the nature of right and wrong as to an effort to describe and justify the proper approach to life and life's challenges that a wise person takes.

In this regard Royce distinguished three stages of ethical maturity. In the first and least mature stage, the moral agent acts more or less naively, aiming their efforts at achieving goals. As a moral being, the agent attempts to be loyal to loyalty, and so to fulfil their duties and in general live a responsible life. But the agent has not yet confronted the difficulties life has to offer, its pains, frustrations, anxious cares, crushing burdens, demoralizing defeats. With such features of life the ethical agent still must learn to contend.

At the second, somewhat more mature, ethical stage the agent responds to the pains of life by achieving a kind of quiet resignation, turning inwards onto the self, that is to say towards meditation, self-control and self-alteration. But in this resignation to suffering, the agent ceases to attempt to alter the external world, or indeed anything in their relation to the external world other than the self. Indeed, this approach is broadly the stance of the mystic, the introvert, the meditator. Royce associates the second stage of ethical existence with some of the disciplines of oriental philosophy and religion.

At the third and highest stage of ethical maturity,

the agent has transcended both the naive stance of the first stage and the quietistic resignation of the second. Once again the agent is an active agent attempting to change the external world and not merely the self. But now the agent is fully aware of life's sufferings and of the fact that very probably most of their efforts, perhaps even all of them, will be in vain. Nevertheless, the agent acts, not expecting that the efforts will be rewarded with success. At this third stage, the object of acting is moral action in itself.

Royce's late ethics has a great deal in common with certain strains of twentieth-century thought in what has been called 'existentialism'. In particular it has a great deal in common with that variety of existentialism labelled 'absurdism' by the French philosopher Albert Camus. For Royce, just as for Camus, the mature life of bliss is to be found not in achievements but rather in strivings, not in what is accomplished but rather in the manner and quality of what is attempted (see EXISTENTIALISM). Only in the ethical life of striving while remaining free of all expectations regarding results is an agent immune from the frustrations of the first ethical stage and from the introspective isolation of the second.

3 Metaphysics

Royce's position in metaphysics was his own particular brand of idealism, which, despite its unique features, naturally had affinities with other forms of idealism. It had, for example, affiliations with the so-called 'subjective idealism' of Berkeley, whose principal doctrine was that all things are either minds or the contents of minds. Royce's idealism also in many key respects resembled the so-called 'transcendental idealism' of Kant, whose principal doctrine is that the objects of experience have no intelligibly conceivable existence outside of experience. In other respects Royce's position resembled the so-called 'metaphysical idealism' of Hegel, whose principal doctrine is that the world as we understand it is the evolutionary unfolding of a mental principle that we can call 'Spirit' (see BERKELEY, G. §3; HEGEL, G.W.F. §4; IDEALISM; KANT, I. §5).

The chief feature of Royce's early idealism that set it apart from other varieties of idealism was his doctrine of the existence of what he called a 'Universal Consciousness' or 'Absolute Mind'. He conceived this as a kind of overarching, all-embracing mind or consciousness in which all particular thoughts, as well as all the objects of these thoughts, along with all finite minds, are in some fashion 'contained'. This doctrine of the 'Universal Consciousness' was the burden of Royce's first major book *The Religious Aspect of Philosophy* of 1885, the year of his appointment at Harvard to an assistant professorship. In his doctrine of the Universal Consciousness, Royce aimed to capture in philosophical terms a sense of the radically immediate presence of the Divine Being. The spiritual thrust of Royce's philosophizing remained a steady feature of it throughout his career.

Despite the religious import of the doctrine of the Universal Consciousness, however, Royce tried in his work of 1885 to base this doctrine entirely on a semantical and logical analysis of the concepts of knowledge and truth. He began with two initially plausible assumptions. The first was that knowledge and truth presuppose reference. The second was that reference is to be analysed in such a way that objects of reference are completely determined purely by the referential intentions of referring minds. We may call this latter assumption the assumption of pure referential intentionalism.

Pure referential intentionalism has the consequence that all objects of reference are internal to minds. In particular, objects of reference are internal to the minds that achieve reference to such objects simply by means of having the referential intentions that they do. This consequence obviously involves an idealist commitment of some sort. But in order to see the particular form of idealism that Royce elicited from it, let us consider that the consequence raises a number of problems. How, for example, given this consequence, can two different minds refer to (and thus know) one and the same thing? Indeed, how even can one mind refer to (and thus know) one and the same thing on two different occasions? How can anyone ever make an error in judgment (since even in making a mistake in judging one must, it would seem, surely know that to which one refers)? Royce argued that the doctrine of the Universal Consciousness was required in order to solve these and other such problems, in particular that of the possibility of error.

With only minor changes this doctrine of the Universal Consciousness persisted in Royce's writings through his turn-of-the-century Gifford Lectures that were published as the two-volume work *The World and the Individual* (1899–1901).

The theory of knowledge and truth defended by Royce was soon to be attacked by William James in his works on pragmatism. Indeed, James's own pragmatic theory of truth was a direct response to the Roycean idealist challenge (see JAMES, W. §5). James's main task was that of accounting for reference and truth without committing himself to an idealism that he considered absurd. Thus his task was to account for reference and truth on some basis other than pure referential intentionalism. Ultimately his pragmatism took a position according to which

reference is determined not purely by referential intentions but also and more importantly by unbroken chains of causal connection stretching from referential intentions to objects of reference. Such objects, then, need not have a purely mental status but may consistently be regarded as being outside minds and in the external world. Not surprisingly, Royce and James enjoyed almost daily debates with one another on the topics of reference and truth until James's death in 1910. One of the most important of the historical consequences of Royce's thought is this influence on the development of James's version of pragmatism.

Not only was Royce an original philosopher – in particular an original idealist philosopher – in his own right: he was also a serious student of the history of philosophy. Indeed, although the bulk of his work was devoted to his own philosophical creation, still great portions of it were almost entirely devoted to the history of philosophy, for example almost all of *The Spirit of Modern Philosophy* and *Lectures on Modern Idealism*. His interest in the history of philosophy was simply a part of his interest in history more generally, and he devoted several years to writing on the history of his native state, California. Royce's interest in the history of thought led him to become accomplished in a wide variety of subjects, among them even such specialized subjects as the Sanskrit language.

4 Mathematical logic

A little-known side of Royce's intellectual life is his deep interest in mathematical logic and his extensive work in this area. Indeed, Royce introduced the topic of mathematical logic into the curriculum at Harvard, and by means of his own efforts and later those of his student C.I. Lewis, logic remained one of the mainstays of the Harvard philosophical experience. Royce's interest in logic was present as early as 1881, when he wrote for the benefit of his students at Berkeley his *Primer of Logical Analysis*. At this time he evidenced in his private diaries his concern to develop a logic that would be relevant to the theory of space. In this project Royce was aligning himself with the Kantian idea of a 'transcendental logic', that is to say a logic in which the structure of space and time plays a major role.

Royce seems to have left his logical concerns to lie dormant, however, until they were revived by Charles S. Peirce in 1898, when Royce attended Peirce's Cambridge Conference Lectures entitled *Reasoning and the Logic of Things* (see PEIRCE, C.S. §8). In these lectures Peirce showed that the forms of logic were in fact intimately connected with the forms of spatial structure; indeed, Peirce presented in the lectures a geometric form of logic that he had invented, called 'Existential Graphs'. Thus Peirce showed that Royce's earlier ideals with regard to logic were capable of detailed, technical fulfilment.

Peirce also fired Royce's logical and mathematical imagination in other ways. For example, he introduced Royce to the thought of the English mathematician A.B. Kempe, who had been a student of Augustus de Morgan, and who in the 1890s was an officer and leading figure in the London Mathematical Society. Kempe was considered by Peirce to be the world's greatest logician. As early as 1890, Kempe had published a number of works in which he had attempted to reduce all mathematical form to certain special forms, and in which he had attempted to show deep similarities between the most basic structures of logic and the fundamental geometrical structures. Of particular interest to Royce was Kempe's paper 'The Relation between the Logical Theory of Classes and the Geometrical Theory of Points'.

From the time of Peirce's Cambridge Conference Lectures until at least as late as 1910, Royce worked assiduously on mathematical logic, indeed with a fierce enthusiasm. His goal was in accord with his earlier, ultimately Kantian ideals, namely to amalgamate mathematical logic with the theory of space. By the second volume of *The World and the Individual*, composed around 1900, Royce was already utilizing the fruits of his own original mathematical and logical researches, for example in describing space as a certain kind of logical order. By 1905 he had developed what he called his 'System Sigma'. This mathematical system was similar to Kempe's system for analogizing logic and geometry, but it attempted to remove various imperfections that Royce perceived in Kempe's theory, the most important of which concerned the notion of an individual.

Royce had a subsidiary and ancillary mathematical interest in what were called Boolean functions. In connection with this subject Royce studied A.N. Whitehead's researches into Boolean algebra. Royce was one of the first mathematical thinkers to discuss what are now called 'Boolean rings'. Another of his interests was the mathematical and logical paradoxes, including 'Russell's Paradox', and the foundations of set theory (see RUSSELL, B.A.W. §§4–7). By 1905 Royce had proposed a set theory that would be 'non-foundational', that is to say, a set theory in which it is allowable to have infinitely descending (ordered by the relation of set membership) sequences of sets.

5 Ultimate position

During the last years of his life, Royce was beset by various health and family problems, but his philosophical production was undiminished. Indeed, *The Problem of Christianity*, which is widely regarded as his greatest work, was published only in 1913. In this work, under the influence of Peirce, Royce modified his earlier idealism into a powerful philosophical position, not unlike that of the later Wittgenstein in that its major themes are language and in particular the social functions of language. Central to the development in this work of Royce's own theory of the community is his employment of Peirce's ideas concerning the 'triadic' character of the notion of interpretation. For Royce the community is in essence a community of interpretation. It is an organic whole whose parts are individual persons, in which each of the parts has its place in a crisscrossing series of interpretations: each member interprets (things) to each other member. The resultant network of interpretation is the community. This idea is Royce's most mature expression of the idealistic thesis that was expressed in his earlier work by employing the metaphysical notion of the Absolute Consciousness. For the philosophical role played earlier by the Universal Consciousness comes to be assumed by the 'Community of Interpretation'. In this down-to-earth, as it were 'naturalized', version of idealism, the spiritual concerns that had driven Royce's earliest idealistic thought were unattenuated: indeed, as the title of his master work indicates, these concerns were made even more conspicuous in that work than ever before.

See also: ABSOLUTE, THE; HEGELIANISM §5; LOGIC IN THE 19TH CENTURY; PRAGMATISM

List of works

Royce, J. (1885) *The Religious Aspect of Philosophy*, Boston, MA: Houghton Mifflin. (Royce's first major work on ethics and metaphysics.)

—— (1886) *California from the Conquest in 1846 to the Second Vigilance Committee in San Francisco [1856]: A Study of the American Character*, Boston, MA: Houghton Mifflin. (Royce's history of California in the state's early days.)

—— (1887) *The Feud of Oakfield Creek: A Novel of California Life*, Boston, MA: Houghton Mifflin. (Royce's only novel.)

—— (1892) *The Spirit of Modern Philosophy: An Essay in the Form of Lectures*, Boston, MA: Houghton Mifflin. (An exposition of the major idealist themes presented in *The Religious Aspect of Philosophy*.)

—— (1897) *The Conception of God*, New York: Macmillan. (An exposition of Royce's idealism with a special emphasis on the nature of god and the finite individual.)

—— (1898) *Studies of Good and Evil*, New York: D. Appleton. (An analysis of fundamental ethical ideas.)

—— (1899–1901) *The World and the Individual*, New York: Macmillan, 2 vols. (One of Royce's greatest works: his two-volume set of Gifford Lectures.)

—— (1908a) *The Philosophy of Loyalty*, New York: Macmillan. (Royce's systematic presentation of his ethical theory based on loyalty.)

—— (1908b) *Race Questions, Provincialism, and Other American Problems*, New York: Macmillan. (Miscellaneous ethical and social-philosophical essays.)

—— (1911) *William James and Other Essays on the Philosophy of Life*, New York: Macmillan. (A collection of essays on various topics.)

—— (1912) *The Sources of Religious Insight*, New York: Charles Scribner's Sons. (Royce's treatment of religious epistemology.)

—— (1913) *The Problem of Christianity*, Chicago, IL: University of Chicago Press, 1968. (One of Royce's greatest works: his transformation of his early idealism into a theory of thought that is socially and communally based.)

—— (1914) *War and Insurance*, New York: Macmillan. (Royce's effort to promote world peace.)

—— (1916) *The Hope of the Great Community*, New York: Macmillan. (A further work on the topic of community.)

—— (1919) *Lectures on Modern Idealism*, ed. J. Loewenberg, New Haven, CT: Yale University Press. (Text of Royce's lectures of 1906.)

—— (1920) *Fugitive Essays*, ed. J. Loewenberg, Cambridge, MA: Harvard University Press. (A posthumously published set of miscellaneous essays.)

McDermott, J.J. (ed.) (1969) *The Basic Writings of Josiah Royce*, Chicago, IL: University of Chicago Press, 2 vols. (An extensive anthology of Royce's writings.)

Clendenning, J. (ed.) (1970) *The Letters of Josiah Royce*, Chicago, IL: University of Chicago Press. (An excellent edition of Royce's letters.)

References and further reading

Clendenning, J. (1985) *The Life and Thought of Josiah Royce*, Madison, WI: University of Wisconsin Press. (The definitive biography of Royce, very carefully and elegantly presented. It is a natural starting place for anyone interested in Royce's life, times and thinking.)

* Kempe, A.B. (1889–90) 'The Relation between the Logical Theory of Classes and the Geometrical Theory of Points', *Proceedings of the London Mathematical Society* 21: 147–82. (An exposition of fundamental similarities among the topics of set theory, logic and geometry.)

Kuklick, B. (1985) *Josiah Royce: An Intellectual Biography*, Indianapolis, IN: Hackett Publishing Company. (A general account of Royce's life and thought, written by a historian rather than a philosopher.)

Oppenheim, F.M. (1993) *Royce's Mature Ethics*, Notre Dame, IN: University of Notre Dame Press. (An account of Royce's ultimate ethical position.)

—— (1987) *Royce's Mature Philosophy of Religion*, Notre Dame, IN: University of Notre Dame Press. (An interpretation of Royce's *The Problem of Christianity*.)

—— (1980) *Royce's Voyage Down Under: A Journey of the Mind*, Lexington, KY: The University Press of Kentucky. (An account of Royce's recovery from a nervous breakdown by means of travel to Australia.)

* Peirce, C.S. (1992) *Reasoning and the Logic of Things*, ed. K.L. Ketner, Cambridge, MA: Harvard University Press. (This is a recent edition, indeed the only adequate edition, of Peirce's Cambridge Conference Lectures of 1898, the lectures that inspired Royce to return to mathematical logic with vigour. This edition includes an extremely valuable introduction by Kenneth Laine Ketner and Hilary Putnam.)

ROBERT W. BURCH

ROZANOV, VASILII VASIL'EVICH (1856–1919)

Vasilii Rozanov, a prominent spokesman of the Russian Religious-Philosophical Renaissance, is known for his writings on sex, marriage and the family, his attacks on Christian asceticism, and his love–hate attitude to Judaism. He termed Judaism a religion of life because it sanctified sex and the family, and Christianity a religion of death because it exalted celibacy. But Rozanov also charged that Judaism mandated ritual murder and that Jews were feeding off Russians. In Apokalypsis nashego vremeni (The Apocalypse of Our Time) (1917–18), he apologized for his anti-Semitic pronouncements and blamed the Bolshevik Revolution on Christian otherworldliness and sexlessness. In private life, Rozanov was a pillar of the Church, which he regarded as a haven of beauty, warmth, and spiritual succour.

Rozanov's writings contain brilliant insights, contradictions, distortions and outright lies. 'Falsehood never tormented me', he wrote, 'and for a strange reason. What business is it of yours precisely what I think?' He championed conservative policies in articles published under his own name and radical policies under a pseudonym. It is clear, however, that Rozanov was deeply religious and that he associated sex and the family with God. 'Dirty diapers and a naked wife: this is the truth of Bethlehem around you.'

Rozanov's interpretations of Dostoevskii, Gogol' and other Russian authors were original and perceptive. His collections of aphorisms Solitaria *(1912) and* Opavshie list'ia *(Fallen Leaves, 2 vols) (1913b, 1915), are considered masterpieces of Russian style.*

1 **Biography and early works**
2 **Sex, marriage and the family**
3 **Christianity and Judaism**

1 Biography and early works

Rozanov was born in Vetluga, Kostroma province. The death of his father, a minor forestry official, when Rozanov was 5 plunged the family into poverty. His mother was too overworked to provide the love and attention that he craved. Rozanov was 13 when she died; his first reaction was that now he could smoke openly. He attended gymnasia in Kostroma, Simbirsk and Novgorod, and the Historical and Philological faculty at Moscow University, graduating from the latter in 1881. In his third year he married Apollinaria Suslova, Dostoevskii's former mistress and twenty years Rozanov's senior, in a bizarre attempt to be close to the great writer. Suslova left him in 1888, but cruelly refused consent to a divorce. In 1889, Rozanov met Varvara Rudneva, a young widow. Two years later they were married in an unofficial church ceremony which was conducted secretly lest he be prosecuted for bigamy. He had to adopt their five children formally.

Between 1880 and 1893 Rozanov taught history and geography in provincial gymnasia, hating every moment and writing in his spare time. His articles appeared in a variety of newspapers including the ultra-conservative *Novoe vremia* (New Times). His first book, *O ponimanii* (On Understanding) (1886), an attack on positivism, was ignored by the critics and sold very few copies. But *Legenda o velikom inkvizitore F. M. Dostoevskogo* (*Dostoevsky and the Legend of the Grand Inquisitor*) (1891) attracted the attention of the influential literary critic Nikolai Strakhov (1828–96) who found Rozanov a minor bureaucratic job in St Petersburg, thereby enabling him to leave teaching. In 1899, Rozanov became a staff writer for *Novoe*

vremia. His next books – *Literaturnye ocherki* (*Literary Sketches*) (1899), *Sumerki prosveshcheniia* (*The Twilight of Enlightenment*) (1899), *Religiia i kul'tura* (*Religion and Culture*) (1899) and *Priroda i istoriia* (*Nature and History*) (1900) – were collections of previously published articles, most of which had a conservative Slavophile bent. He was then seeking a Christian metaphysic of culture. Later on, he publicly endorsed the Holy Synod's excommunication of Tolstoi, but he criticized its impersonal and bureaucratic handling of the matter. Rozanov would have preferred that Tolstoi be 'driven out of the Church' by a band of outraged peasants whose religious sensibilities he had offended.

Around the turn of the century, Rozanov began to associate with Symbolists and Decadents even though he disapproved of their 'unnatural' writings. He published in *Mir iskusstva* (The World of Art), had a regular column, 'In My Own Corner', in *Novyi put'* (New Path), and was a prominent member of the Religious-Philosophical Society of St Petersburg. Instrumental in obtaining permission for the meetings, he was the only founding member who was a personal friend of some of the clerics.

In 1905–6, Rozanov wrote pro-revolutionary articles under a pseudonym (Varvarin) for *Novoe slovo* (New Word) in which he associated revolution with youth and described the autocracy as a 'weakening fetish'. He reprinted these articles under his own name in *Kogda nachal'stvo ushlo* (When the Authorities Went Away) (1910). In *Fallen Leaves II*, he wrote, 'Politics must be destroyed, apoliticism established ... by confusing all political ideas. ... By making "red" "yellow" and "white" "green"'. Laura Engelstein maintains that Rozanov was consciously trying to 'disorganize' public discourse by 'wreak[ing] havoc with the conventions of serious prose and responsible argument' (1992: 314).

Rozanov welcomed the First World War as the beginning of Russia's renaissance. He hailed the February Revolution and was going to 'compose an ideology' for it, but the Bolshevik Revolution was a disaster for him. When the Bolsheviks closed *Novoe vremia* he moved, with his family, to Sergeev Posad, near the Holy Trinity Monastery. He died of starvation and exhaustion, after having the priests administer the last rites nine times. At his request he was buried next to Konstantin Leont'ev (1831–91) in the monastery cemetery.

Leont'ev, Dostoevskii and Nietzsche were the major intellectual influences on Rozanov (see LEONT'EV, K.N.; DOSTOEVSKII, F.M.; NIETZSCHE: IMPACT ON RUSSIAN THOUGHT). He and Leont'ev corresponded in 1890–1, drawn together by mutual hostility to positivism, liberalism and democracy, and by concern for the future of Russia and of Christianity. But Leont'ev ridiculed the 'rosy-coloured' Christianity of Dostoevskii and Tolstoi and regarded Old Testament Judaism as a religion of fear. Rozanov pictured Jehovah as a father, a giver of life and a founder of families. Both writers were called the 'Russian Nietzsche' – Leont'ev because of his elitist aestheticism and Rozanov because of his diatribes against Christianity and his unabashed amoralism. 'Morality', Rozanov wrote, 'I don't even know how to spell it'. In sharp contrast to Nietzsche, Rozanov idealized domesticity and found supreme beauty in the face of Jesus and in church rituals. Trotsky called Rozanov the 'poet of the cosy corner'.

2 Sex, marriage and the family

Rozanov's first writings about sex, marriage and the family were motivated by his personal situation. *Semeinyi vopros v Rossii* (The Family Question in Russia) (1903), treated the legal and social status of the family, interspersing letters, newspaper reports and statistics with his own commentary. Rozanov considered the increase in illegitimacy, abortion, and prostitution symptoms of the decay of marriage, which he blamed on the Church. He advocated easy divorce as a way to revitalize the family and urged that the very concept of illegitimacy be abolished. An earlier work, *V mire neiasnogo i nereshennogo* (In the World of the Obscure and Unresolved) (1901), was banned as pornographic because it included a letter from a correspondent who claimed that circumcision had improved his sexual performance. In articles published in *Mir iskusstva*, Rozanov praised the sun-worshipping (life-affirming), phallic religions of the Ancient Near East.

Throughout his life, Rozanov proclaimed the sanctity of family life and the metaphysical and religious significance of the sexual act. He believed that during intercourse the couple's souls come into contact with other worlds and create a new soul, and that pregnancy was a sacred state. Contrasting the two poles of Christianity, Bethlehem (childbirth) and Golgotha (death), Rozanov maintained that by concentrating on Golgotha, the Church has turned Christianity into a religion of suffering, sorrow and death. He wanted Christians to resurrect the spirit of Bethlehem and for Christianity itself to become phallic, 'at least in part'. Independently of Freud, he extolled a good sex life as essential to physical and mental health.

3 Christianity and Judaism

Around 1905–6 Rozanov went through a religious crisis. Soon after, he began to attack Christianity *per se* as a religion more suited to funerals than to weddings, a religion that teaches man *'to live for death and to die for life'*. No Christian conception of the family exists, he argued. Monasticism was the Christian ideal – denial of life and love, rejection of the world and the family, renunciation of pleasure of any kind for the sake of heaven. One cannot even imagine any of the apostles or their young wives in love. Only love of Jesus is allowed. Through love of 'the sweetest Jesus', the fruits of this world tasted bitter. The Gospels were a religiously cold, even religiously indifferent book, in which the stamp of sadness is ever present. Jesus never laughed, never sang, never danced, and did not marry. Christian monks and nuns were akin to the castrated priests of the Phoenician gods Moloch and Astarte. 'And this hard crystal [monasticism] is indissoluble in Christian civilization. Moreover, it is slowly leading the Christian peoples...and Christianity itself to disunion, destruction and to leaving behind on earth [only] the "chosen few"'. (see Roberts 1978: 194).

Rozanov expressed these ideas in 'On Sweetest Jesus and the Bitter Fruits of the World' (1907), published in *Tëmnyi lik. Metafizika khristianstva* (Dark Face: The Metaphysics of Christianity) (1911a), *Liudi lunnogo sveta. Metafizika khristianstva II* (People of the Moonlight: The Metaphysics of Christianity II) (1911b) and *Apokalypsis nashego vremeni* (The Apocalypse of Our Times) (1917–18).

Rozanov termed ascetics 'lunar types' who live outside the family and do not procreate. Some ascetics had a weak or non-existent sex drive, but most were repressed homosexuals. As examples, Rozanov gave Jesus, Plato, Solov'ëv, monks and nuns, career women, and secular radicals from 'that half Urning' (homosexual), Chernyshevskii to the present. Rozanov associated atheism and socialism with 'seedlessness', non-procreation. Homosexuals and lesbians were a 'third sex'. They have contributed greatly to society and culture and should not be persecuted. But Rozanov also claimed that because they have no children, they are indifferent to the future, including their country's future.

Rozanov admired the sex-positive teachings of Judaism, the strong family life of contemporary Jews, and Jewish survival in the face of centuries of persecution. But he found Jewish energy menacing, and attributed it to their sex-positive religion and to circumcision. He portrayed certain Jewish rituals in eerie, other-worldly terms and described Jews as spiders feeding off Russian blood and as destroyers of Russian culture. During the Beiliss Case (1911–13) – the government's frame-up of a Jew, Mendel Beiliss, for ritual murder – Rozanov falsely claimed that ritual sacrifice was and remains the most essential aspect of Judaism. Denying that he was exacerbating anti-Semitism in a land rife with pogroms, Rozanov declared that he wanted to move the case from politics to a higher 'religious' plane. Some of his writings were so scurrilous that even *Novoe vremia* refused to print them. Because of them Rozanov was expelled from the Religious-Philosophical Society.

In *Apokalypsis nashego vremeni*, Rozanov's response to the Bolshevik Revolution, he wrote that the Gospels have led humanity to a 'blind alley of castration and death' and called *Revelations* an anti-Christian book, because it was based on birth ('The Woman Clothed in the Sun'). He claimed that the masses have abandoned Christianity because it is impotent. 'Despite all the beauty of Christianity', it cannot provide bread. Christianity's dissolution has left 'huge voids' into which 'all humanity is falling'. Rozanov also criticized Russian literature, especially nihilism, Gogol' and himself, for causing Russians to lose sight of reality. And he apologized to the Jews for defaming them, lauded their positive role in history and in Russian society, and condemned pogroms.

Rozanov's diatribes against Christianity and Christ were motivated as much by love as by hate. His writings also contain innumerable positive statements about them. For example: 'only in the Church is it warm'; 'of course I will *nevertheless die in the Church, of course I need the Church incomparably more than literature*'; and 'I need only consolation, and therefore I need only Christ... Paganism and Judaism do not even come to mind' (see Roberts 1978: 304–10; original emphases). His writings constitute an extreme example of the revaluation of Christian dogma that was a feature of the Religious-Philosophical Renaissance.

See also: RUSSIAN RELIGIOUS-PHILOSOPHICAL RENAISSANCE

List of works

Rozanov's writings, consisting of over twenty books and 2,500 articles, have never been collected.

Rozanov, V. (1886) *O ponimanii* (On Understanding), Moscow: E. Lissiev & Iu. Roman.

—— (1891) *Legenda o velikom inkvizitore F.M. Dostoevskogo* serialized in *Russkii vestnik*, Moscow: Nikolaev, 1894; repr. of St Petersburg 1906 edn, Munich: W. Fink, 1970; trans. S. Roberts, *Dostoevsky and the Legend of the Grand Inquisitor*, Ithaca, NY: Cornell University Press, 1972.

—— (1899a) *Literaturnye ocherki* (Literary Sketches), St Petersburg: Merkushev.

—— (1899b) *Religiia i kul'tura* (Religion and Culture), St Petersburg: Merkushev.

—— (1899c) *Sumerki prosveshcheniia. Sbornik statei po voprosam obrazovaniia* (Twilight of Enlightenment. A collection of articles about education), St Petersburg: Merkushev.

—— (1900) *Priroda i istoriia* (Nature and History), St Petersburg: Pertsov.

—— (1901) *V mire neiasnogo i nereshennogo* (In the World of the Obscure and Unresolved), St Petersburg: Merkushev; 2nd edn, 1904; repr. Moscow: Respublika, 1995.

—— (1903) *Semeinyi vopros v Rossii* (The Family Question in Russia), St Petersburg: Merkushev, 2 vols.

—— (1906) *Okolo tserkovnykh sten* (Near the Church Walls), St Petersburg: Vaisberg i P. Gershunin, 2 vols.

—— (1910) *Kogda nachal'stvo ushlo* (When the Authorities Went Away), St Petersburg: Suvorin.

—— (1911a) *Tëmnyi lik. Metafizika khristianstva* (Dark Face: The Metaphysics of Christianity), St Petersburg: Vaisberg i Gershunin.

—— (1911b) *Liudi lunnogo sveta. Metafizika khristianstva II* (People of the Moonlight: The Metaphysics of Christianity II), St Petersburg: Merkushev; 2nd edn 1913; repr. of 2nd edn, Wurzburg, 1970, with intro. by G. Ivask; repr. of 2nd edn Moscow: Druzhba narodov, 1990.

—— (1912) *Uedinënnoe*, St Petersburg: Suvorin; trans. S.S. Koteliansky, *Solitaria*, London: Wishart, 1927.

—— (1913a) *Lituraturnye izgnanniki* (Literary Exiles), St Petersburg: Suvorin.

—— (1913b, 1915) *Opavshie list'ia* (Korob pervyi, Korob vtoroi), St Petersburg: Suvorin, 2 vols; trans. of 1st vol., S.S. Koteliansky, *Fallen Leaves, Bundle One* London: Mandrake, 1929.

—— (1914a) *Sredi khudozhnikov* (Among the Artists), St Petersburg: Suvorin.

—— (1914b) *Oboniatel'noe i osiazatel'noe otnoshenie evreev k krovi* (The Attitude of the Jews towards the Smell and Touch of Blood), Petrograd: Suvorin; repr. Stockholm: n.p., 1932.

—— (1915) *Voina 1914 g. i russkoie vozrozhdenie* (The War of 1914 and the Russian Renaissance), Petrograd: Suvorin.

—— (1917–18) *Apokalypsis nashego vremeni* (The Apocalypse of Our Time), Sergiev Posad: Ivanov.

—— (1990) *V.V. Rozanov*, Moscow: Nauka, ed. E.V. Barabanov, 2 vols. (Volume 1 contains Religiia i kul'tura, Russkaia tserkov', L.N. Tolstoi i Russkaia tserkov', and Tëmnyi lik. Metafizika khristianstva. Volume 2 contains Liudi lunnogo sveta, Uedinënnoe and Opavshie list'ia, both bundles.)

References and further reading

Banerjee, M. (1971) 'Rozanov and Dostoevsky', Slavic and East European Journal 15: 411–24. (Focus on Rozanov's The Legend of the Grand Inquisitor.)

Crone, A.L. (1978) Rozanov and the End of Literature, Würzburg: Arnult Liebing. (Part I – Rozanov's aphorisms as a polyphony of eight voices; Part II – Rozanov on literature and his use of literary forms.)

—— (1986) 'Nietzschean, All Too Nietzschean? Rozanov's Anti-Christian Critique', in Nietzsche in Russia, ed. B.G. Rosenthal, Princeton, NJ: Princeton University Press, 95–112. (Argues that Nietzsche influenced Rozanov.)

* Engelstein, L. (1992) 'Sex and the Anti-Semite: Vasilii Rozanov's Patriarchal Eroticism', in The Keys to Happiness, Ithaca, NY: Cornell University Press, 299–333. (Emphasizes gender issues.)

Fateev, V.A. (ed.) (1995) V.V. Rozanov: Pro et contra, St Petersburg: Izdatel'stvo russkogo Khristianskogo gumanitarnogo instituta, 2 vols. (Anthology of writings by Russian thinkers and scholars about Rozanov's life and work.)

Glouberman, E. (1976) 'Vasilii Rozanov: The Anti-Semitism of a Russian Judaephile', in Jewish Social Studies 38 (2): 117–44. (Argues that Rozanov's anti-Semitism is endemic to Christianity.)

Gollerbakh, E.V. (1922) Rozanov: Lichnost' i tvorchestvo, Petrograd: Poliarnaia zvezda. (Reminiscences and bibliography of works about Rozanov to 1922.)

Hutchings, S. (1993) 'Breaking the Circle of the Self: Domesticiation, Alienation, and the Question of Discourse in Rozanov's Late Writings', in Slavic Review 52 (1): 67–86. (Emphasizes genre issues.)

Kline, G.L. (1968) 'Religious Neo-Conservatives: Leontyev and Rozanov', 35–72. (Synopsis and comparision of their views of Christianity.)

Kornblatt, J.D. (1997) 'Russian Religious Thought and the Jewish Kabbala', in The Occult in Modern Russian and Soviet Thought, ed. B.G. Rosenthal, Ithaca, NY: Cornell University Press, 75–95. (Includes section on Rozanov's misuse of the Kabbala to 'prove' ritual murder in the Beiliss Case.)

Nikoliukin, A.N. (ed.) (1995) V.V. Rozanov. O pisatel'stve i pisateliakh (V.V. Rozanov. On Writing and Writers), Moscow: Respublik. (Anthology of Rozanov's essays on the subject.)

Putnam, G. (1971) 'Vasilii Rozanov: Sex, Marriage, Christianity', in Canadian Slavic Studies 3: 301–26. (A pioneering study of these subjects.)

Roberts, S. (1978) Four Faces of Rozanov: Christianity, Sex, Jews, and the Russian Revolution, New York: Philosophical Library. (Introductory and concluding essays by the editor; translation of 'On Sweetest Jesus', excerpts from Liudi lunnogo sveta and Apokalypsis nashego vremeni.)

Romanoff, J. (1974) 'Vasilij Rozanov, the Jurodivij of Russian Literature', Ph.D. dissertation, Stanford University. (Detailed study of Rozanov's life and thought.)

Stammler, H. (1984) Vasilij Vasil'evic Rozanov als Philosoph (Vasilii Vasil'evich Rozanov as Philosopher), Giessen: W. Schmitz. (Contains extensive bibliography of works by and about Rozanov.)

BERNICE GLATZER ROSENTHAL

RUFUS, RICHARD see RICHARD RUFUS OF CORNWALL

RUGE, ARNOLD (1802–80)

Arnold Ruge was the most influential liberal writer and activist of the radical wing of Young Hegelianism. For him philosophy was a challenge to translate the humanist ideals of emancipation and self-determination into the realities of moral, cultural and political practice. As editor of powerful intellectual journals such as 'Hallesche und Deutsche Jahrbuecher' (1838–43) with Theodor Echtermeyer, 'Anekdota zur neuesten deutschen Philosophie und Publizistik' (1843), 'Deutsch-Franzoesische Jahrbuecher' (1844) with Karl Marx, and 'Die Akademie' (1850), he became the leading promotor of liberal philosophy and civic emancipation in Germany. Ruge represented the citizens of Breslau in the Frankfurt Paulskirche parliament in 1848–9 and worked briefly with Alexandre Ledru-Rollin and Guizeppe Mazzini in establishing a short-lived 'European Democratic Committee' in London in 1849.

Ruge understood his critical educational, cultural and political activities as a direct calling from the heritage of European enlightenment and German idealism, thus transforming idealistic theory and vision into the realities of political practice and agitation. In this manner he promoted such radical figures as Bruno Bauer, Max Stirner, David Friedrich Strauss and Ludwig Feuerbach.

1 **Philosophy and revolution**
2 **Protestantism and romanticism**
3 **Religion of humanism**

1 Philosophy and revolution

Arnold Ruge, born 9 September 1802 in Bergen on the German island of Rügen, died in 1880 in Brighton, England after thirty-one years of exile. One of the most influential and radical German liberal intellectuals and democrats, he had to take refuge first in Paris and London in 1843 where he worked with Karl Marx, and again after 1849 in London and Brighton. Ruge was a successor to the tradition of academic philosophy which runs from the Enlightenment through KANT, FICHTE and HEGEL. But Kant's concept of autonomy and Hegel's model of emancipation still were only theoretical and academic: 'Today we have to resolve not only the theoretical, but also the practical conflicts. Only the unity of free thought and free will, only the dissolution of the conflict between free thought and un-free mankind will result in the complete realisation of liberty' (Ruge 1852: 18). Times have changed: 'Our times are political, and politics work for the liberty of this world', he wrote in 1842 (1985 vol. 2: 254) in his influential critique of Kant's and Hegel's reluctance to address real practical matters of political change.

It is by free and reasoning people that the unconscious self-determination of humankind will be elevated to self-conscious self-determination. Only the free person is the true person; the realization of liberty lies in emancipation and humanization – that is, in humanism. Ruge held that the humanism of the future will translate traditional principles of existing and historic religions into the 'humanistic religion', determined to realize the 'essence of man through knowledge, beauty, and liberty'. Means to achieve these goals are 'a constitution of society rooted in self-determined development, free communities, schools and academies of the sciences and arts' resulting in a humanism which is characterized by 'true religious practice in ethics and the education of all humans to their true essence in equal, political, and economic community' (Ruge 1852: 26, 45).

2 Protestantism and romanticism

Contrary to Hegel's complex and consensus-oriented hermeneutical interpretation of dialectical processes in personal development and in the history of ideas and in world history, Ruge in 1842 identified only two conflicting forces in history as well as in personal development: Protestantism and romanticism. Protestantism is the progressive and evolutionary progress of political, cultural and personal development, a self-reforming and self-emancipating principle, 'free and autonomous as science which is an offspring of protestant reasoning'. Romanticism, the contradict-

ing principle, dwells on emotions and sentiments, on 'inwardness' ('Innerlichkeit') which defines itself in antagonistic and dualistic terms against the outside world and its challenges (Ruge 1985 vol. 2: 128). Modern 'romantic inwardness' itself must be understood as a product of Protestant emancipation of individual conscience from heteronomous religious, metaphysical or political powers. In political terms, romanticism can easily be identified as the anti-emancipatory and reactionary force, and is politically represented by the suppressive and reactionary political powers on the European continent. While German Protestantism, in Ruge's assessment, does not live up to its calling and heritage any more as it has become a part of the reactionary powers of romanticism, the principle of Protestantism has already emigrated into liberal philosophy and radical political theory. Ruge's conflict theory – influenced by Bruno Bauer's Manichean model of antithetical progress in philosophy and politics (see BAUER, B.) – becomes the blueprint for Marx's concept of ideational antithetics between materialism and idealism, and of political and economic antithetics between capitalism and proletarism. It marks the departure of radical and confrontational antithetical Hegelianism from the non-confrontational dialectical method of Hegel.

3 Religion of humanism

Ruge regards his political vision of a socialist and democratic republic of responsible and freely contracting individuals as the manifestation of free religion, the religion of humanism. In *Die Loge des Humanismus* (The Lodge of Humanism) (1852) and *Unser System* (Our System) (1850) he outlines his cultural, social and political programme of the religion of humanism as the logical consequence of the history of visions, ethics and economics. He holds that religious principles such as work-ethics and virtues, love and solidarity, altruism and mutual understanding have to be released from the bondage of established churches and religious sects in the same way as individuals have to be freed from the dominating powers of heteronomous tutelage by reactionary and elitist models of government. Not only individuals, but also the institutions of society must be driven by self-determination and self-emancipation.

Ruge calls for free education, free religious societies, academies for the arts and sciences, for free speech and free public opinion, and a free economic market within a socialist framework guided by a culture of work ethics, justice, solidarity and equality. But such a vision, in his understanding, does not exclude the 'organisation' of free institutions of learning, arts, and crafts, of a system of labour organisational and distribution by state authorities. Heine called Ruge the grim doorkeeper of Hegelian philosophy; to be a philosopher for Ruge meant not only to analyse the good and to argue for it but also to will it and to fight for it.

See also: HEGELIANISM §3; HUMANISM; STIRNER, M.; STRAUSS, D.F.

List of works

Ruge, A. (1985–) *Werke und Briefe*, ed. H.-M. Sass, Aalen: Scientia, 12 vols. (To date the following volumes have been published: volume 2 (1988) *Philosophische Kritiken 1838–1846* ; volume 3 (1988) *Literarische Kritiken (1838–1846)*; volume 4 (1988) *Politische Kritiken 1838–1846* ; volume 10 (1985) *Briefwechsel und Tagebuchblaetter 1825–1847*; volume 11 (1985) *Briefwechsel und Tagebuchblaetter 1848–1880*.)

—— (1846–8) *Saemtliche Werke*, 10 vols, Mannheim: J.P. Grohe. (annotation?)

—— (1842) 'Hegels Rechtsphilosophie und die Politik unserer Zeit', *Deutsche Jahrbücher für Wissenschaft und Kunst* 189, 190; trans. J.A. Massey as 'Hegel's Philosophy of Law and the Politics of Our Times', in L. Stepelevich (ed.) *The Young Hegelians*, New York: Cambridge University Press, 1983, 211–37. (Offers a critique of Hegel from a Young Hegelian standpoint.)

—— (1843) 'Eine Selbstkritik des Liberalismus', *Deutsche Jahrbücher für Wissenschaft und Kunst* 1843 (1); trans. J.A. Massey as 'A Self-Critique of Liberalism', in L. Stepelevich (ed.) *The Young Hegelians*, New York: Cambridge University Press, 1983, 237–60. (annotation?)

—— (1852) *Die Loge des Humanismus* (The Lodge of Humanism), Bremen: Arnold Ruge. (Ruge's thoughts on liberalism and humanism.)

—— (1850) *Unser System* (Our System), Leipzig: Verlagsbureau; repr. Frankfurt: Neuer Verlag, 1903. (Detailed presentation of Ruge's philosophical ideas.)

—— (1854) *New Germany, its Modern History, Literature, Philosophy, Religion and Art*, London: Holyoake & Co. (Identical to *Die Loge des Humanismus*, 1852.)

—— (1868) *Eight Lectures on Religion*, St Louis, MO: (publisher?). (German edition was published in Berlin in 1869.)

References and further readings

Brazill, W.J. (1970) *The Young Hegelians*, New Haven, CT, and London: Yale University Press. (Concentrates on the interpretation of the 'young Hegelian metaphysic' (27–70) and Ruge's role in promoting Young Hegelian politics (227–60); includes a bibliographical essay (283–96).)

Eßbach, W. (1988) *Die Junghegelianer. Soziologie einer Intellektuellengruppe (The young Hegelians: Sociology of an Intellectual Movement)*, Munich: Fink. (An intellectual history of the ideas of Young Hegelian thought and their mode of argumentation.)

Loewith, K. (1964) *From Hegel to Nietzsche. The Revolution in Nineteenth Century Thought*, trans. D. Green, New York: Holt, Rinehart & Winston. (Classic contribution on Young Hegelian theory-formation and the process of radicalization within the movement.)

Neher, W. (1933) *Arnold Ruge als Politiker und politischer Schriftsteller (Arnold Ruge as politician and political writer)*, Heidelberg: Winter. (Describes Ruge's political theory in the context of his political activities.)

Sass, H.-M. (1960) *Untersuchungen zur Religionsphilosophie der Hegelschule (Studies on the religion philosophy of the Hegelian School)*, Phil. Diss. Münster: Universität Münster. (Dissertation, discussing Ruge's humanist and liberal theory within the context of the Young Hegelian movement, also Ruge's political role as editor of influential critical journals.)

Walter, S. (1995) *Demokratisches Denken zwischen Hegel und Marx. Die politische Philosophie Arnold Ruges (Democratic thinking between Hegel and Marx: the political philosophy of Arnold Ruge)*, Düsseldorf: Droste. (Reconstructs and analyses Ruge's political philosophy, and analyses his liberal ideas of transnationalism, international peace, European unity and democracy.)

Zanardo, A. (1970–1) *Arnold Ruge giovane hegeliano 1842–1849 (The young Hegelian Arnold Ruge 1842–1849)*, Contributo bibiografico Annali Istituto Giangiacomo Feltrinelli, 12, Milano: Istituto Feltrinelli. (Comprehensive annotated bibliograph, 1842–9.)

HANS-MARTIN SASS

RULE OF LAW (RECHTSSTAAT)

The 'rule of law' most simply expresses the idea that everyone is subject to the law, and should therefore obey it. Governments in particular are to obey law – to govern under, or in accordance with, law. The rule of law thus requires constitutional government, and constitutes a shield against tyranny or arbitrary rule: political rulers and their agents (police and so on) must exercise power under legal constraints, respecting accepted constitutional limits. The British and US conceptions of this ideal find a parallel in the Germanic concept of the Rechtsstaat, *or 'state-under-law', where the state as an organized entity is conceived to be limited by laws and by fundamental principles of legality, rather than being a purely political organization that can dispense with law in the interests of policy. Such concepts play an essential part in the political philosophy of liberalism; yet, characteristically, their more detailed exposition and indeed their nature and meaning are contested and controversial.*

In a wider sense, the rule of law articulates values of procedural fairness or due process which affect the form *of legal rules and govern the manner of their application. Those values both enhance the utility of legal regulation and also acknowledge underlying ideas of human dignity and autonomy. In a further sense, the rule of law refers to the faithful application of those rules and principles which constitute the law of a particular legal system. It expresses the idea that legal obligation should always be determined in particular cases by analysis of existing law – as opposed to* ad hoc *legislation by judges – even where disagreement may exist about the true meaning or content of the law.*

The connection between the rule of law and justice is complex. The rule of law cannot itself guarantee justice, but it forms an essential precondition. In so far as it imposes formal constraints on the laws enacted or enforced, which ensure that they are capable of being obeyed and that they are fairly administered, the rule of law assumes a conception of moral personality – of how individuals should be treated, as responsible human beings, capable of a sense of justice – which links the idea with the values of freedom and autonomy, and the ideal of equality.

1   **Constitutionalism and the separation of powers**
2   **Justice and liberty**
3   **Judicial obligation and legal decisions**

1   Constitutionalism and the separation of powers

Constitutional government entails some form of separation of powers. Although the law may be changed by the exercise of political power, it may be altered only in compliance with established constitutional procedures; and all acts of government and public officials must respect the requirements of the law which apply at the time of acting. The legislative, executive and judicial powers of the state must not be simultaneously exercised by the same persons or the same institutions, without appropriate restraints. The independence of the judiciary is fundamental. Although various arrangements for the division of legislative and executive powers may suffice – the rule of law does not necessarily require complete institutional independence – the judicial power must be wholly distinct. Both government and legislature must act in accordance with the existing law – as ultimately interpreted by the judiciary – until it is altered by lawful (constitutional) means.

F.A. Hayek, however, defended a more rigorous interpretation. The law constituted a shield against arbitrary rule by virtue of its generality. If the political rulers were obliged to govern within the constraints of general laws, they could not single out particular persons for special treatment. John Locke also emphasized the importance of rule by general laws, as opposed to 'arbitrary decrees' tailored to the circumstances of particular cases.

Hayek objected that the rule of law had been undermined by the modern blurring of the legislative and executive functions. Every coercive act of government should be authorized by law in the sense of a 'universal rule of just conduct' – a general rule which was also abstract in the sense that it was not directed to the attainment of any specific policy objective or desirable set of circumstances. Hayek considered that the executive government should always respect the ordinary rules of private law, applicable to the actions of private citizens. The authorization by the legislature of particular acts of government which would otherwise be unlawful permitted the executive to escape the constraints of general laws. Acting as a representative assembly, whose majority is committed to the support of an administration or of schemes for the use of public resources, the modern legislature fulfils a primarily executive role in breach of the theory of separation of powers.

A.V. Dicey attributed similar importance to the subservience of government to the ordinary private law. In his analysis of the rule of law as a principle of British constitutional law, Dicey stressed the idea of equality, in the sense of the equal subjection of everyone – public official as well as private citizen – to the civil and criminal law. The rule of law meant not only the absence of arbitrary or even discretionary governmental power, but also that constitutional law was the product of the courts' decisions in ordinary litigation involving public officials.

It is now widely considered that Dicey gave exaggerated emphasis to private law, at the expense of public law. It is not possible for government to accomplish necessary tasks of economic control and social administration without special powers conferred by, and subject to independent principles of, public law. None the less, Dicey's famous repudiation of 'administrative law' or *droit administratif* reflected the underlying rationale of the rule of law. Hayek distinguished between rules regulating the activities of governmental agencies, or regulations made by such agencies, on the one hand, and 'administrative powers over persons and property', on the other. The latter entailed the exercise of discretion and permitted discrimination between persons. The pursuit of 'social justice', if that involved treating the citizen and his property as objects of administration, was not compatible with a free society under the rule of law.

Constitutionalism means more than adherence to a purely formal concept of legality which satisfies the principle of separation of powers. If there were no limits on the nature and scope of government powers – because the laws permitted the exercise of unfettered discretion – there would be no safeguard against arbitrariness, and individual freedom would be constantly in peril. Hans Kelsen's 'pure' theory of law seems deficient in this respect (see KELSEN, H.). Kelsen identified the 'state' with the legal order, in the sense that the state was a 'personification' of the 'unity' of the legal order. Acts could be imputed to the state where they were performed by persons or institutions occupying certain superior positions within the hierarchy constituted by the legal order. The law of a state consisted of those norms whose validity could be logically derived from acts of will by the ultimate authority, which was itself empowered by the 'basic norm' necessarily presupposed by lawyer and 'legal scientist'. It was not necessary, then, that 'law' should have any particular content, provided only that it was enacted or laid down by the appropriate authority. In this minimal sense, every state is a *Rechtsstaat* – a state defined and regulated by law. It is apparent, however, that in this sense the rule of law has no value as a principle of constitutionalism, or safeguard of liberty. The contemporary German conception of *Rechtsstaat* postulates observance of fundamental principles of legality and proportionality, and respect for guaranteed constitutional rights expressing the inviolability of human dignity. Kelsen's formalism is largely rejected.

2 Justice and liberty

The special process-values which are closely associated with the rule of law, in its wider conception, were articulated by Lon FULLER. Fuller argued that the rule of law was the special virtue of law, in the sense that the existence of a legal system – as opposed to the exercise of unbridled power – involves compliance with the 'inner morality of law'. In addition to the requirement of generality – the exercise of power must be constrained by rules – the laws must be published so that the citizen can know their content. Obedience is possible, moreover, only if the laws are clear, and not contradictory. Legality is equally frustrated by laws requiring the impossible. Laws imposing strict liability for civil wrongs pose special problems; and strict criminal liability, whereby someone can be punished despite acting innocently and with due care, undermines the rule of law.

Laws should be prospective for similar reasons, although a retroactive statute might sometimes be needed as a curative measure to correct lapses in other requirements of the law's internal morality. The precept *nulla poena sine lege* expresses the widely shared condemnation of *ex post facto* criminal laws. There must also be reasonable constancy of law through time; and the actions of officials must conform to the rules declared. The rules of 'natural justice', or 'procedural due process', assist in achieving such congruence by ensuring that the law is correctly applied in particular instances.

Although Fuller asserted a connection between procedural legality and the moral quality of the law enforced, he failed to establish a necessary connection. Other writers have observed that legality is compatible with great iniquity because it places no limitations on the substantive content of law (see LEGAL POSITIVISM §1). It excludes certain sorts of arbitrary power, but fails to guarantee respect for human rights, civil liberties or social equality. The rule of law has been likened to a sharp knife – an efficient instrument for governance, but morally neutral between different purposes. In this respect, attempts to associate the rule of law with a wider vision of political liberty and social justice have been criticized for dissolving its discrete contribution to political theory in more diffuse and contentious philosophical claims.

A connection between the rule of law and the moral quality of law may, however, be made by paying closer attention to the underlying rationale of legality. Adherence to the rule of law acknowledges human dignity and autonomy by treating people as capable of using the law as a guide in determining their actions. Where the rule of law exists, citizens may take account of legal requirements in formulating their plans; and their powers of self-determination are not frustrated by the unpredictable exercise of political authority. John Finnis has observed that the rule of law recognizes the intrinsic importance of a certain quality of interaction between ruler and ruled, expressing values of reciprocity and procedural fairness whose preservation may often justify sacrifices in efficiency or other political ends (see NATURAL LAW §4).

Moreover, Fuller emphasized the likelihood of frequent conflict between the various canons of legality – there could be no utopia in which all the desiderata were always fully satisfied. The rule of law may therefore be thought to embrace an approach to the resolution of such conflicts, in any particular case, which itself respects the values of dignity and autonomy constituting its essential point. In this respect, the coherence of the 'inner morality' of law ultimately depends on considerations which cannot be regarded as wholly instrumental.

It is also mistaken to regard the rule of law merely as a fetter on the exercise of political power. The law does not serve merely to execute the will of political rulers, but to provide a stable framework within which each person may pursue their own ends while respecting a similar freedom in others. In this way, adherence to the rule of law serves to protect legitimate expectations, formed in reliance on private as well as public law and affording secure grounds for individual planning and independent action.

John RAWLS has made a similar connection between justice and the rule of law. The regular and impartial administration of public rules – or 'justice as regularity' – is a necessary condition of a just scheme of social cooperation. The more perfectly a legal order fulfils the precepts of the rule of law, the more securely is liberty protected and the more effective is the organization of social conduct. The boundaries of our liberty are uncertain if laws are vague and imprecise, or the rules of natural justice are neglected. The principle of responsibility, whereby criminal liability should not exist in the absence of *mens rea*, also serves to protect individual liberty (JUSTICE, EQUITY AND LAW; LAW AND MORALITY).

3   Judicial obligation and legal decisions

The separation of powers assumes that judges are bound by existing law even when its application to particular cases presents questions of interpretation, whose proper resolution may be controversial. The ideal of the rule of law would seem to be seriously compromised if, in doubtful cases, judges were free to usurp the legislative function and create new law according to their own perceptions of justice or public policy.

Ronald DWORKIN has offered a theory which seeks to explain the sense in which every judicial decision is determined by existing law, even in cases where good lawyers may reasonably disagree about what the law requires. The principle of separation of powers is reflected in Dworkin's distinction between principle and policy. Questions of policy are those which concern the public good or the general welfare, and they are primarily the province of government or legislature. Judicial decisions should be grounded mainly on principle, which concerns the scope and content of individual rights. When accepted rules do not clearly determine questions about legal rights, the judge must resort to analysis of underlying principle. He is bound by law in the sense that he must decide each case in accordance with the scheme of principle which best explains and justifies existing legal rules and practices. Since Dworkin supposes that, in any highly developed legal system, a sufficiently rigorous analysis would display good reasons of morality or consistency for judicial decision, even when the outcome may be controversial, he claims that there is in principle a correct answer to every question of law.

Argument about the requirements of the rule of law, in this further sense, focuses on the content of existing law, properly understood, rather than on more formal criteria which are independent of any particular legal system. Dworkin's account has the merit of showing the importance of the individual conscience in making judgments about the content of law. It is part of the idea of the rule of law that legal obligation is ultimately a matter of reason, and is therefore susceptible of understanding and intelligent obedience by every citizen. The identification of legal analysis with moral reasoning and political principle, however, makes the content of law closely dependent on controversial criteria of justice and fairness. It may be argued, none the less, that the values of autonomy and individual responsibility, which underlie formal accounts of the rule of law, assume precisely the kind of independent moral judgment which Dworkin's theory makes central to legal analysis.

The concept of 'integrity', which expresses Dworkin's model of judicial reasoning, represents an accommodation between conflicting values of justice, concerning individual rights, and fairness, in the sense of the appropriate distribution of political power. Integrity requires that the law should reflect a consistent and coherent body of principles, in order that everyone is treated alike. The analysis therefore reveals the importance of equality as an ingredient of the rule of law. Dworkin shows that the formal equality which is ensured by the uniform and consistent application of legal rules – the least controversial feature of the rule of law – must be supplemented by a more thoroughgoing consistency of legal principle. The ideal of equality before the law ultimately assumes a substantive equality of legal protection for the rights and interests of every citizen.

See also: LAW, PHILOSOPHY OF; SOCIAL THEORY AND LAW

References and further reading

Altman, A. (1990) *Critical Legal Studies: A Liberal Critique*, Princeton, NJ: Princeton University Press. (A sophisticated but lucid defence of the liberal ideal of the rule of law against contemporary critics.)

Dworkin, R. (1977) *Taking Rights Seriously*, London: Duckworth. (Series of essays which challenge positivist conceptions of law; some assume a background knowledge of other works.)

—— (1985) *A Matter of Principle*, Oxford: Oxford University Press. (Essays on various aspects of legal philosophy which, though closely argued, do not generally assume specialized knowledge.)

—— (1986) *Law's Empire*, London: Fontana. (More difficult, but elaborates the author's theory of law as integrity.)

Finnis, J. (1980) *Natural Law and Natural Rights*, Oxford: Oxford University Press, 270–6. (Short, readable discussion, but proper appreciation requires wider study of the work as a whole.)

Fuller, L. (1969) *The Morality of Law*, revised edn, New Haven, CT: Yale University Press. (Very readable and easily understood explanation of procedural legality.)

Hayek, F. (1960) *The Constitution of Liberty*, London: Routledge & Kegan Paul; Chicago, IL: University of Chicago Press. (Easily readable; no specialized knowledge required.)

—— (1973–9) *Law Legislation and Liberty*, vol 1: *Rules and Order* (1973), vol 2: *The Mirage of Social Justice* (1976), vol 3: *The Political Order of a Free People* (1979), London: Routledge & Kegan Paul; Chicago, IL: University of Chicago Press. (Perhaps more difficult, but no previous study of philosophy necessary.)

Kelsen, H. (1945) *General Theory of Law and the State*, trans. A. Wedberg, Cambridge, MA: Harvard University Press, 1949. (For the specialist reader: full statement of the author's conception of legal positivism.)

Locke, J. (1690) *Two Treatises of Government*, P. Laslett (ed.), Cambridge: Cambridge University Press, vol. 2, chaps 9–12, 1960. (Early and readable treatment of separation of powers.)

Loughlin, M. (1992) *Public Law and Political Theory*, Oxford: Clarendon Press. (An analysis of the evolution of modern British public law in response to conflicting traditions of thought about political theory and the nature of law.)

Lucas, J. (1966) *The Principles of Politics*, Oxford: Oxford University Press, 78–143. (Accessible to the general reader; the rule of law is set in the context of other associated ideas and principles.)

Rawls, J. (1972) *A Theory of Justice*, Oxford: Oxford University Press, 235–43. (Straightforward account, but should be read in the light of the author's wider theory of law and justice.)

Raz, J. (1977) 'The Rule of Law and its Virtue', *Law Quarterly Review* 93, 195–211; repr. in J. Raz, *The Authority of Law*, Oxford: Clarendon Press, ch. 11, 1979. (Good general discussion which does not assume specialized knowledge.)

T.R.S. ALLAN

RULES AND LANGUAGE
see MEANING AND RULE-FOLLOWING

RUSSELL, BERTRAND ARTHUR WILLIAM (1872–1970)

Bertrand Russell divided his efforts between philosophy and political advocacy on behalf of a variety of radical causes. He did his most important philosophical work in logic and the philosophy of mathematics between 1900 and 1913, though later he also did important work in epistemology, metaphysics and the philosophy of mind, and continued to contribute to philosophy until the late 1950s. He wrote relatively little on ethics. His political work went on until his death.

In the philosophy of mathematics his position was logicism, the view that all of mathematics can be derived from logical premises, which he attempted to establish in detail by actual derivations, creating in the process what is essentially now the standard formulation of classical logic. Early in this work he discovered the self-referential paradoxes which posed the main difficulty for logicism and which he eventually overcame by the ramified theory of types.

Logic was central to Russell's philosophy from 1900 onwards, and much of his fertility and importance as a philosopher came from his application of the new logic to old problems. Among his most important logical innovations were the modern theory of relations and the theory of descriptions. The latter enabled him to reparse sentences containing the phrase 'the so-and-so' into a form in which the phrase did not appear. The importance of this theory for subsequent philosophy was that it enabled one to recast sentences which apparently committed one to the existence of the so-and-so into sentences in which no such commitment was suggested. This laid the basis for a new method in metaphysics (widely pursued by Russell and others in the first half of the century) in which theories about items of a given kind are reformulated so as to avoid reference to items of that kind.

Logicism itself offers just such a treatment of mathematics and in his later work Russell used the method repeatedly, though the reformulations he suggested were rarely so explicit as the ones he had offered in mathematics. In 1914 he proposed a solution to the problem of the external world by constructing matter out of sensibilia. After 1918 he proposed to construct both mind and matter out of events. After 1940 he treated all particulars as bundles of qualities. In each case his motivation was to avoid postulating anything that could be constructed, thereby eliminating ontological commitments which had no independent evidential support. Outside mathematics, his starting-point was the empirically given and he attempted to make his constructions depend as little as possible upon items not given in experience. He was not, however, a strict empiricist, since he did not think that empirical evidence alone would be sufficient for the constructions and he was always prepared to supplement it in order to obtain them. He wanted to construct, not those items which were empirically warranted, but those which were required by the relevant scientific theories, for he regarded science as the best available, though by no means an infallible, source of truth. The task, in each case, was therefore to reveal the least amount of apparatus that would have to be assumed in addition to the empirical data in order for the constructions required by science to be possible. This methodology, which he pursued throughout his career, gives an underlying unity to what, more superficially, appears as a series of abrupt changes of position.

1 Life
2 Early work
3 Logicism
4 Absolute realism
5 Solutions to the paradoxes: the zig-zag theory
6 Solutions to the paradoxes: the substitutional theory
7 Solutions to the paradoxes: the theory of types
8 Problems with ramified types
9 The theory of incomplete symbols
10 Theories of truth and judgment
11 Logical atomism
12 Our knowledge of the external world
13 Neutral monism
14 Later epistemology

1 Life

Russell was born into the Whig aristocracy and inherited many of the values of its most radical wing. His grandfather, a prominent Whig reformer of the 1830s, had twice been prime minister. Russell was orphaned before he was 4 and was brought up by his grandmother who had him educated at home. In 1890 he went to Trinity College, Cambridge, to study mathematics. He gained a first in mathematics in 1893 and then turned to philosophy for his fourth year.

In 1894 he married Alys Pearsall Smith and spent part of his honeymoon in Berlin working on his first book, *German Social Democracy* (1896). The following year he published *An Essay on the Foundations of Geometry*, a revised version of his dissertation for which he had been awarded a six-year fellowship at Trinity. This was the first of a projected series of books on the sciences. After some aborted work on physics, he turned to pure mathematics and logic, producing many of his most important contributions in the period to 1913. While doing so, he lived mainly off unearned income, but in 1910, his capital depleted, he took up a lectureship at Trinity where he taught until 1916.

Though Russell had been born with an interest in politics, it had not hitherto occupied much of his time (despite his study of the German Marxists and vigorous interventions on behalf of free trade and women's suffrage). With the outbreak of war in 1914, however, his interest in philosophy lessened and he threw himself into writing, speaking and organizing on behalf of the pacifists. A conviction under the Defence of the Realm Act led to his dismissal from Trinity in 1916; a further conviction led to his being jailed in 1918. After 1916 he had only relatively short periods of academic employment and was dependent upon writing to make his living – a fact which only partially explains his huge subsequent output.

After the war he visited Russia to see the work of the Bolshevik government, but was disillusioned with its authoritarianism. In 1920–1 he spent a year at the University of Peking (Beijing). Returning to England he married Dora Black in 1921, just in time to legitimize his son; a daughter was born in 1923. Parenthood led him to take an interest in education and with his wife he started an experimental school. It was not, in Russell's eyes, a success, and it was very expensive to run, requiring that he undertake regular lecture tours of the USA to raise money. His involvement with it ended, along with his marriage, in 1932, though Dora continued to run it on her own until 1943.

Through the 1920s and early 1930s Russell wrote prolifically on an astonishing range of topics, producing (among much else) books on Russia, China, relativity, history, education, sexual morality, international relations, religion and the future of society. Though much of this activity was necessary to make ends meet, Russell was a tireless advocate of progressive causes. By the mid-1930s, however, tiring of the precariousness of this way of life and needing now to support two families (he had remarried in 1936 and a third child was born in 1937), he hoped to return to academic life. This was not easy: positions were scarce and Russell was a controversial figure. In 1938 he lectured at Oxford, followed by visiting appointments at Chicago and UCLA and finally an offer of a permanent position at City College, New York. This last, however, provoked opposition from New York's Catholic community and the appointment was overturned in a celebrated court case.

In 1940, therefore, Russell found himself unemployed and marooned in America by the war. At this point, the eccentric millionaire Albert Barnes came to his rescue with a five-year appointment to lecture on the history of philosophy at the Barnes Foundation in Philadelphia. Although Barnes fired Russell at the end of 1942, he permanently solved Russell's financial problems, for not only did Russell collect a sizeable sum for breach of contract but the lectures he gave for Barnes became the basis for his hugely successful *History of Western Philosophy* (1945).

Russell returned to England in 1944 to take up a fellowship at Trinity College, where he completed his last great philosophical work, *Human Knowledge* (1948). His return marked not only a mending of his relations with Trinity but also with the British establishment. His continued condemnation of communism in general and the Soviet government in particular was well suited to the beginnings of the cold war and Russell enjoyed a period of unaccustomed respectability. Throughout the 1950s he continued to write prolifically, including a philosophical autobiography, *My Philosophical Development* (1959). He married for a fourth time in 1952.

His respectability was short-lived. After the death of Stalin his hatred of the Soviet government moderated, and the threat of nuclear war came to dominate his thoughts. He wrote extensively on the danger of war during the 1950s but increasingly felt the need for action and in 1958 helped found the Campaign for Nuclear Disarmament, and then the more militant Committee of 100. In 1961 he was jailed once more for inciting demonstrators to civil disobedience. The 1960s were a time of hectic political work for Russell. He lent support to many causes and was especially active in opposing the Vietnam War. His last political statement, on the Middle East, was written two days before his death.

2 Early work

As an undergraduate Russell came under the influence of the neo-Hegelianism which then dominated British philosophy, especially the work of J.M.E. McTAGGART, James Ward and F.H. BRADLEY. His earliest logical views were influenced most by Bradley, especially Bradley's rejection of psychologism. But, like Ward and McTaggart, he rejected Bradley's metaphysical monism in favour of monadism. Even as an idealist, he held that scientific knowledge was the best available and that philosophy should be built around it. Through many subsequent changes, this belief about science and his pluralism remained constant.

In 1895 he conceived the Hegelian plan of writing an encyclopedia of the sciences, together with another series of books on social and political issues, the two to be united in a synthesis of theory and practice. He followed this plan long after its Hegelian inspiration had passed, and in old age he noted that he had written as much of both series as could have been expected – except for the final synthesis, which still eluded him. As a system, the encyclopedia was to be dialectical, with supercessions between the individual sciences. Within each science, however, transcendental arguments were used to establish its a priori elements. In *An Essay on the Foundations of Geometry*, for example, he attempted to show that projective geometry was a necessary condition for the possibility of external experience. At the same time, he argued that geometry gave rise to contradictions which could only be resolved by a supercession to kinematics. From geometry he turned to arithmetic (which preceded it in the dialectic) and to physics (which followed it), though what he wrote on these subjects remained largely unfinished (see 1983–: vol. 2).

Two main problems caused Russell to abandon this work. First, there was (as G.E. MOORE pointed out) a lingering psychologism associated with his use of transcendental arguments. Second, the contradictions which supposedly arose in the special sciences generally were not eliminated by the transition to a new science, but merely reappeared in a new form. They resulted from the use of asymmetrical relations, but only if these relations were treated as internal.

Russell resolved both problems in 1898 by abandoning idealism (including internal relations and his Kantian methodology). He called this the one real revolution in his philosophy (see HEGELIANISM §5; TRANSCENDENTAL ARGUMENTS).

3 Logicism

The new philosophy was little help with Russell's immediate task – an analysis of the concept of number – until, in 1900, he discovered Peano's symbolic logic. Significantly, Russell's first contribution to Peano's logic was a formal theory of relations on the basis of which he was able to define the cardinal number of a class u as the class of classes coextensive with u and produce a theory of progressions which formed the basis for ordinal arithmetic (1901).

Using the new logic Russell propounded logicism, the view that the whole of pure mathematics can be derived deductively from logical principles, a position he arrived at independently of Frege, who held a similar but more restricted view (and who had anticipated Russell's definition of cardinals in 1884) but whose work Russell discovered only later (see FREGE, G. §8). Russell's first full statement of logicism was published in *The Principles of Mathematics* (1903). The interest of this work is mainly philosophical: it contains none of the actual derivations of mathematical results from logical principles. The latter was to be carried out in a projected second volume to be written in collaboration with A.N. Whitehead (see A.N. WHITEHEAD §2). Their work expanded over the next ten years and resulted in the three-volume *Principia Mathematica* (1910–13), in which detailed derivations were given for Cantor's set theory, finite and transfinite arithmetic (including an elegant generalization of ordinal arithmetic called 'relation-arithmetic') and elementary parts of measure theory (see CANTOR, G.). A fourth volume, by Whitehead alone, on geometry (including complex number theory) was never completed. As a demonstration of logicism, therefore, *Principia* depends upon much prior arithmetization of mathematics, for example, of analysis, which is not explicitly treated. Even with these allowances much is still left out, such as abstract algebra and statistics (see NUMBERS §6).

4 Absolute realism

The philosophy which Russell had adopted after abandoning idealism in 1898 and which underlay his early logicism was an extreme realism (to which Moore also subscribed). It was fully stated in *The Principles of Mathematics* and had been anticipated in *A Critical Exposition of the Philosophy of Leibniz* (1900) and in unpublished writings (see 1983–: vol. 2).

In Russell's absolute realism, everything which can be referred to or made the subject of a proposition is a term which has being (though not necessarily existence). Terms are either things, which can occur in a proposition only as its subject(s), or concepts, which may occur as subjects but which may also occur as relations. A proposition is a complex of terms related to each other. All complexes are propositions; all propositions are terms. Terms are neither linguistic nor psychological, but objective constituents of the world. The first task of philosophy is the theoretical analysis of propositions into their constituents. The propositions of logic are unique in that they remain true when any of their terms (apart from logical constants) is replaced by *any* other term.

In 1901 Russell discovered that this position fell prey to self-referential paradoxes. For example, if the combination of any number of terms is a new term, the combination of *all* terms is a term distinct from any term. This paradox is related to the greatest cardinal paradox which arose in Cantor's transfinite arithmetic. Cantor had shown that the power-set, $\wp(S)$, of any set S has a higher cardinality than S. But if S is the set of all cardinals, the cardinality of $\wp(S)$ will then be a cardinal greater than any in S. While thinking about this problem Russell came upon an even more troubling contradiction, now known as Russell's paradox, which affected the foundations of set theory itself. It seems natural to suppose that some sets are, but most sets are not, members of themselves. If we consider, however, the set of all sets that are not members of themselves and ask whether this set is a member of itself we arrive at Russell's paradox. For supposing that it is a member of itself, then it lacks the defining property of the set and so is not a member of itself. But if it is not a member of itself then it has the defining property of the set and so is a member of itself. The paradox is simply proven given the unrestricted comprehension axiom of naive set theory, that for any property (or propositional function) ϕ there is a set $\{x: \phi x\}$ of just those things that satisfy ϕ; that is to say, $a \in \{x: \phi x\} \equiv \phi a$. Let ϕx be $\sim(x \in x)$ and let a be $\{x: \sim(x \in x)\}$, then substituting in the comprehension axiom gives:

$$\{x: \sim(x \in x)\} \in \{x: \sim(x \in x)\}$$
$$\equiv \sim(\{x: \sim(x \in x)\} \in \{x: \sim(x \in x)\}).$$

These paradoxes in set theory are related to other self-referential paradoxes. The best-known is the liar paradox, generated by the person who says 'I am lying': if what they say is true, it is a lie; if it is a lie then they speak the truth. The long delay in the publication of *Principia* was largely due to the difficulty of devising a logic which was both paradox-free and strong enough to support pure mathematics (see PARADOXES OF SET AND PROPERTY §4; CANTOR'S THEOREM; CONTINUUM HYPOTHESIS).

5 Solutions to the paradoxes: the zig-zag theory

In *The Principles of Mathematics* Russell offered no firm solution to the paradoxes, but in the next few years he tried a variety of approaches. The first was what he called the 'zig-zag theory'. The intuitive idea behind it was simple: only 'fairly simple' propositional functions determine classes; 'complicated and recondite' functions do not (1906a: 145–6). The problem was to specify the degree of complexity which marked the divide. Russell's only published remarks on the theory were in a survey article written after he had abandoned the theory and are vague on this point (1906a). Unpublished writings reveal that he tried a number of formulations (1983–: vol. 4). The chief difficulty is to find an appropriately restricted comprehension axiom: versions with weak constraints permit new contradictions to be derived, but if the constraints are too strong, logicism (for example, Russell's definition of cardinal number) is undermined. Russell found no way of showing that a comprehension axiom strong enough to support logicism would be paradox-free.

The zig-zag approach has some affinity to Quine's 'New Foundations' theory (Quine 1937) and some more recent type-free theories (Feferman 1984), but the former imposes quite different constraints on comprehension, while the latter is inconsistent with logicism.

6 Solutions to the paradoxes: the substitutional theory

Russell's next attempt went considerably further. It occupied him from 1905 to 1906 and started from the theory of incomplete symbols he had devised in 1905 (see §9 below). Under the substitutional theory Russell eliminated classes, relations and predicates as terms over which variables ranged. Variables now range over entities, which are either simple individuals or complexes (including propositions). The fundamental notion of the theory is that of substituting one entity for another in a complex to yield a new complex. This is written '$p\frac{b}{a}!q$' and read 'p with b substituted for a yields q', where p and q need not be propositions, though in the interesting cases they will be. '$p\frac{b}{a}!q$' will always be true or false whatever p, a and b are. If a does not occur in p then $p\frac{b}{a}!p$. Propositional functions and classes of individuals are expressed by matrices, for example, 'p/a', in which p is called the prototype and a the argument. b is a member of the class represented by 'p/a', if $p\frac{b}{a}!q$ and q is true. Propositional functions of propositional functions (or classes of classes) are expressed by the matrix '$q/(p/a)$'. Russell hoped to avoid the paradoxes because the application of a matrix to itself, which generates many of them, is impossible in the system. For example,

$$p\frac{\dfrac{p/a}{a}}{}$$

is ill-formed, because 'p/a' is an incomplete expression, not the name of an entity, and thus there is nothing which is substituted for a. Thus one can express with matrices everything that could previously be expressed by means of classes or functions except, as Russell puts it, for 'certain limiting cases... [which] are precisely those that lead to contradictions' (1906b: 171–2).

The ability to capture an iterative concept of classes by substitutional means preserved Russell's definition of cardinal number and thus permitted the logicist programme to proceed. Russell spent much of 1906 developing logicism on a substitutional basis (see 1983–: vol. 5). The above account illustrates the lengths he was prepared to go to in order to preserve the unrestricted variables of the *Principles*. However, the fact that the theory allowed propositions as substituends permitted a propositional paradox to be derived. After several attempts to eliminate it and finding that, each time, it returned in more complicated forms, Russell reluctantly abandoned the substitutional theory.

7 Solutions to the paradoxes: the theory of types

In 1906 Russell adopted the solution which appears in *Principia*, namely the theory of types which banned self-reference by stratifying terms and expressions into complex hierarchies of disjoint sub-classes. The expression 'all terms', for example, is then meaningless unless restricted to terms of specified type(s), and a combination of terms of a given type is a term of different type; functions are of a different type to their arguments; classes of a different type to their members.

Ironically, a simple version of the theory had appeared in *The Principles of Mathematics* (appendix B). There, propositional functions are assigned a range of significance, 'a range within which x must lie if $\phi(x)$ is to be a proposition at all' (1903: 525). Significance ranges form types in that 'if x belongs to the range of significance of $\phi(x)$, there is a class of objects, the *type* of x, all of which must belong to the range of significance of $\phi(x)$' (1903: 525). Every significance range either is a type or is the union of several types. Types are hierarchically arranged: individuals constitute the lowest type, classes of individuals the next, classes of classes of individuals the next after that, and so on. Two-place relations (in extension) form a different hierarchy, three-place relations yet another, and so on. The theory bears resemblance to Chwistek's simple type theory (Chwistek 1921), though there are important differences, notably that in Russell's theory all ranges form a type, and propositions and numbers form distinct types outside the hierarchy. Since propositions are not stratified into types, Russell's theory yields a propositional version of the contradiction (1903: 527).

Russell anticipated that the type theory of the *Principles* would have to be 'transformed into some subtler shape before it can answer all difficulties' (1903: 523). One reason he did not pursue this immediately was due to his reluctance to abandon the unrestricted variables of the *Principles* upon which his account of logic depended (see Urquhart 1989). Only when other avenues had been explored did he return to type theory. In the type theory of the *Principles* the type of a function had been determined exclusively by the type(s) of its argument(s). The 'subtler shape' of the theory Russell developed after 1906 – the 'ramified theory of types' – was obtained by adding order distinctions within each type based upon the form of the function. In a controversy with POINCARÉ, Russell had acknowledged that all the paradoxes involved violations of the 'vicious circle principle': No totality can contain members defined in terms of itself; or, in the formulation Russell preferred, 'whatever involves an apparent [bound] variable must not be among the possible values of that variable' (1906c: 198). The ramified theory of types was designed to build order-restrictions into the bound variables themselves in such a way that violations of the vicious circle principle would be prevented by the symbolism itself.

Functions are significant only when their arguments for each argument-place are drawn from a specified range of items appropriate to that place. Russell expresses this by saying that a function presupposes a totality for each of its argument-places; such a totality is the significance range for that argument-place. As before, individuals constitute the lowest such totality. First-order functions take only individuals as arguments; second-order functions take either first-order functions or individuals as arguments; third-order functions take either second-order functions, first-order functions or individuals as arguments; and so on. All the arguments of any function must be of a lower order than that of

the function. If an nth-order function has an argument of order $n-1$, the function is said to be *predicative*. Non-predicative functions all involve quantification over functions of lower order. (For example, if Russell is an individual, 'Russell is clever' employs a first-order predicative function of individuals, whereas 'Russell has all the (first-order) qualities of a great philosopher' employs a non-predicative function of second-order involving the quantification $(\phi)(x$ is a great philosopher $\supset \phi x)$, where the variable ϕ ranges over the totality of first-order functions. All bound variables range over only one such totality.)

Propositions form a similar hierarchy: *elementary* propositions have only individuals as terms; first-order propositions are either elementary or involve quantification over individuals; second-order propositions involve quantification over first-order propositions; and so on. First-order propositions presuppose no totality except that of individuals and, in general, propositions of nth-order presuppose totalities only of propositions of order $n-1$. The hierarchy of propositions can be derived from the hierarchy of functions since a proposition involving a totality of nth-order propositions can be reduced to one involving a totality of nth-order functions. Observing the restrictions imposed by these hierarchies ensures that no violations of the vicious circle principle can occur. The liar paradox is avoided, for instance, because what the liar asserts is '(p)(I affirm p and p is false)'. For this to be significant the bound variable 'p' must range over propositions of some specified order, while the proposition the liar asserts will be of a higher order and thus not among the propositions the liar asserts to be false.

In 1908, Russell sketched the development of logic and set theory up to the definition of cardinal and ordinal numbers on the basis of the ramified theory, a process that is completed in *Principia*. There are some differences between the 1908 presentation followed above and that in *Principia*: for instance, in *Principia* elementary propositions are not included among first-order propositions and propositional quantification is avoided. This is related to a more important change, namely Russell's treatment of propositions in *Principia* as incomplete symbols (see §10) which requires a radical distinction between elementary propositions and those involving first-order quantification and is the basis for his claim that the propositional hierarchy is derived from the functional one. Some elements of the substitutional theory survive into ramified type theory, indeed Landini (1993) goes so far as to call the 1908 version a 'modification' of the substitutional theory. As in the substitutional theory, classes remain incomplete symbols, and Russell presents the hierarchy of functions in explicitly substitutional terms (see THEORY OF TYPES).

8 Problems with ramified types

Russell's reluctance to embrace the ramified theory of types was well-motivated, for it raised serious obstacles to logicism. In the first place, Russell's definition of a cardinal number as the class of all similar classes is no longer admissible. There is no longer a class of all similar classes, but only a class of all similar first-order classes, a class of all similar second-order classes, and so on. (Strictly, of course, the definition will proceed in terms of the hierarchy of functions, but the class terminology is more familiar and admissible as a *façon de parler*.) There then ceases to be a unique cardinal 2, for example, but a different 2 at each level of the hierarchy; ordinary talk about 2 is typically ambiguous between these different cardinals. Similar problems affect the statement of logical principles which, strictly, would need to be stated for each order. In *Principia* this is avoided by the use of free variables which are typically ambiguous. Thus $\vdash . \phi x \vee \sim \phi x$ asserts the law of excluded middle for monadic propositions of undetermined order; whereas $\vdash . (\phi) . \phi x \vee \sim \phi x$ asserts it for those of some particular order. These results are untoward but not intolerable.

A similar, but more troubling difficulty threatened Russell's treatment of the continuum, for on the ramified theory the least upper bound of a bounded set of real numbers is a number of a higher level. The most serious difficulty, however, concerns the principle of mathematical induction: namely, that any function satisfied by 0, and satisfied by $x + 1$ if satisfied by x, is satisfied by all natural numbers. These two difficulties threaten the logicist programme for transfinite and finite arithmetic respectively. Russell surmounted them by making the assumption that for every nonpredicative function there is an equivalent predicative function in the same variables. This is his 'axiom of reducibility': $(\exists f)(\phi x \equiv_x f!x)$ (1910–13: *12.1).

It has often been objected that the axiom of reducibility undoes all the good that ramifying type theory achieved, on the grounds that it renders the ramified theory equivalent to the simple theory, thereby readmitting all the paradoxes ramification was designed to prevent (Ramsey 1925; Copi 1950). Myhill (1979) shows that this objection is ill-founded.

Frank RAMSEY (1925) proposed that the paradoxes should be divided into those which belong to logic and set theory and those which are semantical or linguistic and that logic need solve only the former. Since the simple theory of types solves the logical paradoxes, the ramified theory is not needed in logic. This suggestion has been very influential. However, it still leaves the semantic paradoxes to be dealt with and Ramsey's demarcation between the two kinds is hardly adequate. His suggestion that the semantic paradoxes are in some way empirical is neither clear nor plausible. Moreover, the fact that both types of paradox arise from self-reference suggests a uniform treatment. Above all, Ramsey's distinction does little justice to Russell's appealing intuition that the same underlying logic should be applied universally. It is clear now that semantics is capable of just as rigorous, formal treatment as set theory and the suggestion that the proper formal treatment of each requires different logical principles lacks *prima facie* plausibility (see SEMANTIC PARADOXES AND THEORIES OF TRUTH §2).

Under the influence of WITTGENSTEIN, Russell came to accept the view that logical propositions were all tautologies. From this point of view the axiom of reducibility is clearly unsatisfactory (Wittgenstein 1922). From much the same point of view, Ramsey argued that it was not only contingent but a contingent falsehood – though it is not clear that his counterexample is a good one (Ramsey 1925). In the second edition of *Principia*, therefore, Russell tried to dispense with the axiom. He conceded that much of transfinite arithmetic would be lost as a result, but hoped none the less to save the theory of natural numbers by proving a version of the principle of mathematical induction within the constraints of the ramified theory and without the axiom of reducibility. Gödel (1944) noted the flaw in the proof and Myhill (1974) has since shown it to be irremediable. It follows, therefore, that even finite arithmetic cannot be logicized within the constraints of the ramified theory without the axiom of reducibility.

9 The theory of incomplete symbols

Both the substitutional theory and ramified type theory were closely linked to one of Russell's most important contributions to logic: his theory of definite descriptions and the more general theory of incomplete symbols it presaged. The theory of descriptions arose out of problems in Russell's theory of denoting in *The Principles of Mathematics*. It is plain that 'I met Quine' and 'I met the author of *Quiddities*' are different propositions, even though Quine is the author of *Quiddities*. In the *Principles*, the first proposition contains Quine, while the second contains a 'denoting concept' (expressed by the definite description 'the author of *Quiddities*') which denotes Quine. When Quine occurs in a proposition the proposition is about Quine, but when a denoting concept occurs the proposition is not about the concept but what the concept denotes. This theory, if it is to be statable, requires that there be some way in which a denoting concept, rather than its denotation, can be denoted. After much effort, Russell in 'On Denoting' (1905) concluded that this was impossible and eliminated denoting concepts as intermediaries between denoting phrases and their denotations by means of his theory of descriptions.

Russell showed in a broad (though not comprehensive) range of cases how denoting phrases could be eliminated in favour of predicates and quantified variables by providing an analysis of the sentence in which they occurred. This advance was made possible by Russell's study of Frege, whose theory of quantification replaced the intricate but unavailing theory of the *Principles*. Russell analysed sentences containing definite descriptions, such as, 'The successor of 1 is even', thus:

(1) $(\exists x)(x$ succeeds 1 & (y)
   (y succeeds $1 \supset y = x)$ & x is even)

The three conjuncts in this analysis ensure, respectively, that a successor of 1 exists, that there is at most one successor of 1 and that whatever succeeds 1 is even.

In cases where the definite description does not denote, the sentence gets the value *false* on account of the falsity of the first conjunct of its analysis. This enabled Russell to treat as meaningful sentences containing non-denoting definite descriptions without having to suppose either that nonexistent objects were denoted (as in Meinong's theory of objects) or that there were such things as denoting concepts (as in Russell's 1903 theory) or Fregean senses. The subsequent literature has emphasized the first point, but it was the second which motivated Russell.

Some counterintuitive consequences of Russell's analysis were removed by his introduction of scope distinctions among the occurrences of descriptions within sentences. Not all problems are thus removed, however, and there have been many subsequent attempts to do better either through improvements to Russell's theory, or through 'free logics', or by means of Meinongian theories which permit quantification over nonexistent objects.

Obviously the theory will not permit the use of definite descriptions as substitution-values for the variables in (1) and this leads to a sharp distinction in Russell's philosophy of language between definite descriptions and names. Since Russell thought that most ordinary names were in fact disguised definite descriptions, he distinguished between descriptions and 'logically proper names' which alone could be substituted for variables. (The latter were names of objects of acquaintance – represented in ordinary language by 'this' and 'that'.) By treating ordinary names as descriptions he could use the theory of descriptions to account for the informative nature of identity statements such as 'Hesperus = Phosphorus'.

The principle of contextual definition employed in the theory of descriptions, which allowed sentences containing a description to be reparsed to eliminate the description, led Russell, after 1905, to make a sharp distinction between the grammatical and the logical form of a proposition. He applied similar techniques to other kinds of expression (for instance, to class names and to propositions). Russell held that the expressions thus eliminated, which he called 'incomplete symbols', had meaning only in the context of a sentence and were meaningless in isolation. The various ways in which they were eliminated constituted his 'theory of incomplete symbols' (see DESCRIPTIONS; EXISTENCE §2; FREE LOGICS §§1, 3; PROPER NAMES §4; SENSE AND REFERENCE; STRAWSON, P.F. §2).

10 Theories of truth and judgment

The theory of incomplete symbols made possible Russell's substitutional theory, in which class names and relations were treated as incomplete symbols. The appearance of a propositional paradox in the substitutional theory convinced Russell that propositions should also be treated as incomplete symbols. This was accomplished by his multiple relation theory of judgment which became part of the philosophical underpinnings of ramified type theory. In Russell's early realism, true and false propositions alike were treated as subsistent complexes and belief as a relation between a mind and a proposition. This leaves it obscure why we prefer to believe true propositions. In the multiple relation theory, belief and other 'propositional' attitudes were treated as many-place ('multiple') relations between a mind and the individual constituents of the erstwhile proposition. Thus 'm believes that aRb' has the form '$B(m, a, R, b)$', not '$B(m, p)$'. Apparent references to propositions are eliminated by subsuming their constituents within an actual psychological complex including a mind and related by some 'propositional' attitude. Propositions thus become fabrications of the mind. The belief represented by '$B(m, a, R, b)$' will be a true belief just in case there is a complex a-R-b.

Russell had considered such a theory as early as 1906, but put it aside while he worked on the substitutional theory in which propositions were needed as entities. The theory was taken up again and developed in writings from 1910 to 1913. The final development of the theory, in *Theory of Knowledge* (1913), was left unpublished by Russell because of criticisms from Wittgenstein, then his student at Cambridge. Wittgenstein's criticisms are perhaps most simply expressed as a dilemma. Either the constituents of a belief (*a*, *R* and *b* in the example above) are assigned to types or they are not. If they are not, then the 'propositions' fabricated by thought will not be subject to the ramified type hierarchy (it will be possible to judge nonsense, as Wittgenstein puts it) and the paradoxes will reappear. If they are, then they must be assigned to types by some prior judgment, to which the same considerations apply, and an infinite regress results (Sommerville 1981; Griffin 1985).

11 Logical atomism

Russell used the name 'logical atomism' for all his philosophical work after 1898, though now it is used mainly to describe his position from 1905 to 1919. The philosophy was atomistic because it took items in certain categories to be basic; it was logical because it sought to construct items in other categories by rigorous logical means. This involved a two-fold process: an analysis of concepts in ordinary or scientific use to discover which items were basic, followed by a logical reconstruction of the science from the basic items up. Although Russell's early logicist constructions were clearly along these lines, this analytic methodology came fully into its own only with the advent of the theory of incomplete symbols in 1905.

One important consequence of the theory of incomplete symbols was that the ontological commitments of a theory could be reduced by reformulating the theory to remove expressions which apparently denoted problematic entities. It was unnecessary to posit the existence of items which could be logically constructed. This formed the basis for what Russell called the 'supreme maxim in scientific philosophizing', his version of Ockham's razor: 'Wherever possible, logical constructions are to be substituted for inferred entities' (1983–: vol. 8, 11).

Parallel results held in epistemology. The theory of incomplete symbols showed how knowledge of a wide range of items could be achieved by knowledge (by acquaintance) of a much narrower range. Acquaintance was a direct, two-place cognitive relation, and objects of acquaintance were epistemically basic. Knowledge of other items was obtained by description, which always depended upon knowledge by acquaintance (1911). The distinction between knowledge by acquaintance and knowledge by description first appeared in 'On Denoting', where Russell first formulated his 'principle of acquaintance': 'in every proposition that we can apprehend . . . all the constituents are really entities with which we have

immediate acquaintance' (1983–: vol. 4, 427). All other apparent constituents were to be eliminated by analysis. These innovations in 1905 marked the end of Russell's extreme realism, though he remained a Platonist in that he included universals among the objects of acquaintance (see KNOWLEDGE BY ACQUAINTANCE AND DESCRIPTION; LOGICAL ATOMISM §2; ONTOLOGICAL COMMITMENT).

12 Our knowledge of the external world

Russell has traditionally been regarded as the direct heir of the British empiricists, yet his work prior to 1910 belongs more naturally to the continental rationalist tradition. None of the thinkers who influenced him during this period – Kant, Bradley, Cantor, Peano, Frege – were empiricists, and it was not until 1912, when he was commissioned to write a short introduction to philosophy, *The Problems of Philosophy*, that he undertook a serious study of the British empiricists, especially BERKELEY and HUME. Hume's influence appears directly in the chapter on induction (and in a paper of 1912, 'On the Notion of Cause'); Berkeley's was more indirect (since Russell rejected his idealism) and appears in Russell's treatment of the external world.

In *Problems* Russell held that empirical knowledge is based on direct acquaintance with sense-data and that matter itself, of which we have only knowledge by description, is postulated as the best explanation of sense-data. He soon became dissatisfied with this idea and, inspired by his logicist constructions of mathematical concepts, proposed instead that matter be logically constructed out of sense-data, thereby obviating dubious inferences to material objects as the causes of sensations. The actual data of sense, however, are too fragmentary for the construction of items with the expected properties of matter (such as permanence). To solve this problem Russell was led to postulate unsensed sensibilia in addition to sense-data. It is important to realize that for Russell, unlike most sense-datum theorists, sense-data were physical, located in physical space at varying distances from the place at which common sense located the material object. It is thus logically, though not practically, possible for more than one mind to be acquainted with the same sense-datum at the same time. Sense-data are merely sensibilia with which a mind happens to be acquainted, so properly speaking matter is constructed out of sensibilia rather than sense-data. In addition to matter, Russell also sought to construct space and time. All the sense-data with which a single mind is acquainted are located within a perspective, a private space peculiar to that mind. Similar spaces exist at every point at which a mind could be located.

These private spaces Russell calls perspectives. Physical space is the set of all such perspectives. The arrangement of perspectives in physical space is achieved by the variation in the qualities of the sensibilia (such as their size and shape) as they appear in the perspectives: for instance, if the sensibilia in perspectives P_1 and P_2 are more similar than those in perspectives P_3 and P_4, P_1 and P_2 will be located closer together in physical space than P_3 and P_4.

This theory received its fullest expression in *Our Knowledge of the External World* (1914), though it remained in programmatic form; detailed constructions along similar lines were undertaken by Carnap (1928) (see CARNAP, R. §1). Although Russell hoped that eventually a correlation between sense-data and the differential equations of physics would be forthcoming, it is difficult to see how this would ever be possible. Many of the standard objections to sense-data do not apply to Russell's theory, but it is still difficult to see how the gap between experiential evidence and physical theory could be bridged in the deductively rigorous way Russell wanted. For example, it is difficult to see how perspectives could be uniquely arranged in physical space when no sensibile occurs in more than one perspective. Nor is it clear how sensibilia could be grouped together to form the material objects required by either common sense or physics. Moreover, since sensibilia are physical and objective it would seem that they are still subject to misapprehension by the mind, thereby reintroducing the difficulties with illusion which had allegedly made material objects unviable as objects of acquaintance (see PERCEPTION, EPISTEMIC ISSUES IN).

13 Neutral monism

Before 1919 Russell wrote little about the philosophy of mind, though his dualism was evident in his analyses of judgment and acquaintance. By 1919, however, he came to think that mind, like matter, should be constructed out of more primitive material, a view akin to James's neutral monism (see JAMES, W.). This change is somewhat puzzling, since Russell had criticized James's theory in some detail in *Theory of Knowledge* (1913) and, more tentatively, in 'The Philosophy of Logical Atomism' (1918). He was influenced partly by Hume's arguments for the unintrospectability of the self, but most importantly by Wittgenstein's treatment of belief, which 'shows...that there is no such thing as the soul' (Wittgenstein 1922: 5.5421).

Russell's neutral monism began with a new theory of belief in 'On Propositions' (1919a). He identified the contents of beliefs with images ('image-propositions') and words ('word-propositions'), understood

as certain sorts of events – now the basic elements of his construction – which are neutral in the sense of being neither physical nor mental. Truth was analysed in terms of resemblance and causal relations. Wider issues are treated in *The Analysis of Mind* (1921), where the influence of contemporary trends in psychology, especially behaviourism, is evident. He never fully embraced behaviourism (for example, he did not attempt a behaviourist elimination of images), but he was prepared to push it as far as he thought it would go. He offered, for example, a behaviourist account of desire, about which he subsequently had doubts.

On Russell's neutral monism, minds and matter are constructed out of events and differ only in that they are organized by different causal laws: material objects by those of physics, minds by 'mnemic' causal laws, in which a past state of the mind is among the proximate causes of its current state. The theory is a precursor of later mind–brain identity theories.

In 1927, Russell returned to the problem of matter – this time, paying more attention to contemporary physics. Part I of *The Analysis of Matter* is devoted to relativity and quantum theory, and Part III deals with the causal and spatiotemporal order of events. In Part II, starting from a causal theory of perception, Russell asks what can be inferred from percepts (considered as events occurring within one's head) about the nature of their supposed external causes. Using the dictum that like causes have like effects, Russell answers that we can infer only the structure of the external world from the structure of our percepts – a doctrine known as structural realism.

Russell quickly abandoned structural realism when M.H.A. Newman (1928) showed that any set with the right cardinality could be arranged so as to have the same structure as the world – a result analogous to that claimed in Putnam's model-theoretic argument against realist theories of reference (Demopoulos and Friedman 1989). Russell, however, never abandoned neutral monism, though he left the theory incomplete. Constructions were suggested rather than provided (the fullest sketches offered were the treatment of belief in the second edition of *Principia* (1925) and a 1936 paper on temporal order). Moreover, while Russell had much to say about consciousness, he said very little about intentionality and (more surprisingly) personal identity. On the physics side, the breakdown of causality in quantum theory was a serious problem, given the importance Russell attached to causal relations in his constructions, but in 1927 it was perhaps not yet so well-established a fact as to demand explanation (see NEUTRAL MONISM).

14 Later epistemology

Russell's penchant for reductive analysis was taken further in *An Inquiry into Meaning and Truth* (1940) where the terms of atomic facts, hitherto sense-data or events, are construed as bundles of compresent qualities. These qualities are the meanings of object-words, and bundles of them are denoted by logically proper names. This position was retained in *Human Knowledge* (1948); it marks the culmination of Russell's long battle with substance/attribute metaphysics. Despite its title, the *Inquiry* was more concerned with metaphysics and epistemology than with semantics. The meaning theory proposed there was causal and (in inspiration) behaviourist, though once again Russell did not expect a purely behaviourist analysis to be adequate.

Russell's allegiance to empiricism, like behaviourism, was never very strong and by 1936 he was writing on 'The Limits of Empiricism'. Even in *The Analysis of Matter* there are clear indications that he thought pure empiricism would render science impossible. In the *Analysis* he thought that Berkeleyan scepticism about matter could be avoided by construction, but that Hume's scepticism about induction was so far untouched. He tackled induction most thoroughly in *Human Knowledge* (1948), which contains his only extended treatment of probability. The problem for this book was set in 'The Limits of Empiricism', where he asked what non-empirical principles must be assumed in order for science to be possible. Originally, he thought that induction itself would be sufficient. In *Human Knowledge*, however, he showed that inductive inference was not always truth-preserving (for reasons later popularized by Nelson GOODMAN as 'the new riddle of induction') (see INDUCTION, EPISTEMIC ISSUES IN §1).

In place of induction, he proposed five 'postulates of non-demonstrative inference' as the minimum extra-logical, non-empirical apparatus required for science. His methodology here returned to that which had guided his work on *Principia* where he had sought the minimum logical apparatus necessary to support mathematics. It even had some resemblance to his earlier Kantian methodology, though Russell pointed out that he proposed his postulates as scientific hypotheses, not as synthetic a priori truths. The postulates, unfortunately, were vaguely stated in *Human Knowledge*, and Russell left more detailed work on them unpublished, probably on account of the frosty reception the book received.

By the time *Human Knowledge* was published linguistic philosophy was at its height and Russell's work had become very unfashionable. Russell had no time for Wittgenstein's later philosophy, nor for the ordinary language philosophy it inspired. He continued to think that understanding the world, rather than language, was the chief task of philosophy and his last philosophical writings, in the 1950s, were unavailing attempts to stem the tide of linguistic philosophy (see ORDINARY LANGUAGE PHILOSOPHY, SCHOOL OF §§1–3).

See also: ANALYTICAL PHILOSOPHY §§1–3; IDEALISM §§5, 7; LOGICISM; MONISM; MOORE, G.E. §4

List of works

Russell, B.A.W. (1983–) *The Collected Papers of Bertrand Russell*, The McMaster University Edition, various editors, 30 vols anticipated, London: Routledge. (The definitive edition of Russell's shorter writings and unpublished works. His philosophical papers are to be found in volumes 1–11.)

—— (1896) *German Social Democracy*, London: Allen & Unwin, 1965. (Russell's first book. A study of German Marxism.)

—— (1897) *An Essay on the Foundations of Geometry*, New York: Dover, 1956. (The first instalment of the encyclopedia of the sciences. An attempt to rehabilitate a Kantian philosophy of geometry in the light of non-Euclidean geometry.)

—— (1900) *A Critical Exposition of the Philosophy of Leibniz*, London: Routledge, 1992. (For long an influential work on Leibniz, it also contains early intimations of Russell's own realist philosophy.)

—— (1901) 'Sur la logique des relations avec des applications à la théorie des séries' (The Logic of Relations with Some Applications to the Theory of Series), *Revue de mathématiques* 7: 115–48; trans. R.C. Marsh, in Russell (1983–), vol. 3: 314–49. (The formalization of Russell's theory of relations in Peano's logical notation; an early statement of logicism which includes the Frege–Russell definition of cardinal number.)

—— (1903) *The Principles of Mathematics*; 2nd edn, 1937; London: Routledge 1992. (A philosophical prolegomena to logicism.)

—— (1905) 'On Denoting', *Mind* 14: 479–93; repr. in Russell (1983–), vol. 4: 415–27. (The first published statement of Russell's theory of definite descriptions.)

—— (1906a) 'On Some Difficulties in the Theory of Transfinite Numbers and Order Types', *Proceedings of the London Mathematical Society* series 2, 4: 29–53; repr. in Russell (1974), 135–64. (A survey of different approaches to solving the paradoxes.)

—— (1906b) 'On the Substitutional Theory of Classes and Relations' in Russell (1974), 165–89. (A survey of Russell's substitutional theory, prepared for publication but withdrawn in the face of Russell's discovery of new paradoxes.)

—— (1906c) 'Les Paradoxes de la Logique', *Revue de métaphysique et de morale* 14: 627–50; trans. 'On "Insolubilia" and their Solution by Symbolic Logic', in Russell (1974), 190–214. (A defence of logicism against criticisms by Poincaré. In it Russell recognizes violations of the vicious circle principle as the source of the paradoxes.)

—— (1908) 'Mathematical Logic as based on the Theory of Types', *American Journal of Mathematics* 30: 222–62; repr. in Russell (1956), 59–102. (The first version of ramified type theory with which Russell finally hoped to eliminate the paradoxes.)

Whitehead, A.N. and Russell, B.A.W. (1910–13) *Principia Mathematica*, Cambridge: Cambridge University Press, 3 vols; 2nd edn, 1925–7. (The definitive statement of Russell's logicism, containing detailed derivations of cardinal and ordinal arithmetic including Cantor.)

Russell, B.A.W. (1911) 'Knowledge by Acquaintance and Knowledge by Description', *Proceedings of the Aristotelian Society* 11: 108–28; repr. in Russell (1983–), vol. 6: 148–61. (An early epistemological paper by Russell, dominated by insights gained by his theory of descriptions.)

—— (1912a) *The Problems of Philosophy*, Oxford: Oxford University Press, 1974. (A popular introduction to philosophy, with the emphasis on epistemology.)

—— (1912b) 'On the Notion of Cause', *Proceedings of the Aristotelian Society* 13: 1–26; repr. in Russell (1983–), vol. 6: 193–210. (A sceptical, neo-Humean account of causation, and a denial of its importance for science.)

—— (1913) *Theory of Knowledge*, in Russell (1983–), vol. 8. (A major unfinished work on epistemology. Extant parts give detailed discussion of acquaintance and belief.)

—— (1914) *Our Knowledge of the External World*, London and Chicago, IL: Open Court; 2nd edn, London: Allen & Unwin, 1926; London: Routledge, 1993. (A deductivist treatment of the external world, programmatically proposing to construct material objects out of sensibilia.)

—— (1918) 'The Philosophy of Logical Atomism', *The Monist* 28: 495–527; 29: 32–63, 190–222, 345–80; repr. in Russell (1983–), vol. 8: 160–244. (A summary of Russell's philosophical development to date with a survey of outstanding problems.)

—— (1919a) 'On Propositions: What They Are and How They Mean', *Proceedings of the Aristotelian Society* supplementary volume 2: 1–43; repr. in Russell (1983–), vol. 8: 278–306. (The first statement of Russell's neutral monist theory of belief.)

—— (1919b) *An Introduction to Mathematical Philosophy*, London: Routledge, 1993. (A popular introduction to the logic of *Principia*.)

—— (1921) *The Analysis of Mind*, London: Routledge, 1992. (The fullest statement of Russell's neutral monism.)

—— (1927) *The Analysis of Matter*, New York: Routledge, 1992. (The definitive statement of Russell's structural realism about the external world.)

—— (1936a) 'The Limits of Empiricism', *Proceedings of the Aristotelian Society* 36: 131–50. (An admission that pure empiricism is an insufficient basis on which to construct science.)

—— (1936b) 'On Order in Time', *Proceedings of the Cambridge Philosophical Society* 32: 216–28; repr. in Russell (1956), 347–63. (A formal construction of temporal order based on Russell's event ontology.)

—— (1940) *An Inquiry into Meaning and Truth*, London: Routledge, 1992. (As much metaphysics and epistemology as semantics. An important statement of Russell's later position.)

—— (1945) *A History of Western Philosophy*, London: Routledge, 1993. (A popular, entertaining and brilliantly witty history. Scholars may sneer, but it's well worth reading.)

—— (1948) *Human Knowledge: Its Scope and Limits*, London: Routledge, 1992. (Russell's last major statement in epistemology.)

—— (1956) *Logic and Knowledge: Essays 1901–1950*, ed. R.C. Marsh, London: Routledge, 1992. (A collection of important essays, edited by Marsh in collaboration with Russell.)

—— (1959) *My Philosophical Development*, London: Routledge, 1993. (Russell's philosophical autobiography.)

—— (1967–9) *The Autobiography of Bertrand Russell*, London: Allen & Unwin, 3 vols. (The full autobiography of Russell's life and times, including his political activism.)

—— (1974) *Essays in Analysis*, ed. D. Lackey, London: Allen & Unwin. (Further essays, with more of a bias towards logic. Contains a very useful three-part bibliography.)

References and further reading

* Carnap, R. (1928) *Der Logische Aufbau der Welt*, trans. R.A. George, *The Logical Structure of the World*, London: Routledge, 1967. (The only serious attempt actually to furnish the logical constructions proposed in Russell (1914). Technical.)

* Chwistek, L. (1921) 'Antynomje logiki formalnej', *Przeglad Filozoficzny* 24: 164–71; trans. 'Antinomies of Formal Logic' in S. McCall (ed.) *Polish*

Logic, Oxford: Oxford University Press, 1967, 338–45. (Proposes a simple type theory reminiscent of that of Russell's *Principles of Mathematics*. Technical.)

Clark, R.W. (1975) *The Life of Bertrand Russell*, London: Cape and Weidenfeld & Nicolson. (The standard biography.)

* Copi, I. (1950) 'The Inconsistency or Redundancy of *Principia Mathematica*', *Philosophy and Phenomenological Research* 11: 190–9. (Claims that ramified type theory with the reducibility axiom is equivalent to simple type theory.)

—— (1971) *The Theory of Logical Types*, London: Allen & Unwin. (A simple introduction to simple type theory.)

* Demopoulos, W. and Friedman, M. (1989) 'The Concept of Structure in *The Analysis of Matter*', in C.W. Savage and C.A. Anderson (eds) *Rereading Russell. Essays on Bertrand Russell's Metaphysics and Epistemology*, Minneapolis, MN: University of Minnesota Press, 183–99. (An excellent account of Newman's criticism of the *Analysis of Matter* and its ramifications.)

* Feferman, S. (1984) 'Towards useful Type-free Theories', *Journal of Symbolic Logic* 49: 75–111. (Theories with some resemblance to Russell's zig-zag theory are proposed – though the Frege–Russell definition of cardinal number fails in them.)

* Gödel, K. (1944) 'Russell's Mathematical Logic', in P.A. Schilpp (ed.) *The Philosophy of Bertrand Russell*, La Salle, IL: Open Court, 1989, 123–54. (Still one of the best things written on Russell's logic.)

Grattan-Guinness, I. (1977) *Dear Russell – Dear Jourdain. A commentary on Russell's logic based on his correspondence with Philip Jourdain*, London: Duckworth. (Difficult and technical, but an important and fascinating source on Russell's logic.)

Grayling, A.C. (1996) *Russell*, Past Masters series, Oxford: Oxford University Press. (A very concise popular introduction to Russell's thought, including his politics.)

* Griffin, N. (1985) 'Russell's Multiple Relation Theory of Judgment', *Philosophical Studies* 47: 213–47. (An account of the development of the multiple relation theory and its collapse under Wittgenstein's criticisms.)

—— (1991) *Russell's Idealist Apprenticeship*, Oxford: Clarendon Press. (A detailed survey of Russell's neo-Hegelian work and the reasons that led him to abandon it.)

Jager, R. (1972) *The Development of Bertrand Russell's Philosophy*, London: Allen & Unwin. (The most comprehensive book on Russell – including his

social and political thought. Sometimes superficial, but a useful survey for the beginner.)

Hylton, P. (1990) *Russell, Idealism, and the Emergence of Analytic Philosophy*, Oxford: Clarendon Press. (One of the best books on some of the central themes of Russell's philosophy to 1913. Not introductory, but not technical.)

Landini, G. (1987) 'Russell's Substitutional Theory of Classes and Relations', *History and Philosophy of Logic* 8: 171–200.

* —— (1993) 'Reconciling *PM*'s Ramified Type Theory with the Doctrine of the Unrestricted Variable of the *Principles*', in A.D. Irvine and G.A. Wedeking (eds) *Russell and Analytic Philosophy*, Toronto, Ont.: University of Toronto Press, 361–94. (Landini's two articles offer the best and most detailed account of Russell's substitutional theory. Both are technical, but those new to the subject should begin with the first.)

Monk, R. (1996–) *Bertrand Russell*, London: Jonathan Cape, 2 vols. (An important, insightful and controversial biography.)

* Myhill, J.R. (1974) 'The Undefinability of the Set of Natural Numbers in the Ramified *Principia*', in G. Nakhnikian (ed.) *Bertrand Russell's Philosophy*, London: Duckworth, 19–27. (Proves the impossibility of Russell's attempt in the second edition of *Principia* to derive a principle of mathematical induction within the constraints of ramified type theory without the axiom of reducibility. Technical.)

* —— (1979) 'A Refutation of an Unjustified Attack on the Axiom of Reducibility', in G. Roberts (ed.) *Bertrand Russell Memorial Volume*, London: Allen & Unwin, 81–90. (A refutation of the claim in Copi (1950). Technical.)

* Newman, M.H.A. (1928) 'Mr. Russell's Causal Theory of Perception', *Mind* 37: 137–48. (The definitive refutation of the structural realism of Russell (1927).)

Pears, D.F. (1967) *Bertrand Russell and the British Tradition in Philosophy*, London: Fontana. (The classic statement of the traditional view of Russell as the heir of the British empiricist tradition. Intricate in places, but not technical.)

—— (1972) *Bertrand Russell: A Collection of Critical Essays*, Garden City, NY: Doubleday. (Though dated, the essays are generally of high quality. Contains an exceptionally useful, though now somewhat dated, bibliography.)

* Quine, W.V. (1937) 'New Foundations for Mathematical Logic', *American Mathematical Monthly* 44: 70–80; repr. in W.V. Quine, *From a Logical Point of View*, Cambridge, MA: Harvard University Press, 1953, 80–101. (Includes a proposal, like that in

Russell's zig-zag theory, to avoid the paradoxes by restricting comprehension – though Quine's restriction differs from any proposed by Russell.)

* Ramsey, F.P. (1925) 'The Foundations of Mathematics', *Proceedings of the London Mathematical Society* series 2, 25: 338–84; repr. in F.P. Ramsey, *Foundations: Essays in Philosophy, Logic, Mathematics and Economics*, ed. D.H. Mellor, London: Routledge, 1978, 152–212. (Contains the influential proposal to distinguish logical from semantic paradoxes and to solve only the former within logic, thereby obviating the need for ramified, as distinct from simple, type theory. An important original contribution to logic in the Russellian tradition.)

Ryan, A. (1988) *Bertrand Russell: A Political Life*, London: Allen Lane. (A survey of Russell's political engagements; more narrative than analysis.)

Savage, C.W. and Anderson, C.A. (eds) (1989) *Rereading Russell: Essays in Bertrand Russell's Metaphysics and Epistemology*, Minneapolis, MN: University of Minnesota Press. (Several useful papers on Russell's early logic and his later epistemology.)

Schilpp, P.A. (ed.) (1944) *The Philosophy of Bertrand Russell*, La Salle, IL: Open Court; 5th edn, 1989. (An old collection of essays of variable quality – Gödel's is superb and Weitz's is still worth reading. The collection is of special value because Russell replies to the papers – but not, unfortunately, to Gödel's.)

* Sommerville, S.T. (1981) 'Wittgenstein to Russell (July, 1913): "I am very sorry to hear...my objection paralyses you"', in *Language, Logic and Philosophy: Proceedings of the 4th International Wittgenstein Symposium*, Vienna: Holder-Pichler-Tempsky, 182–8. (The first paper to identify Wittgenstein's objections to Russell's multiple relation theory.)

* Urquhart, A. (1989) 'Russell's Zig-Zag Path to the Ramified Theory of Types', in I. Winchester and K. Blackwell (eds) *Antinomies and Paradoxes. Studies in Russell's Early Philosophy*, Hamilton, Ont.: McMaster University Library Press, 82–91. (An excellent, concise account of Russell's attempts to solve the paradoxes between 1903 and 1908 and why he was so reluctant to embrace ramified type theory. Not difficult.)

Watling, J. (1970) *Bertrand Russell*, Edinburgh: Oliver & Boyd. (An admirably concise and clear book concentrating on Russell's less technical work to 1914. The best 100-page introduction to the topic.)

* Wittgenstein, L.J.J. (1922) *Tractatus Logico-Philosophicus*, trans. D.F. Pears and B.F. McGuinness, London: Routledge & Kegan Paul, 1966. (An astonishing and exceedingly difficult work by the other logical atomist, cited here for its criticisms of the logical foundations of *Principia*.)

Russell: The Journal of the Bertrand Russell Archives (1971–) publishes articles on all aspects of Russell's life and work.

NICHOLAS GRIFFIN

RUSSIAN EMPIRIOCRITICISM

Russian empiriocriticism was an ephemeral movement within Russian Marxism of the early twentieth century. Its brief existence and deep involvement in politics invite the judgment, 'of historic interest only'. But that pat phrase dodges the problem of comprehending history and acting appropriately, which obsessed such thinkers as A.A. Bogdanov (1873–1928) and A.V. Lunacharskii (1875–1933), the best-remembered of the Russians who looked to Mach and Avenarius for philosophic support of Marx. In its German origins empiriocriticism was an academic effort to avoid metaphysics while analysing experience as the source of knowledge. In Russia the focus moved outside of academic cloisters. How is one to relate action to social understanding, if one knows that action and understanding shape each other within an overwhelming process of socioeconomic transformations? Analysis of 'experience' or 'practice' in the Russian context – a 'backward' society under a tyrannical state in an age of total war – nullified the academic calm of Mach and Avenarius. Their Russian admirers wanted to justify Marx's claims of social knowledge that would be both scientific and revolutionary; they rejected philosophies that merely interpret the world in different ways, while the task, described in Marx's final 'Thesis on Feuerbach', is to change it.

1   Philosophy and politics
2   Bogdanov
3   Lunacharskii and others

1   Philosophy and politics

Insistence on a revolutionary fusion of philosophy, social science and political action was a common feature of Russian radicals, offered in justification of diverse philosophical and political positions. 'Orthodox' believers in 'dialectical materialism', a name that PLEKHANOV devised in 1891, were Menshevik as well as Bolshevik (the two wings of the Russian Marxist party, which split into antagonistic parties by 1912). Countercurrents of 'revisionist' philosophy emerged on both sides of the split, though mostly among the Bolsheviks, perhaps because the greater wilfulness of Bolshevik politics invited some drastic revision of 'materialist fatalism', some turn to schools of philosophy which privileged 'experience' and 'will'. LENIN denounced them all as 'subjective idealism', in *Materializm i èmpiriokrititsizm* (Materialism and Empiriocriticism) (1909), but his polemic did not end their linkage with Bolshevism. Even after the 1917 Revolution Bogdanov defended his mixture of Marxism and empiriocriticism within the Communist Academy. Lunacharskii, who was the Soviet Commissar of Education until 1929, Pokrovskii, the chief of higher education, and Bukharin, the major communist ideologist of the 1920s, showed their partiality more discretely, for confession of orthodoxy was becoming obligatory within the communist state (see MARXIST PHILOSOPHY, RUSSIAN AND SOVIET §§1–3).

'Revisionism' in philosophy should not be equated with 'reformism' in politics just because a few of Marx's German disciples proposed that equation at the turn of the century. It was formally rejected even in Germany, where the Marxist party was becoming reformist in political action while clinging to a professed faith in orthodox revolutionary theory. In Russia virtually all Marxists disdained political reformism both in theory and in practice; they took for granted an inevitable lower-class upheaval, and split on political strategies and theoretical justifications for guiding the working classes through revolution to democracy and socialism.

Such tangles of political and philosophical issues have preoccupied scholarly interest in Russian empiriocriticism, with a chronic temptation to impose simplistic correlations – such as the linking of Bolshevik wilfulness with radical positivism or Nietzschean voluntarism. The Russian Marxists themselves, whether orthodox or revisionist, were sufficiently open-minded to restrain that temptation during their first four decades, from the 1890s until Stalin's 'revolution from above' in 1929–32 (see MARXIST PHILOSOPHY, RUSSIAN AND SOVIET §4). His 'great break' initiated a strict party line in philosophy; before that violent establishment of uniformity Russian Marxists usually took for granted some variety of debatable correlations between philosophical views and political positions.

Nevertheless a difference in mentalities was emerging in those first forty years. Whether Menshevik, Bolshevik or in between, the Marxists who were not embarrassed to call themselves 'orthodox', though they rejected traditional religions and were closing their minds to new developments in philosophy. Their critics within the Marxist movement were trying to adapt it to the new positivism, which was retreating from the visionary claim that science yields a guiding plan of human history. Some of the critical Marxists were also succumbing to the new Romanticism, as we may call the insistence by Nietzsche and James that beliefs precede the reasoned inquiry which serves them, that action is the ground of human being and reason its ancillary. Goethe's blasphemous inversion of Genesis – 'In the beginning was the deed' – was a favourite quote within all Marxist trends; they divided on ways to confess such irrationality and still to justify their claims of rationality. The orthodox way was to barricade the mind within a confessional creed, favouring defensive apologetics rather than critical inquiry, claiming to be rational critics of their own beliefs while actually shutting off the possibility. The revisionist way was to resist that closing of the Marxist mind; revisionists would neither quit the movement nor quit criticizing it.

The movement – parties committed to Marxism – was swiftly growing in Germany and in Russia, while grand philosophical systems were disintegrating, obliging thoughtful militants to decide whether they were committed to a grand system, to a cluster of particular theories claiming scientific justification, to a mode of inquiry for the guidance of action, or to some combination of all three – with the possible admixture of an irrational will to power. Orthodox Marxists, such as Plekhanov and Lenin, tended to beat down such questions in polemics against those who asked them, in vehement defence of vague generalities. For example, they denounced positivism in name and praised dialectical materialism, but tended to favour the notion that a queenly discipline of philosophy withers away as each branch of knowledge becomes a genuine science. The Russian Marxists who scoffed at dialectical materialism and studied empiriocriticism were less content with generalities, and more receptive to the corrosive inquiry that disintegrates grand schemes. Yet they wound up, paradoxically, doing more system-building than their orthodox opponents.

2 Bogdanov

The paradox was most evident in BOGDANOV, known as the chief 'Machist' among Russian Marxists, though he repudiated the label. He created 'empiriomonism', which was supposed to overcome, unlike Mach's empiriocriticism (see MACH, E. §2), the fragmentation of modern knowledge and the surrender to history as blind process or 'elementalism'. (The Russian word, *stikhiinost'*, is commonly mistranslated as 'spontaneity', though the root is Greek *stoicheion*, element, and the Russian meaning is not free agency but mindless process.) Seeking a unified science of all sciences, which would bring organized consciousness to the 'elemental' upheaval of the lower classes, Bogdanov drew first on Ostwald's 'energeticism'. He liked its vision of science as the monistic inquiry that studies energy in its transformations, culminating in human consciousness with its capacity for rational organization. But he criticized Ostwald for confusing the unity of scientific method with a notion of energy as metaphysical substance, and found in Mach's analysis of experience complete escape from metaphysics into methodology. Yet Bogdanov's Mach was ancillary to his Marx, methodology to worldview, for he insisted that human experience is collective, historically developing, organized by evolving 'ideology', Bogdanov's umbrella category for all forms of knowledge and art at all stages of human development, which he brought to order in empiriomonism.

Bogdanov claimed, in effect, to be creating a system that was not a system. 'Empiriomonism' indicated both 'the final philosophical goal, the ideal of cognition' and 'the way to it, the effort to give as coherent a world picture as possible for our time and for that social class to which I have devoted myself'. To support that version of Marxism he relied not only on contemporary positivists. Zarathustra's declaration, 'Man is the bridge to the superman', served as epigraph to an early article, gesturing towards a future transcendence of present values. But a subsequent explanation pointed backward in time:

The ideal of a complete and powerful, harmonious and all-victorious life, which is expressed in the sculptures of the ancient world, and in the statues of their gods, is clearer and, I would suggest, deeper than Nietzsche's 'superman' in philosophy.

(Bogdanov 1911: 17)

He did not examine in depth the implicit clash between Romanticism and classicism, that is, between a vision of human values in open-ended creation and a vision of endless striving towards a changeless ideal. Bogdanov's eclectic mixture was still Marxism, he insisted, for various philosophies were 'materials' for his theorizing, but 'the social philosophy of Marx...has been the regulator and the method of my work'. He disagreed with revisionists who argued that Marx's social theorizing lacked philosophical justification. Bogdanov found it in Marx's vision of the historical process, which, in his rendition, resembled Comte's three-stage scheme: first an authoritarian social system justified by religious thought; then an individualist stage with an exchange economy and speculative systems of thought; finally the collective stage and scientific thought, which were coming together in the proletarian struggle for emancipation within industrial society (see COMTE, A.). Out of that struggle Marx had distilled a guiding consciousness, which needed further development as 'empiriomonism' or 'universal organizational science' or 'tectology'. Bogdanov moved from one term to the next in the course of his prolific writing from the 1890s to the 1920s. (He borrowed the word 'tectology' from another scientific monist of the period, Ernst HAECKEL, who grounded his grand system in biological rather than social science.)

Some scholars have interpreted Bogdanov as a thinker like Sorel, who declared social theorizing to be myth-making that justifies the wilful behaviour of social groups. Others have narrowed Bogdanov's vision of organizational science to mathematical modelling of 'systems', and picture him as a forerunner of cybernetics. Still others, the present author included, take due note of Bogdanov's strenuous *resistance* to the separation of mythopoeic from scientific modes of thought, of subjective from objective aspects of experience. That resistance sustained his old-fashioned positivist faith in science as unified knowledge that reveals the whole pattern of history, while he ostensibly confronted the downfall of such pretensions, the rising critical insistence that knowledge is irremediably partial, in both senses of the word: limited and biased. Bogdanov tended to evade the version of this antinomy that was most distinctive of Marx, the striving for a history of socioeconomic formations that would be simultaneously particular and universal, true to the variegated past of human societies and predictive of an authentically human future for all. A dreamy abstraction marked the 'general task' that Bogdanov set for 'empiriomonism': 'to find the way by which it would be possible to systematically reduce all the discontinuities [*pereryvy*] of our experience to a principle of continuity [*nepreryvnost'*]' (1905–7: vol. 1, 173).

Bogdanov's disagreements with Lenin have sometimes been interpreted as a clash between freedom and authoritarianism within emergent communism, though both agreed, while founding the Party, that it must bring disciplined collective 'consciousness' to the 'elemental' struggle of the lower classes. Bogdanov distinguished between authentic revolutionary consciousness, a free collectivism that he attempted to encourage in the movement for 'proletarian culture', and the false consciousness of a social group in bondage to 'verbal fetishism' or 'vampirism'. Those were his favourite cursewords for blind worship of dead formulas, idolatrous cults that feed on the revolutionary movement. Since he published such criticism of the Leninists as they took power, he has been praised as an original Bolshevik who tried to keep alive the yearning for 'utopia' as present consciousness, endlessly disturbing to those whose chants of a distant 'utopia' soothe the slaves of 'verbal fetishism'. That praise may not be compatible with tributes to him as a prophet of 'systems theory' and computerized society – or with the view of him as 'the red Hamlet', tragically baffled by the conflicting demands of thinking and doing. It remains to be seen which view of Bogdanov, or indeed whether any significant interest in him, will survive the collapse of the state that turned Russian Marxism into a petrified orthodoxy.

3 Lunacharskii and others

The same question hangs over the other theorists who tried to keep Russian Marxism alive by infusion of new philosophies. In the Soviet period Lunacharskii seemed to have a lasting hold on posterity, but the reasons may have been more political than intellectual. He had been expelled from Lenin's party along with Bogdanov in 1909, but he rejoined in 1917, as Bogdanov did not. He was Commissar of Education for the first twelve years of the Soviet state, died before the wild destruction of 'old Bolshevik' survivals in the late 1930s, and enjoyed a revival in the post-Stalin efforts to revitalize the communist vision. His flood of publications was more varied than Bogdanov's, with artistic flair to draw readers in and less abstractness to tax their patience. Literary critic and playwright as well as philosophical essayist and revolutionary boss, Lunacharskii was, like Trotsky, a spectacular analogue to the men of letters who played major roles in the 'bourgeois' revolutions of an earlier age. Yet these Russian stand-ins for Jefferson and Condorcet, however energetic and creative, were at odds with their era, which splinters the intellect into specialized disciplines and puts the label 'superficial' or 'dilettante' on those who cling to the tradition of the universal mind.

Lunacharskii studied with AVENARIUS at the University of Zürich, but grinding at the self-doubts of academic positivism could not confine a spirit captivated very early, as he confessed, by 'religious and artistic expressions of man's life of the heart'. They became his 'authentic *life's problem*' after an 'ecstatic "conversion to Marxism"'. Most Marxists recoiled against such talk, insisting that their doctrine was not religion but science. Lunacharskii argued that it was both. Marx had endowed the socialist faith with knowledge of the historical process, but that 'cognition of the world' still needed an appropriate 'evaluation of the world', which projected human preferences into an otherwise indifferent universe. Thus Lunacharskii became a leader of 'God-building', as a sympathetic Maksim Gorkii named the

effort to create a faith out of human aspirations, to connect each ephemeral life with a progressive reality larger than itself.

> To live the life of a human being means to see and to feel the past as one's own, even before one's day of birth, and the future as one's own, *really one's own*, even beyond the grave; this means to be conscious of oneself as a mortal part of an immortal element [*stikhiia*] – of the collective life.
>
> (1909: 87)

Lunacharskii dismissed the similarity with Comte's religion of humanity, which he considered a ridiculous imitation of Catholicism. He derided 'Plekhanovist' orthodoxy as 'materialist fatalism', an unacknowledged religion that invoked cosmic processes for assurance of human progress, culminating in socialism. Not mindless atoms and indifferent galaxies, he insisted, but evolving social practice was the ground of Marx's theorizing, and therefore Bogdanov was 'the sole Marxist philosopher continuing the pure philosophical tradition of Marx'. Lunacharskii ridiculed 'the guards at the Marxist museum ... who have raised cries of heresy', while they reviled the demand for clear distinctions between the true faith and taboo beliefs. Such mockery was part of his serious argument that knowledge of humanity's progress towards socialism must be charged with intense feeling if the movement is to go forward as our knowledge tells us it must.

Lunacharskii's aesthetic theorizing also rested on insistence that knowledge and feeling are necessarily intermixed. He joined Nietzschean versions of that theme with biologistic talk, taken from Avenarius and SPENCER, of nerve energies raised towards a destructive level, and released in some life-enhancing way. He distinguished two types of that aesthetic discharge: art as play and art as mobilization of emotion for work or struggle. Thus, as early as 1904, he came to a formula for a kind of art that would be called 'socialist realism' in the Soviet period:

> To beautify the people's life as much as possible, to draw pictures of the future gleaming with happiness and perfection, and along with that [to picture] the repulsive evil of the present, to develop the sense of tragedy, the joy of struggle and of triumph, of promethean striving, of stubborn pride, of unyielding courage, to join hearts in a general feeling of the urge toward the superman [see NIETZSCHE: IMPACT ON RUSSIAN THOUGHT §3].
>
> (1967: vol. 7, 99)

Such formulaic prescriptions were at odds with Lunacharskii's enthusiasm for modernist revolts against prescriptive formulas, for art as experience reshaped in unpredictable forms. Praise of modernist writers flowed continuously from his pen, whether in theatre reviews for a pre-revolutionary newspaper or in lectures on West European literature at a communist university in the 1920s. Indeed, an enthusiastic preface to a Soviet translation of Proust was the last thing he wrote, in 1933, just before his heart stopped. Yet his aesthetic theorizing anticipated the formulaic rigidity of 'socialist realism', and so did the aesthetics of other Russian Marxists, both revisionist and orthodox. (See especially essays by Lunacharskii, Trotsky, Bazarov, Iushkevich and so on, attacking 'literary decadence' in *Literaturnyi raspad*, 1908–9). The anarchic creativity of the artistic avant-garde and the mobilization of political commitment by the revolutionary vanguard were at odds within Lunacharskii's mind, as in Russia at large. He tried to reconcile the contrary currents, ultimately without success. He was committed to action on behalf of a revolution that was drifting into cultural petrifaction, a dreadful position for one who held social practice to be the criterion of truth.

The same can be said of nearly all the Russian thinkers who tried to enrich Marxism with new forms of positivism or Nietzscheanism. After the Soviet revolution most of them tried to work for the new regime. N. Valentinov – pen-name of N.V. Vol'skii (1879–1964) – who went West and turned against the whole revolutionary project, was exceptional, and even he tried to serve the Soviet cause for twelve years. V.A. Bazarov – pen-name of Rudnev (1874–1939) – hung on, tried to bend socialist economic theorizing towards realism, and was condemned for 'wrecking' in 1931. Ia.A. Berman (1868–1933) seems to have suffered a similar fate. P.S. Iushkevich (1873–1945), creator of 'empirio-symbolism', singled out by a recent historian as 'the most eloquent and outspoken protestor against dogmatism' before 1917, survived afterward as a translator.

The experience of these thinkers must have some lesson for philosophies that claim 'experience' or 'practice' as the criterion of knowledge, but it may be impossible to specify the lesson without falling into vicious circularity – claiming to know how ongoing experience will work out – or leaping beyond historical experience, to romantic claims of transcendent knowledge. If the social process to be comprehended is both a determinant and a product of the action to be taken, claims of comprehension may be masks of interests to be served, or worse yet, of interests poorly served, by a rash will to power or a cowardly fatalism, or by some confused fluctuation between the two extremes. Such issues, which threaten vicious circularity for all believers in the primacy of experience or practice, become painful dilemmas when would-be

activists confront economic backwardness, tyranny, catastrophic wars, lower-class revolts and national conflicts, such as the Russian Empire and the USSR experienced in the twentieth century.

List of works

Bogdanov, A.A. (1905–7) *Èmpiriomonizm; stat'i po filosofii* (Empiriomonism: Articles on Philosophy), 3 vols, Moscow: Dorovatovskii & Charushnikov; 2nd and 3rd edns, 1906–8. (See BOGDANOV for detailed bibliography.)

—— (1911) *Kul'turnye zadachi nashego vremeni* (The Cultural Tasks of Our Time), Moscow: Dorovatovskii & Charushnikov. (A pamphlet arguing for 'cultural revolution', and against the interpretation of Marxism by Plekhanov and Lenin.)

Lunacharskii, A.V. (1908–11) *Religiia i sotsializm* (Religion and Socialism), vols 1 and 2, St Petersburg. (His major work on religion.)

—— (1909) *'Dvadtsat' tretii sbornik "Znaniia"'* (The Twenty-third Collection of 'Knowledge'), in *Literaturnyi raspad; Kriticheskii sbornik* (Literary Decadence; a Critical Collection), vol. 2, St Petersburg: EOS, 1908–9. (Lunacharskii's contribution to a major attack on modernistic literature.)

—— (1964) *A.V. Lunacharskii o literature i iskusstve: bibliograficheskii ukazatel', 1902–1963* (A.V. Lunacharskii on Literature and Art: Bibliographical Index), ed. K.D. Muratova, Leningrad. (Bibliography of Lunacharskii's works on literature and art.)

—— (1967) *Sobranie sochinenii* (Collected Works), vol. 7. (Includes the 1904 article 'Osnovy pozitivnoi estetiki' (Foundations of Positive Aesthetics).)

Sborniki (collections) with articles by empiriocriticists:

Ocherki realisticheskogo mirovozzreniia; sbornik statei po filosofii obshchestvennoi nauke i zhizni (Essays on the Realistic Worldview: A Collection of Articles on Philosophy, Social Science and Life) (1904) St Petersburg: Dorovatovskii & Charushnikov.

Ocherki po filosofii marksizma (Essays on the Philosophy of Marxism) (1908) St Petersburg.

Literaturnyi raspad: kriticheskii sbornik (Literary Decadence: A Critical Collection) (1908–9) St Petersburg: Izdatel'skoe biuro.

Ocherki filosofii kollektivizma; sbornik pervyi (Essays on the Philosophy of Collectivism; First Collection) (1909) St Petersburg: Znanie.

References and further reading

Bailes, K.E. (1967) 'Sur la "théorie des valeurs" de A.V. Lunacharskij' (On A.V. Lunacharskii's Theory of Values), in *Cahiers du monde russe et soviétique* 8: 223–43. (A revealing analysis, using archival sources.)

Kelly, A. (1981) 'Empiriocriticism: A Bolshevik Philosophy?' in *Cahiers du monde russe et soviétique* 22 (1): 89–117. (A richly documented argument for an affirmative answer.)

Kline, G. (1968) '"Nietzschean Marxism" in Russia', in *Boston College Studies in Philosophy II: Demythologizing Marxism*, The Hague: Nijhoff. (The Nietzschean elements in Bogdanov *et al.*)

Kolakowski, L. (1978) *Main Currents of Marxism II: The Golden Age*, Oxford: Clarendon Press. (Ch. 17 analyses the conflict over empiriocriticism.)

Lebedev, A.A. (1970) *Ėsteticheskie vzgliady A.V. Lunacharskogo* (A.V. Lunacharskii's Aesthetic Views), Moscow: Iskusstvo. (A Soviet effort to rescue Lunacharskii's aesthetics from orthodox hostility.)

* Lenin, V.I. (1909) *Materializm i ėmpiriokrititsizm: kriticheskie zametki ob odnoi reaktsionnoi filosofii* (Materialism and Empiriocriticism: Critical Notes on a Reactionary Philosophy), Moscow: Zveno. (Many republications and translations in the Soviet era.)

Plekhanov, G.V. (1957) *Izbrannye filosofskie proizvedeniia* (Selected Philosophical Works), vol. 3, Moscow: Gosizdat. (Polemics against Bogdanov *et al.*)

Read, C. (1979) *Religion, Revolution and the Russian Intelligentsia, 1900–1912*, London: Macmillan. (Includes Marxist issues in larger debates about religion.)

Rosenthal, B.G. (ed.) (1986) *Nietzsche in Russia*, Princeton, NJ: Princeton University Press. (Part 3: 'Nietzsche's Influence on Russian Marxism'.)

Scherrer, J. (1978) 'La crise de l'intelligentsia marxiste avant 1914: A.V. Lunacharskij et le *bogostroitel'stvo*' (The Crisis of the Marxist Intelligentsia before 1914: A.V. Lunacharskii and God-building), in *Revue des études slaves* 51: 207–15. (Lunacharskii's role in God-building.)

Tait, A.L. (1984) *Lunacharskii, Poet of the Revolution, 1875–1907*, Birmingham: University of Birmingham Press. (Richly informed analysis of Lunacharskii's early development.)

Utechin, S.V. (1958) 'Bolsheviks and Their Allies after 1917: The Ideological Pattern', in *Soviet Studies* 10: 113–35.

Williams, R.C. (1986) *The Other Bolsheviks: Lenin and His Critics, 1904–1914*, Bloomington, IN: Indiana University Press. (A history that emphasizes political issues.)

DAVID JORAVSKY

RUSSIAN LITERARY FORMALISM

Russian literary Formalism, an active movement in Russian literary criticism from about 1915 to 1929, approached the literary work as a self-referential, formed artefact rather than as an expression of reality or experience outside the work. It asked the question, 'How is the work made?' rather than 'What does the work say?' Its founding assumption, that poetic language differs from the language of ordinary communication, spawned numerous investigations of what the Formalists called 'literariness' – the qualities that make a work artistic. This distinction between practical and poetic language also allowed the Formalists to argue that literature was an autonomous branch of human activity, evolving according to its own immanent laws rather than as a consequence or reflection of historical events. Proceeding from this theoretical model, the Formalists viewed literary works as responses to previous literature rather than to the outside world.

In their literary theory and their interpretations of particular literary works, the Formalists were reacting to the predominant tendency of Russian literary criticism to draw direct correspondences between lived experience and the literary work. Boris Eikhenbaum, Roman Jakobson, Viktor Shklovskii, Boris Tomashevskii, Iurii Tynianov and other Formalists questioned accepted correspondences between life and art, casting doubt upon realist interpretations of Russian authors such as Gogol' and Tolstoi, and examining the narrative structure of non-Russian works such as Tristram Shandy and O. Henry's short stories. Their analyses showed how intonation, word order, rhythm and referential meaning interact within a literary work, and they argued that literary works are less a reflection of life than an attempt to refresh conventional perceptions. The influence of Russian literary Formalism is felt in more recent theoretical schools such as semiotics, structuralism, deconstruction, feminist criticism and new historicism, in so far as all of these take account of the particular use of language in any literary work.

1 Practical versus poetic language
2 Literariness
3 Literary evolution
4 Autonomy of literature

1 Practical versus poetic language

Russian literary Formalism can be roughly divided into three periods. From 1915 to 1919, it sought to establish the distinction between practical and poetic language; from 1919 to 1921 it investigated the use of poetic language in particular literary works; and from 1921 until 1929 it examined literary works as responses to previous literary history. The movement began as part of the avant-garde experimentation in the arts in the years surrounding the Bolshevik revolution of 1917. Its practitioners formed two groups: the Moscow Linguistic Circle, which included Roman Jakobson, Pëtr Bogatyrev, N. Trubetskoi and Grigorii Vinokur; and its sister group in St Petersburg, the Society for the Study of Poetic Language (*Opoiaz*), whose members included Osip Brik, Boris Eikhenbaum, Lev Iakubinskii, Evgenii Polivanov, Viktor Shklovskii, Boris Tomashevskii and Iurii Tynianov. This collaboration between linguists and literary scholars addressed language as the focal point of literature. Verbal texture was examined as the artistic medium of literature, which contributed to message. In seeking to build an objective theory of literature, Russian literary Formalism ignored authorial intention, biography and social and historical conditions, the better to focus on the work itself.

Taking its cue from the sound experiments of Russian Futurist poetry, early Formalism drew attention to the non-referential aspects of language, particularly to the role of sound. In 'Voskreshenie slova' (The Resurrection of the Word) (1914), which may be considered the inaugural work of Russian literary Formalism, Viktor Shklovskii declared that the expressive impact of words was dulled by habitual usage and that the purpose of literature was to restore to words a sense of newness and to stimulate new perceptions. In 'Iskusstvo kak priëm' (Art as Device) (1916), Shklovskii introduced the concept of *ostranenie* ('defamiliarization') to refer to the ways in which literary works may overturn conventional perceptions.

The whole edifice of Russian Formalist theory rests on the differentiation between practical and poetic language, formulated by Iakubinskii in his 1916 article, 'O zvukakh stikhotvornogo iazyka' (On the Sounds of Verse Language). Iakubinskii argued that the goals of ordinary speech and poetic language were fundamentally opposed. Everyday utterances were aimed at rapid, efficient communication, and to that end they employed readily recognizable formulations. This 'automatized' language, as the Formalists termed it, grown familiar through repeated, habitual use, had attained a narrow functionality at the expense of its vitality and richness. The goal of poetic speech was to restore the palpability of language that is lost with quick recognition. Poetic language, said Iakubinskii, retards the process of comprehension while making it multilayered, bringing out a wealth of accumulated meanings. Where practical language is highly referential, pointing unambiguously to objects and ideas, poetic language is largely self-referential, drawing attention to the verbal pattern of the work.

In their preoccupation with the renewal of automatized perceptions and with the properties of language, the Formalists were influenced by Andrei Belyi and Henri-Louis BERGSON. Belyi's 1910 book, *Simvolizm* (Symbolism), had attempted to establish an 'anatomy of style' by counting syllables, accents and parts of speech in thousands of lines of verse. Following Belyi, the Formalists took an almost scientific approach to literary analysis.

Until about 1919, Russian literary Formalism was occupied with attempts to characterize poetic language, investigating the question of how the renewal of automatized language was achieved. Studies by Brik, Polivanov and Shklovskii showed that in poetry and other short genres words were selected for their auditory properties no less than for their referential meaning. They explored sound patterns in literary texts, showing that meaning resides in sound as well as in semantics. Shklovskii in particular identified literary 'devices', such as retardation (the intentional slowing down of plot development to create suspense), parallel story lines and repetitions. Plot development itself was shown to be a device: the chronology of a narrative could be rearranged to achieve particular effects. The presumed chronological order of events in a narrative the Formalists termed *fabula* (frequently translated as 'story'); the artistic rearrangement of events for purposes of narration they called *siuzhet* (usually rendered as 'plot'). As with the distinction between practical and poetic language, here too the Formalists cast matters in terms of an opposition between the non-literary (*fabula*) and the literary (*siuzhet*).

2 Literariness

The Formalists' emphasis on the device and their attention to arrangement and selection of verbal elements were an attempt to account for what Jakobson termed the *literariness* of the work. Message was necessarily affected by presentation, so that a work's literariness was an integral and inseparable part of its message or content. Instead of seeing form as a covering imposed on a pre-existing content, the Formalists rejected the dichotomy of content and form, seeing words, syntax and intonation as simultaneously both content and form. The literary work consisted exclusively of formed content.

Formalist theory and practice were part of a strident literary debate with Russian Marxist critics, and many Formalist statements were deliberately polemical and one-sided. Formalism shared its polemical stance and emphasis on form with Russian Futurist poetry, which emphasized sounds in isolation from meaning; the 'self-valuable' word; neologisms; and shock value. Shklovskii's widely publicized statement, 'art is the sum of its devices', was an example of the polemical nature of Formalist utterances, as were his assessment of Laurence Sterne's *Tristram Shandy* as the most typical novel of world literature, and his categorical statement that a literary work is nothing but form.

In spite of such catchwords and slogans, the Formalist emphasis on form in no way dismissed meaning. Eikhenbaum's study of verse intonation in his book *Melodika russkogo liricheskogo stikha* (Melody in Russian Lyric Verse) (1922) examined the interaction of lexical meaning and syntax in dozens of poems, showing that literary interpretation rested on the blend of the semantic and the formal. Formalism sought to displace the usual explanation of content as a reflection of the non-literary world, replacing it with an approach to content as a literary component of a work. What the Formalists objected to (like the American New Critics after them) was the attempt to paraphrase a work's content, extracting it from the verbal blend. The problem with the content–form dichotomy was that it implicitly equated content with meaning.

With the distinction between poetic and practical language in place, the Formalists began to examine the workings of poetic language in specific literary texts. This middle stage of Formalism, lasting from about 1919 to 1924, treated the literary work as a 'dynamic system' in which contrasting and often conflicting features competed for primacy. Instead of matching each other and forming a congruous whole, elements such as rhythm, syntax and intonation were shown often to be at odds, forcing concessions from one another in a struggle for dominance. At the heart of poetic language the Formalists saw not harmony but dissonance, incongruity and struggle. This followed logically from their premise of automatization: the need for poetic language constantly to renew and defamiliarize meant the creation of new, unexpected combinations of linguistic and semantic material. Borrowing from the German aesthetician Broder Christiansen the concept of the *dominanta*, Tynianov in *Problemy stikhotvornogo iazyka* (Problems of Verse Language) (1924) theorized that the prevailing element in this struggle deformed the others. Tynianov introduced the term 'constructive principle' to refer to the relationship between the *dominanta* and the other elements in a work. Shklovskii's catch-phrase 'art is the sum of its devices' was now shown to be an oversimplification: art was far more than the mere *sum* of its parts, because the

meaning of each part was dependent on the whole context created by the work. Each element served to place the others in relief.

To view the literary work as a 'system' was to see it as a self-created world rather than an imitation of outside reality or referent. In this the formalist concept of the literary work paralleled the work of Ferdinand De SAUSSURE (§2) on the sign. Saussure's sign, which consisted of mental concept (signified) and word (signifier), took no account of the referent, which was completely outside the sign. Similarly, for the Formalists 'content', like referent, was completely outside the literary work, which consisted of aestheticized meaning – the interaction of all components of the literary work.

Since the goal of poetic language was to renew familiar, automatized language, and since what was familiar changed over time, it followed that what constituted poetic language in one epoch would cease to be poetic in the next. Poetic language itself was susceptible to automatization through repeated usage in different works, thereby losing its poeticity. Writers trying to overcome the automatized conventions of their literary 'fathers' would turn to works by their 'grandfathers' or 'uncles' for devices that might revitalize exhausted genres. In 'Noveishaia russkaia poéziia' (Modern Russian Poetry) (1919), Jakobson stated that new literary forms arise to replace previous literary forms that have become exhausted. This position, for which the Formalists found precedent in the work of the nineteenth-century Russian ethnographer Aleksandr Veselovskii, contrasted with the widely held view of the nineteenth-century civic critics and the Bolsheviks that new forms in literature are needed to express a new content, such as a change in the structure of society.

3 Literary evolution

In building change into its model of poetic language, Russian literary Formalism differed from theories that applied a formulaic description to all works of a given genre. Poetic language was by definition *new* language. In 'O literaturnoi évoliutsii' (On Literary Evolution) (1927), Tynianov described this process of renewal and change in poetic language as a four-step cycle of literary evolution: (1) a new constructive principle arises to replace the previously dominant one that has finally become automatized; (2) the new constructive principle gains currency in new literary works; (3) it becomes more widespread; (4) it becomes automatized and evokes opposing constructive principles.

The concept of a constructive principle within a dynamic system whose elements are constantly colliding allowed the Formalists to challenge accepted interpretations of major literary works, especially those widely characterized as examples of realism. Eikhenbaum's seminal article on Gogol''s short story 'The Overcoat' called into question the consensual interpretation of that story as a portrayal of the humble man disdained by his colleagues and superiors in an inhumane society. Eikhenbaum argued that the 'realist' passages, including the famous words 'I am your brother', universally interpreted as a plea for recognition of human dignity, constitute only one strand of Gogol''s narrative, and that they are undercut by another, comic strand woven out of sheer linguistic play. When a realist narrative is placed in the context of a linguistic game, Eikhenbaum argued, its meaning is altered.

Eikhenbaum's article reflected the Formalist bias that realistic mimesis was not the main business of literature. Having established that each work constituted an aesthetic system, the Formalists now had an approach to literature that could be offered as an alternative to realist readings. A system of interacting elements meant that the function of a device could change depending on its context. Furthermore, the workings of this dynamic system, the demands of artistic presentation, worked against an accurate reflection of the world. Aesthetic requirements conflicted with factual accuracy; literary works on historical themes might need to sacrifice historical accuracy in the interests of aesthetics.

4 Autonomy of literature

The differentiation between practical and poetic language, as well as the notion of system, allowed the Formalists to claim that literature was an autonomous activity not chained to economic, social or political reality. The Formalists thus liberated literary studies from the mimetic orientation that sees the work as a reflection of the world. Such harnessing of the literary work to the outside world had been the practice of mainstream Russian literary criticism. It characterized the radical civic critics of the mid-nineteenth century, who pressed literature into the service of social justice; the academic critics of the cultural-historical and cultural-psychological schools; and also the Marxist critics who gained legitimacy after the Bolshevik Revolution and with whom the Formalists engaged in bitter polemics. Russian literary Formalism set out to make literary criticism into a scholarly discipline by constructing an 'objective' theory of literature, centred on the work itself, that would not subordinate the study of literature to other disciplines. Most of the Formalists' theoretical concepts, such as their early emphasis on sound and the palpability of the word, pointed to the work itself rather than to the cultural context that produced it.

The case for literary autonomy was a major achievement of Formalism while simultaneously containing the germ of its demise. The notion on which autonomy rested – that of a poetic language whose definition lay in the revitalization of automatized forms – accounted merely for the fact of literary change, not for the actual direction of change at any given time. By the mid-1920s, it became clear that the automatization/revitalization dynamic, while at least partly valid, left too many questions unanswered, and that the answers were to be found in the non-literary contexts that Formalism had dismissed as irrelevant to literariness and aesthetics. Within the confines of the purely work-centred poetics, no further insights were possible.

In an attempt to incorporate some of these contexts without sacrificing the literary autonomy for which Formalism had fought so hard, Tynianov proposed a modification of Formalist theory. His article of 1927, 'On Literary Evolution', put forth a model of culture presenting its various aspects – economic, social, political, religious, linguistic, literary – as parallel, autonomously developing lines, or 'series'. Tynianov's model preserved the Formalist premise of literary autonomy, since each series had its own immanent development that was not directly affected or 'caused' by any other series. Indirect influences from other series, however, could occur, passing vertically from one series to the next as though through a porous membrane. The most significant influence, Tynianov suggested, would come from the neighbouring series; influences from more distant series, which would have to pass through the intervening series, would be modified along the way and more difficult, if not impossible, to trace. Initially Tynianov maintained that the literary series had as its closest neighbour the linguistic series; subsequently, in a collaborative article of 1928, 'Problems in the Study of Literature and Language', Tynianov and Jakobson proposed that the series change their positions, so that in different eras the literary series might border on the economic, the social or the political.

At the same time that the model of the parallel series was intended to reinvigorate the increasingly repetitive practice of Formalist criticism by admitting a select amount of extra-literary information into literary interpretation, it also challenged the Marxist model of economic base and cultural superstructure (see MARX, K §8). Tynianov's model, in providing for immanent development within each series, conferred on literature and all other activities an autonomy that was incompatible with the notion of a base reflected in a superstructure.

With the rigid controls imposed on literature, philosophy and theory at the close of the 1920s when Stalin consolidated his power, the Formalists had to abandon the attempt to open their literary theory to include extra-literary factors. Those Formalists who remained in Russia by and large omitted theoretical issues from their subsequent writings. The tendency of post-structuralist literary theories to place literary works in their broader cultural context addresses an omission of Formalism; but these same critical schools have internalized the founding Formalist assumption that the construction of the linguistic/ literary utterance is central to meaning.

See also: DECONSTRUCTION §1; SEMIOTICS; STRUCTURALISM; STRUCTURALISM IN LITERARY THEORY

References and further reading

Any, C. (1994) *Boris Eikhenbaum: Voices of a Russian Formalist*, Stanford, CA: Stanford University Press. (See ch. 3 for analysis of Formalist theory.)

* Belyi, A. (1910) *Simvolizm: Kniga statei* (Symbolism: A Book of Articles), Moscow: Musaget. (Referred to in §1.)

Bennett, T. (1979) *Formalism and Marxism*, London: Methuen. (Examines Formalism with respect to Saussure, Bakhtin, Althusser and post-Althusserians.)

* Eikhenbaum, B. (1922) *Melodika russkogo liricheskogo stikha* (Melody in Russian Lyric Verse), St Petersburg: Opoiaz. (Contrasts the melodic intonational structure of poems by Zhukovskii and Lermontov with unmelodic poems of Pushkin, Tiutchev and Fet.)

—— (1919) 'Kak sdelana "Shinel'" Gogolia'; trans. R. Maguire, 'How Gogol's "Overcoat" Is Made', in R. Maguire (ed.), *Gogol from the Twentieth Century: Eleven Essays*, Princeton, NJ: Princeton University Press, 1974, 269–92. (The classic example of Russian Formalism, showing how syntax and word play can undermine conventional semantics.)

Erlich, V. (1981) *Russian Formalism: History – Doctrine*, New Haven, CT: Yale University Press. (Fourth edn of Erlich's definitive 1955 work on Russian Formalism, with full bibliography.)

Gorman, D. (1992) 'A Bibliography of Russian Formalism in English', in *Style* 26 (4): 554–76. (Thorough listing of anthologies, works by individual Formalists, and works about Formalism.)

Hansen-Löve, A. (1978) *Der russische Formalismus*, Vienna: Akademie der Wissenschaften. (Written after Erlich's study and assumes greater knowledge of Formalism.)

* Iakubinskii, L. (1916) 'O zvukakh stikhotvornogo iazyka' (On the Sounds of Verse Language), in *Sborniki po teorii poèticheskogo iazyka* (Collected Articles on the Theory of Poetic Language), Petrograd: Opoiaz, vol. 1. (Referred to in §1.)

* Jakobson, R. (1919) 'Noveishaia russkaia poèziia'; trans. E. Brown, 'Modern Russian Poetry: Velemir Khlebnikov', in E.J. Brown (ed.) *Major Soviet Writers: Essays in Criticism*, New York, NY: Oxford University Press, 1973, 58–82, 413–14. (A Formalist study of the Futurist poetry of Velemir Khlebnikov.)

* Jakobson, R. and Tynianov, Iu. (1928) 'Problemy izucheniia literatury i iazyka'; trans. H. Eagle, 'Problems in the Study of Literature and Language', in L. Matejka and K. Pomorska, eds, *Readings in Russian Poetics: Formalist and Structuralist Views*, Cambridge, MA: MIT Press, 1971, 79–81. (Written when Russian Formalism had exhausted its possibilities, this brief outline suggests new directions for literary theory.)

Jameson, F. (1972) *The Prison-House of Language: A Critical Account of Structuralism and Russian Formalism*, Princeton, NJ: Princeton University Press. (Theoretical analysis for knowledgeable readers.)

Shklovskii, V. [Shklovsky] (1914) 'Voskreshenie slova'; trans. R. Sherwood, 'The Resurrection of the Word', in S. Bann and J. Bowlt, (eds), *Russian Formalism: A Collection of Articles and Texts in Translation*, Edinburgh: Scottish Academic Press, 1973, 41–7. (The first work of Russian Formalism argues that a poet's task is to make us perceive familiar words in a new way.)

* —— (1916) 'Iskusstvo kak priëm'; trans. B. Sher, 'Art as Device', in V. Shlovskii [Shklovsky], *Theory of Prose*, Elmwood Park: Dalkey Archive, 1990. (How literary works renew conventional perceptions.)

Shukman, A. (1977) 'A Bibliography of Translations of Formalist Writings', in *Russian Poetics in Translation*, vol. 4, *Formalist Theory*, eds L. O'Toole and A. Shukman, 100–8. (123 titles in English, French, German and Italian. Includes a category on 'Bakhtin and his School'.)

Steiner, P. (1984) *Russian Formalism: A Metapoetics*, Ithaca, NY: Cornell University Press. (Argues for metaphorical basis of Formalist theory, which variously approaches literature as machine, organism or system.)

Striedter, J. (1989) *Literary Structure, Evolution, and Value: Russian Formalism and Czech Structuralism Reconsidered*, Cambridge, MA: Harvard University Press. (Ch. 1 explicates Formalist theory of prose and evolution; ch. 2 examines relationship of Russian Formalism with the Prague School.)

* Tynianov, Iu. (1924) *Problemy stikhotvornogo iazyka*; trans. M. Sosa and B. Harvey, *Problems of Verse Language*, Ann Arbor, MI: Ardis, 1981. (Distinguishes literary criteria for poetry versus prose.)

* —— (1927) 'O literaturnoi èvoliutsii'; trans. C. Luplow, 'On Literary Evolution', in L. Matejka and K. Pomorska, (eds), *Readings in Russian Poetics: Formalist and Structuralist Views*, Cambridge, MA: MIT Press, 66–78. (Theoretical discussion of how new literary genres eventually become automatized.)

CAROL ANY

RUSSIAN MATERIALISM: 'THE 1860s'

No tradition of philosophical materialism existed in Russia until the years conventionally called 'the 1860s' – roughly, the period from the death of Tsar Nicholas I in 1855 to the attempted assassination of Tsar Alexander II in 1866. During that time philosophical freethinking, under the delayed influence of the French Enlightenment and the contemporaneous influence of post-Hegelian German materialism, came together with political radicalism to create a major social and intellectual movement with a broadly materialist philosophical foundation.

The theoretical underpinnings of the movement were elaborated in Russia (as far as tsarist censorship would permit) by Nikolai Chernyshevskii, Dmitrii Pisarev, Nikolai Dobroliubov, Ivan Sechenov and others, and more freely in emigration by Mikhail Bakunin. Their 'materialism' was less a precisely articulated ontological position than a grand, science-worshipping worldview that sought to undermine both religion and the state; its elements included naturalism and universal causal determinism in metaphysics, empiricism in epistemology, reductionism in the philosophy of mind, 'rational egoism' in ethics, revolutionary socialism in political philosophy and realism in aesthetics. Because of their extreme opposition to established authority and traditional values, the representatives of this movement came to be called 'nihilists', and under that name they were portrayed in best-selling novels of the day by Ivan Turgenev and Fëdor Dostoevskii.

Government repression after 1866 put an end to the open development of this materialist movement, but the writings of its leaders proved to be an inspiration to Georgii Plekhanov and Vladimir Lenin, the founders of Russian Marxism. Under Communism, the materialists

of 'the 1860s' were honoured in Russia as great philosophers and important precursors of Marx.

1 **Intellectual lineage**
2 **Philosophical content**
3 **Sociocultural significance**

1 Intellectual lineage

Although Soviet Marxist historians of philosophy laboured for decades to find a native materialist tradition in Russian philosophy extending back to the eighteenth century, no such tradition is discernible until the mid-nineteenth. The influence of the French Enlightenment, encouraged in Russia for a time by Catherine the Great, can be seen in the thought of Aleksandr Radishchev (1749–1802) and the 'Russian Voltairians', but none of them actually advanced a materialist ontology or significantly influenced the later Russian thinkers who did, and the same is true of other alleged early 'materialists' such as Mikhail Lomonosov (1711–65) and the theoreticians of the abortive Decembrist uprising of 1825. The eighteenth-century Enlightenment affected only a small stratum of Russian society and did little to change the overall religious, idealistic direction of Russian philosophical thought – a direction that was reinforced with a vengeance by the repressive measures of Nicholas I, the 'Tsar-disciplinarian', upon his accession to the throne in 1825 (see ENLIGHTENMENT, RUSSIAN).

Materialism came to Russia in the nineteenth century as it had come to Germany – as a reaction against German Idealism; and in both countries the trend was initiated by Ludwig FEUERBACH. Among the liberally minded, Western-oriented Russian intelligentsia, brief but intense infatuations with Schelling, Hegel and Fichte (see SCHELLINGIANISM; HEGELIANISM, RUSSIAN; FICHTE, J.G.) were followed by enthusiasm for Feuerbach, whose views became known in Russia shortly after the publication of his *Das Wesen des Christentums* (Essence of Christianity) in 1841, despite official prohibition of his writings. But the materialist trend in philosophy that Feuerbach inspired did not become a broad movement in Russia until the death of Nicholas I in 1855 and the end of the Crimean War a year later. When it did, its tone was set more by the German 'scientific materialists' who had succeeded Feuerbach – Ludwig BÜCHNER, Jacob Moleschott and Karl Vogt (see MATERIALISM §3).

The bitter experiences of the Crimean War persuaded many Russians of the need for radical social reform, and the accession of Alexander II offered hope of movement in that direction. Censorship was eased somewhat, and as a consequence new books were available and new journals appeared. A vigorous progressive spirit arose, leading in 1861 to the long-sought emancipation of the serfs. Philosophically this new spirit was manifested in a secular, empiricist attitude that put its trust in reason and science to sweep away the accumulated evils of the past and set society on the path of progress. It was the Enlightenment revisited. Indeed, since Russia's eighteenth-century Enlightenment was so shallow and limited that Nicholas could easily obliterate it, this was in effect the true Russian Enlightenment. Leon Trotsky called 'the 1860s' 'our short-lived eighteenth century' (see Lampert 1965: 6).

If the German materialists were the Diderot and Holbach of the delayed Russian Enlightenment, Büchner's notorious *Kraft und Stoff* (Force and Matter) (first published in German in 1855) was its *Encyclopédie*. Called 'the Bible of the German materialism of the present day' by the historian of philosophy Friedrich Ueberweg, the book was no less a sensation in Russia than in Germany. Like the works of Feuerbach, it was never published legally in pre-Soviet Russia; but beginning about 1859, Russian university students became *samizdat* pioneers in the translation and reproduction of prohibited books. It was *Kraft und Stoff* that the 'nihilist' younger generation in Ivan Turgenev's novel *Otsy i deti* (Fathers and Sons) (1862) recommended to the 'fathers'.

These Russian materialists made little distinction between the views of Feuerbach and the 'scientific materialists', whose impact on most of them was concurrent. Like Feuerbach they often referred to themselves as 'realists' rather than 'materialists', but this was at least in part owing to the fact that the typical Russian censor found 'realism' less alarming than 'materialism'. They appear to have regarded the two terms as synonymous, and they looked upon the intellectual movement from Feuerbach to Büchner, Moleschott and Vogt not (as some critics did) as a degeneration of philosophical materialism but as the productive elaboration of a common philosophical core. CHERNYSHEVSKII singled out Feuerbach for special praise, but he never explicitly criticized the later thinkers or pointed to differences between their outlook and Feuerbach's. Pisarev enthusiastically endorsed the views of Büchner and company, but without rejecting Feuerbach. Among Russians who developed materialist views in 'the 1860s', only BAKUNIN (writing abroad, apart from the active domestic scene) expressed reservations about the scientistic extremes of materialist thought.

The philosophical manifesto of '1860s' materialism – Chernyshevskii's essay 'Antropologicheskii printsip v filosofii' ('The Anthropological Principle in Philosophy') (1860) – is sometimes considered a Russian popularization of the ideas of Feuerbach. Much of its content is indeed reminiscent of Feuerbach, but it is also reminiscent of Büchner, and in fact Chernyshevskii's central idea of the organic connection between all human activity and an integral, physical human nature was already expounded in his diary in 1848, before he had read Feuerbach, not to mention Büchner. Others have pointed to La Mettrie and Holbach (especially the latter's *Système de la nature*) as Chernyshevskii's sources. In the end, specific influences on particular works of Chernyshevskii or the other Russian materialists cannot be pinpointed. All of them were stimulated by Feuerbach, impressed by the further advances of the German 'scientific materialists', influenced directly or indirectly by various thinkers of the French Enlightenment (Chernyshevskii, for one, was fascinated by the figure and the thought of ROUSSEAU); but they were also guided by their own reactions both to modern European philosophy and to the social and intellectual realities of their immediate Russian environment.

2 Philosophical content

The actual content of the 'materialism' preached by the radicals of 'the 1860s' is not always clear. As indicated, they often avoided the term itself for reasons of censorship, and when they used it they often did so without delineation of its scope. At the same time, they did subscribe to a loose constellation of ideas that can be identified as a materialist philosophical programme. Its fullest legal expression in Russia came in the published writings of Chernyshevskii, Sechenov and Pisarev (especially Chernyshevskii's 'Antropologicheskii printsip v filosofii'); more explicit presentation of these ideas may be found in some unpublished writings such as a series of letters Chernyshevskii wrote from his Siberian exile and a number of essays by Bakunin published abroad.

The clearest and most succinct expression of the materialists' ontology was provided by Chernyshevskii in a letter from Siberia: 'That which exists is matter. Matter has properties. The manifestations of properties are forces. What we call laws of nature are the modes of action of forces' (see Scanlan 1970: 78). With this basic outlook and with its most immediate implications, all the Russian materialists of 'the 1860s' would agree. Those implications include, first, the ontological thesis that nothing immaterial, such as a supernatural supreme being or an immortal spiritual soul, exists; second, the epistemological thesis that only empirical investigation, not faith or pure reason, can provide knowledge; and third, the reductionist thesis that all human functions or 'forces' (including of course what we call mental operations) are properties of matter.

Because outright denial of God's existence or rejection of faith as a source of knowledge could not readily be camouflaged to avoid censorship, the attention of Chernyshevskii, Sechenov and others in their works published in Russia in 'the 1860s' was directed primarily towards establishing the reductionist thesis – that is, towards demonstrating that all human functions, from the most 'animal' to the most refined, are materially based and can be exhaustively comprehended by the natural sciences. Chernyshevskii's apparent rambling in 'Antropologicheskii printsip v filosofii' is actually a sustained defence of this thesis, following two complementary lines of argument: that other animals possess all the traits sometimes thought to be restricted to man, and that human behaviour is explicable solely and completely in the same physiological and ultimately chemical terms used to explain processes in the 'lower' orders of nature (Chernyshevskii implies, for example, that because thinking can be reduced to processes of sensation, which is a form of assimilation comparable to digestion, thinking is a chemical process like digestion). The physiologist Sechenov's contribution to this argument is evident from the alleged subtitle (struck out by the censors) of his work *Refleksy golovnogo mazga* (Cerebral Reflexes) (1863): 'An Attempt to Reduce the Mode of Genesis of Psychical Phenomena to Physiological Bases'. Pisarev contributed some of the more imaginative applications of the reductionist thesis, such as his contention that the intellectual vitality of eighteenth-century Europe was attributable to the introduction of the stimulants tea and coffee.

A corollary of the reductionist approach is that the laws of nature apply to acts of the human will just as they do to all other natural 'forces', and this determinist thesis is vigorously championed by Chernyshevskii, Sechenov and Bakunin. Pisarev, on the other hand, offers an inconsistent mixture of materialistic reductionism and 'subjectivity': he attributes an undefined but supremely important 'individual autonomy' to human beings. Bakunin, too, is concerned to retain a place for human freedom in a deterministic universe, but he does so by locating 'freedom' in the conscious awareness that one is determined *only* by natural laws and not by the will of another; thus 'materialism denies free will and ends in the establishment of liberty' (Bakunin [1870–1] 1970: 48).

Their determinism did not prevent most of the materialists of 'the 1860s' from espousing an ethical theory, despite their expressed abhorrence of 'mor-

ality' and 'ideals'. Chernyshevskii and Pisarev, in particular, advanced a form of ethical egoism, holding that people ought to act in accordance with their own best interests or true needs. This theory was said to be 'scientific' because it was based on the elementary truth of *psychological* egoism – that is, on the supposed 'natural law' that people invariably *do* act in accordance with what they *think* is their own best interest, with their *perception* of their needs. The task, then, is simply to bring perceptions of needs into line with genuine needs and provide social arrangements for their satisfaction; once people are shown what their true needs really are, and are allowed to pursue them, psychological egoism guarantees that they will do so. The materialists were not worried that a society of perfect egoists would be chaotic or conflictual, because they were convinced that the true, 'natural' needs of all people are harmonious and mutually reinforcing. Hence 'rational egoism', as they called it, would coincide in practice with altruism.

In its most general terms, the social ideal of all these thinkers, including Bakunin, was a society consisting of institutions that allowed the expression of 'natural' human needs rather than generating 'false' or 'artificial' needs such as acquisitiveness and hostility. Because existing institutions were so distant from this ideal, so 'unnatural', an initial posture of revolutionary destruction was called for, expressed most vehemently by Pisarev when he wrote: 'What can be smashed should be smashed. What withstands the blow is fit to survive. What flies into pieces is rubbish. In any case, strike out right and left; no harm can come of it' (see Edie *et al.* 1965: vol. 2, 65). The exact contours of what was expected to survive were never fully elaborated, though it was widely assumed that the society attuned to people's true needs would be secular, socialist and non-authoritarian (to the point of anarchism, in the case of Bakunin).

An important place in the materialists' worldview was occupied by their philosophy of art. This was the first element of their outlook to receive broad public attention after the publication of Chernyshevskii's essay 'The Aesthetic Relation of Art to Reality' in 1855. In opposition to the prevailing idealist theories, Chernyshevskii argued that the purpose of art is simply to reproduce reality critically – that is, to portray what exists in such a way as to explain it, identify its shortcomings and project a more desirable future, all in the service of true human needs. The notion that art is subordinate to life and is justified only to the extent that it contributes to social progress was carried to an extreme by Pisarev, who under the banner of 'the destruction of aesthetics' rejected almost all art of the past on the ground that it catered to false, artificial needs.

3 Sociocultural significance

The Russian materialism of 'the 1860s' is less important for the philosophical content of its ideas than for their influence on Russian society and culture. Materialism in Russia, as it was in France in the eighteenth century and in Germany around 1848, was closely allied with the revolutionary movement. It opposed, in the words of T.G. MASARYK, both 'theology and theocracy' – both God and the autocratic state ruled in God's name (Masaryk [1913] 1919 vol. 2: 48). It offered not merely an alternative philosophical perspective but a system of values and purposes that were radically different from traditional attitudes and that required the sweeping rejection of existing institutions. The challenge to construct a new life both personally and socially was taken up by throngs of restive Russians, most of them young and many with little interest in philosophy. Called 'nihilists' because of their seemingly total denial of standards of thought and behaviour, they were in fact dogmatically committed to their own antireligious, antitraditionalist and anti-authoritarian standards.

By 1861 the radicals were disappointed by the slow pace of reform, and especially by the illiberal terms of the emancipation of the serfs in that year. Disturbances were answered with intensified repression; both Chernyshevskii and Pisarev were arrested and imprisoned in 1862. Earlier hopes of change from above grew into a determination to bring change about by force, and a 'nihilist' student, Dmitrii Karakozov, effectively ended the relatively open decade of 'the 1860s' by his unsuccessful attempt on the life of Alexander II in 1866. Thereafter, Russian materialism evolved into a philosophy of revolutionary activism, soon with Marxist overtones. A disciple of Chernyshevskii named Pëtr Nikitich Tkachëv (1844–86 NS), one of the first Russian writers to come under the influence of Marx, brought elements of Marxist historical materialism into his literary criticism in the mid-1860s; subsequently, writing abroad, Tkachëv became an extreme advocate of revolutionary terrorism and the violent seizure of power.

Among the enduring cultural influences of the Russian materialists' worldview was its impact in the field of literature. The Russian tradition of 'civic criticism', inaugurated by Vissarion BELINSKII, was developed further by Chernyshevskii, Pisarev, Dobroliubov and others, in part because the discussion of literature offered them a relatively protected forum for the social critique they could not publish directly. Creative literature, too, felt the powerful impact of 'nihilism'. The very term was popularized by Turgenev in *Otsy i deti* (Fathers and Sons), in which the character Bazarov is the quintessential '1860s' materialist, bent on saving the world through studying the physiology of frogs. A more sympathetic, if aesthetically less successful, portrayal of the 'new people' of the day was presented in Chernyshevskii's own widely read novel, *Chto Delat'?* (What Is to Be Done?) (1863). The deepest literary impact of the movement, albeit a negative one, came in the works of Fëdor DOSTOEVSKII. His *Zapiski iz podpol'ia* (Notes From Underground) (1864) is a frontal assault on the determinism and 'rational egoism' of Chernyshevskii, and all of Dostoevskii's great novels deal in one way or another with the materialist outlook and what Dostoevskii took to be its pernicious implications; in *Besy* (The Possessed) (1871–2) he paints a highly unflattering portrait of 'nihilist' revolutionaries.

Although the writings of the materialists of 'the 1860s' inspired one of the liveliest intellectual debates in nineteenth-century Russia, the debate did not result in the philosophical refinement of their materialist outlook (except to some degree in Chernyshevskii's unpublished and publicly unknown letters from Siberia of 1876–8). In 1861 and 1862, the religious philosopher Pamfil Danilovich Iurkevich (1826–74) published a series of essays containing careful and philosophically sophisticated criticism of materialism and especially of Chernyshevskii's 'Antropologicheskii printsip v filosofii'. Because of censorship, however, Chernyshevskii could not reply substantively to the charges against him; his side of the philosophical argument was effectively proscribed, and he and his supporters resorted to invective and crude personal attacks on Iurkevich. The only strictly philosophical legacy of the materialists came in the form of their influence on Russian Marxism. Georgii Plekhanov and Vladimir Lenin, the two thinkers most responsible for the development of Marxism in Russia, credited Chernyshevskii with having, respectively, 'massive' and 'overwhelming' influence on them (see Scanlan 1970: 65). During the communist period of Russian history, the principal 'nihilist' theoreticians were officially lionized under the designation 'Russian revolutionary democrats' and were called the most important materialist thinkers in the history of philosophy before Marx.

See also: NIHILISM, RUSSIAN

References and further reading

* Bakunin, M. (1870–1) *God and the State*, ed. P.

Avrich, New York: Dover, 1970. (Referred to in §2. The most popular of Bakunin's writings, a lively statement of his worldview.)

* Büchner, L. (1855) *Kraft und Stoff* (Force and Matter), Frankfurt. (Referred to in §1. A presentation, highly influential in Russia, of extreme reductive materialism.)

* Chernyshevskii, N. (1855) *Esteticheskie otnosheniia iskusstva k deistvitel'nosti* (The Aesthetic Relation of Art to Reality), St Petersburg. (Referred to in §2. Chernyshevskii's statement of a realist philosophy of art.)

* —— (1860) 'Antropolgicheskii printsip v filosofii' (The Anthropological Principle in Philosophy), in *Sovremennik*, vol. 4, 329–36, vol. 5, 1–46. (Referred to in §§1–3. Chernyshevskii's principal philosophical essay.)

* Edie, J.M. *et al.* (eds) (1965) *Russian Philosophy*, Chicago, IL: Quadrangle Books, 3 vols. (Referred to in §2. A comprehensive anthology of Russian philosophy containing extensive selections from the writings of the thinkers discussed in this entry, as well as bibliographies of their works.)

* Feuerbach, L. (1841) *Das Wesen des Christentums*, trans. M. Evans (George Eliot) as *Essence of Christianity*, 1854; new edn, intro. K. Barth, foreword H.R. Niebuhr, New York: Harper & Row, 1957. (Feuerbach's most influential work, referred to in §1.)

* Lampert, E. (1965) *Sons against Fathers: Studies in Russian Radicalism and Revolution*, Oxford: Clarendon Press. (Referred to in §1. A highly readable and thorough study of the Nihilist movement, with major chapters on Chernyshevskii, Pisarev and Dobroliubov.)

* Masaryk, T.G. (1913) *The Spirit of Russia: Studies in History, Literature and Philosophy*, trans. E. and C. Paul, 2 vols, London: Allen & Unwin, 1919. (Referred to in §3. An older but still useful intellectual history of Russia with a lengthy chapter on 'Realism and Nihilism' (vol. 2, 1–114).)

* Scanlan, J.P. (1970) 'Nicholas Chernyshevsky and Philosophical Materialism in Russia', in Journal of the History of Ideas 8 (1): 65–86. (Referred to in §§2–3. Expansion of many of the points in this entry.)

* Sechenov, I. (1863) *Refleksy golovnogo mazga* (Cerebral Reflexes), Moscow. (Referred to in §2. A Russian physiologist's influential statement of reductive materialism.)

JAMES P. SCANLAN

RUSSIAN PHILOSOPHY

Russian thought is best approached without fixed preconceptions about the nature and proper boundaries of philosophy. Conditions of extreme political oppression and economic backwardness are not conducive to the flowering of philosophy as a purely theoretical discipline; academic philosophy was hence a latecomer on the Russian scene, and those (such as the Neo-Kantians of the end of the nineteenth century: see NEO-KANTIANISM, RUSSIAN) who devoted themselves to questions of ontology and epistemology were widely condemned for their failure to address the country's pressing social problems. Since Peter the Great's project of Westernization, Russian philosophy has been primarily the creation of writers and critics who derived their ideals and values from European sources and focused on ethics, social theory and the philosophy of history, in the belief that (as Marx put it in the first 'Thesis on Feuerbach') philosophers had hitherto merely interpreted the world: the task was now to change it. This passionate social commitment generated much doctrinaire fanaticism, but it also inspired the iconoclastic tendency made philosophically respectable by Nietzsche: the revaluation of values from an ironic outsider's perspective. The principal contribution of Russian thinkers to world culture has so far consisted not in systems, but in experiments in the theory and practice of human emancipation. Some of these led to the Russian Revolution, while others furnished remarkably accurate predictions of the nature of utopia in power. Like Dostoevskii's character Shigalëv who, starting from the ideal of absolute freedom, arrived by a strict logical progression at the necessity of absolute despotism, Russian philosophers have specialized in thinking through (and sometimes acting out) the practical implications of the most seductive visions of liberty that Europe has produced over the last 200 hundred years.

1 The development of Russian philosophy

What Berdiaev called the 'Russian Idea' – the eschatological quest that is the most distinctive feature of Russian philosophy – can be explained in terms of Russian history. The Mongol yoke from the twelfth to the fourteenth century cut Russia off from Byzantium (from which it had received Christianity) and from Europe: it had no part in the ferment of the Renaissance. Its rise as a unified state under the Moscow Tsardom followed closely on the fall of the Orthodox Byzantine Empire, and the emerging sense of Russian national identity incorporated a messianic element in the form of the monk Philotheus' theory of

Moscow as the 'Third Rome', successor to Rome and Constantinople as guardian of Christ's truth in its purity (see MEDIEVAL PHILOSOPHY, RUSSIAN). 'There will not be a fourth', ran the prophecy: the Russian Empire would last until the end of the world. Russian thought remained dominated by the Greek patristic tradition until the eighteenth century, when the Kievan thinker SKOVORODA (sometimes described as Russia's first philosopher) developed a religious vision based on a synthesis of ancient and patristic thought. He had no following; by the mid-century Russia's intellectual centre was St Petersburg, where Catherine the Great, building on the achievements of her predecessor Peter, sought to promote a Western secular culture among the educated elite with the aid of French Enlightenment ideas. But representatives of the 'Russian Enlightenment' were severely punished when they dared to cite the *philosophes'* concepts of rationality and justice in criticism of the political status quo (see ENLIGHTENMENT, RUSSIAN). The persecution of advanced ideas (which served to strengthen the nascent intelligentsia's self-image as the cultural and moral leaders of their society) reached its height under Nicolas I (1825–55), when philosophy departments were closed in the universities, and thought went underground. Western ideas were the subject of intense debate in small informal circles of students, writers and critics, the most famous of which in Moscow and St Petersburg furnished the philosophical education of such intellectual leaders as the future socialists Herzen and Bakunin, the novelist and liberal Ivan Turgenev, the literary critic Belinskii (from whose 'social criticism' Soviet Socialist Realism claimed descent), and the future Slavophile religious philosophers Kireevskii and Khomiakov (see SLAVOPHILISM). As a critic has noted: 'In the West there is theology and there is philosophy; Russian thought, however, is a third concept'; one which (in the tsarist intellectual underground as in its Soviet successor) embraced novelists, poets, critics, religious and political thinkers – all bound together by their commitment to the goals of freedom and justice.

In the 1830s these beleaguered individuals encountered German Idealism: an event of decisive significance for the future development of Russian thought. The teleological structures of idealist thought provided Russian intellectuals with a redemptive interpretation of their conflicts and struggles as a necessary stage in the dialectical movement of history towards a transcendent state of harmony. Idealism (notably in its Hegelian forms: see HEGELIANISM, RUSSIAN) left its mark on the vocabulary of subsequent Russian philosophy, but its principal legacy was the belief, shared by the vast majority of Russian thinkers, that an 'integral worldview', a coherent and unified vision of the historical process and its goal, was the essential framework both for personal moral development and social theorizing. The question of history's goal became a matter for intense debate among the intelligentsia with the publication in 1836 of Chaadaev's 'Philosophical Letter', which posed Russia's relationship to the West as a central philosophical problem, maintaining that Russia's historical separation from the culture of Western Christianity precluded its participation in the movement of history towards the establishment of a universal Christian society. Chaadaev's version of the march of progress was much indebted to French Catholic conservatism, while the nationalist riposte to his ideas drew heavily on the Romantics' critique of the Age of Reason and Schelling's organic conception of nationhood: the Slavophiles held that Western culture was in a state of terminal moral and social decline, suffering from an excess of rationalism, which had led to social atomization and the fragmentation of the individual psyche (see CHAADAEV, P.IA.; SCHELLINGIANISM). These divisions could be healed only by religious faith in its purest form, Russian Orthodoxy, whose spirit of organic 'togetherness', uncontaminated by Western rationalism, they presented as a model for Russian society and a beacon for mankind. They thereby laid the foundations of a distinctively Russian tradition of cultural and religious messianism which includes Dostoevskii's political writings, the Pan-Slavist and Eurasian movements (see DOSTOEVSKII, F.M.; PAN-SLAVISM and EURASIAN MOVEMENT), and the apocalyptic vision of Berdiaev, whose philosophy was highly popular among the Soviet underground.

Secular and Westernist thinkers tended to be scarcely less messianic in their response to Chaadaev's pessimism. The first philosophers of Russian liberalism (see LIBERALISM, RUSSIAN) interpreted their country's past and future development in the light of Hegel's doctrine of the necessary movement of all human societies towards the incarnation of Reason in the modern constitutional state, while the Russian radical tradition was shaped successively by the eschatological visions of the French utopian socialists, the Young Hegelians and Karl Marx. Herzen defined the distinctive characteristic of Russian radical thought as the 'implacable spirit of negation' with which, unrestrained by the European's deference to the past, it applied itself to the task of freeing mankind from the transcendent authorities invented by religion and philosophy; and the radical populist tradition that he founded argued that the 'privilege of backwardness', by permitting Russia to learn both from the achievements and the mistakes of the West, had placed it in the vanguard of mankind's movement towards liberty.

Russian religious philosophers tended to see themselves as prophets, pointing the way to the regeneration of human societies through the spiritual transformation of individuals. Vladimir SOLOV'ËV (regarded by many Russians as their greatest philosopher) believed that his country's mission was to bring into being the Kingdom of God on Earth in the form of a liberal theocracy, which would integrate knowledge and social practice and unite the human race under the spiritual rule of the Pope and the secular rule of the Russian tsar. His metaphysics of 'All-Unity' was a dominant force in the revival of religious and idealist philosophy in Russia in the early twentieth century, inspiring an entire generation of thinkers who sought to reinterpret Christian dogma in ways that emphasized the links of spiritual culture and religious faith with institutional and social reform, and progress in all other aspects of human endeavour. Among them were leading Russian émigré philosophers after 1917, such as Semën FRANK, BULGAKOV (who sought to create a new culture in which Orthodox Christianity would infuse every area of Russian life), BERDIAEV (who was strongly influenced by the messianic motifs in Solov'ëv), and HESSEN, who offered a Neo-Kantian and Westernist interpretation of the notion of 'All-Unity'. A number of émigré philosophers (notably IL'IN and VYSHESLAVTSEV) interpreted Bolshevism as the expression of a spiritual crisis in modern industrialized cultures. Many blamed the Russian Revolution on infection from a culturally bankrupt West which (echoing the Slavophiles, Dostoevskii and LEONT'EV) they presented as corrupted by rationalism, positivism, atheism and self-centred individualism (although few have gone as far as the fiercely polemical LOSEV who, up until his death in the Soviet Union in 1988, maintained that electric light expressed the spiritual emptiness of 'Americanism and machine-production'). Most maintained a historiosophical optimism throughout the catastrophes of the first half of the twentieth century, which Berdiaev saw as a precondition for messianic regeneration, while Hessen believed that religious and cultural values would emerge triumphant from the carnage in a dialectical *Aufhebung*.

2 Major themes in Russian philosophy

The main impetus of Russian philosophy has always been towards the future, as its representatives strained to discern the features of the 'new man' (the term favoured by the left from the 1860s, with the addition of the adjective 'Soviet' after 1917), or the 'integral personality', as Slavophiles and neo-idealists preferred to describe the individual who would one day be free from the cognitive and moral defects that had hitherto prevented mankind from realizing its potential. The nature of these flaws and the specifications of the regenerated human being were the subject of bitter disputes between rival movements. Even on the left, models of the 'new man' varied widely, from the narrow rationalist who was the ideal of the 'nihilists' of the 1860s (see NIHILISM, RUSSIAN; RUSSIAN MATERIALISM: 'THE 1860S') and subsequently of LENIN and PLEKHANOV, to Bakunin's eternal rebel, who would embody the spontaneous spirit of freedom in defiance of all established authorities and orders. At the end of the nineteenth century, in the cultural ferment produced by new movements in philosophy and the arts emanating from the West, radical thinkers began *en masse* to renounce their predominantly rationalist models of the individual and society (see RUSSIAN RELIGIOUS-PHILOSOPHICAL RENAISSANCE). Nietzsche's Superman had a pervasive influence on the ensuing 'revaluation of values', undertaken with the aim of formulating moral and social ideals that would embrace the manysidedness of human creativity (see NIETZSCHE: IMPACT ON RUSSIAN THOUGHT). Some radical philosophers (such as Berdiaev and Frank), in the process of moving from Marxism to neo-idealism, sought to reconcile Nietzsche's aesthetic immoralism with Christian ethics, while the 'Empiriocriticist' group of Bolsheviks attempted to inject Russian Marxist philosophy with an element of heroic voluntarism by synthesizing it with Nietzschean self-affirmation and the pragmatism of Ernst Mach (see RUSSIAN EMPIRIOCRITICISM). Nietzschean influences combined with the mechanistic scientism of Soviet Marxism in the Soviet model of the 'new man' (whose qualities Lysenko's genetics suggested could be inherited by successive generations). In the post-Stalin 'thaw' some Soviet philosophers, including IL'ENKOV and MAMARDASHVILI, began a critical rereading of Marx's texts from an anthropocentric standpoint which emphasized the unpredictable and limitless potential of human consciousness (see MARXIST PHILOSOPHY, RUSSIAN AND SOVIET).

This open-ended view of progress (officially encouraged in the Gorbachev period) is uncommon in Russian philosophy, where epistemological scepticism is more often to be encountered in uneasy combinations with eschatological faith. Like other rootless groups, Russian intellectuals were drawn to compensating certainties that seemed capable of resisting their corrosive critique. The radical humanism of much Russian thought placed it at the forefront of the developing critical insistence on the context-dependent nature of truth; but many thinkers who attacked the claims of systems and dogmas to encompass and explain the experience and creative needs of living individuals in specific historical contexts, nevertheless retained a belief in a final, ideal state of being in which the fragmentation of knowledge would be overcome and all human purposes would coincide: a condition for whose principles some looked to science, others to religious revelation. The nihilists, who rejected metaphysics and all that could not be proven by rational and empirical methods, fervently believed that progress would inevitably lead to the restoration of a natural state of harmony between the individual and society. The empiriocriticist movement within Russian Marxism opposed the idolatry of formulas with the claim that experience and practice were the sole criteria of truth, but the group's leading philosopher, BOGDANOV, looked forward to a metascience that would unify the fragmented world of knowledge by reducing 'all the discontinuities of our experience to a principle of continuity', predicting that under communism, when all would share the same modes of organizing experience, the phenomenon of individuals with separate mental worlds would cease to exist. Solov'ëv's pervasive influence on subsequent Russian religious idealism owed much to the charms of his vision of 'integral knowledge' and 'integral life' in an 'integral society'. Religious and socialist motifs were combined in some visions of an earthly paradise, such as Bulgakov's 'Christian Socialism', or Gorkii's and Lunacharskii's creed of 'God-building', which called for worship of the collective humanity of the socialist future. In the revolutionary ferment of the first two decades of the twentieth century many religious and radical philosophers, together with Symbolist writers and poets, envisaged the leap to the harmonious future in apocalyptic terms: the novelist and critic Merezhkovskii prophesied the coming of a 'New Christianity' which would unite Christian faith with pagan self-affirmation in a morality beyond good and evil (see NIETZSCHE: IMPACT ON RUSSIAN THOUGHT§1; RUSSIAN RELIGIOUS-PHILOSOPHICAL RENAISSANCE §§3–4). In the aftermath of 1917 some thinkers (notably Berdiaev and members of the Eurasian movement) found consolation in apocalyptic fantasies of a new light from the East shining on the ruins of European culture.

Herzen memorably ascribed such doctrinaire utopianism to the Russian tendency to march 'in fearless ranks to the very limit and beyond it, in step with the dialectic, but out of step with the truth'. The most original and subversive Russian thinker, he was the first of a significant minority who directed the iconoclastic thrust of Russian philosophy against all forms, without exception, of messianic faith. Contending that there was no basis in experience for the belief in a purposeful universe on which the great optimistic systems of the nineteenth century were built, he urged his contemporaries to adapt their categories to the flow of life, to accept (and even welcome) the dominant role of contingency in human existence, on the grounds that individual freedom and responsibility were possible only in an unprogrammed world. Herzen's critique of the claims of metaphysical systems to predict or regulate the course of history was echoed by the 'subjective sociology' developed by MIKHAILOVSKII and LAVROV in opposition to the deterministic scientism of the dominant Russian radical tradition. TOLSTOI pointed to the chanciness of life and history in order to demonstrate the inadequacy of all attempts to formulate general rules for human societies; Dostoevskii confronted the systematizers with the lived experience of human freedom as the ability to be unpredictable; in their symposium of 1909 (frequently cited in the West as a pioneering analysis of the psychology of political utopianism) the neo-idealists of the *Signposts* movement explored the ways in which obsession with an ideal future impoverishes and distorts perception of the historical present (see SIGNPOSTS MOVEMENT).

Under the Soviet system a few representatives of this anti-utopian tradition ingeniously evaded the pressure on philosophers (backed up by the doctrine of the 'partyness' of truth – see PARTIINOST') to endorse the official myths of utopia in power. The history of the novel form was the vehicle for Bakhtin's reflections on the 'unfinalizability' of human existence (see BAKHTIN, M.M.); similar insights were expressed by the cultural-historical school of psychology established by VYGOTSKII, who drew on Marx to counter the mechanistic determinism of Soviet Marxist philosophy with a view of consciousness as a cultural artefact capable of self-transcendence and self-renewal. In the 1960s Soviet psychologists and philosophers such as Il'enkov helped to revive an interest in ethics with their emphasis on the individual as the centre of moral agency, while in its historical studies of culture as a system of semiotic signs, the MOSCOW-TARTU SCHOOL brought a richly documented and undoctrinaire approach to important moral and political topics.

The insights of some of these individuals and movements into the attractions and delusions of utopian thought are lent added conviction by their own often spectacularly unsuccessful efforts to overcome what Nietzsche called 'the craving for metaphysical comfort'. Tolstoi was torn all his life bween his pluralist vision and his need for dogmatic moral certainties, while Dostoevskii in his last years preached an astonishingly crude variety of religio-political messianism. The humanism of some later religious philosophers (including the *Signposts* authors Berdiaev and Bulgakov) is hard to reconcile with their eschatological impatience.

See also: ASMUS, V.F.; CHERNYSHEVSKII, N.G.; FËDOROV, N.F. ; FLORENSKII, P.A.; KROPOTKIN, P.A.; LOSSKY, N.O.; POSITIVISM, RUSSIAN; ROZANOV, V.V.; RUSSIAN LITERARY FORMALISM; SHESTOV, L.; SHPET, G.G.; TROTSKY, L.

Further reading

Berlin, I. (1978) *Russian Thinkers*, London: The Hogarth Press. (Essays in nineteenth-century Russian thinkers, including Tolstoi, Herzen, Bakunin and Belinskii.)

Edie, J.M.; Scanlan, J.P.; and Zeldin, M.B. (eds) (1966) *Russian Philosophy*, Chigaco, IL: Quadrangle Books, 3 vols. (A selection of texts, well annotated and introduced, from the beginnings of Russian philosophy until the Soviet period.)

Masaryk, T.G. (1955) *The Spirit of Russia. Studies in History, Literature and Philosophy*, trans. E. and C. Paul, with additional chapters and bibliographies by J. Slavik, London: Allen & Unwin, 3 vols. (First published in German in 1913, and still an excellent introduction to Russian philosophy.)

Walicki, A. (1980) *Russian Thought From the Enlightenment to Marxism*, Oxford: Clarendon Press. (Covers the main movements in Russian thought from the eighteenth to the early twentieth century.)

Zenkovsky, V. (1948–50) *Istoriia russkoi filosofii*, Paris: YMCA-Press, 2 vols; 2nd edn 1989; trans. G.L. Kline, *A History of Russian Philosophy*, London and New York: Routledge & Kegan Paul and Columbia University Press, 1953. (A general history.)

AILEEN KELLY

RUSSIAN RELIGIOUS-PHILOSOPHICAL RENAISSANCE

The Russian Religious-Philosophical Renaissance was created by lay intellectuals who found rationalism, positivism and Marxism inadequate as explanations of the world or guides to life. They were deeply engaged in finding solutions to the problems of their time, which they saw as moral or spiritual/cultural in nature. Some were already devout Christians; others became so later on. Collectively known as the God-seekers, they propounded their ideas in numerous publications and in the Religious-Philosophical Societies of St Petersburg and Moscow. The meetings of these societies attracted capacity audiences and helped disassociate religion from reaction. Branches were founded in Kiev and Vladimir. The founding members were mainly Symbolist writers and idealist philosophers. Both groups sought a new understanding of Christianity, but the Symbolists emphasized psychological and literary/aesthetic issues and the idealists focused on ethics, epistemology and political and social reform. The Revolution of 1905 was a watershed for all of them. The hitherto apolitical Symbolists perceived it as the start of the apocalypse and championed anarchistic political doctrines. The idealists continued to champion reform. After the revolution, some of them called for a new religious intelligentsia that respected culture and the creation of wealth, spiritual/cultural and material. Both groups began to talk about national identity and destiny. The Bolshevik Revolution signalled the end of the Religious-Philosophical Renaissance. In 1922–3, over 160 non-Marxist intellectuals were forced into exile, where they continued their work. Inside Russia private religious-philosophic study circles carried on illegally.

The Religious-Philosophical Renaissance had a profound impact on Russian thought and culture. It inspired attempts to ground metaphysics and political doctrines in Christianity, demands for church reform, visions of a new culture, sophiology, religious existentialism and new interpretations of Orthodox ritual and dogma. Its proponents made people aware of the needs of the 'inner man', the soul or the psyche, and the importance of art and myth. Symbolism became the dominant aesthetic, shaping literature, poetry, painting and theatre. Theorists of Symbolism tried to make it the basis of a new cosmological worldview. The Religious-Philosophical Renaissance was rediscovered by Soviet intellectuals in the 1960s, nourished the dissident movement from then on, and is extensively discussed in Russia today.

1   **The leading figures**
2   **The Religious-Philosophical Society meetings**
3   **Merezhkovskii's 'new religious consciousness'**
4   **Symbolism as a worldview**
5   **The idealists**
6   **Responses to the Bolshevik Revolution**

1   The leading figures

The leading figures of the Religious-Philosophical Renaissance opted for spirituality over materialism, art over utility, and mysticism or idealism over positivism. Focusing on spiritual, psychological and cultural transformation rather than social engineering, they debated issues such as the relevance of Christianity to the political and social order, Christian attitudes to sex, philosophy and the law, art and cognition, the intelligentsia and the people, and the essence of 'Russianness'. Although they argued about the same problems and were occupied in a common search for new values, their approaches were somewhat different so that in essence there were two groups. The first group included the Symbolist writers Dmitrii Merezhkovskii (1865–1941), his wife Zinaida Gippius (1869–1945), Dmitrii Filosofov (1872–1940), Nikolai Minskii (real name Vilenkin, 1855–1937), Andrei Belyi (1880–1934), Aleksandr Blok (1880–1921), Vyacheslav Ivanov (1866–1949) and Aleksei Remizov (1877–1957). Associated with them were Fëdor Sologub (Teternikov, 1863–1927), Vasilii Rozanov (1856–1919) and Aleksandr Benois (1870–1960), of the journal *Mir iskusstva* (The World of Art) (1899–1904). The Symbolist writer Valerii Briusov (1873–1924) was not a God-seeker, but he used their terminology and published their works in his journal *Vesy* (The Balance) (1904–9). Influenced by Nietzsche and Wagner, and in some cases by Solov'ëv, this group was primarily concerned with art, self-expression, and personal freedom (see NIETZSCHE: IMPACT ON RUSSIAN THOUGHT; SOLOV'ËV, V.S.). Once they became politicized most of them favoured anarchism but, except for the mandate to feed the hungry, they ignored economic issues and were indifferent or hostile to industrialization. The second group included the contributors to the symposium *Problemy idealizma* (Problems of Idealism) (1902), Pavel Novgorodtsev (1866–1924), Sergei Trubetskoi (1861–1905), Evgenii Trubetskoi (1863–1920), Nikolai BERDIAEV (1847–1948), Sergei BULGAKOV (1871–1944), Semën FRANK (1877–1950), and Pëtr Struve (1870–1944). Influenced by Neo-Kantian idealism and by theories of natural law, they advocated economic growth if it be guided by ethical considerations, self-discipline and a sense of responsibility for one's actions (see NATURAL LAW; NEO-KANTIANISM, RUSSIAN §5). The idealists were also influenced by Solov'ëv, but they highlighted different writings. Neither group was homogeneous. The Trubetskoi brothers objected to the Nietzscheanism of Berdiaev's and Frank's essays in *Problemy idealizma*. Belyi and Rozanov defended the symposium *Vekhi* (Signposts) while Merezhkovskii attacked it (see SIGNPOSTS MOVEMENT). Berdiaev and Bulgakov ultimately rejected Kant. Ivanov, a proponent of Mystical Anarchism during the Revolution of 1905, contributed to the idealists' anti-Bolshevik symposium *Iz glubiny* (Out of the Depths) (1919). Another leading figure, the philosopher Lev SHESTOV (1866–1938) was neither a Symbolist nor an idealist. The philosopher-priest Pavel FLORENSKII (1882–1937) was a God-seeker in the early twentieth century.

2 The Religious-Philosophical Society meetings

The Religious-Philosophical Society of St Petersburg was founded by Merezhkovskii, Gippius and Filosofov. After obtaining permission from the Overprocurator of the Holy Synod Konstantin Pobedonostsev, they held the first meeting in November 1901. Bishop Sergei (Stragorodskii), Rector of the Theological Academy of St Petersburg (university level), was the President and a different Bishop Sergei, Rector of the Theological Seminary (secondary-school level) was Vice-President. Also presiding over the meetings were V.M. Skvortsov, editor of *Missionerskoe obozrenie* (Missionary Survey), Merezhkovskii, Gippius, Filosofov, Minskii, Benois, Valentin Ternavtsev, the secretary of the Holy Synod, and two professors from the Theological Academy, Anton Kartashev and Vasilii Uspenskii.

At the meetings a paper was read and discussed; the discussion sometimes continued for several sessions. The minutes were published serially in the Merezhkovskii's revue *Novyi put'* (New Path) (1902–4). Ternavtsev's keynote address, 'The Clergy and the Intelligentsia', was a call for their reconciliation. To combat atheistic socialism, he argued, the Church must find Christian solutions to the problems of everyday life, not ignore them. Several sessions were devoted to Merezhkovskii's studies of the life and work of Tolstoi, Dostoevskii and Gogol' and their contemporary relevance. Sessions devoted to the relation of church and state, to Christian attitudes to sex, and to whether or not Orthodox dogma is complete were particularly stormy. Outraged at the excommunication of Tolstoi by the Holy Synod in 1901, Merezhkovskii called for a re-opening of the issue of the Synod's authority and charged that by excommunicating Tolstoi it had alienated everyone who believes in freedom. Father Mikhail Semënov's paper on Christian marriage, which maintained that sexual desire must be expressed only in marriage and for the purpose of begetting children, inaugurated a particularly stormy series of sessions on 'the mystery of the flesh'. Rozanov argued that the sexual act is itself holy and denied the right of the Church to regulate marriage and divorce (see ROZANOV §2). Merezhkovskii talked about 'holy flesh', the permeation of flesh by spirit. Uspenskii's paper on Christian dogma provoked challenges to the authority and position of the clergy as its sole interpreter. Some members denied the need for any dogma at all. Others

423

maintained that new dogma was necessary and that laymen must share in its creation. In April 1903 Pobedonostsev ordered that the society be closed down. From his point of view the 'mission to the intelligentsia' had failed. But he could not surpress the rethinking of Orthodoxy that the society had stimulated. The meetings, twenty-two in all, provided a platform for new religious views and forced clergymen to defend their positions. This hitherto unprecedented spectacle encouraged more challenges to clerical authority and, during the Revolution of 1905, demands for a Church council (*Sobor*). The St Petersburg society was revived in 1907 but without the clergy.

The Solov'ëv Moscow Religious-Philosophical Society (1906–17) was founded by Berdiaev, Bulgakov, Florenskii, Vladimir Ern (1881–1917) and others. Social and political issues dominated the agenda, as they did that of the revived St Petersburg society (sometimes the same paper was presented to both), but issues such as Christian asceticism and church reform were also on the agenda. In 1906, members or former members of these societies formed two short-lived groups: The Group of Thirty-Two, priests who demanded various reforms, and the Christian Brotherhood of Struggle, which preached a kind of liberation theology (see LIBERATION THEOLOGY). Bulgakov attempted, unsuccessfully, to form a Union of Christian Politics.

3 Merezhkovskii's 'new religious consciousness'

Merezhkovskii was the dominant figure in the original St Petersburg society, which he founded to proselytize his 'new religious consciousness' and his quest for a new Christianity. In the 1890s, he had initiated the Symbolist movement and popularized Nietzsche's thought. In the early twentieth century, he shaped the framework of the Religious-Philosophical Renaissance and, as he had done for Symbolism, defined the issues which others treated in a more sophisticated manner. He propounded his views in a trilogy of historical novels (about Julian the Apostate, Leonardo da Vinci and Peter the Great), in studies of Tolstoi, Dostoevskii and Gogol', and in numerous articles about current social, political, cultural and religious issues.

Merezhkovskii taught that 'historical Christianity' (Christianity as taught by the churches) was becoming obsolete; he expected a New Revelation, a Third Testament, to be granted by Christ himself, whose Second Coming was imminent. At that point, the joyousness of Jesus' Resurrection will prevail over the suffering of Golgotha and the hitherto proscribed pagan values of sensuality, worldly beauty, and self-affirmation will be sanctified. Russians were to prepare for His Advent by studying all religions and by joining Merezhkovskii in his religious quest. At first Merezhkovskii envisaged a new church developing out of the Orthodox Church. Later on, he advocated a complete break with it.

When Merezhkovskii began to preach his 'new religious consciousness', religion was so unpalatable to the intelligentsia that he found it necessary to expend a great deal of energy arguing that people need religion and that surrogate religions – whether scientism, aestheticism or socialism – were inherently unsatisfactory. Religion, he said, begins when man realizes that he is mortal. Therefore, personal immortality, the resurrection of both the body and the soul, is the heart of religion. All other aspects, including ethics, are mere by-products. Faith nourishes the soul just as food nourishes the body. Individuals are part of a culture shaped by religious faith; when the faith breaks down the culture loses its unity and individuals are left isolated and alone. The effects of spiritual deprivation are nameless fear and loneliness, and the sufferers do not even know what ails them. Western civilization was nourished by the sap of Christianity, but rationalism has destroyed that sap. Only a 'Christian renaissance' would enable contemporary humankind to overcome despair and decadence. Merezhkovskii also argued that Nietzsche's objections to Christianity applied only to 'historical Christianity'. True Christianity is not life-denying; it is the supreme affirmation of life. Christianity does not teach a slave morality but a new morality beyond conventional notions of good and evil. And Jesus Christ is the Superman that Nietzsche sought in vain.

Previously, in his essay 'Pushkin' (1896), Merezhkovskii had argued that Christianity and paganism (really Nietzscheanism) represented the 'truth of heaven' (personal immortality and love) and the 'truth of the earth' (worldly pleasures) respectively. Each constituted half of a yet unknown greater truth. Merezhkovskii's search for this truth led him to postulate that the Old Testament was the Revelation of God the Father and the New Testament of God the Son. A Third Revelation will be of the Holy Spirit. In emigration, Merezhkovskii maintained that the Holy Spirit was feminine.

In *Tolstoi i Dostoevskii* (1900–1), written in the first flush of his 'new religious consciousness', Merezhkovskii reformulated the 'two truths' as polarities *within* Christianity. Comparing the Russian giants with each other and with Nietzsche, Merezhkovskii argued that Dostoevskii represented 'the spirit' and Tolstoi represented 'the flesh' which 'historical Christianity' denied. Merezhkovskii attributed Tolstoi's asceticism to an unconscious preoccupation with the flesh, accused him of hypocrisy and of a 'flight from culture', and claimed that Tolstoi's real religion was Buddhism. But Merezhkovskii also saw an unconscious 'pagan holiness' in Tolstoi's *The Cossacks* and he praised Tolstoi's courage in defying the Orthodox Church. Even so, he preferred Dostoevskii, seeing him as the prophet of the spiritualization of the flesh and of a new humanity united by 'evangelic love'. Even though Dostoevskii was not always faithful to his own insights, even though he had the Grand Inquisitor advocate the slavery of 'miracle, mystery, and authority' in *Brat'ia Karamazovy* (*The Brothers Karamazov*), Elder Zosima's message in the same book showed that Dostoevskii anticipated the coming Christ. Merezhkovskii believed that the Grand Inquisitor and Elder Zosima voiced contradictory aspects of Dostoevskii's incompletely integrated worldview, but that Elder Zosima and his disciple Alësha Karamazov represented Dostoevskii's truly prophetic insights. A decade later, Merezhkovskii described his attempt to reconcile Christianity and paganism as dangerous heresy. As he distanced himself from Nietzsche, his admiration for Tolstoi grew correspondingly (see DOSTOEVSKII, F.; TOLSTOI, L.N.).

To Merezhkovskii, beauty outranked sex as the greatest worldly pleasure and beauty was incarnated in the statues of Venus or Aphrodite that the early Christians destroyed. Hence his objection to Tolstoi's *Chto takoe iskusstvo?* (*What is Art?*) (1898), which subjugated art to moralism. In a study of Gogol' (1903) Merezhkovskii portrayed his confessor, Father Matvei (Konstantinovskii), as the personification of Christian asceticism, and blamed him for Gogol's ruin. Merezhkovskii's interpretation of Tolstoi, Dostoevskii and Gogol' as religious thinkers rather than social critics inspired other 'religious' interpretations.

Novyi put' provided an outlet for other Godseekers. Blok made his debut there. Rozanov had a regular column, as did Bulgakov who came on board with Berdiaev in mid-1904. Ivanov's influential study, 'Ellinskaia religiia stradaiiushchego Boga' (The Hellenic Religion of the Suffering God) (1904), which treated Dionysus as a precursor of Christ, first appeared in *Novyi put'*. Florenskii published some early articles in it. Berdiaev and Bulgakov became co-editors of its successor journal *Voprosy zhizni* (Questions of Life) (1906), which featured essays by Symbolists and idealists.

During and after the Revolution of 1905, political and other disputes fractured the Symbolist group and created a breach between them and the idealists. Merezhkovskii advocated a 'religious revolution' that would institute the Kingdom of God on Earth and proclaimed that the atheistic intelligentsia, not the Orthodox Church, was the carrier of Christ's message: 'They are not yet with Christ but Christ is with them'. Ivanov supported Mystical Anarchism, a doctrine that advocated the abolition of government, law and morality. Love (*eros*), ritual and myth would be the social cement. The idealists continued to champion reform. Members of both groups predicted that 'Socialism as Religion' would lead to despotism.

4 Symbolism as a worldview

Russian Symbolism was not just an artistic school but a worldview, based on a mystical epistemology which held that the empirical world is but a reflection of a higher reality, and that art, imagination and intuition, rather than reason and science, are the means to new psychological and religious truths. The Symbolists saw themselves as creators of a new culture of freedom, beauty and love, which was opposed in all respects to contemporary materialist and positivist-utilitarian culture, including such 'bourgeois' institutions as constitutions and parliaments.

Basic to Russian Symbolism were the Orthodox concepts of transfiguration and incarnation, and the Orthodox belief that man is called upon to fulfil the divine Plan – to be co-creator with God. Also basic, especially to Ivanov, Belyi and Blok, were Solov'ëv's apocalypticism, and his concepts of all-unity (*vseedinstvo*), Godmanhood (*Bogochelovechestvo*) and Sophia (divine wisdom, the 'eternal feminine', or the World Soul) (see SOLOV'ËV, V.S. §§1–2). Melding these concepts with ideas derived from Nietzsche, Wagner, Dostoevskii, FËDOROV and occult doctrines, the Symbolists regarded art as a theurgical activity that would transfigure the world and human beings. The poetic word was itself a symbol, bearing the transparent reflection of the eternal in the temporal. The Symbolist poet had a divine mission, the articulation of a new saving word which would generate a new world. Within this broad framework, each Symbolist had special themes. Blok wrote poems to 'the Beautiful Lady' and to 'the Stranger', a fallen Sophia. Ivanov advocated self-transcendence in the mystical ecstasy of the Dionysian rites. Maintaining that poetry requires a special hieratic language, he was interested in the roots of language and the origins of myth and cult. Merezhkovskii opposed all attempts to subvert individual integrity and used language that ordinary people could understand. Belyi tried to make Symbolism the basis of a new religious worldview that encompassed art, philosophy and science. Briusov, however, maintained 'Symbolism was and always wanted to be only art'. He made this statement in 1910, during the 'crisis of Symbolism'. After the crisis, individual Symbolists remained creative but went their separate ways. *Vesy* and *Zolotoe runo* (Golden Fleece) (1906–9) had ceased publication, but they had access to mainstream journals such as *Russkaia mysl'* (Russian Thought) and to a new religious journal *Trudy i dni* (Works and Days) (1912–16).

The Symbolists refused to defer to 'necessity', including the 'laws of nature'. Ivanov titled one of his essays 'On the Non-Acceptance of the World' (after Ivan Karamazov's refusal to accept the world that God has created) and praised 'struggling with God' (*Bogoborchestvo*), by which he meant rejection of that which exists in the name of a higher ideal. Some Symbolists, and Berdiaev, rejected the traditional family (husband, wife, children). They counterposed resurrection to procreation and separated sex from procreation in the hope of breaking the endless cycle of birth and death. Their ideal human being was an androgyne, which implies the end of the sexual act.

The Symbolists' sociopolitical ideal, which they borrowed from the Slavophiles and Solov'ëv, was *sobornost'*, originally an ecclesiastical concept that pertained to the unity of all believers in the mystical body of Christ (see SLAVOPHILISM §3). To the Symbolists and to most idealists as well, *sobornost'* connoted a society united by love and common ideals whose members retain their individuality, as opposed to individualism which they rejected as self-affirmation against or apart from society. They also rejected impersonal collectivism.

As the eschatological expectations aroused by the Revolution of 1905 died down, the Symbolists and some idealists condemned the 'pagan' Renaissance and romanticized the medieval West. Ivanov made Dante Alighieri into a Symbolist and equated Beatrice with Sophia. Paradoxically, the very same people pontificated about Russia's cultural/national identity and destiny. Ivanov tried to articulate the 'Russian Idea' – that which distinguishes Russia from other nations – insisting that it was a Christian idea and that only Christianity could provide the spiritual integration that Russia needed. He urged the intelligentsia to 'descend' to the people in the spirit of Christian humility and self-sacrifice. Merezhkovskii objected to Ivanov's view on various grounds, but he shared Ivanov's belief that Russia stood at a crossroads and must choose between 'the beast' and Christ. Blok began to write about an anthropomorphized Russia, at once mother and wife, and to prophesy the destruction of the Westernized intelligentsia. The latter was also the theme of Belyi's novel *Serebrianyi golub'* (The Silver Dove) (1909), the first of a projected trilogy on the collision of East and West. *Petersburg* (1911) was the second. The third novel, which Belyi never wrote, was to be about the

legendary city of Kitezh which sank to the bottom of Lake Svetloiar at the time of the Mongol invasion and would rise at the end of time. Reports at Religious-Philosophical Society meetings included attempts to distinguish between 'nationality', love of one's own land and culture, and aggressive, self-aggrandizing 'nationalism'. Ivanov maintained that the 'sin' of Slavophilism was its inclusion of spiritually extraneous factors such as the state in its metaphysics. He viewed the nations of humanity as members of a cosmic *sobornost'*.

Nevertheless, Ivanov welcomed the outbreak of the First World War as the start of a new constructive era, as did most other Religious-Philosophical Society members. Merezhkovskii was a notable exception. During the war, Ern gave a lecture 'From Kant to Krupp' in which he argued that Kant's philosophy leads inevitably to a drive for world hegemony. In another lecture, Ern proclaimed that 'the time is slavophilizing'. In his major philosophical work *Struggle for the Logos* (1911), Ern distinguished between the Logos, a real entity, and abstract rationalism, associating the latter with the West.

5 The idealists

The symposium *Problemy idealizma* was a foundational work of the Religious-Philosophical Renaissance. All the contributors emphasized the importance of the individual person, grounded this tenet in a metaphysical worldview, and attacked positivism, materialism and determinism. They came from different milieus. Novgorodtsev, who was also the editor, and the Trubetskoi brothers were devout Christians and long-standing members of the Moscow Psychological Society (founded 1885). Berdiaev, Bulgakov, Frank, Struve and S.A. Askoldov had been 'legal Marxists' in the 1890s. All the idealists were indebted to Kant, and most of them to Solov'ëv as well. Berdiaev and Frank were also captivated by Nietzsche. Novgorodtsev, a liberal and a founding member of the Kadet (Constitutional Democratic) Party, did not write about religion *per se*. Rather, he argued for moral renewal based on 'the principle of the unconditional significance of the person'. Novgorodtsev based his respect for the individual person on Christian and Kantian ethics, which he viewed as compatible, even though he recognized a certain tension between Christian personalism and Kantian rationalism (see KANTIAN ETHICS). He regarded the rule of law as a safeguard against arbitrary political power and as a precondition for the development of individuality, and argued that for law to be respected it must accord with morality and justice. Novgorodtsev never gave a paper or participated in the Religious-Philosophical discussions, but he knew about them. During the Revolution of 1905 he argued that political and social reform could not, by themselves, bring about a good society; the prerequisites were moral regeneration and self-perfection. Convinced that there would always be tension between the personal and the political, he wanted to keep them separate. Novgorodtsev did not contribute to *Signposts*, but he sympathized with its critique of revolutionism and gave it his qualified support. In *On the Social Ideal*, serialized 1911–16, he warned that utopianism could lead to despotism. Only in exile did Novgorodtsev write about subjects such as 'The Essence of the Russian Orthodox Consciousness' (1923).

Sergei Trubetskoi held that philosophy must be based on a metaphysics that is deeply rooted in Christianity. He claimed that rationalism, empiricism and mysticism each omit essential aspects of reality, and hoped to unite their insights in 'absolute all-unity'. He called his philosophy 'concrete idealism'. One of its tenets was the communal (*sobornyi*) nature of human consciousness. His most important books are two studies of the history of philosophy, *Metaphysics in Ancient Greece* and *The Doctrine of the Logos*, and three works in which his own views are stated: *On the Nature of Human Consciousness*, *The Foundations of Idealism* and *The Belief in Immortality*. One of Trubetskoi's concerns was to overcome Solov'ëv's pantheism. Another was to resist the 'mystical alogism' of Berdiaev, Bulgakov, and Florenskii by arguing that 'Revelation itself is inseparable from the Logos and is subject to its valuation'.

Evgenii Trubetskoi is best known for his two volume study of Solov'ëv's worldview (Mirosozertsanie Solov'ëva) (1912) which describes the collapse of Solov'ëv's utopianism, but he also wrote about early Christianity, epistemology, and Russian icons. In his newspaper, *Moskovskii ezhenedel'nik* (Moscow Weekly) he argued that Christianity did not mandate either socialism or anarchism, but was compatible with several political systems. He was a co-director of the publishing house Put', which specialized in books and articles about Orthodox philosophy and its contemporary applications.

Signposts was the high-water mark of the former legal Marxists' liberalism and Kantianism. Soon after, their thought took a different direction. Berdiaev and Bulgakov rejected Kant. Frank continued to grapple with 'Kantian' ideas, but was no longer a Neo-Kantian. Struve advocated a mystique of the state, nationalism and imperial expansion.

6 Responses to the Bolshevik Revolution

Merezhkovskii considered Bolshevism the reign of the Anti-Christ and worked against it in Russia and in emigration. Rozanov bewailed 'the apocalypse of our time' and attributed it to the Church's neglect of everyday life. By contrast, Belyi and Blok perceived the Bolshevik Revolution as part of a spiritual revolution that would culminate in a non-materialistic, artistically creative new man. Ivanov regarded it as a religious trial, a Golgotha which would eventually result in Resurrection. In 'Our Language', his contribution to *Iz glubiny*, Ivanov attacked the Bolshevik orthographic reform as a secularizing measure. In their contributions, Berdiaev, Bulgakov, Novgorodtsev, Frank and Struve blamed the Revolution on the secular intelligentsia. Struve emigrated soon after. Berdiaev, Bulgakov, Frank and Novgorodtsev were expelled in 1922. Ivanov left voluntarily in 1924.

Soviet intellectuals discovered the God-seekers in the 1960s. By 1980 there was so much interest that the government began publishing books that debunked them. In 1988–9, however, Gorbachev permitted official publications of their works. Interest grew rapidly and continues to the present day.

References and further reading

Edie, J.M.; Scanlan, J.P. and Zeldin M.B. (eds) (1965) *Russian Philosophy*, vol. 3, Chicago, IL: Quadrangle Books. (This anthology includes critical commentary on twentieth-century Russian philosophers, edited with the collaboration of G.L. Kline.)

Hughes, R.P. and Paperno, I. (eds) (1994) *Christianity and the Eastern Slavs, vol. 2, Russian Culture in Modern Times*, Berkeley, CA: University of California Press. (Based on papers presented to two conferences commemorating the centennial of the Christianization of Rus.)

Khoruzhii, S. (1994) *Posle pereryva. Puti russkoi filosofii* (After the Break. Paths of Russian Philosophy), Moscow: Aleteiia. (Interpretation of the distinctive aspects of the Russian religious-philosophical tradition by a contemporary philosopher.)

Kornbatt, J.D. and Gustafson, R. (eds) (1996) *Russian Religious Thought: Contexts and New Perspectives*, Madison, WI: University of Wisconsin Press. (Articles on Bulgakov, Florenskii, Frank and Solov'ëv.)

Kuvakin, V. (ed.) (1994) *A History of Russian Philosophy*, Buffalo, NY: Prometheus Books, vol. 2, part 9, 'Idealism and New Systems'. (Articles on Neo-Kantianism, Rozanov, Berdiaev, Shestov,

Bulgakov, Florenskii, Lossky and Frank, by academics at Moscow State University and other Russian institutions.)

Lossky, N.O. (1951) *History of Russian Philosophy*, New York: International Universities Press. (Chapters on the leading religious philosophers, except for Rozanov.)

Pachmuss, T. (1971) *Zinaida Hippius: An Intellectual Profile*, Carbondale, IL: Southern Illinois University Press. (Emphasizes the Christian aspects of Gippius' life and work.)

Poltoratzskii, N. (ed.) (1975) *Russkaia religiozno-filosofskaia mysl' xx veka* (Russian Religious-Philosophical Thought of the Twentieth Century), Pittsburgh, PA: University of Pittsburgh Press. (Articles about the major figures and themes of the Religious-Philosophical Renaissance by American scholars.)

Putnam, G. (1977) *Russian Alternatives to Marxism: Christian Socialism and Idealistic Liberation in Twentieth Century Russia*, Knoxville, TN: University of Tennessee Press. (This work takes the sociology of knowledge approach, viewing Bulgakov and Novgorodtsev as examples of the claims of the Church and the academy to the moral leadership of Russia.)

Pyman, A. (1994) *A History of Russian Symbolism*, Cambridge: Cambridge University Press. (Analyses the works of the major Symbolists from a literary perspective; includes some discussion of underlying philosophical and religious issues.)

Read, C. (1979) *Religion, Revolution, and the Russian Intelligentsia, 1900–1912: The Vekhi Debate and its Intellectual Background*, London: Macmillan. (Describes the intelligentsia's turn to religion and its debate about the revolutionary tradition.)

Rosenthal, B.G. (1975) *D.S. Merezhkovsky and the Silver Age: The Development of a Revolutionary Mentality*, The Hague: Martinus Nijhoff. (Merezhkovskii's evolution from Symbolist, to God-seeker, to revolutionary.)

Rosenthal, B.G. and Chomiak, M.B. (eds) (1990) *A Revolution of the Spirit: Crisis of Value in Russia, 1890–1924*, Bronx, NY: Fordham University Press. (Translations of Merezhkovskii's 'Revolution and Religion', Belyi's 'Revolution and Culture', Ivanov's 'The Crisis of Individualism', Berdiaev's 'Socialism as Religion', Bulgakov's 'An Urgent Task', Novgorodtsev's 'The Essence of the Russian Orthodox Consciousness' and other important essays.)

Scanlan, J.P. (ed.) (1994) *Russian Thought After Communism: The Rediscovery of a Philosophical Heritage*, Armonk, NY: M.E. Sharpe. (Articles on the Religious-Philosophical Renaissance by Western and Russian scholars.)

Scherrer, J. (1973) *Die Religios-Philosophischen Vereinigungen* (The Religious-Philosophic Unions), Wiesbaden: Otto Harrassowitz. (The first and still the most complete study of the Religious Philosophical Societies.)

Walicki, A. (1992) 'Pavel Novgorodtsev: Neo-Idealism and the Revival of Natural Law', in *Legal Philosophies of Russian Liberalism*, Notre Dame, IN: Notre Dame University Press, 291–341. (Shows that Novgorodtsev was indebted to Solov'ev as well as to Kant.)

Zenkovsky, V.V. (1948–50) *Istoriia russkoi filosofii*, Paris: YMCA-Press, 2 vols; 2nd edn 1989; trans. G.L. Kline, *A History of Russian Philosophy*, vol. 2, London: Routledge & Kegan Paul and New York: Columbia University Press, 1953, 760–80. (Chapters on the leading religious philosophers.)

Zernov, N.N. (1963) *The Russian Religious Renaissance of the Twentieth Century*, London: Darton, Longman & Todd. (The pioneering work on the subject.)

BERNICE GLATZER ROSENTHAL

RYLE, GILBERT (1900–76)

Alongside Wittgenstein and Austin, Ryle was one of the dominant figures in that middle period of twentieth-century English language philosophy which became known as 'Linguistic Analysis'. His views in philosophy of mind led to his being described as a 'logical behaviourist' and his major work in that area, The Concept of Mind *(1949), both by reason of its style and content, has become one of the modern classics of philosophy. In it Ryle attacked what he calls 'Cartesian dualism' or the myth of 'the Ghost in the Machine', arguing that philosophical troubles over the nature of mind and its relation with the body arose from a 'category mistake' which led erroneously to treating statements about mental phenomena in the same way as those about physical phenomena. For Ryle, to do something was not to perform two separate actions – one mental, one physical – but to behave in a certain way.*

Much of Ryle's work had a similar theme: philosophical confusion arose through the assimilation or misapplication of categorically different terms, and could only be cleared up by a careful analysis of the logic and use of language. He later became preoccupied with the nature of reflective thinking, since this stood as an example of an activity which seemed to evade the behaviouristic analysis that he recommended. Ryle was also a considerable Plato scholar, though his work in this area has been less influential.

1   **Early influences**
2   *The Concept of Mind*
3   *Dilemmas* **and 'Le Penseur'**
4   **The return to Greek philosophy**

1   Early influences

Gilbert Ryle was born in 1900 in Brighton, England, and went to the Queen's College, Oxford, as a Scholar in Classics. He read Literae Humaniores (Classics and Philosophy) and then Modern Greats (Philosophy, Politics and Economics). In 1924 he became a Lecturer in Philosophy at Christ Church, Oxford, and was to remain at Oxford University for the whole of his academic life.

In a deliberate attempt to avoid sinking into what he felt was a rather parochial philosophical atmosphere at Oxford, in the first few decades of the twentieth century Ryle deliberately directed his academic gaze outwards. He travelled to Cambridge to hear Moore, Russell and Wittgenstein, and set himself the task of reading Wittgenstein's *Tractatus Logico-Philosophicus* as well as dipping into Russell's *Principia Mathematica*. Ryle also set out to gain some knowledge of contemporary continental European philosophy. He taught himself German and read Husserl's *Logische Untersuchungen*, as well as some Croce, Gentile, Meinong, Brentano, Bolzano and Frege. Against the prevailing fashion he offered at Oxford 'an unwanted course of lectures, entitled "Logical Objectivism: Bolzano, Brentano, Husserl and Meinong"', which became known as 'Ryle's three Austrian railway stations and one Chinese game of chance'. Indeed Ryle's first published pieces of philosophical writing were book reviews of works by the Polish philosopher Ingarden (a follower of Husserl) and Heidegger.

As with the Cambridge school, so with the Continentals, Ryle was principally interested in their philosophical logic, and this is reflected in the titles of his earliest papers, 'Negation' (1929), 'Are There Propositions?' (1930) and following shortly after, 'Imaginary Objects' (1933a), 'About' (1933b) and 'Internal Relations' (1935).

In the introduction to his *Collected Papers*, Ryle remarks that 'to elucidate the thoughts of a philosopher we need to find the answer not only to the question "What were his intellectual worries?" but, before that question and after that question, the answer to the question "What was his overriding worry?"' (1971: ix). Ryle himself declared that his overriding worry concerned the nature and function of philosophy itself. This question has arisen from time to time in philosophy but, through the influence both of the scientistic doctrines of logical positivism

and Wittgenstein's *Tractatus*, and also because of the remarkable inroads which natural science seemed to be making into the subject matter of philosophy, the question became particularly insistent in the 1920s.

Ryle gave his answer in the seminal paper, 'Systematically Misleading Expressions' (1932). His uncompromising and restricted view of philosophy, as 'the exercise of systematic restatement', became one of the major influences on the style and content of mid-century English-speaking philosophy. It led to those who felt sympathetic to Ryle's (and to some extent Wittgenstein's) view of philosophy being dubbed 'Ordinary Language Philosophers' and to their movement, if it could be called that, being called 'Linguistic Analysis' (see ORDINARY LANGUAGE PHILOSOPHY, SCHOOL OF §§2–3).

When Ryle came to the task of working out his programme of 'systematic restatement' in more detail, it turned out to consist mainly of two subsidiary tasks, a positive and a negative one. The negative task was concerned with exposing and correcting conceptual mistakes perpetrated by philosophers' mishandling of ordinary language in the course of propounding and defending philosophical theories. The positive task consisted in what he later described as 'conceptual cartography' or the job of getting clear about the basic categories that were or should be operative in some area of knowledge.

These views were among the influences that shaped the style of English-speaking philosophy in the twentieth century. He believed that the 'growing passion for ratiocinative rigour' was to be satisfied by ever more careful, step-by-step conceptual analysis. Great emphasis was to be placed on getting clear about the exact meaning of terms and, in consequence, on the exact usage of them. Ryle's views about the nature of philosophy also influenced the subject matter of philosophy, because he felt, with Wittgenstein, that philosophers should eschew theorizing and be content with the logico-linguistic analysis of concepts. In turn, this meant that for several decades philosophy in much of the English-speaking world became heavily weighted towards the analysis of language.

For most of the Second World War Ryle was engaged in intelligence work. In 1945, he was elected to the Waynflete Chair of Metaphysical Philosophy at Oxford, which had lain vacant since R.G. Collingwood's death in 1943. In his Inaugural Lecture, entitled 'Philosophical Arguments', Ryle expanded on his views about the nature of philosophy. 'Philosophical reasoning,' he proclaimed, 'separates the genuine from the erroneously assumed logical powers of abstract ideas by using the *reductio ad absurdum* argument as its flail and winnowing fan,' and philosophers of genius are those who have the insight to see, then flail and winnow, new abstract ideas which then become the core of some new area of enquiry or some new way of making sense of an old area of enquiry.

2 The Concept of Mind

In 1947, Ryle became editor of *Mind*, then the most influential philosophy journal in the English-speaking world, and set about turning its gaze outwards as well. A few years before, in 1945, he was beginning to crystallize his ideas about a number of issues in the philosophy of mind. The outcome of this, in 1949, was *The Concept of Mind*. As he himself readily admitted, *The Concept of Mind* was 'a sustained piece of analytical hatchet-work' on Cartesian dualism, whose view of mind he gleefully lampooned as an account of 'the life of a ghostly Robinson Crusoe' and as 'the dogma of the Ghost in the Machine'. Strictly speaking, his target was not so much Descartes himself as Cartesian doctrines which he believed had lain more or less unmolested in the philosophy of mind up to that time.

Ryle believed that Cartesian dualism was one large category mistake – an incorrect assignment of the terms of our common-sense psychological vocabulary to one logico-linguistic category or type when they should be assigned to another. After careful philosophical analysis it would be discovered that our mental terms, such as 'mind', 'thought' or 'belief', are not words which refer to or describe an inner private mental world of faculties with their proprietary activities but are mostly to be analysed as dispositional terms whose attribution depends on the ordinary observation of ordinary human behaviour. For dispositions are nothing but an ability, propensity, liability or capacity to do things of a certain type in certain specifiable circumstances. To be intelligent is to be disposed to accomplish successfully such tasks as doing mathematical problems or intelligence tests; it is not to provoke an inner Cartesian faculty, called 'the intellect', into producing its private and proprietary mental acts (see DUALISM §1).

Even attributions about what seem to be the most 'inner' and 'private' of mental activities are still to be cashed out in a behaviouristic way. Thus imagining is paradigmatically an outward performance, such as when a boxer imagines, in an afternoon's shadow-boxing performance, how the fight will go that evening. So imagining in one's head should also be analysed in relation to ordinary 'outer' behaviour. To imagine my childhood nursery is not to engage in inner Cartesian performances, but simply to realize, anticipate or expect what I would be seeing if I were once again in my nursery. It is to be disposed to see something *if . . .*

To take another example, to introspect is not to observe inwardly, in some non-sensuous manner with our 'mind's eyes', some item in our streams of consciousness. Rather, it is to 'retrospect' in memory some behaviour of our own, covert or public, which we have perceived in the past with our ordinary 'outer' senses, and then to make some overall dispositional claims about what we have been able to recall. Indeed, Ryle notoriously asserted in *The Concept of Mind* that 'the sorts of things that I can find out about myself are the same as the sorts of things that I can find out about other people, and the methods of finding them out are much the same' (1949: 155)

It was conclusions such as these which led many to describe Ryle as a logical behaviourist. In *The Concept of Mind* at least, he seemed to arrive at much the same conclusions as did the psychological behaviourists, but his reasons were logico-linguistic, not methodological. On the other hand, it is probably true to say that both those who assent that Ryle was a logical behaviourist and those who deny it find support for their arguments in *The Concept of Mind* (see BEHAVIOURISM, ANALYTIC).

3 Dilemmas and 'Le Penseur'

In 1953, Ryle gave the Tarner Lectures at Cambridge; they were published the following year as *Dilemmas*. The paradigmatic type of dilemma which Ryle had in mind, and which he believed would yield to the right sort of philosophical analysis, was that which arose when answers to different questions were mistakenly taken to be answers to one and the same questions and so to be in competition with one another. The solution to such dilemmas was to demonstrate that the purported answers cannot in fact be answers to one and the same question because they are of a different logical type or category. Thus, for example, the neurophysiologist's account of perception, the philosopher's account and the ordinary person's account are not in competition with each other, though they might at first appear to be so. When examined closely, each account has been generated in response to quite different questions. The neurophysiologist's question is 'What are the mechanisms of perception?', the philosopher's 'What is perception?', and the ordinary person's 'What is perceived?'

Ryle dealt with other dilemmas by analysing them as arising through the misinterpretation of some unproblematic and innocuous proposition, such that the misinterpretation then emerges as a rival to the common-sense view of the matter. For example, a dilemma occurs when the dictum, 'That whatever is, was to be' is misinterpreted by the Fatalist as 'That for whatever takes place, it was antecedently true that it was going to take place', instead of being given the quite innocuous interpretation, 'That for everything that happens, if anyone had at any previous time made the guess that it would happen, the guess would have turned out correct'. The misinterpretation occurs, Ryle suggested, when the term 'true' is incorrectly assigned to the category of 'property' when it should be assigned to the category of 'verdict'.

Though less spectacular and on the whole less successful than in *The Concept of Mind*, the Tarner Lectures were a further display of his view that many philosophical problems can be solved by 'systematic restatement' through 'the replacement of category-habits by category-disciplines'. This in turn meant that category mistakes are to be corrected by having misapplied terms and the misunderstood concepts underlying them reassigned to their correct categories or types. It was not an idle comment of Ryle's when he said that Russell's Theory of Types had been an important influence on his work (see CATEGORIES §2).

Between 1949 and 1954 Ryle wrote a further series of influential papers on philosophical logic, including '"If", "So" and "Because"' (1950a), 'Heterological-ity' (1950b), 'Thinking and Language' (1951), and 'Ordinary Language' (1953). At about the same time Ryle also embarked on the first in the series of papers on the theme which was to occupy him on and off for the rest of his life: the nature of thinking, in particular reflective or contemplative thinking. Indeed, he believed that an inadequate account of this latter aspect was one of the major omissions in *The Concept of Mind*.

Ryle acknowledged that mental activities such as doing mental arithmetic or composing a tune in one's head or, in general, doing whatever it was that 'Le Penseur' (Rodin's 'Thinker') was doing posed a particular problem for his approach to the analysis of mind. Such activities were circumstance-disengaged and behaviour-free, and thus there was nothing of which a dispositional analysis could take hold. Eventually Ryle toyed with the idea of giving 'an adverbial account'. Such an account worked well enough in the context of practical thinking. Thinking, Ryle argued, was often doing something, such as playing chess or driving a car, 'thinkingly' or 'wittingly', that is, 'with initiative, care, patience, pertinacity and interest'. However, to give an adverbial account of what 'Le Penseur' is doing, one must first nominate some inner activity of which thinking is the modification. This, Ryle admitted, he was never able satisfactorily to do, and he was still wrestling with the problem at the time of his death in 1976. The

record of his struggles with this problem – in the case of true contemplative thinking, of 'finding the peg' on which to hang the adverbial modifications – was published posthumously as *On Thinking* (1979) (see MENTAL STATES, ADVERBIAL THEORY OF).

4 The return to Greek philosophy

Besides his collected papers, the other major work published by Ryle after *Dilemmas* was a series of articles on Plato which culminated in his book *Plato's Progress* (1966). This was a reappraisal of the chronology of Plato's dialogues, and included the provocative claim that the dialogues had been written for dramatic performance. In the following year his magisterial entry on Plato appeared in Paul Edwards' *Encyclopedia of Philosophy* (1967). These essays in Greek philosophy were not the sign of a change of direction in the last part of his life, but a reversion to one of his earliest philosophical interests. His interest in Greek philosophy, which encompassed both Plato and Aristotle, had never waned. In the 1930s he had immersed himself in Plato's later dialogues; this concentration culminated in his paper on the Parmenides (1939) and in a review of Cornford's book on the same dialogue. These works initiated a revolution in the philosophical interpretation of Plato's later work. In the 1950s Ryle was still enthralling undergraduates with a detailed series of lectures on the Theaetetus; he was a powerful lecturer – tall, firm-voiced, dryly humorous and incisive. When Ryle died in 1976, among his 'work in progress' there was a paper on Plato's *Meno*.

List of works

Ryle, G. (1971) *Collected Papers*, London: Hutchinson, 2 vols. (These two volumes comprise all the papers, except for a few very minor pieces, such as reviews and obituary notices, which Ryle published before 1971. Of the papers mentioned in the body of this entry (with their original dates of publication in brackets, but given here with the pagination of their most accessible form, in the *Collected Papers*) – namely 'Negation' (1929: 1–11), 'Are There Propositions?' (1930: 12–38), 'Systematically Misleading Expressions' (1932: 39–62), 'Imaginary Objects' (1933a: 63–81), 'About' (1933b: 82–4), 'Internal Relations' (1935: 85–100), 'Plato's Parmenides' (1939: 1–44), 'Review of F.M. Cornford: Plato and Parmenides' (1939: 45–53), 'Philosophical Arguments' (1945: 194–211), '"If", "So" and "Because"' (1950a: 234–49), 'Heterologicality' (1950b: 250–7), 'Thinking and Language' (1951: 258–71), and 'Ordinary Language' (1953: 301–18) – all appear in volume 2, with the exception of the two papers on the *Parmenides*, which are reprinted in volume 1.)

—— (1949) *The Concept of Mind*, London: Hutchinson. (In this, his *magnum opus*, Ryle sets out to dispel 'The Cartesian Myth' on account of which both philosophy and psychology since Descartes have been haunted by the distinction between the inner and outer world. Ryle makes explicit the traces of Cartesianism in traditional theories of will, feeling, imagination, perception and thought, and tries to obliterate those traces. In place of the myth, he proposes an alternative behaviouristic account of our mental vocabulary.)

—— (1954) *Dilemmas: The Tarner Lectures 1953*, Cambridge: Cambridge University Press. (Ryle sets out to resolve certain false dilemmas wherein the ordinary person's account of the world or of their knowledge of it, in terms of, for example, the concepts of pleasure or motion or perception, is made to look as if it is opposed to and so inferior to some technical or scientific view of the world. These resolutions are a practical demonstration of Ryle's view that many philosophical problems are just cases of conceptual confusion which can be dissolved by 'systematic restatement' through 'the replacement of category habits by category disciplines'.)

—— (1966) *Plato's Progress*, Cambridge: Cambridge University Press. (A provocative intellectual history of Plato, in which Ryle questions the accepted chronology of Plato's dialogues and suggests that by and large they were composed for public recitation at the great Hellenic festivals. He also disputes whether Aristotle was in any meaningful sense ever a disciple of Plato.)

—— (1979) *On Thinking*, ed. K. Kolenda, Oxford: Blackwell. (This collection of eight papers on topics of thinking encompasses most of Ryle's papers which were published after his *Collected Papers* went to press. It also includes an interesting preface by Geoffrey Warnock as well as a very brief appendix, entitled 'On Bouwsma's Wittgenstein'.)

—— (1993) *Aspects of Mind – Gilbert Ryle*, ed. R. Meyer, Oxford: Blackwell. (Includes some of Ryle's previously unpublished 'publishable' papers, most of which were written between the late 1950s and the late 1960s. Among them is a paper on Plato's *Meno*, a short piece tracing the development of Oxford Philosophy in the mid-century, a set of notes of Ryle's lectures and a seminar taken by

Meyer, and two tributes to Ryle. In his 'Annotations', Meyer mentions that 'when he retired as Waynflete Professor of Magdalen College in 1967, Ryle donated his books and some papers to Linacre [College, Oxford]. The collection consists of about 1,100 books, some papers, rough notes and letters'.)

References and further reading

Lyons, W. (1980) *Gilbert Ryle: An Introduction to His Philosophy*, Brighton: Harvester Press, and Atlantic Highlands, NJ: Humanities Press. (This is a critical introduction and guide, written for students, to the central themes in Ryle's philosophical work. It contains also a short biographical chapter plus a bibliography of works which discuss topics in Ryle's philosophy.)

Magee, B. (1971) 'Conversation with Gilbert Ryle', in *Modern British Philosophy*, London: Secker & Warburg. (This transcript of a conversation with Ryle about his own philosophical work is part of a book that originated in a series of conversations with contemporary British philosophers about their own or others' work which were first broadcast on BBC radio during the winter of 1970–1.)

Passmore, J. (1957) *A Hundred Years of Philosophy*, London: Duckworth, ch. 18. (This chapter, entitled 'Wittgenstein and Ordinary Language Philosophy', rightly places considerable emphasis on the work of Ryle and in a very scholarly way places his work in context.)

Quinton, A.M. (1964) 'Contemporary British Philosophy', in *A Critical History of Western Philosophy*, ed. D.J. O'Connor, New York: The Free Press. (This extended essay gives a synoptic account of the period leading up to Ryle and of that in which Ryle flourished.)

Rée, J. (1993) 'English Philosophy in the Fifties', *Radical Philosophy* 63. (This essay covers much the same ground as Quinton (1964) but puts an interestingly different and more sceptical slant on things.)

Wood, O.P. and Pitcher, G. (eds) (1970) Ryle, *Modern Studies in Philosophy series*, ed. A. Rorty, London: Macmillan. (This is a large collection of articles and reviews on Ryle's work and remains the best secondary source.)

WILLIAM LYONS

S

SA SKYA PAṆḌITA (1182–1251)

The philosophical importance of Sa skya Paṇḍita (Sagya Paṇḍita) lies in his clarification of the tradition of logic and epistemology established by Dharmakīrti. He actively promoted the study of Dharmakīrti's thought in Tibet as a propaedeutic to the study of other systems of Buddhist philosophy as well as to a Buddhist account of knowledge; knowledge is a crucial element in the Buddhist tradition, for ignorance is considered the main obstacle to liberation, the summum bonum of the tradition. Like Dharmakīrti, Sa skya Paṇḍita held that the only two types of knowledge are perception and inference. Perception presents us with real individual objects, while inference enables us to consider these individuals in a conceptual way, in terms of universals; however, it is a mistake to regard these universals as real.

Sa skya Paṇḍita (Sagya Paṇḍita), whose name is often shortened to Sa-paṇ, is a dominant Tibetan figure whose accomplishments go well beyond the domain of philosophy. Politically, he was the first ruler of a unified Tibet after the collapse of the Tibetan empire in 842. He was chosen by the Mongolian Prince Godan to govern Tibet under Mongolian supervision, and was summoned to the Mongolian court, where he spent his last years. Religiously, Sa skya Paṇḍita was the fourth leader of the school named after the monastery of Sa-skya in southwestern Tibet. He played an important role in bringing the monastic and Tantric aspects of Tibetan Buddhism together, furthering Atīśa's attempt to harmonize these two traditions by describing the practice of Tantra from a monastic perspective in his *ldom gsum rab byed* (Differentiation of the Three Vows).

Sa skya Paṇḍita is important philosophically for his contribution to the tradition established by DHARMAKĪRTI, which was introduced into Tibet by rNgog lō tsa ba Blo ldan shes rab (Ngok lodzawa loden shayrap, 1059–1109) and Phya pa Chos kyi seng ge (Chaba Chögyi sengge, 1109–69). Through these two thinkers, an important indigenous tradition of logico-epistemological study developed, based on realist principles. Its orientation was actually quite different from Dharmakīrti's antirealist philosophy, as Sa skya Paṇḍita discovered while studying with the recently exiled Indian pandit, Śākya Śrībhadra

(1127–1225). To expose and correct the revisionism of rNgog, Phya pa and their followers (among which the later dGe-lugs tradition is included), Sa skya Paṇḍita wrote his famous *Tshad ma rigs gter* (Treasure on the Science of Valid Cognition).

Sa skya Paṇḍita interprets Dharmakīrti as espousing a conceptualist view of universals, in opposition to Phya pa's realist interpretation, which allows for the existence of real universals. In the Buddhist tradition, reality is composed of momentary and causally effective objects set apart from the realm of unreal conceptual entities. For Sa skya Paṇḍita, only individuals can be real, since an entity can be considered real if, and only if, it has its own distinctive essence (*rang bzhin; svabhāva*). The term 'specifically characterized phenomenon' (*rang mtshan; svalakṣaṇa*) used by Dharmakīrti indicates quite well the individual nature of real entities. For Sa skya Paṇḍita, the distinctive essence corresponds to clear identity conditions, spelled out in terms of definite spatio-temporal location. Only things clearly located in space and time are real. Tested this way, individuals pass, while universals do not.

Abstract entities such as properties or universals are described by Dharmakīrti as 'generally characterized phenomena' (*sāmānyalakṣaṇa; spyi mtshan*). They are conceptually superimposed onto reality and hence are without the power to produce an effect. This does not mean, however, that they are completely nonexistent. Although less than real, universals have a minimal ontological status as objects of concepts. They are quasi-entities, whose existence does not rest on any extra-mental reality and is presupposed by thought.

Sa skya Paṇḍita's epistemology reflects his parsimonious ontology. Following Dharmakīrti, he asserts the existence of only two types of knowledge, perception (*pratyakṣa; mngon sum*) and inference (*anumāna; rjes dpag*). These two types of cognition are distinguished on the basis of their objects and their modes of operation: whereas perception is nonconceptual and relates to real objects through experience, inference apprehends unreal conceptual constructs on the basis of reasoning.

It would be a mistake, however, to think that Sa skya Paṇḍita's view of perception is that of a straightforward empiricist who would hold perception to be cognitive by itself. For Sa skya Paṇḍita, we do not know things only by sensing them, for we need concepts to identify them. Since perception is non-conceptual, it cannot deliver fully articulated objects, but only initiates a contact that becomes cognitively relevant through categorization. Perception passively holds an object and induces the appropriate conceptual judgement, thereby creating a fully cognitive situation. Whether or not the perceiver adequately ascertains the situation depends less on the perception than on the perceiver's conceptual state.

The other form of knowledge is inference, which is conceptual. This is the more active form of knowledge, which categorizes the objects perceived and synthesizes them on the basis of a reason. In this way it brings signification to the bare data apprehended by perception, and extends knowledge beyond the purview of the evident. Unlike perception, conception does not mirror the reality of individuals, but relates to universals, which it mistakenly projects onto the former. In this way, conceptuality constructs the universe of meaning in which humans live. Sa skya Paṇḍita's conceptualist and constructivist bent also concerns language, which like thought is based on conceptual activity.

The process of conceptual construction, which characterizes thinking and language, is negative in nature: conceptual constructs are formed by eliminating their contradictories. For example, the concept of tree is constructed by eliminating the non-tree. This process requires thought to create a dichotomy between a conceptually constructed property (being a tree) and its contradictory (not being a tree). By eliminating this contradictory, a property is constructed. Such a quasi-entity is just an elimination of others (*anyāpoha*; *gzhan sel*); it does not exist in reality and is merely superimposed by thought. In this way, the strict distinction between the real and the conceptual is maintained.

See also: MOMENTARINESS, BUDDHIST DOCTRINE OF §§1, 5; NOMINALISM, BUDDHIST DOCTRINE OF; rGYAL TSHAB DAR MA RIN CHEN; TIBETAN PHILOSOPHY; UNIVERSALS, INDIAN THEORIES OF §3

List of works

Sa skya Paṇḍita (1182–1251) *ldom gsum rab byed* (Differentiation of the Three Vows), Complete Works of the Great Masters of the Sa sKya Sect, Tokyo: Toyo Bunko, 1968, V.297.1.1–323.2.6. (This work, which has been central to the Tibetan tradition, seeks to conciliate exoteric and esoteric aspects of Buddhism. It also contains a fierce polemic against the views of some of Sa skya Paṇḍita's contemporaries.)

—— (1182–1251) *mkhas pa rnams 'jug pa'i sgo* (The Door of the Wise People), Complete Works of the Great Masters of the Sa sKya Sect, Tokyo: Toyo Bunko, 1968, V.183.3.4– 154.4.6. (Sa skya Paṇḍita's statement concerning Buddhist scholarship and its philosophy.)

—— (1182–1251) *thub pa'i dgongs pa'i rab gsal ba* (Revealing the Thought of the Muni [the Buddha]), Complete Works of the Great Masters of the Sa sKya Sect, Tokyo: Toyo Bunko, 1968, V.1.1.1–50.1.6. (A presentation of the main practices of the Buddhist path, an example of Gradual Path (*lam rin*) literature.)

—— (1182–1251) *tshad ma rigs gter* (Treasure on the Science of Valid Cognition), Complete Works of the Great Masters of the Sa sKya Sect, Tokyo: Toyo Bunko, 1968, V.155.1.1–167.1.6. (A masterful summary in mnemonic verses of Dharmakīrti's logico-epistemological system.)

—— (1182–1251) *tshad ma rigs gter rang 'grel* (Autocommentary to the Treasure on the Science of Valid Cognition), Complete Works of the Great Masters of the Sa sKya sect, Tokyo: Toyo Bunko, 1968, V.167.3.1–264.2.6. (Sa skya Paṇḍita's own commentary on the previous text.)

References and further reading

Dreyfus, G. (1996) *Recognizing Reality*, New York: State University of New York Press. (A philosophical discussion of Sa skya Paṇḍita's epistemology in the context of the Tibetan reception of Dharmakīrti.)

Jackson, D. (1987) *The Entrance Gate for the Wise*, Vienna: Arbeitkreis für Tibetische und Buddhistische Studien. (No complete study of Sa skya Paṇḍita's work is available, but this is the best historical overview. Also contains a translation of part of Sa skya Paṇḍita's work on scholarship.)

—— (1990) 'Sa-skya Paṇḍita the "Polemicist": Ancient Debates and Modern Interpretations', *Journal of the International Association of Buddhist Studies* 13 (2):17–116. (A sympathetic view of Sa skya Paṇḍita's polemical activities.)

—— (1994) 'The Status of Pramāṇa Doctrine according to Sa-skya Paṇḍita and Other Tibetan Masters: Theoretical Discipline or Doctrine of Liberation?', in T. Skorupski and U. Pagels (eds), *The Buddhist Forum*, London: School of Oriental and African Studies, vol. 3: 85–129. (A discussion of Sa skya Paṇḍita's view of the religious implications of Dharmakīrti's works.)

Jackson, R. (1982) 'Sa-skya Paṇḍita's Account of the bSam yas Debate: History as Polemic', *Journal of the International Association of Buddhist Studies* 5:

89–99. (A particular example of Sa skya Paṇḍita's polemical activity.)

Kuijp, L. van der (1983) *Contributions to the Development of Tibetan Epistemology*, Wiesbaden: Franz Steiner. (An exploration of some of the philosophical and historical details of Sa skya Paṇḍita's epistemology.)

GEORGES B.J. DREYFUS

SAADIAH GAON
(*fl.* early 10th century)

Saadiah Gaon al-Fayyumi was the first systematic philosopher of Judaism and a pioneering exegete, grammarian, lexicographer, liturgist and chronologist. His Kitab al-mukhtar fi 'l-amanat wa-'l-'i'tiqadat *(Book of Critically Chosen Beliefs and Convictions) uses reason, experience and tradition to elaborate a monotheistic theology and pluralistic ethics.*

Organized in ten thematic treatises, the work, familiarly known by the title of its Hebrew translation, Sefer Emunot ve-De'ot *(The Book of Beliefs and Convictions), opens with a striking epistemological prelude laying out the sources of knowledge in sense experience, reason and (for the recipients of Scripture) tradition. Saadiah defends sense experience on the grounds that scepticism is self-undermining. He defends reason as the basis of critical and scientific knowledge; and he defends the Jewish sources of traditional learning on the grounds of the continuity and trustworthiness of their transmission. He treats tradition not as an independent source of knowledge but as a means of preserving primary knowledge acquired in the past.*

The ten treatises of the work defend creation against alternative cosmological theories, argue for God's unity and incorporeality, explain the human situation as a trial designed to test and reward human goodness, defend God's justice and the substantiality and immortality of the soul, affirm the national restoration promised by the prophets of Israel, and lay out the constituents of the good life, which Saadiah argues is undermined by excessive attention to any one of the varied goods available to us. Committed to reason, science, free will and God's ultimate justice, Saadiah champions the veracity of Scripture using his formidable philological skills and learning to find appropriable interpretations of biblical language whenever the apparent textual sense to be ruled out by reason, science, another text, or a sound tradition. In keeping with the Rabbinical and Biblical outlook, he upholds the value of this life on the grounds that only here are authentic choices possible. Saadiah's philosophy profoundly influenced Maimonides and later Jewish thinkers; his biblical commentaries are still consulted for their philosophical and philological insights.

1 Life and works
2 *The Book of Critically Chosen Beliefs and Convictions*
3 The good life

1 Life and works

Born in Egypt well and educated in Scripture and Rabbinic law, Saadiah published his first Hebrew–Arabic lexicon in 913, expanding it gradually to over one thousand entries. He sought a philosophical correspondence with the Jewish Neoplatonist Isaac ISRAELI. His polemics against the Karaites evidently led to his removal from Egypt. Living in Palestine, Iraq and Syria, he deepened his knowledge of history, philosophy and Scripture, studied with Abu Kathir Yahya al-Katib of Tiberias, and absorbed the ideas of the Jewish philosopher/*mutakallim* (dialectical theologian) Daud AL-MUQAMMAS and the Masoretes of Tiberias. His writings show a thoughtful acquaintance with the Arabic texts of Plato and Aristotle.

Gaining repute for his successful defense of the traditional Hebrew calendar against proposed alterations, Saadiah was appointed an *alluf* (master) of the ancient Talmudic academy of Pumpedita, now, like its sister academy of Sura, relocated in Baghdad. In 928 the Exilarch David ben Zakkai made Saadiah head of the Sura academy, with the traditional title Gaon (eminence). Ben Zakkai was not put off but only piqued when warned that Saadiah seemed to fear no one. By 930 the two men were at loggerheads over Saadiah's refusal to sign a testamentary judgment in which ben Zakkai had improperly awarded himself a fee from the proceeds. Bans, depositions, factions and even riots ensued.

Refusing a bribe from a jealous rival, the Khalif assigned the case to 'Ali ibn 'Isa, 'the good wazir', as 'Ali was known, restored Saadiah to office and was seeking to reconcile the rival leaders when the Khalif was killed in a coup d'etat and 'Ali's government was prorogued. When the new and impecunious Khalif al-Qahir ascended the throne, Saadiah was deposed. At length a reconciliation was achieved, consummated in a moving ceremony in 937. The anathemas were withdrawn and Saadiah restored to office with approval of the new Khalif al-Radi and the reinstated 'Ali ibn 'Isa.

Deprived of judicial authority for seven years, Saadiah pursued scholarship and philosophy. His commentary in 931 on the Kabbalistic *Sefer Yetzirah*

435

(Book of Creation) adopts a scientific cosmology. Like the Muslim savants of his day, he knows that the earth is round; he has no use for a flat-earth cosmology and refuses to prop it up against Scripture. Philosophy and history, he urges, are the proper work of man, in which God will aid us, 'disclosing deep things' (Job 12: 22). By 933 Saadiah completed his chief philosophic work, opening with a critical epistemology, a constructive, rationalistic empiricism, buttressed by a subdued Platonism and enriched by a chastened traditionalism that relies on trustworthy ancestors for their histories and hermeneutics but does not treat tradition as a source of knowledge independent of reason and experience.

Saadiah finds little use for the Neoplatonic 'active intellect' (see NEOPLATONISM). Yet, his naturalism and rationalism do not exclude mysticism. Prophets and the blessed derive comfort and inspiration from a 'created light' that is no rival to God's absoluteness but allows the immanence of divine action. Anchoring what would later become a central Kabbalistic tenet, reciprocity between the human and the divine, Saadiah systematically glosses ascriptions to God of emotions like yearning, satisfaction and joy, as transferred epithets whose logical subject is a human being. The approach finds consummate expression in the liturgical phrase applied to Jacob, and thus to all Israel: 'whom Thou didst love with Thine own love and rejoice with Thine own joy'. SPINOZA later uses the same idea in explaining how the Infinite can care for finite individuals.

Saadiah's books on language, surviving only in fragmentary form, include the earliest known Hebrew grammar. He composed the first scholarly *Siddur* or Hebrew prayerbook. Most of his liturgical poetry is lost, but his didactic poem on the Ten Commandments and his penitential and petitionary prayers, found in the Cairo Geniza, convey the flavour: highly allusive writing of the philological type favoured in his day. His prose prayers are more straightforward, and his Arabic prayers and translations of Hebrew prayers reveal his expressive powers.

Saadiah's Arabic Bible translations and commentaries assign each book a thematic title and include an introduction explaining the book's problematic and complementing the linear commentary to reveal the higher order argument. The commentaries are openly philosophical and typically fight shy of midrashic embroideries.

Most of Saadiah's *halakhic* contributions are lost, but in the fragmentary corpus that survives, thematic introductions and conceptual organization reveal the role of philosophy in structuring Saadiah's thought. Saadiah's lost *Kitab al-ta'rikh* (Chronology), apparently was intended as a summary of history from the creation. As Franz Rosenthal (1968: 139) showed, the work represented the movement towards linear historiography that was ongoing in Saadiah's time. Saadiah's goal was to situate Biblical and other events chronologically. His exegetical writings show a similar interest in geographical orientation.

2   The Book of Critically Chosen Beliefs and Convictions

Saadiah's philosophical *chef d'oeuvre* is commonly known by the Hebrew title, *Sefer Emunot ve-De'ot* (The Book of Beliefs and Opinions). But in what seems to be his final revision it bears the title *Kitab al-mukhtar fi 'l-amanat wa-'l-'i'tiqadat* (The Book of Critically Chosen Beliefs and Convictions), 'And rightly so', Joseph Kafih explains. 'For our teacher did not set out simply to gather a compendium of beliefs and convictions, but to demonstrate which beliefs were worthy of choice and which convictions were true in his estimation' (Kafih 1970: 1). Like Aristotle and Plato, Saadiah surveys and criticizes rival views, choosing one to be accepted. As in *kalam* (dialectical theology), he answers objections and arrays arguments, scriptural and rational, against the rejected views and in support of the view he deems orthodox; but the enterprise is never purely apologetic, since what passes muster cannot remain unaffected by the demands of critical scrutiny.

The work comprises ten 'treatises'. The introduction lays out Saadiah's epistemology. Doubt is a natural concomitant of our finitude but can be overcome by subduing its causes, ignorance and impatience. Subjectivism is absurd, since opinions do not determine reality; nor does disbelief exempt us from our obligations. Saadiah defends perceptual knowledge, arguing that systematic scepticism about perception itself is self-destructive. He goes on to urge that the methods needed to render perceptions trustworthy lead inevitably to general theories and thus to the sciences. Only the superstitious forbid speculation, fearing for the faith. Such fears are as irrational as the fantasy of the ignorant that whoever travels to India will grow rich.

Treatise 1 defends creation as the bulwark of theism, warning against attempts to explain the ultimate Cause found by reason. 'Explaining' the ultimate in terms, for example, of sensory phenomena would reduce God to the very facts that creation was invoked to explain. The revolution of the heavens proves the cosmos finite; its finitude and compositeness, the temporality of all accidents in nature, the inability of finite particulars to cause their own existence, all prove the world to have been created. True, nothing comes from nothing, but for that very reason, creation provides the best explanation for nature's existence.

Neoplatonic attempts to derive the physical from the ideal explain the obscure by the more obscure and bring matter and spirit no closer together than does the sheer Biblical creation. Materialism, by contrast, hides a tendency to confuse cause with effect. Our aim is not to deny causality; but proximate causes are just part of the cosmic system. They are insufficient without the ultimate cause. Thus, when Aristotelians ascribe the cosmic order to the celestial motions, Saadiah emphasizes that circular motion is natural to the heavenly bodies, and is thus part of what we are seeking to explain.

Against the idea that chance is the ultimate cause, Saadiah argues that chance could not produce a stable system. Besides, chance can be defined only relative to a natural order; so it is incoherent to treat it as the ultimate cosmic principle. The idea that nature has always been as we observe it, by contrast, extrapolates our experience to the wholly unknown.

Treatise 2 derives God's unity from his incorporeality as the absolute creator, from his oppositeness to the world's multiplicity, and from the economy of explanations: one cause is sufficient, more would be redundant and would require proof beyond the sole proof we have, the act of creation. Dualists and polytheists have no way of limiting divinities once they begin; in the end they cannot help making a god of every element or principle. If God needed help or cooperation to make or rule the world, he would be powerless; and if some other god were not his aide but free to contradict him, the two would either limit one another's power, making neither divine, or overrule each other – so that the same object, for example, could have contradictory characteristics.

As for attributes, God's life, power, knowledge and transcendent goodness are known from the act of creation. However, God's attributes represent a single reality; they differ only in our understanding. Thus they are figures, like the Biblical anthropomorphisms, not to be taken literally. Paradigmatically, the ascription of loves and hates to God expresses normative intentions. God's speech is a created sound, and God's 'back', as seen by Moses, is his created glory.

God created the world, Treatise 3 explains, to allow humans to earn blessedness. Earned desert is far more precious than mere bliss, but the effort to earn blessedness entails real risks: trials of our mettle, accountability for our choices, sufferings that may be warnings or chastisements, or 'sufferings of love', whose purpose, which we cannot know when we undergo them, is enhancement of our reward in the hereafter through recompense for preserving our integrity. The chief vehicle of our test, for which the world was created, is the system of our obligations. The most basic of these are well known to reason, as when we recognize the wrongfulness of causing bloodshed or pain, fornicating, stealing or lying. But many of the commandments are known to us only because they are revealed. Their performance is our obligation not because of any intrinsic value in the acts they involve but because they function symbolically, as expressions of gratitude, a fitting means of honouring our Creator.

The rational commandments are not derivable from hedonism or from any merely empiric naturalism. Hedonism will make the same act, such as a theft, both good and evil, since it brings pain to the victim and pleasure to the thief. But if we recognize the need to differentiate ourselves from animals (and so do not fornicate), understand that misrepresentation is a grotesque perversion of creation (and so do not lie), and see that bloodshed thwarts fulfilment of God's plan (by violating the potentials God imparted to be realized), we discover the values underlying some of the precepts of the Law. We can even find the rational basis for the ritual commandments, those that would have had no strict standing as obligations had they not been commanded. Reason demands a response to generosity, and all the ritual commandments, although they may yield benefits (Sabbath rest, Levitical purity), are ultimately expressions of gratitude. Such laws, then, have a purpose, but that purpose alone does not define, but as we might put it today, underdetermines their content. Prophets are needed to spell out God's expectations. Miracles corroborate the claims of prophets, and tradition preserves their message, vouching for its authenticity, but also interpreting it. Just as reason is prior to revelation, tradition is posterior to it; none of the three can stand alone.

Treatise 4 presents man as the object of creation, at the centre of the cosmos, endowed with moral freedom. Our bodies are small, but are the best that could be given mortal beings; and the human soul is vaster than the cosmos, which its knowledge embraces. That cosmos was created in our interest, not for our pleasure. Life is short, but the choices made while choice is possible are of absolute significance. As with any growth, dead wood must be cleared away. Thus there is capital punishment in this world and hellfire in the next, where the very light that comforts the blessed torments the damned. God gives us the capacity to act and choose, but some choices may diminish our degrees of freedom. What God forms is our underlying nature; our character is our own work.

We are judged, Treatise 5 teaches, by the preponderance of our good or evil actions, whose inner worth God knows irrefragably. Reconciling virtue ethics with command ethics, Saadiah finds each act significant, but insists that one act is not our character. Thus penitence is possible, fulfilling regret, just as action fulfills intent. The weight of our choices, however, precludes redemption of every act: once choices have sealed our character they have sealed our destiny, and even penitence becomes impossible. Prayer goes nowhere when it is insincere or intransigent; it is bootless in one who is actively neglectful of the Torah or the poor, mired in embezzlement or impurity. Three sins will not be expiated: slander, misleading others and retention of ill-gotten gains. Three merits are rewarded in this world, even for those who reject God's service: filial piety (Exodus 20: 12), kindness to animals (Deuteronomy 22: 7) and honest dealing (Deuteronomy 25: 15). Like MAIMONIDES after him, Saadiah derives not merely the commandment (and its reward) but the generalized theme of each precept: not simply releasing the mother bird, but kindness to animals; not simply fair weights and measures, but honest dealing.

The soul, Treatise 6 argues, is created on completion of the body with which it is united. Neither soul nor body is impure; sin results only from our own wrong choices. Like the heavenly spheres, the soul draws luminosity from God, gaining life and consciousness, which allow it to animate a body that would otherwise be passive and inert. Once its destiny is complete, it returns to God, who allowed it to act through the body's intermediacy. When the tally of souls God destined for existence is complete, all are reunited with their bodies and judged. Those whose lives were cut short or who suffered undeservedly are recompensed, including the slain infants of Israel's ancient conquest, and even any animals that suffered unduly in the Temple sacrifices.

The soul is not an accident; it is not a function of the body or adjunct of the blood. Nor is it a self-moving number, an entelechy or an epiphenomenon. The world was not created for the sake of an accident. The soul is not made of fire or air, for it lacks their qualities. It is not of two parts locatable in the head and heart, for the soul would be what enables these to interact. Nor are there three separate souls, as suggested by Plato. Appetite, ire and reason are faculties of one soul, called alive in virtue of the immortality to which it is heir. The demands of theodicy may give colour to the theory of metempsychosis, but understanding that God's grace and justice assure us of recompense for all unrequited sufferings and retribution for all unpunished wrongs deflates the appeal of the notion of transmigration.

Treatises 7–9 differentiate resurrection, redemption and requital. Resurrection reunites body and soul here in the world. All monotheists will share in it, but Israel will have the leading role because of her long sufferings. God did not include resurrection in the first redemption, the exodus from Egypt, but promised it for the future, because Israel's present bondage is heavier than the Egyptian enslavement.

Redemption is the historical vindication of God's promises to Israel: the ingathering of her exiles, the return of prophecy and the restoration of the Davidic monarchy. But the ultimate requital must be otherworldly, to respond to transcendent human goodness and suffering, sin and cruelty. In this world, Saadiah argues, following AL-RAZI, pains outweigh pleasures, the wicked often triumph, and suffering innocents are not requited. God's mercy must remedy life's defects. Were it not for future requital, fire and brimstone would surely have fallen on the earth long ago, as they did on Sodom and Gomorrah.

But the hereafter is not an earthly place. Only metaphorically is it called Tofet or Eden. Time itself will be transmuted in the new heaven of which Isaiah spoke. The most striking transcendence will be moral: our trials over, there will be no more need, or chance, for choices, but the infinite consequence of our decisions in this world will be played out to eternity.

3 The good life

Treatise 10 concerns the good life, defined in moral terms, for we do not know the reward of the ritual commandments even in this life, still less in the hereafter. Saadiah's eudaimonism is pluralistic, based on the complexity of human nature. Like PLATO, he sees the good life as a balancing of interests (see GOOD, THEORIES OF THE §5). He does not break these down into intellectual, appetitive and spirited, but elicits his own list from Scripture and from observation of human nature: abstinence, eating and drinking, sex, passionate love, wealth, progeny, agrarian and urban development, longevity, power, vengeance, knowledge, worship and rest. Each of these (even vengeance) is in some sense a good, but none, as devotees might imagine, offers a fulfilling life. To make one of them our sole object is to cheat ourselves of the rest.

Self-denial is a valuable discipline, but the pure ascetic is misanthropic and embittered; his isolation feeds his envy and deprives him of the piety he may have sought. Food and drink sustain body and mind and foster reproduction, but the gourmand is bloated, unhealthy, selfish, foggy-headed and licentious. Sex is a unique delight, countering melancholy, cementing human relations and well accepted by the prophets, but the lascivious are unhealthy and typically adulterous. Passionate love has its place, sustaining the marital relationship; but, as a way of life, it is an absurd obsession, often a source of regret or hatred. Progeny perpetuate the world and give solace and joy, but offspring are also a hardship and source of anxiety; they are not sufficient to give meaning to our lives. Development is useful and satisfying; but taken beyond human need and made our overriding object, it distracts us from intellectual and spiritual goals and becomes a source of anxiety and compulsion. Longevity too is a means to an end, allowing us to attain our spiritual and worldly goals, but the valetudinarian must know that even the vigorous often die young, and there are higher goals than maintenance of the body.

Power or authority is necessary to the ordering of the world; but, if made all-sufficient, it promotes arrogance and injustice and becomes self-destructive, transforming a ruler's ebullience from overconfidence to the tyrant's suspicions and hatred of humanity. Vengeance is the most specious of *prima facie* goods. It gives momentary satisfaction, but the scheming it engenders fosters anxiety and ruthlessness. Hatred cannot be made a way of life. Vengeance may spur us in pursuit of justice, but vengeance is not justice. Like all other *prima facie* goods, it becomes an actual good only when mitigated by the rest.

Knowledge is a good, but even the quest for knowledge can be excessive; pursued to the exclusion of all else, our appetite for knowledge would ruin our health, even dull our mind. Worship is a fitting expression of gratitude; but, as an exclusive goal, it is self-undermining. How can we fulfil the commandment to keep just weights and measures if we eschew all social engagement and economic activity? Pietists may aspire to devote themselves wholly to God, but their neglect of their bodies and their offspring cannot be condoned. Finally, rest is needed, and is prescribed for sabbaths and holy days. But rest is possible and valuable only through work; laziness is destructive. Rest imparts a taste of the world to come, but our obligations are for this world.

Saadiah underlines his integrative pluralism with a brief discussion of aesthetics. Blending, he argues, is the key to beauty. Tastes, colours, sounds, even smells are beautiful when mingled; rough, even injurious, when left simple. All goods – and Saadiah acknowledges more *prima facie* goods than he has listed – have their proper place and context, and this can be found, if one is not simply rationalizing one's appetites and desires but inquiring after the truth with humility and sincerity. The Torah lays out a way of life that enables us to balance the goods pertinent to our nature, allowing none to usurp the place of reason.

See also: BIBLE, HEBREW; GOOD, THEORIES OF THE

List of works

Saadiah Gaon (early 10th century) *Kitab 'usul al-shi'r al-'ibrani* (*Ha-Egron*, The Book of the Roots of Hebrew Poesy), ed. N. Allony, Jerusalem: The Academy of the Hebrew Language, 1969. (This is Saadiah's dictionary, presented here in a modern, critical edition.)

—— (early 10th century) *Kitab al-mukhtar fi 'l-amanat wa 'l-'i'tiqadat* (The Book of Critically Chosen Beliefs and Opinions), trans. J. Kafih, *Sefer ha-Nivar ba-Emunot uva-De'ot*, Jerusalem: Sura, 1970; trans. S. Rosenblatt, *The Book of Beliefs and Opinions*, New Haven, CN: Yale University Press, 1948. (Kafih provides Arabic text with a modern Hebrew translation. Rosenblatt's English translation is in need of reworking.)

—— (early 10th century) *Kitab al-ta'dil* (The Book of Theodicy), trans. L.E. Goodman, New Haven, CN: Yale University Press, 1988. (Saadiah's commentary and translation of the Book of Job.)

References and further reading

Cohen, B. (ed.) (1943) *Saadiah Anniversary Volume*, New York: American Academy for Jewish Research. (Includes papers by Salo Baron, Solomon Gandz, Harry Wolfson, A.S. Halkin and others.)

Efros, I. (1974) *Studies in Medieval Jewish Philosophy*, New York: Columbia University Press, 1–137. (These pages represent a monograph on Saadiah's philosophy.)

Finkelstein, L. (ed.) (1944) *Rab Saadia Gaon*, New York: Arno Press; repr. 1988. (Symposium volume, includes papers by A. S. Halkin, Ben Zion Bokser, Robert Gordis and others.)

Goodman, L.E. (1976) 'Saadya Gaon on the Human Condition', *Jewish Quarterly Review*, new series 67: 23–9. (Explains Saadiah's views about the prevalence of suffering in this life and the warrant he gives for deriving an afterlife from the recognition of God's justice.)

—— (1990) 'Saadiah Gaon's Interpretive Technique in Translating the Book of Job', in *Translating Scripture, Jewish Quarterly Review* supplement, Philadelphia, PA: Annenberg Research Institute, 47–76. (Analyses Saadiah's exegetical method with concrete examples of their application and explication of their philosophical and hermeneutical import.)

—— (1996) *God of Abraham*, New York: Oxford University Press. (Chapter 6, 'Monotheism and Ritual', contains a detailed examination and defence of Saadiah's treatment of the ritual commandments, arguing against the widely held view that Saadiah differentiated these, or any class of *mitzvot*, as non-rational.)

Heschel, A.J. (1944) *The Quest for Certainty in Saadia's Philosophy*, New York: Feldheim. (Early study of Saadiah's epistemology.)

Katz, S. (ed.) (1980) *Saadiah Gaon*, New York: Arno Press. (A collection of classic papers in English, French and German, by David Neumark, Georges Vajda, Alexander Altmann and others.)

Malter, H. (1969) *Saadiah Gaon: His Life and Works*, New York: Hermon Press. (Reprint of the edition of 1926.)

Neuman, A.A. and Zeitlin, S. (eds) (1943) *Saadiah Studies*, Philadelphia, PA: Dropsie College. (Includes the epistemological studies of Heschel and Efros, along with papers by Solomon Skoss, Harry Wolfson, Louis Ginzburg (on Saadiah's *Siddur*) and the two editors.)

Rosenthal, E.I.J. (1943) *Saadya Studies*, repr. New York: Arno Press, 1980. (Includes papers by Alexander Altmann, Chaim Rabin, Simon Rawidowicz and the editor, among others.)

* Rosenthal, F. (1968) *A History of Muslim Historiography*, Leiden: Brill, 2nd revised edn. (This general work on the development of Islamic writing about history contains a brief discussion of Saadiah's lost work on history, situating it against the background of Islamic works of world history and chronology.)

Skoss, S. (1955) *Saadia Gaon, The Earliest Hebrew Grammarian*, Philadelphia, PA: Dropsie College Press. (A detailed analysis of Saadiah's pioneering work in the grammar of the Hebrew language.)

Vajda, G. (1967) 'Autour de la Théorie de la Connaissance chez Saadia' (On Saadiah's Theory of Knowledge), *Revue des Études Juives* 126: 375–97. (Classic investigation of Saadiah's epistemology.)

Ventura, M. (1934) *La Philosophie de Saadia Gaon*, Paris: Vrin. (A detailed commentary on the theses and arguments of Saadiah's *Book of Critically Chosen Beliefs and Convictions*.)

L.E. GOODMAN

AL-SABZAWARI, AL-HAJJ MULLA HADI (1797/8–1873)

Al-Sabzawari was the most influential nineteenth-century Iranian philosopher. His reputation rests in part on his Sharh al-manzuma, *a commentary on his own* Ghurar al-fara'id *(The Blazes of the Gems), a didactic poem (*manzuma*) encapsulating in a systematic fashion an exposition of the existentialist philosophy of Mulla Sadra. He was also the most sought-after teacher of philosophy in his day, and many students travelled to Sabzavar to be taught by him. Famous for his saintliness as well as his erudition, he set the tone for much of twentieth-century Iranian philosophy.*

Al-Hajj Mulla Hadi al-Sabzawari, the most famous of the philosophers of the Qajar period in Iran, was born in AH 1212/AD 1797–8 in Sabzavar in northeastern Iran. He studied logic, mathematics, law and metaphysics in Mashhad, where he moved at the age of ten after completing his preliminary education in Sabzavar. He pursued his interests in philosophy by moving to Isfahan to study for seven years with, among others, Mulla 'Ali Nuri (d. AH 1246/AD 1830–1), the foremost interpreter of his day of the philosophy of Mulla Sadra. He returned to Mashhad to teach for five years, and then accomplished the pilgrimage to Mecca (*hajj*). On his way back from pilgrimage he spent a year in Kirman, where he married, before returning to Sabzavar where he spent the rest of his life devoted to teaching and writing. A remarkable number of students of philosophy came to study with him, not only from Iran but from Arab countries and India as well. So great was his reputation that Nasir al-Din Shah, for whom he wrote his *Asrar al-hikam* (Secrets of the Wisdoms), came to visit him in AH 1284/AD 1867, but al-Sabzawari's pious and ascetic way of life (several minor miracles are attributed to him), led him to refuse direct royal patronage. He died in AH 1289/AD 1873, having turned Mulla Sadra's legacy into the predominant philosophical school of the nineteenth and twentieth centuries.

Al-Sabzawari's fame rests primarily on one work, his *Ghurar al-fara'id* (The Blazes of the Gems), a poem in which he gives a systematic and complete presentation of the philosophy of the school of Mulla Sadra, together with the *Sharh al-manzuma*, his own commentary on this poem, which he composed despairing of the philosophical ignorance of his contemporaries. The merit of this work lies not so much in any radically new theories, but in its plan and organization, which have made it the standard text for students of philosophy in Shi'i *madrasa*s until the present day. The situation is now changing and new teaching texts are appearing, but most of these are still influenced by the *Sharh al-manzuma* in both structure and content.

In the centuries after Mulla Sadra, philosophers were on the whole inclined to write on specific topics, thus leaving a gap in so far as there was no text that treated the whole of post-Sadrian philosophy in a systematic and assimilable fashion to which students could turn. Al-Sabzawari filled this gap, first with his didactic poem, which was to be memorized, and second with his commentary, which elaborates the poem in the manner of a traditional teacher in the Islamic religious sciences. The completeness of the work can be gauged by its contents, which give a good idea of what subjects philosophy encompasses for the contemporary religious student in a Shi'i *madrasa*.

The first part is on logic, with the commentary separately subtitled *al-La'ali al-muntazima* (The Well-Ordered Nights). The second part (with commentary subtitled *Ghurar al-fara'id*), is divided into seven sections: (1) general principles (*al-umur al-'amma*), covering existence and related matters (unity, systematic ambiguity, modality, actuality and so on), quiddity and causality; (2) substance and accident; (3) metaphysical theology (*al-ilahiyyat bi-'l-ma'na al-akhass*), God's essence, attributes and acts; (4) natural philosophy, including discussions of matter and motion and a section on psychology; (5) certain supernatural phenomena, including dreams, miracles and prophecy; (6) the resurrection (*ma'ad*); and (7) ethics (*akhlaq*), with a brief treatment of spiritual values. It should be noted that (2) is essentially part of (1), that (1–4) form the core of the work, and that (5–7) are relatively short sections.

The commentary is amply provided with proofs and arguments, but there is also a marked emphasis on intuitive and mystical perception. This aspect of al-Sabzawari's thought is even more evident in his other works, which included commentaries on two of the key supplications in Shi'i devotional literature and the above-mentioned *Asrar al-hikam*, in Persian, in which eschatology is elucidated through metaphysical theology, psychology, ethics and the law (*shari'a*). This latter work is threaded through with poetic quotations. Al-Sabzawari was not only a poet in his own right (he has a Persian *diwan*, or collection of poems), but he also produced an elaborate metaphysical commentary on passages from Jalal al-Din al-Rumi's *Mathnavi* which amply reflects his own spiritual preoccupations.

Because of the elegance of his exposition of the entire scope of the Sadrian philosophy of his time, al-Sabzawari has attracted the attention of a number of modern scholars who, under the influence of his manifestly esoteric outlook, have tended to emphasize the mystical approach in nineteenth-century Iranian philosophy. Although this influence has tended to obscure other philosophical currents of the time and their legacy to twentieth-century Iranian philosophy, it cannot be denied that al-Sabzawari was the most significant philosopher of this period and the one who, through the large number of his students, exerted the most powerful effect on later generations.

See also: ISLAMIC PHILOSOPHY, MODERN; MULLA SADRA; MYSTICAL PHILOSOPHY IN ISLAM

List of works

In addition to the works listed below, al-Sabzawari wrote glosses on several works by Mulla Sadra. Those on the *Asfar* can be found in the footnotes of the printed edition of that work (see MULLA SADRA).

al-Sabzawari (1826–45) *Sharh al-manzuma* (commentary on the didactic poem (*manzuma*), the *Ghurar al-fara'id*), ed. H.H. al-Amuli and M. Talibi, Tehran: Nab, 1995, 3 vols; *Sharh-i manzuma*, lithograph editions in Arabic. (This edition is so far incomplete. The only complete text is provided by numerous printings of the lithographed texts, the most common being the so-called 'Nasiri' lithograph. In the published edition, Volume 1 contains the logic, *al-La'ali al-muntazima*; Volume 2 is sections 1 and 2 of the metaphysics of the *Ghurar al-fara'id*; Volume 3 contains the remainder of the metaphysics. The text is in Arabic with glosses by H.H. al-Amuli, but there is an English introduction to Volume 3. An earlier Arabic edition of the metaphysics is *Sharh ghurar al-fara'id*, ed. M. Mohaghegh and T. Izutsu, Tehran: McGill University Institute of Islamic Studies, Tehran Branch, 1969. This edition also contains extracts from the commentaries of Muhammad Taqi Amuli and Akhund-e Hidaji, and has a useful Arabic–English glossary of al-Sabzawari's philosophical terminology.)

—— (1867–70) *Asrar al-hikam* (Secrets of the Wisdoms), ed. H.M. Farzad, Tehran: Intisharat-e Mawla, 1982. (Arabic text, not a critical edition.)

References and further reading

Akhtar, W. (1984) 'Sabzawari's Analysis of Being', *al-Tawhid* 2 (1): 29–65. (Makes a strong case for Sabzawari's originality as a thinker, and situates the *Sharh al-manzuma* within a history of ontology; useful comparative analysis.)

Izutsu Toshihiko (1971) 'The Fundamental Structure of Sabzawari's Metaphysics', in Izutsu Toshihiko (ed.) *The Concept and Reality of Existence*, Tokyo: Keio Institute of Cultural and Linguistic Studies, 57–149. (A discussion of existence and quiddity in peripatetic and illuminationist philosophy, as the background to understanding al-Sabzawari's thought.)

Izutsu Toshihiko and Mohaghegh, M. (1983) *The Metaphysics of Sabzawari*, Delmar, NY: Caravan.

(An English translation of the first section of the *Ghurar al-fara'id*.)

Nasr, S.H. (1966) 'Renaissance in Iran (continued): Haji Mulla Hadi Sabziwari', in M.M. Sharif (ed.) *A History of Muslim Philosophy*, Wiesbaden: Harrasowitz; repr. Karachi, 1983. (A good introduction to the content of al-Sabzawari's *Sharh al-manzuma*.)

JOHN COOPER

SACRAMENTS

The Christian theory of 'sacraments' underlies ideas of a general 'sacramentality' in the universe whereby ordinary things have religious significance by their own nature or by virtue of some hidden power within them. The pre-Christian Latin word sacramentum *meant a non-returnable gift marking the taking on of some binding obligation; more informally it meant an oath, and later a secret or mystery. Latin theology turned it to Christian use, initially in rough translation of the Greek* mysterion, *applied to the Church, to the Scriptures and to Old as well as New Testament rites. The word then became the predominant medieval and modern term specifically designating those rites in permanent use in the Church which human authority was conceived not to be free to abolish, add to or change in their essentials.*

Each such rite presupposes that the creaturely things used have some aptitude which allows or invites the particular ritual use concerned, that is, which presupposes some more general sacramental potential in natural things. The conceptual tools developed in Catholic theology – 'effective sign', 'matter and form', 'sacrifice', 'authority', 'power' and 'institution' – sharpen enquiry into the phenomenology of rituals within many different religious traditions.

1 **Explaining early conceptions: the 'seven sacraments'**
2 **The Eucharist: presence and sacrifice**
3 **Post-medieval developments**
4 **General sacramentality of the universe**

1 Explaining early conceptions: the 'seven sacraments'

The so-called seven sacraments existed in the Church long before being classified together as 'sacraments' to distinguish them from other Church rituals, and long before any discussion of their precise number or

what they had in common – what it is to be a 'sacrament'.

The Fourth Lateran Council (1215) set forth the Western Catholic conception of seven sacraments: two of initiation – Baptism and Confirmation; the Eucharist, the central action supposed constitutive of the Church, around which the others are grouped (commonly referred to as the Mass or the Divine Liturgy, or, among Protestants, Holy Communion or the Lord's Supper); two of healing – Reconciliation (absolution from sin, commonly referred to as Confession or Penance) and the Anointing of the Sick (Extreme Unction); Ordination, conveying authority to celebrate the Eucharist and to teach; and Marriage, which is unique as the context of cooperation with God in his creation of new persons, and gives grace enabling marriage to imitate the mystery of the love between Christ and the Church. The Eastern Orthodox Churches generally agree in the same list. Protestants tend to similar conceptions of which rites are integral to the life of the Church, but regard only baptism and the Eucharist as instituted by Christ himself, and so only these as sacraments in the strict sense (although Luther initially ranked confession as a third). All agree on the higher status of baptism and the Eucharist.

Catholic theological tradition saw a sacrament as essentially an action that is effective in communicating grace, the action being such as to signify what is being done. The philosophical concept of 'effective sign' defined what the seven rites had in common.

How was effectiveness viewed? God alone (acting immediately, not deputing his power) gives grace inwardly in the sacraments, with Christ himself acting as principal agent through the Holy Spirit; the ministers of the sacraments are essentially instruments. In this conception, it is primarily Christ who baptizes, absolves, celebrates the Eucharist, heals, joins in marriage, ordains and so forth – a view echoed in the Anglican archbishop William Temple's insistence that in ordination the minister acts as the representative of Christ, not of the Church. The effectiveness of the sacraments seems an immediate corollary of this conception, so that, if there is no obstacle on the side of the recipient, then the appropriately intended performance of the rite by ministers with appropriate authority must be effective for God to give grace, in the traditional phrase *ex opere operato* (that is, effective simply 'out of the work's having been worked'), although the fruitfulness of the grace is affected by the dispositions and prayer of the persons concerned.

This belief in effectiveness was what first made the notion of 'institution by Christ' pivotal, since evidently no merely human authority could arrogate to a human ritual (even granted appropriate intentions and ministers) certainty of being thus instrumental to an action of God. This consideration made Thomas Aquinas reject earlier ideas that some sacraments might have been instituted by the apostles or by the Church. He argued that such lesser authorities could no more do this than institute or alter the essential constitution of the Church. The list of sacraments was supposedly compatible with many different explanations of how and when they were instituted. Aquinas, for example, distinguished the institution of a sacrament (the establishment of its power), its being published (perhaps by Christ instructing the apostles before his Ascension) and its being promulgated (made known to the whole world); the promise of the Holy Spirit without measure implied the completion of baptism in confirmation and the elevation of marriage, instituted at the beginning of mankind, to a sacramental means of grace. Which rites were actions of Christ and therefore effective was not held in doubt, only their mode of establishment.

The notion of 'sign' seems less problematic, and customarily two aspects were distinguished: matter (water, bread, wine, oil, the laying on of hands – that is, certain materials and actions with them) and form (what indicates the meaning of the actions, including the kind of minister required). But how the matter/form distinction applies in the cases of confession and marriage is obscure; where both the laying on of hands and the application of oil are used, which is essential has been disputed; and the Eucharist presents another difficulty, described in §2 below. Plainly, the form is paramount; but many obscurities arise of the kinds philosophy often finds in the areas of law and action (for example, how to distinguish the publicly recognizable context of words or actions, which determines 'the intention of the rite' – that is, the character of the action – from the private intentions of ministers or recipients). Problems are resolvable only by regarding the essence as lying in some action, an action by the doing of which grace is given, not in the applicability of this matter/form distinction. These distinctions, problems and approaches to resolution arise in considering the rituals of almost every religion.

The list of seven has a rationale in its relation to the universal structure of human life. However, its significance has always lain partly in what it excludes, for example, kings being anointed or crowned, monks and suchlike taking vows, places and objects being dedicated (except in the Eucharist). It also excludes all other public or private ritual postures, acts, ceremonies and processions, including those centred on sacred icons, statues or images. To distinguish them

from the sacraments, they all are commonly grouped as 'sacramentals', along with various uses of candles, incense, ashes or water (except in baptism) – the last sometimes associated with natural springs and wells.

2 The Eucharist: presence and sacrifice

The Eucharist is described by Aquinas as the greatest of the sacraments because 'it contains Christ substantially'. According to ancient Catholic and Orthodox tradition, what is sacramentally present and received under the forms of bread and wine is not bread and wine as such, but Christ himself, mysteriously present in his complete humanity. Receiving Christ's body and blood is not itself the grace received, but only the means of grace. The aim is not cannibalism: Christ's body is said to be present but 'not in the way a body is in a place in its own dimensions' (Summa theologiae IIIa, q.76, aa.3–6); therefore it is not available so as to be altered and consumed in physical nutrition. Rather the grace given is that of being 'nourished with the divine life', 'divinized', 'made partakers of the divine nature' (2 Peter 1: 4). Anscombe (1981) argues that it is a secondary question whether Christ, as wholly present in the sacrament, is thus present really or only symbolically or only in the act of reception; the primary datum is that in the Eucharist it is Christ himself – mysteriously present in body, blood, soul and divinity – who is the matter or means of grace, whereas in other sacraments it is only water, oil, the laying-on of hands, and suchlike. Describing the matter of the sacrament as 'bread and wine' is oversimple.

The philosophical difficulties in Catholic and Orthodox teaching are signalled by the absence of any positive ways of describing Christ's mode of presence (the word 'sacramentally' tells us no more than the word 'mysteriously') or of describing the conversion of the bread and wine into Christ's body and blood (denied to be an annihilation), beyond saying that they constitute a change in 'reality' or 'substance' (a 'transubstantiation'). The use of the term 'transubstantiation' (Greek, metaousiosis) was ancient, recurring in the Fourth Lateran Council (1215), and not tied to Aristotelian doctrine, let alone to the contrast between essential and accidental predicates. The Council of Trent (1547–63) used the term 'appearance' (species), not the term 'accident', thereby implying no more than that the change concerned is knowable by faith alone.

However, such philosophical difficulties have been exacerbated by considering the aspect of presence out of its original context, namely that of a memorial (Greek, anamnesis). The Jewish conception of memorial is not of individuals gathered in an assembly each, in their individual minds, remembering the thing being remembered, but rather of laying this out in front of other people, the world or God – in the case of an action, it is more like re-enacting it than doing anything merely psychological (etymologically, 're-member-ing' is putting parts together again). Memorial is also the context for conceiving the Eucharist as a 'sacrifice', not in the modern sense of killing or mutilating something, but still in the sense of an offering, not just of 'ourselves', but of Christ – it involves pleading again in an unbloody manner the one bloody sacrifice of Christ on the cross. Dummett (1987) argues that the reality of the presence of the risen Christ is a condition of the objectivity of the memorial made, so we cannot make sense of the ancient understanding that the primary action of the Eucharist is the making of this memorial without registering that it was understood to require a real presence. The generic meaning of the word 'sacrifice' as 'making holy' or 'separating from human use for divine use' adds nothing, except in being one of a whole family of features anticipated in Jewish as well as pagan rites. In the Eucharistic memorial, Christ as having been sacrificed is presented, now risen, before the Father under the forms of food and drink; these forms mark this action as to be completed by Christ's being received by the participants as food and drink, with all the symbolism of a shared meal and of being nourished, the participants being thereby also set apart for divine use.

Roman Catholic and Orthodox Christians reckon the Eucharist to contain, not just the pledge, but the reality of the incarnate Christ now risen, and so to represent and embody the change in the world brought about by the Incarnation – in Athanasius' words, 'God's being made man in order that man might be made divine'. It was thus that the Eucharist with its many aspects first became envisaged as the Mystery constitutive of the Church.

3 Post-medieval developments

The primary feature of Protestant accounts was, while retaining the notion of outward signs of inward grace, to repudiate any *ex opere operato* effectiveness, and to make the receiving of grace wholly dependent on the faith of the recipient, the minister being the representative of the congregation rather than of Christ. Institution by Christ was now important only because obedience to explicit Scripture required it, not because the sacraments were actions of Christ in the Church. In the Protestant conception, a sacrament was a human work, of no intrinsic merit, so that efficacy lay only in faith in God, who instituted the

sacrament; in the Catholic conception, by contrast, a sacrament was in itself a divine work, so that reliance on it constituted direct reliance on God rather than on one's own psychological state.

Philosophical conceptions varied: Luther's consubstantiation might seem only a slight variation on transubstantiation (the body of Christ co-present with the bread, as fire in molten iron, instead of taking its place), except it was conceived more as a temporary indwelling than a real change, the change not conceived as persisting after the ceremony; Calvin's doctrine involves only a power (*virtus*) in the bread and wine, a power realized only in their being received in faith; Zwingli began by regarding the bread and wine as symbols of Christ's body and blood, but later considered only the ceremony as a whole as significant, emphasizing its aspect as a community meal. Recent Catholic theology has added other nonrealistic theories, such as transignification (criticized by Anscombe (1981) and Dummett (1987)), as well as attempts to explain how the non-empirical change of bread into Christ's body can be ontological and real without being physical (for example, Schillebeekx 1968; Dummett 1987).

Twentieth-century Catholicism, transformed by Pius X's drive for 'frequent and even daily communion' and Pius XII's systematic emphasis on the people's participating in more ways in every part of the liturgy, is now experiencing the resultant vernacularization initiated by Vatican II. This has dramatized the character of the sacraments as bringing people into relation to one another as well as to God. Each sacrament relates people to the Church in the same act as relating them to Christ, so that (for example) being joined or reconciled to Christ is being joined or reconciled to the Church. The Eucharist presents itself as constitutive of the Church. Vatican II situates both sacraments and sacramentals within the context of the Church as 'Sacrament or instrumental sign of intimate union with God and of the unity of all humanity.'

4 General sacramentality of the universe

Their realistic standpoint with regard to the Eucharist, despite the absence of any satisfactory account of it, constitutes the high point in Catholic and Orthodox resistance to the desacralization of the world. In the lesser sphere of 'sacramentals', the numinous significance of icons for the Orthodox presents a dramatic case of the same resistance.

In the theistic perspective, God, as cause of being, immediately present in and upholding everything, is never an absentee. Therefore, within the world thus loaded with his presence and activity, there is always the possibility, through the Holy Spirit, of God's presence and activity taking forms beyond mere causation, forms richer in personal significance and power, and instanced not only in the sacraments but more widely. This perception appears in Donald Baillie's emphasis on the sacramentality of the universe (1957), and is given vivid expression in Gerard Manley Hopkins' poem 'God's Grandeur' (1877). The way God's immanence in all things makes all potentially open to religious significance has also been important for Christian understanding of very differently expressed ideas – for example, in Hinduism. It is the background for the permanent potential that nature and particular places have to arouse religious awe, a sense of the 'numinous'.

In the Catholic conception, relationship to God in any such rich mode of presence in creation is constitutive of relationship to the Church. God's giving grace is not limited to the sacraments, but the symbolism they embody signifies or explains the direction of the grace which he may give without them. What happens when a person receives grace by a sacrament is representative of what happens when the same grace is given without sacrament.

Within a dualist framework of thought, identifying the spiritual with the immaterial, the sacraments have been thought of as an accommodation of God's mode of action to the lowly body-and-imagination-bound character of the human soul, as if human worship and its expression were ideally purely verbal or intellectual. However, the sacraments can be thought of as reflecting God's express purpose in creating the physical universe; the human being's unitary psychophysical nature is not a weakness or a privation, but a source of enrichment, modes of worship include a physical aspect, and voluntary physical action often provides the most definitive expression of the human heart. Light, heat, the air, the sea, the heavens, food and water provide images pregnant with religious meaning, not to be disparaged in a false body/mind dualism, but integral to a rounded communication between God and the human race, the background to sacrament and sacramental alike.

See also: GRACE; RITUAL

References and further reading

* Anscombe, G.E.M. (1981) 'On Transubstantiation', in *Collected Papers, III: Ethics, Religion and Politics*, Oxford: Blackwell. (A modern philosopher discusses a key mislocation of the problem of the nature of the Eucharist.)
Aquinas, T. (1266–73) *Summa theologiae* IIIa, qq.60–90, London: Blackfriars, vols 56–60, 1961–70; also the Supplement, qq.1–68, in *Summa theologiae*, London: Burns & Oates, 2nd edn, vols 18–20, 1941. (The Supplement was compiled after Aquinas' death from earlier writings to complete his plan for the whole *Summa*. See especially qq.64–6, 72, 75–7 and Suppl. qq.29, 41–2. Of special philosophical interest are q.75, on 'transubstantiation', and q.76 and q.77, a.7, on the peculiar mode of Christ's spatial presence.)
* Baillie, D. (1957) *The Theology of the Sacraments*, London: Faber & Faber. (Part II gives an eirenic Protestant view – in Lecture 1, of the general sacramentality of the universe, in Lecture 2, of the rooting of Christian sacraments in the Incarnation and in Lecture 4, of the meaning of the Eucharist.)
Calvin, J. (1536) *Institutes of the Christian Religion*, ed. J.T. McNeill, trans. F.L. Battles, London: SCM, 1960, bk IV, chaps 14, 17–19. (This systematic Protestant masterwork treats the sacraments in general in chapter 14, the Eucharist in chapters 17–18 and lesser rites in chapter 19.)
* Dummett, M. (1987) 'The Intelligibility of Eucharistic Doctrine', in W.J. Abraham and S.W. Holtzer (eds) *The Rationality of Religious Belief: Essays in honour of Basil Mitchell*, Oxford: Oxford University Press. (A modern analytic philosopher examines the difficulties of Eucharistic doctrine.)
* Hopkins, G.M. (1877) 'God's Grandeur', in *Poems and Prose*, ed. W.H. Gardner, London: Penguin, 1953. (Displays the principle of Hopkins' poetry, a world whose every feature is pregnant with meaning.)
Luther, M. (1520) 'The Babylonian Captivity of the Church', *Luther's Works*, vol. 36, *Word and Sacrament II*, Philadelphia, PA: Fortress Press, 1959. (A pioneer elaboration of a Protestant view; see especially pages 18, 28–41, 51–7, 62–8.)
* Schillebeekx, E. (1968) *The Eucharist*, London: Sheed & Ward. (An attempt to give a phenomenological interpretation of a realist view of the Eucharist.)

DAVID BRAINE

SAGYA PAṆḌITA/ SAGYPAṆḌITA *see* SA SKYA PAṆḌITA

SAGYABA *see* TIBETAN PHILOSOPHY

SAINT/ST. *see* UNDER NAME OF PERSON

SAINT-CYRAN *see* PORT-ROYAL

SAINT-SIMON, CLAUDE-HENRI DE ROUVROY, COMTE DE (1760–1825)

An influential French social theorist, Saint-Simon propounded a philosophy of history and an account of the future organization of industrial society. He predicted a 'golden age', where harmony between individual capacities and social structures, reflected in a reordering of 'temporal' and 'spiritual' power, would overcome disorder and banish idleness. He has been variously portrayed as a utopian socialist, the founder of sociology and a prescient madman.

Saint-Simon's life was eventful, even if the more apocryphal details of the hagiography transmitted by his followers – including his descent from Charlemagne, being tutored by d'Alembert, childhood imprisonment, and marriage proposal to Madame de Staël – are omitted. As a commissioned French officer he participated in the American Wars of Independence, was wounded and imprisoned by British forces, and commended for bravery by the American government. Following his release, Saint-Simon pursued an unsuccessful canalization project in Panama before returning to France. During the Revolution, he (prudently) renounced his title, underwent a 'republican baptism', and made (and subsequently lost in litigation) a fortune speculating on the property market – his brief incarceration during the Terror was the result of mistaken identity. From 1802 Saint-Simon devoted his energies to developing and promoting his distinctive views on social organization in a torrent of books, pamphlets, prospectuses, articles and letters. The interpretative difficulties created by the diversity of these projects are compounded by the frequency of joint and disputed authorship, his opportunistic willingness to adapt his emphasis to imagined audiences as varied as the European proletariat and the French king, and the indifference to consistency that accompanied his predilection for descriptive detail. His productivity was punctuated by an unconsummated and hastily terminated marriage, a period in a private mental hospital, trial and acquittal on charges of subversion, and a suicide attempt (involving seven shots to his head) which resulted in the loss of his right eye.

In advocating a 'science of social organization', Saint-Simon depicted himself as emulating physiology in applying the methodology of the natural sciences – basing arguments on 'observed and examined facts', rather than revelation or deductions from reason – to the study of humankind. History, he claimed, was driven by the progression of the human mind, in which successive advances in understanding are embodied in a (twelve-stage) chronological narrative. In its most schematic form – as promulgated by Saint-Amand Bazard – history is structured into 'organic' epochs (in which ideas and institutions are in harmony) divided by 'critical' interludes (where social arrangements lag behind the progress of intellect). Development proceeded from the ancient and Christian worlds (grounded in polytheism and theism respectively), through the contemporary period of transition, to a final 'golden age' of industrialism (founded on positive science). The role of human agency was limited to hastening the arrival, rather than determining the content, of 'the perfection of the social order' that lay ahead.

'Social physiology' revealed inequalities in human nature, both between 'Africans' and 'Asians' (the 'descendants of Cain') on the one hand and 'Europeans' (the 'children of Abel') on the other, and within the latter category, where one of three capacities – emotive, rational and motive – would typically predominate within any particular individual. This psychology motivates the class structure of industrialism in which social differentiation according to capacity – into artists, scientists and 'industrials' (the latter group including wage labourers and owners of capital) – is functional to both the individual aim of fulfilment (since 'every citizen must naturally tend to confine himself to the role for which he is most suited') and the social goal of production (which requires the invention, examination and execution of useful projects). Saint-Simon portrays the shared ends of industrial society in moral terms, but reduces morality to the general happiness which is in turn identified with productivity – 'work is the essence of all virtues'. The same reductive strategy defines society as 'the ensemble and union of men engaged in useful work', describes individuals as free when they are 'unrestricted in productive work', and reveals 'true equality' as consisting in an individual's right to benefits 'exactly proportionate' to the contribution of that person (and their capital) to productivity.

The universal human drive to seek power would in future be sublimated, deflected away from immoral and destructive expression in conflict between individuals and into a cooperative victory over nature.

Politics would be transformed into a positive science, developing 'laws of hygiene' to eradicate idleness ('a state of sickness in man'), whilst 'government' would transmogrify into a much reduced 'administrative' structure facilitating production (divided accordingly into Chambers of Invention, Examination and Execution). His scientism and belief in natural inequality led Saint-Simon to assign 'temporal power' to those most competent to exercise it (the most successful 'industrials'). 'Spiritual power' would be the responsibility of a clerisy of scientists and artists, providing the moral and educational leadership necessary for social stability. Initially Saint-Simon advocated a 'Religion of Newton', with its own forms of worship and dogma, as an alternative to Christianity (optimistically suggesting that existing clergy might retrain for the new order). Increasingly, however, he portrayed his 'holy enterprise' as embodying the 'true spirit' of a Christianity uncontaminated by the heresies of the Church. This 'New Christianity' would utilize rhetoric, music and imagery to 'fill the souls of the faithful with feelings of terror or joy' designed 'to direct their ardour...towards works of general utility'. Institutionalized cooperation between the 'temporal' and 'spiritual' powers of Europe would lead to a confederation 'without wars, catastrophes or political revolution', in which a 'new family sentiment of Europeanism' would supersede competing patriotisms.

Saint-Simon's legacy resists summary. Any adequate account would include and assess his impact on his distinguished and estranged secretaries (Auguste COMTE, Augustin Thierry) and claims of influence upon a succession of renowned social and political theorists (John Stuart Mill, Karl Marx), writers (Heinrich Heine, George Sand) and musicians (Franz Liszt, Hector Berlioz). The Saint-Simonian 'movement' did not survive intact in France, but fractured into the worldly and messianic currents that Saint-Simon had sought to incorporate. The achievements of the former, a distinguished group of engineers, mathematicians, economists and bankers, include the Suez Canal Company, the Paris-Lyon-Méditerranée railway and the Crédit mobilier. The latter, a more wayward group under Père Enfantin, scandalized Paris with the elaborate public rituals of their community at Ménilmontant and talk of an androgynous (and seemingly lascivious) God, before embarking on a crusade to North Africa in search of the 'Female Messiah'.

See also: HISTORY, PHILOSOPHY OF; POSITIVISM IN THE SOCIAL SCIENCES §1; SOCIALISM; UTOPIANISM

List of works

Saint-Simon, C.-H. de R., Comte de (1966) *Oeuvres de Claude-Henri de Saint-Simon*, Paris: Éditions Anthropos, 6 vols. (The most complete modern edition of Saint-Simon's writings.)
—— (1975) *Selected Writings on Science, Industry and Social Organisation*, trans. and ed. K. Taylor, London: Croom Helm. (An extensive and useful collection of excerpts in translation from Saint-Simon's writings.)
—— (1976) *The Political Thought of Saint-Simon* ed. G. Ionescu, Oxford: Oxford University Press. (A selection of excerpts in translation from Saint-Simon's writings focusing on his political ideas.)

References and further reading

Carlisle, R.B. (1987) *The Proffered Crown. Saint-Simonianism and the Doctrine of Hope*, Baltimore, MD: Johns Hopkins University Press. (A sympathetic historical account of the Saint-Simonian movement.)
Durkheim, É. (1958) *Socialism and Saint-Simon*, ed. A.W. Gouldner, Yellow Springs, OH: Antioch Press. (An interpretation of Saint-Simon as the founder of a positivist science of society by the renowned French sociologist.)
Manuel, F. (1956) *The New World of Henri Saint-Simon*, Cambridge, MA: Harvard University Press. (An erudite and interesting general work on Saint-Simon.)

DAVID LEOPOLD

SALVATION

For there to be such a thing as salvation, there must be someone to be saved, something from which they need to be saved, and some way in which they can be saved from it. 'Salvation' is primarily a religious term, and religious traditions typically assume that there is some basic religious problem that all people face. Monotheistic religions (for example, Judaism, Christianity, Islam, Viśiṣṭādvaita and Dvaita Hinduism) whose central doctrine concerns God conceived as Creator and Providence take this basic problem to lie in the fact of sin. Human persons have sinned (knowingly acted against the will of God) and sinning has become habitual. Thus there is need for forgiveness and reformation, which are available only in God's gracious pardon and restorative power. People can receive forgiveness and reformation through repentance and faith. Salvation by sheer self-effort is impossible.

Nonmonotheistic traditions (for example, Buddhism, Jainism, Advaita Vedānta Hinduism) take a particular sort of ignorance to be the basic problem. The ignorance in question involves having false beliefs about the nature of persons and their cosmic environment. The proper treatment and cure is the achievement of an esoteric religious experience in which calm and bliss are accompanied by an understanding of the true nature of reality. The different traditions give very different accounts of what this nature is. Thus religious traditions differ greatly in the ways in which they conceive persons, their basic religious problem, and the proper treatment and cure. Secular notions of salvation, as in classical Marxism, tend to be secularizations of one or another religious conception – in the Marxist case, of the notion of the Kingdom of God.

1 **Indian Buddhism**
2 **Jainism**
3 **Advaita Vedanta**
4 **Monotheistic traditions**
5 **Agreements and disagreements**

1 Indian Buddhism

According to Indian Buddhism, there is a cycle of birth and rebirth in which every person participates; the cycle is beginningless and, unless one becomes enlightened, endless. There is a law of karma: one's misdeeds yield bad consequences for oneself, and one's good deeds yield good consequences for oneself. These consequences frequently come in a later life than that in which one performed the original action. Life in this cycle is inherently unsatisfactory, so the basic religious problem is that of escaping the round of birth and rebirth. The way to do so is through having a pre-*nirvāṇa* enlightenment experience in one's present life, which prepares one for release from the cycle and entry into *nirvāṇa* upon one's (next) death.

To prize anything in the reincarnation cycle more than escape from that cycle is, for reincarnation traditions, the height of folly. A person who enjoys the best of earthly conditions and fails to see that they are momentary and meaningless compared to the value of escape and enlightenment is desperately ignorant.

The natural world (roughly, the set of objects of sensory experience) does not consist of mind-independent, enduring physical objects. Rather, it consists of either physical (nonconscious) states or mental (conscious) states with perceptual content; in Theravāda Buddhism – the 'tradition of the elders' – it is held to consist of both, whereas in Mahāyāna Buddhism – the 'greater vehicle' (as contrasted to Hīnayāna, the 'lesser vehicle', Mahāyāna's term for

Theravāda) – it consists only of mental states. Perhaps more importantly, persons themselves are nothing more *at* a given time than a bundle of states (conscious and nonconscious for the Theravādin, only conscious for the Mahāyānin), and *over* time they are nothing more than a series of such bundles. The idea seems to be that were persons more than this, enlightenment and escape from the reincarnation and karma cycle would be impossible. This tells us, then, the nature of what requires salvation according to Indian Buddhism, and what it needs salvation from (see BUDDHIST PHILOSOPHY, INDIAN §§1–2).

The nature of salvation is another matter. What is it to be in the condition of having been saved? Buddhist salvation is a matter of becoming enlightened in this lifetime, which involves having an esoteric religious experience in which one comes to recognize the truth of the Buddhist account of reality, particularly concerning persons, and experiences calm and bliss. This experience in turn allows one release from the reincarnation cycle at death. For the Theravāda tradition, as for Buddhism generally, there is nothing permanent – nothing endures. Everything noncomposite that exists at a given moment exists only at that moment and everything composite either exists only at one moment or else is composed of elements each of which exists at only one moment. Further, every state or condition that can enter into the composition of a person is inherently unsatisfactory. Given these doctrinal claims, it follows that continued existence as a person inevitably involves continuing to have the basic problem that attaining *nirvāṇa* is intended to solve. Hence *nirvāṇa* will be extinction as a person; it will involve extinction or annihilation of any state or series of states that could enter into the composition of a person. This is what Theravāda doctrine entails and what various texts seem to teach. This interpretation, however, is controversial, and *nirvāṇa* is sometimes said to be ineffable. For part of the Mahāyāna tradition, achieving a pre-*nirvāṇa* enlightenment state involves achieving a condition in which one is still composed of conscious states, but states which are not unsatisfactory. Hence the earlier claim that every state or condition that can enter into the composition of a person is inherently unsatisfactory is rejected. On this view, one who becomes enlightened will indefinitely postpone entering final *nirvāṇa* until the time at which everyone is able to do so, and it is sometimes held that this time will never come. Thus, on this account, whatever personal identity holds regarding a person within one lifetime can also hold over lifetimes after one has become enlightened, and over enlightened lifetimes in which none of one's composing bundles contains anything unsatisfactory. By contrast, Mahāyāna voidist tradition denies that even such persons as Mahāyāna idealism allows are anything other than illusory, and so takes the solution to one's religious problem to be that the problem, and those who have it, are themselves only illusory (see BUDDHIST CONCEPT OF EMPTINESS).

2 Jainism

Jainism holds that there exist a great number both of real (nonillusory) self-conscious substances and non-self-conscious substances. To be a substance is to be a possessor of properties, not to be a property oneself, to endure over time and to remain numerically the same through qualitative change. Indeed, Jaina mental substances are permanent and indestructible, and their goal is to escape being embodied because embodiment causes ignorance, namely the false beliefs that we depend on other things for our existence and could be destroyed, and that our knowledge is inherently limited. Each person or soul is eternally distinct from every other and from any physical (nonconscious) substance. Though the Jainas believe in individual immortality, they do not believe in a supreme deity (see JAINA PHILOSOPHY §1).

The depth and importance of the difference between Buddhism and Jainism concerning the nature of persons is illustrated by one of their more important disputes. The Jaina objection to the Buddhist account of persons and karma essentially runs as follows. Justice requires that the same person who performs an action must reap the positive or negative karmic consequences that follow from it. According to the Buddhist tradition, a person at a time is but a momentary bundle composed of momentary states. Call this a single-time person; all there is to any person at any time is a single-time person. According to the Buddhist tradition, a person over time is a series of momentary bundles – a series of single-time persons – and so is what we might call a multiple-time person. Every action is performed at some time, and so is done by some single-time person. Every consequence is received at some time, and so by a single-time person. But since consequences typically take time to come along, the same single-time person does not both perform the action and receive the consequences, and justice is not served.

The obvious Buddhist answer is that it is enough to serve justice that the same multiple-time person include both the doer of the deed and the receiver of the consequences thereof. The Jaina response is that all there is to the multiple-time person at the time of the action is the single-time person who then exists, and all there is to the multiple-time person at the time of the consequences is the single-time person who

then exists; multiple-time persons are agents or patients only in so far as their component single-time person parts act or receive. Single-time persons must *be* persons, or else agents are not persons. But then multiple-time persons are not persons in the sense in which agents are persons, but are classes of persons; single-time persons are persons in one sense (the basic) and multiple-time persons are persons in another (derivative) sense. If the person-in-the-basic-sense who acts is different from the person-in-the-basic-sense who receives the consequences of the action, then justice is not served.

Jainas, like Buddhists, hold that salvation requires the having of an enlightenment experience; this involves feelings of calm and bliss, and essentially includes a recognition of the correctness of the Jaina view of reality, particularly concerning persons. One who has such a this-life experience is released from embodiment and karmic obligations upon death. Personal identity is retained.

3 Advaita Vedānta

For Advaita Vedānta, a nonmonotheistic variety of Hinduism, ultimate reality, which does not depend on anything else for its existence, is nonpersonal and eternal, unchanging and permanent. The real self (*ātman*) of each person is identical to this ultimate reality (Brahman-without-qualities). Having an enlightenment experience (*mokṣa*) involves realizing this truth, thereby escaping the reincarnation cycle, losing all individuality, and being 'absorbed' into Brahman. Here, in contrast to Jainism, personal identity is not retained. What was you, or seemed to be, no longer exists as you when final enlightenment occurs. Critics of this view point out that it means that there can be neither persons who have a basic religious problem, nor a problem for them to have – nor, of course, on this view can persons exist problemless (see VEDĀNTA §1). Viśiṣṭādvaita Vedānta (whose major figure is Rāmānuja) and Dvaita Vedānta (whose greatest representative is Madhva) are monotheistic varieties of Hinduism that offer a very different account of the sacred texts to which Śaṅkara, the most influential Advaita Vedānta philosopher, appeals.

4 Monotheistic traditions

Monotheistic traditions typically hold that God, an omnipotent, omniscient and morally perfect being, depends for existence on nothing else, and everything else that exists depends on God for its existence. Whether beginningless, or created *at* a time, or *with* time, the world exists by divine courtesy. Persons resemble God in ways that nonpersons do not, having some degree of knowledge, power and (potential) goodness. God is unique and holy, and, typically, in some sense the source of morality. For at least Semitic (Jewish, Christian and Islamic) as well as Hindu monotheism, God is characterized by unselfish love (see GOD, CONCEPTS OF §§1–6).

According to these traditions, the basic religious problem all human beings face is that they have sinned – that is, they have knowingly acted wrongly against God's will, and overrated their own significance while undervaluing the worth of others. Sin is not merely manifested in individual actions, but comes from a disposition towards wrong action that comes to lie deep in our nature. Our individual and collective existence is plagued by it; sin has social and institutional as well as individual manifestations. Thus there is a need for human repentance, for sorrow for one's sins that includes the resolve not to repeat them, and for prayer for divine forgiveness. This prayer God graciously answers, enabling forgiven sinners to love others as they love themselves. Love in this sense is primarily volitional, not emotional, and involves concern for the ultimate good of the beloved, for which one is prepared to act sacrificially (see SIN §§1–2). Human individuality, then, is viewed as real, not illusory, and good. Finite persons typically are viewed, as in Jainism, as mental substances, but also, as in Buddhism, as not indestructible.

In Christianity, it is the incarnation, death and resurrection of Jesus Christ, God incarnate, that brings salvation. Christ lived a perfect human life as our example, died for our sins to make a just forgiveness possible and rose from the dead; the power to forgive and to progressively free us from the domination of sin is exercised through Christ's life, death and resurrection (see INCARNATION AND CHRISTOLOGY §1; ATONEMENT).

Sin is not seen as the violation of arbitrary laws, but as a disposition (realizing itself in action) that thwarts one's potential to realize one's capacity to become as like God as is possible for a creature, and hence to fulfil one's nature. It is in worship, obedience and service that one both shows love to God and becomes fully oneself. Creation in God's image involves having an intrinsic worth that God sustains in existence. Hence, in the monotheistic traditions, personal identity is typically fully retained in the afterlife. Union with God is a matter of oneness of purpose, not of being. Salvation is seen as resulting in a personal relationship with God that occurs in the context of a redeemed community.

5 Agreements and disagreements

Semitic and Hindu monotheism, generally speaking, agree on these matters. For both sorts of monotheism, God is providential, though in Hindu monotheism this involves God governing the course of reincarnation and distributing karma with a justice tempered by mercy, whereas for Semitic monotheism, God's being providential involves such actions in history as calling Abraham to be father of the nation of Israel, giving the law to Moses, sending the Old Testament prophets, becoming incarnate in Jesus Christ (for Christianity) and revealing the Qur'an to Muhammad (for Islam). (There are traditions associated with particular Hindu temples that Krishna, for example, appeared to someone and commanded that a temple be built at a particular place, but there is not the robust notion of God acting in history that characterizes the Semitic traditions, and no notion of God moving the course of history towards the Kingdom of God). For each sort of monotheism, worship is not a preliminary religious experience to be later transcended; its appropriateness is built into the nature of the distinction between Creator and creature, which is not a dissolvable distinction. In Semitic, but not Hindu, monotheism central religious doctrines make essential reference to certain persons and events. For Christianity, God's becoming incarnate in Jesus Christ to die for our sins and be raised from the dead for our justification is an essential objective basis for divine forgiveness of the repentant.

There are similarities between Indian monotheistic religious traditions and Indian nonmonotheistic traditions. They agree that there is no movement of history towards an end or fulfilment. For Advaita Vedānta and Buddhist voidism, temporal and historical processes are illusory. For Buddhist idealism, historical events are all states within the minds of persons – parts of transitory bundles. For earlier Indian Buddhism, historical events include physical or nonconscious states, many of which do not belong to bundle-persons, but, like Jainism and Hindu monotheism, it denies that a providence guides those events to any historical conclusion or goal. All the Indian perspectives initially agree that the doctrines of reincarnation and karma are true, though some of them so radically reinterpret these doctrines as in the end to reject them. For no Indian tradition does basic religious doctrine essentially concern certain persons or contain essential references to places.

There are also differences between Indian monotheistic and nonmonotheistic perspectives. For the nonmonotheistic traditions, the basic religious problem is ignorance, not sin (there is no God to sin against), and the basic religious need is for enlightenment, not for forgiveness (there is no God to forgive). For Indian monotheism, it is sin that is our problem, and God's active forgiveness that solves it. For the nonmonotheistic traditions, religious knowledge is gained through meditation and through sacred texts that have no nonhuman personal source, not through revelation (there is no God to offer revelation). For Indian monotheism, Brahman is the source of all religious knowledge, scriptural or experiential. For the nonmonotheistic traditions, salvation comes through one's own efforts (there is no God to help). These are do-it-yourself religions: however necessary the aid of a teacher, guide or guru prior to one's enlightenment, it is one's own efforts that ultimately succeed or fail. For all of these traditions, it is in an enlightenment experience that one is said to learn the ultimate religious truth, and by having the experience one learns it in such a manner that one is transformed. But the truths that one is alleged to learn cannot all be true; at most one is. The claim is that enlightenment experience yields saving religious knowledge, not merely that it provides psychological certainty or great comfort. For monotheistic traditions, salvation requires that one repent of one's sins and seek God's forgiveness, and is constituted by one's flourishing in a community that lives in God's presence.

See also: HEAVEN; JUSTIFICATION, RELIGIOUS; REINCARNATION

References and further reading

Brandon, S.F.G. (1962) *Man and his Destiny in the Great Religions*, Manchester: Manchester University Press. (Brandon's Wilde Lectures, delivered 1954–7 at Oxford, dealing widely with notions of salvation.)

—— (1963) *The Saviour God*, Manchester: Manchester University Press. (Collection of essays covering many notions of religious salvation.)

Carman, J.B. (1974) *The Theology of Ramanuja*, New Haven, CT: Yale University Press. (The classic discussion in English of Rāmānuja's theology.)

—— (1994) *Majesty and Meekness*, Grand Rapids, MI: Eerdmans. (Comparative study of concepts of God.)

Denney, J. (1912) *The Death of Christ*, London: Hodder & Stoughton. (A classic statement of the Christian understanding of salvation through Christ.)

Lott, E. (1980) *Vedantic Approaches to God*, London: Macmillan. (Excellent discussion of Indian monotheism.)

McGrath, A.E. (1986) *Iustitia Dei*, Cambridge: Cam-
bridge University Press, 2 vols. (A history of the Christian doctrine of justification.)

—— (1994) *Christian Theology: An Introduction*, Oxford: Blackwell. (Comprehensive, accessible introduction to Christian theology.)

Sharma, N.K. (1902) *Philosophy of Madhacarya*, Delhi: Motilal Barnasidas. (Major study of the philosophy and theology of Madhva.)

Smart, N. (1964) *Doctrine and Argument in Indian Philosophy*, London: Allen & Unwin. (Clear general discussion of Indian philosophy.)

—— (1968) *The Yogi and the Devotee*, London: Allen & Unwin. (Comparison of Indian and Catholic theology.)

Wood, T.E. (1990) *The Mandukya Upanishad and the Agama Sastra*, Honolulu, HI: University of Hawaii Press. (Discussion of Advaita Vedānta.)

—— (1991) *Mind-only: A Philosophical and Doctrinal Analysis of the Vijnavada*, Honolulu, HI: University of Hawaii Press. (A lucid and superb discussion of early Buddhism with some reference to later Buddhism.)

KEITH E. YANDELL

ŚAṂKARA *see* ŚAṄKARA

SĀṂKHYA *see* SĀṄKHYA

SAṂSĀRA *see* KARMA AND REBIRTH, INDIAN CONCEPTIONS OF

SAMYAY *see* TIBETAN PHILOSOPHY

SANCHES, FRANCISCO (1551–1623)

Francisco Sanches was a sceptical philosopher and a professor of medicine at the University of Toulouse in southern France in the late sixteenth and early seventeenth century. He was born in Spain to a family of Jewish ancestry that had been forcibly converted to Catholicism, but he was brought up in France. Though he was a distant cousin of the sceptic Michel de Montaigne, he independently advanced what was perhaps the strongest sceptical critique of Aristotelianism and Platonism. In addition he developed a scepticism about mathematical knowledge claims. At the same time, he offered the first form of constructive scepticism, a way of solving intellectual problems without antecedently overcoming the sceptical challenge to traditional kinds of knowledge. He thus presented science as a way of dealing with experience, rather than as a way of gaining knowledge, and in this his views anticipate some twentieth-century philosophies. Sanches was also an important empirical medical practitioner, who presented the newest medical findings in his courses at Toulouse. His sceptical-critical views were influential in the first half of the seventeenth century, and were still being studied in Leibniz's time.

1   **Life and works**
2   **Attacks on Aristotle and Plato**
3   **Constructive scepticism**
4   **Influence**

1   Life and works

Francisco Sanches (or Sánchez, though he is not to be confused with Francisco Sánchez de la Brozas (1523–1600), also known as Sanctius) was born in 1551 on the Spanish-Portuguese border to a family which had been very influential in Spain before the Expulsion of the Jews in 1492, and were now Marranos or New Christians (Jews who had been forcibly converted to Christianity). They first moved to Portugal and then, in 1564, to southern France in order to escape religious and political persecution by the Inquisition. The young Sanches studied at the Collège de Guyenne in Bordeaux, the same school that MONTAIGNE had attended. After these studies he travelled in Italy for a while, visiting various universities there, and then settled in Rome. After two years of study at Rome with leading medical innovators who brought him into contact with new medical discoveries and theories, he went to the University of Montpellier, where he received a degree in medicine in 1574. After several years as a successful medical practitioner he was appointed first as professor of philosophy at the University of Toulouse in 1585, and then in 1612 as professor of medicine at the same university. He continued to work there until his death in 1623.

Sanches wrote extensively. The first of his philosophical writings that has survived is a letter to the Jesuit mathematician, Father Christopher Clavius, who had just edited Euclid's works, and whom Sanches had met in Rome. In the letter, Sanches offered a sceptical attack on the possibility of attaining genuine truth in mathematics. This was followed by his most famous writing, *Quod nihil scitur* (*That Nothing is Known*), composed between 1574 and

its first publication in 1581. Soon thereafter he wrote *Carmen de Cometa*, published in 1578, a critical examination in poetic form of the astrological interpretations of the comet of 1577. He also wrote some commentaries on portions of Aristotle's writings, as well as many medical works. Sanches criticized various Renaissance naturalistic views, such as those of CARDANO (§§3, 6), and he may have actually debated with Giordano BRUNO in person.

Limbrick's introduction to *That Nothing is Known* stresses how much of Sanches' limited sceptical view grew out of his lifelong medical work: 'it is the combination of two approaches to the theory of knowledge, the philosophical and the medical, which distinguishes Sanches' contribution to the history of ideas in the sixteenth and seventeenth centuries' ([1581]1989: 25–6).

2   Attacks on Aristotle and Plato

The most important work of Sanches, *That Nothing is Known*, is perhaps the best technical exposition of philosophical scepticism produced during the sixteenth century (see SCEPTICISM, RENAISSANCE §5). Unlike other philosophers who were diffuse and digressive in their presentations of scepticism, appealing to the history of human stupidity and the variety of theories that have been accepted, Sanches instead systematically developed a radical sceptical critique of the Aristotelian theory of knowledge (see ARISTOTLE §6), pointing out its many errors and inconsistencies. All sciences, he declared, begin with definitions. But these definitions are arbitrarily assigned to things without having any definite relation to them, and so they do not state the nature of things. Moreover, names keep changing. Hence when we think we are saying something about the nature of things by means of combining words and definitions, we are unfortunately just fooling ourselves.

This nominalistic thesis, when applied to Aristotle's view that science consists of knowledge that is certain, acquired by syllogistic demonstrations from true definitions, leads quickly to a scepticism about whether such knowledge can be achieved. As already seen, we do not possess true definitions, but only arbitrary ones. In fact, the particulars about which we are trying to demonstrate are better known than the general terms in the premises. Further, the syllogistic method of reasoning does not lead to any new knowledge. There is a vicious circularity in any knowledge claims based on demonstrative syllogisms, for the conclusion that is being proved actually constitutes part of the evidence for the premises. In order to demonstrate that Socrates is mortal, it is argued that all men are mortal and that Socrates is a man. However, the premises involve the conclusion, since the particular, Socrates, is needed in order to have a conception of man and of mortality. This criticism was later given by both GASSENDI (§3) and J.S. MILL (§2) in their discussions of Aristotelian logic. Moreover, one could not have a true definition of the terms involved in the syllogism without already knowing their meaning, in which case one would not need the syllogism. On the basis of all this, Sanches said of Aristotle's notion of science, 'Do you call this science? I call it ignorance!'

Next Sanches contended that in a formal sense anything can be proved syllogistically if one just begins with the proper premises. Thus the fact that one can construct a syllogistic demonstration constitutes no indication that the conclusion of such a demonstration is true, for if the initial premises are carefully chosen, both true and false propositions can be proved in this manner.

Finally he attacked the Aristotelian claim that true knowledge is knowledge of things in terms of their causes. In order to know something in this manner one would have to know the cause of the cause as well, and the cause of the cause of the cause, and so on *ad infinitum*.

In his letter to Clavius, Sanches attacked a form of the Platonic theory of knowledge (see PLATO §10). We cannot gain knowledge of things through mathematical study, since the objects studied by mathematics are not the natural real ones encountered in human life. Rather these objects are ideal, or perhaps even impossible ones, like points and lines. The mathematical relations that are demonstrated about such objects do not help explain anything in nature or experience, unless we happen to know independently that the experienced objects have mathematical properties, and also know that the principles of mathematics are in fact true. We cannot learn this from mathematics itself. So far as we can tell, mathematics is just conjectural or hypothetical until we can independently determine the nature of things.

3 Constructive scepticism

To replace the approaches that Sanches regarded as false conceptions of science, he insisted that true science is perfect knowledge of a thing ('Scientia est rei perfecta cognitio'). This conception, Sanches contended, was perfectly clear. Genuine knowledge is the immediate, intuitive apprehension of all of the real qualities of an object. Therefore true science will deal with particulars, each of which will somehow have to be understood individually. Any generalizations that go beyond this level of scientific certainty will introduce abstractions, fictions and so on.

Scientific knowledge in its ideal form for Sanches would then consist of the experiential apprehension of each particular thing in and by itself.

None the less Sanches casts doubt on the possibility of such an experiential apprehension. At the beginning of *That Nothing is Known*, Sanches had said that he did not know if he actually knew anything at all. After casting doubt on whether anything can be known by using Aristotle's theory of science, Sanches then analysed his own view, and showed that in a strict sense humans are incapable of reaching any certainty at all. A full apprehension of objects which are known only one by one cannot be reached, in part because of the nature of objects, and in part because of the human being's nature. Everything is related to everything else, and therefore cannot be known individually. And there are an unlimited number of things, all of which are different, so they could never all be known. And, to make matters worse, things change. Thus they cannot be truly known since they never reach a final or complete state.

Turning to the human side of the question, Sanches spent much time discussing the difficulties that prevent human beings from obtaining true knowledge. Our ideas are dependent on our senses which are only capable of perceiving the surface aspects of things, the accidents, and never the substances. Appealing to his medical information Sanches was able to indicate how unreliable sense information is, how it changes as our state of health changes, and so on. The many imperfections and limitations that God has seen fit to leave us with do, in fact, prevent our senses and our other faculties and powers from ever reaching true knowledge. All that we can attain is a quite limited, imperfect knowledge of some things which are present in our experience through observation and judgment. And, as Sanches seems to have found out through his medical studies and work, few scientists in fact make use of experience, and few persons actually know how to judge.

Sanches' sweeping negative conclusion that 'nothing is known' (*nihil scitur*), goes far beyond the Pyrrhonian balancing of opposing views and suspension of judgment offered by his distant cousin Montaigne. Yet Sanches' conclusion is the result of a most careful epistemological examination of the nature of our knowledge. Unlike the scepticism presented by AGRIPPA VON NETTESHEIM (§3), which is destructive in its tendencies, Sanches attempted to state precisely what genuine knowledge would be, and then to show why it is not possible to attain this knowledge. He differs from both MONTAIGNE (§§2–3) and Agrippa in that there is also a positive side to his work. He put forward a procedure which was not aimed at gaining knowledge, but at developing a way of dealing constructively with human experience. This procedure, which Sanches explicitly called scientific method ('método universal de las ciencias'), consists in patient, careful empirical research and cautious judgment and evaluation of the data observed. This would not provide, as his contemporary Francis BACON (§§3, 6) thought, a key to knowledge of the world, but it would allow us to obtain the best information available. In advancing this limited or constructive view of science, Sanches was the first Renaissance sceptic to conceive of science in its modern form, as the useful activity concerning the study of nature that remained after one had given up the search for absolutely certain knowledge of the nature of things (see SCIENTIFIC METHOD).

Unlike other Renaissance sceptics, Sanches only briefly raises the fideistic solution to sceptical difficulties, the appeal to knowledge gained by religious faith alone. This lack of a serious presentation of fideism has led José Faur (1992) to suggest that Sanches was really secretly putting forth a non-Christian message, an assertion of his ancestral Jewish faith rather than the Christianity of the other fideists. Faur shows that Sanches' use of biblical material, together with his knowledge of early Jewish non-biblical literature could be taken to suggest that he was indicating his real beliefs. However, the fact that two of his sons became priests may be more indicative of Sanches' actual views.

4 Influence

Sanches had a good deal of influence in his own day and throughout the seventeenth century. *That Nothing is Known* was reissued several times up to 1665, and he is mentioned by quite a few authors, including Leibniz, who refers directly to some of Sanches' views from both *That Nothing is Known* and the letter to Clavius. People have seen possible influences on DESCARTES (§4), GASSENDI (§3), MERSENNE (§2) and SPINOZA (§8), among others. However, in general it is hard to determine his exact influence as distinct from that of Montaigne, Sextus Empiricus, Cicero, Charron, and other available sceptical sources that were read by most intellectuals of the time.

See also: MONTAIGNE, M. DE §§2–3; SCEPTICISM §1; SCEPTICISM, RENAISSANCE

List of works

Sanches, F. (c.1570–1623) *Opera philosophica* (Philosophical Works), ed. J. de Carvalho, Separata da Revista de Universidade de Coimbra 18, Coimbra,

1955; repr. 1957. (The only complete edition of Sanches' philosophical works.)

—— (1578) *Carmen de Cometa*, in J. de Carvalho (ed.) *Opera philosophica*, Coimbra, 1955. (Poetic analysis of different interpretations of the 1577 comet.)

—— (1581) *Quod nihil scitur*, ed. and trans. E. Limbrick and D.F.S. Thomson, *Franciscus Sanches: That Nothing is Known*, Cambridge: Cambridge University Press, 1989. (A systematic sceptical critique of Aristotelian epistemology; Sanches' most important work. Includes Limbrick's excellent introduction (referred to in §1).)

References and further reading

* Faur, J. (1992) *In the Shadow of History, Jews and Conversos at the Dawn of Modernity*, Albany, NY: State University of New York Press. (Referred to in §3. Chapter 6, 'Francisco Sanchez and the Quest for a New Rationality' is an attempt to see Sanches' contribution in terms of Jewish intellectual developments resulting from forced conversions.)

* Limbrick, E. and Thomson, D.F.S. (eds) (1989) *Franciscus Sanches: That Nothing is Known*, Cambridge: Cambridge University Press, 1989. (Translation of Sanches' most important work, *Quod nihil scitur*, with an extensive bibliography that includes secondary literature in Portuguese. Limbrick's introduction, referred to in §1, gives an excellent overall presentation of Sanches' life, thought and influence.)

Popkin, R.H. (1979) *The History of Scepticism from Erasmus to Spinoza*, Berkeley, CA: University of California Press. (Places Sanches in the context of the development of scepticism in the Renaissance.)

RICHARD H. POPKIN

SANCTIFICATION

Sanctification, the process of becoming holy, is closely connected to justification, although Roman Catholic and Protestant theologians differ on how closely. According to the Roman Catholic Church, sanctification takes place in justification. In justification, sins are forgiven and there is an infusion of sanctifying grace, whereby one is made just and holy; this is what it is to be sanctified. In this state of grace, one merits heaven. Nonetheless, there is room for spiritual growth in the Christian life (though this is not called sanctification, as it would be in Protestantism) because concupiscence remains and appetites are still not fully under control. Justification is the beginning of a new life (the life of grace) in which we may grow towards integrity, the proper use of appetites; moreover, the gifts of faith, hope and charity, which enable one to perform meritorious works, can also increase. The state of grace, which is the result of justification, can be lost by mortal sin, but can be fully restored through the sacrament of penance.

Protestants teach that in justification one's sins are forgiven and one is fully reconciled to God, but that one is not wholly sanctified (that is, renewed or made holy). Luther's formula that we are simul iustus et peccator *(both just and sinner) is widely accepted by Protestants. Justification is only the beginning of sanctification, which, most Protestants believe, is never completed in this life. The exceptions are Methodists and members of some holiness churches (groups that either broke away from Methodism or were influenced by it).*

1 **The influence of Eastern Orthodoxy on the Western Church**
2 **The Christian life in Roman Catholicism**
3 **Protestant views: Luther, Calvin and Wesley**
4 **Pastoral psychology and sanctification**

1 The influence of Eastern Orthodoxy on the Western Church

The Orthodox Fathers never engaged in controversies over justification and sanctification comparable to those of the Western churches. Their debates concerning humanity's salvation focused on the nature and person of Christ, that is, on what Christ must be in order to effect salvation. At the Council of Nicaea (325) it was affirmed that Jesus is fully God and fully man. At the Council of Chalcedon (451) it was made clear that Jesus is the mediator between God and humanity because Jesus has two natures, a divine one and a human one. God saves his followers through the work of Christ, which is brought to fullness by the Holy Spirit. The teachings of these two councils were accepted as definitive by both the Roman Catholic and the Protestant churches. The outlook of the Eastern Church was summarized by Saint Athanasius in his *Incarnation*: 'He was made man that we might be made divine' (ch. 54: 3). That is, human beings, while remaining human, are able through union with the crucified and risen Christ to participate in the eternal (uncreated) life of God.

The Christian life, whether Roman Catholic, Protestant or Orthodox, begins with baptism, which remits sin and enables one to participate in the death and life of the risen Christ. What distinguishes the Orthodox Church is its focus on the Christian life as the increase of one's participation in the uncreated life of God; this process is referred to as *theiopoiesis*

(divinization). The liturgy of the Eucharist (Holy Communion) is an eschatological event at which the present world and the world to come intersect. The congregation, in the presence of the risen Christ, the prophets, the apostles and the saints, has a foretaste of heaven. The Eucharist is often referred to as the 'medicine of immortality', whereby one is increasingly healed of the effects of original sin, which introduced death into human life, and is increasingly enabled to participate in the eternal life of God.

Eastern Orthodoxy deeply influenced the spirituality of the Western churches, largely through the ascetic practices of the Desert Fathers and Mothers (from the third century) and the mystical theology of Pseudo-Dionysius, who was active in the sixth century. Evagrius of Pontus summarized their ascetic practices in his *Praktikos* (Practice). He distinguished eight deadly thoughts (gluttony, lust, avarice, anger, sadness, sloth, vainglory and pride), which are said to assail every Christian and which must be mastered so that one may obey Christ's commandment to love one's neighbour. Reading, vigils, prayer, almsgiving and fasting are particularly recommended as effective remedies for the passions they arouse. Once sufficiently freed of the distractions of the eight deadly thoughts by the development of *apatheia* (understood as purity of heart, and not as lack of feeling, as in Stoicism), Christians are able to practise the contemplative life. Contemplative prayer in particular increases knowledge and love of God, culminating, as Paul taught, in knowledge of God face to face (1 Corinthians 13: 12). The sixth-century Pope Gregory the Great, through his knowledge of John Cassian, a disciple of Evagrius and other Desert monastics, recast Eastern ascetic teaching for the Western Church; the eight deadly thoughts, for instance, became the seven deadly sins (lust, gluttony, avarice, sloth, wrath, envy and pride).

The teachings of Pseudo-Dionysius, first through Maximus the Confessor and then, from the tenth century, through a direct knowledge of some of his writings, brought into the Western Church the practice of an elaborate spiritual ascent into God, said to culminate for a very few Christians in mystical ecstasy. Some of the most important Western spiritual teachers that Pseudo-Dionysius influenced are Bernard of Clairvaux, Bonaventure (§§2–3) and Saint John of the Cross. John particularly stressed Pseudo-Dionysius' *via negativa,* in which all images and concepts of God are set aside as inadequate, and the 'dark nights' of purification, which enable one to ascend into mystical union with God. The most influential alternative to this speculative spirituality ('speculative' meaning knowledge of God as reflected in God's works and culminating in direct mystical knowledge of God) is the practical spirituality of Ignatius Loyola's masterpiece, *Spiritual Exercises*. Its practical nature lies in the stress on the discernment and pursuit of God's will for one's individual life.

All Christian spirituality uses the distinction between the active or ascetic life, and the contemplative life (see ASCETICISM). Thanks mostly to the influence of Pseudo-Dionysius, the contemplative life is usually subdivided, yielding the famous threefold way: the purgative way of ascetic practices, and the illuminative and unitive ways of contemplation. The way of illumination is an indirect knowledge of God through contemplation of God's two books: the book of nature, which reflects God's power, wisdom and goodness, and the book of Scripture, usually interpreted allegorically for hidden spiritual wisdom. The unitive way is a direct knowledge of God through such practices as the *via negativa* and prayer. The thirteenth-century writer Hugh of Balma's widely used terms, beginner, proficient and perfect, more or less correspond to the threefold way (to asceticism, the illuminative way and the unitive way respectively).

2   The Christian life in Roman Catholicism

The Roman Catholic Church clearly affirms that Christians grow in their participation in the divine life. Nonetheless, it placed its emphasis on the other aspect of the Christian life, namely the forgiveness of sin, which, by renewing one, puts one in a state of grace that merits heaven. The tradition of spirituality, with its stress on ascent to God, is primarily for those who have a special vocation. Even so, the central concern for all Catholics is to obey the teachings of Christ, which is possible through the infused grace of the sacraments. It is by participation in the sacraments that one grows in faith, hope and charity, and achieves greater integrity. But since one is not granted the gift of stability in the restoration from the Fall, there is a continuing concern to preserve the state of grace and to restore it whenever it is lost by mortal sin.

There is a strong emphasis on the objective character of the sanctifying grace that justifies. In justification, one is actually renewed and is just or holy regardless of one's psychological state. That is, one does not have to experience grace in order for sanctifying grace actually to have changed one's state from that of sin to that of grace. This affects pastoral practice, since there is a marked distance between the ontological condition of holiness and the actual experience of Christians. Although there is no theoretical incompatibility between doctrinal teaching on justification, spirituality and pastoral practice, the strong interpersonal nature of the Christian life with God (made possible by the indwelling of Christ) is in

practice in danger of being neglected by the stress on sanctifying grace as objective, since the personal appropriation, however desirable, is not necessary.

In justification, one is just or holy by the standard of justice, because one has been actually renewed and made innocent. In the state of grace, one is able to perform actions which are meritorious (worthy of reward) according to the standard of justice; this is called condign merit. By good deeds, one may also merit an increase of grace in this life and a greater glory (degree of beatitude) in the next life (see HEAVEN §3); this is called congruous merit and, in contrast to condign merit, stems from divine liberality rather than justice. One may congruously merit special graces for oneself and for others, including the sanctifying grace of justification. These views on merit underlie the propriety of prayer for others.

3   Protestant views: Luther, Calvin and Wesley

Martin LUTHER has been widely misunderstood by both Roman Catholics and Protestants (including Lutherans) as teaching a view of justification that has no place whatsoever for sanctification. For Luther, in justification we are forgiven because Christ's righteousness is imputed to us. But unlike Roman Catholic teaching, we are not made holy or sanctified. Luther formulated his view as *simul iustus et peccator* (both just and sinner). But in theological polemics, it is little noticed that Luther held that justification is the beginning of sanctification, the beginning of the reception of God's promise in Christ to establish his kingdom or rule in his followers. The coming of this eschatological fact into their lives is how Luther conceived of sanctification. Although they are forever inadequate according to the law (that is, they remain sinners because they are incapable of making themselves acceptable to God by their efforts), God in Christ makes life with God and in God possible. Whenever and wherever that life manifests itself, sanctification occurs. One has regeneration of one's life, with the eschatological reality of God's kingdom breaking into one's life.

Luther's conceptions of ordinary occupations as genuine spiritual vocations (with the rejection of the monastic or priestly life as spiritually superior) and justification by faith are hallmarks of Protestantism, marking it as sharply different from ancient and medieval conceptions of the Christian life. Furthermore, in order to avoid any suggestion that righteousness (justice, holiness) could be achieved by one's own efforts (by works), Luther also rejected any scheme of stages of growth for achieving sanctification. For Luther, there is no path or course that describes the Christian journey, a position which would include a rejection of the pre-eminently influential Protestant account, Bunyan's *The Pilgrim's Progress*. Yet Luther did not repudiate spirituality entirely, despite the rejection of stages of growth and of monasticism. On the contrary, he deeply admired *Theologica germanica*, an anonymous classic of spirituality written in the fourteenth century, and wrote that, next to the Bible and Augustine, he had read nothing more helpful and true.

John CALVIN (§4) was in essential agreement with Luther, but unlike Luther he wrote extensively on sanctification. For Calvin, the issue of one's salvation is firmly and completely settled with justification. Although one's primary concern is to discern and do the will of God, one is still under the power of sin, with a will that resists God's will. Sanctification consists of the conflict between sin and grace, flesh and spirit, which lasts until the will becomes wholly subject to Christ's will. One then becomes free of the tyranny of sin and finds perfect freedom. In this struggle to become holy, one realizes how much one is utterly dependent on God's mercy. So although one can do good deeds, they are acceptable to God only because of God's liberality (this corresponds to 'congruous merit' rather than 'condign merit' in Roman Catholic theology). Calvin makes it clear that sanctification (actual regeneration and holiness), no less than justification (the gift of Christ's right-eousness), comes to the believer from Christ. The two are distinct, but are not to be disjoined, since they both result from one's union with Christ.

Both Luther and Calvin agreed that, even though one is justified apart from the law, there are three valid uses of the law: enforced by the civil government, it permits civil society; it convicts one of sin; and it guides the life of believers in discernment of God's will. Both were opposed to an antinomianism in which it was inferred that since one is saved by faith alone, the law is not binding; however, both believed that through justification, one is motivated by love and not by compulsion to obey the law. The extensive debate between Lutherans and Calvinists over the third use of the law appears in retrospect to have been based on misunderstanding.

Unlike Luther and Calvin, John Wesley agreed with the Roman Catholic view that the gift of salvation can subsequently be lost. However, his main concern was the completion of salvation by achieving freedom from all effects of the Fall ('entire sanctification'). For him, the sanctification described by Roman Catholic teaching is not entire because one is not freed from all effects of sin (concupiscence remains), nor does one achieve perfection. It is difficult to tell what Wesley meant by the perfection he believed attainable in this life, but this belief divides him from Luther and Calvin, and Roman Catholicism. He clearly thought that there is an experience of sanctification in which there is a total death to sin and a complete renewal of the image of God. His various qualifications concerning the nature of perfection did not, however, weaken the Methodist stress that one must press on towards perfection in this life. Much of the social activism of Methodism sprang from this stress.

4 Pastoral psychology and sanctification

The nineteenth-century camp meeting revivals, with their stress on a 'born again' experience led Horace Bushnell to champion Christian nurture as the normal path to godliness. Through his reliance on modern pedagogical principles, including elementary psychology, he became the father of the Christian education movement. In Protestantism, Christian education continues to be the primary means for promoting spiritual growth.

In post-war years, the psychology of Sigmund Freud and, to a lesser extent, that of Carl Jung was adapted for the purposes of understanding and promoting spiritual development, especially in US Protestantism. It is generally held that the pastoral psychology movement has become increasingly in danger of complete secularization, losing a transcendent dimension. Since about 1970, this has provoked a marked resurgence of interest in spiritual classics, because of their explicit stress on the work of the Holy Spirit in renewal, as well as new attempts to integrate spirituality and psychology.

See also: GRACE; JUSTIFICATION, RELIGIOUS

References and further reading

* Anon. (14th century) *Theologica germanica*, New York: Paulist Press, 1980. (A spiritual classic that emerged from a movement known as the Friends of God.)

Aquinas, T. (1266–73) *Summa theologiae*, New York: McGraw-Hill, 1964. (A compact statement of Roman Catholic teaching on justification and sanctification; book III, section 4 is particularly useful.)

* Athanasius (*c*.335) *Incarnation*, New York: Macmillan, 1946. (A classic statement of our redemption by Christ.)

Berkouwer, G.C. (1952) *Faith and Sanctification*, Grand Rapids, MI: Eerdmans. (A major Reformed study from Calvin to Barth, with comparisons to Lutheranism.)

* Bunyan, J. (1678) *The Pilgrim's Progress from This World to That Which is to Come*, ed. J.B. Wharey,

Oxford: Clarendon Press, 1960. (The most influential Protestant treatment in the English-speaking world of the Christian life.)

* Calvin, J. (1957) *Institutes of the Christian Religion*, trans. H. Beveridge, London: James Clarke, bk III. (The most important and influential work in Reformed theology.)

* Evagrius of Pontus (c.400) *Praktikos and Chapters on Prayer*, trans. J.E. Bamberger, Spencer, MA: Cistercian Publications, 1972. (The most influential work on ascetic theology.)

Flew, R. (1934) *The Idea of Perfection in Christian Theology*, London: Oxford University Press. (Especially valuable for the account of Wesley.)

Forde, G.O. (1984) 'The Christian Life', in C.E. Braaten and R.W. Jensen (eds) *Christian Dogmatics*, Philadelphia, PA: Fortress, vol. 2. (A thorough discussion of Luther and Lutheranism on justification and sanctification.)

Imbelli, R. (1994) 'Catholic Identity after Vatican II', *Commonweal* (11 March): 12–16. (A progress report on Jozef van Beeck's theology, which seeks a new spiritual–pastoral–theological synthesis in response to Vatican II.)

* Loyola, I. (1548) *Spiritual Exercises*, New York: Paulist Press, 1991. (The major statement of a practical – in contrast to a speculative – spirituality.)

Luther, M. (1516) *Commentary on the Epistle to the Romans*, Grand Rapids, MI: Zondervan, 1954. (A major account of Luther's development of what became the Protestant doctrine of justification, with indications of his views on sanctification.)

Pseudo-Dionysius (c.500) *Theologia mystica*, West Park, NY: Holy Cross Press, 1944. (The classic account of the spiritual ascent into divine ecstasy.)

Stump, E. (1993) 'Sanctification, Hardening of the Heart, and Frankfurt's Concept of Free Will', in J.M. Fischer and M. RaVizza (eds) *Perspectives on Moral Responsibility*, Ithaca, NY: Cornell University Press. (An account of how a good God could sanctify some people and not others, and how sanctification is compatible with free will.)

Veith, G.E., Jr (1985) *Reformation Spirituality*, Lewisburg, PA: Bucknell University Press. (A valuable study of sanctification, through the poetry of George Herbert.)

Wingren, G. (1957) *Luther on Vocation*, Philadelphia, PA: Muhlenberg. (A presentation of the Protestant view of the spiritual value of ordinary occupations.)

DIOGENES ALLEN

ŚAṄKARA (early 8th century)

Śaṅkara has been a highly influential figure in Hindu philosophy and religion from his lifetime (early eighth century; traditionally 788–820) to the present day. He is the most renowned teacher of nondualist (Advaita) Vedānta, which emphasizes realizing the nondual reality, Brahman, through hearing and contemplating the Upaniṣads, sacred knowledge which reveals the nature of human existence and the cosmos. Unlike many Western thinkers, who consider themselves forward-looking individuals putting forth new insights, Śaṅkara is self-consciously part of an ongoing tradition committed to scriptural exegesis. He honours prior teachers (such as Gauḍapāda), and his own writings are primarily explanatory commentaries on sacred Vedānta texts. Śaṅkara also requires certain purifying qualifications to pursue liberation, and vigorously contests other views prevailing in his time.

1 Life and works
2 Śaṅkara on Brahman
3 Qualifications for pursuing liberation
4 Śaṅkara on other Indian schools

1 Life and works

The traditional Advaitic account of the life of Śaṅkara (Śaṅkarācārya) is as follows: born a Brahman in Kaladi, South India, he was a worshipper, and reputedly an incarnation, of Śiva. Becoming a renunciant when still a youth despite his mother's wishes, he went to Banaras to study and teach. During extensive travels, he set up monasteries in the four corners of India and founded an ascetic order with ten divisions. He debated with (and often converted) scholars of other religious sects and philosophical schools, both Hindu and Buddhist. Although he is said to have died at the age of 32, his Advaita Vedānta philosophical school and the renunciant Brahmanical tradition continues, from immediate followers such as Sureśvara and Padmapāda to contemporary teacher-leaders called Śaṅkarācārya ruling most prominently at the Śṛṅgeri and Kanchipuram monasteries in South India.

Śaṅkara's primary writings include commentaries on a number of Upaniṣads (such as the Bhadārayaka, Chāndogya and Taittirīya), Bādarāyaṇa's *Brahmasūtra* (concise aphorisms on Brahman which attempt to explain and show the coherence of Upaniṣadic teachings while refuting other views), and the *Bhagavad Gītā*, the immensely influential poetic discourse found in the *Mahābhārata*. He also wrote an independent philosophical work, the *Upadeśasāhasrī*, and is said to have composed many devotional hymns (*stotras*) to Śiva, though his authorship of these writings is contested by many scholars.

2 Śaṅkara on Brahman

Throughout his writings, most notably in comments on *Brahmasūtra* 1.1.1–4, Śaṅkara holds that Vedāntic texts teach that the basis of reality is nondual Brahman, which is eternal, qualityless (*nirguṇa*) and pervades everything without limitation. It is the single, efficient, substantial and conscious cause of existence. Brahman is identical with our true un-qualified and unchanging self (*ātman*), which is immediate, self-luminous and distinctionless consciousness. The *ātman* is 'intuited' as that pure subject prior to all particular contents of consciousness (and free from the limitations which condition waking and dreaming); it is sometimes called *sākṣin*, the self-luminous and unconditioned but passive witness. The self is undeniable and self-authenticating; one who doubts it in fact presupposes it.

Śaṅkara's Advaita teaches that human beings normally suffer bondage to transmigratory existence (*saṃsāra*), which requires experiencing the fruits of all one's actions (karma) and thus repeatedly entering the cycle of rebirth. The delusive manifestation of diversity and change (*māyā*) appears due to beginningless ignorance (*avidyā*), which is the superimposition (*adhyāsa*) of illusory phenomenal diversity on *nirguṇa* Brahman. Brahman is, however, unaffected by the superimposition of objects and conditions upon it. The knowledge that *ātman* and Brahman are identical removes ignorance, and this removal brings liberation (*mokṣa*) from *saṃsāra*. Liberation is knowing *and* being Brahman, our original nature. Liberation has no beginning, end or degrees; it is not a place or an attainment. It is solely a change in understanding through the removal of ignorance, not a product or result of any action.

Śaṅkara's well-known introduction to the *Brahmasūtra* commentary states that ignorant beings such as ourselves have a general sense of the pure subject, nondual Brahman, but then, from the memory of a thing previously experienced elsewhere, we erroneously superimpose objective limiting conditions on Brahman, and properties of Brahman on limited, unconscious objects. We begin to identify all things as 'I/mine' or 'other', oblivious to the ultimate nondifference of subject/object and knower/known. Through this natural and eternal *adhyāsa*, we falsely suppose that we are finite and embodied agents and enjoyers (called *jīvas*), but neither *jīvas* nor the world are truly real. Śaṅkara calls the *jīva* a reflection of the self, like an image of the sun reflected in a pool of water; changes or imperfections in the reflection do not affect the source. Inquiry into Brahman is necessary and proper because Brahman is now known imperfectly, and there are many mistaken opinions about it (such as regarding it as a body, agent or momentary entity). Śaṅkara concludes that Vedānta study should be begun to remove the error of superimposition and to realize the unity of the self.

An obvious problem here is how to explain the common-sense perception of duality. Śaṅkara relies on the idea of two levels of truth, one apparent, known as practical or 'everyday' worldly activity (*vyavahāra*), and the other the higher nondual reality indicated in the Upaniṣads. Śaṅkara does not merely dismiss the everyday activity of *vyavahāra*, sphere of reasoning and experience. He claims that despite lacking ultimate reality, objects appear – thus, they are neither existent nor nonexistent. *Vyavahāra* is real as far as it goes; those in it should follow the ritual and social order according to *dharma* (though without attachment to results) to prepare properly for liberating knowledge. He often describes delusive everyday appearance as being like a rope mistakenly seen as a snake due to superimposition – the snake is never there and never different from the rope (see ERROR AND ILLUSION, INDIAN CONCEPTIONS OF §1). Still, unreal imaginings (snake, *vyavahāra*) are based on a real substratum (rope, Brahman). Śaṅkara's 'realism' also asserts that waking experience is normally true on its own terms, and dreams are mental creations less real than, and largely derived from, waking. On the other hand, both these states are shown to be false by the highest truth, and he praises deep sleep as suggestive of Brahman: luminous, serene and objectless bliss.

For Śaṅkara, then, we are always Brahman, but do not know it – just as the 'snake' is always the rope, but we realize that only after being told. Still, according to Śaṅkara, some things in the realm of ignorance, such as the Upaniṣads and wise teachers, can move us towards higher knowledge. One can in fact be liberated while living, but the knower remains in a body as long as needed to experience currently manifesting fruits of actions, as one temporarily continues trembling even after realizing the 'snake' is but a rope.

Perhaps one of Śaṅkara's strengths is that he does not feel obliged to resolve all the difficult philosophical problems his outlook raises. This is but one manifestation of his reservations about reasoning and the need for reliance on scripture. He is not deeply concerned with how diversity arises from unity, and he acknowledges that why superimposition takes place, or exactly how Brahman and ignorance are related, is ultimately inexplicable. Neither does he resolve whence ineluctable karma arises, or whether karma

459

limits Brahman. He asserts that such issues are only relevant to those caught in *vyavahāra* and cannot be understood until ignorance ends.

3 Qualifications for pursuing liberation

Śaṅkara holds that one must be qualified to attain liberation. In commenting on *Brahmasūtra* 1.1.1, he describes four personal or psychological requirements for pursuing knowledge of Brahman: discriminating between non-eternal and eternal things, detachment from enjoyments here or in the afterlife, serenity and control of mind and senses, and desire for liberation. He implicitly endorses the later formula which states that one must hear, reflect on and meditate on Vedic texts.

In addition, and contradicting modern claims of Advaitic inclusivism, Śaṅkara held that access to the Veda (the source of liberating knowledge) is externally or socially restricted. That is, in everyday reality Śaṅkara remains committed to Brahmanical orthodoxy, which stresses the caste system and the importance of Vedic duties and right action according to *dharma* as a preliminary leading to renunciation and knowledge. Since only higher-caste males can hear the Veda, no women, low-caste or outcaste men may get the proper training which brings liberation, a state that Śaṅkara generally seems to hold can only be gained as a male Brahman renunciate.

4 Śaṅkara on other Indian schools

While Brahman is one, it has many manifestations. Śaṅkara recognizes a lower Brahman 'with qualities' (*saguṇa*), often called *īśvara* ('lord'). *Īśvara* is omnipotent and omniscient, and the efficient and material cause of world appearance, creating due to motiveless play. Despite *īśvara*'s relative inferiority, Śaṅkara holds that belief in and devotion to *īśvara* is acceptable as a preliminary to, and helpful auxiliary on, the path to liberation. Worshipping a god may lead one to the path of the gods, but not to liberation; that is, it may lead to the heavens and a better rebirth as a high-caste renunciate, well-placed to pursue *mokṣa*, but it does not lead directly to the ultimate end.

Śaṅkara's Vedānta is sometimes called the later (*uttara*) Mīmāṃsā, or Exegesis (of Brahman), to differentiate it, but show its indebtedness to, earlier (*pūrva*) Mīmāṃsā (of *dharma*), which explains duties described in the ritual-oriented portions of the Veda (see MĪMĀṂSĀ). Śaṅkara repeatedly rejects the Pūrva Mīmāṃsā view that actions are necessary or sufficient to bring liberation; he argues that the works portion of the Veda, which contains injunctions about rituals and social duties, is inferior to the knowledge portion, which makes statements about Brahman. As stated earlier, release comes from knowledge of nondual Brahman alone (and this knowledge is not an action); actions cannot affect or purify the self. Performing Vedic rituals and caste duties may, like worship, lead to prosperity, increased purity or better rebirth (which make one eligible for knowledge). Still, only Brahman knowledge, eternally present and not dependent on human activity, can bring final liberation. Even yogic meditation, which stills the mind, cannot bring liberation; it is a humanly dependent action and presupposes duality.

Despite major philosophical differences with Pūrva Mīmāṃsā, Śaṅkara largely shares its commitment to textual exegesis, its modes of argumentation, and its understanding of the means of knowledge (*pramāas*). For the highest truth, Śaṅkara holds that the most important means is Vedic text (*śruti* or *āgama*), which is eternal and transcends human senses and reason. While *pramāṇas* like sense perception and reasoned inference are generally valid and legitimate in their own (duality-based) sphere, they are relevant only to the ignorant *vyavahāra*-bound being, and cannot reveal nondual Brahman on their own. Although Brahman is not directly communicable in language, even by scripture, the Vedāntic texts are vital since they inform us about Brahman and evoke an immediate intuition of it through identity statements like *tat tvam asi*, 'you (*ātman*) are that (Brahman).'

Śaṅkara's writings reveal him to be a superb debater and polemicist. He generally puts forth the opponent's view (*pūrvapakṣa*) and then counters with his response, which brings the correct conclusion (*siddhānta*). His commentaries often include critiques of other philosophical schools of his time, attempting to show Advaita's coherence and the incoherence of his opponents, particularly Sāṅkhya and the Sarvāstivāda and Vijñānavāda schools of Buddhism. He focuses on issues concerning causality. For example, Śaṅkara generally agrees with the Sāṅkhya view (called *satkāryavāda*) that an effect pre-exists in a cause (like a pot is 'in' a lump of clay); otherwise, events could happen randomly and anything could arise anywhere. However, unlike Sāṅkhya, Śaṅkara holds that change in form is not real transformation, but only appearance; that is, the unchanging cause (Brahman, clay) merely appears as an effect (*māyā*, pot), and is unaffected by the latter's impurities (see CAUSATION, INDIAN THEORIES OF §§3–4; SĀṄKHYA §5).

Later schools, within and outside Vedānta, engage extensively with Śaṅkara's ideas (see RĀMĀNUJA; MADHVA). There are also many modern interpreters of Śaṅkara's Advaita; some, such as Swami Vivekananda and Sarvepalli RADHAKRISHNAN, have been influenced by Western thought, and claim Śaṅkara as an ecumenicist, reformer and 'philosopher' (see RAMAKRISHNA MOVEMENT). While it should be acknowledged that great thinkers allow for many readings, readers should be wary of how some modernize Śaṅkara's views to fit the temper of other times.

See also: BRAHMAN; MONISM, INDIAN; VEDĀNTA

List of works

Śaṅkara (early 8th century) *Brahmasūtrabhāṣya*, in G.F.W. Thibaut (trans.) *The Vedānta Sūtras of Bādarāyaṇa with the Commentary of Śaṃkara*, Sacred Books of the East 34, 38, New York:EDover, repr. 1962; trans. Swami Gambhirananda, *Brahma-sūtrabhāṣya of Śrī Śaṃkarācārya*, Calcutta: Advaita Ashrama, 1965. (Thibaut's is the standard translation, with a good introduction comparing Śaṅkara's and Rāmānuja's commentaries; however, Gambhir-ananda's largely accurate translation is more lucid than Thibaut's.)

—— (early 8th century) *Upadeśasāhasrī*, ed. and trans. Sengaku Mayeda, *A Thousand Teachings (The Upadeśasāhasrī of Śaṃkara)*, Tokyo: University of Tokyo Press, 1979; Albany, NY: State University of New York Press, 1992. (A translation of Śaṅkara's major independent work with an introduction to his thought.)

References and further reading

Clooney, F.X. (1993) *Theology After Vedanta*, Albany, NY: State University of New York Press. (Includes an exceptionally informative close reading of Śaṅkara's *Brahmasūtrabhāṣya*.)
Pande, G.C. (1994) *Life and Thought of Saṃkarācārya*, Delhi: Motilal Banarsidass. (Includes much historical context and uses a wide variety of sources, but is sometimes insufficiently analytical.)
Potter, K.H. (ed.) (1981) *Encyclopedia of Indian Philosophies*, vol. 3, *Advaita Vedānta up to Śaṅkara and his Pupils*, Princeton, NJ: Princeton University Press. (Includes summaries of Śaṅkara's works and a thorough introduction to Advaita philosophy.)

ANDREW O. FORT

SĀNKHYA

Considered one of the oldest classical Hindu schools by Indian tradition, Sāṅkhya is most famous in Indian philosophy for its atheism, its dualist model of puruṣa *(passive, individual consciousness) and* prakṛti *(non-conscious, cognitive-sentient body) and its theory that effects pre-exist in their cause. In its classical formulation the* puruṣa-prakṛti *model is analysed into twenty-five components (*tattva*) intended to encompass entire metaphysical, cognitive, psychological, ethical and physical worlds in terms of their embodiment as individual constituents and the creative and interpretive projection of those worlds as experience by and for individuals. Both the world and the individual, in other words, are considered a phenomenological refraction and projection of the underlying and constitutive components of the conscious body.*

Falsely identifying with the cognitive and sensory components of prakṛti *(which according to orthodox Sāṅkhya performs cognitive and sentient operations, but is bereft of consciousness;* puruṣa *alone is conscious), Sāṅkhyans believe themselves to be the agents of their actions, rather than recognizing that actions are processes lacking any selfhood. Sāṅkhyans claim that liberation from the suffering of repeated rebirths can only be achieved through a profound understanding of the distinction between* puruṣa *and* prakṛti*. The latter is not abandoned after liberation, but continues to operate, observed with detachment by* puruṣa*. However, according to some versions of Sāṅkhya,* prakṛti *eventually becomes dormant. Puruṣa and* prakṛti *both are considered to be eternal and to have no beginning. Since liberation is achieved through knowledge, Sāṅkhya stresses the importance and efficacy of knowledge over ritual and other religious endeavours.*

Sāṅkhya is cognate to saṅkhyā, *meaning 'to count' or 'enumerate'. Thus Sāṅkhya seeks to enumerate the basic facts of reality so that people will understand them and find liberation. Basic Sāṅkhyan models and terms appear in some Upaniṣads and underlie important portions of the epic Mahābhārata, especially the Bhagavad Gītā and Mokṣadharma. No distinct Sāṅkhyan text prior to Īśvarakṛṣṇa's Sāṅkhyakārikā (c.350–c.450) is extant. It enumerates and explains the twenty-five components and a subsidiary list of sixty topics (*ṣaṣṭitantra*), which are then subdivided into further enumerative lists. Most of the subsequent Sāṅkhyan literature consists of commentaries and expositions of the Sāṃkhyakārikā and its ideas, which continued to be refined without major alterations well into the eighteenth century. Sāṅkhyan models strongly influenced numerous other Indian schools, including Yoga, Vedānta, Kashmir Shaivism and Buddhism.*

1   **Historical overview**
2   *Puruṣa* and *prakṛti*
3   *Buddhi*

4   Orthodox epistemology
5   Causal theory
6   Soteriology

1   Historical overview

Sāṅkhya claims origins in remote antiquity, identifying its founders with names found in the Vedas – the earliest Indian texts (c.2000–c.800 BC) – such as Kapila and Āsuri, but nothing in the early material points to these people as having particularly Sāṅkhyan views. Some Sāṅkhya texts assert that its teachings predate the Vedas. Kauṭilya's *Arthaśāstra* (c.300 BC) mentions Sāṅkhya as one of the leading teachings of the day. The epic *Mahābhārata* (c.400–200 BC) contains sections revealing a sophisticated, elaborate Sāṅkhyan system. In one section, the *Mokṣadharma*, the basic system of twenty-five components is already found, along with a twenty-six component system, adding a universal single *puruṣa* as the twenty-sixth item. This universal, cosmic *puruṣa*, or 'ultimate self', was retained in the Yoga school, which in many other respects developed parallel to Sāṅkhya. The *Mahābhārata*'s most famous section, the *Bhagavad Gītā*, not only presents a detailed discussion of early Sāṅkhya theories, but structures its characters and plot to reflect those models. Both sections, emphasizing the indispensability of knowledge, use the terms 'field' and 'knower of the field' as synonyms for *prakṛti* and *puruṣa* respectively. The Buddhist poet Aśvaghoṣa, in his *Buddhacaritam* (Life of the Buddha) (first to second century), treats Sāṅkhya thought as one of the formative teachings studied by the Buddha on his way to enlightenment, suggesting that by Aśvaghoṣa's time there already existed a developed Sāṅkhyan tradition considered ancient and influential even by its opponents.

Orthodox Sāṅkhya begins with Īśvarakṛṣṇa's *Sāṅkhyakārikā*, which synthesized centuries of conflicting Sāṅkhyan speculation. Its seventy verses (although the number varies in different commentaries) concisely presents the models, terminology, arguments and systematic configurations that were to be definitive for Sāṅkhya from that time on. Virtually every subsequent Sāṅkhya text is a commentary on either the *Sāṅkhyakārikā* or the *Sāṅkhyasūtra* (about fifteenth century). The latter itself is considered to be an expanded, reorganized version of the *Sāṅkhyakārikā*. The many dozens of commentaries written over the centuries reflect the changing concerns and growing sophistication of Indian thought. While some of the commentaries display clever strategies and great erudition, and minor points are continually being redefined and reinterpreted, the basic parameters set by Īśvarakṛṣṇa are scrupulously followed. The same stock arguments and examples invariably appear century after century in every commentary (Mainkar 1964; Raja 1963) – sometimes with embellishments – but there are no truly creative innovations to the system itself.

The earlier commentaries endeavour to deploy the latest developments in Indian epistemology and argumentative discourse to defend the statements of the *Sāṅkhyakārikā* from actual and possible objections. The later commentaries make increasing concessions to non-Sāṅkhyan ideologies, often to the point of subverting or reversing the point of distinctive Sāṅkhyan teaching while attempting to retain the terminology and basic structure established by Īśvarakṛṣṇa. While orthodox Sāṅkhya claimed individuals possessed their own distinct *puruṣa*, later commentators sought to ground this multiplicity of selves in a universal single self. Orthodox Sāṅkhya denied the existence of God, but some later commentators reinstated God, or encouraged their readers to reject Sāṅkhya's atheistic claims. These later concessions, whose most important advocates were Vācaspati Miśra (ninth to tenth century), Aniruddha (fifteenth century) and Vijñānabhikṣu (sixteenth century), were not so much efforts to change or reform the Sāṅkhya system as attempts to make Sāṅkhya palatable to contemporary audiences or promote reforms in the non-Sāṅkhyan ideologies of the day to which these commentators owed their true allegiance. They may have been emboldened by the Yoga School (whose classical text is Patañjali's *Yogasūtra*), which unlike Sāṅkhya, accepted the existence of God who was identified as the best of the *puruṣas*. Yoga also rejected the Sāṅkhyan duality of *puruṣa* and *prakṛti*, claiming instead that ultimately the latter dissolves into the former.

2   *Puruṣa* and *prakṛti*

The term *puruṣa* originally meant 'person' and is used in the *Ṛg Veda* to signify the primordial, cosmic person from whom the universe is created (*Puruṣasūkta* 10.90). As *Ṛg Veda* states, 'Two birds, inseparable companions, have found refuge in the same sheltering tree. One incessantly eats from the peepal tree; the other, not eating, just looks on' (I.24.7). This image of an inseparable dyad, one part actively engaging its appetites and appropriational desires and the other passively observing the activity of the first part, prefigures the notion of *puruṣa* and *prakṛti*.

In Sāṅkhya *puruṣa* signifies the observer, the 'witness'. *Prakṛti* includes all the cognitive, moral, psychological, emotional, sensorial and physical aspects of reality. It is often mistranslated as 'matter' or 'nature' – in non-Sāṅkhyan usage it does mean 'essential nature' – but that detracts from the heavy Sāṅkhyan stress on prakṛti's cognitive, mental, psychological and sensorial activities. Moreover, subtle and gross matter are its most derivative by-products, not its core. Only prakṛti acts. Puruṣa and prakṛti are radically different from each other, although both are considered to be eternal, without a beginning and ultimately inseparable. Every person is constituted of conjoined puruṣa-prakṛti. Misunderstanding how these two aspects function and interrelate is the root cause of all problems. Liberation arises from properly distinguishing between them such that one ceases falsely to identify with the components of prakṛti as one's self and instead correctly understands that puruṣa is a dissociated watcher of the activities of one's prakṛti.

Primordially, prakṛti is composed of three primary strands or qualities (guṇa): sattva, which is light, clear, tranquil, joyous, kind; rajas, which is passionate, moving, dynamic, agitated, angry; and tamas, which is dull, inert, dark, depressed, stupid. Everything in the universe (except puruṣa) is composed of varying proportions of these three qualities. Physical objects, mental and emotional states, moral qualities, types of food and personality, for example, are all definable according to which quality predominates. Rajas and tamas signify the inertia of motion and rest, respectively. Sattva signifies the clarity and tranquillity that comes from 'rising above' the negative properties of the other two qualities. For example, by shaking up or moving (rajas) something sedimented, depressed, stuck (tamas), it may either return to tamas (resediment) or remain dynamic (rajas), or it may purify and become sattvic. A clear and peaceful condition, if disturbed by passion or violent activity, can transform into reciprocal anger and violence, or produce stupidity, depression and stubbornness. Such dynamics can be applied to psychology, politics, physics, soteriology, or any other field. The three qualities undergo perpetual transformation, those transformations being the empirical universe. The essence of the three qualities remains unmanifest, acting as the cause of the empirical world (manifest prakṛti) which, as effect, shares the same nature as its cause. Sāṅkhyakārikā characterizes their function thus: sattva is illuminating, rajas is activating or unfolding and tamas imposes limitations and restrictions. They are inseparable, like the wick, oil and flame of a lamp (tamas, rajas and sattva, respectively). Sattva and tamas are comparable to the Chinese principles of yang and yin, with rajas as the catalyst and dynamic agent that keeps the other two active.

Orthodox Sāṅkhya analyses puruṣa-prakṛti into twenty-five fundamental components. One is puruṣa; the remaining twenty-four are aspects of prakṛti, each a further development or transformation of the three qualities. These twenty-five components account for the totality of the universe, as well as the components of each individual. The second component consists of the three qualities taken together, also called 'fundamental prakṛti' and the 'unmanifest'. The remaining components, lumped together as the 'manifest' are all formed from combinations of these three. The third of these components is known as buddhi which represents reflective discernment and discrimination. Puruṣa is most directly connected to buddhi through which it is aware of the activities of prakṛti. It is buddhi's task to distinguish effectively between puruṣa and prakṛti. Ahaṃkāra, the fourth component, is literally the 'I-maker' or 'the constructor of the "I am"'. The 'I-maker' refracts the three qualities to generate the sensorium, which it then appropriates for itself, thus constructing a sense of subjective selfhood. Thus, it interprets the activities of the three qualities in such a way that it sees itself as the agent or origin of the experience or interpretive theory. It experiences the results as 'my experience'. The intensity of its sense of self-concern disrupts and obscures buddhi's understanding of its relation with puruṣa. The fifth component is the empirical mind (manas), which interprets the sensorium and coordinates the discrete sense fields, such as audition and vision, into coherent experience. The next five components are the sense capacities, namely, hearing, touching, seeing, tasting and smelling. The eleventh to fifteenth components are the five activity capacities, such as speaking, grasping, mobility, excreting and procreating. The next five are the subtle elements, such as sound, tactility, colour, form, taste and smell. The five gross elements, ether, air, fire, water and earth, represent the final five components.

3 Buddhi

Buddhi alone among the twenty-four components of prakṛti directly interacts with puruṣa. Orthodox Sāṅkhya wishes to maintain a radical distinction between puruṣa and prakṛti, as well as a prakṛti that is fully cognitive, intellective, sensorially aware and active. At the same time it must also be nonconscious (acetana). The question of how buddhi can be rational, discerning, reflective, discriminative and cognitive and yet lacking consciousness is an interesting one. Buddhi must provide both the linkage or communication between puruṣa and prakṛti and yet generate the discernment that realizes their ultimate separation. Since Sāṅkhyan soteriology relies on *buddhi* to discern that separation, and the relation between the radically incommensurate *puruṣa* and *prakṛti* resides in the function of *buddhi*, the coherence of the entire system rests on the coherence of the notion of *buddhi*.

Prakṛti is not 'insentient', since the senses and their functions operate entirely within *prakṛti*. The five sense capacities are said to possess 'bare awareness' of their objects (see SENSE PERCEPTION, INDIAN VIEWS OF). The empirical mind is described as both a sense organ and a conceptualizer. The 'I-maker' generates the sense of subjectivity. *Buddhi* discriminates, decides, reflects and provides certainty.

Reserving conscious knowing exclusively for *puruṣa*, while assigning all cognitive, psychological and sensory activities to *prakṛti* only seems confusing, argues *Sāṅkhyakārika*. This is because we transfer mistakenly the properties of one to the other due to their proximity: *prakṛti* seems to be conscious and *puruṣa* seems to be active, but in fact they are not. Iron becomes hot when in proximity with heat, but heat is not in its nature, they argue. *Puruṣa* and *prakṛti* support each other and are compared to the symbiosis of a blind man and a lame man. In order to travel, the blind man (that is, *prakṛti*), who cannot see where he is going can carry the lame man (that is, *puruṣa*), who cannot walk but can see and direct the blind man. Since directing a blind man may be construed as an activity and the blind man must be sentient to cooperate with and be useful to the lame man, this example confuses rather than clarifies the problem.

In the later Yoga system, which also adopted a version of the twenty-five components, *puruṣa* shines a light into *buddhi* which *buddhi* then disperses throughout the rest of *prakṛti*. In other words, *puruṣa* infuses *prakṛti*. Thus the 'light' of reason, sensation and cognition in *prakṛti* is the refracted vision of *puruṣa*. Enlightenment and liberation are produced by realigning *buddhi* such that *puruṣa*'s light is reflected back into *puruṣa*, producing 'self-illumination'. This structure, however, is not entertained by Sāṅkhya, according to which *puruṣa* is passive and thus can illuminate nothing. *Sāṅkhyakārika* 33–7 explains its relation to *buddhi* in terms of a distinction between the internal organs (*buddhi*, the 'I-maker' and empirical mind) and the external organs (the ten capacities, that is, five sense capacities and five activity capacities). The external organs only perceive objects in the present; the internal organs can also perceive objects in the past and future. All objects perceived by the external organs are also perceived by the internal organs. Although each organ is different as each is derived from distinct differentiations of the three qualities, together 'like a lamp', they illumine *buddhi* for the sake of *puruṣa*. This is so *buddhi* can provide *puruṣa* with every experience and differentiate the subtle otherness between *puruṣa* and *prakṛti*. Thus, *Buddhi*, both causes *puruṣa*'s suffering and effects its liberation (see AWARENESS IN INDIAN THOUGHT).

4 Orthodox epistemology

Sāṅkhyakārikā, like Buddhism and many other Indian schools, claims that the root problem as experienced is a profound sense of dis-ease and dissatisfaction (*duḥkha*) that can only be cured by knowledge. Some commentaries say this knowledge concerns the difference between *puruṣa* and *buddhi*; some say it is knowing the twenty-five components or the list of sixty topics. Sacrifice, ritual and scriptural remedies, the usual methods for an orthodox Hindu, are declared ineffective for anything except temporary rebirth in heaven. Moreover, those methods cannot guarantee success (for example, even authentic prayer and religious observance may not cure barrenness) and they often involve 'impurity' (the killing during sacrifice, the caste requirements to have intercourse with one's mate). Heavenly births and impurities both perpetuate the cycle of life and death rather than resolving it. Like Buddhists, Sāṅkhyans consider existence in any realm into which one is reborn, whether human, or heavenly, to be transitory.

Sāṅkhya accepts three means of acquiring knowledge: perception, inference and reliable testimony. Descriptions of all three vary. Among Īśvarakṛṣṇa's predecessors, Vārṣagaṇya (*c*.300–*c*.100 BC) reportedly defined perception as the function of sense organs; Vindhyavāsin (*c*.400–*c*.300 BC) added that valid perception was devoid of mental or linguistic construction. Īśvarakṛṣṇa added that perception ascertains specific and definite objects. The *Yuktidīpikā*, one of the fullest and most sophisticated of the commentaries on *Sāṅkhyakārika*, further asserts that the instrumentality of perception (that is, the *pramāṇa*) is located in *buddhi*, but its results occur in *puruṣa*.

The discussions of inference also vary across the commentaries, reflecting developments in Indian logic (see INFERENCE, INDIAN THEORIES OF). *Sāṅkhyakārikā* cryptically states that inference is threefold, based on a mark and its antecedent mark. The *Sāṅkhyavṛtti* (author and date unknown) describes the three types of inference as inferring from what precedes, for example, imminent rain from storm clouds; inferring the whole from a part, for example, inferring all sea water is salty by tasting one drop; and generalization, for example, inferring that because one tree is in bloom others must be likewise. The *Suvarṇasaptati*, a *Sāṅkhyakārikā* commentary that only survives in a

Chinese translation made by Paramārtha in the sixth century, states that inference is dependent on perception. It redefines the three types in the following terms: inference from what precedes means to infer an effect from the perception of a cause, that is, rain from a black cloud; inferring the whole from the part means to infer a cause from the perception of an effect, such as previous rain from a flood; and examples for generalization are self-evident. Gauḍapāda (sixth century) in his commentary *Sāṅkhyakārikābhāṣya*, for 'generalization' or 'general correlation' gives as an example seeing someone first in one place and then another, which denotes movement although the moving itself may not have been perceived.

This last example is important as orthodox Sāṅkhya argues that merely because something is not perceived, this does not mean that it does not exist, as when one knows the Himalayas have a top without actually seeing it. Imperceptibles may be proven to exist through inference. Since Sāṅkhyans are atheists, it is not God whose existence they are trying to prove but rather *puruṣa* and unmanifest *prakṛti*. *Sāṅkhyakārikā* 8 states that *prakṛti* is too subtle to be perceived, but it is 'perceived through its effects'. Sāṅkhyan arguments for the knowability of imperceptibles by means of inference are disappointing since they fail to distinguish between what is not perceived but in principle perceptible, and what is genuinely imperceptible. All their examples address the former variety. Even when the *Yuktidīpikā* records this objection from a Buddhist, its response continues to ignore the distinction.

The most repeated 'proof' for the existence of *puruṣa* is a questionable argument from design (for example, *Sāṅkhyakārikā* 17). It states that the body, or *prakṛti*, like a bed, is composite in nature (implying it was put together), therefore it must be for something other than itself. The only existent other than *prakṛti* is *puruṣa*, therefore *prakṛti* and its operations must be for the benefit of *puruṣa*. There is a usual argument offered to prove that the imperceptible unmanifested three qualities are the cause of the manifest world. It is that an effect must be of the same nature as its cause and the effects of the three qualities are observable everywhere in the manifest world, as everything can be seen as varying proportions of the three qualities. This is illustrated by an analogy of cloth and thread. Thread when woven becomes cloth, although in nature there is no difference between thread and cloth. Since for the Sāṅkhyans the qualities function as material causes as well as efficient causes, they were satisfied with this argument, although the thread does not transform the manner posited of *prakṛti*. The *Yuktidīpikā* states that

fundamental *prakṛti*, because it is too subtle lacks the 'function of movement', but instead has the 'function of transformation'. Transformation, it says, is when an object obtains new qualities without deviating from its essence. An example might be found in the way a piece of black *palāśa* wood becomes yellow because of exposure to heat and yet never stops being *palāśa* wood. However, the change from threads to cloth is certainly not a transformation in this sense.

The *Yuktidīpikā* describes the ten factors that constitute logical proof. These include five psychological 'conditions for an inference': desire to know, doubt, purpose, examining alternative possibilities, removal of doubts; and the five parts of an actual syllogism: thesis, reason, example, application and conclusion. The *Māṭharavṛtti*, another *Sāṅkhyakārikā* commentary, discusses the later Indian three- and five-part syllogisms in a manner consistent with their explication in Nyāya and Buddhism.

As for testimony or reliable authority, like most Hindu schools Sāṅkhya accepts scripture and the testimony of a reliable person as valid means to knowledge. The *Yuktidīpikā*, for example, asserts that the legendary ancient preceptors of Sāṅkhya, such as Pañcaśikha (mentioned in the *Mahābhārata*), actually perceived the effect in the cause so that the Sāṅkhyan causal theory rests on their authority (see TESTIMONY IN INDIAN PHILOSOPHY).

5 Causal theory

Sāṅkhyakārikā holds that the effect pre-exists in the cause (*satkāryavāda*) in a latent or potential state, arguing that since something cannot arise from nothing, the effect must pre-exist. It further claims that all effects rely on a material cause. Things do not arise indiscriminately from just anything: certain types of causes produce certain types of effect, for example, cows do not give birth to puppies. Something can only produce what it is capable of producing and a producer can only produce what is capable of being produced; the nature of the cause is in the effect. The same text says elsewhere that all manifest things must have a single ultimate cause to avoid an infinite regress of causes and effects. This ultimate cause is *prakṛti*.

Other causal notions are found in the commentaries. Gauḍapāda's commentary states that each of the three qualities produces conditions conducive to the other two, as well as to itself: 'thus *sattva*, like a beautiful woman, is a joy to her husband, a trial to her co-wives and arouses passion in other men' (*sattva*, *tamas* and *rajas*, respectively). The *Sāṅkhyasaptativṛtti* discusses two types of cause: productive causes, which entail fundamental *prakṛti*, *buddhi* , the 'I-maker' and the subtle elements and cognitive causes, which includes five types of misconception, twenty-eight types of dysfunction (of the sense and activity capacities, mind and *buddhi*), nine contentments, eight types of attainment and the cognitive constructions of the eight predispositions.

There are also various discussions on material, efficient and instrumental causes, but these are merely adopted from other Indian schools. Sāṅkhya seemed more interested in specific causal sequences and correlations between its various enumerated lists than in an elaborate theory of causality itself. The *Yuktidīpikā* criticizes Buddhist 'momentariness' and the causal theories of Vaiśeṣika and Nyāya, but the arguments shed little light on causal theory in general (see CAUSATION, INDIAN THEORIES OF).

6 Soteriology

Sāṅkhyakārikā states that the purpose for which the experiential world is created by the conjoining of *puruṣa* and *prakṛti* is so that the former can 'see' the latter, and the latter can liberate or isolate the former. Everything *prakṛti* does, she does for the liberation of *puruṣa*: 'just as unaware milk operates as an efficient cause to nourish a calf, so does *prakṛti* operate as an efficient cause for the liberation of *puruṣa*' (*Sāṅkhyakārikā* 57). As a dancer stops dancing once the audience has seen the performance, so does *prakṛti* stop after having illumined *puruṣa*. She, like a self-sacrificing mother, does everything for the sake of *puruṣa*, while *puruṣa* lends no assistance whatsoever.

The *Sāṅkhyasaptativṛtti* declares that *buddhi* enlightens and attains liberation for *puruṣa*. Critics of Sāṅkhya have been quick to point out that *puruṣa* is defined in *Sāṅkhyakārikā* 19 as inherently liberated and indifferent to pain and pleasure, thus it should be in no need of liberation. Sāṅkhya's response to this criticism again hinges on *buddhi*, but with an additional notion known as the 'predispositions' (*bhāva*). The predispositions that bind and liberate are classified into three types and into eight types: the three are innate, natural and acquired; the eight are *dharma* (meritorious action), which leads to rebirth in a higher life, adharma (demerit), which leads to lower births, knowledge, which leads to liberation, ignorance leading to bondage, detachment leading to dissociation from the activities of *prakṛti*, attachment producing the cycle of birth and death, power conducive to controlling circumstances and impotence leading to loss of control. Innateness, acquisition, detachment leading to dissociation from activities of *prakṛti* and power conducive to controlling forces are considered sattvic; their opposites are considered tamasic.

The *Sāṅkhyasaptativṛtti* defines the innate predispositions as *dharma*, knowledge, detachment and power; the natural predispositions are latencies that emerge at certain times in one's life and the acquired dispositions are derived from learning the truth from a teacher. Gauḍapāda defines the innate as the eight predispositions constituting one's inherent nature; nature is the eight dispositions resulting from previous lives and the acquired is the eight predispositions obtained by hearing the truth from a teacher. He adds that the predispositions reside in *buddhi* and shape the (gross) embryo. Of the eight, knowledge alone leads to liberation. To the extent that the other seven contribute to knowledge they are conducive to liberation, but only knowledge can effect release.

The predispositions and the subtle body cannot operate without each other. The subtle body is composed of the internal organs, the ten capacities and the five subtle elements. It does not experience anything, but is the repository that holds the predispositions. Impelled by these predispositions, the subtle body is reborn from life to life until the predispositions are eliminated by knowledge. The subtle body is neither a self nor invariant since it is perpetually being modified by the predispositions influenced by the fluctuations of *prakṛtic* experience.

Puruṣa, prior to liberation, watches *prakṛti*'s transformations and suffers the pain of old age and death. But those transformations are merely an unconscious movement, a dance designed to show *puruṣa* that in its own nature it is never bound or liberated. At the next stage, while 'standing aside like a spectator, *puruṣa* views *prakṛti* who, having fulfilled her purpose, stops, turning her back on the seven forms' (v.65), that is, all the predispositions except knowledge. Although *puruṣa* and *prakṛti* are still conjoined, no new creation is generated and no new predispositions are created. By the attainment of correct knowledge, the seven predispositions cease to cause further embodiment and yet, 'like a potter's wheel that continues to spin even after the potter has stopped applying force', embodiment continues for a while. Having fulfilled its purpose, *prakṛti* ceases functioning, sometimes understood to mean that the qualities return to an equilibrium from which no further transformations emerge. Attaining separation from the body, *puruṣa* attains everlasting 'isolation' or 'freedom' (*kaivalya*).

See also: DUALISM; KARMA AND REBIRTH, INDIAN CONCEPTIONS OF; SELF, INDIAN THEORIES OF

References and further reading

Āraṇya, Svāmī Harihdrānanda (1977) *The Sāṃkhya-Sūtras of Pañcaśikha and the Sāṃkhyatattvāloka*, Delhi: Motilal Banarsidass. (Includes the Sanskrit text in Devanagri with an English translation, although the English leaves much to be desired.)

Chakravarti, P. (1951) *Origin and Development of the Sā ṃkhya System of Thought*, Calcutta: Metropolitan Printing and Publishing House Ltd. (A substantial treatment of the early sources.)

Chapple, C. (1986) *Karma and Creativity*, Albany, NY: State University of New York Press. (Deals with Sāṅkhyan models found in several texts, including the *Mahābhārata* and *Yogavāsiṣṭha* in an insightful and lucid manner.)

De Nicolas, A. (1976) *Avatāra: The Humanization of Philosophy Through the Bhagavad Gītā*, New York: Nicolas Hays. (Penetrating, original interpretation of the *Gītā* that includes a superior English translation.)

Johnston, E.H. (1937) *Early Sāṃkhya*, London: Royal Asiatic Society. (An important examination of the early Sāṅkhya tradition.)

Larson, G. (1979) *Classical Sāṃkhya*, Delhi: Motilal Banarsidass. (Includes review of earlier scholarship, an analysis of *Sāṅkhyakārikā* with romanized Sanskrit text and translation in an appendix.)

Larson, G. and Ram Shankar, B. (eds) (1987) *Sā ṃkhya: A Dualist Tradition*, Princeton, NJ: Princeton University Press. (A volume in the *Encyclopedia of Indian Philosophies*, this is the most comprehensive English work to date on the subject. Includes historical and philosophical overviews, summaries of every major text and thinker in the tradition and a careful delineation of all the major and minor terms and lists.)

* Mainkar, T.G. (trans.) (1964) *The Sāṃkhyakārikā of Īśvarakṛṣṇa with the Commentary of Gauḍapāda*, Poona: Oriental Book Agency. (An interesting translation.)

* Raja, C.K. (1963) *The Sāṃkhyakārikā of Īśvarakṛṣṇa*, India: V.V. Research Institute. (Translation with romanized Sanskrit text, includes the translator's commentary drawn from Gauḍapāda and Vacāspati Miśra.)

Takakusu, M. (1904) 'La *Sāṃkhyakārikā* étudiée à la lumière de sa version chinoise (II)' (The *Sāṅkhyakārikā* Studied in the Light of the Chinese Version), *Bulletin de l'École Française d'Extrême Orient* 4: 978–1064. (French translation of the commentary translated into Chinese by Paramārtha.)

DAN LUSTHAUS

ŚĀNTARAKṢITA *see* BUDDHISM, MĀDHYAMIKA: INDIA AND TIBET

SANTAYANA, GEORGE (1863–1952)

George Santayana was a philosopher, essayist, novelist and poet. Born in Spain, he moved to America as a child and attended Harvard, studying under William James and Josiah Royce. The philosophical world first took note of Santayana for his work in aesthetics. The Sense of Beauty (1896), his attempt to give a naturalistic account of the beautiful, remains influential. He wrote exquisitely crafted essays on literature and religion, viewing both as articulating important symbolic truths about the human condition. His mature philosophical system is a classical edifice constructed out of positions adopted from Plato and Aristotle, which he modified in light of the naturalistic insights of his beloved Lucretius and Spinoza and steeped in pessimism reminiscent of Schopenhauer. Although in close touch with the philosophical developments of his day, he always viewed human life and its problems in a calming cosmic perspective.

1　Life and works
2　Santayana's realism
3　Values and spirituality

1　Life and works

George Santayana was born Jorge Augustin Nicolas Ruiz de Santayana in Madrid, Spain, on 16 December 1863. At nine years of age, he accompanied his mother on her move to Boston. He attended Harvard University and studied with William James and Josiah Royce. Upon receiving his doctorate, he joined his former teachers on the faculty and rose to professor of philosophy. He never married, took early retirement from his teaching post and spent the last forty years of his life travelling and writing in Europe. He died in Rome on 26 September 1952.

Santayana's philosophical work is best understood in the context of the rejection of idealism at the beginning of the twentieth century. He was a realist in every significant sense of the word, believing that the world exists independently of human cognitive efforts and that not even the themes of thought we entertain depend for their reality on the human mind. Although his early, five-volume *The Life of Reason* (1905–6) has been compared to Hegel's *Phenomenology of Spirit*, the two works are fundamentally different. Santayana's philosophical edifice lacks Hegel's optimistic teleology, his devotion to totality and his structuring commitment to the power of consciousness (see HEGEL, G.W.F. §5).

Beginning around 1920, Santayana developed an ontology designed to identify fundamentally different types of being. In *Scepticism and Animal Faith* (1923) and the much-misunderstood four-volume *Realms of Being* (1927–40), he attempted to show the ways in which essence, matter, truth and spirit differ from one another and are jointly adequate to account for everything in human experience and in the world. The terms in which Santayana cast his system derive from the great Western philosophical tradition. References to essence and substance may even make his writing appear scholastic. His message, however, is thoroughly modern, even postmodern, in its rejection of essentialism, of the possibility of certainty, and of a universal hierarchy of values.

2 Santayana's realism

Scepticism is irrefutable, Santayana argues, as long as knowledge is supposed to involve certain possession of its object. Such a stringent demand as this, however, commits us to a wrong-headed standard for cognition. In the affairs of life, we neither seek nor need assurance of the highest order. Accordingly, scepticism is defeated not by its logical weaknesses but by the irrelevance of the criterion it imposes on knowledge.

Santayana issues a call for honesty in philosophy, meaning by this the refusal to believe in our reflections what we would never countenance in daily life. This opens the door to a new method of doing philosophy and to a resultant system of ideas we might call 'the philosophy of animal faith'. The method consists of taking animal action as a starting point and attempting to disentangle the beliefs implicated in it. When animals eat, for example, they take the independent existence of their food for granted. Consciously or otherwise, they believe that what they eat is not a part of themselves, that it continues to exist even after it slips from sight, that they have the power to engulf it and that doing so is beneficial. The existence of a dynamic and enduring environment consisting of differentially powerful and desirable items is thus one of the beliefs involved in and justified by activities in which we all engage. The job of philosophy is to identify these beliefs and to present them as a coherent system of common sense.

What Santayana calls 'the discovery of essence', however, is often thought to be anything but common-sensical. But criticisms of the infinity of the forms of which the realm of essence consists are based largely on misunderstandings. The essences he distinguishes do not *exist*: they are the qualities and relations, the structures and the event-types that may gain embodiment in the world. Santayana focuses on the ways in which these forms are different from the flux of physical events. As objects of thought, features of existence and terminal points of change, they remain free of the ravages of time. Their eternal self-identity renders them beacons in the turning world: they make temporal process possible without sharing its fate.

Essences are what the tradition has called 'universals'. But since every distinguishable characteristic and the object of every possible thought is an essence, generic forms and the forms of natural kinds enjoy no privilege. This disintegrates the metaphysical, epistemic and axiological prerogatives of essences: if forms set the standards for being, knowing and the good, the infinity of essences means that we must choose which of a very large number of possible norms to embrace. Santayana accepts Aristotle's idea that nature determines perfection. He thinks, however, that human nature is not defined by a single generic form, consisting instead of a vast continuum of the variously resembling forms of individuals. This leaves ample room for diversity and calls for choice in deciding which essence to enact.

Embodiment is the work of matter – a restless, mindless, impersonal force. Existence consists of a jostle of miscellaneous events: its external relations result from instantiating a shifting and arbitrary collection of essences. Santayana refers to the force of embodiment as a 'whirlwind' that creates 'an insane emphasis'. Why there is something rather than nothing and why this world exists rather than some other are, therefore, questions that admit of no intelligible answer. Existence is a surd whose ultimacy cannot be eliminated by imagining a God who confers it as an expression of benevolence.

The realm of truth consists of all the essences that have been, are being and will be actualized in the history of the world. Truth is, in this way, a complete record of the agency of matter. Even if this realm contains an infinite number of forms, there remains an infinity never actualized. For if there is a monstrously complex essence that contains the form of everything that ever happened in the history of the world, there is another, unembodied essence differing from it in a tiny particular. In addition, there is an infinity of other forms that differ from it in indefinitely many ways.

Although this view of truth makes it eternal and unchanging, Santayana thinks that its tie to time cannot be severed. All truths relate to the changing world: only those essences that matter endows with external relations are members of the realm of truth. Santayana calls the truth about a fact its 'standard, comprehensive description'. He does not mean by this, however, that it involves some actual description by a living being and thus that it belongs in the sphere of language or discourse. On the contrary, though it may be difficult to know, it is altogether objective and independent of what anyone says or thinks. It is the standard against which such thoughts are measured and is a 'description' only in the sense of being the total embodied form that may be described.

3 Values and spirituality

'Spirit' is Santayana's word for consciousness, which he thinks is a product of biological causes. The immediate objects of consciousness are the nontemporal qualities and relations that belong to the realm of essence. Animal eagerness takes the presence of such themes in consciousness as signs of surrounding things. Perception and the knowledge of the world it makes possible are, therefore, always symbolic: they involve the use of present essences in deciphering the nature and causal powers of the substances on which our weal and woe depend. Such knowledge is never certain. Continued experience can correct it and successful action serves as its final criterion. The growth of knowledge in this way expresses the interests of the animal and not the intrinsic nature of awareness.

Consciousness in its purity pays no heed to animal life and knowledge. It finds no essences more worthy of attention than any others; it enjoys the presence of every form with equal readiness. By the claim that spirit is intrinsically spiritual Santayana means that it naturally transcends the concerns of daily life to engage in the carefree contemplation of eternal forms. This is 'pure intuition', a moment of aesthetic vision in which, as he puts it, the ultimate becomes immediate.

The spiritual life is not an existence that rivals successful rational life in this world. It consists of pure intuitions that can be had anywhere because their objects may be any of the infinity of essences. The only requirement of this achievement is that we liberate ourselves from animal concern and attend to the intrinsic features of what is present, rather than to its causal or cognitive properties. This stress on the enjoyment of immediacies connects Santayana to the long history of spirituality and to such modern advocates of aesthetic immediacy as Schopenhauer (see SCHOPENHAUER, A. §5).

What generates and justifies this account of ultimate human satisfaction is Santayana's view of the impotence of consciousness. He thinks that awareness is epiphenomenal, a 'lyric cry in the midst of business'. Although a product of the human nervous system, it is ontologically different from anything material and can wield no formative power. Its only function is to light up the realm of forms and, in the process, to enable us to enjoy things under the form of eternity. The transcendence it offers has a material ground and natural limits: spirituality is a perfection of this life, not the promise of another (see EPIPHENOMENALISM).

Intuition of essence does not yield knowledge. The immediate objects of consciousness are universals and it takes animal faith to convert the colours and sounds that appear to us into signs of a surrounding world. Perception is veracious when the direct object of mind is an apt symbol of the features and movements of matter. This critical realism sees the identity of the essence we intuit with the essence embodied as a limiting case of knowledge; it is not necessary for cognition, we can probably not achieve it, and even if we did, we could have no valid evidence of it. There is little need of literal knowledge so long as the symbols we use help us live successfully.

Santayana's conviction that one's good is determined by one's nature is not enough to lead him back to Greek virtue ethics. He rejects the tidy universality that imposes a single perfection on all humans or even on all the members of a community. Working on the assumption that the role of the moral philosopher is to understand, not to condemn, he insists on the internal justification of every coherent life and unified set of values. The personal good is relative to the nature of the individual and the social good to the natures with which a community endows its members. The great problems of human life derive not from wickedness but from the clash of incompatible commitments, from internal confusion about the good and from the militancy that attempts to impose alien values.

By the time of his death, the loss of interest in systematic philosophy fostered by logical empiricism sent Santayana's popularity into decline. But the last two decades of the twentieth century witnessed the rediscovery of his thought. He is valued not only for his sharp insights, but also for his tolerant understanding of the varieties of human perfection. His naturalistic ontology is strikingly contemporary and his realism can serve as a welcome counterweight to prevailing historicist and constructivist positions. His categories offer a sensible and unified picture of the world, along with an account of human life that is free of illusions. His greatest contribution may be the way in which he combined an uncompromising naturalism with the highest demands of spirituality.

See also: SPAIN, PHILOSOPHY IN §8

List of works

Santayana, G. (1896) *The Sense of Beauty*, New York: Charles Scribner's Sons; New Critical Edition, ed. W. Holzberger and H. Saatkamp, Cambridge, MA: MIT Press, 1988. (Naturalistic aesthetics, arguing that beauty is objectified pleasure.)

—— (1900) *Interpretations of Poetry and Religion*, New York: Charles Scribner's Sons; New Critical Edition, ed. W. Holzberger and H. Saatkamp, Cambridge, MA: MIT Press, 1990. (Literature and religion as symbolic of the struggles of the human spirit.)

—— (1905–6) *The Life of Reason*, New York: Charles Scribner's Sons, 5 vols. (Elegant account of the development of human ideas and institutions.)

—— (1913) *Winds of Doctrine*, New York: Charles Scribner's Sons. (Contains important essays on Bergson, Russell and others.)

—— (1923) *Scepticism and Animal Faith*, New York: Charles Scribner's Sons. (Central text for understanding Santayana's relation to scepticism and his philosophy of animal faith.)

—— (1927–40) *Realms of Being*, New York: Charles Scribner's Sons, 4 vols. (Full development of Santayana's mature ontology.)

—— (1936) *Obiter Scripta: Lectures, Essays, and Reviews*, New York: Charles Scribner's Sons. (Philosophical and literary essays.)

—— (1946) *The Idea of Christ in the Gospels*, New York: Charles Scribner's Sons. (Naturalistic interpretation of the Gospels.)

—— (1951) *Dominations and Powers*, New York: Charles Scribner's Sons; New Critical Edition, ed. J. McCormick, New Brunswick, NJ: Transaction, 1995. (Santayana's ideas on social and political life.)

—— (1969) *Physical Order and Moral Liberty*, ed. J. Lachs and S. Lachs, Nashville, TN: Vanderbilt University Press. (Selections from Santayana's unpublished manuscripts.)

References and further reading

Arnett, W.E. (1984) *Santayana and the Sense of Beauty*, Magnolia, MA: Peter Smith. (Presents Santayana as a philosopher of disillusionment.)

Jones, J. and Saatkamp H. (1982) *George Santayana: A Bibliographical Checklist, 1880–1980*, Bowling Green, OH: Philosophy Documentation Center. (Exhaustive listing of works on Santayana.)

Kerr-Lawson, A. and Saatkamp, H. (eds) *Overheard in Seville*, College Station, TX: Texas A&M University. (Journal devoted to Santayana studies.)

Lachs, J. (1988) *George Santayana*, New York; Macmillan. (Introduction to Santayana's system of philosophy.)

Leitz, R.C. (ed.) (1991) *Critical Essays on George Santayana*, New York: Macmillan. (Essays on Santayana as literary artist.)

Levinson, H. (1992) *Santayana, Pragmatism, and the Spiritual Life*, Chapel Hill, NC: University of North Carolina Press. (Lively discussion of Santayana's moral and political views.)

McCormack, J. (1988) *George Santayana: A Biography*, New York: Paragon House. (Detailed but controversial biography.)

Singer, B. (1970) *A Rational Society*, Cleveland, OH: The Press of Case Western Reserve University. (Perceptive account of Santayana's social and political views.)

Sprigge, T.L.S. (1995) *Santayana: An Examination of His Philosophy*, New York: Routledge, 2nd edn. (Fine assessment of Santayana's philosophical contributions.)

Woodward, A. (1988) *Living in the Eternal*, Nashville, TN: Vanderbilt University Press. (Appreciation of Santayana's spirituality.)

JOHN LACHS

SA-PAN *see* SA SKYA PAṆḌITA

SAPIR, EDWARD *see* SAPIR-WHORF HYPOTHESIS

SAPIR-WHORF HYPOTHESIS

The Sapir-Whorf Hypothesis is a widely used label for the linguistic relativity hypothesis, that is, the proposal that the particular language we speak shapes the way we think about the world. The label derives from the names of American anthropological linguists Edward Sapir and Benjamin Lee Whorf, who persuasively argued for this idea during the 1930s and 1940s – although they never actually characterized their ideas as an 'hypothesis'. In contrast to earlier European scholarship concerned with linguistic relativity, their approach was distinguished by first-hand experience with native American languages and rejection of claims for the superiority of European languages.

Early in the twentieth century, American anthropologist Franz Boas (1858–1942) inaugurated an important expansion of scientific investigation of the languages of native North America. As part of a broad critique of nineteenth-century evolutionary arguments he stressed the equal value of each language type and their independence from race and cultural level. He argued that each language necessarily represents an implicit classification of experience, that these classifications vary across languages, but that such variation probably has little effect on thought or culture.

His student Edward Sapir (1884–1939) accepted the main thrust of Boas' position but came to feel that the closely knit system of categories in a language could represent incommensurable analyses of experience with effects on speakers' conceptual view points and aesthetic interpretations. Gestalt and psychoanalytic psychology and Sapir's own literary efforts also played a role in his thinking on this issue. Sapir's concern was not with linguistic form as such (for example, whether a language uses inflections or not), nor with linguistic content or meaning as such (for example, whether a language could refer to a particular referent), but rather with the formal organization of meaning characteristic of a language, the regular ways meanings are constructed (for example, grammatical categories and patterns of semantic composition). Despite the suggestiveness of his formulation, Sapir provided few specific illustrations of the sorts of influences he had in mind.

Benjamin Lee Whorf (1897–1941), a gifted amateur linguist independently interested in these issues as they related to the nature of science, came into contact with Sapir in 1930 and began developing these views in a more systematic way. He analysed particular linguistic constructions, proposed mechanisms of influence, and provided empirical demonstrations of such influences on belief and behaviour. However, his views on this issue are known to us largely through letters, unpublished manuscripts and popular pieces, which has led to considerable debate about his actual position. In this context, the one article on this issue prepared for a professional audience must be given special weight (see Whorf 1956).

Whorf argued that each language refers to an infinite variety of experiences with a finite array of formal categories (both lexical and grammatical) by grouping experiences together as analogically 'the same' for the purposes of speech. These categories also interrelate in a coherent way, reinforcing and complementing one another, so as to constitute an overall interpretation of experience. Languages vary considerably not only in the basic distinctions they recognize, but also in the assemblage of these categories into a coherent system of reference. Thus the system of categories which each language provides to its speakers is not a common, universal system, but one peculiar to the individual language, and one which makes possible a particular 'fashion of speaking'.

But speakers tend to assume that the categories and distinctions of their language are natural, given by external reality. Further, speakers make the tacit error of assuming that elements of experience which are classed together on one or another criterion for the purposes of speech are similar in other respects as well. The crux of Whorf's argument is that these linguistic categories are used as guides in habitual thought. When speakers attempt to interpret an experience in terms of a category available in their language they automatically involve the other meanings implicit in that particular category (analogy) and in the overall configuration of categories in which it is embedded. And speakers regard these other meanings as being intrinsic to the original experience rather than a product of linguistic analogy. Thus, language does not so much blind speakers to some obvious reality, but rather it suggests associations which are not necessarily entailed by experience. Ultimately, these shaping forces affect not only everyday habitual thought but also more sophisticated philosophical and scientific activity. In the absence of another language (natural or artificial) with which to talk about experience, speakers will be unlikely to recognize the conventional nature of their linguistically-based understandings.

The ideas of Sapir and Whorf have attracted widespread attention in the humanities and social sciences. Their views have been important in leading many students into comparative linguistics and played a crucial role in giving rise to the field of psycholinguistics in the 1950s. Despite this wide currency, their views have not been subjected to much empirical research. In large part, acceptance or rejection of their proposals has had more to do with the personal and professional outlook of the investigator and the prevailing temper of the times than with any solid evidence. In particular, philosophical responses, whether sympathetic or derisive, have rarely engaged with real linguistic phenomena (that is, how languages actually differ) or with practical cognition (that is, what kinds of effects one might expect). Instead debate centres on the logical (im)-plausibility of linguistic incommensurability and determinism.

Existing empirical research on Whorf's claims has consisted primarily of tests for a relationship between lexical or grammatical categories (for example, words for colour, number marking) and experimental assessments of patterns of memory and classification.

There have also been some attacks on Whorf's particular evidence, especially his claims about the Hopi language. This empirical research remains controversial, but some results clearly support Whorf's proposals and none decisively contradicts them. Another important strand of thinking has considered whether diverse uses of language (in particular the specialized discursive forms associated with language standardization, literacy and formal education) might have effects on thinking either in their own right or by mediating the structural effects proposed by Sapir and Whorf. This research often focuses on the cognitive importance of decontextualized speech and on the nature of speakers' conscious awareness and control of language – this latter an issue of concern to Whorf himself. Direct empirical research on such possible discursive effects remains quite limited.

There is also a growing body of research exploring the historical development of Sapir and Whorf's views, including intellectual biographies, more complete collections of their works, and accounts of the relation of their views to earlier European thinkers, especially in Germany. It seems certain that they were aware of this earlier work: Boas trained in Germany, Sapir wrote a Masters paper on Herder, and both Sapir and Whorf explicitly reject Humboldt's main substantive thesis, though not by name (see HERDER, J.G.; HUMBOLDT, W. VON). However, their work is better understood, as with the rest of twentieth-century American anthropology, as an innovative departure from Europeanist views stimulated by direct first-hand contact with native American languages and cultures in a context of an emerging non-hierarchical view of culture.

See also: AUSTIN, J.L.; CASSIRER, E.; CONDILLAC, E.B. DE; DETERMINISM AND INDETERMINISM; DIDEROT, D.; HAMANN, J.G.; LANGUAGE, PHILOSOPHY OF; PUTNAM, H.; QUINE, W.V.; RADICAL TRANSLATION AND RADICAL INTERPRETATION; RELATIVISM; SEARLE, J.R.; WITTGENSTEIN, L.

List of works

Sapir, E. (1921) *Language: An Introduction to the Study of Speech*, New York: Harcourt, Brace & Co. (Classic treatment of language from an anthropological perspective; important for his early views; chapters 1, 4, 5, 10 and 11 deal with matters relevant to language and thought.)
—— (1924) 'The Grammarian and His Language', repr. in D.G. Mandelbaum (ed.) *The Selected Writings of Edward Sapir in Language, Culture,*

and Personality, Berkeley, CA: University of California Press, 150–9. (States his views on the diversity among languages as systems.)
—— (1929) 'The Status of Linguistics as a Science', repr. in D.G. Mandelbaum (ed.) *The Selected Writings of Edward Sapir in Language, Culture, and Personality*, Berkeley, CA: University of California Press, 160–6. (States his view, especially on page 162, that language differences shape a speaker's view of reality.)
—— (1931) 'Conceptual Categories in Primitive Languages', repr. in D.H. Hymes (ed.) *Language in Culture and Society: A Reader in Linguistics and Anthropology*, New York: Harper & Row, 1964, 128. (Dense, one-page summary of the shaping power of language at several levels.)
—— (1933) 'Language', repr. in D.G. Mandelbaum (ed.) *The Selected Writings of Edward Sapir in Language, Culture, and Personality*, Berkeley, CA: University of California Press, 7–32. (Important for the explicit dismissal of nineteenth-century views of the Humboldtian sort regarding the correlation of language type, such as inflectional or isolating, with cultural type or level.)
Whorf, B.L. (1956) *Language, Thought, and Reality: Selected Writings of Benjamin Lee Whorf*, ed. and intro. J. Carroll, Cambridge, MA: MIT Press. (The basic source for Whorf's writings on language and thought. Reprints 'The relation of habitual thought and behavior to language' his most important work for a professional audience (pages 134–59), several articles written for a popular audience (pages 207–70), and important unpublished manuscripts (pages 57–125). Carroll's introduction provides a brief intellectual biography and a bibliography of published and unpublished works.)

References and further reading

Aarsleff, H. (1988) 'Introduction', in W. von Humboldt, *On Language: The Diversity of Human Language-Structure and its Influence on the Mental Development of Mankind*, trans. P. Heath, Cambridge: Cambridge University Press, vii–lxv. (Useful summary of eighteenth- and nineteenth-century European views on linguistic relativity making clear en route their differences from contemporary views.)
Bertefflany, L. von (1955) 'An Essay on the Relativity of Categories', *Philosophy of Science* 22: 243–63. (Sympathetic treatment of the Sapir-Whorf hypothesis as analogous to other, commonly accepted types of incommensurability.)
Black, M. (1959) 'Linguistic Relativity: The Views of Benjamin Lee Whorf', *The Philosophical Review* 68:

228–38. (Influential article attacking Whorf's views as logically flawed.)

Boas, F. (1911) 'Introduction', *Handbook of American Indian Languages, Bureau of American Ethnology Bulletin* 40 (1): 1–83. (Classic statement of the Boasian view of language; see especially §2 on diversity among languages; various reprints available.)

Hymes, D. (1964) 'Two Types of Linguistic Relativity', in W. Bright (ed.) *Sociolinguistics, Proceedings of the UCLA Sociolinguistics Conference*, The Hague: Mouton, 114–65. (Early effort to consider the implications of work on language use or pragmatic function for Whorf's ideas.)

Gipper, H. (1972) *Gibt es ein sprachliches Relativitäts- prinzip? Untersuchungen zur Sapir-Whorf- Hypothese*, Frankfurt am Main: S. Fischer; trans. R. Pinxton, 'Is There a Linguistic Relativity Principle?', in R. Pinxton (ed.) *Universalism versus Relativism in Language and Thought*, The Hague: Mouton, 1977, 217–28. (Contemporary German view on the Sapir-Whorf hypothesis, partly reproduced in translation.)

Gumperz, J.J. and Levinson, S.C. (eds) (1996) *Rethinking Linguistic Relativity*, Cambridge: Cambridge University Press. (Collection of contempor- ary anthropological research on issues related to renewed interest in the Sapir-Whorf hypothesis. Includes a review by Lucy of approaches suggesting relativity due to differences in language use.)

Koerner, E.F.K. (1992) 'The Sapir-Whorf Hypothesis: A Preliminary History and a Bibliographic Essay', *Journal of Linguistic Anthropology* 2: 173–8. (Useful brief introduction to the various historical studies of the Sapir-Whorf tradition and its various precursors. Good bibliography.)

Lee, P. (1996) *The Whorf Theory Complex: A Critical Reconstruction*, Amsterdam: John Benjamins. (Close intellectual history of Whorf and those who have worked on his ideas; makes heavy use of archival materials; extensive bibliography.)

Lucy, J. (1992) *Language Diversity and Thought: A Reformulation of the Linguistic Relativity Hypothesis*, Cambridge: Cambridge University Press. (Close textual analysis of the views of Boas, Sapir and Whorf and a critical analytic review of subsequent empirical research. Extensive bibliogra- phy of the social science literature.)

—— (1992) *Grammatical Categories and Cognition: A Case Study of the Linguistic Relativity Hypothesis*, Cambridge: Cambridge University Press. (Outlines a method for investigating the Sapir-Whorf hypoth- esis and provides an extensive empirical investiga- tion.)

Penn, J. (1972) *Linguistic Relativity versus Innate*

Ideas: The Origins of the Sapir-Whorf Hypothesis in German Thought, The Hague: Mouton. (Traces important historical connections with earlier work.)

Rollins, P. (1972) *Benjamin Lee Whorf: Transcenden- tal Linguist*, unpublished Ph.D dissertation, Har- vard University, Cambridge, MA. (Biographical information on Whorf's intellectual interests. Volume 3 reprints some of Whorf's unpublished materials. The main arguments are reworked in *Benjamin Lee Whorf: Lost Generation Theories of Mind, Language, and Religion*, Ann Arbor, MI: University Microfilms, 1980.)

Silverstein, M. (1979) 'Language Structure and Linguistic Ideology', in P. Clyne, W. Hanks and C. Hofbauer (eds) *The Elements: A Parasession on Linguistic Units and Levels*, Chicago, IL: Chicago Linguistic Society, 193–247. (Influential extension of Whorf's arguments to questions of language use and native-speaker ideology.)

JOHN A. LUCY

SARASWATI, SWAMI DAYANAND *see* ARYA SAMAJ

SARTRE, JEAN-PAUL (1905–80)

Sartre was a philosopher of paradox: an existentialist who attempted a reconciliation with Marxism, a theorist of freedom who explored the notion of predestination. From the mid-1930s to the late-1940s, Sartre was in his 'classical' period. He explored the history of theories of imagination leading up to that of Husserl, and developed his own phenomenological account of imagination as the key to the freedom of consciousness. He analysed human emotions, arguing that emotion is a freely chosen mode of relationship to the outside world. In his major philosophical work, L'Être et le Néant (Being and Nothingness) (1943a), Sartre distinguished between consciousness and all other beings: consciousness is always at least tacitly conscious of itself, hence it is essentially 'for itself' (pour-soi) – free, mobile and spontaneous. Everything else, lacking this self-consciousness, is just what it is 'in- itself' (en-soi); it is 'solid' and lacks freedom. Consciousness is always engaged in the world of which it is conscious, and in relationships with other consciousnesses. These relationships are conflictual: they involve a battle to maintain the position of subject and to make the other into an object. This battle is inescapable.

Although Sartre was indeed a philosopher of freedom, his conception of freedom is often misunderstood. Already in Being and Nothingness *human freedom operates against a background of facticity and situation. My facticity is all the facts about myself which cannot be changed – my age, sex, class of origin, race and so on; my situation may be modified, but it still constitutes the starting point for change and roots consciousness firmly in the world. Freedom is not idealized by Sartre; it is always within a given set of circumstances, after a particular past, and against the expectations of both myself and others that I make my free choices. My personal history conditions the range of my options.*

From the 1950s onwards Sartre became increasingly politicized and was drawn to attempt a reconciliation between existentialism and Marxism. This was the aim of the Critique de la raison dialectique) *(Critique of Dialectical Reason) (1960) which recognized more fully than before the effect of historical and material conditions on individual and collective choice. An attempt to explore this interplay in action underlies both his biography of Flaubert and his own autobiography.*

1   **Background**
2   **Early philosophy**
3   ***Being and Nothingness***
4   **Literary works**
5   **Later philosophy**

1   Background

Sartre's prestige as a philosopher was at its peak, in France at least, in the late 1940s, in the aftermath of the Second World War, when a philosophy of freedom and self-determination fitted the mood of a country recently liberated from the Occupation. It was at its nadir in the late 1960s and 1970s when structuralism had discredited, temporarily, both humanism and existentialism, and proclaimed 'man' to be no more than a locus of forces traversed and indeed produced by social and linguistic structures (see STRUCTURALISM). The British analytic tradition has never had much time for the literary and dramatic aspects of existentialism and phenomenology, though some recent critics, such as Phyllis Morris (1974) and Gregory McCulloch (1994), have attempted to take Sartre seriously as a philosopher and to assess his contribution in terms more accessible to analytically trained minds.

The emotive responses tend in their different ways to distort Sartre's arguments and to focus, for

example, on one of the poles of the many paradoxes which his philosophy implies. For Sartre is indeed a philosopher of paradox – deliberately facing his readers with logically 'impossible' or self-contradictory statements in order to force them to think beyond the confines of the binary oppositions to which common sense and analytic reason have accustomed them. For example, 'Man is what he is not and is not what he is' (1943a: 97), provocatively compels the reader who perseveres to confront the difficult issues of the relationship between essence, existence and negation. 'Man is what he is not', that is to say, man is a being without an essential nature, a being who operates through negation, who cannot be identified with his past, or indeed his present self, and so 'who is not what he is'.

1940s Paris overestimated Sartre's faith in human freedom and lauded him for it; 1960s Paris made the same mistake and discarded him along with all other relics of mid-century humanism. Neither period read Sartre carefully enough to recognize the constraints and limits within which freedom was, from the outset, deemed to operate.

2   Early philosophy

Sartre's first published philosophical works were *L'Imagination* (1936a), a history of theories of imagination up to the theory of Edmund HUSSERL, and 'La Transcendance de l'ego' (*The Transcendence of the Ego*) (1936b). *The Transcendence of the Ego* shows hostility to any kind of essentialism of the self. In it Sartre argues (against Husserl) that the ego is not transcendental but transcendent, that is, it is not an inner core of being, a source of my actions, emotions and character, but rather a construct, a product of my self-image and my image in the eyes of others, of my past behaviour and feelings. Sartre maintains that consciousness is not essentially first-person but is impersonal, or at most pre-personal, and that it is characterized by intentionality, that is to say it is always directed at something other than itself. In this context Sartre positions himself in relation to the Kantian 'unity of apperception', arguing that although the 'I think' must be able to accompany all my representations, it does not always do so, at least explicitly. I may turn my attention at any moment away from what I am doing and direct it towards myself as agent, but this reflexivity is not a permanent, thetic feature of consciousness. Later, in *L'Être et le Néant* (Being and Nothingness) (1943a), Sartre claims that it is precisely this very reflexivity – the self-consciousness of consciousness – that personalizes consciousness and constitutes the human subject, but in *The Transcendence of the Ego* such a notion is absent and he is more concerned to argue against the identification of consciousness with self-hood than to explore the ways in which consciousness relates to the notion of subject.

In his *Esquisse d'une théorie des émotions* (*Sketch for a Theory of Emotions*) (1939) Sartre turns his attention to another area of human experience in order to show that this, in its turn, cannot be described in essentialist terms. Emotions, in Sartre's account, are chosen rather than caused: emotion involves a 'magical' attempt to transform reality by changing what can be changed (my own feelings) rather than what is less easily malleable, that is, the outside world. In the face of extreme danger I may faint from fear: the danger has not disappeared but I am no longer conscious of it. Sartre here takes a radical position which he maintained but modified in later years, as his recognition of the degree to which we are formed by external conditions gradually increased. He is careful to distinguish between various areas related to emotion – passion, feeling and so on. Emotion is not sustainable continuously through time, but is subject to fluctuations of intensity, and may at times be replaced by alternative feelings. In this sense too Sartre rejects essentialism: like Proust he believes in the 'intermittances of the heart': love, for example, is not a continuous emotional state, but an amalgam of affection, desire, passion, as well as, perhaps, jealousy, resentment and even occasionally hatred. Love is not the permanent compelling state we may like to imagine: it is the product of a decision and a commitment (see EMOTIONS, NATURE OF §4; EMOTIONS, PHILOSOPHY OF §4).

These two works form the grounding for Sartre's early theory of human freedom along with a second work on the imagination. In *L'Imaginaire, psychologie phénoménologique de l'imagination* (The Psychology of the Imagination) (1940) Sartre picks up the threads of Husserl's theory of imagination and develops it further by showing how phenomenological psychology works in practice. Unlike traditional empirical psychology it is not based in a positivist methodology in which evidence depends on an accumulation of examples. The phenomenological method operates through a particular type of introspection or intuition in which the phenomenologist examines a single example, or a series of examples, of the phenomenon to be analysed (here imagination) and deduces from the example the general principles and features of the phenomenon. In this way Sartre describes what he calls the 'poverty' of the image – the fact, that is, that I can never find in it any more than I have already put there. If, say, I do not know the number of columns in the Parthenon, I can count them if I look at the temple in reality; if I merely imagine the temple the number of pillars will depend not on the real building but merely on my own implicit estimate. I cannot learn anything from imagination as I can from perception. But the reverse of this 'poverty' of the imagination is its *freedom* – in imagination I am not constrained as I am in perception by the material world around me. Indeed, imagination is not merely image formation – in Sartre's account it is itself constitutive of the freedom of consciousness. Without imagination we would be 'stuck in the real', unable to escape from the present moment of time and our immediate surroundings. It is imagination that allows us to step back from our material environment and take up an (imaginary) distance from it, in Sartre's terms to 'totalize' it, to see it as a 'world' with order and pattern. In *Being and Nothingness* Sartre will also maintain that the imagination is the source of the purpose and finality we see in the world, but *The Psychology of the Imagination* concentrates rather on the different functions of imagination and image formation in the narrower sense (see IMAGERY; IMAGINATION §2).

3 *Being and Nothingness*

Being and Nothingness sets out the main philosophical tenets of the 'classical' Sartre. Being is subdivided, as it were, into two major regions – being for-itself (*l'être pour-soi*) or consciousness, and being-in-itself (*l'être en-soi*) which is everything other than consciousness, including the material world, the past, the body as organism and so on. To being-in-itself Sartre devotes no more than six of his 660 pages; there is little to be said about it other than it is, it is what it is, and it is 'in itself'. Only through the 'for-itself' of consciousness does the 'in-itself' become a world to speak of. Indeed, Sartre argues, we cannot know anything about being as it is, only about being as it appears to us. It is through consciousness that the world is endowed with temporality, spatiality and other qualities such as usefulness. This is where the imagination in its broadest sense may be seen as primary: 'imagination is the whole of consciousness as it realizes its freedom' (1940: 236). Imagination makes a world of the 'in-itself', it totalizes and 'nihilates' it. Nihilation (*néantir*) is a term that is specific to Sartre, and means not annihilation but rather the special type of negation that consciousness operates when it 'intends' an object: it differentiates the object from its surroundings and knows itself *not* to be that object. But consciousness is not alone in the world it has created from the brute 'in-itself', indeed it has not created the world individually, but rather as part of an intersubjective community. And other people, or their consciousnesses, are not an afterthought for Sartre.

Like HEIDEGGER he sees man as always already engaged in relationships with others; unlike Heidegger he sees these not in terms of *Mitsein* (Being-with), but in terms of conflict in a manner reminiscent of the account given by HEGEL of the relationship between masters and slaves. The other is in permanent competition with me. I wish to be a subject and make of the other an object, while he or she attempts to make me an object in my turn. In Sartre's account, this battle is the key to all human relationships, and not merely those which might appear conflictual, but also those of sexual desire and even love. Consciousness is engaged in a permanent struggle to maintain its freedom in the face of onslaughts from all sides.

These aspects of Sartre's early philosophy are probably the best known. Less familiar but no less significant are his accounts of the limits within which human freedom operates. The battle of consciousnesses is not disembodied, and my own body constitutes not only the condition of possibility but also one of the major constraints on my freedom. Consciousness and imagination are free, but they are free against a background of facticity and situation. Facticity in particular is rarely given due weight by exegetes of Sartre's philosophy. My facticity is all the facts about myself which cannot be changed – my age, sex, height, class of origin, race, nationality, for example. (Later Sartre comes to include in facticity more psychological elements of genetic or environmental origin.) One's situation may be modified, but it still constitutes the starting point for any change, and roots consciousness firmly in the world about it. All this means that the Sartrean philosophy of freedom is less idealized than it might at first appear. I am not free to change a whole multiplicity of aspects of my condition, and those I am free to change may not prove easy. As I live I create a self which does not bind me but which certainly makes some courses of action easier and more attractive than others. My own self-image and the image others hold of me also condition the range of possibilities open to me. I make a character for myself over the years, and though it is always open to me to act 'out of character' – after all it is a self I have constituted, not an essence I was born with – such a decision is not usually easy. Sartre describes this self-constitution in terms not so much of character as of 'project', each person having a fundamental project of being, which is not necessarily the result of a conscious decision, and possibly elaborated gradually over time. This project forms the core of a whole nexus of choices and behavioural decisions which form the totality that constitutes my self. My actions form a meaningful whole, each act relates to others before and since, and so the decision to make significant changes always comes up against resistance from already existent patterns and structures. Discussing, for example, an episode when a man gives up on a long hike declaring he is 'too tired' to continue, Sartre discusses the abandonment of the walk in terms of a project which does not put persistence in the face of setbacks at much of a premium. He 'could have acted differently, of course,' Sartre comments, 'but at what cost?' (1943a: 531). Our personal history does not eradicate our freedom, but in practice it is often easier to deny our freedom than to employ it. We hide behind the selves we have constructed, fearing change and convincing ourselves that our choices are limited. Freedom is threatening to us, it opens up a range of possibilities which we find daunting, and we flee from it in what Sartre calls 'bad faith'. Ideally we would like the positive aspect of liberty – free choice, a lack of constraints – together with the security and comfort of a fixed character or nature. The two are incompatible, and our desire to combine them is termed by Sartre a 'useless passion' (see SELF-DECEPTION, ETHICS OF §2).

In 1943, then, Sartre already sets freedom firmly against a background of constraint – constraints which arise from the features of the material world, from other people whose projects may not coincide with mine, from bodily existence, from facticity and from fear of freedom itself. Freedom is always within and starting from situation, and it is on the determinants and conditioning power of situation that Sartre increasingly focuses in his later writings.

4 Literary works

The 1940s were the period of Sartre's most prolific literary production. From *La Nausée* (Nausea) (1938) which explores the relationship of contingency and necessity in life and art through the experiences of Roquentin, Sartre moves on in the war years to a contemporary trilogy *Les Chemins de la liberté* (The Roads to Freedom) (1945–9). The trilogy (or unfinished quadrology?) portrays the lives of a varied group of Parisian intellectuals at the outbreak of war, and in particular the ways in which they hide their freedom from themselves while convincing themselves that it is their ultimate goal. Mathieu, a university academic, is the main focus for such ambivalence as he tries to find money for an abortion for his long-term mistress Marcelle.

Sartre also wrote several very successful plays in this period – *Les Mouches* (The Flies) (1943b), a wartime allegory of resistance to German occupation, which uses the Orestean myth to explore the power of human liberty in the face of oppression. *Huis Clos* (In Camera) (1944) shows the deadly consequences of conflictual human relations and self-deception in a hell comprising three characters doomed to remain together for ever in a Second Empire drawing room. *Les Mains Sales* (*Dirty Hands*, or *Crime Passionel*) (1948) debates the issues of realism and idealism, means and ends, truth, lies and political commitment in Illyria, an imaginary Communist country in Eastern Europe. This finely balanced and complex play received an unexpectedly positive response from the bourgeois press who interpreted it, against Sartre's intentions, as predominantly anti-communist. In consequence Sartre felt obliged to ban its production for about ten years.

5 Later philosophy

The increasing politicization of Sartre's postwar writing meant that he left both literature and philosophy to one side in the 1950s as he became increasingly engaged as a writer, lecturer and public figure in concrete political issues and endeavours. His next major philosophical work, the *Critique de la raison dialectique* (Critique of Dialectical Reason), did not appear until 1960 and is clearly marked by his increasing intellectual engagement with MARX. The *Critique* is an attempt to do the impossible: to reconcile existentialism and Marxism; to revivify Marxism, which Sartre believed was becoming sclerotic, by reawakening its awareness of individual and collective subjectivity; and to bring existentialism into closer contact with the material conditions of historical existence. Sartre examines social and political issues such as group action, historical change, revolution and behaviour in the face of material scarcity of resources. He modifies his radical position on the extent of human freedom by recognizing more fully than before the effect of historical and material conditions on individual and collective choice. He takes as his own the famous slogan of Engels: 'Men make history on the basis of what history has made them.' We are not pawns or cogs in a machine, nor do we simply participate in processes of internalization and externalization: we are free agents, but agents who are profoundly and inescapably situated in specific social and material conditions. Indeed Sartre later uses the (Jansenist) term 'predestination' to explain how his views differ from positivist theories of human determinism. Material conditions set up the environment in which we operate. They do not causally determine our behaviour, but they do prescribe the (limited) range of options open to us. A white bourgeois male in a prosperous suburb has a vastly wider range of choices on which to exercise his freedom than an elderly black women living in the poverty of an inner city ghetto. Both are free in the ontological sense, but their

possibilities for making use of that freedom are not comparable. And in 1960 Sartre is as concerned with the restrictions imposed on freedom by the material world as with human liberty itself.

It is this preoccupation with the absolute and yet circumscribed nature of human freedom that underpins Sartre's two last major works: his autobiography, *Les Mots* (Words) (1963), a brief and finely wrought literary masterpiece, and *L'Idiot de la famille* (The Idiot of the Family) (1971–2), a 3000-page biography of Flaubert which draws on a vast range of different disciplines. 'What can one know of a man, today?' was the question Sartre set out to answer in his account of Flaubert, and in it he synthesizes not only existentialism, phenomenology and Marxist theory and method, but also psychoanalysis, sociology, history of literature, aesthetics and anthropology. What did Flaubert make of what was made of him? Educated in a family embodying the historical conflicts of its age, second son of a doctor and expected to become a lawyer, the young Gustave Flaubert constructed a very different career for himself. Resistant to adult pressures to perform, he learned to read late (hence the *Idiot* of the title), lived in his elder brother's shadow and opted out of law school through a hysterico-epileptic crisis ('intentional' but not 'deliberate', in Sartre's terms) which made him an invalid – the 'hermit of Croisset' – and thus permitted him to live in the family home and become a writer. Sartre's account of his own choice of the same career is more succinct and more ironic: the Sartre and Schweitzer (maternal grandfather) families are not spared in the biting and witty descriptions of the 'family comedy' which made of young Jean-Paul a precocious charlatan, writing to please adults, writing for future fame – a superman author – and finally writing as a professional. The gap between choice and destiny is shown to be very small, but it has not closed. Even when analysing with cruel perspicacity his own formation, Sartre maintains the framework he set up thirty years earlier: freedom within situation, even when the situation may leave little room for manoeuvre. Subjectivity is now defined as the *décalage* or difference between the processes of internalization and externalization; liberty may be no more than the 'play' in the mechanism, but the permanent dialectic between the poles of freedom and conditioning remains untotalized.

See also: BEAUVOIR, S. DE; CAMUS, A. ; EXISTENTIALISM; EXISTENTIALIST ETHICS; MERLEAU-PONTY, M.; PHENOMENOLOGICAL MOVEMENT

List of works

Sartre, J.-P. (1936a) *L'Imagination*, Paris: Alcan; trans. F. Williams, *Imagination, a Psychological Critique*, Ann Arbor, MI: University of Michigan Press, 1962. (A history of theories of the imagination leading up to Husserl.)

—— (1936b) 'La Transcendance de l'ego, Esquisse d'une description phénoménologique', *Recherches Philosophiques* 6; repr. in *La Transcendance de l'ego, Esquisse d'une description phénoménologique*, ed. S. le Bon, Paris: Vrin, 1965; trans. F. Williams and R. Kirkpatrick, *The Transcendence of the Ego. An Existentialist Theory of Consciousness*, New York: Noonday, 1962. (A phenomenological account of the ego.)

—— (1938) *La Nausée*, Paris: Gallimard; trans. L. Alexander, *Nausea, or The Diary of Antoine Roquentin*, New York: New Directions, 1949; trans. R. Baldick, *Nausea, or The Diary of Antoine Roquentin*, Middlesex: Penguin, 1965. (Novel in diary form about the discovery by Antoine Roquentin of the contingency of existence.)

—— (1939) *Esquisse d'une théorie des émotions*, Paris: Hermann; trans. B. Frechtman, *The Emotions: Outline of a Theory*, New York: Philosophical Library, 1948; trans. P. Mairet, *Sketch for a Theory of the Emotions*, London: Methuen, 1962. (Study of the psychology of the emotions.)

—— (1940) *L'Imaginaire, psychologie phénoménologique de l'imagination*, Paris: Gallimard; trans. B. Frechtman *The Psychology of the Imagination*, New York: Philosophical Library, 1948. (A phenomenological study of imagination.)

—— (1943a) *L'Être et le Néant. Essai d'ontologie phénoménologique*, Paris: Gallimard; trans. H.E. Barnes, *Being and Nothingness: An Essay of Phenomenological Ontology*, New York: Philosophical Library, 1956; London: Methuen, 1957. (Sartre's major philosophical work: a study of the relationship between consciousness and the world, and between consciousness and other consciousnesses.)

—— (1943b) *Les Mouches*, Paris: Gallimard; repr. Paris: Livres de Poche, 1971; trans. S. Gilbert, *The Flies*, in *No Exit and Three Other Plays*, New York: Vintage Books, 1949. (Resistance play based on the Greek myth of Orestes.)

—— (1945) *Huis Clos*, Paris: Gallimard; repr. Paris: Livres de Poche, 1971; trans. S. Gilbert, *In Camera*, in *No Exit and Three Other Plays*, New York: Vintage Books, 1949. (Drama of existence in which three people are trapped together for eternity.)

—— (1945–9) *Les Chemins de la liberté* (The Roads to Freedom): vol. 1, *L'Âge de raison*, Paris: Gallimard, 1945; trans. E. Sutton, *The Age of Reason*, New York: Knopf, 1947; vol. 2, *Le Sursis*, Paris: Gallimard, 1945; trans. E. Sutton, *The Reprieve*, New York: Knopf, 1947; vol. 3, *La Mort dans l'âme*, Paris: Gallimard, 1949; trans. G. Hopkins, *Troubled Sleep*, New York: Vintage Books, 1951. (Trilogy of novels set in Paris of the early 1940s.)

—— (1946) *L'Existentialism est un humanisme*, Paris: Nagel; trans. B. Frechtman, *Existentialism*, New York: Philosophical Library, 1947, and Citadel, 1957. (A lecture purporting to present existentialist philosophy as a humanism – later repudiated by Sartre as over-simple.)

—— (1948) *Les Mains Sales*, Paris: Gallimard; trans. L. Abel, *Dirty Hands*, or *Crime Passionel*, in *No Exit and Three Other Plays*, New York: Vintage Books, 1949. (Political play opposing realism and idealism.)

—— (1960) *Critique de la raison dialectique, précedé de Questions de methode, I, Théorie des ensembles pratiques*, Paris: Gallimard; repr. in new annotated edn, 1985; first essay trans. H.E. Barnes, *Search for a Method*, New York: Knopf, 1963; main text trans. A. Sheridan-Smith and ed. J. Rée, *Critique of Dialectical Reason*, London: New Left Books, 1976, and Atlantic Highlands, NJ: Humanities Press, 1976. (A lengthy attempt to reconcile existentialism and Marxism within a philosophy of history.)

—— (1963) *Les Mots*, Paris: Gallimard; trans. B. Frechtman, *The Words*, New York: Braziller, 1964; trans. I. Clephane, *Words*, London: Hamish Hamilton, 1964. (Sartre's (ironic) account of his childhood.)

—— (1971–2) *L'Idiot de la famille, G. Flaubert de 1821 à 1857*, Paris: Gallimard; trans. C. Cosman, *The Idiot of the Family*, Chicago, IL: University of Chicago Press, 3 vols, 1981, 1987, 1989. (A three-volume existential biography of Flaubert, intended to answer the question, 'What can we know of a man today?')

—— (1983a) *Les Carnets de la drôle de guerre*, Paris: Gallimard; trans. Q. Hoare, *The War Diaries of Jean-Paul Sartre*, New York: Pantheon Books, 1984. (Sartre's diaries at the onset of the Second World War.)

—— (1983b) *Cahiers pour une morale* (Notebooks for an Ethic), Paris: Gallimard. (Notebooks attempting a sketch for an ethics with which Sartre was never fully satisfied.)

—— (1985) *Critique de la raison dialectique, tome II (inachevé), L'Intelligibilité de l'Histoire* (Critique of Dialectical Reason, vol. 2 (incomplete), The Intelligibility of History), ed. A. Elkaim-Sartre, Paris: Gallimard. (Volume 2 of the *Critique*, focusing in particular on the question of the intelligibility of history.)

Contat, M. and Rybalka, M. (1970) *Les Ecrits de Sartre*, Paris: Gallimard; trans. *The Writings of Jean-Paul Sartre*, Evanston, IL: Northwestern University Press, 1973. (A full bibliography of Sartre's works up to 1969. Later supplements are given in the English translation, and in *Obliques* (1979) 18–19, ed. M. Sicard.)

References and further reading

Aronson, R. (1980) *Jean-Paul Sartre: Philosophy in the World*, London: New Left Books. (A lively critical account.)

Caws, P. (1979) *Sartre*, London: Routledge & Kegan Paul. (A clear and comprehensive study.)

Chiodi, P. (1976) *Sartre and Marxism*, trans. K. Soper, Hassocks, Sussex: Harvester, and New York: Humanities Press. (A lucid critical discussion of Sartre's *Critique*, from a Marxist perspective.)

Cohen-Solal, A. (1987) *Sartre: A Life*, New York: Pantheon, and London: Heinemann. (Much the best biography of Sartre so far; well-informed and not uncritical.)

Danto, A. (1975) *Sartre*, Modern Masters, London: Fontana. (Short and entertaining account.)

Fell, J. (1965) *Emotion in the Thought of Sartre*, New York: Columbia University Press. (The best study of Sartre's early phenomenological psychology.)

—— (1979) *Heidegger and Sartre*, New York: Columbia University Press. (A well-informed comparison of Sartre and Heidegger.)

Howells, C. (1988) *Sartre: The Necessity of Freedom*, Cambridge: Cambridge University Press. (A study of both literature and philosophy.)

—— (ed.) (1992) *The Cambridge Companion to Sartre*, Cambridge: Cambridge University Press. (A stimulating collection of essays by American and European specialists.)

Jeanson, F. (1947) *Le Problème moral et la pensée de Sartre*, Paris: Seuil; trans. R. Stone, *Sartre and the Problem of Morality*, Bloomington, IN: Indiana University Press, 1980. (An early discussion by a close friend of Sartre, especially good on Sartre's early ethical theory.)

* McCulloch, G. (1994) *Using Sartre*, London: Routledge. (An attempt to connect Sartre's early philosophy with themes from analytical philosophy.)

Merleau-Ponty, M. (1945) *Phénoménologie de la Perception*, Paris: Gallimard; trans. C. Smith, *Phenomenology of Perception*, London: Routledge, 1962. (A major work of philosophy in its own right, part 3 contains penetrating criticisms of *Being and Nothingness*.)

* Morris, P. (1976) *Sartre's Concept of a Person*, Amherst, MA: University of Massachusetts Press. (An account of Sartre from an analytic perspective.)

Olafson, F. (1967) *Principles and Persons*, Baltimore, MD: Johns Hopkins University Press. (A well-informed critical discussion of Sartre's ethical theory.)

—— (1965) *The Philosophy of Sartre*, London: Hutchinson, and New York: Hillary House. (A classic, if now out-of-date, account.)

Warnock, M. (ed.) (1971) *Sartre: A Collection of Critical Essays*, New York: Anchor. (An early collection of essays, many of them still well worth reading.)

Wilcocks, R. (ed.) (1988) *Critical Essays on Jean-Paul Sartre*, Boston: G.K. Hall. (An excellent collection of essays.)

CHRISTINA HOWELLS

SARVĀSTIVĀDA *see* BUDDHISM, ĀBIDHARMIKA SCHOOLS OF

SA-SKYA-PA *see* TIBETAN PHILOSOPHY

SAUSSURE, FERDINAND DE (1857–1913)

Though he made a major contribution to the comparative and historical studies which dominated nineteenth-century linguistics, Saussure is best known today for the development of a radically different conception of language and of the methodology of linguistics which became central to twentieth-century structural linguistics. According to this conception a language is a system of signs which are radically arbitrary, so that their significations are determined only by the historically constituted systems of conventions to which they belong – such a system Saussure called 'la langue'. It follows, therefore, that a linguistic study is first and foremost one of la langue, that is, of the conventional relations obtaining at a given time between signs belonging to the same system, rather than one of the development of linguistic forms over time, as the comparativists had maintained.

1   **The primary object of linguistic study**
2   **Language as a system of signs**
3   **Semiology and structuralism**

1   The primary object of linguistic study

In the nineteenth century linguistics was dominated by comparative and historical studies the primary aims of which were to compare forms in different languages and to trace their development. The Swiss linguist Ferdinand de Saussure made a major contribution to these studies at the age of twenty-one in his *Memoires sur le système primitif des voyelles dans les langues indo-européenes* (Memoir on the Primitive System of Vowels in Indo-European Languages, 1878). However, he became increasingly dissatisfied with the assumptions made by these studies. In particular, they failed to ask fundamental questions: 'What is the primary object of a linguistic study?' and 'What is the nature of the object studied?' Saussure proposed novel answers to these questions in three lecture courses given in Geneva between 1906 and 1911. Unfortunately, he died in 1913 before he was able to publish his conclusions; the text by which he is best known, *Cours de linguistique générale* (*Course in General Linguistics*), was reconstructed from his lecture notes by two of his pupils and published in 1916.

Saussure's argument about the nature of the object of linguistics is a complex one, in the course of which he develops a conception of a language as a social institution which is, at the same time, radically arbitrary. The starting point of the argument is a claim that for each language one can make a distinction between *la langue* (the language itself, for example, French or German) and *le parole* (its uses, the primary one for Saussure being speech). *La langue* is a system of conventions the knowledge of which enables speakers to communicate. It both logically precedes and is more abstract than *le parole*, since speech sounds, while being the primary means of its articulation, are nevertheless only one of its instruments. The existence of other instruments, such as writing, or the signs of a language for the deaf, show that what is natural to man is not 'oral speech but the faculty of constructing a language' (1916 (1977): 26). Thus, to concentrate attention on speech sounds, or indeed on any other instrument of articulation, would be to neglect the underlying system (*la langue*) which makes articulation possible and is, therefore, both more fundamental and more abstract than any of its instruments of expression; in short, it is 'a form not a substance' (1977: 113). Since *la langue* is a system of conventions, it is inherently social, but it has no architect and so is not an intentional product. On the other hand, aspects of *le parole* – the uses of that system – such as the production of speech sounds, written texts or speech acts and so on, are individual acts or products which are typically intentional. Nevertheless, they are logically parasitic on the existence of an underlying system; for instance, without a conventional way of naming days of the week (a fact about *la langue*), one could not assert that today is Tuesday by uttering the words 'It is Tuesday'. So, Saussure argues, the fundamental study is one of *la langue*: '*from the very outset we must put both feet on the ground of language (*la langue*) and use language as the norm of all other manifestations of speech*' (1977: 9; original emphasis).

To appreciate the importance of Saussure's claim, and the distance which he had moved from the position of historical linguistics, it is necessary to consider at this point the other major distinction he introduced; that between 'synchronic' and 'diachronic' linguistics. One way in which he presents this distinction seems relatively unproblematic, involving no more than a difference, created by the inquirer's point of view, between studying something at a moment in time (a synchronic study) and studying it as it changes over time (a diachronic study). But his account of the distinction is misleading if it suggests that what is studied from the two perspectives is one and the same thing. On the contrary, Saussure maintains that one can study *la langue* only from the first perspective. By contrast, diachronic linguistics is the study of changing relations between individual items which, though they may impact on *la langue*, are not designed or intended by anyone to do so. They do not, therefore, form a system, so that 'there is no such thing as "historical grammar"' (1977: 134). Moreover, Saussure argues, before one can compare items belonging to different stages of a language one first needs to establish what the respective systems of conventions are or were, so that a synchronic study logically precedes a diachronic one. For instance, it is a synchronic fact that a number of English nouns mark the plural with a vowel change: 'tooth'/'teeth', 'goose'/'geese' and so on. This is a fact about the conventions of contemporary English, which is psychologically real for native speakers. On the other hand, it is a diachronic fact that this way of marking the plural was made possible by a series of purely phonetic changes which occurred previously; changes which were in no way designed or intended to make possible the modern way of forming a plural in the cases in question. So if we want to understand how plural forms are generated within a language, we can do so only by studying the language synchronically: 'the linguist can neither describe it nor draw up standards of usage except by concentrating on one state' (1977: 82). Hence Saussure's conclusion that the fundamental linguistic study is a synchronic one of *la langue* – a root-and-branch rejection of the assumptions of nineteenth-century historical linguistics.

2 Language as a system of signs

Central to the argument underpinning this conclusion is Saussure's theory of signs. For him each sign has two aspects, one acoustic, the other conceptual, and he designates them by the terms 'signifier' and 'signified' respectively. For example, an acoustic impression of an utterance of 'cat' is the word's signifier, and, *as a first approximation*, its signified is the concept *cat* (see comments on values below). It is a fundamental principle that signs are arbitrary: 'the signified "ox" has its signifier *b-ö-f* [*boeuf*] on one side of the border and *o-k-s* (*Ochs*) on the other' (1977: 67). Saussure's principle implies, of course, that the connection between a signifier and its signified is contingent; but it asserts more than that, namely that there are no extra-linguistic facts which determine either the existence of, or the relation between, a signifier and a signified. For instance, it is not because of facts about the structure of our eyes that we have the colour vocabulary that we have, nor because of facts about the structure of thought that we employ the linguistic categories we do. Thought without language is amorphous, so that 'nothing is distinct before the appearance of language' (1977: 112). The development of language does not involve, as some think, a naming ceremony at which signifiers are invented to correspond to pre-existing signifieds. Rather, the differentiation of distinct signifiers and signifieds has to proceed together.

However, Saussure argues, the differentiation has to proceed systematically: 'the principle of the arbitrariness of the sign would lead to the worst sort of complication if applied without restriction' (1977: 133). Numerical signs illustrate this point: 'twenty-one', 'thirty-one' and so on are constructed in a systematic way, and if this were not so it would not be possible to learn them all. Moreover, Saussure maintains that it is because a sign has a unique position in a system that we can identify occurrences of it. What makes two spoken occurrences of 'Gentlemen!' the same is not identity of sound or content, but the fact that each differs in the same way from instances of other English words – 'in language there are only differences *without positive terms*' (1977: 120; original emphasis). These differences depend on two kinds of relations that signs can enter into, called 'syntagmatic' and 'associative' respectively. The first kind of relation holds between a sign and the elements which can precede or succeed it; for

example, there is a syntagmatic relation between 'talk' and 'ing' in 'John is talking.' The second relation holds between items which by virtue of a similarity in form or meaning can be substituted for each other in a range of contexts. For instance, 'talking' and 'walking' are associatively related because of similarities in form, while 'talking' and 'speaking' are related because of similarities in meaning. And since the *only* way to identify a sign is by identifying the syntagmatic and associative relations it has to other signs – so we know what it is not – signs present themselves as elements of a system and cannot be identified independently of it.

Hence, Saussure argues, signifieds cannot be identified, as we did as a first approximation, with concepts, for that would suggest that they have a content independent of the linguistic system to which they belong. Instead, they should be thought of as values which are wholly dependent on the system to which they belong. Colour words provide an illustration; for example, the English word 'brown' has no exact equivalent in French, since it can be translated as 'brun', 'marron' or even 'jaune' depending on context (Lyons 1968: 56). This makes it clear why a synchronic study of *la langue* is the primary study, since a study of values is a study of the system to which they belong.

3 Semiology and structuralism

The contention that linguistic units can only be identified as terms of a system is the central tenet of European structural linguistics (see STRUCTURALISM IN LINGUISTICS), a movement for which Saussure's work provided the foundations. However, not least because they were work in progress, his theories leave much scope for interpretation and for further development; for instance, there is no serious theory of *le parole* in *Course in General Linguistics*, though one was promised, and there is no *formal* account of the relations which signs can enter into, something which is particularly serious in the case of associative relations given the vagueness of the idea of a similarity of form or meaning. So there was much work still to be done by linguists both to develop and to explore the limitations of Saussure's ideas.

As well as its importance for the development of European structural linguistics, Saussure's work also had a much wider influence. The central importance which he gave to the theory of the linguistic sign led him to speculate whether that theory were not in fact an instance of a more general study of signs of any kind that express ideas: '*a science that studies the life of signs within society* is conceivable; it would be a part of social psychology and consequently of general psychology; I shall call it *semiology* (from the Greek *sēmeîon* "sign")' (1977: 16; original emphasis). This claim was programmatic, but, albeit belatedly, it undoubtedly affected and enriched the thought of many who tried to adapt the methodology of structural linguistics as a model for that of the study of cultural signs in general, including such thinkers as Merleau-Ponty, Lévi-Strauss, Barthes and Lacan. So the impact of Saussure's work has to be measured not only in terms of its effects on the development of linguistics, especially European structural linguistics, but, more widely, in terms of its impact on the development of a methodology for the study of the social sciences in general.

See also: SEMIOTICS; STRUCTURALISM IN SOCIAL SCIENCE; STRUCTURALISM IN LITERARY THEORY

List of works

Saussure, F. de (1878) *Memoires sur le système primitif des voyelles dans les langues indo-européenes* (Memoir on the Primitive System of Vowels in Indo-European Languages), Leipzig: Teubner. (Saussure's contribution to comparative and historical linguistic studies; not available in English.)
—— (1916) *Cours de linguistique générale*, ed. C. Bally and A. Sechehaye, with the collaboration of A. Riedlinger, Lausanne and Paris: Payot; trans. W. Baskin, *Course in General Linguistics*, Glasgow: Fontana/Collins, 1977. (The key source of Saussure's ideas.)
—— (1993) *Saussure's Third Course of Lectures in General Linguistics (1910–1911): From the Notebooks of Emile Constantin*, Language and Communication series, vol. 12, trans. and ed. E. Komatsu and R. Harris, Oxford: Pergamon. (This account of Saussure's final lecture course was compiled from notes not available to the editors of the original 1916 publication. It contains new material and gives a more advanced picture of Saussure's final ideas.)

References and further reading

Culler, J. (1976) *Saussure*, Glasgow: Fontana/Collins. (A good general introduction, with an excellent account of Saussure's impact on structuralist thought.)
Ducrot, O. and Todorov, T. (1981) *Encyclopedic Dictionary of the Sciences of Language*, trans. C. Porter, Oxford: Blackwell. (As well as a sympathetic essay on Saussure, there are very helpful separate essays on all the main Saussurean themes.)
Harris, R. (1987) *Reading Saussure*, London: Duckworth. (A good recent detailed critique by a linguist.)
Holdcroft, D. (1991) *Saussure: Signs, System, and Arbitrariness*, Cambridge: Cambridge University Press. (A lengthier exposition of the themes of this essay.)
* Lyons, J. (1968) *An Introduction to Theoretical Linguistics*, Cambridge: Cambridge University Press. (Includes a sympathetic discussion of the main Saussurean theses.)

DAVID HOLDCROFT

SAVIGNY, FRIEDRICH KARL VON (1779–1861)

Friedrich Karl von Savigny was a powerfully influential student of Roman law both in its medieval manifestations and in the contemporary 'Pandektenrecht' (law based on Justinian's Pandects, or Digest) of nineteenth-century Germany. His contributions to the philosophy of law are in the spirit of the Romantic movement, and lay stress on the organic character of the legal experience of a people, hence favouring customary law over statute law, and opposing the contemporary movement towards codification. A founder of what is sometimes called the 'historical school' in the philosophy of law, he argues that law is to be understood always in its historical setting, the result of a process of historical development, not simply as the arbitrary command of a – perhaps transitory – sovereign power.

Savigny was a nobleman whose family roots were in Lorraine; his decision to become an academic was unusual for one of his class. His doctoral thesis of 1803, on 'Possession', made his reputation; analysing the civilian texts, he advanced the thesis that possession in law requires both physical control and an appropriate intention, namely the intention to hold the object in question for oneself. In 1810, he was called to his chair in Berlin, and taught there until 1842. Appointed then to be Prussian Minister for Legislation, he served until 1848. His two major scholarly works, the first on the The History of the Roman Law during the Middle Ages, the second on the *System of Modern Roman Law*, were published in the years 1815–21 and 1840–49 respectively. Especially in the analysis of personality in law, and in relation to contractual obligations, he had influence beyond the German-speaking world; at a time of revival in academic legal studies in England and

America, his works had considerable influence in the common-law world.

His historicist view of law was most famously expressed in a pamphlet of 1814, *Zum Beruf unser Zeit für Gesetzgebung und Rechtswissenschaft* (*On the Vocation of our Age for Legislation and Jurisprudence*). This was a polemic against a proposal by Thibaut for codification of law in the Germanic states along the lines of the already-celebrated Code Napoléon; as the German states emerged from their conquest and domination by Napoleonic France, Savigny issued his critique of the positivistic view implicit in the codification project. Law, he argued, emerges from the 'spirit of the people', the *Volksgeist*, and develops organically like language. As society becomes more advanced, there has to develop a special profession of lawyers, and it is their customs, including their practices of interpretation of received texts such as the *Pandects*, that express the people's spirit so far as concerns technical law. As a protest against what F.A. Hayek was later to dub 'constructivist rationalism' in law, Savigny's theory makes an important point; in awakening legal studies to the significance of history (and in founding a legal-historical journal that survives to this day), Savigny made an enduring contribution. His rather mysterious and holistic *Volksgeist* is, however, less convincing, and coloured by an unacceptable ethnic nationalism.

See also: COMMON LAW; JURISPRUDENCE, HISTORICAL §1; JUSTINIAN; LAW, PHILOSOPHY OF; ROMAN LAW

List of works

Savigny, F.K. von (1814) *Zum Beruf unser Zeit für Gesetzgebung und Rechtswissenschaft*, trans. A. Hayward, *On the Vocation of our Age for Legislation and Jurisprudence*, Birmingham, AL: Legal Classics Library, 1986. (Savigny's most celebrated single contribution to legal theory, where he developed his theory of the customary and popular or national character of law, in opposition to Thibaut's proposals for codifying German law.)

—— (1815–21) *Geschichte des römischen Rechts in Mittelalter*, trans. E. Cathcart, *The History of the Roman Law during the Middle Ages*, repr. West Port, CT: Hyperion Press, 1979. (Reprint provides an accessible modern edition.)

—— (1840–49) *System des heutigen römischen Rechts* (System of Modern Roman Law), Berlin: O.L. Heuser. (The full text of Savigny's most enduringly influential work, in which the theory of the *Volksgeist* is stated.)

References and further reading

Cohen, M.R. and Cohen, F.S. (1952) *Readings in Jurisprudence and Legal Philosophy*, New York: Prentice Hall. (A student's reader, containing at pp. 386–93 some well-chosen excerpts from translations of Savigny, set in a helpful context of related readings.)

Guthrie, W. (1880) *Private International Law, and the Retrospective Operation of Statutes*, 2 vols, Edinburgh: T. & T. Clark. (A treatise on the conflict of laws and the limits on their operation in respect of space and time, translating and working from one of Savigny's most influential contributions.)

Paton, G.W. and Derham, D.P. (1972) *Jurisprudence*, 4th edn, Oxford: Clarendon Press. (A useful textbook of jurisprudence, containing at pp. 19–21 a discussion of Savigny's stance and influence in legal theory.)

Perry, Sir E. (1848) *Treatise on Possession, or the Jus Possessionis of the Civil Law*, 6th edn, London: Sweet. (Savigny's elaborate discussion of the physical and mental elements of possession considered as a right set the tone for analytical jurisprudence in this domain for a century to follow.)

Rattigan, W.H. (1884) *Jural Relations, or the Roman Law of Persons as Subjects of Jural Relations*, London: Sweet. (Translation of book 2 of Savigny's *System of Modern Roman Law*; this gives Savigny's view on the nature of personhood in law.)

Stone, J. (1966) *Social Dimensions of Law and Justice*, London: Stevens and Sons. (See pp. 86–101, for a sympathetic and revealing discussion of Savigny's historicist legal theory, set in the context of contemporary debate and also against the background of a discussion of the development of sociological approaches to law.)

NEIL MacCORMICK

SCANDINAVIA, PHILOSOPHY IN

The three countries of Scandinavia – Sweden, Denmark and Norway – share much of their history and culture with Finland and Iceland, and it is natural to treat all five Nordic countries together in any philosophical survey. The first universities in this region were founded more than 500 years ago, in Sweden at Uppsala in 1477, and in Copenhagen, the Danish capital, two years later. Over the years, the main trends of philosophical thought, from Descartes and Locke to Hegelianism, existentialism and logical positivism have all impinged upon philosophy in these countries. A unique feature of philosophy in Norway and Iceland, and until 1971 also in Denmark, is that all university students, including students in law, medicine and dentistry, spend all or most of their first semester preparing for a compulsory exam in philosophy which comprises some philosophy of science and philosophy of language, and some history of philosophy and history of science. This requirement has meant much for recruiting and employment opportunities for philosophers. Thus, for example, the University of Oslo has sixty-five tenured philosophers, while Denmark has suffered a dramatic reduction in the number of philosophical positions since the requirement was abolished. In Sweden philosophy is a compulsory subject in some branches of study in secondary schools.

That philosophers from the Nordic countries have gained a reputation for broad interests and familiarity with several philosophical traditions may largely be due to two factors: small countries *increase the likelihood that they will get involved in popularization and public affairs, and* small language communities *induce the learning of other languages, notably English, German and French, which makes developments in other countries more accessible.*

1   **From the Middle Ages to *c*.1870**
2   **Sweden**
3   **Denmark**
4   **Finland**
5   **Norway**
6   **Iceland**

1   From the Middle Ages to *c*.1870

Philosophy in the Nordic countries began in the eleventh and twelfth centuries with the introduction of Christianity and the establishment of monasteries. Many went abroad to study at the leading universities, and some made notable contributions, such as the Swedish Averroist BOËTHIUS OF DACIA who, together with SIGER OF BRABANT, taught at the University of Paris until they were both condemned in 1277. Boëthius ended his days in the 1290s as canon in Linköping.

When the first universities were set up in the late fifteenthth century, Aristotelianism continued to be the main philosophical pursuit. The University of Copenhagen, founded in 1479, almost perished during the Reformation and was re-established in 1537 as a Lutheran institution. The University of Uppsala was suppressed from 1515 to 1593. After the Reformation, a short period of interest in Ramism was followed by a rise in Cartesianism, due in no small way to the fact that in 1649 DESCARTES came to Stockholm as Queen Christina's personal tutor. A

widespread interest in natural law culminated with Samuel PUFENDORF leaving his chair in Heidelberg in order to serve as Professor of Natural Law at the University of Lund during its first nine years. He thereafter went to Stockholm where he spent ten years writing a thirty-three-volume history of Sweden.

The mid-1700s were marked by the influence of WOLFF, especially in Sweden and Finland. Subsequently, interest in LOCKE became prevalent in Finland and Sweden due to the work of Henrik Hassel (1700–76) and Henrik Gabriel Porthan (1739–1804) in Turku and Pehr Niclas Christiernin (1725–99) in Uppsala. Kant was introduced into Danish discussion by Børge Riisbrigh (1731–1809), and Kant's ethics and philosophy of law had a strong influence on the lawyer and politician Anders Sandøe Ørsted (1778–1860) and through him on Danish law. In Sweden, Kant was introduced by Daniel Boëthius (1751–1810), while in Finland the poet and professor Franz Mikael Franzén (1772–1847) and others developed various versions of Kantianism. Kant had little impact in Norway, mainly as a consequence of the criticism of Niels Treschow (1751–1833), the first professor of philosophy at the new university of Oslo (founded 1813). Treschow, who developed a Spinozistic conception of evolution, was born in Norway and held a chair in Copenhagen from 1803 until taking up the appointment in Oslo. He left the university after just one year to go into government.

SCHELLING had some influence in Denmark, mostly due to Henrik Steffens (1773–1845). Born in Norway, Steffens studied in Copenhagen and went on to hold professorships in Halle, Breslau and Berlin. The dominant influence on philosophy in the Nordic countries in the late 1800s was, however, HEGEL. In Uppsala, Benjamin Höijer (1767–1812) anticipated in interesting ways the post-Kantian developments of Fichte and Schelling. He is for this reason often called 'Sweden's Fichte'. However, his later development was influenced by Hegel. The Uppsala professor of history Erik Gustaf Geijer (1783–1847), in opposition to Hegel, developed a personalistic philosophy, arguing that self-consciousness is possible only in interaction with other individuals: 'No you – no I'. In Turku the philosopher and statesman Johan Vilhelm Snellmann (1806–81), who has been honoured as the 'national philosopher' of Finland, transformed Hegel's idea of absolute spirit into a doctrine of national spirit expressed through a nation's language and literature. Snellman gave philosophy a central public role in Finland, that it has retained since. In Denmark and Norway the influence of Hegel went so far as to become extremely oppressive, and KIERKEGAARD reacted strongly to Hegelianism and every other 'system philosophy'. In Norway Hegelianism was introduced by the Danish philosopher and poet Poul Martin Møller (1794–1838), who taught philosophy at the University of Oslo from 1827 to 1831. However, it was through Marcus Jacob Monrad (1816–97), who became professor in Oslo at age 29 and retained the position for more than fifty years, that Hegelianism became more protracted in Norway than in any of the other Nordic countries. Following this period of widespread Hegelianism, philosophy developed in a different directions in each country.

2 Sweden

Christopher Jacob Boström (1797–1866), professor of practical philosophy in Uppsala from 1842 to 1863, developed a kind of personalism which combined elements of Plato's theory of ideas, Leibniz's monadology and Berkeley's idealism (see PLATO; LEIBNIZ, G.W.; BERKELEY, G.). Boström (who has been called 'Sweden's Plato') exercized a strong influence on Swedish intellectual life in the latter part of the nineteenth century, acquiring a dominance similar to that of Hegel in the other Nordic countries. After Boström's death, three of the four philosophy chairs in Sweden were held by his students: the chair of theoretical philosophy in Lund was held by a Hegelian.

The Uppsala school. In the first decade of the twentieth century the dominance of Boströminianism was broken by what was to become the most remarkable philosophical movement to come out of Sweden: the Uppsala school of philosophy, which flourished until the Second World War. This was the result of the work of two gifted philosophers, Axel HÄGERSTRÖM and his student and later colleague Adolf Phalén (1884–1931). In 1905 Hägerström started to develop the idea that was to become basic for the Uppsala school, that moral sentences express emotions and contain an imperative element. They may in addition have a descriptive ingredient, but their emotive component is the proper topic of ethics, which is an investigation into the noncognitive nature of moral sentences.

Hägerström expanded this view into philosophy of religion and philosophy of law. He rejected metaphysics and studied the ways in which language deceives us into thinking that there are values and that moral statements are true or false. While there are many similarities between the Uppsala school and later logical empiricism, there are also important differences: the Uppsala school combined moral subjectivism with epistemological objectivism, it rejected the view that the subject has immediate knowledge solely of its own experiences, and placed a strong emphasis on the history of philosophy. These

historical studies were particularly important for Phalén. Whereas Hägerström maintained and supported his theses with great intensity, Phalén explored with calm objectivity the various possible ways in which the major philosophers have tried to deal with the contradictions in common-sense notions of time, motion, reality, knowledge and so on. This work started in 1910 with a criticism of subjectivism and continued in his large dissertation on Hegel two years later. Historical analysis is also evident in his works on space and time and other systematic issues, as well as in his lectures (unpublished until 1973–8). Phalén's main interest, however, was epistemology, where his position resembles that of HUSSERL in some respects, and in 1911 he was the first philosopher in Scandinavia to write on Husserl's phenomenology. After the Second World War, philosophy in Sweden became much more varied both in theme and perspective.

History of philosophy. The two most notable Swedish philosophers in the generation that succeeded the Uppsala School were Konrad Marc-Wogau (1902–91), professor of theoretical philosophy in Uppsala from 1946 to 1968, and Anders Wedberg (1913–78), professor of theoretical philosophy in Stockholm from 1949 to 1976. Marc-Wogau published a number of books and essays on Plato, Descartes, Marx, Hägerström and other figures in the history of philosophy and on contemporary Soviet thought. He also wrote a logic text and several studies of systematic issues, including a book on psychoanalysis. Together with his two prewar great books on Kant and his 1945 work *Die Theorie der Sinnesdaten* they establish him as one of Scandinavia's most notable philosopher-scholars. Wedberg's few, but high-quality publications, on a broad spectrum of topics, are mostly historical. He had a strong interest in BOLZANO, which has been followed up by Jan Berg (1928–), since 1969 in Munich. Wedberg was above all a great systematic philosopher, and his works set a high standard for his students, the foremost of whom were Kanger, Berg and Prawitz.

In Lund, all the major philosophers during that period worked in the history of philosophy. Particularly important was Hans Larsson (1862–1944), professor of theoretical philosophy from 1901 to 1927, who wrote on Kant and Spinoza, and whose work earned him one of the eighteen places in the Swedish Academy. Åke Petzäll (1901–57) introduced logical empiricism in Sweden and founded the journal *Theoria.* His successor in the chair of practical philosophy, Manfred Moritz (1909–90) was Sweden's foremost expert on Kant's ethics after Hägerström. He also further developed Wesley Hohfeld's system of basic legal concepts, as did Kanger later.

Philosophical logic. The most prominent Swedish contributions to philosophy today are within the field of philosophical logic. Sören Halldén (1923–), who held the chair in theoretical philosophy in Lund from 1964 to 1988, produced the first major work in this field in Sweden in his Uppsala dissertation of 1950. His later contributions include one of the first studies of preference logic, several books on decision logic and its bearing on epistemology, and a number of other books and articles within several areas of philosophy. Together with the legal scholar Per Olof Ekelöf (1906–90) in Uppsala and the philosopher of science Martin Edman (1945–) in Umeå, Halldén has been working on the evaluation of evidence, particularly in courts, and developed the important notion of evidentiary mechanisms and the evidentiary value model.

A most significant Swedish contribution to philosophical logic was the dissertation which Stig Kanger (1924–88) wrote in Stockholm for Wedberg in 1957. Kanger here presented the key ideas of what has later come to be called 'Kripke semantics' for modal logic, named after Saul Kripke who published them in 1959 and 1963. Although Hintikka and Kripke discovered this type of semantics independently, it would be appropriate to call it Kanger-Kripke semantics. Kanger also made several further important and original contributions to logic and its applications and to the theory of measurement. He also developed and refined Hohfeld's system of basic legal terms. In 1968 he succeeded Marc-Wogau in the chair in theoretical philosophy in Uppsala.

Dag Prawitz (1936–) also wrote his dissertation with Wedberg and in 1976 succeeded Wedberg in the chair of theoretical philosophy in Stockholm, after five years as a professor in Oslo. In his 1965 dissertation he was the first to prove Gentzen's *Hauptsatz* directly for certain systems of natural deduction. Prawitz has extended this result and has also written on causality, utilitarianism and a number of other topics, and has developed a Dummett-inspired theory of meaning. Similar work on meaning has been done by Per Martin-Löf (1942–), research professor in logic in Stockholm. Martin-Löf has also developed an intuitionistic-type theory and has done important work on the foundations of probability theory.

A main contributor to modal logic is Krister Segerberg (1936–), who in 1990 succeeded Kanger in Uppsala. Among his many results are a generalization of Lemmon and Scott's 'filtration method', a way of replacing complicated models with simple ones. Bengt Hansson (1943–), who succeeded Halldén in Lund in 1989, has worked in modal logic, preference logic, philosophy of science and philosophy of language. Among the many other philosophers in Sweden who have worked on logic and its applications, Per Lindström (1936–) in Gothenburg has done particularly important work in model theory. In 1969 he proved what has become known as Lindström's theorem.

Ethics. Among Swedish postwar philosophers, the best known to the general public has been Ingemar Hedenius (1908–82) who, from 1947 to 1974, held the chair once held by Hägerström. Hedenius' 1941 *Om rätt och moral* (On law and morality) exerted a strong influence on legal philosophy and ethics in Sweden, while his 1949 work *Tro och vetande* (Faith and knowledge) played an extraordinary role in the debate on religion in Scandinavia. Hedenius also developed a version of utilitarianism and wrote several articles and books on ethics and the history of ethics (Berkeley, Hume and Plato) as well as on other topics. His successor in Uppsala was Lars Bergström (1935–), who produced his dissertation under the direction of Ofstad and Wedberg in 1966. In 1987 he left Uppsala for Stockholm. Most of Bergström's work has been in ethics, much of it connected with his very precise statement of utilitarianism in his dissertation, but he has also written articles on other areas. In Lund, Göran Hermerén (1938–) has written on *Influence in Art and Literature* (1975) and other topics in aesthetics, is now professor of medical ethics.

Decision theory. Among Hedenius' and Bergström's many gifted students some have turned to decision theory and related fields. Sven Danielsson (1939–), who succeeded Bergström in Uppsala, and Wlodek Rabinowicz (1947–), professor of practical philosophy in Lund, have together with Peter Gärdenfors (1949–), professor of cognitive science in Lund, and Nils-Eric Sahlin (1954–) done important work on decision theory, group preferences and distributive justice. Gärdenfors and Sahlin have also worked on many other topics, including dynamic models of belief and empirical evidence.

Other activities. The fields that have been mentioned are particularly vigorous in Sweden, but there is also activity in many other fields. Gothenburg, in particular, has had two philosophers with highly distinctive profiles. Ivar Segelberg (1914–87), professor of philosophy from 1951 to 1979, wrote several phenomenological studies inspired by Phalén, and has in turn stimulated a third generation of Swedish phenomenologists. Segelberg's successor, Mats Furberg (1933–) has written extensively on speech-act theory, and has in recent work attempted a reconciliation between speech-act theory and hermeneutics. However, his most distinctive contribution is a number of exceptionally engaging books in Swedish, on topics such as death, the meaning of life and the riddle of the world.

3 Denmark

Harald Höffding (1843–1931) was the dominant figure in Danish philosophy from the 1870s until he retired in 1915 after thirty-two years as professor in Copenhagen. His humanistic naturalism was inspired by, among others, the positivism of COMTE and the empiricism of John Stuart MILL and Herbert SPENCER. He defended a double-aspect theory of mind and body, and in a somewhat eclectic way, via utilitarianism and religion, he transposed ideas from the Danish idealist tradition into the framework of naturalism. Jørgen Jørgensen (1894–1969), professor in Copenhagen from 1926 to 1964, favoured Russell's logic and the logical positivist movement, and criticized 'metaphysical' assumptions in the sciences. In his later works Jørgensen developed a psychologistic understanding of epistemology and logic, and maintained that nerve processes, behaviour and ideas are different aspects of the same thing. In meta-ethics he defended an emotivist version of noncognitivism and in consequence a radical distinction between values and facts. A similar positivistic view on values was introduced in jurisprudence by Alf ROSS, professor of law in Copenhagen from 1938 to 1969. Having studied under Hans KELSEN in Vienna, Ross adopted his tutor's interpretation of propositions in law as predictions of the behaviour of a judge in court.

Partly under Jørgensen's influence, several Danish philosophers have taken up philosophy of science, notably Johannes Witt-Hansen (1908–86), professor of philosophy in Copenhagen between 1959 and 1978, who wrote on Eddington, on matter, on generalization and on historical materialism. David Favrholdt (1931–), who in 1966 became the first professor of philosophy at the University of Odense, wrote his dissertation on Wittgenstein's *Tractatus*, but has been working on Niels BOHR. So has Jan Faye (1947–), who received his doctorate in Odense in 1981 with a dissertation in which he argued that backward causation is possible in principle. A major issue between Favrholdt and Faye is to what extent Harald Höffding had a decisive influence on Bohr's interpretation of quantum mechanics.

In ethics, a most influential Danish contribution has come from Knud Ejler Løgstrup (1905–81), professor of theology at the University of Aarhus. In the 1950s, inspired by the phenomenological philosophy of Hans Lipps, he developed an ethical theory which is widely studied in several countries, notably among theologians. Mogens Blegvad (1917–), professor of philosophy in Copenhagen from 1964 to 1987, has written on the naturalistic fallacy, action explanation and a variety of other topics.

The later WITTGENSTEIN has influenced philosophy in Denmark mainly through Justus Hartnack (1912–), who dominated the philosophical scene in Aarhus during his time there as professor (1954–72). Peter Zinkernagel (1921–) argued that all language-use presupposes the truth of certain language rules embedded in ordinary language. These rules include substantial philosophical claims, for example that there is an external physical world. Thus phenomenalism and other traditional philosophical views which run counter to common sense turn out to be self-refuting.

The abolition of the compulsory philosophy exam in 1971, together with a negative attitude to universities among politicians, has been disastrous for Danish philosophy. In Copenhagen the number of chairs in philosophy was reduced from four to one. However, several young Danish philosophers went abroad to study and many of them have returned, bringing with them a conception of philosophy as a discipline with fundamental systematic ambitions and introducing the works of Donald Davidson, Michael Dummett and Saul Kripke into Danish philosophy. Among these is Finn Collin (1949–), associate professor in Copenhagen who, after a dissertation on sensations in Berkeley, has written books on interpretive social science and on the construction of social fact. He has also written on causality and explanation, on phenomenology and hermeneutics, and on philosophy of language. His Copenhagen colleague Peter Sandøe (1955–), who studied in Frankfurt and Oxford, has written about moral realism.

History of philosophy. The most notable Danish contributions to philosophy in recent decades have come within the history of philosophy, most of them from Copenhagen, which is a centre for the study of ancient and medieval philosophy. Karsten Friis-Johansen (1930–) has followed his early important Plato studies with work on Democritus and on Kierkegaard, and has also written a monumental first volume of a four-volume history of philosophy. In the Classics Department, Johnny Christensen has written *An Essay on the Unity of Stoic Philosophy* (1962) and has produced several other works. In the theological faculty Troels Engberg-Pedersen (1948–) has written *Aristotle's Theory of Moral Insight* (1983) and *The Stoic Theory of Oikeiosis* (1990).

In medieval philosophy, Jan Pinborg (1937–1982) published a number of important studies on semantics and logic in the Middle Ages. Several of his articles were co-authored with Sten Ebbesen (1946–), whose main work is his three-volume *Commentators and Commentaries on Aristotle's Sophistici Elenchi* (1981). Niels Jørgen Green-Pedersen (1942–) has also written *The Tradition of the Topics in the Middle Ages* (1984).

In Aarhus, at the Institute for the History of Science, Olaf Pedersen (1920–) and his colleagues have produced a number of renowned studies on ancient and medieval history of science, mathematics and technology, among them Pedersen's *Early Physics and Astronomy* (1974) and his *Galileo and the Council of Trent* (1983).

Modern philosophy is studied in Copenhagen by Carl Henrik Koch (1938–), who has written the large third volume (from the Reformation to the Enlightenment) of a four-volume history of philosophy. Koch has also written a survey of eighteenth century philosophy for the *Cambridge History of 18th Century Philosophy*. Knud Haakonssen (1947–), who took his doctorate in Edinburgh on what later became the book *The Science of a Legislator. The Natural Jurisprudence of David Hume and Adam Smith* (1981), is now teaching at Boston University.

4   Finland

Like other countries, Finland experienced a reaction against Hegelianism towards the end of the nineteenth century, inspired in part by Höffding in Denmark. Particularly important was Edward Westermarck (1862–1939), whose work on ethical relativism reflects his combined interest in ethics and sociology. He divided his time between a chair of sociology in London and a professorship of philosophy in Helsinki, and later in Turku (Åbo). Westermarck and the aesthetician Yrjö Hirn (1870–1952) were the first Finns to influence international philosophical discussion.

In the 1930s, Eino Kaila (1890–1958) had an important influence on Finnish philosophy. He participated in the meetings of the Vienna Circle and wrote on the philosophy of psychology and the philosophy of physics (see VIENNA CIRCLE). He introduced symbolic logic and logical empiricism as well as Gestalt psychology and empirical psychology to Finland. Ultimately, however, he went more in the direction of philosophy of nature than philosophy of science. His students included Erik Stenius (1911–90), Oiva Ketonen (1913–) and Georg Henrik VON WRIGHT, all of whom did some of their work in logic. Ketonen, who succeeded Kaila at the University of Helsinki in 1948 when Kaila was appointed to the Academy of Finland, has written influential works in Finnish on science policy and university affairs, as well as on general cultural issues. Stenius wrote his dissertation on paradoxes in logic and set theory. He later worked on the Presocratics, epistemology, logic and philosophy of language, but is best known for his incisive interpretation and defence of Wittgenstein's picture theory of language (1960).

Jaakko Hintikka (1929–) is, together with his teacher von Wright, among the leading figures on the international philosophical scene. Like so many Finnish philosophers, Hintikka came to philosophy from mathematics and did his first work in logic, developing further von Wright's idea of distributive normal forms, which continues to play a role in his later work. In 1957 Hintikka – independently of the slightly earlier proposal by Kanger and of the later one by Kripke – presented the basic idea of possible worlds semantics for modal logic. There is not room here to enumerate Hintikka's many important and seminal contributions to modal, epistemic and deontic logic, to model theory, the interpretation of quantifiers, game theoretic semantics, to philosophy of science, epistemology and philosophy of language and to the history of philosophy from Plato and Aristotle, through the medievals, Descartes, Leibniz, Kant, and Husserl to Wittgenstein.

Hintikka has attracted a large number of talented students who, in the United States and in Finland, work in all the different areas of philosophy in which Hintikka has been working. His Finnish students are main contributors within all the three most active fields of philosophy in Finland today: philosophy of science, philosophy of language and the history of philosophy.

Philosophy of science. Two of Hintikka's earliest students teach at the University of Turku: Risto Hilpinen (1943–) and Juhani Pietarinen (1938–). Both wrote their dissertations on inductive logic. Hilpinen has also written on deontic logic, norms and imperatives and their connection with action theory, and on C.S. PEIRCE, in particular his theory of 'indeterminate reference'. Several of Hilpinen's latest publications explore a question-theoretic approach to scientific inquiry.

Raimo Tuomela (1940–) in 1970 was appointed to the newly established chair in the methodology of the social sciences in Helsinki, having received his Ph.D. at Stanford the previous year. He has worked mainly on action theory, particularly social action. Together with Ilkka Niiniluoto (1946–), he has written on theoretical concepts and hypothetico-deductive inference. Niiniluoto's later works, on scientific progress and especially truthlikeness, establish him as a leading philosopher of science. Niiniluoto has also contributed to inductive logic. He has published several studies on research policy and the evaluation of research, and has also branched into ethics and law, as in. In 1975 he became the first to hold a chair in the foundations of mathematics in Helsinki.

Jan von Plato (1951–) is working on the foundations of probability, particularly as applied in statistical physics and in dynamical systems. He has also written outstanding historical studies on the foundations of probability.

Philosophy of language. Hintikka's many ideas in the philosophy of language have been followed up by several of his students, in particular game-theoretic semantics, which has been applied to the study of quantifiers, partially ordered connectives, and anaphora. Hintikka-Åqvist's logic of questions has been applied to throw light on explanations.

History of philosophy. A characteristic of Finnish philosophy has been to combine historical and systematic work. Finnish systematic works are rich in historical references, and all the main Finnish historians of philosophy have made contributions to contemporary systematic discussion. Kaila had historical interests, but the combination of high-quality historical scholarship and systematic discussion starts with von Wright, Stenius and Hintikka. Greek philosophy has been studied by all three, especially Stenius and Hintikka. Important contributions have also come from Mårten Ringbom (1934–) and the classicists Rolf Westman (1927–) and Holger Thesleff (1924–). Simo Knuuttila (1946–) in the theological faculty in Helsinki has written on Greek philosophy, but his main work has been on medieval philosophy, to which he is one of the main contributors in Scandinavia. His 1976 dissertation showed that the assumptions concerning modality that Hintikka had attributed to Aristotle, were commonplace throughout most of the Middle Ages. Knuuttila has written on modality in *The Cambridge History of Later Medieval Philosophy* and has also produced numerous articles on subjects ranging from Plato to Descartes.

Finland also has a leading Descartes scholar, Lilli Alanen (1941–). As well as her books and articles on Descartes she is taking up systematic issues in the philosophy of mind and is directing a research group on intentionality. In 1997 she was appointed to a new chair in the history of philosophy at the University of Uppsala in Sweden. Another prominent woman philosopher in Finland is Leila Haaparanta (1954–), who has written a number of books and articles on Frege, Husserl, Peirce and other nineteenth-century thinkers.

Wittgenstein studies are particularly strong in Finland. In addition to the publications of Stenius, von Wright and Hintikka, important contributions have come from some of von Wright's and Stenius' students, notably Lars Hertzberg (1943–) and Heikko Kannisto (1945–). Two other philosophers who have been influenced by von Wright and Stenius are Ingmar Pörn (1935–) and Ghita Holmström-Hintikka (1936–). Pörn has written on action theory and social science, on deontic logic and also on power, Kierke-gaard, the emotions and on health, health care and medical ethics, while Holmström-Hintikka has developed a theory of action and will, and applied it to the philosophy of law and in the analysis of medieval discussions, notably in Augustine and Ockham. She has also written on the philosophy of law and on medical ethics.

5 Norway

Monrad's long Hegelian reign was followed by a combination of philosophy and psychology, typical of the time. This combination culminated with Harald Schjelderup (1896–1974) who became professor of philosophy at age 26, but had his chair changed to psychology in 1928. From then until 1954 there remained only one professorship in philosophy in Norway. This was held from 1908 to 1937 by Anathon Aall (1867–1943), who was opposed to Hegelianism and combined empirical psychology, Greek philosophy and the history of Christian thought. Aall was succeeded in 1939 by Arne Næss (1912–), an appointment opposed by many who felt that empirical tendencies were a danger to philosophy. However, fortunately for the openness and the international orientation of Norwegian philosophy, Næss was appointed.

Although it is more than hundred years since philosophy became compulsory for all university students, there have been few teaching positions. In Oslo the situation has improved greatly during the last fifteen years. The philosophy department in Oslo now has sixty-five full-time permanent faculty members spread over most main areas of philosophy. The other universities are following suit. Areas of particular strength at present include logic, philosophy of science and the history of philosophy, notably Greek philosophy, Kant, Kierkegaard and Husserl. There is also an effort to build up pure and applied ethics and to attract more women to philosophy.

Logic and philosophy of language. The earliest international contributions to philosophy from Norway came in logic, starting with Axel Thue (1863–1922) and culminating with Thoralf Skolem (1887–1963). Oslo now has six professors of logic, three in the mathematics department and three in linguistics. Jens Erik Fenstad (1935–) has taught most of them.

In the Philosophy Department in Oslo, Dagfinn Føllesdal (1932–) started out as a student of Skolem, but went to Harvard to take a Ph.D. in philosophy with Quine, and now concentrates mainly on philosophy of language and phenomenology. Also in the Philosophy Department in Oslo is Andrew Jones (1947–), who is working in deontic logic and also in philosophy of mind, philosophy of language, artificial intelligence and particularly the philosophy of law. Jones has also been advisor to an impressive number of doctoral students. Olav Gjelsvik (1956–), also in Oslo, received his D.Phil. in Oxford 1986 and is working in the philosophy of mind, philosophy of language and action theory. In Trondheim Ingemund Gullvåg (1925–) has written on definiteness of intention, and in his later work has explored a wide variety of ideas in epistemology, metaphysics and philosophy of logic.

Philosophy of science. Philosophy of science, including philosophy of the humanities and the social sciences, is a main theme in the compulsory philosophy exam at the Norwegian universities. This has led to considerable activity within this field.

Jon Elster (1940–), based at Columbia University, has written an impressive number of widely read and highly regarded books on Marx and Leibniz, but mostly on issues relating to rationality and deviations from rationality, including addiction. He has also published empirical studies of justice. Nils Roll-Hansen (1938–), who combines philosophy of science with history of biology, has written on Pasteur, Wilhelm Johannsen and Lysenko, arguing from detailed analysis of historical case studies that there is a basis for objectivity and rationality in empirical science.

In Bergen, Gunnar Skirbekk (1937–) and Ragnar Fjelland (1947–) have established a centre for the study of the sciences and humanities. Fjelland, who came from engineering to philosophy, is working on philosophical issues connected with science and technology, while Skirbekk has written several books in French, English and German, on political philosophy, rationality and other topics. Together with Nils Gilje (1947–) he has written a history of philosophy, which has been translated into several languages. Erik Brown (1943–) in Bergen and Magne Dybvig (1940–) and Sverre Sløgedal (1930–) in Trondheim are working in epistemology, while Audun Øfsti (1938–) in Trondheim and several of the philosophers in Troms, the world's northernmost university, are working in transcendental pragmatics.

Greek philosophy. The study of Greek philosophy in Norway is concentrated in Oslo, which has a special chair. Egil Wyller (1925–), who has written on Plato's Parmenides and worked out a Plato-inspired philosophy of unity called 'henology', has been succeeded in this chair by Eyjólfur Kjalar Emilsson (1943–), a native of Iceland. Emilsson, whose main work has been on Plotinus, now has two younger colleagues who, like himself, each received their Ph.D. in Greek philosophy from Princeton.

Kant. Several philosophers are working on Kant and German transcendental philosophy, among them two women in Oslo, Hjørdis Nerheim (1940–) – Norway's only woman professor in philosophy – and Camilla Serck-Hanssen (1960–), who has her Ph.D. from the University of California, San Diego. She worked there with Henry Allison (1937–), who since 1995 has been Professor at the University of Oslo.

Kierkegaard studies. Alastair Hannay (1932–) came to Oslo from London in 1961. He served as professor in Trondheim from 1975 to 1985 before returning to Oslo, where he was appointed professor in 1990. He has written extensively on Kierkegaard and has translated several of Kierkegaard's works into English. He has also written on the philosophy of mind, and since 1971 has been editor of the journal *Inquiry*, which was founded by Arne Næss in 1958.

Husserl's phenomenology. In Norway, the study of phenomenology started in Oslo in the 1950s and then spread to the other universities. In 1956 Dagfinn Føllesdal wrote his M.A. thesis on Husserl and Frege, and the following year Hans Skjervheim (1926–) wrote his on 'Objectivism and the study of man'. Skjervheim, who was professor in Bergen from 1982 until he retired, criticized various tendencies to 'objectivize' mental and social phenomena and not recognize their intentionality. Skjervheim has been important for an anti-positivist movement in Norway. There are now several young philosophers in Norway, chiefly in Oslo, working in phenomenology and related fields.

Wittgenstein. WITTGENSTEIN had his hut in Skjolden, one of the inner branches of the Sogne Fjord north of Bergen. Appropriately, the University of Bergen has taken the responsibility for The Norwegian Wittgenstein Project, whose aim is to register Wittgenstein's *Nachlaß* in electronic form.

Ethics. Ethics is an area of rising activity, and the central figure here has been Knut Erik Tranøy (1918–), professor in Bergen from 1959 to 1978, and in Oslo from 1978 to 1986. Tranøy was the first professor of medical ethics in Oslo (1986–8). In 1989 a centre for medical ethics was founded in Oslo on Tranøy's initiative. Tranøy has written on ethics, on science as a norm-guided activity, on Aquinas and on Wittgenstein. Also Tore Nordenstam (1934–) in Bergen has written extensively on ethics and also on aesthetics, as has Kjell S. Johannesen (1936–). In Oslo, Jon Wetlesen (1940–) has been a main contributor to ethics.

To build up more competence in ethics in Norway, the Norwegian Research Council started a ten-year ethics programme in 1991, which has thirty people working towards doctorates in ethics. Most concentrate on applied ethics and already have a doctorate or similar background in the field whose ethics they are studying.

There is also an effort to bring more women into philosophy. In addition to those mentioned above, there is Vigdis Songe-Møller (1949–) in Bergen, who has written on Parmenides and on women's issues. Also Else Viestad (1940–) is working on women's issues, as well as Else Barth (1928–), professor emeritus of analytic philosophy in Groningen.

6 Iceland

Iceland, with a population of merely 266,000, has two universities: the University of Iceland in the capital, Reykjavik, founded in 1911, and a small university in Akureyri in the north, established in 1987. At both universities the compulsory 'philosophicum' is taught. This has led to there now being five professorships in philosophy in Reykjavik and several lectureships there and in Akureyri. Since its beginning, Icelandic philosophy has been internationally oriented, and Icelandic philosophers have usually gone abroad for their doctorates. However, after their return to Iceland much of their effort has gone into making classical and contemporary philosophy accessible to Icelanders through translation and popular publications, and they have published relatively little for an international public. They have been working in all the central areas of philosophy, and also in the history of philosophy, on Plotinus, Descartes, Hume, Nietzsche, Husserl, Heidegger, Ingarden and Ricoeur.

References and further reading

General surveys

Bostad, I. and Svenneby, E. (1994) *Gender – an Issue for Philosophy?*, Oslo: Nordic network for women in philosophy. (Articles by women philosophers from the Nordic countries, with a roster of Nordic women philosophers and their work.)

Burr, J.R. (ed.) (1980) *Handbook of World Philosophy: Contemporary Developments Since 1945*, Westport, CT: Greenwood Press. (Articles on philosophy in the Nordic countries by Wedberg, Hintikka, Hartnack, Næss and Hellesnes.)

Embree, L. (ed.) (1997) *Encyclopedia of Phenomenology*, Dordrecht: Kluwer. (The article on Scandinavia surveys work in phenomenology.)

Klibansky, R. and Pears, D. (eds) (1993) *La philosophie en Europe*, Paris: Gallimard. (The article 'Pays nordiques' (Nordic countries) is a guide to young philosophers and their work.)

Olson, R.E. and Paul, A.M. (1972) *Contemporary Philosophy in Scandinavia*, Baltimore, MD: Johns Hopkins University Press. (Articles by Scandinavian philosophers, with an excellent survey of philosophy in Scandinavia by Georg Henrik von Wright.)

Sweden

* Bergström, L. (1966) *The Alternatives and Consequences of Action*, Stockholm Studies in Philosophy, Stockholm: Almqvist & Wiksell. (A very precise, critical discussion of some of the basic notions in utilitarianism.)

Dahlquist, T. (1976) 'Theoretical Philosophy, Practical Philosophy. Some pages from the History of Philosophy in Uppsala', *Uppsala University 500 years*, 5: Faculty of Arts at Uppsala University: History, Art and Philosophy, 129–46. (A brief survey of the history of philosophy in Uppsala.)

Halldén, S. (1986) *The Strategy of Ignorance: From Decision Logic to Evolutionary Epistemology*, Library of Theoria 17, Stockholm: Thales. (How decision logic helps us to understand the wisdom of living beings.)

Henschen-Dahlquist, A.-M. (1993) *En Ingemar Hedenius bibliografi*, Stockholm: Thales, 1993. (A bibliography of one of Sweden's publicly most visible philosophers.)

* Kanger, S. (1957) *Provability in Logic*, Stockholm Studies in Philosophy, Stockholm: Almqvist & Wiksell. (Dissertation, supervised by Wedberg, which anticipated Kripke.)

Marc-Wogau, K. (1967) *Philosophical Essays*, Library of Theoria 11, Lund: Gleerup. (Contains a bibliography of the writings of Konrad Marc-Wogau.)

Ofstad, H. (1990) *Our Concept of Weakness*, Stockholm: Almqvist & Wiksell. (Major study of Nazism by a former Professor of Practical philosophy in Stockholm.)

Phalén, A. (1914) *Zur Bestimmung des Begriffs des Psychischen*, Skrifter utgifna af K. Humanistiska Vetenskaps-Samfundet i Uppsala, Leipzig: Harrassowitz. (A critical discussion of various attempts to define consciousness, settles for a Husserl-inspired conception of consciousness as directedness.)

Prawitz, D. (1965) *Natural Deduction. A Proof Theoretical Study*, Stockholm Studies in Philosophy, Stockholm: Almqvist & Wiksell. (Dissertation, supervised by Wedberg, which was the first to prove Gentzen's Hauptsatz directly for certain systems of natural deduction.)

Sahlin, N.-E., and Segerberg, K. (eds) (1993) *The Philosophy of Sören Halldén*, (*Theoria* vol. 59),

Stockholm: Thales. (Contains a bibliography of the writings of Sören Halldén.)

Wedberg, A. (1955) *Plato's Philosophy of Mathematics*, Stockholm: Almqvist & Wiksell. (One of Wedberg's few, but high-quality publications.)

—— (1982–4) *History of Philosophy*, vols 1–3, Oxford: Oxford University Press. (A history of philosophy where the arguments stand in focus.)

Denmark

Blegvad, M. (1972) 'The Philosophy of Value of Harald Höffding', in R.E. Olson and A.M. Paul, *Contemporary Philosophy in Scandinavia*, Baltimore, MD: Johns Hopkins University Press, 1972. (The author's major works in ethics are all written in Danish.)

Collin, F. (1985) *Social Reality*, London: Routledge & Kegan Paul. (Clarification of key issues in contemporary social science by a young Copenhagen philosopher.)

Favrholdt, D. (1965) *An Interpretation and Critique of Wittgenstein's 'Tractatus'*, Copenhagen: Munksgaard. (Important dissertation which earned its author the first professorship in Odense.)

Hartnack, J. (1995) *Hegels Logik*, Frankfurt: Peter Lang. (The latest book by the prominent Aarhus philosopher.)

Jørgensen, J. (1964) 'Bibliography', *Danish Yearbook of Philosophy*, vol. 1, Copenhagen: Munksgaard, 183–96. (The bibliography is the last section of a Festschrift for Jørgensen.)

Løgstrup, K.E. (1997) *The Ethical Demand*, Notre Dame, IN: University of Notre Dame Press. (The main work of Denmark's most influential theologian/philosopher.)

Sandelin, K. (ed.) (1932) *Harald Höffding in Memoriam*, Copenhagen: Munksgaard. (Comprehensive bibliography of works by and on Höffding.)

Finland

Aarnio, A. (1983) *Philosophical Perspectives in Jurisprudence*, Helsinki: Acta Philosophica Fennica 36. (Starts with a forty-page survey of the development of legal theory and philosophy of law in Finland; extensive bibliography.)

Alanen, L. (1982) *Studies in Cartesian Epistemology and Philosophy of Mind*, Helsinki: Acta Philosophica Fennica 33. (Dissertation of Scandinavia's foremost Descartes-scholar.)

Bogdan, R. (ed.) (1987) *Jaakko Hintikka*, Profiles 8, Dordrecht: Reidel. (Essays on Hintikka's philosophy, with responses by Hintikka and a bibliography of his writings.)

Hintikka, J. (1996–) *Selected Papers*, Dordrecht: Kluwer. (Volume 1, *Ludwig Wittgenstein* and volume 2, *Lingua Universalis vs. Calculus Ratiocinator*, are the first of a multivolume edition of Hintikka's papers.)

Kaila, E. (1979) *Reality and Experience: Four Philosophical Essays*, Vienna Circle Collection, Dordrecht: Reidel. (One of the most characteristic works of the philosopher who inspired von Wright, Stenius and Ketonen.)

Niiniluoto, I. (1993) 'From logic to love: The Finnish tradition in philosophy', *Proceedings of the Estonian Academy of Sciences, Humanities and Social Sciences* 42 (4): 369–77. (A brief history of philosophy in Finland.)

Plato, J. von (1994) *Creating Modern Probability: Its Mathematics, Physics and Philosophy in Historical Perspective*, Cambridge: Cambridge University Press. (A major contribution to the history of probability theory by a young Finnish philosopher.)

Pörn, I. (1984) *The Philosophy of Erik Stenius*, (*Theoria* vol. 50), Stockholm: Thales. (With a bibliography of the writings of Erik Stenius.)

* Stenius, E. (1960) *Wittgenstein's Tractatus*, Oxford: Oxford University Press. (Incisive interpretation and defence of Wittgenstein's picture theory of language.)

Norway

Elster, J. (1979) *Ulysses and the Sirens: Studies in Rationality and Irrationality*, Cambridge: Cambridge University Press. (One of the author's many influential books on rationality and deviations from rationality.)

Hannay, A. (1990) *Human Consciousness*, London: Routledge. (The author's most recent book on the philosophy of mind.)

Roll-Hansen, N. (1979) 'Experimental Method and Spontaneous Generation: The Controversy between Pasteur and Pouchet 1859–64', *Journal of the History of Medicine and Allied Sciences* 34: 273–92. (Combines the history and the philosophy of biology in a way characteristic of the author.)

Skirbekk, G. (1993) *Rationality and Modernity: Essays in Philosophical Pragmatics*, Oslo: Universitetsforlaget. (Essays by a productive Bergen philosopher.)

Tranøy, K.E. (1988) *The Moral Import of Science*, ed. A.J.I. Jones, Bergen: Sigma. (With a bibliography of the writings of Knut Erik Trany.)

Iceland

Emilsson, E.K. (1988) *Plotinus on Sense Perception*, Cambridge: Cambridge University Press. (A main work by an Icelandic philosopher who is now professor in Oslo.)

Karlsson, M.M. (1978) 'Doubt, reason and Cartesian therapy', in M. Hooker (ed.) *Descartes: Critical and Interpretive Essays*, Baltimore, MD: Johns Hopkins University Press. (One of the most influential articles from Iceland.)

DAGFINN FØLLESDAL

SCEPTICISM

Simply put, scepticism is the view that we fail to know anything. More generally, the term 'scepticism' refers to a family of views, each of which denies that some term of positive epistemic appraisal applies to our beliefs. Thus, sceptical doctrines might hold that none of our beliefs is certain, that none of our beliefs is justified, that none of our beliefs is reasonable, that none of our beliefs is more reasonable than its denial, and so on. Sceptical doctrines can also vary with respect to the kind of belief they target. Scepticism can be restricted to beliefs produced in certain ways: for example, scepticism concerning beliefs based on memory, on inductive reasoning or even on any reasoning whatsoever. And sceptical views can be restricted to beliefs about certain subjects: for example, scepticism concerning beliefs about the external world, beliefs about other minds, beliefs about value and so on. Solipsism – the view that all that exists is the self and its states – can be seen as a form of scepticism based on the claim that there are no convincing arguments for the existence of anything beyond the self.

The philosophical problem of scepticism derives from what appear to be very strong arguments for sceptical conclusions. Since most philosophers are unwilling to accept those conclusions, there is a problem concerning how to respond to the arguments. For example, one kind of sceptical argument attempts to show that we have no knowledge of the world around us. The argument hinges on the claim that we are not in a position to rule out the possibility that we are brains-in-a-vat being artificially stimulated to have just the sensory experience we are actually having. We have no basis for ruling out this possibility since if it were actual, our experience would not change in any way. The sceptic then claims that if we cannot rule out the possibility that we are brains-in-a-vat, then we cannot know anything about the world around us.

Responses to this argument often fall into one of two categories. Some philosophers argue that we can rule out the possibility that we are brains-in-a-vat. Others argue that we do not need to be able to rule out this possibility in order to have knowledge of the world around us.

1   **The philosophical problem of scepticism**
2   **Responses to scepticism**
3   **Relevant alternatives fallibilism**
4   ***Modus ponens* fallibilism**
5   **The role of intuitions**

1   The philosophical problem of scepticism

Most contemporary discussions of scepticism have focused on scepticism concerning the external world. We can use this type of scepticism to illustrate the broader philosophical problem, as many of the arguments we consider can be applied *mutatis mutandis* to other types of scepticism.

One type of scepticism denies that we know anything about the external world. The view is not simply that, for example, by gathering more evidence we could come to know. Rather, it is that we are unable to attain knowledge. On the plausible assumption that knowledge entails justified belief, scepticism concerning knowledge follows from scepticism concerning justified belief – the view that justified belief about the external world is unattainable.

Scepticism is of philosophical interest because there appear to be very strong arguments that support it. This presents us with the problem of how to respond to these arguments. One way would be to accept their conclusion. Of course, very few philosophers are willing to do this. There are very few actual sceptics. So the problem of scepticism is how to refute or in some way neutralize or deflate the force of these arguments.

In the history of philosophy, some sceptical arguments have been based on the unreliability or relativity of our senses (see PYRRHONISM), or upon the inability of reason to produce non-question begging arguments for our beliefs (see HUME, D. §2). Nearly all sceptical arguments exploit sceptical hypotheses or alternatives. Sceptical alternatives suppose that the world is very different from what we would normally believe on the basis of our sensory evidence. This entails that our sensory evidence is radically misleading. More precisely, suppose we claim to know a proposition q on the basis of evidence e. Let (proposition) h be an *alternative* to q just in case h is incompatible with q (q and h cannot both be true). Then h is a *sceptical alternative* to q provided h is an alternative to q compatible with e. An alternative of this kind has sceptical force precisely because it is compatible with the evidence we claim gives us knowledge of *q*. For example, ordinarily, I would claim to know on the basis of my visual evidence that I am currently looking at my computer monitor. One sceptical alternative, introduced by Descartes (1641), is that the world of familiar objects does not exist and that I am being deceived into thinking it does by a powerful demon. The demon causes me to have just the sensory experiences I would have if the world of familiar objects existed (see DESCARTES, R. §4). According to a modern version of this alternative, I am a brain-in-a-vat being artificially stimulated to have all the experiences I would have if I had a body and interacted, in the normal way, with the world of familiar objects. These alternatives are incompatible with what I claim to know about the familiar world around me since according to those alternatives, that world does not exist. Moreover, since these alternatives entail that it appears to me as if that world exists, they are compatible with my evidence.

Sceptical alternatives provide the basis for very powerful sceptical arguments. Exactly how they do this is a matter of some controversy. The quickest route to scepticism is through what I will call the entailment principle:

S knows *q* on the basis of (evidence) *e* only if *e* entails *q*

Since a sceptical alternative is, by definition, a proposition incompatible with *q* but compatible with *e*, it follows from the mere existence of sceptical alternatives of the kind we have been considering that we do not know those empirical propositions we ordinarily claim to know. But, this argument is only as good as the entailment principle. Should we accept this principle? In effect, the principle says I can know *p* only if my evidence precludes the possibility of error. Though many philosophers concede that this principle has considerable intuitive force, most have thought, in the end, that it should be rejected. This position is sometimes called fallibilism (see COMMONSENSISM §§1–2; FALLIBILISM). Of course, few philosophers believe that scepticism should be avoided at all costs. But when given a choice between scepticism and fallibilism, most philosophers opt for fallibilism (at the expense of the entailment principle).

Does fallibilism beg the question against scepticism? After all, precisely what the sceptic claims is that the existence of alternatives consistent with our evidence undermines our claims to know. Fallibilists merely respond that the alternatives the sceptic has invoked do not undermine our knowledge claims: that is, we can know even when there are such alternatives. Since this is the point at issue, fallibilists seem to need an argument in support of this crucial claim.

Here, fallibilists can appeal to our strong intuition that in many cases we do know things, despite the existence of sceptical alternatives. And it is not clear that the sceptic can undermine those intuitions except by appealing to the entailment principle – which is itself undermined by those very intuitions. Thus neither side of the debate may be able to defend its position without begging the question.

Unfortunately scepticism is not so easily dispatched. The sceptic can turn the appeal to our ordinary intuitions against fallibilism. For some of those intuitions can provide the basis for a new sceptical argument. This argument begins by claiming, quite plausibly, that whatever else we may say about the significance of sceptical alternatives, we cannot claim, plausibly, to know they are false. For example, we cannot claim, plausibly, to know that we are not brains-in-a-vat being artificially stimulated to have exactly the same experience we would have as normal human beings. None of our evidence counts against this hypothesis since if it were true, we would have precisely that evidence.

But how, exactly, does this permit the sceptic to conclude we do not know the propositions we ordinarily claim to know? At this point, the sceptic appeals to a very intuitive principle that is weaker than the entailment principle. This principle says that the set of known (by *S*) propositions is closed under known (by *S*) entailment:

If *S* knows *q*, and *S* knows that *q* entails not-*h*, then *S* knows not-*h*

While one could quibble with some details about this principle, it (or something very much like it) seems compelling (see DEDUCTIVE CLOSURE PRINCIPLE). From this principle and the claim that we fail to know sceptical alternatives are false, it follows that we fail to know the propositions we ordinarily claim to know (since we know those propositions entail the falsity of sceptical alternatives).

2 Responses to scepticism

This argument presents problems for fallibilism, as I have characterized it, since the argument at no point presupposes the entailment principle. The sceptical argument we are now considering merely exploits the fallibilist position that permits the existence of alternatives to known propositions.

Fallibilist responses come in two forms, each of which corresponds to the denial of one of the two premises of the sceptical argument. One response denies the closure principle. For example, Dretske (1970) has argued that the fact that we do not know the falsity of sceptical alternatives shows that the closure principle is false, since we do know the truth of many empirical propositions that (we know) entail the falsity of sceptical alternatives. According to this view, certain alternatives are not relevant to whether one knows a proposition: one does not have to know such an alternative to q is false in order to know q. So, for example, one can know that one sees a zebra without knowing that the alternative – that one sees a cleverly disguised mule – is false, because that alternative is not relevant. This version of fallibilism is sometimes called the 'relevant alternatives' view.

The other fallibilist response to the sceptical argument agrees with the sceptic that the closure principal is true. But, against the sceptic, these fallibilists deny the claim that we fail to know the falsity of sceptical alternatives. One version of this fallibilist response uses the closure principle along with the claim that we do have knowledge, to reject the claim that we do not know that sceptical alternatives are false. They argue from the premise that we know some ordinary proposition q and the premise that if we know q then we know any proposition that we know is entailed by q (the closure principle), to the conclusion that we know that we are not seeing a cleverly disguised mule. We can call this view '*modus ponens* fallibilism'.

3   Relevant alternatives fallibilism

As we have noted, the sceptic attempts to undermine our claims to know by calling attention to sceptical alternatives. The relevant alternatives response to this sceptical manoeuvre is to deny that these alternatives are relevant. An alternative, h, to q, is relevant just in case we need to know h is false in order to know q. So if h is not a relevant alternative, we can still know q even if we fail to know h is false. This view entails that the deductive closure principle is false.

There are two ways to argue for this view. The direct way is to cite alleged counterexamples to the deductive closure principle. Some philosophers have done this by appealing both to our intuition that we know many propositions about the external world and to our intuition that we fail to know the falsity of sceptical alternatives. So my strong intuition that I know I am looking at my computer monitor and my strong intuition that I fail to know I am not a brain-in-a-vat constitute the basis for such a counter-example.

A more indirect way to argue for this view is to construct a theory of knowledge that has as a consequence, the failure of the closure principle, as in Nozick (1981). The basic idea of these kinds of theories is that knowing requires the truth of certain subjunctive conditionals. On one (simplified) version, my knowing q requires that:

(S) If q were false, I would not believe q

This requirement for knowledge precludes my knowing I am not a brain-in-a-vat. For I would still believe I am not a brain-in-a-vat, even if I were a brain-in-a-vat. But, this requirement allows me to know I see a computer monitor. For it seems plausible to claim that I would not believe I see the computer monitor if I were not seeing it.

A significant difficulty for the direct way of arguing for the relevant alternatives view – the appeal to counterexamples to the closure principle – is that the intuitions that support the counterexamples seem no more compelling than the intuitions in favour of the closure principle. Many think that the closure principle expresses a fundamental truth about our concept of knowledge. So much so that if a certain theory of knowledge entails the falsity of the closure principle, some philosophers are inclined to take the fact as a *reductio ad absurdum* of that theory.

But this presents problems for the indirect way of arguing for the relevant alternatives view: some philosophers reject theories that endorse condition (S), for the very reason that it entails the falsity of the closure principle. Moreover, there are other difficulties for theories that endorse conditions like (S). One problem for these theories is that they seem to preclude our knowing much of what we take ourselves to know inductively. Consider an example where you leave a glass containing some ice cubes outside on an extremely hot day (Vogel 1987). Several hours later, while you are still inside escaping the heat, you remember the glass you left outside. You infer that the ice must have melted by now. Here we have an ordinary case of knowledge by inductive inference. According to the theories we are now considering, my knowing that the ice cubes have melted requires the truth of this subjunctive conditional:

(S′) If the ice cubes had not melted, I would not believe that they had

But (S′) looks false. It seems plausible to claim that had the ice cubes not melted, it might have been for some reason (for example, someone putting them in a styrofoam cooler) that would still leave me believing they had melted. Thus, it looks as if theories which endorse this condition are too strong. If this is correct, then the anti-sceptical results afforded by condition (S) come at the cost of scepticism about certain kinds of inductive knowledge.

We should note, however, that there is some controversy over the evaluation of subjunctive conditionals like (S′). But I think it is fair to say that standard semantics for subjunctive conditionals would render (S′) as false (see DEDUCTIVE CLOSURE PRINCIPLE §§2–3).

4 *Modus ponens* fallibilism

Modus ponens fallibilists accept, along with the sceptic, the deductive closure principle. But they attempt to turn that principle against the sceptic. Like relevant alternatives fallibilists, they take as a starting point the strongly intuitive claim that we do know many things about the world. They then note that, given the closure principle, it follows that we know the falsity of sceptical alternatives. For example, I now know that I am looking at my computer monitor. I also know that my looking at a computer monitor precludes my being a brain-in-a-vat. It follows by the closure principle that I know I am not a brain-in-a-vat.

Is this piece of reasoning legitimate? One might challenge those who reason in this way to explain how we know sceptical alternatives are false. How, for example, do I know I am not a brain-in-a-vat? After all, the sceptical problem arises because we seem to lack any reason for believing sceptical alternatives are false. These alternatives are constructed so as to make it impossible for our evidence to count against them. Presumably, our recognition of this explains, at least in part, our intuition that we fail to know sceptical alternatives are false.

One way for the *modus ponens* fallibilist to try to meet this challenge is to claim that I can know:

not-*h*: I am not a brain-in-a-vat

by inferring it from:

q: I am looking at my computer monitor

According to this way of proceeding, even though none of my evidence for *q* counts in favour of not-*h*, it does not follow that I have no reason to believe not-*h*. For that reason can be *q* itself. Since I know *q* (on the basis of my visual evidence) and I know that *q* entails not-*h*, I can infer not-*h* from q and thereby come to know not-*h*.

Is this reasoning legitimate? Let's compare it with another case. Suppose I park my car in front of the market and go inside. Although I am not currently looking out the window I can still know:

p: My car is parked in front of the store

Can I then come to know:

r: My car has not been towed away

simply by inferring it from *p*? Notice that *p* entails *r*. It seems, none the less, that I would already need to have

sufficient evidence to know *r* before I could infer *p*. And if my initial evidence is insufficient for me to know *r*, I cannot infer *p* and so I cannot infer *r* from *p*.

The *modus ponens* fallibilist reasoning concerning sceptical alternatives looks suspicious because it seems like the reasoning in the parked car case. Intuitively, I need to have reason to believe not-*h* before I can infer (and thereby come to know) *q*. Thus I cannot first infer *q* and then go on to infer (and thereby come to know) non-*h*.

Another version of fallibilism argues for the claim that we know sceptical alternatives are false by appealing to principles of inductive inference. One version of this view argues that the hypothesis that the familiar world of objects exists is the best explanation of our sensory evidence (and so a better explanation than sceptical alternatives). This licenses an inference from our sensory evidence to the familiar-world hypothesis (see INFERENCE TO THE BEST EXPLANATION). We can thereby come to know that this familiar world exists. And since we know that the familiar-world hypothesis rules out the sceptical alternatives, it follows by the closure principle that we know sceptical alternatives are false.

The burden for this view is to say why the familiar-world hypothesis is a better explanation of our sensory evidence than any sceptical alternative. This is not easy to do since sceptical alternatives are designed to explain our sensory evidence. Proponents of the view that sceptical alternatives provide inferior explanations often appeal to pragmatic considerations like simplicity and conservatism. But there are several problems with this approach. Even if we could establish that the familiar-world hypothesis is, for example, simpler than any sceptical alternative, why should we think that this supports the claim that the hypothesis is true? Unless this crucial link can be made, it is not clear how this response to the sceptic can succeed (see THEORETICAL (EPISTEMIC) VIRTUES).

Moreover, often arguments that the familiar-world hypothesis is the best explanation of our sensory data are quite sophisticated and complex. This raises the worry that only those who are philosophically sophisticated enough to follow such an argument can have knowledge of the external world.

5 The role of intuitions

Many fallibilist responses to the sceptic take as their starting point our ordinary intuitions about knowledge or our everyday pattern of knowledge attributions. But how exactly can our everyday pattern of knowledge attributions have force against sceptical arguments, since the sceptic is calling into question precisely these attributions?

The reason our ordinary intuitions about knowledge have force against the sceptic is that these intuitions persist even in the face of sceptical arguments. When we confront a sceptical argument, even though we may not be able to say where the argument goes wrong, we are reluctant to withdraw our everyday knowledge attributions. This is the basis of G.E. Moore's famous response to sceptical arguments. Moore claimed to be more sure that he knew some things, for example, that he has a hand, than he is that the sceptical argument is sound. So even though he could not say where the sceptical argument goes wrong, he thought it more rational to suppose that there is a mistake in the sceptical argument than to suppose that the conclusion of the argument – we fail to know anything – is true (see MOORE, G.E. §3; COMMONSENSISM).

The sceptic could try to dismiss the significance of our reluctance to withdraw our everyday knowledge attributions as nothing more than the persistence of old habits. This persistence of our habitual ways of thinking about knowledge even after we have been confronted with sceptical arguments was noticed by Descartes and by Hume.

But in response, we can note that, often, we find our everyday pattern of knowledge attributions compelling even while we are in the midst of sincere philosophical reflection. The fact is that when we think about sceptical arguments, we often find ourselves pulled in two directions. We feel the pull of the sceptical argument and yet we remain reluctant to give up our claims to know. This phenomenon cannot be dismissed as nothing more than an unreflective habit. So the fallibilist can maintain that our everyday knowledge attributions reflect deep-seated intuitions about our concept of knowledge. Since our intuitions are a kind of data that any theory of knowledge must explain, they present a formidable challenge to the sceptical position.

Nevertheless, there is something unsatisfying about rejecting scepticism just because it conflicts with our intuitions about knowledge. For, again, it is hard to deny the force of the sceptical argument. And just as our intuitions about our everyday knowledge attributions present a problem for scepticism, so our sceptical intuitions present a challenge to our everyday knowledge attributions. If scepticism is a strongly counterintuitive view, then why do sceptical arguments have any grip on us at all? Why do we not immediately respond to sceptical arguments by objecting, for example, that sceptical hypotheses are too remote and fanciful to undermine our knowledge claims? (Either we can know that sceptical alternatives are false or we need not know they are false in order to know things about the external world.) Sometimes we are inclined to do just that. But the sceptical problem arises precisely because we cannot always sustain that attitude. Sometimes, when we consider sceptical arguments, we begin to worry that sceptical alternatives really do threaten our knowledge claims.

What we are confronting here is a paradox – a set of inconsistent propositions, each of which has considerable independent plausibility:

(1) We know some ordinary empirical propositions.
(2) We do not know that sceptical alternatives are false.
(3) If S knows q, and S knows that q entails not-h, then S knows not-h.

One of these propositions must be false (on the assumption that we know q entails not-h). Yet each of them is very difficult to deny. This is what explains our vacillation over scepticism. The arguments for scepticism and for fallibilism attempt to exploit the intuitions favourable to them. The sceptic appeals to (2) and (3), and concludes that (1) is false. Relevant alternatives fallibilism appeals to (1) and (2), and concludes that (3) is false. *Modus ponens* fallibilism appeals to (1) and (3), and concludes that (2) is false. Because each member of the set has independent plausibility, it seems arbitrary and unsatisfying to appeal to any two members of this triad as an argument against the third. Such a strategy does not provide what any successful resolution of a paradox should provide, namely an explanation of how the paradox arises in the first place. Any satisfying resolution of the paradox that defends our claims to know against the sceptic must explain the appeal of sceptical arguments. For it is that very appeal that gives rise to the paradox.

This is where Moore's response to the sceptic goes wrong. Many philosophers think that Moore begged the question against scepticism. In a way he did, but no more so than the sceptic begs the question against him. Still, there is something quite unsatisfying, philosophically, about Moore's treatment of the sceptical argument. But the problem with it is not that it begs the question against the sceptic. Rather the problem is that it fails to explain the dialectic force of sceptical arguments. Though it is possible that the apparent cogency of sceptical arguments is explained by some very subtle error in our reasoning, the simplicity of these arguments suggests that their appeal reveals something deep and important about our concept of knowledge. That is why we can learn much about the nature of knowledge by grappling with the problem of scepticism.

See also: CAUSATION, INDIAN THEORIES OF §2;
INDUCTION, EPISTEMIC ISSUES IN; INTERNALISM AND
EXTERNALISM IN EPISTEMOLOGY; JUSTIFICATION,
EPISTEMIC §6; KNOWLEDGE, CONCEPT OF §8;
KNOWLEDGE, INDIAN VIEWS OF §4; PERCEPTION,
EPISTEMIC ISSUES IN; PHENOMENOLOGY, EPISTEMIC
ISSUES IN; RATIONAL BELIEFS §2; RELIABILISM;
SCEPTICISM, RENAISSANCE; SOLIPSISM

References and further reading

Cohen, S. (1988) 'How to be a fallibilist' in J. Tomberlin (ed.) *Philosophical Perspectives*, 2, Atascadero, CA: Ridgeview, 91–123. (This contributor's treatment of scepticism.)

Cornman, J. (1980) *Scepticism, Justification, and Explanation*, Dordrecht: Reidel. (Defends inference to the best explanation response – see §4.)

* Descartes, R. (1641) *Meditations on First Philosophy*, in E. Haldane and G.R.T. Ross (eds) *The Philosophical Works of Descartes*, Mineola, NY: Dover Publications, 1955. (Meditation I contains a classic statement of the sceptical problem.)

* Dretske, F. (1970) 'Epistemic Operators', *Journal of Philosophy* 67: 1007–23. (Argues against the deductive closure principle for knowledge.)

Klein, P. (1981) *Certainty*, Minneapolis, MN: University of Minnesota Press. (Detailed defence of *modus ponens* fallibilism.)

Moore, G.E. (1959) 'Certainty', in W. Doney (ed.) *Descartes: A Collection of Critical Essays*, Garden City, NY: Doubleday, 1967. (Classic statement of *modus ponens* fallibilism.)

* Nozick, R. (1981) *Philosophical Explanations*, Cambridge, MA: Harvard University Press. (Detailed defence of a theory that endorses condition *S* – see chapter 3.)

Unger, P. (1975) *Ignorance*, New York: Oxford University Press. (Influential defence of scepticism.)

* Vogel, J. (1987) 'Tracking, Closure and Inductive Knowledge', in S. Luper-Foy (ed.) *The Possibility of Knowledge: Nozick and His Critics*, Totowa, NJ: Rowman & Littlefield. (Critical discussion of condition *S*.)

Wittgenstein, L. (1921) *Tractatus Logico-Philosophicus*, trans. D.F. Pears and B.F. McGuinness, London: Routledge & Kegan Paul, 1961. (Interesting treatment of solipsism.)

STEWART COHEN

SCEPTICISM, MORAL
see MORAL SCEPTICISM

SCEPTICISM, RENAISSANCE

Ancient Greek scepticism was revived during the Renaissance, and played an important role in the religious and philosophical controversies of the time. There is little evidence that ancient scepticism was known directly during the Middle Ages, or that its perplexing questions played any significant role in medieval thought. It was indirectly known from the writings of Augustine; some manuscripts of the texts of Cicero and Sextus Empiricus were available; and occasionally vague reference to some sceptical details appears in medieval discussions. However, the interests of scholastic philosophers were, by and large, far removed from the questions about the sources, reliability and certainty of knowledge claims that concerned the ancient sceptics. With the humanistic revival of interest in ancient literature there came a rediscovery of scepticism as presented in the writings of Cicero, Sextus Empiricus and Diogenes Laertius. Cicero's Academics *(*Academica*) was read from the fourteenth century on;* Life of Pyrrho *by Diogenes Laertius was rediscovered in the early fifteenth century; and Greek manuscripts of the writings of Sextus were brought from Constantinople into Italy in the mid-fifteenth century. These treasuries of sceptical argumentation were used in many ways in the Renaissance. At first they were seen largely as sources of information about the ancient world, but gradually more attention was paid to the actual arguments they contained. Some saw these arguments as a basis for rejecting Aristotelian philosophy, as well as other ancient dogmatic claims about nature and humanity. Others used them as ammunition in the great religious controversies between Catholics and Protestants. A full-fledged scepticism about knowledge claims was developed in the second part of the sixteenth century, through the work of Sanches and Montaigne. Montaigne was particularly inspired by the first published Latin translations of the writings of Sextus Empiricus. Scepticism in all its forms was closely associated with fideism. If it is impossible to acquire knowledge of anything through the senses and reason, then it is impossible to acquire knowledge of God in these ways, and one can argue that religious truth must be accepted on the basis of faith in divine revelation. The weak recommendation of ancient sceptics to suspend belief while accepting local customs as the guide for conduct was thus turned into a strong recommendation to adopt Christian beliefs. Only later* *did epistemological scepticism become associated with scepticism about religious beliefs themselves. Renaissance scepticism in its various guises was a major intellectual force in the transition from scholasticism to modern thought.*

1 **Recovery of ancient texts**
2 **Informal sceptical currents**
3 **Early scepticism and the Reformation**
4 **Scepticism and anti-scholasticism**
5 **Philosophical scepticism: Sanches, Montaigne, Charron**
6 **Impact of Renaissance scepticism**

1 Recovery of ancient texts

The most important direct sources of ancient scepticism are Cicero's philosophical dialogue, *Academics* (*Academica*), written in Latin (see CICERO §3); *Outlines of Pyrrhonism* and *Against the Professors* (*Adversus Mathematicos*) by SEXTUS EMPIRICUS, both written in Greek; and the *Life of Pyrrho* which DIOGENES LAERTIUS, included in his *Lives of the Philosophers*, also written in Greek. Through these works Renaissance authors became acquainted with two types of scepticism, both of which employed arguments and dialectical puzzles to cast doubt on sense perception and reason as sources of knowledge and on the possibility of formulating any reliable criterion for judging knowledge claims. Academic sceptics (whose views were formulated from the third to the first century BC), at least as interpreted during the Renaissance, were those who denied the possibility of any knowledge, thus adopting negative dogmatism. They were also said to have allowed probable judgments, a stance criticized by MONTAIGNE (§3) who said 'Either we can judge absolutely, or we absolutely cannot.' Pyrrhonian sceptics, who were followers of PYRRHO, preferred to say that judgment should be suspended altogether. This epistemological stance had moral implications, for the sceptic was then exhorted to live peacefully in accordance with the laws and customs of society.

During the Middle Ages, scepticism was known only indirectly through Augustine's attack on Academic scepticism in his *Contra Academicos* and *De Trinitate* (see AUGUSTINE §2). The *Life of Pyrrho* was not available at all, and while there are some medieval manuscripts of Cicero's *Academics* and some early fourteenth-century manuscripts of a partial Latin translation of *Outlines of Pyrrhonism* by Sextus Empiricus, there is no evidence that anyone made use of this material. Only in fourteenth-century Byzantium was there any interest in ancient scepticism. Nor was there any independent development of

scepticism. Neoplatonic doubts about sense perception as a basis for knowledge, various types of mysticism, and fourteenth-century discussions both of intuitive cognition and of God's absolute power certainly allowed opportunity for such development, but the opportunity was not taken. The main factor in the revival of scepticism was the recovery of the ancient texts.

These texts first became known in Italy through the work of the humanists, though after the 1520s the focus of attention shifted to northern Europe. Cicero's *Academics* was the first to be read, though it never became very popular. While it had been available before the fourteenth century, it became better known after Petrarch (see PETRARCA, F.) referred to it. It was printed with the other works of Cicero in 1471, but the first separate printed text only dates from 1535 and the first commentary from 1536. Diogenes Laertius' *Lives of the Philosophers* (including the *Life of Pyrrho*) was widely known and studied from the early fifteenth century in Latin and Italian translations, and the first Greek text was printed in 1533. It was used to supplement the information available from Latin sources.

The most important ancient source is Sextus Empiricus. His work was almost unknown until the mid-fifteenth century, when manuscripts from Constantinople began to circulate in Italy. By the end of the century Greek manuscripts were available in Rome, Venice and Florence, especially in the library of the convent of San Marco where Girolamo Savonarola was the prior. At first, Sextus Empiricus seems to have been regarded as a literary, philological and historical source, rather than as a source of epistemological problems. Serious philosophical attention was paid to him in northern Europe after the publication of two Latin translations. His *Outlines of Pyrrhonism* was published by the Protestant Henri Estienne in 1562, and his *Against the Professors* was published (along with Estienne's translation of *Outlines of Pyrrhonism*) in 1569 by the Catholic Counter-Reformer Gentian Hervet. The Greek texts were not printed until 1621.

The term 'sceptic' itself comes from the recovery of the ancient texts, for *scepticus* and its Latin cognates became an accepted part of the intellectual lexicon only during the fifteenth century.

2 Informal sceptical currents

Many developments in the Renaissance raised problems and questions about accepted beliefs, and gave rise to an informal scepticism about previous knowledge claims in many areas. One important factor was the European discovery of America and the first voyages round Africa to India, China and Japan which led to the discovery of new cultures, civilizations and religions all over the planet. Information brought back by the explorers and later by Jesuit missionaries, raised doubts about all previous claims about geography, and even about the nature of the human being. Could one still accept the biblical view about human origins? Where did all these different people come from? Were they truly human? Attempts were made to fit everybody into the biblical framework by referring to possible migrations after the Flood and after the Tower of Babel episode. But could this really account for how people crossed wide oceans, and had such different ways of living? Some hardy souls suggested that the American Indians were, perhaps, pre-Adamites, peoples who had an independent origin. If this were the case then the Bible could no longer be considered the complete history of humanity. Thomas Harriot, who accompanied Sir Walter Ralegh to Virginia, is supposed to have presented an 'atheist' lecture on his return in which he said that American Indian history was 16,000 years old, while biblical history was supposed to have started only in 4004 BC. Giordano Bruno suggested that there were three original protoplasts from which three different kinds of human being developed. In the seventeenth century, Isaac La Peyrère (1596?–1676) in his book *Prae-Adamitae* (1655) offered the hypothesis that there were humans before Adam who were not created by God, but were part of an eternal universe. Only Adam was divinely created as a way of starting divine history, the history of the Jews, but not the rest of humanity.

Another source of informal scepticism was the influence of humanism on Bible scholarship. The increased use of Greek and Hebrew raised serious sceptical questions as to whether the biblical text is correct, complete and accurate. ERASMUS questioned whether the doctrine of the Trinity was really in the original version of the New Testament. Others, especially those using Jewish materials, questioned the accepted Christian readings of the text. Some, like Michael Servetus, who was burned at the stake in 1553 by John Calvin and his followers, even suggested that the Bible had to be understood contextually, in terms of what was going on in ancient pre-Christian times, rather than in terms of foreshadowings of the New Testament. Scholars began questioning the authenticity of some of the canonic writings and the status of the Apocrypha (see HUMANISM, RENAISSANCE §6).

Along with the growing knowledge of Hebrew during the Renaissance came the awareness of a wholly different way of understanding Scripture and the cosmos, namely that presented in the Jewish Kabbalistic writings. The Kabbalah was a series of medieval Jewish treatises containing Neoplatonic and Gnostic elements (see KABBALAH). The treatises purported to contain an ancient wisdom and to offer non-rational ways of understanding the world. Many thinkers combined the study of the Kabbalah with the study of the *Corpus Hermeticum*, a body of writings from the second and third centuries AD (see HERMETISM). These too contained a mixture of Neoplatonic, Gnostic, Jewish and other elements, and they purported to record a wisdom which predated Greek philosophy. These sources influenced such authors as Giovanni PICO DELLA MIRANDOLA, Leone Ebreo and AGRIPPA VON NETTESHEIM. The mix of Kabbalistic learning with Neoplatonism gave rise to a wide variety of new religious interpretations, some of them like those of Guillaume Postel and Giordano Bruno, definitely heretical, and sceptical of accepted Christianity.

Another, originally less intellectual, critique of accepted Christianity was offered by Spanish mystics (usually Jewish forced converts) who claimed to be directly illuminated by God. At the beginning of the sixteenth century, some Spanish women with no theological training began offering a version of what they considered pure Christianity, gained through special non-rational practices. Despite persecution by the Spanish Inquisition, the mysticism of the *alumbrados* became a most important spiritual force, especially as expressed by Teresa of Avila and Juan de la Cruz (John of the Cross), and led many to scepticism about accepted Christian theology and the efficacy of Church practices (see MYSTICISM, HISTORY OF §6).

Developments in science challenged accepted views in medicine, astronomy and physics. PARACELSUS (§3) presented a new view of the role of medicine in relation to human nature and the cosmos; COPERNICUS raised questions about the accepted geocentric theory of the universe; and BRUNO (§§4–5) and others cast doubt on Aristotelian science.

Some people (for example, Jardine 1983) have suggested that humanist dialectic, in placing an emphasis on techniques of persuasion and probable argumentation, was influenced by Academic scepticism as presented by Cicero. However, Lorenzo VALLA (§4) rejected such nonstandard argument forms as *sorites*, and later humanist logicians failed to present a genuine informal logic of probabilities (see LOGIC, RENAISSANCE §4).

All these currents none the less created an informal kind of scepticism that was pervasive in the late Renaissance world. As John Donne put it, 'new philosophy calls all in doubt'. This informal general scepticism was often combined with an informal use of the ancient sceptical texts. References to items that appear in Sextus and Cicero are in many authors of the period. RABELAIS (§2), for instance, introduced a Pyrrhonian professor as a comic foil to Pantagruel in a discussion of whether Panurge should marry. The Pyrrhonian professor uses the terms of ancient scepticism without really developing the view. Other thinkers contented themselves with a general attack on the possibility of knowledge. For instance, AGRIPPA VON NETTESHEIM (§3) in his *De incertitudine et vanitate scientiarum et artium* (Of the Vanity and Uncertainty of Arts and Sciences) (1526) – a most popular work of the time, translated into many languages – attacked all kinds of intellectual activity and knowledge claims in a way that is anecdotal rather than systematic, though he did draw materials from both Cicero and Sextus.

3 Early scepticism and the Reformation

The first use of Greek scepticism in the religious controversies of the time appears in the views of Girolamo Savonarola and his leading disciple, Gianfrancesco Pico della Mirandola (1469–1533), the nephew of the great fifteenth-century humanist Giovanni Pico. Savonarola was a Dominican monk and philosophy teacher in Florence who pressed for reform of the Catholic Church. Although he campaigned against pagan philosophy, he apparently suggested the reading of Sextus as an introduction to Christian faith, and he wanted his monks to prepare a Latin translation of Sextus' works. This did not happen, as he was condemned as a heretic and burned at the stake in 1498. His disciple, Gianfrancesco Pico, presented Sextus' arguments for the European audience in his anti-Aristotelian work, *Examen vanitatis doctrinae gentium* (An Examination of the Emptiness of Pagan Learning) (1520). Like Savonarola, he saw Sextus' attacks on all forms of intellectual pursuits as a way of making people accept religious revelation as the sole basis for knowledge. He made serious use of Sextus' arguments against various ancient schools of philosophy, and he attacked Aristotelian sense-based epistemology. Pico's work had some influence on various Renaissance thinkers, and was known to GASSENDI (§3) and LEIBNIZ (§10). It was used along with Sextus' arguments by a Venetian rabbi in the early seventeenth century as a means of getting Jews to accept the Torah as the sole source of truth.

The early use of scepticism in the religious controversies of the Reformation is illustrated by the debate between Desiderius ERASMUS (§§4, 6) and Martin LUTHER. Erasmus was interested in Academic scepticism as presented by Cicero. In his *In Praise of Folly* (1511), where he criticized all kinds of philosophical views, Erasmus said that he found the Academic sceptics 'the least surly' of all the philosophers because they had the good sense not to dogmatically assert anything. Erasmus' own *philosophia Christi* was an acceptance of the spirit of Christ's teachings without buttressing them with any metaphysical principles or systems.

When Luther challenged the Church of Rome's unique claim to determine Christian truth, Erasmus was initially supportive of this challenge to an apparently overbearing authority, but as Luther himself became more and more dogmatic in his pronouncements, Erasmus slowly withdrew his support and remained within the Catholic Church. He was urged by Catholic leaders to speak out against the Reformation and finally did so in his *Discourse on Free Will* (1524), which challenged Luther. Erasmus contended that the subject was too complicated for human beings to understand, and the Scriptures were too difficult to interpret on the matter. Because of this Erasmus recommended that one adopt the sceptical attitude of suspending judgment while accepting the traditional view, that of the Church, undogmatically.

Luther found Erasmus' gentle scepticism, offered as a reason for remaining a Catholic, totally unacceptable. Christians, Luther insisted, cannot be sceptics, since they must be certain rather than dubious of their beliefs, given that salvation is at stake. Faith and scepticism are incompatible, for a Christian must 'delight in assertions'. Luther declared that his erstwhile friend, Erasmus, could remain a sceptic if he wished, but he should be aware that Judgment Day was coming and that *Spiritus Sanctus non est scepticus* ('The Holy Ghost is not a sceptic').

The Erasmus–Luther debate raised a fundamental sceptical problem: how does one establish what criterion to employ in determining religious truth? Luther had challenged the Church's traditional criteria (the Pope, Church councils, Church tradition), and he defiantly appealed to Scripture alone. But people's readings of Scripture varied, and Luther then appealed to Scripture as interpreted by the Holy Spirit. This introduced what was in effect a subjective private criterion – the dictates of the Holy Spirit to each person's conscience. In the on-going battle between Catholics and Protestants, the problem of the criterion raised by the ancient sceptics thus became a living issue, and the texts of Cicero and Sextus became a vital part of the argument.

Both Estienne and Hervet in their prefaces to their translations of Sextus said that this ancient treasury of sceptical arguments would be useful for those engaged in the religious debates of the time. In fact Hervet, who was the secretary of the Cardinal of

Lorraine and a participant at the Council of Trent, said that ancient scepticism would provide the perfect answer to Calvinism, then making great inroads in France. If nothing can be known, then Calvin's knowledge claims cannot be known; the Reformers made the same claim about Catholicism. Each side then proposed a sceptical fideism, or a Christian Pyrrhonism. If sceptical difficulties about knowledge cannot be resolved, then religious views must be accepted on the basis of faith alone.

4 Scepticism and anti-scholasticism

The sceptical texts were also used in the anti-scholastic controversies. Cicero's *Academics* and commentaries upon it were appealed to in support of Petrus Ramus' drive for a new non-scholastic method of understanding and teaching various subjects, and in support of Francesco Patrizi's 1581 blast against all forms of Aristotelianism (see RAMUS, P.; PATRIZI DA CHERSO, F. §2). Some of these writers were accused of being, or were labelled by themselves, *nouveaux académiciens* or *nouveaux pyrrhoniens*, and some traditionalists decried the menace of these new sceptical groups.

An important figure in this context was Omer Talon, a close associate of Petrus Ramus in Paris. In 1547 (with a reissue in 1550) he published Cicero's *Academics* with a lengthy introduction and a commentary. Whether or not Talon was a *nouveau académicien*, as he was accused of being, he used ancient scepticism to show the need for less dogmatism and for free inquiry in philosophizing. This would make the entrenched scholasticism of the universities less powerful, and so clear a path for Ramism.

Talon's work was attacked by Pierre Galland, Professor at the Collège Royal, who published a polemical oration in 1551 in favour of the schools of Paris against 'the new Academy of Petrus Ramus'. The aim of Ramus and Talon, according to their critic, was to attack the Gospel after having destroyed all of philosophy! Galland's long oration was apparently taken sufficiently seriously that Rabelais saw fit to ridicule it. Another criticism of the *nouveaux académiciens* was written by Guy de Brués, a friend of Ramus, and a member of the group of writers, La Pléiade, connected with the great poet, Pierre Ronsard. In 1557, he published a set of dialogues in which four actual writers of the time discuss scepticism, and the sceptic finally is led to abandon his doubts, saying 'O miserable Pyrrho, who has made all into opinion and indifference!' In his preface De Brués claimed he was writing in order to prevent young people from giving up religion because of sceptical doubts. The dialogues do not really bring out either the strong force of Greek sceptical arguments, or the struggle to answer them, but they indicate the importance intellectuals of the time gave to the presence of scepticism.

Another work which should be mentioned is the *Academica* of Pedro de Valencia (1596) which gives a favourable historical analysis of the development of Academic scepticism, and which ends on a fideist note, saying that God is the only source of truth.

5 Philosophical scepticism: Sanches, Montaigne, Charron

Modernized versions of ancient philosophical scepticism were advanced by two distant cousins, Francisco SANCHES and Michel de MONTAIGNE. Both were educated, though not at the same time, at the Collège de Guyenne in Bordeaux, and both also studied at the University of Toulouse, then a centre of the ferment of new philosophical and religious ideas. Sanches then studied medicine at Montpellier and Rome and became professor of philosophy and later of medicine at the University of Toulouse. Montaigne studied law and became a political figure in Bordeaux, serving as mayor of the city and a councillor to Henri de Navarre, the Protestant leader who later turned Catholic and became King Henri IV. There is no evidence that they ever knew each other or read each other's writings, but each produced his version of modern scepticism at about the same time. Montaigne wrote the major part of his longest and most sceptical essay, 'The Apology for Raymond Sebond', in 1575–6, when Sanches was already at work on his book *Quod nihil scitur* (That Nothing is Known), published in 1581.

As the title of his book suggests, SANCHES (§2) was most influenced by Academic scepticism, and indeed, he makes no explicit reference to Sextus Empiricus. The main thrust of his work was an attack on Aristotelian science, viewed as a demonstrative process that employs definitions to give necessary reasons or causes for natural events. He used sceptical arguments to show that neither definitions nor syllogistic reasoning could produce knowledge, and that the appeal to knowledge of an object's causes leads to an infinite regress. His own view was that knowledge would have to deal with particulars, each understood individually, but, he argued, human beings are incapable of reaching any certainty about individuals, both because of the unlimited and changing nature of reality, and because of our own imperfections. As a result, nothing can be known. However, again following the spirit of Academic scepticism, Sanches did allow some constructive results. Patient, careful empirical research combined with cautious judgment and evaluation of observed data will not give us certain knowledge, but it will allow us to obtain the best information available, and give us a useful way of dealing with human experience.

Montaigne explicitly rejected Academic scepticism. He regarded the claim that nothing could be known as just the kind of dogmatic assertion the sceptic should reject, and he did not approve of any appeal to probable judgment, as that too involves assertion. He preferred to follow the road of Pyrrhonian scepticism as presented by SEXTUS EMPIRICUS. In 'The Apology for Raymond Sebond' he developed in a gradual manner the many kinds of problem that make people doubt the reliability of human reason. He cast doubt on human intellectual pretensions by comparing human abilities to those of animals; and he drew on the reports of ancient philosophers and modern explorers concerning the great variety of customs and behaviour in different parts of the planet to suggest that there was no way of determining right or true standards. He argued that even scientists were merely offering personal opinions that were likely to be replaced by other people's opinions. Finally, he considered in more detail the unreliability of the information gained by the senses or by reason, and the inability of human beings to find a satisfactory criterion of knowledge. He concluded that people should suspend judgment on all matters, and that they should follow customs, traditions and social rules undogmatically, while being tolerant of other people's views. He combined these conclusions with fideism. The state of complete doubt and suspension of judgment leaves the human mind 'a blank tablet prepared to take from the finger of God such forms as he shall be pleased to engrave on it'. Religious beliefs should be based solely on faith rather than on dubious evidence (see MONTAIGNE, M. DE).

Montaigne's Pyrrhonian scepticism was presented and popularized in didactic form by Pierre CHARRON (§3). In his *De la Sagesse* (On Wisdom) (1601), a work often republished during the seventeenth century, he advanced a fideistic defence of religious thought which was based on accepting complete scepticism while appealing to faith alone as the source of religious knowledge.

6 Impact of Renaissance scepticism

Renaissance scepticism, in both its informal manifestations and especially as put forth by Sanches, Montaigne and Charron, played a most important role in the development of modern thought. Seventeenth-century thinkers either accepted scepticism,

offered ways of living with it, or tried to refute it. Scepticism was used by MERSENNE (§2) and GASSENDI (§§3–5) to attack Renaissance naturalism, astrology and alchemy, and as the basis for proposing a constructive or mitigated scepticism, a way in which the emerging modern mechanical science could be accepted hypothetically rather than as a necessarily true picture of the world. Others, such as René DESCARTES (§4), demanded some certainty that no sceptics could challenge, and so developed the first modern philosophical systems.

See also: CICERO §3; DIOGENES LAERTIUS; HUMANISM, RENAISSANCE; MONTAIGNE, M. DE; PYRRHONISM; SANCHES, F.; SCEPTICISM; SEXTUS EMPIRICUS

References and further reading

Floridi, L. (1995) 'The Diffusion of Sextus Empiricus's Works in the Renaissance', *Journal of the History of Ideas* 56: 63–85. (Floridi surveys the manuscripts of Sextus that were available in the fifteenth and sixteenth centuries, and argues that the failure of the humanists to use Sextus' sceptical arguments was due more to lack of interest than to ignorance.)

* Jardine, L. (1983) 'Lorenzo Valla: Academic Skepticism and the New Humanist Dialectic', in M. Burnyeat (ed.) *The Skeptical Tradition*, Berkeley, CA, and London: University of California Press, 253–86. (Referred to in §2. A controversial discussion of links between scepticism, humanist logic and probable argumentation.)

Popkin, R.H. (1979) *The History of Scepticism from Erasmus to Spinoza*, Berkeley, CA: University of California Press. (Basic study of the development of scepticism from the early sixteenth century on; substantial bibliography.)

—— (1993) 'The Role of Scepticism in Modern Philosophy Reconsidered', *Journal of the History of Philosophy* 31: 501–17. (An examination of how the work of Popkin and Schmitt has stood up, and directions for future investigations.)

—— (1993) 'Scepticism and Modernity', in T. Sorell (ed.) *The Rise of Modern Philosophy*, Oxford: Clarendon Press, 15–32. (Recent evaluation of how sceptical thought helped bring about 'modernity'.)

—— (1996) 'Scepticism and Prophesy', *British Journal for the History of Philosophy* 4: 1–20. (On Savonarola and Gianfrancesco Pico and the use of scepticism to advance prophetic religion.)

Popkin, R.H. and Schmitt, C.B. (eds) (1987) *Scepticism from the Renaissance to the Enlightenment*, Wolfenbütteler Forschungen Band 35, Wiesbaden:

Harrassowitz. (Several relevant articles, including Schmitt on the development of the historiography of scepticism.)

Schmitt, C.B. (1969) *Gianfrancesco Pico della Mirandola (1469–1533) and His Critique of Aristotle*, The Hague: Martinus Nijhoff. (The only study of Gianfrancesco Pico's philosophy, especially his sceptical work.)

—— (1972) *Cicero Scepticus: A Study of the Influence of the Academica in the Renaissance*, The Hague: Martinus Nijhoff. (A study of the role played in the Renaissance by Cicero's *Academics* (*Academica*).)

—— (1983) 'The Rediscovery of Ancient Skepticism in Modern Times', in M. Burnyeat (ed.) *The Skeptical Tradition*, Berkeley, CA, and London: University of California Press, 225–51. (The best available information on how ancient scepticism entered Renaissance thought; good bibliography.)

RICHARD H. POPKIN

SCHELER, MAX FERDINAND (1874–1928)

Max Scheler, usually called a phenomenologist, was probably the best known German philosopher of the 1920s. Always an eclectic thinker, he was a pupil of the neo-idealist Rudolph Eucken, but was also strongly influenced by the life-philosophies of Dilthey and Bergson. While teaching at Jena he regularly met Husserl, the founder of the phenomenological movement, and his mature writings have a strongly phenomenological, as well as a Catholic, stamp. Later he turned towards metaphysics and the philosophical problems raised by modern science.

Scheler's interests were very wide. He tried to do justice to all aspects of experience – ethical, religious, personal, social, scientific, historical – without doing away with the specific nature of each. Above all, he took the emotional foundations of thought seriously. Many of his insights are striking and profound, and sometimes his arguments are very telling, but his power to organize his material consistently and to attend conscientiously to the business of justification is poorly developed.

Scheler is best known for his anti-Kantian ethics, based on an a priori emotional grasp of a hierarchy of objective values, which precedes all choice of goods and purposes. He himself describes his ethics as 'personalist', and makes personal values supreme, sharply distinguishing the 'person' from the 'ego', and linking this with his analysis of different types of social interaction. In epistemology he defends a pragmatist approach to science and perception; thus philosophy, as

the intuition of essences, requires a preparatory ascetic discipline. His philosophy of religion is an attempt to marry the Augustinian approach through love with the Thomist approach through reason. In his later work, to which his important work on sympathy provides the transition, he defends a dualist philosophical anthropology and metaphysics, interpreting the latter in activist terms as a resolution of the tensions between spiritual love and vital impulse.

1 **Life**
2 **General characteristics of his philosophy**
3 **Philosophy and other forms of knowledge**
4 **Ethics**
5 **The person and society**
6 **Religion**
7 **Sympathy**

1 Life

Scheler was a Bavarian, born at Munich on 22 August 1874 to a Protestant father and a Jewish mother. He was three times married and twice divorced. He died at Frankfurt am Main, 19 May 1928.

Between 1894 and 1899 he studied at the universities of Munich, Berlin (under DILTHEY), Jena (under Rudolph Eucken), and Heidelberg (to hear Max WEBER). Both his doctoral promotion and habilitation were achieved under Eucken. He was baptised a Catholic on 20 September 1899.

While lecturing at Jena, he had several meetings with Husserl, who helped him transfer to Munich in 1906. He quickly won a leading role among the Munich phenomenologists (see HUSSERL, E.; PHENOMENOLOGICAL MOVEMENT). However, irregularities in his private life led the university authorities to withdraw his license to teach. There followed a period of unofficial lecturing at Göttingen in 1910–11, thanks to the phenomenologists there, and then also in Berlin from 1912, where his first mature works began to appear: *Zur Phänomenologie und Theorie der Sympathiegefühle und von Liebe und Haß* (On the Phenomenology and Theory of Sympathy and of Love and Hate) (1915), *Der Formalismus in der Ethik und die materiale Wertethik* (*Formalism in Ethics and Non-Formal Ethics of Values*) (1913, 1916) and *Vom Umsturz der Werte* (The Subversion of Values) (1915a). Poor eyesight disqualified him from active service in the war, but he was employed by the state to give propaganda lectures.

In 1918 he was called to the chair of Philosophy and Sociology and the Directorship of the Institute of Social Sciences at Cologne, where he published *Vom Ewigen im Menschen* (On the Eternal in Man) (1921), *Die Wissensformen und die Gesellschaft* (Society and the Forms of Knowledge) (1926) and *Die Stellung des Menschen im Kosmos* (The Place of Man in the Cosmos) (1927). In 1928 he was called to Frankfurt, but died of a heart attack before he could take up office. *Philosophische Weltanschauung* (Philosophical Perspectives) was published in 1929.

2 General characteristics of his philosophy

Scheler's work is usually divided into three periods. His few early writings show the influence of Eucken's neo-idealism, and are separated by about eight years from a productive period beginning around 1912, with his second marriage, and lasting till about 1922. Scheler is here at his most phenomenological and Catholic. But in the early 1920s, at Cologne, he begins to pay less attention to what is timeless in human experience, and more to what is changing and evolving. Theism gives place to pantheism. This change is first apparent in his sociologically inclined writings, but then dominates his metaphysics. This late work only reached the stage of partial sketches before his death.

Scheler's philosophy is hardly ever academic or dry. Like Eucken, he thought that philosophy should change people's lives, and this gives his phenomenology a very different feel from that of Husserl. Even when not primarily engaged in some critique of the modern world, as in many of his minor works, he often seems to be trying to create a change of heart in the reader. Even his metaphysics is conceived in terms of 'engagement' for the full unfolding of the deity, in which he sees the meaning of the developing universe. He never preaches, but his writings have a vital, passionate and challenging quality.

One formal key to his thought is his use of the categories of higher and lower. Like Greek and medieval thinkers, he is always revealing hierarchies: of values, forms of social relating, levels of consciousness and embodied existence, of types of being. These often furnish an effective instrument in the critique of other philosophical positions. They culminate in his late philosophical anthropology, where the hierarchical structure of human being, now focused on the duality of spirit and drive (a dualism nearer to Kant than Descartes), becomes the key to the metaphysics.

Scheler's thought is highly eclectic. His receptive mind could not help learning even from those he most strongly criticized, above all Kant. But he also took much from Spinoza, Hegel, Schopenhauer, Nietzsche and Dilthey. Even his conscious borrowings (from Augustinianism, Malebranche, Pascal, Maine de Biran, for example) are always thoroughly assimilated. He took nothing that he could not experience

for himself. It is this that gives his work its ultimate unity.

Scheler made an extremely powerful impression on his contemporaries, both academic and lay, especially as a lecturer and teacher, but also as a writer, clearing the ground in many spheres and making new beginnings or revivals possible. Had it not been for the twelve-year Nazi ban on his work, his influence on later generations would probably have been much greater. In fact, many related thinkers, including Heidegger and the early Sartre, owe more to him than is often acknowledged, and his influence in the social sciences was considerable, and is growing once more. Both the sociology of knowledge and philosophical anthropology received their initial impetus from his later work. But perhaps his greatest achievement was to re-open people's eyes to a world where vital, spiritual and religious values and phenomena (essences and necessary relations between them) could all be acknowledged in their own right, free of the monistic reductions of psychologism or positivism, or the anthropocentric distortions of Neo-Kantianism.

3 Philosophy and other forms of knowledge

Although Scheler also called himself an ethical personalist, he implies that he was already thinking along phenomenological lines when he met Husserl, by whom he was clearly influenced. However, he differs from him in important respects. Apart from a lack of interest in method as such and a refusal to follow him in his 'idealist' turn, Scheler has a different approach to the intuition of essence, the question 'what exactly is given in experience?'. Husserl saw 'phenomenological reduction', which enabled us to investigate essences without the distractions of real objects and states of affairs, as a 'bracketing' of existence, a purely intellectual operation. But Scheler interpreted existence as 'resistance to striving'. It is 'given' to us (though never known) at the lowest level of psychic functioning (analogous to Aristotle's 'vegetable soul'), where our vital impulses blindly encounter something that confines them. Thus phenomenological reduction must be an inhibition of impulse. This removes the barriers to spiritual cognition of all kinds. Philosophy thus requires a moral culture of humility, self-knowledge and self-control.

This account of philosophy occurs in *On the Eternal in Man*. Later he calls it *Bildungswissen*, or knowledge for 'formation', since spiritual persons are 'formed' by the essences and values that become part of them. All knowing is, in Greek and Scholastic fashion, 'having a share in' an object without changing it. The object known, *qua* essence, is henceforward 'in' the mind of the knower. Philosophy is also a 'desymbolization of the world'. Our natural, self- or group-centred 'vital' approach to things (later writers talk of the 'life-world') rests on a classification according to vital importance. Perception itself thus selects from the totality of the given. The partial aspects of an object's nature that we take in (the redness of a cherry, for example) function as symbols of the object both as it essentially is and as it relates to our purposes. But the philosophical inhibition of impulse enables us to get beyond the screen of concepts to the entire essential nature, and see what 'can only be seen'.

The 'natural worldview' given in culture and language is the basis for control over our environment. Knowledge from this viewpoint can, however, be as adequate as that of philosophy or, at the other extreme, science. But its objects are relative to the concerns of the human species (with cultural modifications). Scientific objects, on the other hand, are relative to those of living beings as such, since science transcends the limits of human sensory equipment, and thus the range of human concerns. The world as reduced by science, largely unintelligible in terms of our sensory imaginations, is an almost pure (and largely probabilistic) schema of the world, from which the essential content of things has almost disappeared. The schema is structured as a device for control, the world of pure pragmatism. Scientific knowledge is thus *Leistungswissen*, or knowledge for achievement.

The third form of knowledge is *Heilswissen*, or knowledge for salvation. In Scheler's Catholic period, salvation concerns moral and religious knowledge and practice, and the salvation of the spiritual individual as member of the 'community of love'. But in the last period *Heilswissen* is metaphysics, and salvation itself concerns the resolution of all tensions and oppositions in the absolute being, whose spirit is the sphere of emergent essences and whose body is the material universe. Human beings provide the arena where this reconciliation of the spiritual and the material takes place. Thus metaphysics is engagement for the deity, an active spiritual love of essences and values together with an ecstatic participatory 'yes' to the blind processes of material and vital energy. The *Nachlaß* volumes which supplement the last lectures and papers show us something more of this grand conception, but very little is worked out in any detail.

4 Ethics

Scheler's ethics depends on his theory of value, which did not change in his last years. His first phenomeno-

logical and Catholic works are, *inter alia*, concerned to defend the objectivity of values and a less materialistic approach to the world. Among his particular targets are NIETZSCHE, with his attack on Christian morality, and the utilitarian or calculating attitude to morals, based on an all-devouring resentment ('Das Ressentiment im Aufbau der Moralen' (Resentment in the Structure of Morals) (1915)) and the elevation of hedonic values above those of vitality. His great ethical treatise, *Formalism in Ethics and Non-Formal Ethics of Values*, rich in subtle analyses and distinctions, is primarily intended as a refutation of Kantian ethics, together with the philosophical assumptions Kant uses to justify his position (see KANTIAN ETHICS). The huge, rambling, but immensely impressive work has six parts, each criticizing some specific Kantian theme.

In the course of it Scheler defends his thesis that values are the intentional objects of feeling. They are qualities felt in or on objects, and are hence inaccessible to the understanding. They constitute an 'emotional a priori', since the phenomena of goods and purposes, and even the attractions of pleasure, presuppose them. Far from being formal, they are given to us, in positive and negative forms, in distinct kinds of material and in a hierarchical order, with the hedonic or sensory values at the bottom, then those of vitality, then spiritual values of beauty, justice and assent to pure (non-pragmatic) truth, and lastly the values of holiness. A separate category of welfare values is sometimes inserted between the hedonic and the vital. There are also other hierarchies of 'relatively formal' values, depending on the nature of the value-bearers concerned. But moral values are personal and of a logically second order. A person's act has moral value when it intends the realization of a first-order value intrinsically higher than the given alternatives. Since choice of value depends on the structure of one's loving, the main foundation of personal being (see *Bildungswissen* above), Scheler's ethics has something in common with virtue ethics, and a corresponding distaste for moral obligation, though this is accepted as a regrettable necessity. It also contains illuminating discussions of ethical relativism (where he defends the absoluteness of values as such against various relativities of ethos, ethic, moral code and moral conduct), levels of the emotional life, and retribution and punishment.

5 The person and society

The last section of *Formalism in Ethics and the Non-Formal Ethics of Values* is a long treatise on the person as individual and social being. The influence of Kant is strong in the first part, though Scheler insists that the spiritual person is not just a rational or intellectual being, but also performs emotional acts, acts of will and, above all, acts of love. These depend on the otherwise 'automatic' mental functioning of the 'ego', 'through' which the 'functional unity' of the person acts, thereby raising ego-functioning to a higher level, where questions of meaning and validity are inescapable.

The analyses of forms of social relating begin from the distinction between community and association, but are illuminatingly extended, and integrated with the value-philosophy and analysis of the individual person. Scheler's interesting treatment of the problem of 'other minds' comes in *Wesen und Formen der Sympathie* (The Nature of Sympathy) (see OTHER MINDS). He here argues that the acquisition of knowledge is, *inter alia*, a matter of filling with particular content and in a definite order the initially empty spheres of being which are given to human consciousness as such. The social sphere (a possibly unfulfilled experience of 'we') is, in fact, filled before the sphere of individuality. Hence the main assumption of the 'problem' of other minds, that self-awareness must come first, is the false insinuation of 'individualism'. Our actual knowledge of the ego-functioning of other egos depends on the 'universal grammar of expression' to which we have access as living beings; in so far as this behaviour is raised to the dignity of spiritual activity, we can know it by performing the acts 'with' or 'after' the persons concerned.

6 Religion

The theory of spheres of being goes with a theory of specific spiritual acts relating to the typical contents of each sphere. In *On the Eternal in Man* Scheler argues that at some time or other we all perform religious acts, which include repentance, petitionary prayer, thanks, praise and worship, in relation to the absolute sphere. It is only through performing such acts that we fully grasp the meaning of holiness, the highest value. This gives us a key to answering the most fundamental question: whether our own religious acts are directed to an adequate object, or only to an idol, such as knowledge, fame or comfort. He also held that the absolute sphere of being is the first to be given some determinate content. Since religious acts presuppose the absoluteness and holiness of their object, which for Scheler denotes the supreme Good, our first and most deeply bedded experiences are of perfect objects and absolute qualities.

This religious, or 'Augustinian', road to God, open to all who try to work out their salvation in practical life, has its counterpart in a philosophical road, which

starts from wonder and a concern to grasp the nature of ultimate reality. Scheler briefly expounds the 'three fundamental philosophical truths' in 'Probleme einer Soziologie des Wissens' (*Problems of a Sociology of Knowledge*) (1926). They are, first, that there is 'something and not nothing', second, that existing beings must either be absolute or dependent on something else for their own being, and third, that all being has both essence and existence. Scheler insists that the first two have an emotional content, which can only be grasped in wonder, humility and reverence, and a shuddering glance into the abyss of absolute nothingness. The absolute being which can thus be directly cognized is in complete 'conformity' with the perfect being encountered in religious acts. The two approaches to God are complementary.

7 Sympathy

We may finally return to *The Nature of Sympathy*, which many critics have considered his best work. The general importance of the emotional in Scheler's thought is clear, but this work also contains some excellent phenomenological analysis of the different types of sympathy itself, ignored by most writers of 'sympathy ethics'. He goes on to discuss metaphysical theories of sympathy, especially Schopenhauer's, and devotes much attention to *Einsfühlung* ('feeling one with'), which is needed for the 'engagement' of the later metaphysics. The second part of the work contains an analysis of love and hate. Love is the key to the spiritual and personal, since only love opens up the world of essences and values. Humanity is, for Scheler, the *Ens amans*, the being that loves. His own analysis of love as a creative movement of the heart which brings out the higher values of its objects (hatred is destructive, working in a contrary direction) is difficult but profound. The metaphysical writings introduce us to *Eros* or vital love, which plays an important role in his account of evolution, and in the metaphysical reconciliation between spirit and drive.

List of works

Scheler, M.F. (1954) *Gesammelte Werke* (Collected Works), Bonn: Bouvier Verlag. (Vols 10–14 contain papers and fragments from the *Nachlaß*.)
—— (1899) *Beiträge zur Feststellung der Beziehungen zwischen den logischen und ethischen Prinzipien* (On the Relations between Logical and Ethical Principles), Jena: Vopelius; in *Gesammelte Werke*, vol. 1. (Aspects of the opposition between thought and action, the true and the good.)
—— (1900) *Die transcendentale und die psychologische Methode* (The Transcendental and Psychological

Methods), Jena: Dürr; in *Gesammelte Werke*, vol. 1. (Dialectical critique of the transcendental and psychological methods in philosophy and establishment of the 'noological'.)

—— (1913) *Zur Phänomenologie und Theorie der Sympathiegefühle und von Liebe und Haß* (On the Phenomenology and Theory of Sympathy, and of Love and Hate), Halle: Max Niemeyer. (Phenomenology and theories of sympathy and love; essay on 'other minds'.)

—— (1913, 1916) *Der Formalismus in der Ethik und die materiale Wertethik*, Halle: Max Niemeyer; in *Gesammelte Werke*, vol. 2; trans. M.S. Frings and R. Funk, *Formalism in Ethics and Non-Formal Ethics of Values*, Evanston, IL: Northwestern University Press, 1973. (Scheler's own position on values and goals, the a priori, consequentialism, imperatives, eudaimonism and the person discussed in opposition to Kant.)

—— (1915a) *Vom Umsturz der Werte* (The Subversion of Values), Leipzig: Verlag der weißen Bücher, 2 vols; in *Gesammelte Werke*, vol. 3. (A collection of ethical and phenomenological papers on virtue, ressentiment, human nature, self-knowledge and other topics. Includes 'Das Ressentiment im Aufbau der Moralen', trans. W. Holdheim, ed. Lewis A. Coser, *Ressentiment*, New York, The Free Press of Glencoe, 1961.)

—— (1915b) *Der Genius des Krieges und der deutsche Krieg* (The Spirit of War and the German War), Leipzig: Verlag der weißen Bücher; in *Gesammelte Werke*, vol. 4. (Philosophical discussion of war, with special application to the First World War.)

—— (1917) *Die Ursachen des Deutschenhasses* (Why the Germans are Hated), Leipzig: Kurt Wolff; in *Gesammelte Werke*, vol. 4. (A moral-pedagogical call to the nation on the basis of psychological analysis.)

—— (1921) *Vom Ewigen im Menschen*, Leipzig: Neue Geist; in *Gesammelte Werke*, vol. 5; trans. B. Noble, *On the Eternal in Man*, London: SCM Press, 1960. (The nature of philosophy, religion and Christian love.)

—— (1923) *Wesen und Formen der Sympathie*, Bonn: Friedrich Cohen; in *Gesammelte Werke*, vol. 7; trans. P. Heath, *The Nature of Sympathy*, London, Routledge & Kegan Paul, 1954. (As (1913) with much additional material on the metaphysics of sympathy.)

—— (1923–4) *Schriften zur Soziologie und Weltanschauungslehre* (Papers on Sociology and the Theory of Worldviews), Leipzig: Neue Geist; in *Gesammelte Werke*, vol. 6. (Subjects include suffering, love and knowledge, national characteristics in thinking, and Christian social problems.)

—— (1926) *Die Wissensformen und die Gesellschaft* (Society and the Forms of Knowledge), Leipzig: Neue Geist; in *Gesammelte Werke*, vol. 8. (Contains 'Probleme einer Soziologie des Wissens', trans. M.S. Frings, ed. K.W. Stikkers, *Problems of a Sociology of Knowledge*, London, Routledge & Kegan Paul, 1980. Also contains the important 'Knowledge and Work: the limits of the pragmatic approach in our world-knowledge'.)

—— (1927) 'Idealismus-Realismus', in *Philosophischer Anzeiger II*, Bonn: Friedrich Cohen; in *Gesammelte Werke*, vol. 9. (Unfinished; includes material on the metaphysical foundations of knowledge.)

—— (1928) *Die Stellung des Menschen im Kosmos*, Darmstadt: Otto Reichl; in *Gesammelte Werke*, vol. 9; trans. H. Meyerhoff, *Man's Place in Nature*, New York, Noonday Press, 1961. (Important summary of Scheler's work in philosophical anthropology.)

—— (1929) *Philosophische Weltanschauung*, Bonn: Friedrich Cohen; in *Gesammelte Werke*, vol. 9; trans. O. Haac, *Philosophical Perspectives*, Boston, MA, Beacon Press, 1958. (Papers on forms of knowledge, history, the future of man, Spinoza.) >

References and further reading

Dunlop, F. (1991) *Scheler*, in *Thinkers of our Time* series, London: The Claridge Press. (A short, clear and untechnical introduction to Scheler's life and thought.)

—— (1978) 'Scheler's Theory of Punishment', *The Journal of the British Society for Phenomenology* 9 (3): 167–74. (Gives a short, easy introduction to the social philosophy. The same issue also contains a bibliography of English translations of works by Scheler and five other articles on aspects of his thought.)

Dupuy, M. (1959) *La Philosophie de Max Scheler: son évolution et son unité*, Paris: Presses Universitaires de France, 2 vols. (An excellent introduction to Scheler's thought, including the early works.)

—— (1959) *La Philosophie de Religion chez Max Scheler*, Paris: Presses Universitaires de France. (A full-length study of Scheler's philosophy of religion.)

Frings, M.S. (1965) *Max Scheler: a Concise Introduction into the World of a Great Thinker*, Pittsburgh, PA: Duquesne University Press. (Good coverage of the later work.)

—— (1974) *Max Scheler: Centennial Essays*, The Hague: Nijhoff. (Contains continuation of Hartmann's bibliography.)

Gabel, M. (1991) *Intentionalität des Geistes* (What Does Scheler Mean by Intentionality?), Leipzig: St Benno Verlag. (A good recent work.)

Good, P. (ed.) (1975) *Max Scheler im Gegenwartsgeschehen der Philosophie* (Reactions to Scheler by Contemporary Thinkers), Bern: Francke Verlag. (A useful collection of papers, especially on Scheler's phenomenology and anthropology. Good bibliography.)

Hartmann, W. (1963) *Max Scheler: Bibliographie*, Stuttgart-Bad Canstatt: Friedrich Frommann Verlag. (Thorough list of works by and about Scheler, including translations, up to 1963.)

Mader, W. (1980) *Max Scheler: in Selbstzeugnissen und Bilddokumenten* (Max Scheler's Life, on the Basis of Autobiographical and Pictorial Sources), Reinbek bei Hamburg: Rowohlt Taschenbuch Verlag. (Illustrated. Especially good on the relation between the life and the work.)

Spiegelberg, H. (1971) *The Phenomenological Movement: A Historical Introduction*, 2nd edn, The Hague: Nijhoff. (Contains a substantial section on Scheler's place in the phenomenological movement.)

* Stegmüller, W. (1970) *Main Currents in Contemporary German, British and American Philosophy*, Bloomington, IN: Indiana University Press. (Contains a good critical chapter on Scheler, 101–32.)

FRANCIS DUNLOP

SCHELLING, FRIEDRICH WILHELM JOSEPH VON (1775–1854)

Like the other German Idealists, Schelling began his philosophical career by acknowledging the fundamental importance of Kant's grounding of knowledge in the synthesizing activity of the subject, while questioning his establishment of a dualism between appearances and things in themselves. The other main influences on Schelling's early work are Leibniz, Spinoza, J.G. Fichte and F.H. Jacobi. While adopting both Spinoza's conception of an absolute ground, of which the finite world is the consequent, and Fichte's emphasis on the role of the I in the constitution of the world, Schelling seeks both to overcome the fatalism entailed by Spinoza's monism, and to avoid the sense in Fichte that nature only exists in order to be subordinated to the I. After adopting a position close to that of Fichte between 1794 and 1796, Schelling tried in his various versions of Naturphilosophie *from 1797 onwards to find new ways of explicating the identity between thinking and the processes of nature, claiming that in this philosophy 'Nature is to be invisible mind, mind*

invisible nature'. In his System des transcendentalen Idealismus *(System of Transcendental Idealism) (1800) he advanced the idea that art, as the 'organ of philosophy', shows the identity of what he terms 'conscious' productivity (mind) and 'unconscious' productivity (nature) because it reveals more than can be understood via the conscious intentions that lead to its production. Schelling's 'identity philosophy', which is another version of his* Naturphilosophie, *begins in 1801, and is summarized in the assertion that 'Existence is the link of a being as One, with itself as a multiplicity'. Material nature and the mind that knows it are different aspects of the same 'Absolute' or 'absolute identity' in which they are both grounded. In 1804 Schelling becomes concerned with the transition between the Absolute and the manifest world in which necessity and freedom are in conflict. If freedom is not to become inexplicable, he maintains, Spinoza's assumption of a logically necessary transition from God to the world cannot be accepted.* Philosophische Untersuchungen über das Wesen der menschlichen Freiheit und die damit zusammenhängenden Gegenstände *(Of Human Freedom) (1809) tries to explain how God could create a world involving evil, suggesting that nature relates to God somewhat as the later Freud's 'id' relates to the developed autonomous 'ego' which transcends the drives which motivate it.*

The philosophy of Die Weltalter *(The Ages of the World), on which Schelling worked during the 1810s and 1820s, interprets the intelligible world, including ourselves, as the result of an ongoing conflict between expansive and contractive forces. He becomes convinced that philosophy cannot finally give a reason for the existence of the manifest world that is the product of this conflict. This leads to his opposition, beginning in the 1820s, to Hegel's philosophical system, and to an increasing concern with theology. Hegel's system claims to be without presuppositions, and thus to be self-grounding. While Schelling accepts that the relations of dependence between differing aspects of knowledge can be articulated in a dynamic system, he thinks that this only provides a 'negative' philosophy, in which the fact of being is to be enclosed within thought. What he terms 'positive' philosophy tries to come to terms with the facticity of 'being which is absolutely independent of all thinking' (2 (3): 164). Schelling endeavours in his* Philosophie der Mythologie *(Philosophy of Mythology) and* Philosophie der Offenbarung *(Philosophy of Revelation) of the 1830s and 1840s to establish a complete philosophical system by beginning with 'that which just exists ... in order to see if I can get from it to the divinity' (2 (3): 158), which leads to a historical account of mythology and Judeo-Christian revelation. This system does not, though, overcome the problem of the 'alterity' of being, its irreducibility to a philo-*

sophical system, which his critique of Hegel reveals. The direct and indirect influence of this critique on Kierkegaard, Nietzsche, Heidegger, Rosenzweig, Levinas, Derrida and others is evident, and Schelling must be considered as the key transitional figure between Hegel and approaches to 'post-metaphysical' thinking.

1 **Transcendental philosophy and** *Naturphilosophie* **(1795–1800)**
2 **Identity philosophy (1801–c.1808)**
3 **The** *Ages of the World* **(1809–c.1827)**
4 **Positive and negative philosophy, and the critique of Hegel (c.1827–54)**

1 Transcendental philosophy and *Naturphilosophie* (1795–1800)

Schelling was born in Leonberg, near Stuttgart, on 27 January 1775. He attended a Protestant seminary in Tübingen from 1790 to 1795, where he was close friends with both Hegel and Friedrich Hölderlin. He moved to Leipzig in 1797, then to Jena, where, via Goethe's influence, he took up his first professorship from 1798 to 1803. From 1803 to 1806 he lived in Würzburg, whence he left for Munich, where he mainly lived from 1806 onwards, with an interruption from 1820 to 1827, when he lived in Erlangen. He moved to Berlin in 1841 to take up what had been Hegel's chair of philosophy. He died on 20 August 1854 in Ragaz, Switzerland.

Schelling's early philosophy was inspired by the French Revolution and by the revolution in philosophy inaugurated by KANT, particularly as interpreted in the work of J.G. FICHTE. The tensions in Schelling's philosophy of this period, which set the agenda for most of his subsequent work, derive from a series of related sources. In the view of the early Schelling, Kant failed to explain the nature of the subject's knowledge of itself: in Kantian terms knowledge could only result from judgments, the synthesis by the subject of intuitions which were given to it from the external world. Although the subject was the condition of possibility or ground of *knowledge*, it seemed unable to ground itself. Kant regards the condition of possibility of the syntheses of knowledge as a 'spontaneity', as cause of itself rather than as the result of other natural causes, but does not succeed in explicating this spontaneity. Along with Kant's approach to the question of grounding knowledge, the most significant other approaches to the issue for Schelling were those of F.H. JACOBI and Fichte.

In 1783 Jacobi became involved in the 'Pantheism controversy', an influential dispute with the Berlin Enlightenment philosopher Moses Mendelssohn over

the claim that G.E. Lessing had admitted to being a Spinozist, an admission which at that time was regarded as tantamount to an admission of atheism. In his *Über die Lehre von Spinoza in Briefen an den Herrn Moses Mendelssohn* (On the Doctrine of Spinoza in Letters to Herr Moses Mendelssohn) (1785; 2nd, revised edition 1789), which was influenced by his reading of Kant's first *Critique*, Jacobi revealed a problem which recurs in differing ways throughout Schelling's work. Jacobi's interpretation of Spinozism was concerned with the relationship between what he termed the 'unconditioned' and the 'conditioned', between God as the ground of which the laws of nature are the consequent, and the chain of the deterministic laws of nature. Cognitive explanation relies, as Kant suggested, upon finding a thing's 'condition'. Jacobi's question is how this can ultimately ground the explanation, in that the explanation leads to a regress in which each condition depends upon another condition *ad infinitum*. Any philosophical system thus 'necessarily ends by having to discover *conditions* of the *unconditioned*'. For Jacobi this led to the need for a theological leap of faith if philosophy were to be grounded. In the 1787 Introduction to the first *Critique* Kant maintains that this problem can be overcome by acknowledging that, while reason must postulate the 'unconditioned ... in all things in themselves for everything conditioned, so that the series of conditions should thus become complete', by restricting knowledge to appearances, rather than 'things in themselves', the contradiction of seeking conditions of the unconditioned can be avoided.

The condition of the knowledge of appearances for Kant was the 'transcendental subject', but what sort of 'condition' was the transcendental subject? This problem initially united Schelling and Fichte. Fichte insisted in *Wissenschaftslehre* that the establishing of the unconditioned status of the I was required for Kant's system to legitimate itself. He asserts that 'It is ... the ground of explanation of all facts of empirical consciousness that before all positing in the I, the I itself must previously be posited', thereby giving the I the founding role which he thought Kant had failed adequately to explicate. Fichte does so by suggesting that the cognitive activity of the I, via which it can reflect upon *itself*, cannot therefore be understood as part of the causal world of appearance and must therefore be part of the noumenal realm, where Kant had located the 'unconditioned'.

Schelling takes up the problems posed by Jacobi and Fichte in two texts of 1795: *Vom Ich als Prinzip der Philosophie oder über das Unbedingte im menschlichen Wissen* (Of the I as Principle of Philosophy or on the Unconditional in Human Knowledge), and

Philosophische Briefe über Dogmatismus und Kriticismus (Philosophical Letters on Dogmatism and Criticism). He reinterprets Kant's question as to the condition of possibility of synthetic judgments a priori as a question about why there is a realm of judgments, a manifest world requiring syntheses by the subject, at all. In *Of the I* Schelling puts Kant's question in Fichtean terms: 'How is it that the absolute I goes out of itself and opposes a Not-I to itself?'. He maintains that the condition of knowledge, the 'positing' by the I of that which is opposed to it, must have a different status from what it posits: 'nothing can be posited by itself as a thing, that is, an absolute/unconditioned thing (*unbedingtes Ding*) is a contradiction'. However, his worry about Fichte's position already becomes apparent in the *Philosophical Letters*, where he drops the Fichtean terminology: 'How is it that I step at all out of the Absolute and move towards something opposed [*auf ein Entgegengesetztes*]?'. The problem Schelling confronted was identified by his friend J.C.F. HÖLDERLIN, in the light of Jacobi's formulation of the problem of the 'unconditioned'. Fichte wished to understand the Absolute as an I. For something to be an I, though, it must be conscious of an other, and thus in a relationship to that other. The overall structure of the relationship could not, therefore, be described from only one side of that relationship. Hölderlin argued that one has to understand the structure of the relationship of subject to object in consciousness as grounded in 'a whole of which subject and object are the parts', which he termed 'being'.

Schelling sought a philosophical way to come to terms with the 'ground' of the subject's relationship to the object world, which avoided the fatalist consequences of Spinoza's system by taking on key aspects of Kant's and Fichte's transcendental philosophy and yet which did not fall into the trap Hölderlin identified in Fichte's conception of an absolute I. In his *Naturphilosophie* (Philosophy of Nature), which emerges in 1797 and develops in the succeeding years, and in the *System des transcendentalen Idealismus* (System of Transcendental Idealism) (1800) Schelling wavers between a Spinozist and a Fichtean approach to the problem of the 'unconditioned' (see NATURPHILOSOPHIE; SPINOZA, B. §§2–4). In the *Naturphilosophie* the Kantian division between the appearing world of nature and nature in itself results from the fact that the nature theorized in cognitive judgments is wholly objectified in opposition to the knowing subject. This fails to account for the living dynamic forces in nature, including those in our own organism, with which Kant himself became concerned in the third *Critique* and other late work, and which had played a role in Leibniz's account of nature.

Schelling thinks of nature in itself as a 'productivity': 'As the object [*qua* conditioned condition] is never absolute/unconditioned (*unbedingt*) then something *per se* non-objective must be posited in nature; this absolutely non-objective postulate is precisely the original productivity of nature'. The Kantian dualism between things in themselves and appearances is a result of the fact that the productivity can never appear as itself and can only appear in the form of 'products', which are the productivity 'inhibiting' itself. The products are never complete in themselves: they are like the eddies in a stream, which temporarily keep their shape, despite the changing material flowing through them.

Schelling then tries to use the insights of transcendental philosophy, while still avoiding Kant's dualism, to explain our knowledge of nature. Given the fact of knowledge, things in themselves and 'representations' cannot be absolutely different:

> One can push as many transitory materials as one wants, which become finer and finer, between mind and matter, but some time the point must come where mind and matter are One, or where the great leap that we so long wished to avoid becomes inevitable.

(1797, 1 (2): 53)

The *Naturphilosophie* includes ourselves within nature, as part of a necessarily interrelated whole, which is structured in an ascending series of 'potentials' that entail a polar opposition within themselves. The model is a magnet, whose opposing poles are inseparable from each other, even though they are opposites. As productivity, nature cannot be conceived of as an object, since it is the subject of all possible real 'predicates', but its 'inhibiting' itself means that the 'principle of all explanation of nature' is 'universal duality', an inherent difference of subject and object which prevents nature from ever reaching stasis. The sense of nature as an absolute subject links it to the spontaneity of the thinking subject, which is the condition of the syntheses required for the constitution of objectivity. The problem for Schelling lies in explicating how these two subjects relate to each other.

In the *System of Transcendental Idealism* Schelling returns to Fichtean terminology, though he soon finally abandons it. He endeavours to explain the emergence of the thinking subject from nature. This emergence is thought of in terms of an absolute I coming retrospectively to know itself in a 'history of self-consciousness'. The *System* recounts the history of which the transcendental subject is the result. A version of the model Schelling establishes was to be adopted by Hegel in the *Phenomenology of Mind*.

Schelling conceives of the whole process in terms of the initially undivided I splitting itself in order to articulate itself in the syntheses, the 'products', which constitute the world of knowable nature. The founding stages of this process, which bring the world of material nature into being, are 'unconscious'. These stages then lead to organic nature, and thence to consciousness and self-consciousness. Schelling claims that the resistance of the noumenal realm to theoretical knowledge results from the fact that 'the [practical] act [of the absolute I] via which all limitation is posited, as condition of all consciousness, does not itself come to consciousness'. He prophetically attempts to articulate a theory which comes to terms with the awareness that thought is driven by forces which are not finally transparent to it, of the kind later to become familiar in psychoanalysis. How, though, does one gain access by thought to what cannot be an object of consciousness?

Schelling adopts the idea from the early Romantic thinkers Friedrich Schlegel and Novalis, whom he knew in Jena at this time, that art is central to understanding what cannot appear as an object of knowledge. Philosophy cannot represent nature in itself because access to the sphere of the unconscious must be via what appears to consciousness in the realm of theoretical knowledge. The work of art is an empirical object, but if it is not more than what it is *qua* determinable object it cannot be a work of art, which requires the free judgment of the subject. Although the *System* depends upon the transition from theoretical to practical philosophy, which involves breaking Jacobi's chain of 'conditions', Schelling is concerned to understand how the highest insight must yet be into reality as a product of the interrelation of both the 'conscious' and the 'unconscious'. It is not, therefore, a re-presentation of the latter by the former. Whereas in the *System* nature begins unconsciously and ends in consciousness, in the work of art: 'the I is conscious according to the production, unconscious with regard to the product'. The product cannot be understood via the intentions of its producer, as this would mean that it became a 'conditioned' object, which would lack that which makes mere craft into art. Art is 'the only true and eternal organ and document of philosophy, which always and continuously documents what philosophy cannot represent externally'. The particular sciences can only follow the chain of conditions, via the principle of sufficient reason, and must determine the object via its place in that infinite chain. The art object, on the other hand, manifests what cannot be understood in terms of its knowable conditions, in that an account of the materials of which it is made does not constitute it as art. It shows what cannot be

said. Philosophy, therefore, cannot positively represent the Absolute, because 'conscious' thinking operates from the position where 'absolute identity' has always already been lost in the emergence of consciousness.

2 Identity philosophy (1801–c.1808)

Although the period of Schelling's 'identity philosophy' is usually dated from the 1801 *Darstellung meines Systems der Philosophie* (Presentation of My System of Philosophy) until some time before the 1809 *Philosophische Untersuchungen über das Wesen der menschlichen Freiheit und die damit zusammenhängenden Gegenstände* (Of Human Freedom), the project of that philosophy is carried on in differing ways throughout his work. The identity philosophy derives from Schelling's conviction that the self-conscious I must be seen as a result, rather than as the originating act as it is in Fichte, and thus that the I cannot be seen as the generative matrix of the whole system. Again, the problem is to articulate the relationship between the I and the world of material nature, without either reverting to Kantian dualism or falling into the traps of idealism and materialism.

Schelling's mature identity philosophy, which is contained in *System der gesammten Philosophie und der Naturphilosophie insbesondere* (System of the Whole of Philosophy and of the Philosophy of Nature in Particular), written in Würzburg in 1804, and in other texts between 1804 and 1807, breaks with the model of truth as correspondence:

> It is clear that in every explanation of the truth as a correspondence [*Übereinstimmung*] of subjectivity and objectivity in knowledge, both, subject and object, are already presupposed as separate, for only what is different can agree, what is not different is in itself one.
>
> (1804a, 1 (6): 138)

The crucial problem is explaining the link of the subject and object world, which is what makes judgments possible. For there to be synthetic judgments at all, what is split must, Schelling contends, in some way already be the same (see TRUTH, CORRESPONDENCE THEORY OF). This has often been understood as leading Schelling to a philosophy in which, as Hegel puts it in the *Phenomenology*, the Absolute is the 'night in which all cows are black', because it swallows all differentiated knowledge in the assertion that everything is ultimately the same. This is not a valid interpretation of Schelling's argument.

In order to get over the problem in monism, of how the One is also the many, Schelling introduces the notion of 'transitive' being, which links mind and matter as predicates of itself. Schelling explains this 'transitivity' via the metaphor of the earth:

> You recognize its [the earth's] true essence only in the link by which it eternally posits its unity as the multiplicity of its things and again posits this multiplicity as its unity. You also do not imagine that, apart from this infinity of things which are in it, there is another earth which is the unity of these things, rather *the same* which is the multiplicity is also unity, and *what* the unity is, is also the multiplicity, and this necessary and indissoluble One of unity and multiplicity in it is what you call its existence...Existence is the link of a being [*Wesen*] as One, with itself as a multiplicity.
>
> (1806a, 1 (7): 56)

'Absolute identity' is the link of the two aspects of being, which, on the one hand, is the universe, and, on the other, is the changing multiplicity which the knowable universe also is. Schelling insists now that 'The *I* think, *I* am, is, since Descartes, the basic mistake of all knowledge; thinking is not my thinking, and being is not my being, for everything is only of God or the totality': the I is 'affirmed' as a predicate of the being by which it is preceded.

Schelling is led to this view by his understanding of the changing and relative status of theoretical knowledge. It is the inherent incompleteness of all finite determinations which reveals the nature of the Absolute, as is evident in his description of time: 'time is itself nothing but *the totality appearing in opposition to the particular life of things*', so that the totality 'posits or intuits itself, by not positing, not intuiting the particular'. The particular is determined in judgments, but the truth of claims about the totality cannot be proved because judgments are necessarily conditioned, whereas the totality is not. Given the relative status of the particular, though, there must be a ground which enables us to be aware of that relativity: this ground must have a different status from the knowable world of finite particulars. At the same time, if the ground were wholly different from the world of relative particulars the old problems of dualism would recur. As such the Absolute *is* the finite, but we do not *know* this in the manner in which we know the finite. Without the presupposition of 'absolute identity', therefore, the evident relativity of particular knowledge becomes inexplicable, since there would be no reason to claim that a revised judgment is predicated of the same as the preceding – now false – judgment.

Schelling summarizes the theory of identity as follows:

> For being, actual, real being is precisely self-disclosure/revelation (*Selbstoffenbarung*). If it is to be as One then it must disclose/reveal itself in itself; but it does not disclose/reveal itself in itself if it is not an other in itself, and is *in* this other the One for itself, thus if it is not absolutely the living link of itself and an other.
>
> (1806a, 1 (7): 54)

The link between the 'real' and the 'ideal', the physical and the mental, cannot, Schelling maintains, be seen as a causal link. Although there cannot be mental events without physical events, the former cannot be causally reduced to the latter: 'For real and ideal are only different views of one and the same substance'. Schelling wavers at this time between a position of the kind which Hegel soon tried to articulate, in which, in Schelling's terms, 'the sameness of the subjective and the objective is made the same as itself, knows itself, and is the subject and object of itself', in the 'identity of identity and difference', and the sense that this position cannot finally circumscribe the structure of the Absolute. The structure of reflection, where each aspect mirrors itself and then is mirrored in the other, upon which this account of the identity of subject and object relies, must be grounded in a being which carries it:

> Reflection...only knows the universal and the particular as two relative negations, the universal as relative negation of the particular, which is, as such, without reality, the particular, on the other hand, as a relative negation of the universal...something independent of the concept must be added to posit the substance as such.
>
> (1804a, 1 (6): 185)

Without this independent basis, subject and object would merely be, as Schelling thinks they are in Fichte, relative negations of each other, leading to a circle 'inside which a nothing gains reality by the relation to another nothing'. Schelling prophetically distinguishes between the cognitive – reflexive – ground of finite knowledge, and the real – non-reflexive – ground that sustains the movement of negation from one finite determination to another. As a two-sided relationship, reflection alone always entails the problem that the subject and the object in a case of reflection can only be *known* to be the same via that which cannot appear in the reflection: if I am to recognize *myself* in a mirror, rather than a random object in the world, I must already be familiar with myself before the reflection. This means a complete system based on reflection is impossible, because, in order to ground the system, it must presuppose as external to the system what it claims is part of it. From the 1820s onwards, Schelling raises

513

this objection against Hegel's system of 'absolute reflection'.

Schelling's own dissatisfaction with his early versions of identity theory derives from his rejection of Spinozism. Spinoza saw the move from God to the world of 'conditions' as a logical consequence of the nature of God. Schelling becomes convinced that such a theory gives no reason why the Absolute or the 'unconditioned' should manifest itself in a world of negative 'conditions' at all. Schelling is confronted with the task of explaining the transition from the Absolute to the finite world. In *Philosophie und Religion* (Philosophy and Religion) (1804), he claims, like Jacobi, that there is no way of mediating between conditioned and unconditioned, and already makes the distinction between 'negative' and 'positive' philosophy, which will form the heart of his late work. Explicating the structure of the finite world leads to 'negative philosophy', but much has already been gained by the fact that the negative, the realm of nothingness, has been separated by a sharp limit from the realm of reality and of what alone is positive'. The next stage of his philosophy will become concerned with the transition between infinite and finite.

3 The *Ages of the World* (1809–c.1827)

Schelling's work from his middle period is usually referred to as the philosophy of *Die Weltalter* (Ages of the World). It begins with *Philosophische Untersuchungen über das Wesen der menschlichen Freiheit und die damit zusammenhängenden Gegenstände* (Of Human Freedom) (1809), written in Stuttgart, and lasts until the late 1820s. The *Weltalter* philosophy is an attempt to explain the emergence of an intelligible world at the same time as coming to terms with the inextricable relation of mind to matter. The initial concern is to avoid Spinoza's fatalism, which renders the human freedom to do good *and* evil incomprehensible. Schelling's crucial objection is to the idea that evil should be understood as merely another form of negativity, which can therefore be understood by insight into a necessitated totality, rather than as a fact relating to the nature of human freedom. He now sees the fundamental contradictions of the *Naturphilosophie* in terms of the relationship of the intelligibility of nature and ourselves to a ground without which there could be no intelligibility, but to which intelligibility cannot be reduced. In *Of Human Freedom* he introduces, against both Spinoza and Fichte, a conception of 'willing', which was later influential for Schopenhauer's conception of the 'Will': 'In the last and highest instance there is no other being but willing. Willing is primal being, and all the predicates of primal being only fit willing: groundlessness,

eternity, being independent of time, self-affirmation' (1809, 1 (7): 350). Schelling establishes a more antagonistic version of the structure of the identity philosophy. The 'ground' is now in one sense 'groundless', that is, uncaused: it must be understood in terms of freedom, if Spinozism is to be avoided. At the same time there must be that against which freedom can be manifest for it to be freedom at all. The theory is based on the antagonisms between opposing forces which constitute the 'ages of the world'. He argues, though, that the world whose origins the *Weltalter* wishes to understand must entail the *same* conflicting forces which still act, though not necessarily in the same form, in this world, of which the mind is an aspect: 'Poured from the source of things and the same as the source, the human soul has a co-knowledge/con-science (*Mitwissenschaft*) of creation'. Schelling suggests that there are two principles in us: 'an unconscious, dark principle and a conscious principle', which must yet in some way be identical. The same structure applies to what Schelling means by 'God'. As that which makes the world intelligible, God relates to the ground so that the 'real', which takes the form of material nature, is 'in God' but 'is not God seen absolutely, that is, in so far as He exists; for it is only the ground of His existence, it is "nature" in God; an essence which is inseparable from God, but different from Him'. The point is that God would be meaningless if there were not that which God transcends: without opposition there is no life and no sense of development.

Wolfram Hogrebe has convincingly claimed that the *Weltalter* philosophy is a theory of predication (1989). In it, being is initially One, is not manifest and has no reason to be manifest: Hogrebe terms this 'pronominal being'. The same being, given that there is now a manifest world, must also be 'predicative being' (ibid.), which 'flows out, spreads, gives itself'. The contradiction is only apparent. Schelling maintains in line with the identity philosophy that the 'properly understood law of contradiction really only says that the same cannot be *as the same* something and also the opposite thereof, but this does not prevent the same, which is A, being able, as an other, to be not A'. One aspect of being, the dark force, which he sometimes terms 'gravity', is contractive, the other expansive, which he terms 'light'. Dynamic processes are the result of the interchange between these ultimately identical forces. If something is to be *as* something, it must both be, in the positive sense in which everything else is, which makes it indeterminately positive, and it must have a relationship to what it is not, in order to be determinate. In the *Weltalter* the One comes into contradiction with itself and the two forces constantly vie with each other. Differences must be grounded in unity, however, as otherwise they could not be manifest at all as differences. The ground is, though, increasingly regarded as the source of the transitory nature of everything particular, and less and less as the source of tranquil insight into how we can be reconciled to finite existence.

The abandonment of his residual Spinozism leads Schelling to a growing concern with the tensions which result from contradictions which we also embody. The ages of the world are constituted by the development of forms and structures in the material and the mental world. The development depends upon the expanding force's interaction with the contracting force's slowing of any expansion, which allows transient but determinate forms to develop. This process gives rise most notably to language, which Schelling sees as the model for the development of the whole world:

> It seems universal that every creature which cannot contain itself or draw itself together in its own fullness, draws itself together outside itself, whence, for example, the elevated miracle of the formation of the word in the mouth belongs, which is a true creation of the full inside when it can no longer remain in itself.
>
> (1946: 56–7)

Language as 'contracted' material signifier, and 'expanding' ideal meaning repeats the basic structure of the *Weltalter* philosophy. This interaction between what is contained in itself and what draws something beyond itself is also what gives rise to consciousness, and thus to an inherent tension within consciousness, which can only be itself by its relation to an other. Hegel uses a related model of subjectivity, particularly in the *Phenomenology*, but Schelling later rejects this model. Schelling's later philosophy will present a subject whose origin in nature prevents it from ever achieving the 'self-presence' Hegel thinks he can explicate via the completed structure of 'self-reflection' in the other. Schelling's *Weltalter* philosophy is never completed: its Idealist aim of systematically unifying subject and object by comprehending the real development of history from the very origins of being founders on problems concerning the relationship between philosophical system and historical contingency which do not admit of solutions.

4 Positive and negative philosophy, and the critique of Hegel (*c.*1827–54)

Schelling has usually been understood to provide the transitional 'objective idealist' link between Fichte and Hegel. By regarding Hegel's system as the culmination of German Idealism this interpretation fails to do justice to Schelling's real philosophical insights. Many of these insights, particularly in the later philosophy, directly and indirectly influenced the ideas of thinkers, such as Feuerbach, Kierkegaard, Nietzsche and Heidegger, who were critical of Hegel's attempt at a complete philosophical system (see HEGELIANISM §2).

The differences between Hegel and Schelling derive from their respective approaches to understanding the Absolute. For Hegel the Absolute is the *result* of the self-cancellation of the finite. It can therefore be presented in the form of the successive overcoming of finite determinations, the 'negation of the negation', in a system whose end comprehends its beginning. For Hegel the result becomes known when the beginning moves from being 'in itself' to being 'for itself' at the end of the system. Schelling became publicly critical of Hegel while working on a later version of the *Weltalter* philosophy in Erlangen in the 1820s, but made his criticisms fully public in lectures given in Munich in the 1830s, and in the 1840s and 1850s as professor in Berlin. The aim of the Idealist systems was for thought to reflect what it is not – being – as really itself, even as it appears not to be itself, thereby avoiding Kant's dualism. The issue between Schelling and Hegel is whether the grounding of reason by itself is not in fact a sort of philosophical narcissism, in which reason admires its reflection in being without being able to articulate its relationship to that reflection. Schelling's essential point is that it is not the particular manifestation of knowledge which tells me the truth about the world, but rather the necessity of movement from one piece of knowledge to the next. This much can be construed in Hegelian terms. However, a logical reconstruction of the process of knowledge can, for Schelling, only be a reflection of thought by itself: the real process cannot be described in philosophy, because the cognitive ground of knowledge and the real ground, though inseparable from each other, cannot be shown to *reflect* each other.

Dieter Henrich characterizes Hegel's Absolute as follows: 'The Absolute is the finite to the extent to which the finite is nothing at all but negative relation to itself' (1982). Hegel's system depends upon showing how each limited way of conceiving of the world cannot grasp the whole, because it has an internal contradiction. This necessarily leads thought to more comprehensive ways of grasping the world, until the point is reached where there can be no more comprehensive way, because there is no longer any contradiction to give rise to it. The very fact of the limitations of empirical thought therefore becomes what gives rise to the infinite, which, in Hegel's terms, is thought that is bounded by itself and by nothing else.

Schelling accepts such a conception, to which he substantially contributed in his early philosophy, as the way to construct a 'negative' system of philosophy: it explains the logic of change, once there is a world to be explained. It does not, though, explain why there is a developing world at all, but merely reconstructs in thought the necessary structure of development. Schelling's own attempt at explaining the world's facticity led him to a 'philosophical theology' which traces the development of mythology and then of Christian revelation in his *Philosophie der Mythologie* (Philosophy of Mythology) and *Philosophie der Offenbarung* (Philosophy of Revelation), which like all his substantial works after 1811, were not published in his lifetime. The failure of his philosophical theology does not, though, invalidate his philosophical arguments against Hegel. The alternative to the 'common mistake of every philosophy that has existed up to now' – the 'merely logical relationship of God to the world' – Schelling terms 'positive philosophy'. The 'merely logical relationship' entails reflexivity, in which the world necessarily follows from the nature of God, and God and the world are therefore the 'other of themselves'. Hegel's system removes the facticity of the world by understanding reason as the world's immanent self-articulation. Schelling insists that human reason cannot explain its *own* existence, and therefore cannot encompass itself and its other within a system of philosophy. We cannot, he maintains, make sense of the manifest world by beginning with reason, but must begin with the contingency of being and try to make sense of it with the reason which is only one aspect of it.

Schelling contends that the identity of thought and being cannot be articulated *within* thought, because this must presuppose that they are identical in a way which thought, as one side of a relation, cannot comprehend. By redefining the 'concept' such that it is always already both subject and object, Hegel's aim is to avoid any presuppositions on either the subject or the object side, allowing the system to complete itself as the 'self-determination of the concept'. Schelling presents the basic alternative as follows:

For either the concept would have to go first, and being would have to be the consequence of the concept, which would mean it was no longer absolute being; or the concept is the consequence of being, then we must begin with being without the concept.

(1842–3, 2 (3): 164)

Hegel attempts to merge concept and being by making being part of a structure of self-reflection, rather than the ground of the interrelation of subject and object. He invalidly assumes that 'essence', which is one side of the relationship between being and essence, can articulate its identity with the other side in the 'concept', because the other side is revealed as being nothing until it has entered into a relation which makes it determinate as a moment of the whole process.

The problem that Hegel does not overcome is that this identity cannot be known, because, as Schelling argues of his concept of being, 'existing is not here the consequence of the concept or of essence, but rather existence is here itself the concept and itself the essence'. The problem of reflection cannot be overcome in Hegel's manner: identifying one's reflection in a mirror as oneself (understood now as a metaphor for essence) entails, as we saw above, a prior non-reflexive moment if one is to know that the reflection *is* oneself, rather than a random reflected object. How far Schelling moves from any reflexive version of identity philosophy is evident in the following from the *Einleitung in die Philosophie der Offenbarung oder Begründung der positiven Philosophie* (Introduction to the Philosophy of Revelation or Foundation of the Positive Philosophy):

Our self-consciousness is not at all the consciousness of that nature which has passed through everything, it is precisely just *our* consciousness... for the consciousness of man is not = the consciousness of nature... Far from man and his activity making the world comprehensible, man himself is that which is most incomprehensible.

(1842–3, 2 (3): 6–7)

Schelling refuses to allow that reason can confirm itself via its reflection in being:

what we call the world, which is *so completely contingent* both as a whole and in its parts, cannot possibly be the impression of something which has arisen by the *necessity of reason*... it contains a *preponderant* mass of *unreason*.

(1832–3: 99)

Schelling is, then, one of the first philosophers seriously to begin the destruction of the model of metaphysics based on the idea of representation, a destruction which can be seen as one of the key aspects of modern philosophy from Heidegger to the later Wittgenstein and beyond. At the same time, he is committed, unlike some of his successors, to an account of human reason which does not assume that reason's incapacity to ground itself should lead to the abandonment of the question of truth.

See also: GERMAN IDEALISM; ROMANTICISM, GERMAN

List of works

Schelling, F.W.J. (1856–61) *Friedrich Wilhelm Joseph Schelling's Sämmtliche Werke*, ed. K.F.A. Schelling, Division 1 (10 vols), Division 2 (4 vols), Stuttgart: Cotta. (An easily accessible, substantial selection of the complete works has been published as *Friedrich Wilhelm Joseph von Schelling, Ausgewählte Schriften*, ed. M. Frank, Frankfurt: Suhrkamp, 1985, 6 vols.)

—— (1946) *Die Weltalter*, ed. M. Schröter, Munich: Biederstein. (This has other versions than the version from 1813 printed in the *Sämmtliche Werke*.)

—— (1976–) *Historisch-kritische Ausgabe, im Auftrag der Schelling-Kommission der Bayerischen Akademie der Wissenschaften*, ed. H.M. Baumgartner, W.G. Jacobs and H. Krings, Stuttgart. (This is still a long way from completion, but will become the new standard edition.)

—— (1794) *Über die Möglichkeit einer Form der Philosophie überhaupt*, trans. and with commentary by F. Marti, On the Possibility of an Absolute Form of Philosophy, in *The Unconditional in Human Knowledge: Four early essays 1794–6*, Lewisburg, PA: Bucknell University Press, 1980. (Argues the need for an 'absolute founding proposition' in philosophy in the light of Reinhold's attempt to establish the foundations Kant had failed ultimately to provide.)

—— (1795a) *Vom Ich als Prinzip der Philosophie oder über das Unbedingte im menschlichen Wissen*, trans. and with commentary by F. Marti, Of the I as the Principle of Philosophy or on the Unconditional in Human Knowledge, in *The Unconditional in Human Knowledge: Four early essays 1794–6*, Lewisburg, PA: Bucknell University Press, 1980. (Attempts in a mainly Fichtean manner to establish the 'unconditioned' for philosophy in the wake of Kant.)

—— (1795b) *Philosophische Briefe über Dogmatismus und Kriticismus*, trans. and with commentary by F. Marti, Philosophical Letters on Dogmatism and Criticism, in *The Unconditional in Human Knowledge: Four early essays 1794–6*, Lewisburg, PA: Bucknell University Press, 1980. (Schelling's attempt to reconcile a Spinozist and a Fichtean account of the Absolute.)

—— (1796–7) *Abhandlungen zur Erläuterung des Idealismus der Wissenschaftslehre* (Essays in Explanation of the Idealism of the Doctrine of Science), in *Friedrich Wilhelm Joseph Schelling's Sämmtliche Werke*, ed. K.F.A. Schelling, Stuttgart: Cotta, 1 (1) 345–452. (Further exploration of Kantian and Fichtean questions concerning the foundation of philosophy.)

—— (1797) *Ideen zu einer Philosophie der Natur als Einleitung in das Studium dieser Wissenschaft*, trans. E.E. Harris and P. Heath, with intro. by R. Stern, *Ideas for a Philosophy of Nature: Introduction to the Study of This Science*, Cambridge: Cambridge University Press, 1988. (First version of a system of *Naturphilosophie*, which begins to move away from Fichte.)

—— (1799) *Erster Entwurf eines Systems der Naturphilosophie* (First Plan of a System of the Philosophy of Nature), in *Friedrich Wilhelm Joseph Schelling's Sämmtliche Werke*, ed. K.F.A. Schelling, Stuttgart: Cotta, 1 (3) 5–268. (Further attempt to develop a systematic *Naturphilosophie*.)

—— (1800) *System des transcendentalen Idealismus*, trans. P. Heath, with intro. by M. Vater, *System of Transcendental Idealism* Charlottesville, VA: University Press of Virginia, 1978. (Remarkably internally consistent account of the history of self-consciousness, using a model which Hegel will adopt in the *Phenomenology*. Sees art as the 'organ of philosophy'.)

—— (1801a) *Darstellung meines Systems der Philosophie* (Presentation of My System of Philosophy), in *Friedrich Wilhelm Joseph Schelling's Sämmtliche Werke*, ed. K.F.A. Schelling, Stuttgart: Cotta, 1 (4) 107–212. (First, clearly flawed, presentation of the 'identity philosophy'.)

—— (1801b) *Über den wahren Begriff der Naturphilosophie und die richtige Art, ihre Probleme zu lösen* (On the True Concept of the Philosophy of Nature and the Right Way to Solve its Problems), in *Friedrich Wilhelm Joseph Schelling's Sämmtliche Werke*, ed. K.F.A. Schelling, Stuttgart: Cotta, 1 (4) 81–103. (The text in which Schelling clearly distances his philosophy from that of Fichte for the first time.)

—— (1802) *Bruno oder über das göttliche und natürliche Prinzip der Dinge*, trans. and with intro. by M. Vater, *Bruno, or On the Natural and the Divine Principle of Things*, Albany, NY: State University of New York Press, 1984. (Further explorations of questions of *Naturphilosophie* and 'identity philosophy'.)

—— (1802–3) *Philosophie der Kunst*, trans. *The Philosophy of Art*, Minneapolis, MN: Minnesota University Press, 1989. (The first work ever to carry this title: a systematic presentation of the philosophical significance of the differing forms of art. Particularly impressive in relation to music.)

—— (1803) *Vorlesungen über die Methode des akademischen Studiums*, trans. E.S. Morgan, ed. N. Guterman, *On University Studies*, Athens, OH:

517

Ohio University Press, 1966. (Texts concerned with the nature of university study which relate to the foundation of new German universities at this time.)

—— (1804a) *System der gesammten Philosophie und der Naturphilosophie insbesondere* (System of the Whole of Philosophy and the Philosophy of Nature in Particular), in *Friedrich Wilhelm Joseph Schelling's Sämmtliche Werke*, ed. K.F.A. Schelling, Stuttgart: Cotta, 1 (6) 133–577. (The most coherent and important version of the 'identity philosophy'. The philosophical reflections are among Schelling's most important: the account of *Naturphilosophie* is at times merely bizarre.)

—— (1804b) *Philosophie und Religion* (Philosophy and Religion), in *Friedrich Wilhelm Joseph Schelling's Sämmtliche Werke*, ed. K.F.A. Schelling, Stuttgart: Cotta, 1 (6) 13–70. (Text in which Schelling first makes the distinction between 'negative' and 'positive' philosophy. Also signals the beginning of the move away from the Spinozist aspects of the 'identity philosophy'.)

—— (1806a) *Darlegung des wahren Verhältnisses der Naturphilosophie zu der verbesserten Fichteschen Lehre* (Explanation of the True Relationship of the *Naturphilosophie* to the Improved Fichtean Doctrine), in *Friedrich Wilhelm Joseph Schelling's Sämmtliche Werke*, ed. K.F.A. Schelling, Stuttgart: Cotta, 1 (7) 3–126. (Contains important formulations of the principles of identity philosophy.)

—— (1806b) *Aphorismen zur Einleitung in die Naturphilosophie* (Aphorisms as an Introduction to the Philosophy of Nature), in *Friedrich Wilhelm Joseph Schelling's Sämmtliche Werke*, ed. K.F.A. Schelling, Stuttgart: Cotta, 1 (7) 140–197. (Further important development of the mature identity philosophy.)

—— (1807) *Über das Verhältnis der bildenden Künste zur Natur* (On the Relationship of the Fine Arts to Nature), in *Friedrich Wilhelm Joseph Schelling's Sämmtliche Werke*, ed. K.F.A. Schelling, Stuttgart : Cotta, 1 (7) 291–329. (Further development of Schelling's conception of art.)

—— (1809) *Philosophische Untersuchungen über das Wesen der menschlichen Freiheit und die damit zusammenhängenden Gegenstände*, trans. and with critical notes by J. Gutmann, *Of Human Freedom*, Chicago, IL: Open Court, 1936. (The text which inaugurates a major change in Schelling's thought, which is concerned with the question of evil and its relation to human freedom, and with God's relationship to nature.)

—— (1810) *Stuttgarter Privatvorlesungen* (Stuttgart Private Lectures), in *Friedrich Wilhelm Joseph Schelling's Sämmtliche Werke*, ed. K.F.A.

Schelling, Stuttgart: Cotta, 1 (7) 419–84. (Takes up some of the themes from *Of Human Freedom*, developing them in a more systematic manner.)

—— (1811–15). *Die Weltalter*, trans. and with intro. and notes by F. de W. Bolman, Jr, *The Ages of the World*, New York: Columbia University Press, 1967. (Schelling's attempt to give a metaphysical account of why the world becomes intelligible at all, and how the conflicts in reality can be grasped within philosophy. Contains vital remarks on the question of predication and identity.)

—— (1820–1) *Initia Philosophiae Universae*, ed. H. Fuhrmans, Bonn: Bouvier, 1969. (Important text which begins Schelling's move away from Idealist philosophy. Contains key account of the problem of 'reflection', which paves the way for the critique of Hegel. Contains *Ueber die Natur der Philosophie als Wissenschaft*.)

—— (1821) *Ueber die Natur der Philosophie als Wissenschaft* (On the Nature of Philosophy as a Science), in *Friedrich Wilhelm Joseph Schelling's Sämmtliche Werke*, ed. K.F.A. Schelling, Stuttgart: Cotta, 1 (9) 209–46. (Also contained in *Initia Philosophiae Universae*.)

—— (1827–8) *System der Weltalter* (System of the Ages of the World), ed. S. Peetz, Frankfurt: Klostermann, 1990. (Development of *Die Weltalter*. Contains one of the earlier attacks on Hegel's system.)

—— (1830) *Einleitung in die Philosophie* (Introduction to Philosophy), ed. W.E. Ehrhardt (Schellingiana, vol. 11), Stuttgart: Frommann-Holzboog, 1989. (Further evidence of Schelling's move away from the Idealist paradigm towards the 'positive philosophy'.)

—— (1832–3) *Grundlegung der positiven Philosophie* (Foundations of the Positive Philosophy), ed. H. Fuhrmans, Turin: Bottega d'Erasmo, 1972. (First extant systematic account of the 'positive philosophy', contains vital remarks against Hegel's account of reason.)

—— (c.1833–4) *Zur Geschichte der neueren Philosophie*, trans. and with intro. by A. Bowie, *On the History of Modern Philosophy*, Cambridge: Cambridge University Press, 1994. (Uniquely valuable account of the history of philosophy from Descartes to Schelling himself, covering Spinoza, Leibniz, Wolff, Kant, Fichte, Jacobi, and containing the most extensive extant critique of Hegel. A text which anticipates many of the major themes in European philosophy after Schelling.)

—— (1841–2) *Philosophie der Offenbarung* (Philosophy of Revelation), ed. M. Frank, Frankfurt: Suhrkamp, 1977. (Illegally transcribed, but clearly accurate outline of the whole of the *Philosophy of*

Revelation. Contains vital remarks on Hegel and positive philosophy. Excellent introduction.)

—— (1842) *Philosophie der Mythologie* (Philosophy of Mythology), in *Friedrich Wilhelm Joseph Schelling's Sämmtliche Werke*, ed. K.F.A. Schelling, Stuttgart: Cotta, 2 (2) 3–674. (Remarkable historical account of the emergence and development of mythology: contains important methodological reflections on the study of mythology that influenced many subsequent thinkers.)

—— (1842–3) *Philosophie der Offenbarung* (Philosophy of Revelation), in *Friedrich Wilhelm Joseph Schelling's Sämmtliche Werke*, ed. K.F.A. Schelling, Stuttgart: Cotta, 2 (3) 3–530. (The official version of *Philosophy of Revelation*, compiled by Schelling's son. The first ten lectures contain some of Schelling's most brilliant critical remarks on modern philosophy.)

—— (between 1847 and 1852) *Philosophische Einleitung in die Philosophie der Mythologie oder Darstellung der reinrationalen Philosophie* (Philosophical Introduction to the Philosophy of Mythology or Presentation of the Purely Rational Philosophy), in *Friedrich Wilhelm Joseph Schelling's Sämmtliche Werke*, ed. K.F.A. Schelling, Stuttgart: Cotta, 2 (1) 255–572. (Important further reflections on negative and positive philosophy. Contains some of Schelling's most significant remarks on ontology, particularly in relation to Aristotle and the question of being and non-being.)

References and further reading

Bowie, A. (1990) *Aesthetics and Subjectivity: from Kant to Nietzsche*, Manchester: Manchester University Press. (Contains a chapter on Schelling which characterizes him in relation to Hölderlin and to Romantic and post-Romantic theories of aesthetics, and as a theorist of subjectivity who does not rely on the idea of self-presence.)

—— (1993) *Schelling and Modern European Philosophy: An Introduction*, London: Routledge. (The first full-length account of Schelling in English to consider him as a major philosopher in his own right, rather than as a pendant to Hegel. Connects Schelling to issues in contemporary analytical and European philosophy.)

* Fichte, J.G. (1971) *Werke* (Works), Berlin: de Gruyter, 1, 1. (The standard edition of Fichte's writings; referred to in §1.)

Frank, M. (1975) *Der unendliche Mangel an Sein* (The Unending Lack of Being), Frankfurt: Suhrkamp. (The classic modern account of Schelling's critique of Hegel: a dense, very difficult, but indispensable work.)

—— (1985) *Eine Einführung in Schellings Philosophie* (An Introduction to Schelling's Philosophy), Frankfurt: Suhrkamp. (A detailed account of Schelling's early work until the end of the identity philosophy: see §2.)

—— (1991) *Selbstbewußtsein und Selbsterkenntnis* (Self-Consciousness and Self-Knowledge), Stuttgart: Reclam. (Contains a vital essay on Schelling's identity theory, 'Identität und Subjektivität' (Identity and Subjectivity), which sees the theory as a major event in Western philosophy.)

Frank, M. and Kurz, G. (eds) (1975) *Materialien zu Schellings philosophischen Anfängen* (Material on Schelling's Philosophical Beginnings), Frankfurt: Suhrkamp. (Essays on various aspects of Schelling's philosophy between 1795 and 1804, with accompanying historical material.)

Heidegger, M. (1971) *Schellings Abhandlung über das Wesen der menschlichen Freiheit* (Schelling's Essay on the Essence of Human Freedom), Tübingen: Niemeyer. (Dense and difficult, but essential commentary on Schelling's *On the Essence of Human Freedom*, with material from later lectures by Heidegger. Referred to in §3.)

* Henrich, D. (1982) *Selbstverhältnisse* (Self-Relationships), Stuttgart: Reclam. (Important essays on Schelling, Hegel and modern philosophy.)

Heuser-Kessler, M.-L. (1986) '*Die Produktivität der Natur*' *Schellings Naturphilosophie und das neue Paradigma der Selbstorganisation in den Naturwissenschaften* (The 'Productivity of Nature', Schelling's *Naturphilosophie* and the New Paradigm of Self-Organization in the Natural Sciences), Berlin: de Gruyter. (Claims that Schelling's philosophy of nature can be linked to developments in non-linear dynamics and to the theory of self-organizing systems.)

* Hogrebe, W. (1989) *Prädikation und Genesis. Metaphysik als Fundamentalheuristik im Ausgang von Schellings 'Die Weltalter'* (Predication and Genesis. Metaphysics as Fundamental Heuristics Beginning with Schelling's 'The Ages of the World'), Frankfurt: Suhrkamp. (A brilliant, but demanding account of the *Weltalter* as a theory of predication, which uses the tools of analytical philosophy to show how consistent much of Schelling's position is.)

Jähnig, D. (1966, 1969) *Schelling, Die Kunst in der Philosophie* (Schelling: Art in Philosophy), Pfullingen: Neske, 2 vols. (Detailed and impressive account of the importance of art for Schelling's philosophy as a whole.)

Jaspers, K. (1955) *Schelling: Größe und Verhängnis* (Schelling: Greatness and Disaster), Munich: Piper. (An interesting, if outdated, account of Schelling's life and work, which sees Schelling as failing to achieve his philosophical goals.)

Marx, W. (1984) *The Philosophy of F.W.J. Schelling: History, System, Freedom*, Bloomington, IN: Indiana University Press. (General and fairly accessible account, mainly of earlier work by Schelling, as far as *On the Essence of Human Freedom*.)

Sandkaulen-Bock, B. (1990) *Ausgang vom Unbedingten. Über den Anfang in der Philosophie Schellings* (Going Out from the Absolute: On the Beginning in the Philosophy of Schelling), Göttingen: Vandenhoeck & Ruprecht. (Excellent account of Schelling's response to questions posed in particular by Jacobi concerning the grounding of philosophy in the Absolute: historically detailed and very thorough on the early work.)

Sandkühler, H.J. (1970) *Friedrich Wilhelm Joseph Schelling*, Stuttgart: Metzler. (Contains bibliography, which complements that of Schneeberger (1954).)

—— (ed.) (1984) *Natur und geschichtlicher Prozeß* (Nature and Historical Process), Frankfurt: Suhrkamp. (Selection of essays on the philosophy of nature with useful bibliography of writings on that philosophy.)

Schneeberger, G. (1954) *Friedrich Wilhelm Joseph von Schelling. Eine Bibliographie*, Bern: Franke. (The standard bibliography, to be complemented by those cited above.)

* Scholz, H. (ed.) (1916) *Die Hauptschriften zum Pantheismusstreit zwischen Jacobi und Mendelssohn* (The Main Texts in the Pantheism Controversy Between Jacobi and Mendelssohn), Berlin: Reuther & Reichard. (Contains most of the key texts by Jacobi in the Pantheism controversy.)

Schulz, W. (1975) *Die Vollendung des deutschen Idealismus in der Spätphilosophie Schellings* (The Completion of German Idealism in the Late Philosophy of Schelling), Pfullingen: Neske. (The book which reoriented the study of Schelling after the Second World War towards the study of the later work, particularly the critique of Hegel, and linked Schelling to Kierkegaard and Heidegger. Difficult but thought-provoking.)

Snow, D.E. (1996) *Schelling and the End of Idealism*, Albany, NY: State University of New York Press. (Lucid historical and philosophical introduction to Schelling's work from §§1–3. Excellent on the relationship to Jacobi, but does not deal with the Schelling of 'positive philosophy' and the critique of Hegel, §4.)

Tilliette, X. (1970) *Schelling une philosophie en devenir* (Schelling: A Philosophy in Development), Paris: Vrin, 2 vols. (Encyclopedic historical account of the development of Schelling's work: stronger on general exposition and on theology than on Schelling's philosophical arguments.)

—— (1983) *Schelling: Introduction to the System of Freedom*, New Haven, CT, and London: Yale University Press. (Good introduction to Schelling's work as a whole, which tends to focus, though, on its undoubted weaknesses, at the expense of its strengths.)

Zizek, S. (1996) *The Indivisible Remainder. An Essay on Schelling and Related Matters*, London and New York: Verso. (Very wide-ranging, fascinating, but dense and often difficult reflections on the implications of Schelling's relationship to Jacques Lacan and Hegel. Tends to underestimate the radical differences between Schelling and Hegel, but gives a very good sense of why Schelling matters to contemporary philosophy.)

ANDREW BOWIE

SCHELLINGIANISM

Schelling's philosophy, spread by German professors teaching at Russian universities and by Russians who had studied in Germany, some with Schelling himself, had an early and lasting influence in Russia. It was greatest in aesthetic theory and in the philosophy of history, but it was noticeable even in the natural sciences. Schelling appealed especially to Russians who were inclined to reconcile a modern scientific worldview with religious faith or with an exalted view of art. Particularly prominent figures were Odoevskii, Belinskii, Chaadaev, Venevitinov and Solov'ëv.

1 **Schellingianism at Russian universities**
2 **Schellingian aesthetics**
3 **Schellingian philosophies of history**

1 Schellingianism at Russian universities

Danilo Vellanskii (1774–1842), who had studied with SCHELLING in Germany, was a professor of the natural sciences at St Petersburg University from 1805 and published several works on medicine, biology and physics in which he faithfully followed Schelling's *Naturphilosophie* (see NATURPHILOSOPHIE §2). Mikhail Pavlov (1793–1840), another student of Schelling's, was appointed professor of physics and agronomy at Moscow University in 1820. His *Outline of Physics* (1825–36) is clearly under the sway of Schelling's conception of nature. Aleksandr Galich (1783–1848), who had studied in Germany, was made a professor of philosophy at St Petersburg University

520

in 1819. His 'Opty nauki iziashchnogo' (Essay on a Science of the Beautiful) (1825) accurately presents Schelling's aesthetics. Nikolai Nadezhdin (1804–56) won an appointment as professor of fine arts and archaeology at Moscow University in 1831, on the strength of a dissertation (in Latin) on Romantic poetry. Nadezhdin knew Schelling well and used his ideas in developing his own aesthetic theory, which features an organic conception of the social, national and historical aspects of art. The list of professors known to have taught Schellingian ideas may be readily expanded.

The student circle 'Lovers of Wisdom' in Moscow (1823–5), a secret discussion group, was led by Prince Vladimir Odoevskii (1804–69), president, and Dmitrii Venevitinov (1805–27), secretary. It had perhaps a dozen members and sympathizers, among them the Kireevskii brothers, Ivan (1806–56) and Pëtr (1808–56), both students of Schelling, Aleksei Khomiakov (1804–60), Mikhail Pogodin (1800–75) and Stepan Shevyryov (1806–64), all of whom would later become prominent Slavophiles (see SLAVO-PHILISM). The circle was a hotbed of Schellingian ideas, which were launched in the publications of its members.

Odoevskii's *Russkie nochi* (*Russian Nights*) (published 1844, but written largely in the 1820s) has a group of young Russians gather to read their stories and discuss their ideas. Schelling's philosophy is explicity identified as the focus of these discussions. Faust, the discussion leader, presents it as a synthesis of all sciences, an inspired vision of the universe as a living organism in goal-directed flux. The power of a great artist (Bach is the case in point) is seen as in tune with the very rhythm of the cosmos. The idea that ultimate truth, though understood intuitively, eludes rational expression, also appears as a leitmotif in *Russian Nights*. Venevitinov's essays 'Sculpture, Painting, and Music' (1827) and 'Anaxagoras: A Platonic Dialogue' (1830) are poeticized versions of Schellingian conceptions, the former being an allegoric exposition of Schelling's hierarchy of art forms, the second a poetically stylized statement of Schelling's idea that the human spirit passes from a Golden Age of instinct into freedom, as it enters history, and will return to a second Golden Age when all self-will is eliminated and pure reason reigns.

The poet Fëdor Tiutchev (1803–73) might have been among the Lovers of Wisdom, had he not joined the Russian foreign service in 1822. Like them, he later became a Slavophile. While stationed in Munich, he met Schelling and became intimately acquainted with his philosophy. A basic theme of Schelling's thought is dominant in Tiutchev's poetry: nature is an organism possessed of spirit – a cosmos; but when intuition penetrates the surface of this cosmos, it faces chaos and senses man's affinity to it, perceiving the chaos of night as the mother of all things.

A circle led by Nikolai Stankevich (1813–40) at Moscow University in the early 1830s became yet another hotbed of Schellingianism. Among its members and sympathizers were Vissarion BELINSKII (1811–48), Mikhail BAKUNIN (1814–76), Timofei Granovskii (1813–55) and Konstantin Aksakov (1817–60), to mention the most prominent. Stankevich and several members of his circle abandoned Schelling for Hegel around 1838 (see HEGELIANISM, RUSSIAN).

2 Schellingian aesthetics

Schelling's organic aesthetics dominated Russian literary criticism mainly as a result of Belinskii's pervasive influence. Belinskii, a student of Nadezhdin's, turned Hegelian after 1838, but the principles of Schelling's romantic aesthetics were retained by some of his followers, particularly Apollon Grigor'ev (1822–64), who in turn influenced DOSTOEVSKII and even the Symbolists at the turn of the century. These principles were: true art is not *mimesis* but a creative extension of nature; it is inherently symbolic and has cognitive power, expressing the universal through the particular, the ideal through the real, and the eternal through the temporal; it is free, yet it necessarily expresses the truth of life; it is in phase with history, creating the mythology by which nations and societies live. Grigor'ev, who called his method 'organic criticism', defined historical sense as 'an understanding of the organic nature of history, a recognition of eternal, absolute ideals, the presence of which gives meaning to history' ([1858] 1876: 223). He denounced the Hegelian 'historical school' for seeing only the progress of history, rather than the absolute and lasting values created by each stage of the historical process.

3 Schellingian philosophies of history

While the Left of Russian thought followed Hegel and the Left Hegelians once they had become known in Russia, the Right stayed with a Schellingian philosophy of history, essentially in an effort to retain religion as a foundation of national life. This is true of Pëtr CHAADAEV (1794–1856), the first prominent Westernizer. Chaadaev met Schelling in Germany and corresponded with him. He was the first Russian to believe that humankind would enter the millennium through the gates of history, seen as a movement generated by a striving for unity, perfection and universality. Unlike Schelling, he saw Christian religion not as a mere stage of this process, but as its sole generating power.

Slavophiles, specifically Khomiakov and Ivan Kireevskii, and the *pochvenniki* (from *pochva*, 'soil', Schelling's *Boden*) Grigor'ev and Dostoevskii shared Schelling's organic conception of nationhood and saw the historical process in terms of revealed absolute ethical values undergoing temporal metamorphoses through a dialectic of resolved contradictions. The Slavophiles, in particular, stressed the primacy of revealed religion: in a dialectic of material and spiritual values, the burden was on science to raise itself to the level of religion, not vice versa.

Khomiakov perceived history as a dialectic process whose opposite poles are 'Iranian' humanity, guided by ideal (spiritual and aesthetic) values and its 'Kushite' antipodes, guided by material aspirations of power and possessions. Christianity, the culmination of Iranian humanity, amounts to the realization of the idea that man is so godlike – in a spiritual sense – that God could become man: we have a capacity for infinite perfection, which gives us infinite freedom.

Lev Shestov said of Vladimir SOLOV'ËV (1853–1900), Russia's leading academic philosopher, that 'Schelling so permeated him that he apparently lost his ability to distinguish himself from him' (1964: 38). In particular, it was Schelling's *Philosophy of Revelation* that appealed to Solov'ev, who also followed Schelling in incorporating Jakob Boehme's mystic doctrines into his system. Solov'ev's first work was pure Schelling: *'The Mythological Process in the Paganism of Antiquity'* (1873) sees history as a mythmaking and theogonic process. Solov'ev's conception of history is that of a complex, living, personal God, realizing himself through a process of overcoming what is alien to him: chaos, disorder, evil. In his *Opravdanie dobra* (Justification of the Good) (1897), Solov'ev followed Schelling in dealing with the problem of evil: God denies evil as final or ever-lasting, but allows it to exist as a passing condition of freedom. The nature of man is one of divine potential. Once the process of divine revelation is completed, evil will become unreal. Solov'ev also followed Schelling in presenting his historical insights in terms of dialectic potencies. In an essay of 1877, 'Three Powers', the inhuman God of the East is countered by godless man of Western capitalist society, with a synthesis of godly man produced by a union of East and West.

Schellingian ideas appear massively in the writings of Solov'ev's followers, such as Sergei Trubetskoi (1862–1905), Viacheslav Ivanov (1866–1949), and Nikolai BERDIAEV (1874–1948).

References and further reading

* Grigor'ev, A. (1858) 'Kriticheskii vzgliad na osnovy, znachenie i priemy sovremennoi kritiki iskusstva' (A Critical View of the Foundations, Importance and Devices of Contemporary Art Criticism), in his *Sochineniia* (Works), 1876. (Referred to in §2.)

—— [Grigoryev] (1862–4) *Moi literaturnye i nravstvennye skital'chestva*; trans. R.E. Matlaw, *My Literary and Moral Wanderings and Other Autobiographical Material*, New York: E.P. Dutton, 1962.

Lehmann, J. (1975) *Der Einfluss der Philosophie des deutschen Idealismus in der russischen Literaturkritik des 19. Jahrunderts: Die 'organische Kritik' Apollon A. Grigor'evs* (The Influence of the Philosophy of German Idealism in Russian Literary Criticism of the Nineteenth Century: the Organic Criticism of Apollon A. Grigor'ev), Heidelberg: Carl Winter. (Covers Schelling in great detail.)

Leighton, L.G. (1975) 'D.V. Venevitinov: Schellingism and Philosophy; the Poet's Own Feelings', in *Russian Romanticism: Two Essays*, The Hague and Paris: Mouton, 79–84.

* Odoevskii, Prince V. [Odoevsky] (1844) *Russkie nochi*; trans. O. Koshansky-Olienikov and R.E. Matlaw, *Russian Nights*, New York: E.P. Dutton, 1965. (Written in the 1820s. Referred to in §1.)

Setschkareff, W. (1939) *Schellings Einfluss in der russischen Literatur der 20er und 30er Jahre des XIX. Jahrhunderts* (The Influence of Schelling in Russian Literature of the 1820s and 1830s), Leipzig: Harrassowitz; repr. Nendeln/Liechtenstein: Kraus, 1968. (Covers Schelling's influence in all areas (literature, philosophy, the sciences) up to the end of the 1830s.)

* Shestov, L. (1964) 'Umozrenie i apokalipsis: Religioznaya filosofiya Vl. Solov'eva', in *Umozrenie i otkrovenie* (Speculation and Revelation), Paris: YMCA-Press, 23–91. (Written in 1927, this examines Solov'ev's efforts, futile in Shestov's opinion, to prop up revelation with ratiocination. Points out Solov'ev's dependence on Schelling.)

Solov'ev, V. [Solovyov] (1952) *A Solovyov Anthology*, arranged by S. Frank, trans. N. Duddington, New York: Scribner. (Compiled from a broad range of Solov'ev's works.)

Venevitinov, D.V. (1826) 'O sostoianii prosveshcheniia v Rossii'; trans. and ed. L.G. Leighton, 'On the State of Enlightenment in Russia', in *Russian Romantic Criticism: An Anthology*, New York and London: Greenwood Press, 1987, 111–18.

VICTOR TERRAS

SCHILLER, FERDINAND CANNING SCOTT (1864–1937)

F.C.S. Schiller was the outstanding exponent of pragmatism in Britain. His views, which he referred to at various times as humanism, voluntarism and personalism, as well as pragmatism, were strongly influenced by William James, to whom he paid great tribute, although he claimed to have arrived at his opinions independently. Schiller pursued the subjective and personal aspects of James's psychology, whereas Dewey built on its objective and social elements. In taking the process of knowing as central to reality, Schiller was also influenced by Hegel. Schiller's philosophy may be best approached in terms of his opposition to the absolute idealism of the then-dominant British Hegelians (particularly F.H. Bradley, his bête noire); Schiller thought their monism, rationalism, authoritarianism and intellectualism denied the basic insight of Protagoras that it is man who is the measure of all things.

Schiller was born in Schleswig-Holstein and studied at Oxford, where he gained an MA. In 1893 he went to Cornell as a graduate student and instructor. He left there without a doctorate, however, to go to Corpus Christi College, Oxford, where he became senior tutor and fellow. He received the D.Sc. degree in 1906, as well as other academic honours. In 1926 he began to spend part of each year at the University of Southern California, and moved there permanently in 1935 as professor.

Schiller argued that all acts and thoughts are irreducibly the products of human beings, and are therefore inescapably associated with the needs, desires and purposes of the individual actor or thinker. Such concepts as 'reality' and 'truth' do not denote independent and absolute entities; they are permeated by human intentions and activities. The absolute idealists maintained that 'reality' is a seamless logical unity in which all separateness vanishes, and that nothing finite, transitory or changeable is quite real. But, Schiller pointed out, all that exists for us are the bits of matter we encounter, the individual acts we perform and the private thoughts we think. Reality for us is indeed piecemeal, incomplete and plastic. The reality revealed by our active inquiries is not rigid but malleable, not complete but evolving, responsive to our probing and manipulating, and therefore to our needs and purposes. What we call 'real' is what we evaluate as important. It is the result of the kind of activity by which we reduce the chaos about us to order. To be sure, there are patent limits to human

powers, and the world obviously preceded our existence; Schiller later reluctantly accepted the distinction between 'making' the real and 'finding' it, but he reiterated the meaninglessness of the 'real-as-it-is-in-itself'. He used the Greek term '*hyle*' to refer to the indeterminate formless chaos beyond our ability to perceive or manipulate. His metaphysics can thus accommodate Darwinian evolution and the emergence of genuine novelty (always a problem for the absolute idealist). It is a firm foundation for human freedom, and legitimizes human progress. Metaphysical systems reflect personality and temperament, and are thus quasi-ethical, or even aesthetic, in character.

Schiller's doctrine of truth likewise raised British philosophical hackles. The truth of a proposition can be determined only by what follows from it in the court of experience. Truth is a valuation applied as the result of a procedure called verifying, or making true. Since no verifying can establish the absolute truth of a statement, Schiller held that truth is particular, personal and progressive. That which furthers the purpose of our inquiries we call true. 'Truth is that manipulation of [objects] which turns out upon trial to be useful, primarily for any human end, but ultimately for that perfect harmony of our whole life which forms our final aspiration'. Of course it is fallacious to infer 'the useful is true' from 'the true is useful' – all sorts of statements (political propaganda, advertising, outright lies, for example) can be useful, though clearly false. Schiller distinguished seven levels of truth claims. Thus a postulate is a statement which becomes an axiom if it is fully verified, 'serves as principle for a fully established science' and 'rests securely on the solid mass of scientific fact it has been instrumental in eliciting'. There are also methodological assumptions (for instance, determinism) and methodological fictions (for instance, the use of plane geometry in cartography).

Schiller accused traditional formal logic of having 'etherealized' and 'depersonalized' truth in its search for validity. It had become a word game, with no concern for actual thinking processes, or for meaning and context. In two books, *Formal Logic* (1912) and *Logic for Use* (1929), Schiller showed that formal logic, even on its own terms, was not free from ambiguity – how can there be anything in the conclusion of a syllogism not contained in its premises? What is the precise import of the copula in a proposition? How can logic consistently appeal to such psychological notions as the 'necessity' of implication or the 'self-evidence' of axioms? Schiller urged that logic should become a systematic evaluation of actual knowing. His resolute experimentalism led him to claim in 'Axioms as Postulates' (1902) that even the basic Aristotelian principles of identity, contradiction and excluded middle were postulates. He also argued that the 'facts' of the scientist are relative to our senses, memory, language, instruments, aims and hypotheses.

Schiller carried his pragmatism into ethics, social policy (he was a great advocate of eugenics) and religion. He shared with William JAMES and Henri BERGSON an interest in psychical research, and translated James's 'will to believe' into the 'right to postulate'. Schiller was a prolific writer, a sprightly stylist and a spirited polemicist; he rather enjoyed being an *enfant terrible*. He produced a parody of that stately establishment journal *Mind* (which he called *Mind!*), an example of that scarce commodity, philosophical humour.

See also: PERSONALISM; PRAGMATISM; TRUTH, PRAGMATIC THEORY OF §2

List of works

Schiller, F.C.S. (1891) *Riddles of the Sphinx: A Study in the Philosophy of Evolution*, London: Swan Sonnenschein; New York: Macmillan; new and revised edn, subtitled *A Study in the Philosophy of Humanism*, London: Macmillan, 1910. (A traditional discussion of traditional philosophical problems, written before Schiller saw the light of pragmatism; not very useful now. First published under the pseudonym 'A. Troglodyte'.)

—— (1902) 'Axioms as Postulates' in H. Sturt (ed.) *Personal Idealism*, London: Macmillan, 47–133. (A pragmatic and fertile approach to the theory of knowledge.)

—— (1903) *Humanism: Philosophical Essays*, London and New York: Macmillan; 2nd edn, 1912. (Fifteen essays on various subjects, mostly based on or reprinted from lectures or papers in learned or philosophical journals.)

—— (1907) *Studies in Humanism*, London and New York: Macmillan. (Twenty essays on various subjects. Schiller preferred this form to writing a systematic single expository or controversial volume.)

—— (1908) *Plato or Protagoras?*, Oxford: Blackwell; London: Simpkins, Marshall. (Subtitled, 'A Critical Examination of the Protagoras Speech in the *Theaetetus*, with some remarks upon Error'.)

—— (1912) *Formal Logic: A Scientific and Social Problem*, London: Macmillan. (Schiller's basic contention: that you cannot consider the abstract 'forms of thought' apart from their content without losing sight of the fundamental issues of meaning and truth.)

—— (1917) 'Scientific Discovery and Logical Proof', in C.J. Singer (ed.) *Studies in the History and Methods of Science*, Oxford: Clarendon Press, vol. 1, 235–89. (Schiller argues that logic has treated scientific discoveries as illustrations of a preconceived ideal of proof, and thus misunderstands the problem of science.)

—— (1921) 'Hypothesis', in C.J. Singer (ed.) *Studies in the History and Methods of Science*, Oxford: Clarendon Press, vol. 2, 414–46. (Schiller argues for the inter-relationship of 'fact' and 'hypothesis': a good hypothesis does not conform to abstract prior rules, but is made good and knocked into shape by the procedure of verification.)

—— (1924a) *Problems of Belief*, London: Hodder & Stoughton. (Schiller was interested in the problem of immortality and in the methods of science at its periphery, for instance, in psychical research. Here he argues that non-anthropomorphic thought is absurd.)

—— (1924b) *Tantalus, or the Future of Man*, London: Kegan Paul; New York: Dutton. (Part of the 'Today and Tomorrow' series, this is written in a popular style. The survival of the human race is threatened by the progress of science, which helps the weak and least fit to survive.)

—— (1926) *Eugenics and Politics*, London: Constable; Boston, MA: Houghton Mifflin. (Schiller was an advocate of eugenic improvement, before Hitler put it into practice.)

—— (1929) *Logic for Use: an Introduction to the Voluntarist Theory of Knowledge*, London: G. Bell. (A constructive sequel to the destructive *Formal Logic*; here he argues that logic can and should be a theory of actual reasoning, not of empty and abstract forms.)

—— (1934) *Must Philosophers Disagree?*, London: Macmillan. (Collection of essays in popular philosophy. In the title essay Schiller argues that philosophy should be concerned with human actions, not with 'word games'.)

—— (1939) *Our Human Truths*, New York: Columbia University Press. (Twenty-seven essays on various subjects, selected and edited by his widow, Louise S. Schiller.)

References and further reading

Abel, R. (1955) *The Pragmatic Humanism of F.C.S. Schiller*, New York: King's Crown Press of Columbia University. (A critical study of Schiller's philosophy, with an exhaustive bibliography.)

REUBEN ABEL

SCHILLER, JOHANN CHRISTOPH FRIEDRICH (1759–1805)

*Schiller was an artist first – a major poet and the leading dramatist of eighteenth-century Germany – and an aesthetician second. At the height of his involvement in aesthetics, he calls the philosopher 'a caricature' beside 'the poet, the only true human being'. But reflection had deep roots in his nature, to the point where he felt it inhibited his creativity, yet would also have to be the means to restore it. He eventually came to terms with this paradox by devising a typology of 'naïve' and 'reflective' artists that explained his problem – and incidentally the evolution of modern European literature (*On Naïve and Reflective Poetry*, 1796). Schiller was also driven by a passionate belief in the humanizing and social function of art. His early speech* The Effect of Theatre on the People *(1784; later title* The Stage considered as a Moral Institution*) celebrated the one meeting-place where our full humanity could be restored. In the mature essays of the 1790s, an immensely more complex argument cannot hide the ultimate simplicity of his faith in art, even and especially in the midst of historical crisis: his culminating statement on beauty,* On the Aesthetic Education of Man *(1795) is at the same time a considered response to events in France, where a 'rational' Revolution had turned into a Reign of Terror. Schiller proposes an education for humane balance as the only sufficiently radical answer to the violent excesses of impulse, and argues that art is its only possible agent. Schiller's ideas are imaginative, generous and intuitively appealing as an account of what art is and might do. With the authority of his poetic standing and the high eloquence of his prose, they are powerful cultural criticism. Arguably they could have been more effective still and less vulnerable if he had not tried to make them something else by giving them a systematic quasi-Kantian form, as a result of which philosophical commentators have often patronized him while the Common Reader has been scared off.*

1 Life
2 First essays: the sublime and tragedy
3 Beauty and aesthetic experience
4 The *Kallias* Letters
5 *Grace and Dignity* (1793)
6 *Letters on the Aesthetic Education of Man* (1795)
7 *On Naïve and Reflective Poetry* (1796)

1 Life

Schiller was born at Marbach in Württemberg. At fourteen he was placed in the Duke of Württemberg's military academy against the wishes of his parents, and made to study medicine against his own. Apart from an occasional autopsy and some observations of melancholia in a fellow-student, 'medicine' largely meant philosophical speculation on the workings of mind and body. Schiller was fascinated by the problem of mind–body interaction which was to remain central to his aesthetics. His 'medical' dissertations emphasize the effect and value of the physical component, true to the pattern of German eighteenth-century aesthetics which upgrades sense experience and alters the priorities of rationalism. Frustrated by a lowly post as regimental doctor and a ducal prohibition on writing any more drama after his sensational début *The Robbers* (1782), Schiller fled from Württemberg into the dubious freedom of a hand-to-mouth existence. There followed years of editing journals and writing pot-boiler fiction and popular history, necessary means of survival but obstacles to his higher ambition. In 1789 he was appointed Professor at the University of Jena, lecturing on history and aesthetics: a post that brought prestige but little pay. He only became relatively free of financial pressures in the very last years before his premature death. By then at least his fame was secure as poet, dramatist and critic and (from 1794 on) the literary partner and acknowledged equal of Johann Wolfgang Goethe in what came to be known as Weimar Classicism.

2 First essays: the sublime and tragedy

Schiller's first work in aesthetics proper is avowedly derivative from Kant's account of the sublime, except that Schiller takes over this standard eighteenth-century concept as the basis of his definition and practice of tragedy (see KANT, I.). Burke in 1757 had already suggested that sublime objects – towering crags, desert wastes and the like – 'exercise the finer parts of the system' in a virtually physiological way. By 1790 Kant is explaining the pleasures of sublime phenomena by an intricate psychological-cum-moral sequence in which their threat to overwhelm us forces us back on our distinctively human rational nature. By now, too, human actions such as principled self-sacrifice have crept in among the sublimities. The proximity to tragedy is obvious. Schiller locates tragedy in the necessary assertion of 'moral being' (*Sittlichkeit*) in the face of threats from or to the agent's 'sensuous being' (*Sinnlichkeit*). This may seem a reaffirmation of rationalist moral values, but for Schiller 'sensuous being' is not so readily abandoned as in earlier heroic and Christian drama. The pleasure of tragedy is not the simple one of moral triumph at the rejection of something worthless, but the poignant mixed feeling at the necessary sacrifice of something intensely valuable. In his last essay on the sublime (probably late 1790s), the tragic vision has been intensified by European wars, and the primacy of the stoic moral will is even more in the foreground. Yet tragedy still only treats the harsher aspect of life, is only one literary genre, and not for Schiller the highest. This rank he gives to the genre he never worked in, comedy, because of its final harmony and balance. Schiller was the last writer to make significant use of the sublime in its traditional sense before it expired with the century, to be reassumed into a single larger conception of beauty (although the concept recurs with a different function in Hegel's *Aesthetics* and is resurrected in twentieth-century theories of 'Post-Modernism').

3   Beauty and aesthetic experience

On this central theme, Schiller once again starts from Kant, and after following some false trails goes well beyond him. In particular he does fuller justice to the complexity of both the aesthetic object and its reception. Both aspects bear out Schiller's aperçu that it was crucial for a theory of art that the thinker should be a practising artist. Kant's principle that aesthetic experience consisted in 'pleasure without interest' had set the object apart from practical purposes like use or desire, to be dwelt on for its own sake; while the effect of the pure form-percept lay in its power to seem nevertheless mysteriously purposive. This is conventionally seen as a philosophical breakthrough, but it only codified what contemporary writers were already perceiving and demanding in their practice, namely that the work of art and its constituent elements must be free of the constraints, moral, political or religious, placed on utterances in the practical world, and that it had formal laws of its own. Art was a distinct realm of contemplation and representation where the writ of authority did not, or at least should not, run – a recognizable off-shoot of the central Enlightenment principle of independent thought and free public communication. This is not of course to explain away in social terms the new insight that art is a means to hold external demands in suspense while life is inspected with a fresh eye and reshaped by the imagination. To all this, Schiller the writer was deeply committed.

For Kant, however, aesthetic judgment and the very attribution of aesthetic status were subjective, resting on an adjustment of the observer's mode of seeing. This left Schiller dissatisfied. Was there nothing in the constitution of the object that

positively invited such a mode of seeing – more compellingly than Kant's example of the arabesque, which inspired no 'interest' the observer would need to disregard and could thus, by a too simple logic, actually rank higher in beauty than the human form? An equally dubious logic had established Kant's next step. If observers all abstracted from their personal 'interests', then what was left must be common ground, for they had categorically lost the wherewithal to disagree. Ergo, aesthetic judgments were universal. But this was to reduce the beholder to a pure Nobody, emptying both subject and object of the reality that must surely be present – transformed, yes, but not purified out of existence – if art is to matter to anybody.

4   The *Kallias* Letters

Kant's limitations set Schiller's programme. In the never-completed project *Kallias*, sketched in 1793, he tried to establish an objective (but not empirically dependent) definition of beauty. He begins in Kantian spirit by calling it the 'form of a form', that is, a pure percept which is, as it were, permitted by the functional form of objects. (In line with much eighteenth-century aesthetics, he has natural objects in mind at least as much as artefacts.) But where for Kant it was the observer who disregarded purpose, for Schiller the object has itself 'overcome' its purpose, to appear free. Hence beauty is 'freedom in the phenomenon' or 'in appearance'. Though the German *Erscheinung* does not mean 'mere' or 'illusory appearance', Schiller cannot get round the fact that his freedom *is* merely in the eye of the beholder, or even just a metaphor for beauty's effect. Nor is there, incidentally, any clear reason why aesthetic pleasure should stem from the sight of freedom, other than that it offers 'an analogy with the form of the pure will', and that Schiller is avowedly one of those 'for whom freedom is the highest principle'. His fall-back position – that beauty comes about when nothing in the phenomenon too obviously *belies* the appearance of freedom – remains just as open to his friend Körner's objection that the whole theory rested on 'the autonomy which the observer mentally adds to the phenomenon', that is, it was irretrievably subjective.

5   *Grace and Dignity* (1793)

But instead of pursuing this central problem with a changed approach, Schiller keeps his flawed approach and changes the problem, to a secondary one which promised to fit it better. He defines grace as 'beauty in motion': motion at least was objective. Yet, lacking a satisfactory definition of the beauty to be observed in motion, he was (as he admitted) trying to fly before he could walk. 'Grace' moreover, when further unpacked, turned out to depend on the same criterion that had given trouble in *Kallias*: it was 'the beauty of the [human] form [*Gestalt*] under the influence of freedom'. Admittedly freedom in human beings, even if problematic in other ways, is not in doubt as an illusion of the beholder. And it soon becomes clear that Schiller is attempting an aesthetics not just of physical movement *per se*, but of total modes of behaviour in real situations. This might seem to cross the border from aesthetics into ethics altogether. Schiller distinguishes two basic responses to two equally basic types of situation. When human impulses are in harmony with each other and not under pressure from the surrounding world, the agent can freely choose how to act, and as an unconscious effect (Schiller constructs careful provisos against its conscious pursuit) grace may result. In contrast, when the impulses are at war with each other or under attack from the world, so that only a stoic defence is left, dignity may result. The first case shows freedom *in*, the second freedom *from* nature, where 'nature' is both the system of inner purposes that constitute our organic form, and the nexus of outer constraints that shape our lives. Schiller also posits a character type – the 'beautiful soul' or 'fine mind' (*schöne Seele*) – whose serene inner nature entails grace as a constant attribute. Yet even this ideal type cannot be immune to life's tribulations. In adversity, the harmony of mind and body has to be replaced by the freedom of mind *from* body, the 'sublime' quality of dignity. The links with Schiller's theory of tragedy are plain, as is the implication that the *schöne Seele* would be in its literary element as the hero or heroine of comedy or idyll.

The direct claims of morality that had been expelled from eighteenth-century aesthetics seem at first sight to have got in again. Schiller however is asserting a value higher than mere ethical outcomes. This emerges clearly in his discreet rebellion against the moral authority of Kant. If, as Kant had argued, an action can only be accounted moral when duty is kept sharply distinct from inclination, and indeed has normally had to overcome inclination, then there can be no such thing as an inherently moral being. Surely, Schiller argues, the ideal should be an *inclination to* duty? Only then would virtue be a value we embrace with our whole self, and no longer merely an external requirement that we obey in an endlessly repeated struggle with ourselves. Schiller concedes that Kant's rigorism may have been a necessary prescription for their age. But the highest moral norm should surely not be set by emergency; it must lie in the kind of

primal spontaneity of action that defines the *schöne Seele*. Kant'sfootnote to the second edition of *Religion within the Bounds of Mere Reason*, acknowledging Schiller's 'masterly treatise', is a response but hardly an answer. Schiller, diplomatically, hastened to declare himself satisfied. Yet his conception remains a significant challenge to Kant's axiom of pessimistic dualism. It is an appeal to balance spirit with sense, and moral with aesthetic judgment.

6   *Letters on the Aesthetic Education of Man* (1795)

Balancing opposed elements is the central idea of Schiller's major essay. It is the key both to understanding the nature of beauty and to creating a stable free society in some future age. These disparate aims make an unlikely pair, but to Schiller art seemed to offer precisely what the politics of the 1790s cried out for. Imbalance was the common condition in a world already suffering from division of labour. Here Schiller prepares the ground for Hegel and Marx on alienation, drawing a familiar eighteenth-century contrast with the wholeness of the human individual that was possible in Ancient Greece (L6). The added stress of revolutionary upheaval in France had now produced internecine violence. The French had acted with the ruthless rationality of 'barbarians' untouched by feeling, or the crude sensuousness of 'savages' unchecked by spirit (L4), an analysis that incidentally echoes the comments of observers in Paris. The project of an ideal society had failed not through the use of reason to guide reform, as conservatives like Burke held, but through its unmediated use by the unreformed. A force was needed that would smooth and stabilize the transition from sense to reason, exercising the human agent as both sensuous and rational being and strengthening or moderating each element as needed. That, according to Schiller's philosophical poem 'The Artists', was the role beauty had played in human evolution, and it could be repeated now. Art was the only force potentially free from the vicious circle of unregenerate humanity and the society that resulted. Art's highest exemplars fused substance and form and thus could balance and integrate sense and spirit in the beholder. The structural correspondence is clear. Less clear is how art might get a purchase on political reality. Schiller however is not offering a plaster for present ills, but a means to stop them recurring in the long term and so to create a new civic starting-point. There is no question of art's relapsing into didacticism to achieve this. Its effect for any specific purpose is avowedly 'nil'. Yet precisely by nullifying all previous determinations, its effect is 'infinite' because that restores human beings to themselves and sets them free once more to be – 'what they are meant to be' (L21). This is the still undaunted Enlightenment or Rousseauian faith that a new start will necessarily be a start in the right direction. The more pessimistic view, that our only realistic course is to practise a stoic rationality since life will always be crisis, is left for that tailpiece on the sublime (see §2 above) which in a sense completes the programme of aesthetic education.

We are again at frontiers, with ethics, politics, social anthropology. To get there has required new solutions in aesthetics, and it was the pressure of an urgent problem in those areas that drove Schiller to find them. After sketching the crisis and arguing that art alone can help (L1–9), he has analysed human makeup into 'person' and 'condition', the core identity and its changing determinations (L10); and identified two matching drives, a sensuous impulse (*Stofftrieb*) towards realization and involvement in the material world, and a formal impulse (*Formtrieb*) towards moral and intellectual control (L12). These elements are only separable in the abstract; we actually experience them in their various interactions and imbalances. The ideal fulfilment of our dual nature would be to assimilate a maximum of reality but with a maximum of formal coherence. Such a state would bring into being a third drive, the play impulse (*Spieltrieb*), whose concrete object would be a fusion: the material world, or in its broadest sense 'life' (*Leben*), would join with formal structure or 'shape' (*Gestalt*) to produce 'living shape' (*lebende Gestalt*) (L15). More important surely for art's role as a sociopolitical remedy, though Schiller does not say this, would be the reverse sequence: once aesthetic play was in some measure achieved, the two original impulses would be brought into some kind of balance. 'Living shape' meantime becomes Schiller's definition of beauty, and 'play' his account of aesthetic experience. Although he proposes the aesthetic state as the long-term answer to a political problem, in the still longer term he intends it to be self-sufficient. It can be borrowed to meet a need, but is ultimately an ideal (L27). For 'human beings only play when they are human in the fullest sense of the word, and they are only fully human when they play' (L15). The language of the *Letters*, incidentally, enacts the complexities of opposition and reconciliation in a play of its own with a rich and at first confusing array of concepts, all of them however variations on an underlying pattern. Readers will find the game is better played fast for its form than slowly for its detailed content.

Leaving the political application aside, the *Letters* are a great advance on earlier aesthetics, both Schiller's own and Kant's. No longer is an 'objective' theory insisted on, though there are vestiges of it in the original draft of Letter 1. Instead, both the constitution and the effect of beauty are grounded in the psycho-physical constitution and needs of human beings. Whereas Kantian 'disinterestedness' was a passive state that denied individuality, 'play' is an activity that subtly redeploys it. People bring to aesthetic encounters not an 'empty indeterminateness' but their whole past experience in a state of 'active determinability' (L20ff). This ensures, not a depersonalized universality of aesthetic judgment as in Kant, but a deeply personal response to both the forms and the substance of art. It restores reality to the abstractions of aesthetics: a landscape painting works with our accumulated experience of landscapes, a statue of Venus provokes more than an appreciation of assorted arabesques. The notion of 'play' means we take things seriously but not solemnly, in and for themselves, in an act of contemplation and savouring. In Brecht's deceptively simple words, 'In art, people enjoy life'. Such enjoyment involves separating 'appearance' – *Schein* this time, the standard word for illusion – from reality (L26). But it clearly no longer bothers Schiller that this makes his theory a subjective one. It has strong enough roots in the individual experience art springs from and appeals to, while 'play' is universal not as a logical abstraction but as an anthropological phenomenon.

7 *On Naïve and Reflective Poetry* (1796)

Schiller's final large-scale essay is not so much aesthetic theory as literary and cultural history, with sections of brilliant practical criticism. In the wake of long-running European debates on the relative merits of Ancients and Moderns, it traces a movement from the Greeks' oneness with the natural world to the hyperconsciousness of post-Christian Europe where, except for a few outstanding cases like Shakespeare, Molière and now Goethe, reflection necessarily intrudes between the poet and the object. Modern writing is constituted by reflection's many forms, but their underlying constant, and hence the deepest shaping influence on European literature, is an elegiac sense of lost harmony. To restore that harmony and the perfection of artistic form that went with it in antiquity, while managing somehow still to retain the riches of the modern sensibility – a postmodernism of serious substance – is the near-impossible millennial goal. But Schiller was never short on aspiration.

See also: AESTHETICS AND ETHICS; BURKE, E.; CASSIRER, E.; GOETHE, J.W. VON; SUBLIME, THE §§2, 3

List of works

Schiller, J.C.F. (1943–) *Nationalausgabe*, ed. B. von Wiese, L. Blumenthal and N. Oellers, Weimar. (The standard edition of Schiller's works and letters. The philosophical writings are in vols 20–22. There is also a reliable complete edition in 5 vols, ed. H. Göpfert and G. Fricke, Munich, 1958 and reprints.)

—— (1795) *On the Aesthetic Education of Man in a Series of Letters*, trans and with intro. by E.M. Wilkinson and L.A. Willoughby, Oxford, 1967, reprinted in paperback 1982. (German text with facing English translation. Editorial apparatus includes a glossary of concepts, diagrammatic representations of Schiller's thought, and an extensive bibliography.)

—— (1796a) *On Naïve and Sentimental Poetry*, trans. H. Watanabe, Manchester: Carcanet Press, 1981. ('Sentimental' in the normal English sense is not Schiller's meaning, which is why I translate his word 'sentimentalisch' as 'reflective' in this entry.)

—— (1796b) *On Naïve and Sentimental Poetry*, with On the Sublime, trans. J.A. Elias, New York: Ungar, 1966.

—— (1985) *German Aesthetic and Literary Criticism*, ed. H.B. Nisbet, Cambridge. (Reprints the Elias version in a collection of the most important eighteenth-century German aesthetic essays.)

—— (1978) *Medicine, Psychology and Literature*, ed. K. Dewhurst and N. Reeves, Oxford. (Presents in full the young Schiller's medical dissertations, which contain the seeds of his mature thought, along with much editorial material on medicine in the period.)

No reliable translation is available of Schiller's other essays.

References and further reading

* Burke, E. (1757) *A Philosophical Enquiry into the Origin of our Ideas of the Sublime and Beautiful*, Oxford: Oxford University Press, 1990. (See especially Part 4 for Burke's views on the sublime.)

* Cassirer, E. (1916) *Freiheit und Form*, Berlin. (A classic account of the intellectual tradition in which Schiller's thought has its roots.)

Ellis, J.M. (1969) *Schiller's Kalliasbriefe and the Study of his Aesthetic Theory*, The Hague: Mouton. (Acute arguments whose import extends well beyond the named text.)

Mann, T. (1932) 'Goethe and Tolstoy', in *Three Essays*, New York: Knopf. (Elaborates on Schiller's naïve/reflective typology, and applies it to the pair Tolstoy/Dostoevsky as well as to Goethe/Schiller.)

Podro, M. (1972) *The Manifold in Perception. Theories of Art from Kant to Hildebrand*, Oxford: Oxford University Press. (Schiller's theory forms the core of the book, which proceeds from a perceived affinity between painting since Impressionism and classical German aesthetics in which the author finds 'valuable critical ideas quite absent from contemporary philosophical writing'.)

Reed, T.J. (1991) *Schiller*, Past Masters series, Oxford: Oxford University Press. (A concise introduction with emphasis on the historical context and connections in the history of ideas.)

Reiner, H. (1953) *Pflicht und Neigung*, Meisenheim: Anton Hain. (A full and cogent treatment of Schiller's differences with Kant over duty and inclination.)

Schaper, E. (1979) *Studies in Kant's Aesthetics*, Edinburgh: Edinburgh University Press. (The chapter 'Schiller's Kant: a chapter in the history of creative misunderstanding' sees confusions in Schiller's reading of Kantian terminology, but is not dismissive: his early essays point up areas of difficulty in Kant's aesthetics.)

Sharpe, L. (1991) *Friedrich Schiller. Drama, Thought and Politics*, Cambridge: Cambridge University Press. (A substantial and coherent survey of all areas of Schiller's work.)

—— (1995) *Schiller's Aesthetic Essays: Two Centuries of Criticism*, Columbia, SC: Camden House. (A wide-ranging survey of the literature in both English and German.)

Simmel, G. (1904) *Kant. Sechzehn Vorlesungen*, Leipzig: Duncker & Humblot. (Lecture 15 is a classic statement of the essentials of Kant's and Schiller's aesthetic thought.)

Wilkinson, E.M. (1960) 'Reflections on translating Schiller's *Letters on the Aesthetic Education of Man*', in *Schiller Bicentenary Lectures*, ed. F. Norman, London: Institute of Germanic Studies, 45–82. (Illuminates the relation of Schiller's discrete concepts to his underlying binary structures and attempted resolutions.)

T.J. REED

SCHLEGEL, FRIEDRICH VON (1772–1829)

Schlegel was the major aesthetician of the Romantic movement in Germany during its first formative period (1797–1802). In these years he developed his influential concepts of Romantic poetry and irony, created an original approach to literary criticism and edited the journal of the early Romantic circle, Athenäum. *Along with F. von Hardenberg (Novalis), F.W.J. Schelling and F.D.E. Schleiermacher, he was also a guiding spirit in the development of a Romantic metaphysics, ethics and politics. His metaphysics attempted to synthesize Fichte's idealism and Spinoza's naturalism. His ethics preached radical individualism and love against the abstract formalism of Kant's ethics. In his early politics Schlegel was very radical, defending the right of revolution and democracy against Kant. In his later years, however, he became much more conservative. His final works are a defence of his neo-Catholic mysticism.*

Schlegel began his intellectual career as a classical scholar. His *Ueber das Studium der Griechischen Poesie* (On the Study of Greek Poetry) (1797) attempted to write a history of Greek poetry and formulate a neoclassical aesthetics. Schlegel wanted to do for the history of Greek poetry what J.J. Winckelmann had done for the history of Greek sculpture. Like Winckelmann, Schlegel admired the ancient Greeks for attaining a purely 'objective' norm of beauty, which was independent of national taste, personal caprice or even moral and political ends. He criticized modern literature because, rather than observing such a norm, it pandered to national taste with novel and striking gimmicks. Schlegel believed that the artist should attempt to imitate the purity and simplicity of classical models; in the recent works of Goethe he saw promising signs of a new classicism in Europe.

However, as early as 1797, largely under the influence of Friedrich SCHILLER, Schlegel began to have doubts about his neoclassicism. He now started to appreciate some of the distinctive values of modern Christian culture, especially its ideal of the infinite, its ethic of love and its emphasis upon personal freedom. In his *Athenäums Fragmente* (1798) Schlegel then gave a condensed account of his new Romantic aesthetic. The aim of the Romantic artist is to express the characteristic feature of modern culture: the striving for the infinite, the longing for the kingdom of God on earth, the struggle to realize Kant's ideal of the highest good (see KANT, I. §11). What is distinctive of Romantic art in contrast to classical, Schlegel wrote in his *Gespräch über Poesie* (Conversation on Poetry) (1800a), is that it expresses sentiment, especially the feeling of love, which is the longing to realize the infinite. In attempting to express such a grand ideal, the Romantic artist should attempt to cultivate irony, a critical detachment towards his own productions, for any of them are limited and therefore inadequate to express his unlimited ideal.

In several essays of the late 1790s, 'Ueber Lessing', 'Georg Forster' and 'Jacobis Woldemar', Schlegel developed a new method of literary criticism, which he described as 'characterization' (*Charackteristik*).

The aim of this method was to understand a work as a unique whole, to reconstruct an author's characteristic style. Rather than criticize a work according to some norm of objective beauty, Schlegel insisted upon evaluating it according to its own aims and upon exposing its inconsistencies. This internal approach to a work was, according to Wilhelm Dilthey, an important step in the development of hermeneutics (see HERMENEUTICS).

It was also in the late 1790s that Schlegel made his most important contributions to the ethics and politics of Romanticism. His 'Versuch über den Begriff des Republikanismus' (Essay on the Concept of Republicanism) (1796 (1996)), one of the most radical writings of the 1790s in Germany, was a defence of the right of revolution and direct democracy against Kant. His *Athenäums Fragmente* (1798–1800) and *Lucinde* (1799) were also far ahead of their time in championing such progressive causes as sexual liberation and the emancipation of women. Along with SCHLEIERMACHER, Schlegel developed an ethic of love and individuality in reaction to the abstract formalism of Kant's ethics (see KANTIAN ETHICS). He maintained that love cannot be understood as a legal obligation, and that it should involve a sensualization of the spirit as much as a spiritualization of the senses.

Schlegel's contribution to the metaphysics of Romanticism is his *Vorlesungen über die Transzendentalphilosophie* (Lectures on Transcendental Philosophy), delivered as lectures in Jena in 1800. This work is an attempt, several years before Hegel, to develop a synthesis of naturalism and idealism, of SPINOZA and FICHTE. While Schlegel argued that Kant and Fichte had wrongly separated the self from nature and history, he also criticized Spinoza for his static and ahistorical conception of the divine substance.

In the early 1800s the flame of Schlegel's early radicalism dimmed and his thought moved steadily in a conservative direction. He became disillusioned with the French Revolution, which seemed to end in anarchy, commercialism and military dictatorship. Increasingly, he saw the defence of the Catholic Church and the old social hierarchy as the only safeguards against these disturbing trends, and as the only pillars of spiritual and communal values. His growing conservatism culminated in his conversion to the Roman Catholic Church in 1808 and in his diplomatic and literary activity on behalf of Metternich between 1809 and 1818. In his later political writings, especially his *Signatur des Zeitalters* (Sign of the Age) (1820), Schlegel defended a virtually reactionary position: that the basis of all right is tradition, that society should be organized according to estates, and that social order depends upon the restoration of the Church.

His later works are mainly an apology for his neo-Catholic mysticism. His *Philosophie des Lebens* (Philosophy of Life) (1828) taught that the aim of philosophy should be to develop the spiritual life of a person, their receptivity for a divine revelation. His *Philosophie der Geschichte* (Philosophy of History) (1829) held that world history is not a progression towards greater rationality, but an attempt to return to spiritual grace and harmony with the divine. Although this work does give great importance to non-Western cultures, Schlegel still sees European Christianity as the turning point of history and the culmination of civilization.

See also: ROMANTICISM, GERMAN

List of works

Schlegel, F. von (1958–) *Kritische Friedrich Schlegel Ausgabe* (Critical Friedrich Schlegel Edition), ed. E. Behler, J.J. Anstett and H. Eichner, Paderborn: Schöningh. (The standard edition of Schlegel's works.)
—— (1797) *Ueber das Studium der Griechischen Poesie* (On the Study of Greek Poetry), Berlin: Unger. (The chief work of Schlegel's early classical phase.)
—— (1798–1800) *Athenäum. Eine Zeitschrift von August Wilhelm und Friedrich Schlegel* (Athenaeum: A Journal by August Wilhelm and Friedrich Schlegel), Berlin: Vieweg, 3 vols. (The main journal of the Romantic movement.)
—— (1799) *Lucinde*, Berlin: Fröhlich. (Schlegel's first and only novel.)
—— (1800a) Gespräch über Poesie (Conversation on Poetry), in *Athenäum*, vol. 3, 169–87. (Schlegel's reflections on the nature of art and the aims of the Romantic artist.)
—— (1800b) *Vorlesungen über die Transzendentalphilosophie* (Lectures on Transcendental Philosophy), in *Neue philosophische Schriften*, ed. J. Körner, Frankfurt: Schulte Verlag, 1935. (Written as lectures in 1800, these were published only in 1935, and are the main source for Schlegel's early philosophy.)
—— (1808) *Ueber Sprache und Weisheit der Indier* (On the Language and Wisdom of India), Heidelberg: Mohr. (Schlegel's pioneering work on Indian philosophy.)
—— (1820) Signatur des Zeitalters (Sign of the Age), in *Concordia*, Vienna: J.B. Wallishausser, vols 1–4: 3–70, 164–90, 343–98.
—— (1828) *Philosophie des Lebens* (Philosophy of Life), Vienna: Schaumberg. (The main exposition of Schlegel's mature philosophy.)
—— (1829) *Philosophie der Geschichte* (Philosophy of History), Vienna: Schaumberg. (The main work for Schlegel's mature philosophy of history.)
—— (1968) *Dialogue on Poetry and Literary Aphorisms* trans. and ed. E. Behler, University Park, PA: Penn State Press.
—— (1957) *Literary Notebooks 1797–1801*, ed. H. Eichner, Toronto: Toronto University Press.
—— (1971) *Lucinde and the Fragments*, trans. P. Firchow, Minneapolis, MN: University of Minnesota Press. (Translations of Schlegel (1798–1800) and (1799).)
—— (1996) *Early Political Writings of the German Romantics*, trans. and ed. F. Beiser, Cambridge: Cambridge University Press. (Contains 'Essay on the Concept of Republicanism' (1796), *Athenäums Fragments* and parts of *Lectures on Transcendental Philosophy*.)

References and further reading

Ayrault, R. (1961) *La Genèse du romantisme allemand* (The Genesis of German Romanticism), Paris: Aubier. (The most thorough account of the early years of German Romanticism; vol. 4, 279–311 is devoted to Schlegel's Romantic aesthetic.)
Eichner, H. (1970) *Friedrich Schlegel*, Twayne World Author Series 98, New York: Twayne. (A useful introduction to all aspects of Schlegel's thought.)
Haym, R. (1890) *Die romantische Schule* (The Romantic School), Berlin: Gaertner. (The classic account of the young Schlegel and the origins of the Romantic school.)
Silz, W. (1929) *Early German Romanticism*, Cambridge, MA: Harvard University Press. (A useful introductory survey.)
Walzel, O. (1932) *German Romanticism*, New York: Putnam. (A useful and careful survey of early Schlegel and the Romantic movement.)

FREDERICK BEISER

SCHLEIERMACHER, FRIEDRICH DANIEL ERNST (1768–1834)

Friedrich Daniel Ernst Schleiermacher was the most notable German-speaking protestant theologian of the nineteenth century. He gave significant impetus to the re-orientation of theology after the Age of Enlight-

enment (see his speeches Über die Religion *(On Religion) (1799), and also* Kurze Darstellung des theologischen Studiums *(Brief Outline of Theology as a Field of Study) (1811a))* and he enjoyed a wide audience in Berlin both as preacher and Professor of Theology and Philosophy. Throughout his life he was a fervent advocate of the union between the Lutheran and the Reformed Church established in the so-called Old Prussian Union, and his compendium* Der christliche Glaube *(The Christian Faith) (1821, 1822) is held to be the first dogmatics transcending the denominational boundaries between the Reformation Churches. His translation of Plato attained the status of a classic. In his university lectures and academic speeches on philosophy he made a profound and lasting impression on his audience, both in his historical and systematic thought. He also had an important hand in the reform of the German Universities. In theology and philosophy he strove to find an independent and intermediate position between the Enlightenment, German Idealism and Romanticism.*

1 **Life**
2 **Philosophical work**
3 **The system of sciences**
4 **Dialectics**
5 **Ethics**
6 **Psychology**
7 **The philosophy of religion**
8 **Aesthetics**
9 **Hermeneutics**
10 **Pedagogics**
11 **Politics**

1 Life

Schleiermacher was born on 21 November 1768 in Breslau, the second child and eldest son of the Reformed Church chaplain Johann Gottlieb Adolph Schleyermacher and his first wife Elisabeth Maria Katharina Schleyermacher (born Stubenrauch). After a childhood spent in Breslau, Pless and Anhalt (Upper Silesia), Schleiermacher was educated among the Moravians (Herrnhuter Brüdergemeine), a small Lutheran community established by Zinzendorf in 1727. He was a pupil at the *Pädagogium* (grammar school) in Niesky and then went to the *Seminarium* (college) in Barby. After leaving the Moravians, he studied theology and philosophy at the Friedrichs-Universität in Halle an der Saale from 1787 to 1789. From Johann August Eberhard he gained familiarity with ancient and contemporary philosophy. Schleiermacher sought to find his own position within the intellectual dialogue that was being conducted between the Leibniz–Wolff school and Kant's

critical philosophy, which had begun to gain ascendency in Germany. He passed his first Church examination in 1790 and took a post in Schlobitten, East Prussia, as tutor to the family of Count Dohna. After successfully negotiating his second Church examination in 1794, he became a preacher in the Reformed Church, initially at Landsberg an der Warthe; then, from 1796 to 1802, at the Charité hospital in Berlin and eventually at Stolp in Pomerania. In 1804 he was appointed Professor of Reformed Theology in Halle an der Saale, but after the Prussian defeat at the hands of the French and the truce at Tilsit in 1807, he moved back to Berlin. He participated in the literary discussion concerning the reform of the university, the subject of his *Gelegentliche Gedanken über Universitäten in deutschem Sinn* (Occasional Thoughts on Universities in the German Sense) (1808a). In 1809 he married the widow of a friend, Henriette von Willich (born von Mühlenfels), and took up the pastorate of the Reformed Church at the Dreifaltigkeitskirche in Berlin. In the following year Schleiermacher also became Professor of Theology at the newly founded Friedrich-Wilhelms-Universität, and a member of the philosophical section in the Royal Academy of Sciences in Berlin. In this capacity he gave lectures both in theology and philosophy at the university. As secretary of the philosophical section from 1814 and, from 1826, also secretary of the section in history and philology, he undertook the reorganization of the Academy, becoming secretary of the historical-philosophical section in 1827. While Schleiermacher worked actively in the Prussian reform movement after 1807, participating officially in educational reform from 1810–14, he took a stance in opposition to the government during the Restoration era. He continued his official ecclesiastic and academic duties in Berlin until his death on 12 February 1834.

2 Philosophical work

Schleiermacher's main philosophical interest was in the field of ethics. As a member of the Berlin circle of Early Romantics he anonymously published several small essays on ethical themes in the *Athenaeum* journal of the Schlegel brothers (1798–1800) (see SCHLEGEL, F.). His poetical early writings were in part dedicated to the exposition of his ethical views: *Monologen. Eine Neujahrsgabe (Soliloquies) (1800a)* as the manifesto of an individualist ethics, and his *Vertraute Briefe über Friedrich Schlegel's Lucinde* (Letters concerning Friedrich Schlegel's *Lucinde*) (1800b) as the Romantic interpretation of erotic love. His first systematic work was *Grundlinien einer Kritik der bisherigen Sittenlehre* (Principles of a Critique of all Doctrines of Ethics Hitherto) (1803), which was a critical examination of ethical systems from Antiquity to KANT (§§9–11) and FICHTE (§6). Schleiermacher laid the plans for his own exposition of ethics in his lectures, but never published them. Instead he published detailed ethical investigations in the course of his academic treatises (1819–30). Areas to which he directed much philosophical attention were his research into the history of philosophy (for instance, *Herakleitos* (1808b)) and to his translation of Plato's works (1804–28). However, Schleiermacher also undertook comprehensive systematic studies in the course of his lecturing career and it is here that he made his seminal contribution to hermeneutics, pedagogics and psychology. He never managed to work out his rich and diverse lectures on different philosophical disciplines for publication; his philosophical system has to be reconstructed from the relevant posthumously published manuscripts and his students' notes of his lectures.

3   The system of sciences

Schleiermacher's system follows the ancient division of philosophy into dialectics, physics and ethics. His idea of philosophy is the perfection of knowledge in the mutual interpenetration of six basic sciences (*Grundwissenschaften*), four with regard to the material aspects of knowledge and two to the formal. He structures the system of material sciences with the help of the dual opposition between reason and nature on the one hand and essence and existence on the other. The sciences of nature and reason, which differ with respect to their objects, fall under the modal distinction of the speculative and the empirical. The science of nature and the science of reason are thus subdivided into a speculative science of the essence of nature and reason respectively and into an experiential science of the appearance of nature and reason respectively. Schleiermacher calls these four material sciences 'physics' and 'the study of nature' (*Naturkunde*), 'ethics' and 'the study of history' (*Geschichtskunde*). The formal sciences are dialectics and mathematics. Dialectics is the supreme science, which replicates the supreme knowledge formally, just as mathematics is concerned with the form of the particular as such.

Schleiermacher did not explore the natural sciences to any great degree, and in this domain he relied in particular on the work of Henrik Steffens (*Grundzüge der philosophischen Naturwissenschaft*, Berlin, 1806). What he did attempt to reconstruct philosophically was the self-realization of reason in the process of history. The study of history illustrates the doctrine of ethics and the doctrine of ethics structures the study

of history. Since there is no transition, but rather a hiatus between ethics as a science of essence and the study of history as a science of appearances, both ethics and history have to be related to each other in theory and in practice through critical and technical procedures. Critical procedure is investigative, whereas technical procedure is regulative. While critique (*Kritik*) judges the particular appearances as representations of the ideas, technology (*Technik*) gives instructions as to how, under different natural conditions, the production of particular appearances might take place. Psychology, aesthetics, political science and the philosophy of religion belong to the critical disciplines, while hermeneutics, pedagogics and political wisdom belong to the technical disciplines.

4   Dialectics

Schleiermacher's elementary philosophy, which sets out the procedural rules for the production of knowledge, he calls 'dialectics' (first lectures 1811). In his dialectics he expounds the principles according to which speech (both dialogue and monologue) which is aimed at attaining knowledge must proceed, if it is to fulfil its task of developing contested claims into completely accepted, universally valid knowledge. Dialectics is an artificial doctrine, designed to avoid conflict and doubt in the field of pure thought and reach a permanent and harmonious accord. Thus it stands opposed to scepticism. But since dialectics presupposes a conflict about knowledge, it cannot be the beginning of all knowledge. It thus gets its meaning from its intermediary position between the already extant will to know and the perfection of knowledge. The historical and social limitations of dialectics result from the fact that all thought is bound to language.

Schleiermacher's dialectics joins metaphysics (transcendental philosophy) and logic (formal philosophy). In the transcendental part he deals with the fundamental principles, conditions and structures of knowledge, and in the technical part he gives directions as to how knowledge is to be produced. In the first part dialectics is *prima philosophia*, in the second it is a logical apparatus ('organon') for the construction of the totality of knowledge and for the evaluation of individual items of knowledge.

The mutual play of reason and sensuality lies at the root of all knowledge. Reason as an intellectual function gives overall unity and determines the form of thinking. Sensuality as an organic function furnishes the manifold material contents. All concrete perceptions are conceptually structured, and all concepts are saturated with experience. Logic and ontology are parallel. Forms of being and forms of knowledge correspond to one another.

Two transcendental ideas which transgress the limits of real knowledge – the idea of the world and the idea of God – are none the less constitutive of all knowledge. The idea of the world signifies the totality of the oppositions which beset finite beings, and to which real thinking approximates. The idea of God means the unity without oppositions, which is presupposed by all knowledge, and to which knowledge cannot approximate. Schleiermacher pairs the ideas of the world and God, because God without the world would be an empty representation, and the world without God something purely contingent.

5 Ethics

Ethics, or the philosophical doctrine of morals (first lectures 1804–5 (1805–6)), next to which Schleiermacher places the Christian doctrine of morals (first lectures 1806 (1834–64: 1, 12)), is the science of the principles of history. In the ethical process of history, reason appropriates nature in such a way that their opposition is eventually overcome. History is complete when nature has become the organ and symbol of reason, and when what is individual and what is universal have been wholly evened out in a comprehensive process of interaction.

Philosophical ethics is a theory of culture and formulates the essential content of history, in so far as it understands the present as a phase on the way to perfection. Ethics is more descriptive than prescriptive. It tries to avoid the Kantian dualisms of duty and inclination, universal reason and individual will, ought and is (see KANTIAN ETHICS). Its central concern is the productive moral power of the individual, which manifests itself in different social situations. The morality of an individual is embedded in sociality. The moral law becomes analogous to a law of nature and understood as its improvement.

Schleiermacher divides ethics into the doctrine of the good, the doctrine of virtue and the doctrine of duty, and gives precedence to the doctrine of the good, as in ancient philosophy. The doctrine of virtue asks the question, 'Who is good and who does good?' and looks at the moral power of the individual. Following the ancient canon of cardinal virtues Schleiermacher recognizes four main virtues: wisdom, love, prudence and perseverance. The doctrine of duty asks the question, 'What is good?' and looks at the moral deed. It teaches a system of actions and modes of behaviour which shows how everyone can best promote the universal moral goal of the highest good. In the process Schleiermacher looks at the compatibility of the different fields of social action, so that

law, profession, love and conscience might fit together. The doctrine of the good asks after the very concept of moral goods, which human beings produce through their moral powers and which constitute the world of ethical action. The doctrine of the good constructs the concept of the highest good through the interrelation of two pairs of opposites: the action of reason on nature is organizing or symbolizing, and it is individual or universal (identical). Accordingly Schleiermacher divides up the manifold of concrete actions using the following schema: identical (universal) organization is the concern of work, business and economics; individual organization is the concern of property, friendship, sociality and hospitality. Identical (universal) symbolization, which is articulate in speech and in thought, is the concern of science; individual symbolization is the concern of art and religion. These four fields of ethical or moral life become relatively independent through the institutions of the state, the household, the scientific academy and the church. Moral demands on the individual are embedded in the forms of community, within which morality is always already present. Imperatives aim at the development of the highest good and to this extent they can always be based upon the fact that reason has already become in some measure objective.

6 Psychology

Schleiermacher's psychology (first lectures 1818 (1834–64: 3, 6)) complements and concretizes his ethics. The basic structures of ethics are traced to the characteristics of individuals and peoples. Schleiermacher argues that the soul, which must not be isolated from the body, is only present in the context of one's life as a whole. The 'I', the basic structure of the soul, is not thought of as the aggregate of human faculties, but is disclosed through its opposite activities. The receptive activity processes the impressions which are received from outside, while the spontaneous activity is creatively directed towards the outside world. Both these directions of activity are always woven together and increase in determinacy only in the course of their development. The task of psychology is to comprehend both basic activities in terms of their genesis and their different characteristics.

Receptivity is characterized by the activity of the senses. This activity leads to a doubling of all perceptive consciousness into an objective consciousness of things and a subjective self-consciousness. Within objective and subjective consciousness there is a tendency towards ever greater generalization. By dint of its realization in concepts and language, objective consciousness strives towards knowledge in the sense of a rational species-consciousness (*Gattungsbewußtsein*). In subjective consciousness the tendency towards generalization is made manifest in the feeling of sociality and in the formation of an individual consciousness which presages the infinite at the limits of the finite. Spontaneity is likewise analysed in terms of its subjective and objective aspects. The acquisitive appropriation of the external world of nature is juxtaposed to the manifestation of the self in art and science.

7 The philosophy of religion

Schleiermacher conceives the philosophy of religion as a critical discipline, which makes a structural comparison of the various forms of religion from the starting point of the ethical basis of religion. However, he never devoted any of his lectures specifically to the philosophy of religion. In his theological writings, *Kurze Darstellung des theologischen Studiums* (Brief Outline of Theology as a Field of Study) (1811a), *Der christliche Glaube* (The Christian Faith) (1821, 1822) and *Über die Religion* (On Religion) (1799), one can find numerous references to the philosophy of religion. The essence of Christianity can be ascertained from a comparison of the different forms of religion.

Religion is a sense for the infinite and is based on the feeling of absolute dependency in the immediacy of self-consciousness. It is a universal element of life which is based in the universal essence of mankind and it does not conflict with the knowledge through which it is vouchsafed in reason and experience. Christianity, philosophy and the causal sciences are all compatible.

Piety and understanding are the poles between which the life of the spirit unfolds. Philosophy, which remains a kind of negative theology, points towards its opposite pole, which it is unable to attain. Philosophy and Christian piety gravitate together in a continual process of approximation. Philosophy does not offer the foundation for piety, but provides religion with concepts for its exposition.

Theology has no space of its own in the system of sciences. As a positive science, it is functionally constituted through its external task of offering its knowledge and skills for the governing and management of the church. Dogmatic propositions describe the self-consciousness which is germane to Christian piety; their truth is grounded in this self-consciousness.

8 Aesthetics

Schleiermacher understands aesthetics as a critical discipline which speculatively comprehends art in the context of all human activities and encyclopedically grasps the historical occurrence of the different forms of art (first lectures 1819 (1819, 1825)). According to ethics, art is the symbolization of something individual. It is generated from the individual's coming to self-awareness, from the individual's sensitivity for the world and from the expressive power of the individual's imagination. Art is the organ of the representation of what is individual. All human beings are therefore artists in this sense.

Schleiermacher's aesthetics is an aesthetics of production. It begins from the standpoint of the activity of the artist, not from the content of the art work. It looks at art's process of becoming and marks the stages in which feelings become objective in a work. The original datum is the becoming of the original image in the joining together of enthusiasm and temperance. The imagination fashions an internal image into the form of a work. This presentation in the material can then be experienced by others.

Schleiermacher's aesthetics is an aesthetics of expression. It examines the expression of subjective feeling, which at the same time brings to appearance something that is universally human. What is only inchoate in nature is made complete and explicit in artistic activity. In art the productive spirit shows itself to be that which interprets and advances creation.

Schleiermacher's division of the arts follows the fundamental distinction of his psychology between self-consciousness and object-consciousness. The visual arts of painting and sculpture proceed from object-consciousness, by forming and physically realizing representations in free imaginative productions in external media. Music and mimic art proceed from self-consciousness by creatively shaping the articulation of feeling through gesture and sound. Poetry unites both poles, although it is more strongly attracted to the pole of object-consciousness.

9 Hermeneutics

Schleiermacher removes hermeneutics from its traditional contexts of theology, philology and jurisprudence, and develops it into a general theory of understanding (first lectures 1805 (1819)). Hermeneutics allows for thoughts which are articulated in language to be partially understood and partially not, and thus it operates neither on the level of complete knowledge nor on the level of complete ignorance. It claims to reconstruct individual and concrete linguis-

535

tic utterances methodologically, in order to determine the thought which they articulate. Diametrically opposed to dialectics, hermeneutics considers the transition between linguistic communication and universal reason. The process of understanding is open-ended and interminable, like the process of history. Every interpretative act must have a provisional grasp of the whole in order to comprehend the parts, which in their turn reveal the contours of the whole more precisely. Thus hermeneutics does have an ethical orientation, since it participates theoretically and practically in the realization of the highest good, in so far as it furthers successful communication and the formation of the scientific community.

What characterizes Schleiermacher's hermeneutics, which counts as one of the technical disciplines, is that it prescribes a method. The method specifies four procedures with which given speeches or texts have to be reconstructed: grammatical, psychological, comparative and divinatory interpretation. Since every linguistic utterance is both the product of an author and a component of a linguistic system, grammatical (objective) interpretation examines the utterance in the context of language as a whole, while psychological (subjective) interpretation focuses on the context of the individual's production of thoughts. The comparative procedure clarifies obscurities with the help of what is already understood, and to this end it requires particular historical and philological investigations. The divinatory procedure elucidates meaning and context intuitively, and to this end it is based on the autonomous productivity of the interpreter. The four basic procedures are normally put to use in combinations of two. The grammatical method is predominantly comparative, while psychological interpretation is mainly divinatory. Nevertheless, attention should be paid to all four procedures in the course of every interpretation.

The hermeneutic formula of method is complemented by its indication of the goal of inquiry – to understand a given utterance or text as well as its author, and then better than its author. So first of all interpreters have to attempt to put themselves in the position of the author, and then, distancing themselves from this proximity with the author, to make new sense of the text or utterance in the context of the linguistic system.

10 Pedagogics

As a technical discipline, pedagogics inherits its guiding concepts and basic structure from the field of ethics (first lectures 1813 (1834–64: 3, 9)). The ethical relation between individual and community, between nature and reason, provides education with its two guiding perspectives: individual education – the drawing out of the student's individual nature – and social education – the integration of the student into ethical life.

Schleiermacher distinguishes three periods of education: the family upbringing and acquisition of language; school education; and vocational training. The activity of education which is directed towards the formation of character and capacities has to promote good and suppress evil. The intellectual capacities which involve the student's *Weltanschauung* (worldview) are honed on the scientific study of history and nature; the ethical capacities, which concern their *Weltbildung* (their way of making the world) are formed through the undertaking of ethical and human tasks.

Since pedagogics as a technical discipline presupposes that a certain level of culture has already been attained, it imposes the twofold task of preserving the ethical *status quo* and ameliorating what is still ethically imperfect. Schleiermacher puts his pedagogics in the historical situation of Europe after the French Revolution, namely in the conflict between a traditionalism hostile to all reform and a revolutionism hostile to all tradition. His great aim is the overcoming of social inequality, of the division between aristocracy and bourgeoisie. The pedagogics of ethical perfection is supposed to smooth the path of progress without revolutionary force and thus shows itself to be in accord with the Prussian policy of reform.

11 Politics

Schleiermacher conceives politics as a combined critical and technical discipline (first lectures 1808–9 (1980–: 2, 8)). Politics indicates the general perspectives from which existing states are to be appraised. Thus political activity can be harmonized with the level of culture, which for Schleiermacher is characterized above all by the Prussian reform movement and the national uprising against France.

The state is constituted by the distinction between government and people, and by the presence of an accepted law. It is a social institution which regulates identical organization (the communal mastery of nature) and thus guarantees the subsistence of the citizens. The state therefore has a particular orientation towards administration and economics. In this way Schleiermacher downgrades the significance of the military. The progress of culture is furthered by labour. Schleiermacher rejects capital punishment, offensive wars, violent revolutions and enforced colonization.

The state has to overcome the basic tension

between the individual and the universal will; it must take upon itself the task of restraining private interest where it threatens the public good, but must also restrict itself and leave private interest to its own devices where such interest serves the ends of humanity. The state must take appropriate measures to intervene in the labour process, in order to ensure that the universal interest is served. It must not become an economic subject in the process, however, but must guarantee social welfare in the way in which it would uphold a legal duty.

Schleiermacher holds constitutional monarchy to be the most appropriate form of constitution for large, modern nation-states. In a constitutional monarchy the legislative power extends from the people to the king, and the executive power extends from the king to his subjects. Standing above all private interests, the king is in an excellent position to guarantee the universality of freedoms and justice. Aristocracy has the disadvantage that it fixes differences in class and status. Democracy has the disadvantage that public and private interest can come into intractable conflict with each other.

Schleiermacher accords the state no primacy over other forms of community. He rather places the state beside church, household and academy of science, so that religion, free sociality and science are thereby removed from its jurisdiction.

See also: ETHICS; HERMENEUTICS

List of works

Schleiermacher, F.D.E. (1980–) *Kritische Gesamtausgabe (KGA)*, ed. H.-J. Birkner, G. Ebeling, H. Fischer, H. Kimmerle, G. Meckenstock, K.-V. Selge, Berlin and New York: de Gruyter. (New Critical edition of all works, lectures, sermons, translations and letters.)

—— (1834–64) *Sämmtliche Werke* (Collected Works), Berlin: Reimer. (Early thirty-volume edition of the works, sermons and lectures.)

—— (1799) *Über die Religion. Reden an die Gebildeten unter ihren Verächtern*, Berlin: Unger; 2nd edn, revised, 1806; 3rd edn, revised and extended, 1821; 4th edn, 1831; 1st edn trans. R. Crouter, *On Religion. Speeches to its Cultured Despisers*, Cambridge: Cambridge University Press, 1988, new edn, 1996; 4th edn trans. J. Oman, London: Paul, Trench, Trübner, 1893; New York, Harper, 1959. (Classical document of the early Romantic understanding of religion; critical edition in *KGA* 1, 2; 2nd–4th edns in *KGA* 1, 12.)

—— (1800a) *Monologen. Eine Neujahrsgabe* (Soliloquies: A New Years Gift), Berlin: Spener; 2nd edn,

revised, 1810; 3rd edn, revised, 1822; 4th edn, revised, 1829; 1st edn trans. H.L. Friess, *Soliloquies*, Chicago, IL: Open Court, 1926. (Manifesto of an ethics of individuality; critical edition in *KGA* 1, 3; 2nd–4th edns in *KGA* 1, 12.)

—— (1800b) *Vertraute Briefe über Friedrich Schlegel's Lucinde* (Confidential Letters on Friedrich Schlegel's *Lucinde*), Lübeck and Leipzig: Bohn. (Apology for Friedrich Schlegel's erotic novel, which caused a great scandal; critical edition in *KGA* 1, 3.)

—— (1803) *Grundlinien einer Kritik der bisherigen Sittenlehre* (Principles of a Critique of All Hitherto Doctrines of Ethics), Berlin: Realschulbuchhandlung. (Critical analysis of ancient and modern systems of ethics.)

—— (ed. and trans.) (1804–28) *Platon's Werke* (Plato's Works), Berlin: Realschulbuchhandlung and Reimer, 6 vols; introductions trans. W. Dobson, *Introduction to the Dialogues of Plato*, Cambridge: Deighton, 1836. (Classic translation of Plato's dialogues into German with critical introductions.)

—— (1805–6) *Brouillon zur Ethik* (Outline of Ethics), ed. H.-J. Birkner, Hamburg: Meiner, 1981. (Lectures of 1805–6. The introduction contains a bibliography.)

—— (1808a) *Gelegentliche Gedanken über Universitäten in deutschem Sinn. Nebst einem Anhang über eine neu zu errichtende*, Berlin: Realschulbuchhandlung; trans. T.N. Tice and E. Lawler, *Occasional Thoughts on Universities in the German Sense*, San Francisco, CA: Edwin Mellen Press, 1991. (Programmatic work of educational and political significance on the founding of the University of Berlin.)

—— (1808b) *Herakleitos der dunkle, von Ephesos, dargestellt aus den Trümmern seines Werkes und den Zeugnissen der Alten* (Heraclitus the Obscure of Ephesus, reconstructed from the Remnants of his Work and the Testimonies of the Ancients), in *Museum der Alterthums-Wissenschaft* 1, 313–533. (Historical reconstruction of the doctrine of Heraclitus.)

—— (1811a) *Kurze Darstellung des theologischen Studiums zum Behuf einleitender Vorlesungen*, Berlin: Realschulbuchhandlung; 2nd edn, 1830; trans. T.N. Tice and E. Lawler, *Brief Outline of Theology as a Field of Study*, San Francisco, CA: Edwin Mellen Press, 1988. (Functionally structured encyclopedia of theology. 2nd edition heavily reworked and extended.)

—— (1811b) *Dialektik* (Dialectics), ed. A. Arndt, Hamburg: Meiner, 1986. (Lectures of 1811. The introduction contains a bibliography.)

—— (1812–13) *Ethik* (Ethics), ed. H.-J. Birkner, Hamburg: Meiner, 1981. (Lectures of 1812–13. The introduction contains a bibliography.)

—— (1814–15) *Dialektik* (Dialectics), ed. A. Arndt, Hamburg: Meiner, 1984. (Lectures of 1814–15 and a fragment from 1833. The introduction contains a bibliography.)

—— (1819) *Hermeneutik* (Hermeneutics), ed. H. Kimmerle, Heidelberg: Winter, 1974. (Lectures of 1819 and other source texts on hermeneutics.)

—— (1819, 1825) *Ästhetik* (Aesthetics), ed. T. Lehnerer, Hamburg: Meiner, 1984. (Lectures from 1819 and 1825. The introduction contains a bibliography.)

—— (1821, 1822) *Der christliche Glaube nach den Grundsäzen der evangelischen Kirche im Zusammenhange dargestellt* (The Christian Faith according to the Principles of the Protestant Church Expounded in Context), Berlin: Reimer, 2 vols; 2nd edn revised, 1830, 1831; trans. H.R. Mackintosh and J.S. Stewart, *The Christian Faith*, Edinburgh: T. & T. Clark, 1928, 1948; New York, Harper, 1963. (The most significant protestant dogmatics of the nineteenth century.)

—— (1992) *On Freedom*, trans. A.C. Blackwell, Lewiston, NY: Edwin Mellen Press. (Translation of *KGA* 1, 1: 217–356. Detailed analysis of the concept of freedom.)

—— (1992) *On the Highest Good*, trans. H.V. Froese, Lewiston, NY: Edwin Mellen Press. (Translation of *KGA* 1, 1: 81–125. Critical discussion of Kant's *Critique of Practical Reason*.)

—— (1995) *On What Gives Value to Life*, trans. E. Lawler and T.N. Tice, Lewiston, NY: Edwin Mellen Press. (Translation of *KGA* 1,1: 391–471. Phenomenological analysis and moral rating of human life and fate.)

References and further reading

Lehnerer, T. (1987) *Die Kunsttheorie Friedrich Schleiermachers* (Schleiermacher's Theory of Art), Stuttgart: Klett-Cotta. (Systematic exposition of Schleiermacher's theory of art.)

Meckenstock, G. (1988) *Deterministische Ethik und kritische Theologie. Die Auseinandersetzung des frühen Schleiermacher mit Kant und Spinoza 1789–1794* (Deterministic Ethics and Critical Theology: The Early Schleiermacher's Encounter with Kant and Spinoza 1789–1794), Berlin and New York: de Gruyter. (Detailed investigation of the early writings.)

Meckenstock, G. and J. Ringleben (eds) (1991) *Schleiermacher und die wissenschaftliche Kultur des Christenthums* (Schleiermacher and the Scientific Culture of Christianity), Berlin and New York: de Gruyter. (Contains essays on historical, theological and philosophical themes.)

Meding, W. von (1992) *Bibliographie der Schriften Schleiermachers nebst einer Zusammenstellung und Datierung seiner gedruckten Predigten* (Bibliography of Schleiermacher's Writings with a Collection and Chronology of His Published Sermons), Berlin and New York: de Gruyter. (Bibliography of Schleiermacher's works.)

Moxter, M. (1992) *Güterbegriff und Handlungstheorie* (The Concept of the Good and Theory of Action), Kampen: Kok Pharos. (Historical and systematic reconstruction of Schleiermacher's ethics of the good.)

New Athenaeum – Neues Athenaeum (1989–) A Scholarly Journal Specializing in Schleiermacher Research and Nineteenth-Century Studies– Zeistschrift für Schleiermacher-Forschung und für Studien zum 19. Jahrhundert, Lewiston, NY: Edwin Mellen Press. (Contains articles on and translations of Schleiermacher's work.)

Pleger, W. (1988) *Schleiermachers Philosophie* (Schleiermacher's Philosophy), Berlin and New York: de Gruyter. (Introductory survey of the many subjects thematized by Schleiermacher's philosophy.)

Reymond, B. (1984) 'Schleiermacher en Français' (Schleiermacher in French), in *Archivio di Filosofia* 52: 489–97. (Bibliographical list of the French translations and the French Schleiermacher literature.)

Rieger. R. (1988) *Interpretation und Wissen* (Interpretation and Knowledge), Berlin and New York: de Gruyter. (Historical account of Schleiermacher's hermeneutics.)

Scholtz, G. (1984) *Die Philosophie Schleiermachers* (Schleiermacher's Philosophy), Darmstadt: Wissenschaftliche Buchgesellschaft. (Offers a very good introduction to the system and the history of Schleiermacher's philosophy, with all the important earlier literature.)

Selge, K.-V. (ed.) (1985) *Internationaler Schleiermacher-Kongreß Berlin 1984* (International Schleiermacher Congress, Berlin 1984), Berlin and New York: de Gruyter, 2 vols. (Contains essays on philosophical, theological and historical themes.)

Sorrentino, S. (ed.) (1992) *Schleiermacher's Philosophy and the Philosophical Tradition*, Lewiston, NY: Edwin Mellen Press. (Contains essays on various philosophical themes.)

Tice, T.N. (1966) *Schleiermacher Bibliography*, Princeton, NJ: Theological Seminary. (Bibliographical list of Schleiermacher's writings and the Schleiermacher literature, 1800–1964.)

—— (1985) *Schleiermacher Bibliography: Corrections, New Information and Comments*, Princeton, NJ:

Theological Seminary. (Bibliographical corrections to the 1966 list.)

—— (1985) *Schleiermacher Bibliography (1784–1984), Updating and Commentary*, Princeton, NJ: Theological Seminary. (Supplements and additions to the 1966 list.)

—— (1989) 'Schleiermacher Bibliography: Update 1987', in *New Athenaeum – Neues Athenaeum* 1, 280–350. (Supplements and additions to the 1966 list.)

—— (1991) 'Schleiermacher Bibliography: Update 1990', in *New Athenaeum – Neues Athenaeum* 2: 131–63. (Supplements and additions to the 1966 list.)

—— (1995) 'Schleiermacher Bibliography: Update 1994', in *New Athenaeum – Neues Athenaeum* 4, 139–94. (Supplements and additions to the 1966 list.)

Zeitschrift für Neuere Theologiegeschichte – Journal for the History of Modern Theology (1994–), Berlin and New York: de Gruyter. (Articles on and editions of Schleiermacher's work.)

Translated by J.G. Finlayson

GÜNTER MECKENSTOCK

SCHLICK, FRIEDRICH ALBERT MORITZ (1882–1936)

Moritz Schlick is usually remembered as the leader of the Vienna Circle, a group that flourished from the late 1920s to the mid-1930s, and made an important contribution to the philosophical movement known as 'logical empiricism'. Yet many of Schlick's most original contributions to philosophy antedated the hey-day of the Circle, providing the foundations for much of its subsequent development. He started his academic career as a physicist, and his early contributions to philosophy include an influential conventionalist interpretation of general relativity and a new account of the definitions of the basic terms of theoretical science. In the debates that flourished within the Vienna Circle he is famous for his commitment to the Principle of Verifiability and his defence of a correspondence theory of truth. In addition, his works during the final years of the Vienna Circle represent some of the most sober reflections on the problems that vexed the early logical empiricists. Although few of the views identified with logical empiricism currently find favour among philosophers, their approach to philosophy, especially their identification of its central perplexities, still wields enormous influence among contemporary thinkers.

Since Schlick contributed significantly to the form logical empiricism assumed during its period of dominance, there can be little doubt that his thought continues to inspire much philosophical thinking today.

1 **Spacetime and conventionalism**
2 **Epistemology**
3 **The Vienna Circle**
4 **Empiricism**

1 Spacetime and conventionalism

Schlick originally planned a career in physics, and finished his doctorate under the direction of the Nobel prize-winner Max Planck, in 1904. Within a few short years his interests turned to philosophy and he soon he produced a youthfully enthusiastic ethical tract (*Lebensweisheit*) as well as a long essay on the concept of truth. Schlick's work on truth was an impressive achievement, for it not only provided an extensive discussion of the major treatments of truth then prevailing in German academic philosophy, it also contributed an original analysis of the nature of truth. Schlick's basic idea was that truth consists in what he called the 'univocal designation' by a judgment of a situation in the world. Judgments consist of constituents that must be coordinated with elements of reality, in order for the judgment to possess any external significance at all. If the constituents of a judgment are combined in such a way that the judgment as a whole univocally designates a situation in the world, then it is true; if not, the judgment is false. In the prevailing context of German Neo-Kantianism, Schlick's analysis of truth was strikingly innovative. Yet its greatest significance derives from the role it subsequently played in his interpretation of the new physics of relativity theory.

It was Schlick's philosophical interpretation of relativity theory that first brought him to eminence, not only among scientifically-minded philosophers but also in the eyes of prominent physicists. Schlick pioneered the conventionalist understanding of relativity that prevailed in the 1920s and eventually became a cornerstone of logical empiricist philosophy of science. After treating the Special Theory in an article in 1915, he applied his insights to the General Theory in a highly reputed monograph, Space and Time in Contemporary Physics. There Schlick's interpretation results from combining his insights concerning the nature of truth with a geometric conventionalism drawn from Jules Henri POINCARÉ.

Schlick recognized that the system of geometry and physics is not just a series of purely symbolic formulas unrelated to experience; the symbols occurring in geometric and physical expressions must be

539

coordinated with elements of reality. Not only must the geometry and physical principles be chosen, they must be interpreted in experience by coordinating their symbols with identifiable empirical situations, or elements thereof. But once the system of geometry, physics, and symbolic coordinations is in place, there are still choices to be made. For, according to Schlick's work on the concept of truth, the goal is to provide a univocal designation of reality and, as the history of physics has taught, there are often distinct systems, each of which provides an unambiguous representation of reality. The choice among equivalent systems of representation can only be founded on considerations of simplicity, for no other consideration can adjudicate between equivalent systems that univocally designate reality.

A similar line of reasoning had led Poincaré to his own geometric conventionalism. Poincaré reasoned that, since the choice of a geometry can only be guided by considerations of simplicity, physicists will always opt for the simplest geometric system. Moreover, since Euclidean geometry is the simplest, physicists will always choose it over any alternative. Departing from Poincaré's conclusion, Schlick insisted that it is not just geometry that is conventionally selected, but the whole system – including physical principles and empirical coordinations as well. Since, as Kant had already noted, it is never space itself, but only the motion of bodies in space that is the object of perception and measurement, it makes no sense to speak of the geometry of space apart from a specific understanding of the physical principles governing motion. There simply is no fact of the matter concerning which geometry best describes space, independently of a specific understanding of the behaviour of bodies. Consequently, the choice of a particular geometry can never be made apart from the construction of a specific theory (see KANT, I. §5).

Schlick's conventionalist interpretation would eventually prevail as the dominant understanding of the new physics; it was immediately acclaimed by Albert EINSTEIN himself, who aided Schlick's efforts to obtain a position at the University of Kiel, which he assumed in 1921 (see CONVENTIONALISM).

2   Epistemology

Schlick then applied his understanding of physical knowledge to other domains, in his *General Theory of Knowledge* of 1918. There Schlick furthered his claim that his conventionalist epistemology distinguished itself not only from the metaphysics of Kant but from the phenomenalism of Ernst MACH as well. Philosophers like Ernst CASSIRER and Hans REICHENBACH

rejected Schlick's conventionalism, claiming instead that if Kant were 're-worked', his philosophy could comprehend Relativity. But Schlick argued that, once Cassirer had 're-worked' the synthetic a priori (see KANT, I. §4) to fit relativity theory, little was left of what was ingenious about Kant's doctrine. Reichenbach's objection was different: although he explicitly subscribed to many of Schlick's own premises, he could not see how concepts could be formed without the Kantian a priori.

It was at this point that Schlick made a contribution that helped wrest twentieth-century philosophy of science from the grip of the past. Schlick had, in *General Theory of Knowledge*, provided an account of concept-formation by means of the doctrine of implicit definition, and Reichenbach himself had relied on it without fully appreciating its significance. Schlick borrowed the idea of implicit definition from the mathematician David Hilbert, in order to demonstrate how scientific concepts are formed according to a conventionalist philosophy. Hilbert utilized the method for application to geometry, arguing that the geometric primitives were defined by the axioms of the system, whether the system was Euclidean or one of the non-Euclidean geometries. But the philosophical significance of the method was not recognized until Schlick promoted it as a method of concept-formation generally applicable throughout the sciences. Schlick's idea was simply that one function of the most fundamental postulates of any science is to give sense to the key terms occurring in it. Thus generalized, the doctrine of implicit definition not only obviates the need for a Kantian a priori to constitute concepts, it reveals a method of concept-formation distinctly at odds with the 'abstraction and generalization' pattern characteristic of empiricist philosophies, like the phenomenalism of Ernst Mach. Thus Schlick's new epistemology blazed an original trail that departed from time-worn paths.

3   The Vienna Circle

By the time the second edition of *General Theory of Knowledge* appeared in 1925, Schlick had already been exposed to new ideas that would deeply affect his thinking. In 1922, he assumed the prestigious chair of *Naturphilosophie* at the University of Vienna, which had been occupied by such luminaries as Ludwig Boltzmann and Ernst Mach. There he became involved with other scientifically-minded thinkers, including mathematicians and social scientists as well as philosophers. This group, the precursor of the Vienna Circle (see VIENNA CIRCLE), was interested in the latest developments in logic and the foundations of mathematics; indeed, one of their earliest projects was to read and discuss Ludwig WITTGENSTEIN's *Tractatus Logico-Philosophicus*. Soon Rudolf CARNAP would join the faculty at Vienna and provide Schlick with yet another source of innovative ideas.

By the late 1920s, Schlick began meeting with Wittgenstein in Vienna, discussing all sorts of philosophical topics, especially ones that arose from scientific contexts. The result was one of the most thoughtful interchanges on issues in geometry, physics, and philosophy of science between two of the major thinkers of the twentieth century. These discussions, as well as Schlick's interaction with his University colleagues, served as a prelude to the period of greatest activity in his philosophical career. Indeed, it was from the heady intellectual atmosphere created by these exchanges that the Vienna Circle would emerge, and Schlick would become its natural leader. More significant, perhaps, is that it was in this period that Schlick first articulated his own variety of logical empiricism. And though many have cited this period as one in which Schlick abandoned the views of his earlier years, there is a natural continuity that ties his entire career together.

These new influences first became apparent in Schlick's attempts to address the challenge to traditional conceptions of causality raised by microphysics. He envisaged a stratification of principles, ranging from statements describing singular statements of fact, through empirical hypotheses, to philosophical principles. Statements at the lowest level, asserting the existence of individual states of affairs, embody all the evidential content of science. Wittgenstein had suggested that hypotheses are introduced to systematize these singular statements, by providing universalized characterizations of a limitless number of cases. Thus the utility of hypotheses lies in their function in the framing of predictions. From the hypothesis 'All Fs are Gs', along with the knowledge that some particular x is an F, we could predict that x will be a G. Hypotheses may thus be conceived as rules for forming expectations, as Wittgenstein suggested. But, as Wittgenstein further noted, to accept an hypothesis is not just to recognize that it yields accurate predictions, it is also a commitment to the existence of the ontology it posits, to the range of entities described by the terms of the hypothesis. Just employing the term 'electron' and its ilk in an hypothesis commits one to a microphysical ontology. Schlick took Wittgenstein's ideas a step further, and argued that, just as hypotheses may be understood as rules for forming predictions, the causality principle is a rule for framing hypotheses. Analogously to the relation of hypotheses to singular statements, certain philosophical principles control our formation of scientific claims. One such principle

is the causality principle. Although the principle of causality is usually taken to express a claim about the nature of the world, it is really a prescription for framing hypotheses. Taken as such, the principle recommends forming hypotheses that yield absolutely precise predictions. And the new developments in quantum physics show that the utility of the causal principle is limited by discoveries in the submicroscopic domain.

4 Empiricism

Schlick's reasoning was guided by a precept that would play a larger and larger role in his thinking, the Principle of Verifiability. Schlick regarded this principle as the core of his empiricism. And though it has been interpreted in nearly as many ways as there were early logical empiricists, Schlick's understanding of the Verifiability Principle was one of the most liberal. Roughly speaking, what this principle required was that every meaningful statement asserts only what can be verified in experience. Schlick hastened to add that this does not mean that only experience is real, for such a claim would itself be meaningless. Nor did Schlick employ the principle to exclude from significant discourse physical statements which assert more than can be verified in a finite number of immediate experiences. Rather, Schlick used the Verifiability Principle only to dismiss as empty typical philosophical theses that assert the reality of one domain of entities to the exclusion of others, such as the thesis of positivism, construed as the assertion that only immediate experience is real and implying that physical objects are mere constructions out of immediate experience that summarize regularities within the given. Since whether this thesis were true or false would make no difference in our experience, the thesis is meaningless. And the same holds for the realist thesis that only physical objects are real. Like positivism, this thesis purports to assert the reality of one domain while denying others, but does not make any claim that can be verified in experience.

Schlick also deployed the Verifiability Principle to revive, in a somewhat altered form, a distinction already present in his earlier thought. In *General Theory of Knowledge*, he had created a deep division between concepts, formally constituted by means of implicit definitions, and intuitions, the experiences to which concepts must be linked to provide us with knowledge of the world. Later, Schlick identified the conceptual structure of our knowledge with its form, and intuitions as its material content, citing the concurrence of Carnap and Wittgenstein. The structure of our knowledge is embodied in the logic of the language in which we express it, but the intuitions to which each of us connects concepts are purely subjective. Thus, although private experience is the ultimate touchstone of the truth of our beliefs about the world, it can never be expressed, although its structure may be. For what, Schlick asked, would it mean to compare the subjective experiences of distinct individuals, other than to relate the ways in which the individuals have structured those contents? Since there is no means of verifying sameness or difference of the contents of distinct individuals, the question of their comparison cannot be answered. The consequence, which Schlick called 'The Thesis of the Incommunicability of Content', is that content, the ineffable material of experience, can never be expressed.

Although other members of the Circle, especially Carnap, had developed versions of the form–content dichotomy, most had abandoned it by the time Schlick was working out his own ideas on the matter. By then the other Circle members were embracing physicalism: the idea that all scientific discourse could be expressed in the language of physics. In particular, they thought that statements expressing the results of observation, so-called 'protocol sentences', could be expressed in the everyday language of material things. Recognizing that such statements are, by their very nature, fallible, they admitted there was no absolutely secure basis for science. Some members of the Circle even flirted with the coherence theory of truth, the idea that truth consists in the consistency of the statements accepted by the community of scientific practitioners (see TRUTH, COHERENCE THEORY OF). Schlick was adamantly opposed to this last development, for it contradicted his long-standing view that truth is a property of statements that correspond to the facts (see TRUTH, CORRESPONDENCE THEORY OF). In his classic essay, 'On the Foundation of Knowledge' (1934), he acknowledged that coherence was necessary for truth, but denied that it was sufficient. His argument involves little more than pointing out that, if coherence sufficed for truth, a well-crafted fairy tale would have to be accorded the same status as the finest textbooks in physics, chemistry, etc. Schlick then proceeded to sketch his own positive account, in which the correspondence doctrine was substantiated by the idea that the body of knowledge rests on a foundation of beliefs which directly correspond to what is observed. The foundation consists of physicalistic protocol sentences which, as Schlick and the other Circle members recognized, are fallible. But these observation statements are, in turn, grounded in fleeting momentary experiences he called 'affirmations'. Affirmations themselves are absolutely certain, though this epistemic property is not transmitted to the fallible, physicalistic protocols to which they give rise. Naturally, Schlick's claim that affirmations were 'certain' provoked immediate opposition within the Circle, mostly from members who did not understand that, on Schlick's view, affirmations were little more than occasions for the assertion of proper observation reports and, as such, lie outside the system of science.

But the criticism and opposition to Schlick's 'Foundation' essay gave him the opportunity to clarify his views on fundamental philosophical issues. He continued to maintain his earlier conventionalism, though expressed in terms of the choices to be made between alternative languages. He especially emphasized the limits of his conventionalism, denying that it allowed the possibility of adopting languages in which observational statements did not play a privileged epistemic role. This latter qualification was founded on his empiricism, expressed in the form of the Verifiability Principle. Thus, in his last essays, Schlick defended a form of empiricism that acknowledged the limited role of conventions, as well as the fallibility of scientific beliefs, while emphasizing the foundationalist view that observation is the final touchstone – indeed, the only touchstone – of the truth of our claims about the world.

On 6 June 1936, Schlick was on the steps of the University of Vienna when he was approached by one Johan Nelböck. Nelböck had received an advanced degree in philosophy from the University and, for some reason, had been threatening Schlick's life for several years. Indeed, Nelböck had menaced Schlick to the extent that the authorities had committed the former to an asylum, where he was diagnosed as a paranoid schizophrenic, and released after observation. Although the simplest explanation of Nelböck's behaviour is that he was deranged, the only evidence of his *dementia* was his threat against Schlick. But on that June day in 1936, he was in earnest, shooting Schlick four times in the abdomen and leg with an automatic pistol. Schlick died within a few hours.

See also: LOGICAL POSTIVISM; MEANING AND VERIFICATION

List of works

Schlick, M. (1979) *Philosophical Papers*, vols I and II, eds B. v. de Velde-Schlick and H. Mulder, Dordrecht: Reidel. (The best current source of Schlick's writings.)
—— (1908) *Leibensweisheit* (Life wisdom), Munich. (Schlick's youthful ethical treatise.)
—— (1910) 'Das Wesen der Wahrheit nach der modernen Logik', *Vierteljahrschrift für wissenschaftliche Philosophie und Soziologie* 34: 386–477; trans.

P. Heath, 'The Nature of Truth in Modern Logic', in *Philosophical Papers*, vol. I, 41–103. (This highly original essay lays the groundwork for Schlick's subsequent conventionalist interpretation of relativity theory.)

—— (1915) 'Die philosophische Bedeutung des Relativitätsprinzips', *Zeitschrifft für Philosophie und philosophische Kritik* 159: 129–75; trans. P. Heath as 'The Philosophical Significance of the Principle of Relativity', *Philosophical Papers*, vol. I, 153–89. (Schlick's treatment of the special theory of relativity.)

—— (1917) 'Raum und Zeit in der gegenwärtigen Physik: Zur Einführung in das Verständnis der allgemeinen Relativitätstheorie', *Die Naturwissenschaften* 5: 161–7, 177–86; enlarged edn *Raum und Zeit in der gegenwärtigen Physik: Zur Einführung in das Verständnis der Relativität- und Gravitätionstheorie*, Berlin: Springer, 1919; 3rd edn trans. H. Brose as *Space and Time in Contemporary Physics*, New York: Oxford University Press, 1920; enlarged, revised 4th edn, Berlin: Springer, 1922, trans. P. Heath as 'Space and Time in Contemporary Physics', *Philosophical Papers*, vol. I, 153–89. (This work set the standard for the understanding of relativity theory that prevailed in the 1920s among such luminaries as Albert Einstein, Arthur Eddington and Hans Reichenbach.)

—— (1918) *Allgemeine Erkenntnislehre*, Berlin: Springer. A revised, second edition appeared in 1925 and was translated into English by A. Blumberg and H. Feigl as *General Theory of Knowledge*, New York and Vienna: Springer, 1974. (This is a classic text – truly a 'must read' for anyone interested in the origins of analytic philosophy.)

—— (1926) 'Erleben, Erkennen, Metaphysik', *Kant Studien* 31: 146–58; trans. P. Heath, 'Experience, Cognition, and Metaphysics', in *Philosophical Papers*, vol. II, 99–111. (Here Schlick introduced his form–content duality, citing – for the first time – the work of Wittgenstein and Carnap.)

—— (1930) 'Die Wende der Philosophie', *Erkenntnis* 1: 4–11; trans. P. Heath, 'The Turning Point in Philosophy', in *Philosophical Papers*, vol. II, 154–60. (This is the 'lead' article in the first issue of the journal which served as the 'house organ' of the early logical empiricists, edited by Rudolf Carnap and Hans Reichenbach.)

—— (1931) 'Die Kausalität in der gegenwärtigen Physik', *Die Naturwissenschaften* 19: 145–62; trans. P. Heath, 'Causality in Contemporary Physics', in *Philosophical Papers*, vol. II, 176–209. (Schlick presents the idea that results in the investigation of the quantum domain present an insuperable limit

to the applicability of the principle of causality. His view was immediately attacked by Albert Einstein in correspondence.)

—— (1932) 'Positivismus und Realismus', *Erkenntnis* 3: 1–31; trans. P. Heath, 'Positivism and Realism', in *Philosophical Papers*, vol. II, 259–84. (This essay evoked a sharp response from Schlick's mentor, Max Planck, who seems to have misunderstood its central thesis that neither of the positions mentioned in the title was significant.)

—— (1934) 'Über das Fundament der Erkenntnis', *Erkenntnis* 4: 79–99; trans. P. Heath, 'On the Foundation of Knowledge', in *Philosophical Papers*, vol. II, 370–87. (This is the sharp response to developments by Carnap and Neurath that provoked the protocol sentence controversy.)

—— (1936) 'Meaning and Verification', *The Philosophical Review* 45: 339–69; reprinted in *Philosophical Papers*, vol. II. (A full development of Schlick's view of language, which departs significantly from Wittgenstein's at that time.)

References and further reading

Friedman, M. (1983) 'Critical Notice: Moritz Schlick, Philosophical Papers', *Philosophy of Science* 50: 498–514. (This very helpful survey of Schlick's thought throughout his entire philosophical career focuses critically on his later work.)

—— (1993) 'Geometry, Convention, and the Relativized *Apriori*: Reichenbach, Schlick and Carnap', in W. Salmon and G. Wolters (eds) *Logic, Language, and the Structure of Scientific Theories*, Pittsburgh: University of Pittsburgh Press, 21–34.

Lewis, J. (1988) 'Schlick's Critique of Positivism', in *PSA* 1988, East Lansing, MI: The Philosophy of Science Association, vol. 1, 110–17. (Like her subsequent work, this essay addresses problematic aspects of Schlick's epistemology in the context of his commitment to scientific realism.)

—— (1990) 'Hidden Agendas: Knowledge and Verification', in *PSA* 1990, East Lansing, MI: The Philosophy of Science Association, vol. 2, 159–68. (Further development of the author's work on Schlick's epistemology in the context of scientific realism.)

—— (1996) 'Conceptual Knowledge and Intuitive Experience: Schlick's Dilemma', in R. Giere and A. Richardson (eds) *The Origins of Logical Empiricism*, Minnesota Studies in the Philosophy of Science, Minneapolis, MN: University of Minnesota Press, 292–308. (Further addresses problematic aspects of Schlick's epistemology in the context of his commitment to scientific realism.)

McGuinness, B. (ed.) (1967) *Wittgenstein und der*

Weiner Kreis, Berlin: Suhrkamp. (A record of the conversations between Wittgenstein, Waismann and Schlick in the late 1920s and early 1930s.)

—— (ed.) (1988) 'Moritz Schlick', special issue of *Synthèse* 64 (3). (A collection of essays exploring Schlick's philosophy from a variety of viewpoints.)

Oberdan, T. (1993) *Protocols, Truth and Convention*, Studien zur Oesterreichischen Philosophie, vol. 19, Amsterdam and Atlanta, GA: Rodopi. (An extended attempt to integrate Schlick's epistemology into the background of his (largely unpublished) views on the philosophy of language.)

—— (1996) 'Postscript to Protocols: Reflections on Empiricism', in R. Giere and A. Richardson (eds) *The Origins of Logical Empiricism*, Minnesota Studies in the Philosophy of Science, Minneapolis, MN: University of Minnesota Press, 269–91. (Condenses many of the arguments of Oberdan (1993) in order to explore the nature of Schlick's commitment to empiricism.)

Uebel, T. (1992) *Overcoming Logical Positivism from Within: The Emergence of Neurath's Naturalism in the Vienna Circle's Protocol Sentence Debate*, Studien zur Oesterreichischen Philosophie, vol. 17, Amsterdam and Atlanta, GA: Rodopi. (A detailed study of the philosophies of the leading protagonists in the protocol sentence controversy, based on primary sources and unpublished materials.)

—— (1996) 'Anti-Foundationalism and the Vienna Circle's Revolution in Philosophy', *British Journal for the Philosophy of Science* 47: 415–40.

THOMAS OBERDAN

SCHMITT, CARL (1888–1985)

Carl Schmitt was a conservative critic of the Weimar Republic's liberal-democratic constitution. After Hitler's rise to power, he allied himself briefly to Nazism, and despite having fallen from favour and having revised his position even before the war, was never able to rehabilitate himself from the Nazi taint. Interned at Nuremberg in 1945, he was never brought to trial, but was banned from teaching thereafter. His critique of liberalism lay in liberalism's alleged inability to deal with the nature of politics. Schmitt continues to exert a vast influence on German public law, legal theory and political philosophy, as well as on European right-wing thought. His work remains important for liberals and opponents of liberalism for the challenges it poses to the neutrality of the liberal state and its legal order.

Schmitt claims that there is no rational way of deciding political conflict since the characteristic of politics is the distinction between irreconcilable friends and enemies in a pluriverse of ideologies. Liberalism attempts to construct a legal order which gets rid of political conflict by subjecting all individuals to the rule of law, the order of positive law of parliamentary democracy. But liberalism finds itself compelled to adopt a stance of neutrality between individual conceptions of the good, which allows groups of individuals to capture the legal order and thus the liberal state. The only way to end this conflict between private interest groups is for a (dictatorial) leader to reconstruct political and legal order on the basis of the vision he articulates of the substantive homogeneity of the people (*Volk*). Liberalism finds itself unable to preclude this event, since its commitment to legalism disables it from dealing with the 'state of exception', the moment when a sovereign decision is required to resolve a fundamental challenge to the *status quo* (see RULE OF LAW (RECHTSTAAT); LAW AND MORALITY §§1–3).

Schmitt's position is perhaps best explained in a work published in 1938, after he had fallen from Nazi favour. There he meditates on the passage from the publication of Hobbes' *Leviathan* (1651) to his own quite precarious situation.

According to Schmitt, Hobbes saw that the political order and stability of the modern state turned on eradicating political conflict within the state and displacing it to a matter of external affairs; he also saw that such order had to be maintained by a system of positive law founded on the myth of the great monster Leviathan. However, that myth cannot survive Hobbes' attempts to provide in addition a rational justification for political and legal order. Whenever Hobbes appeals to or makes room for individual reason, he subverts his own project (see HOBBES, T.). Hence Schmitt can conclude that what is required is a deeply anti-individualist or anti-liberal myth, which has the consequence that he seems to accept that those who do not fit a particular myth's otherwise arbitrary criteria for inclusion should expect no protection from the state.

Liberal thinkers today are deeply divided on such issues as state neutrality, the nature of legal order, and the proper response to the fact of pluralism and hence to potentially fundamental challenges to the legitimacy of liberal democracy. It may prove fruitful for the friends as well as the enemies of liberalism to take Schmitt seriously.

See also: LAW, PHILOSOPHY OF; RADBRUCH, G.

List of works

Schmitt, C. (1922) *Politische Theologie: vier Kapitel zur Lehre von der Souveränität* , trans. and intro. G. Schwab, *Political Theology: Four Chapters on the Concept of Sovereignty*, Cambridge, MA: MIT Press, 1988. (This work claims that all secular political ideologies are disguised theologies.)
—— (1923) *Die geistesgeschichtliche Lage des Heutigen Parlamentarismus*, trans. and intro. E. Kennedy, *The Crisis of Parliamentary Democracy*, Cambridge, MA: MIT Press, 1998. (Here Schmitt explores an alleged contradiction between liberalism and democracy.)
—— (1928) *Verfassungslehre* (Constitutional Theory), Berlin: Duncker & Humblot, 1989; trans. into French L. Deroche, intro. O. Beaud, *Théorie de la Constitution*, Paris: Presses Universitaires de France, 1993. (Schmitt's most elaborate work on legal theory.)
—— (1932) *Der Begriff des Politischen*, trans. and intro. G. Schwab, *The Concept of the Political*, New Brunswick, NJ: Rutgers University Press, 1976. (Here Schmitt claims that the fundamental distinction of politics is that between friend and enemy.)
—— (1938) *Der Leviathan in der Staatslehre des Thomas Hobbes: Sinn und Fehlschlag eines politischen Symbols*, ed. G. Maschke, Cologne: Hohenheim; *The Leviathan in the State Theory of Thomas Hobbes: Meaning and Failure of a Political Symbol*, trans. G. Schwab and Erna Hilfstein, Westport, CT: Greenwood, 1996. (A translation of Schmitt's commentary on Hobbes' *Leviathan*.)

References and further reading

Note that any evaluation of Schmitt is complicated by the writer's understanding of the relationship between that work and his involvement with Nazism.

Bendersky, J. (1983) *Carl Schmitt: Theorist for the Reich*, Princeton, NJ: Princeton University Press. (A political biography of Schmitt.)
Caldwell, P. (1997) *The Theory and Practice of Weimar Constitutionalism*, Durham, NC: Duke University Press. (This book contains an important discussion of Schmitt's theory in the context of Weimar debates about law.)
Dyzenhaus, D. (ed.) (1997) 'Carl Schmitt', *Canadian Journal of Law and Jurisprudence* 10. (Special issue containing essays on Schmitt's political and legal theory.)
—— (1997) *Legality and Legitimacy: Carl Schmitt, Hans Kelsen, and Hermann Heller in Weimar*, Oxford: Clarendon Press. (A critique of Schmitt's legal and political philosophy.)

McCormick, J. (1997) *Against Politics as Technology: Carl Schmitt's Critique of Liberalism*, New York: Cambridge University Press. (A discussion and critique of the main themes of Schmitt's work.)
Scheuerman, W. (1994) *Between the Norm and the Exception: The Frankfurt School and the Rule of Law*, Cambridge, MA: MIT Press. (This book contains an important discussion and critique of Schmitt's legal theory.)
Schwab, G. (1989) *The Challenge of the Exception: An Introduction to the Political Ideas of Carl Schmitt between 1921 and 1936*, New York: Greenwood Press. (First monograph in English on Schmitt's political and legal theory.)

DAVID LUDOVIC DYZENHAUS

SCHOOL OF NAMES *see* LOGIC IN CHINA

SCHOPENHAUER, ARTHUR (1788–1860)

Schopenhauer, one of the great prose-writers among German philosophers, worked outside the mainstream of academic philosophy. He wrote chiefly in the first half of the nineteenth century, publishing Die Welt als Wille und Vorstellung *(The World as Will and Representation), Volume 1 in 1818 and Volume 2 in 1844, but his ideas became widely known only in the half-century from 1850 onwards. The impact of Schopenhauer's philosophy may be seen in the work of many artists of this period, most prominently Wagner, and in some of the themes of psychoanalysis. The philosopher most influenced by him was Nietzsche, who originally accepted but later opposed many of his ideas.*

Schopenhauer considered himself a follower of Kant, and this influence shows in Schopenhauer's defence of idealism and in many of his central concepts. However, he also departs radically from Kant. His dominant idea is that of the will: he claims that the whole world is will, a striving and mostly unconscious force with a multiplicity of manifestations. Schopenhauer advances this as a metaphysical account of the world as it is in itself, but believes it is also supported by empirical evidence. Humans, as part of the world, are fundamentally willing beings, their behaviour shaped by an unchosen will to life which manifests itself in all organisms. His account of the interplay between the will and the intellect has been seen as a prototype for later theories of the unconscious.

Schopenhauer is a pessimist: he believes that our nature as willing beings inevitably leads to suffering, and that a life containing suffering is worse than nonexistence. These doctrines, conveyed in a literary style which is often profound and moving, are among his most influential. Equally important are his views on 'salvation' from the human predicament, which he finds in the denial of the will, or the will's turning against itself. Although his philosophy is atheist, Schopenhauer looks to several of the world religions for examples of asceticism and self-renunciation. His thought was partially influenced by Hinduism at an early stage, and he later found Buddhism sympathetic.

Aesthetic experience assumes great importance in Schopenhauer's work. He suggests that it is a kind of will-less perception in which one suspends one's attachments to objects in the world, attaining release from the torment of willing (desire and suffering), and understanding the nature of things more objectively. The artistic genius is the person abnormally gifted with the capacity for objective, will-free perception, who enables similar experiences in others. Here Schopenhauer adopts the Platonic notion of Ideas, which he conceives as eternally existing aspects of reality: the genius discerns these Ideas, and aesthetic experience in general may bring us to comprehend them. Music is given a special treatment: it directly manifests the nature of the will that underlies the whole world.

In ethics Schopenhauer makes thorough criticisms of Kant's theory. He bases his own ethical views on the notion of compassion or sympathy, which he considers a relatively rare quality, since human beings, as organic, willing beings, are egoistic by nature. Nevertheless, compassion, whose worldview minimizes the distinctness of what are considered separate individuals, is the only true moral impulse for Schopenhauer.

1   Life
2   Early work
3-6   *The World as Will and Representation*

1   Life

Arthur Schopenhauer was born in Danzig in 1788 into a wealthy and enlightened business family. Following a childhood of sound school education and wide travel in Europe he attended the universities of Göttingen and Berlin, gravitating to philosophy after studying a number of subjects. He was most impressed by the writings of Kant and Plato, but also came across the Hindu Upaniṣads. These three he later claimed as his greatest influences. However,

Schopenhauer's early impressions of the German university system were not favourable. He found the lectures of Fichte in particular to be pretentious and vacuous. While his inheritance from his father allowed Schopenhauer financial security, he developed a contempt for professional university philosophy which eventually became focused on HEGEL, its leading figure.

The most creative period of Schopenhauer's life was the decade 1809–18, when he was in his twenties. He gained his doctorate in 1813 with a dissertation entitled *Über die vierfache Wurzel des Satzes vom zureichenden Grunde* (On the Fourfold Root of the Principle of Sufficient Reason), a work which he always regarded as integral to his philosophy and which he revised substantially for republication in 1847. In 1816 he published a short work *Über das Sehn und die Farben* (On Vision and Colours), which had its origin in a collaboration with GOETHE.

The work which outshines all Schopenhauer's others, *Die Welt als Wille und Vorstellung* (The World as Will and Representation), was published in 1818. It aimed to present a complete philosophical system, starting from a modified Kantian idealism and a metaphysics of the will embracing both the self (the microcosm) and the world (the macrocosm), and moving on to present original doctrines concerning aesthetics, ethics and the nature of human existence. Schopenhauer adhered to the philosophy of this work for the remainder of his life, and revised it for publication in 1844 with the addition of a second volume of elucidatory essays that more than doubled its length. There is little genuine intellectual development in Schopenhauer beyond 1818. His later writings give more reflective expression to the same set of doctrines.

Schopenhauer made an abortive attempt to begin a career at the University of Berlin in 1820, but scheduled his lecture at the same hour as Hegel's and had no audience. His hatred for Hegel's philosophy and the university system became intense. His own work, which he considered a great contribution to philosophy, went almost unnoticed. After a period of instability Schopenhauer settled in Frankfurt am Main in 1833, and remained there, leading a largely solitary life, until his death in 1860. His publications during this period were *Über den Willen in der Natur* (On the Will in Nature) (1836), *Die beiden Grundprobleme der Ethik* (The Two Fundamental Problems of Ethics) (1841), the second, two-volume edition of *The World as Will and Representation* (1844), the second edition of *On the Fourfold Root* (1847) and *Parerga und Paralipomena* (Parerga and Paralipomena) (1851). In the final decade of his life he prepared second editions of *On the Will in Nature* and *The Two Fundamental*

Problems of Ethics, and in 1859 a third edition of *The World as Will and Representation*.

All Schopenhauer's publications from the 1830s onwards were designed to defend and amplify the ideas set out in *The World as Will and Representation*. *On the Will in Nature* attempted to support the metaphysical doctrine of the will with empirical evidence taken from the various sciences. *The Two Fundamental Problems of Ethics* is a compilation of the separately written essays *Über die Freiheit des menschlichen Willens* (On the Freedom of the Human Will) (1839) and *Über die Grundlage der Moral* (On the Basis of Morality) (1840). These were composed as entries to essay competitions set in Norway and Denmark. Because of the anonymity of the competitions, Schopenhauer could not rely on a full exposition of his philosophical system. The result is a pair of well-argued, self-contained essays which make an interesting contribution to ethics.

After the publication of *Parerga and Paralipomena*, a wide-ranging collection containing substantial philosophical essays, polemical pieces and popular aphorisms, Schopenhauer's philosophy was more widely recognized, and in old age he began to enjoy something of the popularity which continued for half a century after his death. During this time he became through his writings one of the greatest intellectual figures in European culture, and his influence may be traced in different ways in, among others, Wagner, NIETZSCHE, Tolstoy, Hardy, Freud, Jung, Proust, Thomas Mann and Wittgenstein.

2 Early work

At university Schopenhauer took greatest interest in the writings of KANT and PLATO, and in certain doctrines of Hinduism. Volume 1 of his surviving *Manuscript Remains* (1966–75) shows that from around 1813 he was trying to produce a critical synthesis of these sources. Schopenhauer worked initially with a dichotomy between 'empirical consciousness' and what he called 'better consciousness'. He associated empirical consciousness with appearance, individuality and suffering, and saw the better consciousness as the experience of a higher reality in which the mind could penetrate beyond appearances, lose its sense of individuality, and enter a state free of suffering. The idea had both religious and aesthetic associations. Kant's influence is present in Schopenhauer's use of the appearance/thing-in-itself distinction and his attempt to characterize the empirical world in terms of the a priori forms of space, time and causality imposed by the subject of experience. The Platonic influence shows in the notion of a higher, pain-free cognition of a timeless reality lying beyond

the empirical. From the Hindu writings he adopted the doctrine of the veil of *māyā*, the view that ordinary consciousness is enmeshed in illusion, and the idea that at a fundamental level the distinctness of individuals is illusory (see MONISM, INDIAN). At this stage Schopenhauer was prone to conflate his disparate sources. For example, he assumed that Kant's thing-in-itself and Plato's Ideas were the same – a mistake which he later corrected, but whose effects his theory never entirely lost (see the opening of *The World as Will and Representation*, Third Book).

During the same period Schopenhauer wrote his dissertation, *On the Fourfold Root*, taking as his theme the principle of sufficient reason which states '*nihil est sine ratione cur potius sit quam non sit*' (nothing is without a ground or reason why it is rather than is not). This principle may concern distinct species of 'reason' or 'ground', and hence different species of explanation. Schopenhauer seeks to clarify matters by mapping out four distinct kinds of explanatory principle, which he calls the sufficient reason of becoming, the sufficient reason of knowing, the sufficient reason of being and the sufficient reason of acting. The framework of *On the Fourfold Root* is Kantian. Schopenhauer uses the dichotomy of subject and object, in which objects are the known and the subject is the knower that can never itself be an object of knowledge. What can be known as objects are representations (*Vorstellungen*) which the subject has. The four kinds of explanation in the dissertation concern different classes of representations and the connections between them.

Schopenhauer follows Kant in describing empirical consciousness as consisting of representations organized by the a priori forms of space and time. The empirical content that fills these forms is matter, appearing to the subject as distinct spatiotemporal objects. Schopenhauer's first kind of connection among representations is the 'principle of the sufficient reason of becoming', which asserts that every state that appears must have resulted from a change that preceded it. This version of the principle is thus the 'law of causality'. Schopenhauer's discussion of causality builds on but also criticizes Kant's, and is the longest and most successful section of *On the Fourfold Root*. Space and time also yield the distinct explanatory principle which Schopenhauer calls the 'principle of the sufficient reason of being'. This is supposed to cover reason-giving in mathematics. Schopenhauer here relies on Kant's idea that mathematics involves non-empirical, a priori intuition of spatial position and temporal succession. Space and time themselves are described as objects or representations for the subject, and the connections in space and time cognized a priori are termed relations of 'mathematical necessity'. Concepts are held to be another distinct class of representations. Schopenhauer calls them 'representations of representations', regarding them as derivative from perception by a process of abstraction. Concepts enable the subject to make judgments, and the 'principle of the sufficient reason of knowing' states that if a judgment is to express knowledge, it must be related to a ground – which may lie in perception, in inference from another judgment, or in the possibility of experience or thought as such. Finally, Schopenhauer states the 'principle of the sufficient reason of acting', or law of motivation, which says that every act of will is related to a motive which causes it. The subject's own will is the unique object of experience which this form of the principle concerns. Schopenhauer later extended his account of the will, but in general regarded his early analysis of the forms of the principle of sufficient reason as indispensable for understanding the rest of his thought.

3 *The World as Will and Representation*, First Book

Schopenhauer divides his main work into four books, both in the original Volume 1 and in the parallel, elucidatory Volume 2. Volume 1 also contains a long appendix entitled 'Critique of the Kantian Philosophy'. Schopenhauer regards himself as a follower of Kant, but he has many criticisms to make. For instance, he is scathing in his attack on Kant's architectonic ambitions, his style of writing and his account of the Ideas of soul, world and God – Ideas of the 'unconditioned' supposedly produced by 'pure reason' itself, but which Schopenhauer finds suspiciously amenable to the parochial Christian tradition. This 'Critique of the Kantian Philosophy' is closely linked to Schopenhauer's concerns in the rest of the work.

In the First Book Schopenhauer is primarily concerned with epistemology. He defends transcendental idealism, a doctrine whose outline and terminology he takes from Kant. Transcendental idealism states that the world of empirical things is a world of objects existing for the subject's experience, not existing in itself; and that the reality of the empirical world (our representations) consists in its being organized in space, time and causality, the necessary principles of connection among representations, whose origin is in the subject. Of the Kantian categories Schopenhauer retains only causality. The empirical world consists of causally efficacious matter filling the forms of space and time.

A feature of Schopenhauer's account which would have been anathema to Kant is his appeal to Berkeley's philosophy. Schopenhauer argues that

Kant's transcendental idealism shares with Berkeley the claim that the world of empirical things is mind-dependent, the difference being that Berkeley's contribution is exhausted by this insight, while Kant adds the account of the a priori conditions of experience to explain objectivity. Schopenhauer had researched Kant's *Critique of Pure Reason* thoroughly, making an extensive comparison of the second edition with the first, which had fallen into neglect. He alleges that Kant's commitment to idealism is more clearly apparent in the first edition but that he wavers in the second, in fear of being classified as a Berkeleyan. Schopenhauer uses a number of arguments for idealism which are variants on arguments found in BERKELEY (§3). He suggests that idealism is the only viable alternative to scepticism about the external world, that to imagine a world existing without the subject is impossible, and that realism commits its proponent to a world existing in the subject's representations and to a parallel, redundant mind-independent world. But he chiefly relies on his concepts of 'subject' and 'object'. All experience requires that there be both – 'No subject without object' and 'No object without subject' are, he says, self-evident truths. Schopenhauer appears confident that this is sufficient to show that material objects would not exist without a subject.

Schopenhauer's account of the subject of experience is significant. This subject, he claims, can never be an object of experience. It is not identical with the person (since persons are, at least in part, bodily, and bodies are objects of experience). It is not identical with any part of the spatiotemporal, empirical world – not any individual thing within the world. Rather, he says, 'each of us finds himself as this subject' ([1818, 1844] 1969: 1, 5). Schopenhauer uses a number of images in describing the subject: it is like an eye that cannot see itself, or the focal point at which light rays are concentrated by a concave mirror.

At the same time Schopenhauer is keen to stress that each person, while 'finding' themselves as this pure subject, is a bodily thing within the world of objects. There is a deliberate tension in his account here. Throughout Schopenhauer's philosophy idealism is set in contrast with a blunt form of materialism. Materialism, he says, cannot be the whole truth because it cannot account for the subject's experience: 'materialism is the philosophy of the subject which forgets to take account of itself'. Yet in the same passage he maintains: 'It is just as true that the knower is a product of matter as that matter is a mere representation of the knower' ([1818, 1844] 1969: 2, 13). From an objective standpoint there is ultimately only matter in space and time – and this is true also of oneself considered from an objective standpoint. But from a subjective standpoint, he thinks, we must embrace transcendental idealism and its conception of the pure, non-objective subject.

Schopenhauer makes a sharp distinction between perceptual and conceptual representations. He claims (heretically, as far as Kant is concerned) that causality, one of the basic organizing forms of experience, is not conceptual. Like space and time, it is for Schopenhauer a form of intuition (*Anschauung*). Intuition or perception is the awareness of particular, causally connected, spatiotemporal objects through the senses. Concepts, for Schopenhauer, are quite different from this. Their role is in discursive thought or judgment which may have linguistic expression, and thus in reasoning. (He accuses Kant, perhaps with some justification, of not clearly separating the discursive role of concepts from their alleged role in organizing perception.) Schopenhauer has a clear view about the distinction between humans and other animals: it is simply that humans alone have concepts, language and reason. Animals have understanding (*Verstand*), however, which is the ability to perceive a world of objects, and is different not in kind but only in degree from human understanding. An interesting sub-theme in Schopenhauer is the kinship of humans and animals, rooted in his conviction that the possession merely of reason provides no grounds for regarding a species as superior. Schopenhauer regards reason (*Vernunft*) as a secondary capacity, whose 'abstract, discursive concepts... have their whole content only from the knowledge of perception, and in relation to it' ([1818, 1844] 1969: 1, 35).

4 *The World as Will and Representation*, Second Book

The Second Book moves away from Kant and brings into play Schopenhauer's conception of the will. He argues that all processes in nature are fundamentally a kind of striving or end-seeking (usually unconscious) for which the term 'will' is the most appropriate. The governing aim here is metaphysical – the will provides Schopenhauer with an account of the nature of the world-in-itself, including the underlying nature of the individual human being. At the same time he believes that evidence from animal behaviour, psychology, the natural sciences and ordinary human experience gives confirmation of his view.

The argument begins with the question: How is one aware of one's own body? Schopenhauer's previous account of the subject in the First Book severed the knower from the known: the possessor of empirical knowledge surveyed the totality of objects comprising the spatiotemporal world, but was at no place within

that world. But if I am such a subject, the body I call mine will be for me simply 'an object among objects', and I will not understand its movements except by the kind of observation and inference I apply to all empirical processes. As Schopenhauer says, this is not how things are: I do not generally relate to my body's movements in this way. I understand them 'from inside', and I understand them as my 'will'.

Schopenhauer's view of action is firmly anti-dualist. 'Act of will' is not, for him, the description of any purely mental event:

> The act of the will and the action of the body are not two different states objectively known, connected by the bond of causality; they do not stand in the relation of cause and effect, but are one and the same thing, though given in two entirely different ways, first quite directly, and then in perception for the understanding.
>
> ([1818, 1844] 1969: 1, 100)

This means that the account Schopenhauer gave earlier of the subject and its relation to a world of objects is now seen as inadequate. As subjects of action, we are bodily: when someone acts, the manifestation of will occurs directly in their body.

Schopenhauer goes further and states that 'the whole body is nothing but objectified will'. Here we must be careful. He calls the process of digestion, for example, one in which will manifests itself. But he does not mean that the digestive system develops and functions in conscious or rational pursuit of a goal. The term 'will' applies equally to 'blind' processes, and Schopenhauer wishes to regard the whole body as an expression of will only in the sense that its processes, such as digestion, can be explained by the end they serve for the organism. This part of his philosophy centres around his conception of the will to life (*Wille zum Leben*). Life is not an end which is consciously or rationally chosen by living things – primarily, this is not even the case with living things that are conscious and rational – but their morphology, behaviour and psychology convince Schopenhauer that life is the end for which they are organized. He paints a vivid picture of the whole of animate nature as forever striving, struggling and competing to live and to further life by producing offspring. Conscious, rationally caused willing in humans is merely the highest sophistication of this will to life that permeates nature.

Since human beings are as much organic expressions of the will to life as any other living thing, Schopenhauer thinks we should not overestimate the fact that we are subjects of knowledge, applying the classifications of space, time and causality, understanding the empirical world and making rational judgments. We are organisms whose brains and other physiological processes enable us to perform these functions, but the innermost core of the human being, as of every organism, is the will. Our mental processes are almost always at a deeper level subservient to the 'blind' will to life. Schopenhauer sees a complex interplay between this will and the conscious intellect. His idea that the intellect is often forced to follow the 'secret purposes' of an underlying will which it cannot control has been seen as a precursor of Freud's view of the unconscious. FREUD also acknowledged that Schopenhauer had prefigured him in his treatment of sexuality. Schopenhauer links sexuality with the drive to reproduce, one principal way in which the will to life manifests itself throughout nature. He is not surprised, therefore, to find that sex is constantly, if 'secretly', present in human behaviour: 'It is the ultimate goal of almost all human effort; it has an unfavourable influence on the most important affairs, interrupts every hour the most serious occupations' ([1818, 1844] 1969: 2, 533).

The doctrine of the will is, however, supposed to extend well beyond animate nature. All natural processes, including those such as magnetism and gravity, are to be seen as manifestations of will: as if, with or without consciousness, with or without life, every bit of the world must be striving for some end or other. It is essential to Schopenhauer's thought that there is no supreme end, no grand design, purpose or meaning. There is no answer to the question why the will wills as it does. Nevertheless Schopenhauer discerns a kind of internal order within the world as will. There are a determinate number of natural kinds: nature is not haphazard but falls into distinct species and repeatable law-like processes. Schopenhauer says that in addition to the individual things and events of the empirical world, there are eternal Ideas, those forms, such as 'lion' or 'oak tree', which may be shared in by many individual lions or oak trees. He calls these Ideas 'grades of the will's objectification'.

Schopenhauer's 'world as will' is an exercise in metaphysics, an attempt to say how the world is in itself. Thus it becomes clear that his idealism has a different purpose from Kant's: he wants to separate the empirical world, existing only in the subject's representations, from the world as it is in itself, in order to give a positive account of the latter. Schopenhauer's 'key' to the will as thing-in-itself is provided by action. The 'inner' awareness I have of my own will manifesting itself in the body supposedly points me towards what exists beyond the realm of representations altogether. My 'inner' awareness shows me that what I *am* in myself is will. Rather than maintain a kind of theoretical egoism (or solipsism) in which I alone have this essence – a view

which he regards as irrefutable but mad – Schopenhauer advocates extending the same insight to the world as a whole.

Schopenhauer uses the expression 'the will', implying that the whole world of objects is the expression (or 'objectification') of one thing-in-itself. There cannot be a plurality of things-in-themselves: space and time are the principle of individuation (*principium individuationis*), but space and time do not apply to the thing-in-itself. Also the relation between the 'in itself' and the empirical cannot be causal, because causality has legitimate application only within the realm of representations. Schopenhauer says instead that the thing-in-itself (the will) 'objectifies itself' as a multiplicity of empirical things. This means simply that the world's experienceable aspect (the world as representation) consists of many spatiotemporal things, whilst considered as it is in itself (the world as will) it is not composed of distinct individuals (see MONISM).

This metaphysical system is beset by problems. Even if it makes sense to say that the same world is, under one aspect, divisible into many empirical things, and under another aspect one single thing, there remain at least two further difficulties. First, it is unclear how Schopenhauer is entitled to any knowledge at all of the thing-in-itself. And second, there is some mystery as to why the thing-in-itself is best called 'will'. Schopenhauer says that our own willing is the nearest we ever come to knowing the 'in itself' of anything, so 'will' is the best term available to describe *the* thing-in-itself. Yet clearly neither the world-in-itself nor the majority of its phenomenal manifestations exhibit will in the way a human agent does. 'Will' threatens to become just a proper name for the world – but that in turn robs Schopenhauer's theory of any power to understand or interpret the world. He sets out to 'solve the riddle' of the thing-in-itself. It remains unclear how that is to be achieved.

5   *The World as Will and Representation*, **Third Book**

Schopenhauer associates the will with misery. The will to life drives us on through an ever-ramifying set of desires and goals, but we reach no ultimate point or final satisfaction. To have desires unsatisfied is to suffer, to have needs is to be vulnerable to deprivation, and – the final irony – to be without needs usually brings only a state of empty boredom waiting to be filled by a further cycle of desires.

Yet there is alleviation of this condition, in the form of aesthetic experience, which is the topic of Schopenhauer's Third Book. The unifying thought in Schopenhauer's aesthetic theory is that one may have perceptual experience while the will is suspended.

Such an occurrence is comparatively rare because the intellect is by nature a tool of the will and not prone to contemplating reality with the objectivity and freedom from desires that aesthetic experience demands. In aesthetic experience one is sunk in contemplation of some object and ceases to impose upon it the usual spatial, temporal and causal connections: 'we no longer consider the where, the when, the why and the whither of things, but simply and solely the *what*' ([1818, 1844] 1969: 1, 178).

Aesthetic experience, whether of nature or of art, has value for Schopenhauer because it is a temporary state of calm will-lessness, from which desire and suffering alike are excluded. But he also sees in aesthetic contemplation a cognitive change and an alteration in one's sense of self. The subject in aesthetic experience becomes unaware of its separateness from that which it experiences: 'the person who is involved in this perception is no longer an individual, for in such perception the individual has lost himself; he is *pure* will-less, painless, timeless *subject of knowledge*' ([1818, 1844] 1969: 1, 179). At the same time, the object of the experience is not merely the individual spatiotemporal thing, but one of the eternal Ideas fixed in nature. Schopenhauer's thinking here is as follows: individual empirical things are experienced when and only when the subject applies to its representations the a priori forms of space, time, and causality. But ordinary empirical knowledge is driven by the will: it consists in brain processes whose occurrence subserves the ends of the organism. Thus, if the intellect breaks away from its service to the will, it must leave behind the forms of space, time and causality. And since we experience individual spatio-temporal things only because we impose these forms, a timeless and spaceless experience must have as its object something beyond individual spatiotemporal things. This doctrine is the descendant of Schopenhauer's earlier thinking about the 'better consciousness'. He believes that, by freeing one's intellect temporarily from the will, one gains a higher form of knowledge, and becomes a pure subject, objectively mirroring reality, and leaving behind one's identification with any individual part of the empirical world.

Although he recognizes that nature provides many opportunities for this kind of elevated contemplation, Schopenhauer's main interest is in art, where the spectator's experience is mediated by the activity of the artist. For Schopenhauer the true artist is a genius, by which he means someone whose intellect – the capacity for perception, not concept-use or reasoning – is abnormally powerful and able to function in greater isolation from the will. The genius can discern the universal in the particular with greater objectivity, as it were on behalf of the rest of us, and convey this

insight in perceptible form. Schopenhauer says emphatically that conceptual thinking, by contrast, is unfruitful in the arts.

Schopenhauer's writing is informed by a wide knowledge and appreciation of the various arts. He discusses architecture, painting of different genres, sculpture, poetry and drama. Each art form has Ideas (or 'grades of the will's objectification') which it is especially able to reveal. This enables Schopenhauer to place the arts in a hierarchy. At the lower end, architecture, for example, enables us to know the fundamental Ideas of gravity, cohesion and rigidity. Landscape painting displays Ideas of inanimate nature and the plant world. Other paintings reveal the Ideas of different species of animals, and finally of human beings – but the highest art form, whose speciality is the Idea of humanity in all its complexity, is poetry.

At the very pinnacle stands tragedy, which has a special significance for Schopenhauer, since the eternal Idea of humanity which it makes known contains the most profound picture of the misery of our condition. Yet tragedy's value for Schopenhauer does not lie solely in this knowledge of what he calls 'the conflict of the will with itself'. He contends that the best tragedies present the hero's will turning away from life and adopting a sublime resignation in the face of suffering – thus exemplifying the attitude which he later argues is the only genuine 'salvation' (see TRAGEDY §5).

Schopenhauer's account of music is especially noteworthy. He suggests that while the other arts all attempt to stimulate knowledge of Ideas by depicting individual things, music 'is as *immediate* an objectification and copy of the whole *will* as the world itself is' ([1818, 1844] 1969: 1, 257). The will expresses itself as the phenomenal world; the same will expresses itself again in music, which bypasses the level of Ideas altogether. Thus Schopenhauer maintains that the appeal of music lies in its copying the patterns of striving and resolution of the will, to which we respond because they resonate with our lives as willing beings. But no personal strivings or sufferings enter into music:

Music does not express this or that particular and definite pleasure, this or that affliction, pain, sorrow, horror, gaiety, merriment, or peace of mind, but joy, pain, sorrow, horror, gaiety, merriment, peace of mind *themselves*, to a certain extent in their abstract nature.

([1818, 1844] 1969: 1, 261)

Hence the value of music to the listener may also be that of a will-less calm (see MUSIC, AESTHETICS OF §6).

6 *The World as Will and Representation*, Fourth Book

The Fourth Book of *The World as Will and Representation* concerns ethics, taken broadly to include questions about the value of human existence, and what kind of happiness or salvation we may hope for. Schopenhauer gives his views here on the nature of morality and the question of free will and responsibility. These views are equally well stated (or perhaps better stated) in *On the Freedom of the Will* and *On the Basis of Morality*. It is only in *The World as Will and Representation*, however, that his conclusions about the human condition and his advocacy of denial of the will are presented with their full power.

Schopenhauer gives an elegant case for determinism, making a distinction between freedom to act, which one has when there are no impediments to one's doing what one wills, and freedom to will. The latter raises the important question: given that one willed to do such and such, could one have willed a different course of action? Schopenhauer suggests that acts of will are caused by a combination of one's permanent unchanging character and motives, which are representations of states of affairs in the world. No act of will could have failed to occur if the same motives and the same character had been present. In this sense there is no free will. Yet the feeling that we are responsible for our actions remains. Schopenhauer tries to account for this by saying that we feel responsible for what we are – for our unchanging, intelligible character, a character which is supposedly what we are beyond the realm of the empirical (see FREE WILL).

This view has a Kantian ancestry. But in his moral theory Schopenhauer is generally critical of Kant. He is unimpressed by the notion of a categorical imperative, seeing it as a relic of the idea that commands are issued by the absolute authority of a divine being. He also questions Kant's linking of morality to rationality; other animals for Schopenhauer should be accorded moral status, and the fact that they lack rationality is irrelevant (see KANT, I.). His own account of morality is simple. The one genuine moral impulse is compassion (or sympathy, *Mitleid*), which he says is present in each human being in some degree. Individuals governed by compassion apprehend the world and their place in it in a superior way, and they and their actions are good.

Each individual's character – which for Schopenhauer is inborn and unchanging – has some combination of the ingredients of egoism, compassion and malice. Malice is the impulse to seek another's harm, egoism the impulse towards one's own well-being and the avoidance of harm to oneself. Egoism is the greater part of most natures, according to Schopenhauer, since as manifestations of the will to life we must strive continually to survive and further ourselves. Pure malice is as much an exception as pure compassion, but both impulses must be accepted as facts of human nature. Compassion is the impulse to seek another's well-being and to prevent their suffering, and is grounded in a vision of the world which sets less store than usual on divisions between individuals: the good man, says Schopenhauer, sees everywhere 'I once more'. The metaphysical foundation for this is the claim that individuation is not an ultimate truth in the universe, since whatever appears as distinct at the empirical level is, at the level of the 'in itself', one and the same will. If individuality is thus illusory, compassion is more profoundly justified than egoism.

The core of Schopenhauer's pessimistic assessment of the value of human life lies once again in the opposition between the individual and the world as a whole. One's existence as a bodily, striving individual emerges not only as illusory (when viewed from the highest metaphysical vantage point), but as pernicious. To be an individual in which will manifests itself is inevitably to be open to suffering. But neither the striving of which the individual's life is full, nor the suffering which accompanies it, nor the temporary achievement of satisfaction which so soon induces boredom, has any higher point or value. Schopenhauer concludes that existence as an individual human being is always a worse alternative than nonexistence. 'In fact,' he proclaims, 'nothing else can be stated as the aim of our existence except the knowledge that it would be better for us not to exist' ([1818, 1844] 1969: 2, 605). He also argues that we inhabit the worst of all possible worlds.

Death is not something to fear, in Schopenhauer's view, since the world-will which expresses itself in this one fleeting individual continues undisturbed; death is 'the great opportunity no longer to be I ... the moment of that liberation from the one-sidedness of an individuality that does not constitute the innermost kernel of our true being' ([1818, 1844] 1969: 1, 507–8). Despite this, Schopenhauer does not approve of suicide, which he regards as a failure to accept life on proper terms. The suicide affirms life, but revolts against the particular sufferings life contains. The contrasting attitude which Schopenhauer advocates is denial of the will to life, an attitude which accepts the state of being alive but acquiesces in the suffering and the non-fulfilment of desires which it brings.

The question arises whether denial of the will to life is, paradoxically, something one can bring about at will. Schopenhauer appears to think not, since he talks of 'those in whom the will has turned and denied itself' and says denial of willing 'is not to be forcibly arrived at by intention or design . . . it comes suddenly, as if flying in from without' ([1818, 1844] 1969: 1, 404). It is as though the will to life is a distinct agency from the individual in whom it dwells. There are two routes to this turning of the will. One is the life of what Schopenhauer calls a saint. Such a person has knowledge of the illusoriness of individuation, and their individual will is 'quieted' thereby. The attitude of saints is one of such overwhelming compassion that they do not seek to further their own ends in distinction from those of others, nor to avoid harm to themselves. The other path leading to the turning of the will is to undergo suffering so great that one's will to life gives out spontaneously, while yet one is still alive. Those in whom the will has turned attain a state which Schopenhauer describes as 'resignation, true composure, and complete will-lessness'. He asks us to consider the blissful state of aesthetic contemplation, and then to imagine it prolonged: such, he claims, is the state of will-less self-denial that is the only genuine 'salvation' for humanity. Since our existence as bodily, striving individuals is one we would have been better without, the only remedy lies in achieving a vision of the world which attaches the lowest possible importance to one's individuality.

See also: ART, VALUE OF; SEXUALITY, PHILOSOPHY OF

List of works

Schopenhauer, A. (1946–50) *Schopenhauers sämtliche Werke*, ed. A. Hübscher, 7 vols, Wiesbaden: Brockhaus. (The definitive edition of Schopenhauer's published works.)

—— (1977) *Arthur Schopenhauer: Zürcher Ausgabe*, ed. A. Hübscher, 10 vols, Zurich: Diogenes. (An accessible paperback version of the above.)

—— (1813, 1847) *Über die vierfache Wurzel des Satzes vom zureichenden Grunde*, trans. E.F.J. Payne, *On The Fourfold Root of the Principle of Sufficient Reason*, La Salle, IL: Open Court, 1974; trans. F.J. White as *Schopenhauer's Early Fourfold Root*, Aldershot: Avebury, 1997. (Schopenhauer's doctoral dissertation, which he later substantially revised, and regarded as integral to his philosophical system. The White translation also provides a commentary on the shorter 1813 version.)

—— (1816) *Über das Sehn und die Farben*; trans. E.F.J. Payne, *On Vision and Colors*, Oxford and Providence, RI, Berg, 1994. (A short work instigated by Goethe's theory of colours, but diverging from it. Not regarded as important to Schopenhauer's philosophy.)

—— (1818, 1844) *Die Welt als Wille und Vorstellung*, trans. E.F.J. Payne, *The World as Will and Representation*, New York: Dover, 2 vols, 1969; ed. D. Berman, trans. J. Berman as *The World as Will and Idea: abridged in one volume*, London: Everyman, 1995. (The main work of Schopenhauer's life, from whose central doctrines he never deviated. The only work containing his whole system of thought. The abridged version is greatly condensed and loses the grand sweep of the original, but makes the remaining argument more accessible to the general reader.)

—— (1836) *Über den Willen in der Natur*, trans. E.F.J. Payne, *On the Will in Nature*, New York and Oxford: Berg, 1992. (Schopenhauer's attempt to corroborate the doctrine of will stated in his main work by finding confirmations in science.)

—— (1841) *Über die Freiheit des menschlichen Willens*, trans. K. Kolenda, *On the Freedom of the Will*, Oxford: Blackwell, 1985. (A clear, self-contained essay on the problem of free will.)

—— (1841) *Über die Grundlage der Moral*, trans. E.F.J. Payne, *On the Basis of Morality*, Providence, RI and Oxford: Berhahn Books, 1995. (Schopenhauer's account of morality as based on compassion, preceded by a critique of Kant's ethics.)

—— (1851) *Parerga und Paralipomena*, trans. E.F.J. Payne, *Parerga and Paralipomena*, Oxford: Clarendon Press, 1974, 2 vols. (A late work containing a mixture of philosophical essays expanding on themes dealt with in earlier works, and various aphorisms and ruminations.)

—— (1966–75) *Schopenhauer: Der handschriftliche Nachlaß*, ed. A. Hübscher, Frankfurt am Main: Waldemar Kramer, 5 vols; trans. E.F.J. Payne, *Manuscript Remains*, Oxford, New York and Hamburg: Berg, 1988–90, vols 1–4. (Schopenhauer's unpublished notes, ranging throughout his career.)

References and further reading

Atwell, J.E. (1990) *Schopenhauer: The Human Character*, Philadelphia, PA: Temple University Press. (Concentrates on action, the will and ethical theory.)

Fox, M. (ed.) (1980) *Schopenhauer: His Philosophical Achievement*, Brighton: Harvester. (A collection of articles written from various points of view.)

Gardiner, P. (1967) *Schopenhauer*, Harmondsworth: Penguin; repr. Bristol: Thoemmes Press, 1997. (A comprehensive account of Schopenhauer's philosophy.)

Hamlyn, D.W. (1980) *Schopenhauer*, London: Routle-

553

dge & Kegan Paul. (A treatment of all major aspects of Schopenhauer's philosophy.)

Higgins, K.M. (1993) 'Arthur Schopenhauer', in R.C. Solomon and K.M. Higgins (eds) *Routledge History of German Philosophy, vol. 6: The Age of German Idealism*, 330–62. (A short introductory essay.)

Jacquette, D. (ed.) (1996) *Schopenhauer, Philosophy and the Arts*, Cambridge: Cambridge University Press. (Essays by various authors on Schopenhauer's aesthetics and its influence.)

Janaway, C. (1989) *Self and World in Schopenhauer's Philosophy*, Oxford: Clarendon Press. (Discusses the self, idealism, subjective and objective standpoints and Kant.)

—— (1994) *Schopenhauer*, Oxford: Oxford University Press. (Written at an introductory level for non-specialists.)

Luft, E. von der (ed.) (1988) *Schopenhauer: New Essays in Honor of his 200th Birthday*, Lewiston, NY: Edwin Mellen. (A varied collection of articles with a thorough bibliography covering works by and on Schopenhauer.)

Simmel, G. (1907) *Schopenhauer and Nietzsche*,trans. H. Loiskandl, D. Weinstein and M. Weinstein, Amherst, MA: University of Massachusetts Press, 1986. (A classic comparative study of the two philosophers.)

White, F.C. (1992) *On Schopenhauer's Fourfold Root of the Principle of Sufficient Reason*, Leiden: E.J. Brill. (A commentary on *On the Fourfold Root*.)

Young, J. (1987) *Willing and Unwilling: A Study in the Philosophy of Arthur Schopenhauer*, Dordrecht: Martinus Nijhoff. (A treatment of all major aspects of Schopenhauer's philosophy.)

CHRISTOPHER JANAWAY

SCHRÖDINGER'S CAT

see QUANTUM MEASUREMENT PROBLEM

SCHUMPETER, JOSEPH ALOIS (1883–1950)

*Schumpeter is best known for his seminal work in economics, but he also made important contributions to the fields of political science and sociology. He aimed to create a broad economic science that he called 'social economics' (*Sozialökonomik*), which was to include not only economic theory but also economic history, statistics and economic sociology. Inspiration for this project came in particular from his colleague Max Weber.*

As an economist Schumpeter is primarily remembered for his theory of the entrepreneur and for his emphasis on the dynamic aspects of economic reality: capitalism, as he saw it, meant first and foremost change. But Schumpeter also made a number of interesting observations about theorizing in economics and the role that vision plays in the work of the economist. His trenchant critique of the conventional theory of democracy and advocacy of a more realistic theory is generally recognized as a major contribution to political theory. Many of Schumpeter's most important ideas on economics and politics can be found in his book Capitalism, Socialism and Democracy *(1942), which has become something of a classic in the social sciences.*

1 **Life**
2 **Early works**
3 ***Capitalism, Socialism and Democracy***
4 **Schumpeter's last work**

1 Life

Joseph Alois Schumpeter was born in the small town of Triesch, part of the Austro-Hungarian Empire. His family was Catholic and belonged to the local elite. At the age of ten Schumpeter moved with his mother and stepfather to Vienna, where he was educated at an exclusive imperial school. As a student at the University of Vienna, he soon focused on economics and received his doctorate in 1906 at a record early age. After a sojourn in England and Egypt (where he worked as a lawyer), in 1908 Schumpeter returned to his native country to pursue an academic career as an economist. Initially very successful, he soon earned a full professorship at the University of Graz – again at a record early age. During the years before the First World War Schumpeter produced three books, which established him as one of the country's most promising young economists. One of these books – *Theorie der wirtschaftlichen Entwicklung* (The Theory of Economic Development) (1911) – is considered to be his most successful work in economic theory.

After the First World War Schumpeter tried his luck first in politics – he was finance minister for a few months in 1919 – and then as a banker and investor. Both of these enterprises ended badly, and by the mid-1920s Schumpeter was happy to return to academia. In 1932 he emigrated for personal reasons to the USA, where he was to teach at Harvard University until his death. While in the USA, Schumpeter produced three major works: the enormous two-volume set *Business Cycles* (1939), the popular *Capitalism, Socialism and Democracy* (1942) and the extensive *History of Economic Analysis*, published posthumously in 1954.

2   Early works

As a young man Schumpeter produced three books: a short history of economics, a study of economics using a conventional static approach and a study of economics using an innovative dynamic approach. The most important and original of these is the third work, which appeared in 1911 and which was translated as *The Theory of Economic Development* in 1934. It is in this work that Schumpeter for the first time presented his famous theory of the entrepreneur. In a dynamic approach to the economy, he argued, one has to assume that there exists a force *within* the economy itself that can account for change and development. This force is embodied in the entrepreneur; and entrepreneurship is defined as 'the carrying out of new combinations' (Schumpeter [1911] 1934: 66). An entrepreneur does not invent, Schumpeter says, but innovates. The original innovation produces huge profits and is soon imitated by others, thereby leading to a wave of economic change that affects the whole economy.

According to Schumpeter, there exist five basic types of entrepreneurship: (1) the introduction of a new good; (2) the introduction of a new method of production; (3) the opening up of a new market; (4) the conquest of a new source of raw materials or half-manufactured goods; and (5) a new way of organizing an industry (Schumpeter [1911] 1934: 66). Schumpeter also emphasized that the entrepreneur is not primarily motivated by the prospect of gain – the textbook image of *homo economicus*. What makes the entrepreneur act is something else: 'the dream and the will to found a private kingdom', 'the will to conquer' and 'the joy of creating' ([1911] 1934: 93).

Finally, it should be noted that the first edition of *The Theory of Economic Development* included a last chapter in which Schumpeter suggested that the basic principles of dynamic economics could also be applied to all other social sciences. Schumpeter even supplied an outline of what such an analysis would look like. The fear of being misunderstood made Schumpeter eliminate this evocative chapter in later editions of his work however.

3   *Capitalism, Socialism and Democracy*

After not having published a book for more than twenty years, Schumpeter's *Business Cycles* finally appeared in 1939. Its reception was a disappointment

to Schumpeter however, and while planning his next work in economics he undertook an interim project: the book that was to become *Capitalism, Socialism and Democracy* (1942). This work contains a provocative analysis of MARX (§12), a novel approach to the theory of democracy and the famous prophecy that capitalism will soon be replaced by socialism: 'Can capitalism survive? No. I do not think it can.' 'Can socialism work? Of course it can' (Schumpeter [1942] 1994: 61, 167).

According to Schumpeter, there existed a number of reasons why capitalism was doomed, including the fact that the entrepreneur was everywhere being replaced by managers, the intellectuals were getting out of hand and the old sense of property was vanishing. Schumpeter was very unhappy about these developments since he personally detested socialism. He did not want his own personal feelings to interfere with his scientific judgement, however, and agreed that it was, in principle, possible to have a democratic form of socialism (see SOCIALISM §§1, 4).

While Schumpeter's approach to Marx and his thesis of the demise of capitalism are still occasionally referred to, it is however his theory of democracy that has survived best. What Schumpeter called 'the classic doctrine of democracy' had, in his mind, a simplistic and naïve approach to politics. He characterized its basic tenets in the following way: 'the democratic method is that institutional arrangement for arriving at political decisions which realizes the common good by making the people itself decide issues through the election of individuals who are to assemble in order to carry out its will' (Schumpeter [1942] 1994: 250). According to Schumpeter, this approach to democracy implied a series of errors. For one thing, there is no such thing as a 'common good' that all people can agree on. Second, if such a common good none the less existed, it would provide no guidance whatsoever in individual cases. And third, the important role that politicians play in the political process tends to disappear if they are seen simply as those persons who carry out the will of the people. A much more realistic attitude to democracy, Schumpeter continued, would be to conceptualize it as a way of selecting those people who are to govern the masses. Schumpeter's 'alternative theory of democracy' is defined in the following way: 'the democratic method is that institutional arrangement for arriving at political decisions in which individuals acquire the power to decide by means of a competitive struggle for the people's vote' (Schumpeter [1942] 1994: 269) (see DEMOCRACY §1).

Some commentators have felt that Schumpeter's own theory of democracy is cynical and elitist since it views democracy as an active enterprise only for those who govern. This view has some truth to it and Schumpeter's book contains many contemptuous remarks about the political capacity of the average person. Other commentators, however, have felt that Schumpeter's approach to democracy is refreshingly realistic and non-ideological. Finally, it should be mentioned that Schumpeter's conception of the politician as a kind of political entrepreneur (a view that has its origins in the work of Max WEBER) has inspired the public choice school (see RATIONAL CHOICE THEORY §7).

4 Schumpeter's last work

When Schumpeter died in January 1950 he had almost completed the extensive history of economics which he had begun work on in the early 1940s. In *History of Economic Analysis*, published posthumously in 1954, Schumpeter tried to summarize his experience of a life as an economist, and his book covers a vast array of topics. It is here, for example, that we find Schumpeter's discussion of what he called an economist's 'vision'. Behind all the great works in economics, Schumpeter said, there is always a specific vision of how the economy works and what its building blocks are. Schumpeter defines vision in the following way: 'a preanalytic act that supplies the raw material for the analytic effort' ([1954] 1994: 41).

It is also in *History of Economic Analysis* that we find Schumpeter's most extensive presentation of his own vision of economics. Inspired very early in his career by Max Weber, Schumpeter envisioned economics as a very broad kind of science, which would encompass not only economic theory but also economic history, economic sociology and statistics. Schumpeter emphasized that 'the all-round economist' must in principle be knowledgable in all of these fields. His statement that if he were to relive his life and could choose only one field, he would chose economic history, shocked his colleagues. A careful reading of Schumpeter's last work shows, however, that its author held economic theory in very high regard. Indeed, *History of Economic Analysis* contains a number of interesting observations about the role that theory plays in economics. Theory, for example, must be closely linked to empirical reality if it is to be useful. Schumpeter also emphasized that creative theorizing has little to do with the testing of hypotheses (this comes at a later stage of the scientific process), but is rather a way of initially conceptualizing economic reality and thereby adding to the economist's 'box of tools'. Thus, despite his many contributions to a variety of fields in the social sciences, Schumpeter's primary interest as an economist was, and always remained, economic theory.

See also: ECONOMICS, PHILOSOPHY OF

List of works

Schumpeter, J.A. (1911) *Theorie der wirtschaftlichen Entwicklung*, Leipzig: Duncker & Humblot; trans. of 2nd edn from 1926 by R. Opie, *The Theory of Economic Development*, Cambridge, MA: Harvard University Press, 1934. (Schumpeter's most famous work in economics, containing his well-known theory of entrepreneurship. Opie's translation is the standard text, although considerably shorter.)
—— (1939) *Business Cycles*, New York and London: McGraw-Hill, 2 vols. (Schumpeter's giant work on business cycles is simultaneously a history of capitalism from 1787 to 1930s.)
—— (1942) *Capitalism, Socialism and Democracy*, London: Routledge, 1994. (Probably Schumpeter's best-known work, with brilliant passages on contemporary capitalism as well as on the problems democracy.)
—— (1954). *History of Economic Analysis*, London: Routledge, 1994. (An enormous history of economic thought which is very useful. Published posthumously.)

References and further reading

Allen, R.L. (1991) *Opening Doors: The Life and Work of Joseph Schumpeter*, New Brunswick, NJ: Transaction Publishers. (An important but somewhat unwieldy biography.)
Harris, S.E. (ed.) (1951) *Schumpeter, Social Scientist*, Cambridge, MA: Harvard University Press. (An excellent anthology of articles by some of Schumpeter's colleagues and pupils.)
Swedberg, R. (1991) *Joseph A. Schumpeter: His Life and Work*, Cambridge: Polity Press. (An intellectual biography of Schumpeter which emphasizes his vision of economics as a very broad kind of science.)

RICHARD SWEDBERG

SCHURMAN, ANNA MARIA VAN (1607–78)

The first woman to attend a Dutch university, Schurman studied ancient languages and theology. Her Latin treatise on the expedience of scholarship for women made this 'Star of Utrecht' the most famous female intellectual in seventeenth-century Europe. She was among the few women to publish views on Counter-Reformation controversies concerning predestination and transubstantiation. Her autobiography served as an apology for the Pietist sect, Labadism.

1   **Philosophical and theological influences**
2   *The Learned Maid...*
3   *De Vitae Termino*

1   Philosophical and theological influences

Anna Maria van Schurman studied theology, Hebrew, Arabic, Chaldanean, Aramaic and Syrian under the mentorship of Gisbertus Voetius, Calvinist theologian of the University of Utrecht. Her first publication, *Amica dissertatio...* (1638), was a scholastic defence of women's fitness for scholarship, which included a correspondence with the Calvinist theologian André Rivet; part of it was translated as *The Learned Maid...* (1659). Her correspondence on the issue of predestination with the physician Johan van Beverwijck was published as *De vitae humanae termino* (1639). This treatise, the *Dissertatio* and selected letters were published in her collected works, *Opuscula...* (1648). Throughout the 1640s, Schurman communicated both with noted philosophers, such as GASSENDI, ELISABETH OF BOHEMIA, Marie le Jars de Gournay and, via Constantijn Huygens, MERSENNE, and with such theologians as Jacob Lydius, Frederick Spanheim, Gisbertus Voetius and Daniel Heinsius. In response to Claude de Saumaise's treatise on transubstantiation, she wrote an epistolary essay commenting on the views of the Church Fathers. Though she had contact with DESCARTES and Queen Christina of Sweden, she came to reject both for religious reasons. During the 1650s, her Pietist leanings led her to abandon all scholarship except the study of Revelation, opting to pursue a life of faith in service to others (see PIETISM). After joining Jean de Labadie's Pietist community in Amsterdam in 1669, she obtained a haven for her persecuted 'household', first via Abbess Elisabeth of Bohemia at Herford in Germany, later at Altona and Wieuwerd. Her autobiography and defence of Labadism appeared in 1673 as *EYKΛHRIA: seu Melioris partis electio....* In response to charges by Huygens, Drechssler and others against Labadism, she published *Korte Onderrichtinge...* and wrote *EYKΛHRIA II*, which, like her biblical criticism, was published posthumously.

2   *The Learned Maid...*

Schurman's scholastic treatise begins by defining and conservatively limiting terms: 'Maid' refers to a Christian woman of 'indifferent good wit', enough wealth to pay a teacher, sufficient free time to devote to study and the following goals for her scholarship: God's glory, personal salvation, virtue, happiness, the instruction of the family, and aid to other women. 'Scholar' refers to one 'given to the study of... all kinds of Learning' and Schurman is among the first to urge that no restrictions be placed on learning for women. By 'may be' she means 'expedient, fit, decent' – a normative notion weaker than 'ought'. She advances fifteen syllogistic arguments, with refutations of adversaries' arguments, to show that: (1) women have the appropriate nature, intellectual powers and desire for all the arts and sciences; (2) study will provide them with 'a similitude of Divine gladness', or pleasure; (3) it is fitting for women to study sciences instrumental to theology, since these lead to greater love of God; (4) scholarship is especially appropriate for those with leisure time to spend at home; and (5) learning will aid women in acquiring virtue and escaping vice and heresy.

The arguments for (1) rely upon the Aristotelian view that the Form of a human being is the rational soul and 'that which is in the whole Species or kind, is in every Individual... in Maids also' (1659: 8). Schurman's assumption that there is no deformation of the rational soul in woman rests, in part, on the argument that since some maids actually learn arts and sciences (together with the Aristotelian assumption that there are no acts without corresponding powers or principles), they must be naturally endowed with the powers or principles for the arts and sciences. The arguments for (2) turn on Aristotle's views about pleasure in the *Nicomachean Ethics*. The arguments for (4) and (5) constitute one of the earliest philosophical responses by a woman to the *querelle des femmes* tradition in moralistic writings of the period (see FEMINISM §2). These writings, derived from the Church Fathers, assume women's inconstancy, vanity, imprudence and small-mindedness; humanist writers such as Erasmus saw these vices as augmented by women's increased leisure time. Because Schurman turns diverse moralist assumptions to her own advantage in the course of her arguments, there are occasional tensions between syllogisms. For example, Argument IV assumes that 'leisure... is... the Mother of wickedness' to conclude that women must have no free time, rather 'continual employment'. Argument V, however, positively depicts the leisurely life of maids as one with the 'Tranquillity and Liberty' conducive to study. But these tensions are inherent in the conflicting positions of the moralists themselves. Schurman's purpose is to show that all roads lead to women's fitness for learning. Indeed, Schurman's very production of this treatise stands as an argument for her conclusion. This work, together with Marie le Jars de Gournay's *Egalité des hommes et des femmes*

(1622), spawned numerous defences of women's intellectual and moral capacities, many by women.

3   De Vitae Termino

This epistolary treatise ('Concerning the Limit of Life') responds to Beverwijck's questions concerning predestination: (1) How can we reconcile God's decree concerning the 'limit of human life' as an event 'fixed and immovable', when, as part of the contingent events of this world, this limit appears 'changeable'? and (2) Of what use are doctors or medicines 'if they have no power at all to delay the death which fate threatens?' ([1648] 1650: 8). In answer to (1), Schurman argues that while a limit for each mortal creature's life has been 'unalterably established' by a decree of God, nevertheless, because this limit is produced 'freely and contingently' by the power of the subordinate causes, 'it can most lawfully be called changeable and movable' ([1648]1650: 6). The decree of God, then, which necessarily determines all future events, also determines the manner in which events are to take place by secondary causes, either contingently or necessarily. So, from the standpoint of a creature, and in relation to secondary causes that could have been different, the limit of life may be called 'contingent'. Like Calvin and Descartes, Schurman none the less admits that no one can understand how 'divine providence bends the wills of men so sweetly and strongly that they freely and willingly choose and pursue that which God has decreed' ([1648] 1650: 23). In reply to (2), Schurman argues that while 'the art of medicine falls short of its own end, and the limit of the dying man is ever the same', still we should take physicians to be 'the instruments or rather "partners" of the very Author of life and health' ([1648]1650: 26). For, the duty of a physician is not to 'cheat the hidden plans of God, but to break the hold of disease, to soothe pains, to restore natural strength, especially when they see that death is surely imminent' ([1648]1650: 25). Versions of Schurman's responses can be found in earlier Reformed authors such as Calvin, Voetius, Rivet and Johannes Wollebius, and in later ones such as Francis Turretin. The treatise's uniqueness lies in the erudition displayed in support of her Calvinist position – ancient Stoic, Sceptic, Ciceronian, Platonic, Aristotelian, Judaic, early Christian, Muslim, Thomist and Italian Renaissance sources – coupled with its authorship by a woman, given its discussion of such controversial points of Calvinist doctrine (see PREDESTINATION).

List of works

Schurman, A.M. van (1638) *Amica dissertatio inter*

noblissimam virginem Annam Mariam a Schurman et Andream Rivetum de ingenii muliebris ad scientias et meliores literas capacitate (A friendly discourse between the renowned Miss Anna Maria van Schurman and André Rivet concerning the suitability of woman's mode of thinking for the arts and sciences), Paris; repr. as *Dissertatio logica...* (A logical discourse...), Leiden, 1641; French trans. as *Question célèbre...* (The celebrated question...), Paris, 1646; English trans. C. B[arksdale] as *The Learned Maid...*, London, 1659. (One of the most important early modern defences of woman's nature and fitness for scholarship; the fifteen syllogisms, with refutations of adversaries' arguments, reproduced in the English translation, are joined with Schurman's correspondence with Rivet on this topic in the Latin and French versions.)

—— (1639) *De vitae humanae termino* (Concerning the limit of human life), Leiden; repr. as *De vitae termino in Opuscula*; Dutch trans. as *Paelsteen van den Tijt onzes Levens*, Dordrecht, 1639. (In response to the physician Beverwijck, this epistolary treatise defends the Calvinist position on predestination, drawing support from ancient pagan, Christian, Judaic, Islamic and Italian Renaissance sources.)

—— (1648) *Nobiliss. Virginis Annae Mariae à Schurman. Opuscula, hebraea, graeca, latina, gallica, Prosaica et metrica* (The works of the renowned Miss Anna Maria van Schurman: Prose and verse in Hebrew, Greek, Latin and French), Leiden, 1650; repr. London, 1649; repr. Utrecht, 1652; new edn, D. Loeber, Leipzig, 1794. (Schurman's collected works, including her *Dissertatio* and *De vitae termino*, a substantial correspondence with noted philosophers, theologians and other intellectuals, some of her poems, and elegies dedicated to her.)

—— (1673) *EYKΛHRIA: seu melioris partis electio brevem religionis ac vitae ejus delineationem exhibens* (Eukleria: or the choice of the better part, as presenting a brief sketch of her religion and life), Altona; repr. Dessau, 1782; Dutch trans. as *Eucleria of Uitkiezing van het Beste Deel*, Amsterdam, 1684, repr. Leeuwarden, 1978; English trans L. Richards as *Choosing the Better Part: Anna maria van Schurman (1607–1678)*, ed. M. de Baar, Dordrecht and London: Kluwer, 1996. (In the tradition of Augustine's *Confessiones*, this work combines Schurman's autobiography and defence of her faith.)

—— (1675) *Korte Onderrichtinge Rakende de Staat en de manier van leven der Personen die god t'samen vergadert en tot sijnen dienst vereenigt heeft door de bedieninge sijnes getrouwen dienstknechts Johannes de Labadie en sijner Broeders en Mede-Arbeiders Petrus Yvon en Petrus Dulignon* (Short instruction concerning the state and the way of life of those persons whom god gathers and has united in his service through the actions of his faithful servant Jean de Labadie and his brothers and fellow-workers Pierre Yvon and Pierre Dulignon), Amsterdam. (In the year following Labadie's death, Schurman published this defence of the Labadist community, which had finally settled in Wieuwerd, Friesland, after being expelled from Herford and Altona in Germany.)

—— (1684) *EYKΛHRIA II*, Amsterdam; Latin edn, Amsterdam,1685. (This posthumously published work, completed in the last days of Schurman's life, resumes the Labadist defence begun in the original *EYKΛHRIA*, responding, in part, to Drechssler's criticisms of that earlier work.)

—— (1699) *Mysterium magnum oder Grosses Geheimnis* (Mysterium magnum or the great mystery), Wesel. (The posthumous publication of Schurman's speculations about the future kingdom of God.)

—— (1732) *Uitbreiding over de drie eerste Capittels van Genesis* (Elaboration on the first three chapters of Genesis), Groningen. (The posthumous publication of an example of Schurman's most cherished intellectual pursuit: Biblical criticism.)

References and further reading

Birch (Pope-Henessy), U. (1909) *Anna van Schurman: Artist, Scholar, Saint*, London: Longmans, Green & Company. (The most comprehensive discussion in English. As Moore notes, 'Schotel, Birch and Douma still provide the foundation of Schurman scholarship'.)

Douma, A.M.H. (1924) *Anna Maria van Schurman en de Studie der Vrouw* (Anna Maria van Schurman and the study of woman), Amsterdam: H.J. Paris. (Treats Schurman on women's education; reviews secondary literature up to 1915.)

* Drechssler, J.G. (1673) *Eukleria Eukeatos seu Melioris Partis Electio rescissa* (Eukleria Eukeatos or the choice of the better part torn apart), Leipzig. (This Lutheran educator accused *EYKΛHRIA* of claiming that internal illumination provides revelation independently of the Scriptures and that the pursuit of the sciences is morally useless.)

* Gournay, M. le J. de (1622) *Egalité des hommes et des femmes* (The equality of men and women), n.p.; English trans. E. O'Neill in J. Sterba (ed.) *Social and Political Philosophy in perspective: Classical Western Texts in a Feminist and Multicultural Perspective*, Belmont, CA: Wadsworth, 1994. (Like Schurman's *Dissertatio*, this is one of the most important early modern philosophical works on the issue of woman's moral and intellectual capacities.)

* Huygens, C. (1670a) *Heusche Vermaaning, aan de doorlugtige en wel-edele juffr. Anna Maria van Schurman, om haar selven te kennen, en af te wijcken van Jean de Labadie* (Serious admonition to the serene and noble Miss Anna Maria van Schurman, to know herself, and to break with Jean de Labadie), Amsterdam. (An anti-Labadist tract by a previous supporter of Schurman.)

—— (1670b) *Sedige en sielveroerende aenspracke aen Juffr. Anna Maria van Schurman, om haer af te trecken van Jan de Labadie* (Modest and soul-stirring appeal to Miss Anna Maria van Schurman, to pull her away from Jean de Labadie), Amsterdam. (Another important anti-Labadist tract by this Dutch poet, musician and correspondent of Descartes.)

Irwin, J.L. (1977) 'Anna Maria Van Schurman: From Feminism to Pietism', *Church History* 46: 48–62. (An examination of Schurman's changing religious views and their relation to their position on what role scholarship should play in a pious life.)

—— (1989) 'Anna Maria van Schurman: Learned Woman of Utrecht', in K. Wilson and F. Warnke (eds) *Women writers of the Seventeenth Century*, Athens, GA: University of Georgia Press. (A survey of Schurman's life and works; excerpts from *The Learned Maid*, translated letters and and translated selection from *EYKΛHRIA* are appended.)

Moore, C.N. (1994) 'Anna Maria van Schurman', in K. Aercke (ed.) *Women Writing in Dutch*, New York and London: Garland. (A survey of Schurman's life and works, a slightly corrupt text of *The Learned Maid*, a translation of a letter to Dorothea Moor and translated selections from *EYKΛHRIA* are appended.)

Schotel, G.D.J. (1853) *Anna Maria van Schurman*, 's-Hertogenbosch: Gebroeders Muller. (Among the first book-length treatments of Schurman, it remains a central secondary source.)

EILEEN O'NEILL

SCHÜTZ, ALFRED (1899–1959)

Alfred Schütz, Austrian-American philosopher and social scientist. Combining ideas from Weber, Bergson and Husserl, Schütz developed a methodology for social science that integrated subjectivist, phenomenological elements with the causal-explanatory aspects of traditional objectivist approaches.

Schütz was born in Vienna, where he studied law, economics and sociology, and subsequently worked as a lawyer for a banking firm while pursuing his scholarly interests in his spare time. He emigrated to the USA in 1939, and was appointed professor at the New School for Social Research in New York in 1956.

Schütz's work stands in the German *geisteswissenschaften* tradition of Wilhelm DILTHEY and Max WEBER (§3), which insists that social science must methodologically reflect the specific nature of its human subject matter. Human and social reality – in particular, human action – is distinctive, in that it springs from the free flow of human subjectivity; hence, a method of interpretation (*verstehen*) of this subjective basis of action is required. Following Weber, Schütz endeavoured to combine *verstehen* with an objectivistic, causal approach. He held, however, that Weber's methodology lacked an adequate philosophical analysis of human subjectivity, a gap which Schütz sought to fill, first with elements from Bergson's doctrine of the flow of consciousness, later with tenets from Husserl's transcendental phenomenology. In turning to Husserl, Schütz broadened the investigation of the subjective springs of action into a phenomenological analysis of the acts of consciousness through which social reality is constituted. Schütz, however, did not conduct a full investigation of this domain within phenomenological brackets in his main work, *Der sinnhafte Aufbau der sozialen Welt* (The Phenomenology of the Social World) (1932), but rather examined the way social reality is grasped by subjects in the everyday, 'mundane' attitude. Indeed, Schütz eventually came to doubt the power of transcendental phenomenology fully to resolve the problems of *verstehen*; instead, in his US period, he strengthened the empirical side of his work by incorporating ideas from Mead and James, among others.

Schütz's phenomenological investigation brought to light certain characteristic structural properties of social reality as grasped by the agent (the agent's social *lebenswelt*). Social reality is organized around the experiencing subject in spheres of increasing concreteness and vividness the closer they are to the subject. Closeness here refers both to an item's spatial proximity to the subject and its relevance with respect to the subject's projects; Schütz stressed the pragmatic nature of our conceptualization of social reality, a nature manifest also in the way that this conceptualization is taken for granted and never exposed to theoretical doubts. The innermost circle of social reality is inhabited by persons with whom the subject is in direct face-to-face contact. This permits a full and detailed grasp of the other's unique individuality, a privileged mode of social cognition of which other

modes are derivatives. Outside this zone lies the world of our contemporaries, people who exist simultaneously with ourselves but beyond our sensory horizon; then the world of our predecessors; and finally the world of our successors, the people who shall live after we are dead. Denizens of these spheres cannot be grasped in their full individuality, but must be understood in terms of general typifying concepts of increasing anonymity the further away they are from their source in the subject's experienced here-and-now. Schütz's analysis of the social *lebenswelt* shows his debt to Bergson in the stark contrast drawn between immediate intuitive experience and abstract conceptual understanding, and is tinged with a distinctly existentialist pathos when the unique significance of the face-to-face encounter is described.

The phenomenological account of the agent's subjective life-world is an indispensable part of social inquiry in its own right and, in addition, provides tools for the construction of an objective and genuinely theoretical stratum of social science. The social scientist must push further the process of typification that is present in inchoate form in the everyday agents' understanding of their life-world, analysing the social world in terms of idealized types that are derived from the agents' own abstract classifying concepts. In expounding a methodology of ideal types, Schütz borrowed heavily from Weber. Weberian ideal types are derived from experience by the one-sided accentuation of certain selected features, which are extrapolated to full logical perfection. Ideal types permit the formulation of law-like generalizations about human action, a paradigm case of which was, for Schütz as well as for Weber, the principles of rational action as found in particular in economics. Schütz also embraced Weber's methodological individualism and his insistence that science be 'value-free'.

The suggested approach is meant to solve what Schütz viewed as the crucial methodological problem for social science, namely how to construct an objective science of the agents' subjective meaning structures. The subjectivist desideratum is satisfied because the concepts used in the proposed science retain a link to the agents' naïve, unreconstructed notions. This link is formally guaranteed in terms of a general principle of methodology, which requires that the ideal concepts be understandable to the agents themselves in terms of everyday interpretations of action. On the other hand, the scientific concepts are refined and idealized, and hence satisfy the usual scientific standards with respect to clarity, consistency and precision.

Schütz conceived of his social theory as a 'sociology of everyday knowledge', but it differs from sociology of knowledge in the Marxist tradition in its lack of critical intent. It simply describes the structure of everyday social knowledge and the way it is utilized in the agents' understanding of their social life-world. Schütz's dual methodology thus offers no directions for the social scientist in the event of a clash between its objective and subjective components, such as a failure of an ideal type to be instantiated in the conduct of the agents, despite their endorsement of the same. This might occur if the agents were the victims of an ideological misconstrual of their own motivations. Indeed, the notion of 'ideology' and related concepts are signally absent from Schütz's methodology. Thus, the compatibility of the subjectivist and objectivist aspects of Schütz's methodology of social science is tacitly assumed, rather than effectively achieved.

See also: EXPLANATION IN HISTORY AND SOCIAL SCIENCE; PHENOMENOLOGICAL MOVEMENT §3

List of works

Schütz, A. (1932) *Der sinnhafte Aufbau der sozialen Welt*, Vienna: Julius Springer; Eng. trans. *The Phenomenology of the Social World*, Evanston, IL: Northwestern University Press, 1967. (Schütz's earliest and most penetrating work, in which he endeavours to ground Weber's interpretive sociological method on Husserlian phenomenology; rather dense.)

—— (1962–66) *Collected Papers*, 3 vols; vol. 1, *The Problem of Social Reality*, 1962; vol. 2, *Studies in Social Theory*, 1964; vol. 3, *Studies in Phenomenological Philosophy*, 1966, The Hague: Martinus Nijhoff. (These volumes chiefly contain material from Schütz's US period. Volume 1 shows the development of Schütz's philosophy of social reality under the influence of US philosophers and social scientists. Volume 2 contains Schütz's essays within empirical social thought. Volume 3 contains Schütz's reflections, at times very critical, on the chief figures of phenomenology.)

—— (1970) *Reflections on the Problem of Relevance*, R.M. Zaner (ed.), New Haven, CT: Yale University Press. (An edited version of a highly fragmentary manuscript found in Schütz's literary remains. Partially overlaps the *Collected Papers* and the 1973 book, but contains some new material on the phenomenology of social action.)

Schütz, A. and Luckmann, T. (1973) *The Structures of the Life-World*, Evanston, IL: Northwestern University Press. (Thomas Luckmann's edition of a manuscript left unfinished at the time of Schütz's death. Offers a more empirical and more accessible,

but often less concise, version of some of the topics covered in the 1932 book.)

References and further reading

Collin, F. (1985) *Theory and Understanding: A Critique of Interpretive Social Science*, Oxford: Blackwell. (Contains a critique of Schütz's methodology.)

List, E. and Srubar, I. (eds) (1988) *Alfred Schütz: Neue Beiträge zur Rezeption seines Werkes* (Alfred Schütz: New Contributions Regarding the Influence of His Work), Amsterdam: Editions Rodopi. (A collection of essays in German and English on the impact of Schütz's work.)

Natanson, M. (ed.) (1963) *Philosophy of the Social Sciences*, New York: Random House. (A selection of texts contrasting interpretive and positivist approaches to social reality.)

Thomason, B. (1982) *Making Sense of Reification*, Atlantic Highlands, NJ: Humanities Press. (Discusses the idealist and realist aspects of Schütz's methodology.)

Wagner, H.R. (1983) *Alfred Schütz: An Intellectual Biography*, Chicago, IL: University of Chicago Press. (Combines biography with a comprehensive treatment of the intellectual influences upon Schütz. Includes a good bibliography.)

FINN COLLIN

SCIENCE AND GENDER
see GENDER AND SCIENCE

SCIENCE AND RELIGION
see RELIGION AND SCIENCE

SCIENCE IN ISLAMIC PHILOSOPHY

Islam attempts to synthesize reason and revelation, knowledge and values, in its approach to the study of nature. Knowledge acquired through rational human efforts and through the Qur'an are seen as complementary: both are 'signs of God' that enable humanity to study and understand nature. Between the second and eighth centuries AH (eighth and fifteenth centuries AD), when Muslim civilization was at its zenith, metaphysics, epistemology and empirical studies of nature fused to produce an explosion of 'scientific spirit'. Scientists and scholars such as Ibn al-Haytham, al-Razi, Ibn Tufayl, Ibn Sina and al-Biruni superimposed Plato's and Aristotle's ideas of reason and objectivity on their own Muslim faith, thus producing a unique synthesis of religion and philosophy. They also placed great emphasis on scientific methodology, giving importance to systematic observation, experimentation and theory building.

Initially, scientific inquiry was directed by everyday practices of Islam. For example, developments in astronomy were influenced by the fact that the times of Muslim prayer were defined astronomically and its direction was defined geographically. In the later stage, the quest for truth for its own sake became the norm, leading to numerous new discoveries and innovations. Muslim scientists did not recognize disciplinary boundaries between the 'two cultures' of science and humanities, and individual scholars tended as a general rule to be polymaths. Recently, Muslim scholars have started to develop a contemporary Islamic philosophy of science by combining such basic Islamic concepts as 'ilm *(knowledge),* khilafa *(trusteeship of nature) and* istisla *(public interest) in an integrated science policy framework.*

1   **Science and metaphysics**
2   **Methodology**
3   **Revival attempts**

1   Science and metaphysics

The Muslim inspiration for the study of nature comes straight from the Qur'an. The Qur'an specifically and repeatedly asks Muslims to investigate systematically natural phenomena, not simply as a vehicle for understanding nature but also as a means for getting close to God. In Surah 10, for example, we read:

> He it is who has made the sun a [source of] radiant light and the moon a light [reflected], and has determined for it phases so that you might know how to compute years and to measure [time]... in the alternative of night and day, and in all that God has created in the heavens and on earth, there are messages indeed for people who are conscious of Him.
>
> (Surah 10: 5–6)

The Qur'an also devotes about one-third of its verses to describing the virtues of reason. Scientific inquiry, based on reason, is thus seen in Islam as a form of worship. Reason and revelation are complementary and integrated methods for the pursuit of truth.

The philosophy of science in classical Islam is a product of the fusion of this metaphysics with Greek philosophy. Nowhere is this more apparent than in Ibn Sina's theory of human knowledge (see IBN SINA §3) which, following AL-FARABI (§3), transfers the Qur'anic scheme of revelation to Greek philosophy. In the Qur'an, the Creator addresses one man – the Prophet – through the agency of the archangel Gabriel; in Ibn Sina's Neoplatonic scheme, the divine word is transmitted through reason and understanding to any, and every, person who cares to listen. The result is an amalgam of rationalism and ethics. For Muslim scholars and scientists, values are objective and good and evil are descriptive characteristics of reality which are no less 'there' in things than are their other qualities, such as shape and size. In this framework, all knowledge, including the knowledge of God, can be acquired by reason alone. Humanity has power to know as well as to act and is thus responsible for its just and unjust actions. What this philosophy entailed both in terms of the study of nature and shaping human behaviour was illustrated by IBN TUFAYL in his intellectual novel, *Hayy ibn Yaqzan*. Hayy is a spontaneously generated human who is isolated on an island. Through his power of observations and the use of his intellect, Hayy discovers general and particular facts about the structure of the material and spiritual universe, deduces the existence of God and arrives at a theological and political system (see EPISTEMOLOGY IN ISLAMIC PHILOSOPHY; ETHICS IN ISLAMIC PHILOSOPHY).

While Mu'tazilite scholars had serious philosophic differences with their main opponents, the Ash'arite theologians, both schools agreed on the rational study of nature. In his *al-Tamhid*, Abu Bakr al-Baquillani defines science as 'the knowledge of the object, as it really is'. While reacting to the Mu'tazilite infringement on the domains of faith, the Ash'arites conceded the need for objective and systematic study of nature. Indeed, some of the greatest scientists in Islam, such as Ibn al-Haytham (d. 1039), who discovered the basic laws of optics, and al-Biruni (d. 1048), who measured the circumference of the earth and discussed the rotation of the earth on its axis, were supporters of Ash'arite theology (see ASH'ARIYYA AND MU'TAZILA).

The overall concern of Muslim scientists was the delineation of truth. As Ibn al-Haytham declared, 'truth is sought for its own sake', and al-Biruni confirmed in the introduction to his *al-Qanun al-mas'udi*: 'I do not shun the truth from whatever source it comes.' However, there were disputes about the best way to rational truth. For Ibn Sina, general and universal questions came first and led to experimental work. He begins his *al-Qanun fi'l-tibb* (Canons of Medicine), which was a standard text in the West up to the eighteenth century, with a general discussion on the theory of drugs. For al-Biruni, however, universals came out of practical, experimental work; theories are formulated after discoveries. But either way, criticism was the key to progress towards truth. As Ibn al-Haytham wrote, 'it is natural to everyone to regard scientists favourably.... God, however, has not preserved the scientist from error and has not safeguarded science from shortcomings and faults' (see Sabra 1972). This is why scientists so often disagree amongst themselves. Those concerned with science and truth, Ibn al-Haytham continued, 'should turn themselves into hostile critics' and should criticize 'from every point of view and in all aspects'. In particular, the flaws in the work of one's predecessors should be ruthlessly exposed. The ideas of Ibn al-Haytham, al-Biruni and Ibn Sina, along with numerous other Muslim scientists, laid the foundations of the 'scientific spirit' as we have come to know it.

2   Methodology

The 'scientific method' (see SCIENTIFIC METHOD), as it is understood today, was first developed by the Muslim scientists. Supporters of both Mu'tazilism and Ash'arism placed a great deal of emphasis on systematic observation and experimentation. The insistence on accurate observation is amply demonstrated in the *zij*, the literature of astronomical handbooks and tables. These were constantly updated, with scientists checking and correcting the work of previous scholars. In medicine, Abu Bakr Muhammad al-Razi's detailed and highly accurate clinical observations in the early third century AH (ninth century AD) provide us with a universal model. AL-RAZI was the first to observe accurately the symptoms of smallpox and described many 'new' syndromes. However, it was not just accurate observation that was important; equally significant was the clarity and precision by which the observations are described, as was demonstrated by Ibn Sina in his writings.

The emphasis on model construction and theory building can be seen in the category of Islamic astronomical literature known as *'ilm al-haya*, or 'science of the structure (of the universe)', which consists of general exposition of principles underlying astronomical theory. It was on the strength of both accurate observation and model construction that Islamic astronomy launched a rigorous attack on what was perceived to be a set of imperfections in Ptolemaic astronomy (see PTOLEMY). Ibn al-Haytham was the first to declare categorically that the arrangements proposed for planetary motions in the

Almagest were 'false'. Ibn Shatir (d. 1375) and the astronomers at the famous observatory in Maragha, Adharbayjan, built in the thirteenth century by Nasir al-Din AL-TUSI, developed the Tusi couple and a theorem for the transformation of eccentric models into epicyclic ones. It was this mathematical model that COPERNICUS used to develop his notion of heliocentricity, which played an important part in the European 'scientific revolution'.

Apart from the exact sciences, the most appropriate and interesting area in which theoretical work played an essential role was medicine. Muslim physicians attempted to improve the quality of *materia medica* and their therapeutic uses through continued theoretical development. Emphasis was also placed on developing a precise terminology and ensuring the purity of drugs, a concern that led to a number of early chemical and physical procedures. Since Muslim writers were excellent organizers of knowledge, their purely pharmacological texts were themselves a source for the development of theories. Evolution of theories and discovery of new drugs linked the growth of Islamic medicine to chemistry, botany, zoology, geology and law, and led to extensive elaborations of Greek classifications. Pharmacological knowledge thus became more diversified, and produced new types of pharmacological literature. As this literature considered its subject from a number of different disciplinary perspectives and a great variety of new directions, there developed new ways of looking at pharmacology; new areas were opened up for further exploration and more detailed investigation. Paper-making made publication more extensive and cheaper than use of parchment and papyrus, and this in turn made scientific knowledge much more accessible to students.

While Muslim scientists placed considerable faith in scientific method, they were also aware of its limitations. Even a strong believer in mathematical realism such as al-Biruni argued that the method of inquiry was a function of the nature of investigation: different methods, all equally valid, were required to answer different types of questions. Al-Biruni himself had recourse to a number of methods. In his treatise on mineralogy, *Kitab al-jamahir* (Book of Precious Stones), he is the most exact of experimental scientists. However, in the introduction to his ground-breaking study *India* he declares that 'to execute our project, it has not been possible to follow the geometric method'; he therefore resorts to comparative sociology.

The work of a scholar of the calibre and prolificity of al-Biruni inevitably defies simple classification. He wrote on mineralogy, geography, medicine, astrology and a whole range of topics which dealt with the dating of Islamic festivals. Al-Biruni is a specific product of a philosophy of science that integrates metaphysics with physics, does not attribute to either a superior or inferior position, and insists that both are worthy of study and equally valid. Moreover, the methods of studying the vast creation of God – from the movement of the stars and planets to the nature of diseases, the sting of an ant, the character of madness, the beauty of justice, the spiritual yearning of humanity, the ecstasy of a mystic – are all equally valid and shape understanding in their respective areas of inquiry. In both its philosophy and methodology, Islam has sought a complete synthesis of science and religion.

Polymaths such as al-Biruni, al-Jahiz, AL-KINDI, Abu Bakr Muhammad AL-RAZI, IBN SINA, al-Idrisi, IBN BAJJA, Omar Khayyam, Ibn Zuhr, IBN TUFAYL, IBN RUSHD, al-Suyuti and thousands of other scholars are not an exception but the general rule in Muslim civilization. The Islamic civilization of the classical period was remarkable for the number of polymaths it produced. This is seen as a testimony to the homogeneity of Islamic philosophy of science and its emphasis on synthesis, interdisciplinary investigations and multiplicity of methods.

3 Revival attempts

At the end of the twentieth century, scholars, scientists and philosophers throughout the Muslim world are trying to formulate a contemporary version of the Islamic philosophy of science. Two dominant movements have emerged. The first draws its inspiration from Sufi mysticism (see MYSTICAL PHILOSOPHY IN ISLAM) and argues that the notions of 'tradition' and the 'sacred' should constitute the core of Islamic approach to science. The second argues that issues of science and values in Islam must be treated within a framework of concepts that shape the goals of a Muslim society. Ten fundamental Islamic concepts are identified as constituting the framework within which scientific inquiry should be carried out, four standing alone and three opposing pairs: *tawhid* (unity), *khilafa* (trusteeship), *'ibada* (worship), *'ilm* (knowledge), *halal* (praiseworthy) and *haram* (blameworthy), *'adl* (justice) and *zulm* (tyranny), and *istisla* (public interest) and *dhiya* (waste). It is argued that, when translated into values, this system of Islamic concepts embraces the nature of scientific inquiry in its totality; it integrates facts and values and institutionalizes a system of knowing that is based on accountability and social responsibility. It is too early to say whether either of these movements will bear any real fruit.

See also: ARISTOTELIANISM IN ISLAMIC PHILOSOPHY; AL-FARABI; GREEK PHILOSOPHY: IMPACT ON ISLAMIC PHILOSOPHY; IBN SINA; ISLAMIC PHILOSOPHY: TRANSMISSION INTO WESTERN EUROPE; NEOPLATONISM IN ISLAMIC PHILOSOPHY; RELIGION AND SCIENCE; SCIENTIFIC METHOD

References and further reading

Bakar, O. (1996) 'Science', in S.H. Nasr and O. Leaman, *History of Islamic Philosophy*, London: Routledge, ch. 53, 926–46. (Discussion of some of the main thinkers and principles of science in Islam.)

* Dani, A.H. (1973) *Al-Biruni's India*, Islamabad: University of Islamabad Press. (Al-Biruni's research on the people and country of India.)

Fakhry, M. (1983) *A History of Islamic Philosophy*, London: Longman, 2nd edn. (A general introduction to the role of reason in Islamic thought.)

Hill, D. (1993) *Islamic Science and Engineering*, Edinburgh: Edinburgh University Press. (The classic work on the practical aspects of Islamic science.)

Hourani, G. (1975) *Essays on Islamic Philosophy and Science*, Albany, NY: State University of New York Press. (An important collection of articles on particular theoretical issues in the philosophy of science.)

—— (1985) *Reason and Tradition in Islamic Ethics*, Cambridge: Cambridge University Press. (A discussion of the clash between reason and tradition in Islamic culture as a whole, especially in ethics.)

* Ibn Tufayl (before 1185) *Hayy ibn Yaqzan* (The Living Son of the Vigilant), trans. S. Oakley, *The Improvement of Human Reason Exhibited in the Life of Hai Ebn Yokhdan*, Zurich: Georg Olms Verlag, 1983. (This translation of *Hayy ibn Yaqzan* was first published in 1708.)

Kirmani, Z. (1992) 'An Outline of Islamic Framework for a Contemporary Science', *Journal of Islamic Science* 8 (2): 55–76. (An attempt at conceptualizing modern science from an Islamic point of view.)

Leaman, O. (1985) *An Introduction to Medieval Islamic Philosophy*, Cambridge: Cambridge University Press. (A general approach to the role of philosophy in Islam.)

Nasr, S.H. (1993) *The Need for a Sacred Science*, Richmond: Curzon Press. (An argument for the significance of religion in any understanding of science.)

Pines, S. (1964) 'Ibn al-Haytham's Critique of Ptolemy', in *Actes du Xe Congrès internationale d'histoire des sciences*, Paris: Ithaca. (One of the most important works in Islamic astronomy.)

* Sabra, A.I. (1972) 'Ibn al-Haytham', in C.C. Gillispie

(ed.) *Dictionary of Scientific Biography*, New York: Charles Scribner's Sons, 6th edn. (An excellent introduction to the thought and work of Ibn al-Haytham.)

Said, H.M. (ed.) (1979) *Al-Biruni Commemorative Volume: Proceedings of the International Congress held in Pakistan, November 26–December 12, 1973,* Karachi: Hamdard Academy. (Contains numerous papers discussing all the major works of al-Biruni.)

Saliba, G. (1991) 'The Astronomical Tradition of Maragha: A Historical Survey and Prospects for Future Research', *Arabic Sciences and Philosophy* 1 (1): 67–100. (A study of a particularly well-developed period of astronomical research in the Islamic world.)

Sardar, Z. (1989) *Explorations in Islamic Science,* London: Mansell. (Some contemporary debates on the nature of Islamic science.)

Young, M.J.L., Latham, J.D. and Serjeant, R.B. (1990) *Religion, Learning and Sciences in the Abbasid Period,* Cambridge: Cambridge University Press. (The leading work on the most important period for science in the Islamic world.)

ZIAUDDIN SARDAR

SCIENCE, MEDIEVAL

see NATURAL PHILOSOPHY, MEDIEVAL

SCIENCE, 19TH CENTURY PHILOSOPHY OF

In the nineteenth century, science was organized, it tested and confirmed positive knowledge of the natural world and achieved remarkable theoretical development and hitherto unimagined practical application. Science drove industry and free enterprise, and became a powerful catalyst in the battle between defenders of knowledge as power and advocates of knowledge as love.

Fruitful scientific theories and observations were plentiful. Darwin, Wallace and Spencer caused a revolution in biology. Faraday, Maxwell and Hertz contributed seminal ideas in electromagnetic theory. Hermann von Helmholtz studied the physiology of tones and discovered a principle of the conservation of force. Lyell's efforts established geology as a science. Ernst Mach argued for the elimination of absolute space in favour of a space and time consisting of observable relations between things, thus providing incentive for Einstein's theory of relativity. Sir John

Herschel added many observed double stars to the growing catalogue of celestial bodies.

These and other observational, theoretical and applied achievements in nineteenth-century science were replete with philosophical consequences. Until the nineteenth century natural philosophy and science coexisted as a single discipline. Now science and traditional philosophy drew apart. Some held that henceforth science would deal with the world revealed in experience, and philosophy with the world existing (if any does) beyond what we experience. Others (including prominent scientists) were unwilling to yield to philosophy licence to speculate beyond the limits of what could be ascertained by means of observation and experimentation: even if science and philosophy were no longer one unified intellectual enterprise, philosophy had a substantial role to play in philosophizing about science.

To satisfy changing expectations, a new intellectual discipline was created in the nineteenth century: the philosophy of science. Unlike previous philosophy, whose subject matter was everything that is (or is not), the philosophy of science had a distinct and determinate subject matter: theoretical texts and experimental and observational reports of scientists (the word 'scientist' having been invented by William Whewell).

Theoretical scientific systems and their logical structure were one focus of attention. Science was also said to discover laws. Were such laws timeless and exceptionless truths about nature, or simply convenient, economical ways of cataloguing information? These laws were discovered (or invented) generalizations that provided tested information about nature. This discovery and confirmation relied upon the method of induction – thought by most nineteenth-century philosophers of science to have a logic – to involve decisions concerning the validity or invalidity of inferences based on knowledge from experience. Was this alleged logic trustworthy? These questions exemplify the complex problems concerning the epistemic reliability of scientific explanation.

1   **'Man is the interpreter of nature, science, the right interpretation'**
2   **'The general property of the age'**
3   **The status of scientific laws**
4   **The logic of induction**
5   **The justification of induction**
6   **'The ultimate problem of all philosophy'**

1   **'Man is the interpreter of nature, science, the right interpretation'**

William WHEWELL provides the aphoristic watch-

565

word expressive of the new nineteenth-century pre-occupation with the success of science. For him, as for many others, certain fundamental scientific theories had achieved the status of complete and unrevisable truths, among them, the physical synthesis of Newton and the wave theory of light. These theories stood as exemplars of what could be achieved in the inductive natural sciences. Study of the historical development of these, and other, sciences reveals the methodological strategies involved in the establishment of theories now seen to be established truth. Above all, the history of the inductive sciences confirms that science is progressive, moving always towards theories that are simpler, more comprehensive and more accurate as instruments of prediction. New sciences may emerge, but the established ones now require, not additional evidential support, but only refinement.

Others, like Ernst MACH, pointed out that the major theoretical triumphs of science should be construed as invitations to strive for completion, for the end of a science is an ideal, not an achievable result. Nevertheless, Mach shared the general acceptance of the fact that science is progressive, that what we know of nature now is somehow more reliably known than heretofore. A completed science may never be attained but this admission need not entail that we have not progressed in our positive knowledge of how the world works.

John Stuart MILL argued for the epistemic ascendancy of science by claiming that because science has discovered some invariable laws of nature, we can justly conclude that all phenomena are governed by such laws. The progress of science is characterized by the discovery of lawfulness.

Progress as completion of theory, as epistemic ideal, as discovery of laws – three complex philosophical versions of the Victorian aphorism: nature as text receives its best reading from the precise and comprehensive testimony of science.

2 'The general property of the age'

John Stuart Mill used this phrase to describe what Auguste COMTE conceived as the concluding phase of human cultural history: entry into a positivistic age in which both religion and metaphysics no longer function as reliable guides to human action. That which transcends human experience is to be replaced forever by a cooperative social reliance upon the facts disclosed by the sciences.

Many of the thinkers of the century can be classed as positivists, not in the sense of those in the Vienna Circle (see LOGICAL POSITIVISM §4; VIENNA CIRCLE) but in the sense of subscribing to the main tenets of a new, although not always explicitly articulated, philo-sophical programme involving five commitments. First, Victorian positivists accepted Whewell's aphor-ism: only science provides reliable knowledge of nature. Second, these philosophers were convinced that metaphysics could no longer be regarded as a trustworthy source of knowledge. Third, for the majority of nineteenth-century philosophers it was almost a truism to hold that, whatever is to count as reliable knowledge must make contact with the world of human experience. Whewell's 'facts', Mach's 'elements', Mill's 'particulars' and Helmholtz's 'perceptions' (see HELMHOLTZ, H. VON §2) form a family of conceptualizations of meaningful human experiences. For these thinkers (Mill may be the exception) the basic units of experience are laden with theory. Whewell's facts come about by means of the controlled imposition of an idea upon given data. Mach's elements are creatures of reflection upon common human episodes. Helmholtz's perceptions are produced by unconscious inferences based upon rememberings. Nevertheless, the implications of an idea can be tested, an abstraction can be decomposed into its participating components and an inference can be found to be valid or invalid. The point is that, if illusions and imperfect conceptual constructions can somehow be accounted for, it will have to be agreed that no legitimate knowledge can proceed from a foundation other than what is directly available in human contact with the environment.

Fourth, mathematics was elevated to a high position both in education and in the work of scientists. The arguments on behalf of the primacy of mathematics came from Whewell and his contemporaries at Cambridge, later from Henri Poincaré, and from the new formal logicians, for example Stanley Jevons, George Boole and Augustus DeMorgan. Fifth, an element of pragmatism became prominent in the thinking of philosophers of science. Part of what is typical of the application of scientific inductive method involves the making of decisions based on considerations of utility, workability and other values not necessarily associated with truth.

Nineteenth-century philosophers of science did not engage the five points as planks in a philosophical platform. There were important exceptions. Not everyone developed an ambiguity-free positivism of the sort described. What is involved is not so much intellectual acceptance of a set of propositions; rather, our philosophers of science in the main assumed the five points as philosophical obligations, matters of trust to be taken to heart if one is to understand science. From a historical perspective the five points ought to be construed as sign posts directing the investigation of how philosophers of the nineteenth century understood science.

3 The status of scientific laws

In an age of sociopolitical empires, when half the known world was being cut up piecemeal by piratical European governments, it was not difficult for philosophers to call attention to the universal tendency of human beings to generalize, to project universal claims on the basis of small samples. Ever since Aristotle, such generalization had been identified as induction. The formula, though vacuous as a classification, persisted: deduction moves from the general to the particular; induction, from the particular to the general (see INDUCTIVE INFERENCE; LOGIC IN THE NINETEENTH CENTURY). Whewell and Sir John Herschel believed they had discovered an inductive 'propensity'. Herschel characterized this tendency as an

> irresistible impulse of the mind to generalize *ad infinitum*, when nothing in the nature of limitation or opposition offers itself to the imagination, [and as an] involuntary application of the law of continuity to fill up, by the same ideal substance of truth, every interval which uncontradicted experience may have left blank in our inductive conclusions.
>
> (1857a: 198)

Whewell was also convinced that 'the mind has a perpetual propensity to consider... individual propositions as cases of more general ones and to frame and contemplate these latter' (1830).

In one of his notebooks, Whewell illustrates this propensity by means of a humorous, if logically badly flawed, example:

[We start with the particular observation that:]

(1) That apple tree is full of fruit;

[and then move from this observation through the following generalizing steps:]

(2) All apple trees of this district are full of fruit;

(3) All the fruit trees of the kingdom are this season full of fruit;

(4) This season is one of great fruitfulness;

(5) All things are at present going on very well;

[to this grand generalized conclusion:]

(6) All things always go on well[!]

(1830)

This propensity provides the nerve centre of inductive logic. The conclusions of generalizing, which in common affairs are maxims or rules of behaviour, in the sophisticated reaches of scientific inference, are laws. For most philosophers of science a law represents a proposition expressing universally invariant regularity of some sort, and possessing what is now called 'counterfactual force' (see COUNTERFACTUAL CONDITIONALS; LAWS, NATURAL §2). Even if no piece of lead is ever again submerged in *aqua regia*, it is still true that 'lead dissolves in *aqua regia*'.

Mill and Whewell, believing as they did that the logic of induction possesses resources for distinguishing valid from invalid inductive inferences, held also that the results of valid inductions, laws, are necessary truths. Herschel provided the conceptual flag carried by the growing regiment of scientific realists who regarded the observed regularities as fixed, 'the laws of nature are not only permanent, but consistent, intelligible, and discoverable with such a modest degree of research, as is calculated rather to stimulate than to weary curiosity' (1830) (see SCIENTIFIC REALISM AND ANTIREALISM §1). Whewell argued that the acceptability of necessary truths was demonstrated by the self-contradictory character of their logical opposites. Mill held a somewhat more complex view of the epistemic status of natural laws.

Pause to reflect. The world could, for all we know, be very different. There is a clear case for concluding that any generalization over items of experience is contingent; it might, again for all we know, be false. More seriously, all known regularities could be replaced, in accordance with a plan or a successful wager on random possibilities. Such logical possibilities led some to propose that natural laws are endowed with a somewhat attenuated epistemic status.

Mill insisted that natural laws are inductively adequate descriptions of observed empirical regularities. Karl Pearson refined this idea: scientific laws, unlike civil laws which are prescriptive, are descriptive. They are valid for all normal human beings, not just for special communities at special times, and are 'unchangeable so long as their perceptive faculties remain at the same stage of development' (1911). A natural law is not descriptive of repeated sequences of events existing outside us, but is what Pearson calls a 'mental formula'. This initially perplexing idea had been given fuller treatment by several earlier nineteenth-century philosophers of science; surprisingly, Mill is one of them.

Although Mill thought that a scientific law can be understood as part of our knowledge of nature, he also thought that a law can be taken to be a 'memorandum for our guidance'. As knowledge of nature, a law 'registers' facts; as a memorandum, it can be used as a guide to inference. Mill wrote: 'General propositions are merely registers of such [inductive] inferences already made, and short for-

567

mulae for making more' (1843). We do not draw inferences *from* generalizations, but *in accordance with* generalizations taken as licensing certain inferences. We arrive at generalizations by collecting resembling particulars. No one of these particulars is specially privileged, and when we conclude that 'all particulars of sort *x* are particulars of sort *y*', and then go on to infer that some specific *x* is a *y*, we are, says Mill, 'merely deciphering our own notes'.

In commenting upon the generally accepted characterization of a law as a description, Mach prefers the term 'restriction on expectations' to point to the biological significance of scientific laws: 'in origin, the "laws of nature" are restrictions that under the guidance of our experience we prescribe to our expectations' ([1905] 1976). More fully:

> A law always consists in a restriction of possibilities, whether as a bar on action, as an invariable course of natural events, or as a road sign for our thoughts and ideas that anticipate events by running ahead of them in a complementary manner. Galileo and Kepler imagine the various possibilities of free fall and planetary motion, trying to guess those that correspond to observation and making them more precise. The law of inertia which assigns uniform rectilinear motion to a body once all forces disappear, selects one of infinitely many possible thoughts as the decisive one for our ideas.
>
> (Mach 1976: 352)

Mach is not denying that laws pick out observed invariable regularities. But human knowers are biological beings whose expectations are motivated by the need for preservation; laws of nature are instruments of orientation, rules of preservation. It is true that the refinement of laws requires abstraction from given experiences, simplification, idealization of facts and mental decomposition of facts into more cognitively manageable units, which allow us to deal with facts more efficiently (see IDEALIZATIONS). Uniform and uniformly accelerated motions of masses, stationary (steady) thermal and electric currents, are examples of such idealized factual simples; as creatures of mind, they never occur in reality. 'Natural science may be viewed as a kind of collection of instruments for the intellectual completion of any partially given facts or for the restriction, as far as may be, of expectations in future cases.' This is one formulation of Mach's famous thesis of the economy of thought.

The instrumentalism of laws argued for by Mill, Pearson and Mach appears entirely consistent with the pragmatic positivism of the time. Instrumentalism is anti-metaphysical – in Mach and Mill it is even anti-theoretical. In stressing the specific human purposes that are to be fulfilled by seeking and employing laws, our three philosophers of science join forces with other nineteenth-century thinkers, who, like Herbert SPENCER and Thomas HUXLEY, provide related arguments on behalf of the thesis that man is a progressive being.

It can be argued that instrumentalism is incoherent because it really cannot state its own case. Were there no ways in which nature invariably worked before the idealizing techniques of science came into play? Yes and no, answers the instrumentalist. Yes (perhaps), but who, as human knower, cares? No, because laws can only be useful for human knowers; laws restrict what we can know and do. Instrumentalism becomes a matter of perspective; it is a manner of viewing the efficacy of known natural law. But the perspective, though it provides orientation and patterns of adaptation, also displays limitations on what we can know if what we can know is truly only what we can successfully use. The laws, in addition, must be construed as mind-dependent, possible only because of the imposition and manipulation of ideas.

4 The logic of induction

The characteristics of inductive inference (as learning from experience) were much discussed by nineteenth-century philosophers of science. Whewell and Mill debated the question of just what constituted proper induction; Herschel provided the first rules of inductive procedure since Francis Bacon; Mach argued that conclusions of inductive arguments are as vacuous as those of deductive arguments; Mach, Pearson and Ernst Friedrich Apelt stressed the role of abstraction in scientific enquiry; James Clerk MAXWELL championed a complex anti-theoretical methodology based on reasoning from analogies.

The core consideration here is the unwavering confidence of some philosophers of science in what they regarded as the logic of induction, a confidence emphatically proclaimed in Mill's statement that 'there are... certain and universal inductions; and it is because there are such, that a Logic of Induction is possible'. Herschel's nine 'general rules' were intended to provide guidance in the search for natural laws (or common causes of similar phenomena), by permitting deliberate experimental manipulation of data in order to disclose the causes or laws. The suggestion is that, properly applied, the rules will generate valid inductive inferences.

Mill appropriates Herschel's rules in his simplified and generalized 'canons of induction', now better known as 'Mill's methods'. Induction, which for Mill is always inference from particular to particular, is based on consideration of sets of data constructed out of empirically noted regularities and similarities. Factors in a set are varied so that agreements and differences are detectable. These features may refer to invariable antecedence or consequence of certain factors, increase or diminution of certain factors, discovered proportionality of certain factors, and the like. In cases of valid inference, the causal analysis of varying factors will lead to discovery of a true cause, or a law of nature.

Mill thus follows one lead from the insightful writings of Herschel on scientific method. Whewell follows another. Herschel's rules and Mill's methods deal with what we might call 'local induction', generalization over known cases, and inference to others of the same kind not now known. Here, the only evidence that an induction is valid is that it covers the known cases, that it is empirically adequate. It had been recognized since the work of David HUME that any inferences beyond the known cases to all cases of the same (and sometimes different) kind (of global inductions), are hazardous at best, logically unwarranted at worst. Herschel suggests a test of such inferences that Whewell makes the cornerstone of his theory of method. Herschel writes:

The surest and best characteristic of a well-founded and extensive induction ... is when verifications of it spring up, as it were, spontaneously, into notice, from quarters where they might be least expected, or even among instances of that very kind which were at first considered hostile to them. Evidence of this kind is irresistible, and compels assent with a weight which scarcely any other possesses.

(1830: 170)

Whewell calls this epistemic phenomenon a 'consilience of inductions', and regards the test as one capable of establishing the validity of some inductive inferences:

The instances in which [consilience] has occurred, indeed, impress us with a conviction that the truth of our hypothesis is certain. No accident could give rise to such an extraordinary coincidence. No false supposition could, after being adjusted to one class of phenomena, exactly represent a different class, where the agreement was unforeseen and uncontemplated. That rules springing from remote and unconnected quarters should thus leap to the same point, can only arise from *that* being the point where truth resides.

(1858a: 88)

Whewell regarded hypotheses (he called them 'colligations') as initiated by a mental act: the imposition of an idea on some body of data. Mach complimented Whewell on what Mach mistakenly thought was Whewell's concession to the role of freely fantasized and intuited hypotheses. But Whewell was more cautious. There are at least two kinds of restraint imposed on the selection of colligating ideas: success in the past employment of similar ideas, and fruitful discussions in the peer group of relevant scientists. Thus constrained, the idea used is to 'save the appearances', to provide a useful conduit to predictions of phenomena of the same kind as are in the original body of data. Successful prediction is thus one evidential test of a hypothesis, but it still operates on the local level, serving only to enlarge the items in the original set of data. Mill argued that successful prediction is of no evidential value; it only provides more items falling under the same description.

Whewell, the arch scientific realist, finally staked everything on global inductions, those successfully colligating *and* consiliating a hypothesis, adequately covering initial data, predictions of data of the same kind, and unexpected data originally thought to be different in kind, but now seen to be data of the same kind as items in the initial set. Recall Newton's hypothesis of universal gravitation, which covers motions of earthly bodies and of heavenly bodies, and the motions of the tides. Mill thought all induction was local induction, induction by enumeration. Although he agreed with Whewell that induction arrives at necessary truths, his comment on the value of consilience was deliberate silence.

A well-recognized feature of deduction is that deductive conclusions from premises convey no new information that is not contained in the premises but merely *analyse* the premises. The test of a valid deductive inference is that one should not be able to deny the conclusion, given the premises, without logical contradiction. It had also been a long-standing view that inductive inferences yield conclusions that convey new information. It was generally thought that induction moves from the known to the unknown. Valid induction is discovery. The problem, underscored by the devastating analysis of causality by Hume, is to understand the respect in which induction can, like deduction, have a logic, for the conclusions of inductive inferences (as generalizations about the world) seem to involve contingent claims. Alternative conclusions are always *logically* possible.

Mach argued that inductive inference, like deductive inference, yields only vacuous conclusions. If it is simply a matter of piling up more and more instances, as in Mill's favoured induction by simple enumeration, then nothing really new is ever learned that could count as a law. All that one learns is that some data sets are larger than others. Mach's objection may apply to local induction of Mill's sort, but what about global induction? Here also Mach thinks no new information is obtained, for although in consilience data of an apparently new kind are involved, the consilience itself shows that they are not really different in kind from the initial data. If consilience really happens, it converts new data to old, and only extends the magnitude of the enumeration.

William Stanley Jevons delivers what looks like a fatal blow to any claim to have a logic of induction. Granting that science yields only approximations of the given in experience, involving as it does those factors stressed by Mach and Whewell – abstraction, simplification, idealization – any perfect fit between theory and observation must be grounds for suspicion that we are wrong, not for confidence that we are right. In the consideration of rival hypotheses, which are always possible in science, Jevons introduced subjectivist probability theory.

How, then, did believers in the possibility of a logic of induction justify induction?

5 The justification of induction

Herschel thought that the risk of error involved in Jevons's challenge is infinitesimal when we are dealing with 'the unbroken experience of all observers, in innumerable instances'. A conclusion from induction can 'enjoy [no] more than a provisional security'. Such a small risk should produce at least a practical, as distinct from a mathematical, certainty, 'in all physical inquiry, and in all transactions of life' (1857b). This pragmatic appeal to limited certainty would satisfy Mach, whose views on science as providing instruments for orientation have been discussed above. It would also satisfy Karl Pearson, and the biologically oriented Herbert Spencer. It would not, however, satisfy Mill or Whewell.

Whewell, the scientific realist, believed that science does establish laws that are universal truths, that contingent claims become necessary ones. The warrant for this belief is partly pragmatic: Whewell does appeal to the success of certain kinds of methodological technique as disclosed by the history of the inductive sciences. He also seeks a metaphysical justification of his scientific realism.

The historical record of attempts to justify induction reveals that for the most part philosophers rested content with an appeal to the principle of the uniformity of nature. Why trust induction? Inductive conclusions are based on invariable sequences of events. Why take them to be invariable? Nature is uniform. But the argument is viciously circular. We can only know that nature is uniform because we observe lots of sequences taken to be invariable. Or

the argument appeals to metaphysical knowledge: nature is uniform because God made it that way. Or, as Herschel thought, the principle of uniformity is 'an axiom drawn from the inward consciousness of our nature, by involuntary generalization. We acknowledge it expressly or impliedly in every instant of life'.

Mill accepts a form of this argument as his justification of induction. We discover what we take to be laws of nature, invariable repeated sequences of events. What is the simplest assumption that can guarantee that we are right in our assumption that we have in fact discovered laws of nature? The assumption that there are laws of nature (that nature is uniform). This argument is not circular. It asks for the simplest assumption from which all of the known laws of nature can be deduced. The assumption is not inductively established, it is posited. Perhaps it is the best we can hope for (see INDUCTION, EPISTEMIC ISSUES IN).

6 'The ultimate problem of all philosophy'

Whewell admitted with characteristic candour that what he called 'the ultimate problem of all philosophy' is profound, and probably unsolvable. This did not stop him from offering a solution. The problem is as old as scepticism: by means of human mental resources, we arrive at what we take to be knowledge of causal connections, of natural necessity, how can we be sure that what we frame in mind exists in reality outside us? Whewell's committed Christianity provided him with the motivation that ensured a solution. The orders of human knowing correspond to real orders because God makes it so. Scientists share God's thoughts when they hit upon natural laws. That those laws involve independent realities is thus assured, since what God thinks, in these cases at least, he enacts.

Whewell's realism thus shifted its troubled burden on to a metaphysics as old as Leibniz's. He carries that burden alone. For Helmholtz, Hertz, Emil DuBois-Reymond and others, mechanism, the view that all natural phenomena conform to the fundamental principles of mechanics, provides the answer. Although there is no qualitative similarity between our sensations and ideas and their causes in the external world, there are the activities of nerve impulses, which mediate between the two. Physiology, as a part of physics, provides the argument for this reductionist position. Our ideas do not directly correspond to external realities, but both these realities and our ideas are, ultimately, to be viewed as the motions of atomic parts over distances.

We know that Mach was strongly opposed to the mechanical philosophy. He was also strongly opposed to considering Whewell's ultimate problem as a genuine one. Taking his cue from biology, he argued for the thesis that science provides human orientation in a complex world, not metaphysical guidance. Science aids us in our efforts to get along in this world, helps us to realize purposes. But there can be no question of identifying the economies of our successful ideas with an established pattern existing independently of us and holding for all time.

Herbert Spencer's similar biological interests led him to hold a view not unlike that of Mach. It may be true that the order of human knowing reflects accurately and without obdurate distortions the order of reality independent of the human mind, but this is because human beings evolve in the direction of better intellectual adaptation; any correlation between experience and law is not fixed. In the biological domain all change is towards equilibrium; this includes changes in knowledge as well as changes in social contexts.

The ultimate problem is basically the problem of scepticism: how can I trust that I know anything at all? Whewell leaves us in perplexity. There are those who will believe that the avenue to God's mind is forever closed for repairs. The same persons will likely also accept that those who coupled pragmatism and biology created, not an avenue, but a naturalistic horizon whose philosophical enticements constitute one of the benefits of later philosophy of science.

See also: DARWIN, C.R.; GEOLOGY, PHILOSOPHY OF §1; HERTZ, H.; WALLACE, A.R.

References and further reading

Butts, R.E. (ed.) (1989) *William Whewell: Theory of Scientific Method*, Indianapolis, IN, and Cambridge: Hackett Publishing Company. (An anthology of Whewell's basic writings in philosophy of science, with an introduction and bibliography.)

—— (1993) *Historical Pragmatics. Philosophical Essays*, Boston Studies in the Philosophy of Science, vol. 155, Dordrecht: Kluwer. (Essays 8–13 supply details of nineteenth-century philosophy of science, especially that of Herschel, Mill and Whewell. The interpretive analyses are sometimes complicated.)

Cannon, W.F. (1961) 'John Herschel and the Idea of Science', *Journal of the History of Ideas* 22: 215–39. (Good background. Not too technical.)

Giere, R. and Westfall, R.S. (eds) (1973) *Foundations of Scientific Method: The Nineteenth Century*, Bloomington, IN: Indiana University Press. (A conference volume, including papers on Whewell, Peirce, Maxwell, Darwin and Bernard. Nontechnical, good bibliographies.)

Helmholtz, H.L.F. von (1921) *Schriften zur Erkenntnistheorie*, P. Hertz and M. Schlick (eds), Berlin: Springer; trans. M.F. Lowe, *Epistemological Writings*, Boston Studies in the Philosophy of Science, vol. 37, Dordrecht: Reidel, 1977. (Major works of Helmholtz on epistemology.)

* Herschel, Sir J.F.W. (1830) *A Preliminary Discourse on the Study of Natural Philosophy*, London: Longman; repr. *The Sources of Science*, no. 17, New York and London: Johnson Reprint Corp., 1966. (Introductory work on philosophy of science.)

* —— (1857a) 'Whewell on the Inductive Sciences', *Essays from the Edinburgh and Quarterly Reviews*, London: Longman, 142–256. (Critical review of Whewell's *Philosophy of the Inductive Sciences.*)

* —— (1857b) 'Quetelet on Probabilities', *Essays from the Edinburgh and Quarterly Reviews*, London: Longman, 365–465. (Excellent statement of Herschel's pragmatic acceptance of natural laws.)

Jevons, W.S. (1874) *The Principles of Science: A Treatise on Logic and Scientific Method*, London: Macmillan; repr. New York: Dover, 1958. (Difficult sections, but a good introduction to his thought.)

Mach, E. (1883) *Die Mechanik in ihrer Entwicklung. Historisch-kritisch dargestellt*, Leipzig; trans. *The Science of Mechanics. A Critical and Historical Exposition of its Principles*, Chicago, IL, and London, 1893. (Difficult, presupposes knowledge of nineteenth-century physics.)

—— (1886) *Die Analyse der Empfindungen und das Verhältnis des Physischen zum Psychischen*, Jena; trans. *The Analysis of Sensations and the Relation of the Physical to the Psychical*, Chicago, IL, 1897. (Technical and involved argument, but essential for understanding Mach.)

* —— (1905) *Erkenntnis und Irrtum*, Leipzig: J.A. Barth; trans. T.J. McCormack and P. Foulkes, *Knowledge and Error*, Dordrecht: Reidel, 1976. (Straightforward and easy introduction to Mach's philosophy of science.)

Mandelbaum, M. (1971) *History, Man, and Reason. A Study in Nineteenth-century Thought*, Baltimore, MD, and London: Johns Hopkins University Press. (An indispensable guide to the history of nineteenth-century ideas. Presupposes some knowledge of the history of philosophy.)

* Mill, J.S. (1843) *System of Logic: Ratiocinative and Inductive; Being a Connected View of the Principles of Evidence and the Methods of Scientific Investigation*, London, Longman; 8th edn, 1872; repr. in J.M. Robson (ed.) *Collected Works of John Stuart Mill*, London: Routledge and Toronto, Ont.: University of Toronto Press, vols 7 and 8, 1991. (Mill's major work on scientific method, including his criticisms of Whewell. The argument is often

involved and difficult. The pagination of volumes 7 and 8 is consecutive; volume 8 begins at page 639.)

—— (1865) *Auguste Comte and Positivism*, London; repr. in J.M. Robson (ed.) *Collected Works of John Stuart Mill*, London: Routledge and Toronto, Ont.: University of Toronto Press, vol. 10, 261–368, 1991. (Invaluable source of Mill's thoughts about positivism. Also contains his critique of Herbert Spencer. Nontechnical.)

* Pearson, K. (1911) *The Grammar of Science*, London; repr. New York: Meridian Books, 3rd edn, 1957. (Presupposes some knowledge of nineteenth-century science, but not a difficult book.)

Santillana, G. de (1950) 'Aspects of Scientific Rationalism in the Nineteenth Century', *International Encyclopedia of Unified Science*, vol. II, no. 8, Chicago, IL: University of Chicago Press. (Valuable nontechnical account of the scientific background.)

Spencer, H. (1855) *The Principles of Psychology*, London: Williams & Norgate; 2nd edn, New York: Appleton, 1871–3, 2 vols. (The two editions comprise Spencer's basic ideas in psychology. Few technicalities.)

—— (1864, 1867) *Principles of Biology*, London: Williams & Norgate, 2 vols; 2nd edn, 1898, 1899. (Spencer's basic ideas on evolution of species predated those of Darwin.)

* Whewell, W. (1830) 'Induction III (I) genl. views/geology/etc', unpublished notebook in black metal chest marked INDUCTION, Wren Library, Trinity College, Cambridge. (A historical treasure with views predating published ones.)

—— (1840) *Philosophy of the Inductive Sciences*, London, 2 vols. (Whewell's *magnum opus* in philosophy of science; relatively nontechnical.)

* —— (1858a) *Novum organon renovatum*, London: J.W. Parker & Sons.

—— (1858b) *History of Scientific Ideas*, London: J.W. Parker & Sons.

* —— (1860) *On the Philosophy of Discovery*, London: J.W. Parker & Sons. (1858a and b and 1860 comprise the 3rd edition of *The Philosophy of the Inductive Sciences*. New material is added. 1860 contains Whewell's 'solution' to the ultimate problem of philosophy.)

Wolters, G. (1987) *Mach I, Mach II, Einstein und die Relativitätstheorie. Eine Fälschung und ihre Folgen* (Mach I, Mach II. Einstein and the Theory of Relativity. A Forgery and its Consequences), Berlin and New York: de Gruyter. (Unfortunately not translated into English. Enlightened understanding of Mach's philosophy of science. Difficult sections.)

—— (1989) 'Phenomenalism, Relativity and Atoms: Rehabilitating Ernst Mach's Philosophy of Science', in J.E. Fenstad, I.T. Frolov and R. Hilpinen (eds) *Logic, Methodology and Philosophy of Science VIII*, Proceedings of the Eighth International Congress of Logic, Methodology and Philosophy of Science, Moscow, 1987, Amsterdam: North Holland, 641–60. (A clear, concise statement of Wolter's reading of Mach's philosophy of science.)

ROBERT E. BUTTS

SCIENCE, PHILOSOPHY OF

1 Historical background and introduction

Science grew out of philosophy; and, even after recognizable, if flexible, interdisciplinary boundaries developed, the most fruitful philosophical investigations have often been made in close connection with science and scientific advance. The major modern innovators – Bacon, Descartes, Leibniz and Locke among them – were all centrally influenced by, and in some cases significantly contributed to, the science of their day. Kant's fundamental epistemological problem was generated by the success of science: we have obtained certain knowledge, both in mathematics and – principally due to Newton – in science, how was this possible? Unsurprisingly, many thinkers who are principally regarded as great scientists, had exciting and insightful views on the aims of science and the methods of obtaining scientific knowledge. One can only wonder why the epistemological views of Galileo and of Newton, for example, are not taught along with those of Bacon and Locke, say, in courses on the history of modern philosophy. Certainly it can be argued very convincingly that the former two had at least as much insight into the aims and methods of science, and into how scientific knowledge is gained and accredited as the latter two (see GALILEI, G. §3; NEWTON, I. §2–3; also see BOYLE, R.; COPERNICUS, N.; KEPLER, J.).

In the nineteenth century, MAXWELL, HERTZ and HELMHOLZ all had interesting views about explanation and the foundations of science, while POINCARÉ who was undoubtedly one of the greatest mathematicians and mathematical physicists, was arguably also one of the greatest philosophers of science – developing important and influential views about, amongst other things, the nature of theories and hypotheses, explanation, and the role of probability theory both within science and as an account of scientific reasoning (also see DUHEM, P.M.M.; FRENCH PHILOSOPHY OF SCIENCE; LE ROY, É.; MEYERSON, É.; SCIENCE, NINETEENTH CENTURY PHILOSOPHY OF).

The period from the 1920s to 1950s is sometimes

seen as involving a movement towards more formal issues to the exclusion of detailed concern with the scientific process itself (see LOGICAL POSITIVISM). While this has been over-exaggerated – CARNAP, HEMPEL, POPPER and especially REICHENBACH for example all show sophisticated awareness of a range of issues from contemporary science (also see BRIDGMAN, P.W.; OPERATIONALISM) – there is no doubt that general attention in philosophy of science has been redirected back to the details of science, and in particular of its *historical* development, by 'post-positivist' philosophers such as HANSON, FEYERABEND, KUHN, LAKATOS and others.

Current philosophy of science has developed this great tradition, addressing many of the now standard philosophical issues – about knowledge, the nature of reality, determinism and indeterminism and so on – but by paying very close attention to science both as an exemplar of knowledge and as a source of (likely) information about the world. This means that there is inevitably much overlap with other areas of philosophy – notably epistemology (the theory of scientific knowledge is of course a central concern of philosophy of science) and metaphysics (which philosophers of science often shun as an attempted a priori discipline but welcome when it is approached as an investigation of what current scientific theories and practices seem to be telling us about the likely structure of the universe). Indeed one way of usefully dividing up the subject would see scientific epistemology and what might be called scientific metaphysics as two of the main branches of the subject (these two together in turn forming what might be called general philosophy of science), with the third branch consisting of more detailed, specific investigations into foundational issues concerned with particular scientific fields or particular scientific theories (especial, though by no means exclusive, attention having been paid of late to foundational and interpretative issues in quantum theory and the Darwinian theory of evolution). Again not surprisingly, important contributions have been made in this third sub-field by scientists themselves who have reflected carefully and challengingly on their own work and its foundations (see BOHR, N.; DARWIN, C.R.; EINSTEIN, A.; HEISENBERG, W.; PLANCK, M.), as well as by those who are more usually considered philosophers.

2   Contemporary philosophy of science: the theory of scientific knowledge

Scientists propose theories and assess those theories in the light of observational and experimental evidence; what distinguishes science is the careful and systematic way in which its claims are based on evidence (see SCIENTIFIC METHOD). These simple claims, which I suppose would win fairly universal agreement, hide any number of complex issues.

First, concerning theories: how exactly are these best represented? Is Newton's theory of gravitation, or the neo-Darwinian theory of evolution, or the general theory of relativity, best represented – as logical empiricists such as Carnap supposed – as sets of (at least potentially) formally axiomatized sentences, linked to their observational bases by some sort of correspondence rules? Or are they best represented, as various recent 'semantic theorists' have argued, as sets of models (see MODELS; THEORIES, SCIENTIFIC)? Is this simply a representational matter or does the difference between the two sorts of approach matter scientifically and philosophically? This issue ties in with the increasingly recognized role of idealizations in science and of the role of models as intermediates between fundamental theory and empirical laws (see CAMPBELL, N.R.; IDEALIZATIONS). It also relates to an important issue about how best to think of the state of a scientific field at a given time: is a scientist best thought of as accepting (in some sense or other) a single theory or set of such theories or rather as accepting some sort of more general and hierarchically-organized set of assumptions and techniques in the manner of Kuhnian paradigms or Lakatosian research programmes? It seems likely that arriving at the correct account of scientific development and in particular of theory-change in science will depend on identifying the 'right' account of theories.

Next concerning the *evidence*: it has long been recognized that many of the statements that scientists are happy to regard as 'observation sentences' in fact presuppose a certain amount of theory, and that *all* observation sentences, short perhaps of purely subjective reports of current introspection, depend on some sort of minimal theory (even 'the needle points to around 5 on the scale' presupposes that the needle and the scale exist independently of the observer and that the observer's perception of them is not systematically deluded by a Cartesian demon). Does this mean that there is no real epistemic distinction between observational and theoretical claims? Does it mean that there is no secure basis or foundation for science in the form of observational and experimental results (see OBSERVATION)? If so, what becomes of the whole empiricist idea of basing scientific theories on the evidence? It can be argued that those who have drawn dire consequences from these considerations have confused fallibility with (serious) corrigibility: that there are observation statements, such as reports of meter readings and the like, of a sufficiently low level as to be, once independently and intersubjectively verified, not seriously corrigible despite being trivially strictly fallible (see MEASUREMENT, THEORY OF). Aside from this issue, experiment was for a long time regarded as raising barely any independent, philosophical or methodological concern – experiments being thought of as very largely simply means for testing theories (see EXPERIMENT). More recently, there has been better appreciation of the extent to which experimental science has a life of its own, independent of fundamental theory, and of the extent to which philosophical issues concerning testing, realism, underdetermination and so on can be illuminated by studying experiments.

Suppose that we have characterized scientific theories and drawn a line between theoretical and observational statements, what exactly is involved in 'basing' theoretical claims 'systematically and carefully' on the evidence? This question has of course been perhaps *the* central question of general philosophy of science in this century. We have known at least since David HUME that the answer cannot be that the correct theories are deducible from observation results. Indeed not only do our theories universally generalize the (inevitably finite) data as Hume pointed out, they also generally 'transcend' the data by explaining that data in terms of underlying, but non-observable, theoretical entities. This means that there must always in principle be (indefinitely) many theories that clash with one another at the theoretical level but yet entail all the same observational results (see UNDERDETERMINATION). What extra factors then are involved over and beyond simply having the right observational consequences? What roles do such factors as simplicity (see SIMPLICITY (IN SCIENTIFIC THEORIES)), and explanatory power (see EXPLANATION), play in accrediting theories on the basis of evidence? Moreover what status do these factors have – are they purely pragmatic (the sorts of features *we* like theories to have) or are they truth-indicating, and if so why? Some have argued that the whole process can be codified in probabilistic terms – the theories that we see as accredited by the evidence being the ones that are at any rate *more probable* in the light of that evidence than any of their rivals (see CONFIRMATION THEORY; INDUCTIVE INFERENCE; PROBABILITY THEORY AND EPISTEMOLOGY).

Finally, suppose we have characterized the correct scientific way of reasoning to theories from evidence, what exactly does this tell us about the theories that have been thus 'accredited' by the evidence? And what does it tell us about the entities – such as electrons, quarks, and the rest – apparently postulated by such theories? Is it reasonable to believe that these accredited theories are *true* descriptions of an underlying reality, that their theoretical terms refer to real, though unobservable entities? (Or at least to believe that they are *probably* true? or *approximately* true? or perhaps probably approximately true?) More strongly still, is any one of these beliefs the *uniquely* rational one? Or is it instead more, or at least equally, reasonable – at least equally explanatory of the way that science operates – to hold that these 'accredited' theories are no more than empirically adequate, even that they are simply instruments for prediction, the theoretical 'entities' they involve being no more than convenient fictions (see CONVENTIONALISM; FICTIONALISM; INCOMMENSURABILITY; PUTNAM, H.; SCIENTIFIC REALISM AND ANTIREALISM)? One major problem faced by realists is to develop a plausible response to once accepted theories that are now rejected either by arguing that they were in some sense immature – not 'fully scientific' – or that, despite having been rejected, they nonetheless somehow live on as 'limiting cases' of current theories (see ALCHEMY; CHEMISTRY, PHILOSOPHICAL ASPECTS OF §2; FIELD THEORY, CLASSICAL; MECHANICS, ARISTOTELIAN; MECHANICS, CLASSICAL; OPTICS; VITALISM).

Clearly an antirealist view of theories would be indicated *if* it could convincingly be argued that the accreditation of theories in science is not simply a function of evidential and other truth-related factors or even of epistemic pragmatic factors, but *also* of broader cultural and social matters. Although such arguments are heard increasingly often, many remain unconvinced – seeing those arguments as based *either* on confusion of discovery with validational issues *or* on fairly naïve views of evidential support (see CONSTRUCTIVISM; DISCOVERY, LOGIC OF; GENDER AND SCIENCE; MARXIST PHILOSOPHY OF SCIENCE).

3 Contemporary philosophy of science: 'scientific metaphysics'

Suppose that we take a vaguely realist view of current science, what does it tell us about the general structure of reality? Does a sensible interpretation of science require the postulation, for example, of natural kinds (see NATURAL KINDS) or universals? Does it require the postulation of a notion of physical necessity to distinguish natural laws from 'mere' regularities (see LAWS, NATURAL)? What is the nature of probability (see PROBABILITY, INTERPRETATIONS OF) – is a probabilistic claim invariably an expression of (partial) ignorance or are there real, irreducible 'objective chances' in the world? What exactly is involved in the claim that a particular theory (or a particular system described by such a theory) is deterministic (see DETERMINISM AND INDETERMINISM), and what would it mean for the world as a whole to be deterministic?

Does even 'deterministic' science eschew the notion of *cause* (as Russell argued)? Does this notion come into its own in more 'mundane' contexts, involving what might be called 'causal factors' and probabilistic causation? What exactly is the relationship between causal claims – such as 'smoking causes heart disease' – and statistical data (see CAUSATION)? How should spacetime be interpreted (see SPACETIME): as substantive or as 'merely' relational? Does current science plus whatever ideas of causality are associated with it unambiguously rule out the possibility of time travel (see TIME TRAVEL), or does this remain at least logically possible given current science?

Finally, and most generally, what is science (or, perhaps more significantly, the *direction* of scientific development) telling us about the overall structure of the universe – that it is one simple system governed at the fundamental level by one unified set of general laws, or rather that it is a 'patchwork' of interconnected but separate, mutually irreducible principles (see UNITY OF SCIENCE; REDUCTION, PROBLEMS OF)? Although it is of course true – despite some exaggerated claims on behalf of 'theories of everything' – that science is very far from reducing everything to a common fundamental basis, and although it is of course true that, even in cases where reduction is generally agreed to have been achieved, such as that of chemistry to physics, the reduction is *ontological* (that is, chemistry has been shown to need no essential, non-physical primitive notions) rather than *epistemological* (no one would dream of trying actually to *derive* a full description of any chemical reaction from the principles of quantum mechanics), some would nonetheless still argue that the overall *tendency* of science is in the reductionist direction (see CHEMISTRY, PHILOSOPHICAL ASPECTS OF §5).

These are examples of the more or less general, and impressively varied, 'metaphysical' issues informed by science that have attracted recent philosophical attention.

4 Contemporary philosophy of science: foundational issues from current science

Many of the most interesting issues in current philosophy of science are closely tied to foundational or methodological concerns about current scientific theory. One fertile source of such concerns is quantum theory. How much of a revolutionary change in our general metaphysical view of the world does it require? Is the theory irreducibly indeterministic or do 'hidden variable' interpretations of some sort remain possible despite the negative results? What does quantum mechanics tell us about the notion of cause? Does quantum mechanics imply a drastic

breakdown of 'locality', telling us that the properties of even vastly spatially separated systems are fundamentally interconnected – so that we can no longer think of, for example 'two' spatially separated electrons as separate, independent 'particles'? More directly, is there, in view of the 'measurement problem' a coherent interpretation of quantum mechanics at all? (It has been argued that when the theory is interpreted universally so that *all* systems, including 'macroscopic' ones, such as measuring apparatuses, are assigned a quantum state then the two fundamental principles of quantum theory – the Schrödinger equation and the projection postulate – come into direct contradiction (see BELL'S THEOREM; FIELD THEORY, QUANTUM; QUANTUM MEASUREMENT PROBLEM; QUANTUM MECHANICS, INTERPRETATION OF; also see RANDOMNESS; STATISTICS).)

Although perhaps attracting relatively less attention than quantum theory, the other two great theories that form the triumvirate at the heart of contemporary physics – relativity (both special and general) and thermodynamics – pose similarly fascinating problems. In the case of relativity theory, philosophers have raised both ontological issues (for example, concerning the nature of spacetime) and epistemological issues (concerning for example the real role played in Einstein's development of the theory by Machian empiricism, the role of allegedly crucial experiments such as that of Michelson and Morley (see CRUCIAL EXPERIMENTS), and the evidential impact on the general theory of the Eddington star-shift experiment). There are also important issues about the consistency of relativity and quantum theory – issues that in turn feed into the more general questions concerning the unity of science and realism (see GENERAL RELATIVITY, PHILOSOPHICAL RESPONSES TO; RELATIVITY THEORY, PHILOSOPHICAL SIGNIFICANCE OF).

Thermodynamics raises issues about, amongst other things, probability and the testing of probabilistic theories, about determinism and indeterminism, and about the direction of time (see THERMODYNAMICS; DETERMINISM AND INDETERMINISM; DUHEM, P.M.M. §2; TIME). Other current areas of physics, too, raise significant foundational issues (see CHAOS THEORY; COSMOLOGY).

For a long time, philosophy of science meant in effect philosophy of *physics*. A welcome broadening-out has occurred recently – especially in the direction of philosophy of biology. The central concern here has been with foundational issues in the Darwinian theory of evolution (or more accurately the neo-Darwinian synthesis of natural selection and genetics). Questions have been raised about the testability and, more generally, the empirical credentials of that theory, about the scope of the theory (in particular what it can tell us about humans and human societies), about the appropriate 'unit of selection' (individual, gene, group), about what exactly are genes and what exactly are species, and about whether evolutionary biology involves distinctive – perhaps even in *some* sense 'teleological' – modes of explanation (see DARWIN, C.R.; ECOLOGY; EVOLUTION, THEORY OF; FUNCTIONAL EXPLANATION; GENETICS; HUXLEY, T.H.; LIFE, ORIGINS OF; LINNAEUS, C. VON; SOCIOBIOLOGY; SPECIES; TAXONOMY; WALLACE, A.R.). More recently philosophy of biology has started to widen its own scope by considering issues outside of evolutionary theory (see MOLECULAR BIOLOGY; MEDICINE, PHILOSOPHY OF), where, however, issues of reductionism and of the possibility of distinctive modes of explanation still loom large.

See also: ARCHAEOLOGY, PHILOSOPHY OF; ATOMISM, ANCIENT; COLOUR, THEORIES OF; COMPUTER SCIENCE; CONSERVATION PRINCIPLES; DECISION AND GAME THEORY; DEMARCATION PROBLEM; DEMOCRITUS; ELECTRODYNAMICS; FACTS; FEMINISM AND SOCIAL SCIENCE; GEOLOGY, PHILOSOPHY OF; HEIDEGGERIAN PHILOSOPHY OF SCIENCE; INFORMATION THEORY; JUNG, C.G.; KEYNES, J.M.; KOYRÉ, A.; MATTER; MEAD, G.H.; NATURALIZED PHILOSOPHY OF SCIENCE; PARANORMAL PHENOMENA; POSTCOLONIAL PHILOSOPHY OF SCIENCE; PROCLUS §10; PTOLEMY; RELIGION AND SCIENCE; RESPONSIBILITIES OF SCIENTISTS AND INTELLECTUALS; RISK ASSESSMENT; SCIENCE IN ISLAMIC PHILOSOPHY; SCIENTIFIC REALISM AND SOCIAL SCIENCE; SPACE; TECHNOLOGY, PHILOSOPHY OF; THOUGHT EXPERIMENTS

Further reading

Kitcher, P. (1993) *The Advancement of Science: Science without Legend, Objectivity without Illusions*, New York, and Oxford: Oxford University Press. (Thorough and illuminating account of the general issues surrounding theory-change in science; also useful as an introduction to the methodological issues raised by Darwinian theory.)

Maudlin, T. (1994) *Quantum Non-Locality and Relativity*, Oxford, and Cambridge, MA: Blackwell. (Given its subject matter, an exceptionally clear, accessible account of some of the foundational issues in quantum theory, especially concerning its reconcilability with relativity theory.)

Papineau, D. (ed.) (1996) *The Philosophy of Science*, Oxford Readings in Philosophy, Oxford: Oxford University Press. (Recent collection of articles, especially on the realism/antirealism issue, but also on issues of empirical support.)

Salmon, M.H. *et al.* (1992) *Introduction to the Philosophy of Science*, Englewood Cliffs, NJ: Prentice Hall. (A text written by members of the internationally celebrated History and Philosophy of Science Department at the University of Pittsburgh and covering general philosophy of science, as well as philosophy of physics, of biology, and of the behavioural and social sciences.)

JOHN WORRALL

SCIENTIFIC METHOD

Procedures for attaining scientific knowledge are known as scientific methods. These methods include formulating theories and testing them against observation or experiment. Ancient and medieval thinkers called any systematic body of knowledge a 'science', and their methods were aimed at knowledge in general. According to the most common model for scientific knowledge, formulated by Aristotle, induction yields universal propositions from which all knowledge in a field can be deduced. This model was refined by medieval and early modern thinkers, and further developed in the nineteenth century by Whewell and Mill.

As Kuhn observed, idealized accounts of scientific method must be distinguished from descriptions of what scientists actually do. The methods of careful observation and experiment have been in use from antiquity, but became more widespread after the seventeenth century. Developments in instrument making, in mathematics and statistics, in terminology, and in communication technology have altered the methods and the results of science.

1   'Method' and 'science'
2   Ideas of method from the Greeks to Thomas Kuhn
3   Scientific method in scientific practice

1   'Method' and 'science'

'Method' comes from the Greek *meta* (after) plus *hodos* (path or way). A method is a way to achieve an end; a scientific method is a way to achieve the ends of science. What those ends are depends on what science is or is taken to be. The word 'science' now means primarily natural science, examples of which are physics, astronomy, biology, chemistry, geology and psychology, and it applies secondarily to social sciences such as economics and sociology. Discussions of method focus on the cognitive aims of science, which may include knowledge, understanding, explanation, or predictive success, with respect to all or part of nature or to some domain of natural or social phenomena. Abstractly described, scientific method is the means for attaining these aims, especially by forming models, theories, or other cognitive structures and testing them through observation and experiment (see EXPERIMENT; MODELS; OBSERVATION; THEORIES, SCIENTIFIC). Investigations of scientific method may describe the methods actually employed by scientists, or they may formulate proposals about the procedures that should be followed to achieve scientific knowledge (see NATURALIZED PHILOSOPHY OF SCIENCE).

The main features traditionally ascribed to 'the scientific method' – including clear statement of a problem, careful confrontation of theory with fact, open-mindedness, and (potential) public availability or replicability of evidence – are common to many cognitive endeavours, including much work in the humanities. Although there is no single method that distinguishes science from other intellectual practices, the following features are characteristic of the natural and social sciences: the use of quantitative data and of theories formulated mathematically; the use of artificially created experimental situations; and an interest in universal generalizations or laws (see DEMARCATION PROBLEM; LAWS, NATURAL §1; UNITY OF SCIENCE). (But note that biological taxonomies are not intrinsically quantitative, and that neither astronomy nor economics is based primarily on experiment.) In both the natural and social sciences, the formation of models or theories may involve skills in mathematical computation and derivation, in evaluating consistency, in imagining new theoretical possibilities, in assessing the structure of a taxonomy, or in relating one area of investigation to other areas. The means for testing theories or generating new empirical knowledge vary widely, and include systematic observation, unsystematic observation, checks against background theories or knowledge, and various experimental procedures, including sophisticated statistical techniques, the construction of special instruments or apparatus and the use of specially bred laboratory animals.

2 Ideas of method from the Greeks to Thomas Kuhn

Because 'science' originally meant any systematic body of knowledge, ranging from mathematics to theology, the method of science was the method for obtaining, or perhaps merely for presenting and teaching, knowledge in general. Methods varied in relation to beliefs about what there is to be known.

The writings of Plato and Aristotle embody contrasting conceptions of both the objects of knowledge and the method for knowing them. In *Republic* VI, Plato divided the objects of knowledge into two realms: the visible and the intelligible (see PLATO §14). He considered the former to include the objects of the senses, about which only opinion but not genuine knowledge is possible, and the latter to include geometry and astronomy, in which investigators assume the existence of their objects (such as geometrical objects) and reason from them as from hypotheses. In the highest reaches of the intelligible realm, reason attempts to reach 'the first principle of all that exists', from which it then 'comes down to a conclusion ... proceeding by means of Forms and through Forms to its conclusions which are Forms', without any reference to the visible world. Plato conceived the sensible world as a dim reflection of the intelligible Forms, and he held that the Forms themselves are best known through direct intellectual contemplation, independent of sensory experience. The notion of an intelligible world behind the sensible world, and especially of a world described by mathematics, has played an important role in physical science since Plato's time.

ARISTOTLE rejected Plato's intelligible realm because it removed the objects of mathematical sciences such as astronomy from the sensible world, where he believed the forms of things are to be found. He carried out extensive observations (including dissections) in biology and developed a preliminary taxonomic scheme. Aristotle's principal discussion of method is the *Posterior Analytics*, a founding work in the philosophy of science. He accepted the Platonic distinction between a direction of cognition that is going 'to the forms' and the direction of cognition (as in syllogistic demonstration) that proceeds 'from the forms', but he conceived these processes as starting from sensible objects and arriving at knowledge of the common natures or essences of things as existing in those objects. Such knowledge (for instance, of the essence of a specific kind of mineral, or kind of living thing) yields a set of core propositions in each science, from which other knowledge is to be deductively derived.

Medieval philosophers, including Roger BACON, John DUNS SCOTUS and William of OCKHAM, commented extensively on Aristotle's methodological writings, which were later discussed at the University of Padua together with those of GALEN. A central topic was the distinction between analysis and synthesis, or, as it was sometimes called, between resolution and composition. In the analytic phase of inquiry, one resolves the object of investigation into its basic constituents or least elements so as to determine its first principles. In the synthetic phase, one explains a subject matter from its first principles, or presents a body of knowledge by deriving it from such principles. In a common example, the analytic phase would include the search for the axioms, postulates and definitions of geometry; the synthetic phase the demonstration of theorems from those axioms and postulates. Bacon suggested that the first principles achieved in the analytic or inductive phase can be tested by deducing and checking new consequences (a feature of 'hypothetico-deductive' tests of theories). Scotus outlined a method of agreement, in which a possible cause for an effect is found by listing the circumstances that co-occur with the effect and looking for one that is present every time. Ockham suggested a method of difference, in which a circumstance that is present when the effect is present and absent when it is absent is considered as a possible cause for the effect.

The seventeenth century, a time of fundamental change in physics and astronomy, saw continuing attention to method within the inductive-deductive framework established by Aristotle. Francis BACON outlined inductive procedures in detail, calling for extensive collections of data (named 'histories') which are to be culled systematically for general principles or laws. Galileo urged that mathematical descriptions be fitted to natural phenomena through observation and experiment (see GALILEI, G.). Descartes wrote in *Discourse on the Method* (1637) that the derivation of an effect from a cause may serve as an explanation of the effect, and also as an empirical 'proof' of the posited cause (see DESCARTES, R. §6). Newton, in *Mathematical Principles of Natural Philosophy* (1729), laid down several 'hypotheses' or 'rules' for reasoning in natural philosophy. He advised investigators to avoid multiplying causes in relation to effects, to generalize from properties found in bodies that have been observed to all bodies in the universe, and to accept inductively supported propositions as 'accurately or very nearly true' until new observations improve upon their accuracy or limit their scope (see NEWTON, I. §4).

During the nineteenth century, the 'philosophy of science' or the 'logic of science' became, in the writings of William WHEWELL, John Stuart MILL and others, a main staple of philosophy (see PHILOSOPHY OF SCIENCE IN THE NINETEENTH CENTURY). Whewell's *Philosophy of the Inductive Sciences* (1840) analyses scientific knowledge of 'external' nature (excluding the mind itself). Whewell held that scientific knowledge is based upon sensations and ideas, the former being the 'objective' element (caused by objects), the latter a 'subjective' element (provided by the knowing subject). Consciously entertained facts and theories correspond to sensations and ideas,

but not completely, because all facts implicitly include ideas (and so, possibly, theory). Whewell divided the methods of science into methods of observation, of obtaining clear ideas, and of induction. The methods of observation include quantitative observation (as in chemistry or astronomy) and the perception of similarities (as in natural history); observation includes both the collection and classification of facts. Clear ideas result from intellectual education (including both the mathematical sciences and natural history), and from discussion, including (sometimes metaphysical) discussions of definitions, such as whether uniform force acting in free fall should be defined relative to space or to time. Science proceeds by 'induction', including the use of quantitative techniques to smooth out the irregularities of observation (that is, the 'method of curves' by which a curve is fitted to data points, the 'method of means' and the 'method of least squares') and the formation and empirical testing of tentative hypotheses. Laws of phenomena are usually formed first, but theories of true causes are desired, such as (Whewell explained) have been found in physical astronomy, physical optics, and geology, and might be found with respect to heat, magnetism, electricity, chemical compounds and living organisms.

In *A System of Logic* (1846), Mill analysed the methods of science even more fully than had Whewell, now including psychology and the social sciences (also known as the 'mental' and 'moral' sciences). In his analysis of experimental method, Mill included the methods of agreement and difference already mentioned, and added the method of residues, which directs the investigator to look for the (as yet unknown) causes of those effects that remain after all other effects have been assigned to known causes, and the method of concomitant variations, according to which those phenomena that vary regularly in quantitative degree with one another are assumed to be causally related. Like Whewell, Mill emphasized the role of new or pre-existing concepts and names in scientific observation, and the role that classification plays in induction. He proposed that psychology and the social sciences should adopt the explanatory structures of the natural sciences, a proposal frequently criticized since his time, notably by the Neo-Kantians Wilhelm DILTHEY, Heinrich Rickert and Ernst CASSIRER, who discussed methods pertaining to the 'social' or 'human' sciences, and who included the humanities as a form of 'science' (in German, *Wissenschaft*) (see NEO-KANTIANISM; POSITIVISM IN THE SOCIAL SCIENCES).

Philosophers in the first half of the twentieth century, especially the Vienna Circle and Karl POPPER, sought to analyse science and to reconstruct scientific reasoning using the new symbolic logic or the new theory of probability (see VIENNA CIRCLE). They continued the investigation of theory confirmation, focusing on recent theories in physics (see CONFIRMATION THEORY). Rudolph CARNAP attempted unsuccessfully to develop a quantitative theory of inductive support. Carl HEMPEL, who favoured a hypothetico-deductive account of scientific confirmation (involving the testing of theories by their deductive consequences), revealed certain paradoxes that result when the relation between scientific generalizations and confirming instances are expressed in predicate logic and certain (plausible) assumptions are made. Popper concluded that the defining feature of the empirical methods of science is that statements are always subjected to falsification by new data.

In the second half of the twentieth century philosophical analyses of scientific method broadened to again include sciences such as biology and geology, and paid greater attention to the history of science. N.R. HANSON recalled the often implicit role of theory in observation, questioning the notion of a theory-neutral observation language (see OBSERVATION §4). Thomas S. KUHN emphasized the social nature of scientific communities and the common training that produces a shared vocabulary and set of experimental procedures. Kuhn and Paul FEYERABEND stressed the need to distinguish the idealized accounts of scientific method given by some scientists and philosophers from the actual methodological practices of scientists. In studying the latter, historical and sociological investigation supplements the participatory acquaintance with scientific research possessed by scientists themselves and by some philosophers.

3 Scientific method in scientific practice

The methods of careful observation and description (including quantitative description) and of controlled experiment arose in antiquity and were practised by Greek, Hellenistic and Islamic investigators (see PHILOSOPHY OF SCIENCE IN ISLAM §2). Examples include Aristotle's biological observations, the many Greek and Arabic (and earlier Babylonian) tables of astronomical data, Ptolemy and Alhazen's careful studies of binocular vision and distance perception, and Galen's use of the ligature and other experimental techniques in physiology.

From antiquity, instruments aided the precision of observation in astronomy and optics. In the early seventeenth century Johannes KEPLER used Tycho Brahe's precise astronomical data (obtained with improved instruments) to establish the elliptical orbits of the planets and to determine the relations among the sizes and periods of those orbits. In 1609 Galileo used the newly invented telescope to observe previously unseen heavenly bodies (including the moons of Jupiter). Later in the century the microscope opened new fields of observation. The nineteenth and twentieth centuries have seen the development of refined and often complex instrumentation in all branches of natural science, including biology, chemistry and psychology, ranging from improved balances to the electron microsope and the space telescope. Photography has been used to record data in nearly every field. The computer permits collection and manipulation of larger bodies of data than was previously practical. In psychology, the computer allows generation of precisely controlled stimuli and the recording of data with highly accurate temporal measurement.

The development of mathematics, including probability and statistics, has yielded new forms of theory statement and new descriptions of observational or experimental data. Mathematical sciences from antiquity to the seventeenth century used geometry almost exclusively. The development of algebraic geometry and of the calculus permitted new statements of Newtonian mechanics in the eighteenth century, and opened up new possibilities (theoretical as well as experimental) for describing and investigating functional relations among quantities. In the nineteenth and twentieth centuries, new mathematics has been demanded by or has facilitated mathematical physics. Thus, the discovery of non-Euclidean geometries opened up hitherto unforeseen theoretical possibilities in physical cosmology. The development of probability and statistics permitted the formulation of statistical laws, as in mathematical genetics, quantum physics and sociology (see PROBABILITY, INTERPRETATIONS OF; STATISTICS; STATISTICS AND SOCIAL SCIENCE). Inferential statistics is widely used in the analysis of quantitative data in psychology and other sciences.

Clear and precise terminology is an important feature of scientific methodology. Astronomy, optics (as the science of vision), natural history and medicine developed technical vocabularies in antiquity. Newton profoundly altered the terminology of physics, which continues to change as theories change. Carl von LINNAEUS invented important taxonomies in botany and zoology; after Darwin's theory of natural selection gained acceptance, evolutionary history influenced biological taxonomy (see EVOLUTION, THEORY OF; TAXONOMY). Molecular biology has produced another new terminology (see MOLECULAR BIOLOGY). In psychology, long-standing mentalistic terminology was purged by twentieth-century behaviourists (see BEHAVIOURISM, METHODOLOGICAL AND SCIENTIFIC), and has since been reintroduced, partly under the influence of the computer metaphor for mental processes (see MIND, COMPUTATIONAL THEORIES OF). Likewise, economics, anthropology and sociology use refined technical vocabularies.

A sense of the various instruments and techniques of data collection and analysis now used can be gleaned from the materials, methods and results sections of scientific journals. Journals and other means of communication are themselves of methodological significance. The available methods for presenting observational data were radically altered by the development of printing (for both text and images), and again through computer-generated images and electronic communication. The mass production of standardized illustrations and printed data permits worldwide dissemination, utilization and hence testing of scientific findings.

The structure of scientific research groups and their interaction with scientific institutions, including the processes for deciding whether to fund research or to publish results, are also part of the method of science (broadly conceived). The methodological effectiveness of science can be evaluated at various scales, including the individual experiment, the individual investigator, the laboratory group, or the institutional structures by which collective instruments such as particle accelerators are administered. One might further examine the normative consequences of having relative homogeneity of methodological and theoretical belief across an active science, as opposed to the hedged bet of methodological and theoretical diversity. The student of scientific methods may investigate any aspect of the linguistic, conceptual, psychological, instrumental, social and institutional features of the sciences that affects their cognitive products.

See also: CRUCIAL EXPERIMENTS; DISCOVERY, LOGIC OF; EXPLANATION; INDUCTIVE INFERENCE; FEMINISM AND SOCIAL SCIENCE; GENDER AND SCIENCE; HEIDEGGERIAN PHILOSOPHY OF SCIENCE; OBJECTIVITY; PHILOSOPHY OF SCIENCE IN ISLAM; POSTCOLONIAL PHILOSOPHY OF SCIENCE

References and further reading

* Aristotle (c.mid-4th century BC) *Posterior Analytics* (Analytica Posteriora), in J. Barnes (ed.), *Complete Works of Aristotle*, vol. 1, Princeton, NJ: Princeton University Press, 2 vols, 1984. (A founding work in philosophy of science.)

Bacon, F. (1620) *Novum organum*, London: Longmans; repr. in T. Fowler (ed.) *Bacon's Novum organum*, Oxford: Clarendon Press, 1888; trans. P.

Urbach and J. Gibson, Chicago, IL: Open Court, 1994. (Seminal statement of an empirical methodology for investigating nature.)

* Descartes, R. (1637) *Discours de la méthode pour bien conduir sa raison et chercher la vérité dans les sciences plus la dioptrique, les meteores, et la geometrie, qui sont des essais de cete methode* (Discourse on the Method for Properly Conducting Reason and Searching for Truth in the Sciences, as well as the Dioptrics, the Meteors, and the Geometry, which are essays in this method), in J. Cottingham, R. Stoothoff, D. Murdoch and A. Kenny (eds and trans.) *The Philosophical Writings of Descartes*, vol. 1, Cambridge: Cambridge University Press, 1984–91, 2 vols. (Seminal statement of a programme for investigating all of nature.)

Hanson, N.R. (1958) *Patterns of Discovery*, Cambridge: Cambridge University Press. (Important study of fundamental concepts in science, with reference to actual historical cases.)

Jardine, N. (1984) *Birth of History and Philosophy of Science: Kepler's 'Defence of Tycho against Ursus', with Essays on Its Provenance and Significance*, Cambridge: Cambridge University Press. (Detailed analysis of an early modern work in philosophy of science.)

Kitcher, P. (1993) *The Advancement of Science: Science without Legend, Objectivity without Illusions*, New York: Oxford University Press. (Advanced work in philosophy of science, relevant to method.)

Kuhn, T. (1962) *Structure of Scientific Revolutions*, Chicago, IL: University of Chicago Press; 2nd edn, 1970. (Widely read analysis of the historical development scientific knowledge.)

Losee, J. (1993) *Historical Introduction to the Philosophy of Science*, Oxford: Oxford University Press, 3rd edn. (An introduction, with references, to many topics in the philosophy of science.)

* Mill, J.S. (1846) *A System of Logic*; repr. in J.M. Robson (ed.) *Collected Works of John Stuart Mill*, London: Routledge and Toronto, Ont.: University of Toronto Press, 1991. (Lengthy but readable and important nineteenth-century examination of the structure and empirical basis of scientific knowledge.)

* Newton, I. (1687) *Philosophiae naturalis principia mathematica*, London: Joseph Streater (for the Royal Society); 2nd edn, Cambridge, 1713; 3rd edn, London: Guil. & Joh. Innys (for the Royal Society), 1726; repr. in A. Koyré and I.B. Cohen (eds) with assistance of A. Whitman *Isaac Newton's Philosophiae naturalis principia mathematica* (3rd edn 1726, with variant readings), Cambridge, MA: Harvard University Press, 1972, 2 vols. (Newton's

monumental contribution, forever transforming science. Contains the 'Rules of Reasoning in Philosophy'.)
* Plato (*c*.380–367 BC) *Republic*, trans. G.M. Grube, revised by C. Reeve, Indianapolis, IN: Hackett Publishing Company, 1992.(Contains a discussion of knowledge and methods of knowing.)
* Whewell, W. (1840) *The Philosophy of the Inductive Sciences Founded upon their History*, London: J.W. Parker, 2 vols. (Difficult but seminal work in philosophy of science.)

GARY HATFIELD

SCIENTIFIC REALISM AND ANTIREALISM

Traditionally, scientific realism asserts that the objects of scientific knowledge exist independently of the minds or acts of scientists and that scientific theories are true of that objective (mind-independent) world. The reference to knowledge points to the dual character of scientific realism. On the one hand it is a metaphysical (specifically, an ontological) doctrine, claiming the independent existence of certain entities. On the other hand it is an epistemological doctrine asserting that we can know what individuals exist and that we can find out the truth of the theories or laws that govern them.

Opposed to scientific realism (hereafter just 'realism') are a variety of antirealisms, including phenomenalism and empiricism. Recently two others, instrumentalism and constructivism, have posed special challenges to realism. Instrumentalism regards the objects of knowledge pragmatically, as tools for various human purposes, and so takes reliability (or empirical adequacy) rather than truth as scientifically central. A version of this, fictionalism, contests the existence of many of the objects favoured by the realist and regards them as merely expedient means to useful ends. Constructivism maintains that scientific knowledge is socially constituted, that 'facts' are made by us. Thus it challenges the objectivity of knowledge, as the realist understands objectivity, and the independent existence that realism is after. Conventionalism, holding that the truths of science ultimately rest on man-made conventions, is allied to constructivism.

Realism and antirealism propose competing interpretations of science as a whole. They even differ over what requires explanation, with realism demanding that more be explained and antirealism less.

1   **Arguing for realism**
2   **Piecemeal realisms**
3   **Alternatives to realism**
4   **The constructivist challenge**

1   Arguing for realism

Late nineteenth- and early twentieth-century debates over the reality of molecules and atoms polarized the scientific community on the realism question. Antirealists like MACH, DUHEM and POINCARÉ – representing (roughly) phenomenalist, instrumentalist and conventionalist positions – at first carried the day with a sceptical attitude towards the truth of scientific theories and the reality of the 'theoretical entities' employed by those theories (see PHENOMENALISM; CONVENTIONALISM). Led by the successes of statistical mechanics (see THERMODYNAMICS) and relativity (see RELATIVITY THEORY, PHILOSOPHICAL SIGNIFICANCE OF), however, PLANCK and EINSTEIN helped turn the tide towards realism. That movement was checked by two developments. In physics the quantum theory of 1925–6 quickly ran into difficulties over the possibility of a realist interpretation (see QUANTUM MECHANICS, INTERPRETATION OF) and the community settled on the instrumentalist programme promoted by BOHR and HEISENBERG. This was a formative lesson for logical empiricism whose respect for developments in physics and whose positivistic orientation led it to brand the realism question as metaphysical, a pseudo-question (see LOGICAL POSITIVISM, PHILOSOPHY OF). Thus for a while empiricist and instrumentalist trends in science and philosophy eclipsed scientific realism.

The situation changed again in the 1960s, by which time science and its technological applications had become a ubiquitous and dominant feature of Western culture. In this setting philosophers like Smart (1963) and Putnam (1975) proposed what came to be known as the 'miracles' argument for scientific realism (see SMART, J.J.C. §3; PUTNAM, H. §2). They argued that unless the theoretical entities employed by scientific theories actually existed and the theories themselves were at least approximately true of the world at large, the evident success of science (in terms of its applications and predictions) would surely be a miracle. It is easy to see, at least with hindsight, that the most one could conclude from scientific success, however impressive, is that science is on the right track. That could mean, as the argument concludes, on the track to truth or it could just mean on the track to empirical success, perhaps with deeply flawed representations of reality. The 'miracles' argument is inconclusive. Nevertheless, during the next two decades it was compelling for many philosophers. Indeed, during this period realism became so identified with science that questioning realism was quickly put down as anti-science.

Realist orthodoxy found support in Popper's attack on instrumentalism, which he criticized as unable to account for his own falsificationist methodology (Popper 1956) (see POPPER, K.R. §2). Broadening this line, Boyd developed an explanationist version of the 'miracles' argument that focused on the methods of science and tried as well to give proper due to the human-centred (constructivist and conventionalist) aspects of science emphasized by KUHN and FEYERABEND. Boyd asks why methods crafted by us and reflecting our interests and limitations lead to instrumentally successful science. Contrasting realism with empiricism and constructivism, he finds that realism offers the best (indeed, the only) explanation. That is because, he argues, if we begin with truths or near-truths the methods we have crafted for science produce even more of the same. Since it is only realism that demands the truth of our scientific theories, then realism wins as giving the best explanation for the instrumental success of science. Hence, like a scientific hypothesis, realism is most likely to be true and we should believe in it.

The explanationist argument is carefully framed so that we ask only about the instrumental success of science; that is, success at the observational level. To take science as successful (for example, truth-producing) at the theoretical level would beg the question against empiricism and instrumentalism. Once this is recognized, however, we can see a significant gap in the reasoning. The argument is driven by a picture of science as generating new truths from old truths, but the explanatory issue raised is only about truths at the level of observation, not about truths in general. Antirealists might well reject this as an illegitimate request for explanation. If they accept it, there is an obvious empiricist or instrumentalist response: namely, that our scientific methods are made by us to winnow out instrumentally reliable information. If we begin with fairly reliable statements, the methods we have crafted for science will produce even more. Thus the explanation for scientific success at the instrumental level need not involve the literal truth of our scientific principles or theories, just their instrumental reliability. This move nicely converts the argument for realism as the best explanation of scientific success into an argument for instrumentalism.

There is a second problem with the explanationist tactic, perhaps even more serious. The conclusion in support of realism depends on an inference to the best explanation (see INFERENCE TO THE BEST EXPLANATION). That principle, to regard as true that which explains best, is a principle that antirealisms (especially instrumentalism and empiricism) deny. Van Fraassen, for example, regards being the best explanation as a virtue, but one separate from truth. (He reminds us that the best may well be the best of a bad lot.) Although not required, there could perhaps be an instrumentalist principle of inference to the best explanation. It would not infer to the truth of the explanation but to its instrumental reliability (or empirical adequacy) – precisely the strategy pursued above where we infer instrumentalism from the instrumental success of science. Thus the explanationist argument uses a specifically realist principle of inference to the best explanation and, in so doing, begs the question of truth versus reliability, one of the central questions at issue between realism and antirealism.

2 Piecemeal realisms

Inference to the best explanation promised the most cogent version of the 'miracles' argument. Its inadequacy hastened a retreat from realism's original undertaking as a global interpretation of science. Retreat was fostered by two other antirealist developments. One was the pessimistic meta-induction to the instability of current science, a conclusion based on the repeated overthrow of scientific theories historically and the consequent dramatic alterations in ontology. The other was a sharpening of the underdetermination thesis associated with Poincaré and Duhem, suggesting that there may be empirically equivalent theories between which no evidence can decide (see UNDERDETERMINATION). Both developments tended to undermine claims for the reality of the objects of scientific investigation and the truth of scientific theories.

Pursuing a salvage operation, several philosophers suggested that realism could confine itself to being a doctrine about the independent existence of theoretical entities ('entity realism') without commitment to the truth of the theories employing them. Hacking (1983) proposed an 'experimental argument' for this entity realism; roughly, that if you can deploy entities experimentally to discover new features of nature (for example, use an electron gun to learn about quarks), then the entities must be real whether or not the covering theories are true (see EXPERIMENT §3). Cartwright (1983) suggested that the strategy of inference to the best explanation be confined to an inference to the causes of phenomena, since causes are unquestionably real. To the antirealist, however, these related strategies seem far from compelling. For one thing, it is not clear that one can so neatly disengage theoretical entities from their covering theories. Moreover, in both cases, we can see that the basis on which one is asked to draw a realist conclusion need support no more than a conclusion about utility or reliability. In Hacking's case one need conclude only that electrons are a useful theoretical construct (perhaps a useful fiction?) and in Cartwright's that certain causal hypotheses are reliable in certain domains.

Faced with these difficulties realism has fragmented even further. Sometimes it takes an historicist turn, countering the pessimistic meta-induction by endorsing as real only those fruitful entities that survive scientific revolutions. Sometimes realism becomes highly selective in other ways; for example, looking only at what seems essential in specific cases of explanatory or predictive success, or at entities that stand out as supported by only the very best scientific evidence. Although each of these principles locates matters of scientific significance, it is not clear that such criteria overcome the general strategies that have undone global realist arguments. In particular they do not seem to discriminate effectively between what is real and what is merely useful (and so between realism and instrumentalism).

3   Alternatives to realism

Several alternatives to realism have developed in the course of these debates. Principal among them are Putnam's 'internal realism' (1981) (see PUTNAM, H. §8), van Fraassen's 'constructive empiricism' (van Fraassen 1980) and what Fine (1986) calls 'the natural ontological attitude', or NOA. In a chameleon-like move, Putnam switched from being realism's champion to its critic. Rejecting what he called 'metaphysical realism' (associated with a 'God's eye view'), Putnam proposed a perspectival position in which truth is relative to language (or conceptual scheme). He could then allow scientific claims to be true in their proper domain but deny that they tell the whole story, or even that there is a whole story to tell. His picture was that there could be other truths – different stories about the world – each of which it may be proper to believe. Van Fraassen's constructive empiricism eschews belief in favour of what he calls commitment. He takes the distinguishing features of realism as twofold: realism seeks truth as a goal, and when a realist accepts a theory it is accepted as true. Constructive empiricism, by contrast, takes empirical adequacy (not truth) as the goal of science, and when it accepts a theory it accepts it as empirically adequate. This involves commitment to working within the framework of the theory but not to believing in its literal truth. Unlike these others, Fine's NOA is not a general interpretive scheme but simply an attitude that one can take to science. The attitude is minimal,

deflationary and expressly local. It is critically positive, looking carefully at particular scientific claims and procedures, and cautions us not to attach any general interpretive agenda to science. Thus NOA rejects positing goals for science as a whole, as realists and constructive empiricists do. NOA accepts 'truth' as a semantic primitive, but rejects any general theories or interpretations of scientific truth, including the perspectivalism built into internal realism and the external-world correspondence built into realism itself. NOA is perhaps better classified as a nonrealism than as an antirealism.

It is interesting to contrast how these positions respond to good science. Realism accepts good science as true of an observer-independent world; internal realism accepts it as true relative to our scheme of things; constructive empiricism accepts it only as empirically adequate. NOA simply accepts it. This brings out two significant features of the recent debates. One is that they are more about the reach of evidence (what kind of acceptance is warranted) than about the metaphysical character of the objects of belief. The contrast also shows that major contenders, whether realist or not, share a basically positive attitude towards science. This has not always been acknowledged and a contrary suspicion still attaches to constructivism, which is frequently regarded as anti-science.

4   The constructivist challenge

Contemporary developments in the history and sociology of science have revived constructivist approaches (see CONSTRUCTIVISM). Sharing with instrumentalism and other forms of pragmatism an emphasis on science as an activity, constructivism borrows the Marxist vocabulary of the 'production' of ideas (see MARXIST PHILOSOPHY OF SCIENCE) to place science among the manufacturing institutions. Specifically, what science makes is knowledge, which includes concepts and theories, along with things and even facts. Constructivism also emphasizes that science is open-ended. It highlights the role of unforced judgment in scientific practice, challenging the picture of a strict scientific method and of decision-making forced by rationality at every turn. The upshot is to see science as a form of human engagement like others; just people doing their own thing as best they can. Many regard this placement of science as a displacement, demoting science from its privileged position as the paradigm of rational and objective inquiry.

The emphasis on human constructions may challenge the mind-independence that is the hallmark of realist metaphysics. The respective roles of the social order and of nature in shaping these constructions, however, differ among constructivists, making for strong idealism at one pole (see IDEALISM) and pragmatic realism at the other. Despite these differences, constructivism challenges the unique position that realism marks out for itself with respect to ongoing science. If we look beyond the relatively sophisticated arguments for realism rehearsed above, perhaps realism's major hold on our attention is its claim to offer the only viable setting for understanding scientific practice. We are told that unless we take scientists to be engaged in finding out about a world not of their own making we cannot begin to understand how science works. The major constructivist challenge is right here. The heart of constructivism consists in richly detailed studies of science in action. These studies set out to understand how science actually proceeds while bracketing the truth-claims of the area of science under investigation. Instead, constructivists typically employ little more than everyday psychology and an everyday pragmatism with respect to the common objects of experience. To the extent to which these studies succeed they paint a picture of science quite different from realism's, a constructivist picture that may undermine not only the arguments but also the intuitions on which scientific realism rests.

See also: DEWEY, J.; EMPIRICISM; FICTIONALISM; PRAGMATISM; REALISM AND ANTIREALISM; THEORIES, SCIENTIFIC

References and further reading

* Cartwright, N. (1983) *How the Laws of Physics Lie*, New York: Clarendon Press. (Advances the causal argument mentioned in §2.)

Devitt, M. (1983) 'Realism and the Renegade Putnam', *Nous* 17: 291–301. (Critical discussion of Putnam's 'internal realism' of §3.)

* Fine, A. (1986) *The Shaky Game: Einstein, Realism and the Quantum Theory*, Chicago, IL: University of Chicago Press. (Elaborates on NOA of §3. The Afterword of the 2nd edition, 1996, brings the discussion up to date.)

* Fraassen, B.C. van (1980) *The Scientific Image*, Oxford: Clarendon Press. (The 'constructive empiricism' of §3.)

Galison, P. and Stump, D. (eds) (1996) *The Disunity of Science: Boundaries, Contexts, and Power*, Stanford, CA: Stanford University Press. (Essays by leading figures touching the constructivist themes of §4.)

* Hacking, I. (1983) *Representing and Intervening*, Cambridge: Cambridge University Press. (Advances the 'experimental argument' mentioned in §2.)

Leplin, J. (ed.) (1984) *Scientific Realism*, Berkeley, CA: University of California Press. (Significant essays that signalled a turning away from realism. The essay by Boyd expands on the material of §1, that of Laudan responds to the 'miracles' argument of §1, and purses the pessimistic meta-induction referred to in §2, while the essay by McMullin develops the fruitfulness line mentioned in §2.)

Miller, R.W. (1987) *Fact and Method*, Princeton, NJ: Princeton University Press. (Book-length defence of a piecemeal realism, as in §2.)

Papineau, D. (ed.) (1996) *The Philosophy of Science*, Oxford: Oxford University Press. (Essays by leading figures touching on many of the themes related to §2 and §3.)

* Popper, K. (1956) 'Three Views Concerning Human Knowledge', in H.D. Lewis (ed.) *Contemporary British Philosophy*, London: Allen & Unwin; repr. in *Conjectures and Refutations*, London: Routledge & Kegan Paul, 1972, 97–119. (Contains the attack on instrumentalism mentioned in §1.)

* Putnam, H. (1975) *Mathematics, Matter and Method*, vol. 1, Cambridge: Cambridge University Press. (The 'miracles' argument of §1 occurs on page 73.)

* —— (1981) *Reason, Truth and History*, Cambridge: Cambridge University Press. (The 'internal realism' of §3.)

Rosen, G. (1994) 'What is Constructive Empiricism?', *Philosophical Studies* 74: 143–78. (Critical discussion of van Fraassen's 'constructive empiricism' of §3.)

Rouse, J. (1996) *Engaging Science: How to Understand its Practices Philosophically*, Ithaca, NY: Cornell University Press. (Critical discussion of Fine's NOA of §3, and the constructivism of §4.)

* Smart, J.J.C. (1963) *Philosophy and Scientific Realism*, London: Routledge & Kegan Paul. (Defence of realism by means of the 'miracles' argument of §1.)

ARTHUR FINE

SCIENTIFIC REALISM AND SOCIAL SCIENCE

A central issue in the philosophy of the social sciences is the possibility of naturalism: whether disciplines such as sociology, anthropology, economics and psychology can be 'scientific' in broadly the same sense in which this term is applied to physics, chemistry, biology and so on. In the long history of debates about this issue, both naturalists and anti-naturalists have tended to accept a particular view of the natural sciences – the 'positivist' conception of science. But the challenges to this previously dominant position in the philosophy of science from around the 1960s made this shared assumption increasingly problematic. It was no longer clear what would be implied by the naturalist requirement that the social sciences should be modelled on the natural sciences. It also became necessary to reconsider the arguments previously employed by anti-naturalists, to see whether these held only on the assumption of a positivist conception of science. If so, a non-positivist naturalism might be defended: a methodological unity of the social and natural sciences based on some alternative to positivism. That this is possible has been argued by scientific realists in the social sciences, drawing on a particular alternative to positivism: the realist conception of science developed in the 1970s by Harré and others.

1 **Realist *v.* positivist views of science**
2 **The nature of a realist social science**
3 **Scientific realism and anti-naturalism**

1 Realist *v.* positivist views of science

Within the philosophy of science, scientific realists criticize positivism both on philosophical grounds, and for failing adequately to represent the nature of scientific theories and their historical development. Rejecting the positivists' deductive-nomological model of explanation as unable to distinguish predictive from explanatory power, realists argue that scientific explanation consists in describing the processes through which observable phenomena, and whatever regularities obtain between them, are generated by the operation of (typically unobservable) underlying structures and mechanisms. In doing so, they likewise reject the regularity view of causation and defend a concept of natural necessity together with a Lockean view of causal powers.

This view of explanation brings with it a far less restrictive attitude towards the ontological commitments of scientific theories than positivism permits. For although (most) positivists accept what may be termed the 'minimal realist' claim that science aims at knowledge of an external world whose existence and nature are independent of the knowing subject (see REALISM AND ANTIREALISM), scientific realists criticize the positivists' tendency to limit what can be said to exist to what is observable, directly measurable, and so on. They therefore reject both operationalist and instrumentalist interpretations of the cognitive status of theoretical concepts, instead regarding them as having, at least potentially, a straightforwardly referential function (see THEORIES, SCIENTIFIC). Further, whereas for positivists, scientific progress is largely a matter of the increasing scope and hence

predictive-explanatory power of universal laws, for scientific realists it consists primarily in increasing theoretical depth, with each level of causally operative structures and mechanisms being successively explained by reference to other, deeper levels. In such developments, existential hypotheses concerning previously unimagined entities – by contrast with the universal hypotheses emphasized by positivists – often play a central role.

Adopting this alternative to the positivist conception of science, realist naturalists have attempted both to articulate the character of a realist social science (§2), and to disarm a number of influential anti-naturalist arguments (§3).

2 The nature of a realist social science

Some realists, notably Bhaskar in *The Possibility of Naturalism* (1979), have seen it as their task to identify the ontological presuppositions of a realist social science, especially the nature of the agency–structure relationship (see CRITICAL REALISM). But others, such as Keat and Urry in *Social Theory as Science* (1975), have pursued more modest aims: to free social science from the unnecessary and impoverishing limitations of positivism, and to indicate what kinds of theoretical work in the social sciences would be consistent with, or suggested by, their being modelled on a realist view of natural science.

Obvious examples of such positivistically inspired limitations are provided by the various forms of behaviourism in psychology and other social sciences (see BEHAVIOURISM, METHODOLOGICAL AND SCIENTIFIC). For realists, mentalistic concepts can be seen as performing a similar function to theoretical concepts in the natural sciences: potentially referring to unobservable entities, structures and processes, and employed in theories that can be tested for their explanatory power like any others. Hence there is no a priori reason either to eliminate them altogether, to provide them with operational definitions in behavioural terms, or to regard them instrumentally, as no more than convenient fictions or predictive devices.

Nor, for the realist, need the realm of the mental be restricted to that of consciousness. Hence, whereas positivists have often regarded psychoanalytic theory as 'unscientific' or even 'metaphysical', realists may view Freud's arguments for the postulation of 'the unconscious' as on a par with those typically adduced in postulating theoretical entities in the natural sciences, and his attempts to specify the nature of its structures and mechanisms as, in principle, a perfectly legitimate exercise in scientific theorizing.

However, none of this should be taken to imply that realists do or must endorse the substantive truth or explanatory power of mentalistic or psychoanalytic theories. A realist philosophy of the social sciences provides no more guidance about the truth or falsity of specific theoretical claims than does realism in the natural sciences. This applies equally to what has been, in the work of many realist naturalists, the main example of a substantive social theory open to a realist interpretation, namely Marx's materialist theory of history and his attempts to identify the underlying structures of the various 'modes of production', such as capitalism and feudalism, and the nature of their respective generative mechanisms, such as their specific means of extracting surplus value.

Since Marxism, psychoanalytic theory and mentalistic psychology all seem to provide bona fide examples of the kinds of theoretical enterprise permitted by realism, its adoption should not be seen as implying commitment to a materialist ontology: not only material but also ideational items (such as beliefs, values and conceptual schemes) may legitimately be referred to by the theoretical concepts of a realist social science. Indeed realism would seem to be consistent even with 'idealism' in the social sciences, that is, with the claim that the social world is exclusively ideational in character: provided, of course, that these ideational items meet the minimal realist requirement of existing independently of the social scientist's supposed knowledge or theoretical representation of them.

There is, however, a quite different sense of 'idealism', according to which the 'objects of knowledge' are themselves constructed or constituted by the knowing subject, and/or by the conceptual frameworks within which specific scientific theories are articulated (see IDEALISM). Idealism in this latter sense is clearly incompatible not just with scientific realism in the social sciences, but with any minimally realist view of either the social or natural sciences. These two senses of 'idealism' are often confused in debates about the social sciences: in particular, by some post-structuralist social theorists who adopt both forms of idealism without noticing their inconsistency in doing so.

3 Scientific realism and anti-naturalism

In its most general form, the anti-naturalist claim is that there is something about the character of the social world that makes it an impossible or inappropriate object of inquiry modelled upon the natural sciences. What realist naturalists try to show, in effect, is that this 'something', while excluded by a positivist social science, can find a suitable home in a realist one.

The most influential versions of anti-naturalism focus on the distinctively 'meaningful' character of social phenomena, and argue that these require, in place of scientific explanation, some form of 'understanding': the so-called 'understanding v. explanation' thesis. According to one version of this thesis, such understanding consists in identifying the reasons that people have for their actions, and/or in relating these to social rules of various kinds. To this the realist may respond by claiming that, once positivistic restrictions on theoretical entities are removed, there are no grounds for excluding such 'meaningful' items from the social sciences, nor for rejecting the possibility of causal relations obtaining between them. Thus such 'understanding' of actions can be seen as a form of causal explanation, with agents' reasons as the mental causes (beliefs, desires and so on) of their behaviour. Correspondingly, the distinction between (physical) behaviour and (meaningful) action, much cited by anti-naturalists, may be interpreted by realists as one between observable phenomena and a theoretical redescription of these referring to their presumed causal determinants, something that is commonplace in the natural sciences.

But there are other versions of the understanding v. explanation thesis, especially those associated with the hermeneutic tradition, that are less obviously open to this naturalist rejoinder from a realist standpoint (see HERMENEUTICS). Here the concern is not with the nature of the relationship between reasons/rules and actions, but with the epistemological and methodological character of the 'interpretive' process through which the identification of these reasons and rules itself takes place.

Consider, for example, the claim that agent A's reason for action X is their belief that P, where P is some proposition. Even if, as the realist maintains, A's believing that P can in principle be seen as (part of) the cause of their doing X, there remains the question of what exactly is involved in the identification of P itself. There is surely some process of 'interpretation' here, through which the meaning or content of this proposition is grasped or understood; and similarly for social rules and the like. Nor need this interpretive process stop at 'surface' meanings: one may also go further, through various 'depth-hermeneutic' procedures, to arrive at more fundamental levels of belief, meaning and so on.

Admittedly, there is also a necessary role for such interpretive processes in the conduct of the natural sciences, namely in the communicative interactions that take place between members of a scientific community. But there, it would seem, such interpretive procedures play no part in identifying or understanding the objects of scientific inquiry themselves. For these, unlike their counterparts in the social sciences, are essentially non-meaningful in character.

The scientific realist may respond to such claims by arguing that provided the structures of meaning arrived at in this way meet the minimal realist requirement of existing independently of the interpretive procedures employed – something that is accepted by some, though by no means all hermeneutic theorists – a qualified form of naturalism remains defensible. For the interpretation of meanings may then be seen, not as replacing the explanatory aims of a realist social theory, but rather as serving to identify the nature of the entities to which reference must be made in pursuing that explanatory project. Thus interpretation, while necessary given the distinctive nature of social phenomena, is not by itself enough: it must be combined with causal explanation of a recognizably 'scientific' kind.

However, this partial concession by the realist is unlikely to satisfy most anti-naturalists. Many would deny, for example, the possibility of objective hermeneutic interpretation, or would view with suspicion the realist's attempt to assimilate the 'unobservability' of structures and mechanisms in nature and that of meanings in the social world. At this point, perhaps, what is required is a more nuanced and discriminating account of naturalism and anti-naturalism themselves, to make clear just what it is that the natural and social sciences are being asserted or denied to have in common.

See also: NATURALISM IN SOCIAL SCIENCE; POSITIVISM IN THE SOCIAL SCIENCES; SCIENTIFIC REALISM AND ANTIREALISM

References and further reading

Benton, T. (1977) *Philosophical Foundations of the Three Sociologies*, London: Routledge & Kegan Paul. (Includes a realist interpretation of Marxist theory.)

* Bhaskar, R. (1979) *The Possibility of Naturalism*, Brighton: Harvester Wheatsheaf, 1989. (Defends a qualified naturalism based on a philosophically distinctive form of scientific realism.)

Harré, R. (1970) *The Principles of Scientific Thinking*, London: Macmillan. (A key statement of the realist alternative to positivism in the natural sciences.)

—— (1986) *Varieties of Realism*, Oxford: Blackwell. (A useful guide to different forms of realism in science.)

Keat, R. (1981) *The Politics of Social Theory*, Oxford: Blackwell. (A realist response to Habermas' critique of positivism, including discussion of the scientific status of psychoanalytic theory.)

* Keat, R. and Urry, J. (1975) *Social Theory as Science*, London: Routledge, 2nd edn, 1982. (A statement of the case for realism in the social sciences.)

Outhwaite, W. (1987) *New Philosophies of Social Science*, London: Macmillan. (A succinct and informative comparison of realism, hermeneutics and critical theory.)

—— (1990) 'Realism, Naturalism and Social Behaviour', *Journal for the Theory of Social Behaviour* 20: 365–77. (Reviews much of the literature on realism in the social sciences over the preceding twenty years.)

Sayer, A. (1984) *Method in Social Science*, London: Hutchinson. (Develops the implications of Bhaskar's realism for research methods in the social sciences.)

Stockman, N. (1983) *Antipositivist Theories of the Sciences*, Dordrecht: D. Reidel. (Criticizes scientific realism from a standpoint sympathetic to Habermas' critical theory; extensive bibliography.)

RUSSELL KEAT

SCIENTIFIC THEORIES
see THEORIES, SCIENTIFIC

SCIENTISTS, RESPONSIBILTIES OF
see RESPONSIBILITIES OF SCIENTISTS AND INTELLECTUALS

SCOPE

Scope is a notion used by logicians and linguists in describing artificial and natural languages. It is best introduced in terms of the languages of formal logic. Consider a particular occurrence of an operator in a sentence – say, that of '→' in (1) below, or that of the universal quantifier '∀' in (2) below.

(1) A → (B & C)

(2) ∀x(Bxy → ∃ yAxy)

Speaking intuitively, the scope of the operator is that part of the sentence which it governs. The scope of '→' in (1) is the whole sentence; this renders the whole sentence a conditional. The scope of '&', on the other hand, is just '(B & C)'. In (2), the scope of the quantifier '∀' is the whole sentence, which allows it to bind every occurrence of x. The scope of '∃' is only '∃yAxy'. Since 'Bxy' is outside its scope, the 'y' in 'Bxy' is left unbound.

Although the importance of scope is semantic, it is usually identified with a syntactic relation between an occurrence of an expression in a sentence and a part of that sentence. In sentence and quantifier logic, the scope of an occurrence of an operator in a sentence S is usually defined as the smallest sub-sentence of S containing the occurrence. This ensures that for any two (occurrences of) operators with overlapping scope, exactly one is in the other's scope. In '$A \rightarrow (B \& C)$', for example, '$\&$' is in the scope of '$\rightarrow$', and not vice versa. When the scope of one operator includes that of a second, the first is said to have wider scope than the second; the second's scope is narrower than that of the first.

Many semantically significant properties are characterized in terms of scope. The main logical operator of a sentence is the operator with the whole sentence as its scope. Thus conjunction, universal quantification, necessitation and so on are defined in terms of scope. A variable is bound whenever it occurs in the scope of a quantifier on it. A *de re* sentence is a sentence, such as '$\exists x$ I believe that x is a spy', in which a variable in the scope of a non-extensional operator (like 'believes' or 'necessarily') is bound by a quantifier outside that operator's scope. *De dicto* sentences are ones which do not involve such 'quantifying in' (see DE RE/DE DICTO).

Differences in relative scope can affect a sentence's truth-conditions. 'Many hate a few' has an interpretation, in which 'many' gets wide scope, on which it says that many have the property 'hating a few'. It has a quite different reading in which 'a few' gets wide scope, on which it says that a few have the property 'being hated by many'. If the quantifier 'someone' in 'I believe that someone is a spy' has a narrower scope than 'believes', the sentence does not imply that there is some individual whom I think is a spy; if the quantifier's scope is wider, it does imply this.

In a well-designed formal language, the relative scope of operators is indicated by surface syntax, but this is not inevitably true in natural language. A natural language sentence with n operators has potentially $n!$ (n factorial: $n(n-1) \ldots 3 \times 2 \times 1$) readings, since there are in principle that many ways of ordering the scopes of the operators. (Not all such orderings need be linguistically possible, of course.) Such ambiguities need to be resolved by an interpretive process, or a user's intentions, before the sentence can be evaluated for truth. Some syntactic theories posit a stage in sentence generation ('logical form') at which quantifier scope ambiguities are

resolved by moving quantifiers so that their relative positions encode their scope (see LOGICAL FORM).

A quantifier's scope should be the domain in which pronouns 'anaphoric on' (referring back to) the quantifier behave as variables bound by it. For example, the occurrence of 'her' in

(1)   Every woman knew a man who loved her,

if anaphoric on 'every woman', behaves as a bound variable, since (1) is then understood as equivalent to

(1') $\forall x(x$ is a woman $\rightarrow x$ knew a man who loved x),

and the scope of 'every woman' is therefore the whole sentence.

Observe that only some uses of pronouns anaphoric on quantifiers behave like variables bound by those quantifiers. For example, consider the sentence

(2)   Garth bought some dogs and Wayne vaccinated them.

Even when anaphoric on 'some dogs', 'them' in (2) cannot be treated as a bound variable. If it were a bound variable, then the sentence as a whole would be equivalent to

(3)   There are some dogs Garth bought which Wayne vaccinated,

but (3) does not imply that Wayne vaccinated *all* the relevant dogs, as (2) does. (Gareth EVANS (1985) seems to be the first person to have noticed this.) So 'them' is to be excluded from the scope of the quantifier 'some dogs'. In accounts of natural language grammar which identify sentences with tree structures, quantifier scope is often identified with a structural relation between tree parts called c-command. While an expression in one sentence may be anaphoric on one in another, it is not possible for an expression in one sentence to c-command an expression in another. In particular, 'some dogs' in (2) does not c-command 'them'. It follows, on such accounts, that not all pronouns anaphoric on a quantifier are bound thereby.

Russell (1910–13) speaks of the scope of a description in giving his 'definition in use' for (that is, method for eliminating) definite descriptions. When the scope of a description 'the F' in a sentence S is a sub-sentence 'T(the F)' of S, Russell says S is equivalent to the result of substituting (a formalization of) 'there is exactly one F, and T(it)' for 'T(the F)' in S. For example, if, in 'Possibly, the mayor is mad', the scope of the description is the whole sentence, the sentence is equivalent to 'There is exactly one mayor and possibly it is mad'. If the scope of the description is just 'The mayor is mad', the sentence is equivalent to 'Possibly: there is exactly one mayor and it is mad'.

Russell's account makes the definite article semantically analogous to a binary quantifier.

Expressions other than quantifiers and connectives also have scope. Variable binders (such as function abstractors) and verbs which take sentential complements (for example, 'to believe') are examples. Standard definitions extend straightforwardly here.

One hears it said that proper names 'always take wide scope'. This seems intended as the claim that what is said by a use of a sentence $S(n)$, with n a proper name, is what would have been said by an appropriately related use of a sentence of the form 'n is such that S(it)', with 'it' anaphoric on n.

See also: ANAPHORA; DESCRIPTIONS; QUANTIFIERS, SUBSTITUTIONAL AND OBJECTUAL

References and further reading

* Evans, G. (1985) *Collected Papers*, Oxford: Oxford University Press. (Essays 4, 5 and 8 discuss the interpretation of pronouns as bound variables. Somewhat difficult.)
Higginbotham, J. (1980) 'Pronouns and Bound Variables', *Linguistic Inquiry* 14: 679–708. (Proposes identifying Russell's notion of scope with c-command. Difficult.)
Neale, S. (1990) *Descriptions*, Cambridge, MA: MIT Press. (Discusses and defends Russell's account of descriptions. Also discusses contemporary accounts of binding and anaphoric relations. A good introduction to these topics.)
Russell, B. (1905) 'On Denoting', *Mind* 14: 479–93. (Russell's first presentation of his account of definite descriptions.)
* Russell, B. and Whitehead, A.N. (1910–13) *Principia Mathematica*, Cambridge: Cambridge University Press, 3 vols; 2nd edn, 1925–7. (Volume 1 includes a formal treatment of descriptions and the scopes thereof.)

MARK RICHARD

SCOTUS, JOHN DUNS *see* DUNS SCOTUS, JOHN

SEARLE, JOHN (1932–)

John Searle was a pupil of J.L. Austin at Oxford in the 1950s. He is the Mills Professor of Mind and Language at the University of California, Berkeley, where he has taught philosophy since 1959. According to Searle, the primary objects of analysis in the philosophy of language are not expressions but the production of expressions, speech acts, in accordance with rules. Learning a language involves (often unconsciously) internalizing rules that govern the performance of speech acts in that language. Speech-act theory aims to discover these rules and is itself a part of action theory, which concerns intentional states directed at or about something. It follows that speech-act theory is part of a more comprehensive theory of intentionality.

1 Speech acts and intentionality
2 Defending common sense

1 Speech acts and intentionality

Searle's career has primarily been devoted to developing a general theory of intentionality, beginning with *Speech Acts* (1969), moving deeper into his analysis in *Intentionality* (1983). Pursuit of questions about how words relate to the world crystallized for Searle questions about how the mind relates to the world. The conditions of satisfaction of speech acts derive from the conditions of satisfaction of corresponding psychological states. In *The Rediscovery of the Mind* (1992), Searle reaffirms his general picture. A theory of language is incomplete without an account of the relation between mind and language and of how meaning – the derived intentionality of linguistic elements – is grounded in the more biologically basic intrinsic intentionality of the mind/brain.

Searle's view that intentional states are related to a network of other intentional states, though not indisputable, is nevertheless in the mainstream. Commitment to the network is a form of holism; only relative to a vast range of other intentional states does any single intentional state have conditions of satisfaction. His view that intentional states function only against a background of skills is less widespread. These skills cannot be reduced to rules, nor can they be explicated by appeal to intentional states themselves, for they do not function as representations. But understanding literal meaning, and in particular, metaphor, requires this background. An oddity of the background is that, though the network fades off into it, the background itself is not intentional, but still involves some kind of stance towards the world (see HOLISM: MENTAL AND SEMANTIC).

Underlying Searle's general approach is the view that any divide between the mental and the physical is logical, not ontological, since in his view intentional states are caused by, and realized only in, physical structures. However, unlike mainstream philosophers of mind who worry how physical phenomena can have intentional properties, Searle since the late 1970s has been saying that the mind–body problem has a simple solution. Instead of this problem, Searle takes consciousness to be the central issue in the philosophy of mind. He has been successful in recruiting lots of others to refocus philosophical attention on consciousness (see CONSCIOUSNESS).

In *The Construction of Social Reality* (1995) Searle promotes his view about collective intentional behaviour. There is a difference between a group of people merely running around a field and a group playing football. According to Searle, this difference cannot be analysed as the sum of the behaviour of individuals. Since bodily movements can be (type-)identical in both cases, Searle infers that the difference lies in their minds. For those playing football, each has a collective intention of the form 'we intend to play football', distinct from, and irreducible to, individual intentions of the form 'I intend to run downfield twenty yards' or even 'I intend to play football'. Rejecting any suggestion that collective intentions are the product of a mysterious Hegelian communal mind, Searle incorporates collective intentions into his individualistic theory of intentionality. Since all mental phenomena are caused by operations of the brain and realized in its structure, there too must collective intentions lie.

2 Defending common sense

Though §1 sketches some of Searle's contributions to philosophy to date, it fails to reveal his greatest impact. He has enraged the philosophical community simply by defending the unexceptional. Here is a sampling of views he fiercely and proudly defends in the face of so-called academic achievement in fields as diverse as literary criticism, artificial intelligence, cognitive science, animal and child psychology, and of course, contemporary continental and analytical philosophy: the physical world is independent of its inhabitants and would continue to exist even if they did not (see REALISM AND ANTIREALISM); the world comprises facts which make statements and beliefs about it true or false (see TRUTH, CORRESPONDENCE THEORY OF); some statements are true solely because of what they mean, others because of the way the world is (see ANALYTIC AND SYNTHETIC); some translations are correct, others are incorrect; because and only because linguistic expressions have meaning, they can determinately apply to things in the world (see REFERENCE); thoughts are in the head (internalism); because thoughts are (individuated by factors) in the head, it is (logically) possible that we are radically deceived about (the nature of) the external world (see SCEPTICISM); I am (or can be) consciously aware of my thoughts and feelings in a way that others cannot (see INTROSPECTION, EPISTEMOLOGY OF); small children and some animals think and feel; one couldn't have a mind in virtue of running a computer program (see CHINESE ROOM ARGUMENT); mental phenomena are just biological phenomena - that is, higher-level features of the brain - and so, studying the mind is studying the brain (biological naturalism); but since Searle maintains a logical distinction between mental and neurophysiological predicates, neurophysiology wouldn't give one any philosophical or conceptual insight into mental phenomena.

That it has become fashionable to contradict the views Searle defends might amaze a novice to philosophy. Even more amazing is that, though speech act theory has become academically fashionable (more in linguistics than in philosophy), it is Searle's defence of the unexceptional that has won him the reputation of philosophical maverick. Some have branded Searle an iconoclast sans argumentation, as philosophically unsubtle and obtuse. But with unflinching commitment, Searle defiantly rejects any philosophy that controverts the commonplace. Searle, not unlike J.L. AUSTIN, WITTGENSTEIN and MOORE before him, looks to philosophy for analytic clarification, not metaphysical reduction or elimination.

See also: INTENTIONALITY; SPEECH ACTS; ANALYTICAL PHILOSOPHY; ORDINARY LANGUAGE PHILOSOPHY

List of works

Searle, J.R. (1969) *Speech Acts: An Essay in the Philosophy of Language*, Cambridge: Cambridge University Press. (Develops a theory of how language is an expression of thought.)
—— (1979) *Expression and Meaning: Studies in the Theory of Speech Acts*, Cambridge: Cambridge University Press. (Further development of his theory of speech acts.)
—— (1983) *Intentionality: An Essay in the Philosophy of Mind*, Cambridge: Cambridge University Press. (Develops a theory of intentionality.)
—— (1984) *Minds, Brains and Science*, Cambridge, MA: Harvard University Press. (Criticizes the very idea of artificial intelligence; includes famous 'Chinese room argument'.)
——(1987) 'Indeterminacy, Empiricism, and the First Person', *The Journal of Philosophy* LXXXIV: 123–46. (An important critisism of Quine's indeterminancy thesis.)
——(1992) *The Rediscovery of the Mind*, Cambridge,

MA: MIT Press. (Criticizes the dominant traditions in the philosophy of mind– in particular, materialism and dualism.)

——(1995) *The Construction of Social Reality*, New York: Free Press. (Examines the structures of the world that are facts only by human agreement.)

References and further reading

LePore, E. and van Gulick, R. (eds) (1991) *John Searle and his Critics*, Oxford: Basil Blackwell. (A useful collection of essays with a reply by Searle).

ERNIE LEPORE

SECOND- AND HIGHER-ORDER LOGICS

In first-order predicate logic there are symbols for fixed individuals, relations and functions on a given universe of individuals and there are variables ranging over the individuals, with associated quantifiers. Second-order logic adds variables ranging over relations and functions on the universe of individuals, and associated quantifiers, which are called second-order variables and quantifiers. Sometimes one also adds symbols for fixed higher-order relations and functions among and on the relations, functions and individuals of the original universe. One can add third-order variables ranging over relations and functions among and on the relations, functions and individuals on the universe, with associated quantifiers, and so on, to yield logics of even higher order. It is usual to use proof systems for higher-order logics (that is, logics beyond first-order) that include analogues of the first-order quantifier rules for all quantifiers.

An extensional n-*ary relation variable in effect ranges over arbitrary sets of* n-*tuples of members of the universe. (Functions are omitted here for simplicity: remarks about them parallel those for relations.) If the set of sets of* n-*tuples of members of a universe is fully determined once the universe itself is given, then the truth-values of sentences involving second-order quantifiers are determined in a structure like the ones used for first-order logic. However, if the notion of the set of all sets of* n-*tuples of members of a universe is specified in terms of some theory about sets or relations, then the universe of a structure must be supplemented by specifications of the domains of the various higher-order variables. No matter what theory one adopts, there are infinitely many choices for such domains compatible with the theory over any infinite universe. This casts doubt on the apparent clarity of the notion of*

'all n-*ary relations on a domain': since the notion cannot be defined categorically in terms of the domain using any theory whatsoever, how could it be well-determined?*

1   **Standard second-order logic**
2   **Alternative semantics**
3   **Metamathematics**

1   Standard second-order logic

Only second-order quantification over relations will be discussed here. Higher-order quantification and quantification over functions can be treated in an entirely parallel way. Symbols for higher-order relations and functions will be omitted for simplicity. Supplement the language of first-order predicate logic (see PREDICATE CALCULUS) with variables X_n^m for m-ary relations, for all natural numbers m and n. Add to the definition of a formula of first-order predicate logic that, for all natural numbers m and n, $X_n^m t_1 \ldots t_m$ is an atomic formula, where each t_i is a constant symbol or first-order variable; and that if ϕ is a formula, then so are $(\forall X_n^m)\phi$ and $(\exists X_n^m)\phi$. Free and bound second-order variables are defined in exact parallel to the definitions for first-order variables, and a sentence is a formula with no free variables of any order.

It will be convenient always to require of any given language that there be infinitely many relation symbols of each possible number of places and infinitely many constant symbols not in it. The definition of truth in a structure for first-order predicate logic is extended to the *standard semantics* for second-order logic by supplying additional clauses for second-order quantification as follows. Consider a structure $\mathfrak{A}$ with language $\mathcal{L}$. Let P be some definite m-placed relation symbol not in $\mathcal{L}$, and define $\psi(P)$ to be the sentence which results from replacing every free occurrence of X_n^m in ψ by P.

(1)   If the sentence ϕ is of the form $(\forall X_n^m)\psi$ for some m and n, then the truth-value of ϕ is T if the truth-value of $\psi(P)$ is T in every expansion of $\mathfrak{A}$ to a structure for the language that includes every member of $\mathcal{L}$ and also P. It is F otherwise.

(2)   If the sentence ϕ is of the form $(\exists X_n^m)\psi$ for some m and n, then the truth-value of ϕ is T if the truth-value of $\psi(P)$ is T in at least one expansion of $\mathfrak{A}$ to a structure for the language that includes every member of $\mathcal{L}$ and also P. It is F otherwise.

Once given the standard semantics a logical truth is defined to be a sentence true in every structure for the language of the sentence and a valid argument to be

591

one such that there is no structure in which all the premises are true and the conclusion false, as for first-order logic. Moreover, since the notion of structure is unchanged from first-order logic, standard model-theoretic notions such as isomorphism and categoricity can be taken over unchanged from the model theory of first-order logic. (Two structures are said to be isomorphic if, roughly, there is a one-to-one correspondence between their universes that takes the interpretations of constant and relation symbols in one to the corresponding interpretations in the other. A theory is said to be categorical if all its models are isomorphic.)

It is natural to turn now to a deductive system for second-order logic to characterize logical truths and valid arguments. This does not work out nearly so well for second-order logic as for first-order.

The core of any deduction system for second-order logic will be a first-order system supplemented with quantifier rules for the second-order quantifiers that exactly parallel those for the first-order ones, with n-placed relation symbols playing the role constant symbols did for first-order quantification in the case of second-order quantification over n-ary relations.

In standard second-order logic one assumes that for any formula ϕ with all of its free variables from the list $v_1, \ldots, v_m, v_{m+1}, \ldots, v_{m+n}$ and for any n individuals $b_1, \ldots, b_n$, there exists an m-ary relation comprehending exactly those m-tuples of individuals $a_1, \ldots, a_m$ which are such that

$$\phi[a_1, \ldots, a_m, b_1, \ldots, b_n]$$

holds, where the square brackets indicate that v_1 is replaced everywhere it occurs free in ϕ by a new constant symbol interpreted by a_1 in an expanded structure, and so on. The relation is said to be defined by ϕ with parameters $b_1, \ldots, b_n$. More precisely, one assumes that the following axiom schema of comprehension holds:

$$(\forall v_{m+1}) \ldots (\forall v_{m+n})(\exists X_1^m)$$
$$(\forall v_1) \ldots (\forall v_m)(X_1^m v_1 \ldots v_m \leftrightarrow \phi),$$

where m and n are natural numbers and ϕ is a formula with all of its free variables among $v_1, \ldots, v_{m+n}$. If the variables $v_1, \ldots, v_m$ do not occur in the formula ϕ, then the comprehension axiom entails that the empty m-ary relation is in the domain of the second-order variables when ϕ does not hold of $b_1, \ldots, b_n$, and that the universal m-ary relation is in the domain of the second-order variables when it does hold.

It is enough for many purposes to consider only the predicative axiom schema of comprehension, which requires additionally that ϕ be a formula that does not contain any second-order quantifiers.

One might add other axioms to a deduction system for second-order logic. However, there is no usable system of axioms that yields all the logical truths as theorems: if a deduction system for second-order logic is *sound* (that is, if it cannot be used to derive sentences that are not logical truths) and the theorems are recursively enumerable (that is, there are effective procedures for listing the axioms and checking deductions – see COMPUTABILITY THEORY), then it is incomplete in the sense that there is a logical truth that cannot be deduced in it.

The impossibility of providing a complete deduction system for second-order logic follows from Gödel's incompleteness theorems (see GÖDEL'S THEOREMS §§3–4) and the fact that there is a second-order sentence that is a categorical axiomatization of arithmetic (that is, an axiomatization such that any model is isomorphic to a model with universe the set of natural numbers with, say, for definiteness, the relation 'strictly less than' and the addition and multiplication operations – in less technical terms, this is an axiomatization that characterizes the natural numbers completely for all mathematical purposes). (A sentence that is a categorical axiomatization of arithmetic is described and discussed in §3 below.) Suppose the sentence Φ is a categorical axiomatization of arithmetic. A truth of arithmetic is just a sentence true of the natural numbers. Thus, a sentence ϕ is a truth of arithmetic just if it is true in every model of Φ, that is, just if the argument from Φ to ϕ is valid. But that means that a complete deduction system for second-order logic would yield a decision procedure for the truths of arithmetic: ϕ is true if deducible from Φ and not true if $\neg\phi$ is deducible from Φ, and a systematic enumeration of all possible deductions from Φ will eventually decide which of these is the case. Gödel's incompleteness theorem entails that no such decision procedure is possible, and so no such deduction system is possible.

2 Alternative semantics

Instead of requiring, as in the standard semantics, that second-order variables range over all relations on a domain, one can be more explicit about their range by specifying as part of a structure the domains of the second-order variables in addition to that for the first-order variables. A Henkin structure for second-order logic is, by definition, an ordinary structure (with a universe and an interpretation function) supplemented by a third component: a domain function $\mathcal{D}$ on the natural numbers that takes each natural number n to a set of n-ary relations on the universe of the structure. For each natural number n, the set $\mathcal{D}(n)$ must contain every n-ary relation that is the interpretation of an n-placed relation symbol in the language of the structure. (This condition is frequently omitted. But no use is ever made of the Henkin structures that do not satisfy it.)

Let $\mathfrak{A}$ be a Henkin structure with language $\mathcal{L}$, and let P and $\psi(P)$ be as above. In Henkin semantics, the clauses of the definition of truth for the quantifiers will be

(1') If the sentence ϕ is of the form $(\forall X_n^m)\psi$ for some m and n, then the truth-value of ϕ is T if the truth-value of $\psi(P)$ is T in every expansion of $\mathfrak{A}$ to a Henkin structure for the language that includes every member of $\mathcal{L}$ and also P and interprets P by a member of $\mathcal{D}(n)$. It is F otherwise.

(2') If the sentence ϕ is of the form $(\exists X_n^m)\psi$ for some m and n, then the truth-value of ϕ is T if the truth-value of $\psi(P)$ is T in at least one expansion of $\mathfrak{A}$ to a Henkin structure for the language that includes every member of $\mathcal{L}$ and also P and interprets P by a member of $\mathcal{D}(n)$. It is F otherwise.

One can define a Henkin logical truth to be a sentence true in every Henkin structure for the language of the sentence and a Henkin valid argument to be one such that there is no Henkin structure in which all the premises are true and the conclusion false. If one were to restrict attention to *full* Henkin models – in which for each n the value of $\mathcal{D}(n)$ is the set of all n-ary relations on the domain – one would recover the logical truths and valid arguments of standard second-order logic. There are possibilities intermediate between considering all Henkin structures and considering only full ones: for example, that of restricting attention to Henkin structures that are models of the comprehension schema.

The second-order quantification of Henkin semantics resembles first-order quantification in that the universe of quantification is specified. That suggests going even further – to a first-order semantics for (syntactically) second-order logic. The domains of n-ary relations of Henkin structures are here replaced by perfectly arbitrary domains of objects – no longer required to be relations on the universe of individuals – and the atomic formulas of the form $X_n^m t_1 \ldots t_m$, which are now just of the semantic form of a list of $m+1$ first-order constants and variables, are interpreted using what are called 'predication relations' (which should really be called 'relation relations' but are not, for obvious reasons). For example, $X_n^m v_1 \ldots v_m$ becomes $P_m X_n^m v_1 \ldots v_m$, where P_m is the predication relation for m-ary relations, which may be read 'the relation X_n^m holds of $v_1, \ldots, v_m$'.

Once there are predication relations, there is no need to introduce any other relations, except as objects in the first-order domains – all the relations can be taken to be members of the universes of the second-order variables. It is therefore possible to assume that the only relation symbols in a first-order structure for second-order logic are those for the predication relations and equality. This is not absolutely essential, but it does simplify matters considerably. A *first-order structure for second-order logic* will be constituted, as usual, of a non-empty universe of individuals, a domain function $\mathcal{D}$ on the natural numbers that takes each number to a non-empty set, and an interpretation function. The interpretation function interprets constant symbols as members of the various universes, and it interprets each predication relation symbol P_n as a relation that can hold only between a member of $\mathcal{D}(n)$ and n members of the universe of individuals, that is, the interpretation of each P_n is a set of $n+1$-tuples with first members from $\mathcal{D}(n)$ and all other members from the universe of individuals.

A Henkin structure can be converted into a first-order structure for second-order logic as follows. The domain function $\mathcal{D}$ is simply the domain function of the Henkin structure. The predication relations are based on membership relations: the nth predication relation holds between $R \in \mathcal{D}(n)$ and n objects just if the n-tuple formed by the n objects is a member of R. Each n-placed relation symbol must be replaced by a constant symbol that has the same interpretation, now viewed as a member of $\mathcal{D}(n)$. The semantics for second-order logic with first-order structures is just a standard first-order semantics for a multi-sorted structure, that is, one with many universes. The variables associated with a given universe (in our example, variables X_m^n are associated with $\mathcal{D}(n)$) are only interpreted by (or replaced by constant symbols interpreted by) members of that universe. The device of using many universes instead of one involves less than meets the eye: it is possible using entirely elementary methods to replace structures with many universes with ordinary single-universe structures that are equivalent in a suitably strong sense.

One can make use of intensional first-order structures for second-order logic, but here we restrict our attention to extensional ones, which are, by definition, those that are models of the following schema:

$$(\forall X_1^n)(\forall X_2^n)((\forall v_1) \ldots (\forall v_n)$$
$$(X_1^n v_1 \ldots v_n \leftrightarrow X_2^n v_1 \ldots v_n) \to X_1^n = X_2^n).$$

The schema says that relations that hold of the same n-tuples are identical.

In extensional first-order structures for second-order logic, the set of n-tuples of which a relation holds fully determines the relation, and so extensional first-order structures for second-order logic might as well just be Henkin structures: every such structure $\mathfrak{A}$ gives rise to a Henkin structure by dropping the predication relations and, for each n, replacing each member R of $\mathcal{D}(n)$ by the set of all n-tuples $(a_1, \ldots, a_n)$ such that $(R, a_1, \ldots, a_n)$ is in the nth predication relation of the first-order structure. Constant symbols that stand for objects in $\mathcal{D}(n)$ must be replaced by n-placed relation symbols that are interpreted as the relations corresponding to the given objects. The resulting Henkin structure, converted to a first-order structure by the procedure described above, yields a first-order structure suitably similar to the original structure $\mathfrak{A}$.

3 Metamathematics

Dedekind observed that a set is finite if and only if there is no one-to-one correspondence between the set and any of its proper subsets. Thus, the following formula, $\Psi(X_1^1)$, on the standard semantics, expresses that the predicate X_1^1 holds of finitely many things:

$$(\forall X_1^2)(((\forall v_1)(X_1^1 v_1 \rightarrow (\exists v_2)(X_1^1 v_2 \wedge X_1^2 v_1 v_2))$$
$$\wedge (\forall v_1)(\forall v_2)(\forall v_3)(X_1^1 v_1 v_2 \wedge X_1^2 v_1 v_3 \rightarrow v_2 = v_3)$$
$$\wedge (\forall v_1)(\forall v_2)(\forall v_3)(X_1^2 v_1 v_3 \wedge X_1^2 v_2 v_3 \rightarrow v_1 = v_2))$$
$$\rightarrow (\forall v_2)(X_1^1 v_2 \rightarrow (\exists v_1)(X_1^1 v_1 \wedge X_1^2 v_1 v_2))).$$

Using this formula one can categorically axiomatize the natural numbers as a discrete linear order with a least element and no greatest element ('discrete' means that every element that has a predecessor (successor) has an immediate predecessor (successor)) in which the set of elements less than any element is finite. One can then supplement this with standard first-order axiomatizations of, for example, addition and multiplication. It is straightforward to give a first-order axiomatization of the discrete linear orders with a least element and no greatest element. The only second-order part of the categorical axiomatization is the use of the notion of finitude. That is our main concern here.

Note that on the Henkin interpretation of second-order logic $\Psi(X_1^1)$ does not define finitude: in order for the definition to work, it is crucial that the domain of the variable X_1^2 include relations that yield *all* one-to-one correspondences from X_1^1 to itself. To give a trivial example, $\Psi(X_1^1)$ holds vacuously of any set – including an infinite one – in a Henkin structure in which there simply are not any binary relations that relate objects in the set to other objects in the set. It is

clear that this example may in some sense be taken to be artificial. Indeed, the constraints we have placed on which Henkin structures are to be allowed exclude ones in which there are no binary relations whatever on some part of the universe. But if constraints are to be imposed axiomatically – that is, by restricting attention to Henkin models of some set of axioms – then no constraints help to ensure that Ψ, or indeed any other formula, characterizes finitude. Any suitable axiomatic constraints would, as was in effect shown in §2, carry over into first-order axiomatic constraints such that finitude could be characterized over the first-order structures for second-order logic that satisfy them.

But the notion of finitude cannot be characterized axiomatically in first-order logic, since first-order logic is *compact*. The compactness theorem for first-order logic states that if every finite subset of a set of sentences of first-order logic has a model, then so does the whole set. Suppose a set S of sentences of first-order logic has models in which the interpretation of a predicate symbol P is of arbitrarily large finite size. Let S' be the set of sentences including those in S plus sentences of first-order logic formalizing 'There is at least one thing v such that $P(v)$', 'There are at least two things v such that $P(v)$', and so on. Then every finite subset of S' has a model. But then by the compactness theorem the whole set has a model, in which the extension of P must be infinite. So if a set S of sentences of first-order logic has models in which the interpretation of P is of every finite size then it has a model in which the interpretation of P is infinite. It fails to characterize finitude. (See MODEL THEORY.) Thus, the notion of finitude cannot be axiomatically characterized in second-order logic interpreted using either first-order or Henkin structures.

By a contraposition of this argument, since finitude can be characterized in standard second-order logic, standard second-order logic is not compact. Thus, a sentence of standard second-order logic can be a logical consequence of infinitely many sentences of standard second-order logic without being a consequence of any finite subset of them. This is a very strong failure of the very idea of having a deduction system for standard second-order logic.

In §1, it was shown that no deduction system captured the logical truths of standard second-order logic. It now follows that standard second-order logic is also difficult to characterize in a second sense: the Henkin structures that are associated with standard second-order logic – the full Henkin structures – cannot be characterized axiomatically, in the sense that there is no set of axioms, not even the set of all the logical truths of standard second-order logic, that hold of all and only the full Henkin structures. That follows because if there were such a set of axioms (since finitude can be characterized in standard second-order logic) they could be used to characterize axiomatically the notion of finitude.

The situation is entirely similar with many other familiar mathematical notions: like finitude, many notions that mathematicians seem to feel they understand have adequate definitions in standard second-order logic but not in first-order logic.

See also: LOGICAL AND MATHEMATICAL TERMS, GLOSSARY OF; SECOND-ORDER LOGIC, PHILOSOPHICAL ISSUES IN

References and further reading

Church, A. (1956) *Introduction to Mathematical Logic*, Princeton, NJ: Princeton University Press. (An influential introduction to second- (and first-) order logic.)

Ebbinghaus, H.-D., Flum, J. and Thomas, W. (1984) *Mathematical Logic*, Berlin and New York: Springer, 2nd edn, 1994. (The mathematical results about second-order logic found in this article are proved in detail. Results characterizing first-order logic – and hence distinguishing it from second-order and other logics – are presented in an unusually accessible manner.)

Field, H. (1994) 'Are our Logical and Mathematical Concepts Highly Indeterminate?', in P.A. French, T.E. Uehling, Jr and H.K. Wettstein (eds) *Midwest Studies in Philosophy*, vol. 19, *Philosophical Naturalism*, Notre Dame, IN: University of Notre Dame Press, 391–429. (The ways in which second-order logic does and does not help in the determination of our logical and mathematical concepts are analysed in some detail, and a number of arguments and positions are carefully laid out.)

Hilbert, D. and Ackermann, W. (1928) *Grundzüge der theoretischen Logik*, Berlin: Springer, 2nd edn, 1938; trans. L.M. Hammond, G.G. Leckie and F. Steinhardt, *Principles of Mathematical Logic*, ed. R.E. Luce, New York: Chelsea, 1950. (A classic introduction to logic, including second-order logic; quite clear and detailed.)

Lavine, S. (1994) *Understanding the Infinite*, Cambridge, MA: Harvard University Press. (Though the main focus of this work is the theory of sets, it includes a detailed discussion of how a part of second-order logic plays a role in fixing mathematical concepts.)

Monk, J.D. (1976) *Mathematical Logic*, Graduate Texts in Mathematics 37, New York: Springer. (This text includes a concise but readable introduction to the basics of the syntax and semantics of second- and higher-order logic.)

Moore, G.H. (1988) 'The Emergence of First-Order Logic', in W. Aspray and P. Kitcher (eds) *History and Philosophy of Modern Mathematics*, Minneapolis, MN: University of Minnesota Press, 95–135. (A stellar synoptic treatment of the emergence of first-order logic – and hence, as a sort of residue, second-order logic – from earlier systems of logic that classified things rather differently. This article provides an excellent entry point into the modern history of the subject, with a very useful bibliography.)

Shapiro, S. (1991) *Foundations without Foundationalism*, Oxford: Clarendon Press. (A comprehensive work on basics of second-order logic and the ways in which it is relied on in much of ordinary mathematical practice. Extensive bibliography.)

SHAUGHAN LAVINE

SECONDARY QUALITIES

Primary qualities are generally defined as those properties that objects have independently of being perceived. Standard examples would include properties of shape, weight, position, electric charge, atomic structure. These properties characterize the way the world is in itself, separately from mind. Secondary qualities, by contrast, are defined as those properties that incorporate sensory responses in their conditions of application, so that the idea of a perceiver is built into their nature. It is more controversial which properties, if any, belong to this category, since not all philosophers agree that the standard alleged examples of secondary qualities – colours, sounds, tastes, smells, feels – are really correctly so classified. Some thinkers hold that objects have only primary qualities. Let us note the significance of the question, concentrating on the case of colour, which is the one most frequently discussed.

Objects appear to have both shape and colour in equal measure, but is this really how things are? Depending upon how we answer this question, we get very different pictures of the relation between appearance and reality. If both sorts of property are equally out there, equally objective, then what appears to us in perception is reality itself. When we see a material object we see something that exists independently of our seeing it, and we see the object as it is whether or not there are (or even could be) any perceivers. But if the colour of the object is inherently dependent upon our sensory responses, then the question arises as to whether what we see is really in some way itself mental. If colour is a secondary quality, in other words, do we see things as they really are? What is it that bears colour if colours are in some way mentally constituted? Do we indeed see anything at all, as distinct from introspecting the features of our own subjective states?

1 **Some theories**
2 **Assessment**
3 **Consequences**

1 Some theories

To the question, 'what is color?' a number of answers might be given; we shall mention five, and then offer some evaluation of them.

(1) An answer that appeals to the disciple of science is that to be red is to instantiate some physical property of surfaces and media – as it might be, reflecting or transmitting light of a particular wavelength. That is, whatever science says is the primary quality basis of colour in the object is literally identical with that colour. The case is thus analogous to other theoretical identifications with which we have become familiar, say heat with molecular motion or light with volleys of photons. Science has, on this view, discovered what redness really is, deep down in its hidden nature. Possibly, there is no one physical property to which redness reduces, since different types of red object might not be unified by any single physical property; in which case the proponent of the current theory will opine that it is the disjunction of each of the many physical properties that underlie redness in different objects with which redness is identical. When we see an object as red, then, we are seeing the relevant physical property as presenting a certain sensory appearance; but the redness itself has a nature that is not given to us in the sensory presentations we record with the word 'red'. Redness thus has an invisible nature, not revealed to ordinary perception. The seen is but the appearance of the unseen.

(2) Discomfort with a reducibility thesis of the previous kind is apt to prompt a claim of irreducibility. Just as some philosophers have felt that there is no alternative to accepting the ultimate irreducibility of mental states, so it might be thought that colour properties simply are what they are and not anything else: to be red is to be, precisely, red – period. Nothing more can be said, nor need it be. There is no doubt an operative causal basis of colour in objects, where this basis explains how light of certain wavelengths reaches the human eye; but it is not true that colour is simply identical with that basis. There are no informative identities of the kind envisaged by the previous theory. As with so many other concepts, colour concepts pick out their corresponding properties in the only way they can be picked out. Nothing is hidden in the nature of colour itself: how we see redness is how it is, *in toto*. Colours are not physical properties at all, save in the trivial sense that physical objects have them; they form an irreducible family of properties, not assimilable to properties of other kinds. In an important sense, they are inexplicable, primitive aspects of the way things are.

(3) Sensing a subjective ingredient in colour, some thinkers have gone to the extreme of denying outright that external objects are coloured; what bear colour properties are rather perceptual experiences themselves, episodes in the mind. Just as it is mental states to which the predicate 'pain' properly applies (see BODILY SENSATIONS), so it is states of mind that are rightly said to be red or green. Seeings themselves are what is coloured; or, put less bluntly, we must introduce items called 'sense-data' to serve as the bearers of colour, where sense-data are construed as inherently mind-dependent (see SENSE-DATA). When we say that a tomato is red we make an error of projection, spreading the mind upon the world. This type of view will then naturally go all the way and accept that the shapes of things we see are also not properties of external objects, since the shaped object we see is surely identical with the coloured object we see – it is not like a case of one object lying behind another. It will turn out then that we are not perceptually acquainted with objects in the external world at all but only with items that dwell in our minds. If there are any external objects, we do not see them; indeed, given that we do not see them, we must face the question of what point there is in assuming their existence. Hence idealism – the denial of anything aside from minds and their states. Because of colour the ordinary world gets extinguished (see IDEALISM).

(4) A radical move now might be to deny that anything is ever coloured: not any physical object, because colour is too sense-dependent; and not any mental object, because then the objective world becomes invisible to us, at best a lurking presence shrouded in deep shadow. We are, to be sure, acquainted with colours in experience, but it is a mistake to think that anything has them, in the way that primary qualities are had. To experience a red tomato is like having a red after-image: there is colour in the offing in the latter case, but no physical thing is thereby red and nor is any mental thing. Colour might be compared with a medium through which you see things; it is not a property of what is seen or of the seeing of it. Colour is like perspective, a mode of seeing rather than a thing seen. When we say that the tomato is red we can only mean that it is presented

though the medium of redness – from that chromatic perspective, as it were – not that it literally instantiates a property. Colour terms are more like adverbs of seeing than adjectives of objects: just as we see things clearly, so we see things redly (see MENTAL STATES, ADVERBIAL THEORY OF).

(5) The final theory has been historically the most popular: it attempts to register the subjectivity inherent in colour while not denying that external objects are the proper bearers of colour. By situating colours as deftly as possible between the external object of perception and the inner experience of seeing, the theory aims to preserve as much as possible of our common-sense view of the world. Colours, on this theory, are dispositions that objects have to cause sensory responses in perceivers under appropriate conditions of lighting and perceptual receptivity. Objects have physical properties that interact with light and thence with our nervous systems to produce colour experiences in us: for an object to have a given colour is then for it to have a certain complex relational property – that of having the physically grounded capacity to produce specific modes of experience in suitably placed perceivers. To be red is to have the disposition or ability to appear red to perceivers in virtue of properties that do not themselves include the property of being red – such as reflecting certain wavelengths of light. Colours are thus like such properties as fragility, digestibility, potency – powers to produce specific effects. They are indeed in objects, since it is the object that has the disposition, but they are defined by reference to the sensory effects that objects produce, so that an element of subjectivity is introduced. In effect, they are higher-order psychophysical properties – logical constructions from a (possibly variable) physical basis and a specific sensory type. The mistake of the other theories was to regard colours as monolithic non-relational properties; once we recognize their complex psychophysical relational character colours can be everything we want them to be. Out there, yes; but also rooted in what is in here.

2 Assessment

We shall mention here just a few of the salient problems with each approach. Theory (1) suffers from two main problems: first, it makes our knowledge of the nature of colour overly conjectural and empirically vulnerable; second, it imposes an absoluteness on colour concepts that they cannot plausibly bear. Thus, to take the first, if red is constituted by some underlying micro-property, then we do not know the true nature of red until we know the identity of that micro-property; and we do not know how red relates

logically to other colours until we know how the underlying micro-properties relate. But both of these consequences are highly counterintuitive. And, secondly, when we consider a hypothetical case in which the same micro-property systematically interacts with various nervous systems so as to produce different types of experience from case to case, we find that our intuitions favour the idea that in such circumstances the perceivers in question would speak truly in predicating of the objects a colour property that matches their experience, not one that matches the experience of some other privileged group of perceivers. Less cumbrously put, if things that look red to us look green to Martians, in virtue of our different sensory systems, then Martians speak truly when they describe as green what we describe (truly) as red. Truths about colour are relative, while micro-properties are absolute, so the former cannot be identical to the latter. To be more exact, given that a particular colour is essentially the colour it is – which seems hard to deny – we cannot allow that different micro-properties might constitute the same colour or the same micro-property different colours.

Theory (2) ventures little and so risks little: its chief failing, viewed as offering the whole truth, is that it turns its face against a plain conceptual connection, namely that between the colour of an object and how it appears to perceivers. As we have just noted, colour truths are sensitive to the facts of sensory response, and simply declaring them irreducible does nothing to accommodate that constitutive connection. The dispositional theory, by contrast, explicitly builds the link to experience into its definition of colour, thus acknowledging what the simple irreducibility theory ignores.

The trouble with theory (3) has already been indicated: it cuts us off perceptually from the real world, by making the proper objects of sight purely mental. And there is this correlative problem: if mental items are what bear colour, and if what bears colour is the same as what bears shape, then we are committed to holding that mental items instantiate primary qualities too. Not only are bits of my mind red – they are also spherical and hollow and heavy. But that is surely false, even a category-mistake: no experience of a red sphere can itself be a red sphere, on pain of cramming the mind with spatially extended objects, with all that that implies. The theory roundly conflates what an experience is of with the experience itself, with the absurd result that the mind comes to be credited with all the properties of the physical world.

Theory (4) is an obscure and desperate attempt to wriggle out of the kinds of problem just rehearsed. No matter where we put the colour property we get into trouble, so put it nowhere! Here the difficulty is immediate: surely it is excessively revisionary to maintain that colour words are incapable of predicating properties of anything. Grammatically they are just like other predicates, and we have no hesitation in saying that what we are seeing is red, just as it is spherical. When you perceive a multi-coloured expanse you surely experience something as having various colours; so your experience itself would have to be grossly delusory if this were, in truth, not so. Your experience is certainly not as of there being colourless things viewed through a coloured filter (whatever that might mean). The phenomenology of colour experience, as well as the language of colour, is powerfully object-ascriptive – as much so as for primary qualities.

The dispositional theory aims to preserve this feature of colour by identifying colours with relational properties of objects, while not severing the link with sensory response. It also allows us to accord the right kind of epistemological status to our knowledge of colour, since we know our own experiences with an immediacy that is not vulnerable to empirical upset. Relativity to perceivers is explicitly registered, as is the need for a categorical physical base in the object. Theory (5) thus appears to paint colour in the right hues, locating it at the appropriate juncture between subjective and objective.

But there is a fly in the ointment, which concerns the phenomenology of colour experience. For ordinary visual experience does not, on the face of it, present colours to us in the way they intrinsically are according to that theory: a red object does not look as if it instantiates a complex relational disposition in respect of appropriate perceivers; it looks, rather, as if it instantiates a simple monadic property of the object's local surface. Indeed, dispositions do not in general look any way at all (consider solubility), while colour is paradigmatically perceptual, seeming to inhere firmly in the seen object and nowhere else. This would not be such a problem if we did not hold that you can tell the nature of colours just by seeing them – that they are transparent to perception. But that axiom of common sense is put under pressure if their nature is declared to be intrinsically relational, since this is not how they appear. Should we then give up the assumption of the perceptual transparency of colour, or should we conclude that the dispositional theory gets the colours wrong? Neither alternative delights the spirit. What we need, ideally, is a way to retain the benefits of the dispositional theory while avoiding its revisionary consequences. How can colours be dispositions and yet not look like them, given that they have to look the way they are?

This may seem a difficult feat to accomplish; the authority of colour vision seems to set an impossibly high standard for the dispositional theory to meet. But there does, happily, appear to be a way through the problem, which requires but a little delicacy in formulating the purport of the dispositional theory. Typically, the theory is propounded in a strong form, as maintaining an identity thesis as between the property of being red and the property of having a categorically based disposition to appear red in certain circumstances to perceivers. The problem, then, is that this putative identity is not borne out by colour experience itself, which sets a condition of adequacy for any account of the kind of property redness is. Might we weaken the theory so as to relinquish any claim of identity while preserving the conceptual link we want to respect? We might indeed: let us say that being red is *dependent* upon the corresponding disposition but not identical with it. Or, to bring out the analogy with a similar strategy in the philosophy of mind, let us say that colour properties are supervenient upon the corresponding dispositions but they are not reducible to those dispositions – in somewhat the way that pain is supervenient on brain states yet is not reducible to them (see SUPERVENIENCE; SUPERVENIENCE OF THE MENTAL). Moreover, let us add that the dependence in question is conceptual, so that we can recognize it to hold a priori. Thus nothing else has to be true of an object for it to be red than that it instantiates the right disposition, but it does not follow from this – and is not true – that the colour is the disposition. In other words, we combine an irreducibility thesis about the colour property itself, after the fashion of theory (2), with a dependency claim about what disposition that property necessarily covaries with. Accordingly, the colour essentially depends upon the relational disposition but it does not thereby inherit all the logical features of what it depends upon. And this allows us to say that the colour is itself a simple monadic property of surfaces, which is precisely how it appears, while its instantiation is wholly controlled by a complex disposition that has no perceptual counterpart (is not seen). Note that the disposition does not constitute the hidden nature of the colour, since it is not identical to it; rather, it provides an extrinsic condition that nevertheless completely fixes the distribution of colours across the world. It is indeed a conceptual truth that colours map on to dispositions to appear, but we need not infer that we have any collapse of the former into the latter. Insisting on this logical gap enables us to respect colour experience to the hilt while recognizing the important vein of truth in the dispositional theory. Here, as elsewhere, holding philosophical explication to the strict standard of reduction – with the identity relation prized as the only respectable relation to invoke – leads to implausibility in our account of the concept at issue. Beguiling to the philosophical imagination though identity is, it is not the only relation that can serve our philosophical purposes. We need to acknowledge a hierarchy of distinct properties here – from categorical physical basis in the object to perceiver-relative disposition to simple colour property – instead of just so many descriptions of a single property.

3 Consequences

Having canvassed the options and hit upon the most lissom one, let us satisfy ourselves that matters have worked out as we would wish. Does the non-reductive dispositional theory leave us where we are content to rest? For it does have one large metaphysical implication that some may find disturbing, namely that the world cannot be divided exhaustively into a mental part and a physical part. On the pure dispositional theory, colour properties turn out to be constructions from physical bases in the object and sensory responses in perceivers, so that a fundamental metaphysical dualism is observed. But if colour properties are strictly irreducible to such dispositions, then there are properties in the world that are neither mental nor physical nor a combination of both. These properties belong to a third great category, not reducible to the other two. True, colours depend upon properties from the other two categories, but that is by no means the same as belonging to them; they are, as it were, emergent with respect to mental and physical properties. Thus, if we are asked whether colours are inherently subjective on the theory in question, the only correct answer is that strictly speaking they are not; though they may be rated as subjective in the weak sense that their conditions of instantiation include subjective facts. Metaphysically, then, colours force a pluralism of properties into our ontology, exceeding the limits of the mental and the physical.

This result has consequences for a general materialism (see MATERIALISM). It is commonly assumed, by those who favour a dispositional theory of colour, that colours would come within a materialist ontology if experiences themselves could be brought within that ontology. But that is not quite right if colours are construed according to the weaker dispositional theory, since even if experiences themselves were wholly physical it would not follow that the colours they fix are themselves physical, on account of the non-identity of colours with their corresponding dispositions. Materialism would fail even for material objects, even if it could be made to work for the mind.

Colour logic comes out satisfactorily under the weak dispositional theory, perhaps even more so than under the strong version. For the weak version allows us to hold on fully to the idea that we know, ahead of doing any science, what the intrinsic nature of each colour is, and hence how the various colours relate to each other in terms of exclusion, similarity, and the like. No knowledge of the underlying micro-properties is needed; nor indeed are we required to translate colour talk into sensory disposition talk. What we know of colour logic is thus derived directly from our acquaintance with colours as they are presented to us in all their simplicity; there is no call to reformulate such necessities into other terms (though there is a sense in which they have their origin in experiential necessities).

See also: COLOUR, THEORIES OF; PRIMARY–SECONDARY DISTINCTION

References and further reading

Hardin, C.L. (1988) *Colour for Philosophers*, Cambridge, MA: Hackett Publishing Company. (Relates the philosophical issues to the empirical facts about colour vision.)

Johnston, M. (1992) 'How to Speak about the Colours', *Philosophical Studies* 68: 221-63. (Fine recent discussion.)

Locke, J. (1690) *An Essay Concerning Human Understanding*, ed. P.H. Nidditch, Oxford: Clarendon Press, 1975, esp. bk II, ch. viii. (Classic source for the distinction between primary and secondary qualities.)

McGinn, C. (1983) *The Subjective View*, Oxford: Oxford University Press. (Sets the discussion in the context of the relationship between the world as it is independently of the mind and the world as it is presented to the mind.)

McGinn, C. (1996) 'Another look at colour', *The Journal of Philosophy* 93: 537-53. (Discusses the phenomenology of colour experience and the dispositional theory of colour.)

Smith, A.D. (1990) 'Of Primary and Secondary Qualities', *Philosophical Review* 99: 221-55. (Fine recent discussion.)

COLIN McGINN

SECOND-ORDER LOGIC, PHILOSOPHICAL ISSUES IN

Typically, a formal language has variables that range over a collection of objects, or domain of discourse. A language is 'second-order' if it has, in addition, variables that range over sets, functions, properties or

relations on the domain of discourse. A language is third-order if it has variables ranging over sets of sets, or functions on relations, and so on. A language is higher-order if it is at least second-order.

Second-order languages enjoy a greater expressive power than first-order languages. For example, a set S of sentences is said to be categorical if any two models satisfying S are isomorphic, that is, have the same structure. There are second-order, categorical characterizations of important mathematical structures, including the natural numbers, the real numbers and Euclidean space. It is a consequence of the Löwenheim–Skolem theorems that there is no first-order categorical characterization of any infinite structure. There are also a number of central mathematical notions, such as finitude, countability, minimal closure and well-foundedness, which can be characterized with formulas of second-order languages, but cannot be characterized in first-order languages.

Some philosophers argue that second-order logic is not logic. Properties and relations are too obscure for rigorous foundational study, while sets and functions are in the purview of mathematics, not logic; logic should not have an ontology of its own. Other writers disqualify second-order logic because its consequence relation is not effective – there is no recursively enumerable, sound and complete deductive system for second-order logic.

The deeper issues underlying the dispute concern the goals and purposes of logical theory. If a logic is to be a calculus, an effective canon of inference, then second-order logic is beyond the pale. If, on the other hand, one aims to codify a standard to which correct reasoning must adhere, and to characterize the descriptive and communicative abilities of informal mathematical practice, then perhaps there is room for second-order logic.

1   **First-order and second-order logic compared**
2   **Defence**
3   **Prosecution**
4   **Settlement?**

1   First-order and second-order logic compared

The downward Löwenheim–Skolem theorem states that if S is a set of first-order sentences that has an infinite model, then S has a model whose domain is at most countably infinite (or the cardinality of S, whichever is larger). The upward Löwenheim–Skolem theorem states that if S is a set of first-order sentences such that, for each natural number n, S has a model whose domain has at least n elements, then for every infinite cardinal κ, S has a model whose domain has cardinality at least κ. It follows that no set of first-order sentences that has an infinite model is

categorical. (A set of sentences is said to be categorical if any two models satisfying it are isomorphic.)

There is a complete, sound and effective deductive system D for first-order logic (see PREDICATE CALCULUS). That is, if S is a set of sentences and ϕ is a single sentence, then ϕ is deducible from S in D if and only if ϕ holds in every structure that satisfies every member of S. Finally, first-order logic is compact, in that for every set S of first-order sentences, if every finite subset of S has a model, then S itself has a model.

(In standard semantics for second-order languages, the set or predicate variables range over the entire power set of the domain. It follows that the domain of discourse determines the range of the other variables. There is an alternative semantics, due to Leon Henkin (1950), in which this does not hold. Each model consists of not only a domain of discourse, but also separate ranges for the predicate, relation and function variables. With Henkin semantics, second-order logic is complete and compact, and the Löwenheim–Skolem theorems hold. In effect, with Henkin semantics, second-order languages are treated as multi-sorted first-order languages. The foregoing discussion presupposes standard semantics.)

Second-order logic has none of the above properties. The upward Löwenheim–Skolem theorem fails because there is a categorical characterization AR of the natural numbers. Every model of AR is countably infinite. The downward Löwenheim–Skolem theorem fails because there is a second-order categorical characterization AN of the real numbers. Every model of AN has the cardinality of the continuum, and so is uncountable (see CANTOR'S THEOREM; CONTINUUM HYPOTHESIS). A corollary of these features, and Gödel's incompleteness theorem, is that second-order logic is not complete (see GÖDEL'S THEOREMS §1). There is no effective, sound and complete deductive system for second-order logic. Likewise, second-order logic is not compact.

The sentence AR characterizing the natural numbers is a straightforward formalization of common informal axiomatizations of arithmetic. The 'second-order' item is the induction principle, stating that if a property (set) P of numbers holds for (contains) zero and is closed under the successor function, then P holds for (contains) all natural numbers. In symbols,

$$\forall P[(P0 \,\&\, \forall x(Px \to Psx)) \to \forall x Px].$$

In first-order arithmetic, this principle is replaced by a scheme. Every instance of

$$[\phi(0) \,\&\, \forall x(\phi(x) \to \phi(sx))] \to \forall x \phi(x)$$

in which ϕ is a formula in the language of first-order

arithmetic, is an axiom. Thus, first-order arithmetic has infinitely many axioms.

In the characterization AN of real analysis, the second-order item is the principle of completeness, stating that every non-empty set of real numbers with an upper bound has a least upper bound:

$$(\forall P)\{(\exists x Px \ \& \ \exists x \forall y (Py \rightarrow y \leqslant x))$$
$$\rightarrow \exists x [\forall y (Py \rightarrow y \leqslant x) \ \&$$
$$\forall z (\forall y (Py \rightarrow y \leqslant z) \rightarrow x \leqslant z)]\}$$

First-order real analysis is obtained by replacing the completeness axiom with the completeness scheme,

$$(\exists x \phi(x) \ \& \ \exists x \forall y (\phi(y) \rightarrow y \leqslant x))$$
$$\rightarrow \exists x [\forall y (\phi(y) \rightarrow y \leqslant x) \ \&$$
$$\forall z (\forall y (\phi(y) \rightarrow y \leqslant z) \rightarrow x \leqslant z)]$$

one instance for each formula ϕ that contains neither x nor z free.

The difference between, say, second-order real analysis and its first-order counterpart is that in the former one cannot directly state that every non-empty bounded set has a least upper bound. Instead, there is a separate principle for each such set which is definable by a formula in the language of first-order analysis. Since there are sets which are not definable, the first-order theory has models which are not isomorphic to the real numbers. Such structures are called 'nonstandard models' (see LÖWENHEIM--SKOLEM THEOREMS AND NONSTANDARD MODELS).

One common characterization of finitude, due to Richard Dedekind, is that a set is finite if there is no one-to-one function from the set to a proper subset of itself. This can be rendered as a second-order sentence with no non-logical terminology:

$$\text{FIN}(X): \sim \exists f [\forall x (Xx \rightarrow Xfx) \ \&$$
$$\forall x \forall y ((Xx \ \& \ Xy \ \& \ fx = fy) \rightarrow x = y)$$
$$\& \ \exists z (Xz \ \& \ \forall x (Xx \rightarrow fx \neq z))]$$

It follows from the compactness property that there is no first-order characterization of finitude.

2 Defence

It is widely held, often implicitly, that mathematicians succeed in describing various structures, up to isomorphism, and in communicating information about them. When various mathematicians refer to 'the natural numbers', 'the real numbers', 'Euclidean space' and so on, they are talking about the same structures. Similarly, there is little doubt that such mathematical notions as finitude and well-foundedness are clear, definite and unequivocal. In short, it is

agreed that the *informal* language of mathematics is sufficient for ordinary description and communication of the basic structures and notions.

One purpose of logic, model theory in particular, is to 'model' the semantics of the informal languages of mathematics. Thus, one desideratum is that logic should somehow register the successful description and communication of mathematical structures and notions. As we have seen, first-order logic falls short of this. As Barwise and Feferman put it, 'As logicians, we do our subject a disservice by convincing others that logic is first-order and then convincing them that almost none of the concepts of modern mathematics can really be captured in first-order logic' (1985: 5).

A further claim is that it is unnatural to rely on infinitely many axioms, when a single second-order axiom is available. For example, if someone is asked why they believe that the second-order completeness axiom holds for the real numbers, the reply might be that the principle characterizes the numbers, perhaps citing the categoricity result. However, if asked why they believe every instance of the first-order completeness scheme, the answer is not that simple. One cannot claim that the scheme characterizes the real numbers since, as we have seen, the scheme does not characterize the numbers. Georg Kreisel suggests that the reason that mathematicians believe the instances of the various schemes is that they are consequences of the respective second-order axiom (1967). Indeed, in common deductive systems for second-order logic, each instance of each scheme can be deduced from the corresponding axiom. An opponent might retort that one can see from the scheme itself that all of its instances are true. This might be called a 'metalinguistic' move, since it invokes the scheme itself at the level of justification. Notice that this manoeuvre involves a generalization, since it refers to *all* instances of the scheme. It remains to be seen whether this generalization is any more problematic than the generalization over predicates, properties or sets. Notice also that the scheme itself is an infinite structure, and cannot be characterized in a first-order metalanguage.

Another problem with the schemes is that each one is tied to the ingredients of the particular language in use at the time. For example, if the induction scheme is formulated in a language whose only non-logical term is the successor symbol, then a very weak, decidable theory results. To obtain a richer system, closer to classical arithmetic, symbols for addition and multiplication must be added, and the induction scheme must itself be expanded to include instances with the new terminology. On the other hand, the second-order induction axiom, which contains only the successor symbol, is sufficient to characterize the natural numbers. Moreover, addition and multiplication can be defined in second-order arithmetic, as can any recursive function. Beyond that, new terminology can be added as needed, without having to modify the very definition of the natural numbers. This fits the intuition that one cannot tell in advance what resources, and thus what terminology, are needed to shed light on the natural numbers, even after the structure has been characterized.

In short, 'the natural numbers' has an informal interpretation that outruns what is captured in first-order arithmetic, and this informal interpretation plays a central role in actual mathematical practice. Alonzo Church agrees:

> our definition of the consequences of a system of postulates...can be seen to be not essentially different from [that] required for the...treatment of classical mathematics.... It is true that the non-effective notion of consequence, as we have introduced it...presupposes a certain absolute notion of ALL propositional functions of individuals. But this is presupposed also in classical mathematics, especially classical analysis
> (1956: 326)

3 Prosecution

A number of authors have either rejected second-order logic outright, or else claimed that it is not logic, but rather an obscure form of mathematics. One broad attack is aimed at 'traditional' versions of second-order and higher-order systems that have variables ranging over intensional items such as properties, attributes and propositional functions (see INTENSIONAL ENTITIES). There is no consensus on which properties, attributes and so on exist, and there is no consensus on when two properties are identical or distinct. These sticky metaphysical matters should not interfere with serious work in the foundations of mathematics, the argument goes. Mathematics itself is reasonably clear, and we should not invoke obscurity in order to develop foundations for it.

This argument does not affect contemporary systems. The items in the range of the second-order variables in standard semantics are extensional – they are sets or classes. For any collection C of elements of the domain of discourse, there is an item in the range of the 'property' variables whose elements are the members of C. The development of modern set theory shows that the extensional notion of class is at least relatively clear (see SET THEORY).

The problem now, however, is that by invoking set-theoretic notions in the model theory, we may have crossed a border from logic into mathematics. W.V. Quine calls second-order logic 'set theory in disguise' and 'set theory in sheep's clothing'. The metaphor suggests that, unlike grizzly mathematics, logic is, or ought to be, a mere 'sheep'.

Quine and others have brought a number of arguments for this judgment. One involves ontological commitment (see ONTOLOGICAL COMMITMENT). A first-order theory, with an intended interpretation, has variables ranging over a given domain of discourse. A second-order theory, with standard semantics, has variables ranging over the entire power set of the domain, a larger collection. Moreover, the usual metatheory for second-order languages, where we turn for information about the power set operation, uses Zermelo–Fraenkel set theory (see SET THEORY, DIFFERENT SYSTEMS OF §3), which does have a vast ontology. As Quine puts it, 'Set theory's staggering existential assumptions are...hidden...in the tacit shift from schematic predicate letter to quantifiable set variable' ([1970] 1986: 68).

Because of the expressive resources of second-order languages, including the terminology for sets, there are a number of rather substantial mathematical statements that can be formulated in second-order languages. There is, for example, a sentence that is a logical truth if and only if the generalized continuum hypothesis is true, and there is a sentence that is a logical truth if and only if the axiom of choice holds. But it is on the face of it counterintuitive to hold that these statements are logically true or logically false.

It follows from Gödel's completeness theorem that the consequence relation of first-order logic is effective. The set of first-order logical truths, for example, is recursively enumerable. On the other hand, the set of second-order logical truths is not. The set is not even definable in (second-order) arithmetic, although it is definable in set theory. Again, we seem to be beyond the purview of logic (see NON-CONSTRUCTIVE RULES OF INFERENCE).

In summary, many of those who hold that second-order logic is not logic seem to agree that the *informal* language of mathematics is somehow adequate to describe and communicate the various structures and notions, but they add that logic must fail where informal mathematics succeeds. There is another line of argument, less popular today, that rejects the presupposition that the mathematical structures and notions in question are unequivocal. Accordingly, the Löwenheim–Skolem theorems indicate that there is no unambiguous notion of 'finite', 'countable', 'natural number' and so on. All of these notions are relative to a background (first-order) set theory. This sceptical view is sometimes called 'Skolemite relativism'. Advocates of it adopt first-order logic because they claim that its model theory accurately reflects the ontological/epistemic/semantic situation. There is nothing unequivocal to capture or describe with either formal or informal languages of mathematics.

4 Settlement?

By itself, a border dispute concerning mathematics may not be all that interesting. The deeper matters here concern the role and purposes of logical theory. Why do we develop logical systems in the first place? Historically, a number of goals have been articulated. One of these is to present a calculus, a deductive system to codify or serve as a canon of correct reasoning. In light of incompleteness, this goal is not served by the consequence relation of second-order logic (as long as a system must be effective, or recursive, in order to qualify as a calculus; see CHURCH'S THESIS). There are, to be sure, good deductive systems for second-order languages, but they are all incomplete for standard semantics.

On the other hand, it is widely held that deductive systems must themselves adhere to a prior notion of logical consequence. This notion is often understood in modal terms. Near the beginning of the *Prior Analytics*, Aristotle defines a 'syllogism' to be 'a discourse in which, certain things having been supposed, something different from the things supposed results *of necessity*' (see LOGIC, ANCIENT §§1–3). In advance of reflection, there is no reason to expect that the pre-theoretic, modal notion of logical consequence is effective, and that there is a complete deductive system for it. Advocates of second-order logic claim that the second-order consequence relation captures an underlying notion of logical consequence, one to which deductive systems must answer.

There is a trend in philosophy to understand at least some modality in terms of language. In particular, it is held by many that necessities are grounded in the meanings of terms. In this spirit, logical consequence is sometimes defined in terms of the meanings of a certain collection of terms, the so-called 'logical terminology'. This is consonant with the slogan that logical consequence is a matter of 'form'. The logical terminology of a discourse is what marks its form, while the non-logical items determine content. From this perspective, the issue of second-order logic is whether the membership (or predication) relation and bound variables ranging over classes are logical. This, of course, is another border dispute. It should be settled by examining the various systems, to determine which are the most useful and insightful accounts of logical consequence. Perhaps

one can be eclectic (see LOGICAL CONSTANTS; LOGICAL FORM).

Second-order, and even higher-order, languages have found applications outside of logic and the foundations of mathematics. Two noteworthy examples are Montague grammar, for natural language (1974; see MONTAGUE, R.M.), and Aldo Bressan's higher-order modal logic for the language of science (1972). Although, as noted, many logicians have come to see first-order logic as too weak, it is still widely held that the consequence relation of second-order logic is too intractable for useful mathematical study. A growing research programme in mathematical logic is to develop and study alternatives which are, in a sense, intermediate between first-order and second-order.

See also: CONSEQUENCE, CONCEPTIONS OF; LOGICAL AND MATHEMATICAL TERMS, GLOSSARY OF; SECOND- AND HIGHER-ORDER LOGICS; SECOND- AND HIGHER-ORDER LOGICS; THEORY OF TYPES

References and further reading

* Barwise, J. and Feferman, S. (eds) (1985) *Model-Theoretic Logics*, New York: Springer. (Extensive treatment of many logics, some of which are intermediate between first-order and second-order. Quite technical, for the most part. Extensive bibliography.)
* Bressan, A. (1972) *A General Interpreted Modal Calculus*, New Haven, CT: Yale University Press. (An extensive, higher-order modal logic, put to a number of philosophical uses.)
* Church, A. (1956) *Introduction to Mathematical Logic*, Princeton, NJ: Princeton University Press. (Still an excellent introduction to both first-order and second-order logic.)
  Heijenoort, J. van (ed.) (1967) *From Frege to Gödel*, Cambridge, MA: Harvard University Press. (Collection of many original papers in logic, translated into English. Includes papers by Frege, Peano, Dedekind, Cantor, Hilbert, Russell, Zermelo, Löwenheim, Skolem, Weyl, Ackermann, von Neumann, Bernays and Gödel.)
* Henkin, L. (1950) 'Completeness in the Theory of Types', *Journal of Symbolic Logic* 15: 81–91. (Henkin's alternative semantics, which treats second-order languages as multi-sorted first-order languages, with separate ranges for the predicate, relation and function variables.)
  Hilbert, D. and Ackermann, W. (1928) *Grundzüge der theoritischen Logik*, Berlin: Springer; trans. L. Hammond, G. Leckie and F. Steinhardt, *Principles*

of Mathematical Logic, New York: Chelsea, 1950. (Historical source; quite readable.)

* Kreisel, G. (1967) 'Informal Rigour and Completeness Proofs', in I. Lakatos (ed.) *Problems in the Philosophy of Mathematics*, Amsterdam: North Holland, 138–86. (Among other things, a multifaceted philosophical defence of the use of higher-order languages in foundational studies. Moderate difficulty.)

* Montague, R. (1974) *Formal Philosophy*, ed. R. Thomason, New Haven, CT: Yale University Press. (Higher-order logic, put to linguistic use. The start of an extensive research programme.)

* Quine, W.V. (1970) *Philosophy of Logic*, Englewood Cliffs, NJ: Prentice Hall; 2nd edn, Cambridge, MA: Harvard University Press, 1986, esp. ch. 5. (Argument against second-order logic. Lucid.)

Shapiro, S. (1991) *Foundations Without Foundationalism: A Case for Second-Order Logic*, Oxford: Oxford University Press. (Extensive development and justification for higher-order logic. Philosophical, mathematical and historical treatment. Most of the book requires some background in logic. Extensive bibliography.)

STEWART SHAPIRO

SELDEN, JOHN (1584–1654)

Antiquarian, philologist, parliamentarian, legal historian and practising lawyer, John Selden was a major figure in the renaissance and systematization of common law. In jurisprudence, his importance lies in his attempt to develop certain elements of an epistemology of common law. He made use of history to criticize current legal doctrines, and developed a philosophical methodology in relation to the interpretation of precedent.

Educated at Oxford, Selden joined Clifford's Inn (1602) and Inner Temple (1604) and was called to the Bar in 1612. A friend of the historian William Camden and the antiquary Sir Robert Cotton, his historical writings were in large measure responses to the Reformation and to the vernacularization of English law.

Selden's work was in essence a nascent form of common law hermeneutics, a critical interpretation of legal texts and institutions. His use of philology to reconstruct the development of common law indicated not only that it was a member of the European tradition of law but also that, conceived as a tradition of judgment, English law was far more complex and diverse a cultural form than the insular profession of his day would allow. In his extra-legal writings, most notably in his posthumously published *Table Talk*, Selden did much to indicate the cultural significance of legal institutions.

In common with the historical and classicist tendencies of the Elizabethan era, Selden was concerned primarily to collect for posterity what he termed the neglected and fragmentary evidence of antique common law. In an early and in many respects exemplary work on the ancient constitution, *Jani Anglorum facies altera* (The Other Face of the English Janus) (1610a), he thus traced the inhabitants and laws of England through an imaginative and remarkably wide-ranging study of sources as diverse as mythology, literature, etymology and statuary inscriptions. The work explicitly placed the common law under the ambivalent sign of Janus and indicated in detail the diversity of nationalities and of languages that had played a part in the development of common law. The constitution was in his view plural and in many respects uncertain. The histories of English law which Selden subsequently wrote concentrated upon detailing the foreign influences and jurisdictions which subsisted within the common law. In his history of *The Duello or Single Combat* (1610b), he showed the importance of French law to English custom. In his *Titles of Honour* (1614) and in his editions of the early treatises *Fleta* and *De Laudibus Legum Angliae* (In Praise of the Laws of England) he indicated the pervasiveness of Roman influence. In *Mare Clausum* (The Enclosed Sea) (1636), his polemical tract directed against the famous treatise by Hugo Grotius on the freedom of the seas, Selden urged the use of natural law, while in *De Diis Syris* (Of Syrian Gods) (1617b) and in the *History of Tythes* (1618), his last major work, he argued for the importance of divine law (*ius divinum*). In each case the importance of historical research lay not simply in rectifying the neglect of evidence and precedent but also and more remarkably in providing a tool for the criticism of England's 'dulling custom' and of some of its substantive faults. He argued thus in *Jani Anglorum* for the recognition of the right of women to inherit public office, while elsewhere he urged reform of the law of tithes and more broadly supported an expansion of the historical method and sources of common law judgment.

It was Selden's lifelong belief that what he coined, in a work on *Titles of Honour*, as 'the Lady Common Law' could not lie alone but was rather to be understood as a member of a family of legal traditions whose ancestry could be traced across Europe and whose reason was both divine and human.

See also: COMMON LAW; LAW, PHILOSOPHY OF; LEGAL DISCOURSE; LEGAL HERMENEUTICS

List of works

Selden, J. (1610a) *Jani Anglorum facies altera* (The Other Face of the English Janus), trans. R. Westcot, London: T. Bassett, 1683. (Study of the other face or 'backface' of English law, concerned particularly with fragments and evidence of female rule and female lawgivers.)

—— (1610b) *The Duello or Single Combat*, London: I. Helme. (History of the law of duels, with particular attention to the comparative and civilian sources from which English practice developed.)

—— (1614) *Titles of Honour*, London: W. Stansby. (Extended analysis of the civilian *ius imaginum*, the law of nobility and lineage, as applied within the common law.)

—— (1617a) *Table Talk*, London: E. Smith, 1689. (Selden's most popular work, an aphoristic collection of moral conversations concerned with Christian manners.)

—— (1617b) *De Diis Syris* (Of Syrian Gods), Lipsiae: L.S. Corneri, 1672. (Treatise in two volumes addressing the history of pagan gods and the laws against idolatry.)

—— (1618) *History of Tythes*, BL 517.b.4, London: Private Circulation. (History of the canon, civil and common law relating to tithes, the tenth part of the annual increase of the profits of land, originally due to the Church. Published privately, available from the British Library.)

—— (1636) *Mare Clausum* (The Enclosed Sea), London: published by Royal Command, repr. and trans. M. Needham, 1652; a further edn, 1663. (Polemical tract attacking the international lawyer Grotius, and the argument that the seas be kept free.)

References and further reading

Christianson, P. (1985) 'John Selden, the Five Knights Case, and Discretionary Imprisonment', *Criminal Justice History* 6: 65–87. (Interesting account of Selden in his capacity as lawyer and politician at a dangerous time.)

Kelley, D.R. (1990) 'English Developments: The Common Law', in *The Human Measure: Social Thought in the Western Legal Tradition*, Cambridge MA: Harvard University Press. (This contains a discussion of Selden's part in giving relatively early definition to common law and the character of common law thinking.)

Ogg, D. (1925) 'Introduction', in *Ioannis Seldeni Ad*

Fletam Dissertatio, Cambridge: Cambridge University Press. (This gives a very helpful scholarly account of Selden's work as a legal historian and antiquary.)

Tuck, R. (1979) *Natural Rights Theories*, Cambridge: Cambridge University Press. (Selden's work is placed in its context in a historical discussion of ideas of natural law and natural right.)

PETER GOODRICH

SELF, INDIAN THEORIES OF

Hindu thought traces its different conceptions of the self to the earliest extant Vedic sources composed in the Sanskrit language. The words commonly used in Hindu thought and religion for the self are jīva (life), ātman (breath), jīvātman (life-breath), puruṣa (the essence that lies in the body), and kṣetrajña (one who knows the body). Each of these words was the culmination of a process of inquiry with the purpose of discovering the ultimate nature of the self. By the end of the ancient period, the personal self was regarded as something eternal which becomes connected to a body in order to exhaust the good and bad karma it has accumulated in its many lives. This self was supposed to be able to regain its purity by following different spiritual paths by means of which it can escape from the circle of births and deaths forever.

There is one more important development in the ancient and classical period. The conception of Brahman as both immanent and transcendent led to Brahman being identified with the personal self. The habit of thought that tried to relate every aspect of the individual with its counterpart in the universe (Ṛg Veda X. 16) had already prepared the background for this identification process. When the ultimate principle in the subjective and objective spheres had arrived at their respective ends in the discovery of the ātman and Brahman, it was easy to equate the two as being the same spiritual 'energy' that informs both the outer world and the inner self. This equation had important implications for later philosophical growth.

The above conceptions of the self-identity question find expression in the six systems of Hindu thought. These are known as āstikadarśanas or ways of seeing the self without rejecting the authority of the Vedas. Often, one system or the other may not explicitly state their allegiance to the Vedas, but unlike Buddhism or Jainism, they did not openly repudiate Vedic authority. Thus they were āstikadarśanas as opposed to the others who were nāstikadarśanas. The word darśana for philosophy is also significant if one realizes that philosophy does not end with only an intellectual knowing of one's self-identity but also culminates in realizing it and truly becoming it.

1 Vedic literature
2 The Upaniṣadic view
3 *Dharma*, karma, human goals and transmigration
4 Six schools of Hindu thought
5 Nyāya-Vaiśeṣika
6 Sāṅkhya-Yoga
7 Mīmāṃsā and Vedānta

1 Vedic literature

Hindu thought traces most of its philosophical ideas to the time of the Vedas (*c*.2000–1000 BC) composed in Sanskrit. While the corpus called Vedic literature cannot be accurately classified, it is by convention considered to comprise the four Vedas (*Ṛg Veda, Atharva Veda, Yajur Veda, Sāma Veda*) along with the *Brāhmaṇas* (liturgical works), *Āraṇyakas* ('books composed in the forest') and Upaniṣads (philosophical literature) attached to each of the Vedas. The *Ṛg Veda*, which is uniformly considered to be the most ancient contains statements that formed, in some way, the basis of important notions of the self that were developed in the philosophical schools later (*c*.200–600 AD). By the time of the early Upaniṣads (*c*.800–400 BC) the different words used for the self were entrenched in Hindu thought. All the different genres of Vedic literature collectively enjoy a sacrality which is denoted by designating them as 'not the work of humans' (*apauruṣeya*) and by the fact that they were never written down at their time of origin. They were 'heard' (*śruti*) and are considered to be the result of the intuitive insight of the Vedic wise sages (*ṛṣis*); they were handed down orally from generation to generation and many methods were devised to preserve the accuracy of the texts.

There are many terms used to denote the individual self in Hindu thought; some of them are *jīva* (from the root *jīv* – to live, be alive), *ātman* (from the root *an* – to breathe), *jīvātman* (combining the first two), *puruṣa* (from the root *puri śete* – lying in the body, embodied), *kṣetrajña* (from *kṣetram jānāti* – one who knows the body, embodied self). Thus, it can be seen that the self in all these meanings differs from the usual notion of ego: what a person is, their identity, etc., with which one associates the self in ordinary understanding. While we cannot believe that Vedic literature, as it exists today, contains early thought pertaining to the question of personal identity, what we do have is fairly representative of the directions this inquiry took. More importantly, these meanings persisted and were standardized in the course of time,

so that in the later schools of philosophy (*c*.200–600 AD), as well as in popular Hinduism, these were accepted as words that convey the idea of the self.

The inquiry in the Upaniṣads was mainly speculative. It had the dual purpose of finding the ultimate principle that was the basis of the universe and the true nature of the individual self. The first inquiry led to the postulation of Brahman (from root *bṛh* – to expand, burst forth) as the source behind the universe. This was the culmination of the trend set in hymns like *Ṛg Veda* 1.164.46, 10.81, 10.90, 10.129, where different ideas are expressed regarding the ultimate source of the universe. This concept finally settled down with the notion of Brahman being described both as immanent in the cosmos (Chāndogya Upaniṣad 3.14.1, 7.25.2) and as transcending the same (Bṛhadāraṇyaka Upaniṣad 3.8).

The other inquiry was directed towards discovering the identity of the self by analysing the inner nature of the human being. Having arrived at the conclusion that the individual self cannot be identified with any one of the senses (both motor and cognitive), through a process of elimination (Kena Upaniṣad 3.4) the mind as being the self was also ruled out as it was obvious that all mental states had something other than the mind as their referent which was also constant. While this form of inquiry was a process from the gross to the subtle elements, another feature was the observation that the 'sense-of-I' (personal identity) was invariably associated with consciousness (self-awareness) and knowledge. This, combined with the persistence of the 'sense-of-I' in all the three states of waking, dreaming and deep sleep led to the postulation of the *ātman* being the inner self, which is the ultimate principle (Bṛhadāraṇyaka Upaniṣad 4.3 and 4).

There were other trends which were growing in the same period which would contribute to the enrichment of the concept of *ātman*. By the time of the Upaniṣads the concepts of *dharma* (from root *dhṛ* – to sustain, support, behave in a human way) and that of karma (from root *kṛ* – to act (ritually)) had evolved into metaphysical principles. The goals of life called *puruṣārthas* had also been formulated by this time as the pursuit of *dharma*, artha (economic goal constituting *dharma*), *kāma* (sensual fulfilment within *dharma*) and finally *mokṣa* (liberation from bondage, or to a state of one's true nature).

All these ideas working on the self meant that good karma will result in a good life on earth, while its opposite will lead to a bad life. Since one single life could not adequately explain the inequalities present in life, the same self came to be considered eternal, taking birth repeatedly after the fall of the body (death) until such time as it realizes the futility of this worldly existence (see KARMA AND REBIRTH, INDIAN CONCEPTIONS OF). The way to realize that was to overcome the ignorance of identifying the self with the body through experiencing the true nature of the self, either by following the path of knowledge, of disinterested action (action for its own sake without thinking of the result or reward), or the path of devotion. In the course of time these came to be the famous threefold paths of *jñāna mārga* (knowledge path), *karma mārga* (action path) and *bhakti mārga* (devotion path). Yoga also came to be recognized as a path by the time of the *Bhagavad Gītā* (*c*.200 BC). The state of liberation was called variously *mokṣa*, *apavarga*, *nirvāṇa*, *kaivalya*, *sāyujya* and so on.

2 The Upaniṣadic view

By pursuing a methodology that mainly combined perception, inference, experience and speculation the Upaniṣads reach a startling and bold conclusion. This was the identification of the ultimate truth underlying the universe called Brahman with the inner self of all beings called the *ātman*. It was the same *ātman* that was present in all living beings, the differences seen being attributed to the nature of the respective body it occupies (see BRAHMAN). The journey that ended in this equation can be described in a twofold manner: one that approached the question in an objective, external direction; the other which turned its attention to the inner nature of oneself, or adopted a subjective approach.

The objective search went through the exercise of finding the ultimate principle that underlies the universe (*Ṛg Veda* 10.31.7). But significant to the *ātman*–Brahman equation is the tendency to find a correspondence between the individual and the universe in a 'micro–macro' paradigm that manifests itself very early in the period, for example, in the *Ṛg Veda* 10.90, 10.16, *Atharva Veda* 11.4, Aitareya Upaniṣad 1, Chāndogya Upaniṣad 3.16.1, 5.11–18. This came to be known as the affinity (*bandhutā*) theory. Side by side there was the tendency to assign the world an inferior status compared to the transcendent nature of Brahman (*Ṛg Veda* 10.129).

The subjective approach, on the other hand, analysed the inner person in a twofold manner. One was the approach from the gross to the subtle and the other was from the point of view of knowledge and the principle of consciousness. The first approach led to the elimination of all motor senses and the senses of knowledge as being the self (Kena Upaniṣad 3, 4). Even the mind was ruled out as the enduring self for it was obvious that all mental states referred to something other than themselves as a basis for those states and also this referent was a constant factor under-

lying all mental states, as in the Kaṭha Upaniṣad 2.2.1, 3.5, 3.10. and the Kena Upaniṣad 1.4.8. It was also observed that the self was always associated with any event of cognition.

Another interesting discovery was the fact of the persistence of the 'sense-of-I' in the three states of waking, dreaming and deep sleep. The deep sleep identity was explained by the fact that the person who gets up from such a slumber recognizes their own identity as the one who had that experience of sleep. As these three states were still within the realm of worldly existence, *ātman* was viewed as transcending these three states and reaching its pure form in a fourth stage which is identified with the state of freedom (Chāndogya Upaniṣad 8.6, Māṇḍūkya Upaniṣad 1).

The affinity phenomenon, combined with the immanent and transcendent nature of both *ātman* and Brahman, made it easy to equate the one with the other. Thus by the time of the Upaniṣads the *ātman* was established as the self in any living being, it was of the nature of pure consciousness, it was identified with Brahman very often denoted by the word *paramātman* (highest self) and was of the nature of both immanence and transcendence (Bṛhadāraṇyaka Upaniṣad 2.4.14, Taittirīya Upaniṣad 2.1–5). As for the question of whether this *ātman* can be known like any other event in knowledge, the Upaniṣads seem to suggest only an intuitive realization of the self which is different from knowledge understood in everyday life (Kena Upaniṣad 2.2, Kaṭha Upaniṣad 2.23).

3 *Dharma*, karma, human goals and transmigration

There were many other ideas which reached maturity during the time of the Upaniṣads and which led to the theory of the permanent nature of the *ātman*. The Brahman–*ātman* equation and their status as the final truth in an interchangeable manner posed a problem for the philosopher; if something is existent in an absolute sense it cannot be negated at any time or in any sense. Thus, in order to preserve the immutable nature of *ātman* it was conceived as being a permanent entity, existing even after the fall of the body (Māṇḍūkya Upaniṣad 4.40, Kaṭha Upaniṣad 2.18, *Bhagavad Gītā* 2.16).

The concepts of *dharma* and karma had evolved into metaphysical principles that held sway over the lives of individual selves on this earth. It is not possible to trace all the nuances of meaning that *dharma* went through before it settled down to mean virtue, merit, good conduct and also to be raised to the status of the first of the goals of human beings. These goals were four in number, called *dharma*, *artha* (pursuit of economic ends within *dharma*), *kāma* (legitimate sensual pleasure within *dharma*) and *mokṣa* (liberation from repeated births to deaths).

Karma meanwhile had also grown into a fully fledged theory out of the necessity to explain inequalities seen in the world. It was a theory of ethics relating one's life on earth to the kind of deeds one had done in past lives (Kaṭha Upaniṣad 2.2.7). In this way, since the inexplicable details of a single life could not be explained, the self came to be accepted as a permanent entity that transmigrates from one birth to another until it realizes its true nature. This realization could come through knowledge, disinterested action or devotion. Later Yoga also came to be recognized as a means to the final goal.

We now get a concept of the self which is eternal, connected with a body due to its own good or bad deeds, capable of realizing its true nature by following the spiritual path best suited to itself, which finally escapes the circle of births and deaths attaining *mokṣa*. The nature of *mokṣa* that the self attains will depend on the kind of ontological status assigned to the final truth in each philosophical system. Some retain a theistic, cosmic view of the ultimate while others favour a monistic, acosmic perception. While the goal of *mokṣa* may be defined variously depending on the nature of Brahman, the self is viewed in the same way in practically all schools of Hindu thought.

4 Six schools of Hindu thought

The six schools of Hindu thought are collectively called the *āstikadarśanas*. *Āstika* stands for that which does not reject the authority of Vedic literature and *darśana* literally means vision. Thus, *darśana* is the equivalent of philosophy in the Hindu context. It also indicates that philosophy does not end with just an intellectual understanding of what the 'self' is, but it culminates in 'seeing it' or 'becoming it'.

The six *darśanas* are Nyāya, Vaiśeṣika, Sāṅkhya, Yoga, Mīmāṃsā and Vedānta. While each of these systems had an independent beginning, some came to be designated jointly as twin systems because of certain affinities in their metaphysical theories. Thus, after the grouping, the six systems are referred to as Nyāya-Vaiśeṣika, Sāṅkhya-Yoga and Mīmāṃsā-Vedānta in the philosophical treatment of the schools. Each of these developed its own extensive theories regarding both ontological and epistemological categories, but all were in agreement regarding the eternal nature of the individual self and in its ultimate liberation from births and deaths, however they may differ in detail. These schools can also be viewed as representing different philosophical approaches to the understanding of the ultimate categories. They range from the most realistic (Nyāya-Vaiśeṣika) to the most idealistic (Advaita Vedānta) in the way they approach the theory of the *ātman*.

5 Nyāya-Vaiśeṣika

As the name signifies Nyāya (reasoning) lays emphasis on the method of critical reasoning. Vaiśeṣika, on the other hand, is derived from the word for particularity (*viśeṣa*) which is one of its ultimate categories. It conveys a sense of differentiation even between things which cannot be otherwise differentiated. Among the six schools Nyāya-Vaiśeṣika is the most realistic as it believes in the independent existence of objects in the world. All objects of experience are divided into seven classes in the Vaiśeṣika: one of them is known as substance (*dravya*). We will pay attention only to the substances, of which there are nine, one of which is *ātman*; the other eight are earth, water, light, air, ether, space, time and the mind. The Nyāya has a scheme of sixteen ultimate philosophical topics and the seven of Vaiśeṣika come under its second topic called knowable things (*prameya*) (see ONTOLOGY IN INDIAN PHILOSOPHY).

Since the treatment of *ātman* is similar in both Nyāya and Vaiśeṣika, henceforth it will be treated as a single school for purposes of the *ātman* problem. The *ātman* is unique, eternal, all-pervading and there are as many selves as there are bodies associated with them. Consciousness is not intrinsic to *ātman*, but it is only one of the many qualities that the self has. It is not only an essential quality but also an adventitious attribute along with desire, volition, pleasure, pain, love, aversion, virtue and vice.

The system is in agreement with the general theory of the bondage of the *ātman* in the round of births and deaths. The reason for this state is lack of true knowledge of the self as distinct from all other things, which is the reason for pain. When correct knowledge dawns through study of the sacred books and by the practice of Yoga, there is the destruction of ignorance and the achievement of the goal of liberation. The fact that the self does not also have the attribute of consciousness in liberation means that the self is not conscious of its own freedom. Although a Supreme self known as the Lord (*Īśvara*) is admitted in the school, it is restricted to being the efficient cause of the world and does not extend to the sphere of liberation of the individual self. Nyāya and Vaiśeṣika do not believe in liberation while still in an embodied state as some of the other systems do (see NYĀYA-VAIŚEṢIKA).

6 Sāṅkhya-Yoga

The school of Sāṅkhya-Yoga recognizes two ultimate ontological categories called *prakṛti* (material nature) and *puruṣa* (personal self). The selves are also many as in Nyāya and Vaiśeṣika. While Sāṅkhya and Yoga agree in this classification, Yoga also believes in God, who is described as a unique person different from both material nature and the personal selves in bondage; God has never been subject to the bondage of births and deaths (see GOD, INDIAN CONCEPTIONS OF §4). The evolution of the universe takes place from material nature, which is composed of three material qualities. Material nature is perpetually in motion and replicates itself when there is an equilibrium of the constituent qualities. When this balance is upset evolution is set in motion and leads to the unfolding of the different principles. In Sāṅkhya the basis for the evolution to start is the presence of the *puruṣa*: it is not clear whether one self or many selves are intended here, but some kind of connection with karma seems to be suggested. It is this difficulty that Yoga tries to overcome by postulating a God who effects the association of material nature with the unseen karma of selves and starts the process of evolution. However, the concept of a Supreme self over and above the other selves seems more a practical necessity and does not serve any philosophical purpose.

In Sāṅkhya-Yoga the self is characterized by pure consciousness, unlike in Nyāya and Vaiśeṣika, where consciousness is only one of the attributes of the soul. It is the false identity of the *puruṣa* with material nature (which in its psychological and bodily effects are represented by intellect, ego-sense, mind, five motor senses, five senses of knowing, five subtle elements, the five gross elements of earth, water, fire, wind and ether), which is called ignorance that causes bondage to the self. This false identification comes about due to the capacity of the intellect to reflect *puruṣa* onto itself as a mirror, which then imagines itself to be the experiencer of all that happens. This false knowledge has to be rectified by true knowledge. This is the stage when discriminate discernment as to the true nature of *puruṣa* and material nature dawns. There is a difference in the way this stage is described in Sāṅkhya and Yoga, but both generally agree to it in essence.

It is perhaps in the means that one adopts for liberation that the two still retain their distinctiveness. The Sāṅkhya does not elaborate on it and mentions only meditation on the difference between material nature and *puruṣa* as the means (*Sāṅkhyakārikā* 64). This resembles the Nyāya and Vaiśeṣika approach through study, reflection and applied meditation. On the other hand, Yoga lays down an elaborate plan of psychological preparation which will result in isolating *puruṣa* from its entanglement with material nature through an eightfold path of Yoga.

While Sāṅkhya describes this state of liberation as *apavarga* (escape from pain), Yoga calls it *kaivalya* (the self abiding alone in its own nature). Both Sāṅkhya and Yoga believe that this liberation can be attained while still living in the world. The second liberation is that which comes on the fall of the body and is termed *videhamukti* (see SĀṄKHYA).

7 Mīmāṃsā and Vedānta

These two systems can be discussed together as they have some common understanding of the Vedas, although they differ in their basic philosophy. Of all the six systems, the Mīmāṃsā assigns a paramount position to the ritualistic portion of the Vedas (*brāhmaṇas*). Ritual is the pivot around which its ontology and epistemology are built. As it accords an inferior status to the Upaniṣads (that come at the end of the Veda and are known as Vedānta), it is called Pūrva Mīmāṃsā (reflection on the earlier portion of the Veda). Opposed to this is the Uttara Mīmāṃsā, for whom the Upaniṣads are the quintessence of philosophy.

The selves in Mīmāṃsā are eternal, all-pervasive, have knowledge as their attribute, are many and are completely under the control of ritualistic activity (karma), which is also at the back of the formation of the world of objects. As karma is self-sufficient to explain both the world and the selves there is no belief in the existence of God. It is thus a realistic school which postulates the continuation of the self after death in another world until it returns to the earth after reaping the fruit of its ritual acts in the previous life.

Virtue (*dharma*) and vice (*adharma*) are called together *apūrva* (something never known before) and are the result of ritual action. *Dharma* is defined in the school as an injunction to perform a deed (sacrifice), and *adharma* is its opposite. One learns of what is *dharma* and *adharma* from the Vedas. Karma in this scheme is described mainly as threefold: first, done to obtain some desired result, like the gaining of heaven after death; second, prohibited, as its indulgence will lead to undesirable results; third, mandatory, the performance of which is for its own sake (see DUTY AND VIRTUE, INDIAN CONCEPTIONS OF).

If one then acts as instructed by the Veda, the highest result of liberation (which in its earlier stages was equivalent to attaining heaven through *dharma*, or even equivalent *dharma* per se) would be accomplished. This is now understood, like all the other systems, as an end to the round of births and deaths for the individual self and a cessation of its relation to the world. In liberation all attributes of the self, including that of consciousness, also disappear. Thus it resembles Nyāya-Vaiśeṣika in the state of liberation, except that it retains the potential to manifest these qualities. However, once liberation is achieved, according to the Mīmāṃsā view, there will be no need for the self to manifest such attributes as consciousness. Again as in Nyāya-Vaiśeṣika and Sāṅkhya-Yoga, the state of liberation is described negatively as *apavarga*, an escape from worldly existence (*saṃsāra*). As in Nyāya-Vaiśeṣika, liberation is also only obtained on the fall of the body and there is no belief in being liberated while still alive (see MĪMĀṂSĀ).

Vedānta is based on the three works the *Brahma-sūtra*, the Upaniṣads and the *Bhagavad Gītā*. These three together are known as the Three Texts and at least six schools of Vedānta, along with many variations, have sprung up, divided according to the way the Three Texts have been interpreted. While these schools differ in the ultimate ontological categories and in the relationship of the ultimate being to the individual self, they do not differ substantially in their understanding of the nature of the self.

Since Advaita is the earliest of the Vedānta schools, we can start with the nature of the self given in it. This system pursues relentlessly the logic of monism in the Upaniṣads and maintains the nondual nature of the ultimate truth called Brahman, which is identified with *ātman* (individual self) and is the only reality, all others including the world being explained as a superimposition on Brahman due to ignorance. Brahman is intrinsically without attributes, but it is of the essence of existence, consciousness, and bliss, and it is infinite (Taittirīya Upaniṣad 2.1). Even God is only a superimposition and is brought in to make sense of the world of objects. The individual self, which in all other systems is an ultimate entity, is here a complex of Brahman characterized as an eternal witness and the objective internal organ (see MONISM, INDIAN).

This complex called the living soul (*jīva*) serves to explain among other things the notion of ego that is superimposed on the pure witness. The living soul is caught up in the world of births and deaths due to beginningless karma and identifies itself with the body and the senses. Since the self is really Brahman, only in association with the internal organ, liberation is not some state to be achieved but is to be realized in experience. The obstacle of ignorance has to be removed and this makes Advaita assign paramount importance to knowledge as the only means to liberation.

Such knowledge, which results in an identity experience with Brahman, can only be of a rare kind. Although the direct means is knowledge, there is a preliminary training which strengthens detachment from the world and cultivates a strong desire for liberation. Then comes the rigorous study under a *guru*, someone who has realized the truth of the Upaniṣads. Next there is the following of the instructions introspectively through reasoning and finally the aspirant must engage in constant meditation on the truth reasoned out. Such a course will result in an immediate experience of the identity with Brahman in the form *aham brahma asmi* ('I am Brahman' (Bṛhadāraṇyaka Upaniṣad 1.4.10)). This is possible while still in the body. When the body falls, the self, being disassociated from ignorance, stays as Brahman.

The other Vedānta schools consider the self not in the complex way that Advaita does; they essentially differ in recognizing a personal god as the ultimate entity; the self is eternal, characterized by knowledge and bliss in all these schools; in addition the Dvaita school also believes that each living soul is different from every other. All the schools believe in the bondage of the selves due to karma and ignorance; they are all in agreement about devotion to God being the highest means to liberation. But the liberation is one in which duality persists; they also do not believe in liberation during life, as the ontology assumes attainment of liberation in another world, in which one's God resides (see VEDĀNTA).

See also: BUDDHIST CONCEPT OF EMPTINESS; BUDDHIST PHILOSOPHY, INDIAN; HEAVEN, INDIAN CONCEPTIONS OF; HINDU PHILOSOPHY; MIND, INDIAN PHILOSOPHY OF; RĀMĀNUJA; ŚAṄKARA; SOUL, NATURE AND IMMORTALITY OF THE

References and further reading

Belvakar, S.K. and Ranade, R.D. (1927) *History of Indian Philosophy*, Poona: Bilvakunja Publishing House. (An excellent background to Indian philosophy.)

* *Bhagavad Gītā* (Song of God) (*c.*200 BC), trans. F. Edgerton, *The Bhagavad Gītā*, Harvard Oriental Series 38–9, Cambridge, MA: Harvard University Press, 1944. (A fairly accurate translation of the most important text of Hinduism.)

Chatterjee S. and Datta, D. (1960) *An Introduction to Indian Philosophy*, Calcutta: University of Calcutta. (A good introduction to the six schools.)

Das Gupta, S.N. (1975) *A History of Indian Philosophy*, vols 1, 3 and 5, Delhi: Motilal Banarsidass. (Has detailed information on the six schools.)

Hiriyanna, M. (1952) *Outlines of Indian Philosophy*, London: George Allen & Unwin. (One of the best books in Indian philosophy both for undergraduate and graduate students.)

R.E. Hume (trans.) (1931) *The Thirteen Principal Upaniṣads*, 2nd edn trans. R.E. Hume, London: Oxford University Press, 2nd edn. (Gives a good introduction to Upaniṣadic thought.)

Radhakrishnan, S. (1966) *Indian Philosophy*, vols 1 and 2, London: George Allen & Unwin. (Detailed approach to philosophical schools along with comparisons to Western thought where relevant. As a general survey of Indian thought these two volumes are still the best.)

Griffith, R.T.H. (trans.) (1987) *Hymns of the Ṛg Veda*, revised 3rd edn with popular commentary, New Delhi: Munshiram Manoharlal, 2 vols. (Provides a good background to Vedic poetry.)

* *Sāṅkhyakārikā of Īsvara-kṛṣna*, trans. T.G. Mainkar, Poona: Oriental Book Agency, 1964. (Deals with the Sāṅkhya school and has a good translation of the kārikās.)

* Upaniṣads (800–300 BC), trans. P. Olivelle, *Upaniṣads*, Oxford: Oxford University Press, 1996. (A new translation that may well be the best; readable and accurate.)

T.S. RUKMANI

SELF, POSTMODERN CRITIQUE OF *see* SUBJECT, POSTMODERN CRITIQUE OF

SELF-AWARENESS IN INDIAN PHILOSOPHY *see* AWARENESS IN INDIAN THOUGHT

SELF-CONTROL

A human person or self possesses powers that can come into conflict. Reason may have to struggle to overcome contrary desire. Self-control may be characterized as the ability to regulate or resolve such conflict correctly. A well-ordered self has self-control; a disordered self lacks it. When an agent lacks self-control, inner conflict often results in the victory of evil over good. Philosophers such as Plato, Aristotle, and Kant have painted portraits of the disordered self. They are alike in portraying its actions as stemming from appetites or desires that are not properly ruled by some 'higher part' of the self. These philosophers have also proposed accounts of the well-ordered self. They are alike in depicting it as a self in which a part of the self connected with reason or wisdom governs a 'lower part' associated with appetites or desires.

1   **The disordered self**
2   **The well-ordered self**

1   The disordered self

According to PLATO, a disordered self is a soul whose parts or components are in conflict. The *Phaedrus* likens the soul to the union of powers in a pair of horses and their charioteer. One of the horses struggles against control by the charioteer. If the rebellion were to succeed, the soul would do something evil the charioteer does not want to do. In Plato's *Republic*, the soul is divided into rational, spirited and appetitive parts. A struggle for control between the rational part and the spirited part or the appetitive part occurs in a disordered self.

For ARISTOTLE, a disordered self is an incontinent or akratic self (*Nicomachean Ethics*). It suffers from weakness of will or *akrasia* (see AKRASIA). Suppose some people on a diet ought not to eat sweets. Knowing this, when they perceive that this piece of cake is sweet, their practical reasoning should move them to reject it. But if they are incontinent, an appetite for pleasure may make another line of reasoning more salient. In the presence of an appetite for pleasures of taste, if they believe that all sweet things are pleasant, their perception that the piece of cake is sweet may move them to eat it. Though they are aware that they ought not to eat sweets, they eat the cake because their reasoning is unduly influenced by an appetite.

Aristotle recognized two kinds of incontinence: the weak deliberate about what to do but fail, on account of their passions, to stand by their conclusions; the impetuous fail to deliberate, in some cases because they are too quick to make up their minds and in others because their appetites are too strong. Both the weak and the impetuous are apt to be aware of the general practical principle that should determine their actions. Hence, as Aristotle observes, the incontinent are likely to repent, acknowledging in retrospect that they have done something they should not have done.

According to Kant (1793), the disordered self suffers from a radical evil in human nature. Influenced by the Christian doctrine of original sin, Kant believed that there is a propensity to evil deep in all of us. We bring it upon ourselves by freely adopting a policy for acting that does not respect the proper order of the incentives for the will. The incentives provided by our inclinations or sensuous desires always ought to be subordinated to the incentive of respect for the moral law in the maxims on which we act. A policy that does not respect this order manifests itself in particular cases in the frailty, impurity, or wickedness of the human heart. The frail are those in whom the incentive of respect for moral law proves in practice to be weaker than their inclinations; they want to act morally but do not do so. The impure are those by whom dutiful actions are done not purely for duty's sake; they act in accord with the moral law but from mixed motives because respect for the law is not a sufficient incentive for their wills. The wicked neglect the incentive of respect for moral law altogether; even when they act in accord with the moral law, they do the right thing for the wrong reasons and so are corrupt in their cast of mind (see SIN §3).

These three pictures of the disordered self have something in common. They portray its actions as flowing from appetites or desires that have not been subordinated properly to the rule of some higher part or aspect of the self. Bad or evil action results when the self allows unruly appetites or desires to get out of hand.

2   The well-ordered self

For Plato, the remedy for lack of self-control consists of establishing the mastery of the rational part of the soul and rendering docile the other two parts. The rational part of the soul is described in the *Republic* as the ruling principle: the self is well-ordered when reason's two subjects are agreed that reason ought to rule and so do not rebel against it.

As Aristotle sees it, practical wisdom determines the right rule for action. Since an incontinent person is one who allows bodily appetites to move them to act contrary to the right rule, a continent person will be one who possesses such appetites but does not allow them to have such motivating force. Aristotle tells us that the continent person does nothing contrary to the rule for the sake of the bodily pleasures. A person who is merely continent will have bad appetites and will feel pleasure contrary to the right rule but not be led by it to act contrary to the rule. Hence, Aristotle's initial remedy for lack of self-control is continence. A continent self is well-ordered because it has self-control with respect to action. For Aristotle, however, merely being continent is not the ideal state of the self; it is better to be temperate. Like the continent agent, the temperate agent does nothing contrary to the rule for the sake of bodily pleasures. But the temperate agent does not have bad appetites

and does not feel pleasure contrary to the right rule. In such a self not only actions but also appetites and feelings are in accord with the rules specified by practical wisdom. Thus, Aristotle's ultimate remedy for lack of self-control is the virtue of temperance. Yet it is doubtful that temperate people should be thought of as having self-control. Lacking bad appetites, they seem to have nothing unruly within them that needs to be kept under control. It appears, then, that a person who has self-control is one who achieves continence but falls short of temperance (see VIRTUES AND VICES §§2–3).

According to Kant, the remedy for radical evil in human nature that manifests itself in frailty, impurity, and wickedness is a moral revolution in character in which one freely adopts a policy for acting that respects the proper order of incentives for the will. There is in all of us a capacity for respect for the moral law to serve by itself as a sufficient incentive for the will, and this capacity is not destroyed by our propensity to evil. Kant thought it can be restored to its original purity if we reverse, in a single unchangeable decision, the evil policy of not always subordinating the incentives of inclination or sensuous desire to the incentive of respect for the law. Kant did not profess to know how such radical character change is possible. He was confident, however, that we can bring it about because he was persuaded both that it is our duty to do so and that whatever we ought to do we can do. And such a moral revolution will, he thinks, set us on a path of continual progress from bad to better in our actions. So the Kantian remedy for lack of self-control is a revolution in character that results in respect for the moral law, which is the legislation of our own practical reason, being restored to its dominant place in the hierarchy of our incentives for action.

These three accounts of self-control resemble one another to a considerable extent. In all of them, self-control consists of a 'higher part' of the self, associated with reason or wisdom, governing a 'lower part' of the self, associated with bodily appetite, sensuous desires, passions or feelings. Though such rationalistic accounts of self-control have been dominant in philosophy, they have not escaped criticism. Few philosophers would consider unbridled wantonness or self-indulgence virtuous. But many contemporary feminists, for example, are apt to suspect gender bias in the thought of the self as a monarchy ruled by reason. Such critics are motivated to construct more democratic models of the well-ordered self in which parts of the self cooperate, reason need not always be in control, and the cultivation and expression of feeling are valued (see FEMINIST ETHICS).

See also: EMOTIONS, PHILOSOPHY OF; MORALITY AND EMOTIONS

References and further reading

* Aristotle (*c.* mid 4th century BC) *Nicomachean Ethics*, trans. with notes by T. Irwin, Indianapolis, IN: Hackett Publishing Company, 1985, VII. (Discusses incontinence and continence.)
* Kant, I. (1793) *Die Religion innerhalb der Grenzen der blossen Vernunft*, trans. T.M. Greene and H.H. Hudson, *Religion Within the Limits of Reason Alone*, New York: Harper & Row, 1960, I. (Presents the doctrines of radical evil and moral revolution.)
* Plato (*c.*380s–370s BC) *Phaedrus*, trans. R. Hackforth, Cambridge: Cambridge University Press, 1952; repr. in *The Collected Dialogues including Letters*, ed. E. Hamilton and H. Cairns, Oxford: Oxford University Press, 1975. (Compares the human psyche to a charioteer and two horses.)
* —— (*c.*380–367 BC) *Republic*, trans. P. Shorey, Cambridge, MA: Harvard University Press, 1930; repr. in *The Collected Dialogues including Letters*, ed. E. Hamilton and H. Cairns, Oxford: Oxford University Press, 1975, IV. (Presents the theory of the tripartite psyche.)
Rorty, A.O. (1980) '*Akrasia* and pleasure: *Nicomachean Ethics* Book 7', in A.O. Rorty (ed.) *Essays on Aristotle's Ethics*, Berkeley and Los Angeles, CA: University of California Press. (Useful discussion of *akrasia* or weakness of will.)
Wood, A.W. (1970) *Kant's Moral Religion*, Ithaca, NY: Cornell University Press, ch. 6. (Discusses radical evil and its remedy.)

PHILIP L. QUINN

SELF-CULTIVATION IN CHINESE PHILOSOPHY

Chinese philosophy may be viewed as disciplined reflections on the insights of self-cultivation. Etienne Balazs asserted that all Chinese philosophy is social philosophy and that, even if Chinese thinkers dwell upon metaphysical speculation, they will sooner or later return to the practical issues of the world here and now. This concern for the concreteness of the life-world gives the impression that the social dimension of the human condition features so prominently in the Chinese world of thought that the idea of the group takes precedence over conceptions of the individual self. The anthropological studies that contrast the Chinese sense of shame with the Western sense of guilt further enhance the impression that external social approval, rather than internal psychological sanction, defines the moral fabric of Chinese society. The prevalent sociological literature on the mechanism of 'saving face' as a key to understanding Chinese interpersonal relationships also stresses the centrality of external conditioning in Chinese ethics.

If we follow this line of thinking, it is easy to assume that Chinese philosophers are preoccupied with neither the transcendent referent nor the inner psyche. They are not particularly interested in questions of ultimate reality such as the creator, the origin of the cosmos or the existence of God. Nor are they engrossed in problems of the mind such as consciousness, self-identity or moral choice. Indeed, Chinese philosophy as social philosophy seems exclusively immersed in issues of correct behaviour, familial harmony, political order and world peace. Even strands of thought that emphasize the aesthetic experience of the self are all intimately bound up with the highly ritualized world of human-relatedness. Actually the spirit of spontaneity, as a liberation from social constraints, should be appreciated in terms of a conscious reflection on and critique of society and thus inherently sociological.

However, this widely held opinion of Chinese philosophy is seriously flawed. While it offers a common-sense picture of where the strength of Chinese thought lies, it does not address the underlying reasons or the actual processes that define the main trajectory of the Chinese modes of thinking. Wing-tsit Chan suggests a more comprehensive characterization of Chinese philosophy as humanism: 'not the humanism that denies or slights a Supreme Power, but one that professes the unity of man and Heaven' (Chan 1963: 3).

It is crucial to note that 'humanism' so conceived is diametrically opposed to secular humanism as a distinctive feature of the Enlightenment mentality of the modern West. Western humanism emerged as a thorough critique of spiritualism and a radical departure from naturalism, or a sense of affinity with nature; it was the result of secularization. Chinese humanism, on the other hand, tends to incorporate the spiritual and naturalist dimensions in a comprehensive and integrated vision of the nature and function of humanity in the cosmos.

The advantage of characterizing Chinese philosophy as humanistic rather than sociological is to open the possibility of allowing aesthetic, religious and metaphysical as well as ethical, historical and political perspectives to shape the contours of the Chinese reflective mind. This synthetic approach better captures the spirit of Chinese thought because it was historical and social change, rather than speculation, which was instrumental in the outgrowth of humanism as a defining characteristic of Chinese philosophy.

1 Chinese philosophy: the beginning
2 Philosophy as a spiritual quest: Confucius
3 Ultimate justification: Mencius
4 Cultural transformation: Xunzi
5 The root for human flourishing
6 The embodiment of the Way: the Daoist approach
7 An anthropocosmic vision
8 Discipline of the mind: the Buddhist insight
9 The cultivation of the body
10 Learning to become a sage: the neo-Confucian Way
11 Modern significance

1 Chinese philosophy: the beginnings

The advent of Chinese philosophy was not marked by rupture from a mythic, religious world of shamanistic panpsychism to 'rational' reflection, but by a moral discourse on the interplay between the Mandate of Heaven and human virtue. As the pre-Confucian *Shijing* (Book of Odes) notes, the establishment of the Zhou civilization in twelfth century BC was the result of virtuous deeds:

Don't you mind your ancestors!

Cultivate your virtue.

Always strive to be in harmony with Heaven's Mandate.

Seek for yourselves the many blessings.

(*Shijing*, in Chan 1963: 7)

The idea of cultivating virtue as a human endeavour to harmonize with Heaven's Mandate and to seek blessings provides a root metaphor for self-cultivation.

2 Philosophy as a spiritual quest: Confucius

This lack of differentiation between religious commitment and intellectual reflection, as implied in this idea of self-cultivation, has profound implications for our understanding of the nature of Chinese philosophy, which is a spiritual discipline directed toward human flourishing. The realms of abstract theory, devoid of significance for practical daily living, are rejected as the proper domain for the life of the mind. Indeed, the insistence that thinking must be grounded in the lived concreteness of the human condition is based on the 'anthropocosmic' vision that human beings, through self-effort, can fully realize their nature as co-creators of the cosmic process.

Confucius' pithy account of his life history is a paradigmatic example that self-cultivation is pivotal in each stage of his learning to be human:

At fifteen, I set my heart on learning.

At thirty, I took my stand.

At forty, I came to be free from doubts.

At fifty, I knew the Decree [Mandate] of Heaven.

At sixty, my ear was attuned.

At seventy, I followed my heart's desire, without overstepping the line.

(*Analects* 2.4)

The very fact that Confucius located the beginning of his spiritual journey at fifteen indicates the conscious choice to shape the direction of his life through learning as awakening, and marks the definitive boundary between givenness and wilful transformation. Meaningful life begins when one has made a conscious choice to learn to become human through self-effort. The ability to 'plant one's feet firmly on the ground' and find a proper niche in society implies that the inherently personal undertaking of self-cultivation necessarily involves a social dimension. However, despite the commitment that learning as awakening entails the internalization of social norms in every facet of ordinary daily living, the inner strength of self-knowledge does not depend upon standards superimposed from the outside. Indeed, when one is free from 'perplexities', there is a depth of self-awareness which engenders a profound sense of direction.

The transcendent dimension at the age of fifty, instead of a departure from the 'humanist' quest for self-realization, offers a new insight on the human condition. The significance of the evocation of the Mandate of Heaven is twofold: on the one hand, it indicates a critical, if not tragic, recognition of the structural limitations inevitably imposed by aging; at the same time, it also symbolizes a transcendental breakthrough in self-awareness. The former shows that since we are merely human; we cannot but come to terms with our mortality. As Confucius said, to know what we do not know is wisdom; we may analogize that to accept fully the responsibility for what we cannot do is a sign of courage. This 'transcendental breakthrough', then, implies that despite our conditionality, what we do and what we become as humans has cosmological significance.

The deliberate choice of aural rather than visual perception as a way of depicting Confucius' stage of self-cultivation at sixty is profoundly meaningful. The art of listening requires the calmness of the heart and the patience to receive all the messages without prejudging any of them. As an accomplished listener, the dynamic temporality broadens and deepens one's awareness of the outside world without affecting inner tranquillity. The harmony between what one does out of natural impulse and what one ought to do as dictated by moral obligations is, therefore, a further refinement on training the ear to be docile. Within this context, the spirit of spontaneity and freedom that Confucius experienced at seventy, as the result of decades of continuous self-cultivation, has become a standard of inspiration in Chinese moral philosophy.

While Confucius' life history is itself a lesson of self-cultivation through exemplary teaching, it is not meant to be a rigid model for human flourishing. Confucius' attainments depended so much on a confluence of conditions involving economic circumstances, social class, political situation and cultural milieu that it is unique and unrepeatable (see CONFUCIUS). Confucian followers rejected the idea of imitating Confucius but insisted upon the relevance of his example for emulation (see CONFUCIAN PHILOSOPHY, CHINESE). The best way to emulate Confucius is to practise his way of learning to be human through our own self-cultivation. A commitment to internalize the central values of his teachings and integrate them into our daily life is required. However, this does not mean that we have to suspend our rational thinking and critical judgment in order to embrace the Confucian project. The fusion of intellectual inquiry and spiritual transformation suggests that the philosophy of self-cultivation is predicated on an experiential understanding of how it actually works; acceptance of any unexamined dogmas or implicit doctrines is not a precondition.

In response to the query, 'is there a single saying that one can act upon all day and every day?' Confucius said, 'Perhaps the saying about reciprocity: "Never do to others what you would not want them to do to you".' What is the status of this 'golden rule' in Confucian moral philosophy? On the surface, it seems to be a dogma and a doctrine, yet, as presented, it does not have the force of 'thou shall not do otherwise.' It is an observation, a suggestion, a recommendation. The implicit message is: put this 'rule' into practice in your ordinary interpersonal relationships, and see how it actually works. Assuming that this emphasis on considerateness is sometimes unworkable because the anticipated sympathetic response is absent, should the practice be continued? As concrete practice rather than abstract principle, a realistic assessment of the situation is critical in the application of the Confucian golden rule. When Confucius was asked about the merit of repaying malice with kindness, instead of encouraging the student to cultivate what may be called a higher morality of considerateness, Confucius retorted, how are we to repay kindness? If our reciprocal response to malice is kindness, we may have difficulty responding appropriately to kindness. The recommendation that we repay malice with justice and kindness with kindness is to encourage

attention to the specificity of the situation in formulating a measured response.

However, it is mistaken to characterize Confucian self-cultivation as a form of situational ethics. As a virtue-centred moral philosophy, an overriding concern is the cultivation of a personality through character-building that will be able to respond to all situations with dignity and openness:

> The profound persons have nine areas for which they are mindful. In seeing they are mindful of seeing clearly; in hearing they are mindful of hearing distinctly; in looks they are mindful of being good-natured; in their manners of being reverential; in their words of being trustworthy; in their works of being diligent. When in doubt they are mindful of asking for information; when angry they are mindful of the consequences, and when they see a chance for gain, they are mindful of whether the pursuit of it would be consonant with rightness.
>
> (*Analects* 16.10)

Concrete situations provide the opportunity to put general principles, such as the golden rule, into practice, but self-cultivation as a way of learning to be human takes as its primary purpose the fostering of balanced personalities:

> When there is a preponderance of native substance over acquired refinement, the result will be churlishness. When there is a preponderance of acquired refinement over native substance, the result will be pedantry. Only a well-balanced admixture of these two will result in gentlemanliness.
>
> (*Analects* 6.18)

It should be noted that the self in Confucian self-cultivation is not an isolated or even isolatable individual, but a centre of relationships. As a centre, there is a unique configuration of social roles evolving around the autonomous and independent self. The self as an end, rather than a means, can never be reduced to these roles. Confucius' injunction that the profound person is not a vehicle clearly shows that the dignity of the person cannot be fully appreciated by referring merely to their role and function in society. The paradox is of course that each social role (that is, parent, child, teacher, student, patron, client, employer, employee, farmer, worker, merchant, business executive, lawyer, doctor, journalist, artist, writer or computer programmer) provides an opportunity for self-realization. As a centre of relationships, the self is enriched and empowered by a continuous interaction and interchange with other selves. Nevertheless, balanced personalities are not simply well-adjusted to the vicissitudes of the external environment; an inner core of self-knowledge serves as a spring of rich spiritual resources.

3 Ultimate justification: Mencius

The great contribution that MENCIUS made to the Confucian project is precisely locating this inner core in human nature:

> A profound person [gentleman] steeps himself in the Way because he wishes to find it in himself. When he finds it in himself, he will be at ease in it; when he is at ease in it, he can draw deeply upon it; when he can draw deeply upon it, he finds its source wherever he turns. That is why a profound person wishes to find the Way in himself.
>
> (*Mengzi* 4B14)

There is a paradox in the assertion that profound persons, intent on finding the Way in themselves, steep themselves in the Way. If the Way is already in us, all we need to do is to find it through introspective self-examination. Indeed, Mencius seems to believe that is the case:

> All the myriad things are present in me. There is no greater joy for me than to find, on self-examination, that I am true to myself. Try your best to treat others as you would wish to be treated yourself, and you will find that this is the shortest way to humanity.
>
> (*Mengzi* 7A4)

However, by steeping ourselves in the Way, we are enjoined to make a conscious effort to realize that, if we follow our original nature, we are intrinsically congenial to the Way. By implication, since we are not necessarily what we ought to be, we may easily mistake that part of us which is contrary to the Way as the true self. The art of self-cultivation, then, is to know the difference and to act accordingly. Mencius straightforwardly articulates what he observes as the central *Problematik* in self-cultivation:

> When our senses of sight and hearing are used without thought and thus become obscured by material things, the material things act on the material sense and lead them astray. That is all. The function of the mind-and-heart is to think. If we think, we will get the principles of things. If we do not think, we will not get them. This is what Heaven has given us. If we first build upon the 'great body' of our nature, then the 'small body' cannot overcome it. It is this which makes human beings great.
>
> (*Mengzi* 6A15)

Although we are not what we ought to be, the process by which we learn to become so can be initiated from the very structure of what we are here and now. The assumptive reason is that the ultimate justification for self-cultivation lies in the feeling, willing, knowing, and sensing capacities of the heart-and-mind. As long as our heart-and-mind can feel the suffering of others, there is the authentic possibility of self-cultivation. Human beings so defined are primarily sentient beings. Our sensitivity, which includes rationality, enables us to experience directly the sympathetic and reciprocal resonances with other human beings and the world at large.

Yet, it is necessary that we know the difference between the 'great body' and the 'small body' in our nature. We must not allow our desires, especially appetite and sex, to dominate, or we will be obsessed with the demands of the small body. As a result, our behaviour can be easily defined in terms of the rules of the game common to all animals: survival and procreation. On the other hand, if we cultivate our great body in order to realize that 'all the myriad things are present in me', the potential for our interconnectedness is immense. Mencius' art of nourishing the flood-like vital energy addresses this in seemingly mythical terms:

> [The flood-like vital energy] is the sort of vital energy which is utmost in vastness and utmost in strength. If through uprightness you nourish it and do not interfere with it, it fills the space between heaven and earth. It is the sort of vital energy which matches rightness with the Way. Without these it starves. It is generated by the accumulation of right deeds, and is not the sporadic right deeds that one might make a grab at. If anything in conduct is dissatisfying of the heart, it starves.... You must work at it and never let it out of your mind. At the same time, while you must not let it out of your mind, you must not forcibly help it either.
>
> (*Mengzi* 2A2)

Viewed from this perspective, Mencius' thesis that human nature is good provides an ultimate justification for self-cultivation. The reason that we can cultivate ourselves is because the feeling, willing, knowing and sensing capacities of the heart-and-mind are inherent in our nature (see XIN (HEART AND MIND)). Virtues of humanity, rightness, wisdom and propriety can be cultivated by appealing directly to the basic manifestations of human sensitivity: sympathy, empathy, the feeling of shame and dislike, the ability to know the difference between right and wrong and a sense of appropriateness.

4 Cultural transformation: Xunzi

While XUNZI, the great Confucian thinker of the third century BC, shares Mencius' vision that the human condition is improvable through self-effort and that moral education is absolutely necessary for the maintenance of social order, he doubts that human nature will automatically generate the creative process for human flourishing. He insists that the coercive power of the law, the influence of ritual and music, the authority of the ruler, the guidance of the teacher, and the enduring presence of good customs are all necessary for the harmonious functioning of society. His justification for self-cultivation is twofold: it is sociologically necessary on the one hand, and psychologically and epistemologically possible on the other.

Xunzi subscribes to an evolutionary theory of the advent of the human species with particular emphasis on its sociality. He observes that whereas all modalities of being have vital energy, plants have life and animals have consciousness, human beings alone possess rightness. A distinctive feature of the human sense of rightness is the ability to know the need and the intelligence to design the structure to organize human communities for survival and flourishing. Self-cultivation is central to the stability and solidarity of any human community. Human desires are numerous, but the material goods to satisfy them are limited. If desires are not properly channelled, social order cannot be maintained. Although coercive measures from the outside are necessary, in the long run the surest way is still moral self-cultivation. To be sure, human nature suffused with the passions of appetite, sex and aggression cannot in itself generate the mechanism for the development of pro-social sentiments, but the cognitive function of the mind has the capacity to make distinctions and intelligent choices.

Xunzi compares the mind to a pan of water: 'If you guide it with reason, nourish it with clarity, and do not allow external objects to unbalance it, then it will be capable of determining right and wrong and of resolving doubts' (*Xunzi*, in Liang 1996: 222). Understandably, an important concern of Xunzi's moral education is to free the mind from obsessions:

What are the sources of obsession? One may be obsessed by desires or hates, by the beginning of an affair or the end, by the far away or close by, by breadth of knowledge or by shallowness, by the past or by the present. When one makes distinctions among myriad beings of creation, these distinctions all become potential sources of obsession. This is the danger in the use of the mind which is common to all human beings.

(*Xunzi*, in Liang 1996: 222)

However, despite the mind's vulnerability, three distinctive qualities it possesses enable it to save humanity from self-destruction: emptiness, oneness and tranquillity.

The mind's receptivity is inexhaustible; no matter how much information it receives, there is always room for new. The emptiness of the mind offers a great capacity for learning. Xunzi believes that although human beings, as compared with other animals, are weak in physical strength, through learning they can be socialized to become the most intelligent. The mind also has the synthetic power to integrate fragmented ideas into a coherent pattern, and can do so without losing sight of its own inner identity. Similarly, while the mind responds dynamically to external stimuli, it can always maintain its internal tranquillity. These qualities enable the mind to exercise its cognitive function to control the passions of human nature.

Consequently, what Xunzi recommends as the central task of self-cultivation is to use the mind to govern human nature. Specifically, he recognizes the necessity of artfully constructed cultural forms to help the mind do this work. Law, ritual, music, norms and customs are all critically important in helping the mind to transform human passions so that their destructive influence on society can be minimized. Both Mencius and Xunzi see the need to control desires. They do not advocate asceticism, but they are fully aware that the best way to nourish the mind is to make desires few.

5 The root for human flourishing

The centrality of self-cultivation in classical Confucian humanism is captured in a pithy statement in the *Daxue* (Great Learning):

From the Son of Heaven on down to the common people, all must regard cultivation of the personal life as the root. There is never a case where the root is in disorder and yet the branches are in order. There has never been a case that what is treated with great importance becomes a matter of slight importance or what is treated with slight importance becomes a matter of great importance.

(*Daxue* 1)

It is profoundly significant that the root and importance of self-cultivation is extended to the family, state and the world. It is not only a subject in moral education of the young but also the major concern of the body politic as a whole:

The ancients who wished to manifest their clear character to the world would first bring order to

617

the states. Those who wished to bring order to their states would first regulate their families. Those who wished to regulate their families would first cultivate their personal lives. Those who wished to cultivate their personal lives would first rectify their minds. Those who wished to rectify their minds would first make their wills sincere. Those who wished to make their wills sincere would first extend their knowledge. The extension of knowledge consists in the investigations of things.

(*Daxue* 1)

Self-cultivation so conceived occupies a pivotal position in the link between the self and the community mediated by a variety of political, social and cultural institutions. At the personal level, it involves a complex process of empirical studies and mental disciplines. In terms of the whole project of human flourishing, it serves as the foundation of stable families, ordered states and a peaceful world.

The Confucians may have been particularly concerned about the social and political implications of self-cultivation, but self-cultivation features so prominently in all Chinese philosophy that it is central to Chinese modes of thinking in ethics, aesthetics, metaphysics and epistemology. In the Chinese life of the mind, the primary concern in ethics is how to establish the standards of inspiration for the young through exemplary teaching, in aesthetics how to acquire the real taste of beauty through rigorous discipline, in metaphysics how to understand ultimate reality from within, and in epistemology how to know in the spirit of impartiality and mutuality. Indeed, the centrality of self-cultivation compels Chinese thinkers to ground ethics in practice, aesthetics in experience, metaphysics in wisdom and epistemology in communication. The Chinese equivalent of the Greek dictum that an unexamined life is not worth living is that an uncultivated person is not yet human. A defining characteristic of learning to be human is to engage in a ceaseless process of self-cultivation. Philosophy so conceived is neither abstract theorizing nor speculative thinking but a spiritual discipline. As a spiritual discipline, the love of wisdom is a transformative act.

6   The embodiment of the Way: the Daoist approach

Self-cultivation for the Daoists requires the art of unlearning (see DAOIST PHILOSOPHY). While in the pursuit of knowledge one gains by day, in the quest for the *dao* one must let go, lose and be silent:

To rarely speak – such is the way of Nature.

Fierce winds don't last the whole morning.

Torrential rains don't last the whole day.

Who makes these things?

If Heaven and Earth can't make these last long –

How much more is this true for man!

(*Daodejing* 23, in Liang 1996: 223)

The constant and enduring way of nature is therefore undramatic, nonviolent, peaceful, tranquil and colourless. The precondition to emulate this is to acknowledge our fatal flaw of not knowing that we do not know:

To know you don't know is best.

Not to know you don't know is flaw.

Therefore, the Sage's not being flawed

Stems from his recognizing a flaw as a flaw.

Therefore, he is flawless.

(*Daodejing* 71, in Liang 1996: 222)

Having acknowledged our ignorance, we begin to appreciate that, in the spirit of the *dao*, self-cultivation does not take the form of action:

The softest, most pliable thing in the world runs roughshod over the firmest thing in the world.

That which has no substance gets into that which has no spaces or cracks.

I therefore know that there is benefit of taking no action.

The wordless teaching, the benefit of taking no action –

Few in the world can realize these!

(*Daodejing* 43, in Liang 1996: 222)

Even though the *dao* is ineffable, it can be experienced. The tacit 'knowledge' of non-action can help us to embody it. To experience the *dao* or to acquire a taste of it is the focus of Daoist self-cultivation:

To know the constant is to be all-embracing;

To be all-embracing is to be impartial;

To be impartial is to be kingly;

To be kingly is to be like Heaven;

To be like Heaven is to be one with the Dao;

If you're one with the Dao, to the end of your days you'll suffer no harm.

(*Daodejing* 16, in Liang 1996: 223)

ZHUANGZI describes vividly how, for the Daoists, an experiential understanding of the *dao* is the most efficacious way of realizing the *dao* in our ordinary daily living. The relationship between the perception of what the dao is, and the spiritual journey through which the *dao* is embodied, is articulated by the language of nature symbolizing spontaneity, constant flux and incessant transformation:

Tao [Dao] has reality and evidence but no action or physical form. It may be transmitted but cannot be received. It may be obtained but cannot be seen. It is based in itself. Before heaven and earth came into being, Tao existed by itself from all time. It gave spirits and rulers their spiritual powers. It created heaven and earth. It is above the zenith but it is not high. It is beneath the nadir but it is not low. It is prior to heaven and earth but it is not old. It is more ancient than the highest antiquity but is not regarded as long ago.

(*Zhuangzi*, in Chan 1963: 194)

The spiritual implications for this perception of the *dao* are equalizing all things and opinions, abandoning selfishness of all descriptions and attaining enlightenment by moving into the realms of 'great knowledge' and 'profound virtue'. In Zhuangzi's own style of expression, the person who has learned *dao* is able to transcend this world, all material things and all life:

Having transcended all life, he became as clear and bright as the morning. Having been as clear and bright as the morning, he was able to see the One. Having seen the One, he was able to abolish the distinction of past and present. Having abolished the past and present, he was then able to enter the realm of neither life nor death. Then, to him, the destruction of life did not mean death and the production of life did not mean life. In dealing with things, he would not lean forward or backward to accommodate them. To him everything was in the process of destruction, everything was in the process of perfection. This is called 'tranquillity in disturbance'. Tranquillity in disturbance means that it is especially in the midst of disturbance that [tranquillity] becomes perfect.

(*Zhuangzi*, in Chan 1963: 195)

This remarkable convergence of an ontological reading of the *dao* and an existential interpretation of the true person suggests a fruitful interplay between the aloofness and elusiveness of the *dao*, and the concreteness and practicality of the Daoist experience. The *dao* as an idea is conceptually forever inaccessible, and as a way of life is experientially always present.

7 An anthropocosmic vision

It is easy to assume that the Confucians, being politically concerned, socially engaged and culturally sensitive, take self-cultivation as a this-worldly value-orientation, whereas the Daoists, being disinterested in politics, society and culture, define self-cultivation in other-worldly terms. In a deeper sense, however, Confucians and Daoists are both immersed in the same *Problematik*: how can we respond to the vicissitudes of a constantly changing world in the spirit of spontaneity without losing the inner tranquillity of the mind? In the words of a syncretic text of the Han dynasty, how can we transform together with external things but not lose our true nature? A classical formulation of this central issue is found in the *Zhongyong* (Doctrine of the Mean):

When emotions, such as pleasure and anger and sorrow and joy, have not been aroused, the state is called that of centrality. When these emotions are aroused and each and all attain due measure and degree, it is called the state of harmony. The state of centrality is the great root and the state of harmony is the far-reaching way of all existence in the world. Once centrality and harmony are realized, Heaven and Earth take their proper place and all things receive full nourishment.

(*Zhongyong* 1)

The 'anthropocosmic' vision embedded in this statement is both Confucian and Daoist. Indeed, it is predicated on an ontological commitment in the 'Appended Remarks' of the *Yijing* (Book of Changes): the great transformation of the cosmos is the highest standard of inspiration for human self-cultivation, and human beings can assist in the transforming and nourishing processes of Heaven and Earth and thus form a trinity with Heaven and Earth through personal self-realization. By implication, what we do in the privacy of our homes and in the practical living of our everyday existence is profoundly meaningful in a cosmological as well as in a psychological sense.

8 Discipline of the mind: the Buddhist insight

This central and enduring motif of self-cultivation philosophy has been greatly enriched by the introduction of Buddhism from India (see BUDDHIST PHILOSOPHY, CHINESE). The most obvious Buddhist contribution to Chinese self-cultivation philosophy is the discipline of the mind. An early Buddhist master, Huisi (514–77), remarked that, through concentration, we can realize the pure mind; insight derived from the realization of the pure mind enables us to perceive that all sentient beings are 'harmoniously identified to form one body of a single character' (Liang 1996: 225). The power of concentration helps us not only to attain calmness, stillness and purity of the mind, but also to function without the form of functioning, and to act without the form of acting. This resembles the Daoist idea of acting in the spirit of non-action.

The introduction of Buddhism was accompanied by a host of spiritual disciplines hitherto unavailable to the Daoist practitioner. Furthermore, its new perceptions of the human condition fundamentally reshaped the basic tenets of Chinese self-cultivation philosophy. The issue of 'attachment' loomed large in the new configuration. As Jizang (549–623) notes, 'if there is an attachment (in the mind), there is a fetter, and one cannot obtain release from birth and old age, sickness and death, care and sorrow, pain and suffering.' To rise above attachment and perceive things as they are, a combined effort of meditation and wisdom is required. Yet, as Huineng noted, meditation and wisdom are a unity, rather than two separate disciplines:

> Calmness [stillness] itself is the substance of wisdom; wisdom itself is the function of meditation. At the very moment when there is wisdom, then meditation exists in wisdom; at the moment when there is meditation, then wisdom exists in meditation. Good friends, this means that wisdom and meditation are alike.
>
> (Chan 1963: 433)

The use of substance and function to define the relationship between meditation and wisdom is instructive. The penetrating insight which emerges from the meditative practice is itself an illumination of the mind. Since our original nature is the source of wisdom, the meditative practice as a way of clarifying the mind enables our original nature to present itself. As long as that happens, wisdom is there. Meditation is therefore a return and discovery of the original nature whereas wisdom is the character of the purified mind. Huineng insists that the internal and sudden approach is the authentic method of true awakening (see PLATFORM SUTRA). If we do not place our trust in external practices but cultivate right views in regard to our original nature in our own minds, self-awakening is always possible. Unfortunately, our deluded minds compel us to seek wisdom by external practice and thus prevent us from awakening to our true nature.

It seems on the surface that Huineng is oblivious to the 'weakness of the will' problem. Where is the source of strength for this sudden awakening? His rival, Shenhui (670–762), offered a reasonable gradualist solution with emphasis on the power of good habits:

> After a master founder has smelted and refined the material, gold and the mineral will presently be differentiated. The more refined, the purer the gold will become, and with further smelting, the residual mineral will become dust. The gold is analogous to Buddha-nature, whereas minerals are analogous to afflictions resulting from passions. Afflictions and Buddha-nature exist simultaneously.
>
> (Liang 1996: 226)

This is the reason that, in his famous verse of self-cultivation, Shenhui perceived the body as the 'tree of perfect wisdom' (*bodhi*) and the mind as 'the stand of a bright mirror' (Chan 1963: 431). The method of self-cultivation is analogous to diligently wiping the mirror at all times so that it will never become dusty.

This common-sense approach, however, was emphatically rejected by Huineng as inadequate. Instead, he advocated sudden enlightenment as not only a more efficacious but also the only true way to understand how the mind actually works in spiritual self-cultivation. Sudden awakening is possible even for those sentient beings filled with passions and sentiments:

> It is like the great sea which gathers all flowing streams, and merges together the small and large waters into one. This is seeing into your own nature. Such a person does not abide either inside or outside; he is free to come or go. Readily he casts aside the mind that clings to things, and there is no obstruction to his passage.
>
> (Liang 1996: 226)

The freedom one experiences as the result of sudden awakening, presumably occasioned by the combined effort of meditation and wisdom, is neither cumulative nor sequential; it happens all at once. Understandably, Huineng's verse, as a response to Shenhui's formulation, is to deny the authenticity of a gradualist approach to self-cultivation:

> The mind is the tree of perfect wisdom.
>
> The body is the stand of a bright mirror.
>
> The bright mirror is original clear and pure.
>
> Where has it been defiled by any dust?
>
> (Chan 1963: 432)

However, in a deeper sense, the strength of Chinese Buddhist self-cultivation philosophy lies in its integrated thinking as the basis for guiding practical living in ordinary daily existence. The fruitful interaction between the gradualist and suddenist approaches enabled the Buddhist teachers, especially Chan masters, to subscribe to suddenist insight as ontological wisdom without losing sight of the gradualist effort as an existential discipline. FAZANG (643–712), for example, offered the merging of the one and many as an ontological insight:

When the feelings have been eliminated and true substance revealed, all becomes an undifferentiated mass. Great function then arises in abundance, and whenever it does, there is surely Perfect Reality. All phenomena are in great profusion, and are inter-fused but not mixed. The all is the one, for the relation between cause and effect is perfectly clear. As the power of the one and the function of the many embrace each other, their expansion and contraction are free and at ease.

(Chan 1963: 410)

What Fazang propounded here is both an attained state of the mind and the true nature of ultimate reality such a mind perceives. With regard to self-cultivation, Fazang's ontological insight is not at all in conflict with the recommendation of Huangbo (d. 850) of the concrete steps for purifying the mind:

First, learn to be entirely unreceptive to sensations arising from external forms, thereby purging your bodies of receptivity to externals.

Second, learn not to make any distinctions between this and that arising from your sensations, thereby purging your bodies of useless discernments between one phenomenon and another.

Third, take great care to avoid discriminating in terms of pleasant and unpleasant sensations, thereby purging your bodies of vain discrimina-tions.

Fourth, avoid pondering things in your mind, thereby purging your bodies of discriminatory cognition.

(Liang 1996: 227)

Surely, the Buddhist thinkers, by their rigour of ascetic practices, persistent meditation and profound wisdom, fundamentally reshaped the spiritual land-scape of self-cultivation in China, but the distinctive Buddhist traditions that emerged in the Zhongtu (the Middle Country) assumed new forms significantly different from their Indian origins. Chan Buddhism, which exemplifies the creative transformation of Buddhist teaching in China, is a paradigmatic case. The recognition that buddha-hood is inherent in our human nature, that our physical bodies are capable of fully realizing our nature and that we can attain buddha-hood in this life extends the Buddhist community to embrace the world at large and instills a sense of urgency, a heightened temporality, among the Chan practitioners. The simple and direct method Master Yixuan (d. 867) employed to inspire his disciples is a case in point:

Time is precious. Don't make the mistake of following others in desperately studying meditation

or the Path, learning words or phrases, seeking after the Buddha or patriarchs or good friends. Followers of the Path, you have only one father and one mother. What else do you want? Look into yourselves. An ancient sage said that Yanjnadatta thought that he had lost his head and sought after it, but when his seeking mind was stopped he realized he had never lost it.

(Liang 1996: 228)

Huineng pointedly remarked that our self-nature, which entails the Three Bodies of Buddha (the Dharma-body, the Reward-body, and the Transfor-mation-body), is in our physical bodies. In the classical theory of the Three Bodies, the Dharma-body is the Buddha-body in its true original self-nature that is empty (no bodily existence at all). The Reward-body is the enlightened body with real insight into the 'thusness' of things in its eternal bliss of self-enjoyment, and the Transformation-body is the compassionate manifestations of buddha-hood ap-pearing in various forms to save people. Although the three bodies are in one, are present in all buddhas, and are potentially realizable by all human beings, the conditions for their realization are so complex and the time required so long that it is beyond imagination that any physical body has a chance to attain them in its own life time. Reflecting on the implications of Huineng's insistence that 'the Three Bodies are inherent in one's physical nature', Wing-tsit Chan commented:

The doctrine of 'becoming Buddha in this very body' is a far cry from the original Indian idea that the body is a hindrance to freedom. One cannot help recalling that the Confucianists have always regarded the body as a gift from parents and as such it is a sacred trust and therefore to be well taken care of, and that for centuries the Taoist [Daoist] religion had tried in many ways, including medicine, diets, exercise, sex technique, and breath control to make the body suitable for everlasting life on earth. These are some of the roots that make Zen [Chan] essentially Chinese.

(Chan 1963: 437)

9 The cultivation of the body

The Chinese heritage as a whole takes our physical nature, the body, absolutely seriously. Self-cultivation, as a form of mental and physical development and rejuvenation is an ancient Chinese art involving such exercises as rhythmic bodily movements and breath-ing techniques. Understandably, the classical Chinese conception of medicine focuses on healing rather than merely curing illness because its primary function is not only preventing sickness but also restoring vital energy essential for the wholeness of the body. Since the level of vital energy required for health varies according to the specific conditions of a particular person, the wholeness of body is situationally defined as a dynamic process rather than a static structure. The maintenance of health, accordingly, involves a delicate balance among a wide range of environmental, dietary, physiological and psychological factors. The rhythm of the living body is seasonal, for the body is temporal as well as spatial. The temporalization of the body as budding (spring), growing (summer), withdrawing (autumn) and preserving (winter), symbolizes longevity as both an attainment and a natural process.

Our bodies are not merely physiological entities; they are energy fields rather than conglomerates of discrete organs. Indeed, their functions are analogous to 'power stations' and 'communication centres'. The body is, therefore, a conduit through which we communicate with all modalities of vital energy in order to realize the ultimate meaning of life in ordinary human existence. Religious Daoism, especially the cult of immortality, has developed one of the richest traditions of cultivating the body as a spiritual discipline.

10 Learning to become a sage: the neo-Confucian Way

To the neo-Confucians, the central problem in self-cultivation philosophy is how to learn to become a sage (see NEO-CONFUCIAN PHILOSOPHY). This is founded on the faith in the perfectibility of human nature. ZHOU DUNYI (1017–73), having responded positively to the question whether or not sagehood can be learned, succinctly outlined a course of action for the spiritual journey:

> The essential is to concentrate on oneness. By concentrating on oneness is meant having no desire. Having no desire, one is vacuous while tranquil, and straightforward while in action. Being vacuous while tranquil, one becomes intelligent and hence penetrating; being straightforward while active, one becomes impartial and hence all embracing. Being intelligent, penetrating, impartial, and all-embracing, one is almost a sage.
>
> (Chan 1963: 473)

Sagehood, as the most authentic manifestation of humanity, is the result of self-cultivation. Indeed, the state of being desireless is existentially impossible for any human being to attain. This is because we observe the human condition from the perspective of the senses. If we focus our attention on the heart-and-mind rather than the senses, we can experientially understand that it is possible to rise above all desires, if only for a moment. If we can experience this even once, we recognize that sagehood, far from being an unattainable ideal, can be a standard of inspiration for daily practical living. As ZHANG ZAI (1020–77) notes, if we are not encumbered by the perceptions of the senses and engage ourselves in realizing fully the inner abilities of the heart-and-mind, we will appreciate sagelike qualities in our own ordinary experience.

This distinction between what we ontologically are, and what we existentially can be and must strive to become, is critical for self-cultivation philosophy. All three teachings – Confucianism, Daoism and Buddhism – share a profound faith in human nature as a necessary and sufficient condition for self-realization (see XING). Since ontologically sagehood, dao or buddha, is inherent in our nature, we are potentially sages, true persons and buddhas. Existentially, however, no matter how hard we try we can never fully realize sagehood, dao, or buddha. There is always room for improvement. Yet, although we are not what we ought to be, the ideals of what we must strive to become are inherent in our nature, indeed our bodies.

This non-dualistic thinking offers a radically different approach to the mind/body problem. The deliberate and arbitrary split of the self into res cogitans and res extensa is absent (see MIND, PHILOSOPHY OF). The body is never reduced to a reified corporeality, nor are the thinking and reflecting functions of the living person totally subsumed under the category of the mind. The sharp contrast between the mental and the physical totally undermines the affective dimension, feeling, as an essential feature of being human. Surely human beings are capable of willing, sensing and knowing, but feeling underlies all mental and physical activities. No expression of willpower, sense of appropriateness or cognition can be devoid of feeling. It requires a stretch of our imagination to believe that we can will, sense or know independent of how we feel. It is human to feel. Natural feelings that arise in response to the suffering of others defines who we are.

The cultivation of moral values such as humanity, rightness, propriety, wisdom, and faithfulness depends upon the nourishment of the appropriate feelings: commiseration for humanity, shame and dislike for rightness, deference for propriety and a sense of right and wrong for wisdom. CHENG HAO (1032–85) addresses this issue in his commentary on Mencius:

> Humanity implies impartiality, that is, to make (the moral principle) human. Rightness means what is proper, the standard for weighing what is of greater or smaller importance. Propriety means to distin-

guish (to determine ranks and functions). Wisdom is to know. And faithfulness (belief) means 'We have it'. All things have nature. These Five Constant Virtues are nature. As to commiseration and so forth (the sense of shame, the sense of deference and compliance, and the sense of right and wrong), they are all feelings. Whatever is aroused is called feeling.

(Chan 1963: 537)

This integrated vision of virtues and feelings in the context of human nature and the heart-and-mind enabled the neo-Confucians to practice self-cultivation on a daily basis. For example, Cheng Hao remarked: 'When I practice calligraphy, I am very reverential. My purpose is not that the calligraphy must be good. Rather, my practice is the way of moral training.'

CHENG YI (1033–1107) made it clear that self-cultivation can be conceived as the site of a contest between nature and emotions, but since nature also reveals itself in feelings, it is the contest between feelings such as commiseration, shame, deference and a sense of right and wrong, and emotions such as pleasure, anger and sorrow (see XIN):

As the physical form appears, it comes into contact with external things and is aroused from within. As it is aroused from within, the seven emotions – called pleasure, anger, sorrow, joy, love, hate, and desire – ensue. As emotions become strong and increasingly reckless, his nature becomes damaged. For this reason the enlightened person controls his emotions so that they will be in accord with the Mean. He rectifies his mind and nourishes his nature. This is called turning emotions into original nature. The uncultivated person does not know how to control them. He lets them loose until they are depraved, fetter his nature, and destroy it. This is therefore called turning one's nature into emotions.

(Chan 1963: 548)

Following Cheng Yi's teaching, ZHU XI (1130–1200) singled out reverence as the psychological state most congenial to self-cultivation. As a gradualist, Zhu Xi strongly advocated the necessity of a cumulative process for nurturing the right beliefs, attitude and behaviour. He urged his students to cultivate their hearts-and-minds as a daily routine:

The mind is that with which man rules his body. It is one and not a duality, is subject and not object, and controls the external world instead of being controlled by it. Therefore, if we examine external objects with the mind their principles will be apprehended.

(Liang 1996: 230)

While he believed that when it is in a state of reverence, the mind will naturally nourish the proper dispositions for human flourishing, he insisted that the advancement of learning lies in the extension of knowledge. By implication, the investigation of things, a kind of empirical study, is relevant to and essential for moral self-cultivation.

WANG YANGMING (1472–1529), however, criticized the Cheng–Zhu line of thinking for its failure to fully comprehend the true nature of moral knowledge. His perception that, in the actual practice of self-cultivation, knowing entails a transformative act serves as the basis for this doctrine of the unity of knowledge and action:

In their learning people of today separate knowledge and action into two different things. Thereupon when a thought is aroused, although it is evil, they do not stop it because it has not been translated into action. I advocate the unity of knowledge and action precisely because I want people to understand that when a thought is aroused that it is already action. If there is anything evil when the thought is aroused, one must overcome the evil thought. One must go to the root and go to the bottom and not allow that evil to lie latent in the mind. This is the basic purpose of my doctrine.

(Chan 1963: 670)

On the surface, Wang's theory is basically therapeutic; its primary purpose is to bring about concrete results in moral behaviour. However, despite its remedial function, the inseparability of knowing and acting is predicated on the centrality of 'primordial awareness' in self-cultivation.

'Primordial awareness' (liangzhi), variously referred to as 'innate knowledge', 'the knowledge of the good', 'conscientious consciousness' or simply 'conscience', is what Wang takes to be the true function of human nature and the ultimate reality of all beings. This form of knowing is inherently creative; such knowledge in itself engenders new realities. Strictly speaking, 'primordial awareness' is not a reflection or meditation on external objects. Rather, it is an awareness which arises through embodying the inner patterns of things in an ever-expanding sensitivity of the heart-and-mind. Self-cultivation so conceived involves the extension of one's 'primordial awareness' through analogical thinking. The quality of the heart-and-mind is vitally important. Regardless how much empirical knowledge one accumulates, one's ethical intelligence will only be enhanced when the mind is properly cultivated. Therefore, in Wang's self-cultivation philosophy, the sincerity of the will, as an effort to purify one's motivation, takes precedence over the investigation of things.

In the thought of Liu Zhongzhou (1578–1645), Zhu Xi's painstaking effort to ritualize the body through reverence and Wang Yangming's 'direct and immediate' approach to the self-illumination of the heart-and-mind reaches a new synthesis. Liu recommends on the one hand that we dwell in vigilant solitude in order to strengthen the roots of our intentions; on the other hand, he also recommends that this emphasis on the interiority of self-cultivation be supplemented by focused attention to the details of our daily behaviour. The authentic way of learning to be human is through examining and correcting mistakes. Self-cultivation combines the purification of an ever-deepening subjectivity with the rectification of all the mistakes made in ordinary practical living. This interplay between alertness of the subtle, incipient activation of the heart-and-mind and rigour in the ritualized discipline of the body offers a balanced programme for self-cultivation.

An elaborate project defining self-cultivation as a nine-stage effort to purify the mind was designed by the seventeenth century syncretist Lin Chao'en as an attempt to integrate the Three Teachings (Confucianism, Buddhism and Daoism) into one coherent idea of human flourishing. Lin enunciated his doctrine in a language richly textured by the symbolism of the *Yijing*. This claim that the microcosmic process in the physical body directed by the heart-and-mind actually emulates the macrocosmic process of the Heaven and Earth is characteristic of virtually all forms of self-cultivation in popular religion.

11 Modern significance

The primacy of experience, the centrality of exemplary teaching, and the necessity of personal commitment beyond reason may imply that, while such an approach is religiously meaningful, it is not philosophically significant. However, the pervasiveness of self-cultivation in all strata of Chinese society and all periods of Chinese history, clearly indicates that it is reasonable to characterize Chinese philosophy as disciplined reflections on the insights of self-cultivation. Even in Chinese Marxist literature, self-cultivation is assumed to be an integral part of the political ideology (for example, Liu Shaoqi's essay on 'How to be a Good Communist') (see MARXISM, CHINESE). Feng Qi's philosophy of wisdom, arguably one of the most original Chinese contributions to Marxism, focuses on the transformation of praxis into virtue-centred ethics. Self-cultivation provides the necessary background for Feng's thought. Self-cultivation also features prominently in New Confucian Humanism. Indeed, a defining characteristic of New Confucians in the twentieth century is the prominence of the moral discourse on the learning of the heart-and-mind in their styles of philosophy.

Feng Youlan [Fung Yu-lan] (1895–1990), a major thinker under the influence of New Realism, characterized philosophy as a reflection on the human spirit, self-reflexivity and thinking about thinking. In a highly original philosophical move, he constructed his New Learning of the Principle around four cardinal concepts: principle, vital energy, substance of the *dao*, and the Great Whole. He also described Wang Yangming's 'primordial awareness' (*liangzhi*) as a basic philosophical postulate. Feng's use of propositional language in defining 'primordial awareness' as a postulate was severely criticized by Xiong Shili (1885–1968), one of the founders of New Confucian Humanism. Xiong insisted that 'primordial awareness' as an experience is a manifestation, indeed a realization of the human spirit. If it is defined merely as a postulate, the advantage of philosophical impartiality will be offset by its spiritual irrelevance. How could a mere postulate generate a profound sense of commitment to its full realization? On the surface, the difference between Feng and Xiong lies in the choice between an analytical reflection and an ethico-religious assertion. The former belongs to philosophy, whereas the latter smacks of religious or theological advocacy. At stake, however, is the role and function of self-cultivation in our definition of philosophy.

If philosophy is itself a spiritual quest and its purpose is self-knowledge, the disciplined reflection on insights ought to lead to wisdom necessary for human flourishing. 'Primordial awareness', the innate knowledge and innate ability that enables us to cultivate ourselves through our own effort, should not be affirmed merely as a postulate. Rather, it should be demonstrated as a presence and experienced as a reality. The danger of the propositional language is not only the misleading impression that the whole exercise is noncommittal but also the mistake in confusing the really real with an imagined possibility. We may detect a dogmatic streak in presenting the 'primordial awareness' as a true presence and an experienced reality. However, the purpose is to show that philosophers must share their insights the way they experientially understand them to be. If 'primordial awareness' is what philosophers believe to be a genuine insight on the human condition (both Feng and Xiong, as Confucian thinkers, certainly did), then to them it must be more than a postulate.

On the surface, this may appear to be a conflict between different styles of philosophizing. Feng seems justified in having made 'primordial awareness' a mere postulate before he fully demonstrated its validity. After all, he could follow a series of assumptive reasons until he finally arrived at the conclusion that without 'primordial awareness' his whole philosophical enterprise would fall. Nevertheless, Xiong would contend that this style of philosophizing cheapens the seriousness of the spiritual exercise; it can be reduced to an inconsequential intellectual wordplay.

An underlying conviction of the New Confucian Humanists is that philosophy rooted in self-cultivation, far from being an academic discipline confined to a coterie of professionals in the ivory tower, is available to and necessary for all people. To paraphrase a statement in the *Daxue*, from the ruling minority and cultural elite to people in the street, all should regard self-cultivation as the root. If the root is not established, the Way cannot prevail; all the moral, social and political institutions instrumental for human flourishing (family, school, community, state and the world) depend upon self-cultivation for their stability, regularity, governance and peace. This personalist approach to morality, society and politics is based on the simple notion that the health of the whole is determined by the vitality of its constitutive parts. Ultimate human flourishing means that each and every member of the family, school, community, nation and the world is well-cultivated. Yet, to understand the significance of self-cultivation simply as a means to serve the ends of community well-being is one-sided. It is also an end in itself. Indeed, the justification for regulated families, functioning schools, ordered communities, governed states and a peaceful world is that they provide a wholesome environment for self-cultivation.

What is the relevance of self-cultivation philosophy to a complex modern society? A smooth functioning of the market, a vibrant democracy and the societal respect for the dignity of the person all depend upon the quality of the people involved. As we become increasingly self-interested, profit-oriented, litigious, competitive and individualistic, the need to develop a sense of public-mindedness, rightness, civility, trust and group spirit is compelling. The philosophy that enjoins us to elevate our common sense to good sense and transform the private ego into an open, dynamic and creatively transformative selfhood is vitally important for our life of the mind.

Perhaps the most enduring contribution of self-cultivation to the current style of philosophizing with emphasis on the analytical technique is to broaden the scope of rigorous thinking to include reflection on things at hand, meditation on ultimate concerns and examination of practical matters of daily living. Philosophy so conceived is no longer the privilege of a small coterie of trained professionals. Rather, it is a cultivated art accessible to all reflective, meditative and examining minds in the human community. While highly complex abstract reasoning may still characterize what teachers and researchers of philosophy do, the philosophical enterprise of self-knowledge is then an open invitation to all who cherish the value of the life of the mind. Surely, the degree of sophistication and refinement in self-cultivation varies from individual to individual and, like art, literature or music, the difference in proficiency and accomplishment between an initiating student and a virtuoso can be immense; but, to the extent that philosophy is viewed as self-cultivation, it is accessible to all members of the human community. While there is no need to delink philosophy from logic, epistemology and natural sciences, philosophy as self-cultivation or self-cultivation philosophy (they are of course distinguishable) must involve scholars in the humanities and social sciences. Indeed, for philosophy to regain the meaning and vitality as the 'love of wisdom' it once possessed, it must also transcend the boundaries of the ivory tower. Attention to self-cultivation is essential for such a task.

See also: BUDDHIST PHILOSOPHY, CHINESE; CHINESE CLASSICS; CHINESE PHILOSOPHY; CONFUCIAN PHILOSOPHY, CHINESE; CONFUCIUS; DAO; DAODEJING; DAOIST PHILOSOPHY; DAXUE; MENCIUS; NEO-CONFUCIAN PHILOSOPHY; XIN; XING; YIJING; ZHONGYONG

References and further reading

Balazs, E. (1964) 'Political Philosophy and Social Crisis', in H.M. Wright and A.F. Wright (ed. and trans.) *Chinese Civilization and Bureaucracy*, New Haven, CN: Yale University Press. (A collection of essays on Chinese institutions, history and thought.)

* Chan Wing-tsit (ed. and trans.) (1963) *A Source Book of Chinese Philosophy*, Princeton, NJ: Princeton University Press. (A survey of original sources in translation.)

* Confucius (551–479 BC) *Analects*, trans. D.C. Lau, *Confucius: The Analects*, Harmondsworth: Penguin, 1979. (An authoritative translation.)

Cua, A.S. (1982) *The Unity of Knowledge and Action: A Study in Wang Yang-ming's Moral Psychology*, Honolulu, HI: Unversity of Hawaii Press. (A study of Wang's doctrine in light of present inquiry concerning the relation between moral thought and action.)

Ivanhoe, P.J. (1993) *Confucian Moral Self Cultivation*, New York: Peter Lang. (A study of major Confucian thinkers that aims to provide a philosophically sensitive account of Confucian moral self-cultivation.)

* Liang Congjie (1996) *The Great Thoughts of China*, New York: Wiley. (A source book on Chinese philosophy.)

* Mencius (4th century BC) *Mengzi*, trans. D.C. Lau, *Mencius*, Harmondsworth: Penguin, 1970. (An authoritative translation.)

Tu Wei-ming (1979) *Humanity and Self-Cultivation*, Berkeley, CA: Asian Humanities Press. (A collection of articles on Confucian self-cultivation.)

—— (1985) *Confucian Thought: Selfhood as Creative Transformation*, Albany, NY: State University of New York Press. (A collection of articles on Confucian thought.)

—— (1989) *Centrality and Commonality: An Essay on Confucian Religiousness*, Albany, NY: State University of New York Press. (Although focused primarily on the *Zhongyong*, this monograph provides understanding of moral self-cultivation in light of Confucian religious thought.)

* Xunzi (*c.*298–238 BC) *Xunzi*, trans. B. Watson, *Hsün Tzu: Basic Writings*, New York: Columbia University Press, 1966. (An authoritative translation of selected chapters.)

TU WEI-MING

SELF-DECEPTION

Philosophical work on self-deception revolves around a trio of questions. What is self-deception? Is self-deception possible? How are cases of self-deception to be explained? The extent to which self-deception is analogous to interpersonal deception is controversial, partly because certain analogies threaten to render the possibility of self-deception deeply problematic. The problems concern both the mental state of self-deceived individuals at a particular time (static problems) and the dynamics of self-deception (dynamic problems). For example, in normal interpersonal deception the deceivers know something, p, or at least believe truly that p, while getting their victims to believe the opposite, ~ p. So if self-deception is strictly analogous to (normal) interpersonal deception, self-deceivers know or believe truly that p while getting themselves to believe that ~ p. If this entails simultaneously believing that p and believing that ~ p, self-deception may seem impossible. (For example, how can I believe that someone will read this entry while also believing that no one will read it?) Moreover, even if this state is possible, the suggestion that people can get themselves into it by deceiving themselves is problematic. It may seem, for instance, that any project describable as 'getting myself to believe what I now know to be false' is bound to be self-defeating. Self-deception may be dynamically impossible.

1 **Intentional self-deception and partitioning strategies**
2 **Departing from interpersonal models and related issues**

1 Intentional self-deception and partitioning strategies

Philosophers who deem self-deception conceptually or psychologically impossible typically contend that deceiving, by definition, is an intentional activity and that putative self-deceivers, therefore, must intentionally deceive themselves. In various time-lag scenarios, intentionally deceiving oneself clearly is possible. Paul, a pudgy prankster who has intentionally deceived others about their weight by secretly adjusting their bathroom scales, now intends to deceive himself into believing that he is lighter than he in fact is. Cognizant of his forgetfulness, the prankster adjusts his own scales for this purpose and counts on eventually forgetting that it was done. In this way, Paul may intentionally bring it about that he believes himself to be lighter than he is. In problematic cases, there is no such time lag. Rather, at some point during agents' intentional efforts to deceive themselves, they succeed in so doing. Some contend that such cases are impossible and that self-deception, therefore, is nonexistent. (These theorists suppose that self-deception is essentially intentional and involves no time lag.) Others defend the possibility of such cases. Yet others argue that intentional self-deception is remote from garden-variety self-deception and that even if the hard cases are impossible, that leaves the reality of self-deception intact.

Some philosophers propose to account for the possibility of self-deception by postulating a partitioned mind. Partitioning strategies range from postulating full-blown sub-agents with their own motives and intentions to employing modest distinctions among kinds or levels of awareness (see MODULARITY OF MIND; COGNITIVE ARCHITECTURE). In general, partitioners accept a strict interpersonal model of self-deception and seek to locate the requisite divisions within a single mind. A seriously divided mind may contain both a deceiving agent and a deceived subject. The deceiver (D) may believe that p while intentionally causing the subject (S) to believe that $\sim$ p. To the extent to which a divided mind is analogous to a pair (or group) of persons, static problems seem manageable. As you may believe that p while I believe that $\sim$ p, D may believe that p while S believes that $\sim$ p. Dynamic problems would be equally manageable. The basic idea of a representative dynamic problem has two major components. First, given that self-deceivers intentionally deceive themselves, they must intentionally follow a plan in so doing. Second, setting aside time-lag scenarios, any attempt at such plan-following would be self-defeating: just as I will not deceive you during a temporal span t, if you know what I am up to throughout t, you will not deceive yourself during t, if you know what you are up to throughout t. In a radically divided mind, S may have no idea what D is up to, and the problem vanishes.

Radical partitioners are often charged with substituting a species of 'other-deception' for self-deception. The criticism is that no human beings both deceive and are deceived by themselves on the radical view; rather, a sub-agent is the deceiver and something else is deceived. Further, the mental condition of radically partitioned persons strikes some theorists as disturbingly similar to multiple personality disorder. Surely, ordinary self-deceivers need not be so fragmented? Arguably, more modest proposals can account for self-deception.

Less radical partitioners eschew appealing to internal agents. Normally, however, their partitioning hypotheses are designed specifically to handle static problems, and dynamic counterparts remain. It has been proposed, for example, that a person may simultaneously believe that p and believe that $\sim$ p, because the true belief may be possessed only unconsciously and therefore need not pre-empt the simultaneous holding of a contrary belief (see UNCONSCIOUS MENTAL STATES). However, this does not answer the charge that intentional processes logically required for self-deception are necessarily self-defeating.

2 Departing from interpersonal models and related issues

Another approach to defending the possibility of self-deception is to motivate a departure from strict interpersonal models of the phenomenon. The assumption that deceiving is, by definition, an intentional activity drives many familiar puzzles about self-deception; and it is false. Using deceived in the passive voice, we properly say such things as 'Unless I am deceived, I left my keys in my car'. Here 'deceived' means 'mistaken'. In a corresponding use of 'deceive' in the active voice, to deceive is 'to cause

to believe what is false'; and not all instances of this are intentional. Your father accidentally misreads an encyclopedia article, taking it to report that p. He then tells you that p, intending to report something true but actually uttering something false. If you believe him, he has caused you to believe a falsehood: he has deceived you, in one legitimate sense of the word, but not intentionally.

This point has been exploited. When we know that people accidentally caused themselves to believe a falsehood (by innocently misreading an encyclopedia article, for example), we do not charge them with self-deception. However, when motivation enters the causal story in certain ways, a charge of self-deception seems warranted. Ordinarily, people who allegedly deceive themselves into believing that p want p to be true. For example, people who deceive themselves into believing that their spouses are not having extramarital affairs normally want it to be true that they are not so engaged, and parents who deceive themselves into believing that their children were erroneously convicted of a crime normally want it to be true that they are innocent. Owing significantly to the influence of relevant desires, Edna falsely believes that her husband, Ed, is not having an affair, in the face of strong evidence to the contrary. Is it likely that Edna first comes to believe that Ed is having an affair and then forms the intention to get herself to believe that he is not so engaged – which intention, perhaps after a bit of means/end reasoning, she successfully executes? Or is it more likely that, owing partly to her desire that Ed not be having an affair, Edna acquires or retains a false belief that he is innocent of infidelity without having come to believe that he is guilty and without intending to deceive herself?

A proper understanding of the dynamics of self-deception requires an appreciation of the ways in which motivation may bias reasoning and the formation, perseverance, and revision of beliefs. How might it happen that Edna believes that Ed is innocent of infidelity even though an impartial person, presented with the same evidence, reasonably concludes that he is guilty? Owing to her desire for Ed's innocence, Edna may misinterpret data, reasoning, for instance, that if Ed were having an affair he would hide it and that his seemingly intimate meetings with his apparent lover in local taverns and cinemas consequently indicate that he is not sexually involved with her. Edna may even recruit Ed (in effect) in her motivated interpretive activities, by asking him for an explanation of the data, or by suggesting for his approval some acceptable hypothesis about his conduct. Further, again owing to her desire, Edna's attention may be selectively attracted by evidence of Ed's innocence. There is considerable empirical evidence that what we believe tends to be affected by the salience of our data; and Edna's desire for Ed's innocence may render corresponding data more salient than they would otherwise be. Edna may even set out to conduct an impartial investigation, but, owing to her desire, locate and focus on less accessible support for Ed's innocence while overlooking more readily attainable support for his guilt.

All this can happen without Edna's intending to deceive herself. Still, given the motivated way in which Edna's pertinent belief is produced or sustained, even in the face of stronger evidence to the contrary, Edna is plausibly regarded as self-deceived. She is deceived as a consequence of her motivationally biased cognitive conduct.

The alleged requirement that self-deception be intentional is separable from another putative requirement – namely, that the person who is self-deceived in believing that p also knows or believes, at some level, that ~ p. Some allege that self-deceived individuals characteristically behave in ways that clash with their sincere assertions and that this is explained by their knowing the truth at some level, which knowledge manifests itself in their overt behaviour. This is disputable. Edna, for instance, arguably is self-deceived even if she does not know or believe, at any level, that Ed is having an affair – even if her self-deception consists, in part, in a motivated failure to acquire the true belief that Ed is guilty of infidelity. Further, if Edna's behaviour towards Ed has become cool, and if she has begun to enquire regularly of his whereabouts, this may be explained on the less demanding hypothesis that she suspects that Ed may be having an affair. Edna may believe that Ed is faithful while also believing that there is a significant chance that she is wrong about this: 'I believe that p, but I may be mistaken' is utterly intelligible. In a thoroughly self-deceived person, beliefs of the latter sort presumably are absent. A self-deceived person – like a person deceived by someone else into believing that p – may be fully confident that p.

In garden-variety instances of self-deception, on this view, we do not deceive ourselves with the intention of so doing, or with the intention of causing ourselves to believe (or to cease believing) something. The absence of such an intention does not, however, preclude personal responsibility for garden-variety self-deception. Often, we are properly held responsible for unintended deceiving: for example, when we should have taken more care to get the facts straight, or to express them clearly. Sometimes, when we should have been more vigilant, we are justifiably held accountable for being

deceived. This is so even when the deceiving and deceived persons are one and the same.

A thorough understanding of self-deception would clarify such related issues as the nature of belief, the influence of motivation on belief, and the structure of human minds. Certain controversial views about self-deception contravene the popular idea that belief is essentially exclusive, in the sense that a person's believing that p is incompatible with the person's simultaneously believing that ~ p. Various discussions of the dynamics of self-deception illuminate the influence of motivation on belief. The literature also features a lively debate about the extent to which the human mind is unified and about the range of entities (sub-agents, for example) to which such mental items as beliefs, desires and intentions are plausibly attributed.

See also: ACTION; SELF-DECEPTION, ETHICS OF

References and further reading

All items cited are comprehensible by advanced undergraduates.

Davidson, D. (1985) 'Deception and Division', in E. Lepore and B. McLaughlin (eds) *Actions and Events*, New York: Blackwell. (Advances a much-discussed partitioning account.)

Demos, R. (1960) 'Lying to Oneself', *Journal of Philosophy* 57: 588-95. (Seminal paper advancing modest partitioning.)

Fingarette, H. (1969) *Self-Deception*, London: Routledge & Kegan Paul. (Emphasizes the dynamic nature of self-deception and develops an action-oriented response to familiar worries about the possibility of self-deception.)

Haight, M. (1980) *A Study of Self-Deception*, Sussex: Harvester Wheatsheaf. (Defends the impossibility of self-deception.)

Lockard, J. and Paulhus, D. (eds) (1988) *Self-Deception: An Adaptive Mechanism?*, Englewood Cliffs, NJ: Prentice-Hall. (Useful collection of literature in psychology and related fields.)

McLaughlin, B. and Rorty, A. (eds) (1988) *Perspectives on Self-Deception*, Berkeley, CA: University of California Press. (Useful collection; extensive bibliography.)

Martin, M. (ed.) (1985) *Self-Deception and Self-Understanding*, Lawrence, KS: University of Kansas Press. (Useful collection of philosophical and psychological literature; extensive bibliography.)

Mele, A. (1987) *Irrationality: An Essay on Akrasia, Self-Deception, and Self-Control*, New York: Oxford University Press. (Criticizes partitioning and advances an alternative resolution of the static and dynamic problems.)

Pears, D. (1984) *Motivated Irrationality*, Oxford: Oxford University Press. (Advocates radical partitioning.)

Sartre, J-P. (1943) *L'être et le néant*, Paris: Gallimard; trans. H. Barnes, *Being and Nothingness*, New York: Washington Square Press, 1956. (Includes an influential discussion of bad faith, a phenomenon sometimes identified with self-deception.)

A.R. MELE

SELF-DECEPTION, ETHICS OF

Self-deception is complicated and perplexing because it concerns all major aspects of human nature, including consciousness, rationality, motivation, freedom, happiness, and value commitments. In a wide sense, 'self-deception' refers to intentional activities and motivated processes of avoiding unpleasant truths or topics and the resulting mental states of ignorance, false belief, unwarranted attitudes, and inappropriate emotions. Deceiving oneself, like deceiving other people, raises a host of questions about immorality. These include whether self-deception is always immoral or only when it conceals and supports wrongdoing; whether self-deception about wrongdoing and character faults compounds or mitigates guilt for causing harm; how important the value of authenticity is, and whether it can be sacrificed in an attempt to cope with reality; what the relation is between self-deception and responsibility; and whether groups can be self-deceived. Ultimately, the moral status of any instance of self-deception depends on the particular facts of the case.

1 **Explaining wrongdoing**
2 **Authentic values**
3 **Healthy coping**
4 **Ambiguous responsibility**
5 **Collective self-deception**
6 **Conclusion**

1 Explaining wrongdoing

The activities and the mental states involved in self-deception – especially the suggestion that we can wilfully get ourselves to believe the opposite of what we know is true – seem paradoxical in ways that have generated a large literature in epistemology and philosophy of mind (see SELF-DECEPTION). That literature is germane to the moral issues, especially as it serves to clarify the extent of voluntariness in deceiving ourselves.

Self-deception is objectionable when it camouflages and supports greed, cruelty and other forms of wrongdoing. Moreover, often the first step towards self-reform is to remove self-deception about our character faults. And we would make fairer appraisals of other people if we were less self-deceiving about condemning them and excusing ourselves. Or so traditional ethicists have contended.

In his discussion of this in two early lectures (1722), Joseph BUTLER focused on two contexts. First, when moral rules are vague we tend to interpret them in ways convenient to ourselves. For example, we employ legalistic ruses in narrowly interpreting duties to help others and prohibitions against corruption. Second, we excuse our overt violations of clear duties so as to make them 'sit a little easy' in conscience. In both contexts, our motives might be general selfishness or specific passions. Our tactics include rationalization, wilful ignorance, and systematic ignoring. Having (and using) suspicions and partial knowledge of our faults, we avoid further inquiry, closing 'the eyes of the mind' as easily as those of the body. Because the avoidance is intentional, Butler concludes that self-deception compounds rather than lessens guilt for harming others and for corrupting our own consciences. It makes us hypocrites before others and also 'inner hypocrites' who culpably pretend to ourselves that we are better persons than we are.

Kant (1797) went further in suggesting that self-deception about virtually any topic – not just immorality – can indirectly cause violations of duties to others, either by making us ignorant of morally-relevant information or by encouraging habits of self-deception. Kant's view is implausible regarding many examples but it has some plausibility regarding general habits of engaging in self-deceit.

David Pears (1984) and Alfred R. Mele (1987), among others, have explored parallels and interactions between self-deception and moral weakness (see AKRASIA). Self-deception explains many instances of acting against our better judgment by revealing how we blur that judgment or ignore morally relevant information. Even when moral weakness is fully conscious, self-deception causes a loss of moral perspective that might have prevented it. Conversely, some self-deception may itself qualify as moral weakness in so far as we voluntarily violate our standards of morality and rationality.

2 Authentic values

No philosopher was harsher in condemning self-deception ('bad faith') than Jean-Paul SARTRE (§3).

His condemnations were made despite and partly because of his renunciation of traditional beliefs in objectively justifiable values (see EXISTENTIALIST ETHICS §3).

Sartre (1943) defined authenticity as fully acknowledging our complete freedom to choose values and to interpret the world in light of them (see EXISTENTIALIST ETHICS §§1–2). By definition, authenticity is incompatible with self-deceptive excuses and evasions. The worst self-deception is the direct denial of freedom of consciousness because it leads to violating other persons' freedom of conduct, for example through anti-Semitism or political oppression. Yet self-deception about all topics, not just about freedom in general, implies a cowardly refusal to acknowledge our freely chosen mental states and actions. Tactics of self-deception include quick oscillations of attention towards pleasing aspects of our lives and away from anxiety-producing ones. For example, we affirm our freedom ('transcendence') in so far as it promises happiness, but we appeal to hard facts ('facticity') whenever it assuages the anxieties in admitting responsibility for 'authoring' our choices. The fundamental strategy ('original project') in self-deception is to distort the standards of rationality for belief by exaggerating favourable evidence for what we want to believe, disregarding contrary evidence, and resting content with minimal evidence for pleasing beliefs. Sartre's discussion is often insightful, but he conflates key distinctions such as those between free consciousness and free conduct and between causal responsibility and moral accountability.

Nietzsche (1888) offered a more nuanced critique of self-deception than Sartre (see NIETZSCHE, F. §9). Certainly he could be equally harsh in condemning traditional beliefs in the objectivity of moral values, with the possible exceptions of honesty and courage. Perhaps inconsistently, however, he praised the need for some self-deception in asserting our 'will to power' in developing and living according to authentic value-perspectives.

A more traditional approach to authentic values and personal identity retains the traditional faith in objective moral values by reference to which authenticity is understood. This approach does not entail dogmatism and leaves room for a pluralistic conception of diverse forms of goodness from which we choose in creating meaningful lives (see MORAL PLURALISM). On this view, the authentic self is honestly responsive to general moral requirements, attuned to the particular goods we care most deeply about, and courageous in dealing with ineluctable realities such as death.

3 Healthy coping

Despite claims of neutrality, psychologists and social scientists who discuss self-deception frequently presuppose evaluative perspectives. Those who focus on mental illness emphasize the harmful aspects of self-deceiving 'defence mechanisms'; those who focus on healthy behaviour stress the value of self-deception as an adjustment mechanism.

Although Sigmund Freud (1920) rarely used the term 'self-deception', many of his followers interpret defence mechanisms (such as repression, projection, and sublimation) as strategies of self-deception. Using these strategies, the ego (the coping part of the mind) defends itself against onslaughts from the id (unconscious sexual and aggressive desires), the superego (socially instilled values), and external reality. In his early work Freud portrayed the ego as entirely conscious, but later he emphasized that an unconscious part of the ego engages in defence.

Cognitive psychologists have explored the positive roles of self-deception in promoting mental wellbeing, especially in maintaining healthy self-esteem by exaggerating our virtues, supporting optimism by playing down risks and creating illusions of control, and coping with traumatic events and threatening uncertainties. Similarly, sociobiologists hypothesize that we evolved as creatures who compete more successfully when we can deceive ourselves into believing the falsehoods we perpetrate on others (in order not to betray the deception with behavioural signals). These scientists provide needed correctives to one-sided condemnations of self-deception by Kant and Sartre.

4 Ambiguous responsibility

Responsibility for self-deception is obscure and ambiguous because the notion suggests a self divided against itself, rather than a unified agent, accountable for its voluntary choices.

In *Self-Deception* (1969), Herbert Fingarette linked self-deception to wider issues about personal identity and divided selves. In his view, self-deceivers pursue 'engagements' (ways of participating in the world) that they disavow. Disavowal implies a refusal to become explicitly conscious of engagements and also of the activities involved in concealing them. More fundamentally, disavowal constitutes a refusal to integrate disavowed engagements into the network of other engagements that comprise the dominant aspects of one's personality. Isolated and without rational supervision, disavowed engagements can wreak havoc on oneself and others. We are responsible for initiating disavowal, but responsibility becomes ambiguous in so far as we lose control over disavowed engagements.

Fingarette has been criticized for being too sympathetic to psychoanalysis and insufficiently rooted in more empirical psychology (although it should be noted that his book inspired many subsequent empirical studies of self-deception). It has also been noted that he unhelpfully plays down cognitive terms like 'belief' and 'knowledge' as he shifts to action-oriented terms like 'avow' and 'disavow'. Finally, he has been accused of over-generalizing about the moral ambiguities of (all) self-deception, rather than attending to the moral variety of particular cases.

5 Collective self-deception

Collective self-deception is self-deception by entire groups who share false beliefs and unwarranted attitudes. Charges of collective self-deception are both provocative and contentious. Thus, Marxists portray workers who accept capitalism as suffering from 'false consciousness', that is, illusions about the economic origins and political implications of economic 'ideologies' (see MARX, K. §10; IDEOLOGY §1). Some feminists portray satisfied homemakers as having 'internalized' patriarchal ideologies. Religious and nonreligious thinkers criticize each other's perspectives as self-deceiving. And in *1984* (1949), George Orwell suggested that political oppression is sustained by fostering widespread 'doublethink', a process he described in terms reminiscent of Sartre's description of bad faith.

Some charges of collective self-deception are illuminating, although troublesome in thinking about personal and collective responsibility (see RESPONSIBILITY). In so far as my self-deception is pressured or encouraged by strong social forces, am I less blameworthy because my autonomy is lessened, or is my responsibility compounded because I allowed myself to be a passive conspirator? (In *Invisible Man* (1947), Ralph Ellison suggests that both may be true, in different respects.) Nevertheless, allegations of collective self-deception are easily abused and tend to degrade the concept of self-deception into a rhetorical weapon that undermines tolerance. Ascriptions of self-deception about morality are rooted most firmly where values are clear and well-justified; they are best avoided in contexts where morally reasonable persons interpret and balance values in alternative ways.

6 Conclusion

Self-deception is morally complex for two main reasons. First, in evaluating particular instances and in ascribing responsibility for their consequences, attention must be paid to an array of contextual factors: what the self-deception is about, what motivates it, which obligations it threatens, the degree of harm it causes to oneself and to others, the vital needs it may serve, how much control an individual has in initiating and sustaining it, what help is available to overcome it, and whether it is episodic or habitual. When motives are good and consequences are desirable, self-deception may be excusable, forgivable, desirable, or simply comic, depending on the circumstances. When motives and consequences are evil, as they were in the self-deception that Albert Speer ascribes to himself in his memoirs, *Erinnerungen* (*Inside the Third Reich*) (1969), self-deception becomes a form of cruelty and callous moral negligence.

Second, different moral emphases can be brought to bear in understanding self-deception. We may agree that honesty (with oneself and others) is an important virtue, but exactly how important relative to other virtues is open to dispute and reasonable disagreement (see TRUTHFULNESS). The insistence that honesty is always paramount and forbids all self-deception can result in inhumane neglect of other important values such as love and self-respect. Indeed, idealistic demands for perfect honesty can themselves be permeated with self-deceptive self-righteousness, as playwrights remind us: see Molière's *Le Misanthrope* (*The Misanthrope*) (1666), Henrik Ibsen's *Vildanden* (*The Wild Duck*) (1884), and Eugene O'Neill's *The Iceman Cometh* (1957). It is equally clear, however, that love and self-respect are themselves undermined when habitual self-deception distorts caring for others and for oneself.

References and further reading

Ames, R.T. and Dissanayake, W. (eds) (1996) *Self and Deception*, Albany, NY: State University of New York. (Essays contrasting Western and non-Western views of self-deception.)

* Butler, J. (1722) 'Upon Self-Deceit' and 'Upon the Character of Balaam', in *The Works of Bishop Butler*, Oxford: Oxford University Press, 1896. (Insightful sermons that focus on the corruption of conscience.)

Dilman, Ï. and Phillips, D.Z. (1971) *Sense and Delusion*, New York: Humanities Press. (Argues that self-deception undermines meaningful life.)

* Ellison, R. (1947) *Invisible Man*, New York: Vintage Books. (A novel about a young man's search for authenticity in a racist society.)

* Fingarette, H. (1969) *Self-Deception*, London: Humanities Press. (Focuses on personal identity,

integrating ideas of Sartre, Kierkegaard and Freud.)

* Freud, S. (1920) *A General Introduction to Psychoanalysis*, New York: Liveright. (Readable and lively overview of the role of unconscious motives.)

Haight, M.R. (1980) *A Study of Self-Deception*, London: Humanities Press. (Explores paradoxes of freedom, determinism, and the divided self.)

* Ibsen, H. (1884) *Vildanden*, trans. D.B. Christiani, *The Wild Duck*, New York: W.W. Norton, 1968. (A play unmasking dangerous illusions about human pretensions.)

* Kant, I. (1797) *Metaphysische Anfangsgründe der Tugendlehre*, trans. M.J. Gregor, *The Doctrine of Virtue: Part II of The Metaphysics of Morals*, Philadelphia, PA: University of Pennsylvania Press, 1964. (Early reflections on the divided self.)

Lockard, J.S. and Paulhus, D.L. (eds) (1988) *Self-Deception: An Adaptive Mechanism?* Englewood Cliffs, NJ: Prentice Hall. (Psychological studies of self-deception as a coping device.)

Martin, M.W. (1986) *Self-Deception and Morality*, Lawrence, KS: University Press of Kansas. (Discussion of four moral perspectives: inner hypocrisy, authenticity, moral ambiguity, and vital lies.)

—— (ed.) (1985) *Self-Deception and Self-Understanding*, Lawrence, KS: University Press of Kansas. (Philosophical and psychological essays on ethics, paradoxes, and mental structures of self-deception.)

* Mele, A.R. (1987) *Irrationality: An Essay on Akrasia, Self-Deception and Self-Control*, Oxford: Oxford University Press. (Explores interconnections between weakness of will and self-deception.)

* Molière, J-B.P. (1666) *Le Misanthrope*, trans. R. Wilbur, *The Misanthrope*, New York: Harcourt Brace, 1954. (Comic exploration of the idea that honesty threatens personal relationships unless constrained by common decency.)

* Nietzsche, F. (1888) *Ecce Homo*, trans. W. Kaufmann and R. Hollingdale in *Basic Writings of Nietzsche*, New York: Modern Library, 1968. (Wide-ranging epigrams dealing with knowledge and values.)

* O'Neill, E. (1957) *The Iceman Cometh*, New York: Vintage Books. (Drama that exposes the violence in personal relationships camouflaged by 'pipe dreams'.)

* Orwell, G. (1949) *1984*, New York: New American Library, 1961. (Nightmarish vision of a totalitarian government which uses mind control centred around 'doublethink'.)

* Pears, D. (1984) *Motivated Irrationality*, Oxford: Oxford University Press. (Studies the parallels between self-deception and other forms of irrationality.)

Pines, C.L. (1993) *Ideology and False Consciousness*, Albany, NY: State University of New York Press. (Introduction to Marxist conceptions of collective self-deception.)

* Sartre, J-P. (1943) *L'Être et le Néant. Essai d'ontologie phénoménologique*, Paris: Gallimard; trans. H.E. Barnes, *Being and Nothingness: An Essay of Phenomenological Ontology*, New York: Washington Square, 1966, 86–116. (Famous chapter on 'bad faith' that sparked extensive philosophical interest in self-deceit.)

* Speer, A. (1969) *Erinnerungen*, trans. R. Winston and C. Winston, *Inside the Third Reich*, New York: Avon, 1970. (Memoirs of Hitler's leading bureaucrat, who explains his cruelty by ascribing to himself self-deception.)

MIKE W. MARTIN

SELF-REALIZATION

'Self-realization' is the development and expression of characteristic attributes and potentials in a fashion which comprehensively discloses their subject's real nature. Usually, the 'self' in question is the individual person, but the concept has also been applied to corporate bodies held to possess a unitary identity.

What constitutes the self's 'real nature' is the key variable generating the many conceptions of self-realization. These can be grouped broadly into two types: (1) the 'collectivist', in which the self-realizing lifestyle, being either the same for all or specific to a person or subgroup of people, is ultimately definable only in the context, and perhaps with reference to the common purposes, of a collective social body; (2) the 'individualist', in which a person's self-realization has no necessary connection with the ends of a particular community.

As an ethic, self-realization can be proposed as the means to achieve a life identified as good by some criterion independent of the self-realizing process, or held to be that which actually defines the good. Its critics typically argue that human nature is such that any equation of 'self-realization' and 'goodness' is implausible or undesirable.

1   **Collectivist self-realization**
2   **Individualist self-realization**
3   **Further problems**

1 Collectivist self-realization

Aristotle's moral and political work, especially *Nicomachean Ethics*, is an enormously influential example of a self-realizationist theory, which holds that the development and expression of people's potentials is the goal for the best moral – and, for Aristotle, political – life (see ARISTOTLE §§20–6). Using 'self-realization' as much to describe the good society as the good person, he proceeds from the belief that humans naturally possess a unique, essential state of being – the life of reason-guided activity – to argue that achievement of this state is the goal (*telos*) towards which normal human development aims (see HUMAN NATURE §1). Subsequently, he identifies those personal dispositions and social institutions necessary for securing this end.

Aristotelian self-realization is collectivist not only in the sense of its essence being a shared characteristic but also in its requirement that it be achieved within a very particular form of social life: the polis or city-state. Theoretically, it permits some diversity across the range of self-realizing lives. Other versions of collectivist self-realization can be much stricter in detailing exactly what form of life is required, tying the 'real nature' of the self to specific social roles or the performance of onerous moral duties. Often, these doctrines adopt a version of positive liberty by characterizing self-realization as 'true freedom', which facilitates their descriptions of non-self-realizing lifestyles as not 'really' wanted by people despite any 'mistaken' preferences to the contrary (see FREEDOM AND LIBERTY).

The sustainability of collectivist conceptions in Western thought was weakened significantly (particularly from the seventeenth century onwards) with the emergence of more atomized, individualistic notions of the self, generated not least by a growing appreciation of human diversity. This distinctively modern form of identity self-consciously sought individuation, conceptualizing the self and its ends apart from any particular, metaphysically independent moral order. Increasingly, people were seen as empowered to direct their own lives according to their own desires. The postulation of substantive shared natures and comprehensive collective purposes, and the equation of their realization with human freedom and morality, became much less credible. Indeed, for some, such conceptions were downright pernicious in their attempt to attribute an artificial uniformity to human nature.

That some versions of collectivist self-realization remained vibrant in the nineteenth and twentieth centuries was due largely to Hegel and his intellectual heirs, but the transformation in the concept of the individual left its mark on them (see HEGELIANISM). Reflecting high Enlightenment optimism over the goodness of human potential and the continuing reconcilability of freedom, morality and social order, their theories held that self-realization involved the expression of full individuality and a unification of every self with each other in a qualitatively new, yet genuinely communal, form of social life (see ENLIGHTENMENT, CONTINENTAL). Marxism became the most influential exponent of this approach, viewing self-realization as based upon the capacity for free creative labour supposedly shared by all and insisting that, under full communism, the free self-realization of each would ultimately be dependent upon the free self-realization of all (see MARX. K.).

2 Individualist self-realization

Romanticism was the prime influence in bequeathing conceptions of self-realization to the individualized notions of selfhood, prompting a view of the self as invested with a capacity to develop – freely and creatively – a naturally given potential to lead a morally worthy, aesthetically stimulating life (see ROMANTICISM, GERMAN). This was distinguishable from the collectivist variant in that the self-realizing lifestyle was held to be unique to each individual and no longer required reference to the purposes of a larger whole for its full meaning. Many individualistic conceptions nevertheless stressed self-realization's dependence upon specific forms of community as necessary means for its achievement, retaining the concept's potential as critic of degenerate societies and inspiration for social and political reform. The emphasis had nevertheless switched to the individual's uniqueness as the end in itself and in some other versions, notably that of the later Rousseau, modern society is seen as so irredeemably corrupt as to require virtual abandonment by the self seeking realization (see also ROUSSEAU, J.-J.).

The 'individualistic' label should not obscure the fact that these conceptions generally reaffirm the idea that there are certain features common to everyone's self-realization: similar kinds of potential, for example. This preserves the viability of 'self-realization' as something identifiably separate from other ways of living. Yet the same sensitivity to human diversity which undermined the collectivists' credibility poses serious challenges here, too. One may doubt that even the relatively minimal shared features specified by these conceptions really exhaust all cases of what self-realization might legitimately involve. One may believe there is no warrant for characterizing self-realization as anything other than however individuals would like to live, in which case the need for –

perhaps even the very intelligibility of – the concept as distinct from, say, mere 'autonomy' must be questioned (see AUTONOMY, ETHICAL).

Alternatively, if self-realization is still defined in sufficiently substantive terms to avoid a content-draining equation of it with 'whatever one chooses to be or do', but one also desires to respect individuals' autonomy (as individualistic conceptions usually profess to do), self-realization very readily reduces simply to one lifestyle option among many which might be chosen by free people. Though this need not force a denial that it is the best form of life, preference for self-realization over respect for autonomy as a social and political ethic consequently seems to lose justification.

3   Further problems

The concept's detractors may also be critical of its presentation as an ethical standard, in which self-realization is defined by some independent specification of goodness or is deemed to be what actually yields the criterion of goodness itself (see PERFECTIONISM). Arguing that humanity's behaviour reveals nothing good in people's potentials, they may contend that self-realization is far from the best route to goodness and patently unsatisfactory as a defining characteristic of the good. Alternatively they may urge that, even if it is not intrinsically bad, self-realization creates a 'culture of narcissism', encouraging those forms of selfhood which, while perhaps harmless enough in themselves, nevertheless fail to show respect for others and threaten to enervate social life itself.

Critics also claim that the self-realization of people with morally positive natures might still entail struggle, frustration and disillusionment, which could be worse (in hedonistic or any other terms) than the outcome of a non-self-realizing life. Equating 'good' directly with 'self-realization' theoretically dissolves such worries ('whatever pain it may cause, self-realization remains the best by definition'). Yet this move seems eminently resistible if we consider the gamut of human potentials to be profoundly ambivalent in character. There are both good and bad potentials, with some people possessed of a surfeit of one and most, perhaps, laden with a mixture of both. To yield this plausible discrimination, we clearly need to conceptualize 'good' independently of 'self-realization'. However, the same ambivalence militates against the thought that self-realization is the best way to achieve an independently defined good: the latter might require the restraint of at least part of one's nature.

Furthermore, the very concept of the self as possessed of a given identity capable of realization has been challenged in postmodernist thinking (see SUBJECT, POSTMODERN CRITIQUE OF THE). While many conceptions of self-realization readily accept that the 'givenness' of the self's nature does not preclude its fluidity and revisability, postmodernism wants to resist any such fixity and, accordingly, prefers putatively distinct notions of self-*creation*.

Yet 'self-realization' can be revised to insist that the highest realizable values must spring from part of human nature, urging that we learn to identify with that part which promises the most fulfilling and sustainable form of personal and social life, and fashion our lifestyles accordingly. Green moral and political thought has utilized the concept thus, interestingly de-emphasizing its usual 'activist' insistence upon personal striving in a reconciliation of the self with nature which is more reminiscent of the spiritual, contemplative self-realizationist ethics in Eastern philosophy (see ENVIRONMENTAL ETHICS §2; BUDDHIST PHILOSOPHY, INDIAN §1).

If it can, then, be rendered a distinctive and attractive concept, 'self-realization' might plausibly continue to be a central concept in critiques of those ways of life and forms of society which leave people unfulfilled and alienated.

See also: DAODEJING; HAPPINESS; JAPANESE PHILOSOPHY §§8–9; LIFE, MEANING OF; NIRVĀṆA; SELF-CULTIVATION IN CHINESE PHILOSOPHY; SELF-DECEPTION, ETHICS OF

References and further reading

Aristotle (*c.* mid 4th century BC) *Nicomachean Ethics*, trans. with notes by T. Irwin, Indianapolis, IN: Hackett Publishing Company, 1985. (Arguably the single most influential text in Western self-realizationist thinking.)

Berlin, I. (1969) 'Two Concepts of Liberty', in *Four Essays on Liberty*, Oxford: Oxford University Press. (Describes self-realization as a version of positive freedom, which it attacks for its totalitarian potential.)

Elster, J. (1986) 'Self-Realization in Work and Politics: The Marxist Conception of the Good Life', in E.F. Paul, F.D. Miller, Jr, J. Paul and J. Ahrens (eds) *Marxism and Liberalism*, Oxford: Blackwell. (A clear exposition and defence of a self-realizationist ethic loosely inspired by Marx.)

Lasch, C. (1978) *The Culture of Narcissism*, New York: W.W. Norton. (Attacks what it considers to be a pervasive and overly indulgent, narrow-minded obsession with oneself which self-realization has been accused of promoting.)

Naess, A. (1995) 'Self-Realization: An Ecological

Approach to Being in the World', in G. Sessions (ed.) *Deep Ecology for the 21st Century*, Boston, MA: Shambala Publications. (Representative of the contemporary Green interest in conceptions of self-realization.)

Taylor, C. (1979) *Hegel and Modern Society*, Cambridge: Cambridge University Press. (A compact discussion not only of the Hegelian but also the Romantic and Marxist versions of self-realizationist theory.)

—— (1993) *The Ethics of Authenticity*, Cambridge, MA: Harvard University Press. (Using 'authenticity' synonymously with 'self-realization', an ideal introduction to a contemporary moral and political theory based upon the concept.)

MARK EVANS

SELF-RESPECT

Persons are said to respect themselves when they have an appropriate sense of their own worth either as persons generally or as individuals occupying particular roles. In respecting themselves as persons, people may recognize their worth as persons ('recognition' self-respect) or value the positive aspects of their character ('evaluative' or 'appraisal' self-respect). On the 'subjective' view of self-respect, persons have self-respect so long as they value themselves according to their own standards of worthiness. On the 'objective' view, there are certain attitudes or actions that show self-respect, regardless of whether the agents exhibiting them are conforming to their own standards. Self-respect plays a central role in the ethical philosophy of Kant and the political philosophy of Rawls. Kant maintains that persons have a duty to respect themselves, which consists in regarding themselves as equal in moral status to other persons. Rawls holds that a just society must provide the social bases of self-respect for all citizens, for without self-respect, their lives are severely diminished. In this same spirit, some critiques of oppression emphasize the injustice of robbing people of their self-respect, which is often a consequence, it is claimed, of being oppressed.

1 The concept of self-respect
2 Self-respect in moral and political philosophy

1 The concept of self-respect

Self-respect is a multifaceted notion involving a constellation of attitudes, beliefs, desires, dispositions, commitments, expectations, actions and emotions that express or constitute one's sense of one's worth. It includes a recognition and understanding of one's worth, as well as a desire and disposition to protect and preserve it. One can respect oneself as a person, as when one stands up for one's rights, or in a specific role or capacity, as when one adopts the code of ethics associated with one's work or profession. One may also merit one's own respect, as a person or as the occupier of a role, by conducting oneself honourably or by living up to one's standards. Since philosophers tend to be concerned with respect for oneself as a person, 'self-respect' will henceforth be assumed to have persons as such as its object.

Most writers on self-respect agree that it can be divided into two kinds, according to its appropriate grounds. Robin Dillon (1992a) calls these two kinds 'recognition' self-respect and 'evaluative' self-respect. The latter kind is also widely referred to as 'appraisal' self-respect (see RESPECT FOR PERSONS §1). Recognition self-respect is a type of regard towards oneself that all persons are obliged or entitled to acquire. Unworthy attitudes or conduct, such as servility or needless self-deprecation, are viewed as evidence of, or as constitutive of, its absence. The label 'recognition self-respect' derives from the fact that the attitude to which it refers consists primarily in recognizing that one is a person and weighing appropriately this fact in deliberation and action. Such recognition is not to be understood as mere acknowledgement of the fact that one is a person. It also includes appreciating the special status one has as a person and that this status may require certain kinds of responses, conduct, or restraint. One is obliged or entitled to respect oneself in virtue of the fact that one is a person.

The concept of recognition self-respect relies heavily on a normative conception of the person. Moreover, one must have some sense of what that conception entails to understand what would count as respecting or showing disrespect to persons. It follows that we can infer much about philosophers' understanding of the nature and status of persons from their accounts of the content of recognition self-respect. The notion of the person that is presupposed by most contemporary discussions of recognition self-respect is either strictly Kantian, or Kantian in spirit (see RESPECT FOR PERSONS §2). On this view, persons are essentially autonomous rational agents who possess a special worth grounded in their capacity for moral agency and who enjoy a status of moral equality with other persons on the basis of this special worth (see AUTONOMY, ETHICAL). Recognition respect for oneself as a rational autonomous agent involves acknowledging and appreciating one's autonomy, one's rationality, the value one has in virtue of having these capacities, and the moral status of equality that is grounded in this shared value (see KANTIAN ETHICS).

In contrast with recognition self-respect, which all persons are required or entitled to secure, evaluative self-respect is a kind of self-respect that individuals may or may not merit and may merit in varying degrees. Where the presence of recognition self-respect prompts us to engage in worthy conduct or refrain from engaging in unworthy conduct, the presence of evaluative self-respect results from an assessment of conduct already undertaken. Because persons must earn evaluative self-respect by conforming their actions, emotional responses, attitudes and so on to certain standards of worthiness, not everyone is entitled to evaluative self-respect, and some people's evaluative self-respect is unwarranted. Likewise, some people's lack of evaluative self-respect is also unwarranted. The normative ground of evaluative respect is the quality of one's moral character and those actions that reflect it. One merits evaluative self-respect, in other words, not in virtue of *being* a person, but because of the virtue *of* one's person.

Self-respect is distinct from self-esteem, though the latter notion bears some resemblance to evaluative self-respect. Both evaluative self-respect and self-esteem involve having a favourable opinion of oneself that arises from an assessment of one's traits or actions. Moreover, both attitudes can be undeserved as well as deserved but absent. None the less these two notions differ in their respective normative grounds. A favourable regard for oneself based upon features that do not bear directly upon one's moral character, such as one's sense of humour or one's having won a chess match, is self-esteem. Evaluative self-respect involves the positive regard one has for oneself based upon one's moral character. Although this method of distinguishing self-respect from self-esteem is by no means uncontroversial, it has the advantage of allowing us to distinguish clearly the positive attitudes towards oneself that are directly relevant to morality and those that are less so. Evaluative self-respect, since it involves one's moral character, is certainly an appropriate subject for moral theorizing. Self-esteem, in contrast, if it is relevant to morality, is so indirectly.

On the preceding account, recognition self-respect was described as an objective notion. That is, it was assumed that there are certain attitudes, dispositions and responses that a person *must* have in order to be adequately self-respecting. Those who propound an objective view would probably claim, for instance, that persons who habitually ingratiate themselves with others for personal gain are lacking in recognition self-respect. According to the subjective view, on the other hand, so long as such persons do not *themselves* regard ingratiation for personal gain as objectionable or

'beneath them', their self-respect is intact. It is compromised only if they behave in ways that *they* judge to be inappropriate. When moral philosophers claim that all persons ought to have recognition respect for themselves, they are generally treating self-respect as an objective concept. Their claim expresses the idea that all persons, regardless of those persons' own views of what is fitting, ought to value their rights, assert their needs when appropriate, formulate and commit themselves to ideals and goals worthy of them as persons, abstain from self-destructive behaviour, avoid subordinating themselves to others unnecessarily and take responsibility for their conduct.

Evaluative self-respect can also be viewed either as an objective or as a subjective notion. Regarded as an objective concept, evaluative self-respect is judged to be warranted only if the standards by which one has appraised oneself positively are morally worthy. As a subjective concept, evaluative self-respect is seen to be warranted so long as one's positive self-assessment is based upon standards that one deems worthy of oneself.

2 Self-respect in moral and political philosophy

Though many philosophers have remarked upon self-respect, or related notions such as pride, integrity and dignity, self-respect figures most prominently in the work of Kant and Rawls. In *Die Metaphysik der Sitten* (*Metaphysics of Morals*) (1797), Kant claims that persons have a duty to respect themselves. Self-respect, on his view, is a valuing stance that one wilfully adopts or neglects to adopt towards oneself. It consists in an understanding and appreciation of the equal moral status one shares with other persons and a disposition to act in ways that express this understanding and appreciation. The requirement that persons regard and treat themselves as the moral equals of others is grounded in Kant's contention that all rational beings have a special moral value, which he calls 'dignity', that is itself rooted in our capacity for autonomous rational agency. Since every person as such has dignity, each person as such is equal in basic moral status to every other person and ought to appreciate this fact and act accordingly.

Our special moral worth, Kant claims in *Grundlegung zur Metaphysik der Sitten* (*Groundwork of the Metaphysics of Morals*) (1785), requires that all persons be treated and treat themselves as ends in themselves and never merely as a means to another's ends. In other words, the capacity of rational agents to set ends freely for themselves should be treasured and respected by all (see KANT, I. §§9–11). This duty, which is one formulation of the categorical imperative, has been interpreted by some philosophers as a duty to respect others and to respect oneself. For Kant, the requirement that we respect ourselves consists not only in a duty to regard ourselves as having the same moral standing as others, but also in an array of duties requiring us to value our autonomy and rational agency and to treat ourselves in accordance with our special moral status.

In contrast to Kant, John RAWLS views self-respect as an entitlement rather than a duty. In *A Theory of Justice* (1971), he maintains that justice requires that self-respect, or more precisely its social bases, be provided for all members of a society. Moreover, he sees self-respect not as an attitude that individuals may wilfully adopt, but as a social good that can be secured by individuals only when certain social and political conditions prevail. He defines self-respect as a conviction that one's plan of life is worth pursuing accompanied by the belief that one is well-suited to pursue it. The value of self-respect, Rawls claims, lies in the fact that no one can carry out or achieve their aims adequately without it.

For Rawls, civil equality is the key to citizens' acquiring and maintaining adequate self-respect. In the absence of civil equality, those with fewer rights and privileges will regard their life plans as less worthwhile than the life plans of citizens with more rights and privileges, for, by depriving certain citizens of goods essential to the effective pursuit of their ends, a society implies that the ends of those so deprived have a lesser value. Since self-respect is fundamental to the basic wellbeing of all persons, it follows that principles prescribing the design of basic social structures are just only if they foster or do not hinder civil equality. The two principles of justice proposed by Rawls, the equal liberty principle and the 'difference principle', are designed to ensure civil equality and hence help guarantee self-respect for all citizens.

Influenced by Rawls' realization that self-respect is largely a product of one's social and political circumstances, some political theorists have employed the notion of self-respect in their critiques of the oppression of white women, people of colour, and gays and lesbians. These writers point to the damage done to the self-respect of members of groups that are marginalized, stigmatized or exploited by the dominant culture. Oppressed people may internalize the disparaging images and views of them produced by the dominant culture and hence come to see themselves as inferior or as undeserving of equal treatment. Some writers discuss the ways in which both individual and collective resistance to oppressive institutions, actions and images can empower those who suffer from oppression, thereby augmenting and

reinforcing their sense of worth. Boxill (1976), for example, claims that oppressed people can have faith in their worth only if they protest against injustices done to them. In the course of discussing the relation between oppression and self-respect, some theorists have attempted to reconceive traditional conceptions of self-respect so as to expunge from them features that are judged to reflect or champion objectionable aspects of the dominant culture. Dillon (1992b), for example, has argued that the Kantian notion of the person as an independent, autonomous, self-legislating will that underlies most conceptions of self-respect is androcentric (see FEMINIST ETHICS §4).

Recent philosophical explorations of self-respect have thrown into relief its value and significance. They have shown that self-respect is a central component of human wellbeing, since its absence is painful and debilitating, and illustrated its connection with many other important moral and social values such as rights, autonomy, dignity, freedom and equality.

See also: AUTONOMY, ETHICAL; EQUALITY; FREEDOM AND LIBERTY; RIGHTS

References and further reading

* Boxill, B. (1976) 'Self-Respect and Protest', *Philosophy & Public Affairs* 6: 58–69. (Argues that those whose self-respect is at risk must protest against injustices done to them in order to be confident that they are self-respecting.)

* Dillon, R. (1992a) 'How to Lose Your Self-Respect', *American Philosophical Quarterly* 29: 125–39. (Explains the distinction between 'evaluative' and 'recognition' self-respect and identifies a variety of failures of self-respect.)

* —— (1992b) 'Toward a Feminist Theory of Self-Respect', *Hypatia* 7: 52–69. (A feminist evaluation of traditional conceptions of self-respect.)

Hill, T.E., Jr. (1973) 'Servility and Self-Respect', *Monist* 57: 12–27. (Extensively anthologized discussion of the concept of self-respect from a Kantian perspective.)

* Kant, I. (1785) *Grundlegung zur Metaphysik der Sitten*, trans. with notes by H.J. Paton, *Groundwork of the Metaphysics of Morals* (originally *The Moral Law*), London: Hutchinson, 1948; repr. New York: Harper & Row, 1964. (Develops an ethical theory centred around a principle of morality that emphasizes the absolute worth of rational agents.)

* —— (1797) *Die Metaphysik der Sitten*, trans. M.J. Gregor, *The Metaphysics of Morals*, Cambridge: Cambridge University Press, 1991. (Presents the various duties, including the duty of self-respect, which are derived from the supreme principle of

morality established in *Groundwork of the Meta-physics of Morals.*)

Massey, S. (1983) 'Is Self-Respect a Moral or a Psychological Concept?', *Ethics* 93: 246–61. (Offers a distinction between 'objective' and 'subjective' conceptions of self-respect and endorses the latter.)

Mohr, R. (1988) 'Dignity vs. Politics: Strategy When Justice Fails', in *Gays/Justice: A Study of Ethics Society and Law*, New York: Columbia University Press: 315–7. (Argues that the gay and lesbian rights movement ought to adopt strategies that promote the dignity and self-respect of gays and lesbians.)

* Rawls, J. (1971) *A Theory of Justice*, Cambridge, MA: Harvard University Press. (Presents a theory of distributive justice according to which self-respect is a prominent social good.)

Thomas, L. (1978) 'Rawlsian Self-Respect and the Black Consciousness Movement', *Philosophical Forum* 9: 303–14. (Argues that the black consciousness movement was in part a call for African-Americans to respect themselves as persons.)

CYNTHIA A. STARK

SELLARS, WILFRID STALKER (1912–89)

Wilfrid Sellars was among the most systematic and innovative of post-war American philosophers. His critical destruction of the 'Myth of the Given' established him as a leading voice in the Anglo-American critique of 'the Cartesian concept of mind' and in the corresponding shift of attention from the categories of thought to public language. His own positive views were naturalistic, combining a robust scientific realism with a thoroughgoing nominalism which rejected both traditional abstract entities and ontologically primitive meanings. In their place, Sellars elucidated linguistic meaning and the content of thought in terms of a sophisticated theory of conceptual roles, instantiated in the linguistic conduct of speakers and transmitted by modes of cultural inheritance. He combined this theory with a form of 'verbal behaviour-ism' to produce the first version of functionalism in the contemporary philosophy of mind. Besides his pro-foundly original philosophical contributions, his long career as a distinguished teacher and influential editor earned him justified acclaim as one of the definitive figures of the post-war period.

1   **Life and works**
2   **Ontological perspectives**
3   **Epistemological perspectives**

1   Life and works

As the son of the eminent Critical Realist philosopher Roy Wood Sellars, Wilfrid Sellars' own philosophical calling was almost preordained. Educated at the University of Michigan and as a Rhodes Scholar at Oxford, he held positions at the University of Iowa, the University of Minnesota and Yale University before becoming University Professor of Philosophy and Research Professor of the Philosophy of Science at the University of Pittsburgh, where he remained from 1963 until his death. In 1950, with Herbert Feigl, he founded the first scholarly journal explicitly devoted to analytic philosophy, *Philosophical Studies*, edited jointly until 1971 and by Sellars alone for three more years.

Sellars saw post-war philosophers as confronted with two 'images', each of which laid claim to being a (potentially) complete picture of man-in-the-world – the 'manifest image', which had been the focal concern of 'perennial philosophy' from Plato and Aristotle to Strawson and Austin, and the 'scientific image', a complex understanding of man-in-the-world still in the process of emerging from the fruits of theoretical reasoning. Philosophy was challenged to explore the possibility of a 'stereoscopic understand-ing', in which the two images would become 'fused' into a single synoptic vision. Sellars' writings are consequently dialectical and synthesizing, typically undercutting or evading accepted dichotomies and attempting to mediate conflicting intuitions. They are shaped by the standing conviction that it is a philosopher's duty not merely to show that a received position has gone wrong, but also to explain why and how it could ever have appeared to be right.

2   Ontological perspectives

Along with WITTGENSTEIN, Sellars figured among the pre-eminent contributors to the twentieth cen-tury's thoroughgoing critique of Descartes' picture of first-person privileged access to the states of a thinking substance (see DESCARTES, R.; PRIVACY). Unlike Wittgenstein, however, Sellars proceeded to develop a positive reconception of the problem space traditionally centred on a dualism of bodies and minds as a transposition of a more fundamental dualism of facts and norms (see DUALISM; FACT/VALUE DISTICTION). Kant's analysis of the distinct contributions of the sensibility and understanding in perceptual experience became the guiding thread for Sellars' further sharp separation of problems regard-ing 'raw feels' from questions regarding intentional (object-directed) thought.

Along with QUINE, but without his global rejection

of semantic, mental and modal contexts, Sellars helped consummate the shift of semantic attention from the categories of thought to those of public language. Sellars differs from Quine, too, in that his own rejection of Cartesian models of the mind never issued in a correlative (radically behaviourist) abandonment of inner episodes *per se*. Instead, Sellars' critique of the positivist picture of scientific theories enabled him to develop an alternative, thoroughly realistic, understanding of sophisticated scientific inquiry in terms of which the status of concepts pertaining to inner episodes could be constructively understood on the model of theoretical discourse (see SCIENTIFIC REALISM AND ANTIREALISM; THEORIES, SCIENTIFIC).

Sellars' fundamental metaphysical conviction that the distinguishing mark of the real is the power to act or be acted upon was reflected in his thoroughgoing naturalism. This, in turn, imposed strong nominalistic constraints, not only on the overall synoptic project, which consequently needed to find a place for mind that did not require independent ontological status for intentional entities, but also on traditional categorial ontology, which could legitimately maintain the reality of abstract entities only if it were possible simultaneously to supply an adequate account of their place within the causal order, broadly conceived. Sellars' response to both of these naturalistic challenges was to develop a sophisticated theory of conceptual roles at the heart of which was the idea that one and the same item could be at once both a causally evoked response to the environment and a normatively significant item in a rule-governed network of reasons. On Sellars' view, a person's grasp of a concept, for example, the concept 'red', consists precisely in their differential disposition to produce such inferentially articulated responses to red things (see SEMANTICS, CONCEPTUAL ROLE).

Sellars consequently proposed to interpret both categorial ontological idioms and mentalistic intentional contexts in terms of a semantic discourse fundamentally conceived in terms of the inferential roles of public 'natural linguistic objects'. Like Rudolf CARNAP, Sellars embraced a form of 'linguistic nominalism', which treated traditional categorial discourse as the classificatory discourse of a functional metalanguage transposed into the 'material mode of speech'. Unlike Carnap, however, he refused to identify the extensional constructs of 'pure' formal syntax or semantics with their corresponding 'descriptive' pre-philosophical counterparts, arguing that to do so is to fail to acknowledge properly the irreducibly normative aspects of syntactical and semantical words functioning as such.

In the philosophy of mind, Sellars adopted 'psychological nominalism', the denial that any sort of commerce with abstract entities is an essential ingredient of mental acts, and espoused instead what he came to call 'verbal behaviourism', according to which the primary sense of (occurrently) thinking that-*p* is a 'thinking-out-loud that-*p*', that is, in first approximation, an event of candidly and spontaneously saying *p* (see BEHAVIOURISM, METHODOLOGICAL AND SCIENTIFIC; LANGUAGE OF THOUGHT). The conceptual framework of inner episodes was to be understood as built upon the semantical characterization of overt verbal episodes in a manner analogous to the way in which, for instance, the framework of molecules is built on the observable behaviour of gases. On Sellars' account, the concept of a thought is fundamentally the concept of a causally mediating logico-semantic (inferential) role player, the determinate intrinsic ontological (empirical) character of which is left open. The identification of such intentionally-characterized inner episodes with, for instance, occurrences in an organism's central nervous system thus generates no ontological tension, and the manifest image's conception of persons as thinkers can fuse smoothly with the scientific image's story of complex material organisms. These proposals constituted the original version of functionalism in the contemporary philosophy of mind, the subsequent manifold varieties of which were both facilitated and directly or indirectly inspired by the theoretical space of philosophical options they had opened (see FUNCTIONALISM).

As in the case of thoughts, Sellars argued that talk about sensations ('raw feels') can also usefully be interpreted on the model of a species of theoretical discourse. Since, however, with Kant and contrary to the Cartesian tradition, Sellars viewed sensations as *non*-intentional items, his account both of their place within the manifest image and their ultimate relocation within the scientific image differs essentially from his ontologically noncommittal functionalist picture of occurrent thoughts. Sellars proposed that it is the job of analogical thinking to construct new forms of concepts pertaining to theoretical entities. Within the philosophically refined manifest image, sensation concepts pick out non-intentional states of individual perceivers, 'sensings', whose intrinsic characters are analogically indicated by adverbial transpositions of qualitative predicates of objects. In a series of essays stretching over a period of forty years and widely regarded as among his most difficult and challenging works, however, Sellars argued further that, because the manifest image's unitary perceiving subjects have ontological pluralities as their scientific image counterparts, the fusion of the two images at the point of sensations will in fact require the postulation of further (theoretically) basic entities which actually ontologically instantiate qualitative sensory contents conceived in yet another analogically constructed categorial guise distinct from both 'properties of objects' and 'manners of sensing'. In particular, he concluded, sensory contents can be non-epiphenomenally integrated into the scientific image only after it has as a whole been transposed from its classical 'thing-like' (particulate) form into a categorially monistic framework all of whose fundamental entities are 'event-like' absolute processes (see EPIPHENOMENALISM; MENTAL STATES, ADVERBIAL THEORY OF; QUALIA).

3 Epistemological perspectives

Sellars' key nominalistic strategies could succeed only if the notion of a linguistic item's having a semantic or inferential function could itself be explicated without recourse to irreducibly platonistic or mentalistic conceptions. One of the greatest strengths of his systematic philosophy is the exquisite care with which he proceeded to locate the normative conceptual order within the causal order and to interpret the modes of causality exercised by linguistic rules. For Sellars, inference itself is always a normative affair, a matter of the judgments one ought to or is entitled to make. He defuses the circularity which threatens such an account by arguing that our knowledge of what implies and follows from various claims is, in the first instance, a *practical* ability to discriminate, that is, to respond differentially to, good and bad inferences. Rule-governed linguistic behaviour develops out of multiple repertoires of 'pattern-governed behaviour', behaviour which exhibits a pattern because the propensity to produce behaviour belonging to that pattern has been selectively reinforced and contrary propensities selectively extinguished (see LANGUAGE, SOCIAL NATURE OF; MEANING AND RULE-FOLLOWING). The pattern-governed behaviour characteristic of language includes 'language-entry transitions', propensities to respond to non-linguistic states of affairs (such as sensory stimulations) with appropriate linguistic activity; 'language-departure transitions', propensities to respond to a subset of linguistic representings (for example, such first-person future-tensed conduct-ascriptions as 'I shall now raise my hand') with appropriate corresponding behaviour; and 'intra-linguistic moves', propensities to respond to linguistic representings with further linguistic episodes (only) in patterns corresponding to valid theoretical and practical inferences. Linguistic roles or functions, Sellars suggested, are ultimately individuated in terms of the structures of positive and negative

uniformities generated in the natural order by such pattern-governed activities.

In the Kantian tradition Sellars insisted that, in contrast to the mere capacity to be sensorily affected by external objects, *perception* of how things are requires not only systematic differential response dispositions but also the ability to respond to sensory stimulation with a *judgment*, that is, the endorsement of a claim (see PERCEPTION, EPISTEMIC ISSUES IN). Sellars went on, however, to propose that reports of how things look or seem, rather than employing 'more primitive' concepts, result instead from withholding these characteristic endorsements. This account enabled him to explain the incorrigibility of 'seems' judgments that Cartesianism takes as its fundamental datum. Their incorrigibility is simply a matter of their tentativeness; a 'seems' judgment expresses a perceptual ascription without endorsing it. It follows that 'seems' judgments do not express a special class of immediate cognitions. Applying the concept 'looks red' requires the same mastery of inferential articulations, the same inferential 'know how', as does applying the concept 'is red'.

Sellars' analysis of the Cartesian incorrigibility of perceptual 'seemings' is one strand of the philosophical dialectic most frequently associated with his name, his comprehensive critique of the 'Myth of the Given'. Basic to this critique is his insistence on the irreducibly normative character of epistemic discourse. Characterizing an episode or state in epistemic terms is not giving an empirical description of it but rather placing it within a social framework of justifications, of having and being able to give reasons for what one says. All knowledge that something is the case – all 'subsumption of particulars under universals' – presupposes intersubjective learning and concept formation. It follows that the ability to be (epistemically) aware of a sort of thing rests upon a *prior* command of the concept of that sort of thing and cannot account for it – and this holds equally true for concepts pertaining to 'inner episodes'. The first-person reporting role of such concepts, a use Cartesians interpret as evidencing the 'privacy' of the mental and one's 'privileged access' to one's own mental states, is necessarily built upon and presupposes their intersubjective status.

The idea that a language necessarily contains a stratum of claims any of which, on various occasions, can occur either as a report (an unmediated causally evoked response) or as the conclusion of an inference (mediated by other linguistic-conceptual representations) suggests the possibility of a further stratum of purely inferential claims. That is how Sellars proposes that we understand theoretical claims, that is, as claims that one can *de facto* become entitled to endorse only as the conclusion of an inference. On this view, the difference between theoretical objects and observables is not ontological but methodological. It is not a matter of the kind of thing our claims are about; it is a matter of how we come to be entitled to make them – and, as our technological sophistication increases, this can change. Once it is recognized that there is no epistemically privileged stratum of judgments with which to respond to one's sensory environment, and that such a 'language-entry' response is what 'observation' is, it follows that nothing is in principle unobservable. Noninferential and purely inferential claims can both be about the same kind of object (see OBSERVATION).

Sellars' holistic view of justification implied that the reasonableness of accepting even first principles is a matter of the availability of good arguments warranting their acceptance. Since it is definitive of first principles that they cannot be derived by sound theoretical reasonings from still more basic premises, Sellars located the requisite arguments in a stratum of 'vindications', practical reasonings in which the adopting of specific principles (an epistemic conduct) is demonstrated to contribute to the realization of non-arbitrary epistemic ends. From the ontological point of view, however, such practical cognitions – intentions and volitions – are simply species of occurrent thinkings whose unique conduct-structuring functional role is to be understood in terms of their special ('language-exit') relationships to non-linguistic behaviour (see JUSTIFICATION, EPISTEMIC).

For Sellars, it is finally practical thinking which lies at the centre of the framework of persons as such (see PERSONS). To think of an entity as a person is to think of it as actually or potentially a member of a community, and it is the most general common intentions of a community – its 'we-intentions' – that fundamentally define the structure of norms and values, crucially including those which make meaningful discourse and rationality itself possible, in terms of which the conducts of its members come to be appraised. A genuinely synoptic vision of man-in-the-world, Sellars concluded, can therefore be achieved only by enriching the scientific image with the language of individual and shared intentions.

See also: CATEGORIES; CONCEPTS; FOUNDATIONALISM; INTENTIONALITY; NOMINALISM; ONTOLOGY

List of works

Sellars, W.S. (1963) *Science, Perception and Reality*, London and New York: Routledge & Kegan Paul; repr. Atascadero, CA: Ridgeview, 1991. (Contains Sellars' best-known essays, including his classical critique of the 'Myth of the Given', 'Empiricism and the Philosophy of Mind', and his metaphilosophical manifesto, 'Philosophy and the Scientific Image of Man'.)

—— (1967) *Philosophical Perspectives*, Springfield, IL: Charles C. Thomas; repr. Atascadero, CA: Ridgeview, 1977, 2 vols. (Work from the 1950s and early 1960s. Part 1 consists of historical essays on Plato, Aristotle and the Rationalists. Part 2 includes important original essays in metaphysics and the philosophy of mind.)

—— (1968) *Science and Metaphysics: Variations on Kantian Themes*, The John Locke Lectures for 1965–6, London and New York: Routledge & Kegan Paul; repr. Atascadero, CA: Ridgeview, 1992 (Based on his John Locke Lectures for 1965–6. The most systematic presentation of Sellars' views on perception, intentionality, representation, truth and the metaphysics and ethics of persons, developed in relation to the work of Kant, Peirce and the early Wittgenstein.)

—— (1974) *Essays in Philosophy and Its History*, Dordrecht: Reidel. (A rich collection of historical interpretive and systematic essays from Sellars' most productive years. Includes his presidential address to the American Philosophical Association on the Kantian text 'this I or he or it (the thing) which thinks...', as well as significant contributions to the philosophy of language, metaphysics and the philosophy of science.)

—— (1980) *Naturalism and Ontology*, Atascadero, CA: Ridgeview. (Sellars' John Dewey Lectures for 1973–4 present his mature views on the interrelationships of language, logic and ontology. The most systematic defence of his 'linguistic nominalism'.)

—— (1981a) *Pure Pragmatics and Possible Worlds*, ed. and with intro. by J.F. Sicha, Atascadero, CA: Ridgeview. (A comprehensive collection of Sellars' earliest works (1947–53). These richly textured and dialectically complex early essays are difficult to access, but, besides offering a developmental perspective on Sellars' overall corpus, they include a number of interesting ideas and theses not explicitly developed in his later work.)

—— (1981b) 'Foundations for a Metaphysics of Pure Process', *Monist* 64: 3–90. (A special issue of the *Monist*, containing Sellars' Carus Lectures from 1977–8. This is the most developed and systematic presentation of Sellars' unique views in the philosophy of mind. The title reflects his conviction that sensible qualities can be satisfactorily accommodated within a naturalistic worldview only in the context of a (speculatively-envisioned) ontology of 'pure processes'.)

—— (1989) *The Metaphysics of Epistemology: Lectures by Wilfrid Sellars*, ed. P.V. Amaral, Atascadero, CA: Ridgeview. (This posthumously published work reproduces a series of university lectures given by Sellars in 1975 on central topics in epistemology and metaphysics. In sharp contrast to his densely written essays, Sellars' classroom presentations tended to be discursively relaxed and informal. This charmingly illustrated book is consequently a good first introduction to his complex views regarding perception, knowledge, minds, meaning and representation.)

References and further reading.

Castañeda, H.-N. (ed.) (1975) *Action, Knowledge, and Reality: Critical Studies in Honor of Wilfrid Sellars*, Indianapolis, IN: Bobbs-Merrill. (A collection of critical studies of Sellars' work by his students and colleagues. The book also contains two important pieces of original Sellarsiana, his intellectual autobiography and 'The Structure of Knowledge', a systematic treatment of epistemological themes based on Sellars' 1971 Machette Foundation Lectures at the University of Texas.)

Delaney, C.F., *et al.* (1977) *The Synoptic Vision: Essays on the Philosophy of Wilfrid Sellars*, Notre Dame, IN: University of Notre Dame Press. (Interpretive and critical essays on Sellars' views and contributions in epistemology, ontology, philosophy of science, philosophy of mind and ethics by members of the philosophical faculty of Notre Dame University. The title echoes Sellars' thesis that contemporary philosophy is challenged with fusing two comprehensive worldviews, the 'manifest image' and the 'scientific image' into a single 'synoptic' picture.)

Pitt, J.C. (ed.) (1978) *The Philosophy of Wilfrid Sellars: Queries and Extensions*, Dordrecht: Reidel. (Fourteen interpretive and critical essays deriving from a Workshop on the Philosophy of Wilfrid Sellars held at the Virginia Polytechnic Institute and State University in 1976.)

Seibt, J. (1990) *Properties as Processes: A Synoptic Study of Wilfrid Sellars' Nominalism*, Atascadero, CA: Ridgeview. (The first full-scale, systematic, book-length study of Sellars' philosophy, written by one of his last doctoral students and described by Sellars himself as 'one of the best essays on my work that I have ever seen'. This presentation of Sellars as 'a unique example of radical and systematic nominalism' is indispensable for any serious student of his views.)

JAY F. ROSENBERG

SEMANTIC PARADOXES AND THEORIES OF TRUTH

The Cretan philosopher Epimenides said that Cretans always lie. Assuming, for the sake of argument, the mendacity of all other statements by Cretans, we get a paradox: if what Epimenides said was true, it must have been a lie, whereas if what he said was a lie, it would have made his statement true. The citizens of Crete have long since forgiven the insult, but semantics has never recovered.

Alfred Tarski perceived the consequences of Epimenides' paradox with particular clarity. Our commonsense intuitions about truth follow the paradigm: 'Snow is white' is true if and only if snow is white. As Tarski rigorously shows, if the language we are describing (the object language) is the same as the language in which we are formulating our theory (the metalanguage), this paradigm will be inconsistent with the rudimentary laws of syntax. The conclusion Tarski drew was that, if we are to develop a satisfactory theory of truth, our metalanguage must be essentially richer in expressive power than the object language. Since there is no human language essentially richer than English (or any other natural language), there can be no satisfactory theory of truth for English.

One earnestly hopes that this is not the end of the matter. Tarski's analysis leaves open the prospect that we can develop a fully satisfactory theory of truth for a substantial fragment of English; also the prospect that we can develop a theory of truth for English as a whole which, while not fully satisfying our intuitions, is none the less useful and illuminating.

Both prospects have been substantially advanced by Saul Kripke's 'Outline of a Theory of Truth', which exploits the idea that there are truth-value gaps, statements which are neither true nor false, and that Epimenides' insult was one of them.

Invocation of truth-value gaps does not resolve the paradox in any straightforward way. If we let the phrase 'the simple liar sentence' refer to the sentence 'The simple liar sentence is false', we see that we can readily account for the paradoxical features of the sentence by declaring the sentence neither true nor false; but if we let the strengthened liar sentence be 'The strengthened liar sentence is not true', we get a sentence we cannot dispose of so tidily. If the strengthened liar is neither true nor false, then it is not true; but that it is not true is precisely what the sentence says.

Truth-value gaps have not vanquished the liar paradox. Nor have any of the alternatives, the most prominent of which are a contextualist account, which sees the English word 'true' as radically ambiguous, and so-called 'revision theory', which investigates the cyclic reasoning that occurs when we try to evaluate the simple liar sentence: if the sentence is true, then it must be false; but if, then, it is false, it must be true; and so on. While these approaches have not eliminated the paradox, they have opened new approaches that have greatly improved our prospects for finding a comfortable way to live with it.

1 **Tarski's requirement of a richer metalanguage**
2 ***Principia Mathematica* and its successors**
3 **Kripke's theory of truth**
4 **The fixed-point theorem**
5 **Classical-logic versions of Kripke's theory**
6 **Revision theory**
7 **English as an object language?**

1 Tarski's requirement of a richer metalanguage

Kurt Gödel (1931) proved the incompleteness of a version of Peano Arithmetic by associating a code number, denoted $\ulcorner \phi \urcorner$, with each sentence ϕ of the language of arithmetic, then constructing a sentence χ which denied that $\ulcorner \chi \urcorner$ was the code of a theorem (see GÖDEL'S THEOREMS). Tarski (1935) used Gödel's construction to give a formalized version of the liar paradox. If $Tr(x)$ were a formula of the language of arithmetic which represented the set of code numbers of true sentences, we would expect to have

(T) $Tr(\ulcorner \phi \urcorner) \leftrightarrow \phi$

for each sentence ϕ. But Gödel's methods can be used to construct a sentence λ such that $\lambda \leftrightarrow \neg Tr(\ulcorner \lambda \urcorner)$ is a theorem. We conclude that there is no formula of the language of arithmetic which represents the set of code numbers of true sentences of the language of arithmetic. Indeed, this result holds not only for the language of arithmetic but for any language which includes the language of arithmetic.

Arithmetic plays an inessential role here. Quine (1946) shows that we can encode the language of arithmetic into any language which can provide a rudimentary theory of syntax. We are forced to conclude that, if $\mathcal{L}$ is a language that is able to describe its own syntax, then there is no open sentence $Tr(x)$ of $\mathcal{L}$ such that the schema (T) is consistent with the laws of syntax; here $\ulcorner \phi \urcorner$ is a standard name of ϕ which describes the sentence in terms of its syntactic structure. On the other hand, any semantic theory which adequately represents our intuitive understanding of truth must surely imply all the (T)-sentences. We conclude that there is no possibility, consistent with the laws of syntax, of finding an open sentence of $\mathcal{L}$ which adequately represents the set of truths of $\mathcal{L}$. The conclusion Tarski drew, and which nearly everyone has accepted,

is that, to develop a satisfactory theory of truth for $\mathcal{L}$, we must work within a metalanguage richer than $\mathcal{L}$ in expressive power.

2 *Principia Mathematica* and its successors

Whitehead and Russell responded to Epimenides' paradox by proposing a layered multiplicity of notions of truth. Simple statements of fact enjoy the first order of truth; attributions of truth at order one will be true or false at order two; and so on. An attribution of nth order truth must always have order higher than n. In this way (though they did not give details), Whitehead and Russell were able to develop the semantics of *Principia Mathematica* without contradictions. *Principia Mathematica* was designed to resolve a variety of paradoxes in addition to the liar. Here we shall follow contemporary practice in separating the semantic from the set-theoretic paradoxes (as recommended by Ramsey 1925), and in focusing on the liar as our paradigmatic representative of the former.

Tarski's approach to the liar was similar to Whitehead and Russell's, but simplified from the intricacies of the theory of types. Tarski spoke of a hierarchy of languages. The ground language has no semantic predicates, while the $(n+1)$th language is derived from the nth language by adding a predicate true$_n$ whose extension is the true sentences of the nth language.

Whitehead and Russell proposed to apply their analysis to natural languages by treating the English word 'true' as ambiguous; contradictions arise from failing to recognize the ambiguity.

Their proposal has been vigorously pursued, by Tyler Burge (1979), Charles Parsons (1974), Jon Barwise and John Etchemendy (1987) and others, who have treated 'true' as an indexical term, like 'here' and 'now', whose extension is determined in part by the context of utterance. If everything Plato says is either true$_{12}$ or false$_{12}$, the use of 'true' in 'Everything Plato says is true' will be contextually determined to mean 'true$_{13}$'. One quickly requires transfinite indices, going beyond the finite levels of *Principia Mathematica*.

Paradoxes arise when the customary rules for placing subscripts falter. Ordinarily, the subscript taken by 'false' in the sentence 'Everything a Cretan says is false' will be greater than the subscripts supplied to any occurrence of 'true' or 'false' in any utterance by a Cretan. But it is not possible to observe this rule when the sentence is uttered by a Cretan. If we take the word 'false' in Epimenides' statement 'Everything a Cretan says is false' to mean 'false$_\alpha$', we find that his statement is neither true$_\alpha$ nor false$_\alpha$, since the predicates 'true$_\alpha$' and 'false$_\alpha$' only apply to sentences with subscripts less than α.

From a higher level of reflection of which Epimenides himself was in principle incapable, we can see that, since Epimenides' statement that everything a Cretan says is false$_\alpha$ is not false$_\alpha$, we can make out a sense in which the sentence 'Everything a Cretan says is false' is false, namely, 'Everything a Cretan says is false$_\alpha$' is false$_{\alpha+1}$. We should not say, however, that what Epimenides said was false after all, rather, the sentence Epimenides uttered expresses something false when we say it, though in Epimenides' mouth it was neither true nor false.

Talk of levels of reflection is something the theorist engages in when describing the language, but not something speakers of the language engage in. If this were not so, Epimenides could say 'Nothing a Cretan says is true at any level of reflection' and reinstate the paradox. Thus we still submit to Tarski's requirement that the metalanguage have expressive powers not available in the object language. Again, the theorist can make the subscripts under 'true' and 'false' explicit, and use variables as subscripts. The speakers of the language cannot do this, otherwise they could get a contradiction by formulating the explicit liar ('The explicit liar is not true$_\alpha$, for any α'). Contextualists have not overturned Tarski's requirement that the semantics of a language be developed in a richer metalanguage, nor, for the most part, have they attempted to do so. Instead they have tried to show that, contrary to first impressions, Tarski's requirement is relaxed enough to make room for virtually everything speakers of English want to say.

3   Kripke's theory of truth

We have been pretending that, apart from one notorious remark by Epimenides, everything ever said by a Cretan is outright false. This pretence is, of course, contrary to fact, and, once we drop the pretence, Epimenides' statement is no longer problematic. If we hear a Cretan remark that snow is white, we can conclude at once that not all Cretans always lie, hence Epimenides' statement is false. To reach this judgment, it is not necessary to examine everything a Cretan has ever said; it is enough to find one Cretan truth.

The assignment of levels we get from *Principia Mathematica* is unnecessarily extravagant. It is based upon the idea that, to determine the truth of 'Everything a Cretan says is false', we need to take account of everything any Cretan ever says, so it tries, unsuccessfully, to assign to the sentence a level higher than the level assigned to any Cretan statement. But to determine that Epimenides' statement is false, we do not need to take account of everything a Cretan ever says, we only need to find one truth uttered by a Cretan. So, if some Cretan statement is true at the first level, we can declare Epimenides' statement false at the second level, without waiting to examine a raft of irrelevant further statements.

This adjustment in the assignment of levels effects a remarkable simplification and clarification of the hierarchical structure. In describing the construction, we shall utilize a first-order language with primitive connectives 'and', 'not' and 'all', other connectives defined as usual. All terms other than 'Tr' are assumed already to have a fixed meaning. We assume that our universe of discourse is a set, and we suppose that every member of the universe is named by some constant, expanding the language if necessary to ensure this. (Alternatively, we could define truth in terms of satisfaction, as Tarski does; but this would complicate matters.) We assume that the language can describe its own syntax, either directly or via a Gödel coding.

A non-semantic atomic sentence will be either true$_0$ or false$_0$.

A sentence of the form $Tr(c)$ is true$_{\alpha+1}$ if c denotes a sentence which is true$_\alpha$, and false$_{\alpha+1}$ if c denotes a sentence which is false$_\alpha$. If the individual denoted by c is not a sentence, $Tr(c)$ is false$_0$.

If ϕ is true$_\alpha$ and ψ is true$_\beta$, the conjunction $(\phi \wedge \psi)$ will be true$_{\max(\alpha,\beta)}$. If either conjunct is false$_\gamma$ for some γ, the conjunction is false$_\gamma$ for the least such γ.

A negation is true$_\alpha$ if the negatum is false$_\alpha$ and false$_\alpha$ if the negatum is true$_\alpha$.

A universally quantified sentence is true$_\alpha$ if α is the least ordinal such that every substitution instance of the sentence is true$_\beta$ for some $\beta \leqslant \alpha$. If some substitution instance of $\psi(x)$ is false$_\gamma$, then $(\forall x)\psi(x)$ is false$_\gamma$ for the least such γ.

Kripke's proposal (1975) is that a sentence be regarded as true if it is true$_\alpha$ for some α, false if it is false$_\alpha$ for some α, and undetermined otherwise. Applying his construction to a suitably regimented fragment of English, we find that it manages narrowly to skirt the edge of paradox without falling into contradiction, and the truth-values it supplies, when it supplies truth-values, are invariably the intuitively correct ones. For example, suppose that Socrates says only

Everything Plato says is true.

while Plato says

Not everything Socrates says is true.

Everything Epimenides says is true.

and Epimenides says

Nothing a Cretan says is true.

Snow is white.

Epimenides' second statement is true$_0$, so his first statement is false$_1$. Hence Plato's second statement is false$_2$, Socrates' statement is false$_3$, and Plato's first statement is true$_4$.

Not only does Kripke's theory get the right truth-values, but, more importantly, it explains them. Sentences declared true are true because they are grounded in the non-semantic facts. Thus a sentence is true$_\alpha$ for some α just in case it is derivable from true atomic and negated atomic non-semantic sentences by the following rules, while a sentence is false$_\alpha$, for some α, just in case its negation is derivable:

'Tr'-introduction: If c denotes a sentence ϕ, infer $Tr(c)$ from ϕ.

'$\neg Tr$'-introduction: If c denotes a sentence ϕ, infer $\neg Tr(c)$ from $\neg\phi$. Also, if c denotes a non-sentence, you may write $\neg Tr(c)$.

Conjunction introduction: Infer a conjunction from its conjuncts.

Negated conjunction introduction: Infer the negation of a conjunction from the negation of either conjunct.

Double negation introduction: From a sentence, infer the negation of its negation.

Universal quantification introduction: Infer a universal quantified statement from all of its instances. (This is an infinitary rule.)

Negated universal quantification introduction: Infer the negation of a universally quantified statement from the negation of any of its instances.

4 The fixed-point theorem

We have been speaking of 'true' as an ambiguous predicate. It is perhaps simpler, and certainly closer to Kripke's original way of thinking, instead to regard 'true' as a univocal predicate in a language with a nonclassical logic. We employ Kleene's 'strong three-valued logic' (see Kleene 1952: §54), according to which a predicate has an 'extension', consisting of those things to which it is determined that the predicate applies, and an 'anti-extension', consisting of those things to which it is determined that the predicate does not apply. The two cannot overlap, but there may be things to which it remains unsettled whether the predicate applies. An atomic sentence $Rc_1 \ldots c_n$ is true if the n-tuple consisting of the things denoted by c_1 to c_n lies in the extension of R, false if it lies in the anti-extension, and truth-valueless other-wise. A conjunction is true if both conjuncts are true and false if either conjunct is false. A negation is true if the negatum is false and false if the negatum is true. A universally quantified statement is true if every instance is true and false if at least one instance is false.

In the application we are interested in, all the terms other than 'Tr' already have a fixed interpretation in which the anti-extension is the complement of the extension, so all we need to determine is the extension and the anti-extension of 'Tr'. Where A and B are non-overlapping sets, let $\Gamma(A, B)$ be the pair $\langle C, D \rangle$, where C is the set of sentences which are declared true if A is assigned as the extension of 'Tr' and B as its anti-extension; and D is the union of the set of non-sentences and the set of sentences declared false when A is assigned as the extension of 'Tr' and B as its anti-extension. $\langle A, B \rangle$ is a 'fixed point' if and only if $\langle A, B \rangle = \Gamma(A, B)$.

Kripke's construction can now be succinctly characterized. Let C be the set of sentences which are true$_\alpha$ for some α, and let D be the set consisting of the non-sentences and the sentences which are false$_\alpha$ for some α. Then $\langle C, D \rangle$ is the smallest fixed point; that is, it is a fixed point included in every other fixed point. (We say $\langle A, B \rangle$ is included in $\langle C, D \rangle$ if $A \subseteq C$ and $B \subseteq D$.)

The existence of fixed points is startling. The liar paradox shows that, within the context of classical two-valued logic, it is not possible to assign an extension to 'Tr' in such a way that, for any sentence ϕ, ϕ is true or false according as $Tr(\ulcorner\phi\urcorner)$ is true or false. We can, however, solve the analogous problem for three-valued logic. At a fixed point, we assign an extension and an anti-extension to 'Tr' in such a way that, for any sentence ϕ, ϕ is true, false or unsettled according as $Tr(\ulcorner\phi\urcorner)$ is true, false or undecided.

There are fixed points other than the smallest. If A and B are non-overlapping sets with $\langle A, B \rangle \subseteq \Gamma(A, B)$, then there is a smallest fixed point which contains $\langle A, B \rangle$. The extension of 'Tr' in this smallest fixed point consists of the sentences which are derivable from the true atomic and negated atomic non-semantic sentences, together with the sentences in A and the negations of the sentences in B.

Fixed points other than the smallest are useful in describing the different sorts of pathological behaviour we find among self-referring sentences. Tarski's sentence λ, which asserts its own untruth, is viciously paradoxical; whether we declare it true or false, we fall into contradiction (see GÖDEL'S THEOREMS). By contrast, if we formalize the construction of the truth-teller sentence ('The truth-teller sentence is true'), getting a sentence τ which is provably equivalent to $Tr(\ulcorner\tau\urcorner)$, we again get a sentence which is paradoxical, but in a more compliant fashion; whether we declare the sentence true or false, the sentence is amiably willing to go along, but no such classification has any basis in extra-semantic reality.

The difference between these two sorts of pathologies is reflected in the structure of the fixed points. There are no fixed points in which λ is assigned a truth-value. By contrast, there are some fixed points in which τ is true, others in which it is false, and still others in which it lacks a truth-value.

There are a great many fixed points; if the language has κ sentences, there will be 2^κ of them. The fixed points constitute a complete lower semi-lattice, that is, a partially ordered set in which every non-empty subset has a greatest lower bound. If $\mathcal{K}$ is a non-empty collection of fixed points, the union of all the fixed points which are included in every member of $\mathcal{K}$ will be a fixed point, so it will be the greatest lower bound of $\mathcal{K}$.

5 Classical-logic versions of Kripke's theory

Where Kripke's construction assigns a truth-value, the value it assigns invariably agrees with our intuitive understanding of the everyday application of 'true'. However, there are many sentences to which the construction fails to assign a truth-value but about which ordinary intuition fails to detect even a whiff of paradox. For example, 'A conjunction is true if both its conjuncts are true' is, according to intuition, harmlessly and obviously true, yet the construction fails to give it a truth-value. Indeed, the construction fails to provide even the simplest semantic generalizations, withholding its assent from such harmless platitudes as 'Every true sentence is a true sentence'; since $Tr(\ulcorner\lambda\urcorner)$ is truth-valueless, so is $(Tr(\ulcorner\lambda\urcorner) \to Tr(\ulcorner\lambda\urcorner))$, hence $(\forall x)(Tr(x) \to Tr(x))$ falls into the gap between truth and falsity.

This limitation is easily remedied by extending the rules of inference to encompass classical logic and taking as axiomatic the principle that, if a conditional and its antecedent are both true, the consequent is also true. Thus the variant construction treats a sentence as true just in case it is derivable from true atomic and negated atomic non-semantic sentences, together with instances of the schema

$$(Tr(\ulcorner\phi \to \psi\urcorner) \to (Tr(\ulcorner\phi\urcorner) \to Tr(\ulcorner\psi\urcorner))),$$

by 'Tr'-introduction, '$\neg Tr$'-introduction, universal quantification introduction, and the laws of classical logic.

According to this variant construction, all classically valid sentences are true, in particular, $(\forall x)(Tr(x) \to Tr(x))$. For each ϕ and ψ, the conditional

$$((Tr(\ulcorner\phi\urcorner) \wedge Tr(\ulcorner\psi\urcorner)) \to Tr(\ulcorner\phi \wedge \psi\urcorner))$$

is derivable from the fact that 'Tr' distributes over conditionals, and the generalization that a conjunction is true if both its conjuncts are true follows by universal quantification introduction. Indeed, we can show that an inference schema is valid in classical logic if and only if all substitution instances of the schema are truth-preserving.

There is a price to pay. In the original construction, truth is unmistakably grounded in the non-semantic facts. In the alternative construction, this is not so evident, since we want an explanation of the truth of the laws of classical logic. In the original construction, the truth of a disjunction was based upon the truth of one of its disjuncts, but, in the alternative construction, this is no longer so.

Another construction with much the same effect employs Bas van Fraassen's method of 'supervaluations' (1966) in place of Kleene's three-valued logic; this is the method suggested by Kripke himself. The sentences declared true in $\Gamma(A, B)$ will be those sentences true in all the classical models we get from the original model by taking the extension of 'Tr' to be a consistent set of sentences, closed under first-order consequence, which contains A and is disjoint from B; the sentences declared false will be those whose negations are declared true. A sentence is regarded as true if it is declared true in the smallest fixed point.

The two constructions give similar results. Indeed, if the language is countable (which implies, since everything has a name, that the universe of discourse is countable), they give precisely the same results.

The classical-logic versions of Kripke's theory capture a great many of our common-sense intuitions about truth and paradox, but there remain fundamental intuitions that they leave aside. Notably, the intuition driving the theory is that the paradoxical sentences are neither true nor false. But the statement that the strengthened liar sentence is neither true nor false, while formalizable in the language, is never accepted as true. That the strengthened liar sentence is neither true nor false is something we can only see from the perspective of an essentially richer metalanguage. Within the object language, we can only recognize a sentence as untrue if at some stage it is declared false; only from the external vantage point of the metalanguage can we regard a sentence as untrue because it is never declared true.

6 Revision theory

There are other proposals for obtaining an unambiguous truth predicate within a classical framework, notably the 'revision theory' of Hans Herzberger (1982), Anil Gupta (1982) and Nuel Belnap (1982), which sees the paradoxes as arising because the processes by which we ordinarily introduce new terms into the language, as seen in ordinary explicit definitions and in inductive definitions, partially break down when the (T)-sentences are taken to define 'Tr'. The processes fail to stabilize upon a single choice for the extension of 'Tr'. Instead, if V_0 is a candidate for the extension of 'Tr' we get another candidate, at least as good, by taking the extension of 'Tr' to be the set V_1 of sentences true in the classical model obtained by setting the extension of 'Tr' equal to V_0. We get another good candidate by taking the extension of 'Tr' to be the set V_2 of sentences true in the model in which the extension of 'Tr' is V_1. The process never settles down. Whereas Plato's first statement above is in V_n for all $n > 5$, if the simple liar sentence is in V_n, it is outside V_{n+1}, but it is back inside V_{n+2}. The process continues into the transfinite, and, as it proceeds, we get better and better candidates for the extension of 'Tr'. The process must eventually repeat itself, and, after it starts to do so, the candidates we get are all optimal candidates for the extension of 'Tr'. Because the starting point V_0 was arbitrary, there are many different revision sequences. Count a sentence as 'stably true' if there is an ordinal level after which it always appears at every stage in every revision sequence.

The details of extending the process into the transfinite – what exactly to do at limit stages – is a matter of some disagreement among the three authors mentioned above, but all agree that a sentence is in V_λ, for λ a limit, if it is in all V_α, for α a sufficiently large ordinal less then λ, and a sentence is outside V_λ if it is outside V_α for sufficiently large $\alpha < \lambda$.

Revision theory still requires a richer metalanguage. We can only construct the revision sequences when the universe of discourse of the original language is a set, so we cannot carry out the construction for the language of set theory or for English, languages whose universe of discourse is not a set. (In those languages, we can talk about all sets, and there is no set that includes all sets.) The hope is that, in spite of this limitation, the fragments of English amenable to revision-theoretic treatment will be rich enough so that their study will cast a useful light upon our ordinary conception of truth in English.

7 English as an object language?

Most of the recent work on the paradoxes has been aimed at explicating the intuitions that govern ordinary speakers' usage of the word 'true'. For such purposes, a theory which only takes account of a fragment of the natural language may well suffice. For some theoretical purposes, however, one would like a global semantic theory, which takes full account of the linguistic practices of English speakers. Should it turn out, on the contrary, that a comprehensive theory of language is inherently impossible, so that part of our language lies irretrievably beyond the reach of linguistic inquiry, this would severely curtail the hopes of science, and it would also gravely undermine the prevalent mood of metaphysical naturalism, according to which human language is a part of the natural order, not intrinsically more mysterious or less comprehensible than the planetary orbits.

Hopes for a comprehensive theory are greatly discouraged by the liar paradox, but, if our optimism persists, we have only two alternatives: either to restrict classical logic or to restrict schema (T) (see §1 above). Restricting the logic does not seem to help. If we replace classical logic with Kleene's three-valued logic, we still do not get the (T)-sentences. Indeed, Feferman's investigations (1984) would seem to show that we do not get the (T)-sentences within any reasonable logic.

We might hope to preserve at least one direction of schema (T), but even here our hopes are thwarted by Montague's theorem (1963) that any logical system that includes the left-to-right direction of (T) together with the 'Tr'-introduction rule will be inconsistent with the laws of syntax. A dual result shows that the right-to-left direction is incompatible with '$\neg Tr$'-introduction and also that it is incompatible with 'Tr'-elimination, which is the converse of 'Tr'-introduction.

Another possibility, recommended by Vann McGee (1991), is to replace schema (T) with a system of rules of inference: 'Tr'-introduction and -elimination and '$\neg Tr$'-introduction and -elimination. The paradoxes are diagnosed as arising from the misapplication of these rules of inference within conditional proofs. The classical-logic versions of Kripke's theory can be employed to show that this system of rules is consistent.

As this consistency proof shows, Kripke's construction is a highly versatile tool, which can be usefully applied to a wide variety of philosophical purposes.

See also: INDUCTIVE DEFINITIONS AND PROOFS; LOGICAL AND MATHEMATICAL TERMS, GLOSSARY OF; PARADOXES OF SET AND PROPERTY; TARSKI'S DEFINITION OF TRUTH; THEORY OF TYPES

References and further reading

* Barwise, J. and Etchemendy, J. (1987) *The Liar*, New York: Oxford University Press. (A mathematically and philosophically sophisticated development of the thesis that the referent of 'true' depends on context, developed within situation semantics, as found in Barwise and Perry (1983).)

Barwise, J. and Perry, J. (1983) *Situations and Attitudes*, Cambridge, MA: MIT Press. (Situation semantics, utilized in Barwise and Etchemendy (1987).)

* Belnap, N. (1982) 'Gupta's Rule of Revision Theory of Truth', *Journal of Philosophical Logic* 11: 103–16. (Proposed modifying Gupta's revision theory by changing the procedure for limit stages, a proposal accepted by Gupta.)

* Burge, T. (1979) 'Semantical Paradox', *Journal of Philosophy* 76: 169–98; repr. in Martin (1984), 83–117. (Lucid and highly influential development of a context-dependent conception of truth.)

* Feferman, S. (1984) 'Toward Useful Type-Free Theories, I', in Martin (1984), 237–87. (Careful investigation of a variety of unified approaches to semantic and set-theoretic paradoxes.)

* Fraassen, B.C. van (1966) 'Singular Terms, Truth Value Gaps, and Free Logic', *Journal of Philosophy* 64: 464–95. (Invented supervaluations, used in §5.)

* Gödel, K. (1931) 'Über formal unentscheidbare Sätze der *Principia Mathematica* und verwandter Systeme I', *Monatshefte für Mathematik und Physik* 38: 173–98; trans. 'On Formally Undecidable Propositions of *Principia Mathematica* and Related Systems', in J. van Heijenoort (ed.) *From Frege to Gödel: A Source Book in Mathematical Logic, 1879–1931*, Cambridge, MA: Harvard University Press, 1967, 592–617. (In proving the incompleteness of Peano arithmetic, Gödel developed the fundamental tools of modern logic.)

* Gupta, A. (1982) 'Truth and Paradox', *Journal of Philosophical Logic* 11: 1–60; repr. in Martin (1984), 175–235. (Gupta and Herzberger independently discovered revision theory.)

Gupta, A. and Belnap, N. (1993) *The Revision Theory of Truth*, Cambridge, MA: MIT Press. (Extends the revision theory of truth, according to which 'true' is defined by the (T)-sentences, to an illuminating general theory of circular definitions.)

* Herzberger, H. (1982) 'Notes on Naïve Semantics', *Journal of Philosophical Logic* 11: 61–102; repr. in Martin (1984), 133–74. (Herzberger and Gupta independently discovered revision theory.)

* Kleene, S.C. (1952) *Introduction to Metamathematics*, New York: Elsevier, 1971. (An invaluable textbook. Three-valued logic is in §54.)

* Kripke, S.A. (1975) 'Outline of a Theory of Truth', *Journal of Philosophy* 72: 690–716; repr. in Martin (1984), 53–81. (The centre of all contemporary discussion of the liar paradox.)

Martin, R. (ed.) (1984) *Recent Essays on Truth and the Liar Paradox*, New York: Oxford University Press. (A collection of the most important papers.)

Martin, R. and Woodruff, P. (1985) 'On Representing "True-in-*L*" in *L*', *Philosophia* 5: 213–17; repr. in Martin (1984), 47–51. (First proved the existence of fixed points, independently of Kripke.)

* McGee, V. (1991) *Truth, Vagueness, and Paradox*, Indianapolis, IN: Hackett Publishing Company. (Explores prospects for a theory of truth developed without recourse to a richer metalanguage.)

* Montague, R. (1963) 'Syntactical Treatments of Modality, With Corollaries on Reflexion Principles and Finite Axiomatizability', *Acta Philosophica Fennica* 16: 153–67. (A version of the liar paradox with 'necessary' in place of 'true'.)

* Parsons, C. (1974) 'The Liar Paradox', *Journal of Philosophical Logic* 3: 381–412; repr. in Martin (1984), 9–45. (Insightfully develops a unified approach to the semantic and set-theoretic paradoxes, based upon the context dependence of both the extension of 'true' and the domain of quantification.)

* Quine, W.V. (1946) 'Concatenation as a Basis for Arithmetic', *Journal of Symbolic Logic* 11: 105–14. (Codes arithmetic into the theory of syntax.)

* Ramsey, F.P. (1925) 'The Foundations of Mathematics', *Proceedings of the London Mathematical Society* 25: 338–84; repr. in *Philosophical Papers*, Cambridge: Cambridge University Press, 1990, 164–224. (Distinguishing semantic from set-theoretic paradoxes, Ramsey effects a great simplification in the theory of types by neglecting the former.)

* Tarski, A. (1935) 'Der Warheitsbegriff in den formalisierten Sprachen', *Studia Logica* 1: 261–405; trans. J.H. Woodger (1956), 'The Concept of Truth in Formalized Languages', in *Logic, Semantics, Metamathematics: Papers from 1923 to 1938*, ed. J. Corcoran, Indianapolis, IN: Hackett Publishing Company, 2nd edn, 1983, 152–278. (Virtually all modern work on the logic of truth takes this fundamental paper as its starting point.)

* Whitehead, A.N. and Russell, B.A.W. (1910–13) *Principia Mathematica*, Cambridge: Cambridge University Press, 3 vols; 2nd edn, 1925–7; repr. 1994. (The development of all of mathematics on a single axiomatic basis. Discussion of the semantic paradoxes is in the introduction, 41–47 and 60–65.)

VANN McGEE

SEMANTIC VIEW OF THEORIES *see* MODELS; THEORIES, SCIENTIFIC

SEMANTICS

Semantics is the systematic study of meaning. Current work in this field builds on the work of logicians and linguists as well as of philosophers. Philosophers are interested in foundational issues in semantics because these speak to the nature of meaning, as it embeds in our thinking and in our relations to each other and to the world. Of special interest are questions about how a semantic theory should respect the connections of meaning to truth and to understanding. In addition, numerous semantic problems concerning particular linguistic constructions bear philosophical interest, sometimes because the problems are important to resolving foundational semantic issues, sometimes because philosophical problems of independent interest are expressed using the constructions, and sometimes because clarity about the semantic function of the constructions enables clarity in the development of philosophical theories and analyses.

1   **Historical sources and goals**
2   **Contemporary semantical traditions**
3   **Issues and problems in semantics**

1   Historical sources and goals

Systematic theorizing about meaning in language always has been of philosophical interest. In addition to being a science with interesting foundational problems, semantics interests philosophers because of their special interests in the nature of meaning and in the meaning of particular sorts of language, notably the language that serves as our primary means of expressing philosophically interesting concepts and thoughts (see LANGUAGE, PHILOSOPHY OF).

Contemporary semantics owes a great deal to work in formal logic by Gottlob FREGE, Bertrand RUSSELL and Alfred TARSKI, among others (see LOGIC, PHILOSOPHY OF). This work has provided techniques for constructing *formal systems* – abstract systems of symbols and sets with rigorously defined logical and structural relationships (see FORMAL LANGUAGES AND SYSTEMS). Ludwig WITTGENSTEIN and logical positivists such as Rudolf CARNAP found these techniques so compelling that they took certain formal, logical systems to reveal the kind of structure that any coherent language – in particular, any language suited to serious science – must possess at its roots (see LOGICAL POSITIVISM). A less extreme but more enduring view is that many aspects of natural languages are aptly *modelled* by formal systems – whether formal systems devised independently by logicians or designed expressly to reveal the systematic structure of the languages in question.

Recently, semantics has profited from the development, under the aegis of Noam CHOMSKY, of systematic accounts of natural language syntax (see SYNTAX). Chomsky regards the grammar of a person's language as a partly innate theory that is implicitly mastered in acquiring the language (see LANGUAGE, INNATENESS OF). The linguist's task is to make this theory explicit, guided by the person's spontaneous judgments about which constructions are grammatically acceptable, by experimental evidence about their cognitive faculties, and by general evidence about innate constraints on human grammars. Armed with this conception of the linguist's task, Chomsky and others have developed powerfully sophisticated theories of natural language grammar. Contemporary semanticists find this work useful for a number of reasons. Many semanticists now view their task in a Chomskian light: to uncover partly innate, cognitively real theories. Also, most contemporary semantic theories begin with something very like a grammar: a systematic account of the way sentences of the language in question are constructed from their meaningful parts – and it is quite reasonable to expect that the semantically relevant kind of sentence-structure bears a close relation to the correct grammar for the language.

2   Contemporary semantical traditions

The meaning of a statement is a matter of how things are, according to the statement; and the meaning of any expression is what users attach to it in their competent understanding of it. Semantics, then, ought to respect the outward-looking aspect of meaning: meaning fixes the representational and descriptive powers of language. And semantics must also respect the cognitive and epistemological aspect of meaning: meaning is cognized – it is grasped, known, understood.

A language (whether it be a shared social entity such as English, a narrower dialect, or even an individual's own 'idiolect') contains reusable words and expressions such as words and sentences. These are called expression-types because different tokenings of the expressions (different utterances or inscriptions of them) are importantly similar – they are of the same type (see TYPE/TOKEN DISTINCTION). Expression-types in a language have 'timeless' meaning that is drawn on in the various tokenings of the expressions. However, meanings can be expressed in the tokenings that complete, or go beyond, the timeless meanings of the expressions used. For instance, a particular utterance of the sentence 'That was worse' would express a meaning to do with a particular subject matter ('that') and would involve (because of 'was worse') a gesture to another subject matter and to a dimension of evaluation. An attractive principle is that the timeless meaning of an expression simply is a matter of the expression's distinctive potential for expressing meanings in particular tokenings. The discipline of pragmatics (whose border with semantics is notoriously porous) seeks to understand the relations between the timeless meaning of expression-types and the meanings achieved by tokenings, as well as the variety of ways tokenings (or speech acts) can achieve communicative and other purposes (see PRAGMATICS; PRESUPPOSITION; PROPOSITIONS, SENTENCES AND STATEMENTS; SPEECH ACTS).

A fact about natural languages that is no less impressive for being obvious is that every natural language issues in infinitely many sentences with different meanings. In English, 'Ann ate a pear' differs in meaning from 'Ann ate a pear, and then Ann ate a pear', which differs too from 'Ann ate pear, and then Ann ate a pear, and then Ann ate a pear', and so on. Any acceptable semantic account of a natural language will reveal its meanings as depending systematically on its repeatable, recombinant features (features of its expression-types and of their tokenings). One way to accomplish this is to show how meanings of complex expressions are generated from the meanings of simpler expressions, according to how the simpler expressions are combined. Such a strategy might employ a notion of *semantic values* of the meanings that are assigned to the simpler expressions (or tokenings) in the generation of the meanings of the more complex. That structure of a linguistic expression which, on these accounts, provides the key to the compositional derivation of its meaning sometimes is called the expression's *logical form*, because of assumptions about the nature of meaning to which we now turn (see COMPOSITIONALITY; LOGICAL FORM).

The representational side of meaning has led many semanticists to take as their primary goal systematic accounts of the *truth-conditions* of sentences, as well as accounts of such related phenomena as the conditions of true application of predicates (such as 'is a horse') and the conditions of the denotation or reference of various noun phrases (such as proper names, definite descriptions like 'the last Tsar', and demonstratives like 'this'). It is immediately plausible

that conditions of truth, applicability and reference are proper subjects for a semantic theory. For instance, the meaning of 'is a felucca', very plausibly, is a matter of what it is for a thing to be a felucca, which, again plausibly, is given by revealing what it takes for a thing to be truly described as a 'felucca'. Similarly, the meaning of 'In Syracuse there are many feluccas' is elucidated by characterizing how things would have to be to be truly so described (see MEANING AND TRUTH).

Because of the widespread view that a complete semantic account of a language must include systematic explanations of what it takes for its expressions to be true, to refer, or to apply truly, the central foundational issues in semantics include the nature of truth and reference, as well as the proper explanation and use within a semantic theory of the notions of truth- and applicability-conditions. Since truth- and application-conditions stand to each other in logical relations such as consistency and entailment, accounts of these conditions can serve what is regarded as another important goal in semantics: to explain the logical relations among linguistic expressions (and among their tokenings) (see TRUTH, COHERENCE THEORY OF; TRUTH, CORRESPONDENCE THEORY OF; TRUTH, DEFLATIONARY THEORIES OF; TRUTH, PRAGMATIC THEORY OF; SEMANTIC PARADOXES AND THEORIES OF TRUTH; REFERENCE; SENSE AND REFERENCE).

A style of contemporary semantics that can be traced to Frege and Russell employs as semantic values abstract 'universals' such as *propositions* and *properties* – entities that embody truth- or application-conditions, in that (unlike linguistic expressions) they are not intrinsically tied to any particular language and have their truth- or application-conditions timelessly and essentially. Thus, some semantical frameworks start with conceptions of the nature of propositions and properties; within these frameworks the principal task in giving a semantical description of a given language is to discover the principles governing which expression-tokenings have as their semantic values which propositions and properties (see PROPOSITIONS, SENTENCES AND STATEMENTS; UNIVERSALS; INTENSIONAL ENTITIES).

Some of these frameworks employ devices from the logical theory of models, in which the meanings of expressions are represented by set-theoretical structures (see MODEL THEORY). A particularly influential tradition in semantics deriving from the work of Carnap, Saul Kripke and Richard Montague, uses or imitates the notion of a 'possible world': the meaning of a statement is given by the sets of possibilities it excludes and allows, and the meanings of smaller expressions are their contributions to this semantic function of the sentences in which they figure (see SEMANTICS, POSSIBLE WORLDS; CARNAP, R.; MONTAGUE, R.M.; KRIPKE, S.A.; SEMANTICS, SITUATIONAL). Among the philosophical insights claimed for this work is the idea that in addition to revealing a statement's simple truth-condition (the condition that the utterance must meet if it is to be true), a semantical theory ought further to reveal its *modal content*, which determines what sorts of possible situation the utterance correctly describes. Focus on this distinction has promoted intense debate about metaphysical necessity and possibility, in particular, on whether certain devices of natural language (such as proper names) presuppose substantive views about necessity and essence, and on whether these views are seriously tenable (see PROPER NAMES; ESSENTIALISM; KRIPKE, S.A.).

A somewhat different tradition in semantics has been pioneered by Donald DAVIDSON, employing techniques due to Tarski (see TARSKI'S DEFINITION OF TRUTH). The goal in offering a Davidsonian semantics for a given language is to find an appropriate 'truth theory', thought of as a deductive system whose axioms and rules issue in 'T-sentences' such as 'The sentence "Schnee ist weiss" is true if and only if snow is white'. An appropriate truth-theory will not only be correct and complete, but also will in some sense explain the language-user's competence by revealing what it is that the speaker knows in knowing the language (see MEANING AND TRUTH; MEANING AND UNDERSTANDING §2).

Recently, too, philosophers, linguists and cognitive scientists have developed systematic semantic accounts based on algorithmic or procedural conceptions of meaning. These traditions borrow from the logical theory of proof (see SEMANTICS, GAME-THEORETIC; PROOF THEORY).

All semantical traditions, even those that focus heavily on truth-conditions, must aim as well at least for compatibility with satisfactory explanations of the cognitive/epistemological aspects of meaning, including understanding (see MEANING AND UNDERSTANDING; MEANING AND VERIFICATION; SENSE AND REFERENCE). One strategy is to keep issues about understanding at a remove from detailed semantic theorizing, by viewing understanding as involved not so much in the nature of meaning as in the uses to which meaning is put in thought and communication. David Lewis, for instance, proposes that a semantic account of a language is simply a correct description of the abstract function that assigns to statements in the language sets of possible worlds as meanings; understanding enters the picture only when we consider what constitutes the language's actually being used. For Lewis, the competent use of a particular language amounts to participation in a certain sort of conventional practice (see LANGUAGE CONVENTIONALITY OF; LEWIS, D.K.). Other strategies take semantic theorizing to be more directly focused on what the competent understanding of a language consists in. Some accounts in the Davidsonian tradition, for instance, submit truth-theories to constraints of cognitive plausibility: a truth-theory must not employ conceptual resources beyond those plausibly required of a competent language-user. Other accounts allow alien concepts in a semantic description of a language and employ a notion of *tacit knowledge* to explain how the semantic description represents what the language-user knows (see KNOWLEDGE TACIT). Also heavily cognitive in orientation are accounts within the Chomskian paradigm; these take the primary goal of semantics to be the discovery of the cognitive capacities and structures underlying linguistic competence (see CHOMSKY, N.). Some semantic accounts take as their task the explanation of how linguistic meaning is fixed by the meaning of mental items such as concepts and thoughts; for the ultimate source of meaning, these accounts defer to theories of cognitive semantics (see MIND, PHILOSOPHY OF; GRICE, H.P.; COMMUNICATION AND INTENTION; CONCEPTS; LANGUAGE OF THOUGHT; SEMANTICS, CONCEPTUAL ROLE; SEMANTICS, INFORMATIONAL; SEMANTICS, TELEOLOGICAL).

3 Issues and problems in semantics

Some debates about the semantic features of particular sorts of expression arise only within particular semantic traditions. Questions of *reference*, in contrast, are of very broad interest, since reference is widely taken to be a semantically central notion. Philosophers have hotly pursued questions about the nature of reference, about the proper role of reference in semantic theories and about how the reference of particular kinds of linguistic item is determined (see REFERENCE; SENSE AND REFERENCE). Receiving special attention have been proper names, natural kind terms (like 'tiger' and 'gold'), context-dependent terms (such as the demonstrative 'that' and the indexical 'today') and theoretical terms of science (such as 'mass' and 'oxygen') (see PROPER NAMES; NATURAL KINDS; DEMONSTRATIVES AND INDEXICALS; SCIENTIFIC REALISM AND ANTIREALISM). Among the questions under heavy discussion are the extent to which the determinants of reference are settled by intrinsic features of a speaker's cognition, rather than being settled by features of the speaker's society and environment (see LANGUAGE, SOCIAL NATURE OF; CONTENT: WIDE AND NARROW; METHODOLOGICAL INDIVIDUALISM).

Issues about the semantical or logical structure of various locutions, in contrast, are often discussed in the context of particular traditions of semantic theory (see LOGICAL FORM). Still, a number of such issues have interest that is not confined to any one semantic tradition. Among these are the proper treatment of definite descriptions such as 'the short spy'. Definite descriptions resist easy assimilation either to that of the paradigm of proper names or to that of quantifying phrases such as 'all circles' and 'three dogs' (see DESCRIPTIONS; QUANTIFIERS). Also of persisting interest is the behaviour of 'anaphoric' pronouns – ones which in one way or another 'refer back' (or even ahead) – such as occur in 'The dog is happy; he is wagging his tail' and 'Probably some dogs can climb trees; it is likely that they are small'. Difficulties in providing systematic explanations of the roles of anaphoric pronouns has led to a number of theories according to which semantic accounts of sentences must view their semantically relevant structure as inextricable from the larger discourse in which the sentences figure (see DISCOURSE SEMANTICS; ANAPHORA). Even the logical form of apparently simple subject–predicate sentences has been debated. For instance, Davidson proposes that the logical form of 'Bill is running' involves not the simple predication of an attribute to Bill, but rather an existence claim about an event (perhaps: an event exists, which is a running, which is in progress, and of which Bill is the agent). This account is meant to cohere with a straightforward account of adverbs, in which, for instance, it is clear why 'Bill is running' is entailed by 'Bill is running slowly' (see PREDICATION; EVENTS; ADVERBS).

So-called propositional-attitude ascribing statements (such as 'Sue believes that oranges are expensive') also have prompted extensive discussion. An ancient puzzle still has received no widely accepted solution: how is it that Hesperus and Phosphorus are one and the same entity, and yet 'Hammurabi believed that Hesperus is bright' might be true while 'Hammurabi believed that Phosphorus is bright' is false (see PROPOSITIONAL ATTITUDE STATEMENTS; INDIRECT DISCOURSE; INTENSIONALITY)?

Another source of fascinating, but inconclusive, debate among semanticists is the treatment of conditionals (if/then sentences), including indicative conditionals like 'If Oswald didn't shoot Kennedy, then someone else did' and subjunctive, counterfactual conditionals like 'If Oswald hadn't shot Kennedy, then someone else would have'. Concerning indicative conditionals, one current view is that their truth-conditions are aptly modelled on those of the material conditional of formal logic, while another is that indicative conditionals have no truth-conditions at all

but only conditions of proper assertion (see INDICATIVE CONDITIONALS). Counterfactual conditionals have been linked to metaphysical issues about necessity, causation and natural law, and debates about their interpretation are enmeshed with metaphysical debates (see COUNTERFACTUAL CONDITIONALS).

Also among the issues that bear on semantic theories are questions about necessity and possibility, the nature and ontological acceptability of intensional entities, tense, metaphor, vagueness and language apparently about nonexistent and fictional entities (see MODAL OPERATORS; MODAL LOGIC, PHILOSOPHICAL ISSUES IN; INTENSIONAL LOGICS; INTENSIONAL ENTITIES; TENSE AND TEMPORAL LOGIC; METAPHOR; VAGUENESS; EXISTENCE; FICTION, SEMANTICS OF; FICTIONAL ENTITIES; NECESSARY TRUTH AND CONVENTION).

See also: AMBIGUITY; ANALYTICITY; EMOTIVE MEANING; IMPERATIVE LOGIC; INTUITIONISTIC LOGIC AND ANTIREALISM; LOGICAL CONSTANTS; MASS TERMS; MEANING, INDIAN THEORIES OF; MEANING IN ISLAMIC PHILOSOPHY; ONTOLOGICAL COMMITMENT; QUESTIONS; SEMIOTICS; STRUCTURALISM IN LINGUISTICS

References and further reading

Larson, R. and Segal, G. (1995) *Knowledge of Meaning*, Cambridge, MA: MIT Press. (A lucid and philosophically sophisticated introduction to semantics developing a broadly Davidsonian approach.)

Chierchia, G. and McConnell-Ginet, S. (1995) *Meaning and Grammar*, Cambridge, MA: MIT Press. (An excellent introduction to semantics in the tradition of Montague grammar.)

MARK CRIMMINS

SEMANTICS, CONCEPTUAL ROLE

According to conceptual role semantics (CRS), the meaning of a representation is the role of that representation in the cognitive life of the agent, for example, in perception, thought and decision-making. It is an extension of the well-known 'use' theory of meaning, according to which the meaning of a word is its use in communication and, more generally, in social interaction. CRS supplements external use by including the role of a symbol inside a computer or a brain. The uses appealed to are not just actual, but also counter-

factual: not only what effects a thought does *have, but what effects it* would *have had if stimuli or other states had differed. Of course, so defined, the functional role of a thought includes all sorts of causes and effects that are non-semantic, for example, perhaps happy thoughts can bolster one's immunity, promoting good health. Conceptual roles are functional roles minus such non-semantic causes and effects.*

The view has arisen separately in philosophy (where it is sometimes called 'inferential' or 'functional' role semantics) and in cognitive science (where it is sometimes called 'procedural semantics').

1   Motivations for CRS
2   Two-factor CRS
3–4 Criticisms of CRS
5   Framework, not theory

1   Motivations for CRS

There are two quite different projects that go by the name 'semantics'. One, which we might call *linguistic* semantics, deals with the meanings of particular expressions in particular languages and how they fit together to make up meanings of larger expressions. The second project, *metaphysical* semantics, is one of investigating the fundamental nature of meaning, especially what it is about a person that gives their words or thoughts whatever meanings they have in the first place. Conceptual role semantics (CRS) is in the domain of metaphysical semantics: it says that the nature of meaning is functional. It does not have anything very informative to say about linguistic issues, about particular languages or about how a language user works out the meanings of sentences on the basis of the meanings of their component words. But if correct, it can contribute to these enterprises by discouraging false and confused foundational views (see SEMANTICS).

One major motivation for CRS is a functionalist approach to the mind generally (see FUNCTIONALISM). Functionalism says that what makes a state a mental state and what gives a mental state the specific content that it has is the role it plays in interacting with other mental states in a creature's psychology.

This idea motivates a reply to theories that insist that a mind requires something more. For example, Searle (1980) has argued that computers cannot understand language in virtue of their programs or, more generally, by manipulating symbols in a certain way. He rests his case on a thought experiment, the Chinese room, in which a non-Chinese speaker manipulates Chinese symbols by following rules that do not require him to understand the meanings of the symbols he is manipulating. The rules are so devised

that he produces sensible responses in Chinese to any Chinese inputs. Searle says that none the less he does not understand Chinese: he is just mindlessly manipulating symbols. CRS motivates the 'systems reply': if we can programme a computer to be intelligent, it will not be the central processing unit (CPU) all by itself that is intelligent or that understand the symbols, but rather all the complex relations between the CPU and other subsystems of the mind, for example, for perception, reasoning and decision making. So the whole system understands Chinese even if the person who is simulating the CPU does not (see CHINESE ROOM ARGUMENT).

Approaching the matter from the point of view of language rather than thought, what makes CRS plausible is the fact that many terms seem definable only in conjunction with one another. For example, in learning the theoretical terms of Newtonian mechanics – 'force', 'mass', 'kinetic energy', 'momentum' and so on – we do not learn definitions outside the circle. There are no such definitions. We learn the terms by learning how to use them in our thought processes, especially in solving problems. Indeed, CRS explains the fact, noted by Thomas Kuhn (1962), that modern scientists cannot understand the phlogiston theory without learning elements of an old language that express the old concepts. The functional role of, for example, 'principle' as used by phlogiston theorists is very different from the functional role of any term or complex of terms of modern physics, and hence we must acquire some approximation of the eighteenth-century functional roles if we want to understand their ideas (see DEFINITION; SCIENTIFIC METHOD).

Moreover, CRS does seem to give a plausible account of the meanings of the logical connectives. For example, we could specify the meaning of 'and' by noting that certain inferences – for example, the inferences from '*p*' and '*q*' to '*p* and *q*', and the inference from '*p* and *q*' to '*p*' – have a special status (they are 'primitively compelling', in the terminology of Peacocke 1992).

A further motivation for CRS is that it explains a reasonable version of a principle of charity according to which we cannot rationally attribute irrationality to a person without limit (see CHARITY, PRINCIPLE OF §4). Attributing unexplainable irrationality leads to a poor match of roles. If the best translation yields poor enough matches, then the alien conceptual system is not intelligible in ours.

2   Two-factor CRS

Putnam (1975) raised what might seem to be a powerful objection to any CRS. He pointed out that many natural kind concepts, such as 'water' and 'gold', depend in part for their meaning upon something other than the role of a representation in a person's head, namely upon what happens to be in their external environment (see CONTENT: WIDE AND NARROW; METHODOLOGICAL INDIVIDUALISM).

Some proponents of CRS have responded by favouring a 'two-factor' version of CRS. On this view, meaning consists of an internal, 'narrow' aspect of meaning – which might be handled by functional roles that are within the body – and an external referential/truth-theoretic aspect of meaning, which might be handled by some other metaphysical theories of meaning (for example, a causal one). According to the external factor, 'Superman flies' and 'Clark Kent flies' are semantically the same since Superman = Clark Kent; it is the internal factor that distinguishes them. But the internal factor counts 'Water is more greenish than bluish' as semantically the same in my mouth as in the mouth of my twin on twin earth (see CONTENT: WIDE AND NARROW §2); in this case, it is the external factor that distinguishes them.

Two-factor theories gain some independent plausibility from the need for them to account for *indexical* thought and assertions, assertions whose truth depends upon facts about when and where they were made and by whom (see CONTENT, INDEXICAL). For example, suppose that you and I say 'I am ill'. One aspect of the meaning of 'I' is common to us, another aspect is different. What is the same is that our terms are both used according to the rule that they refer to the speaker; what is different is that the speakers are different. White (1982) generalized this distinction to apply to the internal and external factors for all referring expressions, not just indexicals.

In a two-factor account, the conceptual roles stop at the skin in sense and effector organs; they are 'short-arm' roles. But CRS can also be held in a one-factor version in which the conceptual roles reach out into the world – these roles are 'long-arm'. Harman (1987) has advocated a one-factor account which includes in the long-arm roles much of the machinery that a two-factor theorist includes in the referential factor, but without any commitment to a separable narrow aspect of meaning.

3 Criticisms of CRS

Error. Actual conceptual roles involve errors, even dispositions to err. For instance, in applying the word 'dog' to candidate dogs, one will make errors, for example, in mistaking coyotes for dogs (see Fodor 1987). This problem arises in one form or another for all naturalistic theories of truth and reference, but in the case of CRS it applies to erroneous inferences as

well as to erroneous applications of words to things. Among all the conceptual connections of a symbol with other symbols, or (in the case of long-arm roles) with the world, which ones are correct and which ones are errors? Saul Kripke (1982), for example, wonders what distinguishes someone who mistakenly says '57 + 65 = 5' from someone who says it correctly, meaning by '+' a function that agrees with addition except in yielding a value of 5 with 57 and 65 as arguments. The answer a person gives in the two cases could be the same, correct in one and erroneous in the other.

Some think we can solve the problem by appealing to dispositions to 'correct' previous answers, or to 'correct' those corrections. But others wonder why all these dispositions could not be the same for two persons who use '+' to designate different functions. (The problem of error is sometimes said to be the problem of specifying semantic 'norms', although norms in this sense should not be confused with norms in the sense of how one ought to apply a word; see Horwich 1994.) Another line of reply is to attempt to specify some sort of naturalistic idealization which specifies roles that abstract away from error, in the way that laws of free fall abstract away from friction.

Words/world. Fodor criticizes a computer-oriented form of CRS for confusing what words denote with the words themselves. The functional roles in the target version of CRS stress searching data banks and manipulating representations, and this Fodor says is like claiming that the meaning of 'Napoleon won at Waterloo' is a set of instructions for finding that sentence in a book in the New York Public Library. All such a search yields is more words: we never get the semantic values of those words, namely Napoleon or Waterloo. But, the CRS theorist says in response, long-arm roles include causal chains outside the machine. And the two-factor version of CRS relies on a second factor, the referential factor, to explain the relation between the word 'Napoleon' and Napoleon.

CRS is often criticized from the point of view of truth-conditional theories of meaning (see MEANING AND TRUTH). If the meaning of a sentence is its truth-conditions, then the meaning cannot be its conceptual role. But with the two-factor theory, proponents of CRS have the option of counting meanings as the same or different in accordance with whether the external factor specifies truth-conditions that are the same or different. Further, there is reason to suppose that meaning is more fine-grained than truth-conditions. For example, the truth-conditions of 'I am happy' and 'Ned is happy' are the same (since I am Ned), but the meanings of those sentences differ. The further machinery involved in the internal factor can capture the differences among sentences with the same truth-conditions.

Sensory properties. Fodor also criticizes CRS for giving the wrong account of how I and Helen Keller (who was blind and deaf from an early age) can mean the same thing by, for example, 'Water tastes great'. After all, none of her thoughts bears the same relation to the evidence of sight and sound that mine do. But here Fodor assumes that CRS only has the resource of appealing to similarity in *inferential* role, which is entirely internal. He disparages such an account in favour of a referential view: we mean the same because our concepts of water are concepts of the same *thing*. But a two-factor CRS, relying in part on a referential component, has the option of giving exactly the same account as can a long-arm one-factor account.

What glues the two factors together. Fodor and LePore (1992) object to the two-factor account, wondering what glues the two factors together. Why can there not be a sentence that has the inferential role of 'Water is greenish' but is true if and only if 3 is a prime number? But there is nothing in the CRS approach that dictates that there is any restriction at all on what roles can go with what truth-conditions. This is an independent question that both proponents and opponents of CRS can ask. Everyone who accepts the existence of inferential roles and truth-conditions should find the question meaningful, whether or not they think these are two factors of meaning.

4 Criticisms of CRS (cont.)

Holism. CRS is often viewed as essentially holistic, but the CRS theorist does have the option of regarding some proper subset of the functional roles in which an expression participates as the ones that constitute its meaning. Thus the subset could be taken to be those that are analytic (or 'true by virtue of meaning'); or as the primitively compelling inferences (Peacocke 1992) plus those generated by them; or the explanatorily basic regularities (Horwich 1994).

One natural and common view of what distinguishes the meaning-constitutive roles is that they are analytic, or played by an expression by virtue of its meaning, as in the case of an inference from 'bachelor' to 'male'. Proponents of CRS are thus viewed as having to choose between accepting holism and accepting that the distinction between the analytic and synthetic is scientifically respectable, a claim that has been seriously challenged by Quine (1954) (see ANALYTICITY). Indeed, Fodor and LePore (1992) argue that, lacking an analytic/synthetic distinction, CRS is committed to semantic holism,

regarding the meaning of any expression as depending on its inferential relations to *every* other expression in the language (see HOLISM: MENTAL AND SEMANTIC). This, they argue, amounts to the denial of a psychologically viable account of meaning.

Proponents of CRS can counter as follows. First, there is a question of whether a meaning-constitutive inference is thereby analytic. *If* what is meaning-constitutive is analytic, then holistic versions of CRS need analyticity too, since they regard all inferences as meaning-constitutive. But if what is meaning-constitutive is *not* thereby analytic, then neither holistic nor non-holistic versions of CRS need analyticity. So analyticity is not the issue between holistic and non-holistic versions of CRS.

Second, proponents of CRS can reply that the view is not committed to regarding what is meaning-constitutive as analytic. In terms of our earlier two-factor account, they can, for example, regard the meaning-constitutive roles as those that are explanatorily basic in a *narrow* psychology: they are the rules that explain other rules of use and determine *narrow* content (Horwich 1994). Narrow content does not involve *truth*-values; these arise only with regard to *wide* content, and so *a fortiori* it does not involve any commitment to *truth by virtue of meaning alone.*

A third approach to accommodating holism with a psychologically viable account of meaning is to substitute close enough similarity of meaning for strict identity of meaning. That may be all we need for making sense of psychological generalizations, interpersonal comparisons and the processes of reasoning and changing one's mind.

Compositionality. Fodor and LePore (1992) raise a further worry that links the metaphysical semantic issue with a linguistic one: a CRS would seem to risk violating 'compositionality', that is, the requirement that the meaning of a complex expression be a function (in the mathematical sense) of the meanings of its parts (see COMPOSITIONALITY). It is widely thought that such a property of both language and thought is required to explain how human beings seem to able to grasp indefinitely many ever more complicated thoughts, and how they can learn to understand complex sentences on the basis of simple ones. CRS threatens this principle, since, Fodor and LePore say, the conceptual role of a complex non-idiomatic representation is not always a function of the conceptual roles of its parts. Someone who thinks that rattling snakes, especially, are dangerous is disposed to infer 'This is dangerous' from 'This is a rattling snake' for reasons that may not depend at all on any inferences they are disposed to make from 'This is rattling' or 'This is a snake' separately.

Advocates of non-holistic versions of CRS should

regard the argument's assumption that all inferences are to be included in inferential roles as question-begging. Non-holistic versions of CRS can deal with compositionality by counting only a subset of inferences as meaning-constitutive. As mentioned above, these inferences could be identified as the analytic ones, the explanatorily basic ones, or as those that are primitively compelling or generated by them. The threat to compositionality can be avoided by not counting the inference from 'This is a rattling snake' to 'This is dangerous' as part of the meaning-constitutive roles of either sentence.

Advocates of holistic versions of CRS may wish to go along with Fodor and LePore in assuming that all inferences are part of inferential roles. They should point out that the inferential role of 'rattling' and 'snake' is a matter not just of their roles in *isolation* from one another, but also their roles in contexts involving 'rattling' and 'snake' *together*. The 'rules of use' of these terms are context-sensitive, not context-free.

Once we allow context-sensitive rules of use, compositionality can be trivially satisfied. For example, we can characterize the meaning of a word as an ordered pair, $\langle X, Y \rangle$, where X is the set of inferences *to* sentences containing the word and Y is the set of inferences *from* sentences containing the word. This is a holistic version of the view, for it includes the inference from 'rattling snake' to 'dangerous' in the meaning of 'rattling' and 'snake', and this example stands proxy for the inclusion of *every* inference in the meaning of every word involved in those inferences. Now the roles just mentioned satisfy the requirements of compositionality from a metaphysical point of view without being a psycholinguistic or a linguistic theory of the representations on the basis of which language is learned or sentences are understood.

5 Framework, not theory

CRS is more of a framework for a theory than an actual theory. There is no agreement among proponents of this framework about how the roles are constituted. By actual causal interactions among thoughts? All? Some? If some, which ones? And what about systematically mistaken inferences (for example, the 'gambler's fallacy')? Do widespread cognitive illusions contribute to the determination of meaning? Or are the roles normative? If the roles are idealized to avoid mistakes, how is the idealization supposed to be understood? Inference can be understood in intentional terms or in purely causal terms, and the latter would be preferable from the point of view of avoiding circularity in specifying roles. And is there any way to distinguish correcting an old practice from

changing to a new one (Kripke 1982)? Many successful philosophical theories are quite sketchy. Some say that CRS is no worse than many of them, but others say that the problems in filling in these details involve difficulties that are fatal to the whole project.

See also: CONCEPTS

References and further reading

Block, N. (1987) 'Functional Role and Truth Conditions', *Proceedings of the Aristotelian Society* 61: 157–81. (Argues that two-factor and one-factor theories do not differ substantively.)

Field, H. (1977) 'Logic, Meaning and Conceptual Role', *Journal of Philosophy* 69: 379–408. (Two-factor version of CRS based in conditional probability.)

* Fodor, J. (1987) *Psychosemantics: The Problem of Meaning in the Philosophy of Mind*, Cambridge, MA: MIT Press. (Raises the 'error' or 'disjunction' problem for theories of meaning.)

* Fodor, J. and LePore, E. (1992) *Holism: A Shoppers' Guide*, Oxford: Blackwell. (A critique of arguments for holism. Chapter 3 is concerned with CRS.)

* Harman, G. (1987) '(Non-Solipsistic) Conceptual Role Semantics', in E. LePore (ed.) *New Directions in Semantics*, London: Academic Press. (A defence of a one-factor CRS.)

* Horwich, P. (1994) 'What it is Like to be a Deflationary Theory of Meaning', in E. Villanueva (ed.) *Philosophical Issues*, vol. 5, *Truth and Rationality*, Atascadero, CA: Ridgeview. (Shows how use theories can accommodate the truth-conditional, normative and compositional aspects of meaning.)

* Kripke, S. (1982) *Wittgenstein: On Rules and Private Language*, Oxford: Blackwell. (Influential discussion of the 'error' problem, which Kripke claims to find in Wittgenstein.)

* Kuhn, T. (1962) *The Structure of Scientific Revolutions*, Chicago, IL: University of Chicago Press. (A famous argument that the history of science is a series of routine periods punctuated by revolutions in which the scientific community changes its conception of the problems and of what the criteria are for a solution.)

Miller, G. and Johnson-Laird, P. (1976) *Language and Perception*, Cambridge, MA: MIT Press. (A CRS proposal in psychology.)

* Peacocke, C. (1992) *A Theory of Concepts*, Cambridge, MA: MIT Press. (A CRS-oriented account of the nature of concepts.)

* Putnam, H. (1975) 'The Meaning of "Meaning"', in

K. Gunderson (ed.) *Minnesota Studies in the Philosophy of Science*, vol. 7, *Language, Mind and Knowledge*, Minneapolis, MN: University of Minnesota Press. (The source of the famous twin earth thought experiment.)

* Quine, W.V. (1954) 'Carnap and Logical Truth', in *Ways of Paradox and Other Essays*, Cambridge, MA: Harvard University Press; 2nd edn, 1976, 107–32. (Challenges the claim that the distinction between the analytic and synthetic is scientifically respectable.)

* Searle, J. (1980) 'Minds, Brains and Programs', *Behavioral and Brain Sciences* 13 (4): 610–42. (Presentation of the 'Chinese room argument' against computational theories of mind and meaning.)

* White, S. (1982) 'Partial Character and the Language of Thought', *Pacific Philosophical Quarterly* 63: 347–65. (The source of the view of narrow meaning based on Kaplan's theory of demonstratives.)

Wittgenstein, L. (1953) *Philosophical Investigations*, Oxford: Blackwell. (Source of the view that 'the meaning of a word is its use', an important inspiration for CRS.)

Woods, W. (1981) 'Procedural Semantics as a Theory of Meaning', in A. Joshi, B. Webber and I. Sag (eds) *Elements of Discourse Understanding*, Cambridge, MA: MIT Press. (A CRS proposal in artificial intelligence.)

NED BLOCK

SEMANTICS, GAME-THEORETIC

Game-theoretic semantics (GTS) uses concepts from game theory to study how the truth and falsity of the sentences of a language depend upon the truth and falsity of the language's atomic sentences (or upon its sub-sentential expressions). Unlike the Tarskian method (which uses recursion clauses to determine satisfaction conditions for nonatomic sentences in terms of the satisfaction conditions of their component sentences, then defines truth in terms of satisfaction), GTS associates with each sentence its own semantic game played on sentences of the language. This game defines truth in terms of the existence of a winning strategy for one of the players involved. The structure of the game is determined by the sentence's structure, and thus the semantic properties of the sentence in question can be studied by attending to the properties of its game.

For each sentence S of the language, there is a semantic game $G(S)$ between two players, the defender of S and the attacker. S is true when the defender has a way of winning the game, no matter what the attacker does – that is, when the defender has a winning strategy in $G(S)$. S is false when the attacker has a winning strategy. The defending player defends a disjunction by selecting a disjunct to defend, since the truth of a disjunction requires only a single disjunct to be true. Since the truth of a conjunction requires both its conjuncts to be true, the attacker attacks a conjunction by selecting a conjunct for the defender to defend. This means that the defender must be able to defend both conjuncts, if the conjunction is to be true. To defend a negation $-S$, it suffices to show S false, so the defender of $-S$ is the attacker of S, and vice-versa.

A play of $G(S)$ eventually comes down to a single atomic sentence A. Since the truth-values of nonatomic sentences depend on those of atomic ones, $G(S)$ is played against the background of a specified assignment of truth-values to the language's atoms. If A is true according to the given assignment, the defender of A wins this play of $G(S)$, but if it is false, the attacker wins. Truth of A is not necessary in order for the initial sentence S to be true; for instance, the defender may defend a disjunction unwisely by picking a false disjunct, even if the disjunction is true. S is true when the defender of S has a winning strategy, which means that there is a way to force any play of $G(S)$ to end in victory for that player.

To show an existential quantification to be true, it suffices to find a single true instance. To show a universal quantification false, it suffices to find a single false instance. Thus the defender of an existential sentence selects an individual as an instance of the existential claim, and the attacker of a universal selects an instance of that universal. Again, the universal is true only if the defender can defend every instance that the attacker might select.

When applied to an ordinary first-order language (with no restrictions imposed on strategies available to the players), the assignment of truth-values to sentences produced by game-theoretic semantics (GTS) – on the basis of an assignment of values to the atoms – coincides with the results of the more familiar semantic frameworks. The usefulness of GTS appears when attention turns to natural language, and also when restrictions are imposed on available strategies in games for formal languages.

Unlike most formal languages, English is structurally ambiguous in ways that a semantics must treat (see AMBIGUITY). For instance, 'Everyone loves someone' is ambiguous between two readings, $(\forall x)(\exists y)(x \text{ loves } y)$ and $(\exists y)(\forall x)(x \text{ loves } y)$, with the former reading strongly preferred. This ambiguity arises in GTS because there are distinct games for the sentence. In one game, the universal quantifier 'everyone' is processed first, thus receiving a wide-scope interpretation so that the first reading is produced. In the second, the existential quantifier 'someone' is processed first. The first reading is preferred because 'everyone' commands 'someone' in the sentence. ('Command' refers to the structural relation of the two quantifiers: the first is 'higher' in the sentence than the second). Thus GTS for English involves a principle that commanding operators must be processed first. This is an 'ordering principle' which governs the structures of semantic games so as to produce preferred readings of ambiguous sentences. Some ordering principles can be absolute, others (like the example above) can be defeasible. Another defeasible ordering principle is that operators should be processed following the left-to-right order of their occurrence in the sentence in question. This principle also applies to 'Everyone loves someone'.

Unlike many approaches to the semantics of English, GTS is not compositional. The interpretation of a sentence need not be determined in a 'cumulative' way based on the predetermined meanings of its components. This allows GTS to treat various semantic phenomena that do not respond to compositional semantic analysis (see COMPOSITIONALITY).

GTS applied to English yields interesting and novel treatments of such well-known semantic problems as anaphora (determining the conditions for co-reference of pronouns and related singular terms and quantifiers), conditionals, intentional identity, negation and nonstandard informational relationships among operators in a sentence. This can be seen in so-called 'branching quantifiers' and in the interpretation of relational questions. For example, the branching sentence:

$$\begin{matrix} \forall x \exists y \searrow \\ \qquad\qquad Fxyzw \\ \forall z \exists w \nearrow \end{matrix}$$

has y within the scope of x and w within the scope of z, but y is not within the scope of z, nor w within the scope of x. This pattern of quantifier relationships cannot be represented in a linear first-order quantifier prefix. The semantic game for this sentence is like the game for $\forall x \exists y \forall z \exists w Fxyzw$, except that the game for the branching sentence is a game of imperfect information. The defender of the sentence is ignorant of certain previous moves in the game, whereas the defender of the linear sentence knows what has transpired in the game for that sentence (see QUANTIFIERS §2).

Branching quantification is a well-understood

example of informational independence of operators. Informational independence is currently the object of intense study in GTS, which has led to the formulation of 'independence-friendly' logics and the discovery of conditions governing informational variability. Other areas currently of great interest include negation in English and the role of subgames in interpretation. The subgame of a semantic game is a self-contained game serving as a component of the larger game, so that the larger game involves results of the subgame in its play. For example, interpretation of a conditional requires information concerning the semantic game for its antecedent, in order to interpret pronominal connections between the antecedent and consequent. Recent developments have generalized the subgame idea, using 'tangent games' to provide a semantics of relative clauses and to link them to homophonic embedded questions.

See also: DECISION AND GAME THEORY; SEMANTICS

References and further reading

Hand, M. (ed.) (1994) *Synthèse* 99 (3), special issue. (Special GTS issue containing important new work on negation, informational variability, games with chance moves and other topics.)

Hintikka, J. (1976) *The Semantics of Questions and the Questions of Semantics*, Amsterdam: Acta Philosophica Fennica. (An early, extensive semantic investigation of questions.)

—— (1983) *The Game of Language: Studies in game-theoretical semantics and its applications*, Netherlands: Kluwer. (Papers by Hintikka – some in collaboration with Kulas – on negation, tense and other topics.)

Hintikka, J. and Kulas, J. (1985) *Anaphora and Definite Descriptions*, Dordrecht: Reidel. (A GTS account of pronominal relations.)

Hintikka, J. and Sandu, G. (1990) *On the Methodology of Linguistics*, Dordrecht: Reidel. (Focuses largely on a GTS account of pronominal relations.)

Saarinen, E. (1979) *Game-Theoretical Semantics*, Dordrecht: Reidel. (A collection of early papers in GTS, including Hintikka's influential discussions of branching quantification, Hintikka and Carlson's original discussion of subgames in the semantics of conditionals, Saarinen on backward-looking operators and intentional identity, and Rantala's urn models.)

MICHAEL HAND

SEMANTICS, INFORMATIONAL

Information-theoretic semantics (ITS) attempts to provide a naturalistic account of the conditions under which a psychological state such as a belief or desire has a particular mental content: what it is by virtue of which, say, a psychological state is a belief 'that it is raining' or a desire 'that it stop raining'. Because of the complexities of an entirely general account, ITS typically attempts to provide merely a sufficient naturalistic condition for a belief content of the sort normally acquired by perception (for example, that it is raining). It is expected that other sorts of mental contents may require that ITS be supplemented in various ways.

ITS was inspired by Claude Shannon's theory of 'information' (1948), which provided a mathematical measure of the amount of information carried by a signal. Employing a notion of 'natural meaning' discussed by Peirce (1931) and Grice (1957), Dretske (1981) supplemented Shannon's work with an account of what information a signal carries. The intuitive idea is that a signal carries the information 'that p' *if and only if it naturally means (that is, indicates) that* p, *as when smoke 'means' there is fire.*

Natural indication is a key ingredient in ITS accounts of mental content. In their accounts, Stampe (1977) and Stalnaker (1984) appeal to the notion of what a state indicates under 'optimal' conditions. Fodor (1987) appeals to 'asymmetric dependencies' between the meaning-forming and the non-meaning-forming indication conditions in the causation of psychological states. Dretske (1988) appeals to the idea that, via operant conditioning, a state can acquire a functional role vis-à-vis *behaviour because it naturally indicates 'that* p' *and thereby can acquire the natural function of indicating 'that* p'.

1   **Content and indication**
2   **Two problems**
3   **Three proposals**
4   **Two-factor theories**

1   Content and indication

In an early proposal, Dretske (1981) maintained that a state, S, carries the information 'that p' (that is, has the informational content 'that p') if and only if the probability of S, given p, is equal to 1 (see INFORMATION THEORY). One issue this proposal raises is whether the probability is 'objective' or 'subjective' (a matter of degrees of belief) (see PROBABILITY, INTERPRETATIONS OF). If the notion of information content

is to be suitable for a naturalistic account of mental content, the notion of probability invoked must be objective. But, as Dretske himself pointed out, the relevant notion of probability is not relative frequency. Moreover, it seems not to be propensity either: the direction of propensity is the direction of causation; but the conditional probability Dretske would have us consider is the opposite direction: the probability of there being 'fire', given that there is 'smoke'. In a later proposal, Dretske (1988) employed a counterfactual: the occurrence of a state, S, carries the information that p if and only if S would not have occurred unless p. He claimed that such counterfactuals express objective, mind-independent facts.

2   Two problems

Error. A state carries the information 'that p' if and only if it indicates (or naturally means) 'that p'. But a state indicates 'that p' only if p is indeed the case. So information, in the sense of natural indication, does not admit of misinformation, or error. However, belief does: one can believe 'that p' even when p is false. How can information-theoretic semantics (ITS) accommodate this fact?

Fine-grained individuation. Moreover, even when a belief 'that p' indicates 'that p', the indication relation will not uniquely pair the belief with p. The belief 'that p' can differ from the belief 'that q', even when p and q are logically equivalent. For example, the belief that 'there is a chair in the room' has a different content from the belief that 'there is a chair in the room and it is either an antique or not an antique', even though these contents are logically equivalent. However, if a state indicates p, then it indicates anything that is logically equivalent to p. Indeed, if a state indicates 'that p', then it indicates anything that is merely nomologically equivalent to p: for example, anything that indicates the presence of a renate (creature with kidneys) indicates the presence of a cordate (creature with a heart). Moreover, if something indicates 'that p', then it indicates anything that logically or even nomologically follows from p: anything that indicates that something is a cow indicates that it is a herbivore. Yet the belief that something is a renate is different from the belief that it is a cordate, a belief that something is a cow is different from the belief that it is a herbivore.

3   Three proposals

Optimal conditions. Stampe (1977), Fodor (1990b) and Stalnaker (1984) try to accommodate the possibility of error or misrepresentation by maintaining that the content of a psychological state is what the state would indicate under 'optimal' conditions. Stalnaker's proposal is that a belief state has the content 'that p' if and only if, in optimal conditions, the state indicates p, and the subject is in the state because p or because of something that entails p. The idea is that in cases of false belief, conditions are not optimal (see IDEALIZATIONS).

One problem is that it is by no means clear that the notion of ideal conditions is suitably naturalistic. Belief fixation is holistic: what someone would come to believe in some situation depends on what they already believe about other things. Even in a good light, someone presented with a horse might not think it is one if they think appearances are misleading. If optimal conditions must include the subject's being in belief states with certain contents, then, as an account of belief content, ITS is circular.

Asymmetric dependencies. FODOR (1987) formulates his ITS theory as one for mental symbols – expressions in a 'language of thought' (see LANGUAGE OF THOUGHT). He calls tokens of mental symbols meaning 'cow' that are caused in the absence of cows 'wild', and calls the property whereby symbols can mean things that on occasion are not causes of their tokening 'robustness'. He points out that in solving problems of robustness and error, ITS needs to solve the 'disjunction' problem: given that among the causes of a symbol's tokenings, there are both meaning-forming and wild causes, what distinguishes them? In particular, what makes it true that some symbol F means [horse] and not [horse or cow on a dark night] or [horse or cow on a dark night or w_2 or w_3 or...] (where each w_i is a property the exemplification of which could cause the tokening of F)?

Fodor speculates that a state's being caused by wild conditions depends upon its being caused by meaning-constitutive ones, but not vice versa: ill-lit cows causing horse thoughts depends upon well-lit horses causing them, but well-lit horses causing them does not similarly depend upon the ill-lit cows doing so (getting things wrong depends upon getting things right in a way that getting things right does not depend upon getting things wrong). Fodor draws from this speculation the proposal that mention of ideal conditions is inessential: the structure of this asymmetric causal dependency alone, abstracted from any specific conditions or causal chains, can do all the work.

One problem with this suggestion is that there are many asymmetric dependencies even within meaning-forming cases: for example, small horses causing horse thoughts might asymmetrically depend upon all horses doing so, but not vice versa. If this were so, Fodor would be committed to claiming that 'horse' meant 'non-small horse'.

Another problem is that, in avoiding any mention of mentality, the account risks gratuitous meanings that are brought about by the physics of the world but have no cognitive significance for the agent: electrical stimulation by a poking neurosurgeon, or by cosmic rays, causing tokenings of a mental state in one set of circumstances (for example, when potassium levels were high), might depend upon their lawfully causing those tokenings under other circumstances (when sodium levels were low, for example), but not vice versa. Fodor's view would seem to be committed to treating these further phenomena as meanings, albeit of no cognitive relevance to the agent.

Fodor (1987, 1990a) has replied to these objections with considerable ingenuity. However, what is needed is not only to rule out cases one-by-one, but some general reason to believe that the relevant notion of asymmetric dependency can be explicated without appeal to any mentalistic notions.

Indicator functions. Dretske's most developed ITS proposal is that a mental state has the content 'that p' if and only if it is has the *function* of indicating p. This distinguishes a proper subset of natural indications; moreover, errors arise when the state fails to indicate what it has the function of indicating. The problem of consequences is handled by observing that from the fact that a state has the function of indicating 'that p', and p implies q, it does not follow that the state has the function of indicating that q (see SEMANTICS, TELEOLOGICAL; FUNCTIONAL EXPLANATION).

The main burden of this approach is to say what makes it the case that a state has a certain indicator function. Dretske offers an account of how a state can acquire such a function, and uses it to offer an account of what he calls 'proto-beliefs' and 'proto-desires'. Suppose that a state B of an organism indicates that some property or kind F (for example, water) is present in the organism's vicinity, and that a state D of the organism renders it receptive to a reward R. Then, when in D, the organism's behaviour can be reinforced by R. Suppose further that when B and D jointly contribute to producing a movement M in circumstances in which F is present, this results in the organism's receiving R. Then, through a process of operant conditioning, B and D can come to have the 'control' duty of producing M. State B can thus acquire the control duty because it indicates F, and D can thus acquire this duty because it is a state of receptivity for R. According to Dretske, if B and D were recruited in this way for the control duty of producing some movement, B has the natural function of indicating that F is present, and D counts as a proto-desire for R.

A problem for this account is whether it can be naturalistically supplemented to yield an account of beliefs and desires themselves, since pairs of beliefs and desires do not generally have a specific control duty *vis-à-vis* movements: desiring water and believing there is some in the brook, does not necessarily give rise to any specific behaviour. And, of course, this account is inapplicable for beliefs and desires not acquired by operant conditioning (see BEHAVIOURISM, ANALYTIC; BEHAVIOURISM, METHODOLOGICAL AND SCIENTIFIC).

Moreover, appeals to function arguably fail to solve the problem of fine-grained individuation. If *p* and *q* are logically equivalent or even nomologically equivalent, then the mechanisms of operant conditioning will be insensitive to their difference (see INTENTIONALITY; PROPOSITIONAL ATTITUDE STATEMENTS). Consequently, a state will have the natural function of indicating 'that *p*' if and only if it has the natural function of indicating 'that *q*'. Indeed, whenever *p* and *q* are such that the mechanisms of operant conditioning are insensitive to their difference, whatever has the natural function of indicating *p* has the natural function of indicating *q*. Thus, if, for instance, such mechanisms are insensitive to the difference between the presence of a 'rabbit' and the presence of 'undetached rabbit parts' (to borrow a famous example from Quine 1960), it seems that a state will have the function of indicating that a rabbit is present if and only if it has the function of indicating that undetached rabbit parts are present.

4 Two-factor theories

Since BRENTANO, it has seemed to many philosophers undeniable that the mind makes more distinctions than even all possible worlds provide: the mind can conceive the impossible, and distinguish among even necessarily co-instantiated properties (like 'being an equiangular triangle' and 'being an equilateral triangle'). 'Two-factor' theories claim that there is something about a mental state in addition to what is captured by ITS that supplies the additional distinctions, notably, its structure or its conceptual role. Fodor (1990a), doubting that conceptual roles can be specified in a way immune to Quine's criticisms of the analytic/synthetic distinction, holds that what distinctions are needed can be captured by structures specified in a language of thought. Others (Block 1986, for example) think that once conceptual roles are specified purely internally, independently of issues of truth, Quine's criticisms are no longer a worry. Most defenders of ITS agree that capturing the contents of logically complex, non-perceptual beliefs (for example, that 'not every particle retains charge if divided') requires reference

to some internal factor (see SEMANTICS, CONCEPTUAL ROLE §3; CONCEPTS §10).

See also: CONTENT, NON-CONCEPTUAL; INFORMATION THEORY; INFORMATION THEORY AND EPISTEMOLOGY; SEMANTICS; SEMANTICS, TELEOLOGICAL

References and further reading

* Block, N. (1986) 'Advertisement for a Semantics for Psychology', in P. French, T. Uehling, Jr, and H. Wettstein (eds) *Midwest Studies in Philosophy*, vol. 10, *Studies in the Philosophy of Mind*, Minneapolis, MN: University of Minnesota Press. (Defence of a 'two-factor' theory of content, allowing for information-theoretic semantics and conceptual role semantics.)

Boghossian, P. (1989) 'The Rule-Following Considerations', *Mind* 98: 507–50. (Raises the holism objection to information-theoretic semantics accounts that appeal to optimal conditions, and argues that ITS accounts cannot capture the normativity of mental content.)

* Dretske, F. (1981) *Knowledge and the Flow of Information*, Cambridge, MA: MIT Press/Bradford Books. (Dretske's original proposal of information-theoretic semantics.)

* —— (1988) *Explaining Behavior: Reasons in a World of Causes*, Cambridge, MA: MIT Press/Bradford Books. (Dretske's later development of information-theoretic semantics.)

Fodor, J. (1984) 'Semantics, Wisconsin Style', *Synthese* 59: 231–50. (Criticism of Stampe- and Dretske-style theories (see Stampe 1977; Dretske 1981) from a fellow endorser of the information-theoretic semantics strategy.)

* —— (1987) *Psychosemantics*, Cambridge, MA: MIT Press/Bradford Books. (Source of the 'asymmetric dependency' proposal referred to in §3.)

* —— (1990a) *A Theory of Content and Other Essays*, Cambridge, MA: MIT Press. (Criticisms of conceptual role theories of content and a defence of his asymmetric dependency proposal.)

* —— (1990b) 'Psychosemantics, or Where Do Truth Conditions Come From?', in W. Lycan (ed.) *Mind and Cognition: A Reader*, Oxford: Blackwell, 312–38. (A vigorous defence of an 'optimal conditions' version of information-theoretic semantics; widely circulated as a manuscript in 1980 and published in 1990 despite Fodor's repudiation of the view (see Fodor 1987).)

Gates, G. (1996) 'The Price of Information', *Synthese* 107: 325–47. (Forceful criticism of information-theoretic semantics on the basis of the argument of Quine 1960.)

* Grice, H. (1957) 'Meaning', *Philosophical Review* 80: 377–88. (Famous effort to distinguish 'natural' from 'non-natural' meaning, aimed against ITS-style theories.)

Loewer, B. (1986) 'From Information to Intentionality', *Synthese* 2: 287–317. (Makes the point about objective probability and natural meaning made in §1; raises the holism objection to accounts using information-theoretic semantics that appeal to optimal conditions.)

Loewer, B. and Rey, G. (eds) (1991) *Meaning in Mind: Fodor and His Critics*, Oxford: Blackwell. (Criticisms by a number of philosophers of Fodor's theory of mind generally, but especially of his 'asymmetric dependency' theory of content; with replies by Fodor and a useful introduction to his theory by the editors.)

McLaughlin, B. (1986) 'What is Wrong With Correlational Psychosemantics', *Synthese* 2: 271–86. (Raises the holism objection to accounts using information-theoretic semantics that appeal to optimal conditions; points out that such accounts cannot cover mental contents that are satisfied by conditions that cannot obtain in optimal conditions, and thus cannot account for beliefs such as that one is not in optimal conditions.)

—— (ed.) (1991) *Dretske and His Critics*, Oxford: Blackwell. (Contains several essays on Dretske's information semantics and his replies to these essays.)

Peirce, C.S. (1931) *Collected Papers*, ed. C. Hartshorne and P. Weiss, vol. 2, Cambridge, MA: Harvard University Press. (Perhaps the earliest proposal of an information-theoretic semantics.)

Quine, W.V. (1960) *Word and Object*, Cambridge, MA: MIT Press. (A highly influential discussion of meaning that contains a limited, behaviouristic version of information-theoretic semantics, raising (in chapter 2) the famous 'gavagai' problem for any such theory: how could, for example, 'rabbit' be distinguished from 'undetached rabbit parts'.)

Shannon, C.E. (1948) 'The Mathematical Theory of Communication', repr. in C.E. Shannon and W. Weaver, *The Mathematical Theory of Communication*, Chicago, IL: University of Illinois Press, 1949. (Presents a mathematical theory of *quantity* of information.)

Stalnaker, R. (1984) *Inquiry*, Cambridge, MA: MIT Press/Bradford Books. (Defends a version of information-theoretic semantics that appeals to optimal conditions.)

Stampe, D. (1977) 'Toward a Causal Theory of Linguistic Representation', in P. French, T. Uehling, Jr, and H. Wettstein (eds) *Contemporary Perspectives in the Philosophy of Language*, Minneapolis, MN: University of Minnesota Press, 81–102. (One of the original proposals of information-theoretic semantics.)

BRIAN P. McLAUGHLIN
GEORGES REY

SEMANTICS, POSSIBLE WORLDS

Possible worlds semantics (PWS) is a family of ideas and methods that have been used to analyse concepts of philosophical interest. PWS was originally focused on the important concepts of necessity and possibility. Consider:

(a) Necessarily, 2 + 2 = 4.
(b) Necessarily, Socrates had a snub nose.

Intuitively, (a) is true but (b) is false. There is simply no way that 2 and 2 can add up to anything but 4, so (a) is true. But although Socrates did in fact have a snub nose, it was not necessary that he did; he might have had a nose of some other shape. So (b) is false.

Sentences (a) and (b) exhibit a characteristic known as intensionality: *sentences with the same truth-value are constituent parts of otherwise similar sentences, which nevertheless have different truth-values. Extensional semantics assumed that sentences stand for their truth-values, and that what a sentence stands for is a function of what its constituent parts stand for and how they are arranged. Given these assumptions, it is not easy to explain the difference in truth-value between (a) and (b), and hence not easy to give an account of necessity.*

PWS takes a sentence to stand for a function from worlds to truth-values. For each world, the function yields the truth-value the sentence would have if that world were actual. '2 + 2 = 4' stands for a function that yields the truth-value 'true' for every world, while 'Socrates had a snub nose' stands for a different function that yields 'true' for some worlds and 'false' for others, depending on what Socrates' nose is like in the world. Since these two sentences stand for different things, sentences that have them as constituents, such as (a) and (b), can also stand for different things.

This basic idea, borrowed from Leibniz and brought into modern logic by Carnap, Kripke and others, has proven extremely fertile. It has been applied to a number of intensional phenomena in addition to necessity and possibility, including conditionals, tense and temporal adverbs, obligation and reports of informational and cognitive content. PWS spurred the development of philosophical logic and led to new applications of logic in computer science and artificial intelligence. It revolutionized the study of the semantics of natural languages. PWS has inspired analyses of many concepts of philosophical importance, and the concept of a possible world has been at the heart of important philosophical systems.

1 Intensions demeaned
2 Modal logic
3 Other applications
4 Temporal logic
5 Conditional logic
6 Quantified modal logic
7 Index theory and intensional logic
8 Montague semantics
9 Intensions triumphant
10 All the intensions we need?

1 Intensions demeaned

Traditionally, the 'intension' of a predicate was distinguished from its 'extension'; the former is a property, the latter is a set. The predicates 'is a featherless biped that is not a plucked chicken' and 'is human' have (one can imagine) the same extensions but different intensions. (The example is from Bertrand Russell.) Gottlob Frege's concepts of *Sinn* and *Bedeutung* extend this idea: the *Sinn* of a singular term is an identifying condition (or 'individual concept'), the *Bedeutung* the individual designated. The *Sinn* of a sentence is a proposition, the *Bedeutung* a truth-value. Frege defended his choice of truth-values as the *Bedeutung* of sentences on systematic grounds (see FREGE, G.; SENSE AND REFERENCE).

As model theory was developed by Tarski and others, a version of Frege's choices for *Bedeutung* became the standard values in 'extensional semantics'. The extension of an *n*-place predicate is the set of *n*-tuples of objects of which the predicate is true (thus, the extension of 'gives' might be the set of those four-tuples containing two persons, an object and a time, such that the first person gives the object to the second person at that time). The extension of a singular (object-denoting) term is the object it designates. The extension of a sentence is a truth-value (see MODEL THEORY). The packaging together of the predicate calculus with an extensional semantics proved adequate for important work in mathematical logic and overshadowed older approaches to logic. In contrast, no understanding of intensions emerged that is generally agreed on. In the middle part of the century interest in intensional phenomena waned. In fact, the success of extensional logic led to

somewhat uncharitable attitudes towards any non-extensional phenomena. In Quine's influential view non-extensional constructions are not suited for scientific work; they are more in need of regimentation than straightforward analysis (see QUINE, W.V.). (Non-extensional constructions are those that apparently distinguish between different phrases or sentences used to complete them, even though the phrases or sentences have the same extensions. One example is 'Elwood believes that...'. 'Elwood believes that Stanford is east of Hawaii' might be true, while 'Elwood believes that Stanford is east of Berkeley' might be false, even though 'Stanford is east of Hawaii' and 'Stanford is east of Berkeley' both have the same extension (the truth-value 'true'). 'Intensional' is sometimes used simply to mean 'non-extensional', and is sometimes given a narrower meaning.)

2 Modal logic

A number of philosophers and logicians continued to attempt to provide straightforward analyses of intensional phenomena, however. Until the 1950s, the emphasis was on syntactic approaches. A key figure was C.I. LEWIS, whose dissatisfaction with the extensional treatment of 'if..., then...' as the material conditional led him first to the logic of 'strict implication', then to 'modal logic', the logic of necessity and possibility (see Lewis and Langford 1932). The modal operators (typically translated 'necessarily' and 'possibly', and usually symbolized as $\Box$ and $\Diamond$) are not truth-functional, and so require intensional analysis.

The language of propositional modal logic (ML) consists of the language of propositional logic, plus the rule that if ϕ is a well-formed formula (wff), then so are $\Box\phi$ and $\Diamond\phi$. Lewis and others worked out a number of axiom systems for ML and studied and compared them proof-theoretically.

More semantically oriented approaches to intensionality emerged later in the century, beginning with CARNAP (1946, 1947). One of the most important of Carnap's many contributions to the study of intensionality was to recruit Leibniz's idea that necessary truth was truth 'in all possible worlds' to the task of building an intensional semantics. This is the guiding idea of possible worlds semantics (PWS). Carnap's version of this idea, less straightforward than those that were to follow, relies on linguistic representations of possible worlds which he called 'state-descriptions'.

The basics of the now-standard treatment came in the late 1950s and early 1960s with results obtained by Stig Kanger (1957; also Føllesdal 1994) and Saul KRIPKE (1959, 1963a, 1963b; also Hintikka 1957,

Montague 1974a). We shall look briefly at **K**, **S4** and **S5**, three among the plethora of axiom systems for modal logic that have been studied.

S5 includes:

- all propositional tautologies and *modus ponens*,
- the definition $\Diamond\phi =_{df} \neg\Box\neg\phi$,
- the rule of necessitation ($\vdash\phi / \vdash\Box\phi$, that is, if ϕ is deducible from the null set of premises, then so is $\Box\phi$),
- the axioms

    [*K*]: $\Box(\phi \rightarrow \psi) \rightarrow (\Box\phi \rightarrow \Box\psi)$

    [*T*]: $\Box\phi \rightarrow \phi$

    [*4*]: $\Box\phi \rightarrow \Box\Box\phi$

    [*B*]: $\Diamond\Box\phi \rightarrow \phi$

If we drop *B* we have **S4**; if in addition we drop *4* and *T* we have **K**, Kripke's minimal system.

A modal model structure is a pair $\langle K, R \rangle$. K is the set of worlds; R we will consider later. A modal model will tell us which atomic sentences of the base language L are true at which worlds of K. For the connectives of propositional logic the rules remain unchanged. To extend the system to include $\Box$ it is natural, on the Leibnizian conception, to use the rule (we symbolize 'ϕ is true in w' as $\phi[w]$):

$\Box_A$: $\Box\phi[w]$ iff $\forall w'\phi[w']$.

Given the definition of $\Diamond$ we have:

$\Diamond\phi[w]$ iff $\exists w'\phi[w']$.

The reader can check that on this conception, all of the axioms for **S5** are valid, that is, true in every world of every model. Consider *B*, for example. Suppose the antecedent is true at w. Then $\exists w'\forall w''\phi[w'']$. Since the existential quantification is vacuous, this reduces to $\forall w'\phi[w']$. Then, by Universal Instantiation (U.I.), we have $\phi[w]$.

Note that the $\Diamond$ was vacuous; $\Diamond\Box\phi$ collapsed into $\Box\phi$. This is characteristic of **S5**: iterated modalities collapse to the right.

S5 is a natural logic for metaphysical necessity, which was doubtless the conception Leibniz had in mind. But there are other coherent concepts of necessity, for which some of the axioms of **S5** do not seem correct, and for which distinctions among iterated modalities are significant (see MODAL LOGIC).

Consider physical necessity. We have $\Box\phi[w]$ if ϕ is true in every world that obeys the laws of physics of w. Suppose w' is a world which has all of our laws and more. Certain events may be ruled out by the physics of w' that are not ruled out by our physics, so our world is not physically possible relative to w'. Suppose, for example, that it is a law of physics in

w' that no golf ball travels more than 200 yards. Then even though w' is physically possible (it obeys our laws) and 'No golf ball travels over 200 yards' is necessary in w', it is not true that no golf ball travels over 200 yards. So Axiom *B* is incorrect for physical necessity.

T is intuitive in the case of metaphysical and physical necessity, but not for 'deontic logic', in which '$\Box\phi$' is interpreted as 'It ought to be the case that ϕ' (see DEONTIC LOGIC).

In discussing these alternative conceptions of necessity and possibility, we move from an absolute to a relative conception of possibility, the idea that the set of worlds relevant to issues of necessity varies from world to world. This is the information given by the second member of the model structure above. R is a relation on K, the 'accessibility relation'. Different accessibility relations correspond to different conceptions of necessity. We replace our absolute rule $\Box_A$ with a relative rule:

$\Box_R$: $\Box\phi[w]$ iff

$\forall w'$, if w' is accessible from w, then $\phi[w']$

The axioms that characterize the various systems of modal logic correspond to the logical properties of the relation R. The axiom K places no restrictions on it; T requires reflexivity; 4 requires transitivity; and B symmetry. Thus absolute necessity, captured by **S5**, is the case where the accessibility relation is an equivalence relation.

3 Other applications

The semantical apparatus developed for modal logic has been used to investigate a number of other logical systems.

In 'epistemic logic', for example, a knowledge operator, indexed by knowers, is patterned after $\Box$; $K_\alpha\phi$ means 'ϕ holds in all of α's epistemic alternatives' (Hintikka 1962; see EPISTEMIC LOGIC).

It is important for the philosophically oriented reader to keep in mind that for the purposes of developing and applying semantical treatments of intensional languages, for example, in completeness proofs, the possible worlds of PWS need not be invested with any important metaphysical properties; they are just indices for models. The basic apparatus has been used to study a number of areas in which the metaphor of a possible world is inapplicable. In dynamic logic, for example, the apparatus of modal logic is applied to programs. The 'worlds' are states of a machine. Accessibility relations are indexed by programs. Where α is a program, $\Box[[\alpha]]\phi$ means 'ϕ holds after every terminating execution of α' (see Pratt 1976; DYNAMIC LOGICS).

The interplay between semantic structures and logical systems involved in these investigations constitute a development in logic comparable to the move in geometry away from Euclidean geometry, conceived as the one true system, to geometry as the study of alternative axiom systems for spaces with diverse properties.

4 Temporal logic

The apparatus of modal model structures works nicely to provide a semantics for temporal logic – the logic of operators modelled after the tense and temporal adverb systems of natural languages. Let 'G' mean 'It will always be the case' and 'F' mean 'It will sometimes be the case'; 'F' can be defined as '$\neg G \neg$'. Thus G is a universal operator, analogous to $\Box$, and F is an existential operator, analogous to $\Diamond$. Similarly, let 'H' mean 'It has always been the case' and define 'P' as '$\neg H \neg$'. Then instead of a set of worlds and an accessibility relation, take a model structure to be a set of moments of time and an ordering relation between them. The need for an accessibility relation is rather more intuitive here than in the case of necessity and possibility since, unlike worlds, we usually think of times as ordered by the relation of 'before'. As with modal logic, different logics correspond to different conceptions of the ordering relation. One minimal tense logic (Benthem 1988) contains the axioms:

- $G(\phi \rightarrow \psi) \rightarrow (G\phi \rightarrow G\psi)$
- $H(\phi \rightarrow \psi) \rightarrow (H\phi \rightarrow H\psi)$
- $\phi \rightarrow GP\phi$
- $\phi \rightarrow HF\phi$

and the rules *modus ponens* and the analogue to necessitation, sometimes called 'eternity':

- $\vdash \phi / \vdash G\phi$
- $\vdash \phi / \vdash H\phi$

As with modal logic, there is a precise correspondence between ordering conditions and additional axioms. For example $PP\phi \leftrightarrow P\phi$, which seems plausible enough, requires that the structure of moments be transitive (if t is before t' and t' is before t'', t is before t'') and dense (if t is before t', there is a t'' between them, that is, after t and before t') (see Prior 1967; Benthem 1988; TENSE AND TEMPORAL LOGIC).

5 Conditional logic

As we noted, dissatisfaction with the material conditional as an explication of the ordinary-language conditional was an early complaint against extensional logic. There is some connection between the antecedent and the consequent that the semantics

for the material conditional misses. For one thing, $\phi \rightarrow \psi$ is true whenever ϕ is false, making all counterfactual conditionals trivially true. Let us use '$\Rightarrow$' as a symbol for a better approximation. Another key way in which $\Rightarrow$ should differ from $\rightarrow$ is that it should not always permit *strengthening the antecedent*. We have:

$(\phi \rightarrow \psi)$ only if $(\phi \wedge \chi \rightarrow \psi)$

but not:

$(\phi \Rightarrow \psi)$ only if $(\phi \wedge \chi \Rightarrow \psi)$.

For example:

ϕ: I put water in my canteen when I start my hike.
ψ: I have water when I stop for a rest.
χ: There is a hole in my canteen.

Robert Stalnaker's version of Frank Ramsey's test for evaluating conditionals is 'make the minimal revision of your stock of beliefs required to assume the antecedent. Then, evaluate the acceptability of the consequent on the basis of this revised body of beliefs' (Ramsey 1931). Stalnaker (1968) and David Lewis (1973) have proposed analyses that implement this idea within the possible worlds framework:

Stalnaker: $\phi \Rightarrow \psi[w]$ iff ψ holds in the ϕ-world that is closest to w.

Lewis: $\phi \Rightarrow \psi[w]$ iff ψ holds in *all* ϕ-worlds which are closest to w.

These analyses require a relation of overall similarity or closeness among worlds. (It can be argued that the relation of overall similarity of worlds is vague and context sensitive; it is replied that this captures the vagueness and context sensitivity of the ordinary conditional.)

On either analysis, strengthening the antecedent fails for $\Rightarrow$, because when the antecedent is strengthened, different worlds might be the closest in which the antecedent is true.

The choice between Lewis' definition and Stalnaker's depends on such issues as whether there is always a unique closest world. One important principle that turns on this is 'conditional excluded middle',

$(\phi \Rightarrow \psi) \vee (\phi \Rightarrow \neg\psi)$

which Stalnaker endorses and Lewis rejects (see INDICATIVE CONDITIONALS; COUNTERFACTUAL CONDITIONALS).

6 Quantified modal logic

In 1946, Ruth Barcan Marcus and Rudolf Carnap independently published systems of quantified modal logic (QML), in which principles like the following were considered:

$$\forall x \square \phi(x) \rightarrow \square \forall x \phi(x)$$

This is the 'Barcan formula', attractive to those who would reduce *de re* to *de dicto* necessity (see DE RE/DE DICTO).

Kripke (1963b) has provided a semantics for these systems. A quantificational modal structure $\langle K, R, \Psi \rangle$ adds a function Ψ which assigns a domain of individuals to each possible world in K. A model assigns extensions to each predicate at each world. On the natural, 'world-bound' interpretation of universal quantification, $\forall x \phi(x)$ is true in a world w if and only if in w $\phi(x)$ is true of every member of the domain of w.

If we suppose, as is natural, that worlds have varying domains (that objects that might have been in our world, for example, actually exist in other worlds), then it seems the Barcan formula is not valid. Even if every object we find in the actual world is ϕ in all possible worlds, there could be objects in other possible worlds that are not ϕ. But the formula can be validated if we interpret quantifiers as ranging over all possible objects, or if we suppose that the domain is constant across worlds; each of these alternatives have found proponents.

'Quantifying in' (that is, quantification across modal operators as in the antecedent of the Barcan formula) was deemed by Quine to put us in danger of a commitment to 'essentialism'. Suppose Quine is in the extension of 'is a Kantian' in some possible world w. This fact about the realm of possibility is not a fact about the necessary or possible truth of some sentence, so there is some commitment to *de re* modality. Note however that accepting such facts as these does not commit one to a view that Quine must have an essence that distinguishes him from all other objects, one natural understanding of 'essentialism' (Føllesdal 1986) (see MODAL LOGIC, PHILOSOPHICAL ISSUES IN §3).

7 Index theory and intensional logic

Starting in the late 1960s, PWS began to find a role beyond providing semantics for particular logical systems. One development was the development of 'intensional logics' that combined modal, temporal and other operators (see INTENSIONAL LOGICS).

We can think of time and possible worlds, for example, as two dimensions along which the truth of a sentence can vary; from this point of view, it is natural to provide a semantics for a system in which sentences are true in worlds at times, and that contains both temporal and modal operators. Thus, for example,

$$\square(H\phi)$$

will be true in world w at time t if and only if in every world w' accessible to w, at every time t' earlier than t, ϕ is true at w' and t'.

But there are also other factors relative to which the truth of sentences can vary. In particular, sentences containing indexicals (such as 'I', 'you', 'here' and 'now') will vary in truth depending on who says them, to whom, where and when.

Thus we could think of:

I will walk to the shop

as being true at a world w, time t and person a, if in w, a walks to the shop at some time subsequent to t.

Following the advice of Dana Scott, Montague, Lewis and others developed and explored versions of 'index theory', systems in which sentences were true at an index, where indices were n-tuples of worlds, times, speakers and other factors (see Scott 1970; Montague 1974b; Lewis 1970).

Kamp's 'double-indexing' (1971), Segerberg's 'two-dimensional modal logic' (1973) and Kaplan's 'logic of demonstratives' (1989) provide alternatives to index theory. These authors emphasize the difference between *reliable* sentences such as 'I am here now', that, even if they express contingent propositions, cannot be uttered falsely, and sentences such as 'either there are cats or there are not', that are valid in the standard sense, of being true in every world in every modal model.

8 Montague semantics

Richard MONTAGUE was a leader in the development of intensional logic. In his early papers, he developed PWS as a tool for investigating a number of phenomena of philosophical interest, such as sense-data and events. In later work he developed PWS as a powerful tool for model-theoretic treatments of the semantics of English and other natural languages. Montague's work has had a profound influence in linguistics (see Partee 1989).

As the body of Montague's work developed, intensional phenomena were increasingly seen not as exceptional and marginal, but as at the core of the way language works. In modal logic, intensionality derives from special operators added onto a base language that works on extensional principles. In Montague semantics, intensionality is a ubiquitous phenomenon; there are not only intensional operators, but intensional verbs, adjectives, adverbs and so on. In Montague's later work, intensionality is basically the default case, with special postulates to guarantee extensionality (1974c).

By using intensional logic and PWS to give a precise semantics for constructions of natural language, Montague developed an important new sub-discipline of linguistics, often simply called 'Montague Grammar'.

9 Intensions triumphant

PWS provides philosophy with a toolkit of entities for the analysis of intensional phenomena:

- For individual concepts: functions from worlds to individuals.
- For properties: functions from worlds to extensions.
- For propositions: functions from worlds to truth-values (or sets of worlds).

Note that these functions are themselves extensionally understood, and so analysable within the framework of set theory, and (in that sense at least) free of obscurity.

By the 1970s, philosophers were availing themselves of these tools to talk in disciplined ways about many traditional and some new issues, issues often not directly connected with the interpretation of systems of logic. A few of these are:

- Quantified modal logic has been at the heart of a productive rethinking of issues involved in the distinction between *de dicto* and *de re* necessity, beginning with Quine's charge that quantified modal logic commits us to essentialism (see Føllesdal 1986; ESSENTIALISM).
- PWS provides two models for the semantics of names. On the possible worlds version of the Frege–Russell–Searle descriptive account of names, the meaning of a name is an individual concept. An alternative is to model names on variables directly assigned to individuals, the same for all worlds, irrespective of their properties in the worlds. Marcus (1961) suggested the latter possibility, and in *Naming and Necessity* (1980), Saul Kripke has mounted a full-scale challenge to the descriptive account, arguing that names are 'rigid designators' (referring to the same object in all worlds), and providing a causal account of the link between name and thing as an alternative to the descriptive account (see PROPER NAMES).
- David Kaplan, whose lectures, seminars and unpublished writings stirred much interest in PWS throughout the 1970s, worked out an account of indexicals and demonstratives in the context of index theory. This has led to a clarification of a number of issues involving the semantics and epistemology of indexicals (see Kaplan 1989; DEMONSTRATIVES AND INDEXICALS).
- David LEWIS has used the apparatus of PWS to make significant contributions to our understanding of convention, the semantics of natural language, the understanding of counterfactuals (see above) and many other issues in metaphysics, epistemology and the philosophy of science (see Lewis 1970, 1973, 1979).

Lewis' own view of possible worlds maintains that possible worlds are alternative concrete realities; they are actual for their inhabitants, as ours is for us. The inhabitants of other worlds are not identical with the inhabitants of the actual world (that is, our world), but are their *counterparts*; Lewis' account of quantification is based on the counterpart relations rather than identity.

10 All the intensions we need?

Can PWS supply philosophy with all the intensions that are needed to understand intensional phenomena? Can all intensions be understood as functions from worlds to appropriate sets?

One of the most difficult challenges is the problem of propositional attitudes. The basic problem is that PWS supplies only one necessary proposition (the set of all worlds) and only one contradictory proposition (the null set). This seems to pose a severe problem for dealing with mathematical knowledge. Given usual principles of compositionality, we could infer from 'Elwood knows that $7 + 5 = 12$' to 'Elwood knows that S' for any true mathematical sentence S or any other necessary truth for that matter.

Robert Stalnaker (1984) has given an careful and extended defence of the use of PWS in epistemology. He argues that the concept of content needed for propositional attitudes is grounded in pragmatic relations and such informational relations as indication. The problem of mathematical knowledge, he argues, can be resolved by seeing a linguistic element in our knowledge of mathematical truths.

Advocates of situation semantics have argued, however, that the possible worlds analysis of indication is also vitiated by the problem of the single necessary proposition. Where P is a contingent proposition and N is the necessary proposition, $P = P \& N$. So if the tree rings indicate that the tree is one hundred years old, they also indicate that it is one hundred years old and $7 + 5 = 12$. But indication appears to distribute over conjunction, so we could infer that the tree rings indicate that $7 + 5 = 12$ (see Perry 1993; SEMANTICS, SITUATION).

While these and other problems have stimulated great interest in other approaches to intensionality in recent years, it seems fair to say that PWS has had by far the most impact on the disciplined investigation of intensional phenomena and that no alternative treatment yet devised provides as natural and comfortable a scheme for thinking about intensional matters.

See also: INTENSIONAL ENTITIES; POSSIBLE WORLDS

References and further reading

* Benthem, J. van (1988) *A Manual of Intensional Logic*, Stanford, CA: Center for the Study of Language and Information. (A survey of modal logic, tense logic and other applications of the possible worlds framework.)
* Carnap, R. (1946) 'Modalities and Quantification', *Journal of Symbolic Logic* 11: 33–64. (Introduces quantifiers into modal logic.)
* —— (1947) *Meaning and Necessity*, Chicago, IL: University of Chicago Press. (Carnap's classic work; explains his system of intension and extensions, and presents a version of possible worlds semantics.)
* Føllesdal, D. (1986) 'Essentialism and Reference', in L.E. Hahn and P.A. Schilpp (eds) *The Philosophy of W.V. Quine*, Library of Living Philosophers, La Salle, IL: Open Court, 97–115. (Discusses Quine's charge that quantification into modal contexts involves essentialism; argues that it is valid in a relatively benign sense of 'essentialism', but not valid in other senses.)
* —— (1994) 'Stig Kanger In Memoriam', in D. Prawitz, B. Skyrms and D. Westerståhl (eds) *Logic, Methodology and Philosophy of Science IX*, Uppsala: Elsevier Science, 885–888. (Discusses the contributions by Kanger, Kripke and others to the semantics of modal logic.)
* Hintikka, J. (1957) 'Quantifiers in Deontic Logic', *Societas Scientiarum Fennica, Commentationes humanarum litterarum* 23 (4). (An early use of the idea of relative necessity.)
* —— (1962) *Knowledge and Belief: An Introduction to the Logic of the Two Notions*, Ithaca, NY: Cornell University Press. (Explores the logic of knowledge and belief within a version of the possible worlds framework.)
* Kamp, H. (1971) 'Formal Properties of "Now"', *Theoria* 37: 227–74. (Develops two-dimensional version of index theory to treat temporal indexicals.)
* Kanger, S. (1957) *Provability in Logic*, Stockholm

Studies in Philosophy 1, Stockholm: Almqvist & Wiksell. (Basic completeness results in modal logic using accessibility relations.)
* Kaplan, D. (1989) *Demonstratives*, in J. Almog, J. Perry and H. Wettstein (eds) *Themes from Kaplan*, 481–563, New York: Oxford University Press. (Classic treatment of indexicals within a possible worlds framework; discussions of related philosophical and semantical issues.)
* Kripke, S.A. (1959) 'A Completeness Theorem in Modal Logic', *Journal of Symbolic Logic* 24: 1–15. (Uses possible worlds semantics to prove the completeness of S5.)
* —— (1963a) 'Semantical Analysis of Modal Logic I, Normal Propositional Calculi', *Zeitschrift für mathematische Logic und Grundlagen der Mathematik* 9: 67–96. (Uses possible worlds semantics with accessibility relations to obtain a number of completeness results.)
* —— (1963b) 'Semantical Considerations on Modal Logic', *Acta Philosophical Fennica* 16: 83–94. (Provides possible worlds semantics for quantified modal logic.)
* —— (1980) *Naming and Necessity*, Cambridge, MA: Harvard University Press. (Groundbreaking work on the semantics of proper names, arguing that they are 'rigid designators'.)
* Lewis, C.I. and Langford, C.H. (1932) *Symbolic Logic*, New York: The Century Company. (Includes a survey of modal logics.)
* Lewis, D.K. (1970) 'General Semantics', *Synthèse* 22: 18–67. (Possible worlds semantics in the index style applied to problems in natural language.)
* —— (1973) *Counterfactuals*, Cambridge, MA: Harvard University Press. (Proposes an analysis of conditionals within the possible worlds framework.)
* —— (1979) 'Attitudes *De Dicto* and *De Se*', *Philosophical Review* 88: 513–43. (Treats problems of indexicality and self-knowledge within a possible worlds framework.)
* Marcus, R.B. (1946) 'A Functional Calculus of the First Order Based on Strict Implication', *Journal of Symbolic Logic* 11: 1–16. (Introduces quantifiers into modal logic; identifies crucial principles.)
* —— (1961) 'Modalities and Intensional Languages', *Synthèse* 13: 303–32. (Discussion of philosophical issues in the interpretation of quantified modal logic; argues that names are like tags rather than descriptions.)
* Montague, R.M. (1974a) 'Logical Necessity, Physical Necessity, Ethics and Quantifiers', in R. Thomason (ed.) *Formal Philosophy: Selected Papers of Richard Montague*, New Haven, CT, and London: Yale University Press, 71–83. (Notes quantificational

structure of various operators; uses a relative notion of necessity.)

* —— (1974b) 'Pragmatics and Intensional Logic', in R. Thomason (ed.) *Formal Philosophy: Selected Papers of Richard Montague*, New Haven, CT, and London: Yale University Press, 119–147. (Develops an index-style treatment of indexicality within an intensional language.)

* —— (1974c) 'English as a Formal Language' and 'The Proper Treatment of Quantification in Ordinary English', in R. Thomason (ed.) *Formal Philosophy: Selected Papers of Richard Montague*, New Haven, CT, and London: Yale University Press, 188–221, 247–70. (In these two classic papers Montague develops a formal semantics for significant fragments of a natural language.)

* Partee, B. (1989) 'Possible Worlds in Model-Theoretic Semantics: A Linguistic Perspective', in S. Allen (ed.) *Possible Worlds in Humanities, Arts and Sciences. Proceedings of Nobel Symposium 65*, Berlin and New York: de Gruyter, 93–123. (Survey of the contribution that possible worlds semantics has made to the field of linguistics.)

* Perry, J. (1993) *The Problem of the Essential Indexical and Other Essays*, New York: Oxford University Press. (This collection includes papers on indexicality and critiques of possible worlds semantics.)

* Pratt, V.R. (1976) 'Semantical Considerations on Floyd–Hoare Logic', *Proceedings of the Seventeenth Annual IEEE Symposium on Foundations of Computer Science*, 109–21. (A seminal work in the logic of programs.)

* Prior, A.N. (1967) *Past, Present and Future*, Oxford: Oxford University Press. (The classic presentation of temporal logic.)

* Ramsey, F.P. (1931) *The Foundations of Mathematics*, London: Routledge & Kegan Paul. (Collection of Ramsey's philosophical writings.)

* Scott, D. (1970) 'Advice on Modal Logic', in K. Lambert (ed.) *Philosophical Problems in Logic*, Dordrecht: Reidel. (An important work in the development of index theory.)

* Segerberg, K. (1973) 'Two-Dimensional Modal Logic', *Journal of Philosophical Logic* 2: 77–96. (Develops a version of index theory in which the accessibility relation holds between pairs of indices.)

* Stalnaker, R. (1968) 'A Theory of Conditionals', in N. Rescher (ed.) *Studies in Logical Theory*, Oxford: Blackwell. (Proposes an analysis of conditionals within the possible worlds framework.)

* —— (1984) *Inquiry*, Cambridge, MA: MIT Press. (An analysis of basic epistemological concepts within possible worlds semantics.)

JOHN R. PERRY

SEMANTICS, SITUATION

Situation semantics attempts to provide systematic and philosophically coherent accounts of the meanings of various constructions that philosophers and linguists find important. It is based on the old idea that sentences stand for facts or something like them. As such, it provides an alternative to extensional semantics, which takes sentences to stand for truth-values, and to possible worlds semantics, which takes them to stand for sets of possible worlds.

Situations are limited parts or aspects of reality, while states of affairs (or infons) are complexes of properties and objects of the sort suitable to constitute a fact. Consider the issue of whether Jackie, a dog, broke her leg at a certain time T. There are two states of affairs or possibilities, that she did or she did not. The situation at T, in the place where Jackie was then, determines which of these states of affairs (infons) is factual (or is the case or is supported). Situation theory, the formal theory that underlies situation semantics, focuses on the nature of the supports relation.

Situation semantics sees meaning as a relation among types of situations. The meaning of 'I am sitting next to David', for example, is a relation between types of situations in which someone A utters this sentence referring with the name 'David' to a certain person B, and those in which A is sitting next to B. This relational theory of meaning makes situation semantics well-suited to treat indexicality, tense and other similar phenomena. It has also inspired relational accounts of information and action.

1   **History of situation semantics**
2   **Situations**
3   **Meaning**
4   **Accomplishments**

1   History of situation semantics

Situation semantics was originally conceived as an alternative to extensional model theory and possible world semantics especially suited to the analysis of various problematic constructions, including naked-infinitive perception verbs (Barwise 1981) and belief-reports (Barwise and Perry 1981) (see MODEL THEORY; SEMANTICS, POSSIBLE WORLDS). In its earliest forms, the central ideas were:

• *Partiality.* Situations are contrasted with worlds; a world determines the answer to every issue – the truth-value of every proposition. A situation corresponds to the limited parts of reality we in fact perceive, reason about, and live in. What goes on in these situations will determine answers to some issues, but not all. In 'Scenes and Other Situations' (1981), reporting his initial work on situation theory, Jon Barwise represents scenes, the situations we perceive, as partial first-order models.

- *Realism.* Basic properties and relations are taken to be real objects – uniformities across situations and objects – not bits of language, ideas, sets of *n*-tuples, or functions. In *Situations and Attitudes* (Barwise and Perry 1983), 'courses of events' are partial functions from sequences of locations, relations and objects to truth-values. Complex properties and relations, and various types of objects were full-fledged objects, entering into courses of events.
- *The relational theory of meaning.* The meaning of an expression ϕ is conceived as a relation between a discourse situation, a connective situation and a described situation, written:

$$d,c[[\phi]]_e$$

The meaning of 'I am sitting next to David', for example, would obtain between courses of events *d*, *c* and *e* if there are individuals *a* and *b* such that (1) in *d*, *a* is the speaker of the sentence; (2) in *c*, *a*'s use of 'David' is used to refer to *b*; and (3) in *e*, *a* is sitting next to *b*.

A number of trenchant criticisms were made of *Situations and Attitudes* (see especially Soames 1985). In reaction to them, Barwise and Perry (1985) recognized the need to rethink the foundations of situation semantics. Two main developments bridge the early versions of situation semantics and the later ones which emerged from this rethinking:

(1) In early versions, situation semantics was developed within standard set theory; this led to foundational problems. In the mid-1980s, Barwise and others developed various versions of 'situation theory', in which all of the various entities that had become necessary were treated axiomatically (Barwise 1989; Devlin 1991; Westerståhl 1990) or within Peter Aczel's version of set theory (Barwise and Etchemendy 1987).
(2) The concept of a constraint, developed in *Situations and Attitudes* as an adjunct to the relational theory of meaning, has become central to the development of situation semantics as a general account of informational and intentional content (Barwise 1993; Israel and Perry 1990; Perry 1993).

2 Situations

The basic idea of situation semantics is that in thought and action we use complexes of objects and properties to classify 'directly' and 'indirectly' parts and aspects of reality, or 'situations'. This sort of realistic classification is more basic than linguistic classification, and it underlies linguistic classification. Consider a simple dialogue:

'What happened in the woods this afternoon?'
'Jackie broke her leg.'

The question concerns a certain situation, a bit of reality: the events in the woods this afternoon. The answer directly classifies the situation in terms of an object (the dog Jackie) and a property (acquiring a broken leg). We classify situations by what goes on in them, by which properties objects have, and by the relations they stand in to one another in virtue of the events that comprise the situation.

Consider the issue of whether Jackie broke her leg at a certain time *t*. There are two dual possibilities or 'states of affairs', corresponding to whether her leg was broken or not, which we can represent as:

$$\sigma: \langle\langle \text{breaks leg}, t, \text{Jackie}; 1 \rangle\rangle$$

and

$$\sigma\prime: \langle\langle \text{breaks leg}, t, \text{Jackie}; 0 \rangle\rangle$$

Of course, what goes on in the whole world (if we assume there is such a totality) will determine whether or not Jackie broke her leg, but this will also be determined by much smaller situations. Let *s* be the situation in the woods this afternoon. Then,

$$s \models \sigma$$

that is, *s supports* σ, or (in more traditional philosophical terms) *s makes it the case that* σ, or *makes* σ *factual.*

In situation theory, various objects are built from the basic interplay of situations and states of affairs, permitting complex and abstract ways of classifying situations, including complex states of affairs, properties and relations. A key concept is a 'type of situation', such as the type of situation in which a dog breaks its leg (call it *S*) and the type of situation in which a dog does not run (call it *S'*).

There are states of affairs involving these abstract objects. In particular, one type of situation may involve another: if there is a situation of the first type, there will also be one of the second type. *S* involves *S'*: dogs with broken legs do not run. These sorts of states of affairs are 'constraints'.

3 Meaning

Constraints give rise to the possibility of 'indirect classification': classifying situations by what they mean. That is, classifying situations not by the states of affairs they support, but by the types of situations they involve, relative to some constraint.

Indirect classification is how situation semantics conceives of informational and intentional content. Classifying situations by their contents is what organisms do under the influence of what Hume calls 'custom': confronted with a situation, they form expectations, or at least contemplate possibilities, on the basis of what the situation involves relative to some constraint, factual or not, to which they have become attuned. Situation semantics interprets informational and intentional content as a system that exploits such indirect classification. Situations are indirectly classified relative not only to laws of nature and other actual constraints (informational content), but also to conventions, rules, customs, plans and other constraints, both factual and fictional, of human contrivance (intentional content).

Consider:

(1) Jackie has a broken leg.

(2) The x-ray shows that Jackie has a broken leg.

(3) The vet said that Jackie had a broken leg.

In (1), we have direct classification; in (2) and (3), indirect classification. In the latter a common pattern is discernible, involving three types of situation and a constraint:

- A local situation.
- Connections between objects in that situation and other objects, the 'subject matter'.
- A remote situation, the content, involving the subject matter.
- A constraint according to which a combination of situations of the first two types involves a situation of the third type.

In (2) the local situation is the x-ray having certain characteristics. The x-ray is connected to Jackie: it was taken of her. The complex type of situation, in which an x-ray taken of a certain dog exhibits those features, involves a situation in which the dog has a broken leg. Given the connections between the x-ray and Jackie, its having those characteristics shows that she has a broken leg. Here the constraint is factual and the content is informational.

In (3) the local situation is the utterance, in which the vet utters the words 'Jackie has a broken leg'. The vet's use of the word 'Jackie' is connected through various mental and conversational links to the dog Jackie. The rules of English provide the constraint: given the characteristics of the utterance and its connections, it is true if and only if Jackie has a broken leg. English speakers are attuned to these constraints, not in the sense that they automatically form expectations when they hear utterances, but in the sense that they grasp the type of situation meant. Here the content is intentional.

Situation semantics then conceives of meaning as a relation between types of situations. A key advantage of this conception is that it allows us to see how different information can be gleaned from the same 'signal' given different starting points.

In the case of (2), we think naturally of a case in which an experienced vet in a well-organized office studies an x-ray known to be of Jackie, and learns that she has a broken leg. In another case, an experienced vet in a poorly organized office might infer from the x-ray and the fact that Jackie is the only dog in the place with a broken leg, that it was of her. And a would-be vet might learn how to read x-rays, knowing that the x-ray is of Jackie and that she has a broken leg.

Similarly, in (3) we think of a person who knows to which dog the vet refers when he says 'Jackie' and knows English, learning that Jackie has a broken leg. But attunement to the same constraint and a different starting point might allow someone to learn which of the dogs in the office was named 'Jackie'.

4 Accomplishments

Situation semantics has been used to analyse a wide variety of linguistic phenomena (see, for example, Gawron and Peters 1990; Cooper 1992), the liar paradox (Barwise and Etchemendy 1987), heterogeneous reasoning and representation (Barwise and Etchemendy 1991), diagrammatic reasoning (Shin 1990), the nature and structure of information and action (Israel and Perry 1990; Devlin 1991; Barwise 1993), and a number of other issues involving language, representation and computation.

It is probably fair to say, however, that up to this point situation semantics has been more successful in terms of adoption of its broad themes than in terms of adoption of its specific formalism and proposals. The main themes of early situation semantics (partiality, realism and the relational nature of meaning; see §1) have been incorporated into the (generally) received wisdom of philosophy and linguistics. But situation semantics remains only one of a number of alternative semantical frameworks that exhibit these virtues in various ways, from which a theorist may choose.

References and further reading

* Barwise, J. (1981) 'Scenes and Other Situations', *Journal of Philosophy* 77: 369–97; repr. in *The Situation In Logic*, Stanford, CA: Center for the

Study of Language and Information, 1989. (In this paper Barwise describes his original idea of a scene semantics, a precursor of situation semantics in which partial first-order models are used to provide an analysis of naked-infinitive perception reports.)

* —— (1989) *The Situation In Logic*, Stanford, CA: Center for the Study of Language and Information. (The papers in the collection developed many of the basic ideas of later versions of situation theory.)

* —— (1993) 'Constraints, Channels, and the Flow of Information', in P. Aczel, D. Israel, Y. Katagiri and S. Peters (eds) *Situation Theory and Its Applications*, Stanford, CA: Center for the Study of Language and Information, vol. 3, 3–27. (In this paper Barwise develops an abstract theory of information flow based on the idea of constraints.)

* Barwise, J. and Etchemendy, J. (1987) *The Liar*, New York: Oxford University Press. (Barwise and Etchemendy provide an analysis of the liar paradox in terms of situation semantics.)

* —— (1991) 'Visual Information and Valid Reasoning', in W. Zimmerman (ed.) *Visualization in Mathematics*, Washington, DC: Mathematical Association of America, 9–27. (Barwise and Etchemendy use a situation-based concept of information to defend the view that reasoning using diagrams and reasoning that combines diagrams and sentences can provide valid proofs and can be studied model-theoretically.)

* Barwise, J. and Perry, J. (1981) 'Semantic Innocence and Uncompromising Situations', in P. French, T. Uehling and H. Wettstein (eds) *Midwest Studies in the Philosophy of Language*, Minneapolis, MN: University of Minnesota Press, vol. 6, 387–403. (In this article, which announced situation semantics, Barwise and Perry criticize a famous argument used by Church, Davidson and others to show that facts cannot be the semantic values of sentences.)

* —— (1983) *Situations and Attitudes*, Cambridge, MA: MIT Press/Bradford. (This book developed a version of situation theory within set theory, and applied it to linguistic meaning, the propositional attitudes and the semantics of mental states.)

* —— (1985) 'Shifting Situations and Shaken Attitudes', *Linguistics and Philosophy* 8: 105–61. (Responding to the criticisms of Soames and others, Barwise and Perry recognize that their theory (1983) has serious problems and explore strategies for repairing it.)

* Cooper, R. (1992) 'A Working Person's Guide to Situation Theory', in S. Hansen and F. Sørensen (eds) *Semantic Representation and Interpretation*, Fredericksberg: Samfundslitteratur. (A lucid introduction to situation theory for the working cognitive scientist.)

* Devlin, K. (1991) *Logic and Information*, Cambridge: Cambridge University Press. (Devlin's book explains the basics of the current version of situation theory and applies it to a number of problems in linguistics and psychology.)

* Gawron, J.M. and Peters, S. (1990) *Anaphora and Quantification in Situation Semantics*, Stanford, CA: Center for the Study of Language and Information. (Situation semantics is used to explain the certain aspects of anaphoric relations.)

* Israel, D. and Perry, J. (1990) 'What is Information?', in P. Hanson (ed.) *Information, Language, and Cognition*, Vancouver, BC: University of British Columbia Press, 1–19. (Israel and Perry develop a distinction between pure and incremental information within situation theory.)

* Perry, J. (1993) *The Problem of the Essential Indexical and Other Essays*, New York: Oxford University Press. (A collection of Perry's essays on situation semantics and related topics.)

* Shin, S.J. (1990) *The Logical Status of Diagrams*, Cambridge: Cambridge University Press. (Situation theory is used to provide a precise analysis of reasoning with Venn diagrams.)

* Soames, S. (1985) 'Lost Innocence', *Linguistics and Philosophy* 8: 59–71. (A trenchant critique of Barwise and Perry (1983).)

* Westerståhl, D. (1990) 'Parametric Types and Propositions in First-Order Situation Theory', in R. Cooper, K. Mukai and J. Perry (eds) *Situation Theory and Its Applications*, Stanford, CA: Center for the Study of Language and Information, vol. 1, 193–230. (A subtle analysis of the role of parameters in situation theory.)

JOHN R. PERRY

SEMANTICS, TELEOLOGICAL

Teleological/biological theories of meaning use a biological concept of function to explain how the internal states of organisms like ourselves can represent conditions in the world. These theories are controversial, as they have the consequence that an organism's history affects the content of its present thoughts. These theories have advantages over other naturalistic theories of meaning in the task of explaining the possibility of error and unreliable representation.

1 **Basic ideas**
2 **Related theories**
3 **Current debates**

1 Basic ideas

Teleological/biological theories (hereafter, 'teleological theories') of meaning claim that certain internal states of organisms represent particular external conditions because of the biological *functions* of these inner states and mechanisms that interact with them. These functions derive from evolutionary history, or from some other history of selection; something's function is (roughly) the thing it does which explains why it is there (Wright 1973). For example, the function of the heart is pumping blood, as that is the thing hearts do that explains why they are there. Teleological theories of meaning, such as those theories of Millikan (1984) and Papineau (1987), apply this strategy of analysis to inner representational states (see FUNCTIONAL EXPLANATION).

These theories claim that inner states that help an organism coordinate its behaviour with its environment can represent environmental conditions that have played a certain causal role in the organism's history. For example, an animal may be put together in such a way that when a dark shadow appears overhead, an inner state occurs which causes the animal to hide. This inner state has the content 'Predator!' (or perhaps 'Danger!') if it is the presence of predators (or danger) on past occasions of this type that explains this pattern of inner wiring being favoured by natural selection. Similarly, though a frog might snap at any small dark object in its visual field, if the pattern of wiring responsible for this behaviour has been selected over alternatives because of past occasions in which this behaviour resulted in frogs obtaining food, then 'Food!' or perhaps 'Edible insect!' is the content of the inner state that is caused by the dark spot and which causes the behaviour. To use the language of Ruth Millikan (1984), who has developed the most sophisticated teleological theory, the inner state represents the environmental condition that must obtain for the state to help the parts of the organism that make use of (or 'consume') it to perform their functions in a historically normal way.

This type of explanation accounts for the content of belief-like states. The content of desire-like states can be explained in terms of satisfaction conditions. A desire's satisfaction condition is the condition in the world that the desire is supposed to bring about (see BELIEF; DESIRE).

Teleological theories do not hold that all beliefs or concepts have a specific evolutionary history. First, these theories can explain some novel beliefs as novel combinations of old concepts. Second, there can be teleological explanations of concepts that are not innate. Millikan explains the semantic properties of learned concepts in terms of the biological functions of parts of the cognitive system that are designed to adapt the organism to novel conditions by means of learning. An alternative approach, defended by Papineau (1987, 1993), is to view learning as a selection process itself, one akin to natural selection across generations, and an independent source of biological functions. In principle there are also other mechanisms which could bestow functions of the relevant sort, such as cultural evolution and deliberate design.

Though Millikan and Papineau give general analyses of all mental representation in these terms, it is also possible to use these ideas in less ambitious ways. A teleological theory could be used to explain only the most basic types of internal representation. Other theories of meaning could then make use of the representational abilities explained by the teleological theory (Sterelny 1990). For example, we might explain a basic stock of primitive concepts in teleological terms, and see more complex concepts as logical constructions out of these (an old-fashioned possibility). Or the teleological view might explain how it is possible for organisms to represent basic environmental features, including other organisms, and then social factors could be used to assign semantic properties to more complex thoughts and public representations. Either way, the teleological view would then be part of a package of different theories which work together in explaining meaning.

2 Related theories

One way to motivate the teleological view is by contrasting it to other naturalistic semantic theories. Indicator theories explain representation in terms of the existence of a reliable correlation, in certain conditions, between an inner state and its object (see Dretske 1981; Fodor 1990; SEMANTICS, INFORMATIONAL). These theories have difficulty explaining error and unreliable representation. Teleological theories are attractive to some because they allow an organism to represent something that it cannot, in principle, reliably detect. Suppose an organism's means of detecting predators is not reliable, as it is prone to 'false alarms'. No matter how unreliable it is, if this inner wiring was selected because it enabled organisms to escape predators, the inner state in question can be seen, on a teleological view, as about predators. For an indicator theory, the content of the inner state must be something weaker, which is reliably correlated with the inner state, such as dark shape. Although most teleological theories do assign these 'ecologically salient' states as contents of representations – 'Predator!' rather than 'Dark shape!' – this is not strictly necessary. Neander (1995) has defended a theory which is teleological in structure, but which converges with indicator theories in the contents it assigns in these cases.

Indicator theories are 'upstream-looking' theories; they link a representation to its object by looking to the processes involved in the bringing about of the representational state. They are based upon the organism's powers of discrimination by means of perception. Teleological theories look instead to connections 'downstream' of the representational state, connections going via behaviour and its consequences. In this respect there is a kinship between the teleological approach and some older ideas about thought associated with pragmatism (see PRAGMATISM). A simple way to link behaviour and belief content is to suppose that the truth condition of a belief is the condition such that actions based on the belief will be successful if and only if that condition obtains. The teleological approach is one way of developing this idea. It replaces the problematic notion of 'success' with a precise concept based upon natural selection. In some respects the debate between the indicator view and the teleological view is an expression of a more general opposition concerning the relative importance of perception and behaviour in understanding the mind. However, there have also been attempts to combine the indicator and the teleological approaches, such as the theory defended by Dretske (1988). For Dretske an inner state represents predators if it has the 'function to indicate' predators; both reliable correlation and function are required.

3 Current debates

Teleological theories of representation have been the subject of lively debate. I will discuss three types of objection.

First, these theories claim that organisms can only represent the world in virtue of facts about their history. Some find this unacceptable, as it entails that a molecule-for-molecule replica of you (such as the 'swampman' of Davidson 1987) which arose instantly by sheer chance would not have thoughts with any semantic content. Millikan's response is simply to embrace this result. Note that while an evolutionary history is required for content on Millikan's view, a more moderate line can be taken by theories such as Papineau's, which treat individual learning as an independent source of functions. Then a swampman would have no thoughts with content initially, but could acquire them within its lifetime.

Second, Jerry Fodor (1990) has argued that teleological theories cannot account for the 'opacity' of attributions of content (see INTENTIONALITY;

PROPOSITIONAL ATTITUDE STATEMENTS). Fodor claims that if all *F*s are *G*s in some environment, then anything that was selected in that environment for responding to *F*s was selected also for responding to *G*s. If so, attributions of content based on biological function cannot distinguish in such cases between representing the presence of an *F* and representing the presence of a *G*. Millikan replies that 'selection for' is a causal matter, and hence that attributions of function have as much opacity as causal explanations in general. Then teleological theories will distinguish between representing the presence of an *F* and representing the presence of a *G*, when all *F*s happen to be *G*s. The theories will only fail to distinguish between these two if the properties of being an *F* and being a *G* are indistinguishable in their causal powers. Then the question becomes whether a teleological theory ought to distinguish, for example, thoughts about equilateral triangles from thoughts about equiangular ones (see CAUSATION; PROPERTY THEORY).

Lastly, suppose an organism avoids predators by avoiding some totally different environmental condition, such as sunrise, which happens to be reliably correlated with danger from predation (Pietroski 1992). Teleological theories say that the condition in the world with explanatory importance is the object of representation. So an animal that instinctively flees the sun and hence avoids predators is representing to itself 'Predator!' rather than 'Sun!'. This can be so even if the animal has no ability to detect predators when they are right in front of it. This is a problem for most teleological views, including Millikan's and Papineau's, although not for Dretske's 'mixed' view nor Neander's theory. The problem is hard for standard teleological views because on such views there is not supposed to be a sharp distinction between the object of a representation and the object which explains the representational practice. These theories are explicitly aimed at assimilating the former to the latter.

See also: EVOLUTION, THEORY OF; FUNCTIONAL EXPLANATION; SEMANTICS

References and further reading

* Davidson, D. (1987) 'Knowing One's Own Mind', *Proceedings and Addresses of the American Philosophical Association* 60: 441–58. (Introduces 'swampman'.)
* Dretske, F. (1981) *Knowledge and the Flow of Information*, Cambridge, MA: MIT Press. (Classic text for the 'indicator' approach.)
* —— (1988) *Explaining Behavior*, Cambridge, MA:

MIT Press. (Defends a view which combines the teleological approach and the indicator approach.)

* Fodor, J.A. (1990) *A Theory of Content and Other Essays*, Cambridge, MA: MIT Press. (Attacks the teleological approach and defends an indicator theory.)

Godfrey-Smith, P. (1994) 'A Continuum of Semantic Optimism', in S. Stich and T.A. Warfield (eds) *Mental Representation: A Reader*, Oxford: Blackwell. (Surveys teleological theories, and other theories which use a link between meaning and success.)

* Millikan, R.G. (1984) *Language, Thought, and Other Biological Categories*, Cambridge, MA: MIT Press. (The most sophisticated teleological theory.)

—— (1993) *White Queen Psychology, and Other Essays for Alice*, Cambridge, MA: MIT Press. (Various papers defending and developing Millikan's theory; includes 'Biosemantics', the best introduction to her view, and her response to Fodor, 'Speaking up for Darwin'.)

* Neander, K. (1995) 'Misrepresenting and Malfunctioning', *Philosophical Studies* 79: 109–41. (Presents a teleological theory and defends it against Fodor, Pietroski and others.)

* Papineau, D. (1987) *Reality and Representation*, Oxford: Blackwell. (Defends a teleological theory and discusses connections to debates about realism.)

* —— (1993) *Philosophical Naturalism*, Oxford: Blackwell. (A further development of Papineau's teleological theory.)

* Pietroski, P. (1992) 'Intentionality and Teleological Error', *Pacific Philosophical Quarterly* 73: 267–82. (An interesting criticism of the teleological approach.)

* Sterelny, K. (1990) *The Representational Theory of Mind: An Introduction*, Oxford: Blackwell. (A more 'modest' teleological approach.)

* Wright, L. (1973) 'Functions', *Philosophical Review* 82: 139–68. (Classic article on functions.)

PETER GODFREY-SMITH

SEMIOTICS

As the study of signification, semiotics takes as its central task that of describing how one thing can mean another. Alternatively, since this philosophical problem is also a psychological one, its job could be said to be that of describing how one thing can bring something else to mind, how on seeing 'x' someone can be induced to think about 'y' even though 'y' is absent.

A person in whose head 'y' has been brought to mind may be responding to an 'x' someone else has transmitted with the intention of its signifying 'y'; or, mistakenly, responding to an 'x' someone has transmitted in the guileless expectation of its signifying some 'z'; or, often, responding to an 'x' that comes to his notice without anybody's apparent intention at all. Words, for example, generally signify because someone intends them to, and ideally (though not always) they signify what is intended; whereas clouds signify – a coming storm, a whale – because we so interpret them, not because they shaped themselves to convey some meaning.

Obviously the study of signification forms an integral part of the study of thinking, since no object can itself enter the brain, barring fatal mischance, and so it must be represented by some mental (that is, neural) 'x' that signifies it.

Signifiers are equally essential for creatures far lower than humans, as when a chemical signal 'x' emitted by some bacterium signifies to one of its colleagues some 'y' such as 'there's a dearth of food hereabouts'.

There are a number of ways in which an 'x' can signify some 'y', but for humans these are chiefly: by physical association; by physical resemblance; and/or by arbitrary convention.

When we take some 'x' as signifying some 'y' we are often guessing; our guess is subject to checking by interpretative (re)appraisal.

1   **The signifier, the signified, the appraisal**
2   **Modern developments**
3   **Signifying by association, by resemblance, by convention**
4   **Systematicity**
5   **The field**

1   The signifier, the signified, the appraisal

In what might be called the standard version of semiotic theory, which in most essentials we owe to the American polymath Charles S. PEIRCE, our knowledge of the external world, in fact all thinking of any kind, is composed of chains and skeins of linked representations or signifiers ('signs' for short). The world enters our consciousness as highly processed sense-reports, which begin as representations (for instance, the electro-chemical signals into which our light-receptors transform the light striking the retina). So the world is understood, to the extent that it is, via signs, many of which stand for still other signs, each bound to what it signifies by interpretative (re)appraisals, which take account of such things as general knowledge and immediate context. An illustrative example of such a skein of signs is provided by the various ways in which an English word can be encoded. In Morse code the word 'card' is '— · — · · — · — · —··', where, to take just the first Morse letter, '— · — ·' stands for:

(1) the relatively long and short electrical impulses we call 'dash, dot, dash, dot' (thus sequenced);
(2) the relatively long and short audible beeps we call 'dash, dot, dash, dot' (thus sequenced);
(3) the words 'dash, dot, dash, dot' (thus sequenced);
(4) the Roman letter 'C';
(5) the sound that 'C' spells in the context '-ard', namely /k/.

Each of these stands, in turn, for any or all of the others. Even this is but a bare beginning, since the entire word 'card', however expressed, stands ultimately for a concept, which interpreted or appraised in a particular context might be a playing card, a visiting card, an index card or part of a machine for carding wool.

Though he had many eminent predecessors, it was Peirce who first undertook, in plangent insights scattered over his (mostly unpublished) eighty-odd volumes of papers, to build a comprehensive discipline of semiotics within which all varieties and manners of signification could be given a unified explanation. He entered his final decline with this mighty task unachieved, but he had at least clearly delineated the framework within which almost all semiotic issues, even the semiotic investigations of antiquity, are currently best understood. In particular, it was Peirce who first definitively gave equal triadic footing to the signifier, what it signifies and its interpretative (re)appraisal.

The two greatest semiotic theorists of antiquity were ARISTOTLE and AUGUSTINE, with other important contributions from PLATO and the Greek Stoics, especially CHRYSIPPUS (see LANGUAGE, ANCIENT PHILOSOPHY OF). Taken as a group, these philosophers distinguished with some care, first, between 'x' the signifier and 'y' what it signifies and, second, between the signified 'y' and, where at issue, the object in the putatively real world that 'y' represents (Plato, primarily in *Cratylus*; Aristotle, most importantly in *De Interpretatione* (*Perihermenias*); Chrysippus; and Augustine in *De Doctrina Christiana*). In addition Aristotle established in the *Prior Analytics* that in the process by which sign is tied to signified, the determination of what the sign signifies is often a probabilistic guess. If I interpret the apparent fact that 'That weathervane is pointing north' as signifying that 'The local wind is a northerly', I am jumping from premise to conclusion without invoking the universal premise ('A north-pointing weathervane *always* signifies that the local

wind is a northerly') that would clinch this enthymeme as a syllogism. (Note that here, as so often, 'signifies' functions like 'implies'.) In fact this missing universal premise is quite properly omitted, since it is false. Weathervanes sometimes mislead. They can be rusted in place; be under the control of mischievous children; be indicating, in the absence of any more recent wind, the direction from which it blew a day ago. In short, once a sign like a weathervane's pointing north has been guessed to be signifying a current local northerly, there is much room left for an interpretative (re)appraisal of such vital facts as the presence or apparent absence of mischievous children.

Chrysippus nicely demystified the tie between the signifier and what it signifies by arguing that any such tie is made in the mind. (He so emphasized this point, in fact, as to hold that the tie itself is the *only* mental entity, since for him both signifier and signified – his *semenon* and *semenomenon* – were real things in the real world. Whereas nowadays we recognize that it is not the weathervane itself that signifies to us, but our mental image of it. If its image is lacking, the weathervane has not even been seen.)

It was well recognized in antiquity that, while words may be the archetypical signifiers, many signifiers are not words. Aristotle, for instance, mentions in the *Prior Analytics* that a woman's lactating constitutes a sign (it signifies that she is pregnant); and Augustine, to take another instance, writes in *De Doctrina Christiana* of footprints as signs (of the passage of whoever owned the feet). In this fashion the groundwork was laid for a general science of signs, that is, for semiotics.

Interest in signs and their relations continued during the medieval and early Renaissance periods, notably among the many who seem to have devoted the bulk of their waking hours to writing exegeses of Aristotle. These activities centred, for reasons partly accidental, in Iberia: in Portugal (FONSECA, P. DA and JOHN OF ST THOMAS, also known as Jean Poinsot) and, in an earlier and more arcane outbreak, in Catalonia (LLULL, R.). Although this work retains much historical interest, it added little to semiotic theory, perhaps because so much of it was devoted to weighing in on one or another of the theological or quasi-theological debates that in those days took the place of free inquiry. With the full Renaissance, however, and the rebirth of interest in everything human, interest in semiotic problems occasionally took a different and more organized turn, notably in the work of George Dalgarno of Scotland (*c.* 1619–87).

2 Modern developments

The next important advances came in the late nineteenth and twentieth centuries. First, Charles S. Peirce codified Aristotle's notion of enthymemic signification into the trivium: 'sign' (signifier) + signified objective (which Peirce unfortunately shortened to 'object') + 'interpretant'. It is worth especial notice that Peirce's 'interpretant' plays an essential role in his system, since for him (as for Aristotle) many and perhaps most signs are understood to be tied to their object(ive)s by probabilistic guesswork – by the intuitive leap that Peirce called 'abduction' – requiring the amplification and partial (de)confirmation available, with luck, from an appraising interpretant. More importantly, in Peirce's codification each such interpretant is often itself a sign and so in turn is tied to some signified object, or perhaps to more than one such, each being in need of a still further interpretant, and so on, in some cases *ad infinitum*. In this fashion Aristotle's enthymemic sequence of (minor premise) + (consequent) + (probabilistic substitute for the missing major premise) is converted into a unified chain of signs, each engaged in a triadic structure of sign + object + interpretant.

The three most important theorists since Peirce have been Charles Morris (1901–79), Thomas A. Sebeok (b.1920), and Umberto Eco (b.1932).

Morris' chief contribution was to put living flesh on Peirce's 'interpretant', which for Peirce was a discarnate or at least incorporeal activity – 'pure mind' perhaps – but which for Morris was an interpreter with a brain and a body. This is a gain, since who or what produces and interprets signs has a physical shape that can influence how signs are shaped and related to other signs. (Simple example: the deaf 'speak' their signs with their hands, face and torso; and, compared to vocal signs, the signs of the deaf are predictably different in form, in their modifiability, in their mutual resemblances, and in the ways in which they can mimic what they signify.) Similarly, the primary signs that begin the process of someone's assigning to some sign some significance – the process that is nowadays called 'semiosis' – are for Morris real and observable 'sign-vehicles' of interest in their own right. Both points are important, because how signs are emitted and received by physical entities (such as bodies and brains), and how the signs of a given system (such as the English language) are structured and inter-related, are topics to which Peirce himself gave short shrift. The distinction between corporeal and discarnate semiosis can be summed up in two terms: 'pragmatics' versus 'pure rhetoric',

respectively Morris' and Peirce's terms for the study of how signs are related to their interpretants.

Thomas Sebeok's effect on semiotics as a field of study has been pervasive, and is universally recognized. He was co-founder (with Margaret Mead) of the modern semiotic discipline (in 1962); he was founding editor of the defining journal *Semiotica* (from 1968); and he has been the guiding mentor to the entire field. His theoretical contributions are likely to prove just as lasting. He has steadily broadened the scope of semiotic inquiry, for instance by delving into zoösemiotics (the study of infrahumans' signifying activities, in both fact and myth, and of their 'prefigurations of art') and into the sub-area of endosemiotics (the study of signifying among microbiota, neurons included). He has sharpened some of Peirce's most basic notions (see §3) and he has opened the eyes of many to the necessity of defining the logical nature of the basic connective 'signifies' (or 'is a sign of'), as by noting that that connective must be at least potentially reflexive and symmetric.

Umberto Eco, besides having written the 'semiotic' novels that have brought him deserved fame, has been deeply involved in the development of semiotic theory since the late 1960s. He is the author of well-known basic texts, has written on the history of semiotic inquiry and has striven to refine some of Peirce's fundamental concepts.

Among the many other twentieth-century scholars who have also made noteworthy contributions to this burgeoning field are Ferdinand de SAUSSURE, Jacob von Uexküll (1864–1944), Karl Bühler (1879–1963), Roman Jakobson (1896–1982) and Louis Hjelmslev (1899–1965) (see STRUCTURALISM IN LINGUISTICS).

3 Signifying by association, by resemblance, by convention

A given sign may do its signifying in different ways: in the widely used terminology laid down by Peirce, it may signify by physical association with what it signifies (such signifiers are called 'indexes'); by mimicry, that is, by physical resemblance to it ('icons'); and/or arbitrarily and merely by convention ('symbols'). For instance the sketchy representation of a man found on certain urgently sought doors in airports indicates by physical association (location) that this and not the next one is the door to the men's toilet; it indicates by recognizable physical resemblance to a man that this door leads to the men's facility (and not the women's); and it indicates the latter fact partly by convention, since generally it is a stick-figure with a pumpkin head and bears little resemblance to an actual person.

This three-way distinction of types of sign was first

drawn by Augustine (*De Doctrina Christiana*), though the distinction between imitative icon and arbitrary symbol, or between symbol and associative index, had been hinted at earlier, respectively by Plato (especially *Cratylus*) and Aristotle (*Prior Analytics*). The distinctions are clear enough in theory, but their application is sometimes aporetic, as when deciding the extent to which a word like 'ding-dong' is imitative (hence 'iconic' in Peirce's sense) or arbitrary (hence 'symbolic'). Indeed, as Plato showed, albeit inadvertently, such discussions are often inconclusive or plain silly. (He argued in *Cratylus* that no Greek noun could be wholly arbitrary, unless imported from Phrygian or some other barbarian language, since any native Greek word could be partitioned, in the crackpot philology of the time, into meaningful subsegments.)

The ternary division of sign-types has a broad acceptance, though alternatives are possible. Certainly a binary division is conceivable – for instance, into Saussure's 'arbitrary' and 'non-arbitrary' types, the latter including both the iconic and the indexical – and it is not difficult to add a fourth or even fifth sign-type. One such is the sign that signifies by modelling the physical process of producing its real object, as the characters of the Korean Hangul writing-system do (they model the mouth in the act of articulating the characters' corresponding sounds).

On the other hand, Peirce's basic tripartite division of sign-types seems quite robust in comparison with some of the other categorizations that have been proposed. For example, in George Dalgarno's tripartite typology, the earliest fully coherent one (in *Didascalocophus* (1680)), three kinds of signification are defined, but by such a hotchpotch of criteria as to leave the categories leaking rather badly. Dalgarno reserves 'conventional' signs (Peirce's 'symbols') for the exclusive use of humans, and 'natural' signs (Peirce's 'indexes') for infrahumans; supernatural signs, such as 'dreams' and 'apparitions' (these correspond to nothing in Peirce's basic typology) he reserves for the use of 'Almighty God'. (This last category is consistent with the pervasive belief in theurgy typical of Dalgarno's day, but it may have sprung from one of the more bizarre passages in *Cratylus*, where Plato avers that the gods have their own language. Proof: they call 'Xanthus' the river that humans call 'Scamander'.) Dalgarno would thus implicitly deny to humans the ability to signify anything by indexes (such as by correctly placing the 'men's toilet' sign) or, presumably, by such humanly transmitted 'apparitions' as plays or films.

4 Systematicity

Signs typically fall into sets, each sign sharing with its fellows distinctive properties of similarity of form and/or function. Thus the words of English are similar in their partaking of the English sound-system (so that a French word, if properly pronounced, cannot be an English word). Again, any arrangement of signs properly called a sentence is only the overt aspect of one or more covert underlying structures. The sentence: 'Politicians who hold floozies to be congenial are likely to be denounced from the pulpit', can be assigned either of two rather different structures and corresponding meanings. In one, certain politicians embrace floozies in order to be congenial; in the other, it is to the floozies that congeniality is attributed, by certain politicians (see AMBIGUITY). Such structures have been paid far more attention by linguists than by other semioticists, partly because they are presumably more intricate in language than elsewhere; but, clearly, some other systems of signification have intricacies of their own (think of a map of the London Underground), and much remains to be done.

Another way in which signs are parts of systems is this: the connective 'signifies' has logical or functional properties, which when well defined may be uniform. While the colloquial verb 'signifies' does not map neatly into a single logical connective, any more than the colloquial verb 'implies' does, much is gained by pondering this issue. As a defined propositional connective, 'signifies' is functionally equivalent to 'implies' or even 'if and only if'. For instance, when 'signifies' is narrowly defined then '(p signifies q) & (q signifies r)' signifies 'p signifies r'. (Let 'p' = 'that weathervane points southward', 'q' = 'the local wind is southerly', and 'r' = 'it will soon warm up'.) However, 'signifies' as a nominal connective is rather different. From 'this drawing signifies that cloud' & 'that cloud signifies an impending storm' it certainly does not follow that therefore 'this drawing signifies an impending storm'. Two different meanings of 'signifies' are being played on here – 'represents' and 'betokens' – and mixing them must often produce nonsense.

This said, it remains to observe that the construction of a comprehensive semiotic calculus is very much a work-in-progress.

5 The field

As presently constituted, the field of semiotics exists less as a discipline than as a speciality. The process by which someone receives or emits a sign, and interprets or conceives it – the process generally called 'semiosis' – is investigated by both semioticists and psychologists, mainly in a domain such as the processing of language, whether written or spoken. (In earlier semiotic work issues of semiosis were rather slighted, apart from some inconclusive remarks by Peirce on, for example, the 'firstness' (roughly, accessibility without mediation) of sense-impressions. This is nice, but it sharpens only slightly Augustine's pellucid definition of a sign as 'a thing which, over and above the impression it makes on the senses, causes something else to come into the mind as a consequence of itself' (*De Doctrina Christiana* 2.1.1).) The functioning of signs in literature, music, architecture, painting and drama is mainly pursued by semioticists who are also students of those respective arts. Examples of work in these and other areas of semiotics can be found in the references.

See also: LANGUAGE, PHILOSOPHY OF; MOSCOW-TARTU SCHOOL

References and further reading

* Aristotle (*c.* mid-4th century BC) *The Complete Works of Aristotle*, ed. J. Barnes, Princeton, NJ: Princeton University Press, 1984, 2 vols. (Contains *De Interpretatione*, which discusses signification, among other topics. Also contains *Prior Analytics*)
* Augustine (396–426) *De Doctrina Christiana* (On Christian Instruction), New York: Cima, 1947. (Brilliant and clear-headed discussion of signs and their function.)
  Bréhier, E. (1951) *Chrysippe et l'ancien stoïcisme*, Paris: Presses Universitaires de France. (The best introduction to Chrysippus.)
* Dalgarno, G. (1680) *Didascalocophus*, Menston: The Scolar Press, 1971. (Odd but fascinating early attempt to categorize signs.)
  Deely, J. (1982) *Introducing Semiotic*, Bloomington, IN: Indiana University Press. (Especially good on medieval work.)
  Eco, U. (1979) *A Theory of Semiotics*, Bloomington, IN: Indiana University Press. (On semiotics as a study of communicative codes.)
  Eschbach, A. and Trabant, J. (eds) (1983) *History of Semiotics*, Philadelphia, PA: John Benjamins. (The study of signs from Plato to Wittgenstein.)
  Harris, W.V. (1983) 'On Being Sure of Saussure', *Journal of Aesthetics and Art Criticism* 41: 387–97. (A nice account of Saussure's views on the arbitrariness or conventionality of the signs of language.)
* Plato (427–347 BC) *Works*, trans. T. Taylor, London, 1804; repr. New York: Garland, 1984. (Contains *Cratylus*, with notes, which discusses signification, among other topics.)
  Posner, R. (1982) *Rational Discourse and Poetic Communication*, Berlin: Mouton. (On the semiotic study of language and literature.)
  Ross, W.D. (1965) *Aristotle's Prior and Posterior Analytics*, Oxford: Clarendon Press. (Excellent introduction to Aristotle's insights into signification in relation to logic.)
  Sebeok, T.A. (1989) *The Sign and Its Masters*, Lanham, MD: University Press of America. (Authoritative account of modern semiotics.)
  Tarasti, E. (1994) *Musical Semiotics*, Bloomington, IN: Indiana University Press. (The standard work in the field.)
  Watt, W.C. (ed.) (1994) *Writing Systems and Cognition: Perspectives from Psychology, Physiology, Linguistics, and Semiotics*, Dordrecht: Kluwer Academic Press. (Modern work within the intersection of semiotics and psychology.)

W.C. WATT

SEN, KESHUB CHUNDER
see BRAHMO SAMAJ

SENECA, LUCIUS ANNAEUS (4/1 BC–AD 65)

Lucius Annaeus Seneca, Roman statesman and Stoic philosopher, is the earliest Stoic of whose writings any have survived intact. Seneca wrote, in Latin, tragedies and a wide range of philosophical works. His philosophical and literary work was carried out in the intervals of an active political career. He is most important for his ethics and psychology, although natural philosophy was not neglected. Unlike many Stoics he showed little interest in logic or dialectic. His most influential work was on the psychology of the passions, the nature of the human will and techniques of moral education; he also wrote extensively on social and political issues from a distinctively Stoic perspective.

1   **Life and works**
2   **Psychology**
3   **Ethics, physics, logic**
4   **Seneca and philosophy in the first century** AD
5   **The *Letters***

1   Life and works

Seneca was born into a wealthy family of the equestrian class at Cordoba in Spain. His father, the Elder Seneca, saw to it that his son was educated at Rome, where he rose to become a senator. Exiled and recalled by the emperor Claudius, Seneca became the teacher and advisor of the emperor Nero. His influence on Nero was considerable until AD 62; Seneca eventually withdrew from active politics, but nevertheless was compelled to commit suicide in AD 65 for his presumed support of a conspiracy against Nero.

Seneca's Stoicism was affected by his early adherence to the Sextian school of philosophy (see NEO-PYTHAGOREANISM), which emphasized asceticism and moral training. His Stoic education was thorough, and his works reveal the influence of PANAETIUS, Hecaton and POSIDONIUS as well as the early heads of the school (see STOICISM §1). He rethought many aspects of Stoic philosophy and continued the work of CICERO in developing a Latin philosophical vocabulary. His prose writings display a balance between his personal contribution and inherited school doctrine. He was a part of contemporary literary culture, famous for his distinctive rhetorical prose style and as the author of justly admired tragedies. The relationship between his philosophical convictions and the tragedies is controversial, as is the question of the impact of his philosophical convictions on his political activity.

Many of Seneca's works are lost, including a biography of his father, speeches, letters and a late treatise entitled *Moral Philosophy*. His surviving prose works include three consolatory works, *To Marcia*, *To Polybius* and *To Helvia* (his mother). Most of his treatises on ethics were dedicated to close friends or family members, although *On Mercy* was addressed to Nero. Also of political note is a viciously witty satire on the dead emperor Claudius, the *Pumpkinification*. Late in his career Seneca wrote a lengthy work on physics, the *Natural Questions*.

The other extant ethical works are: *On Anger* (in some ways a companion piece to *On Mercy*); *On the Brevity of Life*; *On the Steadfastness of the Wise Man*; *On Mental Tranquillity*; the fragmentary *On the Private Life*; *On the Happy Life*; the long treatise *On Favours*, which deals with social relations as well as personal ethics; the fragmentary *On Providence*; and his most influential work, the *Letters to Lucilius* (more correctly *Letters on Ethics*, henceforth *Letters*).

Seneca is important for the history of Stoicism because he is the earliest professed Stoic any of whose works survive in complete form. It is not his aim to report on the history of the school, and his evidence for its early period must be used with care. His treatises confirm and elaborate on what is known about early Stoicism from other sources, but divergences and changes of emphasis are not uncommon.

Examples of this include the treatment of a political figure, Cato the Younger, as a sage; an emphasis on suicide as the ultimate expression of personal freedom; and a humane application of the traditional Stoic view that there are no natural slaves.

Seneca's philosophical works have been persistently influential, first on Latin Church Fathers and again in the Renaissance; Montaigne's *Essays* owe much to Seneca's *Letters* (see PATRISTIC PHILOSOPHY; MONTAIGNE, M.E. DE; RENAISSANCE PHILOSOPHY).

2 Psychology

Seneca's greatest contribution is in moral psychology. In numerous works it is apparent that personal moral decision (*voluntas* or 'will') is given greater emphasis than it received in earlier Stoicism. The treatise *On Anger* (especially book II) also suggests (although this is a controversial point) that he has rethought the earlier Stoic theory of assent and reassessed its role in the explanation of passions. He treats assent as a consciously made decision, a moment of personal self-assertion which shapes (rather than just reveals) our moral character. Will, for Seneca, has become the focus of individual moral freedom, much as *prohairesis* was to be for EPICTETUS (§3). It would be extreme to say that Seneca has posited a distinct faculty of 'will'; but he certainly took some steps in that direction and inspired others, such as AUGUSTINE, to go even further.

His views on the relationship between reason and the passions are also of note. He held to the view that passions are produced by the rational mind when it makes errors about the values of things, and denied the claim of PLATO (§14) and ARISTOTLE (§§22–3) that they are rooted in a non-rational part of the soul. Seneca did, however, take an interest in the complexity of the interactions between bodily reactions to external stimuli and our mental responses to them. His psychology may sometimes seem Platonic, but if there is 'dualism' in his theory, it is the body–soul dualism of Plato's *Phaedo* rather than the psychological dualism of the *Republic* (see PLATO §§13–14). Hence Seneca rejected the Peripatetic view (see PERIPATETICS) that passions should merely be moderated; *apatheia*, complete freedom from passions, remained the ideal.

3 Ethics, physics, logic

Seneca emphasizes that he is not himself a wise man, but merely a *prokoptōn*, a person making moral progress. Like other Stoics of the first century AD and like Panaetius two centuries earlier, he focuses on the moral needs of his audience of imperfect but serious students of philosophy, rather than on the somewhat abstract deductions of earlier theorizing. The paradoxical technicalities of Stoic ethics are not unknown to Seneca, however; in the treatise *On Favours* he applies them effectively to serious ethical questions.

Seneca's attitude to physics is typical of his time, and is important as background to ethics: one must grasp the basic outlines of a providentially organized cosmos held together by a divine plan with which mankind is in harmony, but detailed debate about physics and cosmology is not worth much effort. Specific phenomena, such as those explored in the *Natural Questions*, are dealt with out of scientific curiosity or as illustrations of the divine rationality of the world we inhabit. Logic and dialectic are almost entirely neglected by Seneca. He was aware of work in this area, but comparison with Epictetus shows Seneca's limitations in logic (see EPICTETUS §2).

4 Seneca and philosophy in the first century AD

Seneca's works provide us with an invaluable picture of philosophical life in Rome in the first century AD. His reaction to Epicureanism (which ranges from selective appreciation in the early books of the *Letters* to the hostile denunciations of *On Favours* 4) shows that the school was still to be taken seriously. Similarly, *Letters* 58, 65 and 89 show that Seneca was familiar with the more technical doctrines of contemporary Platonic and Aristotelian philosophy, just as *Letters* 121 and 124 display his detailed knowledge of the technical side of Stoic ethics. Cynic philosophy was important in Rome, and Seneca anticipates Epictetus in his attitude to it: a Cynic (such as Seneca's friend Demetrius) can be presented as a paradigm of the wise person, despite the Cynic rejection of physics and logic as areas of study.

5 The *Letters*

The *Letters to Lucilius* have proved the most influential of Seneca's works. The dedicatee, Lucilius, was a real person, but the letters are fictitious, philosophical open letters modelled on those of Epicurus and designed to emulate the published correspondence of Cicero. Seneca plays the role of a moral advisor to Lucilius, whose progress can be followed through the sequence of letters. The tone and style of the letters also owes much to the rhetorical form known as the diatribe (see CYNICS §3), and is often similar to that of his moral treatises; but there is a greater fluidity and intimacy. Although the facade of epistolary realism is often dropped, Seneca's pretence of writing to a close personal friend draws the reader into a personal engagement with Stoicism

that could not otherwise be achieved; finely judged autobiographical revelations and confessions sustain a sympathy for Seneca as a moral teacher which is not evoked by the rest of his works. The *Letters*, in fact, paved the way for the development of the personal philosophical essay as a genre.

The *Letters* as we have them culminate with an investigation of a technical problem in Stoicism: is 'the good' grasped by the senses or by the intellect? Beginning with a quotation from Virgil, Seneca guides the reader through the complexities which establish that the genuine good is grasped by the mind and can only be found in a rational soul. That rational virtue is the only good is a view fundamental to Stoic ethics, yet detailed physical and metaphysical argument is required to establish it. The reader is soothed by the literary grace of Seneca's style; the strategy of personal address promotes personal conviction. Seneca goes beyond LUCRETIUS, who claimed to mask the bitterness of philosophical technicality with the honey of his poetry. However, Seneca used the tools of his literary art not to disguise the philosophy we must swallow, but to draw us as willing participants into its inner workings. Like the best of Plato's dialogues, Seneca's letters exploit the illusion of personal dialogue to make us partners in his own search for wisdom.

List of works

The dating system used below follows Griffin (1992); *On Providence*, being fragmentary, is hard to date with accuracy.

Seneca, L.A. (late 30s AD) *Consolation to Marcia*, trans. J.W. Basore, Loeb Classical Library, Cambridge, MA: Harvard University Press and London: Heinemann, 1932. (Latin text with facing translation; addressed to the daughter of the historian Cremutius Cordus.)

—— (40s AD, during his exile) *Consolation to Polybius* trans. J.W. Basore, Loeb Classical Library, Cambridge, MA: Harvard University Press and London: Heinemann, 1932. (Latin text with facing translation; in part an attempt to regain favour at the court of Claudius.)

—— (40s AD, during his exile) *Consolation to Helvia*, trans. J.W. Basore, Loeb Classical Library, Cambridge, MA: Harvard University Press and London: Heinemann, 1932. (Latin text with facing translation; addressed to his mother, concerning his own exile.)

—— (before AD 52) *On Anger*, trans. J.W. Basore, Loeb Classical Library, Cambridge, MA: Harvard University Press and London: Heinemann, 1917–25, 10 vols. (Latin text with facing translation; especially important for Stoic theory of passions.)

—— (*c*. AD 48–55) *On the Brevity of Life*, trans. J.W. Basore, Loeb Classical Library, Cambridge, MA: Harvard University Press and London: Heinemann, 1928. (Latin text with facing translation; life is long enough for one guided by philosophy.)

—— (*c*.50s) *On the Steadfastness of the Wise Man* (*De constantia sapientis*), trans. J.W. Basore, Loeb Classical Library, Cambridge, MA: Harvard University Press and London: Heinemann, 1928. (The wise man is immune to insult and injury.)

—— (*c*.50s) *On Mental Tranquillity*, trans. J.W. Basore, Loeb Classical Library, Cambridge, MA: Harvard University Press and London: Heinemann, 1932. (Latin text with facing translation; Stoic rationality as the key to contentment.)

—— (*c*.50s) *On the Private Life*, trans. J.W. Basore, Loeb Classical Library, Cambridge, MA: Harvard University Press and London: Heinemann, 1932. (Latin text with facing translation; on the relation between political and philosophical life.)

—— (*c*.50s) *Pumpkinification* (*Apocolo-cyntosis*), trans. W.H.D. Rousé, Loeb Classical Library, Cambridge, MA: Harvard University Press and London: Heinemann, 1917–25, 10 vols. (Latin text with facing translation; satire on the emperor Claudius.)

—— (*c*.50s) *On Mercy*, trans. J.W. Basore, Loeb Classical Library, Cambridge, MA: Harvard University Press and London: Heinemann, 1928. (Latin text with facing translation; important for political theory as well as ethics.)

—— (*c*.50s) *On the Happy Life*, trans. J.W. Basore, Loeb Classical Library, Cambridge, MA: Harvard University Press and London: Heinemann, 1932. (Latin text with facing translation; a vigorous defence of the Stoic conception of life according to nature.)

—— (*c*. AD 56–62) *On Favours* (*De beneficiis*), trans. J.W. Basore, Loeb Classical Library, Cambridge, MA: Harvard University Press and London: Heinemann, 1935. (Latin text with facing translation; general theory of social relations and ethically appropriate action.)

—— (by AD 64) *Natural Questions*, trans. T. Coscoran, Loeb Classical Library, Cambridge, MA: Harvard University Press and London: Heinemann, 1971–2. (Latin text with facing translation; essays on a range of topics in natural philosophy with ethical digressions.)

—— (*c*. AD early 60s) *Letters*, trans. R.M. Gummere, Loeb Classical Library, Cambridge, MA: Harvard University Press and London: Heinemann, 1917–25, 10 vols. (Latin text with facing translation.)

—— (*c*. mid 1st century BC) *On Providence*, trans. J.W. Basore, Loeb Classical Library, Cambridge, MA: Harvard University Press and London: Heinemann, 1928. (Latin text with facing translation.)

References and further reading

Arnold, E.V. (1911) *Roman Stoicism*, Cambridge: Cambridge University Press. (Standard work, somewhat dated but still useful.)

Chaumartin, F.-R. (1989) 'Quarante ans de recherche sur les œuvres philosophiques de Sénèque (Bibliographie 1945–1985)' (Forty years of research on Seneca's Philosophical Works), in W. Haase (ed.) *Aufstieg und Niedergang der römischen Welt*, Berlin and New York: de Gruyter, II.36: 3, 1545–1605. (Well articulated bibliography, arranged chronologically within each topic.)

Cooper, J.M. and Procopé, J.F. (1995) *Seneca: Moral and Political Essays*, Cambridge: Cambridge University Press. (Better translations of *On Anger, On Mercy, On the Private Life*, and *On Favours* 1–4, plus excellent introduction and commentary.)

Griffin, M. (1992) *Seneca: A Philosopher in Politics*, Oxford: Clarendon Press, 2nd edn. (Definitive historical treatment; offers a likely order of composition for Seneca's works.)

Grimal, P. (1979) *Sénèque, ou la conscience de l'Empire*, Paris: Les Belles Lettres. (A general assessment of his philosophical work and the historical context.)

—— (1989) 'Sénèque et le stoïcisme romain', in W. Haase (ed.) *Aufstieg und Niedergang der römischen Welt*, Berlin and New York: de Gruyter, II.36: 3, 1962–92. (An assessment of Seneca's relation to the early Stoics.)

BRAD INWOOD

SENGHOR, LEOPOLD

see AESTHETICS, AFRICAN; AFRICAN PHILOSOPHY, ANGLOPHONE ETHNOPHILOSOPHY, AFRICAN; AFRICAN PHILOSOPHY, FRANCOPHONE

SENGZHAO (AD 384?–414)

Sengzhao was one of the first native Chinese thinkers to develop a distinctive version of Buddhist philosophy. He blended the dialectical logic of Indian Mādhyamika Buddhism with ideas and terms often borrowed from Chinese Daoism. His collected treatises, the Zhaolun, *argued that language is inadequate for capturing reality. There is a need for an intuitive insight to penetrate reality in its nonlinguistic form as a means to understanding the process and limitations of subsequent conceptualization.*

Born in Changan (present day Xian) in AD 384 (or possibly 374), Sengzhao was from a poor family and found work as a copyist, an occupation that gave him broad exposure to a variety of literatures. Originally enamoured of the neo-Daoism popular at the time, Sengzhao converted to Buddhism after reading a copy of the *Vimalakīrti Sūtra*. As a Buddhist monk in northwestern China and then in Changan, he studied under the famous Indian Buddhist translator and commentator Kumārajīva (AD 344–413). Kumārajīva introduced Sengzhao to Mādhyamika thought, known in China either as the 'Four Treatise School' or the 'Three Treatise School' (see BUDDHISM, MĀDHYAMIKA: INDIA AND TIBET). As a chief disciple of Kumārajīva, Sengzhao achieved great eminence and his writings have been regarded as foundational to the Sinicization of Indian Buddhism.

Sengzhao's contribution to Chinese philosophy had multiple dimensions. First, he introduced a new form of rhetoric for philosophical argument. In this regard, Sengzhao often used models of argumentation taken from the second-century founder of Indian Mādhyamika philosophy, NĀGĀRJUNA. Nāgārjuna had developed a form of dialectical analysis to show that opposing concepts could only be understood in relation to each other. Yet, the realities to which they referred were typically considered ontologically discrete. For example, the concepts of 'past', 'present' and 'future' are understood in terms of each other, yet the realities to which they supposedly refer cannot temporally coexist and, therefore, cannot be directly related. So, Nāgārjuna argued that the way concepts interrelate cannot mirror the way their supposed referents interrelate. Sengzhao assimilated aspects of this form of argument in analysing pairs of concepts. However, he did not always analyse the same pairs of concepts as had Nāgārjuna. Often his arguments seemed to address issues more central to the indigenous concerns among the neo-Daoist philosophers, for example. In this regard, it is important to note that some of Sengzhao's dialectical style of analysing opposing pairs of concepts also resembled the form of argument in Chapter Two of *Zhuangzi*, the famous Daoist philosophical classic (see ZHUANGZI). Therefore, Sengzhao was developing a form of argumentation that drew on both Indian and indigenous Chinese traditions. This may account for the almost immediate reaction of his contemporaries that he had introduced a new and important style of philosophical argument.

Second, and closely related to the first point, Sengzhao's writings heightened the Chinese awareness of the logical structure of argumentation. Sengzhao did not seem to have a logician's grasp of the principles involved in Mādhyamika argumentation, sometimes making invalid inferences in his arguments. It is likely that he did not have access to Indian logical treatises. Therefore, without the help of theoretical explanation, he probably developed his logical arguments by trying to mimic the style of Mādhyamika writings. Despite this limitation, he often formulated arguments with a logical tightness that had not been attained previously by Chinese writing in their native language. This set the stage for further Chinese developments in this area as the Chinese Buddhists learned more of the Indian forms of rhetoric and logical analysis.

Third, Sengzhao gave the Mādhyamika idea of intuitive insight (*prajñā* in Sanskrit; *banru* in Chinese) a new explication. As in the Indian tradition, this intuitive insight was considered an immediate, perhaps mystical, grasp of reality without the intervention of conceptual understanding. One important difference from the Indian tradition, however, was that Sengzhao associated this intuitive insight with the Chinese tradition of the sage. In various indigenous philosophies, the Chinese sage had been described as having extraordinary powers of insight into reality. Sengzhao identified this quality with the Buddhist ideal of intuitive insight. This had the effect of making Chinese Buddhism, like Daoism and Confucianism, a 'sage religion'. Furthermore, it reinforced the indigenous idea that an immediate experience of reality was possible. Sengzhao stressed that since this intuitive insight did not have a conceptual object, it could not be a form of knowledge. It was something more 'spontaneous' or 'natural' than conceptual modes of apprehension. This emphasis on merging with the natural gave the Buddhist idea a distinctively Daoist flavour (see DAOIST PHILOSOPHY §1; ZHI).

Lastly, although Sengzhao stressed the primacy of intuitive insight, he also stressed the dual-layered character of reality. On one level, there is a natural, organic source that can be grasped immediately. On another level are the functions of that source as the realm of conceptual expression, yielding a necessary but limited grasp of truth. This gave Sengzhao's Chinese Buddhism an emergent or process form of ontology describing how the non-conceptual became conceptualized. This organic model of reality was not present in the Indian Mādhyamika tradition and was much closer to ideas in Daoism and such ancient Chinese classics as the *Yijing* (see YIJING).

Because of these varied dimensions to Sengzhao's work, scholars disagree about the best way to classify his own philosophical perspective. Was Sengzhao essentially a product of the Chinese, fundamentally neo-Daoist worldview who managed to graft on to the tradition some new rhetorical structures imported through Indian Buddhism? Or was he a convert to the Indian philosophy of Mādhyamika Buddhism who was able to stretch his native language and indigenous ideas to accommodate the new way of thinking he had adopted? Or was he a creative, syncretistic thinker who developed his own distinctively cross-cultural philosophy? Because his writings are not extensive and because he was breaking out of the boundaries of the traditional styles of writings, some critical points are open to multiple interpretation. What is undisputed, however, is Sengzhao's impact on the ensuing Chinese philosophers of various schools.

See also: BUDDHIST PHILOSOPHY, CHINESE; DAOIST PHILOSOPHY; BUDDHISM, MĀDHYAMIKA: INDIA AND TIBET

List of works

Zhaolun (Treatises of Zhao) (AD *c.*384–414); ed. and trans. Tsukamoto Zenryū, *Jōron kenkyū* (Studies of the Zhaolun), Kyoto: Hōzōkan, 1955; ed. and trans. W. Liebenthal, *Chao Lun: The Treatises of Seng-chao; A Translation with Introduction, Notes and Appendices*, Hong Kong: Hong Kong University Press, 1968. (Tsukamoto provides the best critical edition of the original Chinese text as well as a Japanese translation and philological essays in Japanese. Liebenthal is a full English translation of the *Zhaolun* with commentary emphasizing the Chinese, rather than Buddhist, nature of the text.)

References and further reading

Cai Zongqi (1993) 'Derrida and Seng-Zhao: Linguistic and Philosophical Deconstructions', *Philosophy East and West* 43 (3): 389–404. (Interesting comparison of the deconstructive strategies in the language use of Jacques Derrida and Sengzhao.)

Fung Yu-lan (1953) *A History of Chinese Philosophy*, vol. 2, trans. D. Bodde, Princeton, NJ: Princeton University Press. (A classic survey of Chinese philosophy with a section (pages 258–70) devoted to a summary of the three central fascicles of the *Zhaolun*.)

Robinson, R.H. (1965) *Early Mādhyamika in India and China*, Madison, WI: University of Wisconsin Press. (Good scholarly study of the Mādhyamika tradition, including a chapter on Sengzhao and a translation of three fascicles of the *Zhaolun*. In contrast to Liebenthal, Robinson emphasizes Sengzhao as a continuation of the Indian Mādhyamika tradition.)

THOMAS P. KASULIS

SENG-CHAO *see* SENGZHAO

SENNERT, D. *see* ARISTOTELIANISM IN THE 17TH CENTURY

SENSATIONS, BODILY
see BODILY SENSATIONS

SENSE AND FORCE
see PRAGMATICS (§8)

SENSE AND REFERENCE

The 'reference' of an expression is the entity the expression designates or applies to. The 'sense' of an expression is the way in which the expression presents that reference. For example, the ancients used 'the morning star' and 'the evening star' to designate what turned out to be the same heavenly body, the planet Venus. These two expressions have the same reference, but they clearly differ in that each presents that reference in a different way. So, although coreferential, each expression is associated with a different 'sense'. The distinction between sense and reference helps explain the cognitive puzzle posed by identity statements. 'The morning star is the evening star' and 'The morning star is the morning star' are both true, yet the sentences differ in cognitive significance, since the former may be informative, whereas the latter definitely is not. That difference in cognitive significance cannot be explained just by appeal to the references of the terms, for those are the same. It can, however, be naturally accounted for by appeal to a difference in sense. The terms 'the morning star' and 'the evening star' used in the first sentence, having different senses, present the referent in different ways, whereas no such difference occurs in the second sentence.

The distinction between sense and reference applies to all well-formed expressions of a language. It is part of a general theory of meaning that postulates an intermediate level of sense between linguistic terms and the entities the terms stand for. Senses give significance to expressions, which in and of themselves are just noises or marks on a surface, and connect them to the world. It is because linguistic terms have a sense that they can be used to express judgments, to transmit information and to talk about reality.

1 Sense, reference and cognitive significance
2 The sense and reference of different types of expressions
3 The multiple roles of sense
4 Compositionality and substitutivity
5 Non-customary contexts

1 Sense, reference and cognitive significance

The distinction between sense and reference was originally drawn by Gottlob Frege in his 1892 article 'Über Sinn und Bedeutung' ('On Sense and Reference'; see FREGE, G. §3). According to Frege, associated with each meaningful expression of a language there is a 'sense' (*Sinn*) that makes the expression significant and determines its 'reference' (*Bedeutung*), that is, the entity the expression applies to or designates. ('*Bedeutung*' is also translated as 'designation', 'designatum', 'denotation' and 'nominatum'. It is also sometimes translated as 'meaning'. This can create confusion, since some of Frege's contemporaries, including Russell, used 'meaning' as the translation of '*Sinn*', most likely on the assumption that the notion corresponding to '*Sinn*' is that of cognitive meaning or significance.) Before 1892, Frege had espoused the view that the significance or content of an expression is given exclusively by that which the expression designates or stands for (what he came to regard as the 'reference'). Observe that on such a view two coreferential terms, such as 'Cicero' and 'Tully', are supposed to have the same content or significance. But if that is so, it seems impossible to explain the obvious difference in cognitive significance between, say, 'Cicero is Cicero', a trivially true and uninformative statement, and 'Cicero is Tully', a potentially informative sentence. The problem of how to explain differences in cognitive significance is not restricted exclusively to statements of identity. 'Cicero was an orator' and 'Tully was an orator' also differ in cognitive significance, since it is possible for a competent speaker to accept one of the statements while rejecting the other. Without postulating a difference in the content or significance of the terms 'Cicero' and 'Tully', it would seem impossible to explain the differences between those two pairs of sentences. The distinction between sense and reference provides for a natural explanation: although the two names are coreferential, they are associated with different senses and those senses present the referent in different ways (see PROPER NAMES §1).

2 The sense and reference of different types of expressions

The distinction between sense and reference is intended to apply to all meaningful expressions of a language, whether simple or complex. In the case of definite descriptions it is an extremely natural distinction since it is obvious that different descriptions of one and the same object present that object in different ways. In the case of proper names, the reference is the bearer of the name and the sense is traditionally conceived as some sort of condition satisfied uniquely by the referent. There is no unanimity, however, regarding how to understand such a uniquely identifying condition. Frege suggests (1892) that the sense of a proper name is some descriptive information that applies uniquely to the bearer. Thus, some philosophers interpret Frege's suggestion as entailing the claim than each proper name is synonymous with some definite description. Others, including John Searle (1958), view the sense of a given proper name as a cluster of descriptive information that speakers associate with the name, and the referent as whatever satisfies most of the attributes in the cluster. Other semanticists do not uphold the descriptive nature of the senses of proper names. For example, David Kaplan (1969) has argued that on Frege's view the sense of a name may be seen as a representation of the referent and so the relation between the sense of a name and its reference is much like the relation between picture and pictured object. Finally, Michael Dummett (1981) is the foremost representative of the view that regards the sense of a proper name, as the sense of any expression, as a mechanism or procedure that, under ideal circumstances, would enable a competent speaker to single out the referent.

The reference of a general term is traditionally taken to be the extension of the term in question. Thus, for example, in the case of a predicate such as 'red' the extension is the set of red things, that is, the set of things to which the predicate correctly applies. And the extension of a relational verb such as 'is taller than' is a set of ordered pairs (since 'being taller than' is a relation between two things) such that the first member of each pair is taller than the second member of the pair. The sense of a general term is a mode of presentation of the set and is responsible for the cognitive content or cognitive significance of the term.

Although it is traditional to represent the reference of a general term as a set, such a choice is strictly incorrect, from the standpoint of pure Fregean orthodoxy. Frege distinguished sharply between concepts and objects. Only the latter are, on his view, 'saturated' entities; entities that subsist on their own. People and artefacts, also numbers and sets, are saturated entities. On the other hand, concepts are 'unsaturated'; they do not have an independent existence, but can only subsist as completed by a saturated entity. On Frege's view, the reference of a general term is a concept, and thus an unsaturated entity. Thus, the reference of a general term is not a set, for the latter is a saturated entity. Still, in the posthumously published comments on 'Über Sinn und Bedeutung' (1892–5), Frege himself stresses that any two general terms refer to the same concept just in case their extension is the same. So, it seems that, even for Frege, equality of extension is a criterion of identity for concepts, so taking the reference of a general term to be a set is not a radical departure from the standard Fregean theory.

Finally, according to the theory, whole sentences express complete thoughts. The 'thought' or sense associated with a sentence is the claim or assertion, traditionally called the 'proposition', expressed by the sentence. In 'Über Sinn und Bedeutung' Frege argues that the sentence's reference is its truth-value. The relation between a sentence and its truth-value should therefore be understood in terms of the relation between a name and its bearer or a definite description and the individual it designates. A true sentence is like a name for 'True', so that all the true sentences (like all the false ones) have one and the same reference; however, since different, non-synonymous sentences express different thoughts, they present that reference in different ways. Frege's argument relies on the assumption (see §4 below) that the reference of a complex expression does not change if components with the same reference are intersubstituted. Thus, for example, if we substitute the coreferential 'the orator who denounced Catiline' for 'Cicero' in the complex expression 'the father of Cicero', the reference of the expression (whoever fathered the famous orator) does not change. In this vein Frege asks what it is that remains constant when we intersubstitute coreferential components in a sentence, for that should be the reference, if anything is. He observes that the thought cannot be the reference, for typically the thought expressed by the

sentence is altered: 'Cicero was an orator' and 'The orator who denounced Catiline was an orator' clearly express different thoughts. The truth-value of the sentence is what remains constant in spite of the substitution, so that should be the reference.

3 The multiple roles of sense

The sense of an expression, as we have seen, embodies its cognitive value and is solely responsible for its significance. A term that lacks a sense is therefore not a meaningful constituent of a language; however, an expression may have a sense (that is, be meaningful) and still lack reference. For example, 'the least integer' is a meaningful expression even if there is no object to which it refers. The sense of an expression determines the referent (if the expression has a referent) but, as Frege points out, there is no road back from reference to sense. Aristotle, for example, is the referent of many different terms; there is no mechanism, no procedure that would single out a sense only on the basis of what the reference is.

The sense of a sentence – the thought or proposition it expresses – determines a truth-value as reference. But truth-value typically depends on specific features of the world. Thus, given the way the world is, the sense of the sentence 'Aristotle was a philosopher' determines (we suppose) 'True' as reference. Had Aristotle never thought about philosophical questions, the sense of that sentence would determine 'False' as reference. It is the role of the sense of a sentence to determine truth-value on whatever conditions obtain, thus the sense accounts for the truth-conditions of a sentence. Because the thought expressed by a sentence is a function of the senses of the component expressions, the sense of an expression is that expression's contribution to the truth-conditions of the sentences in which it figures.

Senses are also what speakers grasp when they understand words. Hence, language learning and linguistic competence are a matter of grasping senses. Moreover, speakers communicate linguistically with one another by grasping the same thoughts. So senses, although mentally graspable entities, should not be confused with private images or ideas. Senses are objective, so that different speakers can grasp the same senses and transmit a given thought to other speakers.

4 Compositionality and substitutivity

The Fregean theory of sense and reference espouses two basic and closely connected semantic principles: the principle of compositionality and the law of substitutivity.

The principle of compositionality states that the reference of a complex expression is a function of the references of its components, plus the way in which those components are combined (see COMPOSITIONALITY). Similarly, the sense of a complex expression is a function of the senses of the component expressions. Thus the reference of the sentence 'The Eiffel Tower is taller than the Empire State Building', a truth-value, is determined exclusively by the references of the meaningful components and their combination. The mode of combination is important, since a different reference would be determined if the components were combined differently, as with the sentence 'The Empire State building is taller than the Eiffel Tower'.

Since, by compositionality, the references of the parts are solely responsible for the reference of the whole, it obviously follows that coreferential terms are intersubstitutable without altering the reference of the complex expressions in which they occur. The latter is known as the law of substitutivity, which states that an expression which figures as part of another expression can be replaced with a coreferential one, and the reference of the complex will remain the same. However, the *sense* of a complex is typically altered when coreferential components are intersubstituted, if they have different senses. Thus, for example, 'Aristotle was Greek' and 'The tutor of Alexander the Great was Greek' express different thoughts but, since the latter sentence results from the exchange of coreferential terms, the reference of the two sentences is the same. (The sense of a complex remains the same if components with the same sense are intersubstituted.)

5 Non-customary contexts

The law of substitution seems to have obvious counterexamples. For example, although 'Cicero' and 'Tully' are coreferential names, the reference of sentences such as 'Mary said that Cicero was a historian' or 'John said, "Cicero was a historian"' may be altered if 'Tully' is substituted for 'Cicero'. But, according to the standard theory of sense and reference, some contexts cause shifts in the sense and reference of the expressions that occur in them. Thus the alleged failure of substitutivity is only apparent, for in the contexts in question the terms being substituted do not have their customary reference. The Fregean theory of sense and reference is essentially contextual: what an expression refers to and what its sense is depend on the context in which the expression occurs.

Consider the sentence 'The word "Cicero" contains six characters'. The reference of a word within quotation marks is not the customary referent, but rather the word itself (see USE/MENTION DISTINCTION AND QUOTATION). In our example, the occurrence of 'Cicero' does not refer to Cicero but to the word 'Cicero'. Clearly, the substitution of 'Tully' for 'Cicero' in that context would alter the truth-value of the sentence in question. But since 'Tully' and 'Cicero' are different words, the terms of the attempted substitution are not coreferential in that context, and therefore the observed phenomenon does not violate the principle of substitutivity.

Something similar occurs in the case of indirect quotation, such as 'Mary said that Cicero was a historian' (see INDIRECT DISCOURSE), and belief ascriptions, such as 'John believes that Cicero was a historian' (see PROPOSITIONAL ATTITUDE STATEMENTS §§1–2). Here too the intersubstitution of what seem to be coreferential terms may alter the reference of the sentence. And here again, the breakdown of substitutivity is only apparent, for, according to the theory of sense and reference, expressions in contexts such as these, which Frege called 'oblique', have a non-customary referent. The non-customary referent in these cases – the oblique referent – is the customary sense of the expression. In oblique contexts the reference of the embedded clause is the thought which that clause customarily expresses, and the reference of each of the clause's component expressions is its customary sense. So, the reference of 'Cicero' in the two sentences considered above is not Cicero but rather the sense 'Cicero' has in customary contexts such as 'Cicero was an orator', 'Cicero was a historian' and so on. In oblique contexts expressions have in turn an oblique sense, whose role is precisely to determine the oblique reference. It is an open question whether the semantic treatment of more complex embeddings requires that expressions have a higher-order sense that determines the oblique sense as reference in the context in question.

See also: INTENSIONAL ENTITIES §1

References and further reading

Burge, T. (1990) 'Frege on Sense and Linguistic Meaning', in D. Bell and N. Cooper (eds) *The Analytic Tradition: Meaning, Thought and Knowledge*, Philosophical Quarterly Monographs series, vol. 1, Oxford and Cambridge, MA: Blackwell, 30–60. (Proposes a nontraditional interpretation of the notion of sense.)

Church, A. (1951) 'A Formulation of the Logic of Sense and Denotation', in P. Henle, H. Kallen and S. Langer (eds) *Structure, Method and Meaning*, New York: Liberal Arts, 3–24. (A formal development of Frege's ideas. Church argues for the need for an infinite hierarchy of senses.)

Donnellan, K.S. (1972) 'Proper Names and Identifying Descriptions', in D. Davidson and G. Harman (eds) *Semantics of Natural Language*, Dordrecht: Reidel, 356–79. (A criticism of the Fregean theory of sense and reference as applied to proper names.)

* Dummett, M. (1981) *Frege: Philosophy of Language*, Cambridge, MA: Harvard University Press. (A comprehensive discussion of various aspects of the theory of sense and reference.)

Evans, G. (1982) *The Varieties of Reference*, Oxford: Clarendon Press. (A contemporary Fregean approach to sense and reference. Chapter 1 has a thorough exposition and discussion of the doctrine of sense and reference for proper names.)

—— (1985) 'Understanding Demonstratives', in *Collected Papers*, Oxford: Oxford University Press. (Applies the theory of sense and reference to indexicals.)

Frege, G. (1879) *Begriffsschrift, eine der arithmetischen nachgebildeten Formelsprachen des reinen Denkens*, Halle: Nebert; trans. 'Conceptual Notation', in *Conceptual Notation and Related Articles*, ed. T. Bynum, Oxford: Clarendon Press, 1972, 101–203. (A sample of Frege's thought before the distinction between sense and reference. §8 gives Frege's first attempted solution to the problem posed by true and informative identity sentences.)

* —— (1892) 'Über Sinn und Bedeutung', *Zeitschrift für Philosophie und philosophische Kritik* 100: 25–50; trans. and ed. P.T. Geach and M. Black, 'On Sense and Meaning', in *Translations from the Philosophical Writings of Gottlob Frege*, Oxford: Blackwell, 3rd edn, 1980, 56–78; trans. H. Feigl, 'On Sense and Nominatum', in H. Feigl and W. Sellars (eds) *Readings in Philosophical Analysis*, New York: Ridgeview, 1982, 85–102. (This is the essay in which Frege introduces the distinction between sense and reference.)

* —— (1892–5) 'Ausführungen über Sinn und Bedeutung', in *Nachgelassene Schriften*, ed. H. Hermes, F. Kambartel and F. Kaulbach, Hamburg: Meiner, 1969–76; trans. P. Long and R. White, 'Comments on Sense and Meaning', in *Posthumous Writings*, ed. H. Hermes, F. Kambartel and F. Kaulbach, Chicago, IL: Chicago University Press, 1979, 118–25. (A posthumously published discussion of some of the major themes of 'Über Sinn und Bedeutung'. Frege focuses specially on the application of the notions of sense and reference to general terms.)

—— (1918) 'Der Gedanke: eine logische Untersuchung', *Beiträge zur Philosophie des deutschen Idealismus* 1: 58–77; trans. A.M. and M. Quinton,

'The Thought: A Logical Inquiry', *Mind* 65: 289–311; trans. P.T. Geach and R. Stoothoff, 'Thoughts', in *Collected Papers*, ed. B. McGuinness, Oxford: Blackwell, 1984. (Frege's defence of the objectivity of the realm of sense. It also includes a few remarks on the sense of indexicals.)

Furth, M. (1968) 'Two Types of Denotation', *Studies in Logical Theory*, American Philosophical Quarterly Monograph series, vol. 2, Oxford: Blackwell, 9–45. (Discusses unsaturated entities and the reference of general terms.)

* Kaplan, D. (1969) 'Quantifying In', in D. Davidson and J. Hintikka (eds) *Words and Objections*, Dordrecht: Reidel, 178–214. (A discussion of Frege's treatment of oblique contexts. Argues for the representational conception of the sense of proper names.)

Parsons, T. (1981) 'Frege's Hierarchies of Indirect Senses and the Paradox of Analysis', in P.A. French, T.E. Uehling, Jr and H.K. Wettstein (eds) *Midwest Studies in Philosophy*, vol. 6, 37–57. (Contends, against Church, that just one level of oblique sense and reference is sufficient to provide an adequate semantic treatment of all contexts.)

Perry, J. (1977) 'Frege on Demonstratives', *Philosophical Review* 86: 474–97. (Criticizes the theory of sense and reference as applied to indexicals.)

Salmon, N. (1986) *Frege's Puzzle*, Cambridge, MA: MIT Press. (A critical discussion of the puzzle of cognitive significance.)

* Searle, J.R. (1958) 'Proper Names', *Mind* 67: 166–73. (On the cluster conception of the sense of proper names.)

Sluga, H. (ed.) (1993) *The Philosophy of Frege*, vol. 4, *Sense and Reference in Frege's Philosophy*, New York: Garland. (Large collection of articles about the topic.)

GENOVEVA MARTÍ

SENSE PERCEPTION, INDIAN VIEWS OF

Sense perception is considered in classical Indian thought in the context of epistemological issues – in particular, perception as a source of knowledge – and of psychological and metaphysical issues, for example, the relations of sense experiences to objects, to language and to the perceiving self or subject. The Sanskrit word used most commonly in philosophical investigations of sense perception is pratyakṣa, *a compound of* prati, *'before', and* akṣa, *'eye' or any 'organ of sense'; thus it* should be understood as 'being before the eyes' or 'experientially evident' as an adjective, and 'immediate experience' or 'sense experience' as a noun. The meaning 'sense perception' is normal within philosophical inquiries. But just how many sense modalities there are is not to be taken for granted. In addition to the five types of sense experience commonly identified, 'mental' perception (as of pleasures, pains and desires), apperception (awareness of awareness) and extraordinary or yogic perception are sometimes counted as pratyakṣa.

Views about the psychology of perception or, more broadly, about perception considered as part of the world are developed in religious and soteriological literature (literature about enlightenment and liberation) predating classical philosophical discussions. In Upaniṣadic, Buddhist and Jaina texts over two millennia old, perception is painted in broad strokes within spiritual theories of self and world that promote ideas of the supreme value of a mystical experience. Sense perception is usually devalued comparatively. Later, the psychology of perception becomes very advanced and is treated in some quarters independently of soteriological teachings.

Classical Indian philosophy proper is marked by tight argumentation and self-conscious concern with evidence. The justificational value of perception is recognized from the outset, in so far as any justifiers, or knowledge sources, are admitted at all. Nāgārjuna and others challenge the epistemological projects of Nyāya and other positive approaches to knowledge, prompting deep probing of perception's epistemic role. Views about veridicality, fallibility and meaningful doubt become greatly elaborated.

What do we perceive? Throughout classical thought, sharp disagreements occur over the perceptibility of universals, relations, absences or negative facts (such as Devadatta's not being at home), parts versus wholes, and the self or awareness itself. Issues about perceptual media (such as light and ether, ākāśa, the purported medium of sound), about occult or spiritual perceptibles and about the very existence of objects independently of consciousness are hotly debated. A Buddhist phenomenalism is polemically matched by a Mīmāṃsā and Nyāya realism on a range of concerns.

Probably through the influence of mysticism, verbalization of experience, however simple and direct, becomes suspect in comparison with experience itself; this suspicion is evident in concerns over the value of each in presenting reality, as well as in other, sometimes rather indefinite, ways. The judgment is prevalent that what prevents a person from living in an enlightened or liberated state is thinking – verbalizing experience, calculating, planning, and so on – instead of having pure experience, perceptual and otherwise, and thus living

with a 'silent mind'. This attitude emerges in treatments of sense experience, reinforcing what is perhaps a natural tendency among philosophers to find the relations of experience and language problematic. Even in the root text of Nyāya, where the influence of yoga and mysticism is not so strong, perception is said to be a cognition that is nonverbal, avyapadeśya, although there is considerable dispute about precisely what this means. The relations between various modes of experience and the language used with respect to them remains an ongoing concern of the very latest and most complex classical Indian philosophy.

1–2 Psychology of perception
3   Epistemology of perception
4–5 Perception and the world
6   Perception and language

1 Psychology of perception

This entry is concerned with classical Indian views of perception. The reflections of modern philosophers not writing in Sanskrit (such as Aurobindo Ghose, whose innovative theory has not been sufficiently explored) and academic philosophers fall outside its purview. In this section, four topics will be discussed: (a) views of perception as episodic, along with the role of psychological dispositions, called saṃskāra, in recognition and related cognitive processes; (b) internal perception and the internal instrument, the manas or 'mind'; (c) peculiarly Indian views about the operation of sense organs; and (d) the relation of perception to consciousness. With the first three topics, labelling according to school – Buddhist Yogācāra, Nyāya, Mīmāṃsā, and so on – or individual thinker is done incidentally, mainly to provide minimal historical context. Most of the positions are pan-Indian, common across periods as well as the usual metaphysical divides, although not invariably. With the fourth topic, the stances of individual schools are discriminated, since there is much disagreement about consciousness.

In early Buddhist texts, discussion of sense perception occurs within the context of the doctrine of 'no-self', an-ātman (in Pāli, anatta), which is advanced by the Buddha apparently to facilitate disidentification with desires and other phenomenal presentations – such disidentification being considered crucial to the attainment of a mystical enlightenment. Varieties of consciousness are listed by the Buddha's interpreters in efforts to analyse the make-up of the false conglomerate commonly thought to be a self. Thus emerges a picture of streams of experience integrated into an ego that is erroneously thought to endure. Perception is considered episodic in character; a perceptual moment lasts only an instant and is followed by a distinct occurrence.

So, too, throughout the approximately two-thousand-year history of Nyāya-Vaiśeṣika and most other classical schools is found a view of perception as episodic. (The vṛtti notion used in Sāṅkhya and Advaita Vedānta, roughly 'modification', is a change to be understood temporally.) Despite the realism of some of these philosophies, standing in sharp opposition to the most prominent Buddhist schools, there is agreement that sense experiences occur as brief episodes in a temporal series, or as an intersection of multiple series (a sense experience results from both physical and psychological factors, according to some views). Much classical Indian psychology of perception traces a complex of causal factors giving rise to particular types of awareness, with sense experiences included within the broader project.

Some of these analyses are intricate. For example, with the phenomenon of recognition (as in 'This is that Devadatta whom I saw yesterday') a perceptual factor and a memory factor are identified. The memory factor is analysed in terms of saṃskāra, dispositions or subconscious traces formed by a blend of past experiences and actions. Disputes centre on how the perceptual factor (expressed by 'this' in the verbalization 'This is that Devadatta') fuses with or relates to the memory dispositions. In later thought, it is well recognized that verbalizable perceptual awareness always, or almost always (or on almost all analyses), contains an admixture of concepts understood dispositionally. What some Western thinkers would call beliefs are talked about in these same terms, namely, with reference to saṃskāra, as is a whole range of cognitive phenomena, such as doubting, planning, expecting, and so on.

2 Psychology of perception (cont.)

Dispositions, or subconscious traces, are not the only internal factors talked about in analyses of perceptual awareness. Though there is much controversy about the nature of a cognizer or self, there is surprising consensus about an internal perceptual organ called the manas, commonly translated 'mind' (and here rendered as 'sense mind'), and sometimes also called antaḥkaraṇa, the 'internal organ'. Phenomenologically, perceptions of pleasures, pains and desires are similar to perceptions of colours, sounds, tastes, and so forth. In the latter cases, sense organs mediate, or deliver, the perceptions; thus it would appear that there must be an organ for 'internal' perceptions, too. Moreover, awarenesses originating through different sense media are synthesized – or channelled or

bundled together – in such a way that a person at least seems to get a multidimensional view of the self and the world, a presentation informed by multiple senses, including the internal colourings of hedonic tone and appetitive hue. The sense mind is postulated to serve the dual function of grasping desires and the like and bundling the displays of the external senses. It is normally considered 'internal' with respect to the physical organs, as somehow nearer the seat of consciousness, but 'external' to the self or consciousness itself. It is an instrument of awareness, but, as Sāṅkhya philosophers stress, it is part of nature, not of consciousness, nor is it in itself conscious, except according to some Buddhist theorists (see SĀṄKHYA §2).

The nature of manas is filled out differently according to different schools. One important difference concerns the apparent synthesis of the deliverances of the distinct senses. In Nyāya-Vaiśeṣika, it is held that the appearance of a synthesis is an illusion comparable to the firebrand that appears to be a circle but is really a single torch whirled around rapidly. Similarly, the sense mind, which is considered atomic and capable of delivering to the self only one bit of sense-mediated information at a time, moves very rapidly among the organs and internal occurrences, giving the impression of a unified, multidimensional moment of consciousness, whereas the mosaic is really a rapid series of perceptions (see NYĀYA-VAIŚEṢIKA §6). Again, this fuller view is by no means held by all schools, although a core theory or simple postulation of a sense mind is.

What relations hold between sense organs and the objects they grasp? According to some, all the organs come into direct contact with their objects, while others maintain that direct contact is the operative relation only with certain organs and certain objects. Most parties agree that touch operates by direct contact, also taste and smell, and most hold that the sense mind, or internal organ, works similarly too. A prominent view, though less universally espoused, is that with the seat of vision being the eyes, the visual organ itself is a ray that goes out of the body as swiftly as light (which carries it), comes into contact with objects at a distance and spreads over their illuminated surfaces. To obvious objections, proponents come up with ingenious rejoinders. Concerning hearing, there are advocates of a travelling organ, but a more prominent view is that sounds are transmitted in a special element called ether, ākāśa, alternatively through air, reaching the organ located in the hole in the ear. Some hold that the ether as delimited by the earhole is the sense organ.

There are issues about the relation to the grasping sense organ of objects not plausibly in direct contact with it, such as the colour and shape of a pot. We touch a pot, but not its shape, at least not directly. The visual organ may come into direct contact with the pot, but colour is not the sort of thing with which there could be direct contact, contact being a relation that holds between substances. Such issues are not pressing for Buddhist phenomenalists, since they hold that there is no essential difference between the means to awareness and awareness itself: talk of 'organs' is just a manner of speaking. But on almost all other views, considerable attention is paid to the nature of the operative relation for each type of object perceived, for example, substance, quality (and different types of quality – colours, sounds, and so on), motion, universal or absence.

Finally, the major schools take distinct positions on the question of the consciousness in perception. Yogācāra Buddhists (Buddhist phenomenalists) generally hold that every perception is conscious in itself. To postulate an additional cognizer would be otiose. Sāṅkhya-Yoga propounds a strict dualism of consciousness and nature, with all perceptual apparatus as well as content regarded as part of nature. Consciousness is purely a witness, with no further, thicker relation to that which it beholds. Advaita Vedānta takes a similar view: consciousness has no relation to the modifications of the internal organ other than to be their witness. Mīmāṃsā and Nyāya-Vaiśeṣika philosophers uphold a more integrated position. In Mīmāṃsā (or, more precisely, the Mīmāṃsā of Kumārila and followers), awareness is considered a personal act, creating the quality of 'being-perceived' in an object perceived. Nyāya-Vaiśeṣika thinkers view awareness, perceptual and otherwise, as a quality or attribute of the self, a quality of brief duration, as explained above, and the result of complex causal processes. In philosophy, an awareness may be verbalized in abstraction from the person to whom it belongs, but there are no free-floating awarenesses. Nor are selves conscious except in possessing awarenesses (see AWARENESS IN INDIAN THOUGHT).

3 Epistemology of perception

It is difficult to appreciate classical views on the epistemic value of perception in isolation from fuller epistemological projects where perception is identified as one of several sources of knowledge (see KNOWLEDGE, INDIAN VIEWS OF). The Sanskrit word *pratyakṣa* is normally used with an implication of veridicality; a nonveridical sense experience is not counted as *pratyakṣa*. Westerners are prone to react to this by suspecting classical Indian thinkers of missing crucial issues by presupposing too much in how they understand a term. But it is the translation 'perception' that is a little misleading. The English term 'knowledge' is normally used to imply truth of a belief. If what was considered a bit of knowledge is discovered to be in fact a false belief, then it is said that there was no knowledge in the first place, only a belief that was considered true. The same logic holds for *pratyakṣa*, substituting veridicality for truth and awareness for belief: if what was considered a perceptual awareness is discovered to be in fact nonveridical, then it is said that there was no perception in the first place, only an awareness that was considered veridical.

Little is to be gained in epistemology from semantic reflections. There is, however, a nice tie between the veridicality presupposition in the use of the term *pratyakṣa* and an important point about default justification, fallibility and the burden of proof that is central to much classical Indian epistemology. This is that doubt, like all awareness, has grounds, indeed causal grounds (as is brought out lucidly in later reflection), such as one's inability to discern a distant object that appears, say, to be perhaps a post, perhaps a person. Disagreement can be a cause for doubt, as can other sorts of cognitive tension. In such situations, we are called to look to reliable sources of information to resolve the doubt. But when the conditions for such meaningful doubt do not obtain – regarding sense experience, when conditions for doubting the reality of what we see or otherwise perceive do not obtain – then we proceed, and have every right to proceed, assuming the experience's veridicality. Veridicality is the default assumption. And the defeasibility, or fallibility, of perceptual judgments, contributes to this right, to the default being an assumption of veridicality (along with an assumption of the truth of perceptual judgments). Were we to claim infallibility, or certitude, then the burden of proof would be on our shoulders; that is to say, the conditions for meaningful doubt would be a lot less stringent. Much of this position is worked out by members of the Nyāya school in response to epistemological scepticism advanced by the Buddhist Nāgārjuna and others. But it is also developed by the Yogācāra Buddhist Dharmakīrti and some of his followers.

Perception, *pratyakṣa*, is held to be the fundamental knowledge source, the 'eldest' (*jyeṣṭa*) source, by philosophers belonging to several distinct schools. The Cārvāka sceptic – who, with Nāgārjuna and his school and the later dialectical Advaita Vedānta of Śrīharṣa, is a common target of those with positive epistemological projects – accepts the epistemic value of perception; what the Cārvāka questions is the authority of inference and other putative knowledge sources. Nyāya itself is concerned with inference only in so far as it is to provide knowledge of the world, holding that any correct inference must have a perceptual premise. Moreover, inferential cognitions that are *prima facie* correct can be overridden by perception. This is clearly made out. Less clearly discerned, and often not at all, is the importance of inference to show the nonveridicality of a sense experience. The Dharmakīrti school, however, does propound a combination of coherentism and experiential foundationalism where considerations of coherence are viewed as potential overriders and weighted more heavily than any perceptual judgment (see DHARMAKĪRTI; EPISTEMOLOGY, INDIAN SCHOOLS OF §1).

4 Perception and the world

A perceptual awareness is intentional; that is to say, it has an object or content, namely what it is *of*. But just what types of things is perception capable of revealing, and – because much of perception's epistemic value hangs on the following refinement – just what is it capable of *directly* revealing?

Yogācāra Buddhists, who are nominalists as well as phenomenalists, hold that what perception reveals is invariably unique and particular (see NOMINALISM, BUDDHIST DOCTRINE OF §§1–2). Dharmakīrti develops this stance into a pragmatism about concept-formation, justification and truth, finding inferential relations to hold only on the level of our mental fictions, not among things (or events) themselves. Indian realists, in contrast, paint a much richer picture of what we directly perceive.

To take up a highly contentious example, on the issue of how, according to the realists, an inference-underpinning pervasion, *vyāpti* (every locus of *F* as also a locus of *G*), is known, the view is that universals or class characters (natural kind characters) and relations among them are presented perceptually. To counter such objections as that from knowing the universal we should be acquainted with things strewn throughout all time, realists admit that internal factors are relevant to what in perception we are capable of verbalizing and acting upon. Of course, not everything *F* or *G* is known perceptually; what is known is *F*-hood and *G*-hood and the relation between them. A child may not be able to recognize cowhood in its generality, though the universal is available in the presence of Bessie the family cow; there is a difference between seeing cowhood and seeing it as cowhood (see §6). The realists stress their fallibilism, as well as the training often required to recognize something for what it is. Thus the relation between smokiness and fieriness, for example, may

not be recognized; or we may think we perceive a connection, and a future counter-instance proves us wrong. It is wide experience (*bhūyo-darśana*) of correlations of things *F* and *G* that gives us confidence. Nevertheless, since a pervasion is a natural occurrence, one can be grasped on a single occasion. To use less technical terms, can we not know from a single witnessing that smoke is caused by fire? (Causal relations are important types of pervasion, on the realists' view, but not the only types.)

Other important ontological issues fought over with reference to direct perceptibility are relations (in particular that which the realists find between a property and a property-bearer – there is no such distinction, claim the Buddhists and, for different reasons, the Advaita Vedāntins), absences or negative facts, and the self or awareness itself (see ONTOLOGY IN INDIAN PHILOSOPHY §§1–2, 10–11; NEGATIVE FACTS IN CLASSICAL INDIAN PHILOSOPHY). However, the focus here will be on the debates about the reality of wholes and the very existence of objects independently of consciousness; these stand close to the heart of the Buddhist–realist controversy, where so much of the best of classical Indian argument over perception is to be found.

The Buddhist tradition that the great Dharmakīrti defines, both by summarizing the arguments of his predecessors and by setting the terms of the debate for his followers, finds a chasm between what experience directly presents and conceptual constructions. VASUBANDHU (*c.*400) entertains the possibility of a universal illusion – the world as presented perceptually does not differ from the presentations of a dream – to land in a phenomenalism of event-instants. These presentations (atomic events of colour-shape, of sound, of feeling, and so on) are common to illusions and veridical experiences, common to dreaming and to waking. Wholes are mentally or imaginatively constructed (*kalpanā* is the key term: 'imagination' in classical aesthetics) out of these parts, as are enduring objects. And though important variations among Buddhists appear (whole schools are differentiated by Vasubandhu and others), generally speaking it is a mark of our spiritual ignorance that we take our constructions to be real. The only true difference between dreaming and waking is that between individual and mass delusion, between an imaginative construction or projection due to individual karma (dispositions built from past actions) and projections due to common karma. (Dharmakīrti says the nature of our constructions are due to our desires.)

With this view as background, Buddhists find an easy target in the realist view of wholes (such as in Nyāya), for the claim is not only that a whole, such as a tree, is in itself a reality other than the totality of its parts, but that when we perceive a tree we directly perceive the whole. (How ridiculous! Are the roots then directly perceived?) The deep issue is what counts as basic evidence. The Buddhists maintain that it is the atomic-event presentations common to illusions and veridical experiences. Nyāya philosophers counter that we see wholes, and they do not mean to use a different sense of 'see': we directly perceive wholes; perception of wholes is the basic evidence.

5   Perception and the world (cont.)

The *Nyāyasūtra* (2.1.33–5) presents two nonphenomenological lines of argument to shore up the position (phenomenological appeals, at this point, would beg the question). The first is that the view that we see a part presupposes that we see a whole – a part of what? Moreover, if we see only parts, then presuming a part is a macro object, it must have parts, and so *it* turns out not to be seen. Or if it is partless, it is so minute as to be imperceptible (some Buddhists do admit that, strictly speaking, the event-instants are not consciously perceived). Thus if we cannot see wholes, we can see nothing at all. The second line of argument is that only by assuming a whole can we explain holding and pulling. Only wholes, not parts (at least of some things), can be moved about. The realists also purport to have an answer to the Buddhist argument about a common core to veridical and illusory experiences in their theory of nonveridical awareness (see ERROR AND ILLUSION, INDIAN CONCEPTIONS OF §§1–2). Concerning objects' independence of consciousness, they continually invoke considerations of intersubjectivity and then, in later periods, supplement such arguments with an appeal to parsimony (*lāghavatva*, theoretic 'lightness') as the decisive advantage of their position.

The Buddhists, for their part, seem driven by an idealism that is tied to an understanding of what makes *nirvāṇa* experience possible: if objects were independent of experience, there could be no enlightenment, no consciousness of a single interdependent reality as is taught by the Buddha. On the other hand, Dharmakīrti achieves a pragmatism built on a more moderate view of a fundamental reality, indeed a sophisticated scepticism. That is, what is fundamentally real may be problematic, but as far as our everyday activities are concerned, all we need take to be real is what is capable of satisfying our desires. Our perceptions are to be understood as revealing things that are in this way causally efficient, so long as they cohere with other bits of knowledge.

Backing away from extreme idealist statements would seem an advantage polemically. But the realists get the last word in the debate with the Buddhists, for

Nyāya and Mīmāṃsā as schools outlast Buddhist philosophy in India by several centuries. In the later period, many Buddhist arguments and positions are, however, taken over by Advaita Vedāntins.

Concerning what some call yoga-born perception and the spiritual matters putatively revealed by it, many philosophers addressing the topic do not seem themselves to have been yogins, and the views presented involve only minor extensions of common positions in the psychology of perception. Through yoga and the accumulation of religious merit, the organs of perception are modified, particularly the sense mind (*manas*), such that spiritual matters, or things subtle, remote or normally hidden, are directly perceived. Such speculation is supposed to show how extraordinary perception is possible; given the possibility, an epistemic parallelism between ordinary and extraordinary perception is upheld.

6   Perception and language

A range of views about the relation, or multiple relations, between perception and language-mediated thought – running alongside it, unfolding concepts implicit in it, perverting it, abstracting from it, referring to things revealed by it – occurs in classical Indian schools. We shall begin with a quick look at the panoply of positions and views in an abbreviated and general form.

BHARTṚHARI, an astute grammarian and psychologist of the fifth century, appears to embrace a metaphysics where all awareness would be manifestation of a primordial Word, with several gradations or levels of ideas/language. He more than anyone else is responsible for provoking classical philosophers to suspect that there is no non-language-mediated consciousness. But Patañjali too, the author of the *Yogasūtra* (*c*.400), promotes the view that short of the highest mystic trance, the ultimate liberation and enlightenment, all mentality is shot through with seeds of concepts and speech. As mentioned, it is in Buddhist traditions that we find views of perception as utterly foreign to language: the mind-stream runs alongside perception or alters it so that it is no longer in its language- and concept-free native state. The realists are influenced on this score by their opponents, and the *Nyāyasūtra* pronounces perception to be nonverbal. Nevertheless, as a knowledge source, perception is taken not only to reveal things but to warrant judgments about the things that it reveals. Dharmakīrti himself, though in a hedged and qualified manner, accords perception a similar role. Moreover, it seems all the later philosophers come to recognize that it is only speech behaviour, *vyavahāra*, reflecting experience (presumably), that is of any use in philosophical debate. Universally, the need is felt to be able to account for, or at least take into consideration, common perceptual judgments and a wide range of speech acts.

The fourteenth-century Navya-Nyāya ('New Logic') philosopher GAṄGEŚA (§2) accepts as a first principle of verbalizable awareness – that is, awareness reflected in speech behaviour and useful in our lives – that whatever an awareness is of, namely a qualificandum, is cognized as something or other: anything x is known as some predicate ϕ, a qualifier. But in order to be able to recognize and talk about a qualificandum as ϕ, we have to have a prior awareness of ϕ; otherwise, we would not be able to see or talk about the object as ϕ. Thus it would seem that ϕ has to be cognized as something or other, and an infinite regress of qualification looms. In other words, Gaṅgeśa views even the simplest verbalizable awareness as having an object that is ontologically complex. Such an awareness is *viśiṣṭa*, 'qualified', by which he means that a qualificandum is cognized through a qualifier. Thus in order to avoid an infinite regress of qualification (the qualifier$_1$ of qualificandum$_1$ as itself a qualificandum, qualificandum$_2$, to be known through another qualifier, qualifier$_2$, *ad infinitum*), Gaṅgeśa posits indeterminate awareness, where qualifiers are directly cognized. To cognize Bessie as a cow presupposes acquaintance with cowhood, that is, awareness of the ground for application of the term 'cow'. Thus there appears a danger of an infinite regress: *how* is the qualifier cognized? And so qualifiers such as cowhood must be directly available – in what Gaṅgeśa calls, borrowing a Buddhist term, indeterminate (or non-propositional) awareness, which may be considered as a first phase of the causal process that results in a determinate, verbalizable awareness. Thus, in sum, there are two phases of sense perception according to New Logic, an indeterminate one where qualifiers are directly grasped in an immediate and nonverbalizable way, followed by determinate perception, which is propositional in content and verbalizable in terms that capture a fact perceived (that is, given that the perception is veridical).

Seeing cowhood and seeing it *as* cowhood are not the same. The ground for recognizing the universal would be 'cowhoodness', which is, according to Gaṅgeśa's followers, not an additional real. But here we threaten to pass into ontological and logical matters that occupy the latest of the New Logicians, and to exceed the confines of our charge.

See also: BUDDHISM, YOGĀCĀRA SCHOOL OF §§3–8; MĪMĀṂSĀ §2; MIND, INDIAN PHILOSOPHY OF; PERCEPTION

References and further reading

Bhattacharya, G. (trans.) (1976) *Tarkasaṃgrahadīpikā on Tarkasaṃgraha by Annaṃbhaṭṭa*, Calcutta: Progressive Publishers. (Lucid presentation of Nyāya views related to perception – through the vehicle of translation and explanation of a Nyāya textbook.)

Bhattacharyya, S. (1993) *Gaṅgeśa's Theory of Indeterminate Perception*, New Delhi: Indian Council of Philosophical Research. (Translates Gaṅgeśa on indeterminate awareness.)

Dasgupta, S. (1922) *A History of Indian Philosophy*, vol. 1, Cambridge: Cambridge University Press, repr. 1969. (Remains probably the best overall introduction to classical Indian systems.)

Dignāga (c.500) *Pramāṇasamuccaya* (Collected Writings on the Acquisition of Knowledge), ch. 1 trans. Masaaki Hattori, *Dignāga, On Perception*, Cambridge, MA: Harvard University Press, 1968. (Dignāga is the most important Yogācāra Buddhist philosopher except for Dharmakārti, who saw himself as Dignāga's follower.)

Matilal, B.K. (1986) *Perception: An Essay on Classical Indian Theories of Knowledge*, Oxford: Oxford University Press. (A modern classic by a premier scholar and philosopher.)

Mukhopadhyay, P.K. (1984) *Indian Realism*, Calcutta: K.P. Bagchi. (A modern defence of the spirit – and often the letter as well – of Nyāya realism.)

* *Nyāyasūtra* (c.150), trans. M. Gangopadhyay, *Nyāyasūtra with Vātsyāyana's Commentary*, Calcutta: Indian Studies, 1982. (A readable and accurate translation.)

Sinha, J. (1969) *Indian Epistemology of Perception*, Calcutta: Sinha Publishing. (Probably too difficult for those unfamiliar with Sanskrit philosophical terminology, but a storehouse of information and astute commentary on classical views.)

Warder, A.K. (1970) *Indian Buddhism*, Delhi: Motilal Banarsidass, 2nd edn, 1980. (A classic historical study.)

STEPHEN H. PHILLIPS

SENSE-DATA

A philosophical theory of perception must accommodate this obvious fact: when someone perceives, or seems to perceive something, how things appear may differ from how they are. A circular coin tilted will look elliptical. A stick partially immersed in water will look bent. Noting that appearance and reality do not always coincide, some philosophers have given the following account of the contrast between the two. Suppose someone seems to see a book with a red cover. Whether or not there is any book to be seen, the individual seeming to see the red book will be aware of something red. What they are aware of is called a sense-datum. According to a sense-datum theory, any perceptual experience involves awareness of a sense-datum whether or not it is an experience of a physical object.

Some philosophers link a sense-datum theory with certain views about knowledge. According to foundationalists all knowledge of the external world must rest on a foundation of beliefs that are beyond doubt. We can always be mistaken about what physical objects are like. On the other hand, we cannot be mistaken about what sense-data are like. So, all knowledge about the external world rests on beliefs about sense-data. In this way a sense-datum theory is supposed to do double duty in contributing towards an account of perception, and an account of knowledge based on perception.

1 **Sense-datum theories**
2 **Arguments for the existence of sense-data**
3 **The relation between sense-data and physical objects**
4 **Objections to sense-data**

1 Sense-datum theories

The term 'sense-datum' was coined early this century by Bertrand Russell. However, sense-datum accounts of perception go back much further. When Locke, Berkeley and Hume refer to ideas of sense, sensible qualities or impressions of sense frequently they appear to be referring to what we would now call sense-data.

In this century early advocates of sense-data intended the term 'sense-datum' to be neutral. Philosophers adopting opposed views about perception were supposed to be able to agree that any case of perceiving involves an awareness of sense-data, even if they then disagreed about what sense-data actually are and how they relate to the physical. A sense-datum may be a physical object, or it may be non-physical; it may exist only when perceived, or exist unperceived; it may be an event, or belong to some other category; it may be perceivable by only one individual, or more than one. But, however these issues are resolved, it is said to be undeniable that I am aware of a circular gold sense-datum. In this way sense-data, understood neutrally, are supposed to provide the foundation on which to erect competing theories of perception.

Sense-data are supposed to explain how perceptual experiences can fail to match reality. The book appears red even though it is some other colour.

How can this be? Because the individual looking at it is aware of a red sense-datum. The coin appears elliptical even though it is circular: the individual looking at it is aware of an elliptical sense-datum. Sense-data, it is said, are what one is aware of in virtue of having perceptual experiences.

Call a perceptual experience veridical just in case in having it one seems to perceive an object with those qualities. I have a perceptual experience as of seeing a grey surface. My experience is veridical because I am seeing a grey surface. Now consider someone who is having a non-veridical experience. Consider the alcoholic who has an experience as of seeing a pink rat. According to the sense-datum theorist, even if not seeing a pink rat, the alcoholic is having an experience as of seeing something pink because they are aware of something pink. The alcoholic is aware of a pink sense-datum. Hence, sense-datum theorists are committed to:

(i) Every perceptual experience involves an awareness of a sense-datum.

G.E. Moore once toyed with the idea that a sense-datum can appear to have characteristics it lacks. However, allowing that sense-data may not be as they appear undermines a central role that sense-data are supposed to play in perception. Sense-data are appealed to, in part, to explain how the apparent characteristics of a physical object can differ from its actual characteristics. That explanation would be undermined if the apparent characteristics of a sense-datum could, likewise, differ from its actual characteristics. For that reason, sense-datum theorists are also committed to:

(ii) At least for a certain range of characteristics, it is impossible for a sense-datum to appear to have a characteristic that it lacks.

A physical object can appear red or round without being red or round. A sense-datum cannot appear red or round without being red or round.

Apart from (i) and (ii) other features have commonly been attributed to sense-data. Some say that sense-data are private: it is metaphysically impossible for more than one individual to be aware of the same sense-datum. Some say that sense-data are transient: it is metaphysically impossible for one sense-datum to be perceived discontinuously. Some say that sense-data are self intimating: for a restricted range of characteristics, a sense-datum must appear to have any characteristic that it has. These features, privacy, transience, mind dependence, and self intimation are optional in the following sense. Lacking any of the features in question will not disqualify sense-data from playing a role in the theory of perception.

A.J. Ayer proposed an unorthodox interpretation

of sense-datum theories. His interpretation has become known as the alternative language view. Ayer accepts that a sense-datum theory is not open to empirical confirmation or disconfirmation. Since that is so, he is reluctant to treat a sense-datum theory as a theory about the existence of a special class of entities called sense-data. Instead, he views advocacy of a sense-datum theory as a recommendation to use language in a particular way. Consider again the coin that first appears circular to Jayne, then elliptical. She could describe the perceptual facts by saying that she was aware first of a circular sense-datum, then of an elliptical sense-datum. Alternatively, she could describe them by saying that the coin she perceived changes from being circular to being elliptical. Which description is correct? In Ayer's view neither. Which description Jayne selects, the sense-datum description or the one that has implausible implications about the stability of objects, is simply a matter of convenience.

2   Arguments for the existence of sense-data

I will use 'sense-datum' to refer to things that, at least, satisfy (i) and (ii). What reason is there to think that there are sense-data? Many arguments have been offered, but all depend on contestable assumptions that are rarely defended in the literature.

The perception of parts argument One cannot perceive an object unless one perceived every part of it. Whenever one looks at a physical object one does not perceive every part of it. So, whenever one looks at a physical object, one perceived something distinct from it: a sense-datum. This argument is only as plausible as its first premise, which to many people does not seem plausible at all.

The certainty argument Suppose one takes oneself to see a tomato. One cannot be certain that one is seeing a tomato. Nevertheless, one can be certain that one is seeing something that looks red, round and bulgy. So, the red-, round- and bulgy-looking thing one is certain of seeing is not the tomato, or any part of it. It is a sense-datum.

This argument depends on three assumptions. First, it is assumed that, in the case of seeing the tomato, one cannot be certain that a tomato exists. Second, it is assumed that one can be certain that a red-, round-, and bulgy-looking thing exists. Finally, it is assumed that if I am certain that a red-, round- bulgy-looking thing exists but uncertain that a tomato exists, then the red-, round- bulgy-looking thing is not the tomato. In general, however, it does not follow from someone being certain that **a** exists, and uncertain that **b** exists, that **a** is not identical with **b**.

The causal argument Perception involves a causal chain extending from a physical object to a perceiver.

What is really perceived is only what is at the end point of the causal chain: a sense-datum. This argument depends upon the unwarranted assumption that only the end point of a causal process which enables one to see something can be perceived.

The time lag argument When someone perceives a very distant object, for example a star, light takes a long time to reach their perceptual apparatus. Because it does so, the star may have ceased to exist by the time the silvery speck taken to be the star is perceived. Hence, the silvery speck is not identical with the star. It is a sense-datum. This argument depends upon the assumption that nothing can be perceived unless it exists at the same time that it is perceived.

The argument from analysis Any case of veridical or non-veridical perception involves having a perceptual experience and, it is agreed, having a perceptual experience is best analysed as awareness of an object. The object in question is a sense-datum.

Why should we think that having a perceptual experience is best analysed as awareness of an object? Suppose someone sees a red after-image against a white wall. Surely that individual is aware of *something* red which is both an after-image and sense-datum. After all, there seems to be something, an after-image, obscuring part of the wall in much the way that a physical red patch would do.

Or consider the following three cases. In the first someone is looking at some yellow curtains through blue tinted spectacles. In the second someone is looking at the same curtains without anything impeding or distorting that person's vision. In the third someone is hallucinating a yellow surface without seeing any physical surface with that colour. The second and third cases share something is common which they do not share in common with the first. In the first someone in aware of some yellow curtains without being aware of their colour. In the second and third someone is aware of the colour, yellow, which is in fact the colour of the curtains. How can someone be aware of the colour of the curtains in the third case, unless they are aware of *something*, a sense-datum, with that colour?

The problem with the argument from analysis is that it relies on the sense-datum theorist's analysis of having a perceptual experience being superior to any other. However, alternative analyses have been defended in the literature. One implies that perceptual experiences invariably have objects, but treats the objects of perceptual experiences as intentional (see INTENTIONALITY). Another treats perceptual experiences as dispositions to believe (see PERCEPTION). According to a third, the adverbial analysis (see MENTAL STATES, ADVERBIAL THEORY OF), perceptual experiences need not have objects. For example, if it is said that someone is experiencing a red after-image, the expression 'red' is used to specify how the person is experiencing rather than a quality of an experienced object.

Frank Jackson has recently argued for the superiority of a sense-datum analysis over these competitors. For example, he argues that an analysis of perception in terms of sense-data can, in contrast to an adverbial analysis, explain the validity of certain incontestably valid arguments concerning appearances.

3 The relationship between sense-data and physical objects

Direct realists (see PERCEPTION §4) hold that in perception one is often directly or immediately aware of the surfaces of physical objects. The famous argument from illusion has been used to refute direct realism and is said to show that sense-data are never identical with the surfaces of physical objects. Suppose Jayne looks at the same surface of a coin over an interval of time during which it is rotated. At first the coin looks circular. Later it looks elliptical. Since the coin does not change shape, the elliptical items that Jayne is later aware of are, presumably, not identical with the surface of the coin. As the coin rotates Jayne is aware of a series of things. The first member is circular, and the last elliptical. It is implausible to maintain that the first member of the series is a physical surface, and the later elliptical members things of a totally different kind. We should allow that, as the coin rotates, all of the differently shaped things Jayne perceives are sense-data. In general, one immediately perceives only sense-data whenever one perceives a physical object.

What is the relationship between immediately perceived sense-data and physical objects? According to representative realists, sense-data interpose between the physical world and the perceiver's awareness of it and represent physical objects to the perceiver in virtue of standing in an appropriate relation, usually though of as causal, to those objects (see PERCEPTION §2). According to one version of idealism physical objects are collections of mind dependent sense-data (see IDEALISM §2). According to one version of phenomenalism statements about physical objects are analyzable as statements about the sense-data one would have if one were suitably located (see PHENOMENALISM).

It should be noted that, of the above views about the relationship between sense-data and physical objects, only representative realism requires reference to sense-data for its formulation. There are versions of idealism and phenomenalism that make no mention of sense-data. On the other hand, any version of representative realism will have to incorporate reference to sense-data.

4 Objections to sense-data

A multitude of objections have been raised against sense-data, to which, naturally, sense-datum theorists have replies.

The individuation objection When I see something am I aware of a single visual sense-datum, or a number of sense-data? How can I tell whether I am aware of the same sense-data at different times? These questions, it is said, are unanswerable since we lack criteria for the identity of sense-data.

This objection presupposes that lack of precise criteria for individuating sense-data constitutes an objection to their existence. However, we lack precise criteria for individuating many things we believe in such as persons or ships.

The private language objection If sense-data exist, we can refer to them. Sense-data are essentially private objects. Hence, sense-data can only be referred to using a private language. However, it is agreed, private languages are impossible (see PRIVATE LANGUAGE ARGUMENT). This objection presupposes that sense-data must be private, and, more dubiously, that one cannot refer to private objects using a public language.

The intelligibility objection For a sense-datum theory to be intelligible certain distinctions have to be grasped such as the distinction between sense-data and material objects, or the distinction between direct and indirect perception. However, these distinctions are not really intelligible when they are applied as the sense-datum theorist wishes to apply them. For example, it only makes sense to say that something is directly perceived if it is possible to indirectly perceive it. According to the sense-datum theorist, a sense-datum can only ever be directly perceived.

This objection appears to rest on much disputed theses about the nature of language, and in particular on the thesis that an expression only meaningfully applies to something if there could be a thing of the same kind to which the expression does not apply.

The indeterminacy objection If something exists it must be determinate in the sense that, for any property, it either has or lacks that property. But sense-data are not determinate. I see a hen which appears to have a certain number of speckles. Despite that, for any number of speckles, the hen does not appear to have that number of speckles. So, the sense-datum I am aware of when I see the hen is speckled without having any particular number of speckles. It is indeterminate.

This objection assumes that, not only must a sense-datum be as it appears, but a sense-datum must appear in every respect as it is. Unless this is so, the sense-datum of the speckled hen may, like the hen itself, have a determinate number of speckles without appearing to have that number of speckles.

See also: FOUNDATIONALISM; PERCEPTION, EPISTEMIC ISSUES IN §5

References and further reading

Armstrong, D.M. (1961) *Perception and the Physical World*, London: Routledge & Kegan Paul. (A critique of sense datum theories combined with an alternative analysis of perception in terms of the acquisition of belief.)

Austin, J.L. (1962) *Sense and Sensibilia*, Oxford: Oxford University Press. (A sustained attack on sense datum theories.)

* Ayer, A.J. (1964) *The Foundations of Empirical Knowledge*, London: Macmillan. (An exposition and defence of Ayer's alternative language view.)

* Jackson, F. (1977) *Perception: A Representative Theory*, Cambridge: Cambridge University Press. (An ingenious defence of a sense datum analysis of perception in the context of defending a representative theory of perception.)

* Price, H.H. (1932) *Perception*, London: Methuen. (A classic and detailed exposition of a sense datum theory.)

Sprigge, T.L.S. (1970) *Facts, Words, and Beliefs*, London: Routledge & Kegan Paul. (Chapter I contains an excellent response to the objections raised to sense data by Austin and others.)

Swartz, R.J., ed. (1965) *Perceiving, Sensing, and Knowing*, New York: Doubleday. (A collection on perception which includes an excellent selection of pieces on sense data in section II entitled Sensing, Sense Data, and Appearing.)

ANDRÉ GALLOIS

SENTENCES *see* PROPOSITIONS, SENTENCES AND STATEMENTS

SEQUENTS/SEQUENT CALCULI *see* NATURAL DEDUCTION, TABLEAU AND SEQUENT SYSTEMS

SERGEANT, JOHN (1623–1704)

John Sergeant was the last of the Blackloists – the faction of English Catholics who followed the thought of Thomas White in the middle decades of the seventeenth century. As such his major philosophical concern was with a refutation of scepticism, and to that end he adopted a synthesis of Aristotelianism and aspects of the new philosophy. Sergeant is now best remembered as the main Catholic protagonist in the theological 'rule of faith' debates, when he engaged with such eminent Anglicans as Tillotson and Stillingfleet to argue the cause of religious certainty, attainable only through Catholic tradition. Turning later to the need for certainty in philosophy and science, he formulated his own 'solid philosophy': within an essentially Aristotelian framework, he incorporated aspects of the new thought that had been earlier adopted by Thomas White and Kenelm Digby.

John Sergeant's conversion to Catholicism took place after his graduation from St John's College, Cambridge, in 1643. Having then spent some twelve years at the English Catholic College at Lisbon, he returned to England in 1655, and acted as Secretary to the English Catholic Chapter during the height of its Blackloist influence, until 1667. His reputation as a disciple of the discredited Thomas WHITE, and his own incrimination in the 'Popish Plot', have resulted in long historical neglect. He remains, however, not only of theological importance, but also of considerable philosophical interest. In particular, his two late works, *The Method to Science* (1696) and *Solid Philosophy Asserted* (1697), are significant as purporting to provide the means for a last-ditch defence against encroaching scepticism.

Sergeant is essentially a late Aristotelian, and he specifically opposes such proponents of new thought as DESCARTES and LOCKE. The trouble with these 'ideists' is that they reduce our ideas or conceptions to mere representations or similitudes. We are then left without criteria for distinguishing which similitudes are true and which false, and we are reduced to predicating reality only of the contents of our own minds; and this is to be reduced to scepticism. The remedy is to ground one's knowledge in empiricism: simple notions are to be assumed, which leave bodies and enter through our sense-organs into our minds. Such notions are actual physical entities, actual parts of the original body; so that our apprehension of them is incontrovertible, inasmuch as they do not *represent* the external object, but actually *are* a part of that object.

With notions thus conceived as sense-data, with respect to which there is no room for misunderstanding, some solid foundation has been laid for the acquisition of certain knowledge. Admittedly, there is room for subsequent misunderstanding, as cognition consists in linking together those notions in an orderly way, such that there is 'conformity of the understanding to the thing'; but, by taking care to avoid misunderstanding and linguistic ambiguities, we may proceed to certain knowledge. Whereas 'ideists' ground their philosophical work on abstractions which have a dubious relationship with the object they purport to represent, Sergeant claims that his own empirically-based philosophy is founded on direct knowledge of 'things themselves'. From that secure starting-point, further knowledge can be attained by means of traditional Aristotelian syllogistic reasoning.

Sergeant's position, then, is derived in part from Aristotle, for whom direct apprehension of external objects gave clear though necessarily limited knowledge, and for whom syllogistic reasoning provided the subsequent path to truth. But Sergeant is indebted also to his Blackloist friends Thomas White and Kenelm DIGBY, who had earlier adopted a 'mechanical' theory of perception, in terms of which material particles were directly received by our sense-organs, having emanated from bodies in an imperceptible but material 'effluvium'.

Sergeant's philosophy is ultimately underpinned by his theology. In this his prime concern is with asserting the necessity of Catholic tradition to ensure certainty, but he also reveals the religious foundations of his assumed philosophical certainties. Thus, the self-evident propositions on which his logic is to be based are themselves derived from a deity who justifies the most supremely self-evident proposition that 'self-existence is self-existence'. Without God's self-existence, the whole of logic itself might be suspect; and without belief in a God who created an orderly nature, our assumption of a correlation between our logical theories and the natural world would be further undermined. 'An atheist can have no perfectly certain knowledge or evidence of anything'; and such a sceptical outcome has by all means to be resisted.

See also: ARISTOTELIANISM IN THE 17TH CENTURY

List of works

Sergeant, J. (1665) *Sure-footing in Christianity*, London. (Sergeant's first major contribution to the 'rule of faith' debate, in which he argues in favour of Catholic tradition.)
—— (1667) *Faith Vindicated from Possibility of Falsehood*, Louvain. (An assertion of the 'firmness and certainty' of Catholic faith.)
—— (1696) *The Method to Science*, London. (A spirited attempt to refute scepticism by establishing grounds for philosophical certainty.)
—— (1697) *Solid Philosophy Asserted against the Fancies of the Ideists*, London; repr. New York: Garland, 1984. (An anti-sceptical treatise, which includes in particular a criticism of Locke's *Essay*.)
—— (1698) *Non Ultra: or a Letter to a learned Cartesian*, London. (A criticism of Cartesian claims for certainty, and a recommendation of syllogistic reasoning.)

References and further reading

Bradish, N.C. (1929) 'John Sergeant: a forgotten critic of Descartes and Locke', *Monist* 39: 571–628. (An early attempt to resuscitate Sergeant as a critic of canonical philosophers.)
Cooney, B. (1973) 'John Sergeant's criticism of Locke's theory of ideas', *Modern Schoolman* 50: 143–58. (Discusses relationship of Sergeant's anti-Lockean epistemology with his theory of mind–body interaction.)
Krook, D. (1993) *John Sergeant and his Circle: A Study of Three Seventeenth Century English Aristotelians*, ed. and intro. B.C. Southgate, Leiden: E.J. Brill. (Analyses Sergeant's philosophy as essentially Aristotelian; includes bibliography.)
Phemister, P. (1993) 'Locke, Sergeant, and Scientific Method', in T. Sorell (ed.) *The Rise of Modern Philosophy: The Tension between the New and Traditional Philosophies from Machiavelli to Leibniz*, Oxford: Clarendon Press. (Compares Sergeant with Locke in relation to scientific method.)
Southgate, B.C. (1998) '"Beating down scepticism": the solid philosophy of John Sergeant, 1623–1707', in M.A. Stewart (ed.) *English Philosophy in the Age of Locke*, Oxford: Clarendon Press. (Outlines Sergeant's anti-sceptical philosophy and argues for Blackloist influence.)

BEVERLEY SOUTHGATE

SERRES, MICHEL *see* FRENCH PHILOSOPHY OF SCIENCE (§7)

SET THEORETIC PARADOXES *see* PARADOXES OF SET AND PROPERTY

SET THEORY

*In the late nineteenth century, Georg Cantor created mathematical theories, first of sets or aggregates of real numbers (or linear points), and later of sets or aggregates of arbitrary elements. The relationship of element a to set A is written $a \in A$; it is to be distinguished from the relationship of subset B to set A, which holds if every element of B is also an element of A, and which is written $B \subseteq A$. Cantor is most famous for his theory of transfinite cardinals, or numbers of elements in infinite sets. A subset of an infinite set may have the same number of elements as the set itself, and Cantor proved that the sets of natural and rational numbers have the same number of elements, which he called $\aleph_0$; also that the sets of real and complex numbers have the same number of elements, which he called **c**. Cantor proved $\aleph_0$ to be less than **c**. He conjectured that no set has a number of elements strictly between these two.*

In the early twentieth century, in response to criticism of set theory, Ernst Zermelo undertook its axiomatization; and, with amendments by Abraham Fraenkel, his have been the accepted axioms ever since. These axioms help distinguish the notion of a set, which is too basic to admit of informative definition, from other notions of a one made up of many that have been considered in logic and philosophy. Properties having exactly the same particulars as instances need not be identical, whereas sets having exactly the same elements are identical by the axiom of extensionality. Hence for any condition Φ there is at most one set $\{x|\Phi(x)\}$ whose elements are all and only those x such that $\Phi(x)$ holds, and $\{x|\Phi(x)\} = \{x|\Psi(x)\}$ if and only if conditions Φ and Ψ hold of exactly the same x. It cannot consistently be assumed that $\{x|\Phi(x)\}$ exists for every condition Φ. Inversely, the existence of a set is not assumed to depend on the possibility of defining it by some condition Φ as $\{x|\Phi(x)\}$.

One set x_0 may be an element of another set x_1 which is an element of x_2 and so on, $x_0 \in x_1 \in x_2 \in \ldots$, but the reverse situation, $\ldots \in y_2 \in y_1 \in y_0$, may not occur, by the axiom of foundation. It follows that no set is an element of itself and that there can be no universal set $y = \{x|x = x\}$. Whereas a part of a part of a whole is a part of that whole, an element of an element of a set need not be an element of that set.

Modern mathematics has been greatly influenced by set theory, and philosophies rejecting the latter must therefore reject much of the former. Many set-theoretic notations and terminologies are encountered even outside mathematics, as in parts of philosophy:

pair	$\{a,b\}$	$\{x|x = a \text{ or } x = b\}$
singleton	$\{a\}$	$\{x|x = a\}$
empty set	$\emptyset$	$\{x|x \neq x\}$
union	$\cup X$	$\{a|a \in A \text{ for some } A \in X\}$
binary union	$A \cup B$	$\{a|a \in A \text{ or } a \in B\}$
intersection	$\cap X$	$\{a|a \in A \text{ for all } A \in X\}$
binary intersection	$A \cap B$	$\{a|a \in A \text{ and } a \in B\}$
difference	$A - B$	$\{a|a \in A \text{ and not } a \in B\}$
complement	$A - B$	
power set	$\wp(A)$	$\{B|B \subseteq A\}$

(In contexts where only subsets of A are being considered, $A - B$ may be written $-B$ and called the complement of B.)

While the accepted axioms suffice as a basis for the development not only of set theory itself, but of modern mathematics generally, they leave some questions about transfinite cardinals unanswered. The status of such questions remains a topic of logical research and philosophical controversy.

1   **The axioms of set theory**
2   **Ordinal numbers and ordinal arithmetic**
3   **Cardinal numbers and cardinal arithmetic**
4   **Combinatorial set theory**
5   **Point sets**
6   **New axioms for set theory: large cardinals and determinacy**
7   **Models of set theory**

1   The axioms of set theory

The axiom of *extensionality* states that sets having exactly the same elements are identical. The axiom of *foundation* states that there is no infinite descending sequence of sets $\ldots \in x_2 \in x_1 \in x_0$. The basic Zermelo–Fraenkel axioms (ZF; see ZERMELO 1908) consist of the axioms of extensionality and foundation and existence axioms stated below. The accepted axioms ZFC consist of ZF plus the axiom of choice (AC): given a partition or set x of sets that are nonempty (each has at least one element) and disjoint (no two have a common element), there exists a choice set y having exactly one element in common with each element of x.

The intuition behind the axioms is that sets lie in a

hierarchy of levels (see SET THEORY, DIFFERENT SYSTEMS OF §5), and when $x \in y$, then x lies below and y, above. At the lowest level there is just $\emptyset$ (though a variant of the standard notion allows at this level 'individuals' or items that have no elements and are not sets but may be elements of sets of any level). There is no highest level (though a variant allows a top level of 'classes' or items that may have sets of any level as elements but are not themselves sets nor elements of anything). If set x lies at one level then the 'successor' of x, $x^{\#} = x \cup \{x\}$ lies at the next higher level. The levels continue into the infinite, so that above $\emptyset$, $\emptyset^{\#} = \{\emptyset\}$, $\emptyset^{\#\#} = \{\emptyset, \{\emptyset\}\}$, ... lies the set $\{\emptyset, \{\emptyset\}, \{\emptyset, \{\emptyset\}\}, ...\}$, whose existence is asserted by the axiom of *infinity*. The hierarchy is supposed to be as 'tall' and as 'wide' as possible, an intuition (only) partly expressed by the remaining existence axioms. These consist of axioms asserting the existence of the pair, union and power sets, along with infinitely many further axioms of each of two kinds. First, for any condition $\Phi(x)$ there is an axiom asserting that, for any set u, *separation* from u of those elements x for which $\Phi(x)$ holds forms a set:

$$\{x \in u | \Phi(x)\} = \{x | x \in u \text{ and } \Phi(x)\}$$

Second, for any binary condition Ψ there is an axiom asserting that if for every x there is a unique $y = \psi(x)$ such that $\Psi(x,y)$ holds, then for any set u, *replacement* of each element x of u by $\psi(x)$ forms a set:

$$\{\psi(x) | x \in u\} = \{y | \Psi(x,y) \text{ for some } x \in u\}$$

(In a rigorous formalization, the vague, intuitive notion of 'condition' would be explained in terms of a precise, logical notion of a 'formula' of a symbolic language.)

To develop mathematics on the basis of these axioms, for each system of numbers, points or other mathematical objects, a system of set-theoretic objects must be specified to serve as substitutes. Usually the system of set-theoretic substitutes is easy to specify intuitively, in terms of the relationship of the substitutes to the original objects, but it may be less easy to define formally, in terms taken only from the language of set theory. Set-theoretic counterparts to the basic operations on the original objects must also be defined in the language of set theory, and the counterparts of the basic laws for these operations deduced from the axioms of set theory. When this is done, the set-theoretic substitutes are thereafter called by the name of the mathematical objects in question, which are said to have been 'identified with' their set-theoretic substitutes.

No more can be done here than to describe intuitively for the natural, integral, rational, real and complex numbers the related sets with which

these numbers are identified. First, each natural number $n \in \mathbb{N}$ is identified with the *set* of natural numbers less than n, so that $0 = \emptyset$, $1 = \{0\} = \{\emptyset\}$, $2 = \{0,1\} = \{\emptyset, \{\emptyset\}\}$, and so on; and $\mathbb{N}$ itself with the set whose existence is asserted by the axiom of infinity (above). For other kinds of numbers, one needs the identification of the ordered pair (a,b) of a,b with the set $\{\{a\}, \{a,b\}\}$, which allows one to define

$$A \oplus B = \{(0,a) | a \in A\} \cup \{(1,b) | b \in B\}$$
$$A \otimes B = \{(a,b) | a \in A \text{ and } b \in B\}$$
$$B^A = \{F \subseteq A \otimes B | \text{ for all } a \in A \text{ there is}$$
$$\text{a unique } b \in B \text{ with } (a,b) \in F\}$$
$$\text{dom}(F) = \{a | (a,b) \in F \text{ for some } b\}$$
$$\text{ran}(F) = \{b | (a,b) \in F \text{ for some } a\}$$
$$F \upharpoonright C = \{(a,b) \in F | a \in C\}$$
$$F[C] = \{b | (a,b) \in F \text{ for some } a \in C\}$$
$$F^{-1}[C] = \{a | (a,b) \in F \text{ for some } a \in C\}$$

and to define a relation on A or a function from A to B to be a subset of $A \otimes A$ or an element of B^A, respectively, so that, intuitively, a relation R or function F is identified with the set of pairs (a,b) such that aRb or $F(a) = b$. (Then the notions $\text{dom}(F)$, $\text{ran}(F)$, $F \upharpoonright C$, $F[C]$ and $F^{-1}[C]$ agree with certain customary notions from mathematical analysis, where they are called the 'domain' (or set of arguments), 'range' (or set of values), 'restriction', 'image' and 'pre-image'.)

Now an integer w can be identified with the set of pairs of naturals whose difference is w; a rational x with the set of pairs of integers whose quotient is x; a real y with the set of rationals $x < y$ or, alternatively, with the set of functions f from naturals to rationals such that $f(x)$ for larger and larger x gives a better and better approximation to y; and a complex z with the ordered pair of its real and imaginary parts (each a real number). Ultimately any hypothesis that can be stated in conventional mathematical language can be stated in the language of set theory, and any theorem provable by conventional mathematical methods can be proved from the axioms ZF, with AC, or one of its many known implications, such as 'dependent choice' (DC), being needed in certain branches of higher mathematics. (DC asserts that if R is a relation on A such that for every $a \in A$ there exists at least one $b \in A$ with aRb, then there exists a function F from $\mathbb{N}$ to A with $F(n)RF(n+1)$ for all $n \in \mathbb{N}$.)

2 Ordinal numbers and ordinal arithmetic

One equivalent of AC that is widely used in mathematics is called 'Zorn's lemma'. A 'partial order' on a set A is a relation R such that for all $a, b, c \in A$ one has

aRa	(reflexivity)
If aRb and bRa then $a = b$	(antisymmetry)
If aRb and bRc then aRc	(transitivity).

R is an 'order' (also called a 'total order' or 'linear order') on a given $C \subseteq A$ if for any $a, b \in C$ either aRb or bRa (dichotomy). If R is an order on (all of) A, one often writes ' $\leqslant$ ' ('less than or equal to') for R, and uses the common notations and terminology ' $<$ ', ' $\geqslant$ ', ' $>$ ' and so on in the usual way. Even if R is only a partial order on A, one can use such notions as that of an 'upper bound' d for $C \subseteq A$ (cRd for all $c \in C$), but one must be careful to distinguish the notion of a 'maximum' element ($d \in C$ such that cRd for all $c \in C$) from that of a 'maximal' element ($d \in C$ such that, for any $c \in C$, dRc implies $c = d$), and similarly for 'minimum' and 'minimal'.

Zorn's lemma states that if R is a partial order on A and every $C \subseteq A$ on which R is a total order has an upper bound, then A has a maximal element.

The equivalent of AC most widely used in set theory is the 'well-ordering' principle, which asserts that every set can be well-ordered. A 'well-order' on a set A is a total order which also has the property that every non-empty subset of A has a minimum element (groundedness).

Cantor introduced two kinds of transfinite numbers: cardinal and ordinal. The cardinal (number) of a set is concerned only with the 'size' of the set; an ordinal also with the relationship of its elements. To define an ordinal, we must first define isomorphism. A function $F : A \to B$ is a 'bijection' (that is, a one-one, onto mapping) if for every $b \in B$ there is exactly one $a \in A$ with $F(a) = b$. Given (total) orders R, S on sets A, B, a function $F : A \to B$ 'preserves order' if for any $a, a' \in A$ one has aRa' if and only if $F(a)SF(a')$. An 'isomorphism' is a bijection that preserves order. The 'order type' of an order R is written $|R|$. $|R| = |S|$ if there is an isomorphism from R to S, and $|R| \leqslant |S|$ if there is an isomorphism from R either to S or to an initial sub-order of S, $S_b = S \lceil B_b$. An 'initial sub-order' is the order on the 'initial subset' $B_b = \{b' \in B | b'Sb \text{ and } b' \neq b\}$, for some $b \in B$. An 'ordinal' is the order type of a well-order.

If ρ is the ordinal of a well-order on a set of cardinality α, then ρ will also be said to be of cardinality α. By the well-ordering principle, every cardinal is that of some ordinal; and it follows from the definitions that if ordinals ρ, Σ are of cardinality α, β and $\rho \leqslant \Sigma$, then $\alpha \leqslant \beta$. (To avoid confusion arising from the traditional use of the same notations for both cardinal and ordinal numbers, we will use the letters α, β, γ for cardinals, and ρ, Σ, τ for ordinals.)

Cantor proved that the order on the ordinals (defined above) is a well-order. Hence there is a least or zero ordinal. For every ordinal ρ there exists a greater ordinal and hence, again by the definition of a well-order, a *least* greater ordinal, called its successor, $\rho^{\#}$. For every set T of ordinals there is an ordinal greater than or equal to each of its elements, hence a least such ordinal, called its 'supremum', $\sup T$. (Note this implies that there can be no set of all ordinals.) A 'limit' (ordinal) is one that is neither zero nor a successor.

The ordinals 0, $1 = 0^{\#}$, $2 = 1^{\#}, \ldots$ less than the least limit are called 'finite', and the least limit $\sup\{0, 1, 2, \ldots\}$, the ordinal of the natural order on the natural numbers, is called ω_0 or simply ω. It follows from the definitions that if Σ is the ordinal of a well-order S on a set B, then there is an isomorphism F from S to the order on the set $\{\rho | \rho < \Sigma\}$ of ordinals less than Σ (namely, $F(b) = |S_b|$ for $b \in B$). It is now customary to identify the ordinal Σ with this set of lesser ordinals (generalizing what was done in the case of finite ordinals – natural numbers – in §1). With this identification, it is easy to describe explicitly $\rho^{\#}$ and $\sup T$: they are just $\rho \cup \{\rho\}$ and $\cup T$, respectively. Thus

$$\omega^{\#} = \{0, 1, 2, \ldots, \omega\}$$
$$\omega^{\#\#} = \{0, 1, 2, \ldots, \omega, \omega^{\#}\}$$

and so on; and the next limit is

$$\omega^{\dagger} = \{0, 1, 2, \ldots, \omega, \omega^{\#}, \omega^{\#\#}, \ldots\}.$$

Addition and multiplication for order types can be defined as follows. Given linear orders R, S on sets A, B, one defines orders $R \oplus S$, $R \otimes S$ on $A \oplus B$, $A \otimes B$ by

$(a, b)(R \oplus S)(c, d)$	if $(a = c = 0$ and $bRd)$
	or $(a = 0$ and $c = 1)$
	or $(a = c = 1$ and $bSd)$
$(a, b)(R \otimes S)(c, d)$	if bSd
	and (if $b = d$ then aRc).

Intuitively, $R \oplus S$ is like a copy of A in the R order, followed by a copy of B in the S order, while $R \otimes S$ is like a copy of B but with each element replaced by an entire copy of A. Then $|R| + |S| = |R \oplus S|$ and $|R| \cdot |S| = |R \otimes S|$.

For ordinals the methods of proof by transfinite induction and definition by transfinite recursion, analogous to the ordinary methods of induction and recursion in higher arithmetic or number theory, are available. To prove by transfinite induction that $\Phi(\rho)$ holds for all ordinals ρ, one must prove, as in finite induction, that $\Phi(0)$ holds and if $\Phi(\rho)$ holds then $\Phi(\rho')$ holds, and additionally that if τ is a limit and $\Phi(\Sigma)$ holds for all $\Sigma < \tau$, then $\Phi(\tau)$ holds.

Similarly, to define by recursion $\psi(\rho)$ for all ordinals ρ, one must define (1) $\psi(0)$, (2) $\psi(\rho')$ in terms of $\psi(\rho)$, and (3) $\psi(\tau)$ in terms of $\psi(\Sigma)$ for $\Sigma < \tau$ at limits τ. Equivalent, more convenient, definitions of addition and multiplication, plus a definition of ordinal exponentiation, can be given for ordinals by transfinite recursion:

$$\rho + 0 = \rho \qquad \rho + (\Sigma^{\#}) = (\rho + \Sigma)^{\#}$$
$$\rho \cdot 0 = 0 \qquad \rho \cdot (\Sigma^{\#}) = (\rho \cdot \Sigma) + \rho$$
$$\rho^{0} = 1 \qquad \rho^{(\Sigma^{\#})} = (\rho^{\Sigma}) \cdot \rho$$

and at the limits:

$$\rho + \tau = \sup\{\rho + \Sigma | \Sigma < \tau\}$$
$$\rho \cdot \tau = \sup\{\rho \cdot \Sigma | \Sigma < \tau\}$$
$$\rho^{\tau} = \sup\{\rho^{\Sigma} | \Sigma < \tau\}.$$

If ρ, Σ both have cardinality α, then so do $\rho + \Sigma$, $\rho \cdot \Sigma$ and even (in contrast to cardinal exponentiation) ρ^{Σ}. Note $\rho^{\#} = \rho + 1$. Also $\omega^{\#}$, $\omega^{\#\#}$ and $\omega^{\dagger}$ are $\omega + 1$, $\omega + 2$, $\omega + \omega$.

3 Cardinal numbers and cardinal arithmetic

The cardinal number ('size') of a set is written $\|A\|$. The order '$\leqslant$' on the cardinals is defined as follows. $\|A\| = \|B\|$ if there is a bijection from A to B, and $\|A\| \leqslant \|B\|$ if there is a bijection from A to a subset of B. This order also has the properties of a well-order, by its connection with ordinal order. Hence there is a least or zero cardinal. Cantor proved that for any cardinal α there is a greater cardinal and hence a least greater cardinal, its successor, α^+ (an explicit description is given below). For every set C of cardinals there is a cardinal greater than or equal to each of its elements, hence a least such cardinal, the supremum of C, $\sup C$. If $C = \{\beta | \beta = \|B\|$ for some $B \in X\}$, then $\sup C = \|\cup X\|$. (Note this implies there can be no set of all cardinals.) A limit (cardinal) is one that is neither zero nor a successor.

As with ordinals, the cardinals $0, 1 = 0^{\#}, 2 = 1^{\#}, \ldots$ less than the least limit are called finite, and the least limit $\sup\{0,1,2,\ldots\}$, the cardinal of the natural numbers, is called $\aleph_0$ ('aleph-nought' or 'aleph-null'). Sets of cardinality $\aleph_0$ are called 'countable'. $\aleph_0^+$ is

called $\aleph_1$, and the least ordinal of cardinality $\aleph_1$ is called ω_1 or Ω. $\aleph_1^+, \aleph_1^{++}, \ldots$ are called $\aleph_2, \aleph_3, \ldots$, and the next limit cardinal $\sup\{\aleph_0, \aleph_1, \aleph_2, \ldots\}$ is called $\aleph_{\omega}$, while the least ordinals of these cardinals are called $\omega_2, \omega_3, \ldots, \omega_{\omega}$. There is only one ordinal of each finite cardinality (since there is an isomorphism between any two orders on a finite set). Not so for infinite cardinals, since the ordinals $\omega^{\#}, \omega^{\#\#}, \ldots, \omega^{\dagger}$ can also be described as the ordinals of certain unnatural well-orders on the natural numbers, namely

$$1, 2, 3, \ldots, 0$$
$$2, 3, 4, \ldots, 0, 1$$
$$1, 3, 5, \ldots, 2, 4, 6, \ldots, \ldots$$

and hence all have cardinality $\aleph_0$. Indeed, Cantor gave an explicit description of α^+ by proving that it is the cardinal of the set of ordinals of cardinality α. It is now customary to identify a cardinal with the least ordinal of that cardinal, so that $\aleph_0 = \omega_0$, and so on.

Cardinal addition, multiplication and exponentiation are defined as follows: $\|A\| + \|B\| = \|A \oplus B\|$, $\|A\| \cdot \|B\| = \|A \otimes B\|$ and $\|A\|^{\|B\|} = \|A^B\|$. These agree with the usual arithmetic notions on natural numbers, and some of the usual arithmetic laws generalize from the finite to the infinite (the associative, commutative and distributive laws of addition and multiplication, and the laws of exponents). But there are some differences. Bijections from $\mathbb{N}$ to $\mathbb{N} \oplus \mathbb{N}$ and to $\mathbb{N} \otimes \mathbb{N}$ are suggested by the following.

$(0,0)$	$(0,0)$
$(1,0)$	$(0,1)$
$(0,1)$	$(1,1)$
$(1,1)$	$(1,0)$
$(0,2)$	$(0,2)$
$(1,2)$	$(1,2)$
$(0,3)$	$(2,2)$
$(1,3)$	$(2,1)$
$(0,4)$	$(2,0)$
$(1,4)$	$(0,3)$
$\vdots$	$\vdots$

This shows that $\aleph_0 + \aleph_0 = \aleph_0 \cdot \aleph_0 = \aleph_0$. This result can be generalized in two directions to show (1) that a union of countably many countable sets is countable and (2) that

$$(\aleph_0)^n = \aleph_0 \cdot \ldots \cdot \aleph_0 = \|\mathbb{N} \otimes \ldots \otimes \mathbb{N}\| = \aleph_0$$

for all $n \in \mathbb{N}$, and hence (3) writing $\mathbb{N}^{<\omega}$ for the set of all finite ordered sequences (pairs, triples, ...) of natural numbers and $\aleph_0^{<\omega}$ for $\sup\{(\aleph_0)^n | n = 0, 1, 2, \ldots\}$, one has

$$\aleph_0^{<\omega} = ||\mathbb{N}^{<\omega}|| = \aleph_2.$$

These 'abstract' results have 'concrete' counterparts for the sets $\mathbb{Z}$, $\mathbb{Q}$ and $\mathbb{A}$ of integers, rational and algebraic numbers (these last being the real numbers that are roots of polynomial equations with rational coefficients); namely,

$$||\mathbb{Z}|| = ||\mathbb{Q}|| = ||\mathbb{A}|| = \aleph_0.$$

Finally, there is the generalization that $\alpha + \alpha = \alpha \cdot \alpha = \alpha^{<\omega} = \alpha$ for all infinite α, and $\alpha + \beta = \alpha \cdot \beta = \sup\{\alpha, \beta\}$ for all infinite α, β, so cardinal addition and multiplication trivialize.

Exponentiation is not trivial. A bijection between subsets of A and functions from A to $\{0,1\}$ is obtainable by relating a subset B with its 'characteristic function', χ_B.

$$\chi_B(a) = \begin{cases} 1 & \text{if } a \in B \\ 0 & \text{if } a \notin B \end{cases}$$

Thus $||\wp(A)|| = 2^{||A||}$. Cantor proved that $||A|| < 2^{||A||}$. (Indeed, no function $F : A \to \wp(A)$ can be a bijection, since $F(a) \neq \{x \in A | x \notin F(x)\}$ for any a.)

The cardinal $\mathbf{c}$ (for 'continuum') is defined to be $||\mathbb{R}||$, where $\mathbb{R}$ is the set of real numbers (or points in the line). By the general result $||A|| \cdot ||A|| = ||A||$, $\mathbf{c}$ is equal to $||\mathbb{R} \otimes \mathbb{R}||$ or $||\mathbb{C}||$, where $\mathbb{C}$ or $\mathbb{R} \otimes \mathbb{R}$ is the set of complex numbers (or points in the plane). It can also be shown to be equal to $||\wp(\mathbb{N})||$ or $2^{\aleph_0}$, and by the general result $||A|| < 2^{||A||}$ one has $\aleph_0 < \mathbf{c}$. A 'concrete' consequence of this 'abstract' result is that there exist transcendental (that is, non-algebraic real) numbers.

The 'generalized continuum hypothesis' is the conjecture that $2^\alpha = \alpha^+$ for all cardinals α. The 'continuum hypothesis' (CH) is the special case for $\alpha = \aleph_0$. Equivalently, CH asserts there is no intermediate cardinal α with $\aleph_0 < \alpha < \mathbf{c}$. The most interesting alternatives to CH include the hypotheses CH': that there is just one such intermediate; and CH#: that there are $\mathbf{c}$ intermediates. Where CH asserts that $\mathbf{c} = \aleph_1$ and CH' asserts that $\mathbf{c} = \aleph_2$, CH# implies that $\mathbf{c} > \aleph_1, \aleph_2, \ldots, \aleph_\omega$, and more. Assuming the generalized continuum hypothesis, exponentiation simplifies.

$$\alpha^\beta = \begin{cases} \alpha & \text{if } \beta < \mathrm{cf}\alpha \\ \alpha^+ & \text{if } \mathrm{cf}\alpha \leq \beta < \alpha \\ \beta^+ & \text{if } \mathrm{cf}\alpha < \beta \end{cases}$$

Otherwise, one must distinguish between a cardinal α being a limit, meaning that $\beta^+ < \alpha$ whenever $\beta < \alpha$, and α being a 'strong limit', meaning that $2^\beta < \alpha$ whenever $\beta < \alpha$.

The 'cofinality' $\mathrm{cf}\alpha$ of a cardinal α is the least β such that there is a set B of sets with $\beta = ||B||$ and $||b|| < \alpha$ for all sets $b \in B$, but $||\cup B|| = \alpha$. α is 'regular' or 'singular' according as $\mathrm{cf}\alpha$ is equal to or less than α. $\aleph_0$ is regular (otherwise $\mathrm{cf}\aleph_0$ would be finite, but a union of finitely many finite sets is finite), $\aleph_1$ is regular (otherwise $\mathrm{cf}\aleph_1$ would be $\aleph_0$, but a union of countably many countable sets is countable), and generally α^+ is regular. $\aleph_\omega$ is singular, with $\mathrm{cf}\aleph_\omega = \aleph_0$ (a union of countably many sets with cardinality $\aleph_0$, $\aleph_1$, $\aleph_2$ and so on has cardinality $\aleph_\omega$). It can at least be proved that $\mathbf{c} \neq \aleph_\omega$, and more generally that $\mathrm{cf}2^\alpha > \mathrm{cf}\alpha$.

4 Combinatorial set theory

Analogous to finite combinatorics based on the ordinary arithmetic of the natural numbers there is an extensive 'combinatorial' set theory or infinitary combinatorics based on the transfinite arithmetic of cardinals and ordinals. A typical cardinal result is the 'delta system' theorem: if A is an uncountable set of finite sets, then there is a fixed finite set b and an uncountable $B \subseteq A$ such that $b' \cap b'' = b$ for all $b', b'' \in B$.

A typical ordinal result is the 'pressing down' theorem. Let A be a set of ordinals. A is called 'unbounded' in τ if $\sup(A \cap \tau) = \tau$, or for every $\rho < \tau$ there exists $\Sigma \in A$ with $\rho < \Sigma < \tau$. Given an uncountable regular cardinal α, A is called 'closed' in α if $\tau \in A$ whenever $\tau < \alpha$ and A is unbounded in τ. $B \subseteq \alpha$ is called 'stationary' in α if for all sets A that are closed and unbounded in α, $B \cap A \neq \emptyset$. The theorem asserts that if F is a function from α to α and $\{\rho < \alpha | F(\rho) < \rho\}$ is stationary, then there is a $\Sigma < \alpha$ such that $\{\rho < \alpha | F(\rho) = \Sigma\}$ is stationary.

Also included in combinatorial set theory are results about order types other than ordinals, beginning with the theory of the order types η, θ of the usual orders on $\mathbb{Q}$ and $\mathbb{R}$. Given a linear order ' $\leq$ ' on a set A, an 'open' interval is a set of the form $]a,b[= \{x | a < x < b\}$ for $a < b$ and a 'closed' interval is a set $[a,b] = \{x | a \leq x \leq b\}$, $a \leq b$. $B \subseteq A$ is 'dense' if it is disjoint from no open interval and 'bounded' if it is a subset of some closed interval. $\leq$ is 'separable' if there exists a countable dense subset B, and satisfies the 'countable chain condition' (or 'is CCC') if there exists no uncountable set of disjoint open intervals. (Separability implies CCC since each of a set of disjoint open intervals must contain a distinct element of the countable dense set.) ' $\leq$ ' is 'complete' if every chain of closed intervals has a non-empty intersection. $\mathbb{Q}$, $\mathbb{R}$ are each unbounded and dense in themselves, and $\mathbb{Q}$ is dense in $\mathbb{R}$ (and countable), so $\mathbb{R}$ is separable and CCC. $\mathbb{R}$ is complete, but $\mathbb{Q}$ is not (for example, the intervals

...$[1.414, 1.415] \subseteq [1.41, 1.42] \subseteq [1.4, 1.5] \subseteq [1, 2]$
have intersection $\{\sqrt{2}\}$). Cantor proved that any unbounded, dense linear order on a countable set has order type η. Similarly, any unbounded, dense, separable, complete linear order has order type θ. The 'Suslin hypothesis' is that the latter result holds with CCC in place of separability.

5 Point sets

The oldest part of set theory and the part most closely connected with the rest of mathematics (analysis, topology) is the theory of sets of points in the line, plane and so on (identified with $\mathbb{R}$, $\mathbb{R} \otimes \mathbb{R}, \ldots$). Modern analysis and topology consider more complicated functions and sets than traditional calculus and geometry. A function $F : \mathbb{R} \to \mathbb{R}$ is 'continuous' if $F^{-1}[U]$ is open for every open $U \subseteq \mathbb{R}$, where an 'open' set is a union of open intervals and a 'closed' set is the complement of an open set. The Cantor 'discontinuum', the complement in the unit interval $[0, 1]$ of the union of the open intervals $]\frac{1}{3}, \frac{2}{3}[$, $]\frac{1}{9}, \frac{2}{9}[$, $]\frac{7}{9}, \frac{8}{9}[$, $]\frac{1}{27}, \frac{2}{27}[$, $]\frac{7}{27}, \frac{8}{27}[$, $]\frac{19}{27}, \frac{20}{27}[$ and so on, is a famous example of a closed set (see CONTINUUM HYPOTHESIS §2) more complicated than any considered in traditional mathematics. Sets obtainable from open sets by iterated application of complementation and countable union are called 'Borel' sets. They occur ubiquitously in modern mathematics (as in the rigorous formulation of probability theory), while sets beyond Borel occur sporadically.

An 'analytic' set is the image of a Borel set under a continuous function, a 'co-analytic' set is the complement of an analytic set, a 'pro-co-analytic' (PCA) set is the image of any set under a continuous function, and a 'co-pro-co-analytic' (CPCA) set is the complement of a pro-co-analytic set. Sets obtainable from Borel sets by iterated application of continuous image and complementation are called 'projective'. Projective sets are rather special compared with arbitrary sets. It can be shown that there are only $\mathbf{c}$ projective sets, whereas there are $2^{\mathbf{c}}$ subsets of $\mathbb{R}$. The study of such special classifications of sets is called 'descriptive' set theory. In one notation, open sets are denoted Σ^0_1, closed sets, Π^0_1, unions of countably many closed sets, Σ^0_2 and their complements, $\Pi^0_2, \ldots$. Analytic, co-analytic, PCA and CPCA sets are denoted, respectively, Σ^1_1, Π^1_1, Σ^1_2 and $\Pi^1_2, \ldots$ sets.

Central to attempts to define integration for complicated functions, and length, area and so on for complicated linear, planar, ... sets, is the notion of a (complete probability) 'measure' on a set or 'space' X. Such a measure is a function μ from the set of '(μ-)measurable' subsets of X to the unit interval

$J = [0, 1]$, $\mu(A)$ being called the (μ-)measure of $A \subseteq X$. μ has the following properties: (1) 'normality' – the whole space has measure one; (2) 'non-triviality' – any one-point set has measure zero; (3) 'completeness' – any subset of a set of measure zero has measure zero; (4) 'complementarity' – the complement of a measurable set is measurable; and (5) 'additivity' – the union of a countable set of measurable sets is measurable and, if the sets are disjoint, the measure of their union is the sum of their measures. The analogue of additivity with 'countable set' replaced by 'set of cardinality less than that of the whole space' may be called (5') 'superadditivity'. If we restrict ourselves to the unit interval, the 'translation' of $A \subseteq J$ by $t \in J$ is defined to be $\{a \# t | a \in A\}$, where $x \# y$ is defined to be whichever of $x + y$, $x + y - 1$ is an element of J, and one may consider the further property (6) 'invariance' – a translation of a measurable set is measurable, and its measure is the same. The key positive result is the existence of a unique measure on J with properties (1)–(6), called 'Lebesgue measure'. (Analogues can also be defined on $\mathbb{R}$, $\mathbb{R} \otimes \mathbb{R}$ and so on.) For Lebesgue measure, $\mu(A)$ intuitively represents the probability that a point randomly chosen from J will be an element of A. One respect in which the discontinuum is 'pathological' is that it is large in the sense of having cardinality $\mathbf{c}$ but small in the sense of having Lebesgue measure 0. (Like some other positive results, the existence and uniqueness of Lebesgue measure require for their proof only DC (see §1 above), not full AC.)

To mention a negative result, the hypothesis that all sets are Lebesgue measurable (AM) fails. Let S be a choice set for $\{y \in J | (y - x) \in \mathbb{Q}\}$. If S were measurable, then using invariance it would follow that the disjoint sets of form $\{y \in J | y \# p \in S\}$ for $p \in \mathbb{Q}$, whose union is all of J, would all have the same measure ε. But then using additivity, $\mu(J)$ would have to be $\varepsilon + \varepsilon + \varepsilon + \ldots$, which is 0 or ∞ according as $\varepsilon = 0$ or > 0. The failure of AM leads to consideration of some alternative hypotheses, notably the hypothesis (known to imply $\sim$CH and $\sim$CH') of the existence of a measure with properties (1)–(5) for which all sets are measurable, or the hypothesis (known to imply CH#) of the existence of a measure with properties (1)–(4) and superadditivity for which all sets are measurable. A more positive result using AC may also be mentioned. Given $Q \subseteq \mathbb{R}$, and a continuous F from $\mathbb{R}$ to $\mathbb{R}$, a uniformization for Q, F is a choice set P for $\{\{y \in Q | F(y) = F(x)\} | x \in Q\}$. AC immediately implies the existence of a uniformization for any Q, F.

The failure of AM also leads to consideration of some restricted hypotheses: for Γ one of the special classifications considered above, 'Γ-measurability' is the hypothesis that all sets in Γ are measurable. Similarly, 'Γ-uniformization' is the hypothesis that for any $Q \in \Gamma$ and any continuous F there is a uniformization $P \in \Gamma$. It can be shown that while Σ_p^1-measurability and Π_p^1-measurability imply each other for the same p, Σ_p^1-uniformization and Π_p^1-uniformization cannot both hold for the same p. Positive results of descriptive set theory obtained by the end of the 1930s include Σ_1^1- and Π_1^1-measurability, an example of a 'regularity' theorem or result of the form 'Every set in Γ has some "nice" property', and also Π_1^1- and Σ_1^1-uniformization, an example of a 'structure' theorem or result of the form 'For every set in Γ there is another set in Γ related to it in some "nice" way'. All attempts to prove Σ_2^1- and Π_2^1-measurability, and Σ_3^1- or Π_3^1-uniformization have failed.

6   New axioms for set theory: large cardinals and determinacy

Beginning in about 1940, many conjectures Δ (including those mentioned at the end of §5) have been proved by mathematical logicians to be 'undecidable' relative to ZFC, meaning that it has been shown that if ZFC is consistent, then so are both ZFC + Δ (relative consistency of Δ) and ZFC+ $\sim\Delta$ (relative independence of Δ). Note that the consistency of ZFC, let alone of ZFC + Δ (or ZFC+ $\sim\Delta$), cannot be proved within ZFC itself, by celebrated results of mathematical logic (see GÖDEL'S THEOREMS), and hence cannot be proved by ordinary mathematical methods, since these can be developed within ZFC. The most one can hope to prove is the *relative* result that if a contradiction could be deduced from ZFC + Δ (or ZFC+ $\sim\Delta$), then a contradiction could be deduced from ZFC. There are two basic methods for proving relative consistency. A first method was used by Kurt Gödel to prove the consistency of CH relative to ZFC (and of AC relative to ZF) (see CONSTRUCTIBLE UNIVERSE). A second method was used by Paul Cohen to prove the independence of CH relative to ZFC (and of AC relative to ZF) (see FORCING). Both methods have been widely applied since.

For some hypotheses, however, there can be no hope of a proof of relative consistency, namely for any hypothesis that itself implies the consistency of ZFC. An example is the hypothesis of the existence of an 'inaccessible' or regular strong limit cardinal α (IC). (How IC implies the existence of a model of ZFC, and hence the consistency of ZFC, will be indicated in §7.) Even in such cases there may be heuristic or inductive evidence of consistency (failure to deduce a consequence in years of work with the hypothesis). In order to decide questions undecidable in ZFC, new axioms have from time to time been advocated. The two kinds

most often advocated (which unfortunately still leave CH undecided) have been 'large cardinal' and 'determinacy' axioms. The former, which pertain to sets larger than any encountered in ordinary mathematical practice, are often advocated on the intrinsic ground that they are further expressions of intuitions only partly expressed by the ZFC axioms (to the effect that the hierarchy of sets is 'tall'). The latter, which pertain to special classifications of sets of linear, plane, . . . points, and are connected with problems in analysis and topology, are often advocated on the extrinsic ground that their consequences are 'nice'.

Large cardinal axioms include IC and also MC, the hypothesis that there exists a measurable cardinal β. Here β is measurable if there is a superadditive measure (as defined in §5), taking only the two values 0 and 1, for which all subsets of β are measurable. It follows from non-triviality and superadditivity that any subset of cardinality $< \beta$ will have measure 0, and by superadditivity again that any union of a set of cardinality $< \beta$ of such subsets will still have measure 0, whence β is regular. It also follows that if $\alpha < \beta$ and F is a function from β to $\wp(\alpha)$, then for any $\rho < \alpha$ one of the sets

$$D^+(\rho) = \{\Sigma < \beta | \rho \in F(\Sigma)\}$$
$$D^-(\rho) = \{\Sigma < \beta | \rho \notin F(\Sigma)\}$$

will have measure 0, the other, measure 1, and by superadditivity the union D of the ones with measure 0 will have measure 0. But for $\Sigma, \tau \notin D$ one has

$$F(\Sigma) = F(\tau) = \{\rho < \alpha | \mu(D^+(\rho)) = 1\}$$

so F is not a bijection, $2^\alpha = ||\wp(\alpha)|| < \beta$, and β is a strong limit. So a measurable cardinal β is inaccessible, and indeed it can even be shown that $\{\alpha < \beta | \alpha$ is an inaccessible cardinal$\}$ has cardinal β, so MC is a much stronger hypothesis than IC. Still stronger is the hypothesis (SC) that there exists a 'supercompact' cardinal γ. For such a γ there is for any $\delta > \gamma$ an analogue of a measure as above for the subsets of δ of cardinality γ.

Determinacy axioms pertain to certain infinite games considered in mathematical game theory. Given $A \subseteq J$ there is a game for two players I, II: they alternately pick the terms in the decimal expansion of a real x, and I or II wins according as x is or is not an element of A. A 'strategy' for a player is, intuitively, a rule telling the player how to play as a function of the opponent's previous moves, and is winning if by so playing the player will win the game, no matter what the opponent's moves. A is 'determinate' if one or other player has a winning strategy. Π_1^1-AD, PD and AD (to add to the notation set up in §5) are, respectively, the hypotheses that all Π_1^1, projective or arbitrary sets are determinate. AD is refutable using AC, among other reasons because AD implies AM, while, by essentially the same proof, PD implies projective measurability, and various other regularity theorems. Similarly, PD implies projective uniformization and various other structural theorems. Π_1^1-AD yields, correspondingly, Σ_2^1- and Π_2^1-measurability and Π_3^1-uniformization.

Despite superficial differences, there are deep connections between large cardinals and determinacy. By the 1970s it was established that a large cardinal axiom somewhat weaker than MC implies a conclusion somewhat stronger than Π_1^1-AD, with the partial converse that such a determinacy hypothesis implies the consistency of such a large cardinal hypothesis. In the 1980s an analogous relation between SC and PD was established. So the cases for large cardinal and for determinacy axioms reinforce each other. The search for further axioms to decide CH continues.

7 Models of set theory

In Gödel's method for proving relative consistency of a conjecture Δ, one seeks a formula $\Xi(x)$ and proves that for any axiom of ZFC + Δ and hence for any finite conjunction Ψ of such axioms, Ψ^Ξ is provable in ZFC, where Ψ^Ξ is the result of replacing each quantifier 'for all x' or 'for some x' in Ψ by the 'restricted' quantifier 'for all x such that $\Xi(x)$' or 'for some x such that $\Xi(x)$'.

Supposing this had been done, if a contradiction could be deduced from ZFC + Δ, the deduction would use only finitely many of the axioms of ZFC + Δ, and so a contradiction Θ and $\sim\Theta$ could be deduced from some finite conjunction Ψ of axioms of ZFC + Δ and, restricting quantifiers, a contradiction Θ^Ξ and $\sim\Theta^\Xi$ could be deduced from Ψ^Ξ. By exhibiting the deduction of a contradiction from Ψ^Ξ, $\sim\Psi^\Xi$ would be provable in ZFC, and hence a contradiction (both Ψ^Ξ and $\sim\Psi^\Xi$) would be deducible in ZFC. Such a Ξ (and derivatively, the 'universe' of all x such that $\Xi(x)$ holds) is said to constitute an 'inner model'.

In Cohen's method for proving relative consistency, one assumes the existence of a set X that is a model of ZFC in the sense that for any axiom of ZFC, and hence for any finite conjunction Φ of such axioms, Φ^X holds, where Φ^X is the result of replacing each quantifier in Φ by the restricted quantifier (as above). One then proves the existence of a set Y that is a model of ZFC + Δ, but in such a way that for any finite conjunction Ψ of axioms of ZFC + Δ, the proof that Ψ^Y holds depends only on the assumption that Φ^X holds for some finite conjunction $\Phi = \Phi_\Psi$ of axioms of ZFC. Supposing this done, one uses the fact that while the existence of a model X of all of ZFC cannot be proved in ZFC (since this would imply the consistency of ZFC), for any finite conjunction Φ of axioms of ZFC the existence of a model of Φ can be proved in ZFC (as will be indicated below). It follows that the existence of a model for any finite subset Ψ of ZFC + Δ is provable in ZFC. Then if a contradiction could be deduced from ZFC + Δ, a contradiction could be deduced from some finite conjunction Ψ of axioms of ZFC + Δ, and by exhibiting this deduction the non-existence of any model of Ψ could be proved in ZFC, and hence a contradiction (existence and non-existence of a model of Ψ) could be proved in ZFC.

The general theories of set models X (as in the second method) and formula models Ξ (as in the first method) are closely parallel, and only the theory of set models will be sketched here. For applications it suffices to consider only sets X that are 'transitive' in the sense that whenever $u \in v \in X$, then $u \in X$. Informally, if Φ^X holds, it will be said that it 'appears' to X that Φ holds, or that Φ holds 'inside' X. Central to the theory of models is the determination of sufficient conditions for various axioms of ZFC to hold inside X. Central to this determination are considerations of absoluteness, where a formula Φ is called 'absolute' for X if for any $u, v, \ldots \in X$, $\Phi(u, v, \ldots)$ appears to X to hold if and only if it really holds. This will always be so if Φ is a 'limited' formula, mentioning only u, v, and their elements, elements of elements and so on, since by transitivity these will all be elements of X.

For instance, the condition 'u, v have different elements' or 'For some w, either $w \in u$ and $w \notin v$ or $w \in v$ and $w \notin u$' is limited, and so $u, v \in X$ appear to X to have different elements if and only if they really do have different elements, and so the axiom of extensionality, 'For every u, v, if $u \neq v$ then u, v have different elements', holds inside X for any transitive X. Similarly, it can be shown that the axiom of foundation holds inside X for any transitive X. As for pairing, the condition '$w = \{u, v\}$' or '$u \in w$ and $v \in w$ and for all $z \in w$, $z = u$ or $z = v$' is limited, and so w appears to X to be the pair $\{u, v\}$ of u, v if and only if it really is that pair, and so the axiom of *pairs*, 'For every u, v there exists a w such that $w = \{u, v\}$', holds inside X if and only if $\{u, v\} \in X$ whenever $u, v \in X$, or, as is said, if and only if X is closed under the pairing operation $\{\,,\,\}$. Similarly it can be shown that the axiom of *union* holds in X if and only if X is closed under the union operation '$\cup$'; that the axiom of infinity holds in X if and only if $\omega \in X$; and that the axiom of choice holds in X if and only if every partition in X has a choice set in X.

As for power, u appears to X to be a subset of v if

and only if it really is, but w appears to X to be the set $\wp(v)$ of all subsets u of v if and only if w really is the set $\wp(v) \cap X$ of all subsets u of v with $u \in X$. Thus the axiom of *power* appears to X to hold if and only if X is closed under the operation of forming $\wp(v) \cap X$ from v, which may be the case even if X does not contain all subsets of v and therefore is not closed under the operation of forming $\wp(v)$ from v. Similarly, a necessary and sufficient condition for separation to hold inside X is that for each condition Φ, X is closed under the operation that applies to any v forms $\{u \in v | \Phi^X(u)\}$. Similarly, a necessary and sufficient condition for replacement to hold inside X is that for each condition Φ such that for every $x \in X$ there is a unique $y = \psi^X(x) \in X$ such that $\Phi^X(x,y)$ holds, X is closed under the operation that applied to v forms $\{\psi^X(u) | u \in v\}$. X is 'supertransitive' if whenever $u \subseteq v \in X$, then $u \in X$. For supertransitive X, $\wp(v) \cap X = \wp(v)$ for any $v \in X$, so the necessary and sufficient condition for power to hold is just that X is closed under the power operation $\wp$. Supertransitivity is a more than sufficient condition for separation to hold. Similarly, a more than sufficient condition for replacement to hold is that whenever $u \subseteq X$, $||u|| = ||v||$ and $v \in X$, then $u \in X$.

One kind of model of a large part of ZFC is obtained as follows. For any x let the 'transitivization' $t(x)$ of x be $\cup\{x, \cup x, \cup \cup x, \dots\}$, the set of all elements, elements of elements and so on of x. For any uncountable cardinal α, let $H(\alpha)$ be $\{x | \alpha > ||t(x)||\}$. It follows from the definition that $H(\alpha)$ is supertransitive, and it can be checked, using the necessary and sufficient conditions indicated above, that $H(\alpha)$ is a model of all axioms of ZFC except perhaps power and replacement. Moreover, if α is a strong limit, then $H(\alpha)$ will be closed under $\wp$ and hence a model of power; while if α is regular, then one will have $u \in H(\alpha)$ whenever $u \subseteq H(\alpha)$, $||u|| = ||v||$, $v \in H(\alpha)$ and $H(\alpha)$ will be a model of replacement. (Thus if α is inaccessible, $H(\alpha)$ is a model of the whole of ZFC.)

Another kind of model of a large part of ZFC is obtained as follows. The hierarchy of levels of sets, intuitions about which underlie the axioms (as in §1), can be defined by transfinite recursion.

$$V(0) = \emptyset$$

$$V(\rho + 1) = \wp(V(\rho))$$

$$\text{at limits } V(\tau) = \cup\{V(\Sigma) | \Sigma < \tau\}$$

That $V(\rho)$ is supertransitive can be proved by transfinite induction. Given the other axioms of ZFC, the principle of replacement can be proved equivalent to the following principle of 'reflection': for any formula Φ there are arbitrarily large ordinals ρ such that Φ is absolute for $V(\rho)$. In particular, for any finite conjunction Φ of axioms of ZFC there are arbitrarily large ordinals ρ such that Φ holds in $V(\rho)$.

While both the $V(\rho)$ (for $\rho > \omega$) and the $H(\alpha)$ (for $\alpha > \aleph_0$) are uncountable, it can be shown that if a ZFC or some variant set theory has a transitive model, then it has a countable transitive model, using a celebrated result of mathematical logic (see LÖWENHEIM–SKOLEM THEOREMS AND NONSTANDARD MODELS). Since the uncountability of the power set of the set of natural numbers is a theorem of set theory, the existence of a countable model for set theory is sometimes considered paradoxical, and called the 'Skolem paradox'. There is, however, no genuine contradiction. (For the conditions '$x = \wp(\omega)$' and '$||x|| > \aleph_0$' are not absolute: the former holds inside a model X if $x = \wp(\omega) \cap X$, which may well be countable even though $\wp(\omega)$ is uncountable; the latter holds inside the model X if there is no surjection $F \in X$ from ω to x, which there may well not be even if there is such an $F \notin X$.)

See also: CANTOR'S THEOREM; LOGICAL AND MATHEMATICAL TERMS, GLOSSARY OF

References and further reading

Barwise, J. (ed.) (1977) *Handbook of Mathematical Logic*, Amsterdam: North Holland, 317–522. (A standard reference including surveys on a generous scale of the different branches of set theory, with attribution of results to their original authors and references to the original technical literature.)

Benacerraf, P. (1965) 'What Numbers Could Not Be', *Philosophical Review* 74: 47–73; repr. in P. Benacerraf and H. Putnam (eds) *Philosophy of Mathematics: Selected Readings*, Cambridge: Cambridge University Press, 2nd edn, 1983. (A philosophical puzzle about 'identification' as in §1.)

* Cantor, G. (1895, 1897) 'Beiträge zur Begründung der transfiniten Mengenlehre', *Mathematische Annalen* 46: 481–512, 49: 207–46; trans. P.E.B. Jourdain (1915), *Contributions to the Founding of the Theory of Transfinite Numbers*, New York: Dover, 1955. (The original source for §§2–3, with an introduction setting the work in its historical context.)

Halmos, P. (1960) *Naive Set Theory*, New York: Van Nostrand. (A perennially popular elementary textbook, expounding for students of mathematics the development of mathematics on the basis of ZFC mentioned in §1.)

Jech, T. (1977) 'About the Axiom of Choice', in J. Barwise (ed.) *Handbook of Mathematical Logic*, Amsterdam: North Holland, 345–70. (Surveys all aspects of AC mentioned here, and many more besides.)

Kunen, K. (1977) 'Combinatorics', in J. Barwise (ed.) *Handbook of Mathematical Logic*, Amsterdam: North Holland, 370–402. (Surveys at length combinatorial set theory as mentioned in §4; and, briefly, large cardinals as in §6.)

Maddy, P. (1988) 'Believing the Axioms', *Journal of Symbolic Logic* 53: 481–511, 736–64. (Surveys axioms old and new as in §§1, 6; especially advances made in the 1980s.)

Martin, D.A. (1977) 'Descriptive Set Theory', in J. Barwise (ed.) *Handbook of Mathematical Logic*, Amsterdam: North Holland, 783–818. (Surveys theory of projective sets (as in §§5–6) through the 1970s.)

Shoenfield, J.R. (1977) 'Axioms of Set Theory', in J. Barwise (ed.) *Handbook of Mathematical Logic*, Amsterdam: North Holland, 321–44. (Surveys material mentioned in §§1–4, 6.)

* Zermelo, E. (1908) 'Untersuchungen über die Grundlagen der Mengenlehre, I', *Mathematische Annalen* 65: 261–81; trans. S. Bauer-Mengelberg, 'Investigations in the Foundations of Set Theory', in J. van Heijenoort (ed.) *From Frege to Gödel: A Sourcebook in Mathematical Logic*, Cambridge, MA: Harvard University Press, 1967, 200–15. (The original source for the axiomatization of set theory, with an introduction setting the work in its historical context.)

JOHN P. BURGESS

SET THEORY, DIFFERENT SYSTEMS OF

To begin with we shall use the word 'collection' quite broadly to mean anything the identity of which is solely a matter of what its members are (including 'sets' and 'classes'). Which collections exist? Two extreme positions are initially appealing. The first is to say that all do. Unfortunately this is inconsistent because of Russell's paradox: the collection of all collections which are not members of themselves does not exist. The second is to say that none do, but to talk as if they did whenever such talk can be shown to be eliminable and therefore harmless. This is consistent but far too weak to be of much use. We need an intermediate theory.

Various theories of collections have been proposed since the start of the twentieth century. What they share is the axiom of 'extensionality', which asserts that any two sets which have exactly the same elements must be identical. This is just a matter of definition: objects which do not satisfy extensionality are not collections. Beyond extensionality, theories differ. The most popular among

mathematicians is Zermelo–Fraenkel set theory (ZF). A common alternative is von Neumann–Bernays–Gödel class theory (NBG), which allows for the same sets but also has proper classes, that is, collections whose members are sets but which are not themselves sets (such as the class of all sets or the class of all ordinals).

Two general principles have been used to motivate the axioms of ZF and its relatives. The first is the iterative conception, according to which sets occur cumulatively in layers, each containing all the members and subsets of all previous layers. The second is the doctrine of limitation of size, according to which the 'paradoxical sets' (that is, the proper classes of NBG) fail to be sets because they are in some sense too big. Neither principle is altogether satisfactory as a justification for the whole of ZF: for example, the replacement schema is motivated only by limitation of size; and 'foundation' is motivated only by the iterative conception.

Among the other systems of set theory to have been proposed, the one that has received widespread attention is Quine's NF (from the title of an article, 'New Foundations for Mathematical Logic'), which seeks to avoid paradox by means of a syntactic restriction but which has not been provided with an intuitive justification on the basis of any conception of set. It is known that if NF is consistent then ZF is consistent, but the converse result has still not been proved.

1 **Virtual collections**
2 **Real collections**
3 **Zermelo–Fraenkel set theory**
4 **Von Neumann–Bernays–Gödel class theory**
5 **Other axiomatizations**
6 **Anti-foundation axioms**
7 **Quine's systems**

1 Virtual collections

Sometimes when we speak of collections it is just a manner of speaking and no more: if we say that Sarah belongs to the collection of all linguists, we might just as well say straight away that she is a linguist; nothing seems to be lost in the translation. This way of regarding collections is quite old: it is how Peano conceived of them in the 1880s. If we already have before us some formal theory which does not have collection-talk in it, then we can add it straightforwardly. If $\Phi(x)$ is a formula of the theory in question, we introduce a new term $\{x: \Phi(x)\}$ (called a 'collection term') into the language. Collection terms are subject to the following two rules:

(1) If $\Phi(x)$ is a formula then $x \in \{y: \Phi(y)\}$ is an abbreviation for $\Phi(x)$.

709

(2) If $\Phi(x)$ and $\Psi(x)$ are both formulas of the theory then $\{x: \Phi(x)\} = \{x: \Psi(x)\}$ is an abbreviation for $\forall x(\Phi(x) \leftrightarrow \Psi(x))$.

We permit the use of collection terms only in contexts from which these two rules allow them to be eliminated. Collections used harmlessly in this way have been called 'virtual' by Quine and we shall follow this terminology here. Let us introduce the convention that lower-case Greek letters stand schematically for collection terms. So the second re-writing rule allows us to assert, for instance, the following *extensionality schema*:

$$\forall z(z \in \alpha \leftrightarrow z \in \beta) \rightarrow \alpha = \beta.$$

By this schematic device we generate a considerable amount of the naïve theory of collections. We can, for instance, introduce the usual Boolean operations as follows:

$$\alpha \cap \beta = \{x: x \in \alpha \wedge x \in \beta\}$$
$$\alpha \cup \beta = \{x: x \in \alpha \vee x \in \beta\}$$
$$\emptyset = \{x: x \neq x\}$$
$$V = \{x: x = x\}$$
$$\{x\} = \{y: y = x\}$$
$$\{x,y\} = \{x\} \cup \{y\}$$

and so on. The theory thus generated is elegant enough in itself, but it is difficult to be satisfied with it for long. (We have to remember, for instance, that in this theory expressions such as $\{x,y\}$ are merely notational devices and do not, despite the appearance to the contrary that their 'explicit' definitions might suggest, have any meaning on their own.) Collection terms stand in sentences in some of the places where the grammar leads us to expect proper names; schematic letters stand where we might expect variables. There is a drive to objectify at work here; to suppose that collection terms can stand in *all* the places where names can occur. It is of course this step which, if carelessly done, leads straight to contradiction. How to do it without contradiction will be the subject of the rest of this entry.

2 Real collections

In the virtual theory just discussed the relation of membership is defined contextually. In the real theory with collections regarded as objects in their own right membership is taken by almost all authors as primitive. (Lewis (1991) is a rare exception.) Formally, this means that the language in which the theory is couched contains, in addition to the usual logical constants, a binary predicate symbol '$\in$'. It will be convenient to introduce a few notational conventions straight away. Upper-case Greek letters such as Φ and Ψ will stand for formulas. The notation $\Phi(x)$ stands for a formula in which the variable x occurs free: it does not indicate that no other variable occurs free in the formula. If Φ is a formula, we write $\Phi^{(a)}$ for the 'relativization' of Φ to a, that is, the formula obtained from Φ by replacing each quantifier $\forall x$ or $\exists x$ by $(\forall x \in a)$ or $(\exists x \in a)$, as the case may be. We write $x \subseteq y$ as an abbreviation for $\forall z(z \in x \rightarrow z \in y)$. We introduce ordered pairs by means of the device

$$(x,y) = \{\{x\}, \{x,y\}\}.$$

In the virtual theory, the question of whether there are any objects which are not collections is scarcely an issue: since there are not really any collections, if there is nothing else then there is nothing at all; the theory therefore collapses into vacuity. In any non-trivial real theory things are different: there are plenty of collections to talk about, whether or not there are any non-collections. Since this issue arises uniformly for all the real theories we shall be discussing, it is best to address it now. The objects of a theory which are not collections are called 'atoms', 'individuals' or (even in some non-German texts) '*Urelemente*'. If we are to allow for their presence, we need a primitive unary predicate $\text{atom}(x)$ to represent that x is an atom. We then introduce as an axiom the *axiom of extensionality* (*applied form*):

$$\forall x \forall y(\text{atom}(x) \vee \text{atom}(y) \vee$$
$$\forall z(z \in x \leftrightarrow z \in y) \rightarrow x = y).$$

This asserts no more than that objects which are not atoms are collections, since (as we have already observed) it is part of what we mean by a collection that it is completely determined by its members. If the atoms are to play any role in the theory at all, we shall also need the *collection axiom*, which states that the atoms form a collection:

$$\exists y \forall x(x \in y \leftrightarrow \text{atom}(x)).$$

If, on the other hand, it is pure collections that interest us, then the beginnings of the theory are a little more concise. We do not need the predicate '$\text{atom}(x)$' nor the collection axiom, and we can use the simpler *axiom of extensionality* (*pure form*):

$$\forall x \forall y(\forall z(z \in x \leftrightarrow z \in y) \rightarrow x = y).$$

Throughout what follows we shall state theories in their pure form and adopt the convention that if T is a pure theory (that is, one which includes the pure form of the axiom of extensionality) then TU is the corresponding applied theory (that is, the one obtained from T by deleting the pure form of extensionality and substituting the applied form together with the collection axiom). In the virtual theory we had collection terms defined contextually, provided that they occurred in certain positions (on the right of the '$\in$' symbol or on either side of the '$=$' symbol). Now that we are regarding collections as real we cannot be so indiscriminate. Let us say that a formula $\Phi(x)$ is 'collectivizing' in x for a theory T if

$$T \vdash \exists y \forall x(x \in y \leftrightarrow \Phi(x)).$$

Suppose now that T includes extensionality among its axioms. If $\Phi(x)$ is collectivizing in x for T then, by extensionality, we have uniqueness:

$$T \vdash \exists! y \forall x(x \in y \leftrightarrow \Phi(x)).$$

It is therefore legitimate to introduce a term $\{y \colon \Phi(y)\}$ with the property that

$$\forall x(x \in \{y \colon \Phi(y)\} \leftrightarrow \Phi(x)).$$

We thereby retrieve the virtual theory of §1 but limited to collectivizing formulas. What remains is to specify which formulas are collectivizing; it is this that is dealt with differently in the various competing theories.

3 Zermelo–Fraenkel set theory

In 1908 Ernst Zermelo published the first axiomatization of set theory. His choice of axioms seems to have been driven largely by his desire to ground a proof of the well-ordering theorem (see Axiom of choice §2; Set theory §2), which he published in the same year. Zermelo's axioms were those of ZCU^- (that is, the applied form of Z^- plus the axiom of choice) except that the axiom of infinity was replaced by Zermelo's own form (see below).

Although Zermelo's system is strong enough for many mathematical purposes, it is weaker than ZCU^- in one important respect: in it, it is impossible to develop a satisfactory theory of ordinal numbers (see Set theory §2). During the 1920s this problem was solved in two ways: ingenious methods were found, principally by Kuratowski (1921), of achieving without ordinals what is most naturally done with them; and Zermelo's system was strengthened, principally by Fraenkel and Skolem, so as to permit the theory of ordinals to be embedded in it. Zermelo–Fraenkel set theory (ZF) was the result.

We start by listing the axioms of a fragment of Zermelo–Fraenkel set theory called Z^-.

Axiom of extensionality:

As before.

Axiom schema of separation. If $\Phi(x)$ is a formula in which y does not occur free, then this is an axiom:

$$\forall z \exists y \forall x(x \in y \leftrightarrow x \in z \wedge \Phi(x)).$$

Empty set axiom:

$$\exists x \forall y \, y \notin x.$$

Pairing axiom:

$$\forall x \forall y \exists z(x \in z \wedge y \in z).$$

Union set axiom:

$$\forall a \exists x \forall y \forall z((z \in y \wedge y \in a) \rightarrow z \in x).$$

Power set axiom:

$$\forall x \exists y \forall z(z \subseteq x \rightarrow z \in y).$$

Axiom of infinity:

$$\exists x(\emptyset \in x \wedge \forall y \forall z((y \in x \wedge z \in x) \rightarrow y \cup \{z\} \in x).$$

To get Z we add:

Axiom of foundation:

$$\forall x(x \neq \emptyset \rightarrow (\exists y \in x)x \cap y = \emptyset).$$

(See Set theory §1 for an alternative formulation.) To get ZF we add:

Axiom schema of replacement. If $\Phi(x,y)$ is a formula in which z does not occur free then this is an axiom:

$$\forall a((\forall x \in a)\exists! y \Phi(x,y) \rightarrow$$
$$\exists z(\forall x \in a)(\forall y \in z)\Phi(x,y)).$$

To get ZFC we add:

Axiom of choice:

$$\forall a \exists b(\forall x \in a)(x \neq \emptyset \rightarrow \exists! y(y \in x \cap b)).$$

Many other variants are possible. Below are some examples.

(1)   In the presence of the replacement schema the exact form of the axiom of infinity is not critical: any axiom asserting the existence of a set which can be proved to be infinite will do. Two popular choices are the following.

Axiom of infinity (weak form):

$$\exists x(\emptyset \in x \wedge \forall y(y \in x \rightarrow y \cup \{y\} \in x).$$

Axiom of infinity (Zermelo's form):

$$\exists x(\emptyset \in x \wedge \forall y(y \in x \rightarrow \{y\} \in x).$$

(2)   In ZF^- (that is, ZF without foundation) and stronger theories the pairing axiom is redundant.

(3)   The separation and replacement schemata and the union set axiom can be amalgamated into the following single schema.

Axiom schema of selection and union. If $\Phi(x,y)$ is a formula in which a and b do not occur free, then this is an axiom:

$$\forall y \exists a \forall x (\Phi(x,y) \to x \in a) \to$$
$$\forall b \exists z \forall x (x \in z \leftrightarrow (\exists y \in b) \Phi(x,y)).$$

4 Von Neumann–Bernays–Gödel class theory

Zermelo–Fraenkel set theory is adequate for almost all mathematical purposes. However, its restrictions can sometimes be inconvenient. Mathematicians who use ZF and its variants are therefore accustomed to using the device of virtual sets (see §1 above), except that in order to distinguish virtual sets from the real thing they are called virtual *classes*. If we stop there, we have a good compromise: the technical simplicity of ZF plus the convenience of virtual classes when we need them. However, the urge to treat virtual objects as real is strong, and there is a popular alternative, von Neumann– Bernays–Gödel class theory (NBG), which allows us to say the same things but with classes treated as real.

Before we state the axioms of NBG we need to express what it is for a relation to be 'functional': we do this by writing func(r) as an abbreviation for the formula $\forall x \forall y \forall z (((x,y) \in r \wedge (x,z) \in r) \to y = z)$.

Axiom of extensionality:

As before.

Axiom of classes:

$$\exists x \forall y ((\exists z\ y \in z) \to y \in x).$$

Empty set axiom:

$$\exists x (\forall y\ y \notin x \wedge \exists z\ x \in z).$$

Pairing axiom:

$$(\forall x \in \mathbf{V})(\forall y \in \mathbf{V})(\exists z \in \mathbf{V})$$
$$\forall u (u \in z \leftrightarrow u = x \vee u = y).$$

Axiom schema of class existence. If Φ is any formula with free variables $v_1, v_2, \ldots, v_n$ then this is an axiom:

$$(\forall v_1, v_2, \ldots, v_n \in \mathbf{V})$$
$$\exists z \forall x (x \in z \leftrightarrow (x \in \mathbf{V} \wedge \Phi^{(\mathbf{V})})).$$

Union set axiom:

$$(\forall x \in \mathbf{V})(\exists y \in \mathbf{V}) \forall u (u \in y \leftrightarrow$$
$$\exists v (u \in v \wedge v \in x)).$$

Power set axiom:

$$(\forall x \in \mathbf{V})(\exists y \in \mathbf{V}) \forall u (u \in y \leftrightarrow u \subseteq x).$$

Axiom of infinity:

$$(\exists x \in \mathbf{V})(\emptyset \in x \wedge (\forall u \in x)(\forall v \in x)(u \cup \{v\} \in x)).$$

Axiom of replacement:

$$(\forall x \in \mathbf{V}) \forall r (\text{func}(r) \to$$
$$(\exists y \in \mathbf{V}) \forall u (u \in y \leftrightarrow (\exists v \in x)(v,u) \in r)).$$

Axiom of foundation:

As before.

Most of these axioms are unexciting transcriptions of the axioms of ZF. However, there is one striking difference: the axiom schema of replacement has turned into a single axiom. Even more surprisingly, the axiom schema of class existence can also be replaced by a finite list of axioms, such as the following.

$$\exists a (\forall x, y \in \mathbf{V})((x,y) \in a \leftrightarrow x \in y)$$
$$\forall a \forall b \exists c \forall x (x \in c \leftrightarrow (x \in a \wedge x \in b))$$
$$\forall a \exists b (\forall x \in \mathbf{V})(x \in b \leftrightarrow x \notin a)$$
$$\forall a \exists b (\forall x \in \mathbf{V})(x \in b \leftrightarrow (\exists y \in \mathbf{V})((x,y) \in a))$$
$$\forall a \exists b (\forall x, y \in \mathbf{V})((x,y) \in b \leftrightarrow x \in a)$$
$$\forall a \exists b (\forall x, y, z \in \mathbf{V})((x,y,z) \in b \leftrightarrow (y,z,x) \in a)$$
$$\forall a \exists b (\forall x, y, z \in \mathbf{V})((x,y,z) \in b \leftrightarrow (x,z,y) \in a)$$

So NBG is finitely axiomatizable. This is quite striking since, by contrast, ZF cannot be finitely axiomatized (if it is consistent). And yet NBG and ZF are of equal strength, in the sense that if Φ is any formula in the language of set theory then

$$\text{ZF} \vdash \Phi \text{ if and only if } \text{NBG} \vdash \Phi^{(\mathbf{V})}.$$

And moreover, NBG is consistent if and only if ZF is consistent.

Once we have taken the step of regarding classes as objects, it is puzzling why we should constrain the class existence schema by insisting that the formula defining a class can mention only sets, not proper classes. So if we are serious about the reification of proper classes, we should replace the class existence schema with the following.

Morse–Kelley schema. If $\Phi(x)$ is any formula in which y does not occur free then this is an axiom:

$$\exists y \forall x (x \in y \leftrightarrow (x \in \mathbf{V} \wedge \Phi(x))).$$

The system thus obtained is known as Morse–Kelley class theory (MK; see Kelley 1955). It is (if consistent) a genuine extension of NBG, even with respect to sets. In other words, there are formulas Φ such that $\text{MK} \vdash \Phi^{(\mathbf{V})}$ but $\text{NBG} \nvdash \Phi^{(\mathbf{V})}$. However, the difficulty now is to know why we should stop: if classes are sufficiently real to occur legitimately in the definitions of sets, there seems no good reason why they should not be members of still more collections. As long as we refrain from calling the new collections thus countenanced 'sets' or 'classes', there is no fresh danger of inconsistency. Theories arranged in this way are not popular, though, despite their practical convenience.

5   Other axiomatizations

So far we have said little about the motivation for the axioms. Two principles have guided traditional accounts of this question: the iterative conception; and the doctrine of limitation of size. However, it is not easy to justify all the axioms of ZF on the basis of either principle on its own: for example, the replacement schema is motivated only by limitation of size; and foundation is motivated only by the iterative conception.

Other axiomatizations have been given which are closer in spirit to these principles. Here we shall describe two. The first is Scott's way of axiomatizing the iterative conception of set, according to which sets are divided up into 'levels' (see Scott 1974). The set of all levels belonging to a given level is called its 'history'. The formal details are as follows. First define the 'accumulation' of a set to be the set of all the elements and subsets of its members (if this set exists):

$$\mathrm{acc}(a) = \{x \colon (\exists b \in a)(x \in b \vee x \subseteq b)\}.$$

Next define the predicate 'history(a)' to be an abbreviation for

$$(\forall b \in a)b = \mathrm{acc}(b \cap a).$$

Then define 'level(b)' to be an abbreviation for

$$\exists a(\mathrm{history}(a) \wedge b = \mathrm{acc}(a)).$$

Now adopt the convention that the variables V, V', V'' are restricted to range over levels, so that, for instance, $\forall V \ldots$ is an abbreviation for $\forall V(\mathrm{level}(V) \to \ldots)$. Then the axioms of Z' are as follows:

Axiom of extensionality:

As before.

Axiom schema of separation:

As before.

Axiom of creation:

$$\forall x \exists V \ x \in V.$$

Axiom of infinity:

$$\exists V(\forall V' \in V)(\exists V'' \in V)(V' \in V'').$$

The axioms of ZF' are as follows:

Axiom of extensionality:

As before.

Axiom schema of separation:

As before.

Axiom schema of reflection. If $\Phi(x)$ is any formula then this is an axiom:

$$\exists V(\forall x \in V)(\Phi(x) \to \Phi^{(V)}(x)).$$

Then Z' is equivalent to Z and ZF' is equivalent to ZF.

The second theory we shall describe is due to Ackermann (1956). It takes **V** as a primitive constant. The axioms of the system A are as follows.

Axiom of extensionality:

As before.

Axiom schema of separation:

As before.

Axiom of transitivity:

$$\forall x \forall y(x \in y \wedge y \in \mathbf{V} \to x \in \mathbf{V}).$$

Axiom of subsets:

$$\forall x \forall y(x \subseteq y \wedge y \in \mathbf{V} \to x \in \mathbf{V}).$$

Ackermann's schema. If Φ is a formula in which the free variables are $v_1, v_2, \ldots, v_n$ and in which **V** does not occur, then this is an axiom:

$$(\forall v_1, v_2, \ldots, v_n \in \mathbf{V})(\forall x(\Phi(x) \to x \in \mathbf{V})$$
$$\to (\exists y \in \mathbf{V})\forall x(x \in y \leftrightarrow \Phi(x))).$$

The motivation for A is not that of the iterative conception; rather, it is based on the idea that anything formed solely from sets is itself a set. The modified system A* is something of a hybrid: it grafts onto A the following axiom, which is derived from the iterative conception and cannot be justified by the motivating idea of A:

Axiom of foundation:

$$(\forall x \in \mathbf{V})(x \neq \emptyset \to (\exists y \in x)(y \cap x = \emptyset).$$

If Φ is a formula in which the constant **V** does not occur, then

(1)   if $Z^- \vdash \Phi$ then $A \vdash \Phi^{(\mathbf{V})}$;

(2) $A^* \vdash \Phi^{(\mathbf{V})}$ if and only if $ZF \vdash \Phi$.

6 Anti-foundation axioms

We have already mentioned that not all the axioms of ZF can be motivated by any one account of the notion of sethood. In particular, the axiom of foundation cannot be sustained solely on the basis of the doctrine of limitation of size. But without it where do sets get their individuation? To tell whether two sets are equal we compare their members; if necessary, we compare *their* members, and so on. In the presence of the axiom of foundation, this process cannot go on indefinitely; in its absence, it can. Now if the pattern of membership exhibited by the two sets is the same, then it seems reasonable to say that they are equal: they have done all that can be expected of them, as sets, to be regarded as identical. We are therefore led to the following principle.

Axiom of extensionality (strong form). If two sets have isomorphic $\in$-graphs, then they are equal.

(The $\in$-graph of a set is the membership relation restricted to the set, its members, their members, and so on.) As we have already noted, this assertion is provable in ZF, but in ZF^- (ZF without foundation) we need to add it as an axiom. It ensures, for instance, that there is at most one set Ω such that $\Omega = \{\Omega\}$ (since any two such sets would have to have isomorphic $\in$-graphs). However, it does not guarantee that there *is* such a set. Aczel (1988) and others have studied the consequences of adding to ZF^- not only the strong extensionality axiom just mentioned (which is essentially limitative) but also a permissive axiom generating non-well-founded sets (which can be thought of as limit points in much the same way that irrational numbers are limits of rational numbers). The most natural of the axioms that have been studied is the following *anti-foundation axiom*:

Every graph is the $\in$-graph of some set.

7 Quine's systems

Another, more radical strand in attempts to resolve the set-theoretic paradoxes (see PARADOXES OF SET AND PROPERTY) is represented by the various forms of the theory of types (see THEORY OF TYPES). We cannot, in any of the systems we have been describing so far, collect together all the objects to form another object, but we can certainly quantify over them; in the theory of types we cannot. Objects are stratified into 'types', which are not cumulative but otherwise resemble the levels of Scott's theory; variables are labelled with superscripts to indicate the type they range over. The formula $x^m \in y^n$ is taken to be well-formed only if $n = m + 1$. Now type theory is not, according to the strict definition adopted here, a form

of set theory, because it does not have the axiom of extensionality. What it has instead is a schema of axioms, one for each type:

$$\forall x^{n+1} \forall y^{n+1} (\forall z^n (z^n \in x^{n+1} \leftrightarrow z \in y^{n+1})$$
$$\rightarrow x^{n+1} = y^{n+1}).$$

Not to call this the axiom of extensionality may seem a pedantic cavil, particularly if the device of 'typical ambiguity' is introduced, whereby formulas are written with superscripts omitted and taken to stand schematically for any way of adding superscripts which produces a grammatical result. Thus the extensionality schema above is usually represented

$$\forall x \forall y (\forall z (z \in x \leftrightarrow z \in y) \rightarrow x = y).$$

Nevertheless, we maintain, this is not the axiom of extensionality. Typical ambiguity is not true generality. To see the difference, consider the formula $\exists y \forall x \, x \in y$: taken as typically ambiguous this stands schematically for such formulas as

$$\exists y^{n+1} \forall x^n \, x^n \in y^{n+1}$$

and is therefore true; taken as a formula in its own right it is false. The restrictions on what can be said in the theory of types have struck many writers as too severe. However, the means by which the theory avoids paradox are as secure as those of iterative set theories. Quine has proposed a system which uses type theory's method of paradox-avoidance but abandons its grammatical restrictions. Specifically, he regards formulas as genuine, not typically ambiguous, but calls a formula 'stratified' if it is possible to decorate it with superscripts so as to make it well-formed according to the theory of types. The system, which is known as NF because it was proposed in an article called 'New Foundations for Mathematical Logic' (1937), has the following axioms.

Axiom of extensionality:

As before.

Axiom schema of stratified comprehension. If $\Phi(x)$ is any stratified formula in which y does not occur free then this is an axiom:

$$\exists y \forall x (x \in y \leftrightarrow \Phi(x)).$$

NF is very different from ZF. For one thing NF is finitely axiomatizable. Moreover, since the formula $x = x$ is stratified, it follows at once that there is a set of all sets: if we denote it V then $V \in V$. The axiom of choice is provably false in NF. When we come to arithmetic, it is possible in a natural way to define zero and the successor operation in NF, and then to define the set of natural numbers to be the intersection of all sets containing zero and closed under successors. This works well up to a point, but gives us mathematical induction only for stratified formulas. Unfortunately some useful formulas are not stratified. For example, we cannot prove in NF, and are therefore forced to add as an axiom, the *axiom of counting*:

If n is a natural number then it has exactly n predecessors.

In an effort to overcome this inconvenience Quine has proposed a second system called ML which stands to NF in somewhat the same relation that NBG stands to ZF. The second system takes **V** as a primitive constant and has the following axioms.

Axiom of extensionality:

As before.

Axiom schema of class existence. If $\Phi(x)$ is a formula in which y does not occur free then this is an axiom:

$$\exists y \forall x (x \in y \leftrightarrow y \in \mathbf{V} \wedge \Phi(x)).$$

Axiom schema of set existence. If $\Phi(x, v_1, v_2, \ldots, v_n)$ is a stratified formula in which no variables other than those listed occur free, then this is an axiom:

$$\forall v_1, v_2, \ldots, v_n \exists y \in \mathbf{V}$$

$$\forall x (x \in y \leftrightarrow \Phi^{(\mathbf{V})}(x, v_1, \ldots, v_n)).$$

In contrast to NF, ML is not finitely axiomatizable if it is consistent. If Φ is any formula in which **V** does not occur then

$$\text{NF} \vdash \Phi \text{ if and only if } \text{ML} \vdash \Phi^{(\mathbf{V})}.$$

Thus ML is consistent if and only if NF is consistent. However, it is still not known whether ML and NF are consistent if ZF is consistent. If we define the natural numbers in superficially the same way as in NF, we get mathematical induction even for non-stratifiable formulas, obviating the need for an axiom of counting. However, this time we cannot prove that the class of natural numbers is a set (if ML is consistent). So now we have to add *this* as an axiom. Thus neither NF nor ML suffices without supplementation as a basis for mathematics.

See also: LOGICAL AND MATHEMATICAL TERMS, GLOSSARY OF

References and further reading

* Ackermann, W. (1956) 'Zur Axiomatik der Mengenlehre' (On the Axiomatization of Set Theory), *Mathematische Annalen* 131: 336–45. (The source for the system A mentioned in §5.)
* Aczel, P. (1988) *Non-Well-Founded Sets*, Stanford, CA: Center for the Study of Language and Information, Stanford University. (An account of anti-foundation axioms, aimed at the mathematically aware.)
  Boolos, G. (1989) 'Iteration Again', *Philosophical Topics* 17 (2): 5–21. (An interesting but fairly technical discussion of the iterative and limitation-of-size conceptions of set.)
  Bourbaki, N. (1968) *Theory of Sets*, New York: Addison-Wesley. (A development of set theory in a system equivalent to ZF⁻ together with a strong form of the axiom of choice. The system is notable for its employment of the axiom schema of selection and union referred to in §3.)
  Forster, T.E. (1992) *Set Theory with a Universal Set*, Oxford: Oxford University Press. (A survey of work on NF, well written but aimed at logicians.)
  Fraenkel, A.A. (1922) 'Zu den Grundlagen der Cantor–Zermeloschen Mengenlehre' (On the Foundations of Cantor–Zermelo Set Theory), *Mathematische Annalen* 86: 230–7. (This paper is the reason Fraenkel's name is associated with the standard formulation of set theory.)
  Fraenkel, A.A., Bar-Hillel, Y. and Levy, A. (1958) *Foundations of Set Theory*, Amsterdam: North Holland; revised 2nd edn, 1973. (Detailed discussions of most of the systems of set theory mentioned here and a wealth of historical information and references.)
  Gödel, K. (1940) *The Consistency of the Continuum Hypothesis*, Princeton, NJ: Princeton University Press, 1994. (The definitive formulation of NBG.)
  Hallet, M. (1984) *Cantorian Set Theory and Limitation of Size*, Oxford: Clarendon Press. (A detailed study of the early history of set theory.)
  Heijenoort, J. van (ed.) (1967) *From Frege to Gödel: A Source Book in Mathematical Logic, 1879–1931*, Cambridge, MA: Harvard University Press. (It is possible to trace the historical development of ZF and NBG through the papers reprinted here.)
* Kelley, J.L. (1955) *General Topology*, Princeton, NJ: Van Nostrand. (The appendix includes the first published version of MK.)
* Kuratowski, K. (1921) 'Sur la notion d'ordre dans la théorie des ensembles' (On the Notion of Order in Set Theory), *Fundamenta Mathematicae* 2: 161–71. (Mentioned in §3.)
* Lewis, D.K. (1991) *Parts of Classes*, Oxford: Blackwell. (An entertaining, non-technical discussion of a way of separating the hierarchical from the non-hierarchical part of set theory.)
  Morse, A. (1965) *A Theory of Sets*, New York: Academic Press. (A treatment of the theory of classes based on a version of MK.)
  Neumann, J. von (1925) 'Eine Axiomatisierung der

Mengenlehre' (An Axiomatization of Set Theory), *Journal für die reine und angewandte Mathematik* 154: 219–40; trans. in J. van Heijenoort (ed.) *From Frege to Gödel: A Source Book in Mathematical Logic, 1879–1931*, Cambridge, MA: Harvard University Press, 1967. (The first formulation of an axiomatization similar to what is now called NBG.)

Potter, M.D. (1990) *Sets: An Introduction*, Oxford: Oxford University Press. (An account of set theory based on a Scott-type axiomatization; intended for the mathematically-minded.)

* Quine, W.V. (1937) 'New Foundations for Mathematical Logic', *American Mathematical Monthly* 44: 70–80. (Principally of historical interest. For up-to-date information about NF consult Forster (1992).)

—— (1940) *Mathematical Logic*, Cambridge, MA: Harvard University Press; revised edn, 1951. (Very technical, but includes a wealth of information.)

—— (1963) *Set Theory and its Logic*, Cambridge, MA: Harvard University Press; revised edn, 1969. (Rather idiosyncratic but extremely clear and well written.)

* Scott, D. (1974) 'Axiomatizing Set Theory', in *Axiomatic Set Theory*, Proceedings of the Symposium of Pure Mathematics 13 (2), Providence, RI: American Mathematical Society, 207–14. (The primary source for Scott's axiomatization of ZF' described in §5.)

Skolem, T. (1923) 'Einige Bemerkungen zur axiomatischen Begründung der Mengenlehre', in *Matematikerkongressen i Helsingfors den 4–7 Juli 1922, Den femte skandinaviska matematikerkongressen, Redogörelse*, Helsinki: Akademiska Bokhandeln, 217–32; trans. S. Bauer-Mengelberg, 'Some Remarks on Axiomatized Set Theory', in J. van Heijenoort (ed.) *From Frege to Gödel: A Source Book in Mathematical Logic, 1879–1931*, Cambridge, MA: Harvard University Press, 1967, 291–301. (The first precise formulation of the axiom schema of replacement and of Zermelo's notion of 'definite property'.)

* Zermelo, E. (1908) 'Untersuchungen über die Grundlagen der Mengenlehre I', *Mathematische Annalen* 65: 261–81; trans. S. Bauer-Mengelberg, 'Investigations in the Foundations of Set Theory', in J. van Heijenoort (ed.) *From Frege to Gödel: A Source Book in Mathematical Logic, 1879–1931*, Cambridge, MA: Harvard University Press, 1967, 200–15. (The first published axiomatization of set theory.)

MICHAEL POTTER

SEUSE, HEINRICH *see* SUSO, HENRY

SEXTUS EMPIRICUS
(*fl. c.* AD 200)

*Sextus Empiricus is our major surviving source for Greek scepticism. Three works of his survive: a general sceptical handbook (*Outlines of Pyrrhonism*), a partly lost longer treatment of the same material, and a series of self-contained essays questioning the utility of the individual liberal arts.*

Little is known about the life of Sextus Empiricus, our major source for Pyrrhonism. He was a doctor of the Empirical school, a sceptically-minded medical sect (see HELLENISTIC MEDICAL EPISTEMOLOGY), and wrote some (lost) medical treatises. He also wrote three treatises on scepticism. *Outlines of Pyrrhonism*, is a three-volume handbook of sceptical arguments. The first covers the nature of Pyrrhonism and its distinction from other philosophies, the proper interpretation of the sceptic's characteristic expressions (see PYRRHONISM §§3, 6), and the general form of sceptical argument (see PYRRHONISM §2). The second deals with the Pyrrhonian attack on dogmatic logic and epistemology, in particular with the issue of the criterion, and the nature of signs and proof (see PYRRHONISM §4). The third is on physics, attacking dogmatic notions of cause, motion, generation, space and time, number, and so on (see PYRRHONISM §5), and ethics (see PYRRHONISM §2).

A fuller treatment of the same material is standardly known as Books VII–XI of *Against the Professors* (sometimes called *Against the Mathematicians*). These break down into three subsections: *Against the Logicians* (Books VII–VIII), *Against the Physicists* (Books IX–X) and *Against the Ethicists* (Book XI), which contain the material to be found in Books II and III of *Outlines of Pyrrhonism*, as well as a reworking of some of the contents of *Outlines of Pyrrhonism* I 210–41. As Janáček (1963) has shown, *Against the Professors* VII–XI is incomplete, lacking at least one preliminary book corresponding to the bulk of Book I of *Outlines of Pyrrhonism*.

Finally, Sextus composed a series of treatises against the dogmatists' conceptions of the liberal arts (grammar, rhetoric, geometry, arithmetic, astrology and music: *Against the Professors* I–VI), the scepticism of which seems a good deal more moderate in tone, and whose arguments owe much to Epicureanism.

Sextus makes no claims to originality as a thinker,

and he clearly owes a great deal to AENESIDEMUS, and to subsequent Pyrrhonist systematizers, especially AGRIPPA. However, the Pyrrhonism he outlines is clear, consistent and rigorous; and, while the quality of the argumentation it contains is, as Sextus himself admits (*Outlines of Pyrrhonism* III 280), uneven, the Sextan version of scepticism became canonical. Diogenes Laertius (IX 116) mentions him as a prominent Pyrrhonian; and in the fourth century St Gregory of Nazianzus excoriates him in the same breath as Pyrrho himself, as the originator of 'the vile and malignant disease' of scepticism (*Orations* XII 21).

In 1564, Henri Étienne (better known as 'Stephanus') published a Latin translation of *Outlines of Pyrrhonism*; it was read with eagerness by MONTAIGNE, and the ghost of Sextan argument can often be discerned behind Montaigne's elegant and discursive prose. More importantly still, Greek scepticism came by this route to influence DESCARTES, and to provide the ultimate stimulus for his search for an epistemological foundation of knowledge and science proof against sceptical assault; as such, Sextus has had, albeit indirectly, a profound impact on the development of modern philosophy.

List of works

Sextus Empiricus (*c.* AD 200) *Outlines of Pyrrhonism*, trans. J. Annas and J. Barnes, *Outlines of Scepticism*, Cambridge: Cambridge University Press, 1994. (Fine translation with introduction and notes.)
—— (*c.* AD 200) *Against the Professors*, trans. R.G. Bury, *Against the Logicians*, *Against the Physicists*, *Against the Ethicists* and *Against the Professors*, Loeb Classical Library, Cambridge, MA: Harvard University Press and London: Heinemann, 3 vols, 1935, 1936, 1949. (Parallel Greek text and English translation with minimal notes.)

References and further reading

* Diogenes Laertius (*c.* early 3rd century AD) *Lives of the Philosophers*, trans. R.D. Hicks, *Diogenes Laertius Lives of Eminent Philosophers*, Loeb Classical Library, Cambridge, MA: Harvard University Press and London: Heinemann, 1925, 2 vols. (Parallel Greek text and English translation; IX 61–116 is devoted to Pyrrhonism.)
House, D.K. (1980) 'The Life of Sextus Empiricus', *Classical Quarterly* 30: 227–38. (Stresses how little we actually know about Sextus Empiricus.)
* Janáček, K. (1963) 'Die Hauptschrift des Sextus Empiricus als Torso erhalten?' (Does Sextus Empiricus' Principal Work survive as a Torso?), *Philologus* 107: 271–7. (Establishes that our text of *Against the Professors* is incomplete.)

R.J. HANKINSON

SEXUALITY, PHILOSOPHY OF

The philosophy of sexuality, like the philosophy of science, art or law, is the study of the concepts and propositions surrounding its central protagonist, in this case 'sex'. Its practitioners focus on conceptual, metaphysical and normative questions.

Conceptual *philosophy of sex analyses the notions of sexual desire, sexual activity and sexual pleasure. What makes a feeling a sexual sensation? Manipulation of and feelings in the genitals are not necessary, since other body parts yield sexual pleasure. What makes an act sexual? A touch on the arm might be a friendly pat, an assault, or sex; physical properties alone do not distinguish them. What is the conceptual link between sexual pleasure and sexual activity? Neither the intention to produce sexual pleasure nor the actual experience of pleasure seems necessary for an act to be sexual. Other conceptual questions have to do not with what makes an act sexual, but with what makes it the type of sexual act it is. How should 'rape' be defined? What the conceptual differences are, if any, between obtaining sex through physical force and obtaining it by offering money is an interesting and important issue.*

Metaphysical *philosophy of sex discusses ontological and epistemological matters: the place of sexuality in human nature; the relationships among sexuality, emotion and cognition; the meaning of sexuality for the person, the species, the cosmos. What is sex all about, anyway? That sexual desire is a hormone-driven instinct implanted by a god or nature acting in the service of the species, and that it has a profound spiritual dimension, are two – not necessarily incompatible – views. Perhaps the significance of sexuality is little different from that of eating, breathing and defecating; maybe, or in addition, sexuality is partially constitutive of moral personality.*

Normative *philosophy of sex explores the perennial questions of sexual ethics. In what circumstances is it morally permissible to engage in sexual activity or experience sexual pleasure? With whom? For what purpose? With which body parts? For how long? The historically central answers come from Thomist natural law, Kantian deontology, and utilitarianism. Normative philosophy of sex also addresses legal, social and political issues. Should society steer people in the direction of heterosexuality, marriage, family? May the law regulate sexual conduct by prohibiting prostitution or homosexuality? Normative philosophy of sex includes nonethical value questions as well. What is good sex? What is its contribution to the good life?*

The breadth of the philosophy of sex is shown by the variety of topics it investigates: abortion, contraception, acquaintance rape, pornography, sexual harassment, and objectification, to name a few. The philosophy of sex begins with a picture of a privileged pattern of relationship, in which two adult heterosexuals love each other, are faithful to each other within a formal marriage, and look forward to procreation and family. Philosophy of sex, as the Socratic scrutiny of our sexual practices, beliefs and concepts, challenges this privileged pattern by exploring the virtues, and not only the vices, of adultery, prostitution, homosexuality, group sex, bestiality, masturbation, sadomasochism, incest, paedophilia and casual sex with anonymous strangers. Doing so provides the same illumination about sex that is provided when the philosophies of science, art and law probe the privileged pictures of their own domains.

1 **Conceptual analysis**
2 **Sexual activity**
3 **Social constructionism**
4 **The metaphysics of sex**
5 **Aquinas and natural law**
6 **Kant's sexual ethics**
7 **Contemporary Kantians**
8 **Consent and coercion**
9 **Utilitarianism**
10 **Sadomasochism and love**

1 Conceptual analysis

The philosophy of sex investigates conceptual, metaphysical and normative questions, although the boundaries between these three are hardly firm. Metaphysical and normative philosophy of sex are well developed, stretching back to Plato and Augustine (see PLATO §12); sexual ethics has a famous history, and the contemplation of the place of sexuality in human nature is central to Christianity. The analysis of sexual concepts, by contrast, is in its infancy. The subjects of analysis are these core concepts and the logical relationships among them: sexual desire, sensation, pleasure, act, arousal and satisfaction. Derivative sexual concepts, which presuppose an understanding of the core concepts, are also the subject of analysis. Among these are rape, sexual harassment, sexual orientation, sexual perversion, prostitution and pornography (see PORNOGRAPHY).

Consider adultery. It can be defined as a sexual act that occurs between two persons, at least one of whom is married but not to the other. The definition should also mention, as a necessary condition, willing and knowledgeable consent. Suppose X coerces Y, who is married to Z, into coitus. Y did not commit adultery, because Y did not have the proper frame of mind; Y never intended to commit adultery or engage in intercourse at all. Or suppose X and Y engage in coitus, both believing, on the basis of good evidence (but falsely), that X's spouse Z died years ago; or the unmarried X has good reason to think (but falsely, due to Y's deception) that Y, too, is not married. Has X committed an adulterous sexual act, unwittingly and so, perhaps, not culpably; or is X's lack of *mens rea*, X's ignorance of the true state of affairs, incompatible with adultery?

We cannot fully understand the derivative sexual concept 'adultery' until we have defined 'sexual act'. If X and Y send to each other sexually arousing messages through the Internet, have they engaged in a sexual act ('cybersex')? Is their exchange of messages sexual enough, quantitatively or qualitatively, to be adulterous, if one of them is married? Here we can see the intertwining of conceptual and moral matters. A lack of clarity about 'sexual act' allows the exoneration of adultery by a convenient redescription of what occurs between X and Y – it was only 'fooling around', not 'real' sex. Another, quite opposite, manoeuvre, is possible. Theologians often define adultery in the spirit of Matthew 5: 28, making a sexual fantasy sufficient, even in the absence of physical contact: X commits adultery if X thinks lustful thoughts about Y.

2 Sexual activity

Our interest in defining 'sexual act' is not merely philosophical; it is also practical. Precise definitions of 'sexual act' are needed for social scientific studies of sexual behaviour and orientation (to be used in the consideration of questions about, for example, who engages in homosexual acts and whether this correlates with genetics, and how often people engage in sex) and for legislation in the areas of child abuse, rape, harassment and adultery.

Sexual acts might be defined as those involving sexual body parts. The sexual parts of the body are first catalogued; acts are sexual if and only if they involve contact with one of these parts. 'Sexual act', on this view, is logically dependent on 'sexual part'. But do we clearly understand 'sexual part'? Two people might shake hands briefly, without the act being sexual; they could, alternatively, warmly press their hands together and feel a surge of sexual pleasure. Sometimes, then, the hands are used nonsexually and sometimes they are used sexually.

Are the hands a sexual part? Whether the hands are a sexual part depends on the activity in which they are engaged. Hence, instead of an act's being sexual because it involves a sexual body part, a body part is sexual because of the sexual nature of the act in which it is used. We might say that a genital examination is not a sexual act even though the genitals are touched; hence contact with a sexual part is not sufficient for an act to be sexual. But we could also say that not even the genitals are sexual parts in the requisite sense; for in the medical context the genitals are not being treated as sexual parts.

The morality of sexuality has been understood by some in terms of its procreative function (see §5). Alternatively, the procreative nature of sexual activity might be employed analytically rather than normatively. Sexual acts, on this view, are those having procreative potential in virtue of their biological structure. The principal case of such an act is heterosexual intercourse. This analysis, then, is too narrow, if taken as stating a necessary condition. Here is a more plausible formulation: sexual acts are (1) acts that are procreative in structure and (2) any acts that are the physiological or psychological precursors or concomitants of acts that are sexual by (1). This version casts a wider net, but not wide enough. Masturbation, which is not a procreative act and not often a precursor or concomitant of coitus, turns out not to be a sexual act. Another emendation suggests itself: sexual acts are also (3) acts that bear a close physical resemblance to the acts judged sexual by (1) or (2). This vague condition does not save the proposed analysis. Some sexual perversions (such as fondling shoes) are sexual even though they bear no reasonable resemblance to coitus or its concomitants. This analysis also suggests that homosexual acts, all of which are nonprocreative, are sexual just because they sufficiently resemble heterosexual acts. That seems to be the wrong reason for the right conclusion.

Another view is that both homosexual and heterosexual acts are sexual in virtue of the type of pleasure or sensation they produce. Thus it seems reasonable to propose that sexual acts are those that produce sexual pleasure (Gray 1978). But if pleasure is the criterion of the sexual, pleasure cannot be the gauge of the nonmoral quality of sex acts. The couple who have lost sexual interest in each other, and who engage in routine coitus from which they derive no pleasure, are still performing a sexual act. We are forbidden, by this analysis, from saying that they engage in sex but that it is (nonmorally) bad sex. Rather, we can say, at most, that they tried to engage in sex, and failed. Furthermore, in this analysis 'sexual act' is logically dependent on 'sexual pleasure', so we cannot say that sexual pleasure is the pleasure produced by sexual

acts. Then how might we distinguish sexual pleasure or sensations from others? This problem also arises for a more complex analysis: sexual acts are those acts that tend to satisfy sexual desire, where sexual desire is taken to be the desire for the pleasure of physical contact (Goldman 1977). 'Pleasures of physical contact' might not specify sexual pleasure accurately enough. An additional complication is that a gender difference in the experience and conceptualization of sexual pleasure might exist. Additionally, someone might experience sexual desire yet have no idea what to do as a result of having it, no idea that physical contact, or what kind of physical contact, is the next, but hardly mandatory, step. Sexual desire, as argued by Jerome Shaffer (1978: 186–7), might not be a desire *for* something or *that* something at all. What, then, are the features of a desire that make it sexual? Sexual desire is distinguished, on Shaffer's account, by being accompanied by sexual excitement and arousal. We can, in turn, ask what sexual excitement and arousal are, as opposed to other kinds of excitement and arousal. For Shaffer, sexual arousal is 'directly sexual in that it involves the sexual parts, viz., the genital areas'. Have we gone full circle?

Finally, sexual acts might be understood as those involving a sexual intention. But an intention to produce or experience sexual pleasure, for example, might be neither necessary nor sufficient for an act to be sexual. A couple engaging in coitus, both parties intending only that fertilization occur and neither concerned with sexual pleasure, performs a sexual act. Maybe this is not the correct sexual intention. But the intention to procreate is not it: gays and lesbians experience desire and arousal and engage in sex without any procreative intent. Furthermore, intentions are arguably irrelevant in making sexual acts sexual. Rape can be sexual whether the rapist intends to get sexual pleasure from it, to humiliate his victim, or to assert his masculinity. From the fact that in some rapes, rapists intend to degrade their victims, to dominate and exert power over them, it does not follow that the act is not sexual. Indeed, the rapist might have chosen a sexual act quite on purpose as his method to humiliate and degrade. His victim is degraded exactly by the sexual nature of the act endured; the victim experiences a shame that accompanies a forced sexual act but would not accompany sexless assault.

3 Social constructionism

What, then, are sexual acts? Maybe they have no transcultural or ahistorical essence, and the analytic project is doomed. Acts involving the same body parts are sometimes sexual, sometimes not. Some touches and movements are deemed sexual in one culture but not in others; the fragrances, mannerisms and costumes that are sexually arousing vary among places and times. No lowest common denominator exists that makes all sexual acts sexual. Bodily movements acquire meaning – as sexual, or as something else – by existing within a culture that attaches meaning to them. There are, then, only variable social definitions of the sexual.

Such is the view known as social constructionism (or anti-essentialism). As one proponent puts it, 'the very meaning and content of sexual arousal' varies so much among genders, classes, and cultures that 'there is *no* abstract and universal category of "the erotic" or "the sexual" applicable without change to *all* societies' (Padgug 1979: 54; original emphasis). Nancy Hartsock elaborates:

> We should understand sexuality not as an essence or set of properties defining an individual, nor as a set of drives and needs (especially genital) of an individual. Rather, we should understand sexuality as culturally and historically defined and constructed. Anything can become eroticized.
>
> (1983: 156)

Hartsock's expression 'anything can become eroticized' must mean 'anything can be linked to sexual arousal and pleasure'. That might be true; after all, unusual items bring paraphiliacs sexual joy. If so, however, there seems to be a common denominator after all, an essential even if narrow core to the sexual: an unchanging, culturally invariable subjective experience of sexual pleasure.

The history of sexuality is the history of our discourse about sex, as Michel FOUCAULT might have put it. We create things by using words. There really is no such thing as masturbatory insanity or nymphomania – no medical condition, no psychological character trait, no underlying pathology. Well, there is, but only because we have picked out some behavioural patterns and made up a word to name them, not because masturbatory insanity and nymphomania have, like the moon, an existence independent of our words, our observations, and our evaluations of it. Social facts, such as the existence of 'peasants', 'witches' and 'yuppies' (Edward Stein's examples), have an odd, plastic, fuzzy nature. Similar considerations apply to 'perversion', 'philanderer' and 'homosexuality'. Thus the title of David Halperin's social constructionist monograph, *One Hundred Years of Homosexuality* (1990). It did not exist before the word 'homosexual' was coined by Károly Mária Benkert in 1869.

Adrienne Rich asserts that even heterosexuality is a 'man-made institution'. Heterosexuality is 'forcibly and subliminally imposed on women', 'designed to keep [them] within a male sexual purlieu' (1986: 34–57). Ti-Grace Atkinson similarly claims that 'sexual intercourse is a political construct, reified into an institution' (1974: 13). People have been engaging in sexual intercourse because doing so serves not their own individual needs, but a political purpose: to keep the species (and the system) going by replenishing the population. People have been groomed by society to perform the act of intercourse, their desire-pleasure apparatus manipulated, even created, to serve this purpose. Hence, when the development of brave-new-world reproductive technology eliminates the social function of coitus, individuals' 'sexual "drives" and "needs" would disappear' as well (20), there not being any reason to keep the grooming in operation. The end of biological reproduction is also the end of sex, or at least of sex as we know it. Whether that possible state would be a cause for celebration or despair is unclear.

4 The metaphysics of sex

In sex we are vulnerable to another's enticing words and seductive touch. Our wills are weak, so we are dominated as much by our desires as by the other's physical strength or alluring beauty. Engulfment or invasion of our bodies by the other's gaze and flesh is hazardous. In exchange for exquisite pleasure, we make ourselves susceptible to embarrassment, anguish, betrayal (see VULNERABILITY AND FINITUDE §2). This psychology of sex provides reason for taking sex, and so sexual ethics, seriously. Its consequences – transmission of disease, the existence of a new human being – do so as well. If procreation is a couple's contribution to God's ongoing work of creation, if it is the sacred ground where humans and God engage in a shared project, then sexuality must be protected by stringent ethics. Or if sexual personality resides at the core of moral personality, if the training of sexuality impinges on developing character in such a way that the failure to learn to control the pursuit of sexual pleasure undermines the achievement of virtue, then the moral education of the body is crucial.

In light of sexuality's intricate psychology and far-reaching consequences, sexual activity might be justifiable only by weighty nonsexual considerations. Consider the hostility of Christianity to sex, as in Augustine's *De nuptiis et concupiscentia* (On Marriage and Concupiscence), where we hear the strains of Plato's *Phaedrus*:

> A man turns to good use the evil of concupiscence... when he bridles and restrains its rage... and never relaxes his hold upon it except when

intent on offspring, and then controls and applies it to the carnal generation of children... not to the subjection of the spirit to the flesh in a sordid servitude.

(I 9)

Neither is Immanuel Kant kind to sexuality: 'Sexual love makes of the loved person an Object of appetite.... Taken by itself it is a degradation of human nature' (1780–81: 163). If sexual desire objectifies, in virtue of pushing us to seek pleasure without regard for our partners, if sexual urges engender deception and manipulation, then sexuality is morally suspicious. Only special circumstances could make acting on these desires morally right. For these gloomy reasons, many conservative and religious thinkers, but also some feminists, believe that sexual activity is redeemed only by love or marriage.

In contrast, sexual liberals suppose that sexuality is a wholesome bonding mechanism that allows persons to overcome the psychological and moral tension between egoism and benevolence (see EGOISM AND ALTRUISM). Sexual activity involves pleasing the self and the other at the same time; these exchanges of pleasure generate gratitude and affection. Further, sexual pleasure is a valuable thing in its own right, the pursuit of which does not require external or nonsexual justification. And sexuality is a cardinal affirmation of the goodness of bodily existence. There is no contradiction in presuming that a virtuous person can lead a life in which sexual pleasure is sought for its own sake – in moderation, of course. Weak, not stringent, moral rules apply to sex.

The claim that sexual pleasure is valuable does not mean we should not condemn sexual misconduct. We often do, however, pardon sexually motivated misconduct when we would not excuse similar conduct motivated otherwise (see Pausanias in Plato's *Symposium* 182e-183c). Does sex warrant this exculpation? If the most intense way we relate to another person is sexually, then maybe forgiveness for sexual offences should be graciously forthcoming. But sexuality is hardly unique in the depth of the personal relationship it elicits; think about mutual hatred. Nor is there much intensity in the dull coitus of a long-married couple. According to another line of thought, sexuality has a peculiar ability to thwart reason: sexual impulses make us temporarily deranged (recall the dark horse of Plato's *Phaedrus*). We are to be excused because in sexual matters we cannot control ourselves. But the lures of politics, ambition and money are just as powerful and devilish as the anticipations of the flesh. In none of these respects does sexuality seem unique or significant enough to deserve special attention.

Perhaps sexual desire – as a component of love and as opposed to mere 'horniness' – latches on to particular objects (I want *Jennifer*), in a way hunger does not (I want a sausage, and any fat, juicy one will do). Genuine *eros* makes us desire a particular person; crude desire is satisfiable by fungible bodies. But the distinction between *eros* and lust is a fine one, and in many instances doubtful; we only deceive ourselves that this person is not replaceable by others in our affections. As Roger Scruton puts it, 'a metaphysical illusion resid[es] in the heart of sexual desire' (1986: 95). Sexual passion misleads us; it makes it *appear* that we are ontologically more than we are, transcendental selves rather than mere material beings (1986: 130).

Plato, in the *Symposium*, also issued a warning: what we think we are seeking is not really what we want; our *eros* for bodies is really *eros* for truth and beauty. Augustine similarly thought that the search for God was hidden beneath the search for sensual pleasure in another's body. And for Arthur Schopenhauer, the beauty of the object of sexual desire was nature's way of tricking us (men?) into thinking that the satisfaction of our erotic love for our beloveds is for our own individual good. To the contrary, sexual love benefits only the species, for the good of which nature makes mere use of us (1844: 538–40) (see SCHOPENHAUER, A. §4). This naturalist vision of sex is not far removed from Atkinson's anti-essentialism; both see its purpose in terms of the species and not of the individual.

5 Aquinas and natural law

For Aquinas, sexual acts are morally wrong in two different ways (*Summa theologiae* IIaIIae.154.1) (for an introduction to his ethical views, see AQUINAS, T. §13). First, 'when the act of its nature is incompatible with the purpose of the sex-act [procreation]. In so far as generation is blocked, we have unnatural vice, which is any complete sex-act from which of its nature generation cannot follow.' Aquinas gives four examples (IIaIIae.154.11) of sexual acts that are unnatural vice because not procreative: 'the sin of self-abuse', 'intercourse with a thing of another species', acts 'with a person of the same sex', and acts in which 'the natural style of intercourse is not observed, as regards the proper organ or according to other rather beastly and monstrous techniques'. Second, 'the conflict with right reason may arise from the nature of the act with respect to the other party', as in incest, rape, seduction and adultery.

Sexual sins in the first category are the worst: 'unnatural vice flouts nature by transgressing its basic principles of sexuality, [so] it is in this matter the gravest of sins' (IIaIIae.154.12). Aquinas is replying to an interlocutor who argues that unnatural vice is *not* the morally worst sex. 'The more a sin is against charity', says the interlocutor, 'the worse it is. Now adultery and seduction and rape harms our neighbour, whereas unnatural lust injures nobody else, and accordingly is not the worst form of lust.' Aquinas rejects this thinking. Seduction, rape and adultery violate only 'the developed plan of living according to reason' that derives from humans living in society, while 'unnatural sins', which violate the plan of creation, are an 'affront to God'. If some sexual acts are unnatural, they are morally wrong, in Thomistic ethics, just for that reason. To the list of reasons sexual acts might be wrong – they are dishonest, cruel, unfair, manipulative, coercive, exploitative, selfish or negligently dangerous – a Thomist adds 'unnatural'. Not so the sexual libertarian. Mutual consent is, in the absence of third-party harm, sufficient for the morality of sexual acts, and no law of God or nature need supplement this basic principle of proper relations among humans.

In arguing that sexual behaviour ought to conform to human nature within God's plan, one must be able to justify particular conceptions of that nature and his intentions. Augustine and Aquinas knew, or thought they did, that God wanted sexuality to be the mechanism of procreation. Aquinas displays confidence in his account of human nature:

It is evident that the bringing up of a human child requires the care of a mother who nurses him, and much more the care of a father, under whose guidance and guardianship his earthly needs are supplied and his character developed. Therefore indiscriminate intercourse is against human nature. The union of one man with one woman is postulated, and with her he remains, not for a little while, but for a long period, or even for a whole lifetime.

(IIaIIae.154.2)

Christine Gudorf (1994), however, argues for a new, non-Augustinian yet Christian understanding of the body. Basing her view in part on the existence of the clitoris, an organ that on her view has only a pleasure-producing function and no procreative function, Gudorf argues that God designed the human body foremost for sexual pleasure.

Although he appeals to biology and not the Lord's plan, Michael Levin concludes, in agreement with Aquinas, that homosexual acts 'involve the use of the genitals for what they aren't for' (1984: 253). Homosexual anal intercourse is unnatural because being inside another man's rectum is not what a man's penis is 'for'; it is for penetrating a woman's vagina. This kind of Thomism is susceptible to mockery

(Does a man's masturbation misuse the penis, or the hand? Does heterosexual cunnilingus misuse the tongue?) but it has also received serious discussion (see Murphy 1987). In deriving ethical judgments directly from nature, the problem is to come up with a coherent, plausible account of the 'natural'. Whereas Aquinas claims that a man's 'indiscriminate intercourse is against human nature', much recent biology claims that promiscuity in men is perfectly natural, the result of evolutionary mechanisms. In this way, science has the power to turn philosophical or theological reliance on nature on its head (see EVOLUTION AND ETHICS §§2–3). Thus, if the current research suggesting that homosexual orientation has a substantial genetic basis is vindicated, the Western religions might have to concede that such sexual desires and behaviour are, after all, part of the design of nature. Patricia Jung and Ralph Smith (1993) offer a Christian defence of loving, homosexual marriages, in part based on the idea that being homosexual is little different from being left-handed.

6 Kant's sexual ethics

Most philosophers have had something to say about sex; with a little digging, one can uncover the unsystematic sexual thoughts of Aristotle, Descartes and Hume. Others – such as Schopenhauer, KIERKEGAARD and SARTRE – took sexuality more seriously. And for some, most notably Plato and FREUD, the sexual was nearly the heart and soul. But in Kant's sexual philosophy, the conceptual, the metaphysical and the ethical are most provocatively combined; and in Kant, contemporary philosophical problems and disputes about sex can be glimpsed clearly.

Aquinas' fame (or notoriety) rests with his natural law sexual ethics; Kant is important as the author of a sexual ethics of respect (see RESPECT FOR PERSONS). For Kant, human sexual interaction involves one person's merely using another for the sake of pleasure:

there is no way in which a human being can be made an Object of indulgence for another except through sexual impulse.... Sexual love makes of the loved person an Object of appetite.... Sexual love... by itself and for itself... is nothing more than appetite.... As an Object of appetite for another a person becomes a thing and can be treated and used as such by every one. This is the only case in which a human being is designed by nature as the Object of another's enjoyment.

(1780–81: 163)

If all sexual acts – not only rape, or those in which consent is absent – are objectifying and instrumental, is not celibacy required? Kant thinks not. Following

Paul ('The wife hath not power of her own body, but the husband: and likewise also the husband hath not power of his own body, but the wife', 1 Corinthians 7: 4), Kant lays down a stringent rule:

> The sole condition on which we are free to make use of our sexual desire depends upon the right to dispose over the person as a whole.... If I have the right over the whole person, I have also the right... to use that person's *organa sexualia* for the satisfaction of sexual desire. But how am I to obtain these rights over the whole person? Only by giving that person the same rights over the whole of myself. This happens only in marriage. Matrimony is an agreement between two persons by which they grant each other equal reciprocal rights, each of them undertaking to surrender the whole of their person to the other with a complete right of disposal over it.... If I yield myself completely to another and obtain the person of the other in return, I win myself back.... In this way the two persons become a unity of will.... Thus sexuality leads to a union of human beings, and in that union alone its exercise is possible.
>
> (1780–81: 166–7)

Mary Ann Gardell, instead of sensing the Pauline 'marriage debt' in the Kantian exchange of rights, reads Kant as benignly claiming that 'marriage transforms an otherwise manipulative masturbatory relationship into one that is essentially altruistic in character' (1987: 11). But Kant speaks of marriage as a contract, an exchange of rights of access to the body. So he might be claiming that the marital pledge, the voluntary assumption of the terms of an agreement, assures that the spouses are not treating each other only as means, but also as ends, in the marriage bed. Or Kant might be justifying marital sex by abolishing the mere possibility of instrumentality: after the ontological union of two persons into one by marriage, there cannot *be* any use of one person by another (Baker and Elliston 1984: 26–7). This is why Kierkegaard found such views not benign but pernicious. 'All pleasure is selfish. The pleasure of the lover... is not selfish with respect to the loved one, but in union they are both absolutely selfish, inasmuch as in union and in love they constitute one self' (1845: 56).

Kant's idea that marriage cleanses sex of instrumentality apparently implies that homosexual marriage would similarly cleanse same-sex sexuality. Kant sidesteps this conclusion, asserting that homosexuality is one of the *crimina carnis contra naturam*:

> Onanism... is abuse of the sexual faculty.... By it man sets aside his person and degrades himself below the level of animals.... Intercourse between *sexus homogenii*... too is contrary to the ends of humanity; for the end of humanity in respect of sexuality is to preserve the species without debasing the person.
>
> (1780–81: 170)

The homosexual 'no longer deserves to be a person'. Kant, following Augustine and Aquinas, condemns nonprocreative sex as unnatural, even if it is, in his own sense, noninstrumental.

Kant's notion of marriage, in which a person obtains rights over a person and their genitals, might itself reduce the spouses to sex objects, unless the voluntary agreement of the spouses to the arrangement is sufficient to eliminate mere use. But if we emphasize the voluntary nature of the exchange of rights that occurs in marriage, Kant's contention that sex is permissible only in marriage is undermined, because two people – gay or straight – can grant each other reciprocal rights to dispose over their persons for a limited period of time (as in the casual sex of one evening). Nothing in the idea of an exchange of rights seems to entail that the exchange must be forever or exclusive. Is there something irreversible about *this* exchange of rights? If not, Kant's defence of monogamous, lifelong marriage in terms of a 'unity of will' is no more convincing than Aquinas' appeal to human nature.

7 Contemporary Kantians

From the various strands of Kant's sexual philosophy, twentieth-century sexual conservatives and liberals have fashioned their own brands of Kantian sexual ethics.

Libertarian sexual ethics. If oral and anal sex, gay and lesbian sex, bisexual and group sex, contraceptive coitus, wearing lingerie and cosmetics, adultery, prostitution, making or viewing pornography, and the paraphilias – the things often condemned by conservative sexual ethics – can be carried out without harm befalling the participants or others, by consenting adults who know what they want, how could they be morally wrong? According to libertarian sexual ethics, as long as the persons involved are participating voluntarily, they are not merely using each other for their own purposes; the free and informed consent of each to the acts that occur is sufficient to eliminate mere use and thus to make sexual activity, of whatever flavour, morally permissible (see LIBERTARIANISM). The paradigmatically wrong sexual act is not buggery, but rape, in which the absence of consent makes the mere use obvious. Consensual participation in sexual activity implies

723

that each person is respecting the other as an autonomous agent capable of making up their mind about the value of the activity. Furthermore, as Alan Goldman claims, sexual partners, by recognizing each other's 'subjectivity', can satisfy Kant's 'second formulation':

> Even in an act which by its nature 'objectifies' the other, one recognizes a partner as a subject with demands and desires by yielding to those desires, by allowing oneself to be a sexual object as well, by giving pleasure or ensuring that the pleasures of the act are mutual.
>
> (1977: 87)

It follows that neither marriage nor heterosexuality nor love are necessary for salvaging sex, and the acquisition of the right of bodily access can be temporary and reversible.

The Vatican. Although the Church embraces natural law ethics, it has also invoked Kant. In his 1968 encyclical 'Humanae Vitae', Paul VI argued against the permissibility of the use of contraceptive devices. 'Each and every marriage act... must remain open to the transmission of life' (sect. 11), and therefore 'conjugal acts made intentionally infecund' (sect. 14) are immoral. In Kantian style, he warned that the use of contraceptive devices makes husbands 'lose respect' for their wives. Since using contraception implies the act is primarily for pleasure, the husband sees his wife as 'a mere instrument of selfish enjoyment' (sect. 17). Karol Wojtyla (later John Paul II) has expressed a similar thought:

> When the idea that 'I may become a father'/'I may become a mother' is totally rejected in the mind and will of husband and wife nothing is left of the marital relationship, objectively speaking, except mere sexual enjoyment. One person becomes an object of use for another person.
>
> (1960: 239)

Rejecting the libertarian view that consent is sufficient, John Paul also asserted that only love eliminates the sexual use of one person by another, since love is a unification of persons achieved through the mutual gift – rather than a Kantian contractual exchange – of their selves. Marriage might by its nature be indissoluble (irreversible) if, once a person makes a gift of self to another, that gift cannot, for logical reasons, be taken back or returned.

Conservative sexual philosophy. John Finnis (1993: 12) argues that there are morally worthless sexual acts in which 'one's body is treated as instrumental for the securing of the experiential satisfaction of the conscious self'. In masturbating or in being sodomized, the body is just a tool of satisfaction and, as a result, one undergoes 'disintegration'. 'One's choosing self [becomes] the quasi-slave of the experiencing self which is demanding gratification.' As in Kant, the worthlessness and disintegration attaching to masturbation and sodomy attach to 'all extramarital sexual gratification'. This is because only in married, heterosexual coitus do 'their reproductive organs... make them a biological (and therefore a personal) unit'. Finnis begins with the Kantian intuition that sexual activity involves treating the body instrumentally, and he concludes with the Kantian intuition that sex in marriage avoids disintegrity since the couple is a unit: 'the orgasmic union of the reproductive organs of husband and wife really unites them biologically'.

8 Consent and coercion

Sexual activity between an adult and a child – 'intergenerational' sex – is considered morally wrong in many cultures. The arguments against it claim that it is physically and psychologically harmful to the child and violates canons of consent. Children are not able to consent to sex in the same way they are not able to consent to surgery, or to what school they attend; in these areas parents are empowered to decide for them. Defenders of intergenerational sex reply that depending on the age of the child and the acts performed, sex is not physically harmful, and it is psychologically harmful only to the extent that society condemns it. In addition, children are able to consent to sex in the same way they are able to give consent, or withhold it, to what they eat, wear, or the films they see. Thus whether children are able to give meaningful consent to sex depends on its significance – whether sex is more like eating pizza or contributing to the 'grand design'. (Analogous views are possible about sex between humans and animals: Is it harmful to the nonhuman creatures? Can they consent? Does it matter?) Intergenerational sex thus suggests separate and pressing issues about the nature of consent.

In the 1920s, Bertrand Russell admonished: 'the intrusion of the economic motive into sex is always... disastrous. Sexual relations should be a mutual delight, entered into solely from the spontaneous impulse of both parties.' In employing this principle, Russell found prostitution lacking. He also observed, prophetically, that it applied elsewhere, to married women who have economic reasons for acquiescing to the sexual demands of their husbands (1929: 121–2; see Engels 1884). Russell was voicing something close to Robin Morgan's feminist definition of rape:

> How many millions of times have women had sex 'willingly' with men they didn't want to have sex with?... How many times have women wished just

to sleep instead or read or watch the Late Show?... Most of the decently married bedrooms across America are settings for nightly rape.

(1977: 166)

The fundamental idea is that genuinely consensual participation in sex, without a hint of coercion, requires substantial economic, social and psychological equality between the persons involved. A society characterized by both poverty and wealth is one in which people are exposed to economic coercion, even if it appears that they freely consent to what they do. If some groups have less economic and social power than others, their members will be exposed to sexual coercion, among other kinds. Women's consent to heterosexual sexual activity might be largely chimerical also in virtue of systematic male dominance. If women's consent to heterosexual acts within an oppressive patriarchal society is not genuine, this will be especially true of prostitution, which can be seen as rape perpetrated by men employing economic or psychological power rather than physical assault or the threat of a knife.

An extreme view is that the presence of any pressure is coercive and morally objectionable. In 'Nonviolent Sexual Coercion' (1991), Charlene Muehlenhard and Jennifer Schrag list, among other things, 'status coercion' (women are coerced into sex or marriage by a man's occupation) and 'discrimination against lesbians' (which compels women into sexual relationships with men) as objectionable forms of coercion. Depending on the kind of case we have in mind, it might be more accurate to say either that some pressures are not coercive (a husband who constantly nags for sex) or that some pressures are coercive but not morally objectionable (a woman who marries for economic reasons). This last point might hold as well for sexual objectification: is it all wrong? Why is sexual objectification condemned, when other objectification is not?

Other questions about consent to sex are analogous to those that arise in medicine, business and law (see MEDICAL ETHICS, §3). How *specific* must consent be in order that a person engage voluntarily in subsequent sexual behaviour? Because consenting is opaque, when one person agrees 'to have sex' with another, the first has not necessarily consented to any sensual caress or coital position the second has in mind. How *explicit* must consent be in order to be an indication of voluntary choice? Whether consent can be implied reliably by nonverbal behaviour, and whether anyone should take nonverbal cues as showing decisively that another has consented to sex, are questions that arise in discussions of acquaintance rape. And how *informed* must consent

be? Do sexual partners have a duty to reveal their marital or immunological status? Conventional wisdom thinks so, but there is dissent (see Mayo 1996).

9 Utilitarianism

It seems likely that the John Stuart Mill who wrote *On Liberty* would have defended libertarian sexual ethics on general utilitarian grounds, insisting that the consent of the participating parties is morally sufficient as long as significant harm to third parties is avoided (see UTILITARIANISM). Do as you will in your experiments in living, he might have said; neither the law nor public opinion should be brought to bear unless, say, violations of assignable duties occur. Kantians and Thomists agree that the interests of third parties and society might be adversely affected by sexual activity, even if the sexual act occurring between two persons embodies genuine respect for each or is fully natural.

The difficult question concerns which of the ubiquitous effects on third parties or society are significantly harmful. Is a person harmed by becoming nauseous when noticing two homosexuals (or heterosexuals) kiss in public? Is a spouse harmed by the infidelity about which he or she knows nothing? Is someone harmed merely by knowing that immoral or offensive conduct is occurring? This area of social philosophy has been especially contentious, since decisions about 'harm' have profound implications. A narrow notion of harm yields a permissive (sexual and nonsexual) ethics and provides little justification for using the criminal law to interfere with sexual behaviour; a broad notion of harm implies the opposite. Mill and James Fitzjames Stephen squared off against each other over this issue in the nineteenth century; in the twentieth century, the debate was revived, initially by Patrick Devlin and H.L.A. Hart (see LAW AND MORALITY §§1–3; LAW, LIMITS OF). Utilitarian sexual ethics can in any event be restrictive *or* permissive, depending on the truth of empirical assertions about the consequences of sexual behaviour, or about the consequences of trying to prevent it. In addition to depending on contestable notions of wellbeing, the empirical claims underlying utilitarian judgments are difficult to verify. Similar problems plague claims that the existence of pornography helps maintain a social environment inimical to the wellbeing of women (see PORNOGRAPHY).

10 Sadomasochism and love

Sadomasochism has long been scorned by moralists. Nonlibertarian Kantians think that sadomasochistic sexual activity is wrong because it violates the personhood of the participants; humiliating and demeaning attitudes retain their character even when the sexual acts are consensual. A utilitarian might conclude that this activity, or legally permitting it, does more harm than good (as in some utilitarian arguments against permitting active euthanasia). And for a moral paternalist, it is wrong for one person to harm another, even if the latter is willing, or for persons to allow themselves to be harmed. For other utilitarians and Kantians, however, sadomasochism can be engaged in lovingly, or while fully respecting one's sexual partner, and without significant harm being done to nonparticipants.

Sadomasochism has been gaining in visibility, especially in homosexual culture. The radical libertarian sons of Kant have even given birth to the daughters of de Sade. Thus the debate over sadomasochism is especially heated among feminists, for whom there are strong partisan differences in the moral and political assessment of both heterosexual and homosexual sadomasochism (see FEMINIST ETHICS §3). About lesbian sadomasochism in particular, Claudia Card says, on the positive side, that its 'participants generally wish each other well and respect each other's choices'. But Card also worries about such activities: 'the only things distinguishing the behavior of [a top] from battery and other abuse may be the motivations of the parties and the consent of the [bottom]' (1995: 221) – and, for Card, neither the consent nor the motivation (for example, sexual pleasure) seem to turn battery and abuse into anything other or better than battery and abuse. But what more could we want in distinguishing respectful sadomasochism from battery, other than the consent to experience mutual pleasure? To say that consent is not enough, that the persons must be married, committed to each other, 'in love', or must avoid uncommonly repugnant acts, is to jeopardize all unconventional sex, not just sadomasochism. The task for a defender of this position is to deny that marriage is essential for legitimate sexuality and to bless a great deal of human sexual interaction on the basis of consent (such as homosexuality), without adopting a libertarianism so thin that it condones sadomasochism. There are well-founded doubts that that project can be successfully completed.

Unwoolly accounts of the ingredient that is required beyond consent are hard to come by, but the idea that something is required has often recommended itself:

> Avoiding deceit and coercion are only the core of treating others as persons in sexual relationships. In avoiding these we avoid... obvious ways of using as (mere) means. But to treat another as a person in an intimate, and especially an intimate sexual, relationship requires far more. These further requirements reflect the intimacy rather than the specifically sexual character of a relationship. However, if sexual relationships cannot easily be merely relationships between consenting adults, further requirements for treating another as a person are likely to arise in any sexual relationship. Intimate bodies cannot easily have separate lives.
> (O'Neill 1985: 269–70)

If the quest for sexual pleasure threatens the self's wholeness (Finnis), the other's personhood (John Paul II), and society's viability (Devlin), if it insults the human spirit (Augustine), the natural order of things, and God (Aquinas), then love – be it a dose of *agape* or *caritas* (an uplifting sort of *eros*), or the trendy 'intimacy' – is necessary, and perhaps (as in some versions of romanticism) also sufficient, for sexual relations to be licit.

The thought that love is the magical ingredient has immediate application to homosexuality: gay and lesbian sex can be justified within loving, monogamous homosexual marriages. Whether sadomasochism can genuinely express or involve love seems to be an empirical question, as long as we have a workable operational definition of 'love'. What kind of domestic arrangement do these sex partners have – is it much different, aside from the sadomasochistic sex, from Ozzie and Harriet's? Furthermore, love as the extra ingredient makes defending the use of contraception easy: sex acts, including the nonprocreative, express and bolster the love spouses have for each other. Given these rhetorical benefits, it might not be surprising that natural science cements the link between sex and love: 'Nature has emotionally enriched the human reproductive impulse through love, and in doing so she has immensely increased our enjoyment of both' (Walsh 1994: 371). In one biological swoop, a perplexing question has been answered, namely, 'why species survival, the means of impregnation, and emotional/erotic relationships should ever have become so rigidly identified with each other' (Rich 1986: 35; see Hume 1739/40: section 11). If you prefer God to nature, try Paul VI's answer: there is an 'inseparable connection, established by God, which man on his own initiative may not break, between the unitive significance and the procreative significance which are both inherent to the marriage act' (1968: §12).

See also: FAMILY, ETHICS AND THE; FRIENDSHIP; GENETICS AND ETHICS; KANTIAN ETHICS; LOVE; MORALITY AND EMOTIONS; REPRODUCTION AND ETHICS

References and further reading

The most challenging items on this list are the books by Boswell, Foucault, Halperin, Hartsock, MacKinnon, Price and Scruton, plus some of the essays in the collections edited by Murphy, Soble, Stein and Stewart.

* Aquinas, T. (1266–73) *Summa theologiae* (Synopsis of Theology), ed. T. Gilby, Cambridge: Blackfriars, 1968, vol. 43, IIaIIae.153–4. (Classic natural law sexual ethics.)

* Atkinson, T-G. (1974) *Amazon Odyssey*, New York: Links. (A famous piece of radical feminism that condemns the political 'institution' of heterosexuality.)

* Augustine (419–21) *De nuptiis et concupiscentia* (On Marriage and Concupiscence), in *Works*, vol. 12, Edinburgh: T. & T. Clark, 1874. (Early Christian sexual ethics and metaphysics: concupiscence is sinful; sexual intercourse is forgiven in marriage; children thereby produced contract original sin. See also *The City of God* [vols 1–2] and *Confessions* [vol. 14].)

* Baker, R. and Elliston, F. (eds) (1975) *Philosophy and Sex*, Buffalo, NY: Prometheus Books; 2nd edn, 1984, editorial introduction, 11–36. (Introductory textbook, which includes papers on marriage, abortion, contraception, pornography, homosexuality and paedophilia, and contains an enormous bibliography compiled by W. Vitek.)

Boswell, J. (1980) *Christianity, Social Tolerance and Homosexuality*, Chicago, IL: University of Chicago Press. (A book of history rich in intelligent philosophical discussion of the definition of homosexuality, social constructionism, and Aquinas' natural law.)

* Card, C. (1995) *Lesbian Choices*, New York: Columbia University Press. (Discusses lesbian ethics, culture, friendship and sexuality.)

Davis, M. (1983) *Smut: Erotic Reality/Obscene Ideology*, Chicago, IL: University of Chicago Press. (Insightfully divides the metaphysical terrain into Jehovanist, Naturalist and Gnostic philosophies of sex.)

* Engels, F. (1884) *Der Ursprung der Familie, des Privateigentums und des Staats*, trans. *The Origin of the Family, Private Property and the State*, New York: International Publishers, 1972. (The Marxist alternative to Augustine's theory of original sin.)

Finnis, J.M. (1994) 'Law, Morality, and "Sexual Orientation"', *Notre Dame Law Review* 69 (5): 1049–76. (Lays out a Catholic case against the toleration of homosexuality by the law; criticizes M. Nussbaum's understanding of Greek homosexuality. Occasionally woolly.)

* Finnis, J.M. and Nussbaum, M. (1993) 'Is Homosexual Conduct Wrong? A Philosophical Exchange', *The New Republic* 15 November: 12–13. (Finnis presents a Kantian-Catholic argument for the moral inferiority of homosexuality; Nussbaum finds the argument unconvincing.)

Foucault, M. (1978, 1985, 1986) *The History of Sexuality*, vol. 1, *An Introduction*, New York: Vintage Books; vol. 2, *The Use of Pleasure*, New York: Pantheon; vol. 3, *The Care of the Self*, New York: Vintage Books. (Provocative ruminations on sexuality and its history by the purported instigator of the academic furore over social constructionism.)

* Gardell, M.A. (1987) 'Sexual Ethics: Some Perspectives From the History of Philosophy', in E.E. Shelp (ed.) *Sexuality and Medicine*, Dordrecht: D. Reidel, vol. 2, 3–15. (A brief introduction to the history of sexual ethics.)

* Goldman, A. (1977) 'Plain Sex', *Philosophy and Public Affairs* 6 (3): 267–87; repr. in A. Soble (ed.) *The Philosophy of Sex*, Savage, MD, Rowman and Littlefield, 2nd edn, 1991, 73–92. (This straightforward, sensible paper combines conceptual analysis of 'sexual activity' and 'sexual desire' with Kantian, libertarian sexual ethics.)

* Gray, R. (1978) 'Sex and Sexual Perversion', *Journal of Philosophy* 75 (4): 189–99; repr. in A. Soble (ed.) *The Philosophy of Sex*, Totowa, NJ: Rowman and Littlefield, 1980, 158–68. (Conceptual analysis of 'sexual perversion' and 'sexual act'.)

* Gudorf, C.E. (1994) *Body, Sex and Pleasure: Reconstructing Christian Sexual Ethics*, Cleveland: Pilgrim Press. (Sexual pleasure is a gift from God; the fundamental ethical principle governing sexual relations is 'mutuality'.)

* Halperin, D. (1990) *One Hundred Years of Homosexuality*, New York: Routledge. (Scholarly treatment of homosexuality, social constructionism, and Plato's *Symposium*.)

* Hartsock, N.C.M. (1983) *Money, Sex and Power: Toward a Feminist Historical Materialism*, New York: Longman. (Develops a feminist-Marxist theory; ch. 7, 'Gender and Power', discusses sexuality.)

Herman, B. (1993) 'Could it Be Worth Thinking About Kant on Sex and Marriage?' in L.M. Antony and C. Witt (eds) *A Mind of One's Own*, Boulder, CA: Westview, 49–67. (Taking the answer to this question to be 'Yes, it could', this paper explores intriguing similarities between Kant's sexual philosophy and that of C. MacKinnon.)

* Hume, D. (1739/40) 'Of the Passions', in *A Treatise of Human Nature*, ed. L.A. Selby-Bigge, Oxford: Clarendon Press, 1986, book 2, part II. (Focuses

on love and hate; section 11 discusses sexual desire as a 'compound passion'.)

* Jung, P. and Smith, R. (1993) *Heterosexism: An Ethical Challenge*, Albany, NY: State University of New York Press. (Argues that an unbiased, that is, nonheterosexist, reading of Scripture points in the direction of Christian homosexual marriage.)

* Kant, I. (1780–81) *Lectures on Ethics*, trans. L. Infield, New York: Harper & Row, 1963. (Traditional sexual metaphysics and ethics from someone whose accomplishments in other areas boggle the mind.)

* Kierkegaard, S.A. (1845) *Stadier Paa livets Vej*, trans. W. Lowrie, *Stages on Life's Way*, Princeton, NJ: Princeton University Press, 1945. (Includes 'In Vino Veritas' ('The Banquet') (25–93), Kierkegaard's [or William Afham's] splendid variation on the *Symposium* theme. To be read right after *Either/Or*.)

* Levin, M. (1984) 'Why Homosexuality is Abnormal', *The Monist* 67 (2): 251–83. (Builds a secular case for the nonmoral inferiority of homosexuality.)

Linden, R.R., Pagano, D., Russell, D.E.H. and Star, S.L. (eds) (1982) *Against Sadomasochism: A Radical Feminist Analysis*, East Palo Alto, CA: Frog in the Well. (Collection of essays aimed at refuting the defence of lesbian sadomasochism made in the work edited by *SAMOIS, Coming to Power.*)

MacKinnon, C.A. (1989) *Toward a Feminist Theory of the State*, Cambridge, MA: Harvard University Press. (The 'unmodified feminist' legal and social analysis of heterosexuality, rape and pornography.)

* Mayo, D.J. (1997) 'An Obligation to Warn of HIV Infection?', in A. Soble (ed.) *Sex, Love and Friendship*, Amsterdam: Editions Rodopi, 447–53. (Argues that HIV-positive persons do not have a moral duty to warn sexual partners of the health hazards of contemplated sexual acts.)

* Morgan, R. (1977) *Going Too Far: The Personal Chronicle of a Feminist*, New York: Random House. (Her collected *oeuvre*; includes 'Theory and Practice: Pornography and Rape'.)

* Muehlenhard, C.L. and Schrag, J.L. (1991) 'Nonviolent Sexual Coercion', in A. Parrot and L. Bechhofer (eds) *Acquaintance Rape: The Hidden Crime*, New York: John Wiley, 115–28. (A catalogue of ways women are [or might be] coerced into sexual activity without being forced violently.)

* Murphy, T.F. (1987) 'Homosexuality and Nature: Happiness and the Law at Stake', *Journal of Applied Philosophy* 4 (2): 195–204. (A thorough critique of M. Levin's 'Why Homosexuality is Abnormal'; the essay focuses on the arguments from nature and happiness and rebuts their purported legal implications.)

* —— (ed.) (1994) *Gay Ethics: Controversies in Outing, Civil Rights and Sexual Science*, New York: Haworth Press. (Introductory-to-advanced collection of essays on such issues as outing, gay marriage, gays in the military, affirmative action, and the science of sexual orientation.)

Nagel, T. (1969) 'Sexual Perversion', *Journal of Philosophy* 66 (1): 5–17; revised version repr. in *Mortal Questions*, Cambridge: Cambridge University Press, 1979, 39–52. (Sophisticated analysis of 'sexual perversion' that draws on Sartre and Grice in formulating an account of natural human sexual psychology.)

Noonan, J.T. (1965) *Contraception: A History of Its Treatment by the Catholic Theologians and Canonists*, Cambridge, MA: Harvard University Press, enlarged edn, 1986. (Excellent history of the philosophical and theological arguments surrounding the use of methods to prevent conception during heterosexual intercourse.)

Nussbaum, M. (1995) 'Objectification', *Philosophy & Public Affairs* 24 (4): 249–91. (Analyses seven distinct types of sexual objectification; some are benign, others malignant. Occasionally pornographic.)

* O'Neill, O. (1985) 'Between Consenting Adults', *Philosophy & Public Affairs* 14 (3): 252–77. (An essay on what it is – and what it is not – to treat someone as a person, with respect; the account is applied to sexual relations.)

* Padgug, R. (1979) 'Sexual Matters: On Conceptualizing Sexuality in History', *Radical History Review* 20 (Spring/Summer): 3–23; repr. in E. Stein (ed.) *Forms of Desire*, New York: Routledge, 2nd edn, 1992, 43–67. (Social constructionism with a Marxist gloss: hunger is hunger, but not all hunger is the same, as Marx put it in the *Grundrisse*.)

* Paul VI (1968) 'Humanae Vitae', *Catholic Mind* 66 (September): 35–48; repr. in R. Baker and F. Elliston (eds) *Philosophy and Sex*, Buffalo, NY: Prometheus Books, 2nd edn, 1984, 167–83. (This papal encyclical is Paul VI's post-Vatican II affirmation of the doctrine that the use of contraception is morally illicit.)

Pineau, L. (1989) 'Date Rape: A Feminist Analysis', *Law and Philosophy* 8: 217–43. (A lucid discussion of what it is for one person to have a *reasonable belief* that another person has consented to engage in sexual activity.)

* Plato (*c*.386–380 BC) *Symposium*, trans. R. Waterfield, Oxford: Oxford University Press, 1994. (Plato's brilliant, moving, sometimes hilarious, and endlessly discussable account of *eros*.)

Price, A.W. (1989) *Love and Friendship in Plato and Aristotle*, Oxford: Clarendon Press. (Of the vast writings on love, sex and friendship in Plato and Aristotle, this absorbing treatise is one of the best places to start.)

Primoratz, I. (1993) 'What's Wrong With Prostitution?' *Philosophy* 68 (264): 159–82. (The answer according to this essay is 'Not much'. An uncompromising libertarian view of prostitution, which rebuts feminist objections.)

* Rich, A. (1986) 'Compulsory Heterosexuality and Lesbian Existence', in *Blood, Bread and Poetry*, New York: W.W. Norton, 23–75. (A classic item of radical feminist sexual philosophy.)

Ruse, M. (1988) *Homosexuality: A Philosophical Inquiry*, New York: Blackwell. (A comprehensive philosophical treatment of ethical and scientific questions about homosexuality.)

* Russell, B.A.W. (1929) *Marriage and Morals*, London: Allen & Unwin. (A little book of liberal common sense that caused Russell untold trouble.)

SAMOIS (ed.) (1981) *Coming to Power*, Palo Alto, CA: Up Press; 2nd edn, Boston, MA: Alyson Publications, 1982. (A brave collection of essays defending lesbian sadomasochism; especially noteworthy is G. Rubin's 'The Leather Menace'. *SAMOIS* is the name of a lesbian/feminist sadomasochism collective.)

* Schopenhauer, A. (1844) *Die Welt als Wille und Vorstellung*, vol. 2, Leipzig: Brockhaus; trans. E.F.J. Payne, *The World as Will and Representation*, vol. 2, Indian Hills, CO: Falcon's Wing Press, 1958. ('The Metaphysics of Sexual Love' appears as ch. 44 in the supplements to book 4. A cynical – or just hard-nosed – naturalistic view of human sexuality in which we are mere pawns in a larger game and our personal dreams and intentions are illusions.)

* Scruton, R. (1986) *Sexual Desire: A Moral Philosophy of the Erotic*, New York: Free Press. (A conservative theory of sex thick with Kantian themes; Scruton's favourite notion is 'individualising intentionality' (see 384). Readers are also recommended to see M. Nussbaum's tart review of this essay, 'Sex in the Head', *New York Review of Books*, 18 December 1986, 49–52.)

* Shaffer, J. (1978) 'Sexual Desire', *Journal of Philosophy* 75 (4): 175–89; repr. in A. Soble (ed.) *Sex, Love and Friendship*, Amsterdam: Editions Rodopi, 1997, 1–12. (Sophisticated conceptual analysis of 'sexual desire'; a gem of an example of what the philosophy of sex – or philosophy – can be.)

Singer, I. (1984–7) *The Nature of Love*, Chicago, IL: University of Chicago Press, 3 vols. (A magnificent history of the philosophy of love and sex, from Plato right through twentieth-century psychology.)

Soble, A. (ed.) (1980) *The Philosophy of Sex*, Totowa, NJ: Rowman and Littlefield; 2nd edn, Savage, MD: Rowman and Littlefield, 1991. (Introductory-to-advanced textbook; topics covered in the 2nd edn include pornography, adultery, prostitution, rape, homosexuality, sadomasochism and perversion.)

—— (ed.) (1989) *Eros, Agape and Philia*, New York: Paragon House. (Introductory-to-advanced textbook, a mixture of historical [Plato, Aristotle, Montaigne, Descartes, Pascal] and contemporary pieces [G. Vlastos, L. Kosman, D. Hamlyn, S. Mendus, W. Newton-Smith].)

—— (1996) *Sexual Investigations*, New York: New York University Press. (A work of sexual ethics, politics and conceptual analysis.)

—— (ed.) (1997) *Sex, Love and Friendship*, Amsterdam: Editions Rodopi. (Introductory-to-advanced collection of sixty contemporary essays that discuss Plato, Aristotle, Spinoza, Kant, Sade, Kierkegaard, Heidegger, and diverse topics, including sexual objectification, abortion, sexual perversion, love and sex, pornography and gay rights.)

* Stein, E. (ed.) (1990) *Forms of Desire*, New York: Garland; 2nd edn, New York: Routledge, 1992. (Advanced collection of essays explaining, defending and criticizing social constructionism.)

Stewart, R.M. (ed.) (1995) *Philosophical Perspectives on Sex and Love*, New York: Oxford University Press. (Comprehensive advanced textbook on sex, love [of various kinds] and friendship; sexual topics discussed include pornography, prostitution, sexual objectification, perversion, homosexuality, sadomasochism, rape and adultery.)

Sullivan, A. (1995) *Virtually Normal: An Argument About Homosexuality*, New York: Alfred A. Knopf. (An iconoclastic neoconservative political philosophy applied to questions revolving around homosexuality; Sullivan argues that the linchpin of gay liberation is access to civil marriage.)

Vannoy, R.C. (1980) *Sex Without Love: A Philosophical Exploration*, Buffalo, NY: Prometheus Books. (Argues that sexual activity is morally and nonmorally sound without being attached to love; provides conceptual analyses of 'sexual perversion' and 'love'.)

Verene, D. (ed.) (1972) *Sexual Love and Western Morality*, New York: Harper & Row; 2nd edn, Boston, MA: Jones and Bartlett, 1995. (Introductory textbook; 2nd edn includes Plato, Aristotle, Augustine, Aquinas, Luther, Kant, Schopenhauer, Nietzsche, Hegel, Sartre, Freud, Sade and Foucault.)

* Walsh, A. (1994) 'Love and Sex', in V.L. Bullough and B. Bullough (eds) *Human Sexuality: An Encyclopedia*, New York: Garland, 369–73. (An introduction, with an evolutionary bent, to the relationship between love and sex.)

Weithman, P. (1997) 'Natural Law, Morality, and Sexual Complementarity', in D. Estlund and M. Nussbaum (eds) *Sex, Preference, and Family: Essays on Law and Nature*, New York: Oxford University Press, 227–46. (A meticulous explication, analysis and critique of John Finnis' sexual ethics.)

Wertheimer, A. (1996) 'Consent and Sexual Relations', *Legal Theory* 2 (1): 89–112. (Sharp, insightful conceptual analysis of the moral and legal force of 'consent' in, especially, sexual contexts.)

* Wojtyla, K. (later John Paul II) (1960) *Miłość I Odpwiedzialność*, Krakow: Wydawnicto, Znak; trans. H.T. Willetts, *Love and Responsibility*, New York: Farrar, Strauss & Giroux, 1981. (A Kantian-Catholic sexual ethics, written before Wojtyla, a professor of philosophy, was elected pontiff; his *official* view is expressed in, for example, 'Evangelium Vitae', *Origins* 24 (42): 689–727, 1995.)

ALAN SOBLE

SHAFTESBURY, THIRD EARL OF (ANTHONY ASHLEY COOPER) (1671–1713)

Shaftesbury, whose influence on eighteenth-century thought was enormous, was the last great representative of the Platonic tradition in England. He argued that by natural reason we can see that the world is an intelligible, harmonious system. In reflecting on our character traits we will inevitably approve of those which contribute to the good of humanity and of the whole system. These same personal qualities are also needed for a happy life, so virtue and happiness go hand in hand.

Shaftesbury is often seen as the founder of the moral sense or 'sentimentalist' school in ethics, whose members held that morality was based on human feeling rather than on reason. Although leading sentimentalists, such as Hutcheson and Hume, made use of many of his ideas, Shaftesbury himself has more in common with the rationalists, who held that there are eternal moral truths which we can know by the use of reason.

1   Life and influences
2   Teleology
3   Ethics

1   Life and influences

Anthony Ashley Cooper, Third Earl of Shaftesbury, was born in February 1671. Superintendence of his education was handed over to no less a personage than John LOCKE, with whom Shaftesbury seems to have had an ambivalent relationship. While honouring him as his 'friend and foster father', Shaftesbury came not only to reject, but even to detest, much of Locke's philosophy. He played a full part in English political life, first in the Commons and then in the Lords, though ill health forced occasional retreats to the Continent. He devoted the latter portion of his life to writing; his published work was eventually brought together in his three-volume *Characteristics of Men, Manners, Opinions, Times* (1711), a work very widely read in the eighteenth century.

Shaftesbury was deeply influenced by Greek and Roman thought, in which he distinguished two strands. The first presupposes that we live in an ordered and intelligible universe; the second that everything came into being by chance and that nothing has any meaning. It is to the former strand that Shaftesbury owes allegiance. It proceeds through Plato, Aristotle, the Neoplatonists and Platonized Christianity to the Cambridge Platonists of the seventeenth century (see CAMBRIDGE PLATONISM; NEOPLATONISM). Shaftesbury's notebooks reveal in particular the marked influence of the Stoics, especially EPICTETUS and MARCUS AURELIUS (see STOICISM).

2   Teleology

Shaftesbury's conception of the world is thoroughly teleological. By the use of unaided natural reason, we can come to see that the universe forms a well-ordered, intelligible, harmonious system, in which humans have their proper place. To understand the nature of anything, including ourselves, is to know what functions are natural and proper to it, and which ones are unnatural and perverted. This knowledge is practical as well as theoretical. In the Platonic tradition to which Shaftesbury belongs, to know the good is to love it. Shaftesbury is thus an apostle of intellectually disciplined enthusiasm; rational beings cannot help but be moved once they are aware of this universal harmony, which Shaftesbury celebrates in glowing and lyrical terms. To live in accordance with nature, to have one's inner harmony attuned to the outer, is to be both virtuous and happy. Virtue is its own reward; the virtuous life is in itself the most fulfilling there is.

The passions that disturb our lives stem from false values, from a wrong assessment of what is good and bad. Once we see that our good is to be found in the part we play in the good of the whole then we can face hardship and even death with equanimity. For we find our true good not in externals, such as wealth or reputation, which can be taken from us, but in a balanced and harmonious mind, which cannot be overthrown by anything except our folly. Moreover, the goods of the mind are superior to any goods we find in nature or in human art. As Shaftesbury explains in *The Moralists, A Philosophical Rhapsody* (1709), mind is not only the source of harmony, beauty and goodness (which for him are essentially one and the same), but is itself better and more beautiful than its products. To value any external good more highly than inner harmony is to prefer a secondary beauty to its primary source, to prefer the shadow to the reality.

Shaftesbury stresses the immanence of the divine mind rather than its transcendence. Shaftesbury often pictures God's relation to the world as more like that of the soul to the body than it is like that of the watchmaker to his watch. We see this in *The Moralists* (part III, section 1) where we find an unusual variant of the argument from design which starts from the issue of personal identity (see GOD, ARGUMENTS FOR THE EXISTENCE OF §§4–5). Among all the changes to both body and mind which any person undergoes in the course of life, it is undeniable that there is something which unites these stages and makes them all properties of the same person. We cannot give a coherent account of the metaphysical status of this self, but that there is such a continuing self which governs and superintends one's life is undeniable. Since nature is also self-regulating and orderly, it too must be governed by a mind, which bears the same relation to the world and its activity as our mind does to our body and actions, even if we can give no clear indication of its metaphysical status.

In spite of his token orthodoxy Shaftesbury is a true parent of the Enlightenment in his willingness to question authority and in his advocacy of liberty. In thought and discussion there should be freedom of speech (at least among educated gentlemen!). No subject is too grave that it may not be subject to jest; for raillery, Shaftesbury contends, is a test of truth. Error cannot withstand mockery. Art and culture only flourish in conditions of freedom. Genuine patriotism can only spring from an identification with the body politic which cannot be found in tyrannies.

3 Ethics

The core of Shaftesbury's philosophy, however, is his moral theory, which is most fully and systematically expounded in his *Inquiry Concerning Virtue or Merit* (1699), his earliest work. In the first part he delineates what goodness and virtue are. Every creature, and every species, is part of a wider system to which it

contributes. Each system is itself part of a wider system, until we reach the universe, the complete system which incorporates all the subsystems. Each individual (or species) is to be judged by its contribution to the good of its system and, ultimately, by its contribution to the good of the whole.

In judging an individual creature we are concerned with its character, with what Shaftesbury calls its affections – its, desires, motives and enjoyments. A good creature is one whose affections will, in the normal course of events, cause it to act in a way that will be for the good both of itself and of the system of which it is a part. While animals can be good or bad, humans alone can be virtuous or vicious, for humans alone are self-conscious and capable of reflecting on their own actions and affections so that these can in their turn become the object of an affection, this time of approval or disapproval. We are naturally and ineluctably led to approve of what is natural and honest and to disapprove of what is dishonest and corrupt. Our capacity for reflection, however, enables us to be self-governing, and thus virtuous or vicious, for we can choose whether to indulge our good or our bad inclinations (see AUTONOMY, ETHICAL).

We might note that Shaftesbury departs from the Stoic model in one respect. For those in the Socratic tradition the four cardinal virtues are wisdom, courage, temperance and justice. Benevolence, pity or compassion receive less emphasis. Epictetus concedes that we should behave sympathetically towards the unfortunate; but we should not disturb our stoic tranquillity by pitying them. Shaftesbury, by contrast, puts the social virtues of love, friendship and universal benevolence at the forefront of his theory (see VIRTUES AND VICES §1).

Shaftesbury proceeds in the second half to ask what reason we have to be virtuous. He assumes without argument that the only reason we can offer is that it is in our interests – a virtuous life will be a happy one. He is thus a rational egoist, for he holds that questions of the rational justification of a way of life must appeal to self-interest. But he is not a psychological egoist, for he holds, as against Hobbes, that agents have altruistic as well as egoistic motives (see HOBBES, T. §8). Nor is he an ethical egoist, for morality requires us to be motivated by concern for others (see EGOISM AND ALTRUISM §1).

Shaftesbury then argues, ingeniously if not always persuasively, that the qualities of character needed to live a good life are the very same as those needed to live a virtuous one. In particular, proper development of the social affections, which are directed to the good of others, gives a degree and type of satisfaction not otherwise available.

It is customary to view Shaftesbury as the source or

founder of the moral sense or sentimentalist school of ethics, whose foremost members were Hutcheson and Hume (see MORAL SENSE THEORIES). It is true that they were much influenced by him, but in the great eighteenth-century debate as to whether morality is founded on reason or on sentiment, Shaftesbury should, I think, be counted on the rationalist side in so far as he holds that there are eternal moral truths, existing independently of us, and revealed to us by the use of reason.

List of works

Shaftesbury (1995) *The Shaftesbury Collection*, Bristol: Thoemmes, 4 vols. (Comprehensive recent collection.)

—— (1699) *An Inquiry Concerning Virtue or Merit*, ed. D. Walford, Manchester: Manchester University Press, 1977. (In the first part of his major work on ethics Shaftesbury discusses what virtue is, and in the second part he argues that it is in our interest to be virtuous.)

—— (1709) *The Moralists, A Philosophical Rhapsody*, in *Characteristics of Men, Manners, Opinions, Times*, vol. 2, ed. J.M. Robertson, London: Grant Richards, 1900; repr. in *The Shaftesbury Collection*, vol. 2, Bristol: Thoemmes, 1995. (A philosophical dialogue, in which the claim that the world is the product of an intelligent and beneficent Mind is examined and defended.)

—— (1711) *Characteristics of Men, Manners, Opinions, Times*, ed. J.M. Robertson, London: Grant Richards, 1900, 2 vols; repr. in *The Shaftesbury Collection*, vols 1 and 2, Bristol: Thoemmes, 1995. (Contains all important works published by Shaftesbury in his lifetime.)

—— (1900) *The Life, Unpublished Letters, and Philosophical Regimen of Anthony, Earl of Shaftesbury*, ed. B. Rand, London: Swan Sonnenschein; repr. in *The Shaftesbury Collection*, vol. 3, Bristol: Thoemmes, 1995. (Contains Shaftesbury's important personal notebooks and a fairly full selection of his letters.)

—— (1914) *Second Characters, or The Language of Forms*, ed. B. Rand, Cambridge: Cambridge University Press; repr. in *The Shaftesbury Collection*, vol. 4, Bristol: Thoemmes, 1995. (Contains Shaftesbury's uncompleted proposed work on aesthetics, including his long and fascinating instructions to the artist on the composition of 'The Judgement of Hercules', which he commissioned while in Italy.)

References and further reading

Darwall, S. (1995) *The British Moralists and the Internal 'Ought'*, Cambridge: Cambridge University Press, 176–206. (A lucid and authoritative discussion of Shaftesbury's ethics in relation to his predecessors.)

Fowler, T. (1882) *Shaftesbury and Hutcheson*, London: Sampson Low, Marston, Searle, & Rivington, 1–167. (A clear summary of Shaftesbury's main views with numerous quotations.)

Grean, S. (1967) *Shaftesbury's Philosophy of Religion and Ethics*, Athens, OH: Ohio University Press. (Discusses whole of Shaftesbury's work with particular emphasis on his advocacy of enthusiasm.)

Klein, L. (1994) *Shaftesbury and the Culture of Politeness*, Cambridge: Cambridge University Press. (Examines political context of Shaftesbury's writings in some detail and places emphasis on rhetorical structure of his writings.)

McNaughton, D. (1996) 'British Moralists of the Eighteenth Century: Shaftesbury, Butler and Price', in S. Brown (ed.) *Routledge History of Philosophy*, vol. 5, *The British Enlightenment*, London: Routledge, 203–27. (Expansion of the material in this entry.)

Taylor, C. (1989) *The Sources of the Self: The Making of the Modern Identity*, Cambridge, MA: Harvard University Press, 248–59. (A brief sketch, placing Shaftesbury firmly in his contemporary philosophical context.)

Trianosky, G. (1978) 'On the Obligation to be Virtuous: Shaftesbury and the Question, Why be Moral?', *Journal of the History of Philosophy* 16: 289–300. (A penetrating discussion of book II of *An Inquiry Concerning Virtue or Merit*.)

Voitle, R. (1984) *The Third Earl of Shaftesbury*, Baton Rouge, LA: Louisiana State University Press. (The definitive biography, with an excellent bibliography.)

DAVID McNAUGHTON

SHAH WALI ALLAH (QUTB AL-DIN AHMAD AL-RAHIM) (1703–62)

Shah Wali Allah of Delhi, the greatest Muslim scholar of eighteenth-century India, made an immense contribution to the intellectual, economic, social, political and religious life of the Muslim community in India, the effects of which persist to the present day. He lived during a time when the Muslim empire was losing ground on the Indian subcontinent, with the Muslim community divided and at odds. Seeking to give theological and metaphysical issues a new rational interpretation and labouring to harmonize reason and revelation, he tried to reconcile the various factions of the Indian Muslims, thereby protecting the empire from collapse.

Shah Wali Allah contended that the root cause of the downfall of the Indian Muslims was their ignorance of the sacred scripture of Islam. He initiated a movement with the theme 'Back to the Qur'an', and translated the Qur'an into Persian to facilitate its understanding among all the Muslims of India. It is believed to be the first complete translation of the Qur'an from the Arabic by an Indian Muslim scholar.

1   Life
2   Intellectual and metaphysical contribution
3   Political contribution

1   Life

Qutb al-Din Ahmad ibn 'Abd al-Rahim, known as Shah Wali Allah, was born in AH 1114/AD 1703 near Delhi, a member of a distinguished intellectual and religious family. He received a highly structured education and spiritual instruction at the *madrasa* (religious school) established by his father, Shah 'Abd al-Rahim, at Delhi. As well as the Qur'an, he studied Arabic and Persian grammar and literature and the higher philosophical, theological, metaphysical, mystical and juridical texts. He graduated from the school when he was barely fifteen years old; in the same year, his father initiated him into the famous Naqshbandi order. He began his career as a teacher at the Madrasa-e-Rahimiyya under the tutelage of his father; after the death of the latter in AH 1131/AD 1719, Shah Wali Allah became the head of the *madrasa*, teaching all the current sciences at the school for about twelve years. During the same period he continued his own studies, growing in stature as a teacher and attracting students to his circle.

In AH 1143/AD 1731, Shah Wali Allah went on the *hajj* (pilgrimage to Mecca), after which he remained in Mecca and Medina, the sacred cities of Islam, for about fourteen months, studying *hadith* (accounts of the Prophet) and engaging in intellectual discussions, meditation and spiritual perfection. During this time, he saw the forty-seven spiritual visions which form the subject matter of his famous mystical work *Fuyud al-haramayn* (Emanations or Spiritual Visions of Mecca and Medina). After making his second *hajj*, Shah Wali Allah returned home to Delhi in AH 1144/AD 1732. He spent the rest of his life teaching *hadith* literature and metaphysics and writing. All but one or two of his works were produced during his later years. He died in AH 1176/AD 1762.

2   Intellectual and metaphysical contribution

Shah Wali Allah wrote in both Arabic and Persian. He published between fifty and seventy works, including five collections of letters and epistles. His writings played a major role in the intellectual and spiritual life of the Muslims in the Indo-Pakistan subcontinent, a role which continues today. Some of these works have greatly changed the Muslim approach to the study of the Qur'an.

In addition, Shah Wali Allah tried to reshape Islamic metaphysics in greater conformity with the teachings of the Qur'an and the *sunna* of the Prophet. He adopted a more rational approach to the controversial issues of metaphysics, which led to greater harmony among subsequent Islamic metaphysical thinkers. He was careful to give a balanced criticism of some of the views of his predecessors and contemporaries. His constructive and positive approach to those issues was always considered a sincere attempt at reconciliation.

Shah Wali Allah made the first attempt to reconcile the two (apparently) contradictory doctrines of *wahdat al-wujud* (unity of being) of IBN AL-'ARABI and *wahdat al-shuhud* (unity in conscience) of Shaykh Ahmad Sirhindi. Shaykh Muhyi al-Din ibn al-'Arabi, the advocate of *wahdat al-wujud*, was of the opinion that being in reality is one and God. All other actual and possible beings in the universe are manifestations and states or modes of his Divine Names and Attributes. By the act of creation through the word *kun* (be), Ibn al-'Arabi means the descent of Absolute Existence into the determined beings through various stages. This gradual descent of the Absolute Existence is called *tanazzulat al-khamsa* (five descents) or *ta'ayyunat al-khamsa* (five determinations) in Sufi terminology. On the other hand, according to Shaykh Ahmad Sirhindi, the exponent of the doctrine of *wahdat al-shuhud*, God and creation are not identical; rather, the latter is a shadow or reflection of the Divines Name and Attributes when they are reflected in the mirrors of their opposite non-beings (*a'dam al-mutaqabila*). Shah Wali Allah neatly resolved the conflict, calling these differences 'verbal controversies' which have come about because of ambiguous language. If we leave, he says, all the metaphors and similes used for the expression of ideas aside, the apparently opposite views of the two metaphysicians will agree. The positive result of Shah Wali Allah's reconciliatory efforts was twofold: it brought about harmony between the two opposing groups of metaphysicians, and it also legitimized the doctrine of *wahdat al-wujud* among the *mutakallimun* (theologians), who previously had not been ready to accept it.

Shah Wali Allah wrote about thirteen works on

metaphysics, which contain his constructive and balanced metaphysical system. One of the most important is *al-Khayr al-kathir* (The Abundant Good). This work is divided into ten chapters, each called a *khizana* (treasure). The first four chapters deal with the reality of *wujud* (being), knowledge of God, the relationship between God and the universe, and human knowledge. From the discussion of human knowledge, Shah Wali Allah turns to the discussion of the reality of prophecy and the prophethood of Muhammad. In the seventh *khizana*, he deals with the rules and principles of sainthood and mysticism. The eighth and ninth chapters contain details about practical aspects of Islam, the *shari'a*, as well as the eschatological view of Islam. In the tenth *khizana*, Shah Wali Allah explains his theological view which, according to him, is in full accord with Ash'arite theology.

Altaf al-quds fi ma'rifat lata'if al-nafs (The Sacred Knowledge) is another metaphysical work concerned with the inner dimensions of human personality. Here Shah Wali Allah deals with the important questions of mystical intuition (*kashf*) and inspiration (*ilham*). He examines systematically the reality of both the external and internal perceptive qualities of a human being as the heart, the intellect, the spirit, the self, the secret (*al-sirr*) and the ego. A separate chapter is devoted to the metaphysical teachings of Shaykh Junaid Baghdadi, wherein he presents a brief historical account of mysticism. The last chapter deals with the subtle question of 'thoughts and their causes'. Shah Wali Allah specifies various external and internal causes which affect the human mind and produce thoughts.

Sata'at (Manifestations) is a systematic division of *wujud* (being), representing Shah Wali Allah's view concerning the *tashkik al-wujud* (hierarchy or gradation of being). Existence, in relation to determined being, is composed of existence and essence and has many grades, stages and modes. The particular beings in the universe provide the foundation for the claim of the *tashkik* (gradation) and *kathrat* (multiplicity) of being. Each grade or stage covers a certain area of determination and each stage is related to the next, not in a way that a material being is connected to another material being, but in *ma'nawi* (conceptual) manner. He describes the relationship between the various stages of being as like that between the lights of various lamps in a single room. The lights of these lamps are apparently mingled and are one, and are difficult to differentiate from one another; but in reality, they are distinguishable from one another because of the number of the lamps.

Shah Wali Allah's 'magnum opus' is his *Hujjat Allah al-baligha* (The Profound Evidence of Allah).

This comprehensive work deals with both intellectual and practical aspects of Islam. The first part deals with metaphysics, scholastic theology, the gradual development or evolution of human society and the philosophy behind the divine injunctions. The second part is devoted to ethics, politics, rituals and the social life of Islam.

Al-Tafhimat al-ilahiyyah (Instructions or Clear Understanding) is one of his most comprehensive metaphysical works. The work is divided into sections called *tafhim* (instruction). Both Arabic and Persian languages are used for the expression of ideas and concepts in this work. These *tafahim* (plural of *tafhim*) are actually Shah Wali Allah's mystical visions and experiences, and his letters and articles written to various people at various times in different contexts. The famous epistle called *Maktub al-madani* (Madinian Epistle) to Isma'il Afandi is a part of the second volume of the book. This article is a detailed description of *wahdat al-wujud* and *wahdat al-shuhud*, along with Shah Wali Allah's attempt at reconciliation concerning this controversial issue. In addition to the ontological discussions, the work also includes the author's cosmological, anthropological and theological views.

Another important metaphysical work is *al-Budur al-bazigha* (The Full Moons Rising in Splendour). The introduction deals with basic metaphysical issues such as *wujud* in general, the unity of God, the essence and existence of God and the relationship between God and the universe. Shah Wali Allah considers the universe to be a manifestation of the Divine Attributes. In the first chapter, he deals with the study of humanity with respect to its social and rational being. The second chapter is devoted to humanity's relationship with the Creator. At the end of the work, Shah Wali Allah describes in detail the reasons and causes for the development and evolution of the various *shara'i'* (religions or religious laws) and *milal* (religious communities).

Shah Wali Allah also tried to provide a basis for bringing the four schools of law closer to each other. His commentaries on the *Mu'atta* (a collection of the Prophet's sayings) of Imam Malik, called *al-Musawwa* (Arabic) and *al-Musaffa* (Persian), were written with a view to finding common orthodox ground for the reconciliation of different schools of Islamic law. Likewise, he wrote *'Aqd al-jid fi akham al-ijtihad wa'l-taqlid* with the proposal that the door of *ijtihad* (judgement) is open. According to him, the experts of Islamic knowledge (*'ulama'* (religious scholars) and *mujtahidin* (legists) have the right to respond effectively to new situations instead of being perpetually bound to previous solutions.

3 Political contribution

A hallmark of Shah Wali Allah was his ability to reconcile opposing points of view to the satisfaction of each side. Standing behind this aspect of his teachings is the unity of the Muslim community or *umma*. His powerful abilities as a reconciler enabled him to provide common ground and a strong basis for co-operation and harmony between the Sunni and Shi'i.

Shah Wali Allah lived during a time of political and moral decline, chaos and destruction in the Mughul empire. His vantage point near the centre of the Muslim state gave him a clear view of the situation. He did his best to bring stability to the tottering empire and protect the Indian Muslims from disaster. Through his writings, especially his letters, he appealed to the Muslim rulers, nobles and intelligentsia to be aware of the dreadful situation and its possible consequences. His correspondence reveals many factors of Indian politics in the eighteenth century. His detailed letter to Ahmad Shah Abdali, the founder and ruler of Afghanistan, contained a comprehensive picture of the political situation in India. Ahmad Shah Abdali heeded Shah Wali Allah's call to invade India and restore Muslim power to the country, culminating in the defeat of the Marathas and their allies at the battle of Panipat in 1761. Shah Wali Allah himself left a rich intellectual legacy in the form of literary works, well-trained disciples including his four sons – who also became eminent scholars – and one of the greatest educational institutions of the time.

See also: ISLAM, CONCEPT OF PHILOSOPHY IN; ISLAMIC PHILOSOPHY, MODERN; ISLAMIC THEOLOGY; MYSTICAL PHILOSOPHY IN ISLAM

List of works

Shah Wali Allah (1703–62) *Altaf al-quds* (The Sacred Knowledge), ed. D. Pendlebury, trans. G. Jalbani, *The Sacred Knowledge*, London: Octagon, 1982. (A general account of the metaphysics of Shah Wali Allah.)

—— (1703–62) *al-Khayr al-kathir* (The Abundant Good), trans. G. Jalbani, Lahore: Ashraf, 1974. (Comprehensive discussion of the links between metaphysics and theology.)

—— (1703–62) *Hujjat Allah al-baligha* (The Profound Evidence of Allah), Lahore: Shaikh Ghulam Ali and Sons, 1979. (A detailed discussion of the links between theoretical and practical philosophy.)

—— (1703–62) *Sata'at* (Manifestations), trans. into Urdu by S.M. Hashimi, Lahore: Idarah Thaqafat Islamiyya, 1989; trans. into English by G. Jalbani, *Sufism and the Islamic Tradition: the Lamahat and Sata'at of Shah Waliullah*, London. (A systematic and highly influential account of being.)

—— (1703–62) *Lamahat* (Flashes of Lightning), Hyderabad: Shah Wali Allah Academy, 1963; trans. G. Jalbani, *Sufism and the Islamic Tradition: the Lamahat and Sata'at of Shah Waliullah*, London, 1980. (One of the important writings on Sufism.)

—— (1703–62) *Fuyud al-haramayn* (Emanations or Spiritual Visions of Mecca and Medina), Delhi: Matba' Ahmadi, no date. (A collection of pure mystical and metaphysical experiences and visions received during his stay in Mecca and Medina.)

—— (1703–62) *al-Tafhimat* (Instructions or Clear Understanding), Dabhail, 1936, 2 vols. (One of the most comprehensive metaphysical works.)

—— (1703–62) *al-Budur al-bazighah* (The Full Moons Rising in Splendour), Dabhail: Madinah Barqi Press, 1354 AH. (Important metaphysical work.)

References and further reading

Hermansen, M. (1986) 'Shah Wali Allah of Delhi's *Hujjat Allah al-baligha*: Tension Between the Universal and the Particular in an 18th Century Islamic Theory of Religious Revelation', *Studia Islamica* 63: 143–57. (A clear account of Shah Wali Allah's major work.)

Kemal, R. and Kemal, S. (1996) 'Shah Waliullah', in S.H. Nasr and O. Leaman (eds) *History of Islamic Philosophy*, London: Routledge, ch. 37, 663–70. (Account of the life, times and influence of the philosopher.)

Malik, H. (1973) 'Shah Wali Allah's Last Testament', *Muslim World* 63: 105–18. (A useful summary of his basic philosophical principles.)

Rizvi, S. (1980) *Shah Wali Allah and His Times*, Canberra: Ma'rifat Publishing House. (A discussion of the links between Shah Wali Allah's philosophical views and the renewal movement in India.)

HAFIZ A. GHAFFAR KHAN

SHAH WALIULLAH OF DELHI

see SHAH WALI ALLAH (QUTB AL-DIN AHMAD AL-RAHIM)

SHAME *see* MORAL SENTIMENTS

SHAO YONG (1012–77)

One of the founders of neo-Confucianism, Shao Yong was a Chinese philosopher best known for his use of numerical ideas to illustrate natural patterns of change. His thought encompassed a variety of concerns including knowledge, language and self-cultivation, and has received differing interpretations.

Shao Yong (styled Yaofu, called Kangjie) was considered one of the five founders of the Song dynasty (960–1279) philosophical movement called the learning of the Way, widely known as neo-Confucianism. His family was from north China, and he established his home in Loyang. While friendly with scholars and officials, Shao never took the examinations and declined several official recommendations. His major works were *Huangji jingshishu* (Book of the Supreme Ultimate Ordering the World) and *Yichuan jirangji* (Collection of Yichuan's Beating on the Ground), a collection of poetry. His supposed authorship of *Yuqiao wendui* (Conversation between the Fisherman and Woodcutter) and *Wuming gongzhuan* (Biography of Mr No Name) has not been verified.

Combining aspects from different traditions, Shao focused on natural patterns of change in the universe and the experience of sagely knowledge. Called the 'Prior to Heaven learning', his ideas regarding universal regularities belonged to the learning of images and numbers, based on the *Yijing* (Book of Changes) and emphasizing correlations. His views on knowledge, language and self-cultivation drew on Daoist thinking (see DAOIST PHILOSOPHY). While accepting Confucian thought, Shao stressed that political history, individual behaviour and the natural universe shared identical patterns. Buddhist influence is suggested in his ideas on sagely perception (see BUDDHIST PHILOSOPHY, CHINESE).

Shao viewed the universe as characterized by constant change, occurring according to regular patterns. Composed of *qi* (matter-energy) (see QI), the universe and cosmological development were described in terms of theoretical levels, from the extrasensory original unity to all the things/events of human experience. Although cycles of twelve and thirty were important, most critical were the binary and quaternary patterns of change. Original unity (the Supreme Ultimate) gives rise to *yin* and *yang* which in turn interact to produce divisions of four, eight (the trigrams) and eventually sixty-four (the hexagrams) (see YIJING; YIN–YANG). Production and completion, and movement and response, illustrate the binary pattern while the four seasons, four directions and four classics illustrate the quaternary pattern.

Representable by numbers and images, patterns were unknowable without things, the two largest of which were the heavens and earth. Changes in one realm were correlated with those in the other, according to a quaternary pattern that systematically classified all things/events. For instance, the heavens were symbolized by three, five, seven, nine and the sun, moon, stars and celestial markers, while earth was symbolized by two, four, six, eight and water, fire, earth and stone. The relationships among the categories explained all kinds of activity, and numbers reflected the regularity of change.

Shao urged people to overcome their limited perspectives, but only a sage perceived things from the viewpoint of the whole. Admired as a principled Confucian recluse, eccentric, teacher and poet, Shao was respected for his numerological formulations, predictive abilities and ideas about the sage. Shao's numerical ideas have been misinterpreted as bad astronomy and as a deterministic view of human behaviour.

See also: DAOIST PHILOSOPHY; NEO-CONFUCIAN PHILOSOPHY; YIJING

List of works

Shao Yong (1050s–70s, self-preface 1066) *Yichuan jirangji* (Collection of Yichuan's Beating on the Ground), Sibu congkan edition, Daozang edition. (Collection of most of Shao's extant poems written over a period of about thirty years.)

—— (1060s–70s) *Huangji jingshishu* (Book of the Supreme Ultimate Ordering the World), Sibu beiyao edition, Siku quanshu edition, Daozang edition. (Contents emphasize cosmological, historical and numerous other topics and include writings by Shao, his (possible) comments recorded by others, and charts, diagrams and writings by others.)

—— (11th–12th century) *Wuming gongzhuan* (Biography of Mr No Name), Siku quanshu edition; trans. A.J. Berkowitz, 'Biography of the Gentleman with No Name', in V.H. Mair (ed.) *The Columbia Anthology of Traditional Chinese Literature*, New York, Columbia University Press, 1994, 751–6. (Translation of Shao Yong's autobiography; but attribution uncertain, possibly authored by Shao's son or students.)

—— (11th–12th century) *Yuqiao wendui* (Conversation between the Fisherman and the Woodcutter), Siku quanshu edition; trans. K. Lundbaek, *Dialogue Between a Fisherman and a Woodcutter*, Hamburg: C. Bell Verlag. (Includes a short helpful introduction and the Chinese text to accompany the English translation. Attribution uncertain, possibly authored by Shao's son or students.)

References and further reading

Berkowitz, A.J. (1083) 'On Shao Yong's Dates (21 January 1012–27 July 1077)', *Chinese Literature: Essays, Articles, Reviews* 5: 91–4. (Analysis of various writings to determine Shao Yong's dates.)

Birdwhistell, A.D. (1982) 'Shao Yung and His Concept of Objective Observation (fan-kuan)', *Journal of Chinese Philosophy* 9 (4): 367–94. (Theoretical analysis of Shao's concept of objective observation, or reflective perception.)

—— (1989) 'The Philosophical Concept of Foreknowledge in the Thought of Shao Yung', *Philosophy East and West* 39 (1): 47–65. (Epistemological analysis of Shao's concept of foreknowledge.)

—— (1989) *Transition to Neo-Confucianism: Shao Yung on Knowledge and Symbols of Reality*, Stanford, CA: Stanford University Press. (Emphasizes epistemological analysis of Shao's philosophy; has general comments on historical context and extensive bibliography.)

Black, A.H. (1989) *Man and Nature in the Philosophical Thought of Wang Fu-chih*, Seattle, WA: University of Washington Press. (Includes extensive treatment of Wang's seventeenth-century views of Shao Yong and Song thought.)

Freeman, M.D. (1982) 'From Adept to Worthy: The Philosophical Career of Shao Yung', *Journal of the American Oriental Society* 102: 477–91. (Discussion of Shao's life and thought from perspective of intellectual history.)

Ryan, J.A. (1993) 'The Compatibilist Philosophy of Freedom of Shao Yong', *Journal of Chinese Philosophy* 20 (3): 279–91. (Argues for a compatibilist position on freedom, with comparison to Leibniz.)

—— (1996) 'Leibniz' binary system and Shao Yong's *Yijing*', *Philosophy East and West* 46 (1): 59–90. (Compares Shao Yong and Leibniz from an implicit positivist position, thus seeing Shao's position as proto-science.)

Smith, Jr, K., Bol, P.K., Adler, J.A. and Wyatt, D.J. (1990) *Sung Dynasty Uses of the I Ching*, Princeton, NJ: Princeton University Press. (Discusses the thought of Shao and three other thinkers in a Song historical context.)

Wyatt, D.J. (1984) 'Shao Yung: Champion of Philosophical Syncretism in Early Sung China', unpublished Ph.D. dissertation, Harvard University. (General introduction to Shao's life and thought.)

—— (1985) 'Chu Hsi's Critique of Shao Yung: One Instance of the Stand Against Fatalism', *Harvard Journal of Asiatic Studies* 45 (2): 649–66. (Analysis from perspective of intellectual history.)

ANNE D. BIRDWHISTELL

SHAO YUNG *see* SHAO YONG

SHARI'A LAW *see* LAW, ISLAMIC
PHILOSOPHY OF

SHEM TOV FAMILY

The ibn Shem Tov family included four Jewish intellectuals of fifteenth century Spain whose philosophical, theological, homiletical and polemical works followed the persecution of 1391 and the ensuing mass apostasy of Jews. Responding to these traumatic events, the Shem Tovs rethought the place of philosophy in traditional Judaism. Although the pater familias *reacted sharply to the spiritual crisis by criticizing Maimonides and endorsing Kabbalah, his offspring charted a more moderate course that enabled Jewish intellectuals to cultivate philosophy and the kindred arts and sciences while asserting the ultimate primacy of their revealed faith over philosophy, and its philosophical superiority to Christianity.*

1 Shem Tov ibn Shem Tov
2 Joseph and Isaac ibn Shem Tov
3 Shem Tov, son of Joseph ibn Shem Tov
4 Theology, preaching, hermeneutics and polemics

1 Shem Tov ibn Shem Tov

Shem Tov ibn Shem Tov (*c.* 1380–1441) witnessed the destruction of Spanish Jewry in his youth. Like Hasdai CRESCAS and Shlomo Alami, he responded by comprehensively re-examining Judaeo-Hispanic culture. In *Sefer ha-'Emunot* (The Book of Beliefs) he held Jewish rationalists responsible for the mass defections that followed the persecutions. He charged his chief targets, Abraham IBN EZRA and Moses MAIMONIDES, with denying cardinal tenets of rabbinic Judaism including divine retribution, bodily resurrection, personal providence, miracles and individual immortality. They had accorded Jewish Law merely instrumental value, had made human perfection dependent on knowledge of philosophy, equated prophecy with natural human knowledge and reduced the Torah to a popular allegory of philosophic profundities.

Shem Tov conceded to philosophy sound knowledge of the natural world, knowledge that can aid us in grasping the plain sense of the Torah, but he found philosophy inherently unreliable in metaphysics and subordinated it to revelation, whose salvific truths are beyond the ken of natural reason (see REVELATION). Revelation itself requires authoritative interpretation through a tradition that, for Shem Tov, includes the teachings of Kabbalah (see KABBALAH). In a work still extant in manuscript on the subject of the Sefirot – originally Neo-Pythagorean hypostases but later understood to be aspects of the divine pleroma – he places Kabbalistic theosophy above philosophy.

Shem Tov's endorsement anticipated by over a century the rise of Kabbalah to centrality in Jewish theology, but he failed to diminish the stature of Maimonides or to discredit Judaeo-Hispanic rationalism. His own sons, Joseph (c. 1400–c. 1460) and Isaac (d. c. 1489) and his grandson, Shem Tov ben Joseph (fl. 1480s), perpetuated Jewish Aristotelianism and defended Maimonides, although they agreed that philosophy cannot secure salvation alone; it must be perfected by revelation and tradition. They accepted Kabbalah as integral to Judaism but did not displace philosophy, instead incorporating Kabbalistic ideas into their rationalism. For example, they identified the Sefirot with the 'attributes of action' allowed to God in Maimonidean negative theology.

2 Joseph and Isaac ibn Shem Tov

Joseph, the most illustrious of the Shem Tovs, was a court physician and auditor of accounts in the courts of King John II and Henry IV of Castile until he was deposed in 1456. A prolific exegete, Joseph wrote commentaries, extant in manuscript, on Aristotle's *On the Soul* and *Nicomachaean Ethics*, Averroes' now lost epistle on the possibility of conjunction (in both longer and shorter formats), his epistle on the nature of material intellect, his commentary on Alexander of Aphrodisias' *On the Intellect*, and Moses Narboni's commentary on al-Ghazali's Avicennan summary, *Maqasid al-falasifa* (The Intentions of the Philosophers). No longer extant are commentaries on Porphyry's *Isagōgē* and Aristotle's *Economics*. The surviving manuscripts show a deep familiarity with Judaeo–Muslim Aristotelianism and, strikingly, with Christian scholasticism.

Joseph's younger brother Isaac, a popular teacher of Aristotelian philosophy in Aguilar di Campaha,

Castile, wrote four supercommentaries on Averroes's middle commentary on Aristotle's *Physics*, as well as treatments (now lost) of Averroes' long commentaries on *On the Soul* and *On Generation and Corruption* and on al-Ghazali's *Maqasid al-falasifa*. In the *Physics* supercommentaries, Isaac rebutted Crescas' attack on the twenty-five theses of Aristotelian philosophy which Maimonides had laid out as the premises of Aristotelian proofs of the existence, unity and incorporeality of God. Crescas' aim had been to liberate Judaism from Aristotelian philosophy. A loyal Maimonidean, Isaac dismissed Crescas' critique as ill-taught philosophy. He failed to grasp the originality and subtlety of Crescas' views, but pondered the origin of the universe and other metaphysical questions in his lost *'Etz ha-Da'at* (The Tree of Knowledge).

3 Shem Tov, son of Joseph ibn Shem Tov

The last known member of the family, Shem Tov, son of Joseph ibn Shem Tov, also taught philosophy in commentaries. He wrote a supercommentary on Averroes' middle commentary on Aristotle's *Physics* and *On the Soul*, Hebrew philosophical works on the distinction between matter and form, and a work on teleology. The technical virtuosity of these works, written to preserve a worldview that had come under increasing attack, attests to the abiding appeal of philosophy in Spain until the very end of the Jewish presence there, but they show little novelty. Intellectually, the movement was a spent force. The real creativity of the Shem Tovs (and of other Jewish thinkers of their day) lay in theology and philosophical hermeneutics.

4 Theology, preaching, hermeneutics and polemics

The major vehicle of Jewish theology in fifteenth-century Spain was commentary on Maimonides' *Guide to the Perplexed* (see MAIMONIDES, M.) Joseph ibn Shem Tov's commentary on the highly controversial 68th chapter of Part I survives in manuscript. Isaac commented on the entire *Guide* (the commentary on Part I is extant), and Joseph's son Shem Tov's linear commentary on the entire *Guide* is still printed in traditional editions. By seeking to fathom Maimonides' original intent, these commentaries ranged over the full repertoire of medieval Jewish philosophy, including God's existence and attributes, creation, providence, miracles, prophecy, human knowledge and the ultimate human goal. The works also defended Maimonides against charges of heresy and inconsistency. Like other Maimonideans (Abraham Shalom, Abraham Bibago and Moses Alashkar), the

Shem Tovs ascribed their own moderate views to Maimonides and projected upon him a synthesis they had developed from their own Maimonidean reflections on Averroes (see IBN RUSHD), Avicenna (see IBN SINA), AL-GHAZALI, IBN BAJJA and IBN TUFAYL.

Joseph ibn Shem Tov's systematic treatises develop his moderate synthesis of religion and philosophy. In *Kevod Elohim* (The Glory of God), he follows Meir Alguades' Hebrew translation of the Latin *Nicomachaean Ethics*, seeking to harmonize Aristotle's idea of happiness with rabbinic values. Taking his cue from Thomas AQUINAS, Joseph argues that Aristotle delineates the supreme temporal good, whereas eternal happiness can be known only through revelation. Like Aquinas, Joseph understood this ultimate felicity as a beatific vision by the immortal soul of God's essence; but only those who live by the precepts of the Torah can attain such eternal bliss. Joseph's narrowing of philosophical universality by the specification of this requirement clearly aimed to strengthen the faith of despairing Spanish Jews.

In his *Moznei ha-'Iyyun* (The Scales of Speculation), Joseph developed these themes further and sought to explain the mass apostasy of Spanish Jews as the outcome not of philosophical study but of weak character and superficial intellectual commitment, which had allowed his countrymen to succumb to the material blandishments of Christianization. From Talmudic sources, he showed that there was no religious prohibition against philosophy, which was in fact highly beneficial in understanding of the revealed canon. Addressing another oft-cited cause of mass apostasy, Joseph composed *Da'at 'Elyon* (Knowledge of the Supernal) attacking the determinism of Abner of Burgos, a famous Jewish apostate and Christian theologian (see VOLUNTARISM, JEWISH §1). Finally, he wrote a commentary on Yeda'aiah Berdersi's *Behinat 'Olam* (Examination of the Universe), a popular fourteenth-century poetic summary of Jewish Aristotelianism. These two works are no longer extant.

The Shem Tovs all engaged in sacred hermeneutics. The elder Shem Tov commented on Mishnah Avot and the Passover Haggadah; Joseph commented on Lamentations, Job and Genesis, and on Tractate *Ketubot* of the Babylonian Talmud. Shem Tov ben Joseph published homilies on the Torah based on his sermons. Preaching was the major vehicle for the dissemination of Jewish theology, and Joseph was not only a popular preacher (fifteen of his sermons survive in manuscript) but the author of the earliest known Hebrew manual on homiletics, *'Eyn ha-Qore* (The Eye of the Reader). Inspired by a humanist concern for eloquence, it sought to improve the quality of Jewish preaching and counter the appeal its Christian counterpart.

Like other polemicists of his day, Joseph defended Judaism as a rational religion grounded in the revelation of God's perfect wisdom. Christianity was philosophically inferior, based on irrational beliefs and paradoxes. To aid the resistance to conversionary pressures and rebut Christian claims to spiritual superiority, he translated Hasdai Crescas' *Bittul 'Iqqarey ha-Notzrim* (Refutation of Christian Principles) from the Catalan original into Hebrew and wrote a commentary that preserves the only extant version of this influential text (see CRESCAS, H.). He also commented on Profiat Duran's epistle *Al Tehi ka-Avotekha* (Be Not like Your Fathers), known to Christians under the distorted title *Alteca Boteca*. Duran had mocked the apostasy of the epistle's addressee by satirizing Christian dogmas (see DURAN, P.). Joseph's commentary sought to ensure that Jews understood the irony of the original polemical work, but it had the unintended effect of alerting the Inquisition to the work's genuine intent.

See also: ARISTOTELIANISM, MEDIEVAL; MAIMONIDES, M.

References and further reading

Davidson, H. (1983) 'Medieval Jewish Philosophy in the Sixteenth Century', in B.D. Cooperman (ed.) *Jewish Thought in the Sixteenth Century*, Cambridge, MA: Harvard University Press, 106–45. (The first part of this essay portrays the conservative stance of fifteenth-century Jewish philosophers, among them Joseph ibn Shem Tov.)

Gottlieb, E. (1976) 'Al Darko shel Shem Tov ibn Shem Tov La-Qabbalah' (The Path of R. Shem Tov ibn Shem Tov towards Kabbalah), in J. Hacker (ed.) *Studies in the Kabbalah Literature*, Tel Aviv: Tel Aviv University, 347–56. (Discusses the shift of Shem Tov ibn Shem Tov from rationalism to Kabbalah and lists the manuscripts of his Kabbalistic works.)

Guttmann, J. (1913) 'Die Familie Shem Tob in ihren Beziehungen zur Philosophie' (The Shem Tov Family and its Relationship to Philosophy), *Monatschrift für Geschichte und Wissenschaft des Judentums* 57: 177–95, 326–40, 419–51. (To date, this is still the only comprehensive study of the entire Shem Tov family.)

Ibn Shem Tov, Shem Tov (*c.*1420?) *Sefer ha-'Emunot* (The Book of Beliefs), Ferrara, 1556; photomechanical reproduction, Jerusalem, 1969. (Attacks Ibn Ezra and Maimonides, whom Ibn Shem Tov holds responsible for defections from the faith following Christian persecutions.)

Ibn Shem Tov, Joseph (1442) *Kevod Elohim (The Glory of God)*, Ferrara, 1556; photomechanical reproduction, Jerusalem, 1969. (Work on ethics, following Aristotle's *Nicomachean Ethics*.)

—— (1451) *Sefer Bittul 'Iqqarey ha-Nozrim*, ed. D.J. Lasker, *Sefer Bittul Iqqarei ha-Nozrim: Translation of (Crescas' work by) Joseph Ben Shem Tov*, Ramat Gan and Beer Sheva: Bar Ilan University Press and Ben Gurion University, 1990; trans. D.J. Lasker, *The Refutation of the Christian Principles by Hasdai Crescas*, Albany: State University of New York Press, 1992. (Translation of the original by Hasdai Crescas, on the refutation of Christian principles.)

Ibn Shem Tov, Shem Tov ben Joseph (1489) *Derashot 'al ha-Torah* (Sermons on the Torah), Salonica, 1525. (Religious work by the last known member of the family.)

Lasker, D.J. (1977) *Jewish Philosophical Polemics Against Christianity in the Middle Ages*, New York: B'nai B'rith Publications. (An excellent study of the Jewish–Christian polemics which climaxed in the fifteenth century; explains how Jewish polemicists used Aristotelian philosophy against Christian claims to spiritual superiority.)

Regev, S. (1983) 'Teologiah u-Mysticism Rationali be-Kitvey R. Yosef ibn Shem Tov' (Theology and Rational Mysticism in The Writings of R. Joseph ben Shem Tov), unpublished Ph.D. dissertation, Hebrew University. (In Hebrew with an English summary. The most systematic analysis of Joseph ibn Shem Tov's works and his moderate rationalism; analyzes his theory of prophecy and its Averroian epistemological background; comprehensively discusses the relationship between philosophy and religion in his theological compositions, and lists all the known manuscripts of his works.)

—— (1986) 'Ha-Mahshavah ha-Rational-Mystit ba-Hagut ha-Yehudit ba-Me'ah ha-Tet-Vav' (Rational-Mystical Thought in Jewish Philosophy of the Fifteenth Century), *Jerusalem Studies in Jewish Thought* 5: 155–89. (Presents Joseph ibn Shem Tov as a typical example of Jewish philosophy in the fifteenth century, and shows how he sought to reconcile rationalist philosophy and Kabbalah.)

—— (1988) 'Le-Ba'ayt Limud ha-filosofia be-Hagut ha-Me'ah ha-Tet-Vav: R. Yosef ibn Shem Tov ve-R. Abraham Bibago' (On the Problem of the Study of Philosophy in 15th-Century Thought: R. Joseph ibn Shem Tov and R. Abraham Bibago), *Daat* 16: 57–86. (Considers the debate on the status of philosophy in Jewish culture during the fifteenth century in the wake of the mass apostasy of Iberian Jews. By focusing on Ibn Shem Tov and Bibago, who wrote commentaries on Averroes, the author shows how the philosophers argued for the superiority of Kabbalah over philosophic knowledge.)

Saperstein, M. (1989) *Jewish Preaching: 1200–1800*, New Haven, CN: Yale University Press, 167–79, 180–201. (This anthology includes scholarly translations of sermons by Joseph ibn Shem Tov and his son, Shem Tov, locating them in the context of Jewish biblical exegesis and homiletics.)

Schwartzmann, J. (1991) 'Perushu shel Yitzhaq ibn Shem Tov le-'Moreh Nevukhim'' (Isaac ibn Shem Tob's Commentary on 'The Guide of the Perplexed'), *Daat* 26: 43–59. (Based on an unpublished doctoral dissertation, this essay summarizes the major themes of Isaac ibn Shem Tov's religious philosophy in ontology, cosmology, theology, rational psychology and the interactions of reason and revelation.)

Sirat, C. (1985) *A History of Jewish Philosophy in the Middle Ages*, Cambridge: Cambridge University Press, 381–4. (The chapter on Jewish philosophy in the fifteenth century includes important summaries of Joseph and Isaac ibn Shem Tov's chief works and ideas.)

Tirosh-Rothschild, H. (1997) 'Human Felicity – 15th Century Perspectives on Happiness', in B. Cooperman and A. Seeff (eds) *Iberia and Beyond: Hispanic Jews Between Two Cultures*, Willmington, DE: University of Delaware Press. (Discusses Joseph ibn Shem Tov's view of human happiness, the reception of Aristotle's *Ethics*, Jewish–Christian polemics and Joseph's debt to Aquinas.)

Wolfson, H.A. (1977) 'Isaac ibn Shem-Tob's Unknown Commentaries on the Physics and His Other Unknown Works', in I. Twersky and G.H. Williams (eds) *Studies in the History of Philosophy and Religion*, Cambridge, MA: Harvard University Press, vol. 2, 479–90. (This essay was the first to identify Isaac ibn Shem Tov as the author of the four commentaries on Aristotle's *Physics* that rejected Crescas's critique of Aristotle.)

HAVA TIROSH-SAMUELSON

SHESTOV, LEV (YEHUDA LEIB SHVARTSMAN) (1866–1938)

A major though atypical figure of the Russian Religious-Philosophical Renaissance, Shestov taught that reason and science can neither explain tragedy and suffering, nor answer the questions that matter most. A maximalist, a subjectivist and an anti-dogmatist, Shestov regarded philosophical idealism as an attempt to gloss over the 'horrors of life' and attacked morality and ethics as inherently coercive. He maintained that science ignores the contingent, the unique and the ineffable, that philosophy cannot be a science, and that necessity depersonalizes and dehumanizes the individual. Philosophy and revelation are incompatible because God is not bound by reason, nature or autonomous ethics. To God 'all things are possible', even undoing what has already happened. God even restored Job's dead children to him – the same children, not new ones, Shestov insisted.

In Dobro v uchenii gr. Tolstogo i Fr. Nitshe *(The Good in the Teaching of Tolstoy and Nietzsche) (1900) and* Dostoevskii i Nitshe *(Dostoevsky and Nietzsche) (1903) Shestov attacked philosophical idealism and attributed his subjects' philosophies to a defining personal experience: Tolstoi's horror at urban poverty, Nietzsche's illness, and Dostoevskii's Siberian exile, respectively. These books established Shestov as a major literary critic and interpreter of Nietzsche. Around 1910 he turned to philosophy and religion. In his magnum opus* Athènes et Jerusalem *(1938) Shestov preached a religious existentialism centred on the living God of Abraham, Isaac and Jacob, and argued that evil came into the world with knowledge. Adam and Socrates were fallen men because they opted for knowledge over life and faith. Socrates, Aristotle, the Scholastics, Descartes, Spinoza, Kant, Hegel and Husserl were all faith-destroying. Shestov preferred the anti-rationalism of Dostoevskii, Nietzsche, Tertullian, Luther, Pascal and Kierkegaard. He wanted to restore the primordial freedom of Adam before the Fall. Although Shestov quoted the Gospels and certain Christian theologians approvingly, he was not a Christian. Neither was he an adherent of traditional Judaism.*

A brilliant stylist, Shestov used reason and knowledge to combat reason and knowledge. He distinguished between the empirical realm where they applied and the metaphysical realm where they did not. But since he philosophized only about the metaphysical realm he comes across as an irrationalist.

1   **Life**
2   **Early writings**
3   **A leap into faith**
4   **Religious existentialism**

1   Life

Son of a wealthy Jewish family, Shestov was born Yehuda Leib Shvartsman in Kiev. As a student, he was primarily interested in political and social questions. Because of his radical political views, he

had to transfer from a gymnasium in Kiev to one in Moscow. He studied science and mathematics and then law at Moscow University, but completed his studies at Kiev University. His doctoral dissertation was on factory legislation; because it described the appalling condition of the workers it was rejected by the Board of Censors in Moscow as revolutionary. Shestov graduated with the degree of Candidate, not Doctor, of Law in 1889. He was licensed to practise law, but never did. He joined the army and then entered his father's textile business. In 1895, he had a nervous breakdown brought on by a combination of business pressures (he saved the firm from bankruptcy) and unhappy romantic involvements with two Gentile women, one after another, whom his father would not allow him to marry. To recover his health, Shestov went abroad in the spring of 1896. In Rome, he fell in love with a Russian Orthodox medical student, Anna Elezarovna Berezovskaia. They lived together and had two daughters. In 1907, they were married in London. Shestov did not tell his parents about Anna and the children until 1914, living apart from them, sometimes in different cities, for months at a time. Shestov also had an illegitimate son, who lived in Moscow with his mother. Shestov supported them and was a real father to his son.

In 1898, Shestov returned to Russia, bringing two completed manuscripts with him: *Shekspir i ego kritik Brandes* (Shakespeare and his Critic Brandes) and *Dobro v uchenii gr. Tolstogo i Fr. Nitshe* (*The Good in the Teaching of Tolstoy and Nietzsche*). He lived in St Petersburg and Moscow and then resumed working in his father's business in Kiev. Shestov's acquaintance with Merezhkovskii, ROZANOV, Diaghilev and Ivanov, and his lifelong friendships with BERDIAEV, BULGAKOV and Remizov date from this time (see RUSSIAN RELIGIOUS-PHILOSOPHICAL RENAISSANCE §1). Early in 1906 he came close to another nervous breakdown. He was then forty years old and still unable to live as he pleased. *Apofeoz bezpochvennosti* (The Apotheosis of Groundlessness) (1905) and *Nachala i kontsy* (Beginnings and Endings) (1908) reflect the hopelessness and despair that overwhelmed him. Between 1910 and 1914 he lived in Switzerland with his family and worked on *Sola Fide* (By Faith Alone) and *Vlast' kliuchei* (The Power of the Keys). When the First World War broke out, they returned to Russia and settled in Moscow. In mid-1918, they fled to Kiev, then under German control. He gave a course on Greek philosophy at the University of Kiev and was awarded an honorary doctorate by the University of Simferopol. In February 1919, Kiev was 'liberated' by the Red Army.

The Bolsheviks considered Shestov a revolutionary writer and offered to publish *Potestas Clavium* if he would add a brief introduction defending Marxist doctrine, but he refused. In the autumn of 1919 the Shestovs emigrated, reaching Paris by a round-about route in 1920. Shestov was almost unknown there, but three articles, published in French, on Dostoevskii, Tolstoi and Pascal, brought him a European-wide reputation. The German Nietzsche Society elected him its honorary president and he was invited to lecture all over Europe. He was also elected to the Kant Society. His books were translated into French, German and other European languages. He taught at the Institut des Etudes Slaves and in the extension division of the Sorbonne, and associated with leading European intellectuals, including Husserl, who became one of his best friends despite their intellectual differences. It was at Husserl's urging that Shestov read Kierkegaard. Shestov's last article, 'In Memory of a Great Philosopher', was a tribute to Husserl, who had just died.

Politically Shestov was a liberal or a moderate socialist. After all, politics and economics belonged to the empirical realm. In 'Chto takoe bol'shevizm?' (What is Bolshevism?) (1920), he described Soviet rulers as reactionary, destructive and parasitical, emphasized their hostility to freedom, and pointed to the 'paradox of idealists who believe only in crude physical force'. In 'Menacing Barbarians of Today' (1934), Shestov compared the Nazis to the Tartars and maintained that civilization entailed the triumph of the spirit over force.

There is a personal dimension to Shestov's lifelong campaign against reason and morality – the double life he led for seventeen years and long-standing tensions with his father. At 12 or 13 Shestov was kidnapped by radicals and held for ransom. Apparently, this was a hoax to raise funds and Shestov was involved in the plot. Perhaps suspecting this, his father refused to pay. After six months Shestov was released unharmed. The battle of wills between father and son is significant, especially since Shestov lost. It is almost as if his writings were an outlet for his rage, not only against his father but against authority and 'necessity' in any form. Shestov's interpretation of the authors he treats is highly personal. He highlighted episodes or statements that resonated with his own experience, repeated them over and over again, and omitted others of equal or even greater importance.

2 Early writings

Shestov's early writings treated issues that were to occupy him all his life. In his first book, *Shekspir i ego kritik Brandes*, Shestov discussed the meaning of tragedy, the limits of positivism and Kantianism, and the indifference of science to life, giving as an example

a brick that falls on someone's head and kills him. The law of gravity can explain why the brick fell, he said, but not why it fell on that particular man, nor does it care. Disputing Brandes' contention that tragedy is meaningless, Shestov argued that tragedy has a higher purpose – spiritual development or moral edification. He rejected this idealist interpretation in his books on Nietzsche, but came back to it, in a way, later on. A tenet of Shestov's religious existentialism is that suffering is the beginning of awakening. He also stated that philosophy begins in despair, not in wonder, as the Greeks believed.

Shekspir i ego kritik Brandes begins and ends with a quotation from Nietzsche, but Shestov had not yet assimilated Nietzsche's ideas. On first reading, Shestov did not understand *Beyond Good and Evil*. He found *The Genealogy of Morals* profoundly disturbing and searched for ways to combat Nietzsche's 'terrible, pitiless thought'. But then he learned about Nietzsche's sickness; 'on this day, I understood'. Reading Nietzsche sensitized Shestov to 'Nietzschean' qualities in Dostoevskii and accelerated Shestov's rejection of philosophical idealism and moralism (see DOSTOEVSKII, F.; NIETZSCHE, F.).

In *The Good in the Teaching of Tolstoy and Nietzsche*, Shestov contrasted Nietzsche's passionate search for truth 'beyond good and evil' with Tolstoi's 'cowardly' submission to idealist pieties (see TOLSTOI, L.N.). As Shestov tells it, Tolstoi was appalled by the poverty he saw in Moscow, but rather than admit his helplessness, he retreated to his estate to perfect himself. From then on, Tolstoi preached the identity of goodness and God, and tried to impose his self-denying morality on others. By contrast, Nietzsche's sickness led him to realize the futility of lofty ideals. The sickness was unjustified; Nietzsche had lived a virtuous life, but that was Shestov's point – great suffering is inexplicable and arbitrary. From personal experience Nietzsche learned that nature is cruel and that God (goodness) is dead. But then Nietzsche lost his nerve and created a new idol – the Superman. Nevertheless, Shestov concluded: 'Nietzsche has shown the way. We must seek what is *higher* than compassion, what is *higher* than good. We must seek God' ([1900] 1969: 140).

In his next book, Shestov treated Dostoevskii and Nietzsche as 'underground' thinkers and spiritual twins. Dostoevskii's defining experience was hard labour and exile in Siberia, followed by his discovery of his own egoism upon his return to St Petersburg. In *Zapiski iz podpol'ia* (Notes From Underground) (1864) the protagonist declares that the whole world could 'go to pot' as long as he had his regular cup of tea. In *Crime and Punishment* Raskol'nikov asserts that there are two moralities, one for ordinary people, the other for extraordinary people like himself. Therefore, he was entitled to murder a 'useless' old woman because he needed her money. Nietzsche's 'underground' was illness, physical pain and loneliness. Like the protagonist of *Notes From Underground*, Nietzsche honestly and openly admitted that the happiness of humanity did not interest him. Both writers realized that egoism negates reason, conscience and idealism. Theirs was a '*morality of tragedy*', as distinct from a '*morality of commonplaceness*'. Circumstances, not innate nobility, forced them into it.

Shestov believed that social changes will never banish tragedy from life and that to deny suffering is to deny reality. Philosophy's task, therefore, was not to preach humility, submission, renunciation or self-sacrifice, but to teach people not 'to transfer all the horrors of life into the sphere of the *Ding an sich*'. In *Apofeoz bezpochvennosti*, a compilation of 168 numbered sections, Shestov wrote: 'The business of philosophy is to teach men to live in uncertainty – man who is supremely afraid of uncertainty, and who is forever hiding behind this or the other dogma' ([1905] 1920: §11). In 'Creation From the Void', an essay published in *Nachala i kontsy* (Beginnings and Endings) (1908), Shestov praised Chekhov precisely because he did not offer a consoling ideal; his protagonists were people who lost all hope. In 'The Gift of Prophesy', Shestov pointed to prophecies of Dostoevskii, Tolstoi and Solov'ëv that did not come true. In *Velikie kanuny* (Great Vigils) (1911), Shestov interpreted the life and work of Sologub, Ibsen, William James and Tolstoi (as creator and destroyer of worlds) and criticized Kantian and positivist theories of knowledge.

Nietzsche was one of Shestov's lifelong reference points. He seconded Nietzsche's attack on Socratic rationalism (for different reasons), and claimed that it was Spinoza who murdered God. Shestov praised 'extraordinary' people who were given a second pair of eyes by the angel of death, or who thought in a second dimension. His protest against undeserved suffering turned into a conviction that for salvation 'works' don't matter. Shestov viewed Luther as a tragic figure like Nietzsche. He interpreted Nietzsche's 'will to power' as a variant of Luther's 'sola fide' and emphasized their mutual hostility to reason, righteousness and law (see LUTHER, M.). Dostoevskii was another lifelong reference point. When discussing people's willingness to give up their freedom for bread, security, and happiness, Shestov often alluded to 'The Grand Inquisitor' (see DOSTOEVSKII, F.M. §4). When Shestov claimed that all metaphysical systems begin with freedom and end in necessity, he probably had Shigalëv's confession (in *The Possessed*)

in mind. But he never invoked Dostoevskii's ideal of a community of faith. There is no church or synagogue in Shestov's philosophy. Focused on the solitary individual, Shestov rejected Solov'ëv's ideals of 'all-unity' and a supra-personal 'Godmanhood' (see SOLOV'ËV, V.S.). Moreover, Solov'ëv's orientation was too rational for him.

3 A leap into faith

Shestov's leap into faith is evident in *Sola Fide* (written 1911–14), *Vlast' kliuchei* (The Power of Keys) (1923), and *Na vesakh Iova* (In Job's Balances) (1929). Shestov considered *Sola Fide* a personal statement and did not publish it in his lifetime. The two sections, 'Greek and Medieval Philosophy' and 'Luther and the Church', reveal Shestov's immersion in Western philosophy and religion from the pre-Socratics to Husserl as well as Shestov's turn to the Bible. Describing Christian disputations on law and grace and on faith and works, Shestov pointed out that theologians attracted to Hellenic rationalism, ignored or denied miracles and mystery. *Vlast' kliuchei* reflects Shestov's horror at the First World War, not only because of the unprecedented mass slaughter, but because his beloved son was killed at the front. The title is an allusion to the keys that open and close the gates of heaven that Jesus gave to Peter. But, Shestov argued, Socrates and his successors also claimed the keys to heaven, substituting autonomous reason and autonomous virtue for the gods and maintaining that the virtuous man can be happy in a torture device (the bull of Phalaris). The Medieval Church wrested the keys away from the pagan philosophers; making the fatal mistake of trying to reconcile faith and reason, it ended up subordinating Scripture to reason. Now the keys are being claimed by science, a development Shestov deplored. He blamed the war on Europeans' sacrilegious attempt to deify themselves and their reason in place of God. In 'Memento Mori', Shestov attacked Husserl for relying on self-evidences and logic, arguing that the law of identity, A = A, and the law of non-contradiction apply only to 'the middle zones of human and universal life, which do not at all resemble the polar and equatorial zones. The truths of one zone are not the truths of the other'. God's truths are not man's truths.

The epigram to *In Job's Balances* is Job's lament that his grief and calamity were heavier than the sands of the sea (Job 4: 2–3). Shestov's point was that human suffering weighs more than 'objective' truth. The foreword, 'Science and Free Inquiry', was about the limitations of science. Part I, 'Revelations of Death', comprises two essays: 'The Conquest of the Self-Evident: Dostoevsky's Philosophy', and 'The

Last Judgment: Tolstoi's Last Works'. Dostoevskii and Tolstoi, Shestov argued, blunted their unique visions, by trying to fit them into the framework of commonplace truths. Dostoevskii transformed his insight that people actually like to suffer into the idea that suffering must 'buy' something, or redemption through suffering. Tolstoi, however, finally realized when he wrote 'The Death of Ivan Il'ich', 'Master and Man' and 'Father Sergei', that 'works' don't matter, that goodness isn't God. Shestov regarded death as an escape from 'omnitude' (allness, the One, total unity) to self-consciousness because everyone faces death alone.

Part II, 'Revolt and Submission', is comprised of fifty-two numbered sections. In the section about medieval debates on why God became a man, Shestov opposed the usual explanation, that there was no other way to save man, with his own: 'supernatural interference was only necessary because man had to be supported in his "mad endeavor", in his *unreasonable* audacity and self-affirmation' ([1929] 1975: 177; emphasis added).

Part III, 'On the Philosophy of History', comprises the essays 'Children and Stepchildren of Time: Spinoza in History', 'Gethsemane Night: Pascal's Philosophy' and 'Words That are Swallowed Up: Plotinus's Ecstasies'. Shestov held that there is no immanent Idea, or development in history, as Hegel maintained; it is all contingency. Pascal's method of seeing 'by lamentation' (Pascal was always in pain) he considered superior to Spinoza's dictum 'not to laugh, not to weep, not to curse, but to understand'. Spinoza was referring to human action and to the passions; Shestov, to misfortune. The essay on Plotinus emphasized the ecstatic insights that enable one to soar above knowledge, and Plotinus' resistance to the world-renunciation preached by the Gnostics. 'Suddenly' was one of Shestov's (and Dostoevskii's) favourite words; he used it to describe both tragedy and epiphany and associated 'suddenly' with the absurd, in other words, not part of the regular order.

4   Religious existentialism

In *Athènes et Jerusalem* (1938) Shestov summed up and developed ideas set forth in his previous works, including *Kierkegaard et la Philosophie Existentielle* (1936). His major theme was that philosophy and biblical revelation are incompatible. Therefore people must make an either/or choice between faith and knowledge. To this theme Shestov subordinated others: knowledge enslaves man; evil came into the world with knowledge; salvation is by faith alone; man must choose between the tree of knowledge and the tree of life; and God's freedom is infinite. Quoting

Peter Damian's assertion that God can 'make what happened not to have happened' and Kierkegaard's *Fear and Trembling*, Shestov proclaimed that God can violate or suspend the laws he has established, be they the laws of nature or the Ten Commandments. For example, God commanded Abraham to kill Isaac. God can restore Job's children and undo Socrates drinking the hemlock and Nietzsche's madness (see KIERKEGAARD, S.).

Shestov associated the impossible with the absurd, attacked religions of consolation and claimed that both Christian and Jewish theologians have abandoned Scripture. As an example, he contrasted Isaiah's prophecy that the lion will lie down with the lamb with Aquinas' dictum, 'grace does not abolish nature'. One of Shestov's favourite biblical quotations was 'What things soever ye desire ... ye shall have them' (Mark 11:24).

According to Shestov reason and morality demand resignation while the absurd and faith sanction daring. In this context, he quoted Kierkegaard on the difference between a 'knight of faith' and a 'knight of resignation', as well as Kierkegaard's admission that if he himself really had faith he would not have broken his engagement to Regina.

Shestov maintained that Western philosophy has struggled against the 'I', against individual existence, from its very beginning. Thales declared that all is God. Anaximander considered voluntary separation from the 'all' as a great sin, which doomed the individual to the greatest punishment, to death. This dreadful law inseparably links birth and death. Necessity, uniformity, regularity and the depersonalizing philosophy of Descartes, Spinoza and Hegel all stem from it. By contrast, the Living God of Abraham, Isaac and Jacob, created man 'in his own image and likeness'. For man, as for God, everything is possible, including immortality, provided that he tear himself away from the seduction of reason. Not all questions can be answered, Shestov opined; God hides his truths in mystery.

To Shestov, the sin of Adam and Eve was choosing knowledge over life, not disobedience, as is usually maintained. Before the Fall they did not have to choose between good and evil, because there was no evil. Everything that God created was good. But the serpent deceived Eve. Knowledge does not increase human power but diminishes it. Evil and sin came into the world with knowledge. Shestov defined 'religious philosophy as the final supreme struggle to recover original freedom and the divine "very good", which was hidden in this freedom and which, after the Fall, was split into powerless good and our destructive evil' ([1938] 1966: 70). Now, instead of the creative 'Let there be!', there is only the plane of the petrified 'is'. And in the same spirit: faith abolishes reason. Faith is given to man to make him master in the world established for him by the Creator. Faith enables man to break through the self-evidences of reason and reach the freedom in which the impossible becomes the reality.

People subordinate God to reason and morality because they fear an omnipotent and capricious God, Shestov argued. Fear of the unknown leads people to take refuge in dogmatism. Luther created new catechisms and made Scripture the ultimate authority. Nietzsche deferred to necessity in the form of *amor fati*. Kierkegaard had all sorts of 'you musts'. Shestov denied any intention of attributing 'authority' to the Bible; he believed that Scripture 'decisively rejects the idea of authority'. God does not coerce man. Distinguishing between God's truth (freedom) and coercive truth (dogma), Shestov maintained that coercive truth destroys communication and leads to eternal hatred.

The utopianism and antinomianism of Shestov's *magnum opus* place him in the mainstream of the Religious-Philosophical Renaissance. On the other hand, despite his paeans to biblical revelation, his discussion of the Incarnation and his invocations of Christian theologians, he was not a Christian.

See also: EXISTENTIALISM; NIETZSCHE: IMPACT ON RUSSIAN THOUGHT; RUSSIAN RELIGIOUS-PHILOSOPHICAL RENAISSANCE; TRAGEDY

List of works

Shestov, L. (1911) *Sobranie sochinenii* (Collected Works), St Petersburg: Shipovnik, 6 vols. (Contains all listed works to 1911.)

—— (1898) *Shekspir i ego kritik Brandes* (Shakespeare and his Critic Brandes), St Petersburg: Mendelevich.

—— (1900) *Dobro v uchenii gr. Tolstogo i Fr. Nitshe – filosofiia i propoved'*, St Petersburg: Stasiulevich; 1st edn repr. Paris: YMCA-Press, 1971; trans. S. Roberts, introduction by B. Martin, The Good in the Teaching of Tolstoy and Nietzsche, part I of Dostoevsky, Tolstoy and Nietzsche, Athens, OH: Ohio University Press, 1969.

—— (1903) *Dostoevskii i Nitshe – filosofiia tragedii*, in *Mir iskusstva*; St Petersburg: Shipovnik; 1st edn repr. Paris: YMCA-Press, 1971; trans. S. Roberts, Dostoevsky and Nietzsche: The Philosophy of Tragedy, Part II of Dostoevsky, Tolstoy and Nietzsche, Athens, OH: Ohio University Press, 1969.

—— (1905) *Apofeoz bezpochvennosti* (The Apotheosis of Groundlessness), St Petersburg: Obshchestven-

naia pol'za; repr. of 2nd edn, Paris: YMCA-Press, 1971; trans. S.S. Koteliansky, All Things Are Possible, London: M. Secker, 1920, introduction by D.H. Lawrence; repr. with additional introduction by B. Martin, Athens, OH: Ohio University Press, 1977. (The 1977 edition does not include the essays on Julius Caesar and Dmitrii Merezhkovskii.)

—— (1908) *Nachala i kontsy* (Beginnings and Endings) St Petersburg: Stasiulevich; 1st edn repr. Ann Arbor, MI: Ardis, 1978; Penultimate Words and Other Essays, London: M. Secker, 1920; also published as Anton Chekhov and Other Essays, introduced by S. Monas, Ann Arbor, MI: University of Michigan Press, 1966. (Neither translation includes 'Pokhvala gluposti' (In Praise of Folly), a review of Berdiaev's book *Sub specie aeternitatis*.)

—— (1910) *Velikie kanuny* (Great Vigils), St Petersburg: Shipovnik.

—— (1920) 'Chto takoe bol'shevizm?' (What is Bolshevism?), Berlin: Skify.

—— (1923) *Vlast' kliuchei* (The Power of the Keys), Berlin: Skify; trans. B. Martin, Potestas Clavium, Athens, OH: Ohio University Press, 1968. (The translation does not include 'Vyacheslav velikolepnyi' (Viacheslav the Magnificent) about Viacheslav Ivanov.)

—— (1929) *Na vesakh Iova*, Paris: Sovremennye zapiski; repr. Paris: YMCA-Press 1973; trans. C. Coventry and C.A. Macartney, In Job's Balances, London: Dent & Sons, 1932; repr. Athens, OH: Ohio University Press, 1975, introduction by B. Martin. (The 1975 edition was translated from the German and collated with the Russian.)

—— (1934) 'Menacing Barbarians of Today', in *The Aryan Path*, August, Bombay; 'Ugrozy sovremennykh varvarov', *Vestnik R. Kh. D.*, Paris (1976), 119. (*The Aryan Path* was a monthly philosophy journal.)

—— (1936) Kierkegaard et la Philosophie Existentielle; trans. T. Rageout and B. de Schloezer, Paris: Vrin; *Kirgegard i ekzistentsial'naia filosofiia*, Paris: Dom knigi i sovremennye zapiski, 1939; repr. Moscow: Progress-Gnozis 1992, includes Russian translation of Czeslav Milosz' essay 'Shestov, or the Purity of Despair' (1973) from the French rather than the original English; trans. E. Hewitt, Kierkegaard and the Existential Philosophy, Athens, OH: Ohio University Press, 1969.

—— (1938) Athénes et Jerusalem, trans. B. de Schloezer, Paris: Vrin and Athen und Jerusalem, trans. H. Ruoff, Graz: Schmidt-Dengler; *Afiny i Ierusalim*, Paris: YMCA-Press, 1951; trans. B. Martin, *Athens and Jerusalem*, Athens, OH: Ohio

University Press, 1966. (The 1966 translation contains bibliographical footnotes.)

—— (1964) *Umozrenie i otkrovenie*, Paris: YMCA-Press; trans. B. Martin, Speculation and Revelation, Athens, OH: Ohio University Press, 1982. (Includes Shestov's essay on Husserl, 'In Memory of a Great Philosopher', trans. George L. Kline.)

—— (1966) *Sola fide–tol'ko veroiu* (By Faith Alone), Paris: YMCA-Press. (Written 1910–14.)

—— (1993) *Lev Shestov*, Moscow: Nauka, 2 vols, A.V. Akhutina, ed. and author of introduction, 'Odinokii myslitel''. (Vol. 1 contains *Vlast' kliuchei* and *Afiny i Ierusalim*. Vol. 2 contains Na vesakh Iova.)

References and further reading

Baranova-Shestova, N. (1983) *Zhizn' L'va Shestova* (The Life of Lev Shestov), Paris: La Presse Libre, 2 vols. (Shestov's life through correspondence and memoirs.)

Erofeev, V. (1975) 'Ostaëtsia odno: Proizvol' (Only One Thing Remains: Arbitrariness), in *Voprosy literatury* 10: 153–88. (Argues that the idea of justice is implicit in Shestov's protest but that this idea contradicts his conception of God as arbitrariness and undermines his entire religious philosophy.)

Fondane, B. (1982) *Rencontres avec Léon Chestov*, Paris: Plasma. (An intellectual biography and reminiscences of Shestov by his only disciple. Fondane died in a Nazi concentration camp in 1944; the texts were collected and edited by Natalia Baranoff and Michel Carassou.)

Gal'tseva, R.A. (1992) *Ocherki russkoi utopicheskoi mysli xx veka* (Essays in twentieth-century Russian Utopian Thought) , Moscow: Nauka, ch. 2, 77–119. (Views Shestov as an existentialist before existentialism and contrasts his sympathy for the defeated and the suffering with Nietzsche's immoralism.)

Hill, K.R. (1976) 'The Early Life and Thought of Lev Shestov: 1866–1903', unpublished MA thesis, University of Washington. (Detailed analysis of Shestov's first three books and early articles.)

—— (1980) 'On the Threshold of Faith: An Intellectual Biography of Lev Shestov from 1901 to 1920', Ph.D. thesis, University of Washington. (Argues that Shestov never found the faith he so avidly sought.)

Kline, G.L. (1968) 'Religious Existentialists Shestov and Berdyaev', in *Religious and Anti-Religious Thought in Russia*, Chicago, IL: University of Chicago Press, 73–102. (Discussion of similarities and divergences in their religious existentialism.)

—— (1975) 'Spor o religioznoi filosofii: L. Shestov protiv V. Solov'ëva' (Arguments about Religious Philosophy: L.Shestov against V. Solov'ëv), in *Russkaia religiozno-filosofskaia mysl' xx veka*, ed. N. Poltoratzky, Pittsburgh, PA: University of Pittsburgh, 37–53. (Examines Shestov's 'existentialist' and 'irrationalist' critique of Solov'ëv's idealist speculative system.)

Maia Neto, J. (1995) 'After the Christianization of Pyrrhonism: Shestov's Irrationalism', in *The Christianization of Pyrrhonism. Scepticism and Faith in Pascal, Kierkegaard, and Shestov*, Dordrecht: Kluwer, 55–109. (Argues that Shestov's philosophy is informed by his responses to Neo-Kantianism.)

Shein, L. (1991) *The Philosophy of Lev Shestov (1866–1938), A Russian Religious Existentialist*, Lewiston, NY: Mellen. (Published posthumously. Shestov's early works, including *Sola fidei*. Vol. 2 would have included works written in emigration.)

Steinberg, A. (1991) 'Shestov', *Druz'ia moikh rannikh let (1911–28)* (Friends of My Early Years (1911–28)), Paris: Sintaksis, 217–65. (Personal recollections.)

Valevicius, A. (1993) *Lev Shestov and his Times. Encounters with Brandes, Tolstoi, Dostoevsky, Chekhov, Ibsen, Nietzsche, and Husserl*, New York, NY: Peter Lang. (Argues that Shestov developed his thought in response to the above.)

Wernham, J. (1968) *Two Russian Thinkers: Berdyaev and Shestov*, Toronto, Ont.: University of Toronto Press, 57–109. (Views them as existentialists; emphasizes their responses to Dostoevskii.)

Zakydalsky, T. (1994) 'Lev Shestov and the Revival of Religious Thought in Russia', in *Russian Thought After Communism: The Recovery of a Philosophical Heritage*, ed. J.P. Scanlan, Armonk, NY: M.E. Sharpe, 153–164. (Discussion of Russian studies of Shestov from the thaw to the present.)

BERNICE GLATZER ROSENTHAL

SHI *see* LEGALIST PHILOSOPHY, CHINESE

SHINRAN (1173–1263)

Shinran lived in thirteenth-century Japan, an age of socio-political turmoil, when the old order represented by imperial rule, aristocratic culture and monastic Buddhism was in the process of internal disintegration, and a vibrant age of military clans, popular culture and new schools of Buddhism, appealing to the disenfranchised, was beginning to emerge. Although Shinran's name is not found in the historical records of the period, he left many writings, including original works, commentaries, poetry and letters that contain religious and philosophical insights which had a great impact on subsequent Japanese life. His place in history was secured when in 1921 a collection of his wife's letters, attesting to their relationship over the years, was discovered in the archives of Nishi Hongwanji in Kyoto.

Shinran inherited the pious strain of Pure Land devotional Buddhism, a strain that existed in various subsidiary forms within the great monastic schools such as Tendai, Shingon, Hossō, Kegon and Sanron. In 1175, however, his teacher Hōnen made a radical break from tradition and declared the establishment of an independent Pure Land (Jōdo) School. As a consequence, the movement suffered societal criticism and political persecutions. Among Hōnen's followers, it was Shinran who deepened and expanded the Pure Land insights within the context of Mahāyāna Buddhist thought. His basic teaching may be summarized by such concepts as self-power and Other Power, the various stages of religious life, Amida Buddha as Other Power, and birth in the Pure Land.

The terms 'self-power' and 'Other Power' were first used by Tanluan (476–542) and developed by both Hōnen and Shinran as central concepts in Pure Land praxis. Self-power refers to the belief in one's capacity to attain enlightenment; it is rooted in the unconscious attachment to the ego-self in which every thought, act and speech aims at self-gratification. In contrast, Other Power, according to Shinran, is 'that which is free of calculation'. While self-power is manifested within the subject–object dichotomous mode, Other Power is an awakening to a non-dichotomous reality, such that one sees things, including the self, free of myopic self-centredness. Religiously, Other Power is symbolically represented by Amida, the Buddha of Immeasurable Life and Light. Ultimately, self-power cannot be recognized apart from appreciating Other Power, and the latter cannot be fully realized without exerting the former to its utter, breaking limits. The contrast between the two is not unrelated to Heidegger's distinction between calculative and meditative thinking (see HEIDEGGER, M.), although they are not religious categories; calculative thinking is epitomized in science and technology, and meditative thinking in poetry as a form of disclosure.

The aim of the Pure Land path, then, is abrogating self-power for Other Power as the center of one's life. This transformation involves the proper understanding of Amida and Pure Land, whereby the 'other' is not to be understood in the conventional subject-object sense. Shinran explicates the two in the opening lines of the chapter on True Buddha and True Land of his major work, *Kyogyoshinsho* (Teaching, Practice, Faith and Realization), as follows:

> Reverently contemplating the true Buddha and the true land, I find that the Buddha is the Tathāgata of inconceivable light and that the land also is the land of immeasurable light.
>
> (*Kyogyoshinsho*, in Ueda 1987, III: 395)

While the Buddha and Pure Land may appear to be objectified realities seen within a subject-object framework, true appreciation for both occurs when the reality of karma-bound self is illuminated through their working. It is not the case that there exists a being called Buddha who emanates rays of light, nor is there a place called Pure Land radiating light in all directions; rather, light which is regarded as 'the form taken by wisdom' (*prajñā*) illuminates the 'darkness of ignorance' (*avidyā*) within, thereby liberating the self from its binding powers. When this light is personified, it is called Amida Buddha; and when it is localized, the Pure Land. This dynamic working of reality in the midst of *samsāra* accords with the basic definition of Buddhahood traditionally given in East Asia: 'self-awakening and awakening of others, the activity of awakening unfolding without end' (*jikaku-kakuta kakugyō-gūman*).

The transformation of a samsaric being of ignorance to a person of true awakening in the Pure Land mode involves a spiritual evolution which Shinran called the 'transformation through the three stages' (*sangan-ten'yu*), based on the praxis stipulated in three basic vows among the forty-eight vows fulfilled by Amida Buddha: the 19th, 20th and 18th vows. To adapt the language of Kierkegaard's stages of life's way (see KIERKEGAARD, S.A.), the 19th may be called the ethical, the 20th religiousness 'A', and the 18th religiousness 'B'. The 19th vow requires of a devotee a deep commitment to enlightenment, good works and sincere desire for birth in the Pure Land. When such self-power activities are recognized ultimately as fruitless for the truly religious life, one turns to the 20th vow, devised for those resigned to their lack of spiritual capacity and relying wholly on the sole invocation of *nembutsu* (the holy name of Amida), a religious act said to be 'planting the roots of merits'. But sooner or later, this act too is recognized for what it is: another calculation (*hakarai*) of self-power, unconsciously rooted in the ego-self and prideful of cumulative invocation. The realization of the futility of spiritual fulfillment according to the prescriptions in the 19th and 20th vows opens up the self to the working of Other Power, a transformation experienced within the parameters of the 18th vow. The person now experiences a 'leap' (*ōchō*) not from the relative to the relative but from the relative to the absolute; the primary impetus originates with the absolute, whether it is called true compassion, Other Power or Amida Buddha (see ABSOLUTE, THE). As a consequence, one is endowed with a trusting heart and mind (*shinjin*).

Such a person attains 'birth in the Pure Land', which for Shinran had two implications. First, at the moment of being endowed with a trusting heart one attains a new life, here and now. It is said that although our defiled bodies remain within *samsāra*, our hearts and minds play in the Pure Land. Second, when the karmic life on this earth is exhausted at death, one attains birth in the Pure Land, which is simultaneous with attaining Buddhahood. This means that now, as a fully awakened being of wisdom and compassion, one returns to the world of *samsāra* to work for the deliverance of all existence. 'Birth in the Pure Land' understood in these two ways manifests the dynamic relationship between time and timelessness. Since the Pure Land symbolizes timelessness (eternity), it is inseparable from time (*samsāra*) and manifests itself in time. A person thus can have an experience of timelessness while remaining in time as a karma-bound being. But when karmic life is exhausted and Buddhahood realized (timelessness), one cannot help but identify with every moment of time (*samsāra*) (see ETERNITY).

Going to the Pure Land and returning to *samsāra* are the fullest expressions of the life of *bodhisattva*, philosophically expressed as the simultaneous activity of ascent and descent. Both are made possible not by any human calculation but by the working of Other Power. This powerful working leads to the releasement of self-power, manifested in a person as humility, repentance and gratitude which form the core of a truly ethical life, established on the basis of interdependence and interconnectedness of all existence, both animate and inanimate.

See also: BUDDHIST PHILOSOPHY, JAPANESE

List of works

Shinran (1173–1263) *Kyogyoshinsho* (Teaching, Practice, Faith and Realization), ed. and trans. Ueda Yoshifumi, *The True Teaching, Practice and Realization of the Pure Land Way*, Shin Buddhism Translation Series, Kyoto: Hongwanji International Centre, 1983–90, 4 vols. (This series contains Shinran's complete works, including his letters. Alternate translations are found in the Ryukoku Translation Series, published at Kyoto: Ryukoku University Translation Centre, 1961–86.)

References and further reading

Bloom, A. (1965) *Shinran's Gospel of Pure Grace*, Tucson, AZ: University of Arizona Press. (Outdated but still the only good one-volume work on Shinran available in English.)
Ueda Yoshifumi and Hirota, D. (1989) *Shinran: An Introduction to His Thought*, Kyoto: Hongwani International Center. (Outline of Shinran's thought, including original text and interpretations, based on the publications of the Shin Buddhism Translation Series.)
Unno Taitetsu (1996) *Tannisho: A Shin Buddhist Classic*, 2nd revised edn, Honolulu, HI: Buddhist Study Center Press. (An introduction to the thought of Shinran as recorded by one of his disciples.)

TAITETSU UNNO

SHINTŌ

Shintō means the 'way of the kami *(gods)' and is a term that was evolved about the late sixth or early seventh centuries – as Japan entered an extended period of cultural borrowing from China and Korea – to distinguish the amalgam of native religious beliefs from Buddhism, a continental import. Shintō embraces the most ancient and basic social and religious values of Japan. It is exclusively Japanese, showing no impulse to spread beyond Japan. The exportation of Shintō would in any case be exceedingly difficult since its mythology is so closely bound to the creation of Japan and the Japanese people, and since many of its deities are believed to make their homes in the mountains, rivers, trees, rocks and other natural features of the Japanese islands.*

Shintō comprises both great and little traditions. The great tradition, established in the mythology that was incorporated into Japan's two oldest extant writings, Kojiki *(Record of Ancient Matters) and* Nihon Shoki *(Chronicle of Japan), both dating from the early eighth century, is centred on the imperial institution. According to the mythology the emperorship was ordained by the sun goddess, Amaterasu, who sent her grandson from heaven to earth (Japan) to found a dynasty 'to rule eternally'. The present emperor is the 125th in a line of sovereigns officially regarded, until Japan's defeat in the Second World War, as descended directly from Amaterasu.*

Shintō's little tradition is a mixture of polytheistic beliefs about kami, *manifested in nature worship (animism), ancestor worship, agricultural cults, fertility rites, shamanism and more. Lacking a true scriptural basis, Shintō derives from the faith of the people, and from earliest times has had its roots firmly planted in particularistic, localistic practices. Thus it has always been strongest in its association with such entities as families, villages and locales (for example, mountains thought to be the homes of certain kami or, indeed, to be the* kami *themselves).*

1   *Kami*, people and nature
2   Worship of the *kami*
3   Purification
4   Shintō and Buddhism
5   The imperial institution
6   The shrine

1   *Kami*, people and nature

In Shintō belief there is no sharp distinction between *kami* and people – indeed some people, such as emperors, great heroes and ancestors, are regarded as *kami* – and both *kami* and people are joined together by their common habitation in the natural environment of the Japanese islands (although some *kami* in the mythology, including the sun goddess Amaterasu, reside in heaven). The human, natural and sacred realms merge. As the great eighteenth-century Shintō scholar MOTOORI NORINAGA observed, '...the *kami* are spirits that abide in and are worshipped at the [Shintō] shrines. In principle human beings, birds, animals, trees, plants, mountains, oceans – all may be *kami*. According to ancient usage, whatever seemed strikingly impressive, possessed the quality of excellence, or inspired a feeling of awe was called *kami*' (quoted in Agency for Cultural Affairs 1972: 38).

Through Shintō, the Japanese people express their respect for all life as well as their appreciation of the beauties and powers of nature. And because certain elements and phenomena of nature, such as the sun, the moon, the wind and mountains, are regarded as *kami* and because nature as a whole is the principal home of the *kami*, nature is seen as 'good'. The Shintō view of nature has given a powerful stimulus to the arts and aesthetic tastes of the Japanese. Regarding nature as both beautiful and good, the Japanese have celebrated its qualities – especially the perishable beauties of the changing seasons, such as the cherry blossoms of spring and the maple leaves of autumn – in countless poems, paintings and other artistic media. Although Buddhism has also influenced the Japanese understanding of nature, the natural environment of Japan is first and foremost a world of Shintō (see AESTHETICS, JAPANESE).

2   Worship of the *kami*

Kami are, for the most part, beneficent entities, requiring only that they be properly and respectfully attended to. Through worship, the people provide this attention and express their gratitude to the *kami*. The principal form of worship is the presentation of offerings to the *kami*, which can be rendered privately at home or publicly at a Shintō shrine. Items used as offerings include rice, other foods, *sake* and money.

People also say prayers and address petitions to the *kami*. The formal prayers, recited in archaic language by priests at shrines, typically praise the *kami* and express thanksgiving for the benefits they have bestowed. They may also include accounts of the lineages of the *kami* and describe the offerings being made to them. In their personal prayers and petitions, people make requests for such things as good health and personal success.

3   Purification

Shintō is a religion of rituals (see RITUAL), and one of the central rituals is purification. The importance attached to purification in Shintō is readily observable, for example, in the procedures followed in preparing for worship and in worshipping. In approaching a shrine, one first performs 'external' or 'outer' purification – thus making oneself ready to enter the presence of the *kami* – by rinsing the mouth and hands with water at an ablution basin. Inside the shrine, the priest performs 'internal' or 'inner' purification in the form of exorcism by reciting prayers and waving a wand. Reflecting primitive, pre-ethical attitudes, Shinto regards both manifest defilements – such as bleeding, disease and death – and acts of evil or wrongdoing as 'pollutions' that must be ritually cleansed. Purification effects renewal: through purification, things are returned to their original states and proper identification with the *kami* is re-established.

Manifestations of the concern for purity and purification, deriving primarily from Shintō, can be observed in countless aspects of Japanese behaviour and life even today. The great attention given by the Japanese to bathing and general cleanliness is the most obvious of these manifestations, but they can also be found in such practices as the scattering of salt – a form of ritual purification – by sumo wrestlers before their bouts and the constant 'cleansing' of the utensils used in the tea ceremony. Although the tea ceremony, as it evolved during the medieval age, is generally thought to derive its spiritual essence from Buddhism, especially Zen, it is also thoroughly infused with Shintō or, more precisely, Shintō-like rituals of purification. We see this not only in the cleansing of the utensils but also in the precise and careful handling of water and fire, both of which are important agents of purification.

4 Shintō and Buddhism

According to the *Nihon Shoki* (Chronicle of Japan) in the early eighth century, Buddhism was introduced to Japan from Korea in 552. Undoubtedly the Japanese knew about Buddhism from a much earlier time, but it was in the middle or late sixth century that Buddhism was formally established in Japan, becoming in fact a principal carrier of continental culture during the long period of borrowing from China and Korea from the late sixth to mid-ninth centuries. It appears, as mentioned above, to have been the introduction of Buddhism to Japan that prompted the Japanese to coin the word Shintō for their native religious beliefs and practices. The construction of Buddhist temples in Japan also apparently inspired the Japanese to build sacred structures – which we call shrines – for Shintō (although there may have been some shrine construction from an earlier period). The continental architecture of Buddhism influenced Shintō architecture in various ways, particularly in later centuries. However, the structures of Shintō shrines (see §6) are based primarily on native styles and tastes that set them quite distinctively apart from Buddhist temples.

In addition to the architectural wonders of its temples, Buddhism also brought to Japan new types of religious paintings and statuary. Buddhist iconography is extremely rich and varied, and became a major component of art in Japan in succeeding centuries. Yet this is an area in which Buddhism exerted little influence on Shintō, for Shintō, with only minor exceptions, has not conceived of its deities in visual terms: that is, it has made virtually no attempt to portray the *kami* as entities based on, say, anthropomorphic or zoomorphic prototypes.

Buddhism's view of the world could scarcely differ more from that of Shintō. Whereas Shintō celebrates life – and hence this existence – in all its manifold forms and creative vitality, Buddhism looks upon the world with the deepest pessimism as a place of incessant suffering. Suffering is caused because all things in the world are in flux, in a constant process of change (see MUJŌ). People seek to acquire things, to hold onto them, but this is impossible because of the impermanence of everything: nothing is substantial, nothing real. The result of human acquisitiveness is, inevitably, suffering. Although the various sects of Buddhism differ in the methods and the paths they recommend to their followers, they share the goal of achieving release from the cycle of life and death and hence from suffering (see SUFFERING, BUDDHIST VIEWS OF ORIGINATION OF).

It is certainly an oversimplification to say, as has often been said, that Shintō is concerned with life and Buddhism with death, but there is a rough truth to this statement. Although Shintō mythology describes an underworld to which people must go upon death, essentially it has developed no theology about the afterlife. Death is a form of pollution, which like other pollutions requires ritual purification. Very likely a major reason why Shintō did not develop a theology of the afterlife is because Buddhism, upon its arrival in Japan, pre-empted this field. In any case, Buddhism handles death – through funerals and periodic rites of mourning – to the point where its priests have in recent times been unflatteringly labelled the 'undertakers of Japan'.

One reason, then, why Shintō and Buddhism have been able to coexist in Japan through the centuries is because they deal with essentially different realms, roughly categorizable as life and death. Another reason is that they have been partially syncretized. Syncretism is characteristic of East Asian religion and thought in general, and is certainly observable in Buddhism where, for example, we find the ninth-century founder of Shingon (True Word) Buddhism, KŪKAI, writing a tract entitled *Jūjūshinron* (The Ten Stages of Religious Consciousness), in which he ranks Confucianism, Daoism, and various sects of Buddhism in a hierarchy of ascending 'consciousness' culminating, at the highest level, in Shingon.

In both India and China, Buddhism recognized the 'deities' of other religions or systems of belief, including Confucianism and Daoism in China, by considering them as avatars of buddhas and bodhisattvas (see BUDDHIST PHILOSOPHY, INDIAN; BUDDHIST PHILOSOPHY, CHINESE). It did this according to the concept of *honji suijaku* (original substance manifests traces), which became particularly important in Japan in regard to the association of Buddhism and Shintō. From the standpoint of Japanese Buddhists, *honji suijaku* meant that the deities of Buddhism (the substance) manifested themselves as the *kami* (traces) of Shintō. Thus, for example, the sun goddess Amaterasu was thought to be the 'trace' of Shingon's cosmic Buddha, known in Japanese as Dainichi (Great Sun).

Fundamental to *honji suijaku* thought during the early centuries after its introduction to Japan was the belief that the buddhas and bodhisattvas were primary and the deities of Shintō were secondary. In the medieval age (1185–1573), however, there arose a movement within Shintō – as part of a larger Shintō revival – that sought to reverse this relationship, declaring the Shintō deities to be primary and the buddhas and bodhisattvas secondary. A good example of this reversal of the *honji suijaku* relationship can be observed in the late thirteenth century, when two attempts by forces of the Mongol dynasty of China to invade Japan, in 1274 and 1281, were defeated by typhoons that devastated the Mongol fleets. The Japanese believed these storms were *kamikaze*, 'winds of the gods', that were sent to protect Japan in times of greatest peril. Whereas for centuries the guardian deities of Buddhism had been looked upon as the principal protectors of the state, the function of state protection was thereafter shifted to the *kami* of Shintō.

5 The imperial institution

The mythology of Shintō proclaims that the sun goddess Amaterasu mandated her grandson – his name was Ninigi – to descend to Japan and establish a dynasty to rule the country eternally (although the actual dynastic founder and first emperor was Ninigi's grandson, Jimmu). In any case, belief that Japan would be ruled forever by a single royal line became one of the most powerful myths in Japanese history, a myth that retained its potency as a tool of rule until it was shattered by Japan's catastrophic defeat in the Second World War. Although through most of Japanese history the emperor has in fact functioned more as a 'sacred legitimizer' than an actual ruler (he has reigned rather than ruled), he, more than any other person or thing, has through the centuries symbolized 'Japan'.

The significance of the imperial institution to Japan and the Japanese was given important new definition during the Shintō revival in the early medieval period. Following upon the assertion that the *kami* of Shintō, rather than the deities of Buddhism, provided protection for the state at the highest level, the fourteenth-century courtier Kitabatake Chikafusa declared in the opening lines of his history of Japan, *Jinnō Shōtōki* (Chronicle of the Direct Descent of Gods and Sovereigns):

> Great Japan is the divine land. The heavenly progenitor founded it, and the sun goddess bequeathed it to her descendants to rule eternally. Only in our country is this true; there are no similar examples in other countries. This is why our country is called the divine land.

(Varley 1980: 49)

Here Japan is extolled as a country superior to others because it has been 'ruled' from its founding by an unbroken dynastic line of sovereigns. As Chikafusa observed, other countries– such as India and China –

have often been without sovereigns or have suffered frequent dynastic changes. The belief in the superiority of Japan and the Japanese centred on Japan's 'unique' imperial institution, implicit in Chikafusa's declaration, was sustained into the modern age, becoming the core of the *kokutai* (national polity) ideology that was officially promoted by Japanese governments until the end of the Second World War (see SOVEREIGNTY).

6 The shrine

Probably the best known symbol of Shintō is the *torii* or 'bird perch' entranceway to a shrine. This entranceway supposedly has its origins in the mythology, where we read that a perch was erected for a cock to crow and signal the commencement of entertainment organized by the other gods in order to lure Amaterasu out of a cave in which she had secluded herself.

Shintō shrines are of a great variety, constructed in many diverse locations. At the base of society, in the villages and towns, shrines are found primarily in natural settings removed from most human habitation. These shrines seem to merge with nature in the same way that the human realm merges with the natural and sacred realms (see §1).

Shrines are the homes of *kami* and the places where offerings are made and prayers recited. Although some shrines are quite elaborate, comprising many buildings and covering extensive areas, the shrine at its simplest has an inner sanctuary, where the symbol of the resident *kami* (or symbols, if the shrine houses more than one *kami*) is housed, and an outer area for offerings and prayers. All shrines also have an ablution basin (see §3) where worshippers perform external purification. Worshippers do not enter the shrine buildings; only priests are allowed in them.

Although it may be difficult to perceive it in those located in congested cities, the shrine is always designed to evoke a sense of mystical unity with the *kami* and indeed with the land of Japan itself, the home of the *kami*. Shintō, represented by the shrine, constitutes the very basis of Japanese civilization.

See also: AESTHETICS, JAPANESE; BUDDHIST PHILOSOPHY, JAPANESE; JAPANESE PHILOSOPHY; MOTOORI NORINAGA; RELIGION, PHILOSOPHY OF

References and further reading

* Agency for Cultural Affairs (ed.) (1972) *Japanese Religion*, Tokyo: Kodansha. (Introduction to Japanese religion.)

Grapard, A.G. (1983) 'Shintō', *Kodansha Encyclope-*

dia of Japan, vol. 7, Tokyo: Kodansha. (Good introduction to the subject.)

Ono Sokyo (1962) *Shintō, the Kami Way*, Tokyo: Charles E. Tuttle Co. (More detailed description of Shintō.)

* Varley, H.P. (trans.) (1980) *A Chronicle of Gods and Sovereigns: The Jinnō Shōtōki of Kitabatake Chikafusa*, New York: Columbia University Press. (Translation of Kitabatake's history of Japan.)

PAUL VARLEY

AL-SHIRAZI, SADR AL-DIN MUHAMMAD *see* MULLA SADRA (SADR AL-DIN MUHAMMAD AL-SHIRAZI)

SHŌTOKU CONSTITUTION

The Shōtoku Constitution is the earliest fundamental political document of Japan. Promulgated in AD 604, it is ascribed to the regent Shōtoku, who was also a devout Buddhist and philosopher. The document reflects the influences of Confucianism, Buddhism, Daoism and Legalism in its various provisions; it is strongly marked by Chinese thought rather than being influenced by Shintō. Not a constitution in the modern sense, the document is rather a set of ideals, guiding principles and basic requirements for those in government. As well as helping to lay the foundation for a unified Japan, the Constitution also marks the beginning of a period of assimilation of Chinese culture and philosophy.

The Shōtoku Constitution was, according to tradition, promulgated in AD 604. Also called the Constitution in Seventeen Articles, it is ascribed to Shōtoku (574–622), a philosopher and a devout Buddhist as well as a statesman, who served as regent of Japan under the Empress Suiko. Before this time, Japan had not existed as a nation but had been divided into autonomous regions and clans, whose chiefs vied with one another for hegemony. With his Constitution, Shōtoku sought to establish Japan as a unified nation under the sole authority of the imperial throne, and to ground its conduct of government upon universal principles which he found in Buddhism and classical Chinese philosophy.

The Shōtoku Constitution is not a constitution in the modern and technical sense of a set of principles formally limiting the extent of legislation and formally grounding the legality of other laws. It is instead a set of ideals, guiding principles and basic requirements for the officials who exercise governmental powers.

The Constitution consists of seventeen articles, as follows:

Article 1 declares harmony to be a principle of governance within a hierarchical order and promotes the discussion of public affairs.

Article 2 exhorts the reverence of the Three Treasures of Buddhism, namely the Buddha, the Law and the Community of Practitioners, as 'the final refuge of all living beings' and 'the ultimate foundation of all nations'.

Article 3 compares the lord to Heaven, the vassal to Earth and enjoins the vassal to obey the imperial commands scrupulously.

Article 4 enjoins the ministers and functionaries to base their conduct upon decorum.

Article 5 warns against the settling of law-suits under the influence of bribery.

Article 6 emphasizes the importance of moral integrity on the part of officials, and admonishes them not to resort to self-promoting deceptions.

Article 7 lays down the policy of honouring the wise in the management of bureaucracy.

Article 8 seeks to impress officials with the importance of diligence and punctuality.

Article 9 declares trustworthiness among vassals to be 'the basis of righteousness' on which the success or failure of government depends.

Article 10 calls for the cessation of anger, resentment and self-righteousness: 'For everybody has a heart, and every heart has its own attachment. Their right is our wrong, our right, their wrong.'

Article 11 stresses the importance of reward and punishment according to deserts.

Article 12 forbids provincial governors and district administrators to levy taxes for themselves, and reserves taxation as a prerogative of the sovereign.

Article 13 commands the officials to execute public affairs responsibly, stating that their absence, for reasons official or personal, does not excuse them from their duties.

Article 14 points out the evils of envy at the sight of the promotion of those with superior intelligence or ability.

Article 15 calls for the setting aside of private motives, which otherwise would lead to resentment and discord.

Article 16 states that the conscription of labour for public works should not interfere with the peasants' agricultural production.

Article 17 points out the need of public discussions of weighty public affairs.

In this set of principles the influence of Confucianism is prominent. Harmony, decorum and trustworthiness, which are the bases of Articles 1, 4 and 9, are central elements of Confucian ethics (see CONFUCIAN PHILOSOPHY, JAPANESE; CONFUCIAN PHILOSOPHY, CHINESE). Article 2 is striking in its commitment to Buddhism; Buddhists vow to take refuge in the Three Treasures (see BUDDHIST PHILOSOPHY, JAPANESE). Articles 5, 11 and 12, concerned respectively with the fair enforcement of laws, reward and punishment, and taxation, betray the influence of Legalism (see LEGALIST PHILOSOPHY, CHINESE). The call to abandon desires in Article 5 and the relativity of conventional valuation in Article 10 sound Daoist (see Daoist philosophy). In contrast with the marked presence of Chinese thought in the Constitution, the influence of Shintō, the indigenous folk religion, is characteristically absent.

The philosophical interest and significance of the Shōtoku Constitution lie primarily in the following three areas:

(1) Exactly what universal principles of East Asian continental thought were applied, and how were they applied, to the political situation in the southwestern half of the Japanese archipelago at the formative stage of Japan in the early seventh century? Did the urgent practical need for political reform dictate the utilizations of ideas and ideals of political philosophy as instruments, or did the political situation serve as the medium through which to implement the ideas and ideals?

(2) How are the ideas and ideals culled from the different sources of Mahāyāna Buddhism, Daoism, Confucianism and Legalism related one to another in the ways in which they inform the Constitution? Do the influences of Confucianism and Buddhism, for instance, simply coexist side by side, or are they reconciled with each other and integrated into some coherent pattern? If so, what is that pattern?

(3) How did the Constitution, the earliest politically authoritative articulation of an ideology, set a precedent for the subsequent development of Japanese thought and culture?

On these three issues, no clear scholarly consensus has yet emerged. However, scholars have to a considerable extent overcome healthy scepticism concerning the prior issues about the date and the authorship of the Constitution, and have canvassed a vast body of Chinese literature, including Chinese versions of Mahāyāna sūtras, in order to identify the sources of verbal borrowings, echoes and allusions with which the text of the Constitution abounds. The entire text of the Constitution, written in highly stylized classical Chinese, has been preserved as a quotation in the Nihon shoki (Chronicles of Japan), and is there attributed to Shōtoku.

Among other achievements of the Shōtoku regency are the construction of Buddhist temples, the writing of commentaries on three Mahāyāna sūtras, the institution of the Twelve Cap–ranks of bureaucracy and the inauguration of official envoys to China. The Constitution, together with these achievements, contributed much to the transition of Japan from a divided tribal society to a united nation, the adoption and assimilation of Chinese civilization including philosophy, and the transformation of Japan into a land of Buddhism.

See also: BUDDHIST PHILOSOPHY, JAPANESE; BUSHI PHILOSOPHY; LEGALIST PHILOSOPHY, CHINESE; CONFUCIAN PHILOSOPHY, JAPANESE; DAOIST PHILOSOPHY; JAPANESE PHILOSOPHY; SHINTŌ

References and further reading

The text of the Shōtoku Constitution is in *Nihon shoki* (Chronicles of Japan) (AD 720), ed. Ienaga Saburō, Inoue Mitsusada, Ōno Sususmu and Sakamoto Tarō, Tokyo: Iwanami, 1968, vol. 2, 180–7; trans. in W.T. de Bary, D. Keene and Tsunoda Ryūsaku, *Sources of Japanese Tradition* (1958) New York: Columbia University Press, 1958, 49–53. (The latter gives an English translation of the Shōtoku constitution.)

Anesaki, M. (1930) *History of Japanese Religion*, London: Kegan Paul, Trench, Trubner, 57–65. (Sees the Constitution, an expression of Shōtoku's political philosophy, as an application of Buddhist ideals.)

de Bary, W.T (ed.) (1969) *The Buddhist Tradition in India, China and Japan*, New York: The Modern Library, 255–65. (Articulates the views of Anesaki (1930).)

Kitagawa, J.M. (1987) *On Understanding Japanese Religion*, Princeton, NJ: Princeton University Press. (Studies of the patterns of blending of Buddhism, Chinese schools of thought, and Shintō in Japan.)

Sansom, G. (1958) *A History of Japan to 1334*, Stanford, CA: Stanford University Press, 40–81. (Includes a history of Japanese thought from the fifth to the seventh century, inclined to deny Shōtoku's authorship of the Constitution.)

Sonoda, K. and Brown, D.M. (1993) 'Early Buddha Worship', in J.W. Hall, M.B. Jansen, Madoka

Kanai and D. Twitchett (eds) *The Cambridge History of Japan*, vol. 1, *Ancient Japan*, Cambridge: Cambridge University Press. (An up-to-date and judicious survey of scholarly opinions on Shōtoku's authorship of the 'Injunctions' and also on the issue of priority among the diverse strands of thought involved. The context of this survey is the placement of Shōtoku in the early phase of the history of Buddhism in Japan.)

Umehara, T. (1993) *Shōtoku Taishi* (Prince Shōtoku), Tokyo: Shūei-sha, 4 vols. (A close study of the structure of the Constitution with a view to determining the pattern of conceptual integration underlying the document; see especially vol. 2, 340–533.)

YUKIO KACHI

SHPET, GUSTAV GUSTAVOVICH (1879–1937)

Gustav Shpet was the first Russian philosopher to take up Edmund Husserl's idea of pure phenomenology as prima philosophia *and develop it in several directions. Thus, in his most important phenomenological work* Iavlenie i smysl *(Appearance and Sense) (1914), he outlined his 'phenomenology of hermeneutic reason' on the basis of Husserl's* Ideas 1. *In this theoretical framework he formulated, between 1914 and 1918, hermeneutic and semiotic problems, which in the 1920s he elaborated more specifically within the fields of philosophy of language and theory of art. In doing so he took up ideas from other philosophical movements, particularly Dilthey's hermeneutics and Wilhelm von Humboldt's philosophy of language.*

Shpet's reception of phenomenology has to be seen in the context of Russian intellectual and cultural life during the first two decades of the twentieth century. The Platonic 'Moscow Metaphysical School' (which included V. Solov'ëv and S. Trubetskoi) provided the intellectual atmosphere in which his turn to Husserl's phenomenology took place, and his ideas on theories of language and signs are close to ideas of the contemporary movement of Russian Formalism. Through his phenomenological and structural theories he influenced Prague structuralism via the 'Moscow Linguistic Circle', and is seen as a precursor to Soviet Semiotics.

1 Life
2 Development towards phenomenology
3 Concept of phenomenology
4 Hermeneutics, philosophy of language and poetics
5 Turning away from Husserl's concept of language

1 Life

Gustav Shpet, founder of a phenomenological movement in Russia, was born in Kiev. He studied there at the Vladimir University from 1901–5 and finished his studies with a monograph entitled *Problema prichinnosti v Iume i Kante* (The Problem of Causality in Hume and Kant). In 1907 he moved to Moscow, and taught at Moscow University from 1910 onwards. During a stay in Göttingen (1912–13) where he studied with HUSSERL he turned to Husserl's transcendental phenomenology. His first phenomenological publication *Iavlenie i smysl* (Appearance and Sense) (1914) marked the beginning of a productive reception of Husserl's phenomenology in Russia. In 1916 he had his viva on his Master's thesis *Istoriia kak problema logiki* (History as a Problem of Logic. Part I). In 1918 he finished his manuscript on *Germenevtika i eë problemy* (Hermeneutics and its Problems), in which he critically presented the problems of hermeneutics as they have developed throughout history from antiquity (especially in Origen and Augustine) to modern times, thereby at the same time elaborating the basic outline of his 'hermeneutical philosophy': a philosophy which is caught in the field of tension exerted, on the one side, by Husserl's 'Phenomenology of Reason' and, on the other, by Dilthey's 'Philosophy of Life'.

After the Revolution of 1917, Shpet was active in many different fields. He received a professorship of philosophy at Moscow University. In 1920 he joined the 'Moscow Linguistic Circle' (MLK), a centre of Russian Formalism (see RUSSIAN LITERARY FORMALISM), and in 1921 was appointed director of the Institute for Scientific Philosophy, a new research institute at Moscow University. Expelled from there in 1923 for political reasons, he concentrated his activities on the State Academy of the Arts (GAKhN), whose vice-president he was until 1929, and whose Department of Philosophy he temporarily led.

His most important contributions to the theory of art and language are his *Ėsteticheskie fragmenty* (Aesthetic Fragments), published in 1922 and 1923 in Petrograd, and *Vnutrenniaia forma slova* (The Internal Form of the Word) (1927). *Ėsteticheskie fragmenty* includes a phenomenology of 'living discourse' and an analysis of those rules which determine the constitution of meaning in poetic discourse. These phenomenological and structural analyses of language, which aim to construct a poetics, were further developed through a critical assessment of Humboldt's philosophy of language in Shpet's last substantial work *The Internal Form of the Word*.

During a 'cleansing' of the GAKhN in 1929, Shpet was forced to retire, but was still able to work for a while as a translator, editor and critic. It was then that he translated Dickens, Byron and Shakespeare into Russian. In March 1935 he was arrested by the NKVD and charged with having led an anti-Soviet group during his time at the GAKhN in the 1920s. After a lengthy detention he was exiled for five years to Eniseisk, later to Tomsk. Here in 1937 he finished his Russian translation of Hegel's *Phenomenology of Spirit*. In October of the same year he was again arrested and shot by the NKVD.

2 Development towards phenomenology

Representative of Shpet's notion of philosophy before his turn to phenomenology (and of expectations he then had for a future reform of philosophy and psychology) is his article 'Odin put' psikhologii i kuda on vedët' (One Method of Psychology and Where It Leads To), published in 1912. He criticized the prevailing trend of an experimental and explanatory psychology for having replaced 'lively and concrete facts' with 'empty schemata and abstractions'. Only a descriptive psychology which focuses on the pure data of consciousness would be able to fathom psychic life in its concreteness and totality. He saw the basis for such a new direction in psychological thinking in Wilhelm Dilthey's *Ideas on a Descriptive and Analytical Psychology* (1894) (see DILTHEY, W.) and he argued that there was a particular style of philosophizing, that would correspond to this new type of philosophy which takes into account the totality of psychic life: a 'realistic metaphysics' whose task it would be to grasp 'the real in its true essence and its totality'. Shpet thought that such a philosophy, which draws on the evident facts of 'inner experience', had been realized in important movements of nineteenth and early twentieth century Russian philosophy. Philosophers of the 'Moscow Metaphysical School' are mentioned as typical exponents of this trait in Russian thought (see SOLOV'ËV. V.S.).

Another, no less important, influence on Shpet's reception of Husserl was his interest in the logic of the historical sciences. During his stay in Göttingen (1912–13) he found in Husserl's phenomenology the theory he had been looking for, and his hermeneutical interest motivated him to try to develop Husserl's 'Phenomenology of Reason', as outlined in *Ideas Pertaining to a Pure Phenomenology, volume 1* (referred to as *Ideas 1*) into a theory of hermeneutic reason which focuses on the problem of understanding signs.

Although the ideas Shpet encountered in Göttingen primarily concerned *transcendental* phenomenology – the seminar on 'Nature and Spirit', which Shpet attended with other influential phenomenologists like Roman Ingarden and Hans Lipps, certainly met his hermeneutical interests – on the other hand, the *ontological* trend in the intellectual atmosphere among Husserl's fellow students in Göttingen also has to be taken into account (see PHENOMENOLOGICAL MOVEMENT §§3–4).

3 Concept of phenomenology

Shpet's encounter with Husserl's phenomenology in the light of his expectation of a reform of philosophy and psychology leads to a peculiar notion of phenomenology, which is documented in *Iavlenie i smysl* (*Appearance and Sense*) (1914). On the one hand, the Russian phenomenologist tries to reconstruct Husserl's noetic-noematic studies within the framework of an ontological question, based on the Neoplatonism of the 'Moscow Metaphysical School'; on the other he demonstrates the incompleteness of Husserl's analyses of objects, as given in *Ideas 1*, and completes these analyses with his own. The 'noematic sense' intended in acts of consciousness, as presented by Husserl, presupposes for Shpet a class of intentional experiences hardly dealt with in *Ideas 1*; acts of consciousness through understanding, which play a role in the constitution of all classes of concrete objects. The structure of these 'hermeneutic acts' is illustrated by a range of phenomena which are only of minor importance in *Ideas 1*: by the mode of appearance of items of practical use, the specific character of historical sources and the understanding of linguistic utterances. Thereby Husserl's 'Phenomenology of Reason' meets Shpet's endeavour to find a basis for historical cognition in scientific logic, and eventually to prepare a grounding of the humanities, in other words, to prepare an analysis of their conceptual frameworks and most important methods.

Appearance and Sense marks the early phase of Shpet's reception of Husserl. Here he outlines his project of a 'phenomenology of hermeneutical reason'. The ensuing works on hermeneutics, philosophy of language and theory of art, published or written between 1916 and 1927, can be seen as a further development of such a hermeneutical phenomenology, whose leading idea is the correlation of signs (as combinations of expression and meaning) and sign-interpreting consciousness.

Shpet also characterizes his project as a semiotic 'Philosophy of Culture' in which language, art, myths and manners are to be described as systems of signs. He develops the basic model of a sign out of Husserl's concept of linguistic expression, which acts as prototype for all other forms of signs. The idea of a 'purely logical grammar', which formulates laws for the grammatical meanings of natural languages, should be applied analogously to all the other cultural systems.

4   Hermeneutics, philosophy of language and poetics

The concrete form of Shpet's phenomenology of hermeneutical reason in his philosophy of language and his poetics was also much influenced by Dilthey's 'Philosophy of Life'. In his hermeneutical philosophy, as outlined in the manuscript *Germenevtika i eë problemy* (Hermeneutics and its Problems), he worked with Schleiermacher's, Boeckh's and Dilthey's theories of understanding (see HERMENEUTICS §§2–4; SCHLEIERMACHER, F.D.E.). Above all, he tried to deepen and refine Dilthey's late grounding of the humanities – then the culmination in the development of hermeneutics – with insights in the domain of semiotic theories, which he found not only in Husserl's first *Logical Investigation* on *Expression and Meaning*, but also in other semantic works of the Brentano School (Marty and Meinong especially). A combination of Husserl's semantics with Dilthey's hermeneutics would be an enrichment for both sides, as Shpet wrote at the end of the manuscript. The theory of understanding could find a new answer to the question of the mutual relation of the different methods of interpretation, whereas semantics would experience in this combination a 'philosophically lively and concrete embodiment'.

This actualization of Husserl's semantics, with a hermeneutical intention, has left its traces in Shpet's *Èsteticheskie fragmenty*. With this tripartite work he entered the contemporary discussions on literary theory, as initiated by Russian Formalism. He was particularly concerned with the definition of the specific character of poetical discourse as opposed to others, be they scientific, rhetorical or everyday discourses. If one puts this question phenomenologically, one has to ask under what condition a linguistic utterance appears as artistic or poetic to a listener or reader. Since a poetic utterance is experienced only as a contrast to everyday use of language, one has to analyse first the reception of everyday language. This is the procedure Shpet follows in the second part of *Èsteticheskie fragmenty*. In the description here of the various forms and aspects of the understanding of language, the difference between understanding the message and understanding the author of the message plays a pivotal role.

Here only the description of the understanding of language is called a phenomenological analysis. In opposition to this, Shpet presented his description of the structure of linguistic expression as 'ontology of the word', which he, in turn, subsumed under a general theory of semiotics. In this confrontation between a phenomenological inquiry, which is confined to the side of experience, and an ontology, which focuses on the object, the ever increasing influence of Husserl's early concept of phenomenology on Shpet becomes visible. In Shpet's 'ontology of the word' a particular concept of structure is of central importance. 'The structure is a concrete construction whose individual parts can vary in their extent and even in their quantity, but not a single part of the whole *in potentia* can be removed without destroying this whole' (1922–3: II, 11). By 'structure of the word' Shpet did not mean the morphological, syntactic or stylistic construction, in short, not the arrangement of linguistic units 'in the plain', but 'the organic, depthwise, as it were, arrangement of the word – from the sensually conceivable wording to the eidetic object' (1922–3: II, 11). Therefore the word-structure consists not only of the relations between wording and meaning, but also of the relations between meaning and 'object' (the latter, as ideal object, being ontologically distinguished from concrete individual things).

When Shpet spoke of the structure of the *word*, he took it in the wide sense of the Russian expression for 'word', namely 'slovo'. 'Slovo' is used not only for words but also for groups of words, sentences and combinations of sentences, even for literary texts and for the whole of a natural language. Shpet used it with all these different meanings, yet was mainly concerned with the 'communicating word': meaningful discourse able to convey something to another person. Thereby Shpet took up Plato's definition of predicative statements, as the 'shortest and most simple *logos*'. Shpet saw its structure as follows:

In a simple predication the expression in subject position denotes a concrete, individual object; the predicate indicates a property belonging to this object. How such a sentence, consisting of a proper name (or other denominations) and a predicate, can have a sense and refer to objects, is clarified by Shpet through an analysis of the use of these expressions. In denoting speakers refer to a thing, in predication they say something about it. What can be said about this thing, and, conversely, which predications are impossible, is determined by the species to which the thing belongs. Therefore an act intending this species, which Shpet called also the 'eidetic object', is constitutive for the construction of a meaningful predication.

The central point of Shpet's theory of predication is that the meaning of the predicate can only be given in the act of predication, in so far as an assertion of meaning only happens in the interplay of the denoting of individuals and the act intending an eidetic object.

With these definitions Shpet outlined the 'word's'

structure, which is common to factual or scientific communicating, to rhetorical and to poetic discourse. The key to the specification of this general structure in the artistic and literary usage and formation of words, sentences and combinations of sentences, is to be found in Shpet's theory of linguistic functions; a theory which he developed through a critical assessment of Husserl's and Marty's philosophy of language. He started from three different functions of language which can be fulfilled by each type of discourse. Thereby in each case one function dominates the others. These three functions are the factual-communicating, the expressive and the poetic, in other words, the function working through the creative formation of language. (The idea of the creative character of language, which is most obvious in poetic discourse, is common to both Russian Formalism and Shpet's poetics, and can be traced back to Wilhelm von Humboldt's concept of language as *Energeia*' (see HUMBOLDT, W. VON).

Depending on which of the three functions is dominant, discourse is either scientific (concerned with factual communication), rhetorical (concerned with influencing the emotions), or poetic (primarily concerned with the arrangement of linguistic expressions as such). The predominance of one of the three functions implies in each case a different mutual relation between the parts of the word-structure. Whereas, for example, in everyday language the arrangement on the level of expression aims primarily at structuring the expressed meaning, and thereby at the communication of facts, in poetic discourse all levels gain a relative importance on their own. The rhythmic forms and syntactic particularities of this discourse should be noticeable as such. On the other hand, the meaning expressed in poetic discourse is more dependent on those external forms of language: whereas the meaning of a factual – above all scientific – communication is not affected by each change of wording and syntactic arrangement, the 'poetic meaning' is far more sensitive to such changes.

5 Turning away from Husserl's concept of language

By giving pure logic, which deals with the condition of the possibility of science, a phenomenological foundation, Husserl excluded important aspects of living discourse. Shpet's project was more extensive than Husserl's in that he analysed scientific discourse as a possible form of discourse next to poetic, rhetoric and everyday discourse. This widening of the horizon entails a turning away from (not only a modification of) Husserl's concept of language. This becomes obvious when Shpet questioned a central presupposition of *Logical Investigations* – that scientific dis-

course can be marked off from living discourse. These two kinds of discourse are only tendencies, as Shpet emphasized; they are not fully realized in any empirical speech sample: 'Figurativeness is not only a trait of "poetry"...it is a general property of language, which belongs to scientific discourse, too'. 'The figurative and the literal can only be distinguished by tendency' (1922–3: III, 32).

The thesis of the irreducibility of figurative-ambivalent discourse has to do with Shpet's emphasis on the fact that thought is inseparably bound to language. With this concept of language as 'formative organ of thought', as outlined by Shpet in his interpretation of Humboldt of 1927, he turned away most clearly from Husserl's *Logical Investigations*, according to which 'the fact of being expressed is arbitrary for the meanings'.

List of works

Shpet, G. (1907) *Problema prichinnosti v Iume i Kante* (The Problem of Causality in Hume and Kant), Kiev: Universitet St Vladimira. (Shpet's first work, a monograph.)

—— (1912) 'Odin put' psikhologii i kuda on vedët' (One Method of Psychology and Where It Leads To), in *Filosofskii sbornik L.M. Lopatinu*, Moscow, 245–64. (Representative of Shpet's notion of philosophy before his turn to phenomenology.)

—— (1914) *Iavlenie i smysl. Fenomenologiia kak osnovnaia nauka i eë problemy*, Moscow; trans. T. Nemeth, *Appearance and Sense. Phenomenology as the Fundamental Science and its Problems*, Dordrecht, Boston, London: Kluwer Academic Publisher, 1991. (Shpet outlines his 'phenomenology of hermeneutical reason'.)

—— (1916) *Istoriia kak problema logiki* (History as a Problem of Logic), Moscow. (Shpet's master's thesis.)

—— (1918) *Germenevtika i eë problemy* (Hermeneutics and Its Problems), in *Kontekst*, Moscow; German translation, A. Haardt and R. Daube-Schackat (eds), *Die Hermeneutik und ihre Probleme*, Freiburg, Munich: Alber, 1993. (Critical presentation of the problems of hermeneutics as they have developed throughout history.)

—— (1922–23) *Ėsteticheskie fragmenty I-III* (Aesthetic Fragments), Petrograd: Kolos; 2nd edn in *Sochineniia* (Works), Moscow: Pravda, 1989, 343–472. (Shpet's contribution to the theory of art and language.)

—— (1927) *Vnutrenniaia forma slova* (The Internal Form of the Word), Moscow: GAKhN. (A critical assessment of Humboldt's philosophy of language.)

References and further reading

Haardt, A. (1993) *Husserl in Rußland. Phänomenologie der Sprache und Kunst bei Gustav Shpet und Aleksej Losev* (Husserl in Russia. Phenomenology of Language and Art in Gustav Shpet and Aleksei Losev), Munich: Fink. (Essential background reading for an understanding of the Phenomenological Movement in Russia).

Translated by P. Schnyder.

ALEXANDER HAARDT

SHU *see* LEGALIST PHILOSOPHY, CHINESE

SHVARTSMAN, YEHUDA LEIB
see SHESTOV, LEV

SIDDHĀRTHA GAUTAMA
see BUDDHA

SIDDHASENA DIVAKARA
see TIBETAN PHILOSOPHY

SIDGWICK, HENRY
(1838–1900)

Henry Sidgwick was a Cambridge philosopher, psychic researcher and educational reformer, whose works in practical philosophy, especially The Methods of Ethics *(1874), brought classical utilitarianism to its peak of theoretical sophistication and drew out the deep conflicts within that tradition, perhaps within the age of British imperialism itself. Sidgwick was profoundly influenced by J.S. Mill, but his version of utilitarianism – the view that those social or individual actions are right that maximize aggregate happiness – also revived certain Benthamite doctrines, though with more cogent accounts of ultimate good as pleasure, of total versus average utility, and of the analytical or deductive method. Yet Sidgwick was a cognitivist in ethics who sought both to ground utilitarianism on fundamental intuitions and to encompass within it the principles of common-sense ethics (truthfulness, fidelity, justice,*

etc.); his highly eclectic practical philosophy assimilated much of the rationalism, social conservatism and historical method of rival views, reflecting such influences as Butler, Clarke, Aristotle, Bagehot, Green, Whewell and Kant. Ultimately, Sidgwick's careful academic inquiries failed to demonstrate that one ought always to promote the happiness of all rather than one's own happiness, and this dualism of practical reason, along with his doubt about the viability of religion, led him to view his results as largely destructive and potentially deleterious in their influence.

1 Life
2 Ethics and utilitarianism
3 The dualism of practical reason
4 Epistemology and other works

1 Life

Henry Sidgwick's entire life fell within the reign of Queen Victoria and his entire career within the domain of Cambridge University, where he went from a brilliant undergraduate performance at Trinity College to become Knightbridge Professor of Moral Philosophy in 1883. He began his career as a classicist, but throughout his life extended his research and teaching into new disciplines: primarily moral theory, epistemology and metaphysics, political economy and political theory. His impact on the moral sciences at Cambridge was profound, and he was the guiding spirit behind Newnham College, one of England's first women's colleges. A long-standing member of the elite Cambridge discussion group, the Apostles, Sidgwick taught in a style that was, as W.R. Sorley put it, 'a training in the philosophical temper – in candour, self-criticism and regard for truth'. His best-regarded work has always been *The Methods of Ethics* (1874), but he also wrote major treatises on *The Principles of Political Economy* (1883) and *The Elements of Politics* (1891), as well as a primer on the history of ethics and numerous essays and reviews. Various posthumous works also appeared, thanks to the efforts of Eleanor Mildred Sidgwick (née Balfour), whom he had married in 1876 and who collaborated with him on many projects.

The sole interruption in Sidgwick's Cambridge career came in 1869, when he resigned his fellowship because he could no longer in good conscience subscribe to the Thirty-Nine Articles as required by law. Although he kept a lectureship and the tests were abolished in 1871, this was a formative event in his life, both stimulating and prefiguring his struggles with the foundations of ethics – as shown by his pamphlet on *The Ethics of Conformity and Subscription* (1870). His years of 'storm and stress' over religious questions led him from historical biblical criticism to philosophy and psychic research. He was a founder and the first president of the Society for Psychical Research, and his scientific investigations of purported psychical phenomena complemented his philosophical investigations into the 'deepest problems of human life', since he thought that evidence for personal survival of death might provide rational grounds for religious belief and ethical conduct.

2 Ethics and utilitarianism

In composing *The Methods*, Sidgwick thought of himself as emulating Aristotle, whose *Ethics* had 'reduced to consistency by careful comparison' the common-sense morality of Greece, treated not from the outside but as what he and others thought upon reflection. He wants to 'do the same for *our* morality here and now, in the same manner of impartial reflection on current opinion'. His aim is less practice than knowledge, merely 'to expound as clearly and as fully as my limits will allow the different methods of Ethics that I find implicit in our common moral reasoning; to point out their mutual relations; and where they seem to conflict, to define the issue as much as possible'.

Sidgwick's reflections often clash with earlier traditions, including utilitarianism, the empiricism, psychological egoism and reductionism of which he rejected. He maintains that the basic concept of morality – 'ought' or 'right' – is unique and irreducible, *sui generis*. Also, moral approbation is 'inseparably bound up with the conviction, implicit or explicit, that the conduct approved is "really" right – that is, that it cannot, without error, be disapproved by any other mind'. He describes these 'dictates' or 'imperatives' in a largely internalist fashion as 'accompanied by a certain impulse to do the acts recognized as right', though other impulses are likely to conflict. Despite such debts to Butler, Clarke and Kant, Sidgwick saw the issue of free will v. determinism (and other metaphysical issues) as largely irrelevant to ethics, since it is usually impossible, in deliberation, to regard the mere absence of adequate motive as 'a reason for not doing what I otherwise judge to be reasonable' (see MORAL MOTIVATION §1; PRAISE AND BLAME).

Judgments of ultimate good, rather than right, do not involve definite precepts to act or the assumption that we are capable of doing so, and leave it open 'whether this particular kind of good is the greatest good that we can under the circumstances obtain'. 'Ultimate good on the whole,' Sidgwick suggests, if 'unqualified by reference to a particular subject, must be taken to mean what as a rational being I should

desire and seek to realize, assuming myself to have an equal concern for *all* existence' – in contrast to taking my own existence alone to be considered, as in 'ultimate good on the whole for me'. With greater Benthamite consistency than Mill, he argues that happiness (whether for the egoist or the utilitarian) should be interpreted hedonistically in terms of pleasure or desirable consciousness, and that this yields the best account of ultimate good (see GOOD, THEORIES OF THE; HAPPINESS; HEDONISM).

Although not preoccupied with the moral faculty as such, Sidgwick is specially concerned with moral reasoning. A 'method' of ethics is not simply a principle or theory, but a rational procedure 'for determining right conduct in any particular case', for determining the rightness of an individual's actions by seeing whether the acts in question possess some property, which, on the basis of principle, provides the ultimate reason for the rightness of acts. The plain man, he holds, uses a jumble of different methods, insufficiently reflected upon. Though many think that conscience delivers immediate judgments on the rightness of particular acts ('perceptional' or 'ultra' intuitionism), Sidgwick has 'no doubt that reflective persons, in proportion to their reflectiveness, come to rely rather on abstract universal intuitions relating to classes of cases conceived under general notions'. But this 'dogmatic' intuitionism, on which 'the practically ultimate end of moral actions' is their 'conformity to certain rules or dictates of Duty unconditionally prescribed' and discernible with 'really clear and finally valid intuition', can also be subjected to further reflection and found wanting. In synthesizing its precepts, and 'without being disposed to deny that conduct commonly judged to be right is so, we may yet require some deeper explanation *why* it is so', yielding a third phase of Intuitionism:

> which, while accepting the morality of common sense as in the main sound, still attempts to find for it a philosophic basis which it does not itself offer: to get one or more principles more absolutely and undeniably true and evident, from which the current rules might be deduced, either just as they are commonly received or with slight modifications and rectifications.
>
> (*The Methods of Ethics* 1907: 102)

Thus Sidgwick famously reconciles intuitional or common-sense morality – the nineteenth-century opponent to utilitarianism – with utilitarian principles. There are self-evident practical principles, but they 'are of too abstract a nature, and too universal in their scope, to enable us to ascertain by immediate application of them what we ought to do in any particular case'. As reflection is followed out, apprehension changes; the 'self-evidence' of particular maxims of duty fades beside that of such abstract principles as 'what is right for me must be right for all persons in precisely similar circumstances' and 'I ought to prefer the greater good of another to my own lesser good'. The dogmatic intuitionist discovers that such rules as veracity, fidelity and justice require both qualification and further systematization by higher principles, which will also resolve the conflicts between and variable formulations of such rules. Utilitarianism can sustain the 'general validity' of such rules and correct for 'the defects which reflection finds in the intuitive recognition of their stringency'; it also 'affords a principle of synthesis, and a method for binding the unconnected and occasionally conflicting principles of common moral reasoning into a complete and harmonious system'. If reflection thus reveals utilitarianism as the view to which common morality 'naturally appeals for that further development of its system which this same reflection shows to be necessary, the proof of Utilitarianism seems as complete as it can be made' (see INTUITIONISM IN ETHICS §2; MORAL JUSTIFICATION; UTILITARIANISM).

Sidgwick allows that current morality should not be accepted *en bloc* as the middle axioms of utilitarianism. But he insists that in both ethics and politics, utopian speculation is an 'illimitable cloud-land', and we must start

> with the existing social order, and the existing morality as a part of that order: and in deciding the question whether any divergence from this code is to be recommended, must consider chiefly the immediate consequences of such divergence, upon a society in which such a code is conceived generally to subsist.
>
> (*The Methods of Ethics* 1907: 474)

Besides, it is not self-evident that universal benevolence 'is the right *means* to the attainment of universal good', since this end may be 'self-limiting; may direct its own partial suppression in favour of other impulses'. Indeed, Sidgwick notoriously countenanced the idea of an 'esoteric morality', since in less than ideal utilitarian circumstances, a utilitarian could reason that 'some of his conclusions should be rejected by mankind generally; or even that the vulgar should keep aloof from his system as a whole, in so far as the inevitable indefiniteness and complexity of its calculations render it likely to lead to bad results in their hands' – a view that, Sidgwick admitted, is itself perhaps best kept esoteric. Such arguments continue to inspire both utilitarians and their critics, and suggest the difficulties of finding in Sidgwick's focus on method any great confidence in the normal person's capacity for moral self-direction.

A 'method' straddles the distinction between ethical standards and decision-procedures; it admits of indirect (or two-level) utilitarianism, and only in this way addresses act v. rule utilitarianism, motive utilitarianism, and so on (see CONSEQUENTIALISM; MORAL EXPERTISE).

It is ironic that Sidgwick assimilated both the epistemology and much of the social conservatism for which utilitarians had long castigated such intuitionists as Whewell: 'Adhere generally, deviate and attempt reform only in exceptional cases in which...the argument against Common Sense is decisive'. As D.G. Ritchie noted, Sidgwick's ethics and politics were decidedly 'tame and sleek' – the 'method is Bentham's; but there is none of Bentham's strong critical antagonism to the institutions of his time'. Sidgwick even downplayed his own critical insights, if they veered too far from common sense. *The Methods* provides a clear and original defence of classical against average utility calculations in relation to optimal population size and future generations, but *The Elements* elides the issue in the search for common ground, a manoeuvre also made with respect to women's equality and the utilitarian critique of nationalism.

3 The dualism of practical reason

Sidgwick's philosophical intuitionism houses a number of presumptively compatible, abstract, self-evident truths: a universalizability principle, a principle of rational prudence to the effect that, *ceteris paribus*, one should be equally concerned with all temporal parts of one's life, and the principle of rational benevolence, the basis for utilitarianism (somewhat questionably derived by enjoining aiming at good generally and taking the good of each as equally important). He anticipates many recent utilitarians in interpreting the universalizability principle, derived from Kant, as purely formal, meaning simply that whatever 'is right for me must be right for all persons in similar circumstances' and therefore as compatible with utilitarianism (see IMPARTIALITY). However, such concordances notwithstanding, the conflict between the methods of utilitarianism and egoism, unlike that between intuitional morality and utilitarianism, is real. In an essay on *The Methods*, he explains that along with

> (a) a fundamental moral conviction that I ought to sacrifice my own happiness, if by so doing I can increase the happiness of others to a greater extent than I diminish my own, I find also (b) a conviction – which it would be paradoxical to call 'moral', but which is none the less fundamental – that it would

be irrational to sacrifice any portion of my own happiness unless the sacrifice is to be somehow at some time compensated by an equivalent addition to my own happiness.

('Some Fundamental Ethical Controversies' 1889: 483)

Each of these convictions has as much clearness and certainty 'as the process of introspective reflection can give' as well as a preponderant, if implicit, assent 'in the common sense of mankind'.

Excepting the criterion of mutual consistency, both convictions could pass the most demanding tests for self-evident truths: careful reflection, clarity and precision, and consensus among competent judges. Sidgwick therefore regards this as a 'fundamental contradiction in our apparent intuitions of what is Reasonable in conduct' and concludes, in the first edition of *The Methods*, that unless a way be found to reconcile 'the Individual with the Universal Reason', the 'Cosmos of Duty is thus really reduced to a Chaos: and the prolonged effort of the human intellect to frame a perfect ideal of rational conduct is seen to have been foredoomed to inevitable failure'.

Whether Sidgwick regarded egoism as a matter of ethics or simply of rationality is hardly to the point; for him, the problem was to frame a rational way to live. He would have been dismayed to learn that the consistent (agent-relative) egoist would still challenge moral theorists at the close of the twentieth century.

In later editions and works, Sidgwick downplayed this dilemma, but his journal and letters reveal that he was always troubled by it. He had turned to ethics hoping to establish it as independently rational, perhaps a show of God's order; his inquiry drove him to the conclusion that ethics was incoherent unless the utilitarian could infer 'the existence of Divine sanctions' that would 'suffice to make it always every one's interest to promote universal happiness to the best of his knowledge'. Evidence for the personal survival of death might help, but by 1887 he was concluding 'that we have not, and are never likely to have, empirical evidence of the existence of the individual after death'. In a singular revelation, he explained that

When I was writing my book on Ethics, I was inclined to hold with Kant that we must *postulate* the continued existence of the soul, in order to effect that harmony of Duty with Happiness which seemed to me indispensable to rational moral life. At any rate I thought I might *provisionally* postulate it, while setting out on the serious search for empirical evidence. If I decide that this search is a failure, shall I finally and decisively make this postulate? Can I consistently with my whole view of truth and the method of its attainment?

(*Henry Sidgwick, A Memoir* 1906: 467)

His crisis of faith had proved enduring.

4 Epistemology and other works

Sidgwick also explored the epistemological issue of whether such a postulate was unwarranted. If physical science is indeed based on self-evident premises, then practical philosophy should seek such a foundation as well. However,

We find that in our supposed knowledge of the world of nature propositions are commonly taken to be universally true, which yet seem to rest on no other grounds than that we have a strong disposition to accept them, and that they are indispensable to the systematic coherence of our beliefs, – it will be more difficult to reject a similarly supported assumption in ethics, without opening the door to universal scepticism.

(*The Methods of Ethics* 1907: 509)

His intuitionism was scarcely unthinking or mystical – he was only converted to it by the claim that mathematics could find no other basis – and was based on the view that inferential knowledge presupposes significant non-inferential knowledge. And as such works as 'Criteria of Truth and Error' show, he rejected any 'simple infallible criterion' for ultimate knowledge and favoured a sophisticated fallibilist criterion for 'the humbler task' of 'excluding error'. For this, he advanced a threefold test: intuitive or Cartesian verification (clarity and certainty on careful examination), discursive verification (system and coherence) and ecumenical verification (consensus). The second test, he allows, 'is of special and preeminent importance', since 'the ideal aim of philosophy is systematization – the exhibition of system and coherence in a mass of beliefs which, as presented by Common Sense, are wanting therein', but, he adds, 'the special characteristic of *my* philosophy is to keep the importance of the others in view'.

Sidgwick has been cast as both an early practitioner of Rawlsian reflective equilibrium and a prescient critic of it, but such attempts to dress his moral methodology for contemporary debates often read him selectively and out of his historical context. He was moved by the intellectual, cultural and political tensions of the Victorian era; religious scepticism, moral scepticism and the threat of egoism in theory and practice came to form an unholy trinity against which he would contend in one arena after another. Even *The Methods* does not fully convey the

761

persistence and ingenuity with which he engaged 'the deepest questions of human life' or the way in which his meta-ethics were at once intuitionist and fallibilist, commonsensical and dialectical.

Indeed, Sidgwick's work is rarely appreciated even as a comprehensive account of utilitarianism, covering political, legal and economic theory. *The Principles* gives a penetrating treatment of distributive justice from the utilitarian standpoint, and *The Elements* and *The Development of European Polity* carry the classical tradition far beyond the simplicities of Austinian jurisprudence and ahistorical Benthamism, with a complex approach to the art of politics that balances analytic, historical and comparative methods. Such works reveal how, for Sidgwick, egoism was hardly a potentially cogent alternative for reformulating morals and politics, but was rather the view capable of inspiring most of what he found politically abhorrent: class or party conflict at home and neo-Machiavellianism in foreign policy.

In the end, Sidgwick's inquiries into epistemology and politics were, in his eyes, no more successful than his inquiries into religion, ethics and psychic research. Yet beyond his enduring accomplishments in clarifying utilitarianism and advancing substantive moral and political theory, it is perhaps the very tension between his subtle, penetrating scepticism and his longing for a rational faith and morality that make him one of the most fascinating representatives of his age.

See also: COMMON SENSE SCHOOL; COMMONSENSISM; ETHICS; MILL, J.S. §§8–12; MORALITY AND ETHICS ; MORAL SCEPTICISM; TELEOLOGICAL ETHICS; UNIVERSALISM IN ETHICS

List of works

The Sidgwick Papers, Wren Library, Trinity College, Cambridge, form the most extensive collection of original manuscript materials, but there are many other archival resources. The most comprehensive edition of Sidgwick's works, including all of his major works (with both the first and seventh editions of *The Methods*) and a wide range of his previously unpublished lectures and correspondence, is a database: (1997) 'The Complete Works and Select Scholarly Correspondence of Henry Sidgwick', ed. B. Schultz, Past Masters series, Charlottesville, VA: InteLex Corporation.

Sidgwick, H. (1870) *The Ethics of Conformity and Subscription*, London: Williams & Norgate. (This extremely important pamphlet marks Sidgwick's first serious attempt to show how common-sense

morality is incomplete and requires something like utilitarianism.)

—— (1874) *The Methods of Ethics*, London: Macmillan; later edns, 1877, 1884, 1890, 1893, 1901, 1907. (Sidgwick's masterpiece, in which classical utilitarianism is given its most sophisticated formulation and reconciled with common-sense morality, though not with egoism. *The Methods* set the agenda for much of the substantive ethical theory and metaethics of the twentieth century. Changes made for the second and third editions were also published separately as supplements. Sidgwick wrote a number of commentaries on his book, including 'Some Fundamental Ethical Controversies', (1889) *Mind* 56; 'Prof. Calderwood on Intuitionism in Morals', (1876) *Mind* 4; and 'The Establishment of Ethical First Principles', (1879) *Mind* 13.)

—— (1883) *The Principles of Political Economy*, London: Macmillan; later edns, 1887, 1901. (Sometimes dismissed as inappreciative of the marginalist revolution, Sidgwick's political economy was in fact informed by the work of Jevons, Marshall and Edgeworth, and his discussion of distributive justice and the role of the state provides an essential complement to the arguments of *The Methods*.)

—— (1885) *The Scope and Method of Economic Science*, London: Macmillan. (Sidgwick's presidential address to the Economic Science and Statistics section of the British Association is a clever exposition of the limits of *laissez-faire* and the absurdities of the grandiose sociologies of Comte and Spencer (reprinted in *Miscellaneous Essays*).)

—— (1886) *Outlines of the History of Ethics for English Readers*, London: Macmillan; later edns, 1888, 1892, 1896, 1902, 1931. (May well remain the best work of its kind; with succinctness and accuracy, Sidgwick surveys the entire range of philosophical ethics from its origins down to his own time.)

—— (1891) *The Elements of Politics*, London: Macmillan; later edns, 1897, 1908, 1919; student edn, ed. B. Schultz, Cambridge: Cambridge University Press, 1998. (Sidgwick's second most important book, this massive volume provides another vital complement to *The Methods* by setting out Sidgwick's utilitarian politics and distinguishing his analytical approach from that of Bentham, Austin and the Mills. The student edition contains helpful secondary material, as well as new primary sources.)

—— (1898, 1909) *Practical Ethics: A Collection of Addresses and Essays*, London: Swan Sonnenschein. (Essays and addresses delivered before various 'Ethical Societies' which aimed at 'the intelligent study of moral questions with a view to elevate and purify social life'. 'The Ethics of Religious Conformity' and 'Clerical Veracity' show the significance of this issue in Sidgwick's life and thought.)

—— (1902) *Lectures on the Ethics of T.H. Green, H. Spencer and J. Martineau*, ed. E.E. Constance Jones, London: Macmillan. (Sidgwick came to think that *The Methods* did not do enough to address critically the transcendentalist and evolutionist positions, and this posthumous work thus provides a useful supplement to *The Methods* by giving detailed criticisms of key representatives of these schools as well as further material on Martineau.)

—— (1902) *Philosophy, Its Scope and Relations*, ed. J. Ward, London: Macmillan. (A succinct, precise articulation of his epistemology and its bearing on cognate fields of inquiry, mainly psychology, history and sociology.)

—— (1903) *The Development of European Polity*, ed. E.M. Sidgwick, London: Macmillan. (A lucid historical survey of political doctrines, this posthumous volume provides the inductive, historical approach to politics that Sidgwick regarded as a necessary supplement to the analytical and deductive approach of *The Elements*.)

—— (1904) *Miscellaneous Essays and Addresses*, ed. E.M. Sidgwick and A. Sidgwick, London: Macmillan. (Contains many of Sidgwick's best short works, including discerning literary studies of Clough and Shakespeare, sober critiques of Arnold and perfectionist educational theories, various probing assessments of socialism, and a witty essay on 'Bentham and Benthamism'.)

—— (1905) *Lectures on the Philosophy of Kant and Other Philosophical Lectures and Essays*, ed. J. Ward, London: Macmillan. (Contains some of Sidgwick's most significant metaphysical and epistemological work, and conveys some sense of his plan for his projected study of 'Kant and Kantism in England'. Includes 'Criteria of Truth and Error'.)

Seeley, J. (1896) *Introduction to Political Science*, ed. H. Sidgwick, London: Macmillan. (In editing the work of his colleague Seeley, an ideologue of British imperialism, Sidgwick perhaps unwittingly demonstrated the severe limitations of academic Victorian political theory.)

References and further reading

Broad, D.D. (1930) *Five Types of Ethical Theory*, London: Routledge & Kegan Paul. (An extensive, sympathetic, philosophically sophisticated account that is marred by various confusions concerning Sidgwick's notion of a method, which is treated as equivalent to a theory.)

Frankena, W. *et al.* (1974) '*Monist* Symposium: Henry Sidgwick', *Monist* 58. (Commemorates the centenary of the publication of *The Methods*; Frankena's paper is especially important for understanding Sidgwick's internalism and Singer provides a provocative defence of intuitionism against reflective equilibrium.)

MacIntyre, A. (1990) *Three Rival Versions of Moral Enquiry*, Notre Dame: Notre Dame University Press. (Contains a critique of Sidgwick's 'encyclopedist' version of enquiry from the perspective of a traditionalist.)

Moore, G.E. (1903) *Principia Ethica*, Cambridge: Cambridge University Press. (Moore was an ungenerous critic who largely begged the question of the dualism of practical reason, but was effective in diminishing Sidgwick's reputation.)

Parfit, D. (1984) *Reasons and Persons*, Oxford: Oxford University Press. (Important work in moral theory revealing a deep indebtedness to *The Methods*, with many astute asides on Sidgwick's critique of common-sense morality, his account of ultimate good and his view of the person.)

* Ritchie, D.G. (1891–2) 'Review: *The Elements of Politics*', *International Journal of Ethics* 2: 254–7. (A witty, critical and very widely-cited review of Sidgwick's *magnum opus* on politics.)

Schneewind, J.B. (1977) *Sidgwick's Ethics and Victorian Moral Philosophy*, Oxford: Clarendon Press. (The most important work on Sidgwick's ethics, or indeed, on Sidgwick. Schneewind situates Sidgwick's work within the broader context of English moral theory, and is especially concerned to construe *The Methods* as a piece of systematic moral theory rather than simply as a brief for utilitarianism. Contains an excellent bibliography.)

Schneewind, J.B. and Schultz, B. (1998) 'Henry Sidgwick, A Bibliography', *The Cambridge Bibliography of English Literature*, Cambridge: Cambridge University Press, 3rd edn. (The most comprehensive bibliography of works by or on Sidgwick published before 1920.)

Schultz, B. (ed.) (1992) *Essays on Henry Sidgwick*, Cambridge: Cambridge University Press. (A wide-ranging collection of articles, many new, covering most of the current interpretive controversies.)

—— (1996) 'Sidgwick, Henry', *Dictionnaire d'éthique et de philosophie morale*, ed. M. Canto-Sperber, Paris: Presses Universitaires de France, 1391–99. (A short but up-to-date introduction that both surveys Sidgwick's philosophy and points to his larger cultural significance, including his connections to such controversial figures as J.A. Symonds and F.W.H. Myers.)

—— (1998) *Eye of the Universe: Henry Sidgwick and*

the Victorian Quest for Certainty. (The only comprehensive treatment of Sidgwick's practical and theoretical philosophy, this book brings out the overall unity of Sidgwick's writings and the central role of scepticism and the dualism of practical reason in his life and work.)

* Sidgwick, E.M. and Sidgwick, A. (1906) *Henry Sidgwick, A Memoir*, London: Macmillan. (The essential biographical treatment, with a good bibliography; Sidgwick's widow and brother drew from his letters and journal, though they excluded excessively technical or personal material.)

Williams, B. (1982) 'The Point of View of the Universe: Sidgwick and the Ambitions of Ethics', *Making Sense of Humanity*, Cambridge: Cambridge University Press. (A wonderful introduction to Sidgwick, with a penetrating critical overview that gives special currency to the interpretation of Sidgwick as a 'Government House' utilitarian, but compares him favourably to Moore.)

BART SCHULTZ

SIGER OF BRABANT
(*c.*1240–*c.*1284)

Born probably circa *1240 in the Duchy of Brabant, Siger of Brabant studied philosophy in the arts faculty at the University of Paris and became regent master there in the 1260s. Various positions which he defended were included in Bishop Etienne Tempier's condemnations of 1270 and 1277, and he appears to have fled France when cited to appear before the French inquisition. He probably spent his final days in Italy, and died there before November 1284.*

As a professional teacher of philosophy, Siger regarded it as his primary mission to lecture on Aristotle and other philosophers and to present their views on the points at issue. Early in his career he defended some of the positions condemned by Bishop Tempier, but after 1270 he often nuanced his exposition of such views by noting that he was only presenting the views of the philosophers or of Aristotle, or that he was proceeding philosophically in these discussions. Often regarded as a leading Latin 'Averroist', he agreed with Averroes that there is only one human intellect, though he eventually reversed his view on this. His personal philosophy is strongly Aristotelian, but with various elements derived from Neoplatonism.

On the relationship between essence and existence in created beings, Siger denies that existence is something added to a thing's essence and holds that the existence of such entities belongs to their essence. He holds that

one can demonstrate God's existence, but insists that Aristotle's physical argument for a First Mover must be completed by metaphysical argumentation. While denying that human beings in this life enjoy any direct knowledge of the divine essence, he seems open to Averroes' view that they can reach some knowledge thereof.

1   **Life and works**
2   **Philosophy and religious belief**
3   **Metaphysics: the science of being as being**
4   **Essence and existence**
5   **Philosophical knowledge of God**
6   **Procession of created reality from God**
7   **Eternity of the universe**
8   **Unicity versus plurality of the human intellect**

1   Life and works

Siger studied philosophy in the arts faculty at the University of Paris and became regent master in that faculty in the 1260s, perhaps *circa* 1263–5. Some of his views were included in a condemnation of thirteen propositions by Etienne Tempier, Bishop of Paris, in December 1270, and many more were included in Tempier's much broader condemnation of 219 propositions on 7 March 1277. Little is known about Siger's final years, but it is certain that in November 1276 he and two colleagues from the arts faculty were cited to appear before the French inquisition in January 1277. Apparently he and the others had already departed from France. He probably spent his final years in Italy and died some time before November 1284, murdered perhaps by a secretary. Although his name has long been associated with the radical Aristotelian movement in the arts faculty at Paris known by some as Latin 'Averroism' (see AVERROISM), he was never found guilty of heresy. Scholars have been intrigued by the fact that Dante ALIGHIERI places him in Paradise, and has Thomas AQUINAS introduce him.

Most of his surviving writings date from after 1270. Many of his works were reports taken down by others at his lectures, although some of these were later revised by Siger. Other works were originally composed by Siger himself, and some of these were probably based on prior scholarly disputations. A number are commentaries on works by Aristotle, or in one case, on the *Liber de causis*, written in the form of questions occasioned by the text (see LIBER DE CAUSIS).

2   Philosophy and religious belief

By Siger's time at Paris, the faculty of arts had become in fact a faculty of philosophy. This was owing in large measure to the recovery in Latin translation in the twelfth and thirteenth centuries of a large amount of philosophical literature of non-Christian origin originally written in Greek or in Arabic (see TRANSLATORS). There had been initial reservations and even prohibitions early in the thirteenth century on the part of Church authorities at Paris against incorporating some of this newly available material into teaching in the arts faculty at the University. By 1255, however, the situation had changed to the point where the statutes for that faculty required students to read all the known works of Aristotle. Thus Siger regarded it as his primary mission to lecture on Aristotle and the other philosophers, and gave great weight to them.

Siger did this with such enthusiasm in two early works that some of his positions alarmed Bishop Tempier and were condemned in 1270. Thus in his *Quaestio utrum haec sit vera* he had accepted the eternity of the human species (and hence of the world) (see ETERNITY OF THE WORLD, MEDIEVAL VIEWS OF), and in his *Quaestiones in Tertium De anima* (Questions on Book III of Aristotle's *On the Soul*), the view associated with Averroes that the human intellect is only one for the entire human race and exists apart from individual human beings (see IBN RUSHD). Particularly offensive to ecclesiastical authorities was the implication following from this that individual souls are not immortal (see SOUL, NATURE AND IMMORTALITY OF THE).

In addition to Tempier's condemnation of these views, Thomas Aquinas sharply attacked the Averroistic and Sigerian defence of the unicity of the intellect in his *De unitate intellectus*, also of 1270. In subsequent works, when dealing with theologically sensitive issues, Siger became more circumspect and struggled to find a satisfactory resolution for the faith–reason problem. When dealing with points defended by Aristotle or Averroes or other philosophers which contradict Christian teaching, he often remarks that he is simply presenting such positions as the view of the philosophers, or according to the mind of the philosophers, or that he is speaking philosophically. In his final works, especially his *Quaestiones super Librum de causis* (Questions on the *Liber de causis*), he moves still further in the direction of religious orthodoxy. In sum, while he never works out a fully satisfactory solution to the faith–reason problem, he appears to be sincere in his repeated protestations of religious belief and in his gradual movement toward more orthodox positions. At the same time, along with other colleagues in his faculty, especially BOETHIUS OF DACIA, he strongly defends the autonomy of philosophy within its own sphere, and the right of the philosopher, even though

Christian, to draw conclusions from philosophical principles wherever they may lead. If these conclusions contradict religious belief, the Christian, being aware of the fallibility of human reason, should regard the teachings of faith as true. Siger does not defend the 'double-truth theory', according to which two contradictory propositions, one taught by philosophy and one taught by faith, could both be true at the same time (see ARISTOTELIANISM, MEDIEVAL).

3 Metaphysics: the science of being as being

Siger is familiar with Aristotle's description in *Metaphysics* IV of a science that studies being as being and his contrast between this and more particular sciences which study the attributes of only particular parts of being. Siger also recalls Aristotle's presentation of three theoretical sciences in *Metaphysics* VI, physics, mathematics, and a divine science that studies separate and immobile (and divine) entities (see ARISTOTLE). Avicenna denies that God can be regarded as the subject of this science, for he maintains that it belongs to metaphysics and not to physics to demonstrate God's existence. Since no science can demonstrate the existence of its subject, the subject of metaphysics is not God, but being as being (see IBN SINA). Averroes affirms that it belongs to physics to demonstrate the existence of the First Mover or God, and that in referring to being as being as the subject of metaphysics, Aristotle really means that its subject is the primary instance of being, or God (see IBN RUSHD). In agreement with Avicenna, Siger holds that the subject of metaphysics is not God but being as being. However, he adopts an intermediary position on the issue of a physical or metaphysical proof of God's existence. The middle term used by Aristotle to prove God's existence in his *Metaphysics* is taken from his *Physics* (see GOD, ARGUMENTS FOR THE EXISTENCE OF).

4 Essence and existence

Much contested during Siger's time and thereafter was the issue of the relationship between essence and existence in created entities (see EXISTENCE). It was generally granted that they are identical in God. To account for the metaphysical structure of finite beings, AQUINAS defends a composition of two distinct principles in such beings, an essence and a corresponding act of being (*esse*), often referred to by others as existence. GILES OF ROME defends a seemingly more extreme version of this approach, and by 1276 HENRY OF GHENT sharply criticizes the real distinction between essence and existence, especially as presented by Giles; he postulates an 'intentional' distinction between them, that is, one that is less than real but more than purely mental.

In his *Quaestiones in Metaphysicam* (Questions on the *Metaphysics*) Siger asks whether in caused beings existence (*esse*) belongs to their essence. Against this claim he cites Boethius and Avicenna, and then as a leading critic of distinction between them, Averroes. Among contemporaries he presents ALBERT THE GREAT as holding that existence is added to a thing's essence, and rejects this position. Siger presents as intermediary the view of Aquinas (in the latter's commentary on the *Metaphysics*) that existence is something added to a thing's essence, which does not belong to its essence and yet is not an accident but is, as it were, 'constituted' from the principles of the essence. Siger agrees with Aquinas that existence is not an accident, but complains about the way he formulates his position. For Siger, if existence belongs to a thing it must either be a part of that thing's essence, like matter and form, or something composed of those principles, or an accident. For Aquinas to say that it is added to the essence without being any of these is for him to postulate a fourth nature among entities. Siger concludes that the existence of such entities belongs to their essence and is not something superadded. The terms which he now uses to signify essence and existence, 'thing' (*res*) and 'existing entity' (*ens*), do not signify different intentions but rather one and the same essence in different ways, one as potentiality (*res* = essence), and the other as actuality (*ens* = existing entity).

In responding to various arguments he had offered for real distinction between essence and existence, Siger notes that one especially moved Aquinas. Everything other than the First Being (God) must be composed. Because created pure spirits lack matter–form composition, they must be composed of essence and *esse*. To this Siger proposes two responses, though he does not assert the first definitively. First, it is enough to say that things other than God recede from him as pure actuality and are multiplied by approaching potentiality. This suffices to distinguish them from God without postulating different 'essences' within them. Second, even if one concedes Aquinas' claim that to be distinguished from God created entities must somehow be composed, Siger finds it sufficient to appeal to substance–accident composition in created spirits. Even in them, there is a distinction between their substance and the intelligible species they use in thinking.

Interestingly, in his final work, *Quaestiones super Librum de causis* (Questions on the *Liber de causis*), while discussing the kind of infinity enjoyed by the First Cause, Siger notes that in created spiritual

entities existence (*esse*) is not limited by matter. Yet their existence is limited to their nature which receives it and is related to it as potentiality to actualization. Perhaps Siger now accepts Aquinas' position on essence and the act of being.

5 Philosophical knowledge of God

Reference has been made to Siger's insistence on incorporating Aristotle's physical argument for a First Mover into metaphysical argumentation for God's existence. For Siger, one cannot stop with a purely physical proof but must in metaphysics establish the existence of a supreme being which is unique, and which is the cause of being for all other entities. At different points in his *Quaestiones in Metaphysicam* he attempts to show that the First Mover is the creative cause of all other entities, including separate – that is, immaterial – substances. He also offers a series of arguments to show that there is only one first and uncaused cause (see CAUSATION).

Presupposed for all his reasoning from effects to God as the first cause is Siger's conviction that in this life human beings do not enjoy a direct knowledge of God's essence. However, on one occasion in his *Quaestiones in Metaphysicam*, Siger comments favourably on Averroes' view that human beings can arrive at some kind of knowledge of the divine essence. Siger himself here suggests that one who is truly expert in philosophy may be able to form an adequate idea of the divine essence. Also in his *Quaestiones super Librum de causis* he offers a series of arguments for and another series against the claim that the essence of the First Cause can be grasped by the human intellect. Unfortunately, his resolution of this question is missing from the text.

6 Procession of created reality from God

In his *De necessitate et contingentia causarum* (On the Necessity and Contingency of Causes), Siger presents God as the immediate, necessary and eternal cause of the first intelligence, but as only the mediate cause of other effects. He supports this by appealing to the Neoplatonic axiom that from the one simple being (God) only one thing can proceed immediately. This view is at odds with traditional Christian belief both in affirming the eternal existence and the necessary production of various created realities, and in denying that God is the immediate creator of anything but the first intelligence. However, Siger also states twice in the course of his discussion that this is so according to the mind of the philosophers. Hence he may not have adopted this as his own position, although he does offer a sympathetic presentation of necessary emanation in one version of his *Quaestiones in Metaphysicam*. However, he clearly rejects the theory of mediate emanation or creation in his *Quaestiones super Librum de causis*.

7 Eternity of the universe

While their religious faith required Christian participants in this discussion to believe that the world began to be, much disagreement existed concerning whether this could be demonstrated philosophically. Bonaventure, at least as he is usually interpreted, defends this possibility. Aquinas denies that human reason can prove this and in his final treatment of the issue goes so far as to hold that an eternally created world is possible, philosophically speaking. As already noted, in a work written before 1270, Siger defends the eternal existence of the human race. After the condemnation of 1270, when he presents argumentation for an eternal world or some eternally produced creature, he usually qualifies this by saying that this is so according to the mind of Aristotle or according to the mind of the philosophers and is careful not to defend the eternity of the world in his own name. Like Aquinas, he denies that human reason can prove that the world began to be (see ETERNITY OF THE WORLD, MEDIEVAL VIEWS OF).

8 Unicity versus plurality of the human intellect

In his *Quaestiones in Tertium De anima* from the 1260s, Siger defends the view that there is only one separate intellect (including both the agent and the receiving or possible intellect) for the entire human race. The agent and possible intellects are two powers of one separate substance, and not two separate substances, as Averroes holds in his Long Commentary on the *De anima*. After the condemnation of 1270 and Aquinas' attack that same year, Siger deals with this issue very carefully. In his *De anima intellectiva* (The Intellective Soul) of *circa* 1273, after much discussion he declares himself unable to resolve this issue on purely philosophical grounds. He concludes that in such a matter one must follow the teaching of faith. In his final work, his *Quaestiones super Librum de causis*, he strongly argues on philosophical grounds that the intellective soul is a perfection of each individual human body, and that it is multiplied as are human beings themselves. His position is now perfectly orthodox.

See also: AQUINAS, T.; ARISTOTELIANISM, MEDIEVAL; AVERROISM; BOETHIUS OF DACIA; CAUSATION; GOD, CONCEPTS OF; IBN RUSHD

List of works

Siger of Brabant (*c.*1265) *Compendium magistri Sugeri super De generatione et corruptione* (Compendium of Master Siger on Aristotle's *On Generation and Corruption*) ed. B. Bazán, *Siger de Brabant. Écrits de logique, de morale et de physique*, Louvain: Publications universitaires, 1974. (Commentary on Aristotle.)

—— (*c.*1269 or earlier) *Quaestiones in Tertium De anima* (Questions on Book III of Aristotle's *On the Soul*), ed. B. Bazán, *Quaestiones in Tertium De anima, De anima intellectiva, De aeternitate mundi*, Louvain: Publications universitaires, 1972. (Questions on *On the Soul*.)

—— (before 1270) *Sophisma Omnis homo de necessitate est animal* (The Sophisma 'Every Human Being is Necessarily an Animal'), ed. B. Bazán, *Siger de Brabant. Écrits de logique, de morale et de physique*, Louvain: Publications universitaires, 1974. (Edition of the sophisma.)

—— (before 1270) *Quaestio Utrum haec sit vera: homo est animal nullo homine existente* (Is the Proposition 'A Human Being is an Animal' True When No Human Being Exists?), ed. B. Bazán, *Siger de Brabant. Écrits de logique, de morale et de physique*, Louvain: Publications universitaires, 1974. (Edition of the question.)

—— (*c.*1270–1) *Quaestiones in Physicam* (Questions on Aristotle's *Physics*), ed. A. Zimmermann in B. Bazán (ed.) *Siger de Brabant. Écrits de logique, de morale et de physique*, Louvain: Publications universitaires, 1974. (Edition of the questions.)

—— (*c.*1272) *De necessitate et contingentia causarum* (The Necessity and Contigency of Causes), ed. J.J. Duin, *La doctrine de la providence dans les écrits de Siger de Brabant*, Louvain: Institut supérieur de philosophie, 1954, 14–50. (Work on causation.)

—— (*c.*1272) *De aeternitate mundi* (The Eternity of the World), ed. B. Bazán, *Quaestiones in Tertium De anima, De anima intellectiva, De aeternitate mundi*, Louvain: Publications universitaires, 1972. (Siger's work on eternity.)

—— (*c.*1272) *Quaestiones logicales* (Logical Questions), ed. B. Bazán, *Siger de Brabant. Écrits de logique, de morale et de physique*, Louvain: Publications universitaires, 1974. (Edition of the questions.)

—— (*c.*1272) *Impossibilia*, ed. B. Bazán, *Siger de Brabant. Écrits de logique, de morale et de physique*, Louvain: Publications universitaires, 1974. (Edition of the work.)

—— (*c.*1272–3) *Quaestiones naturales* (Natural Questions) (Paris), ed. B. Bazán, *Siger de Brabant. Écrits de logique, de morale et de physique*, Louvain:

Publications universitaires, 1974. (Edition of the questions.)

—— (*c.*1273) *De anima intellectiva* (The Intellective Soul), ed. B. Bazán, *Quaestiones in Tertium De anima, De anima intellectiva, De aeternitate mundi*, Louvain: Publications universitaires, 1972. (Siger's work on the intellect.)

—— (*c.*1273–4) *Quaestiones morales* (Moral Questions), ed. B. Bazán, *Siger de Brabant. Écrits de logique, de morale et de physique*, Louvain: Publications universitaires, 1974. (Edition of the questions.)

—— (*c.*1273–4) *Quaestiones naturales* (Natural Questions) (Lisbon), ed. B. Bazán, *Siger de Brabant. Écrits de logique, de morale et de physique*, Louvain: Publications universitaires, 1974. (Edition of the questions.)

—— (*c.*1273–4) *Quaestiones in Metaphysicam* (Questions on Aristotle's *Metaphysics*) (Munich and Vienna), ed. W. Dunphy, Louvain-la-Neuve: Institut Superieur de Philosophie, 1981. (These may repeat one or more sets of oral lectures.)

—— (*c.*1273–4) *Quaestiones in Metaphysicam* (Questions on Aristotle's *Metaphysics*) (Cambridge and Paris), ed. A. Maurer, Louvain-la-Neuve: Institut superieur de philosophie, 1983. (These may repeat one or more sets of oral lectures.)

—— (*c.*1275–6) *Quaestiones super Librum de causis* (*Questions on the Liber de causis*), ed. A. Marlasca, *Les Quaestiones super Librum de causis de Siger de Brabant*, Louvain: Publications universitaires, 1972. (Edition of the questions.)

References and further reading

Bianchi, L. (1990) *Il vescovo e i filosofi. La condanna Parigina del 1277 e l'evoluzione dell'aristotelismo scolastico* (The Bishop and the Philosophers: The Condemnation of 1277 at Paris and the Evolution of Scholastic Aristotelianism), Bergamo: Pierluigi Lubrina Editore. (Contains many references to Siger and a very full bibliography concerning the events surrounding the condemnation of 1277.)

Hissette, R. (1977) *Enquête sur les 219 articles condamnés à Paris le 7 mars, 1277* (An Investigation Concerning the 219 Articles Condemned at Paris on 7 March, 1277), Louvain: Publications Universitaires, Paris: Vander-Oyez. (Indispensable for the condemnation of 1277 and also for Siger's implication therein.)

Mandonnet, P. (1908–11) *Siger de Brabant et l'averroïsme latin au XIIIe siècle* (Siger of Brabant and Latin Averroism in the Thirteenth Century), Les Philosophes Belges VI–VII, Louvain: Institut supérieur de philosophie, 2 vols. (Though now

badly dated, this was a seminal work for much earlier twentieth-century scholarship on Siger.)

Putallaz, F.-X. (1995) *Insolente liberté – controverses et condamnations au XIIIe siècle* (Insolent Liberty: Controversies and Condemnations in the Thirteenth Century), Fribourg: Éditions Universitaires de Fribourg Suisse. (See especially pages 15–50 on Siger's explanation of the roles of the intellect and the will in accounting for human choice.)

Van Steenberghen, F. (1931–42) *Siger de Brabant d'après ses oeuvres inédites* (Siger of Brabant According to His Unedited Works), Les Philosophes Belges XII–XIII, Louvain: Institut supérieur de philosophie, 2 vols. (The major work of its day calling for a re-evaluation of Siger, although now surpassed by its author's later works.)

—— (1977) *Maître Siger de Brabant* (Master Siger of Brabant), Louvain: Publications universitaires, Paris: Vander-Oyez. (The most definitive work yet to appear on Siger's life, career, works and doctrine.)

—— (1991) *La philosophie au XIIIe siècle* (Philosophy in the Thirteenth Century), 2nd edn, Louvain: Éditions Peeters. (See Chapter VIII especially for the author's most recent overview of Siger.)

Wippel, J.F. (1995) *Medieval Reactions to the Encounter Between Faith and Reason*, Milwaukee, WI: Marquette University Press. (See pages 14–18 on Siger's implication in the 1270 and 1277 condemnations at Paris, and pages 33–59 on Siger's views on the faith–reason issue.)

JOHN F. WIPPEL

SIGNPOSTS MOVEMENT

The symposium Signposts *(Vekhi, sometimes translated* Landmarks*), published in 1909, was a succès de scandale which provoked a long debate of extraordinary intensity and scope on the nature and outlook of the Russian intelligentsia. The discussion continued after the 1917 Revolution among intellectuals in exile, and was resumed in Russia with the republication of the volume in the Gorbachev era.*

The contributors to Signposts *were the philosophers N.A. Berdiaev (1874–1948), S.N. Bulgakov (1871–1944) and S.L. Frank (1877–1950); M.O. Gershenzon (1869–1925), a well-known critic and historian of literature; A.S. Izgoev (pseudonym of A.S. Lande, 1872–1935), a journalist active in the liberal Constitutional Democratic (Kadet) Party; B.A. Kistiakovskii (1868–1920), a specialist in constitutional law; and P.B. Struve (1870–1944), an eminent* economist and editor, and a member of the Kadet Party's Central Committee. They argued that the 1905 Revolution had revealed the despotic potential in the intelligentsia's traditional materialist faith, and urged it to re-examine its values, which were based on a misunderstanding of human nature and threatened the existence of Russian culture.

The shock caused by the volume owed much to the fact that, unlike most of the intelligentsia's critics, the authors were not of the political right. The majority were former Marxists who had moved to forms of liberalism based on idealist positions in philosophy. But although many intelligentsia groups were also reassessing their values in the wake of the 1905 Revolution, for political reasons liberals closed ranks with the left in an overwhelming condemnation of Signposts as a betrayal of the cause of freedom. The famous Signposts debate (which was pursued in exile after 1917 as a discussion on the meaning of the Russian Revolution) was not a dialogue, but rather a succession of dogmatic professions of faith by mutually hostile political groups. Western historians have commonly stressed the symposium's significance as a prophetic indictment of Russian radical messianism from the standpoint of liberal pragmatism. But Signposts was not an ideological unity: as well as its dominant liberal Westernism it contained a strong strand of nationalistic messianism which had affinities with traditions on both the Russian left and the right. In this respect the volume reflects a fundamental tension in Russian thought between dogmatic utopianism and radical humanism.

1   From Marxism to idealism
2   Utopianism versus humanism
3   *Signposts*
4   The debate
5   The sequels

1   From Marxism to idealism

Signposts' critique of the intelligentsia's outlook was grounded in the revival of metaphysical idealism in Russia at the beginning of the twentieth century. A major part in this was played by Struve, BERDIAEV, BULGAKOV and Frank, who had been leading exponents of Marxism in Russia in the 1890s, stressing its superiority over previous radical ideologies because of its 'scientific' demonstration of the historical inevitability of Russia's progression through capitalism to socialism. But, influenced by German Marxist revisionism, they began to lose faith in the predictive powers of Marx's revolutionary dialectic, and came to believe that the phenomenal world of law and necessity did not exhaust reality: there was also an inner world of goals and ideals. In 1901 a long

preface by Struve to Berdiaev's *Sub"ektivizm i individualizm v obshchestvennoi filosofii* (Subjectivism and Individualism in Social Philosophy) outlined the general position on which all four were then converging as a result of their critique of the empirical and logical defects of deterministic materialism: a Kantian dualism that placed human goals and values in a transcendental realm, the source of the categorical imperative that the individual be regarded always as an end in himself and never as a means (see KANT, I. §9; NEO-KANTIANISM, RUSSIAN §5). They argued that in their pursuit of material goals the Russian radical intelligentsia had ignored mankind's metaphysical thirst for good, truth and beauty, and neglected what should be the ultimate aim of the fight for progress: the creation of a new human type, spiritually reborn, the bearer of ideal values.

In finding the positivist and materialist tenets of the Russian radical tradition inadequate as explanations of the world or guides to action, the four thinkers represented a widespread mood that found expression in the Russian Religious and philosophical renaissance and the cultural ferment of the 'Silver Age' (see RUSSIAN RELIGIOUS-PHILOSOPHICAL RENAISSANCE). In 1903 they contributed with eight other writers to the symposium *Problemy idealizma* (Problems of Idealism), which sketched out idealist positions in the fields of ethics, sociology, the philosophy of history and law, in which to ground a systematic defence of the proposition that the individual was not just a cog in society but the source of its values. The contributors stressed the symposium's practical purpose: like the new movements in literature and the arts, it was a response to a 'striving for moral renewal' among large numbers of the intelligentsia who believed that commitment to narrow political ideologies had stunted their personal growth and distorted their moral vision: the 'new man' of the future, they hoped, would be a many-sided 'integral personality', morally, intellectually and aesthetically developed. But while some contributors held that such a type would possess an 'integral worldview', in which knowledge and faith would be harmonised in the perception of the historical process as a movement to a transcendent goal, others were moving towards a humanistic idealism incompatible with a dogmatic metaphysics. The former included Berdiaev and Bulgakov, the latter Struve and Frank. Their diverging paths would lead to irreconcilable positions in *Signposts* on the question of the goals of progress in Russia and the intelligentsia's role in their attainment.

2 Utopianism versus humanism

In his book *Sub"ektivizm i individualizm v obshchestvennoi filosofii*, Berdiaev declared the need for 'an organically whole, positive view of the world; at this historical moment scepticism can only serve reactionary purposes' (1901: 24). He and Bulgakov both believed that disenchantment with the millenarian promises of Marxism had left a vacuum that must be filled by a new faith to inspire the fight against autocracy. They found the source of this faith in the messianic vision of Vladimir Solov'ëv, who was a major influence on the revival of idealism in Russia at that period. Solov'ëv taught that alienation and social conflict were the results of the divorce of reason from religious faith. The spiritual unity of the psyche would be restored only when philosophy, science and theology were united in the pursuit of the supreme aim of knowledge: an understanding of the 'total-unity' of all existence through communion with its source, God (the Absolute) to which it is destined to return. The historical process was a movement to this final goal: an era when mankind would live an 'integral life' within an 'integral society' – a utopia both humanistic and theocratic, uniting East and West, Church and state. Like the Slavophiles, Solov'ëv believed that Russia's destiny was to fulfil a religious mission: to be the first bearer of the new life among mankind (see SLAVOPHILISM; SOLOV'ËV, V.S.).

Berdiaev and Bulgakov saw no contradiction between their defence of the individual's right to self-direction against the encroachments of collectivistic social doctrines and their belief in a form of historical determinism that drew heavily on Solov'ëv. In *Problemy idealizma* Bulgakov defines historical progress as the march of the Absolute towards its goal. All nations and individuals have their particular historical mission, 'foreordained in the moral world order', which can be discovered by consulting conscience, the voice of the Divine Will within each individual. Bulgakov's religious evolution was already leading him away from historical to theological concerns (he became an Orthodox priest in 1918). Berdiaev on the other hand was involved in all aspects of the Russian cultural renaissance. He was active in discussions in which representatives of the Church and the intelligentsia sought a *rapprochement* on questions of morality and culture, and until 1908 was part of the circle of Symbolist writers and religious thinkers grouped around D.M. Merezhkovskii and his wife, the poet Zinaida Gippius. He shared their enthusiasm for Nietzsche's ideas and adopted Merezhkovskii's theory of the imminent coming of a 'New Religious Consciousness' based on a 'Third Testament' which would teach a morality reconciling Christ and AntiChrist, the flesh and the spirit, Nietzschean self-affirmation and Christian brotherhood (see NIETZSCHE: IMPACT ON RUSSIAN THOUGHT §1). He greeted the 1905 Revolution as an apocalypse that signalled the advent of a religious utopia, but, disillusioned by its failure to achieve the goal of political liberty, concluded that the attainment of freedom was not possible in the material world, and broke with Merezhkovskii's group, taking up a stance of spiritual revolt against the irredeemable philistinism of human societies, a position much influenced by Nietzsche, and which he described as mystical anarchism. He warned the intelligentsia that Russia's cultural backwardness could not be overcome by a historical leap – a view that was hard to reconcile with the belief that he also expressed at that period, that Russia was destined to bring about a universal spiritual regeneration by assimilating Western culture and combining it with Orthodox spirituality.

Berdiaev and Bulgakov were intransigent utopians who (as their memoirs reveal) had been attracted to Marxism by its promise of a wholly emancipated mankind. In contrast, Struve records that he had been drawn to Marx's economic analysis by the light it shed on the practical problems of achieving civil and political liberties in an undeveloped economy. In 1900 he moved from Social Democracy to liberalism, and in 1906 became a member of the Central Committee of the newly formed Kadet Party and subsequently editor of a leading liberal journal, *Russkaia mysl'* (Russian Thought). He was followed to liberalism by Frank, who had become a close friend. Both regarded their political allegiance as an expression of their religious humanism, basing their defence of gradualism and compromise on their belief in the inseparability of the material and spiritual elements in human creativity, and its roots in the continuity of national life. They stressed the interdependence of freedom and culture, which they defined as the embodiment of eternal values in the economic and social structures, artefacts and everyday activities of historical existence. They regarded the Russian left's faith in the principle of destruction as anti-cultural and thereby antilibertarian, and devoted their journalism between 1905 and the First World War principally to a campaign against all forms of radical and religious messianism that, in the expectation of an historical leap to a state of ideal freedom, ignored the importance of historical continuity and of the everyday tasks of social construction and cultural creation.

3 Signposts

While the four ex-Marxists often aired their differences in print, they were agreed in holding the intelligentsia principally to blame for the anarchy and destruction of the 1905 Revolution and its failure to attain its objectives. For this reason the literary historian M.O. Gershenzon invited them to contribute to a symposium on that theme, together with two liberals concerned with similar issues, B.A. Kistiakovskii (who had contributed to *Problemy idealizma*) and A.S. Izgoev.

In his introduction to *Signposts* Gershenzon outlines the reasons for the project. The intelligentsia's traditional values had been tested by the Revolution and found wanting. The volume's aim was to contribute to the process of self-examination that had ensued among the intelligentsia by offering its own diagnosis of their malaise. Despite differences of principle among the authors, they shared a common platform: recognition of the theoretical and practical primacy of the individual's inner spiritual life over the external forms of community. They believed that the intelligentsia's outlook, which rested on the opposite principle – recognition of the unconditional primacy of social forms – was erroneous in theory and harmful in practice.

Although the essays were written without prior consultation among the authors, they had a number of themes in common, chief among which was a critique of the intelligentsia's moral relativism and its utilitarian approach to all values as means to political ends. Kistiakovskii points to the traditional contempt of Russian radicals for legal principles, which they perceived as impediments to revolutionary change. Berdiaev notes their indifference to philosophical truths which could not be used for social purposes. Frank defines their outlook as 'nihilistic moralism': a rejection of objective and universally binding moral standards combined with a deification of the subjective interests of the masses which (identified with the goals of a specific class or party) had been invoked to sanction violence and criminality during 1905. Gershenzon pointed out that the intelligentsia's preoccupation with revolutionary agitation had led them to neglect the skills and capacities needed for the task of social construction. Izgoev noted that the supreme criterion of virtue among young radicals was readiness to die for the cause; Bulgakov argued that the left's idolatrous worship of the revolutionary hero was the root cause of its preference for extreme positions over compromise in all cases. But he and Berdiaev differed from the other contributors in discerning positive qualities in the intelligentsia's maximalism, arguing that its ascetic hostility to bourgeois culture and values expressed an unconscious religious thirst for the Kingdom of God on Earth which had close affinities with the religious and

cultural messianism of the Slavophiles, Dostoevskii, and Vladimir Solov'ëv. They placed their hopes for Russia's political and cultural progress on a future synthesis of the religious and secular traditions of Russian thought whereby the intelligentsia, having renounced its atheism, would apply itself to the elucidation of Russia's spiritual mission in the world.

Struve's essay, however, rejects the theory of the intelligentsia's unconscious religiosity as a myth. He and Frank unambiguously condemn its ideological intransigence, in which they see the seeds of despotism and mob rule. Struve argued that the intelligentsia's traditional opposition to the state had led it to ignore the problem of education in politics and social reform: it had appealed to the instincts and passions of the masses in 1905 instead of using the concessions forced out of the government as a means of schooling the people in the habits of democracy. Frank attacks the cult of 'simplicity' common to Russian radicalism and Tolstoism: a puritanical hostility to all cultural values that were alien to the traditional life of the Russian peasant. Berdiaev and Bulgakov discerned an admirable otherworldliness in the intelligentsia's aversion to the bourgeois culture of the West; Struve and Frank looked forward to its embourgeoisement, when it would cease to exist as a separate cultural category with its own traditions and fanatical faiths, and would turn its attention from the redistribution of material goods to the creation of cultural values.

As Struve remarked after *Signposts'* publication, it reflected the traditional division in Russian thought between Westernizers and Slavophiles. (The latter included Gershenzon who, unlike the other contributors, had little interest in politics but shared the Slavophiles' concern with spiritual 'integrality'.) *Signposts* pointed simultaneously in opposing directions.

4 The debate

The symposium was the sensation of the year. It was pronounced on by public figures and passionately discussed in newspapers and journals throughout the Russian Empire. It generated three counter-symposia; meetings and speeches were devoted to it, and it soon ran into five editions.

To the authors' embarrassment, the volume was fulsomely praised by the conservative right which interpreted it as a political attack on the left. The great majority of the intelligentsia took the same view, representing the authors as the government's agents or its unconscious tools. In the words of the Socialist Revolutionary leader Viktor Chernov *Signposts* was 'the most reactionary book of the decade'. A Kadet symposium on the volume argued that while some of its criticism was valid, the intelligentsia's shortcomings were a consequence of Russia's economic backwardness and the Signposts authors themselves were not immune from its diseases. Among Russian writers only the Symbolist poet and novelist Andrei Belyi and the essayist Vasilii ROZANOV publicly expressed solidarity with its critique of the values of the left, whose battle against metaphysics, aesthetics and religion had, in Rozanov's view, resulted in the loss of its 'spiritual sight'.

The intelligentsia's overwhelming hostility to *Signposts* has been cited by historians as evidence of its dogmatic adherence to its traditional revolutionary mystique. But the experiences of 1905 had led to a widespread questioning of that mystique in the radical movement, notably among the leadership of the Socialist Revolutionary Party, who had begun a fundamental re-examination of their moral assumptions, while writers sympathetic to the left, such as D. Merezhkovskii, commented on the role of religious and philosophical ideas in the transformation of its outlook. The closing of the intelligentsia's ranks against *Signposts* was due to the belief that their criticism came from a hostile camp and would strengthen conservative political forces. In the Kadets' case there was a tactical reason (the desire to preserve a coalition with the left) for distancing themselves from *Signposts*. The party's leader, Miliukov, even found it necessary to undertake a lecture tour around Russia for the purpose of attacking the volume: this did not prevent Lenin from labelling *Signposts* 'an encyclopedia of liberal apostasy'.

The *Signposts* authors failed to spark off a discussion of the intelligentsia's self-image on their own terms; but the volume may be seen as part of a wider mood of self-examination among the Russian intelligentsia which sprang from the philosophical and religious revival of the early twentieth century, and which, in the last decade before the Revolution, was reflected in a growing moral opposition to the outlook of the Bolsheviks from other parties on the left.

5 The sequels

In 1918, as the Bolshevik dictatorship began to hunt down its critics, while civil war raged in the south of Russia and the countryside was ravaged by anarchy and famine, *Signposts*' predictions of a national catastrophe seemed tragically prophetic. Struve, living clandestinely in Moscow, conceived the idea of a sequel which could discuss the causes and meaning of the 1917 Revolution. He brought together all the *Signposts* authors except Gershenzon and Kistiakovskii, and six others, including P.I. Novgorodtsev, who had been the editor of *Problemy idealizma*, and the Symbolist poet Viacheslav Ivanov. All had been prominent in Russian intellectual life before the Revolution.

The new symposium's title, *Iz glubiny* (*Out of the Depths*), was taken from the 130th Psalm. It was confiscated before it could be distributed and only two copies found their way to the West. It was virtually unknown until it was reprinted in Paris in 1967. The authors interpret the Revolution as a vindication of *Signposts'* warnings. The essays fall into two main categories: those primarily concerned with what Struve called the 'ultimate religious questions' of human existence, including such topics as the 'Russian soul'; and those that focus on more concrete social and political issues. The two approaches are exemplified in the contributions of Berdiaev and Struve respectively. Struve points to the contradiction between socialism's rational theory and destructive practice, while Berdiaev contends that the Revolution revealed a dark side of the Russian soul: the anarchic nihilism first diagnosed by Gogol' and Dostoevskii.

All the contributors express the hope for a spiritual rebirth of the Russian people based on national and religious values, but are unspecific on the form this should take. Berdiaev was then engaged in developing a philosophical interpretation of the Russian Revolution as the prelude to the end of European civilization, which would be apocalyptically transformed into a new universal culture which Russian thinkers like himself (whose spiritual make up, he believed, represented a synthesis of East and West) were destined to reveal to the world. In his book *The Philosophy of Inequality*, published in Berlin in 1923, he would attack the 'tyranny of democracy', and call for 'total freedom', which he admits is unrealizable on earth. In *Out of the Depths* as in *Signposts*, the aims of religious utopians conflict with those of liberal humanists, such as Struve, who defends the right to property and economic liberty and the principles of individual responsibility and initiative, although (as in earlier writings on this theme) he emphasizes the importance of a strong and unified state as the guardian of the national culture.

In 1921 the debate over *Signposts* was taken up in emigration with the publication in Prague of a volume of essays entitled *Smena vekh* (*Change of Signposts*), the manifesto of a short-lived movement later known as 'National Bolshevism'. Its proponents, mainly former Kadets who claimed to be inspired by the nationalist strand in *Signposts*, called for reconciliation with the Bolsheviks on the grounds that in its sweeping destruction the Revolution had been an authentically Russian phenomenon, an expression of the people's instincts. A counter-symposium, *O smene vekh* (*On Change of Signposts*) (1922), whose authors included Izgoev, appeared inside Russia, protesting against what they saw as this group's distortion of the principles of *Signposts*: as the embodiment of revolutionary nihilism, Bolshevik ideology could not be the basis of a new national culture. Struve (by then in emigration) also strongly repudiated the new movement as intellectually and morally contemptible.

This marked the end of the public debate over *Signposts* in emigration, although the work frequently figured in émigré literature. Its central themes were echoed in the work of two *Signposts* authors in particular: as editor of a succession of émigré periodicals, Struve devoted much of his writing to the question of the meaning of the Russian Revolution, while Berdiaev (who as a philosopher became the best known of the *Signposts* authors in the West) produced interpretations of Russian thought for a Western audience.

Mention of *Signposts* in official Soviet historiography was confined to a recapitulation of Lenin's attack on it, but in the post-Stalin period Russian dissidents who were rediscovering pre-revolutionary Russian philosophy and religious thought found its critique of the intelligentsia's values highly relevant to their own time. In 1974 the exiled Solzhenitsyn, with a number of intellectuals who were still in Russia, published a collection of essays modelled on *Signposts* whose title *Iz-pod glyb* (*From under the Rubble*) was a phonetic echo of the Russian words for *Out of the Depths*. Although differing from *Signposts* on some issues, the collection cites it as a vision of the future which sheds light on the spiritual bankruptcy of the Soviet elite.

One of the first fruits of the new press freedoms under Gorbachev was the republication of *Signposts* and *Out of the Depths*. The lively interest of post-Soviet Russian intellectuals in *Signposts* (which has since gone into several reprints) suggests that it may now play a role in the intelligentsia's self-examination that was denied it in 1909. Recent commentaries on *Signposts* in the West have linked it with Mikhail Bakhtin's subsequent critique of dogmatic thought, as part of a minority current in the Russian intellectual tradition which refused to regard all moral questions as political ones, and which is enjoying a significant revival today.

See also: LIBERALISM, RUSSIAN §3; MARXIST PHILOSOPHY, RUSSIAN AND SOVIET §2

List of works

Berdiaev, N.A. (1901) *Sub"ektivizm i individualizm v obshchestvennoi filosofii. Kriticheskii ètiud o N.K. Mikhailovskom, s predisloviem P.B.Struve* (Subjecti-

vism and Individualism in Social Philosophy. A critical study of N.K. Mikhailovskii, with a preface by P.B. Struve), St Petersburg: Popova. (A critique of the radical intelligentsia's philosophical outlook from an idealist perspective.)

Novgorodtsev, P.N. (ed.) (1903) *Problemy idealizma. Sbornik statei* (Problems of Idealism. A Collection of Articles), Moscow: Moskovskoe psikhologicheskoe obshchestvo. (Essays on aspects of the future Signposts movement's philosophy.)

Vekhi. Sbornik statei o russkoi intelligentsii (1909) Moscow: I.N. Kushnerev; 5th edn, 1910; trans. M.S. Shatz and J.E. Zimmerman, *Signposts. A Collection of Articles on the Russian Intelligentsia*, Irvine, CA: Charles Schlacks Jr, 1986. (Contains an informative introduction and a bibliography of the debate.)

Iz glubiny: Sbornik statei o russkoi revoliutsii (1918) Moscow; 2nd edn Paris: YMCA-Press, 1967; trans. W.F. Woehrlin, *Out of the Depths. A collection of articles on the Russian Revolution*, Irvine, CA: Charles Schlacks Jr., 1986. (Distribution of the 1918 printing was suppressed for political reasons. The collection survived only because two copies reached the West. The 1967 edition, based on one of these copies, represents its first publication.)

Smena vekh: Sbornik statei (Change of Signposts: A Collection of Articles) (1921) Prague: Politika. (A pro-Bolshevik response to *Signposts*.)

O smene vekh (On Change of Signposts) (1922) Petrograd: Logos. (A reassertion of the principles of *Signposts* against *Smena vekh*.)

Solzhenitsyn, A. *et al.* (1974) *Iz-pod glyb: Sbornik statei*, Paris: YMCA-Press; trans. A.M. Brock *et al.*, *From under the Rubble*, Boston: Little, Brown, 1975. (A collection of essays by Russian intellectuals modelled on *Signposts*.)

References and further reading

Burbank, J. (1986) *Intelligentsia and Revolution. Russian Views of Bolshevism 1917–1922*, Oxford: Oxford University Press. (Chs 5 and 6 on the intellectual background to *Out of the Depths* and *Change of Signposts*.)

Kelly, A.M. (1998) *Towards Another Shore: Russian Thinkers between Necessity and Chance*, New Haven, CT: Yale University Press. (Includes an essay on the conflict between utopian and anti-utopian positions in *Signposts*.)

Kindersley, R. (1962) *The First Russian Revisionists*, Oxford: Clarendon Press. (On the early thought of the *Signposts* authors.)

Mendel, A.P. (1961), *Dilemmas of Progress in Tsarist Russia*, Cambridge, MA: Harvard University Press.

(A subtle study of the early philosophical evolution of Berdiaev, Bulgakov and Struve.)

Morson, G.S. (1993) 'Prosaic Bakhtin: Landmarks, Anti-Intelligentsialism, and the Russian Counter-Tradition', *Common Knowledge* 2 (1): 35–74. (Approaches *Signposts* as part of a tradition antithetical to the intelligentsia's.)

Oberländer, E. (1968) 'Nationalbolschewistische Tendenzen in der russischen Intelligentz: Die 'Smena Vech'-Diskussion 1921–1922' in *Jahrbücher für Geschichte Osteuropas* 16 (2): 194–211. (On the *Change of Signposts* controversy.)

—— (1965) *Die Vechi-Diskussion 1909–12*, Köln: Ph.D. dissertation. (A summary of positions in the debate.)

Read, C. (1979) *Religion, Revolution and the Russian Intelligentsia 1900–1912: the Vekhi Debate and its Intellectual Background*, London: Macmillan. (Focuses on the role of religious belief in the Signposts debate.)

Schapiro L. (1955) 'The Vekhi Group and the Mystique of Revolution' in *Slavonic and East European Review* 34 (82): 56–76. (Interprets *Signposts* as a liberal critique of the Russian left).

AILEEN KELLY

AL-SIJISTANI, ABU SULAYMAN MUHAMMAD (*c.*932–*c.*1000)

Al-Sijistani was one of the great figures of Baghdad in the fourth century AH (tenth century AD). He assembled around him a circle of philosophers and litterateurs who met regularly in sessions to discuss topics related to philosophy, religion and language. As a philosopher with a humanistic orientation, his concerns went beyond subjects of strictly philosophical nature. His philosophical ideas displayed Aristotelian and Neoplatonic motifs. He considered philosophy and religion to be totally different in nature and method, so that the two could not be reconciled. God is only prior to the world in essence, rank and nobility, not in time. Al-Sijistani insisted that in no way should one attribute to God the imperfections of created things. According to him, the soul is simple by nature and natural reason is capable of attaining a state of pure knowledge that enables one to distinguish between good and evil. Reason, if taken as a guide, could ensure happiness.

1 Life and works
2 Doctrines

1 Life and works

Abu Sulayman Muhammad al-Sijistani, known as al-Mantiqi (the Logician), was born, *c.*AH 320/AD 932. His formative years were spent in Sijistan (now Sistan in Iran) but the mature phase of his career took place in Baghdad. He became one of the great figures of the Islamic humanist movement that flourished during the fourth century AH (tenth century AD) in Baghdad. He dominated his generation by the enlightenment of his judgments and the breadth of his knowledge. He was especially interested in ancient philosophy and its transmission into the world of Islam. He assembled around him a circle of friends, philosophers, scientists and litterateurs of various ethnic and religious affiliations. The circle met in regular sessions (*majalis*) and with open and critical minds discussed topics related to philosophy, religion, science and language. Al-Sijistani died *c.*AH 391/AD 1000.

Those of al-Sijitani's works that have reached us are not numerous. One of the most important attributed to him is *Siwan al-hikma* (Vessel of Wisdom), from which only selections have survived. The attribution to al-Sijistani of this collection of dicta and anecdotes of Greek and Islamic philosophers has been challenged by W. al-Qadi (1981), but Joel Kraemer (1986) believes that the work emanated from al-Sijistani's school, based upon classroom notes and texts. In addition to *Siwan al-hikma*, al-Sijistani wrote short treatises on the first mover, the fifth nature of the celestial spheres, the perfection peculiar to the human species, principles of being, dream omens and logic.

In a Socratic fashion, al-Sijistani preferred oral instruction over writing. We owe to his student and protégé Abu Hayyan AL-TAWHIDI most of the information concerning his philosophical ideas and doctrines. Al-Tawhidi recorded the sessions of al-Sijistani's circle in his works *al-Muqabasat* (Conversations) and *al-Imta' wa-al-mu'anasa* (Book of Pleasure and Conviviality), which remain the major sources of information on the life and thought of al-Sijistani. Consequently we have to look at his teachings through the window of his pupil's writings.

2 Doctrines

As a philosopher with a humanistic orientation, al-Sijistani's concerns went beyond subjects of strictly philosophical nature. His philosophical ideas displayed Aristotelian and Neoplatonic motifs and touched on a wide range of subjects such as politics, aesthetics and friendship, among others. However, his chief preoccupation, and that of the circle members as reflected in al-Tawhidi's recordings, centred on the relations between philosophy and religion, the mind–body problem – why the soul was susceptible to virtues and vices, good and evil – the question of God's relation with and action in the universe, and finally the individual and society.

Al-Tawhidi represents his mentor as a man of deep religious sentiments but who regarded both religion and philosophy as true and valid. The two are independent and should not and cannot be reconciled. They differ in method and substance. In religion there are things which cannot be fathomed or understood but are to be accepted and assented to; the end of religion is proximity to God, whereas the aim of philosophy is contemplation. Al-Sijistani objected to the attempt by the Brethren of Purity to harmonize religion and philosophy, and lashed out at the Islamic theologians (al-mutakallimun) who claimed that their methodology was rationalist when in reality it was false rationalism (see IKHWAN AL-SAFA'; ISLAMIC THEOLOGY).

For al-Sijistani the universe is divided into the terrestrial and the intelligible according to the Platonic system, but God acts in accordance with the Aristotelian concept of first mover. Having accepted the view that matter is eternal, he held that this does not detract from the perfection of God since in the final analysis everything depends on his will. One should not attribute to God the imperfections of the created world. God is prior to the world in essence, rank and nobility, but not in time.

Knowledge implies two types: natural and supernatural. There are four degrees of knowledge: sensible knowledge possessed by non-reasoning animals; absolutely and exclusively intelligible knowledge possessed by the celestial bodies; the sensible–intelligible knowledge tied up with the imagination of those who have not reached perfect purity; and the intelligible–sensible knowledge which has been arrived at through rational and speculative investigation. This is the highest knowledge humans, including such persons as philosophers, augurs (kahins) and prophets, can acquire. Intuition, however, is the noblest kind of knowledge because it presents itself by itself in the soul and is not subject to generation and corruption. Through reason we overcome all obstacles to reach God through the intellect, which is the medium between human beings and the supernatural world. Reason has the power to contact the super-sensible beings until it reaches the First Being.

Having been greatly interested in the body–soul relationship, al-Sijistani distinguished between soul (nafs) and spirit (ruh), considering the soul to be a simple substance imperceptible to the senses and not subject to change or corruption. According to him, human beings are so by virtue of having a soul and

not by the possession of a body, although the soul cannot make a human being by itself. The soul is the principle of knowledge, the body the principle of action. Because of the rival elements, nature versus reason, that constitute a human being and pull him in opposite directions, it is important to take reason as a guide. It alone can ensure our ultimate happiness, namely the knowledge of God and the good which he has reserved for the virtuous. One should aim high towards the celestial world in order to reach eternal life (see SOUL IN ISLAMIC PHILOSOPHY).

See also: ARISTOTELIANISM IN ISLAMIC PHILOSOPHY; GREEK PHILOSOPHY: IMPACT ON ISLAMIC PHILOSOPHY; NEOPLATONISM IN ISLAMIC PHILOSOPHY; AL-TAWHIDI

List of works

al-Sijistani (c.932–c.1000) *Siwan al-hikmah wa-thalath rasa'il* (Vessel of Wisdom and the Three Treatises), ed. A. Badawi, Teheran: Bunyad Farhang, 1974; ed. D.M. Dunlop, *The Muntakhab Siwan al-Hikmah of Abu Sulaiman as-Sijistani, Arabic Text, Introduction and Indices*, The Hague: Mouton, 1979. (The Badawi edition includes, in addition to introductions in Arabic and French, the following treatises: *Fi anna al-ajram al- ulwiya tabi'atuha tabi'a khamisa* (The Nature of the Celestial Bodies is a Fifth Nature); *Fi al-muharrik al-awwal* (On the First Mover); and *Fi al-kamal al-khass bi-naw' al-insan* (On the Perfection Peculiar to the Human Species). Dunlop contains fragments, especially on medicine, that are not in the Badawi edition. He believes that sections dealing with the Greek philosophers are derived from Porphyry's *History of Philosophy*.)

—— (c.932–c.1000) *Fi mabadi' al-mawjudat* (On the Principles of Beings), ed. and trans. G. Troupeau, *Pensamiento* 25, 1969: 259–70. (Discusses the ranks of the first beings and the attributes by which the first essence is qualified.)

—— (c.932–c.1000) *Fi al-kamal al-khass bi-naw' al-insan* (The Perfection Peculiar to the Human Species), ed. and trans. into French by M. Kügel-Turker, *Pensamiento* 25, 1969: 207–24. (By using the intellect, man reaches perfection.)

References and further reading

Jadaane, F. (1971) 'La philosophie de Sijistani', *Studia Islamica* 33: 67–95. (A general introduction to al-Sijistani's philosophical ideas and their Greek sources.)

* Kraemer, J.L. (1986) *Philosophy in the Renaissance of Islam, Abu Sulayman al-Sijistani and His Circle*,

Leiden: Brill. (Major work which examines the extent to which al-Sijistani and his circle were conversant with technical discussions of philosophical issues treated in Greek and late antiquity.)

Leaman, O. (1996) 'Islamic Humanism in the Fourth/ Tenth Century)', in S.H. Nasr and O. Leaman (eds) *History of Islamic Philosophy*, London: Routledge, ch. 10, 155–64. (Analysis of the nature of this important period of Islamic philosophy, concentrating on the ethical thought of the period.)

* al-Qadi, W. (1981) '*Kitab Siwan al-Hikmah*: Structure, Composition, Authorship and Sources', *Der Islam* 58: 87–124. (Based on some internal evidence, concludes that the real author is the little known Abu al-Qasim al-Katib.)

* al-Tawhidi (*c.*930–1023) *al-Imta' wa-al-mu'anasa* (Book of Pleasure and Conviviality), ed. A. Amin and A. al-Zayn, Beirut: al-Maktaba al-'Asriyya, 2nd edn, 1953, 3 vols. (A record of night sessions in Baghdad in which al-Sijistani participated in discussing philosophical questions.)

* —— (*c.*930–1023) *al-Muqabasat* (Conversations), ed. T. Husayn, Baghdad: Matba'at al-Irshad, 1970. (A collection of 106 conversations on various philosophical subjects.)

GEORGE N. ATIYEH

SILVESTRI, FRANCESCO (1474–1528)

A Thomist philosopher and theologian, Silvestri composed, along with Aristotelian commentaries and polemical works, a vast commentary on Aquinas' Summa Contra Gentiles *which, from the first, has been recognized as its classic exposition. Silvestri imitated the method (*expositio formalis*) of Cajetan's commentary on Aquinas'* Summa Theologiae, *but disagreed with Cajetan on key points of Thomistic doctrine and proposed interpretations generally closer to the letter of Aquinas. Chief among these are the doctrines of analogy, abstraction and the rational demonstrability of the soul's immortality.*

Francesco Silvestri was born in Ferrara and, hence, is commonly known as Ferrariensis (or as Francis Sylvester of Ferrara). He entered the Dominican Order in 1488 and completed his initial studies in Bologna in 1497. In 1498 he was appointed lector in Mantua. From 1503–8 he lectured in Milan and from 1509–11 in Bologna. He spent 1511–3 as bachelor of the *Sentences* in Milan and subsequently returned to Bologna where he graduated as master of theology in

1516. He was then elected prior of the convent in Ferrara, and also taught at the university. In 1519 he was appointed inquisitor in Bologna and in 1521–4 he was regent master of the Dominican *studium generale* there. In 1524 he was elected prior of the convent in Bologna and, soon after, Pope Clement VII named him vicar general of the order. He was elected master general at the general chapter held in Rome in 1525 and continued in this office until his death.

Silvestri's doctrine of analogy is presented in his commentary on Aquinas' *Summa contra gentiles* as a critical supplement to that of CAJETAN (§2). Unlike the latter, Silvestri is more concerned with accurate exegesis of Aquinas' text than the refutation of Scotism and is, accordingly, more attuned to the determination of analogy's logical structure than to its metaphysical implications. Starting from Aquinas' affirmation that analogy is the predication of terms according to an order of priority and posteriority (see AQUINAS §9), he makes a clear distinction between such an order (1) as operative in the psychological process of naming, and (2) as holding in reality and representing the relative positions of things in the hierarchy of being.

Two features are essential to every instance of analogy: first, secondary analogates bear some kind of reference to the primary analogate (*ordo ad unum*); second, the proper notion (*ratio propria*) of the primary analogate enters the definition of secondary analogates. From this follows a division of analogy foreign to Aquinas: analogy may be founded on the relation (or resemblance) which holds between either a plurality of things and one other thing (*duorum ad tertium*) or between one thing and another (*unius ad alterum*). The latter kind is further divided into analogy founded on a direct, fixed relation between one thing and another (analogy of proportion) and analogy founded on an indirect, loose relation between one thing and another (analogy of proportionality). Unlike Aquinas and Cajetan, Silvestri distinguishes between these two latter types of analogy in psychological rather than mathematical terms. The analogical predication of names of God and creatures cannot be of the kind *duorum ad tertium* because there is no prior 'third thing' to which both God and creatures are related (or that both God and creatures resemble), so as to justify the imposition of common terms. It can only be the analogy of proportionality that permits one to talk meaningfully about God and that, unlike analogy of proportion, safeguards the divine transcendence (see LANGUAGE, RENAISSANCE PHILOSOPHY OF §4).

Silvestri proposed a personal theory of abstraction in a critique of Cajetan's explanation (*In Contra Gentiles Commentaria* II c.77). He argues that Cajetan attributes to the phantasm features of the intelligible object (universality, immateriality), transforming it into a direct object of intellection and rendering the agent intellect redundant. For Silvestri the agent intellect performs a 'radical and fundamental' illumination. It acts upon both the phantasm and the possible intellect, and acts in conjunction with the imagination (*phantasia*) to produce the impressed intelligible species.

Silvestri is original on several other epistemological and metaphysical issues. The possible intellect has the capacity to form a proper concept of the singular sensible object in addition to, and after, the formation of the universal concept which represents the common nature. Numerical multiplication is possible within species of immaterial substances. The individuation of material substances is effected by matter in so far as it is quantified by determined dimensions.

Silvestri has been considered fundamentally a disciple, albeit at times critical, of Cajetan. He should rather be counted a member of the Bolognese Thomist school founded by Peter of Bergamo (d. 1482) and represented during the early sixteenth century by such figures as Sylvester Prierias (1456–1527), Chrysostom Javelli (1470–1543) and Bartholomeo de Spina (d. 1545). Generally opposed to Cajetan on speculative issues, their differences came to the fore during the Pomponazzi affair (see POMPONAZZI, P. §2). This is the context of Silvestri's own defence of the rational demonstrability of the soul's immortality. Especially in need of correction is the explanation of the Bolognese Thomists' opposition to Cajetan (and Pomponazzi) in terms of an inability to distinguish between philosophy and Aristotelianism (Laurent 1938; Nardi 1958). This distinction is, in fact, stressed by all of them, including Silvestri.

See also: AQUINAS, T.; ARISTOTELIANISM, RENAISSANCE; CAJETAN; POMPONAZZI, P.

List of works

Silvestri, F. (1517) *Adnotationes in libros Posteriorum Aristotelis et S. Thomae*, Venice. (Commentary on Aristotle's *Posterior Analytics* and Aquinas' commentary on the same.)

—— (1524) *In libros s. Thomae Aquinatis Contra Gentiles Commentaria* (Commentary on Aquinas' *Summa contra gentiles*), Venice; in T. Aquinas, *Opera Omnia*, Editio Leonina, vols 13–15, Rome: Typis Riccardi Garroni, 1918–30. (Begun in 1508 and completed in 1517, the first edition of *In Contra Gentiles Commentaria* appeared in 1524.)

—— (1525) *Apologia de convenientia institutorum Romanae Ecclesiae cum evangelica libertate* (Apology for the Appropriateness of the Institutions of the Roman Church for Evangelical Freedom), Rome; ed. G. Sestili, Rome: F. Pustet, 1906. (Polemical work against Luther.)

—— (1535) *Quaestiones in III libros De Animae* (Questions on the Three Books of Aristotle's *On the Soul*), Venice. (Focuses on the most controversial aspects of Aristotle's *On the Soul*.)

—— (1535) *Quaestiones in libros Physicorum* (Questions on Aristotle's *Physics*), Venice. (Focuses on disputed points of Aristotle's *Physics*.)

References and further reading

Bellerate, B.M. (1960) 'L'analogia tomista nei grandi commentatori di S. Tommaso' (Thomistic Analogy in the Great Commentators on Aquinas), Rome: Salesian University, 73–95. (Abstract of a Ph.D. thesis that gives the most detailed account of Silvestri's theory of analogy.)

Giacon, C. (1944) *La seconda scolastica* (The Second Scholasticism), Milan: Bocca, vol. 1, 37–52, 80–2, 91–114, 130–2, 146–62. (Overview of Silvestri's developments of Aquinas and disagreements with Cajetan.)

Hegyi, J. (1959) *Die Bedeutung des Seins bei den klassischen Kommentatoren des heiligen Thomas von Aquin: Capreolus, Silvester von Ferrara, Cajetan* (The Meaning of Being in the Classic Commentators on Aquinas: Capreolus, Silvestri and Cajetan), Pullacher Philosophische Forschungen 4, Pullach bei München: Berchmanskolleg, 53–106. (Account of Silvestri's metaphysics.)

Lauchert, F. (1912) *Die italienischen literarischen Gegner Luthers*, Freiburg: Herder, 269–78. (Account of Silvestri's anti-Luther polemics.)

* Laurent, M.-H. (1938) 'Introductio', in Cajetan, *Commentaria in De Anima Aristotelis*, ed. P.I. Coquelle, Rome: Institutum Angelicum, vol. 1, xlvii–li. (Influential, but erroneous, evaluation of Silvestri.)

Lohr, C. (1988) 'Silvestri (de Silvestris) Ferrariensis, Franciscus O.P.', *Latin Aristotle Commentaries: II, Renaissance Authors*, Florence: Olschki, 422–3. (Not entirely accurate bio-bibliography, lists editions of commentaries on Aristotle.)

Mortier, A. (1911) *Histoire des maîtres généraux de l'ordre des Frères Prêcheurs*, Paris: Picard, vol. 5, 260–84. (Account of Silvestri's activities as Dominican master general.)

McInerny, R.M. (1961) *The Logic of Analogy*, The Hague: Nijhoff, 23–31. (Brief account of Silvestri on analogy.)

* Nardi, B. (1958) *Saggi sull'Aristotelismo Padovano*

(Essays on Paduan Aristotelianism), Florence: Sansoni, 222–3. (Appropriates Laurent's evaluation of Silvestri.)

Sestili, G. (1923) 'Francesco Silvestri', *Gli scienziati italiani*, Rome: Nardecchia, vol. 1, 128–37. (Most thorough bio-bibliography, not entirely reliable.)

MICHAEL TAVUZZI

SILVESTRIS, BERNARDUS
see BERNARD OF TOURS

SIMMEL, GEORG (1858–1918)

Georg Simmel was a prolific German philosopher and sociologist, who was one of the principal founders of sociology in Germany. His philosophy and social theory had a major impact in the early decades of the twentieth century, both among professional philosophers and sociologists and within the cultural and artistic spheres. This is true of his foundation for sociology, his philosophy of art and culture, his philosophy of life and his philosophy of money. His thought ranged from substantive issues within the philosophical tradition to a concern with the everyday world and its objects.

Although he insisted on many occasions that he wished to be recognized as a philosopher and despite his extensive philosophical writings, Simmel is today still largely known as one of the founders of German sociology at the turn of the nineteenth century.

Simmel taught at Berlin University from 1885 to 1914 until he obtained a chair in philosophy at Strasbourg University, which he held until his death. Although he studied philosophy (under Eduard Zeller and Friedrich Harms), history and ethnology at Berlin University, Simmel regarded his most significant teacher to be the *Völkerpsychologist* Moritz Lazarus. Simmel's writings, especially in the early period, manifest a wide range of influences: DARWIN, Herbert SPENCER, Gustav FECHNER, Lazarus, KANT, SCHOPENHAUER and others. Not surprisingly he was subsequently categorized as a positivist, pragmatist, Neo-Kantian, the 'German Bergson', a philosopher of life and a relativist.

His doctoral dissertation of 1881 on Kant's monadology indicated the commencement of a critical confrontation with Kantian philosophy, but despite his later contact with leading Neo-Kantians, such as Heinrich Rickert, it is not easy to subsume Simmel's philosophy under that of the Neo-Kantian tradition (see NEO-KANTIANISM, §2). His early monographs displayed seemingly diverse theoretical interests. *Über sociale Differenzierung* (On Social Differentiation) (1890) contained Simmel's first attempt to ground sociology methodologically as an independent discipline, as well as applications of his sociological method. *Die Probleme der Geschichtsphilosophie* (*The Problems of the Philosophy of History*) (1892) argued against the existence of universal historical laws, but it was its second (totally rewritten) edition of 1905 which had a significant impact upon methodological discussions within the social sciences on historical method and problems of interpretive understanding. The two-volume *Einleitung in die Moralwissenschaft* (Introduction to Moral Science) (1892–3) was devoted to rejecting universal ethical concepts and principles as an a priori formalistic grounding for moral philosophy in favour of a critical, psychological, sociological and historical investigation of the diversity of ethical norms in their everyday practice.

If several of these early works did not receive substantial acclaim, the same cannot be said of Simmel's most sustained philosophical study *Philosophie des Geldes* (*The Philosophy of Money*) (1900). If, as stated in its preface, one of philosophy's aims is to bring together the fragments of knowledge into a totality, then money serves as an instance for the presentation of relations between the most diverse and often fortuitous objects and for the possibility of discovering in each of the details of life the totality of its meaning. The philosophy of value appropriate for money as the universal equivalent of all values is some version of relativism or relationism. Simmel's wide ranging philosophy of money makes important contributions to the theory of value, to the philosophy of social action within a means/end framework, to a theory of the individual person and individual freedom, and to the aesthetics of modern society. Money as symbol of the eternal flux of interrelations between the most diverse phenomena serves to generate a theoretically grounded relativism. Many of Simmel's contemporaries viewed this rich synthesis as a philosophy of specifically 'modern' times and its author as possessing an instinct for the philosophical exploration of modernity.

In the period after publication of *The Philosophy of Money*, Simmel intended working on a volume on the philosophy of art and aesthetics, a project which, despite an extensive number of essays in this area on landscape, the picture frame and other aesthetic themes, never came to fruition. However, he did publish his highly popular and influential introductory lectures on *Kant* (1904) and on *Schopenhauer und Nietzsche* (1907) – both volumes serving as testimony to the impact of these philosophers upon Simmel's own development.

The work which did have a major influence was his *Soziologie* (Sociology) (1908), the culmination of more than a decade's concern with explicating his version of sociology. There, numerous substantive applications of his sociological method were preceded by Simmel's most elaborated foundation of sociology as the study of the forms of sociation and social interaction. The concept of interaction or reciprocal effect (*Wechselwirkung*) which pervades his philosophical writings lies at the centre of his foundation of sociology, focusing on the analysis of forms that social relations take. Human sociation is created in social interactions and Simmel's programme for sociology opens up the study of any and all forms of sociation as a basis for understanding how society is possible. This accounts for the extensive breadth of Simmel's sociological – and philosophical – investigations, an insistence upon the fundamental interrelatedness of all phenomena, a relational sociology and philosophy.

The necessary abstraction and separation of form from content which his sociology requires is itself indicative of more fundamental separations pervading his philosophy as a whole, but most fully developed in his later writings, namely between subjective and objective culture and between life and form. Explorations of the dialectical relationship between subjective and objective culture are at the heart of Simmel's philosophy and sociology of culture; the investigation of the opposition between life and form is at the centre of his philosophy of life (*Lebensphilosophie*). (See LEBENSPHILOSOPHIE).

Simmel's theory of culture radicalized the widening gap between subjective, individual culture and a more rapidly expanding objective culture – both material and non-material. This problematic of cultural alienation, in which human subjects must still realize themselves within an objective culture from which they are estranged, had a significant influence upon cultural and social theorists (especially in the tradition of critical theory). At the same time, essay collections such as *Philosophische Kultur* (Philosophical Culture) (1911) revealed a concern to develop not merely a philosophy of *culture* but also a *philosophical* culture capable of analysing this and other problematics.

Simmel's later writings also developed a philosophy of life grounded in the opposition of life and form in which life as a dynamic dimension struggled against rigidified form in a dialectical tension. This suggested affinities with Bergson's vitalism (see BERGSON, H.-L.), but also significantly influenced contemporary artistic movements, notably German Expressionism.

List of works

Simmel, G. (1988–) *Gesammelte Werke* (Complete Works), ed. O. Rammstedt, Frankfurt: Suhrkamp, 24 vols. (A recent critical edition of Simmel's complete works.)

—— (1890) *Über soziale Differenzierung* (On Social Differentiation), ed. H.J. Dahme, Frankfurt: Suhrkamp, 1989.

—— (1892) *Die Probleme der Geschichtsphilosophie*, Leipzig: Duncker & Humblot, 1905; trans. and ed. G. Oakes, *The Problems of the Philosophy of History. An Epistemological Essay*, New York: Free Press, 1977.

—— (1892–3) *Einleitung in die Moralwissenschaft. Eine Kritik der ethischen Grundbegriffe* (An Introduction to Moral Science. A Critique of Basic Ethical Concepts), ed. K.C. Köhnke, Frankfurt: Suhrkamp, 1989, 1991.

—— (1900, 1907) *Philosophie des Geldes*, Leipzig: Duncker & Humblot; *The Philosophy of Money*, London: trans. T. Bottomore and D. Frisby, London: Routledge, 1978.

—— (1904) *Kant*, Leipzig: Duncker & Humblot.

—— (1906a) *Kant und Goethe*, Berlin: Bard, Marquardt.

—— (1906b) *Die Religion*, Frankfurt: Rütten & Loening.

—— (1907) *Schopenhauer und Nietzsche*, Leipzig: Duncker & Humblot; trans. H. Loiskandl, D. Weinstein and M. Weinstein, *Schopenhauer and Nietzsche*, Amherst, MA: University of Massachussetts Press, 1986.

—— (1908) *Soziologie*, ed. O. Rammstedt, Frankfurt: Suhrkamp, 1992; partly trans. K.H. Wolff, *The Sociology of Georg Simmel*, New York: Free Press of Glencoe, and London: Collier-Macmillan, 1964.

—— (1910) *Hauptprobleme der Philosophie* (Key Problems of Philosophy), Leipzig: Göschen.

—— (1911) *Philosophische Kultur. Gesammelte Essais* (Philosophical Culture. Collected Essays), Leipzig: W. Klinkhardt.

—— (1922) *Zur Philosophie der Kunst. Philosophische und kunstphilosophische Aufsätze* (On the Philosophy of Art. Articles on Philosophy and Philosophy of Art), ed. G. Simmel, Potsdam: Kiepenheuer.

—— (1987) *Das individuelle Gesetz. Philosophische Exkurse* (The Individual Law. Philosophical Excursions), ed. M. Landmann with afterword by K.C. Köhnke, Frankfurt: Suhrkamp.

—— (1959) *Georg Simmel, 1858–1918. A Collection of Essays with Translations and a Bibliography*, ed. K.H. Wolff, Columbus, OH: Ohio State University Press.

—— (1968) *The Conflict in Modern Culture and Other Essays*, trans. and ed. P.K. Etzkorn, New York: Teachers College Press.

—— (1971) *On Individuality and Social Forms. Selected Writings*, ed. D.N. Levine, Chicago, IL: University of Chicago Press.

Lawrence, P.A. (ed.) (1976) *Georg Simmel: Sociologist and European*, trans. D.E. Jenkinson *et al.* and with intro. by P.A. Lawrence, Sunbury: Nelson.

Simmel, G. (1980) *Essays on Interpretation in Social Science*, trans. and ed. G. Oakes, Manchester: Manchester University Press.

Frisby, D. and Featherstone, M. (eds) (1996) *Simmel on Culture: Selected Writings*, with intro. by D. Frisby, London: Sage.

References and further reading

Frisby, D. (1984) *Georg Simmel*, London: Tavistock. (An introduction to his social theory.)

—— (1992) *Simmel and Since*, London: Routledge. (Essays on Simmel's social theory.)

—— (ed.) (1994) *Georg Simmel. Critical Assessments*, London: Routledge, 3 vols. (Assessments of most aspects of Simmel's work and key early reviews.)

Kaern, M., Phillips, B. and Cohen, R.S. (eds) (1990) *Georg Simmel and Contemporary Sociology*, Dordrecht, Boston, MA, and London: Kluwer. (A valuable collection, also containing essays on aspects of Simmel's philosophy.)

Köhnke, K.C. (1996) *Der junge Simmel* (The Young Simmel), Frankfurt: Suhrkamp. (The first systematic examination of Simmel's early philosophical writings.)

Kracauer, S. (1995) 'Georg Simmel' in *The Mass Ornament*, Cambridge, MA: Harvard University Press, 225–7. (A brief introduction to Simmel's philosophy by one of his students.)

Poggi, G. (1993) *Money and the Modern Mind*, Berkeley, CA, and London: University of California Press. (An introduction to Simmel's *Philosophy of Money*.)

(1991) 'A Special Issue on Georg Simmel', *Theory, Culture & Society* 8 (3). (Contains translations and essays largely on culture.)

Weingartner, R.H. (1962) *Experience and Culture: The Philosophy of Georg Simmel*, Middletown, CT: Wesleyan University Press. (Looks especially at his later philosophy.)

Weinstein, D. and Weinstein, M. (1993) *Postmodern(ized) Simmel*, London: Routledge. (Relates Simmel's philosophy to postmodern theorists.)

DAVID FRISBY

SIMPLE TYPE THEORY *see*
THEORY OF TYPES

SIMPLICITY (IN SCIENTIFIC THEORIES)

In evaluating which of several competing hypotheses is most plausible, scientists often use simplicity as a guide. This raises three questions: what makes one hypothesis simpler than another? Why should a difference in simplicity make a difference in what we believe? And how much weight should simplicity receive, compared with other considerations, in judging a hypothesis' plausibility? These may be termed the descriptive, the normative, and the weighting problems, respectively. The aesthetic and pragmatic appeal of more simple theories is transparent; the puzzle is how simplicity can be a guide to truth.

1   **Curve-fitting, parsimony and unification**
2   **Bayesian approaches**
3   **Popper**
4   **Akaike**

1   Curve-fitting, parsimony and unification

Considerations of simplicity play a role in the *curve-fitting problem*, depicted in the figure. Suppose a scientist wants to discover what general relationship obtains between the independent variable x and the dependent variable y, and pursues this question by gathering a set of observations, each of which corresponds to a point.

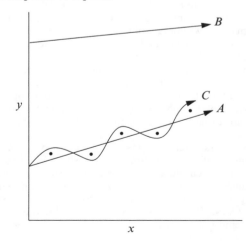

What role might the data play in evaluating different competing hypotheses, each of which corresponds to a curve? If observational error is impossible, then any curve that fails to pass exactly through the data points must be false. However, error is always possible. This means that the true curve may fail to pass exactly through the data points. How, then, are the data to be used?

The standard scientific procedure is to use the concept of 'goodness-of-fit'. Consider Curve A. For each data point, compute the squared distance from the observed y-value to the y-value that Curve A predicts. The 'sum of squares' (SOS) measures how far the curve is from the data. If SOS measures how well the data support the curve in question, then the data in the figure support Curve A better than they support Curve B.

The rationale for SOS as a measure of evidential support is not far to seek. Curves that are close to the data are more likely, in the technical sense defined by R.A. Fisher (1925). Curve A is more likely than Curve B (given standard assumptions about the probability of error) because A confers on the data a higher probability than B does: P(Data | Curve A) > P(Data | Curve B). It is important in this context not to confuse likelihood and probability. The conclusion is not that A is more probable – that is, that P(Curve A| Data) > P(Curve B| Data).

Although likelihood as measured by SOS helps discriminate between Curve A and Curve B, it says nothing concerning how A compares with Curve C. They have the same SOS values. It is at this point that simplicity is said to be relevant. Curve A is smooth and Curve C is bumpy. Curve A seems more simple. If simplicity guides our judgements about which curve is more plausible, we will conclude that Curve A is superior to Curve C, given the data at hand.

If curve-fitting is subject to the twin criteria of goodness-of-fit and simplicity, the descriptive, normative, and weighing problems must all be addressed. The last of these is quite fundamental. In general, the goodness-of-fit of a hypothesis can be improved by making it more complicated. In fact, with n data points, *perfect* goodness-of-fit (an SOS of zero) can always be secured by a polynomial of degree n (that is, an equation of the form $y = a_1 + a_2x + a_3x^2 + \ldots + a_nx^{n-1}$). If there are just two data points, a straight line will fit them perfectly; if there are three, a parabola can be found with an SOS of zero, and so on. The practice of science is to view goodness-of-fit as one consideration relevant to evaluating hypotheses, but not the only one. The problem is to understand that practice.

Simplicity considerations play a role in other inferential contexts. Ockham's razor, the principle of parsimony, says that hypotheses that postulate fewer entities, causes or processes are better than hypotheses that postulate more. In addition, the preference for simpler hypotheses finds expression in the idea that a unified theory that covers two bodies of phenomena is sometimes more plausible than a disunified theory that treats them as separate and independent. An adequate account of the role of simplicity in curve-fitting should bring in its wake an understanding of the value that science seems to place on parsimonious and unified theories.

2   Bayesian approaches

Bayes' theorem shows how the posterior probability $P(H \mid O)$ of a hypothesis – the probability that H has, given that the observation O has been made – is related to the probability $P(H)$ the hypothesis had prior to the observation: $P(H \mid O) = P(O \mid H)P(H)/P(O)$ (see PROBABILITY, INTERPRETATIONS OF §5; STATISTICS §2). When two hypotheses, H_1 and H_2, are evaluated in light of the observations O, the theorem entails that $P(H_1 \mid O) > P(H_2 \mid O)$ if and only if $P(O_1)P(H_1) > P(O \mid H_2)P(H_2)$. That is, if H_1 has the higher posterior probability, then it must have the higher likelihood or the higher prior probability (or both).

Let us apply the Bayesian framework to the curve-fitting problem represented in the figure. How could Curve A have a higher posterior probability than Curve C, relative to the data depicted? There are two possibilities to explore, and one of them will not help. We have already noted that the two curves have the same likelihoods. This means that a Bayesian must argue that Curve A has the higher prior probability.

However, if prior probabilities are to be assigned to curves, a problem arises. The straight lines in the x–y plane are not denumerable. Apparently, they are equally simple. If their prior probabilities are to reflect just their simplicity, then they must be assigned the same prior probability – namely, zero. But hypotheses assigned a prior probability of zero cannot increase in probability when favourable evidence is obtained.

An alternative approach would be to assign probabilities, not to specific curves, but to families of curves. For example, the straight lines comprise a family of curves (LIN), each having the form $y = a_1 + a_2x$, while (PAR) is the family of parabolas, each having the form $y = a_1 + a_2x + a_3x^2$. In these equations, the a_i terms are *adjustable parameters*; members of the family are specified by assigning values to these parameters.

If the assignment of prior probabilities is limited to a denumerable set of such families, with simpler families receiving higher values, it is possible to construct an infinite series of positive prior probabilities that converges on a sum that is not greater than unity. This is the approach that Harold Jeffreys (1957) adopts.

It is important to take care that the families in this series are disjoint. For example, since (LIN) is included in (PAR), (LIN) cannot have a higher probability. With nested families of curves, more complex families have higher probabilities. One solution is to define the family (PAR'), which is the subset of (PAR) in which all adjustable parameters are nonzero. No contradiction ensues if one assigns (LIN) a higher prior than (PAR').

However, a problem now arises, one that concerns Bayesianism in general. If prior probabilities merely report an agent's subjective degrees of belief, then there is no reason why we should assign (LIN) a higher prior than (PAR') rather than doing the reverse. And once this normative question is addressed, it must puzzle the Bayesian why (LIN) should be more probable than (PAR'). After all, (LIN), in effect, sets the parameter $a_3 = 0$, while (PAR') stipulates that $a_3 \neq 0$. What could show that the former is more probable than the latter?

Bayesians may reply that their goal is to describe the practice of science, not to justify it. Another option is to abandon the goal of analysing the complexity of families of curves and to focus exclusively on some denumerable set of curves with no adjustable parameters. A third would be to theorize about the likelihoods of families of curves as a measure of their simplicity (Rosenkrantz 1977).

3 Popper

Karl POPPER (1959) turns the Bayesian approach on its head. For him, the goal of science is to find highly *im*probable hypotheses. Hypotheses should be valued for their falsifiability – for their saying more, rather than less. Popper conjoins this requirement with the idea that we should reject hypotheses that have been falsified. So the two-part epistemology he proposes is that we should prefer hypotheses that are unfalsified though highly falsifiable. This means that we should prefer (LIN) over (PAR) if neither has been falsified by the data. (LIN) is more falsifiable, says Popper, because at least three data points are needed to falsify it; for (PAR) to be falsified, at least four observations are required.

One problem for Popper's proposal arises when it is applied to equations that contain no adjustable parameters. If we consider, not (LIN) and (PAR), but some specific straight line and some specific

parabola, then each can be falsified by a single observation. All specific curves are equally falsifiable.

A further limitation in the Popperian approach should be noted. A purely deductivist methodology cannot explain why scientists reasonably decline to reject curves that fail to pass exactly through the data points. The three curves in the accompanying figure are all 'falsified' by the data. However, as Popper sometimes intimates, a more adequate assessment of the fit of hypotheses to data is afforded by the concept of likelihood; rather than considering the yes/no question of whether a hypothesis has been falsified, we need to consider the quantitative issue of the degree to which a hypothesis says that the observations were to be expected. It is arbitrary to impose on that continuum a cut-off point that separates the stipulated categories of 'falsified' and 'unfalsified'. However, once likelihood is substituted for the concept of deductive falsification, the weighting problem arises as a significant issue.

4 Akaike

The statistician, H. Akaike and his school have developed a set of theorems that show how the predictive accuracy of a family of curves may be estimated (1973).

The predictive accuracy of a family reflects how well it does in predicting new data when its parameters are estimated from an old data set. Consider (LIN) as an example. First find the member of (LIN) that best fits the available data, D_1. This straight line is the likeliest member of that family; call it L(LIN). Then obtain a new set of data, D_2, from the true (and unknown) underlying curve, and measure how well L(LIN) fits D_2. Now imagine repeating this process, first finding the best fitting member of (LIN) with respect to one data set and then using that curve to predict new data. The average performance of (LIN) defines its predictive accuracy, which also might be termed its closeness to the truth.

Akaike's theorem says that the following provides an *unbiased* estimate of the distance from the truth of family F:

Estimate (Distance from the truth of family F)

$$= \mathrm{SOS}[L(F)] + 2k\sigma^2 + \text{constant}$$

Here k is the number of adjustable parameters in F, and σ^2 is the error variance – the degree of dispersion of observations around the true curve. The third addend disappears when hypotheses are compared with each other, and so may be ignored.

The second addend in the displayed equation gives simplicity its due: the complexity of a family is measured by how many adjustable parameters it contains. It is important to note that the number of adjustable parameters is not a syntactic feature of an equation. Although the equations '$y = ax + bx$' and '$y = ax + bz$' may each seem to contain two parameters (a and b), this is not the case. The former equation can be *reparameterized*. Let $a' = a + b$; now the first equation can be restated as '$y = a'x$'. In fact, the first equation contains one parameter, while the second contains two.

The second term in Akaike's theorem, besides adverting to the number of adjustable parameters, also mentions the error variance. When this variance is large, this second term plays a larger role in estimating the family's distance from the truth; when observations are largely free of error, it makes only a negligible contribution. Simplicity cannot matter when observational error is impossible; it matters more and more as the data become noisier.

Akaike's theorem applies to one of the most famous examples of the role of simplicity considerations in hypothesis evaluation – the dispute between Copernican and Ptolemaic astronomy. In Ptolemy's geocentric model, the relative motion of the earth and the sun is replicated within the model for each planet; the result is a system containing a very large number of adjustable parameters. Copernicus decomposed the apparent motion of the planets into their individual motions around the sun and a *common* sun–earth component, thereby drastically reducing the number of adjustable parameters. In *De revolutionibus*, Copernicus argued that the weakness of Ptolemaic astronomy derives from its failure to impose principled constraints on the separate planetary models. Thomas Kuhn (1957) and others have claimed that the greater unification and 'harmony' of the Copernican system is a merely aesthetic feature. The Akaike framework offers a quite different diagnosis: since the Copernican system fitted the data then available about as well as the Ptolemaic system did, Akaike's theorem entails that the former had an *astronomically* superior degree of estimated predictive accuracy.

See also: CONFIRMATION THEORY; INDUCTIVE INFERENCE; INFERENCE TO THE BEST EXPLANATION; SCIENTIFIC REALISM AND ANTIREALISM; STATISTICS; THEORETICAL (EPISTEMIC) VIRTUES

References and further reading

* Akaike, H. (1973) 'Information Theory and an Extension of the Maximum Likelihood Principle', in B. Petrov and F. Csaki (eds) *Second International Symposium on Information Theory*, Budapest: Akademiai Kiado, 267–81. (Develops the Akaike information criterion for estimating a model's predictive accuracy.)

* Fisher, R.A. (1925) *Statistical Methods for Research Workers*, Edinburgh: Oliver & Boyd. (Presents likelihood as a measure of the degree to which a set of observations supports a hypothesis.)

Forster, M. and Sober, E. (1994) 'How to Tell when Simpler, More Unified, or Less *Ad Hoc* Theories will Provide More Accurate Predictions', *British Journal for the Philosophy of Science* 45: 1–36. (Provides exposition and application of Akaike's ideas, as well as criticism of some other proposals.)

Hesse, M. (1967) 'Simplicity', in P. Edwards (ed.) *The Encyclopedia of Philosophy*, New York: Macmillan, vol. 7, 445–8. (A useful overview of philosophical accounts.)

Howson, C. (1988) 'On the Consistency of Jeffreys's Simplicity Postulate and its Role in Bayesian Inference', *Philosophical Quarterly* 38: 68–83. (Defends Jeffreys' approach against Popper's criticisms, but concludes that it is ultimately unworkable.)

* Jeffreys, H. (1957) *Scientific Inference*, Cambridge: Cambridge University Press, 2nd edn. (Presents a Bayesian solution to the problem of understanding the role of simplicity in hypothesis evaluation.)

* Kuhn, T. (1957) *The Copernican Revolution*, Cambridge, MA: Princeton University Press. (Argues that the appeal to 'harmony' that Copernicus made in defence of his hypothesis invoked a merely aesthetic consideration.)

* Popper, K. (1959) *The Logic of Scientific Discovery*, London: Hutchinson. (Defends the idea that the simplicity of a hypothesis reflects its degree of falsifiability, and for this reason is relevant to the task of hypothesis evaluation.)

* Rosenkrantz, R. (1977) *Inference, Method, and Decision*, Dordrecht: Reidel. (A Bayesian proposal in which simplicity is connected with the idea of average likelihood.)

Sober, E. (1988) *Reconstructing the Past: Parsimony, Evolution and Inference*, Cambridge, MA: MIT Press. (Explores why common cause explanations are superior to separate cause explanations in the context of the evolutionary problem of phylogenetic inference.)

—— (1994) 'Let's Razor Ockham's Razor', in E. Sober (ed.) *From a Biological Point of View*, Cambridge: Cambridge University Press, 136–57. (Argues that invoking the principle of parsimony is a surrogate for an assumed background theory, which, once stated explicitly, renders appeal to parsimony superfluous.)

ELLIOTT SOBER

SIMPLICITY, DIVINE

To be complex is to have many parts. To be simple is to have few. Theists of all religious traditions have asserted that God is completely simple – that is, has no parts of any sort. A contemporary statement of this doctrine of divine simplicity would add that God is identical with each of his intrinsic attributes. Thus if God is omnipotent and omniscient, for example, then he is identical with omnipotence and omniscience (and so these attributes are also identical). The doctrine's popularity across traditions may rest on theists' shared convictions that God is the ultimate reality, perfect, and creator of all that is not himself, and on the fact that many theists have thought that each of these claims entails the doctrine of divine simplicity. It may also rest on strands of mystical experience common to many traditions.

The doctrine has played an important part in ontological arguments for the existence of God because of its assertion of the identity of God with God's nature (if the latter in some sense exists, so must the former). Indeed, divine simplicity is near the conceptual core of classical theism; it is one chief reason classical theists think God immutable, impassible, timeless and wholly distinct from the universe. Many who oppose divine simplicity do so because of these other doctrines it entails. Other recent critics have charged that divine simplicity makes God a mere abstract entity or requires him to have all his attributes necessarily or all contingently.

1 **The popularity of simplicity**
2 **The case for simplicity**
3 **Challenges to simplicity**

1 The popularity of simplicity

The claim that God is simple asserts that God has no parts of any sort. Different thinkers have had different inventories of kinds of part. But the doctrine of divine simplicity claims that *whatever* kinds of part there are, God lacks them. (This is why Trinitarian Christians have been able to accept divine simplicity: whatever the Trinity's persons are, they are not parts of God (see TRINITY).) So thinkers' beliefs in different kinds of part need not give them different versions of divine simplicity. Medieval friends of divine simplicity treated intrinsic accidental attributes and essential attributes distinct from their subject as among its parts (see, for example, *Summa theologiae* Ia 3, 3 and 6). So the doctrine of divine simplicity led them to say that God lacks these, that is, that God is not distinct from his essential attributes and has no intrinsic accidents. Given divine simplicity, then, if God is

essentially omnipotent, God is identical to omnipotence. 'Omnipotence' *seems* to pick out an essential attribute God has, but *really* refers just to God. Further, if God is essentially omniscient, God is identical to omniscience, and so omniscience is identical to omnipotence.

But there is a question as to how we interpret these attribute-identities. Most medieval thinkers before Duns Scotus held that, save for 'proper accidents' (of which a simple God has none), if necessarily whatever is *F* is *G* and whatever is *G* is *F*, *F*ness and *G*ness are identical. But these thinkers used a concept of necessity weaker than broadly logical necessity (see Knuuttila 1993). As they use the term 'necessary', it can be the case that necessarily whatever is *F* is *G* and vice versa even if it is *logically* possible that something be *F* but not *G*. On their modal views, then, it can be logically possible that something be *F* but not *G* and yet be the case that *F*ness and *G*ness are identical. So if pre-Scotus medieval philosophers say that intrinsic divine attributes are identical, they may make a weaker claim than we would make by these words. If *we* say that *F*ness is identical to *G*ness, we imply that nothing can be *F* but not *G*. If medieval philosophers who say that *F*ness is identical to *G*ness do not imply this, then our concept of identity may not correctly represent their claim. Thus medieval versions of divine simplicity may not identify all of God's intrinsic attributes, but only those *F*s and *G*s for which they would say that nothing can be *F* but not *G* or *G* but not *F*. So perhaps divine simplicity's medieval partisans would let God have logically contingent attributes distinct from his essence (Stump and Kretzmann 1985). Still, many medieval arguments which deny that God has intrinsic accidents work as well against the claim that God has logically contingent attributes (see, for example, *Summa theologiae* Ia, 3, 6). So it is likely that the modal theory medieval philosophers employ betrays their intent, and that they *meant* to identify God with all of God's intrinsic attributes.

Divine simplicity has been in the mainstream of Western theism at least since ARISTOTLE (§16). It moved from Middle Platonism into Judaism through Philo of Alexandria. The doctrine entered Christianity through such Church Fathers as Athenagoras, Irenaeus and Clement of Alexandria (see PLATONISM, MEDIEVAL §§1–2). It became orthodox in AUGUSTINE (§7) and reigned unchallenged through to the time of Duns Scotus. The key to Plotinus' theology, and so to the change from Middle Platonism to Neoplatonism, is his making divine simplicity the core of his account of the One, the supreme God; as Stoicism and Epicureanism faded away, versions of Platonism embodying divine simplicity became the theology of late paganism (see PLOTINUS §3; NEO-PLATONISM §3). Divine simplicity was the main point at issue in one of the earliest Islamic theological debates, that over the status of the divine attributes. This debate later became that between orthodox Islamic theologians and partisans of Aristotle, and so enlisted Ibn Sina, al-Ghazali and Ibn Rushd (see ISLAMIC THEOLOGY §3). Given the ties between medieval Arabic and Jewish philosophy, divine simplicity naturally became a prime topic of medieval Jewish theology as well. Mystics of all periods, East and West, have claimed divine simplicity as a direct deliverance of their experience.

2 The case for simplicity

One may well wonder why (save for mystical experience) theists of so many traditions and times concur in the doctrine of divine simplicity, or even care about so abstract a claim. One reason is that basic theistic intuitions seem to converge on divine simplicity. The intuition that God is the ultimate reality (see GOD, CONCEPTS OF §1) suggests divine simplicity, for anything composed of parts (or having distinct attributes) is less basic than they and depends on them (*Summa contra gentiles* I, 18). The intuition that God is creator of all that is distinct from himself suggests divine simplicity, for if God was composed of parts or had essential attributes distinct from himself, these would be distinct from him, yet he could not have created them without creating himself. The intuition that God is perfect suggests divine simplicity, for (at least to classical theists) it suggests that God is maximally self-sufficient. Whatever has parts or essential attributes distinct from itself depends on these and so is less self-sufficient than a simple being.

A second reason for divine simplicity's popularity has been that it is a fertile source of further claims about God; it yields a strong, interesting theological theory. First, if God is simple, then:

(N) necessarily, whatever is God is simple.

For if God is simple, the attribute of being divine is identical to the attribute of being simple. (N) entails that whatever is God is:

Unique. There can be at most one God. For suppose that there are two simple beings, *A* and *B*. *A* and *B* must differ in some attribute, else they would be identical. So suppose that *A* and *B* differ in that *A* has and *B* lacks an attribute *F*. If *F* is the attribute of being simple, then if *A* and *B* are both simple, both *A* and *B* have it. But *A* and *B* differ in *F*. So *F* is not being simple. But then if *A* has *F*, *A* has two distinct attributes, *F* and being simple. Whatever has two distinct attributes is not simple; all of a simple being's

attributes are identical, as all are identical with the simple being itself. Hence if *A* has *F*, *A* is not simple. So only *B* is simple. Thus there can be at most one simple being. So given (N), there can be at most one God: divine simplicity guarantees monotheism. This helped draw Jews and Muslims to divine simplicity, given their creedal emphasis that God is one; Maimonides was so enthusiastic as to argue that monotheism entails divine simplicity (see *The Guide for the Perplexed*). The tie to monotheism may also have commended divine simplicity to Trinitarian Christians facing charges of tritheism (see MONO-THEISM).

Immaterial. Whatever has matter in its make-up contains that matter's parts. Divine simplicity thus guarantees God's complete distinctness from the universe, or his transcendence.

Immutable. Whatever changes becomes different in a part or attribute (else there was no change), yet is the same in some parts or attributes (else there was not change, but a thing's disappearing and being replaced by another). So what has no parts or distinct attributes cannot change (see IMMUTABILITY §§1–2). Aquinas and many others argue that any immutable substance is:

Timeless. It has no past or future, its life neither containing nor located in any series of earlier and later events (*Summa theologiae* Ia, 9, 1 and 10, 2). So if this is right, divine simplicity entails timelessness (see ETERNITY).

If nothing created God, divine simplicity guarantees that God is:

A se. God is entirely independent. For if God has no parts or distinct attributes, nothing can make a causal contribution to his existence except by making him *ex nihilo*, or out of no prior material. If God is *a se*, he is:

Impassible. He is completely unaffected by other things. If other things affected God, putting him in a state *S*, God would depend on those things for *S* and so not be wholly *a se*. Further, given divine simplicity, God would be identical with *S*. So whatever caused *S* to exist would have caused God to exist.

Given appealing assumptions, divine simplicity entails that God is:

Necessarily existent. If he exists, he cannot fail to exist. Assume that:

(a) God exists,

(b) if *P* is actual, then necessarily, *P* is at least possible (the Brouwer axiom), and

(c) entities have attributes only if they actually exist.

Given (a) and (b), then necessarily, it is possible that God exists. On (c), if possibly God exists, this is because some entity has an attribute which makes this true: presumably because God's nature exists and is possibly exemplified. So given (a)–(c), necessarily, God's nature exists. On divine simplicity, God is identical to God's nature. So if God's nature exists necessarily, God exists necessarily. So given (b), (c) and divine simplicity, if God exists, God exists necessarily (see NECESSARY BEING §§1–2).

Divine simplicity explains the common theistic claim that God is present as a whole wherever he is present (see OMNIPRESENCE §4): what has no parts is present as a whole if at all. Again, given divine simplicity, God's psyche is peculiarly simple. This can help to explain God's moral perfection. Traditionally, this includes *impeccability*, or inability to sin (see, for example, *Summa theologiae* Ia, 25, 3 *ad.* 2). If God is simple and wants to do good, then God is impeccable. For given divine simplicity, all God's desires are identical with God's desire to do good. So if nothing can be both a desire to do good and a desire to do evil, God cannot have a desire to do evil. But his necessary omniscience guarantees that he cannot do evil through ignorance, and his necessary omnipotence guarantees that nothing can force him to do evil. So divine simplicity, a desire to do good, necessary omnipotence and necessary omniscience yield impeccability. Again, if God's psyche is simple, his knowing is identical to his willing. This generates appealing theories about God's relation to morality and modality (Mann 1989), as does divine simplicity's implication that God is identical to God's nature (Kretzmann 1983).

Divine simplicity implies all these conclusions, but most do not in turn entail divine simplicity. Thus divine simplicity is one of the strongest, most basic assertions of theologies in which it appears; it is near the conceptual roots of the classical theist's concept of God (see GOD, CONCEPTS OF §6).

A third reason for divine simplicity's popularity has been its connection with efforts to prove God's existence. Historically, Aristotelians inferred divine simplicity directly from their cosmological arguments (for example, *Summa theologiae* Ia, 3, 1–7) (see GOD, ARGUMENTS FOR THE EXISTENCE OF §1). Given actualism, 'possibly God exists' entails 'God's nature exists', and given divine simplicity, God is identical to God's nature. So given divine simplicity plus actualism:

(P)   'possibly God exists' entails 'God exists'.

(P) is a key premise of many ontological arguments for God's existence (see GOD, ARGUMENTS FOR THE EXISTENCE OF §§2–3). Good prospects (as they thought) for proving a simple being's existence likely gave Western religious thinkers further reason to

embrace divine simplicity; by so doing, they believed, they could help give theism rational warrant.

3   Challenges to simplicity

Islam rejected divine simplicity in reacting against Aristotelianism; some Jewish philosophers (for example, Crescas) also rejected it. Within Christianity, divine simplicity's first real challenge was Duns Scotus' positing of a 'formal distinction' between divine attributes, faculties, and so on. Other challenges arose in Leibniz, Spinoza, Hegel, and nineteenth- and twentieth-century theology. Some reject divine simplicity because it implies other doctrines they question: it has been a casualty in revolts against divine immutability, impassibility, timelessness and distinctness from the universe. Thus one must in part pursue the case against divine simplicity in cases against these other doctrines.

Recent discussion in analytic philosophy has focused on divine simplicity itself. Some philosophers (for example, Plantinga 1980) reject divine simplicity on the grounds that since it entails that God is identical to God's attributes, it entails that God *is* an attribute, an abstract object. But this need not follow: it may follow only that the one thing which is both God and an attribute has divine attributes and also some attributes typical of abstract objects, a claim theists endorse anyway.

Some philosophers (for example, Morris 1985) raise a problem of modal uniformity: if all God's attributes are identical, God has all attributes necessarily or all contingently. But God seems to have both necessary and contingent attributes: he is necessarily omnipotent, but only contingently the creator of Adam (since he need not have created Adam). Perhaps divine simplicity need not face this problem; as we have seen, the medieval philosophers may not have meant to identify all of God's attributes. But if they did, advocates of divine simplicity can perhaps counter by distinguishing attributes from predicates. Even if God has just one intrinsic attribute, that attribute, coupled with God's *relations* to other things, may let God satisfy some predicates necessarily and others contingently. God necessarily satisfies '… is omniscient', because every possible world contains only truths God would know if he created that world. God contingently satisfies '… is Creator of Adam' because only in some possible worlds is there an Adam. The difference in modality rests on entities outside God and their relations to God.

If God cannot have logically contingent intrinsic attributes but has created Adam, it may follow that the inner intrinsic state of God by which he knows and has created Adam might instead have not known and not created Adam, without itself being intrinsically any different. Is this conceivable? Consider a complex entity consisting of God plus the world he makes. If this complex entity contains the world, it is different if the world is different, but it does not follow that God himself is different. On an 'externalist' view of divine mental content, this complex entity could be God's mind. On the more usual picture, God's mind is wholly internal to God, and a difference in God's mind is prior to and explains a difference in the world. On an 'externalist' picture of God's mind, a difference in God's mind *includes* a difference in the world, but may not include a difference in God himself. If divine intrinsic simplicity does preclude God's having logically contingent intrinsic attributes, perhaps its price is that we are always in God's mind.

See also: NATURAL THEOLOGY; NEGATIVE THEOLOGY

References and further reading

* Aquinas, T. (1259–65) *Summa contra gentiles* I, trans. A. Pegis, Notre Dame, IN: University of Notre Dame Press, 1975. (Classic statement of classical theism built around divine simplicity.)
* —— (1266–73) *Summa theologiae*, trans. Dominican Fathers, New York: Benziger Brothers, 1948. (Classic statement of divine-simplicity-centred classical theism.)
  Aristotle (mid 4th century BC) *Physics*, trans. R. Hardie and R. Gaye, in R. McKeon (ed.) *The Basic Works of Aristotle*, New York: Random House, 1941. (Gives his argument for God's existence, and ties it to divine simplicity.)
  Athenagoras (177) *An Embassy for the Christians*, trans. B. Pratten, in A. Roberts and J. Donaldson (eds) *Ante-Nicene Fathers*, vol. 2, Peabody, MA: Hendrickson, 1994. (Second-century Christian adopts divine simplicity; see page 132.)
  Clement (194–201) *Stromata*, trans. A. Coxe, in A. Roberts and J. Donaldson (eds) *Ante-Nicene Fathers*, vol. 2, Peabody, MA: Hendrickson, 1994. (Rambles through many topics, including divine simplicity; see page 464.)
  Hughes, C. (1989) *On a Complex Theory of a Simple God*, Ithaca, NY: Cornell University Press. (Excellent extended critique of divine simplicity. Rigorous but not technical.)
  Irenaeus (182–8) *Against Heresies*, trans. A. Coxe, in A. Roberts and J. Donaldson (eds) *Ante-Nicene Fathers*, vol. 1, Peabody, MA: Hendrickson, 1994. (Early Christian adopts the doctrine of divine simplicity; see page 374.)
* Knuuttila, S. (1993) *Modalities in Medieval Philosophy*, New York: Routledge. (Gold mine of information on evolving concepts of necessity. Occasionally technical.)
* Kretzmann, N. (1983) 'Abraham, Isaac and Euthyphro', in D. Stump (ed.) *Hamartia*, Toronto, Ont.: Mellen, 27–50. (Divine simplicity and meta-ethics. Very clear.)
* Maimonides, M. (*c.*1190) *The Guide for the Perplexed*, trans. M. Friedlander, New York: Dover, 1956. (Jewish version of classical theism; extended treatment of divine simplicity and its implications.)
  Mann, W. (1982) 'Divine Simplicity', *Religious Studies* 18 (4): 451–71. (Reply to Plantinga, exposition of divine simplicity. Criticized by Morris (1985).)
  —— (1983) 'Simplicity and Immutability in God', *International Philosophical Quarterly* 23 (3): 267–76. (Rebuts a number of objections to divine simplicity.)
  —— (1988) 'God's Freedom, Human Freedom, and God's Responsibility for Sin' in T. Morris (ed.) *Divine and Human Action*, Ithaca, NY: Cornell University Press, 182–210. (Clear discussion of surprising connections between these issues and divine simplicity.)
* —— (1989) 'Modality, Morality and God', *Noûs* 23 (1): 83–99. (Elegant discussion of divine simplicity's implications for meta-ethics and God's relation to necessary truth.)
  Miller, B. (1996) *A Most Unlikely God*, Notre Dame, IN: Notre Dame University Press. (Defends divine simplicity, skilful but idiosyncratic.)
* Morris, T. (1985) 'Of God and Mann', *Religious Studies* 21 (3): 299–318. (Forceful, clear reply to Mann (1982); poses modal uniformity problem.)
  Philo (first half of first century AD) *Legum allegoria*, in F. Colson and G. Whitaker (trans) *Philo*, vol. 1, Cambridge, MA: Loeb Classical Library, Harvard University Press. (Jewish Platonist adopts divine simplicity; see page 225.)
* Plantinga, A. (1980) *Does God Have a Nature?*, Milwaukee, WI: Marquette University Press. (Criticizes the doctrine of divine simplicity during a broader treatment of God's relation to necessary truth.)
* Stump, E. and Kretzmann, N. (1985) 'Absolute Simplicity', *Faith and Philosophy* 2 (4): 353–82. (Careful reading of Aquinas' version of divine simplicity as allowing contingent intrinsic attributes. Relates divine simplicity to divine freedom and issues in philosophical theology.)
  Wolfson, H. (1977) *The Philosophy of the Kalam*, Cambridge, MA: Harvard University Press. (Largely about the medieval Islamic debate over divine simplicity.)
  —— (1979) *Repercussions of the Kalam in Jewish*

Philosophy, Cambridge, MA: Harvard University Press. (Largely about the medieval Jewish debate over divine simplicity.)

Wolterstorff, N. (1991) 'Divine Simplicity, in J. Tomberlin (ed.) *Philosophical Perspectives V: Philosophy of Religion*, Atascadero, CA: Ridgeview, 531–52. (Accessible account of divine simplicity and the medieval writers' treatment of attributes as parts of their subjects.)

BRIAN LEFTOW

SIMPLICIUS (*fl.* first half 6th century AD)

Simplicius of Cilicia, a Greek Neoplatonic philosopher and polymath, lived in the eastern part of the Roman Empire. He is the author of the most learned commentaries on Aristotle produced in antiquity, works which rest upon the accumulated accomplishments of ancient Greek philosophy and science. In them he gives numerous illuminating references and explanations that not only lead to a fuller understanding of Aristotle, but also allow one to reconstruct the history of the interpretation and criticism of Aristotelian doctrines in antiquity. The main principle that guides Simplicius' exegesis is the conviction that most Greek philosophers, including some Presocratics, can be brought into agreement with Neoplatonism. Simplicius adduces copious quotations to prove his point, thereby supplying us with substantial fragments from lost works of thinkers like Parmenides, Empedocles, Anaxagoras, Eudemus and the Stoics. A devout pagan, Simplicius sought to defend traditional Greek religion and philosophy against the oppressive dominance of Christianity. His commentaries have influenced the reception and interpretation of Aristotle's philosophy ever since.

1. Life and writings
2. Hermeneutics and ethics
3. Physics
4. Logic and mathematics
5. Influence

1 Life and writings

The circumstances of Simplicius' life are largely unknown. He was probably slightly older than his great rival, the Christian commentator and theologian John PHILOPONUS. Simplicius studied first at Alexandria under AMMONIUS, SON OF HERMEAS, the influential philosophical head of the school there, and later under DAMASCIUS, the last head of the Neoplatonic school at Athens. The course of Simplicius' life and career underwent dramatic change in 529, when, in the wake of the empire's anti-pagan policies, the Emperor Justinian I closed the Athenian school of philosophy. During the crisis, seven Athenian philosophers, among them Simplicius, Damascius and Priscian, emigrated to Persia where Chosroës I enjoyed a reputation as a philosopher-king. Their sojourn was disappointing and brief. The philosophers left the Persian court when, in a peace treaty between Persia and Byzantium in 532, Chosroës' diplomacy secured them the liberty to live on Roman territory without fear of persecution, although they were presumably barred from public teaching. Arabic sources, in conjunction with inconclusive evidence in Greek texts, suggest however that some of them were active in the Mesopotamian town of Carrhae (Harran), a pagan stronghold near the Persian border. Whether Simplicius belonged to this group, or returned to Athens, or indeed went elsewhere, is a matter of considerable controversy (see also ARISTOTLE COMMENTATORS).

Simplicius wrote his major works after the Persian adventure. With the exception perhaps of the relatively late commentary on Aristotle's *Categories*, these are pieces of scholarship to be read, rather than lectures delivered in class. There seem to be no further treatises extant in manuscript form. Works on Iamblichus and on Hermogenes' rhetoric are lost, and perhaps even a commentary on Aristotle's *Metaphysics*, which is referred to in the commentary on Aristotle's *On the Soul*. This latter work bears Simplicius' name, but is of inferior quality and has plausibly been attributed to Simplicius' contemporary Priscian. If this is correct, evidence for a *Metaphysics* commentary by Simplicius becomes slim.

2 Hermeneutics and ethics

Simplicius makes his hermeneutic position explicit in the commentary on the *Categories*, a set book for philosophical beginners. The scholars of the sixth century (Ammonius, Philoponus, Olympiodorus, Elias and Simplicius) all discuss, in the introductions to their lectures on the *Categories*, ten questions regarding Aristotle's philosophical corpus as a whole, its structure and its end. One of these questions concerns the qualifications and attitude of the proper exegete of Aristotle. The stock answer is that the interpreter, in addition to being knowledgeable, must strive to discern the truth and, if necessary, prefer it to Aristotle. Philoponus seems to have been the only one to put this maxim to practical use. Characteristically, Simplicius glosses over this requirement and emphasizes instead that rather than voice his own philosophical convictions the exegete should seek out the agreement between Plato and Aristotle. Likewise, the student should refrain from quibbling with Aristotle. Simplicius is convinced that the 'truth' can be found in the harmony of Plato, Aristotle and other inspired thinkers. Thus, he is prepared to accept doctrines on the basis of authority, especially if they can be shown to agree with the fundamental ideas of Neoplatonism (see NEOPLATONISM).

Simplicius' earliest surviving work, *On Epictetus' Manual*, is a commentary on the *Manual* (*Enchiridion*) of the Stoic philosopher EPICTETUS. In general, Neoplatonists scorned the materialist outlook of the Stoics (see STOICISM §3). Stoic ethics, however, conforms to the lowest level of the Neoplatonic system of moral instruction, which requires the practice of, in ascending order, political, purificatory and contemplative virtues. In the Preface, Simplicius explains that Epictetus' aphorisms and maxims are beneficial to those who want their bodies and desires to be ruled by rationality. A training in the political virtues resulting in a moderation of one's emotions initiates the ascent of the embodied soul through philosophy. The aim is the pure contemplation of intelligible Forms. This separation of the soul from the concerns of the body is also the road to salvation, and Simplicius conceives of his works simultaneously as intellectual and spiritual exercises. In a political atmosphere that increasingly suppressed and eradicated the remnants of paganism, his commentaries also protested against what he perceived as the blasphemy of the new religion.

3 Physics

The text that exemplifies this aspect most clearly is the commentary on Aristotle's *On the Heavens*. In one respect, it is a scholarly exegesis of Aristotle's cosmological treatise, enriched with invaluable information on ancient astronomy. A prominent feature, however, is the polemic against the renegade John Philoponus, a Christian Neoplatonist trained in Alexandria. At the very time when the Athenian philosophers were struggling for survival, Philoponus launched an attack on the Aristotelian-Neoplatonic doctrine of the eternity of the world by rejecting, among other points, Aristotle's theory of the existence of a celestial fifth element, aether (*On the Heavens* I.2–4). In an unprecedented spirit of criticism, Philoponus called the cogency of Aristotle's reasoning into doubt and argued that the supra- and sub-lunary regions are in fact of the same corruptible nature. In his reply, Simplicius offers the last defence in antiquity of Aristotle's controversial theory of aether. However, in the course of his counter-attack Simpli-

cius loses sight of the crucial point – Aristotle's postulate of a fifth elementary body that naturally displays circular motion. Simplicius interprets Aristotle as meaning something approximating Plato's theory (*Timaeus* 40a, 58c–d) that the heavens consist of a mixture of the purest grades of the four elements, in particular luminous fire (*On Aristotle's On the Heavens* 12.27–13.3; 85.7–15). Moreover, Simplicius holds that celestial motion is not caused by nature but rather by the agency of a celestial soul (78.17–80.13), a position Aristotle at one point explicitly rejected (*On the Heavens* II.1, but see also 285a29). Despite considerable reinterpretations such as these, the commentary turns into a grandiose reaffirmation of the divinity and eternity of the heavens and the universe as a whole. The sincere prayer to the creator-intellect with which Simplicius ends his work underscores the vital link, so characteristic of Neoplatonism, between philosophy and spirituality.

A less elevated work is the monumental commentary on Aristotle's *Physics*, which modern scholars have culled primarily for its invaluable reports and quotations from earlier philosophers, most importantly the Presocratics. Recent scholarship, however, has shown that here too Simplicius occasionally comes forward with original interpretations of fundamental concepts of Aristotle's natural philosophy. For example, ever since PLOTINUS (§4), many Neoplatonists had interpreted Aristotle's prime matter as incorporeal, formless and devoid of magnitude, an elusive entity capable of accepting the property of indefinite extension and thus becoming the substrate for all physical forms. In the sixth century, both Philoponus and Simplicius revised this idea and paved the way for a conception of matter as mass. Philoponus polemically rejected the notion of prime matter as incoherent and superfluous, positing three-dimensional extension as the lowest level of the physical world. Without entering into any kind of polemic, Simplicius chose to interpret the Aristotelian prime matter in a very similar way, calling it an extension and an indefinite diffusion (*Physics* commentary, 537.22–538.14).

This notion of prime matter is not easily distinguished from that of space. Like many thinkers before him, Simplicius finds fault with Aristotle's definition of a thing's place (*topos*) as the adjacent boundary of the containing body (*Physics* 212a2–6). However, he also rejects the notion of space (*chōra*) as empty extension, and in the so-called 'corollary on place' (*On Aristotle's Physics* 601–45) he conflates, much like Aristotle, the idea of 'extension' with that of 'location'. On the one hand, Simplicius speaks of place *qua* extended space as a substance that is both animate and immobile (623.19–21). On the other hand, he defines place as incorporeal but perceptible in bodies, an ordering of the position of each thing relative to others (642.14–21). Significantly, it is place that facilitates order in the physical universe, since it provides the physical images of the intelligible paradigms with structure and allows them to be similar to the paradigms (626.28–32).

A further example of Simplicius stepping beyond the bounds of mere exegesis is his discussion of time. Aristotle began his analysis in *Physics* (4.10) by presenting two arguments suggesting, paradoxically, that time is unreal. The premises (1) that the past exists no longer, (2) that the future exists not yet, and (3) that the present, being an instant, cannot be considered a 'part' of time (for as the temporal analogue of a point, it cannot serve as a measure of any length of time) seem to entail the unreality of time. Moreover, the view of the present as an instant renders mysterious how the present ever ceases to exist, for this can neither take place *at* the present instant nor *at* some later instant. In the so-called 'corollary on time' (*On Aristotle's Physics* 773–800) Simplicius points out that Aristotle's paradoxes arise only if one regards as existent that which is in fact always and only in a process of becoming. He reiterates the view of Damascius that time does not exist in actuality, as a sensible object might exist, but that 'it has its being in becoming'. His solution that time is never actual, but always potential, may seem to yield too much to the claim that time is unreal. However, on Simplicius' Neoplatonic view, passing time is only an image of 'primary time', which is a stable intermediate between the fleeting time of the physical realm and unparticipated eternity (784.17–785.10).

4 Logic and mathematics

On Aristotle's Categories is probably the latest authentic work of Simplicius we possess. One question that particularly interested Neoplatonists was the subject matter, or *skopos*, of Aristotle's treatise: is it about words, things or concepts? (See PORPHYRY §2; CATEGORIES §1; ARISTOTLE §7). Simplicius explains that the treatise concerns itself with human language and, more precisely, with its simple, primary and generic utterances (*phōnai*) in so far as they signify concrete objects (*pragmata*). It instructs us about such objects, but also about the concepts (*noēmata*) through which the utterances gain signification (*On Aristotle's Categories* 13.11–15). In the course of this study of language the soul is once again being prepared in an ideal way for its ascent to the noetic world.

Like most Neoplatonists, Simplicius had a keen interest in mathematics. *On Aristotle's Physics* contains an extensive discussion of geometry including an extract from Eudemus' *History of Geometry* concerning the quadrature of lunes by Hippocrates of Chios. These passages bear witness to the oldest Greek mathematical work and present important material for a reconstruction of the history of pre-Euclidean mathematics. Fragments of a commentary by Simplicius on the definitions, postulates and axioms of book I of Euclid's *Elements* are extant in Arabic.

5 Influence

Through his work, Simplicius shaped the reception and interpretation of Aristotle for centuries. The bibliographies of Ibn an-Nadim and Ibn al-Qifti show that his commentaries were at least partially known in the Arab world (see ARISTOTELIANISM IN ISLAMIC PHILOSOPHY). The first Latin translations by Robert GROSSETESTE and William of Moerbeke date from the thirteenth century and had an immediate impact on Thomas AQUINAS and his circle. Later, Simplicius is one of the pillars of Renaissance Aristotelianism (Galileo, in the *Dialogue*, names his Aristotelian straw man 'Simplicio'), and even today his work is indispensable for any serious student of Aristotle or the history of Greek philosophy.

List of works

Simplicius (*c.*533) *On Epictetus's Manual*, ed. I. Hadot, *Simplicius – Commentaire sur le 'Manuel' d'Épictète. Introduction et édition critique du texte grec*, Leiden: Brill, 1996. (The volume includes a long general introduction to Simplicius as well as a good bibliography.)

— (*c.*536) *On Aristotle's On the Heavens*, ed. I.L. Heiberg, *Commentaria in Aristotelem Graeca VII*, Berlin: Reimer, 1894. (A commentary on Aristotle's cosmological treatise and vigorous defence of the pagan notion of the divinity of the heavens.)

— (after 538) *On Aristotle's Physics*, ed. H. Diels, *Commentaria in Aristotelem Graeca IX– X*, Berlin: Reimer, 1882–5; parts available in translation, as follows: B. Fleet, *Simplicius on Aristotle's Physics 2*, London: Duckworth, 1997; J.O. Urmson and L. Siorvanes, *Simplicius, Corollaries on Place and Time*, London: Duckworth, 1992; J.O. Urmson and P. Lautner, *Simplicius, On Aristotle on the Void*, London: Duckworth, 1994; D. Konstan, *On Aristotle Physics 6: Simplicius*, London: Duckworth, 1989; C. Hagen, *On Aristotle's Physics 7: Simplicius*, London: Duckworth, 1994; C. Wildberg, 'Simplicius, Against Philoponus on the Eternity of the World', in D. Furley and C. Wildberg, *Place, Void, and Eternity*, London: Duckworth, 1991, 95–134. (Diels gives Greek text only; the others are translations with notes.)

— (after 538) *On Aristotle's Categories*, ed. C. Kalbfleisch, *Commentaria in Aristotelem Graeca VIII*, Berlin: Reimer, 1907; trans. and ed. I. Hadot, *Simplicius: Commentaire sur les Catégories*, Leiden: Brill, fasc. I and III, 1990, fasc. II, 1996; trans. *Simplicius, Commentaire sur le Catégories d'Aristote, traduction de Guillaume de Moerbeke*, ed. A. Pattin and W. Stuyven, *Corpus Latinum Commentariorum in Aristotelem Graecorum III*, Paris: Éditions Béatrice–Nauwelaerts, 1971. (The Hadot text contains French text with comments by different authors; the Patton and Stuyven text is the standard translation of the medieval Latin translation.)

— (*c.*540) *On Aristotle's On the Soul*, ed. M. Hayduck, *Commentaria in Aristotelem Graeca XI*, Berlin: Reimer, 1882; trans. in part, J.O. Urmson and P. Lautner, *Simplicius, On Aristotle's On the Soul 1.1–2.4*, London: Duckworth, 1995. (The authorship of this work is disputed, the date uncertain.)

References and further reading

Cameron, A. (1969) 'The Last Days of the Academy at Athens', *Proceedings of the Cambridge Philological Society* 195, new series, 15: 7–29. (Argues that the school continued to exist in Athens after 529 and that Simplicius returned there; for the opposing view see Hadot's *Commentaire sur le 'Manuel' d'Épictète*.)

Gätje, H. (1982) 'Simplikios in der arabischen Überlieferung' (Simplicius in the Arabic Tradition), *Der Islam* 59: 6–31. (A discussion of bibliographical references to Simplicius in Arabic texts.)

Hadot, I. (ed.) (1987) *Simplicius – Savie, son œuvre, sa survie* (Simplicius – His Life, Work and Influence), Berlin and New York: de Gruyter. (A collection of articles on Simplicius' biography, his doctrine, the textual transmission of his work and its influence in the Renaissance.)

— (1990) 'The Life and Work of Simplicius in Greek and Arabic Sources', in R.R.K. Sorabji (ed.) *Aristotle Transformed*, London: Duckworth, 275–303. (This article owes much to the pioneering work by Michel Tardieu; the whole volume is an excellent guide to philosophy in late antiquity, offering an extensive bibliography.)

Hoffmann, P. (1987) 'Simplicius' Polemics. Some Aspects of Simplicius' Polemical Writings against John Philoponus: From Invective to a Reaffirmation of the Transcendency of the Heavens', in R.R.K. Sorabji (ed.) *Philoponus and the Rejection of Aristotelian Science*, London: Duckworth, 57–83. (A discussion of Simplicius' rhetoric of invective and piety in the commentary on Aristotle's *On the Heavens*.)

Knorr, W.R. (1986) *The Ancient Tradition of Geometric Problems*, Boston, MA: Birkhäuser. (Chapter 2 offers a discussion of the mathematical passages in the *Physics* commentary.)

Sonderegger, E. (1982) 'Simplikios: Über die Zeit. Ein Kommentar zum Corollarium de tempore' (Simplicius: On Time. A Commentary on the 'Corollary on Time'), *Hypomnemata* 70, Göttingen: Vandenhoeck. (A detailed analysis of Simplicius' 'Corollary on Time' in the *Physics* commentary.)

Sorabji, R.R.K. (1988) *Matter, Space and Motion*, London: Duckworth, ch. 1. (A discussion of Simplicius' interpretation of Aristotle's prime matter as extension.)

Tardieu, M. (1986) 'Sabiens coraniques et "Sabiens" de Harran' (The Sabieans of the Koran and the Sabians of Harran), *Journal Asiatique* 274: 1–44. (A masterly article establishing the thesis that the Athenian Neoplatonists continued their work in Carrhae/Harran.)

CHRISTIAN WILDBERG

SIMULTANEITY

see CONVENTIONALISM; RELATIVITY THEORY, PHILOSOPHICAL SIGNIFICANCE OF; TIME; TIME TRAVEL

SIN

The most archaic conception of human fault may be the notion of defilement or pollution, that is, a stain or blemish which somehow infects a person from without. All the major religious traditions offer accounts of human faults and prescriptions for dealing with them. However, it is only when fault is conceived within the context of a relationship to a personal deity that it makes sense to speak of it as an offence against the divine will. The concept of sin is the concept of a human fault that offends a good God and brings with it human guilt. Its natural home is in the major theistic religions of Judaism, Christianity and Islam.

These religious traditions share the idea that actual or personal sins are individual actions contrary to the

will of God. In the Hebrew Bible, sin is understood within the context of the covenantal relation between Yahweh and his chosen people. To be in covenant with Yahweh is to exist in holiness, and so sin is a deviation from the norms of holiness. In the Christian New Testament, Jesus teaches that human wrongdoing offends the one whom he calls Father. The Qur'an portrays sin as opposition to Allah rooted in human pride.

According to Christian tradition, there is a distinction to be drawn between actual sin and original sin. The scriptural warrant for the doctrine of original sin is found in the Epistles of Paul, and the interpretation of Paul worked out by Augustine in the course of his controversy with the Pelagians has been enormously influential in Western Christianity. On the Augustinian view, which was developed by Anselm and other medieval thinkers with considerable philosophical sophistication, the Fall of Adam and Eve had catastrophic consequences for their descendants. All the progeny of the first humans, except for Jesus and his mother, inherit from them guilt for their first sin, and so all but two humans are born bearing a burden of guilt. The Augustinian doctrine of original sin is morally problematic just because it attributes innate guilt to humans. It was criticized by John Locke and Immanuel Kant.

1   **Actual sin**
2   **Augustinian original sin**
3   **Modern philosophical critiques**
4   **Contemporary philosophical critiques**

1   Actual sin

Actual or personal sins are individual human actions that are offensive to God. Since God is conceived of in the major theistic religions as morally perfect, all wrongdoing will be offensive to God and hence will be sinful. Most theists hold that some things would be morally wrong even if there were no God; only theological voluntarists suppose that nothing would be morally wrong if God did not exist (see RELIGION AND MORALITY §1; VOLUNTARISM). On the majority view, much of morality is independent of the existence and will of God; divine prohibitions do not make such things as murder, torture or rape wrong. Divine commands to refrain from doing such things serve to reinforce an independent morality. Murder becomes, so to speak, doubly wrong when forbidden by God. It is a wrong against the victim and it is a wrong against God, but it would still be wrong even if, on account of the nonexistence of God, it were not sinful. Actions of this kind are such that their moral wrongness is independent of their sinfulness.

However, not all actions are of this kind. It is commonly thought that we have a moral duty to express gratitude to our benefactors. If God created us and conserves us in existence and if the gift of life is on the whole good, then we have a duty to express gratitude to God. It would be morally wrong and hence sinful not to do so. But if there is no God, we do not owe such a debt of gratitude, and so it would be neither morally wrong nor sinful not to express gratitude to God. So some actions are such that both their moral wrongness and their sinfulness depend on the existence and actions of God. For such actions moral wrongness is not independent of sinfulness.

A third possibility worth considering is that there are distinctively religious duties which are not also moral duties. It seems to be morally indifferent whether one worships God on one day rather than another, or using one ritual rather than another. But God may have prescribed the form worship is supposed to take. If so, it would be offensive to God and hence sinful not to worship in the prescribed manner. Yet it is at least arguable that it would not be immoral to fail to worship in the prescribed manner even if, because of a duty of gratitude to God, it would be morally wrong not to express reverence to God in some manner. So perhaps there are also actions or omissions that are sinful even though they are not morally wrong.

There are thus at least two varieties of actual sin. There are actions or omissions that are morally wrong whether or not God exists but are also sinful if God exists. And there are actions or omissions that are neither morally wrong nor sinful if God does not exist but are both morally wrong and sinful if God exists. In addition, there may be actions or omissions that are neither morally wrong nor sinful if God does not exist but are sinful yet not morally wrong if God exists.

A distinction can be drawn between objective and subjective actual sin. If people do what is objectively offensive to God, they sin objectively and acquire objective guilt. If people do what they believe to be offensive to God, they sin subjectively and acquire subjective guilt. If God exists, there will be cases in which people sin both objectively and subjectively, cases in which people sin objectively but not subjectively, and cases in which people sin subjectively but not objectively. The guilt of actual sin renders the sinner liable to punishment by God if appropriate conditions on responsibility are satisfied. A person who sins both objectively and subjectively and whose true beliefs about what is offensive to God are well warranted may deserve severe punishment. A person who sins objectively but not subjectively and whose lack of true beliefs about what is offensive to God are not the result of culpable ignorance may deserve little or no punishment. In general, the relations among actual sin, guilt before God, responsibility and desert of punishment in the theistic religions are similar to and no more problematic than the relations among wrongdoing, moral guilt, responsibility and desert of sanctions in common morality. This is not the case for Augustinian original sin.

2 Augustinian original sin

The roots of the doctrine of original sin lie in the story of the Fall of Adam and Eve. When they disobey a divine command and eat the forbidden fruit, God punishes them with toil, suffering and death. Being subject to such things is part of a legacy we inherit from them. But the story does not force us to conclude that they are also to be thought of as punishments in our case. Nor does it clearly suggest that we have also inherited from the first humans a burden of guilt. That suggestion derives from the Epistles of Paul.

Seeking to appropriate the contents of the Hebrew Bible for Christianity, Paul reads it as full of foreshadowings of things that only come to fruition in the life and death of Jesus Christ. In Romans, he powerfully contrasts Adam and Christ, beginning as follows: 'Therefore, just as through one man sin entered the world and with sin death, death thus coming to all men in as much as all sinned' (5: 12). He concludes: 'Just as through one man's disobedience all became sinners, so through one man's obedience all shall become just' (5: 19). The obedience (good action) of Christ is said to be that through which all shall become just (have positive moral status); this completely contrasts with the disobedience of Adam, through which all became sinners. The implication is that everyone acquired the negative moral status of being sinners through Adam's disobedience, which would be easily explained on the assumption that guilt is somehow transferred from Adam to his progeny in a way that parallels the transfer of justice from Christ to those who benefit from his atonement.

AUGUSTINE (§§6, 9) explicitly makes this assumption. He tells us that 'when the first couple were punished by the judgment of God, the whole human race, which was to become Adam's posterity through the first woman, was present in the first man' (*De civitate Dei*, book 13: 271). All humans were present in Adam because human nature was present in Adam's semen. So we are all born in the condition of being soiled by sin, doomed to death and justly condemned (such is our nature), and this condition is part of what we would today refer to as our genetic endowment because it propagates biologically from Adam to his posterity by means of semen. As *The New-England Primer* neatly summarizes this doctrine of innate sin and guilt: 'in Adam's fall, we sinned all'. When he tries to defend it against his Pelagian opponent Julian of Eclanum, who rejects it, Augustine frequently appeals to the authority of Pauline texts such as Romans 5: 12 and 5: 19 (see PELAGIANISM).

Many scholars doubt the legitimacy of the appeal to Romans 5: 12. As they see it, Augustine misinterpreted that verse because he read it in Latin rather than in the original Greek. Apparently he took it to say that through one man sin entered the world and with sin death, death thus coming to all men, *in whom* all sinned; he mistakenly supposed that the final clause referred back to the one man, Adam, which led him to conclude that Adam's fall brought about not only universal death but also universal sin. But even if this conclusion is not supported by Romans 5: 12, it does seem to be supported by Romans 5: 19, and so the Augustinian doctrine of original sin appears to have a basis in scriptural texts. It was accepted by most Western Christian thinkers for more than a millennium, and it is still accepted by many Christians. It bears a striking resemblance to the archaic account of pollution that infects a person from without.

The Augustinian doctrine of original sin was elaborated in the work of medieval theologians such as ANSELM OF CANTERBURY (§8). According to Anselm, human beings are metaphysical composites that include both a nature, which makes each – like others – human, and a principle of individuation, which makes each a particular person distinct from all others. Original sin is sin that one contracts with human nature at the very origin of one's existence as a person; it is innate and unavoidable. It consists of a will that lacks a proper upright orientation because it is not subject to the will of God. Anselm describes the process by which their descendants derive original sin from Adam and Eve in terms of a principle of causal transmission. It states that 'as what is personal passes over to the nature, so what is natural passes over to the person' (*De conceptu virginali et peccato originali*: 202). By the first half of this principle, the sin Adam and Eve committed when they disobeyed God caused human nature to become sinful; by its second half, sinful human nature in turn causes their descendants to be sinful from the very first moment they possess it. And Anselm draws a shocking conclusion from the Augustinian doctrine. It is that infants who die unbaptized, before having committed any personal sins of their own and so with only the stain of original sin on their souls, are condemned by God, who is morally perfect, to exclusion from the kingdom of heaven (see LIMBO §1). Many of Anselm's successors, including Thomas Aquinas, Martin LUTHER, John CALVIN (§4) and Jonathan Edwards, played other variations on this Augustinian theme.

3 Modern philosophical critiques

Important philosophers of the modern era have been critical of the Augustinian doctrine of original sin. LOCKE (§1) tried to undermine its scriptural support by reinterpreting the Pauline texts cited by Augustine, and KANT (§11) proposed to substitute for it his doctrine of radical evil.

Locke's procedure is to quote a verse, then to offer his own paraphrase of it, and finally to argue in support of the paraphrase in an appended note. The paraphrase of Romans 5: 12 goes as follows:

> Wherefore to give you a state of the whole matter from the beginning. You must know, that as by the act of one man Adam the father of us all, sin enterd into the world, and death, which was the punishment annexed to the offence of eating the forbidden fruit enterd by that sin for that Adams posterity thereby became mortal.
>
> (1707: 523)

Having, in effect, substituted 'became mortal' for 'sinned' at the end of the verse, Locke has blocked both the inference that sin is inherited as well as death and the inference that death is a punishment for sin in Adam's posterity. In the note, he tries to justify this substitution by claiming that Paul is using metonymy, that is, substituting the cause for the effect, sin in Adam being the cause of his mortality and, through him, the cause of the mortality of his posterity.

Similarly, Locke's paraphrase of Romans 5: 19 is this:

> For as by one mans disobedience many were brought into a state of mortality which is the state of sinners soe by the obedience of one shall many be made righteous. i e be restord to life again as if they were not sinners.
>
> (1707: 527)

The justificatory note is terse: '*Sinners*. Here St Paul uses the same metonymie as above ver. 12 putting *sinners* for *mortal* whereby the Antithesis to righteous is the more lively' (1707: 527). We could always paraphrase away talk of Adam's disobedience making his progeny sinners in favour of talk of Adam's disobedience making his progeny mortal, thereby undercutting the scriptural basis for Augustinian original sin, if Locke's metonymy gambit were successful across the board. However, not many biblical scholars are persuaded that it is successful.

Kant flatly rejects the Augustinian doctrine of inherited sin and guilt:

> However the origin of moral evil in man is constituted, surely of all the explanations of the spread and propagation of this evil through all members and generations of our race, the most inept is that which describes it as descending to us as an *inheritance* from our first parents.
>
> (1793: 35)

Yet Kant holds that there is, in a sense, radical evil in human nature because there is in all humans, as far as we can tell, a morally evil propensity to evil. It is this propensity that is the proxy for original sin in his philosophy of religion; he even calls it *peccatum originarium*.

A propensity, Kant tells us, is a predisposition to crave a delight which, when once experienced, arouses in the subject an inclination to it. Those who have a propensity for chocolate, for example, do not desire chocolate before they first taste it, but once they have sampled it they develop a craving for it. Kant describes propensities of this sort as physical because they belong to their possessors considered as beings determined by natural laws. Whatever is determined by natural laws is morally indifferent, and so physical propensities are morally indifferent. If all propensities were physical, then even if there were a propensity for evil in humans it would not itself be morally evil. So there must be nonphysical propensities if a propensity for evil is to make its human possessors morally evil. For Kant, nothing is morally evil but free action and what derives from it, and so a propensity for evil that is itself morally evil has to be a product of the exercise of freedom. Though the propensity for evil can, according to Kant, be represented as innate, it should not be represented merely as innate; it should also be represented as brought by humans upon themselves. It can be represented as innate in its possessors because, as the underlying ground of all morally evil actions, it is to be thought of as present in them antecedent to all such actions and so represented temporally as present in them as far back as birth. It should be represented as brought by humans upon themselves because, being morally evil, it has to be a product of freedom for which its possessors are accountable. And it can be represented as brought by humans upon themselves because it can be thought of as the product of an atemporal act of noumenal freedom.

On Kant's view, there is radical evil in human nature only in the sense that, as far as we can tell on the basis of the available evidence, all humans have brought upon themselves a morally evil propensity for evil. This propensity is not transmitted to us causally from our remote ancestors; it is not part of the genetic endowment that comes to us through sexual procreation. When Kant endorses the formula 'in Adam all have sinned', he means only to say that the story of the sin of Adam and Eve represents in a symbolic fashion something that actually occurs in every human life. Whether the Kantian account of radical evil is an improvement on the Augustinian doctrine of original sin depends heavily on the plausibility of Kant's assumption that there are atemporal acts of noumenal freedom. Many philosophers do not consider it even remotely plausible.

4 Contemporary philosophical critiques

Original sin has not been a major issue in the philosophy of religion of the twentieth century. However, some Christian philosophers have added to the criticism of the Augustinian doctrine of innate guilt.

Richard Swinburne (1989) acknowledges that humans have an innate proneness to sin. It stems from the strong selfish desires that are part of our evolutionary heritage and it is genetically transmitted. Although he describes this proneness to wrongdoing as original sinfulness, he insists that the bad desires in which it consists incline without necessitating and so do not inevitably issue in actual wrongdoing. And he emphatically rejects the doctrine of original guilt according to which all of Adam's descendants are guilty of Adam's original sin. He argues that one cannot be guilty in a literal sense for the sins of another unless one had some obligation to deter that person and failed to do so. Since no one alive today could have had an obligation to deter Adam and Eve, we cannot be guilty for their first sins. Swinburne also cites Scripture to support his view: 'The son shall not bear the iniquity of the father, neither shall the father bear the iniquity of the son; the righteousness of the righteous shall be upon him, and the wickedness of the wicked shall be upon him' (Ezekiel 18: 20). As he sees it, the guilt we acquire when we fail in our obligations to deter others from wickedness is the only literal exception to this sound prophetic claim.

The doctrine of original guilt was taught by the federal theology of the Reformation. According to federalism, Adam was, by covenant with God, the federal head or representative of the whole human race. All of Adam's posterity stood their probation in him, and so guilt for his sin is imputed to them by God in consequence of his having fallen while acting as their covenant head. Federal theologians do not deny that Adam's progeny were seminally present in him or that a proneness to sin is biologically transmitted from Adam to his posterity. However,

they insist that guilt for Adam's first sin extends to his descendants not by way of biological transmission but by way of divine imputation. The Puritan theologian and philosopher Jonathan Edwards (1758) defended the account of original guilt offered by the federal theology. In a critical examination of his views, William Wainwright (1988) explores various models of the moral or legal relations that might be involved in Adam being the covenant head or representative of his posterity. Some of these models permit the transfer of liability from one person to another, but none of them allows for the transfer of guilt. According to Wainwright, the reason for this is that one must have committed an act to be guilty of it and one cannot commit another's act. His conclusion is that 'even though liability can be transferred from one person to another, guilt cannot. Adam's posterity cannot be guilty of Adam's fault unless Adam's act is somehow *literally* their own' (1988: 47). But, of course, none of the acts of any of one's ancestors is literally one's own.

See also: HELL; PURGATORY; SALVATION

References and further reading

Adams, M.M. (1991) 'Sin as Uncleanness', in J.E. Tomberlin (ed.) *Philosophical Perspectives 5: Philosophy of Religion*, Atascadero, CA: Ridgeview Publishing. (Treats sin as ultimately an impropriety in the relation of created persons to God rather than a matter of moral wrongdoing.)

* Anselm of Canterbury (1100) *De conceptu virginali et peccato originali* (The Virgin Conception and Original Sin), trans. J.M. Colleran, Albany, NY: Magi Books, 1969. (Presents the elaboration of the Augustinian doctrine of original sin discussed in §2.)

* Augustine of Hippo (426) *De civitate Dei* (City of God), trans. G.G. Walsh, D.B. Zema, G. Monahan and D.J. Honan, Garden City, NY: Doubleday, 1958. (Book 13 contains the account of original sin discussed in §2.)

* Edwards, J. (1758) *Original Sin*, ed. C.A. Holbrook, New Haven, CT and London: Yale University Press, 1970. (Contains the account of original sin referred to in §4.)

* Kant, I. (1793) *Religion innerhalb der Grenzen der bloßen Vernunft* (Religion within the Limits of Reason Alone), trans. T.M. Greene and H.H. Hudson, New York: Harper & Brothers, 1960. (Book 1 presents the account of radical evil discussed in §3.)

* Locke, J. (1707) *A Paraphrase and Notes on the Epistles of St Paul*, ed. A.W. Wainwright, Oxford:

Clarendon Press, 1987. (Volume 2 contains the Lockean interpretation of Romans 5: 12 and 5: 19 discussed in §3.)

Pagels, E. (1988) *Adam, Eve, and the Serpent*, New York: Random House. (A readable historical and critical study of Augustine's doctrine of original sin.)

Quinn, P.L. (1992) 'On Demythologizing Evil', in F. Reynolds and D. Tracy (eds) *Discourse and Practice*, Albany, NY: State University of New York Press. (Expansion of the material of §§2–3 of this entry.)

Ricoeur, P. (1967) *The Symbolism of Evil*, New York: Harper & Row. (Part 1 is an important study of defilement, sin and guilt from a phenomenological perspective.)

* Swinburne, R. (1989) *Responsibility and Atonement*, Oxford: Clarendon Press. (Chapter 9 contains the criticism of the doctrine of original guilt discussed in §4.)

* Wainwright, W.J. (1988) 'Original Sin', in T.V. Morris (ed.) *Philosophy and the Christian Faith*, Notre Dame, IN: University of Notre Dame Press. (Presents the criticism of Edwards on original sin discussed in §4.)

* Watts, I. (1790) *The New-England Primer*, Newburyport, MA: John Mycall. (There are many editions of this work, which is cited in §2.)

Williams, N.P. (1927) *The Ideas of the Fall and of Original Sin*, London: Longmans, Green & Co. (A classic historical and critical study of the doctrine of original sin.)

PHILIP L. QUINN

SINGULAR TERMS

see REFERENCE

SINN UND BEDEUTUNG

see SENSE AND REFERENCE

SIRHAK

Sirhak refers to the reformist scholarship and thought in Korea during the latter half of the Chosôn (Yi) Dynasty (1392–1910). The term was coined in the twentieth century to refer to the writings of individual scholars from the eighteenth to the mid-nineteenth centuries who were critical of the existing political, social and economic conditions.

As Korea recovered slowly from the devastations suffered from the two major foreign invasions by the Japanese (1592–8) and the Manchus (1636), the ruling Chosôn dynasty was faced with many serious political, social and economic problems, due largely to the political infighting and ineptitude of the ruling circle. At the same time, the traditional emphasis on strict adherence to neo-Confucian orthodoxy created a climate of intellectual rigidity, as the overriding philosophical concerns centred mostly on abstract and metaphysical issues such as debates on the primacy of the principle (*i*; in Chinese, *li*) and the material force (*ki*; in Chinese, *qi*), and on ritual formalities (see CONFUCIAN PHILOSOPHY, KOREAN). It was in reaction to this that *sirhak* (practical learning) scholarship arose. Turning away from the conventional emphasis on abstract issues, the *sirhak* scholars dealt with more practical questions ranging from the classics and political economy to science and agriculture. In general, their encyclopedic writings emphasized four broad areas: the role of the government in promoting and protecting the welfare of the people, the practical use of knowledge, empirical evidence for knowledge and consciousness of Korea's identity.

Mindful of the well-being of the people, the *sirhak* scholars criticized the government and its policies for failing to protect the people adequately and proposed wide-ranging reforms of various institutions and practices. Seeing inequity in land holdings as the primary source of social ills, many proposed land reforms. Yu Hyôngwôn (1622–73) and Yi Ik (1681–1763) made proposals that would assure that farmers had their land to cultivate, while CHÔNG YAGYONG (1762–1836) called for a 'village land system' whereby villagers would jointly own the land and work together, sharing the harvest in proportion to the amount of labor each put in. Along with Yu Suwôn (1694–1755) and other *sirhak* scholars, they severely criticized the rigid social structure that granted privileges to the elite *yangban* social class based on birth. The abusive practices of the civil service examination system were also blamed for contributing to the social ills of the time. Through his satirical novellas, which resemble those of Voltaire, Pak Chiwôn (1737–1805) condemned the hypocritical life led by the *yangban*. Envisaging a more egalitarian society, the *sirhak* scholars wanted to do away with privileges based on birth and to make government more responsive to the needs of the people (see EQUALITY).

The *sirhak* scholars believed in the practical application of knowledge in daily life. Agriculture was of special interest to many *sirhak* scholars, and Pak Sedang (1629–1703), Hong Mansôn (1643–1715),

Sô Hosu (1736–99) and Sô Yugu (1764–1845) wrote extensively on soil conditions, fertilizer, irrigation, horticulture, sericulture, livestock, forestry and similar subjects in order to improve the condition of the peasants. Unlike the conventional Confucian scholar-officials, many *sirhak* scholars recognized the importance of trade and commerce. For Pak Chega (1750–1805), prudent consumption was necessary to create demand for production; he wanted the government to encourage domestic as well as international trade. The introduction of Western science and technology also stimulated the thinking of many *sirhak* scholars. Kim Sôngmun (1658–1735) and Hong Taeyong (1731–83) wrote extensively on mathematics and explained terrestrial movement within a solar system. Based on knowledge acquired from China, Chông Yag-yong devised cranes that were used to construct the new city of Suwôn and developed inoculations for measles and smallpox.

There was also a growing interest in historical and geographical studies of Korea. An Chôngbok (1712–91) rewrote Korean history, emphasizing the legitimacy of the Korean rulers starting from Tangun. In his monumental study of Korean history, Yi Kûngik (1736–1806) tried to present an objective history unhampered by factional biases. Yu Tûkkong (1748–1807) was the first historian to treat the kingdom of Parhae (Po-hai in Chinese) (699–926) as an integral part of Korean history. In historical geography, Sin Kyôngjun (1712–81), Han Chinsô (1777–?) and Chông Yagyong traced Korea's boundaries at various historical periods, while Yi Chunghwan (1690–1752) presented an authoritative study on the cultural and economic characteristics of various regions of Korea. Kim Chôngho (*fl.* 1834) produced several maps of Korea that are remarkably detailed and accurate even by modern standards. These studies enhanced consciousness of Korea's own identity.

Many *sirhak* scholars emphasized that knowledge is founded on empirical evidence. In his studies of the classics, Chông Yagyong wanted to go back to the texts of Han times or earlier for verification, in the belief that the classical canons are not necessarily the final words we must accept in faith, but merely the records of the ancient sages in search of betterment. Perhaps the most articulate proponent of empiricism in Korea was Ch'oe Hangi (1803–79). Upholding the primacy of *ki* (material force) over *i* (principle), Ch'oe emphasized that knowledge is acquired through the perceptions of our senses and that even the Mencian notion of humanity, righteousness, propriety and wisdom is derived from our experience, not from innate knowledge (see MENCIUS). Ch'oe Hangi is often regarded as an intermediary between tradition and modernity in Korea.

As the proposals of the *sirhak* scholars contained certain elements of the modernistic ideas, many Korean scholars tried to characterize them as the forerunners of modern Korea. However, the *sirhak* scholars envisioned their reform ideas within the bounds of the Confucian worldview, and regarded themselves as the heirs of the Confucian tradition.

See also: CHÔNG YAGYONG; CONFUCIAN PHILOSOPHY, KOREAN

References and further reading

Asea munje yôn'guso (ed.) (1974) *Sirhak sasang ûi t'amgu* (Search for Sirhak Thought), Seoul: Hyônmasa. (A collection of the studies on five representative *sirhak* scholars and also on *sirhak* scholars' criticism of Catholicism, by five Korean scholars.)

Baker, D. (1990) 'Sirhak Medicine: Measles, Smallpox and Chông Tasan', *Korean Studies* 14: 135–66. (An interesting study of how Chông Yagyong approached Chinese and Western medicine within *sirhak* tradition.)

Chông Sông-ch'ôl (1974) *Sirhakp'a ûi ch'ôrhak sasang kwa sahoe chôngch'i chôk kyônhae* (Philosophical Thought and Socio-Political View of the Sirhak School), Pyongyang: Sahoe kwahak ch'ulp'ansa. (An extensive survey of *sirhak* focusing on Yi Ik, Hong Taeyong, Pak Chega and Chông Yagyong from a Marxist standpoint by a distinguished North Korean scholar.)

Kalton, M.C. (1975) 'An Introduction to Silhak', *Korea Journal* 15 (5): 29–46. (A useful overview of *sirhak* by an American specialist on Korean intellectual history.)

Kûm Changt'ae (1987) *Hanguk sirhak sasang yôngu* (Study of the Thought of Practical Learning in Korea), Seoul: Chimmundang. (After giving an overview of *sirhak* thought, a well-known Korean specialist examines the philosophical ideas of Chông Yagyong and Ch'oe Han'gi.)

Lee, W. (1975) 'Korean Intellectual Tradition and the Sirhak Thought', in H.W. Kang (ed.) *Traditional Culture and Society of Korea: Thought and Institutions*, Honolulu, HI: University of Hawaii Press. (A Korean specialist examines *sirhak* within the context of Korean intellectual history.)

Palais, J.B. (1996) *Confucian Statecraft and Korean Institutions: Yu Hyôngwôn and the Late Chosôn Dynasty*, Seattle, WA: University of Washington Press. (A massive study of a representative *sirhak* scholar, Yu Hyôngwôn, examining comprehensively various ideas of Yu with a comparative perspective in traditional East Asian history.)

Yôksa hakhoe (ed.) (1974) *Sirhak yôngu immun* (Introduction to the Studies of Sirhak), Seoul: Ilchogak. (A collection of short studies on nine sirhak scholars with Korean translation of their representative works.)

Yu Wôndong (1983) *Hanguk sirhak kaeron* (General Discourse on Sirhak in Korea), Seoul: Chôngôm munhwasa. (A Korean economic historian examines the reform proposals of ten *sirhak* scholars.)

YÔNG-HO CH'OE

SITUATION ETHICS

'Situation ethics' accords morally decisive weight to particular circumstances in judging whether an action is right or wrong. Thus we should examine critically all traditional rules prohibiting kinds of actions. Proponents of these views have exerted their greatest influence in Europe and North America in the twentieth century, although such influence waned by 1980. The views received extensive scrutiny in Christian communities. Three quite different warrants were offered for privileging discrete situations. First, we should remain dispositionally open to God's immediate command in a particular time and place (theological contextualism). Second, we should take the actual consequences of particular actions as morally decisive (empirical situationism). Third, we should be ready to perform actions that compromise moral ideals when doing so improves matters in ways a given situation, with its distinctive constraints, makes viable (mournful realism).

St Augustine's famous dictum, 'Love, and do what you will', summarizes the views that many proponents of situation ethics commend. Doubtless it would distress Augustine to see his dictum employed to support views he himself repudiates. He holds that a motive of love is a necessary condition for a good action, yet denies that it is a sufficient condition. Indeed, he claims that certain actions are wrong in themselves. Those forbidden absolutely include murder, lying, and adultery (see DEONTOLOGICAL ETHICS).

Proponents of situation ethics, for their part, adopt his dictum, but reject his stipulation that there are certain things that are always wrong. They attend instead to the distinctive features of the case at hand. Situation ethics is thus a movement that protests generally against the imposition of unchanging moral absolutes that prohibit everywhere certain classes of conduct. Yet deeper currents contributed to the widespread debates the movement occasioned earlier in the twentieth century (roughly until 1980), both in Europe and North America. Some currents came from secular communities, where existentialist thinkers stressed the importance of 'authentic' personal decisions, and attacked rules that blocked spontaneity and awareness of change (see EXISTENTIALIST ETHICS). Other currents came from Christian communities, where so many of the debates occurred, and where three warrants for concentrating on particular situations proved especially influential.

One warrant – theological contextualism – stems from the claims that Søren KIERKEGAARD advances in *Frygt og Baeven* (*Fear and Trembling*) (1843). He examines the biblical narrative of Abraham's near-sacrifice of Isaac. Kierkegaard insists that Abraham cannot 'love' Isaac if he disobeys God's command, and that Abraham paradigmatically displays a dispositional openness to God's immediate command. We can suppose for the best of human reasons that a given action is wrong, but if God commanded it in a certain context, we should have to change our minds. Twentieth century religious thinkers who extend a case for immediacy include Karl BARTH and Emil BRUNNER. The particular situation has priority over 'code morality' in that it must be *God* who commands in the present moment. We may jeopardise divine sovereignty and be diverted from a personal confrontation with God by claiming to know in advance what we should do and forbear so that we only interpret, apply, and execute this knowledge. The enterprise of 'casuistry' with its subsumption of cases is thought, fairly or not, to afford an opportunity for such diversion (see CASUISTRY). Commended in its place is a kind of act-deontology. God's immediate command, self-interpreting in a particular situation, may sometimes lead us to suspend our antecedent moral judgments.

A second warrant – empirical situationism – jettisons any appeal to immediate divine commands, and proceeds instead to apply directly to each situation the general injunction 'to love your neighbour as yourself'. In *Situation Ethics* (1966), Joseph Fletcher contends that we should determine what action is right in a particular situation by confronting our loving wills with the contextual details of the situation itself. He allies his 'situationism' formally with modified act-utilitarianism (see UTILITARIANISM). Neighbour-love, like utility, is the sole governing criterion that should always guide action. Other subsidiary precepts and rules, including the traditional prohibitions that Augustine takes as absolutes, Fletcher affirms only as 'illuminative maxims'. They are at most 'statistically preponderant generalizations', based on past cases and cumulative experience that inform us of the kinds of action that typically produce good or bad consequences. But we should suspend or reject maxims whenever it seems more loving to do so, that is, whenever we effect more good by breaking them than by adhering to them. If a traditional maxim proves unloving in this situation, we should disregard it, without remorse, and without a sense of conflicting obligations.

A final warrant – mournful realism – accents the moral compromises a particular situation may exact. In *The Nature and Destiny of Man* (1949), Reinhold Niebuhr laments that a particular situation may present us with unwanted choices, and induce us to consider doing things we may judge repellent, or at least things we would never do for their own sake. But he justifies making choices we do not want to make, when the alternative is to acquiesce to corrupt forces that threaten altogether the conditions for a tolerable community.

This third warrant is like the second in several ways. It judges that immediate divine commands are not possibilities to be taken routinely into account. Neighbour-love remains insuperable. No one subsidiary precept or rule binds absolutely, whatever the consequences. Contextual details may assume effective priority in determining what actions are appropriate. There are, however, some differences. Fletcher is too complacent when he maintains that the greatest moral good possible in a situation is the most loving thing to do. For what is possible often demands compromise that leaves us morally dissatisfied. Compromise never becomes *all right*. Fletcher also goes wrong in weighing all considerations from the ground up each time we decide. While subsidiary precepts and rules are not exceptionless or always decisive, they should never be omitted from consideration in any situation in which they are relevant. Some carry a presumption in their favour. They are not to be disregarded but only overridden, with compunction, and with a sense of competing obligations.

Although situation ethics as a self-conscious movement with its own internal debates faded, the importance of the issues it addressed persists. It still has lessons to teach.

See also: INTUITIONISM IN ETHICS; MORAL JUDGMENT; MORAL REALISM; MORAL SENSE THEORIES

References and further reading

Augustine (416) *In ioannis evangelium tractatus* (Homilies on the Gospel of John), ed. and trans. J. Burnaby, *Ten Homilies on the First Epistle of St John*, in *Augustine: Later Works*, Library of Christian Classics, Philadelphia, PA: The Westminster Press, London: SCM, 1955, vol. 8, 316. (Love is the theme of his exhortations throughout, as it is the theme of this epistle.)

* Fletcher, J. (1966) *Situation Ethics*, Philadelphia, PA: The Westminster Press. (A popular summary of key propositions.)

Frankena, W.K. (1964) 'Love and Principle in Christian Ethics', in A. Plantinga (ed.) *Faith and Philosophy*, Grand Rapids, MI: Eerdmans, 203–25. (An essay that shapes the terms of the debate.)

* Kierkegaard, S.A. (1843) *Frygt og Baeven*, trans. H.V. Hong and E.H. Hong, *Fear and Trembling*, Princeton, NJ: Princeton University Press, 1983. (Defends the possibility of a 'teleological suspension of the ethical'.)

Mahoney, J. (1987) *The Making of Moral Theology: A Study of the Roman Catholic Tradition*, Oxford: Clarendon Press, ch. 5. (Describes situation ethics in Roman Catholic discussions.)

* Niebuhr, R. (1949) *The Nature and Destiny of Man*, New York: Charles Scribner's Sons. (The full dress account of Christian realism.)

Outka, G. (1972) *Agape; An Ethical Analysis*, New Haven, CT: Yale University Press, chaps 4, 6. (Discusses senses of situation ethics.)

Outka, G. and Ramsey, P. (eds) (1968) *Norm and Context in Christian Ethics*, New York: Charles Scribner's Sons; London: SCM. (Contains original theological and philosophical essays covering a spectrum of Protestant and Roman Catholic views.)

GENE OUTKA

SITUATIONAL SEMANTICS
see SEMANTICS, SITUATION

SKINNER, BURRHUS FREDERICK (1904–90)

B.F. Skinner advocated a philosophy of psychology, called 'radical behaviourism', as well as a substantive psychological theory, 'scientific behaviourism'. Radical behaviourism restricted psychology to establishing lawful links between the environment and behaviour, rejecting the 'mind' as a 'needless way station' mediating the two. Scientific behaviourism proposed specific links, the laws of 'operant conditioning', whereby behaviours are 'reinforced' by the consequences they have had in an animal's past. Although Skinner brought to psychology new standards of experimental rigour, and managed to train animals to do remarkable things, there are serious limits to the range of behaviours scientific behaviourism can explain. Both it and radical behaviourism have been obviated by the development of a computational theory of mind.

Influenced by reading Bertrand Russell, Skinner become an adherent of Watson's thesis that 'everything that can be known about man is discoverable by the method of external observation' (1925), that is, that none of our knowledge depends upon introspection; a doctrine called 'methodological behaviourism'. Skinner went further and concluded from this that any serious psychology should therefore confine itself to finding lawful relations between externally observable stimuli and responses, rejecting internal mental states as 'needless way stations' (1963), a doctrine called 'radical behaviourism' (see BEHAVIOURISM, METHODOLOGICAL AND SCIENTIFIC). Skinner often identified mentalism with dualism, which he thought entailed that the mental was essentially 'private'. Alternatively, he sometimes endorsed a version of 'analytical' behaviourism, according to which the meaning of mental talk is be *analysed* in terms of (dispositions to) overt, publicly observable behaviour. Sometimes he even seemed to abandon behaviourism for mere physicalism, allowing psychology to refer to mental events so long as such terms as 'being hungry' or 'thinking to oneself' were physical events in the brain.

Skinner made two very important contributions to the more substantive theory, scientific behaviourism. First, he broadened Pavlov's work (1927) on 'classical conditioning' to include not only elicited, but spontaneous behaviours (what he called 'operants', since they operated in the environment), subsuming them all under Thorndike's 'law of effect' (1911). This says, roughly, that the probability of a response R, given a stimulus S, is increased/decreased if R following S has been paired with a positive/negative reinforcement F (for example, a reward or a punishment) in the past. Thus, for example, if a baby says 'Ma' [R] in front of its mother [S], and the mother hugs the child [F], the probability of the child saying 'Ma' in front of the mother again increases. Skinner believed that by suitable patterns of conditioning one could explain all the intelligent behaviour of people and animals, which, moreover, could be 'shaped' into almost any form. He wrote popular works expounding this view, most notably his utopian novel, *Walden Two*, and a philosophical tract, *Beyond Freedom and Dignity*, in which he draws the kinds of consequences for the ordinary conception of freedom that are drawn by many other determinists (see FREE WILL).

Second, Skinner brought to light surprising facts about the patterns (or 'schedules') of reinforcement, for example, that they were more effective when they were intermittent, rather than constant, and that punishments were often ineffective in delicately shaping behaviour (see Ferster and Skinner 1957; Skinner 1969). These findings remain interesting even for those who reject behaviourism.

Problems with scientific behaviourism arose primarily in explaining the very behaviour of rats in mazes that was supposed to be the theory's parade example. Rats can learn 'latently' (without reinforcement, when they have been sated) or 'passively' (without emitting responses, as when they are wheeled through a maze in a wagon), and can improvise new, appropriate behaviour that has not been reinforced (for example, rats trained to run a maze will swim it when it is flooded). Both this and other ethological evidence suggests that animals in general navigate not by associating stimuli with responses, but by exploiting some sort of internal 'map' (Tolman 1948), and/or computation on vectors that indicate how long they have moved in a certain direction (Gallistel 1990).

One of Skinner's reasons for spurning the mental had to do with a philosophically motivated rejection of 'intervening variables' in an explanation. His complaint here was not that the mind did not *exist*, but that it was *irrelevant* to scientific explanation.

> We cannot account for the behaviour of any system while staying wholly inside it; eventually we must turn to forces operating on the organism from without. Unless there is a weak spot in our causal chain so that the second link is not lawfully determined by the first, or the third by the second, then the first and third links must be lawfully related.
>
> (1953: 35)

Hempel (1965) discussed this issue generally as 'the theoretician's dilemma' (see EXPLANATION).

The argument assumes that in the usual case there is a three-term causal relation consisting of some set E of environmental events causing some set P of psychological/neural events, which in turn cause some set R of behavioural responses. The transitivity of 'cause' suggests that the middle link can be dropped. However, this begs several questions. It assumes that explanation is concerned only with predicting observable phenomena, for example, that it is only R that needs explaining. But what if we want to know what explains P, for example, why some organism is thinking to itself or wants to eat? Surely P cannot be dropped in that case.

More crucially, there is the further important assumption, inherited from classical empiricism, that most interesting causal chains start in the environment. However, some behaviour may result in part from endogenous features of an individual's neurochemistry or from maturational patterns determined by biological evolution. Some species of bird are disposed to learn about the positions of stars *only* when they are young and unable to fly, and become *unable* to learn about them when mature (Emlen 1969). One of Skinner's most penetrating critics, Chomsky (1959), argued that the remarkable rapidity with which children learn their first language requires that substantial knowledge of 'universal grammar' be innate (see CHOMSKY, N.; LANGUAGE, INNATENESS OF).

Scientific behaviourism brought to psychology a higher standard of experimental rigour than it had previously enjoyed, and led to more disciplined tests for even non-behaviourist claims. However, apart from his findings about schedules of reinforcement, few of Skinner's claims remain influential. Scientific behaviourism has been eclipsed by the rise of cognitive and computational theories in psychology that, moreover, obviate the strictures of radical behaviourism, since these theories are compatible with materialism, and are entirely open to public verification.

See also: BEHAVIOURISM, ANALYTIC; BEHAVIOURISM, METHODOLOGICAL AND SCIENTIFIC; OPERATIONALISM

List of works

Skinner, B. (1938) *The Behavior of Organisms: An Experimental Analysis*, New York: Appleton-Century-Crofts. (Skinner's first major presentation of his views.)
—— (1948) *Walden Two*, New York: Macmillan. (Skinner's utopian novel about a community organized according to behaviourist principles.)
—— (1953) *Science and Human Behavior*, New York: Macmillan. (An early popular presentation of behaviourism.)
—— (1957) *Verbal Behavior*, New York: Appleton-Century-Crofts. (Skinner's sketch of a behaviouristic theory of language.)
Ferster, C. and Skinner, B. (1957) *Schedules of Reinforcement*, New York: Appleton-Century-Crofts. (A technical presentation of the findings regarding the effects of different temporal patternings of reinforcement.)
Skinner, B. (1963) 'Behaviorism at Fifty', *Science* 140: 951–58; repr. with useful commentaries by contemporary philosophers and psychologists in *Behavioral and Brain Sciences* 7 (4): 615–21. (Revealing

discussion of much of the philosophical motivation for behaviourism.)
—— (1969) *Contingencies of Reinforcement: A Theoretical Analysis*, New York: Appleton-Century-Crofts. (Late theoretical presentation of the main scientific behaviourist results.)
—— (1971) *Beyond Freedom and Dignity*, New York: Knopf. (Draws consequences of radical behaviourism for the ordinary conception of the person.)
—— (1974) *About Behaviorism*, New York: Random House. (A late defence of the main claims of behaviourism.)

References and further reading

* Chomsky, N. (1959) 'Review of *Verbal Behavior* (by B.F. Skinner)', *Language* 35: 26–58; repr. in J. Fodor and J. Katz (eds) *The Structure of Language: Readings in the Philosophy of Language*, Englewood Cliffs, NJ: Prentice Hall. (Forceful attack on Skinner's account of language acquisition from a foremost linguist whose work set the stage for the cognitive revolution that has largely replaced behaviourism in psychology.)
Dennett, D. (1978) 'Skinner Skinned', in *Brainstorms*, Cambridge, MA.: MIT Press. (An excellent philosophical examination and critique of Skinner's attack on mentalistic explanation.)
* Emlen, S. (1969) 'The Development of Migratory Orientation in Young Indigo Buntings', *Living Bird* 8: 113–26. (Evidence of quite specific, purely biological constraints on learning.)
Flanagan, O. (1991) *The Science of the Mind*, Cambridge, MA: MIT Press, 2nd edn. (Exposition and critique of Skinner's overall conception of behaviourism as a philosophy of science and mind.)
* Gallistel, C. (1990) *The Organization of Learning*, Cambridge, MA: MIT Press. (Extremely rich discussion of recent research on animal learning and navigation, how it seems to require postulation of internal computations, and resists behaviouristic explanation.)
Gleitman, H. (1995) *Psychology*, New York: Norton, 4th edn. (One of the best textbooks in the field; chapter 4 presents an extended discussion of the experimental literature for and against behaviourism.)
* Hempel, C. (1965) 'The Theoretician's Dilemma: A Study in the Logic of Theory Construction', in *Aspects of Scientific Explanation*, New York: Free Press. (Exploration of the puzzle about the role of 'intervening variables' in a theory.)
MacCorquodale, K. (1970) 'On Chomsky's Review of Skinner's *Verbal Behavior*', *Journal of the Experimental Analysis of Behavior* 13: 83–99. (A defence

of Skinner's *Verbal Behavior* against Chomsky's 1959 criticisms.)

* Pavlov, I. (1927) *Conditioned Reflexes*, Oxford: Oxford University Press. (The theory of 'classical conditioning', on which Skinner's theory of 'operant conditioning' was partly based.)

Pinker, S. (1994) *The Language Instinct*, New York: Morrow. (Superb popular introduction to the revolution occasioned by Chomsky's work in linguistics.)

Rey, G. (1997) *Contemporary Philosophy of Mind: A Contentiously Classical Approach*, Oxford: Blackwell. (A defence of a computational approach to mentalism; chapter 4 includes a summary of the main problems with scientific behaviourism as it concerns philosophy of mind.)

* Thorndike, E. (1911) *Animal Intelligence: Experimental Studies*, New York: Macmillan. (The earliest statement of behaviouristic principles, particularly the 'law of effect'.)

* Tolman, E. (1948) 'Cognitive Maps in Rats and Men', *Psychological Review* 55: 189–208. (Early proposal of an alternative to behaviourism as an explanation of navigation.)

* Watson, J. (1925) *Behaviorism*, New York: Norton. (Early statement of behaviouristic ideas that influenced both Russell and Skinner.)

OWEN FLANAGAN
GEORGES REY

SKOVORODA, HRYHORII SAVYCH (1722–94)

Skovoroda was the first truly independent philosopher produced by Ukraine and the last brilliant exponent of its Baroque culture. Departing from the Aristotelian tradition of the Kiev Academy, he constructed an original synthesis of ancient and patristic thought. Because of his classical aloofness from history, the sociopolitical trauma of Ukraine's absorption by Russia, which he witnessed, is hardly reflected in his writings. His worldview foreshadows the Romantic and religious tendencies in nineteenth-century Ukrainian and Russian thought.

Hryhorii Skovoroda (born in Chornukhy, died in Pan-Ivanivka, Ukraine) interrupted his studies at the Kiev Academy first in 1741–4 to sing in the court choir in St Petersburg and then in 1745–50 to serve as music director at the Russian imperial mission in Tokai, Hungary. Returning to Ukraine, he taught poetics at Pereiaslav College and then resumed his studies in Kiev (1751–3). After serving as private tutor, he taught poetics (1759–60), syntax and Greek (1762–4) and Christian ethics (1768–9) at Kharkiv College. Dismissed because of his unorthodox teachings, he spent the rest of his life wandering from friend to friend and writing. Most of his works belong to this period: over a dozen verses, thirty fables, two treatises, twelve dialogues and over 100 letters. His manuscripts were copied and circulated among his friends; none was published during his lifetime.

Skovoroda's style of writing is largely responsible for the widely differing interpretations of his thought. He conveyed his ideas mostly through imagery, similes, metaphors, fables, myths, parables and proverbs. Even philosophical terms are often defined by images, leading to ambiguity in his doctrines. Little clarity can be gained by seeking logical links among his doctrines: he did not arrange them into a system and rarely made explicit logical connections. His favourite devices of persuasion are analogies and illustrations, not arguments. Often, he ignores the implications of his teachings – the obvious questions and difficulties that follow from his statements. Thus, some scholars have viewed Skovoroda as an eclectic without a coherent body of doctrine. Most, however, agree that there is an inner unity to his thought. But then they differ on how his ideas fit together: some take his metaphysical teachings to be central and treat him as a theologian or mystic, others claim that he is a moral thinker. There are also diverse interpretations of his principal doctrines such as God's relation to the world, personal immortality and the nature of matter.

The purpose of philosophy for Skovoroda is practical – to show the way to happiness; hence the key questions are 'What is happiness?' and 'How can it be attained?'. He defines happiness as an inner state of joy, peace and confidence. To reach this state one must know some basic truths about oneself and the world. Skovoroda limits his metaphysical and anthropological teachings to those he regards as necessary for happiness. He shows no interest in theoretical questions that have no immediate bearing on existence.

Skovoroda divides reality into three worlds: the macrocosm or universe and two microcosms – man and the Bible. All three have a similar dualistic structure: they consist of an inner ideal nature that is spiritual, eternal and immutable and an outer sensible nature that is material, transitory and changing. The inner nature is higher; it imparts being to the outer as a tree supports its shadow. In the macrocosm, the inner nature is God and the outer is the physical universe. This position is panentheist, rather than pantheist, for God is in things through his ideas, not immediately. Although parts of the universe are transitory, the universe as a whole shares in God's eternity; hence matter is eternal.

In man, the inner nature is the spirit, soul, heart or true man; the outer is the body. It is unclear whether Skovoroda takes the true man to be a universal being common to all human beings or something unique in each individual. In any case, the soul can know itself more easily than it can know other souls; thus, all knowledge of spiritual reality begins with self-knowledge.

The symbolic microcosm or Bible consists of images of all the things in the macrocosm. The Bible's inner nature is the symbolic meaning, the higher truth known by the wise men of all ages; its outer nature is the literal meaning, which is often mistaken for truth itself. The purpose of biblical stories is to lead the reader to higher knowledge; the people and events described in the stories are insignificant and the miracles, which are contrary to nature, are fictional. Skovoroda interprets biblical symbols so as to show that the Bible's true meaning is expressed in his philosophy.

From this metaphysical scheme Skovoroda draws a number of practical conclusions. Since what is most valuable in us is eternal, we have no reason to fear death. Nor have we any reason to fear privation in this life, for Providence guarantees the necessities of happiness for all. The principle that what is necessary (for happiness) is easy and what is difficult is unnecessary serves as a criterion of rational need and reasonable expectation. Besides absence of fear, happiness requires self-fulfilment – the active pursuit of one's God-given innate calling or congenial task (*srodnoe delo*). To work in one's vocation, regardless of hardships, is to be happy, while to assume an unnatural task is to suffer hellish torment regardless of external rewards. Furthermore, since vocations are distributed by God in such a way as to ensure social harmony, to evade one's vocation is to introduce disorder into society and to harm others. The doctrine of congenial work is central to Skovoroda's moral system and the foundation of his optimistic attitude to life.

Skovoroda's influence on Ukrainian or Russian philosophy was negligible. His poetry was popular among the common people and valued by the founders of Ukrainian vernacular literature in the nineteenth century. During periods of cultural revival in the twentieth century, Ukrainian writers found inspiration in Skovoroda's ideas and independent personality.

List of works

Skovoroda, H. (1973) *Hryhorii Skovoroda: Povne zibrannia tvoriv u dvokh tomakh* (Hryhorii Skovoroda: The Complete Collection of his Work in Two Volumes), eds V. Shynkaruk *et al.*, Kiev: Naukova dumka; Ukrainian edition 1994. (The first full collection of Skovoroda's works, based on manuscripts and preserving the language he used.)
—— (c.1773) 'Razgovor piati putnikov o istinnom shchastii v zhizni'; abridged trans. G.L. Kline, 'A Conversation Among Five Travellers Concerning Life's True Happiness', in *Russian Philosophy*, vol. 1, eds J. Edie *et al.*, London and New York: Quadrangle Books, 1965, 26–57. (A key source for Skovoroda's moral doctrine.)
—— (1990) *Fables and Aphorisms*, trans. D. Chopyk, New York: Peter Lang. (An entertaining supplement to Skovoroda's dialogues.)

References and further reading

Bird, T. and Marshall, R. Jr. (eds) (1994) *Hryhorij Savyc Skovoroda: An Anthology of Critical Articles*, Edmonton and Toronto: Canadian Institute of Ukrainian Studies Press. (Recent studies of Skovoroda's language, style, literary influence and philosophical ideas, with bibliography.)
Ivan'o, I. (1983) *Filosofiia i styl' myslennia H. Skovorody* (H. Skovoroda's Philosophy and Style of Thought), Kiev: Naukova dumka. (An account of Skovoroda's cultural context, symbolism and literary style in relation to his ideas.)
Zenkovsky, V.V. (1948–50) *Istoriia russkoi filosofii*, Paris: YMCA-Press, 2 vols; 2nd edn 1989; trans. G.L. Kline, *A History of Russian Philosophy*, vol. 1, London: Routledge & Kegan Paul and New York: Columbia University Press, 1953, 53–69. (An exposition and critique of Skovoroda's philosophy.)

TARAS D. ZAKYDALSKY

SLAVERY

The moral, economic and political value of slavery has been hotly disputed by philosophers from ancient times. It was defended as an institution by Plato and Aristotle, but became increasingly subject to attack in the modern period, until its general abolition in the Western world in the nineteenth century.

In the twentieth century our belief that slavery is fundamentally unjust has become a benchmark against which moral and political philosophies may be tested. Both utilitarians and contractarian philosophers have argued against slavery in general and the enforceability of slavery contracts more specifically, although for very different moral reasons. Others have argued that only by viewing slavery from the standpoint of the slave can its moral significance be understood.

1   **Classical views of slavery**
2   **Later views of slavery**

1   Classical views of slavery

Slavery was widely practised in the ancient world, in different forms. In the Old Testament, the practice was generally limited to the women and children of the enemies of the Israelites, and was said to be instituted by God (Genesis 9: 25). The men of defeated cities were all killed (Deuteronomy 20: 13) as, often, were the women and children (2: 34, 3: 6). But women and children could be spared and enslaved by the conquerors (2: 14). Slavery also appears to be sanctioned in the New Testament, where slaves are told to obey their masters (Ephesians 6: 5; Colossians 3: 22; Titus 2: 9).

The Greeks, in contrast, often acquired adult male slaves by military means, and even conceived war as a form of hunting for slaves (Aristotle, *Politics* I.7.1255b37–40). There has been some debate over whether Plato envisaged the ideal state he describes in *Republic* as including the practice of slavery (see Wild 1939 versus Vlastos 1968), but the reference to slaves at *Republic* 433e would appear to leave no doubt in the matter. Certainly, they were included in the state described in Plato's *Laws* (for example, 773e).

PLATO never offers a whole theory of slavery, but it is clear from what he does say that the true slave is one who lacks reason (*Laws* 966b). This Platonic conception of the slave may also be found in what is certainly the most extensive philosophical treatment of slavery in antiquity: Book I of Aristotle's Politics. ARISTOTLE seeks to defend the practice of slavery as a just social institution, on the ground that it is not merely supported by existing laws and conventions, but also by nature itself. Aristotle forms his argument as a direct reply to those who argued that slavery is unnatural (*Politics* I.6). On the contrary, Aristotle is convinced that there do exist natural slaves, who are 'from birth marked out by nature as slaves' (I.5.1254a21–4). Like Plato, Aristotle locates the naturalness of slavery in the natural slave's rational deficiency: the slave, Aristotle says, wholly lacks the deliberative part of the soul (I.13.1260a12), and may even be conceived as no more than a part of the natural master's body (I.6.1255b11–12). Natural slave and natural master are both benefited by the institution of slavery: the master through access to the labour of the slave, the slave through access to the deliberative ability of the master. Aristotle concedes

that purely conventional slavery – where those naturally suited to be masters are enslaved, or those naturally suited to be slaves become masters – is morally indefensible.

Both Plato and Aristotle are highly critical of what they regarded as the excessively lenient treatment slaves received in democracies (*Republic* 563b; *Politics* VI .4.1319b28). Modern thinkers may well wonder at such an assessment in the context of democratic Athens, in which slaves were treated – by modern lights – very harshly indeed: slaves could be beaten at the whims of their owners (MacDowell 1978). But Aristotle also thinks that Plato's conception is excessively harsh, for Plato imagines that even the use of admonition 'spoils' the slave (*Laws* 773e), whereas Aristotle argues that the slave is even more appropriately admonished (as opposed to simply commanded) than is a child (*Politics* I.13.1260b5–7). It is problematical what Aristotle may have thought merited the rationalizations of admonition in the slave given that Aristotle makes his case for the naturalness of slavery precisely on the ground that the slave lacks reason (Smith 1991).

2   Later views of slavery

Later views of slavery through the Middle Ages combined this Aristotelian naturalism with the Christian concept of original sin. AUGUSTINE placed special emphasis on the latter; for him the 'prime cause' of slavery was sin, not nature (*City of God* XIX, 15). AQUINAS leaned in the other direction (*Summa theologaie* Ia.96.4). Could slavery have existed in man's natural state? By likening slavery to old age, Aquinas barely managed to avoid an affirmative answer. Slavery is occasioned by sin, but like old age and death it derives its naturalness from the rational order of being (3.suppl.52.1).

Jean BODIN dissented from early modern apologies for slavery, attacking Aristotelian and Augustinian views on empirical grounds (1606: I.5). Thomas HOBBES, who shared Bodin's preference for absolute sovereignty, took a more hypothetical view. Despite his vociferous attacks on Aristotle and 'the School-men', his own argument that slavery is irrational rests, in part, on the acknowledgement that some people are better at rational deliberation than others. The problem with Aristotle's view is that lacking absolute sovereign power, this particular difference may be less salient than it seems in a more stable society. Hence, Hobbes' 'ninth law of nature' urges individuals in the 'state of nature' not to be proud and to acknowledge one another as natural equals (1651: ch. 15). For less-able deliberators the alternatives to consenting to an absolute sovereign (living as outlaws or being slaves) are worse (Kidder 1983: 142).

Despite Locke's standing as a theorist of individual liberty and his denunciation of slavery as 'so vile and miserable an estate', (1690: I.i), he gave a qualified defence of slavery as part of his conception of a just war. When an unjust aggressor wages war, the just conqueror may enslave the former (II.xxiii.85). But even where an unjust act of aggression occurs, further conditions still must be met. The conqueror cannot enslave his own conquering forces, cannot take more than is needed to repair the damages incurred in waging war, and cannot enslave noncombatants. This last qualification extends to future generations and rules out the confiscation of land because land belongs to future generations by virtue of their inheritance rights (Farr 1986: 272–3) (see LOCKE, J. §10).

Enlightenment philosophers, while not unanimous in their condemnation of slavery, shifted the balance of arguments more in that direction. MONTESQUIEU, sometimes ironically, rejected Aristotle's view but added that in warm climates the threat of slavery may be needed to overcome laziness (1748: 15.7). Unsatisfied with this argument, however, he then wondered whether the laws in such climates are responsible for human laziness, and whether perhaps slavery would not be needed if there were better laws to make people less lazy (15.8). ROUSSEAU made a similar point more forcefully. Human nature can be servile when it is enslaved, but Aristotle 'mistook the effect for the cause' (Rousseau 1762: I.ii). Neither nature nor conquest justifies slavery.

The moral stance taken by the *philosophes* against slavery gave way in the nineteenth century to a complex array of historical interpretations. HEGEL argued that in the dialectical struggle for recognition the master's drive for autonomy breeds dependency upon the slave at the same time as the slave's own labour provides him with a mind of his own (Hegel 1807). Slavery, on this interpretation, is a necessary stage in the history of human emancipation. African slavery is especially necessary and should be eliminated only gradually given the African's stage of moral development (1822–30: 183).

Hegel's emphasis on the transformative power of labour captured Marx's imagination. He saw the wage worker under capitalism as engaged in something akin to the dialectical struggle for recognition between master and slave. As the 'wage-slave' shapes the product of his labour he contributes to the creation of a more self-conscious working class ([1844] 1978: 112) (see ALIENATION; MARX. K. §4). In contrast, NIETZSCHE (§8) argued that the new morality of the slave was not a form of greater,

emancipatory self-consciousness, but *ressentiment* and a base preoccupation with mere existence (1887: I.10). Eventually, however, these 'last men' and their democratic societies would give way to a more noble life (1886: § 202).

John Stuart Mill, against the background of a harmonious philosophy of history, focused more narrowly on the morality of voluntary slavery contracts (1859: ch. 5). Despite his strong stance against paternalism, Mill thought that slavery contracts should not be enforced for two reasons: slavery is always more harmful than freedom and freely choosing not to be free is incoherent. Scholars have questioned both arguments; under certain difficult circumstances, it is neither unreasonable nor most harmful for individuals to agree to be the slaves of benevolent slave-holders (Callahan 1985: 225).

More orthodox utilitarians since Mill have been troubled by the argument that under some conceivable circumstances they would have to permit even non-voluntary slavery. In response they claim that utilitarianism is a morality for the world as it actually is and one that respects all individuals equally (see UTILITARIANISM). Under actual circumstances utilitarian moral reasoning would not justify slavery (Hare 1979). In contrast, contractualists have argued that the problem is not what could conceivably be justified on utilitarian grounds, but the administrative kind of reasons utilitarians give in actual cases. According to contractualists, slavery is wrong because the slave-holders have no moral standing and the practice of slavery would not be accepted by the slaves themselves as a reasonable, permanent form of social cooperation (Rawls 1971a: 260–6), even if in dire circumstances it was temporarily acceptable to them (Rawls 1971b: 248) (see CONTRACTARIANISM §7–8).

Finally, some philosophers have argued that in addition to the question of justification, one can look back through the experience of slavery from the standpoint of the slaves, not the slave-holders, to understand more fully complex moral concepts such as paternalism, forgiveness, citizenship and resistance (McGary and Lawson 1992).

References and further reading

* Aquinas, T. (1266–73) *Summa theologaie*, trans. Fathers of the English Dominican Province, London: Burns Oates & Washburne Ltd, 1912–36. (Passages in Ia and 3, supplement, suggest an Aristotelian interpretation of original sin as the 'prime cause' of slavery.)
Archard, D. (1990) 'Freedom not To Be Free: The Case of the Slavery Contract in J.S. Mill's *On Liberty*', *The Philosophical Forum*, October 40

(160). 453–65. (Defends and clarifies the limits of Mill's arguments against enforcing voluntary slavery contracts.)

* Aristotle (*c*.mid-4th BC) *The Politics*, ed. S. Everson, Cambridge: Cambridge University Press, 1988. (Book I offers Aristotle's theory of natural slavery.)

* Augustine (413–27) *City of God*, trans. M. Dods, New York: Random House, 1950. (Chapter XIX outlines a defence of slavery in terms of original sin.)

* Bodin, J. (1606) *The Six Bookes of a Commonweale*, ed. K.D. Macrae, Cambridge: Harvard University Press, 1962. (Book I, chapter 5 offers an empirical argument against slavery.)

* Callahan, J.C. (1985) 'Enforcing Slavery Contracts', *The Philosophical Forum* 16 (3): 223–36. (Carefully reviews the most prominent arguments for and against enforcement of voluntary slavery contracts.)

Davis, D.B. (1966) *The Problem of Slavery in Western Culture*, Ithaca, NY: Cornell University Press). (Comprehensively reviews the history of the idea and practice of slavery in the West.)

* Farr, J. (1986) "So Vile and Miserable an Estate': The Problem of Slavery in Locke's Political Thought', *Political Theory* 14 (2): 169–88. (Clarifies the Lockean conditions under which slavery is justified against an unjust aggressor.)

Fortenbaugh, W.W. (1977) 'Aristotle on Slaves and Women', in J. Barnes, M. Schofield and R. Sorabji (eds) *Articles on Aristotle 2: Ethics and Politics*, London: Duckworth, 135–39. (Seeks to defend the logical coherence of Aristotle's account in Politics.)

Garver, E. (1994) 'Aristotle's Natural Slaves: Incomplete 'Praxeis' and Incomplete Human Beings', *Journal of the History of Philosophy* 32 (2): 173–95. (Seeks to defend the logical coherence of the Aristotelian account.)

Glausser, W. (1990) 'Three Approaches to Locke and the Slave Trade', *Journal of the History of Ideas* 51 (2): 199–216. (Argues that Locke's position on slavery was not coherent.)

* Hare, R.M. (1979) 'What is Wrong with Slavery?', *Philosophy and Public Affairs* 8 (2): 103–21. (Defends utilitarianism against the charge that it could possibly justify slavery.)

* Hegel, G.W.F. (1807) *Phenomenology of Mind*, trans. J.B. Baillie, London: Allen & Unwin, 1966. (Book IVA discusses the master–slave dialectic.)

* —— (1822–30) *Lectures on the Philosophy of World History: Introduction*, trans. H.B. Nisbet, Cambridge: Cambridge University Press, 1975. (Argues for the gradual elimination of African slavery.)

* Hobbes, T. (1651) *Leviathan*, New York: MacMillan, 1962. (Chapter 15 suggests a prudential argument for submitting to absolute sovereignty.)

Hunting, C. (1978) 'The '*Philosophes*' and the Question of Black Slavery: 1748–1765', *Journal of the History of Ideas* 39 (4): 405–18. (Defends the '*philosophes*' as critics of black slavery.)

* Kidder, J. (1983) 'Acknowledgements of Equals: Hobbes's Ninth Law of Nature', *The Philosophical Quarterly* 33 (131): 133–46. (Reduces the distance between Aristotle's natural theory of slavery and Hobbes's views on equality.)

* Locke, J. (1689/90) *Two Treatises of Government*, ed. P. Laslett, Cambridge: Cambridge University Press, 1960. (In I.i, argues against slavery as a violation of natural rights.)

* MacDowell, D. (1978) *The Law in Classical Athens*, Ithaca, NY: Cornell University Press. (Provides a good summary of the laws concerning slavery in ancient Athens.)

* McGary, H. and Lawson, B.E. (1992) *Between Slavery and Freedom: Philosophy and American Slavery*, Bloomington, IN: Indiana University Press. (Analyses moral concepts related to slavery from the standpoint of the slave.)

* Marx, K. (1844) *Economic and Philosophic Manuscripts of 1844*, trans. M. Milligan, in *The Marx-Engels Reader*, ed. R.C. Tucker, New York: W.W. Norton, 1978. 2nd edn. (Draws an analogy between slavery and wage labour.)

* Mill, J.S. (1859) *On Liberty and Other Writings*, ed. S. Collini, Cambridge: Cambridge University Press, 1989. (Chapter 5 argues against the paternalistic enforcement of voluntary slavery contracts.)

* Montesquieu, C. de Secondat, Baron de (1748) *The Spirit of the Laws*, trans. and ed. A.M. Cohler, B.C. Miller and H.S. Stone, New York: Cambridge University Press, 1989. (Chapter 15 argues ironically and with some hesitation against the Aristotelian theory of natural slavery.)

* Nietzsche, F. (1886) *Beyond Good and Evil*, in *The Basic Writings of Nietzsche*, trans. W. Kaufmann, New York: Random House, 1968. (Section 202 foresees the eventual passing of slave morality.)

* —— (1887) *On the Geneology of Morals*, in *The Basic Writings of Nietzsche*, trans. W. Kaufmann, New York: Random House, 1968. (Contains a criticism of slave morality in I.10.)

* Plato (*c*.mid-4th BC) *Republic*, in *Plato: Collected Dialogues*, ed. E. Hamilton and H. Cairns, Princeton, NJ: Princeton University Press, 1963. (At 433e, appears to take it for granted that the 'ideal state' would use slaves.)

* —— (*c*.mid-4th BC) *Laws*, in *Plato: Collected Dialogues*, ed. E. Hamilton and H. Cairns, Princeton, NJ: Princeton University Press, 1963. (At 773e, shows that slaves also will be included in the 'second-best state.')

* —— (1971a) 'Justice as Reciprocity', in *Mill: Utilitarianism*, ed. S. Gorovitz, Indianapolis, IN: Bobbs-Merrill. (Argues from hypothetical consent against the practice of slavery.)

* Rawls, J. (1971b) *A Theory of Justice*, Cambridge, MA: Harvard University Press. (Notes the circumstances in which slaves themselves might prefer slavery to other likely outcomes.)

* Rousseau, J.-J. (1762) *On the Social Contract*, ed. R.D. Masters, trans. J.R. Masters, New York: St Martin's Press, 1978. (Argues against Aristotle's theory of natural slavery.)

Salter, J. (1992) 'Adam Smith on Feudalism, Commerce, and Slavery', *History of Political Thought* 13 (2): 219–41. (Reviews Smith's views on the decline of slavery and economic development.)

Schutrumpf, E. (1993) 'Aristotle's Theory of Slavery – A Platonic Dilemma', *Ancient Philosophy* 13 (1): 111–23. (Argues that Aristotle's confusion over slavery is a legacy from Plato.)

* Smith, N.D. (1991) 'Aristotle's Theory of Natural Slavery' in D. Keyt and F.D. Miller, Jr (eds) *A Companion to Aristotle's Politics*, Oxford: Blackwell, 142–55. (Argues that Aristotle's theory of slavery in Politics is logically incoherent.)

Smith, S.B. (1992) 'Hegel on Slavery and Domination', *The Review of Metaphysics* 46 (1): 97–124. (Argues for a theological reading of Hegel's critique of Aristotle's theory of natural slavery.)

* Vlastos, G. (1968) 'Does Slavery Exist in the Republic?', *Classical Philology* 63 (4): 291–5. (Argues that Plato included slavery in his 'ideal state.')

* Wild, J. (1953) *Plato's Enemies and the Theory of Natural Law*, Chicago. IL: Chicago University Press. (Denies that Plato included slavery in his 'ideal state.')

STEPHEN L. ESQUITH
NICHOLAS D. SMITH

SLAVOPHILISM

In the Slav countries outside Russia the term 'Slavophilism' is a generic name for all advocates of the 'Slav idea', irrespective of their philosophical views and political commitments. In Russia, however, this term is used, as a rule, to denote one specific ideology, elaborated in the 1840s by the former members of the Schellingian circle of 'Lovers of Wisdom': Ivan Kireevskii (1806–56) and Aleksei Khomiakov (1804–60). Among its other followers, the most creative were the former Hegelians – Konstantin Aksakov (1817–60) and Iurii Samarin (1819–76). Despite some individual differences, all these thinkers shared a coherent view of the world which was expressed in their philosophical, theological and historical ideas. Their importance was not immediately recognized, but after Dostoevskii and Solov'ëv it became clear that they were the most important part of Russia's 'philosophical awakening' in the first half of the nineteenth century.

The words 'Slavophiles' and 'Slavophilism' were originally intended as gibes. The same was true of the words 'Westernizers' and 'Westernism'. All these terms, however, could be interpreted positively and were finally accepted by both sides of the 'Slavophile–Westernizer' controversy. But in the case of the Slavophiles it was a very reluctant acceptance: they felt that the term 'Slavophilism' failed to express the essential nature of their philosophical and religious position. In addition, this term contained a rather misleading suggestion as to their solidarity with non-Russian Slavs: in fact they focused their attention on the 'truly Christian' and 'purely Slav' spiritual heritage of pre-Petrine Russia. An interest in the fates of non-Russian Slavs began to play a role in their ideology only at the time of the Crimean War. This shift of focus transformed the original Slavophilism into a form of imperial Russian Pan-Slavism.

1 **Theory of integral knowledge and integral personality**
2 **Philosophy of history**
3 **Ecclesiology and the concept of *sobornost'***
4 **Ideological evolution and different continuations**

1 Theory of integral knowledge and integral personality

The first sketch of the Slavophile worldview was Kireevskii's unpublished article 'A Reply to Khomiakov' (1839). The most elaborate presentation of its philosophical foundations is Kireevskii's essay 'On the Necessity and Possibility of New Principles in Philosophy', published posthumously in 1856.

Kireevskii's philosophical views revolve around the concept of 'integral knowledge' and 'integral personality', opposed to the disintegrating rationalism and individualism of the West. In the theory of knowledge he accused rationalism of taking an anti-ontological position, separating the knower from the known and thus transforming reality into a scattering of isolated fragments, united only by a cobweb of abstract relations. The power of reason, he claimed, is purely formal and, therefore, cannot attain the 'substantive' penetration of reality; the substantial can be grasped only by substantiality, that is to say, by personality as an integral whole. True knowledge is a result of the harmonious cooperation of all the powers of the personality; the precondition of such knowledge is wholeness of spirit and a living, direct bond between the knower and reality. Hence it must be a kind of revelation, an immediate understanding available through faith. But authentic faith (and therefore knowledge) cannot be experienced by an isolated individual; it must be rooted in the supraindividual, corporate consciousness of community. This supra-individual, communal consciousness had been destroyed in the socially atomized West; it was preserved, however, by the Orthodox Church. In Kireevskii's view, membership of the Orthodox Church made it possible for the Russian thinkers to create an entirely new, truly Christian philosophy, breaking with the legacy of rationalism and providing an effective remedy for the European spiritual crisis.

In his philosophy of man Kireevskii developed the concept of 'integral personality', setting it against the Western concept of the 'autonomous individual'. He described autonomy as a divisive, destructive principle: the autonomy of the individual brings about the atomization of society, the autonomy of reason destroys the harmony of the soul, splitting human personality into separate forces, each of them claiming autonomy for itself. In this way human life becomes fragmented into different aspirations: knowledge, politics and economic activity separate themselves from religion and morality, the state separates itself from the Church, aesthetic values become divorced from moral values, and so forth. Thus the striving for autonomy is incompatible with personal wholeness. The latter can be achieved only through the bringing together of all spiritual forces, through the religious concentration of spirit.

Kireevskii presented his philosophy of 'integralism' as rooted in the Russian Orthodox tradition and derived ultimately from the teaching of the Holy Fathers of Eastern Christianity. There was some truth in this claim: it is easy to see an affinity between Slavophile antirationalism and the programmatic anti-intellectualism of Eastern apophatic theology. Nevertheless it is fair to say that the direct source of Kireevskii's philosophy should be seen rather in the ideas of the German conservative Romantics. At the same time it must be stressed that the main target of Kireevskii's critique of rationalism was not the abstract rationalism of the Enlightenment (as was the case with the early Romantics) but the dialectical, historicized rationalism of Hegel. In a sense, Slavo-phile philosophy was a Russian response to the crisis of Hegelian 'Absolute Idealism'. Kireevskii, along with Khomiakov, saw Hegel as the greatest and most consistent rationalist philosopher, in whom Western thought attained its culminating point; hence the

crisis of Hegelianism was for them the crisis of Western philosophy as such. They sympathized with the aged Schelling whose 'philosophy of revelation' was consciously opposed to Hegelian panlogism. They were convinced, however, that a genuinely new and truly Christian philosophy could spring only from the Russian soil (see HEGELIANISM, RUSSIAN §4; SCHELLINGIANISM).

According to the Slavophile philosophers, Hegelian Absolute Idealism was proof that rationalism provides only an abstract, purely formal, empty knowledge, and attempts to create 'a world without a substratum'. Consequently, their own philosophical standpoint was a consistent ontologism: that is, the view that knowledge is a part and function of an existential penetration of reality. This standpoint was almost universally accepted by Russian religious philosophers of the early twentieth century. Some of them (BERDIAEV, N.A. and Ern) saw in it a distinctive feature of Russian philosophy.

2 Philosophy of history

The best-known part of Slavophile ideology was their philosophy of history. It revolved around two inter-connected antitheses: (1) between the 'ancient' (pre-Petrine) and the 'modern' (post Petrine) Russia, and (2) between Russia and Europe.

According to Kireevskii, Western civilization was composed of three constitutive elements: (1) Christianity, (2) the young barbaric peoples which destroyed the Roman Empire, and (3) the heritage of the ancient pagan world. The main difference between Russia and Western Europe lay in the fact that Russia lacked this ancient Roman heritage. In his pre-Slavophile period Kireevskii saw this difference as a great misfortune for his country; by the end of the 1830s, however, he came to see it as a blessing. Following some conservative German Romantics (especially Franz von Baader and Adam Müller) he saw the essence of Roman civilization in its rationalism, as embodied in the rational and formalized system of Roman law (see ROMANTICISM, GERMAN). Due to this, the ancient Roman society was an aggregate of rationally thinking individuals, motivated solely by individual profit; the only social tie was a bond of interest; the only unity, the unity of a party. There was no real community, but only an association of isolated human beings, lacking any common faith, convictions and customs. In such a situation the only regulator of human relations was legal convention backed by the external force of the state machine.

Kireevskii believed that the juridical rationalism of ancient Rome had exerted a fatal influence upon Western Christianity and, consequently, upon the entire course of Western history. He developed this view with the aid of Khomiakov, the Slavophile theologian and historian of the Church. Rationalism, inherited from ancient Rome, was, they argued, the prime disintegrating factor in the history of Western Christianity. The Roman Catholic Church broke away from the real 'catholicity' of tradition by arbitrary changes of dogma and attempts to prove them in a rational, scholastic way. The Church became a hierarchically organized juridical institution, external and alien to her body of believers. The religious individualism of the Reformation was a justified protest against Catholic authoritarianism; its consequence, however, was atheism and the apotheosis of egoism, which laid the spiritual foundation for the modern, rational and industrial European civilization. Thus, the ancient Roman heritage, the increasing rationalism of the Western Churches, the secularizing effect of the Enlightenment, the French Revolution and, finally, modern industrialism were seen by the Slavophiles as links in one historical process, replacing organic communal ties by legal conventions and paving the way for a completely soulless, mechanical civilization.

Old, pre-Petrine Russia represented an entirely different form of social development. Russian Orthodoxy, not infected by Western rationalism, preserved the teachings of Christ in all their purity. In contrast to the West, whose political systems were formed, as a rule, as a result of conquest, the old Russian state was created by a voluntary act of the people; thus in Russia the relationship between the rulers and the ruled could be based upon mutual confidence and solidarity. The basic cell of the old-Russian social structure was the *mir*, or *obshchina* – a self-governing unit based upon communal ownership of the land, respecting old traditions and managing its affairs according to the principle of unanimity. These elementary cells were united into larger structures ruled by the same basic principles. All 'Holy Russia' was one great *mir*, one great community of land, customs and faith. Thus, unlike the West, it was a society where the integrating factors were not mere interests but moral convictions, not things but values.

Konstantin Aksakov, the most original thinker among the younger Slavophiles, developed these views in the direction of an extreme communitarianism, combining a kind of Christian anarchism with an apologia for autocracy. For him the contrast between pre-Petrine Russia and the West was a contrast between internal and external truth. By 'internal truth' he meant the voice of conscience and a living tradition freely expressed in community life; by 'external truth' he meant juridical and political forms.

In his view law and state represented the sphere of society's self-alienation; they demanded obedience irrespective of moral convictions, under the threat of physical coercion, and were therefore incompatible with morality, which they tried to replace with mere legality. The worst form of government was the modern republic since it demanded from the people an active political participation, that is an active involvement with 'external truth'.

In contrast to the West, pre-Petrine Russia accepted law and the state merely as a sad necessity, never as a principle. Autocracy in the sphere of politics was not only compatible with freedom but even an essential condition of it: it was so because true freedom is not political freedom but freedom from politics, and such a freedom could exist only under an autocratic ruler who could carry the burden of politics on his own shoulders. In Muscovite Russia the relations between the state and the land consisted in mutual non-interference: the people never tried to rule and the monarchs (with the regrettable exception of Ivan the Terrible) did not interfere with the communal life of the land. The idea of the absolute state, the state which can arbitrarily change or destroy the living principles of society, was introduced into Russia by Peter the Great. After his violent Westernizing reforms the educated classes, the 'servants of the state', betrayed their national heritage and only the plain folk preserved in its life the old 'internal truth'. This diagnosis substantiated Aksakov's view that the peasant commune, integrated by moral principles and common ownership of the land, was the only remedy against the deep moral crisis resulting from Westernization, which threatened Russia with a destructive revolution. Hence Russia should regenerate itself through returning to its old ways and bridging the gap between the educated classes and the common people. This was the conclusion of Aksakov's long memoir *O vnutrennem sostoianii Rossii* (On the Internal State of Russia), which he submitted to the new Tsar, Alexander II, in 1855 on his accession to the throne.

3 Ecclesiology and the concept of *sobornost'*

An important part of the Slavophile doctrine was its ecclesiology, developed by Khomiakov. It was an all-embracing theory of the Church as a divine-human organism. Its central concept, corresponding roughly to Kireevskii's 'integrality', was *sobornost'*. This term can be associated with both Church sobor (council) and the verb sobirat' (to gather, unite). According to Khomiakov, the word *sobornost'*, which often occurs in old texts in Church-Slav, exactly corresponded to the Greek concept of 'catholicity', which meant universal unity, the unity of all, personified in the Church council as an organ of the Holy Spirit.

Sobornost', or catholicity, conceived in this way was a category which had an ecclesiological, social and epistemological meaning alike. Khomiakov derived its epistemological sense from the thesis that knowledge is rooted in will and faith, and these in turn depend on the strength of the bonds that link the individual to the Church community. The individual acquires knowledge of the truth only by uniting in love with the universal Church and thus becoming an organ of *sobornost' soznaniia*, that is to say, supraindividual consciousness stemming from the charismatic unity of life. Separation from that community means entering the fatal road of rationalism and individualism. This was the case of the Church of Rome: by arbitrarily changing the Creed (the insertion of the Filioque) it raised the private opinion of Western bishops to the rank of a dogma, violating thereby the fundamental principle of catholicity. From that moment on unity and freedom became incompatible concepts in the West. The history of Europe changed into the history of 'unity without freedom' (Catholic authoritarianism) and 'freedom without unity' (Protestant individualism). The secret of the harmonious reconciliation of unity and freedom was preserved by the Orthodox Church, which remained faithful to the old Christian tradition of *sobornost'*. Hence the Orthodox Church had become the only universal Church, the only depository of the true 'catholicity'.

Khomiakov's ecclesiology, systematically expounded in his treatise *The Church is One* and developed in a number of polemical pamphlets and private letters (including letters to William Palmer, a member of the Oxford Movement whom he tried to convert to Orthodoxy), greatly differed from the standard views of the Russian Church hierarchy of his time. It was radically *pneumatic*, since it defined the essence of the Church as neither an institution, nor a doctrine, but as the charismatic community of tradition that covers all the faithful. It was *immanentist*, since it saw the inner consciousness of the Church as the only criterion of truth and categorically rejected the idea of authority. Its holistic and historicist character expressed itself in the denial that any local church (let alone an individual bishop) could be treated as the authoritative teacher. The whole truth, Khomiakov argued, is known only to the Church taken as a whole, including the laity; it crystallizes in an organic historical process, hence even the decisions of the Church councils need to be confirmed through becoming a part of the universally accepted tradition.

It is understandable that the hierarchy of the Russian Church saw in Khomiakov's theological and ecclesiological works many dangerous ideas and (until 1879) strictly prohibited their publication in Russia. The Slavophiles, however, embraced these ideas with enthusiasm. Samarin wrote in 1867 that future generations would probably treat Khomiakov as a thinker who deserved to be called a Doctor of the Church. This prediction proved to be quite accurate. Despite dissenting voices (among them that of Father Pavel Florenskii), the prominent orthodox theologians of the early twentieth century (such as Father S.N. Bulgakov, Father G. Florovskii and many others) perceived Khomiakov's views as the best insight into the true essence of Orthodoxy, an 'eyewitness account' (Florovskii) of the reality of their Church. In many works Khomiakov is described as an important forerunner of the theological renewal in the Orthodox Church in the twentieth century (see RUSSIAN RELIGIOUS-PHILOSOPHICAL RENAISSANCE), or even as a Christian thinker who anticipated some ideas of the Second Vatican Council.

4 Ideological evolution and different continuations

Classic Slavophilism can be defined as a backward-looking utopianism, a Russian variant of conservative Romanticism, setting itself in opposition to the institutions and values of modern, capitalist civilization. Its utopian quality was not a matter for concern, since under the autocratic rule of Nicholas I no currents of Russian thought were allowed to be expressed in, and tested by, political activities. However, the loosening of political controls under Alexander II made it possible and necessary for the Slavophiles to pass from theory to practice. In these new conditions, Slavophilism was transformed into the right-wing variant of gentry reformism, on the one hand, and into Pan-Slavism, on the other. In both cases Romantic utopianism and emphasis on 'truly Christian' values were replaced by an open commitment to nationalism, accepting, at least tacitly, the need for capitalist modernization of the Russian state.

The main Slavophile ideologists of the gentry-supported movement for reforms were Iurii Samarin and Aleksandr Koshelëv. They took an active part in the emancipation of serfs and because of this earned the reputation of 'liberals', although their attitude towards Western liberalism remained intransigently hostile. The difference between them was that Samarin feared all forms of representative institutions on the national level while Koshelëv wanted an all-Russian Land Assembly with advisory power to be convened in Moscow, to serve as a counterpoise to the St Petersburg bureaucracy. Both men greatly contributed to the preservation of the village commune, defending it as a bulwark against proletarianization and as a supplier of cheap labour for the estates of the gentry. Samarin also became a leading ideologist of the russification policies in Russia's 'western borderlands' and in the Congress of Poland.

The leading figure in the transformation of Slavophilism into Pan-Slavism – an ideology providing 'Slav' arguments for Russia's territorial expansion – was Ivan Aksakov (younger brother of Konstantin Aksakov). He was an influential publicist, demanding the conquest of Constantinople and the establishment of a powerful, Russian-led Slav federation. His nationalism was anti-Semitic and violently anti-Polish, defining Poles as 'renegades of Slavdom'. More sophisticated and philosophically developed was the Pan-Slavism of Nikolai Danilevskii (1822–55), the author of *Russia and Europe* (1869). He grounded the 'Slav idea' on a naturalistic foundation and developed an original theory of 'historico-cultural types' of civilization, anticipating to a certain extent Spengler's philosophy of history. But Danilevskii's links with the founders of Slavophilism were very tenuous: he rejected their political Romanticism, especially the idea of a 'Christianization of politics', claiming that Christian morality applied only to individuals, and that the relation of states and nations could only be based on self-interest and struggle for power (see PAN-SLAVISM §3).

The impact of Slavophile ideas on Russian thought was diverse and profound. The Slavophiles' views on the Russian peasant commune influenced HERZEN and through him other ideologists of Russian populism. The Slavophile critique of the West was taken up by DOSTOEVSKII and set the tone for all currents of Russian anti-Westernism. Slavophile philosophy, especially Kireevskii's 'integralism', was the main influence on Vladimir SOLOV'ËV in the first phase of his philosophical development; in later years he broke with the epigones of Slavophilism protesting against their nationalism and anti-Catholicism, but, none the less, continued to develop quite a few of their philosophical ideas. Russian religious philosophers of the early twentieth century had, as a rule, no doubts that Kireevskii and Khomiakov laid the foundation of a distinctively Russian tradition in philosophy.

See also: ENLIGHTENMENT, RUSSIAN

References and further reading

Berdiaev, N. (1912) *Aleksei Stepanovich Khomiakov*, Moscow. (The classic work on Slavophile philosophy by a famous Russian philosopher of the early twentieth century.)

Bolshakoff, S. (1945) *The Doctrine of the Unity of the Church in the Works of Khomiahov and Moehler*, London. (A detailed analysis of Khomiakov's ecclesiology. The author compares Khomiakov's doctrine with the views of J.A. Moehler, a Romantic Catholic theologian from Tübingen.)

Christoff, P.K. (1961, 1972, 1982, 1991) *An Introduction to Nineteenth-Century Russian Slavophilism*, vol. 1, *A.S. Xomjakov*, The Hague; vol. 2, *I.V. Kireevskii*, The Hague; vol. 3, *K.S. Aksakov*, Princeton, NJ: Princeton University Press; vol. 4, *Iu.F. Samarin*, Boulder, CO: Westview Press. (The most comprehensive historical account of the Slavophile movement in any language.)

* Danilevskii, N. Ia. (1869) *Rossiia i evropa* (Russia and Europe), New York: Johnson Reprint Corporation, 1966. (Referred to in §4.)

Edie, J.M., Scanlan, J.P. and Zeldin, M.B. (eds) (1976) *Russian Philosophy*, vol. 1, 2nd impression, Knoxville, TN: University of Tennessee Press. (Representative selection from the works of I. Kireevskii, S. Khomiakov and K. Aksakov.)

Gleason, A. (1972) *European and Muscovite: Ivan Kireevskii and the Origins of Slavophilism*, Cambridge, MA. (Deserves special mention in the literature on Kireevskii.)

Gratieux, A. (1939) *A.S. Khomiakov et le mouvement Slavophile* (A.S. Khomiakov and the Slavophile Movement), 2 vols, Paris. (The first comprehensive monograph of Slavophilism in a Western language examining Slavophile thought from a Catholic viewpoint.)

Leatherbarrow, W.J. and Offord, D.C. (eds) (1987) *A Documentary History of Russian Thought From the Enlightenment to Marxism*, Ann Arbor, MI: Ardis. (Includes selections from the prominent Russian Slavophiles.)

Müller, E. (1966) *Russischer Intellekt in europäischer Krise: Ivan V. Kireevskij*, Cologne. (A recommended work on Kireevskii.)

Raeff, M. (ed.) (1983) *Russian Intellectual History: An Anthology*, 2nd impression, Sussex: Harvester Wheatsheaf. (Collects writings that have helped shape the social and political consciousness of Russia.)

Walicki, A. (1975) *The Slavophile Controversy: History of a Conservative Utopia in Nineteenth-Century Russian Thought*, Oxford: Clarendon Press. (Analyses the Slavophile philosophy from a comparative European perspective; it deals also with the antecedents of Slavophilism, with the confrontation of Slavophilism and Westernism, and with the different continuations of the Slavophile thought.)

ANDRZEJ WALICKI

SLOVAKIA, PHILOSOPHY IN

Until as late as 1918, social and national circumstances were not favourable to the development of philosophy in Slovakia. The enforced retardation of the country had an obviously negative impact on intellectual and cultural life, and stood in the way of the possibility of diversity. That is why the first important Slovak philosophers such as Bayer and Caban emerged only as recently as the seventeenth century. Following this, philosophers of the Enlightenment such as Karlovský, Laurentzy, Steigel and Feješ started to criticize the anti-scientific ideas which still survived. In the first phase of the National Revival Movement, Jan Kollár created a new philosophy of history by postulating the cultural unity of the Slavs. A specific contribution to this theory came from L. Štúr and his followers (Hurban, Hodža, Kellner) who applied it to practical conditions and stressed the necessity of national emancipation for the Slovak nation. Their influence is evident in all further developments of the national movement and its philosophy.

The end of the nineteenth century saw the replacement of this idea by the philosophy of Thomas Masaryk. Slovak cultural life and philosophy, however, only began to develop fully in the context of an independent Czechoslovak Republic after 1918. The mainstream philosophy of the time was rationalistic, evident in the thought of such thinkers as Sv. Štúr, Koreň and Osuský. Philosophy after 1945 was marked by the achievements of Hrušovský, his students and colleagues, whose initial form of neopositivism took on a Marxist dialectical structurology. The importance of Marxism has recently been gradually declining and the Slovak philosophic scene is independently evolving in an atmosphere more in line with other European countries, particularly since the formation of the Slovak Republic in 1993.

1   History and evolution
2   The seventeenth to nineteenth centuries
3   Twentieth century philosophy

1   History and evolution

As early as the tenth century, Slovakia lost its political independence during the formation of new states in the Danube valley. Subsequently, until 1918, Slovakia was politically subject to Hungary and later was part of the Austro-Hungarian empire. Under these circumstances the Slovak nation had lived through centuries of almost uninterrupted national, economic and cultural oppression by foreign rulers. The feudal atmosphere retarded cultural development, as well as the spread of higher education. Many Slovaks thirsting for knowledge went abroad – many of these never returned.

At the end of the sixteenth century the situation began to change as waves of humanism and later-Reformation thought arrived in Slovakia. The first humanistic scholars from Slovakia are connected with this period. These worked abroad, however, and included Ján Sambocký of Trnava (d. 1584), translator of Plato's dialogues, Vavrinec Benedikti of Nedožiery (d.1615), educational reformer and propagator of the ideas of Petrus RAMUS, and Ján Jessenius (d. 1621), physician and supporter of Renaissance Neo-Platonist natural philosophy.

2   The seventeenth to nineteenth centuries

The Reform School (*kolegium*) in the East Slovak town of Prešov became the country's first important philosophical centre. This school tried to overcome scholasticism by promoting Bacon's inductive empirical methods, thereby hoping to achieve closer connection between philosophy and the natural sciences (see BACON, F.). The leading representatives, who were influenced also by the works of COMENIUS, were Ján Bayer (d. 1674) and Izák Caban (d. 1707). At the Jesuit university in Trnava, centre of the anti-reform movement, some professors, including František Kéri (d. 1768), Andrej Jaslinský (d. 1784), and Ján B. Horvát (d. 1800), were impressed by the methods of current natural science and worked to free Slovak philosophy from orthodox neoscholasticism.

The Enlightenment reached its peak in Slovakia between 1789 and 1820. Here it showed some indications of compromise (particularly in relation to religion) when compared to its western European counterpart. Nevertheless, it also fulfilled an emancipatory function through figures such as Žigmund Karlovský (d. 1821), Ján Laurentzy (d.1819), Michal Steigel (d.1829), and Ján Feješ (d.1823).

National Revival, developing at first in parallel and in cooperation with similar Czech feelings, brought a change in the orientation of philosophy. Abstract metaphysics, ontology and logic were no longer at the forefront. Their place was taken by philosophy of history, an interest in theories of nationhood (in connection with philosophy of language, arts and culture) and, in general, philosophy conceived as the theory of particular social practices. Reform tradition, German neohumanism and philosophers such as Herder, Fries and Hegel stimulated new thought. Theoreticians of the National Revival saw ideological support for their efforts in the 'Slavonic' emergence of Herderian–Hegelian philosophy of history as the highest degree of human development. Ján Kollár (d. 1852) built on this philosophy to produce his own idea of the mutual cultural evolution of Slavs. Ľudovít Štúr (d. 1856) developed the idea in a

Hegelian spirit by stressing the necessity of a specific emancipatory role for the Slovak nation, thus influencing the whole future course of the Slovak national liberation effort. Štúr's contemporaries and followers put forward similar ideas, and this concept achieved a kind of Slavonic messianicism in the thought of some philosophers.

A change is evident in the second half of the nineteenth century with thinkers interested in the particular needs of national society. This work was undertaken by scientists such as D. Štúr, A. Stodola and J.A. Wagner on the one hand, while on the other there was later, from the beginning of the twentieth century, a group of intellectuals, including V. Šrobár, A. Štefánek and J. Lajčiak, gathered round the magazine *Hlas* (Voice) which was inspired by the philosophy of MASARYK.

3 Twentieth century philosophy

When Slovakia became part of the independent Czechoslovak Republic in 1918, a new situation arose. Slovak intellectual life flourished and became the potential repository of a new philosophical culture. Contact with the more progressive Czech philosophy became more intensive (Czech philosophers lectured at the newly founded university in Bratislava). Direct contacts with contemporary European thinkers also increased. The influence of Masaryk's philosophy continued to be strong, particularly in the work of Svätopluk Štúr who also made use of ideas from Benedetto CROCE and J.L. Fischer in his search for a synthetic type of rationalism. Classical positivism prevailed in the work of Jozef Koreň and Samuel Š. Osuský, ideologically influenced by the Protestant tradition.

An important event in Slovak intellectual life was the establishment in 1937 of the Association for Scientific Synthesis which brought together researchers from different scientific fields. This association emphasized the use of methodological principles taken from neopositivism and structuralism. The leading figure was Igor Hrušovský who, even after accepting the basic theses of Marxism after 1945, remained the dominant figure of Slovak philosophy, and created a new concept of dialectical structurology.

When the Communist Party regained power in 1948, a Marxist orientation was enforced and subsequently dominated public Slovak philosophy. Historians of philosophy such as E.Várossová, T. Münz, J. Bodnár, J. Kocka, M. Burica, M. Zigo and others began to free themselves from ideological oppression, and many published valuable works. These were followed by works of authors from other philosophical disciplines, and Slovak translations of philosophical classics achieved important success.

After 1968, in the period of the totalitarian regime, philosophers Milan Šimečka and Miroslav Kusý worked in the dissident movement. Their works, analysing the problems of the time, were published illegally or abroad. In the 1980s, the younger generation of Slovak philosophers began publishing the results of their research on the history of philosophy, the problems of phenomenology, existentialism, analytic philosophy, the Frankfurt School and also on postmodern trends. However, it was only after the fall of the totalitarian regime in 1989 that complete freedom of philosophical activity became possible.

See also: CZECH REPUBLIC, PHILOSOPHY IN

References and further reading

Bodnár, J. (ed.) (1988) *Geschichte des philosophischen Denkens in der Slowakei* (History of philosohical thought in Slovakia), Bratislava: Veda. (Detailed history of earlier Slovak philosophy until 1900.)

Král, J. (1934) *La philosophie en Tchécoslovaquie* (Philosophy in Czechslovakia), Prague: Bibliothèque des problèmes sociaux, 2. (Brief summary of historical development of philosophy in Bohemia, considering also Slovakia.)

Lobkowicz, N. (1961) *Marxismus-Leninismus in der ESR, Die tschechoslowakische Philosophie seit 1945*, Dortrecht: Reidel. (Detailed analysis of Czech and Slovak Marxism considering also other trends.)

Pichler, Tibor and Gašpariková, Jana (eds) (1993) 'Language, Values and the Slovak Nation', *Slovak Philosophical Studies I*, Cultural Heritage and Contemporary Change IV, Washington, DC: The Council for Research in Values and Philosophy. (The history of the development of the sense of national identity, written by a team of authors.)

Zumr, J. (1971) 'Philosophie der Gegenwart in der Tschechoslowakei' (Contemporary philosophy in Czechoslavakia), in R. Klibansky (ed.) *Contemporary Philosophy*, Florence: La nuova italia editrice, 455–73. (Brief summary of Czech and Slovak thought, 1930–69.)

JOSEF ZUMR

SMART, JOHN JAMIESON CARSWELL (1920–)

J.J.C. (Jack) Smart was born in England and studied at Glasgow and Oxford universities before moving to

813

Australia to take up the Chair of Philosophy at Adelaide University. He was one of the earliest and most influential advocates of the mind-brain identity theory, the view that mental states are identical with brain states. He also played a major role in articulating and defending realism in science, the four-dimensional view of time and act utilitarianism in ethics.

1 Biography
2 Mind-brain identity theory
3 Realism, time and ethics

1 Biography

J.J.C. Smart was born on 16 September 1920 in Cambridge, England. At Oxford he was influenced by Gilbert RYLE though he subsequently abandoned Rylean behaviourism in favour of a robust realism about mental states and scientific entities. He took up the Chair of Philosophy at Adelaide University in 1950, and moved to La Trobe University in 1972 before going to the Chair of Philosophy at the Institute of Advanced Studies at the Australian National University in 1976. He has made a number of visits to the United States and probably has had more philosophical influence there and in Australia than in Britain.

A distinctive feature of his writing is the clarity and directness with which he advances his views. This is a trait that he shares with another important Australian philosopher, David Malet ARMSTRONG, and together they have influenced the way a generation of philosophers in Australia write, as well as influencing the doctrines they espouse.

2 Mind–brain identity theory

In a landmark article, 'Sensations and Brain Processes', first published in 1959, Smart defends the view (put forward earlier by his Adelaide colleague U.T. Place) that sensations are brain processes. Sensations are not correlated with or causally connected to, but literally identical with brain processes in the same way that lightning is identical with an electrical discharge. Later he extended the view to encompass intentional states like belief and desire and mental states in general.

An important feature of his version of the identity theory is his topic neutral analysis of sensation reports. He grants that when I report a sensation in a sentence like 'I am in pain' or 'I am having a yellow after-image', I am not making a claim about my brain as such. I may not even know that I have a brain. I am, he argues, making a claim roughly to the effect that something is going on in me like what goes on in me when a pin is stuck in me or a whip is applied to me or... (in the case of pain), and like what goes on in me when I see a lemon or a sunflower or... (in the case of a yellow after-image). The nature of these 'somethings that go on in me' is then a matter for empirical investigation, and his view is that they will turn out to be certain processes in the brain. With the benefit of hindsight we can now see his topic neutral analyses as a precursor of functionalism, for both see mental states as inner states whose mental nature is a matter of their relational properties (see MIND, IDENTITY THEORY OF; FUNCTIONALISM).

3 Realism, time and ethics

The view that mental states are brain states is a species of realism. Mental states are not 'convenient fictions' for the prediction of behaviour. Similarly, Smart argues that the sub-microscopic particles of physics are real. Electron theory is not merely a device for predicting the tracks in Wilson cloud chambers (see FICTIONALISM; SCIENTIFIC REALISM AND ANTI-REALISM). Electrons rather are the causes of these tracks. Otherwise, Smart argues, the regular appearance of the tracks would have to be regarded as a cosmic coincidence. More generally, he argues that only the realist can explain why positing sub-microscopic particles should have such great instrumental value. Smart insists that the situation with electrons and macroscopic entities like tables and the sun is essentially the same: none is to be reduced to patterns of observations or patterns of experiences. They are all independently existing entities to be believed in as the best explainers of the patterns.

Smart views time as a fourth dimension akin to the three spatial ones, and sees this as the only view to hold in light of the Minkowski interpretation of relativity theory. Objects are extended in time as well as space, and accordingly have temporal parts as well as spatial ones. A tree's growing is a matter of later temporal parts of the tree being taller than earlier ones, and the problem of identity over time – of persons, trees, schools or whatever – becomes the problem of finding the right relation to unify different temporal parts to make up a single, temporally extended person, tree, school, or whatever. On this view the present has no special ontological status: what I call 'now' is simply the time of my calling, and the past is simply times before then, and the future times after then.

Smart's position in meta-ethics is a version of noncognitivism: ethical statements are expressions of overriding attitudes, and words like 'good' and 'right' are terms of commendation, not terms that describe (see EMOTIVISM). His position in normative ethics is an uncompromising version of act utilitarianism. The right act is that act out of those available to the agent that would produce the most happiness (or, better, has the greatest expectation of doing so). He famously criticizes rule utilitarianism – the view that the right act is the act in accord with the rule the following of which would produce the most happiness – as involving a kind of 'rule worship' inconsistent with utilitarianism's guiding thought that it is outcomes that matter. In Smart's view the value of keeping promises, distributing goods equitably and not punishing innocent people, is instrumental only. Thus, in (arguably rare) cases where punishing someone innocent would have good results – perhaps it is generally believed the prisoner is guilty so that punishing him would have a deterrent effect on potential wrongdoers – it is straighforwardly right to do so (see UTILITARIANISM).

See also: AUSTRALIA, PHILOSOPHY IN

List of works

Smart, J.J.C. (1961) *An Outline of a System of Utilitarian Ethics*, Melbourne: Melbourne University Press. Revised edn in J.J.C. Smart and B. Williams, *Utilitarianism: For and Against*, Cambridge: Cambridge University Press, 1973, 1–74.
—— (1963) *Philosophy and Scientific Realism*, London: Routledge & Kegan Paul. (One chapter of this book is largely based on 'Sensations and Brain Processes'.)
—— (1968) *Between Science and Philosophy*, New York: Random House.
—— (1984) *Ethics, Persuasion and Truth*, London: Routledge & Kegan Paul.
—— (1987) *Essays Metaphysical and Moral*, Oxford: Blackwell.
—— (1989) *Our Place in the Universe*, Oxford: Blackwell.
Smart, J.J.C. and Haldane J. (1996) *Atheism and Theism*, Oxford: Blackwell.

References and further reading

Pettit, P. *et al.* (eds) (1987) *Metaphysics and Morality*, Oxford: Blackwell. (Good collection of papers on Smart's work, with a list of his publications up to 1986.)

FRANK JACKSON

SMITH, ADAM (1723–90)

Despite his reputation as the founder of political economy, Adam Smith was a philosopher who constructed a general system of morals in which political economy was but one part. The philosophical foundation of his system was a Humean theory of imagination that encompassed a distinctive idea of sympathy. Smith saw sympathy as our ability to understand the situation of the other person, a form of knowledge that constitutes the basis for all assessment of the behaviour of others. Our spontaneous tendency to observe others is inevitably turned upon ourselves, and this is Smith's key to understanding the moral identity of the individual through social interaction. On this basis he suggested a theory of moral judgment and moral virtue in which justice was the key to jurisprudence. Smith developed an original theory of rights as the core of 'negative' justice, and a theory of government as, primarily, the upholder of justice. But he maintained the political significance of 'positive' virtues in a public, non-governmental sphere. Within this framework he saw a market economy developing as an expression of humanity's prudent self-interest. Such self-interest was a basic feature of human nature and therefore at work in any form of society; but commercial society was special because it made the pursuit of self-interest compatible with individual liberty; in the market the poor are not personally dependent upon the rich. At the same time, he recognized dangers in commercial society that needed careful institutional and political management. Smith's basic philosophy is contained in The Theory of Moral Sentiments *(1759), but a major part concerning law and government was never completed to Smith's satisfaction and he burnt the manuscript before he died. Consequently the connection to the* Wealth of Nations *(1776) can only be partially reconstructed from two sets of students' notes (1762–3 and 1763–4) from his* Lectures on Jurisprudence *at Glasgow (Smith [1762–6] 1978). These writings are complemented by a volume of essays and student-notes from lectures on rhetoric and belles-lettres.*

Although a philosopher of public life and in some measure a public figure, Adam Smith adhered to the Enlightenment ideal of privacy to a degree rarely achieved by his contemporaries. He left no autobiographical accounts and, given his national and international fame, the surviving correspondence is meagre. The numerous eyewitness reports of him mostly relate particular episodes and individual traits of character. Just as there are only a few portraits of the man's appearance, there are no extensive accounts of the personality, except Dugald Stewart's 'Life of Adam Smith' (1793), written after Smith's death and designed to fit Stewart's eclectic supplementation of common sense philosophy. While Smith was a fairly sociable man, his friendships were few and close only with men who respected his desire for privacy. David Hume was pre-eminent among them.

1 Life
2 Imagination: scientific and moral order
3 Moral theory
4 Law and politics

1 Life

Adam Smith's date of birth is unknown, but he was baptized in Kirkcaldy in Fife, Scotland, on 5 June 1723. His father, a customs officer, died some months earlier and Smith was brought up as an only child, a circumstance shared with several contemporary Scots literati, as has been emphasized in recent psycho-history (Camic 1983). Smith evidently remained close to his mother., and some will see this as an explanation for the fact that his attraction to female company never stretched to marriage. Otherwise, we have little evidence of the nature of Smith's intimate life.

As was common, Smith attended the local parish school and then went to Glasgow University in 1737, where he was taught moral philosophy by Francis HUTCHESON. In 1740 he went to Balliol College, Oxford, lingering there for six years. He compensated for the lack of organized education – later condemned in the *Wealth of Nations* (1776; henceforth *WN*) – by extensive private study, mainly in Greek, Latin and French literature, turning himself into an extremely well-read man. From 1746–8 Smith seems to have stayed with his mother in Kirkcaldy; but during the following three winters he gave public (non-university) lectures in Edinburgh, sponsored by Henry HOME (later Lord Kames) and his circle. The lectures were on rhetoric and belles-lettres, to which was eventually added a series of lectures on jurisprudence (published subsequently as *Lectures on Jurisprudence* ([1762–6] 1978; henceforth *LJ*)). This performance had the desired effect; in 1751 Smith was appointed professor at Glasgow University, first in logic and, after one year, in moral philosophy. Until his resignation in the middle of 1763–4, Smith gave the basic course in moral philosophy that had been founded by Gershom CARMICHAEL in the 1690s and developed by Francis Hutcheson in the 1730s and 1740s. It encompassed natural religion, ethics and jurisprudence. In addition, Smith gave an advanced class on rhetoric and belles lettres. Hardly a trace of Smith's lectures on natural religion has survived, but those on ethics formed the basis for his first major work, the *Theory of Moral Sentiments* (1759; henceforth *TMS*). Two student-reports on the lectures on

jurisprudence, which include economics, have survived from 1762–3 (incomplete) and 1763–4 (henceforth *LJ(B)* and *LJ(A)*, respectively); see Smith 1762–6: there is also the fragment of a report from earlier in Smith's career ('Anderson Notes'). Finally, there is a student's report on the lectures on rhetoric and belles-lettres from 1762–3 (henceforth *LRBL*; see Smith 1762–3).

Early in 1764 Smith became travelling tutor to the Duke of Buccleuch, a lucrative post that afterwards gave him a pension and an influential connection for life. Travelling in France and Switzerland until 1766, Smith met many of the French Enlightenment's leading thinkers, notably François-Marie Arouet VOLTAIRE and the circle of physiocratic economists led by François Quesnay and Anne Robert Jacques Turgot. Smith admired Voltaire, especially as a dramatist; and he shared the conceptual, empirical and normative concerns of physiocracy, though he reached different conclusions about these matters. Like the physiocrats, he understood the relationship between economics and civil society by postulating ideal–typical stages of social development; and like them, he rejected the common mercantilist analysis of wealth in terms of money and advocated a free economic system to create such wealth. Smith, however, rejected the physiocratic idea of land as ultimate source of wealth.

Smith had begun working on these matters during his Glasgow years, as *LJ* and the 'Early Draft' of the *WN* (reprinted in *LJ*) show. But it took him nearly another decade to develop his own grand theory. He worked until 1773 in seclusion at his mother's house in Kirkcaldy and then spent three years in London revising his manuscript. The *WN* appeared in the spring of 1776 to resounding praise from David Hume and Edward Gibbon, among many, and quickly turned the distinguished moral philosopher into a famous political economist.

1776 was in another respect a turning point for Smith, for in the late summer David Hume died. This led Smith publicly to indicate his religious outlook more clearly than before. He was already assumed, as we see from the cool attitude of James Boswell (once Smith's student) and Samuel Johnson, to be a sceptic concerning revealed religion. But when Smith publicly maintained that the infidel Hume had approached 'as nearly to the idea of a perfectly wise and virtuous man, as perhaps the nature of human frailty will permit', he was widely taken to have declared his own atheism (1777: xlix). In fact, Smith never made explicit his religious beliefs. Much of his work appears to be in the mould of common deism, but often it is unclear whether Smith is analysing deism as a psychological disposition or whether he is accepting it as a doctrine.

In the end his obdurate silence suggests he had accepted the basic lesson of agnosticism. He seems cooler toward religion as he gets older, and his 'obituary' for Hume is a milestone on this road.

In 1777 Smith was appointed Commisioner of Customs in Edinburgh, a lucrative office that he discharged conscientiously until his death. In addition to being in public office, Smith was now a public man of letters, sought by government and politicians for advice on matters of state and policy, such as relations with America and Ireland, trade and taxation. He had been elected to the Royal Society and to the Johnsonian 'The Club' during his stay in London in 1773–6. When he paid a rare visit to London, he was received in the literary circles around the Oyster Club, and although he never ventured abroad again, he remained a name in the Parisian salon-world, where he had been so well received in the '60s. He was also part of the cultural life of the high Enlightenment in Edinburgh, sought out by literary tourists and opening his house to a circle of friends once a week (see ENLIGHTENMENT, SCOTTISH). True to his suggestion that a citizen militia served a moral purpose, he was an officer in the Edinburgh militia. Smith lived with his mother, his cousin, Janet Douglas, and a nephew of the latter, David Douglas, whom Smith made his heir.

During these years Smith kept writing. He revised the *TMS* several times, including a major recasting (6th edn 1790) shortly before his death. The *WN* was revised for the second and, especially, the third editions (1778 and 1784) and saw two more life-time editions. But Smith also undertook new projects. One was a 'sort of theory and history of law and government', announced already in the first edition of *TMS* and still aspired to in the last edition of that work. The *WN* had taken account of 'police, revenue and arms', but the part concerning justice, the theory of jurisprudence, was still lacking (*TMS*, Advertisement: v). Smith's other project was 'a sort of Philosophical History of all the different branches of Literature, of Philosophy, Poetry and Eloquence' (Smith 1977: 287). A few days before he died, Smith requested his sixteen manuscript volumes to be burnt. We can form some idea of the former project from the lectures on jurisprudence and parts of *TMS* and *WN*; the latter was obviously related to the early *Essays on Philosophical Subjects* (henceforth *EPS*), published posthumously in 1795, and to the Glasgow lectures on rhetoric and belles lettres. But the systematic coherence of Smith's work is a matter of reconstruction – some scholars even deny that it has such coherence, despite Smith's declared intentions. Smith died in his house in the Canongate on 17 July 1790 and is buried in the Canongate cemetery.

2 Imagination: scientific and moral order

The single most important influence on Adam Smith was David Hume's philosophy, especially the theory of the imagination as the active mental power that fashions a specifically human world within nature (see HUME, D.). Like Hume, Smith saw imagination as that which enables us to create connections between the perceived elements of both the physical and the moral world, ranging from particular events and things to the cosmos and the system of humanity. For Smith there are two fundamentally different kinds of imagination, one concerning other persons as agents and one concerning things – human beings included – and events. The former is the basis for personal identity and sympathy (in Smith's special sense) and, thus, for the moral world. The latter is the basis for all theoretical activity of the mind, including science and the arts. The activity of the imagination is a spontaneous search for order and coherence in the world; satisfaction of it carries its own pleasure, while frustration brings 'wonder and surprise' and, if prolonged, anxiety and unease. Smith talks of this imaginative striving in aesthetic terms as a concern with beauty and harmony.

The 'theoretical' imagination is invoked for a number of different explanatory purposes. It accounts, according to Smith, for our ability to order things and events so that we can orient ourselves in life. It explains the 'aesthetics' of ordinary living, such as our tendency to order things for no other purpose than the order and arrangement that please, and our desire for machinery, gadgets and other 'systems'. Works of art, as well as of technology, are works of imaginative order. Not least, philosophy and science are products of the imagination's attempt to create order in the chaos of experience. This is expressed in the recurring machine analogies for the natural world and for society; and it is reflected in the human mind's tendency to underpin the perceived orderliness of the world by assuming an orderer with a purpose. In other words, science, deism and natural providence are all parts of the explanatory web that the imagination creates to satisfy its desire for order.

Within this framework Smith writes his remarkable histories of science, notably the essay on the history of astronomy. The basic thesis is that empirical evidence can only play a role as evidence if it fits into an orderly system of beliefs. Smith exhibits a sceptical distance in relation to all absolute truth-claims in both science and religion, epitomized in the famous conclusion to 'The History of Astronomy' in *EPS*:

[Newton's] principles, it must be acknowledged, have a degree of firmness and solidity that we should in vain look for in any other system. The most sceptical cannot avoid feeling this... And even we, while we have been endeavouring to represent all philosophical systems as mere inventions of the imagination, to connect together the otherwise disjointed and discordant phaenomena of nature, have insensibly been drawn in, to make use of language expressing the connecting principles of this one, as if they were the real chains which Nature makes use of to bring together her several operations.

([1795] 1980, IV.76: 105)

When we introduce order into our observations of other people, as opposed to the rest of nature, our imagination takes on a special quality. We are able to 'make sense' of the behaviour of others through imaginative identification – what Smith calls sympathy, a central concept in his philosophy. 'Sympathy' here has no evaluative connotations; it does not mean that one person accepts the motives and actions of another as good and right, nor is it a motive for action. Sympathy is the ability to see the point of view of another person so as to be able to accept or reject it as appropriate in *that* person's situation. This native ability is the key to Smith's social theory of the self and, through that, to his theory of the moral world.

Inclination and need lead people to interact; interaction depends on observation and appreciation of others and their situation, and this is facilitated by the universal tendency sympathetically to adopt the position of the other and compare reactions. Observation of others will bring awareness that oneself is the object of other people's observation and assessment. Society is the mirror in which individuals see their own nature. Further, in observing that one is being observed one has the basis for such mutual adjustment of behaviour as is necessary for all social living. Each individual is generally led to pre-empt this assessment by others through self-observation and self-assessment. In short, people internalize the spectator, and the internal spectator has the force to prompt such adjustment of behaviour as would otherwise be demanded by external spectators in order to satisfy the inclination to, or the need for, agreement or conformity.

The process of mutual adjustment through the sympathetic search for a common standpoint often fails, of course, leading to moral and social disorder. Thus we are led to imagine an ideal judgment and an ideal judge, transcending the limitations of knowledge, bias, and so forth of those actually involved. Once we establish a dialogue with this imagined ideal of an impartial spectator, we have a moral conscience.

With this social theory of moral personality Smith rejects the idea of Hutcheson and others that moral agency hinges on a special moral sense, offering instead explanations based on empirical features of the mind. Like Hume, Smith rejects the suggestion of Samuel CLARKE and others that moral judgment and motivation are forms of rational inference. And he ignores religious ideas of conscience as infusion (inspiration) by the deity or a response (fear) to the deity's might perceived. For Smith, formation of the moral self begins with others.

3 Moral theory

By means of this theory of the self, Smith produces a complex analysis of moral life. Moral judgment is inevitably an assessment of propriety – first of the motives of an agent in a given situation, then of the motives of the person who is the 'object' of the agent's actions. But our inclination towards orderliness leads us to classify actions just as our search for impartiality suggests general and impersonal points of view; and on this basis we develop general rules of behaviour which, once given social acceptance, significantly influence our assessment of the propriety of particular motives and actions. Sympathy ties us to the particularity of the situation, while the impartial spectator calls for the generality of rules. Similarly, while we have great difficulty making a moral assessment of motives and associated behaviour on the basis of their outcome, we tend to allow utility and disutility to influence our perception of propriety.

In a different mode from that of the analysis of moral judgment, Smith gives a complex account of moral virtue. At one level he looks on the moral and social ideas that make the world go round from the elevated standpoint of the stoic sage (see STOICISM §19). Smith was attracted by the stoic ideal of tranquility as the end of moral life; yet his account of moral psychology showed everything distinctive about the life of the human species to be due to people's inability to live in tranquility. The exercise of our productive powers, as portrayed in the *WN* and in the *TMS* as emulative vanity, is only the most dramatic illustration of an inescapable restlesness pervading our lives. In Smith's view a dialectic tension between tranquility and activity is bound to be a permanent feature of human life, and the implication is clearly that it would be futile for the philosopher to attempt to defend the one over the other.

At another level, Smith looks at morality from an historical point of view, and combines this with a theory of the cardinal virtues. The features of personality and courses of action people approve and disapprove of in others and in themselves vary from one culture and period to another. Accordingly, a major task for philosophy is to look at humanity historically and comparatively. This reveals that in one sphere of human response there is a great deal that is common to all humankind, namely in the sphere of *moral* approval and disapproval (as opposed to, say, the aesthetic or religious response). The moral philosopher can identify a number of basic virtues and vices, the tone and composition of which may vary significantly, but which are nevertheless universally recognizable and comparable.

One way of organizing this field is by means of the cardinal virtues, though Smith, like Hume, is more interested in distinguishing 'positive' from 'negative' virtues, – benevolence from justice. The distinction is based upon spectator reactions. When the spectator, whether the actual or the imagined impartial one, sympathetically enters into the situation of an agent, the result is approval or disapproval of the agent's judgment and action. When the agent tries to promote the good of someone, whether of self or of other, the spectatorial approval or disapproval tends to vary from person to person. For while we tend to agree on what is good in broad outline, we have great difficulty agreeing on what is good for particular persons in specific situations, unless we are connected in some moral community. By contrast, we tend to agree on what is harmful not only in general but in each case, and the pattern of reaction to harmful behaviour therefore has a high degree of uniformity, known as resentment.

4 Law and politics

The negative virtue of avoiding harm or injury is, according to Smith, *justice*, which is the foundation of law and the subject of jurisprudence. The positive virtues encompass the life of the private sphere, but, in addition, they are the basis for a public sphere that is neither political nor administrative in modern terms. By maintaining a system of justice, the government protects both private life and the non-political public sector of human activity, and one of the most striking features of the modern world of commerce is, in Smith's eyes, that by doing so government has made it possible for economic behaviour to be transformed from private to public.

The personal attributes and actions that are protected in each person when others show them justice, that is abstain from injuring them, are their rights. A *right* is a sphere of freedom to be or do or have something that the individual can maintain against all others because the spectatorial resentment towards infringement of this sphere is so strong that it has been institutionalized in the form of the legal system. This line of argument puts Smith in a tradition of thinking about rights that goes back to

GROTIUS, HOBBES and some religious covenanters. In this tradition the primary moral characteristic of the individual is self-assertion *vis-à-vis* the rest of humanity, so that all common or social morality arises through 'negotiation' between conflicting claims. Natural *law* is a secondary concept to that of *right*, in contrast to the ideas of the mainstream of thinking about natural law. While Hume was in some respects close to this tradition, he never found a way of accommodating the concept of rights within his sentimentalist theory of morality. This was left to Smith's theory of the spectatorial regulation of our moral sentiments (see NATURAL LAW; RIGHTS).

'Rights', 'injury', and 'personality' are linked. The imagination depends on social experience and hence varies from one stage of society to another; consequently the idea of moral personality must vary. This is the core of Smith's historical approach to justice and law. Smith rejects the idea of a state of nature as a device for understanding human nature. The moral life of the species is unavoidably social, since only the social mirror lends us humanity. All consideration of our moral characteristics must therefore include the social setting; this applies not least to rights as the primary characteristic. Even so, certain minimal rights are universal to all social living. A social group is only viable if it recognizes rights to physical, moral and some kind of social personality; these may accordingly be considered universal, 'natural' rights. Beyond this minimum, we have to look to the historical circumstance in order to understand rights.

In Smith's view, humanity can be divided into four broad stages of social development according to the extension of the concept of the person and, consequently, the scope of rights recognized. Hunters and gatherers recognize little beyond what immediately sustains the physical and moral person (food, shelter, personal freedom and social recognition). Dramatic extensions of personhood are produced by nomadic 'shepherds', with the recognition of property in food and tools much beyond what is required for each individual and their immediate dependents; and, further, in the agricultural stage, with recognition of property in land. The most abstract extension of the concept of personality occurs in commercial society, with the full development of contractual entitlements and ownership of purely symbolic property (paper money, credits) as parts of what a person is.

Each of these developments requires stronger government to protect its new rights, and, accordingly, the four-stages theory also accounts for the growth of government and law. However, the four stages are not to be understood as the actual steps of the past; they are 'ideal types'. The historical past has deviated greatly from this conjectural model, mainly due to forceful and tyrannical behaviour by rulers and conquerors. The modern world was thus, for Smith, decisively shaped by the emergence of commerce before agriculture was properly developed, due largely to an alliance of monarchs and city-burghers forged for the purpose of breaking the power of feudal nobility. The resulting alliance of modern government with commerce and finance is the unholy alliance targeted in *WN*.

The *WN* is the greatest working-person's tract ever written. Central to its argument is that in the modern world even the working poor can enjoy personal liberty because the modern economy enables them to sell their labour without selling themselves. With the deepening of the division of labour, each piece of work becomes more 'abstract', less tied to personal abilities, and more easily assessed in monetary terms. The labourer can therefore sell his labour-power to anyone, without the personal dependence of traditional service-relationships. But this will only be effective if the labourer's freedom to sell his labour is protected by government as a right, against traditional monopolistic restrictions.

The liberation of labour from 'servility' is central to the transformation of productive life from the private, familial sphere to the public market, from household oeconomy to political economy. This can only take place when the immoral exaggeration of the virtue of prudent self-interest, namely avarice, can be rendered innocuous in the eyes of society. This happens when the problem of distribution begins to be solved through the market. In pre-commercial society, owners can only use their property by consuming it, and this they can do only by maintaining dependents, typically in the extended family. In commercial society they can spend their riches via the anonymous other of the public market. Accumulation of wealth becomes not only compatible with but dependent upon the freedom of the poor, which leads to a distribution of goods that, while unintended, is as equal as is realistic among humanity.

> [The rich] are led by an invisible hand to make nearly the same distribution of the necessaries of life, which would have been made, had the earth been divided into equal portions among all its inhabitants, and thus without intending it, without knowing it, advance the interest of the society, and afford means to the multiplication of the species.
>
> ([1759] 1976, IV.1.10: 184–5)

There is a price for this freedom, namely the danger of moral corruption. The rich are constantly tempted to undermine the system that creates their wealth by seeking protection against competition. And the poor are exposed to the stupification of mechanical work,

rendering them incapable of taking charge of their lives and making them useless as citizens and soldiers. In both areas protection is to be sought from government; in the former through anti-monopoly legislation and policy, in the latter through basic education funded in part by the public and through freedom of religious worship, both of which tend to establish a moral community of spectators within which the labourer can develop a moral character.

In addition to the economy that springs from self-interest, and the system of law that institutes the virtue of justice, Smith thus operates within a purely political sphere. Politics concerns 'police, revenue and arms', which means various municipal services and major construction works that the market cannot provide, and which facilitate commerce, plus defence. But under 'revenue' Smith also includes educational and cultural policies that are concerned with 'positive' virtues, or at least with facilitating such virtues. Smith is wary of stretching this function of government too far, because of the danger of tyranny in enforcing specific ideas of the good life. This, however, is not the limit of the role of positive virtue in public life: it extends also into an important public, non-political sphere.

Smith has much to say about the importance of a wide variety of social virtues – liberality, probity, generosity, courage, leadership, indeed justice in a distributive sense; or 'public spirit', as he often sums it up. But while these are virtues associated with public office, they are not the virtues that provide the very rationale of government in the way that justice does. Nor are these desirable qualities simply the private virtues of public figures, though they are certainly also that. Integral to Smith's society was a public sphere that was in some sense political, yet was not governmental. This was the world of the local elite, lairds and landlords with significant leadership in local affairs that today are matters of public policy. At the pinnacle of this world were the members of Parliament, whose work overwhelmingly consisted in dealing with private members' bills – often concerned with local matters – rather than with the business of executive government. The proper basis for these public roles was provided by the kind of positive virtues indicated above. While Smith wanted to exclude, or at least severely limit, these virtues in the function of government proper, he never doubted their essential role in a non-political public sphere. Today this sphere has largely been subjected to politics in a development that Hegelians might think of as the politicization of civil society; but it is anachronistic to use this sense of civil society in reading Smith: the public virtues and behaviour he is concerned with are not defined *vis-à-vis* the state.

Smith was not simply an advocate of a particular political and economic scheme. From his Humean perspective, there was little point in advocating things unless they were within the limits of people's imagination. The task was to extend that imagination by informing it of the full complexity of its situation. People who are thus informed may become impartial in judging their society. Smith had educated himself to be an impartial spectator who saw the injuries or injustices done to classes of people in the name of political exigencies that had long since passed. An appeal to the universal virtue of negative justice and an explanation of how and why it was being infringed in this particular historical situation was therefore the backbone of his history and theory of law and government; but he did not thereby reduce all moral life to the administration of justice. At his best he combined the psychological perspicuity of Jane Austen, the historical richness of Gibbon and the philosophical acumen of Hume.

See also: ECONOMICS AND ETHICS; ECONOMICS, PHILOSOPHY OF; JUSTICE; MARKET, ETHICS OF THE; MORAL SENSE THEORIES; PROPERTY; WORK, PHILOSOPHY OF

List of works

Smith, A. (1759) *The Theory of Moral Sentiments*, ed. D.D. Raphael and A.L. Macfie, Oxford: Clarendon Press, 1976, vol. 1. (The Glasgow Edition of the Works and Correspondence of Adam Smith.)

—— (1762–3) *Lectures on Rhetoric and Belles-Lettres*, ed. J.C. Bryce, Oxford: Clarendon Press, 1983; vol. 4. (The Glasgow Edition of the Works and Correspondence of Adam Smith.)

—— (1762–6) *Lectures on Jurisprudence*, ed. R.L. Meek, D.D. Raphael and P.G. Stein, Oxford: Clarendon Press, 1978, vol. 5. (The Glasgow Edition of the Works and Correspondence of Adam Smith.)

—— (1776) *An Inquiry into the Nature and Causes of the Wealth of Nations*, ed. R.H. Campbell and A.S. Skinner, Oxford: Clarendon Press, 1976, vol. 2. (The Glasgow Edition of the Works and Correspondence of Adam Smith.)

—— (1777) 'Letter from Adam Smith, LL.D. to William Strahan, Esq.', Appendix to *The Life of David Hume, Esq., Written by Himself*, London: Strahan & Cadell; repr. in D. Hume, *Essays Moral, Political and Literary*, ed. E.F. Miller, Indianapolis, IN: Liberty Classics, 1985, xxxi–xli.

—— (1795) *Essays on Philosophical Subjects*, ed. W.P.D. Wightman and J.C. Bryce, Oxford: Clarendon Press, 1980, vol. 3. (The Glasgow Edition of the Works and Correspondence of Adam Smith.)

—— (1977) *Correspondence of Adam Smith*, ed. E.C. Mossner and I.S. Ross, Oxford: Clarendon Press; vol. 6. (The Glasgow Edition of the Works and Correspondence of Adam Smith.)

—— (1976) 'Anderson Notes', in R.L. Meek, 'New Light on Adam Smith's Glasgow Lectures on Jurisprudence', *History of Political Economy*, 8: 439–77. (From John Anderson's Commonplace Book, Andersonian Library, University of Strathclyde, volume 1.)

References and further reading

Brown, V. (1994) *Adam Smith's Discourse: Canonicity, Commerce and Conscience*, London: Routledge. (Uses the literary theory of Bakhtin in an analysis that suggests less systematicity in Smith's work than argued in other recent work.)

* Camic, C. (1983) *Experience and Enlightenment: Socialization for Cultural Change in Eighteenth-century Scotland*, Edinburgh: Edinburgh University Press.

Campbell, R.H. and Skinner, A.S. (1982) *Adam Smith*, London: Croom Helm.

Campbell, T.D. (1971) *Adam Smith's Science of Morals*, London. (Stresses the scientific intention of Smith's work.)

Copley, S. and Sutherland, K. (eds) (1995) *Adam Smith, The Wealth of Nations: New Interdisciplinary Essays*, Manchester: Manchester University Press.

Cropsey, J. (1957) *Polity and Economy: An Interpretation of the Principles of Adam Smith*, The Hague: Nijhoff. (Smith in the tradition of modern political thought from Machiavelli onwards.)

Fitzgibbons, A. (1995) *Adam Smith's System of Liberty, Wealth and Virtue: The Moral and Political Foundations of the Wealth of Nations*, Oxford: Clarendon Press. (The ethics of the economics.)

Haakonssen, K. (1981) *The Science of a Legislator: The Natural Jurisprudence of David Hume and Adam Smith*, Cambridge: Cambridge University Press. (Reconstruction of Smith's philosophical system with jurisprudence at the centre.)

—— (1996) *Natural Law and Moral Philosophy: From Grotius to the Scottish Enlightenment*, Cambridge: Cambridge University Press. (Smith's theory of rights (chapter 4) and the role of his project in the later Scottish Enlightenment.)

Hollander, S. (1973) *The Economics of Adam Smith*, Toronto, Ont.: Toronto University Press. (Difficult for non-economists.)

Jones, P. and Skinner, A.S. (eds) (1992) *Adam Smith Reviewed*, Edinburgh: Edinburgh University Press.

Justman, S. (1993) *The Autonomous Male of Adam Smith*, Norman, OK: University of Oklahoma Press. (The tension between the femininity of virtue and the masculinity of stoicism.)

Malloy, R. P. and Evensky, J. (eds) (1994) *Adam Smith and the Philosophy of Law and Economics*, Amsterdam: Kluwer.

Minowitz, P. (1993) *Profits, Priests and Princes: Adam Smith's Emancipation of Economics from Politics and Religion*, Stanford, CA: Stanford University Press. (Thesis suggested by subtitle.)

Mizuta, H. and Sugiyama, C. (eds) (1993) *Adam Smith: International Perspectives*, New York: St Martin's Press. (The international reception of Smith.)

Muller, J.Z. (1993) *Adam Smith in His Time and Ours: Designing the Decent Society*, New York: The Free Press. (General, introductory survey.)

Rae, J. (1895) *Life of Adam Smith*; repr. with additional material by J. Viner, New York: Kelley. (Standard biography for the past century.)

Raphael, D.D. (1985) *Adam Smith*, Oxford: Oxford University Press. (Introductory survey of the whole of Smith's life and works.)

Ross, I.S. (1995) *The Life of Adam Smith*, Oxford: Clarendon Press. (General biography.)

Scott, W.R. (1937) *Adam Smith as Student and Professor*, Glasgow: Jackson.

Shapiro, M.J. (1993) *Reading 'Adam Smith': Desire, History and Value*, London: Sage.

Skinner, A.S. (1979/1996) *A System of Social Science: Papers Relating to Adam Smith*, Oxford: Clarendon Press. (Stresses the systematic coherence between the *WN* and the rest of Smith's work.)

Skinner, A.S. and Wilson, T. (eds) (1975) *Essays on Adam Smith*, Oxford: Clarendon Press.

* Stewart, D. (1793) 'Account of the Life and Writings of Adam Smith LL.D.', in D. Stewart, *Collected Works*, ed. Sir William Hamilton, 1854–60, 11 vols.; facsimile repr. with an introduction by K. Haakonssen, Bristol: Thoemmes, 1994, vol. 10, 1–98.

Teichgraeber, R.F. (1986) *'Free Trade' and Moral Philosophy. Rethinking the Sources of Adam Smith's Wealth of Nations*, Durham, NC: Duke University Press. (Close study of links to Hutcheson and Hume.)

Werhane, P.H. (1991) *Adam Smith and His Legacy for Modern Capitalism*, New York: Oxford University Press.

Winch, D. (1978) *Adam Smith's Politics: An Essay in Historiographic Revision*, Cambridge: Cambridge University Press. (The nature of Smith's *political*, as opposed to economic, theory.)

—— (1996) *Riches and Poverty: An Intellectual History of Political Economy in Britain, 1750–1834*, Cambridge: Cambridge University Press. (Approaches Smith via the debate on the connections between luxury and inequality, stressing the realistic qualities of his science of the legislator.)

Wood, J.C. (ed.) (1983–84) *Adam Smith: Critical Assessements*, London: Croom Helm, 4 vols.

KNUD HAAKONSSEN

SMITH, JOHN *see* CAMBRIDGE PLATONISM

SMITH, NORMAN KEMP
see KEMP SMITH, NORMAN

SOCIAL ACTION

Most of our actions take place in a social context and are, accordingly, in one way or another, dependent on the existence of other persons and their relevant actions, social institutions, conventions, or the like (for example, saluting, voting, drawing money from one's bank account, using lipstick, buying something). But people also perform actions jointly or collectively, to achieve some joint goal. Thus they may jointly sing a duet, play tennis, build a house, or conserve energy. This is collective social action in its most central sense. Such action is based on the participants' mutually known joint intention ('joint plan') to perform it. In weaker kinds of collective social action the participants are interdependent – as to their actions or thoughts – in some other ways.

This entry shall concentrate on collective social action, indeed on the central case: joint action based on joint intentions. Thus, you and I may form the joint intention to paint the house together and agree upon some method of doing it, for instance, that you paint the front while I paint the back of the house. We also agree upon which paint to use and other similar things. Carrying out our joint intention, we come to paint the house jointly. This kind of intentional joint action can be characterized more generally as follows, taking a joint action to be an action divisible into single-agent parts, that generate a purported outcome: the participants have formed a joint plan for a joint action; the plan is taken to involve a relevant joint intention, entailing for each participant the intention to perform their part of the joint action. The participant is assumed to believe that the various conditions for the success of the joint action will be fulfilled at least with some probability, and also to believe that this is mutually believed by the participants. The performance of a joint action can be regarded as agreement-based if the plan has been accepted by the participants and if they have appropriately communicated their acceptances to the others so that a joint obligation to perform the joint action has come about. Joint action in the fullest sense can be argued to be based on either explicit or implicit agreement (in a wide sense) (see INTENTION).

Over and above the standard sense of joint action based on the participants' joint intention we may also speak of joint action in a somewhat wider sense not necessarily involving joint intention. For example: some persons, seeing a car starting to slide down a hill, together start pushing it up the hill. I am passing and form the intention to push the car together with the others, an intention with a collective action as its content, and take part in the pushing. There may even be a belief among all the pushers that I also am participating. All this can take place without these car-pushers (or at least all of them) having a joint intention (joint plan) to push the car together with the others. So understood, we do not have here more than joint action in a wide sense – namely joint activity based on shared collective intention but not full-blown joint intention. The participants' intentions, when the participants are mutually aware of them, can still be regarded as social attitudes ('we-attitudes' in the sense of Tuomela 1994). Ideally, a person has such a social attitude (for example, an intention to do something together) relative to their group if and only if they (1) have (or share) this attitude, (2) believe the group members have it, and also (3) believe that there is a mutual belief that the members have this attitude. The broadest sense of joint action can be taken to be collective action performed because of a shared social attitude.

Joint action in this wide sense excludes such 'mere co-action' as people acting simultaneously in the direction of the same goal but (possibly) independently of each other (for instance, Max Weber's example of people simultaneously opening their umbrellas when it starts to rain). Such co-action does not deserve to be called social action at all.

We can, however, include among social action the following two kinds of collective action with social features – although they do not quite amount to collective social action in our previous sense:

(1) Collective action which is merely accompanied by (but not performed because of) a social attitude (we-attitude). The participants may be performing an action (for example, selling shoes at a department store) either separately or 'together' as their parts of a collective project (or believed project), planned or structured by them or by somebody else.

(2) Collective action consisting of separate individual actions directed towards and performed because of a shared, possibly merely personal goal (the realization of which normally requires several agents' participation).

In the literature on collective action either social action in the strict sense or cases of the kind (1) and even of the kind (2) may be involved. In those cases there is often a public good to which individual actions contribute, although they normally are relatively costly to the contributors. It is worth noting, too, that the interaction (either 'parametric' or 'strategic' interaction) is typically present in joint action in the wide sense and sometimes also in cases of the kinds (1) and (2).

The participants' preference structures in a joint action can be fully cooperative (for example, carrying a table) or they can be to some extent noncooperative (for example, chess, buying and selling). Furthermore, joint action can be physical (for example, carrying a table) or it can involve a conventional or normative element such as transfer of rights (for instance, toasting a national victory, making a business deal, getting married).

Joint action as collective action performed because of a social attitude and social action in the broader senses (1) and (2) are all cases of collective social action and seem to make the classification exhaustive.

See also: ACTION; SOCIAL NORMS

References and further reading

Coleman, J. (1990) *Foundations of Social Theory*, Cambridge, MA and London: The Belknap Press of Harvard University Press. (Gives a comprehensive classification of social action using conceptual and mathematical tools familiar from economics.)

Elster, J. (1989) *The Cement of Society*, Cambridge: Cambridge University Press. (Contains classifications of collective action and discussions of the kinds of motivation of collective action.)

Holmstroem-Hintikka, G. and Tuomela, R. (eds) (1997) *Contemporary Action Theory*, vol. 2 *Social Action*, Synthese Library, Dordrecht and Boston: Kluwer. (Volume two contains papers about social action.)

Miller, S. (1992) 'Joint Action', *Philosophical Papers* XXI: 275–97. (Presents an account of social action based on collective ends.)

* Tuomela, R. (1994) *The Importance of Us: A Philosophical Study of Basic Social Notions*, Stanford, CA: Stanford University Press. (Gives a comprehensive account of social action, including actions performed by social groups; special emphasis is given to the view that full-blown social action involves explicit or implicit agreement to perform the action.)

RAIMO TUOMELA

SOCIAL CHOICE

Social choice theory is the branch of economics concerned with the relationships between individual values, preferences and rights and collective decision making and evaluation. Social choice theory therefore provides connections between the formal analysis of rational choice, the debate on political process, and ethics. A central theme in social choice theory has been the aggregation of individual preferences into either a social decision rule or a social evaluation rule. The most famous result in social choice theory – Arrow's impossibility theorem – is that such aggregation is impossible if individual preferences are conceived as ordinal in nature, and if the aggregation procedure is to satisfy certain apparently reasonable conditions. This result implies that neither a voting system nor a system of moral evaluation can be found that satisfies all of the required conditions. Further impossibility theorems arise from attempts to model the role of individual rights.

Much of social choice theory is concerned with interpreting, extending and questioning these impossibility theorems in a variety of contexts. This discussion has generated an extensive interchange at the margins of economics and ethics on topics such as the commensurability of values and the relationship between morality and rationality.

1 **Impossibility theorems**
2 **Interpretation and critique**
3 **Economics and ethics**

1 Impossibility theorems

Arrow's theorem concerns the aggregation of a set of individual orderings to form a social or collective ordering. The word 'ordering' is used in its technical sense to indicate an ordinal relation that is reflexive, transitive and complete. The objects of the ordering are not specified by the theorem but, following Arrow, social choice theorists refer to orderings of social states; that is, alternative complete descriptions of the world. Similarly, the nature of the individual orderings is not specified by the theorem, but social choice theorists refer to individual preferences. On this standard interpretation, the theorem concerns the possibility of aggregating a set of individual preference orderings over states of the world into a single social ordering.

Arrow (1951) investigated four conditions that impose requirements on the process of aggregation. Condition U, the condition of unrestricted domain, requires the process of aggregation to operate for arbitrary sets of individual orderings. Condition P, the weak Pareto principle, requires that if every individual ranks α above β, then society must rank α above β. Condition I, the independence of irrelevant alternatives, requires that the social ordering over any pair of alternatives depends only on individual orderings over that pair of alternatives. Condition D, nondictatorship, requires that there be no individual whose ordering becomes the social ordering regardless of the orderings of all other individuals. The four conditions were viewed by Arrow as necessary but insufficient conditions for rational social choice. The theorem is that there exists no process of aggregation which satisfies all four conditions.

Much of normative economics is welfarist in the sense that it takes individual utilities to be the only admissible information, and Paretian in the sense of Arrow's condition P. In fact welfarism can be thought of as the combination of Arrow's conditions U, P, and I; so the Arrow theorem can be seen as demonstrating the impossibility of nondictatorial welfarism.

A second impossibility theorem highlights the tension between the weak Pareto condition and a weak concept of individual rights. The relevant concept of a right is that an individual is decisive in the choice between a particular pair of alternative social states – a pair that might differ only in some respect deemed to be private to that individual – so that individual A has a right with respect to social states α and β if and only if A's ranking of α and β is causally sufficient to determine the social ranking of α and β.

Sen (1970a) shows the impossibility of a Paretian liberal by proving that no social choice rule can simultaneously satisfy the weak Pareto condition and grant at least two individuals rights over (distinct) pairs of alternatives.

2 Interpretation and critique

Sen (1977) offers four settings in which the Arrow

result may be considered: (1) the aggregation of individual interests into overall ethical judgments of social welfare, (2) the aggregation of individual ethical judgments into overall ethical judgments of social welfare, (3) the aggregation of individual interests into social decisions, (4) the aggregation of individual ethical judgments into social decisions. Settings (1) and (2) cast social choice theory in terms of ethics, while settings (3) and (4) cast social choice theory in terms of politics. Alternatively, settings (1) and (3) focus on the aggregation of private interests or utilities, while settings (2) and (4) focus on the aggregation of broader judgments of overall value. While the theorem applies equally in each of these settings, its interpretation and significance varies.

The now standard interpretation of the theorem in setting (1) is that simple personal preference orderings cannot in themselves provide sufficient information to ground social evaluations. Further information may take either of two forms; it might be more detailed information concerning the welfare of individuals, or it might relate to non-welfare aspects of individuals. Within the confines of welfarism, the two most obvious types of further information arise from the cardinality of individual utility and the interpersonal comparability of utility. In fact, if cardinality is allowed, but incomparability maintained, the Arrow result is not seriously affected. But once interpersonal comparability is allowed, the nature of the feasible social orderings depends upon the measurability of utility and the extent of interpersonal comparability. Thus, if ordinalism is retained alongside full comparability, social orderings such as that generated by the maximin criterion are feasible. Of particular interest is the simple utilitarian ordering in which social states are ranked by reference to the simple sum of individual utilities. Such utilitarianism requires at least cardinal scale measurability and at least unit comparability.

If welfarism is breached, so that further categories of information are allowed, the feasibility of social orderings depends on the answers to similar questions concerning the measurability of the new aspect of wellbeing, and its commensurability both across individuals and with utility.

In setting (2) we move from individual utility to individual judgments of social welfare, and it is here that the Arrow theorem is most persuasive. There can be no appeal to additional information in this case, since individual judgments may be taken to be all-things-considered judgments. However, the novelty and practical significance of the theorem may be relatively slight in this setting. It is hardly a surprise to find that different value systems (individuals' judgments of social welfare) are, in general, incompatible with each other.

In settings (3) and (4) we move from ethics to politics in viewing social decision-making rules based on individual interests or individual ethical judgments; we are concerned with the more practical matters of the design of voting systems or committee procedures. One general point to be made is that in these settings we are often not concerned with generating a full social ordering over the alternatives, but with selecting a winner (or set of joint winners). This fact allows us to weaken the requirements placed on the aggregation process slightly and so formally escape from the impossibility theorem. But this escape is more apparent than real. If we require the choices made by our voting rule to satisfy even rather weak consistency conditions, new impossibility results arise.

In these settings the Arrow theorem extends and generalizes the results on specific voting mechanisms associated with Condorcet and Borda, most famously that simple majority voting over at least three alternatives can yield intransitivities or cycles – so that even if all voters have well-behaved preferences over the alternatives, and each votes in accordance with those preferences, alternative α can be majority-preferred to alternative β, alternative β majority-preferred to alternative γ, and alternative γ majority-preferred to alternative α. A further result which follows from the Arrow theorem when interpreted in terms of social decision making relates to the manipulability of voting mechanisms. Broadly, the result is that all feasible voting schemes will, in general, provide incentives for individuals to vote strategically; that is, to misrepresent their true preferences in an attempt to manipulate the outcome of the vote.

The debate on the impossibility of a Paretian liberal has been voluminous. Topics considered include a variety of conceptions of individual rights – the contrast between the right to determine an aspect of a social outcome and the right to determine the individual's own strategic behaviour, for example; the extent to which preferences might be laundered to exclude the meddlesome preferences of one individual over matters deemed to be private to another individual; the extent to which the ability to trade rights might eliminate the results, and so on. Whatever the modifications to Sen's original structure, it seems that if aspects of individuals other than their preferences or values are to be included in the process of social evaluation or decision making, further conflicts await.

A fundamental criticism of the basic enterprise of social choice theory first put by Buchanan (1954) argues from an individualistic perspective that it is simply inappropriate to investigate social evaluation or social decision making against criteria of collective rationality. This approach suggests that while individuals may be able to articulate evaluative orderings over alternative states of the world, there is no sense in the idea of a social or aggregate evaluative ordering. Furthermore, if collective decision making rather than evaluation is the focus of attention, we must attend to the question of how individuals might agree on decision-making procedures. In a commonly used example, we might agree to a process of simple majority voting in certain contexts without any commitment to the idea that the outcome of this political procedure is in any aggregate sense best. The claim is that the appropriate framework for the study of collective action problems is provided by the model of voluntary exchange between individuals. This position is strongly linked to a generally contractarian view of both politics and ethics (see CONTRACTARIANISM).

3 Economics and ethics

Social choice theory has stimulated considerable work in the intersection of economics and ethics. In part this is because of the detailed, formal attention paid to questions such as the measurability and comparability of welfare, or the specification of individual rights; in part because of the implications of the theory for the classic debates between consequentialist and non-consequentialist moralities, or between liberalism, utilitarianism and contractarianism; and in part because of the illumination of the relationships between rationality and morality. It is not too difficult to justify the claim that social choice theory has had a major impact on both normative economics and moral theory – but most especially on the interaction between the two.

The debate in normative theory is in sharp contrast to the earlier orthodoxy within economics, when economics was seen as a predominantly technical study divorced from value judgments. Traditional neoclassical economics of the type captured in the textbooks of the mid twentieth century might be caricatured as depending on the twin ideas of a simple conception of self-interested, utility-maximizing individual rationality and an equally simple welfarist conception of the public interest. Initially social choice theory challenged the assumed link between these two ideas, but much of the continuing contribution of social choice theory lies in the more detailed re-examination of each idea. In the same way, while many of the relatively early contributions to social choice theory might be seen as technical exercises in aggregation theory, the more lasting contributions are those which engage with the substantive issues in ethics or political philosophy. In this way social choice

theory has provided the basis for contributions which draw on the technical apparatus of economics in addressing topics of perennial interest to philosophers, while at the same time opening up the possibility of a reverse flow of ideas from philosophy into economics.

See also: ECONOMICS AND ETHICS; RATIONAL CHOICE THEORY; RIGHTS; UTILITARIANISM; WELFARE

References and further reading

* Arrow, K.J. (1951) *Social Choice and Individual Values*, New Haven, CT: Yale University Press, rev. edn, 1963. (Classic source for the Arrow impossibility theorem.)
* Buchanan, J.M. (1954) 'Social Choice, Democracy and Free Markets', *Journal of Political Economy* 62: 114–23. (Individualist criticism of social choice approach – included in Rowley, 1993.)
  Hamlin, A.P. (ed.) (1996) *Ethics and Economics*, Aldershot: Edward Elgar. (A two volume collection of major contributions with a substantive introduction.)
  Rowley, C.K. (ed.) (1993) *Social Choice Theory*, Aldershot: Edward Elgar. (A three volume collection of major contributions to social choice theory.)
* Sen, A.K. (1970a) 'The Impossibility of a Paretian Liberal', *Journal of Political Economy* 78: 152–7. (A classic impossibility theorem – included in Rowley, 1993.)
  —— (1970b) *Collective Choice and Social Welfare*, San Francisco, CA: Holden-Day. (Still the best book-length introduction to the ideas and techniques of social choice theory.)
* —— (1977) 'Social Choice Theory: A Re-examination', *Econometrica* 45: 53–89. (Review of literature emphasizing the informational context – included in Rowley, 1993.)
  —— (1987) *On Ethics and Economics*, Oxford: Blackwell. (Introductory lectures with an extensive bibliography.)

ALAN HAMLIN

SOCIAL CONSTRUCTIVISM
see CONSTRUCTIVISM

SOCIAL CONTRACT
see CONTRACTARIANISM

SOCIAL DEMOCRACY

The idea of social democracy is now used to describe a society the economy of which is predominantly capitalist, but where the state acts to regulate the economy in the general interest, provides welfare services outside of it and attempts to alter the distribution of income and wealth in the name of social justice. Originally 'social democracy' was more or less equivalent to 'socialism'. But since the mid-twentieth century, those who think of themselves as social democrats have come to believe that the old opposition between capitalism and socialism is outmoded; many of the values upheld by earlier socialists can be promoted by reforming capitalism rather than abolishing it.

Although it bases itself on values like democracy and social justice, social democracy cannot really be described as a political philosophy: there is no systematic statement or great text that can be pointed to as a definitive account of social democratic ideals. In practical politics, however, social democratic ideas have been very influential, guiding the policies of most Western states in the post-war world.

1   Social democracy *c.*1880–1940
2   Social democracy *c.*1940–

1   Social democracy *c.*1880–1940

In its earliest phase, social democracy became the leading form of socialism in Western societies (see SOCIALISM). It emerged from a fusion between the ideas of revisionist Marxists such as Eduard BERNSTEIN and those of 'new' liberals such as L.T. Hobhouse who had come to believe that some form of socialism was necessary in order to realize liberal ideals. It differed from the Marxism promulgated by Lenin and his followers in the international communist movement in three main respects. First, in place of the belief that the economic collapse of capitalism was inevitable, the social democrats held that capitalism could only be transformed by the political will of the people; it was important, therefore, to emphasize not only class struggle, but the aims and ideals of socialism. Second, the transformation would not occur in a single revolutionary moment but over an extended period of time, with changes in economic structure being guided by social democratic parties holding political power. Third, the social democrats accepted the procedures and constraints of parliamentary democracy: confident that they could, in due course, win majority support, they saw the route to power lying through open elections.

In this phase, therefore, the final aim of social democracy was to replace private ownership of industry with state or social ownership, but the means were to be those of parliamentary democracy.

2   Social democracy *c.*1940–

In the second, mainly post-war, phase, social democrats came to believe that their ideals and values could be achieved by reforming capitalism rather than abolishing it. They favoured a mixed economy in which most industries would be privately owned, with only a small number of utilities and other essential services in public ownership. Their reformism expressed itself in four main directions.

(1) Under the influence of Keynes, they believed that, by controlling the level of public expenditure, the state could also control the level of aggregate demand, thereby preventing the expansion–recession cycles of uncontrolled capitalism (see KEYNES, J.M. §2). In this way, steady economic growth and full employment were achievable.
(2) The state should provide welfare services (health, education and so forth) free of charge to all who needed them, and should also create a social insurance scheme for those temporarily unable to find work. Together these initiatives would create a social minimum that every citizen would be guaranteed regardless of personal circumstances.
(3) Workers' rights should be protected by legislation and the formation of trade unions, and the state should encourage workers' participation in the management of firms through co-determination schemes and the like. There should be (some degree of) economic democracy alongside democracy in the state itself.
(4) The first three measures would together serve to create considerably more social equality than was possible under unreformed capitalism. But, in addition, the state could legitimately use its powers of taxation and public provision to correct the distribution of resources still further, for instance by taxing incomes at progressive rates and using the proceeds to provide subsidies for the poor (such as cheap housing).

Social democrats argued that in these circumstances the old debate about the ownership of industry had become an irrelevance. Properly controlled, capitalism could be relied upon to produce the resources that social democratic governments could then use to advance their ideals practically. These ideals were a widening of democracy beyond the state to encompass economic and social organizations; social justice, in the sense of equal opportunity to achieve positions of advantage, together with the guaranteed social minimum as outlined above; and, less tangibly, a greater sense of community among citizens to offset the atomizing effects of the market economy.

In the last quarter of the twentieth century, the most powerful challenge to these ideals has come not from socialists but from libertarians, who argue that regulation of the market and redistribution of its proceeds are not only morally illegitimate but also likely to be self-defeating (see LIBERTARIANISM). Their cause has been aided by increasingly intense international economic competition, which has narrowed the range of policy options open to social democratic governments. Yet the ideals of social democracy have retained their popularity, and much recent political philosophy can be seen as an attempt to formalize and ground these ideals (see DWORKIN, R.; RAWLS, J. §4).

See also: DEMOCRACY; JUSTICE

References and further reading

Bernstein, E. (1899) *Die Voraussetzungen des Sozialismus und die Aufgaben der Sozialdemokratie* (The Premises of Socialism and the Tasks of Social Democracy), Dietz: Stuttgart; trans. and ed. H. Tudor, *The Preconditions of Socialism*, Cambridge: Cambridge University Press, 1993. (Seminal text for the earlier generation of social democrats.)

Crosland, C.A.R. (1956) *The Future of Socialism*, London: Cape. (Important statement of social democratic principles by a leading member of the British Labour Party.)

Gay, P. (1952) *The Dilemma of Democratic Socialism*, New York: Columbia University Press. (A full-length study of Bernstein's philosophical and economic thought.)

Levine, A. (1988) *Arguing for Socialism*, London: Verso. (Recent attempt by a philosopher to restate the basic arguments for democratic socialism.)

Tilton, T. (1991) *The Political Theory of Swedish Social Democracy*, Oxford: Clarendon Press. (Surveys the thinking of the leading figures in what has perhaps been the most successful of all social democratic parties.)

Vaisey, J. (1971) *Social Democracy*, London: Weidenfeld & Nicolson. (An introductory survey of social democratic ideas and movements.)

Wright, A. (1986) *Socialisms*, Oxford: Oxford University Press. (Accessible introduction that places social democracy within the socialist tradition as a whole.)

DAVID MILLER

SOCIAL EPISTEMOLOGY

Social epistemology is the conceptual and normative study of the relevance to knowledge of social relations, interests and institutions. It is thus to be distinguished from the sociology of knowledge, which is an empirical study of the contingent social conditions or causes of what is commonly taken to be knowledge. Social epistemology revolves around the question of whether knowledge is to be understood individualistically or socially.

Epistemology has traditionally ascribed a secondary status to beliefs indebted to social relations – to testimony, expert authority, consensus, common sense and received wisdom. Such beliefs could attain the status of knowledge, if at all, only by being based on first-hand knowledge – that is, knowledge justified by the experience or reason of the individual knower.

Since the work of the common sense Scottish philosopher Thomas Reid in the mid-eighteenth century, epistemologists have from time to time taken seriously the idea that beliefs indebted to social relations have a primary and not merely secondary epistemic status. The bulk of work in social epistemology has, however, been done since Thomas Kuhn depicted scientific revolutions as involving social changes in science. Work on the subject since 1980 has been inspired by the 'strong programme' in the sociology of science, by feminist epistemology and by the naturalistic epistemology of W.V. Quine. These influences have inspired epistemologists to rethink the role of social relations – especially testimony – in knowledge. The subject that has emerged may be divided into three branches: the place of social factors in the knowledge possessed by individuals; the organization of individuals' cognitive labour; and the nature of collective knowledge, including common sense, consensus and common, group, communal and impersonal knowledge.

1   Reliance on testimony
2   Conditions of knowledge
3   The organization of cognitive labour
4   Collective knowledge
5   The social construction of knowledge

1   Reliance on testimony

The epistemological status of testimony and received wisdom is the topic in social epistemology which is most extensively treated in classical texts and contemporary discussion, and the only topic for which we have a detailed history (Coady 1991) (see TESTIMONY). The central question here is whether testimony is a source of individual knowledge not derived from a non-social source like perception. According to *strong* individualism, to which John Locke subscribes, all knowledge must be first-hand; no belief can be epistemically justified on the basis of testimony (where epistemic justification is the kind of justification required for knowledge – see JUSTIFICATION, EPISTEMIC §1). The objection to this view is that it entails a broad scepticism, excluding my knowledge of such matters as my own date of birth and the proposition that a cloudless sky is usually blue. According to *weak* individualism, a belief may be justified on the basis of testimony, but any such belief must ultimately be justified on the basis of non-testimonially justified beliefs. There are at least three versions of weak individualism:

(1) On the *inductive* version, to which David Hume subscribes, a belief based on testimony (call it a 'testimonial belief') is justified on the basis of the non-testimonially justified belief that the testimony is trustworthy or reliable (that is, tends to be true), which in turn is justified by induction from non-testimonially justified beliefs (see TESTIMONY §3). The most significant objection to the inductive version is that we rely on testimony for many of the beliefs that would have to serve as the non-testimonial basis of the induction to the reliability of testimony. It is practically impossible to check at first-hand more than a tiny fraction of the reports given by testimony. Hence, the basis for an induction is too slim to justify the belief in reliability.

(2) On the a priori version of weak individualism, a testimonial belief is justified by appeal to an epistemic parity between my own beliefs and those of others. The idea that one person is epistemically no better than another is ancient and was assumed by Sextus Empiricus in the following maxim, which he used to argue for Pyrrhonian scepticism: where others disagree with me, I ought to suspend judgment. The present appeal to parity reverses the sceptical strategy of Sextus. A priori, I have no more reason to trust my own beliefs than I do those of others. Consequently, if I may trust my own beliefs, I may also trust others' beliefs, and thus I am justified in my testimonial beliefs. An objection to this version is that it equivocates on 'trust'. Perhaps I must trust others in the same sense in which I must trust myself. But why suppose that it follows that others' beliefs are trustworthy or reliable in a sense relevant to *my* being justified in having the same beliefs, rather than in a sense relevant to *their* being justified in these beliefs? There is no reason a priori to suppose that my epistemic position is similar to theirs in a way that makes these beliefs justified for me as they are for them. Thus it does not follow that my testimonial beliefs are justified.

(3) On the coherence version, a testimonial belief is justified by its coherence with non-testimonially justified beliefs. The trouble with this proposal is that the objection to the inductive version shows that there is very little coherence between any given testimonial belief and the non-testimonially justified beliefs that might form the basis of an induction to the reliability of the testimony. No doubt testimonial beliefs are often unsurprising and in this sense fit with non-testimonial beliefs. But the epistemic force of this lack of surprise depends on antecedent generalizations about the world, and these in turn depend on prior testimony. Nor can the proponent of the coherence version retreat to the idea that testimonial beliefs are justified by the coherence of all beliefs together, testimonial as well as non-testimonial. For this is no longer a version of weak individualism, since testimonial beliefs are no longer justified on the basis of non-testimonially justified beliefs alone. True, it still counts as a version of individualism. But since we currently have no idea how all these beliefs are supposed to cohere, it seems we lack an individualist account of the justification of testimonial beliefs.

What is the alternative to individualism? Reid proposed that we take the justification of testimonial beliefs to be underived, on a par with the justification of perceptual beliefs (see REID, T. §7). The justification of testimonial beliefs is governed by a first (that is, underived) principle, 'That there is a certain regard due to human testimony in matters of fact, and even to human authority in matters of opinion' (Reid [1785] 1969: 640). Conformity to this principle is made possible by certain innate dispositions of the human constitution: the principle of veracity, which disposes us to tell the truth, and the principle of credulity, which disposes us to believe what is said. First principles are not susceptible to proof, though they can be supported by recognizing their similarity to other first principles, under various desiderata, including common assent, conformity to the human constitution and practical necessity. In the terms of subsequent epistemology, Reid appears to have proposed that testimonial beliefs are *prima facie* justified in a manner analogous to the *prima facie* justification of perceptual beliefs. They are, at least early on, basically (that is, non-inferentially) justified and can be defeated by the subject's other testimonial and non-testimonial beliefs.

2 Conditions of knowledge

Reid incorporates social factors into the conditions of justification by adding a principle of testimony. Others have proposed that the conditions of knowledge are in some sense social throughout. In particular, the content of the concept of knowledge is inherited from the social function of the concept of knowledge. Not all social functions of a concept are manifested in the content of the concept, but if the concept of knowledge has what we might call a social *epistemic* function, then perhaps it also has a social content. There are several examples of this approach.

Edward Craig (1990) has argued that the concept of knowledge is used in testimony as a tag to identify good informants. The concept of knowledge is not identified with the notion of a good informant itself, since knowing does not require being able to communicate to others the proposition believed, as does being a good informant. Rather, the proposal is that the concept of knowledge is an 'objectivization' of the notion of a good informant – a concept in which some of the features of a good informant that serve specific uses are stripped away. An analogous idea is that the concept of justification is used to identify *justifiers* – people able to justify a claim to an audience. On the most straightforward version of this view, suggested by David Annis (1978), one is justified in a belief (or claim) (relative to an audience) just in case one is able to justify it to the audience – or at least to hold one's own in a conversation in which the claim is challenged. With regard to all such approaches, one worries that they have singled out a particular use of the concept of knowledge at the expense of other uses, uses that demand a different conceptual content (see JUSTIFICATION, EPISTEMIC §7).

3 The organization of cognitive labour

Traditional epistemology has little to say on the matter of how individuals should coordinate and institutionalize their inquiry to enhance their prospects of obtaining individual or group knowledge. In recent years, epistemologists have taken an interest in this matter, especially as it applies to science. One question concerns the obligations of individuals to disseminate information to or withhold it from others. A.I. Goldman (1992) has argued for *epistemic paternalism*, the view that individuals should sometimes withhold information to enhance the prospects that recipients will arrive at knowledge or true belief – as, for example, when evidence of a crime is ruled inadmissible in a court of law to prevent the jury from being misled. A second question is what features interpersonal argumentation should have if it is to serve the development of knowledge. A third question is whether, to enhance the prospects of scientific group knowledge, individuals (or subgroups) should pursue lines of inquiry that are unpromising or based on improbable theories. A fourth question is whether individuals' cognitive biases induced by their social interests, such as ambition for professional credit, may steer individual research and belief-formation in such a way as to enhance the prospects of proper group belief-formation.

4 Collective knowledge

The key question of collective knowledge – of common, group and communal knowledge – is whether it reduces to individual knowledge or amounts to something over and above individual knowledge. A related question is whether individual knowledge must in some way be assimilated to communal knowledge (that is, the knowledge possessed by a community). The pragmatist C.S. Peirce argued for an affirmative answer to the latter question on the ground that the aim of proper method must be understood socially (see PEIRCE, C.S. §2). Peirce (1955) took the aim of proper method not to be true belief but relief from doubt. He then argued that the aim must be common rather than individual relief from doubt, since the 'social impulse' will drive people to think that others' opinions are as good as their own, and thus differences of opinion will induce doubt. One might question whether it follows from the claim that relief from doubt depends psychologically on common relief from doubt, that the aim of proper method is common relief from doubt. But Peirce could reply that there is no point in taking relief from individual doubt as the aim when we will in any case have to aim at common belief. Clearly, Peirce's argument for a common aim of proper method carries more weight for beliefs that are publicized, as in the case of science, than for beliefs that tend not to be exposed to the doubts of others (for example, beliefs about the details of one's private life).

It is natural to think that Peirce's argument, if successful, undermines a sharp distinction between individual and common knowledge, since a lone individual evidently cannot employ a method that aims at common beliefs; the coordinated efforts of many individuals are required. But whether Peirce's argument goes this far depends on what a proper method involves. If it involves only accumulating the evidence that would suffice to dispel doubt, rather than including the social actions that actually dispel doubt, then an individual on their own may still employ a proper method.

There are other accounts of individual justification that in some way assimilate it to communal justification. In *On Certainty*, Wittgenstein suggests that an individual's belief is justified by appeal to certain communally accepted claims. On a multi-perspectival view of justification, an individual is justified in believing *p* only if *p* is accepted from each perspective represented in the individual's community. Another view is that a belief is justified only if it conforms to communally accepted rules (see CONTEXTUALISM, EPISTEMOLOGICAL).

Even if individual knowledge is not assimilated to communal knowledge, there remains the question of whether common or group knowledge stands over and above individual knowledge or, instead, reduces to it. *Common* or *mutual* knowledge does reduce to individual knowledge: it obtains when two or more individuals know a proposition, know that each of the others knows, and so on. Common knowledge has proved an essential ingredient in the analysis of social conventions and group knowledge, but whether it amounts to group knowledge is a matter of controversy.

The simplest individualistic account of group justification is a *summative* account: a group is justified in believing a proposition just in case most (or all) of its members are justified in believing the proposition. Opposed to an individualistic account is a *joint* account, on which group justification is not a matter of group members being justified in believing *p*, but of members jointly possessing a good reason to believe *p*, where members jointly possess a reason for *p* just in case they openly express a willingness to treat it as a reason for *p*. The joint account characterizes group justification in terms of the actions and attitudes of the group members. It thus avoids requiring for group justification that there be some group mind over and above the minds of the members of the group.

5 The social construction of knowledge

There are three senses in which it has been claimed that knowledge is socially constructed (see CONSTRUCTIVISM). (1) Some sociologists of science (for example, Bruno Latour 1987) have proposed that the facts reported in scientific journals are fabricated by the manipulation of inscriptions involving 'modalities' (that is, ways of embedding sentences in other sentences). It has also been proposed (Joseph Rouse 1987) that many scientific laws strictly apply only to artificially created laboratory phenomena and extend to phenomena in nature only by analogy; thus, a law implicitly refers to the social conditions in which laboratory phenomena are created. (2) It has been proposed (again by Rouse) that the conditions of scientific communal knowledge are social. The argument is that the standards of knowledge to which scientific theories and experimental results are held

(for example, the degree of confirmation required) depend on the uses to which the theories are put, and these uses are in turn determined by research needs, hence by the social conditions that determine those needs. (3) Finally, it has been claimed, particularly by those associated with the 'strong programme' in the sociology of science, that scientific theoretical and observational communal knowledge, or at least beliefs that are esteemed knowledge, are caused by social, economic and political interests. This sociological causal claim contrasts with *rationalism* about the causes of scientific theory choice, according to which theory choices are caused by rational reasoning on the basis of observations and theoretical desiderata, except where noncognitive factors (such as desires, emotions, peer pressure and the like) interfere with rational choices and pre-empt them.

One argument for the sociological causal claim is a priori: theories are underdetermined by observations and so choice is not caused by observations alone but by social interests (see UNDERDETERMINATION). Nor can rationalists appeal to theoretical desiderata like simplicity and explanatory power to explain theory choice in the face of underdetermination, since these desiderata are merely rationalizations of theory choice, not rationally supported independently of choice. This objection to rationalism underestimates the theory-independent grounds for desiderata like simplicity – such grounds as that simpler theories carry less information than complex theories and thus accepting them entails less exposure to the risk of error (see THEORETICAL (EPISTEMIC) VIRTUES). These grounds for deciding between theories are sometimes said to be theory-laden, leaving the choice of theory once again unexplained. But even if this is so, the way in which these grounds are selected may depend on metaprinciples relating grounds and theories.

Sociologists have also supported the sociological causal claim by appeal to historical case studies of the role of interests in theory choice (see GENDER AND SCIENCE §3; MARXIST PHILOSOPHY OF SCIENCE; POSTCOLONIAL PHILOSOPHY OF SCIENCE; SOCIOLOGY OF KNOWLEDGE). But the poverty of the historical materials makes it difficult to establish that interests cause, and are not merely correlated with, theory choice in these cases. However, a correlation between interests and theory choice, even if not shown to be causal, may be hard to reconcile with rationalism, since we would not expect interests to be correlated with rational choices.

See also: FEMINIST EPISTEMOLOGY; NATURALIZED EPISTEMOLOGY

References and further reading

* Annis, D. (1978) 'A contextualist theory of justification', *American Philosophical Quarterly* 15: 213–19. (Argues that justification is relative to an audience and to the social role of the subject.)

Brown, J.R. (1987) *The Rational and the Social*, London: Routledge. (Critical review of the philosophical claims of the 'strong programme' in the sociology of scientific knowledge.)

* Coady, C.A.J. (1991) *Testimony: A Philosophical Study*, Oxford: Oxford University Press. (Comprehensive historical and philosophical study of epistemological issues about testimony.)

* Craig, E. (1990) *Knowledge and the State of Nature: An Essay in Conceptual Synthesis*, Oxford: Clarendon Press. (Explains various features of the concept of knowledge by deriving it from the notion of a good informant.)

Gilbert, M. (1989) *On Social Facts*, London: Routledge. (The most systematic account of collective concepts yet attempted, with an extensive discussion of common knowledge and group belief.)

* Goldman, A.I. (1992) *Liaisons: Philosophy Meets the Cognitive and Social Sciences*, Cambridge, MA: MIT Press. (Includes articles on epistemic paternalism and – with M. Shaked – on the role of credit in fostering true belief in science.)

Hume, D. (1748) *An Enquiry Concerning Human Understanding*, in *Hume's Enquiries*, ed. P.H. Nidditch and L.A. Selby-Bigge, Oxford: Oxford University Press, 1975. (The discussion of testimony appears in §88.)

Kitcher, P. (1990) 'The division of cognitive labor', *Journal of Philosophy* 87: 5–22. (Argues that pursuing lines of inquiry based on improbable theories can foster the cognitive goals of science.)

* Latour, B. (1987) *Science in Action*, Cambridge, MA: Harvard University Press. (Argues for the first kind of social constructivism defined in §5 above.)

Lehrer, K. and Wagner, C. (1981) *Rational Consensus in Science and Society*, Dordrecht: Reidel. (Contains an account of the conditions in which an individual is committed to accepting the consensus of a group.)

Locke, J. (1689) *An Essay Concerning Human Understanding*, ed. A.C. Fraser, New York: Dover, 2 vols, 1959. (The remarks about testimony appear at Book I, page 58 and Book IV, chapters 15 and 16, §§10 and 11.)

Longino, H. (1990) *Science as Social Knowledge*, Princeton, NJ: Princeton University Press. (A multiperspectival account of scientific knowledge.)

* Peirce, C.S. (1955) 'The fixation of belief', in *Philosophical Writings of Peirce*, ed. J. Buchler, New York: Dover. (The argument for common relief from doubt as the aim of proper method appears on pages 12–13.)

* Reid, T. (1785) *Essays on the Intellectual Powers of Man*, ed. B. Brody, Cambridge, MA: MIT Press, 1969. (The material on testimony appears in Essay VI, chapter 5.)

* Rouse, J. (1987) *Knowledge and Power: Toward a Political Philosophy of Science*, Ithaca, NY: Cornell University Press. (Defends the first two versions of social constructivism about knowledge mentioned in §5 above.)

Schmitt, F.F. (ed.) (1987) *Synthèse* 62, special issue on social epistemology. (Collection of articles on diverse topics in social epistemology.)

—— (ed.) (1994) *Socializing Epistemology*, Lanham, MD: Rowman & Littlefield. (An anthology containing articles on topics in all branches of social epistemology, with an introduction that expands on §§1 and 5 of this entry and an extensive bibliography.)

Sextus Empiricus (c.200) *Outlines of Pyrrhonism*, in *Sextus Empiricus*, vol. 1, trans. R.G. Bury, Loeb Classical Library, Cambridge, MA: Harvard University Press, 1933. (The maxim of epistemic parity among persons is assumed in the second through fifth and in the tenth modes in book I, chapter 14.)

Solomon, M. (1994) 'Social empiricism', *Nous* 28: 325–43. (Argues that biases resulting from scientists' training and professional preoccupations may foster the cognitive goal of empirical adequacy.)

* Wittgenstein, L. (1969) *On Certainty*, ed. G.E.M. Anscombe and G.H. von Wright, trans. D. Paul and G.E.M. Anscombe, New York: Harper. (Suggests that beliefs or claims are justified on the basis of communally accepted propositions.)

FREDERICK F. SCHMITT

SOCIAL LAWS

Social science has always aspired to be like natural science (Hawthorn 1976). And since natural science claims to discover laws of nature, social science has always claimed to discover laws of society. There are two important problems raised by such social laws. What makes the laws social in the appropriate sense? And if they really obtain, does that mean that human beings are not as autonomous as one might have thought: that we are pawns in a game that the laws control?

We may take laws here in a more or less unanalysed fashion as reliable regularities, usually reliable causal regularities, in the succession of events on one another. The statement of a causal law will postulate that whenever an event of a certain type is realized then an event of another type is also going to be realized, perhaps so close in time that they overlap, perhaps at some temporal distance. Or, more plausibly, it will postulate a probabilistic and bounded version of that sort of linkage. The linkage will be probabilistic to the extent that the first sort of event is held to raise the chance of the second sort occurring, not to make it inevitable. And it will be bounded so far as it is assumed to obtain only under certain boundary conditions: only when other things, usually other unspecified things, are equal.

What are the laws of the social realm that the social science project envisages? They cannot by all accounts be just the sorts of laws that empirical psychology, or the sort of psychology employed in microeconomics, postulates. They cannot just be regularities in the way people's individual beliefs and desires, probabilities and utilities, are formed and develop. They must be distinctively social laws (Brown 1984).

A law will be a distinctively social law, we may presume, just where the properties that it involves are, or at least include, some social properties. But what is it for a property to be social? There are many rival accounts (Ruben 1985). One simple one holds that a property is social just where it cannot be realized unless a number of intentional subjects, usually interactive intentional subjects, hold by certain attitudes or exhibit certain actions. The property of an individual that they are a judge or a celebrity, the property of a place that it is a country or a football field, the property of a group that its members meet on Sundays or that they generally go to sleep before midnight: these are all social properties on this generous account.

There is little doubt but that there are social laws, under this account of social laws (Pettit 1993). It is a putative law, however probabilistic and bounded, that urbanization leads to secularization, that an increase in unemployment leads to a rise in crime, and that commercial firms tend to approach the profit levels of their rivals. Such laws indeed are social in quite a strong sense. While the properties involved cannot be realized without a number of people displaying certain intentional actions or attitudes – that is what makes the properties social – still the laws are not just an extension of the body of psychological laws. They do not introduce factors that might be thought to interact with the variables of established psychological laws, thereby extending the laws causally. Nor do they involve patterns that are logically secured just by the fact that certain psychological laws obtain: they

are logically as well as causally discontinuous with psychological laws.

Do social laws, so understood, threaten the sense that we human beings have of ourselves as relatively autonomous thinkers and agents? Those who espouse a collectivist or structuralist vision of social science, for example many in the tradition of Durkheim, tend to say that they do; they tend to take social science, in particular the discovery of social-structural laws, as a challenge to our ordinary common-sense view of ourselves. The idea is that whereas common sense represents us as forming attitudes and actions in response to familiar, more or less rational pressures, social science reveals that we are destined, perhaps even determined, to behave in the manner that certain aggregate social laws require. We are the unknowing dupes of those impersonal dictators (see STRUCTUR-ALISM IN SOCIAL SCIENCE §1).

But this vision of dictatorship by social law – this version of the 'death of the subject' – is uncompelling. It is more plausible to think of social laws as related to intentional or psychological laws – the laws that ensure our relative autonomy – in an architecture of the following kind (Pettit 1993). A higher-level social law relates an antecedent which is variously realizable at the intentional level to a consequent that is variously realizable at the intentional level: so urbanization or secularization may come about via any of an indeterminate number of actions, and any of an indeterminate variety of attitudes, on the part of individuals. If the antecedent is related in a law-like way to the consequent, that is because the intentional realizers of the antecedent, no matter what they are, are more or less bound to lead, under the intentional laws, to the realization of the consequent. The realization of the antecedent 'programmes' for the realization of the consequent helps to ensure the realization of the consequent in a manner that depends on more or less familiar psychological regularities, not in a manner that imposes an alien order on the intentional realm.

This architecture is attractive, because it would enable us to see how social science may discover surprising laws without undermining our image of ourselves as more or less autonomous agents. It would also enable us to see how such laws can be logically discontinuous from the body of psychological laws. The laws may obtain, not just in virtue of psychological laws, but also in virtue of the boundary conditions under which those laws rule. If unemployment leads to crime, that may be a result, not just of the way human psychology works, but also of contingent features of the world in which it works: in a world where the unemployed could always have recourse to wild fruit and warm beaches, for example, the regularity might well break down.

See also: NATURAL LAW; SOCIAL SCIENCES, PHILOSOPHY OF

References and further reading

* Brown, R. (1984) *The Nature of Social Laws*, Cambridge: Cambridge University Press. (Discusses the history of the notion of social law.)
* Hawthorn, G. (1976) *Enlightenment and Despair: A History of Sociology*, Cambridge: Cambridge University Press. (Discusses the aspiration of social science to be science and discover genuine laws.)
* Pettit, P. (1993) *The Common Mind: An Essay on Psychology, Society and Politics*, New York: Oxford University Press. (Chapter 3 characterizes social laws and argues in support of the programme-architecture.)
* Ruben, D.-H. (1985) *The Metaphysics of the Social World*, London: Routledge. (Discusses the meaning of 'social' thoroughly.)

PHILIP PETTIT

SOCIAL NATURE OF LANGUAGE *see* LANGUAGE, SOCIAL NATURE OF

SOCIAL NORMS

A social norm may be defined as the rule of a particular social group. That men are to open doors for women, for instance, may be the rule of a particular group. But what is it for a group to have a rule, according to our everyday understanding? Philosophers have disagreed on this point. An important general issue is whether a group's having a rule is a matter of some or all of its members individually conforming to the rule or individually accepting the rule as a standard of behaviour for the group. An alternative type of account invokes the idea of the group's members jointly, rather than individually, accepting the rule, in effect agreeing to conform to it. It can be argued that this less individualistic account better explains the way in which people criticize deviations from social norms.

1   Lewis' game-theoretic account of social convention
2   Hart's practice theory of social rules
3   Gilbert's joint acceptance account of social rules

1   Lewis' game-theoretic account of social convention

Lewis (1969), following Schelling (1960), proposed an account of (social) convention such that underlying every convention is a recurring 'coordination problem' that will be solved by members' regular conformity to a certain pattern of behaviour (see LEWIS, D.K.). A typical coordination problem occurs when a telephone conversation is cut off. Each party wants the call reconnected. If both call back, however, or if both wait, no reconnection will take place. There is a need for coordination of behaviour in order that the result both prefer occurs.

Lewis' proposal is roughly this: by definition, there is a convention when and only when a suitable regularity in behaviour arises within a coordination problem, accompanied by expectations of conformity. He argues that conventions in his sense are 'norms': we believe that those with such a convention ought to conform to it, since otherwise they go against their own and the other parties' preferences (1969: 97). That may be so, but the question remains whether conventions according to Lewis are social norms in the sense of group rules (see DECISION AND GAME THEORY).

Critics argue that Lewis has not captured the vernacular concept of a social convention, as he hoped (see, for instance, Gilbert 1989, ch. 6). Among other things, conventions do not only arise in the context of coordination problems. Further, it can be argued that from an intuitive point of view social conventions are a class of group rules. According to Lewis' definition, conventions do not amount to group rules intuitively. Among other things, if a convention were a group rule, the parties would understand they had reason to conform irrespective of their personal preferences and expectations.

2   Hart's practice theory of social rules

Hart's account of social or group rules runs roughly as follows: for there to be a social rule, a certain pattern of behaviour must be regularly conformed to within a given group. In addition, members of the group must regard the pattern as a standard by which group members' behaviour may be judged correct or incorrect. They must believe that, all equal, members ought to conform to it. Further, group members must believe they are justified in pressuring one another to conform. In typical cases, such pressure will be imposed on deviants and those who threaten deviance (see HART, H.L.A.).

These conditions seem not to rule out cases like the following. The individual members of a group believe that lying is wrong. They also believe that members are justified in pressuring one another not to lie. In the situation as described, however, the rule proscribing lying does not seem to be a genuine group rule, as opposed to a rule that everyone individually accepts (and deems it appropriate for everyone to enforce) (Dworkin 1977; Hart [1961] 1994, postscript). What is missing from this case?

As Hart himself observes, when a group has a rule the members take themselves to be justified in the imposition of pressure on others solely because of actual or threatened violation of a rule of their group. This is so whether or not they take the rule to be a moral one. (Presumably the rule that men are to open doors for women might not be perceived as a moral one.) This suggests that an adequate account of social rules will make clear how, by their nature, they justify the imposition of pressure for conformity.

3 Gilbert's joint acceptance account of social rules

If we are looking for something other than a moral rule to ground an entitlement to exert pressure on others, an obvious candidate is something akin to an agreement. If you and I have agreed to act in a certain way in the future, and I then act differently, we will both understand that I have failed in an obligation I had to you, and that you therefore have grounds for reproving me, whether or not you choose to do so.

Of course group members do not in general get together and agree to conform to certain standards. Commitments of the sort involved in an agreement can be set up, however, without an agreement proper being made. Language can play a role here, as when members accept appeals to 'our' rule, with the attendant commitments that this may imply (Gilbert 1989, ch. 4).

Gilbert (1989, ch. 6) suggests that a social convention as ordinarily understood is a jointly accepted fiat, while a social rule is a jointly accepted rule, that may or may not be of the fiat form. For members of a population jointly to accept a rule is for them to enter a 'joint commitment' to accept that rule together, that is, as a body. A joint commitment is one that is seen by the participants precisely as joint: it is not the sum of the different individual members' independent commitments. Rather, it is our commitment. All are committed through it, but these 'individual commitments' have a single source in the joint commitment, on which they depend. Each member is beholden to the others for release from the commitment. A joint commitment may be said to involve mutual obligations of a particular sort, and to provide grounds for reproof if the commitment is not complied with (Gilbert 1996).

Given this appeal to the notion of a joint

commitment (which she sees as a fundamental intuitive concept) Gilbert argues, in effect, for a more holistic, less individualistic account of social norms than is envisaged by Hart or Lewis. Rules jointly accepted by group members are more aptly referred to as the rules of a group than are rules merely conformed to or individually accepted by group members.

See also: HOLISM AND INDIVIDUALISM IN HISTORY AND SOCIAL SCIENCE; SOCIAL LAWS; SOCIAL ACTION

References and further reading

* Dworkin, R. (1977) *Taking Rights Seriously*, London: Duckworth. (A collection of Dworkin's articles in jurisprudence including 'The Model of Rules II' in which he criticizes Hart's account of social rules.)
* Gilbert, M. (1989) *On Social Facts*, London: Routledge; 2nd edn, Princeton, NJ: Princeton University Press, 1992. (A theory of the structure of everyday collectivity concepts including the concept of a social group and a social convention.)
* —— (1996) *Living Together: Rationality, Sociality, and Obligation*, Lanham, MD: Rowman and Littlefield. (A collection of Gilbert's articles relating to *On Social Facts* (above). Chapter 12, 'Agreements, Coercion, and Obligation', argues for a particular understanding of the obligations of agreements and related phenomena, in terms of a 'joint commitment' underlying agreements.)
* Hart, H.L.A. (1961) *The Concept of Law*, Oxford: Clarendon Press, 2nd edn with postscript, 1994. (A classic account of the nature of law in terms of a union of primary and secondary rules, with special reference to the nature of social rules in general.)
* —— (1982) *Essays on Bentham*, Oxford: Clarendon Press. (Chapter X provides a new account of what it is for there to be a social rule to the effect that a particular 'commander' should be obeyed.)
* Lewis, D.K. (1969) *Convention*, Cambridge, MA: Harvard University Press. (A game-theoretic account of social conventions, according to which they involve coordination problems, intended to throw light on the idea that language involves convention.)
  Raz, J. (1975) *Practical Reason and Norms*, London: Hutchinson; Princeton, NJ: Princeton University Press, 1992. (Chapter 2 focuses on 'mandatory norms', offers a critique of Hart, and argues in relation to the role of norms in practical reasoning that mandatory norms are 'exclusionary reasons', that is, roughly, reasons to disregard other reasons.)
* Schelling, T. (1960) *The Strategy of Conflict*, Cambridge, MA: Harvard University Press. (Suggests

that 'coordination games' underlie the stability of institutions and traditions. Influenced Lewis and others.)

Ullman-Margalit, E. (1977) *The Emergence of Norms*, Oxford: Oxford University Press. (Focuses on three game-theoretically defined structures, including coordination problems, and argues they are apt to give rise to norms.)

MARGARET GILBERT

SOCIAL RELATIVISM

People in different societies have very different beliefs and systems of belief. To understand such diversity is a prime task of the student of society. The task is especially pressing when alien beliefs seem obviously mistaken, unreasonable or otherwise peculiar. A popular response is social relativism. Perhaps beliefs which seem mistaken, unreasonable or peculiar viewed from our perspective, are by no means mistaken, unreasonable or peculiar viewed from the perspective of the society in which they occur. Different things are not just thought true (reasonable, natural) in different societies – rather, they are true (reasonable, natural) in different societies. Relativism recognizes diversity and deals with it even-handedly.

Relativism has absurd results. Consider the view that what is true in society A need not be true in society B. So if society A believes in witches while society B does not, there are witches in A but not in B. Relativism regarding truth drives us to different 'worlds', one with witches in it and another without. This seems absurd: people who live in different societies do not in any literal sense live in different worlds. The challenge is to do justice to social diversity without falling into absurdities such as this.

1   Social diversity
2   Social relativism
3   Proliferation
4   Idealism

1   Social diversity

Social diversity is one of the first and most familiar facts to strike the student of human beings and the societies in which they live. The foregoing treats of the social diversity of belief. Along with different beliefs come differences in behaviour, customs, rituals, traditions, conventions, institutions, political and legal arrangements, and so forth. For instance, some people enact ritual dances to ensure that rain will fall

on the crops, others think that pregnancy has nothing to do with sexual intercourse, yet others blame magical influences for their misfortunes. Here capital punishment is frowned upon, there it is not. Here a particular religion is state-sponsored, there it is not. Many things other than belief-systems are 'relative to' (that is, distinctive of) different societies.

Yet there is good reason to focus on beliefs. The other differences are all constituted by, or sustained by, or at least associated with, differences in belief. Canons of rationality or of value are generally accepted beliefs about what is reasonable or valuable. It is the custom in a society to bury the dead only if sufficiently many members of that society think it is the thing to do and act accordingly. Traditions and institutions are sustained by the beliefs of the participants in them. Actually, there are deep questions regarding exactly how, and to what extent, social phenomena are 'dependent' on beliefs and belief-systems. We cannot enter into those controversies here, but rather focus on the diversity of beliefs, as is customary.

2   Social relativism

An early response to the diversity of beliefs was to distinguish 'primitive societies' (usually African) from advanced ones (usually European). The bizarre beliefs of 'primitive peoples' were just false, the product of irrational, illogical, even 'pre-logical' processes of thought. Then a reaction set in. You cannot really understand a 'primitive' society by viewing it from the perspective of your own and deeming its beliefs and practices false or irrational or pre-rational. Each society should be judged on its own terms. Beliefs deemed false and irrational by our lights may be perfectly sound and rational seen from the perspective of the society which sustains them. Just as belief-systems are socially and culturally bound, so are honorifics like 'true' or 'reasonable' with which they are evaluated. This is social relativism.

Social relativism is not merely the recognition of social diversity or of the difficulty of understanding the arrangements of one society from the perspective of another. Social relativists add that there is nothing to choose between different beliefs and practices. There are no neutral canons of truth or reason which would enable us to do this. Local mistakes remain possible. An incompetent witch-doctor may consult the poison oracle wrongly or have a false belief about the origin of a particular misfortune. An incompetent priest may administer the sacrament wrongly or make a theological mistake. But neither witchcraft nor Christianity can be globally false or irrational. Truth and rationality are themselves relative to societies. No belief or system of belief can be deemed false or irrational *simpliciter*.

3 Proliferation

One worry about social relativism concerns its tendency to proliferate. Societies are pluralistic and ill-defined. One group may enact magical rituals and also spread fertilizers to ensure good crops. Another may keep their cars well-maintained and also bless them with holy water to ensure safe travel. There exists both a Society of Friends and a Society of Accountants. This is no mere pun on the word 'society': the beliefs, traditions, practices, and so on, of these two groups are as diverse as one might wish.

Social diversity proliferates horizontally, across different societies at the same time. It also proliferates vertically, down the same (or different) societies at different times. For, as L.P. Hartley said at the beginning of *The Go-Between*, 'The past is a foreign country – they do things differently there'. Historical diversity is as familiar a fact to the student of history, as social diversity is to the student of society.

One example of historical diversity is particularly important. Some have been tempted to take science and technology as the arbiters of truth and reason, against which all is to be judged. If we want good crops, we know that fertilizing the soil is better than uttering magical incantations over it. We know this because science teaches it. If we have to choose between 'African traditional thought and western science', to cite the title of a famous contribution to these debates, by Robin Horton (reprinted in Wilson 1970), it is clear how we should choose. But is 'western science' the monolithic system of belief and practice which this seems to suppose? Thomas KUHN said not. A glance into the history of science reveals the same kind of diversity of belief and practice, as we see today as we look across different societies. Furthermore, Kuhn seemed to say, there is as little to choose between the different ways of practising 'western science', as there is between the different beliefs and practices we find today in different societies. Far from being a way out of the relativistic impasse, science viewed historically is a part of it.

One response to social diversity is to maintain that, beneath all the diversity and under-pinning it, there are continuities. All social groups are interested in finding solutions to the basic problems of life, usually detailed as food, shelter and procreation. To that end, all social groups are interested in explaining and, so far as they are able, controlling the phenomena of nature. In pursuit of these basic ends, all social groups have an interest in acquiring beliefs that are true and explanations that work.

Thoroughgoing relativists remain unimpressed. They see diversity even concerning the 'basic problems of life'. There are peoples who (it seems) believe that pregnancy has nothing to do with sexual intercourse. A common interest in explanation represents continuity only if proffered explanations are of the same type and are adjudicated by common standards. A common interest in true beliefs represents continuity only if there is a common notion of truth.

Like many general sceptical theses, thoroughgoing relativism threatens to self-destruct. 'All truths are relative to some S' will itself, if true, only be true relative to some S. One can ask in which S relativism is true. And the best answer seems to involve the society or sub-culture of social anthropologists and their various philosophical hangers-on. Alternatively, one can view relativism as an absolute, ahistorical, trans-cultural truth – in which case, it is false.

4 Idealism

Relativism about truth flies in the face of platitudes. For example, it is true that bloodletting cures diseases if, and only if, bloodletting really does cure diseases. Or generally, something or other is true if, and only if, it is really the case. Such platitudes seem to leave no room for the notion that something might be true for A but not for B. These platitudes assume that what is the case does not in general depend upon what people think is the case. It is to suppose that the world, its objects and their features do not in general depend on our ideas, on our thought or talk. Suppose instead that what is true for one society need not be true for another. It follows that inhabitants of different societies inhabit different worlds. In society A it is believed that diseases are brought about by ill-wishing magicians, in society B it is believed that diseases are brought about by bacteria, viruses and other 'natural causes'. Some people might think that both beliefs cannot be true (though both might be false). But this is to fall back upon a monolithic, societally-neutral notion of truth. No, it is true in society A that diseases are brought about by ill-wishing magicians – not just thought to be true (that is, believed) but true. It follows that there really are in the world ill-wishing magicians – for inhabitants of society A. Once monolithic truth is jettisoned, so is a monolithic 'world' to which monolithic truths 'correspond'. No, different peoples inhabit different worlds. The world of the Kalahari bushman is very different from the world of the industrialized European. The world of the Aristotelian scientist is very different from the world of the Newtonian scientist. If truth is socially constructed, so is reality. The world, its objects, and their features depend for their very nature upon what human beings think about the world, its objects, and their features. (And why just human beings? Avoid human chauvinism, and you will have to agree that the world of the chimpanzee or honeybee is worlds apart from the world of Albert Einstein.) This is idealism (see IDEALISM; REALISM AND ANTIREALISM).

Relativistic and idealistic ways of speaking are popular, and may be innocuous. 'That's true for you but not for me' may just be a picturesque way of saying that you think that true but I do not. 'Witches really existed in seventeenth-century Europe' may just be a picturesque way of saying that seventeenth-century Europeans thought that witches really existed. But if we take such locutions literally, they involve us in idealism.

What of logic and rationality – might they be socially relative? Might a people believe that there are witches – and also believe that there are not? Might there be a 'pre-logical' society where the logical law of contradiction breaks down? The matter of rationality is more difficult. Beliefs can be rational yet false, and irrational yet true. Our ancestors once believed that the earth was flat – their belief was false, but reasonable given the evidence and argument available to them. Should we now find a society of flat-earthers, we might declare their belief false yet reasonable, for much the same reasons. Alternatively, we might suspect that they do not really believe this and that we have mistranslated utterances which led us to think that they do. The enterprise of translation, however, seems to presuppose that sincere utterances are thought true, and not thought untrue at the same time.

Cultural relativism and idealism are fuelled by a laudable ambition to be even-handed about the beliefs and practices of others. But we can understand the beliefs and practices of others 'on their own terms' without dismantling the rational unity of humankind. Indeed, the latter is curiously self-defeating. What is more patronizing than the declaration that this or that is true and real – but just for you? The project is 'understanding a primitive society' (to cite the title of another famous contribution to these debates by Peter Winch, reprinted in Wilson 1970). Do you advance that project by claiming that in 'primitive societies' understanding means something quite different to what it means in ours?

See also: EPISTEMIC RELATIVISM; MORAL RELATIVISM; RATIONALITY AND CULTURAL RELATIVISM; RATIONALITY OF BELIEF; RELATIVISM

References and further reading

Hollis, M. and Lukes, S. (eds) (1982) *Rationality and*

Relativism, Oxford: Blackwell. (A useful collection of readings, containing a bibliography.)

Sumner, W.G. (1907) *Folkways: A Study of the Sociological Importance of Usages, Manners, Customs, Mores, and Morals*, Boston, MA: Ayer, 1979. (Sumner's masterpiece, in which he argues that each society has its ultimate 'mores'.)

* Wilson, B.R. (ed.) (1970) *Rationality*, Oxford: Blackwell. (A more recent collection of readings, also containing a helpful bibliography.)

ALAN MUSGRAVE

SOCIAL SCIENCE, CONTEMPORARY PHILOSOPHY OF

Some philosophers think that the study of social phenomena must apply methods from natural science. Researchers should discover causal regularities (whenever C operates, E occurs) and fit them into systematic theories. Some philosophers hold that social phenomena call for an entirely different approach, in which researchers seek to interpret fully the meaning of people's actions, including their efforts to communicate and cooperate. On this view, the nearest that researchers will come to regularities will be to discover rules (whenever the situation is S, everyone must do A). The nearest that they will get to systematic theories will be systematic expositions of rules, like the rules of a kinship system.

Besides the naturalistic school and the interpretive school, the philosophy of social science harbours a critical school. This finds researches endorsed by the other two schools shot through with bias. It inclines to agree with the interpretive school in resisting naturalistic methods. However, its charges against naturalistic researches extend to interpretations. For interpretations may give untroubled pictures of societies in deep trouble, or picture the trouble in ways that serve the interests of the people who profit from it, for example, by leaving current rules about taking workers on and laying them off unquestioned. Here the critical school may itself use naturalistic methods. If it contends that ignoring ways of reassigning authority over employment increases the chances of private enterprises' retaining their present authority, the critical school is talking about a causal connection. There is no rule that says anyone must increase the chances.

Yet the researches sponsored by the three schools are complementary to the degree that researches into regularities and into rules are complementary. Settled social rules have counterparts in causal regularities, which may be expressed in similar terms, although the evidence for regularities need not include intended conformity. Some regularities are not counterparts of rules, but involve rules notwithstanding. If the proportion of marriages in Arizona ending in divorce is regularly one-third, that is not (as it happens) because one-third of Arizonans who marry must divorce. Yet marriage and divorce are actions that fall under rules.

The three schools do more than endorse studies of rules or regularities. The critical school denies that any study of social phenomena can be value-free, in particular on the point of emancipating people from the oppressions of current society. Either researchers work with the critical school to expose oppression; or they work for the oppressors. The interpretive school brings forward subjective features of human actions and experiences that overflow the study of rules. These features, too, may be reported or ascribed correctly or incorrectly; however, the truth about them may be best expressed in narrative texts more or less elaborate.

Postmodernism has generalized these themes in a sceptical direction. Every text can be read in multiple, often conflicting, ways, so there are always multiple, often conflicting, interpretations of whatever happens. Every interpretation serves a quest for power, whether or not it neatly favours or disfavours an oppressive social class. Such contentions undermine assumptions that the three schools make about seeking truth regarding social phenomena. They do even more to undermine any assumption that the truths found will hold universally.

The assumption about universality, however, is a legacy of the positivist view of natural science. Positivism has given way to the model-theoretic or semantic view that science proceeds by constructing models to compare with real systems. A model – in social science, a model of regularities or one of rules – that fits any real system for a time is a scientific achievement empirically vindicated. Renouncing demands for universality, the philosophy of social science can make a firm stand on issues raised by postmodernism. It can accept from postmodernists the point that scientific success happens in local contexts and only for a time; but resist any further-reaching scepticism.

1   The point of distinguishing schools
2   Naturalism recast
3   The several concerns of the interpretive school
4   Critical social theory: effective with or without reduction
5   The impact of postmodernism
6   The relations between the schools re-examined

1   The point of distinguishing schools

Why make anything of a distinction between schools? One could look upon social science as embracing a great number of inquiries on a variety of topics. Some inquiries deal with regularities; some, with rules; some, as much with the one as with the other. They may all be subject to criticism for ignoring other matters, including sometimes their service to current oppressive arrangements.

However, the different contentions of philosophers on the subject of social science demand something like the three-schools distinction. Among the contentions arise exclusive claims for naturalism; interpretation; critical social theory. The three-schools distinction distributes these exclusive claims under appropriate heads, then confronts them. This is worth doing not only to give the contentions in question due attention. It is in order because social scientists themselves carry on inquiries in different styles answering to the differences between the schools.

The three-schools distinction directs attention to important issues. Is any one school to prevail to the exclusion of the others? If all three survive, because all of them correspond to distinctive and worthwhile inquiries, are the schools and inquiries quite separate? Connections – close and extensive connections – between rules and regularities make the schools allies; and individual inquiries frequently mix the several styles. The schools remain allies, furthermore, when aspects of social phenomena come into the picture that demand philosophical attention though they do not explicitly have to do with rules or regularities.

Chief among these further aspects are, first, the basic subjective features – the temporal structures – of human action and experience, in both of which agents behold the present in a perspective established at once by the immediate past and the foreshadowed immediate future. Second, there is the interpretation of actions as texts the true interpretation of which changes, like the significance of judicial decisions, as history goes on and the perspective of interpretation changes. This is the concern of hermeneutics (see HERMENEUTICS). Both of these matters can be assigned to the interpretive school, along with a special interest in narratives, without making the school incoherent.

Similarly, the naturalistic school can digest the model-theoretic view of science, without in any way abdicating from advocacy of naturalistic methods (see MODEL THEORY). On the contrary, the advocacy becomes more plausible, without encouraging exclusive claims. Within the three-schools framework, the model-theoretic approach, once installed in the naturalistic school, invites application also in the interpretive school. The critical school has for its part a visible opportunity to employ models either of rules or of regularities.

With these new matters accommodated, the relations between the schools need re-examination; and re-examination strengthens the case for complementarity. Moreover, the schools framework furnishes a venue for assessing the impact of postmodernism. How far can it be accommodated, and where? Once the relations within and between the schools have been assessed again, with the lessons about postmodernism allowed for, the relations can be redescribed as relations of inquiries – inquiries concerned with rules, concerned with regularities, concerned with texts, concerned with subjective experience. If one likes, the distinction between the schools, having served all the purposes mentioned, can then be left behind as a historical curiosity.

2   Naturalism recast

John Stuart MILL was a strong early advocate of naturalistic methods in the social sciences; but in the twentieth century its chief advocates were for a long time philosophers grouped at least roughly with logical positivists. During its reign in the philosophy of natural science, positivism held that perfected scientific theories embraced universal laws holding for all times and places. This is an exacting prescription for the natural sciences. In the social sciences it has been impossible to fulfil, and a major embarrassment for the naturalistic school (see POSITIVISM IN THE SOCIAL SCIENCES).

The prescription has vanished from the philosophy of natural science with the eclipse of positivism. Yet the revisions that would recast naturalistic doctrines regarding social science to incorporate the now-prevailing model-theoretic view of science have hardly begun. According to this view, as set forth by R.N. Giere (1988), the business of science is accomplished, first, by setting up models with predicates that hold true precisely only of the models and there as a matter of definition; and then showing that the models resemble one range or another of phenomena closely enough to be more useful than other models in prediction and explanation. The predicates may incorporate universally quantified statements ('In our model of a perfectly competitive market, F's [rises in price] will always be followed by G's [increases in supply]'). However, these need hold only for the model or only for the model and (more or less loosely) for some range of phenomena, perhaps just one, strictly circumscribed (markets for pork bellies, given time to raise more pigs). They may also – another important relaxation in scientific standards –

go no further in causal content than to specify causal conditions, necessary or sufficient only in the presence of other conditions, and leaving open questions about underlying causal mechanisms. One could know that the number of pork bellies coming to market in a given year increased only after a rise in prices for pork bellies in some earlier year, without having worked out how one thing led to the other or how quickly.

At one stroke, the model-theoretic approach relieves social science of the burden of finding regularities that hold for all societies. There may be such regularities; in spite of many disappointments it may be worth looking for them; but social science is already working in perfect keeping with the current conception of natural science whenever it works out a model that fits the regularities of just one society, for example, one with money and an organized national market for agricultural commodities. (Indeed, social science does not even have to produce models to work in keeping with scientific standards: it does so just by identifying rules or regularities not identified before, or even just by deploying statistical skills to establish whether the rates of crime or of unemployment are changing.)

Models may originate in attempts, given a mass of information about various societies or various social practices, to draw a simple picture of what those cases have in common. They may be produced with a direct aim of giving a simplified or idealized account of one real case, for example, the economy of Ireland in the late nineteenth century. But then the perspective in which the model is treated is the same as if it condensed a variety of cases. It is carried from one range of phenomena to another to see where it fits.

When statements that would otherwise be taken to be statements by a theory about the world become statements describing a model, it is no longer worrisome whether they are strictly speaking true. We make them true by definition, by postulating a model that answers to the description; and we can make the model as abstract and idealized as we like. If science is in the business of producing models, then it can easily be accepted that the models will often be idealized and will not quite fit any real phenomena. It suffices for a model to come quite close, as it may do in the social sciences as well as in the natural ones, to fitting the phenomena that we want to predict and explain. We do not have to leave the meaning of being close unduly vague. We can count a model as having been improved on when we advance to making more precise predictions of the variables that specially interest us.

The model-theoretic view is also called the semantic conception because the relation of statements describing models to the models is a matter of semantics (while positivism, preoccupied with universally quantified forms of statements, inclined to emphasize the syntax of theories). Models are non-linguistic, even when they are defined in language (maybe mathematical language), without constructing anything tangible to embody the definition. A tangible model can often be furnished if it is demanded. When it is not furnished, diagrams can serve as one-dimensional or two-dimensional physical models. However, models are sometimes clearly not physical at all; logicians use the integers or the positive numbers as models. In any case, models actually produced would belong with items that language refers to rather than with items of language, just as toy trucks or table-top maps would belong with sharks and trees, not with the words 'toy truck', 'map', 'shark', 'tree'.

An important philosophical issue on which different positions have arisen in the naturalistic school turns on whether all the findings of social science about groups can be reduced to findings about individual persons. Mill held that they can; chief to say that they cannot was the French philosopher and sociologist Émile DURKHEIM (§2), who contended strongly for a social science oriented to the discovery on the social level of facts that constrained people's actions and did not simply combine them. Important as this issue is, it does not compel us to divide the naturalistic school into two. Division on the issue is entirely compatible with the pursuit of causal regularities, though on one view these will be (always) reducible to findings about individual persons and on the other (sometimes) irreducibly regularities about groups.

3 The several concerns of the interpretive school

Giambattista VICO (§§4–6), the pioneer of the interpretive school, held that human beings should have every confidence in their ability to understand social phenomena, because the phenomena are all of their own making. 'Understand' can be taken here in the broad sense in which we understand celestial phenomena better when we grasp what the red shift implies about the movement of the stars. However, it can also be taken in the sense in which we understand another person's actions when we appreciate the hopes and fears that led to them. Max WEBER (§3), highlighting 'understanding' of this sort (*Verstehen*), thought it went hand in hand with explanation. Indeed, any sort of understanding would, though some champions of interpretation, drastically shrinking the scope of the term, use 'explanation' only for attempts at explanation in the naturalistic school.

The study of rules, which are surely of human

making, invites Vico's confidence as much as other concerns of the champions of interpretation. Widely practised, it is continually reinvigorated by new techniques like game theory and by recurrent demands for treating the state and other institutions as systems of rules (March and Olsen 1989; Ostrom 1990). It may serve as a distinguishing mark of the interpretive school. Concern with the study of rules, however, does not do much to identify the other concerns agitating the school, which in its eyes may be much more profound matters.

One such matter, which has found philosophical expression in Edmund HUSSERL and Martin HEIDEGGER and their followers, is concern that the basic subjective features of human experience receive attention and respect. What does an action mean to the person doing it? This is not a question that is to be answered just by referring to the rules under which the action falls. Simple actions have subjective meanings for the people doing them, consisting of temporal structures in which their awareness of what they are doing shifts from one aspect of it to another (Carr 1986). What agents are aware of as just having done in starting up the action (moving to the door when the doorbell rings) gives way to what they are aware of doing now (turning the doorknob and swinging the door open) and this in turn to what they will be aware of having done when they finish (welcoming the person who has come to the door). Even simpler temporal structures may be embedded in these; they in turn are embedded in more elaborate ones.

A structure does not have to be very elaborate to take on aspects of a narrative. Agents may tell themselves a story as they enact it about how they started, how far they have gone, and towards what outcomes they are headed. (I left a sister behind in East Germany twenty years ago; it is she, I believe, who has just rung the doorbell; if all goes well in the reunion I shall take her into my household.) No references to rules may appear in the telling. The stories may have engrossing meaning for the agents without being for them a story about rules at all.

Narratives are examples of texts. Complex events and actions become texts themselves when the notion of texts is extended in a way that hermeneutics encourages. What do texts mean, judiciously interpreted? This is again a question that does not prima facie make references to rules prominent. It would seem, certainly at first sight, to have much more to do with exploring the larger narratives surrounding a text. (The sister's coming is a story that fits in a number of intercrossing ways into other stories – family histories; the recent history of Germany; the history of the Cold War.) Hermeneutics as Hans-Georg GADAMER (§3) conceives it is concerned with interpreting texts under a 'fusion of horizons'. When the texts are actions, only as much place goes to what the actions meant to the agents from what they could see at the time of doing them (with the narratives going on then) as is consistent with giving due weight also to the interpreters' own horizon of meaning (and the narratives now current). That horizon embraces not only what has happened since the action was done, but also present expectations regarding its further consequences.

A clear example is an opinion delivered by the US Supreme Court, in *Planned Parenthood of Southeastern Pennsylvania* v. *Casey* (1991), a case on abortion. In that opinion Justice Sandra O'Connor held that whatever stand one might have taken at the time that *Roe* v. *Wade* (1973), the crucial previous case, was decided, one must recognize that millions of US women had been assuming for some twenty years that abortion was their legal right. This made a crucial difference now both to the issue and to how the previous case was to be understood.

Concern with the study of rules can be made more congenial to the other concerns at stake in interpretation by fully expressing the complexity of the concern. The interpretive school will be interested (since this is essential to discovering which rules are socially settled ones) in rules that elicit observable conformity. But social scientists who fall in with the school are not to be thought preoccupied with conformity. They are as much interested in the abuse of rules, and in violations. They are interested in rules half-formed and merely advisory precepts. Not least in importance, they are interested in the variable space that a structure of settled social rules may leave for spontaneous, inventive, and innovative action. (Professors have been lecturing in academic gowns; but some begin coming to class in sweaters and blue jeans; they get away with it.) Thus the interpretive school endorses, not so much questions about 'What rules do given actions fall under?', but rather 'In what ways are social phenomena related to the presence or absence of rules?'. That allows considerable room for satisfying other interpretive concerns in the very course of studying rules. Subjective experience and narratives at all levels of generality reflect the impact of current rules, sometimes to a point of saturation or obsession, sometimes to a point of outrage and defiance.

It is important philosophically to make the point that if social science disregards the subjective forms of experience utterly (as naturalistic inquiries often do), or disregards any of the ways in which their content escapes the study of rules, social science is bound to give an impoverished picture of human life. Yet it would not follow from this that social science could make anything of the subjective forms of experience.

Social science seeks generalizations, whether they are generalizations identifying rules or generalizations identifying regularities. For a closer, more exciting approach to the subjective forms of experience people might have to go to biography, fiction, drama, poetry.

In fact social science can make something of the subjective forms of experience. Naturalistic social science conducts surveys, sometimes more penetrating in conception, sometimes less, of people's feelings. Are people confident enough about holding their jobs to feel satisfied with the government? Confident enough to buy consumer durables? Matters like these are not mere matters of curiosity. Generalized predictions of decline or recovery in the economy may be founded upon them; and incorporating some of them in the models that political scientists have developed for explaining election results may be indispensable. Models taking into account only 'objective' variables like income, the rate of unemployment, housing starts, and so on, may not work.

Naturalistic social science working hand in hand with interpretive social science has something to gain from investigating narratives. Narratives shared by whole communities figure in explanations of how the respective communities are formed and maintained. It is already itself a generalization of social science that communities cannot be formed or maintained without such narratives. This generalization, moreover, opens up a branch of inquiry into comparisons of narratives. What sorts of narratives are effective with what sorts of peoples and in what sorts of contexts? If the Japanese had other equally strong sources of community feeling, they might be readier to accept the hypothesis that their imperial family was Korean in origin. Effective narratives might share certain plot-elements across cultures (like Claude Lévi-Strauss' myth-forms, of which descent of the emperors from a divinity – the Sun-Goddess, in the Japanese case – may be an instance) (see LÉVI-STRAUSS, C. §§5–6).

4 Critical social theory: effective with or without reduction

Does asserting that critical social theory ask naturalistic questions about regularities and interpretive questions about rules imply a 'reduction' of it to a combination of naturalistic and interpretive views? The term 'reduction' has unwanted overtones. Nevertheless, even in the strong form of saying that in its methods critical social theory is either naturalistic or interpretive, the assertion is strictly compatible with honour for other characteristic features of critical social theory. Distinctive questions, pursued with a distinctive commitment to emancipation, do not imply distinctive sorts of questions or distinctive sorts of methods.

A systematic enumeration of the components of critical social theory would include: (1) distinctive questions, for example, about ideological bias; (2) the thesis that there is no attempt at social science without commitments to political values; (3) commitment, inherited from Karl MARX (§12), to the project of social emancipation; (4) distinctive critical findings respecting both current social arrangements and the limitations of conventional social science. The components may include (5) the thesis that the very phenomena (objects) that critical social theory conceives to be suitable for study in the social sciences differ from those that conventional social science purports to study, and this thesis might extend to implying that the standards of inquiry must differ, too. Further possible components, like an abstract philosophical argument for presupposing a certain ideal of communication (the ideal speech-situation (see HABERMAS, J.)) as a condition of productive discourse, can be disregarded for present purposes.

Whether much remains of (5), the thesis about studying distinctive phenomena, when due allowance has been made for the other components, and for the full operation of interpretive concerns in social science, is doubtful. For these things do bring in the subjective forms of experience; and value-commitments, displayed in the simplest actions, which are done to reach goals that the agents value. Thus, if critical social scientists wish to say that social phenomena at every level are loaded with value-commitments (which naturalistic social science sometimes ignores), this point is accommodated once interpretive social science gets its place alongside social science with a naturalistic cast.

Suppose, however, this reflection is not enough to convince the proponents of critical social theory that social phenomena as they view them are treated adequately by the combination of the inquiries that the other schools have in view. (The combination might not be sufficiently intimate or harmonious.) We could have a robust critique of current society and current social science resting on the first four components of critical social theory alone. Call this 'para-critical social theory'. If it would accomplish substantially the same things in practical political criticism and policy guidance, how much importance attaches to the thesis about distinctive objects?

Some critical social theorists, at some stages of their thinking, would not temporize with social science done under other auspices. They would invoke the thesis of ubiquitous commitment to political values (2); and add that much of current social science is committed not to emancipation but to oppression.

Social science that is not committed to emancipation should be eliminated, by vigorously criticizing it, by setting new examples, by supersession. But para-critical social theory could do this work, too.

True, even if peaceful supersession is all that is in prospect, elimination would not be cheerfully accepted in every quarter. A lot of researchers dissent from the position that a thorough-going social transformation is desirable; or favour social transformations that are not (like the project of emancipation) socialist in inspiration. Moreover, a reasonable critical social theorist would concede that criticisms from these quarters of policies at first sight attractive to socialists and emancipators sometimes make useful points, for example, in advancing market solutions to resist unnecessary expansions of bureaucracy.

The demand for elimination is excessive in other ways. The thesis about inevitable commitment to political values is an indispensable argument for elimination. This thesis, however, cannot be put through unless omitting to invoke certain values counts as favour for values opposed to them. Grant this; otherwise there are too many examples of studies or findings that do not mention the values on one side or another, much less explicitly endorse them. It does not follow that the findings coming forward with these omissions deserve no respect. One can think party competition under a capitalist regime no better than a masquerade. Findings about the effects on party competition of single-member district representation as against various schemes for proportional representation advance knowledge notwithstanding. Such findings may even turn out to have useful applications in a transformed society, supposing that such a society will leave room for contested elections and party competition.

If it will not, many political scientists would argue that the project of emancipation will lead to less freedom rather than more, and less democracy. They would not be alone. Postmodernist philosophers, reflecting on how the Marxist project of emancipation miscarried in Bolshevik hands to produce a totalitarian regime, would decry any tendency to eliminate dissent in the name of the project, or reduce the variety of inquiries, whether the elimination is to occur after the project is carried to an end or beforehand. Critical social theorists could agree. They did not contemplate repressing other sorts of inquiry. They carried on a variety of inquiries themselves. Habermas, their chief heir, has made an explicit endeavour to find a place for all the sorts of inquiry sponsored by the three schools.

5   The impact of postmodernism

Disillusion with the project of emancipation surfaced in critical social theory itself as an aspect of disillusion with the Enlightenment. The Enlightenment fostered expectations of progress in many dimensions – not just in emancipation, but also in science, in technology, in material comforts, in rational and efficient social arrangements. It thus sponsored a number of what the postmodernist philosopher Jean-Francois LYOTARD (§2) calls 'grand narratives', all of which postmodernists categorically repudiate. Michel FOUCAULT did the same. Without ranking himself among postmodernists, Foucault was nevertheless a major source of ideas for them and an ally. Together he and Lyotard do as much as anyone to bring postmodernist ideas to bear upon the philosophy of social science.

Foucault and Lyotard draw points from the philosophy of language and the theory of knowledge to attack, along with grand narratives, 'globalizing' discourses of all kinds, and with them any claim to speak for, or even to aim at, a unified and comprehensive scientific view of the world. The most that can be hoped for, they say, are limited narratives and local bodies of knowledge, confined to transient social practices. Foucault has made ambitious and arresting studies of some of these, like psychiatry, clinical medicine, and penology. To combine his terminology with Lyotard's, such practices are so many language games in which genres of discourse figure, perhaps more than one in a given instance, and employ locutions drawn from various 'regimes' of locutionary acts (phrases). Thus clinical medicine employs declaratives (from one regime), interrogatives (from another), and imperatives (from a third) in discourse that is in genre both cognitive and therapeutic. The rules from the different regimes apply, and so do the rules distinctive of the different genres. In addition, the practice itself brings in rules, for example, a rule requiring that doctors make their diagnoses public before pathologists report on dissections in the same cases.

The knowledge gained within such a practice cannot be generalized. It would be out of place in another practice; and the findings of different practices cannot as they stand be accommodated at more general levels of knowledge. Foucault, for a time at least, went along with Nietzsche in treating every claim to knowledge as a demand for power. Disputes in social science, like disputes about knowledge in other connections, become conflicts of power, or of 'wills to truth'. Lyotard comes back repeatedly to disputes about knowledge turning upon issues (*différends*) that cannot be settled without (he holds) short-

changing the ideas on one side or another. Researchers from one practice confront researchers from another; no general discourse is automatically available to mediate between them.

Some postmodernists might be content with taking guerrilla action against received views, darting out to attack generalizing pretensions whenever they parade by. Given the incessant tendency for styles of inquiry to congeal into rule-bound orthodoxy, disrupting them in this way can be useful and important. It does something to restore the nonchalance about rules and creative playfulness that in the young can be mistaken for mere fecklessness.

The guerrilla role would not suit Foucault, since at stake in his theory of knowledge are his own notable contributions to the histories of practices. Let us distinguish (1) what he does in these accounts; (2) what he describes himself as doing; (3) what he has to say in general about the character of knowledge and possibilities in the social sciences. Some of what he says in (2) may be at odds with (1); some of what he says in (3) may be at odds with (1) and (2) as well, at least in part. Yet the accounts brought forward under (1) come with claims of truth, or at least some approximation of truth. It is, for example, set forth as a truth that punishment as a practice of awe-inspiring spectacles gave way late in the eighteenth century to the practice of systematic imprisonment and surveillance. Moreover, an abundance of passages falling under (2) support saying that he describes himself as aiming to discover truths (in some sense opposed to overall scepticism) in his researches into practices.

Suppose that different views do mask the wills to truth and power of different persons and groups. Suppose, as Foucault maintains repeatedly, the views of the powerful prevail and other views are subjugated, though now and then there is a change in who holds power or a change in the assortment of views. A range of situations answers to this description, from totalitarian domination at one pole to an equal-power situation at the other. Could a general consensus about truth be brought about in an equal-power situation, unlikely though this might be?

It accords with the weight of what Foucault says in (3) that there could be a local and temporary resolution of the conflict. It might take the form of mutual acknowledgements among the contenders of there being 'some truth' in what other groups hold, and a joint statement listing those partial truths. In the intermediate situations, which are much more likely, local and temporary resolutions in the form of mutual acknowledgements could occur, though they would wring only limited concessions from the views of the powerful.

This not only accords with what Foucault says; it is

essential to making sense of his campaign on behalf of 'subjugated knowledges'. Some headway – no doubt short of carrying all the way to the acknowledgements of an equal-power situation – can be made in redressing received patterns of domination in favour of giving at least some attention to the subjugated views. The defects of prevailing views will in consequence abate. If the prevailing view is that solitary confinement induces penitence in prisoners, the subjugated knowledge of the prisoners that solitary confinement enrages and embitters them could be invoked to modify the prevailing view.

Lyotard goes further in making room for advances in knowledge. He may exaggerate the frequency of *différends*. He does not consider at any length how different practices may intersect, as it seems they must do for there to be an issue between them; or how different practices may get along comfortably enough even when inconsistent. Consider astronomers in everyday life speaking of sunrise and sunset, and in poetical moments entertaining the idea of an animate moon ('queen and huntress, chaste and fair'). Yet Lyotard argues that *différends* can be surmounted by conceptual-linguistic innovation that is fair to each of them. Such innovation may have been required to straighten out the foundations of the calculus; and to reconcile quantum physics with logic and the principle of contradiction. One may doubt whether it is required to reconcile naturalistic social science with interpretive, though the spectacle of Weber and Durkheim struggling for a view of social science integrating both might give pause on this point. In any case, Lyotard's idea that even *différends* can be surmounted with conceptual innovation amplifies the conception of local resolutions between conflicting truths in the form of mutual acknowledgements; and makes the conception more credible, wherever it is to be applied.

6 The relations between the schools re-examined

It is not just the furore created by postmodernism that threatens to unsettle the tidy picture of social science given by the three schools framework. A more explicit allowance for the hermeneutical concern with texts and for even more familiar subjective forms of experience has made it harder to see how interpretive studies bear affinities with naturalistic ones. It has made it even harder to see how naturalistic studies are an indispensable supplement. Yet anything lost in this regard can easily be made up.

Postmodernists like Foucault and Lyotard bring back the study of rules, in Foucault's case, with an emphasis more thorough-going than any other philosopher who has touched on the philosophy of social science. But if there can be models of systems of rules just as there can be models of regularities, then how far a model fits a real system, in regard to any universally quantified statement that figures in the model, is a matter for quantitative – statistical – study just as much with rules as with regularities.

With these considerations, the affinity of naturalism with interpretation returns. Not only does the affinity return; it returns in a form that is ready to receive the insistence of postmodern writers on truth being local, a matter of limited context that is always subject to supersession. For a model, if it has any success at all in matching a range of phenomena, may match only the phenomena of one society or one of its subgroups; and its success, moreover, is likely to be temporary. Not only will phenomena change, but what social scientists are looking for as important points of resemblance will change, too.

To which of the three schools should postmodernists be assigned? The rules that Foucault and Lyotard would have studied are rules of discourse, passing into rules of the practices in which the genres of discourse are embodied. Studying them would embrace the study of texts, in both literal and extended senses of the notion of text. Thus Foucault and Lyotard hook up with the interest in texts of the interpretive school and its hermeneutical component. Both Foucault and Lyotard, furthermore, are specially concerned with narratives, and narratives are a species of texts much attended to in the interpretive school.

On the other hand, neither Foucault nor Lyotard has much use for the forms of subjective experience more basic than narratives. Their animus against 'subjects' is directed in some passages against 'transcendental subjects' – ideal observers or agents who Foucault and Lyotard think are implicitly postulated in references to comprehensive knowledge. (Some readers would charge them with acting as transcendental subjects themselves when they make sweeping pronouncements.) In other passages, however, the animus seems to tell against having subjects at all: it is not persons who know or act or contend with one another, but discourses and their ingredients. The interpretive school cannot easily digest this point.

A more congenial home for it can be found in the critical school. The critical school has been all along inclined (though doing so belies some of its own work) to repudiate naturalistic inquiries. What needs to be raised to the critical level in its view has been interpretive social science. Foucault and Lyotard are interpretive enough to qualify; and their campaigns against orthodox views and grand narratives have precedents in the campaigns of the critical school itself against the Enlightenment and against ideology. Foucault and Lyotard generalize the critique: it is not just power reflected in the ideology of the ruling social class that dominates uncritical thinking; it is power everywhere, exerted by various groups and various practices contending with each other, that manifests itself in claims to truth. We can, so far as we can make sense of the idea, think of subjects, both transcendental and personal, as dropping out in the course of generalizing the critique.

Another way of generalizing the critique, which again would leave the three schools standing, along with the variations in them of styles of inquiry, would be simply to demand that every inquiry in social science choose questions that are more useful rather than less so. The standard of usefulness might refer to the urgency of current social problems. On a less intensely moralizing approach, running less danger of reducing the variety of inquiries, the standard might refer also to anomalies or gaps in current theories, or even to unsatisfied curiosity. Broad or narrow, the standard would do more to discriminate between inquiries than postmodernism is able to do given a commitment to variety hard for it to modify. Inquiries that would make only a trivial difference to existing knowledge would fail the test of curiosity.

Some things that Foucault and Lyotard say, along with things voiced elsewhere on the postmodernist scene, are perhaps too devastatingly sceptical in intention or implication to be reconciled with the pursuit of social science in any sense. We may thus have to allow in the philosophy of social science for a school that (unlike any of the three schools in the framework) holds that social science is not possible. We do not have to join it.

See also: EXPLANATION IN HISTORY AND SOCIAL SCIENCE; HOLISM AND INDIVIDUALISM IN HISTORY AND SOCIAL SCIENCE; NATURALISM IN SOCIAL SCIENCE; POST-STRUCTURALISM IN THE SOCIAL SCIENCES; SOCIAL LAWS; SOCIAL NORMS; SOCIAL SCIENCE, HISTORY OF PHILOSOPHY OF; STRUCTURALISM IN SOCIAL SCIENCE; VALUE JUDGMENTS IN SOCIAL SCIENCE

References and further reading

Adorno, T. and Horkheimer, M. (1944) *Dialectic of Enlightenment*, trans. J. Cumming, London: Verso, 1973. (Attacks the Enlightenment within critical social theory, but already in a postmodernist vein.)

Braybrooke, D. (1987) *Philosophy of Social Science*, Englewood Cliffs, NJ: Prentice Hall. (Expounds in detail the distinction between the three-schools and their relations.)

—— (1990) 'How Do I Presuppose Thee? Let Me Count the Ways: The Relation of Regularities to Rules in Social Science', *Midwest Studies in Philosophy* 15: 80–93. (Improves on the 1987 book in treating the relation of regularities to rules.)

Braybrooke, D., Brown, B. and Schotch, P.K. (1995) *Logic on the Track of Social Change*, Oxford: Clarendon Press. (Improves on the 1987 book in defining rules.)

* Carr, D. (1986) *Time, Narrative, and History*, Bloomington, IN: Indiana University Press. (Treats, in a phenomenological perspective, but with a clarity of argument impressive to analytical philosophers, the concept of narrative.)

Durkheim, É. (1895) *Les règles de la methode sociologique*, trans. S.A. Solovay and J.H. Mueller, *The Rules of Sociological Method*, Chicago, IL: University of Chicago Press, 1938. (Puts forward a classical case against an individualistic approach to social phenomena.)

Fay, B. (1996) *Contemporary Philosophy of Social Science*, Oxford: Blackwell. (Relates the interpretive view of social science simultaneously to current conflicts between cultures and to central current debates in philosophy.)

Foucault, M. (1976) 'Two Lectures' in C. Gordon (ed.), trans. K. Soper, *Power/Knowledge: Selected Interviews and Other Writings, 1972–1977*, Brighton: Harvester Wheatsheaf, 1980, 78–108. (With next article referred to, concentrates in short texts Foucault's leading ideas.)

—— (1977) 'Truth and Power', in C. Gordon (ed. and trans.), *Power/Knowledge: Selected Interviews and Other Writings, 1972–1977*, Brighton: Harvester Wheatsheaf, 1980, 109–33. (With previous article referred to, concentrates in short texts Foucault's leading ideas.)

Gadamer, H.-G. (1960) *Truth and Method*, original trans. W. Glen-Doepel, revised by J. Weisheimer and D.G. Marshall, New York: Crossroad, 2nd edn, 1989. (Develops at length the perspective of hermeneutics.)

* Giere, R.N. (1988) *Explaining Science*, Chicago, IL: University of Chicago Press. (Offers the most accessible treatment of the model-theoretic view of science.)

Habermas, J. (1967) *On the Logic of the Social Sciences*, trans. S.W. Nicholson and J.A. Stark, Cambridge, MA: MIT Press, 1988. (Enlarges a perspective received from critical social theory to embrace a variety of approaches in social science.)

Hempel, C.G. (1965) *Aspects of Scientific Explanation*, New York: Free Press. (Sets forth refined positivist views with unparalleled lucidity.)

Hollis, M. (1994) *The Philosophy of Social Science: An Introduction*, Cambridge: Cambridge University Press. (Explores in a lively and imaginative way the relations between naturalistic and interpretive social science.)

Lévi-Stauss, C. (1987) *Anthropology and Myth*, Oxford: Blackwell. (One source for Lévi-Strauss' theory of shared myth-form.)

Little, D. (1989) *Understanding Peasant China: Case Studies in the Philosophy of Social Science*, New Haven, CT: Yale University Press. (Looks into a number of works by social scientists in very different styles and extracts implications for philosophical issues.)

Lyotard, J.-F. (1988) *The Differend: Phrases in Dispute*, trans. G. van den Abeele, Minneapolis, MN: University of Minnesota Press. (Ranked by Lyotard as his fundamental contribution to postmodernist philosophy; very difficult reading.)

—— (1992) *The Postmodern Explained*, trans. D. Barry *et al.*, Minneapolis, MN: University of Minnesota Press. (Briefly and clearly surveys the main points of Lyotard's contributions to postmodernism.)

* March, J.G. and Olsen, J.P. (1989) *Rediscovering Institutions*, New York: Free Press. (Champions the conception of social institutions as systems of rules.)

Marx, K. (1845–6) *The German Ideology: Part I*, trans. S. Ryazanskaya, Moscow: Foreign Languages Publishing House, 1972. (Serves with *The Communist Manifesto* as a prime source for the Marxist conception of ideology.)

Marx, K. and Engels, F. (1848) *The Communist Manifesto*, trans. S. Moore, New York: International Publishers, 1948. (Not only a manifesto, but a brilliant synopsis of Marxist theory.)

Mill, J.S. (1843) *System of Logic*, London: Longman, Green, 1930. (Book VI discusses with great care the 'The Logic of the Moral [Social] Sciences'.)

* Ostrom, E. (1990) *Governing the Commons: The Evolution of Institutions for Collective Action*, Cambridge: Cambridge University Press. (Gives a more rigorously worked-out account of institutions as systems of rules.)

Popper, K.R. (1957) *The Poverty of Historicism*, London: Routledge, 2nd edn, 1961. (In the course of attacking unscientific historical prophecy, provides a classical expression of the naturalistic view of social science.)

Rosenau, P.M. (1992) *Post-Modernism and the Social Sciences*, Princeton, NJ: Princeton University Press. (Surveys in unmatched detail, critically but not unfairly, the whole range of postmodernist thinking as related to the social sciences.)

Runciman, W.G. (1972) *A Critique of Max Weber's Philosophy of Social Science*, Cambridge: Cambridge University Press. (Gives a lucid, brief account of Weber's ideas and a clarified revision of them.)

Vico, G.B. (1744) *The New Science*, trans. T.G. Bergin and M.H. Fisch, Ithaca, NY: Cornell University Press, revised edn, 1984. (Protests with great vigour against all attempts to displace interpretive concerns in favour of a naturalistic treatment of social phenomena.)

Weber, M. (1904, 1905, 1917) *Max Weber on the Methodology of the Social Sciences*, three essays trans. and ed. E.A. Shils and H.A. Finch, Glencoe, IL: Free Press, 1949. (Reflects on the interrelation of interpretation and causal inquiry and on the demand for value-free social science.)

Winch, P. (1990) *The Idea of a Social Science and Its Relation to Philosophy*, London: Routledge, 2nd edn. (Champions the interpretive view with emphasis on the study of rules.)

Wright, G.H. von (1971) *Explanation and Understanding*, Ithica, NY: Cornell University Press. (Classically lucid exposition of the difference between 'explanation' and 'understanding' as key notions in natural and interpretive social science respectively.)

DAVID BRAYBROOKE

SOCIAL SCIENCE, HISTORY OF PHILOSOPHY OF

The history of social science can conveniently be divided into four uneven periods, starting with the beginnings of both western science and philosophy in the ancient Greek polis *(city or state). It is fair to say, with qualifications, that the debate generated by the so-called Sophists, professional teachers of rhetoric in fifth-century Athens, established what would become the central questions for the future. The fundamental issue could be put thus: is society 'natural' or is it 'conventional', a historical product of human activities which vary across time and space? The Sophists, often abused in our standard histories, supported the conventional view. They held that even if it was anthropologically necessary that Homo sapiens live in societies, nature was silent about the character and ends of society. They thus defended what might be called 'cultural relativism'. By contrast Aristotle argued that some men were 'naturally' slaves and that all women were 'naturally' inferior; therefore slavery and patriarchy were dictated by nature, a view that prevailed well into the early modern period.*

Beginning in the sixteenth century we find a host of thinkers who reconceived the problem first raised by the

Sophists. Many of them, for example, Hobbes, Rousseau and Adam Smith, held that 'by nature' humans had similar capacities and powers. Inequalities of power were 'artificial', wholly the result of historically established conventions. These writers also rejected the idea that society was a kind of natural community. For many of them, society existed by consent, the result of a contract.

The rejection of Aristotelianism was inspired by the Copernican revolution and the new physics of Galileo and Newton. This produced a self-conscious effort by early modern writers to articulate the idea of human science, modelled on the new physics. This critical idea was well put by the physiocrat Francois Quesnay: 'All social facts are linked together in the bond of eternal, immutable, ineluctable, inevitable laws, which individuals and government would obey if they were once known to them' (Randall 1940: 323).

The third period, roughly the nineteenth century, is then a battleground over both the idea of science and the idea of a human science. The paradigm provided by celestial mechanics was nearly overwhelming; even so, there was disagreement as regards its character, especially as regards the question of causality and explanation. Until very recently, 'positivists' have tended to prevail. That is, writers have followed Auguste Comte, who gave us the terms 'positivism' and 'sociology', and who held there were social laws which were to be analysed as 'relations of invariable succession': whenever this, then that.

As regards the possibility of a human science, consciousness and the problem of a free will raised the biggest questions. Materialists found nothing special about either; idealists did. Indeed a surprising amount of the most recent debates in the philosophy of the social sciences have their roots in these issues. If, as positivists insist, activity is governed by law, then what of human freedom? On the other hand, if humans have collectively made society and thus can remake it, then what is the nature of a human science?

1 Pre-modern philosophy of the human sciences
2 The late Renaissance and early modern period
3 Machiavelli and Bodin: redefining the polity
4 Two views of society: Hobbes, Locke and Adam Smith; Rousseau and Vico
5 Progress and positivism: Comte and Herder
6 Mill's *Logic*
7 Karl Marx: one human science?
8 Dilthey and historicism
9 Max Weber: human science as concrete
10 Spencer and Engels: two monisms
11 Pareto and Durkheim: two positivisms
12 The twentieth century

1 Pre-modern philosophy of the human sciences

If we are to offer a history of the philosophy of the social sciences which begins prior to the twentieth century, we must admit some anachronism. Prior to this time, perhaps the only term in such a title with its present meaning is 'history'. Only in the nineteenth century was philosophy separated from 'science', and only in the early years of the twentieth century did 'social science' emerge as a set of disciplinary practices which could become the object of 'philosophy'. This is more than a quibble over terms, since issues regarding the nature and methods of acquiring knowledge of the human condition have again and again been contested.

In what follows, we admit the anachronism and sketch what earlier writers said about such inquiry. Moreover, since the lines between a philosophy of social science, a social philosophy, and a social science are also blurred, we consider these matters rather broadly. Until lines were drawn, there were no boundaries – and even today the boundaries are fuzzy.

It is well known that both western science and philosophy began in the West in ancient Greece. The so-called 'nature philosophers', Thales to Democritus, had included in their inquiry concerns about humankind and 'society'. But this was the special concern of the Sophists, who emerged in fifth-century democratic Athens as teachers who prepared men for political careers with instruction not only in rhetoric but also in 'wisdom' (*sophia*) and in 'virtue' (*aretē*). It was in this context that the *physis/nomos* debate arose.

Nomoi (norms, laws, customs or conventions) establish what behaviour is to be sanctioned by the community. *Physis* (nature) was the object of inquiry of the Ionian 'scientists' but it also referred to the particular characteristics of things, for example, the nature or 'essence' of man. ARISTOTLE summarized the debate: 'Some people [for example, the Sophists] think that all rules of justice are merely conventional, because whereas a law of nature is immutable and has the same validity everywhere, as fire burns both here and in Persia, rules of justice are seen to vary' (1968: 295). The implications are many: If humans are alike 'by nature', then why do *nomoi* treat them differently? Do *nomoi* originate from 'agreements', from the acts of legislators, or from gods? What is the *physis* of man? Is understanding *physis* sufficient for human society, or should we follow the sophist Protagoras, who argued that since *physis* could offer no clear prescriptions, human societies require humanly constructed *nomoi*? And if, as he also argued, all men are capable of sharing in the political (social) virtues, then perhaps the Athenians were right to allow every man to offer his advice regarding the *nomoi* of the city? (See PROTAGORAS.)

For complicated historical reasons, the Sophists acquired a very bad name. Against them, PLATO insisted that experience could not sustain an understanding of human society, still less an objective set of norms for the good human life. Plato did indeed raise some challenging problems for an empirical philosophy of humankind and elements of what we call 'platonism' still reverberate in discussions on the human sciences. Against the Sophists, Aristotle sought to found the human sciences in nature. He insisted that 'the *polis* exists by nature' and 'a man that is by nature...cityless is either low in the scale of humanity or above it' (1977: 9).

Although Aristotle offers immense insight relevant to the idea of a human science, particularly his overall 'naturalistic' approach to inquiry, his most striking and probably most influential appeals to nature were, perhaps, those that reinforced the prejudices of his time. For example, 'to rule or to be ruled (*archai kai archesthai*) are conditions not only inevitable but also expedient; in some cases things are marked out from the moment of birth to rule or to be ruled' (1977: 19). Those to be ruled were 'barbarians' and all women.

Most of the current vocabulary of the social sciences comes from Greek and Latin, however we must be careful about changing meanings. For example, 'democracy' and 'economics' share but faint resemblences to their original senses. Many other critical terms derive from Latin appropriations of Greek terms, for example, republic (*res publica*, *politeia*) and citizen (*civitas*, *politeian*). By the time of Polybius' *Histories* (*c*.150BC), the Roman republic was huge by Greek standards. Similarly, Roman citizens bore little resemblance to the Greek original. Roman citizens had what we would call 'civil rights', but lacked utterly what defined a citizen for a Greek: as Aristotle had put it, a right 'to participate in ruling and judging'.

We must forego examination of both Roman and medieval discussions of matters relevant here, except to notice that because in the Augustinian eschatology, redemption depended on grace rather than knowledge, historical modes of explanation were rejected. The Arabic reintroduction of Aristotle found expression, especially in the writings of Thomas AQUINAS and Marsiglio of Padua. With Aquinas, it was impossible 'for the truth of faith to be contrary to principles known by natural reason'. Aquinas and Marsiglio shared with Aristotle the idea that existing things are arranged in natural hierarchies, including therefore humans and their communities. All had 'natures' which seek their *telos* or end. Finally, Renaissance humanism sought to recover, in Christian terms, the Roman concept of *virtus*, total human

excellence. For early modern thinkers, Rome became an important case study.

2 The late Renaissance and early modern period

A great structural change had begun sometime in the late medieval period. It would ultimately produce modernity: the modern state and a capitalist social order. This would be the condition and problem for all subsequent social thinkers. These remarkable changes forced reconsideration of the problems of the human condition and especially, reconsideration of what are the prime philosophical questions of relevance here: what is the object of inquiry in the human sciences and how do we study it?

We identify two major shifts, which both represent efforts to break with the past. First, there was a rejection of the set of ideas which presumed that human associations were 'natural communities' which existed for the sake of realizing human virtues, secular or saintly. The introduction of the terms 'society' and 'state' suggest this. Several points of difference between the new states and older organizations can be noted. These new states had 'governments', itself a new term, which became increasingly concerned to maintain their autonomy not only versus other organizations of similar types, but also as regards organizations within their territories. With the development of the idea of government, the problem of legitimation arose in new forms. Similarly, *societas* acquired a new sense. Originally, a voluntary coming together for some purpose, 'civil society' could be used instead of 'community', or 'republic' which carried ancient connotations.

The second huge shift regarded the aims of 'science' (knowledge) and a new concern with method. The modern writers sought 'inductively grounded' practical knowledge. God was still maker of the universe, but he was to be known through his works, not through contemplation and faith. Similarly, if everything was 'governed' by law, 'prevision' and thus control was possible. Method-conscious Descartes well expressed the Faustian aspect of the new learning:

> it is possible to attain knowledge which is useful in life, and that, instead of that speculative philosophy which is taught in the Schools, we may find a practical philosophy by means of which, knowing the force and the action of fire, water, air, the stars, heavens and all other bodies that environ us, we can in the same way employ them in all those uses to which they are adapted, and thus render ourselves the masters and possessors of nature.
>
> ([1637] 1931: 119)

3 Machiavelli and Bodin: redefining the polity

Exemplifying these changes, MACHIAVELLI was perhaps the first modern 'social scientist'. Proceeding 'inductively' and convinced that men of virtue could tame *fortuna*, he began his *Discourses* with the complaint that for all their admiration of the ancient writers, his generation had failed to appreciate the examples provided by antiquity. But he departed sharply from ancient writers as regards the aims of political organization. It was, he insisted, securing the 'liberty' (independence) and 'security' of the body politic. Today an uncritical given, he seems to be the first to hold that this was the defining condition of associated life.

Machiavelli suggested a choice between two sorts of republics, one that 'desires to extend its empire, as Rome', the other, as Sparta or Venice, that 'confines itself merely to its own preservation'. But in the new environment, the only real choice was Rome.

It is in this context, as well, that his more famous *Prince* should be understood. As Machiavelli had said in his *Discourses*: 'A wise mind will never censure any one for having employed extraordinary means for the purpose of establishing a kingdom or constituting a republic' (1950: 138–9). The message of the *Prince* is technical, not moral. For the Greek, the citizen was the government, for citizens ruled. But Machiavelli assumed that the state (government) and 'the people' are distinct. Public persons constitute a government which exists to serve the governed persons in their private lives. Government may do this well or badly, but it cannot do it well if decisions are persistently opposed, and if it cannot act for the body as a whole. As he put the matter: government is the management of citizens so that 'they are neither able nor disposed to oppose you' (1950: 358). Accordingly, the governors of any well-ordered state will and should quite normally employ measures which, from the standpoint of common morality, are immoral.

What, however, was the character of this new kind of entity? Writing in 1576, Bodin answered:

> Ancient writers have called Common weals, Societies of men assembled to live well and happily together. Which as it may serve for a description of a Citie, so can it not stand for a true definition of a Commonweale.
>
> ([1576] 1962: 3)

It was not necessary that members of a commonwealth live 'happily' or even that they be well governed. Moreover, as individuals pursue many ends, so do commonwealths. The proper definition of a commonwealth required only that members be 'governed by a puissant sovereign of one or many rulers; albeit that they differ in lawes, language, customes, religions, and diversity of nations' ([1576] 1962: 49). Missing entirely is the idea that a polity is a natural community, a 'family' with common ends.

4 Two views of society: Hobbes, Locke and Adam Smith; Rousseau and Vico

The *nomos/physis* debate anticipated what we can now clearly identify as the two fundamentally different and still competing metatheoretical assumptions regarding human associations, one 'holistic', the other 'individualist'. The former idea will not lose its persuasiveness, recurring in variant forms in Vico, Rousseau, Herder, Hegel's variant descendants, and Durkheim. The newer conception, associated with liberal or 'utilitarian' social theory is presupposed by Hobbes, Locke, Adam Smith, Bentham, Mill, Herbert Spencer, Pareto, and in its modern recent variations, rational choice theory (including here modern microeconomics). The choice between the two entails a host of other important differences.

The idea that society is but an aggregation of individuals united by agreements to accept the authority of certain conditions for acting is brilliantly developed by Thomas HOBBES, who also broke decisively with the past in postulating both a universal human nature and the idea that 'by nature' humans differ little in terms of their powers and abilities. Postulating endless desire, individuals everywhere and everywhen 'seek power after power'. Accordingly, the 'natural condition of mankind' is a condition of war. But if individuals alienate their 'right to all things' to a sovereign power, peace can be secured. Since this is the 'rational' thing for mutually self-interested individuals to do, civil society is 'explained' and sovereign power is justified as the cement of society. Hobbes was, accordingly, the first 'law and order' theorist.

Hobbes, Locke and Rousseau are thought of as 'contract' theorists, but the differences are critical. Perhaps Locke's greatest achievement, usually not acknowledged, was his 'explanation' of private property, which, it seems, is the only one available that is also a serious defence (see LOCKE, J. §10). Locke believed that God had 'given the earth to Mankind in common', but he rejected Hobbes' idea that the right to property was merely conventional. If our bodies and, thus, our labour was ours, what we 'mix our labour' with is ours. Although this is a highly problematic idea, neither Proudhon, who believed that property was theft, nor Marx would have cause to disagree. The problem comes when the two moral conditions imposed on the free appropriation from nature are put into question. We should not waste, nor can we appropriate when such appropriation puts others at a disadvantage. Locke argued that money was introduced by our consent. This allowed unlimited appropriation. What is produced in excess of need can be sold to those who are unable to appropriate freely from nature. Since it is their right to sell their labour power to landowners, no one, presumably, is put at any disadvantage. Class inequality, accordingly, was an unintended consequence of the voluntary introduction and use of money. And all this prior to the 'consent' which constituted civil society.

Rousseau's views stand in marked contrast. He shared with Vico the view that one could not 'explain' society in terms of the 'contract' and he further suggested that the psychological qualities attributed to mankind by Hobbes and the liberals who followed him were social constructions (see ROUSSEAU, J.-J.). In his *Discourse on the Origins of Inequality* (1755), Rousseau bitterly criticized his predecessors on just these grounds. For him, 'society' emerged 'naturally', the result of the development of language. The true founder of civil society, he ironically wrote, was the person who having staked out an area of land, declared, 'This is mine' and found people 'simple enough' to believe him. Rousseau seems to have been the first to argue that human history is largely the product of unintended consequences, and he is one of the very few who insisted that the changes were not progressive. For him, humans had unwittingly forged chains which imprisoned them. This was largely the result of the interdependence which genuine humanness had brought. The solution was the social contract. Since sovereignty was for him inalienable, and governments had only executive power, Rousseau, a radical democrat, insisted that unless people take collective control of the conditions of their lives, tyranny is quite inevitable (see CONTRACTARIANISM §6).

We can here compare Vico's *The New Science* (1725). For Vico, culture and its artefacts are all creations of human consciousness. He thus insisted, anticipating Dilthey, that humans can understand themselves and all that they have created. Like Rousseau, but no democrat, Vico rejected 'contract' theory as incapable of explaining society. He argued that history, which was cyclical, set different problems for different ages (see VICO, G.). Marx was impressed by Vico's view that an 'inductive' historical 'science' could emancipate people by emancipating them from superstition and by displaying their true nature.

Adam Smith's rational individualism puts him in direct opposition to Vico and Rousseau (see SMITH, A.). If for Hobbes statutory law turns the violent competition of 'the natural condition' into peace, and

if for Rousseau, the division of labour is the fundamental cause of human self-alienation, for Smith, by means of 'the invisible hand', the division of labour gives 'self-love' distinctly beneficial unintended consequences. Indeed, Smith made the effort to explain the division of labour with one universal psychological principle: the 'propensity to truck, barter and exchange'. By this time, Smith could take private property for granted, along with the idea, still uncritically assumed, of the market.

If Smith was the founder of political economy, it is also important to notice that he did not conceive of its domain narrowly. When *The Wealth of Nations* was published in 1776, 'political economy' referred to 'the art or practical science of managing the resources of nations'. This is why some 60 per cent of *The Wealth of Nations* is historical and sociological, and why from the point of view of modern economic thinking this portion is utterly irrelevant.

John Stuart Mill's 1829 essay, 'On the definition of political economy; and the method of investigation proper to it' (1844) settled several of the then unsettled questions. Thereafter, political economy would be thought of as an abstract, ahistorical science which treats the 'laws' that regulate the production, accumulation and distribution of commodities (see ECONOMICS, PHILOSOPHY OF).

5 Progress and positivism: Comte and Herder

Auguste Comte was an heir to the French Enlightenment, but between Turgot and Montesquieu and Comte's *Cours de Philosophie Positiv* (*The Positive Philosophy of Auguste Comte* [1830–42]) came the French Revolution and the rumblings of anarchism and communism. Not only was the thought of Rousseau and Montesquieu rendered irrelevant, but the events raised the question of whether there could be both order and progress. Comte said yes – if politicians would accept the truths of science, understood by him in distinctly positivist terms (see COMTE, A.).

Comte held that there are three fundamental 'epochs of the mind of the race', three stages: the theological or fictitious, the metaphysical or abstract, and the scientific or positive. The theological mind 'supposes all phenomena to be produced by the immediate action of supernatural beings'. The metaphysical mind 'supposes, instead of supernatural beings, abstract forces...inherent in all things, and capable of producing all phenomena'. The positivist mind, by contrast, has not only 'given over the vain search for Absolute notions, the origin and destination of the universe', but also 'the causes of phenomena'. Instead, it 'applies itself to the study of their laws –

that is, their invariable relations of succession and resemblance' (Comte [1830–42] 1875: I, 2).

There is here a clear contrast between a positivist sense of law and causality and a distinctly realist conception – causes as productive powers. A realist conception, 'metaphysical' for the positivist, is common to ordinary thinking, and shorn of what are, today, unwelcome teleological commitments, it has been given increasing attention since the 1970s. According to positivists, we do not observe productive powers 'inherent in things'. Following Hume, we 'observe' relations of succession: if this, then that. A realist and teleological view was argued by Aristotle and in the tradition which followed him. It is beautifully illustrated, with many of its problems, in the writings of Johann HERDER, one of those who articulated a philosophy of human science which fell by the wayside.

Influenced by Rousseau and Montesquieu, Herder expressed a desire to be 'the Newton of history'. He begins with the realist idea that 'whenever we observe a power (*Kraft*) in operation, it is inherent in some organ and in harmony with it'. But 'power as such is not open to investigation, at least not by our senses. It exists for these by its manifestations…'. This is then applied: 'The human essence – *Humanität* – is not ready made, yet is potentially realizable' ([1794–91] 1969: 266). As with individuals, linguistically interacting people – *Völker* – have environments, 'climates', with which they epigenetically transact. Moreover, 'whatever the climatic influence, every human being, every animal, every plant has a climate of its own; for each absorbs and adapts to external influences in its own organic manner' (Barnard 1965: 120). A multiplicity of equally valuable *Völk*, each in transaction with its 'climate', has created a human world, many concrete realizations of our shared *Humanität*. Indeed, there are no races since 'complexions run into each other… *in toto* they are, in the final analysis, but different shades of the same great picture which extends though all ages and all parts of the earth' (Herder [1794–1] 1969: 284). Herder's vision was anarchist and cosmopolitan, not statist and chauvinist: each *Völk* has its own 'spirit', its own 'genius'. Herder emphatically rejected Eurocentric notions of progress, which for him were but 'figments', constructed from 'embroidered or invented facts'.

Herder lost, Comte's Eurocentrism and positivist conception of a human science carried the day. Comte articulated what are, appropriately, the defining ideas of positivism: not only should we reject the search for causes as productive powers, but also, 'what is now understood when we speak of an explanation of facts is simply the establishment of a connection between single phenomena and some general facts…' (Comte 1875: I, 2) – what is now called 'the covering law model of scientific explanation'.

But not all of Comte's views carried the day. Since humans are essentially social, there is no science between physiology and sociology. Second, not only is society not 'decomposable into individuals' but 'there can be no scientific study of society, either in its conditions or its movements, if it is separated into portions, and its divisions are studied apart' (Lenzer 1975: 228). Comte would not have approved of the present disciplinary division of the human sciences, nor its characteristic 'methodological individualism' (see POSITIVISM IN THE SOCIAL SCIENCES §1).

6 Mill's *Logic*

This is not true of J.S. MILL, who was writing his *System of Logic* (1843) when he read Comte. While he accepted the inevitability of progress, he was dissatisfied with Comte's law of progress. If it was a law, then, it had to be 'invariant' and therefore there had to be as Comte had said, 'a necessarily invariable development of all humanity'. Mill could not see how this was possible.

Mill distinguished 'laws of nature' from 'empirical laws'. With Comte, Mill would leave to the metaphysicians any talk about 'the ultimate mode of production of phenomena, and of every other question regarding the nature of "Things in themselves"' ([1843] 1930, III, ch. V). But if 'empirical laws' are 'uniformities which observation and experience has shown to exist', what makes them different from laws? Mill distinguishes 'ultimate' from 'derivative laws'. Derivative laws are the result of 'a collocation of causes'. Derivative laws are 'resolved' into ultimate laws and are, by subsumption, explained by them. The law of inertia is 'ultimate', an unexplained explainer. Kepler's laws are derivative.

This may not do, especially if the covering law model of explanation is rejected. One might ask, for example, whether there are any empirical uniformities which are not the product of a collocation of causes? And, if so, perhaps the problem resides in the analysis of causality?

Mill affirmed that there were 'laws of society', but they 'can be nothing but the laws of the actions and passions of human beings' ([1843] 1930, VI, ch. VII). In addition, then, to the universal 'laws of the mind', there were 'derivative laws', the object of 'ethology', Mill's science of character. History, then, can only be explained as 'collocations of causes', a point made by Weber who with greater consistency also emphatically rejected the covering law model of explanation.

7 Karl Marx: one human science?

Although every author discussed in this entry has been variously interpreted, the situation is especially difficult as regards Marx's philosophy of the human sciences (see MARX, K.). Not only were many of his important texts unknown until this century, but different interpretations give rise to different Marxist politics. Two widely diverging interpretations are first, the conventional understanding, shared by the mainstream on both sides of the historic confrontation between capitalism and Marxian socialism, and the second which became prominent in the 1970s.

On the 'orthodox' view, Marxism is a positivism and a materialism. As a positivism, it has a deterministic theory of history in which societies must pass through stages. As a materialism, it holds that 'the economic structure of society [is] the real foundation on which arises the legal and political superstructure and to which corresponds definite forms of social consciousness'. A 'dialectic' then explains change. Thus, 'at a certain stage of development, the material productive forces of society come into contact with existing relations of production... From forms of development of the productive forces these relations turn into fetters. Then begins an era of social revolution' ([1859] 1904:12). As in Comte, agency drops out.

On the alternative interpretation, Hegel is taken far more seriously, but on this reading, Marx rejects the idealism/materialism problematic, offering instead a naturalism that acknowledged the active constitutive side of idealist epistemology while holding to the causal demands of the independently existing 'material' reality. On this view, Marx rejected the reified abstractions of idealism. Thus, superstructural properties, for example, law and ideology, have no independent existence and, versus the 'ideologists', there can be no independent histories of law and ideas. There are only 'real individuals, their activity and the material conditions under which they live, both those which they find already existing and those produced by their activity' (1947: 7). This text, from *The German Ideology*, published only in 1883, along with the much later published *Paris Manuscripts* and *Grundrisse* offer the best textual support for this strongly agency-centred reading of Marx's philosophy of social science. It is summarized in the oft-quoted text from Marx's *Eighteenth Brumaire*: 'Men make their own history, but they do not make it just as they please; they do not make it under circumstances chosen by themselves, but under circumstances directly encountered, given and transmitted from the past' ([1852] 1963: 15). Similarly, 'stage theory' is rejected: As Marx wrote in response to a reviewer of *Capital*: 'my critic... feels that he absolutely must metamorphose my historical sketch of the genesis of capitalism in Western Europe into an historico-philosophical theory of the general path every people is fated to tread, whatever the historical circumstances in which it finds itself... But I beg his pardon' ([1877] 1942: 354).

Following on this interpretation is a strongly realist reading of *Capital*. Volume 1 provides an abstract model of capitalist reproduction, shorn of all the particularities and contingencies which shape concrete capitalist societies. For example, it is a system-law that by virtue of the structural relations which define capitalism, there will be a tendency for the falling rate of profit. But this tendency may not be actualized, just as the inertial tendency of a planet to move rectilinearly is not realized. There are other causes at work in the world: For example, capitalists, struggling to reduce costs (and thus reducing the rate of exploitation) will move capital where labour is cheaper.

Finally, since conscious beings make history, it becomes critical to consider how their understanding enters into social reproduction/transformation. In all societies, production is social and people are more or less interdependent. But the form which products take when production is organized for generalized exchange is the commodity. Under this condition, however, 'the relations connecting the labour of one individual with that of the rest appear, not as direct social relations between persons at work, but as what they really are, material relations between persons and social relations between things' ([1867] 1970: I, 1). Such 'fetishism' is essential to capitalist reproduction, and on this reading, its analysis is continuous with his earlier analysis of 'alienation'.

8 Dilthey and historicism

Marx and Engels asserted that 'we know only one science, the science of history'. But as 'naturalists', this did not require a fundamentally different epistemology. The writings of Wilhelm DILTHEY are in the background of most subsequent 'anti-naturalisms' in the philosophy of the social sciences.

For him, the natural sciences had emancipated themselves from metaphysics – in positivist fashion. This would not do for *Geisteswissenschaften*, a term introduced into German as a translation of Mill's 'moral sciences'. In the *Geisteswissenschaften* we are not dealing with 'representations' of an unknowable external reality, but with the objects of consciousness themselves. As Iggers writes: 'Understanding [*Verstehen*] is possible... because life "objectivates" itself in such institutions as the family, civil society,

SOCIAL SCIENCE, HISTORY OF PHILOSOPHY OF

state and law, art, religion and philosophy. As products of life and spirit, these institutions can be understood' (1983: 139).

This 'solution' to the problem of the foundations of knowledge in the human sciences is not without difficulties, which is acknowledged by Dilthey. Thus, 'this task led me to the most general problems; a seemingly insoluble contradiction arises if we pursue historical consciousness to its last consequences. The finitude of every historical phenomenon, whether it be a religion, an ideal, or a philosophic system, hence the relativity of every sort of human conception about the connectedness of things, is the last word of the historical world view' (Iggers 1983: 143–4).

For Hegel, 'spirit' was 'objective' and constituted a specific stage in historical development. This could overcome both subjectivism and relativism, but while Dilthey seems to have moved in this direction, it is doubtful that he finally did overcome the 'seemingly insoluble contradiction'.

9   Max Weber: human science as concrete

A consequence of the Cold War was the view that Marx and Weber polarize on the idealism/materialism dichotomy. There is good reason, however, to believe that Weber, influenced by Neo-Kantian philosophy also rejected this dichotomy. For him, *Verstehen* (understanding) was unproblematic, 'a transcendental assumption' of both everyday life and of any attempt to understand it. Like Marx, Weber rejected Hegelian versions of history in which concrete reality 'emanated' from abstract ideas which had independent existences. Finally, while Weber rejected the reductionist monocausal understanding of history put forward by the Second International, one of the most important aims of the journal he edited was 'the advancement of the economic interpretation of history'.

Weber made a central distinction between two kinds of sciences: abstract or nomothetic and concrete or historical, a distinction which in variant forms begins with Otto Ranke and is found in Dilthey, Rickart, Menger, Simmel and Windelband, who gave us the pair, 'nomothetic/idiographic'.

For Weber, the two kinds of science satisfy different interests and require different methodologies, but crucially the distinction does divide the natural and human sciences. The purpose of 'nomological science' is 'generalized abstraction' and the elimination of 'purely contingent facts'. Its concepts are 'generic'. Thus, the laws of pure mechanics are true of everything; but such knowledge is none the less 'worth knowing'. The human sciences could be nomological, but assertions true of all societies would

not be interesting. Indeed, 'the theses that the ideal of science is the reduction of empirical reality to "laws" is meaningless'. The concrete sciences have as their aim 'the descriptive reproduction of reality in its full actuality'. We want knowledge of things 'which we regard as essential because of their individual peculiarities' (Weber [1903–6] 1975: 57). In the human sciences, we need, not generic concepts, but ideal-type concepts, rich in intention and particular in extension. An ideal-type is 'like a utopia which has been arrived at by the analytical accentuation of certain elements of reality', including 'typical modes of action' (Weber [1904] 1949: 90). The construction of such concepts is the main task of sociology. Ideal-types solve the problem of causal explanation because they enable us 'to become aware of the characteristic meaning of single, concrete cultural elements together with their concrete causes and effects' (Weber [1904] 1949: 65). It follows also that explanation is not by subsumption under law.

10   Spencer and Engels: two monisms

While Darwin's *Origin of Species* (1859) surely established 'evolution' as a prominent way of thinking, Herbert SPENCER was already insisting that evolution ensured that 'progress... is not an accident, but a necessity'. Spencer 'induced' one evolution 'going on everywhere after the same manner....There is a change from an incoherent homogeneity to a coherent heterogeneity, accompanying the dissipation of motion and the integration of matter' ([1862] 1976: 325). As regards society, this issued in an ever-perfecting functional harmony: 'As surely as the tree becomes bulky when it stands alone, and slender if one of a group... so surely must the human faculties be moulded into complete fitness for a social state... so surely must man become perfect' ([1850] 1897: 32).

Spencer's views could be classified as both positivist and monistic naturalist. They compare in this regard to those of his contemporary, Friedrich Engels. The 'old materialists' (Dühring, Büchner) could not explain novelty. This could be overcome with a 'dialectical' materialism: 'the science of the general laws of motion and development in nature, human society and thought' (Engels [1885] 1939: 155). These laws 'reduce' to three: 'the law of the transformation of quantify into quality, and vice versa; the law of the interpenetration of opposites; [and] the law of the negation of the negation' ([1927] 1940: 26). These are all in Hegel, but his 'mistake lies in the fact that these laws are foisted on nature and history and laws of thought, and not deduced [inferred] from them' ([1927] 1940: 26).

Engels, like Spencer, is aware that his super-generalizations are abstract and do not 'say anything concerning the particular processes of development' ([1885] 1939: 154), nor for the same reason, do they say anything about the particular mechanisms of these processes. But if so, then as with Spencer, the most obvious problem is their vacuousness.

11 Pareto and Durkheim: two positivisms

Gustav Schmoller lost the *Methodenstreit* (dispute of methods) to Karl Menger and the new neoclassical economists. As Schumpeter (1954) has argued, for all the technical innovations, marginalism did not represent a paradigm shift from earlier classical political economy. Three differences, all consequences of a more self-conscious positivism, can be noted. First, hints of realism as regards causality largely disappear. Second, as Pareto put the matter, 'establishing a theory is something like passing a curve through a number of fixed points' ([1906] 1971: 31); and third, 'normative propositions' must be sharply distinguished from 'existential propositions'.

Durkheim and Pareto both accepted positivist versions of law and theory. In consequence, both contributed to the idea that quantitative social research was the main task of the social scientist. Both thought of a society as a system although they differed fundamentally on its character.

Pareto argued that 'the form of society is determined by all the elements acting upon it, and it, in turn, reacts upon them' ([1915–19] 1935: para. 2060). The economic system, the domain of 'rational' behaviour, is a subsystem of the social system, embedded in a natural environment. But features of this are accounted for indirectly, since their effects are felt on individuals, the units of the social system. Individuals are possessed of 'sentiments', Pareto's term for the various manifestations of non-rational behaviour, so that action is a joint outcome of the 'rational' and 'non-rational'. Generalizing general equilibrium theory, Pareto warmly endorsed the dream of positivist social science:

In order thoroughly to grasp the form of society in its every detail it would be necessary to know what all the very numerous elements are, and then to know how they function – and that in quantitative terms...The number of equations would be equal to the number of unknowns and would determine them exhaustively.

([1915–19] 1935: para. 2062)

In contrast to Weber (and more recent complexity theory), the social system, like the system of planets, is a closed system. Accordingly, the 'laws' of society can be mathematical functions of variables. This vision, usually unspoken, still pervades inquiry in social science.

Émile DURKHEIM saw no usefulness in economics, nor for that matter in any of the 'utilitarian' sorts of theory which Hobbes had initiated. He agreed with Comte, also, that 'since it does not call for one social form rather than another', psychology cannot explain any of them ([1895] 1938: 108). Instead, there are irreducible 'social facts' – that is, 'ways of acting or thinking with the peculiar characteristic of exercising a coercive influence on individual consciousness' ([1895] 1938: liii). Social facts are 'external' and depend on the collective consciousness which has its own laws. This road, which connects also to Platonism, leads directly to twentieth-century structuralism.

Durkheim was a functionalist, but he was also a critic of the functionalism which he attributed to Comte and Spencer (see FUNCTIONALISM IN SOCIAL SCIENCE). Once having shown that some social form was 'useful' in so far as it satisfied some 'need', they were content. Missing was an account of 'how it originates or why it was what it is' ([1895] 1938: 90). Moreover, a social fact can exist without being useful at all. But Durkheim did not escape the progressivism of Comte and Spencer. Societies, like organisms, have a lawful 'development'. *'Anomie'* was 'abnormal', the product of the breakdown of religion and authority which had subordinated modern industry. Indeed, 'what is needed if social order is to reign is that the mass of men be content with their lot...And for this, it is absolutely necessary that there be an authority whose superiority they acknowledge and which tells them what is right' (1959: 200).

12 The twentieth century

Employing available intellectual materials and exploiting the new opportunities in the new institutions of higher education in the USA, Americans constructed the prevailing disciplinary division of the human sciences (Manicas 1987). By the early 1920s these were reconstituted on a manifestly positivist reading of 'hard science'. This was then profoundly reinforced by 'logical positivism', imported from Vienna.

By the 1950s, the philosophical debate had polarized between positivists and a minority of anti-naturalists who rejected the idea of a human science, at least as understood by positivists (Natanson 1963). Thus Popper, Hempel, Brodbeck and others continued to defend the relevance of the covering law model for social science, even while it was being attacked by sympathetic critics. Except for marginalized Marxists and a few non-Marxist dissenters, for example C.W.

Mills (1959), it was business as usual in the departments of the academy.

Kuhn (1967) devastated foundationist epistemology and generated a radical sociological challenge to it (Barnes 1982), but he did not raise questions about either causality or explanation. A third alternative, a non-positivist, realist understanding of science, did. Hinted at by Toulmin, Scriven, Sellers, Hanson and others, it was given perhaps its first clear expression by Harré (1970) and then by Bhaskar (1975). It was applied to social science by Harré and Secord (1973) and influenced by the fresh readings of Marx, by Keat and Urry (1975), Benton (1977), Bhaskar (1979) and Outhwaite (1983).

This enabled a reconsideration of the ancient ontological debate regarding the nature of society. It continued to be polarized across two dimensions, on the one hand between 'methodological individualists' standing in the tradition of Hobbes (Gellner 1956; Watkins 1957; Homans 1967) and functionalist 'holists', generally influenced by Durkheim (Mandelbaum 1955). On the other hand between 'subjectivist' approaches in, for example, Schütz (1966) and Garfinkel (1967) and variant 'objectivist' structural approaches which included the very different views of, for example, Lévi-Strauss (1962), Althusser (1965) and Alexander (1987).

The more or less explicitly realist efforts to reconcile these turned on re-examining the status of 'agents' as conscious beings engaged in practical activity, an extended gloss on Marx's remark that persons make history but not with materials of their choosing. On Bhaskar's 'transformational model of social action', social forms predate the actions of agents which reproduce and transform them. Giddens' 'structuration' view (1976; 1980), less explicitly realist, defines social structure in terms of the 'rules and resources' available to agents in acting. Social structure thus has but 'virtual existence'.

Some of the same polarities were confronted in re-examining the question of culture (Foucault 1969; Bourdieu and Passeron 1970; Williams 1977). Feminist voices (Harding and Hintikka 1983) were also increasingly important. In turn, 'cultural studies' was being influenced by developments in 'postmodern' theory, including here a 'decentring of the subject' and a strongly anti-naturalistic turn towards 'discourse' (Lacan 1977; Derrida 1970). As regards the philosophy of the social sciences, by the 1990s the hegemony of positivism could no longer be taken for granted.

See also: EXPLANATION IN HISTORY AND SOCIAL SCIENCE; HOLISM AND INDIVIDUALISM IN HISTORY AND SOCIAL SCIENCE; IBN KHALDUN §2;

NATURALISM IN SOCIAL SCIENCE; NATURE AND CONVENTION; SOCIAL LAWS; SOCIAL SCIENCE, CONTEMPORARY PHILOSOPHY OF; SOCIETY, CONCEPT OF

References and further reading

* Alexander, J. (1987) *Theoretical Logic in Sociology*, 4 vols, Berkeley, CA: University of California Press. (Alexander begins his extended review with an account of positivism, proceeds in vol. 2 to discuss Marx and Durkheim and then in the following volumes, what he sees to be two efforts at synthesis: Weber and Parsons. Extensive bibliography.)

* Althusser, L. (1965) *For Marx*, trans. B. Brewster, New York: Vintage, 1970. (The critical book in provoking the idea that there is a decisive 'break' in the thought of Marx; introduces the idea of 'structure in dominance'.)

* Aristotle (*c*. mid 4th century BC) *Politics*, trans. H. Rackham, Cambridge, MA: Harvard University Press, 1977. (This is certainly the most important of Aristotle's work as regards the nature and organization of human associations.)

* —— (*c*. mid 4th century BC) *Nichomachean Ethics*, trans. H. Rackham, Cambridge, MA: Harvard University Press, 1968. (Contains much of interest as regards Aristotle's influential views on human nature and conduct. Still relevant.)

* Barnard, F.M. (1965) *Herder's Social and Political Thought*, Oxford: Clarendon Press. (A very useful selection of key texts.)

* Barnes, B. (1982) *T.S Kuhn and Social Science*, New York: Columbia University Press. (Barnes, an originator of the so-called 'strong programme' in the sociology of science, shows why Kuhn's work was important to a sociological understanding of social science.)

* Benton, T. (1977) *Philosophical Foundations of the Three Sociologies*, London: Routledge. (Discusses 'positivism', 'humanism' (or anti-naturalism in social science) and an alternative which derives from Marx.)

Berlin, I. (1976) *Vico and Herder*, New York: Viking. (An accessible and sensitive comparison.)

* Bhaskar, R. (1975) *A Realist Theory of Science*, Atlantic Highlands, NJ: Humanities Press, 2nd edn, 1978. (A systematic effort at 'realist' theory of science, versus Humean causality and the covering law model of explanation.)

* —— (1979) *The Possibility of Naturalism*, Atlantic Highlands, NJ: Humanities Press. (Applies 'realism' to develop a 'critical naturalist' theory of social science in which 'society is both the ever-present *condition* (material cause) and the con-

tinually reproduced *outcome* of human agency' (p. 43).)

* Bodin, J. (1576) *Six Books of a Commonweale*, ed. with an intro. by K.D. McRae, Cambridge, MA: Harvard University Press, 1962. (A facsimile reprint of the English translation of 1606. Offers the earliest radical reconceptualization of the political association as that had been derived from the Greeks. Spellings of the citations in §3 have been modernized from the old English.)

* Bourdieu, P. and Passeron, C. (1970) *Reproduction in Education, Society and Culture*, trans. R. Nice, London: Sage, 1977. (An alternative to the dominating assumption that 'culture' and 'society' are analytically distinguishable.)

Carver, T. (1983) *Marx and Engels: The Intellectual Relationship*, Brighton: Wheatsheaf Books. (The best treatment of the very critical differences in their respective philosophies.)

* Comte, A. (1830–42) *The Positive Philosophy of August Comte*, freely trans. and condensed by H. Martineau, London: Trubner and Co., 2 vols, 2nd edn, 1875. (Comte's philosophy is the first and perhaps most influential effort to define social science as science, conceived as the search for invariant lawful regularities.)

* Darwin, C. (1859) *Origin of Species*, New York: Cambridge University Press, 1981. (The classic of modern evolutionary theory.)

* Derrida, J. (1970) 'Structure, Sign and Play in the Discourse of the Human Sciences', repr. in *A Postmodern Reader*, ed. J. Natoli and L. Hutcheon, Albany, NY: State University of New York Press, 1993. (Although so-called 'post-modernism' is a highly contestable notion, Derrida's work is surely critical. This is an accessible essay which argues against most of the deep assumptions of mainstream social science.)

* Descartes, R. (1637) *Philosophical Works of Descartes*, vol. 1, trans. E.S. Haldane and G.R.T. Ross, New York: Dover Publications, 1931. (Descartes' *Discourses* powerfully influenced thinkers of the modern age who sought to break away from the inherited legacy of Aristotle and the Schools.)

Dilthey, W. (1910) *Pattern and Meaning in History*, trans. unacknowledged, ed. H.P. Rickman, New York: Harper & Row, 1962. (A useful, if brief collection.)

* Durkheim, É. (1895) *The Rules of Sociological Method*, New York: Free Press, 1938. (A book which, perhaps, most influenced the main strands of post Second World War sociological thought.)

* —— (1958) *Socialism and Saint Simon*, Yellow Springs, OH.: Antioch Press; London: Routledge & Kegan Paul, 1959. (From lectures given from November 1895 to May 1896. A critique of the 'founders' of socialist theory which in some ways, at least, attempts a reproachment of Comte and Marx.)

* Engels, F. (1885) *Herr Eugen Dühring's Revolution in Science*, New York: International Publishers, 1939. (This book, along with *The Dialectics of Nature* (below) established the dominating conception of Marxian social science as a 'dialectical materialism'. See Carver 1983.)

* —— (1927) *Dialectics of Nature*, New York: International Publishers, 1940. (The best statement of Engels' philosophy of science.)

* Foucault, M. (1969) *The Order of Things: An Archaeology of the Human Sciences*, New York: Pantheon, 1970. (In this influential, but very difficult book, Foucault, another of those who have propelled 'postmodernism', aims to show how different 'discourses' – of life, labour and language – get 'structured' and why we view them as providing the universals of social life – a view which he emphatically rejects.)

Frisby, D. and Sayer, D. (1986) *Society*, London and New York: Tavistock. (The best introductory account of the 'career' of the concept of society. Though brief, all the major figures are intelligently and clearly explicated.)

* Garfinkel, H. (1967) *Studies in Ethnomethodology*, Englewood Cliffs, NJ: Prentice Hall. (A fundamental critique of the 'normative model' which has dominated sociology since Parsons.)

* Gellner, E. (1956) 'Holism Versus Individualism', repr. in *Readings in the Philosophy of the Social Sciences*, ed. M. Brodbeck, New York: Macmillan, 1968. (This volume well represents the hegemony of positivist philosophy of social science during this period.)

* Giddens, A. (1976) *New Rules of Sociological Method*, London: Hutchinson. (In this rather brief book, Giddens discusses critically the main themes and some of the main figures of philosophy of social science: Schütz, Garfinkel, hermeneutics, Durkheim, Parsons and Marx and concludes with a criticism of positivism.)

* —— (1980) *The Constitution of Society*, Berkeley, CA: University of California Press. (Giddens' most thoroughgoing statement of his 'structuration' theory – his effort to resolve the continuing dichotomies of social theory. Important.)

* Harding, S. and Hintikka, M. (eds) (1983) *Discovering Reality*, Boston, MA: Reidel. (One of the better collections of interventions in epistemology by feminists.)

* Harré, R. (1970) *The Principles of Scientific Thinking*, Chicago, IL: University of Chicago Press. (Perhaps

a 'Copernician revolution' in the philosophy of science; it provoked a range of new 'realist' thinking.)

* Harré, R. and Secord, P. (1973) *The Explanation of Social Behavior*, Oxford: Blackwell. (The 'ethnogenic' approach of this book offered a clear alternative to most mainstream conceptualizations.)

* Herder, J.G. (1794–91) *J.G. Herder on Social and Political Culture*, trans. ed., and with an intro. by F.M. Barnard, Cambridge: Cambridge University Press, 1969. (Very useful for the general student.)

Hobbes, T. (1651) *Leviathan*, New York: E.P. Dutton, 1950. (The source of much modern political theory. Indispensable.)

* Homans, G. (1967) *The Nature of Social Science*, New York: Harcourt Brace. (An important work by a recent 'behaviouralist' critic of 'holistic' (structuralist) views of sociology.)

* Iggers, G.G. (1983) *The German Conception of History: the National Tradition of Historical Thought from Herder to the Present*, Middletown, CT: Wesleyan University Press. (An excellent overview of this critical history.)

* Keat, R. and Urry, J. (1975) *Social Theory as Science*, London: Routledge & Kegan Paul. ('Realist' theory.)

Kerferd, G.B. (1981) *The Sophistic Movement*, Cambridge: Cambridge University Press. (Gives a sympathetic account of the central issues discussed in §1, above.)

* Kuhn, T. (1967) *The Structure of Scientific Revolution*, Chicago, IL: University of Chicago Press, enlarged edn, 1970. (A book which upset the long legacy of empiricist, positivist thinking about the nature of science, including social science. Essential reading.)

* Lacan, J. (1977) *Ecrits, A Selection*, trans. J. Sheridan, New York: Norton, 1977. (A 'decentring of the subject' which draws on Freud's theory of the unconscious. Often cryptic.)

* Lenzer, G. (ed.) (1975) *Auguste Comte and Positivism: The Essential Writings*, New York: Harper, 1975. (A very convenient student's edition. Judicious editing.)

* Lévi-Strauss, C. (1962) *The Savage Mind*, Chicago, IL: University of Chicago Press, 1966. (A strongly 'structuralist' but anti-functionalist approach to social science.)

Locke, J. (1690) *Two Treatises of Civil Government*, with an intro. and *appartus criticus* by P. Laslett, 2nd edn, Cambridge: Cambridge University Press, 1967. (The foundation of modern constitutionalism and liberalism.)

* Machiavelli, N. (1515, 1527) *The Prince and the Discourses*, New York: Modern Library, 1950. (The

Discourses are less well known than *The Prince* since it was the latter which has shocked readers; but contrary to widespread opinion, for reasons set out in *The Discourses*, most leaders of modern states have learned from Machiavelli.)

Makkreel, R.F. (1975) *Dilthey: Philosopher of the Human Studies*, Princeton, NJ: Princeton University Press. (Perhaps the most important recent commentary on Dilthey.)

* Mandelbaum, M. (1955) 'Societal Facts', *The British Journal of Sociology* 6 (4): 305–17. (A 'classic' defence of 'holism' against 'methodological individualism'.)

—— (1971) *Reason, Man and History*, Baltimore, MD: Johns Hopkins University Press. (Perhaps the best review of nineteenth-century writers relevant to the human sciences. Important and accessible.)

* Manicas, P.T. (1987) *A History and Philosophy of the Social Sciences*, Oxford: Blackwell. (A fuller treatment of the history beginning with the eighteenth century.)

* Marx, K. (1852) *The Eighteen Brumaire of Louis Bonaparte*, New York: International Publishers, 1963. (Probably the best concrete discussion of class and its role in social change in the corpus of Marx's voluminous writings.)

* —— (1859) *A Contribution to the Critique of Political Economy*, Chicago, IL: Charles H. Kerr, 1904. (The 'Preface' has been extremely influential in defining the character of Marx's 'historical materialism'.)

* —— (1867) *Capital*, vol. 1, London: Lawrence & Wishart, 1970. (Certainly one of the most influential books of social science, very much incorporated into current theory – by Marxists and non-Marxists alike.)

* Marx, K. and Engels, F. (1883) *The German Ideology*, New York: International Publishers, 1947. (For many interpretators, this is the most critical text in gaining an understanding of 'historical materialism'.)

* Marx, K. and Engels, F. (1877) *Marx and Engels Selected Correspondence*, New York: International Publishers, 1942. (One of several collections.)

* Mill, J.S. (1844) *Essays on Some Unsettled Questions of Political Economy*, 2nd edn, Clifton, NJ: Augustus Kelly, 1974. (Now little read, these lively essays show that Mill would not have approved of subsequent developments in the philosophy of 'economics'.)

* —— (1843) *System of Logic*, 8th edn, London: Longman, 1930. (A monumental, influential and still useful effort to set out the 'logic' of the human sciences. Introduces his famous 'methods'.)

Mills, C.W. (1959) *The Sociological Imagination*, Harmondsworth: Penguin. (The title, now very much in the literature, is often hardly taken seriously; a hardnosed attack on 'abstracted empiricism' and 'grand theory', both still very much in evidence.)

* Natanson, M. (ed.) (1963) *Philosophy of the Social Sciences*, New York: Random House. (The editor made his selections based on the assumption that there were two polar positions underlying the social sciences, an 'objective' versus a 'subjective' point of view. Contains most of the most important essays which define this debate. Very influential.)

* Outhwaite, W. (1983) *New Philosophies of Science: Realism, Hermeneutics and Critical Theory*, New York: St Martins Press, 1987. (Parallels in some ways Benton 1977.)

* Pareto, W. (1915–19) *Mind and Society*, New York: Harcourt, 1935. (This massive and often tedious work is now largely forgotten even while there is a considerable residue of its driving vision.)

* —— (1906) *Manual of Political Economy*, New York: Kelly, 1971. (A clear statement of Pareto's philosophy of social science.)

Passmore, J. (1957) *A Hundred Years of Philosophy*, Harmondsworth: Penguin, 1968. (Certainly the best account of the often ignored late nineteenth-century 'philosopher/physicists' whose views powerfully influenced the idea of science which was appropriated by the emerging modern social sciences. Passmore is a reliable expositor of all the figures he treats.)

* Randall, J.H. (1940) *The Making of the Modern Mind*, Cambridge, MA: Riverside Press. (Randall gives a superb account of how thinking about society shifted from the medieval period to modernity. Very readable.)

Ross, D. (1991) *The Origins of American Social Science*, Cambridge: Cambridge University Press. (A detailed study of the critical period, 1870–1929, of the constitution of US disciplinary social science.)

* Rousseau, J.-J. (1755) *The Social Contract and Discourses*, trans. G.P.H. Cole, New York: E.P. Dutton, 1950. (Rousseau's writings are essential, but are less often read in terms of philosophy of social science.)

Sayer, A. (1984) *Method in Social Science: A Realist Approach*, 2nd edn, London: Routledge, 1992. (A very useful realist textbook on method.)

* Schumpeter, J.A. (1954) *History of Economic Analysis*, New York: Oxford University Press. (A rich historical source, but not helpful as regards the *Methodenstreit*.)

* Schütz, A. (1966) *The Collected Papers*, 3 vols, The Hague: Niijhoff. (Schütz was central in the effort to restore 'subjectivity' to social scientific understanding – versus the reigning positivism. Difficult.)

Shanley, M.L. and Pateman, C. (eds) (1991) *Feminist Interpretations and Political Theory*, College Park, PA: Pennsylvania State University Press. (An excellent collection of feminist re-examinations of many of the figures discussed in this entry.)

Skinner, Q. (1978) *The Foundations of Modern Political Thought*, 2 vols, Cambridge: Cambridge University Press, 1978. (A detailed study with attention to the development of the concept of the modern state, a datum for all subsequent social scientific thinking.)

* Smith, A. (1776) *An Inquiry into the Nature and Causes of the Wealth of Nations*, eds R.H. Campbell, A.S. Skinner and W.B. Todd, Oxford: Clarendon Press, 2 vols, 1976. (A classic, but as much sociological and historical as economic.)

* Spencer, H. (1850) *Social Statics*, New York: Appleton, 1897. (Spencer's best effort to defend '*laissez-faire*'.)

* —— (1862) *First Principles*, Westport, CT: Greenwood Press, 1976. (Aims to show that nature and history may be understood in terms of fundamental, evolutionary principles.)

* Vico, G.B. (1725) *The New Science*, trans. T.G. Bergin and M. Fisch, Ithaca, NY: Cornell University Press, 1948. (Usually ignored, Vico's work is strikingly modern in many ways.)

* Watkins, J.W.N. (1957) 'Historical Explanation in the Social Sciences', *British Journal for the Philosophy of Science* 8: 104–17. (Perhaps the 'classic' statement of 'methodological individualism'.)

* Weber, M. (1903–06) *Roscher and Kneis: The Logical Problems of Historical Economics*, trans. with an intro. by G. Oakes, New York: Free Press, 1975. (This book contains Weber's most systematic effort to think through problems in the philosophy of social science, but it is not often read. Hard going.)

* —— (1904) '"Objectivity" in Social Science', in *The Methodology of the Social Sciences*, trans. E.A. Shils and H.A. Finch, New York: Free Press, 1949. (This volume contains the more famous of Weber's discussions of social science.)

* Williams, R. (1977) *Marxism and Literature*, Oxford: Oxford University Press. (A very influential effort to overcome the 'reductionism' of much Marxist theory.)

PETER T. MANICAS

SOCIAL SCIENCE, METHODOLOGY OF

Each of the sciences, the physical, biological, social and behavioural, have emerged from philosophy in a process that began in the time of Euclid and Plato. These sciences have left a legacy to philosophy of problems that they have been unable to deal with, either as nascent or as mature disciplines. Some of these problems are common to all sciences, some restricted to one of the four general divisions mentioned above, and some of these philosophical problems bear on only one or another of the special sciences.

If the natural sciences have been of concern to philosophers longer than the social sciences, this is simply because the former are older disciplines. It is only in the last century that the social sciences have emerged as distinct subjects in their currently recognizable state. Some of the problems in the philosophy of social science are older than these disciplines, in part because these problems have their origins in nineteenth-century philosophy of history. Of course the full flowering of the philosophy of science dates from the emergence of the logical positivists in the 1920s. Although the logical positivists' philosophy of science has often been accused of being satisfied with a one-sided diet of physics, in fact their interest in the social sciences was at least as great as their interest in physical science. Indeed, as the pre-eminent arena for the application of prescriptions drawn from the study of physics, social science always held a place of special importance for philosophers of science.

Even those who reject the role of prescription from the philosophy of physics, cannot deny the relevance of epistemology and metaphysics for the social sciences. Scientific change may be the result of many factors, only some of them cognitive. However, scientific advance is driven by the interaction of data and theory. Data controls the theories we adopt and the direction in which we refine them. Theory directs and constrains both the sort of experiments that are done to collect data and the apparatus with which they are undertaken: research design is driven by theory, and so is methodological prescription. But what drives research design in disciplines that are only in their infancy, or in which for some other reason, there is a theoretical vacuum? In the absence of theory how does the scientist decide on what the discipline is trying to explain, what its standards of explanatory adequacy are, and what counts as the data that will help decide between theories? In such cases there are only two things scientists have to go on: successful theories and methods in other disciplines which are thought to be relevant to the nascent discipline, and the epistemology

and metaphysics which underwrites the relevance of these theories and methods. This makes philosophy of special importance to the social sciences. The role of philosophy in guiding research in a theoretical vacuum makes the most fundamental question of the philosophy of science whether the social sciences can, do, or should employ to a greater or lesser degree the same methods as those of the natural sciences? Note that this question presupposes that we have already accurately identified the methods of natural science. If we have not yet done so, the question becomes largely academic. For many philosophers of social science the question of what the methods of natural science are was long answered by the logical positivist philosophy of physical science. And the increasing adoption of such methods by empirical, mathematical, and experimental social scientists raised a second central question for philosophers: why had these methods so apparently successful in natural science been apparently far less successful when self-consciously adapted to the research agendas of the several social sciences?

One traditional answer begins with the assumption that human behaviour or action and its consequences are simply not amenable to scientific study, because they are the results of free will, or less radically, because the significant kinds or categories into which social events must be classed are unique in a way that makes non-trivial general theories about them impossible. These answers immediately raise some of the most difficult problems of metaphysics and epistemology: the nature of the mind, the thesis of determinism, and the analysis of causation. Even less radical explanations for the differences between social and natural sciences raise these fundamental questions of philosophy.

Once the consensus on the adequacy of a positivist philosophy of natural science gave way in the late 1960s, these central questions of the philosophy of social science became far more difficult ones to answer. Not only was the benchmark of what counts as science lost, but the measure of progress became so obscure that it was no longer uncontroversial to claim that the social sciences' rate of progress was any different from that of natural science.

1   **Testability**
2   **Methodological individualism versus functionalism**
3   **Intentionality laws and the philosophy of psychology**
4   **Reflexivity and historicism**
5   **Facts, values and dangerous knowledge**

1   Testability

As in natural science, for a long time one leading aim of many philosophers of social science was to improve and ensure the 'scientific' character of theories in social and behavioural science by increasing their testability. The demand for testability was characteristic of logical positivist philosophy of social science. Philosophers like Neurath insisted that much which passes for social science was pseudoscience because there was no empirical evidence which could bear on its truth or falsity (see POSITIVISM IN THE SOCIAL SCIENCES §2). Even more vigorously, Karl POPPER and his followers long wielded the requirement that scientific theories be in principle falsifiable as a litmus test to find fault with Freudian psychodynamic theory, Marxian economics, and functional sociological theory. Operationalists following Bridgman insisted that for any term introduced in a scientific theory, there be specified operations to tell whether the term applied to something or not (see OPERATIONALISM). Empiricist-oriented social scientists, behaviourists in psychology or sociology like B.F. Skinner or G. Homans, neoclassical economists like P. Samuelson, or Milton Friedman, biologically inspired anthropologists like M. Harris, and a whole host of behaviouralists in political science, attempted to reorient theory in order to meet the positivist demand that it be possible to state explicitly what sort of evidence would confirm or disconfirm it (see BEHAVIOURISM IN THE SOCIAL SCIENCES §§1, 3). One result of the demand for testability was a suspicion of theoretical terms, neologisms, and metaphorical expressions invoked without definitions that could link them to observations providing these terms with empirical content.

Positivism as a philosophy of science receded largely because the positivists and their students were unable to provide an account of empirical testability which satisfied their own standards of adequacy. All specific formulations were found either too narrow – excluding as untestable such scientifically indispensable concepts as 'positive charge' or 'acid', or too broad – including as testable such pseudoscientific concepts as 'the absolute'. With no adequate criterion of testability, the demand that theories satisfy strictures on empirical verifiability came gradually to be surrendered in the philosophy of social science. With the surrender of the search for such principles, the inclination to stigmatize some social theories as meaningless declined and the prescriptive role of the philosophy of social science weakened as well. Nevertheless, there remains among some philosophers and many social scientists a healthy suspicion of explanatory terms and theories embodying them, when these theories lack significant predictive power.

Among some social scientists, especially economists, the supposition that there is a test for scientific as opposed to non-scientific discourse or metaphysics

or pseudoscience lasted far longer than it did among empiricist philosophers of science. And though the demand for testability may have had a salutary effect on the minimization of cant and circumlocution, it could no more be honoured by significant theory in social science than it could in physics or chemistry. This has made much of the official philosophy of science of disciplines like neoclassical economics particularly schizoid. Among economists Popper's demand that theory be falsifiable has long held sway in the methodological volumes while being steadily ignored in actual economic theorizing. The demand for falsifiability, like that of testability, has been shown to be a 'will-o'-the wisp', in large part because falsifying evidence always impugns a large set of hypotheses, not just the particular one the scientist sets out to test. Falsification casts doubt as well on all the auxiliary hypotheses governing the behaviour of measuring instruments, establishing the character of the boundary or initial conditions under test, and assuring the reliability of the data of a test as a reflection of the phenomena under study.

The failure of various principles of testability to be reflected in the actual scientific practice of economics and other disciplines, increasingly resulted in a greater interest by philosophers in the actual character of theory appraisal as pursued by social scientists in the several sciences than in the methodological expressions of opinion by social scientists. This increased attention to what social scientists do, as opposed to what they say they should do, has characterized post-positivist philosophy of social science.

2 Methodological individualism versus functionalism

The question of what the objects of social theories are emerged from the controversy over testability, but has taken on a life of its own. Even before DURKHEIM, historians had adverted to groups, institutions, and organizations whose existence and behaviour could not be exhaustively analysed into or explained by appeal to the existence and behaviour of the individual agents who participate in them. From Durkheim onward such hypostasis was based on the explanatory role and apparently autonomous coercive powers such wholes seemed to have (see HOLISM AND INDIVIDUALISM IN HISTORY AND SOCIAL SCIENCE).

To those who were sceptical about the notion that there were, in Durkheim's terms, social facts above and beyond individual ones, the slogan that the whole is greater than the sum of its parts was simply mystery-mongering provocation. Foremost among social scientific opponents of this holism were the economists, whose own theory rigorously rejected any dispensation from the obligation to explain all economic phenomena by derivation from the rational choices of individual agents. Empiricist philosophers of social science make common cause with such social scientists: since social wholes, facts, institutions, and so on, cannot be directly observed, and since ontologically their existence depends wholly on the existence of agents who compose them, it is tempting to claim that such wholes must be reducible by definition or by explanation to the behaviour of individuals. Allowing such wholes autonomous existence is not only metaphysically bootless, but epistemically gratuitous.

With the demise of demands for testability much of the force of the purely epistemological argument against holism must fade. Thus contemporary debates about methodological individualism versus holism turn on the explanatory indispensability of the appeal to trans-individual entities within social science and biology.

When asking the question 'why biology?' it is important to bear in mind that over the second half of the twentieth century lessons and morals drawn from biology and the philosophy of biology have bulked large in disputes within the philosophy of social science. Just as philosophers have become more interested in the actual practice of social science, so too have they acquired an interest in biology's methodological agenda. The reasons for this interest overlap those of the philosopher of social science. Examination of biological methodology must shed light on the adequacy of a philosophy of science drawn from the examination of physics, and differences between biology and physics will show that prescriptions drawn from physics are inapplicable in biology. This will reinforce the argument that such inapplicability in social science shows the irrelevance of methodological strictures drawn from physical science beyond its official writ. This is a point to which we return below.

Meanwhile, as in social science, evolutionary biology seems to countenance holistic theories, ones which postulate the existence and causal role of family groups, inter-breeding populations, species and ecosystems independent of the individual organisms that compose them. If such postulation is legitimate in biology, the argument proceeds, it should be equally legitimate in social science. On the other hand, some methodological individualists argue the very reverse: first they show that evolutionary explanation in biology is implicitly or explicitly individualist, and then they argue that it must be so in social science as well.

Whether the argument from biology tells in favour of or against the methodological individualist in social science hinges on the correct understanding of teleological explanation and functional analysis in biology. This is another reason why philosophers of social science closely follow or participate in debates among philosophers of biology.

Durkheim was among the earliest explicitly to attribute functions to social institutions above and beyond those individuals ordain or recognize. Durkheim and functionalist social scientists who follow him hold that social wholes exist in order to fulfil certain functions and that the fact that they fulfil such functions can actually explain their existence. Their argument for this view simply followed biological precedent: such explanations are widespread and universally accepted in life science. For example, the presence of the heart is explained by citing its function, the pumping of blood. By contrast the presence of the appendix in humans is problematical, just because it has no function. *Mutatis mutandis* in social theory: social structures exist in order to curb anomie, minimize alienation, optimize social integration, or fulfil some other function vital to the society's survival or well being.

At least since Spinoza philosophers and others have been suspicious of functional and other forms of purposive explanation just because they seem to reverse the order of causation (see FUNCTIONAL EXPLANATION; FUNCTIONALISM IN SOCIAL SCIENCE). To explain the presence of the heart by appeal to its pumping the blood is to cite an effect to explain its cause. As Spinoza said, this is to reverse the order of nature. Worse, many things with functions do not fulfil their purposes. For instance, most sperm cells fail to fertilize any egg, yet that is their function. Can we explain the presence of a particular sperm cell by adverting to a function it fails to perform? Add to this the difficulty of identifying functions, both in the biological case and the social one: what exactly is the function of the peacock's plumage, or matrilineal marriage rules in a patrilateral society? Many empiricist philosophers of biology have looked to the theory of natural selection to legitimize, eliminate and minimize the ontological excesses of functional explanation in biology, and by parity of reasoning the problematical role of such explanation in social science. The theory of natural selection is sometimes invoked to legitimate functional explanation and sometimes to show that teleology is a mere appearance – an overlay we place on purely causal processes. Either way the analysis is roughly the same: the appearance or the reality of adaptation is the result of a long and slow process of random variation in hereditary traits subjected to the culling of nature in the struggle for survival. In a relatively constant environment over a long period of successive generations, variants that are fortuitously advantageous will be selected and will increase their proportion in the whole of a population until the variants become ubiquitous. Thus, to say mammals have hearts in order to pump blood is true and explanatory because the heart exists in mammals now as the result of a long process of selection for blood pumps.

Once teleology is legitimated in biology, it is mere cavilling to withhold it from the social sciences. The trouble is that proponents of its legitimacy in social science are obliged to establish close analogies between mechanisms of biological and social evolution. Here the problem for the methodological holist is that functional explanations in biology are widely held to substantiate a version of methodological individualism. By and large there is agreement among evolutionary biologists that selection does not operate at the level of the group, but only at the level of the individual, that the mechanism of hereditary transmission operates exclusively at the level of the individual and that group properties must be fully explained by appeal to the properties and interactions of individuals. Functional explanation in biology seems resolutely individualist.

This result is disturbing for holists. Their best argument for the existence of social wholes and their properties is the explanatory role of social roles and their properties. But these properties – say kinship rules – are usually accorded a functional role, for example, that of enhancing social integration, and their existence is explained by citing these functions. If functions have explanatory force only to the extent that their existence can in turn be given a thoroughly individualist foundation, then for the holist the game is not worth the candle. The best a holist can hope for is that the drift of the debate in the philosophy of biology, which has long favoured the individualist, may turn in the other direction. Short of that, holists have no other recourse but to repudiate the relevance of biology in the justification of social methodology. To do this is of course to surrender 'naturalism' – the doctrine that the methods of natural and social sciences should be broadly similar. This is an approach many social scientists have further independent reason to contemplate, as we shall now see.

3 Intentionality laws and the philosophy of psychology

As noted above, perhaps the central questions in the philosophy of social science are whether the social sciences do or should employ the same methods as the natural sciences. The thesis that the social sciences should and can do so is traditionally labelled naturalism (see NATURALISM IN SOCIAL SCIENCE). Its denial has been borne by a succession of move-ments in social science and its philosophy: structuralism, semiotics, ethnomethodology, hermeneutics, interpretationalism, and more recently deconstruction, postmodernism, and rhetoric (see POST-STRUCTURALISM IN THE SOCIAL SCIENCES §2; STRUCTURALISM IN SOCIAL SCIENCE). These approaches differ from each other in crucial ways. But they share in common a rejection of naturalism.

The issue on which naturalism and anti-naturalism have longest contended is that of the nature of human action and its explanation. All parties agree that social science shares a presumption, along with history and common sense, that much human behaviour – the displacement of the human body – is action, that action is explained by the joint operation of desires and beliefs, and that action and its consequences are the concern of the social sciences. This is a theory which, on the one hand, is so obvious as to go unmentioned in history and biography, and, on the other hand, has been transformed into the economist's formalization as rational choice theory: each individual has a set of preferences – that is desires – which set is complete, transitive, and continuous, and a set of expectations – beliefs – about available means of satisfying these preferences, and each individual is rational – that is, chooses that action which, in the light of expectations, will attain the object of strongest desire (see RATIONAL CHOICE THEORY). If explanation of human action is common sense and all the social sciences appeal to this principle, formalized or not, then the vindication of naturalism or its refutation turns on whether some version of the theory of rational choice is a causal law or not. Similarly the adequacy of anti-naturalism hinges on whether such explanations' force lies in some non-causal power to illuminate their explanans.

This is because scientific explanation is held crucially to involve derivation of the explananda from causal laws and initial or boundary conditions. Though this analysis of explanation in science has been significantly qualified and circumscribed over the years, the notion that explanation involves systematizing laws and/or causality remains a fixed point in the philosophy of natural science. Accordingly, if a principle of rational action is indispensable in social explanation, then naturalism requires that the principle's explanatory force rests on a causal or nomological understanding. It will have to be a causal law that:

L (x) (if x desires d, and x believes that all things considered doing action a is the most efficient means of attaining desire d, then x does a).

Or if this is not a law, it had better be improvable in the direction of a law of human behaviour. The requirement that a principle of rational choice must be treated as a causal regularity has been common to naturalists in the social sciences at least since it was implicitly embraced by Max Weber. Treating rational choice theory as at least a body of incipient laws is especially crucial to any attempt to make sense of the actual practice of economic theory. Given the predictive weakness of economic theory and its resolute attachment to rational choice theory as its explanatory core, it becomes crucial to economists' claims for their science to show that this core can be retained as a body of laws or approximations to them in the face of apparent empirical disconfirmation.

However the debate on whether a principle like L embodies a law or not is a chapter of what was once the philosophy of mind and has become the philosophy of psychology. For, as Hume long ago noted, for L to be a law, beliefs, desires, and actions must behave in the way that causes and effects recognized in the natural sciences behave. They must be logically independent of one another and it must be possible to establish that each of a particular package of belief, desire and consequent action, obtain without having to establish that the other two obtain. However, the logical connection between these states is something that has long been recognized in the philosophy of psychology. Beliefs and desires have what Brentano unmetaphorically described as 'aboutness', or content or intentionality (see INTENTIONALITY §1). Beliefs are about actual or (in the case of false beliefs) non-actual states of the world, as are desires; actions are distinct from mere bodily motion only because they are the effects of desires and beliefs. Thus, action too is imbued with intentionality. Intentionality is an obstacle to a naturalistic treatment of the psychological for two reasons. First, beliefs and desires are identified and distinguished from one another by their intentional content; but the only way to establish the content of a person's beliefs, given their actions, is to have prior knowledge of all their desires and all other beliefs, and vice versa. Moreover, in order to infer desire and belief from action one must be able to distinguish the action which the combination of the desire and belief cause from mere behaviour, and this cannot be done unless we can establish that the body's motion constitutes action – that is movement caused by belief and desire. We are thus caught in an intentional circle. There is no way independent of the effects of action to establish that its causes obtain, and vice versa. But causes and effects must be logically distinguishable from each other; more than that they must be methodologically distinguishable. Otherwise there will be no way to test the claim that some combination of desire and belief causes some particular action, and consequently no way to

systematically apply our theory of rational choice in the prediction of actions with any hope of improvement over common sense.

Of course if we could establish when a certain combination of desires and beliefs obtain independent of the actions they cause, for example by reading mental states off from the neurological states of the brain, we could in principle identify causes and effects independently. Alas, philosophers and psychologists from Descartes to Skinner have rejected this course as unavailing either in principle or in practice. Despite the scientific conviction that the mind is the brain, no one has yet overcome Descartes' arguments against this claim, nor shown to general satisfaction how intentional states could be physical states. And even were this obstacle overcome, as Skinner long argued, neuroscience can provide no real help in establishing the boundary conditions to which intentional generalizations like those of rational choice are applied for explanation and prediction.

In the latter half of the twentieth century the philosophy of social science was dominated by the dispute about whether the intentional explanations of common sense, history, cultural anthropology, a good deal of political science and sociology, or their economic and psychological formalization, are or could be causal laws. Naturalists proclaimed that they were, but with the coming of Wittgenstein's influence in the philosophy of mind, this view came increasingly under attack. The gist of this attack on naturalism was that since intentional states and actions are logically connected with one another, explanations that appealed to them could not be causal. Instead the explanatory force of such explanations had to have different non-naturalistic foundations. As Wittgenstein wrote in the *Philosophical Investigations*, 'In psychology there are experimental methods and conceptual confusions' (1953, part XIV, p. 2325). The conceptual confusion was to treat belief and desire as the causes of action, and to approach the generalization which links them as an empirical generalization which might be improved and refined so as to become a law. In fact, beliefs and desires are linked to actions as their reasons, and the linkage is established by rules. It is to this confusion of rules for regularities that the sterility and vacuity of much social science is attributable. Rules are learned by asking the right questions, not by making experimental observations of behaviour. When we attempt to apply empirical methods to what is in essence a conceptual inquiry the result is bound to be unsatisfactory.

Opponents of naturalism before and since Wittgenstein have been animated by the notion that the aims of social science are not causal explanation and improving prediction, but uncovering rules that make social life intelligible to its participants (see EXPLANATION IN HISTORY AND SOCIAL SCIENCE). For these purposes there is no alternative to 'folk psychology', the account of action and its sources implicit in our every day beliefs and ubiquitous in all cultures. Folk psychology is what enables us to 'interpret' the behaviour of others, to show it rational or reasonable by our own lights. If we fail to so understand the actions of others, then by and large the fault is not in our 'theory' but in our application of it. We have misdiagnosed the beliefs and the desires of those we seek to understand. From this view the goal of social inquiry is to be understood on the model of the cultural anthropologist 'going native' in order to learn the meaning of day-to-day life for the participant of the culture under study (see ANTHROPOLOGY, PHILOSOPHY OF §1). These meanings are embodied in rules. Indeed the principle of rationality is but a rule which may characterize only western culture. Note that rules may be broken, and when they are there are further rules which dictate the sanctions to be imposed, and so forth. The social scientist's objective is to uncover these rules which render what happens in a society intelligible, though they never make social life predictable beyond limits set by common-sense folk psychology.

That social science is a search for intelligibility will explain why its theories ought not be construed causally and why it neither embodies nor needs explanatory and predictive laws. Thus, the failure of empirically inspired social science to uncover generalizations about human action that seem reasonable candidates for laws or even their rough and improvable precursors is explained not by the complexity of human behaviour and its intentional causes, but by the fact that such a search for laws misunderstands the aim of social science and the role which concepts like rationality sometimes play in attaining this aim. This aim is an interpretation of actions and events which gives them meaning – sometimes the participant's meaning, sometimes a 'deeper' meaning, but always one which presupposes a significant overlap in most of the broader beliefs and desires of the participants and observers as well. However, by adapting the arguments of Quine, anti-naturalists have concluded that the sort of interpretation sought is inevitably underdetermined by the evidence, defeasible, and is a construction subject to negotiation among interested parties.

Under various names this anti-naturalist view of the aims and claims of social science has waxed and waned in fashion along with naturalism from Dilthey and Weber to the present. There is, however, a third alternative to asserting or denying that beliefs and desires work together to explain behaviour as action through causal laws. Eliminativism is an empiricist philosophy of social, behavioural and cognitive science which adopts the interpretationalist conclusion that under their intentional characterizations beliefs and desires cannot be linked to behaviour via laws; so much the worse for beliefs and desires (see ELIMINATIVISM). Since our goal in social science is causal explanation and improving precision and scope of prediction, we should surrender any hope of explaining behaviour as action caused by intentionally characterized psychological attitudes. Instead we should adopt a neuroscientific or some other sort of non-intentional perspective on individual behaviour, and we should seek aggregate generalizations about social processes while remaining agnostic as to their psychological foundations.

Eliminativism has found few defenders in either social science or its philosophy. Faced with the Scylla of interpretationalism and the Charybdis of eliminativism, most naturalists among social scientists and philosophers participating in this debate have challenged a presumption shared by both eliminativists and interpretationalists: the claim that on its naturalistic interpretation rational choice theory cannot reasonably be construed as embodying empirical generalizations with any prospect of being improved into causal laws. Instead naturalists point with pride to relatively controversial and certainly limited successes whether in economics or political science or sociology. More to the present point, naturalists dispute the philosophical theses from which the interpretationalist and the eliminativists draw their pessimistic conclusions about the prospect for intentional laws. Some naturalists dispute the requirement that the description of causes be logically distinct from those of their effects. Others argue that despite ineliminable *ceteris paribus* clauses, the status of the rationality principle as a general law is unimpeachable, or at least no more problematical than *ceteris paribus* laws elsewhere, in biology for example. These philosophers of social science continue to seek the obstacles to predictive power in the social sciences in the complexity and interdependence of human behaviour, and in the openness of social processes to interference by exogenous forces. Others seek the limitations on predictive strength of social science in the reflexivity of social phenomena.

4 Reflexivity and historicism

One set of problems that the social sciences do not share with the natural sciences stem from the fact that the subjects of social science are themselves epistemic agents, that can be influenced by their own beliefs about the generalizations, the input and the output of social theory (see SOCIAL SCIENCES, PREDICTION IN). It is well known that the publication of an economic prediction can result in its being falsified by the action of agents who act on the prediction, or again that the publication of polling results can make their predictions self-fulfilling. This fact has led to an entire movement in macroeconomics, 'rational expectations' theory, which accords the subjects of economic theory – individual rational agents – at least as much knowledge of economic theory as it accords government policy makers. Under this assumption it can be shown that implementing certain policies predicated on the truth of Keynesian theory will cause that theory to be falsified.

Theories and predictions whose dissemination can effect their confirmation are known as 'reflexive' ones. Some philosophers and social scientists have held that theories in social science must be different in kind from those of natural science because the former are potentially reflexive when the latter are not. One extreme version of this view denies that social theory can improve prediction beyond certain narrow limits, and so constitutes a serious obstacle to a naturalistic social science uncovering a succession of improvable causal generalizations. Among advocates of critical theory the doctrine is held not so much to limit knowledge, but to burden it with a special responsibility. Critical theorists hold that since theory can influence social behaviour it ought to, or at least the social scientist has the responsibility of framing and disseminating theory in a way that will emancipate people by showing them the real meaning of social institutions and freeing them from false and enslaving beliefs about themselves and their communities (see CRITICAL THEORY). Critical theorists adopt an empiricist account of natural science, but they insist that the reflexive character and normative aims of social science make for important differences in its methods and epistemology: social science is a search for emancipative intelligibility, not laws, or even rules. Its methods are social criticism of ideologies masquerading as fixed truths, mere interpretations which are to be unmasked as social constructs, not the inevitable result of natural forces.

As critical theory and other anti-naturalistic doctrines give way to more radical doctrines, even its concessions to the empirical character of natural science are withdrawn, in favour of an inference from the non-empirical character of social science to the ideological, negotiated non-cumulative character of natural science. Postmodernism, helping itself to a radical interpretation of Kuhn's theory of scientific change, not only denies that the social sciences have a methodology or an epistemology, but also that

natural science yields objective information about the way the world or even observable phenomena are.

These more extreme anti-naturalistic doctrines share with nineteenth-century philosophy of history a commitment to 'historicism' (see HISTORICISM). The natural sciences have traditionally been viewed as ahistorical in a number of different senses. Natural laws are typically time symmetrical: given laws and initial conditions for a closed deterministic system, we can retrodict past events as well as future ones. There is no causal action at a temporal distance: a past event can only influence a future one transitively through their intermediate effects at each intervening event between the cause and its ultimate effect. If there are causal laws their writ runs across all places and all times: a regularity confirmed in one spatio-temporal region and disconfirmed in another is not a law in either region, it is at best a local empirical regularity to be explained by some exceptionless universal law.

Historicism in social science involves the denial that one or another of these three theses characterizes the social sciences. Typically historicists argue that social processes reflect the operation of asymmetrical principles which mandate a fixed order of events: thus capitalism could not have come into existence without the prior appearance of feudalism; and adult neurosis could not have come into existence without the prior frustration of infantile sexuality. Historicism sometimes also embodies the thesis that each historical epoch operates in accordance with its own distinct explanatory laws, and that sometimes the discovery of such laws can usher in a new era with new laws – whence the connection between historicism and reflexivity.

Reflexivity raises important methodological questions: Can we minimize the obstacles to empirical testing that self-fulfilling prophesies and suicidal predictions make? If not, how do we assess the cognitive status of explanations embodying reflexive theories? Historicism raises metaphysical questions of an even more fundamental sort: Suppose historicism is true, what is it about human action, social institutions, and large scale historical events that makes them so different from causal processes governed by symmetrical causal laws, and how can events reach out to produce much later ones without going through normal causal chains? These questions either go unanswered in contemporary debates or lead us back to problems about the intersection of the philosophy of social science and the philosophy of psychology: problems about the nature of intentionality and the mind. For the answers given to these questions about the historical character of social inquiry invariably appeal to agency, action, will and thought.

5   Facts, values and dangerous knowledge

One traditional set of questions distinctive of the social sciences reflects their special relevance to normative questions about individual and social policy (see VALUE JUDGMENTS IN SOCIAL SCIENCE). Well confirmed theories of human behaviour provide the means to ameliorate, or to worsen human life. This fact raises questions about how this knowledge should be employed. In addition, in choosing which research questions to examine, and which hypotheses to test, the social scientist makes value judgments about the interest, importance, significance of alternatives. However these questions are in principle no different from those raised by advances in theoretical physics. Different questions are raised by the fact that well-confirmed social theories would enable us to control and manipulate individual and aggregate human behaviour. A further distinctive problem is raised by the need to employ human subjects in order to test some theories of human behaviour. Whether it is permissible to treat humans in the way we treat laboratory animals, or even animals in field studies, is an issue social scientists face along with medical researchers.

Additionally, there is the problem of potentially dangerous knowledge. Some inquiries are best left unmade, or so it is alleged. Studies of the correlation of criminality and chromosomal abnormality, or the heritability of intelligence, or the dynamics of jury deliberation, will be condemned on the ground that disseminating the findings may be harmful whether they are scientifically significant or not. Over the last half century this claim has been made with special force in regard to studies of the statistical heritability of IQ among various groups. Some philosophers have attacked such studies on cognitive grounds, arguing that IQ is not a measure of intelligence, and that heritability shows little about genetic inheritance. They have also held that the examination of such questions should be forsworn because merely pursuing them is socially inflammatory and the results, even of well-conceived and well-executed studies, are likely to be misused. Whether this prospect raises special questions beyond those faced in research on toxic chemical substances or harmful disease vectors that might be inadvertently released is one the philosopher of social science needs to debate.

Beyond the normative issues to which social science is relevant, there is the further debate among philosophers of social science about whether claims in the social sciences are themselves explicitly, implicitly, inevitably evaluative, normative, prescriptive, or otherwise 'value laden'. Arguments for this claim often turn on the allegedly evaluative meaning of certain descriptive and explanatory concepts indispensable to varying social theories. For example, the term 'rational' has positive connotations, as do expressions like 'functional', or 'adaptational'. No matter what meaning is stipulated for these terms they may nevertheless convey attitudes or obstruct certain questions without the social scientist recognizing their normative role. More fundamentally, the very treatment by social science of institutions and norms as subjects of objective scientific exploration may unwittingly suggest the naturalness, inevitability and immutability of social arrangements which are in fact artificial, constructed and subject to negotiation. As noted above, it is the responsibility, some will hold, of social scientists to unmask the character of oppressive or exploitative institutions; this is made more difficult by the failure to recognize the implicit normative dimension of social theories and methods.

On a traditional view of the normative dimension of social science *qua* science there is a distinction between facts and values, and by scrupulousness about this distinction the social scientist *qua* scientist can and should avoid making normative claims implicitly or explicitly. The normative force of this claim rests on the view that scientists should be as objective as possible. For the value of scientific knowledge and its further accumulation is jeopardized by the appearance of partiality. Radically opposed to this view is the claim that objectivity is impossible in any science, social or natural, that 'knowledge' is a coercive term that obscures the partiality and negotiated social constructions of physical science, and in any case, as Kuhn is taken to have shown, there is no real accumulation or progress in the history of science. Ironically, on this radical view, the problem of normative versus positive theory is not at all a distinctive one for the philosophy of social science. Either it is a problem for the philosophy of all the sciences or for none of them.

See also: ECONOMICS, PHILOSOPHY OF; SOCIAL SCIENCE, CONTEMPORARY PHILOSOPHY OF; SOCIAL SCIENCE, HISTORY OF PHILOSOPHY OF

References and further reading

Beauchamp, T., Faden, R.R., Wallace, R.J. and Walters, L. (1982) *Ethical Issues in Social Science Research*, Baltimore, MD: Johns Hopkins University Press. (An introduction to moral problems of controlled inquiry.)

Churchland, P. (1981) 'Eliminative materialism and the propositional attitudes', *Journal of Philosophy* 78: 67–90. (Argues for elimination of intentional variables in explanation of behaviour.)

Dennett, D. (1969) *Content and Consciousness*, London: Routledge & Kegan Paul. (Influential treatment of the problem of intentionality in psychology.)

Durkheim, E. (1951) *The Rules of the Sociological Method*, New York: Free Press. (Arguments presented for holism and functionalism by the founder of empirical sociology.)

Friedman, M. (1953) *Essays in Positive Economics*, Chicago, IL: University of Chicago Press. (The *locus classicus* for instrumentalist accounts of social science.)

Geuss, R. (1981) *The Idea of Critical Theory*, Cambridge: Cambridge University Press. (An introduction to the role of reflexivity in critical theory's philosophy of social science.)

Harris, M. (1979) *Cultural Materialism*, New York: Random House. (Defends empiricist approaches in anthropology.)

Hausman, D. (1992) *The Inexact and Separate Science of Economics*, Cambridge: Cambridge University Press. (A complete treatment of the philosophical problems of economics, includes an introduction to the philosophy of science with a lengthy bibliography.)

Hempel, C. (1965) *Aspects of Scientific Explanation*, New York: Free Press. (A collection of influential essays in the philosophy of social and natural science.)

McIntyre, L. and Martin, M. (1994) *Readings in the Philosophy of Social Science*, Cambridge, MA: MIT Press. (The newest and most complete collection of important papers in the philosophy of social science.)

Neurath, O. (1941) 'Philosophy of social science', in *International Encyclopedia of Social Science*, Chicago, IL: University of Chicago Press. (An early logical positivist exposition.)

Popper, K. (1957) *The Poverty of Historicism*, London: Routledge & Kegan Paul. (An attack on historicism and anti-empiricist philosophies of social science, expounds Popper's doctrine of falsifiability.)

Rosenberg, A. (1988) *The Philosophy of Social Science*, Boulder, CO: Westview Press. (An introduction to the philosophy of social science.)

Skinner, B.F. (1953) *Science and Human Behavior*, New York: Macmillan. (A defence of behaviourism and eliminativism in psychology.)

Sober, E. (1993) *The Philosophy of Biology*, Boulder, CO: Westview Press. (An introduction to the philosophy of biology, with relevance to social science.)

Taylor, C. (1964) *The Explanation of Behaviour*, London: Routledge & Kegan Paul. (A defence of an anti-empiricist philosophy of social science.)

Weber, M. (1949) *The Methodology of the Social Sciences*, New York: Free Press. (A historically influential argument for compatibility of causal and intentional explanation in social science.)

Winch, P. (1958) *The Idea of a Social Science*, London: Routledge & Kegan Paul. (The earliest sustained application of Wittgenstein's views to attack the possibility of empirical social science.)

* Wittgenstein, L.J.J. (1953) *Philosophical Investigations*, ed. G.E.M. Anscombe and R. Rhees, trans. G.E.M. Anscombe, Oxford: Blackwell. (The most polished and worked over of all Wittgenstein's later work; it contains the presentation of his ideas on meaning and philosophical psychology with which he was most nearly satisfied.)

ALEX ROSENBERG

SOCIAL SCIENCES, PHILOSOPHY OF

Although some of the topics and issues treated in the philosophy of social science are as old as philosophy itself (for example, the contrast between nature and convention and the idea of rationality are dealt with by Aristotle), the explicit emergence of a subdiscipline of philosophy with this name is a very recent phenomenon, which in turn may itself have stimulated greater philosophical activity in the area. Clearly, this emergence is tied to the development and growth of the social sciences themselves.

Historical approach

There are, perhaps, four distinct ways in which to gain an understanding of the subdiscipline. These ways are, of course, complementary. First, just as with most other areas of philosophy, one might approach the philosophy of the social sciences historically, by studying major schools or philosophers of an earlier period. There is much to recommend this approach (see SOCIAL SCIENCE, HISTORY OF PHILOSOPHY OF). There are a number of classical texts (by Weber and Durkheim, for example) of which any interested student of the philosophy of the social sciences should be aware, much as there is in epistemology or ethics. This provides an interesting contrast with the philosophy of the natural sciences; far less could be said in favour of gaining an understanding of the latter in this way.

Compared with other areas of philosophy, the

history of the philosophy of the social sciences is somewhat truncated, since it can only begin properly with the earliest attempts at social science, in the late eighteenth and early nineteenth centuries, first in the Scottish Enlightenment and subsequently in Germany. Prior to this period, there had been speculation about the nature of society, some of it quite rich and rewarding (Hobbes and Vico provide two examples of this), but it is only in the period of the Scottish Enlightenment and after that writers begin to reflect the first systematic attempts to study and understand society.

There is no clear line of demarcation between philosophers of social science and of society on the one hand and social theorists on the other, especially in this early period. Conventionally, to select only a few examples, G.W.F. Hegel, Wilhelm Dilthey, F.H. Bradley and T.H. Green are considered to be examples of the former, and Adam Smith, Karl Marx, Émile Durkheim, and Max Weber, are considered as examples of the latter, but the line is sometimes somewhat arbitrary (see HEGEL, G.W.F.; MARX, K.; DILTHEY, W.; BRADLEY, F.H.; GREEN, T.H.; SMITH, A.; DURKHEIM, É.; WEBER, M.).

Problems

A second way in which to gain an understanding of the philosophy of social science is through the study of the issues and problems that these writers, and their contemporary counterparts, address (see SOCIAL SCIENCE, METHODOLOGY OF). Many of these problems arise in ordinary as well as in more scientific discussions of and thought about the social realm. It is not only social scientists who think about the social world; all of us do, a great deal of the time. Even in those cases in which the social scientist introduces neologisms, for example, 'demand curves' or 'anomie', they seem closely connected to, and sometimes only a refinement of, concepts already grasped by the lay person.

This nonscientific reflection arises quite apart from any specialized scientific work. It is, to a certain extent, misleading to think of the field as only the philosophy of the social *sciences*. Since so much of the motivation for critical discussion of the problems in this area comes from philosophical reflection on these quite ordinary modes of thought and understanding, the field should perhaps be called 'the philosophy of *society*', to reflect this nonscientific, as well as the scientific, interest in those problems.

Most of the things that social science is about, social structures (like families or society itself), norms and rules of behaviour, conventions, specific sorts of human action, and so on, are items that find a place in

the discourse of the ordinary lay person who has as good a grasp of common talk about social class and purchase, voting and banking, as does the social scientist. This raises, in a direct way, metaphysical questions about the nature of these things. Are these social structures anything more than just individuals and their interrelations? Many philosophers, in the grip of the ideal of the unity of science, have held out the prospect that social science can be derived from, and is therefore reducible to, psychology (the latter eventually being reducible to chemistry and physics). For such thinkers, the world is ultimately a simple place, with only many different ways in which to speak about it. Other thinkers have been struck by the reality and integrity of the social world, and how it seems to impress itself on the individual willy-nilly (see SOCIETY, CONCEPT OF; SOCIAL NORMS; HOLISM AND INDIVIDUALISM IN HISTORY AND SOCIAL SCIENCE).

What is an action, and how does it differ from the mere movement of one's body? It seems hard to say in what this difference consists in a way that remains plausible and true to what action is like. Whatever an action is, what makes some actions *social* actions? One might think that an action is social in virtue of its causal consequences on others. Another line of thought holds that an action is social in virtue of its intrinsic character, quite apart from the question of its effects. Much of the philosophical discussion of action arose in the philosophy of history, over the explanation of historically important action, but has now been absorbed into a separate area of philosophy, the theory of action (see HISTORY, PHILOSOPHY OF; ACTION; SOCIAL ACTION).

The alleged contrast between nature and convention occurs to those who think about humankind and its development, whether they be scientists and philosophers or not. Anyone who has travelled widely and noticed the social differences between peoples and cultures may have wondered whether all social practice was rational in its own terms, wherever found and no matter how apparently peculiar by our home-grown lights. Or perhaps, on the other hand, there are some universal standards of rationality, in the light of which evaluation of social practices and criticism of some of them can be mounted (see NATURE AND CONVENTION; RATIONALITY AND CULTURAL RELATIVISM; SOCIAL RELATIVISM).

The relationship between scientific theory and ordinary modes of thought is, of course, interactive, since many of the concepts or issues that have become part of ordinary lore have their roots in earlier scientific theory (our modern, and by most accounts, confused, concept of race might be an example of this; see RACE, THEORIES OF).

Another set of problems arise in thinking through

the nature of the social scientific enterprise itself. What standards must full explanation in social science meet? Causal explanation is a mode of explanation in natural science that is, relatively speaking, well understood. Explanations of a ritual or practice in society do not appear to be causal explanations, nor do explanations of human action. The first are often functional explanations (for example, a certain ritual exists because it produces such-and-such) and this appears to be an explanation of something by its effects rather than by its causes. Explanations of human action are intentional explanations, whereby an action is explained by the goal or end at which it is directed. This also appears not to be causal. But perhaps appearances are deceptive, and these can be recast as causal explanations after all (see EXPLANA-TION IN HISTORY AND SOCIAL SCIENCE; FUNCTION-ALISM IN SOCIAL SCIENCE).

Natural scientists believe that their work is ethically neutral. To be sure, their work can be put to good and bad uses, but this presumably reflects on the users rather than on the content of the science itself. The relationship between social science and the values of the social scientist seems far more immediate and direct than this, and this alleged contrast has been the subject for continuing discussion and debate (see VALUE JUDGMENTS IN SOCIAL SCIENCE).

Is social science like natural science in important ways? In the developed natural sciences, there are controlled experiments and predictions. Neither seem available to the social scientist. Natural scientists attempt to formulate the laws that govern the phenomena they study. Is this a reasonable goal for the social scientist? Certainly, there are not many candidate laws for the social sciences one can think of. Does the social scientist use statistical evidence in the same way as the natural scientist? (See EXPERIMENTS IN SOCIAL SCIENCE; SOCIAL SCIENCES, PREDICTION IN; SOCIAL LAWS; STATISTICS AND SOCIAL SCIENCE.) Finally, in natural science, we distinguish between theory and observation in a relatively sharp way, and we believe that a rational person should accept that theory which is best confirmed by observations. It is not clear that we can make the same distinction in the social sciences, nor that theory is supported by observation in just the same way. Our observations of the social world seem even more coloured by the theory we employ than is the case in the natural sciences (see THEORY AND OBSERVATION IN SOCIAL SCIENCES.)

Contemporary movements

A third way in which to approach the subject is through the study of either contemporary movements

and schools of philosophy, or specific philosophers, who bring a specific slant to the subdiscipline. Controversy marks the natural as well as the social sciences, but observers have noted that there seems to be even less consensus, even less of an agreed paradigm at any particular time, in the latter than in the former.

Critical reflection on society, or on social science, or both, is very different in France and Germany from the way it is in the English-speaking world. The problems are the same, but the traditions and the manner in which the discussions proceed are markedly distinctive. The hope is that each tradition may learn something from the other (see SOCIAL SCIENCE, CONTEMPORARY PHILOSOPHY OF; BEHAVIOURISM IN THE SOCIAL SCIENCES; CRITICAL REALISM; EVOLU-TIONARY THEORY AND SOCIAL SCIENCE; LÉVI-STRAUSS, C.; NATURALISM IN SOCIAL SCIENCE; POSITIVISM IN THE SOCIAL SCIENCES; POST-STRUC-TURALISM IN THE SOCIAL SCIENCES; SCIENTIFIC REALISM AND SOCIAL SCIENCE; SOCIOLOGY OF KNOWLEDGE; STRUCTURALISM IN SOCIAL SCIENCE; SYMBOLIC INTERACTIONISM; SYSTEMS THEORY IN SOCIAL SCIENCE; BOURDIEU, P.; MACINTYRE, A.; SCHÜTZ, A.).

Specific social sciences

Fourth and finally, one might approach the philo-sophy of the social sciences by studying the philo-sophical problems that arise specifically within each of the social sciences. Some, although not all, of the social sciences have thrown up philosophical indus-tries all their own. Economics is the most salient example. In many ways, it is the most developed of all the social sciences, and this may be the reason why some of the best-defined controversies in the philo-sophy of social science arise from within it. Questions about the philosophical foundations of economics touch on the philosophically central issues of rationality, choice and the nature of wants or desires and their connection with action (see ECONOMICS, PHILOSOPHY OF; SOCIAL CHOICE; RATIONAL CHOICE THEORY). But other social sciences have also given rise to specific problems, including history, psychology, sociology, and anthropology (see PSYCHOLOGY, THE-ORIES OF; SOCIOLOGY, THEORIES OF; ANTHROPOL-OGY, PHILOSOPHY OF).

See also: FEMINISM AND SOCIAL SCIENCE

References and further reading

Martin, M. and McIntyre, L. (eds) (1994) *Readings in the Philosophy of Social Science*, Cambridge, MA:

MIT Press. (A useful collection of recent and contemporary articles, grouped around some of the main issues in the philosophy of social science.)

Root, M. (1993) *Philosophy of Social Science*, Oxford: Blackwell. (Argues that some of the most prominent research programmes in the social sciences flout the ideal of moral and political philosophy.)

Ruben, D.-H. (1998) The Philosophy of Social Sciences, in A. Grayling (ed.), *Philosophy 2: Further Through the Subject*, Oxford: Oxford University Press, vol. 2. (A discussion of the main problems in the philosophy of social science, intended for the philosophy student. Assumes some prior knowledge of philosophy.)

DAVID-HILLEL RUBEN

SOCIAL SCIENCES, PREDICTION IN

Prediction is important in science for two reasons. First human beings have a practical interest in knowing the future. Therefore, all science is potentially predictive in the sense that its results may be used as a basis for expectations. Second, a test of our beliefs is the truth of the predictions we can derive from them. In the social sciences, however, predictions are often supposed to create specific philosophical and methodological problems, the roots of which are the following: the phenomena studied in the social sciences are so complex and so interrelated that it is practically impossible to formulate law-like generalizations about them; human beings are supposed to possess free will; and the predictions may themselves modify the phenomena predicted.

Some phenomena are deterministic; they obey invariable laws. Some other phenomena are stochastic; they obey laws that could be expressed only in statistical terms. Finally, some phenomena – most notably human actions – are claimed to be free. According to the incompatibilist philosophers, free actions are not subjects of either deterministic or stochastic laws (see FREE WILL §2).

As regards predictability, we should note that (1) predictability does not imply determinism, because we may have statistical predictions concerning stochastic phenomena. (2) nor does determinism imply predictability, for the following reasons: some phenomena are deterministic but chaotic in the sense that changes which are undetectably small can sometimes produce large changes; some phenomena are so complex that it is humanly impossible to describe all the relations

and interrelations relevant for predictions; and in some cases it is practically impossible to acquire the information relevant for making informed predictions. From (2) it follows that unpredictability does not imply freedom. All the limitations mentioned in (2) may be relevant in regard to the study of social phenomena. But they can also be relevant in other areas. For example, financial markets may function chaotically, but the same is true of meteorological phenomena. Individual human beings, as well as human societies, are extremely complex entities, but so are animals. Moreover, it is possible for phenomena having extremely complex internal structures to exhibit a predictable pattern in their general behaviour. We may be able to predict the movements of the whole without being able to describe or predict the movements of the parts. Some philosophers have claimed that we cannot find general laws of human societies because all societies are essentially open systems. Unlike in a laboratory experiment, or an astronomical observation, we cannot eliminate the possible influence of outside factors. Thus, we are never entitled to say that phenomena are caused by those particular factors we are experimenting with. Again, all this is equally true in many natural sciences (for example, in meteorology).

It seems that the only philosophical problem specifically relevant to social predictions is the question of free will. However, this supposed freedom does not prevent us making predictions in our everyday life. Usually, we predict without the help of any (systematic) scientific knowledge: we ascribe certain aims and beliefs to our fellow beings, derive rough predictions of how they are going to behave, and form our own expectations accordingly. Similarly, social scientists may postulate general motives, for example, profit maximization, and shared beliefs, for example, correct beliefs about present market prices, deriving useful predictions regarding general trends. Even if the postulates are not true in respect of every individual, individual idiosyncrasies may cancel each other out, or, in particular contexts, there may be pressures among individuals to conform to the postulates. For example, entrepreneurs who do not try to maximize their profits and to use adequate information are soon out of business. The structure of the choice situation may create a predictable pattern.

There is, however, one further problem peculiar to the social sciences only. Mutually held expectations are essential for our social life. Most institutions can work effectively only because people conform to certain predictable patterns, and they conform to these patterns partly because they expect that institutions (for example, banks, governments or courts) will work effectively. When forming expectations, human beings try to take into account information concerning the future, including the information produced by the social sciences. Thus, predictions about the future rate of inflation affect the actual rate of inflation by influencing the expectations of firms and trade unions. Social predictions may possess a self-modifying (reflexive) force: they may make themselves true or untrue. Social scientists may try to take into account the possible effect of their predictions, but the subjects of the predictions may, in turn, react to such attempts. It appears that in certain circumstances a social theory cannot describe and predict the consequences it has for the people it describes and predicts. This result does not presuppose a metaphysical notion of free will. People may react to the content of a theory T1 in a deterministic way, and this deterministic process can be predicted by another theory T2. T2 cannot predict its own effects, but they can be predicted by T3, and so on.

In some research contexts, the self-modifying potential of predictions can be ignored. First, some issues studied, for example, in psychology, are not really of a social nature. They are closely related to the physiological processes of human beings, setting the necessary conditions and limitations of human agency.

Second, in many cases the predictions produced by social scientists are not available or comprehensible to the subjects of the predictions, for various reasons. This solves the reflexivity problem, but only at an ethical cost. For it means that in such contexts, successful predictions presuppose an informationally superior position.

Third, the predicted social situation may be moving towards a unique equilibrium. Here, equilibrium is a technical notion, meaning that the relevant actors (individuals, firms, states and so on) do not simultaneously possess motive and ability to deviate from the predicted pattern. No new information can change the outcome. In a trivial case (for example, an idealized market situation), all or most agents have only a single feasible option.

The self-modifying effect is likely to appear in situations where no equilibria exist, or where there are several – for example, in imperfect markets, in multiparty politics and in multipolar international systems. In such contexts, the agents have an on-going motive to acquire information and to try to outguess each other's future actions. Hence, the ability of the social sciences to predict is dependent on the distribution of knowledge in societies.

See also: EXPLANATION IN HISTORY AND SOCIAL SCIENCE; SOCIAL LAWS

References and further reading

Bicchieri, C. (1987) 'Rationality and Predictability in Economics', *The British Journal for the Philosophy of Science* 38: 501–13. (A relatively technical critique of recent economic theories.)

Friedrichs, R.W. (1970) *A Sociology of Sociology*, New York: Free Press. (The sociological aspects of the prediction problem are discussed on pages 177–95.)

Goldman, A. (1970) *A Theory of Human Action*, Pinceton, NJ: Princeton University Press. (Chapter 6 provides an excellent discussion of the problems of prediction of human actions.)

Henschel, R.L. (1978) 'Self-altering Predictions', in J. Fobles (ed.), *Handbook of Futures Research*, Westport, CT: Greenwood Press, 99–123. (Contains an interesting discussion on the self-modifying effects of predictions; bibliography is excellent.)

—— (1982) 'The Boundary of the Self-fulfilling Prophecy and the Dilemma of Social Prediction', *The British Journal of Sociology* 33 (4): 510–28. (A discussion on the extent of the prediction problem and on the conditions under which it is *not* likely to emerge.)

Hutchison, T.W. (1977) *Knowledge and Ignorance in Economics*, Oxford: Blackwell. (A non-technical and polemical discussion.)

Lagerspetz, E. (1988) 'Reflexive Predictions and Strategic Actions', *Social Science Information* 27: 307–20. (Emphasizes the ethical and political implications of the problem.)

MacIntyre, A. (1981) *After Virtue: A Study in Moral Theory*, London: Duckworth, 2nd edn, 1985. (Chapter 8 of the book is a good philosophical introduction to the subject.)

Rosenberg, A. (1993) 'Scientific Innovation and the Limits of Social Scientific Prediction', *Synthèse* 97: 161–82. (Concentrates on Karl Popper's arguments, which are not discussed above, but relates them to our themes.)

Sen, A.K. (1986) 'Prediction and Economic Theory', *Proceedings of the Royal Society*, A 407: 3–23. (On the role of predictions in economics.)

EERIK LAGERSPETZ

SOCIAL THEORY AND LAW

Social theory embodies the claim that philosophical analyses, reflections on specific historical experience and systematic empirical observations of social conditions may be combined to construct theoretical explanations of the nature of society – that is, of patterned human social association in general and of the conditions that make this association possible and define its typical character. Social theory, in this sense, can be defined broadly as theory seeking to explain systematically the structure and organization of society and the general conditions of social order or stability and of social change. Since law as a system of ideas can also be thought of as purporting to specify, reflect and systematize fundamental normative structures of society, it has appeared as both a focus of interest for social theory and, in some sense, a source of competition with social theory in explaining the character of social existence.

The relation of legal thought to social theory is, thus, in important respects, a confrontation between competing general modes of understanding social relationships and the conditions of social order. In one sense, this confrontation is as old as philosophy itself. But as an element in modern philosophical consciousness it represents a gradual working-out in Western thought, over the past two centuries, of the implications of various 'scientific' modes of interpreting social experience, all in one way or another the legacy of Enlightenment ideas.

From the late eighteenth century and throughout the nineteenth century, criteria of 'scientific' rationality were carried into the interpretation of social phenomena through the development of social theory. These criteria also significantly influenced the development of modern legal thought. The classic social theory of the late nineteenth and early twentieth centuries, which established an enduring vocabulary of concepts for the interpretation of social phenomena, treated law as an object of social inquiry within its scope. It sought scientific understanding of the nature of legal phenomena in terms of broad systems of explanation of the general nature of social relationships, structures and institutions.

In the late twentieth century the relationship between social theory and law has been marked by fundamental changes both in the outlook of social theory and in forms of contemporary regulation. On the one hand, social theory has been subjected to wide-ranging challenges to its modern scientific pretensions. It has had to respond to scepticism about claims that social life can usefully be analysed in terms of historical laws, or authoritatively interpreted and explained in terms of founding theoretical principles. On the other hand, the inexorable expansion of Western law's regulatory scope and detail appears, sociologically, as largely uncontrollable by moral systems and relatively unguided by philosophical principles. Hence, in some postmodern interpretations, contemporary law is presented as a system of knowledge and interpretation of social life of great importance, yet one that has ultimately evaded the Enlightenment ambition systematically to impose reason and principle – codified by theory – on agencies of political and social power.

1 Civil society and modernity
2 Science of law and science of society
3 Law in classic social theory
4 Law and recent social theory
5 Images of contemporary law

1 Civil society and modernity

Social theory aims to develop systematic theoretical understandings of the nature of social phenomena or of 'society' treated as a specific object or focus of inquiry. Intellectual sources of social theory are found in speculations throughout the history of philosophy on the foundations of social order, the character of human association and the essence of human nature. Nevertheless, social theory as a distinct intellectual enterprise is best understood as originating with the Enlightenment. Emerging out of social philosophy, its concerns are closely implicated with general philosophical issues of individuality, rights, authority, responsibility and community. Its establishment as an intellectual field depended on three main developments: first, the identification of an analytically distinct field of the 'social'; second, the acceptance of the necessity of a grounding for social speculation in evidence about social experience in specific historical contexts; and, third, a conception of social change as theoretically explicable, suggesting a qualitative differentiation between 'modern' and 'pre-modern' societies or characteristics of social life.

The identification of a distinct field of the 'social' is associated with the conceptualization, especially derived from Hegelian thought, of civil society as an autonomous realm of social interaction, differentiation, organization and institutions. One consequence of this conceptualization was to identify such institutions as contract, property and social class and the processes and effects of the administration of civil justice as foci for theoretical analysis, not in terms of their ethical implications or their significance for political theory but as components of a cohesive social fabric requiring explanation in terms of its integrative structure and historical dynamics.

The specification of the 'social' also entailed the development of distinctive approaches to analysis and, eventually, the establishment of an intellectual enterprise of sociology claiming its own theory, methods and aims. Beginnings of these processes can be seen in Montesquieu's L'Esprit des lois (The Spirit of the Laws) (1748) which attempts to link typical social and political structures with characteristics of the types of natural and historical environments in which these structures emerge. Climate, geography and population size are related to law and political institutions, and law is seen as a consequence of natural conditions and the culture they inspire as well as a force acting upon them (see MONTESQUIEU, C. §3).

A further element essential to the project of social theory but not present in Montesquieu is a conception of modernity; that is, a conception of a general historical transition from characteristic earlier forms of society or of social relationships to a specifically modern form, which could be generalized as both qualitatively distinct from earlier forms and also typical of the most advanced or developed actual societies of the present. The theme of such a transition pervades the major literature of nineteenth-century social theory. One of its most striking expressions is Ferdinand Tönnies' distinction (1887) between *Gemeinschaft* and *Gesellschaft*; that is, between, on the one hand, multi-faceted, long-term, often emotionally or traditionally sanctioned social relationships typical of close-knit community or family life and, on the other hand, instrumental, specific and limited, often short-term and frequently changing social relationships based on agreement or the negotiation of rapidly changing patterns of social interaction. Tönnies' concepts abstractly present ubiquitous elements of social relationships unrelated to any particular historical context, but the inspiration for their formulation was undoubtedly a sense of the increasing prominence of *Gesellschaft* relations in the conditions of mobile, diverse and dynamic 'modern' society.

Modernity is characterized variously in the most prominent forms of social theory developed by the end of the nineteenth century: for example, in Herbert Spencer's emphasis on functional differentiation and reintegration in modern society; in Émile Durkheim's characterization of complex industrial societies as morally diverse yet also morally integrated by functional interdependence; in Karl Marx's identification of the anatomy and pathology of capitalist society as a distinct historical form; and in Max Weber's ambivalent exploration of the progress of numerous forms of rationalization culminating in the bureaucratized technical consciousness and morally compartmentalized social environments of late nineteenth-century Western capitalist societies.

Many of these presentations of modernity in social theory rely on analyses of law and legal history. Law's doctrinal history provided documentary materials that could be treated as empirical sources in plotting trajectories of social change. Both Tönnies and Durkheim used legal materials – including the jurist Henry Maine's evolutionary legal history (see JURISPRUDENCE, HISTORICAL §2) – extensively in devel-

oping their accounts of the contrast between social modernity and pre-modernity. And Weber's discussion of political and economic structures and modes of thought characteristic of developed capitalism is strongly flavoured by his sophisticated understanding of the nature of modern Western legal thought.

2 Science of law and science of society

A further condition for the emergence of social theory was an emphasis on the need for systematic empirical inquiry about social phenomena and an explicit conception of the nature of scientific method in social analysis (see SOCIAL SCIENCES, PHILOSOPHY OF §1; POSITIVISM IN THE SOCIAL SCIENCES §2). Here it is important to see both a parallel with developing ideas in legal analysis and a challenge to those ideas. Long before the idea of a rational 'science of society' began to establish itself (especially through the writings of Henri de Saint-Simon and Auguste COMTE early in the nineteenth century), legal thought presented itself as a professional 'artificial reason' authoritatively conceptualizing social reality. English common law thought, as elaborated by such as Edward Coke and Matthew Hale in the seventeenth century, embodies conceptions of community that underlie legal doctrine's interpretations of the normative structure of society.

Late eighteenth-century and nineteenth-century movements for scientific rationalism in legal thought did not necessarily suggest the need for theory that would locate law in a wider terrain of empirical social knowledge. The initial demand was, at least in the English context, for more systematic conceptual analysis of legal doctrine than that allowed by the pragmatic methods of judge-made common law. Nevertheless, utilitarian reformers demanded that romantic or mythical common law conceptions of community and of an ancient unchanging constitutional order be replaced with more realistic understandings of the nature of modern government, of the sources of legal authority and of the political processes of creation and application of law.

Comte's identification of a specific science of society, which in 1838 he named sociology, is almost contemporaneous with the jurist John Austin's powerfully influential outline of a modern 'science of law', requiring no support from the moralistic speculations of natural law theory (see AUSTIN, J.). The appeal to 'science' made by many nineteenth-century jurists was usually to some general model of rigorous, rational, objective and systematic thought, such as geometry. The contribution of an emerging social theory, during the nineteenth century, was to help bring into legal analysis a self-consciousness about empirical resources for legal speculation and, eventually, a limited recognition that many resources necessary to an adequate theoretical understanding of law must be found, beyond the scope of the lawyer's traditional structures of reason, in systematically ordered data derived from the observation and recording of social experience.

Social theory in the late nineteenth and twentieth centuries shows an increasing attention to the dilemma of the meaning of 'science' in social analysis. The Durkheimian injunction at the end of the nineteenth century to treat social facts as if they were things (objects of science) to be analysed by means of the observational techniques of natural science (see DURKHEIM, É. §2) was confronted and challenged by contemporaneous claims that the methods of the natural and the social sciences are necessarily radically opposed and that the latter require distinctive methods of interpreting the subjective meaning of social acts for those involved in them if the patterns of social life are to be intelligible to the scientist (see WEBER, M. §3).

The often-quoted dictum that sociology was born in a state of hostility to law can be understood as a recognition that in establishing its empirically-oriented, systematic, generalizing modes of analysis of social life, social theory challenged the prerogatives of such established enterprises of social interpretation as those of law. It sought to replace the normative, evaluative social interpretations that legal analysis offered with explanatory, descriptive and ostensibly non-judgmental analyses of social phenomena, including legal phenomena.

In so far as social theory founded itself on conceptions of modernity and sought to explain patterns of social development theoretically, it challenged common law assumptions about the timeless stability of the community whose immanent normative framework the common lawyers purported to understand and interpret. And, in its unending questioning of the nature of 'science' in social analysis, social theory provided material that would eventually challenge lawyers' claims to possess a secure and autonomous 'science of law'. As long as law was admitted to be a social phenomenon, legal theory would eventually have to take account of debates on social interpretation and analysis that social theory presented. In this way, the advent of modernity in law and in social theory raised the possibility that legal science would become dependent on and subordinate to social theory.

3 Law in classic social theory

The bodies of social theory that have exerted most long-term and widespread influence in social analysis and still provide the main vocabulary of concepts for considering the social character of modern Western law are the systems of thought associated with Karl Marx, Émile Durkheim and Max Weber (see MARXISM, WESTERN). Their contribution to legal scholarship is especially significant because each devotes considerable attention to law within a wider project of social theory, and because each views law, at least in part, as comprising distinctive systems of doctrine or modes of reasoning. They thus indicate the prospect of directly confronting, in social theory, juristic understandings of the nature and significance of legal doctrine.

In these respects, the contributions of this classic social theory to legal scholarship are broader than is suggested by its use in much of the research in sociology of law. Empirical sociology of law is often behaviourally oriented (focusing on the explanation of activity in legal settings – for example, police practices – rather than on legal discourse or doctrine itself). It tends to be strongly influenced by the present organization of social science disciplines and therefore to reflect their perspectives. Partly as a consequence of this organization which largely excludes law, treating it as an independent and external discipline, sociology of law is often viewed as peripheral by the social science disciplines (especially academic sociology and anthropology) to which it relates. At the same time, sociology of law's respect for disciplinary boundaries of academic social science has often deterred it from engaging effectively with the disciplinary outlook of lawyers and the concerns of legal philosophy.

Marxist theory's main influence on legal analysis has been to highlight the need to relate legal doctrine and legal thought systematically to specific social interests which law promotes and to see law as a focus of political struggle often obscured by the technicality of professional legal discourse. While the link between law and social class interests was recognized long before Marx wrote, Marxist theory has focused attention on the devices by which law's class character may be obscured. It radically challenges the idea that law can attain a level of principled generality that gives it a moral and political autonomy above the endless struggle and compromise of conflicting economic and social interests. Marxist theory does not generally engage with the arguments over legal principle and legal foundations that legal philosophy pursues. Rather it regards legal philosophy's moral arguments as being largely conducted on the terrain of ideology. Marxist social theory's most important contribution to legal analysis is the effort to develop a coherent theory of the nature of ideology; a theory that can be used consistently to relate patterns of legal ideas to broader social, economic and political developments while also explaining the mechanisms and conditions under which legal discourse in advanced capitalist societies consistently proclaims its own moral, intellectual and political autonomy from the conflicting social forces that it purports to regulate.

By contrast, Weber, trained in law and viewing his legal studies as central to his overall project of interpreting the social character of Western capitalism, emphasized aspects of modern law different from the mystificatory or ideological elements and repressive structures that Marx had treated as essential. For Weber, modern law's importance lies primarily in its distinctive forms of rationality, which correspond to certain rational requirements of modern Western state structures. This rationality also underpins forms of purposive social action which are especially highly developed in and important to modern capitalist societies, and it contributes to the stability and legitimacy of modern political systems. Weber's acute sensitivity to changing forms of legal reasoning and decision-making allows him to provide important insights into the social and political conditions of existence of the *Rechtsstaat* (see RULE OF LAW (RECHTSSTAAT) §1). Unlike Marx, who views legal ideas consistently from the external standpoint of a demystifier and critic of ideology, Weber interprets these ideas in lawyers' terms, understanding both their social importance and the technical processes by which they evolve. Yet he contextualizes this interpretation, explaining, for example, intimate relationships between changing forms of legal reasoning and conditions for the expansion of capitalistic economic activity; and between these legal forms and the kinds of legitimacy claims that political and other authorities are able to make in specific historical conditions.

Because Weber's social theory is informed by a deeper understanding of the technicalities of legal thought than is Marx's, it offers a more nuanced view of the ambiguities of legal modernity. Its complexity of outlook and its ambivalence about modernity in general, and about the rationalization processes at work in modern law, also make the consequences of Weberian social theory for legal philosophy's concerns harder to define than is the case with Marxist theory. In general, despite its richness and a large secondary literature on its legal aspects, Weber's work still remains insufficiently assimilated in legal scholarship. The explanation lies partly in his methods, which reject the possibility of discovering scientific laws in history and celebrate in often dense, much-qualified argument the variety of perspectives that can be brought to light by using provisional, pragmatically chosen interpretive concepts. Beyond this, however, Weber poses profound challenges – rather like Maine in an earlier era – to the jurist to ignore disciplinary demarcations and recognize law's place as one strand of understandings in a vast, complex, cultural matrix of values and beliefs, modes of reasoning and interpretation.

Among the classic social theorists of law, Durkheim has so far exerted least direct influence on legal theory, perhaps because the emphasis of his legal thought, with its almost complete silence on questions about the relations of law and power (social, economic or political), has seemed naïve to legal scholars who absorbed some of the claims of Marx or Weber about the political or economic conditions of existence of law. The emphasis of Durkheim's legal theory is on law's intimate relations with morality and on the problem of defining the moral foundations of law in modern, secular, functionally and socially differentiated societies. In these societies, shared values, if they can be held to exist, are necessarily greatly limited in scope and significance by comparison with the situation in simpler, more socially uniform and close-knit societies, or those where strong and universal religious commitment underpins unifying social values.

Law was an important focus of study for Durkheim and his school of associates but the more limited impact of his ideas on legal theory by comparison with those of Marx and Weber is understandable in so far as the Durkheimian approach seemed to deny what legal scholars, no less than social analysts, came to sense as one of the major characteristics of modernity – the disintegration of moral unities and the emergence of law as a mechanism by which modern society might endlessly remake itself. The Durkheimian idea of law as a reflection of moral conditions has seemed less appropriate than Marxist and Weberian perceptions of law as a shifting element in complex articulations of economic and political interests in rapidly changing modern society. It has generally seemed more useful to view law as an instrument of political action and a system of ideas integrated with dynamic social forces determining the pace and direction of change and the conditions of social stability.

4 Law and recent social theory

During the last decades of the twentieth century, social theory increasingly rejected or radically modified the three assumptions or claims – a distinct realm of the 'social', distinctive 'scientific' methods of analysis of social phenomena, and the experience of modernity as the ever-present context of analysis – underpinning its original development. This phase of the relationship between social theory and Western legal thought is characterized by a more ambiguous theoretical recognition of the field of the 'social', by a widespread hesitancy about theoretically defending not only distinctive methods of social analysis but also the validity of the social knowledge that they produce, and by a correspondingly greater difficulty in identifying a distinct field of social theory. Thus, relationships between legal scholarship and social theory are increasingly replaced by complex connections between legal theory and various theoretical projects associated with a wide range of intellectual traditions that are not unified by any shared conception of the nature or scope of the 'social' as a research focus.

These developments can be considered in terms of their impact on legal analysis. Of all forms of social theory, Marxist theory probably has had the most direct influence on the study of modern law. Its appeal has depended on its claim to provide a materialist explanation of legal developments; an explanation that showed them as the predictable outcome of a theoretically explicable historical process. Radical legal scholarship in various Western countries, especially from the 1970s, used Marxist theory to develop the idea of law as a site of political struggle, and especially of ideological struggle, following the insights of the Marxist philosophers Antonio Gramsci and Louis Althusser.

The idea of law as a site of ideological conflict, and more generally an emphasis on law's rhetorical significance and its power to shape consciousness, has been retained and developed in current radical or critical legal theory. But, reflecting recent tendencies in social theory, critical approaches in contemporary legal scholarship – in no way limited to those associated with the international Critical Legal Studies movement – now typically resist any idea of objective laws of history or general long-run mechanisms of social change. While ideology remains an important concept, ideology is not to be considered as a distinct object of social analysis but rather as an aspect of intersubjective practices. The idea of society – or any other large-scale social phenomenon – as an object of inquiry has been widely discarded in favour of the study of specific social and political practices and the rhetorics (in which legal ideas often play a prominent part) that accompany them.

Many related tendencies in contemporary social theory are encapsulated in these kinds of scepticism. A distrust of what J.-F. Lyotard (1979) has called 'grand narratives' – theories or perspectives purporting to encapsulate in general terms large swathes of human experience – is founded on a recognition that the ultimate validity of these narratives is necessarily untestable, as well as on a widespread conviction that knowledges adequate to confront the complexities and variety of social experience will necessarily be local rather than general. More specifically, the idea of 'science' as a mark of appropriate social analysis has lost much of its resonance and become associated – perhaps unjustly – with positivist social science and with a lack of sensitivity to the unquantifiable, subjective, transient, immanent but powerful cultural ambiences of social life. It has been associated with the contested claim that clear lines can be drawn between valid and invalid social knowledges, or between truth and falsity in interpretation of social life and social phenomena. Naturalistic models of science have been displaced in favour of models of practice – hermeneutics, literary interpretation, arts of rhetoric, aesthetics, semiotics and linguistic analysis – that offer the prospect of escape from social-scientific protocols of testability and relevance, and promise access to ineffable knowledges that capture the intricacy and indeterminacy of contemporary social experience.

In legal analysis, the issue of the nature of interpretation of legal doctrine remains central and it does so in conditions in which legal regulation proliferates inexorably, assuming a very wide variety of forms. As legal scholarship has accommodated itself to the increasing difficulty of portraying law as an integrated doctrinal system, its concern has focused more sharply on problems of understanding practices of interpretation of doctrine in these conditions. Classic social theory offered, in the main, accounts of the social origins and consequences of particular historical interpretations of legal materials. But it is often charged with failing to explore legal interpretive or discursive processes themselves. Hence literary theory and other bodies of ideas concerned with the nature of interpretation and its contexts have tended to usurp space previously occupied by social theory as a resource for supplementing and illuminating legal inquiry.

5 Images of contemporary law

The most important forms of late twentieth-century social theory that have been imported into legal scholarship have achieved influence mainly because they relate directly to contemporary problems of legal analysis in grappling with law's perceived unprincipled doctrinal complexity and bulk. Michel Foucault's writings describe the development of particular sociological and psychological discourses that have brought new forms of scientific rationality into governmental regulatory practices (see FOUCAULT, M.). Foucault sees this development as part of the very process that, by merging disciplinary power with claims to expert knowledge, has created the immense diversity of contemporary regulation and made the idea of legal sovereignty sociologically problematic. Law, which Foucault treats as the coercive instrument of sovereign authority, has found its prerogatives of social control engulfed and usurped by numerous new regulatory forms and mechanisms that gain their authority specifically from technical knowledge and practice, developed especially in the social and human (for example, psychiatric) sciences.

Other writers emphasize contemporary law's embodiment in systems that not only float free of the moral groundings that Durkheim sought for legal regulation, but also confound 'modern' views of law as a steering mechanism of social life. Thus, Niklas Luhmann (1989) insists that the complex differentiation of society into a range of distinct, self-sustaining systems of communication condemns law to inhabit only its own discursive system, rather than to have the ability to steer all of society's systems – economic, scientific, cultural, political, for example – in the way that modernity's aspirations for rational government proposed.

Contemporary social theory's image of law and society tends to be one of fragmentation and diversity and of the ungroundedness of social knowledge; an image of specific social spheres governed by values and understandings that have no foundations except in the experience and perspectives of the local milieux in which they arise. The old, 'modern' project of a science of society is seen as embodying untenable assumptions about the generalizability of social experience, and about the possibility of agreement on truth claims underpinning universal systematic knowledge of the nature of society. Thus, the tenets of modernity have increasingly been replaced by postmodern conceptions of law and society (see POSTMODERNISM).

It would, however, be wrong to see the Enlightenment project of social theory as dead. Jürgen Habermas' highly influential work has, in large part, been concerned to find the basis of an underlying rational and moral foundation of social life – in his terms, a communicative rationality – despite the recognition that, in many vital respects, the fragmentation of social life in contemporary Western societies into disparate systems has destroyed possibilities for this kind of moral and rational grounding (see HABERMAS, J. §4; COMMUNICATIVE RATIONALITY; LEGAL REASONING AND INTERPRETATION §4). Habermas' analysis of law treats it as precariously balanced between its technical role in mediating economic, political and other systems within society and its moral potential as a set of institutions

expressing the values and understandings that arise in the lived experience and interactions of individuals.

Whether or not Habermas' approach is the most appropriate means of pursuing the search for general theory postulating an underlying rationality of legal and social experience, there are good grounds for claiming that this search is unlikely to cease with a postmodern recognition of its complexity and contradictions. Nor is the invocation of science in the interpretation of social phenomena necessarily rendered inappropriate by critiques of positivist science, 'scientific' interpretations of history, or other kinds of 'grand narratives'. The search for a science of society applicable to legal analysis is best understood as an ongoing commitment to make explicit the partial character of all existing understandings of social (including legal) phenomena and to subject these understandings to unending systematic questioning in the light of broadening social observation and ongoing historical experience. Viewed in this way legal and social theory remain interdependent and the project of social theory appears no less vital, if very much more complex and ambiguous and less coloured by optimism, than in the heyday of the classic social theorists.

See also: CRITICAL LEGAL STUDIES §§3–4; LAW, PHILOSOPHY OF; LEGAL DISCOURSE

References and further reading

Cain, M. and Hunt, A. (eds) (1979) *Marx and Engels on Law*, London: Academic Press. (Collects and introduces Marx's and Engels' essential texts on law.)

Foucault, M. (1975) *Surveiller et punir: naissance de la prison*, Paris: Gallimard; *Discipline and Punish*, trans. A. Sheridan, London: Allen Lane, 1977. (Presents Foucault's analysis of aspects of disciplinary regulation exemplified by the emergence of the prison.)

Habermas, J. (1986) 'Law as Medium and Law as Institution', in G. Teubner (ed.), *Dilemmas of Law in the Welfare State*, Berlin: de Gruyter. (Sets out a view of law in terms of Habermas' developed social theory.)

Kelly, D.R. (1990) *The Human Measure: Social Thought in the Western Legal Tradition*, Cambridge, MA: Harvard University Press. (Explores interpretations of the character of society developed through the traditions of Western legal thought.)

* Luhmann, N. (1989) 'Law as a Social System', *Northwestern University Law Review* 83: 136–50. (Outlines Luhmann's view of the social character of law as a communication system.)

Lukes, S. and Scull, A. (eds) (1983) *Durkheim and the Law*, Oxford: Martin Robertson. (Collects and introduces many of Durkheim's essential texts on law.)

* Lyotard, J.-F. (1979) *La Condition postmoderne: rapport sur le savoir*, Paris: Éditions de Minuit; *The Postmodern Condition: A Report on Knowledge*, trans. G. Bennington and B. Massumi, Manchester: Manchester University Press, 1984. (A *locus classicus* of claims about the status and situation of knowledge and theory in postmodernity.)

* Montesquieu, C. de (1748) *L'Esprit des lois* (*The Spirit of the Laws*), trans. T. Nugent, London: Collier Macmillan, 1949. (A pioneer text of the emerging project of social theory, reinterpreting established structures of Western legal thought. This edition contains an important introduction by Franz Neumann.)

* Tönnies, F. (1887) *Community and Association*, trans. C.P. Loomis, London: Routledge & Kegan Paul, 1955. (Develops the contrast between *Gemeinschaft* and *Gesellschaft* referred to in §1 above.)

Weber, M. (1922) *Wirtschaft und Gesellschaft* (*Economy and Society*), trans. E. Fischoff *et al.*, Berkeley, CA: University of California Press, 1978. (Weber's posthumous *magnum opus*, including his extensive writings on sociology of law.)

ROGER COTTERRELL

SOCIALISM

While socialist ideas may retrospectively be identified in many earlier forms of protest and rebellion against economic injustice and political oppression, socialism both as a relatively coherent theoretical doctrine and as an organized political movement had its origins in early nineteenth-century Europe, especially in Britain, France and Germany. It was, above all, a critical response to early industrial capitalism, to an unregulated market economy in which the means of production were privately owned and propertyless workers were forced to sell their labour power to capitalists for often meagre wages. The evils of this system seemed manifest to its socialist critics. Not only was the relationship between workers and capitalists inherently exploitative, and the commodification of labour an affront to human dignity, but it generated widespread poverty and recurrent unemployment, massive and unjust inequalities of wealth and economic power, degrading and soul-destroying work, and an increasingly atomized and individualistic society.

Socialists were not alone in criticizing some of these features of industrial capitalism and its accompanying ideology of economic liberalism. In particular, antipathy towards individualism was also a characteristic of conservative thought. But whereas conservatives found their inspiration in the hierarchically structured organic communities of the past, and were deeply hostile to the political radicalism of the French Revolution, socialists looked forward to new forms of community consistent with the ideals of liberty, equality and fraternity. For them, the evils of capitalism could be overcome only by replacing private with public or common ownership of the means of production, abolishing wage labour and creating a classless society where production geared to capitalist profits gave way to socially organized production for the satisfaction of human needs. In such a society, the human potential for a genuinely 'social' mode of existence would be realized, with mutual concern for others' wellbeing rather than unbridled pursuit of self-interest, with cooperation for common ends rather than competition for individual ones, and with generosity and sharing rather than greed and acquisitiveness – a truly human community.

For most nineteenth-century socialist theorists, the historic task of creating such a society was assigned to the organized industrial working class; most notably by Marx, the pre-eminent figure in the history of socialism. It was Marx who (along with Engels) provided the socialist movement not only with a theoretically sophisticated economic analysis of capitalism and a biting critique of its social consequences, but also, through his scientific, materialist theory of historical development, with the confident belief that the inherent contradictions and class antagonisms of capitalism would eventually give birth to a socialist society.

In marked contrast to such earlier optimism, contemporary socialists are faced with the continued resilience of capitalist societies and the collapse of at least nominally socialist regimes in the USSR and elsewhere, regimes in which state ownership and centralized planning have been accompanied by political repression and economic failure. For those who reject the idea that a suitably regulated form of welfare capitalism is the most that can be hoped for, the task is to construct some alternative model of a socialist economy which is preferable to this yet avoids the evils of centralized state socialism.

1 Defining socialism
2 Efficiency, planning and markets
3 Wellbeing and the human good
4 Democracy, power and freedom
5 Distributive justice
6 The future of socialism

1 Defining socialism

The term 'socialism' was first used by Owenites in Britain and by Saint-Simonians in France in the 1820s and 1830s, and soon became widely adopted to refer both to a body of ideas critical of capitalism and to the future society that would or should replace it. But disputes about the meaning of 'socialism' – itself sometimes contrasted with 'communism', at other times taken to include it as a subcategory (see COMMUNISM) – have been endemic to its history, even more so than with its two main ideological counterparts, liberalism and conservatism. An enormous variety of theoretical positions and political movements have been termed 'socialist', by proponents and critics alike. Particular versions may be indicated by some qualifying term – as in state socialism, market socialism, guild socialism, revolutionary socialism, scientific socialism, ethical socialism, even national socialism (fascism); but there is no agreed classification of types since the relevant basis for this is itself subject to dispute. For some, what is crucial is the political means through which the desired future is to be achieved – for example, revolution or reform; for others, the specific nature of socialist economic institutions – for example, state planning or decentralized producer democracy; and so on.

An especially significant issue is whether socialism is to be defined normatively or institutionally: in terms of a set of values or ideals which socialists aim to realize, and which provide the basis for their critique of capitalism; or of the specific character of the economic institutions of a socialist society. The latter option has the obvious disadvantage of leaving unmentioned just why this institutional form should be seen as preferable to capitalism, and what makes it a system worth fighting for. The former option, by leaving the institutional requirements for socialism entirely unspecified, makes it a purely empirical question whether, as many who are now termed 'social democrats' would claim, capitalism can be modified so as to realize socialist values: there would then be no logical contradiction in calling such a capitalist society 'socialist'. But given the socialist tradition's opposition to capitalism on the grounds that no such modification is possible, it seems preferable to regard this social democratic thesis, if true, as a refutation of socialism, rather than as consistent with it (see SOCIAL DEMOCRACY).

So it seems best to include in the definition of socialism both normative and institutional elements. For the socialist, the economic institutions of capitalism embody certain features and/or generate certain consequences that are objectionable from the standpoint of certain values; and there are possible alternative forms of economic organization which would either fully realize those values, or at least be markedly preferable to capitalism when judged in these terms. This, of course, is little more than a definitional schema, and leaves room for many varieties of socialism with respect both to the specific values involved and the specific form which a socialist economy might take.

On the latter question, while socialists have typically argued for the replacement of private by social, public or common ownership of the means of production, they have differed about what exactly this should involve – ownership by the state, by functional associations or local communities, by the members of producer cooperatives, and so on – and indeed about whether it is ownership or control that is crucial. Likewise, different solutions to the problems of economic coordination and allocation have been proposed: centralized planning by the state, decentralized planning, or even a market system shorn of its distinctively capitalist property relations. These different proposals are themselves often related to different views as to precisely what it is about capitalism that is objectionable and/or causally responsible for its ills: whether all relations of market exchange are undesirable, or only those involving the sale and purchase of labour power; whether it is private ownership of the means of production that is chiefly responsible for unjust inequalities in the distribution of economic goods, or the operation of a competitive market; and so on.

On the former question, of the specific character of socialist values, perhaps the main source of variation is the attitude taken towards political liberalism (see LIBERALISM). Some socialists have seen their task as engaging in an immanent critique of liberal democracy, broadly endorsing its declared values of freedom and equality but trying to show that their distinctively liberal interpretation is unduly narrow and restrictive: for example, by arguing for the extension of individual rights to include social and economic ones, and of democracy to include control over economic decisions. From this standpoint, liberal democracy is to be transcended – in the Hegelian sense of 'going beyond yet preserving' – rather than totally rejected; and the ideal of community is understood to involve harmonious relations between individuals who respect and enjoy one another's freedom. For others, by contrast, political liberalism – including its emphasis on the rule of law – is no more than an ideological facade of capitalism, so that, for example, its conception of legally enforceable individual rights has no place in a socialist society; and the value of community is understood in a more holistic manner.

With these broad points about the definition and

variations of socialism in mind, we can proceed to examine some of the main arguments for socialism and the critical responses to these, focusing in turn on debates about economic efficiency, human wellbeing, democracy and power, and distributive justice. While the case for socialism typically begins by attributing various ills to capitalism, it depends also on being able to show that there is some alternative system in which these would be absent or greatly reduced. Correspondingly, critics of socialism may deny either that the supposed ills are properly regarded as such, or that they are attributable to capitalism intrinsically rather than to contingent features of particular capitalist societies; and/or they may argue that the proposed socialist alternative fails to overcome these ills, or that it does so only at the cost of producing further ones of its own.

2 Efficiency, planning and markets

Socialist critics of capitalism have frequently pointed to its economic failings. Its reliance on anarchic market forces makes it liable to cycles of booms and slumps, subjects workers to recurrent periods of unemployment and permanent insecurity, and fails systematically to make effective use of human and natural resources. For all its dynamism in producing goods to satisfy increasingly exotic consumer preferences, it leaves many basic needs unmet. It underprovides public goods, cannot incorporate the social costs of economic activity and is destructive of environmental and other preconditions of long term economic development. For many socialists the solution has been seen to lie in a centrally planned economy in which resources can be effectively and rationally directed to satisfy human needs while also meeting other social and ethical objectives.

This case against the market and in support of planning has been met by three main kinds of argument: neoclassical, motivational and epistemic. Neoclassical economic theorists claim that a market economy is demonstrably 'efficient' in the sense of being Pareto-optimal: the outcomes it produces cannot be departed from without at least some individual(s) experiencing a reduced level of preference satisfaction (see ECONOMICS AND ETHICS §3). Admittedly this can be shown only for 'ideal' markets: for example, where there are no public goods or externalities. But such cases of (actual) 'market failure', it is claimed, can be dealt with either by limited forms of state intervention, or by assigning property rights to currently unowned goods and resources.

The motivational argument is that socialism must fail because it makes unrealistic demands on the potential altruism of economic agents. Workers must be expected to perform their tasks without the promise of differential material rewards, and planners to put aside their own interests in making economic decisions. But humans are by nature primarily self-interested beings: the supply of altruism is strictly limited and cannot be relied upon as the basis for economic organization. The market takes advantage of this fact by providing incentives for workers and managers that ensure the allocation of resources to those spheres of production where they will be most beneficially employed. Without such incentives, socialist alternatives to the market will inevitably fail.

The epistemic argument, developed in the Austrian school of economics and especially by Hayek, is that only the market can solve the economic problem of ignorance (see HAYEK, F.A. VON §2). This problem is due to the division of knowledge in society – its dispersal among different economic agents; and to the practical nature of much of this knowledge (knowledge 'how' rather than knowledge 'that'), which cannot be articulated in propositional form, and hence cannot in principle be acquired by a centralized planning agency. Thus no economic plan can gain access to and utilize all the knowledge relevant to economic decisions. By contrast, the price mechanism manages to distribute the knowledge relevant for economic coordination while allowing individual agents to rely on their own 'local' knowledge in the decisions that concern them.

Two main responses to these arguments may be made by socialists. The first is broadly to accept them, but to argue that they do not amount to a defence of capitalism but only of the market, which may itself take either capitalist or non-capitalist forms. This is the line taken by market socialists. The market is, ceteris paribus, the most efficient and dynamic economic mechanism, but it can be constructed in a form compatible with socialism by eliminating its distinctively capitalist features, notably private ownership in the means of production and wage labour. Among numerous versions of market socialism, probably the closest to traditional socialist aspirations involves social ownership in the form of workers' cooperatives whose assets are either directly owned by their members or leased to them by the state.

The second response is to challenge those arguments for the economic superiority of the market. For example, the neoclassical concept of efficiency may be criticized for defining this in relation to the satisfaction of individual wants or preferences, whatever their specific content or rationale. To show that markets are efficient in this sense is to show very little: it ignores the distinction between wants and needs, and fails to discriminate between preferences in terms of their contribution to human flourishing or wellbeing.

To the motivational argument that socialism makes unrealistic demands on altruism, there are several possible replies. One is to say that egoism is not a part of human nature, but the product of living in a capitalist society: a far greater degree of altruism can be expected in the different institutional context of socialism, either because such altruism is itself natural to humans, but inhibited by capitalism, or because human motivations are highly malleable in this respect. Alternatively, the ways in which self-interest and altruism are typically conceived and contrasted in these debates may be challenged. Actions oriented towards the wellbeing of others, and the relationships within which these take place, are often themselves a significant source of wellbeing to those concerned (see HUMAN NATURE §3). The kinds of self-interest the market relies upon are unduly narrow and restrictive in character: socialism does not require self-sacrificial forms of altruism, but instead makes possible the satisfaction of a more extensive and fulfilling range of interests. But the problem remains of how workers in a non-market economy are to be motivated to move to where they are most needed.

Against the epistemic argument for the market it may be objected that the market's informational virtues are much exaggerated. The price mechanism by no means distributes all the information relevant for economic coordination: indeed competitive pressures often generate disincentives to communicate relevant information about other producers' plans, scientific and technical innovations, and so on. Nor is the information required for coordination the only information relevant for economic activity, as the frequent exclusion of environmental impacts from market decisions illustrates. Admittedly, even if such criticisms of the informational virtues of the market can be sustained, there remains a strong epistemic case against centralized economic planning. Yet there may be institutional forms superior both to markets and to centralized planning for at least some tasks, such as those involved in the organization of scientific communities. Whether these provide plausible models for economic coordination is unclear.

3 Wellbeing and the human good

The replies to both the neoclassical and motivational arguments for the market involve claims about the nature of the human agent and of human wellbeing. In doing so they express a recurrent concern on the part of its socialist critics with the market's failure to establish the necessary conditions for human flourishing, and its encouragement of attitudes, motivations and character traits damaging both to those who acquire these and to those affected by them. For example, it is claimed that the market issues in such vices as competitiveness, avarice, egoism, possessiveness and vanity, all at the expense of the proper virtues of character and the humanly beneficial social relationships of community; that the pleasures of private consumption are mistakenly privileged over the more fulfilling demands of public life; and that capitalist forms of production deny to workers the exercise both of their active and creative capacities in work and of their deliberative capacities in the democratic control of the productive process (see WORK, PHILOSOPHY OF §2).

Marx's critique of capitalism as a condition of 'alienation' is typical here (see ALIENATION), but similar arguments against capitalism for its development of particular kinds of human character and social relationships incompatible with human wellbeing are to be found amongst other socialist theorists, from Morris and Tawney in the British tradition to Fromm and Marcuse in the continental. In current philosophical terminology such criticism is 'perfectionist' in form: it claims that social and political institutions should be judged by reference to a specific conception of the human good (see PERFECTIONISM). It is often broadly Aristotelian in content, seeing human wellbeing as consisting of the development and exercise of species powers and capacities. Hence it rejects, *inter alia*, the utilitarian, preference-based accounts of wellbeing that often underpin the neoclassical concept of efficiency: economic institutions are to be assessed not by their ability to satisfy given preferences, but in terms of the nature and value of the preferences they themselves encourage and make it possible to satisfy (see WELFARE §1).

Two kinds of response may be made to such claims. The first, which is typical of much modern liberal thought, is to reject perfectionist arguments altogether. It is a mark of liberal institutions that they be neutral between different conceptions of the good (see NEUTRALITY, POLITICAL). Such neutrality is especially desirable given the pluralistic character of modern societies, in which diverse and irreconcilable conceptions of the good are espoused. In this situation, perfectionism must imply the imposition of a contested conception of the good by coercive means, and hence a political practice which is paternalistic or even authoritarian. By contrast, the market is consistent with liberal neutrality. It provides an economic framework in which individuals with quite different ends and beliefs about the good can pursue these through mutually beneficial free exchanges.

The second response accepts the legitimacy of perfectionist arguments but denies that markets are incompatible with the human good. This may be argued either by denying that the market necessarily has the ill effects that socialists attribute to it, or by attributing to the market effects deemed highly desirable in terms of some alternative conception of the good. In the latter case it may be claimed, for example, that the market has the great merit of fostering individual autonomy; although socialists may respond to this by arguing that the development of such autonomy in fact requires the existence of certain kinds of social relationships which the market tends to undermine.

4 Democracy, power and freedom

The claim that socialism produces the conditions for the realization of liberal political values has been central to arguments for socialism that appeal to the values of democracy and freedom. The argument can take both weaker and stronger forms. The former asserts that many of the standard liberal rights and freedoms are empty without the material conditions for their effective exercise, which the market systematically fails to guarantee. This view is sometimes stated in terms of a criticism of 'negative' conceptions of liberty as the absence of coercion, proposing instead that these material conditions should be included in the definition of liberty itself (see FREEDOM AND LIBERTY §3). Alternatively it may simply be argued that if (negative) liberty is valuable, then so too are the conditions for its exercise. In response to the objection that the market's unequal distribution of material conditions is the unintended consequence of a spontaneous order, and hence should not be seen as a constraint on freedom, the socialist may argue that the market is not the outcome of natural events but of social decisions aimed at its creation and/or maintenance, that its distributive consequences are both foreseeable and alterable, and that there is no justification for restricting one's conception of liberty to the absence of intentional constraints.

The stronger form of the claim that socialism realizes liberal values is that it represents their consistent application to the economic sphere. A version of this position can be found in Marx's early writings, in which the 'ideal' community of the liberal democratic polity is contrasted with the egoistic realm of modern civil society; correspondingly, the rights of citizens exercised through their participation in the political community are set against the 'rights of man' exercised by the private individuals of civil society. The project of socialism is then expressed as bringing the ideal world of the polity down to reality through the democratic transformation of economic life. This strategy of pointing to the divergence between the rights and freedoms of the ideal liberal political order and their absence in the economic sphere has also been employed in other contexts: for instance, by contrasting democratic participation in the political system with the authoritarian nature of power relationships within the capitalist firm.

To such claims that socialism represents the completion of the democratic project, two main responses may be made: the liberal and the radical. The first denies that there is a conflict between the capitalist economic order and the liberal polity: rather, the existence of a market order, in which individuals enter freely into voluntary contractual relations, is itself a condition of the political rights and freedoms that define the liberal polity. It is not a sufficient condition: authoritarian states are compatible with capitalism. However, it is a necessary condition: political liberties are only to be found in free market economies. The socialist order, by concentrating economic, social and political power, destroys the space of civil society in which individuals enter into voluntary relations independent of the state, and which provides the cultural and social conditions for opposition to state power (see CIVIL SOCIETY). This objection applies primarily to centrally planned socialist economies with state ownership of the means of production, and is often endorsed by market socialists as a further reason to support their own proposals. Alternatively, it may be argued that the existence of such concentrations of economic and political power is compatible with restraint in its exercise, and that the absence of liberal political rights in state socialist societies such as the erstwhile USSR can be explained by reference to factors other than the absence of markets – for example, to the lack of liberal democratic institutions prior to their revolutionary transformation.

The second, radical response is concerned not so much with the cogency of the socialist critique of liberalism but with its completeness. In effect it extends the socialist criticism of liberalism to socialism itself. By placing its emphasis on the economic sphere, socialism has been blind to other sources of power, in particular those concerned with race and gender. Thus the feminist criticism of traditional socialism: that by confining its attention to the 'public' sphere of economic and political life it fails, like liberalism, to address the primary origin and location of women's oppression, in the 'private' sphere of the family and in 'personal', including sexual, relations between men and women (see FEMINIST POLITICAL PHILOSOPHY §4). Two replies may be made by socialists to this kind of critique. The first is to claim that these other asymmetries of power can themselves be explained in terms of the organization of economic production. The second is to accept the existence of diverse sources of social power and to re-conceptualize the traditional socialist project in the economic sphere as simply one component of a wider programme of human emancipation.

5 Distributive justice

The final set of arguments for socialism to be considered here are distributive ones. Capitalism is criticized for the unequal and/or unjust distribution of material, social and cultural goods. But this criticism takes a number of different forms. For some socialists, the preferred distributive principle is strict equality, either contrasted with justice or regarded as its proper interpretation. Others espouse some not necessarily egalitarian principle of justice: distribution according to need is the most common, as in the well-known principle, 'from each according to their ability, to each according to their needs'; but appeal may also or instead be made to a principle of desert, such as reward in proportion to contribution. While the last of these is rarely proposed as the sole distributive principle for a socialist society, it has often figured in socialist criticisms of capitalism, especially in the claim that capitalist profits are undeserved and hence unjust. But there is disagreement among socialists about whether the distribution of goods in a non-capitalist market economy would be unjust from this standpoint.

Defenders of capitalism have sometimes argued that it can be shown to be just by reference to a principle of desert: for example, by arguing that profits are a deserved reward for risk-taking. But more commonly they reject altogether the legitimacy of desert-based, need-based, egalitarian or any other so-called 'patterned' principles of justice in judging economic systems, on the grounds *inter alia* that any attempt to realize such patterns will involve unjustifiable and systematic coercion by the state. Instead, it is argued, justice should be understood as a purely 'procedural' concept: distributions are just if they are the outcome of fair or appropriate procedures, whatever the resulting pattern may be. An especially favoured procedure is voluntary exchange between free and equal parties. It is then claimed that since capitalist market transactions consist exclusively of such exchanges, capitalism is a just system (see LIBERTARIANISM; NOZICK, R. §2).

For socialists, such procedural definitions illicitly reduce the concept of justice to that of (negative) liberty. But it may also be argued that even if adopted, they would fail to show that the outcomes of the

transactions between capitalists and workers are just. For although the sale of labour power in return for wages is a transaction between formally or legally free and equal parties, there is an absence of substantive freedom on the part of workers, coupled with marked asymmetries of power. In addition, socialists may point to the historical origin of most current capitalist holdings of private property in past acts of theft, fraud, violence or state coercion.

While arguments for socialism couched in terms of distributive justice and equality have been widely employed, they have often been criticized by Marxists, partly for assuming that the crucial defect of capitalism lies in the improper distribution of goods in the sphere of exchange, rather than in the power relations in the sphere of production consequent upon capitalist property relations. Hence emphasis is placed instead on the concept of exploitation, understood as the extraction by capitalists of surplus value from workers which accrues to the capitalist in the form of profits – something that cannot be remedied by higher wages but only by the abolition of wage labour. Whether this concept of exploitation and its associated theory of value can be sustained is much disputed amongst socialist theorists, some of whom have argued instead for a purely distributional interpretation of the concept: for example, that someone is exploited if they would be better off than they now are had there been an initially egalitarian distribution of ownership rights over the means of production.

6 The future of socialism

The near universal collapse of nominally socialist regimes since the late 1980s has led many critics of socialism to proclaim its death. But these regimes have always had their socialist critics also, for many of whom these historic events may prove welcome, not least in undermining the previously hegemonic status of Marxist-Leninism in socialist theory and practice, and the marginalization of other significant traditions of socialist thought. Thus one response to the political and economic failures of state socialism has been to return to some of these earlier, non-centralist socialist traditions, and attempt to re-work them for contemporary purposes. One such attempt is that of the 'associational socialists' who, taking their inspiration from nineteenth- and early twentieth-century guild socialism and syndicalism, propose independent and self-governing functional associations as the units of political and economic authority, rejecting both state and market.

By contrast, as noted earlier, the project of 'market socialism' is to construct a non-capitalist market system operating within liberal democratic political institutions. This position has the virtue of being able to provide a relatively well-articulated alternative to capitalism which takes account of the powerful objections to centralized planning. Yet its acceptance of market forces, of individual self-interest and relationships of exchange and competition, makes it appear to non-market socialists a poor substitute for the 'truly human' community to which they aspire. To this its proponents may reply that one should not aim at a single, monolithic ideal of community for society as a whole, but accept instead a more differentiated conception of social existence in which different forms of human wellbeing are realized within different spheres or domains, of which the economic is but one. Yet it remains unclear whether market economies are compatible with, or inimical to, the flourishing of significant forms of community outside the economic sphere (see COMMUNTY AND COMMUNITARIANISM).

Further, like any market system, market socialism is subject to a range of objections from an ecological or environmental perspective. The market fails to take account of the environmentally destructive consequences of economic growth; it is unable to incorporate the interests of those who cannot engage in market transactions – whether the poor, members of future generations, or non human beings; and it encourages people to misidentify the primary source of wellbeing as the endless pursuit of consumer satisfactions. Indeed, whilst the environmental movement has presented a serious challenge to the tendency of much socialist thought to conceive of human emancipation as requiring the subordination of nature to human ends, it has also given new life to many traditional socialist objections to the market: its remarkable ability to generate collectively irrational outcomes from individually rational behaviour, including the underproduction of public goods and the overproduction of public ills. For both political ecologists and socialists, there is a vast range of social problems which require collective rather than individual action for their solution, and a continuing need for forms of ethical and political commitment that the market both fails to recognize and may often undermine (see GREEN POLITICAL PHILOSOPHY).

See also: BAKUNIN, M.A.; BERNSTEIN, E.; ENGELS, F.; GRAMSCI, A.; KAUTSKY, K.J.; LASSALLE, F.; LENIN, V.I.; LUXEMBURG, R.; MARKET, ETHICS OF THE §§1–3; MARX, K.; MARXISM, WESTERN; MARXIST PHILOSOPHY, RUSSIAN AND SOVIET; POLITICAL PHILOSOPHY, HISTORY OF; PROUDHON, P.-J.

References and further reading

Berki, R. (1975) *Socialism*, London: Dent. (A sophisticated analysis including discussion of Third World socialism and historical uses of the terms 'socialism', 'communism' and 'social democracy'.)

Bottomore, T. (1990) *The Socialist Economy*, New York: Harvester Wheatsheaf. (A short and readable survey of different theoretical and practical forms of socialist economy and debates about their defensibility.)

Buchanan, A. (1985) *Ethics, Efficiency and the Market*, Oxford: Clarendon Press. (Includes a relatively non technical account of neoclassical defences of the market and their problems.)

Cohen, G.A. (1988) *History, Labour and Freedom*, Oxford: Clarendon Press. (Contains several essays providing sympathetic analytical reconstructions of central normative concepts in Marx's work, including exploitation, coercion and freedom.)

Cole, G.D.H. (1953–60) *A History of Socialist Thought*, London: Macmillan, 5 vols. (A monumental and still unsurpassed history of socialist thought, especially in Europe.)

Fried, A. and Sanders, R. (eds) (1992) *Socialist Thought: A Documentary History*, New York: Columbia University Press. (An extensive collection of extracts from the work of major nineteenth- and twentieth-century socialist theorists, including non-European writers.)

Gray, J. (1993) *Beyond the New Right*, London: Routledge. (An accessible account of epistemic objections to socialism combined with a perfectionist defence of the market pointing also to its limitations.)

Hayek, F.A. (1973–9) *Law, Legislation and Liberty*, London: Routledge, 3 vols. (Arguably the major work of the most influential twentieth-century defender of markets and critic of socialism.)

Hirst, P. (ed.) (1989) *The Pluralist Theory of the State: Selected writings of G.D.H. Cole, J.N. Figgis and H.J. Laski*, London: Routledge. (A selection of writings by associational theorists, with a useful editorial introduction.)

Kolakowski, L. (1978) *Main Currents of Marxism*, Oxford: Oxford University Press. (An influential, informative and highly critical analysis of the main forms of Marxist thought through the nineteenth and twentieth centuries.)

Levine, A. (1988) *Arguing for Socialism*, London: Verso. (Argues that socialism can be justified by reference to values central to liberal political thought.)

Lichtheim, G. (1983) *A Short History of Socialism*, London: Fontana. (A classic history of socialist thought and the socialist movement in Europe and the USA.)

McLellan, D. (ed.) (1977) *Karl Marx: Selected Writings*, Oxford: Oxford University Press. (A useful collection of Marx's work, including his early critiques of alienation and the separation of state and civil society.)

Miller, D. (1989) *Market, State and Community*, Oxford: Oxford University Press. (A defence of market socialism responding both to traditional socialist objections to the market and contemporary liberal objections to socialism.)

Phillips, A. (1993) *Democracy and Difference*, Polity Press: Cambridge. (A sympathetic but critical discussion of socialism's failure to develop an account of democracy which recognizes forms of oppression based on gender, race, and so on.)

Polanyi, K. (1957) *The Great Transformation*, Boston, MA: Beacon Press. (A broadly socialist but non-Marxist historical account of the emergence of the market economy.)

Roemer, J.E. (1988) *Free to Lose: An Introduction to Marxist Economic Philosophy*, London: Century Hutchinson. (A rational choice reinterpretation of Marxist theory, presenting exploitation as the outcome of unequally distributed economic assets.)

Rubel, M. and Crump, J. (eds) (1997) *Non-Market Socialism in the Nineteenth and Twentieth Centuries*, London: Macmillan. (A collection of sympathetic essays on the main currents of non-market socialism.)

Ryle, M. (1988) *Ecology and Socialism*, London: Century Hutchinson. (Argues that neither ecological politics nor socialism can do without one another.)

Sypnowich, C. (1990) *The Concept of Socialist Law*, Oxford: Clarendon Press. (Argues that legal rights and the rule of law have a positive role in socialism, rather than being tied to market societies.)

Wright, A. (1987) *Socialisms: Theories and Practices*, Oxford: Oxford University Press. (Perhaps the best brief introduction, emphasizing the diversity of socialist thought and sympathetic to the ethical socialism of the British tradition.)

RUSSELL KEAT
JOHN O'NEILL

SOCIETY, CONCEPT OF

The term 'society' is broader than 'human society'. Many other species are described as possessing a social way of life. Yet mere gregariousness, of the kind found in a herd of cattle or a shoal of fish, is not enough to constitute a society. For the biologist, the marks of the social are cooperation (extending beyond cooperation between parents in raising young) and some form of order or division of labour. In assessing the merits of attempts to provide a more precise definition of society, we can ask whether the definition succeeds in capturing our intuitive understanding of the term, and also whether it succeeds in identifying those features of society which are most fundamental from an explanatory point of view – whether it captures the Lockean 'real essence' of society.

One influential approach seeks to capture the idea of society by characterizing social action, or interaction, in terms of the particular kinds of awareness it involves. Another approach focuses on social order, seeing it as a form of order that arises spontaneously when rational and mutually aware individuals succeed in solving coordination problems. Yet another approach focuses on the role played by communication in achieving collective agreement on the way the world is to be classified and understood, as a precondition of coordination and cooperation.

1   **Defining social interaction**
2   **Game theory and social order**
3   **Society as a system of communication**
4   **Social groups**

1   Defining social interaction

Max WEBER defines social action as 'action in which the meaning intended by the agent or agents involves a relation to another person's behaviour' (1978: 7), and a social relationship exists 'when several people reciprocally adjust their behaviour to each other with respect to the meaning they give to it' (1978: 30) (see SOCIAL ACTION). Thus several people acting in a similar way need not be engaging in social action, but two cyclists who try to give way to each other are. Weber excludes non-human animals from the realm of the social on the grounds that they are not capable of the intentions that might give meaning to their behaviour. (His paradigm of 'meaningful action' is the rational pursuit of a consciously chosen goal.) In that respect, Weber's definition of the social may seem unduly narrow, but it also seems to be over-inclusive. A population of individuals who took account of each other's behaviour only to the extent of seeking to avoid collisions would not on that account qualify as living a social way of life, not at least by any intuitive criterion. We may also find it odd that cooperation is not a necessary feature of society on Weber's account.

Alfred Schütz (1932) seeks to improve on Weber's definitions, telling us that we have a social relationship where there is mutual awareness of the way each sees the other (see SCHÜTZ, A.). This requirement identifies an important feature of human interaction, but it is still not clear that it captures what makes it 'social' interaction. A sophisticated form of the predator–prey relationship, in which the predator is aware that the prey is aware of it and vice versa, would seem to qualify as a social relationship by this criterion. More promising is Schütz's definition of 'social interaction', which involves, in addition to the requirement of mutual awareness, an attempt by one party to affect the consciousness of the other. Thus social interaction is defined as an attempt to affect another's state of mind in which the other is aware of one's intentions and is also aware that one knows that they are aware of one's intentions. Schütz also notes that this is what we call communication. The work of H.P. Grice develops this approach to communication, invoking yet more complex levels of mutual awareness. Though Grice himself is not concerned to define the social, the kind of mutual awareness to which he appeals is clearly not confined to linguistic interaction, and the idea that communication is a central feature of social interaction has proved fruitful (see §3 below).

2 Game theory and social order

The effect of an exclusive focus on social interaction as a relationship between individuals is to make social order seem a merely incidental and inessential feature of social life. Intuitively that is odd. More recent individualist approaches employing the resources of game theory (see RATIONAL CHOICE THEORY §2) have taken it for granted that both social order and cooperation are defining features of social life, and have seen it as their task to demonstrate that these features can be understood as the outcome of interactions between individuals pursuing their own individual purposes.

In some respects, game theory represents a further refinement and idealization of the assumption of mutual awareness. Individuals are assumed to be instrumentally rational in that they are seeking to maximize the satisfaction of their preferences. This need not mean that they are selfish, but it does mean that the goals they are pursuing are their own and not, for example, a collective goal. It is also 'common knowledge' between them that they are rational. (This amounts to saying that each knows that the others know this, and knows that the others know that they know this, and so on *ad infinitum*.) It is also assumed that there is common knowledge of the possible choices of action open to each party and of the payoffs attached to possible outcomes. There is to be no communication between individuals, but each is

able to assess what it would be rational for others to do and can take that into account in deciding what it is rational for them to do. The claim is that, given these assumptions, where there is a mutual interest in coordination (for example, in everyone driving on the same side of the road), individual rational choices will give rise to uniformities in behaviour without the need for explicit agreement or social sanctions. Lewis (1969) makes this thought the basis of his definition of 'convention' as – very crudely – a regularity in behaviour that everyone keeps to because it is in their interest to do so given that everyone else does (see SOCIAL NORMS §1). Using this account of convention, Lewis seeks to account for linguistic and other forms of communication as forms of game-theoretically rational action with the complexity of levels of mutual awareness to which Grice appeals.

The game-theoretic approach promises not just an explanation of social order but an account of what social order is, for clearly not just any regularity in the behaviour of a population will count as an example of social order. Social order arises, on this view, when rational and sufficiently mutually aware individuals succeed in solving coordination problems. However, it is controversial whether the rational agents of game theory can ever do this, and it is in any case widely conceded that there are aspects of social order that cannot be understood in this way. There are many circumstances in which, though the collective interest would be served by everyone obeying a rule, it is in the individual's interest to break it. In these circumstances game theory predicts that no one will obey the rule and so all will lose out. This is known as the 'free-rider' problem. It does not help to appeal to sanctions against rule breakers, for we then need to explain how it could be rational for one individual to seek to impose sanctions on another, and the free-rider problem arises all over again. Thus the game-theoretic approach fails to explain a form of cooperation that is central to human social life.

One way of responding to this failure is to modify our assumptions about individual motivation, for example by building in a degree of concern for the interests of others, though interestingly it is not clear that this is enough. Elster (1989) argues that we also need to invoke a respect for social norms, but this suggestion faces a dilemma. Either we appeal to a respect for norms in general along the lines of Kant's categorical imperative (see KANT, I. §11), whose implications threaten to be insufficiently determinate to help with our problem, or else we appeal to the respect individuals feel for the norms of their particular society, in which case we beg the question of the explanation of social order by treating social norms as already given.

3 Society as a system of communication

For G.H. Mead and for the Durkheimian tradition, especially as it has been developed in anthropology, the key feature of social interaction is communication (see MEAD, G.H.; DURKHEIM, É.). Not just language but action in general is seen as having communicational or expressive significance, and its function is not simply to transmit useful information but to get agreement on the way the social world is to be classified and understood. A shared way of interpreting and defining reality, sustained by its expression in language, ceremony and ritual, is on this view a precondition, not only of mutual intelligibility, but of the kind of coordination and cooperation between individuals that game theory has such difficulty in explaining. Communication is also an important feature of animal social life, and it is possible to see it as having a similar function there too, even if the forms of expression and the schemes of classification involved are much more restricted.

Even so, it is clear that not just any system of communication constitutes society. The simple transmission of information, as in alarm calls in flocks of birds, is not enough. Nor is it enough that communication yields a shared scheme of classification or definition of reality. The defence of territorial boundaries, for example, yields an agreed definition of reality that is consistent with relationships between individuals being wholly antagonistic. It seems best to say that we have something we can call society only when the agreed definition of reality provides for the possibility of cooperation; though if we are to avoid seeing cooperation between parents in raising offspring as in itself amounting to a social way of life, we must add that the agreement on ways of defining reality must extend beyond two individuals. This is not an arbitrary restriction, for beyond that number agreement becomes significantly more difficult to achieve. Inevitably, questions of classification will sometimes be a matter for dispute, making claim and counterclaim endemic to social life. Thus while cooperation is, by this definition, a necessary feature of social life, so too is a distinctively social form of conflict.

For the Durkheimian tradition, the key distinguishing feature of human society is the normative dimension, the existence of shared standards of correct thought and behaviour. This means not simply the fact of general conformity to standards of correct thought and behaviour but the fact of those standards being collectively policed. For Durkheim, the authority behind social norms is the authority of the collective viewed as an organized group, but Mead's idea of 'the generalized other' suggests a different view. In the absence of shared standards of correctness and legitimacy, agreement emerges, if it emerges at all, from the play of power in disputes between interested parties, supported perhaps by friends and allies. The existence of shared standards means that parties in dispute can appeal to the disinterested jury of others in general, and that they will tend to accept the verdict of that jury. Some standards, of course, are likely to be policed in a more organized way (for example the criminal law), but more generally, and more fundamentally, shared standards are policed by the authority of others in general. For Mead, it is by taking up the point of view of others in general that an individual comes to possess their own sense of what is correct and legitimate, and also a sense of themselves as an individual.

If communication is to be seen as the basis of society, it cannot be viewed as a form of instrumentally rational action of the sort modelled by game theory (see §2 above). Communication must be capable of operating independently of, and at a more primitive level than, the degree of rationality and mutual awareness assumed by game theory. As social beings, we must be supposed to possess an urge to express our own view of things, and also a tendency to be influenced by the way others see things, that is prior to our rationality and which constitutes a distinctive source of motivation in its own right. Thus Jürgen HABERMAS (§2) distinguishes between instrumental action which is 'oriented to success', and communicative action which is 'oriented to reaching understanding'. Habermas also stresses that, in a context of shared standards of correctness, acts of communication take on the force of legitimacy claims. The anthropologist Mary Douglas (1977) makes a similar distinction between instrumental action and expressive action, but emphasizes the competitive aspect of social communication. Our expressive activity reflects a need to give meaning to the world, a need, in fact, to construct an intelligible world as a condition of remaining sane. But my attempts to win agreement to my interpretations of reality may conflict with yours. To see society as a system of communication is to see it as a battleground of conflicting interpretations of reality in which the price of failure to win agreement is exclusion from social interaction.

4 Social groups

For methodological individualists like Weber, talk of social collectivities can only be a way of talking about 'actual or possible social actions of individual persons' (see HOLISM AND INDIVIDUALISM IN HISTORY AND SOCIAL SCIENCE). Elster (1989) offers one way of putting flesh on this idea, defining a society as a geographical area for which there is a local maximum of the number of transactions between the individuals in the area divided by the total number of transactions in which those individuals are involved. Shorn of the reference to a geographical area, this could serve as a definition of social class, for class boundaries are certainly barriers to social interaction, but most social groups are thought of as having a greater degree of unity than this.

For Georg Simmel (1908), the unity of a social group consists in the fact that its members think of it as possessing a unity. Gilbert (1989) develops this idea in a way that recalls Rousseau's distinction between the general will and the will of all (see ROUSSEAU, J.-J. §3). Appealing to what she argues is the central use of the first person plural 'we', she defines a social group as a 'plural subject' constituted by the fact that each of a number of individuals finds it appropriate to use 'we' in attributing purposes, activities, beliefs, and so on, to themselves jointly rather than severally. The idea of a plural subject offers us a less individualist conception of social cooperation than that which emerges from game theory, though seen from a communication system perspective (see §3 above), the idea that 'we' constitute a plural subject is just one of the agreed ways of defining reality which can serve to facilitate coordination and cooperation.

See also: ANTHROPOLOGY, PHILOSOPHY OF; BUSHI PHILOSOPHY; CONFUCIAN PHILOSOPHY, CHINESE; CONFUCIAN PHILOSOPHY, JAPANESE; IBN KHALDUN; NEO-CONFUCIAN PHILOSOPHY; WATSUJI TETSURŌ

References and further reading

* Douglas, M. (1977) 'Why do people want goods?' in S. Hargreaves Heap and A. Ross (eds), *Understanding the Enterprise Culture*, Edinburgh: Edinburgh University Press, 1992. (An example of the Durkheimian approach described in §3.)
—— (1987) *How Institutions Think*, London: Routledge, chaps 1–4. (An example of the Durkheimian approach described in §3.)
Durkheim, É. (1895) *Rules of Sociological Method*, trans. W.D. Halls, New York: Free Press, 1982. (The classic statement of Durkheim's position.)
* Elster, J. (1989) *The Cement of Society*, Cambridge: Cambridge University Press. (An example of the game-theoretic approach described in §2. Also contains the definition of 'social group' referred to in §4.)
* Gilbert, M. (1989) *On Social Facts*, London: Routledge. (The account of social groups as plural subjects described in §4.)
Grice, H.P. (1957) 'Meaning', *Philosophical Review* 66: 377–88. (Definition of 'communication' in terms of mutual awareness, referred to in §1.)
Habermas, J. (1981–2) *The Theory of Communicative Action*, vols 1 and 2, trans. T. McCarthy, Boston, MA: Beacon Press, 1984–7. (Seeks to integrate a Weberian social action approach with a Durkheimian communication system approach, see especially chapters III and V.1.)
* Lewis, D.K. (1969) *Convention*, Cambridge, MA: Harvard University Press. (An example of the game-theoretic approach described in §2.)
Mead, G.H. (1934) *Mind, Self and Society*, Chicago, IL, and London: University of Chicago Press. (A seminal account of the communication perspective.)
* Schütz, A. (1932) *The Phenomenology of the Social World*, London: Heinemann, 1972. (Definition of 'social relationship' and 'social interaction' in terms of mutual awareness, referred to in §1. See especially chapter 4.)
* Simmel, G. (1908) 'How is society possible?' in *Georg Simmel: On Individuality and Social Forms*, ed. D.N. Levine, Chicago, IL and London: University of Chicago Press, 1971. (Contains definition of 'social group' referred to in §4.)
Ullman-Margalit, E. (1977) *The Emergence of Norms*, Oxford: Oxford University Press. (An example of game-theoretic approach described in §2.)
* Weber, M. (1978) 'The nature of social action' in *Max Weber: Selections in Translation*, ed. W.G. Runciman, Cambridge: Cambridge University Press, ch. I, §1. (Seminal definition of social action quoted in §1.)

ANGUS ROSS

SOCINIANISM

Socinianism was both the name for a sixteenth- and seventeenth-century theological movement which was a forerunner of modern unitarianism, and, much less precisely, a polemic term of abuse suggesting positions in common with that 'heretical' movement. Socinianism was explicitly undogmatic but centred on disbelief in the Trinity, original sin, the satisfaction, and the natural immortality of the soul. Some Socinians were materialists. Socinians focused on moralism and Christ's prophetic role; the elevation of reason in interpreting Scripture against creeds, traditions and church authority; and support for religious toleration. The term was used polemically against many theorists, including Hugo Grotius, William Chillingworth, the Latitudinarians, and John Locke, who emphasized free will, moralism, the role and capacity of reason, and that Christianity included only a very few fundamental doctrines necessary for salvation.

1 The Socinian movement
2 The Trinity and satisfaction
3 Original sin, mortalism and materialism
4 Reason and toleration
5 'Socinianism' as an accusation and John Locke

1 The Socinian movement

Socinianism was founded by Laelius and Faustus Socinus, and was the name given to an unorthodox evangelical theological movement which originated in Italy and spread first to Poland, and then to the Netherlands and England. At its height the academy of the Socinian Minor Church in Racov had over a thousand students, and its press published works which were disseminated in many languages and countries. In many countries, however, Socinians were punished or executed as 'heretics' or forced into exile, and the Socinian church was crushed in Poland in 1660. Many Socinians then settled in the Netherlands. The leading Socinian authors in the generations after Faustus Socinus were Johann Crell, Johann Völkel, Johann Von Wolzogen, Andreas Wiszowaty and Samuel Przypkowski.

2 The Trinity and satisfaction

Socinianism was explicitly undogmatic, and many of its beliefs changed over time, but throughout it centred on disbelief in the Athanasian Trinity of three co-eternal consubstantial persons in one Godhead in favour of the belief that Jesus was a divinely inspired man who brought the definitive revelation or Word of God, and that the Holy Spirit was a power or energy of God. Jesus was distinguished from the rest of mankind by his perfect holiness of life, by being conceived by the Holy Spirit and by being endued with divine wisdom. At his resurrection he had been given power to rule over the world. Some Socinians argued that a plurality of infinite persons in one God was impossible. Intimately connected to denial of the Trinity was denial of orthodox Calvinist accounts of Christ's satisfaction. It was held by many Socinians that Christ had not paid an equivalent for humanity's sins in order to satisfy God's justice; his mission was centrally prophetic rather than priestly. God forgave sins, rather than receiving payment for them.

3 Original sin, mortalism and materialism

Socinians denied original sin and held the 'mortalist'

belief that human souls were not naturally immortal. For Socinians, Adam's sin had not corrupted the power of his posterity to choose good over evil. They maintained that humans had free will, and opposed predestination, in part to protect God from responsibility for sin. They simultaneously maintained that humans were sinful, by emphasizing both that individuals were responsible for their own sins and that all generations had engaged in extensive sinning. They depicted naturally mortal humans as left to their natural mortality unless saved by the power of the Spirit in following the commandments of Jesus. They denied both the natural immortality of the soul and the resurrection of the earthly body in favour of belief that there would be a selective resurrection of the saved providing them with immortality in celestial bodies. The eternity of punishment for sin was denied in favour of belief in an eternal fire causing annihilation of the damned. Some Socinians combined mortalist belief with materialism and held that matter was coexistent and coeternal with God; Faustus Socinus himself held that the world had been made from pre-existent matter. Many Socinians depicted Christ as bringing information about an afterlife and a promise of immortality inaccessible by reason alone, with Christ's resurrection itself serving as a central testimony to immortality.

4 Reason and toleration

Socinians placed a heavy emphasis on the role of reason or 'right reason' as the sole and final interpreter of Scripture, and on Scripture as the definitive revelation of God's will. Scripture was said to be perspicuous to reason and Socinians attacked the authority of traditions, church authority and creeds. By the mid-seventeenth century Joachim Stegmann was arguing that nothing in the Bible exceeded human understanding. Many in the later generations of Socinianism suggested that contemporary orthodoxy was overly influenced by the Platonic and Neoplatonic philosophy of the early church, depicting this influence as buttressing belief not just in the Trinity but also in the natural immortality of the soul. Elevating reason against church authority, and personally attacked as 'heretics' for their beliefs, Socinians supported religious toleration and argued that the state was dedicated to purely natural ends. Many were pacifists.

5 'Socinianism' as an accusation and John Locke

The polemic accusation of Socinianism was regularly made in the seventeenth century against many thinkers, including Grotius, Chillingworth and

Locke. Grotius' *De Veritate Religionis Christianae* omitted original sin and the atonement, but he published elsewhere in defence of the satisfaction and he believed in the resurrection of the same bodies (see GROTIUS, H.). William Chillingworth and the Latitudinarians emphasized the limited fundamentals of Christianity, the role of reason, and the centrality of morality in Christianity, but explicitly endorsed the Trinity, the atonement, and the immortality of the soul (see CHILLINGWORTH, W.; LATITUDINARIAN-ISM). The most important philosopher accused of Socinianism was John Locke. A series of writers declared his *Reasonableness of Christianity* 'all over Socinianized'. Leibniz described Locke as 'inclined' to Socinianism for his recognition of the possibility that matter might think, because this rendered it impossible, in Leibniz' view, to prove the soul's natural immortality. Bishop Edward Stillingfleet argued that Locke's epistemology 'favoured' Socinianism for his arguments about the limitation of our knowledge about substance, which undercut Trinitarian explications of the consubstantial Godhead.

Locke's library included many Socinian works, some of which he read carefully. His *Reasonableness* was close to Socinianism in a number of ways. It interpreted Adam's Fall as not involving a 'corruption of human nature in his posterity'; discussed Christ's mission as essentially prophetic and especially kingly rather than priestly; avoided the satisfaction; emphasized Christ's promise of and testimony to immortality; and asserted a credal minimalism of belief in Jesus as the Christ without any mention of the Trinity. Yet he never directly attacked the Trinity or satisfaction, and his comments were compatible with a non-essential Trinitarianism or with kinds of Arianism, and with belief in a satisfaction. Locke's *Paraphrase* included one probably anti-Socinian textual explication. His arguments in the *Essay* may have been constructed in part to undercut Trinitarians' extended explanations of the Trinity and, by its final edition, to allow intellectual space for mortalism. These arguments in the *Essay* were, however, compatible with Socinianism rather than definitively Socinian. They could be combined with anti-Socinian views and were epistemological rather than ontological in orientation as observations about the limitations of human understandings of substance, matter, thought and God's power (see LOCKE, J. §7).

See also: DEISM; NATURAL LAW

References and further reading

Bibliotheca Fratrum Polonorum (The Library of the Polish Brethren) (1688), Amsterdam. (Collection of all major Socinian works in 8 volumes; the first 2 volumes are of works by Faustus Socinus.)

Fix, A. (1991) *Prophecy and Reason*, Princeton, NJ: Princeton University Press. (Chapter 6 provides a very informative introduction to Socinianism in the Netherlands.)

* Grotius, H. (1622) *De Veritate Religionis Christianae* (The truth of the Christian religion), London, 1624. (An eirenic work which avoided disputed dogmatic issues and was accused of Socinianism.)

Jolley, N. (1984) *Leibniz and Locke*, Oxford: Oxford University Press. (Chapters 2 and 3 provide an excellent account of Leibniz's accusation of Socinianism against Locke and its contexts.)

* Locke, J. (1689) *An Essay concerning Human Understanding*, ed. P.H. Nidditch, Clarendon Edition, Oxford: Oxford University Press, 1975. (Locke's magnum opus, accused of inclining to Socinianism.)

* —— (1695) *The Reasonableness of Christianity*, London; 2nd edn, 1696; ed. J. Higgins-Biddle, Clarendon Edition, Oxford: Oxford University Press, 1998. (A work arguing that the sole belief necessary to become a Christian was that Jesus was the Christ, emphasizing morality, and stressing Christ's role as king and not as priest; accused of Socinianism.)

* —— (1700–4) *A Paraphrase and Notes on the Epistles of St Paul*, London, 6 vols, 1705–7; ed. A.W. Wainwright, Clarendon Edition, Oxford: Oxford University Press, 2 vols, 1987. (A work of paraphrase and exegesis of Paul's epistles; silent on the Trinity but one textual explication seems anti-Socinian on Christ.)

McLachlan, H. (1951) *Socinianism in Seventeenth Century England*, London: Oxford University Press. (Broad account of the influence of Socinianism in England.)

Katechizm zbory tych ludzi, ktory w Krolestwie Polskim... (1605), Racov; trans. as *The Racovian Catechism*, London: Thomas Rees, 1818. (The first English translation appeared in 1652; the closest work to a standard account of Socinian beliefs.)

Stegmann, J. (1644) *De iudice et norma controversarum fidei* (Of judgment and standards in controversies of faith), Amsterdam. (A work indicating that nothing in the bible exceeded human understanding.)

Sullivan, R. (1982) *John Toland and the Deist Controversy*, Harvard, MA: Harvard University Press. (Chapter 3 provides a useful account of the varieties of Socinianism in late seventeenth-century England.)

Wallace, R. (1850) *Anti-Trinitarian Biography*, London: Whitfield, 3 vols. (Excellent survey of Socinianism and of individual Socinian thinkers.)

Wilbur, E.A. (1946–52) *A History of Unitarianism*, Cambridge, MA: Harvard University Press, 2 vols. (The standard account of unitarianism.)

Williams, G.H. (1980) *The Polish Brethren*, Missoula, MT: Scholars Press, 2 vols. (Collection of Socinian documents.)

Wootton, D. (1989) 'John Locke: Socinian or Natural Law Theorist?', in J. Crimmins (ed.) *Religion, Secularization and Political Thought*, London: Routledge. (A challenging reading of Locke's thought in the light of Socinianism.)

JOHN MARSHALL

SOCIOBIOLOGY

Following Darwin, biologists and social scientists have periodically been drawn to the theory of natural selection as the source of explanatory insights about human behaviour and social institutions. The combination of Mendelian genetics and Darwinian theory, which did so much to substantiate the theory of evolution in the life sciences, however, has made recurrent adoption of a biological approach to the social sciences controversial. Excesses and errors in social Darwinism, eugenics and mental testing have repeatedly exposed evolutionary approaches in the human sciences to criticism.

Sociobiology is the version of Darwinism in social and behavioural science that became prominent in the last quarter of the twentieth century. Philosophical problems of sociobiology include challenges to the explanatory relevance of Darwinian theory for human behaviour and social institutions, controversies about whether natural selection operates at levels of organization above or below the individual, questions about the meaning of the nature–nurture distinction, and disputes about Darwinism's implications for moral philosophy.

1   Altruism
2   Anthropomorphic and adaptationalist fallacies
3   The levels of selection
4   Nature versus nurture
5   Ideological and moral implications

1   Altruism

Sociobiology is a term coined by E.O. Wilson to name that discipline which applies the synthetic theory of evolution – the conjunction of Darwin's claim that nature selects over random variations and the Mendelian theory of genetic inheritance (see EVOLUTION, THEORY OF §1; DARWIN, C.R.; GENETICS §1) – to explain aspects of and differences in individual behaviour and the behaviour of groups of individuals. Sociobiology seeks to explain behaviour by showing that its emergence is to be expected as a strategy adapted to secure the fitness of the individuals that manifest the behaviour and their genes.

Sociobiology's promise, its explanatory strategy and the controversies surrounding it are aptly illustrated in the discussion of human altruism. Wilson (1976: 3) identified altruism as the 'central' theoretical problem of sociobiology: 'how can altruism, which by definition reduces personal fitness, possibly evolve by natural selection?' Altruism, and cooperation in general, are obvious features of human behaviour. Indeed, sociality requires them. But Wilson (1976: 578) notes that altruism is 'self-destructive behaviour performed for the benefit of others'. Therefore altruism reduces fitness. Accordingly, through evolution it should have been expunged not enhanced. So a characteristic feature of human behaviour appears to be not just exempt from the constraint of natural selection, but perhaps inconsistent with it. Once sociobiologists began to show how natural selection might in fact explain the emergence of altruism as a fitness-maximizing strategy, both its theoretical promise and its interest to philosophers grew rapidly.

The problem of cooperation among humans is one Darwin broached in *The Descent of Man* (1871). His answer to the question of how other-regarding behaviour could evolve made an appeal to the group as the unit of selection. Groups in which members cooperated or otherwise behaved altruistically, are likely in the long run to do better in meeting their members' needs than will groups of egoists. Thus, to the extent that behaviour can be controlled or at least encouraged by individual genetic inheritance, in the struggle for survival between groups, groups of altruists will be selected for. The trouble with this argument is that a group of altruists is vulnerable to 'invasion' by an egoist. Suppose mutation turns a single member of a group of altruists into an egoist who free-rides on the cooperation of others, but does not reciprocate. Note that if altruistic behaviour is genetically fixed, altruists will not retaliate against egoists. The egoist of course does better than the altruists, and amasses more resources. Thus its fitness increases, and it will have more and/or stronger offspring than will the average among altruists. Result: over the long run, the proportion of egoistic descendants will increase, since egoism is a genetically coded mutation that is transmitted down the original mutant's line of descent. After enough generations, there are nothing but egoists left in the original altruistic group.

This argument from individual selection's power to overwhelm group selection had two important consequences: it reinforced evolutionary biologists' commitment to methodological individualism, and it made Darwinism seem irreconcilable with the basic social disposition of altruism. It was W.D. Hamilton (1964), who realized how evolutionary theory and genetics could accommodate altruism, and thus gave sociobiology its late-twentieth-century impetus. Hamilton argued that nature will select for that strategy which leaves the largest number of copies of the gene that codes for it. In the case of sexually reproducing organisms this will usually be direct offspring – sons and daughters. Whence the altruism of parents to offspring. Moreover, a strategy that sacrifices a son or daughter to save two siblings, three nephews or nieces, or a parent will ensure the survival of just as many or more copies of the individual's genes as would a strategy of saving a son or daughter. Accordingly, nature will select for 'inclusive fitness' which reflects the organisms' fitness and the fitness of each of its kin – the other organisms with whom it shares copies of the same genes, corrected by some coefficient of relatedness. If nature engages in 'kin selection' by selecting for 'inclusive fitness', then, altruism may emerge as an adaptive strategy for an individual that is part of a group of kin.

A problem arises immediately: why does an altruist provide resources at its own expense to unrelated organisms? This question is crucial for sociobiology. As human society evolves it is characterized more and more by cooperation, and less and less by kinship. So, again, either features of human society cannot be accounted for on the basis of selection for the fittest individual strategies, or else sociobiology needs to find another explanation for the emergence of altruism than its inclusive fitness. Sociobiological solutions to this problem have increased its interest for philosophers.

We may hypothesize that altruism emerges as a reciprocal strategy, in which individuals are cooperative in order to secure cooperation from others on later occasions. 'Reciprocal altruism' (the term was introduced by Richard Trivers (1971)) is, however, vulnerable to disappointment in the same way that unconditional altruism is. For the optimal strategy for a fitness maximizer is to accept altruistic pay-offs, but to decline to make them. Accordingly, altruism in the expectation of reciprocation will be displaced by egoism. Trivers and others had noticed that among animals, including humans, the problem of reciprocal altruism reflects what economists have called a 'prisoner's dilemma'. In this setting, the pay-off to

free-riding, and the cost of being taken for a sucker, exclude altruism as an available strategy to the rational agent maximizing utility. To the extent that nature selects for maximizing fitness, it will discourage altruism and encourage free-riding whenever the pay-offs in nature are like those in the prisoner's dilemma. (see DECISION AND GAME THEORY §§3, 6). The prisoner's dilemma arises whenever there is a chance to be taken for a sucker combined with an opportunity to free-ride: possible cases include signalling the presence of predators or silently fleeing instead, sharing food or hogging it, encroaching on unprotected territory versus respecting it, procreating without remaining to raise the off-spring. In short, opportunities for altruism by one agent are opportunities for free-riding by another, and it appears that the costs and benefits make the latter an adaptational strategy for individuals and the former a maladaptive one.

However, the prisoner's dilemma is a situation animals face over and over again with a relatively small number of other animals. It is in the search for an optimal strategy for repeated or 'iterated' prisoner's dilemma situations that Hamilton and Axelrod (Axelrod 1984) found a potential solution to Wilson's problem of how altruism emerged. They argued that, under certain circumstances, in iterated prisoner's dilemma encounters, the optimal strategy for the individual is one called 'tit-for-tat': cooperate in game one, and then in each subsequent round do what the other player did in the previous round. Thus, if the other player tries to free-ride in round one, the best response is to refuse to cooperate in round two. If in round two the other party changes strategies and cooperates, in round three one should return to cooperating as well. In the long run no strategy generates a higher pay-off than tit-for-tat. Over the long haul, nature will select fitness maximizers employing this strategy, and as a result cooperation or reciprocal altruism will become fixed in populations. Whence altruism is shown to be compatible with natural selection, and may even have emerged through its operation.

This approach to explaining human behaviour raises issues of philosophical interest: the foundations of rational choice theory, the nature of social conventions, the analysis of teleology.

2 Anthropomorphic and adaptationalist fallacies

Sociobiologists have appeal to fitness-maximizing strategies to explain behaviour like altruism, promiscuity, xenophobia, homosexuality; to explain institutions like the incest taboos, preferential marriage rules, sex role differences, social inequality. Each of these is hypothesized to be the result of natural selection by environmental factors for individual fitness maximization. However, it has seemed absurd to opponents of sociobiology that behaviour which is by definition the result of intentions – desires and beliefs of rather complex sorts – could be intelligibly attributable to nonhumans as far down the phylogenetic ladder as birds and fish. Relatedly, it seems equally absurd to suppose that genes could be causally implicated in the occasions on which such intentions are acted on by humans. Both of these assumptions have been attributed to sociobiology and subjected to philosophical scrutiny.

The argument runs: 'altruism' is defined as action that advantages another with the motive of doing so. It is a concept which carries a definitional commitment to an intentional cause. But this motive forms no part of the sociobiologist's stipulative definition of fitness, as Wilson, for example, gives it. The term is then employed to explain both human and nonhuman non-intentional dispositions, and is applied to explain human intentional altruism by a gratuitous anthropomorphism of nonhuman dispositions.

Arguments like this are too strong. Few sociobiologists suppose that the occurrences of intentional actions are explainable by natural selection. Their interest in any case is in explaining the emergence of dispositions to behave in certain ways under certain conditions. Such explanations are neutral about the immediately prior causes that trigger the exercise of the dispositions explained. Indeed, if selection works on behaviour as it does on structure, it is likely that it will select a variety of different causes with similar effects, just because these effects have the same selective advantage. In human altruism these causes may include intentional states, while in nonhuman ones it may involve some much simpler mechanism. Sociobiology aims to explain a genus – the disposition to altruism, whether intentional or not, of which the former is a species. Similarly, nature will select not just individual genes, but packages of them, and in fact competing packages of differing genes so long as these have the same or equally adaptive effects in human and infrahuman dispositions. No one supposes that there is a single gene or a small number of genes that code for intentional behaviour of any sort, or even a large number of genes that do more than provide for the disposition to engage in intentional actions of an adaptive sort.

But why suppose that selection operates so pervasively as to make adaptational explanations appropriate? This is a more fundamental challenge to sociobiology. Like other applications of the theory of natural selection, sociobiology has been accused of an obsession with identifying every salient behaviour

pattern or institution as the adaptational product of pervasive selection. This commitment to adaptationalism is alleged to reflect an unfalsifiable assumption that deprives sociobiology of its scientific status (see DEMARCATION PROBLEM; SCIENTIFIC METHOD). Many sociobiologists along with most evolutionary theorists will plead guilty to the charge of adaptationalism, but defend the practice as one demanded by the theory of natural selection. The adaptational imperative of the theory is no different from principles governing hypothesis selection in any other theory. It can be misused to defend the theory come what may, but it can hardly be eschewed altogether in a theory whose aim is to apply Darwinism to the human sciences.

3 The levels of selection

Among evolutionary biologists the notion that species, populations or interbreeding groups could be selected for has been unpopular for reasons sketched out above: such groups are liable to 'invasion' by individuals who can take advantage of group traits while not contributing to their maintenance, and group selection is always swamped by individual selection. Some sociobiologists have gone further and argued that not even the individual organism is properly viewed as the level on which selection operates. As G.C. Williams has held, considerations of theoretical parsimony require that adaptational significance should not be accorded to a trait at any level above that necessary to explain the persistence of the trait in question. Following this principle, it has been argued that the locus of selection is always the individual gene – so that if altruism among animals is to be given an evolutionary explanation it must be shown how it can be adaptive for the individual gene borne by the individual altruist (see GENETICS §5).

This controversy has drawn philosophers concerned with reductionism into active debates in sociobiology. Genic reductionists argue that attributing purposes or functions in biology is always dangerous, and the risks of anthropomorphism are minimized by restricting their attribution to the lowest level of organization compatible with the evidence: this level is argued to be the individual gene or allele. Holists have argued that some changes at the level of populations cannot be explained by appeal to properties of the individuals or genes themselves.

For instance, given a certain proportion of altruists and egoists in a population, whether the population expands, and how fast are functions of the distribution of altruists and egoists in the subpopulations out of which the whole group is composed. If the structure of the group includes subpopulations in which altruism is heavily represented, then the population as a whole may increase faster than otherwise. But population structure is a group trait, which can be selected for independently of the selection for traits of individual organisms or their particular genes.

Philosophical scrutiny of the claim that the gene is the unique locus of selection has brought sociobiology into contact with fundamental problems in the analysis of probabilistic causation (see CAUSATION §4). Suppose a gene's having a property raises its chances of leaving copies in some contexts but not in others. Then the question arises of how to describe the overall causal power of the trait in all contexts. When we add in the fact that in a structured population of genes, the trait may have probabilistic effects different from those it has when identically but randomly distributed in an unstructured population, the problem of probabilistic causality makes contact with the problem of determining the level of selection.

4 Nature versus nurture

The rise of sociobiology renewed interest in the substantive questions of the relative causal importance of heredity and environment in the distribution of traits. Almost from the first, sociobiology was stigmatized as guilty of 'biological determinism' – the thesis that traits of interest are not subject to human modification because they are genetically fixed. To some extent this charge betrays a fundamental misunderstanding of the synthetic theory of evolution. For Darwinian theory holds that environmental factors select from among hereditary variations; and genetic theory holds that traits – phenotypes – are the product of genetic and environmental factors. Genes alone can fix nothing.

Nevertheless the question remains of how to apportion causal responsibility between environmental and genetic factors. Biologists have done so by linking causality to experimental methods. In an experiment where one can control both environmental variables and the presence or absence of a gene, differences among outcomes enable one to identify the effects of each, and sometimes even apportion the causal responsibility between the environment and the gene. If the presence of a gene has a greater impact on reproductive success than the presence of an environmental factor, then there is some reason to credit it with a predominantly causal role, even though the environmental factor was also causally necessary for any reproduction.

This operational definition of greater or lesser causal responsibility makes it clear that such judgements are always relativized to sets of genes and sets of environmental variables. To say that a trait is mainly under the control of genes will be to make implicit appeal to a range of environmental variables whose presence or absence has lesser effects on the trait's appearance. In other environments, the presence or absence of the same gene may have lesser impact. This difference has led some writers to condemn claims that some traits are innate genetically, or biologically determined, as false or unfounded. For there may always be crucial environmental factors we can almost never vary whose influence on the presence or absence of the trait will be greater than that of the alleged genetic factors.

5 Ideological and moral implications

Some sociobiologists have argued that a Darwinian approach to the evolution of human behaviour can explain the existence of *mores* and moral codes, and the differences among them as the consequence of selection for fitness maximizing over variation in human and prehuman behavioural dispositions. Some writers have gone further (following Herbert SPENCER) and have suggested that Darwinian theory might even underwrite or justify some normative claims (see EVOLUTION AND ETHICS).

Few philosophers have expressed sympathy with the latter view, noting that it is a discredited form of naturalism (see NATURALISM IN ETHICS §1). Moreover, it has been noted that a theory which purports to explain the moral codes and the social mores which characterize different societies as the result of natural selection can easily become rationalizations for these codes and *mores*, can effectively serve as an intellectual obstacle to changes even when the morals and *mores* are in fact not resistant to fundamental changes in them. Scientists' development of evolutionary explanations for human inequalities and differences can and have been misused to argue that these inequalities are biologically determined, and so cannot be ameliorated or eradicated by environmental intervention. As such, sociobiology can serve an unintended ideological function independent of its cognitive status. Philosophers with differing ideological convictions have sought to uncover the improper ideological exploitation of sociobiological theory.

See also: BEHAVIOURISM IN THE SOCIAL SCIENCES; EVOLUTIONARY THEORY AND SOCIAL SCIENCE; HUMAN NATURE; METHODOLOGICAL INDIVIDUALISM; REDUCTION, PROBLEMS OF; SPECIES; UNITY OF SCIENCE

References and further reading

Alexander, R. (1979) *Darwinism and Human Affairs*, Seattle, WA: University of Washington Press. (Develops an account of social institutions as reflecting genetic and environmental factors.)

* Axelrod, R. (1984) *The Evolution of Cooperation*, Ann Arbor, MI: University of Michigan Press. (An accessible account of the problem of altruism and the role of game theory, and computer modelling in sociobiology. Includes original Hamilton and Axelrod paper.)

Darwin, C. (1859) *On the Origin of Species by means of Natural Selection, or the Preservation of Favoured Races in the Struggle for Life*, London: John Murray; repr. Cambridge, MA: Harvard University Press, 1964. (Darwin's contribution to the discussion of group selection and human cooperation.)

* —— (1871) *The Descent of Man and Selection in Relation to Sex*, London: John Murray, 2 vols; repr. Princeton, NJ: Princeton University Press, 1981. (Darwin's main work on human origins, with a long account of sexual selection and an attempt to apply that theory to explain human characters.)

Dawkins, R. (1989) *The Selfish Gene*, Oxford: Oxford University Press, 2nd edn. (A strong defence of the gene as the unit of selection and of its explanatory relevance to human behaviour.)

* Hamilton, W.D. (1964) 'The Genetic Evolution of Social Behaviour', *Journal of Theoretical Biology* Parts I and II, 7: 1–52. (Develops the theory of kin-selection later exploited by Axelrod.)

Kitcher, P. (1985) *Vaulting Ambition*, Cambridge, MA: MIT Press. (A sustained philosophical attack on sociobiology.)

Maynard Smith, J. (1982) *Evolution and the Theory of Games*, Cambridge: Cambridge University Press. (Introduction to biological exploitation of game theory.)

Richarson, P. and Boyd, R. (1985) *Culture and the Evolutionary Process*, Chicago, IL: University of Chicago Press. (A sophisticated treatment of the interaction of environment, heredity and learning in human social evolution.)

Sober, E. (1983) *Conceptual Issues in Evolutionary Biology*, Cambridge, MA: MIT Press; repr. 1994. (An anthology of important papers in the philosophy of biology touching on many of the issues broached above. The 2nd edition of 1994 contains further papers.)

—— (1993) *The Nature of Selection*, Chicago, IL: University of Chicago Press. (A discussion of the controversy surrounding the units of selection and the nature of evolutionary theory.)

* Trivers, R. (1971) 'The Evolution of Reciprocal Altruism', *Quarterly Review of Biology* 46: 35–57. (First development of theory of reciprocal altruism.)

Williams, G.C. (1966) *Adaptation and Natural Selection*, Oxford: Oxford University Press. (Opposes attributions of selection at levels above the gene, subject to close philosophical examination by Sober and others.)

* Wilson, E.O. (1976) *Sociobiology: The New Synthesis*, Cambridge, MA: Harvard University Press. (Introduction to sociobiology among both humans and infrahuman species.)

—— (1978) *On Human Nature*, Cambridge, MA: Harvard University Press. (Defence and extension of theories of Sociobiology: The New Synthesis.)

ALEX ROSENBERG